FICTION CATALOG

THIRTEENTH EDITION

STANDARD CATALOG SERIES

JULIETTE YAAKOV, GENERAL EDITOR

CHILDREN'S CATALOG
FICTION CATALOG
MIDDLE AND JUNIOR HIGH SCHOOL
   LIBRARY CATALOG
PUBLIC LIBRARY CATALOG
SENIOR HIGH SCHOOL LIBRARY CATALOG

FICTION CATALOG

THIRTEENTH EDITION

EDITED BY

JULIETTE YAAKOV

AND

JOHN GREENFIELDT

MANAGING EDITOR

ZAIDA NIDZA PADRÓ

NEW YORK AND DUBLIN
THE H. W. WILSON COMPANY
1996

Editorial Staff

Anne Price, Joan Robertson
Brenda Smith, Janet A. Stripling

Production Staff

Marjorie E. Beaumont, Dorothy Daniel
Barbara Delegal, Cynthia LeBlanc, Geneva Monroe
Olga Rivera, Crystal L. Williams

Printed in the United States of America

ISBN   0-8242-0894-3

PREFACE

Fiction Catalog is a selective list of established and contemporary works of adult fiction either written in or translated into English. This thirteenth edition includes 5,461 titles and 1,820 analytical entries for novelettes and composite works. Analytical entries heighten the usefulness of the Catalog by expanding access to the library's collections. In addition to this volume, four annual supplements cover the years 1996, 1997, 1998, and 1999. They will be supplied without further charge to those purchasing the thirteenth edition.

Scope and coverage. Books listed are hardcover editions that were published in the United States, or published in Canada or the United Kingdom and distributed in the United States. Out-of-print titles have been included in the belief that good fiction is not obsolete simply because it happens to go out of print. Information about an out-of-print title that is reissued between editions of the Catalog will be included in a supplement. The availability of hardcover reprint editions is noted whenever possible. Large print editions published in hardcover are also identified.

Users who seek information about the writer of a work are referred to *Fiction Catalog's* companion publication, *Public Library Catalog: Guide to Reference Books and Adult Nonfiction,* which includes literary criticism, biographies, books on the writing of fiction, and literary history.

Preparation. Titles were selected with the assistance of experienced librarians from public library systems in different geographical areas. Since the voting represented the collective opinion of a number of librarians in each system, the consensus is relatively broad-based. The popularity of a title is not, of course, an infallible guide to its quality as a creative work.

Organization. The Catalog consists of three parts. The first part lists works alphabetically by the name of the author. Prices have been obtained from the publisher and are as current as possible. Notes about related works, a descriptive summary for novels and a contents note for story collections, and, in most cases, an evaluative comment from a quoted source are provided. The sheer number of subject headings assigned to each work precludes the inclusion of subject tracings under entries in part one.

The second part of the Catalog is a Title and Subject Index. The access by subject or theme is one of the Catalog's most important features and is especially valued by reader advisors. Among specific subject headings are those for persons, places, events, historical periods, lifestyles, and legendary characters. Headings for genre, form, and literary technique identify works by type.

Part three is a Directory of Publishers and Distributors.

More detailed information about the arrangement and content of the Catalog will be found in the Directions for Use.

Acknowledgments. The H.W. Wilson Company thanks those publishers who supplied copies of their books and information about editions and prices. The Company is especially indebted to the staff members of the following library systems for participating in the selection process:

PREFACE

Allentown Public Library
Allentown, Pa.

Contra Costa County Library
Pleasant Hill, Calif.

Dayton & Montgomery County
Public Library
Dayton, Ohio

Enoch Pratt Free Library
Baltimore, Md.

Great Falls Public Library
Great Falls, Mont.

Grosse Pointe Public Library
Grosse Pointe, Mich.

Library Association of Portland
Portland, Or.

Onondaga County Public Library
Syracuse, N.Y.

Providence Public Library
Providence, R.I.

Seattle Public Library—
Popular Library
Seattle, Wash.

West Allis Public Library
West Allis, Wis.

Yonkers Public Library
Yonkers, N.Y.

DIRECTIONS FOR USE

Fiction Catalog is arranged in three parts as described below.

Part 1 lists works of fiction in alphabetical order by the last name of the author or by title if it is the main entry. The following bibliographical information is provided: author, title, publisher, date of publication, paging, illustration note, latest known price, out-of-print status, reprint publication data, ISBN designation, and, when available, Library of Congress card or control number. Notes regarding sequels, publication history, and contents of story collections are also supplied. A descriptive summary and, in most instances, an excerpt from a reviewing source conclude the entry.

References are made from variant forms of authors' names, from names of joint authors, and from names of editors or compilers of short story collections. Analytical entries, which are introduced by the word *"In,"* are made for parts of composite works.

Part 2 is a Title and Subject Index. Each book is listed under title, which is followed by the name of the author under which the entry for the book will be found in Part 1. Books are also listed under their main subjects or themes, as well as under headings for genre, form, and literary technique if appropriate. Editions printed in large type can be located under the heading "Large print books." Subject headings and subject cross references are printed in capital letters.

Part 3 is a Directory of Publishers and Distributors that provides full name, address, telephone and Fax numbers, and ordering instructions for publishers of the books listed.

CONTENTS

Preface   v

Directions for Use   vii

Author Alphabet   3

Title and Subject Index   721

Directory of Publishers and Distributors   969

PART 1

AUTHOR ALPHABET

FICTION CATALOG
THIRTEENTH EDITION

200 years of great American short stories;
edited by Martha Foley. Houghton Mifflin
1975 968p o.p.

Analyzed in Short story index
Contents: A pretty story, by F. Hopkinson; Rip Van
Winkle, by W. Irving; Peter Rugg, the missing man, by
W. Austin; The grey champion, by N. Hawthorne; The
big bear of Arkansas, by T. B. Thorpe; The cask of
Amontillado, by E. A. Poe; Bartleby the scrivener, by
H. Melville; Tennessee's partner, by B. Harte; Captain
Kidd's money, by H. B. Stowe; Marjorie Daw, by T.
B. Aldrich; The lady or the tiger, by F. Stockton; Over
on the T'other Mounting, by C. E. Craddock; The revolt
of mother, by M. W. Freeman; One of the missing, by
A. Bierce; The return of a private, by H. Garland; The
real thing, by H. James; The courting of Sister Wisby,
by S. O. Jewett; The open boat, by S. L. Crane; The
man that corrupted Hadleyburg, by S. L. Clemens; The
furnished room, by O. Henry; To build a fire, by J.
London; The strength of God, by S. Anderson; The
teacher, by S. Anderson; The diamond as big as the
Ritz, by F. S. Fitzgerald; Haircut, by R. Lardner; Double
birthday, by W. Cather; Spring evening, by J. T. Farrell;
Masses of men, by E. Caldwell; The gilded six-bits, by
Z. N. Hurston; Silent snow, secret snow, by C. Aiken;
An odor of verbena, by W. Faulkner; The daring young
man on the flying trapeze, by W. Saroyan; The snows
of Kilimanjaro, by E. Hemingway; A tooth for Paul
Revere, by S. V. Benét; Noon wine, by K. A. Porter;
The leader of the people, by J. Steinbeck; Lily Daw and
the three ladies, by E. Welty; Fire and cloud, by R.
Wright; The patterns of love, by W. Maxwell; The ballad
of the sad café, by C. McCullers; Cass Mastern's wedding
ring, by R. P. Warren; The wedding: Beacon Hill, by
J. Stafford; Rain in the heart, by P. Taylor; Gunners'
passage, by I. Shaw; The lottery, by S. Jackson; February
1999: Ylla, by R. Bradbury; The country husband, by
J. Cheever; A good man is hard to find, by F. O'Connor; The Mexican girl, by J. Kerouac; The Pedersen kid,
by W. H. Gass; Seven say you can hear corn grow, by
K. Boyle; Where are you going, where have you been?
by J. C. Oates; Tell me how long the train's been gone,
by J. Baldwin; Son, by J. Updike; Yellow woman, by
L. Silko

A

Aaron, David
Crossing by night; a novel. Morrow 1993
363p $22

ISBN 0-688-09296-9   LC 92-34200
Also available Thorndike Press large print edition

"A fictional account of the adventures of World War
II spy Elizabeth Pack (code name: Cynthia). *Crossing by
night* chronicles Cynthia's brave and heroic deeds in
1930s Europe, climaxing in her plot to smuggle the
famed Enigma coding device out of Hitler's Germany.
At great personal risk, Pack 'left the comfortable world
of a Washington debutante and diplomat's wife to lead
the life of a spy.' Real-life characters include her passionless husband, Arthur Pack; the romantic Count Michael
Lubienski; and spymaster William Stephenson." Libr J
"In Aaron's capable hands, Elizabeth is an irresistible
heroine and her story is the stuff of highest adventure."
Publ Wkly

Abbey, Edward, 1927-1989
The fool's progress; an honest novel. Holt
& Co. 1988 485p o.p.

                           LC 88-4677

The protagonist of this novel, Henry Lightcap, relates
his journey back from Tucson, Arizona, to his boyhood
home in West Virginia where his brother still lives on
the family farm. "On his way home Henry reviews his
own life in a series of flashbacks." N Y Times Book
Rev
"This work is a bitterly humorous commentary on the
foibles of modern society and its impact on nature. .
. . A powerful, often hauntingly beautiful novel." Libr
J

Abbott, Margot
The last innocent hour; a novel. St.
Martin's Press 1991 505p $21.95

ISBN 0-312-06377-6   LC 91-20550
"In 1946, Sally Jackson, an army intelligence officer
working to help prosecute war criminals, returns to a
ruined Berlin. As she spends her days viewing
photographs of Nazi atrocities, she must confront the
ghosts of her past, when she was a naive young daughter
of the American ambassador in Berlin just before Nazi
brutality overran the country. Although memories constantly assault her as she walks amidst the city's rubble,
her past erupts when a series of photos reveals her ex-
husband (a Nazi SS guard) murdering a child. A flashback reveals the awful contrast between pre-war surface
glitter and the brutalities later inflicted on the country
and on the innocent young woman." Libr J
"Protracted and melodramatic recollections and a few
stereotypical characters detract only slightly from this
fascinating psychological drama." Publ Wkly

Abe, Kōbō, 1924-1993
Beyond the curve; translated by Juliet
Winters Carpenter. Kodansha Int./USA 1991
247p $18.95

ISBN 4-7700-1465-1   LC 90-49456

Abe, Kōbō, 1924-1993—*Continued*

Analyzed in Short story index

Contents: An irrelevant death; The crime of S. Karma; Dendrocacalia; The life of a poet; Record of a transformation; Intruders; Noah's Ark; The special envoy; Beguiled; The bet; The dream soldier; Beyond the curve

"Each ingenuously simple tale is shrouded in a haze of paranoia and surrealism, a sort of Kafka-esque atmosphere of uncertainty and conspiracy. Abe's protagonists are victims, trapped in the inevitability of a nightmare. . . . Abe's world is stark and arbitrary. He dramatizes alienation and helplessness with grim humor and finesse, creating poignant satire." Booklist

The box man; translated from the Japanese by E. Dale Saunders. Knopf 1974 178p il o.p.

Original Japanese edition, 1973

This novel "concerns a man who relinquishes normal life to live in a 'waterproof room,' a cardboard box that he wears on his back. Like a medieval Buddhist monk, the man observes society's goings-on but disdains any interaction with the world he has abandoned as a mad place." Merriam-Webster's Ency of Lit

"The novel that convincingly delineates the disintegration of personality may also be read as an intricate comment on modern society versus the sanctity and brazen humor of the individual who chooses to announce both his freedom of choice and his wish for anonymity." Booklist

The woman in the dunes; translated from the Japanese by E. Dale Saunders; with drawings by Machi Abé. Knopf 1964 239p il o.p.

Original Japanese edition, 1962

"Niki Jumpei, a teacher and amateur insect collector, goes on vacation to a remote part of the seacoast, hoping for interesting insects. There he is captured by villagers who put him down in a deep sandpit, where he shares a small house with a widow. His job, and hers, is to shovel incessantly, to keep the house from being engulfed by the advancing sand dunes. This is part of the village's operation for sheer survival. The rope ladder is withdrawn; he is thrown into permanent proximity to the woman who is no beauty or charmer, but the only human being in direct relationship with him." Book Week

The author "follows with meticulous precision his hero's constantly shifting physical, emotional and psychological states. He also presents the most minute descriptions of the trivia of everyday existence in a sandpit with such compelling realism that these passages serve both to heighten the credibility of the bizarre plot and subtly increase the interior tensions of the novel." N Y Times Book Rev

Abrahams, Peter, 1947-

Hard rain. Dutton 1988 374p o.p.

LC 87-18947

"A sinister deal struck at the Woodstock festival in 1969 sends a poor young man to Vietnam in the place of a rich young man, who finds a new life in California. Nearly 20 years later, the now-divorced man and his daughter have disappeared, and Jessie Shapiro, the child's mother, begins a cross-country hunt. Jessie's search ends in Vermont, the home of her husband's family and the location of a commune in which he once lived. Jessie also finds the home of the man who took her husband's place, thought to be killed in action but now returned." Booklist

"Jessie is an appealingly ordinary heroine, a resilient working mother. And each of the characters she encounters on her descent into a violent world of personal and political deception is vividly drawn. 'Hard Rain,' which takes its title from a Bob Dylan song, is infused with a knowing, affectionate feeling for the pop culture of the 1960's." N Y Times Book Rev

Lights out. Mysterious Press 1994 336p $21.95

ISBN 0-89296-482-0   LC 93-28634

"The summer before he was to go to USC on a swimming scholarship, Eddie Nye became innocently involved in a marijuana smuggling scheme and wound up in jail. He should have been out in three or four years, but his response to a brutal prison 'initiation' forced him to serve his full 15-year sentence. Now he is back on the streets, looking for answers. His search is complicated by a powerful drug lord and fellow inmate, who sees in the unwitting Eddie the perfect messenger for some very important information." Libr J

"Abrahams spares the reader nothing, in gritty dialogue and often gruesome detail. Consistently interesting and suspenseful, his thriller's shocking outcome is revealed only on the very last page." Publ Wkly

Abrahams, William, 1919-

(ed) Prize stories, 1919-1995: The O. Henry awards. See Prize stories, 1919-1995: The O. Henry awards

Achebe, Chinua, 1930-

Anthills of the Savannah. Anchor Press/Doubleday 1988 c1987 216p o.p.

LC 87-18708

First published 1987 in the United Kingdom

This novel describes power politics in an imaginary West African country, Kangan, "where a military coup has brought to prominence a Sandhurst-trained officer ill-prepared for political leadership. Before long 'His Excellency' transforms his initial insecurity into paranoid despotism, suspecting even well-meaning allies of disloyalty. This becomes the fate of his two boyhood friends, Chris Oriko, Commissioner for Information, and Ikem Osodi, poet and editor of a national newspaper, who in different ways both refuse to play safe by compromising." New Statesman

"Mr. Achebe is a moralist and idealist, but he rarely allows himself to put a word in; these positions are perfectly integrated in his characters. . . . There is a world in these individuals." N Y Times Book Rev

Girls at war, and other stories. Doubleday 1973 129p o.p.

Analyzed in Short story index

First published 1972 in the United Kingdom

Contents: The madman; The voter; Marriage is a private affair; Akueke; Chike's school days; The sacrificial egg; Vengeful creditor; Dead men's path; Uncle Ben's choice; Civil peace; Sugar Baby; Girls at war

Set in Nigeria, these stories share an underlying theme: "the various collisions between the life of modern, post-agricultural Africa and vestigial tribal beliefs and customs. . . . Achebe's prose is masterfully simple and concise without ever being mannered. It sometimes does

Achebe, Chinua, 1930-—*Continued*
not sound 'written' at all, but rather like some perfectly normal utterance that is simply unfolding before you." Saturday Rev Arts

Things fall apart; with an introduction by Kwame Anthony Appiah. Knopf 1995 xxi, 181p $15

ISBN 0-679-44623-0   LC 94-13429

"Everyman's library"

A reissue of the title first published 1958 in the United Kingdom and 1959 in the United States by McDowell, Obolensky

"The novel chronicles the life of Okonkwo, the leader of an Igbo (Ibo) community, from the events leading up to his banishment from the community for accidentally killing a clansman, through the seven years of his exile, to his return. The novel addresses the problem of the intrusion in the 1890s of white missionaries and colonial government into tribal Igbo society. It describes the simultaneous disintegration of its protagonist Okonkwo and of his village. The novel was praised for its intelligent and realistic treatment of tribal beliefs and of psychological disintegration coincident with social unraveling." Merriam-Webster's Ency of Lit

Ackroyd, Peter

English music. Knopf 1992 399p il $23

ISBN 0-679-40968-8   LC 92-52951

"Outside the hall in 1920s London where Timothy Harcombe, [the protagonist of this novel], works nightly with his father, a sign reads, 'Clement Harcombe. Medium and Healer.' But it is Timothy who seems to have the greater power. Periodically falling into dreamlike states, he enters into 'English music'—here signifying all the great accomplishments of English culture—where he encounters various literary figures, becomes part of a Gainsborough painting, and is instructed in music by William Byrd. Fearful of his son's gift, the father ships him off to his maternal grandparents in the country. But ultimately Timothy rejoins his father—for 'everyone belongs somewhere'—and discovers the true extent of his miraculous powers." Libr J

"In writing about London, Ackroyd's touch is as sure as ever, and his interest in spiritualism, if not in the same league as a Dickens or even a Powell, is always engrossing." New Statesman Soc

Adams, Alice, 1926-

After you've gone; stories. Knopf 1989 229p o.p.

LC 89-45283

Analyzed in Short story index

Contents: After you've gone; 1940: fall; The end of the world; Child's play; Fog; Lost cat; Tide pools; Favors; Ocracoke Island; On the road; A sixties romance; What to wear; Traveling together; Your doctor loves you

"Alice Adams writes fiction in an elegant, fluid style. And even though her literary inclination is to investigate those recesses of the soul where less than noble motives reside, she ultimately brings to the fore the strengths of character that enable people to overcome their darker impulses." Booklist

Almost perfect. Knopf 1993 243p $22

ISBN 0-679-42398-2   LC 92-54797

Also available Thorndike Press large print edition

"To talented but insecure journalist Stella Blake, her intense affair with charismatic advertising entrepreneur Richard Fallon is 'almost perfect.' Richard is startlingly handsome, likes to cook, always brings flowers. Soon, however, it becomes obvious that he is unstable: he drinks too much and flies into rages. Accustomed to disparaging herself as small, dark and dowdy, Stella is astonished that gorgeous Richard is in her bed, and even as her disquietude increases she is helpless to restrain her love." Publ Wkly

"Although the novel is filled with details about San Francisco's social hierarchies (the privileged as well as the working class, the straight and the gay), 'Almost Perfect' is much more than a comedy of manners. Ms. Adams deftly shows how social and business pressures affect her characters and, in the case of Richard Fallon, exacerbate his decline as he plunges into a series of dangerous and destructive acts." N Y Times Book Rev

Beautiful girl; stories. Knopf 1979 c1978 242p o.p.

LC 78-54932

Analyzed in Short story index

Contents: Verlie I say unto you; Are you in love; Alternatives; Winter rain; Gift of grass; Ripped off; The swastika on our door; A jealous husband; Flights; Beautiful girl; Home is where; A pale and perfectly oval moon; Attrition; Roses, rhododendron; What should I have done?; For good

"Love and its loss is a unifying theme in these 16 stories. . . . Set primarily in sharply recalled San Francisco and North Carolina scenes, these stories are written on a plane under the skin and close to the nerve, in spare, polished prose. Special and fine." Libr J

Caroline's daughters. Knopf 1991 307p $22

ISBN 0-394-56825-7   LC 90-52908

Also available G.K. Hall large print edition

This novel, set in San Francisco, depicts the lives of Caroline Carter's five daughters. "Sage, 41, is a ceramist who initially has more luck in attracting unfaithful men than in becoming a successful artist. At 35, Liza is the most dependable and dreams of being a writer instead of fulfilling the desires of her children and sexually demanding husband. Fiona, 33, is a wealthy, hedonistic restaurateur who falls victim to one of Sage's ex-lovers. A . . . 31-year-old lawyer, Jill satisfies her fantasies by indulging in a scandalous pastime. Portia, 25, . . . drifts from housesitting to gardening and writing poems." Libr J

"If this cast of characters and their convoluted scripts sound overwhelming, they may well have been in the hands of a less skillful writer. Alice Adams knows exactly where she is going, and why. She delivers a fluid, meaty, sexy and rewarding novel. . . . And let us not forget one of the stars of Caroline's Daughters: the setting." Women's Rev Books

Families and survivors. Knopf 1975 211p o.p.

In this novel, set in Virginia and California, "the author covers 30 years and perhaps half as many characters, following Louisa Calloway from uneasy adolescence in Virginia through college and then her marriage and second marriage, her affairs, motherhood, her friends and their children, her search for a usable identity. . . . In time, after much unhappiness, Louisa arrives at a kind of accommodation, for she is also 'a born survivor.'" Newsweek

Adams, Alice, 1926-—*Continued*

"Time is the governing element here: the years from 1941 to 1970 spent by individuals on different plateaus of their lives. . . . Adams' unobtrusive foretelling charts the pursuits of self-discovery and provides needed bridges between islands of telling conversation." Booklist

Superior women. Knopf 1984 367p o.p.

LC 84-47507

The author "follows the lives of five women, from their first meeting during Radcliffe freshman orientation week in 1943, through their college years, and on to the rest of their lives up to 1983." Booklist

"The present-tense vignettes which make up the novel—told from the perspective of now one, now another of the friends—allow the author to develop her characters with the necessary mixture of irony and complicity." Libr J

Adams, Douglas, 1952-

Dirk Gently's Holistic Detective Agency. Simon & Schuster 1987 247p o.p.

LC 87-9464

"Is the book about the Electric Monk on a faraway planet; or Reg, the Regius Professor of Chronology; or perhaps Richard, the befuddled computer whiz? Then, of course, there's detective Dirk Gently, a weasly sort, who is more interested in telekinesis than in tailing suspects. That Adams manages to bring together his various scenarios and round up his wandering characters shows his skill as a writer. His insightful commentary on the human condition is the hot fudge on this literary banana split." Booklist

The Hitchhiker's Guide to the Galaxy. Harmony Bks. 1980 215p $14

ISBN 0-517-54209-9   LC 80-14572

First volume in The hitchhiker's series
"Based on a BBC radio series, . . . this is the episodic story of Arthur Dent, a contemporary Englishman who discovers first that his unpretentious house is about to be demolished to make way for a bypass, and second that a good friend is actually an alien galactic hitchhiker who announces that Earth itself will soon be demolished to make way for an intergalactic speedway. A suitably bewildered Dent soon finds himself hitching . . . rides throughout space, aided by a . . . reference book, The Hitchhiker's Guide to the Galaxy, a compendium of 'facts,' philosophies, and wild advice." Libr J

"A bizarre, wildly funny, satiric novel. . . . There are side commentaries on almost everything; lots of in-jokes SF fans will either love or loathe, and a free-floating irreverence which is irresistible." Voice Youth Advocates

Followed by The restaurant at the end of the universe

also in Adams, D. The hitchhiker's quartet

The hitchhiker's quartet. Harmony Bks. 1986 624p o.p.

LC 86-19480

Omnibus edition of the first four titles in the series which are all entered separately

Contents: The Hitchhiker's Guide to the Galaxy; The restaurant at the end of the universe; Life, the universe and everything; So long, and thanks for all the fish

Life, the universe, and everything. Harmony Bks. 1982 227p o.p.

LC 82-15470

Third volume in The hitchhiker's series
In this volume, "Arthur finds himself in a cave on prehistoric earth, awaiting the arrival of his extraterrestrial friend Ford Perfect so that they may resume their travels in time and space. Their mission: to save the universe from a cataclysm." Booklist

"Arthur Dent and his motley crew do tie up most of the loose ends and manage to prevent the destruction of the universe, but the first two novels . . . 'must' be read to understand the situation, and even then it's confusing." Libr J

Followed by So long, and thanks for all the fish

also in Adams, D. The hitchhiker's quartet

The long dark tea-time of the soul. Simon & Schuster 1989 c1988 319p o.p.

LC 89-120700

First published 1988 in the United Kingdom
"An explosion at London's Heathrow Airport, where Kate Schechter is about to board a jet en route to Oslo, lands her instead in a weird nursing home. She befriends another casualty of the explosion, a man of gigantic proportions, and learns that he is Thor, the God of Thunder, come down from Valhalla to cope with a scandal involving his father Odin, who has sold his immortal soul to a couple of human shills. Meanwhile, sleuth Dirk Gently . . . plays a part in the great events, since he is investigating the perfidious pair—a lawyer and an advertiser—to whom Odin is in thrall." Publ Wkly

"If this all sounds wild and woolly, that's because it is—chock-full of action, jokes, fake red herrings, and somehow, suspense." Booklist

Mostly harmless. Harmony Bks. 1992 277p $20

ISBN 0-517-57740-2   LC 92-25457

Fifth volume in The hitchhiker's series
"A Grebulon reconnaissance ship with faulty programming, a news reporter suffering from a bad case of missed opportunities, a fugitive from the new 'improved' offices of the *Hitchhiker's Guide to the Galaxy*, and a hitchhiker lost in a parallel universe come together in grand style in [this] installment of Adams's best-selling 'trilogy.'" Libr J

The restaurant at the end of the universe. Harmony Bks. 1981 c1980 250p $12.95

ISBN 0-517-54535-7   LC 81-6563

Second volume in The hitchhiker's series
First published 1980 in the United Kingdom
"Poor uprooted Arthur Dent finds himself swept along in the wake of Zaphod Beeblebrox, former President of the Galaxy, as Zaphod searches for the man who rules the Universe. They and their companions tumble from one scrape into another, with the erratic aid of Zaphod's dead great-grandfather and Marvin, their perpetually depressed robot. Adams's lively sense of the ridiculous has concocted many hilarious episodes, though the inspired lunacy of the first book has become rather uneven here. Still, this is one of the best pieces of sf humor available." Libr J

Followed by Life, the universe, and everything

also in Adams, D. The hitchhiker's quartet

So long, and thanks for all the fish. Harmony Bks. 1985 204p o.p.

LC 84-19350

Adams, Douglas, 1952-—*Continued*

Fourth volume in The hitchhiker's series

Arthur Dent "returns to a supposedly destroyed Earth to build a hyperspace bypass. The night of his return, Arthur falls in love with a sedated girl (her brother says she's 'barking mad'), only to lose her, then accidentally find her twice more. She is Fenchurch, the girl who in . . . 'Guide' . . . discovered the secret of Earth's potential happiness moments before it was demolished. Her 'madness' stems from the time when Earth should have been destroyed, and wasn't, but when all the dolphins disappeared. . . . The humor is still off-the-wall, but less forced and more gentle than the other books. . . . The series seems to be winding down, but it is still an addictive commodity to its fans." SLJ

Followed by Mostly harmless

also in Adams, D. The hitchhiker's quartet

Adams, Henry, 1838-1918

Democracy; an American novel.

Available from Amereon and Reprint Services Corp.

"A social and political satire based on the corruption of the second Grant administration, the book includes characters modeled on President Hayes and James G. Blaine. A charming and intelligent young widow, Madeleine Lee, moves to Washington 'to touch with her own hands the massive machinery of society.' She finally rejects an offer of marriage from a senator who has compromised his moral integrity for political advantage." Reader's Ency. 3d edition

Adams, Richard, 1920-

Watership Down. Macmillan 1974 c1972 429p il $40

ISBN 0-02-700030-3

Also available from Buccaneer Bks.

First published 1972 in the United Kingdom

"A small number of male rabbits, frightened by the imminent destruction of their warren, embark upon a hazardous exodus across the English downs in search of a new home. . . . These refugees are constantly beset by dangers and temptations, but fortunately they share among them the qualities of bravery, endurance and resourcefulness required for survival. In the course of their wanderings, these rabbits learn to care for each other, learn to work together. In time they find another warren, but the new community, lacking female company, faces the prospect of extinction. The search for female rabbits draws our heroes to a distant rabbit fortress ruled by a Fascist general of military genius. In two great battles our friends' outnumbered troops must prove their cleverness and courage." Newsweek

Adler, Elizabeth

Fortune is a woman. Delacorte Press 1992 433p o.p.

LC 91-24977

Available Thorndike Press large print edition

"Francie Harrison is the poor little rich girl with a misogynistic father in turn-of-the-century San Francisco. She escapes the doll's world he plans for her and finds love, only to have it disintegrate in the earthquake of 1906. Amidst the destruction, she meets Lai Tsin, an illegal Chinese immigrant, and the strong Yorkshire-woman Annie Aysgarth, who, together, help her build a world for herself. All three profit from the alliance and emerge on top of the business world, rich in friendship as well as treasure. . . . Writing and characterization are tight, depictions of Nob Hill and Oriental influence ring true, and pacing is superb." Booklist

Legacy of secrets. Delacorte Press 1993 454p $21.95

ISBN 0-385-30919-8   LC 92-37239

Also available Thorndike Press large print edition

"Irish immigrant Lily Molyneux is more accustomed to sweeping through grand rooms in ball gowns than sweeping floors, but she learns quickly when banished to the states by her infuriated father. Ironically, the man Lily has said is the father of her child escapes to America on the same ship (working in the engine room) and will one day be rich enough to buy the Irish castle and the property his family worked on as peasants. Adler's narrator is Lily's elderly niece, Maudie, who recounts her great aunt's indiscretions and betrayals to a ready audience made up of Shannon Keefe and Ed Sheridan, descendants of Lily and one of her lovers." Booklist

"Spiced with betrayal, revenge, lust and scandal, this is an intoxicating brew, served with panache." Publ Wkly

The secret of the Villa Mimosa. Delacorte Press 1995 375p $21.95

ISBN 0-385-31212-1   LC 94-9774

Also available Thorndike Press large print edition

"Psychiatrist Phyl Foster is intrigued with the unconscious Jane Doe found—having obviously been left for dead—in a San Francisco ravine. When the woman wakes up with amnesia, Phyl helps her try to remember her past and treats her like a kid sister, giving her clothes and a place to stay. The psychiatrist also runs interference for the woman, newly named 'Bea French,' with macho homicide detective Franco Mahoney, who follows every lead toward Bea's true identity, which he hopes will help him discover who tried to kill her. After Phyl finds Bea a job as social secretary to a rich socialite, the anmesiac travels to Paris. When her employer dies suddenly, she is left with a fortune, two orphans, a restored French villa—and a 50-year-old murder mystery. . . . Adler is expert at digging deep into her characters' psyches and showing what makes them tick." Publ Wkly

Adler, Warren

The ties that bind; a Fiona Fitzgerald mystery. Fine, D.I. 1994 220p $19.95

ISBN 1-55611-395-1   LC 93-74479

In this mystery "Fiona Fitzgerald is teamed with another brilliant woman, Gail Prentiss, in the theory that women cops are best suited to solve crimes perpetrated against women. In their first case together, Fiona and Gail find the daughter of a powerful lawyer dead in a room in the Mayflower Hotel, and the main suspect, a man Fiona knows from her college days, is an Associate Justice of the Supreme Court. The partners travel through the labyrinth of upper-crust Washington in pursuit of this powerful man, who may or may not be the killer." Publisher's note

After the king; stories in honor of J.R.R. Tolkien; edited by Martin H. Greenberg; introduction by Jane Yolen. TOR Bks. 1992 438p $22.95

ISBN 0-312-85175-8   LC 91-34382

After the king—*Continued*
"A Tom Doherty Associates book"
Analyzed in Short story index
Contents: Reave the Just, by S. R. Donaldson; Troll bridge, by T. Pratchett; A long night's vigil at the temple, by R. Silverberg; The dragon of Tollin, by E. A. Scarborough; Faith, by P. Anderson and K. Anderson; In the season of the dressing of the wells, by J. Brunner; The fellowship of the dragon, by P. A. McKillip; The decoy duck, by H. Turtledove; Nine threads of gold, by A. Norton; The conjure man, by C. de Lint; The Halfling House, by D. L. McKiernan; Silver or gold, by E. Bull; Up the side of the air, by K. Haber; The naga, by P. S. Beagle; Revolt of the suger plum fairies, by M. Resnick; Winter's king, by J. Yolen; Götterdämmerung, by B. N. Malzberg; Down the river road, by G. Benford; Death and the lady, by J. Tarr

"Although fans of Middle Earth may be disappointed that none of these tales draw directly from Tolkien's world, discerning readers will find the unmistakable stamp of the master concealed in the heart of each story." Libr J

Agee, James, 1909-1955
A death in the family. McDowell, Obolensky 1957 339p o.p.
"Six-year-old Rufus Follet, his younger sister Catherine, his mother, and various relatives all react differently to the unexpected announcement that Rufus's father has been fatally injured in an automobile accident. The poignancy of sorrow, the strength of personal beliefs, and the comforting love and support of a family are all elements of this compassionate novel." Shapiro. Fic for Youth. 3d edition

Agnon, Shmuel Yosef, 1888-1970
Nobel Prize in literature, 1966
The bridal canopy; now rendered into English by I. M. Lask. Doubleday, Doran 1937 373p o.p.
Written 1922 in Hebrew
Reb Yudel, a poor but devout Hasidic Jew, lived in Galicia, Poland in the early years of the nineteenth century. When it came time for his three dowerless daughters to marry, the Rabbi commanded Reb Yudel to roam throughout Galicia in his search for dowries. Richly provided for by his neighbors he set out on his journey, accompanied by the teamster Nuta. The account of their wanderings is spiced with stories, and stories within stories which the two told each other on their way

"The only way Agnon's heroes can be saved from the mockery of fate is to submit to Divine Providence, wherever it shall lead. Such a character is [Reb Yudel] . . . whose survival is made possible by virtue of miraculous occurrences, which elicit astonishment and laughter. . . . The attitude of the narrator to the naïve innocents in the tale vacillates between humor and irony, on the one hand, and forgiveness and restrained compassion, on the other." Ency of World Lit in the 20th Century

Aiken, Conrad, 1889-1973
Blue voyage
In Aiken, C. The collected novels of Conrad Aiken p15-166

The collected novels of Conrad Aiken; Blue voyage, Great circle, King Coffin, A heart for the gods of Mexico [and] Conversation; introduction by R. P. Blackmur. Holt, Rinehart & Winston 1964 575p o.p.
Blue voyage, published 1927, describes the people and incidents of a transatlantic voyage, written mostly in stream-of-consciousness style. Great circle, published 1933, is a psychological novel also written in stream-of-consciousness style in which the central character, fighting alcoholism, fears his wife is untrue to him and his best friend has betrayed him. King Coffin, published 1935, is a psychological horror story which follows the twisted thinking of an intellectual mind rapidly going insane, as he broods over the idea of a perfect crime, the unmotivated murder of a stranger. A heart for the gods of Mexico, written 1939, a portrayal of Malcolm Lowry, takes a woman and two men on a mortal journey across a changing American landscape into a heightened awareness of life and finality. Conversation, published 1940, probes the conflict between art and human relationships in a domestic crisis between man and wife

Conversation
In Aiken, C. The collected novels of Conrad Aiken p473-575

Great circle
In Aiken, C. The collected novels of Conrad Aiken p167-295

A heart for the gods of Mexico
In Aiken, C. The collected novels of Conrad Aiken p415-72

King Coffin
In Aiken, C. The collected novels of Conrad Aiken p297-414

Aiken, Joan, 1924-
Eliza's daughter. St. Martin's Press 1994 316p $20.95
ISBN 0-312-10972-5   LC 94-2669
Also available Thorndike Press large print edition
In this sequel to Jane Austen's Sense and sensibility, "the illegitimate daughter of Colonel Brandon's sister is raised by brutish foster parents, shuttled from one lukewarm relative to another, discovers her parentage, and at last claims her birthright." Libr J
"Where Austen merely suggests the corrupting influence of society on human impulses, Aiken makes much of it and even conceives of a tragedy concealed beneath Austen's shrewd manipulation of plot. Aiken's story is rich with humor, and her language is compelling." Booklist

The haunting of Lamb House. St. Martin's Press 1993 200p $17.95
ISBN 0-312-09060-9   LC 92-34392
Also available Thorndike Press large print edition
First published 1991 in the United Kingdom
A "ghost story set in the English residence of Henry James and later of E. F. Benson. Most of the book is devoted to the diary of Toby Lamb, who describes mysterious events in his own life and his relations with

Aiken, Joan, 1924——*Continued*
his beloved older sister and with his best friend. In this
tale Aiken suggests as much as she reveals about dark
secrets that lead to suicide. The action then shifts to
James's period of residence, which is followed by a first-
person account of Benson's time in Lamb House. Aiken's
mastery of style serves her well in her creation of three
distinct voices. . . . Those familiar with James's writing,
especially *The turn of the screw*, will derive special
enjoyment from this novel." Libr J

Jane Fairfax; Jane Austin's Emma, through
another's eyes. St. Martin's Press 1991 c1990
252p o.p.

LC 90-28532

Available G.K. Hall large print edition
First published 1990 in the United Kingdom
This novel "re-creates the cosy, busy world of High-
bury as seen through the eyes of Emma's only rival.
Jane, the talented niece of the garrulous Miss Bates,
causes a stir in the village upon her return from the
more sophisticated worlds of London and Weymouth."
Libr J
With this "companion novel and a tribute to Jane
Austen's *Emma*, Aiken reaches the height of her craft.
The novel is an uncommonly good imitation of Austen's
witty and evocative use of language and of her powerful
rendering of the manners and mores that shaped
nineteenth-century society." Booklist

Mansfield revisited. Doubleday 1985 c1984
188p o.p.

LC 84-13748

First published 1984 in the United Kingdom
"Aiken has returned to Jane Austen's 'Mansfield Park'
to record the doings of Susan, sister of Fanny Price, who
married Edmund, a clergyman, younger son of Sir
Thomas and Lady Bertram. Sir Thomas having died suddenly in Antigua, Fanny and Edmund journey there to
wind up his business affairs, leaving Susan to tend the
old lady, assist in the recuperation of Tom, the older
son, and avert the barbs of Julia Bertram Yates, whose
manifest contempt for Susan, a mere poor relation, is
exacerbated by the young girl's flashing good looks. The
torpor of their lives is lifted by the advent of Mary
Crawford, her brother Henry, Frank Wadham, come to
preach in Edmund's stead, and his widowed sister. . .
. All of the new arrivals are instantly enamored of young
Susan and it is clear early on that one of the men will
ask for her hand in marriage." Publ Wkly
"Aiken is a capable romance writer and works perhaps
as diligently if not as subtly as Austen to puncture the
overt snobbery of her upper-class characters." Booklist

Morningquest. St. Martin's Press 1993
c1992 223p $17.95

ISBN 0-312-09339-X   LC 93-18508

First published 1992 in the United Kingdom
"Pandora Crumbe reluctantly accompanies her mother
on a visit to a neighboring manor house and, when her
mother suddenly dies, becomes permanently immersed in
the lives of the eccentric Morningquest family. Led by
Sir Gideon Morningquest, a world-famous composer, the
family leads a posh life in London and a rather spartan
one in their country home. Each summer a new project,
such as a folly or a tunnel is undertaken, and all seven
children, even those of college age, are expected to participate. Just as the Morningquests provided sanctuary
for Pandora as a motherless teen, she eventually becomes

a lifeline for them. Aiken's story is funny, romantic, and
filled with exceptional characters." Booklist

Voices in an empty house. Doubleday
1975 310p o.p.
"The story moves back and forth in time, from
England to New York and other places as Thomas Cook
searches for his stepson, Gabriel, who will die without
immediate heart surgery. Thomas had married Gabriel's
mother, greedy and childish Bella, after the death of her
husband. . . . Bella has a sardonic twin brother Bo who,
like her, prefers kinky sex. Though Bella and Thomas
are divorced, she persuades him to search for Gabriel.
All the people concerned (including Bo's lover, a man)
have selfish reasons for saving Gabriel's life; he will
inherit his father's fortune. But the boy is disillusioned
and determined to die. The narration is utterly absorbing
as it bares secrets the characters try to keep hidden, even
from themselves." Publ Wkly

Aird, Catherine
A dead liberty. Doubleday 1987 177p o.p.

LC 86-16753

"Published for the Crime Club"
"Because a blow to the head has almost totally
incapacitated detective inspector Trevor Porrit, detective
inspector C. D. Sloan is obliged to take over a case
involving the poisoning of a civil engineer. It looks to
be fairly open and shut, until Sloan finds himself intrigued by the defendant—she won't say a word." Publ
Wkly

Henrietta who? Doubleday 1968 188p o.p.
"Published for the Crime Club"
"A nicely contrived tale of multiple murders, all according to plan, for depriving a young woman of her
inheritance. Systematic investigation by Inspector Sloan,
red herrings (but not in excess), and a modest touch
of love interest. Rural scene. Miss A . . . writes clearly
and simply, and with an occasional touch of wit." Barzun. Cat of Crime. Rev and enl edition

Last respects. Doubleday 1982 177p o.p.

LC 82-45344

"Published for the Crime Club"
"Fisherman Horace Boller finds the body of a young
man in the river, and an autopsy proves he has been
murdered. [Inspector] Sloan learns that the victim is
Peter Hinton, a friend of Elizabeth Busby and her
widower uncle, Frank Mundill, residents of imposing
Collection House. Finding no motive for Hinton's killing,
Sloan is at a standstill when Boller is also murdered,
and the detective surmises the fisherman has been blackmailing the killer." Publ Wkly

Passing strange. Doubleday 1981 c1980
174p o.p.

LC 80-1120

"Published for the Crime Club"
First published 1980 in the United Kingdom
"An amiable English country mystery complete with
mildly eccentric local characters (including the police) and
a victim whom no one wanted to see dead, because she
was the much loved village nurse, masquerading at the
garden fête as a fortune teller. It is precisely because
nurse Cooper did know so much about the local folk
that she is strangled with a twist of floral wire. However,
Detective Sloan sorts it all out eventually after several
quirky encounters with villagers who mean to be helpful
but possess an infinite capacity to confuse." Publ Wkly

Aird, Catherine—*Continued*

Some die eloquent. Doubleday 1980 c1979 195p o.p.

LC 79-8046

"Published for the Crime Club"

First published 1979 in the United Kingdom

"A mystery that begins with the quiet death, from diabetes, of an old woman. The death attracts police attention, though, when it's discovered that the dead woman, a former chemistry teacher, has left an estate worth a quarter of a million pounds. Detective Inspector C. D. Sloan begins asking himself and others how the woman amassed so much money and whether her death was as peaceful as it seemed." Booklist

Alcott, Louisa May, 1832-1888

The abbott's ghost

In Alcott, L. M. Behind a mask: the unknown thrillers of Louisa May Alcott p209-77

Behind a mask [novelette]

In Alcott, L. M. Behind a mask: the unknown thrillers of Louisa May Alcott p1-104

Behind a mask: the unknown thrillers of Louisa May Alcott; edited and with an introduction and afterword by Madeleine Stern. Morrow 1995 xxxiii, 281p $23

ISBN 0-688-00338-9

Analyzed in Short story index

A reissue with a new afterword of the title first published 1975

A collection of four novelettes which originally appeared in periodicals. Behind a mask (1866) and The abbot's ghost (1867) were published under the pseudonym A. M. Barnard. The first is about an actress who masquerades as a governess and deliberately arouses the passions of the male members of an aristocratic family in order to secure a wealthy titled husband while humbling the proud family. The second, set during a Christmas gathering in a haunted English mansion, brings out the loves, hates, jealousies, friendships and guilty secrets of those present. Pauline's passion and punishment (1862), published anonymously, concerns a woman scorned by her lover who becomes obsessed with revenge. The mysterious key and what it opened (1867) involves the revelation of accidental bigamy. A blind girl who seeks her rightful inheritance surrenders it to her half sister and stepmother after the young man who aided her falls in love with her half sister

"The stories are full of the clichés of 19th-Century melodrama but are told with verve and include some engaging liberated women characters. And, surprisingly, evil isn't invariably punished. Essential for students of Alcott because these are precisely the kinds of stories Jo March of 'Little Women' was writing to support herself." Libr J

A long fatal love chase. Random House 1995 242p $21

ISBN 0-679-44510-2

LC 95-6793

Written in 1866

This novel follows the "misfortunes of Rosamond Vivian, a young, impetuous Englishwoman who escapes a life of lonely dependence on her grandfather by running off with the charismatic adventurer Phillip Tempest. He is all unbridled male dominance and id, as well as a bigamist; Rosamond flees him in horror, from sanctuary to convent to madhouse, pursued relentlessly by Tempest." Libr J

"Alcott's portrayals of the pathological Phillip and of the conflicted Rosamond—who initially clings to her ex-lover, hoping to reform him until she realizes he is a murderous brute—show strong psychological insights. This absorbing novel revises our image of a complex and, it is now clear, prescient writer." Publ Wkly

Louisa May Alcott: a selected fiction; with an introduction by Madeleine B. Stern; edited by Daniel Shealy, Madeleine B. Stern, and Joel Myerson. Little, Brown 1990 xlvi, 478p o.p.

LC 90-34563

Analyzed in Short story index

Contents: The rival painters: a tale of Rome; The rival prima donnas; The Frost-King; or, The power of love; The lady and the woman; Love and self-love; Hope's debut; Thrice tempted; Perilous play; M. L.; A night; The Blue and the Gray: a hospital sketch; Dull, but necessary; At forty; A modern Mephistopheles; The sisters' trial; A modern Cinderella; or, The little old shoe; Merry's monthly chat; A merry Christmas; Secrets; Literary lessons; The valley of the shadow; A fire brand; Ten years later; Positively last appearance; My boys; My girls; Eli's education; A Christmas dream, and how it came true; Sophie's secret; Pansies; Polly's troubles; Uncles; Coming home; Jo's last scrape; Transcendental wild oats; How I went out to service

The mysterious key and what it opened

In Alcott, L. M. Behind a mask: the unknown thrillers of Louisa May Alcott p153-208

Pauline's passion and punishment

In Alcott, L. M. Behind a mask: the unknown thrillers of Louisa May Alcott p105-52

Alding, Peter, 1926-

For works written by this author under other names see Jeffries, Roderic, 1926-

Aldiss, Brian Wilson, 1925-

(ed) Best SF: 1968-1975. See Best SF: 1968-1975

Helliconia spring; [by] Brian W. Aldiss. Atheneum Pubs. 1982 361p o.p.

LC 81-66036

"In this first of a trilogy, Aldiss presents Helliconia, a dual-star system planet that is beginning to thaw from its centuries-long winter. Humans, humanoid protognostics, and the animal-like phagors contend for its sparse resources, and Aldiss relates episodes from the lives of several of the inhabitants." Libr J

Aldiss, Brian Wilson, 1925——_Continued_

"The reader's imagination will be captured by the gossies and fessups, the kaidaw and the innovative language which defies description and comparison. Aldiss has not only written a science fiction novel about another world, he has created another universe complete with it's own language and flavor, peopled with colorful characters (both human and otherwise) who engage sympathy and interest." Best Sellers

Followed by Helliconia summer

Helliconia summer; [by] Brian W. Aldiss. Atheneum Pubs. 1983 398p o.p.

LC 83-45062

"In this second novel in Aldiss's trilogy, the planet Helliconia . . . is presented as an epic miniature of humanity's loftiest aspirations and basest shortcomings. The action takes place on two levels, represented by the geometrical symbol of the planet's supreme god Akhanaba. Some events proceed along the inner rim, driven by incessant racial wars between the cohabitant Helliconian humans and the 'ahuman' Phagors. Along the outermost rim are the concerns of the king of Borlien . . . and the nefarious intrigues of court hangers-on ranging from chancellors to child prostitutes." Publ Wkly

Followed by Helliconia winter

Helliconia winter. Atheneum Pubs. 1985 281p o.p.

LC 84-45607

In this concluding volume of the "trilogy, the planet Helliconia begins its descent into a winter that will last for centuries. Nonhuman phagors, better suited to the changing climate, begin to reclaim their ancient lands, and the plague they bring panics the Oligarchy into ever more repressive measures to stave off a new dark age. As young Luterin Shokerandit learns, however, such civilized willfulness only subverts the grand, interdependent cycles of the natural world." Publ Wkly

"This conclusion to the Helliconia trilogy ranks as a landmark of fictional world-building." Libr J

Man in his time; the best science fiction stories of Brian W. Aldiss. Atheneum Pubs. 1989 328p $19.95

ISBN 0-689-12052-4   LC 89-6934

Analyzed in Short story index

First published 1988 in the United Kingdom with title: Best SF stories of Brian W. Aldiss

Contents: Outside; The failed men; All the world's tears; Poor little warrior!; Who can replace a man?; Man on bridge; The girl and the robot with flowers; The saliva tree; Man in his time; Heresies of the huge god; Confluence; Working in the spaceship yards; Super-toys last all summer long; Sober noises of morning in a marginal land; The dark soul of the night; An appearance of life; Last orders; Door slams in fourth world; The gods in flight; My country 'tis not only of thee; Infestation; The difficulties involved in photographing Nix Olympica

Total environment

_In_ Modern classic short novels of science fiction p221-59

Aldrich, Bess Streeter, 1881-1954

A lantern in her hand. Appleton, D. & Co. 1928 306p o.p. Amereon reprint available $22.95 (ISBN 0-88411-260-8)

"The story of a pioneer woman who, as a bride, followed the covered-wagon trail to the Nebraska prairies and lived there the rest of her eighty years. A devoted wife and mother, Abbie Deal brought a large and united family through poverty and hardship. Denying herself that the children might have the advantages her talented youth had coveted, she went through life with 'courage her lode-star and love her guide, a song upon her lips and a lantern in her hand.'" Open Shelf

Followed by A white bird flying (1931)

Aleichem, Sholem _See_ Sholem Aleichem, 1859-1916

Alexander, Margaret Walker _See_ Walker, Margaret, 1915-

Alfred Hitchcock presents: Stories not for the nervous. Random House 1965 363p o.p.

Partially analyzed in Short story index

This collection of macabre tales includes 20 short stories, 3 novelettes and the complete text of: Sorry, wrong number, a novelization by Allan Ullman from the screen play by Lucille Fletcher, published 1958

Short stories included are: To the future, by R. Bradbury; Rivers of riches, by G. Kersh; Levitation, by J. P. Brennan; Miss Winters and the wind, by C. N. Govan; View from the terrace, by M. Marmar; The man with copper fingers, by D. L. Sayers; The twenty friends of William Shaw, by R. E. Banks; The other hangman, by C. Dickson; Don't look behind you, by F. Brown; No bath for the Browns, by M. Bennet; The uninvited, by M. Gilbert; Dune roller, by J. May; Something short of murder, by H. Slesar; The golden girl, by E. Peters; The boy who predicted earthquakes, by M. St. Clair; Walking alone, by M. A. deFord; For all the rude people, by J. Ritchie; The dog died first, by B. Fischer; Room with a view, by H. Dresner; Lemmings, by R. Matheson; White goddess, by I. Seabright; The substance of martyrs, by W. Sambrot; Call for help, by R. Arthur

Algren, Nelson, 1909-1981

The man with the golden arm; a novel. Doubleday 1949 343p o.p.

"Set in the slums of Chicago, the novel, which won a National Book Award in 1950, tells the story of Frankie Machine (Francis Majcinek) who is said to have a 'golden arm' because of his sure touch with pool cues, dice, his drumsticks, and his heroin needle. Unable to free himself from his slum environment, Frankie is finally driven to suicide." Reader's Ency. 3d edition

A walk on the wild side. Farrar, Straus & Cudahy 1956 346p o.p. Greenwood Press reprint available $47.50 (ISBN 0-313-20294-X)

A novel about the residents of a slum street in New Orleans during the early years of the Depression

Algren, Nelson, 1909-1981—*Continued*

"Algren's vivid writing gives this degenerate cast the power to shock or appall, and if a glimmer of compassion leaks through occasionally it is slapped down before it gets out of hand." Libr J

Allan, John B.

For works written by this author under other names see Westlake, Donald E.

Allbeury, Ted, 1917-

Deep purple. Mysterious Press 1990 c1989 246p $18.95

ISBN 0-89296-401-4   LC 89-43145

First published 1989 in the United Kingdom

"Igor Yakunin—saying he is a major in the KGB and has worked for a year in the U.S. running two networks of agents in Los Angeles and New York—now wants to defect to the British. Eddie Hoggart of MI6, a man fluent in Russian, is the agent picked to debrief Yakunin. The Soviet spy insists that there is a mole in British intelligence. Hoggart has to sort out not only this knotty international problem but some of his own personal ones." Booklist

"As in many Allbeury books, there are spies and counterspies, plus a foxy lawyer who tries to frame the debriefer. The ending is interesting and unusual. Mr. Allbeury is a very deft operative." Publ Wkly

The Judas factor. Mysterious Press 1988 c1984 202p o.p.

LC 87-28275

First published 1984 in the United Kingdom

This novel "is about Tad Anders, an undercover agent who runs a nightclub in London's Soho and who kills when so ordered by his masters. Opposed to him is a Russian agent, also a killer. This Russian has taken out some British operatives in Europe, so Anders is sent into East Berlin to get the assassin and bring him back alive as a message to the K.G.B." N Y Times Book Rev

"Allbeury's bleak view of spycraft is matched by his jaundiced look at the English class system: Anders is simultaneously involved with spoiled, 'upper class' Judy and Candy, definitely a working girl. The characterization is rich and varied, and Allbeury's spare style moves marvelously in this good, solid read." Publ Wkly

A time without shadows. Mysterious Press 1991 c1990 289p $19.95

ISBN 0-89296-432-4   LC 90-44331

Also available Thorndike Press large print edition

First published 1990 in the United Kingdom

"Philip Maclean, an English art student living in France in 1940, escapes to England where he is recruited by British intelligence. He soon returns to France to establish Scorpio, a resistance network. Barely operational, Scorpio is betrayed and Maclean and his followers are rounded up and shipped off to concentration camps. Forty years later British intelligence officer Harry Chapman is assigned to find out who betrayed Scorpio, and why." Libr J

"The title's irony isn't apparent until halfway into the book; by the end, however, its reverberations are breathtaking." Publ Wkly

Allen, Charlotte Vale, 1941-

Dream train. 1988 326p o.p.

LC 87-33335

"When Joanna James, a photojournalist, accepts the assignment to travel from London to Venice on the new Orient Express, she realizes that she faces not only a new adventure, but also the necessity to decide which of two men she truly loves. During the journey she makes new friends and discovers personal insights." Libr J

Dreaming in color. Doubleday 1993 401p $22

ISBN 0-385-41945-7   LC 92-30312

"When her sadistic husband Joe begins menacing their six-year-old daughter Penny, abused and battered Bobby Salton finally flees their upstate New York home. She finds sanctuary in a well-appointed Connecticut house where she is hired to nurse stroke victim Alma Ogilvie, formerly the independent-minded director of a girls school. But Bobby's presence brings out the worst in Alma's sharp-tongued, judgmental niece, Eva Rule, a novelist who disdains Bobby and—blaming the victim—thinks the woman is perhaps responsible for her own abuse. . . . Complex and sharply delineated characters merge with often compelling prose as Allen portrays three uncertain women finding some degree of resolve." Publ Wkly

Leftover dreams. Doubleday 1992 674p o.p.

LC 91-20116

"Quiet and frail Faye and charmingly spirited Louise grow up in Toronto in the 1940s and '50s, blamed by their bitter mother for her imperfect life. With the help of their grandmother, the teenage girls escape their mother's mental and physical abuse and move into a place of their own, seeming none the worse for their experiences, although closer than most sisters. When Faye dies of a botched abortion after being raped, 18-year-old Louise moves to London in order to flee her memories. There she creates a new life, making friends and starting a public relations business. But to find—and accept—happiness and love, Louise must journey back to her roots and answer questions raised by Faye's death." Publ Wkly

Painted lives. Atheneum Pubs. 1990 307p o.p.

LC 89-38607

Available G.K. Hall large print edition

"When frumpy Sarah Kidd is hired as live-in secretary to Mattie Sylvester, prickly widow of a famed painter, she joins a houseful of misfits wounded by life—a foul-mouthed chauffeur struggling with Vietnam flashbacks, a placid cook who was once a stellar forger. Night after night, like a querulous Scheherazade, Mattie recounts her life history to Sarah, telling how, as a willful young artist of great talent in the 1920s, she fell under the sexual spell of Gideon Sylvester, an artistic pretender who took her for all she was worth." Publ Wkly

Allen, Henry W., 1912-1991

For works by this author under other names see Henry, Will, 1912-1991

Allen, Hervey, 1889-1949

Anthony Adverse; decorations by Allan McNab. Farrar & Rinehart 1933 1224p il o.p.

"This vast romantic novel recounts the story of Anthony—born in 1775, illegitimate, orphaned, left to die in a Catholic convent, educated by the Church, and apprenticed to a wealthy Italian merchant whose heir he became. His business interests were world wide; in early manhood a slave trader, he was later connected with the financial interests of Napolean in France, England, Spain, and the new world. Anthony carried with him through life his one link to the past, a beautiful small figure of the Madonna that identified him to others though he himself never learned his identity." Booklist

"Only a scholar could have assembled the enormous knowledge that has gone into the book and only a poet and a critic could have caught so acutely the implications of that knowledge as idea and emotion in human beings. The triumph of the book, however, is that this wealth of fact and feeling is fused by the gusto of the true storyteller." N Y Her Trib Books

Allende, Isabel

Eva Luna; translated by Margaret Sayers Peden. Knopf 1988 271p o.p.

LC 88-45272

Original Spanish edition, 1987

This novel "gives us successive episodes in Eva's life, from illegitimate birth and orphanhood through drifting adolescence to relative stability and success, but also recounts in parallel the biography of Rolf Carle, from his wartime childhood in Austria to his emigration to Latin America, subsequent fame as a controversial documentary film-maker, and finally his encounter and love affair with Eva herself. A third narrative strand deals with the fortunes of Huberto Naranjo . . . guerrilla fighter and [Eva's] transient lover." Times Lit Suppl

The author "has a delicious humor that often punctuates her multifaceted story. She succeeds, too, in introducing us to an ensemble of characters who are offbeat, alien to our ken, but who become part of our sensibilities." West Coast Rev Books

The house of the spirits; translated from the Spanish by Magda Bogin. Knopf 1985 368p $27.50

ISBN 0-394-53907-9   LC 84-48516

Original Spanish edition, 1982

This novel "tells the story of the Trueba family, with its deep loves and hates, following them from the turn of the century to the violent days of the overthrow of the Salvador Allende government in 1973." Christ Sci Monit

"The style is superbly controlled (and/or the translation is marvelously sensitive), balancing detail rich in associations with a deadpan humor that completely demystifies things that would be otherwise inexplicable. In other words, sentimentality never intrudes on the emotions you develop for these hopelessly well-meaning people and their equally errant children." Best Sellers

The infinite plan; a novel; translated from the Spanish by Margaret Sayers Peden. HarperCollins Pubs. 1993 380p $23

ISBN 0-06-017016-6   LC 92-54741

Original Spanish edition, 1991

This is the "story of Gregory Reeves's journey from childhood to middle age and long sought peace and happiness. Gregory's journey is marked by the contending philosophies of his mother's Bahai faith, his father's personally revealed, metaphysical explanation of the universe called 'The Infinite Plan' (the selling of which provides the family's income), and the traditional Catholicism and sense of nostalgia that permeate the Latin barrio where Gregory lives as a child." Libr J

"Allende's intensely imagined prose has clarity and dimension; she describes the exotic and the mundane with equal skill." Publ Wkly

Of love and shadows; translated from the Spanish by Margaret Sayers Peden. Knopf 1987 274p o.p.

LC 86-46164

Original Spanish edition, 1984

"A journalist and a photographer have teamed up to report on a young girl who seems to be inflicted with mystical trances, but their story unexpectedly takes a sinister turn when the girl is seized by the military police. The search for the girl leads the two reporters to a secret mass grave in the countryside that documents a reign of terror; the grave's discovery leads in turn to a government plot for deadly revenge." Booklist

"Ms. Allende skillfully evokes both the terrors of daily life under military rule and the subtler forms of resistance in the hidden corners and 'shadows' of her title, particularly in the churches or in simple unsung acts of solidarity. At the same time the author ably captures the voices of the regime's apologists—the complex lies and clichés of its proud male foot soldiers and the pat false phrases of its rich lady cheerleaders." N Y Times Book Rev

The stories of Eva Luna; translated from the Spanish by Margaret Sayers Peden. Atheneum Pubs. 1991 330p $18.95

ISBN 0-689-12102-4   LC 90-39615

Also available G.K. Hall large print edition

Analyzed in Short story index

Contents: Two words; Wicked girl; Clarisa; Toad's mouth; The gold of Tomás Vargas; If you touched my heart; Gift for a sweetheart; Tosca; Walimai; Ester Lucero; Simple María; Our secret; The Little Heidelberg; The judge's wife; The road north; The schoolteacher's guest; The proper respect; Interminable life; A discreet miracle; Revenge; Letters of betrayed love; Phantom palace; And of clay are we created

"The title character of Allende's *Eva Luna* returns to frame this collection of stories in a Scheherazade-like fashion. . . . Allende covers familiar territory: social warfare between the rich and the poor, sexual battles between men and women, the dissolution of corrupt politicians and macho military leaders, all set within the landscape of contemporary South America." Booklist

Allingham, Margery, 1904-1966

The China governess. Doubleday 1962 282p o.p. Amereon reprint available $16.95 (ISBN 0-89190-192-2)

Set in London this novel finds Albert Campion and his friend Inspector Luke searching for the connection between a wealthy young man of mysterious parentage and a statuette of a governess charged with murder long ago

Crime and Mr. Campion. Doubleday 1959 575p o.p.

"Published for the Crime Club"

An omnibus volume containing the complete texts of three mystery novels all starring the British detective Albert Campion. Death of a ghost (1934) is based on art forgery, Flowers for the judge (1936) is about the murder of a publisher and Dancers in mourning (1937) concerns a group of theatrical characters

Dancers in mourning

In Allingham, M. Crime and Mr. Campion p363-575

Death of a ghost

In Allingham, M. Crime and Mr. Campion p7-175

The fashion in shrouds

In Allingham, M. Three cases for Mr. Campion p9-255

Flowers for the judge

In Allingham, M. Crime and Mr. Campion p177-362

The Gyrth chalice mystery

In Allingham, M. Three cases for Mr. Campion p421-604

More work for the undertaker. Doubleday 1949 253p o.p. Amereon reprint available $19.95 (ISBN 0-89190-180-9)

Albert Campion tried not to become involved, but before the day was out his companion Lugg received a curious note from an undertaker and Campion felt himself drawn into the strange puzzle that was the Palinode family—a family remarkable for plain living, high thinking, and mysterious dying

The return of Mr. Campion; uncollected stories; edited and with an introduction by J. E. Morpurgo; with a tribute to Margery Allingham by Agatha Christie. St. Martin's Press 1990 1989 xxiii, 165p o.p.

LC 89-77816

Available G.K. Hall large print edition

Analyzed in Short story index

First published 1989 in the United Kingdom

Contents: The case is altered; My friend Mr. Campion; The dog day; The wind glass; The beauty king; The black tent; Sweet and low; Once in a lifetime; The kernel of truth; Happy Christmas; The wisdom of Esdras; The curious affair in nut row; What to do with an ageing detective

"A member of England's literary circles and a close friend of Allingham's, Morpurgo gathered these previously uncollected stories in order to display Allingham's skills as they developed from the mid-'20s to her death in 1966. Many of the 13 pieces recall the ineffable gentleman sleuth Albert Campion. . . . Others suggest a tale preserved in lavender: boy-meets-girl stories, perhaps dated but still witty and original." Publ Wkly

Three cases for Mr. Campion. Doubleday 1961 604p o.p.

"Published for the Crime Club"

This omnibus volume of the author's early Albert Campion mysteries includes: The fashion in shrouds (1938); Traitor's purse (1941); and The Gyrth chalice mystery (1931)

"The Gyrth chalice mystery" unravels Mr. Campion's solution to the secret in the locked room of Gyrth Tower; "The fashion in shrouds" involves the theft of dress designs, sixty cages of canaries, and blackmail, as Albert Campion investigates a three-year-old murder; "Traitor's purse" finds Albert Campion, an amnesia victim haunted by an urgency to do something of immense consequence before time runs out

Traitor's purse

In Allingham, M. Three cases for Mr. Campion p257-420

Allison, Dorothy

Bastard out of Carolina. Dutton 1992 309p $20

ISBN 0-525-93425-1   LC 91-34607

"Set in the rural South, this tale centers around the Boatwright family, a proud and closeknit clan known for their drinking, fighting, and womanizing. Nicknamed Bone by her Uncle Earle, Ruth Anne is the bastard child of Anney Boatwright, who has fought tirelessly to legitimize her child. When she marries Glen, a man from a good family, it appears that her prayers have been answered. However, Anney suffers a miscarriage and Glen begins drifting. He develops a contentious relationship with Bone and then begins taking sexual liberties with her. . . . Unaware of her husband's abusive behavior, Anney stands by her man. Eventually, a violent encounter wrests Bone away from her stepfather." Libr J

"The technical skill in both large things and details, so gracefully executed as to be always at the service of the story and its characters and thus almost invisible, is simply stunning, about as close to flawless as any reader could ask for and any writer, at any age or stage, could hope for and aspire to." N Y Times Book Rev

Alther, Lisa

Kinflicks; a novel. Knopf 1976 c1975 503p o.p.

"Virginia Babcock Bliss, having been discovered in a compromising position with a hippie draft deserter, is thrown out of the house by her husband. She returns to her home town in Tennessee to find her mother dying in a hospital bed. . . . [A series of flashbacks reveals Ginny's development from] an impressionable young woman [who] moves from cheerleader through girl of a motorcycle hood, prim collegian, antiwar lesbian, organic farmer, and model housewife to emerge in her present predicament." Libr J

Alther, Lisa—*Continued*

"An ambitious, funny, lucid, and unfailingly honest first novel. . . . While a number of excellent writers have covered various parts of the turf covered here . . . no other writer has yet synthesized this material as well as Miss Alther has." New Yorker

Original sins. Knopf 1981 592p o.p.

This novel depicts "what it was like to grow up in Tennessee for two sisters, daughters of a white mill owner, two brothers, sons of a white foreman in the mill, [and] a black 'boy' whose mother was a maid in the mill owner's house. The growing-up time is in the 1960's." Publ Wkly

"This is an overlong novel, serious and comic, by turns grimacing and guffawing; wildly exuberant and deadly solemn. Alther's forte is social satire in which her Rabelaisian gifts punctuate many of the psychological con games foisted upon us as 'success' or 'real living.'" Best Sellers

Alvarez, Julia

How the Garcia girls lost their accents. Algonquin Bks. 1991 290p $16.95

ISBN 0-945575-57-2   LC 90-48575

This novel "tells the story (in reverse chronological order) of four sisters and their family, as they become Americanized after fleeing the Dominican Republic in the 1960s. A family of privilege in the police state they leave, the Garcias experience understandable readjustment problems in the United States, particularly old world patriarch Papi. The sisters fare better but grow up conscious, like all immigrants, of living in two worlds." Libr J

"This is an account of parallel odysseys, as each of the four daughters adapts in her own way, and a large part of Alvarez's accomplishment is the complexity with which these vivid characters are rendered." Publ Wkly

In the time of the butterflies. Algonquin Bks. 1994 325p $21.95

ISBN 1-56512-038-8   LC 94-15004

This novel is "based on the lives of the four Mirabel sisters (code name: 'Mariposas,' that is, butterflies), three of whom were martyred in 1960 during the liberation of the Dominican Republic from the dictator Trujillo. Through the surviving sister, Dedé, as well as memories of Minerva, Patria, and Maria Teresa, we discover the compelling forces behind each sister's role in the struggle for freedom." Libr J

"Alvarez captures the terrorized atmosphere of a police state, in which people live under the sword of terrible fear and atrocities cannot be acknowledged. As the sisters' energetic fervor turns to anguish, Alvarez conveys their courage and their desperation, and the full import of their tragedy." Publ Wkly

Amado, Jorge, 1912-

Dona Flor and her two husbands; a moral and amorous tale; translated from the Portuguese by Harriet de Onís. Knopf 1969 553p o.p.

Original Portuguese edition published 1966 in Brazil

"Dona Flor has such a harridan of a mother (Dona Rozilda) that you would like her to have her cake and eat it, too, and she very nearly does. Dona Flor's first husband, Vadinho, is a scamp, a prevaricator, and a 'shameless lover.' On Carnival Sunday, at the height of

the gaiety, filled with rum, he drops dead. Dona Flor is desolate but cuts a handsome figure as a widow. She lives through the wake (a gem of a scene) and her mourning quite well, with memories and her cooking school to sustain her. Then suitors appear. None appeal but Dr. Teodoro Madureira, pharmacist and bassoonist, a pillar of propriety. Dona Rozilda is ecstatic, but the well-rounded Dona Flor has her troubles, for alas, Dr. Teodoro is no lover. Dreams haunt her and strange things begin to happen. Thanks to a Yoruba charm, Vadinho returns to ravish our bewildered heroine, and then the fun begins. Bahia in Brazil is the setting for this delectable rum cake of a novel." Publ Wkly

Gabriela, clove and cinnamon; translated from the Portuguese by James L. Taylor and William L. Grossman. Knopf 1962 425p o.p.

Original Portuguese edition published 1958 in Brazil

"Ilhéus, a Brazilian town near Bahia, is fortunate in the wealth it is realizing from its cacao crop. Money flows freely and is spent in cabarets, in bordellos, and on gambling during the period 1925-1926. . . . The removal of a sand bar blocking the harbor is the basis of this fascinating portrait of politics in a provincial Brazilian town. Amado also tells the love story of Nacib, the Arab owner of the most popular café in town, and Gabriela, a child of nature. Amoral rather than immoral, with skin the color of cinnamon and smelling of cloves, Gabriela gives her love readily and freely. Her skillful cooking makes her more valuable to Nacib as a mistress than as a wife. The atmosphere of this entertaining novel is lusty, sensual, and humorous." Shapiro. Fic for Youth. 3d edition

The war of the saints; translated from the Portuguese by Gregory Rabassa. Bantam Bks. 1993 357p $22.95

ISBN 0-553-09537-4   LC 93-5310

As this novel opens "'a statue of St. Barbara of the Thunder, famed for her eternal beauty and miraculous powers'—has just been transported across the Bay of All Saints to Bahia for an exhibition of religious art. Suddenly, just after the ship has docked, the statue takes life and steps from her litter, transformed into the living African deity of St. Barbara Yansan. . . . St. Barbara Yansan has come to rescue the lovely Manela, a young girl who is in love with a taxi driver named Miro, from the puritanical clutches of her equally beautiful but devoutly Catholic (and distinctly coldhearted) aunt, Adalgisa." N Y Times Book Rev

"Amado exploits the Brazilian penchant for mixing fact and myth by including Brazilian celebrities of the period. . . . And by writing in short vignettes—flitting from one character or subject to another—he manages to make reading this novel like attending a particularly raucous Carnival celebration." Publ Wkly

Ambler, Eric, 1909-

The Levanter. Atheneum Pubs. 1972 307p o.p. Amereon reprint available $22.95 (ISBN 0-88411-296-9)

"Michael Howell is 'the Levanter,' a remotely English (in ancestry) businessman, trying to survive and keep the family firm intact in a Syria newly taken over by a nationalist dictatorship. When he and his secretary-mistress are captured by a vicious Palestine splinter group intent on attacking Israel, and using the Howell

Ambler, Eric, 1909-—_Continued_
factories in which to secretly manufacture bombs for that
purpose, it takes all this particular Levanter's ingenuity
to find a way out." Publ Wkly

Waiting for orders; the complete short
stories of Eric Ambler. Warner Bks. 1991
133p $18.95

ISBN 0-89296-241-0   LC 90-50544

Analyzed in Short story index
Contents: The army of the shadows; The case of the
pinchbeck locket; The case of the emerald sky; The case
of the cycling chauffeur; The case of the overheated service flat; The case of the drunken socrates; The case
of the gentleman poet; The blood bargain
"Most of these eight mildly diverting short stories
disinterred from the work of British suspense master
Ambler were written in 1939-1940." Publ Wkly

American voices; best short fiction; by
contemporary authors; with comments by
the authors; selected by Sally Arteseros.
Hyperion 1992 381p o.p.

LC 92-3937

Analyzed in Short story index
Contents: Roses, rhododendron, by A. Adams;
Separating, by J. Updike; 116th Street Jenny, by J. Ros-
sner; The rich brother, by T. Wolff; The swimmers, by
J. C. Oates; Midair, by F. Conroy; Edie: a life, by H.
Doerr; Fenstad's mother, by C. Baxter; Rules of the
game, by A. Tan; The halfway diner, by J. Sayles;
Another marvelous thing, by L. Colwin; Lily, by J.
Smiley; One holy night, by S. Cisneros; Nothing to ask
for, by D. McFarland; Able, Baker, Charlie, Dog, by S.
Vaughn; The church of no reason, by A. Barrett; A
small, good thing, by R. Carver; New African, by A.
Lee; Shiloh, by B. A. Mason; In a father's place, by
C. Tilghman

Amiel, Joseph
A question of proof. Crown 1993 351p
$22

ISBN 0-517-57520-5   LC 92-27230

"In the months before he received a blunt wedgie to
the back of his head, Peter Boelter's life was increasingly
out of kilter. He drank; slept around; deserted wife and
daughter; and to cap the litany of turpitude, intended
to sell his big-city newspaper. Where in the skein of
motivations is the passion that parleyed homicidal desire
into morgue-room fact? Enter Dan Lazar, the city's ace
defense lawyer, whose stock-in-trade is springing muggers,
rapists, and mobsters. The D.A.'s office wants his scalp,
which looks vulnerable as Dan is charged with fixing
a case. The bribe trail leads into the paper's innards,
where Dan discovers the deceased Boelter was not a
popular publisher. But Dan knew that: he's been sleeping
with the widow—whom, incidentally, the police have
placed at the crime scene." Booklist

Amis, Kingsley, 1922-1995
The folks that live on the hill; a novel.
Summit Bks. 1990 246p o.p.

LC 90-36970

Available G.K. Hall large print edition

"Set in a north London suburb, . . . [this novel] centers around the mild-mannered Harry Caldecote, retired
librarian, clubman, [and] epicure. . . . The trouble with
Harry is that his leisurely pursuit of enjoyment is forever
hijacked by his family's multifarious problems. Brother
Freddie is being slowly suffocated by the attentions of
his appalling wife Desirée; errant son Piers is constantly
sponging to finance a shady private life; Fiona, the niece
of an ex-wife, has to be rescued from alcoholic
misadventures; Bunty, stepdaughter of another ex-wife,
needs protecting from a malicious lesbian lover called
Popsy. . . . [And] Harry feels responsible for all of
them." New Statesman Soc
"Tolerance without hypocrisy is what Harry seems to
aim for, in his best moments. Harry is a class act, and
Amis's novel is a vindication of a certain way of being
conservative today." Christ Sci Monit

The Green Man. Harcourt, Brace & World
1970 c1969 252p o.p.

First published 1969 in the United Kingdom
The Green Man is a pub. "It is also a very nasty
thing conjured up by the resident ghost, a 17th-century
diabolist parson, handily capable of destroying his
enemies at a distance. . . . Maurice Allington, owner
of The Green Man and narrator [of the story], neglects
his daughter, ignores his second wife and despises his
mistress—although he spends what energy he can spare
from drinking and ghost-hunting in trying to get the
ignored and despised into bed with him at the same
time." New Statesman
"The dialogue is filled with humor and a chilling
strangeness. Indeed, the success of this short novel
depends very much upon the balance that Amis maintains between laughter and fear." N Y Times Book Rev

Lucky Jim; a novel. Doubleday 1954
c1953 256p o.p.

Available from Amereon and Buccaneer Bks.

First published 1953 in the United Kingdom
"The title is ironic, since the story is about the comic
misfortunes of Jim Dixon, a young lower-middle-class
instructor at an English university. The book satirizes
the academic 'racket' and cultural pretensions." Reader's
Ency. 3d edition

The old devils; a novel. Summit Bks.
1987 294p o.p.

LC 86-23084

"Set in South Wales, [this novel] opens as three
couples at the beginning of their 'golden years' . . . find
their lives turned upside down by the return, after thirty
years, of successful poet Alun Weaver, and his stunning
wife Rhiannon. Alun (born Alan) . . . has made a career
for himself by talking about 'all things Welsh' on the
television." Publisher's note
"The Old Devils has a tough honest crust and scuttling
sideways humor. Nowhere in it does Amis attempt
shapely sentences or lyrical, dying falls. His is an
aesthetic of the anti-beautiful. The book's astringency
feels just right." New Repub

The Russian girl. Viking 1994 c1992 296p
$21.95

ISBN 0-670-85329-1
First published 1992 in the United Kingdom
"Dr. Richard Vaisey is an esteemed scholar at the
London Institute of Slavonic Studies whose wife,
Cordelia, has perfected the art of manipulation. When
Anna Danilova, an obscure Russian poet, asks his help

Amis, Kingsley, 1922-1995—*Continued*

in freeing her brother from a Russian jail by making her 'famous' and thus calling world attention to the brother's plight, Richard finds himself torn between his growing passion for her and his outright dislike of her poetry. Realizing what is going on between her husband and 'the Russian girl,' Cordelia, plots revenge." Libr J

"What makes 'The Russian Girl' such a jolly good read is precisely [its] scathing level of insight, to say nothing of Amis's dazzling virtuosity with the old bons mots. They litter the floor. He also manages to be very, very funny, even when he's being very, very serious." N Y Times Book Rev

Amis, Martin

London fields. Harmony Bks. 1989 470p $19.95

ISBN 0-517-57718-6   LC 89-49558

This novel, set in 1999 London, follows the exploits of Nicola Six, who has the "knack of knowing what will happen next, and what is going to happen on the morning of November the Sixth—her thirty-fifth birthday—is her own murder. One day she walks into a pub where the palely loitering aristocrat Guy Clinch and the [drunken] tabloid dartsman Keith Talent are separately drinking (as is our narrator, a terminally ill American) and recognizes her future murderer. For the rest of the book she manipulates Guy (through a parody of love) and Keith (through a parody of sex) to bring about the end she requires." Times Lit Suppl

"Amis's technical virtuosity is extraordinary. . . . [This is] the most intellectually interesting fiction of the year, and a work beyond the reach of any British contemporary. Amis's figures, like those of Dickens, are caricatures that have their own gigantic reality." London Rev Books

Time's arrow; or, The nature of the offense. Harmony Bks. 1991 168p $18

ISBN 0-517-58515-4   LC 91-4144

This novel "shoots us into the past as it reveals the true identity of a man called Tod Friendly. As Tod lies in a hospital bed, his consciousness distances itself from the present and assesses his life in reverse, like a film run backwards. Every action is reversed and every conversation inverted. This voice, this estranged soul, watches Tod create food and beverages at meals, get paid for bringing items into stores, and grow younger. As his American identity is stripped away, his hideous past as a German doctor and executioner at a Nazi extermination camp is revealed." Booklist

"With Time's Arrow, Amis takes another look at our diseased world. This time he pares the story down to essentials. Though his writing is as fizzy as ever, it doesn't call attention to itself. His artfully contrived structure serves a purpose: to present the horror in a way so unfamiliar it can't be anesthetized." Voice Lit Suppl

Anatoli, A., 1929-

Babi Yar; a document in the form of a novel; [by] A. Anatoli (Kuznetsov). Translated by David Floyd. Farrar, Straus & Giroux 1970 477p o.p. Bentley reprint available $30 (ISBN 0-8376-0432-X)

Original Russian edition published 1966 in censored form under author's former name A. Kuznetsov; English translation by Jacob Guralsky of this version published 1967 by Dial Press

A documentary novel about the period from 1941 to 1943 in which the Germans systematically murdered some 2,000,000 people, including 50,000 Jews, at the ravine on the outskirts of Kiev known as Babi Yar. The author, who was twelve years old at the time, based his work on interviews, newspaper clippings, diaries and other documents

Andersen Nexø, Martin, 1869-1954

Pelle the conqueror: v1 Childhood; translated from the Danish by Steven T. Murray; edited and with an afterword by Tiina Nunnally. Fjord Press 1989 244p $19.95

ISBN 0-940242-41-9   LC 89-7837

"The first of a four-volume Danish classic follows the fortunes of Lasse Karlsson, an impoverished, aging Swede, and his young son, Pelle. Attracted by legendary prosperity . . . they migrate to Denmark in the late 19th century." Publ Wkly

"Andersen Nexo, who was born in the slums of Copenhagen, ultimately developed Pelle into a proletarian epic hero. In this first, largely autobiographical volume, however, there's scant evidence of his strict social realism. Rather, Andersen Nexo's robust sense of life, his convincing evocation of childhood, his moral vision—and, above all, his brave young hero—make this novel generous and grand." N Y Times Book Rev

Pelle the conqueror: v2 Apprenticeship; translated from the Danish by Steven T. Murray & Tiina Nunnally; with an afterword by Niels Ingwersen. Fjord Press 1991 224p $19.95

ISBN 0-940242-49-4

In this volume "Pelle begins the journey the European proletariat undertook when the modern capitalistic society was formed; he goes from rural misery and poverty to the same or worse in an urban setting. As a shoemaker's apprentice in the nearest town, he retains some ties with the past but grows into adolescence in a milieu of different values and new people, establishing solidarity with the poorest. . . . With his faults and virtues, endurance and optimism, Pelle is one of literature's most charming heroes." Libr J

Anderson, Poul, 1926-

Goat song

In The Hugo winners v3 p330-64

Harvest of stars. TOR Bks. 1993 395p $22.95

ISBN 0-312-85277-0   LC 93-15627

Anderson, Poul, 1926-—_Continued_
"A Tom Doherty Associates book"
In this first title of the author's future history series
"North America is dominated by the Avantist police
state, while space is ruled by the vast Fireball corpora-
tion. Founded by entrepreneur Anson Guthrie, Fireball
is devoted to a nearly libertarian ideal of individual
freedom and laissez-faire economics, the antithesis of the
Avantist policy. The original Guthrie is long dead, but
his mind, downloaded into a computer, lives on to direct
Fireball. When the Avantists capture a second copy of
Guthrie, . . . they have the power to destroy Fireball."
Publ Wkly
Followed by The stars are also fire

Harvest the fire. TOR Bks. 1995 190p
$18.95

ISBN 0-312-85943-0   LC 95-30304

In this third title of the author's future history series
"a poet and a revolutionary find themselves in the midst
of a conspiracy to liberate the human spirit from the
benevolent but stifling patronage of the machine intelligence: Teramind. . . . Deceptive in its brevity and
simplicity, this gemlike story of passion and the poetic
soul belongs in most sf collections." Libr J

Hunter's moon

_In_ The Hugo winners v4 p510-50

The longest voyage

_In_ The Hugo winners v1 p279-310

_In_ Modern classic short novels of
science fiction p65-93

Operation Chaos. Doubleday 1971 232p
o.p.

"Doubleday science fiction"
"This is a fast-moving science fantasy, set in a 'world
of if' where magic has been scientifically developed along
with laws of physical science. Steve Matuchek is a
werewolf using his talent for army intelligence in a
strange World War II, and Ginny Graylock is a witch
he meets on a commando raid. The four sections of
the novel carry them forward to a present in which the
cold war is a struggle directly with hell, and irresponsible
use of magic by student protestors threatens to turn
chaos loose in the world. The story is well developed
within its postulates, and has as much hard-boiled
physical action as wand-waving." Libr J

Orion shall rise. Timescape Bks. 1983
463p o.p.

LC 82-19338

"How would earth's reemerging societies change, adapt
and interact many generations after a nuclear armageddon? In his conception of how earthly society might
evolve, Poul Anderson presents a heterogeneous world,
some cultures far more advanced than ours and some
a hundred years behind. The Maurai, a people seen in
previous Anderson novels, are the stewards of a large
part of earth, and their rules and regulations serve to
conserve scarce energy, inhibit pollution and preserve the
ecosystem. This control is insulting to the Norrmen, who
wish to elevate their quality of life and status through
nuclear technology, forbidden by the Maurai. . . . [A
coup among the sky-based] Aerogens, protectors of a
large domain which was once Europe . . . delivers the
novel's hero, Talence Iern Ferlay, to the ground, where

he quickly becomes involved with the Norrmen and
Maurai." Best Sellers

The Queen of Air and Darkness

_In_ The Hugo winners v3 p143-90

The Saturn game

_In_ The Hugo winners v5 p269-325

The sharing of flesh

_In_ The Hugo winners v2 p558-94

The shield of time. TOR Bks. 1990 359p
o.p.

LC 90-38891

"This is Anderson's first full-length novel about the
Time Patrol, a futuristic group of time travelers whose
task it is to control the past in order to preserve their
own future. Like many science fiction concepts of the
previous generation, this one's beginning to show its age.
But Anderson has done a good job delineating his two
protagonists, a Time Patrolman from the future and a
contemporary California woman; his abiding love for history carries the rest of the story's weight." Booklist

Star of the sea

_In_ Anderson, P. The Time Patrol
p291-398

The stars are also fire. TOR Bks. 1994
413p $22.95

ISBN 0-312-85534-6   LC 94-7020

"A Tom Doherty Associates book"
In this second title in the author's future history series
"human governments labor to construct a habitat in
space that will enable Earth's population to exploit the
mineral resources of its moon [while] a small group of
Lunarians, genetically altered for survival in low gravity,
search the past to find a way to preserve their way of
life and their independence. Spanning 500 years, Anderson's . . . novel offers a tale of dynastic intrigue and
high adventure as two distinct visions of human destiny
struggle for ascendancy." Libr J
Followed by Harvest the fire

Tau Zero. Doubleday 1970 208p o.p.
"A malfunctioning starship continues to accelerate as
it nears light speed, and its crew observe relativistic
effects, ultimately being carried beyond the time frame
of the universe, while the cruel circumstances force psychological and interpersonal adaptations. An archetypal
example of hard SF with a visionary element." Anatomy
of Wonder 4

The Time Patrol. TOR Bks. 1991 458p
o.p.

LC 91-21597

"A Tom Doherty Associates book"
This omnibus edition of the author's Time Patrol tales
includes a new novel Star of the sea; the novel The
year of the ransom, first published 1988 by Walker and
the following stories: Time Patrol; Brave to be a king;
Gibraltar Falls; The only game in town; Delenda est;
Ivory, and apes, and peacocks; The sorrow of Odin the
Goth

The year of the ransom

_In_ Anderson, P. The Time Patrol
p399-458

Anderson, Sherwood, 1876-1941

Certain things last; the selected short stories of Sherwood Anderson; edited and introduced by Charles E. Modlin. Four Walls Eight Windows 1992 xxiv, 359p $24.95

ISBN 0-941423-85-9   LC 92-19918

Analyzed in Short story index

"This collection of 30 post-*Winesburg, Ohio* stories includes three previously unpublished and six previously uncollected stories." Libr J

Contents: Certain things last; I want to know why; The other woman; The egg; Brothers; I'm a fool; The man who became a woman; Milk bottles; The man's story; An Ohio pagan; Death in the woods; The return; There she is—she is taking her bath; In a strange town; These mountaineers; A meeting south; The flood; Brother death; In a field; A criminal's Christmas; Virginia justice; The corn planting; Mrs. wife; Pastoral; Not sixteen; Nobody laughed; For what?; The masterpiece; Fred; The red dog

Poor white; a novel. Huebsch, B.W. 1920 371p o.p.

This novel "describes the changes occurring in a Midwestern town when industrialism replaces the old agrarian, craft-centered society. The town itself is the protagonist of the early part of the book, and Anderson successfully depicts its shabbiness, isolation, and sterility. Hugh McVey, the central character, is an introverted inventor who does not become aware until it is too late that his own genius contributes to the corruption of his environment." Reader's Ency

Short stories; edited and with an introduction by Maxwell Geismar. Hill & Wang 1962 289p o.p.

"American century series"

Partially analyzed in Short story index

Stories from "The Triumph of the Egg," "Horses and Men," "Death in the Woods," and "The Sherwood Anderson Reader"

Contents: The dumb man; I want to know why; The other woman; The egg; The man in the brown coat; Brothers; I'm a fool; The triumph of a modern; The man who became a woman; Milk bottles; The sad horn blowers; Death in the woods; There she is—she is taking her bath; The lost novel; Like a queen; In a strange town; These mountaineers; A meeting south; Brother death; The corn planting; Nobody laughed; A part of earth; Morning roll call; The yellow gown; Daughters; White spot; A walk in the moonlight; His chest of drawers; Not sixteen

Tar: a midwest childhood. Boni & Liveright 1926 346p o.p.

Tar is one of the many children born to Dick and Mary Moorehead. Dick is a garrulous, idle, affable fellow, and his wife a darkly beautiful woman, silent but not taciturn. Tar has something of both parents. The story begins when Tar is about four and continues up to early adolescence, describing the incidents in small town life in 19th century Ohio that brought his consciousness to a new focus and marked a new stage in his development

"Unforgettable, and so tenderly told! A childhood well remembered—and yet, one feels the book is not remembrance, but imagination." Boston Transcr

Winesburg, Ohio. Huebsch, B.W. 1919 303p o.p. Amereon reprint available $20.95 (ISBN 0-8488-0417-1)

Analyzed in Short story index

"A series of twenty-three vignettes, *Winesburg, Ohio* is a character study of a small town. It highlights individual residents and scrutinizes who they are and why this reality often conflicts with their dreams. The short stories are linked through George Willard, a young newspaper reporter who is disenchanted with the narrow-mindedness of small towns." Shapiro. Fic for Youth. 3d edition

Andrews, Cecily Isabel Fairfield *See* West, Dame Rebecca, 1892-1983

Andrézel, Pierre, 1885-1962

For works written by this author under other names see Dinesen, Isak, 1885-1962

Andrić, Ivo, 1892-1975

Nobel Prize in literature, 1961

The bridge on the Drina; translated from the Serbo-Croat by Lovett F. Edwards. Macmillan 1959 314p o.p.

The first volume of the Bosnian trilogy; other titles are: Bosnian chronicle (1963) and The woman from Sarajevo (1965)

Original Serbo-Croatian edition, 1945

"This long narrative . . . relates in a series of episodes the history of a bridge near the Bosnian town of Višegrad. That history covers three and a half centuries, through much of which the Bosnians lived under Turkish overlords. This is probably the most important of Andrić's several novels about his native Bosnia." Reader's Ency. 3d edition

Anthony, Evelyn, 1928-

Albatross. Putnam 1983 c1982 239p o.p.
LC 82-20456

First published 1982 in the United Kingdom

"Top agent Davina Graham . . . has ostensibly quit Britain's Secret Intelligence Service for a job in advertising—but this is only a cover for her unauthorized investigation into the identity of a Soviet mole, known as 'Albatross,' apparently infiltrated into the upper echelons of the S.I.S. Suspects, all veteran agents, include Davina's soon-to-retire boss, her brother-in-law and a closet homosexual, and clues are provided by imprisoned KGB agent Peter Harrington, who had caused the death of Davina's Russian defector husband some years before." Publ Wkly

Anne Boleyn. Crowell 1957 310p o.p.

Historical novel, based on the life of Anne Boleyn, the second of the wives of Henry VIII of England. The period covered is from 1526 when Henry met Anne in the garden of her father's castle, to the day of her death on Tower green in 1536

The author "emphasizes Anne's ambition and her vindictiveness so that Anne is not an especially attractive heroine until she gains the reader's sympathies toward the end of the book. . . . A good, straightforward, but not unusual historical novel." Publ Wkly

Anthony, Evelyn, 1928-—*Continued*
The avenue of the dead. Coward, McCann & Geoghegan 1982 288p o.p.

LC 82-1519

First published 1981 in the United Kingdom
"A widowed British agent is summoned from retirement to investigate a former school friend now married to a top U.S. government official. The Russian responsible for her husband's death, now head of the KGB, is running a complex operation to embarrass the new Washington administration by ruining the reputation of the President's closest advisor. The action moves between London, Washington, Moscow, and Mexico as the heroine falls in love with her bodyguard, and the shadows of suspicion move from one character to another." Libr J

"Especially well done are the various inter- and intra-service feuds and rivalries of the three countries. And the exciting ending leaves us with a couple of lovely, ambiguous loose threads." Publ Wkly

The Cardinal and the Queen. Coward-McCann 1968 221p o.p.
Set against the intrigue-ridden glitter of Louis XIII's court, this is the story of the proud, beautiful Anne of Austria, her humiliating marriage to the listless Louis and her passionate affair with Cardinal Richelieu, the King's minister

"The Louvre, Luxembourg Palace, and other royal buildings of seventeenth-century Paris provide much of the authentic background for this historical novel." Booklist

The company of saints. Putnam 1984 c1983 235p $15.95

ISBN 0-399-12895-6   LC 83-23019

First published 1983 in the United Kingdom
"Davina Graham . . . has just been promoted to chief of Anne's Yard, British Intelligence. On holiday with her lover, she is in Venice when the U.S. secretary of defense is killed. Within weeks, the French minister of justice, a British priest and—a stunner—a member of the KGB are also assassinated. Beset by growing mistrust of her lover and the continued hostility of her family, Davina tries to enlist the support of the chiefs of intelligence of the U.S., France and Italy in identifying the killers." Publ Wkly

The Doll's House. HarperCollins Pubs. 1992 271p $20

ISBN 0-06-017981-3   LC 91-58352

Also available Thorndike Press large print edition

"Rosa, an attractive, successful career diplomat recently recruited as a spy, finds herself in over her head on her first mission when she is sent to spy on a group of retired spooks who have set up a school to train terrorists. Harry, a brilliant and equally attractive ex-spy, leads this disenchanted gang." Libr J

"Although it certainly lacks the realism (or realistic feel) of le Carré, Anthony's novel is a swift-paced tale of espionage heavily laced with romance." Booklist

Exposure. HarperCollins Pubs. 1994 c1993 277p $22

ISBN 0-06-017774-8   LC 93-21266

Also available G.K. Hall large print edition

First published 1993 in the United Kingdom
"Julia Hamilton is an aggressive journalist on a top London newspaper whose shrewdly manipulative editor and publisher, Sir William Western, has big plans for her. She is to head an investigative column called 'Exposure,' and her first target is the hugely successful communications tycoon Harold King. . . . As Julia and her boss, Ben Harris (also her lover), travel through Germany and England delving into King's background, they are shaken by the brutal murder of a potential witness and become aware that they themselves are being stalked. . . . Provocative entanglements and some sharply defined politicians and journalists who skirt the edges of decency sustain interest until the finale." Publ Wkly

The house of Vandekar. Putnam 1988 288p o.p.

LC 88-11555

Available G.K. Hall large print edition

"Ashdown, house of the Vandekars, is the stateliest of English homes, its verdant lawns and magnificent facades making it a legend of elegant refinement. But within its vaulting walls, Ashdown reveals its darker aspects: buried desires, deceit, and tortured expiation, played out by three generations of women and the men they love too much." Publisher's note

"Anthony renders her characters' soured romances and dramatic confrontations with compelling realism." Publ Wkly

The Janus imperative. Coward, McCann & Geoghegan 1980 275p o.p.

LC 79-20768

"Political journalist Max Steiner is interviewing a German politician in Paris when the man is assassinated. His dying word is 'Janus.' As a Hitler Youth 25 years earlier, Steiner had heard another dying man utter the same word in Hitler's Berlin bunker in 1945. He persuades his boss to let him do an in-depth story on the assassination and hurries to Germany to dig into Bunker archives for connections between the two Januses. But as he starts interviewing survivors, a terrorist group is proceeding to murder the same survivors. German intelligence and the CIA become involved, and Steiner's quest ends in a convent in Munich, where some unholy violence takes place." Publ Wkly

This novel has "strong, believable characters, clear prose and good description. . . . [The author's] storytelling skills keep the book exciting throughout and deliver a suspenseful climax." West Coast Rev Books

Mission to Malaspiga. Coward, McCann & Geoghegan 1974 320p o.p.
"Katherine Dexter, on the surface, is an ordinary American tourist visiting Florence. As Katherine di Malaspiga Dexter, however, she is an honored visitor to Italy and, as an American cousin, is especially and warmly welcomed to the home of one of Florence's most prestigious families, the Malaspigas. Katherine is genuinely related to this influential family but her visit is no ordinary familial one. She is going as 'Cousin Rose,' a government agent sent to find the drug ring that seems to come from Malaspiga sources. . . . Suspense is well maintained and the plot is fairly tight and compact. The novel is somewhat a mixture of the police procedural mystery and gothic, with the ingredient of foreign entanglement added for the exotic flavor." Best Sellers

The relic. HarperCollins Pubs. 1991 277p $20.95

ISBN 0-06-016101-9   LC 90-55961

Also available G.K. Hall large print edition

Anthony, Evelyn, 1928——*Continued*

"On the death of her Ukrainian émigré father, Lucy Warren is left St. Vladimir's Cross, a priceless relic secretly in his possession. She is to take it to Ukrainian dissident leader Dmitri Volkov, exiled in Geneva. The Cross, ancient symbol of the Czars and Russian Christianity, would be a powerful force in uniting the Ukraine against the Soviet Union. In Geneva, though, Lucy discovers a Volkov worn down by exile and by his wife's clandestine political activities; soon, however, Lucy and Volkov are united by both physical and political passion. Anthony's knack for telling a ripping good story makes this great reading." Libr J

The tamarind seed; a novel. Coward, McCann & Geoghegan 1971 246p o.p.

"Judith Farrow, an attractive young British widow, trying to get over an unfortunate love affair in the Caribbean, meets Feodor Sverdlow, a high-ranking Russian intelligence agent. The pair's quite inadvertent meeting and few days' companionship turns into a 'cause célebre' that rocks Moscow, London, and Washington." Publ Wkly

This "is a clean, unreal, and romantic espionage thriller." Best Sellers

Anthony, Piers

And eternity. Morrow 1990 369p (Incarnations of immortality, bk7) o.p.

LC 89-3418

"Three women (two ghosts and one mortal teenager) join together in a quest that leads them, ultimately, to a replacement for the Incarnation of God, who actually is offstage for the duration of the story. . . . In part, Anthony is using the novel as a platform to speak out on the state of the world—pollution, overpopulation, war, etc.—and about the concepts of good and evil." Booklist

"This grand finale to one of the author's most popular series showcases Anthony's multiple strengths: high humor, appealing characters, serious themes, and a surprising—although, in hindsight, inevitable—conclusion." Libr J

Bearing an hourglass. Ballantine Bks. 1984 293p (Incarnations of immortality, bk2) o.p.

LC 84-3083

"A Del Rey book"

In the second volume of the Incarnations of immortality series, "a grief-stricken Norton assumes the position of the Incarnation of Time but discovers that such a role involves an increasingly deadly duel with Satan." Booklist

"Amid weighty and often convoluted speculations about the nature of good and evil, time and space, and magic and science, Anthony's irrepressible humor asserts itself in unexpected ways." Libr J

Followed by With a tangled skein

Being a green mother. Ballantine Bks. 1987 313p (Incarnations of immortality, bk5) o.p.

LC 87-47742

"A Del Rey book"

In book 5 of the series "a young girl's lifelong pursuit of the 'Llano'—the elusive Song of Nature—leads her to her destiny as the Incarnation of Nature and tricks her into a bargain with the Incarnation of Evil to halt the world's destruction." Libr J

Followed by For love of evil

Blue Adept. Ballantine Bks. 1981 327p il o.p.

LC 80-21754

"A Del Rey book"

In this second book in the Apprentice Adept series "our hero, Stile, is living in both worlds, striving to rise from serf to citizen in one by winning the all-encompassing Game, while he struggles to become a master of magic in the other—through the new Blue Adept. . . . [He] fights a dragon, wins a magic flute, competes in the unicorn olympics and, with the help of his beautiful robot guardian, Sheen, survives in Proton to progress to the Game finals." Publ Wkly

"Although the alteration of fantasy and sf chapters is rather gimmicky, the story maintains its exciting pace with many unexpected twists, and Anthony's humorous touches continue to delight the reader." Libr J

Followed by Juxtaposition

Chaos mode. Putnam 1993 300p $19.95

ISBN 0-399-13893-5   LC 93-3690

"An Ace/Putnam book"

In this third title in the Modes series "Colene has discovered travel on the Virtual Mode, a buffer zone that connects Earth with thousands of alternate realities. With three companions—Darius, Nona and the telepathic horse Seqiro—she meets Burgess, a tentacled being from a world whose evolutionary development differs dramatically from that of Earth. Anthony effectively conveys Burgess's radical otherness through the creature's community-oriented vocabulary." Publ Wkly

For love of evil. Morrow 1988 383p (Incarnations of immortality, bk6) o.p.

LC 88-2975

"Fleeing persecution by the Church, a young sorcerer in medieval France seeks refuge among the Franciscans, dedicating his life to the triumph of good over evil until a strange twist of fate forces him to assume the role of his greatest enemy and take his place among the immortal Incarnations. . . . Anthony tackles sensitive moral issues with his customary high spirits." Libr J

Followed by And eternity

Fractal mode. Putnam 1992 302p o.p.

LC 91-11745

"An Ace/Putnam book"

In this second volume in the Mode series Colene and "her traveling companions continue their trek across the dimensions of reality, they encounter a fractal world where a young woman struggles to change her oppressive society. . . . The author's protagonists are as ingenuous as ever, infusing his story with an innocence that wavers between charming and cloying. His enthusiasm for new ideas, however, is infectious, and his imagination shows no signs of wear." Libr J

Followed by Chaos mode

Isle of woman. TOR Bks. 1993 448p (Geodyssey, v1) $23.95

ISBN 0-312-85564-8   LC 93-25511

"A Tom Doherty Associates book"

In this first volume of the author's Geodyssey series "an archetypal man and woman, joined by their unfulfilled destiny, provide the link in a series of vignettes that explore the panorama of human history. . . . [This] novel is, on one level, a story of reincarnation, as the couple known as Blaze and Ember seek each other through the centuries. On a deeper level, the author identifies those human instincts that at one time guaranteed the species' survival but that now harbor the seeds

Anthony, Piers—_Continued_
of its self-destruction. . . . Well conceived and written
from the heart." Libr J
Followed by Shame of man

Juxtaposition. Ballantine Bks. 1982 358p
il o.p.
LC 81-69507

"A Del Rey book"
In the third book in the Apprentice Adept series, the
hero "Stile achieves his long-sought goal of pluto-cratic
Citizen status on the science-based planet Proton while
further exploring the parallel magic-based world of Phaze,
where he is the Blue Adept. Now, however, the overlapping worlds are drawing apart and unless Stile can overcome the opposition of most of Proton's Citizens and
Phaze's Adepts to correct an imbalance between them,
both worlds could be destroyed. Should he succeed, he
will face the ultimate dilemma of which world to live
in permanently. Fans of this series will find all the action and incidents they've come to expect. . . . Moving
events along a breakneck pace, Anthony efficiently clears
up the mysteries of Stile's life, ties up all the loose ends
and provides a happy ending. Like the first two books,
this is a diverting lightweight science-fantasy adventure."
Publ Wkly
Followed by Out of Phaze

Killobyte. Putnam 1993 304p o.p.
LC 92-16737

"An Ace/Putnam book"
"When paraplegic ex-policeman Walter Toland and
diabetic teenager Baal Curran discover the virtual reality
computer game known as Killobyte, they revel in their
temporary ability to escape their handicaps—until a malicious hacker turns a friendly game into a deadly race
against time. This stand-alone novel by the prolific Anthony features fast-paced action, a pair of engaging
protagonists, and a guided tour through the worlds of
virtual reality." Libr J

On a pale horse. Ballantine Bks. 1983
249p (Incarnations of immortality, bk1) o.p.
LC 83-6043

"A Del Rey book"
In this first volume of the Incarnations of immortality
series "a young man named Zane tries to commit suicide
and winds up killing Death instead, whereupon he has
to take on the job himself. Zane subsequently learns the
responsibilities of his position and deals with an array
of logical complexities." Booklist
Followed by Bearing an hourglass

Out of Phaze. Putnam 1987 288p o.p.
LC 86-25448

"An Ace/Putnam book"
This is the fourth installment in the author's Apprentice Adept series
"The sister worlds of magic-based Phaze and science-
based Proton intersect as a magician's son and a self-
willed machine transfer minds, becoming stranded in
each other's potentially hostile world. . . . [This is] a
tale of adventure and intrigue featuring unicorns, evil
wizards, extraterrestrials, and political tyrants, as well as
two engagingly naîve protagonists." Libr J
Followed by Robot Adept

Phaze doubt. Putnam 1990 303p o.p.
LC 89-24249

"An Ace/Putnam book"
In the concluding volume of the Apprentice Adept
series "the spacefaring Hectare have conquered the planet
and captured its leading citizens. The only Adept left
is Nepe/Flach, the grandchild of Stile and Blue. Following obscure clues from the Oracle, Nepe/Flach must
logically entice a Hectarian spy into switching sides and
helping the loyal underground." Publ Wkly

Robot Adept. Putnam 1988 286p o.p.
LC 87-19148

"An Ace/Putnam book"
In the fifth installment in the author's Apprentice
Adept series "two pairs of star-crossed lovers hold the
fates of magic-based Phaze and its sister-world Proton
in their hands as Adverse Adepts and Contrary Citizens
plot to gain control of an all-knowing computer and its
magical analog. Fans of games, logic problems, and mental conundrums will appreciate the plot permutations that
highlight the adventures of four feisty heroes." Libr J
Followed by Unicorn point

Shame of man. TOR Bks. 1994 380p
(Geodyssey, v2) $23.95
ISBN 0-312-85811-6
LC 94-21747

"A Tom Doherty Associates book"
In this second volume of the Geodyssey series Anthony
"weaves strands that stretch across all human time into
tales that exemplify the changes wrought by evolution
and cultural development. The characters in any one
chapter are reincarnated in the next, so that the main
character here, originally prehuman Hu, becomes Hue
and Hugh and Hu'o and Huu as time and change march
on." Booklist

Split infinity. Ballantine Bks. 1980 372p
il o.p.
LC 79-20282

"A Del Rey book"
In this first volume of the author's Apprentice Adept
series "Stile, the principal character . . . takes his turns
between two parallel worlds. His home world of Proton
is a strictly regulated mechanized society where wealthy
Citizens own serfs who work and compete for them in
the Games. These Games are a central feature of the
novel and range from tiddlywinks to marathon racing.
The fantasy land of Phaze is an organic world into
which he escapes to avoid a mysterious killer. There he
meets a unicorn, . . . who changes into a woman, and
a man who changes into a werewolf, among others. Here
he discovers that he can cast magic spells and sets out
to find his alter ego." Voice Youth Advocates
Followed by Blue Adept

Unicorn point. Putnam 1989 303p $15.95
ISBN 0-399-13433-6
LC 88-18478

"An Ace/Putnam book"
The sixth volume in the author's Apprentice Adept
series witnesses "the parallel wars of wits and politics
on the magical world of Phaze and its technological
sister-world Proton take a bizarre twist as the children
of the Robot Adept Mach and his Phaze-born counterpart Bane play hide-and-seek for keeps to foil the plans
of the Contrary Citizens of Proton and the Adverse
Adepts of Phaze." Libr J
Followed by Phaze doubt

Virtual mode. Putnam 1991 304p o.p.
LC 90-42919

Anthony, Piers—*Continued*

"An Ace/Putnam book"

In this first volume of the author's Mode series "Darius, a Cyng of Hlahtar, had traveled to earth in order to meet his true love, a suicidal teen named Colene, and bring her back to his universe. But in proving to her that other worlds exist, Darius uses up the power of the artifact that would have permitted them to travel, and they must try a slower, more dangerous method: the creation of a four-dimensional universe." Publ Wkly

"Anthony's 'realism' manages to avoid sleaze, and the lighter parts of the narrative, while indeed light, are seldom frivolous. In addition, Anthony's pacing and world building are up to standard." Booklist

Followed by Fractal mode

Wielding a red sword. Ballantine Bks. 1986 297p (Incarnations of immortality, bk4) o.p.

LC 86-7900

"A Del Rey book"

"The fourth book in Anthony's . . . Incarnations of Immortality series describes the recruitment of an Indian prince to become the latest Incarnation of War—serving alongside Death, Time, Nature and others. Mym reluctantly accepts the office as a way to cut through the tangled political web that has produced famine in his homeland and trampled on his private life. As hard as Mym works to keep earthly peace, however, Satan is ahead of him with snares and lures that lead to hell." Publ Wkly

"Anthony is not quite as comfortable with the Indian background or the action scenes as one would wish. Otherwise, this book contains about the best prose and characterization the author has yet produced in a major work." Booklist

Followed by Being a green mother

With a tangled skein. Ballantine Bks. 1985 280p (Incarnations of immortality, bk3) o.p.

LC 85-6179

"A Del Rey book"

In this third volume in the Incarnations of immortality series "the beautiful Irish lass Niobe takes on the duties of one of the three Fates—Clotho, spinner of the thread of life—in order to avenge her dead lover. She finds, however, that she has only begun a duel with the Devil." Booklist

"Much of the fascination of Anthony's book lies in the idea of the Incarnations and their relationship to the world. His universe is meticulously worked out, and the rules are consistently applied. Clotho emerges as a genuinely real and sympathetic woman, and Satan proves to be a compelling deceiver. The story is gripping, and the question of Fate's role in the life of humanity gives the novel an added depth of meaning and interest." Best Sellers

Followed by Wielding a red sword

Appelfeld, Aharon *See* Appelfeld, Aron

Appelfeld, Aron

The age of wonders; [by] Aharon Appelfeld; translated by Dalya Bilu. Godine 1981 270p o.p.

LC 81-47318

Original Hebrew edition, 1978

This novel "tells the story of Bruno A, the son of an assimilated Austrian-Jewish family. In the first part of the novel the A's struggle to carry on as usual while the impending Holocaust daily constricts their lives. . . . In Part 2, a middle-aged Bruno returns to his childhood home, seeking to retrieve what might remain of his past. He finds the village unchanged except that all traces of a formerly large Jewish community have disappeared." Libr J

"In the hands of a writer less subtle and private The Age of Wonders could easily have become a moral fable or a tract. Instead, the tone is plangent, upset, vaguely bewildered; adult lunacy is accepted as just another strange component of vanished childhood, and that, in the end, is far more chilling." N Y Rev Books

Badenheim 1939; [by] Aharon Appelfeld; translated by Dalya Bilu. Godine 1980 148p o.p.

LC 80-66192

Originally published in Hebrew

"Year after year the regular summer guests, most of them comfortably wealthy middle-class Jews, come to the little resort town Badenheim near Vienna to be entertained, to eat strawberry tarts, to find love. Even in 1939, with the Nazis firmly ensconced in Vienna, no one is allowed to worry, and the few who do are declared mad. In the end, Badenheim is closed off; all its people—guests, musicians, pastry chefs, even the dogs and goldfish of the town—are packed into cattle cars. Still the people delude themselves into thinking that they are going 'home,' back to their origins in Poland, and anyone who doubts this is argued down. The novel ends with the closing of the cattle cars' sliding doors." Libr J

"The most shocking thing about this novel is not its satirical humor, but its charm. Appelfeld manages to treat his appalling theme with grace." N Y Rev Books

Katerina; a novel; [by] Aharon Appelfeld; translated by Jeffrey M. Green. Random House 1992 212p o.p.

LC 91-50975

Original Hebrew edition, 1989

This is the "story of Katerina, a Polish housekeeper who works for a succession of Jewish families in the years before WW II. Raised in a culture permeated with virulent anti-Semitism, she must constantly try to overcome the prejudice instilled by her bitter mother, who beat her, and her callous father, who attempted to rape her. One by one, Jewish people who are good to Katerina die: an employer murdered by thugs on Passover; a moody, perfectionistic female pianist. Then her own baby, whom she has raised as a Jew, is snatched from her arms and killed. For knifing her son's murderer, Katerina spends more than 40 years in prison. Other inmates cheer as freight trains take Jews to concentration camps. Released from prison, Katerina lives in a hut on her deceased family's deserted farm and, at age 79, narrates her life story." Publ Wkly

Tzili, the story of a life; [by] Aharon Appelfeld; translated by Dalya Bilu. Dutton 1983 185p o.p.

LC 82-17770

Appelfeld, Aron—_Continued_
Originally published in Hebrew
In this novel, Appelfeld "presents a dull-witted Jewish
girl who inadvertently survives the Holocaust; the scapegoat of her brilliant family, she is left behind when they
flee, and the Polish peasants mistake her for one of the
local prostitute's many daughters." Libr J
"Though it certainly cannot be described as agreeable
reading, Tzili by no means leaves its reader feeling
crushed. Its steadiness of vision and quiet acceptance of
life reduced to an absolute minimum give it, in the end,
a sense of buoyancy the more moving for being apparently effortless." N Y Rev Books

Unto the soul; [by] Aharon Appelfeld;
translated from the Hebrew by Jeffrey M.
Green. Random House 1994 211p $21

ISBN 0-679-40611-5   LC 93-26005

"Caretakers of a mountaintop cemetery consecrated to
Jewish martyrs—the setting is left deliberately vague—
Amalia and her elder brother Gad lead a spartan existence, subsisting on visitors' alms while observing an
age-old covenant to preserve this holy site. Once Gad
seduces Amalia, they succumb repeatedly to an act they
know is sinful, weakened as they are by despair, isolation
and liquor. Through flashbacks we learn how Amalia as
a girl was cruelly beaten by her unloving mother while
her father passively looked on. Her misery extends to
the present when she discovers that she is pregnant by
her brother; predictably, a series of misfortunes
transpires." Publ Wkly
"'Unto the Soul' is one of the most enigmatic of Mr.
Appelfeld's fictions, a story made of shards and fragments, of perplexing gestures and forgotten speech.
Through its broken dialogue and dreamlike scenes, it
sometimes reaches strata of almost mythic feeling. . .
. As an allegory, the novel powerfully evokes the mood
of resignation and waiting for doom." N Y Times Book
Rev

Archer, Jeffrey, 1940-
As the crow flies. HarperCollins Pubs.
1991 617p $22.95

ISBN 0-06-017914-7   LC 90-56105

This novel "tells the story of a poor barrow boy or
street peddler, Charlie Trumper, born in the year 1900
in the slums of London's Whitechapel district. Charlie
. . . rises to become the founder of Britain's first and
most prestigious department store, [and] a member of
the peerage." N Y Times Book Rev
This novel has the "usual Archer signature: fast-moving
plot, romance, high finance, and good natured mockery
of Britain. It uses the conventions of the classic revenge
tale, featuring a feud that continues through two generations and the stock characters of the genre: the resourceful hero, the clever childhood sweetheart, the bastard
son, the nefarious mother. . . . Archer knows what fast-
reading light fiction is all about and dishes it up with
panache." Quill Quire

First among equals. Linden Press/Simon
& Schuster 1984 415p o.p.

LC 84-11267

"Despite radically different family backgrounds and political beliefs, Charles Hampton, Simon Kerslake, and
Raymond Gould all share a fiercely held ambition: to
be prime minister of England. Hampton, the aristocrat,
employs deceit and petty trickery to gain position in
Tory leadership; party archrival Kerslake suffers near
financial ruin in the aftermath of an ill-chosen investment; and Gould, the intellectual Labourite, risks scandal
with his romantic entanglements." Booklist
"Covering their careers from 1964 into the future to
1991, the author manages the labyrinthine British parliamentary system with an adroit hand and generates real
suspense in the race. For there can be only one winner,
and even in the striving each man pays a price. Fast-
paced and satisfying." Libr J

Honor among thieves. HarperCollins Pubs.
1993 381p $23

ISBN 0-06-017945-7   LC 92-56224

In this suspense novel about Saddam Hussein's attempt
to steal the Declaration of Independence "Hamid Al
Obaydi, Hussein's conniving . . . Ambassador to the
United Nations, hires Antonio Cavalli, the ineffably
suave son of a New York Mafia lawyer, to pinch the
parchment. Among the eager participants Cavalli recruits
are an actor who can mimic President Clinton's voice,
a besotted Irish forger, a Hollywood film director convicted of statutory rape and a corrupt Presidential adviser." N Y Times Book Rev
The "deficit in verisimilitude doesn't detract too much
from the novel's entertainment value, ... and some
will be amused that Archer himself good-naturedly joins
in the criticsm." Publ Wkly

Kane & Abel. Simon & Schuster 1980
c1979 540p o.p.

LC 79-23311

First published 1979 in the United Kingdom
A "novel about obsession and ambition. William Kane
is the scion of a wealthy Boston family; Abel Rosnovski
is the illegitimate son of a Polish baron. Both men are
born on the same day in 1906; both are extremely ambitious and intelligent; and both go on—through very different means—to amass great wealth, prestige and power.
This book traces their 60-year rise to the top and the
terrible feud that arises between them." West Coast Rev
Books
"This is a novel of plot. It entertains, as it was meant
to do. . . . It has adventure, war, suspense, surprise,
sex, thwarted young love, and conflict. If things are
manipulated a bit, who cares?" Best Sellers
Followed by The prodigal daughter

A matter of honor. Linden Press/Simon
& Schuster 1986 399p o.p.

LC 86-7405

"Adam Scott is left a most unorthodox bequest in his
father's will that takes him on a terrifying chase across
Europe pursuing a priceless icon and being pursued by
Soviet, American, and British intelligence forces. Archer
cagily impels his well-crafted characters straight into action, then ever so slowly fills in all the dimensions of
the struggle in which they are engaged. . . . Scott's steely
determination to uphold his family's honor holds the
reader's interest, and his skill at eluding the enemy culminates in a master stratagem that gives the story its
final twist. A fast-paced and exciting, though corpse-
riddled, thriller." Booklist

Not a penny more, not a penny less.
Doubleday 1976 230p o.p.

"Harvey Metcalfe, an American entrepreneur with a
continuous string of shady deals to his credit, pulls his
latest one on an assortment of three Englishmen and one
American. These four purchase large numbers of shares

Archer, Jeffrey, 1940-—*Continued*

of stock in Discovery Oil, a bogus company Metcalfe has established. Metcalfe makes a killing, and the four lose a total of a million dollars in the process. . . . One of the four, Stephen Bradley, an American mathematician, decides to contact the others and arrange a counter-swindle. They meet and agree to his plans." Best Sellers

"A jolly good British crime caper, marvelously well plotted, with just the right amounts of romance, wit and savoir-faire, this is fun all the way. Not the least of that fun comes from the knowledge that when the author was a young M.P. he himself was swindled out of a bundle in a trick scheme not unlike the one to which his four stalwart heroes fall victim here." Publ Wkly

The prodigal daughter. Linden Press/Simon & Schuster 1982 464p o.p.

LC 82-15310

"Archer continues the family saga begun in 'Kane & Abel'. The prodigal daughter is Abel's only child and pride of his life. She meets and marries her father's archenemy's only son. This naturally causes a break with both families. However, through her tremendous drive for success, hard work, and good business insight she succeeds in establishing a boutique chain, then reconciled with her father, she heads the hotel empire he started. Later she enters politics, where her honesty and drive lead her eventually to the U.S. presidency." Libr J

A twist in the tale. Simon & Schuster 1988 240p o.p.

LC 88-23250

Analyzed in Short story index

Contents: The perfect murder; Clean sweep Ignatius; A la carte; Not the real thing; Just good friends; The steal; Colonel Bullfrog; Checkmate; Honor among thieves; A chapter of accidents; The loophole; Christina Rosenthal

"True to the collection's title, there is a twist to every tale—a final sentence that sheds a new perspective on the villain or champion. . . . Archer is a keen observer of human behavior and displays that trait to great advantage in these ingenious stories." Booklist

Armstrong, Charlotte, 1905-1969

The Charlotte Armstrong reader; preface by Alice Cromie. Coward-McCann 1970 501p o.p.

The unsuspected, first published 1946, concerns a Hollywood personality who may or may not be a murderer. A dram of poison, first published 1956, combines a chase after a poison bottle and an attempted suicide. The turret room, first published 1965, is a tale of a man accused of being an insane killer, the girl who befriends him, and a strange house

A dram of poison

In Armstrong, C. The Charlotte Armstrong reader p185-341

The gift shop. Coward-McCann 1967 c1966 255p o.p.

A "story about the search for a missing child, the eight-year-old daughter of millionaire Paul Fairchild. A clue to the child's whereabouts is hidden in a gift shop tended by Jean Culiffe, who becomes involved with Paul's son Harry in looking for the child. The frantic chase takes Jean and Harry from Los Angeles to Copenhagen, an Irish castle, and a California ranch as they try to stay ahead of the people who want to use the child to force Paul's governor son to commute a death sentence." Booklist

"You are tough-minded indeed if you can remain unmoved by the exquisite calculation of Miss Armstrong's suspense technique, or by the wonderfully alive people she creates. Credibility gap and all, this is a gem of a thriller." N Y Times Book Rev

The turret room

In Armstrong, C. The Charlotte Armstrong reader p345-501

The unsuspected

In Armstrong, C. The Charlotte Armstrong reader p13-182

Arnow, Harriette Louisa Simpson, 1908-1986

The dollmaker; [by] Harriette Simpson Arnow. University Press of Ky. 1985 c1954 549p $24

ISBN 0-8131-1544-2   LC 85-40073

A reissue of the title first published 1954 by Macmillan

"Gertie Nevels, a courageous and unselfish Kentucky countrywoman who has a talent amounting to a passion for whittling small objects out of wood, is forced by the war to leave the happy, although poverty-stricken, community where she has spent her life and go to Detroit, where her husband has found work in a factory. The meanness, squalor, and lack of privacy of her new surroundings, and the debasing effect of the city on her husband and on some of their children, oppress her, but she maintains her integrity and her fatih in her fellow human beings." New Yorker

"It is hard to believe that anyone who opens its pages will soon forget [Gertie] and her sufferings as traced in Harriette Arnow's long, heavily packed masterwork." NY Times Book Rev

Arteseros, Sally

(comp) American voices. See American voices

Asch, Shalom, 1880-1957

The Apostle; [by] Sholem Asch; translated by Maurice Samuel. Putnam 1943 804p o.p.

"Around the life of St. Paul the author has built a picture of the early spread of Christianity. The novel opens soon after the crucifixion when Paul with others in Jerusalem became aware of the disciples' preachings, and it follows Paul to his death. Religious and social conditions important in the development of Christianity are portrayed, but Paul's work is always the dominant theme." Booklist

In "'The Apostle,' Sholem Asch has written a book which should stand beside 'The Nazarene.' Its erudition, its essential reverence for the two faiths concerned, its scholarly and dramatic portrayal of the Jew who spread the gospel to the gentiles will call forth the respect of every civilized and intelligent reader." N Y Her Trib Books

Asch, Shalom, 1880-1957—*Continued*

Mary; [by] Sholem Asch; translated by Leo Steinberg. Putnam 1949 436p o.p.

This follows the story of the Virgin Mary and her Son from Mary's marriage to Joseph to the Crucifixion and Resurrection

"With the addition of little not inherent in Biblical records, a unique mother-son relationship becomes the basis for a novel of great beauty. From the time when Mary the pure in heart hears heavenly voices proclaiming her as mother of the long promised Messiah, until years later when she beholds Jesus triumphant over death, she experiences all possible maternal pride, humility, anguish. Her early married years comprise most of the book; Jesus' increasing social consciousness, his visions of destiny, and Mary's perplexed awareness are vividly pictured against the background of a devout Jewish home." Libr J

Moses; [by] Sholem Asch; translated by Maurice Samuel. Putnam 1951 505p o.p.

This novel depicts the life of Moses and the Exodus of the Jews from Egypt and their wanderings and sufferings before reaching the Promised Land

"With the deft craftsmanship of a master, Sholem Asch has recaptured the magnificence of Moses and the heroic moment of his epiphany on the pages of Hebrew history. He has assembled . . . facts in the life of the chosen leader of a chosen people, the Orientalia, Scripture, law, customs, traditions, and having assimilated them, he has reassembled them creatively to call to life out of the dusty tomes of the library, a titanic personage, an elect yet human people, an outstanding epoch in the history of man. Here is the historical novel at its literary best." Best Sellers

The Nazarene; by Sholem Asch; translated by Maurice Samuel. Putnam 1939 698p o.p.

A novel based on the life of Christ told from three different points of view. First there is the narrative as a modern Polish Jewish scholar hears it from lips of one who claims to be the reincarnation of the Roman military governor of Jerusalem. Then there is the 'fifth gospel' written by Judas Iscariot, and finally there is the story as the young Jew remembers it when he realizes that he himself is the reincarnation of a disciple of the Pharisee, Rabbi Nicodemon

"Judged purely as a novel, The Nazarene is a superb achievement. Even on the factual side, a work such as Papini's Life is thin beside it. This is because Mr. Asch has taken an infinite amount of trouble to build up an historical background against which the figure of Jesus may move authentically, with that sense of reality which we should expect of fiction as of life." Atlantic

The prophet; [by] Sholem Asch; translated by Arthur Saul Super. Putnam 1955 343p o.p.

This volume tells of the second Isaiah, or Deutero-Isaiah, who supposedly lived during the conquest of Babylon by Cyrus the Persian in the fifth century B.C. At the close of the book the first of the Israelites are about to set out for their homeland

"The story unfolds against a lush . . . background of pagan life in Babylon. All the same, it remains high level fiction of biblical background, about one of the strangest but most inspired of the great prophets of Israel, in her time of troubles." Chicago Sunday Trib

Ashford, Jeffrey, 1926-

For works written by this author under other names see Jeffries, Roderic, 1926-

Ashton-Warner, Sylvia, 1908-1984

Spinster; a novel. Simon & Schuster 1959 c1958 242p o.p.

First published 1958 in the United Kingdom

"An outpost schoolhouse in New Zealand is the setting in which Anna Vorontosov meets with compassion, humor and brilliance the multiple difficulties of teaching seventy small children, most of whom are Maori, and struggles too with the problems of spinsterhood, a young teacher and an old love." Publ Wkly

"Reminiscent in many ways of Margaret Landon's story of Anna Leonowens and the King of Siam, Mrs. Ashton-Warner's account . . . is as delightful, certainly funnier and, at the same time, deeply poetic and strikingly apropos." N Y Times Book Rev

Asimov, Isaac, 1920-1992

The best science fiction of Isaac Asimov. Doubleday 1986 320p o.p.

LC 85-31200

Partially analyzed in Short story index

Includes the following stories: All the troubles of the world; A loint of paw; The dead past; Death of a Foy; Dreaming is a private thing; Dreamworld; Eyes do more than see; The feeling of power; Flies; Found; Franchise; The fun they had; How it happened; I'm in Marsport without Hilda; The immortal bard; It's such a beautiful day; Jokester; The last answer; The last question; My son, the physicist; Obituary; Spell my name with an S; Strikebreaker; Sure thing; The ugly little boy; Unto the fourth generation

This collection contains "28 pieces, including two comic poems . . . and six short-shorts. . . . These selections date mostly from the '50s, the period in which Asimov [was] beginning to explore a variety of ideas and story types." Publ Wkly

The Bicentennial Man

In Asimov, I. The complete robot

In Asimov, I. The complete stories v2

In The Hugo winners v4 p259-99

The caves of steel

In Asimov, I. The rest of the robots p165-362

The complete robot. Doubleday 1982 557p o.p.

LC 81-43134

Analyzed in Short story index

Contents: A boy's best friend; Sally; Someday; Point of view; Think; True love; Robot AL-76 goes astray; Victory unintentional; Stranger in paradise; Light verse; Segregationist; Robbie; Let's get together; Mirror image; The tercentenary incident; First law; Runaround; Reason; Catch that rabbit; Liar; Satisfaction guaranteed; Lenny; Galley slave; Little lost robot; Risk, Escape; Evidence; The evitable conflict; Feminine intuition; . . . That thou art mindful of him; The Bicentennial Man [novelette]

"This massive volume contains 31 of Asimov's robot stories, from 'Robbie' of 1940 to the Hugo and Nebula award-winning 'Bicentennial Man' of 1976. It is far and away the best available single presentation of Asimov's

Asimov, Isaac, 1920-1992—*Continued*

concepts of the robot, which have influenced not only science fiction but to some extent actual thinking about industrial robots." Booklist

The complete stories. Doubleday 1990-1992 2v o.p   LC 90-3136

Volume one published originally in hardcover; v2 in paperback

"A Foundation book"

Analyzed in Short story index

Contents: v1 The dead past; Franchise; Gimmicks three; Kid stuff; The watery place; Living space; The message; Satisfaction guaranteed; Hell-fire; The last trump; The fun they had; Jokester; The Immortal Bard; Someday; Dreaming is a private thing; Profession; The feeling of power; The dying night; I'm in Marsport without Hilda; The gentle vultures; All the troubles of the world; Spell my name with an S; The last question; The ugly little boy; Nightfall; Green patches; Hostess; "Breeds there a man . . . ?"; C-chute; "In a good cause—"; What if—; Sally; Flies; "Nobody here but—"; It's such a beautiful day; Strikebreaker; Insert knob A in hole B; The up-to-date sorcerer; Unto the fourth generation; What is this thing called love?; The machine that won the war; My son, the physicist; Eyes do more than see; Segregationist

v2 Not final!; The hazing; Death sentence; Blind alley; Evidence; The Red Queen's race; Day of the hunters; The deep; The Martian way; The monkey's finger; The singing bell; The talking stone; Each an explorer; Let's get together; Pâté de foie gras; Galley slave; Lenny; A loint of paw; A statue for father; Anniversary; Obituary; Rain, rain, go away; Star light; Founding father; The key; The billiard ball; Exile to hell; Key item; Feminine intuition; The greatest asset; Mirror image; Take a match; Light verse; Stranger in paradise; That thou are mindful of him; The life and times of Multivac; The Bicentennial Man [novelette]; Marching in; Old-fashioned; The Tercentenary incident

Fantastic voyage; a novel; based on the screenplay by Harry Kleiner from the original story by Otto Klement and Joy Lewis Bixby. Houghton Mifflin 1966 239p o.p

"Five people are sent on a rescue mission in a submarine, but this is no ordinary submarine moving through an ordinary sea. The people and the submarine are miniaturized. They are moving through a man's blood vessels to reach and break up a blood clot in his brain. The miniaturization will not last—they have only 60 minutes to do the job and leave the man's body, before they return to ordinary size." Publ Wkly

A "highly entertaining fantasy. Nobody dies but the villian. The characters are pretty much the stock types of gender." Best Sellers

Fantastic voyage II; destination brain. Doubleday 1987 332p o.p   LC 87-5334

"Contrary to what the title might suggest, this is not a sequel to *Fantastic Voyage* but Asimov's endeavor to write his own story (as *Fantastic Voyage* was a novelization of the movie and not completely Asimov's work)." Voice Youth Advocates

"The story concerns Albert Jonas Morrison, a 21st century neurophysicist, and otherwise an ordinary and unheroic man, who is kidnapped and taken to the Soviet Union. A major Soviet scientist, Pyotr Shapirov, is in an irreversible coma, and . . . Morrison goes cold with

fear because the plan calls for him to be miniaturized— along with four Soviet scientists—to sub-molecular size, introducing them into Shapirov's body and, ultimately, into his brain. The snappish relationships between the scientists is wryly depicted, and the mission itself makes fascinating reading as both an action adventure and an intellectually stimulating premise." Publ Wkly

Forward the Foundation. Doubleday 1993 415p $23.50

ISBN 0-385-24793-1   LC 92-46655

"A Foundation book"

This volume and Prelude to Foundation predate the other Foundation novels in terms of internal chronology

"As a galactic empire struggles to hold onto the million worlds it purports to rule, one man conceives of an idea that will preserve human knowledge during the dark ages that will follow the empire's inevitable fall. The man is Hari Seldon. His idea: psychohistory." Libr J

Although "Asimov leans rather heavily on dialogue to carry the story, we are privileged to learn something more of Seldon, whom Asimov regards as his alter ego— intellectually vigorous, witty, vulnerable, and deeply concerned about the fate of his fallible species." Christ Sci Monit

Foundation. Gnome Press 1951 255p o.p.

The first volume in the author's Foundation series

"A story of a Galactic Empire of the future, and its successor in the government of the Milky Way." Publ Wkly

Followed by Foundation and empire

Foundation and earth. Doubleday 1986 356p $16.95

ISBN 0-385-23312-4   LC 86-2130

In the fifth novel of the Foundation series "Golan Trevize rejects the vaunted Selden Plan of Foundation and Empire in favor of a bold experiment in galactic unity. To ferret out the reason for his instinctive decision, Trevize embarks on a journey through uncharted space in search of a legendary planet known as Earth. Asimov's latest entry in his epic series features his usual cast of intelligent, likeable characters and just enough action to give substance to this novel of lucid speculations." Libr J

Foundation and empire. Gnome Press 1952 247p o.p.

In this second volume of the Foundation series "two groups struggle for control of the world's destiny in a future time when mankind has settled in the Milky Way. Then a mutant appears bringing with him a new threat for everyone." Chicago Public Libr

Followed by Second Foundation

Foundation's edge. Doubleday 1982 366p $14.95

ISBN 0-385-17725-9

The fourth novel in the Foundation series "shows us the Seldon Plan at midpoint and still surprisingly on target in spite of the passage of time and unforeseen events. The focus has narrowed to power struggles between the Foundations, both wishing to be the controlling element in the planned Second Galactic Empire, quite unlike Seldon's idealistic vision. And new players have been introduced into the game." Libr J

Followed by Foundation and earth

Asimov, Isaac, 1920-1992—*Continued*

The gods themselves. Doubleday 1972 288p o.p.

"A three-level tale of the 21st century. The first level is told from the point of view of the Earth Scientists who are receiving mysterious messages from the para-Universe that matches Earth's in some unfathomable realm of time and space. The messages have to do with the Electron Pump that transfers matter back and forth between the two Universes. The second level of the story is told from viewpoints of the nonhumans in the 'other' Universe, where the messages are coming from. The third level is many years later at a time when scientists on a moon colony are grappling with the problems of the two Universes." Publ Wkly

"Imagination is the fount of Isaac Asimov's mastery. The suspense he generates . . . is low-key and subtle, and he has a gifted knack for making wild and indescribable superbeings (for he never quite describes them) seem lifelike, though scarcely human." Best Sellers

(ed) The Hugo winners. See The Hugo winners

I, robot. Gnome Press 1950 253p o.p.

Analyzed in Short story index

The book contains nine related science fiction stories about robots: Robbie; Runaround; Reason; Catch that rabbit; Liar; Little lost robot; Escape; Evidence; The evitable conflict

The naked sun

In Asimov, I. The rest of the robots

Nemesis. Doubleday 1989 364p $18.95

ISBN 0-385-24792-3   LC 89-32938

"A Foundation book"

"Using a primitive interstellar drive, an orbital colony reaches a newly discovered nearby star, only to find that it is on a collision course with the Solar System. The leader of the colony, determined to create a utopia, is opposed to doing anything to warn Earth, which, having discovered its own peril, is racing to build a much-improved starship. The scientific problems and characters are both well developed, and the pace is brisk throughout." Booklist

Nightfall; [by] Isaac Asimov and Robert Silverberg. Doubleday 1990 339p o.p.

LC 90-32469

"A Foundation book"

"Science and religion form an uneasy and fractious alliance on the planet Kalgash when a group of astronomers and a cult of religious fanatics predict the inevitable coming of darkness to a world that has never known night. Based on Asimov's short story 'Nightfall,' this joint venture by two of sf's most revered veterans focuses less on characterization than on the exploration of the human psyche's ability to cope with the imminent destruction of civilization." Libr J

Nightfall, and other stories. Doubleday 1969 343p o.p.

"Doubleday science fiction"

Analyzed in Short story index

Contents: Nightfall; Green patches; Hostess; Breeds there a man . . .; C-chute; In a good cause—; What if—; Sally; Flies; Nodody here but—; It's such a beautiful day; Strikebreaker; Insert knob A in hole B; The up-to-date sorcerer; Unto the fourth generation; What is this thing called love?; The machine that won the war;

My son, the physicist; Eyes do more than see; Segregationist

The positronic man; by Isaac Asimov and Robert Silverberg. Doubleday 1993 259p $23.95

ISBN 0-385-26342-2   LC 93-15148

This is an extended version of Asimov's The Bicentennial Man

"A Foundation book"

"Arriving at the home of the wealthy Martin family as a common housekeeping robot . . . NDR-113, otherwise known as Andrew, soon reveals extraordinary artistic abilities arising from his experimental positronic brain. As Andrew outlasts his mortal patrons, his abilities and self-awareness expand, leading him first upon a quest to become the world's first free robot, then to 'upgrading' himself with his own invented human protheses, and finally to being declared fully human. More than a modernized version of *Pinocchio*, this explores, with clarity and tragicomedy, the full range of philosophical problems involved in drawing the line between human and robot." Booklist

Prelude to Foundation. Doubleday 1988 403p $18.95

ISBN 0-385-23313-2   LC 87-33086

"A Foundation book"

This novel and Forward the Foundation are set chronologically prior to other volumes in the Foundation series

"On Trantor, capital world of the Empire, the 32-year-old Seldon, a mathematician of promise who knows nothing of history or politics, attracts the unwelcome attention of the Imperial Government with his speculations about the predictive power of his equations. Before the Imperials can turn the new tool of psychohistory to their own purposes, a journalist named Chetter Hummin helps Seldon disappear into the cultural maze of Trantor—an experience that provides the naïve academic with an education in human diversity and duplicity." N Y Times Book Rev

This "is vintage Asimov, a novel that places ideas ahead of all its other elements but doesn't stint on characterization or entertaining plot lines. It also contains a fair number of mysteries, and . . . all of this is handled in a simple, direct style that never gets between the reader and the story." West Coast Rev Books

The rest of the robots. Doubleday 1964 556p o.p.

"Doubleday science fiction"

Analyzed in Short story index

Contains two science-fiction mystery novels featuring Elijah Baley: The caves of steel and The naked sun, first published 1954 and 1957 respectively

Short stories included are: Robot AL-76 goes astray; Victory unintentional; First Law; Let's get together; Satisfaction guaranteed; Risk; Lenny; Galley slave

Robot visions; illustrations by Ralph McQuarrie. New Am. Lib. 1990 482p il o.p.

LC 90-60121

"A Byron Priess Visual Publications, Inc. book. A ROC book"

Analyzed in Short story index

Stories included are: Robot visions; Too bad!; Robbie; Reason; Liar!; Runaround; Evidence; Little lost robot; The evitable conflict; Feminine intuition; The Bicentennial Man; Someday; Think!; Segregationist; Mirror image; Lenny; Galley slave; Christmas without Rodney

Asimov, Isaac, 1920-1992—*Continued*

Robots and empire. Doubleday 1985 383p o.p.

This "novel opens nearly two centuries after the close of . . . 'Robots of Dawn'. Earth has resumed interstellar colonization on a grand scale, and the Settler worlds are increasingly seen by the roboticized Spacer societies as a deadly threat. Gladia, heroine of 'Robots of Dawn,' must leave Aurora and travel the Galaxy with a descendant of Elijah Baley and the two robots Giskard and R. Daneel Olivaw in order to defeat a plot against Earth." Booklist

This novel "provides a link between Mr. Asimov's well-known Robot stories and his even better-known stories about the fall of the Galactic Empire and the rise of the Foundations that vie for dominance in the Post-Imperial galaxy. . . . Not only has Mr. Asimov once again turned an ethical dilemma into the basis of an exciting novel of suspense, but he has included within the body of the text all the information that readers unfamiliar with his previous books must know in order to follow the action and to appreciate the dilemma." NY Times Book Rev

The robots of dawn. Doubleday 1983 419p o.p.

Another of the author's novels featuring Interstellar police detective Elijah Baley, who is "coerced into solving a crime on alien territory that no one else has been able to crack. Here he takes on not only an unusual case but also a politically charged, hostile environment. However, Baley is by no means a superhero. Asimov has created an ordinary man with middle-class aspirations and mundane concerns. His foibles contrast with the flawless behavior of the numerous robots in the story." SLJ

The author's "narrative technique is more dependent than ever on dialogue, but his plotting is as ingenious as always. The mystery unravels with the polished, logical precision of a robot's program; but even with all the clues at hand, few will beat Baley, and Asimov, to the punch." Publ Wkly

Second Foundation. Gnome Press 1953 210p o.p.

Third book of the Foundation series about the efforts of a group of scientists who are trying to subdue the chaos and conflict of the galactic world. The story centers on fourteen-year-old Arkady Darrell's search for this secret group

Followed by Foundation's edge

Atheling, William, Jr. *See* Blish, James, 1921-1975

Atkins, Jack *See* Harris, Mark, 1922-

Attebery, Brian, 1951-

(ed) The Norton book of science fiction. See The Norton book of science fiction

Atwood, Margaret, 1939-

Bluebeard's egg and other stories. Houghton Mifflin 1986 281p o.p.

LC 86-10336

Analyzed in Short story index

Contents: Significant moments in the life of my mother; Hurricane Hazel; Loulou; Uglypuss; Two stories about Emma; Bluebeard's egg; Spring song of the frogs; Scarlet ibis; The salt garden; In search of the rattlesnake plantain; The sunrise; Unearthing suite

"As Atwood's attitude ranges from the hilarious to the shocking, the reader is introduced to a series of relationships—husband and wife, parent and child, man and woman—in which the characters' inner and outer worlds are beautifully probed, expressed in the author's understated style." Booklist

Bodily harm. Simon & Schuster 1982 266p o.p. Ultramarine reprint available $25 (ISBN 0-671-44153-1)

LC 81-18370

"Renata (Rennie) Wilford, an attractive middle-aged woman journalist, author of fashion, travel and trivia articles for various Toronto 'lifestyle' magazines, abruptly loses part of a breast to cancer, breaks-up with her lover, and goes on a working holiday to a remote Caribbean island in the hope of restoring the 'normal' to her life." Can Forum

"Though this story gets off to a slow start, there is nothing gratuitous here. Margaret Atwood has . . . created a sophisticated, superbly orchestrated allegorical novel. Her characteristically introspective style is greatly enhanced by an unusually cohesive plot and a political theme that manages to steer clear of didacticism. Bodily Harm is Atwood's richest, most fully realized work to date." Saturday Rev

Cat's eye. Doubleday 1989 c1988 446p $18.95

ISBN 0-385-26007-5   LC 88-24345

Also available G.K. Hall large print edition

First published 1988 in Canada

Elaine Risley, the narrator of this novel, "is a Canadian painter of some renown who, at 50, has returned to her childhood city of Toronto for a retrospective of her work. The dull, provincial city of her youth has become world class in the intervening years . . . but in the week she is there her interest in the city's new galleries and restaurants and shops and, in many ways, in the retrospective itself, is only glancing. Her focus, and the novel's, is all on the past, on those images that surface unexpectedly, relentlessly, amid the glitz of the transformed city, images of the dead, of a lost time, and of Cordelia, her childhood friend and tormentor, her double." N Y Times Book Rev

"Atwood's achievement is the decoding of childhood's secrets, and the creation of a flawed and haunting work of art." Time

Dancing girls and other stories. Simon & Schuster 1982 c1977 240p o.p.

LC 82-10308

Analyzed in Short story index

First published 1977 in Canada

Contents: The man from Mars; Betty; Polarities; Under glass; The grave of the famous poet; Hair jewellery; When it happens; A travel piece; The resplendent Quetzal; Training; Lives of the poets; Dancing girls; The sin eater; Giving birth

"All the pieces in this collection offer solid, easily graspable plots, mostly about love relationships. Atwood maintains a steady, low-key pace throughout. No story shines above the rest; all are of high quality and should be attractive even to readers not ordinarily comfortable with the short-story genre." Booklist

Atwood, Margaret, 1939——*Continued*

The handmaid's tale. Houghton Mifflin 1986 311p $18.95

ISBN 0-395-40425-8   LC 85-21944

Also available G.K. Hall large print edition

"Dystopian novel of a world ruled by militaristic fundamentalism in which sexual pleasure is forbidden. Conception and childbirth have become difficult and the handmaid of the title belongs to a specialist breeding stock. The story is annotated by a historian in a further future, whose shape is not revealed." Anatomy of Wonder 4

"A gripping suspense tale, The Handmaid's Tale is an allegory of what results from a politics based on misogyny, racism, and anti-Semitism. What makes the novel so terrifying is that Gilead both is and is not the world we know." Ms

Lady Oracle. Simon & Schuster 1976 345p o.p.

"The heroine, after her staged death by drowning, hides out alone in Rome. A miserable bundle of low self-esteem, she reviews her life to that point. Her several selves—former fat girl, present thin one, secret author of gothic novels, wife of one man, lover of another— each nurtured privately, are jostling for open exposure." Booklist

"The novel ends on an ambiguously affirmative note, as Atwood undercuts the terror she has wrought, suggesting that the dark fears we hold are perhaps less painful than we imagine: the gothic fiend reaching out for our throats is only a curious reporter hunting for a story. The novel thus tests the conventions by which we order reality. Atwood's versatility and maturity show in this novel, which confirms once again the excellence of her craftsmanship." Choice

Life before man. Simon & Schuster 1980 317p o.p.

          LC 79-20281

This novel set in Toronto in the mid-1970's is "about the entangled relationship of three characters: Elizabeth, aggressive and intimidating, mourning the suicide of her lover; Nate, her husband, helpless within and without the marriage, and Lesje, whose work with fossils at the museum is more absorbing and safer than the present, than her affair with Nate." Libr J

This "is a powerful, introspective view of contemporary marriage and the changing roles of the sexes. . . . [This novel] returns to the survival and identity theme of Atwood's early thematic guide to Canadian literature, but at a level that transcends the national. With men and mores rooted in the prehistoric past, Atwood forces us to confront a harrowing present that anticipates an ecologically and culturally doomed future." Choice

The robber bride. Talese 1993 466p $23.50

ISBN 0-385-26008-3   LC 93-24267

This novel "opens on Tuesday, October 23, 1990. . . . Three middle-aged Toronto women—Tony, a military historian; Charis, a flower child; and Roz, an entrepreneur—who have been friends since university, are meeting for lunch in a trendy Queen Street restaurant called The Toxique. The seemingly disparate trio are bonded by their mutual hatred and fear of a fourth classmate, the evil marauder Zenia, who has the power to bridge their defences, steal their lovers, and even to come back from the dead." Quill Quire

"The amoral, spiteful, ruthlessly self-interested Zenia is almost too bad to be true, but she represents all the impulses that Tony, Roz and Charis have repudiated or suppressed. Good women, in Ms. Atwood's view are their own enemies, and whether one agrees with her opinion or not, she has written a brilliantly intelligent novel to support it." Atl Mon

Surfacing. Simon & Schuster 1973 c1972 224p o.p.

"The heroine, her lover, Joe and a married couple, David and Anna, travel from the city towards her family cabin on a remote Quebec lake. Their mission is to investigate the disappearance of the heroine's father. . . . When the father remains lost and they decide to stay on at the lake for a week, the underlying strains of their relationships begin to take effect." N Y Times Book Rev

The author's "frightened and deadened characters are in fact, extremely interesting. Foolish victims, empty of creative introspection, victimizing and dehumanizing one another, they are the same people who glibly promote new game plans for sex, education, love and war in the mass of semi-erudite words that pour daily from the media. Atwood reveals them with skill and wit." Can Forum

Wilderness tips. Doubleday 1991 227p $20

ISBN 0-385-42106-0   LC 91-17086

Analyzed in Short story index

Stories included are: True trash; Hairball; Isis in darkness; The bog man; Death by landscape; Uncles; The age of lead; Weight; Wilderness tips; Hack Wednesday

This is a collection of stories "portraying aspects of contemporary Canadian life, which move forward in time, from the first story set in the '50s to the last set in the present, and shift back and forth in space from urban to wilderness scenes." Can Forum

Auchincloss, Louis

The book class. Houghton Mifflin 1984 212p o.p.

          LC 84-522

"In 1908 a group of Park Avenue debutantes begins to meet once a month to discuss books, past and present. 'The Book Class' endures for 64 years, creating a lasting and telling impression on the son of one of its members, the novel's narrator, Christopher Gates. These pampered and seemingly fragile women, whose lives are filled with great passion, disappointment, and tragedy, exude an aura of power and mystery which fascinates Gates and which he probes throughout his life." Libr J

"Auchincloss may work on a small canvas, but no one excels his finely etched portraits of sophisticates of good breeding and inherited wealth." Publ Wkly

The collected stories of Louis Auchincloss. Houghton Mifflin 1994 465p $24.95

ISBN 0-395-71039-1   LC 94-14364

Analyzed in Short story index

Contents: Maud; Greg's peg; The colonel's foundation; The mavericks; The single reader; Billy and the gargoyles; The gemlike flame; The money juggler; The Wagnerians; The prince and the pauper; The prison window; The novelist of manners; In the beauty of the lilies Christ was born across the sea; The Fabbri tape; Portrait of the artist by another; The reckoning; Ares; The stoic; They that have power to hurt

"Prolific without once cheapening his pristine prose or skimping on his modulations of character and careful

Auchincloss, Louis—*Continued*

rendering of their particular brand of dilemmas, Auchincloss has been called one of America's most underrated writers in spite of some early successes. This strong and varied set of 19 stories will do much to correct any such neglect." Booklist

The dark lady. Houghton Mifflin 1977 246p o.p.

LC 77-3666

"A tale of two women allied in a successful assault on wealth, fame and political power. [One] is Elesina Dart, a beauty of good background who has gone through two marriages and flubbed one promising theatrical career. The [other] is Ivy Trask, a cynical, shrewd middle-aged fashion editor and social arbiter at Broadlawns, the Westchester estate of Judge Irving Stein, banker and art collector. . . . In the three decades spanned by the novel—from late Depression to the mid-'50s—[Ivy] salvages Elesina from failure and alcohol, marries her to Irving and the Stein fortune, and finally launches her toward a seat in the House of Representatives. . . . [But] Elesina grows into the job as mistress of Broadlawns and proves more formidable than her Svengali." Time

"The novel's problems lie in unspontaneous characterizations and an extraneous anti-Semitic subtheme. Its plus is the imaginative Shakespearean tie-in worked out with a measure of success." Booklist

The epicurean

In Auchincloss, L. Three lives

Honorable men. Houghton Mifflin 1985 278p o.p.

LC 85-5257

"'Chip' Benedict, Yale '38, married Alida, the debutante of her year, and they had the mandatory two children. But trust funds and connections do not fend off life and the world. When we meet Chip, Alida has decided to leave him; his daughter, a physician, is a lesbian and an anti-war activist; his son evaded the Vietnam draft by fleeing to Sweden; and Chip himself is now a special assistant to the Secretary of State. Vietnam disturbs him and he suffers a troubled conscience over the 'multitudinous sins' of his earlier life." Publ Wkly

"Auchincloss knows his period and social circle well, and he has put that knowledge to good use here with a perceptive character study of a troubled power broker and the private toll he must pay for success." Booklist

The lady of situations. Houghton Mifflin 1990 274p o.p.

LC 89-26883

"The daughter of a financier ruined in the Depression, Natica Chauncey is hungry for the social status her family has lost. She turns entrapping 'situations' to her advantage, three times marrying men she uses for self-advancement and refusing the idle female existence prescribed by society." Publ Wkly

"Once again, Louis Auchincloss has stirred up the rich broth of our literary tradition, presenting us with another stinging critique of American society and its poisonous snobbery. Set in the sheltered world of New York's wealthy upper crust in the 1930's and 40's, 'The Lady of Situations' has much in common with other distinguished novels of manners and mores." N Y Times Book Rev

Portrait in brownstone. Houghton Mifflin 1962 371p o.p.

Set in the first half of the twentieth century this is a novel about a New York City family, the Denisons: Geraldine, a greedy beauty; Ida, her mousy cousin; Derrick, her husband and Ida's lover; and their children, all of whom live behind their brownstone facades, clinging firmly to their family identity in spite of flaring feuds and the cross-currents of generations

"Derrick, Ida and Geraldine are complex, interesting, if not particularly likable people. Derrick may be cool and ruthless, but what a welcome relief to have a hero of a novel who is not a feckless blob but a man of determination who knows exactly what he wants and goes out to get it. When we come to the Hartley children of the present generation, however, the spark seems to have died out, and Mr. Auchincloss cannot make them nearly so interesting. He is at his best when chronicling a vanished way of life." Atlantic

The realist

In Auchincloss, L. Three lives

The Rector of Justin. Houghton Mifflin 1964 341p o.p.

The rector of a New England Episcopal private school, eighty-year-old Dr. Frank Prescott, is seen through the eyes of both admirers and detractors. The principal narrator is Brian Aspinwall, a shy young English master. Others include former students, Prescott's youngest daughter, Cordelia, and his oldest friend, Horace Havistock

"This is not only a passionately interesting, but a spiritually important study of the American character. . . If Mr. Auchincloss had confined his portrait of Dr. Prescott to the gentle brush strokes of Brian Aspinwall . . . we would never have had the blazing totality of the man that emerges from this book. . . . In revealing both the best and the worst of Dr. Francis Prescott, he has created as inspiring a character as any reader could want." N Y Times Book Rev

The stoic

In Auchincloss, L. Three lives

Tales of yesteryear. Houghton Mifflin 1994 230p $21.95

ISBN 0-395-69132-X   LC 93-33757

Also available Thorndike Press large print edition

Analyzed in Short story index

Contents: The man of good will; They that have power to hurt; The lotos eaters; The Renwick steles; The poetaster; "To my beloved wife . . ."; A day and then a night; Priestess and acolyte

"Depicting the lifestyles of America's wealthiest families, Auchincloss probes beneath surface relationships to explore the depths of human passions." Libr J

Three lives. Houghton Mifflin 1993 213p $21.95

ISBN 0-395-65567-6   LC 92-27588

This book contains three novellas about the lives of "three New Yorkers born to wealth around the turn of the century. 'The Epicurean' is Nat Chisolm, whose life is a constant pursuit of the next pleasureful challenge in sport, art, love, or war. 'The Realist' is Alida Vermeule, an intelligent woman who finds a way to exercise power despite early twentieth-century restrictions upon her gender. 'The Stoic' is principled, austere, and virginal investment banker George Manville, who manages to at-

Auchincloss, Louis—*Continued*

tain everything that most satisfies him, including an heir, despite—or because of—the follies and emotional indulgences of those around him. Each novella is as fine an example of the literature of manners as you're likely to find." Booklist

Auel, Jean M.

The Clan of the Cave Bear; a novel. Crown 1980 468p (Earth's children) $19.95

ISBN 0-517-54202-1   LC 80-14581

Also available Thorndike Press large print edition

"Young Cro-Magnon orphan Ayla is adopted into the Neanderthal Clan of the Cave Bear and grows up mothered by medicine woman Iza and protected by magician Creb. However, her different characteristics and abilities bring her into conflict with the clan time and again. Broud, clan-leader's son, is her chief adversary: to him Alya is an intolerable threat to tradition who must be subdued or die." Libr J

"It's subject matter, its vast research . . . make this fictional excursion into prehistory a thing of wonder. But it's an enjoyable story, too, though leisurely and not notable for the quality of its prose. . . . The depiction of how the cave-dwelling Neanderthals lived—how they performed their totemistic rituals, gathered medicinal plants, slew mammoths and other animals—is solid, convincing and sometimes exciting." Publ Wkly

Followed by The Valley of Horses

The Mammoth Hunters. Crown 1985 645p (Earth's children) $19.95

ISBN 0-517-55627-8   LC 85-17503

Also available Thorndike Press large print edition

Sequel to The Valley of Horses

This novel "tells of Ayla and Jondalar's meeting the Mamutoi of the Lion Camp, a hunting people with whom they are invited to dwell. Living for the first time among a group of people like herself brings Ayla many new experiences. She is attracted to the Negroid artist, Ranec, which arouses Jondalar's jealousy. She enjoys the friendship of Deegie, a woman of her own age with whom she shares interests. She evokes both the adulation and resentment of Lion Camp members when her talents for healing and animal training are demonstrated." Best Sellers

"The story is lyric rather than dramatic, and Ayla and her lovers are projections of a romantic rather than a historical imagination, but readers caught up in the charm of Auel's story probably won't care." Publ Wkly

Followed by The plains of passage

The plains of passage. Crown 1990 760p (Earth's children) $24.95

ISBN 0-517-58049-7   LC 90-38330

Sequel to The Mammoth Hunters

"Ayla and Jondalar begin the long journey back to Jondalar's people, the Zeladonii. Along the way, they meet different groups of people, including members of another clan, and discover the true depths of their love for each other. More than just another adventure storyteller, Auel continues to offer a wealth of information about the prehistoric world. Her detailed descriptions of animal and plant life, of tools and tool-making, and of the general life-styles of prehistoric societies provide a relaxed pacing that not only mirrors Ayla's and Jondalar's journey but makes important anthropological information accessible to the general public." Booklist

The Valley of Horses; a novel. Crown 1982 502p (Earth's children) $19.95

ISBN 0-517-54489-X   LC 82-5123

This sequel to The Clan of the Cave Bear "recounts Ayla's three years of solitude in a cave after being pronounced 'dead' by the Neanderthal clan who had raised the Cro-Magnon girl as their own. Her story alternates with that of Jondalar, a handsome young man of immense sex appeal who is journeying with his brother because he can't seem to find himself. After [various] . . . adventures, the brother is killed by Ayla's pet lion, and she brings the wounded Jondalar back to nurse him to health. Ultimately . . . they fall in love. . . . The book ends with their meeting more of their kind while out of their cave." Voice Youth Advocates

Followed by The Mammoth Hunters

Augenbraum, Harold

(ed) Growing up Latino. See Growing up Latino

Austen, Jane, 1775-1817

The complete novels of Jane Austen. Modern Lib. 1983 1364p $22

ISBN 0-394-60436-9   LC 83-5473

First Modern Library edition, 1933

Contents: Sense and sensibility; Pride and prejudice; Mansfield Park; Emma; Northanger Abbey; Persuasion

Emma.

Available from various publishers

First published 1815

"Emma is a pretty girl of sterling character and more will than she can properly manage. She thinks she knows what is best for everybody, and is a prey to many deceptions. She is imposed upon, and imposes upon herself; it is a long while before she sees things as they are, and recognizes where her own happiness lies. Her hero is one of Jane's sober, clear-eyed, and perfect men. The Fairfax and Churchill subplot furnished a comedy of dissimulation contrasting didactically with Emma's honesty. A formidable snob and vulgarian, Mrs. Elton, and a good-natured bore, Miss Bates, who would be insufferable outside these pages, are among the more laughable characters." Baker. Guide to the Best Fic

"Less brilliant than 'Pride and Prejudice.' 'Emma' is equally rich in humor, in the vivid portraiture of character, and a never-ending delight in human absurdities, which the fascinated reader shares from chapter to chapter." Keller. Reader's Dig of Books

also in Austen, J. The complete novels of Jane Austen

Lady Susan. o.p.

First published 1871

"This story consists of letters, written chiefly between the kindly Mrs Vernon and her mother Lady de Courcy, and between Lady Susan and her London friend Mrs Johnson. The events occur mainly at Churchill, the country house of the Vernons. Lady Susan, the widow of Mr Vernon's brother, is beautiful, selfish, and unscrupulous. She has had to leave the house of the Mainwarings, where both Mr Mainwaring and his sister's suitor Sir James Martin have fallen in love with her. At Churchill she meets Reginald de Courcy, Mrs Vernon's brother, young and gullible, who also succumbs to her superficial charms. Lady Susan's 16-year-old

Austen, Jane, 1775-1817—*Continued*
daughter Frederica is terrorized by her mother, and
becomes so distraught when learning of her mother's plan
to marry her off to Sir James Martin that she begs
Reginald de Courcy to intercede for her." Oxford Companion to Engl Lit

Mansfield Park.
Available from Buccaneer Bks.

First published 1814
"Presents a household of young people in love with
the right or the wrong person. Thru the device of marrying off three sisters into different ranks, upper middle-
class distinctions come in for amusing comparisons."
Lenrow. Reader's Guide to Prose Fic
"Her most considerable piece of work, not in mere
dimensions, but in the mastery of a difficult problem.
. . . In truth, nowhere is the difference between true
comedy and satire better exemplified." Baker. Guide to
the Best Fic

also in Austen, J. The complete novels
of Jane Austen

Northanger Abbey. o.p.
First published 1818
"The heroine is a girl in the first innocent bloom of
youth, whose entry into life is attended by the collapse
of many illusions." Lenrow. Reader's Guide to Prose Fic
"Though not published until 1818, this was written
1798-9 and entitled 'Susan', revised in 1803 and sold
for publication; it may perhaps have been rewritten or
touched up later, before it appeared posthumously. Begun
as a parody of sentimentalism and the romantics, it
developed into the genre which was to be peculiarly Jane
Austen's—the portrayal in sober and faithful tints of the
quiet middle-class life she knew; the satire restrained, the
comedy all-pervasive." Baker. Guide to the Best Fic

also in Austen, J. The complete novels
of Jane Austen

Persuasion.
Available from Buccaneer Bks.

First published 1818
"The heroine, Anne Elliott, and her lover, Captain
Wentworth, had been engaged eight years before the story
opens but Anne had broken the engagement in deference
to family and friends. Upon his return he finds her
'wretchedly altered,' but after numerous obstacles have
been overcome, the lovers are happily united." Gerwig.
Handb for Readers and Writers

also in Austen, J. The complete novels
of Jane Austen

Pride and prejudice.
Available from various publishers

First published 1813
"Concerned mainly with the conflict between the prejudice of a young lady and the well-founded though misinterpreted pride of the aristocratic hero. The heroine's
father and mother cope in very different ways with the
problem of marrying off five daughters. A masterpiece
of gentle humor." Good Read
"In spite of little plot, the interest is sustained through
the book. The characters are drawn with humor, delicacy,
and the intimate knowledge of men and women that
Miss Austen always shows." Keller. Reader's Dig of
Books

also in Austen, J. The complete novels
of Jane Austen

Sense and sensibility.
Available from Buccaneer Bks.

First published 1811
"The story tells of two sisters: Elinor, who has sense;
and Marianne, who has sensibility. Their unfortunate
love affairs form the basis of the narrative. Edward Ferrars, with whom Elinor is in love, is entangled with a
sly, avaricious girl, Lucy Steele. His mother, upon learning this, disinherits him. Lucy, being without scruple,
then jilts him for his younger brother, now the heir.
So Edward returns to Elinor, who takes him back.
Marianne's lover, the handsome and dashing John Willoughby, is a heartless rascal. He leaves her and goes
to London. Romantic by nature, she follows him to the
city, but his insolent conduct soon disillusions her. She
then sacrifices her childish and absurd romanticism for
the joys of a sensible marriage with staid, middle-aged
Colonel Brandon." Haydn. Thesaurus of Book Dig
"A study of character and manners in a very delicate,
precise, miniature style; the characters just everyday
people, drawn as they are without exaggeration; the
minute differences of human nature delicately pencilled;
the satire directed against mere commonplace foolishness,
conceit, and vulgarity, rather than vice or eccentricity.
In truth, the social failings and personal foibles are self-
revealed rather than satirized and make spontaneous
comedy." Baker. Guide to the Best Fic

also in Austen, J. The complete novels
of Jane Austen

Auster, Paul, 1947-
In the country of last things. Viking 1987
188p $15.95
ISBN 0-670-81445-8   LC 86-40257
"Imagine an American city in the near future,
populated almost wholly by street dwellers, squatters in
ruined buildings, scavengers for subsistence. Suicide clubs
offer interesting ways to die, for a fee, but the rich have
fled with their jewels, and those who are left survive
on what little cash trade-in centers will give them for
the day's pickings. This . . . dreamlike fable about a
peculiarly recognizable society, now in the throes of entropy, focuses on the plight of a young woman, Anna
Blume." Publ Wkly
This novel "is distinguished by an uncanny grasp of
the day-to-day realities of homelessness. This is a scary
but highly relevant book." Libr J

Leviathan. Viking 1992 275p $21
ISBN 0-670-84676-7   LC 92-1282
The chief protagonist in this story "is a novelist-
journalist named Benjamin Sachs who impressed just
about 'everyone' as brilliant, witty, and talented. At the
beginning of the novel he is blown to scraps while attempting to manufacture a bomb by the side of a snowy
winter road in Wisconsin. How he came to this abrupt,
untimely end is the ostensible topic being investigated
by the imaginary author of the present novel, one Peter
Aaron, who had known Sachs intimately for some fifteen
years." N Y Rev Books
"Mr. Auster may write about coincidence, but there
is nothing coincidental about his prose, in which
seemingly straightforward information has an allegorical
dimension. . . . Thus in the literary looking glass of
'Leviathan,' in which things are not always what they
seem, our pleasure in reading the story is enhanced by
the challenge of making other connections." N Y Times
Book Rev

Auster, Paul, 1947— *Continued*

Mr. Vertigo. Viking 1994 293p $21.95

ISBN 0-670-85209-0   LC 93-34887

"Walt Rawley recounts his life: an orphan born in 1924 with 'the gift,' he was seized by his master, Mr. Yehudi, a Hungarian Jew who taught him to levitate. Yehudi takes the boy from St. Louis to his own Kansas ménage, which consists of Mother Sioux and Aesop, a young black genius. . . . After harsh training, Walt tours with his mentor as 'the Wonder Boy,' aka Mr. Vertigo." Publ Wkly

"'Mr. Vertigo' is not thick with detail; it travels light, though longer meditations might have expanded and enriched its meanings. Nor does the novel test its dream against other perspectives, systems, fantasies. But the story is witty, inventive in its language and invitingly playful with its metaphors." N Y Times Book Rev

Austin, A. J.

(jt. auth) Bova, B. To save the sun

Axton, David, 1945-

For works written by this author under other names see Koontz, Dean R. (Dean Ray), 1945-

B

Babel', I. (Isaac), 1894-1941

The collected stories; edited and translated by Walter Morison; with an introduction by Lionel Trilling. Criterion Bks. 1955 381p o.p.

Partially analyzed in Short story index

"The text of this volume follows that of the 1934 Russian edition of Babel's stories, which included 'Red Cavalry' [first published in the United States 1929 by Knopf], 'Tales of Odessa,' and all but the last five of the group called 'Stories.'" Translator's note

Contents: Crossing into Poland; The church at Novograd; A letter; The Remount Officer; Pan Apolek; Italian sunshine; Gedali; My first goose; The Rabbi; The road to Brody; Discourse on the "Tachanka"; The death of Dolgushov; The Brigade Commander; Sandy the Christ; The life and adventures of Matthew Pavlichenko; The cemetery at Kozin; Prishchepa's vengeance; The story of a horse; Konkin's prisoner; Berestechko; Salt; Evening; Afonka Bida; In St. Valentine's Church; Squadron Commander Trunov; Two Ivans; The story of a horse, continued; The widow; Zamoste; Treason; Chesniki; After the battle; The song; The Rabbi's son; Argamak; The King; How it was done in Odessa; The father; Lyubka the Cossack; The sin of Jesus; The story of my dovecot; First love; The end of St. Hypatius; With Old Man Makhno; You were too trusting, Captain; Karl-Yankel; In the basement; Awakening; The S. S. "Cow-Wheat"; Guy de Maupassant; Oil; Dante Street; The end of the old folks' home; Through the fanlight; The kiss; Line and color; Di Grasso

Red cavalry

In Babel', I. The collected stories p41-200

Babel', Isaac *See* Babel', I. (Isaac), 1894-1941

Babson, Marian

A fool for murder. Walker & Co. 1984 c1983 176p $12.95

ISBN 0-8027-5571-2   LC 83-42731

First published 1983 in the United Kingdom

"When rich, old Sir Wilmer Creighleigh returns to Little Puddleton from an American author's tour with a teenaged bride, his family and heirs are outraged. Conflict, threats, and murder follow." Wilson Libr Bull

This "is a sort of British comedy of manners and is as much novel as mystery. In many respects, it has elements of Agatha Christie—the house party, the assortment of people, the tensions that arise. . . . The book is full of some rather wonderful cattiness." N Y Times Book Rev

Murder at the cat show. St. Martin's Press 1989 192p o.p.

LC 89-30162

"Doug Perkins describes the larky and suspenseful action at the cat show that he and his partner, Gerry Tate, have been hired to publicize. Their efforts are hardly needed, since media people swarm about the exhibit, but then famous Hugo Verrier's golden cat statue goes missing and show-organizer Mrs. Chesne-Malvern is killed." Publ Wkly

"A very lighthearted and pleasurable mystery, filled with cat-loving eccentrics and disdainful felines." Booklist

Nine lives to murder. St. Martin's Press 1994 188p $18.95

ISBN 0-312-10511-8   LC 93-45286

"A Thomas Dunne book"

In this mystery, "Winstanley Fortescue, 'a Titan of the English Stage,' is pushed off a ladder during play rehearsal and lands on Montmorency, the theater cat. By some weird confluence of metaphysical fields, the head-on collision causes a mind-body exchange that sends Monty to the hospital in Win's battered body—and leaves Win prowling around on all fours, in search of his unknown attacker. There seems no end to Ms. Babson's ingenuity as she puts Win through his hilarious paces as a cat." N Y Times Book Rev

Past regret. St. Martin's Press 1992 c1990 180p $16.95

ISBN 0-312-07763-7   LC 92-130

"A Thomas Dunne book"

First published 1990 in the United Kingdom

American Dee Sawyer arrives in London to search for her daughter, an exchange student who has disappeared from university. Dee battles university red tape and police indifference but doggedly persists unaware that she is not the only party interested in her daughter's whereabouts

Shadows in their blood. St. Martin's Press 1993 c1991 189p o.p.

LC 93-22452

"A Thomas Dunne book"

First published 1991 in the United Kingdom

A mystery revolving around a "second-rate *Dracula* remake. Trixie Dolan, the somewhat scatterbrained narrator, and Evangeline Sinclair, her peevish cohort, were once stars of the silver screen; now they're forced to share a suite in a drafty, gloomy English castle that

Babson, Marian—*Continued*

doubles as the vampire flick's set. . . . After a pompous actor is stabbed to death, Trixie and Evangeline themselves are suspected of being immortal bloodsuckers." Publ Wkly

Bachman, Richard *See* King, Stephen, 1947-

Bagley, Desmond, 1923-1983

Night of error. St. Martin's Press 1987 c1984 314p o.p.

LC 86-26225

First published 1984 in the United Kingdom

"Mike Trevelyan, an English oceanographer, learns that his brother has died in suspicious circumstances while prospecting in the South Pacific. When an attempt is made to steal the few effects shipped back to the family he decides to investigate. With a crew of ex-commandos and the backing of a Canadian tycoon an expedition is launched to investigate the death and look for the rich mineral deposits the brother has apparently discovered." Libr J

"Bagley serves up a tense, fast-paced romp in the South Pacific as two ship-loads of men go after each other and the underwater treasure with no holds barred. The explosive climax adds a good twist to the story, which Bagley, typically, tweaks yet again on the last page." Publ Wkly

Bailey, Charles W. (Charles Waldo), 1929-

(jt. auth) Knebel, F. Seven days in May

Bainbridge, Beryl, 1933-

The birthday boys. Carroll & Graf Pubs. 1994 c1991 189p $18.95

ISBN 0-7867-0071-8   LC 94-1264

Also available Thorndike Press large print edition

First published 1991 in the United Kingdom

"The story of Capt. Robert Scott's second expedition is narrated by Scott himself and the four men who perished along with him in the frigid weather and miserable conditions of Antarctica. Beginning with their June 1910 departure from Cardiff on the *Terra Nova*, and ending with the terrible journey by sled back to the ship in March 1912, the five men consecutively recount their journey through an emotional as well as physical landscape." Libr J

"These five monologues, which contain some of the most convincing and slyly revealing first-person narrative I've ever read, span a remarkable range of voices and dispositions, but what they share is a mesmerizing readability. . . . They present us with a microcosmic society of flawed individuals, pushed and pulled even in a frozen wilderness by the subtle dictates of class, personality and ambition." N Y Times Book Rev

Baker, Dorothy, 1907-1968

Young man with a horn. Houghton Mifflin 1938 243p o.p. Amereon reprint available $17.95 (ISBN 0-89244-025-2)

"Rick Martin is not interested in school but is intrigued by music. Learning how to play the jazz trumpet from black musicians, Rick becomes a genius in the art of 'swing' and quickly rises to fame in the Phil Morrison orchestra. The inability to cope with success, as well as

a bad marriage and gin, lead to his fatal end." Shapiro. Fic for Youth. 2d edition

Baldick, Chris

(ed) The Oxford book of gothic tales. See The Oxford book of gothic tales

Baldwin, James, 1924-1987

Another country. Dial Press (NY) 1962 436p o.p.

This novel is set in "New York City and focuses mainly on Harlem society. The death—perhaps suicide—of the main character, Rufus Scott, is representative of the treatment individuals receive in an environment which is essentially hostile and which erects barriers to their desire for love." Camb Guide to Lit in Engl

Giovanni's room; a novel. Dial Press (NY) 1956 248p o.p.

"We meet the narrator, known to us only as David, in the south of France, but most of the story is laid in Paris. It develops as the story of a young American involved both with a woman and with another man, the man being the Giovanni of the title. When a choice has to be made, David chooses the woman, Hella." N Y Times Book Rev

"Mr. Baldwin has taken a very special theme and treated it with great artistry and restraint." Saturday Rev

Go tell it on the mountain. Knopf 1953 303p o.p.

"Based on the author's experiences as a teenaged preacher in a small revivalist church, the novel describes two days and a long night in the life of the Grimes family, particularly the 14-year-old John and his stepfather Gabriel. It is a classic of contemporary African-American literature. Baldwin's description of John's descent into the depths of his young soul was hailed as brilliant, as was his exploration of Gabriel's complex sorrows. The novel teems with biblical references." Merriam-Webster's Ency of Lit

Going to meet the man. Dial Press (NY) 1965 249p o.p.

Analyzed in Short story index

Contents: The rockpile; The outing; The man child; Previous condition; Sonny's blues; This morning, this evening, so soon; Come out the wilderness; Going to meet the man

If Beale Street could talk. Dial Press (NY) 1974 197p o.p.

"Tish, aged 19, and Fonny, 22 years old, are in love and pledged to marry, a decision hastened by Tish's unexpected pregnancy. Fonny is falsely accused of raping a Puerto Rican woman and is sent to prison. The families of the desperate couple search frantically for evidence that will prove his innocence in order to reunite the lovers and provide a safe haven for the expected child." Shapiro. Fic for Youth. 3d edition

Just above my head. Dial Press (NY) 1979 597p o.p.

"Two years after the death of his younger brother Arthur, Hall Montana is finally able to 'stammer out' the story of Arthur's career as a gospel and soul singer, his homosexual love affairs, and his inglorious death in the men's room of a London pub. He also comes to terms with his own more conventional adventures in love." Libr J

Baldwin, James, 1924-1987—*Continued*

Tell me how long the train's been gone; a novel. Dial Press (NY) 1968 484p o.p.

Leo Proudhammer, a successful black "actor has a serious heart attack on stage. Barbara King, his leading lady . . . and in a strange way his inamorata, stays by his side. In a series of flashbacks . . . Leo relives his past from his Harlem boyhood on. Although he learned early to hate 'the man,' Leo's own betrayal as a man and as a human being is not limited to the white man's corruption. It encompasses his painful relationship with his brother, who lures him into homosexuality. Paralleling this story is the tale of Leo's career. The third thread is his bisexual private life in which the two main figures are white Barbara, his true but unattainable love, and black Christopher, worshipful and available." Publ Wkly

Ball, John Dudley, 1911-1988

In the heat of the night; by John Ball. Harper & Row 1965 184p o.p. Buccaneer Bks. reprint available $18.95 (ISBN 0-89966-916-6)

"Virgil Tibbs is found with a full wallet in the waiting room of a railroad station in Wells, a small town in the Carolinas. Because he is black he becomes the prime suspect for the murder of the town's musical director. The local police chief learns that Tibbs is a homicide expert from the Pasadena police department and enlists his assistance. Tibbs solves the crime, despite the bigotry to which he is exposed." Shapiro. Fic for Youth. 2d edition

Ballard, J. G., 1930-

The best short stories of J. G. Ballard. Holt, Rinehart & Winston 1978 302p o.p.

LC 77-28234

Analyzed in Short story index

Contents: The concentration city; Manhole; Chronopolis; The voices of time; Deep end; The over-loaded man; Billenium; The garden of time; Thirteen for Centaurus; The subliminal man; The cage of sand; End game; The drowned giant; The terminal beach; The cloud-sculptors of Coral D; The assassination of John Fitzgerald Kennedy considered as a downhill motor race; The atrocity exhibition; Plan for the assassination of Jacqueline Kennedy; Why I want to fuck Ronald Reagan

Empire of the Sun; a novel. Simon & Schuster 1984 279p o.p.

LC 84-10630

"The day after Pearl Harbor, Shanghai is captured by the Japanese, and 11-year-old Jim is separated from his parents and spends some months living on his own. Then he is captured and interned in a Japanese prison camp with other civilians. The story of the next four years is one of struggling to stay alive by any means possible." Libr J

"This novel is much more than the gritty story of a child's miraculous survival in the grimly familiar setting of World War II's concentration camps. There is no nostalgia for a good war here, no sentimentality for the human spirit at extremes. Mr. Ballard is more ambitious than romance usually allows. He aims to render a vision of the apocalypse, and succeeds so well that it can hurt to dwell upon his images." N Y Times Book Rev

Followed by The kindness of women

The kindness of women. Farrar, Straus & Giroux 1991 343p $19.95

ISBN 0-374-18110-1   LC 91-73730

This sequel to the title entered above "begins again with a boy's traumatic experiences in Japanese-occupied Shanghai and ends some 40 years later with his viewing a film based on his novel about those experiences. Before this 'last act in a profound catharsis,' however, the narrator Jim stumbles through medical study at Cambridge, trains briefly as an RAF pilot in Canada, marries, and suffers domestic tragedy." Libr J

"For a writer whose inventiveness is so firmly anchored in 20th century-icons . . . Ballard remains firmly ambivalent about our image-led culture. His whole work is a celebration and an excoriation of 'the media landscape' and [this book] comes face to face with the contradictions." New Statesman Soc

The unlimited dream company; a novel. Holt, Rinehart & Winston 1979 238p o.p. Buccaneer Bks. reprint available $18.95 (ISBN 0-89968-391-6)

LC 79-9806

This fantasy novel "concerns a young man who crashes a stolen light aircraft into the River Thames, apparently dies and is reborn, finding himself trapped in the riverside town of Shepperton. . . . The hero discovers the ability to change himself into various beasts and birds, and to transform the sleepy suburb around him into a vivid garden of exotic flowers. More sinisterly, he is able to 'absorb' human beings into his body—before expelling them again, in the apocalyptic climax to the novel. The book is a remarkable fantasy of self-aggrandizement, colourfully and compellingly told." Ency of Sci Fic

Ballard, Mignon Franklin, 1934-

Final curtain; by Mignon F. Ballard. Carroll & Graf Pubs. 1992 223p $18.95

ISBN 0-88184-799-2   LC 92-5388

"Back in 1936, a young actress named Dahlia Brown spent the summer with a drama troupe at the Plumb-Nelly Tavern in Fiddler's Glen, N.C., and came to a tragic end: her body was found in a ravine, the death attributed to a fall. Now, some 50 years later, her grandniece, Ginger Cameron, has returned to the Plumb-Nelly at the insistence of Grandma Kate, Dahlia's sister, who has become convinced that the young woman was murdered and, nearing the end of her own life, desperately wants the case resolved." Publ Wkly

Balmer, Edwin, 1883-1959

After worlds collide

In Balmer, E. When worlds collide

When worlds collide; by Edwin Balmer and Philip Wylie. Lippincott 1950 2v in 1 o.p.

A combined edition of When worlds collide, and its sequel, After worlds collide, first published 1933 and 1934 respectively

When Worlds collide is a "celebrated novel of impending cosmic catastrophe and the attempt to save a favored few from sharing the fate of the doomed world. . . . The sequel deal[s] with the exploits of the survivors on their new world." Anatomy of Wonder 4

Balzac, Honoré de, 1799-1850

At the sign of the Cat and Racket

In Balzac, H. de. The short novels of Balzac

Colonel Chabert

In Balzac, H. de. The short novels of Balzac

A commission in lunacy

In Balzac, H. de. The short novels of Balzac

The country doctor. o.p.

Original French edition, 1833. Part of the series: Scenes from country life

The device with which this character study is held together concerns the visit of Pierre Joseph Genastas, an ex-soldier, who is searching for the saintly doctor Benassis. "A minute description of country life in the hilly region about Grenoble; the agricultural doings, the wretchedness of the peasantry, and M. Benassis' persevering attempts to ameliorate their condition, furnish a good example of Balzac's indefatigable realism. In this practical philanthropist, the reformed sinner who becomes a public benefactor, an ideal figure is created, a great soul, unselfish, full of love for man, unconquerably patient." Baker. Guide to the Best Fic

Cousin Bette; translated from the French by James Waring. Knopf 1991 xliii, 484p $20

ISBN 0-679-40671-9   LC 91-52964

"Everyman's library"

Original French edition, 1846. Part of the series: Scenes of Parisian life

"This powerful story is a vivid picture of the tastes and vices of Parisian life in the middle of last century. Lisbeth Fischer, commonly called Cousin Bette, is an eccentric poor relation, a worker in gold and silver lace. The keynote of her character is jealousy, the special object of it her beautiful and nobel-minded cousin Adeline, wife of Baron Hector Hulot. The chief interest of the story lies in the development of her character, of that of the unscrupulous beauty Madame Marneffe, and the base and empty voluptuary Hulot. . . . Gloomy and despairing . . . [it is] yet terribly powerful." Keller. Reader's Dig of Books

Cousin Pons. o.p.

Original French edition, 1847. Part of the series: Scenes of Parisian life

"Exposes the selfishness, vanity, and corruption of Parisian life with . . . relentless realism, in the lower social world of the minor theatres, lodginghouse keepers, curiosity shops, poor artists and bohemians. Over against this sordid section of society is set the friendship of two old musicians, the sentimental Schmucke and Cousin Pons. . . . Pons is a virtuoso who, in spite of poverty, has collected a treasury of beautiful things." Baker. Guide to the Best Fic

Droll stories; edited by Ernest Boyd; illustrated by Ralph Barton. Garden City Pub. Co. 1935 c1928 2v in 1 o.p.

Analyzed in Short story index

The stories were written between 1832-1833. First published 1928 in a limited edition by Boni & Liveright

Contents: Fair Imperia; Venial sin; King's sweetheart; Devil's heir; Merry jests of King Louis the Eleventh; High constable's wife; Maid of Thilouse; Brother-in-arms; Vicar of Azayle-Rideau; Reproach; Three clerks of St. Nicholas; Continence of King Francis the First; Merry tattle of the nuns of Poissy; How the Chateau d'Azay came to be built; False courtesan; Danger of being too innocent; Dear night of love; Sermon of the merry vicar of Meudon; Succubus; Despair in love; Perseverance in love; Concerning a provost who did not recognize things; About the Monk Amador, who was a glorious Abbot of Turpenay; Bertha the penitent; How the pretty maid of Portillon convinced her judge; In which it is demonstrated that fortune is always feminine; Concerning a poor man who was called Le Vieux par-Chemins; Odd sayings of three pilgrims; Innocence; Fair Imperia married

Eugénie Grandet; translated from the French by Ellen Marriage. Knopf 1992 237p $15

ISBN 0-679-41716-8   LC 92-52896

"Everyman's library"

First appeared 1833. Part of the series: Scenes of Provincial life

"Grandet, a rich miser has an only child, Eugénie. She falls in love with her charming but spoiled young cousin Charles. When she learns he is financially ruined, she lends him her savings. But her father will never consent to her marrying a bankrupt's son. Charles goes to the West Indies, secretly engaged to marry Eugénie on his return. Years go by, Grandet dies and Eugénie becomes an heiress. But Charles, ignorant of her wealth, writes her to ask for her freedom: he wants to marry a rich girl. Eugénie releases him, pays his father's debts, and marries without love an old friend of the family." Haydn. Thesaurus of Book Dig

Gobseck

In Balzac, H. de. The short novels of Balzac

Juana

In Balzac, H. de. The short novels of Balzac

Louis Lambert

In Balzac, H. de. The short novels of Balzac

Maitre Cornélius

In Balzac, H. de. The short novels of Balzac

Old Goriot

Some editions are:

Knopf (Everyman's lib) $15 translated by Ellen Marriage; introduction by Donald Adamson (ISBN 0-679-40535-6)

Norton $29.95 translated from the French by Burton Raffel. Has title: Père Goriot (ISBN 0-393-03620-0)

Original French edition, 1835. Part of the series: Scenes of Parisian life

"Goriot, a retired manufacturer of vermicelli, is a good man and a weak father. He has given away his money in order to ensure the marriage of his two daughters, Anastasie and Delphine. Because of his love for them, he has to accept all kinds of humiliations from his sons-in-law, one a 'gentilhomme,' M. de Restaud, and the other a financier, M. de Nucingen. Both young women are ungrateful. They gradually abandon him. He dies without seeing them at his bedside, cared for only by

Balzac, Honoré de, 1799-1850—_Continued_
young Rastignac, a law student who lives at the same
boarding house, the pension Vauquer." Haydn. Thesaurus
of Book Dig

Paz

> _In_ Balzac, H. de. The short novels of
> Balzac

The secrets of the Princess de Cadignan

> _In_ Balzac, H. de. The short novels of
> Balzac

The short novels of Balzac; with an
introduction by Jules Romains. Dial Press
1948 503p o.p.
"Permanent library series"
Analyzed in Short story index
Contents: Gobseck; At the sign of the Cat and Racket;
Maitre Cornélius; Colonel Chabert; The vicar of Tours;
Louis Lambert; Juana; A commission in lunacy; The
secrets of the Princess de Cadignan; Paz

The vicar of tours

> _In_ Balzac, H. de. The short novels of
> Balzac

Bambara, Toni Cade
Gorilla, my love. Random House 1972
177p o.p.
Analyzed in Short story index
Contents: My man Bovanne; Gorilla, my love;
Raymond's run; The hammer man; Mississippi Ham
Rider; Happy birthday; Playin with Punjab; Talkin bout
Sonny; The lesson; The survivor; Sweet town; Blues ain't
no mockin bird; Basement; Maggie of the green bottles;
The Johnson girls

The salt eaters. Random House 1980 295p
o.p.
LC 79-4806
"Velma Henry has tried suicide and survived and now
sits on a stool in the Southwest Community Infirmary
in Clayborne (a Southern city) listening to faith healer
Minnie Ransom ask a hard question about what she
wants. Fitfully she asks herself some questions, too, and
in the process remembers what happened, fingers the
past, absents herself from her own healing to recollect
other times, other places, other folks, as she mentally
travels abroad in Clayborne in search of answers." Publ
Wkly
This novel "with its beautiful, difficult prose, is a work
at once intensely personal and political that will assure
Bambara's place in black American fiction." Libr J

Banks, Lynne Reid _See_ Reid Banks, Lynne,
1929-

Banks, Oliver T.
The Caravaggio obsession; a novel; by
Oliver Banks. Little, Brown 1984 230p o.p.
LC 83-17497
"When a friend in the art auction business is killed
in New York, [art detective] Amos [Hatcher] tracks art
and murder to Rome. There he is thwarted by the police
and threatened by quasi-radical thugs. Amos soon realizes
that his friend's murderer, the ringleader of the robberies,
is obsessed with that earlier dark genius, the painter

Caravaggio. Banks crams his story with history and lore
in ways that are essential to the plot and fascinating
to even the most culture-resistant reader. The spirit of
Caravaggio and the desperate, beautiful city of Rome
haunt this superlative thriller." Wilson Libr Bull

The Rembrandt panel; a novel; by Oliver
Banks. Little, Brown 1980 268p o.p.
LC 80-11964
"Art investigator Amos Hatcher turns up in Boston
after two murders that just don't make sense. One victim
is a 'runner,' a man who leads a shoestring life and
occasionally is able to provide dealers with minor finds.
The other is Samuel Weinstock, a pleasant, principled
Charles Street gallery owner who prides himself on his
integrity and his careful scholarship. Hatcher, with
Weinstock's assistant Sheila Woods, aided and abetted
by two canny and amusing Boston homicide detectives,
discovers there's much to meet the sophisticated eye in
the case. The plot turns on a long-missing Rembrandt
portrait and also involves a priceless Greek vase.
Museums, dealers, scholars, all have intricate parts to
play." Publ Wkly

Banks, Russell, 1940-
Affliction. Harper & Row 1989 355p
$18.95
ISBN 0-06-016142-6   LC 89-45075
"Wade Whitehouse is a small-town policeman in his
early forties made crazy-desperate by a life of chronic
failure and intractably self-destructive behavior. Like his
father, he's moody, abusive, and a mean drunk. Wade's
got a good heart, and he'd like to change his ways, but
his desire to reform is thwarted by his baser male
instincts. Things just keep getting worse until he finally
can't take it anymore, whereupon he snaps and literally
runs amok in a mad and murderous rage of Oedipal
annihilation before vanishing, ghostlike, into the snow-
covered New Hampshire countryside. Wade's tragic saga
is related by his younger brother, Rolfe, a bookish history teacher who suppresses his own self-destructive tendencies by submerging himself in scholarly pursuits."
Booklist
This novel is "psychological portraiture of a high
order, and like all profound portraits it finds in its subject astonishing contradictions." N Y Times Book Rev

Continental drift. Harper & Row 1985
366p $17.95
ISBN 0-06-015383-0   LC 84-48137
"The novel charts, in alternating chapters, the eventually intersecting paths of two people desperately on the
move: Bob Dubois, a 30-year-old native of Catamount,
N.H., who decides one cold December night in the late
1970's that he wants something better than the life he
has had so far and takes off with his wife and two
daughters for Florida—and Vanise Dorsinville, a Haitian
woman living in a tiny cabin in the hill country near
Port-de-Paix, who leaves the poverty and bitter hopelessness of her island life for the bright promise of America." N Y Times Book Rev
"There are raw edges to Bank's novel, and a numbing
insistence on the powerlessness of its characters, but
there's no denying its almost frightening intensity." Libr
J

Banks, Russell, 1940-—*Continued*
The sweet hereafter. HarperCollins Pubs.
1991 257p $19.95

ISBN 0-06-016703-3   LC 90-56404

In this novel the story "is told by four people: Dolores
Driscoll, a school-bus driver in a small town; Billy Ansel,
father of two of the children on the bus; Mitchell
Stephens, a lawyer; and Nichole Burnell, a student. In
the accident on which the story is centered, Ansel loses
his children and Nichole is paralyzed. Dolores survives
the accident—the plunge of the bus through the guardrail
and into the water-filled quarry—and then tries to survive survival. Mitchell Stephens becomes the attorney for
the group of parents who mount a lawsuit." Christ Sci
Monit

"Banks handles his dark theme with judicious restraint,
empathy and compassion." Publ Wkly

Bannister, Patricia V. *See* Veryan, Patricia,
1923-

Banville, John
The book of evidence. Scribner 1990 219p
o.p.

                LC 89-10985

First published 1989 in the United Kingdom

"Freddie Montgomery is a schizophrenic 38-year-old
ex-scientist. . . . After study in America, Freddie returns
to Ireland to find that his disowning mother has sold
what he believes is part of his inheritance from his late
father, some paintings that include an Old Dutch master
of a woman he thinks regards him with caring, benevolent authority. As he steals it, he murders a maid who
catches him in the act. His lawyer advises him to plead
manslaughter to quash evidence. Instead . . . Freddie
writes the 'book of evidence' that we read." Libr J

"This novel, the inventive testimony of a murderer
more interested in making an impression than escaping
conviction, is . . . hauntingly beautiful and original. .
. . Mr. Banville shows his uncanny ability to make
everything he describes seem new and rare, yet instantly
recognisable." Economist

Barker, Clive
Babel's children
  In Barker, C. In the flesh
The books of blood. Putnam 1988 c1984
462p o.p.

                LC 88-2404

"An Ace/Putnam book"

Volumes 4 and 5 of Books of blood, entered below
under their distinctive titles

Analyzed in Short story index

Omnibus edition of volumes 1-3 of Books of blood
originally published 1984 in the United Kingdom; 1986
in paperback in the United States

Contents: Volume one: The Book of Blood; The midnight meat train; The Yattering and Jack; Pig blood
blues; Sex, death and starshine; In the hills, the cities
.Volume two: Dread; Hell's event; Jacqueline Ess: her
will and testament; The skins of the fathers; New
murders in the Rue Morgue

Volume three: Son of celluloid; Rawhead Rex; Confessions of a (pornographer's) shroud; Scape-goats; Human
remains; The Book of Blood (a postscript): on Jerusalem
Street

Cabal. Poseidon Press 1988 377p o.p.

                LC 88-23308

Analyzed in Short story index

The title novella "tells the story of Boone, a troubled
young man who has never found his place in the world
most people think of as 'real.' After spending years in
therapy, and coming to believe that he is finally getting
well, Boone's therapist convinces him he has been committing hideous murders, without any recollection of the
crimes. Shocked by Dr. Decker's revelations, and
desperate to find a place to hide, Boone takes refuge
in Midian, an underground community whose inhabitants
are no longer—and perhaps never were—human. . . .
Of the four short stories which accompany the novel—
'The Life of Death,' 'How Spoilers Bleed,' 'Twilight at
the Towers' and 'The Last Illusion'— 'How Spoilers
Bleed' is the most unsettling. . . . The muscularity of
Barker's writing and his ability to pull you into his
stories combine to make all of the stories in this book
fiendishly effective." West Coast Rev Books

Cabal [novelette]
  In Barker, C. Cabal
The damnation game. Putnam 1987 c1985
379p o.p.

                LC 86-26478

"An Ace/Putnam book"

First published 1985 in the United Kingdom

"Set in modern Britain, the story thrusts a flawed
'innocent'—parolee Marty Strauss—into an epic conflict
between wealthy Joseph Whitehead and Mamoulian the
Cardplayer, a centuries-old creature with whom
Whitehead had struck a bargain to obtain his wealth and
power. Whitehead reneges, and the resulting struggle is
played out primarily on his fortress-like estate. Barker's
excellent writing makes the graphic, grotesque imagery
endemic to current horror fiction very effective." Libr
J

Everville; the second book of the art.
HarperCollins Pubs. 1994 697p $25

ISBN 0-06-017716-0   LC 94-27296

This second volume in a projected trilogy is about
"several overlapping searches all taking place in and between the parallel worlds of the Cosm (i.e., reality as
we know it) and the land that is bordered by a sea
called the Quiddity. That body of water lies right on
the other side of a door between worlds situated on a
mountain above Everville, Oregon. Opened during the
nineteenth century, the portal has never quite shut; indeed, malevolent forces on the other side will soon come
pouring through to wreak havoc but will also afford the
opportunity for several otherworld exiles to go home."
Booklist

"At times profoundly moving as flawed heroes and
heroines martyr themselves to love or goodness, this
novel confirms the author's position not only as one of
horror's most potent and fertile minds but also as one
of modern fiction's premier metaphysicians." Publ Wkly

The forbidden
  In Barker, C. In the flesh
The great and secret show; the first book
of the art. Harper & Row 1989 550p $19.95

ISBN 0-06-016276-7   LC 89-45787

Barker, Clive—*Continued*

This is the first volume of a projected trilogy

"Nebraska postal clerk Randolph Jaffe works in the Dead Letter Room, opening and inspecting loads of undeliverable U.S. mail. Soon, through a series of cryptic dead letters, he taps into an ethereal network of mysterious revelations which provides access to enormous power channels. . . . [A] battle of light forces versus dark forces commences, with greedy Jaffe heading the latter, and mad yet philanthropic scientist Richard Fletcher representing the former." Libr J

"Like most fantasy novelists, Barker does not feel compelled to be logical or consistent: the dreamlike narrative has a kitchen-sink inclusiveness and cheats the rationalist in that characters turn out in mid-action to be someone else entirely, cunningly disguised. But the images are vivid, the asides incisive and the prose elegant in this joyride of a story." Time

Followed by Everville

Imajica. HarperCollins Pubs. 1991 824p $23

ISBN 0-06-017922-8   LC 90-56405

This fantasy "begins when a rich gent hires a peculiar assassin to off his estranged wife, the tome's female protagonist, whom he'd . . . stolen a while back from the professional art forger who's the male protagonist. The attempt fails but starts the romance's personae plunging back and forth between 'Dominions,' of which there are at least five, the Earth upon which we all dwell being the fifth and seemingly least developed of the lot." Booklist

"Barker's prodigious imagination delivers magicians, doppelgängers, Boschean creatures of staggeringly various descriptions and a pantheon of gods and goddesses seduced by power and redeemed by love in a story of violence, occasional unconventional eroticism and mesmerizing invention." Publ Wkly

In the flesh. Poseidon Press 1987 c1986 221p o.p.

LC 86-20450

Analyzed in Short story index

First published 1985 in the United Kingdom with title: Books of blood v5

This collection contains four novellas. "The title story, the longest in the book, is an absolute knockout, a nightmarish tale of a convict who seeks out, and finds, his long-dead, murderous grandfather. The evocation of the city of the murdered dead is haunting. 'The Forbidden' seems to be an attempt to write in the manner of Ramsey Campbell, and the narrative succeeds at that, and on its own terms. 'The Madonna' is a turgid and somewhat confused horror story, and 'Babel's Children' is an interesting, offbeat thriller of political conspiracy, madness and magic." Publ Wkly

In the flesh [novelette]

In Barker, C. In the flesh

The inhuman condition; tales of terror. Poseidon Press 1986 220p o.p.

LC 86-5086

Analyzed in Short story index

First published 1985 in the United Kingdom with title: Books of blood v4

Contents: The inhuman condition; The body politics; Revelations; Down, Satan; The age of desire

This collection "combines subtle wit with an original style that ignites the very explosive power of horrorfiction." West Coast Rev Books

The Madonna

In Barker, C. In the flesh

Weaveworld. Poseidon Press 1987 584p o.p.

LC 87-18602

This fantasy concerns "the Fugue, a magical land inhabited by descendants of supernatural beings who once shared the earth with humans. The Fugue has been woven into a carpet for protection against those who would destroy it; the death of its guardian occasions a battle between good and particularly repulsive evil forces for control of the Fugue." Libr J

Barker "creates a fantastic romance of magic and promise that is at once popular fiction and utopian conjuring. . . . There is great wit in the struggle that ensues, and keen attention to the facts of poverty and exile." N Y Times Book Rev

Barker, Pat, 1943-

The eye in the door. Dutton 1994 c1993 280p $20.95

ISBN 0-525-93808-7   LC 93-43833

First published 1993 in the United Kingdom

"Revisiting World War I England to explore war and its effects on individuals and society, Barker brings back characters . . . from *Regeneration*, including bisexual war hero Billy Prior and psychiatrist William Rivers. In 1918, the war was not going well for the Allies, and hysteria took root—the targets being pacifists and homosexuals, who were allegedly open to blackmail. Prior has connections to a group of pacifists who are being persecuted, and he also suffers from psychological episodes in which his personality alters dramatically. Dr. Rivers treats both Prior and other homosexuals on 'The 47,000,' a list of all purported gays in Britain." Libr J

This work "succeeds as both historical fiction and as sequel. Its research and speculation combine to produce a kind of educated imagination that is persuasive and illuminating about this particular place and time. . . . The novel's greatest success, however, has to do with the insight it provides into its central doctor-patient relationships." N Y Times Book Rev

Regeneration. Dutton 1992 c1991 251p $20

ISBN 0-525-93427-8   LC 91-41264

"A William Abrahams book"

First published 1991 in the United Kingdom

This novel "blends fact and fiction in relating a pivotal incident in the tragic life of noted English poet Siegfried Sassoon. In 1917, Sassoon, an army officer who had been decorated for his gallantry, was sent to a military sanitarium at Craiglockhart, diagnosed as suffering from shell shock. In fact, he had been assigned to the hospital less for medical reasons than political ones. No longer believing in the government's vaguely stated war aims and haunted by memories of the victims of the carnage he experienced, he had issued a declaration condemning the war. Only the intervention of his friend, poet Robert Graves, prevented a court-martial." Publ Wkly

"'Regeneration' is an antiwar novel, in a tradition that is by now an established one, though it tells a part of the whole story of war that is not often told—how war may batter and break men's minds—and so makes the madness of war more than a metaphor, and more awful." N Y Times Book Rev

Followed by The eye in the door

Barnao, Jack
See Wood, Ted

Barnard, Judith
For works written by this author in collaboration with Michael Fain see Michael, Judith

Barnard, Robert
At death's door. Scribner 1988 200p o.p.
LC 88-11387

"Famous novelist Benedict Cotterel lies old, ill, and helpless upstairs in his house, being cared for by his son and daughter-in-law. One day his illegitimate daughter, the product of a liaison with a celebrated actress, appears on the scene, intending to do research for a vitriolic biography of her mother. Shortly thereafter her actress mother arrives in an attempt to thwart such a biography from being written. Too bad for her—she turns up dead, leaving an intriguing list of murder suspects." Booklist

Bodies. Scribner 1986 198p o.p.
LC 86-11858

Superintendent Perry Trethowan investigates "a multiple murder in a Soho photography studio. Some of the work that came out of it was relatively harmless soft porn; some was pretty raw. The investigation takes Trethowan into the world of pumping iron, and the book has some insights into the narcissistic men and women who torture their bodies for an impossible dream in which every muscle is high-lighted and controlled. Unfortunately, some of these people used their bodies for ignoble purposes." N Y Times Book Rev

The case of the missing Brontë. Scribner 1983 182p o.p.
LC 83-3328

Scotland yard's Perry Trethowan "is relaxing in a village pub with his wife when he meets Edith Wing, a retired schoolteacher. When she shows them a large piece of yellowing paper covered with tiny writing and confides that she has 200 similar pages at home, inherited from a cousin whose family connections with the Brontes go back five generations, it seems apparent that she is in possesion of an invaluable, previously unknown Emily Bronte manuscript. When Perry suggests that she seek expert advice on the manuscript's authenticity from a local professor, he doesn't suspect that he is very nearly sending Edith to her death." Publisher's note

The cherry blossom corpse. Scribner 1987 213p o.p.
LC 86-31619

Published in the United Kingdom with title: Death in purple prose
Superintendent Perry Trethowan is "on vacation in Norway, attending a meeting of the World Association of Romantic Novelists. He is there acting as a squire for his sister, who writes that kind of book. Naturally there is a murder, and Trethowan has to work with the Norwegian police to crack the case. At the end there is the kind of twist that often is a hallmark of the Barnard books." N Y Times Book Rev

A city of strangers. Scribner 1990 287p $20.95
ISBN 0-684-19192-X
LC 90-8499

This novel is set in Sleate, a Yorkshire town. When rumors suggest that Jack Phelan, an alcoholic welfare recipient, and his disreputable wife and offspring, have plans for moving to a nearby middle-class area, the families in the neighborhood are up in arms. And then Jack Phelan dies in a mysterious fire. The verdict is arson

"Barnard, an acute and merciless chronicler of Britain's middle classes, is at his fiercest in showing how the proper bourgeoisie reacts to, and is repeatedly bested by, the convention-scorning Phelans. The story's most intense drama is generated not by the search for the killer, but by the question of whether the one decent-seeming Phelan, an amiable schoolboy, is for real and will stay that way." Time

Corpse in a gilded cage. Scribner 1984 211p o.p.
LC 84-10703

"The death of a distant cousin catapults happy, middle-class Perce and Elsie Spender into the British aristocracy: they become the twelfth earl and countess of Ellesmere and owners of that forbidding Jacobean manse, Chetton Hall. The Spenders want to spend their fortune elsewhere, but their ill-assorted offspring . . . are dazzled by the prospect of living like lords. The family assembles for the earl's sixtieth birthday, tensions become exacerbated, and a body is found under one of the estate's Bernini statues." Booklist
"A delightful romp through the British class system." Publ Wkly

Death and the chaste apprentice. Scribner 1989 211p o.p.
LC 89-4205

This mystery takes place at "the Saracen's Head outside London where performers have gathered since medieval days to re-create, fittingly, Elizabethan entertainments. Under the new management of Des Capper, a 'loathsome know-all,' the inn becomes a crime scene when he is murdered and all present, save one, had cause to kill the bounder." Publ Wkly

Death and the Princess. Scribner 1982 183p o.p.
LC 82-6022

"Perry Trethowan is seconded from the CID to look after Princess Helena of the British Royal Family, because she is an attractive, reckless, and scrape-prone girl, just then involved with a man and a crowd of dubious reputation. Perry and the princess get on very well indeed and many of the scenes they share are hilarious. But the murder is serious and its detection is neat." Barzun. Cat of Crime. Rev and enl edition

Death by sheer torture. Scribner 1982 c1981 186p o.p.
LC 81-14569

First published 1981 in the United Kingdom with title: Sheer torture
The novel "tells of the odd death of a wacky old gentleman in a dingy castle in England: the fellow met his untimely death wearing gauzy spangled tights in a self-manufactured torture machine he had read about in a book on the Spanish Inquisition. . . . On this particular day someone had cut the cable, and the machine and its screwball master plummeted to the floor with fatal consequences. It was murder, all right, and onto the scene came the local detective, [Perry Trethowan] no other than the estranged son of the victim." Best Sellers

Barnard, Robert—*Continued*

"A good, satisfying whodunit made absolutely delicious by the crazed egotists." Publ Wkly

Death in a cold climate. Scribner 1981 c1980 196p o.p.

LC 80-20979

First published 1980 in the United Kingdom

"In the Norwegian town of Tromsø, Professor Mackenzie, an Englishman attached to the local university, finds the body of a murder victim in the snow and Inspector Fagermo begins investigating. The dead man is identified as Martin Forsyth, a visitor with no known connections in Tromsø, a young oil company employee reported missing three months earlier. Questions to habitues of a club frequented by foreigners give Fagermo data that he forms into a picture of Forsyth as a blackmailer, but it is much more difficult to produce evidence against those he had been bleeding." Publ Wkly

Death of a literary widow. Scribner 1980 c1979 192p o.p.

LC 80-13128

First published 1979 in the United Kingdom with title: Posthumous papers

"Two elderly women, Viola and Hilda, live in the same house, avoiding each other like the plague. Both have been married to the same man, the late writer Walter Mackin, who is the object of a sudden, intense renewal of interest—articles are written about him, his books are reissued. The great concern of the two wives is who will profit from Mackin's posthumous reputation. One of the old ladies dies in a fire, leaving everyone wondering whether she went out in an accidental blaze or as the result of someone's murderous rage." Booklist

Death of a perfect mother. Scribner 1981 188p o.p.

LC 81-2815

Published in the United Kingdom with title: Mother's boys

"This 'perfect' British mother is a real pain who is genuinely despised by nearly everyone including her lovers, her friends, her children and, deep down, her doormat husband. Lily's two sons spend countless hours merrily planning Mother's murder. Yet all are shocked when Lily is found strangled on her way back from her lover's house. Pompous and proper Chief Inspector Dominic McHale is promptly called in to solve this less-than-tragic crime." Best Sellers

Death of a salesperson, and other untimely exits. Scribner 1989 200p o.p.

LC 89-6264

Analyzed in Short story index

Contents: The woman in the wardrobe; A business partnership; Little terror; Breakfast television; What's in a name?; Sisters; The injured party; Just another kidnap; Blown up; A process of rehabilitation; Holy living and holy dying; The Oxford way of death; Daylight robbery; Happy release; Death of a salesperson; My last girlfriend

A fatal attachment. Scribner 1992 281p $20

ISBN 0-684-19412-0   LC 92-10431

Also available Thorndike Press large print edition

"An aloof but admired celebrity in her Yorkshire village, Lydia indulges her fantasies by writing popular biographies of historical swashbucklers like Lord Byron and T. E. Lawrence, and by mooning over a dashing explorer she almost married. But when she begins to instill her reckless notions in two impressionable brothers from the village, someone among Lydia's many past conquests gets a mind to strangle her. Two well-matched police detectives handle the murder investigation." N Y Times Book Rev

"The book's pleasure comes from Barnard's easy use of police procedures, his subtle characterization and his eye for village color. Lydia is a delicious monster, and the ambiguous ending delivers an extra kick." Publ Wkly

Fête fatale. Scribner 1985 183p $13.95 o.p.

ISBN 0-684-18469-9   LC 85-14583

Published in the United Kingdom with title: Disposal of the living

"The village of Hexton-on-Weir is run by its women, and a nasty lot they are, barely excepting the narrator-wife of the murdered man, whose tongue can be as acid as those of her enemies. An unlikely murder weapon and a forced ending mar only slightly the pleasure of Barnard's gifts for characterization and local color." Barzun. Cat of Crime. Rev and enl edition

A hovering of vultures. Scribner 1993 231p $20

ISBN 0-684-19625-5   LC 93-19371

Also available Thorndike Press large print edition

"Detective Charlie Peace travels to rural Yorkshire to attend a weekend gathering of devotees of brother-sister writers Joshua and Susannah Sneddon, who in 1932 died in a murder-suicide incident. There's something odd about this convocation, and as we try to figure out why Detective Peace is in attendance in the first place, we observe him persevering in attempting to learn who murdered the organizer of the literary weekend." Booklist

"While skewering literary pretensions, Barnard . . . writes a tale that is both cozily down-home and wittily urbane." Publ Wkly

A little local murder. Scribner 1983 c1976 190p o.p.

LC 82-23027

First published 1976 in the United Kingdom

"When the little English village of Twitching learns that it will be featured in an international radio broadcast, all of its citizens want to be interviewed. Deborah Withens, wife of the local council chairman, decides that she will choose the participants—and she plans to make the most of a chance to exert the ultimate power over her friends and foes. . . . Deborah decides that most of them will appear on the broadcast only over her dead body. And that's what happens . . . a dead body, that is, along with poison-pen letters and a series of other crimes. Inspector George Parrish is called upon to investigate as Twitching becomes famous for all the wrong reasons." Publisher's note

The masters of the house; a novel of suspense. Scribner 1994 214p $20

ISBN 0-684-19728-6   LC 94-5853

Also available Thorndike Press large print edition

"Thirteen-year-old Matthew Heenan and his 12-year-old sister Annie assume control of their shattered household when their mother dies in childbirth and their unemployed father has a breakdown. Annie, who is the managing type, runs the house and takes care of the younger children. It falls to Matthew . . . to hide their father's catatonic state from the neighbors—and to solve the murder of Mr. Heenan's girlfriend, whose body the children bury in a nearby field." N Y Times Book Rev

Barnard, Robert—*Continued*

Out of the blackout. Scribner 1985 c1984 o.p.

LC 85-1694

"An unusual piece of detection in that the central character is searching for himself—who was he before he was taken, with other children, to foster homes in the country during the London blitz? Though the tale is not wholeheartedly crime fiction, a murder is discovered and its ramifications elucidated by the self-searching hero." Barzun. Cat of Crime. Rev and enl edition

A scandal in Belgravia. Scribner 1991 245p $17.95

ISBN 0-684-19322-1   LC 91-8603

Also available Thorndike Press large print edition

"While writing his memoirs, ex-cabinet minister Peter Proctor questions the 35-year-old unsolved murder of Timothy Wycliffe, his good friend and colleague in the Foreign Office. Soon diverted by fond memories of this engaging and fully alive fellow—who happened to be gay—he researches the murder, questions Timothy's friends, family, and lovers, finally reconstructs the murder, and confronts the murderer." Libr J

"Mr. Barnard never loses control of his polished form, even as he does his pretty hatchet job on the last half-century of Conservative Party politics in England." NY Times Book Rev

School for murder. Scribner 1984 c1983 201p o.p.

LC 83-20185

First published 1983 in the United Kingdom with title: Little victims

This novel is a "study of life and death in a second-rate English boys' school. . . . Many perspectives on the school are offered, from that of the headmaster, to that of the jaded and manipulative new head boy, handsome Hilary Frome. As schoolboy pranks escalate to murderous incidents and finally Hilary's death, Superintendent Michael Pumfrey investigates what turns out to be a case betraying the headmaster's poor judgment and his wife's almost Dickensian neglect of her charges." Libr J

The skeleton in the grass. Scribner 1988 c1987 199p o.p.

LC 88-3075

First published 1987 in the United Kingdom

"Young Sarah Causeley has signed on as governess to the Hallams, a family of intellectual and political renown, whose seat is a big country house in Oxfordshire. But the Hallams are of a pacifist persuasion, a position that, given the tenor of the times—the rise of fascism in Germany and the outbreak of civil war in Spain—makes them not too popular with many of the people in their environs. In fact, their unpopularity leads to murder." Booklist

Barnes, Julian

Flaubert's parrot. Knopf 1985 190p o.p.

LC 84-48550

"Geoffrey Braithwaite, widower and retired physician, devotes his final years to a manic examination of literary 'factoids' (to borrow Mailer's term) concerning his favorite author [Gustave Flaubert]. Is Félicité's parrot, immortalized in Un Coeur Simple, the stuffed bird on display at the Hôtel-Dieu, or the one at Crosset? Or is it one of several others stored in the attic of the Museum of Natural History in Rouen? Braithwaite ridicules scholars who pounce upon inconsistencies . . . . but is caught up in the game himself." Libr J

"A minor classic, and one of the best criticism novels ever, because its critic/narrator has some dignity, because his choice of subject makes emotional sense and because the book has a lively, questioning spirit. . . . [Barnes has] written a modernist text with a nineteenth-century heart, a French novel with English lucidity and tact." Nation

A history of the world in 10½ chapters. Knopf 1989 307p $18.95

ISBN 0-394-58061-3   LC 89-45266

"A revisionist view of Noah's Ark, told by the stowaway woodworm. A chilling account of terrorists hijacking a cruise ship. A court case in 16th-century France in which the woodworm stands accused. A desperate woman's attempt to escape radioactive fallout on a raft. An acute analysis of Géricault's 'Scene of Shipwreck.' The search of a 19th-century Englishwoman and of a contemporary American astronaut for Noah's Ark. An actor's increasingly desperate letters to his silent lover. A thoughtful meditation on the novelist's responsibility regarding love. These and other stories make up Barnes's . . . retelling of the history of the world." Libr J

This book "shapes up not only as Barnes's funniest novel but also his most richly cargoed and imaginatively designed. . . . As satirist and story-teller he has few equals at present." New Statesman Soc

Barnes, Linda

Coyote; a Carlotta Carlyle mystery. Delacorte Press 1990 257p o.p.

LC 90-34505

Available G.K. Hall large print edition

"Boston private investigator/part-time cabbie Carlotta Carlyle's search for a frightened woman's green card involves her in an underground world of illegal immigration, labor exploitation, and gruesome mutilation murder." Libr J

"Carlotta is at her best when she focuses on the personal plight of the individuals who make up the nameless legion of potential deportees. While discovering the truth about them, she convincingly provides wisdom and comfort to the child she adores." Publ Wkly

The snake tattoo. St. Martin's Press 1989 290p o.p.

LC 88-30525

Available G.K. Hall large print edition

Private eye Carlotta Carlyle "is faced with two equally difficult cases: finding a missing teenage girl, who seems to have traded posh suburbia for the moral sewer of Boston's Combat Zone, and helping Beantown cop and longtime friend Mooney, who stands accused of assaulting a supposedly unarmed man in a bar fight." Booklist

"Bright, witty, and a touch sarcastic." Libr J

Snapshot; a Carlotta Carlyle novel. Delacorte Press 1993 325p o.p.

LC 92-41734

Available Thorndike Press large print edition

Barnes, Linda—*Continued*

"Carlotta Carlyle, Boston's snappy, redheaded PI, investigates the suspicious death of a woman's daughter after receiving a series of snapshots in the mail. Carlyle also attempts to locate the biological father of her own 'little sister' Paolina. Both cases ultimately involve drugs and conspiracy." Libr J

"Carlotta uses determination, feistiness, and intelligence to outwit the bad guys and solve the crime. . . . The action is gripping, and there are enough surprises to keep readers interested." Booklist

Steel guitar. Delacorte Press 1991 257p $18.50

ISBN 0-385-30013-1   LC 91-14529
Also available Thorndike Press large print edition

After Boston PI Carlotta Carlyle "saves old friend, now blues star, Dee Willis from publicity and prosecution in a dangerous park incident, Dee hires her to find their long-ago mutual heartthrob Davey Dunrobie. Davey claims that Dee has plagiarized several of his songs. When Dee discovers a murdered band member in her bed, she realizes Davey means business. Carlotta—tall, vivacious, sensitive—unravels all the knots with breathtaking verve." Libr J

A trouble of fools. St. Martin's Press 1987 208p o.p.

LC 87-16147
Available G.K. Hall large print edition

"While looking for a missing cab driver, [Carlotta Carlyle] stumbles upon some strange goings on at the taxi company. From the trashing of her client's house to a strange scam involving large sums of money, Carlyle moves through Boston until the threatening violence explodes when least expected." Libr J

Barrett, Julia

Presumption; an entertainment. Evans & Co. 1993 238p $19.95

ISBN 0-87131-736-2   LC 93-5778
Also available Thorndike Press large print edition

This "sequel to Jane Austen's *Pride and Prejudice,* continues the story of the Bennet, Bingley, Wickham, Darcy, and Collins families, focusing mainly on Georgiana Darcy. . . . Georgiana, sister to the formidable Darcy, is suffering from past romantic indiscretions and is determined to remain more rational in her reactions to masculine attention. However, she soon finds her thoughts turning with alarming frequency to a dashing naval officer as well as to the talented architect her brother has hired. Meanwhile, her irrepressible sister-in-law copes with supercilious friends and neighbors—a task made more difficult by the continuing vulgarity of her mother and the imprisonment of her aunt. Barrett expertly captures Austen's ironic voice and subject matter." Libr J

Barrett, William E.

The left hand of God. Doubleday 1951 275p o.p.

Available from Amereon and Buccaneer Bks.

"In a remote corner of China a young American flyer manages to escape from the local war lord by assuming the guise of a Roman Catholic priest. In the mission where he seeks refuge his problems multiply rapidly when he finds himself taking Mass, hearing confession and with every move reluctantly taking advantage of the faith of a simple people. His moral struggle, his love affair, and the manner in which he extricates himself from his difficult situation make an interesting though farfetched story." Ont Libr Rev

The lilies of the field; drawings by Burt Silverman. Doubleday 1962 92p o.p. Buccaneer Bks. reprint available $18.95 (ISBN 1-56849-166-2)

"Homer Smith is an amiable Southern black man. Driving through the Southwest after getting out of the Army, he stops to help four German refugee nuns build a church. After teaching them English and survival skills, he disappears, leaving behind the legend of his faithful help." Shapiro. Fic for Youth. 3d edition

Barrie, J. M. (James Matthew), 1860-1937

The little minister.

Available from Buccaneer Bks.

First published 1891

"A romantic fantasia on the Thrums motive: the love affairs of the Auld Licht [Presbyterian] minister and a beautiful and sprightly 'Egyptian,' who is a lady in disguise. . . . The sketches of character and of Scottish manners and religious sentiments are very humorous, and there are passages of concentrated pathos." Baker. Guide to the Best Fic

"Aside from its intrinsic interest, there is much skilful portrayal of the complexities of Scotch character, and much sympathy with the homely lives of the poverty-stricken weavers, whose narrow creed may make them cruel, but never dishonorable." Keller. Reader's Dig of Books

Barrie, James Matthew *See* Barrie, J. M. (James Matthew), 1860-1937

Bart, André Schwarz- *See* Schwarz-Bart, André, 1928-

Barth, John

Bellerophoniad

In Barth, J. Chimera p135-308

Chimera. Random House 1972 308p o.p.

Contents: Dunyazadiad; Perseid; Bellerophoniad

"Barth's three interlocked novellas are based on the stories of Scheherazade, Perseus, and Bellerophon, combined in a way that suggests an attempt to present the artist as mythic hero." Atlantic

"The protagonists of these witty confessions are walking psyches, at war with ultimate ambivalence. (Far from clarifying what is ambiguous, Barth deepens it—by retelling familiar stories, deploying their unsettled alternatives so as to virtually insist on their unreality). . . . [He] employs literary devices that multiply confusion [including] . . . the removal of all barriers posed by time and history." Libr J

Dunyazadiad

In Barth, J. Chimera p1-56

Barth, John—*Continued*

The end of the road. Doubleday 1958 230p o.p.

"In the story, at once comic, tragic and satirical, Barth made a frontal attack on the excesses of Sartrean existentialism and existential philosophy popular in the 1950's. The hero is Jacob Horner, a Kafkaesque character, whose quack therapist advises him to teach prescriptive grammar as an antidote to his fits of manic depression. Horner takes a job at a small teachers' college in Maryland and meets Joe Morgan, history teacher and Boy Scout troop leader, and his wife, Rennie. Joe and Rennie believe in the perfect existential love relationship, involving endless intellectual probing and analysis." Publ Wkly

"The plot sounds absurd, but beneath the comic surface, questions are being raised regarding choice and meaning in life." Libr J

The floating opera. Appleton-Century-Crofts 1956 280p o.p.

"A 50-year-old bachelor relives the day 10 years before when he decided to commit suicide. He had changed his mind (in true existentialist fashion) only because suicide, just like every other action in his life, would have been without meaning. In retracing the day he fills in the main events of his life as child, student, and lawyer in a sleepy backwater Maryland town." Libr J

"Just as Voltaire's Candide decides to contentedly cultivate his garden after a disillusioning journey, so does Barth's Todd come to terms with life by discovering in time that it is best to choose among the relative values that life offers rather than cynically rejecting all values by way of suicide." N Y Times Book Rev

Giles goat-boy; or, The revised new syllabus. Doubleday 1966 xxxi, 710p o.p.

"The novel's protagonist, Billy Bockfuss (also called George Giles, the goat-boy), was raised with herds of goats on a university farm after being found as a baby in the bowels of the giant West Campus Automatic Computer (WESCAC). The WESCAC plans to create a being called GILES (Grand-Tutorial Ideal, Laboratory Eugenical Specimen) that would possess superhuman abilities. Billy's foster father, who tends the herd, suspects Billy of being GILES but tries to groom him to be humanity's savior and to stop WESCAC's domination over humans." Merriam-Webster's Ency of Lit

The last voyage of somebody the sailor. Little, Brown 1991 573p o.p.

LC 90-44991

"Simon Behler—or Baylor, as he refers to himself in his countless best-selling books of New Journalism—falls overboard during a cruise retracing the legendary voyages of Sindbad the Sailor and is pulled from the water by contemporaries of the real Sindbad. Trapped in the distant past but never at a loss for words, Behler—or Bey el-Loor, as he is now known—amuses his new friends with his exotic tales: boyhood on Maryland's Eastern Shore, first love, early literary success, marriage, and divorce." Libr J

"If the setting is sober, the narrator is not. This is John Barth, . . . after all, and his hero is variously exuberant, obnoxious, funny, self-conscious, and, not sober at all, but thoroughly intoxicated with sex, love, and story telling, especially with their commingling." Commonweal

Lost in the funhouse; fiction for print, tape, live voice. Doubleday 1968 201p o.p.

Partially analyzed in Short story index

Contents: Frame-tale; Night-sea journey; Ambrose, his mark; Autobiography; Water-message; Petition; Lost in the funhouse; Echo; Two meditations; Title; Glossolalia; Life-story; Menelaiad; Anonymiad

"The book's creator-heroes are a small boy, a goat-herd minstrel banished from the court of Clytemnestra, and the author-figure himself. Their lives are seen as a giddily terrifying tour of a Funhouse, an isolated exile on an island, and a long meaningless swim in a vast 'night-sea.'" Newsweek

Perseid

In Barth, J. Chimera p57-134

The sot-weed factor. Doubleday 1967 806p o.p.

Picaresque novel "originally published in 1960 and revised in 1967. A parody of the historical novel, it is based on and takes its title from a satirical poem published in 1708 by Ebenezer Cooke, who is the protagonist of Barth's work. The novel's black humor is derived from its purposeful misuse of conventional litarary devices." Merriam-Webster's Ency of Lit

The Tidewater tales; a novel. Putnam 1987 655p o.p.

LC 86-25486

"Peter Sagamore, novelist, has come down with a bad case of minimalism. Ruthless self-editing leaves him with works only a few words in length, and no readers. His wife is a 'maximalist' oral historian with an MLS. In June 1980 they spend two weeks sailing around Chesapeake Bay in their boat *Story*, telling stories." Libr J

"What is moving about 'The Tidewater Tales' is its frequent and frequently incidental richness as a love story—marital, filial, domestic—and also its love of a place, of a country, even as place and country are scarred by human depredations. Whether the novel's ending—or its various coves and shallows sailed into along the way—give us something more rich and strange than a funhouse may be left to the reader." N Y Times Book Rev

Barthelme, Donald

Sixty stories. Putnam 1981 457p o.p.

LC 81-8646

Analyzed in Short stories index

Contents: Margins; A shower of gold; Me and Miss Mandible; For I'm the boy; Will you tell me; The balloon; The President; Game; Alice; Robert Kennedy saved from drowning; Report; The dolt; See the moon; The Indian uprising; Views of my father weeping; Paraguay; On angels; The Phantom of the Opera's friend; City life; Kierkegaard unfair to Schlegel; The falling dog; The Policemen's Ball; The glass mountain; Critique de la vie quotidienne; The sandman; Träumerei; The rise of capitalism; A city of churches; Daumier; The party; Eugénie Grandet; Nothing: a preliminary account; A manual for sons; At the end of the mechanical age; Rebecca; The captured woman; I bought a little city; The sergeant; The school; The great hug; Our work and why we do it; The crisis; Cortés and Montezuma; The new music; The zombies; The king of jazz; Morning; The death of Edward Lear; The abduction from the Seraglio; On the steps of the conservatory; The leap; Aria; The emerald; How I write my songs; The farewell; The emperor; Thailand; Heroes; Bishop; Grandmother's house

Bass, Rick, 1958-

Field events

In Bass, R. Platte River p45-95

Mahatma Joe

In Bass, R. Platte River p3-42

Platte River. Houghton Mifflin; Lawrence, S. 1994 145p $19.95

ISBN 0-395-68080-8   LC 93-36115

Analyzed in Short story index

A collection of three novellas. The title story "is about an ex-football player who journeys from Montana to speak at a small college in northern Michigan. . . . 'Mahatma Joe,' [is] about a Canadian evangelist who is near death, and who manages one last convert in an embittered young woman trying to find herself in a wilderness valley. . . . 'Field events' [is] about two over-grown teenage boys who spend every spare moment discus throwing." Booklist

Platte River [novella]

In Bass, R. Platte River p99-145

Bassani, Giorgio, 1916-

The garden of the Finzi-Continis. Atheneum Pubs. 1965 293p o.p.

Original Italian edition, 1962

"The Finzi-Continis, a wealthy Jewish Italian family, lived in a beautiful and seemingly secure environment and enjoyed intellectual pursuits. The narrator remembers the family, his unrequited love for the beautiful but cold Micol, and his friendship with her brother, Albert. The novel describes the assimilation of Jews into Italian society and then the changes effected when fascism overtakes Italy and anti-Semitism destroys the family." Shapiro. Fic for Youth. 3d edition

Batchelor, John Calvin

Father's day; a novel. Holt & Co. 1994 528p $23

ISBN 0-8050-3266-5   LC 94-14461

"The time is 10 years from now, when faltering President Theodore Jay is hospitalized for depression and his feisty Texan Vice President, 'Shy' Garland, takes over. When Jay offers himself as ready to return to office, Garland opposes him—and secretly has an Army unit put in place to assassinate Jay if need be. Garland's opposition comes from the family of Maine Governor Jack Longfellow; from Jack; his powerful wife, Senator Jean Motherwell; and Jack's father, Long John, formerly Secretary of Defense and still a power in the land. The political shenanigans are fast-moving, occasionally confusing but always highly entertaining, and the military passages—involving the chairman of the Joint Chiefs and a duty-bound but deeply divided colonel who commands the assassination force—are electrifying." Publ Wkly

Bates, H. E. (Herbert Ernest), 1905-1974

The best of H. E. Bates; with a preface by Henry Miller. Little, Brown 1963 454p o.p. Ayer reprint available $32 (ISBN 0-8369-3967-0)

Analyzed in Short story index

Published in the United Kingdom with title: Seven by five

Contents: The flame; A flower piece; The mower; Time; The mill; The station; The kimono; Breeze Anstey; The ox; Colonel Julian; The lighthouse; The flag; The frontier; A Christmas song; The Major of Hussars; Elaine; The daffodil sky; The good corn; Country society; Across the bay; Chaff in the wind; The evolution of Saxby; Go lovely rose; The maker of coffins; Love in a wych elm; Let's play soldiers; The watercress girl; The cowslip field; Great Uncle Crow; The enchantress; Now sleeps the crimson petal; Where the cloud breaks; Lost hall; Thelma; Mrs. Eglantine

Fair stood the wind for France. Little, Brown 1944 270p o.p.

"An Atlantic Monthly Press book"

A British bomber, returning from a mission over Italy, crashed in occupied France. The members of the crew managed to escape via the underground route, all but the pilot who was too ill. He was cared for by a family of French peasants, whose innate goodness made such an impression on him that when he finally left France he took with him the daughter of the family, as his wife

"An almost unbearable suspense, the romance of the two young people and a true portrait of the little people of France, defenseless but possessed of an enduring power, all these go to make an unforgettable story, beautifully told." Bookmark

Bates, Herbert Ernest *See* Bates, H. E. (Herbert Ernest), 1905-1974

Battle, Lois

The past is another country. Viking 1990 392p $19.95

ISBN 0-670-82576-X   LC 89-40775

Also available Thorndike Press large print edition

"Megan Hanlon is an up-and-coming filmmaker returning to her Australian homeland on business. She encounters her former convent school classmate Greta Papandreou, now a meek homemaker dependent on her unfaithful husband. As much as Megan desires self-validation and Greta is desperate for security, Joan (formerly Sister Mary Magdalene) a nun still teaching at the convent school, dreams of independence from the institution that has fiercely constrained her mind and body. Forced to make life-altering decisions regarding careers and loved ones, all three examine their ties with the past and their Catholic heritage. Battle's quietly heroic characters are beautifully believable, and her evocation of her native Australia adds an estimable dimension to an engrossing novel." Publ Wkly

Southern women. St. Martin's Press 1984 404p o.p.

LC 83-22999

Battle, Lois—*Continued*

This novel "depicts three generations of Southern women represented by the female line of a prominent Savannah family. Eunnonia Grace Hampton, known as Nonnie, is matriarch of the clan; over 70 when widowhood permits her her first real independence. . . . Lucille Hampton Simpkins, her youngest daughter, has devoted her life to cultivating those traditional feminine charms that only fleetingly satisfy her vanity and leave her vulnerable at 50 to a consummate roué. Lucille's daughter, Cordy, 30, wants more from life than her marital bed can provide, and has become a romance novelist. The book begins when Cordy, after leaving Chicago and her husband, returns home to Savannah." N Y Times Book Rev

"The author's characters are the type that readers of light fiction enjoy: they possess ordinary urges and desires overlaid with tinges of nobility, tragedy, and/or glamour. The plot unravels quickly but logically, with no artificial twists and turns." Booklist

Storyville. Viking 1993 435p $22

ISBN 0-670-83867-5   LC 92-50347

Also available Thorndike Press large print edition

"Kate is an innocent country girl who is seduced by a rake and abandoned, with little recourse but to become a woman 'in the life.' Beautiful and appealing, she snares the heart of young Lawrence Randsome, scion of an old, distinguished New Orleans family. Meanwhile, his mother, transplanted Boston blueblood, bluestocking and suffragette Julia Randsome, has discovered that her husband Charles owns whorehouses in the District, and their marriage is damaged by her bitterness and lack of trust. Eventually, tragedy adds another dimension to their domestic squabbling; then Julia befriends the luckless Kate and comes into her own as an activist for women's rights." Publ Wkly

"Battle has great command of her complex plot and its contentious historical context and conflicting passions. As she sets the steamy, jazzy ambience of New Orleans against the chilly propriety of Boston, the self-sacrificing dutifulness of Julia against the glamorous pragmatism of Kate, she gives form to the divided heart of womanhood." Booklist

War brides. St. Martin's Press 1982 359p o.p.

LC 81-16732

This novel "traces the experience of three Australian war brides who come to post-WWII America to begin life with the husbands they have scarcely had time to get to know. . . . [The author writes] of the different ways each of her heroines adjusts to the challenges of an unfamiliar country. . . . Friends on board ship, they keep in touch over the years, and several twists of fate bring them into occasional direct contact with each other." Publ Wkly

"The book has a well-rounded cast, predictable plot, and adequate writing." Libr J

Baum, Vicki, 1888-1960

Grand Hotel; translated by Basil Creighton. Doubleday 1931 309p o.p.

Available from Amereon and Buccaneer Bks.

Original German edition, 1929

The story takes up the many things that happen within the course of two days to some of the people who are stopping at a large hotel in post-World War I Germany. Among the characters who receive, through their contact with fellow-guests such a 'coup de grâce' from life are the timid clerk, Kringelein, the ballet-dancer, Grusinskaya, and the charming Baron Gaigern. In contrast to these beneficiaries of fate are the selfish and scheming capitalist, Herr Preysing, and the disillusioned Dr. Otternschlag, whose cynicism negates the beauty and significance of those who live life fully

"The people who are shovelled in through the hotel's revolving door are a fascinating collection, and all sharply and eagerly visualized. . . . They are drawn in with the quick clear lines that mark the artist." New Statesman

Bausch, Richard, 1945-

Rare & endangered species

In Bausch, R. Rare & endangered species: a novella & stories p155-257

Rare & endangered species: a novella & stories. Houghton Mifflin; Lawrence, S. 1994 257p $22.95

ISBN 0-395-64493-3   LC 94-9528

Analyzed in Short story index

Contents: Aren't you happy for me?; Weather; High-heeled shoe; Tandolfo the great; Evening; Billboard; The person I have mostly become; The natural effects of divorce; Rare & endangered species [novella]

"Most of the stories examine relationships that cross generations, mainly between grown children and their parents. . . . Death, birth, the arcing of love—this is Bausch territory, mapped with a fine, unwavering hand." Publ Wkly

Rebel powers. Houghton Mifflin; Lawrence, S. 1993 390p $21.95

ISBN 0-395-59508-8   LC 93-9194

"Thomas Boudreaux, divorced proprietor of a used-book store in Virginia, writes about his family in 1967, when he was 17 and his father Daniel, an Air Force career man and Vietnam hero, was caught stealing a typewriter from his Maryland base and sentenced to two years of hard labor in Wilson Creek, Wyo. Daniel's surprising act and rapid conviction pitch his family—his wife Connie, Thomas and eight-year-old Lisa—into nearly overwhelming uncertainty. After they move off the base and into a new town, Connie decides that they must go to Wilson Creek. On the train ride across country, they are befriended by young Penny Holt. Thomas's initial interest in Penny becomes obsessive after she moves into their Wilson Creek boarding house, where she will play a central role in the family's drama." Publ Wkly

"The key to the novel's credibility is the unretouched quality of its portraiture. Its characters live in a carefully chronicled American moment when threatening new ideas are beginning to rub up against weighty old certainties." N Y Times Book Rev

Violence. Houghton Mifflin; Lawrence, S. 1992 293p $19.95

ISBN 0-395-59509-6   LC 91-31419

"Expecting their first child, moody, impatient Charles Connolly and his somewhat dismayed young wife Carol travel to Chicago to celebrate Christmas with Charles's mother. During this visit, Charles is temporarily held hostage with a group of customers in a convenience

Bausch, Richard, 1945——*Continued*
store—an incident that ends in bloodshed. This random act of violence shatters the couple's marriage and leaves Charles paralyzed by guilt and fear." Libr J

"For both Charles and the reader, the public tragedy becomes the catalyst that produces a painful awareness of a darker, less immediately visible brutality. Thus Mr. Bausch follows the twists and turns of Charles's psychological journey to the novel's difficult, revelatory and finally transfiguring conclusion." N Y Times Book Rev

Bawden, Nina, 1925-
Family money. St. Martin's Press 1991 250p o.p.

LC 91-21186

Available Thorndike Press large print edition

This is the "story of a woman attempting to come to grips with old age. When sixtyish widow Fanny Pye is mugged after witnessing a street crime, she finds her loss of memory a frightening portent of things to come. No one will take her seriously; her fears that she may have recognized her mugger are treated as irrational. In effect, friends and family have 'just lumped her into a sack labelled OLD WOMEN,' but Fanny fights back." Libr J

"Sharply observed and drawn with precision, Fanny's troubles and their eventual resolution make a compelling read." Publ Wkly

Bayer, William
Mirror maze. Villard Bks. 1994 338p $21
ISBN 0-679-41459-2   LC 93-1438

Lieutenant Frank Janek is "working on two difficult cases. One involves the murder of a man in a hotel room and a ring of women who prey on men looking for one-night stands. The other case is a nine-year-old headache that haunts the NYPD: Janek goes to Cuba to interview a witness who could turn around the conviction of a wealthy man in prison for the brutal murder of his wife. It all seems so straightforward until Janek realizes that each fact is distorted, and each truth hides another. . . . An outstanding novel." Libr J

Pattern crimes; a novel. Villard Bks. 1987 329p o.p.

LC 86-40401

Available Thorndike Press large print edition

This "tale is set in Jerusalem, where David Bar-Lev, head of the Pattern Crimes Unit, is investigating a series of murders in which all the victims have suffered similar slash marks on their bodies. Bar-Lev determines that there is more to the events than mere random violence. In fact, the truth of the bizarre activity involves the modern madness of the Middle East political scene and the ever-present threat of escalated holy war." Booklist

"Incisive prose, memorable characterization, a carefully orchestrated sense of place, and an intricate but lucid plot enhance this superlative, masterfully rendered police procedural. Excellent and provocative fiction." Libr J

Switch. Linden Press 1984 319p $13.95
ISBN 0-317-05158-X   LC 84-7140

"The locale is New York, where two women are murdered and their severed heads switched. . . . In charge of the case is Lieutenant Janek, an introspective, lonely police officer who believes in the psychological approach." N Y Times Book Rev

"The novel rings true with its police jargon and internal bickering, but the ending seems careless, and the hero seems too good, too tough, and too clever to be believed. . . . Still, the bizarre premise catches the reader's attention immediately, and Bayer does a good job of keeping the story moving." Booklist

Bayley, Iris *See* Murdoch, Iris

Beach, Edward Latimer, 1918-
Run silent, run deep; [by] Edward L. Beach. Holt, Rinehart & Winston 1955 364p o.p. Naval Inst. Press reprint available $32.95 (ISBN 0-87021-557-4)

"Commander Beach has taken the exciting material of a submarine war patrol in the Pacific in World War II and woven it into a novel. The author speaks and sees through the eyes of the book's central character, an Annapolis two-and-a-half striper with his first fleet submarine commnd, the Walrus." N Y Her Trib Books

"If ever a book has the ring of reality, this is it. From the moment the reader steps aboard a training boat in New London, Conn., to the time when the submarine Walrus dives deeply to avoid the depth charges of the enemy's destroyers, there is awe and respect for the author who created them." N Y Times Book Rev

Beagle, Peter S.
A fine and private place; a novel. Viking 1960 272p o.p. Buccaneer Bks. reprint available $18.95 (ISBN 0-89968-419-X)

"Mr. Rebeck has lived in a cemetery for 19 years and can talk to ghosts. He has been supplied with food by a cranky and hilariously funny raven who scavenges the city not only for food but for information of the world outside, so that Mr. Rebeck can remain cloistered. A living companion enters his life when Mrs. Kapper, a Bronx widow, begins to make regular visits to the grave of her deceased husband. Rebeck becomes involved also in the growing relationship between two ghosts, a young professor and a bookstore clerk, neither of whom was honest with himself or herself or others until death allowed them that freedom. This fantasy, rich with characters and situations, takes a less grim look at death than we usually encounter." Shapiro. Fic for Youth. 3d edition

The innkeeper's song; a novel. ROC 1993 346p $20
ISBN 0-451-45288-7   LC 93-3800

"Three powerful women (each with her own secret past), a stable boy, a weaver's son, and an innkeeper set in motion a series of events that bring each of them face to face with the forces of magic and the workings of fate." Libr J

"In elegant yet simple prose Beagle illuminates the shifting relationships among the various major and minor players . . . who people this affecting tale." Publ Wkly

The last unicorn. Viking 1968 218p o.p.

"A beautiful and previously happy unicorn learns that she may be the last unicorn left on earth. Wanting not to believe it, she sets off in quest of her fellows. In the course of her journey, she meets a carnival magician of little ability, has encounters with a Robin Hood-like band, a king presiding over a hate-filled and miserable land, with the aid of the mysterious Red Bull, and a glamorous, if previously ineffectual prince." Publ Wkly

Beagle, Peter S.—*Continued*

"Beagle is a true magician with words, a master of prose and a deft practitioner in verse. He has been compared, not unreasonably, with Lewis Carroll and J. R. R. Tolkien, but he stands squarely and triumphantly on his own feet." Saturday Rev

Bear, Greg, 1951-

Anvil of stars. Warner Bks. 1992 434p $19.95

ISBN 0-446-51601-5   LC 91-50411

Sequel to The forge of God

"One alien culture has destroyed Earth; another, called the Benefactors, has offered the survivors a chance for revenge by building a spaceship for a group of young volunteers whose goal is the extermination of their enemy." Libr J

"Bear is superlatively competent in the English language and a master of both technical wizardry and powerful scenes. Throughout the book, he addresses the question of an ethical basis for genocide, leaving the matter sufficiently open to make one wonder whether the story is yet completed." Booklist

The forge of God. TOR Bks. 1987 474p $17.95

ISBN 0-312-93021-6   LC 87-50482

"Three geologists discover an alien artifact in Death Valley and set off a chain of events leading to the discovery that Earth is about to be invaded by two alien races. One race sends out planet-wrecking machines; . . . the other is trying to enlist the survivors of humanity in tracking down and destroying the planet wreckers. The battle over Earth is seen through the eyes of a large cast of well-drawn characters, crowned by a climax of enormous power." Booklist

Moving Mars. TOR Bks. 1993 448p $23.95

ISBN 0-312-85515-X   LC 93-26546

This novel "tells of twenty-second-century success in making Mars habitable for unprotected human life. It is told from the viewpoints of a physicist who, in his pursuit of knowledge, becomes linked with an artificial intelligence and a young woman from one of Mars' first families who embraces revolutionary politics in pursuit of a future for her native world." Booklist

"Bear makes good use of the extended flashback to illuminate the lives of a pair of extraordinary visionaries who struggle to create a new world on an old planet. Contrasts between Earth's wasted potential and Mars's constant promise emerge through strong characterization and compelling prose." Libr J

Beaton, M. C.

Agatha Raisin and the potted gardener. St. Martin's Press 1994 196p $19.95

ISBN 0-312-10927-X   LC 94-6608

Agatha Raisin "returns to quiet Carsely after a lengthy tour to find that a newcomer has supplanted her in the affections of James Lacey, her sleuthing partner and next-door neighbor. This newcomer, a very attractive woman of means, has wriggled her way into the good graces of the villagers. But an upcoming gardening competition reveals hidden animosities and leads to the woman's murder. A simple plot embellished with horticultural

manipulations provides the perfect background for the lovelorn Agatha and her unique brand of humor." Libr J

Agatha Raisin and the quiche of death. St. Martin's Press 1992 201p $17.95

ISBN 0-312-08153-7   LC 92-28381

"Bored with her early retirement and still on the lookout for romance wherever she can find it, Spunky Agatha Raisin, former owner of a London public-relations firm, welcomes the arrival of veterinarian Paul Bladen to her quiet Cotswold village. When the new vet, whose charming con-man exterior conceals a hatred of dogs and cats, dies from an injection from his own hypodermic syringe, Agatha and her neighbor James Lacey decide that Bladen has been murdered—and line up an extended list of possible suspects." Booklist

Death of a charming man. Warner Bks. 1994 215p $18.95

ISBN 0-89296-529-0   LC 93-36318

Scottish detective Hamish MacBeth "meets handsome newcomer, Peter Hynd, whose suave looks send the village womenfolk running to the hairdresser and aerobics classes. Soon they are at each other's throats and queueing up for a place in his bed. The Lothario goes missing and soon the body of one of his conquests is found on the beach, leaving Hamish with two mysteries to solve while his domestic life deteriorates. Beaton's tremendously likable policeman stars herein a tightly wrought tale, with a gem of an ending in which Hamish manages to be both dead right and dead wrong." Publ Wkly

Death of a glutton. St. Martin's Press 1993 152p $16.95

ISBN 0-312-08761-6   LC 92-21220

This "Hamish Macbeth case occurs near a Scottish Highlands hotel, where someone murders an obnoxious, man-chasing fat woman." Libr J

Death of a hussy. St. Martin's Press 1990 164p o.p.

LC 90-36883

"The Scottish village of Lochdubh has a problem: the beloved police constable, Hamish Macbeth has been transferred to Strathbane because of a dearth of local crime. In a successful bid to get him back, the villagers, led by newcomer Maggie Baird, organize a crime wave. On his return Hamish is confronted with a possible murder." Publ Wkly

"Maggie is a devil, all right, but splendid fun as a character. And the mischief she makes in Lochdubh is resolved by Hamish in an easygoing Highland fashion that is no less canny for being so droll." N Y Times Book Rev

Death of a snob. St. Martin's Press 1991 151p o.p.

LC 90-29906

"Detective Hamish Macbeth, with more couth and tenacity than the usual Scottish villager, visits a health farm on the Hebridean island of Eileencraig to investigate a woman's suspicions that someone wants her dead. He joins a holiday house party there, and meets an unconscionable snob who ends up with a broken neck. Hamish suspects more than an accident, and with the aid of an attractive cookbook writer, he nails the culprit. This efficient little caper, full of gentle humor,

Beaton, M. C.—*Continued*

quick character sketches, and easy movement, will endear itself to Hamish fans and newcomers as well." Libr J

Death of a travelling man. St. Martin's Press 1993 151p $17.95

ISBN 0-312-09783-2   LC 93-20797

Scottish policeman Hamish MacBeth "acquires a new sidekick, P.C. Willie Lamont, who has less talent for police work than for cleaning, polishing, and scrubbing. His insistence on keeping the police station spotless is driving MacBeth mad. But Hamish has other troubles: his lady friend, Priscilla, is being standoffish, and a handsome drifter named Sean has arrived in Lochdubh and seems to be a catalyst for evil. When Sean is brutally murdered, Hamish has the difficult task of finding his killer without upsetting Lochdubh's placid way of life *or* his police superiors in Strathbane." Booklist

Beattie, Ann

The burning house; short stories. Random House 1982 256p o.p.

LC 82-5292

Analyzed in Short story index

Contents: Learning to fall; Jacklighting; Girl talk; The Cinderella waltz; Playback; Winter: 1978; Gravity; Sunshine and shadow; Desire; Happy; Waiting; Afloat; Running dreams; Like glass; Greenwich time; The burning house

These "are marvelously written, moving tales, poignant in that they reveal so much about the way we live now, the way we feel now. . . . Beattie's world is grisaille, sharply observed, carefully shaded with nuances of feeling made tangible and almost surreal by brilliant, seemingly offhand, perfectly chosen significant detail. Beattie's fictions are stunning." Publ Wkly

Chilly scenes of winter. Doubleday 1976 280p o.p.

Charles, the protagonist "loves Laura and is waiting for her, as he must; she is married, not well, and he can only wait for her to return to him, if she will. Waiting, he turns 27, works at the dull job he can't afford to leave, endures his grotesquely crazy mother and his well-meaning but stupid stepfather and kills time with his old buddy Sam." N Y Times Book Rev

"Beattie has an instinct for the grotesque that verges on the edge of real wit and pain. She is obviously a first-rate craftswoman with an eye for idiosyncratic detail." Saturday Rev

Falling in place. Random House 1980 342p o.p.

LC 79-3880

This novel is set "in the summer of 1979. Skylab is falling, 'Norma Rae' is showing. . . . John Knapp, a 40-year-old ad-man with three whiny children and a glum wife in Connecticut, is having an affair with 25-year-old Nina. . . . The Knapps' threadbare suburban marriage . . . has worn down to numb, toneless bickering. Nina's affair with John is her best hope of extricating herself from a floating circle of drug-dazed friends from her college days." Newsweek

"Describes with light irony the dilemmas of failed marriages, fragile affairs, sibling rivalry, and the petulance and irresponsibility of spoiled children. Beattie captures the petty conflicts, studied egoism, and pathetic mistakes and misdirections that characterize the Knapp family and those who surround them (friends, lovers, teachers, neigh-

bors). 'Falling in place' is a casual, witty depiction of the broken American dream—the sterility of a middle-class family without purpose or direction." Choice

Love always; a novel. Random House 1985 247p o.p.

LC 84-45749

"A Vermont-based magazine devoted to the last remaining vestiges of the counterculture harbors a number of people who have turned on and dropped out but still haven't quite mellowed out. Beattie observes these characters over the length of a summer as they sort through their myriad distractions and cope with the stresses of an overprivileged country life-style." Booklist

"The story seems to advance aimlessly, as an offbeat cast of characters . . . moves in and out of the action, humorously converging by chance or coincidence. A funny satire of contemporary media culture and its confusion between reality and invention, and a sad story of disaffected lives." Libr J

Picturing Will. Random House 1989 230p $18.95

ISBN 0-394-56987-3   LC 89-42781

"Aspiring photographer Jody, abandoned by husband Wayne—now on his third wife—is deeply devoted to her young son Will but hesitant to commit to lover Mel. Still, she visits Mel in faraway New York City, where Mel's friend, gallery owner Haverford (whose name she can recall only as Haveabud), takes a shine to her work—or to her. When Mel takes Will to visit his father in Florida, Haveabud goes along for the ride, bringing Spencer, a former protegé's son. . . . Meanwhile Wayne demonstrates his continued instability by cheating flagrantly on his new wife, Corky." Libr J

Beattie "has almost as many narrative voices as characters in this book, yet the result is never confusing. . . . 'Picturing Will' would be admirable for its technique alone; what makes it Beattie's best novel is her new and fearless way with emotional complexity." Newsweek

Where you'll find me and other stories. Linden Press/Simon & Schuster 1986 191p o.p.

LC 86-7396

Analyzed in Short story index

Contents: In the white night; Snow; Skeletons; The big outside world; Coney Island; When can I see you again?; Lofty; High School; Janus; Spiritus; Times; Summer people; Cards; Heaven on a summer night; Where you'll find me

"At the risk of repeating herself thematically and stylistically in her latest collection of stories, Beattie sticks to her succinct depictions of middle-class, early middle-age lives. The sense of disaffection that overwhelms these characters produces a somewhat monotonous effect as Beattie offers brief glimpses of people whose dreams and disappointments supposedly represent the Yuppie generation's version of existential angst." Booklist

Beauvoir, Simone de, 1908-1986

The age of discretion

In Beauvoir, S. de. The woman destroyed p9-85

Beauvoir, Simone de, 1908-1986—*Continued*

Les belles images; translated by Patrick O'Brian. Putnam 1968 224p o.p.

Original French edition, 1966

Laurence, the heroine, is an advertising executive married to a rising architect, and the mother of two daughters. The novel considers her involvements with her parents, husband, lover and children

"At first glance, this book has all been done before, and more intensely. But its final effect is cumulative and peculiarly moving. . . . Simone de Beauvoir has the true novelist's gift of selecting detail and creating individuals whilst refusing to sum up situations." New Statesman

The mandarins; a novel. World Pub. 1956 610p o.p.

Original French edition, 1954

This "semiautobiographical novel addressed the attempts of post-World War II leftist intellectuals to abandon their elite, 'mandarin' status and to engage in political activism. The characters of psychologist Anne Dubreuilh and her husband Robert were roughly based on de Beauvoir and her lifelong associate Jean-Paul Sartre; de Beauvoir's account of Anne's affair with the American Lewis Brogan was a thinly veiled account of her own relationship with novelist Nelson Algren." Merriam-Webster's Ency of Lit

The monologue

In Beauvoir, S. de. The woman destroyed p87-120

The woman destroyed; translated by Patrick O'Brian. Putnam 1969 254p $14

ISBN 0-394-71103-3

Original French edition, 1967

"The title story describes the heartjolting experience of a betrayed wife, and her gradual descent into the abyss of absolute estrangement from her husband. In a grimly revealing 'Monologue,' about another lady in deep distress, Mme. de Beauvoir permits her to speak for herself in a shattering rage against the world that has cast her out for her crimes against it. The third story, 'Age of Discretion,' has overtones of autobiography as it takes the reader on a voyage of discovery between the heroine, a writer, and her scientist husband, as they come to share, at last, the bitter knowledge of their son's reputation." Publ Wkly

The woman destroyed [novelette]

In Beauvoir, S. de. The woman destroyed p121-254

Beck, K. K.

The body in the cornflakes. St. Martin's Press 1992 216p $17.95

ISBN 0-312-08146-4   LC 92-24910

"A Thomas Dunne book"

"When Karl Krogstad, silver-haired owner of Galaxy Foods, announces he will marry sexy Ginger Jessup, Galaxy's TV spokeswoman, his entire family is horrified, especially those who had counted on inheriting the successful Pacific Northwest store. . . . At the grand opening, Ginger's body is found among the boxes of cornflakes on special sale." Publ Wkly

This "is light crime fare, pretty funny, filled with sharp detail." Booklist

A hopeless case; a mystery novel. Mysterious Press 1992 265p $18.95

ISBN 0-89296-479-0   LC 91-58023

"In her late 30s and tired of eking out an existence in Europe, expatriate widow Jane Silva is offered a substantial inheritance if she will assume her late uncle's quixotic profession of solving hopeless cases for those who have no other recourse. Seattle, her childhood home, at first seems to provide little scope for the type of situation that would fit the criteria of the will (which mandates absolutely no publicity), but soon Jane is approached by Leonora Martin, a talented young musician who wants to finance her further studies by regaining the substantial amount of money her now-dead hippie mother, Linda, had given years before to a cult called the Fellowship of the Flame. . . . A good, clean writer with an eye for apt description, Beck has created a breezy and modern detective in a relatively little-mined setting." Publ Wkly

Beckett, Samuel, 1906-1989

Nobel Prize in literature, 1969

Dream of fair to middling women; edited by Eoin O'Brien and Edith Fournier; foreword by Eoin O'Brien. Arcade Pub. 1993 xx, 241p il $21.95

ISBN 1-55970-217-6   LC 92-56275

"In Beckett's semi-autobiographical first novel, never before published, a young man named Belacqua pursues lust and learning across Europe

"Beckett's signature fierceness and piercing insight into the lurchings of the mind are already evident in this early yet adept, high-energy, and boisterously libidinous novel. Belacqua is a layabout, a dreamer, and a pouter, simultaneously aroused and disgusted by the physicality of women. His hazy relationships and silly flirtations, drunken conversations and glorious sulks, temper tantrums and bursts of literary affectation are all conveyed with Beckett's famous double-edged humor and tremendous command of language and thought." Booklist

Malone dies

In Beckett, S. Molloy, Malone dies, and The unnamable p241-398

Molloy

In Beckett, S. Molloy, Malone dies, and The unnamable p2-240

Molloy, Malone dies, and The unnamable; three novels. Grove Press 1959 577p o.p.

Original French editions of Molloy and Malone dies published 1951; The unnamable, 1953. These translations published separately 1955, 1956 and 1958, respectively

The trilogy "is concerned with the search for identity, for the true self which can rest from self-caricature; and as a parallel it is concerned with the true silence which is the end of speech. Molloy, Malone and their final unnamable incarnation are paradigms of humanity in general and of the artist in particular. . . .The trilogy seen as a whole composes one of the most remarkable, most original and most haunting prose-works of the century." Times Lit Suppl

Beckett, Samuel, 1906-1989—*Continued*

Murphy. Grove Press 1957 282p o.p.

First published 1938 in the United Kingdom

"The story concerns an Irishman in London who yearns to do nothing more than sit in his rocking chair and daydream. Murphy attempts to avoid all action; he escapes from a girl he is about to marry, takes up with a kind prostitute, and finds a job as a nurse in a mental institution, where he plays nonconfrontational chess. His disengagement from the world is shattered when his fiancée, with a detective and two new lovers in tow, discovers him. He is killed when someone accidentally turns on the gas in his apartment." Merriam-Webster's Ency of Lit

The unnamable

In Beckett, S. Molloy, Malone dies, and The unnamable p400-577

Begley, Louis

Wartime lies. Knopf 1991 197p $19

ISBN 0-679-40016-8   LC 90-53429

This "novel recounts the wounded moral development of its narrator, a Jew who shared with thousands the misfortune of being born in a time and place to grow up during the Nazi occupation of Poland." N Y Times Book Rev

"The reader of this novel by a gifted writer reaches a better understanding of the destruction of the European Jews in a world gone mad. More important, unlike so much Holocaust fiction, *Wartime Lies* neither trivializes nor exploits the horrors of this most inhuman era of our history." Booklist

Bell, Acton *See* Brontë, Anne, 1820-1849

Bell, Christine, 1951-

The Perez family. Norton 1990 256p o.p.

LC 89-25569

This is a "novel about a Cuban ex-prisoner's arrival in America in the Mariel boatlift. . . . Juan Raul Perez was imprisoned 20 years ago for his political views in his native Cuba, while his wife and young daughter fled to Miami. Few letters have gotten through in the ensuing 20 years, and Juan doesn't know what to expect when he finds them again. But before the reunion, Juan must survive the dizzy world of refugee relocation." Libr J

"Christine Bell is much more than a lighthearted comic novelist. She's one of those writers like Flannery O'Connor or Isak Dinesen: she doesn't so much write stories as spin tales. . . . What may have seemed cartoonish in the middle of the book, you now realize, was mythic, archetypal. What you have been reading turns out to be a profound little parable about the redemptive power of love." N Y Times Book Rev

Bell, Currer *See* Brontë, Charlotte, 1816-1855

Bell, Ellis *See* Brontë, Emily, 1818-1848

Bell, Madison Smartt

All souls' rising. Pantheon Bks. 1995 530p $25

ISBN 0-679-43989-7   LC 95-12339

"Set during the struggle for Haiti's independence in the late 1700s, this intensely imagined epic novel of racial hatred and bloody upheaval illuminates the enmities among the astonishingly complex ethnic populations of the Caribbean island. Bell evokes a society caught in the crucible of violence with superb characterizations, ranging from the arrogant *grand blanc* plantation owners to the black slaves—including Toussaint L'Ouverture, the leader of the black revolt." Publ Wkly

Barking man and other stories. Ticknor & Fields 1990 230p o.p.

LC 89-48683

Analyzed in Short story index

Contents: Holding together; Black and tan; Customs of the country; Finding Natasha; Dragon's seed; Barking man; Petit Cachou; Witness; Move on up; Mr. Potatohead in love

"These memorable tales take place in Bell's native South, the streets of New York, London, the French Riviera, and even a mouse's cage. Each setting is fully realized, perfectly expressing the space and pace of each environment. His characters are striking creations: misfits and loners, visionaries and atypical heroes, their lives pulsing with menace." Booklist

Belle, Pamela

Treason's gift. St. Martin's Press 1993 c1992 546p $24.95

ISBN 0-312-08913-9   LC 92-37736

Another title in the author's series set during the English Civil Wars. Previous titles are: Wintercombe (1988); The lodestar (1989); A falling star (1990)

First published 1992 in the United Kingdom

"When the handsome rake Sir Alexander St. Barbe and his captivating wife, Louise, lose their first child, Louise retreats into her grief and Alex has a foolish affair. Though the couple reconcile, Alex's vicious aunt reveals Alex's indiscretion to Louise, causing another breach between them; then Alex's actions during a drunken rage force him to flee the country. In the Netherlands, Alex comes to lead the party that is encouraging their Highnesses of Orange to assume the British throne before James II can relight the fires of Smithfield." Publ Wkly

Bellow, Saul

Nobel Prize in literature, 1976

The adventures of Augie March; with an introduction by Martin Amis. Knopf 1995 xxxvii, 616p $20

ISBN 0-679-44460-2

"Everyman's library"

A reissue of the title first published 1953 by Viking

"It is a picaresque story of a poor Jewish youth from Chicago, his progress, sometimes highly comic, through the world of the 20th century, and his attempts to make sense of it." Merriam-Webster's Ency of Lit

The Bellarosa connection. Penguin Bks. 1989 102p pa original $7.95

ISBN 0-14-012686-4   LC 89-32936

"This is the story of clubfooted, multilingual Harry Fonstein, a lucky refugee from Holocaust Europe, and his grandly obese wife, Sorella. Arrested in Mussolini's Rome, Harry was imprisoned and awaiting deportation when his escape was arranged by an underground group, bankrolled by Broadway bigshot Billy Rose. Harry wants

Bellow, Saul—*Continued*

personally to thank Rose, but all his efforts are rebuffed. Finally, Sorella confronts Rose in Jerusalem, ready to blackmail him into meeting with Harry." Libr J

"The end of 'The Bellarosa Connection' is abrupt, matter-of-fact, almost offbeat. It is a conclusion, perhaps, in which nothing is concluded, . . . but it is appropriate to the overall pitch and voice of this cannily resourceful entertainment." N Y Times Book Rev

also in Bellow, S. Something to remember me by p[1]-89

Dangling man. Vanguard Press 1944 191p o.p.

This story purports to be the journal of a young man living in Chicago, who gives up his job, expecting to be inducted into the army. Owing to technicalities Joseph is left dangling for almost a year. His journal explains his psychological reactions to idleness, how he passes his time, his growing unrest, and finally the relief when the call comes

"The book is an excellent document on the experience of the non-combatant in time of war. It is well written and never dull—in spite of the dismalness of the Chicago background and the undramatic character of the subject. It is also one of the most honest pieces of testimony on the psychology of a whole generation who have grown up during the depression and the war." New Yorker

The dean's December; a novel. Harper & Row 1982 312p $14.95

ISBN 0-06-014849-7   LC 80-8705

This is a "'tale of two cities', both seen through the eyes of Albert Corde, who visits Bucharest to see his dying mother-in-law, where he reflects on the contrasts between the violence and corruption of Chicago and the bureaucratic chill of Eastern Europe; the novel has, like much of Bellow's work, a strongly apocalyptic note." Oxford Companion to Engl Lit

Henderson the rain king; a novel. Viking 1959 341p o.p.

This novel, "designed on a grand and mythic scale, records American millionaire Gene Henderson's quest for revelation and spiritual power in Africa, where he becomes rainmaker and heir to a kingdom." Oxford Companion to Engl Lit

also in Bellow, S. The portable Saul Bellow

Herzog. Viking 1964 341p o.p.

"Beleaguered by the intensity of his introspection, Herzog worries over his life: an intellectual stumped in the middle of his second book—tellingly, an inquiry into Romanticism—a husband brooding over his second failed marriage, and above all a man trying to think his way into clarity, all the while wryly aware that he is the creator of his own paralysis. The epitome of this condition is the spate of letters that Herzog writes—to the living and the dead, to the famous and to his own circle of friends and enemies—but never sends. The letters document Herzog's detailed, vivid, and anxious apprehensions of contemporary American life in Chicago, in New York, and in the more pastoral setting of his retreat in the Berkshires. They also serve as a wonderfully colloquial venue for his irreverent, chatty, but also profound reflections on the fate of the individual in modern society." Benet's Reader's Ency of Am Lit

Him with his foot in his mouth and other stories. Harper & Row 1984 294p $15.95

ISBN 0-06-015179-X   LC 83-48322

Analyzed in Short story index

Contents: Him with his foot in his mouth; What kind of day did you have? [novella]; Zetland: by a character witness; A silver dish; Cousins

"Love totally eludes Katrina Goliger in 'What Kind of Day Did You Have?' The banal title of the story becomes increasingly ironic as Katrina's predicament unfolds. Freshly divorced, under scrutiny by her husband as he waits for an excuse to seize his two daughters, Katrina pursues an affair with a dying intellectual named Victor Wulpy." Best Sellers

"An impressive collection: Bellow's lush, intellectual fiction vigorously confronts ideas and connects individual experience to a broad scheme of life and art and thought." Libr J

Humboldt's gift. Viking 1975 487p o.p.

"The story of Charlie Citrine, a successful writer and academic plagued by women, lawsuits, and mafiosi, whose present career is interwoven with memories of the early success, failing powers, and squalid death of his friend Von Humboldt Fleischer, whose poetic destiny he fears he may inherit, together with his manuscripts." Oxford Companion to Engl Lit

More die of heartbreak. Morrow 1987 335p o.p.

LC 87-5770

"The novel is narrated by Ken Trachtenberg, a Paris-born and -educated 35-year-old professor of Russian. . . . . The main character, Ken's uncle Benn Crader, is a world-famous botanist. After experiencing numerous sexual miseries during his 15 years as a widower, Benn marries a wealthy and beautiful young woman, Matilda Layamon. Between marriages, Benn had been swindled by his uncle, Harold Vilitzer, a crooked political boss. . . . Matilda's father, Dr. Layamon, plans to use Benn to recover a few million from Vilitzer, so that his daughter can live luxuriously and entertain lavishly. . . . [The] subplot describes Ken's attempt to recover his child from his former mistress, Treckie . . . and his courtship of his warm-hearted student Dita." Natl Rev

"Bellow has always been as enthralled by crooks as by the higher realms of thought. His prose mixes soaring meditation with streetsmart wisecracks. The farcical collisions of ill-prepared idealists with hard-as-nails swindlers and connivers give 'More Die of Heartbreak' its juicy vivacity. . . . Our time with Benn and Kenneth is well spent for the sake of the rascals to whom they introduce us. Bellow's comedy is cunningly planned: first we rollick, then we pause to think." Newsweek

Mr. Sammler's planet. Viking 1970 313p o.p.

"Artur Sammler, in his seventies and an escapee from the horrors of Nazi atrocities and the memory of having had to dig himself out of his own grave, theorizes about the possibility of finding a similar escape from the assaults of life in New York City, its muggings, crime, dirt, noise. Living with his bizarre daughter, Shula, also saved from death in Europe but somewhat deranged, perhaps the result of traumas suffered, is not possible, and living with his niece Margotte also has its drawbacks. The most important person to Sammler is his nephew Elya, by whose generosity Sammler and Shula are able to exist. But Elya's escape from the horrors of his own life—his son Wallace's irresponsible behavior

Bellow, Saul—*Continued*
and his daughter Angela's sexually promiscuous behavior—is by way of death. For our desire to find relief from the outrages of life in this decade, Bellow has made a metaphor of man's desire to go to the moon." Shapiro. Fic for Youth. 3d edition

The portable Saul Bellow; with critical introduction by Gabriel Josipovici; compiled under the supervision of the author by Edith Tarcov. Viking 1974 xlvii, 654p o.p.

"Viking portable library"
Contains the complete novels: Seize the day and Henderson the rain king; excerpts from: The adventures of Augie March, Herzog, and Mr. Sammler's planet; and three short stories: Leaving the yellow house, Mosby's memoirs, and The old system

Seize the day; with three short stories and a one-act play. Viking 1956 211p o.p.
Partially analyzed in Short story index
Anthology composed of one novella: Seize the day; three short stories. A father-to-be, Looking for Mr. Green, and The Gonzaga manuscripts; and a one-act play: The wrecker
"Seize the Day, the long title story, is a great one. . . . The other work in the book is much lighter. . . . Seize the Day gives contemporary literature a story which will be explained, expounded, and argued, but about which a final reckoning can be made only after it ripples out in the imagination of the generations of readers to come. I suspect that it is one of the central stories of our day." Nation

Seize the day [novelette]

In Bellow, S. The portable Saul Bellow
In Bellow, S. Seize the day

Something to remember me by; three tales. Viking 1991 222p $21.95
ISBN 0-670-84216-8   LC 91-51059
Analyzed in Short story index
The novellas The Bellarosa connection and A theft, are entered separately; the title short story was first published 1990 in Esquire
Contents: The Bellarosa connection; A theft; Something to remember me by

A theft; a novella. Penguin Bks. 1989 109p pa original $6.95
ISBN 0-14-011969-8   LC 88-29261
It is Ithiel 'Teddy' Regler, the love of Clara Velde's life, "who gave Clara the emerald ring which she had cherished for years as a symbol of their love, and when the ring is lost she goes into a tailspin. It is recovered, only to be lost—or stolen—once again. . . . Its disappearance is related to her Austrian au pair girl, Gina, whose Haitian boyfriend has been lurking ominously around Clara's Park Avenue co-op. The theft of the ring turns out to be the first step on Clara's path to a new self-knowledge—and . . . [an] affirmation of her love for Lucy, her . . . ten year old daughter." New Statesman
"One doesn't read Bellow just for his plots; one reads him for his marvelous characterization, his verbal dexterity, his trenchant observations, and his philosophical speculations." Libr J

also in Bellow, S. Something to remember me by p[91]-181

What kind of day did you have?
In Bellow, S. Him with his foot in his mouth and other stories p61-163

Benchley, Peter
Beast. Random House 1991 349p $21
ISBN 0-679-40355-8   LC 91-10579
Also available G.K. Hall large print edition
"*Jaws* revisited, but this time with a giant squid as villain. *The Beast* eats swimmers and everything else in sight off the Bermuda coast. Benchley contends that greedy fishermen created the condition for the squid's presence. Overfishing the oceans, destroying coral reefs with bleach, using nets and explosives, and trapping protected sea creatures have eliminated the beast's natural enemies." Libr J
"The suspense is consistent and compelling. Mr. Benchley squeezes every act of violence for maximum tension, dragging out the squid's killings until we too are tangled in the story." N Y Times Book Rev

Jaws. Doubleday 1974 311p o.p.
This is a "story about what happens when a great white shark terrorizes a small Long Island town. . . . A woman swimmer is devoured by the shark, and Police Chief Martin Brody insists on closing the beaches. But he's overruled by the town fathers who remind him that the community is dependent on summer visitors for economic survival. Two deaths later, the news can no longer be suppressed and Brody, an oceanographer and a fisherman go after the monster in an exciting chase." Publ Wkly

Benedict, Elizabeth
Safe conduct. Farrar, Straus & Giroux 1993 230p $21
ISBN 0-374-25341-2   LC 92-37077
Documentary photographer Kate Lurie is newly married to Eli MacKenzie. "Mac has told her about his torrid three-week affair with luscious Lida in St. Petersburg, where he was sent by the State Department in 1971. But Kate is unprepared for the shock of an encounter with Lida, who, 15 years after she and Mac had parted, confronts the couple in Brussels and boldly tempts Mac to be unfaithful. . . . Benedict's spare narrative reflects the tension of a frightened woman witnessing what may be the destruction of her happiness." Publ Wkly

Benét, Stephen Vincent, 1898-1943
The Devil and Daniel Webster; illustrated by Harold Denison. Farrar & Rinehart 1937 61p il o.p. Amereon reprint available $10.95 (ISBN 0-8488-0789-8)
"Jabez Stone, a New Hampshire farmer, receives a decade of material wealth in return for selling his soul to the Devil—Mr. Scratch. When the Devil comes to claim Stone's soul, the farmer has the statesman and orator Daniel Webster argue his case at midnight before a jury of historic American villains." Merriam-Webster's Ency of Lit

also in Benét, S. V. Selected works. Volume two: Prose

Benét, Stephen Vincent, 1898-1943 —
Continued
Selected works. Volume two: Prose. Farrar & Rinehart 1942 483p o.p.
Analyzed in Short story index
Contents: Jacob and the Indians; Tooth for Paul Revere; Devil and Daniel Webster; Freedom's a hard-bought thing; O'Halloran's luck; Diehard; Johnny Pye and the fool-killer; Spanish bayonet; Too early spring; Story about the ant-eater; Schooner Fairchild's class; Everybody was very nice; All around the town; Glamour; No visitors; Death in the country; The curfew tolls; King of the cats; Doc Mellhorn and the pearly gates; Last of the legions; Blood of the martyrs; Into Egypt; By the waters of Babylon

Benford, Gregory, 1941-
Matter's end
In Nebula awards 28 p52-94

Timescape. Simon & Schuster 1980 412p o.p.
"As the world lurches toward disaster, scientists in 1998 try to transmit a warning message to 1962 by means of tachyons. Their story is told in parallel with that of the scientists trying to decode the transmission, and the two plots converge on the possibility of paradox. Unusual for the realism of its depiction of scientists at work; admirably serious in handling the implications of its theme." Anatomy of Wonder 4

(jt. auth) Clarke, A. C. Beyond the fall of night

Benson, E. F. (Edward Frederic), 1867-1940
Fine feathers and other stories; selected and introduced by Jack Adrian. Oxford Univ. Press 1994 302p $23
ISBN 0-19-212325-4   LC 93-38186
Analyzed in Short story index
Contents: The lovers; 'Complete rest'; The five foolish virgins; My friend the murderer; Professor Burnaby's discovery; The exposure of Pamela; Miss Maria's romance; The eavesdropper; James Sutherland, Ltd.; Bootles; Julian's cottage; Fine feathers; The defeat of Lady Hartridge; The jamboree; Complementary souls; Dodo and the brick; A comedy of styles; Noblesse oblige; An entire mistake; Mr. Carew's game of croquet; The fall of Augusta; The male impersonator; M.O.M.; The adventure of Hegel Junior; The simple life; Mrs. Andrews's control; George's secret; Buntingford jugs; By the sluice; Atmospherics; Boxing night
"Lovers of Benson's Mapp and Lucia novels should enjoy this compilation of short stories, all published between 1894 and 1931 and collected here for the first time. . . . Relics of a decidedly vanished age, Benson's delightful stories are escapism, pure and simple." Booklist

Lucia in London
In Benson, E. F. Make way for Lucia p179-358

Make way for Lucia. Harper & Row 1986 c1977 1119p $29.95
ISBN 0-06-015678-3   LC 86-45639

A reissue of the omnibus edition of six novels and one short story published 1977 by Crowell
These novels were originally published in the United States by George H. Doran Company and Doubleday, Doran & Company
Contents: Queen Lucia (1920); Lucia in London (1928); Miss Mapp (1923); The male impersonator (1929); Mapp and Lucia (1931); The worshipful Lucia (1935) [published in England with title: Lucia's progress]; Trouble with Lucia (1939)

The male impersonator
In Benson, E. F. Make way for Lucia p535-48

Mapp and Lucia
In Benson, E. F. Make way for Lucia p549-762

Miss Mapp
In Benson, E. F. Make way for Lucia p359-534

Queen Lucia
In Benson, E. F. Make way for Lucia p1-178

Trouble for Lucia
In Benson, E. F. Make way for Lucia p941-1119

The worshipful Lucia
In Benson, E. F. Make way for Lucia p763-940

Benson, Edward Frederic *See* Benson, E. F. (Edward Frederic), 1867-1940

Berent, Mark
Steel tiger. Putnam 1990 399p o.p.
          LC 89-70151
"'Steel Tiger' was U.S. Air Force code for the northern panhandle of Laos, a crucial sector of the Ho Chi Minh Trail. This sequel to *Rolling Thunder* [1989] focuses on the efforts of the Air Force in the summer and fall of 1967 to cut the vital supply line. . . . Fast-paced accounts of strike missions and fighter combat are juxtaposed with an effective subplot describing North Vietnam's air defenses through the eyes of a Soviet pilot." Publ Wkly

Storm flight. Putnam 1993 383p $22.95
ISBN 0-399-13814-5   LC 93-22981
Fifth and final novel in a series that includes: Rolling thunder (1989); Steel tiger (entered above); Phantom leader (1991) and Eagle station (1992)
"In the bitter year of 1972, deep inside Vietnam, American POWs with special knowledge or skills have been secretly removed from camps, their names hidden from official records. After a daring American raid exposes Soviet complicity, American airmen must try to free their comrades. . . . Genre aficionados will relish the wealth of military detail and the technical explanations; all readers will be rewarded by the ultimate mission, when planes, men and tactics are tested to the spine-tingling limits." Publ Wkly

Berger, Thomas, 1924-

Arthur Rex. Delacorte Press/Seymour Lawrence 1978 499p o.p.

LC 78-7241

A "modernization of Malory's 'Morte d'Arthur.' The setting remains ancient Britain, but King Arthur, Merlin, Launcelot, and the knights of the Round Table suffer from 20th-Century maladies; Guinevere and other fair ladies are liberated. Sex and introspection abound. Embellishing the basic tale, Berger adds seriocomic twists, fantasies, and exaggerations." Libr J

This is a "splendid, satiric retelling of the legend of Camelot. . . . The curious truth is that Mr. Berger's revisions are most authentic, most profound, when the admixture of parody is strongest. At those times—a good three-fourths of the book—he is never merely a parodist after all, but also a compelling yarnspinner in his own right." N Y Times Book Rev

Being invisible; a novel. Little, Brown 1987 262p o.p.

LC 86-20897

"Things are not going well for Fred Wagner, a typical Berger victim. His wife has left him, his job as a catalog copywriter is becoming increasingly unsatisfying, and his novel, after six years, has not progressed beyond the opening pages. Wagner discovers, however, that he does have a talent—he can make himself invisible—and the novel recounts his struggle to make the best of this unique gift. But surprisingly, Wagner finds that whether he is trying to bypass a long line, steal from a bank, or avoid his co-workers, invisibility has its drawbacks; rather than improving his situation, each invisible adventure leads to a further mishap." Libr J

"There is much in 'Being Invisible' to celebrate—the pleasures of invention, humor, surprise, of Mr. Berger's enraged, unforgiving view. That so much of his vision seems neither freakish nor admonitory but rather, oddly tonic, says something about the era in which we live. . . . It is a sign of the times that we feel such affection for Thomas Berger's dogged, cranky courage, and for the denizens of his unwelcoming and chaotic corner of the fictional world." N Y Times Book Rev

Crazy in Berlin. Scribner 1958 438p o.p.

"Because of his German background, Reinhart, an American G.I. stationed in Berlin at the conclusion of W.W. II, has strong guilt feelings about the treatment of Jews in Nazi Germany. His guilt is intensified by his relationships with German-Jewish civilians, with Lt. Schild, a Jewish-American Communist agent, and with Schatzi, a black marketeer, Communist courier, and former follower of Ernst Rohm." Libr J

"A story that boasts a memorable gallery of German, Russian, and American characters. Speech and scene are reproduced with deft precision as are the intellectual and emotional intricacies of personal relationships." Booklist

Followed by Reinhart in love

The feud. Delacorte Press 1983 265p o.p.

LC 82-22139

"One autumn Saturday sometime during the Depression, Dolf Beeler goes to Bullard's hardware store to buy paint remover. But instead he is involved in a nasty scene, is threatened at gunpoint, and leaves humiliated and vowing revenge. That night the Bullard store burns down; the next day the Beeler car blows up. A grudge feud has begun—or has it? For the world of 'The Feud' is one of mistaken identities and false impressions, of misunderstandings that chance to have happy endings or sad ones." Libr J

"Readers will have to decide for themselves whether Berger's deadpan rendering of working-class, small-town life in the 1930s is affectionate or scathing or both. It is a funny, seamless fable of an earlier and more innocent time." Publ Wkly

The houseguest; a novel. Little, Brown 1988 240p $16.95

ISBN 0-316-09163-4   LC 87-26108

"Chuck Burgoyne seems, at first, to be the ideal houseguest, according to Audrey Graves, his unsuspecting hostess. He's a gourmet cook, he's congenial company, and he even saves a family member from drowning. Writing in his customary surreal style, Berger creates the quintessential weekend-houseguest horror story, detailing the process that leads to the decision to kill Chuck, when his behavior inexplicably changes." Publ Wkly

"Throughout this peculiar tale, Berger keeps a tight rein on the insanity, leading us along into situations that would make absolutely no sense if presented too abruptly. His characters are so disarmingly natural that it is not until we are committed to finding out what happens to them that we realize that everyone in this book is more than a little strange. And by that time, it's far too late." West Coast Rev Books

Little Big Man. Dial Press (NY) 1964 xxii, 440p o.p. Amereon reprint available $28.95 (ISBN 0-8488-0429-5)

"The author purports to write the story of Jack Crabb, adopted Cheyenne, gunfighter, buffalo hunter, and survivor of Custer's last stand, whom he has located at the Marville Center for Senior Citizens. In the few months before his death at the self-professed age of 111, Crabb recounts *his* version of life in the Old West." Shapiro. Fic for Youth. 3d edition

Neighbors. Delacorte Press/Seymour Lawrence 1980 275p o.p.

LC 79-20307

"The new neighbors drop in for a drink and chaos breaks loose, as Berger records the nightmarish distractions of a day and night among the American middle class. Existential reverses skewer the suburban lifestyle of the bourgeoisie and unleash unkempt fantasies on manicured lawns as a man's mind, life, and home are boldly and cunningly invaded and violated." Booklist

Berger "quickly conditions the reader to expect the unexpected but manages to be consistently surprising nevertheless, introducing new twists and outrages that not even the most warped spectator could have foreseen. The novel adopts a formal, almost fussy style to convey lunacy, as if Berger were describing low deeds to a maiden aunt. . . . [The book] is not at all interested in being socially redeeming, and those who read books to gain warm feelings or philosophic nuggets will come away from this one empty-handed and probably angry. . . .What Berger has produced is a tour de force." Time

Reinhart in love. Scribner 1962 438p o.p.

Sequel to Crazy in Berlin

This novel begins with "Reinhart's discharge from the Army. He goes to the home of his parents in Ohio, eventually gets a job of sorts, and meets and marries a girl; but while he is following this commonplace course, all sorts of extraordinary things happen to him." Saturday Rev

Berger, Thomas, 1924-—*Continued*

"A comic novel. . . . In richness of funny language, freakishness of situation, eccentricities of character, reckless sweep of narrative, all combined, there probably will not be another like it for five years, perhaps ever." Chicago Sunday Trib

Followed by Vital parts

Reinhart's women; a novel. Delacorte Press/Seymour Lawrence 1981 295p o.p.

LC 81-3271

"This is not the Carlo Reinhart of Crazy in Berlin . . . Reinhart in Love . . . and Vital Parts. He has been divorced from the vituperous Genevieve—his wife of 22 years—for a decade. His son Blaine, a mulish, asexual hippie ten years ago, is now a three-piece materialist; a blubbery, myopic Daughter Winona has been transformed into an anorectic fashion model. . . . Reinhart is 'house-father' in Winona's luxury apartment. . . . Hired by high-powered Grace Greenwood to demonstrate gourmet-food preparation in supermarkets, he is shocked to discover that the executive gorgon is Winona's lesbian lover. Blaine's wife has an erotic nervous breakdown in Reinhart's bedroom. Genevieve returns to stage a breakdown of her own. Helen Clayton, his supermarket assistant, bolsters Reinhart's flagging sexuality with motel trysts. A neighbor, Edie Mulhouse, as big as the hero himself, writes manic mash notes." Time

"Although the hilarity is occasionally forced, this uniquely happy novel is certainly worth reading for all it attempts to cover and mostly for sheer manic fun." Libr J

Sneaky people; a novel. Simon & Schuster 1975 315p o.p.

"The time is the 1930's; the setting, a grimly shabby Midwestern town. When used-car impressario Buddy Sandifer plans to have his wife murdered and wed his waitress mistress, he initiates an endearing concatenation of elaborate, mutually cancelling ruses. The designated murderer has plans of his own; the victim-to-be lives a secret life far from what Buddy imagines as sexless stodginess." Libr J

Berger's "style, always good, improves with each novel, refined here to deft economical strokes that describe a person, a time, or even a culture in a few lines, to dialogue that implies a perfect ear. . . . This [is a] marvelously funny and touching story. . . . It depicts anarchic American individuals in a particular time but for all time. Berger may be our best living novelist." Choice

Vital parts; a novel. Baron, R.W. 1970 432p o.p.

Sequel to Reinhart in love

"Down on his luck, over forty, Carl Reinhart is despised by his hippie son, rejected by his wife, and admired only by his overweight, excessively sensitive, teen-age daughter. Anxious to escape domestic problems Reinhart becomes involved with his friend Bob Sweet in a cryogenic experiment, a plan to freeze a person who has died in the hope that a cure for his fatal disease is discovered in the future. The people Reinhart meets in the course of a discursive novel embody most of the anxieties of Middle Western small town life." Booklist

"As Reinhart is pushed further and further into the absurdities he prides himself so successfully on avoiding, the promise of the brilliant opening scenes is not only confirmed but fulfilled by the double takes in plotting and narrative surface." Harpers

Followed by Reinhart's women

Who is Teddy Villanova? Delacorte Press/Seymour Lawrence 1977 247p o.p.

LC 76-42227

"Wren, former English-lit instructor turned private investigator with offices in a crumbling Manhattan loft, dodges his secretary's demands for back pay, is repeatedly zapped, held at gunpoint, and quizzed by cops. The corpse of a 'great big man' keeps turning up, like unclaimed property from a Hammett-Chandler warehouse. But these inconveniences are as nothing compared with . . . Wren's inability to prove he is indeed Russel Wren and not Teddy Villanova, archfiend and international criminal, whom he has been paid a niggardly retainer to track down." Newsweek

"Berger's style, which is one of the greatest pleasures of the book, is something like S. J. Perelman's—educated, complicated, graceful, silly, destructive in spirit, and brilliant—and it is also something like Mad Comics—densely, sensuously detailed, unpredictable, packed with gags. Beyond all this, it makes an impression of scholarship—that is, Berger seems really to know what he jokes about." N Y Times Book Rev

Bermant, Chaim, 1929-

The patriarch. St. Martin's Press 1981 424p o.p.

LC 81-510

This novel "centers around Nahum Rabinovitz, later Raeburn, who is sent at 16 to Glasgow, Scotland. His long life, ending in 1947, is crowded with an extended family and endeavors ranging from moneylending through ship owning to running a cinema chain. As he becomes established, Nahum brings his mother, aunt, and cousin from Russia." Libr J

This is an "absorbing saga filled with humor and pathos, but it is never sentimental. The characters are finely developed and the richness of Jewish life, the extended Jewish family, and Jewish traditions are warmly illustrated. Although the characters are drawn with naturalness and realism this is no ordinary family." Best Sellers

Berry, Wendell, 1934-

Fidelity; five stories. Pantheon Bks. 1992 201p $20

ISBN 0-679-41633-1   LC 92-7139

Analyzed in Short story index

Contents: Pray without ceasing; A jonquil for Mary Penn; Making it home; Fidelity; Are you all right?

"In these five interrelated stories, Berry focuses once again on the fictional town of Port William and on characters like Andrew Catlett, the central figure of his novel The Remembering. . . . Berry's tales are usually engaging and display a quiet but powerful dignity." Libr J

The **Best** American short stories, 1915-1995; selected from U.S. and Canadian magazines. Houghton Mifflin 1915-1995 81v 1915-1994 o.p; 1995 $24.95

ISSN 0067-6233

Analyzed in Short story index

Editors: 1915-1941, Edward J. O'Brien; 1942-1958, 1972-1977, Martha Foley; 1959-1971, Martha Foley and David Burnett; 1978, Ted Solotaroff and Shannon Ravenel; 1979, Joyce Carol Oates and Shannon Ravenel;

The Best American short stories, 1915-1995—*Continued*

1980, Stanley Elkin and Shannon Ravenel; 1981, Hortense Calisher and Shannon Ravenel; 1982, John Gardner and Shannon Ravenel; 1983, Anne Tyler and Shannon Ravenel; 1984, John Updike and Shannon Ravenel; 1985, Gail Godwin and Shannon Ravenel; 1986, Raymond Carver and Shannon Ravenel; 1987, Ann Beattie and Shannon Ravenel; 1988, Mark Helprin and Shannon Ravenel; 1989, Margaret Atwood and Shannon Ravenel; 1990, Richard Ford and Shannon Ravenel; 1991, Alice Adams and Katrina Kenison; 1992, Robert Stone and Katrina Kenison; 1993, Louise Erdrich and Katrina Kenison; 1994, Tobias Wolff and Katrina Kenison; 1995, Jane Smiley and Katrina Kenison

1915-1941 volumes had title: Best short stories

Contents 1995: Orientation, by D. Orozco; Way down deep in the jungle, by T. Jones; The stucco house, by E. Gilchrist; A night's work, by J. Gordon; Pity, by A. Mandelman; Leg, by S. Polansky; The ugliest house in the world, by P. H. Davies; Birthmates, by G. Jen; The drowning, by E. J. Delaney; Honored guest, by J. Williams; The behavior of the hawkweeds, by A. Barrett; Hand jive, by A. Cozine; So I guess you know what I told him, by S. Doybyns; Undertow, by J. C. Cornell; Pagan Night, by K. Braverman; First, body, by M. R. Thon; The angel Esmeralda, by D. DeLillo; The artist, by E. Falco; Chiromancy, by M. Garland; Xuela, by J. Kincaid

The Best American short stories of the eighties; selected and with an introduction by Shannon Ravenel. Houghton Mifflin 1990 393p o.p.

LC 90-30071

Analyzed in Short story index

Contents: The old forest, by P. Taylor; The emerald, by D. Barthelme; The shawl, by C. Ozick; A working day, by R. Coover; Cathedral, by R. Carver; Exchange value, by C. Johnson; Deaths of distant friends, by J. Updike; Sur, by U. K. Le Guin; Nairobi, by J. C. Oates; In the red room, by P. Bowles; Sarah Cole: a type of love story, by R. Banks; Fellow-creatures, by W. Morris; Gryphon, by C. Baxter; Health, by J. Williams; The way we live now, by S. Sontag; The things they carried, by T. O'Brien; Dédé, by M. Gallant; Helping, by R. Stone; The management of grief, by B. Mukherjee; Meneseteung, by A. Munro

The Best from Fantasy & Science Fiction; 1st-20th, 22nd-24th series. Doubleday 1952-1982 23v o.p.

Analyzed in Short story index

24th series published by Scribner. No volume bearing 21st series designation published; Special 25th anniversary volume published instead (entered below)

Editors: 1st-4th series, Anthony Boucher and J. Francis McComas; 5th-8th series, Anthony Boucher; 9th-11th series, Robert P. Mills; 12th-14th series, Avram Davidson; 15th-24th series, Edward L. Ferman.

Collection culled from a journal, founded in 1949, that "continues to publish an unusual number of first stories and award winners, to discover new, literary writers, to maintain a circulation of about half to two-thirds that of the most popular magazines, and to remain the most consistently reliable magazine in the field." New Ency of Sci Fic

The Best from Fantasy & Science Fiction: a 40th anniversary anthology; edited by Edward L. Ferman. St. Martin's Press 1989 xix, 376p $18.95

ISBN 0-312-03293-5   LC 89-215473

Analyzed in Short story index

Contents: The cat hotel, by F. Leiber; Slow birds, by I. Watson; Judgment call, by J. Kessel; The aliens who knew, I mean, everything, by G. A. Effinger; The God machine, by D. Knight; Understanding human behavior, by T. M. Disch; A rarebit of magic, by J. Morressy; In midst of life, by J. Tiptree; Surviving, by J. Moffett; Cage 37, by W. Wightman; While you're up, by A. Davidson; Eidolons, by H. Ellison; Face value, by K. J. Fowler; Buffalo gals, won't you come out tonight, by U. K. Le Guin; The boy who plaited manes, by N. Springer; Out of all them bright stars, by N. Kress; Salvador, by L. Shepard; State of the art, by R. C. Wilson; Black air, by K. S. Robinson; Uncle Tuggs, by M. Shea

The Best from Fantasy & Science Fiction: a 45th anniversary anthology; edited by Kristine Kathryn Rusch and Edward L. Ferman. St. Martin's Press 1994 350p $23.95

ISBN 0-312-11246-7   LC 94-20632

Analyzed in Short story index

Contents: Kirinyaga, by M. Resnick; Touched, by D. Bailey; Mom's little friends, by R. Vukcevich; Cast on a distant shore, by R. Garcia y Robertson; Graves, by J. Haldeman; The dark, by K. J. Fowler; Willie, by M. E. Robins; The last feast of Harlequin, by T. Ligotti; Coffins, by R. Reed; The resurrection of Alonso Quijana, by M. Donnelly; Steel dogs, by R. Aldridge; Abe Lincoln in McDonald's, by J. Morrow; On death and the deuce, by R. Bowes; The honeycrafters, by C. I. Gilman; Ma qui, by A. Brennert; Next, by T. Bisson; The friendship light, by G. Wolfe; Susan, by H. Ellison; Guide dog, by M. Conner

"A superb collection with something to satisfy every kind of taste, from hard sf to fantasy." Booklist

The Best from Fantasy and Science Fiction: a special 25th anniversary anthology; edited by Edward L. Ferman. Doubleday 1974 326p o.p.

"Doubleday science fiction"

Analyzed in Short story index

Stories included are: When you care, when you love, by T. Sturgeon; To the Chicago abyss, by R. Bradbury; The key, by I. Asimov; Ship of shadows, by F. Leiber; The Queen of Air and Darkness, by P. Anderson; Midsummer century, by J. Blish

The Best horror from Fantasy Tales; edited by Stephen Jones and David Sutton. Carroll & Graf Pubs. 1990 264p il o.p.

LC 89-78358

Analyzed in Short story index

Contents: The forbidden, by C. Barker; Dreams may come, by H. W. Munn; The dark country, by D. Etchison; Dead to the world, by A. Ashley; The generation waltz, by C. L. Grant; Don't open that door, by F.

The Best horror from Fantasy Tales —
Continued

Garfield; The frolic, by T. Ligotti; The sorcerer's jewel, by R. Bloch; The strange years, by B. Lumley; Red, by R. C. Matheson; Ever the faith endures, by M. W. Wellman; Extension 201, by C. Simsa; The last wolf, by K. E. Wagner; Tongue in cheek, by M. Grace; In the X-ray, by F. Leiber; The bad people, by S. R. Tem; A place of no return, by H. B. Cave; The terminus, by K. Newman; The green man, by K. Jones; The voice of the beach, by R. Campbell

The Best horror stories; from the Magazine of Fantasy and Science Fiction; edited by Edward L. Ferman and Anne Jordan. St. Martin's Press 1988 403p o.p.

LC 88-1987

Analyzed in Short story index

Contents: Window, by B. Leman; Insects in amber, by T. Reamy; Free dirt, by C. Beaumont; Rising waters, by P. Ferrara; The night of the tiger, by S. King; Poor little warrior!, by B. W. Aldiss; Nina, by R. Bloch; Werewind, by J. M. Reaves; Dress of white silk, by R. Matheson; Gladys's Gregory, by J. A. West; By the river, Fontainebleau, by S. Gallagher; Pride, by C. L. Grant; Longtooth, by E. Pangborn; Glory, by R. Goulart; Bug house, by L. Tuttle; Hand in glove, by R. Aickman; Stillborn, by M. Conner; Balgrummo's Hell, by R. Kirk; The old darkness, by P. Sargent; The night of White Bhairab, by L. Shepard; Salvage rites, by I. Watson; Test, by T. L. Thomas; The little black train, by M. W. Wellman; The autopsy, by M. Shea

Best new horror [1]-4; edited by Stephen Jones and Ramsey Campbell. Carroll & Graf Pubs. 1990-1993 4v v1-3 o.p.; v4 $21.95

Analyzed in Short story index

Contents: v4 The suicide artist, by S. Edelman; Dancing on a blade of dreams, by R. Lannes; The departed, by C. Barker; How to get ahead in New York, by P. Z. Brite; They take, by J. Brunner; Replacements, by L. Tuttle; Under the pylon, by G. Joyce; The glamour, by T. Ligotti; Under the ice, by J. Gordon; And some are missing, by J. Lane; The little green ones, by L. Daniels; Mirror man, by S. R. Tem; Mothmusic, by S. Ash; Did they get you to trade? by K. E. Wagner; Night shift sister, by N. Royle; The dead, by S. Ings; Norman Wisdom and the angel of death, by C. Fowler; Red reign, by K. Newman; Aviatrix, by P. Atkins; Snodgrass, by I. R. MacLeod; The day of the sharks, by K. Wilhelm; Anima, by M. J. Harrison; Bright lights, big zombie, by D. E. Winter; The ghost village, by P. Straub

Best of the Best American short stories, 1915-1950; edited by Martha Foley. Houghton Mifflin 1952 369p o.p.

Analyzed in Short story index

Contents: How the Devil came down Division Street, by N. Algren; I'm a fool, by S. Anderson; The blue sash, by W. Beck; Nothing ever breaks except the heart, by K. Boyle; Horse thief, by E. Caldwell; Sex education, by D. Canfield; The enormous radio, by J. Cheever; The wind and the snow of winter, by W. V. Clark; Boys will be boys, by I. S. Cobb; Christ in concrete, by P.

Di Donato; Hand upon the waters, by W. Faulkner; My old man, by E. Hemingway; The peach stone, by P. Horgan; Haircut, by R. Lardner; Man on a road, by A. Maltz; Prince of darkness, by J. F. Powers; Resurrection of a life, by W. Saroyan; Search through the streets of the city, by I. Shaw; The interior castle, by J. Stafford; How beautiful with shoes, by W. D. Steele; The women on the wall, by W. Stegner; Dawn of remembered spring, by J. Stuart; A wife of Nashville, by P. Taylor; The catbird seat, by J. Thurber; A curtain of green, by E. Welty

The Best of the Nebulas; edited by Ben Bova. Doherty Assocs. 1989 593p $19.95

ISBN 0-312-93184-0   LC 88-38541

"A TOR book"

Analyzed in Short story index

This volume includes the following novellas: He who shapes, by R. Zelazny; Behold the man, by M. Moorcock; Dragonrider, by A. McCaffrey; A boy and his dog, by H. Ellison; Houston, Houston, do you read? by J. Tiptree; The persistence of vision, by J. Varley. Novelettes included are: The doors of his face, the lamps of his mouth, by R. Zelazny; Gonna roll the bones, by F. Lieber; Time considered as a helix of semi-precious stones, by S. R. Delany; Slow sculpture, by T. Sturgeon; Of mist, and grass, and sand, by V. N. McIntyre; and Sandkings, by G. R. R. Martin. Short stories included are: "Repent, Harlequin!" said the Ticktockman, by H. Ellison; Aye, and Gomorrah . . . by S. R. Delany; Passengers, by R. Silverberg; When it changed, by J. Russ; Love is the plan the plan is death, by J. Tiptree; The day before the revolution, by U. K. Le Guin; Catch that zeppelin! by F. Leiber; The grotto of the dancing deer, by C. D. Simak; and Jeffty is five, by H. Ellison

Best SF: 1968-1975. Bobbs-Merrill 1969-1976 8v o.p.

Partially analyzed in Short story index

First collection in this series: Best SF: 1967, published 1968 in paperback by Berkley Publishing Corporation

Volumes 1969-1974 published by Putnam

Each volume contains an introduction by Harry Harrison on the SF year, and a concluding essay by Brian Aldiss. A broad range of SF stories are included, some poetry, and occasional essays. The classics are represented; sources and authors are not limited to genre specialists

Beyle, Marie Henri *See* Stendhal, 1783-1842

Bierce, Ambrose, 1842-1914?

The complete short stories of Ambrose Bierce; compiled with commentary by Ernest Jerome Hopkins. Doubleday 1970 496p o.p.

Analyzed in Short story index

This collection of ninety-three stories which were written between 1882 and 1896 fall into three groups: tales of the macabre and the supernatural, tales of war, and tall tales

Contents: Haïta the shepherd; The secret of Macarger's Gulch; The eyes of the panther; The stranger; An inhabitant of Carcosa; The applicant; The death of Halpin Frayser; A watcher by the dead; The man and the snake; John Mortonson's funeral; Moxon's master; The damned thing; The realm of the unreal; A fruitless assignment;

Bierce, Ambrose, 1842-1914?—*Continued*

A vine on a house; The haunted valley; One of twins; Present at a hanging; A wireless message; The moonlit road; An arrest; A jug of sirup; The Isle of Pines; At old Man Eckert's; The Spook House; The middle toe of the right foot; The thing at Nolan; The difficulty of crossing a field; An unfinished race; Charles Ashmore's trial; Staley Fleming's hallucination; The night-doings at "Deadmans"; A baby tramp; A psychological shipwreck; A cold greeting; Beyond the wall; John Bartine's watch; The man out of the nose; An adventure at Brownville; The suitable surroundings; The boarded window; A lady from Redhorse; The famous Gilson bequest; A holy terror; A diagnosis of death; One of the missing; A baffled ambuscade; The affair at Coulter's Notch; A son of the gods; One kind of officer; A tough tussle; An occurrence at Owl Creek Bridge; Chickamauga; The coup de grâce; One officer, one man; The story of a conscience; Parker Adderson, philosopher; An affair of outposts; Jupiter Doke; Brigadier-General; A horseman in the sky; The mockingbird; George Thurston; Killed at Resaca; Three and one are one; Two military executions; The Major's tale; A resumed identity; A man with two lives; The other lodgers; A bivouac of the dead; An imperfect conflagration; A bottomless grave; The City of the Gone Away; Curried cow; A revolt of the Gods; Oil of dog; The widower Turnmore; The baptism of Dobsho; The race at Left Bower; The failure of Hope & Wandel; A providential intimation; Mr. Swiddler's flip-flap; The little story; My favorite murder; The hypnotist; Mr. Masthead, journalist; Why I am not editing "The Stinger"; Corrupting the press; "The bubble reputation"; A shipwreckollection; The captain of the "Camel"; The man overboard; A cargo of cat

Binchy, Maeve

Circle of friends. Delacorte Press 1991 c1990 565p o.p.

LC 90-3944

Available G.K. Hall large print edition

First published 1990 in the United Kingdom

The author "explores the intertwining bonds of three women as they travel from a small Irish village to university life in Dublin." Libr J

"There is nothing fancy about 'Circle of Friends.' There is no torrid sex, no profound philosophy. There are no stunning metaphors. There is just a wonderfully absorbing story about people worth caring about. And that is a rare pleasure." N Y Times Book Rev

The copper beech. Delacorte Press 1992 345p $22.50

ISBN 0-385-30775-6　　　　LC 92-18601

Also available large print edition $28 (ISBN 0-385-30853-1)

"The eponymous copper beech is a huge tree that shades the tiny schoolhouse in the [Irish] village of Shancarrig. For generations, graduating pupils have carved their initials on the massive trunk, and the book examines what has become of some of them. Though each of the 10 chapters offers the perspective of a single character, Binchy adroitly indicates the ways in which their lives intersect. . . . The result is a charming and compelling series of interlocking stories about ordinary people who are given dimension through Binchy's empathetic insight. While this book is more fragmentary in structure than some of her previous novels, it should leave Binchy's fans wholly satisfied." Publ Wkly

Dublin 4

In Binchy, M. The lilac bus: stories p165-327

Echoes. Viking 1986 c1985 477p $17.95

ISBN 0-670-80938-1　　　　LC 85-40571

Also available G.K. Hall large print edition

First published 1985 in the United Kingdom

"Clare O'Brien, the brilliant, ambitious daughter of an impoverished shopkeeper, attempts to transcend the rigid social strictures that govern her small Irish seaside community by earning a college degree and marrying David Power, the well-to-do son of the local doctor. Unfortunately, the class-conscious residents of Castlebay make it virtually impossible for David and Clare to bridge peacefully the wide cultural gulf that separates them." Booklist

"Sharply drawn, memorable characters and a convincing picture of a small Irish community bring freshness and zest to a familiar tale." Publ Wkly

Firefly summer. Delacorte Press 1988 601p o.p.

LC 88-5412

"When American millionaire Patrick O'Neill returns to his ancestral home in Ireland, his intent is to bring prosperity to Montfern in the form of a luxury hotel built from the ruins of an old estate. Instead, the villagers see their lifestyles irrevocably changed and the town's inner harmonies disrupted in the four years it takes to build O'Neill's hotel." Libr J

"The careful examination of life and culture in a small Irish town during the 1960s will appeal to many readers." Booklist

Light a penny candle. Viking 1983 c1982 542p $17.75

ISBN 0-670-42827-2　　　　LC 82-19132

First published 1982 in the United Kingdom

"Evacuated from London during the Blitz, 10-year-old Elizabeth White is sent to live with her mother's former schoolmate in Ireland. Elizabeth and Aisling, the 10-year-old O'Connor daughter, become close friends immediately; a friendship that lasts. In the end, as young widows, they realize that their friendship has been the sustaining force in their lives and will continue to strengthen them for whatever the future may hold." SLJ

The maturing of the two women "often carried out in each other's company, make[s] touching reading for those who enjoy expansive but not complex plots in which one can linger for many hours of entertainment. Binchy's characters are *not* constructed with hidden dimensions, yet they are easy to identify with and care about." Booklist

The lilac bus

In Binchy, M. The lilac bus: stories p1-163

The lilac bus: stories. Delacorte Press 1991 327p o.p.

LC 91-13765

Analyzed in Short story index

This volume contains two collections: The lilac bus and Dublin 4, first published in Ireland in 1984 and 1982 respectively

Contents: The lilac bus: Nancy; Dee; Mikey; Judy; Kev; Rupert; Celia; Tom

Binchy, Maeve—*Continued*

Dublin 4: Dinner in Donnybrook; Flat in Ringsend; Decision in Belfield; Murmurs in Montrose

"'The Lilac Bus' consists of eight connected stories, each one a revealing portrait of a Dublin worker who goes home to the outlying town of Rathdoon each weekend in Tom Fitzgerald's minibus. . . . The more fully realized stories in *Dublin 4* have only their Dublin setting in common. . . . While not as completely satisfying as Binchy novels . . . this is an absorbing, entertaining read with characters to care about." Libr J

Silver wedding. Delacorte Press 1989 306p $17.95

ISBN 0-385-29826-9   LC 89-1276

The author "uses the story-within-a-story device to introduce the long-absent, oddball friends and relatives who will reunite at Deirdre and Desmond Doyle's silver anniversary in the couple's suburban London home. Among these are the Doyles' three grown children—a failed Irish nun, the much-put-upon eldest daughter, and the prodigal sheepherder son—the snooty yet tragically unmarried maid of honor, and the corporately well-positioned best man (who happens to be both Desmond's friend and nemesis). As celebratory preparations begin, the skeletons in this dysfunctional network are unearthed." Booklist

"An elegant literary construction, a comedy of manners as well as a soap opera. Each chapter has its own story, yet each story connects with all the others to produce a satisfying whole. Add to this a sly, understated tone and you have a book that's an effortless pleasure to read." N Y Times Book Rev

Birmingham, Stephen

The Auerbach will. Little, Brown 1983 430p o.p.

LC 83-9413

"Saga of a mail-order-house family dynasty. The central character is Essie, a Lower East Side Jewish immigrant, who falls in love with Jake Auerbach, the 'renegade' son in a prominent New York mercantile family. Sent off to Chicago after a disapproved-of marriage, Jake founds the nation's first mail-order business under two Christian names (Sears & Roebuck come to mind from beginning to end, though without substantiation). The business flourishes; Jake and Essie—she now a society figure—are restored to familiar respectability but suffer the disenchantments of fading love, mutual infidelities, unhappy children, blackmail, and hollow glory." Booklist

"Birmingham's deft handling of the fabric of family life and shifting patterns of deception, betrayal and tragedy produces a dramatic narrative. Essie is a wonderfully sympathetic figure, and Birmingham moves her gracefully through her bitter-sweet years from determined young girl to passionate woman to sophisticated grande dame." Publ Wkly

Carriage trade. Bantam Bks. 1993 469p $21.95

ISBN 0-553-08135-7   LC 92-39567

This "novel tells the tale of one Silas Tarkington, founder of an exclusive Manhattan department store. . . Tarkington is actually Solomon Tarcher, a Jew from the Lower East Side who once served time for larceny. While retailing was in his blood—Tarkington's grandmother and mother created a successful millinery business back when women wore hats—his brilliant and calculating career was engineered by a nasty shyster named Moe Minskoff. We learn all the dirty secrets of Tarking-

ton's messy life in flashbacks as his spunky daughter, fiesty mother, stunning and resilient wife, and current mistress try to fathom the chaos of the store's financial straits after Tarkington's suspicious death. . . . Birmingham's casting of women as the heroes in this mercantile thriller cum murder mystery is a nice touch." Booklist

The LeBaron secret. Little, Brown 1986 403p o.p.

LC 85-18208

"From her white mansion overlooking San Francisco's Golden Gate Bridge, the widowed Sari LeBaron rules her family-owned wine company, as well as her three grown children, with the assurance of a despot. But in an age of corporate takeovers her matriarchal tenure is far from secure, and Sari's son Eric soon hatches a plot with his oil-rich father-in-law and with his aunt Joanna LeBaron, a New York advertising executive affectionately known as the 'Medea of Medialand,' to wrest away control of the company." N Y Times Book Rev

"The author so skillfully weaves together the many strands of this trite tale that readers will be stunned by the novel's tragic conclusion. Good popular entertainment for the family-saga set." Booklist

The Rothman scandal; a novel. Little, Brown 1991 535p o.p.

LC 90-27554

"At age forty-seven, Alex has become the world's preeminent arbiter of chic. But at the party meant to celebrate her greatest triumph—*Mode's* record-breaking circulation of 5,000,000—her father-in-law, Herbert, with whom she has had a long-running feud, makes a surprise announcement: Fiona Denton, a young unknown Englishwoman, will be coming on board as Alex's co-editor-in-chief. Stephen, Alex's husband, died years ago; and with Ho, Alex's longtime champion, now apparently incapacitated, it is clear that Herb intends to seize control of the company. Alex's difficult choice: whether to fight to hold on to the magazine she has created, or join in a scheme that will ultimately destroy it." Publisher's note

Bisson, Terry

England underway

In Nebula awards 29 p181-202

Black, Mansell, 1920-1995

For works written by this author under other names see Hall, Adam, 1920-1995; Trevor, Elleston, 1920-1995

Black, Veronica, 1935-

My name is Polly Winter. St. Martin's Press 1993 c1992 188p $16.95

ISBN 0-312-08858-2   LC 92-40800

First published 1992 in the United Kingdom

The author "mixes a ghost story with mystery in this . . . tale about a researcher who falls under the spell of an old crime. Social historian Jessica Cameron moves into The Cedars, an old house near Liverpool, as she begins her search for a typical Victorian middle-class family for an exhibition on domestic history. She becomes intrigued by earlier tenants of The Cedars, the

Black, Veronica, 1935—*Continued*
Makins, and the unsolved disappearance in 1859 of Rev. Edward Makin's daughter and her governess." Publ Wkly

A vow of sanctity. St. Martin's Press 1993 192p $16.95

ISBN 0-312-09408-6   LC 93-13349

Sister Joan, "loyal to her order but not exactly bowed down, spends a month-long retreat in a cave overlooking a remote Scottish loch. Despite her physical isolation and her resolve not to meddle in local affairs, she becomes involved in a six-year-old case of adultery, disappearance, and death that brings her into close contact with ancient antipapist prejudice. In this solid work, location permits vicarious experience from a traditional plot." Libr J

Black thorn, white rose; edited by Ellen Datlow & Terri Windling. Morrow 1994 386p $22

ISBN 0-688-13713-X   LC 94-6432

"An AvoNova book"

Analyzed in Short story index

Includes the following stories: Words like pale stones, by N. Kress; Stronger than time, by P. C. Wrede; Somnus's fair maid, by A. Downer; The frog king; or, Iron Henry, by D. Quinn; Near-beauty, by M. E. Beckett; Ogre, by M. Kandel; Can't catch me, by M. Cadnum; Journeybread recipe, by L. Schimel; The brown bear of Norway, by I. Cole; The goose girl, by T. Wynne-Jones; Tattercoats, by M. Snyder; Granny Rumple, by J. Yolen; The Sawing Boys, by H. Waldrop; Godson, by R. Zelazny; Ashputtle, by P. Straub; Sweet bruising skin, by S. Constantine; The black swan, by S. Wade

"An enchanting, witty collection of 18 original stories that in general achieve relevance without losing their patina of magic." Publ Wkly

Blackmore, R. D. (Richard Doddridge), 1825-1900
Lorna Doone; a romance of Exmoor. o.p.

First published 1869

A romantic love-story of Exmoor and the North Devon Coast of England, telling of the outlaw Doones, the maid brought up in the midst of them, and plain John Ridd's herculean power and his service to James II during Monmouth's Rebellion

"The scenic descriptions of the lovely region befits the tale, and many local worthies have their lineaments preserved here. Though 'Lorna Doone' made little stir at the time of its appearance, it has had innumerable imitations since, and it initiated a return to . . . romanticism in historical fiction." Baker. Guide to the Best Fic

Blackmore, Richard Doddridge *See* Blackmore, R. D. (Richard Doddridge), 1825-1900

Blair, Eric *See* Orwell, George, 1903-1950

Blair, Leona
The side of the angels. Bantam Bks. 1992 486p o.p.

LC 91-45510

"Left by her nymphomaniacal mother when she is 12, Kate battles through life desiring but wary of love. Domineering grandmother Polly struggles between the true love she feels for the girl and the desire to live life all over through her. Win Talley, the only man appreciative of Kate's intelligence and capable of arousing true passion in her, wins her love but betrays it with the egoism of his acting career. Kate succeeds as doctor of women's studies and, eventually, college president. She sticks to her southern family and her philosophies despite the skeletons that abound." Booklist

"Rather than churn up the vapid froth that keeps so many commercial novels afloat, Blair solidly builds this one around the old-fashioned South Carolina political machine Polly runs, with ballast from Kate's scholarly treatise on cross-cultural repression of women. Her injections of wit and wicked spice rarely pall." Publ Wkly

Blaisdell, Anne, 1921-
For works written by this author under other names see Linington, Elizabeth, 1921-; Shannon, Dell, 1921-

Blake, Jennifer, 1942-
Arrow to the heart. Fawcett Columbine 1993 325p $19

ISBN 0-449-90824-0   LC 92-55000

A historical romance set in "antebellum Louisiana. Katrine Castlereagh is dutiful wife to the mysteriously incapacitated Giles, whose mad desire for an heir leads to a dastardly scheme to mate her with the victor of his yearly medieval-style tournament. True-hearted Rowan de Blanc comes to the tourney for reasons of his own: believing Katrine to be responsible for this half-brother's death, he wants to learn more about her. Although attracted to each other, the pair refuse to fulfill Giles's plan—so he imprisons them, naked, in a tower on the grounds of his estate. . . . The intriguing combination of passion and intellect in both Katrine and Rowan gives some edge to a story satisfyingly capped by several neat plot twists." Publ Wkly

Wildest dreams. Fawcett Columbine 1992 341p $18

ISBN 0-449-90617-5   LC 91-58328

Also available Thorndike Press large print edition

"When Joletta Caresse inherits her family's perfume shop in New Orleans, she also becomes heir to the mystery that surrounds the firm's most important fragrance, Le Jardin de Cour. The formula for the perfume, discovered during the 19th century by an ancestress named Violet, is lost when the only person who knows the secret dies suddenly without divulging it. Armed with Violet's diary, Joletta sets off for Europe to retrace the trip during which Violet originally discovered the perfume." Publ Wkly

"Love interest Rone Adamson makes a gallant partner for this sensuously scented European grand tour." Booklist

Blake, Patricia, 1927-

For works written by this author under other names see Egleton, Clive, 1927-

Blasco Ibáñez, Vicente, 1867-1928

Blood and sand; a novel; translated from the Spanish by Mrs. W. A. Gillespie. Dutton 1919 356p o.p.

Original Spanish edition, 1908

This is a novel of the Spanish bull ring. No detail of the professional career of Juan Gallardo, who has risen from the lowest ranks of poverty to unprecedented heights of riches and popular favor, is spared. His vanities, his superstitions, his sufferings from fear, his daring attacks, the technique of his killings, his wounds and recoveries, and the final accident that brings his death, as well as the tortures of the beasts and the joyous delight of the populace in this national sport, are related

The four horsemen of the Apocalypse.
Available from Amereon and Buccaneer Bks.

Original Spanish edition, 1916; first United States edition published 1918 by Dutton

"An interpretation of German and French psychology [during World War I] through the reactions of the two branches of a wealthy Argentinian family, who settle respectively in France and Germany before the war. A powerful and well-written novel, giving detailed pictures of French mobilization, the German occupation of Northern France, trench fighting, etc., and enlarging on contrasting views of humanity, liberty, culture and international relations. . . . [The] 'four horsemen' are War, Pestilence, Famine and Death." Cleveland Public Libr

Blatty, William Peter

The exorcist. Harper & Row 1971 340p o.p.

Set in Georgetown, "the central figure is Regan MacNeil . . . the sweet 'normal' eleven-year-old daughter of a famous actress, Chris MacNeil. . . . Overnight, Regan turns from that normal little girl into a grotesque, unrecognizable monster, possessed by a demonic force that has locked her in a life-and-death struggle. Her weird and ugly behavior baffles the best medical experts. . . . [Chris] turns to the Jesuits. Perhaps exorcism will succeed where science has failed. Father Damien Karras, who is a trained psychiatrist, is skeptical, despite his deep knowledge of Satanism and possession. That is, until the last resort is the Church ritual." Saturday Rev

"Blatty has done his homework. He discourses, a bit bookishly, on the history of possession and the relation of autosuggestion to masked guilt. . . . Blatty maintains headlong thrust, slowly increasing Regan's agony until the reader winces; no more, a part of us says, but of course we want more because Blatty handles the horror so well." Newsweek

Bleeck, Oliver *See* Thomas, Ross, 1926-1995

Blish, James, 1921-1975

The Star Trek reader [I]-IV; adapted by James Blish; based on the television series created by Gene Roddenberry. Dutton 1976-1978 4v o.p.

Analyzed in Short story index

Contents: [I] Arena; A taste of Armageddon; Tomorrow is yesterday; Errand of mercy; Court martial; Operation—annihilate; The city on the edge of Forever; Space seed; The trouble with tribbles; The last gunfight; The doomsday machine; Assignment: Earth; Mirror, mirror; Friday's child; Amok time; Spock's brain; The enemy within; Catspaw; Where no man has gone before; Wolf in the fold; For the world is hollow and I have touched the sky

II: Charlie's law; Dagger of the mind; The unreal McCoy; Balance of terror; The naked time; Miri; The conscience of the king; All our yesterdays; The devil in the dark; Journey to Babel; The menagerie; The Enterprise incident; A piece of the action; Return to tomorrow; The ultimate computer; That which survives; Obsession; The return of the Archons; The immunity syndrome

III: Whom gods destroy; The Tholian web; Let that be your last battlefield; This side of paradise; Turnabout intruder; Requiem for Methuselah; The way to Eden; The savage curtain; The lights of Zetar; The apple; By any other name; The cloud minders; The mark of Gideon; Who mourns for Adonais; The changeling; The paradise syndrome; Metamorphosis; The deadly years; Elaan of Troyius

IV: The alternative factor; The empath; The Galileo Seven; Is there in truth no beauty; A private little war; The Omega glory; What are little girls made of; The Squire of Gothos; Wink of an eye; Bread and circuses; Day of the dove; Plato's stepchildren; Spock must die

Blixen, Karen, Baroness, 1885-1962

For works written by this author under other names see Dinesen, Isak, 1885-1962

Bloch, Robert, 1917-1994

Psycho house. TOR Bks. 1990 217p o.p.
LC 89-39881

"A Tom Doherty Associates book"

"Someone in Fairvale couldn't leave well enough alone. They had to rebuild the burnt-down Bates house and motel, hoping to snare tourists intrigued by the butcher-knife murders ol' Norman did 30 years back. And no sooner is the place ready to open than a 11-year-old girls gets hacked down while snooping around. That brings true-crime writer Amy Haines to town to do her own kind of snooping. Fairvalers are not amused nor very helpful, although they are increasingly interested in her presence as more citizens are hacked up. Bloch's second *Psycho* [1959] sequel is more a whodunit than a horror-screamer, but it's a good one that keeps you guessing all the way." Publ Wkly

Block, Lawrence, 1938-
The burglar in the closet. Random House 1978 166p o.p.
"A New York dentist has set . . . [Bernie Rhodenbarr, the gentleman burglar] up to rob his estranged wife, which he does. Embarrassingly, he gets interrupted and locked in a closet while the woman is stabbed to death and the boodle is stolen. In a temper, the burglar investigates, as does a corrupt policeman who wants half the take. Things are sorted out when a suitcase full of counterfeit money turns up and a couple of suspects conveniently die. Amusing and very easy to read." Libr J

The burglar who liked to quote Kipling. Random House 1979 196p o.p.
"Suave Manhattan cracksman Bernie Rhodenbarr, framed for murder after his latest escapade, gets help from Carolyn Kaiser, a lesbian friend and neighbor. She lets Bernie hide out in her apartment where they work undercover to solve the crime resulting from his heist of a reportedly priceless book by Kipling. J. Rudyard Whelkin has hired Bernie to steal the book from Jessie Arkwright and the thief finds that others . . . also want the volume." Publ Wkly
"Block writes with considerable wit and verve and constantly pulls the rug out from reader expectations. . . . [He] paints a crooked world where the thief is refreshingly straightforward." Booklist

The burglar who painted like Mondrian. Random House 1983 253p o.p.
LC 83-45269
Mystery revolving around bookseller/burglar Bernie Rhodenbarr and his "desperate efforts to clear himself of one caper he did *not* commit. . . . While attempting to reveal how he's been framed, Bernie Rhodenbarr must conceal another crime, rescue a friend's kidnapped cat, form a liaison with a mysterious female, and juggle an increasingly number of framed and unframed paintings 'by' Mondrian. A fast-paced farce with gustsy characters and a well-drawn New York City scene." Libr J

The burglar who studied Spinoza. Random House 1980 213p o.p.
LC 80-5288
Bernie Rhodenbarr "runs a used-book store in Greenwich Village. The store loses money, but that's cool, because Bernie steals things like rare coins. He loves being a burglar. He has two partners in crime. One is a lesbian who shampoos poodles. The other is a cop who insists on a commission. The particular coin that Bernie steals, a Liberty-head 1913 V-nickel, shouldn't have been where it was in the first place. Unfortunately, there seems to have been a burglary in the house before Bernie got there, and a murder after he left." Books of the Times
"There is no question that this is an interesting piece. None of the characters is ordinary. Block's style is crisp and humorous." Best Sellers

The burglar who traded Ted Williams; a Bernie Rhodenbarr mystery. Dutton 1994 258p $20.95
ISBN 0-525-93807-9   LC 93-40191
Also available Thorndike Press large print edition
"Rare books dealer-cum-thief Bernie Rhodenbarr decides to pull off one last job and ends up suspected of murder." Libr J

"Notwithstanding his elastic ethics and shady line of work, Bernie is incorrigibly adorable. Although he inhabits the same mean streets of Manhattan as Matt Scudder, the brooding private eye who is Mr. Block's most celebrated hero, Bernie has a whimsical sense of humor that shields him from the achy-breaky *Weltschmerz* of his hard-boiled literary sibling." N Y Times Book Rev

A dance at the slaughterhouse; a Matthew Scudder novel. Morrow 1991 309p $19
ISBN 0-688-10349-9   LC 91-7876
"Unlicensed New York investigator and series protagonist Matthew Scudder seeks to determine if a cable television producer raped and murdered his own wealthy wife. At the same time, Scudder hunts for a brutal man who makes video 'snuff' tapes involving teenage boys and a leather-dressed woman. The two cases merge . . . as Scudder enlists the aid of his motley assortment of interesting friends." Libr J
"The world of Lawrence Block's maverick PI Matt Scudder is a dark one indeed—and we're talkin' Manhattan as cesspool, friend. . . . The conclusion is a bloody, yet satisfying, one, with Matt teetering on the up side of the down side. Strong stuff from a real pro." Booklist

The devil knows you're dead; a Matthew Scudder novel. Morrow 1993 316p $20
ISBN 0-688-12192-6   LC 93-411
New York P.I. Matt Scudder "has a true friend in Mick Ballou, a sidekick in street urchin T.J., and a lover in former hooker Elaine. Hired by the brother of a mentally handicapped vet accused of the murder of attorney Glenn Holtzmann, Scudder finds that the victim was both less and more than he appeared to be." Booklist
"Scudder is burdened by a load of personal baggage, including romantic attachments to three women and regular attendance at A.A. meetings, that inhibits the action and stifles its sense of urgency. But when this droll, streetwise sleuth quits staring out the window at the rain and starts prowling his neighborhood haunts in Hell's Kitchen, he is just about the best there is." NY Times Book Rev

Eight million ways to die. Arbor House 1982 319p o.p.
LC 81-71698
This "novel is both a rousing private-eye story and an extended meditation on the whimsical ways of death—through freak accident, premeditated murder, and self-destruction. Private eye Matthew Scudder solves murders while he battles his own alcoholism. . . . In [this] tale, a 23-year old prostitute, Kim Dakkinen, wants out of 'the life' and asks Scudder to speak to her pimp, Chance. Scudder does, and a few days later Kim is found stabbed to death. Chance does the unexpected by hiring Scudder to find Kim's murderer, and while Scudder investigates, another one of Chance's prostitutes commits suicide; then another slashing occurs. A magnificently plotted, sensitive portrayal of two kinds of death— the kind that comes as an intruder and the kind that comes as an invited guest." Booklist

A long line of dead men; a Matthew Scudder novel. Morrow 1994 285p $20
ISBN 0-688-12193-4   LC 94-5720
"Scudder is summoned to investigate the curious run of deaths that seem to be afflicting the members of a private club. Not just any private club, mind you, but one whose raison d'être, in a sense, is death. Thirty men

Block, Lawrence, 1938-——*Continued*

gather once a year to celebrate, well . . . not having died yet. When they do die, eventually, the last survivor appoints 30 new members to keep the flame burning. The current batch, though, are dropping at an abnormally fast pace. Enter Scudder. Block takes this absolutely wonderful premise and makes the most of it. Like all the best hard-boiled writers in the post-Chandler era, Block knows that character and ambience are the heart and soul of crime fiction, but unlike so many of his brethren, he also maintains a healthy respect for plot." Booklist

Out on the cutting edge; a Matt Scudder mystery. Morrow 1989 260p $18.95

ISBN 0-688-09069-9 LC 89-32420

This Matt Scudder "case, tracking down a missing girl from Indiana, has the PI in and out of several of New York's sleaziest drinking joints. While looking for the girl, Scudder is befriended by another recovering alcoholic, who promptly dies, taking a terrible secret with him to the grave. Matters are further complicated when Scudder finds himself falling in love with the attractive super at the building where the dead man lived." Booklist

"In this riveting mystery, Block's artistry creates a full complement of fully realized characters, each a real person regardless of his or her perhaps tenuous connection to the plot." Publ Wkly

The sins of the fathers; a Matthew Scudder novel; introduction by Stephen King. Dark Harvest 1992 179p $19.95

ISBN 0-913165-66-2

First published 1976 in paperback

This novel introduced the then-hard-drinking ex-cop Matt Scudder. "The father of murdered Wendy Hanniford comes to Scudder to try to find out more about his errant daughter—not to find her killer, who was apparently her living partner, a brittle young man who was found in the street raving and covered with her blood and who killed himself shortly after he was arrested. In his dour, methodical, oddly empathetic way, Scudder finds out a great deal, altering several lives in the process. . . . This is a fine opportunity to get in on the start of what has become one of the most rewarding PI series currently in progress." Publ Wkly

Some days you get the bear. Morrow 1993 302p $20

ISBN 0-688-10820-2 LC 92-16708

Analyzed in Short story index

Contents: By the dawn's early light; Cleveland in my dreams; Some things a man must do; Answers to Soldier; Good for the soul; The Ehrengraf alternative; Someday I'll plant more walnut trees; The burglar who dropped in on Elvis; As good as a rest; Death wish; The Merciful Angel of Death; The Tulsa experience; Some days you get the bear; Passport in order; Something to remember you by; Hilliard's ceremony; The Ehrengraf nostrum; Like a bug on a windshield; A blow for freedom; How would you like it?; Batman's helpers

"Most of the stories [in this collection] are about crime and criminals. . . . Crime fans who favor the short story form will love this one." Booklist

The thief who couldn't sleep. Armchair Detective Lib. 1994 c1966 198p $22

ISBN 1-56287-064-5 LC 93-40996

First published 1966 in paperback

Evan Tanner "hasn't slept a wink since a piece of shrapnel destroyed the sleep center in his brain during the Korean War. Tanner loves lost causes and beautiful women. The FBI has a thick file on him; the CIA taps his phone. And a super-secret intelligence agency wants him to be their man. He never intended to be a spy— any more than he planned to lead a revolution in Macedonia or land in a Turkish jail. But those kinds of things just seemed to happen when Tanner was around—particularly when there were 573 pounds of pure gold waiting to be found and a beautiful blonde counting on him to gain freedom for her native land." Publisher's note

A ticket to the boneyard; a Matthew Scudder novel. Morrow 1990 302p o.p.

LC 90-5710

"This time, former cop, recovering alcoholic, and dick-without-a-license Matthew Scudder is his own case. Twelve years past, in order to protect himself and a hooker friend, Scudder framed a man, James Leo Motley, who had it coming. Motley's out of prison now, and guess what? He hasn't mellowed." Booklist

The author "has a fine nose for the pungencies of New York's after-dark street life, and he gives his hero wonderful opportunities to swap syllables with the city's most articulate riffraff. This is primo stuff, and Scudder doesn't get any sharper than when he's interviewing transvestite hookers, desk clerks in fleabag hotels and bouncers in gay leather bars." N Y Times Book Rev

Time to murder and create; a Matthew Scudder novel; introduction by Jonathan Kellerman. Dark Harvest 1993 c1976 190p o.p.

First published 1977 in paperback

In this novel, Matthew Scudder, "still in his drinking days, is paid by 'Spinner' Jablon, a small-time hood, to hold an envelope for him, with instructions to open it only when he dies, and then do what's necessary. What's necessary turns out to be determining which of Jablon's three eminent blackmail victims did the little man in. . . . The dialogue is, as always, dead on and rivetingly entertaining, and the atmosphere . . . is 'wonderfully morose.' Not to be missed." Publ Wkly

A walk among the tombstones; a Matthew Scudder mystery. Morrow 1992 318p $17

ISBN 0-688-10350-2 LC 91-41334

Also available G.K. Hall large print edition

In this novel Scudder gets involved in assisting "high-level drug dealers whose family members are being kidnapped for ransom and returned in shopping bags. Scudder, who once carried a police detective's gold shield before falling victim to alcoholism, divides his time between AA meetings and stalking the stalkers through all means fair and foul." Booklist

When the sacred ginmill closes. Arbor House 1986 239p o.p.

LC 85-18682

Available G.K. Hall large print edition

In this novel "Scudder solves a New York City bar holdup by prying into the underworld of the city's taverns. Scudder deals with the IRA, murder, and the 'Westies,' a mob of toughs from the west of Ireland that has ruled Hell's Kitchen since the Great Potato Famine." Booklist

Block, Lawrence, 1938----*Continued*

"The writing is realistic in the best sense of the word. There are no artificial heroics, forced lines of dialogue or false moves. Mr. Block knows his New York and the way people speak." N Y Times Book Rev

Bloom, Amy

Come to me; stories. HarperCollins Pubs. 1993 177p $20

ISBN 0-06-018236-9　　　　　LC 92-54725

"Aaron Asher books"

Analyzed in Short story index

Contents: Love is not a pie; Song of Solomon; Sleepwalking; Hyacinths; The sight of you; Silver water; Faultlines; Only you; Light breaks where no sun shines; Semper fidelis; When the year grows old; Psychoanalysis changed my life

The author "considers the complicated dynamics of families with insight, sympathy and verve. . . . Ms. Bloom is entertaining, wise and tolerant. Her work has the power both to disturb and to console." N Y Times Book Rev

Bojer, Johan, 1872-1959

The emigrants; translated from the Norwegian by A. G. Jayne. Appleton-Century 1925 351p o.p. Greenwood Press reprint available $35 (ISBN 0-8371-6194-0)

Original Norwegian edition, 1924

"The story of Erik Foss's colony of Norwegians, who, land-hungry and impoverished at home, came to take up sections in Red River valley, North Dakota, only to fight drought, frost, poverty and isolation in this country. The book is the first to describe from the Norwegian point of view the operations of that pioneer army of Scandinavians who settled so much of the Middle West from Wisconsin to North Dakota. In its zest, vitality and pungent native flavors, 'The emigrants' is happily free from the sogginess of some of our own novels of the soil." Cleveland Public Libr

Böll, Heinrich, 1917-1985

Nobel Prize in literature, 1972

And where were you, Adam?

In Böll, H. The stories of Heinrich Böll p34-152

Billiards at half-past nine; translated from the German. McGraw-Hill 1962 280p o.p.

Original German edition, 1959

"The novel examines the lives of three generations of architects and their responses to the Nazi regime and its aftermath. The present-day action takes place on the 80th birthday of patriarch Heinrich Fähmel, who built St. Anthony's Abbey. At the end of World War II, his son Robert destroyed the abbey to protest the church's complicity with the Nazis; Robert's son, Joseph, is serving his apprenticeship by helping to restore St. Anthony's. All three characters confront their relationship to building and destruction, as well as their personal and historical past. By the novel's end, the three are reconciled and share a birthday cake in the shape of the abbey." Merriam-Webster's Ency of Lit

The clown; translated from the German by Leila Vennewitz. McGraw-Hill 1965 247p o.p.

Original German edition, 1963

This novel revolves around the loss of meaning in the life of Hans Schnier, a twenty-seven-year-old clown and mime who returns home to Bonn after a disastrous performance tour. Flashbacks reconstruct Schnier's life in Hitler's Germany and his bitter experiences of the postwar period

"What Schnier (and the author) seem to be asking is: How can an honest man profess Christianity when Christian culture in the West failed to stop the rise of Nazism . . . and when the Church thrives in a society that worships nothing but the values of the marketplace? Hard questions but embodied in a bitter and brilliant book." N Y Times Book Rev

Group portrait with lady; translated from the German by Leila Vennewitz. McGraw-Hill 1973 405p o.p.

Original German edition, 1971

"A sweeping portrayal of German life from World War I until the early 1970s. . . . The story's anonymous narrator gradually reveals the life—past and present—of Leni Pfeiffer, a war widow who, with her neighbors, is fighting the demolition of the Cologne apartment building in which they reside. Leni and her illegitimate son Lev become the nexus of Cologne's counterculture; they spurn the prevailing work ethic and assail the dehumanization of life under capitalism. In a larger sense, the work attempts both a reconciliation with the past and a condemnation of the pursuit of affluence in present-day Germany." Merriam-Webster's Ency of Lit

The lost honor of Katharina Blum; or, How violence develops and where it can lead; translated from the German by Leila Vennewitz. McGraw-Hill 1975 140p o.p.

Original German edition, 1974

"The novel condemned as irresponsible the coverage of the trial of the Baader-Meinhof group, a German terrorist organization, by the tabloid newspaper *Bild-Zeitung* and rebuked official government attacks on individual civil liberties. Katharina's ordered life falls into ruins after the *News*, a sensationalist local tabloid, falsely accuses her lover of a single night of terrorism and then names Katharina as his accomplice. Hounded by the press and the police, she shoots and kills the journalist who has tried to exploit her sexually and who has written the lies that have destroyed her life." Merriam-Webster's Ency of Lit

The silent angel; translated by Breon Mitchell. St. Martin's Press 1994 182p $19.95

ISBN 0-312-11064-2　　　　　LC 94-2052

Written in 1950; first German edition, 1992

"Amid the charred rubble of Germany just days after World War II ends, cynical, numbed soldier Hans Schnitzler returns to Cologne under an alias to deliver a dead soldier's will to the widow, Elisabeth Gompertz. Hans was supposed to be shot as a deserter, but military court stenographer Willy Gompertz switched jackets with him and was killed instead. So begins what was Nobel-winner Böll's first novel." Publ Wkly

Böll, Heinrich, 1917-1985—*Continued*

"While the bleakness Böll portrays might have made German publishers wary in 1950, the artistry of his portrayal makes 'The Silent Angel' a rich novel, one still pertinent to our own hunger for the bread of meaning amid the rubble of history. Heinrich Böll's gift to us is the skill with which he captures its first pangs." NY Times Book Rev

A soldier's legacy

In Böll, H. The stories of Heinrich Böll p316-81

The stories of Heinrich Böll; translated from the German by Leila Vennewitz. Knopf 1986 685p o.p.

LC 85-40392

Partially analyzed in Short story index

This collection contains the war novel A soldier's legacy (1985), and the following novellas: And where were you, Adam?; The train was on time; When the war broke out, and When the war was over. Short stories included are: Breaking the news; My pal with the long hair; The man with the knives; Reunion on the avenue; Broommakers; My expensive leg; Children are civilians too; At the bridge; In the darkness; Candles for the Madonna; Across the bridge; That time we were in Odessa; Stranger, bear word to the Spartans we . . .; Drinking in Petöcki; What a racket; Parting; Between trains in X; Reunion with Drüng; The ration runners; Lohengrin's death; Business is business; On the hook; My sad face; Adventures of a haversack; Black sheep; My Uncle Fred; Christmas not just once a year; The Balek scales; The postcard; Recollections of a young king; The death of Elsa Baskoleit; A peach tree in his garden stands; Pale Anna; This is Tibten; Daniel the Just; In search of the reader; The tidings of Bethlehem; And there was the evening and the morning . . .; The taste of bread; Murke's collected silences; Monologue of a waiter; Like a bad dream; A case for Kop; Undine's mighty father; In the valley of the thundering hoofs; The thrower-away; Unexpected guest; No tears for Schmeck; Anecdote concerning the lowering of productivity; He came as a beer-truck driver; The Staech affair; Till death us do part; On being courteous when compelled to break the law; Too many trips to Heidelberg; My father's cough; Rendezvous with Margret; Nostalgia; In which language is one called Schneckenröder?

"From World War II experiences as a young man to the characteristic political utterances of his later years, these stories span the late German writer's entire career. Böll's questioning confrontations with life mine the modern European intellect with uncommon distinction, whether in battle-torn settings or in postwar Germany, recovering materially if not spiritually from the experience of war." Booklist

The train was on time

In Böll, H. The stories of Heinrich Böll p165-250

When the war broke out

In Böll, H. The stories of Heinrich Böll p568-81

When the war was over

In Böll, H. The stories of Heinrich Böll p582-96

Bond, Larry

Vortex. Warner Bks. 1991 670p $21.95

ISBN 0-446-51566-3   LC 90-50528

Set in South Africa, this war thriller "has Nazi-like ultraconservative Afrikaners taking over the Pretoria government, then invading bordering Namibia. A Communist counterforce led by Cubans is mounted, as internal revolt and harsh suppression breed domestic chaos. A Boer nuclear attack on the Cubans is answered with nerve gas; only heavy commitments of U.S. and British forces restore order after much battling and destruction. The love interest involves an American TV journalist and a free-spirited daughter of one of the Afrikaner leaders. In the wake of Desert Storm this knowledgeable evocation of the spectacle of modern weaponry and international conflict will reward new and old admirers of military action." Libr J

Bond, Michael, 1926-

Monsieur Pamplemousse. Beaufort Bks. 1985 191p o.p.

LC 84-24444

First published 1983 in the United Kingdom

Pamplemousse is a "gastronomic detective, an undercover critic for a prestigious Gallic dining guide. With his faithful bloodhound, Pommes Frites, Pamplemousse—a former inspector with the Sureté—investigates the cuisine of his favorite hotel-restaurant, La Langoustine. There, misfortune strikes: the specialty of the house is served to him with a man's head inside. . . . Mystery takes a back seat to fine food and hilarious characters in this ribald, side-splitting farce." Publ Wkly

Monsieur Pamplemousse and the secret mission. Beaufort Bks. 1986 c1984 207p o.p.

LC 85-9159

First published 1984 in the United Kingdom

This mystery features "that discerning gourmet, Monsieur Pamplemousse, and his wily pup, Pommes Frites. When Pamplemousse is commissioned to covertly oversee and overhaul the orderless kitchen of a rapidly declining country inn, he becomes embroiled in one riotous predicament after another. Master and dog labor at a chaotic pace to save the inn, while at the same time solving a hilariously titilating mystery involving the indiscriminate distribution of a potent aphrodisiac. A deliciously racy caper." Booklist

Monsieur Pamplemousse investigates. Fawcett Columbine 1990 175p o.p.

LC 89-92562

"When computer theft and forgery threaten to postpone the publication of the annual edition of *Le Guide*, a discriminating index of France's premier restaurants, food critic Aristide Pamplemousse undertakes the investigation. With the ever-able assistance of his precocious pup, Pommes Frites, Pamplemousse dons a hilarious disguise and stalks a malevolent chef with a long-term grudge against the esteemed directory. An epicurean blend of comedy and mystery." Booklist

Monsieur Pamplemousse rests his case. Fawcett Columbine 1991 199p o.p.

LC 91-70650

"M. Pamplemousse, retired from the Sûreté, is representing *Le Guide* magazine in Vichy, where six celebrated American mystery writers are recreating a gourmet feast supposedly once hosted by Alexandre Dumas. The Inspector arrives at the dinner as instructed,

Bond, Michael, 1926-—*Continued*

costumed as D'Artagnan and riding a horse—a wickedly unreliable horse. All too soon he finds himself thrown into a rural ditch, arrested and handcuffed, pursued on foot over the fields, locked in a country brothel (and rescued by his dog Pommes Frites), tucked in a hotel bed with a ravishing American gourmet-magazine publisher. . . . At the same time he's coping with two fake murders and one genuine one." Publ Wkly

Bonner, Cindy, 1953-

Lily; a novel. Algonquin Bks. 1992 336p $17.95

ISBN 0-945575-95-5   LC 91-40237

"Lily DeLony, is 15, hardworking, and dutiful, having taken over the responsibilities of caring for her family after her mother's death. Life on the DeLonys' Texas farm in the 1880s is demanding, and her papa is a stern, humorless man. Lily has just blossomed into young womanhood, and the son of the only well-to-do family in the area has asked her to the church fair, but her heart has already been snared by Marion, the youngest of the notorious Beatty gang. Although Marion, nicknamed Shot, shares his brothers' outlaw life, he's sharp-witted, affectionate, and not without morals. Their attraction is as unavoidable as gravity." Booklist

"A fine first novel, making the timeworn theme of a responsible young girl's falling in love with a ne'er-do-well rascal new and fresh. . . . The book's strongest assets are its verisimilitude, fortified by the wonderful use of the vernacular, and the pure, simple clarity of the writing." Libr J

Followed by Looking after Lily

Looking after Lily. Algonquin Bks. 1994 326p $18.95

ISBN 1-56512-045-0   LC 93-33730

As this sequel "begins, Lily's husband, Marion ('Shot') Beatty, has been sentenced to two years in jail just as his one surviving brother, Haywood, is being released. Shot begs Haywood to take care of Lily, who is pregnant and has nowhere to go. Haywood is appalled. A loner with a taste for whiskey, gambling, and whoring, he wants nothing to do with a pregnant sister-in-law. But gradually, after a series of disastrous misadventures and the near-disastrous birth of his niece, Emmaline Eliza, Haywood begins to grow into his role of guardian. The trouble is, he also falls in love with Lily. As these two tough, laconic, brave, and, yes, noble individuals struggle with the conundrums of passion and the demanding work of pre-industrial daily life, Bonner does more than hold us rapt with her storytelling skills; she also reveals the transforming power of love." Booklist

Borges, Jorge Luis, 1899-1986

The book of sand; translated by Norman Thomas di Giovanni. Dutton 1977 125p o.p.

LC 77-8418

Analyzed in Short story index
Original Spanish edition, 1975
Contents: The other; Ulrike; The Congress; There are more things; The Sect of the Thirty; The night of the gifts; The mirror and the mask; Undr; Utopia of a tired man; The bribe; Avelino Arredondo; The disk; The book of sand

"Borges' short stories combine intriguing ideas with smooth technique. Among these 13, for example, is one in which, at 70, he meets his 20-year-old self on a park bench and discovers they have few points of agreement. In another, a mendicant sells him a book with an infinite number of pages whose beginning and end cannot be located. Like a sleight-of-hand artist, Borges delights in presenting the impossible as fact. Some of these fictions reflect his Argentinian background, others his Norse scholarship." Booklist

Ficciones; edited and with an introduction by Anthony Kerrigan. Grove Press 1962 174p o.p.

Analyzed in Short story index
Original Spanish edition, 1944
Contents: Tlön, Uqbar, Orbis Tertius; The approach to al-Mu'tasim; Pierre Menard, author of Don Quixote; The circular ruins; The Babylon lottery; An examination of the work of Herbert Quain; The Library of Babel; The garden of forking paths; Funes, the memorious; The form of the sword; Theme of the traitor and the hero; Death and the compass; The secret miracle; Three versions of Judas; The end; The sect of the Phoenix; The South

Borland, Hal, 1900-1978

When the legends die. Lippincott 1963 288p o.p.

A story "about a Ute Indian boy, child of outlaws, brought up in the Colorado wilderness in the old ways and in friendship with a bear cub. His boyhood—when he is torn away from his mountains and 'civilized' against his will—and his young manhood are harsh and brutal: he becomes a bronc-buster with a reputation for a murderous riding style. The time is from 1910 up into the 1920's." Publ Wkly

"The moral of the tale (and Mr. Borland is not averse to some explicit moralizing) is that it is good for a people to change but not good for them to forget their past. A good book for adults and a very fine book for young adults." Libr J

Bosse, Malcolm J., 1934-

Fire in heaven; a novel. Simon & Schuster 1985 654p o.p.

LC 85-14347

Sequel to The warlord

"Vera Rogacheva Embree, former mistress of the infamous warlord General Tang, has made successful life in Bangkok as an antiques importer. Her daughter by General Tang, Sonia, is coming of age and is beginning to question not only her Russian-Chinese ancestry but also her place in Thai society. When Sonia takes up with a young member of the Communist party, Vera recognizes her own misguided idealism and tries to stop her daughter from making a terrible mistake. Sonia, however, already is drawn deeply into a romanticized view of Communist ideology. Vera counts on one last person to save her daughter—Phil Embree, Vera's American husband, who has returned from a two-year sojourn in India." Booklist

The author "has written a story of impressive richness and intensity that not only depicts with an expert's understanding an Asia caught in convulsive change, but does so through the private dramas of a half-dozen characters who are not easy to forget." Publ Wkly

Mister Touch. Ticknor & Fields 1991 502p $22.95

ISBN 0-89919-965-8   LC 90-46780

Bosse, Malcolm J., 1934——*Continued*

"Mister Touch is blind, white, a former Wall Street crook, and the leader of the Skulls, the New York survivors of an apocalyptic virus that has killed most of the human race. The Skulls are trying to maintain a semblance of civilization, but there are a few other survivors, too—drug-crazed sex fiends, wild dogs. Breathing and sight problems afflict the Skulls, and Mister Touch decides they should migrate to a better climate—Arizona. Each of the Skulls has been given a new name to forget the past. The escape from New York, the journey across America, and the climax in Arizona are filled with adventure, pop dialog, and philosophical speculations on life, race, religion, law, and survival." Libr J

"Intense, captivating drama filled with dark irony." Booklist

The vast memory of love. Ticknor & Fields 1992 482p il o.p.

LC 92-7590

This historical novel is "set in London in 1753. Journal entries purporting to be Henry Fielding's are interspersed with the tribulations of Ned Carleton. A servant who is no longer able to find a job because of an injured hand, Carleton takes to stealing to support himself. Another linked storyline deals with a group of noblemen [including the Earl of Sandwich] who practice Satanism and pay local girls for their favors. One of the girls is detained for a month and is put on trial when lies about her captivity are exposed. Teeming with activity, the book examines the London lower classes, the causes of crime, the foibles and cruelties of the nobility, the operations of the Bow Street Runners, and the justice system." Libr J

"This is a triumph of fast-paced storytelling as well as a thoughtful commentary on the hypocrisies of high society and the degraded lives of the poor." Publ Wkly

The warlord. Simon & Schuster 1983 717p o.p.

"In the violent, disorganized China of 1927 four people are thrown together. Tang Shan-teh, a successful general, desires unity and modernization but respects and preserves the old values of Confucianism and tradition; Vera Rogacheeva is a sometime prostitute, a White Russian refugee; Erich Luckner sells German guns to bandits and warlords; and Philip Embree is an American missionary who has gone native to the point of enlisting in Tang's army as an axeman." Libr J

"This book is a must for the student of China as well as those interested in human nature. It is a complicated story and cannot be skimmed or read between loads at the laundromat. This story is for those who enjoy 'hunkering down' in the sun and traveling to exotic places, where they must deal with contradictions, love and hate, peace and violence, confusions, and Marxist loyalty, and ultimately betrayal." Best Sellers

Followed by Fire in heaven

Boswell, Robert, 1953-

Mystery ride. Knopf 1993 333p o.p.

LC 92-4495

Available Thorndike Press large print edition

"Brimming with high ideals, Angela and Stephen Landis wed in the '60s and moved to a farm in Iowa, where their daughter Dulcie was born. Later, desperate for a life outside the confines of the farm and its small community, Angela left Stephen. She has remarried, and Dulcie is a rebellious, almost dangerously unstable adolescent

when Angela returns to the farm for the first time in a decade to leave the fractious 15-year-old with her father." Publ Wkly

"With dazzling technical skill, intelligence and moral seriousness, Mr. Boswell mesmerizes us. Full of characters and events too numerous and too organically bound to pull out and list, 'Mystery Ride' is deeply irresistible. Like Dulcie, Mr. Boswell loves extravagance and risk and speed, but he is uncanny in his ability to pull the reader to a dead halt with stunning reflections." N Y Times Book Rev

Boucher, Anthony, 1911-1968

The compleat werewolf

In Boucher, A. The compleat werewolf and other stories of fantasy and science fiction p7-62

The compleat werewolf and other stories of fantasy and science fiction. Simon & Schuster 1969 256p o.p.

Analyzed in Short story index

Contents: The compleat werewolf [novelette]; The pink caterpillar; Q. U. R.; Robnic; Snulbug; Mr. Lupescu; The bite; Expedition; We print the truth [novelette]; The ghost of me

We print the truth

In Boucher, A. The compleat werewolf and other stories of fantasy and science fiction p170-239

Boucolon, Maryse *See* Condé, Maryse, 1937-

Boulle, Pierre, 1912-1994

The bridge over the River Kwai; translated by Xan Fielding. Vanguard Press 1954 224p o.p. Amereon reprint available $19.95 (ISBN 0-89190-571-5)

Original French edition, 1952

A satire "on a certain type of British officer, a colonel who, even in a Japanese prison camp, keeps a stiff upper lip and clings to discipline. Put in charge of building a bridge with prison labor he carries out the job so satisfactorily that when a team of commandos arrives to blow up his handiwork he indignantly exposes them to the Japanese." Publ Wkly

"This is a stirring and imaginative book. Whatever Monsieur Boulle may think of Kipling standards he has, to his advantage, soaked in the Master's atmosphere. Ably seconded by an excellent translation he has achieved something of the brisk yet laconic style, the unforgettable character sketches, the technical details, the storytelling magic, which were part of the Day's Work and Many Inventions." New Statesman

Planet of the Apes; translated by Xan Fielding. Vanguard Press 1963 246p o.p. Buccaneer Bks. reprint available $18.95 (ISBN 0-89968-331-2)

Published in the United Kingdom with title: Monkey planet

"Ulysse Mérou writes of his experiences on an unusual planet where the roles of humans and apes are reversed. Gorillas wear clothing and run businesses, while humans

Boulle, Pierre, 1912-1994—*Continued*
are caged in zoos and are the subjects of scientific
experiments. In the year 2500 a vacationing couple
cruising through space spot a bottle-encased message,
retrieve it, and soon become absorbed in Mérou's tale."
Shapiro. Fic for Youth. 3d edition
"In this Swiftian fable Boulle gives full play to his
not inconsiderable gift for irony and satire." Libr J

Bova, Ben, 1932-
(ed) The Best of the Nebulas. See The
Best of the Nebulas

Challenges. TOR Bks. 1993 348p $21.95
ISBN 0-312-85550-8   LC 93-18413
"A Tom Doherty Associates book"
Partially analyzed in Short story index
Includes the following stories: The man who hated
gravity; Crisis of the month; Sepulcher; Fitting suits; To
touch a star; Brothers; Interdepartmental memorandum;
World War 4.5; Answer, please answer; The mask of the
Rad Death; Bushido; Thy kingdom come
"A collection of 12 science-fiction short stories and 6
essays that address challenges and change. . . . The
dangers of war, ESP, and life in the near future are
among the themes included." SLJ

Cyberbooks. Doherty Assocs. 1989 274p
o.p.
                                         LC 88-33476
"A TOR book"
"A research scientist threatens to revolutionize the publishing industry with his invention—the 'cyberbook'—and
catapults himself into a world of vicious schemers in
this satire on the convoluted world of publishing." Libr
J
"With his usual broad brush, Bova paints one view
of publishing: editorial assistants chortling in the corridor;
a romance editor named Scarlet Dean; another editor
who moonlights as a belly dancer to make ends meet.
He's somewhat more successful and blackly humorous
describing an ineptly automated warehouse where returns
fuel the furnace and falling cartons of books are a
routine hazard for unwary employees." Publ Wkly

Death dream. Bantam Bks. 1994 497p
$22.95
ISBN 0-553-08234-5   LC 93-46463
"Dan Santorini moves his family to Florida for a job
with a young company working to create virtual reality
games. At first, Dan is delighted to be reunited with
his brilliant and eccentric former partner, Jase Lowrey.
Yet Dan finds Jase uncomfortably manic, and Jase's
playful barbs have a new, cruel sting. After Dan's company provides virtual reality teaching chambers to his
daughter's school, his wife begins to observe a sinister
effect on their daughter. Dan ignores his unease with
his new company—and even his daughter's fainting
spells—until two people die in a fighter pilot simulation
he developed with Jase in their previous collaboration.
Bova's suspenseful plot, which revolves around the use
of completely interactive virtual reality for full-scale
baseball games, moonwalks, and magical journeys,
considers what happens when the methods used to enhance the realism become dangerous and the realism
becomes too real." Libr J

Mars. Bantam Bks. 1992 502p $20
ISBN 0-553-07892-5   LC 91-29466

"A Native American geologist finds himself the center
of political controversy as he becomes one of the first
humans to set foot on the red planet. Bova's imaginary
chronicle of the first human mission to Mars offers a
field day for science buffs as his characters experience
the challenges of exploring Earth's nearest neighbor." Libr
J

Millennium; a novel about people and
politics in the year 1999. Random House
1976 277p o.p.
"In 1999, the Colonel in charge of the American moon
base is a quiet, idealistic man who had been glad to
escape the political furors of Earth. With the U.S. and
the U.S.S.R. now on the brink of war, Colonel Kinsman
may be forced to make a life-and-death decision that
will affect all Earth dwellers." SLJ
The author "imparts some life to a well-worn plot:
revolt of a lunar colony. . . . Heavy use of gratuitous
four-letter words mars a competent job." Booklist

Orion and the conqueror. TOR Bks. 1994
350p $22.95
ISBN 0-312-85447-1   LC 93-42545
"A Tom Doherty Associates book"
In this episode of the fantasy series "Orion's mission
is to see that Alexandros, son of Philip of Macedonia,
becomes king and later conquers the world as Alexander
the Great. Orion finds himself serving King Philip as
a palace guard. His respect for Philip and his duty to
protect his life comes in direct conflict with the creator's
desire to see Philip die from an assassin's hand as Alexandros stands ready to take over. Anya is the goddess
who takes on human form because of her love for Orion
and his great love for her." Voice Youth Advocates
"The sounds, the scents and the sensibility of the ancient world permeate this well-wrought adventure." Publ
Wkly

Orion in the dying time. Doherty Assocs.
1990 356p $22.95
ISBN 0-312-93111-5   LC 90-208344
"A TOR book"
Previous titles in series Orion (1984) and Vengeance
of Orion (1988); another title Orion and the conqueror,
entered above
A fantasy "about the hunter Orion, endowed by the
Creators with superhuman powers. The Creators are the
godlike beings into which mankind has evolved 50,000
years from now. Determined to ensure that the continuum does not veer from the path that led to their
existence, they send Orion back to the nexus points in
history to hunt down their enemies." Publ Wkly

To save the sun; [by] Ben Bova and A.J.
Austin. TOR Bks. 1992 383p o.p.
                                         LC 92-25453
"A Tom Doherty Associates book"
"When the Empire of the Hundred Worlds receives
the news that Earth's sun in dying, the aging emperor
supports a young scientist's attempt to save humanity's
seed-world—despite the objections of bureaucrats who
feel that Earth has outlived its usefulness. This collaboration . . . results in a generation-spanning novel of sf
adventure and high intrigue." Libr J

The Trikon deception; [by] Ben Bova and
Bill Pogue. TOR Bks. 1992 309p o.p.
                                         LC 91-37281

Bova, Ben, 1932--—*Continued*
"A Tom Doherty Associates book"
"In 1998, Trikon, a new space station, becomes a center for genetic experiments too dangerous to perform on Earth. Several nations have contributed projects, but they are also ruthlessly spying on one another, which makes life aboard ship interesting and the pace of the book fast and furious. This one should appeal to both space advocacy and technothriller readers." Booklist

Voyagers. Doubleday 1981 389p o.p.
LC 80-2836

"Dr. Keith Stoner, an astrophysicist and former astronaut, connects strange signals coming from Jupiter with an object sighted by the new orbiting telescope. He believes and hopes the object to be an alien craft. The public is kept in the dark while the world's governments, scientists and even the Vatican scramble for answers. An international project is formed and Stoner finds his plan to meet the object in space—not to mention his life—endangered by national, international and internal Soviet intrigue." Publ Wkly
The author "is a sound storyteller who skillfully handles the complex narrative, with its multiple viewpoints, and his knowledge of science, space programs and politics balances the uneven characterization." Booklist

Bowen, Elizabeth, 1899-1973
The collected stories of Elizabeth Bowen.
Knopf 1981 784p $25

ISBN 0-394-51666-4   LC 80-8729

Analyzed in Short story index
First published 1980 in the United Kingdom
Contents: Breakfast; Daffodils; The return; The confidante; Requiescat; All Saints; The new house; Lunch; The lover; Mrs. Windermere; The shadowy third; The evil that men do—; Sunday evening; Coming home; Ann Lee's; The parrot; The visitor; The Contessina; Human habitation; The secession; Making arrangements; The storm; Charity; The back drawing-room; Recent photograph; Joining Charles; The jungle; Shoes: an international episode; The dancing-mistress; Aunt Tatty; Dead Mabelle; The working party; Foothold; The cassowary; Telling; Mrs. Moysey; The Tommy Crans; The good girl; The cat jumps; The last night in the old home; The disinherited; Maria; Her table spread; The little girl's room; Firelight in the flat; The man of the family; The needle case; The apple tree; Reduced; Tears, idle tears; A walk in the woods; A love story; Look at all those roses; Attractive modern homes; The Easter egg party; Love; No. 16; A queer heart; The girl with the stoop; Unwelcome idea; Oh, Madam. . .; Summer afternoon; The inherited clock; The cheery soul; Songs my father sang me; The demon lover; Careless talk; The happy autumn fields; Ivy gripped the steps; Pink May; Green holly; Mysterious Kôr; The Dolt's tale; I hear you say so; Gone away; Hand in glove; A day in the dark
"These stories trace the growth of a remarkable writer who transformed uncertainties of origin, and limitations of convention and form, into a body of work uniquely (because tangentially) English." New Statesman

The death of the heart. Knopf 1939 418p o.p.
"The novel is set chiefly in London in the period between the World Wars. Sixteen-year-old orphan Portia Quayne goes to live with her half brother Thomas and his wife Anna, both of whom are portrayed as urbane and empty. Bored and lonely, Portia falls in love with Eddie, one of Anna's friends; he does not return her love. Weeks later, Portia learns that Anna has been reading her diary. Thoroughly humiliated, Portia preposterously proposes marriage to a kindly family friend, who refuses her and encourages her to return to Thomas and Anna. In the end, Anna and Portia come to terms with each other, and Anna finally sympathizes with Portia's 'frantic desire to be handled with feeling.'"
Merriam-Webster's Ency of Lit

Eva Trout. Knopf 1968 302p o.p. Smith, P. reprint available $18.75 (ISBN 0-8446-6709-9)
In the novel "we see Eva Trout in aching clarity, a big, graceless girl, unloved, unsure, whose relentless pursuit of 'becoming' makes shambles of the lives she touches. To her homosexual guardian, Constantine, she is an awkward burden to maintain until she comes of age; to Henry, the youngest son of a neighboring vicar, she is 'Pippa Passes' in reverse, leaving 'lust and villainy' in her wake; to her former school teacher she is the ruin and salvation of a marriage; and to the deafmute child, Jeremy, she adopts, she becomes the world he cannot gain and so destroys." Libr J
"There is something about Eva that suggests one of Henry Moore's monumental women, a hugeness, a strength (like a 'dedicated discus thrower'), and a rooted stability combined with the instinctive wisdom of an E. M. Forster character." Christ Sci Monit

The heat of the day. Knopf 1949 c1948 372p o.p.
Essentially this novel presents character studies of Stella Rodney, and the two men who loved her. The background is London after Dunkirk, a London of blitzes and buzz bombs; and peaceful Ireland. The two men are Robert Kelway, Stella's lover, and the mysterious Harrison, who betrays Kelway's secret in order to gain Stella for himself
"Miss Bowen's novel expertly flicks the rawness of several unsolved queries concerning loyalty and love and ponders the degree to which human beings are strangers to each other. More densely written than her earlier work, this study of behavior is a soberly shocking, compassionate baring of the confused and vulnerable human heart." N Y Her Trib Books

Bowen-Judd, Sara Hutton *See* Woods, Sara

Bowles, Paul, 1910-
Collected stories, 1939-1976; introduction by Gore Vidal. Black Sparrow Press 1980 c1979 417p $25

ISBN 0-87685-397-1   LC 79-4569

Analyzed in Short story index
The thirty-nine stories in this volume have appeared in the three books: The delicate prey, 1950; The time of friendship, 1967; and Things gone and things still here, 1977
Contents: Tea on the mountain; The scorpion; By the water; A distant episode; The echo; Call at Corazón; Under the sky; Pages from Cold Point; How many midnights; The circular valley; At Paso Rojo; Pastor Dowe at Tacaté; You are not I; The delicate prey; Señor Ong and Señor Ha; A thousand days for Mokhtar; The fourth day out from Santa Cruz; Doña Faustina; The hours after noon; The successor; If I should open my mouth; The frozen fields; Tapiama; The hyena; A friend of the world; The story of Lahcen and Idir; He of the Assem-

Bowles, Paul, 1910- —*Continued*
bly; The wind at Beni Midar; The time of friendship;
The garden; Afternoon with Antaeus Mejdoub; The fqih;
The waters of Izli; Reminders of Bouselhamj; You have
left your lotus pods on the bus; Istikhara, Anaya,
Medagan and the Medaganat; Things gone and things
still here; Allal
"At the top of his art Bowles is an anima; to inhabit
this book is to experience pain and immensity." Time

The sheltering sky. New Directions 1949
318p o.p.
"Port and Kit Moresby, an American couple of independent means, have been traveling aimlessly for 12
years. By the time they reach Morocco they have become
disaffected and alienated. They take up with a series of
unreliable, rootless wanderers. On a trip to the interior
Port contracts typhoid fever—out of apathy he has neglected to be vaccinated—and dies. Kit has an affair with
an Arab and joins his household, but their relationship
soon falls apart. Kit is found and returned to Oran. She
is teetering on the brink of insanity and finds an opportunity to disappear into the crowded bazaar." Merriam-
Webster's Ency of Lit

Boyd, William, 1952-
Brazzaville Beach; a novel. Morrow 1990
316p o.p.
LC 90-47371
"Hope Clearwater lives alone in a beach house in an
unnamed African country, trying to patch together her
shattered life. An ecologist, she had come to Africa to
participate in primate research and to heal the deep
wounds of her marriage to a brilliant English mathematician; but she soon found herself plunged into another
crisis, one that threatened not only her career but also
her life." Libr J
"As befits a protagonist telling her own story, Hope
often doesn't know where she's going until she gets there,
but Boyd's skill in developing her character overrides
some slight confusion about the more picaresque aspects
of her adventure." Publ Wkly

Boyer, Richard *See* Boyer, Rick

Boyer, Rick
The Daisy Ducks; a Doc Adams suspense
novel. Houghton Mifflin 1986 276p o.p.
LC 86-3016
In this novel dentist-cum-detective Doc Adams'
"soldier-for-hire pal Liantis Roantis . . . gives the adventurous surgeon a reason to take a brief hiatus from
impacted wisdom teeth. Roantis needs Doc's help in
finding a Vietnam buddy who has become a fanatic
survivalist and is ensconced in the North Carolina mountains preparing for Armageddon. Amid the action, Boyer
effectively ponders the not-so-romantic reality of life on
the edge versus the sometimes somnambulant comforts
of home." Booklist
"If you like action-suspense novels, Doc Adams could
become addictive. Boyer's smooth style creates a character with charisma and a story that moves like a freight
train at full throttle—powerfully swift." Best Sellers

Yellow bird; a Doc Adams mystery.
Fawcett Columbine 1991 323p $18
ISBN 0-449-90506-3   LC 91-70537

In this mystery Doc Adams and his "wife Mary are
invited to a late autumn Cape Cod party given by an
old med-school chum who has made it big in Texas.
During a stroll on the beach, the Adamses think they
hear a shot from a deserted mansion, but the house
seems empty when they investigate. A few weeks later,
a body, shot, is found in the house, which belongs to
mega-rich Northrop Chesterton; the victim turns out to
be a former neighbor of Doc's on the mainland. A long,
complicated tale involving more murder, drug dealing,
gay and interracial sex and secret identities unfolds to
a fairly satisfactory end." Publ Wkly

Boyle, Kay, 1902-1992
Fifty stories. Doubleday 1980 648p o.p.
LC 78-22151
Analyzed in Short story index
Contents: Episode in the life of an ancestor; Wedding
day; Rest cure; Ben; Kroy Wen; Black boy; Friend of
the family; White as snow; Keep your pity; Security;
Dear Mr. Walrus; Rondo at Carraroe; Natives don't cry;
Maiden, maiden; The white horses of Vienna; Count
Lothar's heart; Major Alshuster; How Bridie's girl was
won; The herring piece; Your body is a jewel box; Major
engagement in Paris; Effigy of war; Diplomat's wife;
Men; They weren't going to die; Defeat; Let there be
honour; This they took with them; Their name is
macaroni; French harvest; Fire in the vineyards; Hotel
behind the lines; Summer evening; The criminal; Fife's
house; The lovers of gain; Army of occupation; Cabaret;
The kill; A disgrace to the family; The lost; Adam's
death; Aufwiedersehen Abend; A puzzled race; The canals
of Mars; The loneliest man in the U.S. Army; Winter
night; Evening at home; The ballet of Central Park;
Seven say you can hear corn grow
This "omnibus includes 29 of the pieces collected in
'Thirty Stories' (published in 1946) and 21 later stories.
Featuring a wide range of settings, the stories are
populated by both Americans and Europeans, many of
whom are affected personally by the hostilities of World
War II and its difficult aftermath." Booklist

Boyle, T. Coraghessan
East is East; a novel. Viking 1990 364p
$19.95
ISBN 0-670-83220-0   LC 89-40804
In this novel Hiro Tanaka, "a young Japanese seaman,
jumps ship off the coast of Georgia and, through a series
of mishaps and cultural misunderstandings, finds himself
hiding out in an artists' colony from the police and
immigration officials." N Y Times Book Rev
"At its best [this book] is an exuberant combination
of proficient adventure writing and burlesque. It is a tall
tale—or more accurately, a spoof of a tall tale. Boyle
has great fun parodying Hemingway, Faulkner and even
Melville. . . . Boyle commands a quirky, ferociously
energetic prose that seems to owe nothing to anyone
writing today." New Leader

If the river was whiskey; stories. Viking
1989 224p $17.95
ISBN 0-670-82690-1   LC 88-40396
Analyzed in Short story index
Contents: Sorry fugu; Modern love; Hard sell; Peace
of mind; Sinking house; The human fly; The hat; Me
cago en la leche (Robert Jordan in Nicaragua); The little
chill; King bee; Thawing out; The Devil and Irv Cher-
niske; The miracle at Ballinspittle; Zapatos; The ape lady

Boyle, T. Coraghessan—_Continued_
in retirement; If the river was whiskey
"Boyle is a master story teller. In this varied collection
of short stories he shows himself to be literate, satiric,
timely, irreverent and wickedly humorous." Shapiro. Fic
for Youth. 3d edition

Road to Wellville; a novel. Viking 1993
476p il $22.50
  ISBN 0-670-83766-0   LC 92-50731

This social satire provides a portrait of 1907 Battle
Creek, Michigan "from three perspectives. The first and
most central is that of Dr. Kellogg himself, high priest
of a sanitarium where the rich and powerful go to be
cured of physical and spiritual 'autointoxication' brought
about by meat eating and sexual activity. Possessed of
a Napoleon complex and an abiding hatred of Post, he
is saluted around the clinic as 'the Chief.' The second
is that of Will Lightbody, a patient at the clinic who
has trouble getting the Kellogg religion. The third viewpoint is that of Charlie Ossining, a shady businessman
who tries to get a piece of the breakfast-cereal action
a little too late." Booklist

The author "evokes the world of the senses with remarkable skill. As always, his prose is a marvel, enjoyable from beginning to end, alive with astute observations, sharp intelligence and subtle musicality. Possibly
as an effect of his highly developed style, Mr. Boyle's
vision has been one of the most distinctive and original
of his generation." N Y Times Book Rev

Water music; a novel. Little, Brown 1981
437p o.p.
                                        LC 81-12423

"An Atlantic Monthly Press book"
A "novel with two protagonists, the book chronicles
the fictionalized misadventures of Mungo Park—an actual
Scottish explorer (1771-1806)—and his counterpart Ned
Rise, a London scalawag. They team up in Africa, where
they attempt to chart the course of the Niger River,
experiencing every conceivable comic mishap and
catastrophe." Choice

The author "bases his first novel in historical fact, but
brings his story to life with an innovative wit and
bawdiness reminiscent of 'Tom Jones'. He peoples the
novel with a colorful cast, involves them in the mishaps
of daily life, and places everything within a specific historical framework. . . . A very funny and well-written
literary work." Booklist

Without a hero; stories. Viking 1994 238p
$21.95
  ISBN 0-670-84963-4   LC 93-35919

Analyzed in Short story index
Contents: Big game; Hopes rise; Filthy with things;
Without a hero; Respect; Acts of God; Back in the
Eocene; Carnal knowledge; The 100 faces of death,
volume IV; 56-0; Top of the food chain; Little America;
Beat; The fog man; Sitting on top of the world
"Most effective of the 16 technically ingenious and
rudely funny, satirical stories . . . are the sketches of
disaffected individuals who take refuge in hermetic surroundings, self-help programs, political causes and
conspicuous consumption to hold at bay the banal world
of convention and compromise." Publ Wkly

World's end; a novel. Viking 1987 456p
$19.95
  ISBN 0-670-81489-X   LC 87-40023

"The sins of the fathers—along with physical afflictions
and other worries—are visited on their children as one
generation relives in contemporary terms the experiences
of the past. Boyle's novel—partly a historical tale and
partly a modern-day re-creation of the same story—
switches from past to near present and mixes
seventeenth-century Dutch settlers and their landlords
with hippie motorcyclists and Indians intent on
reclaiming their territory in the Hudson River valley."
Booklist

"The themes Mr. Boyle develops as his story shuttles
between epochs make us grasp in new terms their
connection with the American social and political experiment. His mastery of history is the secret of the
accomplishment here. Mr. Boyle has lost none of the
qualities that marked him a wit writer before, but now
he has challenged his own disengagement; passion, need
and belief breathe with striking force and freedom
through this smashing good novel." N Y Times Book
Rev

Bradbury, Ray, 1920-
Dandelion wine; a novel. Knopf 1975
269p $24.95
  ISBN 0-394-49605-1
Also available from Buccaneer Bks.

A reissue, with a new introduction by the author, of
the title first published 1957 by Doubleday
A novel about one summer in the life of a twelve-
year-old boy, Douglas Spaulding: the summer of 1928.
The place is Green Town, Illinois, and Doug and his
brother Tom wander in and out among their elders,
living and dreaming, sometimes aware of things, again
just having a wonderful time. Doug's big discovery that
summer was that he was alive
"The writing is beautiful and the characters are
wonderful living people. A rare reading experience." Libr
J

Death is a lonely business. Knopf 1985
o.p.
                                        LC 85-40221

"The sadly dilapidated pier district of Venice, California, serves as an appropriately dismal backdrop for a
series of bizarre homicides involving a number of the
town's most eccentric inhabitants. In an effort to solve
the seemingly senseless crimes, a naive young writer and
a world-weary detective delve into the pathetic pasts of
the hapless victims and uncover a particularly chilling
motive for the brutal murders. . . . A highly gratifying
blend of the mysterious and the macabre from a master
craftsman." Booklist

Fahrenheit 451. Simon & Schuster 1967
192p o.p.
Available from Amereon and Buccaneer Bks.

Analyzed in Short story index
The novelette Fahrenheit 451 was first published 1952
in paperback by Ballantine Books
Contents: Fahrenheit 451; The playground; And the
rock cried out
The title story tells about a bookburner official in a
future fascist state who finds out that books are a vital
part of a culture he never knew. He clandestinely pursues
reading, until he is betrayed
"Here is a different, off-trail book, filled with intimations of a time to come, of regimented men and women,
of a complex atomic age which looms ahead. It is an
ideal book for that reader whose appetite is in danger

Bradbury, Ray, 1920——*Continued*
of becoming jaded, as well as for him who yearns for
something new, some strange adventure in print."
Chicago Sunday Trib

Fahrenheit 451 [novelette]

In Bradbury, R. Fahrenheit 451 p19-150

The golden apples of the sun; drawings by Joe Mugnaini. Doubleday 1953 250p il o.p. Greenwood Press reprint available $37.50 (ISBN 0-8371-5160-0)

Analyzed in Short story index
Contents: Fog horn; The pedestrian; April witch; The
wilderness; Fruit at the bottom of the bowl; Invisible
boy; Flying machine; The murderer; Golden kite, the
silver wind; I see you never; Embroidery; Big black and
white game; Sound of thunder; Great wide world over
there; Powerhouse; En la noche; Sun and shadow; The
meadow; Garbage collector; Great fire; Hail and farewell;
The golden apples of the sun

A graveyard for lunatics; another tale of two cities. Knopf 1990 285p $18.95

ISBN 0-394-57877-5   LC 89-43387

This novel is set in Hollywood in 1954. The narrator
is hired to write a horror movie. "A boyhood friend
has been signed to create the most dreadful monster in
film history. Searching for inspiration, the buddies visit
a cemetery across the street from Maximus Films.
Abruptly, the body of a long-buried mogul passes in
review. Is it an apparition? What about the hideous
beast that begins to haunt the Brown Derby restaurant?
And the performer who has played Jesus Christ in
movies for 25 years: Is he an actor or an authentic
Saviour? Are they all characters in someone else's
movie?" Time
"For anyone who grew up on Bradbury's stories, this
Baedeker to the fantasies of his own youth is like camping out with Santa Claus. Never mind that you can
forecast the ending a mile off, or that the narrator's
voice is too often adolescently shrill. Out of a lot of
wire and paste and cardboard, Bradbury has convincingly
conjured a lost world, 'lovelier than tonight or all the
nights to come.'" Newsweek

Green shadows, white whale; a novel; with drawings by Edward Sorel. Knopf 1992 271p il $21

ISBN 0-394-57878-3   LC 91-58552

"This is Bradbury's comic account of his trip to
Ireland to write the screenplay for Huston's adaptation
of *Moby-Dick*. The movie itself is merely a background
constant that anchors this series of . . . vignettes and
anecdotes. Bradbury describes his awed dealings with the
erratic, eccentric and impulsive director, and his delight
upon being accepted among the regulars at an atmospheric pub called Heeber Finn's. It's a great place
to hoist a wee drop and listen to stories told in the
best Irish brogue." Publ Wkly
"High jinks follow high jinks, some of them quite
funny, others just too Irish for words. It's as rewarding
when dipped into randomly as when plowed straight
through." Booklist

I sing the Body Electric!; stories. Knopf 1969 305p o.p. Buccaneer Bks. reprint available $24.95 (ISBN 1-56849-451-3)

Partially analyzed in Short story index
Contents: The Kilimanjaro device; The terrible
conflagration up at the place; Tomorrow's child; The
women; The inspired chicken motel; Downwind from
Gettysburg; Yes, we'll gather at the river; The cold wind
and the warm; Night call, collect; The haunting of the
new; I sing the Body Electric!; The Tombling day; Any
friend of Nicholas Nickleby's is a friend of mine;
Heavyset; The man in the Rorschach shirt; Henry the
Ninth; The lost city of Mars; Christus Apollo

The illustrated man. Doubleday 1951 251p o.p. Buccaneer Bks. reprint available $25.95 (ISBN 1-56849-084-4)

Analyzed in Short story index
Contents: The veldt; Kaleidoscope; The other foot; The
highway; The man; The long rain; The rocket man; The
fire balloons; The last night of the world; The exiles;
No particular night or morning; The fox and the forest;
The visitor; The concrete mixer; Marionettes, Inc.; The
city; Zero hour; The rocket
"As almost every science fiction fan knows, there is
no writer quite like Ray Bradbury." N Y Times Book
Rev

The Martian chronicles. Doubleday 1950 222p o.p.

Available from Amereon and Buccaneer Bks.
Analyzed in Short story index
"This is an amazing work; its closely interwoven short
stories, linked by recurrent images and themes, tell of
the repeated attempts by humans to colonize Mars, of
the way they bring their old prejudices with them, and
of the repeated, ambiguous meetings with the shape-
changing Martians. Despite the sf scenario, there is no
emphasis on hard technology at all. The mood is of
loneliness, nostalgia; a dying fall lies over the book." Sci
Fic Ency

Something wicked this way comes. Knopf 1983 c1962 307p $24.95

ISBN 0-394-53041-1   LC 82-48732
Also available from Buccaneer Bks.
A reissue of the title first published 1962 by Simon
& Schuster
"It is late in October when the Dark Carnival arrives,
bringing terror to a sleepy little town where two small
boys and a caretaker stand between the townspeople and
the hypnotic pull of damnation." Cincinnati Public Libr
"A night-marish allegory which can stand on its own
merits as a suspense tale and still make a significant
comment on the human situation." Christ Sci Monit

The stories of Ray Bradbury; with an introduction by the author. Knopf 1980 xx, 884p $40

ISBN 0-394-51335-5   LC 80-7655
Analyzed in Short story index
Contents: The night; Homecoming; Uncle Einar; The
traveler; The lake; The coffin; The crowd; The scythe;
There was an old woman; There will come soft rains;
Mars is heavy; The silent towns; The earth men; The
off season; The million-year picnic; The fox and the
forest; Kaleidoscope; The rocket man; Marionettes, Inc.;
No particular night or morning; The city; The fire balloons; The last night of the world; The veldt; The long
rain; The great fire; The wilderness; A sound of thunder;

Bradbury, Ray, 1920-—_Continued_
The murderer; The April witch; Invisible boy; The golden kite, the silver wind; The fog horn; The big black and white game; Embroidery; The golden apples of the sun; Powerhouse; Hail and farewell; The great wide world over there; The playground; Skeleton; The man upstairs; Touched with fire; The emissary; The jar; The small assassin; The next in line; Jack-in-the-box; The leave-taking; Exorcism; The happiness machine; Calling Mexico; The wonderful ice cream suit; Dark they were, and golden-eyed; The strawberry window; A scent of sarsaparilla; The Picasso summer; The day it rained forever; A medicine for melancholy; The shoreline at sunset; Fever dream; The town where no one got off; All summer in a day; Frost and fire; The anthem sprinters; And so died Riabouchinska; Boys! Raise giant mushrooms in your cellar; The vacation; The illustrated woman; Some live like Lazarus; The best of all possible worlds; The one who waits; Tyrannosaurus Rex; The screaming woman; The terrible conflagration up at the place; Night call, collect; The Tombling day; The haunting of the new; Tomorrow's child; I sing the Body Electric!; The women; The inspired chicken motel; Yes, we'll gather at the river; Have I got a chocolate bar for you; A story of love; The parrot who met Papa; The October game; Punishment without crime; A piece of wood; The blue bottle; Long after midnight; The utterly perfect murder; The better part of wisdom; Interval in sunlight; The black ferris; Farewell summer; McGillahee's brat; The aqueduct; Gotcha; The end of the beginning

Bradford, Barbara Taylor, 1933-
Act of will. Doubleday 1986 374p o.p.
LC 86-6185

"The story peruses the lives of a mother and daughter who struggle to give each other what each thinks the other deserves, in the way of opportunity for the daughter Christina and material reward for the mother Audra. The mother works herself very hard in order that the daughter can enjoy the finest art education England has to offer. The daughter, however, decides that her career as a landscape artist cannot provide her with the money she needs properly to repay Audra for her sacrifice. The alternative, therefore, is to become a sudden success in the fashion industry, as Christina of course does. . . . In the end, a granddaughter reverses the cycle by refusing her mother's invitation to the fashion world in order that she may be an artist." Best Sellers

"While written in a comparatively minor key, this is a light, pleasing tale of three generations, marked by ironic twists of fate and finely etched period detail." Publ Wkly

Angel. Random House 1993 382p $23
ISBN 0-394-55959-2   LC 92-56794
Also available large print edition $21 (ISBN 0-679-74726-5)

Rose Madigan is a "world-famous costume designer for the screen and the sister of an undercover policeman named Kevin. In their early youth, the two were part of a circle of six friends who banded together against the vicissitudes of their respective family lives. One has been lost to drugs, one has vanished without a trace, another, Nell Jeffrey, is a high-powered theatrical agent, and the last, Gavin Ambrose, has become a major movie star. . . . Those who thrive on fantasies about the rich and famous will lap this up." Publ Wkly

Everything to gain. HarperCollins Pubs. 1994 361p $24
ISBN 0-06-017723-3   LC 94-13795

This novel's narrator, "New York wife and mother Mallory Keswick, feels she is showered with blessings, but just as the family is making plans to go to London for Christmas, her husband, twin children and dog are murdered in an attempted carjacking. Depressed and contemplating suicide, Mal flees to London, where she slowly learns to accept her losses. Returning to the States, she turns the family's Connecticut weekend retreat into a successful business venture and eventually meets a man who is able to breach her emotional barricades." Publ Wkly

Hold the dream; the sequel to A woman of substance. Doubleday 1985 632p o.p.
LC 84-25993

This novel "revolves around Emma's abdication of power over her far-flung business enterprises in favor of her grandchildren, particularly her favorite and heir, Paula McGill Fairley. As she struggles to keep the vast Harte empire running smoothly, Paula must deal not only with business crises, but with family and personal problems as well, particularly her disintegrating marriage." Libr J

"Bradford is a talented writer who can make even the most contrived situations seem credible, and the novel's only drawback is its overly long passages and slow pace. But even this flaw will appeal to readers who enjoy luxuriating in good escapist fiction." Booklist

Followed by To be the best

Remember. Random House 1991 381p $22.50
ISBN 0-394-55958-4   LC 91-52706
Also available large print edition $25 (ISBN 0-679-40821-5)

"Television war correspondent Nicky Wells is a media superstar, courageous, beautiful, and renowned for her hard-hitting reports from the world's battlefields and trouble spots. But her life is shattered when she loses the only man she has ever truly loved, dashing English aristocrat Charles Devereaux. Nicky finds solace in her work, and in her friendship with photographer Cleeland Donovan, and together they report on the massacre in Beijing's Tiananmen Square during the student protest in 1989. After a romantic interlude in Provence, Nicky wonders if she might finally be able to fall in love again. But suddenly she is forced to remember Charles Devereaux when she is confronted with disturbing suspicions about this remarkable man and his mysterious double life. And so Nicky embarks on a quest to discover the truth about Devereaux." Publisher's note

To be the best. Doubleday 1988 514p o.p.
LC 88-3813

Sequel to Hold the dream
The author "continues the saga of Emma Harte, her descendants, and the far-flung business empire she founded. Now, some 11 years after Harte's death, the story revolves around Paula Amory O'Neill, Emma's granddaughter and principal heir, and the ups and downs faced by her family and friends." Libr J

Voice of the heart. Doubleday 1983 732p o.p.
LC 81-47863

Bradford, Barbara Taylor, 1933- — Continued

"The story of a world-famous movie star and stage actress who returns to New York to seek out six people who years earlier had suffered hurt, pain, and humiliation at her hands. Curiosity makes them decide to see her and thus reopen the old wounds of their past." Publisher's note

"This is a well-written 'woman's novel,' although it tends to drag and the plot is rather formulaic. There are some lively plot twists and a certain mystery about the book that will keep readers glued to it." Libr J

A woman of substance. Doubleday 1979 755p o.p.

LC 77-9231

"A poor Yorkshire girl rises from the servant class to found a department store and eventually head an important business dynasty. As the aged Emma recalls how she has sacrificed love and happiness for success and power, she repudiates the past for the simpler and more enduring pleasures of life." Booklist

"It's a life worth the telling, and Ms. Bradford has told it well, sparing no detail. She writes competently, if not extraordinarily, against an accurate and well drawn historical background." West Coast Rev Books

Followed by Hold the dream

The women in his life. Random House 1990 522p o.p.

LC 89-43432

"Tycoon Maximilian West, workaholic founder of a multinational financial empire, is endowed with 'personal magnetism,' 'fatal charm,' 'charisma' and 'presence' but is emotionally obtuse with the women who adore him. . . . Bradford is more adept at describing opulent furniture, clothing and food, and in providing capsule tours of posh neighborhoods in London, New York, Berlin, Paris, Venice and Morocco than she is in delineating the personalities of her characters. . . . But her legions of readers undoubtedly will be satisfied by the romantic fortunes of the cultured, wealthy and powerful people whose lives she evokes with lavish sentiment." Publ Wkly

Bradford, Richard, 1932-

Red sky at morning; a novel. Lippincott 1968 256p o.p.

"When World War II begins Josh Arnold's father Frank joins the Navy and sends his wife and son from Mobile, Alabama to tiny Sagrado, New Mexico where the family had spent previous summers. Josh's observations of life among the motley Mexican and Anglo inhabitants of Sagrado and his disarming schoolmates and his concern for his Southern mother and for the nearly permanent house guest Jimbob Buel result in a humorous, honest, and affirmative portrayal of a teen-ager's seventeenth summer." Booklist

This novel "is warm and funny and yet has a sharp bite to it, like the snap of fangs crunching through corn pone. The genteel old South hasn't taken such a beating since Sherman's day. . . . But what makes the book a true delight is the dead-pan, irreverent humor with which Josh tells the story." Book World

Bradley, David, 1950-

The Chaneysville incident; a novel. Harper & Row 1981 432p $14.95

ISBN 0-06-010491-0   LC 80-8225

The Chaneysville incident in which thirteen slaves were willfully killed in 19th century rural Pennsylvania trying to escape the South is the historical center of this novel about John Washington, a black historian who "comes home to Chaneysville because Jack Crawley, a friend of Moses' who raised John when Moses died, is himself dying. Jack's death, and John's last conversations about Moses with him, push John into examining his own past and that of his ancestors." West Coast Rev Books

"Washington is an ornery and abrasive character who occasionally digresses into gripes about history and white society. Those who persevere through those passages will find the rest of the book powerful in its sentiments." Libr J

Bradley, Marion Zimmer

The best of Marion Zimmer Bradley; edited by Martin H. Greenberg. Academy Chicago 1985 367p o.p.

LC 85-18517

Analyzed in Short story index

Contents: Centaurus changeling; The climbing wave; Exiles of tomorrow; Death between the stars; Bird of prey; The wind people; The wild one; Treason of the blood; The jewel of Arwen; The day of the butterflies; Hero's moon; The engine; The secret of the Blue Star; To keep the oath; Elbow room; Blood will tell

Black Trillium; [by] Marion Zimmer Bradley, Julian May, and Andre Norton. Doubleday 1990 409p o.p.

LC 89-71544

First in a fantasy series that includes Blood Trillium by Julian May and Golden Trillium by Andre Norton

"A Foundation book"

"Three princesses, Haramis, Anigel, and Kadiya, are the living petals of the Black Trillium, an ancient flower that is the symbol of the kingdom of Ruwenda. At birth they are given magic amulets by the White Lady and warned of a fearsome destiny. Seventeen years later, both the king and the queen are brutally murdered, and the three princesses, trying to escape, are scattered. One by one, they reach the White Lady and are sent on a quest for a talisman to defeat the evil sorcerer who has taken over their kingdom." Booklist

The firebrand; a novel. Simon & Schuster 1987 608p o.p.

LC 87-17283

"Recounts the story of the Trojan War through the eyes of Kassandra, a princess of Troy blessed with 'the sight' yet doomed by a vengeful god to be thought mad in her prophecies of destruction. . . . As a priestess of Apollo who rode with the Amazons in the waning days of their rule, Bradley's Kassandra is caught between the whims of warring gods and greedy mortals, forced to bear witness to the awful destinies of those she loves, but unable to change the course of any life, including her own. Although these mythic figures stumble through some petty, rather too modern dialogue, the dust of the war fairly rises off the page as Bradley animates this rich history and vivifies the conflicts between a culture that reveres the strength of women and one that makes them mere consorts of powerful men." Publ Wkly

Bradley, Marion Zimmer—*Continued*

The forest house. Viking 1994 416p
$21.95

ISBN 0-670-84454-3 LC 93-33686

"The forbidden love of a druid priestess and a Roman
soldier mirrors the clash of cultures in Roman Britain.
. . . The novel evokes an age when three major religions
maintained an uneasy coexistence on the island of Britain. Eilan, a daughter of goddess-worshiping druids, and
Gaius Marcellius, a half-British Roman, live for the
coming of a legendary future king to unite the warring
islanders. Bradley envisions the 'old religion' as a
refreshing blend of classic and revisionist concepts, adding a distinct flavor to her seamless weave of history
and myth." Libr J

The house between the worlds. Doubleday
1980 244p o.p.

LC 79-7800

"An experimental ESP-enhancing drug sends Cameron
Fenton's astral body into a parallel world while his
physical self stays behind in a coma. The world he visits
as a ghost-like 'tweenman' is the home of the Alfar,
beautiful, magical people reminiscent of Tolkien's elves.
They are mortally threatened by the noisome, goblin-like
Ironfolk, invaders from yet another world. Fenton wants
to help the Alfar, but his only hope is to find the
Worldhouse, a 'physical' gateway between the worlds, and
the Worldhouse may not want to be found." Publ Wkly
"This is an excellent book, with all the virtues readers
have come to expect from Bradley: literate writing; excellent characterization; sound, logical plotting; and broad
humanistic sympathies." Booklist

The mists of Avalon. Knopf 1982 876p
o.p.

LC 82-47810

This "retelling of the Arthurian legend is dominated
by the character of Morgan le Fay (here called Morgaine), the powerful sorceress who symbolizes the historical clash between Christianity and the early pagan religions of the British Isles. After serving a kind of
apprenticeship to the high priestess of Avalon—the Lady
of the Lake—Morgaine is directed to sacrifice her virginity during the annual fertility rites . . . and the 'Horned
God' who impregnates her turns out to be her
younger brother, Arthur, as yet uncrowned. Years later
she turns against him, convinced that he has betrayed
his oath to uphold the old religion of Avalon in favor
of Christianity, and the Arthur-Guinevere-Lancelot
triangle is blasted apart by Sir Mordred, the issue of
that incestuous coupling." Publ Wkly

Bradshaw, Gillian, 1956-
The bearkeeper's daughter. Houghton
Mifflin 1987 310p o.p.

LC 87-2924

"To the recorded facts about Justinian I and his empress Theodora, Bradshaw adds an illegitimate son born
to Theodora. John arrives from Arabia seeking the truth
of statements his father made on his deathbed. Afraid
to acknowledge him, Theodora finds a place for John
as secretary to the palace chamberlain. Later, he becomes
involved in court intrigue, riots, and war in Thrace."
Libr J
"This is a deftly plotted and inviting story that will
entertain romantics as well as history buffs." West Coast
Rev Books

Horses of heaven. Doubleday 1991 448p
$19.95

ISBN 0-385-41466-8 LC 90-43095

"Set amidst ancient Greek culture, Bradshaw's . . .
saga revolves around an aging but powerful king, the
foreign beauty who became his wife, and his son who
is torn by love and loyalty." Booklist
"Well-researched, interesting details on the cultural and
religious customs of the period provide background for
the noble characters, who fulfill the promise, good or
evil, of their true natures." Publ Wkly

Imperial purple. Houghton Mifflin 1988
324p o.p.

LC 88-11923

"The slave Demetrias, a beautiful and talented silk
weaver in fifth-century Tyre, seems unable to love either
her devoted husband or her darling young son. When
a petty official forces her into an intrigue involving certain treason and the possible overthrow of Emperor
Theodosius II, she's diverted from these concerns." NY
Times Book Rev
This novel "owes much of its effectiveness to its
author's careful research. Bradshaw provides a wealth of
details and does so without delivering it in unpalatable
lumps. She brings her characters to life with equal skill."
West Coast Rev Books

Bradshaw-Isherwood, Christopher William
See Isherwood, Christopher, 1904-1986

Brady, William S., 1938-
*For works written by this author under
other names see* Harvey, John, 1938-

Brand, Max, 1892-1944
The collected stories of Max Brand;
edited, with story prefaces, by Robert and
Jane Easton; introduction by William Blood-
worth. centennial ed. University of Neb.
Press 1994 xx, 342p $35

ISBN 0-8032-1244-5 LC 93-43938

Analyzed in Short story index
Contents: John Ovington returns; Above the law; The
wedding guest; A special occasion; Outcast breed; The
sun stood still; The strange villa; The claws of the
tigress; Internes can't take money; Fixed; Wine on the
desert; Virginia creeper; Pringle's luck; The silent witness;
Miniature; Our daily bread; Honor bright; The king

Dark Rosaleen

In Brand, M. Max Brand's best western
stories v2

Dust across the range

In Brand, M. Max Brand's best western
stories v1

Fugitives' fire. Putnam 1991 184p o.p.
LC 90-8478

This novel originally appeared 1928 in Western story
magazine as two novelettes: Prairie pawn and Fugitive's
fire
This novel features fugitive plainsman Paul Torridon.
"A prisoner of the mighty Cheyenne Nation, young Torridon lives in pampered misery. The Cheyenne, who call

Brand, Max, 1892-1944—_Continued_
him 'White Thunder,' are convinced of his supernatural
talents and expect him to deliver good luck in battle
and rain in drought. He is richly rewarded for his
'mystical favors,' but he dreads the day his good luck
and horse sense will fail, revealing him as only too mortal—and losing him his scalp in the bargain." Publisher's
note

The gentle desperado. Dodd, Mead 1985
195p o.p.

LC 85-10321

"Silver star westerns"
This novel is comprised of three stories originally
published in Western Story Magazine under the
pseudonym, George Owen Baxter
"Robert Fernald was a deadly fighter, but he didn't
really believe it, not even when he outgunned his opponents. To his enemies, he looked like a kid, too mild-
mannered to be a threat. But then he went after Tom
Gill and his men who were preying on the Larkin ranch,
forcing handsome young Beatrice Larkin into bankruptcy.
Everyone said it would take an army to stop the rustlers
from driving the stolen cattle through the mountain passes—until Fernald faced tough Tom Gill himself in a
showdown." Publisher's note

Max Brand's best western stories; edited
with a biographical introduction by William
F. Nolan. Dodd, Mead 1981-1987 3v o.p.

LC 81-3204

Analyzed in Short story index
Contents v1 Wine on the desert; Virginia creeper; Macdonald's dream; Partners; Dust across the range [novelet-
te]; The bells of San Carlos
v2 Outcasts [novelette]; The fear of Morgon the Fearless; Dark Rosaleen [novelette]; Cayenne Charlie; The
golden day
v3 Reata's peril trek; Crazy rhythm; Dust storm; A
lucky dog; The third bullet; Half a partner; The sun
stood still

Outcasts

_In_ Brand, M. Max Brand's best western
stories v2

The Stingaree. Dodd, Mead 1968 c1930
216p o.p. Bentley reprint available $16
(ISBN 0-8376-0461-3)
"Silver star westerns"
"Jimmy Green is a wild, half-Indian, half-civilized,
thirteen-year-old who is undisputed king of the small
village of Fort Anxious. One day, a tramp wanders into
the village, and ultimately into the life of Jimmy,
changing it from the complacent existence of a boy into
the desperate flight of a fugitive. The stranger, also
known as the Stingaree, has come from Alabama to
revenge the death of his partner by the leading citizen
of Fort Anxious. Although he succeeds in forcing the
man to confess, he is thwarted by the police in his
attempt to kill Stanley Parker. The Stingaree, along with
Jimmy Green, an Indian companion, and a wild dog
is forced to flee into the wilderness, beginning one of
the best chase episodes." Libr J

Brandon, Jay
Rules of evidence. Pocket Bks. 1992 294p
o.p.

LC 91-27380

"Mike Stennett is a grungy undercover cop who works
the predominantly black and Latino sections of San Antonio, Texas. His arrests are often brutal and tend to
be made on black suspects. He's a career cop, dedicated
to the job, with little chance of promotion, no partner,
and few friends inside or outside the force. When he
is suspended with pay after the beating death of a black
derelict, Stennett chooses Boudro, a black lawyer, to
represent him. Boudro has tangled with Stennett before,
and he's not inclined to trust him much. But the case
evolves in strange ways." Booklist
"Brandon develops an interesting contrast between
Stennett, the unsavory but devoted cop, and Raymond,
the skillful and competitive attorney; each considers himself rightful protector of the crime-ridden East Side where
both grew up." Publ Wkly

Braun, Lilian Jackson
The cat who ate Danish modern. Dutton
1967 192p o.p.
The "adventure of Koko, The Siamese, and his Watson, Jim Qwilleran. The 'Daily Fluxion' assigns Jim to
mastermind a new Sunday supplement called, of all
things, 'Gracious Abodes.' But the shocking consequences
of the first few issues makes Jim realize that he is back
in his own field, crime reporting, and that only Koko
can help with the answers." Libr J
"The mystery is mild, the satire on interior decorating
fads and fancies amusing, and the Siamese cat who helps
play detective delightful." Publ Wkly

The cat who came to breakfast. Putnam
1994 254p $19.95

ISBN 0-399-13868-4   LC 93-34059
Also available G.K. Hall large print edition
"Pickax City's Jim Qwilleran and his intuitive Siamese
cats, Yum Yum and Koko, investigate odd accidents
plaguing a glitzy resort recently built on a nearby island
in Moose County. . . . After an episode of food
poisoning and an accidental drowning at the resort hotel,
the owners of the Domino Inn, an already established
bed-and-breakfast, ask Qwill to find out whether disgruntled locals are trying to discourage tourism." Publ Wkly

The cat who knew a cardinal. Putnam
1991 240p o.p.

LC 90-47557

Available G.K. Hall large print edition
Jim Qwilleran and his cats Koko and Yum Yum
"move into an antique apple barn renovated by building
contractor (and amateur actor) Dennis Hough. Concurrently the Pickax Theatre Club stages _Henry VIII_, with
Hilary VanBrook, the unlikable but talented new high
school principal, directing and playing the plum role of
Cardinal Wolsey. . . . When VanBrook is murdered in
his car after a closing night party at Qwill's new home,
Qwill looks into VanBrook's past while the police investigate his death. . . . Koko and Yum Yum once again
help Qwill identify the culprit via whisker twitches and
tail wags." Publ Wkly

The cat who lived high. Putnam 1990
239p o.p.

LC 90-34526

Available G.K. Hall large print edition
"Jim Qwilleran and his Siamese sleuth Koko investigate the recent death of an art dealer, a former
tenant in a once elite apartment building now seemingly
destined for the wrecker's ball." Booklist

Braun, Lilian Jackson—*Continued*

"Full of colorful, eccentric characters, small-town attitudes, and sprightly fun for cat enthusiasts, this should appeal to most mystery readers." Libr J

The cat who moved a mountain. Putnam 1992 239p o.p.

LC 91-14624

Available G.K. Hall large print edition

"Jim Qwilleran, an affable former big-city crime reporter who has just inherited a considerable fortune, heads for a vacation in the rustic Potato Mountains to ponder the future course of his life. Accompanied by his two omniscient felines, Koko and Yum Yum, he takes up residence in the former home of the town's leading citizen, J.J. Hawkinfield, murdered one year ago. . . . Under the pretext of researching Hawkinfield's biography, Qwilleran pries into everyone's business, aided by the garrulous residents, who raise gossip to a new art form. With the help of his unique cats, he uncovers new evidence and brings to a satisfying conclusion a lively, witty tale bolstered by sharply etched characters." Publ Wkly

The cat who sniffed glue. Putnam 1988 207p o.p.

LC 88-4146

"Residing now with Jim Qwilleran, in Pickax City, Moose County, in the apartment above the carriage house of the Klingenschoen estate, the cats [Koko and Yum Yum] live the life of Riley; it doesn't hurt that the local chief of police believes they can solve crimes. And there is quite a crime: Harley and Belle Fitch, son and daughter-in-law of the owner of the town bank, are murdered. Qwilleran, with his journalist's itch, cannot help but speculate on what might have happened and snoops around in his polite and persistent way. Although Braun uses standard plot conventions, her setting, characters, and sense of the absurd guarantee a thoroughly enjoyable read." Booklist

The cat who talked to ghosts. Putnam 1990 239p o.p.

LC 89-33666

Available G.K. Hall large print edition

"Iris Cobb, the resident-curator of the local historical museum, tells Qwill she's hearing ghosts; after she dies of what the coroner says is a heart attack, Qwill and his Siamese cats, Yum Yum and the psychic zany Koko, move in to find out what could have scared her to death. Unearthing old and well-kept secrets in Moose County family histories, Qwill also investigates some newcomers to the area, notably the museum's neighbors down the road at Fugtree Farm, and the deceased's son whose inheritance is considerable." Publ Wkly

The cat who wasn't there. Putnam 1992 238p o.p.

LC 92-11971

Available G.K. Hall large print edition

"Retired newspaperman and heir to the Klingenschoen fortune, Jim Qwilleran accepts an invitation to join a group of Pickax friends on a Bonnie Scots tour, leaving his two Siamese cats Koko and Yum Yum, at home with a catsitter. When the excursion is interrupted by the sudden death of the tour leader and Qwill returns to Pickax with his librarian friend Polly Duncan, he decides that Koko, the extrasensory sleuth, is trying to tell him something." Booklist

"Although the cats play a smaller role in this installment than in previous ones, Braun's descriptions of Scottish lore and the complications of Qwill's love life will enchant fans." Publ Wkly

The cat who went into the closet. Putnam 1993 238p $19.95

ISBN 0-399-13830-7   LC 92-36567

"Reporter Jim Qwilleran's Siamese cat Koko drags items from several closets in Qwill's rented Florida mansion that provide clues to the suspicious death of the mansion's elderly and eccentric owner. A local missing potato farmer with remote ties to the old woman, meanwhile, turns up dead. Moose County's quaint characters and events provide yet again delightful diversion for Qwilleran and reader alike." Libr J

The cat who went underground. Putnam 1989 223p o.p.

LC 88-32185

Available G.K. Hall large print edition

"Koko and Yum Yum . . . lead their guardian, Jim ('Qwill') Qwilleran, on a subterranean chase for a psychotic plumber. When Qwill decides to spend a restful summer at his cabin in Mooseville, he does not anticipate endless home-repair crises. But he is genuinely astonished when Koko reveals why the carpenter never finished the room addition." Booklist

"Qwill's saving grace is that he is properly humble before the superior intelligence of his pets, while the author is shrewd enough to balance the cats' amazing antics with many amusing character studies of the Mooseville natives." N Y Times Book Rev

Brecht, Bertolt, 1898-1956

Short stories, 1921-1946; edited by John Willett and Ralph Manheim; translated by Yvonne Kapp, Hugh Rorrison, and Antony Tatlo. Methuen 1983 242p o.p.

LC 82-14095

Analyzed in Short story index

Contents: Bargan gives up; Story on a ship; The revelation; The stupid wife; The blind man; A helping hand; Java Meier; The Lance-Sergeant; Message in a bottle; A mean bastard; The death of Cesare Malatesta; The answer; Before the flood; Conversation about the South Seas; Letter about a mastiff; Hook to the chin; Müller's natural attitude; North Sea shrimps; Bad water; A little tale of insurance; Four men and a poker game; Barbara; The Good Lord's package; The monster; The job; Safety first; The soldier of La Ciotat; A mistake; Gaumer and Irk; Socrates wounded; The experiment; The heretic's coat; Lucullus's trophies; The unseemly old lady; A question of taste; The Augsburg chalk circle; Two sons

"Brecht fanciers will find these tales, some of them very brief narratives, an interesting sidelight to the dramatic work. Curiously old-fashioned, these stories nonetheless reveal the imagination and concerns that flowered in his work for the stage." Publ Wkly

Brennan, John *See* Welcome, John, 1914-

Brent, Madeleine

Golden urchin. Doubleday 1987 c1986 330p o.p.

LC 86-8959

Brent, Madeleine—*Continued*

First published 1986 in the United Kingdom

This novel "follows 'Mitji,' a white child raised by aborigines in the Australian outback, in her attempts to discover her 'true people.' Leaving the tribe, the girl rescues a homesteader and is in turn taken in by the man and his ailing wife. The rest of the tale deals with Meg, as she is now called, discovering her real identity, the efforts of the villain of the piece to eliminate her, her heroic rescue of a shipwrecked party, and the ultimate happy ending." Libr J

"Somehow Brent manages to carry off this incredible tale in thoroughly charming fashion. An engaging and neatly plotted romance." Booklist

Moonraker's bride. Doubleday 1973 352p o.p.

"Lucy Waring, jailed for stealing to feed orphans in her care at a Chinese mission, meets a fellow prisoner, Nicholas Sabine. Since he's due to be executed in the morning for offending a warlord, he pays Lucy's bribe money and marries her, leaving her his fortune. Out of prison, Lucy is adopted by an English family whose butler turns out to be Nicholas's father. Nicholas turns up alive to fight with neighbor Robert Falcon, for the love of Lucy. Both men are determined to get hold of a cache of emeralds, so go back to China at the height of the Boxer Rebellion. Lucy and father-in-law follow." Publ Wkly

"Brent writes convincingly of the contrasts between Eastern and Western lifestyle and ably holds the reader's interest, though she may try his credulity. A better-than-average example of the genre." Libr J

Stormswift. Doubleday 1985 326p o.p.

LC 84-8128

"After her parents' deaths in an 1879 massacre at the British Mission in Kabul, Afghanistan, young Jemimah Lawley becomes a slave for several years until her last master arranges for her escape with the help of a traveling peddler. Back in England after a perilous journey (during which she saves the life of her companion, who turns out to be a British spy in disguise), Jemimah finds her heritage usurped by imposters." Booklist

"This historical romance . . . relies more on adventure and suspense than breathless passion to keep the reader's interest." Publ Wkly

Tregaron's daughter. Doubleday 1971 306p o.p.

A Gothic romance "that winds its way from a Cornish fishing village at the turn of the century. Caterina Tregaron, named for her mysterious Italian grandmother, needs to know why she is always haunted by dreams of a dark 'palazzo,' and the need becomes more urgent when she sees a painting of the Palazzo Chiavelli in Venice." Libr J

"The story is refreshing in that it presents a central character with integrity and courage. This relieves one of any of the melodrama characteristic of the sentimental, feminine roles often portrayed in early-twentieth-century Gothic romances." Best Sellers

Breslin, Jimmy

The gang that couldn't shoot straight. Viking 1969 249p o.p.

"The only trouble with the Palumbo Mafia 'Family' of Brooklyn is that it isn't very well organized. Kid Sally Palumbo is trying to take over from the big Mafia boss, Baccala. Baccala has his wife start his car for him every morning in case explosives are wired in. Big Mama Palumbo's watchword is 'be sure to steal-a da license plates.' Into this happy milieu wanders Mario, imported from Italy to ride in a six-day bike race that flopped. A natural-born con man himself, Mario has a brief love affair with young Angela Palumbo, and acts as fingerman for the gang in the big attempt to wipe out Baccala." Publ Wkly

"By no means a great work, this is still a strong indictment of American society—police, politicians, criminals, and the 'silent'—that deserves to offend more than Sicilians." Choice

Table money. Ticknor & Fields 1986 435p o.p.

LC 85-28880

This "saga concerning the Morrisons of Queens, New York—from their late-nineteenth-century arrival in the U.S. to the present day—is painfully stereotypical in its depiction of the men (a long line of hard-drinking, male chauvinistic, and irresponsible tunnel workers) and their beleaguered, long-suffering women. Generation after generation repeats the same mistakes—dying too soon from alcoholism, giving birth too early in life—and even when Owen Morrison, the latter-day lad whose story takes up most of the book, wins the Congressional medal of honor in Vietnam, he finds that his hero's badge is virtually worthless on the gray borough streets and in the perilous tunnel that epitomizes his clan's plight." Booklist

Brett, Simon, 1945-

Corporate bodies; a Charles Paris mystery. Scribner 1992 c1991 189p $19

ISBN 0-684-19397-3   LC 91-34304

First published 1991 in the United Kingdom

"No sooner does London actor Charles Paris land the part of a forklift operator in a corporate video than a young woman employee named Dayna is found crushed under the same machine. Paris is the prime suspect until the police determine that he had no motive. . . . Investigating on his own out of curiosity, Paris learns that the victim had filmed her trysts and that she was killed for one of the tapes." Publ Wkly

Dead giveaway. Scribner 1986 c1985 176p o.p.

LC 85-18407

First published 1985 in the United Kingdom

Charles Paris, "none-too-successful actor and amateur sleuth . . . hasn't had an acting assignment in months, but when his agent books him on a celebrity game program, he envisions himself in scintillating repartée with other well-known figures. During the taping, however, the emcee drinks from what he thinks is a glass of gin, and is poisoned. Suspicion points to Chippy, a young assistant from an adjoining studio, who is charged with the murder. Implored by a friend to clear Chippy's name and find the real killer, Charles has a long list of suspects to choose from." Publ Wkly

Brett, Simon, 1945-—*Continued*

Dead romantic. Scribner 1986 c1985 192p o.p.

LC 85-25075

First published 1985 in the United Kingdom

A mystery novel "beginning with murder and traveling backward through the wrenching series of events that lead up to it. The main character, the Jean Brodie-like poetry teacher Madeleine Severn, is 37, beautiful, and a virgin. One of her adolescent students, Paul Grigson, falls madly and badly in love with her, a situation that becomes compounded by other romantic attachments. Throughout, Brett maintains brilliant ironic control, providing glaring home truths and a complete shocker of an ending." Booklist

The dead side of the mike. Scribner 1980 176p o.p.

LC 80-18269

Available G.K. Hall large print edition

"Murder at the BBC. Andrea Gower, a lower-level studio manager, is found dead in a BBC taping room, her wrists neatly slashed. The police suspect suicide, but sometime actor-sometime sleuth Charles Paris, who happens to be on the scene, is nagged by a belief that Andrea was slain." Booklist

Mrs. Pargeter's package. Scribner 1991 224p $18.95

ISBN 0-684-19286-1 LC 90-27463

Also available Thorndike Press large print edition

First published 1990 in the United Kingdom

"On a tour of Greece, the mature and spirited Melita Pargeter . . . takes on a case more substantial than her earlier challenges. When she agreed to join recently widowed Joyce Dover on holiday, Melita knew she was apt to encounter the moodiness of the freshly bereaved. But Joyce appears to be importing a bottle of the Greek liqueur ouzo *from* England, and talks about her husband controlling her from the grave. When she is found dead, an apparent suicide, Melita has even more on her hands than she bargained for." Publ Wkly

"Avoiding the treacly simpering typical of so many British cozy mysteries, Brett keeps us chuckling with a steady stream of dryly noted cultural tidbits, while still supplying a wide-ranging plot that hangs together elegantly." Booklist

Mrs. Pargeter's pound of flesh; a Mrs. Pargeter mystery. Scribner 1993 c1992 207p $20

ISBN 0-684-19565-8 LC 92-30969

First published 1992 in the United Kingdom

Mrs. Melita Pargeter, "widow of a talented and much-loved ex-con takes the waters at a health spa in order to help a friend. Melita starts snooping, however, when she spies men removing a body in the dead of the night. Still using the services of her late husband's criminal cronies, Melita courts disaster as she nears the truth." Libr J

"Most of Mr. Brett's humor is of the all-in-good-fun variety, which invites the reader to indulge the stout-hearted Mrs. Pargeter and her merry band of lovable crooks and con men in another jolly series romp." NY Times Book Rev

Mrs, presumed dead. Scribner 1989 c1988 248p o.p.

LC 88-38044

First published 1988 in the United Kingdom

"Mrs. Pargeter discovers that the young couple from whom she just bought her house has not simply relocated but in fact disappeared. Inquiry on Mrs. Pargeter's part reveals that the wife has been murdered; eventually, she identifies the malefactor. The Mrs. Pargeter mysteries are not nearly as amusing as the Charles Paris books, but Brett's newer hero remains an endearing character, and the author capably maintains reader interest throughout his well-woven plot." Booklist

Murder unprompted; a Charles Paris novel. Scribner 1982 160p o.p.

LC 82-5578

"Here Paris is less drunk than usual, which enables us to believe that he can think as shrewdly as he does. And the situation is delightful: he gets at last a chance to act in a play that may move to a big West End theater if all goes well in the tryouts. The interplay among the cast is splendid, funny, and also touching. Murder in full view, on the first night, might bring good publicity, but other troubles develop—the whole mess handled in masterly fashion." Barzun. Cat of Crime. Rev and enl edition

A nice class of corpse. Scribner 1987 c1986 221p o.p.

LC 86-11820

First published 1986 in the United Kingdom

"The cast of characters are the staff and guests of the genteel Devereux Hotel, whose owner takes in only those who meet certain financial qualifications. S.B. introduces a new detective, Melita Pargeter, the widow of a loving husband whose dubious occupation provided her the best of everything during and after his lifetime. Using the uncommon expertise learned from the late Mr. Pargeter, Melita is agreeably competent at solving the crimes that occur at the Hotel Devereux." Barzun. Cat of Crime. Rev and enl edition

A reconstructed corpse; a Charles Paris mystery. Scribner 1994 c1993 189p $20

ISBN 0-684-19700-6 LC 93-50797

First published 1993 in the United Kingdom

Charles Paris' "agent has just called with some exciting news: Charles' uncanny resemblance to Brighton property developer Martin Earnshaw, who has mysteriously disappeared after leaving home to visit the local pub, has landed Charles a job reconstructing Earnshaw's 'last moments' on the television program *Public Enemies*. As usual, Charles can't stop getting involved in a bit of amateur detecting." Booklist

"Charles's self-loathing has deepened and Mr. Brett's satirical edge has sharpened over the 15 books in this witty but hardly frivolous series. Here the author takes his best jabs at the corrosive power of television." NY Times Book Rev

A shock to the system. Scribner 1985 c1984 255p o.p.

LC 85-2337

First published 1984 in the United Kingdom

"Graham Marshall is furious when the promotion he has taken for granted goes to another person in his company. Out of anger, Marshall pushes a beggar off a bridge to his death, a murder never detected. Suddenly seeing himself as a master criminal, Marshall disposes of his wife in an 'accident,' turns their children over to his sister-in-law and cuts ties with his mother-in-law.

Brett, Simon, 1945——*Continued*

With other human obstacles to his life as a London 'bon vivant' cleverly removed, the sociopath gains the top position he believes was temporarily stolen from him. Then the police present an unbeatable case against Marshall, for the one killing he hasn't committed." Publ Wkly

"Brett dissects his protagonist's guilt, pride, feeling of exclusivity, and power and goes on to show Marshall glorying in his heinous crime. . . . Though it is a bit heavy-handed and long-winded, it remains a fascinating psychological probe." Booklist

What bloody man is that?; a Charles Paris mystery. Scribner 1987 184p o.p.

LC 87-13000

In this novel Charles "Paris is engaged to play any number of small bits in a provincial theater company's production of the badluck play, 'Macbeth'. When a greatly disliked actor is found dead among the beer taps in a liquor storage room, Paris quickly becomes the chief suspect. A must read for its suspense, its theatrical atmosphere, its effortlessly witty dialogue, and its well-delineated characters." Booklist

Brin, David, 1950-

Earth. Bantam Bks. 1990 601p $19.95

ISBN 0-553-05778-2   LC 90-4

"In the mid-21st century, as the world is attempting to reconcile humanity's furious technological progress with its depletion of the planet's vanishing resources, the discovery of a pair of singularities (miniature black holes) deep in the Earth's core abruptly transforms an ongoing struggle for preservation into a desperate battle to prevent the Earth's imminent destruction. Combining the fast pacing of a techno-thriller with a unique array of characters, the author . . . delivers a thoughtful, persuasive message of hope and warning that embraces today's issues and tomorrow's possibilities." Libr J

Glory season. Bantam Bks. 1993 564p o.p.

LC 93-16605

"As a 'var,' or uncloned female, Maia faces a life on the fringe of the stratified, female clone-based society of Stratos unless she can earn the right to found a dynasty of clones or find some way to change the static world in which she lives." Libr J

"A man writing about an avowedly feminist society, Mr. Brin has worked out the details of Stratoin life with considerable ingenuity. Now and again he takes a mischievous pleasure in confounding expectations." N Y Times Book Rev

The postman. Bantam Bks. 1985 294p o.p.

LC 85-47647

This novel opens with the "familiar portrait of an America brought to the edge of extinction by nuclear war. An itinerant storyteller, Gordon Krantz, finds an old postman's uniform and bag and starts traveling across the country, taking people's letters to loved ones and telling tales of a country on the road to recovery. Eventually he becomes a major force for that recovery, as the hope he gives people rallies them." Booklist

"A well-crafted, realistic and often violent novel with diverse elements woven together in expert style. . . . The most enduring aspect of this solid novel is the character of Gordon Krantz himself, not a superhuman with whom we mere mortals cannot identify, but an ordinary man with a powerful sense of responsibility." Best Sellers

Brink, André Philippus, 1935-

An act of terror; [by] André Brink. Summit Bks. 1992 c1991 834p o.p.

LC 91-35990

First published 1991 in the United Kingdom

Thomas Landman, a young Afrikaner photographer, "is drawn into a conspiracy to assassinate the president of South Africa. The attempt fails, leaving black and white bystanders dead in its wake, and he flees consumed with grief but still convinced of the rightness of his actions." Libr J

"Though the novel's interior monologues ring hollow at times, cumulatively they allow Brink to dramatize the real legacy of Thomas's act: not the maimed bodies it leaves behind, nor the blow to the state, but the small significant revolutions of consciousness it produces in everyone he meets." Nation

A chain of voices; [by] André Brink. Morrow 1982 525p o.p.

LC 82-80315

"The setting of this . . . polyphonic novel is the South African interior, 1825. The central voice is Galant, a black slave who might be part white and who, until adolescence, has been treated in some ways as a member of his master's family. When a series of extraordinarily cruel punishments proves to him that he will always be regarded as a slave, he leads a revolt in which his young master is murdered. Brink sees slavery as a sick product of corrupt moral righteousness and suppressed sexuality." Libr J

"This complex and powerful tale of a slave revolt in nineteenth-century South Africa lacks the hard-edged, polemic tone often found in novels that address racial issues. Brink tells his story through a wide assortment of narrators, all of whom comment on the same events but reach widely disparate conclusions. We are left not with a feeling for whose version is right or wrong, but instead, with a sense of utter inevitability, of the past holding total sway over the future." Booklist

Briskin, Jacqueline

Dreams are not enough. Putnam 1987 400p o.p.

LC 86-22685

"The heroine here is movie star Alyssia Del Mar, born Alice Hollister, a migrant worker who gets a break when, at 15, she marries into a powerful Hollywood family. It's aspiring novelist Barry Corinder whom she marries, but it's his brother, director Hap, with whom she falls in love. In the opening scene, Alyssia calls the Corinder family together for an unknown reason. Briskin devotes the rest of the book to flashbacks that tell the story of each of the five Corinder cousins and reveal the impact Alyssia had on their lives." Booklist

The author "hooks the reader in the opening pages, making it near-impossible to stop reading. So if characters are sometimes less than well-rounded, dialogue less than dazzling, and style sometimes stiff, still the story is relentless." Libr J

The other side of love; a novel. Delacorte Press 1991 566p $22

ISBN 0-385-29918-4   LC 90-22032

Briskin, Jacqueline—*Continued*

This novel is "set in World War II Europe and stars the young Kingsmith cousins—Araminta, the auburn-haired British sexpot; Aubrey, her successful writer brother; Käthe, the beautiful German sprinter who wins a gold medal in the 1936 Olympics in Berlin; and Wyatt, the handsome American basketball player who also wins gold during the games. Not only do the two athletes take home medals, they also fall madly in love." Booklist

"Hero and heroine are symbolic, overdrawn figures, but Briskin has created a memorable cast of supporting characters. She also has impressively conveyed a sense of time and place, especially in writing of Hitler's Germany and wartime England." Libr J

Paloverde; a novel. McGraw-Hill 1978 517p o.p.

LC 78-15955

This family saga "begins in the 1880s, focusing on two brothers, Bud and 3Vee, heirs to the huge Los Angeles 'rancho' of Paloverde, and beautiful half-French Amélie, whom they both love. The down-to-earth Bud marries her, after helping her in her vendetta against the Southern Pacific Railroad; but the romantic 3Vee one night drunkenly forces himself upon her and becomes the presumptive father of her daughter Tessa. In time Bud buries his shame and accepts Tessa as his, which leads to complex and painful consequences when she falls passionately in love with 3Vee's son, Hollywood's favorite actor-aviator." Publ Wkly

"Not only is 'Paloverde' an elongated profile of two generations, but it also is a serious historical saga. Los Angeles evolves from dust covered adobes to a rousing oilboom town, to a modern industrial city. . . . Midst the various unrequited loves, the historical vignettes and the sibling rivalries, Briskin draws some fine caricatures." Best Sellers

Too much, too soon. Putnam 1985 477p o.p.

LC 84-26363

"When three impoverished sisters are 'adopted' by a fabulously wealthy uncle, life seems to stretch ahead like a fairy tale. But soon they learn that there are sacrifices to be made even amid limitless wealth. Honora marries the man she loves, only to find herself an outcast. Crystal marries for money at the price of romantic sexual love. Joscelyn sacrifices her brilliant career to further her mediocre, brutal husband's. The book spans 35 years of their separates lives." Libr J

"This scenario may sound run-of-the-mill, but Briskin gives readers more than three paper dolls wearing designer clothes (although there is no shortage of fabulous outfits). The heroines are fully and cleverly depicted, as is Curt Ivory, the attractive and brilliant engineer who plays such an important part in all three women's lives. Set against an international backdrop and featuring the requisite amount of sex, power, greed, and pathos, this well-plotted and evocatively written volume is the perfect choice." Booklist

Bristow, Gwen, 1903-1980

Calico Palace. Crowell 1970 589p o.p.

"San Francisco in the days of the Gold Rush (1849) is the setting for this lengthy, rather old-fashioned novel, which follows Kendra Morgan through two relatively unhappy marriages, the birth and death of a baby, and friendship with Marny, glamorous proprietress of Calico Palace, a gambling hall. In the eventual, traditional happy ending, both girls find true love." Libr J

Celia Garth. Crowell 1959 406p o.p.

This story "takes its background from South Carolina during the Revolutionary War. Its heroine is Celia Garth, a spirited orphan girl working as an apprentice dressmaker in Charleston, who witnesses the British siege of the city and returns during the occupation to become a spy for the rebels." Booklist

"Celia Garth's story is adventurous and romantic, patriotic and sentimental. Miss Bristow's historical novel presents abundant terror, but it is the terror endured by civilians more than the terror of bloody battle." Best Sellers

Deep summer

In Bristow, G. Gwen Bristow's Plantation trilogy p1-258

Gwen Bristow's Plantation trilogy; Deep summer, The handsome road, [and] This side of glory. Crowell 1962 812p o.p.

An omnibus volume of the three titles published originally 1937, 1938 and 1940, respectively

"The historical background material for each book was supplied by the author especially for this volume." Title page

In this trilogy "Judith Sheramy migrates to Louisiana in the 1800s and meets Philip Larne, the son of a wealthy South Carolina family. The two marry and struggle to keep their plantation through the Civil War. After the war, the lives of the wealthy Larnes and the poor Upjohns are followed to the period of the First World War." Jacob. To be continued

The handsome road

In Bristow, G. Gwen Bristow's Plantation trilogy p263-530

Jubilee Trail. Crowell 1950 564p o.p.

The Jubilee Trail was the traders' name for the great Spanish Trail, which in the 1840's led from Santa Fé to Los Angeles. This long novel describes the trek of a gently bred New York girl and her trader husband, along that trail. When she was left a widow and penniless, Garnet and the variety girl she had befriended managed to make their living. The story closes about the time of the California gold discovery

This side of glory

In Bristow, G. Gwen Bristow's Plantation trilogy p535-812

Bromfield, Louis, 1896-1956

Mrs. Parkington. Harper & Row 1943 330p o.p. Amereon reprint available $23.95 (ISBN 0-88411-502-X)

"From the vantage point of her 84 years, Mrs. Parkington looks back over her long life, beginning with that day in Leaping Rock, Nev., when newly orphaned by the mine explosion that killed both her parents, she married Augustus Parkington and set out with him on the buccaneering career that was to make him one of the richest men of his time. These glimpses of the past are interspersed among events of the present, as Mrs. Parkington guides and controls the complicated, often shady, affairs of the later generations of Parkingtons." Wis Libr Bull

Bromfield, Louis, 1896-1956—*Continued*

The rains came; a novel of modern India. Harper 1937 597p o.p. Amereon reprint available $32.95 (ISBN 0-88411-505-4)

"A small state in India, where an enlightened native prince and his wife have labored for fifty years to establish modern standards and to abolish caste and religious antagonisms, is the scene also of the work of British officials, soldiers, American missionaries, and business men. Here Ransome, bitter, disillusioned expatriate, meets again his former mistress, now the wife of a fabulously wealthy nobleman; at the same time he experiences a slight awakening of chivalry when a missionary's daughter falls in love with him. A flood wipes out the ruler's work, cholera and plague follow, and in the desperate week before relief comes tragedy." Booklist

Brontë, Anne, 1820-1849

The tenant of Wildfell Hall. 531p o.p.
First published 1848

"This epistolary novel presents a portrait of debauchery that is remarkable in light of the author's sheltered life. It is the story of young Helen Graham's disastrous marriage to the dashing drunkard Arthur Huntingdon—said to be modeled on the author's wayward brother Branwell—and her flight from him to the seclusion of Wildfell Hall. Pursued by Gilbert Markham, who is in love with her, Graham refuses him and, by way of explanation, gives him her journal. There he reads of her wretched married life. Eventually, after Huntingdon's death, they marry." Merriam-Webster's Ency of Lit

Brontë, Charlotte, 1816-1855

Emma; by Charlotte Brontë and "Another Lady". Everest House 1980 201p o.p.

Fragments of a story left unfinished at Brontë's death form the opening two chapters of this novel completed by Constance Savery

"In the full-blown literary manner and circuitous storytelling characteristic of Charlotte Brontë, . . . an intriguing melodrama unrolls in this tale of wrongs finally righted. Most wronged is adolescent Martina, deprived of her natural mother by the machinations of her stepbrothers, led on by their sister, the cruel, enigmatic beauty Emma. The events that lead to familial reconciliation include Martina's sentence to ladies' boarding school, abduction to a French convent and graveyard visitations before some fancy detective work by an old friend unravels the ingenious but dastardly plot. The author of this Gothic romp is obviously steeped in the period and felicitous style of the brilliant English novelist, providing entertainment on the same grand scale." Publ Wkly

Jane Eyre.
Available from various publishers
First published 1847

"In both heroine and hero the author introduced types new to English fiction. Jane Eyre is a shy, intense little orphan, never for a moment, neither in her unhappy school days nor her subsequent career as a governess, displaying those qualities of superficial beauty and charm that had marked the conventional heroine. Jane's lover, Edward Rochester, to whose ward she is governess, is a strange, violent man, bereft of conventional courtesy, a law unto himself. Rochester's moodiness derives from the fact that he is married to an insane wife, whose existence, long kept secret, is revealed on the very day of his projected marriage to Jane. Years afterward the lovers are reunited." Reader's Ency. 3d edition

The professor. o.p.
First published 1857

"William Crimsworth, an orphan, after trying his hand at trade in the north of England, goes to seek his fortune in Brussels. At the girls' school where he teaches English he falls in love with Frances Henri, an Anglo-Swiss pupil teacher and lace mender, whose Protestant honesty and modesty are contrasted with the manipulating duplicity of the Catholic headmistress, Zoraide Reuter. Crimsworth resists Mlle Reuter's overtures; she marries the headmaster of the neighbouring boys' school, M. Pelet, Crimsworth resigns his post, and, after finding a new and better one, is able to marry Frances." Oxford Companion to Engl Lit. 5th edition

Shirley. o.p.
First published 1849

"Against the background of a changing world at the beginning of the nineteenth century, the story of a spirited heiress, Shirley Keeldar, is told. The author patterned her after her own sister, Emily. Robert Moore, millowner in Yorkshire, introduces labor-saving devices which cause workmen's riots. He persists, in spite of financial and physical hazards, and wins his point with a promise to give more jobs, and provide better housing. Caroline Helstone, his gentle cousin, is seeking a meaning to her life. Dissatisfied with doing nothing, she marries Robert, whom she adores, and finds direction in her decision to help him. Shirley also is a new type of woman. She marries Robert's brother Louis, a tutor, who has as much spirit as she." Haydn. Thesaurus of Book Dig

Villette. Oxford Univ. Press 1936 573p $16.95

ISBN 0-19-250047-3
Also available from Buccaneer Bks.
"The World's classics"
First published 1853

In Villette "Lucy Snowe makes her way by teaching, as she watches unhappily John Breton's infatuation for the flirt Ginevra Fanshawe, then falls in love herself with and transforms the professor, Monsieur Paul Emanuel." Haydn. Thesaurus of Book Dig

"The novel combines a masterly portrayal of Belgian daily life with a highly personal use of the elements of Gothic fiction." Oxford Companion to Engl Lit. 5th edition

Brontë, Emily, 1818-1848

Wuthering Heights.
Available from various publishers
First published 1847

Forced by a storm to spend the night at the home of the somber and unsociable Heathcliff, Mr. Lockwood has an encounter with the spirit of Catherine Linton. He gradually learns that Catherine's father, Mr. Earnshaw, had taken in Heathcliff as a young orphan. Heathcliff and Catherine began to fall in love, but after Mr. Earnshaw's death Catherine's brother treated Heathcliff in a degrading manner and Catherine married rich Edgar Linton. Heathcliff gradually worked his revenge against those who injured him

"The novel's stern power, which disturbed and shocked contemporaries but has impressed later generations of readers, owes much to the deliberately enigmatic portrait of Heathcliff, who places instinct above moral or social obligation and seems the epitome of Romantic values.

Brontë, Emily, 1818-1848—*Continued*

Hardly less remarkable is the way that the tortuous and violent plot, instead of seeming merely melodramatic, is given solidity by the precisely realized Yorkshire locations and subtlety by the shifting narrative viewpoints." Camb Guide to Lit in Engl

Brookner, Anita

Brief lives. Random House 1991 c1990 260p $20

ISBN 0-394-58548-8   LC 90-38904

First published 1990 in the United Kingdom

This "novel covers the nearly 40 years of intertwining lives of two dissimilar, incompatible women. Flamboyant, selfish Julia was once a glamorous actress. Fay arranges her life around men—first her father, then her husband, then her lover—and eventually her friend, none of them her ideal; finally, she is alone." Libr J

"This short, subtle, beautifully organised and orchestrated novel positively gains from the deliberate restraint and detachment of the writing." London Rev Books

A closed eye. Random House 1992 c1991 263p $21

ISBN 0-679-40447-3   LC 91-53110

First published 1991 in the United Kingdom

"Harriet married the affluent but sexually inept Freddie, who is old enough to be her father, in order to save her parents from genteel poverty. . . . Harriet is obsessed with Jack, her best friend [Tessa's] exciting husband, who is almost perpetually abroad on journalist's missions. Surviving middle age and the deaths of both daughter and husband, this concealed passion prompts her disingenuous care for Jack's neglected daughter, Lizzie." Times Lit Suppl

"Brookner's specificity makes her entertaining. The originality of her perceptions and the pain of her insights are modestly but not impenetrably veiled in unemotional diction and sedate, graceful phrasing—a distinguished performance." N Y Rev Books

Dolly. Random House 1994 c1993 260p $22

ISBN 0-679-42318-4   LC 93-14537

Also available G.K. Hall large print edition

First published 1993 in the United Kingdom with title: A family romance

"Jane, a successful young author, prefers a quiet life, unlike her Aunt Dolly, a flamboyant soul always on display and seeking admiration. Utterly dissimilar and not overly fond of each other, the two women are bound together by unexpected events and consequences dating from Jane's early childhood. As Jane narrates the story of their incongruous mutual dependencies, she speculates on the nature of human connections and the female experience." Libr J

"Certainly its first two-thirds are about as wonderful as anything Miss Brookner has ever written. Jane's apparently aimless ramblings, grounded with exacting detail and raised on a structure of steel, seem a faultless demonstration of authorial assurance." N Y Times Book Rev

Family and friends. Pantheon Bks. 1985 187p o.p.

LC 85-6373

"We first see the widowed Sofka Dorn and her children—Frederick, Alfred, Mimi, and Betty—in London between the wars, after they have come from Eastern Europe, and we follow them from the children's adolescence through their middle age." N Y Times Book Rev

"Anita Brookner's prose is impeccably elegant and she is unsentimental with it. . . . There is a closeness of atmosphere, almost claustrophobic, in Family and Friends, as if we were alternating between a discreetly perfumed lady's boudoir and the smoking room of a superior gentleman's club. There is no mistaking the originality as well as the skill and consistency with which the novel so beautifully conforms to its genre and its intentions." N Y Rev Books

Fraud. Random House 1992 262p $21

ISBN 0-679-41606-4   LC 92-20162

"Anna Durrant, immaculately turned out but dauntingly virginal and good, seems to have vanished. The doctor who cared for her and her recently deceased mother is perturbed enough to call the police, who question Mrs. Marsh, an elderly woman for whom Anna occasionally did favors. This precipitates a prolonged flashback and brings us, for a time, into the labyrinth of Mrs. Marsh's impressions and memories. In her eighties, stubborn, judgmental, and proud, Mrs. Marsh dislikes the perpetually cheerful Anna and wonders why she devoted her youth to her pretty but flaky mother, but Mrs. Marsh's real concern is combating the press of old age." Booklist

"Loneliness, deception, and the plight of midlife women are recurring themes in Brookner's novels. Yet 'Fraud' is not depressing. As Brookner explores these themes in her quiet elegant prose, she brings new insight to old dilemmas." Christ Sci Monit

Hotel du Lac. Pantheon Bks. 1985 c1984 184p o.p.

LC 84-20641

First published 1984 in the United Kingdom

"A sedate Swiss Hotel at end-of-season is the scene of Edith Hope's brief, melancholy exile (she's in disgrace for having jilted her fiancé on their wedding day). Edith observes her fellow guests with sympathy and amusement; writes long, unposted letters to her married lover; and works at her latest romantic novel, her life suspended and uneventful. When the worldly Mr. Neville plumbs her 'unused capacity' for mischief, she nearly acquiesces, at 39, to his quaintly treacherous proposal of marriage and respectability without the promise of love." Libr J

The tone of this novel is "oddly detached, very small-scale, faintly humorous. . . . It is by means of this very remoteness that Edith manages to hold our interest throughout this achingly uneventful holiday, with its empty chasms of time, its murmuring respectability, its dining room scattered sparsely with people who mean nothing to her. . . . There are some uncomfortable patches. . . . But generally, the writing is graceful and attractive." N Y Times Book Rev

A private view. Random House 1995 242p $23

ISBN 0-679-43444-5   LC 94-26413

"At 65, George Bland has been looking forward to retirement and the commencement of his long-anticipated journey to the Far East with his good friend, Putnam. When Putnam suddenly dies, George begins to feel old and uncertain of the dull, restrained, responsible way he

Brookner, Anita—*Continued*

has lived his life. Though he never married, he has maintained a life-long friendship with Louise, his placid first girlfriend, who is now a widow and grandmother. His melancholy days of walks in London's parks and afternoons in museums are interrupted when young, brash Katy Gibbs moves into the flat across the hall. At first exasperated by Katy's rude and greedy nature, George becomes consumed by desire for her and her hedonistic lifestyle." Libr J

"Few writers can infuse a scene in which two people stand in a hallway without speaking with the suspense and tremendous intensity and delicacy of feeling Brookner achieves. Indeed, she is the poet of the silent skirmishes that rage behind the facade of dignified lives." Publ Wkly

Brooks, Terry, 1944-

The black unicorn. Ballantine Bks. 1987 286p il $23

ISBN 0-345-33527-9   LC 87-1456

"A Del Rey book"

In this second book in the Magic Kingdom of Landover series "dreams of trouble, missing spell-books, and a black unicorn send Ben Holiday, Landover's newest king, his wizard, Questor, and the sylph, Willow, on three separate quests that converge in a battle for control of their magical kingdom." Libr J

Followed by Wizard at large

The druid of Shannara. Ballantine Bks. 1991 423p $19.95

ISBN 0-345-36298-5   LC 90-42424

"A Del Rey book"

In the second novel in the Heritage of Shannara tetralogy "Walker Boh, the 'Dark Uncle,' embarks on a perilous journey to recover the black Elfstone and restore the lost druid keep of Paranor." Libr J

"Broadening the landscape of his magic world, Brooks has produced a deep and thoughtful fantasy." Publ Wkly

Followed by The elfqueen of Shannara

The elfqueen of Shannara. Ballantine Bks. 1992 403p $22

ISBN 0-345-36299-3   LC 91-73257

"A Del Rey book"

Third volume of the Heritage of Shannara tetralogy. "While Par and Coll Ohmsford seek the lost Sword of Shannara and Walker Boh travels to the hidden city of Paranor to bring the Druids back to the Four Lands, young Wren Ohmsford journeys beyond the boundaries of the known world to fulfill the charge given to her by the shade of the Druid Allanon: to return the Elves to the lands of Men." Libr J

"Brooks's prose becomes more fluid and his world becomes more complex, ambiguous and credible with each volume." Publ Wkly

Followed by The talismans of Shannara

The Elfstones of Shannara; illustrated by Darrell K. Sweet. Ballantine Bks. 1982 469p il $23

ISBN 0-345-30253-2   LC 81-69187

"A Del Rey book"

Sequel to The sword of Shannara

"The Ellcrys Tree is dying and when she dies, hordes of demons will be released for a final epic battle. The Elves, despite the help of Allanon, the last Druid, are hopelessly outnumbered. It is up to Will Ohmsford and Amberle to carry an Ellcrys seed to the blood fire. A new Ellcrys will result and the demons will be banished." Voice Youth Advocates

This novel features "strong, believable women who aren't paper-doll characters, but substantial, important figures." SLJ

Followed by The wishsong of Shannara

Magic kingdom for sale—sold! Ballantine Bks. 1986 324p $16.95

ISBN 0-345-31757-2   LC 85-26865

"A Del Rey book"

In this first novel in the author's Magic Kingdom of Landover series, dissatisfied lawyer "Ben Holliday buys a 'magic kingdom' for a million dollars, then finds that it is afflicted with an assortment of drawbacks, of which bankruptcy is the least important. More significant from Ben's point of view is the presence of a demon prince who challenges all the new human rulers and invariably defeats them." Booklist

"Despite a slow, pretentious beginning, Brooks displays an unexpected flair for light comedy in this not-so-standard fantasy quest." Libr J

Followed by The black unicorn

The scions of Shannara. Ballantine Bks. 1990 465p il $23

ISBN 0-345-35695-0   LC 89-37935

"A Del Rey book"

The first title in the Heritage of Shannara tetralogy finds the descendants of the heroes of the Shannara trilogy "summoned to the Hadeshorn in vivid dreams by the spirit of the Druid Allanon. The shade reveals the tasks they each must accept in order to save the Four Lands from total devastation. Par Ohmsford is ordered to find the missing Sword of Shannara; Wren must search for the Elves who mysteriously disappeared a long time ago, and Walker Boh must bring back the Druids." Voice Youth Advocates

Followed by The druid of Shannara

The sword of Shannara; illustrated by the Brothers Hildebrandt. Ballantine Bks. 1991 726p il $23

ISBN 0-345-37143-7   LC 90-43727

"A Del Rey book"

A reissue of the title first published 1977 by Random House

"This is an epic, Tolkien-like evaluation of good versus evil. Shea Ohmsford, a half-elfin youth, is slowly drawn into a universe-shaking war against the forces of Darkness led by the horrible Warlock Lord. Shea, descendant of a noble race, is the only being alive who can control the Sword of Shannara, the sole weapon that can prevail against the spreading evil. Trolls, wizards, goblins, and all manner of weird creatures participate in Shea's journey, on which he is accompanied by his intrepid allies. The action-packed and violent novel is a prime example of the 'sword and sorcery' genre." Shapiro. Fic for Youth. 3d edition

Followed by The Elfstones of Shannara

The talismans of Shannara. Ballantine Bks. 1993 453p $22

ISBN 0-345-36300-0   LC 92-90377

"A Del Rey book"

The conclusion of the Heritage of Shannara tetralogy. "Having fulfilled the quests imposed upon them by the shade of the druid Allanon, the children of Shannara

Brooks, Terry, 1944-—*Continued*
must now attempt to use their newfound powers and
allies to defeat the Shadowen who are ravaging the Four
Lands. . . . Brooks's appeal lies in his fidelity to tried-
and-true quest fantasy and in his ability to create
engaging protagonists." Libr J

The Tangle Box; a magic kingdom of
Landover novel. Ballantine Bks. 1994 334p
$22

ISBN 0-345-38699-X   LC 93-47013

"A Del Rey book"
In this fourth Magic Kingdom of Landover fantasy
"ex-lawyer Ben Holiday's peaceful reign as king of the
magic realm of Landover takes a decided turn for the
worse with the arrival of con man and conjurer Horris
Kew, an unwitting agent for an evil power that seeks
to control the good folk of the kingdom." Libr J

The wishsong of Shannara; illustrated by
Darrell K. Sweet. Ballantine Bks. 1985 499p
il $23

ISBN 0-345-31823-4   LC 84-24185

"A Del Rey book"
In the concluding volume of the Shannara trilogy, "a
third generation of Ohmsfords answers the druid Allanon's call to fight the forces of evil as Brin and her
brother Jair carry their own version of elven magic—the
wishsong—into the enemy's camp. Like its predecessors,
. . . this fantasy quest features and entertaining variety
of characters, impossible odds, and victory gained only
through sacrifice." Libr J

Wizard at large. Ballantine Bks. 1988 291p
o.p.

LC 88-47805

"A Del Rey book"
In this third Landover fantasy "a spell to restore the
Court Scribe of Landover to human form backfires, and
Landover's King embarks on a quest to his native world
to rescue his friend and retrieve the medallion of King-
ship from the clutches of a greedy wizard." Libr J
Followed by The Tangle Box

Brown, Christy, 1932-1981
Down all the days. Stein & Day 1970
266p o.p.
This semi-autobiographical novel by a writer severely
crippled by cerebral palsy is "an account of life in a
large working-class family in Dublin. Its characters
include a mother who is all patient endurance; a father
who is all drunken violence; two loosely differentiated
elder brothers; an . . . elder sister who runs away to
London . . . and a mass of younger children. The whole
is seen from the point of view of the one cripple among
them, who is dragged about in a boxcart in order to
be part of the events he describes." N Y Times Book
Rev
"It's hard to be dispassionate and coolly critical about
a book when its very existence is testimony to the
miracle of the human spirit. . . . Christy Brown can
overwrite, wax too consciously poetic, get a little heavy
on the adjectives but his people and their lives are
brutally, bawdily, joyfully (and sadly) real. This singing,
seamy picture of the Dublin slums and the indomitable
life within them is one of those wondrous, not quite
sentimental affirmations that Ireland produces once in
a miraculous while." Libr J

Brown, Dale, 1956-
Chains of command. Putnam 1993 479p
$22.95

ISBN 0-399-13822-6   LC 93-7887

"It is the immediate future. Russia makes a low-level
thermonuclear attack on Ukraine, trying to bring it back
in line with the other former Soviet nations. When Turkey agrees to support the Ukrainian army, NATO
becomes involved, and the U.S. Air Force Reserves are
deployed. Brilliant but maligned maintenance officer
Daren Mace joins forces with the beautiful and talented
pilot Rebecca Furness in a last-ditch mission to destroy
the blood-thirsty Russian leader before full-scale atomic
war can erupt." Libr J

Flight of the Old Dog; a novel. Fine, D.I.
1987 347p o.p.

LC 86-46388

"It is not the Reagan Administration that has secretly
been developing a Strategic Defense Initiative in this first
book by retired USAF Captain Brown, but the Soviets,
and as soon as the system comes on line, the Russians
flagrantly attack American intelligence and military craft
with their laser weapon . . . and the U.S. is left
dangerously incapable of detecting a missile launch from
the eastern U.S.S.R. Desperate, they decide to send a
souped-up veteran B-52 bomber, the Old Dog, and its
expert navigator Patrick McLanahan on a crucial mission
into Siberia to neutralize the death ray." Publ Wkly
"Despite spinning his wheels in the opening portions
of the book—labored attempts at developing character,
a stumbling stab at establishing a love interest, a series
of predictable Soviet low blows that bring the world to
the precipice of nuclear war—Dale Brown finally . . .
draws the reader into a tense, compelling adventure tale
of the first order." Booklist

Hammerheads. Fine, D.I. 1990 478p o.p.
LC 89-46026

"Hammerheads are an elite force, part U.S. Coast
Guard and part customs service, that use a powerful
array of weapons, including a V-22C tilt-rotor Sea Lion
(a combination helicopter and fixed-wing aircraft). The
force is stationed on offshore platforms and led by
General Brad Elliott and Major Mac McLanahan, and
its purpose is to stop the operations of the South American drug cartels." Booklist
"This smooth blend of plot, action and gadgetry supports the debatable argument that drug smuggling can
be checked by military methods. But forget ideologies—
Hammerheads is a reader's delight from first page to
last, a model of the genre." Publ Wkly

Night of the hawk. Fine, D.I.; Putnam
1992 462p o.p.

LC 92-14138

Available Thorndike Press large print edition
"Lithuania, seeking to remove the last traces of Soviet
rule, plans to get rid of a secret research facility where
scientists have developed a Stealth-type bomber—with
the involuntary aid of none other than David Luger,
presumed killed in *Flight of the Old Dog* [entered
above]. Luger has instead been captured, brainwashed
and given a new identity, but somehow he has retained
his professional expertise. Informed of his survival, the
U.S. government mounts a rescue." Publ Wkly

Sky masters. Fine, D.I.; Putnam 1991
510p o.p.

LC 90-56053

Brown, Dale, 1956—*Continued*

This novel "is about a confrontation between China and the United States after an overeager Chinese fleet commander lets loose a nuclear bomb in the Pacific." N Y Times Book Rev

"Avid military fiction fans will devour Brown's tale with its plethora of high-tech weapons and futuristic acronyms." Booklist

Storming heaven. Putnam 1994 399p $22.95

ISBN 0-399-13931-1   LC 94-12213

Also available Thorndike Press large print edition

"Henri Cazaux is a terrorist with a grudge against the United States because MPs mistreated him in an army jail. In retribution, he decides to destroy the entire country by blowing up airports and, eventually, the Capitol. He is opposed by misunderstood retired Coast Guard admiral Ian Hardcastle." Libr J

"Over the top? Sure. But the author's view about the vulnerability of U.S. airports to aerial attack reads almost plausibly, and Cazaux is a fascinating monster." Booklist

Brown, Dee Alexander

Creek Mary's blood; a novel; [by] Dee Brown. Holt, Rinehart & Winston 1980 401p il o.p.

LC 79-9060

"Through the words and memories of Dane, grandson of Creek Mary (or Akusa Amayi), we follow the history of the men, children, and grandchildren in the life of that indomitable exemplar of the American Indian. The action—and there is plenty of it—takes place in the period after the Revolutionary War and continues through the nineteenth century. The customs, rituals, courting, fighting, and celebrating are all described in detail. One of the most painful sections of the book depicts the forced removal west of the Mississippi of Indian tribes. . . . The relationships among the various tribes—Creek, Cheyenne, Cherokee, and others—is of great interest. Many famous names are recalled, among them Tecumseh, Andrew Jackson, Teddy Roosevelt, and the great chiefs Crazy Horse and Sitting Bull." Shapiro. Fic for Youth. 3d edition

Killdeer Mountain; a novel; [by] Dee Brown. Holt, Rinehart & Winston 1983 279p o.p.

LC 82-15460

This "is the saga of a reporter for the Saint Louis Herald who sets out for the Dakota Territory in 1866. In his journey, he comes across the subject of Charles Riley, hero of the Civil War and Indian fighter. Reporter Sam Morrison finds conflicting stories as to the character of Major Rawley, thus planting the seeds of a quest for the truth as to the real story of Indian massacres, dishonor in battle, deserted love and planned rescue of an innocent Dakota Chief held captive in a desolate fort." Voice Youth Advocates

"The story of Major Rawley if it is indeed his story and not that of the mysterious stranger masquerading as Rawley—is told in a 'Rashomon'-like interweaving of different eyewitness accounts, and it is an intriguing and exciting tale." Libr J

Brown, Joe David, 1915-1976

Addie Pray; a novel. Simon & Schuster 1971 313p o.p.

"Set during the Depression this . . . picaresque novel follows the adventures of two con artists—the narrator Addie Pray, an eleven-year-old orphan, and Long Boy, her presumptive father. The pair travel the South selling gold-initialed Bibles to new widows, working a wallet-switching trick, and trading in nonexistent cotton, among other outrageous ploys, until they join Major Carter E. Lee in more complicated swindles culminating in a slick scheme to set Addie up as heiress to an enormous fortune." Booklist

"Brown has a special feeling for the Depression-era South. . . . [Addie's speech] is vulgar, pungent country talk, which adds greatly to the book's easygoing charm. Looking at Long Boy with his floozy, she observes that 'he got that silly, dazed grin like a tom cat being choked to death with cream.' Like that extravagant expression, the book is a long tall, oldtime tale. But as Addie might put it, in the right hands that kind of yarn has a lot of prance left." Time

Brown, Morna Doris MacTaggart, 1907-

For works written by this author under other names see Ferrars, E. X., 1907-

Brown, Rita Mae

Dolley; a novel of Dolley Madison in love and war. Bantam Bks. 1994 382p $22.95

ISBN 0-553-08890-4   LC 93-44429

The author re-creates a "critical year in the life of the fourth president's wife, who loved politics and her husband and who had a great gift for friendship. In 1814, Napoleon's war with Britain spilled into its former colonies, and redcoats marching toward under-defended Washington constitute the backdrop of Brown's slice of Dolley Madison's life. Brown vivifies the capital hostess and covert political manipulator's doings by interspersing snippets from an imaginary diary with the main narrative. . . . Brown's Dolley Madison is full-blown and vibrant." Booklist

High hearts. Bantam Bks. 1986 464p o.p.

LC 85-48042

Set in Virginia, this "Civil War saga centers on the war-time experiences of Geneva Chatfield, who disguises herself as a boy and runs off to join her husband fighting on the Confederate side. In the process, Geneva discovers she can amount to something more than just a clinging vine, more than just a helpmeet for a man. Brown's purpose is to show how this terrible conflict had an effect on women and blacks, too—their participation in it, their sacrifices because of it, what they had at stake in the outcome." Booklist

"Although the chain of events is formulaic and the outcome less than surprising, Brown's style is energetic, her message humane, and her characters unconventional and lively." Publ Wkly

Murder at Monticello; or, Old sins; [by] Rita Mae Brown & Sneaky Pie Brown; illustrations by Wendy Wray. Bantam Bks. 1994 298p il $19.95

ISBN 0-553-08140-3   LC 94-16711

Brown, Rita Mae—*Continued*

"Tiger cat Mrs. Murphy and corgi Tee Tucker . . . help Mary Minor 'Harry' Haristeen, postmistress of Crozet, Virginia, solve a nearly 200-year-old mystery. It begins with a skeleton discovered in a slave cabin during restorations at Monticello—and continues with the present-day murder of Kimball Haynes, head of archaeology there, who has discovered secrets of miscegenation recorded in a doctor's long-hidden journals. . . . An entertaining treat for animal-loving mystery/history fans." Booklist

Rest in pieces; [by] Rita Mae Brown & Sneaky Pie Brown; illustrations by Wendy Wray. Bantam Bks. 1992 292p il o.p.

LC 92-7257

Available Thorndike Press large print edition

This murder mystery "finds Mary Minor ('Harry') Haristeen, who is postmistress in the small southern town of Crozet, Virginia, and also runs a 120-acre farm, trying to discover the identity of a dismembered corpse, pieces of which are found on the property of her new neighbor Blair Bainbridge, a male model from New York." Booklist

"Ms. Brown's earthy prose breathes warmth into wintry Crozet and pinches color into the cheeks of its nosy, garrulous residents." N Y Times Book Rev

Six of one. Harper & Row 1978 310p $9.95

ISBN 0-06-010524-0   LC 78-2057

The author "extols the vitality and variety of women by tracing the lives of two sisters, their families, and cronies. The women are rich and poor, heterosexual (mostly) and lesbian, but they are linked by emotional and physical experiences common to all women. . . . Structurally, the novel intersperses vivid scenes from the past with those from the present (1980 in the book). Despite flaws, the narrative is engrossing, as are the women." Libr J

Southern discomfort. Harper & Row 1982 249p $14.45

ISBN 0-06-014928-0   LC 81-47683

In this novel "the focus is on the rigid class and racial divisions of Montgomery, Ala., society during the early decades of this century. . . . Hortensia Banastre, ice goddess, model society matron, falls passionately in love with a young black boxer, and she bears and secretly raises his daughter. . . . Paris, Hortensia's beautiful and hateful son, figures it out—knowledge that figures in his shocking death." Publ Wkly

The author "seems to understand the way in which dark passions and unspeakable desires become magnified among a people segregated by unnatural laws concerning race, class and social position. She portrays well the suffering incurred by trying to defy such a system; she also captures the earthy quality of those who do what they must to get by." Best Sellers

Sudden death. Bantam Bks. 1983 241p o.p.

LC 82-45948

"Carmen Semana, one of the topseeds on the women's tennis circuit, hopes this year to win the Grand Slam. When she is exposed as a lesbian by her archrival (and former lover), Carmen risks losing lucrative commercial endorsements, being deported to her native Argentina, and estrangement from her current lover. This tour of the locker rooms and bedrooms of women's tennis reflects the interest raised by recent scandals." Libr J

Venus envy. Bantam Bks. 1993 355p o.p.

LC 92-39378

"Glamorous Mary Frazier Armstrong—definitely on the 'A' list, with a pedigree stretching back to 1640—has run a successful art gallery in Charlottesville, Va., since leaving Sotheby's some years ago. When medicos tell her she's got only days to live, she fires off a batch of letters telling relatives and friends she's gay. But before they can reach their destinations, she learns she's been—oops!—misdiagnosed. When the missives land, the southern manners and graces of a cast of deliciously drawn characters splatter, and only wise, widowed Aunt Ru and gallery employee Mandy stand by Frazier." Booklist

Wish you were here; [by] Rita Mae Brown & Sneaky Pie Brown; illustrations by Wendy Wray. Bantam Bks. 1990 242p il o.p.

LC 90-1071

"Mary Minor ('Harry') Haristeen, divorce in the works, runs the post office in Crozet, Virginia, with a pet cat and dog at her side. After two spectacularly gruesome murders rock the community, Harry attempts to gather helpful clues, while the pets (who converse with each other) do their best to protect her." Libr J

"Ms. Brown writes with wise, disarming wit about her country-bred characters and their not-always-neighborly ways." N Y Times Book Rev

Brown, Rosellen

Before and after. Farrar, Straus & Giroux 1992 354p $21

ISBN 0-374-10999-0   LC 92-81571

Also available G.K. Hall large print edition

This novel begins "on the day that Carolyn Reiser, a New Hampshire pediatrician with two teenage kids, gets called to the emergency room. A girl has been bludgeoned to death. The chief suspect is Carolyn's son and he has disappeared." Newsweek

Brown is "tenacious in her examination of each major character. Deftly, artfully, she strips away the delicate shelter of conventional relationships." N Y Times Book Rev

Civil wars; a novel. Knopf 1984 419p $16.95

ISBN 0-394-53478-6   LC 83-48866

An "analysis of the falsehoods within the union of Teddy and Jessie Carll. Nearly two decades have passed since the exhilarating activism of the civil rights movement brought Teddy and Jessie together. The growing distance between them is barely realized and not at all defined when an automobile accident suddenly bequeaths the turbulent family with two more children, who have been raised in a racist, segregated environment. The novel alternates between Brown's third-person narration, which focuses on Jessie, and selections from the diary of one of the adopted orphans." Booklist

"This is a very fine novel. Its principal strength lies in the immense detail with which the characters are depicted. This is especially true of Jessie, from whose viewpoint the story is told." Best Sellers

Tender mercies. Knopf 1978 259p o.p.

LC 78-1315

Brown, Rosellen—*Continued*

"In a moment of high spirits, vacationing Dan Courser took the wheel of a powerboat, gunned the motor, and sucked his swimming wife [Laura] into its blades. Nine months later, Dan goes back home with his family—son Jon, daughter Hallie, and quadriplegic Laura, plucked abruptly from a rehabilitation institute—to come to terms with life. Now bright, lovely Laura must live in her head, her most intimate needs attended to by others. And Dan, weighed down with guilt, longs for pain to exceed hers but still needs some space of his own to keep himself and his family on an even keel." Libr J

"What impresses one most about Tender Mercies is its dignity and restraint. While we learn a great deal about the physical details of paralysis, catheters and such, Brown makes no case for any horror of the body, nor does Laura's suffering prompt a garish loathing of the universe. . . . The language is spare and clean, with flashes of quiet poetry, perfectly suited to the plain but by no means simple New Englanders it portrays." Saturday Rev

Brown, Sandra, 1948-

Charade. Warner Bks. 1994 405p $21.95

ISBN 0-446-51656-2   LC 93-38360

Also available Thorndike Press large print edition

Following a successful heart transplant, soap opera star Cat Delaney "abandons stardom and Hollywood for San Antonio, Tex., where she hosts a local TV program featuring children up for adoption. Cat hardly has a chance to enjoy her change of heart and her new heart-throb, bad-boy crime novelist Alex Pierce, because a stalker is after her." Publ Wkly

French Silk. Warner Bks. 1992 403p o.p.

LC 91-50408

Available G.K. Hall large print edition

"Televangelist Jackson Wilde targets the catalog of Claire Laurent's mail-order lingerie business, French Silk, as part of his anti-pornography campaign. When Wilde's body is discovered in a New Orleans hotel room, Laurent becomes the number-one suspect in a murder investigation that also involves her mentally distracted mother, her partner, the beautiful model Yasmine; Wilde's wife and son, both working members of his ministry; and a local senator with a shady private life." Libr J

"Despite occasionally stilted and didactic dialogue, the novel is adroitly plotted and sleekly paced, and has just the right mix of menace and sex to keep pages turning." Publ Wkly

Where there's smoke. Warner Bks. 1993 417p $19.95

ISBN 0-446-51655-4   LC 92-50525

Also available Thorndike Press large print edition

"The Tackett oil clan of Eden Pass in East Texas, dominated by hard-driving widow Jody, managed to weather the sex-scandal disgrace of eldest son, Clark, a congressman, five years ago, and his recent death by drowning. Now Dr. Lara Mallory, the woman involved in Clark's downfall, moves into town to take over the retiring doctor's practice, which Clark bought before his death and willed to her. . . . Brown never lets up on melodramatic tension, twisting her plot and subplots until the unsuspected truth about Clark's scandal and death is revealed." Publ Wkly

Browne, Gerald A.

18mm blues. Warner Bks. 1993 372p o.p.

LC 92-54098

The title of this "thriller refers to the awesome size of rare blue Burmese pearls. . . . When Setsu and Michiko, the divers who located the uncommon treasure, are murdered by Bertin, the sleazy captain of their pearling boat, he's left with fantastic wealth *and* a witness to his crime. Switching locales to San Francisco, Browne homes in on Grady, a gem merchant, and his girlfriend, Julia, who are about to travel to Burma to purchase precious stones. As the tale unfolds, Thailand provides the setting for all manner of intrigue." Booklist

"Despite a dangerously cute love story . . . Browne's tale succeeds, thanks to a violent, satisfying ending and his mastery of fascinating gem lore." Publ Wkly

19 Purchase Street; a novel. Arbor House 1982 432p o.p.

LC 82-72051

This novel "deals with the big business of laundering dirty money. Purchase Street is the headquarters for a scam involving billions of dollars, carried piecemeal across the world. When Gainer's sister is killed while making a delivery for the group, he joins the organization to avenge her death. He becomes a carrier of money, as much as three million dollars at a time, to Europe, to be exchanged for 'clean' bills, that cannot be traced. Gainer becomes deeply entrenched in the workings of the organization, and makes his own plans to get even with the heads of it for causing his sister's death on one of her money-carrying trips." West Coast Rev Books

"Browne handles the material in this thriller of a tale expeditiously, particularly in a spectacular shoot-out in New York harbor, but some of the elaborate if creaky details that the author injects along the way are hardly for the squeamish or fastidious reader." Booklist

Hot Siberian. Arbor House 1989 424p o.p.

LC 88-7561

"Nikolai, a Russian, is assigned to the London bureau of the Soviet diamond export agency; his charge is to deal with the System, a private worldwide diamond company. Events reveal to Nikolai that the Soviet diamond agency is, in fact, supplying the System with the diamonds it supplies to the world market; and he must deal with contraband diamonds interrupting the System's control of the precious commodity issuing from the Soviet Union. Last but not least, Nikolai must deal with the lovely Vivian." Booklist

"Tautly written and absorbing, the thriller bears comparison with *Gorky Park*, which it closely resembles in mood and topical matter. And it's a noteworthy contribution to the subgenre of thrillers in which the heroes are Russians and some of the bad guys Westerners." Publ Wkly

Brownmiller, Susan

Waverly Place. Grove Press 1989 294p o.p.

LC 88-26072

"Brownmiller constructs a portrait of a man's brutality and a woman's destructive dependence. Criminal lawyer Barney Kantor is a psychopathic bully, conman, chiseler and cocaine addict; insecure, self-hating children's book editor Judith Winograd has a need to be dominated and abused; she's also a heroin addict. During the 17 years the couple live together, Kantor establishes a pattern of

Brownmiller, Susan—*Continued*
physical battery followed by grand gestures of contrition. When an adoption scam brings two babies into their lives, the children, especially Melinda, become innocent victims." Publ Wkly

"It would be clear with or without the author's introductory remarks that she has drawn upon the Joel Steinberg/Hedda Nussbaum case for inspiration. The parallels are unmistakable. But it is the colorful prose with which she describes the milieu of Greenwich Village, as well as the skill with which she maintains a balance between objectivity and a touching sense of humanity which make this story more than just investigative journalism disguised as fiction." West Coast Rev Books

Brulard, Henry *See* Stendhal, 1783-1842

Brunner, John, 1934-1995
The crucible of time. Ballantine Bks. 1983 288p o.p.

LC 83-2750

"A Del Rey book"
This novel "spans millennia to tell of an alien race's progress from primitive superstition to the threshold of space. Civilizations rise and fall as radiation, meteorites, disease, famine, ice ages and worldwide flooding all take their toll. Over the centuries, a dedicated few preserve and act upon the knowledge that a way off the planet must be found if the race is to survive the ultimate disaster that is sure to come in the crowded star cluster ahead. Although each of these people is on stage for only one of the book's seven sections, all are memorable characters, historical figures who do great things. Brunner puts them in an appropriate culture that arises naturally from their alien biology, without denying them a humanity with which we can identify." Publ Wkly

A maze of stars. Ballantine Bks. 1991 393p o.p.

LC 90-93527

"A Del Rey book"
"Having seeded some 600 planets with human stock in the largest breeding experiment ever planned, an omnicompetent machine known only as Ship is programmed to retrace its original route over and over, keeping an unobtrusive eye on the evolution of its stepchildren and occasionally rescuing from mortal danger a social outcast whose planetside presence will not be missed." N Y Times Book Rev

"The plot's concept and execution are fascinating: Brunner has built not one but many exotic worlds, each crafted in enough detail to be credible in both physical and societal features, and he has given the whole an immediacy through the interactions between Ship and assorted humans as well as events on various worlds that lead to Ship acquiring another passenger for a time. The conclusion, which reveals Ship's initial and continuing purpose, leaves the reader much to ponder." Booklist

Stand on Zanzibar. Doubleday 1968 505p o.p. Bentley reprint available $30 (ISBN 0-8376-0438-9)

"Doubleday science fiction"
"Extrapolating from current politics, social and sexual mores, the communications revolution, the use of computers, brainwashing, drug use, psychology, philosophy, and sociology, Brunner has fashioned a mammoth work that is an intricate tapestry depicting a possible future.

The dozens of characters interspersed in a complex fashion make the novel difficult to read but well worth the effort. Brunner's brand of cynicism and radical social commentary may not appeal to the taste of all readers, but in the time that has elapsed since the publication of the book, we have seen changes that bear startling similarities to several of Brunner's predictions." Shapiro. Fic for Youth. 3d edition

Buchan, John, 1875-1940
The thirty-nine steps. Doran, G.H. 1915 231p o.p.

Available from Amereon and Buccaneer Bks.

"A bored, well-to-do Englishman, Richard Hannay, returns home to England after growing up in South Africa. Drifting between his club and the sights of London, he is drawn into the confidences of a secret agent in the thick of espionage. The agent is murdered in Hannay's apartment and Richard finds himself on the run from Scotland Yard and the cult of the 'Black Stone.'" Shapiro. Fic for Youth. 3d edition

Buchanan, Edna
Contents under pressure. Hyperion 1992 277p $21.95

ISBN 1-56282-932-7   LC 92-15949
Also available Thorndike Press large print edition

"Blonde, green-eyed and game, Cuban American Britt Montero is, at 31, a respected crime reporter for a Miami daily. Nevertheless, she is stonewalled in her investigation of the death of former pro football player D. Wayne Hudson, a beloved figure in the city's black community who died in a car crash while being chased by officers on the midnight shift. . . . After Britt breaks her story about excessive police violence, the ensuing trial and verdict lead to a breathtaking explosion of arson and sniper fire, from which Britt barely escapes with her life." Publ Wkly

Miami, it's murder. Hyperion 1994 244p $21.95

ISBN 1-56282-802-9   LC 93-4368
Also available Thorndike Press large print edition

Miami police reporter Britt Montero "investigates a series of increasingly violent rapes and a selection of recent Miami murders, all involving old unsolved police cases. The rapist, who likes to powder his victims, writes to Britt and claims voodoo powers; and a retired, terminally ill cop pal of hers determines to bring to justice a powerful politician whom he is sure is guilty of the murder of a child many years before." Publ Wkly

"Buchanan knows crime inside and out: her dialogue is right, her plotting is clever, and her ambience captures every shade of sleaze in Miami's neon rainbow." Booklist

Buchheim, Lothar-Günther, 1918-
The boat; translated from the German by Denver Lindley and Helen Lindley. Knopf 1975 463p o.p.

Original German edition, 1973; first English translation published 1974 in the United Kingdom with title: U-boat

This novel focuses on the experiences of the crew of a German submarine patrolling the Atlantic during the fall and winter of 1941 in search of British convoys

Buchheim, Lothar-Günther, 1918- — *Continued*

"A memorable story of the power of the sea and of the horror of submarine warfare. . . . It is inevitable that his description of the oceans will be compared to Conrad's for example, but Buchheim's prose (with the superb English translation) stands on its own merit for sheer descriptive power. Toward the end there is a disingenuous and unnecessary espionage plot that is not fully developed and leads nowhere. . . . The excitement of the hunt, the chase and the ocean is more than enough to satisfy the most cynical armchair adventurer, and lifts this novel out of the trough of commonplace war stories." New Repub

Buck, Pearl S. (Pearl Sydenstricker), 1892-1973

Nobel Prize in literature, 1938

Dragon seed. Day 1942 378p o.p. Buccaneer Bks. reprint available $19.95 (ISBN 1-56849-133-6)

Set in 20th century China, this novel shows the effects of the Japanese war on a family of sturdy, upright farmers, living not far from Nanking. Ling Tan, his wife, and their sons and daughters, and their families, at first cannot understand this type of war, and are unprepared to grasp its implications. But with the fall of Nanking, and the looting of the countryside, understanding and horror come. Ling Tan's sons take to guerilla warfare, and the family makes valiant attempts to continue some kind of decent life in the midst of chaos

East and West; stories. Day 1975 202p o.p.

Analyzed in Short story index

Contents: Until tomorrow; Fool's sacrifice; The golden bowl; India, India; To whom a child is born; Dream child

East wind: west wind. Crowell 1930 277p o.p.

"A John Day book"

The theme of this novel is the conflict between Chinese traditions and Western ways. "The daughter of a noble family, trained for wifehood in the old customs and traditions and betrothed since childhood, is married to a Chinese of the new era who has received his medical training in America. It is only by adopting the Western habits which her husband esteems, that the little bride finds love and happiness. Her brother's love for an American girl is another phase of the conflict." Cleveland Public Libr

The good earth. o.p.

Available from Amereon and Buccaneer Bks. Large print edition available from G.K. Hall

First published 1931 by Day

This first volume of a trilogy of Chinese life in pre-war days "describes the rise of Wang Lung, a Chinese peasant, from poverty to the position of a rich landowner, helped by his patient wife, O-lan. Their vigor, fortitude, persistence, and enduring love of the soil are emphasized throughout. Generally regarded as Pearl Buck's masterpiece, the book won universal acclaim for its sympathetically authentic picture of Chinese life." Reader's Ency. 3d edition

Followed by Sons

A house divided. Reynal 1935 353p o.p.

"A John Day book"

This concludes the trilogy which opened with The good earth and continued with Sons. China in revolution is its scene, the dilemma of the modern, educated young men and women is its theme. Yuan, son of Wang the Tiger, grandson of Wang Lung, spends some years in America as a student. He returns to find his country greatly changed and torn by the conflict between Eastern and Western forces, with the latter in ascendancy. Yuan marries a girl of his own race and class and resolves to forward the cause of the New China by teaching students modern methods of agriculture

Imperial woman; a novel. Day 1956 376p o.p.

A biographical novel about Tzu-hsi, last Empress of China, known as Old Buddha. Her life is pictured from the day she received the imperial summons to appear before the Emperor, to her death in 1908

"The accuracy or lack of accuracy will probably be of no particular concern to the readers of 'Imperial Woman.' . . . The details of the secluded life in the Forbidden City, the political jugglings of the court, and the increasing pressure from the Western powers as the Manchu Dynasty breaks up—these contribute to the novel's movement." N Y Times Book Rev

Pavilion of women. Day 1946 316p o.p.

On her fortieth birthday Madame Wu, a beautiful upper-class Chinese woman, voluntarily retires from married life. It is her plan to select a concubine for her husband and live a freer life as chief arbitrator of the house of Wu. The difficulties which ensue change the lives within this "pavilion of women"

"It is a searching, adult study of women written with high seriousness and sympathy, which should find a multitude of women readers. Mrs. Buck's grave unaccented prose is well suited to the delicate matters at hand." N Y Times Book Rev

Sons. Day 1932 467p o.p.

This second volume of a trilogy, which began with The good earth, tells the story of Wang Lung's three sons who after the death of their father "are in great haste to divide the many fields he had spent his lifetime accumulating. It is with the third son, fierce, haughty and hungry-eyed, and the use he makes of his patrimony that the story is mainly concerned. His rise and fall as a petty warlord, and his molding of his son to succeed him, only to have him revert to the land of his grandfather, make interesting reading though less gripping than the earlier novel." N Y Libr

Followed by A house divided

Buckley, Christopher Taylor, 1952-

Wet work. Knopf 1991 271p $19.95

ISBN 0-394-57193-2   LC 90-53119

"Bodies pile up in this satirical thriller as its wealthy protagonist goes after the system that provided a fatal drug overdose to his granddaughter." N Y Times Book Rev

"Buckley subtly merges the sheer entertainment of a good travel yarn with the vicious motivations of greed to produce a story that deserves a strong recommendation." Libr J

Buckley, William F. (William Frank), 1925-
Mongoose, R.I.P; a Blackford Oakes novel; [by] William F. Buckley, Jr. Random House 1988 322p o.p.

LC 87-28344

This Blackford Oakes novel is a "retelling of the Kennedy assassination, which links Oswald to the Castro regime. Learning that the Soviets have secretly left behind a single missile after the U.S. challenge, Castro masterminds a scenario that will see Kennedy dead whether by bullet or ballistic missile." Libr J

"The best of the Blacky books, this is an entertainment of the Graham Greene order that truly entertains, excites, and edifies. . . . The story builds with considerable suspense up to Blackford's horrendous dilemma on the day of JFK's assassination." Natl Rev

Tucker's last stand; a Blackford Oakes novel; [by] William F. Buckley, Jr. Random House 1990 256p o.p.

LC 90-53134

Available large print edition $21.95 (ISBN 0-394-58858-4)

In this "novel, Buckley provides an excuse for the U.S. loss of the Vietnam War. Idealism and romance play equally devastating roles as CIA officer Oakes becomes linked with Montana Tucker, a mechanical genius of questionable army origins who has deliberately obscured his involvement in the building of the atomic bomb. Their assignment comes straight from President Lyndon Johnson: 'Find out a way to block the trail those mothers are using.' While Oakes and Tucker are devising some ingenious schemes to defeat the North Vietnamese, Johnson is back in the U.S. scheming to defeat Barry Goldwater." Booklist

"A few sex scenes, a remarkable scenario at sea and fascinating glimpses of such Capitol figures as Abe Fortas, the Bundys and Robert Kennedy are ingredients in a story most memorable for the questions it raises about a still-troubling episode in our political history." Publ Wkly

A very private plot; a Blackford Oakes novel; by William F. Buckley, Jr. Morrow 1994 272p $20

ISBN 0-688-12795-9   LC 93-20978

Also available G.K. Hall large print edition

This "Blackford Oakes adventure brings the Cold War hero into the age of *glasnost* and beyond. The year is 1995. Senator Hugh Blanton, who is framing a bill that would effectively ban all covert intelligence activity, subpoenas the retired Oakes to give evidence about Cyclops, a Reagan-era CIA operation that supposedly nearly drove Gorbachev to start a nuclear war. Interspersed with the narrative of Oakes's adamant refusal to testify is the true story behind Cyclops, which involves Oakes's discovery in the mid-80s that a group of young Russian patriots plan to assassinate Gorbachev." Publ Wkly

The author's "political wisdom and lordly wit insure that 'A Very Private Plot' delivers more than mere routine spy thrills. The plot may lack complexity, but the ethical issues raised along the way receive thoughtful, nuanced treatment." N Y Times Book Rev

Buffett, Jimmy, 1946-
Where is Joe Merchant?; a novel. Harcourt Brace Jovanovich 1992 xx, 382p $19.95

ISBN 0-15-196296-0   LC 92-17136

Frank Bama "runs an air charter service out of the Florida Keys. His habit is to 'leave the earth below when things get too complicated.' And they do . . . as Frank is drawn by a sleazy journalist into a search for a legendary rock guitarist, thought to be dead but rumored to be living in various odd corners of the Caribbean. Frank's former girlfriend, a disgruntled heiress, shows up, and in quick succession treasure hunters, blithe New Age devotees and a deranged soldier of fortune are all involved in the quest for Joe. While his prose is only serviceable, Mr. Buffett . . . does know how to keep a tale moving." N Y Times Book Rev

Bujold, Lois McMaster
Mirror dance; a Vorkosigan adventure. Baen Pub. Enterprises 1994 392p $21

ISBN 0-671-72210-7   LC 93-39663

This science fiction adventure "features the deformed and undersized heir to the strongman of Barrayar, Miles Vorkosigan, who doubles as Admiral Naismith, leader of the Dendarii Mercenaries—and is secretly on the payroll of Barrayaran Imperial Intelligence. The tale begins with Miles' cloned sibling Mark masquerading as Miles in order to take a Dendarii ship to that free enterprise plague spot, Jackson's Whole, on an unauthorized mission to clean out the clone creches where he was raised. The mission goes awry, Miles comes to Mark's rescue, the rescue goes even more wrong. . . . The remaining pages complete as good a story as ever was offered as science fiction." Booklist

Bulgakov, Mikhail Afanas'evich, 1891-1940
The master and Margarita; translated from the Russian by Michael Glenny. Knopf 1992 c1967 xxvii, 446p $17

ISBN 0-679-41046-5   LC 91-53220

Also available from Ardis $35 (ISBN 0-87501-067-9) edition based on a version published 1989 in Russia and translated by Diana Burgin and Katherine O'Connor

"Everyman's library"

Written in the 1930s. Original Russian edition published 1966-67 in censored form. This translation, first published 1967 by Harper, is based on the unexpurgated version that was subsequently published 1973 in the Soviet Union

This novel "juxtaposes two planes of action—one set in Moscow in the 1930s and the other in Jerusalem at the time of Christ. The three central characters of the contemporary plot are the Devil, disguised as one Professor Woland; the 'Master,' a repressed novelist; and Margarita, who, though married to a bureaucrat, loves the Master. The Master has burned his manuscript and gone willingly into a psychiatric ward when critics attacked his work—a portrayal of the story of Jesus. Margarita sells her soul to the Devil in order to obtain the Master's release from the psychiatric ward. A parallel plot presents the action of the Master's destroyed novel, the condemnation of Yeshua (Jesus) in Jerusalem." Merriam-Webster's Ency of Lit

Bulwer-Lytton, Edward *See* Lytton, Edward Bulwer Lytton, Baron, 1803-1873

Bunyan, John, 1628-1688
The Pilgrim's progress.
Available from various publishers

First published 1678

"The 'immortal allegory,' next to the Bible the most widely known book in religious literature. It was written in Bedford jail, where Bunyan was for twelve years a prisoner for his convictions. It describes the troubled journey of Christian and his companions through this life to a triumphal entrance into the Celestial city. Bunyan 'wrote with virgin purity utterly free from mannerisms and affectations; and without knowing himself for a writer of fine English, produced it.'" Pratt Alcove

Burdick, Eugene
Fail-safe; by Eugene Burdick & Harvey Wheeler. McGraw-Hill 1962 286p o.p. Amereon reprint available $21.95 (ISBN 0-8488-0437-6)

"With mounting tension this gripping thriller tells of a possible nuclear holocaust. An American attack squadron is accidentally and irretrievably launched to obliterate Moscow. The frantic U.S. president and the Russian premier begin a dramatic hotline race against time to halt the bombers' flight and prevent disaster. The crisis is seen through the eyes of several characters, and their differing perceptions provide an effective storytelling technique." Shapiro. Fic for Youth. 3d edition

(jt. auth) Lederer, W. J. The ugly American

Burditt, Joyce Rebeta- *See* Rebeta-Burditt, Joyce, 1938-

Burford, Eleanor, 1906-1993
For works written by this author under other names see Carr, Philippa, 1906-1993; Holt, Victoria, 1906-1993; Plaidy, Jean, 1906-1993

Burgess, Anthony, 1917-1993
Any old iron. Random House 1989 360p $19.95

ISBN 0-394-57484-2   LC 88-42828

This novel "takes a panoramic view of recent history, beginning with the sinking of the *Titanic* and continuing through the two world wars, the Spanish civil war, the Russian Revolution, and the founding of Israel. The story placed within this framework concerns the fate and fortunes of two families, one Welsh and one Jewish, who manage to survive through all these momentous events and personal vicissitudes." Booklist

"One would expect a novel with such subject matter to be unrelievedly grim, but in fact the story is full of comedy, unpredictable action, and crackling dialogue. It is also teasingly ambiguous and sticks in the mind." Atlantic

A clockwork orange. Norton 1988 c1962 192p $14.95

ISBN 0-393-02439-3   LC 86-23843
Also available from Buccaneer Bks.

First published 1962 in the United Kingdom; this reissue restores a final chapter omitted from the 1963 United States edition

"A compelling and often comic vision of the way violence comes to dominate the mind. The novel is set in a future London and is told in a curious but readable Russified argot by a juvenile delinquent whose brainwashing by the authorities has destroyed not only his murderous aggression but also his deeper-seated sense of humanity as typified by his compulsive love for the music of Beethoven. It is an ironic novel in the tradition of Zamiatin's and Orwell's anti-Utopias." Sci Fic Ency

The devil's mode; stories. Random House 1989 290p $18.95

ISBN 0-394-57670-5   LC 89-42910

Analyzed in Short story index

Contents: A meeting in Valladolid; The most beautified; The cavalier of the rose; 1889 and the devil's mode; Wine of the country; Snow; The endless voyager; Hun [novella]; Murder to music

The author "is a linguistic gymnast; his stories are courageously playful, abounding in literary and historical allusions; and he is often funny." N Y Times Book Rev

Earthly powers. Simon & Schuster 1980 607p o.p.

LC 80-20978

The "narrator is an octogenarian writer whose novels, plays and stories, though they never aspired to art, have made him rich and world renowned. Kenneth Toomey's homosexuality imposed upon him early in life a triple exile: from his parents, who thought his proclivity willful; from England, which thought it a crime; and from the Roman Catholic Church, whose priests decreed it a sin. As the story begins, Toomey is asked to write an account of a miracle he once witnessed—a miracle performed by a priest who later became Pope and is now to be promoted to saint. Because Carlo Campanati was Toomey's relative by marriage and longtime friend, the request prompts Toomey to re-examine his life." Newsweek

This novel "is full of . . . parodic brilliancies as it is full of caricatured or modified people and events. But if it plays with the processes of fiction, with the transubstantiation of the actual into the preferred, Burgess does the actual itself with all his usual vividness. . . . [This] is a big, grippingly readable, extraordinarily rich and moving fiction." Times Lit Suppl

Hun
In Burgess, A. The devil's mode p152-269

The pianoplayers. Arbor House 1986 208p o.p. Amereon reprint available $20.95 (ISBN 0-8488-1332-4)

LC 86-20559

"In the first half of this fictional memoir Ellen Henshaw recalls her father, a piano player in silent movie houses. With the advent of the talkies the old man's only hope financially was to stage a 30-day nonstop piano marathon—a fatal mistake. In the second half Ellen describes her career as a teenage prostitute

Burgess, Anthony, 1917-1993—*Continued*
and then her opening a 'school of love' where wealthy gentlemen learn to play a woman's body like a musical instrument." Libr J

"First-rate satiric humor from a literary virtuoso." Booklist

Burgess, Trevor, 1920-1995
For works written by this author under other names see Hall, Adam, 1920-1995; Trevor, Elleston, 1920-1995

Burke, James Lee, 1936-
Black cherry blues. Little, Brown 1989 290p o.p.

LC 89-7977

"A former homicide cop is trying to run his fishing business, care for six-year-old orphan Alafair, and come to terms with the violent death of his wife, Annie. A chance encounter with an old friend haunted by a troubling secret sets off a chain of events that leaves Dave framed for murder. Desperate to prove his innocence and protect Alafair, Robicheaux is forced to conduct his own investigation." Libr J

"A stunning novel that takes detective fiction into new imaginative realms. . . . All the main characters in this darkly beautiful, lyric saga carry heavy emotional baggage, and Robicheaux's sleuthing is a simultaneous exorcism of demons of grief, loss, fear, rage, vengeance." Publ Wkly

Dixie City jam. Hyperion 1994 367p $22.95

ISBN 0-7868-6019-7   LC 93-36228
Also available G.K. Hall large print edition

In this Dave Robicheaux adventure the "foe is a neo-Nazi sadist who thinks Dave is the key to finding a German U-Boat that has been bouncing around the Gulf of Mexico since World War II. Threats to Dave's wife and child draw Robicheaux into a violent confrontation." Booklist

"The preposterous plot implodes from . . . wretched excess, but in brief scene-by-scene doses, Mr. Burke's manic style has a life of its own. The sheer energy of his language has an uplifting effect on the characters, inspiring them to new heights of self-expression and new depths of brutality." N Y Times Book Rev

Heaven's prisoners. Holt & Co. 1988 292p o.p.

LC 87-26878

"Ex-New Orleans cop Dave Robicheaux and his wife, Annie, are fishing in the Gulf one afternoon when a small plane crashes nearby. All of the plane's passengers—Nicaraguan refugees attempting to enter the U.S. illegally—are killed except one, a young girl whom Dave rescues. This chance encounter lands the Robicheaux family in the midst of an immigration squabble and then a vicious drug war." Booklist

"There is a pronounced streak of poetry in Mr. Burke's prose. He has the knack of combining action with reflection; he has pity for the human condition, and even his villains can have some sympathetic and redeeming qualities. Mr. Burke writes in an unhurried manner, but the book never loses tension because he is so wrapped up in his characters and their locale." N Y Times Book Rev

In the electric mist with Confederate dead. Hyperion 1993 344p $19.95

ISBN 1-56282-882-7   LC 92-26615
Also available G.K. Hall large print edition

In this Dave Robicheaux mystery, Burke leads his "Cajun detective into a series of dreamlike encounters with a troop of Confederate soldiers under Gen. John Bell Hood. Soon after the severely mutilated body of a young woman is found in a ditch outside the southern Louisiana town of New Iberia, deputy sheriff Robicheaux busts Elrod Sykes, star of a Hollywood movie being filmed nearby, for drunk driving. Sykes says a skeleton wrapped in chains was unearthed during filming in a marsh where, in 1957, Robicheaux witnessed—but remained silent about—the killing of a chained black man by two white men. As the belatedly guilt-stricken detective tries to identify that victim, another young woman is brutally killed." Publ Wkly

"You can't write about Louisiana without at least nodding toward that supernatural realm hovering out there in the morning mist; somehow it seems right that Robicheaux, his eyes always on the past, would be the one to walk through the curtain." Am Libr

A morning for flamingos. Little, Brown 1990 294p $18.95

ISBN 0-316-11721-8   LC 89-77777

"Burke's Cajun detective, Dave Robicheaux, is once again battling personal demons—questions of fear and bravery, violence and compassion, pleasure and pain—and as he stalks an escaped killer and infiltrates the world of a Mafia drug lord, he finds reflections of his own torment wherever he looks. What it means to be Cajun is at the heart of Robicheaux's dilemma." Booklist

"Attentive to language and atmosphere, Burke delivers action on churning Gulf waters, in city streets, in deserted fields and within the souls of his memorable characters—and a fully satisfying resolution." Publ Wkly

The neon rain. Holt & Co. 1987 248p o.p.

LC 86-15222

"New Orleans homicide cop Dave Robicheaux has a passion for fishing. While pursuing his hobby on a back country bayou, Robicheaux finds a body. His discovery pulls him into a network of small-time Mafiosi, Nicaraguan drug dealers, federal Treasury agents and retired two-star generals—all involved in a plot to ship arms to the Nicaraguan contras." Libr J

"With its fine local color and driving action, this novel is both chilling and first-rate entertainment." Publ Wkly

A stained white radiance. Hyperion 1992 305p o.p.

LC 91-34213

"Sadistic villains and interior demons plague Cajun police detective Dave Robicheaux as the murder of a local cop draws him into the painful conflicts of the Sonnier family, with whom he grew up near the bayous." Publ Wkly

In this novel "the 'venal and meretricious' bear the unmistakable stench of the modern world: a drug-dealing mobster out to settle scores, a trio of swastika-sporting members of the Aryan Brotherhood, and, lurking on the respectable fringe, an impeccably coiffed former Klansman intent on snagging a senate seat. . . . Dave tackles them all, of course, and in the end establishes a tenuous calm into which he and his family are able to retreat. But the elegiac tone dominates." Booklist

Burley, W. J. (William John), 1914-
Wycliffe and the cycle of death. Doubleday 1991 c1990 181p $14.95

ISBN 0-385-41800-0   LC 90-23331

Also available Thorndike Press large print edition

"A Crime Club book"

First published 1990 in the United Kingdom

In this Superintendent Wycliffe mystery "a well-to-do bookseller in a quaint Cornish village is found strangled in his office, and all of the family members have means and motive—a possible connection to the disappearance of the victim's wife 17 years before. As always, Burley weaves the familiar threads into an appealing puzzler." Booklist

Wycliffe and the dead flautist. St. Martin's Press 1992 c1991 192p $21.95

ISBN 0-312-07129-9   LC 91-41657

First published 1991 in the United Kingdom

"At the scene of a shotgun death in his Cornish village, Wycliffe surmises that amateur flautist Tony Miller was shot by a panicked killer who clumsily arranged the scene to suggest a suicide. The experienced inspector is suspicious of the inept staging and initiates the various interviews that make up the rest of the plot." Publ Wkly

Wycliffe and the quiet virgin. Doubleday 1986 179p o.p.

LC 86-8856

"Published for the Crime Club"

"Scotland Yard Chief Superintendent Wycliffe is off for what seems an idyllic Christmas in Cornwall. Cornwall can be cold and bleak, however, and the house Wycliffe visits is even bleaker and beset by tensions. A young girl who plays the Virgin Mary in the local church play disappears on Christmas Eve. Then her mother is found murdered on Christmas morning. Burley's canny use of atmosphere—especially the way the sullen house overlooking the sea plays on one's nerves—is a strong point of this eerie tale." Booklist

Burley, William John See Burley, W. J. (William John), 1914-

Burnett, W. R. (William Riley), 1899-1982
The asphalt jungle. Knopf 1949 271p o.p.

Story of the planning and execution of a million-dollar jewel robbery by underworld gangsters in a large Midwestern city. With the cooperation of the press, an honest and persistent police commissioner solves the case and also succeeds in curbing a disastrous local crime wave

Burnett, William Riley See Burnett, W. R. (William Riley), 1899-1982

Burnford, Sheila, 1918-1984
Bel Ria. Little, Brown 1978 c1977 215p o.p.

LC 77-21082

"An Atlantic Monthly Press book"

First published 1977 in the United Kingdom

"A British soldier who is fleeing before the advancing German troops first comes upon a small trick dog in a circus caravan. When its owners are killed he takes on the responsibility for it and a monkey that makes a habit of riding on its back. When he is evacuated from France, even when the ship is sunk and they must remain in the water for hours, the three stick together. Sinclair, however, is badly wounded and must be hospitalized, so he entrusts the animals to a sick berth attendant on the ship. The dog, who soon is named Ria, at first is lonely and afraid, while the monkey quickly adapts, though every effort is made to keep them apart. Back on shore briefly, Ria is left with someone who will return him to Sinclair. That night, however, the town is bombed and Ria winds up saving the life of a 76-year-old woman who has been entombed by the debris. She takes him under her wealthy wing and he changes her life." Publ Wkly

"A realistic portrayal of wartime life, and an unsentimental but delightful picture of a remarkable animal, self-reliant, independent, and loving." Libr J

The incredible journey; with illustrations by Carl Burger. Little, Brown 1961 145p il o.p. Amereon reprint available $16.95 (ISBN 0-88410-099-0)

"A half-blind English bull terrier, a sprightly yellow Labrador retriever, and a feisty Siamese cat have resided for eight months with a friend of their owners, who are away on a trip. Then their temporary caretaker leaves them behind in order to take a short vacation. The lonely trio decides to tackle the harsh 250-mile hike across the Canadian wilderness in search of home, despite the human and wild obstacles the group will encounter." Shapiro. Fic for Youth. 3d edition

Burns, Olive Ann
Cold Sassy tree. Ticknor & Fields 1984 391p $21.95

ISBN 0-89919-309-9   LC 84-8570

"Young Will Tweedy lives in a small Georgia town called Cold Sassy in the early 1900s. He is hard working (when pushed) because he has chores to do at home and work to do at his Grandpa Blakeslee's store. That still leaves him time to plan practical jokes with his pals and to overhear family dramas. The biggest drama begins when Grandpa, only three weeks after the death of his wife whom he had dearly loved, marries Miss Love Simpson—young enough to be his daughter. Miss Love has to face not only the town gossip, but also rejection from Will's Mother and Grandpa's other daughter. The story has humor, excitement, and realistic family confrontations." Shapiro. Fic for Youth. 3d edition

Leaving Cold Sassy; the unfinished sequel to Cold Sassy tree; with a reminiscence by Katrina Kenison. Ticknor & Fields 1992 290p il o.p.

LC 92-5561

Available G.K. Hall large print edition

"As she battled cancer, Burns (1924-1990) completed 14 chapters of a sequel to her 1984 bestseller *Cold Sassy Tree* leaving behind at her death part of a 15th chapter and notes on how she intended to develop the novel's characters and plot. This new visit to the fictional town of Cold Sassy, Ga., features the original novel's protagonist, Will Tweedy, now 25. . . . Encouraged by local matchmakers, Will nervously courts schoolteacher Sanna Klein." Publ Wkly

Burns, Olive Ann—*Continued*

"These 15 chapters hint admirably at Ms. Burns's plans to turn from her first book's exterior small-town universe to the interior limbo of a marriage, from an adolescent's rites of passage to an adult's experience of disappointment and despair." N Y Times Book Rev

Burns, Tex, 1908-1988

For works written by this author under other names see L'Amour, Louis, 1908-1988

Burroughs, Edgar Rice, 1875-1950

A Princess of Mars; illustrated by Frank E. Schoonover. McClurg, A.C. 1917 326p o.p.

Expanded version of the author's Under the moons of Mars

"Faced with death at the hands of Apache Indians, the protagonist, John Carter, literally wills his transmigration to Mars, where he finds the dying Barsoom torn by strife. The plot is simple; Carter literally fights his way across the planet, gaining respect and friendship from everyone because of his military prowess. After many struggles, he and Dejah Thoris, princess of Helium, live happily for nine years, but then the atmosphere plant breaks down so that Barsoom will suffocate. Carter remembers the 'thought waves' by which the plant may be opened, but the stress and lack of oxygen are such that he falls unconscious and wakes in the cave in Arizona where he had been trapped by Apaches. Thus, he does not know what has occured on Mars." Anatomy of Wonder

Busch, Frederick, 1941-

The children in the woods; new and selected stories. Ticknor & Fields 1994 338p $21.95

ISBN 0-395-64724-X   LC 93-5008

Analyzed in Short story index

Contents: Bread; Bring your friends to the zoo; Is anyone left this time of year?; A three-legged race; The trouble with being food; How the Indians come home; Widow water; The lesson of the Hôtel Lotti; My father, cont.; What you might as well call love; The settlement of Mars; Critics; Stand, and be recognized; Ralph the duck; Dog song; One more wave of fear; The world began with Charlie Chan; Extra extra large; The wicked stepmother; Folk tales; Dream abuse; The page; Berceuse

"Busch's magical, moving stories cut to the bone, revealing concealed fears, pains and hopes as he surveys the wreckage of fractured families, embattled marriages, ruptured lives." Publ Wkly

Closing arguments. Ticknor & Fields 1991 288p $19.95

ISBN 0-395-58968-1   LC 90-28144

"Mark Brennan was a Marine pilot who became a prisoner of the Vietcong. Now a lawyer in upstate New York, he confronts a failing marriage, a troubled son, and a dangerously seductive client on trial for murdering her lover in a motel bed." Libr J

The author "delves unflinchingly into the dark, bleakly erotic, and terrifying realm of intimate violence, masterfully peeling back each layer of deception, brutality, and suicidal desire. . . . Busch has ventured boldly and surefootedly out into forbidding territory. A gripping, sorrowful, and potent work." Booklist

Long way from home. Ticknor & Fields 1993 292p $21.95

ISBN 0-395-63415-6   LC 92-40727

"Adopted soon after birth by Lizzie and Will Mastracola, Sarah, now in her early thirties, enjoys a seemingly perfect life until an ad in the personals of the local newspaper asks, 'Am I your mother?' and Sarah answers 'yes.' Responding to the 'emergency feeling' precipitated by the ad, Sarah abandons husband and son to seek out her biological mother, setting into motion a series of events that ultimately ends in tragedy." Libr J

"At once rational and emotional, this book is especially touching, for Busch feels empathy for everyone involved. And to say his writing is elegant is not to suggest it's precious and thin-blooded, but, rather, that it relates exactly what's on his mind with sheer fluency." Booklist

Butler, Gwendoline

Coffin and the Paper Man. St. Martin's Press 1991 c1990 200p $16.95

ISBN 0-312-05835-7   LC 91-4485

"A Thomas Dunne book"

First published 1990 in the United Kingdom

"The brutal murder of a young girl polarizes the inhabitants of the newly gentrified London neighborhood under the jurisdiction of police chief commander John Coffin. . . . Victim Anna Mary Kinver belonged to a working-class family long resident in the area, while one of the suspects, Tim Zeman, is the son of a well-to-do doctor. Although a blood-soaked vagrant seems a more likely suspect at first, anonymous letters signed 'Paper Man' threaten vengeance if the police don't arrest Tim." Publ Wkly

"The author manages the tricky feat of advancing her narrative entirely through understatement: oblique conversations eventually reveal everything. There is nothing overt, yet nothing is left to chance." Booklist

A coffin for Charley. St. Martin's Press 1994 223p $20.95

ISBN 0-312-11466-4   LC 94-12920

First published 1993 in the United Kingdom

A Thomas Dunne book

London policeman John Coffin's "latest case involves his new wife, actress Stella Pinero, who senses she's being followed by a mysterious watcher who could be harmless—or extremely dangerous. Then Annie Briggs, a disturbed young woman who's an admirer of Stella's, also reports being watched. When a young woman is found brutally strangled nearby, and when shortly afterward one of the apprentice actresses in Stella's repertory company is also found dead, Coffin is fearful that the killer may be the same mysterious watcher who has been frightening Stella and Annie. . . . For readers who enjoy literate, intelligent, thoughtful writing and the challenge of a bizarre and twisted plot." Booklist

Coffin in the Museum of Crime. St. Martin's Press 1990 206p $16.95

ISBN 0-312-04282-5   LC 89-78048

"A Thomas Dunne book"

"After a severed head is delivered to detective John Coffin's doorstep, his investigation targets a local theater troupe and a crime museum." Booklist

Butler, Gwendoline—*Continued*
"The tightly constructed narrative offers a perplexing crime, neatly solved, as well as fascinating portraits of intellectuals, children and memorable working-class characters, all interacting believably." Publ Wkly

Coffin on Murder Street. St. Martin's Press 1992 c1991 219p $17.95

ISBN 0-312-07673-8   LC 92-1074

"A Thomas Dunne book"
First published 1991 in the United Kingdom
Scotland Yard's "John Coffin has reached the apex of his career; the revitalized Docklands are his domain. His flat is high above the river, in a converted church, where he shares space with the theater group his half-sister runs and the flat his occasional lover lives in. Still, it is crime that dominates the days and nights of Inspector Coffin. . . . The first crime is the disappearance and poisoning of a coach full of Americans, among them, inexplicably, a local legend—a busybody with a knack of knowing about crime before the coppers do. The second crime starts with threats and ends with violence, as the young son of the theater's leading lady vanishes." Booklist
The author "breathes life and energy into her well-crafted tale, set in the vibrant Second City, an area of London resembling the Docklands." Publ Wkly

Cracking open a coffin. St. Martin's Press 1993 c1992 239p $18.95

ISBN 0-312-09777-8   LC 93-25501
Also available Thorndike Press large print edition
"A Thomas Dunne book"
First published 1992 in the United Kingdom
"London police commander Coffin's investigation of the murder of a young university student takes him into an odd assortment of settings (theaters, hospitals, refuges for battered women, university dormitories) where he encounters plenty of curious characters, many of whom seem guilty, if not of this particular crime, then of something equally dark." Booklist
"Butler deftly integrates the past and present into Coffin's personal and professional lives, portraying him as a pensive character as ready to turn a critical eye on himself as on those whose lives are caught up in the tragedy he hopes to untangle." Publ Wkly

Death lives next door; the first Inspector Coffin mystery. St. Martin's Press 1992 c1960 191p $16.95

ISBN 0-312-08175-8   LC 92-1581
Also available Thorndike Press large print edition
"A Thomas Dunne book"
First published 1960 in the United Kingdom
"Keeping her detective in the wings, [Butler] begins by focusing her narrative on a gang of shabby, bitter academic types in Oxford, at the center of which dysfunctional clique is the famous and slightly mysterious Marion Manning, watched by a man who in time will claim to be her long lost husband. Everything in Marion's past is weird, and as Coffin is drawn out of London into this narrow little world, it is the investigation of this mysterious past that forms the heart of the book. Butler's regulars shouldn't pass up the chance for this peek at Coffin's past." Booklist

Butler, Octavia E.
Adulthood rites. Warner Bks. 1988 277p (Xenogenesis) o.p.

LC 87-34620

In the second novel in the Xenogenesis trilogy "the alien Oankali have rescued the dying remnants of humanity after Earth's nuclear war. Now, though, the children of the two races, called constructs, are resented and feared by the original survivors. This is the story of one such construct, Akin, who possesses an adult mind and voice before he is two years old. Stolen by a barren human community, he grows up knowing both races." Publ Wkly
Followed by Imago

Dawn; [by] Octavia Butler. Warner Bks. 1987 264p (Xenogenesis) o.p.

LC 87-6195

In this first volume in the Xenogenesis trilogy "a band of nuclear holocaust survivors is in the hands of an alien race that offers to save them. The price is high though: the survivors must participate in the evolution of the aliens by bearing children that incorporate some of the aliens' characteristics. Butler is one of the few sf writers who can handle effectively a slow-moving plot that emphasizes characters' emotions. Her command of the language is superior, and her aliens are quite convincing creations." Booklist
Followed by Adulthood rites

Imago. Warner Bks. 1989 c1985 264p (Xenogenesis) o.p.

LC 88-27975

First published 1985 in the United Kingdom
The concluding volume of the Xenogenesis trilogy "considers a post-holocaust humanity whose only chance for survival is to be absorbed by the alien Oankali. Totally uninterested in domination, this race thrives on a symbiosis that Earthlings find difficult to credit. That distrust hampers the narrator, an ooloi (neuter) named Jodahs, as it tries to find life partners in the same ratio as its five parents: a human couple, an Oankali couple and itself, the essential ooloi who joins all five and melds their genetic legacy. Butler's achievement here is less the abstract reassignment of sexual roles than a warmth and urgency that dramatizes and personalizes these conflicts and transformations." Publ Wkly

Parable of the sower. Four Walls Eight Windows 1993 299p $19.95

ISBN 0-941423-99-9   LC 93-8703

"Written in diary form, *Parable* chronicles the sometimes grim adventures of Lauren Olamina, an adolescent girl living in a barricaded village in Southern California amid the rampant socioeconomic decay of the early twenty-first century. After her neighborhood is overrun by a cult of drug-demented pyromaniacs, Lauren takes to the road and bands together with other refugees of violent attacks." Booklist
The author "infuses this tale with an allegorical quality that is part meditation, part warning. Simple, direct, and deeply felt, this should reach both mainstream and sf audiences." Libr J

Survivor. Doubleday 1978 185p o.p.

LC 77-81548

"Doubleday science fiction"
"The title character is Alanna Verrick, a wild human adopted by Missionaries and carried to a distant planet occupied by warring tribes: the Gharkohn and the Tehkohn. The Missionaries are devoted to spreading the sacred God-image of humankind; they find the hair-covered humanoid Kohn repulsive, and naturally they choose to side with the wrong tribe, considering both

Butler, Octavia E.—*Continued*

more animal than human. Too late they discover just how human the Kohn are, human enough to breed with Earthlings." Best Sellers

"The suspense keeps the reader interested and the satire is effective." Libr J

Butler, Robert Olen

They whisper; a novel. Holt & Co. 1994 333p $22.50

    ISBN 0-8050-1985-5   LC 93-38261

"Middle-aged Vietnam vet Ira Holloway is obsessed with women, seeking a connection to life's deeper mysteries through his numerous sexual trysts. While this novel initially seems a mere sexual memoir, it soon becomes clear that Butler is concerned with hunger for God as much as flesh. Holloway recounts the breakdown of his marriage to the troubled Fiona, a woman whose fragile consciousness is held together by an increasingly fanatical devotion to Roman Catholicism. Throughout, Butler explores the contrast between Fiona's austere, guilt-based faith and Ira's search for spiritual meaning through the physical." Libr J

"While the descriptions of erotic love are integral to the plot, the highly charged sensuality, the details of the rising stages of lust and the relentless stream-of-consciousness monologue sometimes grow wearisome." Publ Wkly

Butler, Samuel, 1835-1902

The way of all flesh. Knopf 1992 374p $17

    ISBN 0-679-41718-4   LC 92-52916
    Also available from Amereon and Buccaneer Bks.
    "Everyman's library"
    First published posthumously 1903; first Everyman's library edition 1933

The theme of this semi-autobiographical novel "is the hypocrisy and smug complacency of English middle-class life, and particularly the relationship between parents and children, which is traced through several generations of the Pontifex family. . . . 'The Way of All Flesh' is generally regarded as a very original work: it exercised considerable influence on later English writers. 'It contains records of the things I saw happening rather than imaginary incidents,' said the author. Undoubtedly this novel has a strong vein of autobiography." Haydn. Thesaurus of Book Dig

Butters, Dorothy Gilman *See* Gilman, Dorothy, 1923-

Butterworth, W. E. (William Edmund), 1929-
For works written by this author in collaboration with H. Richard Hornberger see Hooker, Richard

Byatt, A. S. (Antonia Susan), 1936-

Angels and insects; two novellas. Turtle Bay Bks. 1993 c1991 339p $21

    ISBN 0-679-40512-7   LC 92-56806

    First published 1991 in the United Kingdom

"In 'Morpho Eugenia' penniless young entomologist William Adamson has just returned from a 10-year expedition in the Amazon. William is taken in by a titled clergyman with scientific pretensions, and soon marries his benefactor's beautiful daughter. Unable to undertake another Amazon adventure, he studies domestic ant colonies and discovers indecent parallels between the insects and his new family. 'The Conjugial Angel' involves a circle of spiritualists, chief among them Alfred Tennyson's sister Emily, in her youth engaged to Arthur Hallam, the man immortalized in Tennyson's *In Memoriam*. Emily has been branded faithless for having married years after Hallam's death, . . . but she is uncompromising in her pursuit of Hallam's ghost. . . . Complex and captivating, this fluid volume recasts itself on every page." Publ Wkly

The conjugial angel

   In Byatt, A. S. Angels and insects

Morpho Eugenia

   In Byatt, A. S. Angels and insects

Possession; a romance. Random House 1990 555p $22.95

    ISBN 0-394-58623-9   LC 90-8374

The protagonist of this novel, Roland Mitchell, "is a postdoctoral research student. Working in the London Library of the Victorian poet Ash, he comes upon an interchange of letters between Ash and an unknown woman. . . . A series of clues lead him to believe the recipient of Ash's affections might be Christabel Lamotte, a Victorian poet of much interest . . . to feminist critics, and his quest for information about Lamotte leads him to the beautiful scholar Dr. Maud Bailey. Together Roland and Dr. Bailey unearth letters which establish the details of an intense and hitherto unsuspected relationship between these poets, and form one of their own." New Statesman Soc

"Intelligent, ingenious and humane, [this] bids fair to be looked back upon as one of the most memorable novels of the 1990s." Times Lit Suppl

Byatt, Antonia Susan *See* Byatt, A. S. (Antonia Susan), 1936-

C

Cabell, James Branch, 1879-1958

Jurgen: a comedy of justice; with twelve illustrations by Ray F. Coyle. McBride Co. 1919 368p il o.p.

    Available from Amereon, Buccaneer Bks. and P. Smith

This novel "chronicles the adventures of a pawnbroker named Jurgen who, motivated by guilt and gossip, sets off reluctantly in search of Dame Lisa, his loquacious, nagging wife who has been abducted by the Devil. Along the way, Jurgen encounters Dorothy, the love of his youth, who does not recognize him. Through the power granted him by the earth goddess, he relives one day with Dorothy. Jurgen and legendary women such as Guinevere share erotic experiences. Jurgen and his wife are ultimately reunited." Merriam-Webster's Ency of Lit

Cady, Jack, 1932-

The night we buried Road Dog

   In Nebula awards 29 p242-96

Cain, James M. (James Mallahan), 1892-1977

Cain x 3; three novels; with a new introduction by Tom Wolfe. Knopf 1969 465p o.p.

Contents: The postman always rings twice (1934); Mildred Pierce (1934); Double indemnity (1943)

The first story concerns a young vagrant and a restaurant keeper's wife who plan to murder the latter's husband; the second is a study of a grass widow, her husband and a daughter who becomes a monster; the last deals with an insurance salesman who plots the perfect murder

Cain's "violent, sexually obsessed, and relentlessly paced melodramas epitomized the hard-boiled fiction that flourished in the U.S. in the 1930s and '40s." Merriam-Webster's Ency of Lit

Double indemnity

In Cain, J. M. Cain x 3 p363-465

Mildred Pierce

In Cain, J. M. Cain x 3 p103-362

The postman always rings twice

In Cain, J. M. Cain x 3 p1-101

Caldwell, Erskine, 1903-1987

Complete stories of Erskine Caldwell. Little, Brown 1953 664p o.p. Amereon reprint available $34.95 (ISBN 0-88411-455-4)

Analyzed in Short story index

Contents: After-image; August afternoon; Automobile that wouldn't run; Autumn courtship; Back on the road; Balm of Gilead; Big Buck; Blue Boy; Candy-man Beechum; Carnival; Cold winter; Corduroy pants; Country full of Swedes; Courting of Susie Brown; Crownfire; Daughter; Day the presidential candidate came to Ciudad Tamaulipas; Day's wooing; Dorothy; The dream; Empty room; End of Christy Tucker; Evelyn and the rest of us; Evening in Nuevo Leon; First autumn; Fly in the coffin; Girl Ellen; Grass fire; Growing season; Hamrick's polar bear; Handy; Here and today; Honeymoon; Horse thief; Indian summer; It happened like this; Joe Craddock's old woman; John the Indian and George Hopkins; Kneel to the rising sun; Knife to cut the corn bread with; Lonely day; Mamma's little girl; Man and woman; Man who looked like himself; Martha Jean; Masses of men; Mating of Marjorie; Maud Island; Meddlesome Jack; Medicine man; Memorandum; Midsummer passion; Midwinter guest; Molly Cotton-Tail; Negro in the well; New cabin; Nine dollars' worth of mumble; Over the Green Mountains; People v Abe Lathan, colored; People's choice; Picking cotton; The picture; Priming the well; Rachel; Return to Lavinia; The rumor; Runaway; Saturday afternoon; Savannah River payday; The shooting; Sick horse; Slow death; Small day; Snacker; Squire Dinwiddy; Strawberry season; Summer accident; The Sunfield; Swell-looking girl; Ten thousand blueberry crates; Thunderstorm; Uncle Henry's love nest; Uncle Jeff; Very late spring; The visitor; Walnut hunt; Warm river; We are looking at you, Agnes; Where the girls were different; Wild flowers; The windfall; Woman in the house; Yellow girl

God's little acre; foreword by Lewis Nordan. University of Ga. Press 1995 211p $25

ISBN 0-8203-1662-8   LC 94-20454

Also available from Amereon

"Brown Thrasher books"

A reissue of the title first published 1933 by Viking

"A Georgia 'cracker,' Ty Ty Walden, has devoted 15 years to digging for gold on his farm. Always a 'religious man,' he has set aside one acre whose income shall go to the church, but has had to shift 'God's little acre' constantly, so as not to interfere with the digging. Ty Ty's sincere but adaptable morality appears also in the shiftless lives of his children." Oxford Companion to Am Lit. 5th edition

Tobacco road; foreword by Lewis Nordan. University of Ga. Press 1995 184p $25

ISBN 0-8203-1660-1   LC 94-13090

Also available from Bentley and Buccaneer Bks.

"Brown Thrasher books"

A reissue of the title first published 1932 by Scribner

"Jeeter Lester is an impoverished Georgia sharecropper who lives on Tobacco Road with his starving old mother, his sickly wife Ada, and his two children, 16-year-old Dude and Ellie May, who has a harelip. A third child, Pearl, has been married at the age of 12 to Lov Bensey, a railroad worker. When Jeeter's widowed preacher sister Bessie Rice induces Dude to marry her by buying him a new automobile, Dude accidentally wrecks the car and kills his grandmother. Pearl runs away from Lov Bensey; Ellie May happily goes to live with him; and Jeeter and Ada, left alone one night, perish when their shack burns down." Reader's Ency. 3d edition

Caldwell, Taylor, 1900-1985

Answer as a man. Putnam 1981 c1980 445p o.p. Amereon reprint available $27.95 (ISBN 0-88411-143-1)

LC 80-18187

"Set in a small Pennsylvania boomtown in the first decade of the 20th century, . . . this is the story of Jason Garrity, son of devoutly Roman Catholic, Irish immigrants who rises from delivery boy to wealthy resort hotel entrepreneur. In the course of his ascent, Jason confronts religious hypocrisy, political corruption, financial scandal, ethnic prejudice, martial discord, family upheavals." Publ Wkly

Captains and kings. Doubleday 1972 640p o.p. Buccaneer Bks. reprint available $37.95 (ISBN 1-56849-258-8)

This novel follows the growth of an Irish immigrant family from complete poverty to a position of wealth and political power. Joseph Armagh is ruled by the desire for money and overcome by ambition for his children. Along the way the family seems to have acquired a curse, so that the second generation of Armaghs reaps only misfortune and destruction

"Through all this saga one cannot help but find some parallels with the Kennedy saga, set back to the period 1850-1915. Portraits of some characters, rather bitterly slanted, are certainly more than coincidental." Publ Wkly

Caldwell, Taylor, 1900-1985—*Continued*

Ceremony of the innocent. Doubleday 1976 422p o.p.

Set in Pennsylvania and New York City at the turn-of-the-century this is an "allegory in which a naive servant girl (a cross between Candide and Cinderella) marries her Prince Charming. Always the innocent dupe of jealous and evil persons, she is eventually driven to suicide by her own avaricious children. Key to the allegory is a fatally ingenuous America drawn into the stock market crash of 1929 by her enemies." Booklist

Dear and glorious physician. Doubleday 1959 574p o.p. Buccaneer Bks. reprint available $37.95 (ISBN 1-56849-242-1)

This novel about Lucanus, or Luke, "physician and author of one of the Gospels, depicts him as an individual apart, plainly marked out for the service of God in spite of his almost lifelong protest against a deity who inflicted pain on men. Antioch, scene of his boyhood; Rome, where he visited his family in the intervals between his restless travels; Alexandria, where he was educated; and Judaea, where he learned the story of Jesus from his mother Mary and acknowledged him as the Christ, provide a background." Booklist

"Gripping and absorbing reading that illuminates a period and highlights the development of a man being prepared for God's purpose. The sweep and greatness of the story dwarf any defects in style." Wis Libr Bull

Great lion of God. Doubleday 1970 629p o.p.

Based upon the Biblical character, St. Paul, or Saul of Tarshish. "This very long novel covers Paul's life from the time of his birth and ends with his departure from Palestine for Rome, covering too the Biblical story of Jesus as it related to Paul, his first disbelief in the new Messiah and his conversion after the Crucifixion and Resurrection." Publ Wkly

"The book is backed by extensive research, supporting Miss Caldwell's obvious concern and seriousness about its religious and social implications." Libr J

I, Judas; [by] Taylor Caldwell and Jess Stearn. Atheneum Pubs. 1977 371p o.p.

"A first-person narrative which draws heavily on the four Gospel accounts and offers an explanation for Judas' betrayal of Jesus. It presents Judas as the betrayed: by authorities who promise acquittal, and by his own reasoning that the man who demonstrated power over death by raising Lazarus surely could not himself die. Wrong on both counts, his name became synonymous with treachery. By adhering closely to the biblical version in familiar parts of the story, the authors render their interpretation quite plausible and unthreatening to adherents of received word." Booklist

The authors "have dealt brilliantly with the issue of perspective and therein lies the value of their work." Best Sellers

Testimony of two men. Doubleday 1968 605p o.p. Amereon reprint available $27.95 (ISBN 0-88411-171-7)

"Jonathan Ferrier is the central character. He is dedicated to perfection—to perfect asepsis when few doctors yet acknowledged or even knew the need for it in 1901, and to perfect truth in human relations. Ironically, he himself has been tried for the murder of his wife and justly acquitted. The verdict was not acceptable to his community. Since they are incapable of the perfection he vocally demands, the people around him hate him and are delighted by an apparent opportunity to condemn him." Libr J

"Caldwell combines incisive characterization with an absorbing description of nineteenth-century medical practices." Booklist

Calisher, Hortense

The collected stories of Hortense Calisher. Arbor House 1975 502p o.p.

Analyzed in Short story index

Contents: In Greenwich there are many gravelled walks; Heartburn; The night club in the woods; Two colonials; The hollow boy; The rehabilitation of Ginevra Leake; The woman who was everybody; A Christmas carillon; Il ploe:r dã mõ koe:r, If you don't want to live I can't help you; A wreath for Miss Totten; Time, gentlemen; May-ry; The Coreopsis Kid; A box of ginger; The pool of Narcissus; The watchers; The gulf between; The sound of waiting; Old stock; The rabbi's daughter; The middle drawer; The summer rebellion; What a thing, to keep a wolf in a cage; Songs my mother taught me; So many rings to the show; One of the chosen; Point of departure; Letitia, Emeritus; The seacoast of Bohemia; Mrs. Fay dines on zebra; Saturday night; Little did I know; Night riders of Northville; In the absence of angels; The scream of Fifty-seventh Street

"The stories themselves are a remarkably varied lot, for Miss Calisher knows the pitch and flavor of a great many voices, both of the upper- and lower-middleclass sort. Caste and class is her subject, and one nowhere more compellingly grounded than in her sketches of childhood, in which the society of the classroom and the schoolyard is portrayed in all its biting and complex reality." Saturday Rev

Calling the wind; twentieth-century African-American short stories; edited and with an introduction by Clarence Major. HarperCollins Pubs. 1992 xxvi, 622p $30

ISBN 0-06-018337-3   LC 92-52620

"An Edward Burlingame book"

Analyzed in Short story index

Contents: The goophered grapevine, by C. Chesnutt; The ingrate, by P. L. Dunbar; Mary Elizabeth, by J. Fauset; Esther, by J. Toomer; The hands: a story, by M. Bonner; Sanctuary, by N. Larsen; Truant, by C. McKay; A summer tragedy, by A. Bontemps; Miss Cynthie, by R. Fisher; The gilded six-bits, by Z. N. Hurston; Headwaiter, by C. Himes; Bright and morning star, by R. Wright; Jack in the pot, by D. West; Flying home, by R. Ellison; Who's passing for who?, by L. Hughes; The only man on Liberty Street, by W. M. Kelley; Come out the wilderness, by J. Baldwin; Has anybody seen Miss Dora Dean?, by A. Petry; Mother Dear and Daddy, by J. Edwards; Blues for Pablo, by J. Stewart; Son in the afternoon, by J. A. Williams; What's your problem?, by R. Boles; The distributors, by H. Dumas; Wade, by R. Guy; Key to the city, by D. Oliver; The alternative, by A. Baraka; To Da-duh, in memoriam, by P. Marshall; A new day, by C. Wright; Night and the loves of Joe Dicostanzo, by S. R. Delany; The lookout, by C. Colter; A long day in November, by E. J. Gaines; The lesson, by T. C. Bambara; The story of a scar, by J. A. McPherson; Soldiers, by E. Southerland; Roselily, by A. Walker; White rat, by G. Jones; Loimos, by E. N.

Calling the wind—*Continued*

White; The education of Mingo, by C. Johnson; Scat, by C. Major; Now is the time, by C. M. Brown; Damballah, by J. E. Wideman; Kiswana Browne, by G. Naylor; "Recitatif", by T. Morrison; Girl, by J. Kincaid; Chitterling, by H. Van Dyke; Jesus and Fat Tuesday, by C. J. McElroy; The world of Rosie Polk, by A. A. Shockley; Mali is very dangerous, by R. McKnight; Her Mother's prayers on fire, by D. Belton; Wings of the dove, by H. Bennett; Zazoo, by L. Duplechan; Guess who's coming to seder, by T. Ellis; Top of the game, by J. McCluskey; Going to meet Aaron, by R. Perry; Willie Bea and Jaybird, by T. M. Ansa; Screen memory, by M. Cliff; Age would be that does, by P. Everett; Going for the moon, by A. Young; Quilting on the rebound, by T. McMillan.

Calvino, Italo

Cosmicomics; translated from the Italian by William Weaver. Harcourt 1968 153p o.p.

"A Helen and Kurt Wolff book"
Analyzed in Short story index
Original Italian edition, 1965
Contents: The distance of the moon; At daybreak; A sign in space; All at one point; Without colors; Games without end; The aquatic uncle; How much shall we bet; The dinosaurs; The form of space; The light-years; The spiral

These twelve "imaginative and deeply philosophical stories, escape classification into a genre—mathematical formulas, gases, and man's evolutionary ancestors are among the characters; the plot is the creation of the universe." Libr J

If on a winter's night a traveler. Knopf 1993 c1981 254p $15

ISBN 0-679-42025-8   LC 92-54302

"Everyman's library"
Original Italian edition, 1979; this is a reissue of the edition published 1981 by Harcourt Brace Jovanovich
Translated by William Weaver
The novel "begins with a man discovering that the copy of a novel he has recently purchased is defective, a Polish novel having been bound within its pages. He returns to the bookshop the following day and meets a young woman who is on an identical mission. They both profess a preference for the Polish novel. Interposed between the chapters in which the two strangers attempt to authenticate their texts are 10 excerpts that parody genres of contemporary world fiction, such as the Latin-American novel and the political novel of eastern Europe." Merriam-Webster's Ency of Lit

Invisible cities; translated from the Italian by William Weaver. Harcourt Brace Jovanovich 1974 165p o.p.

"A Helen and Kurt Wolff book"
Original Italian edition, 1972
"Marco Polo, the traveler, describes to Kublai Khan (his patron) the various cities of the Khan's vast empire. The cities, which all have women's names, are metaphors for different kinds of people and the varied relationships they may form. . . . They progress from medieval to modern times, growing steadily in complexity and malignancy." Libr J

"Italo Calvino is recognized as one of the consummate stylists among writers today, a novelist whose superbly imaginative mind conjures up metaphorical fables of exquisite beauty to transcribe his personal visions of man and the universe." Choice

Mr. Palomar; translated from the Italian by William Weaver. Harcourt Brace Jovanovich 1985 c1983 130p $12.95

ISBN 0-15-162835-1   LC 85-5490

"A Helen and Kurt Wolff book"
Original Italian edition, 1983
"'A nervous man who lives in a frenzied and congested world, Mr. Palomar tends to reduce his relations with the outside world; and, to defend himself against the general neurasthenia, he tries to keep his sensations under control insofar as possible.' . . . Calvino [seeks to] lead the reader into three levels of experience—visual, cultural, speculative—in the life of Mr. Palomar. We watch Mr. Palomar on vacation, in the city, and silently thinking." Libr J
"There is an almost perfect sense of complementary relationships: Calvino is delicate and strong, his precision is lyric and mathematic; the equation between perceiver and perceived is made infinitely and effortlessly complex but remains exact. The care which Calvino has lavished on the formal arrangement of his book should not, however, lead us to think that it offers only a formal resolution of compositional intricacies, for Mr. Palomor is a work of cunning dialectics that goes beyond the delight in paradoxes for which Calvino is lazily praised." New Statesman

Under the jaguar sun; translated by William Weaver. Harcourt Brace Jovanovich 1988 86p $12.95

ISBN 0-15-192820-7   LC 88-835

"A Helen and Kurt Wolff book"
Analyzed in Short story index
Contents: Under the jaguar sun; A king listens; The name, the nose
"Taste, hearing, and smell become the driving forces behind Calvino's characters in these three stories, which were to have been a part of the late Italian writer's projected series on the five senses. A couple vacationing in Mexico become inflamed by the local cuisine and by certain cannibalistic practices of the Aztecs; a mad monarch's paranoia is piqued by overheard rumblings; and a Parisian dandy goes off on the trail of a beautiful woman identified only by her alluring scent. With their mixture of the ordinary and the exotic, these stories are masterful miniatures." Booklist

Campbell, Bebe Moore

Brothers and sisters. Putnam 1994 476p $22.95

ISBN 0-399-13929-X   LC 94-14196

"Set in the heart of a Los Angeles still troubled by the aftermath of the April riots, the novel draws a . . . portrait of the internal and external conflicts regarding race experienced by characters of varied backgrounds. The story centers on Esther Jackson, an African American with a promising career in banking who is torn between her need to succeed professionally and her loyalty to other people of color." Libr J

Campbell, Bebe Moore—*Continued*

"What makes 'Brothers and Sisters' different from the traditional potboiler is Ms. Campbell's genuine attempt to address the complexities of race in the modern age." N Y Times Book Rev

Your blues ain't like mine. Putnam 1992 332p $22.95

ISBN 0-399-13746-7   LC 91-45518

"In Ms. Campbell's story, a young black man, Armstrong Todd, visiting from Chicago in 1955, is murdered in Hopewell, Miss., by a white man. Reporters from New York are secretly summoned by an influential citizen of Hopewell, and as a consequence of the resulting news media attention there is, uncharacteristically, a trial. After the trial, the novel follows the lives of Armstrong's relatives in Mississippi—and in Chicago, where Armstrong's mother, Delotha Todd, starts a new and difficult life, raising another son. The novel also follows the lives of the murderer, Floyd Cox, and his family." N Y Times Book Rev

"Written in poetic prose, filled with masterfully drawn and sympathetic characters that a less able hand might have rendered in stereotypes, this first novel blends the irony of Flannery O'Connor's fiction and the poignance of Harper Lee's." Publ Wkly

Campbell, R. Wright, 1927-

Boneyards; [by] Robert Campbell. Pocket Bks. 1992 298p o.p.

LC 92-14938

Available Thorndike Press large print edition

"Ex-cop Ray Sharkey has just been released from prison, where he was sent for killing the murderers of Roma Chounard, a black hooker and Sharkey's lover. Back in Chicago for the funeral of his sister, Sharkey turns his thoughts to the past and to the curious chain of events that led to his imprisonment. Mostly, he was a cop gone bad, corrupted by the system and by circumstances, but he was also father, husband, brother, son, and lover, molded by his Irish Catholic upbringing and a master at using 'Irish honey-cake' (sweet talk) to get his way." Booklist

"Mr. Campbell's mournful elegy for Ray Sharkey is both an eloquent character study of a good man gone bad and an indictment of the political corruption that makes his ruination seem inevitable." N Y Times Book Rev

The cat's meow; a Jimmy Flannery mystery; [by] Robert Campbell. New Am. Lib. 1988 199p o.p.

LC 88-9880

"Strange doings abound at St. Pat's church. First the priest's cat dies; then, after Father Mulrooney reports the ghost of the cat haunting the old church at night, the priest himself expires, and his body is found at the altar, surrounded by sacrificial blood and painted pentagrams. Fortunately, Chicago sewer inspector Jimmy Flannery appears on the scene, like an urban white knight rising from the devilish morass." Booklist

"The colorful characters and smooth writing all make for a captivating read. If there isn't a major mystery here, readers won't mind." Publ Wkly

In La-La Land we trust; [by] Robert Campbell. Mysterious Press 1986 528p o.p.

LC 86-47548

"A two-car collision at the rain-slicked corner of Hollywood and Vine results in one dead driver and one headless female corpse. When eyewitness Whistler, down-at-the-heels private eye, discovers a cover-up . . . he starts his own investigation. A blonde TV starlet and a mysterious millionaire are involved. Soon Whistler learns that the starlet, lured to New Orleans with promises of a movie role, is in danger, and he must stop the movie from turning into a 'snuff' film." Publ Wkly

"Although his dialogue can be bawdy, although the situations can be raw and gritty, Mr. Campbell does not play up the sex. All Mr. Campbell has to do, which he does, is have Whistler present a dispassionate account of the activity without any moralizing or indignation. Whistler is in many ways a very modern reincarnation of Hammett's Continental Op. . . . Mr. Campbell is one of the most stylish crime writers in the business." NY Times Book Rev

Nibbled to death by ducks; [by] Robert Campbell. Pocket Bks. 1989 220p o.p.

"Jimmy Flannery, Chicago sewer inspector and Democratic Party Precinct Captain, returns from a vacation with his wife Mary to find that his old friend Delvin is in Larkspur Nursing Home. Delvin's housekeeper has died and the old gentleman has been committed to the nursing home by a mysterious 'cousin,' Francis Carmody. When Jimmy goes to Larkspur to visit Delvin, he gets the distinct feeling that something is amiss. . . . Jimmy is a delightful, colorful character who obviously knows his way around Chicago—in the precincts, sewers, and City Hall." Voice Youth Advocates

Campbell, Ramsey, 1946-

(ed) Best new horror [1]-4. See Best new horror [1]-4

The Count of Eleven. TOR Bks. 1992 310p o.p.

LC 92-1097

"A Tom Doherty Associates book"

"Jack Orchard is not only a clumsy oaf with a genius for the ill-timed and inappropriate joke but also the victim of a stretch of very bad luck. He decides his ill fortune is caused by those who failed to pass on the chain letter he sent them—so he kills them with a blowtorch. Comedy alternates with horror as Jack's personality becomes increasingly split between his own bumbling self and his efficiently murderous alter ego, the Count of Eleven. This novel will appeal to a broad group of readers beyond Campbell's horror-fan base." Libr J

The long lost. TOR Bks. 1994 c1993 375p $22.95

ISBN 0-312-85825-6   LC 94-21751

"A Tom Doherty Associates book"

First published 1993 in the United Kingdom

"On vacation in Wales, David and Joelle Owain discover Gwen, an old woman asleep in a small cottage on a deserted island created by the tides. Amazingly, she claims to be a distant relative and returns with the Owains to Chester. After a backyard barbecue, where Gwen meets the family's friends and neighbors, misfortunes begin to dog the guests, causing David to wonder just who and what Gwen really is. . . . Disturbing and original, this neat mix of contemporary fiction with supernatural undertones is recommended for most collections." Libr J

Campbell, Ramsey, 1946-—*Continued*
Medusa

In Campbell, R. Strange things and stranger places p38-91

The Nameless. Macmillan 1981 229p o.p.
LC 81-8582

"Barbara Waugh's ordeal began with the kidnapping and apparent murder of her four-year-old daughter Angela. Nine years later, now an established literary agent, she starts getting phone calls from a girl claiming to be her daughter. At first she doesn't believe, but events soon compel Waugh's belief. Few will help her, though, and those who do suffer horribly. The trail leads to the Nameless, a group described as 'making the Manson Family look like Disneyland.' Tapping the human need to be part of something larger than the individual self, this cult brutally tortures and murders other human beings. Angela Waugh has a more important role than mere cult member, however, Barbara Waugh doesn't learn the truth until the final chapters." West Coast Rev Books

"After some initial confusion, and although one wishes Barbara were a less passive character, this develops into a quietly mesmerizing tale of terror." Publ Wkly

Needing ghosts

In Campbell, R. Strange things and stranger places p166-256

Strange things and stranger places. TOR Bks. 1993 256p $18.95
ISBN 0-312-85514-1   LC 93-12758
"A Tom Doherty Associates book"
Analyzed in Short story index
Contents: Cat and mouse; Medusa [novella]; Rising generation; Run through; Wrapped up; Passing phase; A new life; The next sideshow; Little man; Needing ghosts [novella]
This collection frequently displays the author's "remarkable talent for twisting the ordinary into the darkly surreal." Publ Wkly

Campbell, Robert, 1927- *See* Campbell, R. Wright, 1927-

Camus, Albert, 1913-1960
Nobel Prize in literature, 1957
Exile and the kingdom; translated from the French by Justin O'Brien. Knopf 1958 213p o.p. Amereon reprint available $19.95 (ISBN 0-8488-0444-9)
Analyzed in Short story index
Original French edition, 1957
Contents: The adulterous woman; The renegade; The silent men; The guest; The artist at work; The growing stone
"Discipline of thought and style characterize [these] six short stories. . . . The distinguishing marks of locales ranging from North Africa to Brazil are etched with telling detail, but it is the landscape of man's inner life which is most important here. The diverse protagonists— and it is intimated all men—are exiled from themselves, others, and the life of the spirit, but now and again a word or an action renews their courage to continue the pilgrimage." Booklist

The fall; translated from the French by Justin O'Brien. Knopf 1957 147p o.p.
Original French edition, 1956
"A former Parisian lawyer explains to a stranger in an Amsterdam bar his current profession of judge-penitent. His bitter honesty prevented him first from winning his own self-esteem through good deeds, then from exhausting his own self-condemnation through debauchery. Knowing that no man is ever innocent, he is still trying to forestall personal judgment by confession, by judging others, and by avoiding any situation demanding action." Reader's Ency. 3d edition

The first man; translated from the French by David Hapgood. Knopf 1995 336p $23
ISBN 0-679-43937-4   LC 95-2668
Original French edition, 1994
"When Camus died in an automobile accident in 1960, a manuscript was found near him. It turned out to be the first chapters of his autobiographical novel. . . . The book covers the first 14 years of the life of Jacques Cormery, a.k.a. Albert Camus. First there is a 'search for the father,' the undercurrent of a boy's quest to fill a tragic vacuum created by his father's death when he is only a year old. The poverty and difficult circumstances in which he grows up in French Algeria make him feel like an outsider, even when he becomes an adult. Yet the memories of the child are filled with energy and physical intensity. The spontaneity of the narrative by an otherwise reserved writer makes this book a unique document for anyone interested in Camus." Libr J

A happy death; translated from the French by Richard Howard; afterword and notes by Jean Sarocchi. Knopf 1972 192p o.p.
Written between 1936 and 1938 and first published 1971 in France
"Meursault, whose life is close to that of Camus in his early 20's, kills a well-to-do . . . amputee Zagreus at the latter's suggestion to secure the means for his own pursuit of happiness. Paradoxically, this conquest of life is a quest for death, first spiritually, then physically. Purifying experiences ensue: alienation and illness in Prague, elevation at the House above the World in Algiers, communion and submission in a seaside retreat near Tipasa. When he is at one with inhuman natural forces, then he is ready for a happy death." Choice

The plague; translated from the French by Stuart Gilbert. Knopf 1948 278p $23
ISBN 0-394-44061-7
Original French edition, 1947
"The Algerian port of Oran is overwhelmed by an epidemic of bubonic plague, although modern medicine does its best to quarantine the city and isolate the stricken and the dead within. The emergency forces many to make character-revealing decisions; yet death plays no favorites, and life continues much the same after the calamity. The doctor Bernard Rieux represents those who, despite everything, simply do what they can for the cause of human life and hope for the possibility of occasional human joy." Reader's Ency. 3d edition

The stranger; translated from the French by Matthew Ward. Knopf 1988 123p $16.95
ISBN 0-394-53305-4   LC 83-48885

Camus, Albert, 1913-1960—*Continued*

Original French edition, 1942; published in the United Kingdom with title: The outsider

This novel "reveals the 'Absurd' as the condition of man, who feels himself a stranger in his world. Meursault refuses to 'play the game,' by telling the conventional social white lies demanded of him or by believing in human love or religious faith. The unemotional style of his narrative lays naked his motives—or his absence of motive—for his lack of grief over his mother's death, his affair with Marie, his killing an Arab in the hot Algerian sun. Having rejected by honest self-analysis all interpretations which could explain or justify his existence, he nevertheless discovers, while in prison awaiting execution, a passion for the simple fact of life itself." Reader's Ency. 3d edition

Canin, Ethan

The palace thief. Random House 1994 205p $21

ISBN 0-679-41962-4   LC 93-26888

Also available G.K. Hall large print edition

Analyzed in Short story index

Contents: Accountant; Batorsag and Szerelem; City of broken hearts; The palace thief

This "book presents us with four beautifully told long short stories. In each, a man muses over his past and realizes how little control he has had over pivotal moments in his life. . . . Canin proves himself adept at articulating moments of profound embarrassment followed by flashes of self-knowledge that are either invigorating or demoralizing. Moving and memorable." Booklist

Cannell, Dorothy

Femmes fatal. Bantam Bks. 1992 298p o.p.

LC 92-10745

Available G.K. Hall large print edition

"What with little twins and a cat hogging most of her time, winsome heroine Ellie Haskell . . . secretly joins a woman's group designed to rejuvenate relationships. Ellie's breathless fascination with romantic possibilities involving her gorgeous husband provides much of the humor here and lightens the horror of murder and attempted murder that plague the group. Ellie somehow manages to figure out what's happening despite the intervention of a buxom housekeeper, a nutty cousin, a plain-Jane organist, and her husband's good intentions. A pleasant romp." Libr J

How to murder your mother-in-law. Bantam Bks. 1994 261p $19.95

ISBN 0-553-07493-8   LC 93-31149

Also available G.K. Hall large print edition

"After insisting that husband Ben's parents celebrate their anniversary with them at Merlin's Court, Ellie [Haskell] is dismayed when her in-laws reveal that their religious differences (she's Catholic, he's Jewish) prevented their legal marriage. . . . Then Ellie's father-in-law is caught skinny-dipping with a female friend, prompting mother-in-law Magdalene to leave him. Ellie seeks solace from friends in the village and discovers that everyone is suffering from a surfeit of mothers-in-law. A commiseration session among the afflicted daughters-in-law results in several vividly imagined murder scenarios—which, unfortunately, begin to happen." Booklist

The thin woman; an epicurean mystery. St. Martin's Press 1984 242p o.p.

LC 83-24565

"Overweight, overwrought interior designer Ellie Simons is reduced to hiring an escort for a family reunion at her Uncle Merlin's estate. Uncle Merlin dies shortly thereafter and leaves a strange will, specifying that Ellie lose 63 pounds, that her escort write a novel, and that they discover the estate's treasure. Their quest soon becomes an investigation into the murder of Uncle Merlin's mother 60 years before." Booklist

The widows club. Bantam Bks. 1988 338p $16.95

ISBN 0-553-05259-4   LC 87-47913

"Ellie Simons has a great deal on her mind: her pending marriage to handsome Bentley Haskell; the opening of his restaurant in the charming English town of Chitterton Fells; the restoration of the castle Merlin's Court, where she and Ben live. Most compelling of all, Ellie must learn to feel comfortable with her newly thin body, celebrated in the first Cannell mystery, *The Thin Woman*. But from the bacchanalian wedding reception on, she runs into trouble. . . . Into her already chaotic life come Hyacinth and Primrose Tramwell, proprietors of Flowers Detection Agency, to enlist her help in an investigation. Chitterton Fells has been marked by a recent rash of murders, the victims all unfaithful husbands." Publ Wkly

Cao Xueqin *See* **Ts'ao, Hsüeh-ch'in, ca. 1717-1763**

Capote, Truman, 1924-1984

Answered prayers; the unfinished novel. Random House 1986 180p $16.95

ISBN 0-394-55645-3   LC 86-10110

"The first chapter, 'Unspoiled Monsters,' introduces the narrator, P. B. Jones, Capote's dark doppelgänger, who skids between high life and low life, working as a male prostitute to finance a promising first novel. The second, 'Kate McCloud,' introduces the odious Mr. Jones to an impossible love object, a mysterious society woman isolated by her sinister, rich husband. The third, 'La Côte Basque,' features Jones lunching *a deux* with a distressed Park Avenue matron who unloads her marital intimacies in a sodden aria of indiscretion. . . . Between the cloudbursts of malice there are flashes of prose in 'Answered Prayers' that bring the aching reminder of a more whole writer, prose that makes the heart sing and the narrative fly. Some of the character riffs are inspired." N Y Times Book Rev

Breakfast at Tiffany's; a short novel and three stories. Random House 1958 179p $13.95

ISBN 0-394-41770-4

Also available from Amereon

Analyzed in Short story index

Short stories included are: House of flowers; A diamond guitar; A Christmas memory

"'Breakfast at Tiffany's' tells the story of haunting and neurotic Holiday Golightly, Texan child-bride, girl-about-New York and friend of gangster czar, Sally Tomato, in a remarkable novelette that bears the Capote trademark of neat prose, multiple dimensions and unusual atmosphere." Ont Libr Rev

Capote, Truman, 1924-1984—*Continued*
Breakfast at Tiffany's [novelette]

In Capote, T. Breakfast at Tiffany's

A Christmas memory. Random House
1966 c1956 45p $19.95

ISBN 0-394-41931-6

Appeared originally in Mademoiselle

An autobiographical story of a small boy's Christmas
in Alabama and the joy of sharing it with his elderly
cousin, Miss Sook Faulk

This book "is particularly a testimonial to the 60-year-
old Miss Sook Faulk, who may not have been quite
bright but who never stinted in her love of the boy she
helped care for. Unpretentious, but touching." Best Sellers

also in Capote, T. Breakfast at Tiffany's

The grass harp. Random House 1951
181p o.p.

"After the death of his parents, Collin goes to live
with his two aunts, Verna and Dolly. The former is
wealthy and practical, the latter, whimsical and romantic.
Dolly produces a cure for dropsy that she bottles and
sells through the mail. Verna is ready to take over the
operation and realize a large profit. To avoid this
scheme, Collin, Dolly, and Catherine, a servant, go off
to live in a treehouse, where they are joined by other
eccentric characters. When Dolly dies, Collin is ready
for his independence, having learned a valuable lesson
about love and nonconformity." Shapiro. Fic for Youth.
3d edition

Other voices, other rooms. Random House
1968 231p $19.95

ISBN 0-394-43949-X

Also available from Buccaneer Bks.

First published 1948

A novel describing the abnormal maturing of a loveless
thirteen-year-old boy who goes to live with his father
in a run-down Louisiana mansion peopled with eccentric
characters

"Much may still be desired in this tale of a pilgrimage
through adolescence whose sources appear to be firsthand and autobiographical despite the apparent influences
of McCullers, Barnes, Faulkner and Proust. 'Other
Voices, Other Rooms' must be reckoned with as a
fascinating experiment in symbols and images . . . notwithstanding the immediate reservations made by those
who prefer obscure substance to definite shadow." Commonweal

The Thanksgiving visitor. Random House
1968 c1967 63p $19.95

ISBN 0-394-44824-3

This autobiographical story is about "Buddy who was
being raised by elderly relatives, and by his spinster
cousin, Miss Sook Faulk. When Buddy is persecuted by
a bully, Odd Henderson, Miss Sook invites him to their
Thanksgiving dinner and precipitates the incident to
teach Buddy compassion

"If this volume seems thin . . . Capote has told his
story with such precise economy that once inside the
covers readers will no longer question the format. This
is storytelling in the classic tradition." Times Lit Suppl

A tree of night, and other stories.
Random House 1949 209p o.p.

Analyzed in Short story index

Eight short stories with psychic or supernatural backgrounds

Contents: Master Misery; Children on their birthdays;
Shut a final door; Jug of silver; Miriam; The headless
hawk; My side of the matter; A tree of night

Caputo, Philip
Horn of Africa. Holt & Co. 1980 487p
$12.95

ISBN 0-03-042136-5   LC 79-27513

"Three men, two Americans and one Englishman, embark on a mission as mercenaries in Africa, involving
gun-running and clandestine warfare. Their capacity for
violence is related to events and drives in their own
lives. Nordstrand, the most amoral of them, is a character that is indelibly drawn as are the horrible experiences
lived through in desert treks. This author has been compared to Joseph Conrad and Graham Greene in his
exploration of the deepest recesses of man's soul."
Shapiro. Fic for Youth. 3d edition

Caras, Roger A.
(ed) Roger Caras' Treasury of great cat
stories. See Roger Caras' Treasury of great
cat stories

(ed) Roger Caras' Treasury of great dog
stories. See Roger Caras' Treasury of great
dog stories

Card, Orson Scott
Alvin Journeyman. TOR Bks. 1995 384p
$23.95

ISBN 0-312-85053-0   LC 95-22693

"A Tom Doherty Associates book"

"In the fourth book in the series, Alvin, frontier mage
in an alternate America, is in his twenties and, indeed,
must go a-journeying. Driven from the Wobbish country
by a girl's false accusation, he returns to his birthplace
in Hatrack River and promptly finds himself on trial
for stealing the golden plough from Makepiece Smith and
also facing lynching for helping fugitive slaves. Meanwhile, Alvin's younger brother, Calvin, is peddling his
own Maker's skills with more profit if many fewer
scruples, both in America and in Europe. . . . From
beginning to end, this novel is full of riches." Booklist

The call of earth. TOR Bks. 1993 304p
il (Homecoming, v2) $21.95

ISBN 0-312-93037-2   LC 92-36971

"A Tom Doherty Associates book"

In this second volume of the Homecoming saga "the
Oversoul must force a respected and brilliant general,
nicknamed Moozh, to take over Basilica. He sets in
motion forces that will destroy the city and thus disperse
the Basilicans to spread the Oversoul's word throughout
Harmony. . . . Although the plot unfolds at a more than
leisurely pace, well-rounded characters keep it viable, and
the dialogue is superb." Publ Wkly

Followed by The ships of earth

Card, Orson Scott—*Continued*

Earthborn. TOR Bks. 1995 378p
(Homecoming, v5) $23.95

ISBN 0-312-93040-2   LC 95-5231

"A Tom Doherty Associates book"

The concluding volume of the Homecoming saga. "Of a group of humans from the distant planet Harmony searching for long-abandoned Earth, only one woman remains. Blessed and cursed with the immortality conferred upon her by the Cloak of the Starmaster, Shedemi watches from her orbiting starship as three Earth-born races struggle to overcome the prejudices that divide them. Card's protagonists confront their moral quandaries with a brutal and compassionate honesty." Libr J

Earthfall. TOR Bks. 1995 350p
(Homecoming, v4) $22.95

ISBN 0-312-93039-9   LC 94-41993

"A Tom Doherty Associates book"

"The fourth volume of Homecoming, Card's grand saga of the human race's far-future return to Earth, takes the characters on a century-long starship voyage back to the old planet. They find it inhabited by two sapient races, one evolved from rats, the other from bats. The two are constantly hostile to each other but also symbiotically linked by their reproductive process. Meanwhile, the long-standing rivalry between the statesmanlike Nafai and the dictatorial Elemak nearly wrecks the voyage, then leads to open violence on Earth, with consequences for relations with the other two sapient Earth races." Booklist

"This action-packed, plot-rich installment features Card's typical virtues—well-drawn characters and a story driven by complex moral issues." Publ Wkly

Followed by Earthborn

Ender's game. TOR Bks. 1985 357p
$21.95

ISBN 0-312-93208-1   LC 85-136148

"A Tom Doherty Associates book"

An expanded version of the author's novella of the same title

"Chosen as a six-year-old for his potential military genius, Ender Wiggin spends his childhood in outer space at the Battle School of the Belt. Severed from his family, isolated from his peers, and rigorously tested and trained, Ender pours all his talent into the war games that will one day repel the coming alien invasion." Libr J

"The key, of course, is Ender Wiggin himself. Mr. Card never makes the mistake of patronizing or sentimentalizing his hero. Alternately likable and insufferable, he is a convincing little Napoleon in short pants." N Y Times Book Rev

Followed by Speaker for the Dead

Lost boys. HarperCollins Pubs. 1992 448p
$20

ISBN 0-06-016693-2   LC 92-25506

"Step Fletcher, his wife DeAnne, and their children have just moved to Steuben, North Carolina, where there has been a rash of mysterious disappearances. Plagued by various problems, the religious Fletcher family slowly adjusts to the community. Eight-year-old son Stevie, however, spends all his spare time with his imaginary friends. Preoccupied with settling in their new home, Step and DeAnne fail to understand the connection between Stevie's friends and the young boys' disappearances. Almost too late, Stevie makes the ultimate

sacrifice to convince his family that his imaginary friends are real." Libr J

"Most of this absorbing novel has the pull of family drama with an overlayer of rising suspense. . . . Though some readers may find the fantastic plot elements jarring, Card's easy and natural prose goes a long way toward authenticating the supernatural intrusion." Publ Wkly

Maps in a mirror; the short fiction of Orson Scott Card. TOR Bks. 1990 675p $22.95

ISBN 0-312-85047-6   LC 90-38896

"A Tom Doherty Associates book"

Analyzed in Short story index

Contents: Eumenides in the fourth floor lavatory; Quietus; Deep breathing exercises; Fat farm; Closing the timelid; Freeway games; A sepulchre of songs; Prior restraint; The changed man and the king of words; Memories of my head; Lost boys; A thousand deaths; Clap hands and sing; Dogwalker; But we try not to act like it; I put my blue genes on; In the doghouse; The originist; Unaccompanied sonata; A cross-country trip to kill Richard Nixon; The porcelain salamander; Middle woman; The bully and the beast; The princess and the bear; Sandmagic; The best day; A plague of butterflies; The monkeys thought 'twas all in fun; Mortal gods; Saving grace; Eye for eye; St. Amy's tale; Kingsmeat; Holy; Ender's game; Mikal's songbird; Malpractice; Follower; Hitching; Damn fine novel; Billy's box; The best family home evening ever; Bicicleta; I think mom and dad are going crazy, Jerry; Gert Fram

The memory of earth. TOR Bks. 1992 xx, 294p (Homecoming, v1) o.p.

LC 91-36596

"A Tom Doherty Associates book"

The first novel of the Homecoming saga "introduces us to the city of Basilica on the far-future planet of Harmony. The Oversoul, the sentient computer that has kept the Harmonians from developing destructive cultural patterns or technology, is deteriorating, and it needs to be returned to Earth for restoration. To accomplish this, the computer must begin the technological and social development of Harmony in the direction of spaceflight. Its chosen method is 'visions,' which are sent to a trader and clan chief and his youngest son, an event that promptly puts the whole family in danger of life and fortune and drives them into exile." Booklist

"As a maker of visions and a creator of heroes whose prime directive is compassion, Card is not to be outdone." Libr J

Followed by The call of earth

Prentice Alvin. Doherty Assocs. 1989 342p o.p.

LC 88-39927

"A TOR book"

In this third Tales of Alvin Maker title "a country schoolteacher and the child of a runaway slave find their destinies entwined with that of Alvin Miller, whose talent for 'making' has marked him for destruction by the evil force known as the Unmaker. Card's epic tale of a magical, alternate America demonstrates his skill in graceful storytelling." Libr J

Red prophet. Doherty Assocs. 1988 311p $17.95

ISBN 0-312-93043-7   LC 87-50873

Card, Orson Scott—*Continued*

"A TOR book"

In this second volume of the Tales of Alvin Maker series "young Alvin Miller's magical talent for making things whole becomes the focus of a desperate race to prevent a bloodthirsty war between the Indians and the white settlers in North America." Libr J

"This novel superbly demonstrates Card's solid historical research, keen understanding of religious experience, and, most of all, his mastery of the art of storytelling." Booklist

Followed by Prentice Alvin

Seventh son. Doherty Assocs. 1987 241p o.p.

LC 86-51490

"A TOR book"

The first title in the author's Tales of Alvin Maker series

A "fantasy set in early nineteenth century of an alternate-world America. Settlers beyond the Appalachians have brought with them powerful folk magic—charms, hexes, petitions—to ease the hard work and danger of everyday life. Into this world is born Alvin Miller, a seventh son carrying powerful magic. Unfortunately, Somebody or Something is determined that Alvin won't grow up." Booklist

"This beguiling book recalls Robert Penn Warren in its robust but reflective blend of folktale, history, parable and personal testimony, pioneer narrative." Publ Wkly

Followed by Red prophet

The ships of earth. TOR Bks. 1994 382p (Homecoming, v3) $22.95

ISBN 0-312-85659-8   LC 93-42549

"A Tom Doherty Associates book"

This third novel in the Homecoming series "is set on the distant planet Harmony, 40 million years after its settlement by control freaks who programmed a supercomputer to keep the peace forever by stunting technological development among their descendants. Now the supercomputer, known as the Oversoul, is breaking down; to carry on its mission, it has recruited a band of humans from the female-dominated city of Basilica to return to Earth for spare parts and perhaps new programming. To reach the long-forgotten space station, this band must travel through a desert wilderness guided only by the Oversoul." N Y Times Book Rev

"Throughout, Card weaves thoughts on such matters as religion, tradition and the needs of the community versus those of the individual, using Biblical allusions to drive home his points." Publ Wkly

Followed by Earthfall

Speaker for the Dead. TOR Bks. 1986 415p $21.95

ISBN 0-312-93738-5   LC 85-51765

"A Tom Doherty Associates book"

In this second title in the series Ender Wiggin becomes "Speaker for the Dead out of remorse over his role in the unnecessary destruction of the Buggers. In his new identity, Wiggin plays a vital role in preventing war when a second nonhuman intelligent race—even more incomprehensible than the Buggers—is discovered. This book lacks the sheer dramatic power of Ender's transformation from child into warlord as portrayed in its predecessor. However, it benefits from increased dramatic unity, a well-developed background and supporting cast on the colony planet Lusitania, and the author's customarily stylish writing." Booklist

Followed by Xenocide

Xenocide. TOR Bks. 1991 394p $21.95

ISBN 0-312-93208-1   LC 90-27108

"A Tom Doherty Associates book"

Third title in the author's distant future series about Ender Wiggin. "As an armed fleet from Starways Congress hurtles through space towards the rebellious planet Lusitania, Ender Wiggin, his sister Valentine, and his family search for a miracle that will preserve the existence of three intelligent and vastly different species. As a storyteller, Card excels in portraying the quiet drama of wars fought not on battlefields but in the hearts and minds of his characters." Libr J

Carr, Caleb, 1955-

The alienist. Random House 1994 496p $22

ISBN 0-679-41779-6   LC 93-32766

"A society-born police reporter and an enigmatic abnormal psychologist—the 'alienist' of the title—are recruited in 1896 by New York's reform police commissioner Teddy Roosevelt to track down a serial killer who is slaughtering boy prostitutes. The investigators are opposed at every step by crime bosses and city's hidden rulers (including J. Pierpont Morgan); they distrust the alienist's novel methods and would rather conceal evidence of the murders than court publicity." Libr J

"This story boasts a veracious historical feel and a tight plot that keeps open the murderer's identity to the end. An original that fits no established mystery niche." Booklist

Carr, John Dickson, 1906-1977

The bride of Newgate. Harper & Row 1950 308p o.p.

"Caroline Ross wants a marriage certificate, but not a husband, so she marries Dick Darwent, a condemned felon. Freed on a technicality, Dick reveals that he is Lord Darwent, and insists on taking up residence at Caroline's house until he can confound the enemies who had him condemned. Duels, riots, swordplay, attempted assassination, Dickensian characters, and a hint of mystery enter into this colorful novel of love and adventure." Booklist

Carr, Philippa, 1906-1993

For works written by this author under other names see Holt, Victoria, 1906-1993; Plaidy, Jean, 1906-1993

The black swan. Putnam 1990 350p o.p.

LC 89-28545

In this Daughters of England novel "Carr continues the story of Lucie, the devoted daughter of Benedict Lansdon, a member of Parliament and close friend of Prime Minister Gladstone—until they differed over the hotly contested issue of home rule for Ireland. Lucie's life is radically altered by the Irish question: it leads to her father's assassination and her marriage to a terrorist in disguise." Booklist

"The family's complex troubles are so deftly presented that readers willingly follow intimations of ghosts, disguises and violent events that bedevil the characters." Publ Wkly

A time for silence. Putnam 1991 349p o.p.

LC 90-20304

Carr, Philippa, 1906-1993—*Continued*

Part of the author's multigenerational saga of the Cornish Farland family. "When Lucinda Greenham and her impetuous friend Annabelinda Denver leave London for finishing school in Europe, neither imagines the trouble to come. It takes many forms: Annabelinda's secret affair; the child she bears out of wedlock; and the German invasion of Belgium. With the Germans one step behind, the girls flee across a stunned Europe on the brink of World War I, to arrive safely in England at last. Picking up the pieces of their lives, they consign Annabelinda's damaging past to secrecy, only to be faced with blackmail so severe it leads to murder." Publisher's note

Voices in a haunted room. Putnam 1984 335p o.p.

LC 84-4220

In this installment in the author's multigenerational Daughters of England series "young Claudine de Tournville further tangles the family tree when she marries one of the twin sons of her stepfather. It is the other twin, however, mysterious and dashing Jonathan, to whom she is drawn and with whom she has an adulterous affair. How Claudine squares her guilt and contributes to the continuation of the comfortable family lifestyle is worked out mainly in an England that resonates with the imminence of Napoleon's sway and its consequences for the French relatives." Publ Wkly

We'll meet again. Putnam 1993 304p $22.95

ISBN 0-399-13805-6   LC 92-32589
Also available Thorndike Press large print edition

This novel in the author's Daughters of England series "begins with the Denver twins—flighty, sunny Dorabella and sane, logical Violetta—living on neighboring Cornwall estates at the outset of WWII. Repetitive first-person flashbacks recount Violetta's engagement and Dorabella's hasty marriage and widowing; subsequently, Dorabella devotes herself to her child while her twin wonders if her fiancé has survived Dunkirk. . . . The war comes even closer when German spies kidnap Dorabella's son in an attempt to force her to steal radar secrets. The eventful plot compensates somewhat for two-dimensional characters and simple, declarative prose." Publ Wkly

Carr, Robyn

Woman's own. St. Martin's Press 1990 425p o.p.

LC 89-48527

"Set in 19th-century Philadelphia, this . . . historical romance follows three generations of women in the Main Line Armstrong family as they are propelled into independence by the men, good and bad, in their lives." Publ Wkly

"Though the plot is predictable at times and the romantic scenes clichéd, the characters are strongly drawn and engage the reader's interest and emotions." Libr J

Carroll, James

The city below. Houghton Mifflin 1994 422p $22.95

ISBN 0-395-59070-1   LC 93-40837

"In this sequel to *Mortal Friends* [1978] we again meet the Doyle brothers, who are no longer inseparable. Coming of age in the turbulent 1960s, Nick has turned to organized crime, while Terry has left the seminary

for the promised Camelot of the Kennedys. Boston is a maelstrom of religion, politics, bigotry, and racism. Indeed, the city itself is the central character in this Cain-and-Abel saga. Terry returns home often as a Kennedy campaign worker and later as an aide to Senator Teddy, and with each return he clashes with the dark under-belly of Boston and with Nick." Libr J

"Mr. Carroll's story is a rich, seductive meld of characters real and fictive, of history and fancy, a tale that substantiates an Irish chestnut: every lie is a truth somewhere in time." N Y Times Book Rev

Family trade. Little, Brown 1982 417p o.p.

LC 82-272

"A college freshman accidentally sees his CIA father meet two women in a Washington art gallery in 1960. His curiosity leads him to face the awful consequences of his uncle's defection to the Soviets. After a dramatic flashback to the brutality of wartime Berlin in the hours of the Russian 'liberation,' the story advances to the present and the contrivance of a daring rescue from East Berlin. The suspense is sustained as the author juggles double and triple crosses, two love themes, family anguish, patriotic ideals, and a sensitive account of transition from adolescence to adulthood." Libr J

Fault lines. Little, Brown 1980 248p o.p.

LC 80-36756

The title of this novel "alludes to the complexities of strained human relationships. David Dolan, once a notorious, draft-dodging radical, returns to the States after eight years in Canada and Sweden teaching contemporary American literature. Disappointment, remorse, guilt, and longing complicate his search for a new beginning as he confronts an old lawyer friend (who cannot help), his aging mother (who can), and his dead (in Vietnam) brother's widow, Eddie, a writer now married to, and estranged from, ultra-movie star Cheney McCoy. The three principals and their lines of fault and guilt converge on Hunter's Island, Maine, where Eddie has sent her son." Libr J

"Mr. Carroll has told his story from all the characters' points of view—which is to say that the narrator's voice jumps from one character's mind to another's even within a single conversation. And by doing so he's made his people too strong and complex to be reduced to mere agents of the action." Books of the Times

Memorial bridge. Houghton Mifflin 1991 495p $22.95

ISBN 0-395-51136-4   LC 90-28730

"An Irish Catholic seminarian who drops out just before final vows, Sean Dillon works in the famed Depression-era Chicago stockyards to finance his way through night law school. He nearly fails to get his law degree when he misses his final exam because he stayed late to pull the corpse of a murdered man from a blood drainage pipe in the slaughterhouse. In seeking justice for the murdered man, Sean finds both the love of his life, Cass Ryan, the victim's niece, and his life's work in the FBI. Finally, as a Pentagon general, he comes to agree with his conscientious objector son that America has created a slaughterhouse in Vietnam and that the war must be stopped." Libr J

"'Memorial Bridge' is meticulously researched, carefully judicious about still-controversial topics and, frequently, wonderfully written." N Y Times Book Rev

Carroll, James—*Continued*

Prince of peace. Little, Brown 1984 531p
o.p.

LC 84-14336

This novel "explores the complex world of faith, action, and personal conviction revealed when 50-year-old Benedictine lay brother Frank Durkin returns to 1982 New York to bury his best friend, renegade ex-priest Michael Maguire. Durkin's narration places Maguire firmly in the forefront—as athletic seminarian in Washington, D.C., as anti-war demonstrator and spokesman, as 'other man' to Durkin's ex-wife Carolyn (an ex-nun), and, finally, as symbol of moral integrity wronged when church authorities forbid his burial in consecrated ground." Libr J

"Carroll's narrative is gracefully rendered, his dialogue usually true, and, despite occasional lapses into left-wing propaganda, he ultimately reaffirms in many ways the hope and timeless resilience of the Catholic church." Booklist

Carter, Angela, 1940-1992

Saints and strangers. Viking 1986 126p
o.p.

LC 85-41072

Analyzed in Short story index
Contents: The Fall River axe murders; The kiss; Our Lady of the Massacre; Peter and the wolf; The cabinet of Edgar Allan Poe; Overture and incidental music for A midsummer night's dream; The kitchen child; Black Venus

"Angela Carter's voice is literary but not precious, deep but not difficult, funny without being superficial, and indifferent to formulas. The humor in the eight stories (better to call them concoctions) in this volume is a blend of English distance and American wackiness." NY Times Book Rev

Wise children. Farrar, Straus & Giroux 1992 c1991 234p $21

ISBN 0-374-29133-0   LC 91-19920

First published 1991 in the United Kingdom
"On their 75th birthday, we meet Dora and Nora Chance, former dancers and illegitimate twin daughters of one of Britain's leading theatrical actors. They relate their colorful and amusing family history as the novel unfolds, describing their often strained relations with the legitimate branch of the family." Libr J

A "giddy souffle of a novel, mock memoir, mock confession, mock romance, a post-modernist parody of a familiar genre. . . . 'Wise Children' may not be Angela Carter's most provocative and arresting work of fiction, but it inhabits its own manic universe, and would probably translate, with the right talent, into a spirited, bawdy musical comedy-farce of the kind in which the Chance sisters themselves performed, long ago." N Y Times Book Rev

Carver, Raymond

Cathedral; stories. Knopf 1983 227p o.p.

LC 83-47779

Analyzed in Short story index
Contents: Feathers; Chef's house; Preservation; The compartment; A small, good thing; Vitamins; Careful; Where I'm calling from; The train; Fever; The bridle; Cathedral

A "Dickensian tension, the sense of holding back a wave of emotionalism, of heartbreak or rage or faith, galvanizes much of Cathedral—with character after character poised on the edge of some abyss, the verge of despair." N Y Rev Books

What we talk about when we talk about love; stories. Knopf 1981 159p o.p.

LC 80-21752

Analyzed in Short story index
Contents: Why don't you dance; Viewfinder; Mr. Coffee and Mr. Fixit; Gazebo; I could see the smallest things; Sacks; The bath; Tell the women we're going; After the denim; So much water so close to home; The third thing that killed my father off; A serious talk; The calm; Popular mechanics; Everything stuck to him; What we talk about when we talk about love; One more thing

"In spare, deft, precise prose, whole lives are portrayed in a single second as Carver briefly exposes his doom-ridden characters to one startling flash of agonizing self-recognition. These disturbing images remain long in the memory even after their immediate impression has disappeared." Booklist

Where I'm calling from; new and selected stories. Atlantic Monthly Press 1988 393p o.p.

LC 87-36778

Analyzed in Short story index
Contents: Nobody said anything; Bicycles, muscles, cigarettes; The student's wife; They're not your husband; What do you do in San Francisco?; Fat; What's in Alaska?; Neighbors; Put yourself in my shoes; Collectors; Why, honey?; Are these actual miles?; Gazebo; One more thing; Little things; Why don't you dance?; A serious talk; What we talk about when we talk about love; Distance; The third thing that killed my father off; So much water so close to home; The calm; Vitamins; Careful; Where I'm calling from; Chef's house; Fever; Feathers; Cathedral; A small, good thing; Boxes; Whoever was using this bed; Intimacy; Menudo; Elephant; Blackbird pie; Errand

"Carver dwells on the commonplace: the outwardly small but personally consequential bad turn of fortune in ordinary lives. His people are the kind other people easily overlook. . . . But Carver, in his flat style, renders them resonant of common human experience: plain folks always having to face adversity." Booklist

Carvic, Heron

Miss Seeton draws the line. Harper & Row 1970 200p o.p.
"A Joan Kahn-Harper novel of suspense"
Miss Seeton, an "elderly drawing-mistress who is on vacation in the little village of Plummergen, England and whose talent for catching in her drawings of people the clues that lead to discovery of hidden qualities, finds herself somewhat beset by an unidentified strangler who has killed six children, a pair of bandits on bikes, and an absconding cashier. Sergeant Delphick of Scotland Yard has faith in the little old lady's extraordinary skill." Best Sellers

Odds on Miss Seeton. Harper & Row 1975 150p o.p. Buccaneer Bks. reprint available $16.95 (ISBN 0-89966-307-9)
"A Joan Kahn-Harper novel of suspense"
In this novel Miss Seeton "is bewigged, bejeweled and beguiled into serving as a decoy at a posh gambling den. Deprived of her famous 'battling brolly,' attended by a young detective who is soon to fall head over heels in love, she makes a great killing at the gaming tables,

Carvic, Heron—*Continued*

purely by accident, of course, whacks a thug on the head with her heavily laden purse, and is off on another case in which organized crime is clearly no match for an English Gentlewoman." Publ Wkly

Cary, Arthur Joyce Lunel *See* Cary, Joyce, 1888-1957

Cary, Joyce, 1888-1957

The horse's mouth; a novel. Harper & Row 1950 311p o.p. Amereon reprint available $22.95 (ISBN 0-88411-311-6)

The third volume in the trilogy that began with Herself surprised (1948) and To be a pilgrim (1949)

First published 1944 in the United Kingdom

Gulley Jimson is an "artist newly released from prison. At 67, he has finally gained some critical acclaim. His aspirations to paint and live comfortably off the fruits of his achievements are thwarted, however, by his own desire to change artistically and by his accidental killing of a former model, Sara Monday. Gulley is a charming and humorous hero, constanly spouting his ideas on art and London and vividly describing the people around him." Shapiro. Fic for Youth. 3d edition

"The book is crammed with characters and picaresque episodes, and its fire and gusto never once flag. It is a comic hymn to life, but it has nobility as well. Depicting low life, it blazes with an image of the highest life of all—that of the creative imagination." Burgess. 99 Novels

Casey, John, 1939-

Spartina. Knopf 1989 375p o.p.

LC 88-45765

"Dick Pierce is an angry man because he has seen property belonging to his family in his fishing village in Rhode Island bought up by affluent people for their summer homes. He works hard, not really making enough for his family, going out for crabs, lobsters, and swordfish. Pierce's relationship with his wife and his two sons is uneasy and his love for the boat he is building (Spartina—named for the tough grass that thrives on salt in marshy water) crowds out all other considerations. His discontent and need for money lead him to dangerous disregard for the law and into a passsionate affair with Elsie Buttrick, an unconventional and independent young woman. A stunning episode in the novel is Pierce's exposing his new boat to the force of a violent hurricane because there is no safe harbor for it." Shapiro. Fic for Youth. 3d edition

It is the author's "fearless romantic insistence on lyric, even mythic symbolism, coupled with the relentless salt-smack clarity of realistic detail, that makes 'Spartina' just possibly the best American novel about going fishing since 'The Old Man and the Sea,' maybe even 'Moby-Dick.'" N Y Times Book Rev

Cassirer, Nadine Gordimer *See* Gordimer, Nadine, 1923-

Cather, Willa, 1873-1947

Death comes for the archbishop. Knopf 1927 303p $19.95

ISBN 0-394-42154-X

Also available from Amereon and Buccaneer Bks.

"Bishop Jean Latour and his vicar Father Joseph Vaillant together create pioneer missions and organize the new diocese of New Mexico. . . . The two combine to triumph over the apathy of the Hopi and Navajo Indians, the opposition of corrupt Spanish priests, and adverse climatic and topographic conditions. They are assisted by Kit Carson and by such devoted Indians as the guide Jacinto. When Vaillant goes as a missionary bishop to Colorado, they are finally separated, but Latour dies soon after his friend, universally revered and respected, to lie in state in the great Santa Fe cathedral that he himself created." Oxford Companion to Am Lit. 5th edition

also in Cather, W. Willa Cather, later novels

Early novels and stories. Library of Am. 1987 1336p $27.50

ISBN 0-940450-39-9   LC 86-10704

Omnibus edition of four novels, entered separately, and a short story collection

The troll garden contains the following stories: Flavia and her artists; The sculptor's funeral; The garden lodge; "A death in the desert"; The marriage of Phaedra; A Wagner matinée; Paul's case

Contents: The troll garden (1905); O pioneers! (1913); The song of the lark (1915); My Ántonia (1918); One of ours (1922)

A lost lady. Knopf 1973 c1923 177p $14.95

ISBN 0-394-48558-0

Also available from Amereon and Buccaneer Bks.

First published 1923

"The story of Marian Forrester is told by Niel Herbert, a Midwestern youth. Married to rugged old empire-builder Captain Forrester, Marian's graciousness sets her much above her commonplace neighbors. She becomes the lover of his friend, Frank Ellinger, however; and after the Captain's death due to a stroke, the lover of Ivy Peters, the man who acquires her home. Peters marries, and the impoverished Marian returns to the West, a 'lost lady' in the eyes of her youthful admirer, Niel. He later hears that Marian, married to a wealthy Englishman, won the respect and admiration of all in her new surroundings." Haydn. Thesaurus of Book Dig

also in Cather, W. Willa Cather, later novels

Lucy Gayheart

In Cather, W. Willa Cather, later novels

My Ántonia; with illustrations by W. T. Benda. Houghton Mifflin 1954 371p il $24.95

ISBN 0-395-07514-9

Also available from Amereon and Buccaneer Bks.

First published 1918

"Told by Jim Burden, a New York lawyer recalling his boyhood in Nebraska, the story concerns Antonia Shimerda, who came with her family from Bohemia to settle on the prairies of Nebraska. The difficulties related

Cather, Willa, 1873-1947—*Continued*

to pioneering and the integration of immigrants into a new culture are clearly portrayed." Shapiro. Fic for Youth. 3d edition

also in Cather, W. Early novels and stories p707-938

O pioneers! Houghton Mifflin 1913 308p o.p.

"The heroic battle for survival of simple pioneer folk in the Nebraska country of the 1880's. John Bergson, a Swedish farmer, struggles desperately with the soil but dies unsatisfied. His daughter Alexandra resolves to vindicate his faith, and her strong character carries her weak older brothers and her mother along to a new zest for life. Years of privation are rewarded on the farm. But when Alexandra falls in love with Carl Linstrum, and her family objects because he is poor, he leaves to seek a different career. After Alexandra's younger brother Emil is killed by the jealous husband of the French girl Marie Shabata, however, Carl gives up his plans to go to the Klondike, returns to marry Alexandra and take up the life of the farm." Haydn. Thesaurus of Book Dig

also in Cather, W. Early novels and stories p133-290

One of ours. Knopf 1922 459p o.p.

This novel "tells of a young man's escape from his oppressive life on a Midwestern farm to vitalizing experiences as a soldier in France during World War I." Oxford Companion to Am Lit. 5th edition

also in Cather, W. Early novels and stories p939-1298

The professor's house

In Cather, W. Willa Cather, later novels

Sapphira and the slave girl. Knopf 1940 295p o.p.

Available Thorndike Press large print edition

This novel "centers on the family's matriarch, Sapphira Colbert, and her attempt to sell Nancy Till, a mixed-race slave girl. Sapphira's plot is foiled by her husband Henry and their widowed daughter Rachel Blake. A confident, strong-willed invalid, Sapphira has earned the respect of many of her slaves despite her subtle cruelty toward Nancy. Henry is a pious miller whose simple upbringing and passivity contrast with the aristocratic and manipulative nature of his wife. Henry's nephew Martin, a suave but lecherous ex-soldier, tries to seduce Nancy. Rachel, who helps Nancy flee to Canada, remains at odds with Sapphira over the issue of slavery until the death of Rachel's daughter reconciles the pair." Merriam-Webster's Ency of Lit

also in Cather, W. Willa Cather, later novels

Shadows on the rock. Knopf 1931 280p o.p. Amereon reprint available $21.95 (ISBN 0-8488-0455-4)

"A product of Cather's interest in Catholicism, this work is an episodic narrative of life in Quebec during the last days of Frontenac, centered upon the life of Cécile Auclair, a child recently emigrated from Old France." Benet's Reader's Ency of Am Lit

also in Cather, W. Willa Cather, later novels

The song of the lark. Houghton Mifflin 1915 580p o.p.

Available from Amereon and Buccaneer Bks. Large print edition available from Thorndike Press

This novel "tells the story of Thea Kronborg, a Colorado girl, the daughter of a Swedish clergyman, who has a talent for music. She goes to Chicago to study, has an unhappy love affair with Fred Ottenburg, a wealthy young man who cannot obtain a divorce to marry her, and eventually becomes a soprano at the Metropolitan Opera House in New York City, famous for her Wagnerian roles." Reader's Ency. 3d edition

also in Cather, W. Early novels and stories p291-706

The troll garden

In Cather, W. Early novels and stories p1-132

In Cather, W. Willa Cather's collected short fiction, 1892-1912, v2

Willa Cather, later novels. Library of Am. 1990 988p $32.50

ISBN 0-940450-52-6   LC 89-64130

An omnibus edition of six novels, the first four are entered separately

Contents: The lost lady (1923); Death comes for the archbishop (1927); Shadows on the rock (1931); Sapphira and the slave girl (1940); The professor's house (1925); Lucy Gayheart (1935)

The professor's house depicts the relationship between an idealistic scholar and his favorite student. Lucy Gayheart is the story of a mid-western girl who sacrifices her career to become mistress of an egotistical concert singer who eventually spurns her

Willa Cather's collected short fiction, 1892-1912; edited by Virginia Faulkner; introduced by Mildred R. Bennett. [Rev. ed.]. University of Neb. Press 1970 3v in 1 $40

ISBN 0-8032-0770-0

Analyzed in Short story index

First published 1965. This edition includes an attributed unsigned story: The elopement of Allen Poole

Contents: v 1 The Bohemian girl; v2 The troll garden [published separately, 1905]; v3 On the Divide

Short stories included are: v 1 The Bohemian girl; Behind the Singing Tower; The joy of Nelly Deane; The enchanted bluff; On the gulls' road; Eleanor's house; The willing muse; The profile; The namesake; v2 The troll garden; Flavia and her artists; The sculptor's funeral; The garden of Phaedra; "A death in the desert"; The marriage of Phaedra; A Wagner matinee; Paul's case; v3 On the Divide; The treasure of Far Island; The Professor's commencement; El Dorado; A Kansas recessional; Jack-a-Boy; The conversion of Sum Loo; A singer's romance; The affair at Grover Station; The sentimentality of William Tavener; Eric Hermannson's soul; The westbound train; The way of the world; Nanette: an aside; The prodigies; A resurrection; The strategy of the Were-Wolf Dog; The Count of Crow's Nest; Tommy, the unsentimental; A night at Greenway Court; On the Divide; "The fear that walks by noonday"; The clemency of the court; A son of the Celestial; A tale of the white pyramid; Lou, the prophet; Peter

Caunitz, William J.

Black sand. Crown 1989 339p o.p.

LC 88-37372

"The action begins with a massacre in a street-front cafe in Greece. Among the dead are two cops and another cop's family. The investigation soon leads to some stolen ancient scrolls, to a copy of *The Iliad* that was once the property of Alexander the Great, and to America, where the priceless scrolls may have found a new home. Soon the bereaved Greek policeman is in New York, working with another cop, also Greek, and learning the ways of the NYPD." Booklist

"The author perhaps overstates his international brotherhood theme by involving a Russian officer with Interpol on the case. But if these buddy relationships strike the reader as simplistic, they are still sweet on their own terms and do not interfere with the genuinely absorbing procedural detail of this adventure." N Y Times Book Rev

Cleopatra Gold. Crown 1993 328p $20

ISBN 0-517-57498-5   LC 93-9966

"Alejandro Monahan is deep, deep undercover for the New York Police Department. A renegade cartel known as Cleopatra Gold has been responsible for the death of three previous undercover infiltrators. Monahan, whose cover is that of an aspiring Latin balladeer, performs in a club frequented by the dopers. In the face of increasing pressure from the various antidrug agencies, the bad guys are looking for a more efficient way to smuggle in their merchandise. Monahan, professing a desire to quit singing and get rich, proposes the use of a radio-controlled parachute drop system perfected by the U.S. military. The bad guys take the bait; Monahan is in." Booklist

"The fascinating, improbable technology makes a highly intriguing hook, which Caunitz exploits skillfully." Publ Wkly

One Police Plaza. Crown 1984 369p o.p.

LC 83-14323

"This story details the tenacious search of a New York police detective for the murderer responsible for a heinous crime. Lt. Dan Malone is called in on the murder and is caught up in the apparent inconsistencies of the case. Despite threats, direct orders and attempts on his life, Malone refuses to back off. His tenacity pays off, . . . and he is able to solve the murder. The murder, though, includes elements of international terrorism and espionage as well as internal departmental vigilante activities." Best Sellers

The author "expertly depicts the stark reality of the police officer's life and work, and his hard-edged prose drives the story to a stunning conclusion." Booklist

Suspects. Crown 1986 374p o.p.

LC 86-13427

"The story begins with a double homicide in which one victim is a lionized police lieutenant and the other is the owner of a neighborhood candy store. But both victims have skeletons in their closets, as Lt. Tony Scanlon soon discovers as he investigates the crime. Lt. Scanlon is a solid character, a handicapped cop who must balance his loyalty to the job—that is, being a cop—with getting to the truth, something his superiors may not want him to discover." Publ Wkly

"The author's prose is not Joseph Wambaugh's, but his knowledge of life inside an urban police force is extraordinary, and his detailed word-pictures of ballistics tests, fingerprint techniques and department stag parties make this arcane blue world come alive." N Y Times Book Rev

Céline, Louis-Ferdinand, 1894-1961

Journey to the end of the night; translated from the French by John H. P. Marks. Little, Brown 1934 509p o.p.

Original French edition, 1932

"Ferdinand Bardamu, the cynical, disillusioned hero, wander aimlessly through war-torn Europe, surrounded by destruction and putrefaction. Man, as Céline portrays him, attempts to flee from the solitude of his existence and the impossibility of helping his fellow humans but succeeds only in embracing evil and death. The novel caused a scandal when it was published because of the coarseness of its language and the unrelieved blackness of its pessimism. Yet the language is a highly original attempt to reproduce the proletarian *argot* that reflects the horror and intimacy of war, and the pessimism shows Céline's desire to arouse the reader and make him aware of his condition." Reader's Ency. 3d edition

Cerf, Bennett, 1898-1971

(ed) Famous ghost stories. See Famous ghost stories

Cervantes Saavedra, Miguel de, 1547-1616

The colloquy of the dogs

In Cervantes Saavedra, M. de. Three exemplary novels p125-217

Don Quixote de la Mancha.

Various editions available

Original Spanish edition, published in two parts, 1605 and 1615. Variant titles: The adventures of Don Quixote; The ingenious gentleman, Don Quixote de la Mancha

"Originally conceived as a comic satire against the chivalric romances then in literary vogue, the novel describes realistically what befalls an elderly knight who, his head bemused by reading romances, sets out on his old horse Rosinante, with his pragmatic squire Sancho Panza, to seek adventure. In the process, he also finds love in the person of the pleasant Dulcinea. Contemporaries evidently did not take the book as seriously as later generations have done, but by the end of the 17th century it was deemed highly significant, especially abroad. It came to be seen as a mock epic in prose, and the 'grave and serious air' of the author's irony was much admired. In the history of the modern novel the role of *Don Quixote* is recognized as seminal." Merriam-Webster's Ency of Lit

Man of glass

In Cervantes Saavedra, M. de. Three exemplary novels p75-121

Rinconete and Cortadillo

In Cervantes Saavedra, M. de. Three exemplary novels p9-71

Cervantes Saavedra, Miguel de, 1547-1616
—*Continued*

Three exemplary novels; translated by Samuel Putnam; illustrated by Luis Quintanilla. Viking 1950 xxi, 232p il o.p. Greenwood Press reprint available $38.50 (ISBN 0-313-23346-2)

Part of a collection first published 1613 in Spain

Rinconete and Cortadillo is a picaresque novella about thieves in early 17th century Seville. Man of glass is a philosophical tale set in 17th century Italy about a man intent on exposing the lie upon which human existence is based. The colloquy of the dogs describes life in 17th century Spain

Chabon, Michael

A model world and other stories. Morrow 1991 207p $18.95

ISBN 0-688-09553-4   LC 90-43081

Analyzed in Short story index

Contents: A model world; S Angel; Ocean Avenue; A model world; Blumenthal on the air; Smoke; Millionaires; The lost world; The little knife; More than human; Admirals; The Halloween party; The lost world

"Each of the stories concerns an individual's adaptation to a changed relationship, be it with wife (or ex-wife), friend, lover, or parent. . . . Chabon writes with intelligence, humor, and an obvious love of language." Libr J

Challans, Mary *See* Renault, Mary, 1905-1983

Chandler, Raymond, 1888-1959

The big sleep. Knopf 1939 277p o.p. Buccaneer Bks. reprint available $29.95 (ISBN 1-56849-261-8)

"A tale of degeneracy in southern California, in which two Hollywood heiresses become mixed up in blackmail and murder; and Philip Marlowe is the private detective, who tells the story." Washington, D.C. Public Libr

also in Chandler, R. Stories and early novels p587-764

Farewell, my lovely

In Chandler, R. Stories and early novels p765-984

The high window. Knopf 1942 240p o.p.

Available Thorndike Press large print edition

"This early exploit of Philip Marlowe's is certainly high in the merit list. The Pasadena scene, the characterization, the tough-yet-literate style match the complex plot, involving counterfeiting and blackmail. Just how the photograph of the victim was obtained is glossed over, but all other details are clearly etched." Barzun. Cat of Crime. Rev and enl edition

also in Chandler, R. Stories and early novels p985-1177

The lady in the lake. Knopf 1943 216p o.p.

Available Thorndike Press large print edition

"A young wife has been missing for a month and Marlowe is hired by the husband whom she is about to leave for another man. The exposition of situation and character is done with remarkable pace and skill. . . . The scene shifts to Little Fawn Lake, where talk between a local woman, the caretaker of the missing wife's cabin, and Marlowe produces speculation about the absent girl, her lover, and also the missing wife of the caretaker; whereupon comes the dramatic discovery of the corpse in the lake. It is 'not' Marlowe's quarry. From then on this superb tale moves through a maze of puzzles and disclosures to its perfect conclusion. Marlowe makes a greater use of physical clues and ratiocination in this exploit than in any other. It is Chandler's masterpiece and true detection." Barzun. Cat of Crime. Rev and enl edition

also in Chandler, R. Later novels and other writings p1-200

Later novels and other writings. Library of Am. 1995 1076p $35

ISBN 1-883011-08-6   LC 94-43705

Contents: The lady in the lake; The little sister; The long goodbye; Playback; Double indemnity; Selected essays and letters

The lady in the lake and The long goodbye are entered separately; The little sister is included in The midnight Raymond Chandler. In Playback (1958), "Marlowe is weakening (by his own standards), since he takes on an impossible girl who is running away from a quite imaginary threat and forces her to trust him. There is some silly back-and-forth with $5,000 of traveler's checks, a double fornication without much zest, and at last a transatlantic phone call summoning Marlowe to marry his true love." Barzun. Cat of Crime. Rev and enl ed

The little sister

In Chandler, R. Later novels and other writings p201-416

In Chandler, R. The midnight Raymond Chandler p201-416

The long goodbye. Houghton Mifflin 1953 316p o.p.

Detective Philip Marlowe provides moral support for Terry Lennox who is running away to Mexico because he thinks he committed a murder

This novel is one of Chandler's "most meticulously plotted and by some stretches his most corrosive. What he gives us here is painful if exciting pleasure." N Y Her Trib Books

also in Chandler, R. Later novels and other writings p417-734

also in Chandler, R. The midnight Raymond Chandler p417-734

The midnight Raymond Chandler; with an introduction by Joan Kahn. Houghton Mifflin 1971 734p o.p.

This collection contains the complete novels The little sister (1949) and The long goodbye (1953) plus four stories: Blackmailers don't shoot, The pencil, Trouble is my business, and Red wine. Chandler's essay on the genre The simple art of murder completes the volume

Chandler, Raymond, 1888-1959—*Continued*
Playback

In Chandler, R. Later novels and other writings p735-871

Poodle Springs; [by] Raymond Chandler and Robert B. Parker. Putnam 1989 268p o.p.

LC 89-10414

When Chandler died he left "behind the opening chapters of this Philip Marlowe private investigator novel set in the 1950s, which Parker has completed. Here, Marlowe has a rich wife . . . and has moved from Los Angeles to the big-buck community of Poodle Springs, where he is hired by the area crime boss to track down a missing local who has run out on a gambling debt." Libr J

"Like Chandler's finest work, Poodle Springs has a haunted quality that comes from somewhere beyond the plot, a sense of things gone fundamentally wrong. . . . Chandler's great artistic flaw was his sentimentalizing of his detective. Parker isn't, even here, the writer Chandler was, but he's not a sentimentalist, and he darkens and deepens Marlowe." Atlantic

Stories and early novels. Library of Am. 1995 1199p $35

ISBN 1-883011-07-8   LC 94-45462

Partially analyzed in Short story index
Contents: Pulp stories; The big sleep; Farewell, my lovely; The high window
The big sleep and The high window are entered separately. Pulp stories includes the following titles: Blackmailers don't shoot; Smart-aleck kill; Finger man; Nevada gas; Spanish blood; Guns at Cyrano's; Pick-up on Noon Street; Goldfish; Red wind; The king in yellow; Pearls are a nuisance; Trouble is my business; I'll be waiting
Farewell, my lovely (1940), a mystery featuring Philip Marlowe, is a "model of complexity kept under control, with a holocaust at the end. Its contents are the now familiar ones of political and personal corruption, double-crossing, and the woman killer." Barzun. Cat of Crime. Rev and enl edition

Chapman, Walker
For works written by this author under other names see Silverberg, Robert

Chase, Joan
During the reign of the Queen of Persia; a novel. Harper & Row 1983 215p $13.95

ISBN 0-06-015136-6   LC 82-48680

This is the "story of three generations of women on a northern Ohio farm in the 1950s, narrated collectively by the two pairs of cousins who make up the third generation. Gram, dubbed 'the Queen of Persia' by a son-in-law, is the tough matriarch, proud of living past 80 and supporting her five daughters (with help from a rich uncle, but little from drinking, brutish Grandad)." Libr J

The author's "language is as rich and as fertile as the farmland she writes about, and her vision so full that, even with the encumbrance of the 'we' narrator, the novel reads like a single unbroken thought, a sentence in need of no punctuation, a long, undying moan. . .

. [This] remarkable novel is too full of life to leave us in despair." Nation

The evening wolves; a novel. Farrar, Straus & Giroux 1989 295p $18.95

ISBN 0-374-15003-6   LC 88-7864

This novel is an "evocation of a family comprising three children, their father, and their stepmother. Told in alternating chapters from the points of view of the offspring and the second wife, this is essentially the story of a man who fears his flakiness will prohibit his family from staying together. And yet, despite his idiosyncrasies, despite his nontraditional fathering, he does manage to raise his children successfully." Booklist

"'The Evening Wolves' has awkward moments and *longueurs*, but it still succeeds in revealing a writer who understands the tyranny of the human heart—and who is not afraid to take risks." N Y Times Book Rev

Chase-Riboud, Barbara, 1939-
The President's daughter. Crown 1994 467p $24

ISBN 0-517-59861-2   LC 93-42499

Sequel to Sally Hemings
"On her 21st birthday, Harriet, the daughter of Thomas Jefferson and Sally Hemings, his slave and mistress, is allowed to run north and pass into white society. Although Harriet's physical characteristics allow her outward passage to occur without difficulty, the psychological divisions she suffers endure for her lifetime. Obsessed by her desire for Jefferson to acknowledge his slave children, tormented by fears that her husband could be prosecuted for miscegenation and her children sold into slavery, Harriet struggles with the same questions that tear apart the Union and plunge the country into civil war." Libr J

The author "vividly captures the look and feel of Philadelphia from the 1820s to the 1870s. Just as in a romance novel, the beautiful and strong-willed Harriet succeeds in whatever arena she chooses. But her story goes beyond that of a feisty heroine in a heaving bodice; with intelligence and immediacy, 'The President's Daughter' illuminates the brutal politics of slavery." NY Times Book Rev

Sally Hemings; a novel. Viking 1979 348p o.p. Buccaneer Bks. reprint available $21.95 (ISBN 0-89966-915-8)

LC 78-12682

"A Seaver book"
A novel about the relationship between Thomas Jefferson and his mistress Sally Hemings, a slave, whom he lived with for thirty-eight years
"If it indeed existed, the relationship must have been much as the author depicts it in this fine first novel: a mixture of love and hate, of tenderness and cruelty, and of freedom and bondage. The book is well researched, well written, insightful, and entertaining." Libr J

Chatwin, Bruce
Utz. Viking 1989 154p $16.95

ISBN 0-670-82497-6   LC 88-40310

This novel details the "existence of one Kaspar Utz, owner of a superb private collection of Meissen porcelain in Prague. The novel is narrated by a writer who goes to the Czech capital in 1967 to research the Holy Roman Emperor Rudolph II's passion for collecting ob-

Chatwin, Bruce—*Continued*

jets d'art. His research—which he hopes will lead him to conclusions about the psychology of the compulsive collector—first leads him to the door of Kaspar Utz. What develops from this meeting affords the narrator a rich opportunity to observe and attempt to fathom human nature." Booklist

"The hero of Mr. Chatwin's provocative short novel is a successful survivor. He is part Jewish but has managed to survive Hitler. . . . [Utz is] required to bequeath the collection to the state, and what he does about that insult to his elegant eighteenth-century companions becomes his own peculiar final solution. Mr. Chatwin has created an intriguing proposition—that obedient passivity can amount to successful rebellion." Atlantic

Chayefsky, Paddy, 1923-1981

Altered states; a novel. Harper & Row 1978 184p $12.95

ISBN 0-06-010727-8   LC 77-11542

This novel tells the "story of an experiment in genetic regression. . . . Edward Jessup is a psychophysiologist with 'an extraordinary if monomaniacal mind'. His wife suspects that her coldly passionate husband may be a genius. . . . After numerous descents into the black water of an isolation tank he at last succeeds in regressing into a small, hairy, proto-human creature that eats gazelles in the university park and experiences 'the primal unity'. He smashes his way out of the laboratory and exults in the taste of warm blood." New Statesman

"What makes this shocking fantasy work is not only Chayefsky's dramatic skill . . . but also the authority of his prodigious research in chemistry, biology, and medicine. . . . The result is a marvelous and exciting work of the imagination." Saturday Rev

Cheever, John, 1912-1982

Bullet Park; a novel. Knopf 1969 245p o.p.

Available Thorndike Press large print edition

"The interplay between [suburbanites] Eliot Nailles, Paul Hammer, and Naille's son Tony forms the structure of a novel . . . embodying many contemporary issues and problems. Using the third person, Cheever depicts Nailles as an open-faced, conscientious man, driven to desperation when his son is ill. Hammer, in a first-person account, is revealed as criminally insane beneath his [middle-class] neighborly exterior. The third part portrays Hammer's attempt to murder Tony Nailles, an act narrowly averted by his father." Booklist

The author "mixes compassion and high comedy brilliantly, holding up to view an America that is fatally schizoid in many of its manifestations. The confrontation that finally comes between Hammer and Nailles is a horrifying dark allegory of our times." Publ Wkly

Falconer. Knopf 1977 211p o.p.

The novel's protagonist, Ezekiel Farragut, "is a well-read college professor, a drug addict convicted of murdering his brother, Falconer. Prison breaks Zeke Farragut of his addiction but embroils him in all the coarse, desperate gambits of prison life." Libr J

"John Cheever uses prison as an emblem for the world in this stunning novel about love, mysticism, and man's relationship with God. . . . The surface events include a prison riot, a massacre of prison cats by an enraged guard who had his steak stolen by one of them, a homosexual love affair, and a couple of breathtaking escapes, one by Farragut's lover, who dons a cassock to escape in a helicopter with a visiting bishop. Woven in and out are threads of Farragut's past life, his relationship to his wife and the other women in his life, the secret behind his hatred for his brother." Choice

Oh, what a paradise it seems. Knopf 1982 99p o.p.

LC 81-48109

"In a novella that focuses on an aging man's regret and anger at the erosion of time on the human body and the environment, John Cheever attempts a modern fable. Lemuel Sears, elegantly elderly, is rejuvenated via an impromptu, lively and offbeat love affair. His energy is galvanized to mount a legal attack on the despoilment by landfill of a once jewel-like pond near the home of his youth. A series of bizarre but somehow connected events, including a homosexual encounter, enhance Sears' appreciation of the mystery of life and the need for renewal in the waning of the 20th century." Publ Wkly

"Ever more boldly the celebrant of the grand poetry of life, Cheever, once a taut and mordant chronicler of urban and suburban disappointments, now speaks in the cranky, granular, impulsive, confessional style of our native wise men and exhorters since Emerson. The pitch of his final page is positively Transcendental." New Yorker

The stories of John Cheever. Knopf 1978 693p $29.95

ISBN 0-394-50087-3   LC 78-160

Analyzed in Short story index

Contents: Goodbye, my brother; The common day; The enormous radio; O city of broken dreams; The Hartleys; The Sutton Place story; The summer farmer; Torch song; The pot of gold; Clancy in the Tower of Babel; Christmas is a sad season for the poor; The season of divorce; The chaste Clarissa; The cure; The superintendent; The children; The sorrows of gin; O youth and beauty; The day the pig fell into the well; The five-forty-eight; Just one more time; The housebreaker of Shady Hill; The bus to St James's; The worm in the apple; The trouble of Marcie Flint; The bella lingua; The Wrysons; The country husband; The Duchess; The scarlet moving van; Just tell me who it was; Brimmer; The golden age; The lowboy; The music teacher; A woman without a country; The death of Justina; Clementina; Boy in Rome; A miscellany of characters that will not appear; The chimera; The seaside houses; The angel of the bridge; The brigadier and the golf widow; A vision of the world; Reunion; An educated American woman; Metamorphoses; Mene, Mene, Tekel, Upharsin; Montraldo; The ocean; Marito in Città; The geometry of love; The swimmer; The world of apples; Another story; Percy; The fourth alarm; Artemis, the honest well digger; Three stories; The jewels of the Cabots

Thirteen uncollected stories; edited by Franklin H. Dennis; introduction by George W. Hunt. Academy Chicago 1994 227p $19.95

ISBN 0-89733-405-1   LC 93-49582

Analyzed in Short story index

Contents: Fall River; Late gathering; Bock beer and Bermuda onions; The autobiography of a drummer; In passing; Bayonne; The princess; The teaser; His young wife; Saratoga; The man she loved; Family dinner; The opportunity

Cheever, John, 1912-1982—*Continued*

"These stories were nearly all published in the 1930s. . . . Several are Depression tales, set in dead mill towns or waterfront diners and informed by leftist politics. . . . Others are set among the Saratoga horse-racing set and appeared in such commercial magazines as *Collier's*. Surprisingly, women are at the center of many of the stories. . . . A fascinating example of one writer's beginning." Libr J

The Wapshot chronicle. Harper & Row 1957 307p o.p.

This often satirical family chronicle follows the fortunes of the Wapshot family of St Botolphs, a once lively New England seaport declining into respectability. Old Captain Leander Wapshot is in love with his ferryboat, which he loses, regains and loses again. His sons, Coverly and Moses, stand to inherit a fortune from their eccentric Aunt Honora if they marry and produce male heirs. They pursue their fortunes in New York and Washington and become involved in various occupational and marital problems

"It is a story ribald and poignant by turn, a tapestry woven from the threads of emotion, tragedy, comedy (or tragicomedy) and the irony so wonderfully evident in the author's short stories. Although his novel might at times seem to be a series of stories placed together as a literary mosaic, his talent is a controlled one, something that never gets out of hand." San Francisco Chron

The Wapshot scandal. Harper & Row 1964 309p o.p.

This sequel to The Wapshot chronicle "continues the tale of the decline of the fortunes of the Wapshot family and of the mythical New England town of St. Botolphs. The 'scandal' is the discovery that Aunt Honora has never paid her income taxes, and the principal disaster stems from the long-standing oversight. The novel also traces the misfortunes of two Wapshot nephews, Coverly, a public relations man at a missile site, and Moses, an alcoholic. Despite the somberness of the main line of events, the book is not depressing; it is lighted by the high gloss of Mr. Cheever's style, by glints of humor, and especially by the warm glow of human fortitude under stress." Libr J

Chekhov, Anton Pavlovich, 1860-1904

Anton Chekhov's short stories; texts of the stories, backgrounds, criticism; selected and edited by Ralph E. Matlaw. Norton 1979 368p o.p.

LC 78-17052

"A Norton critical edition"
Partially analyzed in Short story index
In addition to thirty-four stories written between 1884 and 1902, this edition contains selections from the Russian author's letters, a memoir by Maxim Gorky and eight critical essays
Includes the following stories: Chameleon; Oysters; A living chronology; The huntsman; Misery; The requiem; Anyuta; Agatha; Grisha; A gentleman friend; The chorus girl; Dreams; Vanka; At home; The siren's song; Sleepy; The grasshopper; In exile; Rothschild's fiddle; The student; The teacher of literature; Whitebrow; Anna on the neck; The house with the mansard; The Pecheneg; A journey by cart; The man in a case; Gooseberries; About love; A doctor's visit; The darling; The lady with the dog; The bishop; The betrothed

The best known works of Anton Chekhov. Blue Ribbon Bks. 1936 678p o.p. Ayer reprint available $32.75 (ISBN 0-8369-4198-5)

Partially analyzed in Short story index
First published 1929 by W. J. Black, Inc. with title: The works of Anton Chekhov
Contains the following stories: The kiss; Chorus girl; La cigale; Verotchka; Match; Excellent people; Black monk; Family council; Woe; Women; A husk; Anna round the neck; The incubus; Miss N. N's story; Young wife; The peasants; Shooting party; Terrible night; In exile; The proposal; Who is to blame; Rothschild's fiddle; Sleepyhead; Princess; Fish; Mass for the sinner; The lament; Oysters; Vanka; Zinotchka; Privy councillor; The wager; Cossack; At the manor; Event; Art; Birds; Ward no. 6; At home; An adventure; A father; Two tragedies; Rook; On the way; Children; Head gardener's tale; The runaway; The reed; In the ravine

Chekhov: the early stories, 1883-1888; chosen and translated by Patrick Miles and Harvey Pitcher. Macmillan 1982 203p $14.95

ISBN 0-02-524620-8   LC 82-24893

Analyzed in Short story index
Contents: Rapture; The death of a civil servant; An incident at law; Fat and thin; The daughter of Albion; Oysters; A dreadful night; Minds in ferment; The complaints book; The chameleon; The huntsman; The malefactor; A man of ideas; Sergeant Prishibeyev; The misfortune; Romance with double-bass; The witch; Grisha; Kids; Revenge; Easter night; The little joke; The objet d'art; The chorus-girl; Dreams; The orator; Vanka; Verochka; A drama; Typhus; Notes from the journal of a quick-tempered man; The-reed pipe; The kiss; No comment; Let me sleep

Longer stories from the last decade; [by] Anton Chekhov; translated by Constance Garnett. Modern Lib. 1993 611p $18

ISBN 0-679-60063-9   LC 93-14536

Analyzed in Short story index
Contents: The duel; The wife; Ward no. 6; An anonymous story; The black monk; A woman's kingdom; Three years; The murder; My life; Peasants; In the ravine

Cherryh, C. J., 1942-

Chanur's Legacy; a novel of compact space. DAW Bks. 1992 386p $20

ISBN 0-88677-519-1

Previous titles in the author's Chanur series were published in paperback

"Hilfy Chanur, young captain of the merchant ship *Chanur's Legacy*, accepts a commission from a stsho dignitary on the planet Meetpoint to deliver a religious artifact to nearby Urtur Station. What appears to be a straightforward business arrangement soon becomes a tangle of interstellar intrigue as Hilfy and her crew battle kidnappers, assassins, and smooth politicans while fighting their own inborn prejudices." Libr J

"Cherryh demonstrates a remarkable grasp of alien psychologies—she has mastered the near-impossible trick of creating aliens who think differently from, but just as well as, humans. Very few SF writers could carry off

Cherryh, C. J., 1942——*Continued*
a 400-page novel with no major human characters; Cherryh does so effortlessly." Publ Wkly

Chernevog. Ballantine Bks. 1990 328p o.p.
LC 90-559

"A Del Rey book"
Sequel to Rusalka (1989)
"The young wizard Sasha, his friend Pyetr, and Pyetr's wife Eveshka, who has been restored to life, face a daunting and extremely hazardous challenge." Booklist
"Forest spirits, 'yard things,' and other magical creatures drawn from Russian folklore add a unique flavor to this story of loyalty and courage." Libr J
Followed by Yvgenie

Foreigner; a novel of first contact. DAW Bks. 1994 378p $20
ISBN 0-88677-590-6   LC 94-179662

"Set on an alien world where the descendants of humans marooned in a long-ago starship accident live segregated from the indigenous *atevi* on a remote island, this [novel] . . . addresses the complicated issue of how humans might have to compromise to survive on a planet where they are barely tolerated by the original, humanoid inhabitants." Publ Wkly
"Cherryh plays her strongest suit in this exploration of human/alien contact, producing an incisive study-in-contrast of what it means to be human in a world where trust is nonexistent." Libr J

Heavy time. Warner Bks. 1991 330p $19.95
ISBN 0-446-51616-3   LC 90-50525

In this Merchanter universe novel "a pair of independent claim-seekers in the asteroid belt answer a distress call, discover the remains of a ship and its half-crazed survivor, and tow their salvage to the nearest way station—where their trouble begins." Libr J
"Superbly rendered—with believable social, economic and political backdrops, complex characters, and a tense, well-paced plot—Cherryh's novel proves that high-tech science fiction need not sacrifice literary values." Publ Wkly

Hellburner. Warner Bks. 1992 343p $21.95
ISBN 0-446-51617-1   LC 91-51180

This novel in the author's spacefaring saga set in the Merchanter universe focuses on "a top-secret test pilot program for the military. When Paul Dekker . . . is seriously injured in a suspicious accident, his surly former partner Ben Pollard is called in as next of kin. While Ben investigates, rival military factions fight for control of the program, with the pilots caught in the middle. Cherryh, who evokes more tension and danger in one verbal confrontation than most writers can manage in a dozen space battles, maintains a fast pace throughout." Publ Wkly

Rimrunners. Warner Bks. 1989 327p $19.95
ISBN 0-446-51514-0   LC 88-27755

"Separated from her Freebooter (outlaw) ship, spacer Elizabeth ('Bet') Martin is stranded on Thule Station without papers and with a slim chance of getting hired. Unexpectedly, she secures a berth on the mysterious Union vessel *Loki*, which shows all evidence of being a 'spook' (intelligence-gathering) ship but turns out to be the bait in a dangerous plan to draw out and attack the Freebooters. . . . Cherryh has created a convincing shipboard setting, and her characters act and react realistically to the everyday minutiae and intrigue of life aboard the *Loki*." Booklist

Tripoint. Warner Bks. 1994 377p $19.95
ISBN 0-446-51780-1   LC 93-38247

A title in the author's saga set in the Merchanter universe. "Tom Bowe-Hawkins, young crew member of the family ship *Sprite*, was conceived in rape and is growing up with a chip on his shoulder. He is caught up in the revenge planned by his mother, Marie Kirgov Hawkins, against his father, Austin Bowe, captain of the *Corinthian*, a vessel suspected to be engaged in smuggling and piracy. When the two vessels find themselves docked at the same space station, Tom tries to keep his mother from getting the ship into trouble with station authorities. . . . Cherryh's satisfying novel delves deeply into the relations between families and crew members tied closely together in long and intimate voyages among the stars." Publ Wkly

Yvgenie. Ballantine Bks. 1991 280p $19
ISBN 0-345-36784-7   LC 91-91909

"A Del Rey book"
"The third of Cherryh's novels drawn from Russian folklore brings back Ksvi Chernevog, the evil wizard of the second book. He has returned in incorporeal form, ready to prey on the susceptibility of Eveshka'a now-adolescent daughter, Ilyana. Eveshka, the former *rusalka* (devouring ghost), has a major battle to fight against both magical assault and adolescent rebellion, both of which are depicted with Cherryh's usual knowledge of folklore and skill in characterization. The saga as a whole is emerging as Cherryh's most significant work of fantasy and should have a place in any active collection." Booklist

Chesney, Marion
Back in society. St. Martin's Press 1994 152p (Poor Relation, v6) $18.95
ISBN 0-312-10932-6   LC 94-6398

"As this volume opens, Lady Jane Fremney tries to commit suicide to avoid an unsuitable marriage. Miss Tonks pines for the attention of the actor who has joined the ranks of the Poor Relations, and Colonel Sandhurst tries to convince the originator of the scheme, Lady Fortesque, to retire with him to the country." Booklist
"Chesney closes her popular 'The Poor Relation' series . . . with this frothy tale of Regency England. . . . Fans of the series will appreciate the fact that the author ties up loose ends for all the hotel owners." Libr J

Colonel Sandhurst to the rescue. St. Martin's Press 1994 152p (Poor Relation, v5) $17.95
ISBN 0-312-10444-8   LC 93-45283

This installment in the Poor Relation series "finds Frederica Gray sheltered at the hotel to avoid a marriage of convenience to the disgusting Lord Bewley. Since her father owes money to the hotel, co-owner Colonel Sandhurst hopes to extract a ransom. Of course, the plan goes awry. Bewley lodges at the hotel to win fair Frederica but falls for look-a-like chambermaid Mary Jones instead." Libr J
The author "employs a delightful cast of memorable, unconventional (and fabulously named) characters." Publ Wkly

Chesney, Marion—*Continued*

Deborah goes to Dover. St. Martin's Press
1992 151p $16.95

ISBN 0-312-06952-9   LC 91-41651

An episode in the author's Travelling Matchmaker
series

"During a coach trip to Dover, the intrepid Miss Pym
encounters the hoydenish Lady Deborah Western, who,
dressed as a boy, is being escorted to a prizefight by
her scapegrace twin brother, Lord William. While trying
to keep her footman, Benjamin Stubbs, from taking part
in a boxing match to recover his gaming losses, Miss
Pym gives Lady Deborah some social protection after
she is revealed as a female. . . . Chesney's story is
frothily entertaining." Publ Wkly

Lady Fortescue steps out. St. Martin's
Press 1992 152p (Poor Relation, v1) $17.95

ISBN 0-312-08231-2   LC 92-25158

"Life as a member of England's aristocratic class isn't
easy when one has no money. Advertising one's misfortune—even to relatives—would be considered ill bred.
But after she is caught stealing silver candlesticks from
her wealthy nephew (he thinks she is becoming senile),
Lady Fortescue is desperate. So she begins a search for
others such as herself—genteel, blue-blooded, and poor.
The little band of six she eventually organizes pools its
meager resources and opens a hotel for high society, an
establishment that soon brings excitement and romance
to the lives of its owners." Libr J

Miss Tonks turns to crime. St. Martin's
Press 1993 152p (Poor Relation, v2) $16.95

ISBN 0-312-08846-9   LC 92-41837

"Meek and mousy Miss Tonks bravely sets out to steal
from her wealthy but overbearing sister to get the needed
funds to resurrect the hotel she runs with her com-
patriots. Though they despair of her ability to do so,
Miss Tonks returns not only with the goods, but with
her niece Cassandra as well. Cassandra is fleeing her
domineering mother's attempts to marry her to Lord
Eston." Libr J

"Romance is the final result, but only after plenty of
neatly contrived disasters." Booklist

Mrs. Budley falls from grace. St. Martin's
Press 1993 152p (Poor Relation, v3) $16.95

ISBN 0-312-09342-X   LC 93-17419

"When funds are particularly low at the Poor Relation
Hotel . . . one of the owners is dispatched to a country
home of a distant relative to snitch some gewgaw worth
pawning." Booklist

Sir Philip's folly. St. Martin's Press 1993
148p (Poor Relation, v4) $17.95

ISBN 0-312-09912-6   LC 93-20794

"The owners of the Poor Relation hotel are busy once
again. This time, Sir Philip Sommerville has installed
a vulgar, grasping woman in the hotel, and his co-owners
are frantic to remove her. At the same time, they decide
they must help a young guest find a husband. . . .
Chesney skillfully creates spirited characters, including the
older principals, and places them in a believable period
atmosphere." Libr J

Chesterton, G. K. (Gilbert Keith), 1874-1936

Father Brown mystery stories; selected and
edited with an introduction by Raymond T.
Bond. Dodd, Mead 1962 246p o.p.

Analyzed in Short story index

Contents: The blue cross; The queer feet; The flying
stars; The invisible man; The sins of Prince Saradine;
The absence of Mr. Glass; The dagger with wings; The
oracle of the dog; The insoluble problem

The Father Brown omnibus; with a
preface by Auberon Waugh. Dodd, Mead
1983 993p o.p.

First omnibus edition published 1933; this is a reissue
of the 1951 edition analyzed in Short story index, with
a new preface by Auberon Waugh

These stories originally appeared in the following
collections: The innocence of Father Brown (1911), entered below; The wisdom of Father Brown (1914); The
incredulity of Father Brown (1926); The secret of Father
Brown (1927); and The scandal of Father Brown (1935)

Contents: The wisdom of Father Brown: The absence
of Mr. Glass; The paradise of thieves; The duel of Dr.
Hirsch; The man in the passage; The mistake of the
machine; The head of Caesar; The purple wig; The
perishing of the Pendragons; The God of the Gongs; The
salad of Colonel Cray; The strange crime of John Boul-
nois; The fairy tale of Father Brown

The incredulity of Father Brown: The resurrection of
Father Brown; The arrow of heaven; The oracle of the
dog; The miracle of Moon Crescent; The curse of the
golden cross; The dagger with wings; The doom of the
Darnaways; The ghost of Gideon Wise

The secret of Father Brown: The secret of Father
Brown; The mirror of the magistrate; The man with two
beards; The song of the flying fish; The actor and the
alibi; The vanishing of Vaudrey; The worst crime in the
world; The red moon of Meru; The chief mourner of
Marne; The secret of Flambeau

The scandal of Father Brown: The scandal of Father
Brown; The quick one; The blast of the book; The green
man; The pursuit of Mr. Blue; The crime of the communist; The point of a pin; The insoluble problem; The
vampire of the village

The incredulity of Father Brown

In Chesterton, G. K. The Father Brown
omnibus p433-630

The innocence of Father Brown. Lane
1911 334p o.p. Amereon reprint available
$20.95 (ISBN 0-89190-338-0)

Analyzed in Short story index

Contents: The blue cross; The secret garden; The queer
feet; The flying stars; The invisible man; The honour
of Israel Gow; The wrong shape; The sins of Prince
Saradine; The hammer of God; The eye of Apollo; The
sign of the broken sword; The three tools of death

also in Chesterton, G. K. The Father
Brown omnibus p1-226

The man who was Thursday; a nightmare.
Dodd, Mead 1908 281p o.p.

Available from Amereon and Buccaneer Bks.

"A club of seven anarchists are in a plot to destroy
the world; six of them, after terrific efforts to run each
other to earth and foil the deadly scheme, turn out to
be police officers in disguise. But narrative and talk are
a form of dialectic. The chief detective sitting in the

Chesterton, G. K. (Gilbert Keith), 1874-1936—*Continued*

darkness had given each man his commission. It is all an allegory of human life, the everlasting struggle in which man finds it so hard to distinguish friend from foe, right from wrong; where the whole basis and ultimate sanction of his faith must be an enigma." Baker. Guide to the Best Fic

The scandal of Father Brown

In Chesterton, G. K. The Father Brown omnibus p815-974

The secret of Father Brown

In Chesterton, G. K. The Father Brown omnibus p631-811

The wisdom of Father Brown

In Chesterton, G. K. The Father Brown omnibus p227-431

Chesterton, Gilbert Keith *See* Chesterton, G. K. (Gilbert Keith), 1874-1936

Childress, Alice, 1920-1994

A short walk. Coward, McCann & Geoghegan 1979 333p o.p.

LC 79-14262

"Born in 1900, Cora James arrives in the world without parents: her black mother is dead in childbirth; her white father has disappeared. But Cora's foster father tells her that 'life is just a short walk from the cradle to the grave,' and Cora is determined to fight her way down that road with a free and independent spirit in spite of the obstacles racial discrimination and economic disadvantage may place in her way. Cora's journey from South Carolina to Harlem becomes a symbolic record of black progress and setbacks in twentieth-century America." Booklist

This is "a story about black life in America seldom equalled in immediacy and depth." Publ Wkly

Childress, Mark

Crazy in Alabama. Putnam 1993 383p $22.95

ISBN 0-399-13855-2   LC 92-38334

"Peejoe, a successful screenwriter living in San Francisco, gets a call from his Aunt Lucille, who wants a part in the movie he's writing. Her request launches Peejoe into remembering the series of incredible events in both his and his aunt's lives in the summer of 1965, 'when everybody went crazy in Alabama.'" Booklist

"It is a measure of Mr. Childress's skill as a novelist—not to mention a triumphant example of style over content—that he soon had me eating out of his hand. I don't know how he did it but he managed to confront every cliché, every convention of the genre head on and pound it into submission, so that his novel seems not only fresh and original but also positively inspired." NY Times Book Rev

Tender; a novel. Harmony Bks. 1990 566p o.p.

LC 90-4298

This novel "features a poor Mississippi-born singer who in the 1950's rises to extraordinary fame, whose career is overseen by an eccentric Southern manager, whose greatest test of character occurs when he's drafted and who lives out his later years overweight and frequently in a drugged stupor." N Y Times Book Rev

"We see the world mostly from Leroy's point of view, and see it plain, we are on stage, watching and enticing the screaming girls, we are caught up in the hard work and technicalities of recording sessions, the heady bafflements of success. If we think of the book as trying to understand Leroy, we may find it engaging enough, but rather thin; if we see it as trying to situate him, to hold him up to the light, it seems a bold and rather austere experiment, a line of details refusing easy generalization." Times Lit Suppl

Christie, Agatha, 1890-1976

The A.B.C. murders. Dodd, Mead 1936 248p o.p.

Available G.K. Hall large print edition

This novel is "about a serial killer who announces his apparently unmotivated killings in advance to Poirot; the only clue is a railway guide left at the scene of each crime. In the opinion of many critics, this is one of Dame Agatha's greatest detective novels." Ency of Mystery & Detection

Agatha Christie: five complete novels of murder and detection. Avenel Bks. 1986 734p $10.95

ISBN 0-517-46852-2   LC 86-7861

Contents: Peril at End House (1932); The murder at Hazelmoor (1931) [variant title: The Sittaford mystery]; Easy to kill (1939) [variant title: Murder is easy]; Ten little Indians (1939) [variant titles: And then there were none; Ten little niggers]; Evil under the sun (1941)

Two of the five titles in this omnibus edition are entered below: Evil under the sun and Ten little Indians (which is entered under variant title: And then there were none.) In Peril at End House, set in Cornwall, Poirot is challenged by a clever criminal whom all perceive as the least likely to commit murder. In The murder at Hazelmoor, a disturbing message at a seance opens the possibility of murder in a small village. Easy to kill is a murder mystery with a strong love interest and elements of demonology in the plot

And then there were none. Dodd, Mead 1940 c1939 218p o.p.

First published 1939 in the United Kingdom with title: Ten little niggers. Variant title: Ten little Indians

"A tour de force on the following trapeze: invitations go out to a group of people, all of whom have been responsible for the death of someone by negligence of intent. The island on which the party is gathered is owned by the would-be avenger of all those deaths. The events and the tension produced by the gradual polishing off of the undetected culprits are beautifully done. One improbability, well hidden, makes the whole thing plausible." Barzun. Cat of Crime

At Bertram's Hotel. Dodd, Mead 1966 c1965 272p o.p.

Available G.K. Hall large print edition

"A solid, comfortable, respectable London hotel where Miss Jane Marple is spending a two weeks' vacation is suddenly of intense interest to the police. An elderly absent-minded clergyman has vanished from the hotel,

Christie, Agatha, 1890-1976—*Continued*
and one or two other things seem very odd about the establishment. This London crime tale [is] complete with a clever Chief Inspector who cooperates with Miss Marple . . . [and is] brought to an end with a surprising stroke of horror." Publ Wkly

The body in the library. Dodd, Mead 1942 245p o.p.
Available G.K. Hall large print edition

"The body that turns up in the married colonel's library is that of a dancing hostess from a neighboring seaside hotel. The setting is St. Mary Mead, whence Miss Marple has drawn her knowledge of human evil and duplicity and applies it to the case at hand, predicting a second murder and averting a third." Barzun. Cat of Crime. Rev and enl edition

also in Christie, A. Five complete Miss Marple novels p555-650

The boomerang clue
In Christie, A. Five classic murder mysteries p305-442

By the pricking of my thumbs. Dodd, Mead 1968 275p o.p.
The ingredients of this mystery plot "run all the way from the fancies of some old ladies in a home for the elderly, to dark hints at child murder, the machinations of a clever criminal gang, and the secret life of a supposedly peaceful English village. . . . [Solved by] the husband-and-wife team of Tuppence and Tommy [Beresford]." Publ Wkly

A Caribbean mystery
In Christie, A. Five complete Miss Marple novels p149-262

Curtain. Dodd, Mead 1975 238p o.p.
Amereon reprint available $20.95 (ISBN 0-88411-386-8)
Also available G.K. Hall large print edition

"In this her last book, which contrives Poirot's death *proprio motu*, the old grand master shows that her powers of invention and execution remained strong and fresh till the end. Her villain acts villainous in an entirely new way and from an original yet convincing motive. As for Poirot's performance, it is charged with a new purposefulness, ending in a fine display of moral conscience. The story may have one or two moments of weak writing and even an unparsable sentence, but it is an astonishing piece of work nevertheless." Barzun. Cat of Crime. Rev and enl edition

Death comes as the end
In Christie, A. Five classic murder mysteries p545-671

Death on the Nile. Dodd, Mead 1938 c1937 326p o.p.
First published 1937 in the United Kingdom
Detective Hercule Poirot is aboard a Nile steamer in Egypt when the seemingly motiveless murder of a beautiful newly married young woman occurs. Complications quickly multiply as he investigates the case

Easy to kill
In Christie, A. Agatha Christie: five complete novels of murder and detection

Endless night. Dodd, Mead 1968 o.p.
Available G.K. Hall large print edition
First published 1967 in the United Kingdom
"A sharp break with all her previous work: none of her usual detectives. No résumé would be fair since the impact of the book depends upon a skillfully worked-out *volte-face* involving two characters. The creator of Roger Ackroyd has done it again, in a different way, but without any pretense at detection." Barzun. Cat of Crime. Rev and enl edition

Evil under the sun. Dodd, Mead 1941 260p o.p.
Available G.K. Hall large print edition
The body of beautiful Arlena Marshall is found in a cove and the untangling of the mystery presents Detective Poirot with one of the most baffling and surprising puzzles of his career

also in Christie, A. Agatha Christie: five complete novels of murder and detection

Five classic murder mysteries. Avenel Bks. 1985 671p o.p.
LC 84-24429
An omnibus edition of five novels that were originally published separately. The murder of Roger Ackroyd is entered below
Contents: The secret adversary (c1922); The murder of Roger Ackroyd (c1926); The boomerang clue (c1933) [variant title: Why didn't they ask Evans]; The moving finger (c1942); Death comes as the end (c1944)
The secret adversary involves the amateur couple Tuppence and Tommy Beresford as they begin sleuthing and find themselves entangled in international espionage. In The boomerang clue, a young man becomes curious about a local murder, and finds himself in danger. The moving finger features Miss Marple, as a series of poison pen letters trigger suicide and murder in rural England. Death comes as the end is a murder mystery set in Thebes, Egypt in the year 2000 B.C.

Five complete Miss Marple novels. Avenel Bks. 1980 650p o.p.
LC 80-23686
Omnibus edition of five novels that were originally published separately; The mirror crack'd and The body in the library, are entered separately
Contents: The mirror crack'd (c1962) [variant title: The mirror crack'd from side to side]; A Caribbean mystery (c1964); Nemesis (c1971); What Mrs McGilliicuddy saw! (c1957) [variant titles: The 4:50 from Paddington; Murder she said]; The body in the library (c1942)
A Caribbean mystery has Miss Marple on a West Indian holiday on which she solves two murders, thus preventing a third. In Nemesis, Miss Marple travels a route given her by a dead man in an attempt to solve a murder she knows nothing about. In What Mrs. McGillicuddy saw, a friend on her way to see Miss Marple thinks she sees a woman being strangled on a passing train

Christie, Agatha, 1890-1976—*Continued*

Hercule Poirot's casebook. Dodd, Mead 1984 860p o.p.

LC 84-13488

Analyzed in Short story index

Contents: The adventure of "The Western Star"; The tragedy at Marsdon Manor; The adventure of the cheap flat; The mystery of Hunter's Lodge; The million dollar bond robbery; The adventure of the Egyptian tomb; The jewel robbery at the Grand Metropolitan; The kidnapped Prime Minister; The disappearance of Mr. Davenheim; The adventure of the Italian nobleman; The case of the missing will; The veiled lady; The lost mine; The chocolate box; Dead man's mirror; The incredible theft; Murder in the mews; Triangle at Rhodes; The mystery of the Bagdad Chest; How does your garden grow; Yellow Iris; The dream; Problem at sea; The Nemean lion; The Lernean Hydra; The Arcadian Deer; The Erymanthian boar; The Augean stables; The Stymphalean birds; The Cretan bull; The horses of Diomedes; The Girdle of Hyppolita; The flock of Geryon; The apples of the Hesperides; The capture of Cerberus; The third-floor flat; The adventure of Johnnie Waverly; Four-and-twenty blackbirds; The under dog; The Plymouth Express; The affair at the Victory Ball; The Market Basing mystery; The Lemesurier inheritance; The Cornish mystery; The king of clubs; The adventure of the Clapham cook; Double sin; Wasps' nest; The theft of the royal ruby; The double clue

The Hollow. Putnam 1992 c1974 296p $24.95

ISBN 0-399-13727-0   LC 91-31855

"A Winterbrook edition"

First published 1946; copyright renewed 1974

"A triumph of Christie's art, not so much of characterization—for the detective story does not really permit true character study—but of *motive-building*. That is where A.C. is unrivaled. She knows how to make plausible the divergence between action and motive that maintains uncertainty until the physical clues, the times, and other objective facts mesh with motive to disclose the culprit. The great art is to multiply the ambiguities of feeling, action, and gesture without falling into obvious patterns about greed, revenge, and the like. Here the familiar figure of the able, virile, brilliant man whom women go for is admirably sketched and provided with three possible women murderers and their possibly jealous men. In addition, an elderly *femme folle* very well done—and Poirot." Barzun. Cat of Crime. Rev and enl edition

The mirror crack'd. Dodd, Mead 1962 246p o.p.

Available G.K. Hall large print edition

First published 1962 in the United Kingdom with title: The mirror crack'd from side to side

Miss Jane Marple, whose house in St. Mary Mead is close to the scene of the crime "gives Scotland Yard her gracious cooperation in solving a poisoning that takes place at a village reception where the hostess is a lovely film star." Publ Wkly

also in Christie, A. Five complete Miss Marple novels p1-147

Miss Marple: the complete short stories. Dodd, Mead 1985 346p o.p.

LC 85-10220

Available G.K. Hall large print edition

Analyzed in Short story index

Contents: The Tuesday Night Club; The Idol House of Astarte; Ingots of gold; The bloodstained pavement; Motive v. opportunity; The thumbmark of St. Peter; The blue geranium; The companion; The four suspects; A Christmas tragedy; The herb of death; The affair at the bungalow; Death by drowning; Miss Marple tells a story; Strange jest; The case of the perfect maid; The case of the caretaker; Tape-measure murder; Greenshaw's Folly; Sanctuary

The moving finger

In Christie, A. Five classic murder mysteries p445-542

Mr. Parker Pyne, detective. Dodd, Mead 1934 244p o.p.

Available G.K. Hall large print edition

First published in the United Kingdom with title: Parker Pyne investigates

Includes the following stories: Case of the city clerk; Case of the discontented husband; Case of the discontented soldier; Case of the middle-aged wife; Case of the rich woman; Gate of Baghdad; Have you got everything you want?; House at Shiraz; Oracle at Delphi; Pearl of price

Mrs. McGinty's dead. Putnam 1993 259p $24.95

ISBN 0-399-13823-4   LC 92-32590

"The Winterbrook edition"

First published 1951 in the United Kingdom with title: Blood will tell; first American edition published 1952 by Dodd, Mead

"A Poirot story with Mrs. Oliver thrown in for humor; otherwise, an ingenious plot involving the discovery of one of the offspring of some scandals of 20 years earlier, so as to account for the murder of a charwoman who presumably found an incriminating photograph. Complex and well handled, as well as amusing." Barzun. Cat of Crime. Rev and enl edition

The murder at Hazelmoor

In Christie, A. Agatha Christie: five complete novels of murder and detection

The murder at the vicarage; a detective story. Dodd, Mead 1930 319p o.p.

Colonel Protheroe, the heartily disliked squire of St Mary Mead, is the victim. The fact that his wife is desperately in love with another man seems to have supplied motive for murder on the part of two people at least. But shrewd Miss Marple points out several other possibilities

"The plot of this tale is intricate. . . . But it is well constructed and holds the reader's attention on the problem of who wanted Col. Protheroe out of the way. The byplay between the vicar and his flirtatious wife is also an amusing innovation." Barzun. Cat of Crime. Rev and enl edition

Murder in the Calais coach. Dodd, Mead 1934 302p o.p.

Variant title: Murder on the Orient Express

A man is murdered on a train going from Istanbul to Calais. The famous detective Hercule Poirot happens to be on board and unravels the mystery

Christie, Agatha, 1890-1976—*Continued*

"This is the tour de force in which Agatha makes conspiracy believable and enlivens it by a really satisfying description of the Taurus Express (part of the Orient system)." Barzun. Cat of Crime. Rev and enl edition

A murder is announced. Dodd, Mead 1950 248p o.p.

Available G.K. Hall large print edition

"A well-told story—her 50th—of blackmail and murder in an English village. Miss Marple does the detecting, and the author plays very fair with the reader in the laying down of a trail leading to the unmasking of a most satisfactory least likely person." Barzun. Cat of Crime. Rev and enl edition

The murder of Roger Ackroyd. Dodd, Mead 1926 306p o.p.

"Roger Ackroyd, a retired business man, is found dead in his study shortly after the suicide of the woman he was to have married. Suspicion and the police point to Ackroyd's adopted son as the murderer, but the outcome of the story is a complete surprise. As in others of Miss Christie's tales, the mystery is solved by . . . M. Poirot." Booklist

also in Christie, A. Five classic murder mysteries p161-302

Murder with mirrors. Dodd, Mead 1952 182p o.p.

Published in the United Kingdom with title: They do it with mirrors

Inspector Curry of Scotland Yard and Jane Marple investigate a murder at Stonygates, a rehabilitation center for delinquent boys

The mysterious affair at Styles; a detective story. Lane 1920 296p o.p.

Mrs. Inglethorpe, step-mother of John and Lawrence Cavendish, holds their estate in trust for them, but since a recent marriage to a bounder much her junior, has treated her stepsons with less than her usual generosity. She dies suddenly of strychnine poisoning. A guest in the house sends for Hercule Poirot

The mystery of the blue train. Dodd, Mead 1928 306p o.p.

When Rufus Van Aldin bought the string of rubies containing the famous 'Heart of fire,' a flawless stone of great value, he made the mistake of his life. For he gave the necklace to his daughter, who was the only being whom he loved more than himself, and Ruth was murdered and the jewels stolen. The task of finding the murderer and the thief was given to Hercule Poirot

N or M!; the new mystery. Dodd, Mead 1941 289p o.p.

In the spring of 1940, Tommy Beresford, a middle aged man who once worked for British Intelligence, and his wife Tuppence, who worked with him on several cases, are bemoaning their lack of opportunity to contribute to the war effort. Then Tommy is assigned to track down two German agents who are organizing a Fifth Column which has already penetrated the defense and intelligence establishments. Tuppence quickly discovers Tommy's secret mission by her own means and joins in the hunt

Nemesis

In Christie, A. Five complete Miss Marple novels p263-408

The pale horse. Dodd, Mead 1985 c1961 259p o.p.

LC 85-4368

"The Winterbrook edition"

First published 1961 in the United Kingdom

A story of a Catholic priest who was murdered after hearing a dying woman's confession. "On his body was discovered a list of names, mysterious in that the people had nothing in common; yet when Mark Easterbrook came to inquire into the circumstances of the people named, he began to discover a connection between them, and an ominous pattern." Publisher's note

"This story relies on Mrs. Oliver without Poirot; detection is carried out by an oldish-young scholar called Mark Easterbrook, and what he investigates is superbly organized murder compounded with black magic. A classic treatment of the paralytic suspect-cum-wheelchair is thrown in for good measure." Barzun. Cat of Crime. Rev and enl edition

Peril at End House

In Christie, A. Agatha Christie: five complete novels of murder and detection

A pocket full of rye. Dodd, Mead 1953 211p o.p.

The elder Fortescue was killed by poison, but no one could explain the rye in his pocket or the practical joke of the blackbirds in the pie. Inspector Neele welcomed Miss Marple's appearance on the scene, but it was some time before the identity of the guilty person was discovered

Sad cypress. Putnam 1994 c1940 263p $24.95

ISBN 0-399-13924-9   LC 93-31257

"The Winterbrook edition"

A reissue of the title first published 1940. Copyright renewed 1968

"Mary Gerrard, a sweet, well-liked girl, lies dead of morphine poisoning. The evidence suggests murder, and points directly to the hands of Elinor Carlisle— or so it seems. The keen-minded detective Hercule Poirot is called in to explore the charges against her." Publisher's note

The secret adversary

In Christie, A. Five classic murder mysteries p1-158

The secret of chimneys. Dodd, Mead 1925 310p o.p.

Years before World War I "the pretty little Parisian actress who had long been a member of a gang of international jewel thieves met an amorous Balkan monarch and exchanged her liberty for a few years of uneasy Queenship in a stormy capital. During the brief period before her husband's living subjects hurried him to a blood-stained grave she corresponded with her former associates using a code in which the whereabouts of certain jewels which have been hidden is described. Her letters are stolen; and the author cleverly sets a number of people to work at trying to recover them." Times Lit Suppl

Christie, Agatha, 1890-1976—*Continued*

Sleeping murder. Dodd, Mead 1976 242p o.p.

Available from Amereon; large print edition available from G.K. Hall

In this posthumously published novel spinster sleuth Miss Marple becomes involved "in an eighteen-year-old murder. Young Gwenda Reed buys a house on the coast only to find it seems oddly familiar; in time she realizes that she has lived in this house briefly when a child, and that what she has thought a nightmare was in fact her memory of seeing her stepmother strangled by a man with monkey's paws. Miss Marple warns her of possible danger unless she lets this 'sleeping murder' lie, but Gwenda and her husband are curious." Newsweek

This is not among Christie's "most skillful works, but it displays her personal sense of what she calls 'evil', of murder as an affront and a violation and an act of unique cruelty. She was not an imaginative or original enough writer to explore this, but when Marple tells us here that 'it was real evil that was in the air last night,' Christie makes us feel her curious primitive shiver." N Y Times Book Rev

Ten little Indians

In Christie, A. Agatha Christie: five complete novels of murder and detection

Thirteen at dinner. Dodd, Mead 1933 305p o.p.

Available G.K. Hall large print edition

Published in the United Kingdom with title: Lord Edgeware dies

Hercule Poirot attends a dinner party as the guest of Lady Edgeware. In the course of conversation she speaks of the desirability of getting rid of her husband, who refuses to divorce her, so that she can marry the Duke of Merton. Within twenty-four hours Lord Edgeware is dead. Poirot investigates the murder

Three blind mice

In Christie, A. Three blind mice, and other stories p1-91

Three blind mice, and other stories. Dodd, Mead 1950 c1948 250p o.p.

Analyzed in Short story index

Contents: Three blind mice; Strange jest; Tape-measure murder; The case of the perfect maid; The case of the caretaker; The third-floor flat; The adventure of Johnnie Waverly; Four and twenty blackbirds; The love detectives

A collection of eight stories and one novelette most of the puzzles solved either by Miss Marple or Hercule Poirot. The title story is a novelette, first published 1948, which was also published with the title: The mousetrap, and appeared as a play with that title. It involves a murder at a boarding-house where several people have taken shelter during a snowstorm. After a policeman arrives on skis, another murder takes place

Towards zero. Blakiston 1944 o.p.

Available G.K. Hall large print edition

"Agatha has always liked the combination of the big house on the cliff, the large party composed of relatives and in-laws at odds with one another, plus a couple of mysterious and possibly good-for-nothing male visitors. All these give sufficient reason for fastening the murder(s) upon almost any one of the group. The present brew is one of her best servings, enhanced by almost too

many cleverly arranged clues, some of them laid by the murderer to bring off a double bluff. Poirot functions only to the extent of being wished for by Insp. Battle, who is solid and acceptable." Barzun. Cat of Crime. Rev and enl edition

What Mrs. McGillicuddy saw!

In Christie, A. Five complete Miss Marple novels p409-553

The witness for the prosecution, and other stories. Dodd, Mead 1948 272p o.p.

Available G.K. Hall large print edition

Contents: The witness for the prosecution; The red signal; The fourth man; S. O. S.; Where there's a will; The mystery of the blue jar; Sing a song of sixpence; The mystery of the Spanish shawl; Philomel cottage; Accident; The second gong

Christmas stalkings; tales of yuletide murder; collected by Charlotte MacLeod. Mysterious Press 1991 264p $17.95

ISBN 0-89296-437-5   LC 91-10306

Also available G.K. Hall large print edition

Analyzed in Short story index

Includes the following stories: A political necessity, by R. Barnard; The January sale stowaway, by D. Cannell; The Santa Claus caper, by B. Crider; The fabulous Nick, by M. Friedman; The running of the deer, by R. Hill; Counterfeit Christmas, by C. MacLeod; The only true unraveller, by J. Malcolm; Fruitcake, mercy, and black-eyed peas, by M. Maron; Family Christmas, by P. Moyes; Liz Peters, PI, by E. Peters; Angels, by M. Sale; Miss Melville rejoices, by E. E. Smith; Two in the bush, by E. Wright

"MacLeod's collection is a fun read—and a fine introduction to the work of 13 talented writers." Booklist

Chute, Carolyn

The Beans of Egypt, Maine. Ticknor & Fields 1985 215p o.p.

LC 84-8840

"The Beans are the unworthy poor with a vengeance, and the novel is a sequence of their dismal, cozy or audacious moments with one another and their angry or hapless encounters with outsiders. Between chapters about the Beans, Mrs. Chute narrates the life of the Beans' neighbor, Earlene Pomerleau. . . . Her story—in its entirety—consists of her progress from a childhood dominated by God-fearing Gram and Gram-fearing Daddy to a worse subjugation—through marriage—as a woman among the Beans." N Y Times Book Rev

The author "vividly evokes the substitutions rural poverty must make for everything from drinking glasses to romance, yet her imaginary Egypt can also echo with Old Testament allusions. The writing is uneven: sometimes striking and provocative, but mainly hovering uncomfortably between (perfectly caught) rural Maine speech patterns and a more literary spareness." Libr J

Other titles about the inhabitants of Egypt, Maine are: Letourneau's Used Auto Parts (1988) and Merry men (1994)

Cisneros, Sandra

The house on Mango Street. Knopf 1994
134p $18

ISBN 0-679-43335-X   LC 93-43564

"Originally published by Arte Público Press in 1984"
Verso of title page

Composed of a series of interconnected vignettes, this
"is the story of Esperanza Cordero, a young girl growing
up in the Hispanic quarter of Chicago. For Esperanza,
Mango Street is a desolate landscape of concrete and
run-down tenements, where she discovers the hard realities of life—the fetters of class and gender, the specter
of racial enmity, the mysteries of sexuality, and more."
Publisher's note

"Although the content is at times amateurish, the
volume, a composite of evocative snapshots that manages
to passionately recreate the milieu of the poor quarters
of Chicago, is a pleasurable read." Commonweal

Woman Hollering Creek and other stories.
Random House 1991 165p $20.50

ISBN 0-394-57654-3   LC 90-52930

Analyzed in Short story index

Contents: My Lucy friend who smells like corn;
Eleven; Salvador late or early; Mexican movies; Barbie-Q;
Mericans; Tepeyac; One holy night; My tocaya; Woman
Hollering Creek; The Marlboro Man; La Fabulosa: a
Texas operetta; Remember the Alamo; Never marry a
Mexican; Bread; Eyes of Zapata; Anguiano religious ar-
ticles rosaries statues . . .; Little miracles, kept promises;
Los Boxers; There was a man, there was a woman; Tin
tan tan; Bien pretty

"Unforgettable characters march through a satisfying
collection of tales about Mexican-Americans who know
the score and cling to the anchor of their culture." NY
Times Book Rev

Clair, Maxine, 1939-

Rattlebone. Farrar, Straus & Giroux 1994
213p $20

ISBN 0-374-24716-1   LC 93-50114

Analyzed in Short story index

Contents: October Brown; Lemonade; Water seeks its
own level; Cherry bomb; The roomers; A most serene
girl; The great war; Secret love; The creation; A Sunday
kind of love; The last day of school

"Set in the black Kansas City of the 1950s, these
interconnected short stories engulf readers in lyrical
language, poignant events, and vibrant characters as they
tell the troubles and triumphs of Reenie Wilson's coming
of age. Reenie and the other townsfolk work their way
into readers' hearts via Clair's wonderful writing, making
life in Rattlebone a touching reality." SLJ

Clancy, Tom, 1947-

The Cardinal of the Kremlin. Putnam
1988 543p maps $19.95

ISBN 0-399-13345-3   LC 88-5818

In this novel Jack Ryan "is a CIA adviser to American arms negotiators. The talks are going well, but a
chance sighting by a spy satellite reveals that the Russians are pursuing their own version of Star Wars just
as they are demanding American concessions in that area
at the bargaining table. Ryan and his colleagues hope
for still more intelligence from a highly placed Russian
mole, but the long-operating source is himself threatened
with discovery." Publ Wkly

"Readers expecting the usual Clancy fare of highly-
detailed battle scenes and lengthy descriptions of technology will be disappointed . . . but the details of the
workings of the CIA and KGB will more than make
up for his lack of discourse about hardware." West Coast
Rev Books

Clear and present danger. Putnam 1989
656p $21.95

ISBN 0-399-13440-9   LC 89-10287

Also available Thorndike Press large print edition

"A president decides that drug smuggling has become
a 'clear and present danger' to national security. The
response is a complex and covert military campaign
against the 'Colombian Cartel.' Clancy presents the technology of special operations and the details of light infantry warfare with his usual facility. Superior even to
his descriptions of tools and techniques, however, is
Clancy's analysis of the legal and moral problems of
operating in a twilight zone, where the rules are ambiguous and an open society makes secrecy impossible." Publ
Wkly

Debt of honor. Putnam 1994 766p $25.95

ISBN 0-399-13954-0   LC 94-27313

Also available Thorndike Press large print edition

"Jack Ryan, now the President's National Security Adviser, finds himself embroiled in the buildup to a new
world war—one in which the stock market and national
economic policy are as critical as advanced weaponry.
A power-hungry Japanese financier, still blaming America
for his parents' deaths in WW II, plans to use his immense wealth to purchase his revenge. . . . As always,
Clancy instructs (sometimes didactically) as he entertains,
teaching us about currency trading, Asian business etiquette and the daily life of an American politician." Publ
Wkly

The hunt for Red October. Naval Inst.
Press 1984 387p $19.95

ISBN 0-87021-285-0   LC 84-16569

"Based on a true incident—the attempted defection of
a Soviet destroyer in 1975—the plot concerns the defection of the 'Red October', a Soviet submarine carrying
26 Seahawk missiles able to destroy 200 cities. Russia's
fleet is ordered to find and destroy the sub; the U.S.
Navy wants to find it and get it to an American port.
An 18-day, 4,000-mile hunt across the Atlantic ensues."
Booklist

Patriot games. Putnam 1987 540p $21.95

ISBN 0-399-13241-4   LC 87-6910

"On a visit with his wife and daughter in London,
Ryan stumbles onto an attempt by a new Irish revolutionary group to kidnap the Prince and Princess of Wales
and their eldest son. Using his Marine Corps training,
Ryan saves the royals (which leads to several visits between the Ryans and the residents of Buckingham
Palace), but Ryan becomes the target of the surviving
terrorists." Publ Wkly

Red Storm rising. Putnam 1986 652p
$21.95

ISBN 0-399-13149-3   LC 86-9488

Also available Thorndike Press large print edition

"A team of Moslem terrorists blows up a key Russian
oil installation. Faced with a severe fuel shortage, the
Soviets plan to seize the Persian Gulf, after establishing
an elaborate smoke screen of hostilities against NATO.
The cunning ruses used to justify the sudden Russian

Clancy, Tom, 1947-—*Continued*
attack on Germany, the clever attempts to downplay Soviet firepower, and the subsequent land, sea, and air battles over Eastern Europe and the North Atlantic take up much of this book as the author weaves the various key offensives together." Booklist

The sum of all fears. Putnam 1991 798p $24.95

ISBN 0-399-13615-0   LC 91-11917
Also available Thorndike Press large print edition

"In the late 1990s the world is cautiously emerging from the Cold War; even the Arab-Israeli conflict is being resolved, thanks to the cleverness of Clancy's hero Jack Ryan. But as confrontation yields to cooperation, what becomes of displaced terrorists? Palestinians without a cause and East Germans without a country seek to rekindle U.S.-U.S.S.R. animosity." Publ Wkly

Without remorse. Putnam 1993 639p $24.95

ISBN 0-399-13825-0   LC 93-13940

"John Kelly [introduced in The hunt for Red October] an ex-Navy SEAL in torment over the recent, accidental death of his wife and the murder of a friend (who was mixed up with a drug ring) takes on two free-lance jobs. First, he sets out to eliminate the man or men responsible for the murder by becoming judge and executioner (skip the jury) of any and all drug dealers who can lead him to the responsible party. Second, he agrees to return to Vietnam (this is 1970), where he has already earned three Purple Hearts. He leads a raid into the north where U.S. officers are being held for interrogation by the Soviets." Booklist

Clark, Carol Higgins
Decked; a Regan Reilly mystery. Warner Bks. 1992 230p $17.95

ISBN 0-446-51549-3   LC 91-50639
Also available Thorndike Press large print edition

This mystery, finds "private detective Regan Reilly returning to Oxford for her tenth reunion. Discovery of a dead classmate's body on the estate of a former professor and his eccentric aunt, however, dampens any festivity. Regan accompanies the aunt on a week-long cruise to New York after someone poisons the original companion, but stays in touch with police. Danger lurks on the boat, of course, and Regan figures things out just in time." Libr J

Iced. Warner Bks. 1995 256p $19.95

ISBN 0-446-51764-X   LC 95-7592

"Thirtysomething private investigator Reilly is headed for the ski slopes of Aspen for the Christmas holidays, parents in tow. Mom and Dad are to be houseguests of television actress Kendra Wood while Regan visits with an old friend who's opening a new restaurant. But the Reillys walk into more than just a cheery holiday ski party—Kendra Wood's valuable art collection has been stolen, and her trusted housekeeper, Eben Bean, is missing. That's all Regan needs to know to send her off in pursuit of Eben and the sneaky thieves." Booklist

Snagged. Warner Bks. 1993 227p $18.95

ISBN 0-446-51548-5   LC 92-50568

In Miami for a friend's wedding L.A. based PI Regan Reilly "acquires a new friend in the bride's uncle, Richie Blossom, who has invented 'run-proof, snag-proof' pantyhose. If Richie can sell his patent to a manufacturer,

he'll have the funds to buy the retirement home where he and his friends live. . . . Meanwhile Ruth Craddock of Calla-Lilly Hosiery, who has her hands on a pair of the prototype pantyhose, realizes that Richie's invention could put her out of business. When an aggressive driver nearly mows Richie down, Regan appoints herself his protector." Publ Wkly

Clark, Curt
For works written by this author under other names see Westlake, Donald E.

Clark, Mary Higgins
All around the town. Simon & Schuster 1992 301p o.p. Buccaneer Bks. reprint available $32.95 (ISBN 1-56849-264-2)
                                LC 92-7511

"When four-year-old Laurie Kenyon ventures out into the front yard to wave at a funeral procession against the strict rules imposed by her mother, nightmarish repercussions ensue. She is kidnapped by a child molester who is abetted by his wife. Even though Laurie is released a few years later and returned to her family, the horror is buried within her psyche. . . . A psychiatrist discovers that Laurie has four other personalities." Booklist

"Besides doling out the visceral thrills in well-calibrated increments [Clark] also knows how to translate more complex psychological terrors into simple, scary prose. There is cunning here, and much craft." N Y Times Book Rev

The Anastasia syndrome and other stories. Simon & Schuster 1989 318p o.p. Buccaneer Bks. reprint available $29.95 (ISBN 1-56849-073-9)
                                LC 89-38841

Analyzed in Short story index
Contents: The Anastasia syndrome; Terror stalks the class reunion; Lucky day; Double vision; The lost angel

In the title novella a "noted woman historian sets to work on a study of the British Civil War, juggling her research schedule with a love affair with a rising politician. But her writing is interrupted by strange mental sequences that seem to transport her back to Cromwell's time and involve her in plots against the monarchy. Moreover, these troubling events out of the past are mirrored in the present as a series of terrorist bombings seems to follow the historian's path around England." Booklist

The cradle will fall. Simon & Schuster 1980 314p o.p. Buccaneer Bks. reprint available $25.95 (ISBN 0-89968-448-3)
                                LC 80-121

"The story centers on what assistant prosecutor Katie De Maio may have seen when she was recovering in the hospital from a car accident. Katie believes, but isn't sure, that she saw a doctor load the body of a young woman into the trunk of a car. Katie has seen clearly, but she doesn't know it. The doctor, a fertility expert who murders his unsuccessful experimental subjects, has seen Katie and determines to get rid of her." Booklist

Clark, Mary Higgins—*Continued*

A cry in the night. Simon & Schuster 1982 317p o.p. Buccaneer Bks. reprint available $25.95 (ISBN 0-89968-447-5)

LC 82-10289

"After divorce from a callow actor, Jenny McPartland works hard at a Manhattan art gallery to support her two young daughters. At an exhibition of the works of Erich Krueger, the painter is thunderstruck when he meets Jenny. He is handsome, mature, kind, and he loves her children, so when he proposes, Jenny accepts. At first she is impressed with Erich's magnificent mansion in rural Minnesota; but her new husband soon displays odd traits and jealous possessiveness. When Jenny's ex-husband shows up to scrounge, he quickly disappears; a too friendly stable boy nearly dies of poison; Jenny gives birth to Erich's child, which dies mysteriously—and all signs point to Jenny as either mad or criminal." Publ Wkly

In this neo-Gothic thriller "the clues are so subtle, so delicately woven into the fabric of the heroine's life, that even the reader begins to believe, with the heroine, that she herself is either criminal or insane." West Coast Rev Books

I'll be seeing you. Simon & Schuster 1993 317p o.p.

LC 93-16584

The "heroine is Meghan Collins, a young reporter who's just landed a coveted spot on network news, but her satisfaction is tempered by sadness and worry as the investigation into her father's puzzling death flounders in uncertainty. . . . Then Meghan has a jolting experience while covering a news story at a Manhattan hospital. An unidentified young woman is rushed in, dying from a knife wound to the heart, and—there's no other way to put it—she's a dead ringer for Meghan." Booklist

"The story moves swiftly and plays cunningly on the universal fear of parental loss and abandonment. And by voicing our secret anxieties about designer genetics . . . Ms. Clark raises such horrid possibilities that, like Meghan, we have no patience for some silly killer lurking in the shadows." N Y Times Book Rev

The lottery winner; Alvirah and Willy stories. Simon & Schuster 1994 265p $22

ISBN 0-671-86716-4   LC 94-241491

Analyzed in Short story index

Contents: The body in the closet; Death on the Cape; Plumbing for Willy; A clean sweep; The lottery winner; Bye, Baby Bunting

"For readers who enjoy the nouveau riche approach to crime solving (á la Jonathan and Jennifer Hart or Nick and Nora Charles), these stories may prove . . . entertaining." Booklist

Loves music, loves to dance. Simon & Schuster 1991 319p o.p. Buccaneer Bks. reprint available $32.95 (ISBN 1-56849-265-0)

LC 91-10757

Also available Thorndike Press large print edition

This novel focuses "on two friends, Erin and Darcy, who'd been college roommates and now, in their late twenties and each engrossed in her own profession, remain close. Thinking little of it, they become involved in a research project concerning people who utilize personal ads to meet people of potential romantic interest; but their efforts result in the murder of Erin." Booklist

"This Cinderella story turned sour reaffirms that Mary Higgins Clark deserves her reputation for creating splendid suspenseful fiction. Though the novel's characters are simple in more ways than one . . . the plot—surprisingly upbeat and thoroughly engaging—more than makes up for this flaw." N Y Times Book Rev

Remember me. Simon & Schuster 1994 306p $23.50

ISBN 0-671-86708-3   LC 94-8762

"Just what is the mysterious presence that seems to haunt Menley Nichols and baby Hannah in their spectacular rented Cape Cod mansion? Menley is still trying to recover from the horror of her two-year-old son Bobby's death on the railroad crossing. Lawyer husband Adam is too busy dashing to and from New York, and defending a local hunk suspected of doing away with his wealthy bride, to be much help. And so the presence moves in on Menley, *Rebecca* style, with eerie middle-of-the-night sound effects and rocking cradles. As always with Clark, there are several plots going on at once, which are miraculously blended and resolved in the finale." Publ Wkly

Stillwatch. Simon & Schuster 1984 302p o.p. Buccaneer Bks. reprint available $28.95 (ISBN 1-56849-070-4)

LC 84-14058

"Pat Traymore arrives in the nation's capital to produce a TV documentary on Sen. Abigail Jennings, rumored to be the President's choice to succeed the ailing, retired Vice-President. Disregarding dire warnings, Pat moves back into the house where, when she was a baby, her father had killed her mother and himself and tried to kill her too. The young woman begins to suspect something not quite admirable in Jenning's background as her research gets under way." Publ Wkly

A stranger is watching. Simon & Schuster 1978 c1977 314p o.p. Buccaneer Bks. reprint available $25.95 (ISBN 1-56849-071-2)

"When Steve Peterson's son and girl friend disappear, there is no apparent connection between this event and the murder of Steve's wife several years earlier. The latter crime had supposedly been solved, and, indeed, the convicted murderer is about to be executed. However, the kidnapping, the murder, and the execution are linked, as it turns out, and the common denominator is an expert mechanic and full-time psychopath named Arty." Best Sellers

Weep no more, my lady; a novel. Simon & Schuster 1987 315p o.p. Buccaneer Bks. reprint available $27.95 (ISBN 0-89968-446-7)

LC 87-4760

This novel "is a throwback to the romantic suspense of the thirties and forties. A beautiful leading actress, Leila LaSalle, dies in a fall from her high-rise terrace, leaving behind a wealthy fiancé who is arrested for her murder. Various 'friends' jockey for money and power and alibis, while her inconsolable little sister wanders around unaware that she is next on the killer's hit list." Wilson Libr Bull

Clark, Mary Higgins—*Continued*

"Although this novel is not quite as tightly plotted as other of Clark's best-sellers, . . . the author's legions of fans will find much to enjoy here—characters aplenty, multiple motives, and enough surprises to keep the action chugging along." Booklist

Where are the children? Simon & Schuster 1975 223p o.p. Buccaneer Bks. reprint available $25.95 (ISBN 0-89966-780-5)

This tale is "set against a background of Cape Cod in the dead of winter. Nancy Eldredge's past hides a terrible secret. She was once tried and almost convicted of the murder of her two young children from a first marriage. . . . She is now happily married again with another little boy and girl. When these two children vanish from their front yard in a snowstorm, Nancy's past is raked up and the local police are certain she has killed again. Under medical hypnosis she begins to relive things about the first crime long buried in her subconscious, and a devilish pattern emerges showing the connection between what did happen and what is happening now." Publ Wkly

While my pretty one sleeps; a novel. Simon & Schuster 1989 318p o.p. Buccaneer Bks. reprint available $25.95 (ISBN 1-56849-072-0)

LC 89-6078

"Fashion expert Neeve Kearney wonders why a controversial, unlikable writer, Ethel Lambston, suddenly disappears and is then murdered. Clark assembles a cast of suspects and skillfully juggles the possible motives and clues. As Neeve gathers evidence, a killer is hired to do her in. Meanwhile, Neeve's father, a former police commissioner, is haunted by a threat issued long ago against his daughter. He becomes convinced that the source of the present danger is the same organized crime figure accused of killing Neeve's mother 17 years earlier. Not the best of Clark's thrillers, but certain to be of interest to her widespread audience." Booklist

Clark, Walter Van Tilburg, 1909-1971

The Ox-bow incident. Random House 1940 309p o.p.

Available from Amereon and P. Smith

"Rustlers are systematically stealing cattle near Bridger's Gulch, Nevada, in the late 1880s. After a cattleman is killed, an illegal posse is formed to apprehend the criminals. In a remote valley they surprise three men, hold a makeshift trial, and hang the three. Soon afterward it is discovered that the wrong men have been punished. This is a western with psychological insight." Shapiro. Fic for Youth. 3d edition

Clarke, Arthur C., 1917-

2001: a space odyssey. New Am. Lib. 1968 221p o.p. Buccaneer Bks. reprint available $24.95 (ISBN 0-56849-417-3)

"Based on a screenplay by Stanley Kubrick and Arthur C. Clarke." Title page

"Alien monoliths mysteriously influence human evolution and entice a space mission into the outer solar system, where computer HAL breaks down and the lone survivor undergoes a psychedelic encounter with strangeness: a symbolic transcendence of the human condition." Anatomy of Wonder 4

2010: odyssey two. Ballantine Bks. 1982 291p o.p.

LC 82-6850

"A Del Rey book"

"The Soviet Union and the United States send a joint mission, which includes Dr. Heywood Floyd, to find out what happened to David Bowman, HAL, and the 'Discovery'. . . . Clarke has written a sequel to the movie, not the book, but it doesn't matter. This is another gripping adventure for which there is bound to be much demand." Libr J

2061: odyssey three. Ballantine Bks. 1987 279p o.p.

LC 87-47811

"A Del Rey book"

"Fifty years after the alien message forbidding humans to approach the moon Europa, an expedition to Halley's Comet is forced to violate the prohibition in the name of mercy." Libr J

"Clarke transforms his grasp of science into informed speculation while unleashing, with the understated skill of a master storyteller, several stunning narrative twists." Booklist

Beyond the fall of night; [by] Arthur C. Clarke and Gregory Benford. Putnam 1990 298p o.p.

LC 89-39736

"An Ace/Putnam book"

This volume contains the original text of Clarke's Against the fall of the night (a revised edition entitled The city and the stars is entered below) and Benford's sequel which "takes place many years later: Earth is now under siege by the 'Mad Mind,' a being of pure mentality created by a much earlier galactic Empire. Cley, last of the seemingly primitive 'Urhumans,' initially refuses to help Alvin, Clarke's hero, in battle. But she begins to view her role differently with the aid of Seeker, a furry 'raccoon-creature' whose species avows 'a respect for evolution and one's place in it.'" Publ Wkly

Childhood's end. Ballantine Bks. 1953 214p o.p.

Available from Amereon and Buccaneer Bks.

This novel is "paradigmatic of Clarke's more speculative, transcendental novels. Structured as a succession of apocalyptic revelations, it depicts the sudden metamorphosis of humanity, under the protective midwifery of the alien Overlords, into the next evolutionary stage, a group mind that ultimately merges with the cosmic Overmind, destroying the Earth in the process. . . . The alien other that transcends humanity yet paradoxically represents humanity's destiny is a recurring theme in the author's speculative novels." New Ency of Sci Fic

The city and the stars. Harcourt Brace & Co. 1956 310p o.p. Buccaneer Bks. reprint available $24.95 (ISBN 1-56849-418-1)

Expanded version of the author's Against the fall of night

"Alvin, a young man in the enclosed 'Utopian' city of Diaspar, on Earth in the 'Far Future,' becomes impatient at the stasis of the perfect life, and after many adventures makes his way outside the city, to Lys, another Utopia, of a different kind, which stresses closeness to nature. Ultimately Alvin finds an alien spaceship left behind millennia ago, visits the stars, and finally discovers the true nature of the cosmic perspective which

Clarke, Arthur C., 1917——*Continued*

has been hidden from both Lys and Diaspar. The final passages blend a sense of loss and of transcendence with an almost mystical intensity." Sci Fic Ency

Cradle; [by] Arthur C. Clarke & Gentry Lee. Warner Bks. 1988 293p o.p.

LC 87-37283

"Photojournalist Carol Dawson charters a fishing boat off the Florida coast, ostensibly to investigate mysterious whale behavior but in reality to check out suspicions that the U.S. Navy is searching for a missing test missile. She and her companion-diver find a huge underwater chamber filled with advanced technology; further exploration leads them to alien robots sent out to seed distant planets." Booklist

"Clarke and Lee tell a gripping, exciting story, most of it at the kind of flat-out pace that keeps readers turning pages and fretting over what might happen next." West Coast Rev Books

Earthlight. Ballantine Bks. 1955 186p o.p.

"Two hundred years after the moon had been meticulously explored and made habitable, man has learned the secret of extracting the previous heavy minerals buried 60 miles below its surface. These rich ore reserves trigger a war between Earth and the Federation of colonized planets. A reluctant young Central Intelligence agent is sent out from Earth, and through his eyes we see the moon's terrain and witness a spectacular space battle. This novel was first published 1955, but this well-known scientist and science fiction writer's vivid rendering of the moon's geography is as realistic as a telecast from a Lunar Rover. He imparts masses of scientific information painlessly and maintains suspense with a well-plotted war story." Publ Wkly

A fall of moondust. Harcourt, Brace & World 1961 248p o.p.

"A science-fiction story, timed a century in the future, when men supposedly have been long established on the Moon. The tale is about what happens when a sightseeing vehicle, full of tourists, has an accident and is buried deeply under an enormous pile of fine volcanic dust in one of the Moon's craters, and how the expert technicians race against time in an effort to save the trapped people." Springfield Repub

"The fascination of this simple tale lies in its transferring a universal predicament to surroundings at once alien and possessed of verisimilitude. Mr. Clarke has thought out his Moon; he has thought it out with such thoroughness, consistency and care that we simply must believe him; and believing him, we are engrossed." Times Lit Suppl

The Garden of Rama; by Arthur C. Clarke and Gentry Lee. Bantam Bks. 1991 441p o.p.

LC 91-2888

This is the third title in the Rama saga. "Trapped aboard the massive Raman spacecraft as it leaves Earth's solor system, three cosmonauts begin a 13-year voyage toward an unknown destination. Combining the best of space adventure (as the spacefarers encounter other life forms within the multi-habitat vessel) with human drama (as children are born and raised in an unearthly environment), this third novel in the Rama cycle asks as many questions as it answers." Libr J

Followed by Rama revealed

The hammer of God. Bantam Bks. 1993 226p o.p.

LC 93-22096

Expanded version of a short story that appeared 1992 in Time magazine

"As an asteroid named 'Kali' hurtles toward earth on a collision course that spells the end to life on the planet, a lone spaceship armed with a weapon to alter the asteroid's path attempts to carry out its perilous mission—unaware that others are simultaneously working for earth's destruction." Libr J

This is "vintage Arthur C. Clarke. While he takes pains to persuade readers that the threat of destruction from outer space is real, he is optimistic about humanity's ability to meet any challenge if its keeps its collective head." N Y Times Book Rev

Imperial Earth. Harcourt Brace Jovanovich 1976 303p o.p.

First published 1975 in the United Kingdom

"The story takes place in 2276, when an emissary is sent from Titan, a moon of Saturn, to Earth in commemoration of the U.S. Quincentennial. The emissary is Duncan Makenzie, son of the president of Titan and grandson of the earth-born explorer who helped settle Titan and turn it into an economic force in the solar system." Booklist

Clarke's "novel is crammed with fascinating gimmicks; polyominoes, asymptotic drives, joy machines, gold reefs, very long radio waves, free fall sex as taught by the NASA Sutra, and much else. Each novelty is utterly plausible, as if its introduction into our lives were absolutely inevitable. The administering of those minute fixes of cultural shock is an essential part of science fiction, and no one does it better than Mr. Clarke." Times Lit Suppl

The nine billion names of God; the best short stories of Arthur C. Clarke. Harcourt, Brace & World 1967 277p o.p.

Analyzed in Short story index

Contents: The nine billion names of God; I remember Babylon; Trouble with time; Rescue party; The curse; Summertime on Icarus; Dog star; Hide and seek; Out of the sun; The wall of darkness; No morning after; The possessed; Death and the Senator; Who's there; Before Eden; Superiority; A walk in the dark; The call of the stars; The reluctant orchid; Encounter at dawn; "If I forget thee, oh Earth . . . "; Patent pending; The sentinel; Transience; The star

Rama II; by Arthur C. Clarke and Gentry Lee. Bantam Bks. 1989 420p o.p.

LC 89-15152

In this second installment in the Rama saga "another *Rama* appears in our galaxy with the same shape, the same unearthly vistas, and even more creatures running wild over its spacescapes. A childlike genius, a beautiful medical officer, and a deeply religious military man form the nucleus of the good guys, anxious to explore, befriend the creatures, and discover the true purpose of the spacecraft." Booklist

Followed by The Garden of Rama

Rama revealed; [by] Arthur C. Clarke and Gentry Lee. Bantam Bks. 1994 466p $22.95

ISBN 0-553-09536-6   LC 93-31459

Clarke, Arthur C., 1917—*Continued*

In this conclusion of the Rama cycle "Cosmonaut Nicole Wakefield, the former governor of the human colony housed within the globe-shaped spaceship Rama III, is awaiting execution for opposing the fascistic powers that now run the colony. She is rescued from her cell by small robots sent by her husband Richard, whom she had thought dead. . . . Along with friends and family from the Earth sector, they begin traveling through the different alien environments housed in the vast Raman world." Publ Wkly

"Fans of skillfully crafted hard sf . . . will find plenty of Clarke and Lee's fascinating scientific speculations vividly given form in the marvels of Raman technology." Booklist

Rendezvous with Rama. Harcourt Brace Jovanovich 1973 303p o.p. Buccaneer Bks. reprint available $26.95 (ISBN 0-89968-449-1)

A massive space capsule "is discovered approaching earth in the 22nd century. A team of scientists sent into space to make contact with and explore the monster at first believe it to be a dead artifact launched from an unknown galaxy a million years before. But as the machine approaches solar orbit it comes alive—with light, oxygen and biological life—and human reactions to it are mixed. A religious cult thinks Rama is a rescue ship come to save the faithful, while colonists on Mercury start making a bomb to keep the thing away." Publ Wkly

This work contains "flights of prose where the language fairly purrs. And here too one finds the questioning and probing of man and his place in the cosmos that marks good fiction and good science fiction." Libr J

Followed by Rama II

Classic lines: more great racing stories. See The New treasury of great racing stories

Clavell, James

Gai-Jin; a novel of Japan. Delacorte Press 1993 1038p $27.50

ISBN 0-385-31016-1   LC 92-42129

The sixth volume in the author's Asian saga depicts the political and social intrigue that resulted when Japan slowly opened its doors to foreigners or gai-jin. This novel "opens in 1862 with a fictionalized version of the assassination of a British citizen, Charles Richardson, by samurai traveling with the rebellious lord of Satsuma on the great national highway known as the Tokaido. It ends with the British bombardment of Kagoshima in 1863, a seminal event on the road to the Meiji Restoration, which brought feudal Japan into the modern era." N Y Times Book Rev

Clavell "melds plot-driven storytelling and colorful characterization in vibrant collaboration with an exotic, dynamic setting." Publ Wkly

King Rat. Delacorte Press 1983 c1962 363p $17.95

ISBN 0-385-29211-2   LC 82-19790

Third novel in the author's Asian saga

A reissue of the title first published 1962 by Little, Brown

"A novel about corruption, fear and despair among the prisoners in a Singapore prison camp in World War II. 'King Rat,' so called because he breeds the prison rats and sells them for food, is an American corporal turned gambler and black marketeer. He has bribed his way into a position as real though unofficial ruler of the camp." Publ Wkly

This novel "is strong in narrative detail, penetrating in observation of human nature under stress, and thought-provoking in its analysis of right and wrong." Cincinnati Public Libr

Noble house; a novel of contemporary Hong Kong. Delacorte Press 1981 1206p $29.95

ISBN 0-385-28737-2   LC 80-26889

Fourth novel in the author's Asian saga

"Ian Dunross, head of Struan's, an old and respected China trade firm in Hong Kong, makes his appearance in the middle of a typhoon, and from there to the very end of this . . . saga the action never lets up. This action takes place during one week of 1963, with two plots going, and dozens of participants. . . . Along the way we are treated to the sights, sounds, smells, and history of Hong Kong. There is international finance and banking, the workings of multinational companies, smuggling of narcotics and gold, insight into how the Chinese regard sex, and their marvelously pragmatic view of how the world works." Libr J

Shogun; a novel of Japan. Delacorte Press 1983 c1975 802p $25

ISBN 0-385-29224-4

First novel in the author's Asian saga

A reissue of the title first published 1975 by Atheneum

East and West meet in this "epic of feudal seventeenth-century Japan. When a gale casts John Blackthorne's ship ashore here, the English sea pilot and his crew must learn to sink or swim in an alien culture. Blackthorne's mentor is a feudal lord locked in a power struggle with another for control of all Japan. How Blackthorne makes himself useful and is rewarded with samurai status forms the bulk of this swashbuckler." Booklist

"Clavell creates a world: people, customs, settings, needs and desires all become so enveloping that you forget who and where you are. 'Shōgun' is history infused with fantasy. It strives for epic dimension and occasionally it approaches that elevated state. It's irresistible, maybe unforgettable." N Y Times Book Rev

Tai-Pan. Delacorte Press 1983 c1966 590p $19.95

ISBN 0-385-29218-X   LC 82-18339

Second novel in the author's Asian saga

A reissue of the title first published 1966 by Atheneum

"The time is 1841. England has just won the first Opium War with China and is determined to advance her interests there. Dirk Struan is tai-pan (supreme ruler) of the Noble House, the most powerful trading company in the orient. Struan realizes with a prophetic vision the value of Hong Kong and her port. He feels that England must use this area to branch out over the far East. Opposition to his plan comes from the apathy of politicians in England. Struan must also deal with Chinese pirates and with the multiple entity that is China and her people." Best Sellers

"The backgrounds—Hong Kong, the sailing ships, the trading preserve in Canton—surge with life, and the plot is neatly dovetailed with history. Superb storytelling; an utterly absorbing book." Publ Wkly

Clavell, James—*Continued*
Whirlwind. Morrow 1986 1147p o.p.
LC 86-11293

Fifth novel in the author's Asian saga

"Andrew Gavallan, based in Scotland, runs a helicopter company operating in Iran during the Shah's reign. When Khomeini comes to power, Gavallan must get his pilots and their families, and his valuable helicopters, out of the riot-torn country. Complicating matters is his power struggle with his company's secret owner, the Noble House of Hong Kong. The pilots' escape efforts form the basic story [of the novel]." Libr J

"Clavell has done a fine job . . . of delineating the geography and politics of a country in turmoil. He seems less successful with the characters, however, as many of his Iranians are thinly disguised stereotypes. Still, the novel is rife with corporate and multinational intrigue, political drama, and romance." Booklist

Cleary, Jon, 1917-
Babylon South. Morrow 1990 c1989 382p o.p.
LC 89-12939

First published 1989 in the United Kingdom

"Two decades after High Court judge Sir Walter Springfellow disappeared, hikers uncover a skeleton wearing his signet ring. When [Detective-Inspector Scobie Malone of the New South Wales Police] reopens the inquiry, he finds that Venetia Springfellow has parlayed the fortune her husband left her into an empire her venomous sister-in-law Emma wants to control. Then Emma is killed and Scobie is saddled with two highly sensitive cases that his jumpy superior prefers to leave unsolved." Publ Wkly

Bleak spring. Morrow 1994 c1993 287p $22

ISBN 0-688-12332-5   LC 93-22610

Also available G.K. Hall large print edition

First published 1993 in the United Kingdom

"Inspector Scobie Malone of the Sydney police looks for the killer of his daughter's boyfriend's father, uncovering a secret bank account and a vast plot in the process." Libr J

"Cleary's sure grip on the brisk plot is equaled by his grasp of psychological motivations. This is first-rate storytelling." Publ Wkly

Dark summer. Morrow 1993 c1992 269p $20

ISBN 0-688-11414-8   LC 92-30482

Also available Thorndike Press large print edition

First published 1992 in the United Kingdom

"When Sydney policeman Scobie Malone . . . finds the body of an informer floating in the pool outside his home, it's merely the first in a series of seemingly random killings. Injecting his victims with poison, the murderer also claims a couple of dockside union hoods and an old prostitute. Scobie takes to the docklands, once the stomping ground of his estranged father, and uncovers secret deliveries of drugs." Publ Wkly

"Cleary gives his readers high adventure, a clever plot, plenty of wit and humor, and a motley cast of engaging lowlifes—all that and the charm of daily life Down Under." Booklist

The faraway drums. Morrow 1982 c1981 288p o.p.
LC 81-14091

First published 1981 in the United Kingdom

"The scene is India in 1911. King George and Queen Mary are there to be crowned emperor and empress. A group of religious fanatics wants to assassinate the king. But wait—a handsome British intelligence officer and a beautiful Boston newspaperwoman are out to stop this crime. The story is partially told by the newspaperwoman in the form of a memoir." Booklist

"Writing sensitively and dramatically, Cleary shows us the fatal discrepancies of a doomed society. Always absorbing, this novel so vividly recreates the now-faded glory of the British Empire that the picture lingers after the book is read." Publ Wkly

The High Commissioner. Morrow 1966 284p o.p.

"The adventures of an Australian police detective, Scobie Malone, who goes to London to arrest the Australian High Commissioner for the murder of his first wife. The commissioner's participation in an international conference on Vietnam brings other elements into a case that has a number of ramifications, including a deepening friendship between Scobie and the commissioner." Booklist

Malone "falls into a surprising relationship of friendship and mutual admiration with the man he is supposed to arrest. . . . Though the plot creaks in a few places, it offers a moving picture of a great man's fall from greatness, an acid and entertaining view of diplomatic cocktail parties, [and] some sequences of tingling suspense and drama." Publ Wkly

High road to China; a novel. Morrow 1977 276p o.p.

"It is 1920. Eve Tozer, beautiful daughter of a merchant tycoon, gets word that her father has been kidnapped by a Chinese warlord and faces execution unless Eve reaches China with an ancient statue as ransom. Plucky and determined, Eve buys three war surplus Bristol fighters, and with an English ex-major, a German baron and a Chinese emissary, attempts the 800 mile trip from London to the Middle Kingdom. All manner of thrilling adventures occur as the unlikely troupe of travelers encounter bizarre and wildly colorful characters, including a mad Balkan countess and a Waziri tribal leader who speaks race track English." Publ Wkly

Murder song. Morrow 1990 288p o.p.
LC 90-39931

In this novel featuring Scobie Malone "a psychopath's killings converge with organized-crime efforts to wipe out a crooked financier before he talks." Publ Wkly

"The atmosphere here—low-rent Sydney in the pouring rain—is unusual and evocatively described, and the characterization of the hapless Scobie, battling demons both on the job (a raving psychopath) and off (a cranky spouse), is a delight." Booklist

Now and then, amen. Morrow 1989 c1988 330p o.p.
LC 88-13501

First published 1988 in the United Kingdom

"Sister Mary Magdalene is found murdered on the steps of Sydney, Australia's most expensive whorehouse. [Inspector Scobie] Malone's dogged investigation leads him to Fingal Hourigan, one of the richest and most powerful figures down under and the victim's grandfather." Booklist

Pride's harvest. Morrow 1991 288p o.p.
LC 91-30582

Cleary, Jon, 1917—_Continued_

This mystery finds Sydney detective Scobie Malone attempting to "solve a politically sensitive murder in Australia's cotton country. The victim, Ken Sagawa, ran a Japanese-controlled cotton company in Collamundra. Although the citizens have reaped financial rewards from the company's presence, many are prejudiced against the Japanese. But who would have shot the outgoing Sagawa and dumped his body into the teeth of a cotton gin? Aware that the region needs Japanese investment, the police chief is determined to find the killer and calls on Scobie and his partner." Publ Wkly

"Mr. Cleary's strongest characters are old men swollen with memories, but everyone in this richly populated narrative stands out bold against the landscape." N Y Times Book Rev

Spearfield's daughter. Morrow 1983 c1982 567p o.p.

LC 82-14542

First published 1982 in the United Kingdom

This is a story of "a talented, ambitious young woman struggling to make it on her own in a male-dominated world. In 1968, Australian journalist Cleo Spearfield, working as a correspondent in Vietnam, is shocked when her story about GI atrocities is killed by her editor for being too controversial. She resigns, moving on to England, where she becomes involved with a maverick publisher, and then to Manhattan, where romance and journalism continue to mingle." Booklist

"Although there's too much plot, too many overlapping love affairs and too many attempts on Cleo's life, the novel is continuously entertaining, and one has the feeling of keeping company with intelligent, outspoken, unpredictable and interesting people." Publ Wkly

The sundowners. Scribner 1952 290p o.p. Amereon reprint available $23.95 (ISBN 0-88411-467-8)

A story of one year in the life of a nomadic family in Australia. The chief characters are Paddy Carmody, a sheepdrover and his wife, Ida, and their fourteen year old son, Sean. The year saw ups and downs in their fortunes, hard times and good times, and the growth to maturity and understanding of the young boy

"The book is notable not so much for the action it develops as for the human qualities it depicts." N Y Her Trib Books

Clemens, Samuel Langhorne _See_ Twain, Mark, 1835-1910

Cocteau, Jean, 1889-1963

The impostor; translated from the French by Dorothy Williams. Noonday Press 1957 132p o.p.

Original French edition, 1923; first English translation published 1925 by Appleton with title: Thomas the imposter

The setting of Cocteau's short novel "is the First World War; his imposter, a French youth, too young for the services, who in a borrowed uniform and under a borrowed name succeeds in obtaining a post in a curious nursing unit run by a Polish princess and her daughter. He plays the part he has adopted so well that in the end he succeeds in convincing even himself of his authenticity, and having finally been adopted as their

mascot by a unit of Marines dies in the end a gallant death." Times Lit Suppl

Cody, Liza

Backhand. Doubleday 1992 279p $18.50

ISBN 0-385-42231-8   LC 91-35159

"A Perfect crime book"

London private investigator Anna Lee "flies to the Florida Keys in pursuit of a slippery customer who has run off with a fashion designer's exclusive line of sweaters—along with the designer's dopey teen-age daughter. Too smart to be dazzled by fat Americans who dress 'like Easter eggs' and play tennis with the ruthlessness of contract killers, she is more impressed with the quick and deadly nature of the American criminals she encounters." N Y Times Book Rev

Bucket nut. Doubleday 1993 c1992 236p $18.50

ISBN 0-385-46776-1   LC 92-30366

First published 1992 in the United Kingdom

The protagonist of this novel is "Eva Wylie, a fledgling professional wrestler working in London. Eva supports her new career with work as a security guard for a junkyard and as a courier for a shady Asian businessman. She lives with two protective dogs in a crumbling trailer amid the junk. She's a loner, very bitter, and not averse to working whatever side of the legal fence she finds herself on. Acting in her capacity as a courier, she becomes involved in a conflict between rival protection rackets. Her soul-deep bad attitude serves her well in the ensuing stroll through London's dark side. Eva's unremitting cynicism is certain to appeal to the hardest of the hard-boiled set." Booklist

Head case. Scribner 1986 197p o.p.

LC 85-25077

Working on a missing-person case, private detective Anna Lee "discovers her quarry, 16-year-old genius Thea Hahn, in a Dorset hospital, hysterical and apparently insane. Death has followed in Thea's wake—her tutor met with a fatal accident just before Thea's disappearance; another man is found shot to death in a hotel room—and Lee must sort through the vagaries of Thea's psyche, strange upbringing, and superficially tranquil past to discover whether the girl is victim or victimizer. A chilling, often funny, and finely plotted mystery." Booklist

Rift. Scribner 1988 240p o.p.

LC 88-17556

"Fay Jassahn, the narrator, is a young English freelance wardrobe assistant, who is completing a movie in Kenya in 1974. Deciding to visit Ethiopia, Fay agrees to deliver a letter across the border from a writer to his estranged lover, Natasha Beyer. Unwittingly, she involves herself in a game of dangerous intrigue. What begins as a romantic adventure—and a means of proving her independence—becomes a nightmare for Fay." Publ Wkly

Coe, Tucker

For works written by this author under other names see Westlake, Donald E.

Coetzee, J. M., 1940-
Age of iron. Random House 1990 198p $18.95

ISBN 0-394-58785-5   LC 90-8310

This novel "takes the form of a letter-diary from Mrs. Curren, a former classics professor dying of cancer, to her daughter in America. She details a series of strange events that turn her protected middle-class life upside down. A homeless alcoholic appears at her door, eventually becoming her companion and confessor. Her liberal sentiments and her very humanity are tested as she experiences directly the horrors of apartheid. She comes to recognize South Africa as a country in which the rigidity of both sides has led to barbarism and to acknowledge her complicity in upholding the system." Libr J

"The word 'shame' throbs through the text like a recurrent pain. The principal character thinks she is dying of it. . . . One can, of course, read her death as a metaphor for the doom of liberalism in South Africa. . . . But Age of Iron is about dying as much as it is about apartheid, and that raises it above the level of a political novel or a *roman à thèse*, and gives resonance to the political message." N Y Rev Books

Foe. Viking 1987 c1986 157p $15.95

ISBN 0-670-81398-2   LC 86-40267

First published 1986 in the United Kingdom

"Cast adrift by a mutinous crew, Susan Barton washes ashore on an isle of classic fiction. For the next year, Robinson Cruso sculpts the land while Friday mutely watches Susan intrude upon their loneliness. Life is mere pattern for the two unquestioning castaways, but Susan is not of their story and she pushes Cruso for rationales that don't exist in a world of imagination. Finally rescued and returned to London, Susan leads Friday to Daniel Foe, the author who will write their tale. Foe, however, sees a different story and seeks 'to tell the truth in all its substance.'" Libr J

"In adding to Defoe's repertory company, Coetzee has introduced urgencies that are neither fresh nor illumined, only brilliantly disguised. Flashing back and forward, scattering allusions, adopting a series of poses and styles, the author is less reminiscent of a prior novelist than of contemporary street mimes who build hints until the audience shouts in recognition." Time

Life & times of Michael K. Viking 1984 c1983 184p $13.95

ISBN 0-670-42789-6   LC 83-47860

First published 1983 in the United Kingdom

"Born with a harelip and brought up in an uncaring orphanage, Michael K. struggles through a desperate life in South Africa. When his sick mother persuades him to bring her back to her homeland, he must endure not only the terrible journey, pulling her in a cart he has made, but also risk the dangers of military checkpoints since he does not have the necessary permits. His undying attachment is to the land, but he is not allowed to remain the gardener he wishes to be. The details of Michael's suffering in camps, hospitals, and labor gangs are harrowing and underscore a courage that never forsakes him." Shapiro. Fic for Youth. 3d edition

The master of Petersburg. Viking 1994 250p $21.95

ISBN 0-670-85587-1

"St. Petersburg is poised for revolution as Fyodor Dostoevsky returns from Germany to claim his deceased stepson's papers. Although the police rule Pavel's death a suicide, the famous writer is drawn into a group of shady characters, including the anarchist Nechaev, who is possibly Pavel's killer. Plagued by seizures and tormented by a torrid affair with his stepson's landlady, Dostoevsky struggles to ascertain once and for all a writer's responsibility to his family and society." Libr J

"The book's momentum is dependent finally on idea rather than incident, with the significance of events contingent on one's grasp of Dostoyevsky's complex frame of beliefs. All of which makes 'The Master of Petersburg' dense and difficult, a novel that frustrates at every turn. But despite that difficulty, the figure who emerges from these pages, the master himself, in his tortured unhappiness, his terror of the next epileptic seizure, his restless sexuality and his desperate gambling with God, will seize any imagination still susceptible to the complicated passions of the Slav soul." N Y Times Book Rev

Coffey, Brian, 1945-
For works written by this author under other names see Koontz, Dean R. (Dean Ray), 1945-

Coghlan, Peggie, 1920-
See also Stirling, Jessica

Colegate, Isabel
The shooting party. Viking 1981 c1980 195p o.p.

LC 80-54194

First published 1980 in the United Kingdom

"The time is October 1913, the place an estate in Oxfordshire where Sir Randolph Nettleby and his wife are hosting the biggest shoot of the season. Brought together are the privileged in pursuit of pleasure. For these guests shooting is a special ritual with the shooters, gamekeepers, beaters, and servants all playing specific roles, and the sport is marvelously and meticulously described. Woven through the story are the portrayals of the gentry, the allusions to romantic and adulterous affairs, the relationship between the classes, and the feeling of the vast changes soon to overtake the Edwardian period. The rising tension that accompanies the final hours of the shooting on this day explodes into unexpected tragedy." Shapiro. Fic for Youth. 3d edition

The summer of the royal visit. Knopf 1992 c1991 219p $20

ISBN 0-679-40880-0   LC 91-53118

First published 1991 in the United Kingdom

This novel is "set in Bath in 1876. Told by a modern-day retired schoolteacher who has inherited his grandmother's diary, the story centers on curate Stephen Collinwood, serving the poor district of Bath. A widower who never feels equal to the demands of his faith, Collinwood harbors a passion for a married, do-good parishioner and wonders about the shady doings of

Colegate, Isabel—*Continued*

shyster Caspar Freeling and psychic Madame Sophia."
Libr J

"Although the ornate Powellian syntax can have its appeal, some of the writing is flat and awkward. . . . It remains, however, a challenging and often disturbing novel." Times Lit Suppl

Coleman, Lonnie, 1920-1982

Beulah Land. Doubleday 1973 495p o.p.

This is the first volume of the Beulah Land trilogy
"This panoramic novel of pre-Civil War (1800-1861) life on a Georgia plantation follows the fortunes of the Kendrick family, owners of Beulah Land, through a multitude of births, marriages, and deaths, dished up with a heavy-handed dollop of sex. No subtle nuances here: the good guys and the bad guys are clearly differentiated—black and white—virtue is triumphant, and evil gets its just desserts in the end. One can fault the book only on characterization; Coleman gives us a splendid picture of the times, manners, and customs of the antebellum South." Libr J
Followed by Look away, Beulah Land

The legacy of Beulah Land. Doubleday 1980 430p o.p.

LC 79-7516

"The final volume of Coleman's Beulah Land trilogy finds life on the Kendrick/Davis plantation struggling back to normal during the last quarter of the nineteenth century. New dynastic troubles plague the land, however, as a poor farmer becomes a powerful threat to the family's inheritance. Although a bit of unsubtle soap opera, the novel benefits from a huge cast of characters, a long series of predicaments, and scenes of graphic violence—all of which produce a nonstop epic." Booklist

Look away, Beulah Land; a novel. Doubleday 1977 492p o.p.

LC 76-50759

Sequel to Beulah Land
"Two great Georgia plantations, Beulah Land and the neighboring Oaks, have already been drained of most of their menfolk when the victorious Yankees finally come—to plunder, rape, burn and kill. The Kendricks, the Davis's and their remaining freed slaves begin the painful task of reconstruction, though not before two of them, accompanied by a Yankee deserter now settled at Beulah Land, take revenge on a murderous Union sergeant. The story that unfolds is intricate, encompassing several generations of whites, blacks and mulattoes whose passion-dominated lives, stirred to vigorous drama by the evil ambitions of a vengeful black, reflect the death of an old society and the birth of a new. This intricacy, however, is part of the charm and power of a tale that is history made back into life." Publ Wkly
Followed by The legacy of Beulah Land

Coleman, William Laurence *See* Coleman, Lonnie, 1920-1982

Colette, 1873-1954

Chance acquaintances

In Colette. Gigi. Julie de Carneilhan. Chance acquaintances p225-315

Chéri

In Colette. Six novels p411-534

Claudine and Annie

In Colette. The complete Claudine p516-632

Claudine at school

In Colette. The complete Claudine p1-206

In Colette. Six novels p1-234

Claudine in Paris

In Colette. The complete Claudine p209-364

Claudine married

In Colette. The complete Claudine p367-510

The collected stories of Colette; edited, and with an introduction, by Robert Phelps; translated by Matthew Ward, et al. Farrar, Straus & Giroux 1983 605p $22.50

ISBN 0-374-12629-1   LC 83-16449

Partially analyzed in Short story index
Contents: The other table; The screen; Clouk alone; Clouk's fling; Chéri; The return; The pearls; Literature; My goddaughter; A hairdresser; A masseuse; My corset-maker; The saleswoman; An interview; A letter; The Sémiramis Bar; "If I had a daughter . . ."; Rites; Newly shorn; Grape harvest; In the boudoir; The "master"; Morning glories; What must we look like; The cure; Sleepness nights; Gray days; The last fire; A fable: the tendrils of the vine; The halt; Arrival and rehearsal; A bad morning; The circus horse; The workroom; Matinee; The starveling; Love; The hard worker; After midnight; "Lola"; Moments of stress; Journey's end; "The strike, oh Lord, the strike"; Bastienne's child; The accompanist; The cashier; Nostalgia; Clever dogs; The child prodigy; The misfit; "La Fenice"; "Gitanette"; The victim; The tenor; The quick-change artist; Florie; Gribiche; The hidden woman; Dawn; One evening; The hand; A dead end; The fox; The judge; The omelette; The other wife; Monsieur Maurice; The burglar; The advice; The murderer; The portrait; The landscape; The half-crazy; Secrets; "Châ"; The bracelet; The find; Mirror games; Habit; Alix's refusal; The seamstress; The watchman; The hollow nut; The patriarch; The sick child; The rainy moon; Green sealing wax; In the flower of age; The rivals; The respite; The bitch; The tender shoot [novella]; Bygone spring; October; Armande; The rendezvous; The kepi [novella]; The photographer's wife; Bella-Vista; April
"Includes two novellas that rank as classics, not only in Colette's canon, but in all of 20th century French literature. The Tender Shoot is the story of a singularly nasty middle-aged roué's pursuit of a 15-year-old peasant girl. Upon this squalid tale, Colette lavished her most lyrical language and poetic fancies, heightening the sense of evil. . . . As Colette remarked of her writing, her 'great landscape was always the human face.' No work demonstrates this better than The Kepi, the portrait of a doomed 46-year-old French lieutenant." Time

Colette, 1873-1954—_Continued_

The complete Claudine; Claudine at school, Claudine in Paris, Claudine married, Claudine and Annie; translated by Antonia White. Farrar, Straus & Giroux 1976 632p o.p.

Omnibus edition of four semi-autobiographical novels written by Colette in 1900-1903. The first three appeared under the pen name of her husband and the fourth novel was published under both their names. These translations have copyright dates 1956, 1958, 1960 and 1962 respectively. Variant title for English translation of third volume: Indulgent husband; of final volume: Innocent wife

In the first novel we meet Claudine as a precocious school girl peeping and spying on both her contemporaries and her boarding school teachers. The second novel depicts a girl approaching womanhood discovering the exciting world of Paris and meeting a varied assortment of escorts. Claudine married is not so much the story of the heroine's marriage as the story of Claudine's love affair with Rézi, another married woman. The final volume has Claudine as one of its principal characters, but it is largely the story of an innocent young wife, who during the absence of her domineering husband begins to see more of her sister-in-law and her sophisticated friends and her eyes open to the true ways of life and love

Gigi

_In_ Colette. Gigi. Julie de Carneilhan. Chance acquaintances p9-74

_In_ Colette. Six novels p649-97

Gigi. Julie de Carneilhan. Chance acquaintances. Farrar, Straus & Young 1952 315p o.p.

Gigi is the story of a young girl brought up to be a prosperous demimondaine who maneuvers a marriage proposal from a sophisticated man-about-town. Julie de Carneilhan tells of a much married aristocrat down on her luck who agrees with an ex-husband to blackmail his present wife and split the gain. The final novella concerns Madame Colette's involvement in the amorous schemes of visitors at a country lodge

Julie de Carneilhan

_In_ Colette. Gigi. Julie de Carneilhan. Chance acquaintances p77-222

The kepi

_In_ Colette. The collected stories of Colette p498-531

The last of Chéri

_In_ Colette. Six novels p535-648

Mitsou

_In_ Colette. Six novels p339-410

Music-hall sidelights

_In_ Colette. Six novels p237-337

Six novels. Modern Lib. 697p o.p.

Contents: Claudine at school; Music-hall sidelights; Mitsou; Chéri; The last of Chéri; Gigi

The tender shoot

_In_ Colette. The collected stories of Colette p421-48

Collins, Larry, 1929-

The fifth horseman; a novel; [by] Larry Collins and Dominique Lapierre. Simon & Schuster 1980 478p o.p.

LC 80-14643

"Libyan leader Qaddafi gives a Carter-like President an ultimatum: the U.S. must force Israel to leave the West Bank and East Jerusalem, or a hydrogen bomb hidden in Manhattan will be detonated in less than two days." Libr J

This "novel is as expertly done as any [international thriller] you are likely to read. . . . Collins and Lapierre, a pair of high-powered journalists well known for deep research in their previous nonfiction works . . . have brought all their investigative skills to their first novel and the results are startlingly effective." N Y Times Book Rev

Collins, Michael, 1964-

The man who dreamt of lobsters. Random House 1993 c1992 223p $19

ISBN 0-679-42090-8   LC 92-50552

Analyzed in Short story index

First published 1992 in the United Kingdom with title: The meat eaters

Contents: First love; The butcher's daughter; The meat eaters; Northern summers; The whore mother; The enemy; The Sunday races; Sickness

"In this collection of eight stories of modern Ireland, the author draws on his country's rich leagacy to reveal the cultural myths, romantic illusions, and sentimentalism that handicap his characters, who are caught up in Ireland's ongoing social turmoil. These are stories of economic survival, gaming and drinking, coming of age, the struggle in the North, and family life." Libr J

Collins, Warwick

The rationalist; a novel. Simon & Schuster 1993 251p $21

ISBN 0-671-86939-6   LC 93-8595

As this novel opens "we find cold, controlled Dr. Grange practicing his art in a small seaside town somewhere in 18th-century England, washing his hands assiduously between patients and giving his nights over to the dry pursuit of philosophy. Grange soon finds his calm bachelor routine interrupted by the machinations of Mrs. Celia Quill, a beautiful, mysterious widow." NY Times Book Rev

Collins, Wilkie, 1824-1889

The moonstone. Knopf 1992 473p $17

ISBN 0-679-41722-2   LC 92-52918

Also available from Amereon

"Everyman's library"

First published 1868

This novel "concerns the disappearance of the Moonstone, an enormous diamond that once adorned a Hindu idol and came into the possession of an English officer. The heroine, Miss Verinder, believes her lover, Franklin Blake, to be the thief; other suspects are Blake's

Collins, Wilkie, 1824-1889—*Continued*

rival and three mysterious Brahmins. The mystery is solved by Sergeant Cuff, possibly the first detective in English fiction." Reader's Ency. 3d edition

The woman in white. Knopf 1991 xxxvii, 569p $20

ISBN 0-679-40563-1   LC 91-52971

"Everyman's library"

First published 1860; first Everyman's library edition 1910

"Practically the first English novel to deal with the detection of crime. The plot is based on the resemblance between the heroine and a mysterious woman in white, and involves an infamous attempt to obtain the heroine's money." Lenrow. Reader's Guide to Prose Fic

Colwin, Laurie

A big storm knocked it over; a novel. HarperCollins Pubs. 1993 259p $22

ISBN 0-06-017019-0   LC 92-56219

Also available Thorndike Press large print edition

"For Jane Louise, even Teddy—her wonderful, new, rock-solid husband—and a baby on the way are not enough to stave off plenty of free-floating anxiety. Luckily, she shares her joy and her distress with best friends Edie and Mokie, who have decided to embark on parenthood at the same time. The extended family formed by these two couples must suffice emotionally for each of the four individuals, since not one of the four fits within his or her own family." Booklist

"The novel makes the idea of happy endings for decent people seem entirely plausible, almost inevitable—no small feat for a writer these days and no small pleasure for a reader." N Y Times Book Rev

Family happiness; a novel. Knopf 1982 271p o.p.

LC 82-23

"Polly Solo-Miller is the mainstay of an attractive, well-to-do New York Jewish family, a family so ensconced in society, so sure of itself and its eminently proper, aristocratic view of life that there is never a doubt in the minds of any of them but what the Solo-Miller way of doing things is the best. Polly loves her husband and two children, her parents, her siblings. She is, in fact, the perfect wife, mother, daughter. But underneath there is more than a hint of rebellion seething and when Polly falls headlong in love with a painter, Lincoln, and takes to spending long and very cozy afternoons in his studio, thoroughly enjoying the adulterous affair, her Solo-Miller conscience is sorely beset." Publ Wkly

"What is so striking about this wrenching novel is not the plot itself . . . but, rather, the absolutely convincing way that Colwin portrays Polly's slow awakening to selfhood." Booklist

Goodbye without leaving. Poseidon Press 1990 253p o.p.

LC 90-6797

This novel follows the "progress of Geraldine Coleshares' life, from mediocre graduate student to rock 'n' roll backup singer to wife and mother. She seems happily married to Johnny Miller, a lawyer but a music fanatic at heart. She worries (but not too much) about what she is doing with her life, and what it all means." Libr J

"The tone here is disarmingly light, the humor intimate, and the plot inventive. A cheerfully irreverent look at an identity crisis and its unexpected resolution." Booklist

Happy all the time; a novel. Knopf 1978 213p o.p.

LC 78-2425

Set in New York City, this love story involves four quite normal people, "two men, two women. The men are cousins and close friends, the women are very different from each other, but full of spunk and individuality. Guido and Holly come together first, Vincent and Misty meet later. The men, long-time associates, are terribly nervous about their women liking each other. The women, in turn, eye each other warily. What we, as readers are treated to, however, is one of the most engaging and funniest dual courtships in a long time. The dialogue is sparkling and crisp, the encounter situations perfectly believable and perfectly ridiculous, as these four people, who really are 'happy all the time,' go through the 'angst' of realizing it." Publ Wkly

Combs, Harry

Brules. Delacorte Press 1994 c1992 598p $22.95

ISBN 0-385-31195-8   LC 93-37555

First published 1992 by Lyford Books

"Cat Brules takes up his story in 1867 as a young hellraiser just off a cattle drive to Hays City, Kansas. He kills a man in a bordello and flees through Comanche country. Captured and tortured, he escapes, later losing his best friend to the Comanche. From there, the story is mainly about Brules's prowess as a killer of Indians, but in between the cold-blooded carnage he ably describes the almost mystical attraction of the glorious Western wilderness from Texas to Montana. He sees the demise of the buffalo herds, destruction of the Plains Indians' way of life, and the gradual introduction of civilization. A violent, brutal but well-written view of Western history." Libr J

Condé, Maryse, 1937-

I, Tituba, black witch of Salem; translated by Richard Philcox; foreword by Angela Y. Davis; afterword by Ann Armstrong Scarboro. University Press of Va. 1992 227p $19.95

ISBN 0-8139-1398-5   LC 92-8134

"A Caraf book"

Original French edition, 1986

This historical novel attempts to re-create the life story of the Barbadian slave who was arrested in 1692 "for witchcraft in Salem, Massachusetts. . . . As a child, Tituba sees her mother executed. She is then raised by an old woman who teaches her the African art of healing and communicating with spirits. As a young woman, she is sold to a Puritan minister who leaves Barbados for America. Tituba uses her powers for good purposes, including the healing of her master's family. But her powers are misunderstood by the [Puritans]." Libr J

"Part historical novel, part literary fable, part exploration of the clash of irreconcilable cultures, [this] is most of all an affirmation of a courageous and resourceful woman's capacity for survival." N Y Times Book Rev

Condon, Richard
Prizzi's family. Putnam 1986 284p o.p.
LC 86-9338

Set chronologically prior to Prizzi's honor, the plot of this novel "revolves around Don Corrado Prizzi's granddaughter, Maerose, who aspires to become Donna Maerose of the brotherhood and who intends to use Charley to advance her ambitious plan in an unlikely liaison. Meanwhile, Charley has fallen in love with Mardell, who is not all she pretends to be and who herself is in love with another man." Booklist
An "entertaining depiction of high-level corruption. . . . Condon serves up this zesty mix with good humor, broadside slams at politicians and evangelism, and generous helpings of Sicilian food." Publ Wkly

Prizzi's glory. Dutton 1988 273p o.p.
LC 88-10194

This novel features "Don Corrado Prizzi, granddaughter Maerose, Charley and Angelo Partanna, and financier Edward S. Price, aka Eduardo Prizzi. This time the plot turns on the Don's and Maerose's ambitions for respectability—and a more profitable, less labor-intensive criminal conglomerate. They franchise crime, producing 800-page procedural manuals for drug-dealing and flesh-peddling." Booklist
"The plot gives Mr. Condon ample elbow room for political and social satire that is always funny. Much of it is based on observations from the point of view of Charley Partanna or his cohorts, clear-thinking, pragmatic Sicilians whose values aren't learned from this season's television series. We like them for that, and Mr. Condon doesn't invest his characters with cute, endearing qualities; rather, the Prizzis' charms stem from their complete lack of hypocrisy." N Y Times Book Rev

Prizzi's honor. Coward, McCann & Geoghegan 1982 316p o.p.
LC 81-17366

"Charley Partanna, as enforcer for the Prizzi mob, is devoted to 'The Family,' virtual owners and operators of America. When Irene Walker appears in New York at a Prizzi relative's wedding, Charley falls instantly in love with her and follows her home to Los Angeles, where she operates as a tax consultant. This is a front; Irene is a free-lance killer for the Mafia and has also organized the theft of nearly a million dollars from the Prizzi operation in Las Vegas. Charley's dedication to 'doing the right thing' as a man of respect means killing Irene but he can't endure losing her. For her part, Irene is lethally determined to keep the money and Charley's love as well." Publ Wkly
"This is a book full of action and surprises. The stage is set quickly, and the action begins almost at once. Loaded with excitement, this novel is enthusiastically recommended." Libr J

Prizzi's money. Crown 1994 241p $20
ISBN 0-517-59695-4 LC 93-8983
Also available Thorndike Press large print edition

"Julia Asbury sets out to swipe $800 million by raiding her husband's multinational companies. Supposedly, the money is to provide a ransom for the kidnapping that her husband (with the help of the Mob) organized. Julia, unaware of her husband's Mob connections, is in for a surprise when she is summoned by Don Corrado Prizzi for having stolen money that the Mob planned to steal. With enterprise and audacity, Julia convinces Mob bosses that rather than eliminate her, they should hire her." Booklist

"As is his wont, Condon uses these goings-on as a base from which to take pointed shots at the rich and powerful. . . . It's all great fun, even if the heavy-handed lampoonery goes over the top now and again." Publ Wkly

Conley, Robert J.
Mountain windsong; a novel of the Trail of Tears. University of Okla. Press 1992 218p $19.95
ISBN 0-8061-2452-0 LC 92-54150

The author "chronicles the Trail of Tears—the forced removal of the tribe in the 1830s from its homelands in the southeastern U.S. to alien territory in Oklahoma. He gives this epic drama a human scale by focusing on the story of Oconeechee, daughter of a famous Cherokee chief, and Waguli (Whippoorwill), the young man she loves. Separated by the genocidal march—one-quarter of the participants died en route to Oklahoma—the pair spend much of the novel searching for each other. A young Native American named LeRoy . . . narrates their saga, related to him by his grandfather after he asks about the beautiful 'windsong' he has heard on a North Carolina reservation occupied by descendants of the Cherokees who escaped relocation." Publ Wkly
"Its historical accuracy and its political correctness aside, the novel is a timeless love story about young people buffeted by a changing world over which they have no control." Booklist

Connell, Evan S., 1924-
Mr. Bridge; [by] Evan S. Connell, Jr. Knopf 1969 369p o.p.
This novel is made up "of fragments of experience from the life of a middle-aged suburban couple between the world wars. Brief episodes are juxaposed to reveal the stereotyped values and emotional and spiritual aridity of the prosperous, proper Bridges." Libr J
"Mr. Connell's art is one of restraint and perfect mimicry. His chapters are admirably short, his style is brevity itself. . . . Rarely has a satirist damned his subject with such good humor." N Y Times Book Rev

Mrs. Bridge; [by] Evan S. Connell, Jr. Viking 1959 254p o.p.
"India Bridge is a country club matron in Kansas City. Her husband, a successful lawyer, is seldom home so Mrs. Bridge copes—not too well—with her children, who are very different from one another. Ruth, the eldest, keeps aloft; Douglas, the youngest, is mostly off on his own projects and not interested in the fine rules of behavior that Mrs. Bridge finds essential. She seems able to communicate most easily with Carolyn, the middle child. We follow the family as the children grow. Mrs. Bridge, eager to be a proper upper-middle-class wife and mother, finds no happiness despite her affluence and good intentions." Shapiro. Fic for Youth. 3d edition

Connelly, Michael, 1956-
The black ice. Little, Brown 1993 322p $19.95
ISBN 0-316-15382-6 LC 92-33500
Also available Thorndike Press large print edition

Harry Bosch is a "smart, determined LAPD homicide detective who's driven by an inner sense of justice. This time out he arrives early on the scene of a fellow officer's suicide; then he's told it's not his case: back off.

Connelly, Michael, 1956—_Continued_

Fat chance. Harry senses the officer may have gone over to the bad guys and was killed when he tried to tiptoe back to the right side of the tracks. At every turn, Harry is confronted by dirty cops struggling to save their collective butts by lying and misdirecting the investigation. . . . A powerful novel." Booklist

The concrete blonde. Little, Brown 1994 382p $21.95

ISBN 0-316-15383-4   LC 93-11802

Also available Thorndike Press large print edition

LAPD detective Hieronymous "Harry" Bosch "is Exhibit A in a civil suit against the city filed by the family of a man Bosch killed: a man he and the police believe was the serial murderer of prostitutes and porn stars whom the media dubbed the Dollmaker. As Bosch's trial opens, however, a Dollmaker-style note directs the police to a woman's body buried in concrete, a 'concrete blonde' who turns out to have been murdered with all the Dollmaker's trademarks _after_ Bosch killed the suspect." Booklist

"Mr. Connelly keeps a tight grip on his seesaw structure, boosting the suspense for the courtroom scenes and saving the gruesome details for the procedural work." N Y Times Book Rev

Conrad, Joseph, 1857-1924

Almayer's folly

_In_ Conrad, J. Tales of the East and West p1-128

The complete short fiction of Joseph Conrad; edited with an introduction by Samuel Hynes. Ecco Press 1991-1992 2v ea $24.95

ISBN 0-88001-307-9 (v1); 0-88001-308-7 (v2)
     LC 91-27115

Analyzed in Short story index

Contents: v1 The idiots; The lagoon; An outpost of progress; Karain: a memory; The return; Youth: a narrative; Amy Foster; To-morrow; Gaspar Ruiz: a romantic tale

v2 An anarchist: a desperate tale; The informer: an ironic tale; The brute: an indignant tale; The black mate; Il conde: a pathetic tale; The secret sharer: an episode from the coast; Prince Roman; The partner; The Inn of the Two Witches: a find; Because of the dollars; The warrior's soul; The tale

The duel

_In_ Conrad, J. Tales of land and sea p441-504

The end of the tether

_In_ Conrad, J. Tales of land and sea p505-610

Great short works of Joseph Conrad. Harper & Row 1966 378p o.p.

"A Harper perennial classic"

Analyzed in Short story index

Contents: The lagoon [short story]; The Nigger of the Narcissus (1914); Youth (1903); Heart of darkness (1899); Typhoon (1902); The secret sharer [short story]

Heart of darkness; with an introduction by Verlyn Klinkenborg. Knopf 1993 110p $15

ISBN 0-679-42801-1   LC 93-1855

Also available from Bentley

"Everyman's library"

Originally published 1902 in the United Kingdom in the collection Youth, and two other stories

"Marlow tells his friends of an experience in the (then) Belgian Congo, where he once ran a river steamer for a trading company. He describes the cruel colonial exploitation there. Fascinated by reports about the powerful white trader Kurtz, Marlow went into the jungle in search of him, expecting to find in his character a clue to the evil around him. He found Kurtz living with the natives and brought him away, dying; Kurtz's last words were 'The horror! The horror!' The 'heart of darkness' is the jungle, and the primitive, subconscious heart of man." Reader's Ency. 3d edition

also in Conrad, J. Great short works of Joseph Conrad p175-256

also in Conrad, J. The portable Conrad p490-603

also in Conrad, J. Tales of land and sea p33-104

The lagoon

_In_ Conrad, J. Great short works of Joseph Conrad p5-17

Lord Jim; a tale. Knopf 1992 xxxiii, 437p $17

ISBN 0-679-40544-5   LC 91-53223

Also available from Bentley and Buccaneer Bks.

"Everyman's library"

First published 1899; first Everyman's library edition 1935

"The title character is a man haunted by guilt over an act of cowardice. He becomes an agent at an isolated East Indian trading post. There his feelings of inadequacy and responsibility are played out to their logical and inevitable end." Merriam-Webster's Ency of Lit

The Nigger of the Narcissus. Doubleday 1959 190p $5.95

ISBN 0-385-04328-7

Also available from Amereon and Buccaneer Bks.

First published 1897 with title: Children of the sea

"All life on board the _Narcissus_ revolves around James Wait, a dying black sailor. Other members of the crew include the strong Captain Allistoun; Craik, an Irish religious fanatic; and Donkin, an arrogant, lazy Cockney. The superstitious sailors cater to Wait, even steal food for him, and rescue him when the ship capsizes during a fierce storm. However, he is also the cause of dissension aboard ship, leading to a near mutiny. The novel is notable not only for its vivid picture of life at sea but also as a study of evolving relationships among men amid the most extreme circumstances." Merriam-Webster's Ency of Lit

also in Conrad, J. Great short works of Joseph Conrad p21-140

also in Conrad, J. The portable Conrad p292-453

Conrad, Joseph, 1857-1924—*Continued*

also in Conrad, J. Tales of land and sea p106-210

Nostromo; a tale of the seaboard. Knopf 1992 532p $20

ISBN 0-679-40990-4   LC 91-53185

Also available from Buccaneer Bks.

"Everyman's library"

First published 1904; first Everyman's library edition 1957

"Set in the South American republic of 'Costaguana,' it is an exciting, complicated story about capitalist exploitation and revolution on the national scene and about personal morality and corruption in individuals. Charles Gould's silver mine helps to maintain the country's stability and its reactionary government. Gould's idealistic preoccupation with the mine warps his character and makes him neglect his gentle wife, Dona Emilia. When the revolution comes, Gould puts a consignment of silver in the charge of Nostromo, the magnificent, 'incorruptible' *capataz de cargadores* ('foreman of the dock workers'). A chance happening makes Nostromo decide to bury the silver and pretend that it was lost at sea. He is eventually killed on the island where his riches are buried, when he is mistaken by his fiancée's father for a prowler. . . . Conrad's characterization is strong, his narration is complex and oblique. The story starts halfway through the events of the revolution and proceeds by way of flashbacks and glimpses into the future." Reader's Ency. 3d edition

The portable Conrad; edited, and with an introduction and notes, by Morton Dauwen Zabel. Viking 1947 760p o.p.

"Viking portable library"

Partially analyzed in Short story index

Contains two novels: The Nigger of the 'Narcissus,' and Typhoon; three long stories; six shorter stories; and a selection from Conrad's prefaces, letters and autobiographical writings

Short stories included are: Prince Roman; Warrior's soul; Amy Foster; Outpost of progress; Il Conde; The lagoon; The secret sharer. The novelettes are: Youth; Heart of darkness

Secret agent

In Conrad, J. Tales of the East and West p353-544

Tales of land and sea; introduction by William McFee; illustrated by Richard M. Powers. Hanover House 1953 695p o.p.

Analyzed in Short story index

Contents: Youth; Heart of darkness; The Nigger of the Narcissus; Il Conde; Gaspar Ruiz; The brute; Typhoon; The secret sharer; Freya of the Seven Isles; The duel; The end of the tether; The shadow-line

Tales of the East and West; edited and with an introduction by Morton Dauwen Zabel. Hanover House 1958 xxx, 544p o.p.

Analyzed in Short story index

Contents: Almayer's folly [novelette]; Karain: a memory; The planter of Malata; An outpost of progress; Falk; Prince Roman; The warrior's soul; Amy Foster; The secret agent [novelette]

Typhoon

In Conrad, J. Great short works of Joseph Conrad p259-328

In Conrad, J. The portable Conrad p192-287

In Conrad, J. Tales of land and sea p287-347

Victory; an island tale. Doubleday, Page 1915 462p o.p.

"'Enchanted Heyst,' a detached, introspective Swedish nobleman, lives alone on an island in the South seas. Pity obliges him to rescue a girl from a traveling 'Ladies orchestra' and to take her to his retreat upon which exciting and tragic happenings follow. There is more of action than in most of his books." N Y State Libr

Youth

In Conrad, J. The complete short fiction of Joseph Conrad p151-80

In Conrad, J. Great short works of Joseph Conrad p143-71

In Conrad, J. The portable Conrad

In Conrad, J. Tales of land and sea p7-32

Conroy, Frank, 1936-

Body & soul. Houghton Mifflin; Lawrence, S. 1993 450p $24.95

ISBN 0-395-51946-2   LC 93-5163

Set in New York City in the 1950s, this novel is about "a fatherless street urchin, Claude Rawlings, [who] is blessed with remarkable talent and a nurturing mentor. Finding his true home in music, . . . Claude moves from the Blue Book for Beginners to performing his own prize-winning concerto with the London Symphony Orchestra, from snagging coins through street grates and languishing over condescending rich girls to professional acclaim and a mature capacity for love." Booklist

"It would be all too easy to be irreverent about 'Body and Soul,' with the simplicities of its structure, of its upstanding hero and of its affection for a bygone era. Yet the novel so fully embodies a certain romantic view of our country's past that one's irreverence can turn into something like nostalgia. Whatever its weaknesses, 'Body & Soul' comes across as a legitimate and moving piece of Americana." N Y Times Book Rev

Conroy, Pat

The lords of discipline. Houghton Mifflin 1980 499p o.p.

LC 80-17170

The story is set in the late sixties at the time of the Vietnam War. The narrator, "Will McLean, recounts his four years at 'Carolina Military Institute.' . . . We follow the fates of four roommates and their reactions to the Institute. Will has been given the responsibility of helping the Institute's first black cadet make it through the first year. In doing that Will runs into a mysterious secret society." Libr J

Conroy, Pat—*Continued*

The novel "is engrossing and well written. Pat Conroy . . . writes dialogue that reeks of witty Hollywood repartee, but his descriptions and characterizations are both sensitive and entertaining. He carefully draws Will as the young man who disdains military formalities and defends plebes." Saturday Rev

The prince of tides. Houghton Mifflin 1986 567p $25.50

ISBN 0-395-35300-9   LC 86-10689

"Savannah Wingo, a successful feminist poet who has suffered from hallucinations and suicidal tendencies since childhood, has never been able to reconcile her life in New York with her early South Carolina tidewater heritage. Her suicide attempt brings her twin brother, Tom, to New York, where he spends the next few months, at the request of Savannah's psychiatrist . . . helping to reconstruct and analyze her early life." Libr J

"The ambition, invention and sheer energy in this book are admirable." N Y Times Book Rev

Constantine, K. C.

Joey's case. Mysterious Press 1988 216p o.p.

LC 87-20594

"A young man, shot and killed just outside of [Pennsylvania police chief Mario] Balzic's jurisdiction, had a father who is now driving the police chief crazy, and he finally hounds Balzic into doing something about reopening the case. So Balzic gets permission from the appropriate authorities to take a new look. One thing is certain: the officer in charge of the original murder investigation goofed up in every particular." N Y Times Book Rev

The man who liked slow tomatoes. Godine 1982 177p o.p.

LC 81-47321

This mystery features "Mario Balzic police chief of Rocksburg, Pennsylvania. . . . Wise and funny, Balzic swears profusely, loves his mother, weeps as he arrests a murderer, creatively manhandles a young punk, and vehemently refuses to endure the bureaucratic games of smalltown politics. His personality carries the book; the plot grows slowly and it is not until the last pages that we encounter in quick succession a corpse, a murderer and a pathetic suicide. Until then the suspense is provided by a missing husband, the crazy leitmotif of too-early-ripening tomatoes, and Balzic's mushrooming impatience with contract negotiations. Constantine is a genius with conversation and reproduces various immigrant accents with uproarious accuracy. This is an intelligent, compassionate and moving book, as well as a top-notch entertainment." Publ Wkly

The man who liked to look at himself. Saturday Review Press 1973 156p o.p.

As police chief of Rocksbury, Pa. the novel's central character, Mario Balzic, is "confronted by parts of a body scattered through a hunting ground. As the case is out of his jurisdiction, he has to work with an unlovely specimen of a lieutenant in the state police, said lieutenant being a loud-mouth, a racist and, on top of all that, impulsive and not very smart. Balzic solves the case because he knows the people in his Pennsylvania town." N Y Times Book Rev

"A top-grade blue-collar, small-town mystery. The dialogue is such that it might have been tape-recorded." Barzun. Cat of Crime. Rev and enl edition

Cook, Robin, 1940-

Blindsight. Putnam 1992 429p o.p.

LC 91-30355

Available G.K. Hall large print edition

"Dr. Laurie Montgomery, a forensic pathologist in the NYC Medical Examiner's office, finds a pattern of unrelated cocaine overdose deaths among career-oriented people never known to have used drugs. Despite the obvious evidence that she's onto something, her boss couldn't care less, while the homicide detective she becomes involved with is more concerned about the mob killings, and, like her boss, cannot understand why she is outraged by 'the behavior of two corrupt, thieving uniformed cops in her department." Publ Wkly

Brain. Putnam 1981 283p o.p.

"Young women, repeating visits to the gynecology clinic [at Hobson University Medical Center in New York] because of abnormal Pap smears, develop seizures, blurred vision, and headaches, and smell strange odors. The women all vanish under mysterious circumstances except for Lisa Marino, who dies on the operating table. . . . Dr. Martin Philips, assistant chief of neuroradiology . . . [and] Denise Sanger, resident in radiology, discover—when they 'borrow' her body from the morgue—that someone stole Lisa's brain." Libr J

Coma; a novel. Little, Brown 1977 306p o.p. Buccaneer Bks. reprint available $29.95 (ISBN 1-56849-266-9)

LC 76-52951

"A female medical student uses her charms and femininity to obtain forbidden charts and computer readouts on certain patients who have gone into coma on the operating table and never come out of it, remaining like vegetables due to extensive brain damage. Susan feels there is something wrong and sets out to find what it is. As a second-year med student, she knows practically nothing of medical terms or practices, so spends all of her class time in the library trying to learn the terminology before she can try to solve a mystery that has puzzled the finest surgeons in the hospital. She does manage to uncover a ring of doctors who are selling various organs for transplant from the coma victims as soon as they can declare them dead, and is almost a victim herself for her pains." West Coast Rev Books

Fatal cure. Putnam 1993 447p $22.95

ISBN 0-399-13879-X   LC 93-38171

Also available G.K. Hall large print edition

"Idealistic young doctors David and Angela Wilson take positions at a state-of-the-art medical center in a small Vermont town partly because they see it as an ideal spot for their daughter, who suffers from cystic fibrosis. But the town is not as idyllic as it seems, and the hospital is in a desperate financial bind due primarily to its contract with a local HMO, David's new employer. Worse still, patients are dying unexpectedly almost daily, and no one seems to care very much. . . . Cook raises troubling questions about the conflicts between medical and financial priorities in managed care." Publ Wkly

Godplayer. Putnam 1983 368p o.p.

LC 83-4507

Cook, Robin, 1940——*Continued*

"Someone is playing God on the surgery floor of Boston Memorial Hospital, causing unexplained patient deaths. Pathologist Robert Sieber, with the help of Dr. Cassandra Kingsley, is investigating these 'SSD's,' sudden surgical deaths. Meanwhile Cassi's husband, a top surgeon, is becoming estranged from her, and seems headed for a breakdown. When Cassi herself must be admitted for an eye operation, she isn't aware that she is the Godplayer's next target." Libr J

Harmful intent. Putnam 1990 400p o.p.
LC 89-39756

The story "opens with the operating-table death of a mother and her newborn child during a routine cesarean section in a Boston hospital. Attending anesthesiologist Jeffrey Rhodes is blamed for the tragedy, and he suffers accordingly. First, a group of prominent malpractice attorneys wins a multimillion-dollar settlement against him; then he's convicted of two counts of second-degree murder. Financially ruined and facing a lengthy prison term, Rhodes jumps bail and embarks on a private crusade to prove that the deaths were not his fault." Booklist

Mindbend. Putnam 1985 368p o.p.
LC 84-24954

"Young doctor Adam Schonberg is married to a dancer, Jennifer, who becomes pregnant. The couple isn't ready for parenting. He is in his third year as a medical student and is dependent on her earnings. When Jennifer goes to a doctor for initial examination, she is told that it would be best to abort since there are already signs of malformation in the fetus. Adam, who has quit school and gone to work for a pharmaceutical house, becomes suspicious of the doctor who has given his wife the frightening and devastating news. He is even more suspicious of the tie-in that this doctor has with the company for which he works." West Coast Rev Books

Mortal fear. Putnam 1988 364p o.p.
LC 87-29085

This suspense novel "centers around the startling death of an eminent biomolecular geneticist and the subsequent inexplicable and untimely deaths of a number of Dr. Jason Howard's patients. As Dr. Howard begins to investigate the deaths and even the possible discovery of the scientific breakthrough that the geneticist had made, we are immersed in an intricate journey that includes modern laboratories, seamy nightclubs, the wilds of the Northwest, and most particularly, Boston's erotic, sleazy backstreets." West Coast Rev Books

Mutation. Putnam 1989 367p o.p.
LC 88-31680

Available Thorndike Press large print edition

"Dr. Frank is an infertility expert, and when he learns that his wife can't conceive, he employs in vitro fertilization—but with genetic alterations in order to produce a superintelligent baby. Predictably, the experiment eventually backfires, and the horror begins. Cook marshals all the medical facts necessary to make this situation seem real, and he musters all the quick pacing necessary to keep the reader engrossed." Booklist

Outbreak. Putnam 1987 366p o.p.
LC 86-25390

"Dr. Marissa Blumenthal, pert, pretty, diminutive, is assigned by Atlanta's Centers for Disease Control to investigate a series of outbreaks of a mysterious, untreatable and highly contagious virus that is felling physicians and their patients in several hospitals around the country. Unless contained and checked, the deadly virus poses a threat to the entire populace. Unaccountably hampered by her superiors, Marissa persists in her sleuthing and, to her dismay, comes to suspect the viral contagion is the work of a sinister cabal of ultraconservative doctors trying to undermine the public's faith in prepaid health-maintenance facilities. Marissa finds her career endangered, her very life in peril. As in his previous medical whodunits, Mr. Cook is nimble at stitching together the ingredients of terror, suspense, intrigue and medical expertise." N Y Times Book Rev

Terminal. Putnam 1993 445p o.p.
LC 92-30678

Available Thorndike Press large print edition

"The Forbes Cancer Center in Miami is experiencing unprecedented cure rates for patients stricken with medulloblastoma. Sean Murphy, a bright, brash, Harvard medical student, takes an elective at the center to learn as much as he can about the procedures and treatments. The icy atmosphere that greets him coupled with a warning to stay away from the unit in question fuels Sean's determination to discover why everything is veiled in such secrecy. To carry out his investigation, he enlists the help of his girlfriend, Janet Reardon, a nurse." SLJ

"Cook tells a beautifully woven story—keeping the various individuals and plots in meaningful operation—and winds up with a dramatic . . . denouement." Booklist

Vital signs. Putnam 1991 396p o.p. Buccaneer Bks. reprint available $32.95 (ISBN 1-56849-267-7)
LC 90-46807

Also available G.K. Hall large print edition

"Epidemiologist Marissa Blumenthal, seen before in *Outbreak* now has a successful pediatrics practice near Boston and an affluent health-care-entrepreneur husband. But her inability to become pregnant threatens both her marriage and her career. After unsuccessful visits to a local fertility clinic, she discovers a surprising and suspicious link between her medical records and those of an inordinate number of the clinic's clients. Traveling to Australia to learn more about a worldwide in vitro fertilization organization, Marissa and her friend Wendy are trailed, and tragedy occurs. Marissa, now accompanied by the physician whose work she had come to Australia to investigate, goes to Hong Kong and eventually China—fleeing murderous assailants every step of the way—before a billion-dollar international scam is revealed." Publ Wkly

Cook, Thomas H.

Evidence of blood. Putnam 1991 319p o.p.
LC 91-476

Available Thorndike Press large print edition

"True-crime writer Jackson Kinley returns to his rural Georgia hometown to attend the funeral of longtime friend Ray Tindall, for years the county sheriff. When Tindall's daughter confides to Kinley that her father had recently grown withdrawn and had been doggedly investigating some case (certain files from which are now missing), Kinley decides to turn his own investigative talent toward the pursuit of Tindall's inquiry." Publ Wkly

"Highly satisfying story, strong in color and atmosphere, intelligent and exacting." N Y Times Book Rev

Cookson, Catherine

The black velvet gown; a novel. Summit Bks. 1984 345p o.p.

LC 84-216472

"After her husband's death in a cholera epidemic, the widow Millican and her four children are homeless and nearly penniless, when the entire family is taken under the protection of an eccentric Northumberland bachelor. Eldest daughter Biddy is sent into service as a laundress at a neighboring estate, where she teaches the other servants to read and write, is promoted upstairs as a lady's maid, falls in love, and becomes the center of a family scandal. Cookson spices her story with blackmail, sexual passion, untimely death, and savage violence, but the novel's underlying message—it's not who you are but what you are that determines your destiny—emerges triumphant." Booklist

The Maltese Angel; a novel. Simon & Schuster 1994 c1992 479p $23

ISBN 0-671-89649-0   LC 94-9729
Also available Thorndike Press large print edition
First published 1992 in the United Kingdom

"Hayward Gibson, a nineteenth-century English farmer, finds his Maltese Angel on the stage in Newcastle, falls in love, and marries this dancer who brings beauty, happiness, and, eventually, generations of grief to his life. The woman he marries is not the cause of the sorrow. It is the woman he scorns, a neighboring country girl who had assumed her place would be beside Ward on his freehole farm. This girl, Daisie Mason, is avenged by her brothers, who torment Ward by damaging his farm property. Not content with that, Daisy catapults a stone at Ward's wife, killing her. Left to raise two young daughters, Ward lives only for the youngest, who so resembles her mother. Such preoccupation has chilling effects on the whole family." Booklist

Coonts, Stephen, 1946-

Final flight. Doubleday 1988 387p o.p.
LC 88-12001

Capt. Jake Grafton's "night-flying's over, thanks to failing eyesight. But the fate of the Middle East is hanging in the balance when his F-14 tears off into Mediterranean air-space. Coonts has cast the hero of his first novel, *The Flight of the Intruder*, as a wing commander aboard an aircraft carrier. He has also thrust him into the bulls-eye of an Arab plot to steal the ship's nuclear weapons. . . . The backdrop is Naples, and the well-detailed lives of Navy pilots. *Final Flight* has a long fuse, but its detonation is well worth the wait." Publ Wkly

Flight of the Intruder. Naval Inst. Press 1986 329p $18.95

ISBN 0-87021-200-1   LC 86-16440

"In the autumn of 1972, despite rumors of peace, United States Navy pilots flew A-6 Intruder attack planes in bombing raids over North Vietnam. Some of these pilots were angered by the relative insignificance of their targets—road intersections, sampan repair yards—which mocked the loss of life incurred carrying out the missions. So when the pilot Jake Grafton's best friend, a bombardier, is killed by a rifle bullet fired randomly from the ground, he decides 'to bomb something worth the trip' and plans a solo, unauthorized raid on Communist Party headquarters in downtown Hanoi." N Y Times Book Rev

The Intruders. Pocket Bks. 1994 344p $23

ISBN 0-671-87060-2   LC 94-213081

This Jake Grafton techno-thriller "takes the heroic Navy aviator back to 1973, immediately following the events of his debut in *Flight of the Intruder*. Disillusioned by the killing and dying 'for nothing' that he saw in Vietnam, Jake is at a crossroads. Should he try to find his way in civilian life, or stay in the service and make the demanding transition from hot shot jet jockey to professional Naval officer? He mulls over his decision while flying A-6 Intruders with a Marine squadron assigned to an aircraft carrier in the Pacific. As always with Coonts, the terrors and elations of flying take center stage." Publ Wkly

The minotaur. Doubleday 1989 436p $19.95

ISBN 0-385-26147-0   LC 89-11879
Also available Thorndike Press large print edition

Jake Grafton's new assignment is "overseeing development of a navy stealth bomber. Jake's predecessor, he soon learns, was offed under mysterious circumstances, which the reader (if none of the navy brass) knows has to do with the dead man's top-secret computer-access code having been used by a Soviet mole code-named *Minotaur*." Booklist

The red horseman. Pocket Bks. 1993 344p o.p.

LC 93-1099

Jack Grafton "has been promoted to deputy director of the Defense Intelligence Agency—a desk job, in other words. But when Boris Yeltsin runs into trouble keeping 20,000 nuclear warheads out of terrorists' hands, only Grafton will do to save us all from death or a fate much worse. An ambitious reporter, Jack Yocke, and Grafton's earthy cohort, Toad Tarkington, also figure in the mix." Booklist

"The issues Coonts confronts—the frighteningly unprotected and undermaintained nuclear devices in the former Soviet Union; factionalism in the U.S. intelligence community; unrest in the Middle East—make this one of the most compelling post-*glasnost* thrillers to date." Publ Wkly

Under siege. Pocket Bks. 1990 408p o.p.
LC 90-62714

Available Thorndike Press large print edition

This Jake Grafton novel is set "in contemporary Washington, D.C., where a Colombian drug lord has been brought for trial. His gunmen terrorize the capital with a series of spectacular mass murders while a hired assassin stalks top officials. . . . [Jake] is joined on the front lines by journalist Jack Yocke and undercover narc Harrison Ronald Ford." Publ Wkly

"Mr. Coonts has a tendency to see things in black and white. His heroes are too good to be true, and his villains are darker than a black hole. But in his prose he avoids the dreadful clichés of most of his colleagues. His dialogue is realistic, the story line mesmeric. That is the mark of a natural storyteller." N Y Times Book Rev

Cooper, J. California

The matter is life; stories. Doubleday 1991 227p $18

ISBN 0-385-41173-1   LC 90-25515

Cooper, J. California—*Continued*

Analyzed in Short story index
Contents: The big day; How, why to get rich; Evergreen grass; Friends, anyone?; Vanity; I told him!; No Lie; The Doras

"Most of Cooper's first-person narrators are shrewd black women, and on occasion the stories suffer from sameness in plots, themes, and characters. Usually, however, they are touching without falling into sentimentality and totally honest without becoming crude." Libr J

Cooper, James Fenimore, 1789-1851

The Deerslayer; or, The first war-path, a tale.

Available from various publishers
This is the first title of the author's Leatherstocking saga featuring Natty Bumppo
First published 1841 in two volumes by Lea & Blanchard
Set in New York State this "is a record of Natty Bumppo's early days as a young hunter brought up among the Delaware Indians, engaged in warfare against the Hurons. He helps defend the family of Tom Hutter, a settler, from attack. Judith, who is really not Tom's daughter, but a girl of noble birth, loves Natty Bumppo and begs him not to return to the Iroquois, who have released him on parole from capture. Bumppo does return, but is rescued by the intervention of Judith, who thereafter disappears, and the Delaware Chief Chingachgook, who remains a lifelong friend." Haydn. Thesaurus of Book Dig
Followed by The last of the Mohicans

also in Cooper, J. F. The Leatherstocking tales v2 p483-1030

The last of the Mohicans.

Available from various publishers
First published 1826
The second in the Leatherstocking tales "presents Chingachgook and his son Uncas as the last of the Iroquois aristocracy. Natty Bumppo, the scout Hawkeye, is in the prime of his career in the campaign of Fort William Henry on Lake George under attack by the French and Indians. The commander's daughters, Cora and Alice Munro, with the latter's fiancé Major Duncan Heyward, are captured by a traitorous Indian but rescued and conveyed to the fort by Hawkeye. Later Munro surrenders to Montcalm, and the girls are seized again by Indians. Uncas and Cora are killed, and the others return to civilization." Haydn. Thesaurus of Book Dig
Followed by The Pathfinder

also in Cooper, J. F. The Leatherstocking tales v1 p467-878

The Leatherstocking tales. Library of Am. 1985 2v ea $32

ISBN 0-940450-20-8 (v1); 0-940450-21-6 (v2)
LC 84-25060
An omnibus edition of the five novels of the saga, individual volumes of which are entered separately
Contents: v1 The pioneers; or, The sources of the Susquehanna, a descriptive tale; The last of the Mohicans; a narrative of 1757; The prairie; a tale; v2 The Pathfinder; or, The inland sea; The Deerslayer; or, The first war-path
These novels "are linked together by the career of Natty Bumppo, or Hawkeye, Cooper's inimitable backwoodsman, a romantic embodiment of the virtues of both races, and of Chingachgook, his Indian counterpart, equally idealized. . . . There is little historical background; but the vivid descriptions of wood, lake, and prairie, and of the daily life of Indian and huntsman, gives the finest imaginable picture extant of natural scenes and human conditions that have long passed away." Baker. Guide to the Best Fic

The Pathfinder; or, The inland sea.

Available from various publishers
First published 1840
The third in the Leatherstocking tales "finds Natty Bumppo at the age of forty. A small outpost on Lake Ontario is under attack. Mabel Dunham helps in the defense, and with the aid of Pathfinder, Chingachgook, and Jasper Western, a young sailor, the Iroquois are routed. Lieutenant Muir . . . arrests Jasper as a traitor, but when Muir is revealed as the guilty one, he is killed by Arrowhead, a Tuscarora Indian. Jasper wins the love of Mabel." Haydn. Thesaurus of Book Dig
Followed by The pioneers

also in Cooper, J. F. The Leatherstocking tales v2 p1-482

The pilot; a tale of the sea; edited with an historical introduction and explanatory notes by Kay Seymour House. State Univ. of N.Y. Press 1986 xlvii, 479p il $49.50

ISBN 0-87395-415-7   LC 84-8765
"The Writings of James Fenimore Cooper"
First published 1823 in a two volume edition
John "Paul Jones's adventures suggested the plot; which is, in brief, an attempt during the Revolutionary War to abduct some prominent Englishmen for exchange against American prisoners." Keller. Reader's Dig of Books

The pioneers.

Available from various publishers
First published 1822
In this fourth of the Leatherstocking tales Natty Bumppo "makes his first appearance in print as an older man, who has witnessed the coming of civilization to the wilderness. The story takes place in upper New York State. . . . The central conflict in the book concerns the opposition between the laws of nature, upheld by Natty, and the laws of civilization. Symbolic of this opposition are two incidents: in the first, Natty kills a deer for food, in Indian fashion. The white settlement seeks to punish him for failing to respect the seasonal hunting laws it has established. On the other hand, there is the wholesale slaughter of pigeons by the civilized inhabitants of . . . [the town] with no purpose but sport. . . . [In the end, Natty] heads for the far West to escape confining civilization." Reader's Ency. 3d edition
Followed by The prairie

also in Cooper, J. F. The Leatherstocking tales v1 p1-465

The prairie; a tale; edited, with historical introduction by James P. Elliott. State Univ. of N.Y. Press 1985 xxxiii, 566p il $49.50

ISBN 0-87395-363-0   LC 84-24096
Also available from Buccaneer Bks.

A reissue of the title first published 1827
This final installment in the Leatherstocking tales "centers on the death of the aged Natty Bumppo. Cooper contrasts the noble, disinterested Natty with the squatter

Cooper, James Fenimore, 1789-1851—*Continued*

Ishmael Bush and his family. Lawless and self-seeking, the squatters portend ill for the future of democracy. Cooper's prairie descriptions, which include an effective buffalo stampede and prairie fire, are derived from the *Journals* of Lewis and Clark." Reader's Ency. 3d edition

also in Cooper, J. F. The Leatherstocking tales v1 p879-1317

The spy; a tale of the neutral ground. Wiley & Halsted 1821 2v o.p. Buccaneer Bks. reprint available $28.95 (ISBN 0-89968-161-1)

A story of the American Revolution. The hero, the spy, is a cool, shrewd, fearless man, who is employed by General Washington in service which involves great personal danger and little glory

Covers "the locality 'between the royal barracks in New York City and the American outposts on the Hudson' where a mixed population of loyalists and British sympathisers mistrusted one another. Not many historic figures or events are introduced . . . but the tale well illustrates the later Revolution period, and is full of allusions to such men as Burgoyne, Gates, Tarleton, Sumter, etc." Nield. Guide to the Best Hist Novels & Tales

Corman, Avery

50. Simon & Schuster 1987 254p o.p.

LC 87-4602

"Doug Gardner—a New York City sports columnist, divorced, with joint custody of his two children—is fast approaching 50. In the course of this novel, which takes him to that milestone, Doug is confronted not only with a body that is beginning to fall apart but with emotional upheavals common to many men—his ex-wife becomes more successful than he and marries a younger, wealthy man; his adolescent daughter is pulled toward her stepfather's lifestyle; he loses his job and makes some compromises in his career; his father dies; and just when his son is getting ready for college, the woman he loves wants to get married *and* have a baby." Libr J

This "is that rarest of books, a novel about good, intelligent people attempting to understand the nature of success." N Y Times Book Rev

Kramer versus Kramer; a novel. Random House 1977 233p o.p.

LC 77-5654

"Joanna Kramer's answer to that locked-in feeling was to leave her husband and pre-school son for a life of her own. Ted Kramer tells of his minute-by-minute adjustments to the crises of single parenthood. Just when he has things under control, his wife brings suit to regain custody of the boy, with startling results. An intelligently wrought novel which depicts the role of single parenthood with convincing verisimilitude." Booklist

Prized possessions. Simon & Schuster 1991 320p o.p.

LC 90-22666

"Elizabeth Mason, her Manhattan family's 'prize possession,' is a dedicated student and talented singer who wins acceptance into Layton, a top liberal arts college near Albany, NY. With all her parents' hopes pinned on her, Liz goes off to Layton where, on the first weekend of her freshman year, she is asked to a party by senior Jimmy Andrews, star of the tennis team. They

dance, they drink, they kiss. Then he gets her alone and he rapes her. . . . With Liz's story, Corman takes a tense, disturbing look at the nature of consent and raises critical questions about negative ways in which society still views female sexuality." Publ Wkly

Cornwell, Bernard

Copperhead. HarperCollins Pubs. 1994 375p (Starbuck chronicles, v2) $22

ISBN 0-06-017766-7   LC 93-29421

"Nathaniel Starbuck is a Northerner, the son of a Boston minister who becomes caught up in the South at the start of the Civil War and joins the Rebel cause, captivated more by the challenge and peril of war than the righteousness of either side. New-forged loyalties entice him to stay with the rebels even after his life and his family ties are put at risk when he must act as a spy to save his best friend from charges of espionage. Nate is a beguiling hero and Cornwell's balance of battle, romance, and historic scenes are neatly paced in this novel set against the 1862 battle for Richmond." Booklist

Rebel. HarperCollins Pubs. 1993 308p $20

ISBN 0-06-017713-6   LC 92-53344

Also available Thorndike Press large print edition

First in a projected series, this novel "follows the adventures of Nathaniel Starbuck, the rebellious and discredited son of a famous Boston abolitionist preacher. Nate flees the North after helping a *femme fatale* steal money she claimed was hers, winding up in Richmond as Fort Sumter falls and the Civil War begins. Unable to return home, distrusted by Southerners because of his parentage, Nate is taken under the wing of the mercurial and megalomaniacal Washington Faulconer, obsessed with building an independent army, answerable only to him, to fight for the Confederacy. Spanning the period from Sumter's capitulation in April 1861 to the First Battle of Bull Run in July, the book is well paced and filled with the historical details genre fans demand." Publ Wkly

Followed by Copperhead

Redcoat. Viking 1988 c1987 405p $18.95

ISBN 0-670-81681-7   LC 87-40018

Also available Thorndike Press large print edition

First published 1987 in the United Kingdom

"The setting is Philadelphia and its environs at the time of the Revolution; the principal characters are Sam Gilpin, a Redcoat lured toward the Patriot cause by love, and Jonathan Becket, who is under his fiercely loyalist uncle's thumb until he makes a perilous break for freedom." Publ Wkly

"The grim and gory reality of war is skillfully played out against the gaiety of Loyalist society. Cornwell's fictional characters mingle well with the historical figures of the time." Libr J

Sharpe's company; Richard Sharpe and the Siege of Badajoz, January to April 1812. Viking 1982 280p o.p.

LC 81-69930

"The imaginary hero Captain Richard Sharpe is once again pitted against Napoleon's vast army as he attempts to seize the impenetrable Badajoz fortress in this third novel in the Sharpe series describing the Peninsular War. The battle itself is only one of Sharpe's problems, however, as he is savagely stalked by a figure from his early army days who proves more dangerous than the enemy. Further complications cause Sharpe still more anguish as he discovers that his gazette has not gone

Cornwell, Bernard—*Continued*

through, thus stripping him of his temporary captaincy and separating him from the very men he has trained and come to trust. Cornwell sustains his fine craftsmanship and adds a new realistic dimension to his portrayal of war as he depicts an army of men who fight for survival within their own ranks. Not even the smallest of details escapes the author's keen reconstruction of a series of events that made history more than a century ago." Booklist

Followed by Sharpe's sword

Sharpe's devil; Richard Sharpe and the Emperor, 1820-1821. HarperCollins Pubs. 1992 280p $20

ISBN 0-06-017977-5   LC 91-58360

In this episode Richard Sharpe "finds himself in the Spanish colony of Chile during its fight for independence in 1820-21. Hired by the wife of a Spanish nobleman to locate her kidnapped husband, the captain-general of Chile, Sharpe and friend Patrick Harper sail halfway around the world on a mission complicated by political intrigue and corruption." Libr J

This is a "rousing read, full of invincible characters, deafening broadsides, roaring cannons, and smoking pistols as Cornwell writes of old-fashioned battles, blazing with glory." Booklist

Sharpe's eagle; Richard Sharpe and the Talavera campaign July 1809. Viking 1981 270p o.p. Buccaneer Bks. reprint available $21.95 (ISBN 1-56849-076-3)

LC 80-54081

First volume of a series set during the Napoleonic Wars

"As the Peninsular War against Napoleon is heating up in the summer of 1809, Lieutenant Richard Sharpe of the British 95th Rifles finds himself in Portugal separated from his battalion and in charge of a motley group of 30 men. When a battalion of greenhorn British troops arrives in Portugal, Sharpe and his detachment are put under the leadership of its colonel, a sadistic and incompetent bully. As they march along the Tagus to join their Spanish allies in a campaign against the French and Dutch at Talavera, Sharpe—who has risen from the ranks—finds himself catching more hell from snobbish British officers than from the enemy." Publ Wkly

This "is an engrossing and entertaining book. The action moves swiftly, and the characters are interesting, especially the hero." Libr J

Followed by Sharpe's gold

Sharpe's enemy; Richard Sharpe and the defense of Portugal, Christmas 1812. Viking 1984 351p o.p.

LC 83-47925

In this installment of Sharpe's adventures it is the "winter of 1812 and the Peninsular War is at its height. Sharpe, a major now, is given a dangerous mission: with a handful of men he is to rescue Lady Farthingale, wife of his poltroon of a superior . . . from the clutches of a villainous international band of deserters holed up in a village near the Spanish-Portuguese border." Publ Wkly

The author "writes in gruesome detail of the horrors faced by the dying soldiers and with glowing excitement of the satisfaction of victory. An appended historical note sets an even more realistic perspective on the events he has so smoothly chronicled." Booklist

Followed by Sharpe's honour

Sharpe's gold; Richard Sharpe and the destruction of Almeida, August 1810. Viking 1982 c1981 250p o.p.

LC 81-51908

In this second volume of the series "the time is 1810, and Lord Wellington's Peninsular army is tottering. Devoid of allies—the Spanish forces had been routed by the French—and badly in need of funds, Wellington's only hope for survival before his confrontation with Bonaparte is a cache of 16,000 gold coins hidden in the Portuguese hills. The gold must be stolen, and only one man is up to the task—Captain Richard Sharpe of the South Essex Regiment. The assignment, of course, is fraught with danger and adventure every step of the way." West Coast Rev Books

The author's "crisp, fast-paced style is engagingly suspenseful, and his rendering of characters wittily perspective." Booklist

Followed by Sharpe's company

Sharpe's honour; Richard Sharpe and the Vitoria Campaign, February to June 1813. Viking 1985 320p o.p.

LC 84-40474

"Fighting with Wellington's British forces in Spain, Major Sharpe is framed for murder and consequently court-martialed in an elaborate plot by a French master spy . . . to seal a treaty between Napoleon and King Ferdinand VIII. Sharpe is secretly spared from hanging only to be given the near-suicidal mission of uncovering the facts behind the conspiracy." Booklist

"The climactic battle of Vitoria is brilliantly presented, followed by an extraordinary scene of looting." Publ Wkly

Followed by Sharpe's regiment

Sharpe's regiment; Richard Sharpe and the invasion of France, June to November 1813. Viking 1986 301p $16.95

ISBN 0-670-81148-3   LC 85-29541

"With the campaign against Napoleon about to enter France, Sharpe is informed that his South Essex regiment has been dissolved. Indignant, he returns to England and uncovers a scam of major proportions—the trainees lured into the prestigious South Essex are being sold off to less-popular regiments in the colonies. Sharpe and his Irish sergeant go undercover, posing as new recruits in hopes of determining the extent of the corruption." Booklist

"What really raises this story high above a mere action tale (including Cornwell's usual effectively gritty view of Army life) is the wonderful depiction of Regency London, from gaudy, bawdy Vauxhall Gardens to a reeking, dangerous slum to the perfumed, equally dangerous Royal Court. The book ends with a highly realistic battle that opens Sharpe's way into France." Publ Wkly

Followed by Sharpe's siege

Sharpe's revenge; Richard Sharpe and the peace of 1814. Viking 1989 348p $17.95

ISBN 0-670-80867-9   LC 88-40398

Also available Thorndike Press large print edition

Cornwell, Bernard—*Continued*

"It is early 1814 and Major Richard Sharpe is still with one-eyed Capt. Frederickson and giant Sgt. Maj. Harper. Sharpe's French nemesis Major Ducos, in the first of a series of betrayals, has stolen a fortune from Napoleon and framed Sharpe for the crime. As fugitives from the British Army and the restored French royalist regime, Sharpe, Frederickson and Harper travel across France and into Naples to find Ducos and clear themselves. They must also deal with a loyal Bonapartist general and a rapacious Neapolitan cardinal, both of whom want the treasure." Publ Wkly

"Just when it seems that Cornwell cannot top his last tale featuring audacious, nineteenth-century British soldier Richard Sharpe, he does." Booklist

Followed by Sharpe's Waterloo

Sharpe's rifles; Richard Sharpe and the French invasion of Galicia, January 1809. Viking 1988 304p $17.95

ISBN 0-670-82222-1   LC 87-40641

Also available Thorndike Press large print edition

Set chronologically prior to the action in the earlier titles about Richard Sharpe

This "is the story of Sharpe's first command. He becomes the leader of a force of Rifles cut off behind lines during the disastrous English retreat from Spain and battles not only crack French dragoons but also the fierce winter weather and the hostility of his men. A Spanish major offers aid if Sharpe will help with his own desperate mission to guarantee a Spanish victory. A crackling adventure yarn, sure to delight Sharpe's many fans." Libr J

Sharpe's siege; Richard Sharpe and the winter campaign, 1814. Viking 1987 319p $17.95

ISBN 0-670-80866-0   LC 86-45850

Richard Sharpe "has arrived in France to fight Napoleon's forces on their own territory. Sent to capture a coastal fort as a ruse to distract the French secret service from the real plans of an overland attack, Major Sharpe and his small company of riflemen are endangered by duplicitous Frenchmen, cowardly English officers, and an American ally of the French who puts our hero's moral scruples and battle strategies to the test. It proves to be a valiant and bloody confrontation. Writing with great charm and a touch of irony, Cornwell supplies all the heroics and ingenuity now expected by Sharpe's fans." Booklist

Followed by Sharpe's revenge

Sharpe's sword; Richard Sharpe and the Salamanca Campaign, June and July 1812. Viking 1983 319p il o.p.

LC 82-40371

In this fourth Captain Richard Sharpe novel, the nineteenth-century British infantryman "faces an inhumane adversary, Captain Leroux, who is Napoleon's most trusted and ruthless intelligence officer. While leading his company into numerous skirmishes in the battle of Salamanca, Sharpe must also search for Leroux, who has acquired, through torture and blackmail, the names of the British army's most valuable spies and is eliminating them. Cornwell not only delineates the political turmoil and battle scenes with incredible specificity, but he also draws in any number of other details that give this historical fiction its ghastly realism." Booklist

Followed by Sharpe's enemy

Sharpe's Waterloo; Richard Sharpe and the Waterloo campaign, 15 June to 18 June 1815. Viking 1990 378p o.p.

LC 89-40661

"At Waterloo, Lieutenant-Colonel Sharpe serves as military adviser to the Dutch prince of Orange—a hapless military strategist who sends legions to their deaths before Sharpe takes matters into his own hands. . . . Along the way, Sharpe settles an old score with Lord John Rossendale, who previously cuckolded him and helped deprive him of his hard-earned fortune. Cornwell graphically depicts the grime and horror of the battlefield, including cavalry charges, cannon bombardments, and infantry attacks. A sublime work of historical fiction." Booklist

Followed by Sharpe's devil

Cornwell, David John Moore *See* Le Carré, John, 1931-

Cornwell, Patricia Daniels

All that remains; a novel; [by] Patricia D. Cornwell. Scribner 1992 373p $20

ISBN 0-684-19395-7   LC 91-32457

Also available Thorndike Press large print edition

"Medical examiner Kay Scarpetta, investigates a series of grim murders of young couples. With bone fragments being, in effect, all that remains of badly decomposed corpses, Scarpetta, Richmond homicide detective Pete Marino, ace reporter Abby Turnbull and even psychic Hilda Ozimek must employ their combined expertise—and a good deal of raw courage—to trace the killer. . . . Cornwell demonstrates that clues about character are as vital as physical evidence at the crime scene." Publ Wkly

The body farm; a novel; [by] Patricia Cornwell. Scribner 1994 387p $23

ISBN 0-684-19597-6   LC 94-8595

Forensic pathologist "Dr. Kay Scarpetta is called in to help investigate the brutal slaying of an 11-year-old girl. Scarpetta believes the child may have been the victim of Temple Gault, a macabre, demented serial killer who remains at large despite Scarpetta's determined efforts to track him down. It turns out that Scarpetta is at least partly right about Gault, but the child's death is more complicated and horrifying than even the 'I can't be surprised anymore' Scarpetta can imagine. Cornwell's plot is visceral, graphic, and frightening in a way that's vaguely reminiscent of *Silence of the Lambs*. Her writing is masterful." Booklist

Body of evidence; [by] Patricia D. Cornwell. Scribner 1991 387p $18.95

ISBN 0-684-19240-3   LC 90-34723

"Kay Scarpetta, chief medical examiner of Virginia . . . gets involved in the case of a brutal stabbing death in Richmond of romance writer Beryl Madison. Now Madison's greedy lawyer accuses Scarpetta of losing his client's latest manuscript, an autobiographical exposé of Beryl's early life as protégé of a legendary novelist. As more deaths occur and the killer closes in on her, Kay suffers palpitations over the sudden and devious reappearance of long-lost lover Mark but still finds time to provide forensic details." Libr J

Cornwell, Patricia Daniels—*Continued*

This "is an accomplished novel; with the autopsy gore wisely downplayed, other, quieter narrative strengths are allowed to emerge." Booklist

Cruel & unusual; a novel; [by] Patricia D. Cornwell. Scribner 1993 356p $21

ISBN 0-684-19530-5   LC 92-32684

Kay Scarpetta, chief medical examiner of Virginia is "unnerved by gruesome events following the execution of a killer. She no sooner finishes her autopsy of the criminal than she spots signs of his handiwork on the mutilated body of a dying boy. More fresh corpses with the dead killer's signature are soon stacking up at the morgue, where someone on the doctor's staff is sabotaging her investigation into these bizarre homicides." N Y Times Book Rev

Postmortem. Scribner 1990 293p $21

ISBN 0-684-19141-5   LC 89-10177

Also available G.K. Hall large print edition

This mystery about a serial killer features "Dr. Kay Scarpetta, Chief Medical Examiner for the Commonwealth of Virginia. . . . From the moment that the strangler makes his fourth killing (one of two that figure prominently in the plot), the tension is up. No less than the police, Dr. Scarpetta is baffled by the absence of the usual sick motivational pattern; but she can read the physical evidence, and she has the brains and the gizmos—computers, fingerprint-matching processor, DNA-testing equipment, F.B.I. profiling systems—to give the madman chase." N Y Times Book Rev

Cortázar, Julio, 1914-1984

Hopscotch; translated from the Spanish by Gregory Rabassa. Pantheon Bks. 1966 564p o.p.

Original Spanish edition published 1963 in Argentina
"Considered to be Cortázar's masterwork, it is an open-ended novel; after reading the first 56 chapters, the reader is asked to reread the chapters in a different order. . . . The novel's antihero is Horacio Oliveira, an Argentine existentialist who lives among cultured expatriates in Paris while searching for his telepathic mistress. Returning to Buenos Aires, Oliveira meets Traveler and Talita, who are the doubles of his mistress and himself. None of the characters understands or cares more than superficially about the others, and impulse motivates their choices and actions. Narrative progress in the story is insignificant and its end is inconclusive." Merriam-Webster's Ency of Lit

Coscarelli, Kate

Heir apparent. St. Martin's Press 1993 310p o.p.

LC 93-3681

"Lacey Haines, treasured daughter of California packaged food mogul Jack Gallagher, is stunned when her father's will leaves the control of Gallagher's Best, promised to her, to her beloved but lightweight younger brother Scott. When he winds up dead with her letter opener in his chest, all the evidence points first to Lacey, then to those closest to her." Publ Wkly
"Readers will enjoy this high-speed thriller in spite of some forced and obvious teases of evidence." Booklist

Costain, Thomas B., 1885-1965

The black rose. Doubleday, Doran 1945 403p o.p. Amereon reprint available $27.95 (ISBN 0-8488-0466-X)

This novel set in the 13th century, is the story of a young English nobleman who fights his way to the heart of the Mongol empire and returns to find that he must choose between an English heiress and a girl of the East
"Its background of history is richly furnished with information and local color. . . . [It is] a story that, in spite of the attention given to the romance, derives its major interest from the remarkable tapestry of history against which it is enacted." Christ Sci Monit

The silver chalice; a novel. Doubleday 1952 533p o.p.

The silver chalice was a frame meant to hold the sacred cup from which Christ drank at the Last Supper. This novel, based on legends of the years following Christ's crucifixion, describes the life of Basil, the artisan, who fashioned the silver chalice. The scenes are laid in Antioch, Rome and Jerusalem
"Costain paints a tremendous canvas filled with warm color and life. . . . As those know who have read his many vigorous re-creations of the past, Costain has a magnificent talent for breathing life into history. . . . But over and above this the novel does something else. It will make real for thousands, perhaps for the first time, the whole world of the New Testament." Chicago Sunday Trib

Coughlin, William Jeremiah, 1929-1992

Death penalty; a novel; [by] William J. Coughlin. HarperCollins Pubs. 1992 353p o.p.

LC 92-52680

"Detroit trial lawyer Charley Sloan is defending a doctor accused of helping his patients die—for a fee. At the same time he is asked to handle the appeal in a five-million-dollar lawsuit involving Ford and a man injured in an accident. Sloan, whose reputation for alcohol consumption and legal shenanigans far outweights his current nondrinking, now-honorable self, is approached by a former Appellate judge who offers him a way to win the appeal." Libr J
"The first-person narrative form and wise-cracking humor give *Death Penalty* the flavor of a hard-boiled detective yarn, but the action all takes place on the battlefield of the courtroom. First rate in every respect." Booklist

In the presence of enemies; [by] William J. Coughlin. St. Martin's Press 1993 309p o.p.

LC 92-29876

Also available G.K. Hall large print edition
"A Thomas Dunne book"
In this courtroom suspense novel "Jake Martin, a probate attorney in a make-or-break race for partnership in a prestigious Detroit firm, starts as part of a team handling the estate of banking tycoon Augustus Daren. Daren's last will and testament favor his fourth wife, the sexy, 20-years-younger Elizabeth. The bank's president, Daren's millionaire children, and someone in Jake's firm don't want Elizabeth running things and contest the will based on an incompetency argument. Through twists of fate (maybe), Jake finds himself in a litigation situa-

Coughlin, William Jeremiah, 1929-1992 — *Continued*

tion for the first time. . . . Coughlin's forte is characterization, which carries the reader's interest." Booklist

Shadow of a doubt; [by] William J. Coughlin. St. Martin's Press 1991 390p o.p.

LC 90-27501

Also available G.K. Hall large print edition

"A Thomas Dunne book"

"Attorney Charley Sloan has lost his lucrative Detroit practice, three wives and a considerable fortune—all to demon rum. Narrowly escaping disbarment, he has retreated to AA and the suburbs to pull his life together. Up pops Charley's high school girlfriend, Robin, who has gone from the backseat of his jalopy to the bed of multimillionaire septuagenarian Harrison Harwell. The mogul's daughter has just been arrested for his murder, and Robin offers Charley the chance to represent Angel Harwell—the media case of the decade—and reestablish his legal reputation. But the DA sees the case as a ticket to a congressional seat and drives full-tilt to discredit Charley." Publ Wkly

"A gripping mystery and reflective judicial drama that explores a number of relevant moral, ethical, and legal conundrums." Booklist

Coulter, Catherine

Impulse. New Am. Lib. 1990 390p o.p.

LC 89-77096

"Rafaella Holland, wealthy, shapely, Pulitzer Prize-winning reporter with a powerful karate kick, goes undercover at a Caribbean resort owned by the gangster who seduced and discarded her besotted mother many years before. Rafaella is his daughter. When her mother is hit by a car owned by the gangster's estranged wife, Rafaella decides to expose him for the snake he is." Publ Wkly

Coulter "proves why she has been dubbed the queen of romance. *Impulse* gives us dashing men, beautiful women, sex, intrigue, and international high stakes. It is a thoroughly enjoyable adventure." Booklist

The Nightingale legacy. Putnam 1994 384p $16.95

ISBN 0-399-13970-2   LC 94-5840

Second title in the author's Legacy trilogy

"At age 19, orphan Catherine Dewent-Jones eagerly anticipates taking control of her own financial affairs. Ffalkes, her greedy and unscrupulous legal guardian, attempts to arrange a marriage for her with his weakling son, Owen. Catherine flees and soon meets Lord Chilton. She is immediately attracted to the handsome but grim and brooding lord. She and Chilton eventually marry to protect her from the devious Ffalkes." Libr J

"Not much history, but plenty of romance: Coulter fans will love this frothy, sexy fairy tale." Booklist

The valentine legacy. Putnam 1995 354p $19.95

ISBN 0-399-14094-8   LC 95-14698

Concluding volume in the Legacy trilogy

"Refusing to marry James Wyndham, the man she has loved secretly for years, outspoken, naive Jessie Warfield escapes to England and the estate of James's cousins—and a life as a 'nanny.' However, when James comes to fetch her, a group of delightful meddlers make certain that they end up neatly married instead. Old secrets, a

pirate's legacy, and a cast of wonderful characters are part of this funny, lively, and occasionally mysterious story." Libr J

The Wyndham legacy. Putnam 1994 320p $19.95

ISBN 0-399-13878-1   LC 93-21908

Also available G.K. Hall large print edition

In this first volume of the author's Legacy trilogy the "Earl of Chase's illegitimate daughter Josephina Cochrain, nicknamed "the Duchess" by her antagonistic cousin Marcus Wyndham because of her precocious self-possession, unexpectedly becomes both legitimate and an heiress upon her father's death. His nephew Marcus receives the title but little else; Josephina inherits most of the money but will lose it all unless she weds her obnoxious cousin. The two protagonists are quite predictable, . . . but Coulter surrounds them with memorable eccentrics, and the action never slows." Publ Wkly

Courter, Gay

The midwife; a novel. Houghton Mifflin 1981 559p o.p.

"Hannah Blau, licensed midwife, delivers her first child—the son of a czarist minister—in 1904. Two years later Hannah and her family flee the rising tide of anti-Semitism in Russia to start a new life in New York's Lower East Side. Soon Hannah is delivering children for the rich and for poor Jewish mothers in her area. At the same time she is supporting her ne'er-do-well husband, trying to keep her marriage afloat, and fighting the New York medical establishment, which is determined to wipe out midwifery because it threatens the male-dominated profession of obstetrics." Libr J

"In colorful vignettes of emerging life-styles among the immigrants, Courter gives freshness to traditional characteristics of the Jewish temperament, among them familial cohesiveness, endurance and a recognition of opportunity even in adversity." Publ Wkly

The midwife's advice. Dutton 1992 598p o.p.

LC 92-52869

Sequel to The midwife

This novel about midwife Hannah Sokolow "covers 1913-22. The persistent questions of her patients at Bellevue Hospital drive Hannah to consult privately about sexual behavior. Each chapter/year deals with a different problem; medical or political details often slow this long book. Underlying the sexual and medical conditions are the political events of the day: World War I, the battle for birth control facts, and the Russian revolution. Hannah's love affair during her husband's prolonged absence in Mother Russia adds interest. While Hannah may be atypical in her professional successes . . . her efforts to work, be a wife and mother without much help will be familiar to many." Libr J

Coward, Noel

Bon voyage

In Coward, N. The collected stories of Noël Coward p562-630

The collected stories of Noël Coward. Dutton 1983 630p o.p.

LC 83-5704

Coward, Noel—*Continued*

Analyzed in Short story index

Contents: The wooden Madonna; Traveler's joy; Aunt Tittie; What mad pursuit; Cheap excursion; The kindness of Mrs. Radcliffe; Nature study; A richer dust; Mr. and Mrs. Edgehill; Stop me if you've heard it; Ashes of roses; This time tomorrow; Star quality; Pretty Polly; Mrs. Capper's birthday; Me and the girls; Solali; Mrs. Ebony; Penny dreadful; Bon voyage [novelette]

Cox, Michael, 1948-

(comp) The Oxford book of English ghost stories. See The Oxford book of English ghost stories

Coyle, H. W. (Harold W.), 1952-

Bright star; a novel; by Harold Coyle. Simon & Schuster 1990 432p il $19.95

   ISBN 0-671-68542-2   LC 90-30992

"When U.S. troops are sent to Egypt in a rapid-deployment exercise, the Soviet Union responds with a mini-buildup in Libya. Libyan terrorists turn international brinkmanship into regional conflict with attempts to assassinate the U.S. and Egyptian presidents. Egypt retaliates while Russians and Americans seek to avoid being drawn into another war. Coyle demonstrates mastery of tactical description—especially battalion-level narratives of armored warfare. Unusual in the genre, the women characters are convincing." Publ Wkly

Code of honor; [by] Harold Coyle. Simon & Schuster 1994 379p $23

   ISBN 0-671-77801-3   LC 93-45952

In this near future thriller, the U.S. "has dispatched its (fictional) 11th Air Assault Division to aid Colombia's unstable government in suppressing a Marxist insurgency and, while it's there, to try and damage the region's booming drug trade as well. By the time Brigadier-General Scott Dixon, familiar to readers of . . . *Bright Star* . . . arrives to evaluate the mission one year later, he finds the insurgency growing ever more formidable and the 11th Air crippled by the incompetence of its commander, Major General Charles Lane." Publ Wkly

Coyle, Harold W. *See* Coyle, H. W. (Harold W.), 1952-

Cozzens, James Gould, 1903-1978

By love possessed. Harcourt Brace & Co. 1957 570p o.p. Buccaneer Bks. reprint available $21.95 (ISBN 1-56849-549-8)

This novel concerns "49 hours in the life of Arthur Winner, . . . New England lawyer. The stability of Arthur's private and professional worlds is suddenly shaken both by repercussions of unhapppy and indiscreet episodes from his supposedly well-ordered past and by present events involving himself and those close to him." Booklist

"Cozzens is no peripheral observer of the human situation in which the Man of Reason finds himself; and all the vignettes of life in small-town Brocton involving the noble and the mean, the serious and the ridiculous, are viewed with sheer objectivity, boldly at one time, sensitively and delicately at another." Best Sellers

Craig, Alisa *See* MacLeod, Charlotte

Craig, Kit *See* Reed, Kit, 1932-

Crane, Stephen, 1871-1900

Active service

   In Crane, S. The complete novels of Stephen Crane p429-592

The complete novels of Stephen Crane; edited with an introduction by Thomas A. Gullason. Doubleday 1967 821p o.p.

Partially analyzed in Short story index

Includes: Magggie: a girl of the streets (1893); The red badge of courage (1895); George's mother (1896); The third violet (1897); Active service (1899); The O'Ruddy (1903). The first two titles are entered separately

The complete short stories & sketches of Stephen Crane; edited with an introduction by Thomas A. Gullason. Doubleday 1963 790p o.p.

Partially analyzed in Short story index

"Contains in one volume all of Stephen Crane's 112 sketches and short stories. . . . The chronological collection begins with a brief but enlightening introduction that comments on the difficulties of compilation as well as on Crane's life and writings." Booklist

Contains the following short stories: The king's favor; The camel; Dan Emmonds; Four men in a cave; Travels in New York; The broken-down van; The octopush; A ghoul's accountant; The black dog; Killing his bear; The Captain; A tent in agony; The cry of a huckleberry pudding; An explosion of seven babies; The mesmeric mountain; The holler tree; Why did the young clerk swear; The pace of youth; The reluctant voyagers; A desertion; An experiment in misery; An experiment in luxury; An ominous baby; A dark brown dog; Billie Atkins went to Omaha; Mr. Binks' day off; The men in the storm; Coney Island's failing days; In a Park Row restaurant; Stories told by an artist; When every one is panic stricken; When a man falls a crowd gathers; The duel that was not fought; A Christmas dinner won in battle; A lovely jag in a crowded car; A mystery of heroism; A gray sleeve; One dash—horses; A tale of mere chance; Three miraculous soldiers; A freight car incident; The little regiment; The veteran; The snake; Raft story; An Indiana campaign; In the Tenderloin; The voice of the mountain; Yen-Nock Bill and his sweetheart; Diamonds and diamonds; The auction; A poker game; A man and some others; The open boat; How the donkey lifted the hills; The victory of the moon; Flanagan and his short filibustering adventure; An old man goes wooing; A fishing village; The bride comes to Yellow Sky; Death and the child; The five white mice; The wise men; The monster; His new mittens; The blue hotel; The price of the harness; A self-made man; The clan of no-name; God rest ye, merry gentlemen; The lone charge of William B. Perkins; The angel child; Lynx-hunting; The revenge of the 'Adolphus'; The sergeant's private madhouse; The battle of Forty Fort; The surrender of Forty Fort; "Ol' Bennett" and the Indians; The lover and the telltale; "Showin' off"; Virtue in war; Making an orator; Twelve o'clock; The second generation; An episode of war; Shame; The carriage-lamps; The Kicking Twelfth; The shrapnel of their friends; "And if he wills, we must die"; The upturned face; The knife; The stove; Moonlight on

Crane, Stephen, 1871-1900—*Continued*

the snow; The trial, execution, and burial of Homer Phelps; An illusion in red and white; The fight; This majestic lie; The city urchin and the chaste villagers; Manacled; A little pilgrimage; At the pit door; The squire's madness; The man from Duluth; A man by the name of Mud

George's mother

In Crane, S. The complete novels of Stephen Crane p301-47

In Crane, S. The portable Stephen Crane p89-146

Maggie: a girl of the streets (a story of New York); an authoritative text, backgrounds and sources, the author and the novel, reviews and criticism, edited by Thomas A. Gullason. Norton 1979 258p $20.95

ISBN 0-393-01222-0   LC 78-24596

"A Norton critical edition"

First published privately in 1893 under the pseudonym Johnston Smith

"Maggie Johnson is the daughter of a brutal father and a drunken mother. She goes to work in a collar factory, falls in love with Pete, a bartender who is a friend of her brother Jimmie, and is seduced by him. Her mother disowns her; she becomes a prostitute, and in despair she finally kills herself. Her final degeneration becomes almost an allegory." Reader's Ency. 3d edition

also in Crane, S. The complete novels of Stephen Crane p99-155

also in Crane, S. The portable Stephen Crane p3-74

The O'Ruddy

In Crane, S. The complete novels of Stephen Crane p593-790

The portable Stephen Crane; edited, with an introduction and notes, by Joseph Katz. Viking 1969 xxvi, 550p o.p.

"Viking portable library"

Partially analyzed in Short story index

Contains sixteen short stories, plus sketches, letters, pieces of journalism, some poetry and three novels: Maggie: a girl of the streets (1893); George's mother (1896); and The red badge of courage (1895)

Short stories included are: A great mistake; An ominous baby; A dark-brown dog; The men in the storm; An experiment in misery; An experiment in luxury; An episode of war; The veteran; Flanagan and his short filibustering adventure; The open boat; The bride comes to Yellow Sky; The five white mice; The blue hotel; The monster; His new mittens; The knife

The red badge of courage.

Available from various publishers

First published 1895

"A young Union soldier, Henry Fleming, tells of his feelings when he is under fire for the first time during the battle of Chancellorsville. He is overcome by fear and runs from the field. Later he returns to lead a charge that re-establishes his own reputation as well as that of his company. One of the great novels of the

Civil War." Cincinnati Public Libr

also in Crane, S. The complete novels of Stephen Crane p197-299

also in Crane, S. The portable Stephen Crane p189-318

also in Crane, S. The red badge of courage, and other stories

The red badge of courage, and other stories; with biographical illustrations and pictures of the settings of the stories together with an introduction and captions by Max J. Herzberg. Dodd, Mead 1957 409p il o.p.

"Great illustrated classics"

Contents: The red badge of courage; The veteran; A mystery of heroism; An episode of war; Ouida's masterpiece; The gratitude of a nation

The third violet

In Crane, S. The complete novels of Stephen Crane p349-428

Craven, Margaret

I heard the owl call my name. Doubleday 1973 166p o.p. Buccaneer Bks. reprint available $19.95 (ISBN 0-89966-854-2)

"When Mark Brian's Bishop learns that the young priest is dying of a terminal illness, he assigns Mark to an outpost in British Columbia with the Kwakiutl Indians. Through his experience among these people, Mark comes to an understanding and an acceptance of death as a normal part of one's existence. When he knows that the owl has called his name, he faces the reality of death without fear." Shapiro. Fic for Youth. 3d edition

The author's "writing glows with delicate, fleeting images and a sense of peace. Her characters' hearts are bared by a few words—or by the fact that nothing is said at all." Christ Sci Monit

Crayencour, Marguerite De *See* Yourcenar, Marguerite

Crichton, Michael, 1942-

The Andromeda strain. Knopf 1969 295p il $25

ISBN 0-394-41525-6

Also available from Buccaneer Bks.

"When a contaminated space capsule drops to earth in a small Nevada town and all the town's residents suddenly die, four American scientists gather at an underground laboratory of Project Wildfire to search frantically for an antidote to the threat of a world-wide epidemic." Shapiro. Fic for Youth. 3d edition

The author "reveals his ability to conceive an imaginative idea and construct a plot that is commendable for its scientific and medical verisimilitude. Although, like most science-fiction writers, he fails to create characters of human dimension, he is concerned with moral values, and makes graphic the dangers of exploiting science for such goals as the perfection of chemical- and biological-warfare techniques." Newsweek

Crichton, Michael, 1942-—*Continued*

A case of need; by Michael Crichton, writing as Jeffrey Hudson. Dutton 1993 c1968 319p $18.95

ISBN 0-525-93802-8   LC 93-11277

First published 1968 under pseudonym Jeffrey Hudson by World

Boston pathologist John Berry "supports his colleague, Dr. Art Lee, who has been arrested for Karen Randall's death. The girl's socialite stepmother declares she has proof positive that Lee is guilty of the fatal operation, and her eminent surgeon father wants no mercy shown to him. The prosecutors and police are happy to oblige. Only Berry is willing to dig deeper into the seemingly open-and-shut case to save Lee. As his search for the truth takes him through hospital labs, mansions, and addicts' dens, from the depths of the sex and drug underworld to the heights of Boston society, John Berry meets with the shocking revelation that his own life, like the life of the colleague he is trying to save, is in deadly jeopardy." Publisher's note

Disclosure; a novel. Knopf 1994 397p $24

ISBN 0-679-41945-4   LC 93-34201

Also available large print edition $23 (ISBN 0-679-75143-2)

"Beautiful, bright, and talented Meredith Johnson arrives at Digital Communications Technology company to become the head of a division, a position that Tom Sanders thought was going to be his. Meredith, his former lover, invites him to her office after hours and attempts to seduce him. When he rejects her, she accuses him of sexual harassment. Tom hires Louise Fernandez to defend him and reverses the accusation to name Meredith as the aggressor." SLJ

"On one level Disclosure is a literary pebble tossed into a political pond, and the ripples just might dampen some of the strident howls and emotional spasms that currently dominate discussion of the issue. On another it is a refreshingly uncluttered and sinewy entertainment, free of pretension and eminently readable." Natl Rev

The great train robbery. Knopf 1975 266p o.p. Buccaneer Bks. reprint available $29.95 (ISBN 1-56849-268-5)

"Edward Pierce, a Victorian prince among rogues, meticulously plans the theft of £12,000 in gold bullion from the London-Paris train. The story is based on an actual heist that rocked Victorian England more than a century ago." Shapiro. Fic for Youth. 3d edition

"The caper is fraught with just enough misjudgment and happenstance to maintain constant tension. Crichton's reconstruction of London past, livened with heavy sprinklings of cockney dialect, is serendipitous." Booklist

Jurassic Park; a novel. Knopf 1990 399p $21

ISBN 0-394-58816-9   LC 90-52960

Also available G.K. Hall large print edition

"The Jurassic Park of the title is an amusement park on a fog-shrouded island off the coast of Costa Rica with a startling main attraction: real, live dinosaurs. The people of InGen, a genetic engineering firm, have succeeded in cloning 15 species of the prehistoric creatures and believe that their designer dinosaurs cannot reproduce or survive in the wild. But they're wrong. After some 'accidents,' the head man brings in some 'consultants' to assess the situation." Booklist

"It may sound daunting to say that a reader will encounter recombinant DNA technology, chaos theory, fractal geometry, nonlinear dynamics and even sonic tomography, but Dr. Crichton is adept at making every one of those ingredients comprehensible, often beguiling, frequently exciting." N Y Times Book Rev

Rising sun; a novel. Knopf 1992 355p $22

ISBN 0-394-58942-4   LC 91-53173

Also available large print edition $24 (ISBN 0-679-41017-1)

"On the forty-fifth floor of the Nakamoto Tower in downtown L.A.—the new American headquarters of the immense Japanese conglomerate—a grand opening celebration is in full swing. On the forty-sixth floor, in an empty conference room, the dead body of a beautiful young woman is discovered. The investigation . . . [involves a] conflict in which control of a vital American technology is the fiercely coveted prize." Publisher's note

"That Mr. Crichton effortlessly weaves a mesmerizing mystery comes as no surprise. . . . That he should now write so passionately and engagingly on matters of Japanese culture and the survival of a free and productive America—that is the surprise. . . . For that, indeed, is what he has done." N Y Times Book Rev

Sphere; a novel. Knopf 1987 385p $23.50

ISBN 0-394-56110-4   LC 86-46321

Also available from Buccaneer Bks.

The author "sends a team of civilian experts to the floor of the Pacific to investigate an enormous spaceship that appears to have rested there for some 300 years. In it, they discover a huge sphere, made of a mysterious metal, which they cannot force open despite its having a door. Then, when one of the group inspects the ship on his own, it opens, he enters, and the real fun begins. . . . Crichton's prose, pedestrian but not clumsy, lets the story spin itself out, and few readers who grab its thread will let go until the web is broken in a 'Wizard of Oz'-style ending." Booklist

The terminal man. Knopf 1972 247p il $23

ISBN 0-394-44768-9

Harry Benson "is a brilliant computer expert, who is also an epileptic given to increasingly severe black-outs in which he attacks the nearest person at hand. A team of doctors, including surgeons and an attractive woman psychiatrist, will implant in Harry, literally, a miniature computer aimed at controlling his seizures. There is only one major problem. Harry is also slipping further and further into insanity, convinced that 'machines are taking over the world.'" Publ Wkly

"The book is filled with interesting details on what surely must be the latest in hospital procedure, neurosurgery, computers, and the like. . . . This is a very different piece of science-fiction because the suspense is centered around a hospital, and the battle is a psychological one between humans and machines." Best Sellers

Crichton, Robert

The Camerons; a novel. Knopf 1972 509p o.p.

"Turn-of-the-century Scotland is the setting for this novel of the now-familiar dilemma of modern man in an increasingly complex society. Ostensibly, it is the story of Maggie Drum's ambitions to escape from Pitmungo, an enslaving mining town; but Gillon Cameron, her husband, seems to wrestle the reader's attention from her.

Crichton, Robert—*Continued*

His strength alone carries the family through repeated conflict with the townspeople and the mine owners; his development and sensitivity to others increase as Maggie's remain static and cold. Finally, in one . . . dramatic scene when the Pitmungo miners storm his house, Gillon's humanity overwhelms all who observe; and the ambitions of Maggie and Gillon alike are fulfilled in an unexpected way." Choice

The secret of Santa Vittoria; a novel. Simon & Schuster 1966 447p o.p. Buccaneer Bks. reprint available $21.95 (ISBN 1-56849-149-2)

"Santa Vittoria, an Italian hill town devoted to the making of wine, is the setting for this story of a clash between the Italians and Germans at the close of World War II. Upon the death of Mussolini, the Fascists are thrown out of office and Bombolini, the town clown, elevates himself to the position of mayor. Having read Machiavelli 43 times, he feels able to handle any emergency. When the German occupation is imminent, he organizes the populace to hide their assets, one million bottles of wine. Captain Von Prum, whose mission is to confiscate the wine, cannot believe that these comic villagers can keep such an enormous secret. Their conspiracy in the face of torture and death make heroes of them, and a fool and madman of Von Prum." Libr J

"It takes a lot of courage—and no little craft—to blend the diverse and exotic ingredients that Robert Crichton has brought together in this heady brew of a novel, a mélange of allegory, symbolism, several kinds of comedy including comedies of error and opera bouffe, traces of Don Quixote and John Hershey's Major Joppolo, and a plot involving barely credible incidents of blind fate." N Y Times Book Rev

Crider, Bill, 1941-

The Texas capitol murders. St. Martin's Press 1992 329p o.p.

LC 91-33409

"A Thomas Dunne book"

"A Mexican-American civil servant named Ramona Gonzalez, rumored to be promiscuous and talkative, is found strangled in an Austin, Tex., dumpster. It turns out that Gonzalez was pregnant and had ties to a powerful state senator, his bisexual chief aide and others. The capital city is thrown into turmoil when another body is found the next day. Assigned to the case by the dotty, paranoid governor, Texas Ranger Ray Hartnett must investigate a varied assortment of suspects." Publ Wkly

Crispin, Edmund, 1921-1978

Holy disorders. Lippincott 1946 269p o.p. Amereon reprint available $20.95 (ISBN 0-8488-0468-6)

"Main line mysteries"

First published 1945 in the United Kingdom

"A vacationing Fen summons composer Geoffrey Vintner to the Cathedral town of Tolnbridge to fill in for an organist who's just been mugged. Vintner is willing, but other parties don't want him near Tolnbridge; he gets threatening letters and is attacked several times. Worse awaits him in the form of a haunted cathedral, Nazi spies, and murder." Booklist

Sudden vengeance. Dodd, Mead 1950 247p o.p.

"A Red badge mystery"

Published in the United Kingdom with title: Frequent hearses

"The suicide of film actress Gloria Scott, a stage name, is followed by the murders of Madge Crane and her brothers, Maurice and Nicholas. The Cranes, stars in an epic movie in the making, had reneged on a promise to give Gloria a plummy part, a secret discovered by Inspector Humbleby of Scotland Yard. . . . The investigation takes the Scotland Yard pro and crime hobbyist Fen into dizzying byways before the cases are solved." Publ Wkly

Cronin, A. J. (Archibald Joseph), 1896-1981

The citadel. Little, Brown 1937 401p $16.45

ISBN 0-316-16158-6

"In 1921 Andrew Manson, newly graduated at the top of his medical-school class, accepts his first position as assistant to a dying physician in an impoverished Welsh mining town. Hard-working and conscientious at first, Andrew is promoted to a more socially desirable post in London, where he abandons his principles. A faulty operating-room procedure magnifies his increasing incompetence and jolts him back to a career of integrity." Shapiro. Fic for Youth. 3d edition

The keys of the kingdom. Little, Brown 1941 344p $16.45

ISBN 0-316-16189-6

Also available from Buccaneer Bks.

"A child of Scottish fisher folk, Father Francis Chisholm, even as a young lad, yearned to enter the Catholic priesthood. After graduation from the seminary and a few years of parish work at home, he was sent to China as a missionary. With the years of toil he acquired saintliness and tolerance. Pestilence and famine, bandits and flood, and unappreciative superiors only served to strengthen his character and fortitude. Excellent character delineation." Libr J

A pocketful of rye. Little, Brown 1969 245p o.p. Amereon reprint available $20.95 (ISBN 0-88411-526-7)

Sequel to A song of sixpence

"Laurence Carroll, young British doctor with a background of completely selfish living, tired of medical work in poor districts, has with some fraud secured for himself a pleasant job in a clinic in Switzerland. To the clinic comes widowed Cathy with her ill son Daniel. Cathy had been Laurence's first love, abandoned with his usual disregard, and only gradually does he learn the story of her wretched marriage and that Daniel is his son." Libr J

A song of sixpence. Little, Brown 1964 344p o.p.

Available from Amereon and Buccaneer Bks.

This novel depicts "the despair and joy of a Dickensonian childhood in Scotland at the turn of the century. . . . Its hero Laurence Carroll, is a Catholic and so an outcast in a Protestant Scottish community, but secure in his loving family circle, until his father dies of tuberculosis. After that, life is a struggle . . . but a struggle relieved by some rollicking good times, love for his mother and a pretty cousin, and help and sympathy from unexpected sources." Publ Wkly

Cronin, A. J. (Archibald Joseph), 1896-1981—*Continued*

"Much of the interest of this sympathy-evoking story of a Catholic boyhood lies in the many and varied adult characters who either helped or exploited Laurence. It is told with Cronin's expert professional skill." Libr J

Followed by A pocketful of rye

Cronin, Archibald Joseph *See* Cronin, A. J. (Archibald Joseph), 1896-1981

Cross, Amanda, 1926-

Death in a tenured position. Dutton 1981 156p o.p.

In this "mystery starring professor of literature, sleuth emeritus, and enemy of pomposity Kate Fansler, a millionaire offers Harvard a million if this bastion of male chauvinism will hire a woman English professor. Janet Mandelbaum, the chosen prof, not only shakes up the Harvard community, providing a litmus test for sexism and jealousy, she also invites murderous inclinations. Fansler investigates after Mandelbaum is slain." Booklist

"With its academic setting, literary flavor, and strong feminist point of view, this book won't appeal to everyone, but within its own framework it is a delight—witty and clever and perfectly true-to-life. The language is the best part." Libr J

An imperfect spy. Ballantine Bks. 1995 228p $20

ISBN 0-345-38917-4   LC 94-25357

Academic sleuth Kate Fansler "and husband Reed have each agreed to teach a course at New York's third-rate, racist, and chauvinistic Schuyler Law School, where they investigate the accidental death of the school's only woman professor and try to assist an imprisoned faculty wife who murdered her abusive husband. Highly sophisticated tone, carefully constructed prose, and nicely contrived plot make this a winner." Libr J

The James Joyce murder. Macmillan 1967 176p o.p.

"A Cock Robin mystery"

A village local found murdered practically on Professor Kate Fansler's own doorstep adds to her travail in "trying to unravel, with the help of a graduate student, the papers of a distinguished publisher who first introduced Joyce's writing to America." Publ Wkly

The author has "written a highly attractive specimen of the leisurely and witty academic mystery novel. . . . Not for action enthusiasts, but a happy souvenir of a once more popular school." N Y Times Book Rev

No word from Winifred. Dutton 1986 217p o.p.

LC 85-29334

"Winifred Ashby, remarkably independent, working as a farmhand, left the New England farm, promising her employers that she would return within a week. She arrived in London to settle her 'aunt's' estate. She did not keep an appointment in London nor did she return to the farm. She simply disappeared. Kate Fansler, professor of English was asked to investigate." Best Sellers

"This entertaining and highly literate novel is peopled with strong women and other interesting characters, and is rich with ideas, though at times the plot is a bit unclear. Kate Fansler, who can on occasion be a bit stuffy, is not at all so here." Publ Wkly

The players come again. Random House 1990 229p $17.95

ISBN 0-394-58785-5   LC 90-53122

This is a "mystery replete with feminist and literary ambience. Kate Fansler, English professor and amateur detective, is asked by a major publisher to take on a bit of literary sleuthing for a biography of one Gabrielle Foxx, whose fame is rooted in the fact that she was married to an author of Joycean stature. As Kate debates whether to take on this project, she meets the surviving family members, three women who entice her through a maze of family secrets, dropping hints that Gabrielle's contributions to her husband's work involved far more than playing the roles of muse and housewife." Booklist

"This compelling novel is about motivation, rather than material motives, about the mystery of human character more than the details of a murder." Publ Wkly

Sweet death, kind death. Dutton 1984 177p o.p.

LC 84-1469

"Patrice Umphelby, history professor at Clare College, maverick, and for many a general pain in the ass, has walked into the campus lake in a successful suicide. Her biographers . . . are suspicious, and they solicit the help of English professor cum sleuth, Kate Fansler." Best Sellers

"This likable whodunit is full to the brim with clever talk and literary allusions. Hard-boiled detective fans may find Fansler's book-learning a bit wearisome, but at least she drinks and smokes. On the other hand, for those who prefer their murder mysteries served with a side order of life according to the Bloomsbury Group . . . Amanda Cross remains the reigning champion." Booklist

The Theban mysteries. Knopf 1971 173p o.p.

"Another literate caper for Kate Fansler, now Mrs. Reed Amhearst. Kate, on sabbatical, reluctantly agrees to give a seminar on Sophocles' 'Antigone' for seven seniors at the Theban, that remarkable girls' school in the East 70's in New York where she was once a student." Libr J

A "modern variation on a classical motif. Youthful rebellion, an older generation as uncomprehending as Creon was, and Kate and her district attorney husband, ruefully aware of the problems faced by both conservative elders and exasperating youngsters, add up to what is not really a murder story, but a highly satisfactory mystery, laced with some intelligent ripostes and aphorisms." Publ Wkly

A trap for fools. Dutton 1989 154p o.p.

LC 88-30204

"Kate Fansler, Cross' English professor detective, is asked by her superiors to determine whether a particularly unpopular university professor committed suicide or was murdered. The possible frame-up of a friend causes Kate to take the case. . . . Cross is a whiz at setting up a maze of evidence, dropping literary references, and portraying the ambience of academia." Booklist

Cross, Mary Ann Evans *See* Eliot, George, 1819-1880

Culver, Timothy J.

For works written by this author under other names see Westlake, Donald E.

Cussler, Clive

Cyclops; a novel. Simon & Schuster 1986 475p il o.p.

LC 85-27704

"American scientists secretly send a manned space station to the moon; a Soviet plot to overthrow Fidel Castro erupts on the eve of a groundbreaking alliance between Cuba and America; and an American industrialist embarks on a treasure hunt in an antique blimp, only to disappear off the coast of Florida. The only constant in these seemingly unrelated events is Dirk Pitt, [who is involved] in every aspect of this complicated tale." Booklist

"The writing is brittle, but the reader is not likely to worry about that in a story whose plot resembles a box of exploding fireworks and poses some interesting questions regarding both Cuba and the militarization of space." Publ Wkly

Deep six; a novel. Simon & Schuster 1984 432p il o.p.

LC 84-5291

Salvage expert Dirk Pitt "is assigned by the U.S. Environmental Protection Agency to locate the source of a deadly nerve agent contaminating the ocean off Alaska. In the action-packed scenes that follow, Pitt uncovers an international plot to take over the U.S. Government through the use of mind control devices." Libr J

Dragon; a novel. Simon & Schuster 1990 542p il $21.45

ISBN 0-671-62619-1   LC 90-9650

Also available G.K. Hall large print edition

In this "novel Cussler brings back Dirk Pitt, special projects director of the National Underwater and Marine Agency (NUMA), who has a 'razor hardness about him that even a stranger could sense,' a man who spends 'almost as much time on and under water as he does on land.' The plot involves a crashed B-29 bomber that was carrying a third atomic bomb to Japan in 1945—the nuclear cargo having been buried in the Pacific Ocean for 45 years—and a group of Japanese extremists who seek to blackmail the U.S. with nuclear weapons strategically planted in several large U.S. cities." Booklist

The author "offers a page-turning romp that achieves a level of fast-paced action and derring-do that Robert Ludlum and other practitioners of modern pulp fiction might well envy." Publ Wkly

Inca gold; a novel. Simon & Schuster 1994 537p $24

ISBN 0-671-68156-7   LC 94-6577

Also available G.K. Hall large print edition

"A chance rescue of two divers trapped in a Peruvian sinkhole leads series hero Dirk Pitt . . . into a search for lost treasure that involves grave robbers, art thieves and ancient curses. Cussler's latest adventure novel features terrorists who aren't really terrorists and a respected archeologist who is not what he seems: it all boils down to a race between Pitt and some unscrupulous crooks for a cache of Inca gold hidden away from the Spanish and lost since the 16th century. . . . It's pure escapist adventure, with a wry touch of humor and a certain self-referential glee." Publ Wkly

Night probe! Bantam Bks. 1981 344p o.p.

LC 81-43094

In this novel salvage expert Dirk Pitt's "mission is to work on two separate underwater wrecks: a ship sunk in the St. Lawrence River and a train buried beneath the Hudson River. The year is 1989 and Pitt must recover two copies of a lost treaty signed by the U.S. and England in 1914, which, if found, could have a profound impact on international relations. Alerted to the American plan, the British send in Brian Shaw, an aging but brilliant agent, who is instructed to prevent Pitt from finding the treaty." Publ Wkly

Raise the Titanic! Viking 1976 314p il o.p.

"It is the year 1988. United States scientists need a rare element, byzanium, the only existing supply of which was shipped in the Titanic's hold, to complete a missile defense system. The Russians try by various means to stop them from retrieving it. In order to get to the byzanium, the U.S. sets about bringing the Titanic, which lies under two and a half miles of water after its 1912 rendezvous with an iceberg, to the surface." Christ Sci Monit

"A great adventure thriller . . . [that] spins from one dizzying climax to another, holds its innermost secrets until the very end, and keeps you so audaciously entertained you won't want it to come to a close. . . . Simply super and very cleverly done, with just the right amount of tongue-in-cheek bravado." Publ Wkly

Sahara; a novel. Simon & Schuster 1992 541p o.p.

LC 92-5100

Available G.K. Hall large print edition

"In West Africa, a vicious plot launched by a military dictator and a French industrialist is killing thousands of people and threatening all the creatures in the world's seas with extinction. As Cussler's perennial hero Dirk Pitt hikes off across the Sahara to bring the world news of these evil doings, he discovers the secret behind Lincoln's assassination, hidden aboard a lost Confederate ironclad, and the disappearance of British aviatrix Kitty Mannock in 1931." Libr J

"Pepper the plot with human-rights abuse, cannibalism, state-of-the-art weaponry, espionage, and the evil General Zateb Kazim—and you've got more than enough action to keep the Cussler's thrill-craving fans satiated." Booklist

Treasure; a novel. Simon & Schuster 1988 539p o.p.

LC 88-1951

During a rescue mission in Greenland to recover a sabotaged airliner full of U.N. representatives, salvage expert Dirk Pitt runs across evidence of the location of a fabled Roman treasure, rescued from Alexandria in A.D. 391

"Cussler creates a world that is just believable enough for the reader to accept as true, a necessary prerequisite for audacious fiction such as this. Characters do and say what you'd expect in their situations. The scientific jargon, gadgets, and weaponry all seem authentic and fit smoothly into the plot. . . . Taken as a just-for-fun adventure, the book is solidly entertaining." West Coast Rev Books

Vixen 03. Viking 1978 286p o.p.

LC 78-63035

Available from Amereon and Buccaneer Bks.

Cussler, Clive—*Continued*

"The tale begins in 1954 when a plane loaded with deadly plague bombs crashes into a lake in Colorado, where it remains buried for thirty-four years. It is only discovered by accident when an investigator from a government agency is on vacation and comes across parts of the plane. The government has written it off as having disappeared in the Pacific and all its papers have been falsified to prevent any possibility of salvage because of the deadly cargo. But when the investigator finds the plane, he finds that eight of the cannisters have been stolen and an extra body added to the lost crew! The story goes on to involve a black South African country in the grip of a power struggle, a white farmer, an ex-British navy man, whose family has been massacred and who is out for vengeance. Cussler is an exceptionally fine writer, a master of characterization and his book is filled with suspenseful episodes." West Coast Rev Books

"Some of the treatment of blacks may be offensive to readers, even though the real bad guys are the white South Africans." Publ Wkly

D

Dahl, Roald

Ah, sweet mystery of life; stories; illustrated by John Lawrence. Knopf 1990 179p il o.p.

LC 89-43292

Available G.K. Hall large print edition

Analyzed in Short story index

First published 1989 in the United Kingdom

Contents: Ah, sweet mystery of life; Parson's pleasure; The ratcatcher; Rummins; Mr. Hoddy; Mr. Feasey; The champion of the world

"These seven stories date from the late 1940s when Dahl was living in England's Buckinghamshire countryside and just beginning his career. The remembered people and settings of this rural region come to life vividly, Dahl converting them into a series of tales that explore a surprisingly deep and engagingly humorous vision of humanity. . . . His characters are refreshingly ordinary and full of life." Booklist

Selected stories of Roald Dahl. Modern Lib. 1968 302p o.p.

Analyzed in Short story index

These stories were selected by the author from two of his previous collections: Someone like you, published 1953 and, Kiss, kiss, published 1960

Contents: Lamb to the slaughter; Dip in the pool; The landlady; Taste; Parson's pleasure; Georgy Porgy; Royal jelly; Genesis and catastrophe; Mrs. Bixby and the Colonel's coat; Skin; The ratcatcher; Rummins; Mr. Hoddy; Mr. Feasy; The champion of the world

"These tales by a social satirist and moralist are a pungent blend of the macabre and the humorous." Chicago. Public Libr

Dailey, Janet

Aspen gold; a novel. Little, Brown 1991 364p o.p.

LC 90-27639

"Kit Masters grew up on an Aspen ranch but left her home for Hollywood, where she's labored in the soaps. Now she has her first break: the lead in a big movie with sex symbol John Travis. Kit's retained her integrity—proven by the fact that she has freckles, is a natural blond, and won't dump her agent—and has kindled real heat in the jaded heart of her oh-so-handsome costar. But trouble lies ahead, and the return to her hometown is also the return to scenes of sad memories. . . . Beautiful Kit, always fashionably attired, poised, and perfumed, works her way through a maze of treacheries as Dailey expertly twists the plot into a satisfying conclusion, once again floating her readers on the cushion of fantasy and escape." Booklist

Heiress; a novel. Little, Brown 1987 477p o.p.

LC 86-27538

"Abbie Lawson is 27 when her father, Dean, dies in an auto accident. Fully expecting to inherit millions from his petroleum-related business, Abbie is devastated to discover that not only was Dean in financial trouble, but that he left an enormous trust to his illegitimate daughter, Rachel Farr. Abbie and her mother are forced to sell the family estate, predictably purchased by Rachel, and so begins a bitter rivalry between the sisters, complicating their lives and those of their loved ones." Libr J

"Dailey doesn't hesitate to make full use of the clichés of the commercial fiction genre, but her wit, imagination and creation of a sardonic male romantic lead constitute solid entertainment." Publ Wkly

Masquerade; a novel. Little, Brown 1990 326p o.p.

LC 89-28830

Available G.K. Hall large print edition

This romance is set in the "decay and corruption of New Orleans," where beautiful Remy Jardin returns after being mysteriously knocked on the head at Carnival in Nice. Her sharp wits befuddled by amnesia, Remy sees everyone with newly opened eyes—her loving father, who's surprisingly anxious to pack her off to a deluxe asylum; goodnatured yet slippery brother Gabe; jovial Uncle Marc; and glowering ex-lover Cole Buchanan, who runs the Jardins' shipping company and tears at her heart. While Remy delves into an unsavory insurance scam she'd be safer letting lie, the story moves smoothly between sentimental glories of the past century and the suspenseful present." Publ Wkly

The proud and the free; a novel. Little, Brown 1994 322p $22.95

ISBN 0-316-17165-4   LC 94-14266

"Temple Gordon and The Blade Stuart are a Cherokee couple at odds over the future of the Cherokee Nation in the early 1830s. In the face of all evidence, Temple persists in believing the Cherokee will not be forced from their land. The Blade can see the writing on the wall however, and tries to persuade his . . . wife and her family to head west voluntarily." Libr J

"Dailey's blend of American history and romance will captivate her fans and create new ones." Booklist

Tangled vines; a novel. Little, Brown 1992 363p o.p.

LC 92-10351

Available large print edition $24.95 (ISBN 0-316-17158-1)

Dailey, Janet—*Continued*

"TV journalist Kelly Douglas hides the memories of her unhappy Napa Valley childhood and abuse by her alcoholic father beneath a veneer of polished professionalism. Her career and composure are threatened, however, when she has to return to her hometown to interview the matriarch of California wines, Katherine Rutledge. . . . Dailey does a nice job of weaving wine-industry tidbits, social messages, and rising suspense into an intriguing plot." Booklist

Dalby, Richard

(ed) The Virago book of ghost stories. See The Virago book of ghost stories

Daley, Robert

A faint cold fear; a novel. Little, Brown 1990 450p $19.95

ISBN 0-316-17184-0   LC 90-39021

"A dedicated New York cop, more interested in fighting crime than maintaining the political status quo, Ray Douglas finds himself unwanted in the Drug Enforcement Agency's Colombian field office. His path crosses that of Jane Fox, an ambitious journalist determined to prove that her abilities as a foreign correspondent are in no way limited by her gender. At first each sees the other only as a tool for their respective careers—he as her inside source, she as a means of reminding the NYPD of his existence—but their tentative friendship evolves into a more serious relationship." Libr J

"To say that Mr. Daley has written a wonderful cop novel may mean little. Considering how few writers do it well, however, what is most amazing is how easy Mr. Daley makes it look. This is popular entertainment of a high order." N Y Times Book Rev

Hands of a stranger. Simon & Schuster 1985 397p o.p.

LC 85-8193

"Joe Hearn, an ambitious inspector in the N.Y.P.D., finds himself falling in love with Judith Adler, the assistant district attorney for sex crimes. His neglected wife, Mary, comes close to having an affair but at the last second changes her mind. As she is about to leave an hourly-rate hotel room, Mary is raped. Her husband, ignoring his responsibilities and abusing the resources of the Police Department, obsessively investigates the assault." N Y Times Book Rev

"Part soap opera, part compelling thriller, Daley's excellent novel paints a brutally vivid portrait of the turmoil within the criminal justice system and the humiliation of rape." Booklist

Man with a gun. Simon & Schuster 1988 475p o.p.

LC 87-27695

"Foreign correspondent Phil Keefe has been selected right-hand man to New York Police Commissioner Timothy J. Egan. . . . Keefe is coached by a sergeant who has seen awful cruelties on the streets of New York. He is suspected by top brass who fear their power slipping into his hands. . . . He is in over his head, though, when police officials saddle him with a difficult hostage negotiation that results in the death of a distraught black trucker." Publ Wkly

"While Daley occasionally lets the plot wander as he explores the often dirty world of police politics, his characterizations are ruthlessly perceptive. Unlike many mysteries, all of the actors in this drama are painted in gritty, realistic shades of gray." Booklist

Tainted evidence; a novel. Little, Brown 1993 391p o.p.

LC 92-31904

"A minor hoodlum named Lionel Epps shoots five cops during a botched arrest in Harlem. For political reasons, responsibility for the prosecution falls on assistant DA Karen Henning, who has to deal with allegations of drug dealing and police corruption from Epps's lawyer, veiled threats from the police commissioner and an activist minister, and betrayal within her own department, not to mention domestic problems with her husband and their two kids." Publ Wkly

Wall of brass; a novel. Little, Brown 1994 409p $22.95

ISBN 0-316-17206-5   LC 94-14185

"When New York City Police Commissioner Harry Chapman is shot while jogging on Manhattan's Upper West Side, his former patrol-car partner, Bert Farber, now chief of detectives, is assigned to find the killer. Farber is also one of three top contenders to replace Chapman as commissioner, and his two chief rivals are doing their best to roadblock him in his search for the killer. Complicating the situation . . . [is] Farber's torrid romance with Chapman's wife, Mary Alice." Publ Wkly

"A tightly plotted, involving tale of law and disorder." Booklist

D'Amato, Barbara

Hard case; a Cat Marsala mystery. Scribner 1994 258p $20

ISBN 0-684-19686-7   LC 94-13858

Freelance reporter Cat Marsala is "pleased when her boss asks her to do a feature on big-city trauma centers, figuring it'll be an easy, 'quickbucks' write. She'll spend a few days in one of Chicago's mega-med centers, interview staff, talk to some recovered patients, find an angle for the story, and bang it out. What Cat doesn't count on is getting involved in a murder. Her first day at the trauma center, Cat discovers the body of the director, who's suffocated after a gauze pad was shoved down her throat. Horrified, Cat vows to discover who wanted the director dead. . . . A riveting read." Booklist

Hard luck; a Cat Marsala mystery. Scribner 1992 242p $20

ISBN 0-684-19408-2   LC 91-37412

"Chicago freelance journalist Cat Marsala . . . watches the story of her career land—literally—in front of her when Jack Sligh, an Illinois lottery official, plummets to his death from a skyscraper. Cat recognizes the corpse because she'd made an appointment with Sligh in regard to an article she was writing on the proposed Central States Lottery. Convinced Sligh was pushed, Cat begins an indepth investigation of his co-workers at the Illinois state lottery." Publ Wkly

"D'Amato's descriptions of state lottery problems and procedures are factual and fascinating, and her characters—both series regulars and lottery folk—are lively and believable." Booklist

D'Amato, Barbara—*Continued*

Hard women; a Cat Marsala mystery. Scribner 1993 249p $20

ISBN 0-684-19564-X   LC 92-32697

"Chicago reporter Cat Marsala is asked to do a television segment on hookers, but researching the piece proves difficult and disheartening. Looking for hookers to interview, Cat befriends a call girl named Sandra, who's found murdered a few days later. The police seem to lack enthusiasm for solving the case, so Cat decides she'll do some independent detecting." Booklist

"Although her tale carries a determined social conscience, D'Amato spins an engrossing story, convincing us again that Cat is as likable as she is clever." Publ Wkly

Dangerous visions; 33 original stories; illustrated by Leo and Diana Dillon. Doubleday 1967 xxix, 520p o.p.

"Doubleday science fiction"

Analyzed in Short story index

Edited by Harlan Ellison

Contents: Evensong, by L. Del Rey; Flies, by R. Silverberg; The day after the day the Martians came, by F. Pohl; Riders of the purple wage, by J. P. Farmer; The Malley system, by A. M. DeFord; A toy for Juliette, by R. Bloch; The prowler in the city at the edge of the world, by H. Ellison; The night that all time broke loose, by B. W. Aldiss; The man who went to the moon—twice, by H. Rodman; Faith of our fathers, by P. K. Dick; The jigsaw man, by L. Niven; Gonna roll the bones, by F. Leiber; Lord Randy, my son, by J. L. Hensley; Eutopia, by P. Anderson; Incident in Moderan, by D. R. Bunch; The escaping, by D. R. Bunch; The dollhouse, by J. Cross; Sex and/or Mr. Morrison, by C. Emshwiller; Shall the dust praise thee, by D. Knight; If all men were brothers, would you let one marry your sister? by T. Sturgeon; What happened to Auguste Clarot? by L. Eisenberg; Ersatz, by H. Slesar; Go, go, go, said the bird, by S. Dorman; The happy breed, by J. T. Sladek; Encounter with a hick, by J. Brand; From the government printing office, by K. Neville; Land of the great horses, by R. A. Lafferty; The recognition, by J. G. Ballard; Judas, by J. Brunner; Test to destruction, by K. Laumer; Carcinoma Angels, by N. Spinrad; Auto-da-fé, by R. Zelazny; Aye, and Gomorrah . . . , by S. R. Delany

Dannay, Frederic, 1905-1982

For works written by this author in collaboration with Manfred Lee see Queen, Ellery

Darby, Catherine, 1935-

For works written by this author under other names see Black, Veronica, 1935-

Dark, Larry

(ed) The Literary ghost. See The Literary ghost

(ed) The Literary traveler. See The Literary traveler

Dart, Iris Rainer

I'll be there. Little, Brown 1991 254p o.p.

LC 90-19990

Sequel to Beaches (1985)

"Dart picks up the saga of singer Cee Cee Bloom after the tragic death of beach-pal Bertie Baron, with Cee Cee struggling to raise Bertie's daughter Nina while maintaining her fast-paced Hollywood career." Libr J

The author "keeps the quips coming and the entertainment-world setting prominent, so can there be any doubt that the ending will be yet another tearily satisfying reprise of past successes?" Booklist

The Stork Club; a novel. Little, Brown 1992 400p $21.95

ISBN 0-316-17332-0   LC 92-15612

"At age 50, Rick, a single movie producer and avowed Casanova combatting a midlife crisis, decides to adopt a baby. Ruthie and Shelley, a successful comedy-writing team, resolve to create a child even though he is gay and she is straight. Lainie and Mitch, owners of a chic California clothing boutique, contract with a surrogate mother to produce their child. These parents form the Stork Club led by Barbara, the child psychologist who guides the group as they struggle to make their atypical family circumstances work." Libr J

This novel is "hilarious, maudlin, warmhearted and surprisingly genuine in its emotions." Publ Wkly

Datlow, Ellen

(ed) Black thorn, white rose. See Black thorn, white rose

(ed) Snow white, blood red. See Snow white, blood red

(ed) The Year's best fantasy and horror. See The Year's best fantasy and horror

Davenport, Diana *See* Davenport, Kiana

Davenport, Kiana

Shark dialogues. Atheneum Pubs. 1994 492p $22

ISBN 0-689-12191-1   LC 93-31273

This "multigenerational saga details the history of Hawaii through the experiences of one family. It begins in the 19th century with the dramatic meeting of a young Yankee sailor and a beautiful Tahitian princess. Their descendants, who live in contemporary Hawaii, are four cousins named Vanya, Ming, Rachel, and Jess who have been brought up by Pono, a kahuna, or seer, who has never talked about her mysterious past to her four granddaughters. Davenport deftly includes much information in the narrative—about politics, leprosy, and the racial melting pot that is Hawaiian society—with a minimum of didacticism. She incorporates folklore, history, and myth in a vivid, lush prose style." Libr J

David, Peter

Q-squared. Pocket Bks. 1994 434p (Star trek, the next generation) $22

ISBN 0-671-89152-9   LC 94-65679

David, Peter—*Continued*

This novel focuses on "Trelane, the son of gods from the Q Continuum. The character Q from *The Next Generation* series is his guardian. Trelane gets out of hand in his adolescence, scattering pieces of Q throughout time and inventing a machine in which all dimensions of the universe chaotically intersect. He continues the campaign begun in his childhood, to play with human beings as toys, by collapsing three parallel *Enterprises* into one." Booklist

Davidson, Diane Mott

The last suppers. Bantam Bks. 1994 283p il $19.95

ISBN 0-553-09587-0   LC 94-18886

"Caterer Goldy Bear's wedding would have been perfect except for two minor problems—the priest is killed shortly before the wedding and her fiancé, homicide detective Tom Schultz, is kidnapped from the scene of the crime. Frustrated with waiting for updates from the police, Goldy attempts to find out who ruined her wedding." Booklist

"An appealing mixture of food and crime." Libr J

Davies, L. P. (Leslie Purnell), 1914-

A grave matter. Doubleday 1968 c1967 190p o.p.

"Published for the Crime Club"

First published 1967 in the United Kingdom

"John Morton, idly skimming through a newspaper, reads a brief item about the discovery of two children's skeletons beside a quiet country road. He recalls that the town is Ashmead, where he lived as a boy. He also has a memory, almost buried by time, of having trespassed into a country estate long ago, of having played with a boy and girl and never seen them again. Impelled to investigate on his own, he encounters plenty of trouble before he uncovers the full truth about what happened in the past." Publ Wkly

"Well plotted, well written, it takes one back to the famous British mystery writers. No overtones of sex, no extreme of violence; it is a professional piece of suspense writing." Best Sellers

Davies, Leslie Purnell *See* Davies, L. P. (Leslie Purnell), 1914-

Davies, Robertson, 1913-1995

Fifth business. Viking 1970 308p o.p.

The first volume in the Deptford trilogy, followed by The manticore and World of wonders

"In the year 1908 in the Canadian Midwest, a woman is struck by a poorly aimed snowball. Her son is born prematurely as a result of her fright. Dunstan Ramsay describes his connection with four of his friends whose lives were affected by the incident: Boy Staunton who threw the snowball; Mrs. Amasa Dempster, who was hit by it; Paul, the son born prematurely; and Leola Cruikshank, a local beauty whom Staunton marries. The intertwining of their lives spans 60 years, three continents, and two wars." Shapiro. Fic For Youth. 3d edition

This novel "achieves a richness and depth that are exceptional in a modern novel and rare at any time. On its simplest and most obvious level it is a remarkably colorful tale of ambition, love and weird vengeance. At its deepest, it is a work of theological fiction that

approaches Graham Greene at the top of his form." Book World

The lyre of Orpheus. Viking 1989 472p $19.95

ISBN 0-670-82416-X   LC 88-40311

Concluding volume of the Cornish trilogy

"This fable about the nature of artistic creation has two major plot lines. One thread concerns the production of an unfinished opera said to have been written by E.T.A. Hoffmann. The other concerns the discovery that the famous art collector Francis Cornish actually passed off one of his own paintings as a 16th-century masterpiece." Merriam-Webster's Ency of Lit

The manticore. Viking 1972 310p o.p.

The second volume in the Deptford trilogy

"The central figure is a highly successful Canadian lawyer, David Staunton, son of a Canadian millionaire, who is compelled to submit himself to the Jung Institute in Zurich for analysis when he feels insecure and no longer in command of his actions. Staunton himself relates the course of his Jungian analysis, revealing significant incidents and aspects of his past life and commenting from a different point of view on persons and actions." Booklist

This book "reflects in its style the buoyancy of the quick mind of its hero as well as his pomposity, his over confidence, and egotism. No doubt about it: Robertson Davies is a manipulator of words and he entrances the reader with a flowing flurry of dialogue and narrative. His book is well written, insightful, and a delightful psychological excursion." Best Sellers

Murther & walking spirits; a novel. Viking 1991 357p $21.95

ISBN 0-670-84189-7   LC 91-29844

"Connor Gilmartin ('Gil') is murdered in the novel's first sentence by a co-worker he discovers in bed with his (Gil's) wife. The indignity of being snuffed by 'the Sniffer,' a theater-cum-movie critic, is compounded when Gil is seemingly condemned to spend his after-life seated next to his nemesis at a film festival. But what Gil sees—unlike the rest of the audience—is a series of highly personal films starring an assortment of ancestors." Libr J

"The films convey more than sight and sound, making our hero eerily privy to his relatives' thoughts and feelings. Davies has great fun with this device, giving full rein to his sense of drama, love of gritty, historical detail, and delight in satire." Booklist

The rebel angels. Viking 1982 c1981 326p o.p.

LC 81-51907

First volume in the Cornish trilogy, followed by What's bred in the bone and The lyre of Orpheus

First published 1981 in Canada

"Set in a prominent Canadian university, the novel examines the dual themes of the distinction between knowledge and wisdom and the role of the university in contemporary society." Merriam-Webster's Ency of Lit

"The names of Rabelais and Paracelsus are not gratuitously invoked by the plot. There is a Rabelaisian quality . . . in Mr. Davies's own writing; while the hermetic and heterodox ideas associated with the name of Paracelsus are exploited in a fashion that is at once playful and serious." New Repub

Davies, Robertson, 1913-1995—*Continued*
What's bred in the bone. Viking 1985
436p o.p.

LC 85-40550

"An Elisabeth Sifton book"
Second volume in the Cornish trilogy
"Born in 1909 in the Canadian town of Blairlogie,
Francis [Cornish] inherits a religious and cultural
dichotomy: his mother is Canadian Catholic, his father
English; both are also secret agents, and mostly absent.
After college at Oxford and art school in Paris, Francis
too becomes a spy, gathering intelligence in Hitler's Ger-
many while apprenticed to a brilliant and devious art
restorer. Three ill-fated loves leave Francis alone at the
end, his life a puzzle to his descendants but not to his
'Daiman' and an Angel of Biography who unravel
Francis's character and destiny." Libr J
"This novel nourishes the brain while it beguiles the
senses. Even those who dislike its message must keep
it in mind while they scramble for a rebuttal." Time

World of wonders. Viking 1976 c1975
358p o.p.
Final volume in the Deptford trilogy
"The world's premier illusionist, Magnus Eisengrim,
tells his story to an audience of friends and filmmakers:
his solitary childhood in a small, deeply Calvinistic village in rural Canada; his abduction by a carnival magician and his years of labor as a huckster; his initiation
into the British theater by a grande dame and her husband, an egotistical star whom Magnus all but absorbs
into himself; his work as a master repairman of gadgets,
clocks, and mechanical toys; and finally his triumphant
career on stage." Libr J
"If there is a single dominating theme, it is that we
can never escape the consequences of our actions, and
to ignore them is to be destroyed. . . . Among contemporary novelists, only Graham Greene has trod this
ground and gleaned it so successfully. He and Davies
stand alone, each in his own quarter of the field." New
Repub

Davies, Valentine, 1905-1961
Miracle on 34th Street. Harcourt Brace &
Co. 1947 120p $13.95
ISBN 0-15-160239-5
"Old Mr. Kringle believed he was Santa Claus, and
he looked the part, but the home for the aged decided
the delusion made him ineligible as a permanent resident
so he went to stay with a friend who was a keeper of
Central Park zoo. Quite by accident he became the official Santa Claus in Macy's department store where he
inaugurated a new and profitable policy of good will
between stores, but an irritated personnel manager tried
to have him committed to a mental hospital. The case
went to court and the judge was in a dilemma—what
would happen to his political career if he declared Santa
Claus a myth?" Booklist
"Nice blend of fantasy, fun and humor with the
universal and wholesome appeal of the Christmas spirit."
Libr J

Davies, William Robertson *See* Davies, Robertson, 1913-1995

Daviot, Gordon, 1896-1952
*For works written by this author under
other names see* Tey, Josephine, 1896-1952

Davis, Dorothy Salisbury, 1916-
Lullaby of murder. Scribner 1984 213p
o.p.

LC 84-3116

Hayes "investigates the murder of her boss, gossip
columnist Tony Alexander, a man hated and feared by
many—and deservedly so. Davis has created a fascinating
cast of characters. Not the least of them is Julie, who
grows with each novel in her painful progression towards
full, independent womanhood. The mystery is good, too."
Read Teach

Davis, Lindsey
The iron hand of Mars; a Marcus Didius
Falco mystery. Crown 1993 c1992 305p $20
ISBN 0-517-59240-1

LC 93-19265

First published 1992 in the United Kingdom
"In A.D. 71, the Emperor Vespasian sends his reluctant
agent Marcus Didius Falco to Germany to bring a rebel
chieftain into line and to find a missing legate whose
battle-worn legion had surrendered him to a druidic sorceress." Publ Wkly
"Essential reading for historical mystery buffs and any
lover of a good story." Libr J

Venus in copper; a Marcus Didius Falco
novel. Crown 1992 c1991 277p $20
ISBN 0-517-58477-8

LC 91-37297

First published 1991 in the United Kingdom
A "mystery set in the Rome of Vespasian. Falco, the
ancient equivalent of a private detective, ferrets out information for two nouveau-riche women about a 'professional bride' who wants to marry their husbands' business partner. When someone murders the partner, the
fiancée hires Falco to find the murderer." Libr J
This novel "demonstrates Davis' solid historical knowledge as well as his quick wit." Booklist

Davis, Thulani
1959; a novel. Grove Weidenfeld 1991
297p o.p.

LC 91-24548

"Willie Tarrant is twelve in 1959 and more interested
in hair and boys than the struggle for equality. But then
she is deputed to be the young Martin Luther King's
guide around the black college in Turner, [Virginia],
where her father teaches, . . . and, shortly after, is
singled out as one of the children to integrate the white
high school." Times Lit Suppl
The author has "combined a coming-of-age story with
an evocative portrait of a segregated community on the
cusp of the '60s. What happens when the blacks of
Turner, Va., get fed up with their lot can be read as
a microhistory of the civil-rights movement, and even
a grimly prophetic emblem of the entire African-
American experience." Newsweek

Dawson, Carol, 1951-
Body of knowledge. Algonquin Bks. 1994
471p $22.95
ISBN 1-56512-054-X

LC 94-13355

Dawson, Carol, 1951-—*Continued*

"Narrator Victoria Grace Ransom (named for the British queen) owes her 500-pound weight to a case of hypothalmus-damaging measles at age four. Unexposed to radio, TV and newspapers, Victoria has scarcely emerged from the Ransom estate since her birth in 1947. To pass the time, she listens to her black servant, Viola Lewis, tell tales of Ransom family history. A 1908 business partnership and secret adulterous liaisons create a hate-filled bond between the Ransom clan and the Macafees." Publ Wkly

"Dawson is a wily storyteller. She beguiles you with precise detail while drawing you into a plot bristling with pointed absurdity and sharp satire." Booklist

De Balzac, Honoré *See* Balzac, Honoré de, 1799-1850

De Beauvoir, Simone *See* Beauvoir, Simone de, 1908-1986

De Bernières, Louis, 1954-

Corelli's mandolin. Pantheon Bks. 1994 437p $24

ISBN 0-679-43644-8   LC 94-4783

"Set on the Greek island of Cephallonia, this . . . novel spans five decades beginning in the late 1930s just before the Axis forces occupy the island. . . . Corelli is an Italian army captain, a member of the first extraneous forces to occupy Cephallonia, and the lover of Pelagia Iannis. It is through Pelagia's voice that much of the story is revealed, but the chorus includes her father, various Greek villagers, Italian and Greek soldiers, and a goatherd." Libr J

The novel "has at times the rangy, expansive feeling of legend or saga, at other times the cozy intensities of chamber drama. The piece of Greek history it represents is composed of sufferings large and small, of national catastrophes and household agonies." N Y Times Book Rev

De Blasis, Celeste

The proud breed. Coward, McCann & Geoghegan 1978 571p o.p.

     LC 77-20282

In this three-generational saga of old California, "beautiful Anglo-Spanish Tessa is rescued from a sadistic suitor by a handsome Yankee, Gavin—and theirs is to be a lifelong love affair only interrupted . . . when Gavin consorts with a whore because he can't bear the 'burden' of loving Tessa. They breed 'golden' palaminos on twin 'ranchos,' develop commercial enterprises in turbulent San Francisco (these are the bad old days of the Gold Rush, vigilante committees and anti-Chinese riots) and beget children, who keep the . . . story going by begetting other children." Publ Wkly

A season for Swans. Bantam Bks. 1989 676p o.p.

     LC 88-37614

Concludes the Swan family trilogy

"Much of the action of this historical romance centers on the breeding and racing of thoroughbreds. . . . The novel opens dramatically with main character Gincie Culhane's murder of her brutal half-brother, Mark, followed by Gincie's and her family's flight to avoid prosecution.

Then another tragedy shakes the family's foundation and threatens to destroy forever the family farm, Wild Swan, where many great thoroughbred racehorses were raised. A thoroughly engrossing, crisply told yarn spanning the final years of the nineteenth century, with a fine blend of historical realism and romantic imagination." Booklist

Swan's chance. Bantam Bks. 1985 547p $16.95

ISBN 0-553-05092-3   LC 85-5999

The second volume of the Swan family trilogy, follows Wild Swan (1984)

"Alexandria's world revolves around her beloved husband, her children and her horse farm in Maryland. Thoroughbred horse breeding and racing, carried on successfully after the death of her first husband, are important factors in Alex' life. The five children grow up, leave home to build their own lives and return to Wild Swan to share success, happiness and tragedy with their parents. Opposed to slavery, Alex and Rane run their farm and shipping business with free employees but nevertheless are touched by the political upheaval preceding the Civil War. The war brings hardships, tragedy and divided loyalties but the family is held together by a strong and caring Alex. Readers of family sagas, historic fiction and adult romance will find their preferences all in one very readable book." SLJ

De Crayencour, Marguerite *See* Yourcenar, Marguerite

De Felitta, Frank

Audrey Rose; a novel. Putnam 1975 374p o.p.

"A fortunate young couple, living just off Central Park West in New York, is bedeviled by a stranger who tells them that their ten-year-old daughter is actually the reincarnation of his little girl who was killed in an unfortunate car accident. He becomes so troublesome, and the girl so distressed, what with the lost soul coming forth, that there is a trial . . . to establish legally the actuality of reincarnation." Libr J

De Hartog, Jan, 1914-

The captain. Atheneum Pubs. 1966 434p o.p. Nautical & Aviation reprint available $19.95 (ISBN 0-933852-83-5)

"In 1942 Captain Martinus Harinxma, a Hollander escaped from the Nazis, is given command of a Dutch tugboat slated for convoy duty on the Iceland-Murmansk run. After the death of his liaison officer, complications pile up for the captain who becomes emotionally involved with the officer's widow. He also discovers that his ideas on war and heroism have changed drastically." Libr J

This sea story "is one of those rarities in contemporary fiction, a real spellbinder, a he-man story, full of action, in which the hero is brave and likeable. . . . The exposure and terror of that long and punishing convoy have never been so powerfully depicted. The art of this book lies in its unforced masculinity, for these men are real." Atlantic

Followed by The Commodore

The centurion. Harper & Row 1989 286p $18.95

ISBN 0-06-039094-8   LC 88-45911

De Hartog, Jan, 1914—*Continued*
"A Cornelia & Michael Bessie book"

The third installment in the author's adventure series. "When retired sea captain Martinus Harinxma discovers he possesses a gift for dowsing (using a divining rod), he unravels the peculiar destiny of a fourth-century Roman centurion. Trapped in an irresistible time warp, Martinus determines that his own fate is inextricably entwined with his mystical vision. De Hartog effectively fuses two parallel plots into a spiritual voyage of self-discovery transcending time and space." Booklist

Followed by The outer buoy

The Commodore; a novel of the sea. Harper & Row 1985 406p $19.95

ISBN 0-06-039041-7   LC 84-48591

"A Cornelia & Michael Bessie book"

Martinus Harinxma featured in The captain "now 70 years old, is called from a nine-year-long retirement to guide the Isabel Kwel, the most powerful tugboat in the world, on a voyage that includes murderously antagonistic factions among its Chinese crew, an alcoholic Caucasian first mate, an inscrutable Chinese captain who refuses to captain, an ever hungry canary and—so we are told—a pet rat that cuddles up to Harinxma in bed, politely shares his meals at table and joyfully rides on his shoulder." N Y Times Book Rev

Followed by The centurion

The inspector. Atheneum Pubs. 1960 312p o.p. Amereon reprint available $19.95 (ISBN 0-88411-069-9)

"Story, set in 1946, of a heroic, middle-aged Dutch policeman, Peter Jongman, and a twenty-one-year-old Dutch Jewish girl, Anna Held, who is dying of tuberculosis and of injuries inflicted on her in the medical-research laboratory of the concentration camp from which she has recently been freed, and whose one wish is to see Israel before she dies. The policeman, an Inspector of the Criminal Investigation Division in Amsterdam, undertakes to get the girl to Israel, although he knows that his action will probably cost him his career and may cost him his life." New Yorker

This is also "the story of Peter Jongman's self-immolation and fulfillment as a man. The characters are memorable; even minor ones are distinctive and vivid. The action is dramatic and suspenseful. The almost mystical theme of forgiveness is poignantly and beautifully wrought." Libr J

The lamb's war. Harper & Row; Atheneum Pubs. 1980 443p $13.45

ISBN 0-06-010995-5   LC 78-20201

The second volume in the author's trilogy about the Quakers

"This multifaceted novel . . . starts out in 1942 when the innocent 15-year-old Laura Martens arrives at a German concentration camp and demands to see her father. She does: the commandant rapes her in front of her gentle, Quaker father, who proceeds to attack the guards, who then beat him to death. She goes into shock, becomes amnesiac and lives for the next three years as the loving concubine of the SS doctor. This will always be her terrible, terrible guilt. A Quaker medic saves her from the camp, marries her out of sympathy and brings her to the U.S., where they become missionaries among a tribe of hostile Indians. There she begins to go mad until she learns to channel her rage and bitterness; she devotes the rest of her short life to saving the babies

of the Third World." Publ Wkly

Followed by The peculiar people

The outer buoy; a story of the ultimate voyage. Pantheon Bks. 1994 243p $23

ISBN 0-679-43604-9   LC 94-9780

"A Cornelia & Michael Bessie book"

Completes the author's adventure saga begun in The captain and continued in The centurion and The commodore

"Lying in an isolation chamber in a NASA lab in Houston, octogenarian Dutch ex-sea captain Martin Harinxma attempts to have an out-of-body experience so that his consciousness, floating free from his body, can visit the moon and read the dial on a damaged lunar module. Four other European WWII vets, all navigational experts, have been recruited along with Harinxma for this secret mission, whose ostensible goal is to furnish data to aid in the construction of a space station." Publ Wkly

The peaceable kingdom; an American saga. Atheneum Pubs. 1972 c1971 677p o.p.

This first volume in the author's trilogy about Quaker life "is set in England in 1652-53 and Pennsylvania in 1754-55. . . . In the first section, Margaret Fell, who falls in love with the Quaker preacher George Fox, must exorcise the passion of sexual desire in order to achieve grace. In her encounters she begins the work of reform in prisons, schools and mental institutions; in her progress she loses her property and possessions and is forced into prison. . . . In the second part of the novel, which takes place in colonial Pennsylvania, (there occur) Indian uprisings, massacres of Indians by whites, several murders of black slaves and ritual retribution by the blacks for the murders." N Y Times Book Rev

Followed by The lamb's war

The peculiar people; a novel. Pantheon Bks. 1992 321p $23

ISBN 0-679-41636-6   LC 92-11682

Concluding volume in the author's trilogy on Quaker life begun with The peaceable kingdom and The lamb's war

"A Cornelia & Michael Bessie book"

This novel is "set primarily in the American West of the 1830s, it concerns devout, individualistic members of the Religious Society of Friends . . . who struggle to put their ideals into practice as they confront divisive issues of human injustice. As they respond to the plights of slaves and American Indians—even as these issues divide their church—de Hartog's characters travel on private spiritual odysseys, grappling with doubts and profound personal weaknesses." Publ Wkly

Star of Peace; a novel of the sea. Harper & Row 1984 376p $16.95

ISBN 0-06-039029-8   LC 83-47552

"A Cornelia & Michael Bessie book"

"The hero of this novel, set in the summer of 1939, is Joris Kuiper, owner and captain of the small Dutch freighter 'Star of Peace.' Kuiper finds his recent rebirth through Christianity strongly challenged when his cargo—consisting of 250 Jews forced by the Nazis to emigrate from Germany—is refused admittance at the destination port in Uruguay or anywhere in North or South America. The novelist masterfully describes the tension aboard ship, focusing on key passengers and crew members as they each face the challenge in far different ways." Booklist

De la Mare, Walter, 1873-1956
Collected tales; chosen, and with an introduction, by Edward Wagenknecht. Knopf 1950 xxi, 467p o.p.
Analyzed in Short story index
Contents: The riddle; The almond tree; In the forest; The talisman; Miss Duveen; The bowl; The tree; Ideal craftsman; Seaton's aunt; Lispet, Lispett and Vaine; Three friends; Willows; Missing; The connoisseur; The map; All Hallows; The wharf; The orgy; Cape Race; Physic; The trumpet; The creatures; The vats; Strangers and pilgrims

De la Roche, Mazo, 1879-1961
The building of Jalna. Little, Brown 1944 366p o.p.
"An Atlantic Monthly Press book"
"In this, the first volume, chronologically, in the Jalna series, the author goes back to the year 1850 and shows Adeline, the impulsive young wife with her blazing loyalty, and Captain Whiteoak, who sold his commission in order to migrate to the virgin country on the shore of Lake Ontario. Describes also the building of Jalna and the social life of the community." Ont Libr Rev
Other titles in the Jalna series: Morning at Jalna (1960), Mary Wakefield (1949), Young Renny (1935), Whiteoak heritage (1940), Whiteoak brothers (1953), Jalna (1927, entered below), Whiteoaks of Jalna (1929), Finch's fortune (1931), The master of Jalna (1933), Whiteoak harvest (1936), Wakefield's course (1941), Return to Jalna (1946), Renny's daughter (1951), Variable winds at Jalna (1954), Centenary at Jalna (1958, entered below)

Centenary at Jalna. Little, Brown 1958 342p o.p.
"An Atlantic Monthly Press book"
Concluding volume in the author's Jalna series
"Traces the activities of the Whiteoak clan in the midfifties, a period climaxed by the one-hundredth anniversary celebration of Jalna, the oldest of the family residences. An alienated brother, a neurotic child, and a reluctant bride-to-be play stellar roles in an agreeably related though episodic tale of people to whom family ties and traditions are all-important." Booklist

Jalna. Little, Brown 1927 347p o.p.
"An Atlantic Monthly Press book"
Jalna is the family home of the Whiteoaks. Gathered under its roof are representatives of each generation from the time the grandparents drifted to Canada, via England from India and there built their homestead on a lavish scale. Renny, 37, is the present head of the household which includes Gran—a formidable old lady of 99—two uncles, an aunt, an elderly sister, and four half-brothers. An affectionate, warring group of strong personalities from the old lady down to Wakefield, the youngest, aged nine. Two of the boys marry and bring their wives home

De Lint, Charles, 1951-
Memory and dream. TOR Bks. 1994 400p $22.95
ISBN 0-312-85572-9   LC 94-21752
"A Tom Doherty Associates book"
"This is the story of a young Canadian artist whose paintings free (or unleash) ancient spirits into the modern world. The story moves from the spirit world into the everyday during a 20-year panorama of contemporary Ontario history." Booklist

The author's "multi-voiced, time-shifting narrative . . . beautifully evokes a sense of creative community, making it almost possible to believe that the rarified aesthetic atmosphere might well be capable of conjuring up a spirit or two." Publ Wkly

De Saint-Aubin, Horace *See* Balzac, Honoré de, 1799-1850

De Saint-Exupéry, Antoine *See* Saint-Exupéry, Antoine de, 1900-1944

De Vries, Peter
Consenting adults; or, The duchess will be furious; a novel. Little, Brown 1980 221p o.p.
LC 80-14054
This novel "principally relates Ted Peachum's involvement with three women: a New Woman police officer, Kathy Arpeggio, whom he tries to ravish in her own prowl car; Snooky von Sickle, a sumptuous brewery heiress whom he shares in a ménage à trois with his best friend, Ambrose d'Ambroise; and Ambrose's young sister, Columbine, the virginal Girl Across the Street. . . . [It culminates in a] love affair with a set of triplets, the Peppermint Sisters, whom Peachum possesses en bloc in a hotel room on alternate Saturdays." Publisher's note
The author "demonstrates his unique ability to blend a motley array of absurd aphorisms, one-sentence character sketches, running gags, cosmological musings and inspired word games into a coherent—well, almost coherent—and hugely enjoyable book." N Y Times Book Rev

Reuben, Reuben. Little, Brown 1964 435p o.p.
A satirical novel set in suburban Connecticut. The author "tells his story through three separate characters. . . . The first is Spofford, an old chicken-farmer of literary bent who breaks into the arty-party crowd of the rich and the bored and loses his substance to veneer. The second is the poet McGland, an alcoholic, wenching Welshman who bases his life on his sexuality, hinges his sexuality to his four remaining upper teeth and crumbles into disaster when he loses one of them. The third is the writer-actor Mopworth, who has a hard time keeping his sanity and his manhood because of the women—masculine in their thinking and furiously jealous because of the inescapable physical proof of his sex—who keep telling him he is really a homosexual." America

Slouching towards Kalamazoo. Little, Brown 1983 241p o.p.
LC 83-1026
Anthony Thrasher, a fifteen-year-old genius who was left back one year in school because he spent his time reading Joyce and Proust instead of doing assigned homework, "gets his eighth-grade teacher, Miss Doubloon, in trouble (it happens, fittingly, during their study of 'The Scarlet Letter'). Cast out from their North Dakota town, she returns to Kalamazoo to bear their son Ahab, wearing a T-shirt with a proud 'A plus'—Tony's rating. From there, the story becomes a tangle of secret familial relationships and comedic reconciliations. Tony's clergyman father is fond of debates which provide ample opportunities for satirical takes at sophistry." Libr J

Dean, S. F. X.

Ceremony of innocence. Walker & Co. 1984 196p $12.95

ISBN 0-8027-5583-6   LC 83-40403

"Professor Neil Kelly, [travels] from Boston to England, where he meets two boyhood friends, British Gus Van Duren and Chinese Francis Li. The three had grown up in China where Neil's father had served as a navy commander before World War II. The professor stands as godfather to the Van Durens' newborn son, the 'ceremony of innocence' washed out tragically by the 'blood-dimmed tide,' when thieves murder the baby and people staying with the child. Neil's anguish motivates him to put his own life on the line to catch the killers." Publ Wkly

This novel is "more than a mere adventure/suspense novel. It is written in a most civilized manner and is full of literary allusions (the author knows his Donne and 17th century England); it is sharply observant and throws light on several aspects of Oriental culture. In short, Mr. Dean knows how to use his own unusual background to maximum effect." N Y Times Book Rev

Death and the mad heroine. Walker & Co. 1985 209p $13.95

ISBN 0-8027-5612-3   LC 84-25632

"Professor Neil Kelly visits his college in Oldhampton after two years in England. The Welshman who has been substituting for Kelly has a wife intent on uncovering the truth about a 20-year-old crime: her father disappeared at the same time that Dickie Colrane, promising football star, was shot in the knee." Libr J

It can't be my grave. Walker & Co. 1984 222p $12.95

ISBN 0-8027-5596-8   LC 84-13192

First published 1983 in the United Kingdom

Professor Neil Kelly "is in London for the British publication of his surprise bestseller on the life of John Donne. There an old Oxford chum, now a famous thespian, and his actress wife tell Kelly of the possibility of running their own theater company devoted to lost plays by women writers and funded by tycoon Gordon Fairly. Sir Gordon, a man of power and charm, believes a 16th century female ancestor to have been the author of a newly found play attributed to Shakespeare or Marlowe, and wants to confirm her authorship. He offers Kelly a huge sum to play devil's advocate and prove his theories wrong, but before research can get under way, the rich man is murdered. . . . This mystery is worth reading for the sheer pleasure of its language." Publ Wkly

Nantucket soap opera. Atheneum Pubs. 1987 259p o.p.

LC 86-22296

"Hoping to finish his new book on Nantucket Island, Kelly fumes at movie mogul William Olds, who pesters him with offers of a role in a planned film. Olds's nasty daughter Panda, lush actress Barbara Gold and others involved add their importunities in vain. Kelly's interest in the company is finally aroused by crimes that rock the community: the sexual abuse of a child and three murders. . . . The professor clinches a case against one suspect, then discovers evidence against the guilty party who had used an outrageous means of framing the accused." Publ Wkly

Defoe, Daniel, 1661?-1731

A journal of the plague year.
Available from AMS Press

First published 1722

An account "of the epidemic of bubonic plague in England during the summer and fall of 1665." Reader's Ency

Moll Flanders. Modern Lib. 1994 364p $14.50

ISBN 0-679-60133-3   LC 91-52994

Also available Everyman's library edition $15 (ISBN 0-679-40548-8)

First published 1722. Variant title: The fortunes and misfortunes of Moll Flanders

This picaresque novel "recounts the adventures of a lusty and strong-willed woman who is compelled, from earliest childhood, to make her own way in 17th-century England." Merriam-Webster's Ency of Lit

Robinson Crusoe.
Available from various publishers

First published 1719

"A minutely circumstantial account of the hero's shipwreck and escape to an uninhabited island, and the methodical industry whereby he makes himself a comfortable home. The story is founded on the actual experiences of Alexander Selkirk, who spent four years on the island of Juan Fernandez in the early 18th century." Lenrow. Reader's Guide to Prose Fic

Deighton, Len, 1929-

Berlin game. Knopf 1984 c1983 345p o.p.

LC 83-48104

The first volume of an espionage trilogy; other volumes are Mexico set and London match

British agent Bernard Samson must "help an undercover agent known as Brahms Four escape from East Berlin; unfortunately, a security leak high in the British organization threatens the continued success of the Brahms Four network." Libr J

This novel "is a decent entertainment that rattles swiftly along to its payoff. Two things especially recommend it—a devious contrivance of plot that has probably never been used before in an espionage novel; and the city of Berlin, mecca to spies and spy novelists. The second is the greater asset. Although the book is elaborately plotted, its best moments derive from the setting and from the force of this particular setting upon behavior and psychology." N Y Times Book Rev

also in Deighton, L. Game, set & match

City of gold. HarperCollins Pubs. 1992 375p $20

ISBN 0-06-017937-6   LC 92-52565

Also available Thorndike Press large print edition

"City of Gold is Cairo, and the time is 1942. Rommel is on the move, and the city waits to see what will happen when he arrives. He has conquered Allied forces because somebody is feeding him information about their plans. A British captain is put in charge of an investigation to dig out the mole." N Y Times Book Rev

"Story lines concern not just the war but also blackmarket activities and the efforts of Jewish operatives to arm themselves for the anticipated battle for a homeland. Directing his varied characters and juggling his many subplots, Deighton demonstrates enviable legerdemain." Publ Wkly

Deighton, Len, 1929-—*Continued*

Faith. HarperCollins Pubs. 1995 c1994
337p $24

ISBN 0-06-017622-9   LC 94-24663

First published 1994 in the United Kingdom

First volume of a third spy trilogy featuring Bernard
Samson

This novel "finds Samson leaving California to pick
up VERDI, code name for a high-ranking East German
Stasi officer who may be defecting to Britain's SIS. The
operation goes disastrously wrong during a shoot-out in
East Germany, but Samson manages to get back to London, where he encounters real danger and fighting: the
take-no-prisoners politicking within the SIS, involving
Samson, his duplicitous wife and a slew of internal
enemies and possible friends. Deighton's penchant for
explosive violence, telling detail and throwaway humor
. . . are much in evidence here, and readers will enjoy
some of the finest intramural politicking since C.P.
Snow." Publ Wkly

Funeral in Berlin; a novel. Putnam 1965
c1964 312p o.p.

First published 1964 in the United Kingdom

A spy story in which a British agent is involved in
smuggling a Russian scientist out of East Berlin with the
connivance of a Russian security officer and a German
contact man whose loyalties and motives are questionable

The author "writes well of the circles within circles
at international crossroads where enemies can be closer
than friends, and where horror and humor follow the
agent." Libr J

Game, set & match. Knopf 1989 857p il
o.p.

LC 88-45258

This omnibus edition first published 1986 in the United Kingdom. Each title is entered separately

Contents: Berlin game; Mexico set; London match

The Ipcress file. Simon & Schuster 1963
c1962 287p o.p.

First published 1962 in the United Kingdom

"A British secret-service agent is assigned to help
recover a kidnapped biochemist. The international intrigue, involving brainwashing, spies, and counter-spies
of uncertain loyalties, takes the agent from London to
the Far East, to an atomic test site in the Pacific, and
behind the Iron Curtain." Shapiro. Fic for Youth. 3d
edition

London match. Knopf 1985 i.e. 1986 407p
o.p.

LC 85-40454

In this concluding volume of the Berlin-based trilogy
"Agent Bernie Samson is faced with yet another problem.
While one mole—Bernie's former wife—has been flushed
from the London office, the Soviet defector's debriefing
indicates there may be yet another double agent still
operating. Bernie, of course, is a likely suspect, but this
would be too obvious and, besides, there are numerous
candidates for the office turncoat. Who could it be? Or
could it be a cunning piece of subterfuge to further
disrupt British intelligence gathering?" Booklist

"The strength of (this novel) is not in its plot but
its characterization. . . . Mr. Deighton portrays each
character of his large cast fully and sympathetically.
However, the best character is the city of Berlin. It is
a living presence, and in some of the descriptions one
can almost hear the stones breathing." N Y Times Book
Rev

also in Deighton, L. Game, set & match

Mexico set. Knopf 1985 373p $16.95

ISBN 0-394-53525-1   LC 84-48500

The second volume of the spy trilogy that began with
Berlin game

"Fiona Samson—wife of our hero, British agent Bernard Samson—has defected to the KGB and become a
diabolical alter ego to her husband, anticipating his
moves and countermoves in ways only a spouse can do."
Booklist

"Deighton displays prodigious talent here: while portraying sharply defined, sympathetic, and down-to-earth
characters, he slowly but inexorably revs up the plot for
a thoroughly exciting and satisfying conclusion." Libr J

also in Deighton, L. Game, set & match

Spy hook; a novel. Knopf 1988 291p o.p.

LC 88-11461

Available Thorndike Press large print edition

The first volume in a second spy trilogy featuring
Bernard Samson

"Samson's story begins with a fruitless meeting in
Washington with former colleague Jim Prettyman, who
denies any knowledge of the slush fund Samson has been
ordered to trace. Over half a million pounds is missing
from money allocated to Bret Rensselear of the German
desk by London Central before he was shot in Berlin.
Later, in London, Samson learns at a briefing that Prettyman has been killed, another 'incident' pressuring Samson's superiors to widen his investigation in East and
West Berlin and eventually in France. All the people he
questions—even trusted friends—deepen Samson's fears
that Central is using him to bait their own hook." Publ
Wkly

"The entertainment lies in Deighton's eye for detail—
landscape, fashion, cuisine, idiom—and in the sudden
menace that erupts from the small talk and the brand
names." Booklist

Spy line; a novel. Knopf 1989 291p
$18.95

ISBN 0-394-55179-6   LC 89-45302

Also available Thorndike Press large print edition

Second volume of the trilogy that started with Spy
hook. The novel opens "with Samson in Berlin, a fugitive from England where the intelligence service accused
him of spying for the Soviets. With the CIA and KGB
also menacing him, Samson is suddenly cleared of the
charge of treason and returned to London and to warm
welcomes from colleagues, his lover Gloria and his children. The situation changes, however, when he's sent on
a 'simple' mission to Vienna and a deep-cover meeting
with Fiona." Publ Wkly

Spy sinker. Harper & Row 1990 374p
$21.95

ISBN 0-06-039118-8   LC 89-46568

Also available Thorndike Press large print edition

"A Cornelia & Michael Bessie book"

Final volume of the second spy trilogy featuring Bernard Samson

In this novel Bernard Samson, "steps backstage as his
wife, Fiona, defects to East Germany after being groomed
as a double agent. In place, Fiona is set to implement
a plan facilitating the westward defection of East German
professionals, leaving a gap in the economic structure

Deighton, Len, 1929-—*Continued*
which is expected to defeat the Communist regime." Publ Wkly

SS-GB: Nazi-occupied Britain 1941; a novel. Knopf 1979 343p o.p.

LC 78-14563

First published 1978 in the United Kingdom

"The King of England is a prisoner in the Tower, the Queen and Princesses have fled to Australia, Winston Churchill has been executed by a German firing squad, and the SS is in charge of Scotland Yard. Detective Superintendent Douglas Archer has started work on what seems to be a routine murder case until an SS official from Himmler's own staff comes to supervise the investigation. Archer finds himself involved in a resistance effort involving wealthy collaborators, high-level scientists, rivalry between the German military and the SS factions, and an attempt to remove King George from the Tower of London to the United States." Shapiro. Fic for Youth. 3d edition

Violent ward. HarperCollins Pubs. 1993 305p $23

ISBN 0-06-017938-4　　　　LC 92-56242

This mystery is "set among the rich and famous of Southern California, with L.A. lawyer Mickey Murphy as the hero. . . . The plot goes like this: Murphy's law firm has been bought by Zach Petrovitch, a megarich mogul with fingers in lots of pies. Petrovitch's wife, Ingrid, Murphy's childhood sweetheart, still makes Mickey's heart rate accelerate. But something funny's going on, and Murphy has to figure out whether Zach's trying to kill Ingrid, Ingrid's trying to kill Zach, or one of Zach's associates is trying to kill them both." Booklist

"Told in perfect Dashiell Hammett style, with the clues all noted but never underlined, this novel respects the reader's intelligence and almost begs for a rereading just to savor how skillfully Deighton has woven everything together." Publ Wkly

XPD. Knopf 1981 339p o.p.

LC 80-7629

The plot involves "a face-to-face meeting between Winston Churchill and Adolf Hitler. Time: 1940. Place: a Belgian bunker. Topic: the surrender of Britain. . . . So sensitive is the clandestine rendezvous—one of the terms discussed is Nazi control of Ireland—that even two generations later, anyone who learns of it is marked for XPD—Expedient Demise. When the Führer's minutes of the affair threaten to surface, counter-intelligence launches a relentless search from Hollywood to Hamburg." Time

"Deighton's attention to detail and his appreciation of the delicacies of international politics give his book a plausibility too often lacking in spy novels." Best Sellers

Del Vecchio, John M., 1948-
The 13th valley; a novel. Bantam Bks. 1982 606p il o.p.

LC 81-70920

This first volume in a trilogy about the Vietnam War "tells the story of a major combat assault by an infantry unit during August 1970. The narrative focuses on three men: Brooks, a black lieutenant who has just received divorce papers from his wife; Egan, a cynical platoon sergeant counting the days left in his tour of duty; and Chery, his new radio man, very scared, very eager, and very naive." Libr J

"The novel is almost documentary in style and conveys to an extraordinary degree the very 'feel' of ground combat in I Corps. . . . Two elements in this well-written novel are especially praiseworthy: the depiction of the explosive relations between white and black GIs, and the moral corruption by war of a decent, sensitive young man. . . . Despite the presence of too much historical exposition, this is one of the finest novels to come out of the Vietnam War." Publ Wkly

Followed by For the sake of all living things

Carry me home. Bantam Bks. 1994 719p $22.95

ISBN 0-553-07224-2　　　　LC 93-31585

In this concluding volume of his Vietnam War trilogy "Del Vecchio focuses on veterans who returned home in the late '60s only to find themselves viewed largely as lepers. Back from his second tour in Vietnam, Marine Sgt. Tony Pisano, 20, bears a leg wound, is assigned to burial detail, marries student nurse Linda, tries out college and faces widespread hatred. Tony's story, central to the novel, melds with that of his doomed buddies, who are now rootless 'expatriates' in their own country. More grounded is the also returned Capt. Robert Wapinski, whose Pennsylvania farm becomes a haven for many vets fighting public castigation, post-traumatic stress disorder and the effects of Agent Orange." Publ Wkly

"Unabashedly polemical, often veering off into melodrama, the narrative is redeemed by its passionate affection for these soldiers who are attempting to build new lives." N Y Times Book Rev

For the sake of all living things. Bantam Bks. 1990 790p o.p.

LC 89-28066

In this second volume of the author's trilogy, "Samnang is an 11-year-old Cambodian peasant who is conscripted into the Khmer Rouge and rises, through brutal training and savage combat, to a position of leadership. His sister Vathana is also separated from their father, Chhuon, and grows up to marry a Frenchified heroin addict from Cambodia's upper class. As her country falls deeper and deeper into civil war, she goes to work in a hospital for refugees. There she meets and falls in love with an American Special Forces officer, John Sullivan, an adviser to the Cambodian military who has few illusions about that army's—or indeed his own nation's—ability to win." N Y Times Book Rev

"While interspersed reports filed by Special Forces Cpt. John Sullivan, Vathana's lover, put events in political perspective, this exhaustive, emotionally powerful novel ends on a note of desperate irony that sums up the Kafkaesque absurdity of Cambodia's torment." Publ Wkly

Followed by Carry me home

Delany, Samuel R.
The star pit

In Modern classic short novels of science fiction p164-220

Stars in my pocket like grains of sand. Bantam Bks. 1984 384p $16.95

ISBN 0-553-05053-2　　　　LC 84-45180

Delany, Samuel R.—*Continued*
This far future novel is the "dual story of Rat Korga, a slave and the last survivor of his devastated world, and Marq Dyeth, an industrial diplomat who introduces Korga to a future galaxy consisting of 6,000 human- and alien-inhabited planets." Booklist
"Reading this novel is like learning another language, only to realize how much it teaches you about your own, and how relative it makes your cultural assumptions." Publ Wkly

Time considered as a helix of semi-precious stones

In The Best of the Nebulas p329-57

Delderfield, R. F. (Ronald Frederick), 1912-1972
Give us this day. Simon & Schuster 1973 767p o.p.
Sequel to Theirs was the kingdom
This third volume of the Swann family saga opens with Victoria's centennial celebration and closes with "the beginning of World War I. Against the background of Edwardian social and political history, Delderfield presents a third generation, the offspring of Adam and Henrietta, whose ventures, at times, become almost melodramatic. The characters are very real, especially Adam and his wife who are shown growing older and looking back over the years. In spite of some unneeded repetition of events, this is well written, good entertainment." Libr J

God is an Englishman. Simon & Schuster 1970 687p o.p.
The action, which takes place between 1857 and 1866, centers on the career of Adam Swann who returns from army service in the Crimea and in India to found a network of freight-hauling coaches bearing the name Swann-on-Wheels, and to marry Henrietta Rawlinson, daughter of a local mill owner. The vicissitudes of Swann's life mirror the ambition and enterprise that brought success to some amid the poverty of many during the period
Followed by Theirs was the kingdom

The green gauntlet. Simon & Schuster 1968 475p o.p.
This sequel to A horseman riding by follows the fortunes of the Craddock family from the Second World War through the postwar years, depicting three decades of modern English life

A horseman riding by. Simon & Schuster 1967 c1966 1150p o.p.
First published 1966 in the United Kingdom
Paul Craddock, a young soldier, returns from the Boer War, comes into a substantial inheritance and purchases a rundown Devonshire estate, consisting of seven tenancies. The story concerns the revitalization of the property by the new owner, the vicissitudes of the seven families that are his tenants, and the richly fulfilled life of the Squire, himself, and his family
Followed by The green gauntlet

Theirs was the kingdom. Simon & Schuster 1971 798p o.p.
This sequel to God is an Englishman "relates the careers of Swann, his indefatigable wife, and nine children. . . . Whereas Swann himself had been the dominant figure, the 'God' in 'God is an Englishman',

the sequel turns to his satellites—to his enterprising children, who illustrate various facets of the Victorian scene, and to his business associates, who represent degrees of devotion and repulsion to the inevitability of change." Choice
Followed by Give us this day

To serve them all my days. Simon & Schuster 1972 638p o.p.
Concerns "the boys and masters of a West Country English public school in the years between World War I and II. . . . The central character is David Powlett-Jones, a shell-shocked youngster fresh from the Western Front, when we first meet him; a compassionate headmaster, whose personal life has known its full share of drama, sorrow and love, when we part company with him. In between, Mr. Delderfield has some eminently sane and sensible points to make about what education for life is really like. Academic rivalries, some bitter and vengeful; the loneliness of a small boy whose parents have no real feeling for him, and of a small girl whose mother and twin have died tragically; the development of an intense love affair between a mature man and woman are all elements in the storytelling." Publ Wkly
"Here is a schoolmaster's cavalcade of England between World Wars, told in the author's best stand-up style, and rife with episodes designed to pluck at the heartstrings." N Y Times Book Rev

Delderfield, Ronald Frederick *See* Delderfield, R. F. (Ronald Frederick), 1912-1972

DeLillo, Don
Libra. Viking 1988 456p $19.95
ISBN 0-670-82317-1   LC 87-40649
Also available G.K. Hall large print edition
DeLillo's "novel is his own personal vision—though anchored well enough in historical actuality—of what really was behind Lee Harvey Oswald's gun blasts from the book depository that day in Dallas. DeLillo follows Oswald through the marines and during his defection to the Soviet Union, as well as positing a scenario for how he came to be the vehicle for delivering the anti-Castro blow that resulted in Kennedy's death." Booklist
This novel "provokes the reader with its clever use of history, its dramatic pacing and its immaculate and detailed construction." Publ Wkly

White noise. Viking 1985 326p $16.95
ISBN 0-670-80373-1   LC 84-40375
"An Elisabeth Sifton book"
"The chairperson of the department of Nazi studies at a midwestern college aches to escape the inevitable path of decline and death; a 'toxic event' that releases a dangerous cloud of pollution gives him the chance to break free in previously uncontemplated ways." Booklist
This "is a stunning performance from one of our finest and most intelligent novelists. DeLillo's reach is broad and deep, combining acute observation of the textures of American life and analytic rigor." New Repub

Delinsky, Barbara
For my daughters. HarperCollins Pubs. 1994 290p $20
ISBN 0-06-017618-0   LC 94-2233
Also available G.K. Hall large print edition

Delinsky, Barbara—_Continued_

"When Virginia St. Clair was a young married woman, she fell in love with the gardener of her vacation house in Maine. At the end of the summer, she chose duty to her husband over love and emotionally estranged herself from everyone who entered her life. Her three daughters, born after that summer, suffered the most. Now, at 70, Virginia decides to correct her mistakes. She purchases her former vacation home in Maine and invites her daughters to join her there." Booklist

"Delinsky develops her characters well and creates a strong sense of place with beautiful, evocative descriptions of the landscapes." Libr J

Demetz, Hanna

The house on Prague Street; by Hana Demetz; translated from the German by the author. St. Martin's Press 1980 186p o.p.

LC 79-27312

Original German edition, 1970

This autobiographical novel tells the story of Helene Richter whose 'adolescence in wartime Czechoslovakia coincides with the Holocaust, which intrudes more and more insistently into her life until its . . . violence destroys her romantic dreams. The house on Prague Street symbolizes her loss of innocence. At first the serene family homestead, it eventually shelters survivors of Auschwitz whose only familial ties are their shared memories of horror." SLJ

The journey from Prague Street; [by] Hana Demetz. St. Martin's Press 1990 152p o.p.

LC 89-24278

In this sequel to the title entered above, "Helen Richler (the only member of her large Jewish family to survive the Holocaust) chronicles her life after the war in Prague, Munich, and New York; her motherhood; and her long marriage to a brilliant, self-centered, philandering professor. When he leaves her for a younger woman, Helen picks up the pieces of her life and eventually finds contentment with a caring blind man whose ancestors came from the same region of Czechoslovakia as Helen's family." Libr J

"In choosing to relate the novel with constant changes in points of view, time and setting, Demetz robs her narrative of some coherence. But such is the innate interest of the events she describes that readers will be caught up in an affecting story." Publ Wkly

DeMille, Nelson

The charm school. Warner Bks. 1988 533p o.p.

LC 87-34637

Available G.K. Hall large print edition

"On an unorthodox vacation trip to Russia, Gregory Fisher, a young American tourist, stumbles onto a secret. . . . In a place called Mrs. Ivanova's Charm School, young Russians are being taught to imitate American citizens. And their instructors, none of whom have volunteered for the job, are Americans. . . . _The Charm School_ offers much in the way of action and adventure, but the novel is more than an 'Us vs. Them' shoot 'em up. It is also a fascinating psychological study, one that forces the reader to ponder the true roles of good and evil, in connection with the individual mind as well as with international relations." West Coast Rev Books

The general's daughter. Warner Bks. 1992 454p o.p.

LC 91-51174

Available Thorndike Press large print edition

"Paul Brenner, a warrant officer in the army's criminal investigation unit, reluctantly teams with an old flame, Cynthia Sunhill, to investigate the murder of Captain Ann Campbell. Ann's body has been staked down with tent pegs on a rifle range; she's naked but she hasn't been brutalized. She's the daughter of a famous general, just back from the Gulf War, and she's also the Army's poster girl, a graduate with honors from West Point. And yet her chosen specialty, psychological operations, has raised some eyebrows, and Brenner and Sunhill soon discover other dark secrets about her." Booklist

"Characterization in general is fuzzy, though DeMille captures the often unquestioning regimen of life on a military base." Publ Wkly

The Gold Coast. Warner Bks. 1990 500p $19.95

ISBN 0-446-51504-3   LC 89-40465

"What happens to a priggish, WASPy, disillusioned Wall Street lawyer when a Mafia crime boss moves into the mansion next door in his posh Long Island neighborhood? He ends up representing the gangster on a murder rap and even perjures himself so the mafioso can be released on $5 million bail. . . . Attorney John Sutter has problems that would daunt even Fitzgerald's Jay Gatsby. His marriage is crumbling, despite kinky sex games with his self-centered wife, Susan, who's the mistress of his underworld client Frank Bellarosa. The IRS is after Sutter, and his law firm wants to dump him." Publ Wkly

"What makes 'The Gold Coast' glitter is Nelson DeMille's sharp evocation of the vulpine Bellarosa and of Sutter, a wonderfully sardonic, self-mocking man betrayed by a midlife crisis. In his way, Mr. DeMille . . . is as keen a social satirist as Edith Wharton." NY Times Book Rev

Spencerville. Warner Bks. 1994 481p $23.95

ISBN 0-446-51505-1   LC 94-25759

"Keith Landry, his Cold War intelligence job a victim of the Soviet collapse, returns to the little Ohio town where he grew up and begins to tinker with thoughts of reviving the family farm. A former sweetheart, Annie, despondent after Keith went off to Vietnam, had married aggressive, good-looking Cliff Baxter on the rebound, but Keith and Annie had never ceased to correspond. Now that he's back, the old interest is rekindled in both, but Baxter, now police chief and a womanizing petty tyrant, is fiercely jealous—and the novel takes off as a deadly struggle between a man trained in the arts of deception and one with all the built-in advantages of police power in a remote spot." Publ Wkly

Word of honor. Warner Bks. 1985 518p o.p.

LC 85-40005

A fictional version of the "My Lai massacre and the trial of Lieutenant William F. Calley. Calley's counterpart in this fictional account is Ben Tyson, a much-decorated Vietnam veteran and former Army lieutenant. One morning, on the way to work as an electronics executive in New York City, Tyson learns that a book has just been published about a military massacre at a

DeMille, Nelson—*Continued*

French hospital in Hue, Vietnam. The book unhesitatingly accuses Tyson of staging the attack against nuns, children, and other civilians, and wounded soldiers on February 15, 1968. Based on evidence contained in the book and on testimony given by two of Tyson's former platoon members, the Army recalls Tyson to active duty in order to try him for murder." Booklist

"The flashbacks to Hue, the pre-trial investigation (involving an attractive female major), the court-martial proceedings, the emotions of the principal characters and the soul-sickness wrought by war (which is the story's effective subtext)—all are depicted with marvelous vividness." Publ Wkly

Denker, Henry

Mrs. Washington and Horowitz, too; a novel. Morrow 1993 333p $29.95

ISBN 0-688-12466-6   LC 92-32877

Sequel to Horowitz and Mrs. Washington (1979)

This is a "love story about a cantankerous 70ish widowed businessman and a sixtysomething widow. They become involved through the machinations of the marvelously manipulative black nurse, Mrs. Washington. She bullied Horowitz to recovery after his stroke and now works to help him recover his sense of purpose and self-worth. Harriet Washington involves Horowitz as a volunteer in the neonatal unit of Harlem Hospital, where he cares, sometimes too much, for the unloved, abandoned crack babies. In fact, he almost loses his job. But Mrs. Mendelson's help (engineered by the matchmaking Mrs. Washington) gets him reinstated. When the couple decides to marry, their children react with typical hostility. Mrs. Washington handles this, too. A very warm and true-to-life depiction of older persons." Libr J

Dennis, Patrick

Auntie Mame; an irreverent escapade. Vanguard Press 1955 280p o.p.

Available from Amereon and Buccaneer Bks. Large print edition available from G.K. Hall

"A fond and somewhat baffled nephew reminisces about the aunt who guided his young footsteps in her unorthodox, inimitable fashion. Auntie Mame lived wholeheartedly in phases; whether she was being show girl, shopgirl, Southern belle, tweedy authoress, college widow, or society matron, she played each part to the hilt. Life with Auntie Mame was infinitely entertaining and unpredictable." Booklist

Followed by Around the world with Auntie Mame (1958)

Dershowitz, Alan M.

The advocate's devil. Warner Bks. 1994 342p $22.95

ISBN 0-446-51759-3   LC 94-61318

"The story involves the heroic efforts of Abe Ringel, a Cambridge-based defense lawyer, to get his charismatic client, a superstar with the New York Knicks named Joe Campbell, acquitted on a charge of rape. . . . Ringel's internal struggle between the desire to win this once-in-a-lifetime celebrity case and the gnawing, ever-increasing suspicion that his client is guilty as hell gives the reader a dazzling, often rather graphic, portrayal of . . . legal ethics." N Y Times Book Rev

Desai, Anita, 1937-

Baumgartner's Bombay. Knopf 1989 c1988 229p $18.95

ISBN 0-394-57229-7   LC 88-25753

First published 1988 in the United Kingdom

"Born in Germany, protagonist [Hugo] Baumgartner escapes to Calcutta as a boy after his family suffers the rise of Hitler and the simultaneous fall of the Baumgartner fine-furniture business, as well as the destruction of their Jewish heritage. Imprisoned during the war as a hostile alien, Hugo moves at war's end to Bombay, where the novel—told in flashbacks—begins." Libr J

"What distinguishes the voice of Anita Desai is the physical intensity of her prose, the range of her capacious intelligence, her unsentimental compassion. She has brought it all together with a formidable surge of power in Baumgartner's Bombay, and it is a triumph." New Repub

Clear light of day. Harper & Row 1980 183p o.p.

LC 84-673511

"The novel begins with the triennial visit of the younger sister Tara and her diplomat husband to the old family home, a decaying suburban mansion on the banks of the Jumma outside Old Delhi. Here Bim the older sister, lives with the youngest brother, Baba. Baba is autistic, a childlike, speechless whisp of a man who spends his days playing 'I'm Dreaming of a White Christmas' and 'Donkey Seranade' on an ancient wind-up gramophone. The oldest brother, Raja, has moved away. The book divides itself equally between the present of Tara's visit and the sisters' memories of the past. . . . The visit is a strain—a series of under-the-surface estrangements and rapprochements, with sisterly love ebbing and flowing." Times Lit Suppl

This work "does what only the best novels can do: it totally submerges us. It takes us so deeply into another world that we almost fear we won't be able to climb out again." N Y Times Book Rev

Fire on the mountain. Harper & Row 1977 145p $12.95

ISBN 0-06-011066-X   LC 77-3788

"In this novel set in the hill country of India, Nanda Kaul's great-granddaughter is sent to spend the summer with her, thus breaking the solitude of the old and withdrawn woman, shattering the privacy she prizes most. But Raka, too, is clearly an outsider, a child living in and through her imagination, and one with a talent for disappearing. As Nanda Kaul finds herself attempting to draw out and communicate with the strange and unfathomable Raka, she discovers in the girl more of herself than she would have believed possible. Meanwhile, Nanda Kaul's lone friend, Ila Das, appears and hovers always on the brink of hysteria until that hysteria leads to a shocking rape and murder that is the book's climax." Publ Wkly

"This is a delicate wisp of a story that nevertheless possesses great tensile strength." Booklist

Destouches, Henri-Louis *See* Céline, Louis-Ferdinand, 1894-1961

Dew, Robb Forman

Fortunate lives. Morrow 1992 285p $20

ISBN 0-688-10781-8   LC 91-24943

Also available Thorndike Press large print edition

Sequel to Dale loves Sophie to death (1981)

"The Howells family—Dinah and Martin and their children, 18-year-old David and preadolescent Sarah—have gingerly resumed normal life six years after the accidental death of the middle child, Toby. During one summer in their small college town in the Berkshires, the family prepares for David's departure for Harvard and copes with the intrusion into their daily routines of Netta Breckenridge, a seemingly needy but highly manipulative divorcée, and Owen Croft, the young man whose car killed Toby and whom Martin, a professor and editor of a literary magazine, has agreed to employ." Publ Wkly

"Dew is a masterful observer of small things and their resonance, finding beauty in domestic routines, while her intense characters experience great tides of emotions. She has an unerring sense of the volatile chemistry of families and the intricacies of the soul that both isolate and connect us. A superbly eloquent, perceptive, and haunting novel." Booklist

Dexter, Colin

The jewel that was ours. Crown 1992 c1991 275p il $20

ISBN 0-517-58847-1   LC 91-45245

Also available Thorndike Press large print edition

First published 1991 in the United Kingdom

This mystery finds British Inspector Morse "stymied by the theft of a rare artifact bound for the Ashmolean Museum and by the sudden deaths of both the American woman who owned it and the curator for whom it was intended. Challenged to keep track of several sneaky academics and frisky elderly tourists, the detective noses over British Rail timetables, handwritten notes and a smelly assortment of red herrings." N Y Times Book Rev

"The watertight solution is as tricky as it is dazzling." Booklist

The secret of annexe 3. St. Martin's Press 1987 c1986 218p o.p.

LC 87-17590

First published 1986 in the United Kingdom

"Inspector Morse and Sergeant Lewis investigate a murder committed on New Year's Eve at a hotel in Oxford. Three couples are housed in the hotel annex, and one man, winner of the prize in the fancy-dress contest, is found dead in his room. The first problem facing Morse and Lewis is locating the other five guests, including the victim's wife, all of whom have fled, having registered under fake names and addresses. . . . Engrossed in the story that Dexter tells in his witty and stylish fashion, readers will savor the mystery of the masquerade and the detecting partners' ultimate triumph." Publ Wkly

The way through the woods. Crown 1993 c1992 296p $20

ISBN 0-517-59444-7   LC 92-40762

Also available Thorndike Press large print edition

First published 1992 in the United Kingdom

"A student disappears, and Inspector Morse's only clue is a cryptic poem that the murderer might have sent." Libr J

"To say that the investigation is tricky is only to hint at the technical density of the plot, which, once all the tantalizing enigmas have been packed up, hinges on the most basic human frailties. Dazzling." N Y Times Book Rev

The wench is dead. St. Martin's Press 1990 c1989 200p il o.p.

LC 89-77807

First published 1989 in the United Kingdom

A mystery featuring Chief Inspector Morse of the Oxford police force. "In the hospital for an ulcer made worse by drink, and frustrated by the proximity of so many pretty young nurses, he finds distraction in an apparent case of gang rape and murder unsolved for over a hundred years." Booklist

"Mr. Dexter has fashioned a taxing brainteaser for Morse, whose superior wits and famously foul temper tug the reader into the detective's hospital bed to share his single-minded pursuit of the truth." N Y Times Book Rev

Dexter, Pete, 1943-

Brotherly love. Random House 1991 274p $22

ISBN 0-394-58573-9   LC 91-52666

"Peter Flood is the son of an Irish trade union leader with ties to the Mafia. In the space of a few days, eight-year-old Peter witnesses the death of his baby sister, his mother's mental collapse and removal to an institution, and his father Charley's bloody revenge on the man who set those events in motion, an act that leads to his own demise. Peter's uncle Phil, who betrayed Charley to the Mafia, inherits his brother's union position and his home; he raises Pete with his own son, Michael, encouraging the boys to think of themselves as brothers." Publ Wkly

"What deepens and darkens [Dexter's] writing, so that art is the precise word to describe it, is a powerful understanding that character rules, that we live with our weaknesses and die of our strengths." Time

Deadwood. Random House 1986 365p $17.95

ISBN 0-394-53669-X   LC 85-19635

"Deadwood (is) a vibrant, squalid late-nineteenth-century boomtown nestled in the forbidding Black Hills of the untamed Dakota Territory. When the legendary Wild Bill Hickok guides a wagon train full of prostitutes into the virtually lawless town, he becomes the target of Al Swearingen, a vengeful and cowardly pimp who hires an addlepated sot to kill him. Wild Bill's disquieted final days are spent in the company of a score of rough characters (including a riotously off-color Calamity Jane), each of whom is later bitterly haunted by the freakish circumstances of his murder." Booklist

This novel "is unpredictable, hyperbolic and, page after page, uproarious; a joshing book written in high spirits and a raw appreciation for the past." N Y Times Book Rev

The paperboy. Random House 1995 307p $23

ISBN 0-679-42175-0   LC 94-21523

"Set in the fetid swamps of northern Florida, the novel concerns the legal case of Hillary Van Wetter, who has been condemned to death for the murder of the county sheriff. Nineteen-year-old Jack James, son of the local

Dexter, Pete, 1943-—*Continued*

newspaper publisher and delivery boy for the daily edition, narrates the story, which begins with Charlotte Bless, an interloping southern floozy just past her prime who takes an obsessive interest in Van Wetter's case. Jack's elder brother, Ward, a reporter in Miami, also detects a story in Van Wetter's predicament and returns to his native Moat County to investigate. He brings along the handsome, ambitious writer Yardley Acheman, whose stylistic flash is matched by his willingness to cut ethical corners. The group's inquiry drives this novel's action, taking them through the swamp, to death row, and on to Daytona Beach." Booklist

"Dexter's writing is rock-solid, he offers acute observations about the nature of reporting and his grip on the Southern male psyche is unquestionable." Publ Wkly

Paris Trout. Random House 1988 306p $17.95

ISBN 0-394-56370-0　　　　LC 87-43314

"Paris Trout, the small-town Georgia store owner . . . sleeps with a sheet of lead under his mattress. He's afraid someone is going to hide under his bed and shoot him in the middle of the night—and for no good reason, as Trout sees it. He was only taking care of business, trying to collect on Henry Ray Boxer's debt. That little black girl, Rosie Sayers, who got shot and killed in the scuffle, shouldn't have got in his way, or the woman with Rosie, who still walks around with Trout's bullet in her chest. . . . Mr. Dexter has created a character whose racism is a blunt, unregenerate fact, as primitive and willful as an earthquake or a rainstorm—and just as sealed off from argument, examination or questions of mercy. What the town's polite society takes care to disguise in Sunday-go-to-meeting euphemisms, Paris sets in defiant, ugly relief; he makes it easy for them to believe they are innocent of racism." N Y Times Book Rev

Di Lampedusa, Giuseppe Tomasi *See* Tomasi di Lampedusa, Giuseppe, 1896-1957

Dick, Philip K.

The collected stories of Philip K. Dick. Underwood/Miller 1987 5v set $125

ISBN 0-88733-053-3

Contents: Beyond lies the wub: Stability; Roog; The little movement; Beyond lies the wub; The gun; The skull; The defenders; Mr. Spaceship; Piper in the woods; The infinites; The Preserving Machine; Expendable; The variable man; The indefatigable frog; The crystal crypt; The short happy life of the brown oxford; The builder; Meddler; Paycheck; The great C; Out in the garden; The king of the elves; Colony; Prize ship; Nanny

Second Variety: The cookie lady; Beyond the door; Second Variety; Jon's world; The cosmic poachers; Progeny; Some kinds of life; Martians come in clouds; The commuter; The world she wanted; A surface raid; Project: Earth; The trouble with bubbles; Breakfast at twilight; A present for Pat; The hood maker; Of withered apples; Human is; Adjustment team; The impossible planet; Impostor; James P. Crow; Planet for transients; Small town; Souvenir; Survey team; Prominent author

The father-thing: Fair game; The hanging stranger; The eyes have it; The golden man; The turning wheel; The last of the masters; The father-thing; Strange Eden; Tony and the beetles; Null-o; To serve the master; Exhibit piece; The crawlers; Sales pitch; Shell game; Upon the

dull earth; Foster, you're dead; Pay for the printer; War veteran; The chromium fence; Misadjustment; A world of talent; Psi-man heal my child!

The days of Perky Pat: Autofac; Service call; Captive market; The mold of yancy; The minority report; Recall mechanism; The unreconstructed M; Explorers we; War game; If there were no Benny Cemoli; Novelty act; Waterspider; What the dead men say; Orpheus with clay feet; The days of Perky Pat; Stand-by; What'll we do with Ragland Park?; Oh, to be a Blobel!

The little black box: The little black box; The war with the fnools; A game of unchance; Precious artifact; Retreat syndrome; A terran odyssey; Your appointment will be yesterday; Holy quarrel; We can remember it for you wholesale; Not by its cover; Return match; Faith of our fathers; The story to end all stories for Harlan Ellison's anthology *Dangerous visions*; The electric ant; Cadbury, the beaver who lacked; A little something for us tempunauts; The pre-persons; The eye of the sibyl; The day Mr. Computer fell out of its tree; The exit door leads in; Chains of air, web of aether; Strange memories of death; I hope I shall arrive soon; Rautavaara's case; The alien mind

Dick, R. A. *See* Leslie, Josephine Aimee Campbell, 1898-1979

The **Dick** Francis treasury of great racing stories; edited and introduced by Dick Francis and John Welcome. Norton 1990 c1989 221p o.p.

LC 89-72151

Companion volume to The New treasury of racing stories

Available G.K. Hall large print edition

Analyzed in Short story index

First published 1989 in the United Kingdom with title: Great racing stories

Contents: The dream, by R. Findlay; Silver Blaze, by A. C. Doyle; A glass of port with the proctor, by J. Welcome; Carrot for a chestnut, by D. Francis; The look of eagles, by J. T. Foote; Prime rogues, by M. Keane; The coop, by E. Wallace; The splendid outcast, by B. Markham; I'm a fool, by S. Anderson; Had a horse, by J. Galsworthy; The major, by C. Davy; What's it get you?, by J. P. Marquand; Harmony, by W. Fain; The bagman's pony, by E. de Somerville

Dickens, Charles, 1812-1870

Barnaby Rudge; a tale of the riots of 'eighty; with 76 illustrations by George Cattermole and Hablot K. Browne "Phiz" and an introduction by Kathleen Tillotson. Oxford Univ. Press 1961 634p il $13.95

ISBN 0-19-254513-2

First published 1841

"Gives a lurid account of the mad orgies and incendiarism of the 'No Popery' riots, introducing Lord George Gordon as an actor, the principal events being founded on fact. Intertwined with this is a private story containing a few characteristic traits." Baker. Guide to Hist Fic

Dickens, Charles, 1812-1870—*Continued*
"The plot of this book is one of Dickens' weakest, and the novel's chief interest lies in its depiction of the terrible riots. In exploring causes for the riots, Dickens finds the answer in a government that is heedless of the needs of its poor." Reader's Ency. 3d edition

Bleak House.
Available from various publishers

First published 1853
"The heroine is Esther Summerson or rather Esther Hawdon, the illegitimate child of Lady Dedlock and Captain Hawdon. Esther, whom Lady Dedlock believes dead, is the ward of Mr. Jarndyce of the interminable case of Jarndyce and Jarndyce in Chancery Court, and lives with him at Bleak House. Lord Dedlock's lawyer, Mr. Tulkinghorn, gets wind of Lady Dedlock's secret past; and when Tulkinghorn is murdered, Lady Dedlock is suspected, disappears and is later found dead." Univ Handbk for Readers and Writers
"In this novel, Dickens attacks the delays and archaic absurdities of the courts, which he knew about firsthand." Reader's Ency. 3d edition

A Charles Dickens Christmas; A Christmas carol; The Chimes; The cricket on the hearth; with illustrations by Warren Chappell. Oxford Univ. Press 1976 308p il $19.95
ISBN 0-19-519899-9
Analyzed in Short story index
Omnibus edition of the titles first published 1843, 1845 and 1846 respectively, the first and third of which are entered separately. The chimes is a fable about the fears and aspirations of the London poor. A porter and runner of errands, under the influence of the goblins of the church bells and/or a dish of tripe, has a nightmare or vision of awful misfortunes befalling his daughter, but conditions are ameliorated after he awakens

The chimes
In Dickens, C. A Charles Dickens Christmas p101-202

In Dickens, C. Christmas tales

A Christmas carol.
Available from various publishers

Written in 1843
"This Christmas story of nineteenth century England has delighted young and old for generations. In it, a miser, Scrooge, through a series of dreams, finds the true Christmas spirit. . . . The story ends with the much-quoted cry of Tiny Tim, the crippled son of Bob Cratchit, whom Scrooge now aids: 'God bless us, everyone!'" Haydn. Thesaurus of Book Dig

also in Dickens, C. A Charles Dickens Christmas p3-98

also in Dickens, C. Christmas tales p11-77

also in Dickens, C. The complete ghost stories of Charles Dickens p89-151

Christmas stories; with 13 illustrations by E. G. Dalziel [et al.] and with an introduction by Margaret Lane. Oxford Univ. Press 1956 758p il $13.95
ISBN 0-19-254517-5

"New Oxford illustrated Dickens"
Analyzed in Short story index
Contents: A Christmas tree; What Christmas is as we grow older; The poor relation's story; The child's story; The schoolboy's story; Nobody's story; The seven poor travellers; The holly-tree; The wreck of the Golden Mary; The perils of certain English prisoners; Going into society; The haunted house; A message from the sea; Tom Tiddler's ground; Somebody's luggage; Mrs. Lirriper's lodgings; Mrs. Lirriper's legacy; Doctor Marigold; Mugby Junction; No thoroughfare; The lazy tour of two idle apprentices

Christmas tales; with illustrations by contemporary artists and a foreword by May Lamberton Becker. Dodd, Mead 1947 c1941 414p il o.p.
"Great illustrated classics"
Analyzed in Short story index
Contents: A Christmas carol; The chimes; The cricket on the hearth; The haunted man; A Christmas-tree; What Christmas is as we grow older; The poor relation's story; The seven poor travellers; The holly-tree; Doctor Marigold

The complete ghost stories of Charles Dickens; edited by Peter Haining. Watts 1983 c1982 341p il o.p.
LC 82-13481
Analyzed in Short story index
First published 1982 in the United Kingdom
Contents: Captain Murderer and the Devil's bargain; The lawyer and the ghost; The queer chair; The ghosts of the mail; A madman's manuscript; The story of the goblins who stole a sexton; Baron Koëldwethout's apparition; A Christmas carol; The haunted man and the ghost's bargain; To be read at dusk; The ghost chamber; The haunted house; Mr Testator's visitation; The trial for murder; The signalman; Four ghost stories; The portrait-painter's story; Well-authenticated rappings

The cricket on the hearth; a fairy tale of home. o.p.
First published in 1846
"In this short Christmas fairy tale of a happy English home, the cricket chirps when all is well, and is silent when sorrow enters. Mr. and Mrs. Perrybingle (John and Dot) give refuge to an old stranger, Edward Plummer. John sees the stranger, as a young man, without his disguise, put his arm around Dot. The cricket takes the form of a fairy and counsels him. John does not judge his young wife and is ready to forgive her. However, Edward bursts in with his bride, May Fielding, and explains everything." Haydn. Thesaurus of Book Dig

also in Dickens, C. A Charles Dickens Christmas p205-308

also in Dickens, C. Christmas tales p147-215

David Copperfield.
Available from various publishers

First published 1850
This novel is "admittedly autobiographical. As a small boy David is sent by his cruel stepfather Mr. Murdstone to Mr. Creakle's school, where he is mistreated but meets an older boy, Steerforth, whom he idolizes. After his mothers' death, he is dispatched to London to make his living; here he pastes labels on bottles in a warehouse by day and is the single lodger of the

Dickens, Charles, 1812-1870—*Continued*
poverty-stricken, though optimistic, Mr. Micawber and his family. David finally runs away to his great-aunt Betsy Trotwood, who becomes his guardian. During a further period of school life, he settles down to board with Mr. Wickfield, a lawyer, and finds a warm friend in Wickfield's daughter Agnes. Unaware of Agnes's deep devotion to him, David goes to work for a law firm in London and marries Dora Spenlow, a frivolous, child-like woman, who dies soon after. . . . *David Copperfield* is a devastating exposé of the inhuman treatment of children in 19th-century England." Reader's Ency. 3d edition

Dombey and Son; with forty illustrations by 'Phiz'; introduced by Lucy Hughes-Hallett. Knopf 1994 xlvii, 889p il $23

ISBN 0-679-43591-3   LC 94-4778
Also available Oxford University Press edition with title: Dealings with the firm of Dombey and Son
"Everyman's library"
"The proud, unfeeling Mr. Dombey has but one ambition in life: to have a son that his firm might be called Dombey and Son. When his son Paul is born he promises to fulfill this ambition, which overrides even grief at the death of Mrs. Dombey. Young Paul, a delicate, sensitive boy, is quite unequal to the great things expected of him; he is sent to Mr. Blimber's school and gives way under the strain of the discipline. . . . Mr. Dombey is embittered by Paul's death. Florence, his daughter, lives on with him trying desperately to win his love, but she has succeeded only in incurring his hatred because she lives while her brother died. Dombey marries again, but his second wife, runs off with Mr. 'Carker,' his business manager. Florence marries the kind young Walter Gay. Dombey's firm fails, and alone and miserable, he finds himself longing for the sweet and kind daughter whom he treated so coldly. The two are reconciled, and Dombey tries to expiate his past through his grandchildren." Reader's Ency. 3d edition

Great expectations.
Available from various publishers
First published 1861
"The first-person narrative relates the coming-of-age of Pip (Philip Pirrip). Reared in the marshes of Kent by his disagreeable sister and her sweet-natured husband, the blacksmith Joe Gargery, the young Pip one day helps a convict to escape. Later he is sent to live with Miss Havisham, a woman driven half-mad years earlier by her lover's departure on their wedding day. . . . When an anonymous benefactor makes it possible for Pip to go to London for an education, he credits Miss Havisham. . . . Pips benefactor turns out to have been Abel Magwitch, the convict he once aided, who dies awaiting trial after Pip is unable to help him a second time. Joe rescues Pip from despair and nurses him back to health." Merriam-Webster's Ency of Lit

Hard times. Knopf 1992 299p $17

ISBN 0-679-41323-5   LC 91-58704
"Everyman's library"
First published 1854. Variant title: Hard times for these times
The proprietor of an experimental private school in an English manufacturing town, "Thomas Gradgrind, a fanatic of the demonstrable fact, has raised his children Tom and Louisa in an atmosphere of grimmest practicality. Louisa marries the banker Josiah 'Bounderby'

partly to protect her brother who is in Bounderby's employ, partly because her education has resulted in an emotional atrophy that makes her indifferent to her fate. Tom, shallow and unscrupulous, robs Bounderby's bank and contrives to frame Stephen Blackpool, an honest and long-suffering mill hand. Meanwhile, Louisa's dormant emotions began to awaken, stimulated by disgust for the vulgar Bounderby, and the attentions of the charming, amoral James Harthouse. When she runs away to her father and when Tom's guilt is discovered, Gradgrind realizes how his principles have blighted his children's lives. . . . The novel is Dickens' harshest indictment of practices and philosophical justifications of mid-19th-century industrialism in England." Reader's Ency. 3d edition

The haunted man [variant title: The haunted man and the ghost's bargain]

In Dickens, C. Christmas tales

Little Dorrit.
Available from various publishers
First published 1857
"Little Dorrit was born and brought up in the Marshalsea prison, Bermondsey, where her father was confined for debt; and when about fourteen years of age she used to do needlework to earn a subsistence for herself and her father. . . . Her father, coming into a property, was set free at length, and Little Dorrit married Arthur Clennam, the marriage service being celebrated in the Marshalsea, by the prison chaplain." Univ Handbk for Readers and Writers
"Satirizes the Civil Service under the style of the Circumlocution Office. Also pictures prison life. Little Dorrit's father being Father of the Marshalsea. The melodramatic element appears in the history of the House of Clennam: with the usual complement of originals: Mr. F.'s Aunt, the Meagles, Pancks, Mr. Nanby, Mr. Casby, Flora Finching, Miss Wade, Tallycoram." Baker. Guide to the Best Fic

Martin Chuzzlewit; with forty illustrations by "Phiz"; introduced by William Boyd. Knopf 1994 xlvii, 851p il $20

ISBN 0-679-43884-X   LC 95-136833
Also available Oxford University Press edition with title: The life and adventures of Martin Chuzzlewit
"Everyman's library"
"The story's protagonist, Martin Chuzzlewit, is an apprentice architect who is fired by Seth Pecksniff and is also disinherited by his own eccentric, wealthy grandfather. Martin and a servant, Mark Tapley, travel to the United States, where they are swindled by land speculators and have other unpleasant but sometimes comic experiences. Thoroughly disillusioned with the New World, the pair returns to England, where a chastened Martin is reconciled with his grandfather, who gives his approval to Martin's forthcoming marriage to his true love, Mary Graham." Merriam-Webster's Ency of Lit

The mystery of Edwin Drood; with 12 illustrations by Luke Fildes and 2 by Charles Collins, and an introduction by S. C. Roberts. Oxford Univ. Press 1956 278p il $10.95

ISBN 0-19-254516-7
Also available from Amereon

Dickens, Charles, 1812-1870—*Continued*

"New Oxford illustrated Dickens"

First published 1870

"This novel Dickens left unfinished at his death. The striking opening scene shows John Jasper, precentor of Cloisterham cathedral, in an opium den. He is the uncle of Edwin Drood, and persecutes with his evil passion Rosa Bud, to whom Drood is betrothed by an arrangement made by the late respective fathers of the two orphans. Actually Edwin is cool to Rosa, and it is another orphan, Neville Landless, who is attracted to her. The sinister Jasper foments a quarrel between Edwin and Neville, not knowing that the engagement has already been broken off. The same night Edwin disappears, and there is circumstantial evidence pointing to Neville as his murderer. The latter is arrested, but as no body has been found, is released. There turns up in the neighborhood a white-haired stranger who calls himself Datchery and acts like a detective on the trail of Jasper. Here the story breaks off with no indication as to how it would have ended." Haydn. Thesaurus of Book Dig

The mystery of Edwin Drood, concluded by Leon Garfield; introduction by Edward Blishen; illustrated by Anthony Maitland. Pantheon Bks. 1981 c1980 327p il o.p.

LC 80-8850

This edition of Dickens' novel as concluded by Leon Garfield was first published 1980 in the United Kingdom

"Garfield's 19 chapters use almost all of the loose ends and planted clues without intruding major inventions. The style is less fertile than Dickens' but has nothing to jar, and the conclusion is quite moving. A satisfactory reading version to add to the Dickens collection." Libr J

Nicholas Nickleby; with an introduction by John Carey. Knopf 1993 lvii, 843p il $20

ISBN 0-679-42307-9 LC 93-1856

Also available Oxford University Press edition with title: The life & adventures of Nicholas Nickleby

"Everyman's library"

First published 1839

After Nicholas Nickleby's father dies bankrupt, Nicholas, his sister and their mother go to London to seek aid from Nicholas' uncle, a moneylender. At the scheming miser's insistence, Nicholas "first goes as usher to Mr. Squeers, schoolmaster at Dotheboys Hall, in Yorkshire, but leaves in disgust with the tyranny of Squeers and his wife, especially to a poor boy named Smike. Smike runs away from the school to follow Nicholas, and remains his humble follower til death. At Portsmouth, Nicholas joins the theatrical company of Mr. Crummles, but leaves the profession for other adventures. He falls in with the brothers Cheeryble, who make him their clerk; in his post he rises to success as a merchant, and ultimately marries Madeline Bray." Reader's Ency. 3d edition

The old curiosity shop; with seventy-five illustrations by Cattermole and 'Phiz'; introduced by Peter Washington. Knopf 1995 569p il $23

ISBN 0-679-44373-8 LC 95-75208

"Everyman's library"

First published 1841; first Everyman's library edition 1907

This is the "story of Little Nell Trent and the evil dwarf Quilp. When Little Nell's grandfather gambles away his curiosity shop to his creditor Quilp, the girl and the old man flee London. Nell's friend Kit Nubbles and a mysterious Single Gentleman (who turns out to be the wealthy brother of Nell's grandfather) attempt to find them but are thwarted by Quilp, who drowns while fleeing the law. Little Nell dies before Kit and the Single Gentleman arrive, and her broken-hearted grandfather dies days later." Merriam-Webster's Ency of Lit

Oliver Twist.

Available from various publishers

First published 1837-1838

Variant title: The adventures of Oliver Twist

"A boy from an English workhouse falls into the hands of rogues who train him to be a pickpocket. The story of his struggles to escape from an environment of crime is one of hardship, danger and the severe obstacles overcome." Natl Counc of Teachers of Engl

Our mutual friend.

Available from various publishers

First published 1865

"John Harmon, 'our mutual friend,' will inherit a fortune if he marries Bella Wilfer. He assumes the names of Julius Handford and later John Rokesmith, and his supposed death helps him conceal his identity. John's father's foreman, Nicodemus Boffin, and his wife, Henrietta, help him with the ruse. He enters the employ of Boffin, who has adopted Bella. Bella has had her head turned by wealth, but reforms when her eyes are opened to its evils; she marries Harmon. Other characters are: Jesse Hexam; his son Charley, and daughter, Lizzie; Bradley Headstone, schoolmaster, who is jealous of Eugene Wrayburn's love for Lizzie Hexam; Fanny Cleaver (Jenny Wren), a doll's dressmaker; one-legged Silas Wegg, the villain in the main plot, as Headstone is in the secondary one. Here again Dickens protests against the poor laws through the character Betty Hidger, who fears the workhouse." Haydn. Thesaurus of Book Dig

The posthumous papers of the Pickwick Club; with forty-three illustrations by Seymour and 'Phiz' and an introduction by Bernard Darwin. Oxford Univ. Press 1959 xxiii, 801p il $10.95

ISBN 0-19-254501-9

"New Oxford illustrated Dickens"

First published 1837

"Episodes of the doings and foibles of the Pickwick Club. . . . The book is made up of letters and manuscripts about the club's actions. Among the incidents are: the army parade; trip to Manor Farm; the saving of Rachel Wardle from the villain, Alfred Jingle; trip to Eatonsville; Mrs. Leo Hunter's party of authors, including Count Smorltork and Charles FitzMarshall; ice skating. Pickwick's landlady, Mrs. Bardell, faints in his arms and compromises the unsophisticated gentleman. She sues him for breach of promise and an amusing court trial follows. Pickwick refuses to pay damages and is put in Fleet prison. Sam Weller, his faithful servant, accompanies him. Mrs. Bardell is also incarcerated for not paying the costs of the trial. When Pickwick is released he retires to a house outside London, with Weller, and the latter's new bride, Mary, as housekeeper. He dissolves the club and spends his time arranging its memoranda." Haydn. Thesaurus of Book Dig

Dickens, Charles, 1812-1870—*Continued*

Sketches by Boz. o.p.

Satires on daily life originally serialized in the Old monthly magazine, 1833-1835

The chapters are arranged under the following headings: Our parish; Scenes; Characters; Tales; Sketches of young gentlemen; Sketches of young couples; The Mudfog and other sketches

A tale of two cities.

Available from various publishers

First published in 1859

A novel of the French Revolution. "The two cities are London and Paris. The plot hinges on the physical likeness of Charles Darnay and Sidney Carton, both of whom are in love with Lucie Manette. Lucie loves Darnay, and Sydney Carton, who is a dissipated ne'er-do-well, never pleads his devotion, but it leads him to go to the guillotine in place of Darnay for the sake of Lucie's happiness." Reader's Ency

Dickey, James

Deliverance. Armchair Detective Lib. 1991 236p $19.95

ISBN 1-56287-010-6   LC 91-10975

First published 1970 by Houghton Mifflin

"A relaxing down-river hunting trip in a wilderness area of the South is taken by a group of four businessmen whose personalities are revealingly different from each other. The planned vacation turns into a nightmare when one man is shot and killed by an elusive local man and the other three must fight for their lives." Shapiro. Fic for Youth. 3d edition

"Dickey is to be praised for resisting the temptation of the poet to write 'poetical' prose. . . . He writes in a neat, terse, matter-of-fact prose, level in pitch and perfectly suited to carry the burden of the action." New Yorker

To the white sea. Houghton Mifflin 1993 275p $22.95

ISBN 0-395-47565-1   LC 93-1247

"A Marc Jaffe book"

WWII Air Force gunner Muldrow is shot down over Tokyo shortly before the "fire raid on that city. His position should be hopeless, but the man comes from a remote region of Alaska, where he grew up hunting, trapping, and studying game. His object is to find similarly cold country, and as he lurks and dodges his way north to Hokkaido, he uses every trick of camouflage and predation that he has learned from hare and wolverine." Atlantic

This novel "allows no easy assumption about nature or violence or war. What makes it so haunting, though, what keeps you reading, is the beauty of the prose." Newsweek

Dickinson, Peter, 1927-

Death of a unicorn. Pantheon Bks. 1984 205p o.p.

LC 84-427000

"Lady Margaret Millett, the narrator . . . is a popular romantic novelist recalling 10 months of 'extreme, unrepeatable happiness' as the young mistress of a magazine publisher whom she describes fondly as looking like a toad. The affair took place in 1952 in the creamier social circles of London when Lady Margaret was plucked off the debutante line by her future lover

to write a column for his smart society magazine. The idyll ended in Rio with the publisher's violent, unexplained death. The story resumes 30 years later, giving the heroine the chance to apply mature insight to her lover's murder. . . . Mr. Dickinson remains a challenge for any reader expecting conventionally developed plots. He's quite a treat, though, for admirers of supple prose, acid social commentary and an ever original perspective on the quicksilver nature of time." N Y Times Book Rev

The glass-sided ants' nest. Harper & Row 1968 186p o.p.

"A Joan Kahn-Harper novel of suspense"

"The wealthy daughter of a missionary to New Guinea fetches the remnants of the [Ku] tribe to London and installs them in Flagg Terrace, where the headman is bashed with a wooden owl. C.I.D. Inspector Pibble is plunged into a wash of native custom and lore." N Y Times Book Rev

"An extraordinary criminal yarn . . . [and] one of the most offbeat detective stories to appear in a number of years. The sleuth is a semi-hero who stands halfway between 'Handsome' West and Inspector Dover, both in charm and intelligence. Mr. Dickinson . . . may fudge just a little in his solution, but the fascination of a tribal murder in the heart of London is so great that you won't really mind." Critic

Hindsight. Pantheon Bks. 1983 191p o.p.

LC 83-42816

"A middle-aged novelist recalls a murder unconsciously buried in his memory for 40 years. Paul Rogers is approached by a literary biographer who wishes to learn about the staff of a boys school that Rogers attended, which was relocated during World War II. The biographer is interested in the relationships of several of the staff members to the subject of his work. In answering the query, Rogers sees the fictional possibilities of the material. Soon he is developing two accounts of his days in the English countryside, and eventually he cannot tell which is 'true.'" Booklist

"A novel within a novel may sound like a literary bag of tricks, but Dickinson's elegant fusion of hindsight, hard facts and imaginative reliving of prep school days makes for satisfying reading, especially with his many well-observed descriptions of faculty and students. . . . A piquant blend of intelligence and suspense." Publ Wkly

The last houseparty. Pantheon Bks. 1982 221p o.p.

LC 84-47892

"Pantheon international crime"

"Forty years after the sudden and inexplicable halt to the fabulous weekend parties of Zena, Countess of Snailwood, an elderly gentleman offers to repair the fantastic great clock in the courtyard of Snailwood, its mechanism stopped by fire at that last houseparty. His presence works a strange influence upon Sarah Quinton, the house's present owner, who presses on to uncover and to understand the meaning of those events which have marked her life." Best Sellers

"The author has fragmented (this novel) scattering the pieces from past to present and shamelessly delaying revelation of the episode on which the whole narrative depends. However, one can forgive Mr. Dickinson's structural improprieties for the pleasure of his elegant prose and the skill with which he resurrects the notions and habits of English Society in the 1930's." Atlantic

Dickinson, Peter, 1927-—*Continued*

Perfect gallows; a novel of suspense. Pantheon Bks. 1988 233p o.p.

LC 87-43047

"Sandwiched between the death of a black servant in an English mansion on the eve of D-Day and the bitter recollection of the event by a famous actor 40 years later, Dickinson reprises the formative years of the actor's life. A young orphan brought to live with his wealthy relatives, Andrew dreams of being an actor. As his talent develops, he realizes that acting affords him the opportunity to become a master of illusion, capable of assuming a new life for himself and thus submerging his private self. Even as his personal myth takes shape, however, the legacy of his complex relationship with the black servant, Samuel, continues to fester. . . . Dickinson portrays the war years to poignant effect and offers a compelling cast, but his real gift lies in the quiet, almost casual way he is able to build tension." Booklist

Play dead. Mysterious Press 1992 c1991 282p $17.95

ISBN 0-89296-478-2 LC 91-20214

Also available Thorndike Press large print edition

First published 1991 in the United Kingdom

"Poppy Tasker, a game and warm-hearted 50-year-old divorcée searching for a life on her own, agrees to babysit for her toddler grandson Toby while her Labour Party daughter-in-law pursues a seat in Parliament from their London district. A young man observed watching Toby's play group in the park angers Poppy and the nannies; he is also seen outside Poppy's house the night she comes home with one of the other tots' fathers—a Romanian national whom she met at a concert. When the young man is found murdered in the play center, the nannies come under suspicion." Publ Wkly

"A stylist of subtle brilliance, the author gradually exposes Poppy and her claustrophobic community of women to the violent realities of the world beyond the playground." N Y Times Book Rev

Skeleton-in-waiting. Pantheon Bks. 1989 154p $16.95

ISBN 0-394-58002-8 LC 89-42561

This sequel to King and Joker (1976) "focuses on the same fictional British royal family after the death of heroine Princess Louise's grandmother, Grand Duchess Marie Romanov. Dickinson juggles several subplots—a rumor of possible terrorist action; the odd behavior of Louise's sister-in-law—but concentrates mostly on the Grand Duchess's possibly scandalous letters and the strange woman hired to translate them from Russian." Libr J

This "is a most satisfying story, fast-paced and enthralling as a good detective thriller should be but also a study of extraordinary social and psychological perception." N Y Times Book Rev

The yellow room conspiracy. Mysterious Press 1994 261p $18.95

ISBN 0-89296-556-8 LC 94-1980

Also available Thorndike Press large print edition

"The yellow room was one of about 50 in Blatchards, an old mansion near Bury St. Edmonds. Owned by Lord Vereker, Blatchards was dominated by his five striking daughters whose politics and personal lives in the 1930s and '40s are at the heart of Dickinson's . . . tale. Flashbacks told in alternating chapters by Lucy Vereker, the third daughter, and her lover Paul Ackerley, now near the end of their lives, describe events that culminated in the 1956 fire that destroyed the house, an event that each one thought the other may have, in different ways, engineered. The fire covered up evidence about the death—accident, suicide or murder?—of Gerry Grantworth, the eldest daughter's husband." Publ Wkly

"Like the labyrinthine route one must take to the Yellow Room, the resolution of the mystery is lengthy and winding and delightfully disorienting." N Y Times Book Rev

Dickson, Carr, 1906-1977

For works written by this author under other names see Carr, John Dickson, 1906-1977

Dickson, Carter, 1906-1977

For works written by this author under other names see Carr, John Dickson, 1906-1977

Dickson, Gordon R., 1923-

The cloak and the staff

In The Hugo winners v5 p209-43

The dragon at war. Ace Bks. 1992 375p $18.95

ISBN 0-441-75698-0 LC 91-46350

In this installment of the author's Dragon series "the great mage Carolinus has been struck with a mysterious illness that leaves him despondent and unsure of his powers just as a sorcerous threat to England is developing, which pretty much leaves Jim, the dragon knight, to work his own lesser magic. As usual, Dickson provides a nice mixture of humor, action, and drama, not to mention interesting characters who reflect the medieval turn of mind regarding chivalry and brutality." Booklist

Followed by The dragon, the Earl, and the troll

The dragon knight. Doherty Assocs. 1990 409p o.p.

LC 90-38897

"A TOR book"

Sequel to The dragon and the George (1976)

"Sir James Eckert, a 20th-century academician turned 14th-century baron in an alternate, magical Middle Ages, finds his idyllic existence disrupted by a call to arms to rescue his captive prince from the clutches of the French. Aided by his loyal companions and by the sudden emergence of his latent magical talents, Sir James brings his own modern sensibilities to bear in a confrontation with the forces of darkness." Libr J

"Dickson has further developed the intriguing medieval universe he posited in the first volume of the series . . . giving reality and texture to the actual life of the time while exploring the effects of magic. The scenes describing diplomatic relations among the dragons are particularly fine." Publ Wkly

Followed by The dragon on the border

The dragon on the border. Ace Bks. 1992 393p o.p.

LC 91-21270

Dickson, Gordon R., 1923-—_Continued_

In this title in the Dragon series "Dickson matches his contemporary-American-turned-medieval-knight-dragon against immortal and deadly sorcerers, the Hollow Men, and sets them against a background drawn from the Anglo-Scots border wars of great and bloody memory. The result is a mixture of humor and drama that recalls L. Sprague de Camp. Dickson is a good enough medievalist, humorist, and storyteller to sustain this combination." Booklist

Followed by The dragon at war

The dragon, the Earl, and the troll. Ace Bks. 1994 442p $21.95

ISBN 0-441-00098-3   LC 94-7538

In this Dragon title Sir James must "contend with medieval court intrigues and the Dark Powers and other unworldly wildlife. He is helped by his wife, Angie; his master-in-magic Carolinus; the unforgettable English wolf Aargh; and his other friends. Although the yarn is unquestionably formulaic, that formula is a tried and tested winner allowing, in Dickson's capable hands, a wealth of wit and range of invention not found in the common ruck of thud-and-blunder romances." Booklist

Lost Dorsai

_In_ The Hugo winners v5 p137-206

Wolf and iron. Doherty Assocs. 1990 468p o.p.

LC 90-2953

"A TOR book"

"Fleeing the cities transformed into battlefields by universal economic collapse, Jeebee Walther heads for the Montana wilderness, where he finds himself prey to roaming marauder bands and deadly survivalist villages until a chance meeting with a captive wolf begins a relationship that teaches him the true meaning of survival in the new Dark Age." Libr J

"Dickson has done his homework on wolves, but more, his writing is up to the level that has made him one of the giants of the field." Booklist

Young Bleys. TOR Bks. 1991 456p o.p.
LC 90-48781

"A Tom Doherty Associates book"

A volume in the author's Childe cycle

"Removed from the care of his 'Exotic' mother and sent to the demanding planet of Association (ruled by humans known as 'Friendlies'), halfbreed Bleys Ahrens discovers a covert organization of crossbred humans which provides a focus for his growing sense of destiny." Libr J

"Dickson's work leaves the borders of the genre unchallenged, but reveals some of that genre's traditional strengths." Publ Wkly

Didion, Joan

A book of common prayer. Simon & Schuster 1977 272p o.p.

LC 76-50067

Charlotte Douglas, the novel's heroine, "is the quintessential American innocent. . . . Nothing alters her self-centered perception of events—not two disastrous marriages nor the fact that her daughter has turned overnight into a political outlaw. . . . Charlotte retires to Boca Grande, a shabby banana republic, to wait for things to turn out 'all right.' There she meets Grace Strasser-Mendana, the narrator of the novel, like Char-

lotte a 'norte-americana,' an anthropologist by training, and a local political power by marriage. Grace unwittingly involves Charlotte in a coup d'état. Charlotte in turn provides the subject matter for Grace's final inquiry into human behavior." Atlantic

Didion's "exposition of situations and details adroitly conceals their significance—until much later their meaning flares before our eyes. This is a remarkably good novel." Newsweek

Democracy; a novel. Simon & Schuster 1984 234p o.p.

LC 84-1216

"Inez Christian Victor, the novel's main character, grew up in Hawaii, married United States Sen. Harry Victor, and had two children—Jessie and Adlai. In 1975 Jessie runs away to find a job in Saigon. At this same time Inez's sister, Janet, is killed—perhaps accidentally—by their father, a trauma which, in part, persuades Inez to flee. She leaves her husband and son to search for Jessie. In the course of Inez's search, she is reunited with Jack Lovett, with whom, in 1952 at the age of 17, she had had an affair." Christ Sci Monit

"As ever-present narrator and minor character in her own novel, Didion achieves the immediacy of journalism at the expense of emotional depth in these 'fitful glimpses' into the life of her heroine and 'acquaintance'. . . . Sophisticated political fiction, written with skill and wit—engaging despite the intrusive narrative techniques." Libr J

Play it as it lays; a novel. Farrar, Straus & Giroux 1970 214p o.p.

"Using a phrenetic millieu of drugs, pills, sexual aberrancy, Didion elliptically etches the self-destructive life of Maria Wyeth. Didion with authorial legerdemain skillfully controls the suspense as Maria dangerously exists: she cannot relate and adjust. Her father has told her life was a crap game and to play it as it lays, not the hard way. But Maria plays it the hardest way, trying to anesthetize herself against pain (almost everyone, anything) and pleasure (Kate, her neurally damaged child), and trying to lose herself in the dead-end life around her." Choice

Diehl, William

27. Villard Bks. 1989 559p o.p.
LC 89-40200

"Some of America's richest, most powerful men meet regularly at an exclusive resort on an island off Georgia. A Nazi 'sleeper agent,' code named 27, living in the U.S. since 1933, plans to kidnap these VIPs and hold them hostage in exchange for Roosevelt's guarantee that the U.S. will stay out of the war. Larger-than-life Francis Keegan, a wealthy American ex-bootlegger and friend of FDR, is agent 27's nemesis." Publ Wkly

The author "handles action scenes well, and the story keeps you turning the pages—but it's best while doing so to keep your capacity for willing disbelief in full working order." N Y Times Book Rev

Primal fear. Villard Bks. 1993 418p $20

ISBN 0-679-40211-X   LC 92-5728

This thriller "focuses on the maneuvers of Chicago defense attorney Martin Vail, a prosecutor's worst nightmare. . . . After discovering the mutilated body of Archbishop Richard Rushman in the rectory of his church, police find Aaron Stampler cowering in a confessional, blood-soaked and gripping the murder weapon. It seems

Diehl, William—*Continued*

like an iron-clad case—psycho slasher carves up 'the Saint of Lakeview Drive'—and a hostile judge appoints Vail as pro bono defense attorney, hoping to publicly humble him." Publ Wkly

"Taking the best elements of horror fiction, the psychological thriller, and the legal novel, best-selling author Diehl concocts an especially exciting chiller. . . . The ending may not hold up under a psychiatrist's professional scrutiny, but the general reader will find it an immensely successful finis!." Booklist

Dikty, Julian May *See* May, Julian, 1931-

Dillard, Annie

The living. HarperCollins Pubs. 1992 397p $24

ISBN 0-06-016870-6   LC 91-58376

Also available Thorndike Press large print edition

"The story begins with two pioneering white families from the Midwest battling with the towering Douglas firs of the Washington coast for a bit of sunlight and open land. Generous native Americans help the struggling settlers survive, and both groups are changed by their ongoing interaction as the settlement waxes and wanes and the economy booms and busts." Booklist

"'The Living' is an august celebration of human frenzy and endurance. Her living are hectically alive, her dead recur in furious memory. And Annie Dillard, sometimes by an apparent crabwise indirection but with utter thoroughness, proves herself a fine novelist." N Y Times Book Rev

DiMercurio, Michael

Attack of the Seawolf. Fine, D.I. 1993 352p $21.95

ISBN 1-55611-360-9   LC 92-54981

Attack of the Seawolf "is set in the not-too-distant future when an underground Chinese democratic movement becomes strong enough to militarily challenge the government establishment. In the ensuing civil war, all foreign journalists are expelled and smoking battlefields render satellite intelligence inconclusive. Sent to the Gulf of Chihli to monitor the situation, the submarine U.S.S. Tampa is captured by hard-line forces. Commanding the new state-of-the-art U.S.S. Seawolf, Captain Michael 'Patch' Pacino . . . sets out to rescue the Tampa and its commander, his one-time Annapolis roommate." Publisher's note

"The author knows how to provide the necessary descriptions of modern submarine technology without obstructing his story line." Publ Wkly

Dinesen, Isak, 1885-1962

The angelic avengers; by Pierre Andrézel. Random House 1946 304p o.p.

Original Danish edition, 1944

Dinesen's only novel "is a melodramatic tale of innocents who defeat their apparently benevolent but actually evil captor, but Danish readers saw in it a clever satire of Nazi-occupied Denmark." Merriam-Webster's Ency of Lit

Last tales. Random House 1957 341p o.p.

Analyzed in Short story index

Contents: The Cardinal's first tale; The cloak; Night walk; Of hidden thoughts and of heaven; Tales of two old gentlemen; The Cardinal's third tale; The blank page; Caryatids, an unfinished tale; Echoes; A country tale; Copenhagen season; Converse at night in Copenhagen

Seven Gothic tales; with an introduction by Dorothy Canfield. Modern Lib. 1994 c1934 522p $16.50

ISBN 0-679-60086-8

First published 1934 by H. Smith and analyzed in Short story index

Contents: The deluge at Norderney; The old chevalier; The monkey; The roads round Pisa; The supper at Elsinore; The dreamers; The poet

"Distinguished by a romantic style and an aura of mystery, these tales of nineteenth-century aristocratic life in northern Europe remain favorites of a wide audience. A major plot device in some stories is the revealing of illegitimacy (sometimes of legitimacy), while a strong element of the supernatural is to be found in others." Shapiro. Fic for Youth. 3d edition

Shadows on the grass. Random House 1961 c1960 149p il o.p.

Analyzed in Short story index

Contents: Farah; Barua a Soldani; The great gesture; Echoes from the hills

"These finely drawn autobiographical stories not only re-create the Africans with whom Dinesen shared those years, but also convey, in every description and episode, the quality and texture of a past era in Kenya and in the author's life." Booklist

Winter's tales. Random House 1942 313p o.p.

Analyzed in Short story index

Contents: The sailor-boy's tale; The young man with the carnation; The pearls; The invincible slaveowners; The heroine; The dreaming child; Alkmene; The fish; Peter and Rosa; Sorrow-acre; A consolatory tale

Dixon, Stephen, 1936-

Interstate; a novel. Holt & Co. 1995 374p $25

ISBN 0-8050-2654-1   LC 94-40174

This novel's "eight narratives are alternative replays of a terrible, defining moment that transpires in the book's opening pages: an act of random violence in which a man and his two daughters are shot at by punks in a passing van, and one of the girls is killed. Dixon's dense, plain-spoken prose perfectly mirrors the chaotic workings of a mind riddled with rage and guilt, where every thought and utterance is second-guessed. A timely, disturbing work." Libr J

The stories of Stephen Dixon. Holt & Co. 1994 642p $25

ISBN 0-8050-2653-3   LC 93-38509

Analyzed in Short story index

Contents: The chess house; The new era; Making a break; Mac in love; Last May; Rose; The return; Parents; Man of letters; The Franklin stove; Em; 14 stories; Milk is very good for you; The signing; Love has its own action; Cut; The intruder; Streets; Movies; Layaways; The watch; Stop; Cy; The hole; Joke; The gold car; Darling; The frame; The bench; For a man your age; Goodbye to goodbye; Come on a coming; Time to go; Eating the placenta; The letter; Change; Moving on; The rescuer;

Dixon, Stephen, 1936-—*Continued*

Love and will; Grace calls; Dog days; In time; Said; The postcard; Windows; A sloppy story; The painter; Takes; Gifts; The student; All gone; The batterer; Magna as a child; Only the cat escapes; Frog's nanny; Frog dances; Frog made free; Frog takes a swim; Frog's mom; Man, woman and boy

"This volume contains some of Dixon's best short fiction, written over a 30-year period from 1963 to 1993. . . . Rich with the precise details of ordinary urban life, the stories are gently distorted by the introduction of fantastic and surreal elements." Libr J

Dobyns, Stephen, 1941-

Saratoga backtalk. Norton 1994 221p $19.95

ISBN 0-393-03659-6   LC 93-48029

"Fearing that his wife wants him dead, a wealthy horse owner appeals to private eye Charlie Bradshaw for help. When a horse kicks the man to death shortly thereafter, Charlie and sidekick Victor Plotz uncover a host of bad feelings and nasty characters." Libr J

"With Charlie on jury duty, Victor draws the job of snooping about Logan's farm, and he quickly manages to offend everyone he encounters—except the reader, of course, who will fall totally under the hedonistic spell of the outrageously obscene, pleasure-craving, life-loving, 59-year-old Victor." Booklist

Saratoga bestiary. Viking 1988 256p $16.95

ISBN 0-670-82024-5   LC 88-14280

Detective Charlie Bradshaw is in "Saratoga Springs, where a stolen painting of Man o' War, a heist from an illegal gambling party, and a murdered grocery store owner have something in common. While unearthing the intricate connections—all of which lead to a very nasty villain who arranges pit bull dog fights and snuff videos—Charlie ponders the 'difficulties' of turning 50." Libr J

Saratoga haunting. Viking 1993 207p $19

ISBN 0-670-84581-7   LC 92-50750

"In the backwoods of upstate New York, laconic sleuth Bradshaw ruminates on his passing years, recalling his younger days when he was a brash career cop, married and miserable. The fluid narrative lures the reader into an ease that is rudely shattered by the eruption of two cases from the past." Publ Wkly

"Unlike most fictional detectives, who give the same flawless performance over and over again in a world outside time, Charlie is allowed by his creator to suffer changes and even to age. He is mortal, like us, and his struggles and successes matter." N Y Times Book Rev

Saratoga headhunter. Viking 1985 208p o.p.

LC 84-20955

"A headless corpse is found in Charlie Bradshaw's house. The corpse is that of a former jockey who was about to testify about crooked races before a grand jury. There are many people who wanted to prevent him from naming certain interests. It's said Bradshaw fingered the jock." N Y Times Book Rev

"None of this would be very interesting if it weren't for Bradshaw, who is such a miserable, guilt-ridden specimen that he eventually becomes paradoxically appealing. The Saratoga setting is another asset; buildings, locations and inhabitants are vividly described." Libr J

Saratoga snapper. Viking 1986 260p o.p.

LC 85-41075

Available G.K. Hall large print edition

Charlie Bradshaw's "mother owns the hotel where his friend Victor Plotz photographs a group at the bar. Later, a hit-run driver nearly kills Victor. While he's hospitalized, Charlie begins to unwind the tortured skein of events that are apparently unrelated: a young maid is found dead in the hotel; one of the people in the photo commits suicide; several local liquor stores are robbed. Everything is unexpected in the ingeniously plotted adventure—most of all, the hair-trigger climax and Charlie's way of shielding the pitiful people innocently involved in a shocking crime." Publ Wkly

Doctorow, E. L., 1931-

Billy Bathgate; a novel. Random House 1989 323p $19.95

ISBN 0-394-52529-9   LC 88-42820

"Having grown up poor but ambitious on the Bronx's Bathgate Avenue during the Depression, young Billy is now being educated in the ways of the world. . . . [He] is a gangster-in-training employed by [Dutch Schultz]. . . . Billy falls for 'the Dutchman's' latest lady—a beauty named Drew Preston who eventually reciprocates his youthful passion. Soon Billy is questioning the actions of the mob he was so eager to join as he seeks to protect Drew from its vengeance." Libr J

This is the "story of Billy's education, conducted on an extravagant scale. Doctorow brings a nice sense of moral ambiguity and creates characters who develop or deteriorate at an appropriate pace. His fecund run-on sentences are a pleasure to read. It all adds up to that rarity: a formal literary work that's also hugely entertaining." Newsweek

The book of Daniel; a novel. Random House 1971 303p o.p.

"The trial of Julius and Ethel Rosenberg in 1950-51 for espionage was a cause célèbre during the fifties. The justice of administering the death penalty to that pair is still argued, particularly by the sons of the Rosenbergs. In this novel, which is based on that case, Daniel Isaacson tells of the effect of that execution on his childhood, marriage, and career. The whole period of pre-World War II radicalism, the tyranny of the McCarthy era, the peace march on the Pentagon in 1967, the nature of left-wing politics in the United States are the elements that make this a provocative sociopolitical novel." Shapiro. Fic for Youth. 3d edition

Lives of the poets; six stories and a novella. Random House 1984 145p $14.95

ISBN 0-394-52530-2   LC 84-42513

Analyzed in Short story index

Contents: The writer in the family; The Water Works; Willi; The hunter; The foreign legation; The leather man; Lives of the poets

"The novella 'Lives of the Poets' ponders life and middle-aged love among East Coast literati. Here knowingness is all, with chat about 'Swiss-water-process decaffeinated coffee' overlaying narrator Jonathan's awareness that 'between the artist and simple dereliction there is a very thin line." Libr J

"The stories in this collection show Doctorow as an impeccable stylist, a man who writes with exceptional clarity and precision, who finds fresh, touching metaphors for the human condition. While the times and settings

Doctorow, E. L., 1931—*Continued*

vary, all these tales picture the individual in a disintegrating society in which everyone lives in emotional isolation." Publ Wkly

Lives of the poets [novelette]

In Doctorow, E. L. Lives of the poets p81-145

Loon Lake. Random House 1980 c1979 258p o.p.

LC 79-5526

Set in the 1930's the narrative "covers several picaresque years in the life of a young roughneck from Paterson, the son of wretchedly poor mill hands, who runs away from home, joins a gang of hobos, becomes a carnival roustabout, and stumbles accidentally onto Loon Lake, the vast Adirondack estate of the steel tycoon F. W. Bennett. One of the old industrialist's toys is a gangster's moll who sneaks out of Loon Lake with Joe, and the two settle down for a while in a steel town owned by one of Bennett's many companies. She leaves him, and Joe goes back to Loon Lake [and] is taken in by the old man." Commentary

"Doctorow has written a myth about the inheritance of America. Many techniques enhance the epic feeling. The novel is set in 1936, yet ranges across the first half of the century, even as it shifts viewpoints from the young man's memories to the poet's verses." Books of the Times

Ragtime. Modern Lib. 1994 320p $14.50

ISBN 0-679-60088-4   LC 93-43631

This is a reissue of the title first published 1975 by Random House

"The lives of an upper-middle-class family in New Rochelle; a black ragtime musician who loses his love, his child, and his life because of bigotry; and a poor immigrant Jewish family are interwoven in this early-twentieth-century story. There are cameo appearances by well-known figures of that period: Houdini, anarchist Emma Goldman, actress Evelyn Nesbit, Henry Ford, and J.P. Morgan, whose magnificent library plays an important part in the story. The book mingles fact and fiction in portraying the era of ragtime." Shapiro. Fic for Youth. 3d edition

The waterworks. Random House 1994 253p $23

ISBN 0-394-58754-5   LC 93-44735

"Martin Pemberton, renegade son of rich, unscrupulous Augustus Pemberton and favorite freelance of the persevering editor of the New York *Telegram*, . . . narrates this tale. First, Martin claims to have seen his dead father on a horse-drawn omnibus, and then he disappears. The worried editor contacts Inspector Edmund Donne—the only honest cop in 1870s New York, where the Tweed Ring holds sway—and eventually they discover that the ailing Augustus is part of an experiment by the brilliant Dr. Sartorius to prolong the lives of several old men rich enough to foot the bill." Libr J

Welcome to Hard Times. Simon & Schuster 1960 180p o.p. Buccaneer Bks. reprint available $24.95 (ISBN 1-56849-393-2)

"A novel about a small town in the barren West at the close of the last century. . . . The tale revolves around a bad-man who destroys the town of Hard Times in one day, causally and cruelly; a mayor who is too weak to kill the bad-man but who is hopeful enough to rebuild the town; and a woman of easy virtue who waits, in terror and hatred, for the return of the bad-man." Springfield Repub

Doerr, Harriet

Consider this, señora. Harcourt Brace & Co. 1993 241p $21.95

ISBN 0-15-193103-8   LC 93-21471

This "novel focuses on expatriate Americans in Mexico searching for love, connection and meaning. Three women buy land on the hillside hard by a poverty-stricken village whose inhabitants view them with gentle bewilderment." Publ Wkly

"Doerr instills each of her memorable characters with great dignity and resilience, and bestows upon her entranced readers a deep sense of peace and wonder." Booklist

Stones for Ibarra. Viking 1984 214p o.p.

LC 83-47861

"When Sara and Richard Everton pack up their belongings and mortgage themselves to leave California for a small village in Mexico, their friends think they are crazy. Many of the Mexican natives in the village of Ibarra also consider the two gringos incredible. While Sara restores the house that had belonged to Richard's grandparents, Richard restores a copper mine that had been his family's, and thereby gives employment to many of the villagers. We learn that Richard has leukemia and has been given just a few years to live, but it is the lives of the villagers that are more full of tragedy, religious commitment, and reliance on talismans and prayers. There is a strength among these people and an acceptance of all that life brings which make them memorable. Learning from them, perhaps, Sara finally accepts the inevitability of her husband's death." Shapiro. Fic for Youth. 3d edition

Doherty, P. C.

The assassin in the greenwood. St. Martin's Press 1994 217p $19.95

ISBN 0-312-11554-7   LC 94-3325

First published 1993 in the United Kingdom

"Dispatched to Nottingham to investigate the sheriff's murder, Sir Hugh Corbett, agent of 14th-century King Edward I, learns that Robin Hood has apparently claimed responsibility. Corbett, of course, suspects otherwise." Libr J

"As Doherty's cinematic descriptions zero in on hangings, throat-slittings and torture, with filth, stench and gore galore, Corbett battles his way to a smashing—if predictable—solution." Publ Wkly

The masked man. St. Martin's Press 1991 174p o.p.

LC 91-20033

Doherty, P. C.—*Continued*

This novel "offers a plausible, fact-based solution to the identity of the Man in the Iron Mask. The Duke of Orleans frees imprisoned Englishman Ralph Croft so that the cunning forger can use his underworld contacts to determine the name of the disguised prisoner, now dead some 16 years. Forced to work with a dangerous archivist and a duplicitous soldier, Croft dodges assassins and tangles with secretive Knights Templar as he deciphers ambiguous clues." Libr J

"A tour de force of retrospective detection." Booklist

Doig, Ivan

Dancing at the Rascal Fair. Atheneum Pubs. 1987 405p o.p.

LC 87-18672

Chronologically the first in the author's Montana trilogy

"The settlement of Montana between 1890 and 1919 is recounted through the quiet but compelling life of Angus McCaskill, a young Scotsman who travels with his friend Rob Barclay to Montana's Two Medicine Country to homestead." Libr J

"If the thorny individualism of Rob and Angus results in lives that are never easy, they are rich in incident and growth, beautifully described in Doig's strong, savory prose. America's frontier history comes vividly to life in this absorbing saga filled with memorable characters." Publ Wkly

English Creek. Atheneum Pubs. 1984 339p o.p. Smith, P. reprint available $20.75 (ISBN 0-8446-6608-4)

LC 84-45051

This volume in the Montana trilogy chronologically follows Dancing at the Rascal Fair

"In the summer of 1939, in the high country of western Montana, 14-year-old Jick McCaskill wants to understand who he is and why. He lives in a boy's dream of wilderness, mountains, sheep ranches, national forests, and an amazing variety of small-town characters. His father is a forest ranger, his mother a practical, hard-nosed local woman; his brother wants to forego college for a girl and a cowboy's life. The summer climaxes in a forest fire that leads Jick and his father to discuss and understand some painful hidden events of their personal histories." Libr J

This "is a sensitive coming-of-age story as well as a portrait of a society still looking to its frontier past, but about to be engulfed by the future. The result is both highly personal and deeply engaging." Best Sellers

Ride with me, Mariah Montana. Atheneum Pubs. 1990 324p $18.95

ISBN 0-689-12019-2   LC 90-35834

Also available Thorndike Press large print edition

Concluding volume of the author's Montana trilogy

"To explore the meaning of Montana's century of statehood, 65-year-old Jick McCaskill, his photographer daughter Mariah, and her newspaper columnist ex-husband Riley Wright tour the Treasure State in Jick's Winnebago. While Riley writes on-the-scene dispatches and Mariah takes photos of the places they visit, Jick, the narrator, recounts the state's—and his family's—good and bad times. A lengthy picaresque with innumerable well-crafted vignettes, this leisurely novel could easily serve as a tour guide of Montana's historic places. As the miles go by, Riley and Mariah again fall in and

out of love, and Jick, a widower, unexpectedly finds a new mate." Libr J

The sea runners. Atheneum Pubs. 1982 279p o.p. Smith, P. reprint available $20.50 (ISBN 0-8446-6538-X)

LC 82-45174

"In 1853 many of the pioneers in Russian Alaska were Scandinavians indentured for seven years in the tsar's service. Four of these men, little better than slaves, resolve to steal a boat and escape from New Archangel (now Sitka) to Astoria, at the mouth of the Columbia River. In an open cedar canoe packed with stolen provisions they traverse the most forbidding and beautiful coastline of America." Libr J

"Blending historical detail and believable dialogue with a remarkable ability to describe the natural world, Doig has fashioned a delightful adventure novel. . . . [The author] does a good job establishing the strained relationship between the escapees, and he is equally effective at evoking the immense physical strains of such a seemingly impossible journey." Booklist

Donaldson, Stephen R.

The gap into madness: chaos and order. Bantam Bks. 1994 617p $22.95

ISBN 0-553-07179-3   LC 94-5850

Fourth volume in the author's far-future series; earlier titles are: The real story (1991), Forbidden knowledge: the gap into vision (1991), and A dark and hungry God arises: the gap into power (1992)

"Pursued by a police battle cruiser, by a bounty hunter and by a ship commanded by human agents of the dreaded Amnion, an alien race, Angus Thermopyl heads his ship, *Trumpet,* for an illegal lab hidden in a chaotic asteroid belt. There, Thermopyle, once a fearsome pirate, now a cyborg partially controlled by police programming, plans to have the secret 'antimutagen,' which protects humans against the forced mutation practiced by the Amnion, replicated for mass distribution. . . . [This novel] offers plenty of thrills and an exciting finish." Publ Wkly

The Illearth war. Holt, Rinehart & Winston 1977 407p il o.p.

LC 77-8621

"The chronicles of Thomas Covenant, the Unbeliever, Book 2"

In this second volume, Lord Foul the Despiser continues his attack against the Land with the Illearth Stone. Covenant and the daughter of the High Lord, Elena, undertake a mission into a mountain region, where they hope they will find the ancient gnostic power that will combat the Stone

Lord Foul's bane. Holt, Rinehart & Winston 1977 369p il o.p.

LC 77-73868

"The chronicles of Thomas Covenant, the Unbeliever, Book 1"

Thomas Covenant, a man burdened with a stigma that has isolated him, is suddenly sent to a mysterious magic world known as the Land. The Land has an immortal enemy—Lord Foul the Despiser—who wishes to destroy it. In Thomas, who does not believe in the Land's life-restoring powers, Lord Foul thinks he has found the perfect tool for his purpose

Donaldson, Stephen R.—*Continued*

The One Tree. Ballantine Bks. 1982 475p $14.50

ISBN 0-345-29898-5   LC 81-17596

"A Del Rey book"

This is the central volume of the second trilogy about the Land

"Book two of the Second Chronicles of Thomas Covenant"

"Covenant finds that his role as savior of the Land must be shared with another from our world, Dr. Linden Avery. . . . To stop Lord Foul's terrible concatenation of plagues, the Sunbane, they sail with giants on a granite ship in search of the One Tree. Covenant hopes to fashion from it a new Staff of the Law to restore the natural order Foul has overturned." Publ Wkly

The power that preserves. Holt, Rinehart & Winston 1977 379p il o.p.

     LC 77-10814

"The chronicles of Thomas Covenant, the Unbeliever, Book 3"

In this final volume of the first trilogy Covenant makes his way to the stronghold of Lord Foul the Despiser. He is accompanied by his friend Saltheart Foamfollower, a Giant. But it is Covenant who must meet Foul in final combat, to ensure survival for the Land and to achieve salvation for himself

"Below the stirring adventure tale is a poignant and profoundly religious chronicle of a quest for self-esteem and peace." Booklist

White gold wielder. Ballantine Bks. 1983 485p il $14.95

ISBN 0-345-30307-5   LC 82-20640

"A Del Rey book"

This is the concluding volume of the second trilogy about the Land

"Book three of the Second Chronicles of Thomas Covenant"

"At the end of 'The One Tree,' Covenant failed to create a new Staff of Law to deliver the Land from the Sunbane, so he, Linden Avery, and their companions set out across the northern wastes to Revelstone, where Covenant extinguishes the Banefire. The paradox of white gold and venom has set him against his friends, however; when he faces Lord Foul at Mount Thunder, they believe that he will betray the Land, until that enigmatic created being, Vain, achieves his destiny." Libr J

The wounded Land. Ballantine Bks. 1980 497p il o.p.

     LC 79-20644

"A Del Rey book"

This is the first volume of the second trilogy about the Land

"Book one of the Second Chronicles of Thomas Covenant"

"In the first of the second trilogy of his adventures, leper Thomas Covenant returns to the mysterious Land after nearly 4000 years have passed there (ten years in earth time). Dr. Linden Avery unexpectedly joins him and goes through the same denial and disbelief he had suffered before. Now the Land is suffering from unending plagues called the Sunbane, inflicted by the evil Lord Foul whom Covenant had defeated but not destroyed on his last visit. Although it is not necessary to have read the previous three to appreciate the breadth and scope of this grim fantasy, for those who have 'The Wounded Land' is absolutely compelling." SLJ

Donleavy, J. P. (James Patrick), 1926-

The ginger man. Complete and unexpurgated ed. Delacorte Press/Seymour Lawrence 1965 347p o.p.

Original French edition, 1955; first United States expurgated edition published 1958 by McDowell, Obolensky

"The central character, Sebastian Dangerfield, an American expatriate law student at Dublin's Trinity College, is the brawling outsider who lives in a world of fantasy to escape despair and loneliness. Donleavy uses the third person to describe what Dangerfield does, the first person to reveal his thoughts, enabling him to be both objective and subjective." Reader's Ency. 3d edition

The author's writing "is distinguished by humor, often inelegant, even coarse, but explosive and irresistible. Humor and poetry are his weapons. The whole novel is a wild and unpredictable outburst." Saturday Rev

Donleavy, James Patrick *See* Donleavy, J. P. (James Patrick), 1926-

Donnelly, Gabrielle

For works written by this author in collaboration with Julia Braun Kessler see Barrett, Julia

Donoso, José

A house in the country; a novel; translated by David Pritchard with Suzanne Jill Levine. Knopf 1984 352p o.p.

     LC 83-11975

Original Spanish edition, 1978

"The setting is an unnamed country on an isolated estate where the Ventura family fritters away the summer while outside the oppressed natives work the family's gold mines and bands of (possibly nonexistent) cannibals reportedly roam the countryside. When the adults leave for a day's excursion, the children erupt into rebellion, tearing down the fence that surrounds the estate and joining the natives in an orgy of anarchy and destruction. The return of the adults only intensifies the struggle, and the novel closes with everyone helpless in the face of the deadly annual thistle-down storm that blankets the estate. Parallels with the political situation in Donoso's native Chile are obvious throughout." Publ Wkly

"Donoso's impressive array of styles and techniques, his astonishing imagination melded to a playful, almost frivolous tone powerfully mirror the tragic Latin American experience. Levine's compelling translation is excellent." Libr J

Dorris, Michael

The crown of Columbus; a novel; [by] Michael Dorris, Louise Erdrich. HarperCollins Pubs. 1991 382p $22.95

ISBN 0-06-016079-9   LC 90-55964

"Told in the very different voices of college professor lovers Vivian Twostar, Native American single mother, and Roger Williams, poet of an old New England family, the collaborative effort flows smoothly. Although estranged during Vivian's pregnancy, both are working on academic projects concerning the 500th anniversary of the discovery of North America by Columbus. The

Dorris, Michael—*Continued*
collision of their two lives is funny, vivid, and life-affirming." Libr J

Working men; stories. Holt & Co. 1993 286p $19.95

ISBN 0-8050-2296-1   LC 93-25558

Analyzed in Short story index
Contents: The benchmark; Earnest money; Qiana; Name games; Groom service; Anything; The vase; Me and the girls; Jeopardy; The dark snake; Oui; Layaway; Shining agate; Decoration Day
"Dorris explores the inner terrain of dignified characters graced with exceptional patience and a profound, reflective reticence. In story after story, Dorris examines the power of unspoken emotions, the elusive but invaluable messages of silence, and the unforeseen leaps of faith that change lives and jump start love." Booklist

A yellow raft in blue water. Holt & Co. 1987 343p $16.95

ISBN 0-8050-0045-3   LC 86-26947

"Three American Indian women of three generations tell their stories in a reverse chronology. Rayona, her mother Christine, and her grandmother Ida, share with the reader their troubled lives and Native American culture. Rayona, whose father was black, perhaps has more obstacles to face than her forebears. Although she is the first narrator, the succeeding two chapters explain how she came to be abandoned by her mother and why her mother, Christine, had so dificult a relationship with her own mother, Ida. Christine's brother, Lee, and his best friend, Dayton, are important characters in this compelling story." Shapiro. Fic For Youth. 3d edition

Dos Passos, John
The 42nd parallel. Harper 1930 426p o.p.

First volume of the author's U.S.A. trilogy
The characters "include Fainy McCreary ('Mac'), who eventually joins the Mexican Revolution; the ruthless J. Ward Moorehouse; Eleanor Stoddard, with whom he has an affair; and Charley Anderson, who later becomes a war hero and airplane manufacturer. These various interlocking strands are designed to show the U.S. on the eve of the First World War, rather than the development of particular individuals." Reader's Ency. 3d edition
Followed by 1919

also in Dos Passos, J. U.S.A. v1

1919. Harcourt Brace & Co. 1932 473p o.p. Amereon reprint available $25.95 (ISBN 0-88411-345-0)
In this second volume of the trilogy, the author continues his chronicle of life in America through the war years, giving glimpses of the lives and characters of five young Americans—a low caste sailor, the daughter of a Chicago minister, a young girl from Texas, a radical Jew, a young poet
"'1919' is literally what so many books are erroneously called, 'a slice of life.' With infinite skill that slicing is done by the author, and the raw surface which meets the reader's eye is the actual living, breathing record of a period in its most intense manifestation." Chicago Daily Trib
Followed by The big money (1936)

also in Dos Passos, J. U.S.A v2

The big money

In Dos Passos, J. U.S.A. v3

Manhattan transfer. Harper 1925 404p o.p. Bentley reprint available $22 (ISBN 0-8376-0433-8)
"Dos Passos creates a portrait of New York City in the first quarter of this century by telling the stories of many people. They include the daughter of an accountant, who loses hope for any future happiness when her first love commits suicide; a milkman who rises in status to become a union boss; and an immigrant sailor who starts as a bartender and becomes a wealthy bootlegger during Prohibition. There are happy and unhappy endings to these stories, but always the city plays an important role." Shapiro. Fic for Youth. 3d edition

U.S.A. Harcourt Brace & Co. 1937 3v in 1 o.p.
An omnibus volume containing the trilogy titles: The 42nd parallel, first published 1930; 1919, first published 1932 and The big money, first published 1936. The first two titles are entered separately
"U.S.A. tries to capture, through a diversity of fictional techniques, the variety and multiplicity of American life in the first decades of the 20th cent.; it presents various interlocking and parallel narratives, against a panoramic collage of real-life events, snatches of newsreel and popular song, advertisements, etc., with a commentary by the author as 'The Camera Eye.'" Oxford Companion to Engl Lit

Dostoevskiĭ, Fedor Mikhaĭlovich *See* Dostoyevsky, Fyodor, 1821-1881

Dostoyevsky, Fyodor, 1821-1881
The best short stories of Dostoevsky; translated with an introduction by David Magarshack. Modern Lib. 1992 xxvii, 348p $14.50

ISBN 0-679-60020-5   LC 92-50214

Analyzed in Short story index
First Modern Library edition 1955
Contents: White nights; The honest thief; The Christmas tree and a wedding; The peasant Marey; Notes from the underground; A gentle creature; The dream of a ridiculous man

The brothers Karamazov.
Available from various publishers

Written 1880
"The main plot involves Fyodor Pavlovich 'Karamazov' and his four sons: Dmitry, Ivan, Alyosha, and the bastard Smerdyakov. Fyodor Pavlovich, a depraved buffoon, is Dmitry's rival for the affections of the local siren, 'Grushenka'. Violent quarrels over her and over Dmitry's disputed inheritance ensue until Fyodor Pavlovich is murdered. Dmitry is arrested and brought to trial for the crime. This basic line of action is complicated throughout the novel by a host of other factors masterfully linked to the main plot. . . . The literal, religious, social, and ethical levels of the novel are buttressed by the psychological probings for which Dostoyevsky is well known." Reader's Ency. 3d edition

Crime and punishment.
Available from various publishers

Written 1866
"The novel is a psychological analysis of the poor student Raskolnikov, whose theory that humanitarian ends justify evil means leads him to murder a St. Peters-

Dostoyevsky, Fyodor, 1821-1881—*Continued*
burg pawnbroker. The act produces nightmarish guilt in
Raskolnikov. The narrative's feverish, compelling tone
follows the twists and turns of Raskolnikov's emotions
and elaborates his struggle with his conscience and his
mounting sense of horror as he wanders the city's hot,
crowded streets. In prison, Raskolnikov comes to the
realization that happiness cannot be achieved by a
reasoned plan of existence but must be earned by suffering." Merriam-Webster's Ency of Lit

Demons; a novel in three parts; translated
and annotated by Richard Pevear and
Larissa Volokhonsky. Knopf 1994 xxvii,
733p $25

ISBN 0-679-73451-1   LC 93-33367

Original Russian edition, 1892; first United States edition published 1913 by Macmillan with title: The possessed. Variant title: The devils
"Loosely based on sensational press reports of a
Moscow student's murder by fellow revolutionists, *The
Possessed* depicts the destructive chaos caused by outside
agitators who move into a moribund provincial town.
The enigmatic Stavrogin dominates the novel. His
magnetic personality influences his tutor, the liberal intellectual poseur Stepan Verkhovensky, and the teacher's
revolutionary son Pyotr, as well as other radicals. Stavrogin is portrayed as a man of strength without direction,
capable of goodness and nobility. When Stavrogin loses
his faith in God, however, he is seized by brutal desires
he does not fully understand. in the end, Stavrogin hangs
himself in what he believes is an act of generosity, and
Stepan Verkhovensky is received into the church on his
deathbed." Merriam-Webster's Ency of Lit

The double

In Dostoyevsky, F. The short novels of
Dostoevsky p475-615

The eternal husband

In Dostoyevsky, F. The short novels of
Dostoevsky p343-473

The friend of the family

In Dostoyevsky, F. The short novels of
Dostoyevsky p617-811

The gambler; with Polina Suslova's diary;
[by] Fyodor Dostoevsky; translated by Victor
Terras; edited by Edward Wasiolek.
University of Chicago Press 1972 xxxix,
366p o.p.

Written 1866
"The gambling mania of the tale's hero, Aleksey
Ivanovich, is a reflection of the author's own weakness.
The heroine of the story, Polina, is based on Polina
Suslova, Dostoevski's lover in 1862-1863." Reader's Ency.
3d edition
"The book contains, in addition to the main narrative,
the diary kept by Polina Suslova detailing her affair with
Dostoevskii, which he limns so graphically in the novel,
a short story titled 'The stranger and her lover' also by
Suslova, and a selection of letters exchanged between
Dostoevskii and Suslova among others." Booklist

also in Dostoyevsky, F. The gambler,
and other stories

also in Dostoyevsky, F. The short
novels of Dostoevsky p1-126

The gambler, and other stories; by Fyodor
Dostoevsky; from the Russian by Constance
Garnett. Macmillan 1917 312p o.p.

Analyzed in Short story index
First published 1914 in the United Kingdom
This volume contains two novelettes: The gambler, entered separately above, and Poor people, written 1846,
which has also appeared with the title: Poor folk. It also
contains the story: The landlady
Poor people "tells of an impoverished, elderly clerk's
hopeless struggle for respectability while concealing his
love for an orphaned girl in a sentimentally expressed,
paternal affection. An uncommon insight into the tragic
futility of poor people in love is revealed, people victimized by cruel circumstances of contemporary society."
Ency Britannica

The house of the dead; or, Prison life in
Siberia. o.p.

First published in Russian in 1861-62; in English in
1881 under title: Buried alive. Variant titles: Prison life
in Siberia, Memorials of a dead house and Memoirs
from the house of the dead
"In this autobiography of a Russian landowner condemned to penal servitude in Siberia, Dostoevsky hardly
troubles to disguise his own experiences. He traces the
different effects of imprisonment on the moral nature,
in the life-stories of a group of criminals. It is a terrible
record of the anguish of the prisoner's lot." Baker. Guide
to the Best Fic

The idiot.

Available from Buccaneer Bks.
Written 1868
"Dostoevsky puts into a world of foolishness, vice,
pretence, and sordid ambitions, a being who in childhood
had suffered from mental disease, and who with an intellect of more than ordinary power retains the simplicity
and clear insight of a child. In the 'Idiot,' he tried to
realize his idea of 'a truly perfect and noble man'; this
Prince Myshkin of his, an epileptic like himself, is the
champion of humanity. The deeply absorbing drama in
which he is a protagonist turns on the salvation of a
woman, Nastasya Filipovna who had been corrupted in
young girlhood." Baker. Guide to the Best Fic

Notes from underground; translated and
annotated by Richard Pevear and Larissa
Volokhonsky. Knopf 1993 xxiii, 136p $20

ISBN 0-679-42315-X   LC 92-32581

Written 1864. Variant titles: Letters from the underworld and Memoirs from underground
"The work, which includes extremely misanthropic passages, contains the seeds of nearly all of the moral, religious, political, and social concerns that appear in
Dostoyevsky's great novels. Written as a reaction against
Nikolay Chernyshevsky's ideological novel *What Is to Be
Done?* (1863), which offered a planned utopia based on
'natural' laws of self-interest, *Notes from the Underground* attacks the scientism and rationalism at the heart
of Chernyshevsky's novel. The views and actions of
Dostoyevsky's underground man demostrate that in asserting free will humans often act against self-interest."
Merriam-Webster's Ency of Lit

also in Dostoyevsky, F. The best short

Dostoyevsky, Fyodor, 1821-1881—*Continued*
stories of Dostoyevsky p115-260

also in Dostoyevsky, F. The short
novels of Dostoevsky p127-222

Poor people

In Dostoyevsky, F. The gambler, and
other stories

The short novels of Dostoevsky; with an
introduction by Thomas Mann. Dial Press
1945 xx, 811p o.p.
Partially analyzed in Short story index
Contents: The gambler; Notes from underground;
Uncle's dream; The eternal husband; The double; The
friend of the family

Uncle's dream

In Dostoyevsky, F. The short novels of
Dostoevsky p223-342

Douglas, Carole Nelson
Catnap; a Midnight Louie mystery. TOR
Bks. 1992 241p o.p.

LC 91-33293

"A Tom Doherty Associates book"
"Midnight Louie, whose cat-memoirs bracket the
discovery of a murdered book publisher at the American
Booksellers Association, 'helps' public relations person
Temple Barr discover the murderer's identity. Las Vegas
provides a slightly surreal backdrop for Temple's
'smooth' friends and sly acquaintances, who alternately
provide assistance or muck things up." Libr J
"Douglas's fine-turned sense of humor gives her tame
plot enough of a spin to keep readers entertained." Publ
Wkly

Douglas, Lloyd C. (Lloyd Cassel), 1877-1951
The Big Fisherman. Houghton Mifflin
1948 581p o.p.
"More than a fictional biography of the Apostle, Simon
Peter, this . . . novel re-creates the Biblical background
and personages of the time. Romance and adventure
enter in the form of an Arabian prince who is searching
for a beautiful Jewish-Arabian princess." Cincinnati
Public Libr
"With the exception of the Arabian scenes, the story
follows the biblical account of Peter, necessarily much
condensed. The personalities of Peter and others of the
disciples receive interesting and plausible interpretations;
the modern idiom is used with somewhat startling effect,
and frequent references are made to many persons actual
and fictitious who appeared in 'The Robe'." Booklist

Magnificent obsession. Houghton Mifflin
1929 330p $22.95

ISBN 0-395-07634-X
Also available from Buccaneer Bks.; large print edition
available from Thorndike Press
The "magnificent obsession" that was the secret of the
famous Dr. Hudson's success—a newly interpreted Christian teaching—was put into practice at Dr. Hudson's
death by the young man who became his successor as
a brain specialist, Bobby Merrick. Bobby, by continuing
his 'personality-investments' in the way of secret philan-
thropies, as advocated by Dr. Hudson's formula,
miraculously succeeds, and makes a famous surgical

invention with which he is able to save the life of the
woman he loves
Followed by Doctor Hudson's secret journal (1939)

The robe. Houghton Mifflin 1942 556p
$21.95

ISBN 0-395-07635-8
"The story of Christ's robe and the influence it had
on the wealthy young Roman soldier who won it at dice.
Marcellus' personal affairs and conversion to Christianity
are of chief interest, but with them is given a picture
of the rise of Christianity in the first few years after
Christ's crucifixion." Booklist
"Perhaps the narrative is a bit too diffuse and attempts
to cover too much ground, but on the whole it is an
interesting effort at explaining a time of crisis that has
many points of similarity to our own. It is a skillful
storytelling with high intent." Christ Century

Dove, Rita
Through the ivory gate; a novel. Pantheon
Bks. 1992 278p $21

ISBN 0-679-41604-8 LC 92-4456
"Virginia King, a talented young black woman, returns
to her hometown of Akron, Ohio, as artist-in-residence
at an elementary school. The story moves back and forth
between the present, which finds her teaching puppetry
to children, and her past, which includes memories of
a constricting community and family life and the liberation offered by college and her stint with a communal
puppet theater." Publ Wkly
"Whether she is evoking the look of a landscape or
depicting the nuances of a family quarrel, Dove sees with
the keen eye of an artist and writes with the finely
honed diction of a poet. In Virginia King, she has
created a distinctive, highly individualized heroine."
Christ Sci Monit

Doyle, Sir Arthur Conan, 1859-1930
Adventures of Sherlock Holmes; by A.
Conan Doyle. Harper 1892 307p il o.p.
Buccaneer Bks. reprint available $25.95
(ISBN 0-89966-385-0)
Analyzed in Short story index
Contains the following stories: Scandal in Bohemia;
Redheaded League; Case of identity; Boscombe Valley
mystery; Five orange pips; Man with the twisted lip;
Adventure of the Blue Carbuncle; Adventure of the
speckled band; Adventure of the engineer's thumb;
Adventure of the noble bachelor; Adventure of the Beryl
Coronet; Adventure of the copper beeches

also in Doyle, Sir A. C. The complete
Sherlock Holmes

The best science fiction of Arthur Conan
Doyle; edited by Charles G. Waugh and
Martin H. Greenberg; with an introduction
by George E. Slusser. Southern Ill. Univ.
Press 1981 190p $19.95

ISBN 0-8093-1046-5 LC 81-8884
"Alternatives"
Analyzed in Short story index
Contents: The American's tale; The Los Amigos fiasco;
The great Keinplatz experiment; The adventure of the
devil's foot; The adventure of the creeping man; The
terror of Blue John Gap; Through the veil; The last

Doyle, Sir Arthur Conan, 1859-1930—*Continued*

galley; The great Brown-Pericord motor; The horror of the heights; Danger; The lift; The disintegration machine; When the world screamed

"The 14 pieces inevitably include a couple of Sherlock Holmes stories. They also include 2 of the not-so-readily-available Professor Challenger tales . . . and 10 other stories spread over more than 40 years of the author's career." Booklist

The case book of Sherlock Holmes

In Doyle, Sir A. C. The complete Sherlock Holmes

The complete Sherlock Holmes; with a preface by Christopher Morley. Doubleday 1960 c1930 1122p $25

ISBN 0-385-00689-6

Analyzed in Short story index

First published 1930 by Doubleday, Doran

Contents: Study in scarlet (1887); Sign of four (1890); Adventures of Sherlock Holmes (1892); Memoirs of Sherlock Holmes (1894); Return of Sherlock Holmes (1905); Hound of the Baskervilles (1902); Valley of fear (1915); His last bow (1917); Case book of Sherlock Holmes (1927)

Contents for the short story volumes included in the above are as follows:

Adventures of Sherlock Holmes: Scandal in Bohemia; Red-headed League; Case of identity; Boscombe Valley mystery; Five orange pips; Man with the twisted lip; Adventure of the Blue Carbuncle; Adventure of the speckled band; Adventure of the engineer's thumb; Adventure of the noble bachelor; Adventure of the Beryl Coronet; Adventure of the copper beeches

Memoirs of Sherlock Holmes: Silver Blaze; Yellow face; Stockbroker's clerk; The 'Gloria Scott'; Musgrave ritual; Reigate puzzle; Crooked man; Resident patient; Greek interpreter; Naval treaty; Final problem

Return of Sherlock Holmes: Adventure of the empty house; Adventure of the Norwood builders; Adventure of the dancing men; Adventure of the solitary cyclist; Adventure of the priory school; Adventure of Black Peter; Adventure of Charles Augustus Milverton; Adventure of the six Napoleons; Adventure of the three students; Adventure of the golden pince-nez; Adventure of the missing three-quarter; Adventure of the Abbey Grange; Adventure of the second stain

His last bow: Adventure of Wisteria Lodge; Adventure of the cardboard box; Adventure of the red circle; Adventure of the Bruce-Partington plans; Adventure of the dying detective; Disappearance of Lady Frances Carfax; Adventure of the Devil's foot; His last bow

Case book of Sherlock Holmes: Adventure of the illustrious client; Adventure of the blanched soldier; Adventure of the Mazarin stone; Adventure of the Three Gables; Adventure of the Sussex vampire; Adventure of the three Garridebs; Problem of Thor Bridge; Adventure of the creeping man; Adventure of the lion's mane; Adventure of the veiled lodger; Adventure of Shoscombe Old Place; Adventure of the retired colourman

Conan Doyle's tales of medical humanism and values: Round the red lamp; being facts and fancies of medical life, with other medical short stories; edited with introduction, commentaries, and notes by Alvin E. Rodin and Jack D. Key. Krieger 1992 481p il $48.50

ISBN 0-89464-571-4 LC 90-24909

Analyzed in Short story index

This volume includes the collection Round the red lamp which was first published in 1894

Round the red lamp includes the following stories: Behind the times; His first operation; A straggler of '15; The third generation; A false start; The curse of Eve; Sweethearts; A physiologist's wife; The case of Lady Sannox; A question of diplomacy; A medical document; Lot no. 249; The Los Amigos fiasco; The doctors of Hoyland; The surgeon talks

Other stories included in this volume are: Crabbe's practice; The great Keinplatz experiment; The ring of thoth

Famous tales of Sherlock Holmes. Dodd, Mead 1958 339p il o.p.

"Great illustrated classics"

Analyzed in Short story index

"With biographical illustrations and pictures from early editions of the stories, together with an introduction by William C. Weber." Title page

Contents: A study in scarlet (1887); A scandal in Bohemia; The Red-headed League; The sign of the four (1890); The Boscombe Valley mystery

His last bow

In Doyle, Sir A. C. The complete Sherlock Holmes

The hound of the Baskervilles.

Available from various publishers

First published 1902

This is the "case of the eerie howling on the moor and strange deaths at Baskerville. Sir Charles Baskerville is murdered, and Holmes and Watson move in to solve the crime." Haydn. Thesaurus of Book Dig

"By a miracle of judgment, the supernatural is handled with great effect and no letdown. The plot and subplots are thoroughly integrated and the false clues put in and removed with a master hand. The criminal is superb, Dr. Mortimer memorable, and the secondary figures each contribute to the total effect of brilliancy and grandeur combined. One wishes one could be reading it for the first time." Barzun. Cat of Crime. Rev and enl edition

also in Doyle, Sir A. C. The complete Sherlock Holmes

The lost world. Doran, G.H. 1912 309p il o.p.

Available from Amereon and Buccaneer Bks.

"Two professors and two other Englishmen come across a region in the Amazon valley where the Jurassic period still persists, with its flora and fauna, pterodactyls, dinosaurs, iguanodons, and other beasts that we know only in fossil form, still flourishing. The scientific squabbles of Challenger and the other professor provide incidental comedy." Baker. Guide to the Best Fic

Memoirs of Sherlock Holmes

In Doyle, Sir A. C. The complete Sherlock Holmes

Doyle, Sir Arthur Conan, 1859-1930 —
Continued

The return of Sherlock Holmes; a fac-simile of the stories as they were first published in The Strand Magazine, London; with Sidney Paget's original illustrations and with a new introduction by Samuel Rosenberg. Schocken Bks. 1975 193p il o.p.

Analyzed in Short story index
Originally published 1903-1904 in The Strand Magazine
Contents: The adventure of the empty house; The adventure of the Norwood builder; The adventure of the dancing men; The adventure of the solitary cyclist; The adventure of the Priory School; The adventure of Black Peter; The adventure of Charles Augustus Milverton; The adventure of the six Napoleons; The adventure of the three students; The adventure of the golden pinz-nez; The adventure of the missing three-quarter; The adventure of Abbey Grange; The adventure of the second stain

also in Doyle, Sir A. C. The complete Sherlock Holmes

Round the red lamp

In Doyle, Sir A. C. Conan Doyle's tales of medical humanism and values p15-302

The sign of four; with an introduction by Graham Greene. Doubleday 1977 134p o.p. Buccaneer Bks. reprint available $15.95 (ISBN 0-89966-230-7)

First published 1890 in the United Kingdom. Variant title: The sign of the four
Mary Morstan, the future wife of Dr. Watson, engages Holmes to trace her vanished father. Four years after his disappearance, Miss Morstan began receiving an annual gift of a large and lustrous pearl. Now her unknown benefactor has summoned her to a rendezvous outside the Lyceum Theater. As Holmes unravels the mystery, the Agra pearls are seen to be the center of a grim tale of murder and duplicity, which begins in India and ends in a chase through London's dockland

also in Doyle, Sir A. C. The complete Sherlock Holmes

also in Doyle, Sir A. C. Famous tales of Sherlock Holmes p187-311

A study in scarlet; with an introduction by Hugh Greene. Doubleday 1977 145p o.p. Buccaneer Bks. reprint available $15.95 (ISBN 0-89966-231-5)

First published 1887
"A sensational story in two parts: the first deals with adventures in Utah and the wrong committed by two brutal Mormons on a girl and her lover; the second is the history of a mysterious double murder committed in London and, by the agency of Sherlock Holmes, shown to be the work of the wronged lover, who thus, after many years, attains his revenge." Baker. Guide to the Best Fic

also in Doyle, Sir A. C. The complete Sherlock Holmes

also in Doyle, Sir A. C. Famous tales of Sherlock Holmes p1-131

Tales of terror and mystery; introduction by Nina Conan Doyle Harwood; illustrated by Barbara Ninde Byfield. Doubleday 1977 224p il o.p. Buccaneer Bks. reprint available $16.95 (ISBN 0-89966-429-6)

LC 75-36589

Analyzed in Short story index
Contents: The horror of the heights; The leather funnel; The new catacomb; The case of Lady Sannox; The terror of Blue John Gap; The Brazilian cat; The lost special; The beetle-hunter; The man with the watches; The japanned box; The black doctor; The jew's breast plate; The nightmare room

Uncollected stories; the unknown Conan Doyle; compiled and with an introduction by John Michael Gibson and Richard Lancelyn Green. Doubleday 1984 c1982 xxiii, 456p o.p.

LC 83-45159

Analyzed in Short story index
First published 1982 in the United Kingdom
Contents: The mystery of Sasassa Valley; The American's tale; Bones. The April fool of Harvey's Sluice; Our Derby sweepstakes; That veteran; Gentleman-ly Joe; The winning shot; An exciting Christmas Eve; Selecting a ghost. The ghosts of Goresthorpe Grange; The heiress of Glenmahowley; The cabman's story; The tragedians; The lonely Hampshire cottage; The fate of the Evangeline; Touch and go: a midshipman's story; Uncle Jeremy's household; The stone of Boxman's Drift; A pastoral horror; Our midnight visitor; The voice of science; The Colonel's choice; A sordid affair; A regimental scandal; The recollections of Captain Wilkie; The confession; The retirement of Signor Lambert; A true story of the tragedy of 'Flowery Land'; An impression of the Regency; The centurion; The death voyage; The Parish Magazine; The end of Devil Hawker; The last resource

This collection "runs the time gamut from 1879 to 1930 and includes ten tales never previously identified with Doyle. His work here is somewhat uneven but usually readable and covers a diverse range of styles and subjects. There are occasional Holmesian insights, but there's nary a sleuthing story in the lot." West Coast Rev Books

The valley of fear; a Sherlock Holmes novel; illustrated by Arthur I. Keller. Doran, G.H. 1915 320p il o.p.

Available from Amereon and Buccaneer Bks.
First published 1914
"With the exception of 'The Hound of the Baskervilles,' our favorite among the long tales of Sherlock Holmes. Chapter 1 has in its ten pages some of the best wit and humor to be found anywhere, plus the solution of a cipher, and a stunning punch ending. Nor is there any serious letdown as Holmes, Watson, and Inspector MacDonald investigate the murder of John Douglas at Birlstone Manor in Sussex. The shadow of Moriarty appears early and comes into sharper focus at the end of the story after the long—and gripping—interlude dealing with Douglas' life among the 'scowrers' of the Pennsylvania coalfields." Barzun. Cat of Crime. Rev and enl edition

also in Doyle, Sir A. C. The complete Sherlock Holmes

Doyle, Sir Arthur Conan, 1859-1930 — *Continued*

The White Company; by A. Conan Doyle; pictures by N. C. Wyeth. Morrow 1988 366p il $17

ISBN 0-688-07817-6   LC 87-62625

Also available from Buccaneer Bks.

First published 1891; this is a reissue of the edition published 1922 by Cosmopolitan Book Corporation

"The Hampshire hero joins an English Free Company, and, in the course of much wandering through France and the Pyrenees, meets with stirring adventures and performs many a deed of valour. The historical situation is that arising out of the Black Prince's decision to espouse the cause of Pedro the Cruel of Castile. Edward III, the Black Prince, Chandos, Sir William Felton, Bertrand du Guesclin, Don Pedro and others appear." Nield. Guide to the Best Hist Novels & Tales

Doyle, Conan *See* Doyle, Sir Arthur Conan, 1859-1930

Doyle, Roddy

Paddy Clarke, ha ha ha. Viking 1993 282p $20.95

ISBN 0-670-85345-3

"Set in the working-class environment of an Irish town in the late 1960s, the story is related by bright, sensitive 10-year-old Paddy Clarke, who, when we first meet him, is merely concerned with being as tough as his peers. Paddy and his best friend Kevin are part of a neighborhood gang that sets fires in vacant buildings, routinely teases and abuses younger kids and plays in forbidden places. In episodic fashion, Doyle conveys the activities, taboos and ceremonies, the daring glee and often distorted sense of the world of boys verging on adolescence." Publ Wkly

Doyle's "triumph in this novel is to replenish our sense of how children think and speak and explain the adult world to themselves." London Rev Books

Dozois, Gardner R.

(ed) Modern classic short novels of science fiction. See Modern classic short novels of science fiction

(ed) Modern classics of science fiction. See Modern classics of science fiction

(ed) The Year's best science fiction. See The Year's best science fiction

Drabble, Margaret, 1939-

The gates of ivory. Viking 1992 463p $22

ISBN 0-670-84270-2   LC 91-39421

Concludes the trilogy begun with: The radiant way and A natural curiosity

"Writer Stephen Cox, recently awarded the coveted Booker Prize, sets off for Cambodia after telling his friend, psychiatrist Liz Headleand, that there's nothing to keep him in London. No one hears from Stephen for months, and then Liz receives an odd package of his notebooks, newspaper clippings, manuscripts, and two finger bones. As she tentatively investigates Stephen's disappearance, the novel divides into a web of narratives." Booklist

"What seem mutually exclusive goals are realized: the characters are clear and compelling, objects of particular scrutiny; and the horrors of history are not trivialized by transposition to a tidily wrapped narrative. Drabble's achievement commands awe even as her subject matter rouses immeasurable stores of pity and terror." Publ Wkly

The ice age. Knopf 1977 295p o.p.

LC 77-3319

This novel "tells, in parallel, the stories of a dozen people, of different social and intellectual backgrounds, who are trapped in the economic and spiritual crisis of the mid-1970s. The central character is Anthony Keating, an Oxford graduate and former television producer turned property speculator. On the November day when the novel opens he is . . . facing the probability of bankruptcy. His lover, Alison Murray, is behind the Iron Curtain, in Walachia, where her teenage daughter is in the hospital with a broken leg, awaiting trial on a charge of dangerous driving. Len Wincobank, the big operator whose example first drew Anthony into the business world, is in [prison for fraud]. Drabble traces the progress [of those, and other characters] through the worst of the winter towards chances of recovery and escape." Times Lit Suppl

Jerusalem the golden. Morrow 1967 240p o.p.

Clara Maugham escapes from her grim, petty life in northern England to a college in London, her 'Jerusalem the golden.' She finds herself in a sort of limbo until she meets a wealthy, literary and liberal-minded family. Eventually she has an affair with one of them—handsome, unhappily married Gabriel

This novel "persuades us that we never looked at it closely enough before; the everyday stuff of contemporary middle-class life is both funnier and more serious than one might think." Times Lit Suppl

The middle ground. Knopf 1980 277p o.p.

LC 80-7630

"London life in the 1970's, with traditional British values surviving amidst foreign immigration, terrorism, and inflation, is the setting for [this] . . . novel. Kate Armstrong, daughter of a sewage worker, has become a popular journalist in the women's movement, but, at 40, begins to question her success. A recent failed love affair, an abortion, and exposure to a fiery young Arab radical, coinciding with a proposed documentary on women's choices, lead Kate to visit her old home town and to examine the paths taken by former schoolmates. Through these, and through the lives of Hugo and Evelyn, Kate's friends and co-narrators, Drabble explores . . . ways in which movements of recent decades have and have not changed the options open to men and women." Libr J

"Drabble, humane and wryly observant, has a certain grasp of life's silliness and dignity. She binds her readers to her with the same humorous intimacy that we find in the company of close friends." Harpers

A natural curiosity. Viking 1989 307p $19.95

ISBN 0-670-82837-8   LC 89-40166

In this "sequel to The Radiant Way, three middle-aged women, lifelong friends, continue their halting yet hopeful quest to find the lives they want amid the distractions and discontinuities of modern Britain. 'Life sets us unfair puzzles,' one of them says. 'Puzzles with pieces missing.'

Drabble, Margaret, 1939——*Continued*
Supported by a rich cast of equally uncertain supporting characters, Drabble's women struggle gamely to find their missing pieces." Am Libr
Followed by The gates of ivory

The needle's eye; a novel. Knopf 1972 368p o.p.
"Rose Vassiliou, divorced from her mercurial husband Christopher and raising her children in near penury, is tossed between material needs and the desire to renounce her austere family's wealth and privilege. She comes under the protective, then loving eye of Simon Camish, a . . . barrister who sees Rose's heroic forbearance as a lesson against intrusions of unprinciple into his own tense, unhappy family life." Libr J
"It is hard not to hear these echoes [of Henry James and George Eliot] in the book's fine rendering of the close tangle of love and hate, truth and falsehood, integrity and corruption, in human emotion and human relationships, and its perception of how deeply these intangibles are affected by cruder realities like money—its presence or absence. . . . 'The needle's eye' is a novel that can enrich the reader's sense of his own humanity." Choice

The radiant way. Knopf 1987 407p o.p.
LC 87-45126
This first volume of a trilogy covers five years in the lives of three women who "met at Cambridge in the '50s. Liz Headleand is a Harley Street psychotherapist and mother of a large family; Alix Bowen teaches 'the poor, the dull and the subnormal' in government sponsored programs; Esther Breuer is an art scholar who has pared her life to minimal terms. Among them these women experience divorce, the death of a parent and of a lover, the loss of a job and a resulting sense of dislocation, an intimation of vulnerability as a ghastly murder affects their lives." Publ Wkly
Drabble "charts every hill and dale in the increasingly brighter landscape of middle-class women's roles (a progression that takes place, ironically, as Britain's economic power erodes). Drabble is a master of delicate phrasing set amid a big, robust narrative." Booklist
Followed by A natural curiosity

The realms of gold. Knopf 1975 354p o.p.
"Drabble juxtaposes the lives of distantly-related members of a family. Frances Wingate, middle-aging archaeologist, is a significant female protagonist who is granted intelligence, passion, ambition, foolishness, error, and goodness. The briefer portraits of her cousins Janet, small-town housewife trapped in despair, and David, solitary geologist, counterpoint Frances' struggles, underlining similarities as well as differences." Libr J
This "is an unusually stimulating novel of ideas—and something more. It is rare entertainment, shuttling brilliantly between sandy African waters and tidy English villages. Perhaps as well as anyone now writing, Drabble can weave metaphysics into the homespun of daily life." Time

The waterfall. Knopf 1969 290p o.p.
The book "tells the story of a young wife and mother, newly deserted by her weak husband, whom she has driven away from her, and falling impetuously into an affair with her cousin's dashing husband. The progress of the affair is contrasted with all that has gone before in Jane's life, her ugly middle-class girlhood and the frigidity she knew in her marriage." Publ Wkly

"Filled with the brooding thoughts and emotions of a girl and woman who has been unable to adjust to her world, the story details her development of self-understanding through true communicaton with her lover. . . . Background of other characters serve to sketch in varying modes and manners of English middle-class life." Libr J

Draper, Hastings, 1926-
For works written by this author under other names see Jeffries, Roderic, 1926-

Dreiser, Theodore, 1871-1945
An American tragedy. Boni & Liveright 1925 2v o.p.
Available from Bentley and Buccaneer Bks.
"Clyde Griffiths, product of a poor and pious home, is driven by ambition to acquire money and social status. He is loved by Roberta, a factory coworker, but is dazzled by Sondra, who would be a passport to the country-club set. When Roberta, pregnant and no longer desirable, becomes an obstacle to Clyde's fulfilling his dream, he plans her death, for which he is caught and convicted." Shapiro. Fic for Youth. 3d edition

Jennie Gerhardt; a novel. Harper 1911 430p o.p.
"The fortunes of two families, German and Irish immigrants. Jennie, child of an unsuccessful German, falls a prey to the pleasure-loving son of the enterprising Irishman. Whether of deep-laid purpose or not, the book illustrates the rottenness of a complex social fabric resting on materialism." Baker. Guide to the Best Fic

Sister Carrie.
Available from various publishers
First published 1900 by Doubleday, Page
"A powerful account of a young working girl's rise to the 'tinsel and shine' of worldly success, and of the slow decline of her lover and protector Hurstwood." Oxford Companion to Engl Lit

Drury, Allen
Advise and consent; drawings by Arthur Shilstone. Doubleday 1959 616p il $16.95
ISBN 0-385-05419-X
Also available from Buccaneer Bks.
"Robert A. Leffingwell, a liberal intellectual, is nominated by the President of the United States to be Secretary of State. The lives of four politicians are affected by the fight for his approval in the Senate. A suicide, a surprise witness at the hearings, a vote of censure, and some chicanery highlight the Washington political scene depicted in this novel." Shapiro. Fic for Youth. 3d edition

Preserve and protect; a novel. Doubleday 1968 394p o.p.
"Most of the characters in this novel, and the background of most of the events in it, have appeared in its predecessors, 'Advise and Consent,' 'A Shade of Difference' and 'Capable of Honor.'" Note to the reader
"President Harley Hudson is killed in an air crash after his renomination. In the course of events, the Speaker of the House becomes President and calls the National Committee to select new nominees for the coming election. In an atmosphere of dangerous violence in Washington, Orrin Knox, Secretary of State, is chosen

Drury, Allen—*Continued*

over Ted Jason, Governor of California. Jason, as a compromise, is selected to be the candidate for Vice-President. As the nominees are about to make their acceptance speeches at the Washington Monument, one of them is killed. The theme of this novel is violence in American life—violence promoted, sponsored, and condoned by liberals who are always fools, dupes, or actively evil." Libr J

Du Maurier, Dame Daphne, 1907-1989

Daphne du Maurier's classics of the macabre; illustrated by Michael Foreman. Doubleday 1987 284p il $18.95

ISBN 0-385-24302-2   LC 87-9108

Analyzed in Short story index
Contents: Don't look now; The apple tree; The blue lenses; The birds; The alibi; Not after midnight

Don't look now. Doubleday 1971 303p o.p.

Analyzed in Short story index
Published in the United Kingdom with title: Not after midnight and other stories
Contents: Don't look now; The breakthrough; Not after midnight; A border-line case; The Way of the Cross

The flight of the falcon. Doubleday 1965 311p o.p.

"An Italian tour guide in Rome recognizes a murder victim found on the steps of a Roman cathedral as his old nurse, whom he had last seen in Ruffano, a northern Italian town, when he was eleven. Afraid of being accused of the murder, but obsessed with finding out more about it, he deserts his tour and turns detective in Ruffano, now a university town." Publ Wkly

Frenchman's Creek. Doubleday, Doran 1942 310p o.p. Bentley reprint available $20 (ISBN 0-8376-0412-5)

"The lovely Lady St. Columb fled by coach from the boredom of London society, and an unloved husband to their wild and unused Cornish coast estate. There she discovered an aristocratic French pirate who secreted his ship and crew in the hidden creek and as a game preyed gaily upon the dull Cornish gentry. [The book describes] the love between the two and the thrilling adventure they shared." Booklist

The house on the strand. Doubleday 1969 298p o.p. Buccaneer Bks. reprint available $27.95 (ISBN 0-89968-424-6)

"Richard Young, being in Cornwall as the guest of his biophysicist friend Magnus, takes 'trips' back into the 14th century under the influence of hallucinogens. Richard's absorption in the past, and the contrast with his own life with a difficult spouse and two stepsons, is tellingly portrayed." Barzun. Cat of Crime. Rev and enl edition

Hungry Hill. Doubleday, Doran 1943 402p o.p. Bentley reprint available $20 (ISBN 0-8376-0414-1)

The story "follows a family of Irish mine owners through four generations. Copper John opened the mines on Hungry Hill and brought in Cornish miners, resented by the villagers. Money poured in, but each generation had its tragedy of weak characters and none had Copper John's strength of purpose." Booklist

Jamaica Inn. Doubleday, Doran 1936 332p o.p. Buccaneer Bks. reprint available $17.95 (ISBN 0-89966-432-6)

"A stirring tale of an old inn on the desolate moors of Cornwall, where Mary Yellan, left alone in the world at her mother's death, took refuge with her aunt. Her uncle, the landlord, directed smugglers who wrecked ships on the nearby coast, and the inn was a place of horror and mystery. Mary's hope of rescuing her aunt, and escaping, was soon complicated by her unwilling interest in the landlord's brother, who stole horses but drew the line at murder." Booklist

The King's general. Doubleday 1946 371p o.p.

Historical novel of Cornwall in the days of the parliamentary wars. The hero is Sir Richard Grenville, the heroine Honor Harris, who tells the story many years after the events took place. As a girl Honor was in love with the blustering Sir Richard, when an accident crippled her for life, only a few days before their marriage. The rest of the story is told as it seemed to the still beautiful cripple

My cousin Rachel. Doubleday 1952 348p o.p.

Available from Bentley and Buccaneer Bks.

The scene is Cornwall and Italy, the time probably the eighteenth century. The narrator is Philip Ashley, who had lived happily with his uncle on the family estate in Cornwall, until his uncle's ill health caused him to take a trip to Italy. There Ambrose met and married a distant cousin, Rachel, and not long after he died. Philip receives Rachel at Cornwall, falls under the influence of her charm, and seeks an unconventional way out when he thinks she may have poisoned his beloved uncle

Rebecca. Doubleday 1938 457p o.p.

"Rebecca, lovely and charming wife of English aristocrat Maxim de Winter, dies unexpectedly, and the mystery surrounding her death haunts all who remain at the Manderley country estate. Eight months after the sailing accident in which Rebecca lost her life Maxim remarries. Through his new wife's writing, the reader learns the truth about Rebecca's death and character." Shapiro. Fic for Youth. 3d edition

The scapegoat. Doubleday 1957 348p o.p.

Available from Amereon and Queens House

"John, an Englishman, has just wound up a job of academic research in France. . . . In a station buffet in Le Mans he meets himself, a fantastic likeness, in the person of Jean, the Comte de Gué. . . . John, against his will, is compelled to become the Comte de Gué. In this role, unaided by anything except the clues at which he snatches while everyone takes him for granted, he must cope with a pregnant and unhappy wife, a sick but domineering mother, a religiously obsessed young daughter, a sister and brother who loathe him, a valet-chauffeur devoted to him, and a mistress who gives without demanding." Saturday Rev

Duane, Diane, 1952-

Dark mirror. Pocket Bks. 1993 337p (Star trek, the next generation) $22

ISBN 0-671-79377-2   LC 93-31885

Duane, Diane, 1952——_Continued_

"When Captain Picard investigates a series of mysterious disappearances, he discovers a parallel universe, with a ship carrying a crew exactly like his own—but with less-than-benign intentions." Libr J

Dudevant, Amantine Lucile Aurore Dupin
See Sand, George, 1804-1876

Dumas, Alexandre, 1802-1870

The Count of Monte Cristo; with elegant illustrations, drawn by M. Valentin. Williams, H.L. 1846 422p o.p.

Available from Amereon and Buccaneer Bks.

Original French edition, 1844

"Edmond Dantés, a young sailor unjustly accused of helping the exiled Napoleon in 1815, has been arrested and imprisoned in the Chateau d'If, near Marseille. After fifteen years, he finally escapes by taking the place of his dead companion, the Abbé Faria; enclosed in a sack, he is thrown into the sea. He cuts the sack with his knife, swims to safety, is taken to Italy on a fisherman's boat. From Genoa, he goes to the cavern of Monte Cristo and digs up the fabulous treasures of which the dying Faria had told. He then uses the money to punish his enemies and reward his friends." Haydn. Thesaurus of Book Dig

The iron mask; or, The feats and adventures of Raoul de Bragelonne. Being the final conclusion of "The three guardsmen;" "Twenty years after;" and "Bragelonne, the son of Athos."; translated from the French by Thomas Williams, esq. Peterson, T.B. 1850 420p o.p.

Available from Amereon and Buccaneer Bks.

Original French edition published 1850 as part of Le Vicomte de Bragelonne

The identity of the man in the iron mask—is an unsolved mystery. Dumas' "iron mask episode is found toward the end . . . of the third volume of 'Vicomte De Bragelonne'. . . . The present volume remains essentially the story of the . . . closing years of those four men who had performed such prodigies—attacking armies, assaulting castles, terrifying death itself—Athos, Porthos, Aramis, and their captain, D'Artagnan." Preface for the reader

The Queen's necklace. o.p.

Original French edition, 1848

Based on a scandal during the reign of Louis XVI, this tale of intrigue describes the efforts of Count Cagliostro, Countess Jeanne de la Motte, and Cardinal Rohan to discredit Queen Marie Antoinette. Their plot involves a coveted diamond necklace, an impersonator of the queen, and a web of suspicions of adultery and theft

Short stories. Black, W.J. 1927 10v in 1 o.p. Ayer reprint available $50 (ISBN 0-8369-4212-4)

Analyzed in Short story index

Contents: v1 Courtship of Josephine and Napoleon; Drowner; Blood union; Lady Hamilton and Admiral Nelson; Honor of Von Bulow; Gaetano and gorger; Provisional government; Cannibals; Confession of the district attorney; Vindication; Mme Dubarry; Storming the Bastile; Aurora; Branded; Tragedy of Nantes; Cripple and giant; Louis XIII; Death of Mirabeau; Anne of Austria; Black pearl

v2 Female defender; Great Copt; Scarlet sphynx; Real Bonaparte; Corneille; Wedding night; Bouquet; Tactics of love; Pipe and a man; Marat and Rousseau; Fate of a regicide; Scar of de Guise; Hollow voice; King and courtiers; Frankfort-on-Main; Bitter cup; Smuggler's in; Prodigal's favor; Sword of the Swiss; French breed

v3 Vive le roi; Mademoiselle; Uninvited visitors; Death of Richelieu; Vicomte's breakfast; Drum-head marriage; Sword and pistol; It rains; Melancholy tale; Isabella; Ransom of Isabella; Bridals; On to Rome; His oath; Legend; Some Prussian history; Count von Bismarck; Chalice; Avalanche; Little dog Jet

v4 King cobbler; Sweet smell; Citizen Bonaparte; Grecian slave-girl; Glove of Conde; Luisa San Felice; Chevalier San Felice; Martyr San Felice; Mad method; Historic fete; D'Orsay; Chimney-back; Modern Aspasia; Royal criminologist; Tenth muse; Ball of the victims—a sketch; Conquest of Circe; Inscription; Statistics; Birds of prey

v5 Caracciolo's capture; Wild boar hunt; Historic Banquo; Daughter of the Caesars; Three madames—a portrait; Vertigo; La Fontaine's first fable; Glimpse of Paris; Odoardo, the prisoner; Odoardo, the gentleman; Marseillaise; D'Artagnan, the Gascon; D'Artagnan meets the musketeers; Musketeers meet D'Artagnan; Voice of liberty; Dowry; Black tulip; Perennial Venus; Straw; Carnot and conspiracy

v6 Burgomaster; Sack of the Tuileries; Murat; Diana de Castro; Champion of beauty; Glory of love; D'Artagnan, detective; Narcotic dream; Instinct; Moliere; Moreau; View of the terror; Bismarck—his offer; Spanish surprise; Prison; Madam; Substitute; Man in the iron mask; Lame mendicant; Andre Chenier

v7 Career of a courtesan; Strange ending; People; Crossing the Alps; Battle of Langensalza; Diana de Meridor; Assassination; Fruit, a torch and a bouquet; Gourmand; Surprise; Cabaret; Picture; Bastard of Waldeck; Word of a king; Marie Touchet; Remember; Queen's perfumer; Madame de Sauve's chamber; Boxes; To Rusconise

v8 Saint Jean d'Acre; Men from Marseilles; Regent's letter; Regent's revenge; Marengo; Byron sees Kean; Son of a courtesan; Destiny; Call; Dock fight; Regal love; Balmasque; Chateau d'If; Story of no.27; Story of no.34; Cemetery of Chateau d'If; Madness; Paradise for hell; Battle of Charenton; Mercedes

v9 Death of the king's mistress; Theory of war; Two fugitives; Chastelard; Big spider; Count of Monte-Cristo; Slaughter; Italian lover; Dormice; First consul; Death of Hercules; Act of faith; Bernadotte; Pilgrimage; Conscience's dream; Mariettes dream; Vision of Athos; Le terrain de Dieu; Weird costume; Three against three

v10 Goddess of reason; Portrait; Thief; Jean Ouillier—a study; Eight long days; Gay prince; Remark; Augereau; Sacrifice of beauty; D'Artagnan-Marechal; Duel; Corsican mother; Corsican son; Corsican brother; Printing house—a sketch; Milan; Source of money: Hannibal; Brigand's faith; Mercy and Brigand; Reverses

The three musketeers. o.p.

Available from Amereon and Buccaneer Bks.

Original French edition, 1844; first United States edition published 1846 by Taylor, Wilde and Company with title: The three guardsmen

"D'Artagnan arrives in Paris one day in 1625 and manages to be involved in three duels with three musketeers. . . . Athos, Porthos, and Aramis. They become d'Artagnan's best friends. The account of their

Dumas, Alexandre, 1802-1870—*Continued*
adventures from 1625 on develops against the rich historical background of the reign of Louis XIII and early
part of that of Louis XIV, the main plot being furnished
by the antagonism between Cardinal de Richelieu and
Queen Anne d'Autriche." Haydn. Thesaurus of Book Dig
Followed by Twenty years after

Twenty years after.
Available from Amereon and Buccaneer Bks.

Sequel to The three musketeers
Original French edition, 1845; first United States edi-
tion published 1846 by Taylor, Wilde and Company
"Anne of Austria's regency, the insurrection of the
Fronde, and the execution of Charles I of England mark
out the period (1648-9)." Baker. Guide to the Best Fic
Followed by The Vicomte de Bragelonne (1848-1850)

Dumas, Alexandre, 1824-1895
Camille. o.p.
Original French edition, 1848; first United States edition published 1857 by E.J. Hincken with title: The
camelia-lady. Variant title: Lady with the camellias
Camille "is a beautiful courtesan who has become part
of the fashionable world of Paris. Scorning the wealthy
Count de Varville who has offered to relieve her debts
should she once more become his mistress, she escapes
to the country with her penniless lover Armand Duval.
Here Camille makes her great sacrifice. Giving Armand
whom she truly loves the impression that she has tired
of their life together, but actually at the request of his
family, she returns to Paris and her life of frivolity. The
tale concludes with the ultimate tragic reunion of Armand and the dying Camille." Reader's Ency. 3d edition

Duncan, David James
The brothers K. Doubleday 1992 645p
$22.50
ISBN 0-385-24003-1   LC 91-27058
"The novel is mainly narrated by Kincaid Chance, the
youngest son in a family of four boys and identical twin
girls, the children of Hugh Chance, a discouraged minor-
league ballplayer whose once-promising career was cur-
tained by an industrial accident, and his wife Laura, an
increasingly fanatical Seventh-Day Adventist. The plot
traces the working-out of the family's fate from the
beginning of the Eisenhower years through the traumas
of Vietnam." Publ Wkly
"Like Dostoevsky's Karamazovs, the Chances speculate
on the nature of God, delve into the nuances of what
constitutes moral behavior, experience evil, suffer from
criminal acts, and finally determine that God is love and
love redeems. But these are American boys, and although
their lives contain some terrible moments, this is essentially a comic novel." Libr J

Dunlap, Susan
Death and taxes; a Jill Smith mystery.
Delacorte Press 1992 247p o.p.
LC 91-33109
Jill Smith, the "Berkeley detective is working homicide
when 'one of the most hated employees of the nation's
most-loathed bureaucracy' staggers off his bicycle and
keels over dead, the victim of a poisoned hypodermic
needle lodged in his bicycle seat. Since the I.R.S. field
agent was not your run-of-the-mill public servant, but
a rabid zealot . . . Jill could use a traffic cop to sort

out all the suspects eager to dance on the dead man's
grave." N Y Times Book Rev
"This poignant, suspenseful puzzler establishes Berkeley,
Calif., homicide detective Jill Smith as one of the most
interesting female series detectives." Publ Wkly

High fall; a Kiernan O'Shaughnessy
mystery. Delacorte Press 1994 264p $19.95
ISBN 0-385-31024-2   LC 94-6047
"Nineteen-year-old movie stuntwoman Lark Sondervoil
vows to be the first person in 10 years to attempt the
'Gaige move,' named for the late legendary stuntman
Greg Gaige. Private eye Kiernan O'Shaughnessy, who
once studied gymnastics with Gaige, arrives to watch the
filming of Sondervoil's stunt. It goes wrong. Sondervoil
misses her mark and plunges off a cliff to her death.
Outraged to learn the fall was captured on film and will
probably be used in an upcoming film, Kiernan decides
to find out what went wrong." Booklist
The author "takes research seriously, which pays off
in the uncanny authenticity of the various 'gags' staged
to hair-raising effect by the stunt crew. With the same
finicky attention to detail, she also covers all the technical minutiae necessary on an outdoor movie set where
each day brings a fresh disaster." N Y Times Book Rev

Too close to the edge. St. Martin's Press
1987 215p o.p.
LC 86-27948
"A Jill Smith mystery"
"When Liz Goldenstern, a noted wheelchair-bound political gadfly and activist, is deliberately drowned in the
shallow coastal waters of San Francisco Bay, the
customarily laid-back citizens of Berkeley are shocked by
the inconceivably cruel nature of the crime. Operating
under enormous pressure to solve the high profile case,
detective Jill Smith uncovers a confounding link between
Liz' death and a string of petty crimes involving the
theft of 12 pairs of designer running shoes. A clever
psychological thriller featuring a hair-raising climax."
Booklist

Dunne, Dominick
An inconvenient woman. Crown 1990
458p $19.95
ISBN 0-517-57763-1   LC 90-1602
Also available G.K. Hall large print edition
This novel "concerns billionaire financier and presidential adviser Jules Mendelson; his high-society wife,
Pauline, and fractious stepson, Kippie; a bunch of other
gangsters and Hollywoodites who are either business associates, friends or antagonists; and Flo March, Jules'
curvacious, decidedly nonblueblood mistress, who comes
to know too much about everyone else's less-than-licit
dealings for her own good." Booklist
"This is a smart novel because Dominick Dunne understands the distance between Los Angeles society and
the spicy bazaars of Hollywood. And what makes Mr.
Dunne not only first-rate, but also different from other
writers who write about the very rich in late 20th-
century America, is his knowledge that there's more to
it than getting the labels and the street names right."
N Y Times Book Rev

People like us; a novel. Crown 1988 403p
$19.95
ISBN 0-517-56879-9   LC 88-353

Dunne, Dominick—*Continued*

In this novel about upper-crust New York life, "Loelia Manchester is leaving her husband for shoe designer Micki Mindaros; Hubie Altemous is dying of AIDS; Matilde Stewart is broke. Trying to break into this world are Elias and Ruby Renthal, the richest people in Cleveland, who soon become the toast of the Upper East Side by watching carefully and spending excessively. The story's two culminating events, Elias Renthal's Boesky-like fall and Gus Bailey's thirst for vengeance, shake the fabric of a world where custom and manners rule." Booklist

"Engaging us in his characters' concerns and then pulling multiple story strands into a tight knot, Dominick Dunne demonstrates with wit and accuracy the delicate, merciless distinction between 'people like that' and 'people like us'." N Y Times Book Rev

A season in purgatory. Crown 1993 377p $22

ISBN 0-517-58386-0   LC 92-42352

Also available Random House large print edition

This novel "begins with the jury deliberating in the murder trial of Constant Bradley, a charming, handsome Congressman from an affluent Irish Catholic family in New England. He has been charged with a crime from his prep school days: the death of Winifred Utley, a pretty 15-year-old neighbor of the Bradleys who was clubbed to death with a baseball bat after a dance at the country club." N Y Times Book Rev

"The unforgettable Bradley family, their skeletons . . . and peccadillos offer an allure similar to a sidelong glance at tabloid headlines, though here told with wit and skill. Their machinations prove both fascinating and appalling—and always hypnotically readable." Publ Wkly

The two Mrs. Grenvilles; a novel. Crown 1985 374p o.p.

LC 85-445

"Basil Plant, a semisuccessful novelist tenuously clinging to the fringes of high society, narrates this haunting tale of two women destroyed by the virulence of their own twisted emotions. Alice Grenville, a respected woman of means, is initially appalled when her only son chooses to marry considerably beneath their fashionable set; still, rather than risk Junior's disaffection, Alice grudgingly accepts second-rate actress Ann Arden into her upper-crust family. The pathetic fates of the two Mrs. Grenvilles are sealed when Ann, in a jealous rage, murders her disenchanted husband. In order to avoid the sensationalism of a highly publicized scandal, Alice helps cover up the crime, forever binding herself to the woman she despises most. An affecting and disturbing tragedy replete with vivid portraits of spiritually crippled souls desperately struggling to inject some substance into their empty lives." Booklist

Dunne, John Gregory, 1932-

Playland; a novel. Random House 1994 494p $25

ISBN 0-679-42427-X   LC 94-4344

Hollywood screenwriter Jack Broderick featured in *The Red White and Blue*, "flies to Detroit to research story ideas. In a Michigan trailer park, he discovers a coupon-clipping bag lady named Melba Mae Toolate who claims to have been Blue Tyler, one of the biggest child movie stars of the 1940s. Melba tells Broderick her life story, focusing on her scandalous liaison with Jacob King, a flamboyant gangster and Las Vegas visionary." Libr J

"The most successful part of this novel is its bawdy, admiring portrait of that time and place, filled with jaundiced observations and half-familiar show-business anecdotes." N Y Times Book Rev

The red, white, and blue; a novel. Simon & Schuster 1987 475p o.p.

LC 86-26025

The author exhibits "a fascination with the invisible web that links certain disparate people and events. . . . 'The Red White and Blue' examines the most complicated web yet, a vast network extending halfway around the globe and across the past 20 years or so to encompass left-wing politics, big business, Hollywood and (yes, once again) a few figures in the Catholic Church. Its story line, if one may call it that, is a rambling rumination upon the career of a radical lawyer named Leah Kaye. Its real story is history's habit of ensnaring us in its meshes—even if we're apolitical, even if we're as uninvolved and wryly ironic as Jack Broderick, the narrator." N Y Times Book Rev

"An insightfully provocative slice of Americana." Booklist

True confessions. Dutton 1977 341p o.p.

"A Henry Robbins book"

This novel is "about brotherhood, the loss of innocence, and the frailty of the human condition. Corruption-ridden LA in the late 1940s provides the backdrop for this tale of two brothers, a cop and a priest, who are unable to detach themselves from their Irish Catholic milieu. The bizarre murder of a prostitute provides the focal point but not the main subject matter of this work, which is concerned with policeman Tom's investigation and his discovery of seemingly universal weakness among the multitude of characters." Libr J

Dunnett, Dorothy, 1923-

Checkmate. Putnam 1975 581p il o.p.

Available from Amereon and Buccaneer Bks.

This concluding volume of the Francis Crawford saga "resolves Lymond's final mystery, the prophecy of astrologer John Dee: 'It is not one thing you seek, I fancy, but two. . . . The first you will have: the second you shall never have, nor would it be just that you should.' Lymond, an aggressive player in the political chess game of royalty, is also a key pawn in the quirky game of family bloodlines." Publ Wkly

"A thoroughly romantic action yarn which isn't an insult to the intelligence. Intricately plotted, atmospheric, and peopled with characters of magnetic complexity, this series combines literary quality with can't-put-down entertainment." Libr J

King hereafter; a novel. Knopf 1982 721p o.p.

LC 81-48112

Available from Amereon and Buccaneer Bks.

"Supposing Macbeth, Son (here stepson) of Findlaech, and Thorfinn, Son of Sigurd, to be one and the same person, this historical novel successfully recreates the atmosphere of 11th century Scotland and Europe. The barbaric Viking culture of the northern isles is being transformed into Christian 'civilization,' though not without turmoil. This hybrid Macbeth/Thorfinn, himself a product of two cultures, personifies and for a time controls this struggle to make Scotland a unified nation." Libr J

Dunnett, Dorothy, 1923- —*Continued*

This novel is "by virtue of its length, its authenticity of detail, its steady dramatic tension and its power to transport the reader back across the centuries, an awe-inspiring performance." Publ Wkly

Niccolò rising. Knopf 1986 470p (House of Niccolò) $18.95

ISBN 0-394-53107-8   LC 86-45306

Also available from Buccaneer Bks.

In the first volume of the House of Niccolò series we meet Claus, later known as Niccolò, "an apprentice at the Bruges branch of the Charetty company, run by the widowed owner. Claus is an enigma, seemingly a buffoon getting into scrapes with Felix, the Charetty heir, but also capable of initiating a courier service in connection with the Charetty commercial and mercenary ventures. In an era of economic and political intrigue, Claus makes the most of all opportunities—romantic and business." Libr J

This novel "displays all the author's strengths: strong characterization, subtle wit (with a dash of slapstick), lively action, and labyrinthine plot." Wilson Libr Bull

Followed by The spring of the ram

Pawn in frankincense. Putnam 1969 486p o.p.

Available from Amereon and Buccaneer Bks.

Previous titles in this series of interlocking novels about Scottish adventurer Francis Crawford are: The game of kings (1961); Queen's play (1964) and The disorderly knights (1966)

This installment of Crawford's adventures finds him in "the eastern Mediterranean region searching for his bastard son, who is being held hostage. Plots and counterplots, blood and gore lead to an excruciating climax in the form of a chess contest (a game this is not), in which Crawford and his old adversary Graham Mallett play with living pieces, themselves included. Penalty for capture is death, and Crawford's son, whom he can't recognize, is involved." Libr J

Race of scorpions. Knopf 1990 534p (House of Niccolò) $19.95

ISBN 0-394-57107-X   LC 89-45292

Third volume in the Niccolò series. "At age 21, fifteenth-century Dutch adventurer Niccolò has lost his wife and her inheritance, but he has the rich resources of his personality and potential wealth in a trading business based in Venice to restore his fortunes in short order. Indeed, a dynastic power struggle over control of Cyprus draws him to that island, where both sides eagerly enlist his support and talents. Meanwhile, there are old wounds and debts to settle with the rulers of Anjou who have previously thwarted his ambitions." Booklist

"Through precisely rendered scenes, whether depicting a battle on the high seas, the operations of a dye works, a cleverly plotted ambush (using insects) or the gruesome tactics employed to destroy a proud city under siege, Dunnett furnishes fascinating images while spinning her admirable narrative web." Publ Wkly

Followed by Scales of gold

The ringed castle. Putnam 1972 c1971 521p o.p.

Available from Amereon and Buccaneer Bks.

First published 1971 in the United Kingdom

In this Francis Crawford of Lymond adventure, the swashbuckling Scot "takes his mercenaries to Russia and becomes commander of the Tsar's armies. Then there's his involvement with the Scottish Philippa, his wife 'in name only,' who persists in tangling into his affairs, in politics and war. There are exotic scenes in Turkey and Russia as well as Scotland and England. Among the notable characters are Ivan the Terrible, Bloody Mary Tudor, and Lady Margaret Douglas." Publ Wkly

Scales of gold. Knopf 1992 519p (House of Niccolò) $25

ISBN 0-394-58627-1   LC 91-58554

First published 1991 in the United Kingdom

Fourth book in the House of Niccolò series. "In 1464, adventurer and merchant banker Nicholas van der Pole . . . returns to Venice to find his financial empire in jeopardy due to the Crusades and the onslaught of powerful, unscrupulous competitors. Closely guarding the specifics of his mission, Nicholas sets out for Africa and its gold trade." Publ Wkly

"Set within a rich tapestry of fifteenth-century Europe and Africa that is woven by a master of historical fiction, Nicholas' travels are constantly endangered by the greedy and vengeful figures he has tangled with in the past as well as by the natural hazards of the period." Booklist

Followed by The unicorn hunt

The spring of the ram. Knopf 1988 469p (House of Niccolò) o.p. Buccaneer Bks. reprint available $33.95 (ISBN 0-89966-964-6)

LC 87-37847

In the second volume of the House of Niccolò saga "Plucky 19-year-old Nicholas, fleeing his bitter foe Simon de Pol, journeys via Florence—where he gets funding from the Medicis—to the East. There he hopes to trade with the Emperor of Trebizond. . . . But the seductive Princess Violante, in diaphanous déshabillé, offers Nicholas protection—and much more." Publ Wkly

"Dunnett tells this story of love and money against a well-researched background of historical and cultural detail, taking her readers from Europe to Byzantium." Booklist

Followed by Race of scorpions

The unicorn hunt. Knopf 1994 656p (House of Niccolò) $25

ISBN 0-394-58628-X   LC 93-35692

First published 1993 in the United Kingdom

In the fifth volume of the saga fifteenth century banker/knight Nicholas vander Poele "sails to Scotland, where he confronts his archenemy, Simon de St. Pol, who may be the father of the child whom Nicholas's wife, Gelis van Borselen, is carrying. Months later, back in Flanders, vengeful Gelis, in order to punish Nicholas for fathering an illegitimate child by her sister, hides her newborn boy. Intrigue, betrayal and adventure follow as hardened Nicholas journeys from Florence, full of Medici machinations, to the Tyrol, where he uses a divining rod to find silver." Publ Wkly

"Dunnett's writing style is somewhat complex but rich in information. The reader can feel immersed in the environment she creates; the characters (there are many) have well-developed, unique identities." Libr J

Dunning, John, 1942-

Booked to die; a mystery introducing Cliff Janeway. Scribner 1992 321p $19.95

ISBN 0-684-19383-3   LC 91-26889

Dunning, John, 1942-- —*Continued*

Homicide detective and rare book collector Cliff "Janeway turns in his badge, opens a shop called Twice Told Books on Denver's Book Row and for a time becomes preoccupied with the enchanting lore of his trade. But Janeway discovers that not all book folk are gentlefolk. Two inoffensive book scouts are murdered after making a rare find, and the young clerk in Twice Told Books is dispatched with equal brutality. Thinking like a cop again, Janeway starts suspecting all his new friends on Book Row, including the woman with whom he has fallen in love. . . . This is a soundly plotted, evenly executed whodunit in the classic mode." N Y Times Book Rev

Duras, Marguerite, 1914-

Blue eyes, black hair; translated from the French by Barbara Bray. Pantheon Bks. 1987 117p o.p.

LC 87-46050

Original French edition, 1986

A novella "about a young man and a young woman who know absolutely nothing about each other but ensconce themselves together in one room, because she reminds him of a beautiful man he has only briefly encountered but with whom he believes himself to be hopelessly in love. . . . The days this man and woman spend together prove to be a deeply sensuous, psychologically demanding, draining series of body and mental explorations. The colors, textures, smells, and emotions that fill their room are delineated with rare precision by a master novelist." Booklist

The lover; translated from the French by Barbara Bary. Pantheon Bks. 1985 117p o.p.

LC 84-26321

Original French edition, 1984

"With ruminative tone, yet in short space, the middle-aged narrator remembers her affair with an older Chinese man, which took place when she was a teenage girl living in French-controlled Indochina. The experience holds importance in her mind as the reason for her quick transition from child to adult, a passage she knows is recorded indelibly in every line on her face." Booklist

This "is a book of powerful, conflicting emotions, a lyrical evocation of the parallel decline of a family and an era, a story of cultural displacement, of sibling rivalries, and of an ambivalent mother-daughter relationship. . . . Duras' style is graceful and poetic. She writes of sexual desire and primitive human emotions, but 'The Lover' contains not a trace of obscenity. It is a powerful and entertaining novel that deserves a wide audience." Best Sellers

The North China lover; translated by Leigh Hafrey. New Press (NY) 1992 231p $19.95

ISBN 1-56584-018-6   LC 92-53729

This version of the title entered above began as notes for the film script

Durham, Marilyn

Dutch uncle. Harcourt Brace Jovanovich 1973 303p o.p.

"Rugged, roving Jake Hollander, gunslinger turned card shark, finds himself saddled with two suddenly orphaned youngsters and reluctantly agrees to drop them in Arredondo, New Mexico at their mother's destination, the Golden Moon, which turns out to be a whorehouse. Not rid of the kids and left behind by the stage, a disgruntled Jake accepts the job of marshall for a month and soon is embroiled in the lives not only of the orphans but also of a number of the town's residents, including the newspaper publisher and his spirited sister, both figures out of Jake's past." Booklist

The man who loved Cat Dancing. Harcourt Brace Jovanovich 1972 246p o.p.

"The man who loved Cat Dancing is John Wesley [Jay] Grobart, an ex-army officer who married Cat, a Shoshone squaw, when she was only 14. . . . When we meet Grobart, he is about to rob a train: recently released from prison after serving a 10-year term for the killing of three Indians believed to have raped and killed his wife, he wants money to regain his son. . . . At the same time, we meet Catherine Crocker who is on her way to catch the same train to expedite flight from her husband. Instead of catching the train she is kidnapped by the robbers. . . . The story . . . takes place in the Wyoming Territory of the 1880s." New Repub

Durrell, Gerald M., 1925-1995

Marrying off mother, and other stories; [by] Gerald Durrell. Arcade Pub. 1992 197p $18.95

ISBN 1-55970-180-3   LC 91-30895

Analyzed in Short story index

Contents: Esmeralda; Fred; or, A touch of the warm South; Retirement; Marrying off mother; Ludwig; The jury; Miss Booth-Wycherly's clothes; A parrot for the parson

"These eight droll stories—linked only in that they may or may not have happened to Durrell—are told with the cleverness and wit of an accomplished after-dinner rancouteur who has put away most of a bottle of brandy." Publ Wkly

Durrell, Lawrence

The Alexandria quartet: Justine; Balthazar; Mountolive [and] Clea. Dutton 1962 884p o.p.

Omnibus edition of four titles entered separately

Balthazar; a novel. Dutton 1958 250p o.p.

The second volume of the Alexandria quartet

"Once again [Durrell] writes of Justine, Melissa, Clea, Nessim, Pursewarden, Scobie, Pombal—but from a fresh point of view. The new insights are provided by the psychiatrist, Balthazar, who convinces the narrator that the first volume of the story was almost wholly inaccurate. . . . So this second volume is a correction and an expansion of the first." N Y Times Book Rev

Followed by Mountolive

also in Durrell, L. The Alexandria quartet p205-390

Clea; a novel. Dutton 1960 287p o.p.

Final volume of the Alexandria quartet

"In this novel events are seen from the point of view of the Englishman Darley who, returning to Alexandria to see old friends and lovers, has a passionate affair with Clea, one of the women in the circle of friends. Again, the tone is philosophic, the language frequently overripe, and the characters, though individualistic, are symbolic. Heterosexual and homosexual affairs are prominent in each of the novels." Booklist

Durrell, Lawrence—*Continued*

"'The Alexandria Quartet' is one of the major achievements of fiction in our time, distinguished not only by its power of language, by its evocation of a place, by its creation of character, by the drama of many of its incidents, but also by its boldly original design. 'Clea' perfects the work, as a spire crowns a cathedral, but the spire is not to be judged in isolation." Saturday Rev

also in Durrell, L. The Alexandria quartet p653-884

Constance; or, Solitary practices. Viking 1982 393p o.p.

LC 81-69998

Third volume of the Avignon quintet

In this novel "World War II sweeps over Avignon, scattering the city's English colony. While psychoanalyst Constance resumes her studies in Geneva, her husband Sam and novelist Blanford find themselves in Egypt, where an artillery accident kills the former and cripples the latter. In Egypt, too, Blanford meets the 'real' characters he will write into Monsieur, for Durrell's sequence is a . . . novel-within-a-novel." Libr J

Justine. Dutton 1957 253p o.p.

First volume of the Alexandria quartet

"Set in Alexandria the story concerns the amorous adventures of a penniless young man, a prostitute who lives with him, the rich and beautiful Justine with whom he has an affair, and Justine's husband." Publ Wkly

Followed by Balthazar

also in Durrell, L. The Alexandria quartet p11-203

Livia; or, Buried alive. Viking 1979 c1978 265p o.p.

LC 78-20796

First published 1978 in the United Kingdom

This Avignon quintet title "comes first chronologically, but was written after *Monsieur*. It describes a band of friends and lovers gathered near Avignon in the days between the world wars, including British consul Felix Chatto, the novelist Blanford, and Livia, within whose beautiful body a man is 'buried alive.'" Husband. Sequels. 2d edition

Monsieur. Viking 1975 c1974 305p o.p.

First published volume of the Avignon quintet

First published 1974 in the United Kingdom with title: Monsieur; or, The Prince of Darkness

Set in France, Italy, and Egypt, the story "revolves around a lifelong 'ménage a trois' (an English brother and sister, and a male doctor-friend), their philosophic and amatory quests, and a ritual murder carried out by a cult of Gnostics led by a strange Arab banker." Libr J

Mountolive; a novel. Dutton 1959 c1958 318p o.p.

Third volume of the Alexandria quartet

First published 1958 in the United Kingdom

The perspective is "that of David Mountolive, the British ambassador: and what appeared to be 'the intrigues of desire' are shown to be intrigues motivated by politics. We learn that the beautiful Jewess, Justine, and her Coptic (Christian) husband, Nessim, are passionately united by a common cause: he believes that the formation of a Jewish state will save other minorities in the Arab world from Muslim domination and he is the leader of a group which is smuggling arms to the Jews in Palestine. The discovery of this conspiracy by Nessim's loyal English friends, Pursewarden and the ambassador, and their reactions to it form the plot line of Mountolive." Atlantic

Followed by Clea

also in Durrell, L. The Alexandria quartet p391-652

Quinx; or, The ripper's tale; a novel. Viking 1985 201p o.p.

LC 85-10563

Final volume of the Avignon quintet

The plot "centers on Constance, the psychoanalyst. In the course of the novel, she uncovers a nasty incest story about her brother and sister, finishes mourning a dead lover, gives up an infatuation with a former patient and finds at last her proper union. Bits of other plots straggle toward completion, and all join in what promises to be an illuminating and redemptive final act—the search for the oft-mentioned treasure of the Templars, a medieval Gnostic order of knights." N Y Times Book Rev

"Despite the frequent patches of perfectly exquisite writing—descriptive passages, mostly—the plot is too evasive and the characters too ambiguous for readers unfamiliar with the earlier novels in the quintet. Given that familiarity, though, 'Quinx' makes just the right dreamy conclusion to this impressionistic series." Booklist

Sebastian; or, Ruling passions. Viking 1984 c1983 202p o.p.

LC 83-40207

Fourth volume of the Avignon quintet

First published 1983 in the United Kingdom

"This novel is set mainly in Geneva and its environs, where Constance, a psychoanalyst, practices her profession while trying to come to terms with the end of a passionate love affair. The Egyptian Affad, or Sebastian, realizing that his attachment to Constance is a violation of the gnostic code, returns to Alexandria. There he learns that a letter prescribing his death has been mailed to Geneva and innocently intercepted by Constance. Durrell's story follows the trail of the letter as it falls into the hands of the madman Mnemedis." Publisher's note

Dwyer, K. R., 1945-

For works written by this author under other names see Koontz, Dean R. (Dean Ray), 1945-

E

Eagles, Cynthia Harrod- *See* Harrod-Eagles, Cynthia

Earth song, sky spirit; short stories of the contemporary native American experience; edited with an introduction by Clifford E. Trafzer. Doubleday 1993 495p $25

ISBN 0-385-46959-4   LC 92-44296

Analyzed in short story index

Contents: From aboard the night train, by K. M. Blaeser; The moccasin game, by G. Vizenor; The prisoner of haiku, by G. D. Henry; The day the crows stopped talking, by Harvest Moon Eyes; The well, by

Earth song, sky spirit—*Continued*
N. S. Momaday; Lost in the land of Ishtaboli, by D. L. Birchfield; Faces, by J. L. Russell; Adventures of an Indian princess, by P. Riley; Lucy, Oklahoma, 1911, by C. Womack; Fear and recourse, by M. Kenny; Earl Yellow Calf, by J. Welch; Grandpa Kashpaw's ghost, by L. Erdrich; Sun offering, by A. Hansen; Lead horse, by D. Glancy; Bone girl, by J. Bruchac; Spirit woman, by P. G. Allen; The cave, by J. D. Forbes; Akun, Jiki Walu: Grandfather magician, by D. B. Wilson; Marlene's adventures, by A. Endrezze; The approximate size of my favorite tumor, by S. Alexie; Shadows and sleepwalkers, by C. Featherstone; For her with no regrets, by D. Niatum; Avian Messiah and Mistress Media, by A. Connors; Slaughterhouse, by G. Sarris; Joseph's rainbow, by I. Petersen; The dream, by P. Olson; Silver bass and alligator gar, by R. Salisbury; Danse d'amour, danse de mort, by L. Howe; Clara's gift, by M. Dorris; The return of the buffalo, by L. M. Silko

East, Charles
(ed) The Flannery O'Connor Award: selected stories. See The Flannery O'Connor Award: selected stories

Easterman, Daniel
Brotherhood of the tomb. Doubleday 1990 c1989 295p o.p.

                    LC 89-49463

First published 1989 in the United Kingdom
"In 1968, in Jerusalem, a tomb is discovered that contains the bones of Jesus, his 'brother' James and their mother Mary. At the same time, at Trinity College in Dublin, young American student Patrick Canavan falls in love with Francesca Contarini, who wears a strange cross around her neck. Twenty-four years later, Francesca has apparently drowned, and Canavan, now ex-CIA has returned to Dublin to try to recapture his youthful peace of mind. But events from the past impinge on the present." Publ Wkly
"This is one of those down-to-the-wire books in which the hero accomplishes the impossible. Still, Mr. Easterman manages to carry it off. Perhaps the plotting will not withstand cold scrutiny. No matter. 'Brotherhood of the Tomb' is hard to put down." N Y Times Book Rev

Eberhart, Mignon Good, 1899-
Murder in waiting; [by] Mignon G. Eberhart. Random House 1973 208p o.p. Amereon reprint available $19.95 (ISBN 0-88411-767-7)
"Judge Bartry, retired and working on his memoirs, is murdered. There are almost too many suspects, since numerous characters in the Connecticut village are worried that there'll be something detrimental about them in the memoirs. Romantic interest centers on niece Bea, who has quarreled with the judge about her engagement to a neighbor taking his exams for the Foreign Service." Publ Wkly

Next of kin; [by] Mignon G. Eberhart. Random House 1982 224p o.p.

                    LC 81-28299

"Mady Smith and Hill (Chan) Channing arrive at the swank apartment of his brother Stuart and heiress sister-in-law Lettie after a party in Stuart's honor. Stuart has been appointed to the President's cabinet, but someone has shot him fatally during the party while he retired to his study. Chan, Mady and Lettie find the body and become dangerously involved in the investigation that delves into dark corners where foreign agents lurk, with big money to pay for U.S. government influences." Publ Wkly

Eco, Umberto
Foucault's pendulum; translated from the Italian by William Weaver. Harcourt Brace Jovanovich 1989 641p $22.95
    ISBN 0-15-132765-3   LC 89-32212
"A Helen and Kurt Wolff book"
Original Italian edition, 1988
A "student of philology in 1970s Milan, Casaubon is completing a thesis on the Templars, a monastic knighthood disbanded in the 1300s for questionable practices. At Pilades Bar, he meets up with Jacopo Belbo, an editor of obscure texts at Garamond Press. Together with Belbo's colleague Diotallevi, they scrutinize the fantastic theories of a prospective author, Colonel Ardenti, who claims that for seven centuries the Templars have been carrying out a complex scheme of revenge. When Ardenti disappears mysteriously, the three begin using their detailed knowledge of the occult sciences to construct a Plan for the Templars—only to discover too late that the Plan they have invented is in fact real." Libr J
This book "is not meant to be easy. . . . [But] great are the rewards for those who actually manage to read it. For while it is not a novel in the strict sense of the word, it is a truly formidable gathering of information delivered playfully by a master manipulating his own invention—in effect, a long, erudite joke." N Y Times Book Rev

The name of the rose; translated from the Italian by William Weaver. Harcourt Brace Jovanovich 1983 502p $29.95
    ISBN 0-15-144647-4   LC 82-21286
Also available from Buccaneer Bks.
"A Helen and Kurt Wolff book"
Original Italian edition, 1982
This mystery set in 14th century Italy "centers on William of Baskerville, a 50-year-old monk who is sent to investigate a death at a Benedictine monastery. During his search, several other monks are killed in a bizarre pattern that reflects the Book of Revelation. Highly rational, Baskerville meets his nemesis in Jorge of Burgos, a doctrinaire blind monk determined to destroy heresy at any cost." Merriam-Webster's Ency of Lit
This novel "is an antidetective-story detective story; as a semiotic murder mystery it is superbly entertaining; it is also an extraordinary work of novelistic art." Harpers

Eddings, David
Belgarath the sorcerer; by David Eddings and Leigh Eddings. Ballantine Bks. 1995 644p $25.95
    ISBN 0-345-37324-3

Eddings, David—*Continued*

"A Del Rey book"

The authors "return to the world of their multivolume sagas, *The Belgariad* and *The Malloreon*. This prequel to the earlier books, presented as Belgarath's memoirs, offers an absorbing story line and some memorable characters as, once again, the authors touch all the right fantasy bases, with warring gods, political intrigues, supernatural creatures and appealingly human magicians involved in a titanic war over the course of seven millennia." Publ Wkly

Demon lord of Karanda. Ballantine Bks. 1988 422p (Malloreon, bk3) o.p.

LC 88-47804

"A Del Rey book"

"King Belgarion, his wife Ce'Nedra, and their companions . . . set forth on a journey to save the King's kidnaped son from the menace of the evil priestess Zandramas. Along the way, humans and sorcerers cross paths with fanatics and demons who impede their progress and seek to change the conditions which will fulfill the Prophecy of a final confrontation between the Child of Light and the Child of Dark at the Place Which Is No More." Voice Youth Advocates

Followed by Sorceress of Darshiva

The diamond throne. Ballantine Bks. 1989 448p (Elenium, bk1) o.p.

LC 88-92805

"A Del Rey book"

In this first volume of the "Elenium saga, Sparhawk the warrior, Sephrenia the wizard, and Flute the strange child must begin a quest to find a way of saving Queen Ehlana from a fatal disease before her death allows corrupt priests serving an evil god to rule everything." Booklist

The author combines "heroic yet humorous characters with exotic settings and tangled politics to create a fast-moving fantasy." Libr J

Followed by The ruby knight

Domes of fire. Ballantine Bks. 1993 484p (Tamuli, bk1) $22

ISBN 0-345-37321-9　　　　LC 92-54386

"A Del Rey book"

In a continuation of the Elenium trilogy "the distant Tamul Empire, endangered by civil unrest exacerbated by paranormal (or magical, depending on the point of view) incidents, begs help from Sparhawk, destroyer of the Elder God Azash and savior of the Elenes. Undertaking the long journey to Tamul, the knight, his royal wife, their daughter Princess Danaë and assorted followers encounter unrest in each of the lands through which they pass." Publ Wkly

Followed by The shining ones

Guardians of the west. Ballantine Bks. 1987 454p (Malloreon, bk1) $16.95

ISBN 0-345-33000-5　　　　LC 86-26588

"A Del Rey book"

"A follow-up to Eddings's popular five-book Belgariad series [published in paperback], this novel is the first in [the Malloreon series.] Garion's slaying of the evil god Torak in the last installment left the world peaceful enough for the current chapter to open with Polgara settling down in the bucolic Vale of Aldur with her husband Durnick, her ancient sorcerer father Belgarath and the orphan Errand. Garion himself, now on the Rivan Throne, tends to his responsibilities as Overlord of the West and concentrates on producing an heir. .

. . Eddings once again delivers an appealing central story that is pleasing for the assured, leisurely pace of its narrative flow and the ease and charm with which it incorporates events of mundane life into a tale of gods, kings and adventure." Publ Wkly

Followed by King of the Murgos

The hidden city. Ballantine Bks. 1994 457p (Tamuli, bk3) $23

ISBN 0-345-37323-5　　　　LC 94-4787

"A Del Rey book"

In the concluding volume of the Tamuli trilogy "the Pandion Knight Sparhawk searches for his wife, Queen Ehlana, who has been kidnapped in order to force Sparhawk to turn over Bhelliom, the jewel of power, to the evil god Cyrgon. . . . Eddings continues to reward lovers of great, sweeping fantasies with creative ingenuity in characterization, world building, and magical effects." Booklist

King of the Murgos. Ballantine Bks. 1988 c1987 456p (Malloreon, bk2) o.p.

LC 87-19473

"A Del Rey book"

"As the words of the Prophecy lead the Rivan King Garion and his companions across the lands of the Snake-Queen and the once hostile Murgos, the malignant Zandramas—kidnapper of Garion's son—pursues another prophecy which, if fulfilled, will lead to the triumph of Darkness." Libr J

Followed by Demon lord of Karanda

The ruby knight. Ballantine Bks. 1990 406p maps (Elenium, bk2) o.p.

LC 90-558

"A Del Rey book"

This novel "continues the story of Sparhawk, who comes to the rescue of Queen Ehlana, frozen in crystal after having been poisoned. The key to saving the queen is a magical jewel, the Bhelliom, and Sparhawk and an oddly assorted company of knights set out in search of it." Booklist

"Eddings's strength lies in his ability to create thoroughly likable heroes with personalities that transcend the formulaic fantasy genre. Graceful prose and judicious humor add style to this excellent addition to fantasy collections." Libr J

Followed by The sapphire rose

The sapphire rose. Ballantine Bks. 1991 467p il (Elenium, bk3) $22

ISBN 0-345-37474-6　　　　LC 91-72882

"A Del Rey book"

In the "concluding volume of Eddings' Elenium saga Sparhawk the knight has achieved his quest for the jewel Bhelliom, which will save Queen Ehlana from death by poison. Unfortunately, the possession of this powerful talisman makes him a target for a wide variety of beings, divine and mortal, who are also interested in acquiring Bhelliom and its powers." Booklist

The seeress of Kell. Ballantine Bks. 1991 399p (Malloreon, bk5) $20

ISBN 0-345-33006-4　　　　LC 90-24635

"A Del Rey book"

The final volume in the Malloreon saga "finds Belgarion, the Child of Light, racing to his cataclysmic and long-prophesied meeting with Zandramas, Child of the Dark, which will determine the future of the world. His small band—consisting of, among others, his wife,

Eddings, David—*Continued*

Ce'Nedra; members of his shape-changing family; and his former enemy, Zakath, Emperor of Mallorea—is joined by Cyradis, the blind seeress of Kell, who is foreordained to decide which will win, the forces of Light or those of Dark." Publ Wkly

"There is no shortage of action, suspense, or reader satisfaction at the resolution of the struggle and the end of Garion's wars. Eddings' fertile imagination and ambitious storytelling make this a must purchase for science fiction collections." Booklist

The shining ones. Ballantine Bks. 1993 470p (Tamuli, bk2) $22

ISBN 0-345-37322-7   LC 9254993

"A Del Rey book"

"While the Queen of Elenia plays hostess to the besieged emperor of Tamuli, the Pandion Knight Sparhawk embarks on a peril-filled journey through foreign lands to recover the stone of power known as the Bhelliom from its watery resting place." Libr J

Followed by The hidden city

Sorceress of Darshiva. Ballantine Bks. 1989 406p il (Malloreon, bk4) $19.95

ISBN 0-345-33005-6   LC 89-6705

"A Del Rey book"

"The sorceress Zandramas, now Child of the Dark after the death of the god Torak at the hands of Belgarion (who is the Child of the Light) has stolen Belgarion's young son to use in a ritual prophesied to assure the dominance of the forces of the Dark. They find an original copy of the Ashabine Oracles, written long before Belgarion's birth, which contains a message to him from Torak that directs them to the ancient city of Kell. As they race other interested parties across battle-blasted landscapes, the group encounters warring troops of men and demons, and the Emperor of Mallorea, who joins the party on the orders of a blind seeress." Publ Wkly

"Eddings' mastery of the large-scale story and a cast of dozens is so complete that one ceases to be concerned about lapses of originality." Booklist

Followed by The seeress of Kell

Eddings, Leigh

(jt. auth) Eddings, D. Belgarath the sorcerer

Eden, Dorothy, 1912-1982

The American heiress. Coward, McCann & Geoghegan 1980 251p o.p.

LC 80-15256

The author "tells the tried and true tale of an illegitimate girl who finds her way into the arms of an English lord. Hetty Jervis accompanies her stepsister, Clemency, across the Atlantic. Despite warnings that the voyage aboard the Luisitania could be dangerous, Clemency refuses to listen. She plans to marry Lord Hazzard, swapping her American millions for an aristocratic title. . . . When the Luisitania is torpedoed, Mrs. Jervis refuses to abandon ship until the girls take all the jewels. When an Irish rescue nurse asks Hetty what the gold monogrammed watch stands for, she repeats the name, Clemency Jervis. From that moment, Hetty decides to live the life of an American heiress." West Coast Rev Books

"All of this is melded together with consummate storytelling skill and fine period atmosphere. The surprise bittersweet ending is just right." Publ Wkly

An important family. Morrow 1982 288p o.p.

LC 81-19026

"Irish Kate O'Connor is looking for escape from the tragic death of her fiancé when she becomes a companion to the wife and daughter of Sir John Devenish on a move to New Zealand in 1862. Sir John is a disciple of Edward Wakefield's utopian colony, his wife, Iris, is a frail shadow and his daughter, Celina, must be drugged into quiescence while on board ship. Once arrived in the new land, Kate dreams of marriage to a retired soldier until Celina enthralls him. Kate then fancies herself in love with Sir John. But secret doings in the past haunt the family until Lady Iris dies, and the truth is revealed." Libr J

"Out of all this comes a solidly satisfying novel with memorable secondary characters and a conclusion as dramatic as it is poignant." Publ Wkly

The millionaire's daughter. Coward, McCann & Geoghegan 1974 384p o.p.

This story "centers around the father's obsessive desire to marry his only daughter into the English aristocracy to compensate somehow for his own wretched childhood in the slums of England. Harry Spencer lavishes all of his wealth and attention on his daughter Christabel, who finally does marry an English Earl, only to find him carrying on a homosexual affair." Best Sellers

This novel "zeros in with sympathy, intuition and accuracy on what the role of women was like in turn-of-the-century New York and London. . . . It is good reading, good writing and vastly entertaining." Publ Wkly

Ravenscroft. Coward-McCann 1965 c1964 253p o.p.

First published 1964 in the United Kingdom with title: Bella

In a "romantic novel of Victorian England two orphaned sisters find themselves trapped by procurers in London. A handsome nobleman interested in social reform rescues the girls, marries one in order to quiet gossip, and later has to outwit the vengeful abductors again." Booklist

The Salamanca drum. Coward, McCann & Geoghegan 1977 286p o.p.

LC 76-56143

Matilda Duncastle "is a strong-willed woman, whose whole life is dedicated to honoring and continuing the Duncastle code of military gallantry and sacrifice. Marrying not out of love but out of duty to save the family estate, she is willing to sacrifice her husband's devotion, her sons' lives, as one war after another bleeds Britain half to death, and her daughters' happiness and right to lives of their own—all for a dream of patriotic glory that is almost madness." Publ Wkly

This novel "combines rich characterizations, plenty of action, lush locales (London, Vienna, Ireland), war, love, madness, a mysterious disappearance, thwarted romance." Libr J

Eden, Dorothy, 1912-1982—*Continued*

The vines of Yarrabee. Coward-McCann 1969 381p o.p.

"The story centers on Gilbert Massingham who leaves Suffolk, England, and with a small inheritance establishes a vineyard in New South Wales. His fiancée, Eugenia Lichfield, joins him in three years at his estate Yarrabee and the developing narrative portrays their marriage, their family, and the interweaving of their lives with those of Molly Jarvis, their attractive housekeeper, Colm O'Connor, a portrait painter, and others of their neighbors and friends." Booklist

"The story is plausible. The atmosphere of Australia authentic. The background of wine-growing and wine-making is interesting." Best Sellers

Edgarian, Carol

Rise the Euphrates. Random House 1994 370p $22

ISBN 0-679-42601-9   LC 93-6323

This novel "examines three generations of Armenian American women alternately united and divided by the burdens of history as the narrative moves from early 20th-century Turkey to suburban Connecticut in the 1990s. Grandmother Casard Essayan, who alone of her family survived the 1915 Turkish massacre of Armenians, carries a burden of guilt that drives her daughter Araxie into a marriage with a non-Armenian, George Loon. Araxie's love-hate relationship with her mother fills her with inchoate longing echoed in her daughter, Seta, whose destiny beckons her to relieve her grandmother's guilt and to find the fulfillment that her mother lacks." Libr J

"While perhaps too reliant on the mystical transmission of knowledge . . . the narrative believably renders conflicts and deep affection among parents and children, lovers, husbands and wives." Publ Wkly

Edgerton, Clyde, 1944-

Killer diller; a novel. Algonquin Bks. 1990 247p $17.95

ISBN 0-945575-53-X   LC 90-42778

Also available G.K. Hall large print edition

"This sequel to *Walking across Egypt* focuses on Wesley Benfield, now 24 and a resident at a halfway house associated with a Baptist college, where he teaches masonry to a retarded teenager, starts a gospel-blues band, and wrestles with his feelings of faith and lust." Booklist

"Occasionally, Mr. Edgerton's sense of humor gets the best of him and he pushes a scene until the characters border on the cartoonish. And near the end the plot . . . seems a bit forced. But the bottom line is that there's an affecting story, authenticity of voice and moral complexity here." N Y Times Book Rev

Walking across Egypt; a novel. Algonquin Bks. 1987 216p $14.95

ISBN 0-912697-51-2   LC 86-20645

"Mattie Rigsbee, at 78, is slowing down. She plans her funeral so as not to be a burden; she supports the local Baptist church and entertains herself with hymns at the parlor piano; she tries not to meddle in her children's lives, though she does wish they'd marry; she longs for grandchildren. Then comes Wesley. Reared in an orphanage until he graduated to the reformatory, Wes-

ley touches her heart, revives a life gone to seed. Just as he needs a grandmother's love and stability, so Mattie needs his challenge, dependence, and love." Libr J

This novel is "warm, innocent, and has a charming central character." Booklist

Edmonds, Walter Dumaux, 1903-

Chad Hanna; by Walter D. Edmonds. Little, Brown 1940 548p o.p.

"Circumstances connected with helping a runaway slave escape into Canada, make it advisable for quick-tempered, quick-witted, freckle-nosed young Chad Hanna to vanish from his job as tavern hostler in Canastota, N.Y., one night when a circus is in town. Enamored of 'a lady rider' and her fine black horse, Chad identifies himself with the fortunes and misfortunes of Huguenine's Great and Only International Circus, as it travels the country roads of New York with its menagerie of one miserable old lion, its five wagons and quarreling but loyal little troupe of performers." Bookmark

"Chad is well done; the minor figures are clearly and vividly conceived; and if some of the major ones are not wholly consistent, it is no great matter in a story that moves along with the interest and vitality of this one." Boston Transcr

Drums along the Mohawk; [by] Walter D. Edmonds. Little, Brown 1936 592p o.p. Buccaneer Bks. reprint available $27.95 (ISBN 0-89966-291-9)

A "regional novel about early settlers in the Mohawk river valley in New York state during the Revolutionary war. The little community is made up of . . . individuals to whom Indian raids, British invasions, and militia gatherings are evidences of a distraught world outside. Their own understanding of the difficulties is rather vague. Gil Martin and his wife, clearing their home in the forest, and their not-very-near neighbors, are the main characters." Booklist

Edwards, Anne, 1927-

Wallis; the novel. Morrow 1991 478p o.p.

LC 90-22735

This novel's heroine is "Wallis Warfield Spencer Simpson, the late duchess of Windsor. Born—too soon after her parents' marriage—into the aristocratic clan of Baltimore Warfields, Bessie Wallis finds that her dubious birth certificate . . . and her beautiful mother's many indiscretions prove social barriers. . . . Though a sketchy finishing school education fits her for little more than the role of a social butterfly, she is determined to make Baltimore look up to her. Two bad marriages precede her whirlwind descent on London society, where her wit and verve as a stylish hostess enable her to stalk the popular, playboy prince of Wales." Publ Wkly

"The fictionally rendered story seems in places more lurid than the real one; but Edwards lends a good degree of understanding to the motives, insecurities, needs, and accomplishments of the 'adventuress,' as King Edward's mother, Queen Mary, dismissed Wallis." Booklist

Egan, Lesley, 1921-

For works written by this author under other names see Linington, Elizabeth, 1921-; Shannon, Dell, 1921-

Egleton, Clive, 1927-

A double deception. St. Martin's Press 1992 309p o.p.

LC 92-2753

"As the story opens, in September 1939, aristocratic Andrew Korwin has arranged for his younger sister and brother to leave their Warsaw home before the Nazis march in. The brother is killed, sister Christina gets away and we last see Andrew trying to escape from a burning hospital. In 1967 Christina's American daughter, Stefanie, appears in London in search of her uncle. She enlists the aid of Campbell Parker of the Foreign Office, and clues point to Polish émigré Arthur Kershaw, successful manufacturer of a new laser-equipped gun. Other players include a seedy PI, a German con man, a newly released war criminal and even Simon Wiesenthal." Publ Wkly

Hostile intent. St. Martin's Press 1993 314p $18.95

ISBN 0-312-08812-4   LC 92-21219

"Peter Ashton, a British agent, investigates the death in 1991 of a colleague who was running a Soviet Army office, a woman, who has disappeared. The search for her leads from Europe to the United States, with Ashton having to avoid the members of a Russian hit team. They want the defector as much as the British and the Americans do. . . . The plotting is careful, the action constant but never heavy-breathing, the characters low-key and believable." N Y Times Book Rev

A killing in Moscow. St. Martin's Press 1994 346p $21.95

ISBN 0-312-10487-1   LC 93-44059

British agent Peter Ashton is "sent to the Moscow embassy to appraise the local security efforts, he gets caught up in the investigation of the murder of a British subject. Puzzled by contradictions in the evidence, he enlists the help of a minor Russian functionary, a woman who is beaten and tortured for what she may know. Soon, the trail leads to Seattle and Serbia, where international commerce has been put to corrupt ends. Egleton is never fanciful but always imaginative, and his latest novel is densely plotted and peopled with full and convincing characters." Libr J

Elegant, Robert S.

Dynasty; a novel. McGraw-Hill 1977 625p o.p.

LC 76-58433

This novel "recounts the history of the Sekloongs, an influential Eurasian commercial family based in Hong Kong. The reader meets the Sekloong patriarch, Sir Jonathan (1853-1950), issue of an Irish father and Chinese mother, and observes his children and their children as they go about the business of birth, death, marriage, love affairs, politics, and, most of all, trade. . . . The Sekloong saga is told against the backdrop of larger events, specifically 20th-Century China in revolutionary turmoil." Libr J

Manchu. McGraw-Hill 1980 560p o.p.

LC 80-17452

This "novel of 17th Century China depicts the conquest of the great Ming Empire by the invading Tartars, or Manchus. The story, panoramic in scope, focuses on the life of Francis Arrowsmith, a European who comes to China at a young age in 1624 to serve the Christian cause as 'not a saint but a sinful soldier.' For the next 30 years Arrowsmith's military career places him at the center of tumultuous events." Libr J

The novel "has color and drama aplenty, and authentically captures the splendor, brutality and intrigue of the Ming dynasty in its decadence." Publ Wkly

Mandarin. Simon & Schuster 1983 527p o.p.

LC 83-18696

This "family saga cum historical epic has for background the tumultuous era of the Taiping Rebellion, which shook the Manchu empire to its foundations and led to the destruction by Western troops of Peking's Summer Palace. The principal characters are members of two wealthy merchant families, the Haleevies and the Lees, one Western and one Chinese, but partners in business and both Jewish by faith, and Yehenala, the decadent emperor's favorite concubine, who bears the heir to the throne and becomes de facto ruler of the empire." Publ Wkly

Eliot, George, 1819-1880

Adam Bede.

Available from Amereon and Buccaneer Bks.

First published in 1859

"The title character, a carpenter, is in love with a woman who bears a child by another man. Although Bede tries to help her, he eventually loses her but finds happiness with Dinah Morris, a Methodist preacher. *Adam Bede* was Eliot's first long novel. Its masterly realism—evident, for example, in the recording of Derbyshire dialect—brought to English fiction the same truthful observation of minute detail that John Ruskin was commending in the Pre-Raphaelites. But what was new in this work of English fiction was the combination of deep human sympathy and rigorous moral judgment." Merriam-Webster's Ency of Lit

Middlemarch.

Available from various publishers

First published 1872

A novel "with a double plot interest. The heroine, Dorothea Brooke, longs to devote herself to some great cause and, for a time, expects to find it in her marriage to Rev. Mr. Casaubon, an aging scholar. Mr. Casaubon lives only eighteen months after their marriage, a sufficient period to disillusion her completely. He leaves his estate, with the ill-intentioned proviso that she will forfeit if she marries his young cousin Will Ladislaw, whom she had seen frequently in Rome. Endeavoring to find happiness without Ladislaw, whom she has come to care for deeply, Dorothea throws herself into the struggle for medical reforms advocated by the young Dr. Lydgate. Finally, however, she decides to give up her property and marry Ladislaw. The second plot deals with the efforts and failure of Dr. Lydgate to live up to his early ideals." Reader's Ency. 3d edition

The mill on the Floss. Knopf 1992 597p $20

ISBN 0-679-41726-5   LC 92-52920

Also available from Amereon

"Everyman's library"

First published 1860. First Everyman edition 1908

"Deeply significant tragedy of the inner life, enacted amidst the quaint folk and old-fashioned surroundings of a country town (St. Ogg's is Gainsborough). The conflict of affection and antipathy between a brother and sister, and again in the family relations of their father,

Eliot, George, 1819-1880—*Continued*

is a dominant motive; but the emotional tension rises to a climax in Maggie's unpremeditated yielding to an unworthy lover and betrayal of her finer nature. Brother and sister . . . are purified and reconciled only in death." Baker. Guide to the Best Fic

Romola. o.p.

First published in book form 1863

"Based on a special study of Florentine history in the epoch 1492-1509, the days of Lorenzo de' Medici, and the saintliness and all-conquering energy of Savonarola are finely portrayed. 'Romola' is a sternly tragic novel of temptation, crime and retribution." Baker. Guide to the Best Fic

Silas Marner; the weaver of Raveloe. Knopf 1993 xxx, 206p $15

ISBN 0-679-42030-4   LC 92-54293

"Everyman's library"

First published 1861

"Silas Marner is a handloom weaver, a good man, whose life has been wrecked by a false accusation of theft, which cannot be disproved. For years he lives a lonely life, with the sole companionship of his loom: and he is saved from his own despair by the chance finding of a little child. On this baby girl he lavishes the whole passion of his thwarted nature, and her filial affection makes him a kindly man again. After sixteen years the real thief is dicovered, and Silas's good name is restored. On this slight framework are hung the richest pictures of middle and low class life that George Eliot has painted." Keller. Reader's Dig of Books

Elkin, Stanley, 1930-1995

Her sense of timing

In Elkin, S. Van Gogh's room at Arles: three novellas p1-109

Mrs. Ted Bliss. Hyperion 1995 291p $22.95

ISBN 0-7868-6104-5   LC 95-5413

"After her husband's death, Dorothy Bliss stays on alone in The Towers, their Miami Beach retirement condo. Everyone continues to address her as Mrs. Ted Bliss, as if she had no identity of her own. But Dorothy adapts quickly to change, and soon she is on The Towers's A-list, hob-nobbing with 'Tommy Overeasy,' an elegant South American drug lord, and the building's chief engineer, a Yiddish-speaking Aztec. By the time Hurricane Andrew bears down on southern Florida, a fully self-sufficient Mrs. Bliss simply barricades herself inside and rides out the storm." Libr J

This is a "smart, generous, melancholy, funny, even elegiac work by a prodigious practitioner." N Y Times Book Rev

Town Crier exclusive, Confessions of a Princess manqué

In Elkin, S. Van Gogh's room at Arles: three novellas p113-217

Van Gogh's room at Arles

In Elkin, S. Van Gogh's room at Arles: three novellas p221-312

Van Gogh's room at Arles: three novellas. Hyperion 1993 312p $22.95

ISBN 1-56282-937-8   LC 92-24802

"'Her Sense of Timing' begins with the abrupt end of a long marriage. Professor Schiff's wife leaves him, in spite of the fact that he's nearly 60 and disabled, on the eve of his annual party for his graduate students. . . . In the next tale, Elkin inhabits the wonderfully cynical mind of a young British woman who easily seduces the virginal Prince of England, who then giddily proposes to her at a press conference. '*Town Crier* Exclusive, Confessions of a Princess Manqué' is her tell-all about their brief engagement and her bizarre interaction with the goofy royal family. And, finally, the title piece is a hilarious fish-out-of-water story about an Indiana community-college professor who is awarded a fellowship to spend five weeks in Arles with a group of far more distinguished and artful academics." Booklist

Elkins, Aaron J.

Curses!; [by] Aaron Elkins. Mysterious Press 1989 204p o.p.

LC 88-19525

"Returning to the site of an archaeological dig at Tlaloc on the Yucatan Peninsula, physical anthropologist Gideon Oliver is confronted with mysterious events from the distant and not-so-distant past as well as the present. Closed five years ago amid scandal when the then project director apparently absconded with a recently discovered priceless Mayan codex, the dig had recently resumed only to disclose some unauthorized excavation and an ancient curse, the details of which are being methodically fulfilled in graphic detail. Oliver and his wife, Julie, join forces with the local police to uncover the truth about what happened five years ago and its connection with the current problem." Libr J

Dead men's hearts; [by] Aaron Elkins. Mysterious Press 1994 227p $18.95

ISBN 0-89296-466-9   LC 93-43762

A mystery featuring anthropologist/sleuth Gideon Oliver. "After reluctantly agreeing to help film a documentary promoting Horizon House, a center for Egyptian studies located in the Nile Valley, Gideon and his wife, Julie, are looking forward to a relaxing few weeks. But soon after they reach Luxor, an ancient skeleton unearthed at a Horizon House dig in the 1920s is misplaced, and the illustrious head of the institute, Professor Clifford Haddon, is murdered. . . . A refreshingly funny, clever, entertaining mystery that will appeal to a broad range of readers." Booklist

A glancing light; [by] Aaron Elkins. Scribner 1991 243p $18.95

ISBN 0-684-19278-0   LC 90-25885

Also available Thorndike Press large print edition

"When a stolen masterpiece surfaces in a shipment of inexpensive copies, [museum curator Chris Norgren] verifies its authenticity but questions the involvement of the seemingly innocent importer. During a business trip to Bologna, his suspicions are confirmed when he discovers the renowned art squad of the Italian carbinieri is conducting an investigation of a series of related thefts and forgeries. As the elaborate scam begins to unravel, Chris becomes the target of a desperately cunning colleague. An intelligent and superbly crafted caper." Booklist

Elkins, Aaron J.—*Continued*

Icy clutches; [by] Aaron Elkins. Mysterious Press 1990 294p $16.95

ISBN 0-89296-377-8   LC 89-49554

"Gideon Oliver, a 'skeleton detective' (he deduces how people got dead by examining their bones), thought Alaska would be a great spot for a getaway vacation. When human bones turn up at a 30-year-old avalanche site, however, play becomes work." Am Libr

"Mr. Elkins skates on thin ice with character and dialogue, but give him a mandibular fossa to analyze, or a glacial upheaval to describe, and he's right up there at 90 degrees north—on top of the world." N Y Times Book Rev

Make no bones; [by] Aaron Elkins. Mysterious Press 1991 234p $17.95

ISBN 0-89296-378-6   LC 91-50204

In this mystery Gideon Oliver "receives an invitation to the sixth biennial 'bone bash and weenie roast' of the Western Association of Forensic Anthropologists, to take place at the Whitebark Lodge in Oregon. The last WAFA conference held at the Whitebark Lodge, 10 years earlier, ended tragically when Albert Evan Jasper, irascible mentor to four of the attendees, died in a fiery bus crash on his way out of town. Or did he? As a highlight of *this* conference, Jasper's charred remains will be on display for viewing and study. . . . Readers who like their humor dark and their gumshoes smart are sure to enjoy the 'bone bash.'" Publ Wkly

Old scores; a Chris Norgren mystery; [by] Aaron Elkins. Scribner 1993 242p $20

ISBN 0-684-19551-8   LC 92-38736

"Seattle Art Museum curator Chris Norgren falls prey to the lure of a newly discovered Rembrandt. . . . He also topples head-first out of a second-story window, but the nasty fall is happily blunted by a conveniently located car. Acquiring art isn't usually perilous, but anything is possible when the work is in the care of French dealer René Vachey, notorious for passing off thefts as publicity stunts." Publ Wkly

"Mr. Elkins and his insouciant hero have their witty fun with the *corps d'élite* of the international art establishment while providing some pretty amazing information on the brilliant forgeries and ingenious art scams that give the experts nightmares." N Y Times Book Rev

Ellison, Harlan

Adrift just off the Islets of Langerhans: latitude 38° 54' N, longitude 77° 00' 13 W

In The Hugo winners v3 p547-81

A boy and his dog

In The Best of the Nebulas p359-89

(ed) Dangerous visions. See Dangerous visions

The deathbird

In The Hugo winners v3 p437-68

Ellison, Ralph

Invisible man; preface by Charles Johnson. Modern Lib. 1994 xxxiv, 572p $13

ISBN 0-679-60139-2   LC 94-176953

A reissue of the title first published 1952 by Random House

"Acclaimed as a powerful representation of the lives of blacks during the Depression, this novel describes the experiences of one young black man during that period. Dismissed from a Negro college in the South for showing one of the founders how Negroes live there, he is used later as a symbol of repression by a Communist group in New York City. After a Harlem race riot, he is aware that he must contend with both whites and blacks, and that loss of social identity makes him invisible among his fellow beings." Shapiro. Fic for Youth. 3d edition

Ellroy, James

The black dahlia. Mysterious Press 1987 325p o.p.

LC 87-7952

"Using the basic facts concerning the 1940s' notorious and yet unsolved Black Dahlia case, Ellroy creates a kaleidoscope of human passion and dark obsession. A young woman's mutilated body is found in a Los Angeles vacant lot. The story is seen through the eyes of Bucky Bleichert, ex-prize fighter and something of a boy wonder on the police force." Libr J

"The author manages a gripping re-creation of LA street life in the 1940s, and his characters are powerfully written and terrifyingly real. The bare-bones plot, the slew of false conclusions, and the hazy evocation of the murder victim give the narrative a dreamlike atmosphere, ideal for a tale of immoral heroes and wasted lives." Booklist

Dick Contino's blues

In Ellroy, J. Hollywood nocturnes p13-91

Hollywood nocturnes. Penzler Bks. 1994 229p $20

ISBN 1-883402-54-9   LC 93-40521

Analyzed in Short story index

This volume includes an autobiographical introduction, the novella Dick Contino's blues, and the following stories: High Darktown; Dial Axminster 6-400; Since I don't have you; Gravy train; Torch number

"Set mainly in the 1940s and 1950s, the stories are populated by cops, criminals, floozies, hustlers, and zoot-suited wiseguys. . . . The hero of the longest piece is Dick Contino, the accordian-playing, benny-popping star of the drive-in classic *Daddy-O*. . . . A good introduction to one of crime fiction's grittier masters." Libr J

L.A. confidential. Mysterious Press 1990 496p $19.95

ISBN 0-89296-293-3   LC 89-40523

This novel focuses on three L.A. policemen: "Trashcan Jack Vincennes, a narcotics cop who makes a little cash on the side by setting up indiscreet celebrities for exposure in a Hollywood scandal sheet; Bad Bud White, whose favorite crime-stopping technique is to 'shoot everyone involved, then look for somebody a bit more intelligent to sort out the bodies'; and Ed Exley, a well-connected officer who believes in 'stern, absolute justice, whatever the price,' provided it doesn't impede his political ambitions." N Y Times Book Rev

Ellroy, James—*Continued*

The author "merges raw-edged period detail with sleazy celluloid lore, producing a dark and dazzling descent into the criminal underworld of the 1950s." Booklist

White jazz; a novel. Knopf 1992 349p o.p.

LC 92-52890

This novel unfolds in "the murky, decadent world of Los Angeles in the late 1950s, as seen through the cynical eyes of David Klein, age 42, the commanding officer of the LAPD's vice division. Klein makes up his own rules as he goes along, rules that involve money, mayhem, and murder as necessary. Klein isn't the only one to follow such rules, which apparently are the 'norm' for other members of the force as well. But Klein suffers the unthinkable when he becomes the scapegoat so that other officers can protect their own dirty laundry from the probing eyes of federal agents." Libr J

"Ellroy's clipped, telegraphic style, his use of real people and real events, and his creation of a world horrifyingly devoid of any conventional morality make *White Jazz* a harrowing, remarkable read." Booklist

Elward, James

(jt. auth) Van Slyke, H. Public smiles, private tears

Endō, Shūsaku, 1923-

The final martyrs; translated by Van C. Gessel. New Directions 1994 199p $21.95

ISBN 0-8112-1272-6   LC 94-746

Analyzed in Short story index

Contents: The final martyrs; Shadows; A fifty-year-old man; Adieu; Heading home; Japanese in Warsaw; Life; A sixty-year-old man; The last supper; A woman called Shizu; The box

"This deftly translated collection, comprised of stories written as early as 1959 and as late as 1985, also includes semi-autobiographical tales in which Endo deals with the traumatic impact that his parent's divorce had on his boyhood. He also writes with grace, compassion and gentle humor about old age, love betrayed, Japanese tourists and the marks we leave on the lives of others." Publ Wkly

The samurai; a novel; translated from the Japanese by Van C. Gessel. Harper & Row 1982 272p $12.45

ISBN 0-06-859852-1   LC 82-47851

Original Japanese edition, 1980

This historical novel is "set in the seventeenth century as a Franciscan missionary and a samurai travel to Spanish America and on to Rome as emissaries of the Eastern emperor to the Pope. Their journey begins under a veil of secrecy and subterfuge and ends in futility when the purpose of their lengthy voyage is negated by a twist of Japanese authority that commands a return to political isolation. This is an effective re-creation of both the Eastern and Western aspects of the tale and also a realistic portrayal of the cultural disjunction experienced by both of the main characters." Booklist

Scandal; a novel; translated from the Japanese by Van C. Gessel. Dodd, Mead 1988 261p o.p.

LC 87-27409

Available from Dufour Eds.

At age 65, "the harmony Suguro feels he has finally achieved between his life and work is shattered. . . . A drunken woman accosts him, accusing the venerated writer of frequenting the brothel district of Tokyo. In fact, she tells him a portrait of his degenerate self now hangs in a gallery there. And a journalist, Kobari, a dabbler in literature and Marxism who is intent on exposing the hypocrisy of this Catholic convert and celebrated artist, forces Suguro to pursue this allegation." N Y Times Book Rev

"This provocative, impassioned meditation manages to explore not only the nature of identity, but also the regions of sin, salvation, art and religion, all with the unerring grace that defines a novelist in the fullest command of his craft." Publ Wkly

The sea and poison; a novel; translated and with an introduction by Michael Gallagher. Taplinger 1980 c1972 167p o.p.

LC 80-16867

Original Japanese edition, 1958; this translation first published 1972 in the United Kingdom

"This novel faces the question of personal response to human vivisection, practiced on American POW's during WWII. The background of the doctors and nurses involved is explored, showing the circumstances which brought each one to the seemingly inevitable decision to participate, or to a lack of reason not to participate." Libr J

Silence; translated by William Johnston. Taplinger 1979 c1976 294p o.p.

LC 78-27168

Original Japanese edition, 1966; this translation first published 1969 in Japan

"The story is based on events in early 17th-century Japan, when Japanese Christians and Christian missionaries were brutally persecuted. In the novel, Sebastian Rodrigues, a Portuguese seminarian, journeys to Japan to investigate why his former teacher, a missionary to Japan, has chosen apostasy over martyrdom. Pervading the novel is the belief that Christianity is incompatible with Japanese culture. In the end, seeing the selfishness of martyrdom, Rodrigues also chooses apostasy." Merriam-Webster's Ency of Lit

Ephron, Nora

Heartburn. Knopf 1983 179p o.p.

LC 82-48999

Cookbook author and TV personality Rachel Samstat "is truly in love with her second husband, Mark Feldman, a columnist prone to asking 'Do you think there's something to it?' when scouting daily life for column material. Rachel is seven months pregnant when she finds out Mark's in love with Thelma Rice." Publ Wkly

"Though 'Heartburn' bristles ferociously with wit, it's not entirely lacking in soul." N Y Times Book Rev

Erdrich, Louise

The Beet Queen; a novel. Holt & Co. 1986 338p $16.95

ISBN 0-8050-0058-5   LC 86-4788

Second installment in the author's North Dakota Quartet

This novel "concerns a brother and sister, Karl and Mary Adare, who are abandoned by their mother, who runs away with a barnstorming pilot. Flight is a recurring theme in this . . . tale of loneliness set against a stark

Erdrich, Louise—*Continued*

North Dakota landscape. Karl spends his life as an itinerant salesman, running from his troubled family and his own sexual ambivalence; Mary, who grows up with her aunt and uncle, uses self-reliance as a way of hiding from the pain of human relationships; and Sita, Mary's cousin, retreats into insanity to avoid facing the realization that her idealized dreams of a glamorous life have evaporated. Only Celestine, Mary's friend and the mother of Karl's child, accepts reality on its own terms as she struggles to protect her daughter from the suffering that has engulfed those around her." Booklist

The bingo palace. HarperCollins Pubs. 1994 274p $23

ISBN 0-06-017080-8   LC 93-37684

Final volume in the author's North Dakota Quartet
"Immediately on returning to his North Dakota Chippewa reservation, Lipsha Morrissey—having failed in the outside world—falls head over heels in love with the beautiful Shawnee Ray. She is the fierce and ambitious mother of the illegitimate son of Lyman Lamartine, owner of the Bingo Palace and a powerful force on the reservation. Lyman is determined to marry Shawnee Ray, who is just as determined to elude him and go to college. When Lipsha goes to work for Lyman, he also enters into a battle for Shawnee Ray's affections, calling first on the magic of tribal elder Fleur Pillager, then on luck, and finally on traditional tribal religion." Libr J
"We're often uncomfortable when so much unadulterated feeling is spilled at our feet, but Erdrich is ready for our squeamishness, mixing romance and comedy with the skill of a master alchemist, diluting sentimentality while enhancing the emotional impact of the story." Booklist

Love medicine; new and expanded version. Holt & Co. 1993 367p $24

ISBN 0-8050-2798-X   LC 93-15166

Original version published 1984
First volume in the author's North Dakota Quartet
"The story opens in 1981 when June Kashpaw, an attractive, leggy Chippewa prostitute who has idled away her days on the main streets of oil boomtowns in North Dakota, decides to return to the reservation on which she was raised. Before leaving Williston, N.D., however, June takes on one more client and, afterward, decides to walk back to her home. En route she dies in the freezing Dakota countryside. But her memory and the legacy she passes on to her family prompt various relatives and acquaintances to recall their relationships with her and to reminisce about their own lives." N Y Times Book Rev

Tracks; a novel. Holt & Co. 1988 226p $22.50

ISBN 0-8050-0895-0   LC 88-9321

This third installment in the author's North Dakota Quartet depicts "the escalating conflict between two Chippewa families, a conflict begun when hapless Eli Kashpaw—who has passionately pursued the fiery, elemental Fleur Pillager—is made to betray her with young Sophie Morrissey through the magic of the vengeful Pauline." Libr J
"Ms. Erdrich is, as always, the generous kind of storyteller, passing along not only everything her characters know, but the story of the stories as well. Giving life and shape and sense to what's happened, she lets the designs spring clear." N Y Times Book Rev

(jt. auth) Dorris, M. The crown of Columbus

Esquivel, Laura

Like water for chocolate; a novel in monthly installments with recipes, romances, and home remedies; translated by Carol Christensen and Thomas Christensen. Doubleday 1992 245p $19.95

ISBN 0-385-42016-1   LC 91-47188

Original Spanish edition published 1989 in Mexico
Set in turn-of-the-century Mexico, this novel relates the story of Tita, "the youngest of three daughters. Practically raised in the kitchen, she is expected to spend her life waiting on Mama Elena and never to marry. Her habitual torment increases when her beloved Pedro becomes engaged to one of her sisters. Tita and he are thrown into tantalizing proximity and manage to communicate their affection through the dishes she prepares for him and his rapturous appreciation. Eventually, Tita's culinary wizardry unleashes uncontrollable forces, with surprising results." Booklist
"A poignant, funny story of love, life, and food which proves that all three are entwined and interdependent." Libr J

Esteves, Carmen C., 1952-

(ed) Green cane and juicy flotsam. See Green cane and juicy flotsam

Estleman, Loren D.

Bloody season. Bantam Bks. 1988 231p $15.95

ISBN 0-553-05231-4   LC 87-47573

A fictional retelling "of the gunfight at the O.K. Corral. Opening with the shootout itself, the narrative then recounts both the events leading up to the battle and its legacy, often doing so in a documentary fashion that focuses on the personal histories of the individuals involved." Libr J
"Estleman displays solid historical knowledge and his usual deft writing. The characters—especially Holliday, an alcoholic, tubercular woman-beater, and Wyatt Earp, a dandified womanizer interested mainly in money—spring indelibly to life. The feel, sights and smells of 1881 Tombstone are beautifully etched in this flawed but compulsively readable gem." Publ Wkly

City of widows. Forge 1994 254p $20.95

ISBN 0-312-85667-9   LC 94-4051

"A Tom Doherty Associates book"
"In an act of personal vengeance, Judge Harlan Blackthorne of Montana Territory sends deputy U.S. Marshal Page Murdock to San Sabado, New Mexico, to bring to justice murderers Ross and Frank Baronet. As a cover for his activities, Murdock . . . buys into a friend's saloon. His task is complicated by the fact that Ross is reputed to be dead in Mexico, and Frank is the sheriff of Socorro County, where Murdock's saloon is located." Libr J
The author "shows once again the difference between mere genre writing and artistry displayed in genre form." N Y Times Book Rev

Estleman, Loren D.—*Continued*

Downriver. Houghton Mifflin 1988 210p o.p.

LC 87-16911

"An Amos Walker mystery"

Detroit private detective Amos "Walker's client, Richard DeVries, has just been paroled after serving 20 years on a riot-related arson and armed-robbery charge. He was framed and wants Walker to help him find the culprit. The search extends to an automobile manufacturer's headquarters 'downriver,' in the industrial area south of Detroit. Careful readers will have spotted the bad guy several chapters before the climax, but that only adds to the sense of inevitability, of the past taking its toll, that Estleman so effectively generates." Booklist

Every brilliant eye. Houghton Mifflin 1985 252p o.p.

LC 85-10711

"An Amos Walker mystery"

Private eye Amos Walker is "hired by a Detroit newspaper to find a missing investigative reporter, Barry Stackpole, who has been summoned by the grand jury. Stackpole is also a Vietnam buddy of Walker's, so the case has its personal side. In following Stackpole's trail, Walker uncovers a murder-for-hire ring, unearths a skeleton in his friend's closet, and romances a svelte book editor who hopes to publish Stackpole's novel." Booklist

General murders. Houghton Mifflin 1988 232p o.p.

LC 88-1869

"An Amos Walker mystery"

Analyzed in Short story index

Contents: Greektown; Robbers' roost; Fast burn; Dead soldier; Eight Mile and Dequindre; I'm in the book; Bodyguards shoot second; The prettiest dead girl in Detroit; Blond and blue; Bloody July

"Dating from 1982 to 1987, these [Amos Walker] samplings are good indicators of the pleasures in Estleman's longer works." Publ Wkly

Kill zone. Mysterious Press 1984 237p o.p.

This novel introduces "Detroit hit man Peter Macklin. Macklin is asked to do something unusually delicate, a departure from his ordinary line of work. When terrorists take over the world's largest passenger-carrying steamboat on Lake Erie and demand that the governor release 10 prisoners or the terrorists will kill the 800 hostages on ship, the Detroit mob, the FBI, and the Secret Service want Macklin to handle the negotiations." Booklist

This has "enough action and colorful characters for three ordinary thrillers. . . . Good guys, bad guys and 'ordinary' citizens are all distinctively portrayed, and the plot twists and turns are dazzling." Publ Wkly

King of the corner. Bantam Bks. 1992 294p o.p.

LC 92-742

Concluding volume in the author's Detroit trilogy

This novel is "set in the present day, during an uneasy experiment in minority rule. At the center is Doc Miller, whose pitching days ended with the drug-related death of a girl at a party he was throwing. After doing hard time at the Jackson county jail, he's struggling. Then he finds his way to Maynard Ance, a bail bondsman who makes a swell living bending the rules—putting his money on the poor 'scrouts' of the neighborhood and

making it pay. Ance also has connections to a militant black outfit, the M&Ms, whose members dwell in that troubled world between heroism and terrorist fervor. And when the cops let it be known that they would like the inside dope, Doc isn't in a position to refuse." Booklist

"As a writer, Mr. Estleman plays in the majors. . . . Despite a shocking act of violence that brings his story to its bitter conclusion, the author plays a good clean game." N Y Times Book Rev

Lady yesterday. Houghton Mifflin 1987 194p o.p.

LC 86-27447

"An Amos Walker mystery"

"When Walker is hired by a Jamaican ex-prostitute, Iris, to find her father, an obscure jazz musician, he has no trouble picking up the trail of the missing trombone player. What he does not bargain for are some harshly explicit warnings from the drug czar of Detroit. . . . As usual, Estleman's dark, moody narration and his evocation of the seamy, forlorn ambience of Detroit mark this series with a special stamp." Publ Wkly

Motor City blue. Houghton Mifflin 1980 219p o.p.

LC 80-12716

"The hero is Amos Walker, a wry type who happens to be Detroit's best when it comes to finding murderers. In this case, however, events unfold as he investigates the whereabouts of a young woman, the ward of an aging gangster." Publ Wkly

Motown. Bantam Bks. 1991 292p o.p.

LC 91-6924

Second volume in the author's Detroit trilogy

"Choreographing the movements leading to the August 1966 Detroit riots, Estleman focuses on three main characters: Rick Amery, an ex-cop hired to spy on a Ralph Nader-like consumer advocate; inspector Lew Canada, trying to prevent a war between the Mafia and black gangs, and a likely race riot; and Quincy Springfield, numbers racketeer and 'blind pig' (after-hours club) operator." Publ Wkly

"Estleman seems more intent here on paying homage to the Motor City than on writing a mystery. Place is more important for Estleman than action, though this time several workable plots merge forcefully toward the novel's conclusion." Booklist

Silent thunder. Houghton Mifflin 1989 202p o.p.

LC 88-32295

"An Amos Walker mystery"

Amos Walker "checks into this case when the murdered heir to an industrial fortune is discovered to have been hoarding enough illegal munitions in his whoopee room to wipe out Zambia. Walker's professional interest is in the victim's wife, who has been charged with the murder. . . . Mr. Estleman turns in a tight, well-oiled plot and some catchy characterizations of the leading local merchants in the illegal weapons trade." NY Times Book Rev

Sudden country. Doubleday 1991 182p o.p.

LC 90-48441

This western set in 1890s Texas is "about a 13-year-old boy and a bunch of desperadoes on the trail of stolen gold." Booklist

Estleman, Loren D.—*Continued*

Sugartown. Houghton Mifflin 1985 220p o.p. Ultramarine reprint available $25 (ISBN 0-89366-256-9)

LC 84-12910

"An Amos Walker mystery"

"Amos Walker's first client is a recent Polish immigrant who wants to find her adult grandson. His second client is a Russian writer who thinks his life is being threatened by the KGB. The cases dovetail when the two trails lead to a missing Polish silver cross. The writing includes a few melodramatic passages and unintentionally comic descriptions. . . . However, the story improves as it unfolds, the solution is satisfying, and the city, dirty Detroit, is always pulsing in the background." Libr J

Whiskey River. Bantam Bks. 1990 262p o.p.

LC 90-32895

First volume in the author's Detroit trilogy

This "chronicles the short business life of a young bootlegger named Jack Dance as he slashes his way among the gangs and gangsters that controlled Detroit's politics and economics as a direct result of the 18th Amendment. But this is not so much Jack Dance's story as it is that of his chronicler, a cynical, disillusioned newspaper columnist named Connie Minor, whose vocational rise and fall nearly parallel that of Dance. . . . At every opportunity, 'Whiskey River' strives for authenticity. And the immediacy of its atmosphere never waivers." N Y Times Book Rev

Eugenides, Jeffrey

The virgin suicides. Farrar, Straus & Giroux 1993 249p $18

ISBN 0-374-28438-5   LC 92-33466

"The Lisbon girls, all five of whom committed suicide in the early 1970s, haunt the memories of boys next door in a wealthy Detroit suburb. A nameless narrator, one of the boys, 20 years later collects and weaves together the impressions that friends, neighbors, and parents had of the dead girls. Except for school and group outings to two ill-fated parties, the girls' lives played out confined to their dwelling, a cloistered existence protected by a mother vigilant for their virtue and by a meek father cowed by his feminized surroundings." Booklist

The author's "engrossing writing style keeps one reading despite a creepy feeling that one shouldn't be enjoying it so much. A black, glittering novel that won't be to everyone's taste but must be tried by readers looking for something different." Libr J

Eustace, Robert

(jt. auth) Sayers, D. L. The documents in the case

Evanovich, Janet

One for the money. Scribner 1994 290p $20

ISBN 0-684-19639-5   LC 93-50733

Also available G.K. Hall large print edition

"Stephanie Plum, a New Jersey native, is a laid-off discount lingerie buyer. Desperate for bucks, she decides to pursue a career as an 'apprehension agent,' tracking down scofflaws for her bail bondsman cousin, Vinnie. Her first mission: to bring in Joe Morelli, a cop accused of murder." Booklist

"A wonderful sense of humor, an eye for detail, and a self-deprecating narrative endow Stephanie Plum with the easy-to-swallow believability that accounts for her appeal as heroine. . . . A witty, well-written, and gutsy debut." Libr J

Evelyn, John Michael *See* Underwood, Michael, 1916-

Exupéry, Antoine de Saint- *See* Saint-Exupéry, Antoine de, 1900-1944

F

The **Faber** book of gay short fiction; edited by Edmund White. Faber & Faber 1991 586p $24.95

ISBN 0-571-14472-1   LC 91-173155

Analyzed in Short story index

Stories included are: Trespasses, by P. Bailey; Just above my head, by J. Baldwin; Three wedding ceremonies, by N. Bartlett; Pages from Cold Point, by P. Bowles; The wild boys, by W. S. Burroughs; Good fortune, by S. Burt; In praise of Vespasian, by A. Chester; My Mark, by D. Cooper; BM, by J. M. Estep; Concerning the eccentricities of Cardinal Pirelli, by R. Firbank; Dr. Woolacott, by E. M. Forster; The list, by P. Gale; Denry Smith, by R. Gluck; Forced use, by A. Gurganus; Native, by W. H. Henderson; Sunday morning: Key West, by A. Holleran; The swimming-pool library, by A. Hollinghurst; The novice, by T. Ireland; Mr. Lancaster, by C. Isherwood; The pupil, by H. James; When you grow to adultery, by D. Leavitt; Southern skies, by D. Malouf; The changes of those terrible years, by A. Mars-Jones; Suddenly home, by A. Maupin; The secret of the gentiles, by D. Plante; Dawn, by J. Purdy; Another life, by L. Raphael; Pages from an abandoned journal, by G. Vidal; Darts, by T. Wakefield; When I was thirteen, by D. Welch; Skinned alive, by E. White; Two on a party, by T. Williams

Fain, Michael

For works written by this author in collaboration with Judith Barnard see Michael, Judith

Fairbairn, Ann, 1901 or 2-1972

Five smooth stones; a novel. Crown 1966 756p o.p. Buccaneer Bks. reprint available $46.95 (ISBN 0-89966-805-4)

"Although born in poverty in New Orleans, David Champlin, a young black man, escapes this dreary background with the help of devoted grandparents, a Danish professor, and a scholarship to a Midwestern college. The book details his successful legal and diplomatic career and his love affair and marriage with Sara Kent, a white

Fairbairn, Ann, 1901 or 2-1972—*Continued*
classmate. David becomes involved also in the Civil
Rights movement. The book concludes on a triumphant
but tragic note." Shapiro. Fic For Youth. 3d edition

Fairbairns, Zoë
Stand we at last; a novel. Houghton
Mifflin 1983 609p o.p.

LC 82-15624

"Beginning in 1855 on the windy cliffs that form the
coast of Sussex, [this novel] traces the lives of five
generations of Englishwomen. . . . Moving by decades,
the novel takes us from the Victorian era, when Sarah
Weeks emigrated to Australia under the auspices of the
Ladies' Progress assisted passages, to 1972 when a great-
great-granddaughter returns to London after a sojourn on
a Scottish commune with her own infant daughter." Ms
This book "travels a long way in time and space, and
covers a lot of ideological ground in the process. It gives
a straightforward, if somewhat simplistic, résumé of the
last hundred years of women's struggle for emancipation
while telling a rattling good tale." Times Lit Suppl

Fallaci, Oriana
A man; translated from the Italian by
William Weaver. Simon & Schuster 1980
463p o.p.

LC 80-17838

Original Italian edition, 1979
The hero of this novel, "Allessandro Panagoulis, tries
to assassinate the Greek dictator George Papadopoulis.
He fails, but even after mutilating tortures and years of
imprisonment in a tomblike cell, he never bows his head
to Papadopoulis' dictatorship. His humor and the
freedom that he guards within preserve his pride and
sanity. . . . [This work is a] narration of [the author's]
relationship with Panagoulis and the events that led to
his [alleged] murder by political agents in 1976, told as
if it were fiction." Saturday Rev
"The focus is obsessively fixed on Panagoulis, a brilliantly realized character whom no novelist could ever
have invented. . . . Fallaci is able to select from the
particulars of this one man's life to fashion clearsighted
analyses into the nature of politics and power. . . . [She]
places her subject in the most deeply Greek context of
all, that of ancient tragedy, as she marvelously adduces
one resonant mythic parallel after another on the way
to her lover's final submission to his tragic fate." New
Repub

Fallon, Martin, 1929- *See* Higgins, Jack,
1929-

Famous ghost stories; compiled and with an
introductory note by Bennett A. Cerf.
Modern Lib. 1944 361p o.p. Amereon
reprint available $24.95 (ISBN
0-88411-146-6)

Analyzed in Short story index
Contents: The haunted and the haunters, by E. Bulwer-
Lytton; The damned thing, by A. Bierce; The monkey's
paw, by W. Jacobs; The phantom 'rickshaw, by R.
Kipling; The willows, by A. Blackwood; The rival ghosts,
by B. Matthews; The man who went too far, by E. F.
Benson; The mezzotint, by M. R. James; The open win-

dow, by "Saki"; The beckoning fair one, by O. Onions;
On the Brighton Road, by R. Middleton; The considerate
hosts, by T. McClusky; August heat, by W. F. Harvey;
The return of Andrew Bentley, by A. W. Derleth; The
supper at Elsinore, by I. Dinesen; The current crop of
ghost stories, by B. A. Cerf

Farmer, Philip José
The classic Philip José Farmer, 1952-1964
—1964-1973; edited and introduction by Martin H. Greenberg; foreword by Isaac
Asimov. Crown 1984 2v o.p.

"Classics of modern science fiction"
Analyzed in Short story index
Contents: 1952-1964: Sail on! Sail on; Mother; The
God business; The Alley Man; My sister's brother; The
king of beasts
1964-1973: The shadow of space; Riders of the purple
wage [novelette]; Don't wash the carats; The jungle rot
kid on the nod; The oogenesis of Bird City; The sliced-
crosswise only-on-Tuesday world; Sketches among the
ruins of my mind; After King Kong fell

The dark design. Berkley Pub. Group
1977 412p o.p.

LC 77-5138

The third volume of the Riverworld series
This volume "continues the adventures of explorer Sir
Richard Burton, Mark Twain, and scores of others who
are resurrected along the banks of the multimillion-mile-
long River. . . . In dirigibles and riverboats, through
heroism and treachery, a band of restless explorers attains the headwaters home of the mysterious Ethicals,
who apparently are responsible for creating the Riverworld and resurrecting its confused populace." Booklist
"Some threads in the design are loose or overknotted,
but the dash and grand scope of the project and this
installment of it are compellingly fascinating." Publ Wkly
Followed by The magic labyrinth

Dayworld. Putnam 1985 320p o.p.

LC 84-17978

First volume in the Dayworld trilogy
"In the 35th century, people live only one day a week,
spending the other six days in suspended animation. Jeff
Caird, a policeman in Tuesday's World, is also a 'daybreaker,' illegally living seven different lives as seven
different people—until the week he becomes both hunter
and hunted in a mad chase across seven different cultures." Libr J
This novel "is cleverly crafted, fastmoving, and absorbing. Smooth transitions connect the days and Caird's
various identities through which the author addresses
many philosophical and political issues such as religious
toleration, a classless society, marriage, monitoring of
citizens by the government, and employer/employee relations." Best Sellers

Dayworld breakup. Doherty Assocs. 1990
324p o.p.

LC 90-172386

"A TOR book"
The concluding volume of the Dayworld trilogy
"The infamous 'daybreaker' William Duncan continues
to battle the powers-that-be in a future where humans
live only one day in seven and a select few possess the
knowledge that could overthrow a corrupt world government. This fast-paced conclusion to Farmer's 'Dayworld
Trilogy' celebrates the power of the iconoclast and the
triumph of idealism." Libr J

Farmer, Philip José—*Continued*

Dayworld rebel. Putnam 1987 317p o.p.

LC 86-25432

"An Ace/Putnam book"

Second volume of the Dayworld trilogy

"The New Era, several thousand years in the future, seems a utopia. War, poverty, hunger and pollution are all obsolete. Overpopulation has been handled by dividing the population into seven groups, each fraction living one day a week while the others wait in suspended animation. Farmer's *Dayworld* chronicled the life of a man whose unique abilities allowed him to assume a different identity for each day. As this sequel opens, he has been caught and is being questioned. Escaping from his Manhattan prison, he flees to the wilds of New Jersey, falling in with a rebel group hiding out in caves. Along with them, he journeys to Los Angeles and contacts a larger subversive organization bent on radical change." Publ Wkly

The fabulous riverboat; a science fiction novel. Putnam 1971 253p o.p.

This second novel in the Riverworld series "is set in an 'after-Earthlife' of resurrected people over the age of five from time immemorial. The main character is . . . Sam Langhorne Clemens, alias Mark Twain, who attempts to build a metal riverboat. His goal, not obtained in this novel, is to sail upriver to reach the Misty Tower and discover the secret of its guardians, the Ethicals." Libr J

Followed by The dark design

Gods of Riverworld. Putnam 1983 331p o.p.

LC 83-9552

The fifth volume of the Riverworld series

"The members of the intrepid band that achieved its quest for the end of the River in the previous books now find themselves in command of the Ethicals' polar control center. When they're not trying to track down an unknown enemy, they're building private worlds and resurrecting a few friends. . . . It's the two varieties of god-playing, culminating in a disastrous tea party in Alice Pleasance Liddell's Wonderland, that give the book its interest." Publ Wkly

The magic labyrinth. Berkley Pub. Group 1980 339p o.p.

LC 80-144

In this fourth volume in the Riverworld series "Farmer brings his large and bizarre cast of characters (including King John Lackland of England, Samuel Clemens, Sir Richard Burton, Hermann Göring, and Alice Liddell, who inspired 'Alice in Wonderland') to the end of their quest and reveals the secret of the Riverworld. For readers prepared to accept it on its own terms, this book will be rewarding, even exciting. Farmer's imagination does not flag from beginning to end." Booklist

Followed by Gods of Riverworld

Riders of the purple wage

In Farmer, P. J. The classic Philip José Farmer, 1964-1973 p30-103

In The Hugo winners v2 p388-459

River of eternity. Phantasia Press 1983 205p $17

ISBN 0-932096-28-X

This is the original version of the novel written in 1952 that later formed the basis of the Riverworld series

"In 70,000 words this highly compressed rendering tells the essential story of the amazing Riverworld. It can't replace the later, grander work, but it is quite entertaining and a fascinating footnote to SF history." Publ Wkly

To your scattered bodies go; a science fiction novel. Putnam 1971 221p o.p.

The first volume of the Riverworld series

"The fabulous Riverworld, site of the resurrection of every human being who has died, is one of the great fictional creations. Sir Richard Burton, Victorian explorer and rogue, finds himself reborn and sets off on an epic journey to learn the truth of its existence." Shapiro. Fic For Youth. 3d edition

Followed by The fabulous riverboat

Farrell, James T. (James Thomas), 1904-1979

Judgment day

In Farrell, J. T. Studs Lonigan

Studs Lonigan; a trilogy comprising Young Lonigan, The young manhood of Studs Lonigan, and Judgment day; introduction by Charles Fanning. University of Ill. Press 1993 xxxi, 874p $49.95

ISBN 0-252-02062-6

LC 93-13851

This omnibus edition first published 1935 by Vanguard Press

The author's "experiences as a baseball enthusiast and pupil of Catholic schools on the city's South Side are the basis of *Young Lonigan* (1932). This naturalistic stream-of-consciousness study of an adolescent in a squalid urban environment shows Farrell's chief influences to be Dreiser, Joyce, and Proust, but also exhibits his interest in the common facts of U.S. life, and his indignation at social and economic inequalities. . . . *The Young Manhood of Studs Lonigan* (1934) follows the hero through his moral disintegration as the result of contact with the Chicago underworld, and *Judgment Day* (1935), completing the trilogy, tells of his defeat and death." Oxford Companion to Am Lit. 5th edition

Young Lonigan

In Farrell, J. T. Studs Lonigan

The young manhood of Studs Lonigan

In Farrell, J. T. Studs Lonigan

Fast, Howard, 1914-

April morning; a novel. Crown 1961 184p o.p.

"The spirit of the Revolutionary War, a country coming of age, and the life of a boy passing into manhood are captured in this historical novel. Fast focuses on one day in the life of Adam Cooper as his family and the community of Lexington rise to the events of April 19, 1775. Adam at first is caught up in the excitement, but by the end of the first skirmish the death of his father has brought home the horror and reality of war." Shapiro. Fic For Youth. 3d edition

Fast, Howard, 1914-—*Continued*

Citizen Tom Paine. Duell, Sloan & Pearce 1943 341p o.p.

The author presents a "picture of Paine's mode of writing, idiosyncrasies, and character—generous, nobly unselfish, moody, often dirty, frequently drunken, a revolutionist by avocation." Libr J

The establishment. Houghton Mifflin 1979 365p o.p.

LC 79-1186

The third volume of the Lavette family saga "starts in 1948, when Barbara Lavette's husband Bernie goes on a gun-running mission to Israel and dies at Arab hands. Successful writer Barbara, the main figure in the story, has barely coped with her grief when she gets caught up in the McCarthy witch-hunt and, being too honorable to name the names of certain 'communist suspects,' is briefly jailed. Other prominent figures are the sons of patriarch Dan Lavette—Tom, who has turned into a ruthless powerbroker, and Joe, whose dedication to medicine drives his wife Sally into the arms of Hollywood, where she thrives." Publ Wkly

Followed by The legacy

Freedom road. Duell, Sloan & Pearce 1944 263p o.p.

An historical novel based on the reconstruction period in the South following the Civil War, when for a few years blacks and whites worked together in harmony. Gideon Jackson, the black leader, who rose from illiteracy to be a member of Congress, is the central character. The rise of Gideon, his efforts to help his people, and the little settlement over which he presided is pictured. Then the Northern troops are withdrawn from the South, and disaster for the blacks follows

"It is told simply in the simplest of human terms. These humble men and women, with their children and loves and graspings after the things that would make a good life for them, do not stand about as the supernumeraries of a historical pageant. Their existence is history; they are the parts of which it is the sum." Saturday Rev

The immigrants. Houghton Mifflin 1977 389p o.p.

LC 77-9317

The first volume of the Lavette family saga. The main characters are Dan Lavette, son of French-Italian immigrants who builds a shipping and business empire with little but determination and luck; his overshadowed Jewish partner Mark Levy; his cold and beautiful society "wife Jean; May Ling, the Chinese woman he loves, but cannot marry without losing his empire. Around these people and their children, and against a background of the San Francisco earthquake, World War I and the Depression, Fast constructs a . . . story that ranges from fisherman's bar to tycoon's boardroom and pits the American Dream against the demands of conscience and love. It also underlines some of the bitter lessons of success." Publ Wkly

Followed by Second generation

The immigrant's daughter. Houghton Mifflin 1985 321p o.p.

LC 85-8251

The fifth volume of the Lavette family saga has "as its centerpiece, the campaign of Barbara Lavette for congresswoman from San Francisco's posh 48th district. Although Barbara—at 60 still in all ways breathtaking—loses, she is propositioned (and betrayed) by her Republican opponent, courted by her ex-husband, a newspaper publisher who sends her on assignment to El Salvador, and at book's end is up to her neck in ban-the-bomb plans." Publ Wkly

The legacy. Houghton Mifflin 1981 359p o.p.

LC 81-2906

The fourth volume of the Lavette family saga is set in the turbulent 1960s. Patriarch Dan is felled by a heart attack. "Daughter Barbara, whose psyche has been scarred by a prison sentence during the McCarthy era, is slowly coming to terms with her own volatile, independent nature, while her son and nephews are briefly involved in the civil rights struggle in the South, the Vietnam War, and the Six-Day War in the Middle East. The view of the Sixties is against Nixon, Johnson, big business, and war; and Fast lends . . . [a] wide-screen glamour to events most adult readers can still remember watching on the six o'clock news." Libr J

Followed by The immigrant's daughter

The outsider. Houghton Mifflin 1984 311p o.p.

"Young New Yorker David Hartman returns from the Second World War, marries Lucy Spendler, a U.S.O. volunteer, and accepts a position as rabbi in 'Leighton Ridge,' a small town in Fairfield County, Connecticut (Jewish population: 14) The narrative follows David's life—and world events—from memories of the Holocaust through blacklisting and the Rosenberg trial, civil rights marches in the South, Vietnam War. Through it all, David must respond to the needs of his growing congregation, his wife, son, and daughter, and his own spiritual questions." Libr J

Second generation. Houghton Mifflin 1978 441p o.p.

LC 78-5540

In the second volume of the Lavette family saga the author "traces the further activities of Dan Levette and his family, focusing upon his daughter Barbara, whose total involvement with the troubled times begins with aid to striking dockworkers, and then continues in prewar Nazi Germany and during journalistic encounters in the Eastern theaters." Booklist

Followed by The establishment

Seven days in June; a novel of the American Revolution. Carol Pub. Group 1994 191p $18.95

ISBN 1-55972-256-8   LC 94-20163

"A Birch Lane Press book"

This novel focuses on a "week of profound tension that will erupt in historic carnage at the Battle of Bunker Hill. In June 1775, some six weeks after the armed clashes at Lexington and Concord, the British have increased their force in Boston under General Howe as thousands of disorganized colonial troops gather nearby. At the center of Fast's story stands Evan Feversham, an English surgeon who has married an American and made a fresh start in Connecticut. Having volunteered to aid the revolutionaries, the doctor finds himself at the heart of their preparations for battle. Fast portrays key colonial figures largely through the eyes of Feversham. . . . Fast's accomplished storytelling draws the reader ever faster into the turmoil and ekes genuine suspense from events whose outcome is a matter of historical fact." Publ Wkly

Fast, Howard, 1914-—*Continued*

The trial of Abigail Goodman; a novel. Crown 1993 256p o.p.

LC 93-18043

Available G.K. Hall large print edition

"Sometime in the near future, Abigail Goodman, feminist history professor in a sleepy Southern town and 41-year-old mother of two, finds herself unexpectedly pregnant; she decides, with her husband's approval, to have an abortion. Shortly thereafter, she is indicted under a new state law that retroactively makes abortion after the first trimester an act of murder punishable by death." Publ Wkly

Faulkner, William, 1897-1962

Nobel Prize in literature, 1949

Absalom, Absalom!; corrected text. Random House 1986 313p $25

ISBN 0-394-55634-8　　　　　LC 86-6488

First published 1936

"During the summer of 1910, prior to Quentin Compson's leaving the South for his first year at Harvard, old Rosa Coldfield insists upon a private conference with the youth to divulge her recollections of Thomas Sutpen. Driven by a great plan to become a Southern aristocrat, Sutpen builds a mansion, only to see his life ruined. The title of the book reveals the story's basic tragedy: Sutpen's disappointment in his children. One is a spinster and thus has no offspring to continue the family lineage; the other is a son who has disappeared. Sutpen himself falls victim to a murder for retribution. Faulkner depicts the South before and after the Civil War in this powerfully written novel." Shapiro. Fic for Youth. 3d edition

As I lay dying. [New ed.]. Random House 1964 c1957 250p $22

ISBN 0-394-41581-7

First published 1930 by H. Smith

"Experimental in both subject and narrative structure, this novel treats the events surrounding the illness, death and burial of Addie Bundren, wife of Anse and mother of Cash, Darl, Jewel, Dewey Dell, and Vardaman. It is divided into 59 short interior monologues, predominantly in the present tense, spoken both by the seven members of the family and by various other characters, including the Reverend Whitfield, Dr. Peabody, and the Bundrens' neighbours, Vernon and Cora Tull." Camb Guide to Lit in Engl

Collected stories of William Faulkner. Random House 1950 900p $22.95

ISBN 0-394-41967-7

Analyzed in Short story index

Contents: Barn burning; Shingles for the Lord; Tall men; A bear hunt; Two soldiers; Shall not perish; Rose for Emily; Hair; Centaur in brass; Dry September; Death drag; Elly; Uncle Willy; Mule in the yard; That will be fine; That evening sun; Red leaves; A justice; A courtship; Lo; Ad astra; Victory; Crevasse; Turnabout; All the dead pilots; Wash; Honor; Dr. Martino; Fox hunt; Pennsylvania Station; Artist at home; The brooch; My Grandmother Millard; Golden land; There was a queen; Mountain victory; Beyond; Black music; The leg; Mistral; Divorce in Naples; Carcassonne

A fable. Random House 1954 437p $15.95

ISBN 0-394-42400-X

"Set in France a few months before the end of World War I, 'A Fable' is both an allegory of the passion of Christ and a study of a world that has chosen submission to authority and the secular values of power and chauvinism instead of the individuality and the exercise of free will. The novel centers on the fate of a young corporal . . . [who] with the aid of twelve companions, incites a mutiny in the trenches which results in a temporary armistice. Betrayed by a member of his own regiment, the corporal is executed for cowardice along with two other military criminals, becoming a martyr to his principles and his belief in humanity." Benet's Reader's Ency of Am Lit

Father Abraham; edited by James B. Meriwether; with wood engravings by John DePol. Random House 1984 c1983 70p $16.95

ISBN 0-394-53722-X　　　　　LC 83-43204

First published 1983 in a limited edition by the Red Ozier Press for the New York Public Library

This work was "written in 1926 as the beginning of the novel of which it became an important part, 'The Hamlet.' Several years later, Faulkner recast it in a different form as one of his best-known short stories, 'Spotted Horses.'" Publisher's note

The Faulkner reader; selections from the works of William Faulkner. Random House 1954 682p o.p.

Partially analyzed in Short story index

Contains the following: The sound and the fury [complete] (1929); The bear, excerpt from Go down, Moses; Old man, excerpt from The wild palms; Spotted horses, excerpt from The hamlet; A rose for Emily; Barn burning; Dry September; That evening sun; Turnabout; Shingles for the Lord; A justice; Wash; An odor of verbena, excerpt from The Unvanquished; Percy Grimm, excerpt from Light in August; The courthouse, excerpt from Requiem for a nun

Flags in the dust; edited and with an introduction by Douglas Day. Random House 1973 370p o.p.

This is the uncut and complete version of Sartoris published 1929 and entered below. "The introduction describes the bibliographic history of the narrative and makes clear that the present work is as complete a reproduction as possible of the extant composite typescript. Emphasis of 'Flags in the dust' is extended from the Sartoris family featured in the later novel to the full range of Faulkner's Yoknapatawpha social structure, resulting in a complete fictional documentation of the intense Faulknerian world which saturated all his writings." Booklist

Go down, Moses; introduction by Stanley Crouch. Modern Lib. 1995 367p $15.50

ISBN 0-679-60174-0　　　　　LC 95-4715

A reissue of the Random House edition published 1942 with title: Go down Moses, and other stories which was analyzed in Short story index

"The voices of Faulkner's South—black and white, comic and tragic—ring through this sprawling tale of the McCaslin clan. The tone ranges from the farcical to the profound. As the title suggests, the stories are rife with biblical themes. Although the seven stories were originally published separately, *Go Down, Moses* is best read

Faulkner, William, 1897-1962—*Continued*

as a novel of interconnecting generations, races, and dreams." Merriam-Webster's Ency of Lit

The hamlet. 3rd ed. Random House 1964 366p $16.95

ISBN 0-394-42759-9

First published 1940

First volume in the trilogy about the "Snopes family who descended upon Yoknapatawpha County, Mississippi in the latter years of the nineteenth century. It "tells how Ab Snopes, ex-bushwhacker, horse trader and sharecropper won immunity in Frenchman's Bend because of his reputation as a barn burner and how his son Flem became a clerk in Will Varner's store. Before long other members of the family descend like swarming locusts on the village. . . . Led by Flem, who has set himself up in the world by marrying Eula Varner when she was pregnant with another man's child, they then move on to Jefferson, the county seat." Magill. Masterpieces of World Lit in Dig Form

Followed by The town

also in Faulkner, W. Snopes p1-349

Intruder in the dust. Random House 1948 247p $13.95

ISBN 0-394-43074-3

"When Lucas, an elderly Negro, is accused of murdering a white man, Charles, a 16-year-old white boy, works to save him from being lynched. Charles gets the help he needs in his sleuthing from an old aristocratic lady and a young black boy. The trio visits the church graveyard at night to dig up the corpse of the supposed victim. The book can be read as a mystery and, on a deeper level, as a social commentary on the South." Shapiro. Fic for Youth. 3d edition

Light in August. Random House 1967 c1959 480p $16.95

ISBN 0-394-43335-1

First published 1932 by Harrison Smith & Robert Haas, Inc.

The novel "reiterates the author's concern with a society that classifies men according to race, creed, and origin. Joe Christmas, the central character and victim, appears to be white but is really part black; he has an affair with Joanna Burden, a spinster whom the townsfolk of Jefferson regard with suspicion because of her New England background. Joe eventually kills her and sets fire to her house; he is captured, castrated, and killed by the outraged townspeople, to whom his victim has become a symbol of the innocent white woman attacked and killed by a black. Other important characters are Lena Grove, who comes to Jefferson far advanced in pregnancy, expecting to find the lover who has deserted her, and Gail Hightower, the minister who ignores his wife and loses his church because of his fanatic devotion to the past." Reader's Ency. 3d edition

The mansion. Random House 1959 436p o.p.

The mansion completes the trilogy of the Snopes family. Using his techniques of flashbacks and recombining earlier themes, Faulkner "covers a time span linking Jack Houston's murder with Flem's violent death at the hands of Mink Snopes thirty-eight years later. In this novel, however, much of Flem's trickery and greed for money and power fade into the background and Linda, Eula's daughter becomes the central figure." Magill. Masterpieces of World Lit in Dig Form

"Sometimes the reader grows tired of the tough repetitive monologues and the revelations of Southern decay, but in Faulkner there is a massiveness and even a majesty not easily found elsewhere in the American fiction of this century. . . . Turgid and difficult as he is, Faulkner is worth the trouble." Burgess. 99 Novels

also in Faulkner, W. Snopes p673-1065

The portable Faulkner; edited by Malcolm Cowley. Viking 1946 756p o.p.

"Viking portable library"

Analyzed in Short story index

Contents: A justice; Red leaves; Was; Raid; Wash; An odor of verbena; The bear; Spotted horses; That evening sun; Ad astra; A rose for Emily; Dilsey; Old man; Death drag; Uncle Bud and the three madams; Percy Grimm; Delta autumn

Pylon. H. Smith and R. Haas, Inc. 1935 315p o.p.

The scene is a Southern city where a Mardi Gras celebration is in progress. The action covers four days in the lives of a strange set of people, all of them connected in some way with the airplane contests which are being held in celebration of the opening of a new airport. The main characters are: Shumann, an airplane pilot; Jiggs, his mechanic; Jackson, a parachute jumper; Laverne, Shumann's wife; and a nameless reporter who adopts the group for the time being

The reivers; a reminiscence. Random House 1962 305p $17.95

ISBN 0-394-44229-6

"Told to his grandson as 'A Reminiscence,' Lucius Priest's monologue recalls his adventures in 1905 as an 11-year-old, when he, the gigantic but childish part-Indian Boon Hogganbeck, and a black family servant, Ned William McCaslin, become reivers (stealthy plunderers) of the automobile of his grandfather, the senior banker of Jefferson, Miss." Oxford Companion to Am Lit. 5th edition

Requiem for a nun. Random House 1951 286p $13.95

ISBN 0-394-44274-1

"Written in three prose sections, which provide the background, and three acts which present the drama in the courthouse and the jail, the novel centers on Temple Drake, one of the main characters of *Sanctuary*. In the interval of the eight years separating the events of the two books, Temple has married Gowan Stevens and borne two children; she is being blackmailed by Pete, brother of her lover in *Sanctuary*, and is planning to run away with him when Nancy Manningoe, her black servant, kills Temple's youngest child. Her attempts to gain a pardon from the governor for Nancy finally bring out Temple's own involvement in and responsibility for the crime." Reader's Ency. 3d edition

Sanctuary; the original text; edited, with an afterword and notes, by Noel Polk. Random House 1981 311p $14.95

ISBN 0-394-51278-2

First published 1931 by J. Cape & H. Smith

"Horace Benbow, an ineffectual intellectual, becomes involved in the violent events centering on Temple Drake, a young coed. Temple is raped by Popeye, who murders a man trying to protect her. Carried off to a Memphis brothel by Popeye, Temple later protects him and testifies against Lee Goodwin, who is accused of

Faulkner, William, 1897-1962—*Continued*
the murder. Benbow defends Goodwin at the trial and unsuccessfully tries to give shelter to his common-law wife. Temple's testimony ends all hope for Goodwin, who is lynched by the townspeople." Reader's Ency. 3d edition

Sartoris. Harcourt Brace & Co. 1929 380p o.p.
"A saga of the Sartoris family, the novel deals primarily with young Bayard Sartoris' urge for self-destruction. His beloved twin brother, John, having been killed in World War I, Bayard returns home haunted by the memories of his brother, and becomes involved in a number of accidents. Because of his reckless driving, his grandfather, old Bayard Sartoris, rides with him in an attempt to force him to drive carefully, but young Bayard runs the car off a cliff and his grandfather dies of a heart attack. Unable to face either himself or his family, Bayard goes to Ohio to become a test pilot and is killed. . . . Faulkner picks up the beginnings of the Sartoris family in 'The Unvanquished.'" Benet's Reader's Ency of Am Lit
A more complete version of this novel published with title: Flags in the dust, is entered above

Snopes; The hamlet, The town, The mansion; introduction by George Garrett. Modern Lib. 1994 1065p $21
ISBN 0-679-60092-2
An omnibus volume of three novels entered separately

Soldiers' pay. Boni & Liveright 1926 319p o.p.
"Lieutenant Donald Mahon, an American in the British air force during World War I, is discharged from the hospital where he has been treated for a critical head wound, and makes his way home to Georgia. The wound leaves a horrible scar, and causes loss of memory and later blindness. On the train from New York he is aided by Joe Gilligan, an awkward, friendly, footloose ex-soldier, and Margaret Powers, an attractive young widow whose husband was killed in the war. Margaret, strangely attracted to the dying, subhuman Donald, decides to go home with him, as does Gilligan, who is in love with her. Their reception in the Georgia town reveals the character of the fickle people." Oxford Companion to Am Lit. 5th edition

The sound and the fury. New, corrected ed. Random House 1984 326p $25
ISBN 0-394-53241-4   LC 84-42626
First published 1929
"The story is told in four parts, through the stream of consciousness of three characters (the sons of the Compson family, Benjy, Quentin, and Jason), and finally in an objective account. The Compson family, formerly genteel Southern patricians, now lead a degenerate, perverted life on their shrunken plantation near Jefferson, Miss. The disintegration of the family, which clings to outworn aristocratic conventions, is counterpointed by the strength of the black servants, who include old Dilsey and her son Luster." Oxford Companion to Am Lit. 5th edition

also in Faulkner, W. The Faulkner reader p5-251

The town. Random House 1957 371p $13.95
ISBN 0-394-42452-2

This second volume in the Snopes trilogy "relates through three narrators of varying reliability the story of Flem Snopes' rise to prominence in the fictional Yoknapatawpha County. Flem's coldly calculated vengeance on his wife, Eula, and her lover culminates in Eula's suicide and Flem's rise to power in Jefferson, the county seat. Because Flem longs for respect as well as money, he turns against the clan of shiftless Snopes cousins who have followed him to town and forces them to leave Jefferson. In his hunger for social validation, he denies his own origins, and the book ends with a hint that the cousins' revenge will follow." Merriam-Webster's Ency of Lit
Followed by The mansion

also in Faulkner, W. Snopes p351-671

Uncollected stories of William Faulkner; edited by Joseph Blotner. Random House 1979 716p $17.95
ISBN 0-394-40044-5   LC 78-21803
Analyzed in Short story index
Contents: Ambuscade; Retreat; Raid; Skirmish at Sartoris; The unvanquished; Vendée; Fool about a horse; Lizards in Jamshyd's courtyard; The hound; Spotted horses; Lion; The old people; A point of law; Gold is not always; Pantaloon in black; Go down, Moses; Delta autumn; The bear; Race at morning; Hog pawn; Nympholepsy; Frankie and Johnny; The priest; Once aboard the Lugger (I); Once aboard the Lugger (II); Miss Zilphia Gant; Thrift; Idyll in the desert; Two dollar wife; Afternoon of a cow; Mr. Acarius; Sepulture South; Gaslight; Adolescence; Al Jackson; Don Giovanni; Peter; Moonlight; The big shot; Dull tale; A return; A dangerous man; Evangeline; A portrait of Elmer; With caution and dispatch; Snow

The unvanquished; drawings by Edward Shenton. Random House 1938 293p il o.p.
Analyzed in Short story index
Contents: Ambuscade; Retreat; Raid; Riposte in tertio; Vendée; Skirmish at Sartoris; An odor of verbena
This is "a collection of interlocking stories. . . . Set during the Civil War, these stories deal with the Sartoris family, whose modern history Faulkner recounted in Sartoris. Composed of seven stories, which first appeared separately in magazines, the book centers primarily on the adventures of Bayard Sartoris and his black companion, Ringo. Colonel John Sartoris and Miss Rosa, Bayard's grandmother, also figure prominently." Reader's Ency. 3d edition

Faust, Frederick, 1892-1944
See also Brand, Max, 1892-1944

Fearing, Kenneth, 1902-1961
The big clock. Harcourt Brace & Co. 1946 175p o.p. Amereon reprint available $22.95 (ISBN 0-8488-1000-7)
"A truly brilliant story, laid in a large mass-communication organization where the hero works and is involved amorously with the boss's woman. Circumstances lead to her death, and he is put in the position of obvious murderer. The details by which he is caught and with the aid of which he unwinds himself are chosen and exhibited with genius. Tone and talk are sharp and often bitter—the whole business is a tour de

Fearing, Kenneth, 1902-1961—*Continued*
force worthy of the highest praise." Barzun. Cat of
Crime. Rev and enl edition

Fecher, Constance, 1911-
*For works written by this author under
other names see* Heaven, Constance, 1911-

Feinberg, Bea *See* Freeman, Cynthia, d.
1988

Feist, Raymond E.
Mistress of the empire; by Raymond E.
Feist & Janny Wurts. Doubleday 1992 613p
$20

ISBN 0-385-24719-2   LC 91-24511

"A Foundation book"
Completes the trilogy about Lady Mara
"Lady Mara of the Acoma, consummate player of the
deadly game of intrigue that maintains the stability of
the Tsurani Empire, pits her vision of a transformed
society against an apparently unbeatable foe. . . . Feist
and Wurts have created an exotic fantasy world that is
rich in texture and alive with political machinations."
Libr J

Servant of the empire; [by] Raymond E.
Feist and Janny Wurts. Doubleday 1990
580p o.p.

LC 90-33460

"A Foundation book"
Second in the trilogy about Lady Mara begun with
Daughter of the empire (1987)
"As leader of her noble house, the Lady Mara must
contend with battles on two fronts: in the hotbed of
intrigue and treachery that is the court of Tsurani, and
in her heart, where her affections for a barbarian slave
from the enemy world of Medkemis lead her to question
the principles by which she lives." Libr J
"Characterizations are well developed and their
interrelationships are intricate; and the authors maintain
their carefully constructed world in this complex novel
with nonstop action on all fronts: the political scene, the
battlefield, and bed." Booklist

Shadow of a dark queen; a novel. Morrow
1994 382p (Serpent war saga, v1) $22
ISBN 0-688-12408-9   LC 93-47455

In this first volume of the Serpent War saga "Erik
von Darkmoor, bastard son of the local baron, flees to
the city of Krondor after accidentally killing his
legitimate and sadistic half-brother. Condemned to death,
Eric and his childhood friend, Rupert (Roo) Avery, are
provisionally spared to serve in a desperate mission
against the reptilian Panthathians, who plan to conquer
Midkemia and bring back their goddess, Alma-Lodaka,
one of the ancient Dragon Lords. . . . A sensitive
coming-of-age tale in which brutality and camaraderie are
equally present." Publ Wkly

Feldman, Ellen
See also Villars, Elizabeth, 1941-

Ferber, Edna, 1887-1968
Cimarron. Doubleday, Doran 1930 388p
o.p.
Available from Amereon and Buccaneer Bks.

"Yancey Cravat was a big, handsome man who quoted
Shakespeare and the Bible and knew the law. He started
a newspaper in Wichita, Kansas, in whose pages he
protested the government's treatment of the Indians.
Against the wishes of her family he married Sabra
Venable, daughter of an aristocratic Southern family.
Then, lured by the newly opened frontier, he took off
with her to help settle Oklahoma, where he was
instrumental in establishing law and order. Although he
could have been governor of the state, his restlessness
took him away for weeks, months, and finally years,
leaving Sabra with the responsibility for the newspaper.
In the lives of these two strong-willed people, and of
their son, Cim, Ferber has captured the drama, conflicts,
and rewards of life in pioneer America." Shapiro. Fic
for Youth. 3d edition

Giant. Doubleday 1952 447p o.p.
Buccaneer Bks. reprint available $13.95
(ISBN 0-89966-806-2)
"The story unfolds as Leslie Lynnton, a patrician Vir-
ginian, marries Bick Benedict, a Texas cattle baron. The
reader experiences Texas from Leslie's point of view, as
she attempts to understand and to adapt to the customs
and expansive way of life of Texans. Alongside her vivid
descriptions of the crudeness of the newly rich oil men
and cattle barons, Ferber observes their exploitation of
the impoverished Mexicans who work for them."
Merriam-Webster's Ency of Lit

Ice Palace. Doubleday 1958 411p o.p.
Buccaneer Bks. reprint available $21.95
(ISBN 0-89968-278-2)
"The case for Alaska's statehood is presented in the
story of two ex-sourdoughs, now the leading citizens of
Baranof. Millionaire Czar Kennedy pulls strings on the
mainland to perpetuate Alaska's territorial status, the better to exploit her resources, while his one time partner,
the journalist Thor Storm, crusades for the democratic
rights of the citizens of this last frontier. The public
warfare between these two is epitomized in the private
tug of war for the affections and ideological allegiance
of their granddaughter Christine." Booklist

Saratoga trunk. Doubleday 1941 352p o.p.
Amereon reprint available $20.95 (ISBN
0-89190-323-2)
A "story of an adventuress making her way in the
[18]80's. Clio, daughter of a New Orleans aristocrat and
his French mistress, returned to scandalize New Orleans
and levy a little blackmail from her father's family. A
flamboyant Texas cowboy joined forces with her and
they chose Saratoga in the racing season for their assault
on society and big business, profiting by the rival railroad magnates' warfare." Booklist

Show boat; a novel. Doubleday, Page 1926
398p o.p.
Available from AMS Press and Buccaneer Bks.

Ferber, Edna, 1887-1968—*Continued*

"In this popular book appear three theatrical generations. First there is Captain Andy Hawks, who runs a showboat on the Mississippi and marries Parthy Ann, a prim New England schoolmarm. They have one daughter, Magnolia, who becomes an actress and runs off with the leading man, Gaylord Ravenal. Their daughter Kim is born on the showboat. The captain dies and Parthy Ann takes over; Ravenal takes Magnolia to Chicago, but ultimately leaves her, and she returns to the showboat. Kim meanwhile grows up to be a Broadway star." Benet's Reader's Ency of Am Lit

So Big. Doubleday, Page 1924 360p o.p.
Available from Amereon and Buccaneer Bks.

Selina DeJong would look up from her work and say, 'How big is my man?' Then little Dirk DeJong would answer in the time-worn way, 'So-o-o big!' And he was so nicknamed. Though So Big gives the book its title his mother is the outstanding figure. Until Selina was nineteen she traveled with her gambler-father. At his sudden death she secured a teacher's post in the Dutch settlement of High Prairie, a community of hardworking farmers and their thrifty, slaving wives—narrow-minded people indifferent to natural beauty. Soon Selina married Pervus DeJong, a plodding, goodnatured boy. With her marriage the never-ending drudgery of a farmer's wife began. Through all the years of hardship she never lost her gay indomitable spirit. Unfortunately, she was unable to transmit these qualities to her son

Ferman, Edward L.

(ed) The Best from Fantasy & Science Fiction: a 40th anniversary anthology. See The Best from Fantasy & Science Fiction: a 40th anniversary anthology

(ed) The Best from Fantasy & Science Fiction: a 45th anniversary anthology. See The Best from Fantasy & Science Fiction: a 45th anniversary anthology

(ed) The Best from Fantasy and Science Fiction: a special 25th anniversary anthology. See The Best from Fantasy and Science Fiction: a special 25th anniversary anthology

(ed) The Best horror stories. See The Best horror stories

Ferrars, E. X., 1907-

Answer came there none. Doubleday 1993 c1992 188p o.p.

LC 92-35631

"A Perfect crime book"
First published 1992 in the United Kingdom
"Sara Marriott, a recently divorced young freelance writer, agrees to ghostwrite the autobiography of elderly Gen. Schofield. Moving to the small town of Edgewater, she rents a flat from the General's friend, the widowed Mrs. Cannon, and is immediately drawn into her landlady's quarrel with her middle-aged son who plans to marry and move to Canada. On her birthday Mrs. Cannon . . . dies of poisoning in her bedroom. . . . Ferrars crafts the story well." Publ Wkly

Beware of the dog. Doubleday 1993 c1992 192p o.p.

LC 92-22134

"A Perfect crime book"
First published 1992 in the United Kingdom
A mystery featuring "the amateur detective, con man and chronic liar Felix Freer. . . . The story begins with the death of elderly, well-off Helen Lovelock in the town of Allingford. Survivors are a grandnephew arrived from Australia only a few months earlier, and a grandniece who flies in from America. When the niece is shot in bed soon after the funeral, the deceased's woefully unprovided-for housekeeper calls for help to Virginia Freer, Felix's estranged wife, who is living next door." Publ Wkly

Blood flies upward. Doubleday 1977 c1976 186p o.p.

LC 76-18343

"Published for the Crime Club"
First published 1976 in the United Kingdom
"A young woman, posing as an abandoned wife, replaces her sister as housekeeper of an English country house after the sister disappears. Other members of the staff and the houseguests at first appear merely offbeat, and the puzzle seems to lead nowhere." Booklist

Danger from the dead. Doubleday 1992 188p o.p.

LC 91-26216

"A Perfect crime book"
"English public school teacher Gavin Cleaver agrees to spend a month in the country with his brother Nigel and his semi-invalided novelist sister-in-law Annabel after learning that her sister Caroline will also be there. Caroline is indifferent to him, however, and he soon resolves to leave—plans that change when he finds Caroline shot through the head and Annabel dead of a stroke, the murder weapon near her body. . . . Some genre devotees might guess the identity of Caroline's murderer, but the jumble of persuasive alibis and theories will keep most readers hanging until the last surprise." Publ Wkly

Death of a minor character. Doubleday 1983 183p o.p.

LC 82-23479

"Published for the Crime Club"
"Virginia and Felix Freer, divorced but still chummy . . . meet at a party in London where one of the guests is Jasper Noble, a silversmith. Back in Allingford, the village where Virginia has settled, she learns that Marcus Avery has been murdered in the antique shop he owns in partnership with his wife Rose. The shop sells Noble's distinctive jewelry, a clue that Virginia and Felix pick up as they investigate those present at the party with ties to the widow and the victim. Felix is bludgeoned by a crook with a shocking motive." Publ Wkly
"This is an engaging team of reluctant sleuths; they are perfect foils for one another in personality, ambition and charm." Best Sellers

Sleep of the unjust. Doubleday 1991 c1990 198p o.p.

LC 90-27454

First published 1990 in the United Kingdom
"Physiotherapist Virginia Freer views her estranged husband, Felix, as an untrustworthy, charming crook. But when sudden deaths disrupt the tranquility of the English country house where they are weekend wedding guests, they quickly team up to investigate." Publ Wkly

Ferrars, E. X., 1907- —*Continued*

Smoke without fire. Doubleday 1991 c1989 182p o.p.

LC 90-3544

Available Thorndike Press large print edition

First published 1989 in the United Kingdom

"It's two evenings before Christmas in the comfy Berkshire village home of Colin and Dorothea Cahill, the tea things have been washed, dinner's on the stove and the Cahills are sipping sherry with their customary houseguest for the holidays, widower Andrew Basnett, a retired botany professor in his 70s. Suddenly the tranquility of the scene is shattered by an explosion that kills the Cahills' arrogant, selfish neighbor Sir Lucas Dearden, a retired criminal lawyer. . . . Many red herrings and blind alleys later, unwilling amateur sleuth Andrew . . . comes to a surprising and satisfying conclusion." Publ Wkly

Something wicked. Doubleday 1984 c1983 182p o.p.

LC 83-16297

"Published for the Crime Club"

"Retired botany professor Andrew Basnett borrows his nephew's cottage in the Berkshire village of Godlingham while his London flat is redecorated. Basnett finds himself drawn into the life of the village, a life that seethes with complicated passions and unresolved relationships. One of Godlingham's residents is a reclusive woman suspected of getting away with murdering her husband six years previously." Booklist

Thy brother death. Doubleday 1993 192p $17

ISBN 0-385-47092-4   LC 93-23187

"A Perfect crime book"

"Patrick and Henrietta Carey are visited by a well-mannered Scotswoman who is seeking the money owed her by her estranged husband, who she says is Patrick Carey. All three are bewildered, even after they realize that she had married Patrick's somewhat pathological brother David. The woman leaves before the Careys' planned party begins. Patrick is a university lecturer, and their guest list includes fellow faculty members, an American visitor, Patrick's spurned mentor, an insecure underling and other tweedy academics. That same evening the Scotswoman perishes in a fire at the mentor's home and, not long afterward, the bobbies appear to question Patrick." Publ Wkly

Trial by fury. Doubleday 1989 201p o.p.

"A Crime Club book"

"In this ambient, village mystery, Constance Lawley, a 60-year-old widow who likes 'doing for' people in need of occasional help, is called on to housekeep at the home of elderly Col. and Dorothea Barrows, after Mrs. Barrow's recent hospitalization. Living with the couple is their grandson Colin, a handsome but strange 15-year-old, orphaned since birth, according to local belief. That story is proved a lie when Margot Pauling, the Barrowses' daughter, arrives and outrages Colin by claiming he's her son. Tactful Constance leaves the four to discuss the situation among themselves and, upon her return, finds them fatally shot." Publ Wkly

Woman slaughter. Doubleday 1990 c1989 197p o.p.

LC 89-25971

First published 1989 in the United Kingdom

In this mystery, Virginia Freer receives a "visit from her husband Felix, a rogue she loves but can't live with. Felix, characteristically, arrives at the start of strange doings, set off by the hit-and-run death of Virginia's elderly neighbor. . . . Next, the murders of two women throw the community into an uproar, and force Virginia to suspect Felix, despite her conviction that his idiosyncratic ethical sense would never permit him to commit serious crimes. As she might have guessed, Virginia's secretive spouse has been using his talent for deceit in an effort that pays off with the arrest of the killers. The tale is lively with intrigue and urbane wit." Publ Wkly

Ferrars, Elizabeth, 1907-

For works written by this author under other names see Ferrars, E. X., 1907-

Ferrigno, Robert

The Cheshire moon. Morrow 1993 285p $20

ISBN 0-688-10314-6   LC 92-22573

"When reporter Quinn's friend Andy is found dead after revealing to Quinn that he has observed a murder, the suspense in this novel begins. The victim is a TV producer, who was trying to blackmail a well-known talkshow host. Quinn, who works for a celebrity magazine, along with his friend Jen, a photographer, find themselves the hunted, as the murderer tries to eliminate all witnesses." Libr J

"The mean streets of southern California remain fertile ground for the stylish mystery novel, as demonstrated by Robert Ferrigno's 'Cheshire Moon.' The ingredients are familiar: a world-weary investigative reporter, his hard-as-nails, softer-than-silk love interest; the friend's murder that demands justice; puzzling connections to the Hollywood of the fabled, faded past. Mr. Ferrigno boils the pot tastefully and enjoyably." N Y Times Book Rev

The Horse Latitudes. Morrow 1990 294p o.p.

LC 89-38234

The plot of this novel "revolves around Danny DiMedici's search for his ex-wife Lauren, a celebrity psychologist who has disappeared after a scientist is murdered in her elegant beach house. . . . A former drug dealer, Danny is the prime suspect in the murder of Lauren's lover, Dr. Tohlson, who has found a way to use fetal tissue to preserve youth. To prove his innocence, Danny embarks on a journey through the culture of Southern California." Time

This novel "features superb writing, relentless action, and some memorably despicable characters." Booklist

Fever, Buck *See* Anderson, Sherwood, 1876-1941

Field, Rachel, 1894-1942

All this, and heaven too. Macmillan 1938 596p o.p.

Available from Amereon and Buccaneer Bks.

In fiction form the author tells the life story of her great-aunt by marriage, the French governess who in 1847 became involved in a famous murder trial, in which she was known as Mademoiselle D. Although she

Field, Rachel, 1894-1942—*Continued*

was acquitted, life became so difficult for her in France that Mademoiselle came to America, where she married an American minister and presided over a Gramercy Park salon, frequented by William Cullen Bryant, Harriet Beecher Stowe, Samuel Morse, and Fanny Kemble among others

Fielding, Henry, 1707-1754

The history of Tom Jones, a foundling.
Available from various publishers

First published 1749

"Squire Allworthy suspects that the infant whom he adopts and names Tom Jones is the illegitimate child of his servant Jenny Jones. When Tom is a young man, he falls in love with Sophia Western, his beautiful and virtuous neighbor. In the end his true identity is revealed and he wins Sophia's hand, but numerous obstacles have to be overcome, and in the course of the action the various sets of characters pursue each other from one part of the country to another, giving Fielding an opportunity to paint an incomparably vivid picture of England in the mid-18th century." Merriam-Webster's Ency of Lit

Joseph Andrews; edited by Martin C. Battestin. Wesleyan Univ. Press 1967 xlvii, 389p $50

ISBN 0-8195-3070-0
First published 1742

"Joseph Andrews, a prudent, brawny, pleasant young man, is intended to be the brother of Samuel Richardson's heroine Pamela. His widowed employer, Lady Booby, dismisses him from his position as footman for refusing her advances, and he flees London to rejoin his own true love, Fanny Goodwill. On hearing the news of his disgrace, Fanny rushes to meet him. Both are set upon by thieves but are providentially rescued by Parson Adams, and the three return to their parish, where Joseph and Fanny, after comic-opera reversals and discoveries, are married in triumph. The time of the novel is coincident with *Pamela*, which it parodies and transcends." Reader's Ency. 3d edition

Fielding, Joy

Good intentions. Doubleday 1989 293p o.p.

LC 88-3206

This "novel tells parallel stories—the love troubles of two Florida women, sweet-tempered Lynn Schuster and her stormy lawyer, Renee Bower. Lynn's husband Gary leaves her and their children for flighty Suzette, whose nice-guy spouse Marc in turn makes a play for Lynn. Renee shrewdly counsels client Lynn on running her life, but obtusely lets her own be ruined." Publ Wkly

"If plot turns are occasionally broadly signaled, and some of the minor characters are stock, still the pace is brisk and the appeal and underlying strength of Lynn and Renee prevails." Libr J

See Jane run. Morrow 1991 364p $20
ISBN 0-688-08867-8   LC 90-22603
Also available Thorndike Press large print edition

"Jane finds herself in downtown Boston, her dress covered with blood, nearly $10,000 in her coat pocket, and absolutely no idea of who she is. She seeks help at Boston City Hospital, where she discovers that she is the wife of handsome Michael Whittaker, a renowned surgeon. The doctor seems to be the perfect husband, and as Jane learns the details of their ideal life together she is unable to understand her suspicions of him. However, as Jane's amnesia persists, it becomes clear that her model husband is threatening her sanity in order to conceal a sinister secret." Libr J

"Fielding handles her material with finesse; suspense is maintained at a high level, and the narrative is enriched by Jane's bracing sense of humor and a cast of sharply drawn, articulate characters." Publ Wkly

Tell me no secrets. Morrow 1993 352p $20

ISBN 0-688-08868-6   LC 92-43692

"Prosecutor Jess Koster is still distressed at the disappearance of her mother eight years before, but then her client disappears, and she starts receiving death threats in the mail." Libr J

"When Jess' ex rescues, or seems to rescue, her from the predictably sadistic stalker/rapist, her comment that 'it's just like in the movies' may seem like self-parody. Jess escapes this formula—and becomes not only real, but touching—when she visits her suburban sister and the brother-in-law she despises, when she talks with a woman juror in a rape trial about why the verdict was not guilty, and when we visit with her in her private fear." Booklist

Fifty years of the best from Ellery Queen's Mystery Magazine; edited by Eleanor Sullivan. Carroll & Graf Pubs. 1991 642p o.p.

LC 90-23928

Analyzed in Short story index

Contents: The clue of the red wig, by J. D. Carr; Lost star, by C. D. King; The Bloomsbury wonder, by T. Burke; Dressing-up, by W. R. Burnett; Malice domestic, by P. MacDonald; I can find my way out, by N. Marsh; The fourth degree, by H. Pentecost; Midnight adventure, by M. Arlen; A study in white, by N. Blake; The phantom guest, by F. I. Anderson; As simple as ABC, by E. Queen; Money to burn, by M. Allingham; The gentlest of the brothers, by D. Alexander; One-way street, by A. Armstrong; Murder at the dog show, by M. G. Eberhart; Always trust a cop, by O. R. Cohen; The withered heart, by J. Potts; The girl who married a monster, by A. Boucher; Between eight and eight, by C. S. Forester; Knowing what I know now, by B. Perowne; Change of climate, by U. Curtiss; Life in our time, by R. Bloch; The special gift, by C. Fremlin; A neat and tidy job, by G. H. Coxe; Run—if you can, by C. Armstrong; Line of communication, by A. Garve; Danger at Deerfawn, by D. B. Hughes; The man who understood women, by A. H. Z. Carr; Revolver, by A. Davidson; The eternal chase, by A. Gilbert; Reasons unknown, by S. Ellin; Three ways to rob a bank, by H. R. Daniels; The perfect servant, by H. Nielsen; The marked man, by D. Ely; Flowers that bloom in the spring, by J. Symons; A nice place to stay, by N. Tyre; Paul Broderick's man, by T. Walsh; When nothing matters, by F. V. Mayberry; This is death, by D. E. Westlake; Woodrow Wilson's necktie, by P. Highsmith; The jackal and the tiger, by M. Gilbert; The fix, by R. Twohy; One moment of madness, by E. D. Hoch; Loopy, by R. Rendell; The plateau, by C. Howard; The butchers, by P. Lovesey; Burning bridges, by J. Powell; A good turn, by R. Barnard; Clap hands, there goes Charlie, by G. Baxt; Big Boy, Little Boy, by S. Brett

Finder, Joseph
The Moscow Club. Viking 1991 548p o.p.
LC 90-50407
"The plot concerns a secret group called the Moscow Club, hardliners who want to overthrow Mikhail Gorbachev. Our hero is Charlie Stone, an analyst for the CIA. . . . The assignment is a personal one for Stone because this evil conspiracy is somehow linked to an episode years ago when his father was branded as a traitor by Senator Joseph McCarthy. Stone becomes the target of would-be assassins across the U.S. and Europe, is framed for a murder, but in the end . . . saves the world from global disaster." Booklist
"The story contains as many chases, murders, conspiracies and uncloseted ghosts as any thriller maven could want, as well as a credible love interest; in all, it's a superbly exciting read." Publ Wkly

Finkelstein, Mark Harris *See* Harris, Mark, 1922-

Finney, Jack
From time to time; a novel. Simon & Schuster 1995 303p il $23
ISBN 0-671-89884-1   LC 94-24497
In this sequel to the title entered below "time traveler Simon Morley leaves his voluntary exile in the 19th century to visit the 20th century of his origins and finds himself drawn into a desperate attempt to alter the events of history and prevent the onset of World War I." Libr J
"This mind-stretching escapist adventure is studded with period photos and news clippings that function as an integral part of the story." Publ Wkly

Time and again. Simon & Schuster 1970 399p o.p. 1995 reprint available $25 (ISBN 0-684-80117-5)
The author "re-creates the world of nineteenth-century New York City and at the same time critically appraises modernity. His hero, Simon Morley, agrees to live in the Dakota apartments and, assisted by hypnosis, to share a series of experiences in the year 1882. Eager to cooperate with the U.S. governmental agencies conducting the test Simon observes the manners and mores of the past and falls in love with Julia, a girl of the period. Simon's enthusiasm palls, however, when he is asked to alter historical events in the interest of the agency's evidently nefarious designs." Booklist
Followed by From time to time

Finney, Patricia, 1958-
Firedrake's eye. St. Martin's Press 1992 263p o.p.
LC 92-3293
"In the fall of 1583, Elizabeth Tudor has been Queen of England for 25 years and the target of plots to restore Catholic rule to England for about the same length of time. 'Tom O'Bedlam,' the mad son of a prominent Catholic family, narrates his tale of one such attempt. Roaming the London streets, Tom sees the threads of an assassination plot slowly woven into an ever-tightening net by his own hated brother, a fanatical Catholic. Will Tom be able to aid those trying to destroy the conspiracy?" Libr J

"Set against the cadence of an archaic London, this is a wonderfully atmospheric rendering of an anarchist plot brimming over with vivid details of intrigue." Booklist

Fisher, Clay, 1912-1991
For works by this author under other names see Henry, Will, 1912-1991

Fisher, Vardis, 1895-1968
Mountain man; a novel of male and female in the early American West.
Available from various publishers
First published 1965 by Morrow
The author delves into the story "of Kate Bowden, whose family has been massacred by Indians, and into the life of the trapper Sam Minard who compassionately builds a cabin for Kate and then rides on to take and dearly love a Flathead bride. Sam . . . declares war against the Crow nation after the Crows murder his wife and unborn child." Publ Wkly
"Superb backgrounds, fascinating detail, and consistency of tone elevate this beyond the adventure story; as a picture of a mountain man, his love of nature and struggle to survive, it is a stirring piece of Americana." Libr J

Fitzalan, Roger, 1920-1995
For works written by this author under other names see Hall, Adam, 1920-1995; Trevor, Elleston, 1920-1995

Fitzgerald, F. Scott (Francis Scott), 1896-1940
Babylon revisited, and other stories. Scribner 1960 253p o.p.
Contents: The ice palace; May Day; The diamond as big as the Ritz; Winter dreams; Absolution; The rich boy; The freshest boy; Babylon revisited; Crazy Sunday; The long way out

The Basil and Josephine stories; edited with an introduction by Jackson R. Bryer and John Kuehl. Scribner 1973 xxix, 287p o.p.
Analyzed in Short story index
Contents: Basil; That kind of party; The scandal detectives; A night at the fair; The freshest boy; He thinks he's wonderful; The captured shadow; The perfect life; Forging ahead; Basil and Cleopatra; Josephine; First blood; A nice quiet place; A woman with a past; A snobbish story; Emotional bankruptcy

The beautiful and damned. Scribner 449p $55
ISBN 0-684-15153-7
"Hudson River editions"
First published 1922; copyright renewed 1950
"Anthony Patch pursues and wins the beautiful and sought-after Gloria Gilbert. He decides that they can survive on his limited income until he comes into a large fortune he stands to inherit from his grandfather. Through the ensuing years, their lives deteriorate into mindless alcoholic ennui. Anthony's grandfather makes a surprise appearance at one of their wild parties and, in disgust, disinherits him. After his grandfather's death,

Fitzgerald, F. Scott (Francis Scott), 1896-1940—Continued

Anthony institutes a lawsuit that takes years to settle. Although the Patches eventually win, by then Anthony's spirit is broken, he and Gloria have grown apart, and they care about nothing." Merriam-Webster's Ency of Lit

The Fitzgerald reader; edited by Arthur Mizener. Scribner 1963 xxvii, 509p o.p.

Partially analyzed in Short story index

Contents: The short stories are: Winter dreams; Absolution; "The sensible thing"; Basil and Cleopatra; Outside the cabinetmaker's; Babylon revisited; Crazy Sunday; Family in the wind; Afternoon of an author; "I didn't get over"; The long way out; Financing Finnegan; The lost decade

This representative selection of Scott Fitzgerald's work "includes the whole of his best novel, 'The Great Gatsby,' and considerable parts of his other two important novels, 'Tender Is the Night,' and 'The Last Tycoon.' It also includes two novelettes ('May Day' and 'The Rich Boy'), the four or five best short stories from each period of his career, and his four most famous essays." Foreword

The Great Gatsby. Macmillan 1993 205p $40

ISBN 0-684-19647-6   LC 93-14173

"A Charles Scribner's Sons book. Macmillan/Hudson River edition"

First published 1925

"The mysterious Jay Gatsby lives in a luxurious mansion on the Long Island shore. . . . Nick Carraway, the narrator, lives next door to Gatsby, and Nick's cousin Daisy and her crude but wealthy husband Tom Buchanan live directly across the harbor. Gatsby reveals to Nick that he and Daisy had a brief affair before the war and her marriage to Tom. . . . He persuades Nick to bring him and Daisy together again but ultimately he is unable to win her away from Tom. Daisy, driving Gatsby's car, runs over and kills Tom's mistress Myrtle, unaware of her identity. Myrtle's husband traces the car and shoots Gatsby, who has remained silent in order to protect Daisy. Gatsby's friends and business associates have all desert him, and only Gatsby's father, and one former guest attend the funeral." Reader's Ency. 3d edition

"The power of the novel derives from its sharp and antagonistic portrayal of wealthy society in New York City and Long Island. . . . The 'Jazz Age,' Fitzgerald's constant subject, is exposed here in terms of its false glamor and cultural barrenness." Benet's Reader's Ency of Am Lit

also in Fitzgerald, F. S. The Fitzgerald reader p105-238

also in Fitzgerald, F. S. The portable F. Scott Fitzgerald p1-168

The last tycoon; an unfinished novel. Scribner 163p $25

ISBN 0-684-15311-4

Also available from Amereon

"Hudson River editions"

First published 1941 with The Great Gatsby, and selected stories; copyright renewed 1969

In addition to providing a foreword to this unfinished novel "Edmund Wilson has assembled a tentative outline of the rest of the story as Fitzgerald intended to develop it, and has appended passages from the author's notes dealing with the characters and scenes." Publisher's note

"The work is an indictment of the Hollywood film industry, where Fitzgerald had had a disappointing career as a screenwriter. Monroe Stahr is a studio executive who has worked obsessively to produce high-quality films without regard to their financial prospects. He takes a personal interest in every aspect of the studio. At age 35 he is almost burned out, and the novel is the story of how he loses control of the studio and his life." Merriam-Webster's Ency of Lit

May Day

In Fitzgerald, F. S. The Fitzgerald reader p3-53

The portable F. Scott Fitzgerald; selected by Dorothy Parker; introduction by John O'Hara. Viking 1945 835p o.p.

"Viking Portable library"

Partially analyzed in Short story index

Contents: Novels: The Great Gatsby, and Tender is the night, both entered separately. Stories: Absolution; The baby party; The rich boy; May Day; The cut-glass bowl; The off-shore pirate; The freshest boy; Crazy Sunday; Babylon revisited

The rich boy

In Fitzgerald, F. S. The Fitzgerald reader p239-75

The short stories of F. Scott Fitzgerald; edited and with a preface by Matthew J. Bruccoli. Scribner 1989 775p o.p.

LC 89-6351

Analyzed in Short story index

Contents: Head and shoulders; Bernice bobs her hair; The ice palace; The offshore pirate; May Day; The jelly-bean; The curious case of Benjamin Button; The diamond as big as the Ritz; Winter dreams; Dice, brass-knuckles & guitar; Absolution; Rags Martin-Jones and the Pr-nce of W-les; 'The sensible thing'; Love in the night; The rich boy; Jacob's ladder; A short trip home; The bowl; The captured shadow; Basil and Cleopatra; The last of the belles; Majesty; At your age; The swimmers; Two wrongs; First blood; Emotional bankruptcy; The bridal party; One trip abroad; The hotel child; Babylon revisited; A new leaf; A freeze-out; Six of one—; What a handsome pair!; Crazy Sunday; More than just a house; Afternoon of an author; Financing Finnegan; The lost decade; 'Boil some water—lots of it'; Last kiss; Dearly beloved

Six tales of the jazz age, and other stories. Scribner 1960 192p o.p. Amereon reprint available $18.95 (ISBN 0-88411-597-6)

Analyzed in Short story index

Contents: The jelly-bean; The camel's back; The curious case of Benjamin Button; Tarquin of Cheapside; "O'Russet witch"; The lees of happiness; The adjuster; Hot and cold blood; Gretchen's forty winks

The stories of F. Scott Fitzgerald; a selection of 28 stories; with an introduction by Malcolm Cowley. Scribner 1951 xxv, 473p $50

ISBN 0-684-15366-1

Fitzgerald, F. Scott (Francis Scott), 1896-1940—*Continued*

Analyzed in Short story index
Contents: Diamond as big as the Ritz; Bernice bobs her hair; Ice palace; May Day; Winter dreams; "The sensible thing"; Absolution; Rich boy; Baby party; Magnetism; Last of the belles; Rough crossing; Bridal party; Two wrongs; Scandal detectives; Freshest boy; Captured shadow; Woman with a past; Babylon revisited; Crazy Sunday; Family in the wind; Alcoholic case; Long way out; Financing Finnigan; Pat Hobby himself; Three hours between planes; Lost decade

Tender is the night. Scribner 315p $40

ISBN 0-684-15151-0
Also available from Amereon; large print edition available from G.K. Hall

"Hudson River editions"
First published 1934. Copyright renewed 1962
"In the decadent setting of post-World War I Europe, a wealthy mental patient, Nicole, falls passionately in love with Dick Diver, a young psychiatrist. She finds her cure in marrying him, but as she achieves independence he deteriorates. Nicole leaves him for a man who will be her lover, not her caretaker. Diver is perhaps a reflection of Fitzgerald's painful experiences with Zelda Fitzgerald, his own mentally disturbed wife." Benet's Reader's Ency of Am Lit

also in Fitzgerald, F. S. The portable F. Scott Fitzgerald p169-545

This side of paradise. Scribner 282p $30

ISBN 0-684-15601-6
"Hudson River editions"
First published 1920; copyright renewed 1948
"Immature though it seems today, the work when it was published was considered a revelation of the new morality of the young in the early Jazz Age; and it made Fitzgerald famous. The novel's hero, Amory Blaine, is a handsome, spoiled young man who attends Princeton, becomes involved in literary activities, and has several ill-fated romances. A portrait of the Lost Generation, the novel addresses Fitzgerald's later theme of love distorted by social climbing and greed." Merriam-Webster's Ency of Lit

Fitzgerald, Francis Scott *See* Fitzgerald, F. Scott (Francis Scott), 1896-1940

Flagg, Fannie

Coming attractions; a wonderful novel. Morrow 1981 320p o.p.

This is a "novel in the form of a journal kept by Daisy Fay Harper from her 11th year (1952) to the day she is crowned Miss Mississippi at 17. Daisy has an alcoholic father, who is involved in money-making schemes such as self-taught taxidermy and a phony revival meeting, with hilarious results; a classmate, Vernon Mooseburger, who is withdrawn and self-conscious because he is totally bald; and other friends with names like Pickle Watkins, Mustard Smoot, Peachy Wigham and Ula Sour. . . . This is a lively fictional memoir, full of 50s nostalgia." SLJ

Fried green tomatoes at the Whistle-Stop Cafe. Random House 1987 403p $25

ISBN 0-394-56152-X   LC 87-12813
Also available large print edition $18 (ISBN 0-679-74495-9)

This novel is "set in a rural hamlet outside of Birmingham, Alabama. Bulletins from a gossipy town newsletter produced in the 1940s by Dot Weems are interspersed with the recollections of Mrs. Cleo (Vinnie) Throughgoode uttered (40 years later) in a nursing home to a depressed, menopausal visitor, Evelyn Couch (whose life is rejuvenated by these Sunday afternoon chats). Flagg also supplies basic narrative passages illuminating the news shared by Dot and Vinnie. The pace of the novel is as swift as the life of the small town is slow—at least it seems slow until Vinnie drops hints of a murder and of riotous pranks played upon the local minister. The story is carefully plotted, with the moods and people of pre- and post-World War II Alabama splendidly evoked." Booklist

Flanagan, Thomas, 1923-

The end of the hunt. Dutton 1994 627p $24.95

ISBN 0-525-93681-5   LC 93-36478
"A William Abrahams book"
In this historical novel about Ireland, the author "covers the years following 1916's Easter Rebellion (an event more important to Irish consciousness than World War I), which will culminate in the creation of an Irish Free State and the waging of brutal civil war. Flanagan gives us history as moments, some dull and some dangerous, in the lives of scores of people, some invented and some actual." Libr J

The author manages "to sustain interest in the individual lives of his various characters while creating a sense of the monumental historical drama in which they are all players. . . . But it does more than re-create an era and satisfy the reader's appetite for a well-told tale. 'The End of the Hunt' is, in fact, a significant contribution to the historical interpretation of the period, an interpretation that possesses considerable relevance." N Y Times Book Rev

The tenants of time. Dutton 1988 824p o.p.

LC 87-13632
"A William Abrahams book"
"Set during three pivotal decades of Irish history, the narrative focuses on four men who participate in the short-lived Rising of 1867 and the irrevocable effects on their lives of the battle of Clonbrony Wood. . . . Except for Hugh, who is one of the narrators of this moving story, tragedy stalks each of the veterans of Clonbrony Wood." Publ Wkly

This "novel is enormously long and unfalteringly rich in its delineation of the sometimes thorny connection between the public associations and private needs and loyalties of people who live energetically, and even recklessly, through times of political turbulence." Commonweal

The year of the French; a novel. Holt, Rinehart & Winston 1979 516p o.p.

LC 78-23539

Flanagan, Thomas, 1923-—*Continued*

This historical novel is based on actual events. The year is 1798, when a band of "Irishmen rise up in County Mayo against their English rulers. The French, secure in the success of their own revolution, decide to come to the aid of the Irish, less for the sake of an ideal than to harass the English. Three shiploads of troops, under the brilliant General Humbert, set sail from France. Their arrival in Kilcummin Bay is the signal for the war of liberation to begin. . . . But by fall, disappointed in their hope for more troops from France and confronted by vastly superior forces under Lord Cornwallis, the Irish are doomed." Publisher's note

The author "writes well, taking care to approximate . . . the spoken and written language of the time. The result is, I'm convinced, not only a serious book, free of the irony and satire that informs so many of the more literary historical fictions written today, but a distinguished one as well." Newsweek

The **Flannery** O'Connor Award: selected stories; edited by Charles East. University of Ga. Press 1992 318p $24.95

ISBN 0-8203-1414-5   LC 91-28973

Analyzed in Short story index

Contents: Appetizer, by R. H. Abel; Inside dope, by G. G. Adams; World without end, by T. Ardizzone; Peacock blue, by F. Camoin; Trinity, by D. Curley; Wilbur Gray falls in love with an idea, by P. F. Deaver; Voici! Henri! by A. DePew; Pie dance, by M. Giles; What my mother knows, by C. L. Glickfeld; A country girl, by M. Hood; The mouthpiece, by S. La Puma; Jet stream, by T. M. McNally; The ponoes, by P. Meinke; The source of trouble, by D. Monroe; The expendables, by A. Nelson; Banquet, by S. Neville; La Bête: a figure study, by M. Pritchard; Horror show, by S. Thompson; Skin and bone, by D. Walton; South of the border, by L. A. Wilson; The metal shredders, by N. Zafris

This "book laudably displays the talents of new writers from across the U.S. Their stories cover a wide range of subjects, themes, settings, and times, unified only by a strong focus on character. All the stories also exhibit a fresh perspective and lack the polished refinement of seasoned writers." Booklist

Flaubert, Gustave, 1821-1880

Madame Bovary; patterns of provincial life.

Available from various publishers

Original French edition, 1857

"With flawless style, Flaubert creates the life and fate of the Norman bourgeoise Emma Bovary. Unhappy in her marriage to a good-hearted but stupid village doctor, Emma finds her pathetic dreams of romantic love unfulfilled. A sentimental, discontented, and hopelessly limited person, she commits adultery, piles up enormous debts, and finally takes her own life in desperation. The novel's subject, the life of a very ordinary woman, and its technique, the amassing of precise detail, make Madame Bovary one of the crowning works in the development of the novel." Reader's Ency. 3d edition

Sentimental education; or, The history of a young man. Magee c1904 2v o.p.

Original French edition, 1869

"The background of this novel is the decline and fall of the Monarchy of Louis Philippe and the Revolution of 1848. . . . The hero, Frederic Moreau, has many of the traits of young Flaubert. Madame Arnous, with whom he falls in love, is very like Madame Schlesinger whom Flaubert had admired at Trouville as early as 1836. The subject of the novel is really the futility of existence." Haydn. Thesaurus of Book Dig

Fleming, Ian, 1908-1964

Bonded Fleming; a James Bond omnibus. Viking 1965 439p o.p.

Partially analyzed in Short story index

This volume featuring British Secret Service agent James Bond contains: For your eyes only, a collection of five novelettes: From a view to a kill; For your eyes only; Quantum of Solace; Risico; The Hildebrand rarity, first published 1960, and two novels: Thunderball and The spy who loved me, published 1961 and 1962 respectively

The five stories in For your eyes only, are about dope-smuggling, an assassination, spying and rampaging human emotion. In Thunderball, Bond faces his most dangerous assignment and confronts S.P.E.C.T.R.E. The spy who loved me is the first-person story of a young woman involved with James Bond both romantically and perilously

Casino Royale. Macmillan 1954 c1953 176p o.p.

"Against the background of a French resort the book describes Bond's destruction of the French branch of SMERSH, the Soviet espionage ring. The climax of the story is a tense game of baccarat in which Bond ruins the leader of the ring, Le Chiffre. The girl in the case is a compliant Soviet agent named Vesper Lynd, and there is much closely described violence." Wakeman. World Authors, 1950-1970

Diamonds are forever

In Fleming, I. More gilt-edged Bonds p443-661

Doctor No. Macmillan 1958 256p o.p.

The setting is the Caribbean, where James Bond is trying to trace the disappearance of two agents who had trespassed on the isolated island kingdom of the Eurasian Dr. No. The maniacal doctor, equipped with two pairs of steel pincers for hands, dreams of world conquest and is stockpiling a deadly arsenal for that time. Bond, with female companion in tow, survives a manhunt through the island's mangrove swamps to foil the doctor's plans

For your eyes only

In Fleming, I. Bonded Fleming p189-328

From a view to a kill

In Fleming, I. Bonded Fleming p191-213

From Russia, with love. Macmillan 1957 253p o.p.

James Bond, the British secret agent here meets the Soviet murder organization SMERSH once more. His execution has been ordered but Bond's counter activities seem successful—until the last page

Goldfinger. Macmillan 1959 318p o.p.

"James Bond, British Secret Service Agent 007, must retrieve British gold from a Mr. Auric Goldfinger whose ruthless obsession is suggesting in his goal—personal possession of half the supply of mined gold in the world." Publ Wkly

Fleming, Ian, 1908-1964—*Continued*

"All this is, in some measure, a great joke, but Fleming's passion for plausibility, his own naval intelligence background, and a kind of sincere Manicheism, allied to journalistic efficiency in the management of his récit, make his work rather impressive." Burgess. 99 Novels

The Hildebrand rarity

In Fleming, I. Bonded Fleming p298-328

Live and let die

In Fleming, I. More gilt-edged Bonds p1-218

The man with the golden gun. New Am. Lib. 1965 183p o.p.

This adventure "begins with a brainwashed Bond ready to do the bidding of the K.G.B. in headquarters of the Secret Service, and thrashes through to a climax in Jamaica where the adversary is Scaramonga, the most ruthless death-dealing instrument forged in the 20th century." Libr J

Moonraker

In Fleming, I. More gilt-edged Bonds p219-441

More gilt-edged Bonds. Macmillan 1965 661p o.p.

An anthology of three novels featuring British secret service agent James Bond: Live and let die, first published 1954 in the United Kingdom; Moonraker, and Diamonds are forever, first published 1955 and 1956, respectively

In Live and let die, James Bond, alias Operator 007, meets the powerful criminal Mr. Big of SMERSH in deadly combat. Moonraker describes the agent's quest for a new super-rocket with an immense potential for destruction, and the enigmatic millionaire who is financing the project. In the third escapade, Diamonds are forever, Bond infiltrates the Spangled Mob to learn the motive behind their increased activities in diamond smuggling

On Her Majesty's Secret Service. New Am. Lib. 1963 299p o.p.

James Bond, British secret agent 007, forsakes his bachelorhood for Countess Teresa di Vicenzo, who involves him in another adventure with Ernst Stavro Blofeld, head of an international crime syndicate and architect of an atomic blackmail scheme. The story is set against an Alpine background

Quantum of solace

In Fleming, I. Bonded Fleming p248-66

Risico

In Fleming, I. Bonded Fleming p267-97

The spy who loved me

In Fleming, I. Bonded Fleming p329-439

Thunderball

In Fleming, I. Bonded Fleming p1-188

You only live twice. New Am. Lib. 1964 240p o.p.

"Bond, near-prostrate from his bride's death, is given a Japanese assignment to snap him out of his torpor. . . . [The story] involves Bond's making up as a Japanese and venturing into the den of a foreign 'death collector,' a madman who has set up a poisonous garden complete with noxious plants, volcanic geysers, snakes, and, in a lake, piranha fish. Very grisly and chilling. The ending is an epitome of horror." Publ Wkly

Fleming, Oliver *See* MacDonald, Philip, 1899-1981

Fleming, Thomas J., 1927-

The officers' wives; [by] Thomas Fleming. Doubleday 1981 645p o.p.

LC 80-1063

In this "tale of military life, the overlapping destinies of . . . six characters unfold. Adam and Honor Thayer, Pete and Joanna Burke and George and Amy Rosser. . . . Adam Thayer, who quickly sours on his beautiful but dim wife, establishes himself as a brilliant strategist, serves valorously in the Special Forces in Southeast Asia, but is eventually undone by his peers for his vehement opposition to the Army's inept conduct of the Vietnam War. George and Amy Rosser, model military politicians, scheme their way up through the ranks to become Mr. and Mrs. General, not even daring to wonder if the struggle was worth it. Pete Burke . . . endures the nightmares of combat in Vietnam only to be broken by the failure of his marriage." N Y Times Book Rev

"Sometimes cumbersome, but often passionate or reflective, Fleming's fictional account of the alterations in our attitude toward military service recapitulates the entire course of recent American history." Atlantic

Over there; [by] Thomas Fleming. HarperCollins Pubs. 1992 608p o.p.

LC 91-58364

This saga of World War I is set on the Allied front in France. "Grimly cataloguing countless atrocities there, the novel focuses primarily on the fortunes of nurse's aide Polly Warden as she changes from a wide-eyed, idealistic young woman into a shell-shocked and weary cynic." Publ Wkly

"Chronicling so dramatically an event that changed the way the world thinks is no small task; Fleming hits his target with artistry and insight." Booklist

Time and tide; [by] Thomas Fleming. Simon & Schuster 1987 734p o.p.

LC 87-9896

"Having left the Battle of Savo Island under suspicious circumstances in 1942, the USS *Jefferson City* is a ship haunted by bad joss. Arthur McKay is sent to relieve the cruiser's captain, Win Kemble, also his Annapolis roommate and best friend. Accused of cowardice under fire, the men of the *JC* fight a constant battle to prove their valor to themselves and the rest of the Navy." Libr J

"Fleming performs a masterful job of blending the private, political, and military concerns faced by this huge, disparate crew, which ranges from movie stars to Annapolis graduates." Booklist

Fletcher, Lucille, 1912-

Sorry, wrong number

In Alfred Hitchcock presents: Stories not for the nervous

Foley, Martha, 1897-1977

(ed) 200 years of great American short stories. See 200 years of great American short stories

(ed) Best of the Best American short stories, 1915-1950. See Best of the Best American short stories, 1915-1950

Follett, Ken, 1949-

A dangerous fortune. Delacorte Press 1993 533p o.p.

LC 93-21912

Available large print edition $28.95 (ISBN 0-385-31188-5)

"In 1866, tragedy strikes at the exclusive Windfield School. A young student drowns in a mysterious accident involving a small circle of boys. Among them are scrappy Hugh Pilaster; his older cousin Edward, the weak, dissolute heir to the Pilaster banking fortune; and Micky Miranda, the darkly handsome son of a brutal South American landowner. The drowning and its aftermath initiate a spiraling circle of treachery that will span three decades and entwine many lives." Publisher's note

This novel contains "an authentic sense of history, a wonderfully complex and fascinating plot, mesmerizing characters, and a thoroughly entertaining story." Booklist

Eye of the needle; a novel. Arbor House 1978 313p o.p.

LC 77-90670

"It is 1944 and the Allies are preparing to invade France. Part of the preparations call for a vast deception that will draw the bulk of the German defending forces to the Calais area while the Allies go in at Normandy. Only one of the enemy smells out the fakery, a German spy called Die Nadel (for the stiletto which is his favorite murder weapon). Called variously Faber or Baker, the only spy Hitler trusts, he must get his information back to the homeland. The race by British Intelligence to thwart Die Nadel provides the story drive of the book." Best Sellers

"An absolutely terrific thriller, so pulse-pounding, so ingenious in its plotting, and so frighteningly realistic that you simply cannot stop reading, this World War II espionage tale is right up there with the best of them." Publ Wkly

The key to Rebecca. Morrow 1980 381p o.p. Buccaneer Bks. reprint available $32.95 (ISBN 1-56849-278-2)

LC 80-16760

The story "opens in 1942, when Rommel successfully places a German spy in British-held Cairo. Alexander Wolff, a German of Egyptian nationality, infiltrates Egypt with great difficulty, only to attract the unwelcome attention of British Intelligence by knifing an Assyut corporal who threatens his cover. . . . [Wolff] eludes pursuer Major William Vandam [and] gains access to battle plans crucial to the defense of Tobruk and Mersa Matruh. .

. . Using the call sign Sphinx, he transmits messages coded from a copy of DuMaurier's Rebecca while hidden on the houseboat of a locally famous . . . belly dancer." Libr J

The author "is no literary stylist, but his clean, purposeful prose is more than adequate to the demands of his tightly plotted, fast moving story. More to the point, he knows his people and his territory; his evocation of wartime Cairo is a marvel of concise atmospherics." Newsweek

Lie down with lions. Morrow 1986 333p o.p.

LC 85-25876

This novel is set in "Afghanistan, where the farmers and nomads are battling their Russian invaders. Jean-Pierre, a doctor fresh from residency, has volunteered two years to tend the wounded and offer general medical aid in the Valley of Five Lions; his real motive, however, is to spy on the rebels for the 'KGB'. Jane, his newly pregnant wife, serves as his nurse and his contact with the women of the villages. When local caravans bringing munitions are repeatedly attacked and the men killed, Ellis Thaler, a 'CIA' expert in explosives, arrives to consolidate the rebel's efforts, that he and Jane had been lovers complicates the situation. Separately they deduce Jean-Pierre's treachery. . . . This is fine adventure filled with passion, violence, and tension." Best Sellers

The man from St. Petersburg. Morrow 1982 323p o.p.

LC 81-22550

"Lydia, born a Russian noblewoman, now married happily into the English aristocracy, has carried with her for years the secret that daughter Charlotte was really sired by an anarchist-murderer lover, not by the man she believes to be her father. When that lover, whose freedom from prison and torture Lydia purchased by her 'safe' marriage, turns up in London, his mission to assassinate a visiting Russian prince, the past rises up to torment Lydia and all hell breaks loose. It doesn't take long for nihilist Feliks to figure out that Charlotte is really his child and he sets out to make her acquaintance both to use her as an unwitting accomplice, and because he discovers he is capable of true, unselfish paternal love." Publ Wkly

This "novel beautifully reconstructs the era of pre-World War I London." Libr J

Night over water. Morrow 1991 400p $23

ISBN 0-688-04660-6   LC 91-17701

Also available large print edition $25 (ISBN 0-688-08579-2)

In this World War II-era thriller "the primary action takes place aboard a transatlantic flight of the Pan American Clipper bound for New York. The cast of characters who board the sumptuous seaplane in Southampton includes an aristocratic Nazi sympathizer and his family, a renowned Jewish physicist, an American film star, an affable jewel thief, a bored housewife and her lover, and a Russian princess. The celebrated wayfarers are blissfully unaware that Eddie Deakin, the all-American aviation engineer, is being forced to sabotage the flight in order to necessitate a dangerous crash landing off the coast of Maine." Booklist

"Details of early aviation firmly establish the cast in their era and a tantalizing mosaic of subplots whisks the reader through a whirlwind of romance and intrigue." Publ Wkly

Follett, Ken, 1949——*Continued*
Paper money. Morrow 1987 c1977 216p
o.p.

LC 87-7867

First published 1977 in the United Kingdom under
the pseudonym Zachary Stone
"The novel's action takes place in a single day and
involves gangsters, financiers, politicians, and journalists
deliberately or unwillingly immersed in an oil scam, a
monumental robbery, and a sex scandal." Booklist
"Though painted in broad brush-strokes, the characters
seem compellingly real, as do their professional environments." Publ Wkly

Pillars of the earth. Morrow 1989 973p
o.p.

LC 89-9405

This novel "chronicles the vicissitudes of a prior, his
master builder, and their community as they struggle to
build a cathedral and protect themselves during the
tumultuous 12th century, when the empress Maud and
Stephen are fighting for the crown of England after the
death of Henry I." Libr J
"Follett has skillfully crafted an extraordinary epic buttressed by a succession of suspenseful subplots. A
towering triumph of romance, rivalry, and spectacle from
a major talent." Booklist

Triple; a novel. Arbor House 1979 377p
o.p.

LC 78-73869

"The Egyptians are making nuclear weapons and the
Israelis, in order to do the same, are obliged to steal
100 tons of uranium. A group of old acquaintances at
Oxford in 1947 come together again in different roles:
the Mossad agent who organizes the theft, the disgruntled
Palestinian spying for Egypt, the Russian bureaucrat (actually a KGB colonel), and the American become a
Mafia don. The hijacking plot is elaborate beyond
description." Libr J

Folsom, Allan R.
The day after tomorrow; a novel; by
Allan Folsom. Little, Brown 1994 596p
$24.95

ISBN 0-316-28829-2   LC 93-30344

"A young American doctor haunted by his father's
murder stumbles into a chilling international conspiracy
and crosses paths with, among others, a weary L.A. cop
investigating a series of surgically precise decapitations,
a naïve physical therapist and a hypercompetent German
assassin." Publ Wkly
"In this ambitious and impressive first novel, Folsom
covers vast amounts of territory at breakneck speed. .
. . That Folsom manages to instill some genuine tension
amidst all this is testimony to his skill." Libr J

Ford, Elbur, 1906-1993
*For works written by this author under
other names see* Carr, Philippa, 1906-1993;
Holt, Victoria, 1906-1993; Plaidy, Jean,
1906-1993

Ford, Ford Madox, 1873-1939
The last post
In Ford, F. M. Parade's end
A man could stand up
In Ford, F. M. Parade's end
No more parades
In Ford, F. M. Parade's end
Parade's end. Knopf 1992 906p $20
ISBN 0-679-41728-1   LC 92-52922
"Everyman's library"
A reissue of the title first published 1950
A one volume edition of the author's tetralogy that
includes: Some do not (1924); No more parades (1925);
A man could stand up (1926); and The last post (1928)
This series of novels "describes the adventures in love
and war of Christopher Tietjens, an old-fashioned gen-
tleman of the English governing class. Ford draws a
brilliant picture of the social changes brought about by
the First World War. Before the war, Tietjens is nobly
faithful to his impossible wife. But trench warfare seems
to him a symbol of the disintegration of his whole
society. He has a mental breakdown, goes to live with
a woman he loves, and gives up his position, wealth,
and historic family ties." Reader's Ency. 3d edition
Some do not
In Ford, F. M. Parade's end

Forester, C. S. (Cecil Scott), 1899-1966
Admiral Hornblower in the West Indies.
Little, Brown 1958 329p o.p.
A collection of Horatio Hornblower's adventures set
in the West Indies. "The first belongs chronologically
with 'Lieutenant Hornblower.' The rest are set nearly 15
years later when, as rear admiral in command of His
Majesty's fleet in the West Indies, he faces a new Bonapartist uprising, suppresses the slave trade, stamps out
piracy, and maintains British diplomacy during the South
American revolutions." Booklist
"Recounted with taste, with psychological insight, and
with a sure sense of story. This is top grade adventure
fiction." N Y Her Trib Books

The African Queen. Little, Brown 1935
275p o.p.
Available from Buccaneer Bks. and Queens House.
Large print edition available from G.K. Hall
"At her brother's death Rose Sayer is left alone in
an isolated African mission. She is determined to fight
against the Germans, who have taken her brother's black
converts into custody. She joins forces with a Cockney,
Alnutt, and they take a long and dangerous trip downriver in Alnutt's dilapidated launch in order to reach
the German boat they intend to blow up. The journey
points up the differences between this ill-matched pair,
and their bravery as well." Shapiro. Fic for Youth. 3d
edition

Beat to quarters. Little, Brown 1937 324p
o.p.
A sea story of the British navy in the early nineteenth
century. Essentially it is a portrait of a man, captain
of an English frigate. Hornblower, son of a country doctor, is a man uncertain of his own powers, of his technical skill and of the admiration of his men, yet when
he is sent under sealed orders to the Pacific coast of

Forester, C. S. (Cecil Scott), 1899-1966 —
Continued

Central America, he accomplishes his mission brilliantly, and fights two successful battles with the same Spanish warship

"There is plenty of action. But there is also an unusual character study." N Y Times Book Rev

Followed by Ship of the line

Commodore Hornblower. Little, Brown 1945 384p o.p.

Available from Amereon and Buccaneer Bks.

"Hornblower returns to sea in command of a squadron on a delicate mission to the Baltic, reluctantly taking leave of his lovely wife Lady Barbara. In this expedition he combines brilliant naval strategy with diplomatic cunning to out-maneuver his old, unseen enemy Napoleon." Ont Libr Rev

"It is a spirited piece of work, and full of interesting detail where matters naval, military, and diplomatic in that year of decision are concerned." Times Lit Suppl

Followed by Lord Hornblower

Flying colours. Little, Brown 1939 294p o.p.

Third book in a series which includes Beat to quarters and Ship of the line. Captain Hornblower, his crippled first mate, Bush, and his servant, Brown, escape from their escort on the way to Paris to be tried for piracy. The story is of their recapture of an English vessel and return to England, where they are covered with honors

Followed by Commodore Hornblower

Hornblower and the Atropos. Little, Brown 1953 325p $17.95

ISBN 0-316-28911-6

Also available from Amereon

This is a series of episodes in the early life of the Captain; a journey across England from Gloucester to London by canal; his part in the funeral of Nelson; and his battles on the coast of Turkey, where he recovers a huge treasure from a sunken English ship

Hornblower and the Hotspur. Little, Brown 1962 344p $17.95

ISBN 0-316-28899-3

Also available from Amereon

"From the standpoint of sequence, this . . . title in the Hornblower saga follows 'Lieutenant Hornblower.'" Wis Libr Bull

"The story opens just before Horatio sails on a cruise in his first command. His rank is Commander; his ship something less than a frigate but something more than a sloop; his task to act as the eyes of the Channel Fleet which is to be in position to blockade Brest upon the imminent declaration of hostilities with France. In the course of action Hornblower is detained at sea for almost two years as, in his own inimitable and logically necessary style, he helps cripple the Napoleonic effort to invade England, the last block to conquest of Europe." Best Sellers

Hornblower during the crisis, and two stories: Hornblower's temptation and The last encounter. Little, Brown 1967 174p $17.95

ISBN 0-316-28915-9

"Posthumous novel fragment and two slender stories. The former concerns Hornblower's eventful voyage to London on another man's ship for reassignment on a spy mission to Spain. . . . In one story Mr. Hornblower is almost taken in by a seemingly harmless mission entrusted to him by a young Irishman before his shipboard execution. In the other tale a stranded traveler in distress, helped by Admiral Hornblower and wife, proves to be Napoleon Bonaparte." Booklist

"Because Forester died before completing this novel, the reader is left with a summary sketch and his own imagination for final details of the plot. For Forester devotees, this will not detract from the essential verve and dash of Hornblower's last chase." Christ Sci Monit

The last nine days of the Bismarck. Little, Brown 1959 138p o.p. Amereon reprint available $16.95 (ISBN 0-89190-606-1)

"Forester describes the pursuit and epic bombardment at sea in World War II when the German battleship 'Bismarck' broke into the Atlantic and sailed toward Brest with the whole British Home Fleet after her. Scenes on board the 'Bismarck' and the British ships have been given dialog to make the telling more vivid." Publ Wkly

Lieutenant Hornblower. Little, Brown 1952 306p $17.95

ISBN 0-316-28907-8

Also available from Amereon

This seventh book in the 'Hornblower' series fills part of the gap between 'Mr. Midshipman Hornblower' and 'Hornblower and the Hotspur'

This novel details "Horatio's adventures as a Lieutenant until his promotion to Commander during the early years of the Napoleonic Wars." Best Sellers

The author "interprets the navy, certainly in its Napoleonic period, with the help of a character that represents the navy at its best and action that is grandly exciting without being melodramatic; helped, too, by a sense of order and a mastery of technique that puts his work on a high plane of artistry." Christ Sci Monit

Lord Hornblower. Little, Brown 1946 322p $17.95

ISBN 0-316-28908-6

Also available from Buccaneer Bks.

In this "Hornblower novel Horatio continues his adventures and helps defeat Napoleon by aiding the heir to the Bourbon throne to enter France. Barbara goes to the Congress of Vienna to act as hostess for her brother while Horatio returns to France to visit old friends and renew an old love. When Napoleon escapes from Elba danger threatens Hornblower as he forms a guerrilla band in the south of France. But, saved by the defeat of the French at Waterloo, he returns to the arms of Barbara and new honors as Lord Hornblower." Booklist

Mr. Midshipman Hornblower. Little, Brown 1950 310p $17.95

ISBN 0-316-28909-4

Also available from Buccaneer Bks.; large print edition available from Thorndike Press

Analyzed in Short story index

Chronologically this is the first book of the Hornblower series. "The book details, in a series of incidents, the genesis of the Hornblower career from the day he first stepped aboard ship as a kings-letter man to the day when he received his commission as Lieutenant in a Spanish prison. Actually the story is told as a series

Forester, C. S. (Cecil Scott), 1899-1966—
Continued
of incidents . . . with only a thin thread of continuity connecting them." Best Sellers
Contents: Hornblower and the even chance; Hornblower and the cargo of rice; Hornblower and the penalty of failure; Hornblower and the man who felt queer; Hornblower and the man who saw God; Hornblower, the frogs, and the lobsters; Hornblower and the Spanish galleys; Hornblower and the examination for lieutenant; Hornblower and Noah's Ark; Hornblower, the duchess, and the devil

Ship of the line. Little, Brown 1938 298p o.p.
In this sequel to Beat to quarters, Captain Hornblower is given command of the ship Sutherland and sent to join the forces blockading the Spanish coast in the war with Napoleon
Followed by Flying colours

To the Indies. Little, Brown 1940 298p o.p. Amereon reprint available $18.95 (ISBN 0-88411-926-2)
"The story of Narciso Rich who is lifted suddenly from his quiet life as a successful lawyer to join the swaggering, gold-hungry hidalgos who went with Columbus on his third voyage. He fights Indians at San Domingo, is kidnapped by renegades, shipwrecked off the coast of Cuba, and finally makes his way back to the settlement in time to return on the ship that carried Columbus in chains." Ont Libr Rev

Forester, Cecil Scott *See* Forester, C. S. (Cecil Scott), 1899-1966

Forrest, Felix C., 1913-1966
For works written by this author under other names see Smith, Cordwainer, 1913-1966

Forster, E. M. (Edward Morgan), 1879-1970
The collected tales of E. M. Forster. Knopf 1947 308p o.p.
Analyzed in Short story index
Originally published separately as two distinct collections: Celestial omnibus, and other stories (1911), and The eternal moment, and other stories (1928)
The celestial omnibus: The story of a panic; The other side of the hedge; The celestial omnibus; Other kingdom; The curate's friend; The road from Colonus
The eternal moment: The machine stops; The point of it; Mr. Andrews; Co-ordination; The story of the siren; The eternal moment

Howards End. Knopf 1991 xxxiii, 359p $17
ISBN 0-679-40668-9   LC 91-52997
Also available from Buccaneer Bks.
"Everyman's library"
First published 1910
This novel "deals with an English country house called Howards End and its influence on the lives of the materialistic Wilcoxes, the cultured and idealistic Schlegel sisters, and the poor bank clerk Leonard Bast. The Schlegels try to befriend Bast. Mr. Wilcox, whom Margaret Schlegel later marries, gives him financial advice which ruins him. Helen Schlegal becomes his mistress for a short time and bears his son; thereupon Charles Wilcox thrashes and accidentally kills him. The house passes from intuitive, half-mystical Mrs. Wilcox to her husband's second wife Margaret Schlegel, to Margaret's nephew Leonard Bast's son. Illustrating Forster's motto 'Only connect.' The house brings together three important elements in English society; money and successful business in the Wilcoxes, culture in the Schlegels, and the lower classes in Leonard Bast." Reader's Ency. 3d edition

also in Forster, E. M. A room with a view and Howards End

Maurice. Norton 1971 256p o.p.
Available from Amereon and Buccaneer Bks.
This novel was written between 1913 and 1914. It depicts the steps by which Maurice Hall, a shy, conventional young man, while a student at Cambridge, first discovers and then gradually comes to accept the fact that he is, by nature, sexually attracted to men, not women. "He enjoys a romantic friendship—idyllic, sentimental, chaste—with Clive, a fellow undergraduate at Cambridge. When Clive turns abruptly to women . . . the unhappy Maurice consults his family doctor and a hypnotist who fail to help him. On a visit to the now-married Clive's country estate he falls in love, physically this time, with a young gamekeeper to whom he commits his future on a brief acquaintance." Newsweek
"This posthumous novel with a homosexual theme would have been sensational had it been published when written in 1913. Appearing in the 1970's, it is not sensational, but it is an interesting novel—well written as all of E. M. Forster's works are. . . . It is filled with keen insight and sympathetic character analysis, valuable for an understanding of the author and his works." Choice

A passage to India.
Available from various publishers
First published 1924
"Politics and mysticism are potent forces in India just after World War I. Ronald Heaslop, magistrate of Chandrapore, has asked his mother, Mrs. Moore, to visit him along with his fiancée, Adela Quested. To add to their knowledge of the real India, Dr. Aziz, a young Moslem doctor offers to take them to the Marabar Caves outside the city. The visit is a shattering experience. Mrs. Moore is struck by the thought that all her ideas about life are no more than the hollow echo she hears in the cave. Adela, entering another cave alone, emerges in a panic and accuses Dr. Aziz of having attacked her in the gloom of the cave. The trial that results from her accusation divides the groups in the city so acutely that a reconciliation appears impossible." Shapiro. Fic for Youth. 3d edition
A depiction of the "clash between East and West, and of the prejudices and misunderstandings that foredoomed goodwill. Criticized at first for anti-British and possibly inaccurate bias, it has been praised as a superb character study of the people of one race by a writer of another." Oxford Companion to Engl Lit

A room with a view. Putnam 1911 364p o.p.
Available from Amereon and Buccaneer Bks.
First published 1908
This novel "is set mostly in Italy, a country which represents for the author the forces of true passion. The heroine, upper-middle-class Lucy Honeychurch, is visiting Italy with a friend. When she regrets that her hotel room has no view, lower-middle-class Mr. Emerson offers the

Forster, E. M. (Edward Morgan), 1879-1970—*Continued*

friends his own room and that of his son. Among Lucy's experiences are a street murder at her feet, from which George Emerson rescues her, and getting lost at a picnic, at which George kisses her. On her return to England she becomes engaged to a shallow, conventional young man of her own class. But when she meets George again, she overcomes her own prejudice and her family's opposition and marries him." Reader's Ency. 3d edition

also in Forster, E. M. A room with a view and Howards End

A room with a view and Howards End. Modern Lib. 1993 533p $18

ISBN 0-679-60069-8   LC 93-15340

A combined edition of two titles, both entered separately

Forster, Edward Morgan *See* Forster, E. M. (Edward Morgan), 1879-1970

Forsyth, Frederick, 1938-

The day of the jackal. Viking 1971 380p o.p. Buccaneer Bks. reprint available $32.95 (ISBN 1-56849-279-0)

"Dissident OAS officers hire a mercenary, known by the code name 'Jackal', to assassinate General Charles deGaulle. The officers hope to cash in on the political chaos that would follow. The methodical, ingenious preparations of 'Jackal' are paralleled by the attempts of the combined French law-enforcement agencies to uncover and stop the plot. The suspense is acute." Shapiro. Fic for Youth. 3d edition

also in Forsyth, F. Forsyth's three

The deceiver. Bantam Bks. 1991 480p o.p.
LC 91-13114

This novel presents four linked tales, "each dealing with a different episode in the career of Sam McCready, the head of a department of the British Secret Intelligence Service that is known as Deception, Disinformation and Psychological Operations." Times Lit Suppl

The devil's alternative. Viking 1980 432p o.p.
LC 79-25929

This novel's plot "involves a Russian crop failure, Ukrainian terrorists who assassinate the head of the KGB to embarrass the Soviet premier, a fanatic faction in the Soviet hierarchy that wants to topple the premier and attack the U.S., a plane hijacking, a ship hijacking (and a threat to kill everyone on board and dump tons of crude oil into the sea), the CIA, and a British spy in Moscow. Basically, the good guys want to keep the level-headed Soviet premier in power to avoid World War III. It's a lot to wade through, but Forsyth is one of the best in the genre and worth the trip." Booklist

The dogs of war. Viking 1974 408p o.p.

A "novel about the carefully planned overthrow of the small African state of Zangaro. Behind the coup is a British multimillionaire, seeking control of the mining rites to the platinum within Zangaro's Crystal Mountain. He hires top mercenary Cat Shannon to do most of the planning and to carry out the attack. The bulk of the novel is devoted to each of the detailed transactions of the 100-day operation, from purchasing and smuggling arms to arranging a multitude of clandestine business deals." Libr J

also in Forsyth, F. Forsyth's three

The fist of God. Bantam Bks. 1994 544p $23.95

ISBN 0-553-09126-3   LC 93-47150

"Hero Mike Martin is a British Special Forces agent sent to Kuwait after the Iraqi invasion to assess the situation and build a resistance movement. When the British discover the existence of Saddam Hussein's double agent, Jericho, who had been feeding information to Israel, Martin is smuggled into Baghdad to contact Jericho and learn about Saddam's battle plans. What Martin finds out is that Saddam has a doomsday weapon he is planning to use against the Coalition Allies when they launch Operation Desert Storm." Publ Wkly

The author's "formula, consisting of well-researched backgrounds, technical detail and a dispassionate reportorial approach to fiction, almost always works well, and this book is no exception. There is general excitement without hysteria and plenty of credible action." N Y Times Book Rev

Forsyth's three. Viking 1980 3v in 1 o.p.
LC 80-14790

An omnibus edition of three titles that are entered separately

Contents: The day of the jackal; The Odessa file; The dogs of war

The fourth protocol. Viking 1984 389p o.p.
LC 83-40646

"The narrative reveals a Soviet plan to control England and destroy NATO by swaying the popular vote in England's election: the Russian's best undercover man will detonate a small nuclear device near an American base in Britain, thereby ensuring a wave of antinuclear sentiment." Libr J

This novel "succeeds magnificently on at least two . . . levels: as a scrupulously detailed study of spy 'tradecraft' and as a testament to the virtues of a well-constructed plot. We want to know what happens in this book not only because of the inherently dramatic situation, but also because we anticipate the sense of resolution that comes when the puzzle's last piece clicks securely into place." Booklist

The negotiator. Bantam Bks. 1989 391p o.p.
LC 88-43346

Available G. K. Hall large print edition

In this "thriller, a high-ranking Soviet official and a Texas millionaire find themselves united in their opposition to a proposed 1991 U.S.-Soviet peace treaty. The novel revolves around their vicious, labyrinthine plots to disrupt the actions of President John Cormack. Quinn (the 'Negotiator') is called in to resolve the sinister series of plots and counterplots that stretch from Moscow to Vermont. . . . An electrifying story, with its healthy share of arms dealers, venal politicians, and mercenaries." Booklist

The Odessa file. Viking 1972 337p o.p.

"Young German reporter Peter Miller comes upon the diary of a survivor of a World War II extermination camp at Riga. Its revelations lead him into the deadly pursuit of commandant Roschmann, known as the Butch-

Forsyth, Frederick, 1938——*Continued*

er of Riga. Roschmann is engaged in an international scheme to destroy the Jewish state. The plan is promoted by the Odessa, a secret organization that protects the identities and fortunes of former SS members. Miller infiltrates the organization to find and expose Roschmann." Shapiro. Fic for Youth. 3d edition

"Forsyth skillfully blends fact and fiction into a suspenseful and detailed story which is often downright chilling in its credibility." Libr J

also in Forsyth, F. Forsyth's three

Fowles, John, 1926-

The collector. Little, Brown 1963 305p o.p.

"Frederick Clegg, a collector of butterflies, becomes obsessed with the idea of capturing a young, attractive art student, as he does insects. He finds the perfect, isolated spot for this adventure, and there ensues a tale of horror and suspense. It is told first by Frederick and then by Miranda, as she struggles valiantly, with intelligence and determination, for her freedom, to no avail." Shapiro. Fic for Youth. 3d edition

"Mr. Fowles is a powerful writer; this story has a nightmarish reality and immediacy. Both Miranda and Clegg are completely developed characters; the book is at once horrifying and fascinating." Best Sellers

Daniel Martin. Little, Brown 1977 629p $19.95

ISBN 0-316-28959-0

"Daniel Martin is a middle-aged Englishman, a successful playwright turned screenwriter, who is summoned from Hollywood to Oxford by the imminent death of a long-estranged friend, a Catholic philosopher named Anthony. In their student days, Dan and Anthony had been best friends and had married sisters. . . . [Dan's] marriage had collapsed in bitterness, and with it had gone Dan's friendship with Anthony and Jane. Now, in the unfailingly polite crucible of Anthony's death and a subsequent therapeutic trip up the Nile with his widow, Dan discovers the truth of something he had suspected ever since Jane crept up to his room that once so long ago at Oxford. He had married the wrong sister; Jane had knowingly married the wrong man." Newsweek

"In Fowles' hands [Martin's] pilgrimage becomes thoroughly absorbing, intellectually challenging—and not at all the snappy read his admirers have come to expect." Time

The French lieutenant's woman. Little, Brown 1969 467p $29.95

ISBN 0-316-29099-8

Also available from Buccaneer Bks.

"The setting is Victorian England. The hero is Charles, respectable, well-to-do, thoughtful, progressive. He is engaged to Ernestina, a rich, attractive, but highly conventional girl, but he falls in love with the beautiful, tragic, mysterious Sarah who is known to Lyme Regis (where the action begins) as 'the French lieutenant's woman' because of some disreputable but romantic episode in her past life. The situation, that of the amorous triangle, is familiar in fiction. What makes this book highly original is that it has three possible endings, all different. . . . We have here a highly readable and informative book, compelling, thrilling, erotic, but we are not permitted to relax as if we were reading Dickens or Thackeray. A very modern mind is manipulating us as well as the characters." Burgess. 99 Novels

A maggot. Little, Brown 1985 455p $19.95

ISBN 0-316-28994-9   LC 85-15937

This novel opens on "the final afternoon—the eve of May Day 1736—of a furtive four-day journey by five people on horseback to a small town in the English countryside, where they take lodging for the night. The party consists of a lord in disguise, his servant who cannot speak or hear, a professional actor hired to protect the disguise, a Welshman for a bodyguard and Rebecca the harlot, also hired but for purposes not yet revealed. . . . A few days after, Dick, the servant, is found hanged in a wood, the lord is missing, and the hirelings have also melted away, later to be tracked down by the agents of one Henry Ayscough, a barrister who investigates the case on behalf of the lord's estranged father. The rest of the book records the testimony of witnesses questioned by Ayscough." N Y Times Book Rev

The magus; a revised version; with a foreword by the author. Little, Brown 1978 c1977 656p o.p.

LC 77-17343

Originally published 1966; this version first published 1977 in the United Kingdom

"This novel follows the harrowing misadventures of Nicholas Urfe, a young British schoolmaster who takes a teaching post on a remote Greek island, Phraxos, where he is drawn into an emotional maelstrom of high intrigue." Newsweek

"With the narrative skill and literary sleight of hand . . . Fowles again provides hours of engrossing entertainment for an audience susceptible to a massive blend of sensuous realism, suspenseful romanticism, hypertheatrical mystification, psychic intervention, and a gallery of unusual or exotic characters in the vivid setting of the golden, craggy, threatening beauty of an isolated Greek island." Booklist

Fox, Paula

A servant's tale. North Point Press 1984 321p o.p.

LC 84-060679

"The narrator and heroine of this novel, Luisa de la Cueva, is the illegitimate daughter of a landowner's disinherited son and a servant girl on the fictional Caribbean island of San Pedro. Though her equivocal status bars her from fully entering into any social caste, she loves her homeland, and her father's sudden decision to uproot the family out of fear of an impending revolution is a wrenching blow. Settled in the barrio of Manhattan's Upper West Side, they find no happiness: Luisa's father cannot hold a job, her mother dies of cancer, and she herself is quickly locked into a pattern of defeatism that leads her to drop out of school, despite her lively intelligence, and hire out as a maidservant." Booklist

The author's "precision and grace in describing such things as Luisa's sudden longing to see her mother after the latter's death, the odd loneliness of a spring day and the eccentricities of Luisa's employers are breathtaking; the lives she creates are sharp-edged yet sympathetic." Publ Wkly

Francis, Clare

Night sky. Morrow 1984 c1983 631p o.p.

LC 83-17351

Francis, Clare—*Continued*

First published 1983 in the United Kingdom

"The story, which takes place between 1935 and 1945, concerns several characters whose disparate paths converge in Europe during the war. Julie Lescaux flees her home in England so her friends won't discover that she's pregnant out of wedlock. Julie has 'always thought of herself as an ordinary sort,' but after settling with an aunt and uncle in Brittany she becomes involved with the hazardous covert operation to evacuate Allied servicemen stranded in occupied Europe." N Y Times Book Rev

"The book is excellent and is completely absorbing, despite its length. Many scenes are like great landscapes and mirror the emotions of the characters during the war." Best Sellers

Wolf winter. Morrow 1988 c1987 558p o.p.

LC 87-24209

First published 1987 in the United Kingdom

"When Norwegian mountain climber Jan Johansen is killed in an incident on the Russian-Finnish border, his widow, Ragna, is drawn into a series of events with roots in World War II which set the stage for espionage in the Cold War of the 1960s. Ragna's attraction for two men, Jan's best friend and an Oslo journalist, brings them all together in a violent struggle for truth and survival in Lapland's frozen wastes." Libr J

"The skill with which the author counterpoints her several plot lines to create a mounting sense of tension is exemplary. . . . 'Wolf Winter' has a sure dramatic sense, minutely realized settings and—most important— the sort of casual style that easily delivers the large amounts of information that are essential to this sort of entertainment." N Y Times Book Rev

Francis, Dick

Across the board; a trilogy. Harper & Row 1975 715p o.p.

"A Joan Kahn book"

Contents: Flying finish (1966); Blood sport (1967); Enquiry (1969)

Flying finish and Enquiry are entered separately. Blood sport is concerned with a British intelligence agent who becomes involved in a search for a thoroughbred stallion that has been hijacked somewhere between Kennedy Airport and a Kentucky stud farm

Banker. Putnam 1983 c1982 306p o.p.

LC 82-18122

First published 1982 in the United Kingdom

"The title figure is a young British investment banker who has no knowledge of racing until he becomes involved in the possibility of arranging a loan to buy a supposedly fabulous horse that will be put out to stud and sire a generation of winners. At the same time he is beginning to realize he is falling in love with the wife of an ailing colleague. Sandcastle is the horse, and very soon it becomes apparent that he is surrounded by violent death and some kind of medical manipulation." Publ Wkly

Blood sport

In Francis, D. Across the board p253-493

Bolt. Putnam 1987 318p o.p.

LC 86-25167

Jockey-sleuth Kit Fielding "must help his employer, Princess Casilia and her husband overcome pressure to convert their large industrial holdings to a munitions works. Murder and physical threats against his fiancée, the Princess's niece, force Kit to adopt a dangerous plan of action." Libr J

"As adept on a race-course as he is in an Eaton Square drawing room, Fielding is a match for any menace. . . . In mystery circles, Francis again demonstrates that he is both a win and a nice read." Time

Bonecrack. Harper & Row 1972 c1971 201p o.p.

"A Joan Kahn-Harper novel of suspense"

First published 1971 in the United Kingdom

"A gangster's spoiled son is redeemed through his burning desire to become a jockey." Booklist

"The ending is much too pat, not to say sentimental, but the man writes so agreeably and knowledgeably that 'Bonecrack' is a pleasant way to pass a few hours." NY Times Book Rev

Break in. Putnam 1986 317p o.p.

LC 85-25682

First published 1985 in the United Kingdom

"Kit Fielding, champion steeplechase jockey, comes to the rescue of his twin sister and her husband, horse trainer and estranged son of millionaire Maynard Allardeck. Someone is mounting a massive smear campaign against Allardeck, and his son is caught in the middle. Kit must find a way to make things right." Libr J

This novel "contains all the ingredients of the Francis formula: a well-written, fast-moving narrative; an attractive, likeable hero; and authentic racing scenes and background." Christ Sci Monit

Comeback. Putnam 1991 320p o.p.

LC 91-23903

Available G.K. Hall large print edition

"Peter Darwin, a British First Secretary, is on his way to his new post in England and falls in with an elderly couple also going to England. When they ask for his help on the journey he winds up in Gloucestshire and becomes deeply involved in some murders and the treatment of several race horses who mysteriously die when they were already making satisfactory recoveries. The veterinarian, Ken McClure, is the target for suspicion of bad medical attention until Darwin begins to unearth a conspiracy with old roots. As usual Dick Francis gives the reader a bang-up finale." Shapiro. Fic for Youth. 3d edition

The danger. Putnam 1984 320p o.p.

LC 83-13973

First published 1983 in the United Kingdom

"This thriller follows a professional anti-kidnapping operative named Andrew Douglas as he works against an equally professional kidnapper known as Peter/ Guiseppe. The key 'victim' is an Italian female jockey, whom Douglas works to free and then assists in rebuilding her shattered sense of security and confidence." Wilson Libr Bull

Dead cert

In Francis, D. Three to show p3-216

Decider. Putnam 1993 318p $22.95

ISBN 0-399-13871-4   LC 93-14416

Also available G.K. Hall large print edition

Francis, Dick—*Continued*

"Architect Lee Morris has been a stockholder in Stratton Park racecourse ever since his mother inherited shares as part of a divorce settlement. When track-owner Lord Stratton dies, he leaves his heirs bitterly divided about the park's future. . . . Lee finds himself unwillingly drawn into the family dispute when someone blows up the grandstand. Convinced that one of the Strattons is behind the dastardly crime, Lee is determined to find out which one—and save the racetrack for future racing enthusiasts." Booklist

(ed) The Dick Francis treasury of great racing stories. See The Dick Francis treasury of great racing stories

Driving force. Putnam 1992 318p $21.95

ISBN 0-399-13776-9   LC 92-22793
Also available Thorndike Press large print edition

"Freddie Croft is a 35-year-old former champion steeplechase jockey, knowledgeable about the British racing milieu and tolerant of its denizens, a bit of a loner, keen on honor and notably phlegmatic. His phlegm is sorely tested when two of his drivers—he owns 14 vans that transport racehorses from a Hampshire village—arrive with the body of a hitchhiker who died in the backseat during the ride." Publ Wkly

This novel is "rich in information—about Cockney rhyming slang, the Michelangelo computer virus, intercontinental smuggling and ticks (yes, ticks), among other subjects. Mr. Francis deals with the potential for boredom in exposition, or at least flatness, by putting the more obscure explanations in the mouths of completely charming, completely obsessed eccentrics." N Y Times Book Rev

The edge. Putnam 1989 324p o.p.

LC 88-23806

In this mystery novel, the protagonist Tor Kelsey works "as an undercover investigator for the British Jockey Club. The object of his attention is a man named Julius Apollo Filmer, who's been involved in numerous questionable transactions with Jockey Club members, using any means at his disposal to acquire ownership of certain thoroughbreds. . . . [When the club] learns that [Filmer has] managed to insinuate himself onto the passenger list of the Great Transcontinental Mystery Race Train, which will shortly be crossing Canada on a seven-day junket, Tor Kelsey is assigned to protect both the horses and the passengers." N Y Times Book Rev

"The novel is something of a tour de force, because, until the final explosion, Mr. Francis contrives a steadily high level of interest, comedy, suspense, and surprise from a situation that is basically that of a cat watching a mousehole." Atlantic

Enquiry. Harper & Row 1969 219p o.p.
Available G.K. Hall large print edition

"Jockey Kelly Hughes and trainer Dexter Cranfield have been barred from racing for throwing a race for personal profit. Hughes knows it is a frame-up and refuses to take it lying down, though his investigation nearly has him lying down permanently in a pine box." Saturday Rev

also in Francis, D. Across the board p499-715

Flying finish. Harper & Row 1967 c1966 249p o.p. Armchair Detective Lib. reprint available $19.95 (ISBN 1-56287-002-5)
Also available G.K. Hall large print edition

First published 1966 in the United Kingdom

"The young hero, heir to a title although he insists on working for a living, is both a private plane enthusiast and head groom in a busy operation that flies race horses and brood mares all over the world by cargo plane. There's more behind the operation than meets the eye and he is soon plunged into a terrifying race against time and sure death." Publ Wkly

"The combination of horse knowledge and aviation is excellent, the love story credible, and the hero—though, as usual, a depressed character—emerges triumphant and strong." Barzun. Cat of Crime. Rev and enl edition

also in Francis, D. Across the board p1-249

For kicks. Harper & Row 1965 244p o.p. Armchair Detective Lib. reprint available $18.95 (ISBN 0-922890-57-9)

"The owner of an Australian stud-farm is hired to find out how certain English steeplechase race horses have been doped. . . . He is determined to finish the job in spite of beastly living conditions (he has to masquerade as a stable boy), very real danger, and another kind of trouble from the very enticing promiscuous daughter of a lord." Publ Wkly

Forfeit. Harper & Row 1969 247p o.p.
Available G.K. Hall large print edition

"A Joan Kahn-Harper novel of suspense"

"James Tyrone, sports writer for the 'Sunday Blaze', always needs extra money for things that make life bearable for Elizabeth his almost totally paralyzed wife. He jumps at the chance to do a feature story for a racing magazine, but as he begins to gather rumors about favorites withdrawn just before starting time to upset odds and enrich bookmakers, he also begins to receive odd warnings, and sinister threats." Libr J

Francis possesses the "conventional merits of uproar and bloodshed, plus an attention to practical detail and a shrewd understanding of social maneuver that pull his stories out of that never-never land in which crime novels tend to wander." Atlantic

also in Francis, D. Two by Francis

High stakes. Harper & Row 1976 c1975 201p o.p.

"A Joan Kahn-Harper novel of suspense"
First published 1975 in the United Kingdom

"A novice race horse owner, [Steven Scott, who is also] a rich inventor, fires his trainer [Jody] for a simple but effective swindle. The trainer steals a prize horse in revenge. The owner and his pals are lined up against the trainer and the hierarchy of the British racing elite, and outright war ensues." Libr J

Hot money. Putnam 1988 c1987 324p o.p.

LC 87-19193

First published 1987 in the United Kingdom

The narrator of this mystery novel is Ian Pembroke, a jockey. "The plot revolves around the protagonist's father, a multimillionaire whose many ex-wives and varied progeny [seem to be] after both his money and his life." Quill Quire

Francis, Dick—*Continued*

"Francis is sometimes faulted for wooden characterizations, but here he is believable and chilling as he takes on the pathology of a large, mutually destructive family. The whodunit puzzle at the book's core is unusually good, and its solution, like those the late Ross Macdonald used to devise, takes into account wounds dealt out and suffered decades before." Time

In the frame. Harper & Row 1977 c1976 230p o.p.

Available G.K. Hall large print edition

First published 1976 in the United Kingdom

The death of his cousin's wife Regina in her English country home leads Charles Todd, a young painter of horses, to Australia. Regina "had been murdered, apparently while interrupting thieves. Everything in the house had been stripped—paintings, antiques, even the wine cellar. . . . [Todd] starts following a trail that leads him to Australia and a ring dealing in stolen antiques." NY Times Book Rev

"The first Dick Francis mystery in which horses are only a peripheral part of the action is excitement from start to finish and definitely proves Francis is as much of a winner off the race track as on." Publ Wkly

Knockdown. Harper & Row 1975 c1974 217p o.p.

First published 1974 in the United Kingdom

Shortly after Jonah Dereham, ex-jockey, "buys a horse for a client at the Ascot Sales, he loses the horse and is hit over the head. Then his stable is broken into and a thoroughbred valued at seventy thousand pounds is turned loose on a busy highway. Then his house is set on fire." New Yorker

Longshot. Putnam 1990 320p o.p.

LC 90-41145

Available G.K. Hall large print edition

John Kendall "is an expert on survival, having written several books on the subject before turning to fiction: when Longshot opens, he is awaiting the publication of his first novel, living very frugally, and (with many reservations) about to accept a commission for a biography . . . [of racehorse trainer] Tremayne Vickers." Times Lit Suppl

"Francis remains one of the most incandescent talents in the mystery game. His plot positively shimmers, and his sleuth easily hurdles that always difficult jump from credible character to believable amateur detective. Perhaps best of all, Francis extracts a wealth of weird and wonderful shadings from his suspects." Booklist

Nerve. Armchair Detective Lib. 1990 c1964 313p $18.95

ISBN 0-922890-26-9   LC 90-32358

Reissue of title first published 1964 by Harper & Row

"Rob Finn, a young steeplechase jockey, had been near Art Mathews when Mathews shot himself at the Dunstable races. When asked why the man had killed himself, Finn replied, 'Mr Kellar might know.' Then other jockeys began having trouble and finally Finn was involved." Publisher's note

also in Francis, D. Three to show p219-491

(ed) The New treasury of great racing stories. See The New treasury of great racing stories

Odds against. Harper & Row 1966 c1965 280p o.p. Armchair Detective Lib. reprint available $19.95 (ISBN 0-922890-78-1)

Also available G.K. Hall large print edition

First published 1965 in the United Kingdom

"Before a racing fall crippled one hand, Sid Hailey had been one of England's foremost jockeys. He lost one career and started a new one at the Radnor Agency which . . . investigated anything from missing persons to criminal cads, and boasted a racing section. It was his former father-in-law who got him involved in the fate of the Seabury Racecourse Company when he arranged the strange meeting with the pretentious and sadistic Howard Krayle. That meeting started Sid on a swift and dangerous chase to discover the stock manipulators who wanted to sell the racecourse land for a housing development and who would stop at no odds to carry out their plans." Libr J

also in Francis, D. Three to show p495-774

Proof. Putnam 1985 334p o.p.

LC 84-15940

"Wine merchant Tony Beach is engaged to supply a horse trainer's garden party. During the party a horse van careens into the marquee, bringing disaster. One of the casualties is a restaurant owner suspected of serving cheap liquor under false labels, and Beach, as an expert taster, is enlisted to track the bootleggers. Francis gives the same fascinating and authoritative detail about the liquor trade as he does about the racing world (which figures intermittently in this book as background)." Libr J

Rat race. Harper & Row 1971 214p o.p.

"A Joan Kahn-Harper novel of suspense"

"The hero's occupation in this tale is piloting an air taxi from one race meeting to another; horses are secondary to his rehabilitation as professional man and husband. As usual, the characters and incidents are well thought out, especially the bombing incident." Barzun. Cat of Crime. Rev and enl edition

Reflex. Putnam 1981 295p o.p.

LC 80-23234

"Philip Nore is an ordinary English jockey, suddenly embroiled in extraordinary murder and mayhem. When a racing photographer Nore knows and dislikes is suddenly killed, the jockey acquires, in a most roundabout fashion, the secret photographic files the dead man has been keeping on half a dozen prominent racing figures. As he slowly unravels the threads of the mystery it becomes clear that this evidence could cost him his life." Best Sellers

Risk. Harper & Row 1978 c1977 240p o.p. Buccaneer Bks. reprint available $37.95 (ISBN 1-56849-281-2)

LC 77-11786

Also available G.K. Hall large print edition

"A Joan Kahn book"

First published 1977 in the United Kingdom

"Absentee American owners of horses are being bled of much money by their unscrupulous English trainer, and Roland Britten, accountant and spare-time jockey, latches on to the business and has to be kept out of the way for a time. So he is shanghaied to Minorca, when a friendly schoolmistress helps to get him back to England, for a nicely calculated sexual price. Renewed

Francis, Dick—*Continued*

trouble follows, not just once but twice." Barzun. Cat of Crime. Rev and enl edition

"The book is superbly constructed and the hero persecuted in a way that is mystifying, frightening and beautifully described." Times Lit Suppl

Slayride. Harper & Row 1974 c1973 219p o.p.

First published 1973 in the United Kingdom

"Horse racing in Norway provides the locale for an absorbing first-person narrative related by British Jockey Club investigator David Cleveland. Called to Oslo to learn the facts concerning the theft of receipts from a day's racing, Cleveland enlists the help of Arnie Kristiansen, investigator for the Norwegian Jockey Club. Discoveries prove painful and results are tragic, but justice is served in solution of a murder." Booklist

also in Francis, D. Two by Francis

Smokescreen. Harper & Row 1973 c1972 213p o.p.

"A Joan Kahn-Harper novel of suspense"
First published 1972 in the United Kingdom

"An English film star is persuaded by a dying friend to go to South Africa to see what is the matter with her eleven race horses—horses that could win races if they did not mysteriously collapse just before the finish." Newsweek

"Even given Francis's high standards [this novel is] an elegant construction, in which we see the parts and their potentialities, and are as much excited to discover how he put them together as what happens when he does. . . . A symphony tumultuous with thrills." Times Lit Suppl

Straight. Putnam 1989 323p o.p.

LC 89-36492

Available G.K. Hall large print edition

"When Derek Franklin, a steeplechase jockey nursing a shattered ankle from a bad spill, learns of the death of his older, long-estranged brother Greville, he's stunned to find himself named as both executor of the will and sole heir. But in rapid succession, Derek is mugged, his brother's gemology firm is robbed, and Derek himself is assaulted in another robbery attempt; understandably, he comes to suspect that Greville's death may not have been an accident." Publ Wkly

Three to show; a trilogy. Harper & Row 1969 774p o.p.

"A Joan Kahn-Harper novel of suspense"
An anthology of three mystery-suspense novels involving the racing set in England. The second and third titles are entered separately
Contents: Dead cert; Nerve; Odds against
In Dead cert (first published 1962) Alan York suspects murder, not accident, when a favored racehorse falls and kills his rider. Alan uncovers some unsavory facts about horse races and places himself in danger

Trial run. Harper & Row 1979 c1978 246p o.p.

LC 78-20204

"A Joan Kahn book"
First published 1978 in the United Kingdom

"Randall Drew, an expert steeplechase rider who is no longer able to ride because he wears glasses and cannot tolerate contact lenses, is persuaded to go to Moscow for the Olympics. He is asked to do this in order to insure the safety of a member of the Royal Family who is supposed to ride in the Olympics. There follows a suspenseful story of danger and pursuit. Francis's tautly written books appeal not only to mystery fans but also to those interested in horses and racing." Shapiro. Fic for Youth. 3d edition

Twice shy. Putnam 1982 307p o.p.

LC 81-15814

"Jonathan Derry, a physicist, is handed some cassettes, apparently Broadway musical scores, by a friend who then meets a violent death. The cassettes turn out to be a computer program for handicapped horses—guaranteed to make the user a rich man. When Jonathan tries to track down the tapes' rightful owner he becomes involved with a rough man and his violent son. The latter is brought to justice by Jonathan and then, after his release, he tries to avenge himself on Jonathan's brother. Computer buffs as well as mystery fans will enjoy this one." Shapiro. Fic for Youth. 3d edition

Two by Francis; Forfeit & Slayride. Harper & Row 1983 477p o.p.

LC 82-48488

Combined edition of two titles entered separately

Whip hand. Harper & Row 1980 c1979 293p o.p.

Available G.K. Hall large print edition

"A Joan Kahn book"
First published 1979 in the United Kingdom

In this novel "Sid Halley, a famous ex-jockey crippled in an accident, is laboriously putting his life back together as a private investigator and making do with an artificial hand. Professionally he is successful. A top trainer's horses are failing in the home stretch; the jockey's repellent ex-wife gets caught in a fraudulent mail-order scheme; an aged peer is trapped as a front man in a crooked consortium. The jockey reluctantly agrees to investigate these mysteries, and they lead him into confronting his deepest fears." Libr J

"The book contains moments of breathless suspense, much information about the sport of kings, and perceptive insights into Halley's character that explain some of the reasons for the breakdown of his marriage." Shapiro. Fic for Youth. 3d edition

Wild horses. Putnam 1994 319p $22.95

ISBN 0-399-13974-5   LC 94-27262

"Filmmaker Thomas Lyon is making a movie—based on a best-selling book—of a real-life tragedy in the horse-racing world. Twenty-some years ago, the young, attractive wife of a horse trainer was found hanged. Although her death was ruled a suicide at the time, Thomas' old friend Valentine Clark, a famous racing writer, whispers a puzzling deathbed confession about the years-old mystery. Thomas feels compelled to investigate." Booklist

"Besides providing a many-faceted mystery and the author's trademark insights into the horse world, this novel offers an in-depth, fascinating behind-the-scenes view of filmmaking." Libr J

Frank, Pat, 1907-1964

Alas, Babylon; a novel. Lippincott 1959 253p o.p. Buccaneer Bks. reprint available $25.95 (ISBN 0-89966-744-9)

"Survival after a submarine nuclear attack is the focus of this story of a small group of people in Fort Repose, Florida. Rationing food, reestablishing law and order, and pondering whether there will be any future for the survivors are some of the concerns of organizer-leader Randy Bragg." Shapiro. Fic for Youth. 3d edition

Frank, Pat, 1907-1964—*Continued*

"This is an extraordinarily real picture of human beings numbed by catastrophe but still driven by the unconquerable determination of living creatures to keep on being alive. The writing is simple and straightforward and practical." New Yorker

Franklin, Miles, 1879-1954

The end of my career; the sequel to My brilliant career; with a foreword by Verna Coleman. St. Martin's Press 1981 234p o.p.

First published 1946 in Australia with title: My career goes bung

Protagonist "Sybylla Melvyn, the Australian country girl who narrated My Brilliant Career, explains that while the earlier work was fiction, she will now tell the truth about how she came to write her book and the events that followed. The adventures of her fictional namesake have created a furor. Beyond her rural circle, whose members are indignant about their apparent depiction in My Brilliant Career, are others eager to fete the young author. They prompt a visit to Sydney, where Sybylla finds the supposedly cultured class just as flawed as those left behind." Libr J

"This book is at times a delicious satire on morals and manners. At other times it is a heart-rending tract for feminism. Always it is entertaining and filled with wisdom and universal truths." Christ Sci Monit

My brilliant career. St. Martin's Press 1980 232p o.p.

First published 1901 in Scotland

"The novel's heroine, Sybylla Melvyn, a girl of sixteen, rebels against the stagnant life on her parents' dairy farm at Possum Gully and against the inevitable fate of teaching or marriage that awaits her; both forms of 'slavery' are distasteful to her but she sees marriage as particularly degrading. Rescued temporarily by a period with her affluent grandmother at the congenial station homestead, Caddagat, she faces interwoven problems—her sexual ambivalence which is characterized by strong physical attraction to eligible young squatter, Harold Beecham, and an equally strong physical revulsion." Oxford Companion to Australian Lit

Franklin, Stella Maria Miles Lampe *See* Franklin, Miles, 1879-1954

Fraser, Anthea

The April Rainers. Doubleday 1990 c1989 180p $14.95

ISBN 0-385-41088-3   LC 89-23615

"A Crime Club book"

First published 1989 in the United Kingdom

Scotland Yard's Detective Chief Inspector David Webb aids provincial police in solving a series of linked murders

Death speaks softly. Doubleday 1987 182p o.p.

LC 86-32887

"Published for the Crime Club"

Scotland Yard's Detective Chief Inspector David Webb conducts a search for a missing girl, a flirtatious young Frenchwoman at the local university. The trail leads to murder

Symbols at your door. Doubleday 1991 c1990 181p $15

ISBN 0-385-41685-7   LC 90-49974

"A Crime Club book"

First published 1990 in the United Kingdom

This mystery set in the remote English village of Beckworth finds Detective Chief Inspector Webb investigating a rash of burglaries and murders all linked to the sudden appearance of strange graffitti on the victims' homes

Fraser, Antonia, 1932-

The cavalier case; a Jemima Shore mystery. Bantam Bks. 1991 c1990 228p $17.95

ISBN 0-553-07126-2   LC 90-41943

First published 1990 in the United Kingdom

This mystery "involves the ghost of a 17th-century poet, an upscale tennis club and modern London society. Ms. Fraser writes with zest and verve, and her primary interest is people." N Y Times Book Rev

Cool repentance. Norton 1982 222p o.p.

LC 82-8300

"Actress Christabel Cartwright, after a notorious affair with a young rock star, has returned to her husband and daughters, and even plans to appear in two plays at the local drama festival. Jemima Shore, arriving to televise the festival, discovers that, underneath her cool exterior, Christabel is terrified of someone. And the murders begin." Libr J

Jemima Shore at the sunny grave and other stories. Bantam Bks. 1993 174p o.p.

LC 92-21605

Analyzed in Short story index

Contents: Jemima Shore at the sunny grave; The moon was to blame; The blude-red wine; House poison; Getting to know you; Cry-by-night; Dead leaves; Out for the Countess; The twist

This is a "collection of nine mystery stories, four of which feature 'stylishly presented' sleuth, Jemima Shore." Libr J

Oxford blood. Norton 1985 224p o.p.

LC 85-15265

This "Jemima Shore mystery takes us into the exclusive reaches of Britain's titled aristocracy, as the glamorous TV investigator is drawn into the quest for an heir's true parentage. A nursemaid's deathbed confession of switched babies starts Jemima on her task, but it is a case—with its potentially unwelcome revelations—she would rather avoid. However, the scion in question, rakish Viscount Saffron, Oxford undergraduate and heir to the title of St. Ives, asks Jemima to investigate the matter." Publ Wkly

A splash of red. Norton 1981 213p o.p.

LC 81-9543

This novel starts "off when Jemima agrees to flat-and cat-sit for Chloe Fontaine, an author renowned for her fine but not financially profitable books and notorious for her many amours. Supposedly off to the Continent, Chloe never leaves the building; her mutilated body is found on the premises, whereupon Chloe's latest discarded lover is arrested. But Jemima shrewdly considers the possible guilt of apparently innocent people with links to the victim: the owner of the building where she lived; her noble editor; a woman friend betrayed by

Fraser, Antonia, 1932-—*Continued*
Chloe and others. With the help of the resident cat, Jemima traces clues that lead to evidence against the killer." Publ Wkly

Fraser, George MacDonald, 1925-
Flashman; from the Flashman papers, 1839-1842; edited and arranged by George MacDonald Fraser. World Pub. 1969 256p o.p.
"An NAL book"
The bounder of Thomas Hughes's Tom Brown's schooldays "left some memoirs, it appears, of which this is the first installment. After a true account of the circumstances of his expulsion from school we learn that he obtained a commission in the 11th Light Dragoons, under the Earl of Cardigan. . . . [Sent to fight in India and Afghanistan] he manages by undeviating cowardice and lack of principle to get himself acclaimed a hero." New Statesman
Followed by Royal Flash

Flashman and the mountain of light; from the Flashman papers, 1945-46. Knopf 1991 365p maps o.p.

LC 90-45453

This installment in the Flashman papers is set in "the Punjab as the outnumbered British forces face a formidable Sikh army. Behind the scenes are a glamorous but corrupt maharani (who is bedded by Flashman), her son and various devious pretenders. Flashman, who speaks the lingo, is acting as secret agent on behalf of the British but somehow always gets involved in battles he seeks to avoid. The atmosphere is colorful in the extreme, the battle scenes are splendidly rendered and some decidedly odd British commanders are deftly sketched." Publ Wkly

Royal Flash; from the Flashman papers, 1842-3 and 1847-8; edited and arranged by George MacDonald Fraser. Knopf 1970 257p o.p.
This second installment in the Flashman papers "finds 'Flashy' involved in a complicated intrigue engineered by Otto von Bismarck to topple the balance of power in Europe. Flashman is forced to pose as the double for Prince Carl Gustaf of Strackenz but before long Flashman finds himself a target for assassination. Forced to flee the bedroom for the countryside, Flashman stamps out the opposition and loses a fortune in jewels to Lola Montez before arriving back in England." Best Sellers
Other titles in the series are: Flash for freedom (1972); Flashman at the charge (1973); Flashman in the great game (1975); Flashman's lady (1978); Flashman and the redskins (1982); Flashman and the dragon (1986) and Flashman and the mountain of light, entered above

Frayn, Michael
A landing on the sun. Viking 1992 c1991 248p $21
ISBN 0-670-83932-9   LC 91-37594
First published 1991 in the United Kingdom
This "novel concerns a methodical British civil servant who is jolted out of his glum routine when he is ordered to investigate the death of [Summerchild], another civil servant who fell out of a window fifteen years earlier.

Somebody upstairs has raised questions of espionage." Atlantic
"Michael Frayn is a deeply accomplished writer: his structure and timing are faultless, his control never wavers. The novel is beautifully written, and in places very moving." New Statesman Soc

Freedman, Benedict
Mrs. Mike; the story of Katherine Mary Flannigan; by Benedict and Nancy Freedman; drawings by Ruth D. McCrea. Coward-McCann 1947 312p o.p. Buccaneer Bks. reprint available $25.95 (ISBN 0-89966-396-6)
"At 16, Boston-reared Katherine Mary O'Fallon is sent north to Alberta, Canada, to find relief for the pleurisy from which she has been suffering. While residing with her Uncle John, she falls in love with Mike, a handsome Canadian Mounted Policeman. Life in the wilderness in the early 1900s is harsh, but the newly married couple finds joy and challenge in their adventures." Shapiro. Fic for Youth. 3d edition

Freedman, J. F.
The obstacle course. Viking 1994 351p $21.95
ISBN 0-670-85346-1   LC 93-22915
"In 1957, 14 year-old Roy Poole dreams of escaping his grimy small town life by attending the Naval Academy, where he runs the obstacle course when he is not hustling homework, trading insults with buddies, shoplifting, or robbing washing machine coin boxes. A chance meeting with a retired admiral gives Roy a patron and hope for the future, but it's endangered when he is accused of the one theft he didn't commit." Libr J
"Freedman nails the teenage state of mind, for which being humiliated in math class or laughed at by friends is nothing less than the end of the world, and tells a wonderfully truthful tale about youthful choice and change, examining how each is controlled by adults." Publ Wkly

Freedman, Nancy, 1920-
(jt. auth) Freedman, B. Mrs. Mike

Freeling, Nicolas
Flanders sky. Mysterious Press 1992 207p $18.95
ISBN 0-89296-492-8   LC 91-50844
Published in the United Kingdom with title: The pretty how town
Henri Castang "has been kicked upstairs—or so he thinks. The assignment to the European Community Headquarters in Brussels seems to imply that he won't be needing his carefully honed street smarts. But as Henri ruminates . . . on his forthcoming ennui, his supervisor's wife is found murdered. And the boss is the prime suspect." Booklist
"Mr. Freeling takes the international *policier* to high ground here and does the genre proud." N Y Times Book Rev

Freeling, Nicolas—*Continued*

Sand castles. Mysterious Press 1990 c1989 209p $17.95

ISBN 0-89296-372-7   LC 89-43144

First published 1989 in the United Kingdom

The author "restores to life his well-beloved Dutch detective, Commissaris Piet van der Valk, whom he killed off in 'Auprès de Ma Blonde' (1972). . . . In Groningen (a 'dusty corner of a tight, righteous little land'), van der Valk comes across a sordid child-pornography racket that confirms his belief in the moral hypocrisy beneath the 'stuffy sinless atmosphere' breathed by the Dutch." N Y Times Book Rev

"Like his idiosyncratic hero and heroine—he bashes the Dutch, she the French, for example—Freeling rewards with his oblique, subtly comic style." Publ Wkly

Freeman, Cynthia, d. 1988

Always and forever. Putnam 1990 381p o.p.

LC 89-48519

Available Thorndike Press large print edition

"Recent Barnard graduate Kathy Ross travels to war-ravaged Hamburg in 1945 to aid in resettling refugees. There she meets David Kohn, an idealistic young doctor whose parents died in the Holocaust while he barely escaped to the U.S., and Phil Kohn, David's distant cousin who is in Germany to covertly bring stolen art back to New York. David and Kathy are immediately attracted to one another, but David, deeply disturbed by his return to his native land, is unable to declare his love. Kathy marries Phil and soon is struggling against the demands of Phil's crass and materialistic family. When Phil becomes physically abusive, she takes their young son and leaves for San Francisco and a new, successful life incognito—never, however, forgetting her love for David." Publ Wkly

Because Freeman "pays as much attention to politics as she does fashion, the background of the novel is rich in detail." Booklist

Come pour the wine; a novel. Arbor House 1980 390p o.p.

LC 80-66501

"A naive young woman from Kansas goes to New York City to make a career as a model, but the big city's relentless pace and icy demeanor almost capsize her hopes until Mr. Right comes along to charm, captivate, and wed her. But the couple's happiness is not to last, and marital discord and dissolution threaten. After the divorce a new man appears on the heroine's horizon to stir her to the roots of her latent Jewish heritage and win her anew with warmth, understanding, and passion. A blatantly old-fashioned but emotionally effective story of love lost and found, with a happy ending yet." Booklist

Fairytales; a novel. Arbor House 1977 352p o.p.

LC 76-50340

"Catherine and Dominic Rossi of San Francisco produce seven offspring, establish an affluent household and do their best to live happily with both. So what's the trouble? First, Dominic wants to be a senator while Catherine would rather he paid as much attention to her as to the media. Second, Dominic has to cut short a highly satisfying affair during his early middle years because 'a man doesn't belong to himself when he has

children.' Switch then to a 'fat farm' resort in the desert. There Catherine hides, plotting to embarrass her ambitious spouse and, as headlines mount, she swoops back into town for a disclosure of gripes at a press conference. That Dominic's senatorial hopes self-destruct is not surprising." Publ Wkly

The last princess. Putnam 1988 382p o.p.

LC 87-29096

This novel "takes us from New York to Paris to Israel and a few places in between. It tells the story of Lily Goodhue, who was rejected by her high society parents because she had the poor judgment to be born a girl—and the even poorer taste to be born with red hair. When her adored younger brother is killed in a riding accident, Lily is held responsible and banished to a boarding school in Switzerland. Still, she does her darndest to please her parents—that is, until she abandons her socially correct homosexual fiancé, with his vast family fortune, to take up with a Jew named Harry. That's the last straw, and Lily is promptly disinherited. But, as in all good morality stories, evil exacts a price." N Y Times Book Rev

No time for tears; a novel. Arbor House 1981 411p o.p.

"This is the story of Chavala Landau, her brother and sisters, her husband, David, and their children. Following pogroms in Russia in 1905 the family flees to Palestine, where they aid the British army during World War I. Disillusioned by continued strife, Chavala, her brother, one of her sisters and her son go to the United States, leaving her husband and the rest of the family behind. Hard-working Chavala starts a pawn shop that she eventually expands to a chain of jewelry stores. The Landaus become involved in the establishment of the state of Israel, Chavala helping with money from America, David and their sons fighting for the new state." Libr J

Seasons of the heart. Putnam 1986 399p o.p.

LC 85-30765

"Ann Coulter's dreams of a happy, prosperous future with her husband, Phillip, a recent law-school graduate whom she met at her best friend's wedding, are shattered by World War II. His internment throughout the war in a Japanese prison camp completely saps his strength of character. By the time Ann's determination to improve the family finances by working as a realtor turns her into a millionaire, the marriage is held together only by the couple's mutual devotion to their daughter." Booklist

Freemantle, Brian

The button man. St. Martin's Press 1993 390p $22.95

ISBN 0-312-08716-0   LC 93-17421

"A Thomas Dunne book"

This novel is "about a serial killer in Moscow who knocks off the niece of an important (but hateful) United States senator, clips her hair and cuts the buttons from her clothes. An honest, efficient Russian cop is on the case. Working with him is an American from the F.B.I." N Y Times Book Rev

"Every scene and conversation in this meticulously plotted tale is a fencing match or a chess game; every turn of events threatens to topple the dense edifice of politics, lust, subterfuge, and insanity. A real winner by thriller veteran Freemantle." Booklist

Freemantle, Brian—*Continued*

Charlie's apprentice. St. Martin's Press 1994 c1993 435p $21.95

ISBN 0-312-10951-2 LC 94-2347

Also available G.K. Hall large print edition

"A Thomas Dunne book"

First published 1993 in the United Kingdom

"British intelligence officer Charlie Muffin, renowned for his unorthodox methods, has been grounded. Charlie's new female boss thinks his time is better spent teaching new operatives rather than working in the field. Although frustrated, Charlie does his best to instruct recent graduate John Gower in surviving as an agent—practical, life-saving tips of the trade that are not found in any of the training manuals. Charlie is suspicous when the inexperienced Gower is sent to Beijing on a tricky assignment; later, when Gower is arrested and imprisoned, Charlie is dispatched to China to extricate him." Libr J

"Charlie has a lesser role in this book than in his previous adventures, but when he has to go to China to bail out his apprentice, he demonstrates yet again that as a field operative nobody can touch him." N Y Times Book Rev

Comrade Charlie; a Charlie Muffin novel. St. Martin's Press 1992 c1989 443p $22.95

ISBN 0-312-08166-9 LC 92-26157

"A Thomas Dunne book"

First published 1989 in the United Kingdom

"Muffin has been relegated to a desk job by his superior, a twit who hates him and would love to see him demoted to dogcatcher. . . . Plugging away at his boring job, Charlie happens upon a Kremlin plot just as the Soviet Union is about to come apart. So his old adversaries at the K.G.B. decide to ruin him once and for all. They plan to use his former girlfriend, a Soviet spy, as bait for destruction. Charlie will be framed in what looks like a foolproof scheme." N Y Times Book Rev

"Freemantle is a wonderfully talented writer, a master at taut, fast-paced plots and deft characterizations, with a flair for making every nuance and detail of the dark world of espionage real and intriguing." Booklist

French, Albert

Billy. Viking 1993 214p $20

ISBN 0-670-85013-6 LC 93-14676

Also available G.K. Hall large print edition

"In 1937, in the small town of Banes, Miss., 10-year-old Billy Lee Turner lives with his mother in one of the miserable shanties of the black ghetto called the Patch. Headstrong Billy convinces another youngster to enter the white area of town, where they are attacked by teenaged cousins who are enraged to see black boys in 'their' pond. Seeking to escape, Billy impulsively stabs one of the girls; she dies, and the white community works itself into a paroxysm of rage and violence. Though Billy is too young to comprehend what he has done, he is sentenced to the electric chair." Publ Wkly

"The story, once in motion, gathers momentum like a landslide. . . . 'Billy' is tragedy in the classical mode, mythic in the sense that instead of the surprise, the twists of plot we might discover in a more typical contemporary novel, here we are confirmed in our worst dreads as destiny immutably and shockingly unfolds." NY Times Book Rev

French, Marilyn, 1929-

Her mother's daughter; a novel. Summit Bks. 1987 686p il o.p.

LC 87-7061

"Anastasia narrates her life experiences by blending them with those of her grandmother, mother, and daughter. Each woman has been determined not to make the sacrifices her mother made, instead seeking joy, freedom, and independence. And in doing so, each has become like her mother—emotionally drained, alienated from her children, and alone." Libr J

The author "continues to imbue what used to be dismissed as 'women's issues' with the significance they deserve. . . . Ms. French continues to write about the inner lives of women with insight and intimacy. What she's given us this time is a page-turner with a heart." N Y Times Book Rev

The women's room. Summit Bks. 1977 471p o.p.

LC 77-24918

"Dealing with the interlocking lives of dozens of American women, who know each other at some point of time between the 1950s and the 70s, and concentrating in particular on the evolution of Mira from petted baby girl wife to independent womanhood, it speaks from the heart to women everywhere. . . . [The author's] dialogue, her characterizations, her knowledge of the changing relationships, sexual and otherwise, between men and women in a complex world of shifting values, are all extraordinary. Mira, the suburban housewife and mother, the unexpected divorcee groping her way out of a marriage that she never understood, going back to Harvard at 38 as a graduate student, meeting other women, some tougher, some weaker, coming to terms with herself against all odds, even if it means a bleak and lonely parting from a man she loves, is memorable." Publ Wkly

Friedman, Philip, 1944-

Inadmissable evidence; a novel. Fine, D.I. 1992 548p $23

ISBN 1-55611-330-7 LC 92-53075

"Manhattan prosecutor Estrada is beset by problems. His lover has moved to the West Coast and his career is idling on two-bit cases. Relief arrives when a sensational murder conviction is reversed, and Estrada is drawn into the retrial. He re-investigates the clues and witnesses surrounding the torrid relationship between Roberto Morales—real estate sharpie, popular Latino role model, defendant—and vivacious victim Mariah Dodge." Booklist

"If Friedman's insistence on day-to-day doings occasionally undercuts his novel's sense of drama and consequence, it also invests his story with authority, allowing a clear portrait of the give-and-take of the legal system and affording an even stronger sense of the ambiguities that arise from the pursuit of justice." Publ Wkly

Reasonable doubt; a novel. Fine, D.I. 1990 487p $19.95

ISBN 1-55611-107-X LC 88-45381

The protagonist of this novel "is Michael Ryan, a widowed attorney whose only child, a son, has been murdered. Ryan's daughter-in-law, wealthy and sophisticated Jennifer Kneeland Ryan, is accused of the murder. Confoundingly, she asks Ryan to defend her; reluctantly, he says yes. In the course of the case, Ryan

Friedman, Philip, 1944-—*Continued*

learns chilling and unsavory truths about both his dead son and his explosive daughter-in-law." N Y Times Book Rev

Frost, Mark

The list of 7; a novel. Morrow 1993 368p $20

ISBN 0-688-12245-0   LC 93-12305

Arthur Conan Doyle, "a young doctor with a lively and critical interest in the occult, attends a seance that ends in murder. He flees the scene, pursued by a gang of hooded zombies, and is rescued by a remarkable man named Jack Sparks. Adept at various arcane martial arts and head of a loyal contingent of reformed but still resourceful crooks, Sparks is engaged in a strange and terrifying battle with the forces of evil. His archenemy is none other than his brother, the vilest possible villain. Doyle soon finds himself confronting one supernatural horror after another, from giant leeches to marauding mummies. This is an engrossing cosmic thriller." Booklist

Fuentes, Carlos

Apollo and the whores

In Fuentes, C. The orange tree p148-204

The campaign; translated by Alfred Mac Adam. Farrar, Straus & Giroux 1991 246p $22.95

ISBN 0-374-11828-0   LC 91-9723

Original Spanish edition, 1990

First volume of a projected trilogy about 19th-century revolutionary Spanish America

The focus of this novel is "on Argentina's complicated transition from colonial to free status. The protagonist is one Baltasar Bustos, a young man of certain privilege—the son of a wealthy ranchowner on the pampas—who performs an amazing act of defiance against the Spanish colonial regime. He sneaks into the house of the judge of the superior court of the viceroyalty of La Plata and substitute's the magistrate's newborn child with the child of a black prostitute. In the process, he not only causes the house to catch on fire, killing one of the babies, but also catches a glimpse of the judge's wife and falls in love with her. To assuage himself of guilt and to attempt to gain her love, Baltasar joins the independence army and follows the lady of his dreams all over South America." Booklist

"The novel takes on huge themes: revolution versus justice, the illusion of human perfectibility, the value of tradition against the appeal to reason. Though set in the past, it is not trapped in it. Mr Fuentes might equally be writing about modern revolutions." Economist

Constancia, and other stories for virgins; translated by Thomas Christensen. Farrar, Straus & Giroux 1990 c1989 340p $19.95

ISBN 0-374-12886-3   LC 89-82138

Analyzed in Short story index

Original Spanish edition, 1989

Contents: Constancia; La Desdichada; The prisoner of Las Lomas; Viva mi fama; Reasonable people

"Underneath the irony, the range of literary and historical reference, the brilliant, bawdy Fuentes finish and humanitarian social conscience, these stories are a set of variations on a macho theme of inner emptiness." Times Lit Suppl

The death of Artemio Cruz; translated from the Spanish by Alfred MacAdam. Farrar, Straus & Giroux 1991 307p $30

ISBN 0-374-13559-2   LC 90-43280

Original Spanish edition published 1962 in Mexico; first English translation by Sam Hileman published 1964

"As the novel opens, Artemio Cruz, former revolutionary turned capitalist, lies on his deathbed. He drifts in and out of consciousness, and when he is conscious his mind wanders between past and present. The story reveals that Cruz became rich through treachery, bribery, corruption, and ruthlessness. As a young man he had been full of revolutionary ideals. Acts committed as a means of self-preservation soon developed into a way of life based on opportunism. A fully realized character, Cruz can also be seen as a symbol of Mexico's quest for wealth at the expense of moral values." Merriam-Webster's Ency of Lit

The Hydra head; translated from the Spanish by Margaret Sayers Peden. Farrar, Straus & Giroux 1978 291p o.p.

LC 78-12603

"As Israeli and Arab agents vie for information about Mexico's oil reserves, Felix Maldonado [a Mexican secret agent] tries to foil a plot he does not understand." Libr J

This novel is "a tour de force, but unlike, say, Borges's detective fictions, beneath its impeccable surface lurks serious social content that adds incomparably to its intensity as narrative." New Repub

The old gringo; translated by Margaret Sayers Peden. Farrar, Straus & Giroux 1985 199p o.p. Borgo Press reprint available $23 (ISBN 0-8095-9136-7)

LC 85-16266

Originally published in Spanish

"Fuentes fictionalizes the last days of the life of American journalist and author Ambrose Bierce, involving a mythic figure to the Mexican revolutionaries with whom Bierce fights and representing Bierce of the novel as an implanted, recurrent memory for the young American schoolteacher who witnesses his final passages through time." Choice

"We have in this novel a fastidious American governess stranded in Pancho Villa's revolution, where she attracts the erotic interest of an intellectual fellow countryman and a nature-boy Mexican general. On this inanely trite foundation Mr. Fuentes has erected a narrative of brilliant complexity and sophistication, describing brisk military action and philosophically contrasting national character, or social tradition, or styles of revolt, or regional strengths, weaknesses, and prejudices." Atlantic

The orange tree; translated from the Spanish by Alfred Mac Adam. Farrar, Straus & Giroux 1994 229p $21

ISBN 0-374-22683-0   LC 93-33608

Analyzed in Short story index

Contents: The two shores; Sons of the Conquistador; The two Numantias; Apollo and the whores; The two Americas

"In four of the five pieces here, Fuentes delves into the Hispanic world's past, with effective, even magical, results. The first, 'The Two Shores,' is a first-person narrative by a Spanish conquistador, who functioned as

Fuentes, Carlos—*Continued*

a translator between his troops and the Aztecs; his account of the conquest of Mexico is spoken from the grave, and offers sympathy to the defeated native inhabitants. . . . 'Sons of the Conquistador,' . . . is, as the title indicates, about the two sons of Cortés, both named Martin, one the son of his Spanish wife, the other the illegitimate son of his Indian mistress. . . . In 'The Two Numantias,' the Spain of Roman times is solidly conjured in brief space; and 'The Two Americas' both informs and entertains as it sees Columbus returning to Spain on a jet 500 years after he left. The remaining story, 'Apollo and the Whores,' . . . deals amusingly with an American grade-B movie actor visiting Acapulco and his phantasmagorical death there." Booklist

Sons of the Conquistador

In Fuentes, C. The orange tree p50-100

Terra nostra; translated from the Spanish by Margaret Sayers Peden. Farrar, Straus & Giroux 1976 777p o.p.

Original Spanish edition, 1975

This "novel is several things: an amalgam of the historical and religious consciousness and heritage of Spain; a biblical allegory; a sensuous, erotic and fantastic journey through time. The chief character around whom all this revolves is Felipe, the Spanish king who administers the state and the faith from his yet-to-be-completed seat, El Escorial. Felipe's trials and nemeses are the structural timber of this . . . work." Booklist

This opus "resembles nothing so much as an enormous Hieronymus Bosch collage in words—multitudinous, encyclopedic, rhapsodic, surrealistic, grotesque, and utterly terrifying in more spots than one might wish, largely because Fuentes, like Bosch, sees men of every age as barbaric wherever the veneer of civilization is even slightly scratched." Saturday Rev

The two Americas

In Fuentes, C. The orange tree p205-29

The two Numantias

In Fuentes, C. The orange tree p101-47

The two shores

In Fuentes, C. The orange tree p3-49

Fujiwara, Murasaki *See* Murasaki Shikibu, b. 978?

Fyfield, Frances, 1948-

Deep sleep. Pocket Bks. 1992 227p o.p.

LC 91-41030

"Lawyer Helen West, newly out of hospital, and DCI Geoffrey Bailey become interested in the 'accidental' chloroform poisoning death of a chemist's wife. Denizens of the chemist's London neighborhood include a policeman's estranged wife and insecure son as well as a docile-but-shrewd drug addict, so opportunities for psychological conflict abound. Tensions reach a snapping point with another murder, a bomb threat, and assault. Absorbing and crafted with care, this deserves every consideration." Libr J

G

Gaddis, William, 1922-

A frolic of his own; a novel. Poseidon Press 1994 586p $25

ISBN 0-671-66984-2   LC 93-26098

In this novel "Oscar Crease, middle-aged college instructor, savant, and playwright, is suing a Hollywood producer for pirating his play *Once at Antietam*, based on his grandfather's experiences in the Civil War, and turning it into a gory blockbuster called *The Blood in the Red White and Blue*. Oscar's suit, and a host of others—which involve a dog trapped in an outdoor sculpture, wrongful death during a river baptism, a church versus a soft drink company, and even Oscar himself after he is run over by his own car—engulf all who surround him." Publisher's note

"The medium is exceptionally dense. The mere effort of sorting out the voices, of tracking them, can be exhausting. . . . In any case, I hope the reader will persevere. 'A Frolic of His Own' is an exceptionally rich, even important novel." N Y Times Book Rev

J R. Knopf 1975 725p o.p.

"JR, ambitious sixth-grader in torn sneakers, bred on the challenge of 'free enterprise' and fired by heady mailorder promises of 'success' . . . parlays a deal for thousands of surplus Navy picnic forks . . . into a nationwide, hydraheaded 'family of companies.' The JR Corp and its Boss engulf brokers, lawyers, Congressmen, disaffected school teachers and disenfranchised Indians, drunks, divorcées, second-hand generals, and a fledgling composer." Publisher's note

The book is "frequently as turgid, monotonous, and confusing as the situation it describes. Yet Gaddis has . . . managed to reflect chaos in a fiction that is not itself artistically chaotic because it is imbued with the conserving and correcting power of his imagination." Saturday Rev

The recognitions; a novel. Harcourt Brace & Co. 1955 956p o.p.

"A novel about forgery. In it William Gaddis has attempted a full-scale portrait of our chaotic contemporary world, in all its hypocrisy and lack of love—a world in which the genuine is continually being discarded in favor of a successful facsimile. . . . Scores of characters move back and forth within the design, each one busy in pursuing his own desired deception." Publisher's note

"Rangy in settng, (New England, Greenwich Village, Paris, Spain, Italy, Central America), aswim in erudition, semi-Joycean in language, glacial in pace, irritatingly opaque in plot and character. The Recognitions is one of those eruptions of personal vision that will be argued about without being argued away." Time

Gage, Elizabeth

The master stroke. Pocket Bks. 1991 373p o.p.

LC 91-20762

Available Thorndike Press large print edition

"Soon after naïve, beautiful Francie Bollinger begins to work for Magnus International, her first brilliant idea is stolen by her boss. A little wiser, she offers her second one, a plan to link the European divisions under one computer, to Jack Magnus, son of CEO Anton. She and Jack have a torrid affair and he asks her to marry him, but says they must keep their betrothal a secret. After

Gage, Elizabeth—*Continued*
the computer link is operational, however, Jack marries the girl his father has chosen for him and Francie is fired. Francie starts her own company and plots the Magnuses' destruction." Publ Wkly

Pandora's box. Simon & Schuster 1990 717p o.p.

LC 90-9961

This novel "charts the careers of two alluring women born the same night in 1933. Secretive dark-haired Laura, given to mystical 'rainy day thoughts,' is left pregnant by a promiscuous art history prof at NYU. Nearly destroyed, she resurfaces as an acclaimed fashion designer and the greatest photographer since Steichen. Meanwhile, red-headed corporate climber Tess (aka Liz, Lisa, Bess), cold, bold and deliciously evil, plots her rise through the budding TV industry, then leaps to power in Washington." Publ Wkly

Gaines, Ernest J., 1933-
The autobiography of Miss Jane Pittman. Dial Press (NY) 1971 245p o.p.
"In the epic of Miss Jane Pittman, a 110-year-old ex-slave, the action begins at the time she is a small child watching both Union and Confederate troops come into the plantation on which she lives. It closes with the demonstrations of the sixties and the freedom walk she decides to make. This is a log of trials, heartaches, joys, love—but mostly of endurance." Shapiro. Fic for Youth. 3d edition

The gathering of old men. Knopf 1983 213p $22
ISBN 0-394-51468-8   LC 82-49000
"The story opens with the murder of Beau Boutan, a Cajun farmer, on the Louisiana plantation of Candy Marshall, a headstrong white owner. She claims to have done the shooting because she wished to protect one of her black workers, Mathu, who has been like a guardian to her following the death of her parents. In the plan to stand between Mapes, the local sheriff, and Mathu, Candy has set into motion an idea that has brought together a group of old black men with shotguns (unloaded), all claiming to have done the shooting. The threat of the South's way of punishing blacks by lynching hangs over the story like a pall. It meets opposition from Beau's young brother who has been friends with a black fellow-student and team-mate at his university." Shapiro. Fic for Youth. 3d edition

In my father's house. Knopf 1978 214p o.p.

LC 77-20357

"The sudden and unexpected appearance of his illegitimate son Etienne (or Robert X) throws Reverend Phillip Martin's life into disorder. His position as a religious figure in the community, a civil rights leader, and a stable family man is threatened, but the confrontation also brings to the fore many questions about father and son relationships and the conflict between the more conservative and militant factions in the black community." Shapiro. Fic for Youth. 2d edition

A lesson before dying. Knopf 1993 256p $21
ISBN 0-679-41477-0   LC 92-20335

"The story of two African American men struggling to attain manhood in a prejudiced society, the tale is set in Bayonne, La. . . in the late 1940s. It concerns Jefferson, a mentally slow, barely literate young man, who, though an innocent bystander to a shootout between a white store owner and two black robbers is convicted of murder, and the sophisticated, educated man who comes to his aid. When Jefferson's own attorney claims that executing him would be tantamount to killing a hog, his incensed godmother, Miss Emma, turns to teacher Grant Wiggins, pleading with him to gain access to the jailed youth and help him to face his death by electrocution with dignity." Publ Wkly
"Despite the novel's gallows humor and an atmosphere of pervasively harsh racism, the characters, black and white, are humanly complex. . . . Ernest J. Gaines has written a moving and truthful work of fiction." N Y Times Book Rev

Galbraith, John Kenneth, 1908-
A tenured professor; a novel. Houghton Mifflin 1990 197p o.p.

LC 89-39559

Available Thorndike Press large print edition
"Can a tenured professor of economics at Harvard, creator of a stock forecasting model, put his vast yields toward liberal causes without upsetting the prevailing political-economic system? Montgomery Marvin develops the Index of Irrational Expectations (IRAT) after studying the euphoria which accompanies investment, and with his activist wife Marjie he puts IRAT earnings to such uses as labeling products based on their makers' number of women executives; establishing chairs in peace studies at the military academies; and setting up PRCs (Political Rectitude Committees)." Libr J
The author "juggles four victims in this irreverently satirical tale: Harvard, which is always a fine target for the deflationary knife jab; the mass hysteria that causes investors to assume that up is the only direction; official prattle about the American way; and the eccentricities of his own profession. He is in short, playing fairly as well as funnily." Atlantic

Galdós, Benito Pérez *See* Pérez Galdós, Benito, 1843-1920

Gallant, Mavis
Across the bridge; stories. Random House 1993 198p $19
ISBN 0-679-42213-7   LC 92-27270
Analyzed in Short story index
Contents: 1933; The chosen husband; From cloud to cloud; Florida; Dédé; Kingdom Come; Across the bridge; Forain; A state of affairs; Mlle. Dias de Corta; The Fenton child
"Penetrating and insightful, these tales reflect the sensibilities of conservative Catholic Montrealers and Parisians coping with the crises of modern life." Publ Wkly

In transit; twenty stories. Random House 1989 c1988 229p o.p.

LC 88-29685

Analyzed in Short story index
First published 1988 in Canada
The stories originally appeared in The New Yorker during the 1950s and 1960s
Contents: The wedding ring; The end of the world;

Gallant, Mavis—*Continued*
An emergency case; April fish; The statues taken down; The circus; When we were nearly young; The hunter's waking thoughts; The captive niece; Malcolm and Bea; Vacances Pax; In transit; By the sea; Careless talk; In Italy; Better times; A question of disposal; Good deed; Questions and answers; New Year's Eve

Overhead in a balloon; twelve stories of Paris. Random House 1987 c1985 196p $16.95

ISBN 0-394-54511-7   LC 86-20329

Analyzed in Short story index
First published 1985 in Canada
Contents: Speck's idea; Overhead in a balloon; Luc and his father; A painful affair; Larry; A flying start; Grippes and Poche; A recollection; Rue de Lille; The colonel's child; Lena; The assembly
"Twelve stories interconnected by the appearance of characters who jump from one tale to another, from secondary parts to leading roles, and then to oblivion. Gallant's adopted Parisian milieu is well captured in these pieces, as the bourgeoisie argue the finer points of real-estate law, roommates anguish over domestic arrangements, writers battle over their literary turf, and lovers dip into a bottomless well of ennui." Booklist

Gallico, Paul, 1897-1976

Ludmila

In Gallico, P. Three legends: The snow goose; The small miracle; Ludmila p77-126

Mrs. 'Arris goes to Paris; drawings by Gioia Fiammenghi. Doubleday 1958 157p o.p.
"The unsinkable Mrs. 'Arris, a middle-aged London charwoman, who is fascinated with her wealthy employer's Dior gown, works and saves her money for her own Dior original. When she gets to Paris, she brings happiness to all she meets, and finally gets her dress." Jacob. To be continued
Other titles in the series are: Mrs. 'Arris goes to New York (1960); Mrs. 'Arris goes to Parliament (1965); and Mrs. 'Arris goes to Moscow (1975)

The Poseidon adventure. Coward-McCann 1969 347p o.p. Amereon reprint available $22.95 (ISBN 0-8488-0270-5)
"A large ocean liner converted to a cruise ship, the S.S. Poseidon, is caught by an underwater earthquake and capsizes. As the ship is slowly sinking, a group of survivors, with the help of an American mountaineer, inch their way upward through the bowels of the ship to safety. The interlocking stories of these passengers make for interesting reading." Shapiro. Fic for Youth. 2d edition

The small miracle; illustrated by Reisie Lonette. Doubleday 1952 58p o.p. Amereon reprint available $14.95 (ISBN 0-8488-0494-5)
A brief story of a little Italian war-orphan and his beloved donkey, Violetta. When Violetta became very ill Pepino asked permission to take her into the crypt of St. Francis' church in Assisi, and he persisted until permission was granted by the Pope himself

"This simple poignant tale . . . brings a message of power, of faith and love." Cincinnati Public Libr

also in Gallico, P. Three legends: The snow goose; The small miracle; Ludmila p47-75

The snow goose. Knopf 1940 57p $9.95
ISBN 0-394-44593-7
"In 1930 Philip Rhayader, a hunchbacked painter, moves to an abandoned lighthouse, where he devotes himself not only to his painting but to maintaining a bird sanctuary. Rejected by the world, he is a recluse until Fritha, a young girl, brings him a hurt Canadian snow goose to care for and heal. The bird becomes a bond in their deepening relationship. When Philip is killed in aiding the rescue at Dunkirk, Fritha continues to care for his birds until the lighthouse is destroyed." Shapiro. Fic for Youth. 3d edition

also in Gallico, P. Three legends: The snow goose; The small miracle; Ludmila p21-45

Three legends: The snow goose; The small miracle; Ludmila; illustrated by Reisie Lonette. Doubleday 1966 126p o.p.
Analyzed in Short story index
The first two novelettes are entered separately. Ludmila, first published 1959, tells about a cow in Liechtenstein who wants to be beautiful

Galsworthy, John, 1867-1933
Nobel Prize in literature, 1932

End of the chapter. Scribner 1934 897p o.p.
"The Forsyte chronicles"
Sequel to A modern comedy
Also known as the Cherrell saga (after family connections of the Forsytes) this book contains volumes 7-9 of the larger series, The Forsyte chronicles: Maid in waiting (1931), Flowering wilderness (1932), and Over the river (1933; published with title: One more river)
In Maid in waiting, Denny Cherrell undertakes the vindication of her brother whose army career has been ruined by an American archeological expedition leader's unjust accusations
In Flowering wilderness, Denny falls in love with Wilfred Desert, a young poet back from the East. A meddlesome traveler spreads the rumor that Wilfred accepted Mohammedanism in order to escape death at the hands of Arab fanatics; English club and society people see this as an outrage to the British ruling class' code of honor. Ostracized and tortured by pride, the sensitive poet becomes in truth a coward and disappears, leaving his still loyal fiancée only her memories
In the final volume, Over the river, Denny's chief concern is her younger sister Clare's divorce from a sadistic husband. After learning of Wilfred's drowning in Siam, Denny decides to marry Dornford

Flowering wilderness

In Galsworthy, J. End of the chapter p331-592

Galsworthy, John, 1867-1933—*Continued*

The Forsyte saga; with a preface by Ada Galsworthy. Scribner 1922 xx, 921p o.p. Buccaneer Bks. reprint available $32.95 (ISBN 0-89966-443-1)

Contains volumes 1-3 of the Forsyte chronicles: The man of property (entered separately), In chancery (1920), and To let (1921). Two interludes are included: Indian summer of a Forsyte (1918) and Awakening (1920)

In chancery relates the further fortunes of the Forsyte family. Irene Forsyte's first effort toward emancipation from her husband Soames ended with the accidental death of the architect who loved her. Meeting Irene again, after a separation of fifteen years, awakens in Soames the old desire to possess her, and failing of her consent, files for divorce. This action forces his cousin Jolyon into the role of correspondent. Soames eventually marries Annette Lamotte, who presents him with a daughter, Fleur, instead of a longed-for male heir, Jolyon and Irene marry and have a son, Jolyon or "Jon"

The first interlude, Awakening, is about little Jon until he is eight years old. The second interlude, Indian summer of a Forsyte, goes back in time to the secret visit of Irene to Old Jolyon at Robin Hill, the country place Soames had built for her before their separation. She captivates the older man by her gentleness, and he dies quietly one summer day

To let centers on the romance of Jon and Fleur who are brought together by chance and are ignorant of the enmity between Soames, and Irene and Jolyon. When Fleur proposes a hasty marriage to Jon, his father reluctantly discloses the reason for the feud. After Jolyon's death, Irene and Jon leave for America, and Fleur, disappointed, marries Michael Mont

Followed by A modern comedy

The Galsworthy reader; edited by Anthony West. Scribner 1968 c1967 xxi, 702p o.p.

This omnibus volume includes: The man of property (entered separately); Indian summer of a Forsyte (1918); excerpts from three other novels, four short stories and two plays

Short stories included are: The consummation; The meeting; A stoic; Virtue

In chancery

   In Galsworthy, J. The Forsyte saga p363-639

The Indian summer of a Forsyte

   In Galsworthy, J. The Forsyte saga p313-59

   In Galsworthy, J. The Galsworthy reader p543-86

Maid in waiting

   In Galsworthy, J. End of the chapter p1-330

The man of property. o.p.

First published 1906

"The 'man of property' . . . is Soames Forsyte, a typical member of the Forsyte family. His wife Irene, whom he regards as just another piece of property, falls in love with Philip Bosinney, a young architect. Soames devotes all his money and power to punishing them, and Philip is killed in an accident." Reader's Ency. 3d edition

also in Galsworthy, J. The Forsyte saga p3-309

also in Galsworthy, J. The Galsworthy reader p15-294

A modern comedy; with a preface by the author. Scribner 1987 c1927 722p $50

ISBN 0-02-542370-3   LC 87-14137

"A Scribners/Macmillan Hudson River edition"
Sequel to The Forsyte saga
A reissue of the title first published 1929
This book contains volumes 4-6 of the Forsyte chronicles: The white monkey (1924); The silver spoon (1926); Swan song (1928)

The white monkey concerns Fleur and Michael Mont, and Fleur's father Soames. A son is born to the couple, thus strengthening the marriage which had been weakened by Fleur's affair with an artist and her unrequited love for her cousin Jon

The silver spoon, picks up the story line three years later in 1924 as Soames challenges a rival of Fleur's for calling his daughter a snob. A disagreeable libel suit evolves

As Swan song opens, Soames has mellowed. He guards with special tenderness the welfare of his daughter and son-in-law, but all his watchfulness and devotion are powerless to avert the tragedy of Fleur's deliberate revival of her love affair with Jon Forsyte when he returns to England with his American wife, Anne. The story ends as Soames saves Fleur from death, and in doing so, is killed himself. This sobers the girl and she returns to her husband

"In some respects 'A Modern Comedy' is inferior to 'The Forsyte Saga'; it is much less rich in varied and vivid types of character; it is less successful as the portrait of an age. . . . But in other ways 'A Modern Comedy' has the advantage of its predecessor. It has a more organic unity, a clearer and more symmetrical plan, dominated by one great figure as tragic finally as Père Goriot,—the figure of Soames Forsyte. . . . It is that least showy and attractive of the Forsytes, Soames, the villain, who has proved so strong that, against the will of his somewhat puzzled creator he has become the hero of the cycle." Saturday Rev

Followed by End of the chapter

Over the river

   In Galsworthy, J. End of the chapter p593-897

The silver spoon

   In Galsworthy, J. A modern comedy

Swan song

   In Galsworthy, J. A modern comedy

To let

   In Galsworthy, J. The Forsyte saga p665-921

The white monkey

   In Galsworthy, J. A modern comedy

Gann, Ernest Kellogg, 1910-1991

The aviator; [by] Ernest K. Gann. Arbor House 1981 189p o.p.

                      LC 80-68543

Gann, Ernest Kellogg, 1910-1991 — Continued

"In 1928 flying the mail was an experimental and highly risky business. This short novel concerns an 'Aviator,' a professional flyer whose name we don't learn until near the end of the story. With the unaccustomed load of a passenger, a young girl, he sets out to fly across the Columbia plateau. They go down, she is hurt, a storm grounds the searchers. The Aviator is scarred physically and mentally by an earlier accident for which he feels responsible. In the wreck of the plane, he learns his own worth and the power of love." Libr J

The high and the mighty. Sloane 1953 342p $18.45

ISBN 0-688-01786-X

Also available from Amereon and Buccaneer Bks.

"Story about 20 people on a Honolulu-San Francisco air liner and how they face the strong possibility that the plane will crash." Christ Sci Monit

In the company of eagles; [by] Ernest K. Gann. Simon & Schuster 1966 342p o.p.

This novel set in 1917 "recreates the frantic pace of biplane battles during World War I. A young French aviator swears vengeance on the German ace who flies without fault and kills without mercy." Cincinnati Public Libr

Garcia, Cristina

Dreaming in Cuban; a novel. Knopf 1992 244p $19.50

ISBN 0-679-40883-5   LC 91-20755

Shifting back and forth between Cuba and Brooklyn, this novel "centers on three generations of a family torn apart by Fidel Castro's revolution. Celia del Pino is the matriarch whose passions alternate between a long-lost Spanish lover and service to El Líder. In Brooklyn, Celia's daughter Lourdes runs the Yankee Doodle Bakery. Haunted by the memory of being raped by a revolutionary soldier back home, she is obsessed by her hatred for Castro and communism and her mother's devotion to both. Lourdes's daughter, Pilar, scoffs at her mother's belief that she can 'fight Communism from behind her bakery counter' and plots a return to the island." Newsweek

"While taking very seriously those ideas that have truly riven so many families in recent years, leaving many obsessed with the politics of Cuba, Ms. Garcia also portrays the costliness of such an obsession and the fading of the light between mothers and daughters, between lovers, as communication fails." N Y Times Book Rev

García Márquez, Gabriel, 1928-

Nobel Prize in literature, 1982

The autumn of the patriarch; translated from the Spanish by Gregory Rabassa. Harper & Row 1976 269p o.p.

Original Spanish edition, 1975

"A highly sophisticated novel about an unnamed dictator (the patriarch), who, at the time of his death, is somewhere between 107 and 232 years of age. The patriarch embodies the archtypal evils of despotism, but even more significant is his extreme, and often pathetic, solitude, which becomes increasingly evident with his advancing age and which emerges as the principal theme. Despite its political and psychological overtones, the autumn of the patriarch can best be described as a lyrical novel, whose plot and character development are subordinate to formal design and symbolic imagery." Ency of World Lit in the 20th century

Big Mama's funeral

In García Márquez, G. Collected stories p97-200

In García Márquez, G. No one writes to the colonel, and other stories p65-170

Chronicle of a death foretold; translated from the Spanish by Gregory Rabassa. Knopf 1983 c1982 120p $18.95

ISBN 0-394-53074-8   LC 82-48884

Original Spanish edition published 1981 in Colombia; this translation first published 1982 in the United Kingdom

Set in a provincial Colombian town, this novella "is a reconstruction of an actual episode in which the people of a whole neighborhood, if not in fact a whole town, stood by and did nothing while a couple of drunks planned, announced, and finally carried out a murder. The killers alleged motive was revenge for their sister's loss of honor and this claim, together with normal languor and stupidity, appears to have brought on collective paralysis and even collective complicity among their fellow citizens." Atlantic

This "investigation of an ancient murder takes on the quality of a hallucinatory exploration, a deep groping search into the gathering darkness of human intentions for a truth that continually slithers away." N Y Rev Books

also in García Márquez, G. Collected novellas p167-249

Collected novellas. HarperCollins Pubs. 1990 249p o.p. Borgo Press reprint available $25 (ISBN 0-8095-9051-4)

LC 89-46106

Analyzed in Short story index

English translations of the three novellas included in this volume were first published 1972, 1968 and 1982 respectively

Contents: Leaf storm; No one writes to the colonel; Chronicle of a death foretold

Collected stories. Harper & Row 1984 311p $16.95

ISBN 0-06-015364-4   LC 84-47826

Analyzed in Short story index

This volume includes stories from the author's three previous collections: No one writes to the colonel, and other stories; Leaf storm, and other stories, and Innocent Eréndira, and other stories. All three collections are entered separately

This "is a wonderous mixture of realism and truth-stretching, with humor the glue that holds the two together. Garcia Marquez' writing is both broad shouldered and lovely, and thus irresistible." Booklist

The general and his labyrinth; translated from the Spanish by Edith Grossman. Knopf 1990 285p $19.95

ISBN 0-394-58258-6   LC 90-52957

García Márquez, Gabriel, 1928-—*Continued*
Original Spanish edition, 1989
This novel attempts to portray the last days of Simon Bolívar. "Ousted from the presidency of Colombia while once adoring crowds jeer him as a tyrant, a dying 46-year-old Bolívar journeys to supposed exile. His route on the Magdalena River is a tropical Via Dolorosa, lined by war-ravaged towns, grieving widows, scheming generals and long-ago romances. What Bolívar encounters most, however, are delirious dreams and memories that expose his life's epic contradictions." Newsweek

"Seldom has there been a more fitting match between author and subject. Mr. García Márquez wades into his flamboyant, often improbable and ultimately tragic material with enormous gusto, heaping detail upon sensuous detail, alternating grace with horror." N Y Times Book Rev

In evil hour; translated from the Spanish by Gregory Rabassa. Harper & Row 1979 183p o.p.
Original Spanish edition, 1968
This novel "is set in a squalid river town. . . . The village is weighed down by an immense inertia, the result of the natives' hatred of a corrupt dictatorship and of the seasonal rains that dampen their spirits. The mayor, a hired assassin of the new central government, dreams of wealth, not war. . . . Lampoons begin to haunt the town, in the form of slanderous posters that appear overnight on doors and walls. No one can trace the authors. . . . Prominent citizens become so upset by the ghostly terrorism that the mayor is forced to impose a curfew, which in turn triggers a resurgence of political opposition." Newsweek

"The reader is carried along effortlessly in the current of this gifted storyteller's prose. Both heroes and villains elicit sympathy because their basic human foibles, while true to local circumstances, can be recognized by people of any culture." Libr J

The incredible and sad tale of innocent Eréndira and her heartless grandmother

In García Márquez, G. Collected stories p262-311

In García Márquez, G. Innocent Eréndira, and other stories p1-59

Innocent Eréndira, and other stories. Harper & Row 1978 183p o.p. Borgo Press reprint available $23 (ISBN 0-8095-9052-2)
Analyzed in Short story index
Contents: The incredible and sad tale of innocent Eréndira and her heartless grandmother [novella]; The sea of lost time; Death constant beyond love; The third resignation; The other side of death; Eva is inside her cat; Dialogue with the mirror; Bitterness for three sleepwalkers; Eyes of a blue dog; The woman who came at six o'clock; Someone has been disarranging these roses; The night of the curlews

Leaf storm

In García Márquez, G. Collected novellas p1-106

In García Márquez, G. Leaf storm, and other stories p1-97

Leaf storm, and other stories; translated from the Spanish by Gregory Rabassa. Harper & Row 1972 146p o.p. Borgo Press reprint available $23 (ISBN 0-8095-9053-0)
Analyzed in Short story index
Short stories included are: The handsomest drowned man in the world; A very old man with enormous wings; Blacamán the Good, vendor of miracles; The last voyage of the ghost ship; Monologue of Isabel watching it rain in Macondo; Nabo

The title novella (originally published 1955) covers three generations of boom and decline in the mythical Colombian town Macondo. "The small river town changes with the leaf storm of people—strangers who come there as a result of civil war and the establishment of a banana company. Marquez begins with the end, the death of one mysterious wanderer, a doctor who . . . withdraws from the world. As the narrators, a man, his daughter, her young son, reveal the doctor's story, so too do the tellers' own melancholy lives emerge, symbolic yet specific, representing the everlasting variety of man's inhumanity to man." Publ Wkly

Love in the time of cholera; translated by Edith Grossman. Knopf 1988 348p $18.95
ISBN 0-394-56161-9   LC 87-40484
Original Spanish edition published 1985 in Colombia
"The story, which concerns the themes of love, aging, and death, takes place between the late 1870s and the early 1930s in a South American community troubled by wars and outbreaks of cholera. It is a tale of two lovers, artistic Florentino Ariza and wealthy Fermina Daza, who reunite after a lifetime apart. Their spirit of enduring love contrasts ironically with the surrounding corporeal decay." Merriam-Webster's Ency of Lit

No one writes to the colonel

In García Márquez, G. Collected novellas p107-66

In García Márquez, G. No one writes to the colonel, and other stories p3-62

No one writes to the colonel, and other stories; translated from the Spanish by J. S. Bernstein. Harper & Row 1968 170p o.p. Borgo Press reprint available $25 (ISBN 0-8095-9054-9)
Analyzed in Short story index
This volume contains the title novella (originally published 1961 in Colombia) and eight short stories (originally published together 1962 in Mexico; translated title: Big Mama's funeral)
Short stories included are: Tuesday siesta; One of these days; There are no thieves in this town; Balthazar's marvelous afternoon; Montiel's widow; One day after Saturday; Artificial roses; Big Mama's funeral

One hundred years of solitude; translated from the Spanish by Gregory Rabassa. Harper & Row 1970 422p $30
ISBN 0-06-011418-5
Also available Everyman's library edition
Original Spanish edition published 1967 in Argentina
This novel "relates the founding of Macondo by Jose Arcadio Buendia, the adventures of six generations of his descendants, and, ultimately, the town's destruction.

García Márquez, Gabriel, 1928-—_Continued_
It also presents a vast synthesis of social, economic, and political evils plaguing much of Latin America. Even more important from a literary point of view is its aesthetic representation of a world in microcosm, that is, a complete history, from Eden to Apocalypse, of a world in which miracles such as people riding on flying carpets and a dead man returning to life tend to erase the thin line between objective and subjective realities." Ency of World Lit in the 20th century

Strange pilgrims; twelve stories; translated from the Spanish by Edith Grossman. Knopf 1993 188p $21

ISBN 0-679-42566-7   LC 93-12257

Analyzed in Short story index
Contents: Bon voyage, Mr. President; The saint; Sleeping beauty and the airplane; I sell my dreams; "I only came to use the phone"; The ghosts of August; Maria dos Prazeres; Seventeen poisoned Englishmen; Tramontana; Miss Forbes's summer of happiness; Light is like water; The trail of your blood in the snow
"Exile and loss are the principal subjects of these 12 stories . . . which capture with lyrical precision the emotions of disorientation and fear, coupled with a sense of new possibility, experienced by Latin Americans in Europe." Publ Wkly

Gardner, Erle Stanley, 1889-1970
The blonde in lower six. Carroll & Graf Pubs. 1990 270p o.p.

LC 90-43553

Analyzed in Short story index
This collection of four tales (three written in the late 1920s, one in 1961) includes the following short novels: The blonde in lower six, The wax dragon, Grinning gods, and Yellow shadows
"Classic hardboiled angst served with all the traditional trimmings." Booklist

The blonde in lower six [novelette]

_In_ Gardner, E. S. The blonde in lower six p7-144

The case of the postponed murder. Morrow 1973 220p o.p.
This novel begins "with a girl trying to pass herself off as the younger of two daughters worried about the disappearance of her older sister. But Perry Mason, to whom she goes for help, is intrigued rather than taken in. The girl is accused of forgery, then a murder occurs in which she is a prime suspect." Best Sellers

The case of the sulky girl. Morrow 1933 303p o.p. Amereon reprint available $22.95 (ISBN 0-88411-402-3)
Also available Thorndike Press large print edition
Defense attorney Perry Mason becomes embroiled in a murder case when he is contacted by a young woman worried about her father's will

The case of the worried waitress. Morrow 1966 212p o.p.
"Perry Mason makes the mistake of taking Della to lunch at Madison's Midtown Milestone, and is, thereby, involved with [waitress] Katherine Ellis and the mysterious things that bother and frighten her. The surprise is at the end when Perry and Hamilton Burger, the DA, shake hands, and no mention is made of a fee." Libr J

The cat-woman

_In_ Gardner, E. S. Dead men's letters p105-46

Come and get it

_In_ Gardner, E. S. Dead men's letters p189-227

Dead men's letters. Carroll & Graf Pubs. 1990 275p o.p.

LC 89-20974

Analyzed in Short story index
Contents: Dead men's letters; Laugh that off; The cat-woman; This way out; Come and get it; In full of account

Dead men's letters [novelette]

_In_ Gardner, E. S. Dead men's letters p1-47

Grinning gods

_In_ Gardner, E. S. The blonde in lower six p189-227

Honest money, and other short novels. Carroll & Graf Pubs. 1991 204p $18.95

ISBN 0-88184-683-X   LC 91-12116

Contents: Honest money; The top comes off; Close call; Making the breaks; Devil's fire; Blackmail with lead
"First published in 1932 and 1933 by _Black Mask_ magazine and starring the young crime-fighting lawyer Ken Corning and gutsy secretary Helen Vail, the six stories collected here provide the prototype for the late author's astoundingly successful Perry Mason crime novels." Publ Wkly

In full of account

_In_ Gardner, E. S. Dead men's letters p229-75

Laugh that off

_In_ Gardner, E. S. Dead men's letters p49-104

This way out

_In_ Gardner, E. S. Dead men's letters p147-87

The wax dragon

_In_ Gardner, E. S. The blonde in lower six p145-87

Yellow shadows

_In_ Gardner, E. S. The blonde in lower six p229-70

Gardner, John, 1933-1982
Grendel; illustrated by Emil Antonucci. Knopf 1971 174p il $15.95

ISBN 0-394-47143-1

Gardner, John, 1933-1982—*Continued*

"To the heroes of 'Beowulf,' the monster Grendel, devourer of men, represented chaos and death and pagan darkness. This is Grendel's side of the story. . . . Grendel perceives that what the primeval dragon has told him is true: he is the brute existent by which men learn to define themselves. 'Grendel' may be read for what it says about the human condition, for its implicit comments on men's art, wars, fears, and hopes." Publ Wkly

"The world, Mr. Gardner seems to be suggesting in his violent, inspiring, awesome, terrifying narrative, has to defeat its Grendels, yet somehow, he hints, both ecologically and in deeper ways, that world is a poorer place when men and their monsters cannot coexist." Christ Sci Monit

Nickel mountain; a pastoral novel; with etchings by Thomas O'Donohue. Knopf 1973 312p il o.p.

The hero of this novel, "Henry Soames, is the fat owner of a truck-route diner deep in the forests of the Catskills. . . . A nice girl named Callie who helps in Henry's diner gets pregnant by a rich man's son, who then skips town. Soames marries her out of kindness. They go through the agony of childbirth. As the boy grows up, their domestic peace is variously threatened in small ways." Time

"Against considerable odds, Henry manages to survive with dignity and good conscience, and this is what the novel is really about—the survival of plain human goodness. Given a little thought, that is an exciting theme. Mr. Gardner has made an absorbing and provocative book out of it." Atlantic

October light; illustrated by Elaine Raphael and Don Bolognese. Knopf 1976 433p il o.p.

"One evening James Page, a 72-year-old Vermont farmer, chases his 80-year-old sister Sally upstairs with a piece of stovewood and locks her in her bedroom. James, part savage and part Green Mountain philosopher thinks the country has gone to hell—you can see it all on TV, which is why he shoots Sally's TV set to pieces right before her eyes. Sally is a liberal, believing in New York City and amnesty, and amuses herself in captivity with a 'trashy' novel about marijuana smugglers. . . . In them, Sally sees an allegory of Third World attacks on capitalism, even sees herself as the Third World and her brother as brutish capitalism. . . . At first James won't let Sally out [of her room], then she won't come out. . . . Family and friends gather to preach and cajole." Newsweek

"With splendid invention (including a marvelous novel within the novel), precise and emphatically drawn characters, superb writing, Gardner explores people and a place uniquely American." Libr J

The sunlight dialogues; illustrated by John Napper. Knopf 1972 673p il o.p.

"In 1966, Fred Clumly, age 64, was a stolid, law-and-order police chief in Batavia, a town in western New York. Law and order are disrupted by a bearded, babbling . . . madman, a magician of sorts who paints the word LOVE across one of the town streets. The Sunlight Man, Clumly calls him for lack of any other name, and locks him up. The lunatic stages a magical escape and then returns to free another prisoner, who murders a policeman as they leave. The hunt is on, and so is the pressure put on Clumly, who seems to do nothing right, though in fact the best fictional detectives—Inspectors

Javert, Porfiry Petrovich and Maigret as well as Clumly—know that you catch your man after you have understood him." Newsweek

Gardner, John Champlin *See* Gardner, John, 1933-1982

Gardner, John E., 1926-

Brokenclaw; [by] John Gardner. Putnam 1990 304p o.p.

LC 90-36302

In this thriller "agent 007, James Bond, is recuperating from burnout in San Francisco. But he is soon activated and charged with preventing classified submarine-detection secrets from falling into Chinese hands. And, while he's at it, to stop this post-Tiananmen Square crowd from destroying Wall Street and other financial centers. Masterminding the villainy here is Brokenclaw Lee, a 6'4", sexually insatiable, half Chinese/half Blackfoot Indian with rippling muscles." Publ Wkly

Death is forever; by John Gardner. Putnam 1992 303p o.p.

LC 92-2560

In this "James Bond thriller, the West has lost sight of a joint British-American intelligence network that once operated in the old Eastern Bloc, and the caseworkers assigned to track down the network's underground agents are found dead under suspicious circumstances. When Bond and American counterpart Eazy St. John pick up the trail, they find themselves the target of the shadowy villain who once directed East Germany's secret service." Libr J

License renewed; [by] John Gardner. Marek, R. 1981 285p o.p.

LC 81-1284

This continues the series of "novels about secret agent James Bond, Ian Fleming's literary creation of the 50s and 60s. . . . Bond now drives a Saab, eschewing the low-mileage Bentleys of his past years for one of those economical foreign models. His cigarettes are low tar, and he admits to cutting his alcohol consumption. But his license to kill has been renewed, for there is yet another mad genius loose in the world, one Anton Murik, nuclear physicist who happens to be Scottish laird as well. Anton has hatched an airtight scheme to make six nuclear power plants contract the China Syndrome unless the countries involved pay up." SLJ

Maestro; [by] John Gardner. Penzler Bks. 1993 610p $23

ISBN 1-883402-24-7   LC 93-19364

This novel brings "old agent-runner Big Herbie Kruger out of semiretirement to represent Britain's Secret Intelligence Service in the debriefing of Louis Passau, an internationally renowned conductor. Passau's life is being threatened, probably by people who don't want him to spill important secrets; a botched assassination attempt occurs after the maestro's 90th Birthday Concert at Lincoln Center. Aided by his musical savvy and the sexy young SIS agent Pucky Curtiss, Kruger interviews Passau, learning much about the musician's unpleasant character and equally nasty past." Publ Wkly

Gardner, John E., 1926-—*Continued*
"By turns shocking, humorous, sad, and repulsive. Passau's story has implications that shake the foundations of spydom. *Maestro* is a grand and glorious adventure that will keep readers mesmerized from the first page to the last." Booklist

The man from Barbarossa; [by] John Gardner. Putnam 1991 303p o.p.

LC 90-26402

This novel finds Bond "involved in a globally tense situation that begins when a secret Soviet organization kidnaps a New Jersey man who is supposedly largely responsible for the slaughter of Russian Jews at Babi Yar in 1941. The problem—*one* of the problems, anyway—is that they've nabbed the wrong guy. The organization then demands ransom and the right man to be turned over to them; Bond is called in to save the world from the havoc the group threatens to wreak." Booklist

Never send flowers; [by] John Gardner. Putnam 1993 286p $18.95

ISBN 0-399-13809-9   LC 93-21796

"James Bond and a female Swiss agent pursue the murderer (by poison pellet) of a British Security Service agent across Europe and through EuroDisney." Libr J
"This light, entertaining read doesn't pretend to be anything more than another episode in what has turned into a never-ending adventure." Publ Wkly

The return of Moriarty; [by] John Gardner. Putnam 1974 366p o.p.

The novel is based on the concept that Professor James Moriarty, archrival of Sherlock Holmes, "had been saved from death at the Reichenbach Falls. Moriarty's notes of his criminal activities in the East End of London have recently been discovered and are now being published, together with footnotes. They outline the nefarious activities and the resounding capers of an English gang of the Nineties, its super-criminal leader, and the destruction of a rival gang of hoodlums." Libr J
"Holmes fans will enjoy Gardner's straight-faced humor—footnotes and all—as well as the colorful characters and their 19th century wickedness." Publ Wkly
Followed by The revenge of Moriarty

The revenge of Moriarty; [by] John Gardner. Putnam 1975 289p o.p.

Moriarty, "the arch enemy of Sherlock Holmes returns to London in 1896 with a hefty bankroll amassed in the U.S. He is burning for revenge—against the quartet of Continental supercriminals who betrayed him, and against Holmes and Scotland Yard's Inspector Crow. Simple murder is too good for his foes; he wants them utterly humiliated and ostracized from their professions. And Moriarty has all the time, money and staff he needs to devise complex schemes of retribution. . . . Superficially, the pace seems as leisurely as that of a Conan Doyle story, but a lot more is happening—including lots of bawdy sex—in a lovingly recreated Victorian London." Publ Wkly

Seafire; [by] John Gardner. Putnam 1994 286p $18.95

ISBN 0-399-13938-9   LC 94-20122

"Working with 007 is the lovely Fredericka von Grusse, formerly of Swiss intelligence, who was introduced in *Never Send Flowers*. The plot involves one Maxwell Tarn, a billionaire, and his wife, who are missing. Sir Maxwell, who disappeared while under surveillance, is evil—dealing in illicit arms and munitions. Bond,

'Flicka,' and the Double-O section of the SIS must find out what really happened to Tarn. The outcome is never in doubt, but it's a rollicking ride all the way." Booklist

The secret families; [by] John Gardner. Putnam 1989 415p o.p.

LC 88-32503

Final volume of the Secret generations trilogy
"The story begins in 1964, when evidence surfaces that Sir Caspar Railton, a recently deceased spymaster, was in fact a Russian 'mole' and traitor. Caspar's nephew, Donald ('Naldo') Railton and American cousin Arnold Farthing thereupon embark on a long-term undercover operation inside Russia, aiming to restore the reputations of their families. Though the narrative is often plodding, the persevering reader will be rewarded in later chapters with a series of surprises, reversals and the final recognition that, as Naldo suggests early on, 'We're all traitors to somebody.'" Publ Wkly

The secret generations; [by] John Gardner. Putnam 1985 383p o.p.

LC 85-6520

First volume of the Secret generations trilogy, followed by the Secret houses and The secret families
"A narrative that spans the years 1909-1935. . . . During the course of the novel, virtually every member of the English Railton family becomes involved in intelligence operations, from the ruthless and manipulative Giles to his grandchildren. Double agents, extramarital affairs and a variety of political movements are worked into Gardner's elaborate tale, which ends with an inventive twist." Publ Wkly

The secret houses; [by] John Gardner. Putnam 1987 399p o.p.

LC 87-16218

Second volume of the Secret generations trilogy
"This book takes the Railton and Farthing families into World War II as their French resistance group Tarot is destroyed by a double agent who now is employing his or her skills in setting up a Soviet apparatus in postwar Europe. But the British secret service is right on the trail, using members of both families as witnesses and suspects in their investigation. Casual readers may be puzzled by the large cast of unfamiliar characters, but the suspense is well portrayed both in the accounts of World War II and in the subsequent cold-war exploits." Booklist

Garfield, Brian

Hopscotch. Evans & Co. 1975 284p o.p.

"A middle-aged ex-CIA spy is bored, and to cheer himself up he decides to write a book exposing the CIA's most cherished secrets. The CIA, predictably cross, tries to kill him to prevent the book from being written. This leads to a chase all over the world, the spy being pursued by American, Russian, and British secret agents." Libr J
This is "outrageously clever entertainment. A thriller without violence, a cat-and-mouse game which ends in satisfying stalemate." Publ Wkly

Garfield, Leon

See Dickens, C. The mystery of Edwin Drood, concluded by Leon Garfield

Garwood, Julie

Prince Charming. Pocket Bks. 1994 387p $22

ISBN 0-671-87095-5

"Compelled to action by the death of her adored grandmother, unconventional Lady Taylor Stapleton agrees to marry Lucas Ross, a man she has never met, and accompany him to America temporarily, all in an effort to save her two young nieces from their greedy and lecherous uncle. But all does not go as planned, and when the girls are kidnapped, Taylor and Lucas are forced to continue their matrimonial charade." Libr J

Saving grace. Pocket Bks. 1993 372p o.p.

LC 93-7831

Available G.K. Hall large print edition

"When Lady Johanna is widowed at the age of 16, she is determined never to marry again and become the victim of abuse at the hands of a husband. King John of England, suspecting that Johanna knows a secret that could destroy him, has chosen another brutal baron for her next husband. Johanna's foster brother finds her a suitable hero in the form of Scottish laird Gabriel Mac-Bain, who weds Johanna in order to control the land she brings as a dowry. Johanna must not only adjust to life in the Highlands, but she must also win the respect of MacBain and his recently unified clan." Libr J

"Garwood endows the novel with a first-rate setting, a splendid supporting cast and witty dialogue that more than offsets the rote predictability of Johanna's great beauty and MacBain's forceful charisma." Publ Wkly

Gash, Joe *See* Granger, Bill

Gash, Jonathan, 1933-

Moonspender. St. Martin's Press 1987 280p o.p.

LC 86-26199

"A Joan Kahn book"

In this caper "antiques dealer Lovejoy, perpetually penurious and even more impoverished than usual, finds himself simultaneously appearing on a TV game show, running a big wedding, receiving a job offer from his current lady friend, helping to redecorate a new restaurant and sniffing out antiquities in East Anglia. There are also a couple of antiques-related deaths, one definitely a murder. Lovejoy gets on with his chores, undeterred by a barrage of lawsuits and myriad romantic complications." Publ Wkly

Paid and loving eyes. St. Martin's Press 1993 261p $19.95

ISBN 0-312-09361-6   LC 93-10340

In this novel Lovejoy "inadvertently gets involved with a group of loathsome creatures who use his knowledge of antiques to execute the scam of scams. But when Lovejoy discovers the horrible evil they're perpetrating, he uses every trick in his repertoire to destroy their plan." Booklist

"Like his manic protagonist, Mr. Gash tends to go over the top when he's having fun, and his baroque plot is often as incoherent as Lovejoy's bizarre slang. But whenever the author takes the time to ruminate on wonderful esoterica . . . his erudite passion for 'the shame, the ecstasy of antiques' can really take your breath away." N Y Times Book Rev

The sin within her smile. Viking 1994 c1993 231p $18.95

ISBN 0-670-85608-8   LC 93-50234

Also available G.K. Hall large print edition

First published 1993 in the United Kingdom

"Antiques dealer Lovejoy offers himself as 'Slave for a Day' at a charity auction and subsequently becomes involved in a fraud concerning some Celtic gold." Libr J

"Gash delivers more than a fair share of antiques lore, finely timed comedy and, in this case, a dazzling climax." Publ Wkly

The tartan sell. St. Martin's Press 1986 227p o.p.

LC 86-3754

"A Joan Kahn book"

"East Anglia antique dealer Lovejoy's passion for collecting takes him to the Highlands of Scotland, where he hides at a crossroads expecting the shipment of a fake antique bureau. Instead, he finds a deserted truck at the side of the road. When the driver is later found murdered, Lovejoy becomes the prime suspect, and to clear himself he switches identity and joins a traveling fair, hiding from the police and seeking out the culprits. Lovejoy's cynicism, his dashing way with women, and his superb knowledge of antiques all pull him through." Booklist

The Vatican rip. Ticknor & Fields 1982 c1981 221p o.p.

LC 81-14387

"A Joan Kahn book"

First published 1981 in the United Kingdom

"Antiques dealer Lovejoy is forced into a plan to steal a Chippendale table from the Vatican. After Italian lessons, he goes to Rome, where he takes up with an old lady con artist and works part-time in an antiques shop, while he perfects his heist plan and plots revenge on his boss. Lovejoy has a short temper, few scruples, and an obsession with antiques. His plans are original and fascinating, making a suspenseful caper novel." Libr J

The very last gambado. St. Martin's Press 1990 c1989 275p o.p.

LC 90-37396

First published 1989 in the United Kingdom

"Hollywood comes to East Anglia as Lovejoy is drawn into a high-paying consulting project for a movie spectacular about a theft from the British Museum. Complications are introduced by an aged Russian countess whose collection of family heirlooms sets Lovejoy's divvying heart a-pounding; by a local heavy reportedly sending containers loaded with antiques to America; by the death of an eminent neighborhood forger; and by the disappearance of a dealer." Publ Wkly

Gaskin, Catherine, 1929-

The ambassador's women. Scribner 1986 c1985 537p o.p.

LC 85-26111

First published 1985 in the United Kingdom

"Dena Ponrose and Ginny Clayton meet when they are both in their final month of pregnancy. The English aristocrat and the American heiress cement their friendship by giving birth to daughters on the same night, and Ginny's rich, crusty father-in-law insists on standing godfather to both babies—a license, it seems, to meddle freely in all their lives. Separated from their husbands

Gaskin, Catherine, 1929-—*Continued*
during World War II, the women and their youngest
children retreat to Cornwall, where . . . the charm that
warded off trouble for so long dwindles in strength, and
disasters follow." Publ Wkly

The charmed circle. Scribner 1989 c1988
646p o.p.

LC 88-26401

First published 1988 in the United Kingdom
"The charmed circle of the Seymour family tantalizes
outsiders, but those within it suffer tragedy. During WW
II, Sir Michael Seymour, a renowned actor on the London stage, loses his wife, a concert pianist, when a
fighter plane crashes into their home in southeast
England. The RAF pilot bails out, saved, it seems, for
a contrived, starry-eyed marriage with one of the
Seymour daughters, Julia, a budding actress. When their
idyll ends tragically, the young widow retires to her husband's crumbling Scottish castle to bear their son. Julia's
sister, Alex, a talented journalist, learns that her husband
has died in a Japanese prison camp, and takes up with
a powerful newspaper mogul; only Connie, the third
sister, has the common touch, choosing love with a
stolid civil servant over a career of her own. After Julia
marries an American movie star with a bad temper and
a history of abuse, their glittering lives turn into a protracted nightmare." Publ Wkly

A falcon for a queen. Doubleday 1972
344p o.p.

"The atmosphere and countryside of the Scottish Highlands make a striking background for this turn-of-the-
century gothic containing deft characterizations and a
skillful blending of suspense, romance, and tragedy. Alone
in China after her missionary father dies in a local
uprising Kirsty Howard is drawn to her ancestral home
Cluain where she is reluctantly accepted by her embittered grandfather, owner of a renowned whiskey distillery.
Other main characters include the enigmatic housekeeper,
her handsome illegitimate son to whom Kirsty is strongly
attracted, and the neighboring Campbells, the family from
whom her grandfather won his choice lands." Booklist

Fiona. Doubleday 1970 278p o.p.

Fiona MacIntyre is "the 19-year-old daughter of a
Scots clergyman, cursed with the gift the Scots call 'the
sight,' who finds herself at Landfall, an elegant, haunted
house on San Cristobal, a small Caribbean island, as
governess for young golden-haired Duncan Maxwell, her
distant cousin. The year is 1833, and the danger and
unrest are sharp and definite in that remote outpost."
Libr J

This is a "romantic yarn that turns unexpected corners,
leads to a holocaust and a slave uprising, and ends with
a surprise twist." Publ Wkly

Gear, Kathleen O'Neal

People of the lakes; [by] Kathleen O'Neal
Gear and W. Michael Gear. Forge 1994
608p il $23.95

ISBN 0-312-85722-5   LC 94-7145

"A Tom Doherty Associates book"
Sixth title in the authors' series about life in prehistoric North America
In this novel "an ancient Mask full of dark magic is
found by Mica Bird, a young warrior. The spirit of his
dead grandfather pleads with him not to use the Power
of the Mask for his own gain—it will consume him.
Mica Bird ignores the spirit and uses the Mask to

manipulate, kill and seduce his own tribe and the tribes
around him. But, Mica Bird is not the only one who
wants the overwhelming Power of the Mask. Other clans
want it for their own." Publisher's note

People of the lightning; [by] Kathleen
O'Neal Gear and W. Michael Gear. Forge
1995 414p il $24.95

ISBN 0-312-85852-3   LC 95-34746

"A Tom Doherty Associates book"
Seventh title in the authors' series about life in prehis-
toric North America
This novel about a village of fisherfolk in ancient
Florida focuses on the adventures of a youth with the
ability to foretell the future

(jt. auth) Gear, W. M. People of the river
(jt. auth) Gear, W. M. People of the sea

Gear, W. Michael

People of the river; [by] W. Michael Gear
and Kathleen O'Neal Gear. TOR Bks. 1992
400p o.p.

LC 92-2968

"A Tom Doherty Associates book"
Fourth title in the authors' series about prehistoric life
in North America; earlier titles published in paperback
A "tale of warring clans in a North American location
around present-day Cahokia, Illinois. The time is A.D.
1300, and the Indian culture known as the Mississippians
or Mound-Builders has a beautiful young priestess named
Nightshade. This is her story, as well as the story of
others like Flycatcher, Lichen, and a brave warrior—
Nightshade's kidnapper and future partner—Badgertail.
With a narrative that includes potent descriptions of art
and artifacts (body ornaments, pottery, carvings, and
weavings), this tale should appeal to readers seeking a
novel containing authentic native American history, cultural rites, myths, and symbols." Booklist

People of the sea; [by] W. Michael and
Kathleen O'Neal Gear. Forge 1993 425p il
$22.95

ISBN 0-312-93122-0   LC 93-26556

"A Tom Doherty Associates book"
Fifth title in the authors' series about prehistoric life
in North America
A "saga of prehistoric Native Americans in contemporary Arizona and California. Pregnant with twins by
her lover, Iceplant, Kestrel flees westward from her abusive husband, Lambkill, who carves Iceplant to death
with a hunting knife. Kestrel's only hope for survival
is to travel to the seacoast and seek refuge with
Iceplant's people." Libr J
The authors, "integrating a tremendous amount of
natural and anthropological research into a satisfactory
narrative, have again produced a vivid and fascinating
portrait of early human life in America." Publ Wkly

(jt. auth) Gear, K. O. People of the lakes
(jt. auth) Gear, K. O. People of the
lightning

Gebert, Lizabeth Paravisini- *See* Paravisini-
Gebert, Lizabeth

Genet, Jean, 1910-1986

Our Lady of the Flowers; translated by Bernard Frechtman; introduction by Jean-Paul Sartre. Grove Press 1963 318p o.p.

Original French edition, 1948

This novel "begins in a prison cell, which Genêt has decorated with pictures of notorious criminals, and the narrative constantly returns to that cell, as Genêt awaits a hearing that may set him free. In his imagination, however, he is already free, as he weaves stories around the Parisian homosexuals and petty criminals who are the focus of his yearning and admiration." Ency of World Lit in the 20th century

"The book has the shocking candor of 'graffiti' in a public place. . . . It is the work of a master of words whose insights alternate between those of a naive child and those of a jaded whore." N Y Times Book Rev

George, Elizabeth

For the sake of Elena. Bantam Bks. 1992 388p o.p.

LC 91-34865

Available G.K. Hall large print edition

"When student Elena Weaver jogs across a bridge spanning the River Cam and stumbles into a fatal ambush, a summons goes out to Scotland Yard's Thomas Lynley. . . . With his 'proletarian sidekick' Barbara Havers serving as a foil to the aristocratic dons lurking around the gothic spires of Cambridge U., Inspector Lynley interviews those who knew the victim, who emerges as casting a rather salacious spell on all men who met her." Booklist

"While elements of the plot are somewhat stretched, George's story never fails to engage." Publ Wkly

A great deliverance. Bantam Bks. 1988 305p o.p.

LC 87-47906

Available Thorndike Press large print edition

"Urbane inspector Thomas Lynley—a fascinating mix of public school bravado and appealing sensitivity—is sent to the wilds of Yorkshire, where an obese girl has been found sitting by the headless corpse of her father, covered in his blood and proclaiming her guilt. Pairing the suave Lynley with the plain, utterly charmless sergeant Barbara Havers, George creates a bizarre study in contrasts. . . . This first-rate whodunit has enough psychological interplay and character pyrotechnics to fuel several perfectly good mysteries." Booklist

Missing Joseph. Bantam Bks. 1993 496p $21.95

ISBN 0-553-09253-7   LC 92-35630

This novel "examines relationships—mother-daughter, husband-wife, father-son, loved-lover—and the question of what is right versus what is moral. At the heart of the story are spirited Maggie Spence and her aloof, mysterious mother, Juliet, who's been accused of accidentally poisoning the village vicar. When Deborah St. James and her forensic scientist husband, Simon, visit the Spences' Lancashire village, they hear complaints from the locals that the murder investigation was mishandled, leaving critical questions unanswered and arousing suspicions of a cover-up. When St. James asks his old friend [Detective Inspector Thomas] Lynley to help investigate further, they find that the truth is infinitely complex. . . . This powerful and moving story won't be easily forgotten." Booklist

Payment in blood. Bantam Bks. 1989 312p o.p.

LC 89-426

Available Thorndike Press large print edition

"On a country estate in Scotland, a troupe of actors has gathered to read through a new play. Alas, by dawn the playwright is found dead, impaled on a dirk, and by the time Scotland Yard arrives, the script has been burned and untold other clues have been disturbed. Inspector Thomas Lynley and his rebellious, class-conscious assistant, Sergeant Barbara Havers, have been assigned to the case. The presence of a woman Lynley loves adds complications to his police procedure, and further intrigue emerges within the marital and extramarital relations of the troupe's members. Red herrings abound in this intricate, finely drawn suspense story, which offers much more than the average locked-room mystery." Booklist

Playing for the Ashes. Bantam Bks. 1994 624p $21.95

ISBN 0-553-09262-6   LC 93-50153

Also available Thorndike Press large print edition

"After cricket star Kenneth Fleming is found asphyxiated in a burned cottage on the estate of Miriam Whitelaw, his patron, [Detective Inspector Thomas] Lynley and Havers, with local Detective Inspector Isabelle Ardery, look into the victim's tangled domestic affairs." Publ Wkly

"There's more to think about in George's story than simply whodunit. Readers will be astounded by the ease with which she weaves complex relationships and provocative moral, emotional, and ethical questions into the compelling plot." Booklist

A suitable vengeance. Bantam Bks. 1991 371p o.p.

LC 91-10575

Available Thorndike Press large print edition

When Thomas Lynley, eighth earl of Asherton and a detective inspector of New Scotland Yard, brings his fiancée Deborah Cotton to Cornwall to meet his widowed mother they become embroiled in a series of local murders

Well-schooled in murder. Bantam Bks. 1990 356p $17.95

ISBN 0-553-07000-2   LC 90-117

Thomas Lynley "and Sergeant Havers focus their prodigious talents on uncovering the murderer of a young boy from an exclusive independent school near London. While author George necessarily centers the plot on solving the case, she adroitly plumbs the emotional and psychological depths of fully fleshed characters coping with various forms of personal stress in addition to the murder." Libr J

George, Margaret

Mary Queen of Scotland and the Isles; a novel. St. Martin's Press 1992 870p $24.95

ISBN 0-312-08262-2   LC 92-20975

This biographical novel is set "against the bloody turmoil of the 16th century's religious wars, in which decadence alternates with penitence, persecution and piety. From the luxury of her upbringing in a French palace to the harshness of her later years in Scotland's fortresses and England's royal prisons, Mary lives a tragic

George, Margaret—*Continued*
life. Her syphilitic drunkard husband plans her murder;
her true love is thrown into a dungeon, shackled and
left to rot; her brother and her trusted advisers betray
her repeatedly; the Pope condemns her; and her last
hope, her cousin, Queen Elizabeth, locks her away for
almost 20 years until finally ordering her execution." NY
Times Book Rev
"George enhances fact with both accurate and colorful
embroidery, and the result is a huge but not cumbersome
novel." Booklist

Giardina, Denise, 1951-
The unquiet earth; a novel. Norton 1992
367p $22.95

ISBN 0-393-03096-2   LC 91-46495

This sequel to Storming heaven (1987) focuses on
"West Virginia coal miners from the Depression into the
1990s. Union organizer Dillon Freeman fights against the
increasingly sophisticated tactics of the coal company
while he struggles with his feelings for his cousin Rachel
Honaker. She crosses over into 'enemy territory' when
she becomes entangled with company men, but continues
to help her family and friends as a county public health
nurse. Rachel's daughter Jackie learns of a world beyond
Blackberry Creek when she meets Tom, a priest from
the Peace Corps, who seeks to organize a food co-op
and later works for social justice in Honduras." Libr J
"Narrated in four primary and three lesser voices, this
compelling saga starkly portrays the mining families'
symbiotic, spiritual relationship with nature and their
helplessness in dealing with the ruthless men who control
their lives." Publ Wkly

Gibbons, Kaye, 1960-
Charms for the easy life. Putnam 1992
254p $19.95

ISBN 0-399-13791-2   LC 92-40690

This novel "concerns three generations of strong
Southern women: a grandmother who heals with herbs
and native wisdom, a mother passionately in love with
the wrong man, and the daughter who narrates this tale."
Libr J
"A touching picture of female bonding and solidarity.
Related with the simple, tart economy of a folktale, the
narrative brims with wisdom and superstition, with
Southern manners and insights into human nature." Publ
Wkly

Ellen Foster; a novel. Algonquin Bks. 1987
146p $11.95

ISBN 0-912697-52-0   LC 86-22136

A "novel narrated by an adolescent girl, Ellen, who
relates the day-to-day experiences she endured as a child
in a troubled family. Ellen's mother died young, her
father was abusive, her other relatives were equally bad;
it wasn't until she was taken into a foster home that
she found the sort of peace and freedom to be innocent
that most normal childhoods afford." Booklist
"What might have been grim, melodramatic material
in the hands of a less talented author is instead filled
with lively humor, . . . compassion and intimacy. This
short novel focuses on Ellen's strengths rather than her
victimization, presenting a memorable heroine who
rescues herself." N Y Times Book Rev

A virtuous woman. Algonquin Bks. 1989
158p $13.95

ISBN 0-945575-09-2   LC 88-22026
Also available G.K. Hall large print edition

"Jack Stokes and Ruby Pitt weave this strong, tightly
knit love story in alternating chapters that begin when
Jack, grieving over Ruby's death four months earlier,
evokes the past. In flashbacks, the two richly cadenced
Southern voices explore their vastly differing backgrounds, troubled histories and their unlikely but loving
marriage." Publ Wkly
"A subtle, evocative, and romantic novel." Booklist

Gibson, William, 1948-
Virtual light. Bantam Bks. 1993 325p
$21.95

ISBN 0-553-07499-7   LC 93-7150

This novel focuses on "two young people in a near-
future San Francisco, a bike messenger named Chevette
and a security guard named Rydell, who may actually
have a flesh-and-blood future of their own, together.
Chevette, whose bike is moderately high-tech, gets her
hands on a pair of super-high-tech sunglasses, which contain secrets that some powerful people are willing to kill
for. Rydell, who discovers to his regret that he is working for the same people, eventually calls on a shadowy
band of hackers for help." N Y Times Book Rev
"Rydell and Chevette are sympathetic without being
as well-drawn as one would like. On the other hand,
besides being a fun read, 'Virtual Light' performs the
valuable service of bringing Gibson's social concepts into
higher resolution." Christ Sci Monit

Gide, André, 1869-1951
Nobel Prize in literature, 1947
The counterfeiters (Les faux-monnayeurs);
translated from the French of André Gide
by Dorothy Bussy. Knopf 1927 365p o.p.
Buccaneer Bks. reprint available $18.95
(ISBN 0-89966-957-3)
Original French edition, 1925
"The novelist Edouard keeps a journal of events in
order to write a novel about the nature of reality. The
intrigues of a gang of counterfeiters symbolize the 'counterfeit' personalities with which people disguise themselves to conform hypocritically to convention or to
deceive themselves. The adolescent boys Bernard
Profitendieu and Olivier Molinier, having left home in
order to be free to find and develop their true selves,
encounter many varieties of hyprocrisy and self-deception
in human relationships and barely escape falling into
such poses themselves. Both begin by seeking a close
emotional tie with Edouard. Each, however, comes to
recognize that Edouard is inadequate as an ideal for
emulation, particularly when the novelist cannot recognize
the psychological reality of the schoolboy Boris' useless
suicide, which is an indirect result of the counterfeiters'
machinations." Reader's Ency. 3d edition

The immoralist; translated by Richard
Howard. Modern Lib. 1984 c1970 171p
$12.50

ISBN 0-394-60500-4   LC 83-42856

Gide, André, 1869-1951—*Continued*

Original French edition, 1902. First United States edition, translated by Dorothy Bussy, published 1930 by Knopf; this translation first published 1970 by Knopf

"Michel takes his bride, Marceline, to North Africa, where he develops tuberculosis and becomes hyperconscious of physical sensations, particularly of his attraction to young Arab boys. Back on his French estate after being cured, he is encouraged by his friend Ménalque to rise above conventional good and evil and give free rein to all his passions. When Marceline falls ill with the tuberculosis she caught while nursing him, he takes her south. He neglects her demands on him more and more, however, in order to keep himself free, since his new doctrine demands that the weak be suppressed if necessary for the preservation of the strong. She dies, and he, guilt-ridden and debilitated by his excesses, tries to justify his conduct to a group of friends." Reader's Ency. 3d edition

Strait is the gate (La porte étroite); translated from the French by Dorothy Bussy. Knopf 1924 231p o.p. Bentley reprint available $18 (ISBN 0-8376-0453-2)

Original French edition, 1907

"Jerome woos his cousin Alissa, but, although she accepts and returns his spiritual love, she will not marry him. Alissa says that she prefers to please God by sacrificing her own worldly happiness to that of her sister, but she is fearful, too, of passion. When the sister no longer needs her sacrifice, Alissa fears that God does not think her capable of such holy selfishness and says she must continue to renounce her own happiness—and Jerome's—in order to prove her sincerity. She dies without even coming close to the mystic joy she sought." Reader's Ency. 3d edition

Gifford, Thomas, 1937-

The Glendower legacy; a novel. Putnam 1978 321p o.p.

LC 78-9818

"When the head of Russia's KGB learns of a document proving George Washington a traitor, he plans to use it in a joke against his CIA counterpart. But the agents assigned to find the document don't know it's all in fun and the action becomes deadly for Harvard professor Colin Chandler who is believed to possess the 200-year-old paper. After two people are murdered, Chandler turns to TV-newswoman Polly Bishop for aid. Together they are chased by both KGB and CIA agents who battle each other without knowing what they are after. . . . [A] masterful, irony-filled espionage thriller." Publ Wkly

Gilbert, Michael, 1912-

The black seraphim. Harper & Row 1984 216p o.p.

LC 83-48020

"Dr. James Pirie Scotland, an overworked London pathologist, takes a holiday in the quiet village of Melchester. What he finds, however, is a town embroiled in real estate scandals, with the local cathedral as the focal point of dissension. When the archdeacon dies suddenly, Dr. Scotland disagrees with the coroner's verdict of influenza and investigates a murder." Booklist

The author provides a "likable hero (complete with love interest) and an entertaining, if guessable, murder." Wilson Libr Bull

The empty house. Harper & Row 1979 c1978 245p o.p.

LC 78-69501

"A Joan Kahn book"

First published 1978 in the United Kingdom

"A scientist, a specialist in genetics, blackmailed by the British government into working in a secret laboratory, may have been killed in an accident. An investigator for an insurance firm begins to think that the man has hidden himself, a belief confirmed when a colleague is gruesomely killed after telling of horrifying discoveries. British intelligence then steps in." Libr J

"This is Michael Gilbert at his best: he knows exactly what he is trying to do, and achieves it triumphantly; a solid plot, an intelligent, civilized and witty style, a sympathetic hero, a good West Country background, and a narrative that is intriguing down to the last comma." Times Lit Suppl

The killing of Katie Steelstock. Harper & Row 1980 293p o.p.

LC 79-3409

"A Joan Kahn book"

"Local girl makes good only to be murdered in her hometown. The town of Hannington, England, has one claim to fame; popular TV singer and personality Katie Steelstock. On a visit home, Katie attends a dance, slips out to meet someone, and is discovered later with her head smashed in. An investigation begins, with conflict quickly developing between local Detective Sergeant Ian McCourt and Scotland Yard Chief Superintendent Charlie Knott. Surprises and jolts abound with the story ending in an attempted murder and yet another mystery." Booklist

Gilbert, R. A.

(comp) The Oxford book of English ghost stories. See The Oxford book of English ghost stories

Gilchrist, Ellen, 1935-

The Anna papers; a novel. Little, Brown 1988 277p o.p.

LC 88-12994

This "novel stars Anna Hand, a much-loved, often-divorced writer with terminal cancer. . . . While Anna is not very likable, being self-absorbed, spoiled, and prone to manipulative over-involvement in the lives of her relatives, she is colorful and vital. Childless herself, she works hard to connect with two of her nieces, one pampered, the other unacknowledged by the family. When her illness becomes serious, she leaves lovers and family, opting for suicide. Stuffy sister Helen serves as Anna's literary co-executor, discovering and absorbing some of Anna's free-living style. Good storytelling and memorable people, but not very substantial and often choppy." Libr J

Giles, Janice Holt, 1909-1979

The enduring hills. University Press of Ky. 1988 c1971 256p $28

ISBN 0-8131-1673-2   LC 88-17304

First published 1950 by Westminster Press; this is a reissue of the 1971 Houghton Mifflin edition

The Kentucky mountains around Piney Ridge were home to Hod Pierce, but he longed to explore the world

Giles, Janice Holt, 1909-1979—*Continued*

beyond. He set out once but was called back by his father's illness. The next escape was successful, but this time it was to join a war which would keep him away from Piney Ridge and the people he loved for a long time

Hannah Fowler; with a foreword by Dianne Watkins. University Press of Ky. 1992 219p $28

ISBN 0-8131-1793-3   LC 92-14269

This is a reissue of the title first published 1956 by Houghton Mifflin

Hannah Moore and her father were on their way to Boonesborough in 1778 when Samuel got blood poisoning and died. A chance meeting with a frontiersman took Hannah on to Logan's Fort. There she married and went with her husband to make their own home. Capture by the Indians and an escape are part of the story

Gill, B. M.

Nursery crimes. Scribner 1987 c1986 194p o.p.

LC 86-29776

First published 1986 in the United Kingdom

"Isn't it strange that violent death seems to surround sweet-looking Zanny Moncrief from the time she's a mere child to the brink of young womanhood? Her parents don't want to admit that Zanny has a hand in the murders going on around her—but she does, she definitely does! This is a . . . psychological suspense novel set in Wales in the 1940s." Booklist

"Gill's support characters, which include Zanny's passionate but ineffectual parents and the orphaned evacuee who trades her knowledge of Zanny's crimes for a good education, are absorbing (if not particularly praiseworthy) mortals. Gill uses them well, not only to further her plot, but also to explore class differences in Britain during and just after World War II and to study the inner life of children in a *most* unsentimental way." Wilson Libr Bull

Seminar for murder. Scribner 1986 c1985 $13.95

ISBN 0-684-18651-9   LC 85-24986

First published 1985 in the United Kingdom

This "murder mystery is set at a mystery writers' convention in a Victorian mansion near Bristol. Detective Chief Inspector Tom Maybridge . . . has been invited to speak to the members of the Golden Guillotine Club. His lecture ends with a mild chide: 'Don't let your murders be slipshod. Try to make them a fine art.' The next day, Sir Godfrey Grant, a renowned but declining author, is found dead, a meat skewer in his neck and a note tacked nearby: 'Fault This Murder, Detective Chief Inspector Maybridge, If You Can.' Maybridge, embarrassed by the murderer's taunt, embarks on an investigation of devilishly clever suspects." Booklist

Time and time again. Scribner 1990 c1989 174p o.p.

LC 89-28046

First published 1989 in the United Kingdom

"In this psychological thriller, Maeve Barclay, after serving an 18-month prison term for injuring a policeman during a demonstration, finds herself gradually being drawn into the world of petty crime and violence of one of her former cellmates." Booklist

"The claustrophobic chambers of Maeve's troubled mind, along with the walking-underwater pace of events, make this novel a murkier read than its predecessors. But it presents us with another character of consequence and confirms Ms. Gill's sure skills as a genre author of unusual depth and sensitivity." N Y Times Book Rev

Gill, Bartholomew, 1943-

The death of a Joyce scholar; a Peter McGarr mystery. Morrow 1989 331p o.p.

LC 88-38560

"McGarr, chief superintendent of Dublin's murder squad, is faced with the brutal annihilation of a professor of English literature at Dublin's Trinity College, one Kevin Coyle. Not only was Coyle an expert on the work of James Joyce, he also had hired himself out on the day of his murder to narrate a guided tour of the Dublin neighborhoods that provide the setting for Joyce's *Ulysses*. Coyle had an odd wife—and her friends, to McGarr, seem even odder—and he was known to have aroused contention among the Trinity community for both personal and professional reasons. Investigating the suspects leaves McGarr up to his eyeballs in scholarly tomes and academic politics." Booklist

"An affectionate acquaintance with Joyce's Dubliners adds considerably to the pleasures of this profoundly clever literary mystery, the better to appreciate its careful Joycean parallels in plot and character." N Y Times Book Rev

The death of love; a Peter McGarr mystery. Morrow 1992 320p $20

ISBN 0-688-08715-9   LC 91-27573

"Irish policeman Peter McGarr goes to the Irish resort of Parknasilla to determine whether the digitalis-induced death of a famous and beloved philanthropist, about to turn politician, was planned or accidental. With the aid of his much-younger wife and several undercover detectives, McGarr questions the man's doctor, his athletic ex-wife, his mistress/assistant, and several powerful politicians." Libr J

"Mr. Gill has constructed a devilishly intricate plot to tell this story; but typical of him, he manages to make the moral dilemma even more painful to resolve." N Y Times Book Rev

Death on a cold, wild river; a Peter McGarr mystery. Morrow 1993 251p $20

ISBN 0-688-12881-5   LC 93-7729

"In the opening scene Nellie Millar, 'the best fisher bar none in all of Ireland,' meets her picturesque death while casting for trophy salmon in the swollen floodwaters of the Owenea River. Peter McGarr, the chief of Dublin's murder squad and Nellie's former lover, carries his grief to the village in Donegal where she is being waked, only to discover that the drowning was no accident." N Y Times Book Rev

"Gill writes well, setting the tone for introspective passages with evocations of Ireland's wild coastal landscape on one page, while amusing us with witty pub banter on another. . . Unpredictable, philosophical, funny, and ever so satisfying." Booklist

McGarr and the legacy of a woman scorned. Viking 1986 218p o.p.

LC 85-40627

Gill, Bartholomew, 1943-—*Continued*

"McGarr, on holiday in the Irish county of Wexford, is called in to investigate the death of an old woman, Fionnuala Walton, found with her neck broken at the bottom of the stairs in a gloomy Edwardian mansion. Although the locals are quick to dismiss the fall as an accident, McGarr senses murder." Booklist

"Integral to the daring plot are the author's amazing descriptions of ancient Irish traditions still observed today." Publ Wkly

McGarr on the Cliffs of Moher. Scribner 1978 246p o.p.

LC 78-2645

"McGarr is chief inspector of detectives of the Irish police, and the cliffs of Moher are where the body of May Quirk was found. May, dead of a pitchfork wound, was a local girl (County Clare) who had gone to New York and become a top investigative reporter on the 'News.' What was she doing back in Ireland? Was she on the track of another big story? Would it have something to do with American financing of the I.R.A.? McGarr . . . is the sort of man who asks the right questions and manages always to be in the right (and often risky) place." New Yorker

Gilliatt, Penelope

22 stories. Dodd, Mead 1986 319p o.p.
LC 86-6307

Analyzed in Short story index

Contents: Fred and Arthur; Come back if it doesn't get better; Known for her frankness; The redhead; The tactics of hunger; As we have learnt from Freud, there are no jokes; F.R.A.N.K.; Staying in bed; The position of the planets; Foreigners; Nobody's business; Splendid lives; Phone-in; Catering; Autumn of a dormouse; Stephanie, Stephen, Steph, Steve; Teeth; As is; When are you going back; Dame of the British Empire, BBC; Addio; On each other's time

Gilliat "has culled from her five previous collections of short stories 22 of the very best. With humor and soft-spokenness—yet eschewing abrasive irony and inconclusive plots—Gilliatt writes of the absurdities of life. Some of her stories read like condensed novels: in these cases, she tries to develop too broad a picture, rather than simply isolating a moment of the drama. But all her stories are very accessible and easy to appreciate for their depth and charm." Booklist

Gilman, Charlotte Perkins, 1860-1935

The Charlotte Perkins Gilman reader; "The yellow wallpaper" and other fiction; edited and introduced by Ann J. Lane. Pantheon Bks. 1980 208p o.p. Smith, P. reprint available $23 (ISBN 0-8446-6618-1)

LC 80-7711

Analyzed in Short story index

Contents: The yellow wallpaper; When I was a witch; If I were a man; The girl in the pink hat; The cottagette; The unnatural mother; Making a change; An honest woman; Turned; The widow's might; Mr. Peebles' heart; The crux; What Diantha did; Benigna Machiavelli; Unpunished; Moving the mountain; Herland; With her in Ourland

The editor "has selected representative pieces by the early-twentieth-century American feminist socialist, including her best known (and best) quasi-autobiographical story, 'The Yellow Wallpaper,' plus excerpts from four novels and three writings about utopias." Booklist

Herland; with an introduction by Ann J. Lane. Pantheon Bks. 1979 xxiv, 147p o.p. Smith, P. reprint available $22 (ISBN 0-8446-6611-4)

"Written in 1915, Herland was serialized in Gilman's monthly magazine, 'The Forerunner.'" Introduction

"On the eve of World War I, three American male explorers stumble onto an all-female society somewhere in the distant reaches of the earth. Unable to believe their eyes, they promptly set out to find the men of the society, convinced that, since 'this is a "civilized" country . . . there must be men.' . . . [The novel examines] what is masculine and what is feminine, what is culturally learned and what is biologically determined in our society." Publisher's note

Gilman, Dorothy, 1923-

The amazing Mrs. Pollifax. Doubleday 1970 234p o.p.

Available G.K. Hall large print edition

Mrs. Emily Pollifax, widow and grandmother, takes on international espionage at the request of the C.I.A. in this spy adventure. The scene is Istanbul where Mrs. Pollifax must help a double agent escape. That she does, outwitting the enemy with her own special brand of logic

Caravan. Doubleday 1992 263p o.p.

LC 91-39459

Available Thorndike Press large print edition

"Born into a carnival family at the turn of the 20th century, 16-year-old Caressa Horvath finds her life taking a dramatic turn when she attempts to rob Jacob Bowman, a rich, eccentric anthropologist 20 years her senior. [Undaunted] by their unconventional introduction, he marries her, and they travel to Tripoli to explore the Sahara Desert. Nomadic Tuaregs attack their caravan but spare Caressa's life, launching her three-year adventure in the desert, where she befriends a young boy named Bakuli, gets sold into slavery, and eventually meets her great love, a wandering Scotsman named Jared MacKay." Libr J

"The story is as much a lesson on desert culture as a fine adventure saga and a love story with a delightful, fateful twist." Booklist

The elusive Mrs. Pollifax. Doubleday 1971 240p o.p.

Mrs. Pollifax "the genteel grandmother-heroine swings into action for the CIA by transporting in her hat some forged passports to the Bulgarian underground which turns out to be a group of five amateurs. In her travels Mrs. Pollifax meets some young Americans, one of whom is ostensibly imprisoned for espionage but actually held for ransom, and Mrs. Pollifax involves the underground and a paid informer in a daring rescue plan. Amusing spy adventure with more appeal for readers of light fiction than for espionage buffs." Booklist

Incident at Badamya. Doubleday 1989 204p o.p.

LC 88-16171

"The time is 1950, the place a Burmese village where Genevieve Ferris is orphaned at age 16. Taking the first step toward returning to her native America, Gen meets Neil Hamlin, an undercover agent from the U.S. sought

Gilman, Dorothy, 1923-—*Continued*
by communist soldiers. Gen and Neil become partners, slipping through the jungle, trying to reach the river boat headed for Rangoon, but the girl is alone when she's grabbed by troops under General Wang. Wang's prisoners include a motley group of men and women, all with secrets they gradually disclose to each other during the long days of captivity." Publ Wkly

"If the rigors of captivity seem rather tame, characters emerge distinctly against the authentic background, and there are some nice flashes of excitement when the group escapes, as well as a pleasant element of last-minute surprise." Booklist

Mrs. Pollifax and the Golden Triangle. Doubleday 1988 184p o.p.

LC 87-13082

Available Thorndike Press large print edition

"Emily Reed-Pollifax and her husband, Curtis Reed, have planned a simple, relaxing vacation to Thailand. Their plans are slightly altered when Mr. Carstairs, Emily's boss at the CIA, receives a cryptic message from a mysterious operative in a small Thai village. He asks the pair of senior citizens to pick up a parcel of significant information while enjoying their trip. . . . Gilman is a pro at pacing her fiction, springing exciting surprises and timely coincidences to the very end." Booklist

Mrs. Pollifax and the Hong Kong Buddha. Doubleday 1985 181p o.p.

LC 85-4335

In this novel Mrs. Pollifax, the widow cum CIA operative is in "Hong Kong, and her assignment is to contact a young Chinese, whom she rescued in her previous mission. Intending to get a line on an apparently turncoat agent, she finds that a psychic and a cat-burglar-turned-Interpol-agent (and good friend) are on the same trail. What they turn up, besides murder, is a group of terrorists with a plan to take over and destroy Hong Kong." Booklist

Mrs. Pollifax and the second thief. Doubleday 1993 201p $20

ISBN 0-385-47109-2   LC 93-12160

Also available G.K. Hall large print edition

In this mystery "the redoubtable CIA operative and New Jersey grandmother finds herself in Sicily, where she helps a former colleague who finds himself in danger after agreeing to authenticate a document bearing Julius Caesar's signature." Libr J

"Gilman's smooth storytelling and slyly comic tone make it easy for readers to overlook a somewhat untidy ending." Publ Wkly

Mrs. Pollifax and the whirling dervish. Doubleday 1990 196p o.p.

LC 89-25796

Available G.K. Hall large print edition

"Mrs. Pollifax's present assignment is to pose as the aunt of a C.I.A. agent while the two, in the guise of tourists, verify the bona fides of the informants, matching faces to photographs. To find the seven, Mrs. Pollifax and her escort are expected to spend a week traversing the desert and mountain areas that lie between Fez and the Algerian border. No sooner do they begin their mission than the first informant is murdered—and Mrs. Pollifax herself is in danger of becoming the killer's next victim." N Y Times Book Rev

"The countryside is depicted in great detail, and so are the native people. Gilman's eye for background matches her marvelous sense of adventure." Booklist

Mrs. Pollifax on safari. Doubleday 1977 182p o.p.

Grandmotherly Emily Pollifax is "assigned by the CIA to join a safari in Zambia and take snapshots of others in the group. The intelligence agents hope one of the pictures will lead them to the identity of the international terrorist known only as Aristotle. The 'Unexpected Mrs. Pollifax' finds some unattractive people among the travelers but also a love interest, Cyrus Reed. When Emily is kidnapped and nearly killed, Cyrus rescues her and both are sure they know who Aristotle is. This is a mistake, they discover, when they spot another of their companions aiming a gun at the president of Zambia." Publ Wkly

Mrs. Pollifax on the China station. Doubleday 1983 184p o.p.

LC 82-45972

"Mrs. Pollifax, the widow whose services are often indispensable to the CIA, heads for China to pick up information leading to the escape of an engineer. Vibrant descriptions of China and apt characterizations of fellow travelers add sparkle to a complicated plot involving a double agent, one real murder, a staged death, and the usual series of unforeseen events. Her final interview with the local security chief shows Mrs. Pollifax at her most innocent and provides a tidy conclusion." Libr J

A palm for Mrs. Pollifax. Doubleday 1973 226p o.p.

Available G.K. Hall large print edition

Emily Pollifax "registers as a guest at a posh resort-clinic in Switzerland where the C.I.A. thinks some stolen plutonium has been hidden. In the course of her investigation Mrs. Pollifax discovers the murdered body of her Interpol contact, meets a charming jewel thief who becomes her ally, befriends a frightened little boy who is the son of a leader in a Middle East nation, and escapes through a latrine chute from a mountain top castle where she and the boy are hiding from the killers who intend to use the plutonium to upset the balance of power in the Middle East." Booklist

The tightrope walker. Doubleday 1979 186p o.p.

LC 78-20006

"Inside a hurdy-gurdy among the items in an antique shop she buys, Amelia finds a note by a woman named Hannah. The writer says that 'faceless ones' are keeping her prisoner, have forced her to sign a paper and are about to murder her. With a friend, Joe, Amelia traces the hurdy-gurdy to a small Maine town. Official records reveal that rich, philanthropic Hannah Meerloo had died in a seeming accident, after making a suspicious new will. Circumstances separate the two investigators and leave Amelia alone, vulnerable to the 'faceless ones,' bent on killing her to keep their old crime covered up." Publ Wkly

The unexpected Mrs. Pollifax. Doubleday 1966 216p o.p. Buccaneer Bks. reprint available $22.95 (ISBN 0-89966-873-9)

"Published for the Crime Club"

A "tale of espionage with the chase in Mexico and through the mountains of Albania. Emily Pollifax, a widow of 63, was startled by her doctor's suggestion that the cure for her depression was a job. The only career

Gilman, Dorothy, 1923-—*Continued*

that inspired Emily was spying, and despite her lack of qualifications, off she went to CIA headquarters in Langly, Virginia, to apply. How she became a routine courier, and why unexpected developments brought into play every scrap of skill and knowledge she had acquired in her former secure life, is an exciting discovery for the reader." Libr J

Gipson, Frederick Benjamin, 1903-1973

Old Yeller; [by] Fred Gipson; drawings by Carl Burger. Harper & Row 1956 158p il $22

ISBN 0-06-011545-9
Also available from Buccaneer Bks.

"In the 1880s 14-year-old Travis has to take care of the farm in the Texas hill country with his ma and little brother when his father joins a cattle drive to Abilene. An ornery stray hound dog, Old Yeller, helps ward off the attacks of bears, wild hogs, and a wolf." Shapiro. Fic for Youth. 3d edition
Followed by Savage Sam

Savage Sam; [by] Fred Gipson; decorations by Carl Burger. Harper & Row 1962 214p il o.p.

This is the story of Old Yeller's son. It is set in the East Texas of the 1870's, and deals with Savage Sam's pursuit of the Apaches who have seized Travis, Little Arliss, and Lisbeth

"Although the story is more contrived than its predecessor and overemphasizes the savagery of the Indians, there is good regional background of East Texas during the 1870's and readers will enjoy the fast-paced, sometimes humorous adventure." Booklist

Giroux, E. X.

A death for a dancer. St. Martin's Press 1985 198p o.p.

LC 85-10896

"Barrister Robert Forsythe and his vigilant secretary, Miss Sanderson, are pressed by another barrister into examining a case involving a body found inconveniently in a miniature Chinese Temple on one of England's most sumptuous estates. The victim is con artist Katherine St. Croix, whose demise throws the family of Sir Amyas Dancer into giddy paroxysms of speculation that can only be relieved, claims Dancer, by a private investigator. Enter Forsythe and Sanderson and exit normalcy as the Dancer family surrounds them with their bizarrely eccentric demeanor." Booklist

Death for a dancing doll. St. Martin's Press 1991 244p o.p.

LC 90-29899

"A Thomas Dunne book"
"An idyllic expedition to pick wildflowers near a breathtaking Canadian waterfall turns tragic when a seven-year-old plummets to her death. The child's mother, wealthy Harriet Holly Pulos, blames her niece, Thalia, who was responsible for watching the little girl. Shortly thereafter, Thalia, a promising young dancer, is found dead—an apparent suicide. The bereaved grandmother suspects foul play and hires visiting London barrister/sleuth Robert Forsythe and his secretary/sidekick Abigail Sanderson." Publ Wkly

Death for a dietitian. St. Martin's Press 1988 182p o.p.

LC 87-28622

A mystery starring London barrister Robert Forsythe's secretary "Abigail 'Sandy' Sanderson. On leave from duty as her Robby's maternal secretary, Sandy joins members of a house party on an island where a game of solving a pretend murder mystery becomes real. . . . Then the chief suspect is also murdered, the group is marooned by a storm and the killer cuts the phone line. Red herrings abound in the story that nevertheless serves as a tense diversion with humorous moments leading to the brave and brainy spinster's triumph over the villain." Publ Wkly

A death for a dodo. St. Martin's Press 1993 230p $17.95

ISBN 0-312-08762-4   LC 92-42573

"A Thomas Dunne book"
"Murder in a swank English nursing home provides a neat puzzle for London barrister and criminologist Robert Forsythe, who nearly becomes a victim himself. . . . Convalescing from knee surgery in the Damien Day Health Home (known as DODO to the locals) near Hundarby, the temporarily crippled Forsythe is drawn into an oddly assorted group of well-known and powerful fellow patients. . . . Giroux's well-crafted page-turner has strong elements of suspense and careful characterization embedded in a classical setting." Publ Wkly

A death for a double. St. Martin's Press 1990 202p o.p.

LC 89-24108

"A Thomas Dunne book"
This Robert Forsythe adventure finds the "English barrister summoned to the hideously modernized country house of Anthony Funicelli, a wealthy Italian American. Funicelli is concerned about several threatening letters he has received, the last of which promises death to his young and gorgeous second wife, Lucia. When Funicelli's look-alike cousin Fredo is murdered in the house, Forsythe suspects someone mistook Fredo for Anthony. . . . All in all, a very readable English country-house mystery, effectively updated and neatly plotted." Booklist

Girzone, Joseph F.

Joshua and the children. Macmillan 1989 224p $14.95

ISBN 0-02-543945-6   LC 89-2615
Also available G.K. Hall large print edition
Sequel to Joshua (1987)
"Joshua, an unusual and attractive young man, comes to a village rent by partisan strife (e.g. Catholic vs. Protestant; guerrillas and political agitators) and immediately captures the hearts of the children, enchanting them with gentle stories and amusing sleight-of-hand until they carry his message to the adults." Publ Wkly
"A simple, moving, and inspirational parable presented in an uncomplicated fashion." Libr J

Joshua in the Holy Land. Macmillan 1992 205p o.p.

LC 92-17264

Available G.K. Hall large print edition
As this novel "opens, the simple carpenter Joshua is wandering in the desert in the Middle East. Finding a lost lamb, he returns it to its owner, the prominent sheik Ibrahim Saud, then cures a little girl in the sheik's

Girzone, Joseph F.—*Continued*

encampment of a deadly snakebite, thus gaining the Arab's eternal gratitude. Their ensuing friendship opens the possibility of success for Joshua's true mission, bringing peace to the Middle East. He unites like-minded Jews, Arabs and Christians as the Children of Peace, hoping to end strife by forming personal bonds between peoples." Publ Wkly

The shepherd. Macmillan 1990 246p $15.95

ISBN 0-02-543947-2　　　　　　LC 90-2351
Also available G.K. Hall large print edition

"On the eve of David Campbell's consecration as a Catholic bishop, he has an all-night vision that changes him from a strict observer of church law to a radical reformer." Libr J

"Girzone's story is a neat picture of where many American Catholics wish their church would head, but it may be far too unrealistically drawn to have an impact on real lives." Booklist

Glasgow, Ellen

Barren ground. Doubleday 1925 511p o.p.
Available from Amereon and P. Smith

"Dorinda Oakley, a Virginia farm girl, disappointed in love for young Jason Greylock, matures into a strong-willed, effective, and self-sustaining woman. She finds work in New York, rejects the hand of a young doctor, and returns to the family farm after her father's death. With her energy and managerial skill, and with little help from an invalid mother and lazy brother, she turns the barren ground into a successful dairy farm. Later, she weds a storekeeper in a sexless marriage of convenience and still later takes in her first love, Jason, by then a penniless drunkard. Jason soon dies." Benet's Reader's Ency of Am Lit

In this our life. Harcourt Brace & Co. 1941 467p o.p. Amereon reprint available $21.95 (ISBN 0-89190-152-3)

This novel is an analytical study of the feeling of kinship as it is manifested in the Timberlake family, decayed aristocrats living in a city in Virginia. The story of how two marriages are wrecked and a great wrong done to an innocent Black boy, is told largely as it is viewed by Asa Timberlake, sixty years of age, husband of a hypochondriac wife, father of two daughters, one utterly selfish and feminine, the other courageous and gallant but confused and unhappy. He is despised by the younger generation, but in a crisis only Asa has the moral stamina to meet the situation

Vein of iron. Harcourt Brace & Co. 1935 462p o.p.

"The Fincastle family are old Scotch Presbyterian stock who have lived for five generations in the mountain region of Virginia. An iron vein of strength and resolution in their characters has carried them through difficulties of all kinds, from the hardships of pioneering to those of the depression. The story is concerned primarily with Ada Fincastle and her love for Ralph McBride. The post-war years take the family to the city, where a few years of prosperity are followed by hard times and the familiar struggle with poverty, finally leading them back to their old home in the valley. Life brings them much trouble and sorrow, but through it all they attain a quiet happiness." Booklist

Glendinning, Victoria

The grown-ups. Knopf 1989 243p o.p.
　　　　　　　　　　　　　　LC 89-45300

"Glendinning's tale of the 'flotsam of 1980s Britain' describes the intersecting lives of three women who were once schoolmates. Her protagonists share a passion for the charismatic author-philosopher Leo Ulm. Martha has married him; Alice has married his son; and Clare observes these relationships and wonders if there is any point to marriage at all. Glendinning is caustic in her delineation of the lives of her women, bringing into stark relief their frailties and bombast." Booklist

Godden, Jon, 1906-1985

In her garden. Knopf 1981 181p o.p.
　　　　　　　　　　　　　　LC 80-19849

"Grace Maitland is a self-reliant 75-year-old widow, living in apparent contentment at Setons, the family home in Kent. But Grace is lonelier than she realizes. She falls in love with her newly hired gardener, 30-year-old Ben Halden, and tragedy results." Libr J

The author "delivers this tale as a genteel modern sketch of manners and morals in which good prevails. The writing never swerves from well-crafted simplicity." Booklist

Godden, Rumer, 1907-

The battle of the Villa Fiorita. Viking 1963 312p o.p.

A "novel about the immediate effects of their parent's divorce on two English children who run off to Italy to persuade their mother to return home. She is enjoying a premarital honeymoon, days filled with sun, golden light, quiet and love, with an English film director. The two children crash into this peaceful pattern and the battle lines are drawn, children against adults." Publ Wkly

Godden's "characters live and linger in the mind, and the very feel of golden Italy counterpoints the sharp battle in which both sides so tragically lose." Libr J

Black Narcissus. Little, Brown 1939 294p o.p.

A "story of a small group of Anglican nuns newly settled in a convent, formerly a general's pleasure palace, on a high ledge facing Himalayan winds and snows. How the strange pagan environment and unusual experiences affect each of the Sisters, and how a year's effort to teach and heal the natives come to naught is related in a portrayal impressive for its beauty, poignancy and insight." Bookmark

China Court; the hours of a country house; a novel. Viking 1961 304p o.p.
Available Thorndike Press large print edition

"When young Tracy returns from the United States to England to attend her beloved grandmother's funeral, the family country house, China Court, yields up its past in kaleidoscopic chapters patterned after the medieval Book of Hours." Bookmark

"All the peace that comes from uninterrupted order, from a sense of continuity and service, fills the pages of this book. This is a measure of Miss Godden's success, since she has juggled the time-sequence of the five generations who lived in China Court. . . . Yet the threads stay untangled and the reader unmuddled, his interest unflagging." Christ Sci Monit

Godden, Rumer, 1907-—*Continued*

An episode of sparrows. Viking 1955 247p o.p.

The sparrows of the title are the thin, wispy children of a bombed section of London. Tip Malone was almost thirteen; Lovejoy Mason was only eleven, but she was determined to have a garden. And to the surprise of people in the Square, and the joy of gentle Father Lambert, the children succeeded

"It is a deft, amusing, and touching story of a London neighborhood where wealth adjoins poverty. . . . It is a novel which rests lightly on the yearnings of childhood and the dreams of the unworldly. A false touch would tip it over, but Miss Godden stays this side of sentiment and of undue irony." Saturday Rev

The greengage summer; a novel. Viking 1958 218p o.p.

"The story tells of the summer adventures of a group of English children, in somewhat shadowed circumstances, at a second-rate hotel on the Marne, near the forest of Compiègne. . . . Their mother is taken seriously ill as they are enroute to the hotel Les Oeillets, at Vieux-Moutiers. Upon arrival, she is rushed to the hospital for a long stay. The disconcerted children are stranded at the hotel where neither the proprietress, Mademoiselle Zizi, nor her henchwoman, Mme. Corbet, want them. It is the somewhat mysterious Englishman, Eliot, apparently romantically involved with Mlle. Zizi, who takes them under his wing and casually superintends their stay." N Y Times Book Rev

"There is real evil in Miss Godden's novel as well as real good: sex and theft and even murder intrude upon her dewy world as baldly as on the daily papers. But even violence she handles with consummate delicacy. If she allows a moral to creep in, it is that we lose something valuable in gaining maturity." N Y Her Trib Books

In this house of Brede. Viking 1969 376p o.p.

Available from Amereon and Buccaneer Bks.

The author writes "about a cloistered order of English Benedictine nuns (Roman Catholic), the way of life they follow in the 20th century, the very real problems, human and spiritual, with which they must grapple, and above all, the intense inner faith that infuses everything they do. . . . Her story centers on a successful career woman in her forties who renounces the world to enter Brede monastery, and what happens to her thereafter." Publ Wkly

"The reader gets an excellent insight into the daily life, rules, and rituals of a religious order." Libr J

Pippa passes. Morrow 1994 171p $22

ISBN 0-688-13397-5　　　　　LC 94-18336

Also available Thorndike Press large print edition

"Pippa Fane, is the youngest member of the Midlands City Ballet. Chosen to go with the company on its Italian tour, she becomes fascinated with Venice, confused by romantic overtures from admirers of both sexes, and challenged by the demands of her dancing troupe." Libr J

"In less able hands, these highly romantic goings-on would seem contrived, but Godden's graceful storytelling keeps readers enthralled, with gorgeous Venice and the nitty-gritty of the dance troupe's routine providing a convincing backdrop for her winsome ingenue." Publ Wkly

Thursday's children. Viking 1984 249p o.p.

　　　　　　　　　　　　　　　　　LC 83-40252

Available G.K. Hall large print edition

"Doone Penny, the sixth, the last and almost unwanted son of a London greengrocer and his starstruck wife, is literally born to dance. . . . At home, the center of attention is his only sister, the beautiful Crystal, for whom his mother, a one-time Gaiety girl, has dreams of theatrical grandeur. Following in Crystal's wake to dance classes, the eight-year-old endures the taunts of his macho brothers and the puzzlement of his tradesman father. Doone not only survives but absorbs Crystal's treacheries and other hardships to make his mark as an incandescent dancer." Publ Wkly

The author's "compassion and perceptions remain at perfect pitch. She obviously knows and cares about her children, their parents, the inbred world of ballet aspirants and principal dancers, in this behind-the-scenes fiction. If at times she seems to be speaking to children, perhaps she is addressing the child in each of us." Best Sellers

Godey, John, 1912-

The taking of Pelham one two three. Putnam 1973 316p o.p. Amereon reprint available $22.95 (ISBN 0-88411-649-2)

A suspense novel about a "New York subway train that is hijacked by four desperate men who threaten to murder sixteen passengers unless the mayor pays $1 million ransom. . . . Ryder, the brain behind the caper, is an amoral, asexual fatalist who killed for country in Vietnam and for profit as a mercenary in the Congo and Biafra. Longman, bitter at being sacked from his subway-motorman job, is willing to exploit his intimate knowledge of the transit system. Steever is a . . . hood who follows orders and Welcome is a surly Mafia reject who doesn't." Newsweek

"Brutally realistic and coarse in its details and language, but will be popular with suspense story readers." Booklist

Godwin, Gail, 1937-

Father Melancholy's daughter. Morrow 1991 404p o.p.

　　　　　　　　　　　　　　　　　LC 90-13490

Available Thorndike Press large print edition

This "novel begins in the 1970s in a small Virginia town. Ruth, the Episcopal minister's young wife, leaves her husband and six-year-old daughter Margaret to pursue unfulfilled dreams that she had forsaken by marrying. Margaret and her idealistic father, a victim of recurring depression, find solace in each other as astounded church members look on. The child becomes the parent, assuming the burden of her father's unhappiness. Now, 16 years later and facing her own adulthood, she must come to terms with her conflicted past." Libr J

This novel "does have a number of real satisfactions, namely the characters that surround Margaret and her father. . . . Gail Godwin is almost Chaucerian in her delivery of these people." N Y Times Book Rev

The finishing school. Viking 1985 322p o.p.

　　　　　　　　　　　　　　　　　LC 84-40069

Godwin, Gail, 1937-—*Continued*

"Fourteen, yearning to grow up, and grieving for the world of Southern gentility she left behind when her widowed mother moved them up north to live with a determinedly middle-class aunt, Justin Stokes 'falls in love' that first summer in rural New York. Ursula DeVane, who shares the neighboring old mansion with her reclusive pianist brother, is 44, a sophisticated bohemian who dazzles . . . Justin with her worldliness and her attentions. A cabin in the woods becomes Justin's 'finishing school' as the . . . tale of Ursula's mysterious past unfolds. . . . [This story is] told from the point of view of a grown-up Justin, nearly 30 years later." Libr J

"'The Finishing School' is a strikingly accurate examination of the affinity between adolescence and middle age." N Y Times Book Rev

The good husband. Ballantine Bks. 1994 468p $22.95

ISBN 0-345-37243-3   LC 94-5651

Death "is the metaphorical 'good husband' whom brilliant professor Magda Danvers invokes as she lies dying, a process in which she participates with the same intellectual zest she has brought to her scholarship. While her body wastes away from cancer, she is devotedly tended by her own 'good husband,' Francis Lake, a former seminarian 12 years her junior. They are an unlikely pair: self-effacing Francis is content in his role as house husband and general factotum to flamboyant, iconoclastic Magda. In contrast, the union of Alice and Hugo Henry should constitute marital serenity. Hugo is a 50ish Southern novelist temporarily occupying a chair at Aurelia College; Alice is the empathetic editor who shepherded to publication the work on which his celebrity rests. Yet an icy chill has descended between them after the loss, at birth, of their son. And Hugo's prickly abrasiveness has been exacerbated by writer's block." Publ Wkly

"Godwin's intensely drawn characters are vividly portrayed during the most intimate times of love, marriage, and death." Libr J

A mother and two daughters. Viking 1982 564p o.p.

LC 81-65286

"Suddenly widowed Nell Strickland and her two daughters, reunited in grief, are all on the verge of change as the story begins. Bohemian Cate is twice divorced, almost 40, out of a teaching job and threatened by losses, while younger Lydia, who just left her husband, is winning: a college degree, a new lover, and fame as a TV personality. Ambivalent about accommodation and possibility but 'hospitable . . . to whatever came next,' each has created herself anew by the end. The North Carolina setting is as precisely evoked as [are] the many unusual, amusing characters." Libr J

Mr. Bedford

In Godwin, G. Mr. Bedford and the muses p1-104

Mr. Bedford and the muses. Viking 1983 229p o.p.

LC 83-47870

Analyzed in Short story index
Contents: Mr. Bedford; A father's pleasures; Amanuensis; St. John; The angry-year; A cultural exchange

"The longest story in this collection concerns itself with a group of young people living as boarders in London with an American couple of mysterious background. Each character is most interestingly described and the tensions and interrelationships among them keep the story moving. In other stories a writer is suddenly visited by a young girl who offers her services in the writer's home with a surprising development; a father's love for his son comes into conflict with his attraction to his son's friend; an author finds his life affected by the presence in his village of a woman with the same name as his. Godwin's writing is graceful and humorous." Shapiro. Fic for Youth. 3d edition

The odd woman. Knopf 1974 419p o.p.

This story follows a week in the life of a teacher at a Midwestern university "that involves a trip home for her grandmother's funeral, forces her to reassess what is happening, and brings stabbing insights into her relationships with the people she knows and loves. Her role as a woman and as a person is what's at stake here. Jane finds she must face herself, her tenuous affair with an art historian, the very married Gabriel. The week of Jane's decision, the week of physical and mental traveling brings growth and the idea of reshaping her life." Publ Wkly

A Southern family. Morrow 1987 540p o.p.

LC 87-12381

This novel begins with a visit by Clare Campion, a successful novelist living in New York City, to her family, the Quicks, in Mountain City, North Carolina. During her visit, Clare's half brother Theo dies violently. The book then "focuses separately on each member of the Quick family, as well as some outside it. . . . Characters talk and think out their perceptions of Theo and themselves." N Y Times Book Rev

"Gail Godwin is something of a rarity today—a writer who not only maintains an elegant and suspenseful pace, but also has something worth saying and worth thinking about." Christ Sci Monit

Violet Clay. Knopf 1978 324p o.p.

LC 77-12890

"Violet Clay, when first we meet her, is eking out a New York living doing cover portraits for paperback Gothics. Behind her lie a quasi-romantic southern childhood, replete with half truths insofar as her family is concerned, a timorous marriage without meaning. Violet lives a great deal of the time in vague dreams of becoming a 'real' painter, slipping in and out of love affairs that are more funny and rueful than anything else. Then the uncle she has worshipped all her life kills himself. She must pick up the pieces, come to terms with the mess he has made of his life and the ever-so-gentlemanly southern way he has had of hiding reality from himself and everyone else. In doing so she at last encounters her own identity and the future that really does lie ahead for her. 'Feminist' in the truest sense of word, without being strident—just tough-minded and honest—this is good Godwin." Publ Wkly

Goethe, Johann Wolfgang von, 1749-1832

Novella

In Goethe, J. W. von. The sorrows of young Werther, and Novella p169-201

Goethe, Johann Wolfgang von, 1749-1832
—Continued

The sorrows of young Werther

In Goethe, J. W. von. The sorrows of young Werther, and Novella p1-167

The sorrows of young Werther, and Novella; translated by Elizabeth Mayer and Louise Brogan; poems translated by W. H. Auden; foreword by W. H. Auden. Modern Lib. 1993 c1971 xx, 201p $13.50

ISBN 0-679-60064-7   LC 93-5007

A translation of two of Goethe's works, originally published 1774 and 1828 respectively; this is a reissue of the 1971 edition published by Random House

"Werther is a sensitive artist, ill at ease in society and hopelessly in love with Charlotte, who is engaged to someone else. This novel, with the eventual suicide of the hero, caused a sensation throughout Europe." Oxford Companion to Engl Lit

Novella, is an example of a specific literary genre, the idyll. A tame tiger which escapes during a fire pursues a princess and is killed. The animal trainer and his family, lamenting its death, persuade the prince, who has been out hunting a lion, to let them tame that animal rather than kill it. According to W. H. Auden it is "a parable about the relation between wild nature and human craft"

Gogol', Nikolaï Vasil'evich, 1809-1852

The overcoat, and other tales of good and evil; [by] Nikolai V. Gogol; translated with an introduction by David Magarshack. Norton 1965 c1957 271p o.p.

Available from Amereon and Bentley

Analyzed in Short story index

This collection was first published 1957 in paperback by Doubleday with title: Tales of good and evil

Contents: The terrible vengeance; Ivan Fyodorovich Shponka and his aunt; The portrait; Nevsky Avenue; The nose; The overcoat

Gold, Herbert, 1924-

Family; a novel in the form of a memoir. Arbor House 1981 192p o.p.

LC 81-66964

The author "continues the tribute to his parents that was begun with 'Fathers'. In the present volume, the image of the first-generation Jewish mother trying to impose her Old World standards of love on her American-born son is poignant, occasionally embarrassing, but always affectionate. . . . In the final pages the now middle-aged son is finally willing and able to accept his mother on her own terms." Libr J

Fathers. Random House 1967 c1966 308p o.p.

"Sam Gold, adopting that surname as a symbol of what he hopes to find in America, leaves the old country. He struggles through the Depression and fights racketeers in order to gain some economic security for his family in Cleveland, Ohio. However, he cannot interest his oldest son in following in his father's steps, although the boy yearns for the close relationship he imagines 'real' American fathers have with their sons.

There is humor and pain in this description of the difficulties endured by the immigrant Jew in America." Shapiro. Fic for Youth. 3d edition

A girl of forty. Fine, D.I. 1986 240p $16.95

ISBN 0-917657-63-2   LC 85-82494

"Suki is charming, beautiful, fey, a free spirit who typifies the sunny California outlook. She is also self-obsessed, relentlessly frivolous, so superficial she is dangerous, and casually, blatantly promiscuous. The narrator, Frank, is her sometime bed partner who remains in love with Suki, despite her infatuations elsewhere. Frank has sat on the sidelines all his life, avoiding emotional commitment, but he and Suki are forced to face reality by Suki's son. Peter, a teenager who is as physically perfect and alluring as his mother, has grown up incubating a deep vein of anger against Suki's sexual flaunting. As the darkness in Peter's soul deepens, Gold's depiction of a destructive mother/son relationship gathers a brutal force. This compulsively readable book . . . is a zinger, a cautionary tale of real power and truth." Publ Wkly

Golden, Lilly

(ed) A Literary Christmas. See A Literary Christmas

Golding, William, 1911-1993

Nobel Prize in literature, 1983

Clonk clonk

In Golding, W. The scorpion god: three short novels p63-114

Close quarters. Farrar, Straus & Giroux 1987 281p $16.95

ISBN 0-374-12510-4   LC 87-5351

This second volume of the trilogy begun with Rites of passage is a "tale of the tragic misadventures befalling an 18th century fighting ship now converted to transporting cargo and passengers on the treacherous voyage from England to Australia. The novel is cast as a journal written by Edmund FitzHenry Talbot, a well-meaning, somewhat uncertain, slightly pompous officer and gentleman enroute to Sydney and a career in His Majesty's service. As a result of a green sailor's blunder, the ship's masts shatter, and it founders. Golding's principal achievement is the vivid, detailed depiction of a disintegrating vessel in the tropical seas, its progressive decay, and the wretchedness and despair of its passengers." Publ Wkly

Followed by Fire down below

Darkness visible. Farrar, Straus & Giroux 1979 265p $14.95

ISBN 0-374-13502-9   LC 79-19206

Also available from Buccaneer Bks.

"A child hideously maimed in the bombing of London during World War II grows up to inspire the messianic fantasies of the people with whom he comes in contact. In Golding's dark world the horrors of the physically deformed are mirrored in—but are no match for—the spiritual monsters who inhabit the novel's strange vision of contemporary life. A powerful contemplation of the evil at the root of human behavior." Booklist

Golding, William, 1911-1993—*Continued*
Envoy extraordinary

In Golding, W. The scorpion god: three short novels p115-78

Fire down below. Farrar, Straus & Giroux 1989 313p o.p.

LC 88-18079

This is the concluding volume of the trilogy begun in Rites of Passage and continued in Close Quarters. "Narrated by young Edmund FitzHenry Talbot, the trilogy recounts his voyage from England to Australia on a former man-of-war during the Napoleonic era. The last of the three novels takes the badly damaged ship through several storms, an encounter with a gigantic iceberg (actually the continent of Antarctica, but the crew doesn't know it) and finally to the safe shelter of Sydney Harbor." N Y Times Book Rev

Golding is "translucent and economical. In his writing, allegorical motifs are revealed fleetingly in the everyday and in the ordinary. He is at once a complex and highly readable novelist." Economist

The inheritors. Harcourt Brace & World 1962 c1955 233p o.p.

First published 1955 in the United Kingdom
A narrative "inhabiting the near-animal consciousness of Lok, a Neanderthal man, and describing in his clumsy terms and with great pathos the casual destruction of his species by *Homo sapiens*. The reader is shown his ancestors, already armed, arrogant, murderous, and corrupt—not superior to the Neanderthalers, only more clever and more evil." Wakeman. World authors, 1950-1970

Lord of the Flies; a novel. Coward-McCann 1955 c1954 243p o.p.
Available from Amereon and Buccaneer Bks.

First published 1954 in the United Kingdom
An allegorical novel "about a group of boys stranded on an island after a plane crash. In spite of the efforts of a few leaders to form an organized society, the boys revert to savagery, complete with primitive rites and ritual murder. The book is a powerful combination of child's adventure story, anthropological insights, and the Christian concepts of Eden and Original sin." Reader's Ency. 3d edition

The paper men. Farrar, Straus & Giroux 1984 191p $13.95

ISBN 0-374-22980-5   LC 84-27984

"The 'paper men' are famed English novelist Wilfred Barclay and American university professor Rick Tucker, and the two are engaged in a battle to the death over whether Tucker will write the aging author's biography. What begins as comedy . . . darkens as Tucker inadvertently destroys Barclay's marriage, provokes an alcoholic crackup, and finally pushes Barclay into taking a terrible revenge." Libr J

The author's "approach to this material is highly personal, projecting the portrait of a writer who struggles more within himself than with his craft and who is both victim and charlatan as he searches for a self that has become hidden in his art and altered by public adulation." Booklist

Rites of passage. Farrar, Straus & Giroux 1980 278p o.p.

LC 80-16809

In this first volume of a trilogy the author "is fascinated by what might have occurred on a long sea voyage to the Antipodes (Australia) in the Napoleonic era. The passengers are a motley lot out of Britain; the crew, officers and men, and a tough-minded captain who hates the clergy, find their scapegoat in a pitiable parson who has no idea of his own latent homosexuality. Told partly from the viewpoint of an aristocratic dilettante aboard and then in the words set down by the tormented victim in a journal meant for his sister but becoming almost a confession to God." Publ Wkly

"In a sense the novel seems highly artificial, not only in its careful, detailed recreation of the period, but also in the elaborate system of correspondences and parallels—some clear, some obscure—which underpins the narration. Yet at the same time it is an extremely lively, enjoyable piece of work. Readers who know only the early Golding will be surprised by its humor." Times Lit Suppl

Followed by Close quarters

The scorpion god

In Golding, W. The scorpion god: three short novels p9-62

The scorpion god: three short novels. Harcourt Brace Jovanovich 1972 c1971 178p o.p.

Available G.K. Hall large print edition
Contents: The scorpion god; Clonk clonk; Envoy extraordinary

In the title story "the Liar (a jester in the court of ancient Egypt) confounds the people of the land and reveals himself as the mysterious Scorpion God. In the second story . . . Charging Elephant (a tribal youth in Africa) passes into manhood through the services of She Who Names the Women and becomes the fierce Water Paw Wounded Leopard. In the third story . . . Panocles (an inventor in ancient Rome) impresses the Emperor by building a steamship and is rewarded with the post of Envoy Extraordinary and Plenipotentiary to China." New Yorker

"Entertaining if somewhat didactic, the three allegorical narratives are ironic, clever, and subtle in style and illustrate Golding's penchant for the unusual." Booklist

The spire. Harcourt Brace & World 1964 215p o.p. Buccaneer Bks. reprint available $21.95 (ISBN 1-56849-062-3)

An allegorical story "in which a vision of glory comes to the dean of a medieval cathedral. He dreams of a cathedral spire built higher than anyone has built before. Money comes from a dubious source; the work is started by swarms of worldly craftsmen; there are deaths and warnings; the church is empty because it is unsafe for services; but pride and obsession drive the dean on with the building." Publ Wkly

"Perhaps because of the ecclesiastical context, Golding seems here to have given his revelation of human evil a setting not too far from the theological: the Lord of the Flies, or one of his companion devils, has a place in God's scheme. But of God we know nothing, and of the mystery of evil we have no understanding at all." Burgess. 99 Novels

Goldman, Francisco

The long night of white chickens. Atlantic Monthly Press 1992 450p o.p.

LC 91-44318

Goldman, Francisco—*Continued*

Roger Graetz's "wealthy Guatemalan mother abandoned her Jewish husband when Roger Greatz was a year old, taking him from the U.S. to her native country; three years later, in the '60s, she returned to raise him in a Boston suburb. Roger's obsession with Flor de Mayo Puac, a beautiful Guatemalan orphan who came to live with his family when she was 13, will lead him back to Gautemala after Flor is murdered there in 1983 while directing an orphanage. Determined to discover who killed her, Roger is joined in his inquiry by childhood friend Luis Moya Martinez, an outspoken Guatemalan newspaper columnist." Publ Wkly

The author's "complex and masterful tale loops and turns and doubles back on itself, revealing the transmutablity of truth, the narcosis of obsession, the enigmas of culture, and the irrepressible drive to survive." Booklist

Goldman, William, 1931-

Magic. Delacorte Press 1976 243p o.p.

"Corky Withers made it big as a magician, and the secret of his success is just that—a secret. Corky has a dummy named Fats in his act, but doesn't Fats seem to speak his own mind; doesn't he seem strangely lifelike? Corky's checkered past and present are revealed in a thriller of supernatural tones and colors." Booklist

Marathon man. Delacorte Press 1974 309p o.p.

Available from Amereon and Buccaneer Bks.

"Babe" Levy, a graduate student, spends his free time running, and dreams of being a great marathon runner. The death of his brother in Babe's apartment starts a chain of mysterious and terrifying events. Pursued by government agents and ex-Nazis, Babe struggles to escape being assassinated. The torture scenes may make this suspenseful story an ordeal for some readers." Shapiro. Fic for Youth. 3d edition

The princess bride; S. Morgenstern's classic tale of true love and high adventure. The "good parts" version, abridged. Harcourt Brace Jovanovich 1973 308p o.p.

Available from Amereon and Buccaneer Bks.

"The author claims to have rewritten a story that his father used to read to him when he was a child, recovering from a serious illness. Goldman calls his 'the good parts version.' All long and boring passages have been removed, and only the fighting, captures, evil prince, henchmen, daring and loyal friends, and, of course, a beautiful heroine and a perfect hero are kept. This is a funny spoof that combines a wild adventurous story with comments on love and life." Shapiro. Fic for Youth. 3d edition

Goldreich, Gloria

Four days. Harcourt Brace Jovanovich 1980 355p o.p.

LC 79-3352

"The decision whether or not to abort an accidentally conceived fetus is particularly agonizing for Ina Feldman. At 41, she is head of a thriving business, wife of a successful lawyer, mother of two accomplished older children, and dweller in a fashionable Manhattan apartment and Long Island summer home. She is also a concentration camp survivor, still terrorized by nightmares of death, and embittered by years of being for her parents not a beloved daughter, but an inadequate replacement for the son who died." Libr J

This "novel is so beautifully woven that the reader too is moved to take a stand, to be for or against the abortion, and not just in general or moral terms, but in terms of the Jewish experience, in terms of the Holocaust history, in the terms of the past, the present and the future." West Coast Rev Books

Leah's children. Macmillan 1985 369p o.p.

LC 85-2912

In this sequel to Leah's journey, "each of Leah's children carry on her struggle for freedom and justice. . . . Aaron takes on a secret mission to Hungary, on the eve of its revolution, to rescue a beautiful physicist whose formulas are urgently needed by our government. Michael leaves the security of campus life and becomes a civil rights activist in Mississippi. He becomes seriously involved with Kemala, a proud and beautiful black woman who is determined at any cost to free her people. Later, Mindell, an Auschwitz survivor, comes into Michael's life. Rebecca, who chooses the danger-filled life of a border kibbutz and whose husband is involved in shaping the policies of Israel on the eve of the Six-Day-War, sets out to find herself, her own values, and her special artistic fulfillment." West Coast Rev Books

"Goldreich skillfully entwines her valiant characters in the significant historical events of several turbulent decades." Publ Wkly

Leah's journey. Harcourt Brace Jovanovich 1978 450p o.p.

LC 77-92553

"Fleeing from a pogrom in post-Revolutionary Russia with its horrors (rape, and death of her young husband), Leah marries gentle David and goes with him to New York. After early struggles and a tragic love affair with a labor leader, the story evolves to a chronicle of personal achievement for Leah and her family, passing through involvements in the Hitler years, World War II, and the emergence of the state of Israel." Libr J

The author "is particularly good in evoking the historical and social forces that affect Leah's life and the lives of her family. An absorbing and often moving narrative, this should satisfy readers who enjoy family sagas written with sensitivity and compassion." Publ Wkly

Followed by Leah's children

That year of our war. Little, Brown 1994 356p $22.95

ISBN 0-316-31943-0   LC 93-20561

"For 15-year-old Sharon Grossberg, June 6, 1944, is 'Death Day'—the day she loses her mother to leukemia. Since her father is serving in Europe, Sharon leaves her Boston home to live with relatives in New York City. This novel is a chronicle of the last year of World War II in the lives of this large, extended Jewish family. The story focuses on Sharon as she struggles to cope with her mother's death, her constant anxiety about her father's safety, and her own coming of age." Libr J

"The ordinary life of the family, with their Shabbat dinners and various holiday preparations, is tinged with growing horror as they learn of the extermination of relatives in Europe. Sharon's evaluation of a complex adult world is rendered with skill and power." Publ Wkly

Years of dreams. Little, Brown 1992 464p $21.95

ISBN 0-316-31937-6   LC 91-28962

Goldreich, Gloria—*Continued*

This "saga opens with a familiar scene: four lifelong friends are summoned to the hospital after an accident claims one of their own. All are Jewish women who met in college during the turbulent years following the assassination of John F. Kennedy. Anne, fiercely independent, tenaciously pursues her dream of becoming a physician, despite its great toll on her personal life; Merle, a talented musician, marries a controlling millionaire she'd sooner leave; Rutti, a gentle artist, is a Holocaust survivor whose dreams for her daughter Sarah don't always match Sarah's own; and Nancy, a psychoanalyst, is as human and problem-ridden as some of her patients." Booklist

"Complex and fully realized, the women open windows on the major issues of the 1960s and '70: the war in Vietnam, student protests, Watergate. Particularly compelling are detailed scenes set in Israel during the Six Day and Yom Kippur wars. A rich and satisfying tale with a bitter, angry edge written by an adroit raconteur." Publ Wkly

Goldsborough, Robert

The bloodied ivy; a Nero Wolfe mystery. Bantam Bks. 1988 191p $15.95

ISBN 0-553-05281-0   LC 88-3513
Also available Thorndike Press large print edition

"Rude, self-centered Nero Wolfe is persuaded by Archie Goodwin, the intelligent, good-natured narrator, to investigate the death of a well-known professor at Prescott University. Hale Markham attracted many students, but he also inspired jealousy among several co-workers. When Markham dies on campus, his friend asks Goodwin for help." Libr J

The missing chapter; a Nero Wolfe mystery. Bantam Bks. 1993 229p $19.95

ISBN 0-553-07241-2   LC 93-13714
Also available Thorndike Press large print edition

A publisher hires Nero Wolfe and Archie Goodwin "to investigate the death, labeled a suicide, of Charles Childress, an ill-tempered author who had recently angered several people, including his agent, his editor and the possibly corrupt reviewer who had lambasted the latest Childress novel." Publ Wkly

"The publishing details ring true, and . . . Goldsborough does a masterly job with the Wolfe legacy." Booklist

Goldsmith, Oliver, 1728-1774

The Vicar of Wakefield.
Available from Amereon and Buccaneer Bks.

First published 1776

"The story, a portrait of village life, is narrated by Dr. Primrose, the title character, whose family endures many trials—including the loss of most of their money, the seduction of one daughter, the destruction of their home by fire, and the vicar's incarceration—before all is put right in the end. The novel's idealization of rural life, sentimental moralizing, and melodramatic incidents are countered by a sharp but good-natured irony." Merriam-Webster's Ency of Lit

Goldsmith, Olivia

Fashionably late; a novel. HarperCollins Pubs. 1994 431p $24

ISBN 0-06-017611-3   LC 94-9376
Also available G.K. Hall large print edition

"Prominent designer Karen Kahn has just won the fashion industry's top achievement award. As this . . . novel quickly shows, however, it's all downhill from there. Karen's company, KK Inc., needs a huge infusion of cash to expand, and her handsome but evasive husband, Jeffrey, who handles the finances, pushes for a $50 million buyout by the megacorporation NormCo. But will Karen lose control of her designs? And how ethically does NormCo run its business?. . . . A glittering New York social backdrop, plenty of namedropping, romance, some outstandingly creative characters and a mystic who applies a unique hex add up to a book that fairly hums with excitement." Publ Wkly

The First Wives Club. Poseidon Press 1992 480p o.p.

LC 91-30959

"Annie, Elise, and Brenda are all good wives who have helped their husbands achieve success. Now that their men are at the pinnacle, they find themselves dumped for younger, sleeker 'trophy wives.' So they band together to form the 'First Wives Club' for the purpose of seeing justice done." Libr J

As the women "stylishly, systematically and nonviolently foil the schemes of their callous former partners, they conquer their own weaknesses and find appreciative friends and lovers who complement rather than rule them. Goldsmith's glitzy, addictive and credible first novel is certain to raise smiles." Publ Wkly

Flavor of the month. Poseidon Press 1993 698p $23

ISBN 0-671-79449-3   LC 93-16431

"In the beginning is Mary Jane Moran, a talented New York actress whose lumpish face and figure corral her in the small-time. Then she spends $67,000 on plastic surgery, becomes drop-dead beautiful and moves to L.A. where, reborn as Jahne Moore, she's instantly cast in a sizzling TV series. Co-starring are Lila Kyle, towering bitch-goddess daughter of an aging screen star, and corn-fed Texan Sharleen Smith, who's been on the lam since she and her half-brother Dean left their abusive father for dead. . . . While Goldsmith has little truck with realism, she perfectly conjures up the envy and insecurity, the toadying and backstabbing associated with the celebrity circuit." Publ Wkly

Goodrum, Charles A.

Dewey decimated. Crown 1977 190p o.p.

"A wealthy private library in Washington [receives] a series of anonymous letters [which] cast serious doubt on the value and authenticity of the library's most recherché books, and shortly afterwards the keeper of rare books is found impaled in the stacks. A . . . young public relations officer and a young scholar from Minnesota are joined by a distinguished retired librarian to investigate this murder as well as that of a secretive bookbinder." Libr J

Gordimer, Nadine, 1923-

Nobel Prize in literature, 1991

Burger's daughter. Viking 1979 361p o.p.

LC 78-20831

"A young Afrikaaner woman inherits a heavy burden from her father, a doctor and a leader of the South African Communist Party who is a martyr to the anti-apartheid cause—all the heavier because she shares his moral outrage but neither his confident analysis of a simple wrong and remedy nor his saintly selflessness. In the eyes of Rosa's father's friends (and foes), however, she is 'Burger's daughter'. . . . After her father dies in prison, when Rosa is in her mid-twenties, her secret ambivalence becomes unbearable, and she obtains a passport and leaves South Africa, resolved to discover if there is any other way she can live." New Yorker

"What enobles Gordimer's riveting poetic prose is her intellectual and political honesty—the scrupulous unsentimentality with which she affixes blame or despair, irrespective of color, status, or political orientation." Christ Sci Monit

The conservationist. Viking 1975 c1974 252p o.p.

First published 1974 in the United Kingdom

The author probes "the way of life that exists in South Africa today, and some aspects of the tensions that exist among English and Afrikaaners, Blacks, coloreds, Indian shopkeepers. . . . Mehring is rich, white, bored. His farm is a weekend pleasure place to which he once brought the mistress whose flirtations with left wing causes have now exiled her forever. His teenage son won't even come home for the holidays and wants out of all that South Africa stands for. Mehring is kind enough to his blacks, keeps them in their place, avoids his Boer neighbors with whom he has nothing in common. A loner, living for himself, deliberately isolated from any unpleasantness that might intrude, only gradually does he begin to perceive that there are forces at work in nature, in the closeness between the blacks and the land by which some day his way of life will be forever changed." Publ Wkly

A guest of honor. Viking 1970 504p o.p.

The hero of this novel, James "Bray is a 54-year-old former administrator for one of Her Majesty's former African colonies. . . . He was cashiered for showing too much sympathy for the local independence movement. After independence, Bray accepts an invitation to return as an educational consultant to Miss Gordimer's nameless, composite, new African nation. His professional commitment to the excruciating process of Third World nation building is complicated because the country's opposing political factions—one moderate, the other revolutionary—are led by two of his former protégés." Time

July's people. Viking 1981 160p o.p.

LC 80-24877

"When revolution breaks out against the whites in South Africa, Bamford and Maureen Smales are forced to flee. Their black servant July, loyal to them for fifteen years, takes them away to his people in a bush village. His role changes slowly to one not only of savior but also overseer. The change in their manner of living from the good, clean, well-regulated life of 'the ruling class' to that of the customs of July's people raises havoc within both the white and black families and in the delicate tissue of understanding between the Smales and their servant. There is much to be learned from this powerful story written by an author who lives in South Africa and who writes with authority on a subject that

has import for any society where race relations or colonial conditions are fragile and explosive." Shapiro. Fic for Youth. 3d edition

Jump and other stories. Farrar, Straus & Giroux 1991 256p $20

ISBN 0-374-18055-5 LC 91-2687

Also available G.K. Hall large print edition

Analyzed in Short story index

Contents: Jump; Once upon a time; The ultimate safari; A find; My father leaves home; Some are born to sweet delight; Comrades; Teraloyna; The moment before the gun went off; Home; A journey; Spoils; Safe houses; What were you dreaming?; Keeping fit; Amnesty

This "collection of tales features an insider's intensity about people caught in the savage particulars of southern Africa today; at the same time, the surprise of the stories and the slash of their endings make the words resonate with the revelations of an ever-widening universe." Booklist

My son's story. Farrar, Straus & Giroux 1990 277p $19.95

ISBN 0-374-21751-3 LC 90-83232

"Sonny is a teacher of mixed race. He and his wife are . . . sympathetic to the plight of the 'real blacks,' yet ambitious that they may someday be accepted by the whites. Sonny's political education begins when he's fired for helping black children demonstrate in their township. Jailed for promoting boycotts and participating in illegal gatherings, Sonny meets and falls in love with a blond, blue-eyed woman who works for a human-rights organization. Sonny's adolescent son, Will, tells the story of his father's political and erotic development, the resentments and betrayals that ensue." Newsweek

This is a "thoughtful, poised, quietly poignant novel that not only recognizes the value and cost of political commitment, but also takes account of recent developments in South Africa and Eastern Europe in a way that Gordimer's previous work did not." Christ Sci Monit

None to accompany me. Farrar, Straus & Giroux 1994 324p $22

ISBN 0-374-22297-5 LC 94-7553

"In the final days of the old regime in South Africa, antiapartheid activists are released from prison or return home afters years of exile. Vera Stark, a white legal aid attorney representing the black community, recognizes many familiar faces from her youth, but she is shocked to see that they appear to have aged overnight. This unnerving experience causes her to reexamine her life. Known around her law firm as someone impervious to con games, Vera is ruthless in exposing her own lies and deceptions. She faces unpleasant truths about her marriages, her affairs, and the effect her actions may have had on her children. But rather than cling to the security of a flawed life, Vera finds that the rapidly changing political situation encourages radical personal change." Libr J

"A novel that raises more questions than it answers, 'None to Accompany Me' is an unflinching and perceptive exploration of people living on the brink of changes—political and personal—with little but their own sense of self-reliance to guide them." Christ Sci Monitor

A sport of nature; a novel. Knopf 1987 341p o.p.

LC 86-46150

Gordimer, Nadine, 1923-—*Continued*

This novel traces the adventures of its protagonist, Hillela Capran, a Jewish South African raised by her two aunts, one conventional, the other radical, through a series of love affairs and marriages which lead to her increasing involvement in African revolutionary causes. At the end of the book, she is the wife of the head of state of an African country and witnesses the end of apartheid in her native land

This is "fully a novel, grand-scale, rich and demanding, but it is also a thoughtfully documented history of postcolonial African nations." N Y Times Book Rev

Gordon, Mary, 1949-

The company of women. Random House 1981 c1980 291p o.p.

LC 80-5284

In this novel "Felicitas is nurtured by a large circle of Catholic women. After attending only parochial schools, Felicitas goes to Columbia University, where she becomes sexually involved with a married professor, gives up her studies, and becomes pregnant. She returns to the company of women, gives birth to her baby, and later marries only to provide a father for her child." Merriam-Webster's Ency of Lit

"Given its scope, depth, and the perfection of its lyrical passages (which are the more impressive because of Gordon's natural inclination toward the austere), it is fair to call this a brilliant novel." Saturday Rev

Final payments. Random House 1978 297p o.p.

LC 77-90259

"Isabel Moore spends 11 years almost totally absorbed in caring for her invalid father, who suffered a paralyzing stroke after discovering his daughter in a compromising situation with one of his students. When she is thirty, her father dies; she is freed from responsibility for his welfare but not yet able to accept responsibility for her own life. Her involvement with two men adds complications as, guilt-ridden and filled with religious skepticism, Isabel searches for answers and begins to heal. Two childhood friends, Eleanor, an independent woman, and Liz, a tough married mother of two children, are instrumental in helping Isabel grow toward self-realization." Shapiro. Fic for Youth. 3d edition

Immaculate man

In Gordon, M. The rest of life: three novellas

Living at home

In Gordon, M. The rest of life: three novellas

The other side. Viking 1989 386p o.p.

LC 88-40633

The author "takes on several generations of an Irish American family and their experiences on both sides of the Atlantic. The story unfolds on a single day at the home of Vincent and Ellen McNamara, whose family has gathered for Vincent's return from a nursing home—his wife Ellen, disabled by a stroke, having injured him by pushing him to the floor in a fit of confusion. Using this gathering to explore family history, beginning with Ellen's and Vincent's separate and very different departures from Ireland, Gordon lays bare a legacy of lovelessness and defeat passed from parent to child to grandchild." Libr J

The rest of life

In Gordon, M. The rest of life: three novellas

The rest of life: three novellas. Viking 1993 257p $22

ISBN 0-670-83828-4   LC 92-50753

Also available G.K. Hall large print edition

Analyzed in Short story index

"In 'Immaculate Lover,' a social worker falls in love with a Catholic priest and explains, with tremendous care and tenderness, the circumstances of their precarious relationship. 'Living at Home' is narrated by a doctor who works with autistic children. Her lover is a journalist who risks his life covering revolution and war. Here, Gordon probes the concept of home and the ways we define ourselves. The final novella, 'The Rest of Life,' records a 78-year-old woman's revelation upon returning to her native Italy for the first time since her exile at age 15. Paola was sent away after the boy with whom she'd made a half-hearted suicide pact went through with it on his own, leaving her alive and deeply ashamed." Booklist

"Gordon endows her heroines with a rich sexuality while engaging us in a probing debate about the complex relationship between our bodies, our pasts, and our sense of self." Libr J

Temporary shelter; short stories. Random House 1987 213p o.p.

LC 86-31627

Analyzed in Short story index

Contents: Temporary shelter; The imagination of disaster; Delia; The only son of the doctor; The neighborhood; Watching the tango; Agnes; The magician's wife; Out of the fray; The thorn; Eileen; Now I am married; The murderer guest; The other woman; Billy; Safe; The dancing party; Violation; Mrs. Cassidy's last year; A writing lesson

"The 22 stories that make up this distinguished collection reaffirm Gordon's ability to create fully dimensional characters who speak in a variety of authentic voices. Though the narratives are poetically compressed, Gordon eschews minimalism and uses incident to sustain narrative energy." Publ Wkly

Gorky, Maksim, 1868-1936

Selected short stories; [by] Maxim Gorky; with an introductory essay by Stefan Zweig. Ungar 1959 348p o.p.

Partially analyzed in Short story index

Contents: Makar Chudra; Old Izergil; Chelkash; Afloat: an Easter story; Twenty-six men and a girl; Malva; Comrade; The ninth of January; Tales of Italy; The romancer; The Mordvinian girl; A man is born; The breakup; How a song was composed; The philanderer

Gorman, Ed

Death ground

In Great stories of the American West p197-287

Gosling, Paula

The body in Blackwater Bay. Mysterious Press 1992 293p $17.95

ISBN 0-89296-459-6   LC 91-50845

Also available Thorndike Press large print edition

"Big city cop Jake Stryker is the latest victim of the 'working' vacation; it was supposed to be two weeks on Paradise Island, a sleepy Great Lakes retreat, lying in a hammock and enjoying the ministrations of girlfriend Kate Trevorne. It's not long, however, before one of Kate's high school chums starts complaining that her ex-husband is following her and threatening violence. There's violence soon enough, but it's the ex who winds up dead and the chum who's the number one suspect." Booklist

"Gosling adeptly juggles business intrigue, small-town gossip and psychological trickery. Stryker remains a genuine, low-key pleasure and the islanders represent a beguiling cross-section of society." Publ Wkly

A few dying words. Mysterious Press 1994 344p $18.95

ISBN 0-89296-510-X   LC 94-18826

Also available G.K. Hall large print edition

"A Blackwater Bay mystery novel"

"While bracing for the Blackwater Bay's annual Howl—a traditional Halloween celebration of carnival rides and pranks—Sheriff Matt Gabriel agrees to meet with clearly agitated retired pharmacist, Tom Finnegan. While driving to the sheriff's office, however, Finnegan is run off the road. Matt reaches the older man's side before he dies and hears him whisper 'not an accident.'" Publ Wkly

"Good writing, an inventive plot, and a nice balance of humor and horror make this an appealing mystery." Booklist

Goudge, Eileen

Blessing in disguise. Viking 1994 561p $21.95

ISBN 0-670-84961-8   LC 93-50238

Also available Thorndike Press large print edition

"Grace Truscott's shocking revelations in her biography of her Southern senator father rock her family and, indeed, Georgia to its very foundations. The truth about his affair with his black secretary and the existence of their daughter jolts the community, derailing Cordelia Truscott's efforts to raise money for her husband's memorial library. Evidently, racism is alive and well in Blessing, Georgia; pillars of the community struggle to come to grips with the difference between reality and social rhetoric, and both Grace and her mother are forced to decide between true love and social conventions." Libr J

"The romantic and family entanglements in the novel make the decisions about shocking secrets more understandable and ultimately more intense." Booklist

Garden of lies. Viking 1989 528p o.p.

LC 88-40395

"Sylvia seizes the opportunity offered by a hospital fire to switch infants, taking a newborn whose appearance resembles her husband. Her true child, fathered by Sylvia's lover, is left to make her own way in the world. Rachel, raised in luxury as Sylvia's daughter, becomes a doctor. When her career is jeopardized, she is defended by Sylvia'a real daughter, who has overcome poverty to become a lawyer. The two women of course compete for the same man, as Sylvia herself tries to decide whether to marry Nikos, her former lover." Libr J

"The characters intrigue, the situations hold attention, and the sex scenes simmer near the boiling point." Booklist

Such devoted sisters. Viking 1992 562p $22

ISBN 0-670-83954-X   LC 91-29103

Also available Thorndike Press large print edition

"In 1954, Dolly Drake mails a letter addressed to Senator Joseph McCarthy that contains damning information about her famous film star sister Eve Dearfield. After leaving small-town America for Hollywood, Dolly has had enough of Eve stealing the spotlight. And she can't tolerate Eve stealing her man, either. Ruining the offending sister's career and her life seems the only thing to do. Years later, of course, she's regretting her actions, but Dolly's far away in Manhattan, with her own chocolate store and a lot of money. And it just so happens that Eve's two children, Annie and Laurel, have run away from home looking for Dolly, their long-lost aunt." Booklist

Goudge, Elizabeth, 1900-1984

The bird in the tree. Coward-McCann 1940 339p o.p.

Available from Amereon and Buccaneer Bks.

The action takes place in the fall of 1938 on the Hampshire coast, centering about the eighteenth century home of the Eliots: three children, two dogs, two young lovers, and Grandmother Lucilla Eliot whose personality has merged completely with that of the old house during the passage of the years

Followed by Pilgrim's inn

The child from the sea. Coward-McCann 1970 736p o.p.

"Lucy Walter is the heroine of a richly detailed historical romance set amid the political upheavals of seventeenth-century England. Resourceful, independent, Lucy was born in a remote Welsh castle and became the beloved although secret wife of Charles II before the shifting course of history brought him to the throne; later events led her to Paris where she died at age twenty-eight." Booklist

A city of bells. Coward-McCann 1936 380p o.p.

Available from Amereon and Buccaneer Bks.

Jocelyn Irvin, dispirited because of a wound received in the Boer War, traveled down to the peaceful little English cathedral city of Torminster, there to visit his saintly old grandfather, Canon Fordyce. Practically forced to open a bookshop in a tiny house in the city, Jocelyn became interested in the writings of a former occupant, Ferranti, who had disappeared. In the finishing and producing of a play of Ferranti's, Jocelyn helped himself and others, especially the charming child Henrietta, Canon Fordyce's adopted grandchild

The dean's watch; illustrated by A. R. Whitear. Coward-McCann 1960 383p il o.p. Amereon reprint available $22.95 (ISBN 0-8488-0509-7)

Set "in a mid-nineteenth-century English cathedral town, this is a richly textured, idealistic, and warmly human story of the transforming power of love. It centers on old Isaac Peabody, a simple but talented clock-

Goudge, Elizabeth, 1900-1984—*Continued*
maker, and Adam Ayscough, respected and feared dean of the cathedral. Through their chance meeting and subsequent friendship, Isaac discovers faith in God; the dean, overcoming his shyness and formidable appearance, wins the affection of those whom he serves; and the lives of a great many people in the city are changed." Booklist

Green Dolphin Street; a novel. Coward-McCann 1944 502p o.p.

Published in the United Kingdom with title: Green Dolphin country

This novel is set on one of the English Channel Islands and in frontier New Zealand. "The principal characters are two sisters and the boy who had been their neighbor and companion in Green Dolphin Street on the island. The sisters are Marianne, stern and intellectual, and Marguerite, radiant and beautiful. It is Marguerite whom William loves, but when he writes the letter from New Zealand asking her father for her hand he unaccountably confuses the names and it is Marianne, who comes to be his wife." Wis Libr Bull

The heart of the family. Coward-McCann 1953 337p o.p.

Available from Amereon and Buccaneer Bks.

"Sebastian Weber, an Austrian refugee, once a famous pianist, is the mysterious character in this novel about the Eliot family. By sharing their daily lives, pervaded with a rare religious mysticism, he is purged of the hatred and despair caused by the loss of his family and years of incarceration in a concentration camp. The story is a simple one, yet the author's exquisite portrayal of children, grownups, animals, and the English countryside gives it the refreshing charm for which she is famous." Libr J

Pilgrim's inn. Coward-McCann 1948 346p o.p.

Published in the United Kingdom with title: The Herb of Grace

In this Eliot family novel the "end of the war has left nearly every one of her children and grandchildren with some problem, and Lucilla saw a way to a wholesale solution. Because of her benevolent scheming one branch of the family bought an old pilgrim's inn, and before the year was out the benign atmosphere of the place has straightened out the tangles of both the Eliots and the strangers who came under its influence." Booklist

Followed by The heart of the family

The scent of water. Coward-McCann 1963 348p o.p.

"A quiet novel of a woman's spiritual regeneration and rebuilding of her life in middle age. The heroine retires at age 50 to an inherited house and garden in the English countryside. With the inheritance comes a set of the private journals of the elderly cousin who once owned the property. Reading these journals and helping her neighbors in their problems, the heroine finds serene happiness and wisdom." Publ Wkly

Gould, Judith

Forever. Dutton 1992 453p $22

ISBN 0-525-93495-2   LC 92-52871

"When author Carleton Merlin is found dead, an apparent suicide, his TV journalist granddaughter Stephanie suspects foul play connected to his research into the life of German opera star Lili Schnieder, who supposedly died in 1950. Stephanie's search for the truth takes her from the arms of her photographer lover and sends her to the capitals of Europe and the Brazilian empire of the world's richest man." Libr J

Grady, James, 1949-

Six days of the condor. Norton 1974 192p o.p.

"When a branch of the CIA is mass murdered, Malcolm, the only survivor, becomes the object of an intense chase involving the Washington police, the CIA, the FBI, the NSC, and a host of other intelligence agencies. Trying to stay one jump ahead of his pursuers, Malcolm struggles to find out who within the agency has sold out his comrades." Libr J

Thunder. Warner Bks. 1994 380p $21.95

ISBN 0-446-51765-8   LC 93-11177

"The story opens with two bloody crimes: the apparent terrorist bombing of a Manhattan skyscraper and, two months later in D.C., the death of veteran CIA agent Frank Mathews by what cops and the Company consider a 'stray bullet.' Mathews's partner, John Lang, doesn't buy that explanation, especially not when his superior tries to prevent his continuing Mathews's probe into a mysterious letter concerning the murder of an American in Europe." Publ Wkly

Graeme, Roderic, 1926-

For works written by this author under other names see Jeffries, Roderic, 1926-

Grafton, Sue

"A" is for alibi; a Kinsey Millhone mystery. Holt & Co. 1990 c1982 274p $19.95

ISBN 0-8050-1334-2

Also available from Buccaneer Bks.

A reissue of the title first published 1982 by Holt, Rinehart & Winston

"California private eye, Kinsey Millhone, makes her debut in this story of a murder committed eight years before. Nikki Fife was convicted of killing her husband, but as soon as she's out of prison she hires Kinsey to find the true murderer." Libr J

"Kinsey Millhone is a cut above the usual woman private eye who flounces through fiction. Millhone is neither a sex bomb nor a detached cerebrum, but a believable, straightforward character." Booklist

"B" is for burglar. Holt & Co. 1985 229p $19.95

ISBN 0-8050-1632-5   LC 84-22378

When Kinsey Millhone "is hired to locate Elaine Boldt, a well-to-do widow, she sets the wheels of a routine missing-persons investigation in motion. The bizarre, outlandish behavior of Elaine's sister and brother-in-law leads Kinsey to suspect a murder has been committed, but in order to solve the crime, a corpse must be uncovered." Booklist

Grafton, Sue—*Continued*

"Grafton's plot is solid p.i. procedural, but it is her sense of style that will truly delight readers. Her characters, from a punk dope pusher to a brave and resourceful eighty-eight-year-old woman, are completely convincing, and Grafton's ear for natural dialogue is among the best in the business." Wilson Libr Bull

"C" is for corpse; a Kinsey Millhone mystery. Holt & Co. 1986 243p $19.95

ISBN 0-8050-2818-8   LC 85-24797

Kinsey Millhone "meets a young man, Buddy Callahan, at the gym where she works out and agrees to take his case. He wants her to investigate an auto accident in which he was badly injured because he claims that it was a murder attempt. When a second attempt results in his death, Kinsey, although she no longer has him as a client, pursues the matter and, in a hair-raising finale that takes place in a morgue, she unmasks the murderer." Shapiro. Fic for Youth. 3d edition

"D" is for deadbeat; a Kinsey Millhone mystery. Holt & Co. 1987 229p $19.95

ISBN 0-8050-0248-0   LC 86-25843

"Ex-con and drunken bum John Daggett hires Millhone to deliver a check for $25,000 to a teenage boy whose family was killed in a violent car crash in which Daggett was the offending drunk driver. Daggett's retainer check bounces, and in trying to recoup her losses, Kinsey is swept up in a tangled web of hate, violence, and families torn asunder." Booklist

"Social awareness and human weakness play a great part in the Millhone books, which always manage to finish with a heart-stopping climax." Libr J

"E" is for evidence; a Kinsey Millhone mystery. Holt & Co. 1988 227p $15.95

ISBN 0-8050-0459-9   LC 87-28100

"While private detective and former cop Kinsey Millhone is investigating a possible case of industrial arson involving a company owned by the family of a former schoolmate, someone tries to make it look as if she's on the take. A mysterious $5000 appears in her bank account. She sets out to clear herself, while two or possibly more cases of murder occur, including one by bombing." Publ Wkly

"The plot is just fine and does what a plot ought to in a good detective novel: it keeps us turning pages and serves as a vehicle for the really interesting stuff, an unveiling of the characters' foibles by the worldly-wise but uncorrupt private eye." NY Times Book Rev

"F" is for fugitive; a Kinsey Millhone mystery. Holt & Co. 1989 261p $15.95

ISBN 0-8050-0460-2   LC 88-27284

Kinsey Millhone "becomes involved in ugly doings in a California coastal town, where she attempts to prove a man's innocence on a 17-year-old murder rap. Floral Beach appears to be a cozy little place, but it's a hotbed of dirty secrets, most of them involving the long-dead Jean Timberlake, a confused yet apparently sexually quite precocious teenager. Kinsey's investigation opens closet doors, and some tawdry skeletons jump out." Booklist

"G" is for gumshoe; a Kinsey Millhone mystery. Holt & Co. 1990 261p o.p.

           LC 89-24652

Available G.K. Hall large print edition

Private investigator Kinsey Millhone is hired to find and take "an elderly woman to a nursing home near her daughter. But the lady mysteriously disappears within hours of her arrival. Painfully aware of the fact that a contract has been arranged for her own murder, Kinsey unravels the events of the past." SLJ

"Millhone, whose background has made her believe that all families are dysfunctional, has unwittingly taken on another case of domestic violence. Grafton excels in this milieu. Never morally oblique, here she is slyly didactic about (among other things) attitudes toward the mentally ill." Newsweek

"H" is for homicide. Holt & Co. 1991 256p $17.95

ISBN 0-8050-1084-X   LC 90-25016

Also available G.K. Hall large print edition

Detective Kinsey Millhone is "hired by California Fidelity to investigate a string of fraudulent automobile insurance claims filed by someone named Bibianna Diaz. To track down the elusive Bibianna, Kinsey adopts an undercover identity as Hannah Moore, a wisecracking, reckless vamp. As Hannah, she befriends Bibianna, a sexy young woman on the run. Both are quickly swept up in an evening of kidnapping and gunplay that ends with the two of them in jail. Through her relationship with Bibianna, Kinsey also stumbles onto a much bigger network of crime." N Y Times Book Rev

"I" is for innocent. Holt & Co. 1992 286p $18.95

ISBN 0-8050-1085-8   LC 91-45165

Also available G.K. Hall large print edition

Kinsey Millhone "lands the job of hunting up evidence for a wrongful-death suit against a high-living architect who couldn't be nailed in court for his wife's murder. It's a sobering case, weighted with the survivors' anger and suspicions and darkened by their sordid domestic affairs." N Y Times Book Rev

"J" is for judgment. Holt & Co. 1993 288p $21.95

ISBN 0-8050-1935-9   LC 92-35769

Also available G.K. Hall large print edition

In this mystery, California P.I. Kinsey Millhone is "investigating a fraud case. Wendell Jaffe, a local businessman, set up a fraudulent Ponzi scheme and then disappeared, leaving his wife and business partner to deal with the creditors. His wife had Jaffe declared dead after five years and picked up a half-million-dollar life insurance settlement. Now Jaffe's supposedly been sighted in Mexico. If he's still alive, the insurance company wants its money back and hires Kinsey to find out what's what." Booklist

"Ms. Grafton writes a smart story and wraps it up with a wry twist; but she takes care to sweeten her tart characterizations with amused understanding and, in the case of Jaffe, even affection." N Y Times Book Rev

"K" is for killer. Holt & Co. 1994 284p $22.95

ISBN 0-8050-1936-7   LC 94-1242

"Grieving mother Janice Kepler asks Kinsey [Millhone] to investigate the nearly year-old death of her daughter Lorna. Janice believes Lorna was murdered, even though there were no signs of violence and the police concluded the young woman died of natural causes. Kinsey, always keen for a challenge, agrees to take the case and winds up working one of the oddest mysteries of her career." Booklist

Grafton, Sue—*Continued*

"Despite an abrupt ending that has the reader frantically paging back for missed clues, the sturdily engineered plot drags Kinsey into the kind of joints that never seem to close: bars, nightclubs, diners, hospital emergency rooms. All this night crawling serves as an eye-opening experience for Kinsey, who is physically exhausted but mentally energized by her encounters with sad young prostitutes and other fascinating creatures of the night."
N Y Times Book Rev

Graham, Caroline

Death in disguise. Morrow 1993 c1992 333p $22

ISBN 0-688-09985-8   LC 92-33300

First published 1992 in the United Kingdom
"Murder in a country manor inhabited by a cult of mystics tests the patience and skills of Detective Chief Inspector Tom Barnaby. . . . Graham's competent procedural works most effectively as a wickedly acid yet sympathetic portrayal of a group of society's misfits seeking comfort and a place in the world." Publ Wkly

The killings at Badger's Drift. Adler & Adler 1988 c1987 264p o.p.

LC 87-1284

First published 1987 in the United Kingdom
As Detective Chief Inspector Barnaby and Sergeant Troy "investigate the coniine (hemlock) poisoning death of 80-year-old spinster Emily Simpson, they encounter a bizarre mixture of eccentric village dwellers, starting with the little old cat-lady and gardener friend of the deceased. The murder, of course, causes a commotion in picturesque Badger's Drift, laden with quaint cottages and Georgian manor houses." Libr J

Graham, James, 1929- *See* Higgins, Jack, 1929-

Graham, Vanessa *See* Fraser, Anthea

Graham, Winston

The angry tide; a novel of Cornwall, 1798-1799. Doubleday 1978 c1977 476p o.p.
LC 77-90809

Sequel to The four swans
First published 1977 in the United Kingdom
This is the "seventh novel in the Poldark saga. The darkly entwined destinies of the genteel Poldarks and the 'nouveaux riches' Warleggans, whose interests span the worlds of banking, mining and politics, continue to unfold. Ross Poldark, quick-tempered but agreeable hero of the piece, has now taken George Warleggan's seat in Parliament (for which he's roundly resented), in addition to being in love with George's wife—which is not to say he doesn't love his own wife, Demelza. Subsidiary characters include Demelza's two brothers, both love crossed, and Morwenna, married to an odious church minister who tries to get her put away as insane. There's a duel, a killing, a mine disaster and a near-drowning at sea." Publ Wkly
Followed by The stranger from the sea

The black moon. Doubleday 1974 c1973 424p o.p.

First published 1973 in the United Kingdom
This is the fifth volume in the Poldark saga. Previous titles in the series: Ross Poldark (1951); Demelza (1953); Jeremy Poldark (1954); Warleggan (1955)
Set in Cornwall in the 1790's this "story of fates hanging in the balance: of England, its church, its social structure, and two of its families. Indeed, these fates form concentric circles about the old feud between George Warleggan and Ross Poldark and serve as metaphoric echoes of it." Libr J
Followed by The four swans

The four swans; a novel of Cornwall, 1795-1797. Doubleday 1977 c1976 479p o.p.
LC 76-18347

Sequel to The black moon
First published 1976 in the United Kingdom
As this sixth novel of the Poldark series opens it is a "bumptious era in British history; malcontents upset the country's equilibrium, Napoleon is thought to be mapping an invasion, upperclass cohesiveness falters before industrial expansion. In the middle of these events is Captain Ross Poldark. A respected man in civilian life or under arms, he parries the political ambitions of ruthless bankers and grapples with the emotional demands of four women who keep crisscrossing his career. Chief among them is wife Demelza, a smoldering vixen who never forgets one lost love. Further embellishing the serial-like chapters are revelations about the paternity of children and the discontents of a clergyman troubled by the pleasures of the flesh." Publ Wkly
Followed by The angry tide

The loving cup; a novel of Cornwall, 1813-1815. Doubleday 1985 c1984 440p o.p.
LC 85-4362

Sequel to The miller's dance
First published 1984 in the United Kingdom
In this tenth novel of the Poldark series, "Demelza and Ross Poldark oversees the escapades and marriages of their two oldest children and revel in the childish delights of their two youngest. The closing triumphs of Wellington's army, in which the Poldark cousins participate, are nicely integrated into the domestic drama." Booklist
"Set against a vivid Cornwall landscape, it is a tale high in readability, made even more enjoyable with a knowledge of the lineage explored in the earlier books." Publ Wkly
Followed by The twisted sword

The miller's dance; a novel of Cornwall, 1812-1813. Doubleday 1983 c1982 372p o.p.
LC 82-45596

Sequel to The stranger from the sea
First published 1982 in the United Kingdom
This "ninth novel of life on the Cornish coast in the late 18th century and the fluctuating fortunes of the Poldark family concentrates on the lives and complicated love affairs of the two oldest Poldark children, Jeremy and Clowance, rather than on their parents, Ross and Demelza. The Poldark story has emphasized events over character development, but *Miller's Dance* does so more than previous books. To the reader unfamiliar with the Poldark family, friends, and enemies, the large and varied cast of characters presented immediately and without introduction will be confusing." Libr J
Followed by The loving cup

Graham, Winston—_Continued_

Stephanie. Carroll & Graf Pubs. 1993 c1992 301p $19.95

ISBN 0-88184-939-1   LC 92-42462

First published 1992 in the United Kingdom

"Stephanie Locke is a 21-year-old student at Oxford who has an affair with 38-year-old Errol Colton, a married man. Shortly after she and Errol return from a trip to Goa, Stephanie is found dead in bed, an apparent suicide. At the inquest, Errol testifies that Stephanie became despondent when he decided to stop seeing her, but Stephanie's father knows that something happened during the couple's holiday that so distressed his daughter that she decided to end the affair although she was still very much in love. James Locke refuses to believe his daughter committed suicide, and his determination to investigate makes some people very nervous." Libr J

Graham "has written a dark, sophisticated, taut, and suspenseful story full of the strange ironies, sad coincidences, and small happinesses of life." Booklist

The stranger from the sea; a novel of Cornwall, 1810-1811. Doubleday 1982 c1981 445p o.p. Amereon reprint available $20.95 (ISBN 0-8488-1017-1)

Sequel to The angry tide

First published 1981 in the United Kingdom

The action of this eighth novel in the Poldark series, begins in 1810 with the younger generation coming to maturity. Jeremy, Ross and Demelza Poldark's eldest, is engrossed in designing a steam engine that may expedite reopening a mine once owned by the Poldarks and now held by their longtime rival, George Warleggan. Jeremy and his sister Clowance have several romantic interests. Hers include Stephen Carrington, who is shipwrecked on the shores of Cornwall but whose origins are not altogether clear." Libr J

Followed by The miller's dance

The twisted sword; a Poldark novel. Carroll & Graf Pubs. 1991 c1990 510p o.p.   LC 91-4504

Sequel to The loving cup

First published 1990 in the United Kingdom

The eleventh and concluding novel in the author's Poldark saga, this adventure revolves "around Napoleon's defeat at Waterloo in 1815. When Ross Poldark undertakes a government assignment to assess the strength of Bonapartist sentiment in Bourbon, France, he and his beloved wife, Demelza, are swept into a giddy Parisian social whirl, belying the ominous threat of war. Meanwhile, young Jeremy Poldark, a lieutenant in the British army, and his bride enjoy a carefree honeymoon in Brussels. As fate and fortune conspire to reunite the Poldarks on the bloodiest of battlefields, life among their familiar band of friends and relatives in Cornwall continues to amuse and intrigue." Booklist

The walking stick. Doubleday 1967 278p o.p.

Handicapped Deborah "is persuaded by her lover and his criminal friends to help them rob the elegant London auction house for which she works." Publ Wkly

"What you begin with is a delicate and persuasive study of the sexual awakening of a highly intelligent girl, hitherto trapped into introversion by a withered leg. Almost a satisfactory novella in itself, this situation expands into a moving tragedy that represents one of those rare instances . . . in which formal suspense, technique and serious psychological novel reinforce each other." NY Times Book Rev

Granger, Bill

The el murders. Holt & Co. 1987 246p o.p.

     LC 86-29399

This mystery features "Chicago homicide detective Terry Flynn and his lover, special investigator Karen Kovac. Flynn's case is the mugging-turned-murder of a gay man on an elevated-train platform. Kovac's case is a brutal rape that also takes place on an El platform. Flynn's key witness—the victim's lover—and Kovac's victim prove to be unacceptable witnesses, but neither Flynn nor Kovac retreats from the investigation." Booklist

"The two cases crisscross in this excellent police procedural filled with tough, streetwise characters and swift, rough action." Libr J

Grant, David, 1942-

For works written by this author under other names see Thomas, Craig, 1942-

Grant, John _See_ Gash, Jonathan, 1933-

Grant, Michael, 1940-

Officer down. Doubleday 1993 437p $21.95

ISBN 0-385-41968-6   LC 92-37205

"First a bomb explodes at New York City's police headquarters, killing an officer, then a policewoman is executed. While it is clear that the police are targets of a highly organized group, the motive behind the attacks is kept secret. FBI agent Chris Liberti, DEA undercover agent Donal Castillo, and deputy inspector Dan Morgan form a special task force to identify the people behind the violence. They know a terrorist group known as _Punyo Blanco_ has been formed by the Colombian drug cartels to force the United States to stop pressuring Colombia into action against the drug lords. . . . The plot is timely, the characters realistic, the motive plausible, and the pace electrifying." Libr J

Grass, Günter, 1927-

The call of the toad; translated by Ralph Manheim. Harcourt Brace Jovanovich 1992 248p il $19.95

ISBN 0-15-125743-4   LC 92-20233

"A Helen and Kurt Wolff book"

The events recounted in this novel date from "November 2, 1989, only days before the Berlin Wall began to crumble. A chance encounter between a German art-historian, Alexander, and a Polish art-restorer, Alexandra, . . . [results in a plan to] found and develop a . . . Cemetery Association to enable exiles to opt for burial in their native Polish soil, uniting again those whom recent history has forced apart. . . . The plan snowballs out of control and into the hands of others more entrepreneurial and less naively idealistic than the quaint couple who had thought it all up." Times Lit Suppl

Grass, Günter, 1927- *—Continued***

This book is a "skillful balancing act that juggles some very timely questions about the conflict between calls for ethnic self-determination and calls for international unity and cooperation." Christ Sci Monit

Cat and mouse; translated by Ralph Manheim. Harcourt, Brace & World 1963 189p o.p. Amereon reprint available $15.95 (ISBN 0-8488-0112-1)

Original German edition, 1961

A novel about Mahlke, a teenager growing up in a Baltic port city during World War II who is set apart from his fellows by his huge Adam's apple. When a classmate attracts a cat to this 'mouse' he launches Mahlke on his career. Mahlke becomes an excellent swimmer and athlete, and later a hero to his nation. But the symbolic cat watching him is a society of petty men and Mahlke is eventually doomed

also in Grass, G. The Danzig trilogy

The Danzig trilogy; translated by Ralph Manheim. Harcourt Brace Jovanovich 1987 1030p $29.95

ISBN 0-15-123816-2   LC 87-8725

"A Helen and Kurt Wolff book"

An omnibus edition of three titles entered separately Contents: The tin drum; Cat and mouse; Dog years

Dog years; translated by Ralph Manheim. Harcourt, Brace & World 1965 570p o.p.

"A Helen and Kurt Wolff book"

Original German edition, 1963

"A monumental parable on 'mass man,' materialism, and transcendence, written in the richly encrusted, playful, brutal, ironic, subtle, sensitive, surrealist, erudite, unique modern baroque. . . . [This novel tells] of Eduard Amsel, rumored to be half Jew, designer of fantastic scarecrows, endlessly ingenious and talented; of Walter Matern, athlete and compulsive tooth grinder, Amsel's blood brother, his defender, and helper until association with a Nazi S. A. group leads him to beat Amsel unmercifully; of Hitler's favorite dog Prinz of notable lineage and the howling dog days echoing down the centuries through World War II and aftermath. The cast is large; the canvas is chiefly Danzig and villages along the Vistula; and the scarecrow prevails as dominant symbol." Booklist

also in Grass, G. The Danzig trilogy

The flounder; translated by Ralph Manheim. Harcourt Brace Jovanovich 1978 547p o.p. Smith, P. reprint available $21.75 (ISBN 0-8446-6705-6)

LC 78-53891

"A Helen and Kurt Wolff book"

Original German edition, 1977

"Grass's first-person narrator is the legendary fisherman who caught the magic fish and might have fared well had it not been for the foolishness of his wife Ilsebill. Grass uses the well-known fairy tale as a frame for his chronicler to relate his various lives' experiences (between the late Neolithic and [1970]) . . . to his pregnant wife Ilsebill in the course of nine months. While his story unfolds, the fish is on trial in a feminist courtroom after he has been caught again, this time by three women in West Berlin." Libr J

"It is perhaps best to take this fantasy . . . as a celebration of life in all its gross particularity, with Grass still telling the German people to beware of the abstractions that have too often made them flounder in a nordic mist." Times Lit Suppl

Local anaesthetic; translated by Ralph Manheim. Harcourt, Brace & World 1970 284p o.p.

"A Helen and Kurt Wolff book"

Original German edition, 1969

"At 17 the narrator, Eberhard Starusch, was the leader of a gang of juvenile delinquents in wartime Germany. Now, at the time of the novel, he is a 'quadragenarian schoolteacher' whose 17-year-old students are not at all impressed by the anecdotes of his youth and are preoccupied with their own projects, such as setting fire to a dog to protest the use of napalm in Vietnam. . . . Some or all of the action takes place while Starusch is sitting in a dentist's chair, undergoing [a] set of repairs to his teeth. The action moves forward simultaneously on three or more time-levels; the war period, the time after the war when Starusch was a cement-salesman and courting one Linde Krings, the daughter of an unreconstructed Nazi general, and the present." Christ Sci Monit

The tin drum. Knopf 1993 xxxvii, 551p $20

ISBN 0-679-42033-9   LC 92-54295

Also available from P. Smith

"Everyman's library"

Original German edition, 1959; this translation by Ralph Mannheim first published 1962 in the United Kingdom, 1963 in the United States by Pantheon Bks.

"Oskar Matzerath, born with an unusually sharp mind, describes the amoral conditions through which he has lived in twentieth-century Germany, both during and after the Hitler regime. This strange narrator stops growing when he is three years old and remains three feet tall until some time late, when he decides to grow a few inches more. After the war he escapes to West Germany, where he works in such capacities as an artist's model, a night-club performer, and a black marketeer. Depicted as a freak (Oskar becomes a hunchback later in his life), this character symbolizes the deformed society of this century. It is through his tin drum, which he uses to stimulate recollections of his life, that Oskar describes his past while he is an inmate in a mental hospital." Shapiro. Fic for Youth. 3d edition

also in Grass, G. The Danzig trilogy

Grau, Shirley Ann, 1929-

The condor passes. Knopf 1971 421p o.p.

This novel is set in New Orleans, where Thomas Henry Oliver "a 90-year-old multimillionaire is dying. His two middle-age daughters and the Cajun son-in-law the Old Man handpicked are at his side, and so is [Stanley] the Old Man's chauffeur. . . . In flashbacks we follow the . . . rags to riches rise of the Old Man, from an impoverished middle-western boyhood through adventurous years at sea and then on the make in New Orleans, building up out of brothels and bootlegging a great financial empire that eventually takes on the trappings of respectability. . . . Then we come to the story of the second generation, inevitably weakened and corrupted by sheer force and power of the Old Man's personality and need to dominate." Publ Wkly

The hard blue sky. Knopf 1958 466p o.p.

Grau, Shirley Ann, 1929-—*Continued*

On the Isle aux Chiens off the Louisiana coast "live the witty, resourceful, sometimes inscrutable, always courageous descendants of Louisiana's French-Spanish pioneers. Depending upon the fickle Gulf for their livelihood, they have no illusions about the hazards of life and fortune. They watch, they quarrel, and they love—always beneath a hard blue sky; but they accept with bravery and zest whatever a day brings." Libr J

The keepers of the house. Knopf 1964 309p o.p.

"This multigenerational novel deals with the twentieth-century heirs of a Southern dynasty, their relations to the past, and their involvement in the racial and political complexities of the present. The narrator is Abigail Mason Tolliver, granddaughter of William Howland, whose second wife had been a Freejack Negro. The townspeople have always assumed that she had been no more than William's mistress, but the truth of the legality of their marriage surfaces when Abigail's husband, John Tolliver, enters the race for governor. In addition to leading to Tolliver's defeat, the story of the marriage also incites a mob to burn down the old Howland house. Abigail saves the house but withdraws the economic support that the Howland family has always supplied the town, and lets it 'shrivel and shrink to its real size.'" Shapiro. Fic for Youth. 3d edition

Roadwalkers. Knopf 1994 292p $22

ISBN 0-679-43233-7   LC 93-37262

The author "relates the experiences of Baby, a homeless African American child during the Depression, whose seemingly endless travels eventually bring her success and respectability, and Nanda, Baby's daughter, whose magical relationship with her mother gives her the strength to integrate an exclusive convent school." Libr J

This novel "seduces us with its vigorous prose, enthralls us with its narrative—and disquiets us with its defiance of our expectations. Ms. Grau has taken on large themes in characters whose stories, while placing them in particular times and locations, isolate them from humanity." N Y Times Book Rev

Graves, Robert, 1895-1985

Claudius, the god and his wife Messalina. H. Smith & R. Haas 1935 583p o.p.

"The troublesome reign of Tiberius Claudius Caesar, Emperor of the Romans (born B.C. 10, died A.D. 54) as described by himself; also his murder at the hands of the notorious Agrippina (mother of the Emperor Nero) and his subsequent deification as described by others." Subtitle

"A vivid picture of profligate Rome during the years in which Claudius conquered Britain and instituted many reforms at home. A story complete in itself, though a continuation of 'I, Claudius.'" Booklist

Collected short stories. Doubleday 1964 323p o.p.

Analyzed in Short story index

Contents: The shout; Old Papa Johnson; Treacle tart; The full length; Earth to earth; Period piece; Week-end at Cwm Tatws; He went out to buy a rhine; Kill them! Kill them!; The French thing; A man may not marry his; An appointment for Candlemas; The abominable Mr. Gunn; Harold Vesey at the gates of Hell; Christmas truce; You win, Houdini; Epics are out of fashion; The apartment house; The Myconian; They say . . . they

say; 6 valiant bulls 6; A bicycle in Majorca; The five godfathers; Evidence of affluence; God grant your honour many years; The Viscountess and the short-haired girl; A toast to Ava Gardner; The lost Chinese; She landed yesterday; The Whitaker Negroes

Hercules, my shipmate; a novel. Creative Age Press 1945 464p il o.p. Greenwood Press reprint available $37.50 (ISBN 0-313-20991-X)

"The story of Jason and the Argonauts on their voyage to retrieve the Golden Fleece is retold with realistic detail and from the point of view of a Greek of the second century B.C. who would still believe in the story." Booklist

I, Claudius; from the autobiography of Tiberius Claudius, born B.C. 10, murdered and deified A.D. 54. Modern Lib. 1983 c1934 432p $15

ISBN 0-394-60811-9

Also available from Amereon

First published 1934 by Harrison Smith and Robert Haas; copyright renewed 1961

"Claudius is lame and a stammerer who seems unlikely to carry on the family tradition of power in ancient Rome. Immersing himself in scholarly pursuits, Claudius observes and lives through the plots hatched by his grandmother, Livia, political conspiracies, murders, and corruption, and he survives a number of emperors. He becomes emperor at last and is a just and well-liked ruler, in contrast to those who preceded him." Shapiro. Fic for Youth. 3d edition

Followed by Claudius, the god and his wife Messalina

Gray, Francine du Plessix

Lovers and tyrants. Simon & Schuster 1976 316p o.p.

"Beginning with her lonely childhood under the tutelage of a staid governess, Stephanie has found that love is synonymous with tyranny. Recounting her girlhood in France, coming of age in the U.S., marriage and affairs, she realizes her life has been a 'series of exorcisms from the spells of different oppressors,' but in early middle age, Stephanie perceives the beginning of total freedom from tyrants." Booklist

World without end; a novel. Simon & Schuster 1981 314p o.p.

LC 81-1493

"Sophie, Claire and Edmund, friends since adolescence, are pilgriming in Russia, seeking inspiration to give meaning to the last third of their lives. The novel shuttles back and forth in time to reveal the sources of their discontent. Sophie, the earth-mother of the trio, worships art and beauty so much she cries at concerts. . . . Claire, her opposite, restlessly seeks salvation in social causes in order to forget her privileged Newport legacy. Edmund, a Russian emigre . . . is a painter at odds with his time. . . . What links them together from 1945 to the present is friendship, and the various levels it aspires to—from the specifically sexual to finally the spiritual support system that merges them into one unified consciousness of thought, word and deed." Best Sellers

"Despite an occasional pretentiousness, Gray's skillful handling of character and thoughtful analysis of her protagonists' dilemma . . . create an insightful perspective on the insecurities of middle age." Libr J

Great racing stories. See The Dick Francis treasury of great racing stories

Great stories of the American West; stories by John Jakes [et al.]; edited by Martin H. Greenberg. Fine, D.I. 1994 290p il $22.50

ISBN 1-55611-417-6   LC 94-071113

Analyzed in Short story index

Contents: The bandit, by L. D. Estleman; At Yuma crossing, by B. Garfield; The guns of William Longley, by D. Hamilton; The debt of Hardy Buckelew, by E. Kelton; Lost sister, by D. M. Johnson; The gift of Cochise, by L. L'Amour; The woman at Apache Wells, by J. Jakes; Law of the hunted ones, by E. Leonard; Snowblind, by E. Hunter; The corpse rides at dawn, by J. D. MacDonald; The time of the wolves, by M. Muller; Gamblin' man, by D. V. Swain; Vigilante, by H. A. DeRosso; Markers, by B. Pronzini; In the silence, by P. S. Curry; Wolf night, by B. Crider; Liberty, by A. Sarrantonio; Hacendado, by J. M. Reasoner; Death ground [novelette], by E. Gorman

"This excellent collection of 19 short stories is a suitable introduction to western fiction or a marvelous way to rekindle one's enthusiasm for the genre." Booklist

Greeley, Andrew M., 1928-
Angels of September. Warner Bks. 1986 451p o.p.

LC 85-43157

"A Bernard Geis Associates book"

"Anne Reilly, an attractive, superficially successful career woman plagued by myriad insecurities, reluctantly seeks professional counsel. During the course of her therapy, she unleashes a host of painful memories and repressed emotions, triggering a series of bizarre telekinetic episodes. A cop, a priest, and a psychiatrist join forces to prevent Anne from permanently succumbing to her dark side." Booklist

"A vivid picture of a good woman struggling to come to terms with her family and an old-fashioned Catholicism that is stunning in its repression. Greeley's zestful irreverence is a delight as he gleefully bashes Popes, bishops, cops, pols and professors, most of them Irish." Publ Wkly

Ascent into hell. Warner Bks. 1983 371p o.p.

LC 82-61879

"A Bernard Geis Associates book"

Second volume of the author's Passover trilogy begun with Thy brother's wife

"Hugh Donlon fulfills his parents' wish that he become a Catholic priest. He then wrangles with his superiors, impregnates a nun and leaves the active priesthood to marry her, has numerous extramarital affairs, gets rich in commodities trading, becomes an ambassador, is jailed for shady finanical dealings, and finally must decide whether to return to the active ministry or marry the woman he has always loved." Libr J

"The narrative is packed with substance, strong characterizations and startling insights into Catholic politics, doctrine and attitudes." Publ Wkly

Followed by Lord of the dance

The cardinal virtues. Warner Bks. 1990 449p o.p.

LC 89-40463

"When Father Laurence ('Lar') McAuliffe, pastor of an affluent suburban Roman Catholic church, acquires an unconventional new assistant, reactionary elements within the congregation of St. Finian's show their displeasure. As Lar and young Father Jamie struggle to minister to the disparate needs of their flock, archdiocesan conservatives attempt to undermine their unorthodox methods. In addition to successfully challenging the ecclesiastical hierarchy, the dynamic spiritual duo also double as matchmakers, salvage disintegrating marriages, counsel spirited teens, and, most impressively, vanquish a regressive secret society flourishing within the clergy. Greeley appears more comfortable in this reversion to his pastoral roots than in his more sensationalistic fictional forays." Booklist

Fall from grace. Putnam 1993 367p $22.95

ISBN 0-399-13723-8   LC 92-32587

Also available Thorndike Press large print edition

The author's "protagonists include a lapsed Catholic psychiatrist; the woman he loves; her photogenic husband, who is running for the Senate; and her brother, a Chicago bishop accused of sexual abuse. As the bishop struggles to remain shepherd of his flock, the would-be politician finds himself threatened by a horrible secret." Libr J

"Though the first-person narratives are occasionally disjointed, the story moves swiftly to its somewhat melodramatic conclusion." Publ Wkly

Happy are those who thirst for justice; a Father Blackie Ryan mystery. Mysterious Press 1987 302p il o.p.

LC 87-11139

"Chicago matriarch and real-estate tycoon Violet Harrington Enright has dominated and largely ruined the lives of her daughter and three sons. Only her granddaughter (and heir) Fionna has the gumption to fight back. When Violet is found shot to death on her Lake Michigan yacht, Fionna is also discovered—hysterical and holding the murder weapon. Monsignor John 'Blackie' Ryan, brother to Fionna's psychiatrist, is convinced Fionna is innocent, and he sets out to probe the tangled relationships of Violet's unhappy family and retainers." Publ Wkly

Irish gold. Forge 1994 334p $21.95

ISBN 0-312-85813-2   LC 94-29745

Also available Thorndike Press large print edition

"A Tom Doherty Associates book"

In this first volume of a projected series "Dermot Michael Coyne travels to Dublin to investigate his grandparents' mysterious flight from Ireland to Chicago during the time of the 'Troubles' in 1922. His initial foray produces life-threatening warnings intended to discourage him from delving into Liam and Nell O'Riada's past. In a local pub, Dermot reflects upon the horrifying prospect that Liam might have been a terrorist. Later, he is dazzled by the presence of a 'Celtic goddess,' Nuala McGrail. Thus begins Dermot and Nuala's passionate relationship. As translator of Nell's Irish diary chronicling the Troubles, Nuala subtly guides Dermot as he untangles a nefarious web of murder and intrigue." Libr J

"There's a lot of history to sort through here, but the persistent reader will be rewarded by a rich story." Booklist

Greeley, Andrew M., 1928-—*Continued*
Lord of the dance. Warner Bks. 1984 401p o.p.

LC 83-40342

"A Bernard Geis Associates book"
Concluding volume of the author's Passover trilogy
"This is the story of the Farrell family, successful Irish Catholic contractors in contemporary Chicago. When 16-year-old Noele Farrell is assigned to write a term paper on family history, she becomes interested in the fate of her cousin Daniel, a U-2 pilot whose plane went down in China in the 1960s. Interviews with family members lead Noele to suspect the existence of skeletons in the family closet." Libr J

An occasion of sin. Putnam 1991 351p o.p.

LC 91-2271

Available Thorndike Press large print edition
"Chicago Cardinal John McGlynn is killed in Nicaragua, after which his candidacy for canonization becomes the subject of debate among clergy and laity. Father Laurence McAuliffe [featured in The cardinal virtues] is charged with assessing the saintly evidence and making determinations regarding the prelate's sexual and otherwise possibly nonbeatific activities." Booklist
"Although the elements here are standard Greeley, this novel, besides being entertaining, suspenseful and well researched, is also more serious than it sounds." Publ Wkly

Patience of a saint. Warner Bks. 1987 446p o.p.

LC 86-15742

"A Bernard Geis Associates book"
This novel "is part theological tract, part comedy of manners, and part potboiler. Red Kane, the protagonist, is a cynical, hard-drinking Chicago newspaper columnist who has an unexpected religious experience, an ecstatic encounter with a 'cosmic baseball bat' that changes his life, galvanizing in him a new sexual passion for his wife (whom he has cheated on regularly), a new affection for his daughters (whom he has abused abominably) and a new moral commitment to expose a corrupt, sadistic businessman who rules much of Chicago. . . . 'Patience of a Saint' is learned, provocative and entertaining, with Andrew Greeley's customary zest and moral energy." NY Times Book Rev

St. Valentine's night. Warner Bks. 1989 435p o.p.

LC 89-40029

Available Thorndike Press large print edition
"The story is told through the eyes of Neal Connor, world-famous reporter on the edge of burnout, who has reluctantly returned to 'the neighborhood.' With Father Ryan's prodding, Neal investigates the suspicious death of old friend Alf Lane. There is missing money and rumors that Alf was involved with the Chicago underworld. For Neal, the real attraction is Megan Lane, Alf's widow and Neal's childhood love, the fairy princess to whom he could never quite commit himself. This is really a novel of the heart wrapped around a mystery story. Centered as it is on Neal's reluctance to act, it starts slowly. But it is, as Neal finds out, difficult to resist the warmth and depth of Father Ryan's world." Libr J

Thy brother's wife. Warner Bks. 1982 350p o.p.

LC 81-16239

"A Bernard Geis Associates book"
First volume of the author's Passover trilogy
The author "sets up two brothers, sons of Mike Cronin, an Irish-American power-broker who, from his Chicago mansion, destines one son, Sean, for the priesthood . . . and the other, Paul, for politics. . . . As both fulfill their father's wish—with interludes of doubt and sex along the way, despite Paul's arranged marriage to Nora, his quasi foster-sister—their personal lives are equally unfulfilling. Sean eschews his conservatism after a sojourn in Rome, gives expression to his latent love for Nora before accepting a call to the Chicago archbishopric from Pope Paul. Senator-elect Cronin, with echoes of Kennedy Camelot days, rises to the threshold of the Presidency, famed as a sexual athlete, until his perhaps accidental death." Publ Wkly
This "novel makes strong statements about important matters—love, morality, power, belief and human frailty under the pressure of animal drives." N Y Times Book Rev
Followed by Ascent into hell

Green, Gerald
The last angry man; a novel. Scribner 1957 c1956 494p o.p.

Available from Amereon and Buccaneer Bks.

The last angry man was a Jewish doctor in Brooklyn, who for forty years had lived in the slums, angry at all injustice, carrying on his profession as a general practitioner, believing in medical ethics and living up to his beliefs. A TV studio decided to do the story of his life for a new program, and in the process of setting up the program the story of the life and death of Dr. Samuel Abelman is told

Green, Hannah *See* Greenberg, Joanne, 1932-

Green cane and juicy flotsam; short stories by Caribbean women; Carmen C. Esteves and Lizabeth Paravisini-Gebert, editors. Rutgers Univ. Press 1991 xxix, 273p $35

ISBN 0-8135-1737-0
LC 91-4788

Analyzed in Short story index
Stories included are: Widow's walk, by O. P. Adisa; Little Cog-burt, by P. S. Allfrey; Cotton candy, by D. Alonso; See me in me Benz an t'ing, by H. D. Campbell; They called her Aurora, by A. Cartagena Portalatín; Columba, by M. Cliff; A pottage of lentils, by M. T. Colimon-Hall; Three women in Manhattan, by M. Condé; Hair, by H. Contreras; Piano-bar, by L. Dévieux; Barred: Trinidad 1987, by R. Espinet; The poisoned story, by R. Ferré; Cocuyo flower, by M. García Ramis; How to gather the shadows of the flowers, by A. Hernández; Opéra Station. Six in the evening. For months . . . , by J. Hyvrard; Girl, by J. Kincaid; No dust is allowed in this house, by O. Nolla; Parable II, by V. Pollard; Red flower, by P. Poujol-Oriol; The day they burned the books, by J. Rhys; Lola; or, The song of spring, by A. Roemer; Bright Thursdays, by O. Senior; Tétiyette and the Devil; ADJ, Inc., by A. L. Vega; Of nuns and punishments, by B. Vianen; Passport to paradise, by M. Warner-Vieyra; Of natural causes, by M. Yañez

Green cane and juicy flotsam—*Continued*

"Throughout, [this anthology] the race and class issues unique to Caribbean women are explored but in diverse ways and on a small scale, so that one comes away from the book with a uniquely personal sense of a much larger political phenomenon." Booklist

Greenberg, Joanne, 1932-

Age of consent. Holt & Co. 1987 277p o.p.

LC 87-11911

"A failed attempt on the life of the Archbishop of Malaga kills Dr. Daniel Sanborn, internationally renowned plastic surgeon capable of miraculous restorations among the war-torn and disaster-ridden outreaches of the world. Trying to work through her grief, his adoptive sister Vivian sets herself a quest to learn more about this talented, distant man she has always, and yet never, known. Contacts with his former assistants deepen the enigma." Libr J

"Greenberg portrays every character, especially Vivian, with subtlety and grace. Without being judgmental, she illumines the awesome complexity of those in whom admirable qualities co-exist with terrible flaws." Publ Wkly

The far side of victory. Holt, Rinehart & Winston 1983 250p o.p.

LC 83-6196

"Eric Arnold Gordon, a frivolous bachelor, awakens in a hospital to discover that he has caused the death of a woman's husband and three children. This trauma shocks him into pursuing a new, more purposeful life. However, the widow, Helen Gerson, and Gordon coincidentally move to the same small town, making it inevitable that they meet again. What is not inevitable is their marriage, which Greenberg craftily yet believably devises. . . . Twelve years into his marriage (the same duration as Helen's first union, which ended so tragically), circumstances occur that force Gordon into realizing that he has never really known his wife. His attempt to understand her turns the novel from a merely dramatic piece into a thoughtful character study." Booklist

I never promised you a rose garden; a novel; [by] Hannah Green. Holt & Co. 1964 300p $21

ISBN 0-8050-0872-1

Sixteen-year-old Deborah "is sick of rebelling against the lies she hears, the hatred she feels, and, at a summer camp, the anti-Semitism she suffers. She is schizophrenic: she has invented for herself a mythical kingdom into which she retreats and only when her parents reluctantly commit her to an asylum does she begin with difficulty to face reality." Publ Wkly

"The hospital world and Deborah's fantasy world are strikingly portrayed, as is the girl's violent struggle between sickness and health, a struggle given added poignancy by youth, wit, and courage." Libr J

In this sign. Holt, Rinehart & Winston 1970 275p o.p.

"The life of deaf-mutes Abel and Janice Ryder is followed from their marriage to their old age. After they leave the cloistered world of the institution for those with their handicap, they are plunged, unprepared, into the terrifying world of the hearing. They are never fully assimilated into that society. When they have a daughter who can hear, they gain new perspectives, but poverty and personal tragedy—the death of a son—further separate them from others, even from other deaf people. Greenberg's insights into the lives of the deaf are sensitive and painful." Shapiro. Fic for Youth. 2d edition

No reck'ning made. Holt & Co. 1993 296p $23

ISBN 0-8050-2579-0

LC 93-10198

"Bitterness tinges this story of teacher Clara Coleman. Struggling to overcome a childhood of poverty in a rough Colorado mining town, Clara attends college, then returns to teach in a one-room schoolhouse, later becoming principal. As the decades pass, the valley changes and so, too, do the parents. Ignorant of past struggles and disdainful of old-fashioned methods, they threaten Clara's career with accusations that question her values." Libr J

"Greenberg creates a clear demographic picture to complement her map of the heart. Her unflinching eye and sense of irony prevent a facile or sentimental solution to Clara's and the community's problems. The lure of a good story, artfully told, is augmented here by the empathy and wisdom of the storyteller." Publ Wkly

Of such small differences. Holt & Co. 1988 262p o.p.

LC 88-4424

"Blind since birth and deaf since the age of nine, when his alcoholic father slammed him down in anger, John lives alone in a small, carefully ordered apartment, has a job, and writes poetry. But life is not easy: John's independence is rife with dependencies . . . and with potential everyday danger as he tries to make his way in a sighted-hearing world, whether it's fixing a simple meal at home, eating at a restaurant, crossing a street, or taking a wrong turn in the road. Then he meets and falls in love with Leda Milan, who, while trying to get started as an actress, drives one of the vans that transport the blind to work." Booklist

"Greenberg's accomplishment in this beautifully imagined and sensitive novel is to give us an awareness of how people with sensory handicaps apprehend and measure the world; she does so through the mind of an indelibly appealing character." Publ Wkly

Rites of passage. Holt, Rinehart & Winston 1972 197p o.p.

Analyzed in Short story index

Contents: Rites of passage; Children of joy; The Lucero requiem; Summer people; The Supremacy of the Hunza; Hunting season; And Sarah laughed; To the members of the D.A.R.; Timekeeper; The tyrant; Orpheus an' Eurydice; Upon the waters

A season of delight. Holt, Rinehart & Winston 1981 244p o.p.

LC 80-20421

"Grace Dowben . . . is a middle-aged Jewish woman. The mother of two, she is a volunteer on the local fire-and-rescue squad. She is not quite sure that she is not the cause of her children leaving their small town and their Jewish culture. The daughter is caught up in the women's movement and poverty movements in California, while the son joins the Hare Krishnas somewhere in Illinois. When a handsome, young, bearded Jew-by-birth volunteers and becomes an infatuation for Grace she learns about many of the attitudes that have changed her children. Happily married to Saul for 25 years, she discovers that it is quite possible for a person

Greenberg, Joanne, 1932-—*Continued*
of her age and mentality to fall in love with a younger man. What she decides to do with this newfound knowledge and how it affects her husband, her children, and her friends is the subject of the book." Best Sellers

Simple gifts. Holt & Co. 1986 198p o.p.
LC 86-323

"When a worker from a government agency called the Social, Cultural and Ethnic Life Placement Program visits the impoverished Fleuris on their ramshackle [Colorado] ranch, he urges them to join 'SCELP' in return for financial assistance. To participate in the program, Akin, Mary Beth, and their four youngsters must scuttle all contemporary amenities, live like homesteaders of the 1880s, and allow 'participant-visitors' to vacation on their premises. Akin, a gruff narcoleptic, and Mary Beth, a dreamy eccentric whose walls are festooned with pictures from the 'New York Times,' hospitably introduce their guests to wholesome, hearty Western ways. Unfortunately, one clan's arrival induces mayhem." Publ Wkly

The author "has written a sprightly, thoughtful novel about an age obsessed with the urge to look back and the need to prettify the past." N Y Times Book Rev

With the Snow Queen. Arcade Pub. 1991 321p o.p.
LC 90-44191

Analyzed in Short story index
Contents: With the Snow Queen [novelette]; Offering up; That bitch; The flight into Egypt; Persistence of memory; Family tree; Like a native; Naming the wind; Elizabeth Baird; Stand still, Ute River; Introduction to seismology; Retrieval; Hell is a city much like Seville; Torch song

"The title story deals with time travel and a woman who is allowed to relive her life. . . . Greenberg excels at picking moments out of everyday life and illuminating them with unexpected comparisons or a unique point of view." Libr J

With the Snow Queen [novelette]

In Greenberg, J. With the Snow Queen p3-78

Greenberg, Martin Harry

(ed) After the king. See After the king

(ed) Great stories of the American West. See Great stories of the American West

(ed) The Horror hall of fame. See The Horror hall of fame

(ed) Lovecraft's legacy. See Lovecraft's legacy

(ed) Rod Serling's Night gallery reader. See Rod Serling's Night gallery reader

Greene, Graham, 1904-1991

3: This gun for hire, The confidential agent, The ministry of fear. Viking 1952 3v in 1 o.p.

A one-volume edition of three suspense stories, the last of which is entered separately. The titles were first published 1936, 1939 and 1943, respectively

Brighton rock. Knopf 1993 xxix, 299p $15
ISBN 0-679-42034-7   LC 92-54296

"Everyman's library"
A reissue of the title first published 1938 by Viking

"This novel presents the story of Pinkie Brown, a chilling, utterly evil 17-year-old gang leader who marries the plodding Rose in order to insure her silence about his crimes. Both Pinkie and Rose were reared as Roman Catholics, and that background continues to inform their thoughts, if not their actions. In the end Pinkie dies while attempting to kill Rose; later, a priest tells Rose that her love for Pinkie may have saved her, as the mercy of God may have saved Pinkie." Merriam-Webster's Ency of Lit

A burnt-out case. Viking 1961 c1960 248p o.p.

"The story opens as Querry, a European who has lost the ability to connect with emotion or spirituality, arrives at a leprosarium in the Belgian Congo. His spiritual aridity is likened to a medical burnt-out-case—a leper who is in remission but who has been eaten up by his disease. Querry is invigorated by his contact with the leprosarium and its inhabitants, and he begins to come to life. Parkinson, an opportunistic journalist, discovers that Querry is a distinguished architect with a lurid past and begins to write sensationalized newspaper articles about him. When Querry innocently consoles the wife of the manager of a local factory, he is shot dead by her husband." Merriam-Webster's Ency of Lit

The captain and the enemy. Viking 1988 188p o.p.
LC 87-40664

Available G.K. Hall large print edition

"The novel takes the form of a memoir of a young man named Victor, who recounts how the mysterious 'Captain,' posing as a friend of his father, removed him from school one day and set him up in residence with Liza, a kind but equally inscrutable woman. Victor is renamed Jim, the Captain—an apparent thief, a liar, and prone to jaunts to the Continent—returns only occasionally to give Liza money and 'instruct' Jim on survival in the world, and the boy grows up bewildered but, in time, aware that his position in life has been that of a kind of gift to Liza, who, as his real father's paramour, once underwent an abortion unwillingly." Booklist

The author "wastes not a word in distilling the fictional preoccupations of a lifetime, omitting descriptive padding and elaborate transitions. But stripped down, the narrative runs fast and true across that bleak and poignant emotional landscape that is uniquely, immortally his." Time

Collected stories; including May we borrow your husband? A sense of reality [and] Twenty-one stories. Viking 1973 c1972 561p o.p.

Analyzed in Short story index
Contents: May we borrow your husband?; Beauty; Chagrin in three parts; The over-night bag; Mortmain; Cheap in August; A shocking accident; The invisible Japanese gentlemen; Awful when you think of it; Doctor Crombie; The root of all evil; Two gentle people; Under the garden; A visit to Morin; The blessing; Church militant; Dear Dr. Falkenheim; Dream of a strange land; A discovery in the woods; The destructors; Special duties; The blue film; The hint of an explanation; When Greek meets Greek; Men at work; Alas, poor Maling; The case for the defence; A little place off the Edgware Road; Across the bridge; A drive in the country; The

Greene, Graham, 1904-1991—*Continued*
innocent; The basement room; A chance for Mr. Lever;
Brother; Jubilee; A day saved; I spy; Proof positive; The
second death; The end of the party

The comedians. Viking 1966 309p o.p.
Buccaneer Bks. reprint available $19.95
(ISBN 0-89966-923-9)

This "book concerns a back-slidden Catholic, a native
of Monaco and owner of a rundown tourist hotel in
Haiti; his affair with the German wife of a Latin American ambassador; and his involvement with a rascally
British con man and an American Presidential candidate
and his wife, in Haiti to propagate the cult of
vegetarianism—most of them in varying degrees
comedians on the stage of life, running a bluff, playing
a role, substituting sham for sincerity." Libr J

The confidential agent

In Greene, G. 3: This gun for hire, The
confidential agent, The ministry of
fear

The end of the affair. Viking 1951 240p
o.p.

"The novel is set in wartime London. The narrator
Maurice Bendrix, a bitter, sardonic novelist, has a five-
year affair with a married woman, Sarah Miles. When
a V-1 bomb explodes in front of Bendrix's apartment
and Sarah finds Bendrix pinned beneath the front door,
she believes him dead. She promises a God in whom
she does not believe that she will give Bendrix up if
he is allowed to live. Just then, Bendrix walks into the
room and Sarah begins her religious journey; she breaks
off with Bendrix, railing against God even as she begins
to take religious instruction. Gradually she comes to a
profound religious faith." Merriam-Webster's Ency of Lit

The heart of the matter. Viking 1948
306p o.p. Amereon reprint available $21.95
(ISBN 0-88411-654-9)

"Set in West Africa, its hero is Scobie, an English
Roman Catholic who is torn between his adulterous love
for a young woman and his duty to his wife and his
religion." Reader's Ency. 3d edition

"Major Scobie, the British colonial officer hero of 'The
Heart of the Matter', is a well-meaning, ineffectual and
essentially commonplace man who happens, seemingly
only incidentally, to be a Catholic. He destroys himself
and in that act appears to reject God, but out of the
very violence and meaninglessness of the act arises a
profound spiritual truth—a sense of what François
Mauriac, in a discussion of another of Greene's novels,
calls 'the utilization of sin by Grace.'" Kunitz. Twentieth
Century Authors

The honorary consul. Simon & Schuster
1973 315p o.p.

Available from Amereon and Buccaneer Bks.

This "novel relates the story of the politically
motivated kidnapping of a minor British functionary near
Argentina's Paraguayan border. The novel's major characters exemplify the kinds of personal sacrifices one must
make in order to live in good conscience in a world
where there is too much tyranny and injustice. A minor
machismo novelist endures privation; a priest joins the
radical underground movement; a physician gives up a
lucrative Buenos Aires practice." Libr J

The human factor. Knopf 1992 c1978
xxviii, 338p $17

ISBN 0-679-40992-0   LC 91-53189

"Everyman's library"

A reissue of the title first published 1978 by Simon
& Schuster

"In the British Foreign Service 'the human factor'
becomes a liability for employees and a conduit for
suspense, intrigue, and tragedy. Maurice Castle, head of
a division in which information seems to have been
leaked, presents a very positive image that appears to
assure his innocence, but Davis, directly responsible to
him, is an object of speculation. For a secret agent, the
normal relationships of love and family are fraught with
danger. As is true of many of Greene's novels, there
are questions in this book about the loyalty owed to
a government whose activities are suspect." Shapiro. Fic
For Youth. 3d edition

The last word and other stories. Reinhardt
Bks. 1990 149p o.p.

LC 90-81665

Available G.K. Hall large print edition

Analyzed in Short story index

Contents: The last word; The news in English; The
moment of truth; The man who stole the Eiffel Tower;
The lieutenant died last; A branch of the service; An
old man's memory; The lottery ticket; The new house;
Work not in progress; Murder for the wrong reason; An
appointment with the General

"This modest volume gathers uncollected stories from
the entire range of Greene's career. The earliest dates
from 1923 (!) and the latest from 1989." Libr J

May we borrow your husband?

In Greene, G. Collected stories p1-161

The ministry of fear; an entertainment.
Viking 1943 239p o.p.

"Probably the author's least remembered work, one
showing the Buchan influence most clearly. A group of
Fifth Column Englishmen attempt to corner and murder
a neurotic fellow countryman who possesses a piece of
military intelligence they want to pass on to Berlin."
Smith. Cloak and Dagger Fic

also in Greene, G. 3: This gun for hire,
The confidential agent, The ministry
of fear

Monsignor Quixote. Simon & Schuster
1982 221p o.p.

LC 82-5937

"Father Quixote is a humble parish priest despised by
his bishop. Through an accidental encounter with a
stranded bishop, he is named Monsignor, much to his
bishop's and his discomfort. He sets off on a journey
with the communist ex-mayor of his town. The philosophy and thinking of the ex-mayor, Sancho, are
diametrically opposed to that of the priest, and there
is much provocative discussion between them as they
follow paths similar to those taken by the priest's fictional forebear, Don Quixote. Some of their adventures
bring the priest to some surprising places, such as an
x-rated cinema and a church where religion is being
commercialized and demeaned. There is much humor as
well as theology to involve the reader in this delightful
odyssey." Shapiro. Fic for Youth. 3d edition

Greene, Graham, 1904-1991—*Continued*
Orient Express. Doubleday, Doran 1933
310p o.p.

First published 1932 in the United Kingdom with title:
Stamboul train

This is the story of what happened to a number of
people who board the Orient Express at Ostend to make
the three-day journey across the continent to Constantinople

Our man in Havana; an entertainment.
Viking 1958 247p o.p.

"Set in Cuba before the communist revolution, the
book is a comical spy story about a British vacuum-
cleaner salesman's misadventures in the British Secret
Intelligence Service. Although many critics found fault
with the book's overly farcical style, it was also admired
for its skillful rendering of the Cuban locale." Merriam-
Webster's Ency of Lit

The power and the glory. Viking 1982
c1940 266p o.p. Amereon reprint available
$22.95 (ISBN 0-88411-656-5)

First published 1940 with title: The labyrinthine ways
Set in Mexico, this novel "describes the desperate last
wanderings of a whisky priest as outlaw in his own state,
who, despite a sense of his own worthlessness (he drinks,
and has fathered a bastard daughter), is determined to
continue to function as priest until captured. . . . Like
many of Greene's works, it combines a conspicuous
Christian theme and symbolism with the elements of a
thriller." Oxford Companion to Engl Lit

The quiet American. Modern Lib. 1992
c1955 247p $13.50

ISBN 0-679-60014-0   LC 92-50219
Also available from Amereon

First published 1955 in the United Kingdom; first
United States edition published 1956 by Viking

"The novel is set in Vietnam during the French war
against the Vietminh, and revolves around the death of
Alden Pyle (the Quiet American), a naïve and high-
minded idealist who has arrived in the country as a
member of the Economic Aid Mission. . . . The narrator,
Thomas Fowler, is a middle-aged English journalist,
cynical and detached. . . . Estranged from his wife in
England, Fowler lives with an Annamite girl, Phuong.
The story alternates between the period immediately after
Pyle's murder and the events leading up to it." Camb
Guide to Lit in Engl

"Mr. Greene has always been a master of suspense,
and the particular excellence of 'The Quiet American'
lies in the way in which he builds up the situation
finally to explode the moral problem which for him lies
at the heart of the matter." Times Lit Suppl

A sense of reality

In Greene, G. Collected stories p164-323

The tenth man. Simon & Schuster 1985
157p o.p.

LC 84-29830

This volume also includes film sketches for Jim Braddon and the war criminal, and Nobody to blame

"The Tenth Man is a long forgotten film treatment
that Greene wrote for MGM in 1947. A prosperous
French lawyer is held hostage during World War II by
the Gestapo. He and his fellow prisoners must draw lots
to see who must die. He draws the marked paper and,

panic-stricken, offers everything he has to save his life.
A consumptive young man accepts and leaves his new
found estate to his mother and sister. The war ends and
this lawyer, in disguise, returns to his chateau. It is
occupied by the young man's senile mother, who awaits
the return of her son, and the sister, who hatefully
awaits the return of the man who bought her brother
's life." West Coast Rev Books

"A fatal series of events follows, entwining narrative
excitement with broader questions of identity, fate, and
morality. As always with Greene, the basic plot is
heightened by the novelist's compelling view of the
human condition." Libr J

This gun for hire

In Greene, G. 3: This gun for hire, The
confidential agent, The ministry of
fear

Travels with my aunt; a novel. Viking
1969 244p o.p. Buccaneer Bks. reprint
available $19.95 (ISBN 0-89966-924-7)

"Aunt Augusta, in her late 70's, embroils her bachelor
nephew, an utterly respectable, dahlia-growing retired
bank manager, in a series of wild escapades. The action
moves from London, across the European continent to
Istanbul, and ends in Paraguay. Most of the characters
are from Aunt Augusta's somewhat murky past, although
there are contemporary figures such as a C.I.A. agent
and his hippie daughter, and Wordsworth from Sierra
Leone, who lives with Aunt Augusta as her 'valet.'" Libr
J

"The book unmistakably turns its back on the Orphic
preoccupations with the hereafter that characterized
Greene's Catholic novels, and wholeheartedly embraces
a Bacchic emphasis on the here and now." N Y Times
Book Rev

Twenty-one stories

In Greene, G. Collected stories p325-562

Greenfeld, Josh
Harry and Tonto; [by] Josh Greenfeld and
Paul Mazursky. Saturday Review Press 1974
183p o.p.

"This amusing novel treats a serious subject: what it's
like to be 70 years old in the 1970's. Harry, a retired
schoolteacher, and his aging cat, Tonto, are forcibly
removed from their West Side Manhattan apartment just
before the building is demolished; thus uprooted, they
wander from New York to California seeking a new
home. This journey enables the authors to satirize
various American life styles." Libr J

Greenleaf, Stephen
Blood type; the new John Marshall Tanner mystery. Morrow 1992 283p $20

ISBN 0-688-11268-4   LC 91-40057

San Francisco PI John Marshall Tanner "questions the
supposed suicide of bar-buddy Tom, an ambulance driver
whose beautiful, blues-singing wife has been dating a
corporate raider of dubious integrity. Because he suspects
murder, Tanner delves into Tom's background, tracks
Tom's 'lost' schizophrenic brother, finds a motive, and
uncovers a scheme involving San Francisco blood banks."
Libr J

Greenleaf, Stephen—*Continued*

Greenleaf delivers "incisive social observations, compassionate characterizations and fine writing. . . . As befits an heir of Ross Macdonald, the author maintains his moral grip on what matters." N Y Times Book Rev

False conception; a John Marshall Tanner novel. Penzler Bks. 1994 273p $22

    ISBN 1-883402-87-5   LC 94-17371

"Stuart and Millicent Colbert can't conceive a child, but they have the resources to hire a surrogate mother. San Francisco private eye, Marsh Tanner is employed to investigate the surrogate, Greta Hammond. The catch: Hammond must never know the identity of the Colberts nor that she's being investigated. . . . Tanner novels are never just mysteries; Greenleaf always weaves in a larger human dilemma, and here he does it more successfully than ever before." Booklist

Southern cross; a John Marshall Tanner novel. Morrow 1993 320p $20

    ISBN 0-688-12772-X   LC 93-17031

"John Marshall Tanner is closing the gap on 50 a little too rapidly—a fact made all the clearer by an upcoming college reunion. The reunion turns out to be the usual mix of memories, regrets, laughs, and love rekindled, but more germane is the case Tanner picks up while worrying about how his life stacks up to those of his peers. Former roommate Seth Hartman, long a civil-rights champion, is now an attorney in Charleston. Recently he's been receiving threatening letters from the Alliance for Southern Pride. Troubling Hartman most is his estranged son's involvement with the Alliance. Tanner agrees to help." Booklist

Greenwood, John *See* Hilton, John Buxton, 1921-1986

Gregory, Philippa

Meridon. Pocket Bks. 1990 439p o.p.

                      LC 90-7184

"The conclusion of Gregory's trilogy, which began with *Wideacre* [1987] and continued in *The Favored Child* [1989], tells the fate of a young gypsy called Meridon, whose childhood is spent training horses for her brutal stepfather until she is sold to a traveling circus and trained as a bareback rider. In the back of her mind is a vision of a place she calls 'Wide' and a longing for a real home to replace the seedy caravan she shares with her adoptive family. Meridon's dreamworld becomes a reality when she is discovered to be the lost heiress of Wideacre." Booklist

"The hard-won homecoming in this historical novel is richly developed and impassioned." Publ Wkly

The wise woman. Pocket Bks. 1993 c1992 438p o.p.

                      LC 93-21824

First published 1992 in the United Kingdom

A novel of "passion and witchcraft in 16th-century England. Growing up as an ill-used apprentice to Morach, the much-feared wise woman of the moors, Alys finds respite by joining an order of Catholic nuns. When young Lord Hugo and his men burn the abbey to the ground during a drunken rampage, Alys is the only one to escape; she flees back to Morach. . . . Attracted to Hugo despite his murderous past, Alys begins to practice witchcraft in earnest to rid him of Catherine and become his wife." Publ Wkly

Grey, Zane, 1872-1939

The Arizona clan. o.p.

First published 1958 by Harper

Set in Arizona's Tonto Basin, this novel of feuding clans and illicit whiskey has the main character, Dodge Mercer, in search of the thieves who are making off with the sorghum supplies by night. Nan Lilley, lovely daughter of old Rock, the head of the Lilley Clan, provides romantic interest as Dodge risks his life to solve the mystery

Knights of the range.

Available G.K. Hall large print edition

Copyrighted 1936; first published 1939 by Harper

A girl, born and bred on the East coast finds herself heir to her father's great cattle empire and the problems caused by outlaw bands of cattle rustlers

Riders of the purple sage.

Available from Amereon

First published 1912 by Harper

"Well handled melodramatic story of hair-breadth escapes from Mormon vengeance in southwestern Utah in 1871." Booklist

The trail driver. o.p.

First published 1936 by Harper

This is the story of a great cattle drive from Texas to Kansas in 1871

This book presents a "really solid and absorbing likeness . . . of the Southwest in a paramount phase and period of its turbulent evolution." N Y Times Book Rev

The vanishing American.

Available from Amereon

First published 1925 by Harper

"A young Nopah Indian, stolen from his tribe and educated in an eastern college where he distinguishes himself both in studies and in athletics, returns to help his people. His romance with the girl who comes from the East to share his struggles is set against a background which reflects the tragedy of the Indian people, despoiled by government agent and missionary." Carnegie Libr of Pittsburgh

West of the Pecos. o.p.

First published 1937 by Harper

"Romantic western which tells of Colonel Terrill, broken by the Civil War, and his tomboy daughter, their efforts to get a start in the new world of the west, the Colonel's brutal murder and Pecos Smith's ride to rescue the girl, left alone in a land of desperados." Wis Libr Bull

Griffin, Pauline

(jt. auth) Norton, A. Firehand

(jt. auth) Norton, A. Redline the stars

Griffin, W. E. B.

The aviators. Putnam 1988 409p (Brotherhood of war, bk8) o.p.

                      LC 88-12657

"Protaganist Johnny is a born soldier who distinguishes himself as a helicopter pilot in Vietnam and is promoted to aide-de-camp to the commanding officer of Fort Rucker. In his new post, he finds himself directly involved with the development of the Army's first Air Assault Division—a new force crucial to meet the chal-

Griffin, W. E. B.—*Continued*

lenge of guerrilla warfare in Vietnam. This is the story of Johnny's year of work and crisis, the making and breaking of rules, the development of friendships, and the awakening of love." Libr J

Battleground. Putnam 1991 414p (Corps, bk4) o.p.

LC 91-187551

This installment in the series "takes the U.S. Marines from Midway to Guadalcanal. Navy Cpt. Fleming Pickering travels to various headquarters, reporting events to the secretary of the Navy; recently promoted Cpt. Charley Galloway forms a new fighter squadron; Sgt. John Moore is a Japanese-language expert on a top-secret intelligence assignment. Griffin . . . employs a surprising effective alternative to military fiction's usual foxhole-and-cockpit perspective—he places the characters on the fringes rather than in the thick of the action." Publ Wkly

Close combat. Putnam 1993 383p (Corps, bk6) o.p.

LC 92-34677

Set in 1942 the sixth book in the series "revolves around a war bond tour featuring Marine heroes of the Guadacanal Campaign. Series fans will recognize the central characters, among them Marine general and presidential troubleshooter Fleming Pickering, his fighter pilot son Pick, and movie mogul Homer Dillon, a Marine for the duration. Griffin has Marine Corps lore and trivia down pat, and he uses the bond-tour story line to convey the public-relations aspects of modern war." Publ Wkly

Counterattack. Putnam 1990 444p (Corps, bk3) o.p.

LC 89-10772

Books one and two Semper fi and Call to arms, published in paperback

This volume in The Corps series "covers the period from Pearl Harbor to Guadalacanal. . . . Griffin explores the difficult adjustment of enlisted men suddenly given officers' commissions; the raising of a Marine parachute battalion; the impact of total war on peacetime routines." Publ Wkly

Honor bound. Putnam 1994 c1993 474p $22.95

ISBN 0-399-13862-5   LC 93-36850

This "World War II novel pits U.S. Marine Captain Cletus Frade, late of Guadalcanal, against an ostensibly neutral ship in Buenos Aires in 1942. Naturally, the Nazis are angling for position in this vital South American port, and Clete's mission is to maintain Allied influence with the Argentine navy by destroying the German-controlled ship. Along the way, Clete encounters the father he's never met (now a top officer in the Argentine army), a sympathetic German Luftwaffe officer, and a beautiful Argentine 'virgin princess,' with whom he falls in love." Booklist

"Griffin's feel for the details of life in the military 50 years ago and the humanity of his characters on all sides of the covert war make this a superior war story in an interesting milieu." Libr J

Line of fire. Putnam 1992 414p (Corps, bk5) o.p.

LC 91-29971

Book five in the Marine Corps saga "is centered mainly on the World War II battle for Guadalcanal, from August through September of 1942. But not only Guadalcanal: in keeping with the form of preceding volumes, *Line of Fire* is vast in geographical scope, with action occurring in such diverse and far-flung locations as Australia; the Japanese-held island of Buka in the Solomon Sea; Parris Island, South Carolina; and Washington, D.C. The cast is appropriately large and liberally stocked with brave heroes, beautiful heroines, and assorted tough guys, and their adventures are rendered in the wry, salty narrative voice ex-soldiers like Griffin so often employ when they turn to writing." Booklist

The murderers. Putnam 1994 396p (Badge of honor) $23.95

ISBN 0-399-13976-1   LC 94-34497

Previous volumes in Badge of honor series published in paperback are: Men in blue; Special operations; The victim; The witness and The assassin

This sixth volume in the series, "set in 1975, centers around the murder of Philadelphia policeman Jerry Kellog, perhaps committed by a corrupt cop because Kellog's wife, who's left him for another cop, has revealed that her husband's narcotics unit is dirty. Meanwhile, bar owner Gerry Atchison hires a small-time hit man to kill his cheating wife and his thieving business partner. Finding solutions to the three murders unites Griffin's huge cast of characters, among them high-profile detective Matt Payne and take-charge Sgt. Jason Washington, both of Special Operations." Publ Wkly

"Griffin knows Philly, the Philadelphia PD, and cops, and he fills his novels with vast amounts of detail as proof of that knowledge." Booklist

The new breed. Putnam 1987 398p (Brotherhood of war, bk7) o.p.

LC 87-10570

Previous volumes in series published in paperback are: The lieutenants; The captains; The majors; The colonels; The Berets; The generals

"The scene is the Congo in 1964, and . . . the enemy is a dual one: both the Congolese rebels, who are described in unrelievedly brutal terms, and the 'hand wringers' in the State Department and C.I.A. who prevent fighting Americans from mowing down blacks to rescue American and Belgian hostages." N Y Times Book Rev

Griffith, Bill *See* Granger, Bill

Grimes, Martha

The Anodyne Necklace. Little, Brown 1983 250p o.p.

LC 83-880

"Sixteen-year-old Katie O'Brien, playing her violin in an underground London station to make some money, is mysteriously attacked. From that incident begins a mystery involving the theft of an emeral necklace, the murder of a young man whose fingers have been chopped off, and still another murder. The characters in this absorbing tale include not only the residents of Littlebourne, Katie's village, but some East End Londoners like the Cripps family, whose squalid home and bizarre behavior will not soon be forgotten by the reader. Satirical humor enlivens the careful and patient unraveling done by the special detective featured in Grimes'

Grimes, Martha—*Continued*
mysteries—the attractive Scotland Yard Superintendent Richard Jury." Shapiro. Fic for Youth. 3d edition

The Deer Leap. Little, Brown 1985 236p $15.95

ISBN 0-316-32886-3   LC 85-15916

This "novel is set in a Hampshire village and centralized in the quaint local pub of the title. Scotland Yard's Jury is summoned to Ashdown Dean after local mystery writer Polly Praed discovers a body in a telephone kiosk. The murder ties in with a series of pet poisonings and a controversy over blood sports. More murder follows before the unflappable Jury can sort things out in this satisfyingly cozy, old-fashioned tale that has the elegant/macabre feel of Edward Gorey's drawings." Booklist

The dirty duck. Little, Brown 1984 240p o.p.

LC 83-25629

"When a group of tourists on holiday in Shakespeare country are beset by brutal murder and kidnapping, with the murderer leaving Elizabethan couplets as a calling card, Superintendent Jury of Scotland Yard becomes drawn into work on the case." Libr J

The author is an "elegant writer who has a strong touch of poetry in her. Her prose flows limpidly, distinguished by its accurate dialogue, sophistication and quiet humor. She also has a sympathetic understanding of human foibles." N Y Times Book Rev

The end of the pier. Knopf 1992 229p $22

ISBN 0-679-41126-7   LC 91-58556

"Maud Chadwick spends her days waitressing at the Rainbow Cafe and her evenings sitting by the lake with a bucket of martinis. Brooding over the poetry of Wallace Stevens, she stares across the water at the distant glitter of a summer party that never seems to end. Her occasional companion, [Sam] the county sheriff, indulges Maud's mournful fantasies about the Gatsby crowd dancing to Cole Porter on the other side of the social divide; but his own thoughts turn to the killer who has been stalking lonely misfits like Maud." N Y Times Book Rev

"If the somber longings of Sam and Maud don't make the reader uneasy, then the killer's narrative interruptions—stark lectures on the link between sex and pain—surely will. Uneasy but compelling reading." Booklist

The five bells and bladebone. Little, Brown 1987 299p o.p.

LC 87-3148

"Visiting his friend Melrose Plant in Plant's ancestral village, Jury is at the local antique shop when Simon Lean's body is found in a flaptop desk. The dealer has just bought the piece from Lady Summerston, mistress of the lush estate of Watermeadows where Simon had lived with his wife Hannah, the lady's granddaughter. Questioning the women, Jury sees the strong resemblance between the widow and Sadie Diver, who was murdered in London's notorious Limehouse district. . . . The splendid mystery has a tragic core, but the gloom is offset by the author's quiet humor." Publ Wkly

Help the poor struggler. Little, Brown 1985 225p o.p.

LC 85-109

"An epidemic of child murders brings Jury and Chief Superintendent Macalvie, a local colleague, to reconsider the 20-year-old murder of a woman which had been witnessed by the victim's five-year-old daughter." Libr J

"This fine novel features a plot that startles, characters that convince, and an atmosphere that sparkles." Booklist

The Horse You Came In On. Knopf 1993 331p $21

ISBN 0-679-42523-3   LC 92-55069
Also available large print edition $19 (ISBN 0-679-74770-2)

"Scotland Yard superintendent Richard Jury joins his friend Melrose Plant in Baltimore, where they solve several seemingly unrelated mysteries and investigate the genealogy of a bunch of upstarts who claim to be descendants of Lord Baltimore." Libr J

"Notable for its themes of authorship and authenticity and for the cast of delightfully eccentric characters—who gather each day at a blue-collar bar called The Horse You Came In On—this mystery, with its feathery plot and fey, lighthearted tone, moves in quite a different direction than earlier Jury tales. Not bad, just different." Publ Wkly

I am the only running footman. Little, Brown 1986 206p o.p.

LC 86-15305

"Scotland Yard's wise, kind Superintendent Richard Jury must determine if the case of Ivy Childess, strangled in London, is related to a similar crime in Devon. Ivy had left her sometime lover, David Marr, after a tiff in the Footman, so he heads the list of suspects. Jury's interrogation ends with Marr offering a strong alibi, backed by his prestigious family. Calling on the man's sister and other kin, the superintendent senses private fears behind a gracious facade. Jury is right, but his suspicions produce no evidence of collusion until a shocking truth sends him racing to save the killer's third intended victim. An artist at plotting, Grimes concludes this urbanely humorous, knife-edge thriller with a double twist." Publ Wkly

Jerusalem Inn. Little, Brown 1984 299p o.p.

LC 84-15495

Superintendent Richard Jury "taking a brief holiday a few days before Christmas, meets Helen Minton, a woman seeking answers about her past. Their acquaintanceship has no time to warm to love; Helen dies, of poisoning, it turns out. As Jury assists the local officials in the investigation, he chances upon a tangle of details that leads him to snowbound Spinney Abbey where occur a shot gun murder plus the apparent gradual poisoning of another woman." Best Sellers

The man with a load of mischief. Little, Brown 1981 263p il o.p.

LC 81-8251

"This book takes its intriguing title from the scene of one of several crimes perpetrated by a murderer with a macabre sense of humor and a penchant for depositing corpses in the vicinity or on the premises of English pubs. When a man is found strangled and deposited in a beer vat, likable but cunning Inspector Richard Jury spends his Christmas holidays in the 'picture postcard village' of Long Piddleton, determined to solve the growing number of crimes. Deft characterization and por-

Grimes, Martha—*Continued*

trayal of English pub life add to the appeal of a cleverly contrived tale." Libr J

The Old Contemptibles. Little, Brown 1991 333p $19.95

ISBN 0-316-32894-4   LC 90-48647

Inspector "Jury is considering marriage to recently met widow Jane Holdsworth at the moment her teenaged son Alex finds her dead, apparently a suicide. Alex runs away, and Jury, required, as a suspect, to remain in London, sends old friend Melrose Plant up to the Lakes to learn what he can about the wealthy Holdsworth family, among whom Jane's death is the fourth suspicious one." Publ Wkly

The old fox deceiv'd. Little, Brown 1982 299p $16.95

ISBN 0-316-32881-2   LC 82-7719

"The central mystery that confronts Inspector Richard Jury of Scotland Yard is not whounit, but to whom was it 'dun.' Was the young woman found mutilated with an ice-pick-like instrument Dillys March, the ward of Colonel Titus Crael who left home 15 years previously and recently returned to reclaim her inheritance? Or was the victim Gemma Temple, Dillys' look-alike, who tried to pass herself off as Dillys to gain the inheritance? The tiny English fishing village of Rackmoor is divided and tormented by this mystery, which threatens to rock its social structure." Booklist

The Old Silent. Little, Brown 1989 425p o.p.

     LC 89-31650

Available Thorndike Press large print edition

While vacationing in Yorkshire, at the inn of the title, Jury "observes a well-dressed, self-contained woman shoot her husband. With no question of who murdered whom, Jury is dogged by the whys. Officially off the case, he's irretrievably hooked when he learns that the victim's son, and the woman's stepson, is the musical prodigy presumed dead in a famous kidnapping case years before." Publ Wkly

"The calm moments in this moody mystery about parental ties and family schisms and relationships thicker than blood are as fine as anything Ms. Grimes has written." N Y Times Book Rev

Grisham, John

The chamber. Doubleday 1994 486p $24.95

ISBN 0-385-42472-8   LC 94-11764

Also available large print edition $29.95 (ISBN 0-385-47439-3)

"The chamber in question is the gas chamber at the Mississippi State Penitentiary—and for 69-year-old Sam Crayhall, the road thence has been many years long. Sam was twice tried and twice acquitted for murder after a 1967 Ku Klux Klan scare bombing accidentally killed the twin sons of the intended target; 14 years later he was tried a third time, convicted and sentenced to death row. Now, in 1990, a young Chicago lawyer, employed by the firm that represented Sam but which he has just unceremoniously dumped, wants Sam as a client. Adam Hall, the 26-year-old rookie, is Sam Crayhall's grandson. . . . Though the countdown to an execution is a well-worn plot device, it has seldom been as effective, especially in the novel's last 100 pages." Publ Wkly

The client. Doubleday 1993 422p $23.50

ISBN 0-385-42471-X   LC 92-39079

Also available large print edition $26 (ISBN 0-385-46865-2)

"While sneaking into the woods to smoke forbidden cigarettes, preteen brothers Mark and Ricky find a lawyer committing suicide in his car. Mark tries to save the man but is instead grabbed by him and told the location of the body of a murdered U.S. senator—a murder for which the lawyer's Mafia-connected client is accused. Witnessing the successful suicide sends Ricky into shock and Mark into a web of lies, half-truths, and finally into refusal to tell the confided secret to the police. Mark accidentally but fortuitously hires a lawyer, Reggie Love, who steers him through a maze of FBI agents, legal systems, judges, ambitious lawyers, and hit men." SLJ

The firm. Doubleday 1991 421p $23.50

ISBN 0-385-41634-2   LC 90-3945

Also available G.K. Hall large print edition

"Fresh out of Harvard Law School, Mitchell McDeere is recruited by an elite Memphis law firm. . . . [His colleagues] put in 19-hour days for their front-office clients, while beavering behind the scenes on money-laundering operations for the Mafia. . . . Mitch, in fear for his life, agrees to work undercover for the F.B.I." N Y Times Book Rev

"The aphorism 'between a rock and a hard place' aptly describes the dilemma of a young attorney pressed by the FBI to reveal crime-related secrets of his firm, while also hounded by his employers to simply take his huge salary and zip his lip. No aphorism, though, can convey the suspense, wit, and polished writing of this laser-sharp candidate for the best recent updating of the David and Goliath story." Libr J

The pelican brief. Doubleday 1992 371p $22.50

ISBN 0-385-42198-2   LC 91-33235

Also available large print edition $25 (ISBN 0-385-42354-3)

"Set in the near future, the novel begins with an attention-getting double whammy, as two Supreme Court justices are assassinated within hours of each other. Brainy, self-possessed Tulane University law student Darby Shaw . . . proposes a theory about the murders in a brief that leaves chaos in its wake when it falls into the wrong hands." Publ Wkly

"Mr. Grisham has written a genuine page-turner. He has an ear for dialogue and is a skillful craftsman. Like a composer, he brings all his themes together at the crucial moment for a gripping, and logical, finale." NY Times Book Rev

A time to kill. Doubleday 1993 487p $23.50

ISBN 0-385-47081-9   LC 93-32545

Also available large print edition $27 (ISBN 0-385-47078-9)

A reissue of the title first published 1989 by Wynwood Press

In this novel, set in rural Mississippi, local criminal lawyer Jake Brigance defends a black man on trial for murdering the men who raped his daughter

Gross, Joel

The books of Rachel. Seaview Bks. 1979 440p o.p.

     LC 79-4879

Gross, Joel—*Continued*
"The story follows a family of Jewish diamond merchants through six centuries, connecting its history by two threads: a fabulous diamond and the first-born female child in each generation. The child is always named Rachel, and the diamond becomes both symbol and talisman in each Rachel's personal drama, demanding and absorbing her heroisms, sacrifices, loves and even weaknesses." Best Sellers

"In tracing the fortunes of the family in all parts of the world, Gross exhibits thorough research into the social conditions of each country and period and considerable knowledge of the diamond industry. If the novel is floridly written, full of ponderous foreshadowings and mystical intuitions, it is also imaginative; the plot moves fast and the characters are vivid enough to keep readers involved." Publ Wkly

Prequel The lives of Rachel (1984)

Growing up Latino; memoirs and stories; edited and with an introduction by Harold Augenbraum and Ilan Stavans; foreword by Ilan Stavans. Houghton Mifflin 1993 xxix, 344p o.p.

LC 92-32624

"A Marc Jaffe book"

Analyzed in Short story index

Includes the following stories: Daughter of invention, by J. Alvarez; The moths, by H. M. Viramontes; Un hijo del sol, by G. Gonzalez; An apology to the moon furies, by E. Vega; The ruins, by P. P. Martin; The closet, by D. Chávez; The day the Cisco Kid shot John Wayne, by N. Candelaria; Mr. Mendelsohn, by N. Mohr; On the road to Texas: Pete Fonseca, by T. Rivera; Pocho, by J. A. Villarea; Brother Imás, by R. Hinojosa; Golden glass, by A. Villanueva; People should not die in June in South Texas, by G. Anzaldúa; The monkey garden, by S. Cisneros; The apple orchard, by R. A. Anaya

The twenty-five "essays and stories in this anthology of contemporary Hispanic American writing focus on coming of age within two conflicting cultures." Libr J

Grumbach, Doris
Chamber music. Dutton 1979 213p o.p.
LC 78-13033

"A Henry Robbins book"

"Caroline Newby Maclaren [is] the 90-year-old narrator of Chamber Music. Widow of an American composer who died in his 30's, Caroline has been requested (by a foundation established in her husband's memory) to leave a record of their life together. While they appeared happily married for 13 years, their 'secret lives' differed radically from their public image. Dominated by his mother, Robert was a homosexual who expended no feelings within his marriage. Caroline's only love affair was with Anna, Robert's nurse during his terminal illness." Libr J

"This is an elegant novel. Its style . . . combines clarity with a formal reserve that underplays a nudging eroticism." Newsweek

Guareschi, Giovanni, 1908-1968
Don Camillo and his flock; translated by Frances Frenaye. Pellegrini & Cudahy 1952 250p o.p.

This title and the one entered below are the first two

volumes in the series of novels featuring the parish priest Don Camillo. Other titles are: Don Camillo's dilemma (1954); Don Camillo takes the Devil by the tail (1957); Comrade Don Camillo (1964); Don Camillo meets the flower children (1969)

Thirty-six short episodes recount the continued warfare between an Italian parish priest and the town's Communist mayor

The little world of Don Camillo; translated from the Italian by Una Vincenzo Troubridge. Pellegrini & Cudahy 1950 205p il o.p. Amereon reprint available $17.95 (ISBN 0-89190-215-5)

"In post-war Italy, in the Po Valley, there is a small country village that is a stronghold of Communism. The head of the local unit is Peppone, the Mayor. His favorite adversary is Don Camillo, the parish priest, and vice versa. Peppone cannot be a thorough-going Communist because he is a man of conscience. Don Camillo cannot be a thorough-going Christian because he is all too human. Out of this situation the author has woven a series of anecdotes." Rel Book Club Bull

Guest, Judith
Killing time in St. Cloud; by Judith Guest & Rebecca Hill. Delacorte Press 1988 300p o.p.

LC 88-15068

"When charming psychopath Nick Uhler returns to his hometown of St. Cloud after a 12-year absence, he precipitates a series of deaths and initiates an irrevocable process in which old, unsavory secrets are revealed. Ruthlessly manipulating his former high school lover, Elizabeth, now married to surgeon Simon Carmody and in her ninth month of pregnancy, drug dealer Nick generates tragic tensions among three oldtime St. Cloud families." Publ Wkly

Ordinary people. Viking 1976 263p o.p.

"When his older brother drowns in a boating accident, seventeen-year-old Conrad Jarrett feels responsible and makes an unsuccessful attempt at suicide. After eight months in a mental institution, Conrad returns home to parents whose marriage is crumbling, friends who are wary of him, and a psychiatrist who works with him to help put the pieces together. The pain of adolescent anxiety and fragile family relationships are authentically depicted." Shapiro. Fic for Youth. 3d edition

Second heaven. Viking 1982 320p o.p.
LC 82-70124

"Cat is a depressed 40-year-old wife whose doctor husband has left her for his young office receptionist. Cat's divorce lawyer, fortyish Michael, is tired of his job and still suffers his own post-divorce aches. . . . Gale is a troubled 16-year-old boy who has run away from his abusive father and been taken in by Cat. . . . A court petition by Gale's parents to have their son institutionalized for stealing . . . jolts the three of them out of their separate depressions and despairs." Ms

Guest "has given us a book that is neither pop schlock nor great literature but a work of humanity and good sense to which we can respond with pleasure." Christ Sci Monit

Gulik, Robert Hans van, 1910-1967

The Chinese bell murders; three cases solved by Judge Dee; a Chinese detective story suggested by three original Chinese plots; with 15 plates drawn by the author in Chinese style. Harper 1959 c1958 262p il o.p.

First published 1958 in the United Kingdom

Judge Dee, a legendary magistrate and detective, who is based on a real 7th century Chinese person and was the subject of Chinese detective tales during the 17th and 18th centuries, made his American debut in this murder-rape case. The judge solves three interwoven crimes in the provincial city of Pooyang. A postscript provides information on ancient Chinese detection and court procedure and on the Chinese sources of the story

The haunted monastery; a Chinese detective story; [by] Robert van Gulik; with eight illustrations drawn by the author in Chinese style. Scribner 1969 159p il o.p.

First published 1961 in Malaysia; first United States edition published 1963 in paperback

This mystery "finds Judge Dee and his family and retainers stranded because of a broken axle and a howling storm. He has to spend the night solving three murders and a problem of impersonation before he can proceed on his journey the following day." Ency of Mystery & Detection

The lacquer screen; a Chinese detective story; [by] Robert van Gulik; with ten illustrations drawn by the author in Chinese style. Scribner 1970 180p il o.p.

First published 1962 in Malaysia; first United States edition published 1963 in paperback

This tale is set in 7th century China. Magistrate detective Judge Dee and his lieutenant join the underworld in a district under the Judge's jurisdiction in order to solve three crimes. They share the life of the gangster-boss and his entourage while the underworld people unwittingly help them in their inquiries. The Judge eventually reveals the ugly secret hidden by the panels of a beautiful lacquer screen

The Red Pavilion; a Chinese detective story; [by] Robert van Gulik; with six illustrations drawn by the author in Chinese style. Scribner 1968 173p il o.p.

First published 1961 in Malaysia

Judge Dee, "solves more than one knotty criminal problem, all of them stemming out of the fact that he elects to stay in the infamous Red Pavilion on Paradise Island, not knowing it has been the scene of several mysterious deaths in the past. The Chinese atmosphere is suitably exotic and there is a lovely, mistreated courtesan for the judge to protect." Publ Wkly

The willow pattern; a Chinese detective story; by Robert van Gulik; with fifteen illustrations drawn by the author in Chinese style. Scribner 1965 183p il o.p.

"This adventure of the legendary Judge Dee, of Seventh Century China, is a strange, brooding tale of crime, cholera, and corruption. . . . The emperor and his court have fled the plague-ridden city and left the judge and his Colonels, Ma Joong and Chiao Tai, in charge of affairs. They quickly become involved in three murders: 'The Case of the Willow Pattern', 'The Case of the Steep Stairs', and 'The Case of the Murdered Bond-Maid.'" Libr J

Gurganus, Allan

Blessed assurance: a moral tale

In Gurganus, A. White people p192-252

A hog loves its life: something about my grandfather

In Gurganus, A. White people p139-80

The oldest living Confederate widow tells all. Knopf 1989 718p $21.95

ISBN 0-394-54537-0   LC 88-45870

"Ninety-nine year old Lucille Marsden, confined to a charity nursing home in North Carolina, is an American cousin of Joyce's Anna Livia Plurabelle. Lucy tells the story of her marriage to 'Captain' Will Marsden, ostensibly the Civil War's last survivor, whom she married when she was 15 and he was more than triple her age. She also tells about her husband's experiences in the war and after, the burning of her mother-in-law's plantation by Sherman's men, and the abduction from Africa of a former Marsden slave, midwife to Lucy's nine children as well as her best friend. But this novel is less about the War Between the States than about the war between the sexes." Libr J

"In a way, 'Oldest Living Confederate Widow Tells All' is as much about language and myth-making as it is about love and war. Whether one feels that it succeeds depends on how much leeway one is willing to give to this indomitable 'veteran of the veteran,' as Lucy describes herself." N Y Times Book Rev

White people. Knopf 1991 c1990 252p $21.95

ISBN 0-394-58841-X   LC 90-52943

Analyzed in Short story index

Contents: Minor heroism: something about my father; Condolences to every one of us; Art history; Nativity, Caucasian; Breathing room: something about my brother; America competes; Adult art; It had wings; A hog loves its life: something about my grandfather [novella]; Reassurance; Blessed assurance: a moral tale [novella]

The novella A hog loves its life concerns a grandfather and his boyish grandson, the other novella Blessed assurance: a moral tale "is a funny, sad, confessional tale told by a man reflecting on his traumatic youth, when he collected funeral insurance premiums from poor blacks. Gurganus is a champion storyteller with particularly American roots, in the tradition of Mark Twain. This is a collection to be savored and reread." Publ Wkly

Guterson, David

Snow falling on cedars. Harcourt Brace & Co. 1994 345p $21.95

ISBN 0-15-100100-6   LC 94-7535

"Japanese American Kabuo Miyomoto is arrested in 1954 for the murder of a fellow fisherman, Carl Heine. Miyomoto's trial, which provides a focal point to the novel, stirs memories of past relationships and events in the minds and hearts of the San Piedro Islanders. Through these memories, Guterson illuminates the grief of loss, the sting of prejudice triggered by World War II, and the imperatives of conscience. With mesmerizing

Guterson, David—*Continued*

clarity he conveys the voices of Kabuo's wife, Hatsue, and Ishmael Chambers, Hatsue's first love who, having suffered the loss of her love and the ravages of war, ages into a cynical journalist now covering Kabuo's trial." Libr J

Guthrie, A. B. (Alfred Bertram), 1901-1991

Arfive; [by] A. B. Guthrie, Jr. Houghton Mifflin 1971 c1970 278p o.p.

Another title in the author's loosely connected series of Western novels which began with The big sky

This novel is set in a small town in Montana at the beginning of the twentieth century. "Benton Collingsworth, the recently hired principal of the new town high school, arrives in Arfive by train and stagecoach with his wife and two children from Indiana. His eastern, disciplined determination mixed with Victorianism is met head-on by the loose attitude of the untamed West. This is not a 'western story' of all-conquering heroes and evil hombres quick on the draw. The characters are grey mixtures of virtue and vice from Benton's patient wife, May, to the hardbitten town prostitute, Eva Fox; from the realistic rancher, Mort Ewing, to the sadistic deputy sheriff Sarge Kraker. Benton is a non-hero in whom, taken together with the townsfolk, the reader can see the type that really built the West." Best Sellers

The big sky; [by] A. B. Guthrie, Jr. Sloane 1947 386p o.p. Buccaneer Bks. reprint available $24.95 (ISBN 1-56849-121-2)

"After a quarrel and fight with his father, 17-year old Boone Caudill leaves his home in Kentucky headed for St. Louis and the west, where he hopes to hunt buffalo and shoot Indians. The story follows his adventurous course, by foot and horseback, to the Mississippi, then by keel boat to the land of the big sky at the headwaters of the Missouri, where for 13 years he leads the typical life of a mountain man for his period and in that short times sees the Indian degraded, the game killed off and the life he loved destroyed." Wis Libr Bull

Fair land, fair land; [by] A. B. Guthrie, Jr. Houghton Mifflin 1982 262p o.p.

LC 82-3055

"Chronologically, this novel follows 'The Way West' and covers the years 1845 to 1870, relating the adventures of Dick Summers. At age 49, Summers . . . starts to explore some unspoiled areas of Montana. In the Bitter Root country, he marries a Blackfoot squaw and devotes his life to hunting and trapping. When gold fever hits the West, Dick goes to Wyoming and makes a living selling fresh meat to the miners. As he approaches 70, he finds game becoming scarce and the crowds of new settlers making life unpleasant; so he settles down with his wife's people and watches as tragic changes come to his world." Publ Wkly

The last valley; [by] A. B. Guthrie, Jr. Houghton Mifflin 1975 293p o.p.

"Covering the mid-20s to the mid-1940s, [this novel] is set in the same locale and has some of the same characters as the previous novel, 'Arfive'. It centers on an ex-military man, Ben Tate, who buys the mediocre local weekly and transforms it into a respected, profitable business. It is typical Guthrie fare in its graphic descriptions of the Western countryside, its rendering of the powers of nature exemplified in winds and floods, its gallery of small-town, sometimes eccentric characters, and

its frank dramatizations of man's psychosexual needs. But 'The last valley' is more insistently political than the others in that the small town becomes the microcosm of our contemporary problems: freedom of the press, the influence of large corporations, appropriate and inappropriate modes of patriotism, the need for progress versus the demands of ecology." Choice

These thousand hills. Houghton Mifflin 1956 346p o.p. Buccaneer Bks. reprint available $24.95 (ISBN 1-56849-122-0)

Lat Evans, son of characters in The Way West, leaves his home in Oregon to help drive a herd of cattle to Montana. There he decides to stay and get a ranch of his own. His adventures, his love for the parlor house girl Callie, and his marriage to respectable Joyce, make a novel more conventional than the author's previous successes

The way West. Sloane 1949 340p o.p. Buccaneer Bks. reprint available $32.95 (ISBN 0-89968-305-3)

A story of an emigrant trek from Independence, Missouri, to Oregon in the 1840s. Dick Summers, one of the principal characters of the author's earlier novel, 'The Big Sky' reappears in this novel

"Where most writers of Western fiction concentrate on what their characters do, Mr. Guthrie concentrates on how they think and feel. It is this emphasis which gives his book depth and sense of reality." Christ Sci Monit

Guthrie, Alfred Bertram See Guthrie, A. B. (Alfred Bertram), 1901-1991

Guy, Rosa

A measure of time. Holt & Co. 1983 365p o.p.

LC 82-15461

"Dorine Davis, a sassy black teenager of generous spirit and vulnerable heart, arrives in Harlem in the 1920s with the dream of making it big. . . . She joins a gang of department store 'boosters' and is soon living high on the hog. After a tragic marriage to a mentally disturbed West Indian, Dorine runs afoul of the law and spends five years in prison. The experience fails to dampen her spirits, but when she returns to Harlem soon after the start of World War II she finds nearly everything changed, and not for the better." Publ Wkly

My love, my love; or, The peasant girl. Holt & Co. 1985 119p o.p.

LC 85-8556

"A modern fable set on a Caribbean island . . . Désirée Dieu Donné, a black peasant girl, saves the life of Daniel Beauxhomme, a wealthy mulatto whose family has renounced its black origins. Daniel is returned to his home, but Désirée, convinced that it is the will of the gods, sets out on an arduous quest to find the Palace Beauxhomme. The two fall in love. The peasant girl is not acceptable to the island aristocracy, however, and Daniel consents to wed a woman of his own class. On the day of the wedding, in a vain and dramatic last attempt for recognition by the Beauxhomme family, Désirée is trampled and killed by the celebrating peasants. This allegory abounds in vivid, sensual images and symbols, many of which parallel Hans Christian Andersen's 'Little Mermaid,' on which it is based. The

Guy, Rosa—*Continued*

last scene, however, in contrast to the fairy tale, is devastating in its ugliness." SLJ

Ruby. Viking 1976 217p o.p.

"Ruby Cathy is a young woman from the West Indies who is trying to adjust to life in Harlem, U.S.A. The recent loss of her mother makes the adjustment more difficult. Neither her domineering father nor bookish sister seem aware of her loneliness and desperate need for love. Moreover, the kindness she insists on extending to a teacher who is openly contemptuous of her Black students isolates Ruby from her high school classmates. Alone and alienated, Ruby enters into a relationship with her classmate, Daphne, which involves some sexual activity. After confronting Ruby's father in a battle of wills, Daphne ends the 'affair' with Ruby—who is devastated and attempts suicide." Interracial Books Child Bull

H

Haasse, Hella S., 1918-

In a dark wood wandering; revised and edited by Anita Miller from an English translation from the Dutch by Lewis C. Kaplan. Academy Chicago 1989 574p $22.95

ISBN 0-89733-336-5   LC 89-17814

Original Dutch edition, 1949

This "book, whose action is set against the background of the Hundred Years War, deals with the internecine feuds among the French aristocracy and, in particular, with the life of the poet Charles d'Orléans, nephew of King Charles VI. When his father, the Duke of Orléans, is murdered by agents of Orléans's rival, Jean of Burgundy in 1407, the young, sensitive Charles promises his brokenhearted mother to avenge the deed. But Charles assumes his duties reluctantly; among these are his new conjugal responsibilities to an older cousin who soon dies in childbirth. He then allows himself to be married off to the daughter of Bernard d'Armagnac. . . . In this unlikely marriage Charles finds true love, but his happiness is short-lived. Captured in battle, he spends the bulk of his adult life as a prisoner in England, where he pens his famous poems of love and longing for his wife and homeland." N Y Times Book Rev

"This novel exemplifies historical fiction at its best; the author's meticulous research and polished style bring the medieval world into vibrant focus." Libr J

The scarlet city; a novel of 16th-century Italy; translation by Anita Miller. Academy Chicago 1990 367p il $22.95

ISBN 0-89733-349-7   LC 90-39547

Original Dutch edition, 1952

"Against the turbulent backdrop of the Italian Wars (1494-1559) Haasse traces the lives and struggles of some of Italy's most famous citizens—Michelangelo Buonarroti, Niccolo Machiavelli, Vittoria Colonna—in chapters interspersed with the diary of soldier/adventurer Giovanni Borgia." Libr J

"As deftly translated by Anita Miller, 'The Scarlet City' is rich historical fiction written with panache." N Y Times Book Rev

Haddam, Jane, 1951-

Bleeding hearts. Bantam Bks. 1994 311p il $19.95

ISBN 0-553-08562-X   LC 93-14466

This mystery "focuses on Valentine's Day as it's celebrated on Philadelphia's Cavanaugh Street, home to retired FBI agent Demarkian and a host of fellow Armenian immigrants. Everyone in the neighborhood is surprised when homely Hanna Krekorian turns up with a new man in her life, but Demarkian is especially shocked when he finds that Hanna's friend is none other than Paul Hazzard, who was once suspected of violently murdering his wife. Hazzard may have some kind of twisted motive for courting Hanna—but what?" Booklist

"Never quite cozy and never quite tough, this tale combines the best of both styles to stunning effect." Publ Wkly

Haggard, H. Rider (Henry Rider), 1856-1925

King Solomon's mines. o.p.

First published 1885

"Highly coloured romance of adventure in the wilds of Central Africa in quest of King Solomon's Ophir; full of sensational fights, blood-curdling perils and extraordinary escapes." Baker. Guide to the Best Fic

She. Lovell, J.W. 1887 317p o.p.

First published 1885 in the United Kingdom

"'She,' or Ayesha, is an African sorceress whom death apparently cannot touch. The young English hero, Leo Vincey, sets out to avenge the murder of his ancestor, an ancient priest of Isis. The setting of this weird romance is an extinct volcano." Univ Handbk for Readers and Writers

Haggard, Henry Rider *See* Haggard, H. Rider (Henry Rider), 1856-1925

Hailey, Arthur

Airport. Doubleday 1968 440p $10.95

ISBN 0-385-04139-X

Also available from Buccaneer Bks.

"In the space of a single night at the . . . Lincoln International Airport nearly every imaginable man, machine or function goes wrong. One of the worst snowstorms in history has been raging over the airport for three days. The longest and widest runway is blocked by a mired Boeing 707. A traffic controller is suicidally depressed. And a Rome-bound flight lifts off with a man carrying a bomb in his briefcase. How Airport Manager Mel Bakersfield and a score of other characters cope provides the [plot of this novel]." Time

"Here are many minor conflicts—of love, sex, business, and psychological problems—all building up to the tremendously exciting scenes of a shattered transoceanic plane trying to make its way back to the airport, and a runway that can't, but must, be cleared." Publ Wkly

Hotel. Doubleday 1965 376p $14.95

ISBN 0-385-03222-6

This novel reveals the inner workings of a large hotel during a hectic week. "Among the many events, the hotel changes ownership, royalty staying at the hotel are involved in hit-and-run deaths, there is an attempted rape, there is a racial incident, and a thief makes off with sizable loot. This is also the story of Peter McDermott. As an honest and intelligent assistant general manager of the St. Gregory Hotel, he thinks quickly and effec-

Hailey, Arthur—*Continued*

tively in handling the many problems that beset this gracious old hotel in New Orleans. Yet his personal record is blemished by a single event which may keep him from rising higher in hotel echelons." Libr J

Strong medicine. Doubleday 1984 448p o.p.

LC 84-8019

This novel deals with "the controversial workings of the drug industry. Threaded into the brisk, clean lines of the story of Celia de Grey's rise to the top of a male-dominated, ultraconservative firm, Felding-Roth Pharmaceuticals, are numerous allusions to real-life events and issues, which make for a biting indictment of alarming medical and pharmaceutical practices. Celia seeks to change her firm's unethical and sometimes life-threatening eye-to-the-profit habits. Meanwhile, her husband, Dr. Andrew Jordan, fights his own battle for reform when he learns that his senior partner is a drug addict who, protected by his knowing colleagues, dangerously continues to practice medicine. While achieving their own ambitious goals, these two main characters also learn to compromise without losing their idealism. An inventive and remarkably insightful work." Booklist

Hailey, Elizabeth Forsythe, 1938-

Home free; a novel. Delacorte Press 1991 293p

LC 90-40454

Available large print edition $21.95 (ISBN 0-385-30399-8)

"Protagonist Kate undergoes a maelstrom of transformation—personally and socially—after her film-director husband, Cliff, announces on Christmas Eve that he is leaving her for another woman. That same night, Kate meets, befriends, and eventually behomes a homeless family: Ford, handsome and lithe, with strong faith in God; his wife, Sunny, who, like Kate, is determined to find her place in the world; and their two likable children." Booklist

"Hailey injects a surprising twist in the plot and creates characters who transcend personal crises." Libr J

Joanna's husband and David's wife. Delacorte Press 1986 328p o.p.

LC 85-16117

"As the title implies, this is the chronicle of a marriage. Joanna and David, who meet during their last undergraduate summer, are a believable coupling of haute bourgeoise and white-collar working class, of ambitious young husband and intelligent, self-sacrificing young wife. Their struggles as David establishes himself as a playwright, and later, Joanna as a novelist—all while raising two daughters and dealing with difficult parents—ring true enough. So do the personalities and trials of friends and associates." Booklist

Life sentences; a novel. Delacorte Press 1982 279p o.p.

LC 82-7388

"Lindsay Howard, 42, is a successful New York magazine editor [whose] . . . personal life is a mosaic of disasters: lost friendships, husband paralyzed and hospitalized for 18 years, parents killed in a crash, unsatisfying affairs, and now pregnant as the result of a violent rape. . . . Lindsay decides to carry and keep the child in an effort to redeem the disappointments of her first 40 years. The nine months of her enforced bed rest provide the occasion for introspection and reunion with her college friends and her lover." Libr J

This novel "seems the work of a great talent out of control, veering wildly from preaching to poignancy, from the unlikely to the unforgettable—exasperating, but never boring." Ms

A woman of independent means. Viking 1978 256p $19.95

ISBN 0-670-77795-1   LC 77-28414

This novel consists of letters tracing Bess Steed Garner's "life from childhood to old age, from the tranquility of Honey Grove, Texas, at the turn of the century to the turbulence of the late sixties. . . . Bess shares her triumphs and follies in love and marriage, in childbearing and child rearing, in travel, business, society." Publisher's note

The author "has succeeded in giving us a portrait of a woman, with all her frailties, strengths, failures and victories combining to prove that living a life is an accomplishment." Christ Sci Monit

Halberstam, David, 1934-

One very hot day; a novel. Houghton Mifflin 1968 c1967 216p o.p.

This novel follows a Vietnamese infantry company under mixed command on a day's mission. U.S. Captain "Beaupre is an army pro who has seen his best days as a soldier and man. . . . It is not the war itself he questions, but the odd little men whose language and soldiering he neither understands nor wants to understand. His junior officer, Lieutenant Anderson . . . is West Point, brave and thoroughly engaged. He does want to understand. . . . The Vietnamese opposite numbers are Captain Dang, an unctuous package of self-serving incompetence, and Lieutenant Thuong, a North Vietnamese who has come south to fight the Communists but whose native knowledge and fatalism give an equivocal edge to his loyalties. The story is told through the minds of Beaupre, Anderson, and Thuong." Saturday Rev

The main characters "and several minor characters are excellently drawn and the novel conveys well the feel of battle and of the Asian countryside." Libr J

Haldeman, Joe W., 1943-

The forever war; [by] Joe Haldeman. St. Martin's Press 1975 c1974 236p o.p.

"Earth is battling the aliens from a planet in the constellation Taurus but in Haldeman's chronicle of the career of William Mandella from private to reluctant major, the war becomes an engrossing, poignant epic. Mandella was among the unlucky first recruits for a war that has been fought for 1,000 years." Booklist

"A naturalistic description of a war that lasts more than a thousand years, although the main characters age only a few years because of the relativistic effects of faster-than-light space travel. The situation of the soldiers fighting in this kind of war is complicated, however, by their alienation from their own societies by the time-dilation effect, and their growing disillusionment with the war." New Ency of Sci Fic

Mindbridge; [by] Joe Haldeman. St. Martin's Press 1976 186p il o.p. Ultramarine reprint available $25 (ISBN 0-89366-143-0)

Haldeman, Joe W., 1943-—*Continued*

"Jacque Lefavre, in an initial survey on a distant planet, discovers a simple aquatic creature that can form a psychic bridge between two minds, allowing each to experience directly the thoughts of the other. While scientists puzzle the physiological and evolutionary principles behind the phenomenon, another survey team makes an inauspicious contact with the L'vrai, a vicious extraterrestrial race with whom communication is impossible and was inevitable. The mindbridge, which can produce fatal side effects on users, offers a slim hope." Booklist

"Composed as a clever sequence of straight narrations, reports, excerpts from books (some written long after the events depicted), graphs and so forth, 'Mindbridge' applies techniques originally designed to heighten social verisimilitude to what is essentially a space epic, featuring telepathic toys left on one planet by an extinct race of god-like aliens, a complex from of 'matter transmission,' an intriguing argument about the 'colonization' of other solar systems and another alien race." Sci Fic Ency

Hale, Edward Everett, 1822-1909

The man without a country.

Available from Buccaneer Bks.

First published 1863 in Atlantic Monthly

"This long short-story concerns Philip Nolan, a young officer of the United States Army who is tried for the Aaron Burr conspiracy. During the court-martial he exclaims, 'Damn the United States! I wish I may never hear of the United States again!' The court thereupon sentences him to live out his life on a naval vessel, and never hear news of the United States. The story recounts the mental torments of the countryless prisoner, who after fifty-seven years finally learns that his nation is thriving, and dies happy." Haydn. Thesaurus of Book Dig

Hall, Adam, 1920-1995

For works written by this author under other names see Trevor, Elleston, 1920-1995

Quiller bamboo. Morrow 1991 322p $20

ISBN 0-688-09696-4   LC 90-49142

Also available Thorndike Press large print edition

British agent Quiller is "sent to Hong Kong, where he has to get a Chinese dissident into British hands. Quiller, of course, does his job. But he is thrown off stride when the dissident demands to go to Tibet instead of London." N Y Times Book Rev

"Insistently driving home the conflict between democracy and communism, Hall's characteristically lean prose offers some exciting moments." Publ Wkly

Quiller barracuda. Morrow 1990 261p o.p.

LC 89-29575

British veteran espionage agent Quiller "is sent to Florida on a mission that has something to do with a Presidential election. Certain factors in that election might involve the balance of power between East and West—and somebody is implanting messages in the brains of key people in the campaign." N Y Times Book Rev

"A sure-fire pleaser for espionage fans." Publ Wkly

The Quiller memorandum. Simon & Schuster 1965 224p o.p. Buccaneer Bks. reprint available $24.95 (ISBN 1-56849-396-7)

Published in the United Kingdom with title: The Berlin memorandum

"Quiller is a British 'Shadow executive', employed by 'the Bureau', a government agency assigned to carry out delicate tasks, and it is so secret it does not exist. As we follow Quiller's 'brain-think' sequences we learn that during the Second World War he was an infiltrator who arranged escapes from Nazi concentration camps. Quiller and others like him with specialised skills, do the jobs that M15 and M16 cannot do. Quiller is used only at the authorisation of the Prime Minister. In *The Quiller Memorandum* he exposes a large, well-organised neo-Nazi conspiracy in Berlin." McCormick and Fletcher. Spy Fic

Quiller meridian. Morrow 1993 287p $22

ISBN 0-688-11797-X   LC 92-21853

Also available Thorndike Press large print edition

When British secret agent Quiller is "sent to Bucharest to salvage a botched mission, he finds himself following a Russian agent to Moscow and then to Vladivostok on the Trans-Siberian Express. Working alone, as he always does, he ferrets out a plot that will alter the course of nations if allowed to come to fruition." N Y Times Book Rev

"As ever, narrator Quiller's voice is knowing and insouciant, deftly turning plot points with razor-sharp characterizations and keeping readers on the edges of their seats. The subtleties of the spy trade—and the inadequacies of British intelligence—are nicely limned, as is life in the new Russia." Publ Wkly

Quiller Salamander. Penzler Bks. 1994 247p $23

ISBN 1-883402-40-9   LC 94-17372

British secret agent Quiller, "bored in London, takes on a rogue assignment—one the Bureau has not sanctioned but which is the private effort of one of the 'controls,' the enigmatic Flockhart. The mission: discover what Pol Pot is up to in his ongoing efforts to return the Khmer Rouge to power. Arriving in Phnom Penh, Quiller finds himself attracted to his first contact, a female French photographer who harbors an important secret, and suspicious of his field director. Following a narrow escape from a Khmer Rouge encampment, Quiller uncovers plans for yet another Cambodian bloodbath." Publ Wkly

"Mr. Hall, a master of intense prose and tense situations, has again come up with a story that wil not disappoint his admirers." N Y Times Book Rev

Quiller solitaire. Morrow 1992 286p $20

ISBN 0-688-10730-3   LC 91-31060

Also available Thorndike Press large print edition

"When a fellow agent who has called upon him for protection is murdered before his eyes, an enraged and embarrassed Quiller pressures his superiors into giving him the dead man's assignment to investigate the murder of a British cultural attache in Berlin. The murder is apparently tied to former East German national Dieter Klaus, a madman who wants to gain attention for his terrorist splinter group." Publ Wkly

Hall, James Norman, 1887-1951

(jt. auth) Nordhoff, C. Botany Bay

(jt. auth) Nordhoff, C. The Bounty trilogy

Hall, James Norman, 1887-1951 —
Continued

(jt. auth) Nordhoff, C. The hurricane

(jt. auth) Nordhoff, C. Men against the sea

(jt. auth) Nordhoff, C. Mutiny on the Bounty

(jt. auth) Nordhoff, C. Pitcairn's Island

Hall, Radclyffe, 1886-1943

The well of loneliness; with a commentary by Havelock Ellis. Covici 1928 506p o.p. Buccaneer Bks. reprint available $31.95 (ISBN 0-89966-948-4)

This autobiographical novel traces "the life of the wealthy young woman Stephen Gordon from birth to her full realization that she is a 'congenital invert' (as she terms it), a lesbian by nature. . . . It is the first full, rich portrait of a lesbian in literature. At the time the publication was an act of outstanding bravery." British Women Writers

Halter, Marek

The book of Abraham; translated by Lowell Bair. Holt & Co. 1986 722p o.p.

LC 85-17582

Original French edition, 1983

The author "begins his tome in 70 A.D. in Jerusalem, when a scribe named Abraham flees the conquering Roman army. The author follows the dynasty of scribes descended from Abraham through the centuries, until he links them to his own real-life ancestors, a line of printers, one of whom worked with Gutenberg in Strasbourg. The book ends with death of Halter's grandfather, a printer, in the Warsaw ghetto, in 1943. The chronicle moves among dozens of cities in Asia and Europe, deftly encapsulating the historical events and social milieu of time and place, as each generation of this family hands down the so-called Book of Abraham, a record of births and deaths that also symbolizes the continuity of the collective Jewish memory." Publ Wkly

Hambly, Barbara

Those who hunt the night. Ballantine Bks. 1988 296p o.p.

LC 88-47803

"A Del Rey book"

"Someone is killing the vampires of London and James Asher, an Oxford professor and former British foreign service agent, has been recruited by one of the oldest vampires in London to locate the murderer." Voice Youth Advocates

"The characters are well drawn (in the case of the vampire Don Simon Ysidro, positively compelling) and plausibly motivated, and the historical setting is both well researched and well depicted." Booklist

Hamilton, Jane, 1957-

A map of the world. Doubleday 1994 389p $22

ISBN 0-385-47310-9   LC 93-45723

Also available G.K. Hall large print edition

"Alice Goodwin is caring for her best friend's children when two-year-old Lizzy Collins wanders to the pond on the Goodwin farm and drowns. The consequences of this tragedy reverberate through a small Wisconsin community, which never accepted Howard and Alice Goodwin. Theresa Collins, bereft at losing a child and a dear friend, draws on her Catholic religion and finds forgiveness. Alice, immobilized by guilt and grief and unable to function as a wife or mother to her own two daughters, is charged with abusing children in her part-time job as a school nurse." Libr J

This is "not an easy or light read; indeed, it takes on some of the toughest issues of modern life. But the writer's skill in describing a community and a way of life, as well as her insight into the hearts of her characters, render this story difficult to forget." Christ Sci Monit

Hammett, Dashiell, 1894-1961

The big knockover; selected stories and short novels of Dashiell Hammett; edited and with an introduction by Lillian Hellman. Random House 1966 xxi, 355p o.p.

Analyzed in Short story index

This volume contains nine short stories and an unfinished novel: Tulip, "preceded by the illuminating reminiscences of a lifelong friend. The stories, though unrevised for book publication, show the author's unmistakable genius and fertility." Barzun. Cat of Crime. Rev and enl edition

Contents: The gutting of Couffignal; Fly paper; The scorched face; This king business; The Gatewood caper; Dead yellow women; Corkscrew; Tulip [unfinished novel]; The big knockover; $106,000 blood money

The Continental Op; selected and with an introduction by Steven Marcus. Random House 1974 xxix, 287p o.p.

Analyzed in Short story index

These seven stories represent early Hammett and his cold-eyed no name detective the Continental Op

Contents: The tenth clew; The golden horseshoe; The house in Turk Street; The girl with the silver eyes; The Whosis Kid; The main death; The farewell murder

The Dain curse

In Hammett, D. The novels of Dashiell Hammett p143-292

The glass key. Knopf 1931 282p o.p.

Appointed special investigator in the district attorney's office to track down the murderer of a Senator's son, Ned Beaumont becomes involved with political bosses, bootlegging gangsters and romance

"One of the two best novels by the man who is generally regarded as the creator and still the acknowledged master of the 'hard-boiled' school of detective fiction. Brutal in its subject matter but excellently written." Howard Haycraft

also in Hammett, D. The novels of Dashiell Hammett p441-588

The Maltese falcon. Knopf 1930 276p o.p.

This novel "called the best American detective novel by some critics, opens with Space accepting a case from Brigid O'Shaughnessy, a statuesque redhead masquerading as a Miss Wonderly. Almost immediately, his partner, Miles Archer is killed. Spade hated him and has been

Hammett, Dashiell, 1894-1961—*Continued*
having an affair with his wife, but feels duty-bound to find his killer. He becomes involved with an odd assortment of characters, each searching for a statue of a black bird, about a foot high, said to be worth a fortune." Ency of Mystery & Detection

also in Hammett, D. The novels of Dashiell Hammett p293-440

The novels of Dashiell Hammett. Knopf 1965 726p o.p.

Includes five novels: Red harvest (1929); The Dain curse (1929); The Maltese falcon (1930); The glass key (1931); The thin man (1934); the last three titles are entered separately

In Red harvest, a hard-boiled detective, Henry F. Neill, arrives in the corrupt town of Personville to find his client murdered. He stays to clean up the town. The Dain curse starts with the trivial theft of eight small diamonds only to introduce the detective-narrator, Sam Spade, and the stirring events that follow

Red harvest

In Hammett, D. The novels of Dashiell Hammett p1-142

The thin man. Knopf 1934 259p o.p.

"Nick Charles, a San Francisco detective, is the narrator. He and his amusing wife, Nora (on a visit to New York), take time out from drinking and dancing to solve the problem of what happened to an inventor whose disppearance coincided with the murder of his mistress-secretary. There is the right amount of underworld, and in lieu of the usual tough stuff we are treated to an adolescent (son of the disappeared-and deceased), who battens on the more lurid aspects of toxicology and pathology." Barzun. Cat of Crime. Rev and enl edition

"One of the first works to bring humor, and of a distinctly native brand, to the detective story in this country." Howard Haycraft

also in Hammett, D. The novels of Dashiell Hammett p589-726

Tulip

In Hammett, D. The big knockover p238-74

Woman in the dark; a novel of dangerous romance. Knopf 1988 c1933 75p o.p.

LC 88-45206

First published 1933 in Liberty magazine and issued as a paperback in 1951

This mystery is about the complications that arise when a former criminal comes to the aid of a woman pursued by a pair of enemies

Hammett, Samuel Dashiell *See* Hammett, Dashiell, 1894-1961

Hammond, Gerald, 1926-

Thin air. St. Martin's Press 1994 154p $17.95

ISBN 0-312-11339-0   LC 94-32248

When Keith Calder's "neighbor, foul-tempered tenant farmer Murdo Hemison, dies from an apparent blow to the head, the local constabulary have difficulty establishing how, let alone why. Hemison had offended

virtually everyone who came within earshot through the years. His son, young Murdo, and wife were frequent targets of the old man's wrath, but the list of those he most despised included every one from the local veterinarian to tradesfolk to the tale's narrator, author Simon Parbitter. . . . A clever little mystery complemented by memorable characters and an appealing portrait of Scottish country life." Booklist

Hammond-Innes, Ralph *See* Innes, Hammond, 1913-

Hamner, Earl, 1923-

The homecoming; a novel about Spencer's Mountain; [by] Earl Hamner, Jr. Random House 1970 115p o.p. Buccaneer Bks. reprint available $19.95 (ISBN 0-89966-945-X)

"Fifteen-year-old Clay-Boy of 'Spencer's Mountain' is again the protagonist in this short novel set in Virginia in the early 1930's. The story takes place one snowy Christmas Eve while the family of nine is anxiously waiting for the father to come home from his out-of-town job. It tells of Clay-Boy's trip to the woods for a Christmas tree, of his encounter with a fabled albino deer, and of his adventures with neighbors as he searches for his father, who is delayed by the storm. This picture of everyday happenings in a small mountain community and of close family relationships amid the hardships of the Depression years is painted with simplicity and charm." Libr J

Spencer's Mountain; [by] Earl Hamner, Jr. Dial Press (NY) 1961 247p o.p. Buccaneer Bks. reprint available $25.95 (ISBN 1-56849-022-4)

An "account of a boy's growing up in a large and impoverished family in the Blue Ridge Mountains of Virginia. . . . His chief problems are love and the fact that his father feels that a college education is a waste of money." Publ Wkly

"A novel filled with joie de vivre, frank simplicity, a little sinning, and much human goodness." Libr J

Hamsun, Knut, 1859-1952

Nobel Prize in literature, 1920

Hunger; translated from the Norwegian of Knut Hamsun by George Egerton with an introduction by Edwin Björkman. Knopf 1921 263p o.p.

Original Norwegian edition, 1890

This novel "is the semiautobiographical chronicle of the physical hunger experienced by an aspiring writer in late 19th-century Norway. The unnamed narrator of this plotless, episodic work is an introspective young man whose hunger to succeed as a writer matches his intense physical hunger. He lacks human contact and at times seems demented. Although he has occasional hunger-induced hallucinations, he neither feels sorry for himself nor tries to rectify his situation." Merriam-Webster's Ency of Lit

Hamsun, Knut, 1859-1952—*Continued*

Mysteries; translated from the Norwegian of Knut Hamsun by Arthur G. Chater. Knopf 1927 338p o.p.

Original Norwegian edition, 1892

"A monologue consisting partly of the hero's, Herr Nagel's, thoughts and dreams, and partly of his interminable talk. He loved anyone who would let him talk, and his talk was always a mixture of mysticism, sheer garrulity, and brilliantly piquant criticism. . . . Eventually he contrived to be drowned and so to escape from a world which seemed to him topsy-turvy." New Statesman

"Johan Nilsen Nagel and his mental escapades and unpredictable actions point directly to the stream-of-consciousness technique of later 20th-century fiction." Choice

Han, Suyin

The enchantress. Bantam Bks. 1985 345p $16.95

ISBN 0-553-05071-0   LC 84-45185

"Set in the eighteenth century, in Switzerland, China, and Thailand, the tale concerns the exploits of Colin and his twin sister, Bea, free spirits whose Celtic roots have endowed them with a special ability to commune with nature. As a child in Switzerland, Colin learns from his father how to make automatons, an early version of robots. After their parents' death, Colin and Bea travel to China, where craftspeople are needed to keep the automatons at the emperor's court in operating order. There, and subsequently in Thailand, they become embroiled in numerous affairs of the heart and state." Booklist

"This is an extremely well-told tale of life and love in the 18th Century. History comes alive, and there is a masterful blending of magic and science at a time when the division between the two were not so great." SLJ

Till morning comes; a novel. Bantam Bks. 1982 500p il o.p.

LC 81-19150

"This is a love story set in China during the period from World War II through the years of the Cultural Revolution. Stephanie Ryder, beautiful daughter of a rich Texan oilman, comes to China as a magazine correspondent and falls in love with Dr. Jen Yong, a physician from an upper class Chinese family who sympathizes with the Communist objectives. . . . Stephanie and Yong endure much censure, hardship and repression to sustain their relationship and marriage in the not very tolerant atmosphere of the Communist Revolution." Best Sellers

"Told with sensitivity, this is an engrossing story. Although her sympathies lie with the Communist uprising, Han does not spare that regime in depicting the purges." Libr J

Handke, Peter, 1942-

The left-handed woman; translated by Ralph Manheim. Farrar, Straus & Giroux 1978 87p o.p.

LC 78-5568

Original German edition, 1976

"Marianne, 30, decides that Bruno, her well-to-do executive husband, will some day leave her, so she throws him out on the spot. She takes long walks through nearby woods, through an unnamed West German city and through the halls and rooms of her rented house. A friend asks her to join what seems to be a women's consciousness-raising group, but Marianne does not. She works at a translation of a French book about a woman trying to achieve independence; if there is a message here for Marianne, she does not get it. Friends, relatives and casual acquaintances gather round her and then disperse as aimlessly as they came. At the end, the woman is virtually catatonic." Time

"There are echoes of Beckett, Sartre, and Kafka in this chilly little novel. . . . Handke at his best handles that moribund trinity of modern themes—alienation, failure of communication and absurdity—with quirky originality." Newsweek

Hansen, Joseph

A country of old men; the last Dave Brandstetter mystery. Viking 1991 177p o.p.

LC 90-50550

"While investigating the murder of a drug-dealing musician and the kidnapping of a little boy who witnessed the killing, the gay detective stubbornly ignores the conspicuously poor state of his own health. But even as he drags his creaky bones on an exhausting and dangerous hunt for the killer, his fine, strong mind keeps turning to thoughts of mortality. . . . A cool stylist who never loses control over his emotional voice, Mr. Hansen trusts his lifelike characters to earn our compassion." NY Times Book Rev

Early graves; a Dave Brandstetter mystery. Mysterious Press 1987 184p o.p.

LC 87-15178

"Gay detective Dave Brandstetter tracks down a serial killer whose victims have all been young men dying of AIDS. Dave, in his 60s, has just returned to L.A. from a business trip, having been met at the airport by his young ex-lover, TV reporter Cecil, when he discovers the body of real-estate developer Drew Dodge on his porch steps. The man's death becomes linked to a string of stabbing murders, and it also becomes clear that he was killed first and then dropped at Dave's." Publ Wkly

Gravedigger; a Dave Brandstetter mystery. Holt, Rinehart & Winston 1982 183p o.p.

LC 81-6381

"A Rinehart suspense novel"

Insurance sleuth Dave Brandstetter "investigates the possible murder of a runaway teenage girl, who may have died by her own involvement with drugs, a strange cult, and the wrong kind of people. The missing girl's father, a corrupt lawyer engulfed by scandal, has run away, too, leaving Brandstetter with two cold trails and a lot of questions." Booklist

The little dog laughed; a Dave Brandstetter mystery. Holt & Co. 1986 184p o.p.

LC 86-12115

"A Rinehart suspense novel"

"Called in to investigate the death claims filed on the shooting demise of a globe-striding political journalist, insurance sleuth Brandstetter gets embroiled in international skulduggery. The writer was, of course, no suicide, and his death is linked to that of a young Latino sans green card who is from a Central American republic in turmoil." Booklist

Hansen, Ron

(ed) You've got to read this. See You've got to read this

Hardesty, Sarah *See* Roberts, Nora, 1950-

Hardwick, Elizabeth
Sleepless nights. Random House 1979 151p o.p.

LC 78-21798

"The narrator is a woman, Elizabeth, thinking back on her past, of her childhood home in Kentucky, of time spent in Boston, New York, Amsterdam, Maine. She remembers people she has known, is mystified and moved by their courage and separateness and [portrays them] . . . in vignettes connected by the thread of her own life and thoughts." N Y Rev Books

"Brilliantly poised and confidently daring, 'Sleepless Nights' is a chin-up tightrope walk along the borderline between fiction and autobiography. By calling it a novel, Hardwick challenges our notions about categories. . . . This extraordinary book turns out to have an unannounced theme—unexpected adherences, strange lifelong conjunctions of people who might not be expected to stick together. A lonely, sleepless woman observes them and incorporates them into her own life." Newsweek

Hardwick, Mollie
The dreaming damozel. St. Martin's Press 1991 183p o.p.

LC 90-19457

This mystery features "Doran Fairweather, an English antiques dealer with a knack for discovering murder along with *objets d'art*. . . . Suffering from malaise after a miscarriage and the loss of her business partner to a more lucrative job, Doran hopes to spark new interest in her shop by branching into Pre-Raphaelite work; she is soon surprised to have a number of rare Rossetti drawings fall into her possession. Obsessed with Rossetti's dreaming figures and fascinated by a mysterious, eccentric man who entrusts her with one apparently rare artwork, Doran quickly links the art to murder." Publ Wkly

"The mystery plot seems a slender reed when stripped of its more piquant art-history references; but the story is gracefully written and full of interesting arcana about the antiques trade." N Y Times Book Rev

The Duchess of Duke Street; a novel. Holt, Rinehart & Winston 1977 c1976 303p o.p.

LC 76-29903

First published 1976 in the United Kingdom in two volumes with title The Duchess of Duke Street: Book 1: The way up; Book 2: The golden years

An "adaptation of a BBC television series. . . . The setting is 1900 London. Heroine Louisa Leyton sets out to be the best cook in England and ends up running a residential hotel and a catering service. The cast includes: Edward, Prince of Wales, whose interest in Luisa goes beyond her culinary skills; Augustus Trotter, who becomes Louisa's husband for propriety's sake and assists her as butler; and the Honorable Charles Tyrrel, who befriends Louisa in her post-Edward days. Although the episodic format is still evident in this novelization, it does not impair readability. There is enough adventure

and humor here to entertain the reader willing to settle for a light-hearted if slightly unbelievable story." Libr J

Malice domestic. St. Martin's Press 1986 218p o.p.

LC 86-11376

This is the first novel featuring "Doran Fairweather, a humorously perceptive antiques dealer, and her love, the Reverend Chelmarsh, both of whom live in the isolated village of Abbotsbourne, Kent. A wealthy bachelor takes over the village's long-deserted great house. Events move from cozy to chilling when a series of deaths ensues, including a teen suicide. Graceful writing embellishes this stunning tale of evil." Booklist

Parson's pleasure. St. Martin's Press 1987 199p o.p.

LC 87-4437

This novel takes Doran Fairweather "to Warwickshire to track down the theft of priceless antiques from a rather eccentric elderly member of the aristocracy, Lady Timberlake. What starts off as a working holiday with her boyfriend, the prudish Rodney Chelmarsh, quickly turns serious when one of the leads Fairweather is investigating, a gypsy antiques dealer, is brutally murdered. Chelmarsh is the first to realize that Fairweather's own life may be in jeopardy. Hardwick has managed to breathe fresh life into this fairly conventional mystery. Everything is vaguely familiar, from the cast of dotty characters to the locale, but this only adds to the book's charm." Publ Wkly

Perish in July. St. Martin's Press 1990 205p $15.95
ISBN 0-312-04402-X

LC 89-77956

This Doran Fairweather mystery "finds the antiques dealer and her vicar husband involved in a parish fund-raising theatrical and the murder of its leading lady." Booklist

"Hardwick again writes about believable characters coping not only with murder and other disasters but with a true-to-life marriage." Publ Wkly

Hardy, Thomas, 1840-1928
Far from the madding crowd.
Available from various publishers
First published 1874

"Bathsheba Everdene is courted by Gabriel Oak, a young farmer who becomes bailiff of the farm she inherits, by William Boldwood, who owns the neighboring farm, and by Sergeant Troy, a handsome young adventurer. She marries Troy, who spends her money freely. Troy now accidentally meets his old love Fanny Robin and her child in pitiful condition on the way to the workhouse and the next day finds them both dead. The incident brings about a quarrel with Bathsheba and his departure; and he is swept out to sea. Bathsheba, who believes him drowned, becomes engaged to William Boldwood. When Troy reappears in blustering mood, Boldwood kills him and is sentenced to penal servitude for life. Bathsheba now marries Gabriel Oak." Reader's Ency

"The theme, which occurs in others of Hardy's novels, is the contrast of a patient and generous love with unscrupulous passion." Oxford Companion to Engl Lit

Jude the obscure. Knopf 1992 518p $20
ISBN 0-679-40993-9

LC 92-52925
Also available from Buccaneer Bks.

Hardy, Thomas, 1840-1928—*Continued*

"Everyman's library"

First published 1895

A novel set in rural England which deals "with the mutual love of Jude Fawley and his cousin, Sue Bridehead. They both marry outsiders, but finally secure divorces to live with each other. After some years, young Jude, the son of Jude's former wife Arabella, murders Jude's two younger children and hangs himself to escape from misery. Broken by this tragedy, Sue returns to her husband and Jude to Arabella. Soon afterward Jude dies." Reader's Ency

"Mr. Hardy's rebellious views of life and religion, and leanings towards naturalistic methods, are given full play in this story of a peasant scholar's foiled ambition, which from beginning to end is sombre and in many of the incidents extremely painful." Baker. Guide to the Best Fic

The Mayor of Casterbridge.

Available from various publishers

First published 1886. Variant title: The life and death of the Mayor of Casterbridge

"Michael Henchard, a young hay trusser, while intoxicated at a fair sells his wife and child at auction for five pounds to a man named Newson. Eighteen years afterward when Henchard has become the Mayor of Casterbridge, they reappear, and most of the novel deals with the problems and embitterments of his later life. The girl, Elizabeth Jane, who, he finally learns, is not his own daughter but Newson's marries his business rival, Farfrae." Reader's Ency

The return of the native.

Available from various publishers

First published 1878

"The novel is set on Egdon Heath, a barren moor in the fictional Wessex in southwestern England. The native of the title is Clym Yeobright, who has returned to the area to become a schoolmaster after a succesful but, in his opinion, a shallow career as a jeweler in Paris. He and his cousin Thomasin exemplify the traditional way of life, while Thomasin's husband, Damon Wildeve, and Clym's wife, Eustacia Vye, long for the excitement of city life. Disappointed that Clym is content to remain on the heath, Eustacia, willful and passionate, rekindles her affair with the reckless Damon. After a series of coincidences Eustacia comes to believe that she is responsible for the death of Clym's mother. Convinced that fate has doomed her to cause others pain, Eustacia flees and is drowned (by accident or intent). Damon drowns trying to save her." Merriam-Webster's Ency of Lit

Tess of the D'Urbervilles.

Available from various publishers

First published in complete form 1891

"Tess Durbeyfield, urged by her dissipated father and the necessities of a poverty-stricken household, takes service with the wealthy Mrs. D'Urberville. Here Alec, the son of the house, forces Tess into sexual relations with him, and she becomes pregnant. The child, however, dies in infancy, and Tess hires herself out as a dairymaid on a farm. She falls in love with Angel Clare, a rector's son, and they marry. On their wedding night they indulge in mutual confessions. Though he expects to be forgiven for his own sinful past, Angel cannot forgive Tess for her past, in which she was victimized rather than sinful, and he deserts her. Some time later, Alec, now a preaching fanatic, entreats Tess to return to him, she does so in the belief that Angel will never relent, and in the face of growing poverty. When the repentant Angel returns, and finding Tess with Alec, prepares to leave once again, Tess stabs and kills Alec in desperation. She and Angel hide out for a time, but finally Tess is arrested and sentenced to death." Reader's Ency

"Tess, the author contends, is sinned against, but not a sinner; her tragedy is the work of tyrannical circumstances and of the evil deeds of others in the past and the present, and more particularly of two men's baseness, the seducer, and the well-meaning intellectual who married her. . . . The pastoral surroundings, the varying aspects of field, river, sky, serve to deepen the pathos of stage in the heroine's calamities, or to add beauty and dignity to her tragic personality." Baker. Guide to the Best Fic

Under the greenwood tree.

Available from Amereon

First published 1872

"The first of the Wessex novels proper, the common groundwork of which is a very vivid delineation of the people of Dorset and the neighbouring counties, and of the natural life and scenery. . . . An idyll of village life, in which the members of a carrier's family and the village life choir, a gathering of rustic oddities, furnish a sort of comic chorus to the love-affairs of a rustic boy and girl." Baker. Guide to the Best Fic

Wessex tales.

Available from Amereon

Analyzed in Short story index

First published 1888

Contents: Three strangers; Tradition of eighteen hundred and four; Melancholy Hussar; Withered arm; Fellow-townsmen; Interlopers at the knap; Distracted preacher

Harper, Karen

Circle of gold. Dutton 1992 393p $20

ISBN 0-525-93453-7   LC 91-41488

"In early 19th-century Kentucky, 13-year-old Rebecca Blake feels a young girl's love for Adam Scott, who would rather tend sick animals than his father's distilling trade. After the death of her beloved mother, Rebecca is left by her keelboater father with a kindly Shaker sect, whose beliefs she tries to honor even though she can never fully embrace them. She is rejected by the community when she falls in love with Ramsey Sherborne, a titled British labor activist who is visiting the Shakers. As Lady Sherborne, Rebecca helps villagers on her husband's Dorset estate earn a living by preparing Shaker products. Then she loses her young husband, returns to Kentucky and is reunited with Adam." Libr J

"Harper brings a fresh integrity to this sometimes trite genre of literature." Booklist

Harris, John, 1916-1991

For works written by this author under other names see Hebden, Mark, 1916-1991

Harris, Marilyn, 1931-

Hatter Fox. Random House 1973 241p o.p.

"Hatter Fox, a teenage Navaho girl, is a victim whose past is a series of virtually insufferable physical and mental tortures. As the novel opens, she is in jail for a minor offense. She stabs a young Indian Bureau doc-

Harris, Marilyn, 1931——*Continued*

tor, Teague Summer, and is sent to a reformatory in the middle of New Mexico. The greater part of the story takes place there and describes her gradual and painful rehabilitation under the guidance of Summer. Finally released into his custody and beginning to learn to cope with the outside, Hatter Fox is killed by a tourist bus, her first paycheck still in her hand." Libr J

This is a "very well written and touching novel. . . . Avoiding virtually all of the pitfalls, including the obvious one of a love affair between Hatter and the doctor, Mrs. Harris writes about the relationship among people who come to care about each other in a manner that is infinitely refreshing." Publ Wkly

Lost and found; a novel. Crown 1991 438p $19.95

ISBN 0-517-58333-X   LC 90-22054

"After she is accidentally put on the wrong train in Tulsa, Okla., by her stepbrother, R.C., three-year-old orphaned Belle Drusso seems to vanish, despite all efforts to locate her by her devoted foster mother, Martha. Set during the 1930s Depression and a racially biased America in the '40s and '50s, Belle's misadventures are initially grim. Alighting from the train in California, she endures several months with dogmatic religious fanatics and survives a stint in a carelessly run orphanage. Fortune seems to smile on her in the form of loving Japanese-American foster parents, but with the advent of WWII, they are put into an internment camp. Later Belle witnesses the racial turmoil surrounding school integration in Little Rock, Ark." Publ Wkly

Harris, Mark, 1922-

Bang the drum slowly, by Henry W. Wiggen; certain of his enthusiasms restrained by Mark Harris. Knopf 1956 243p o.p.

Available from Amereon and Buccaneer Bks.

A baseball novel which centers on Bruce, a black catcher, who is slowly dying of Hodgkin's disease. The narrator tries to keep the matter a secret, but eventually it comes out. The rest of the book concerns the loyalty of Bruce's teammates to their doomed member

"Narrated by 'Author' in the raucous speech of the ball park, yet with an elegiac dignity." Booklist

Harris, Robert, 1957-

Fatherland. Random House 1992 338p $21

ISBN 0-679-41273-5   LC 91-51026
Also available Thorndike Press large print edition

This thriller is "based on the premise that Hitler won the war and now rules a vast trans-European empire. On the eve of Hitler's 75th birthday, just when America's President Joseph P. Kennedy is expected in Berlin, the body of a once-important Nazi official washes up along the Rhine. Investigator Xavier March persists in checking out the case, despite orders to the contrary from the Gestapo itself, and soon he discovers a conspiracy whose roots date back to World War II." Libr J

"'Fatherland' is a bleak book. But what concerns the author is the indestructibility of the human spirit, as exemplified by Xavier March. If Hitler's Germany is hell, at least a few angels are floating around." N Y Times Book Rev

Harris, Ruth

Love and money. Random House 1988 437p $18.95

ISBN 0-394-56556-8   LC 87-27246
Also available G.K. Hall large print edition

Spanning four decades, this "is the story of millionaire stock broker Russell Dahlen's two daughters who have never met. One, Deedee Dahlen, is the 'Million Dollar Baby,' born into the Dahlen family with such wealth that she has a silver ladel in her mouth. The other is Lana Bantry, the illegitimate daughter from the wrong side of the tracks. . . . The tie that pulls these ladies together is a bon vivant by the name of Slash Steiner. . . . One woman ends up married to him while the other becomes his business partner and mistress." West Coast Rev Books

"Harris will keep her fans engrossed as she accentuates the riskiness and unpredictability of lives spent obsessed with money, setting them against a backdrop of dizzying social change and a volatile stock market." Publ Wkly

Modern women. St. Martin's Press 1989 439p o.p.

LC 89-35114

"The story centers on three women in their twenties at the time of John F. Kennedy's assassination . . . who dabble in the sexual, cultural, and political freedoms that raucous era thrust upon the new generation. Jane, Elly, and Lincky are almost indistinguishable: all three are well-bred, middle-or upper-middle-class college grads; all end up in New York City's trendy Greenwich Village; each aspires to a writing career and enters some branch of publishing and each leads a confused, unsettled life filled with man troubles." Booklist

Harris, Thomas, 1940-

Black Sunday. Putnam 1975 318p o.p. Buccaneer Bks. reprint available $24.95 (ISBN 0-89966-876-3)

"In retaliation for American aid to Israel, an Arab terrorist group has determined to blow up the Super Bowl. Their prime weapon is Michael Lander, a former Navy pilot, whose own strange psyche, combined with his experiences as prisoner of war in Vietnam, has driven him to seek revenge against a world he believes has savaged him. As the pilot of the Aldrich television blimp that floats above professional football games and a brilliant technician, Lander is uniquely qualified to carry out the act of madness that obsesses him." Publisher's note

"All is neck and neck, quite excitingly to the very end. . . . The action is . . . very violent (violent sexy episodes, too) and the plot is packed with business. Not a bit believable, but successful entertainment." Libr J

Red Dragon. Putnam 1981 348p o.p. Buccaneer Bks. reprint available $24.95 (ISBN 0-89966-877-1)

LC 81-8674

This novel concerns "a psychopathic mass murderer with an intuitive FBI investigator on his trail. . . . [The ex-F.B.I. man] is Will Graham, whose acute perception gives him entree to murderers' minds. With two mass killers to his credit, he's lured from peaceful retirement and happy marriage to hunt the Red Dragon, slayer of two families within a month. A dedicated group of forensic experts and a dogged scandal sheet reporter also

Harris, Thomas, 1940-—*Continued*

pursue the killer—born with a cleft palate, cruelly mistreated as a child, skewed by the sight of a powerful painting, and side-tracked by warm attention from a blind woman." Libr J

"This is a chilling, tautly written, and well-realized psychological thriller. . . . The suspense is sustained by deft characterizations, fascinating crime-lab details, a twisting plot, and understated prose." Saturday Rev

The silence of the lambs. St. Martin's Press 1988 338p o.p.

LC 88-18203

"Agent Clarice Starling of the FBI's behavioral science section is assigned to conduct a psychological profile of Hannibal Lecter, a psychiatrist imprisoned for serial murder. Uncooperative at first, Lecter then says he can help identify a serial killer who has eluded authorities for months. Lecter's aid proves invaluable, and Starling soon finds herself using one madman to catch another." Libr J

"Harris places his clues with precision, and his characterizations . . . are superbly developed and richly complex." Booklist

Harrison, Harry, 1925-

(ed) Best SF: 1968-1975. See Best SF: 1968-1975

Return to Eden; illustrations by Bill Sanderson. Bantam Bks. 1988 348p il $18.95

ISBN 0-553-05315-9   LC 88-10436

The concluding volume of the Eden trilogy "sees contentions growing once more as rabble-rousers on both sides push for war. The pacifist Yilanè Daughters of Life are split while Kerrick's nemesis, the deposed Yilanè leader Vaintè, still seeks vengeance on him." Publ Wkly

"Harrison's conclusion to his alternate prehistory of Earth excels in its detailed depiction of an alien civilization that might have been. " Libr J

The Stainless Steel Rat sings the blues. Bantam Bks. 1994 229p $19.95

ISBN 0-553-09612-5   LC 93-31809

Previous titles in the author's Stainless Steel Rat series are: The Stainless Steel Rat (1961); The Stainless Steel Rat's revenge (1970); The Stainless Steel Rat saves the world (1972); The Stainless Steel Rat wants you! (1978); The Stainless Steel Rat for president (1982); A Stainless Steel Rat is born (1985); The Stainless Steel Rat gets drafted (1987)

"Caught in the act of robbing the new mint on the planet Paskonjak, master thief Jim DiGriz, a.k.a. the Stainless Steel Rat, is offered a deal by the Galactic League: discover a stolen artifact thought to be somewhere on the prison planet Liokukae within 30 days and go free—or die. In the same vein as previous adventures featuring Harrison's irrepressible antihero . . . this latest outing boasts fast-paced action, a hint of melodrama, and a sizable dose of satirical tweaks at modern culture." Libr J

Stainless steel visions; illustrated by Bryn Barnard. TOR Bks. 1993 254p il $18.95

ISBN 0-312-85245-2   LC 92-43879

"A Tom Doherty Associates book"

Analyzed in Short story index

Contents: The streets of Ashkelon; Toy shop; Not me, not Amos Cabot!; The mothballed spaceship; Commando raid; The repairman; Brave newer world; The secret of Stonehenge; Rescue operation; Portrait of the artist; Survival planet; Roommates; The golden years of The Stainless Steel Rat

"Thirteen of Harrison's robust, fast-paced tales. One is a new tale of his best-known hero, Slippery Jim DiGriz, the Stainless Steel Rat. Another is 'Roommates,' the basis for the movie *Soylent Green*. The other 11 range widely over Harrison's 40-year career and many interests (not to mention more than a few prejudices). All reflect Harrison's acknowledged status as heir to the pulp tradition of keeping the story moving forward at all costs." Booklist

West of Eden; illustrated by Bill Sanderson. Bantam Bks. 1984 483p il o.p.

LC 84-6306

First volume of the author's Eden trilogy

"Alternate-history story in which the dinosaurs were not killed off and ultimately produced sentient, humanoid descendants devoted to biotechnology. Their civilized race is ultimately forced into contact and conflict with savage human beings, adding culture shock to crisis. Inventive, fast-paced narrative." Anatomy of Wonder 4

Followed by Winter in Eden

Winter in Eden; illustrations by Bill Sanderson. Bantam Bks. 1986 398p il o.p.

LC 86-14168

In the second volume of the Eden trilogy "the bitter struggle for dominance between the reptilian Yilanes and the human Tanus continues as Vainte, a cunning Yilane enraged by the destruction of her city, vows to annihilate not only her Tanu nemesis, Kerrick, but also the entire Tanu race." Booklist

Followed by Return to Eden

Harrison, Jim, 1937-

The beige dolorosa

In Harrison, J. Julip p185-275

Julip. Houghton Mifflin; Lawrence, S. 1994 275p $21.95

ISBN 0-395-48885-0   LC 93-43961

Analyzed in Short story index

"The protagonists in this collection of three novellas are spunky aberrants who remain appealing despite their sometimes reprehensible behavior. Julip . . . is a fascinating mixture of waiflike innocence and jaded sexuality. Brown Dog, seen earlier in *The Woman Lit by Fireflies* (1990) and revived now in 'The Seven Ounce Man,' was born 'not to cooperate with the world,' and lurches unsteadily from barroom brawls to protests against the desecration of Indian burial grounds. In 'The Beige Dolorosa' a politically incorrect college professor attacks an 'ecocircus' mime but seeks personal salvation by renaming the birds of America. Richly allusive and wickedly funny." Libr J

Julip [novella]

In Harrison, J. Julip p3-82

The seven-ounce man

In Harrison, J. Julip p85-182

Harrison, Payne

Black cipher. Crown 1994 337p $22

ISBN 0-517-58753-X   LC 94-9849

Harrison, Payne—*Continued*

"When Faisal Shaikh, Britain's top cryptanalyst, breaks a complex code that reveals plans for the assassination of a visiting Saudi diplomat, he is stunned when the murder isn't prevented. When he is summarily fired, he knows that his boss, the head of the British equivalent of the National Security Agency, is dirty; but how many other high-level officials are involved? Faisal begins a globe-girdling dash to find out." Booklist

"Despite the improbability of its hero's magic-carpet mobility . . . and his plot-saving good luck, this highly entertaining thriller will keep readers turning its pages long past midnight." Publ Wkly

Storming Intrepid. Crown 1989 473p $19.95

ISBN 0-517-57133-1   LC 88-22905

This thriller "tells the story of a U.S. space shuttle that carries the components for the Strategic Defense Initiative (SDI). Something goes wrong and the U.S. loses control of the craft to the Russians." Booklist

"After building a wonder of technical wizardry high above the earth, Harrison lets his heroes duke it out in a fierce showdown near ground level. This novel hums with vigor." Libr J

Harrison, Sue

Brother Wind; a novel. Morrow 1994 494p $22

ISBN 0-688-12888-2   LC 94-14271

This volume completes the trilogy about "the harsh and dramatic adventures of Kiin, Samiq and other Aleutian Islanders of 9000 years ago. When her husband is killed by Raven (of the Walrus People tribe), Kiin, an accomplished carver, is forced to abandon both her own tribe of the First Men and one of her twin sons and return with the killer to his village. In revenge, Samiq, chief hunter of the First Men and brother of the murdered man, seeks Raven's death. . . . Informed by Native American legends, myths and traditions and replete with convincing recreations of trading practices, seal hunting and vision fasts, this novel offers an emotionally compelling conclusion to a monumental saga." Publ Wkly

Mother earth, father sky. Doubleday 1990 313p o.p.

LC 89-25656

Available Thorndike Press large print edition

The first volume of the author's trilogy set on the prehistoric Aleutian Islands

This is "the story of an Aleutian woman living around 7000 B.C. When her village is destroyed by a hostile tribe, Chagak flees to her grandfather in the Whale Hunter tribe. Along the way, she finds safety with old Shuganan, but her trails do not end there. She endures brutalization and childbirth. . . . Harrison's fine first novel is based on thorough research into the lifestyle and beliefs of ancient Aleutians; exquisite detail imparts great viability to her characters." Booklist

Followed by My sister the moon

My sister the moon. Doubleday 1992 449p o.p.

LC 91-29102

The second volume in the author's trilogy "picks up 16 years after 'Mother EarthFather Sky' leaves off. . . . The beautiful Kiin is promised to Amgigh, but has been in love with his brother Samiq for years. Violently abused by her father, marriage is a relief for Kiin. But her jealous younger brother brutally kidnaps and rapes her and tries to sell her as a slave into a marriage far from their homeland. The brutality and physical and sexual abuses are vividly portrayed, as well as the rigid roles of men and women." Baya Book Rev

Followed by Brother Wind

Harrod-Eagles, Cynthia

Death to go. Scribner 1994 c1993 281p $20

ISBN 0-684-19650-6   LC 93-10374

Also available G.K. Hall large print edition

First published 1993 in the United Kingdom with title: Necrochip

"Detective Inspector Bill Slider is called on when a teenager finds a human finger among the fried potatoes she ordered at a London fish-and-chips shop. Body parts continue to surface as events expand to include a sinister business tycoon, a prostitutes' rooming house, three mysterious Asians, an odd mix of gay men and five murders." Publ Wkly

"Murder provides the foundation for this extraordinary novel, but, it's finally an examination of love, love lost, and ways in which people cope with both." Booklist

Death watch. Scribner 1993 c1992 280p $20

ISBN 0-684-19519-4   LC 92-30924

First published 1992 in the United Kingdom

"Grim reality and intimations of immortality confront London detectives Slider and Atherton when they respond to the arson murder of a womanizing salesman. The victim, a deceptive man of failing business, marriage, and personal aspirations, serves as a foil to Slider (himself unhappily married) and ladies' man Atherton, who bounce theories off each other as they gather information and suspects." Libr J

"This is a fine example of the British procedural—a simmering rather than boiling narrative, plenty of quick wit, and a splash of romantic intrigue, all skillfully written and solidly plotted." Booklist

Orchestrated death; a mystery introducing Inspector Bill Slider. Scribner 1992 c1991 266p $19.95

ISBN 0-684-19388-4   LC 91-29042

Also available Thorndike Press large print edition

First published 1991 in the United Kingdom

"Detective Inspector Bill Slider [is] taken advantage of at work and pummeled verbally at home by his incompatible spouse. His own dissatisfaction leads Slider to become immersed in solving the murder of a beautiful young violin player. With the help of best friend Sergeant Atherton and the sympathetic ear of new-found true love Joanna, Slider uncovers a far-flung conspiracy." Libr J

A novel "remarkable for its rich, romantic tone, assured technique and perfect literary pitch." N Y Times Book Rev

Hart, Carolyn G.

Dead man's island. Bantam Bks. 1993 276p o.p.

LC 93-3107

Available G.K. Hall large print edition

Hart, Carolyn G.—*Continued*

This mystery "introduces Henrietta O'Dwyer Collins, a widowed former reporter whose investigative instincts have not been blunted by retirement. Forty years after their love affair ended, media magnate Chase Prescott calls 'Henrie O' for help in figuring out who tried to kill him with poisoned candy. He invites her and all those he suspects of wanting him dead to his private island off the coast of South Carolina, hoping that Henrie will be able to ferret out the identity of his would-be killer. While a brewing hurricane threatens the island, Henrie faces a full roster of suspects." Publ Wkly

"Hart handles the classic situation (isolated mansion full of colorful suspects) with panache, controlling the melodrama but utilizing monster Hurricane Derek to great effect as plot and storm peak together." Libr J

Scandal in Fair Haven. Bantam Bks. 1994 275p $19.95

ISBN 0-553-09465-3   LC 93-40346
Also available G.K. Hall large print edition

This Henrie O "adventure takes her to Fair Haven, Tennessee, where a local bookstore owner is accused of murdering his wealthy wife. . . . Hart offers a light and lively read with an appealing 'small-town America' ambience, a compelling plot, a potpourri of fascinating characters, and some revealing insights into what makes us humans tick." Booklist

Southern ghost. Bantam Bks. 1992 322p o.p.

LC 92-2543

"According to the news story published in the *Chastain* (South Carolina) *Courier* at the time, leading citizen Judge Augustus Tarrant suffered a fatal heart attack on May 9, 1970, after learning of the accidental shooting death of his 21-year-old son, Ross. What has prompted young Courtney Kimball to hire Max Darling to investigate this family tragedy 22 years later? . . . Hart's southern-gothic mystery offers a wealth of suspects . . . a generous scattering of literary allusions and peripheral ghost stories, and a chain of intriguing flashbacks that will leave most readers puzzled to the end." Booklist

Hart, Harry *See* Frank, Pat, 1907-1964

Hart, Josephine

Damage; a novel. Knopf 1991 195p $18
ISBN 0-679-40135-0   LC 90-53393

The narrator of this novel, "an English paterfamilias and Tory M.P., leads a passionless existence until he meets his son's fiancée, with whom he becomes erotically enthralled." Newsweek

"Erotic obsession is a risky subject for fiction. No matter how besotted the victims of this malady may be, their behavior is likely to strike mere witnesses, i.e., readers, as distasteful, hilarious or both. This first novel . . . sidesteps such unintended responses, thanks to old-fashioned British reserve. . . . The understatement works wonders." Time

Sin; a novel. Knopf 1992 163p $20
ISBN 0-679-41673-0   LC 92-53853
Also available Thorndike Press large print edition

This novel "focuses on the sin of envy, embodied here in the person of narrator Ruth, corrosively jealous of her orphaned cousin Elizabeth, raised and cherished by Ruth's parents as their own daughter. Ruth hates the good, generous, kind Elizabeth and waits for the moment when she will be able to break her rival and take everything." Libr J

"Hart has constructed an arch and streamlined melodrama inlaid with some undeniably shrewd and provocative observations about human nature." Booklist

Harte, Bret, 1836-1902

The best short stories of Bret Harte; edited, and with an introduction, by Robert N. Linscott. Modern Lib. 1947 517p o.p.

Analyzed in Short story index
Contents: The Luck of Roaring Camp; The outcasts of Poker Flat; Tennessee's partner; Brown of Calaveras; Iliad of Sandy Bar; Poet of Sierra Flat; How Santa Claus came to Simpson's Bar; Passage in the life of Mr. John Oakhurst; Heiress of Red Dog; Ingénue of the Sierras; Chu Chu; Devotion of Enriquez; Yellow dog; Salomy Jane's kiss; Uncle Jim and Uncle Billy; Dick Spindler's family Christmas; Esmeralda of Rocky Cañon; Boom in the "Calaveras Clarion"; Youngest Miss Piper; Colonel Starbottle for the plaintiff; Lanty Foster's mistake; Four guardians of LaGrange; Ward of Colonel Starbottle's; Convalescence of Jack Hamlin; Gentleman of La Porte

The Luck of Roaring Camp, and other tales; with pictures of the author and his environment and illustrations of the setting of the book together with an introduction by Louis B. Salomon. Dodd, Mead 1961 309p il o.p.

"Great illustrated classics"
Analyzed in Short story index
Contents: The Luck of Roaring Camp; The outcasts of Poker Flat; Miggles; Tennessee's partner; The idyl of Red Gulch; Brown of Calaveras; High-water mark; A lonely ride; The man of no account; Mliss; The right eye of the Commander; Notes by flood and field; The mission Dolores; John Chinaman; From a back window; Boonder; How Santa Claus came to Simpson's Bar; Wan Lee, the pagan; Two Saints of the foothills; The fool of Five Forks; A ghost of the Sierras; My friend the tramp; The office-seeker

Harvey, John, 1938-

Cold light. Holt & Co. 1994 370p $22
ISBN 0-8050-2046-2   LC 93-6263

This novel finds Charlie Resnick "and his fellow coppers in the industrial English city of Nottingham harried as usual, what with the customary run of Christmastime crimes. Matters take a decided turn for the worse, though, when a Social Services caseworker goes missing; messages from the kidnapper follow, indicating similarity to a previous case and suggesting that the perpetrator is very sick indeed." Booklist

"Nice men, murderers, child batterers, discarded lovers, grieving parents, weary probation officers, cynical cops—they all hurt, they all count and they all speak a kind of poetry in this writer's book." N Y Times Book Rev

Wasted years. Holt & Co. 1993 339p $19.95
ISBN 0-8050-2044-6   LC 93-247

Harvey, John, 1938-—*Continued*

Nottingham "Inspector Charlie Resnick's past comes back to mock him when a gang of armed robbers on a crime spree reminds him of a criminal who is up for parole. Ten years earlier Resnick put him away, under circumstances that cost the detective his marriage and made him a moody man. 'Boxing with shadows' is the police chief's opinion of Resnick's efforts to track his old enemy, resolve the old questions and maybe take back the lost years." N Y Times Book Rev

"By now Harvey's economy of prose is a given, as is his ability to pull together the many composite parts— the interlocking crimes, the boozing, infidelity and Resnick's very human bunch of underlings—that make a Charlie Resnick mystery such satisfying reading." Publ Wkly

Harvey, Kathryn, 1947-

See also Wood, Barbara, 1947-

Stars; a novel. Villard Bks. 1992 460p $21

ISBN 0-394-58798-7   LC 91-50063

Also available large print edition $24 (ISBN 0-679-41356-1)

"Star's is an exclusive Hollywood resort on Mount San Jacinto accessible only by tramway. Once the home of actress Marion Star, the lavish establishment was left empty for decades after Star's husband was found dead and she disappeared. The new owner prefers anonymity but watches carefully over the guests who come with agendas far more complex than skiing or relaxation. Adultery, movie deals, plastic surgery, corporate takeovers, blackmail, and murder are only some of the issues on these wealthy vacationers' minds." Booklist

Hašek, Jaroslav, 1883-1923

The good soldier Svejk; and his fortunes in the World War; translated and introduced by Cecil Parrott; illustrated by Josef Lada. Knopf 1993 800p $20

ISBN 0-679-42036-3   LC 92-54304

Also available from Bentley

"Everyman's library"

Original Czech edition published 1920-1923 in 4 volumes; this translation first published 1973 by Heinemann

"The novel reflected the pacifist, antimilitary sentiments of post-World War I Europe. The title character is classified as 'feeble-minded'; nevertheless, with the advent of World War I he is drafted into the service of Austria. Naive, instinctively honest, invariably incompetent, and guileless, Schweik is forever colliding with the clumsy, dehumanized military bureaucracy. Schweik's naïveté serves as a contrast to the self-importance and conniving natures of his superior officers and is the main vehicle for Hašek's mockery of authority." Merriam-Webster's Ency of Lit

Hassler, Jon

North of hope; a novel. Ballantine Bks. 1990 518p o.p.

LC 90-34162

"Plagued by a dubious sense of vocation, Father Frank Healy requests reassignment to his hometown parish and the nearby Ojibway reservation church. Here he encounters Libby Pearsall, the passionate woman whom he has silently loved since childhood, and she and her troubled daughter soon become his greatest personal and pastoral challenge." Libr J

"Although somewhat slow-going until the halfway mark, this increasingly evocative novel then picks up speed and acquires depth, spinning out an alcohol-soused tale of heartbreak, strained faith and sordid intrigue." Publ Wkly

Hastings, Graham, 1926-

For works written by this author under other names see Jeffries, Roderic, 1926-

Hawk, Alex, 1926-

For works written by this author under other names see Kelton, Elmer, 1926-

Hawkes, John, 1925-

Sweet William; a memoir of Old Horse. Simon & Schuster 1993 269p $20

ISBN 0-671-74057-1   LC 92-40125

In this novel, the author allows his narrator to "tell his own story in his own direct way. The twist is, this narrator is a horse. Called Sweet William in his prime, which didn't last long, and now called Old Horse, this equine character relates a life story full of grief, thwarted passion, fortitude, some humor, and a pinch of misanthropy and bitterness. Sweet William suffers through his adored mother's death, then loses his manhood to the knife when his lustiness inconveniences his owners. His feistiness persists even in his neutered state, leading to the demise of his brief but glorious racing career, and it's all downhill after that." Booklist

"Employing an uncharacteristically courtly tone that may surprise his longtime readers, Hawkes fills this account with rich color and winning detail; indeed, this is a virtuoso performance, with William's voice rendered in masterful prose." Publ Wkly

Hawthorne, Nathaniel, 1804-1864

The Blithedale romance. o.p.

First published 1852

"Blithedale, a Utopian community, is modeled on Brook Farm, the transcendentalist experiment at West Roxbury, Massachusetts, in which Hawthorne had participated ten years before he wrote the novel. Miles Coverdale, the narrator, is a coldly inquisitive observer; in revealing his knowledge of the other members of the community, he reveals himself." Reader's Ency. 3d edition

"The romance is a meaningful blend of reality and the world of the characters' imaginations—a complex unfolding of characters who, in turn, reveal the narrator and themselves." Oxford Companion to Am Lit. 5th edition

also in Hawthorne, N. The complete novels and selected tales of Nathaniel Hawthorne

The complete novels and selected tales of Nathaniel Hawthorne; edited by Norman Holmes Pearson. Modern Lib. 1993 2v v1 $18, v2 $19

ISBN 0-679-60073-6 (v1); 0-679-60074-4 (v2)

LC 93-11202

Hawthorne, Nathaniel, 1804-1864 — *Continued*

First Modern Library edition published 1937 and partially analyzed in Short story index

All novels except Fanshawe are entered separately. Fanshawe, Hawthorne's first novel, is a romance about college students

Contents: v1 Fanshawe (1828); selections from Twice-told tales (1837); selections from Mosses from an old manse (1846); The scarlet letter (1850); v2 The House of the Seven Gables (1851); The Blithedale romance (1852); selections from The snow image (1851); The marble faun (1860)

Complete short stories of Nathaniel Hawthorne. Hanover House 1959 615p o.p.

Analyzed in Short story index

Contains the following stories: Gray champion; Wedding knell; Minister's black veil; Maypole of Merry Mount; Gentle boy; Mr. Higginbotham's catastrophe; Wakefield; Great carbuncle; Prophetic pictures; David Swan; Hollow of the three hills; Vision of the fountain; Fancy's show box; Dr Heidegger's experiment; Howe's masquerade; Edward Randolph's portrait; Lady Eleanore's mantle; Old Esther Dudley; Village uncle; Ambitious guest; The sister years; Seven vagabonds; White old maid; Peter Goldthwaite's treasure; Shaker bridal; Endicott and the Red Cross; Lily's quest; Edward Fane's rosebud; Threefold destiny; The birthmark; Select party; Young Goodman Brown; Rappaccini's daughter; Mrs. Bullfrog; Monsieur du Miroir; Hall of fantasy; Celestial railroad; Procession of life; Feathertop: a moralized legend; New Adam and Eve; Egotism; Christmas banquet; Browne's wooden image; Intelligence office; Roger Malvin's burial; P's correspondence; Earth's holocaust; Passages from a relinquished work; Artist of the beautiful virtuoso's collection; Snow-image: a childish miracle; Great Stone Face; Ethan Brand; Sylph Etherege; Canterbury pilgrims; Man of Adamant; Devil in manuscript; John Inglefield's Thanksgiving; Wives of the dead; Little Daffydowndilly; My kinsman, Major Molineux; Antique ring; Graves and goblins; Dr. Bullivant; Old woman's tale; Alice Coane's appeal; Ghost of Doctor Harris; Young provincial; Haunted quack; New England village; My wife's novel; Bald Eagle

Doctor Grimshawe's secret; edited, with an introduction and notes, by Edward H. Davidson. Harvard Univ. Press 1954 305p il o.p.

Written 1883

"In a New England town in the early 19th century lives Dr. Grimshawe, an eccentric recluse, and two orphans, Ned and Elsie. The children are involved in a secret related to an estate in England, whence the doctor originally came. This estate has lacked a direct heir since the reign of Charles I, when the incumbent disappeared, leaving a bloody footprint on the threshold. After their guardian's death, the children are separated, but meet again years later, in England. Ned, now Edward Redclyffe, is injured while investigating the estate and is befriended by Colcord, his boyhood tutor. Lord Braithwaite, the estate's present owner, invites Edward to live at the Hall, where he meets Elsie, who warns him of a presentiment of danger. He finds the hiding place of an incredibly old man who 'haunts' the Hall, and recognizes him as the Sir Edward Redclyffe of the times of the bloody footprint. When the old man dies, Colcord produces a locket that proves Edward to be the heir." Oxford Companion to Am Lit

Fanshawe

In Hawthorne, N. The complete novels and selected tales of Nathaniel Hawthorne

The House of the Seven Gables.

Available fron various publishers

First published 1851

"Follows the fortunes of a decayed New England family, consisting of four members—Hephzibah Pyncheon, her brother Clifford, their cousin Judge Pyncheon, and other cousin Phoebe, a country girl. At the time the story opens Hephzibah is living in great poverty at the old homestead, the House of the Seven Gables. With her is [her brother] Clifford, just released from prison, where he had served a term of thirty years for the supposed murder of a rich uncle. Judge Pyncheon, who was influential in obtaining the innocent Clifford's arrest, that he might hide his own wrongdoing, now seeks to confine him in an asylum on the charge of insanity. Hephzibah's pitiful efforts to shield this brother, to support him and herself by keeping a scent-shop, to circumvent the machinations of the judge, are described through the greater portion of the novel. The sudden death of the malevolent cousin frees them and makes them possessors of his wealth." Keller. Reader's Dig of Books

also in Hawthorne, N. The complete novels and selected tales of Nathaniel Hawthorne

The marble faun; or, The romance of Monte Beni. Ohio State Univ. Press 1968 cxxxiii, 610p $70

ISBN 0-8142-0062-1

"Centenary edition of the works of Nathaniel Hawthorne"

First published 1860

"The novel's central metaphor is a statue of a faun by Praxiteles that Hawthorne had seen in Florence. In the faun's fusing of animal and human characteristics he finds an allegory of the fall of man from amoral innocence to the knowledge of good and evil. . . . The faun of the novel is Donatello, a passionate young Italian who makes the acquaintance of three American artists, Miriam, Kenyon, and Hilda, who are spending time in Rome. When Donatello kills a man who has been shadowing Miriam, he is wracked by guilt until he is arrested by the police and imprisoned. Both of the women are tainted by guilt." Merriam-Webster's Ency of Lit

also in Hawthorne, N. The complete novels and selected tales of Nathaniel Hawthorne

The portable Hawthorne; revised and expanded edition by Malcolm Cowley. Viking 1969 698p o.p.

"Viking portable library"

First published 1948 and partially analyzed in Short story index

This collection contains The scarlet letter; selections from The House of the Seven Gables, The Blithedale romance, The marble faun, and The Dolliver romance; thirteen short stories; passages from his notebooks; and eleven letters

Hawthorne, Nathaniel, 1804-1864 — *Continued*

Short stories included are: An old woman's tale; The Maypole of Merry Mount; Young Goodman Brown; The Gray Champion; Roger Malvin's burial; My kinsman, Major Molineux; Feathertop; Wakefield; Egotism; Rappaccini's daughter; The artist of the beautiful; The celestial railroad; Ethan Brand

The scarlet letter.
Available from various publishers
First published 1850
"Set in 17th-century Salem, the novel is built around three scaffold scenes, which occur at the beginning, the middle, and the end. The story opens with the public condemnation of Hester Prynne, and the exhortation that she confess the name of the father of Pearl, her illegitimate child. Hester's husband, an old and scholarly physician, just arrived from England, assumes the name of Roger Chillingworth in order to seek out Hester's lover and revenge himself upon him. He attaches himself as physician to a respected and seemingly holy minister, Arthur Dimmesdale, suspecting that he is the father of the child. *The Scarlet Letter* traces the effect of the actual and symbolic sin on all the characters." Benet's Reader's Ency of Am Lit

also in Hawthorne, N. The complete novels and selected tales of Nathaniel Hawthorne
also in Hawthorne, N. The portable Hawthorne p337-546

Twice-told tales. Ohio State Univ. Press 1974 637p $69.50
ISBN 0-8142-0202-0
Also available from Buccaneer Bks.
"Centenary edition of the works of Nathaniel Hawthorne"
Analyzed in Short story index
First published 1837
Contents: The Gray Champion; Sunday at home; The wedding-knell; The minister's black veil; The May-pole of Merry Mount; The gentle boy; Mr. Higginbotham's catastrophe; Little Annie's ramble; Wakefield; A rill from the town-pump; The Great Carbuncle; The prophetic pictures; David Swan; Sights from steeple; The hollow of the three hills; The toll-gatherer's day; The vision of the fountain; Fancy's show box; Dr. Heidegger's experiment; Howe's masquerade; Edward Randolph's portrait; Lady Eleanore's mantle; Old Esther Dudley; The haunted mind; The village uncle; The ambitious guest; The sister years; Snow-flakes; The seven vagabonds; The white old maid; Peter Goldthwaite's treasure; Chippings with a chisel; The Shaker bridal; Night sketches; Endicott and the Red Cross; The lily's quest; Footprints on the seashore; Edward Fane's rosebud; The threefold destiny

Haymon, S. T.

A beautiful death. St. Martin's Press 1994 c1993 223p $19.95
ISBN 0-312-10420-0   LC 93-37005
Also available Thorndike Press large print edition
First published 1993 in the United Kingdom
Inspector Ben Jurnet "plunges into his deepest fit of melancholia to date when his fiancée is blown to bits by a car bomb. . . . Racked with guilt for surviving the attack that was surely meant for him, the English copper stumbles through his grief, enduring the sympathy of his friends and the glee of his enemies, until he bolts for Ireland in pursuit of a neighborhood youth with terrorist clan connections in the old country. Ms. Haymon, an elegant and assured stylist whose esthetic juices are always stirred by a good, gloomy setting, finds the perfect lyric complement for Jurnet's dismal mood in the gray, misty drizzle of County Donegal in November." N Y Times Book Rev

Death of a god. St. Martin's Press 1987 223p o.p.
LC 86-24781
This mystery "opens with Detective Inspector Ben Jurnet in the slow process of converting to Judaism. His girlfriend is Jewish. A rock group—the Second Coming—is in town for a concert. All of the group's songs are based on biblical texts. Its superstar is a local boy. The concert takes place, and Jurnet is moved by it against his will. The next morning the superstar is found dead in the town square, crucified. The investigation proceeds—slowly, because the police have little to work with. The murder elicits peculiar responses among those who knew the superstar. In some cases it is sheer glee; the man, with all his extraordinary charisma, was a monster. Another murder, one obviously related to the first, ensues." N Y Times Book Rev
"A canny mix of history, police procedure, psychology, and horror." Booklist

Death of a warrior queen. St. Martin's Press 1992 c1991 224p $17.95
ISBN 0-312-06950-2   LC 91-34610
First published 1991 in the United Kingdom
This "elegiac whodunit draws Detective Inspector Benjamin Jurnet to a seaside village in Norfolk, where someone has tampered with an extraordinary archeological dig of ancient druid remains associated with Queen Boadicea. Jurnet has further cause to ponder the fierce ways of British women when he discovers the corpse of the missing village tart buried in a sand dune. As baffling to him as the murder itself is the devotion shown to the victim's fully grown retarded son by a local gentlewoman of exquisite refinement." N Y Times Book Rev

Ritual murder. St. Martin's Press 1982 237p o.p.
LC 82-5781
"Arthur Cossey, an angelic choirboy, is murdered and sexually mutilated in imitation of the killing of Little St. Ulf during the 12th century in a small town, Angleby. St. Ulf was believed a victim of Jewish rituals; his death resulted in a vicious wave of anti-Semitism, and [Detective-Inspector] Jurnet fears the persecution of Jews will be repeated, a factor that intensifes his search for the murderer." Publ Wkly
"History serves as an eerie backdrop to present-day terror in this ably plotted tale." Booklist

A very particular murder. St. Martin's Press 1989 224p o.p.
LC 89-30089
"Although Jurnet and almost all of Scotland Yard are on the alert for trouble during a reception for physicist Max Flaschner, a Nobel Laureate, the scientist dies after drinking cyanide-laced orange juice. Beginning his investigation of this extremely complicated case, Jurnet discovers that Flaschner had ordered the juice for Tawno Smith, his beloved protégé, and believes the poison was

Haymon, S. T.—*Continued*
meant for Tawno, perhaps because he is feared as a brilliant scientist, 'tampering with natural laws.'" Publ Wkly
"This thoroughly entertaining British police procedural bears comparison to a P. D. James novel for mood, setting, wit, and plotting, not to mention a surprise ending that really does surprise." Booklist

Hazzard, Shirley, 1931-
The transit of Venus. Viking 1980 337p o.p.

LC 79-21754

This novel centers on "the lives and loves of two Australian sisters who emigrate to England and America in the mid-20th Century. . . . [Focus is on the sister Caro]. Caro's transit is circular: seduction and abandonment, marriage, widowhood, reunion with her betrayer and—at last and fatally—with the astronomer who loved her secretly all along." Libr J
This "is an exceedingly ambitious novel; a stunning and at times bewildering galaxy of ideas. From a literary and intellectual standpoint it is a challenge. . . . Miss Hazzard's greatest achievement in this novel is the suspense she creates from unfinished relationships. Instead of spinning off in different directions through space, these characters collide once again, drawn together by an ineluctable magnetism." Christ Sci Monit

Head, Ann
Mr. & Mrs. Bo Jo Jones. Putnam 1967 253p o.p.
"A marriage of necessity between two pleasant high school youngsters led astray by their emotions barely holds up against unreadiness for love or marriage and differences in family background and families. After their premature baby's death, Bo Jo and young wife July find their separation, schooling, and return to opposite sides of town assumed and arranged for by their parents. They momentarily yield to seeming reasonableness but, gradually realizing the bonds that have grown between them during a year of marriage, pregnancy, and bereavement, decide to work out their destiny and education together." Booklist
"The relations between the youngsters and their parents are well handled and made painfully real." Publ Wkly

Healy, J. F. (Jeremiah F.), 1948-
Foursome; a John Cuddy novel; [by] Jeremiah Healy. Pocket Bks. 1993 344p o.p.
LC 93-20354
"Called to Maine to help in the defense of a young executive who is accused of using a crossbow to kill his wife and the couple who were their best friends, [Boston private eye] Cuddy learns that everyone on the tranquil lake where his client kept a summer home loathed the foursome for exercising their yuppie values so conspicuously in this unspoiled place." N Y Times Book Rev
"Healy carefully mixes the tough-guy ambience of the Spenser novels with an intricate, multilayered mystery. As always, Cuddy is entertaining and satisfying." Booklist

Shallow graves; a John Cuddy mystery; [by] Jeremiah Healy. Pocket Bks. 1992 282p o.p.

LC 91-44059

"On the verge of a big-time modeling career in New York, Boston model Mau Tim Dani is strangled in her apartment. It looks like a burglary gone bad, but her modeling agency, which carried a 'key employee' insurance policy on her with Empire Insurance, wants to know for sure. Boston private eye John Cuddy used to investigate claims for Empire, which is why he's taken aback when the firm hires him to investigate the death." Booklist
"Healy gives his readers an array of distinctive characters while engaging them in a deftly plotted and satisfying story." Publ Wkly

Healy, Jeremiah F. *See* Healy, J. F. (Jeremiah F.), 1948-

Heaven, Constance, 1911-
The wind from the sea. St. Martin's Press 1993 c1991 503p $23.95
ISBN 0-312-08921-X   LC 92-37731
First published 1991 in the United Kingdom
This romance "chronicles the escape of French aristocrats Isabelle deSauvigny and her brother Guy from Revolutionary France and their adventures and loves once upon British soil. Isabelle marries a man who is involved in secret work for the British during the French Revolution and the terror that follows. Her brother smuggles goods to France and nearly loses his life in the bargain." Libr J
"High adventure, passionate romance, hints of incest, mistaken identities and marvelous depictions of the forbidding and mysterious English seacoast add up to a first-rate read." Publ Wkly

Hebden, Mark, 1916-1991
Pel and the missing persons. St. Martin's Press 1991 c1990 238p o.p.

LC 91-745

"A Thomas Dunne book"
First published 1990 in the United Kingdom
Chief Inspector Pel "is unhappy about a series of daring robberies by a motorized gun-toting gang, about losing some of his staff (reassigned due to a rise in the number of missing persons) and about an old man found dead, apparently a hit-and-run victim. Who is the old man? And why, among other anomalies, was there no blood at the scene? . . . Procedural aspects are handled as superbly as ever, although sharp-eyed readers may spot a crucial murder clue before Pel does." Publ Wkly

Pel and the party spirit. St. Martin's Press 1991 202p o.p.

LC 90-49303

"A Thomas Dunne book"
"Chief inspector Evariste Clovis Desire Pel of the Brigade Criminelle . . . investigate[s] a quadruple-header: an old tower wall collapses revealing a modern corpse; a pair of murderous hitchhikers stalk the Route Nationale 6; the daughter of a wealthy family is kidnapped; and a new batch of hard drugs is rumored to be en route to Pel's jurisdiction. . . . A well-crafted police procedural with a solid protagonist and fair amount of droll humor." Booklist

Hegarty, Frances

See also Fyfield, Frances, 1948-

Heggen, Thomas, 1919-1949

Mister Roberts; with an introduction by David P. Smith. Naval Inst. Press 1992 xxii, 200p $29.95

ISBN 1-55750-723-6   LC 92-9422

"Classics of naval literature series"

A reissue of the title first published 1946 by Houghton Mifflin

"Douglas Roberts, First Lieutenant on the *Reluctant*, a U.S. Navy supply ship in the Pacific, is the leading inspiration for the undeclared war between the crew and the unreasonable skipper. The dull life on ship is eased by humorous antics and the resulting rage of the commander. When Roberts is transferred to a destroyer, the crew is saddened by his departure." Shapiro. Fic for Youth. 3d edition

"The leisurely narrative is told in a very few incidents, all centering about an admirable young lieutenant miserably defeated in his desire to get into fighting. A quiet, credible story of the corroding effects of apathy and boredom on men who, in battle, might have been heroes." New Yorker

Heidish, Marcy

A woman called Moses; a novel based on the life of Harriet Tubman. Houghton Mifflin 1976 308p o.p.

This is a fictionalized account of "the life of Harriet Tubman, born in slavery on Maryland's Eastern Shore, who escaped North and spent her life in conducting hundreds of blacks to freedom along the Undergound Railroad prior to the Civil War." Libr J

"This fictional life story, told in the first person, is filled with incandescent raw materials, namely the cruelties of slavery, and the itineraries of escape." N Y Times Book Rev

Heilbrun, Carolyn G., 1926-

For works written by this author under other names see Cross, Amanda, 1926-

Heinemann, Larry

Paco's story. Farrar, Straus & Giroux 1986 209p o.p.

LC 86-19527

"Lone survivor of a Viet Cong night attack that wipes out the 90-plus men of Alpha Company, Paco Sullivan returns to civilian life after much time spent in military hospitals. Narrated by a nameless dead soldier from Alpha Company, this . . . tale interweaves Paco's infantry days in Vietnam with his Valium- and Librium-soothed afterlife as a dishwasher in a smalltown cafe." Libr J

"Mr. Heinemann's carefully crafted, oblique narrative suggests that the right words are not going to be found in ever-more-graphic, frontal approaches to 'gruesome carnage.' Its horrors may be as forcefully conveyed by a haunting scene in a greasy spoon as by the tearing of human flesh." N Y Times Book Rev

Heinlein, Robert A. (Robert Anson), 1907-1988

The cat who walks through walls; a comedy of manners. Putnam 1985 382p o.p.

LC 85-6519

"The plot of [this novel] centers around Col. Colin Campbell, a k a Richard Ames, an old soldier turned hack writer who has a peg leg and a guilty secret (he survived the aftermath of his last battle by eating his late commanding officer), and Hazel Long, a k a Gwen Novak, a brainy, beautiful and bawdy lady. . . . The tale begins in 2188, in a luxury 'habitat' . . . in orbit around the moon, when a mysterious stranger is killed at Campbell's dinner table, and it ends on the moon as Campbell and Long attempt to liberate a sentient computer from the control of two different sets of bad guys." N Y Times Book Rev

"A narcissistic SF ego trip, fascinating fare for psychoanalysts and Heinlein aficionados." Anatomy of Wonder. 3d edition

Citizen of the galaxy. Scribner 1957 302p o.p.

"Although marketed as a juvenile novel, this work was serialized for adults in *Astounding*. The Horatio Alger hero is in an interstellar setting, except that his lad starts out closer to the edge than Horatio's bootblacks and newsboys: he is a slave on a far planet of a despotic empire. He escapes into space with a nomadic trading company and eventually gets back to Earth, where he assumes (by inheritance!) the headship of a giant financial corporation. This is a *bilungsroman*, except that the young hero never really grows up; but Heinlein's knack for creating sociologically plausible cultures is well displayed." Anatomy of Wonder 4

Double star. Doubleday 1956 186p o.p.

"A ham actor is persuaded to impersonate the kidnapped prime minister of Earth's government. The actual politician is rescued but dies, and his double must carry on. In the process of dealing objectively with the moral judgments entailed in parliamentary politics he grows out of his stagestruck self-centeredness. *Double Star* offers convincing description of the way a planet-spanning constitutional monarchy . . . might actually work." Anatomy of Wonder 4

Friday. Holt, Rinehart & Winston 1982 368p il o.p.

LC 81-13221

"An artificially created superwoman, courier for a secret organization, has to fend for herself when the decline of the West reaches its climax; she ultimately finds a new raison d'être on the extraterrestrial frontier. Welcomed by Heinlein fans as action-adventure respite from his more introspective works." Anatomy of Wonder 4

Job: a comedy of justice. Ballantine Bks. 1984 376p o.p.

LC 84-3091

"A Del Rey book"

"Alexander Hergensheimer, a minister from an alternate-world America dominated by Bible Belt fundamentalism, is flipped from one alternate world to another in rapid succession, whereby his faith, his endurance, and his love for his Margrethe are supremely tested. There are occasional patches of discursive philosophical, religious, and ethical ramblings here, which will be familiar territory to most of Heinlein's readers. For

Heinlein, Robert A. (Robert Anson), 1907-1988—*Continued*

the most part, however, this tightly written, provocative, and powerful book, with its large cast of intriguing characters and an irresistibly compelling love story, is eminently readable." Booklist

The moon is a harsh mistress. Putnam 1966 383p o.p.

"Colonists of the Moon declare independence from Earth, and contrive to win the ensuing battle with the aid of a sentient computer. Action-adventure with some exploration of new possibilities in social organization and fierce assertion of the motto 'There Ain't No Such Thing as a Free Lunch.'" Anatomy of Wonder 4

The puppet masters. Doubleday 1951 219p o.p.

"Heinlein's paranoia-laden tale of sluglike creatures, arrived in saucer-shaped craft to enslave humans by the particularly gruesome procedure of growing into each person's nervous system from a position on the upper back of the victim—making his or her profile hump-backed." Anatomy of Wonder. 3d edition

Stranger in a strange land. Putnam 1961 408p $21.95

ISBN 0-399-10772-X

Also available from Amereon and Buccaneer Bks.

"The hero is a human born of space travelers from earth and raised by Martians. He is brought to the totalitarian post-World War III world that is in many ways depicted as a satire of the U.S. in the 1960s, marked by repressiveness in sexual morality and religion. The plot, which tells how the heroic stranger creates a Utopian society in which people preserve their individuality but share a brotherhood of community, made Heinlein and his novel cult objects for young people dedicated to a counterculture." Oxford Companion to Am Lit. 5th edition

Time enough for love; the lives of Lazarus Long; a novel. Putnam 1973 605p o.p.

"Lazarus Long, the protagonist of this science fiction novel, is 2000 years old in the year 4272. He is tired and wants to die. Instead, he is rejuvenated because his memories are needed to re-invigorate a decaying society. Lazarus' many occupations—space captain, king, salesman, merchant, businessman, etc.—are woven into the narrative . . . along with his participation in the creation of a woman, Minerva, who had been a Master Computer. Society, relationships, religion are appraised in excerpts from Lazarus' notebook." Libr J

Heller, Joseph

Catch-22; with an introduction by Malcolm Bradbury. Knopf 1995 xxxix, 568p $20

ISBN 0-671-43722-3   LC 94-13984

"Everyman's library"

A reissue of the title first published 1961 by Simon & Schuster

"A comic, satirical, surreal, and apocalyptic novel . . . which describes the ordeals and exploits of a group of American airmen based on a small Mediterranean island during the Italian campaign of the Second World War, and in particular the reactions of Captain Yossarian, the protagonist." Oxford Companion to Engl Lit. 5th edition

"By way of some of the funniest dialogue ever, Heller takes shots at the hypocrisy, meanness, and stupidities of our society." Shapiro. Fic for Youth. 3d edition

Followed by Closing time

Closing time; a novel. Simon & Schuster 1994 464p $24

ISBN 0-671-74604-9   LC 94-20604

"Just like the original *Catch-22*, this sequel opens with Yossarian in a hospital bed, flirting with the nurses. Now in his seventies, Yossarian is depressed by his perfect health: things can only get worse. He lives alone in a Manhattan apartment not far from most of his old war buddies, including Milo Minderbinder, a defense contractor straight out of *Dr. Strangelove*. Yossarian and company mourn the decline of New York City and American culture in general and look back longingly to the golden age of prewar Coney Island." Libr J

"Heller is richly paranoid about state paranoia, and his winning jokes are more vicious than anything even in Catch-22 itself. Besides which, although Closing Time is too often like an electricity grid in danger of fusing, there are many exchanges that display all the old verve." New Statesman Soc

Good as Gold. Simon & Schuster 1979 447p o.p.

LC 78-23894

"Dr. Bruce Gold, forty-eight-year-old professor (Jewish) of literature (English) and author of many seminal articles in small journals (unread), finds himself facing the prospect of becoming a high Washington official. The offer comes from Ralph Newsome (Protestant), a presidential aide. . . . [Gold accepts] and soon meets Andrea Conover, the tall, beautiful, gifted daughter (also Protestant) of a wealthy, retired career diplomat (anti-Semite), clearly the suitable mate for a man with a potential of becoming the country's (very first Jewish) Secretary of State." Publisher's note

Something happened. Knopf 1974 569p o.p.

The protagonist of this novel "Bob Slocum, works for a large, nameless company that sells something. What, we never learn. Slocum has a wife without a name, a disgruntled 15-year-old daughter and adorable 9-year-old son, both also unnamed, and a retarded child, Derek, who has a name and nothing else. Slocum lives in terror at his office, where 'there are six people who are afraid of me, and one small secretary who is afraid of all of us. I have one other person working for me who is not afraid of anyone, not even me, and I would fire him quickly, but I'm afraid of him.' Slocum carries his anxieties home. . . . 'Only one member of the family is not afraid of any of the others, and that one is an idiot.' Between these dry equations Slocum circles and recircles the question of what went wrong with his life." Newsweek

Helprin, Mark

Ellis Island

In Helprin, M. Ellis Island & other stories p128-96

Ellis Island & other stories. Delacorte Press 1981 196p o.p.

LC 80-18437

Helprin, Mark—*Continued*

Analyzed in Short story index

Contents: The Schreuderspitze; Letters from the Samantha; Martin Bayer; North light; A Vermont tale; White gardens; Palais de Justice; A room of frail dancers; La Volpaia; Ellis Island

This book "consists of a novella (the title story) and ten short stories whose variation in length, content, style, and theme attest to the remarkable versatility of the writer. . . . Written in the first person, 'Ellis Island' is a four-part story—the recollections of an enterprising Jewish immigrant who finds himself temporarily stranded on that famous stepping stone to the New World. His vulnerability to the arbitrary decisions of immigration functionaries, his efforts to keep from being deported, and his attempts to earn a living are adventures told with a whimsical humor by a raconteur with a zest for life." Best Sellers

A soldier of the great war. Harcourt Brace Jovanovich 1991 792p $24.95

ISBN 0-15-183600-0   LC 90-45987

"In summer 1964, a distinguished-looking gentleman in his seventies dismounts on principle from a streetcar that was to carry him from Rome to a distant village, instead accompanying on foot a boy denied a fare. As they walk, he tells the boy the story of his life. A young aesthete from a privileged Roman family, Alessandro Giuliani found his charmed existence shattered by the coming of World War I. The war led to an onerous tour of duty, inadvertent desertion, near-execution, forced labor, service high in the Italian Alps that took advantage of his . . . skill at mountain climbing, capture by the enemy, and return home, dispossessed of most of his friends and family. Along the way, he gains, loses, and eventually rediscovers love." Libr J

"Helprin's big, rumbustious new novel is about four-fifths of a marvel. Helprin has simplified his language, though he still works up a good head of rhetorical steam, and he has moderated his enthusiasm for phantasmagoric set pieces. He has also picked themes—war and loss, youth and age—that suit a large, elaborate style. . . . For a very large chunk of the novel's center, Helprin writes with riotous energy and sustained brilliance." Time

Winter's tale. Harcourt Brace Jovanovich 1983 673p $26.95

ISBN 0-15-197203-6   LC 83-273

This novel "opens in the years just preceding World War I. Peter Lake, a burglar and mechanic with unparalleled skills, attempts to rob the mansion of the wealthy Isaac Penn—and falls in love with Beverly, Isaac's beautiful but sickly daughter. They marry. She dies. He departs on an involuntary journey through time. One hundred years later, he reappears, and with the help of younger Penns and various hangers-on leads the city of New York through the horrible waning hours of the 20th century, into the justice of the third millenium." Christ Sci Monit

The author "describes the impossible with microscopic precision, and he summons the moods and myriad landscapes of the city with breathtaking poetry. . . . Again and again Helprin celebrates selfless love, a devotion to beauty, the desire to explore, and an acceptance of responsibility. . . . Helprin's freewheeling use of fantasy at times eclipses his essential seriousness, diminishing the novel as a whole. Yet there is unquestionable genius in the book's marvelous individual pieces." Saturday Rev

Hemingway, Ernest, 1899-1961

Nobel Prize in literature, 1954

Across the river and into the trees. Scribner 308p $40

ISBN 0-684-15313-0

First published 1950

"This is the story of a peace-time army colonel, closely resembling the author, who comes to Venice on leave to go duck shooting, to see the young Italian countess he loves, and to make a significant pilgrimage to the place where he, Richard Cantwell (and Nick Adams, Frederic Henry, and the author himself), was wounded in World War I. . . . The novel is Hemingway's weakest. It points up sharply the importance of that war injury in the author's life and work, but in some of its postures and mannerisms it seems to read like a parody of his better fiction." Herzberg. Reader's Ency of Am Lit

The complete short stories of Ernest Hemingway; the Finca Vigía edition. Scribner 1987 650p $40

ISBN 0-684-18668-3   LC 87-12888

Analyzed in Short story index

Contents: The short happy life of Francis Macomber; The capital of the world; The snows of Kilimanjaro; Old man at the bridge; Up in Michigan; On the quai at Smyrna; Indian camp; The doctor and the doctor's wife; The end of something; The three-day blow; The battler; A very short story; Soldier's home; The revolutionist; Mr. and Mrs. Elliot; Cat in the rain; Out of season; Cross-country snow; My old man; Big two-hearted river: part I; Big two-hearted river: part II; The undefeated; In another country; Hills like white elephants; The killers; Che ti dice la patria?; Fifty grand; A simple enquiry; Ten Indians; A canary for one; An Alpine idyll; A pursuit race; Today is Friday; Banal story; Now I lay me; After the storm; A clean, well-lighted place; The light of the world; God rest you merry, gentlemen; The sea change; A way you'll never be; The mother of a queen; One reader writes; Homage to Switzerland; A day's wait; A natural history of the dead; Wine of Wyoming; The gambler, the nun, and the radio; Fathers and sons; One trip across; The tradesman's return; The denunciation; The butterfly and the tank; Night before battle; Under the ridge; Nobody ever dies; The good lion; The faithful bull; Get a seeing-eyed dog; A man of the world; Summer people; The last good country; An African story; A train trip; The porter; Black ass at the cross roads; Landscape with figures; I guess everything reminds you of something; Great news from the mainland

A farewell to arms. Scribner 332p $35

ISBN 0-684-15562-1

Also available G.K. Hall large print edition

First published 1929; copyright renewed 1957

This novel "deals with a love-affair conducted against the background of the war in Italy. Its excellence lies in the delicacy with which it conveys a sense of the impermanence of the best human feelings; the unobtrusive force of its symbolism of mountain and plain; above all the vast scope of its vision of war—the retreat from Caporetto is one of the great war-sequences of literature." Penguin Companion to Am Lit

For whom the bell tolls. Scribner 471p $29.95

ISBN 0-684-10239-0

Also available G.K. Hall large print edition

Hemingway, Ernest, 1899-1961—*Continued*

First published 1940; copyright renewed 1968

"This war tale covers four tension-ridden days in the life of Robert Jordan, an American in the Loyalist ranks during the Spanish Civil War. Having accomplished his mission to blow up a bridge with the aid of guerrilla bands, he is injured when his horse falls and crushes his leg. As enemy troops approach, he is left alone to meet their attack. Jordan's love for Maria, a young girl whom the Fascists had subjected to every possible indignity, adds another dimension to a story of courage, dedication—and treachery." Shapiro. Fic for Youth. 3d edition

The garden of Eden. Scribner 1986 247p o.p.

LC 86-3701

A novel Hemingway "began in 1946 and worked on intermittently in the last 15 years of his life and left unfinished." N Y Times Book Rev

This novel is "based on Hemingway's honeymoon with Pauline in May 1927 at Le Grau-du-Roi, a . . . fishing village in the Camargue. David and Catherine Bourne at first lead an idyllic existence—tasting the pleasures of board, bottle, beach, and bed. . . . After the Bournes meet a beautiful . . . young woman, Marita, Catherine sleeps with her, urges Marita to sleep with David, and then become jealous of David's passion for the blank and passive girl. The love triangle brings out the deep-rooted tensions in the Bournes' marriage." Natl Rev

"Whatever its problems, this version of 'The Garden of Eden' deserves publication for what it says about writing and for the short story which Hemingway shows us David writing." Newsweek

The Hemingway reader; selected with a foreword and twelve brief prefaces by Charles Poore. Scribner xx, 652p $60

ISBN 0-684-15164-2

Also available from Amereon

"Hudson River editions"

First published 1953 and partially analyzed in Short story index

This one volume selection includes two complete novels: The sun also rises and The torrents of spring; excerpts from A farewell to arms; Death in the afternoon; Green hills of Africa; To have and have not; For whom the bell tolls; Over the river and into the trees; The old man and the sea; and eleven short stories

The stories included are: In our time; A way you'll never be; Fifty grand; A clean well-lighted place; Light of the world; After the storm; The short happy life of Francis Macomber; Capital of the world; The snows of Kilimanjaro; Old man at the bridge; Fable of the good lion

In our time; stories. Scribner 156p $30

ISBN 0-684-16480-9

"Hudson River editions"

First published 1930 and analyzed in Short story index. Copyright renewed 1958

Contents: On the quai at Smyrna; Indian camp; The doctor and the doctor's wife; The end of something; The three day blow; The battle; A very short story; Soldier's home; The revolutionist; Mr. and Mrs. Elliot; Cat in the rain; Out of season; Cross country snow; My old man; Big two-hearted river

Islands in the stream. Scribner 466p $50

ISBN 0-684-16499-X

"Hudson River editions"

First published 1970

This posthumous novel is divided into three parts: Bimini, Cuba and At Sea. " 'Bimini' is Thomas Hudson in the 1930s entertaining the three sons of his two wrecked marriages; they fish; their love leaves him open to his loneliness, and then the death of two of them leaves him nothing but lonely. 'Cuba' is Thomas Hudson clandestinely war efforting in about 1942; his other son (the eldest) has been killed as a pilot; Thomas Hudson drinks; he meets his first wife who is all he has ever wanted. 'At Sea' is Thomas Hudson commanding the pursuit of some German U-boat survivors; the Germans die, and it may be that the wounded Thomas Hudson is about to too." N Y Rev Books

Men without women. Scribner 1927 232p o.p. Amereon reprint available $16.95 (ISBN 0-89190-663-0)

Analyzed in Short story index

Contents: The undefeated; In another country; Hills like white elephants; The killers; Che ti dice la patria; Fifty grand; A simple enquiry; Ten Indians; A canary for one; An Alpine idyll; A pursuit race; Today is Friday; Banal story; Now I lay me

The Nick Adams stories; preface by Philip Young. Scribner 268p $40

ISBN 0-02-550780-X

"Hudson River editions"

First published 1972 and partially analyzed in Short story index

Contents: Three shots; Indian camp; The doctor and the doctor's wife; Ten Indians; The Indians moved away; The light of the world; The battler; The killers; The last good country; Crossing the Mississippi; Night before landing; "Nick sat against the wall . . ."; Now I lay me; A way you'll never be; In another country; Big two-hearted river; The end of something; The three day blow; Summer people; Wedding day; On writing; An Alpine idyll; Cross-country snow; Fathers and sons

The old man and the sea. Scribner 127p $13.95

ISBN 0-684-10245-5

Also available G.K. Hall large print edition

First published 1952; copyright renewed 1980

"The old fisherman Santiago had only one friend in the village, the boy Manolin. Everyone else thought he was unlucky because he had caught no fish in a long time. At noon on the eighty-fifth day of fishing, he hooked a large fish. He fought with the huge swordfish for three days and nights before he could harpoon it, but the battle came to nought when sharks destroyed the fish before Santiago could get back to the village." Shapiro. Fic for Youth. 3d edition

The short stories of Ernest Hemingway. Scribner 499p $50

ISBN 0-684-15155-3

"Hudson River editions"

First published 1953

Contents: The short happy life of Francis Macomber; The capital of the world; The snows of Kilimanjaro; Old man at the bridge; Up in Michigan; On the quai at Smyrna; Indian camp; The doctor and the doctor's wife; The end of something; The three-day blow; The battler; A very short story; Soldier's home; The revolutionist; Mr. and Mrs. Elliot; Cat in the rain; Out of season; Cross-country snow; My old man; Big two-hearted river; The undefeated; In another country; Hills like white

Hemingway, Ernest, 1899-1961—*Continued*
elephants; The killers; Che ti dice la patria; Fifty grand; A simple enquiry; Ten Indians; A canary for one; An Alpine idyll; A pursuit race; Today is Friday; Banal story; Now I lay me; After the storm; A clean, well-lighted place; The light of the world; God rest you merry, gentlemen; The sea change; A way you'll never be; The mother of a queen; One reader writes; Homage to Switzerland; A day's wait; A natural history of the dead; Wine of Wyoming; The gambler, the nun, and the radio; Fathers and sons

The snows of Kilimanjaro, and other stories. Scribner 154p $35

ISBN 0-02-550940-7
"Hudson River editions"
First published 1961
Contents: The snows of Kilimanjaro; A clean, well-lighted place; A day's wait; The gambler, the nun, and the radio; Fathers and sons; In another country; The killers; A way you'll never be; Fifty grand; The short happy life of Francis Macomber

The sun also rises. Scribner 247p $19.95

ISBN 0-684-10250-1
First published 1926; copyright renewed 1954
"Set in the 1920s, the novel deals with a group of aimless expatriates in France and Spain. They are members of the cynical and disillusioned post-World War I Lost Generation, many of whom suffer psychological and physical wounds as a result of the war. Two of the novel's main characters, Lady Brett Ashley and Jake Barnes, typify this generation. Lady Brett drifts through a series of affairs despite her love for Jake, who has been rendered impotent by a war wound. Friendship, stoicism, and natural grace under pressure are offered as the values that matter in an otherwise amoral and often senseless world." Merriam-Webster's Ency of Lit

also in Hemingway, E. The Hemingway reader p89-289

To have and have not. Scribner 262p $40

ISBN 0-684-15328-9
"Hudson River editions"
First published 1937; copyright renewed 1965
This novel "deals with the effort of Harry Morgan, a native of Key West, to earn a living for himself and his family. He has operated a boat for rental to fishing parties, but, during the Depression of the 1930s, he is forced to turn to the smuggling of Chinese immigrants and illegal liquor. While assisting a gang of bank robbers to escape, he is shot and mortally wounded. He dies gasping, 'One man alone ain't got . . . no chance.'" Reader's Ency. 3d edition

The torrents of spring; a romance novel in honor of the passing of a great race. Scribner 1987 c1926 90p $30

ISBN 0-02-550750-8   LC 87-14448
"A Scribners/Macmillan Hudson River edition"
A reissue of the title first published 1926
"A burlesque of 'Sherwood Anderson' and the 'Chicago school' of authors, this comic novel tells of Yogi Johnson and Scripps O'Neil, workers in a pump factory in Petosky, Michigan; of Scripp's amours with two waitresses in Brown's Beanery, and of Yogi's adventures with the Indians." Benet's Reader's Ency of Am Lit

also in Hemingway, E. The Hemingway reader p25-86

Hennessy, Max, 1916-1991
For works written by this author under other names see Hebden, Mark, 1916-1991

Hennissart, Martha
For works written by this author in collaboration with Mary J. Latsis see Lathen, Emma

Henry, O., 1862-1910
The best short stories of O. Henry; selected and with an introduction by Bennett A. Cerf, and Van H. Cartmell. Modern Lib. 1994 c1945 340p $19.50

ISBN 0-679-60122-8
Analyzed in Short story index
First Modern Library edition published 1945
Contents: The gift of the Magi; A cosmopolite in a café; Man about the town; The cop and the anthem; The love-philtre of Ikey Schoenstein; Mammon and the archer; Springtime à la carte; From the cabby's seat; An unfinished story; The romance of a busy broker; The furnished room; Roads of destiny; The enchanted profile; The passing of Black Eagle; A retrieved reformation; The Renaissance at Charleroi; Shoes; Ships; The hiding of Black Bill; The duplicity of Hargraves; The ransom of Red Chief; The marry month of May; The whirligig of life; A blackjack bargainer; A lickpenny lover; The defeat of the city; Squaring the circle; Transients in Arcadia; The trimmed lamp; The pendulum; Two Thanksgiving Day gentlemen; The making of a New Yorker; The lost blend; A Harlem tragedy; A midsummer knight's dream; The last leaf; The count and the wedding guest; A municipal report

Cabbages and kings

In Henry, O. The complete works of O. Henry p551-679

The complete works of O. Henry; foreword by Harry Hansen. Doubleday 1953 1692p o.p.

Contents: An omnibus volume of 13 short story collections: The four million; Heart of the West; The gentle grafter; Roads of destiny; Cabbages and kings; Options; Sixes and sevens; Rolling stones; Whirligigs; The voice of the city; The trimmed lamp; Strictly business; Waifs and strays. All the collections are analyzed in Short story index

The four million

In Henry, O. The complete works of O. Henry p1-108

The gentle grafter

In Henry, O. The complete works of O. Henry p267-354

Heart of the West

In Henry, O. The complete works of O. Henry p109-266

Options

In Henry, O. The complete works of O. Henry p680-810

Henry, O., 1862-1910—*Continued*
Roads of destiny

In Henry, O. The complete works of
O. Henry p355-550

Rolling stones

In Henry, O. The complete works of
O. Henry p941-1060

Sixes and sevens

In Henry, O. The complete works of
O. Henry p811-940

Strictly business

In Henry, O. The complete works of
O. Henry p1484-1631

The trimmed lamp

In Henry, O. The complete works of
O. Henry p1365-1483

The voice of the city

In Henry, O. The complete works of
O. Henry p1253-1364

Waifs and strays

In Henry, O. The complete works of
O. Henry p1632-92

Whirligigs

In Henry, O. The complete works of
O. Henry p1094-1252

Henry, Sue, 1940-
Murder on the Iditarod Trail. Atlantic
Monthly Press 1991 278p o.p.

LC 90-20925

"After three 'accidental' deaths early in the running
of the torturous Iditarod Trail (from Anchorage to
Nome) dog sled race, Alaskan police and race officials
step up efforts to prevent further mayhem. State trooper
Alex Jensen, single, brooding, handsome, and adept with
physical evidence, falls upon the puzzling events with
relish, comparing lists, visiting checkpoints, searching sled
cargoes, etc. Consulting with race participant Jessie Arnold, he learns some of the inside facts, experiences
delaying blizzards, and becomes emotionally attached."
Libr J

"Henry provides suspense and excitement in this paean
to a great sporting event and to the powerful Alaskan
landscape." Publ Wkly

Henry, Will, 1912-1991
Mackenna's gold. Random House 1963
276p o.p.

A "Western melodrama with a touch of mystery and
superstition. Set in Arizona in 1897, it tells of a tough
young prospector who learns from a dying Apache of
a valley filled with gold, and is then forced to lead a
band of outlaws to the hidden treasure." Publ Wkly

"This Western, much better written and conceived than
most, is an entertaining piece based on a first-rate Southwestern lost mine tale and a very good but little-read
personal narrative." Libr J

Herbert, Frank, 1920-1986
Chapterhouse: Dune. Putnam 1985 464p
o.p.

LC 84-17979

The sixth Dune novel "is set on the planet Chapterhouse, where the Bene Gesserits have installed their
headquarters. They have fled from the slaughtering
Honored Matres (a corrupt version of the Bene Gesserits), with plans to transform Chapterhouse into another
desert planet on which the valuable melange spice can
be produced. The high point of the book is not the
climactic raid on and capture of a group of Honored
Matres, but rather a chapter in which a former Honored
Matre undergoes the ritual spice agony to become a Bene
Gesserit Reverend Mother." SLJ

Children of Dune. Berkley Pub. Corp.
1976 444p o.p.

This third volume in the saga of Dune "centers on
the development of twins Leto and Ghanima and their
decision to assume the mantle of political and religious
leadership spurned by their father. Herbert expands on
many of the questions raised in earlier books, especially
prescience and the evolution of mankind." Booklist
Followed by God Emperor of Dune

Dune. Putnam 1984 c1965 517p $25.95

ISBN 0-399-12896-4   LC 83-16030

First published 1965 by Chilton
The first volume of the Dune series is "the story of
a selectively bred messiah who acquires paranormal
powers by use of the spice that is the main product
of the desert planet Arrakis, and uses these powers to
prepare for the ecological renewal of the world. Politics
and metaphysics are tightly bound into a remarkably
detailed and coherent pattern; an imaginative, tour de
force." Anatomy of Wonder 4
Followed by Dune messiah

Dune messiah. Putnam 1969 220p o.p.

In this second volume of the Dune series "the Bene
Gesserit, a mystic sisterhood, plot to overthrow the god/
emperor Paul Atreides, whom they created by special
breeding but whom they cannot now control. Presented
here via the narrative and quotes from journals and
legends of the people of Dune, the imperial intrigue is
engineered by such diverse characters as Bene Gesserit
Mother Superior, a Tleilaxu face dancer, a 'ghola' re-
creation of Paul's dead friend, and the Princess Consort.
Paul's eventual victory because of his future-vision makes
fascinating reading." SLJ
Followed by Children of Dune

God Emperor of Dune. Putnam 1981
441p o.p.

LC 80-25149

In the fourth title of the Dune saga "Leto II, the God
Emperor, combines melange, a spice drug, with religion
in order to control his people. The scene is the planet
now called Arrakis, since only a remnant of the desert,
Dune, remains. It is 3,500 years after the events of 'Children of Dune,' which ended while Leto was young. After
sacrificing his human body to melange in exchange for
an estimated four-thousand year rule, Leto is still alive.
Gradually the body of Shi-Hulud the Sandworm God
is developing in him, while Leto the Emperor lives in
the bosom of God, or so his followers believe. . . .
His plan for the survival of humanity is the Golden
Path, an enforced tranquility overriding man's desire for
chaos, especially war." Best Sellers
Followed by Heretics of Dune

Herbert, Frank, 1920-1986—*Continued*

Heretics of Dune. Putnam 1984 480p o.p.
LC 83-16040

"The fifth installment of the 'Dune Cycle' follows the lives of the two children on different planets: On Gammu, a young Duncan Idaho trains relentlessly for the moment that will awaken the memories of his former lives; on Rakis, the fremen-child Sheeana discovers her ability to command the fearsome sandworms of the desert—and becomes an object of worship." Libr J

Followed by Chapterhouse: Dune

The white plague. Putnam 1982 445p o.p.
LC 82-7586

"John O'Neill, a molecular biologist visiting Dublin, is driven to awful and brilliant insanity when he sees his wife and children killed by an IRA bomb. He takes revenge with a synthesized disease that kills only women. The plague can't be contained in the areas he has targeted, and civilization rocks as humanity anticipates a whole new kind of doom and a cure is frantically sought." Publ Wkly

"A novel that combines a concrete warning of the abuses of 'gene-splicing' with a suspenseful plot and fine characterization." Best Sellers

Herlihy, James Leo, 1927-1993

Midnight cowboy; [by] James L. Herlihy. Simon & Schuster 1965 253p o.p.

"The story of Joe Buck, a backward 27-year-old out of Albuquerque, who comes to New York to become a professional stud. In his fancy cowboy rig, Joe feels that he should be able to make his fortune. . . . He teams up with a handicapped pickpocket named Ratso Rizzo, who is just about as ineffectual a ponce as Joe is a hustler. . . . Living in an abandoned building with Ratso, he develops the strongest kinship with a human being since grandmother Sally Buck fell off a horse and died. He cares for Ratso when he is sick, steals for him, and tries to take him by bus to Florida, which he fancies as a land of greater opportunity. Eventually, Ratso breathes his last outside of Daytona—and once more Joe is left to face the world alone." N Y Times Book Rev

"An appalling story, told with great skill and important because Joe Buck is a characteristic product of the way we live and yet he cannot be adequately discussed outside of a novel." Saturday Rev

Hersey, John, 1914-1993

Antonietta; a novel. Knopf 1991 304p $20.50

ISBN 0-679-40194-6   LC 90-52905

"The protagonist of Mr. Hersey's title is a violin made by Antonio Stradivari in 1699. The author has traced its subsequent travels from Italy to France to England to Switzerland and to the United States. Tales about the adventures of this fictional violin, which Stradivari names Antonietta, accumulate along the way: its construction is inspired by a sweetheart, Mozart plays it, it is used to teach Berlioz." N Y Times Book Rev

"Hersey's intelligence, wit, and stylishness—not to mention his well-informed musical taste—save the novel from foolishness while letting it exude charm, ribaldry, and humor with symphonic largesse. Symphonic variety, too, as Hersey changes style with each act." Booklist

A bell for Adano. Knopf 1944 269p $22.95

ISBN 0-394-41660-0

Also available from Buccaneer Bks.; large print edition available from Thorndike Press

"The town bell of Adano is transformed into material for a cannon, and its loss symbolizes a moral loss to the very life of the people. When the town falls into the hands of the Americans and the Fascist forces are in retreat, Major Joppolo, a Brooklyn-born Italian, becomes a favorite of the townspeople because of the concern he has for them. Not only does he help Tina find her missing sweetheart, but he finds a replacement for the bell, retrieving it from a U.S. ship named after an Italian-American hero of World War I. To the town's dismay, Major Joppolo is relieved of his command by an American general whose unreasonable orders he ignores." Shapiro. Fic for Youth. 3d edition

Key West tales. Knopf 1994 227p $22

ISBN 0-679-42992-1   LC 93-11094

Analyzed in Short story index

Contents: God's hint; Get up, sweet slug-a-bed; Did you ever have such sport?; The two lives of Consuela Castanon; They're signaling!; A game of anagrams; Cuba libre!; Fantasy fest; Just like you and me; Page two; Amends; Piped over the side; To end the American dream; The wedding dress; A little paperwork

"In this final collection of stories, Hersey focuses on his theme of ordinary people facing momentous events in their lives: death by AIDS, the death of a friend from AIDS, loss of innocence and virginity, meeting the son one had given up for adoption two decades before, or retirement from military service. As interludes, Hersey presents brief, italicized vignettes of the famous or powerful people who have lived in or visited Key West." Libr J

A single pebble. Knopf 1956 181p $19.95

ISBN 0-394-44562-7

Also available Thorndike Press large print edition

"An American engineer's trip by junk up the Yangtze to locate a dam site, as he relates it years later in retrospect, symbolizes the contrast between the Western idea of progress and tempo of living and the passive resignation of China's ancient culture and traditions. With mounting tension, the story brings into focus the subtle relationship between the young engineer and the owner of the junk, his wife, and the head tracker, Old Pebble, in a drama heightened by the physical grandeur of the Great River." Booklist

The wall. Knopf 1950 632p o.p.

"Based on historical fact but using fictional characters and fictional diary entries, the work presents the background of the valiant but doomed uprising of Jews in the Warsaw ghetto against the Nazis. *The Wall* is a powerful presentation, in human terms, of the tragedy of the annihilation of European Jews. The novel relates the lives and actions of many different characters against the background of the Holocaust." Merriam-Webster's Ency of Lit

Hervey, Evelyn *See* Keating, H. R. F. (Henry Reymond Fitzwalter), 1926-

Hess, Joan

Death by the light of the moon. St. Martin's Press 1992 227p $18.95

ISBN 0-312-06949-9   LC 91-37884

"A Claire Malloy mystery"

"Bookstore owner/sleuth Claire Malloy . . . finds little but trouble when she and teenage daughter Caron attend the 80th birthday celebration of Miss Justicia, mother of Claire's late husband, at the family manor in the Louisiana bayous. Feuding relatives, mysterious hints about inheritances and terrible food begin a ghastly first night that will also include the drowning of the matriarch after she is seen careening drunkenly about the garden in her powered wheelchair." Publ Wkly

"Ms. Hess handles the complicated plot logistics with a deft touch, and although her overblown caricatures lack the affection she lavishes on the characters in her 'Maggody' series, she has a warm spot for teen-agers, whose insufferable ways elicit her funniest and kindest satirical swipes." N Y Times Book Rev

A diet to die for. St. Martin's Press 1989 199p o.p.

     LC 89-34855

"A Claire Malloy mystery"

"Maribeth Galleston, heiress to the Farber fortune, is burdened with obesity, a bullying husband, and severe depression, but Claire Malloy's downstairs neighbor intends to help—by getting Maribeth to join the Ultima Diet Center. The diet, coupled with aerobics classes, seems to be succeeding . . . although Maribeth's behavior is becoming peculiar. When her car crashes through the glass door of Ultima, killing an employee, Detective Peter Rosen blames it on severe potassium deficiency caused by the diet, but Claire investigates and soon discovers that everyone involved seems to be having illicit affairs." Publisher's note

Madness in Maggody. St. Martin's Press 1991 231p $16.95

ISBN 0-312-05465-3   LC 90-49306

"Chief of police Arly Hanks, lately of New York City, takes an offhand attitude toward crime or the lack of it in Maggody, Arkansas, until the tamales hit the fan during the grand opening of a supermarket that none of the other merchants in town wants to see succeed. Now Arly's got one death, and reams of rumors to unravel. Although the situation is loaded with humor and small-town high jinks, the solution to the murder shocks Arly so much she promises herself that in the future she will take her job more seriously." Booklist

Maggody in Manhattan; an Arly Hanks mystery. Dutton 1992 266p il $18

ISBN 0-525-93519-3   LC 92-52870

"Police Chief Arly Hanks of Maggody, Arkansas (pop. 755), escaped the urban horrors of New York after an ugly divorce and vowed never to return. It doesn't work out that way, thanks to her crusty Mom, Ruby, who wins an all-expenses paid trip to the Big Apple for the finals of a baking contest. With a pal along for the ride, Ruby gets the full out-of-towner treatment: dirt, muggings, naked men in her barely functioning hotel room, cops with guns, murder, the whole shebang. Naturally poor Arly is called upon to buy a plane ticket and lend a hand." Booklist

The author "sets forth a delectable dish that succeeds both as a spoof of the unrealistic amateur-sleuth story and the pretentious culinary mystery genre." N Y Times Book Rev

Malice in Maggody; an Ozarks murder mystery. St. Martin's Press 1987 178p $13.95

ISBN 0-317-53413-0   LC 86-26307

"Police chief Ariel 'Arly' Hanks of tiny Maggody, Ark., is frustrated in her investigation of a missing EPA bureaucrat. The leading citizens, including the mayor and Arly's mother Ruby Bee (owner of the town's only bar and motel), are less than cooperative. Arly knows they're hiding something but doesn't know what. . . . The story, half of it narrated by Arly, moves at a nice clip and Hess . . . delivers a nice mystery with wry, effective humor." Publ Wkly

Martians in Maggody; an Arly Hanks mystery. Dutton 1994 264p $18.95

ISBN 0-525-93840-0   LC 94-10285

Also available Thorndike Press large print edition

The "residents of Maggody, Ark., flock to Raz Buchanon's corn fields to speculate about the crop circles that have appeared there overnight. Soon TV crews, tabloid reporters and rival UFO scholars join the ranks, finding evidence of otherworldly visitation in the crop circles and a rash of cattle mutilations. . . . But then the assistant to one of the leading ufologists is killed. Police chief Arly Hanks . . . has her hands full as Maggody's inhabitants pursue the possibility of alien life forms and prominence in tabloid headlines. While Arly questions Maggody's citizens and visitors, one of the ufologists is also murdered. Hess aims her barbed (and good-natured) sense of humor at tabloid journalism as well as at the foibles of her rural cast in this spirited mystery." Publ Wkly

Mischief in Maggody; an Ozarks murder mystery. St. Martin's Press 1988 202p o.p.

     LC 88-1867

"Maggody, a little Ozark town where nothing ever happens, has problems. Its first female police chief, Arly Hanks, . . . comes back from vacation to find the community in an uproar . . . local prostitute and moonshiner Robin Buchanon has disappeared, leaving behind five hungry children. . . . Arly manages to foist them onto Mrs. Jim Bob while she goes hunting for the mother, whom she finds with her head blown off in the middle of a marijuana patch. . . . Another death and the public humiliation of two of the town's most righteous citizens take place before peace comes to Maggody once again. Hess writes an engaging tale, although the raunchy characters impart a certain vulgarity to the text." Publ Wkly

Mortal remains in Maggody. Dutton 1991 294p $18.95

ISBN 0-525-93368-9   LC 91-10525

"A small Hollywood movie company specializing in soft porn decides to use Maggody, Arkansas as the location for its current film. The local yokels—an inveterate bunch of gossipy, inbred, and often comically misguided characters—follow the actors and film crew around until murder puts a stop to production. Chief of Police Arly Hanks, whose New York ties lend her credibility, hustles to discover the killer, as well as the arsonist responsible for several barn-burnings." Libr J

Hess, Joan—*Continued*

O little town of Maggody; an Arly Hanks mystery. Dutton 1993 245p $19

ISBN 0-525-93654-8   LC 93-22861

"It's Christmas in Maggody, and the town is all agog over the impending visit of country-western singer Matt Montana, who hopes to jump start a booze-ravaged career with press coverage of his heart-warming return to his hometown. One small problem: Matt's only relative in Maggody is an aging aunt who lives in the county home and has a tendency to listen to aliens from outer space on her hearing aid. . . . The disappearance of Matt's aunt from the home puts something of a wrinkle into the plans, leaving Arly to sort out the mess." Booklist

"There's a sturdy plot and keen satirical point to all this giddy nonsense. But in the spirit of the season, the author is as generous with her affection as she is with her wit." N Y Times Book Rev

Poisoned pins; a Claire Malloy mystery. Dutton 1993 246p $18

ISBN 0-525-93591-6   LC 92-34409

Claire Malloy "finds herself embroiled in the affairs of Farber College's sorority, Kappa Theta Eta, whose house is next door to Malloy's. Suspecting prowlers after she hears a scream emanating from the shabby premises, Claire gains the qualified (and condescending) tolerance of the house's summer occupants: four students and the divorcée housemother. The reappearance of Claire's nemesis, Arnie Riggles, and further prowler sightings culminate in the hit-and-run death of one of the sisters." Publ Wkly

Roll over and play dead; a Claire Malloy mystery. St. Martin's Press 1991 244p o.p.

LC 90-29882

"Claire Malloy . . . finds herself inadvertently involved in the morally suspect . . . practice of collecting and selling stray animals to research labs. Reluctantly agreeing to attend to two drooling basset hounds at the request of a vacationing acquaintance, Claire (no animal lover) bribes her daughter into feeding the animals. However, the dogs disappear under mysterious circumstances—as do the pets of three neighbors." Booklist

Tickled to death; a Claire Malloy mystery. Dutton 1994 216p $18.95

ISBN 0-525-93810-9   LC 93-49595

Claire Malloy's "friend Luanne is having an affair with dentist Dick Cissel, a possible suspect in the recent death of his second wife. Luanne, who hopes Claire will investigate and turn up a more likely suspect, overcomes her friend's reluctance by finding a needed summer job for Claire's daughter Caron—at a bird sanctuary run by the Dunling Foundation. . . . Hess's low-key humor and bull's-eye dialogue are reason enough to read anything she writes; solid plotting and deft characterization make this latest doubly rewarding." Publ Wkly

Hesse, Hermann, 1877-1962

Nobel Prize in literature, 1946

Demian. Boni & Liveright 1923 215p o.p.

Available from Amereon and Buccaneer Bks.

Original German edition, 1919

A novel "featuring young Emil Sinclair. Largely through the crude aggression of a school bully, Sinclair becomes troubled by the realization that life consists of conflicting, opposite forces. His confusion is both cleared and compounded by the appearance of a mysterious older boy named Max Demian. Both Demian and his mother become central influences in Sinclair's life, although their encounters are sporadic. In a letter, Demian tells Sinclair of the devil-god Abraxas, who is the embodiment of a fusion of all good and evil, of destruction and creation. When he is wounded in the war, Sinclair has a vision of Demian, in which his death is implied. From that time on, Sinclair feels himself to be the possessor of the wisdom and understanding he had attributed to Demian. The novel is one of Hesse's most poignant statements of the terrors and torments of adolescence." Reader's Ency. 3d edition

Gertrude; translated by Hilda Rosner. Rev. translation. Boni & Liveright 1969 237p o.p. Buccaneer Bks. reprint available $26.95 (ISBN 0-89966-629-9)

Original German edition, 1910; this translation first published in the United Kingdom

"The story has three major characters: Herr Kuhn, Herr Muoth, and Fräulein Gertrude Imthor, later Frau Muoth. Narrated by the aging Kuhn, the novel recounts his travails as a youth, his success as a composer, his frustrated love for Gertrude Imthor, and his strange friendship with Heinrich Muoth. . . . As a young man Kuhn had his leg crippled in an accident. The physical disability which prevents him from achieving happiness in life, especially with women, measurably accounts as well for his creativity." Saturday Rev

The glass bead game (Magister Ludi); translated from the German by Richard and Clara Winston; with a foreword by Theodore Ziolkowski. Holt, Rinehart & Winston 1969 558p o.p. Smith, P. reprint available $22.50 (ISBN 0-8446-6524-X)

Original German edition, 1943; first published 1949 in the United States with title: Magister Ludi

This "novel follows the intellectual and spiritual odyssey of Josef Knecht, who lives in a utopian society in the 23rd century. The culture is dominated by a glass-bead game, practiced in its highest form (in which beads are not even used) by an intellectual elite. The game represents a balanced fusion of the active and contemplative disciplines; it is a combination of music and mathematics (art and science) but includes elements from virtually every cultural endeavor. Knecht becomes master of the game (Lat, *Magister Ludi*) but has doubts about the virtues of pure intellect. He renounces his order and departs to the outer world, where he eventually dies, the tragic result of a life dedicated entirely to the world of the spirit." Reader's Ency. 3d edition

Narcissus and Goldmund; translated by Ursule Molinaro. Farrar, Straus & Giroux 1968 315p o.p.

Original German edition, 1930; English translation published 1932 with title: Death and the lover; also 1959 in the United Kingdom, with title: Goldmund

"The setting is Germany in the late Middle Ages—dark forests, wandering scholars, sheltered monasteries, flourishing imperial cities, the plague. The problem is the conflict of the intellectual and the sensual, the scholar and the artist. The device is the biographical novel, half picaresque, half philosophical." Choice

Hesse, Hermann, 1877-1962—*Continued*

"Hesse's prose, ranging from lyricism to allegory, and from unabashed sentimentality to an intellectuality of a high order, is not easily rendered into another language. . . . The present version . . . is close to perfection." Saturday Rev

Siddhartha; translated by Hilda Rosner. New Directions 1951 153p $16.95

ISBN 0-8112-0292-5

Also available from Amereon and Buccaneer Bks.

Original German edition, 1923

"The young Indian Siddhartha endures many experiences in his search for the ultimate answer to the question, what is humankind's role on earth? He is also looking for the solution to loneliness and discontent, and he seeks that solution in the way of a wanderer, the company of a courtesan, and the high position of a successful businessman. His final relationship is with a humble but wise ferryman. This is an allegory that examines love, wealth, and freedom while the protagonist struggles toward self-knowledge." Shapiro. Fic for Youth. 3d edition

Steppenwolf; translated from the German by Basil Creighton. Holt & Co. 1929 309p o.p.

Available from Amereon and Buccaneer Bks.

Original German edition, 1927

"The hero, Harry Haller, . . . is torn between his own frustrated artistic idealism and the inhuman nature of modern reality which, in his eyes, is characterized entirely by philistinism and technology. It is his inability to be a part of the world and the resulting loneliness and desolation of his existence that cause him to think of himself as a 'Steppenwolf' (wolf of the Steppes). The novel, which is rich in surrealistic imagery throughout, ends in what is called the magic theater, a kind of allegorical sideshow. Here, Haller learns that, in order to relate successfully to humanity and reality without sacrificing his ideals, he must overcome his own social and sexual inhibitions." Reader's Ency. 3d edition

Stories of five decades; edited and with an introduction by Theodore Ziolkowski; translated by Ralph Manheim. With two stories translated by Denver Lindley. Farrar, Straus & Giroux 1973 c1972 xx, 328p o.p. Amereon reprint available $23.95 (ISBN 0-89190-669-X)

Analyzed in Short story index

Contents: The island dream; Incipit vita nova; To Frau Gertrud; November night; The marble works; The Latin scholar; The wolf; Walter Kompff; The field devil; Chagrin d'amour; A man by the name of Ziegler; The homecoming; The city; Robert Aghion; The cyclone; From the childhood of Saint Francis of Assisi; Inside and outside; Tragic; Dream journeys; Harry, the Steppenwolf; An evening with Dr. Faust; Edmund; The interrupted class

Heyer, Georgette, 1902-1974

Bath tangle. Putnam 1955 312p o.p.

Available Thorndike Press large print edition

"After thoroughly entangling some very ill-matched lovers, this saucy Regency novel [set in Bath] skillfully unravels the tangles, leaving all tidily arranged. Gentle Fanny, a widow at twenty-three, falls desperately in love with Hector, a conventional soul unsuitably betrothed to spirited Serena, Fanny's twenty-six-year-old stepdaughter. Hector returns Fanny's affections, but honor keeps them silent until Serena's impetuous interference in his affairs brings Rotherham, her former fiancé, on the scene to effect a reconciliation." Booklist

Cousin Kate. Dutton 1968 317p o.p. Amereon reprint available $21.95 (ISBN 0-89190-785-8)

In this Regency novel "Cousin Kate, a poor relation [is] brought into the aristocratic English Broome household with a very nasty fate indeed planned for her. . . . Kate, aided by a dashing cavalier and the earthy family of her old nurse, wins out. The Gothic gloom and doom is nicely leavened with the wit, romance and wonderful period slang." Publ Wkly

The grand Sophy. Putnam 1950 307p o.p. Amereon reprint available $23.95 (ISBN 0-8488-0814-2)

Also available Thorndike Press large print edition

"On the Continent, where she had grown up and knew everyone in military, court, and diplomatic circles, Sophy was famous for her delightfully unexpected behavior, and for her irrepressible habit of managing less energetic people for their own good. When she returned to England, Regency London was also amused and startled by her antics, and her Rivenhall cousins, who offered her hospitality, were subjected to a reorganization of their lives. Sophy had learned the value of surprise attack from the Duke of Wellington, and applied it with shock tactics of her own to untangling the eldest Rivenhall cousins from unsuitable engagements, incidentally winning a husband for herself." Booklist

Lady of quality. Dutton 1972 254p o.p.

"The Lady of Quality is a Miss Annis Whychwood: wealthy, independent—and twenty-nine! She is finally mastered by her love for the pseudo-villain who of course reforms in order to win her after she has won his admiration by 'sparring' with him in what he calls a hornet-like manner of conversation." Best Sellers

Penhallow. Doubleday, Doran 1943 309p o.p. Amereon reprint available $23.95 (ISBN 0-89190-646-0)

Also available G.K. Hall large print edition

A "story about a family of terrorizing and oversexed males, embroiled with one or two victimized females, halfwits, illegitimate boot boys, and others. Very British, rural, and somewhat artificially 'tense.' . . . Here technique is equal to all improbabilities." Barzun. Cat of Crime. Rev and enl edition

Hiaasen, Carl

Native tongue. Knopf 1991 325p $21

ISBN 0-394-58796-0   LC 91-52713

This novel is set in the Florida keys. "There, just a few hundred miles south of Disney World, Francis X. Kingsbury, a k a Frankie King, a one time racketeer now enrolled in the Federal witness relocation program, has assembled a giant parcel of Florida real estate. . . . Kingsbury turns some of the property into an amusement park, the Amazing Kingdom of Thrills, and sets about developing the rest into a turf of condominiums, villas and golf links. Trouble is, the ecologically minded grow enraged. . . . [They] set out to destroy Kingsbury and his developments." N Y Times Book Rev

Hiaasen, Carl—*Continued*

"Hiaasen writes to a formula with brilliant success. His books are addictive. . . . One may miss the sour bite of bleaker comedy, found in the best crime stories of a more realistic kind, but for entertainment few can match him." London Rev Books

Skin tight. Putnam 1989 319p o.p.

LC 89-31580

"When Mick Stranahan, a retired investigator, is the attempted victim of murder, he becomes a little curious to find out who wants him dead. He trails the killer to a quack plastic surgeon who was a suspect in a murder case Stranahan investigated four years before. Someone is about to blab that the surgeon had a more than passing interest in the old case and Stranahan gets back in the harness to investigate." West Coast Rev Books

Strip tease; a novel. Knopf 1993 353p $21

ISBN 0-679-41981-0   LC 93-12358

"At the Eager Beaver, a topless bar in Fort Lauderdale, former FBI clerk Erin Grant dances nightly to pay for legal fees in her custody fight for her young daughter. There David Dilbeck, a poorly disguised, somewhat kinky and imbecilic U.S. Congressman owned by the state's sugar interests, is recognized by a sharp-eyed regular who, infatuated with Erin, initiates a blackmail plan meant to influence her court case. The resulting mayhem, occuring in an election year, involves machinations up to the highest state level." Publ Wkly

In among Hiaasen's "freaks and obsessives, his corrupters and corrupted, his brain-dead and his frenetically active, the author has dropped a real honest-to-God human being, an appealing young woman named Erin Grant. Her presence, her history and goals, make the cartoon nastiness around her less cartoony and more nasty than in previous Hiaasen novels." N Y Times Book Rev

Higgins, George V., 1939-

Bomber's law; a novel. Holt & Co. 1993 296p $22.50

ISBN 0-8050-2329-1   LC 93-26006

"A John Macrae book"

"A young detective, Harry Dell'Appa, discovers that his fellow detective and nemesis, Bob Brennan, has become curiously lax in his efforts to nail Short Joey Mossi, an aging Mafia hit man. Dell'Appa, who has been assigned to take over the Mossi case, begins to suspect that Brennan has gotten to know his subject a little too well—or rather, that he sympathizes too fully with Mossi. As the cops sit together in a cold car, waiting for Mossi to appear, Brennan talks on and on, digressing into stories about other criminals and about his own life. Dell'Appa listens fitfully." Commonweal

"A whiz of a stylist with a black belt in dialogue, Higgins lets his characters' conversation carry the story. This is our language as it is spoken, full of false stops and loony poetry." Newsweek

Defending Billy Ryan; a Jerry Kennedy novel. Holt & Co. 1992 245p o.p.

LC 92-7800

"A John Macrae book"

This is Higgins's "third tale about Jerry Kennedy, a frazzled Boston criminal lawyer paid, in this case, a hundred thousand bucks to defend Billy Ryan, a corrupt public official. Billy Ryan, the commissioner of the De-

partment of Public Works, has finally been indicted after many years of sleazy dealings and conflicts of interest. He does not like his lawyer, which is fine with Jerry Kennedy because the feeling is quite mutual. The story is vintage George Higgins." N Y Times Book Rev

The friends of Eddie Coyle. Knopf 1972 c1971 183p o.p.

The action of the story "involves a series of bank robberies. Eddie Coyle is a small-time [Boston] crook who is trying to crash the big time by providing the armament for the robbers. His 'friends' use him, are used by him, and ultimately there is double-crossing all the way along the line." Publ Wkly

"The language is dirty, ungrammatical, and picturesque, the allusions to sex are highly unlikely in their content and graphically ugly. But the whole book seems real." Best Sellers

The Mandeville talent. Holt & Co. 1991 278p o.p.

LC 91-9232

"A John Macrae book"

This book is about "a 23-year-old unsolved murder in Goshen, Mass. When the granddaughter of murder victim James Mandeville is offered a teaching post at Mount Holyoke, her husband, Joe, a young lawyer in a big Manhattan firm, grabs the chance to resign from the corporate rat race, solve the old murder case and set up private practice in the Berkshires. The local law can't help (for diverse reasons) and sends him to retired Defense Department investigator Baldad ('Baldo') Ianucci, who is bored and looking for something to do." Publ Wkly

"The drama in this book comes simply from watching the protagonists' minds work. Higgins makes us believe that the paper trail of contemporary life actually leads not to obfuscation but to clarity." Booklist

The patriot game. Knopf 1982 237p o.p.

LC 81-18655

The novel is set in "Boston's underside with its small-time political hacks, Irish-Catholic ghetto and real lace country clubs. The hero of this piece is a tough-talking Justice Department agent, Pete Riordan. . . . On the path of an IRA gunrunner, Riordan wants to know why so many proper Bostonians are eager to get a convicted murderer out of prison." Publ Wkly

"George Higgins' strength in his previous novels . . . has always been his ear for snappy street dialogue and a penchant for creating gritty, realistic characters. He doesn't disappoint in 'The Patroit Game.' . . . The dialogue is witty and splendidly profane." Best Sellers

Victories. Holt & Co. 1990 298p o.p.

LC 90-38723

"A John Macrae book"

Henry Briggs, the protagonist of this novel, was a character in Trust (1989). The events are set in 1968. "Briggs, retired baseball player now working as game warden in Vermont, is picked by politician Ed Cobb to run for the Democratic seat in a Congressional race. His opponent, Wainwright, is approaching 80 and has been in office for as long as anyone can remember. But various people begin to delve into the past when Russ Wixton, a newspaperman, decides to do features on Briggs and a hometown boy returning in a casket from Vietnam." Libr J

"As the campaign preliminaries unfold, Mr. Higgins discusses small-town grudges, pointless political feuds, rural poverty, greedy bankers, stupid policemen, unreasonable game laws, and arrogant campaign managers,

Higgins, George V., 1939- —*Continued*
throwing in a few other nuisances along the way. These
are all targets worthy of indignant editorials. It is Mr.
Higgins's great skill as a novelist that converts them into
convincing people conducting believable actions with
profane and amusing garrulity." Atlantic

Higgins, Jack, 1929-

Cold Harbour. Simon & Schuster 1990
318p o.p.

LC 89-26198

Available Thorndike Press large print edition

A "tale of deception set in World War II Europe. Cold
Harbour, a tiny village on the English Channel in Cornwall, is being used by the Special Operations Executive
. . . as a base for running secret agents into and out
of occupied France. To safeguard that operation, Englishmen masquerading as Germans patrol the Channel in
a captured German vessel and fly planes bearing Luftwaffe insignia. But these deceptions are just the beginning. At a French chateau occupied by the German High
Command, the resident family—now reduced to an elderly countess and her young niece, AnneMarie—pretend to
be collaborators." N Y Times Book Rev

"A fast-paced World War II story with plenty of intrigue." Booklist

Confessional. Stein & Day 1985 278p o.p.

LC 884-40777

"The hero of this spy-thriller is three people—a KGB
agent, an ordained Catholic priest and an IRA terrorist,
which means that he goes through a lot of cloak-and-
dagger changes as he slips from role to role. In 1958
the Russians set up a mock Irish village in the Ukraine
to train future KGB agents so that they could more
easily blend into the Irish landscape and go about their
nefarious activities of destabilizing English-Irish relations
by working through the IRA. Mikhail Kelly was a first-
rate candidate because his Irish father had been hung
by the British as an IRA activist and he had been raised
by his Russian mother in Ireland." Best Sellers

This novel is "tense. It is riveting. It is what a thriller
should be. If Mr. Higgins's prose is dull and his understanding of humanity shallow, it may only be because
good prose and a deeper understanding would inhibit the
race to the plot's final twist." N Y Times Book Rev

Day of judgment. Holt, Rinehart &
Winston 1979 263p o.p.

LC 78-15043

"The time of the story is Spring 1963, just prior to
President Kennedy's planned visit to Berlin. To discredit
his good-will tour, members of the East German Intelligence have kidnapped a [Jesuit] Catholic priest known
to be a foe of Communism and a member of an organization that has been smuggling refugees from the East
into the West. They imprison him in a castle just fifty
miles inside the East German border, to try to break
his will and make him reveal certain facts that could
prove an embarrassment to the Free World, through
brainwashing. But they reckon without dedicated people,
including members of the Catholic Church and the members of a non-Catholic monastery in the town where they
are holding the priest. The rescuers also have the help
of a Jesuit father, a woman doctor and a British Intelligence Officer." West Coast Rev Books

The author "has used an episode in history to write
a finely crafted thriller with excellent characterization."
Booklist

The eagle has flown; a novel. Simon &
Schuster 1991 335p o.p.

LC 91-4368

Available G.K. Hall large print edition

In this sequel to title entered below, "Devlin is asked
by the Germans to parachute into England and free
Steiner from St. Mary's Priory, where he has been taken
after being held captive in the Tower of London. This
[adventure also] involves a plot to thwart the assassination of Hitler in order to prevent the nation's takeover
by Himmler and the SS." Booklist

"Mr. Higgins is an expert storyteller, and he goes
about 'The Eagle Has Flown' with typical gusto.
Everything is carefully arranged, little pieces fitting into
other little pieces to form an action-packed mosaic." NY
Times Book Rev

The eagle has landed. Simon & Schuster
1991 399p o.p.

LC 90-44042

A revised edition containing the full text of the title
first published 1975 by Holt, Rinehart & Winston

"After intense training a small force of German
paratroopers lands on the Norfolk coast in November
1943, with the aim of capturing Churchill, who is spending the weekend at a neighbouring country house." Times
Lit Suppl

"There are elements of heroism, duplicity, and heavy
irony, plus considerable bloodshed, in this action-oriented
yarn." Christ Sci Monit

Followed by The eagle has flown

Exocet. Stein & Day 1983 260p o.p.

LC 83-580

This is "a novel about the . . . Falkland Islands war
and a desperate struggle to obtain French-made Exocet
missiles for the faltering Argentinian air force. The
principal characters are Gabrielle Legrand, a British
socialite and occasional spy, her ex-husband Major Tony
Villiers, British Secret Intelligence operative, and Paul
Montera, Argentinian air attaché in London. Argentine
diplomats approach the Russians for a source of Exocets
and an elaborate plot develops to hijack missiles from
the French factory and embarrass several governments
in the process. *Exocet* is exciting and well-written adventure. Scenes of military action are especially convincing.
It is a quick read with mild sex, moderate violence, and
lots of action." Libr J

Eye of the storm. Putnam 1992 320p o.p.

LC 91-46736

Available Thorndike Press large print edition

"Early in 1991, while the Gulf war is in full bloom,
operatives of Saddam Hussein hire legendary terrorist
Sean Dillon to take the war to the enemy. A master
of disguise and subterfuge, Dillon began his career with
the IRA, earning the enmity of Liam Devlin—the unforgettable antihero of *The Eagle Has Landed*, who makes
a featured appearance here—and of Martin Brosnan, an
American Special Forces hero and IRA member turned
college professor. After Dillon's attempt to assassinate
former Prime Minster Margaret Thatcher during a visit
to France fails, he decides to go after her successor John
Major. . . . Although readers can be sure that Dillon's
scheme will be foiled, fun remains in the how and why."
Publ Wkly

Followed by Thunder point

Luciano's luck. Stein & Day 1981 238p
o.p.

LC 881-40330

Higgins, Jack, 1929— *Continued*

"It is 1943 and the Allied invasion of Sicily is imminent. General Eisenhower plans to enlist Sicilian Mafia support for the invasion by sending two emissaries into Sicily to sway Luca, the Sicilian 'capo di tutti capi.' Logically, perhaps, one emissary is the chief U.S. capo, Lucky Luciano (who is in prison); the second is Luca's alienated granddaughter. The commando expedition to effect a meeting between these three in German-occupied Sicily forms the basis for a fast-paced, action-crammed plot, suspenseful to the last page. The fictionalized Luciano is sympathetically portrayed, and although the romanticizing of the Mafia figures jars a little, the historical premises are acceptably plausible." Libr J

Night of the fox. Simon & Schuster 1986 316p o.p.

LC 86-29662

"Taking the form of a continuous flashback, 'Night of the Fox' begins with the aftermath of a U-boat attack off the coast of German-occupied Jersey, which results in the wounded body of an American soldier being washed ashore. For the Allies, Hugh Kelso is a dangerous liability; if the Germans learn what he knows about the proposed Normandy invasion, disaster would be inevitable. British agents Harry Martinique and Sarah Drayton secretly enter Jersey, posing as an SS officer and his mistress. Another form of deception is also taking place, as a gifted Jewish actor arrives on the island, impersonating Field Marshall Rommel and covering for the real 'Desert Fox,' who is in France on secret talks. The three imposters join forces in a daring and dangerous mission." Booklist

"Higgins combines powerful narrative with documentary detail in an exceptional tale that relies upon the interweaving histories of the various characters." Libr J

On dangerous ground. Putnam 1994 304p $22.95

ISBN 0-399-13933-8   LC 93-47589

Also available Thorndike Press large print edition

Special agent Sean Dillon is enlisted "to help British intelligence locate the Chungking Covenant, a 1944 document in which Winston Churchill agreed to assist Mao Tse-tung against the Japanese for Mao's promise to extend Britain's lease of Hong Kong for another 100 years, to 2097, should his revolution succeed. For some reason, the Mafia . . . are most interested in exposing the document and thus sustaining their lucrative Asian drug trade another century. However, Britain fears that revealing the convenant would strain already-delicate relations among the UK, China, and the U.S." Booklist

"Amiable nonsense, all of this, but it's told in the author's best style, with never a pause for breath." NY Times Book Rev

A season in hell. Simon & Schuster 1989 334p o.p.

LC 88-32702

"Sean Egan is Irish, well-educated and cynical, trained by the British as a commando who can shoot bad guys between the eyes without blinking. Sarah Talbot is a powerful Wall Street lawyer and a wealthy socialite. This unlikely duo joins forces to avenge the killings of Sean's adoptive sister and Sarah's son, both murdered by a ghoulish heroin smuggling ring." Publ Wkly

In this novel "too much depends upon unlikely coincidences. But Mr. Higgins is a real pro, and he keeps things moving so fast the reader is apt to forget and forgive." N Y Times Book Rev

Storm warning; a novel. Holt, Rinehart & Winston 1976 311p il o.p.

"Late in the Second World War, a German sailing ship disguised as a Swedish vessel sets out from Belém, Brazil, for Kiel, Germany—5,000 miles across the Atlantic—taking home a crew and group of passengers wishing to return to their collapsing fatherland. The trip is arduous, ending when the ship strikes a reef in the Outer Hebrides Islands off the coast of Scotland." Booklist

"What does work, exceedingly well, are the action at sea scenes, building up to the climax. . . . Basically what we have are decent people on both sides of the war, some of whom survive, some of whom do not, who come together in a desperate attempt to save the lives of the Germans aboard the ship who have fought so bravely to make it home." Publ Wkly

Thunder point. Putnam 1993 320p o.p.

LC 93-6518

In this novel Sean Dillon is pressed "into the service of the British government, which reluctantly employs him as the best operative there is to find a sunken German U-boat in which Martin Bormann, a day before Hitler's suicide, supposedly made his escape. He was carrying two briefcases full of documents incriminating numerous British officials for their Nazi ties." Booklist

"Higgins adroitly mixes his usual ingredients (large cast, swiftly moving plot, spare prose, great premise), cooking up a zesty action-adventure novel." Publ Wkly

Touch the devil. Stein & Day 1982 251p o.p.

LC 82-40080

"Charles Ferguson of British intelligence persuades Devlin [featured in the Eagle novels] to join forces with Martin Brosnan, former comrade in the fight for Irish independence, to find and stop (by killing if necessary) another onetime rebel, Frank Barry, now in the pay of the Soviets. Barry, a cold assassin and thief of NATO secret weapons, is a match in cunning for Devlin and Brosnan, and he learns about the plot against him from a mole in Ferguson's office. He knows that Devlin and Brosnan's lover, Anne-Marie Audin, get help from the British to spirit Brosnan from a French prison, as grim as Devil's Island, where his revolutionary activities have landed him. Anne-Marie takes the two men to her secluded farm house in southern France, where Barry and his hirelings lurk in ambush." Publ Wkly

The Valhalla exchange; [by] Harry Patterson. Stein & Day 1976 224p o.p.

The novel "tells the story of Martin Bormann's escape from Berlin and his 'insurance' plan involving U.S. war hero Hamilton Canning, one of five important prisoners of war tucked away in a small Austrian town during the last days of the Third Reich. General Canning tells the story to a correspondent in South America years later as he searches for Bormann or proof of his death." Booklist

Highet, Helen MacInnes *See* MacInnes, Helen, 1907-1985

Highsmith, Patricia, 1921-1995

The boy who followed Ripley. Lippincott & Crowell 1980 291p o.p.

LC 79-29678

Highsmith, Patricia, 1921-1995—*Continued*

In this novel "two people meet casually, but their fates become inextricably, and dangerously, joined. Tom Ripley is an American expatriate living on the outskirts of Paris; he meets a 16-year-old American runaway, who turns out to be the son of a recently deceased food products tycoon. The boy is haunted by guilt over his father's death and pursued through Europe by kidnappers. Engrossing and shiver packed." Booklist

Ripley's game. Knopf 1974 267p o.p.

"Tom [Ripley], an American married to a lovely French woman and living in luxury in country France, is a diabolically clever killer and con artist. What he begins here starts as a fairly vicious practical joke to worry an Englishman who has snubbed Tom. Before the last ploy has been played out, several murders have taken place, the Mafia has embarked on ruthless revenge against Tom and the Englishman, the latter's happy marriage has been hopelessly damaged and Tom has survived as only someone as totally amoral as he can succeed in doing." Publ Wkly

"Highsmith uses a matter-of-fact, almost reportorial, tone to effect her measured, driving pace and to construct her tightly woven web. The second half of this literate and imaginative thriller is especially brilliant—all the way to the dazzling last page." Libr J

Hijuelos, Oscar

The fourteen sisters of Emilio Montez O'Brien; a novel. Farrar, Straus & Giroux 1993 484p $22

ISBN 0-374-15815-0   LC 92-41935

This novel "tells the story of the family of Nelson O'Brien, an Irish immigrant to the U.S. who travels to Cuba as a photographer during the Spanish-American War. There he falls passionately in love and marries the young and beautiful Mariela Montez. After the couple returns to the farm O'Brien owns in a small Pennsylvania town, he works as the local photographer and operates the community's movie theater, while she keeps busy bearing and rearing their 14 daughters and, finally, one son, Emilio Montez O'Brien." Time

"The sprawling narrative is sustained by the author's leniency in enforcing whatever conventions he adopts. Its pace speeds up and slows down, depending as much, it seems, on Mr. Hijuelos's mood as his material. . . . The changing degree of connectedness discernible among the characters and plot lines mirrors nothing so much as family life the way it is actually lived, by both great broods and small." N Y Times Book Rev

The Mambo Kings play songs of love; a novel. Farrar, Straus & Giroux 1989 407p $18.95

ISBN 0-374-20125-0   LC 89-1248

"The Mambo Kings are two brothers, Cesar and Nestor Castillo, Cuban-born musicians who emigrate to New York City in 1949. They form a band and enjoy modest success, playing dance halls, nightclubs and *quince* parties in New York's Latin neighborhoods. Their popularity peaks in 1956 with a guest appearance on the *I Love Lucy* show, playing Ricky Ricardo's Cuban cousins and performing their only hit song in a bittersweet event that both frames the novel and serves as its emblematic heart." Publ Wkly

"The novel alternates crisp narrative with opulent musings—the language of everyday and the language of longing. When Mr. Hijuelos falters, as from time to time he does, it's through an excess of self-consciousness: he strives too hard for all-encompassing description or grows distant and dutiful in an effort to get period details just right." N Y Times Book Rev

Hill, Pamela, 1920-

Artemia. St. Martin's Press 1990 190p o.p.
LC 89-77894

"Artemia, 'a plain, long-nosed woman, with perhaps a certain placidity of temper,' becomes the unlikely center that holds a tempestuous family in balance. Hired as companion for Lady Feldman, a grande dame of the 1850s, the period of the Crimean War, Artemia experiences a *coup de foudre* when she and Edward Feldman, the unhappily married eldest son, first meet. Their illicit union wins the grudging respect of Lady Feldman, produces two daughters and endures lovingly despite the constraints of Edward's public career. Passive and, as she says, 'suffering little from whoredom,' Artemia is an unusual and intriguing creation." Publ Wkly

The sword and the flame. St. Martin's Press 1992 c1991 316p o.p.
LC 91-34909

First published 1991 in the United Kingdom

This novel "tells the tale of Mary of Lorraine, the mother of the famed Mary Queen of Scots. Pregnant with her second child and mourning the sudden death of her husband, Mary was ordered by the French king to marry James V of Scotland. Her refusals were met with dire threats, and thus was the history of Scotland influenced by a strong-minded woman, who eventually ruled her new country after her second husband's death in battle against England. The story of how Mary achieved, and fought to retain, control of the Scottish throne is told here with all the details of court life, warfare, and social upheaval filling Hill's vivid narration." Booklist

Vollands. St. Martin's Press 1991 c1990 186p $15.95

ISBN 0-312-05989-2   LC 90-28632

First published 1990 in the United Kingdom

The author relates the "demise of a 19th-century English family into this . . . historical novel. After her husband's bankruptcy and subsequent suicide, Anna Volland and her eight children rely on the generosity of her wealthy uncle Hubert. But the benefactor's death leaves Anna's sadistic eldest son, James, in charge of the clan. Hubert's corpse is barely cold when James rapes the deceased's beautiful bastard daughter Jenny, whose illegitimate son later vows to avenge his mother's shame." Publ Wkly

Hill, Rebecca

(jt. auth) Guest, J. Killing time in St. Cloud

Hill, Reginald, 1936-

Blood sympathy. St. Martin's Press 1994 c1993 220p $19.95

ISBN 0-312-11249-1   LC 94-26216

Hill, Reginald, 1936—*Continued*

"A Thomas Dunne book"

First published 1993 in the United Kingdom

This mystery "features unlikely hero Joe Sixsmith, a balding, middle-aged, recently laid-off lathe operator from Luton, Bedfordshire, and Joe's partner, Whitey, a curmudgeonly feline that loves beer, pork rinds, and an occasional taste of champagne. Joe decides that if he can't make a living operating lathes, maybe his real calling is private investigation. Before he can have business cards printed, Joe is juggling a mysterious multiple murder, a cache of illicit drugs, his meddling, matchmaking Aunt Mirabelle, and two thugs whose sole aim in life seems to be inflicting pain on Joe." Booklist

Bones and silence. Delacorte Press 1990 332p o.p.

LC 89-48836

"Set in a cathedral city which will host a contemporary enactment of medieval mystery plays, Hill's narrative features the police duo Andrew Dalziel and Peter Pascoe looking into a series of related murders and disappearances tied to a builder who is coincidentally constructing garages for the police station. Meanwhile, the galvanizing director of the mystery plays, Eileen Chung, has cast Dalziel as God and the builder in question as Lucifer." Publ Wkly

"A complex, challenging and diverting novel, from one of the most cogent of detective writers." Times Lit Suppl

Child's play. Macmillan 1987 296p o.p.

LC 86-8712

"A Dalziel-Pascoe murder mystery"

This novel "has two plots. One concerns the will of a dotty, wealthy old woman who leaves her money to a son missing in action since 1944 and presumed dead. Hungry, greedy, angry relatives gather to see what can be done about breaking the will. . . . The other side of the story has to do with a tough cop who lives a secret life as a homosexual. Mr. Hill handles this aspect with grace; there also is a good deal of humor in the way Dalziel goes into action when, on orders from above, he has to track down the homosexual. He takes care of things in his own inimitable manner. Mr. Hill, as always, has a fine time jousting against hypocrisy and the hollow men of the bureaucracy." N Y Times Book Rev

A clubbable woman. Countryman Press 1984 c1970 256p o.p.

LC 84-17604

"A Foul Play Press book"

First published 1970 in the United Kingdom

This police procedural features "police superintendent Andrew Dalziel and the refined, bookish detective sergeant Peter Pascoe. . . . The wife of a onetime rugby star has her head bashed in as she sits watching television. The murder investigation reveals the adulterous and hateful relationships that form the backbone of what seems a peaceful suburban development." Booklist

Deadheads; a murder mystery. Macmillan 1984 c1983 275p o.p.

LC 83-26735

First published 1983 in the United Kingdom

This novel "finds inspectors Dalziel and Pascoe investigating Patrick Aldermann, a young accountant and obsessive rose gardener, whose good fortune in life comes from a series of highly convenient accidental deaths." Libr J

The author "displays a talent for creating enjoyable, believable, and identifiable characters. His dialogue runs smoothly and lucidly." Best Sellers

Dream of darkness; [by] Patrick Ruell. Countryman Press 1991 204p o.p.

LC 90-38677

"A Foul Play Press book"

"In London 18-year-old Sairey Ellis suffers from a recurring, debilitating nightmare that shows the young Sairey viewing the open coffin of her mother in Uganda years ago. That did not happen, say her retired British security officer father, Nigel, and his sister, who raised Sairey after her mother's death. Sairey's analysis-prompted returning memory of the brief time with her mother in Uganda holds the key to her nightmare and seems to threaten family and friend—as does Nigel, who is writing his African memoirs." Libr J

"The story of Sairey's haunted nights and days alternates with selections from her father's memoirs, which detail his diplomatic career in Uganda during the Amin years. Ruell effectively uses these parallel narratives to slowly unravel the mystery of Sairey's mother's death. A gem of a book with a startling finale." Booklist

Exit lines. Macmillan 1985 c1984 262p o.p.

LC 84-20116

"A Dalziel-Pascoe murder mystery"

First published 1984 in the United Kingdom

"Superintendent Andrew Dalziel and Detective Inspector Peter Pascoe of the Mid-Yorkshire CID probe the murders of three old men who were killed the same night—one died in his bath, another was struck by a car, another was bludgeoned to death in a public park." Booklist

Pictures of perfection; a Dalziel/Pascoe mystery in five volumes. Delacorte Press 1994 307p $19.95

ISBN 0-385-31270-9   LC 93-47449

"The intrepid trio of Sergeant Wield and detectives Dalziel and Pascoe are called to the tiny hamlet of Enscombe to investigate the mysterious disappearance of a rookie constable. When they arrive, however, they find there are more problems than just a missing copper; skulduggery, thievery, forgery, lust, lechery, libel, and passion all lie in wait for the three unwitting chaps. This is an intelligent, stylish, scintillating, witty mystery that transcends its cozy trappings." Booklist

Recalled to life. Delacorte Press 1992 359p o.p.

LC 92-1380

Available Thorndike Press large print edition

A mystery set in England and the U.S. "As Inspector Dalziel and partner Pascoe work unofficially to refute new evidence concerning a 1963 case, they threaten to unearth various nasty political secrets." Libr J

"Though Hill relies too much on coincidence, the complex plot here sustains interest. The novel's chief rewards, however, are those of character: Dalziel is a brilliant, bearish delight and the supporting players, including a brash black woman CIA agent, provide a constant parade of pleasures." Publ Wkly

Underworld; a Dalziel-Pascoe murder mystery. Scribner 1988 280p o.p.

LC 88-6479

Hill, Reginald, 1936-—*Continued*

This mystery is "set among the mines and miners of Yorkshire. Who killed little Tracey Pedley? The police marked the seven-year-old girl's case closed when a sales-rep confessed to other, similar crimes. But some of the people of Burrthorpe have always thought that a local man, Billy Farr, killed Tracey. 'Uncle' Billy went walking with the child on the day she disappeared. He was the last person known to have seen her alive. Now Billy is dead, and his son Colin has come home from the navy to clear his father's name. Colin himself has enemies in Burrthorpe, people who would like to see him gone. He also has a friend—Ellie Pascoe, Inspector Peter Pascoe's wife." Publisher's note

Hill, Ruth Beebe

Hanta yo. Doubleday 1979 834p o.p.

LC 77-74792

"The story is a fictional elaboration upon the chronological record kept on a tanned hide by a member of the Mahto band of the Teton Sioux. Hill follows the tribe from 1794 to 1835 in the seasonal moves across the plains. She unfolds . . . the tale of two families, and in particular, the . . . friendship between Ahbleza and Tonweya, the son of a warrior-leader and the son of a hunter." New Repub

"The practice of using the multi-generational family story to reflect changing times and/or historical events is almost a genre unto itself. This is such a novel. . . . The historical accuracy, linguistic acrobatics, and ethnological acuity do not limit the book's appeal. A superb style transcends the few minor flaws, and despite the scholarly impression given by the introduction, chronology notes, and glossaries, this book is first and foremost a well-written story." Libr J

Hill, Susan, 1942-

Mrs. de Winter; a novel. Morrow 1993 349p $20

ISBN 0-688-12707-X   LC 93-5347

Also available Thorndike Press large print edition

"What happened to Maxim de Winter and his second wife after Manderley burned? This suspenseful 'completion' of Daphne du Maurier's *Rebecca* begins with the couple's return to England, following a ten-year, self-imposed exile, for the funeral of Maxim's sister Beatrice. In a voice true to the original story, Hill's Mrs. de Winter chronicles Rebecca's continuing shadow on their life; a mysterious wreath bearing a card with the initial 'R' is discovered near Beatrice's grave, and unwelcome visitors include Jack Favell, who has visions of blackmail, and Mrs. Danvers, who seeks revenge." Libr J

Hillerman, Tony

The blessing way. Armchair Detective Lib. 1990 201p $25

ISBN 0-922890-10-2   LC 89-18623

Also available G.K. Hall large print edition

A reissue of the title first published 1970 by Harper & Row

"When Bergen McKee, a disillusioned anthropologist, goes to the reservation to continue his research on Navajo witchcraft, he finds himself involved in murder, intrigue, adventure, and, worst of all, what appears to be genuine witchcraft. . . . [Also involved is] Lt. Joe Leaphorn of the Navajo Law and Order Division." Libr J

"Here's suspense enough for anyone, but what makes the first mystery by Tony Hillerman outstanding is the wealth of detail about the Navajo Indian—customs, rites, way of life—with which he has crammed his pages." Saturday Rev

also in Hillerman, T. The Joe Leaphorn mysteries

Coyote waits. Harper & Row 1990 292p o.p.

LC 89-46098

Lieutenant Joe Leaphorn of the Navaho Tribal Police is investigating the murder of "his fellow policeman Delbert Nez. Meanwhile, [Jim] Chee, the erstwhile medicine man and Tribal Police officer, is also on the trail of Nez's murderer and believes he has already arrested the culprit in the person of a fellow Navajo, the old shaman Ashie Pinto." N Y Times Book Rev

"The story line has more twists, turns, and bumps than one of the many back-country roads on the Navajo reservation. . . . Hillerman's characters are not just there to provide dialogue for a story that dances along to a clever ending. Leaphorn and Chee each have a past they remember, a present they puzzle over, and a future they anticipate with mixed feelings." Christ Sci Monit

Dance hall of the dead. Armchair Detective Lib. 1991 c1973 242p $25

ISBN 0-922890-73-0   LC 90-23955

Also available G.K. Hall large print edition

A reissue of the title first published 1973 by Harper & Row

Navajo police lieutenant Joe Leaphorn faces a "mystery and possible murder in the disappearance of a Zuni youth and his Navajo best friend shortly before an important annual Zuni religious ceremony." Booklist

"A novel of three-dimensional characters, involving their cultures as well as their emotions, the land as well as the 'place' of the crime, and the collision of mores. The author tells his story so that it is rooted in a rich background setting of Zuni religion, Navajo and Zuni differences, the differences from the whiteman and the differences among the whiteman." Best Sellers

also in Hillerman, T. The Joe Leaphorn mysteries

The dark wind. Harper & Row 1982 214p o.p.

LC 81-47793

Available Thorndike Press large print edition

"Jim Chee of the Navajo Tribal Police is drawn into the mystique of the Hopi tribal ways, which are very different from his own, as he follows a trail that leads him to a father seeking revenge for his son's death, a corrupt lawman and a fortune in cocaine." Publ Wkly

"Fascinating background and atmosphere makes something special out of an otherwise ordinary story." Libr J

also in Hillerman, T. The Jim Chee mysteries

The ghostway. Harper & Row 1985 c1984 213p o.p.

LC 84-48165

Available Thorndike Press large print edition

"A Harper novel of suspense"

Originally published 1984 in a limited edition by Dennis McMillan Publications

"The story concerns Navaho tribal detective Jim Chee's

Hillerman, Tony—*Continued*

pursuit of the men who killed three Navaho of the Turkey clan. Chee solves the murders through his knowledge of the Indian way of life, which is gradually being eroded by white culture. As Navaho rituals help to solve Chee's murders, they also reinforce his doubts about the Indian in him. In an entertaining and fact-filled narrative, Hillerman offers a good look at the plight of contemporary Indians in the West. It is an engrossing and intelligent book for mystery fans and armchair anthropologists alike." Booklist

also in Hillerman, T. The Jim Chee mysteries

The Jim Chee mysteries. HarperCollins Pubs. 1990 566p $20

ISBN 0-06-016478-6

An omnibus edition of three titles entered separately
Contents: People of darkness; The dark wind; The ghostway

The Joe Leaphorn mysteries; three classic Hillerman mysteries featuring Lt. Joe Leaphorn. Harper & Row 1989 499p o.p.

LC 89-45079

An omnibus edition of three titles entered separately
Contents: The blessing way; Dance hall of the dead; Listening woman

Listening woman. Armchair Detective Lib. 1994 c1978 316p $22

ISBN 1-56287-059-9   LC 93-44681

Also available G.K. Hall large print edition

A reissue of the title first published 1978 by Harper & Row

In this novel detective "Joe Leaphorn of the Navajo Tribal Police . . . [is] tracking down the murderer of a harmless old man and searching for a missing helicopter used for the getaway in a Brinks-style robbery pulled off by a militant Indian-rights group called the Buffalo Society. The desecration of some ritual sand paintings and the rumor of a sacred cave lead Leaphorn into a violent confrontation with the fanatical Buffalo Society. The terrorists are plotting to avenge the victims of a long-forgotten atrocity by recreating it—with white children as the pawns—in a vicious kidnapping/mass-murder scheme." N Y Times Book Rev

also in Hillerman, T. The Joe Leaphorn mysteries

(ed) The Mysterious West. See The Mysterious West

People of darkness. Penzler Bks. 1994 c1980 282p $23

ISBN 1-56287-057-2   LC 94-11790

Also available Thorndike Press large print edition

"The Armchair detective library"

A reissue of the title first published 1980 by Harper & Row

"Navajo Tribal Police Detective Jim Chee, constantly confronted by the split between the ways of the Indian and those of the white man, is led into an investigation that challenges and torments him. A wealthy woman asks Chee to find a stolen box of keepsakes, which contains the key to a mysterious Navajo cult called 'The People of Darkness,' a buried Indian, peyote abuse, and danger. Hillerman has written an absorbing mystery and a

fascinating cultural study." Booklist

also in Hillerman, T. The Jim Chee mysteries

Sacred clowns. HarperCollins Pubs. 1993 305p o.p.

LC 91-50470

Available Thorndike Press large print edition

"Lt. Joe Leaphorn and Officer Jim Chee of the Navajo police resolve personal issues as they investigate the murders of a tribal dancer and a white schoolteacher." Publ Wkly

"The author skillfully employs the elements of detection and routine police work while providing readers with an intriguing glimpse of Navajo culture. The relationships between the officers and between the other well-defined characters give depth to the story, which is spiced with both men's romantic interests." SLJ

Skinwalkers. Harper & Row 1987 216p o.p.

LC 86-45600

The author "brings his Navaho policemen Lieutenant Joe Leaphorn and Detective Jim Chee together in a tale involving Indian mysticism and folklore as well as murder. Leaphorn has three unsolved murders to contend with, and then an attempt is made on Chee's life. Much to Leaphorn's dismay bone head figures are the sole clues found, indicating the work of a skinwalker or witch. Hillerman's Leaphorn and Chee novels convey the Navaho culture with all its intricacies set forth in a meaningful way." Libr J

Talking God. Harper & Row 1989 239p o.p.

LC 88-45914

Available Thorndike Press large print edition

This "complex tale hinges on the mysterious murder of a man in shiny old shoes who was apparently killed on his way to an ancient tribal ceremony. Leaphorn and Chee's investigation reveals a conflict over ceremonial masks, which in turn takes them from their familiar New Mexico haunts to Washington, D.C., where they must foil an assassination attempt. As in his previous works, Hillerman combines P. D. James' taut, precise narrative style with a consistently sensitive portrayal of the native American experience. The rural landscapes shimmer with realism, while the plot is crafted with skill and passion, like the masks that figure so strongly in the action." Booklist

A thief of time; a novel. Harper & Row 1988 209p o.p.

LC 87-46147

In this novel "Lieut. Joe Leaphorn and Officer Jim Chee of the Navajo Tribal Police . . . combine forces . . . in the search for a missing archeologist, Prof. Eleanor Friedman-Bernal. A specialist in Anasazi pots, she's on the verge of a major breakthrough—the identification of a specific artist, dead a thousand years—when, beneath a full desert moon, she seems simply to vanish." N Y Times Book Rev

"It is the complex relationship between Leaphorn and Chee and the rich view of Navaho culture that give the book its depth and resonance." Booklist

Hilton, James, 1900-1954

Good-bye Mr. Chips; illustrated by H.M. Brock. Little, Brown 1962 c1934 132p il $17.95

ISBN 0-316-36420-7

Also available from Buccaneer Bks.

"An Atlantic Monthly Press book"

First published 1934

Gentle, humorous Mr. Chipping had been known familiarly to three generations of English schoolboys at Brookfield, as Mr. Chips. As he sat in his pleasant room across from the entrance to the school Mr. Chips recalled his life there, the jokes he had made which had become classics, the thousands he had known and regarded as his boys. And just as gently as he lived he faded smilingly out of life

Lost horizon. Morrow 1933 277p o.p.

Available from Amereon and Buccaneer Bks.

Two Englishmen, a woman missionary and an American fleeing the consequences of shady financial deals are travelling companions. When their plane lands under mysterious circumstances in a remote Tibetan spot, they "find themselves involuntary guests in a lamasery unknown to the world and almost inaccessible. Here one traveler is admitted to the secret. Civilization and learning are being preserved in this retreat, for the lamas are able to prolong life indefinitely, and when the rest of the world becomes chaos, their cultured, urban existence will continue undisturbed. It is a pleasing combination of adventure story and imaginative fantasy." Booklist

Random harvest. Little, Brown 1941 326p o.p.

Available from Buccaneer Bks.

"An Atlantic Monthly Press book"

"Charles Rainier, wealthy business man and M.P., for nearly twenty years unable to recall that period of his life between his World War injury and 1919 suddenly has his memory restored. The dramatic suspense is great as Rainier faces his two pasts, passionately resolved to find the Paula of his lost years, at whatever cost to his present marriage and position. . . . Part of the story is related in the first person by Rainier's secretary and confidante who is interested in psychology." Libr J

Hilton, John Buxton, 1921-1986

Displaced person; A Superintendent Kenworthy novel. St. Martin's Press 1988 c1987 183p o.p.

LC 87-29920

First published 1987 in the United Kingdom

"Some 40 years after serving in World War II, [Superintendent] Kenworthy is retired but asked to cooperate with the French police on a frustrating and delicate matter. The story unfolds in the ex-soldier's memory of adolescent Marie-Thérèse Laniel, an orphan refugee who had clung to his troop detachment, slogging across France and Holland in the wake of the fleeing German army. . . . An old man now, he's reunited with Marie-Thérèse in Paris where she's charged with blackmail and murder. Beautifully written, the novel sweeps from past to present and to the stunning denouement, always holding one in thrall." Publ Wkly

Himes, Chester, 1909-1984

The collected stories of Chester Himes; foreword by Calvin Hernton. Thunder's Mouth Press 1991 429p o.p.

LC 90-25682

Analyzed in Short story index

Contents: Headwaiter; Lunching at the Ritzmore; All God's chillun got pride; A nigger; Let me at the enemy-an' George Brown; With malice toward none; A penny for your thoughts; Two soldiers; So softly smiling; Heaven has changed; Looking down the street; The song says 'Keep on smiling'; Her whole existence; He seen it in the stars; Make with the shape; Dirty deceivers; A modern marriage; Black laughter; A night of new roses; The night's for cryin'; Face in the moonlight; Strictly business; Prison mass; Money don't spend in the stir; I don't want to die; The meanest cop in the world; On dreams and reality; The way of flesh; The visiting hour; The things you do; There ain't no justice; Every opportunity; I'm not trying to hurt you; Pork chop paradise; Friends; To what red hell; His last day; In the rain; The ghost of Rufus Jones; Whose little baby are you?; Mama's missionary money; My but the rats are terrible; The snake; In the night; All he needs is feet; Christmas gift; The revelation; Daydream; Da-da-dee; Marihuana and a pistol; One more way to die; Naturally, the Negro; Winter coming on; Spanish gin; The something in a colored man; Tang; One night in New Jersey; A modern fable; Prediction; Life everlasting

Hitchcock, Alfred, 1899-1980

(ed) Alfred Hitchcock presents: Stories not for the nervous. See Alfred Hitchcock presents: Stories not for the nervous

Hoagland, Edward

Seven rivers west. Summit Bks. 1986 319p o.p.

LC 86-5815

This novel is a "deliberately written account of a trek through the mountains of the West with time taken to appreciate the beauties of nature and to observe the wildlife. Cecil Roop goes west in search of a young grizzly to train for vaudeville. With him is Sutton, a skilled high diver, who seeks gold. As they proceed they acquire companions, human and animal, most of whom fall victim to the dangers of the wild. The characters are fascinating, the writing is excellent. A novel for readers who enjoy nature, with all its beauties and hazards." Libr J

Hoban, Russell

Pilgermann. Summit Bks. 1983 240p o.p.

LC 83-472

In the "heart of medieval Europe, a young Jewish man is castrated for having seduced the local tax collector's wife. Through his agony, he hears a voice telling him to go to Jerusalem. . . . The maimed pilgrim boards a ship at Genoa and then finds his progress stalled. He is captured by pirates and put up for sale at a slave market in Tripoli. His purchaser, a wealthy Turkish merchant, immediately negotiates his freedom and brings him home in friendship to Antioch, that . . . city whose destiny lies between the Crusaders and their goal.

Hoban, Russell—*Continued*

Looking out at the tents of the besieging armies, the German Jew reflects on the oddity of his position: 'I stand on this wall built by a Roman emperor and keep watch on the Franks with a Turkish bow in my hand.' He dies on a night in June 1098, when the soldiers of Christ sweep into the betrayed fortress." Time

"What we have here—pirates, seductive pigs and violent battles to the contrary—is not so much a tale of adventure as a meditation on history, loss and grief, a dark treatise on the mysterious nature of things." N Y Times Book Rev

Riddley Walker; a novel. Summit Bks. 1980 220p o.p.

LC 80-25859

"About 2,000 years before this novel begins, civilization was shattered by a great barm [bomb]—a flash of light followed by centuries of darkness and ignorance. Riddley [the narrator and interpreter] having reached manhood at 12 and having witnessed the crushing of his father during the unearthing of an ancient machine, sets off on foot across the ruined landscape of Inland [England]. Riddley's quest involves the reader in learning a new language based on English . . . a written language in which spelling is a rusty approximation of sounds handed down orally during the dark centuries." Newsweek

"No review can do more than suggest the range and effect of this extraordinary book. It is 'sui generis,' its inspirations both particular and diverse, its references legion, its craft remarkable—contributing to a whole that is vivid, compelling and certainly unforgettable." Encounter

Turtle diary. Random House 1976 c1975 211p o.p.

First published 1975 in the United Kingdom

"Two middle-aged, unattractive, reclusive, and slightly daft idealists, William G. and Neaera H., record in their diaries a shared obsession: to capture from the aquarium of the London Zoo all the mature sea-turtles and set them free in the ocean. Encouraged by George Fairbairn, the head keeper of the zoo, the two conspirators succeed with astonishing ease, then set their dark plans to free the remaining immature turtles at an appropriate time. Otherwise, nothing much else happens to William G.; his brief fling with Harriet lapses into bored neglect. Similarly, Neaera H. continues her drab life, writing uninspired children's books, tending her water-beetle, and mothering her new sleeping partner." Choice

"Turtle Diary is very intelligent and very funny. I know perfectly well that some people will find it whimsical and irritating; and the journal technique makes it all too easy to include a lot of 'writer's diary' observation of people in buses and shops—there is an air of no material being wasted. But no one else could have written this bizarre book, and it is . . . most distinguished and memorable." New Statesman

Hobson, Laura Keane Zametkin, 1900-1986

Consenting adult; [by] Laura Z. Hobson. Doubleday 1975 256p o.p.

"What happens when a truly liberated, middle-aged, professional woman receives a letter from her son that says, 'I am a homosexual'? Since she is also liberated from religion, to whom can she turn for strength and advice? Her husband Ken, is recovering from a stroke, so she feels that she has to hide it from him as long

as possible. Basically, this story is the thirteen-year history of her efforts to cope with this singular event in her family." Best Sellers

"Never patronizing, Hobson exhibits crystal perception in fashioning a cogent statement about homosexuality as viewed from a parental standpoint." Booklist

Gentleman's agreement; a novel; by Laura Z. Hobson. Simon & Schuster 1947 275p o.p.

Available from Amereon and Buccaneer Bks.

"Phil Green, a member of the editorial staff of 'Smith's Weekly,' is assigned to write a series of ariticles about anti-Semitism in America. He decides to pose as a Jew for six months, and he has some extraordinary experiences." Benet's Reader's Ency of Am Lit

Hodge, Jane Aiken

Escapade. St. Martin's Press 1993 231p $18.95

ISBN 0-312-09799-9   LC 93-24278

Also available Thorndike Press large print edition

"Charlotte Comyn, the 17-year-old heir to a banking fortune, rejects the marriage proposal of childhood friend John Thornton and runs away to London. There, Charlotte meets Beth Prior, friend of her mother, actress, and member of the demi-monde. Beth sees Charlotte as the perfect cover for her role as a spy, and the two set off for Palermo, Sicily. In Sicily, the two become embroiled in political intrigue, and Beth begins to question her involvement in British politics. Charlotte and Beth find adventure and romance in Palermo amid the glittering stage lights and hidden agendas of the aristocracy. Hodge captures the soul of an era when women were often the power behind the throne." Booklist

Strangers in company. Coward, McCann & Geoghegan 1973 252p o.p.

"Stella Marten and her hired companion Marian Frenche, members of a guided tour group traveling by bus through Greece, become the chief, though unwilling participants in a ruthless plot to free a political prisoner from a Greek prison by leaving Mrs. Frenche, a lookalike, to take her place." Booklist

The winding stair. Doubleday 1969 c1968 328p o.p.

First published 1968 in the United Kingdom

"A suspenseful Gothic romance set in early nineteenth-century Portugal under threat from Napoleonic France features a likable half-English, half-Portugese heroine. Juana Brett returns from England to the ancestral Portuguese castle to care for her ailing but formidable grandmother who wants Juana to assume her position as handmaiden to a dangerous secret society dedicated to gaining control of Portugal by any means, a position the grandmother has used to spy on the group for the English." Booklist

Windover. St. Martin's Press 1992 266p o.p.

LC 92-7671

Available Thorndike Press large print edition

"Kathryn of Windover is only 16, but she is madly in love with the family's tutor, Mark Weatherby. When they are caught in an embrace by Kathryn's stepfather, Weatherby is beaten and tossed over a cliff. Told that her beloved departed willingly, Kathryn finally marries another man. Hers continues not to be a peaceful life.

Hodge, Jane Aiken—*Continued*

Eventually, she must tangle with a controlling mother-in-law who is under the spell of a mesmerizing preacher, rescue her late husband's overdrafted bank, and run for her life to London when a plot to murder her is overheard." Booklist

"This appealing 18th-century romance serves up a courageous heroine and plenty of drama against an expertly crafted historical backdrop." Publ Wkly

Hodgins, Eric, 1899-1971

Mr. Blandings builds his dream house; illustrated by William Steig. Simon & Schuster 1946 237p il o.p.

"Expanded from a 'Fortune' short story, this book is an amusing tale of a New York advertiser who found his apartment much too small and bought 50 acres and a farmhouse in the country. Mr. Blandings' trials and tribulations from the time when the architect, after spending a great deal of time and money, decided that the farmhouse should be torn down instead of remodelled until the new home was finished at a cost of $45,000 more than they expected make hilarious reading." Ont Libr Rev

Hoeg, Peter

Borderliners; translated by Barbara Haveland. Farrar, Straus & Giroux 1994 277p $24

ISBN 0-374-11554-0   LC 94-18892

Original Danish edition, 1993

"Hoeg portrays the closed world of Biehl's, a Danish private school where a bizarre social experiment is underway. The narrator, Peter, is now a student at Biehl's after spending all of his life in children's homes and reform schools. He is a borderline case, along with Katarina, whose parents both died in the past year, and August, severely disturbed after killing his abusive parents. Although allowed no social interaction, the children conspire to conduct their own experiment to discover what plan is being carried out at Biehl's." Libr J

"The author avoids simple storytelling, preferring instead to explore the nature of time. 'What is time?' are the book's opening words, and later Mr. Hoeg actually provides brief historical passages on the development of theories of time. In a related device, the novel employs a dreamy, associative narrative, moving back and forth through the years, including flash-forwards to the adult Peter's family life. . . . 'Borderliners' is written from the heart, and its portrait of the embittered survivor Peter is moving." N Y Times Book Rev

Smilla's sense of snow; translated by Tiina Nunnally. Farrar Straus Giroux 1993 453p $21

ISBN 0-374-26644-1   LC 93-17742

Original Danish edition, 1992; published in the United Kingdom with title: Miss Smilla's feeling for snow

This novel "is set in Copenhagen and features Smilla Qaavigaaq, a 37-year-old, part-Eskimo, part-Danish heroine who is investigating the death of Isaiah, her young neighbor. Although police officially rule Isaiah's death an accident, Smilla is convinced that he has been pushed off the roof of her apartment building. Discouraged by Danish officials, the tough, persistent,

and resourceful Smilla follows Isaiah's trail to a ship that is docked off the coast of Greenland with a crew that is involved in drug trafficking and mysterious scientific experiments." Libr J

"Selfishness, menace and systematic corruption form the fabric of this mysterious novel. Relationships are all based on suspicion, and love has to be 'like a military operation.'. . . Peter Høeg has a remarkable feeling for sinister surprises." Times Lit Suppl

Hoffman, Alice

At risk. Putnam 1988 219p o.p.

LC 87-33240

Available G.K. Hall large print edition

"The Farrells are your typical New England upper middle class family. Ivan, the father, is an astronomer, and Polly, the mother, is a free lance photographer. Amanda is a typical 11-year old girl with a passion for gymnastics, and Charles is an 8-year old budding biologist, interested in specimens of frogs and insects and books on dinosaurs. Their comfortable lifestyle is shattered when Amanda is diagnosed as having AIDS. The family goes through stages of disbelief, denial, anger, despair, and finally numbing acceptance as Amanda withers away and is hospitalized at the end presumably with death close at hand." West Coast Rev Books

"Such is Ms. Hoffman's tenderness and perceptiveness that we come to care about her creations despite their imperfections the way we would care about those we love despite theirs." N Y Times Book Rev

Illumination night. Putnam 1987 224p o.p.

LC 86-30472

"A young couple's marriage has survived struggles and poverty in a countercultural transplant to the off-season isolation of Martha's Vineyard only to face a more unlikely and dangerous threat. A teen-age girl, who has moved next door to care for her sick grandmother, develops an erotic fixation on the husband. Hoffman probes the mythic connotations of the situation as she supplies convincing portraits of the man and woman and of the young girl who is determined to come between them. . . . All of this is delineated with both depth and clarity in a novel that encapsulates and transforms the characters' experiences into broader symbols of yearning and passion." Booklist

Second nature. Putnam 1994 254p $22.95

ISBN 0-399-13908-7   LC 93-11595

Also available Thorndike Press large print edition

"Robin Moore rescues a wild, unspeaking young man—called the Wolf Man because he was found, injured, in a wolf trap—from impending transfer to a mental hospital. In the process of teaching Stephen how to live in 'civilized' suburban society, she falls in love with him. Meanwhile, neighborhood animals are found with their throats slit, and a teenage girl is murdered; the Wolf Man is naturally a suspect." Libr J

"In the end, Ms. Hoffman suggests that it is love in all its wondrous forms, from a parent's love for a child to the most consuming sexual passion that truly delineates mankind. Her abiding vision of this ineluctable and uniquely human power informs 'Second Nature' with grace and beauty, making it at once her richest and wisest, as well as her boldest, novel to date." N Y Times Book Rev

Seventh heaven. Putnam 1990 256p o.p.

LC 89-28737

Available Thorndike Press large print edition

Hoffman, Alice—*Continued*

"The setting is a Long Island, N.Y., housing development from 1959 to 1960, a place of conforming, happy families where husbands mow the lawns of the tract houses and wives meet for coffee, where 'safety hung over the neighborhood like a net.' The arrival of Nora Silk, a brassy divorcée with two young children, is the catalyst for disturbing changes and events, some of them violent. Plucky, impetuous, innocently seductive and a messy housekeeper, Nora is anathema to the subdivision wives, who ostracize her and whose children torment her eight-year-old clairvoyant son, Billy. But as Nora's presence disturbs the community, it is slowly revealed that behind the identical facades of the houses are secret lives of turmoil, restlessness and longing." Publ Wkly

This is "one of those rare novels so abundant with life it seems to overflow its own pages, these aren't the sort of fictional characters who are all used up by the end of the book; on the contrary, they seem ready to leap straight into another volume." Newsweek

Turtle Moon. Putnam 1992 255p o.p.
LC 91-37222

Available Thorndike Press large print edition

"Julian Cash, policeman, and Lucy Rosen, obit writer, both with hardened shells covering events that shattered their younger selves, are thrown together when they try to solve a murder that endangers Lucy's son and the murdered woman's child. In the ensuing days they gradually draw solace from each other and revisit their pasts in search of the solution to the murder; Lucy to Great Neck, New York where she lived after her parents died when she was 16; Julian to the foster mother who raised him and the gumbo-limbo tree where an imprisoned angel waits, the cousin Julian killed in a car accident 20 years earlier." Libr J

"Hoffman handles romance, suspense, and the healing properties of love and understanding with aplomb and a dash of magic." Booklist

Hogarth, Grace Allen, 1905-
(jt. auth) Norton, A. Sneeze on Sunday

Holland, Cecelia, 1943-
The Bear Flag. Houghton Mifflin 1990 422p o.p.
LC 89-71670

"A Peter Davison book"
This novel is set in California during the 1840s. The protagonist, Catharine Reilly, "loses everything—including her husband—on the brutal trek to California. She reaches Sutter's Fort and falls in love with Count Sohrakoff, a Russian agent for the Mexican dons who rule California. The settlers' uprising in 1846 places Cat and the Count on opposing sides." Libr J

"Holland's splendidly researched historical novel makes the confusion and brutality of the American takeover of California during the Mexican War believable and steadily interesting. Most of her characters are—or were—real people. She is particularly adroit in recreating the subsurface tension between Frémont . . . and his scout, the experienced Kit Carson." Atlantic

The belt of gold. Knopf 1984 305p o.p.
LC 83-48854

"The city of Constantinople in the ninth century A.D. is the setting [of this novel]. Hagen, a Frank of noble blood, is on the return leg of a Holy Land pilgrimage with his brother. Through a chance meeting with Theophano, a maiden in service to Byzantine Empress Irene, Hagen gets embroiled in the political intrigue and personal treachery that mark the government of the empire, as pro- and anti-Irene factions struggle for supremacy." Booklist

"Swiftly moving, plausible and with just the right amount of historical details to make scenes come clear, the novel is an engrossing tale." Publ Wkly

The earl. Knopf 1971 301p o.p.
"With the exception of the family of the Earl of Stafford, his attendants, and some minor figures, the characters are drawn from history. The castle, borough, and earldom of Stafford actually belonged to the Earl of Chester." Introduction

The author "conjures up twelfth-century England, its harshness, its civil war upheaval, and the noblemen's changing ploys and alliances as King Stephen and Henry Plantagenet of Normandy vie for England. The pragmatic, powerful (Fulk), Earl of Stafford and his family dominate the story. His pride, hatred of a treacherous uncle, and other personal antipathies upset an otherwise cool head that wishes to see England at peace, whatever royal compromise this necessitates." Booklist

The firedrake. Atheneum Pubs. 1966 c1965 243p o.p.
A "picaresque tale set in 11th century Germany, Flanders, Normandy and England. The Irish hero, named Laeghaire, the Gaelic spelling of Lear, is a brave, hard-fighting mercenary in the forces of William of Normandy. He is impetuous, brawling, very proud, with a plain and cutting tongue. Laeghaire kills men in battle with no hesitation, but he is haunted with nightmares about an ugly future. He is a restless adventurer, he is briefly a man in love, he is a violent man of action. This vital central character is placed against a colorful medieval background of castles and wild countryside and in the middle of one fight after another." Publ Wkly

The kings in winter. Atheneum Pubs. 1968 c1967 208p il o.p.
This is an historical novel "which concerns an Irish hero, Brian Boru of the Irish royal house of Munster, and his conquests. The book follows Boru's career and his attempts to unite Ireland." Publ Wkly

"Although some geographical confusion and a spattering of Gaelic words and names are mildly distracting, the tale drives ahead with many a grim episode and many a fine evocation of contemporary thought, emotion and codes of conduct." N Y Times Book Rev

Pacific Street. Houghton Mifflin 1992 260p o.p.
LC 91-27314

Available Thorndike Press large print edition

"A Peter Davison book"
This novel creates a "montage of San Francisco in its wild beginnings. The aptly named Frances Hardheart, an escaped slave with a quick wit, a sharp tongue and a knack for using people, has found the Shining Light, a haven for non-whites. With her protégée, the beautiful and white Daisy Duncan, she sets up a stage show and bar, enlisting the aid of such likable characters as good-natured, white Gil Marcus and taciturn, Indian Mitya. Frances, aka Mammy, soon extends her influence to the city's rising political and social elite." Publ Wkly

Holland, Cecelia, 1943-—*Continued*

"The plot's credibility runs a little thin at times, but Holland captures the lawlessness of early San Francisco with style and imagination and tells a story both engaging and romantic." Libr J

Pillar of the Sky; a novel. Knopf 1985 534p $17.95

ISBN 0-394-53538-3   LC 84-48659

The novel is set in prehistoric England, the "central character is Moloquin, who has lived as a wild child since his mother, Ael, was banished from her village by her brother Ladon, the ruler of the People. When Moloquin is adopted by Karella, the clan's storyteller, he joins the tribe, eventually overthrowing Ladon and becoming the People's new chief. Discovering the dark secret of his father's true identity, the demon-possessed Moloquin buries his shame by overseeing the construction of Stonehenge in the Pillar of the Sky, an ancient burial ground." N Y Times Book Rev

"Part Christ figure and part avenger, [Moloquin] is companionable with women, but also amazingly brutal. The tale is full of subtleties and contradictions and depicts a long struggle between the forces of change and those favoring stability. . . . This is more a story of power and customs than of Stonehenge and the early Britons." Libr J

The Sea Beggars. Knopf 1982 305p o.p.

LC 81-48115

"When the Spanish Inquisition reaches Antwerp, the circumscribed Protestant life of teenage brother and sister Jan and Hanneke van Cleef is destroyed when their father is hanged. . . . After killing a Spanish soldier who raped her, Hanneke flees to the German Empire and joins William of Orange. Jan escapes to his Uncle Pieter, a ship's captain whose vessel was confiscated by the Spanish. After stealing the ship back, Jan and Pieter join the Sea Beggars, a ragtag fleet of Lowlanders, noblemen and pirates who are harassing the Spanish. Jan and Hanneke are reunited at The Brill, a city on the North Sea. Hanneke is killed when the rebels defeat the Spanish army but Jan continues the fight for freedom with William of Orange." Voice Youth Advocates

"Bound by historical reality, the characters are drawn with the author's keen sensitivity to the probable personalities reflected by historical reputations and actions." Best Sellers

Holland, Isabelle

Bump in the night. Doubleday 1988 185p $16.95

ISBN 0-385-23891-6   LC 88-3732

"After another night of heavy drinking, Martha Tierney wakes up to find that her eight-year-old son, Jonathan, has failed to show up for school. . . . Martha desperately tries to recall anything Jonathan may have said before he disappeared, but the past is lost to her in an alcoholic haze. The police get their first lead when Jonathan's photograph is traced to a child pornography ring and the search for the little boy leads them through New York's porn shops and photography studios. A fast-paced, well-written mystery." Booklist

A death at St. Anselm's. Doubleday 1984 229p o.p.

LC 83-11668

"An Episcopal church is rocked by the brutal murder of the parish's business manager, Dick Grism. Grism's helplessness as a paraplegic underscores the savagery of the crime, leading New York City police to search for suspects among the drug addicts and mentally unbalanced who frequent St. Anselm's—including the disturbed, anorexic daughter of the female pastor." Booklist

"Holland remains one of the best of modern romantic suspense writers. Her characters (except for her maniacal murderer) are believable, and her settings (in this case, a modern urban church) are uncommon without being wildly exotic." Wilson Libr Bull

A fatal advent. Doubleday 1989 259p $16.95

ISBN 0-385-24815-6   LC 89-11797

Also available Thorndike Press large print edition

"The Reverend Claire Aldington is experiencing an especially busy Advent season at St. Anselm's Episcopal Church in New York City. Not only are the patients she counsels as psychotherapist more troubled than ever, but a visiting bishop from England has been murdered and Claire's husband is Lieutenant O'Neill's chief suspect. Holland uses the church setting deftly and peoples her novel with an arresting array of characters, from choirboys to bankers." Booklist

Holmes, Marjorie, 1910-

The Messiah. Harper & Row 1987 396p o.p.

LC 87-45056

Sequel to Three from Galilee

Holmes "continues the re-creation of the prophet's life journey, starting at the point of his mission, leading to its well-known conclusion. In richly imaginative scenes, Jesus is placed in a large, extended family. . . . The biblical framework is embellished in a respectful, nondoctrinaire narrative, with lively human dimensions." Publ Wkly

Three from Galilee; the young man from Nazareth. Harper & Row 1985 230p o.p.

LC 82-48145

In this "sequel to 'Two from Galilee' (1972), which presented the fictionalized story of Mary and Joseph, Holmes offers her version of Jesus' youth and his initial recognition of his ministry. The . . . portrayal characterizes Jesus not as an only child, but as one surrounded by a multitude of younger siblings, who react with typical curiosity and jealousy over their oldest brother's place in their parent's hearts." Booklist

This "is a respectful, interesting but debatable fictional interpretation, buttressed by the author's acquaintance with archaeological research in Israel." Publ Wkly

Followed by The Messiah

Holt, Hazel

Mrs. Malory, detective in residence. Dutton 1994 180p $18.95

ISBN 0-525-93903-2   LC 94-16393

"Visiting professor Sheila Malory, a rather timid and wimpish import from Taviscombe, England, becomes the 'insider' for a chummy policeman when murder strikes a Pennsylvania college town. Malory gathers hearsay evidence about two odious and universally disliked brothers murdered within days of each other. . . . Though Malory appears to be too naïve for a sleuth,

Holt, Hazel—*Continued*

this marks her fifth adventure and her first appearance in hardcover." Libr J

Holt, Victoria, 1906-1993

For works written by this author under other names see Carr, Philippa, 1906-1993; Plaidy, Jean, 1906-1993

The black opal. Doubleday 1993 275p $22

ISBN 0-385-47024-X   LC 92-33830

In this "romantic mystery, Dr. Marline and his ailing wife adopt young Carmel March after she is found wandering among the azaleas on their estate, Commonwood House. Soon she is on her way to a new life in Australia. When Carmel finally returns as a young woman, she realizes that she was hustled away to shield her from a mysterious murder at Commonwood House, and she is convinced that the wrong man has been convicted for the crime." Libr J

"This multi-layered fiction is pleasant and rife with surprises." Booklist

Bride of Pendorric. Doubleday 1963 288p o.p.

Favel Farrington is a young bride, married to handsome Roc Pendorric. She is fearful that he has chosen her for her money and that she will become another of the legendary brides of Pendorric Castle to die young and tragically

"A fine novel in every sense of the word. It has a fast-moving suspenseful storyline and appealing, believable characters." Best Sellers

The captive. Doubleday 1989 357p o.p.

LC 89-30932

Available Thorndike Press large print edition

"When a ferocious storm off the African coast capsizes the vessel on which she is sailing, Rosetta Cranleigh is rescued by a deckhand who admits, after their lifeboat drifts to a remote island, that he is actually Simon Perrivale, a nobleman's illegitimate child, forced to flee England after being wrongly accused of slaying one of his father's other sons. Taken hostage by pirates, the pair escape after being sold to a Turkish pasha. Because Simon dares not return home, Rosetta tries to identify the real killer by joining the mysterious Perrivale household as governess to Simon's impossible niece." Publ Wkly

"Romance and mystery haunt the pages of an engaging novel sure to please Holt fans." Booklist

Daughter of deceit. Doubleday 1991 376p o.p.

LC 90-23314

Available G.K. Hall large print edition

"When her mother unexpectedly dies, Noelle Tremaston, the cosseted, illegitimate daughter of an infamous Drury Lane actress, is shattered. Horrified to discover that the young man she intends to marry is, in all probability, her own brother, Noelle flees the country and embarks upon a series of shadowy adventures, culminating in the resolution of a murder and the reconciliation of the star-crossed lovers." Booklist

The Devil on horseback. Doubleday 1977 358p o.p.

LC 77-72414

The novel is set "in eighteenth-century England and in France on the brink of the revolution, where a young British schoolmistress becomes involved with an arrogant French count and is caught up in the terror of the opening days of the revolution." Booklist

The India fan. Doubleday 1988 404p o.p.

LC 87-36497

Available G.K. Hall large print edition

"As a motherless girl whose father is totally engrossed in classical history, Drusilla is grudgingly taken in by the Framlings as a companion to Lavinia, a high-spirited young woman with a taste for sexual escapades. Plain, commonsensical Drusilla is sent, along with Lavinia, to boarding school in England, finishing school in France, and finally India, where Lavinia lives as imprudently as ever as the wife of a young man who once intended to marry Drusilla, until he inherited a title and estate." Booklist

The Judas kiss. Doubleday 1981 400p o.p.

LC 81-43138

"Pippa Ewing discovers that her beloved older sister Francine has been murdered as she lay in bed with her husband Baron Rudolph. As evidence accumulates to show that Francine had not married him after all, Pippa is launched on a quest to solve her sister's murder and vindicate her name, a journey that takes her to the duchy of Bruxenstein; a job as a governess; and another encounter with Nordic, handsome Conrad, who had caused Pippa to 'fall down the slippery slope' one romantic evening. Mysteries pile up as two similar midnight fires take the lives of a pious and cruel grandfather and a young countess. . . . Plenty of romance, an agreeable amount of sex, lots of danger and suspense in Gothic and exotic settings ensure that this will please Holt fans." Publ Wkly

Kirkland Revels. Doubleday 1962 312p o.p.

"Kirkland Revels, a magnificent manor house, standing grand and aloof on the Yorkshire moors, hides many secrets from Catherine Rockwell, its newest resident. The strange suicide of her young husband prompts Catherine to try to prove his death murder despite certain danger." Cincinnati Public Libr

The legend of the seventh virgin. Doubleday 1965 326p o.p.

"A beautiful cottage girl of Cornwall with ambitions far beyond her station lives to become mistress of the great house of St. Larnston Abbas, once a convent, only to find that the manipulative course by which she has triumphed threatens to engulf her with a fate which legend ascribes to one of seven sinful nuns of the Abbas of distant times." Booklist

The mask of the enchantress. Doubleday 1980 327p o.p.

LC 79-6088

"Joel Mateland and his lover Anabel take their bastard child Suewellyn from England to primitive Vulvan Island in the South Pacific after Joel has killed his evil brother and fled his ancestral home, Mateland Castle. After many peaceful years, Suewellyn is grown up. She is understandably alarmed when her double, Susannah, Joel's legitimate daughter, shows up to make mischief. While Suewellyn is visiting Australia, the island's volcano erupts, killing everyone, a disaster that impels the survivor to pose as her half sister and claim a place at

Holt, Victoria, 1906-1993—*Continued*
Mateland Castle. The imposture, however, jeopardizes Suewellyn's life." Publ Wkly

Menfreya in the morning. Doubleday 1966 256p o.p.

"Harriet Delvaney, a poor little rich girl who is afflicted with a limp . . . is despised by her father because her mother died at her birth. She marries Bevil Menfrey, the handsome, tawney-haired scion of a high-spirited but impoverished family, and goes to live at Menfreya, a fortress-like mansion on the Cornish coast. Once installed, Harriet is deliriously happy—but . . . what about the beautiful, coolly poised governess. . . . And what about the legend of the tower clock, which stops when somebody is about to die?" Time

Mistress of Mellyn. Doubleday 1960 334p o.p.

In this romantic novel set in late 19th century England, the heroine is an attractive, young English governess. "She takes charge of the motherless child of a handsome, arrogant gentleman who lives in a large creepy mansion in Cornwall. The plot is lively and complicated. Eventually, our bright heroine discovers that her little pupil's mother was murdered and she narrowly escapes being murdered herself." Publ Wkly

My enemy the Queen. Doubleday 1978 348p o.p.

LC 77-11366

This novel of the Elizabethan era is narrated by Lettice Knollys, cousin of the queen and wife of the Earl of Essex. "Aware that Robert Dudley is the favorite of Elizabeth I and of dark rumors about the death of his wife, Lettice becomes one of Dudley's closet strumpets anyhow. When her husband dies, the Countess dares the axe by marrying Robert, but then betrays him by carrying on with a young man who becomes her third husband when Dudley dies. All the events of a momentous age are colored by Lettice's vanity, even the beheading of her own son, the second Essex, who supplants his stepfather in the affections of the queen." Publ Wkly

The pride of the peacock. Doubleday 1976 303p o.p.

"Set in the English countryside and the opal fields of Australia, [the novel] traces the adventures of young Jessica Clavering, the illegitimate off-spring of a once-wealthy family. Anxious to escape her family's resentment, Opal [i.e. Jessica] enters a platonic marriage with Joss Madden, heir to a fortune in opals. They travel to his home in Australia, where Jessica encounters a jealous rival, a missing gem, and a couple of murders." Libr J

The road to Paradise Island. Doubleday 1985 368p o.p.

LC 85-4538

This novel " opens in nineteenth-century England and closes on an island off the coast of Australia. Its protagonist is determined Annalice Mallory, who finds herself both fascinated and repelled when repairs on her ancestral home reveal the walled-up chamber of a woman who was her namesake. Upon further investigation, Annalice discovers a diary and an old map. The diary reveals that her namesake was murdered and that the map shows the site of an island where 'savages are gentle, where love and amity reign . . . where one picks up gold and uses it for cooking pots.'" Booklist

Secret for a nightingale. Doubleday 1986 371p o.p.

LC 86-2206

"In this Victorian romance, Susanna Pleydell loses her husband to drugs and her dearly loved child to her husband's neglect. She develops an obsessive hatred for Damien Adair, the physician she holds responsible for both tragedies. She tries to forget by taking up a nursing career, eventually going to the Crimea. There, working beside Dr. Adair, she finds herself attracted to him despite her hatred. . . . This is one of the better Holt novels, with a well-drawn historical background." Libr J

Seven for a secret. Doubleday 1992 326p $16

ISBN 0-385-42406-X   LC 91-35802
Also available G.K. Hall large print edition

"Frederica Hammond, a spunky and expressive teenager who comes to Harper's Green to live with her Aunt Sophie, forms close bonds with Rachel Grey, a timid orphan, and Tamarisk St. Aubyns, daughter of the local gentry. Frederica immediately falls for Tamarisk's aloof and patronizing brother Crispin, who, at 20, already has a troubled past and a mysterious devotion to his two retired nannies, one of whom is quite mad. Enter debonair Gaston Marchmont, allegedly an heir to French and Scottish estates, who seduces Rachel, weds Tamarisk and terrorizes the elderly nannies before being murdered." Publ Wkly

The silk vendetta. Doubleday 1987 425p o.p.

LC 87-5266

A "novel of one family's two warring branches—the French St. Allengeres and their English counterparts, the Sallongers. These noble families battle to discover a new and better way to manufacture the silk that is their livelihood. When the Sallongers perfect the fabric, however, suspicious tragedies occur. Lovely and stoic Lenore, an illegitimate St. Allengere, married to a Sallonger, is determined to unearth the reasons behind the feud, the course of which allows Holt to depict the glories of the Victorian age." Publ Wkly

Hood, Ann, 1956-

Places to stay the night. Doubleday 1993 275p $19.95

ISBN 0-385-42556-2   LC 92-10526

"Small-town life in Holly, Massachusetts, serves as the backdrop for two family crisis. The lives of former high school classmates Tom and Libby Harper and Renata Handy intersect when beautiful but unhappy Libby decides to leave Tom and their children and Renata the outsider returns. While Libby seeks fulfillment, Renata only wants to give her fatally ill daughter a moment of normalcy. Despite their own confusion and anger, Tom and his teenage children provide a temporary refuge for Renata." Libr J

"Hood, an accomplished scene setter and dialogist, works out the consequences of the characters' confusion of dream with fantasy and their groping return to truth with a wonderful frankness that illuminates the lessons of paradox and our belief in romance. An exceptionally fluent tale about the unending process of growing up." Booklist

Hooker, Richard

MASH. Morrow 1968 219p o.p. Amereon reprint available $18.95 (ISBN 0-88411-198-9)

"Captains Hawkeye Pierce, Duke Forrest, and 'Trapper' John McIntyre, all M.D.'s, are stationed in Korea with the 4077th MASH (Mobile Army Surgical Hospital). The reader is soon involved in many operations and medical jargon. It is, however, the off-duty activities of these three that engages one's attention and laughter. Full of martinis, or bored, or tired, or all three, the men soon start raising hell. . . . Hilarious, occasionally very serious, full of warm, appealing eccentric characters, one could enjoy a very pleasant evening with this sMASHing novel." Libr J

Hope, Anthony, 1863-1933

The prisoner of Zenda; being the history of three months in the life of an English gentleman. Holt & Co. 1894 226p o.p. Buccaneer Bks. reprint available $21.95 (ISBN 0-89966-226-9)

"Rudolf Rassendyll, an Englishman, makes a three month's visit to the kingdom of Ruritania. He arrives on the eve of the coronation of King Rudolf. The king has an enemy in his brother, Duke Michael, who aspires to the throne himself. During the festivities at Zenda Castle, the Duke drugs King Rudolf so that he is unable to attend his own coronation. Later, Rassendyll, . . . succeeds in impersonating the King and is crowned in his stead. In the meantime, Princess Flavia, the king's betrothed, falls in love with Rassendyll, who in turn loves her. After many dramatic and dangerous escapades, duels, and intrigues King Rudolf is rescued from Zenda Castle where he is held prisoner by Duke Michael. Rassendyll and Princess Flavia renounce each other when the King is restored, and Rassendyll returns to England." Haydn. Thesaurus of Book Dig

Horgan, Paul, 1903-1995

A distant trumpet. Farrar, Straus & Cudahy 1960 629p o.p.

A novel of the Southwest in the 1870's. The chief scene of action is at a U.S. Army outpost in Arizona during the Apache Indian Wars. Chief protagonists in the story are Lieutenant Matthew Hazard and his wife, Laura; Major General Alexander Upton Quait, Laura's resourceful eccentric uncle; Colonel and Mrs. Prescott and other officers and their wives; and, White Horn, an Apache scout

"The author evokes the arid landscape of the Southwest with his usual great skill and feeling; in the characterization of a general officer Mr Horgan appears to have accomplished a real tour de force!" Libr J

Whitewater. Farrar, Straus & Giroux 1970 337p o.p.

"Phil Durham, Billy Breedlove, and Marilee Underwood are a tightly woven trio of school friends. Philip is an introspective, budding author, Billy is the prototype of the teenage hero, and Marilee is sought by both but infatuated with Billy. When Phil accidentally causes Billy to fall to his death from a water tower, Marilee, who has just discovered that she is pregnant with Billy's child, commits suicide. The events are seen in retrospect by Durham, now a mature man." Shapiro. Fic for Youth. 3d edition

Hornberger, H. Richard

For works written by this author in collaboration with W. E. Butterworth see Hooker, Richard

Hornsby, Wendy

Bad intent; a Maggie MacGowen mystery. Dutton 1994 295p $18.95

ISBN 0-525-93817-6   LC 93-42405

Amateur sleuth and freelance filmmaker Maggie McGowan is "in a real bind. Maggie must prove that her boyfriend, an LAPD police officer, is innocent of a cover-up—but all the witnesses keep turning up dead." Libr J

"Key questions raised in this timely story are left unresolved, and the strong voices of the opinionated characters are almost drowned out by all the noisy domestic events. But Maggie's convictions about issues that really matter make her a true idealist and an unusually wholesome heroine." N Y Times Book Rev

Horowitz, Eve, 1963-

Plain Jane. Random House 1992 261p $20

ISBN 0-679-41261-1   LC 92-3991

"After her sister's engagement, which leaves her confused and angered by the changes she sees around her, Jane Singer's comfortable world begins to crumble. Her sister's future in-laws appear to be all that her family is not. Yet the real difference is not between New York's Orthodox Jews and Cleveland's suburban reform community but between Jane's memories and the reality of her family relationships. Only by coming to terms with the pain and underlying problems in her family life can Jane break free and face her future." Libr J

"The prickly, wisecracking style of 'Plain Jane' makes it a fast read, and Ms. Horowitz conjures up a host of fresh, well-drawn and believable characters." N Y Times Book Rev

The **Horror** hall of fame; edited by Robert Silverberg and Martin H. Greenberg. Carroll & Graf Pubs. 1991 416p $21.95

ISBN 0-88184-692-9   LC 91-12569

Analyzed in Short story index

Contents: The fall of the House of Usher, by E. A. Poe; Green tea, by J. S. Le Fanu; The damned thing, by A. Bierce; The yellow sign, by R. W. Chambers; The monkey's paw, by W. W. Jacobs; The white people, by A. Machen; The willows, by A. Blackwood; Casting the runes, by M. R. James; The graveyard rats, by H. Kuttner; Pigeons from hell, by R. E. Howard; It, by T. Sturgeon; Smoke ghost, by F. Leiber; Yours truly, Jack the Ripper, by R. Bloch; The small assassin, by R. Bradbury; The whimper of whipped dogs, by H. Ellison; Calling card, by R. Campbell; Coin of the realm, by C. L. Grant; The reach, by S. King

Household, Geoffrey, 1900-1988

Rogue male. Little, Brown 1939 280p o.p. Amereon reprint available $18.95 (ISBN 0-89190-435-2)

"An Atlantic Monthly Press book"

"Although the situation is somewhat incredible, this book convincingly describes the obsession of a well-bred Englishman and sportsman with shooting a European dictator, or at least seeing whether he can get him within target range. When he is caught, he is flung over a cliff but miraculously survives, only to be hunted himself by the dictator's secret agents. We share every ploy he uses to escape his pursuers. He is the 'rogue' hunted by the pack." Shapiro. Fic for Youth. 2d edition

Houston, Pam

Cowboys are my weakness; stories. Norton 1992 171p $19.95

ISBN 0-393-03077-6   LC 91-12920

Analyzed in Short story index

Contents: How to talk to a hunter; Selway; Highwater; For Bo; What Shock heard; Dall; Cowboys are my weakness; Jackson is only one of my dogs; A blizzard under blue sky; Sometimes you talk about Idaho; Symphony; In my next life

"Short stories, mostly first-person, told with verve and perfect pitch by women entangled with wild men in a cruel world." N Y Times Book Rev

Hoving, Thomas, 1931-

Discovery. Simon & Schuster 1989 301p o.p.

LC 89-35437

"Andrew Foster, the 'dashing globe-trotting president' of New York's Metropolitan Museum of Art and his glamorous wife Olivia are invited to Italy by the amoral Count Don Ciccio Nerone to help excavate the Tertullian family palace, buried by a volcanic eruption nearly 2000 years ago. At the dig, there are . . . run-ins with mafiosi and corrupt officials. Andrew wants to cart the treasure back to Manhattan for a blockbuster art show, while Count Nerone schemes to exploit the palace for his own purposes." Publ Wkly

"Arch, nicely crafted, somewhat tongue-in-cheek in a highbrow sort of way, his novel never deviates from being a pleasurably uncomplicated tale of mystery, suspense, and murder." Booklist

Masterpiece. Simon & Schuster 1986 321p o.p.

LC 86-15522

This novel chronicles the reverberations within the art world when an old British noble is about to auction off the family's famed Velázquez, a portrait of the artist's naked mistress. Private collectors and museums vie to own it, with Washington's National Gallery and New York's Metropolitan emerging as the strongest contenders. The two principals are vying for the Met's top job and also happen to become lovers

"A skillfully wrought tale about the intrigues and inner workings of the international art world. . . . For all its pizazz and connoisseurship of the world of art and luxury, Masterpiece is a simple book: it reads too much like a thriller to be credible as a realistic depiction of conspiracy in the museum world and too much like a would-be novel of manners to make for consistently grip-ping fiction. Hoving is perhaps at his best describing the finer points of the competitive aspects of human nature." Art Am

Howard, Elizabeth Jane

Confusion. Pocket Bks. 1994 c1993 341p $22

ISBN 0-671-70911-9   LC 93-45579

Also available G.K. Hall large print edition

First published 1993 in the United Kingdom

This installment of the Cazalet saga opens in March 1942. "Set in London and the English countryside, much of the story focuses on the eldest Cazalet cousins, Louise, Polly and Clary, as they exit their teens and take their first steps into adulthood. Former acting student Louise has been swept into a brilliant but chilly marriage to Michael Hadleigh, a glamorous portrait painter and aspiring Member of Parliament whose life is controlled by his powerful mother. Best friends Polly and Clary leave the cozy confines of the Cazalet's country home to begin what they hope will be terribly grown-up lives in London. . . . Howard creates a nearly palpaple world, peopled with the sort of well-conceived characters that linger long in the reader's mind." Publ Wkly

The light years. Pocket Bks. 1990 434p o.p.

LC 90-7470

This first novel about the Cazalet family is "set in England in 1937 and 1938. The Cazalets are an upper-crust London family comprising the three grown sons of William and Rachel Cazalet and the sons' wives and children. As the novel opens, the extended family is undertaking its summer relocation to the country house in Sussex. During the course of this summer and the next, readers . . . become witness to the public and private selves of the individual family members." Booklist

"Howard is expert at creating detailed physical environments for her characters, habitats that often reveal just as much about the Cazalets as their words or actions do." Libr J

Followed by Marking time

Marking time. Pocket Bks. 1992 405p o.p.

LC 92-8740

This installment in the Cazalet family saga is set in "1939, Britain has entered WWII, and the nine young Cazalet cousins are gathered for the duration under the rural Sussex roof of their grandparents, the indomitable Brig and his wife, Duchy. The . . . characters engage in a series of interrelated plots and subplots, and each family unit acts out a personal drama against the ever-present backdrop of the war." Publ Wkly

This "saga offers an engrossing look at a unique period of history as experienced by a 'typical' English middle-class family whose shared adventures are engaging, sometimes heroic, and always authentic." Libr J

Followed by Confusion

Howard, Maureen, 1930-

Expensive habits; a novel. Summit Bks. 1986 298p o.p.

LC 86-5727

"Margaret Flood enters 'Expensive Habits' at 45, a celebrated novelist dying in New York of a heart disease. Her deeper disease is bitterness, an unlocated anger that her two husbands have let her down, that she has

Howard, Maureen, 1930-—*Continued*

somehow failed her teen-age son, that her editors have been frauds and bullies, that her celebrity has failed to make her happy, or healthy. Her first husband is now a respected cardiologist (conveniently enough), married to a country-club woman hatched from a madras egg, with two daughters, half of them fools. Margaret's second husband, who lives apart from her, a patrician peace activist in the 1960's, is now, in the mid-70's, the alcoholic proprietor of a used-clothes shop near St. Mark's Place." N Y Times Book Rev

"Howard's insightful comments on the phony glamour of political activism and the universality of self-deception . . . add depth to a significant novel." Publ Wkly

Natural history; a novel. Norton 1992 393p il $22.95

ISBN 0-393-03405-4   LC 92-7041

This novel "relates the tortured history of the Brays, an Irish-American family living in Bridgeport, Connecticut, at the close of World War II. As adults, James and Catherine leave home but cannot come to terms with their lives, for they are trapped in the shadow of their bigger-than-life father. . . . [One section of the book] juxtaposes the storyline with facts and myths about Bridgeport notables, among them P.T. Barnum, Robert Mitchum, and Walt Kelly of Pogo fame." Libr J

This is a "novel always in the midst of breaking free of itself, its pages filled with brilliant variations on the screenplay, the encyclopedia, the diary, and, of course, the history book." New Repub

Howatch, Susan

Absolute truths; a novel. Knopf 1995 559p $25

ISBN 0-679-41206-9   LC 94-27510

Sixth in the Church of England series, this novel "is set during the mid-1960s, the period during which the Church of England . . . was rocked by widespread challenges to tradition. Again representing tradition is narrator Charles Ashworth, The Anglican Bishop of Starbridge. . . . Ashworth's archenemy—and doppelgänger—is Neville Aysgarth, the Dean of the Cathedral who is, according to Ashworth, unorthodoxly open to using the trappings of a capitalistic marketplace to benefit the financially deteriorating church building. To make matters worse, Aysgarth is an alleged dipsomaniac and womanizer, who once made a pass at Ashworth's beloved wife, Lyle. When Lyle dies suddenly, the bereaved widower strays dangerously from the fold." Publ Wkly

Cashelmara. Simon & Schuster 1974 702p o.p.

Divided into six sections, each narrated by a different character, this novel charts "the lives of three generations of the Anglo-Irish de Salis family between 1859 and 1891. They move between London homes, a Warwickshire estate, New York and Boston—where two Lords de Salis find their wives—but end always at the great white house on their Irish estate, Cashelmara. In the background are the simmering troubles between starving Irish tenants and callous English landlords." Christ Sci Monit

"With a copiousness of detail studded with adventure, rape, depravity, intrigue, and murder, the story plays out with clarity and brilliance." Best Sellers

Glamorous powers. Knopf 1988 403p o.p.
     LC 88-45347

This "novel, the second in the Church of England series that began with 'Glittering Images,' weaves an intriguing and wholly involving story out of the otherwise sober subject of Christian mysticism in the 20th-century Church of England. Howatch's chief characters are a clerical odd couple, rivals since their Cambridge days: Jonathan Darrow, a 60-year-old Anglo-Catholic monk with 'glamorous' psychic powers, and his Abbot-General, Francis Ingram, a practical, eloquent, urbane man with sophisticated insight into modern psychology. . . . The wisdom of 'Glamorous Powers' lies in the deft way it aligns psychological and spiritual truths to bring about healing in the broadest sense." N Y Times Book Rev

Followed by Ultimate prizes

Glittering images. Knopf 1987 399p o.p.
     LC 87-45130

This, the first in the Church of England series, "takes place in pre-World War II England, just after Edward VIII abdicated to marry the divorced Wallis Simpson. The event is emblematic, for this novel is about marriage and divorce and proper behavior within a religious context. . . . The narrator is a young intellectual cleric, Charles Ashworth, who is sent by the Archbishop of Canterbury to spy on Alex Jardine, the charismatic, liberal Bishop of Starbridge. Ashworth uncovers evidence in Jardine's household—which includes a depressive wife and her pretty female companion—of sexual scandal and a highly irregular interpretation of Anglican dogma. The revelation of the mystery of Starbridge sends Ashworth into a personal crisis of faith." N Y Times Book Rev

"An ambitious and lifelike work of uncommon depth." Booklist

Followed by Glamorous powers

Mystical paths; a novel. Knopf 1992 433p o.p.
     LC 91-58557

Available G.K. Hall large print edition

This novel is fifth in the Church of England series. "At 25, Nicholas Darrow, scion of eminent churchman Jonathan Darrow [featured in Glamorous powers] has inherited his father's psychic gifts, but overconfidence in his abilities and a dangerously frayed relationship with his father lead him close to the edge of an emotional abyss. Asked by the widow of his friend Christian Aysgarth to investigate her husband's death—Christian was drowned when swept overboard while sailing, but she fears that he committed suicide—Nick embarks on a quest that uncovers dark secrets in the linked lives of his friends and family." Publ Wkly

"Although this is all rather formulaic, Howatch has discovered that the Christian story is essentially a romance, and she has exploited this with considerable intelligence." Booklist

Followed by Absolute truths

Penmarric. Simon & Schuster 1971 735p o.p.

Set against the landscape of Cornwall, this novel relates the "life and amours of brutally selfish Mark Castallack through the end of the Victorian era and . . . the lives and amours of his children, legitimate and illegitimate and their progeny." America

"Throughout the story, the author keeps the reader aware of the great historical precedent and parallel for her fiction; the love of Henry II and Eleanor of Aquitaine; preceding each chapter are two pertinent quotations about that royal couple and the king's progeny. It is a neat and useful device, adding piquancy and historical flavor to an interesting tale." Best Sellers

Howatch, Susan—*Continued*

Scandalous risks. Knopf 1990 385p o.p.
LC 90-53076

Available G.K. Hall large print edition

This novel, fourth in the Church of England series, is "narrated by Venetia Flaxton, a young woman of intellect and means but no direction, and centers around her strange affair in 1963 with 61-year-old Neville Aysgarth, dean of Starbridge Cathedral. Related mainly through their letters and conversations, the progress—and explosive dissolution—of their relationship is set in the context of a real-life theological controversy in England crystallized by the publication of *Honest to God*, a best-selling, situational-ethics view of God's relevance to modern man." Publ Wkly

"With sculptor's hands fashioning rich, lustrous three-dimensional characters, Howatch brilliantly shows how and why the situation between Venetia and her 'Mr. Dean' arose, flourished, then died away." Booklist

Followed by Mystical paths

The shrouded walls. Stein & Day 1971 c1968 179p o.p.

"Set at the turn of the nineteenth century this is an entertaining period Gothic with adequate characterizations. To avoid becoming a governess young Marianne Fleury, illegitimate daughter of a wealthy Englishman, agrees to marry Axel Brandson who needs an English wife in order to inherit the family fortune. When Marianne and Axel join his relatives at Haraldsdyke Marianne discovers that her husband's father had been murdered, presumably by a son who disappeared. As Marianne pieces together more facts she realizes Axel is a prime suspect, and soon she has reason to fear for her own life." Booklist

Sins of the fathers. Simon & Schuster 1980 608p o.p.

"A sequel to 'The Rich Are Different,' (1977) this . . . family saga traces the fortunes of the Van Zales of New York City from the late 1940's through the 1960's. Cornelius, head of the clan and president of the Van Zale Bank, has not shed his killer instinct, and habitually uses raw power to mask his personal inadequacies. His cut-throat tactics have far-reaching adverse effects on friends and family, particularly on his vulnerable daughter Vicki. . . . The novel is narrated by six characters in sequence." Libr J

The author, "witty storyteller that she is, picks her way through a mind-boggling tangle of marriages and motives with the greatest of ease, never losing or confusing the reader." Publ Wkly

Ultimate prizes. Knopf 1989 387p o.p.
LC 89-45303

This, third novel in the Church of England series, "is narrated by Neville Aysgarth, an ambitious archdeacon in the fictional English diocese of Starbridge. A brilliant administrator with a firm, practical faith in God and the Church of England, Neville has steadily moved up in life by 'chasing the prizes,' overcoming his humble birth and troubled youth to win for himself a perfect wife, a flock of delightful children and a powerful position, all before age 40. During his climb to success he has kept his mind as tidy as his diocese by relentlessly 'ringing down the curtain'—a mental curtain, that is—on disturbing memories and desires. But alas for Neville, his curtain is shortly to be twitched off its rod, first by an infatuation with a young society girl, then by a death in his family." N Y Times Book Rev

Followed by Scandalous risks

The wheel of fortune. Simon & Schuster 1984 973p o.p.
LC 84-5357

This "saga, based loosely upon the tragedies that beset Edward of Woodstock (the Black Prince) and his descendants, is 'a recreation in a modern dimension.' A cycle of tragedy plagues the descendants of a lecherous Robert Godwin, who allows the glittering family manor, Oxmoon, to disintegrate into rat fodder until his heirs take decisive action. The treasured Welsh estate is restored to its former grandeur, but a legacy of enormous guilt and a pattern of adultery and murder haunt further inheritors of Oxmoon." Booklist

This "absorbing novel convincingly demonstrates that a family saga can be more than the mere 'show and tell' of one generation following another. By using six different narrators to recount five generations of a 20th-century Welsh family, the author deftly supplies multiple viewpoints of events." Libr J

Howells, William Dean, 1837-1920

The rise of Silas Lapham.
Available from Amereon and Buccaneer Bks.

First published 1885

"Silas is a crude, uneducated man who makes his fortune by methods not above criticism, but manly and capable of better things when his conscience is awakened—a compendium of human virtues and vices, drawn with insight, tenderness and humor. The efforts of the prosperous Laphams to get into Boston society, with their mistakes and disillusionments, the sentimental tragi-comedy of the two daughters, in love with the same young man; and Lapham's business troubles, are more or less neatly woven in to make the plot." Baker. Guide to the Best Fic

Hudson, W. H. (William Henry), 1841-1922

Green mansions; a romance of the tropical forest. Putnam 1904 315p o.p. Buccaneer Bks. reprint available $25.95 (ISBN 0-89966-374-5)

"The hero, Mr. Abel, tells the tragic story of his love for the bird girl, Rima, an ethereal maiden whose jungle upbringing has brought her close to the powers and beauty of nature. Abel has just succeeded in awakening the human emotion of love in the half-wild girl when she is killed by a band of savages." Reader's Ency. 3d edition

Hudson, William Henry *See* Hudson, W. H. (William Henry), 1841-1922

Hughes, Langston, 1902-1967

Laughing to keep from crying. Holt & Co. 1952 206p o.p. Amereon reprint available $19.95 (ISBN 0-88411-060-5)

Analyzed in Short story index

Contents: Who's passing for who?; Something in common; African morning; Pushcart man; Why, you reckon; Saratoga rain; Spanish blood; Heaven to hell; Sailor ashore; Slice him down; Tain't so; One Friday morning; Professor; Name in the papers; Powder-white faces; Rouge high; On the way home; Mysterious Madame Shanghai; Never room with a couple; Little old spy;

Hughes, Langston, 1902-1967—*Continued*
Tragedy at the Baths; Trouble with the angels; On the
road; Big meeting

Not without laughter. Knopf 1930 324p
o.p. Amereon reprint available $21.95 (ISBN
0-8488-1055-4)

This novel portrays the lives of a poor black family
in a small Kansas town
"A sympathetic portrayal, unmarred by bitterness or
sentimentality, of a people to whom life, no matter how
hard, was not without laughter." Booklist

Simple speaks his mind. Simon &
Schuster 1950 231p o.p. Amereon reprint
available $20.95 (ISBN 0-88411-061-3)

The central figure, is a Harlem black who expresses
his views on many subjects, but always from the point
of view of his own race. He dislikes whites, and makes
no bones of it. Some of his favorite topics are women,
landladies especially, parties, and beer
"Simple is completely frank in his opinions about
white people; he dislikes them intensely. The race
problem is never absent, but the flow of the book is
light-hearted and easy." N Y Times Book Rev

Simple stakes a claim. Rinehart 1957 191p
o.p.

In this book Simple, of Harlem, speaks his mind on
a variety of subjects, ranging from housing conditions,
to sex magazines

Simple takes a wife. Simon & Schuster
1953 240p o.p.

Available from Amereon and Buccaneer Bks.

"Before Mr. Jesse B. Semple, the untutored philosopher
of the Harlem rooming-house set, can divorce his wife
and espouse the morally impeccable Joyce, he has to
run the gauntlet of many problems. He discourses on
them in Harlem bars over beers he has cadged from
his sympathetic and more literate listener. Under the
folklike humor of 'Simple's' monologs runs a bitter undercurrent of racial consciousness." Booklist

Simple's Uncle Sam. Hill & Wang 1965
180p o.p. Amereon reprint available $18.95
(ISBN 0-88411-709-X)

Partially analyzed in Short story index
Contents: Census; Swinging high; Contest; Empty
houses; The blues; God's other side; Color problems; The
moon; Domesticated; Bomb shelters; Gospel singers;
Nothing but a dog; Roots and trees; For President;
Atomic dream; Lost wife; Self-protection; Haircuts and
Paris; Adventure; Minnie's hype; Yachts; Ladyhood; Coffee break; Lynn Clarisse; Interview; Simply Simple; Gold-
en Gate; Junkies; Dog days; Pose-outs; Soul food; Flay
or pray; Not colored; Cracker prayer; Rude awakening;
Miss Boss; Dr. Sidesaddle; Wigs for freedom; Concern-
ment; Statutes and statues; American dilemma; Promulga-
tions; How old is old; Weight in god; Sympathy; Uncle
Sam

Hugo, Victor, 1802-1885

The hunchback of Notre Dame.

Available from Amereon

Original French edition, 1830. Variant title: Notre
Dame de Paris

The hidden force of fate is symbolized by the superhuman grandeur and multitudinous imageries of the
cathedral. "The first part . . . is a panorama of medieval

life—religious, civic, popular, and criminal—drawn with
immense learning and an amazing command of spectacular effect. These elements are then set in motion in
a fantastic and grandiose drama, of which the personages
are romantic sublimations of human virtues and passions—Quasimodo the hunchback, faithful unto death;
Esmeralda, incarnation of innocence and steadfastness;
Claude Frollo, Faust-like type of the antagonism between
religion and appetite. Splendors and absurdities, the
sublime and the grotesque are inextricably mingled in
this strange romance. The date is fixed at the year
1482." Baker. Guide to the Best Fic

Les misérables; translated by Charles E.
Wilbour. Modern Lib. 1992 1260p $21

ISBN 0-679-60012-4   LC 92-50220

Original French edition, 1862
"A panorama of French life in the first half of the
[nineteenth] century, aiming to exhibit the fabric of
civilization in all its details, and to reveal the cruelty
of its pressure on the poor, the outcast, and the criminal.
Jean Valjean, a man intrinsically noble, thru the tyranny
of society becomes a criminal. His conscience is
reawakened by the ministrations of the saintly Bishop
Myriel . . . and Valjean, reformed and prosperous, follows in the good bishop's footsteps as an apostle of
benevolence, only to be doomed again by the law to
slavery and shame. The 'demimondaine' Fantine, another
victim of society; her daughter Cosette one of those
whom suffering makes sublime; Marius, an ideal of youth
and love; Myriel, the incarnation of Christian charity,
are the leading characters of this huge morality, which
is thronged with representatives of the good in man and
the cruelty of society. Magnificent description . . . scenes
invested with terror, awe, repulsion, alternate with
tedious rhapsodies. Realism mingles with the incredible."
Baker. Guide to the Best Fic

The **Hugo** winners; edited by Isaac Asimov.
Doubleday 1962-1986 5v o.p.

Analyzed in Short story index
Contents: v1 Novelettes are: The darfsteller, by W. M.
Miller; Exploration team, by M. Leinster; The big front
yard, by C. D. Simak; Flowers for Algernon, by D.
Keyes; The longest voyage, by P. Anderson. Short stories
are: Allamagoosa, by E. F. Russell; The star, by A. C.
Clarke; Or all seas with oysters, by A. Davidson; The
Helbound train, by R. Bloch
v2 Novelettes are: The last castle, by J. Vance; Weyr
search, by A. McCaffrey; Riders of the purple wage, by
P. J. Farmer; Gonna roll the bones, by F. Leiber; Nightwings, by R. Silverberg; The sharing of flesh, by P.
Anderson. Short stories are: The Dragon masters, by J.
Vance; No truce with kings, by P. Anderson; Soldier,
ask not, by G. R. Dickson; "Repent, Harlequin!", said
the Ticktock-man, by H. Ellison; Neutron star, by L.
Niven; I have no mouth, and I must scream, by H.
Ellison; The beast that shouted love at the heart of the
world, by H. Ellison; Time considered as a helix of
semi-precious stones, by S. R. Delany
v3 Novelettes are: Ship of shadows, by F. Leiber; Ill
met in Lankhmar, by F. Leiber; The Queen of Air and
Darkness, P. Anderson; The word for world is forest,
by U. K. LeGuin; Goat song, by P. Anderson. Short
stories are: Slow sculpture, by T. Sturgeon; Inconstant
moon, by L. Niven; The meeting, by F. Pohl; Eurema's
dam, by R. A. Lafferty; The girl who was plugged in,
by J. Tiptree; The deathbird, by H. Ellison; The ones

The Hugo winners—*Continued*

who walk away from Omelas, by U. K. Le Guin; A song for Lya, by G. R. R. Martin; Adrift just off the islets of Langerhans: latitude 38° 54' N, longitude 77° 00' 13 W, by H. Ellison; The hole man, by L. Niven

v4 Novelettes are: Home is the hangman, by R. Zelazny; By any other name, by S. Robinson; Houston, Houston, do you read? by J. Tiptree; The Bicentennial Man, by I. Asimov; Stardance, by S. Robinson; The persistance of vision, by J. Varley; Hunter's moon, by P. Anderson. Short stories are: The borderland of Sol, by L. Niven; Catch that Zeppelin, by F. Leiber; Tricentennial, by J. Haldeman; Eyes of amber, by J. D. Vinge; Jeffty is five, by H. Ellison; Cassandra, by C. J. Cherryh

v5 Novelettes are: Enemy mine, by B. B. Longyear; Sandkings, by G. R. R. Martin; Lost Dorsai, by G. R. Dickson; The cloak and the staff, by G. R. Dickson; The Saturn game, by P. Anderson. Short stories are: The way of cross and dragon, by G. R. R. Martin; Grotto of the dancing deer, by C. D. Simak; Unicorn variations, by R. Zelazny; The pusher, by J. Varley

The stories and novelettes included in these volumes won the Hugo Awards from 1939-1982

Hulme, Juliet *See* Perry, Anne, 1938-

Hulme, Kathryn, 1900-1981

The nun's story. Little, Brown 1956 339p o.p.

"Convent life, with its rigors and its compensations, has seldom been as fairly depicted as in this biographical account. An unhappy love affair was one of the reasons why 'Gabrielle Van der Mal' [fictitious name] entered a convent in Belgium, but her love of God and desire to serve her fellow men were also important influences. For 17 years she tried diligently to discipline her analytical and independent mind through prayer and hard work as a nurse, first in a hospital for the insane, then in a Congo mission, and finally in a TB sanatorium in occupied Holland. Ultimately, she faced the bitter truth that the religious life, with its inflexible authority, was not for her, and she was released from her vows." Libr J

Hulme, Keri

The bone people; a novel. Louisiana State Univ. Press 1985 c1983 450p $19.95

ISBN 0-8071-1284-4   LC 85-12937

First published 1984 in New Zealand

"Hulme's novel tells the story of three people in rural New Zealand, Kerewin, a part-Maori woman; Joe, a Maori man; and Simon, Pakeba (European) child whom Joe finds washed up on the shore during a storm. Joe alternately loves the child passionately and thrashes him brutally. Although they are 'different and difficult people,' isolated from those around them, they are drawn into an intense relationship." Choice

"This novel is unforgettably rich and pungent. . . . Set on the harsh South Island beaches of New Zealand, bound in Maori myth and entwined with Christian symbols, Miss Hulme's provocative novel summons power with words, as in a conjurer's spell." N Y Times Book Rev

Humphrey, William

The collected stories of William Humphrey. Delacorte Press/Seymour Lawrence 1985 371p o.p.

LC 84-26046

Analyzed in Short story index

Contents: The Hardys; Quail for Mr. Forester; Man with a family; Sister; The shell; Report cards; The Fauve; In sickness and health; The last husband; Dolce far' niente; The patience of a saint; A fresh snow; The ballad of Jesse Neighbours; A good Indian; A job of the plains; Mouth of brass; A home away from home; The rainmaker; The pump; A voice from the woods; The human fly; The last of the Caddoes

"Vignettes of American lives, particularly those set in the Southwest during the dust bowl era, capture the essence and richness of small-town experiences that expand far beyond regional borders. The author's traditional style also helps to set the mark of a born storyteller on these superb evocations of a burdened yet perservering national character and consciousness." Booklist

The Ordways. Knopf 1965 c1964 326p o.p.

This novel begins "on a 'graveyard working day' in Clarksville, Tex., sometime in the 1930's. Most of the living Ordways have gathered for this annual rite, and from that vantage point, one of the fourth-generation sons reviews the history of the clan. There was Thomas Ordway, who after being blinded at the battle of Shiloh made the heroic trek from Tennessee to Texas. . . . It was this journey that brought the Ordways clan to Clarksville, in northeast Texas, a section that combined elements of the Old South and the prairie-land West. And there was Sam Ordway, the narrator's grandfather, whose quest for his [kidnapped] son Ned constitutes the longest . . . episode in the book." America

"The way Humphrey handles the language is astonishing and individual. Funny, vivid and moving, this is a fine piece of work and a delight to read." NY Times Book Rev

September song. Houghton Mifflin 1992 256p $19.95

ISBN 0-395-58414-0   LC 92-896

Analyzed in Short story index

Contents: A portrait of the artist as an old man; The farmer's daughter; A labor of love; The apple of discord; A weekend in the country; September song; Mortal enemies; The dead languages; The parishioner; Last words; An eye for an eye; A tomb for the living; Buck fever; Ties of blood; Auntie; Vissi d'arte; Virgin and child; Dead weight; Be it ever so humble; A heart in hiding

This collection is about "characters who are aging or near death. . . . Although frequently somber, these stories never become maudlin, and many contain sharp, expertly controlled touches of humor." Libr J

Humphreys, Josephine

The fireman's fair. Viking 1991 263p $19.95

ISBN 0-670-83907-8   LC 90-50575

Also available Thorndike Press large print edition

"Rob Wyatt, unmarried at 32, has quit his job as a lawyer, moved out of a luxury apartment to poor housing, sold his Alfa for a cheap used car, and is looking for a new kind of life. Hurricane Hugo almost

Humphreys, Josephine—*Continued*

devastates the southern town in which he lives and also seems to have swept an uprooting storm through his personal life. His unceasing love for Louise, now married to wealthy Frank Camden, becomes not so firm when Billy Poe, 18 years old and naively innocent (or precociously wise) comes into Rob's life. She is a healer in her innocent wisdom and the novel has an ending especially welcome as a change from many violent and depressing contemporary novels." Shapiro. Fic for Youth. 3d edition

Rich in love. Viking 1987 261p o.p.

LC 86-40611

"Lucille Odom, a highly intelligent 17-year-old, finds her world turned upside down when her mother walks out abruptly on a seemingly happy marriage and her absent sister arrives home, announcing she's pregnant and married. Lucille finds herself taking on serious responsibilities and acquiring a new, but fragile, maturity as she deals with her own emotions and tries to hold together her crumbling family life. This . . . novel is set in South Carolina." Libr J

"The novel could easily have slipped into the trite and saccharine, but once again Humphreys reveals an extraordinary ability to explore inner lives with subtlety, originality, and deadpan humor. Rich in Love avoids banality by ironically exploiting the catalog of clichés about unhappy families." New Repub

Hunter, Evan, 1926-

For works written by this author under other names see McBain, Ed, 1926-

The blackboard jungle. Simon & Schuster 1954 309p o.p. Buccaneer Bks. reprint available $24.95 (ISBN 1-56849-399-1)

A story "of an idealistic young man, facing the bitter realities of being a teacher in the frighteningly brutal world of a big city vocational high school. A near-rape, student sluggings, a knifing—all these plus a strong indictment of the inadequacies of routine teachers college preparation in helping teachers to learn how to discipline near-morons and prospective or actual delinquents." Libr J

"The author has not used his shocking material merely to appall. With a superb ear for conversation, with competence as a storyteller, and with a tolerant and tough-minded sympathy for his subject, he has built an extremely good novel." N Y Her Trib Books

The Chisholms; a novel of the journey West. Harper & Row 1976 208p o.p.

This novel about the early nineteenth-century pioneer experience "tracks Hadley Chisholm and family, leaving their unproductive Virginia homeland to find a better life in California; the journey [which is followed up to their departure from Fort Laramie in Wyoming] is arduous, to say the least, for every member of the household." Booklist

"An affectingly spare, closely seen recreation of the pioneer spirit and what the search for new opportunity signified." Publ Wkly

Criminal conversation. Warner Bks. 1994 384p $21.95

ISBN 0-446-51755-0   LC 93-42307

Also available Thorndike Press large print edition

"Michael Welles, a young assistant district attorney investigating organized crime, stumbles on a lead to the identity of the new boss of the Manhattan mob, and soon orders surveillance of the suspicious Andrew Faviola. Welles's wife, Sarah, drifts into an increasingly intense affair with a romantic but mysterious businessman, Andrew Farrell—who, of course, is Faviola, in the midst of setting up a massive international drug deal. . . . Mr. Hunter's ear for dialogue, be it that of a police officer, a mobster or an Upper East Side yuppie, is unerring. The ironies of the plot are a trifle obvious, but he unfolds them like the master he is." N Y Times Book Rev

Lizzie. Arbor House 1984 430p o.p.

LC 83-15642

"By legend, Lizzie Borden, a New England spinster, axed her father and stepmother to death one summer day in 1892. Writing fictionally about Lizzie and those horrible crimes, popular novelist Hunter uses actual inquest and trial material, but counterpoints the attempted resolution of the murders in that small Massachusetts town with invented events during a European trip that Lizzie took a couple of years previous. It is this trip wherein lie the seeds for the slaying of Mr. and Mrs. Borden, for Lizzie's latent lesbianism surfaces in Europe and leads her to desperate acts when she returns home." Booklist

"The portrait of Lizzie that emerges is fascinating, ultimately sympathetic: a murderess yes, but the victim of the repression and sexual exploitation of her time." Libr J

Hunter, Stephen, 1946-

Dirty white boys; a novel. Random House 1994 436p $21

ISBN 0-679-43751-7   LC 94-15359

"After killing a black inmate, the brutal Lamar Pye breaks out of the Oklahoma State Penitentiary along with his retarded cousin, Odell, and a hapless artist-turned-felon named Richard. They embark on a desperate run across Oklahoma and Texas, pursued by state troopers. The escapees hide out with a convict groupie who has lived alone since murdering her parents as an adolescent. In a parody of domesticity, Lamar embraces these losers as the family he never knew." Libr J

"The blood-soaked packaging of Mr. Hunter's big, mythic theme is thrilling, in the manner of the ancient storytellers, with battles fierce enough for a war and characters crazy enough to fight them to the death. There is no place to run for cover from this author's prose—no glades of pretty writing to cool his vision of a land of lost children, forgotten values and total desolation." NY Times Book Rev

Hurston, Zora Neale, 1891-1960

The complete stories; introduction by Henry Louis Gates, Jr. and Sieglinde Lemke. HarperCollins Pubs. 1995 xxiii, 305p $25

ISBN 0-06-016732-7   LC 91-50438

Analyzed in Short story index

Contents: John Redding goes to sea; Drenched in light; Spunk; Magnolia flower; Muttsy; 'Possum or pig?; The Eatonville anthology; Sweat; The gilded six-bits; Mother Catherine; Uncle Monday; The fire and the cloud; Cock Robin Beale Street; Story in Harlem slang; High John de Conquer; Hurricane; The conscience of the court;

Hurston, Zora Neale, 1891-1960 — *Continued*

Escape from Pharaoh; The tablets of the law; Black death; The bone of contention; Book of Harlem; Harlem slanguage; Now you cookin' with gas; The seventh veil; The woman in Gaul

Huxley, Aldous, 1894-1963

After many a summer dies the swan. Harper 1939 356p o.p. Amereon reprint available $23.95 (ISBN 0-89190-395-X)

"Centered around Jo Stoyte, a Californian oil magnate afraid of old age and death, [this novel] is a satire of some aspects of American life. Jeremy Pordage, working on some old English manuscripts, discovers that an 18th-century earl used the same rejuvenating system Stoyte is experimenting with. They go to England and find the earl, over 200 years old, a filthy ape. Old Mr. Propter is spokesman for Huxley's spiritual philosophy." Reader's Ency. 3d edition

Antic hay. Doran, G. H. 1923 350p o.p. Buccaneer Bks. reprint available $22.95 (ISBN 1-89966-848-8)

This satirical novel is "about a group of London intellectuals and their long, learned, futile conversations, in which everything seems valueless—God, love, art, learning, social reform, science. The central character is timid Theodore Gumbril, Junior, who gives up his job as a teacher to try to sell a new kind of trousers with built-in air cushion seats. He purchases a thick beard to help him act the part of a confident, aggressive man in business and in love." Reader's Ency. 3d edition

Ape and essence. Harper & Row 1948 205p o.p.

"Using the form of a film scenario . . . Aldous Huxley transports us, in dire and dreadful fancy, to the year 2108. The setting is Los Angeles, a century or so after the Third World War. Atomic and bacterial warfare have left it, and nearly all the world, in blighted ruins. From spared New Zealand, a 'Rediscovery Expedition to North America' has been dispatched, and it is from the experiences of Chief Botanist Alfred Poole that we learn about the 22d century way of life." Christ Sci Monit

"Novels like Ape and Essence seem now to be very much products of their time and rather dated. But this is Huxley—clever, brutal, thoughtful, original—and his fictional tract clings to the mind." Burgess. 99 Novels

Brave new world. Harper & Row 1946 xx, 311p $12.95

ISBN 0-06-012035-5

Also available from Amereon

First published 1932 by Doubleday, Doran & Company

"The ironic title, which Huxley has taken from Shakespeare's *The Tempest*, describes a world in which science has taken control over morality and humaneness. In this utopia humans emerge from test tubes, families are obsolete, and even pleasure is regulated. When a so-called savage who believes in spirituality is found and is imported to the community, he cannot accommodate himself to this world and ends his life." Shapiro. Fic for Youth. 3d edition

Collected short stories. Harper & Row 1957 397p o.p.

Analyzed in Short story index

Contents: Happily ever after; Eupompus gave splendour to art by numbers; Cynthia; The bookshop; The death of Lully; Sir Hercules; The Gioconda smile; The Tillotson banquet; Green tunnels; Nuns at luncheon; Little Mexican; Hubert and Mimmie; Fard; The portrait; Young Archimedes; Half holiday; The monocle; Fairy godmother; Chawdron; The rest cure; The Claxtons

Crome Yellow. Harper & Row 1922 307p o.p.

Available from Amereon and Buccaneer Bks.

First published 1921 in the United Kingdom

"The book is a social satire of the British literati in the period following World War I. *Crome Yellow* revolves around the hapless love affair of Denis Stone, a sensitive poet, and Anne Wimbush. Her uncle, Henry Wimbush, hosts a party at his country estate, Crome Yellow, that brings together a humorous coterie of characters." Merriam-Webster's Ency of Lit

Eyeless in Gaza. Harper 1936 473p o.p. Amereon reprint available $28.95 (ISBN 0-89190-396-8)

"The novel is largely autobiographical and charts the career of Anthony Beavis from early childhood in 1902 to his discovery of mysticism in 1935. Through a series of flashbacks, which occupy entire chapters ('August 30th 1933', 'November 6th 1902', 'June 17th 1912', etc.) key moments in Beavis's life are interwoven. Several secondary characters are similarly observed as their relationships with Beavis change over the years, including Brian Foxe (a sensitive and intellectual schoolfriend who later commits suicide), Hugh Ledwidge and his wife Helen (who becomes Beavis's lover), and Mark Staithes (who in adulthood turns to Marxism). The main burden of the novel is to reveal Beavis's increasing sense of the futility and meaninglessness of his life—and by extension, the meaninglessness of contemporary Western society." Camb Guide to Lit in Engl

Island; a novel. Harper & Row 1962 335p o.p. Borgo Press reprint available $23 (ISBN 0-8095-9048-4)

"Farnaby, spiritually crippled journalist, shipwrecks on Pala, 100-year-old experimental island utopia, idyllic, communal, insulated. Inhabitants are psychically whole in transcendental philosophy of love. War and neurosis unknown. Farnaby's guilt-ridden mentality contrasts with serene yogic spirit of Pala. The end will come when Pala is taken over by outside interests for its oil. Buddha was right. Capitalism is the antithesis of love." Anatomy of Wonder. 3d edition

Point counter point. Doubleday, Doran 1928 432p o.p.

Available from Amereon and Buccaneer Bks.

The book "presents a satiric picture of London intellectuals and members of English upper-class society during the 1920's. Frequent allusions to literature, painting, music, and contemporary British politics occur throughout the book, and much scientific information is embodied in its background. The story is long and involved, with many characters; it concerns a series of broken marriages and love affairs, and a political assassination. The construction is elaborate, supposedly based on Bach's 'Suite No. 2 in B Minor.' It is also a novel within a novel. Philip Quarles a leading charac-

Huxley, Aldous, 1894-1963—*Continued*
ter . . . is himself planning a novel, which echoes or 'counterpoints' the events going on round him." Reader's Ency. 3d edition

Huxley, Elspeth, 1907-
Murder at Government House. Harper 1937 282p o.p.

Life at Government House in the African colony of Chania seemed perfectly ordered—but for the trouble between the two regional railways presenting a snag in the Governor's federation plan. Olivia Brandeis, a young anthropologist, senses trouble brewing below the surface. When the Governor is discovered strangled at his desk, Olivia's suspicions are confirmed

"There is wit and humour in the book, and a good deal of satire at the expense of politicians, bureaucrats and the more pretentious side of colonial society. Also, Mrs. Huxley is one of the very few writers who know how to use both American and English idioms correctly and in the mouths of the right people." Times Lit Suppl

Murder on safari. Harper 1938 289p o.p.

The novel begins with "events set afoot by wealthy colonizers at play in Kenya during the bad old days. 'Great white hunter' Danny de Mare persuades CID Superintendent Vachell to join Lord and Lady Baradale's safari when someone steals the lady's jewels from the portable safe in her tent. Posing as an extra guide, Vachell observes members of the party closely, finding no clues although he has several suspects. . . . The narrative twists its way through murders, passed off as accidents, and other elongated incidents, to the rather vague resolution. The novel's main attractions are the vivid descriptions of the terrain and the author's prescient protest against the slaughter of wildlife for fun and profit." Publ Wkly

Hyman, Mac, 1923-1963
No time for sergeants. Random House 1954 214p o.p.
Available from Amereon and Buccaneer Bks.

"After sundry belligerent maneuverings by Pa, Georgia cracker Will Stockdale is drafted, jailed, sent to camp. There with buddy Ben he finds himself in the Air Force, nearly becoming permanent latrine orderly. Assigned to a daffy air crew, he and Ben narrowly miss a plane crash, claim a medal for Ben, thus bumbling ill-fated Sergeant King out of his stripes and, with them, into an infantry transfer." Libr J

I

Ibáñez, Vicente Blasco *See* Blasco Ibáñez, Vicente, 1867-1928

Iguana dreams; new Latino fiction; edited by Delia Poey and Virgil Suarez; with a preface by Oscar Hijuelos. HarperCollins Pubs. 1992 376p o.p.

LC 92-52628

Analyzed in Short story index
Contents: Customs, by J. Alvarez; In search of Epifano, by R. Anaya; The white bedspread, by E. Castedo; On Francisco el Penitente's first becoming a Santero and thereby sealing his fate, by A. Castillo; Chata, by D. Chávez; Salvador late or early, by S. Cisneros; Nellie, by R. G. Fernandez; Tito's good-bye, by C. Garcia; Frazer Avenue, by G. Garcia; Confession, by L. G. Garcia; The useless servants, by R. Hinojosa-Smith; City for sale, by W. Kanastoga; In the South, by J. Lopez; The ingredient, by J. Marzan, Spider's bite, by P. Medina; The coast is clear, by E. Morales; The movie maker, by E. M. Muñoz; American history, by J. Ortiz-Cofer; Martes, by R. Pau-Llosa; My life as a redneck, by G. Pérez-Firmat; Blizzard!!!, by M. H. Ponce; La yerba sin raiz (The weed without a root), by L. V. Quintana; Saturnino el Magnífico, by A. A. Ríos; Roaches, by A. Rodriguez; Abuela Marielita, by C. Rodríguez-Milanés; Settlements, by V. Suarez; The clocks, ribbons, mountain lakes, and clouds of Jennifer Marginat Feliciano, by E. Vega; Fresh fruit, by M. Veiga; Two sketches: "The last minstrel in California" and "The laughter of my father", by J. A. Villarreal

Iles, Greg
Black cross. Dutton 1995 516p $19.95
ISBN 0-525-93829-X   LC 94-34642

This novel "tells the story of a physician from Georgia and a German Jew who manage to forestall Hitler's use of poison nerve gas during World War II by destroying a secret laboratory hidden in a Nazi death camp. The rash plan for infiltrating the camp and destroying the laboratory has been developed by the Allies and led by Winston Churchill and will require nerves of steel, physical and emotional stamina, unparalleled bravery, and incredible luck. If it works, millions of lives will be saved. But there is a horrible price to pay for the larger victory—hundreds of Jewish prisoners interred in the camp may also die. From the very first page, Iles takes his readers on an emotional roller-coaster ride, juxtaposing tension-filled action scenes, horrifying depictions of savage cruelty, and heart-stopping descriptions of sacrifice and bravery." Booklist

Ingram, Willis J. *See* Harris, Mark, 1922-

Innes, Hammond, 1913-
High stand. Atheneum Pubs. 1986 c1985 335p o.p.

LC 86-3477

First published 1985 in the United Kingdom
"A Sussex solicitor, Philip Redfern, is visited by Miriam, the distraught wife of millionaire Tom Halliday, who has recently changed his will and disappeared. Redfern allows himself to be drawn into the search for the rich man, tracing the trail into the Canadian Rockies and the Yukon. Redfern eventually discovers that the Halliday estate is bankrupt, and dangerous encounters in the North American wilderness await him in his search for answers." Booklist

Isvik. St. Martin's Press 1992 c1991 319p o.p.

LC 91-37343

Innes, Hammond, 1913——*Continued*

"A Thomas Dunne book"

First published 1991 in the United Kingdom

"Peter Kettil, a wood preservation specialist struggling to establish his own business, joins an expedition to the Antarctic in search of an ancient frigate whose frozen remains were spotted by glaciologist Charles Sunderby just before his plane crashed in the ice. Moving forces behind the trek are the dead man's widow, Iris, and Iain Ward, a mysterious Scotsman who agrees to provide financing if he can accompany the crew. Unsettling questions arise about the possible connection of Argentina's *desaparecidos* to the hunt for the frigate and about two men who exhibit deep interest in the widow." Publ Wkly

"A smooth, sensitive writer, Mr. Innes never lets the reader down. There is plenty of action, but it is never unbelievable; there is no heavy breathing. British authors at their best can be so *civilized*, and Hammond Innes is one of the best." N Y Times Book Rev

Medusa. Atheneum Pubs. 1988 350p o.p.
LC 88-21943

The author "exploits the archaeology, history, and political tensions of the island of Menorca in the western Mediterranean. Mark Steele, a sailor who runs a chandlery and manages villas for absentee owners, falls in love with a boat—a gorgeous catamaran. He succumbs to its owner's offer to swap a half-finished villa and a trusty fishing craft. Dazzled by his new property, Steele fails to realize he is being lured into arms smuggling, a political assassination, and a military coup." Booklist

Innes "fashions an absorbing narrative rich in character and exotic atmosphere." Publ Wkly

The wreck of the Mary Deare. Knopf 1956 296p o.p.

"When narrator John Sands first sights the freighter 'Mary Deare' from the deck of his salvage boat, she appears to be a ghostly derelict drifting toward the Channel reefs. Boarding her, however, he encounters her specter-ridden captain, Gideon Patch, and becomes dangerously involved in the suspect seaman's desperate attempt to expose the conspiracy behind her last voyage." Booklist

Innes, Michael, 1906-1994

Appleby and Honeybath. Dodd, Mead 1983 198p o.p.
LC 83-11565

"Sir John Appleby, retired commissioner of the Metropolitan Police, and Charles Honeybath of the Royal Academy both attend the same house party as guests of the district's Master of Fox Hounds, Terence Grinton. Honeybath finds a body in an armchair in the library; by the time he's fetched Appleby, the corpse has disappeared." Booklist

"What joy to see a master of his craft at play! . . . This suspense novel is as smooth and enjoyable as Devonshire cream, a delicious and witty treat." Publ Wkly

Appleby and the Ospreys. Dodd, Mead 1987 c1986 185p o.p.
LC 87-9121

Available G.K. Hall large print edition

First published 1986 in the United Kingdom

"A traditional country-house mystery, featuring Innes' tried-and-true sleuth, Sir John Appleby, now retired as commissioner of the metropolitan police. Just a few days after Sir John and his wife share luncheon with an acquaintance, Lord Osprey, his lordship is found murdered in the library of the Osprey ancestral home. The inevitable challenge of a good case draws Sir John back into the detection business. . . . Top-drawer Innes, which makes the novel superior crime fiction indeed." Booklist

Appleby's end. Dodd, Mead 1945 211p o.p.

"A Red badge mystery"

"It is in this story that Appleby, already a DI at Scotland Yard, meets Judith Raven, his future wife, but the tale belongs to the author's fantastic series. So we do not cavil at the betrothal taking place in darkness and in a haystack, the pair having taken off their clothes after dunking in the river. The whole Raven family is mad, likewise the neighbors, who steal statuary and re-enact symbolic deeds with the aid of farm animals and idiot boys. The dose of ludicrous and far-fetched is heavy but often funny and fully explained (after a fashion) at the end." Barzun. Cat of Crime. Rev and enl edition

Innes, Ralph Hammond- *See* Innes, Hammond, 1913-

Irving, Clifford

Final argument; a novel. Simon & Schuster 1993 333p $22

ISBN 0-671-74868-8   LC 92-42693

"Ted Jaffe is a successful lawyer with a nice family, a six-figure income, and an expensive house. Then a series of events changes his life forever. Twelve years earlier, just after Jaffe had ended a torrid affair with rich, sexy Connie Zide, he had successfully convicted a young black man of killing Connie's husband. Now, one of the men who testified at the trial says he was bribed. Jaffe's interest is piqued, but the truth is elusive. Witnesses are reluctant to talk, and when they do, they end up dead. The case quickly becomes an obsession while Jaffe's personal life disintegrates." Booklist

"A fast-moving legal thriller noteworthy for its virtuoso interweaving of story lines, numerous plot twists and superior characterizations. . . . Culminating in an edge-of-the-seat courtroom showdown with plenty of surprises, this superior thriller is a top example of the genre." Publ Wkly

Irving, John, 1942-

3 by Irving. Random House 1980 718p o.p.
LC 79-5536

Contents: Setting free the bears (1969); The water-method man (1972); The 158-pound marriage (1974)

The first of these novels "involves a madcap scheme to liberate zoo animals, the second chronicles the misadventures of a bungling graduate student, and the third features a ménage-à-quatre in academe. . . . Irving's early fictions are noteworthy not only as forerunners to the remarkable *Garp* but also on their own merits. Possessing much of the same narrative inventiveness, zany wit, and sheer verve that so distinguish Irving's best-seller, they also maintain a *Garp*-like balance between the humorous and the macabre." Choice

The 158-pound marriage

In Irving, J. 3 by Irving p561-718

Irving, John, 1942— —*Continued*

The cider house rules. Morrow 1985 560p $18.95

ISBN 0-688-03036-X   LC 84-27195

"Homer Wells wants to be neither an orphan nor an abortionist. But he has little choice in either matter; failing to be adopted, he is fated to always return to Maine's Saint Cloud's Orphanage and his surrogate father, Dr. Larch, head administrator and resident abortionist. Although still in his teens, Homer learns 'perfect obstetrical procedure' while assisting Larch, but his unwillingness to perform abortions eventually leads him away from Saint Cloud's and into a head-on collision with life and its mysterious rules." Libr J

"The book is, to be sure, a novel . . . not a tract; it follows several human lives from youth to maturity, gripping our attention as chronicle rather than argument. But it is also a book about abortion, and the knowledge and sympathy directing Mr. Irving's exploration of the issue are exceptional." N Y Times Book Rev

The Hotel New Hampshire. Dutton 1981 401p o.p.

LC 81-2610

"A Henry Robbins book"

This is "a family chronicle—a tale of generations of parents coping with children and siblings coping with each other. The chief parents are Win and Mary Berry of Dairy, New Hampshire, a couple brought together after high school at a seaside resort where, on summer jobs, they catch a glimpse of a joyous vocation (innkeeping). The Berry union produces five spirited and amusing children. . . . The story covers a quarter-century, beginning round about 1940, and the principal action takes place in three hotels, each called . . . The Hotel New Hampshire. (The hotels are situated in New Hampshire, Austria, and Maine.)" Atlantic

The author "keeps us moving, sacrificing rhetoric to pace, as in the most primitive narrative forms, the fable and the fairy tale. In fiction like this, meaning lies near the surface of the story and in the voice of the storyteller." New Repub

A prayer for Owen Meany; a novel. Morrow 1989 543p $23

ISBN 0-688-07708-0   LC 88-13839

This novel is set in New Hampshire in the 1950s and 1960s. Owen Meany is a short boy with a squeaky voice, who foresees his own death and sees himself as an instrument of God. He hits a baseball that kills the mother of John Wheelwright, the novel's narrator. Because of Owen, John becomes a Christian

"Despite its theological proppings, A Prayer for Owen Meany is a fable of political predestination. As usual, Irving delivers a boisterous cast, a spirited story line and a quality of prose that is frequently underestimated even by his admirers. On the other hand, the novel invites trespass by symbol hunters. . . . To get lost in critical rummage would be to miss the point. Irving's litany of error and folly may strike some as too righteous; but it is effective." Time

Setting free the bears

In Irving, J. 3 by Irving p1-284

A son of the circus. Random House 1994 633p $25

ISBN 0-679-43496-8   LC 93-44750

"At center stage is Farrokh Daruwalla, an alienated, middle-aged, Bombay-born doctor who returns to his birthplace to study circus dwarfs. Farrokh becomes entangled in a case involving a serial murderer who carves the image of a winking elephant on his victims' torsos. This storyline bounces around like the proverbial three-ring circus and features a cast of eunuchs, hippies, movie stars, transsexuals, and clergymen." Libr J

Irving "is at the peak of his powers in this new novel. He plunges the reader into one sensual or grotesque scene after another with cheerful vigour and a madcap tenderness for life. . . . The author knows what he is doing from first to last, and handles the dozens of strands of his plot with exuberant ease." Economist

The water-method man

In Irving, J. 3 by Irving p285-560

The world according to Garp. Dutton 1978 437p o.p.

LC 77-15564

"A Henry Robbins book"

"Jenny Fields is the black sheep daughter of an aristocratic New England family; she becomes, almost by accident, a feminist leader ahead of her time. Her son, T. S. Garp (named for a father he never saw), has high ambitions for his artistic career, but he has an even higher, obsessive devotion to his wife and children. Surrounding Garp and Jenny are a wide assortment of people: schoolteachers and whores, wrestlers and radicals, editors and assassins, transsexuals and rapists, and husbands and wives." Publisher's note

This "is a long family novel, spanning four generations and two continents, crammed with incidents, characters, feelings and craft. The components of black comedy and melodrama, pathos and tragedy, mesh effortlessly in a tale that can also be read as a commentary on art and the imagination." Time

Irving, Washington, 1783-1859

The complete tales of Washington Irving. Doubleday 1975 xxxvii, 798p o.p.

Analyzed in Short story index

Contents: Rip Van Winkle; The spectre bridegroom; The legend of Sleepy Hollow; The stout gentleman; The student of Salamanca; Annette Delarbe; Dolph Heylinger; The hunting-dinner; The adventure of my uncle; The adventure of my aunt; The bold dragoon; Adventure of the German student; Adventure of the mysterious picture; Adventure of the mysterious stranger; The story of the young Italian; Literary life; A literary dinner; The club of queer fellows; The poor-devil author; Notoriety; A practical philosopher; Buckthorne; Grave reflections of a disappointed man; The booby squire; The strolling manager; The inn at Terracina; Adventure of the little antiquary; The belated travellers; Adventure of the Popkins family; The painter's adventure; The story of the bandit chieftain; The story of the young robber; The adventure of the Englishman; Hell gate; Kidd the pirate; The devil and Tom Walker; Wolfert Webber; Adventure of the black fisherman; The adventure of the mason; Legend of the Arabian astrologer; Legend of Prince Ahmed al Kamel; Legend of the Moor's legacy; Legend of the three beautiful princesses; Legend of the rose of the Alhambra; The governor and the notary; Governor Manco and the soldier; Legend of the two discreet statues; Spanish romances; The legend of the enchanted soldier; Wolfert's roost; The Creole village; Mountjoy; The widow's ordeal; The grand prior of Minorca; A con-

Irving, Washington, 1783-1859—*Continued*
tented man; Guests from Gibbet Island; The early experiences of Ralph Ringwood; The Count Van Horn; Don Juan: a spectral research; Legend of the engulphed convent; The phantom island

Washington Irving's Tales of the supernatural; selected and with an introduction by Edward Wagenknecht; illustrated by R. W. Alley. Stemmer House 1982 307p il $17.95

ISBN 0-916144-64-X   LC 80-29313

"A Barbara Holdridge book"
Analyzed in Short story index
This collection contains 16 tales selected from the author's miscellanies: The sketch book, Tales of a traveller, The Alhambra, and Wolfert's roost

Contents: Rip Van Winkle; The legend of Sleepy Hollow; The adventure of my uncle; The adventure of my aunt; The bold dragoon; The spectre bridegroom; Adventure of the German student; The Devil and Tom Walker; Legend of the Arabian astrologer; Legend of Prince Ahmed al Kamel; Legend of the Moor's legacy; Legend of the Rose of Alhambra; The legend of the enchanted soldier; Legend of Don Munio Sancho de Hinojosa; The legend of the two discreet statues; Guests from Gibbet Island

Isaacs, Susan, 1943-

After all these years. HarperCollins Pubs. 1993 343p $23

ISBN 0-06-016768-8   LC 92-56200

"Rose Meyers was just an ordinary Jew from Queens who married her sweetheart, became a teacher, moved to the suburbs, and had two kids. Then her husband's business made him a millionaire. Suddenly, Rose and Richie have a Long Island mansion, a fleet of BMWs, and invitations to all the soirees. Rose is in for a shock, though, when Richie announces he's leaving her for a younger woman. The divorce papers aren't even signed when Rose, stricken with insomnia, goes downstairs one night for a glass of milk and trips over Richie's corpse. The cops immediately peg Rose as the prime suspect, but she knows she didn't kill her husband, and she's determined to find out who did." Booklist

Isaacs "has a field day lampooning upper-class mores . . . but also weaves into this thoroughly diverting caper unexpected moments of genuine tenderness and sly social commentary." Publ Wkly

Almost paradise. Harper & Row 1984 483p o.p.

LC 83-48357

"Nicholas is the scion of a wealthy family, although Jane's bloodline is anything but aristocratic. They marry after Jane convinces Nick that his true talent lies with acting rather than law. In no time Nick is the rage of Broadway and Hollywood. The marriage remains idyllic until Jane develops a fear of crowds so great she is unable to walk to her own mailbox. But she continues to make their Connecticut farmhouse the ideal place for her husband to entertain his many guests. The arrangement works for twenty years, as Nick resists the attempts of countless women to seduce him. Nick finally succumbs to a timid film student and Jane takes up with her shrink." West Coast Rev Books

Close relations. Lippincott 1980 270p o.p.

LC 80-7858

"David Hoffman would appear to be everything a girl could want—and he appears in Marcia Green's life when the politician she writes speeches for is lagging in the gubernatorial primary and her lover Jerry Morrissey is stubbornly resisting the longterm commitment she longs for. But here's one big strike against David: Marcia's family approves of him. Flashbacks to her childhood, her first marriage, her unhappy promiscuity show the reasons for her rebellion. Ultimately, she and David decide they need each other enough to be happy despite the past." Libr J

"Besides being simultaneously romantic, feminist, and political, the novel is also a satire: of Jewish mothers and success-orientation, late-marrying Irishmen, American political campaigns, WASP mores, and human relations." Best Sellers

Compromising positions. Times Bks. 1978 248p o.p.

LC 77-13896

"Judith Singer is a nice, average Jewish housewife—on the surface—but beneath that placid exterior lurks a secret longing for high adventure. . . . When a local dentist-Lothario is murdered in his office and a neighbor who was his last patient is a suspect, Judith cannot resist getting into the act. Meddling, gossiping, she turns detective, and when she learns that the elegant late Dr. Fleckstein was not only bedding virtually every woman in town but getting them to pose for exceedingly porno photos, there's no stopping her. Enter detective Nelson Sharpe, much more attractive than Judith's stodgy husband. The two make a wild pair of sleuths as Sharpe tracks down the murderer and an accomplice and exposes smug suburban hypocrisy." Publ Wkly

Magic hour. HarperCollins Pubs. 1991 412p o.p.

LC 90-55570

Isaacs' setting, "the various sections of Long Island's Hamptons (N.Y.), allows her to depict the tension between the hardworking locals, many of whom live on the edge of poverty, and the snooty summer people, phony Manhattan culture hounds and social climbers. Movie producer Sy Spencer is clearly among the latter, and when he is shot by the side of his glitzy Southampton swimming pool, homicide detective Steve Brady is not surprised to discover plentiful evidence of widespread resentment and hatred of Spencer." Publ Wkly

"Best of all . . . is the subplot, an old-fashioned love story (think 1940s movie) in which Brady falls hard for his leading suspect, the dead producer's first wife. There's no good reason why we should buy into this romance—it rests on a totally improbable premise—but Isaacs sets the hook and reels us in anyway." Booklist

Shining through. Harper & Row 1988 402p o.p.

LC 87-45630

Available G.K. Hall large print edition

"Linda Voss is a 31-year-old secretary to the dreamiest looking man on Wall Street, international lawyer John Berringer, with whom she is secretly and hopelessly in love: she is a poor girl from Queens, and he boasts an Ivy League background along with his perfect profile. When circumstances lead to their unlikely marriage, however, sexual fireworks keep them together. As World War II engulfs Europe, the Berringers move to Washing-

Isaacs, Susan, 1943——*Continued*

ton, where both become involved in undercover work for the COI, soon to become the OSS. Heartbreak, plus a feeling of kinship for the victims of Nazism, leads Linda, whose childhood was spent in a German-speaking household, to volunteer for a dangerous mission in Berlin." Publ Wkly

"Whether completely believable or not, Isaacs' tale of bravery and romance makes exciting, entertaining reading." Booklist

Isherwood, Christopher, 1904-1986

The Berlin stories; The last of Mr. Norris; Goodbye to Berlin; with a preface by the author. New Directions 1954 2v in 1 o.p.

The two titles included in this combined edition were originally published separately; the first in 1935 in the United Kingdom with title: Mr. Norris changes trains and the latter in 1939 by Random House, which is analyzed in Short story index

The last of Mr. Norris "set in Berlin during Hitler's rise to power is the story of the narrator's innocent friendship with odd, corrupt Mr. Norris. While pretending to be a sincere Communist, Mr. Norris is actually selling information to fascists and foreigners. Mr. Norris's masochistic sexual aberrations add to the impression that he is a symbol of the whole corrupt, disintegrating society." Reader's Ency. 3d edition

Goodbye to Berlin contains six short stories or sketches of life in Berlin in the last years before Hitler came to power. Though written in first person by one calling himself Christopher Isherwood, according to the author's statement, the material is not to be regarded as autobiographical. The sketches are entitled: A Berlin diary (Autumn 1930); Sally Bowles; On Ruegan Island (Summer 1931); The Nowaks; The Landauers; A Berlin diary (Winter 1932-3)

Goodbye to Berlin

In Isherwood, C. The Berlin stories v2
The last of Mr. Norris

In Isherwood, C. The Berlin stories v1

Ishiguro, Kazuo, 1954-

An artist of the floating world. Putnam 1986 206p o.p.

LC 85-25759

"Like figures on a Japanese screen, the painter Masuji Ono and his daughters Setsuko and Noriko are fixed in the formal attitudes that even their private conversations reflect. In the postwar 1940s, the father is a relic of traditional Japan, of teahouses, geishas and patterned gardens not yet destroyed by industry and Westernized thinking. He is unable to communicate with his daughters, unsure of the propriety of his wartime nationalism yet unwilling to exchange it for what seem to him doubtful modern values." Publ Wkly

"The tensions stay tight. And this is what makes Mr. Ishiguro not only a good writer but also a wonderful novelist." N Y Times Book Rev

The remains of the day. Knopf 1989 245p $18.95

ISBN 0-394-57343-9   LC 89-80445

"Mr. Stevens is a butler of high quality now employed by the American owner of Darlington Hall. His position as butler was quite different when Lord Darlington was his employer. Then there was a large staff, including Miss Kenton, whose friendly overtures to Stevens were met only by his inability to unbend or find some humor as an outlet offsetting his customary snobbish personality. As Stevens reflects on the past the reader gains insight into Lord Darlington's political connections after World War I with important government officials including Ribbentrop, representive of Germany's movement toward a dictatorship. Questions regarding an employee's unquestioning loyalty toward his employer and awareness of the political situation in the period just before Hitler's rise to power make this a thought-provoking novel." Shapiro. Fic for Youth. 3d edition

The unconsoled. Knopf 1995 544p $25

ISBN 0-679-40425-2   LC 95-15829

In this novel, "prominent concert pianist Ryder is at odds with his surroundings. Ryder arrives in an unidentified European city at a bit of a loss. Everyone he meets seems to assume that he knows more than he knows, that he is well acquainted with the city and its obscure cultural crisis. A young woman he kindly consents to advise seems to have been an old lover and her son quite possibly his own; he vaguely recalls past conversations. The world he has entered is a surreal, Alice-in-Wonderland place where a door in a cafe can lead back to a hotel miles away. The result is at once dreamy, disorienting, and absolutely compelling; Ishiguro's paragraphs, though Proust-like, are completely lucid and quite addictive to read." Libr J

J

Jackson, Charles, 1903-1968

The lost weekend. Rinehart 1944 244p o.p.

Available from Bentley and Buccaneer Bks.

Psychological study of a drunkard. The actual time covered is five days, but in those five days the story of a man's life is told. Don Biram, a sensitive, charming and well-read man, left alone for a few days by his brother, struggles with his overwhelming desire for alcohol, succumbs to it, and in the resulting prolonged agony, goes over much of his life up to and including the long weekend

"It's written with complete lack of literary pretensions; yet Jackson's sheer ability to lick the problems of flashback, stream of consciousness, mind wandering, twisted recollection and alcoholic delirium is spectacular. . . . Its frankness is sometimes shocking but never aimed to shock. The aim, and it is unerring, is always for accuracy and the complete truth." Book Week

Jackson, Shirley, 1919-1965

The bird's nest. Farrar, Straus & Young 1954 276p o.p. Amereon reprint available $20.95 (ISBN 0-317-27727-8)

"Miss Jackson sets forth the predicament of Elizabeth Richmond, a pallid young woman who lives with her aunt in a small New England town. A series of disquieting incidents leads this girl to a psychiatrist, who discovers that her mind is divided among, and tortured

Jackson, Shirley, 1919-1965—*Continued*

by, four separate, strong-willed personalities, each struggling for dominance. These four personalities, which are visible by turns, according to which one is in control, are designated by the doctor as Elizabeth, Betsy, Bess and Beth. Some terrifying experiences and her doctor's patient guidance bring the girl to a state resembling peace." New Yorker

Come along with me; part of a novel, sixteen stories, and three lectures; edited by Stanley Edgar Hyman. Viking 1968 243p o.p. Amereon reprint available $20.95 (ISBN 0-89190-621-5)

Partially analyzed in Short story index

This "posthumous book contains a section of the novel on which Jackson was working at the time of her death in 1965, plus 14 short stories, three lectures on authorship and two stories . . . illustrating points in the lectures." Libr J

Contents: Short stories included are: Janice; Tootie in peonage; A cauliflower in her hair; I know who I love; The beautiful stranger; The summer people; Island; A visit; The rock; A day in the jungle; Pajama party; Louisa, please come home; The little house; The bus; The night we all had grippe; The lottery

The haunting of Hill House. Viking 1959 246p o.p.

Available from Amereon and Buccaneer Bks.

"Dr. John Montague, an anthropologist, is interested in the analysis of supernatural manifestations. He rents Hill House, which is reported to be haunted, and plans to spend the summer there with research assistants. Eleanor Vance, one of the researchers, is at first repelled by the house but soon adjusts. Other people come and signs of psychic activity are rampant, many of them centered on Eleanor. When Dr. Montague insists that she leave to insure her safety, the house does not release her." Shapiro. Fic for Youth. 3d edition

The lottery; or, The adventures of James Harris. Farrar, Straus 1949 306p o.p.

Available from Bentley and Buccaneer Bks.

Analyzed in Short story index

Contents: The intoxicated; Daemon lover; Like mother used to make; Trial by combat; The villager; My life with R. H. Macy; The witch; The renegade; After you, my dear Alphonse Charles; Afternoon in linen; Flower garden; Dorothy and my grandmother and the sailors; Colloquy; Elizabeth; Fine old firm; The dummy; Seven types of ambiguity; Come dance with me in Ireland; Of course; Pillar of salt; Men with their big shoes; The tooth; Got a letter from Jimmy; The lottery

We have always lived in the castle. Viking 1962 214p o.p.

Available from Amereon and Buccaneer Bks.

"Since the time that Constance Blackwood was tried and acquitted of the murder of four members of her family, she has lived with her sister Mary Catherine and her Uncle Julian in the family mansion. Mary Catherine takes care of family chores and Uncle Julian is busy with the writing of a detailed account of the six-year-old murders. Cousin Charles's arrival on the scene disrupts the quiet peace of the family, and Mary Catherine's efforts to get rid of him unloose a chain of events that bring everything down in ruins." Shapiro. Fic for Youth. 3d edition

Jaffe, Rona

Class reunion; a novel. Delacorte Press 1979 338p o.p.

LC 78-25838

"In the Fifties, when rules were rules, college campuses were husband-hunting grounds, and 'going all the way' could ruin a girl's reputation, four Radcliffe students pursue the dream of Mr. Right, Marriage, and Living Happily Ever After. Jaffe builds this book around their 20th reunion, using alternate chapters to flash back through the tales of beautiful Annabel, witty Chris, golden girl Daphne, and insecure Emily. [The author focuses on these women's lives] from college romances to crises which rock them—loveless marriage, divorce, adultery both homosexual and heterosexual, murder, nervous breakdown, birth of a mongoloid child." Libr J

Jakes, John, 1932-

The best western stories of John Jakes; edited by Bill Pronzini and Martin H. Greenberg. Ohio Univ. Press 1991 275p o.p.

LC 90-49427

Analyzed in Short story index

Contents: Shootout at White Pass; The woman at Apache Wells; Hell on the high iron; A duel of magicians; Death rides here!; The winning of Poker Alice; To the last bullet; Little Phil and the daughter of joy; The tinhorn fills his hand; The naked gun; Dutchman

"This collection combines new material with several of Jakes's better efforts published earlier in the pulp magazines of the 1950s." Libr J

California gold; a novel. Random House 1989 658p $19.95

ISBN 0-394-56106-6   LC 89-3779

"Driven by his father's failed California dream, young Mack sets out from an Appalachian coal mine and lands eventually on Nob Hill, becoming a maverick real estate and business tycoon who sets out to challenge the San Francisco establishment. As he's faced with mounting adversity, his affairs begin to crumble, and so, in 1906, does a large chunk of the city. 'California Gold' is the story of one man, one state and three women." N Y Times Book Rev

"The novel potently conveys the raw, irrepressible vitality of California, but the historical backdrop (especially the 1906 earthquake) outshines the conventional rags-to-riches plot. Jake's impressive research . . . enriches the story considerably." Publ Wkly

Heaven and hell. Harcourt Brace Jovanovich 1987 700p $19.95

ISBN 0-15-131075-0   LC 87-17652

The concluding volume of the North and South trilogy "centers on Charles, Orry Main's cousin, a Southerner totally devastated by the Civil War. Displaced and just having lost his beloved Augusta, Charles heads West with his infant son hoping to make a new life. With Charles as the focal point, the narrative continually shifts to all the other family members, including . . . a madman bent on destroying both families." Libr J

"Mr. Jakes sets this fictional action against a meticulously detailed historical backdrop. Although his characters are not as vivid as his storytelling, his portrait of a divided, demoralized nation, inflamed with hatred, still emerges as an enjoyable work of popular historical fiction." N Y Times Book Rev

Jakes, John, 1932----*Continued*
Homeland. Doubleday 1993 785p $25

ISBN 0-385-41724-1   LC 92-43894

First volume in a project saga about the Crown family

"In 1892, a Berlin street urchin named Pauli Kroner, 14 years old, scrapes up steerage fare for America with the help of his dying Aunt Lotte. Pauli is robbed of his papers and what little money he has just before his arrival. But he still manages to pass customs and make his way to Chicago, where his uncle is one of the city's leading brewers. . . . Paul yearns to be a painter, but lacks the skill. George Eastman's recent invention, the Kodak camera, offers him a chance to overcome that problem. When Paul has a chance to assist in the birth of cinematography, his life's course is set." N Y Times Book Rev

"Chockfull of fascinating period detail, Jakes' captivating story brings to life the sounds, smells, and tastes of turn-of-the-century America." Publ Wkly

Love and war. Harcourt Brace Jovanovich 1984 1019p $19.95

ISBN 0-15-154496-4   LC 84-12895

This sequel to North and South "carries forward the entwined sagas of the Hazards of Pennsylvania, industrialists, and the Mains of South Carolina, plantation owners. . . . The story moves from action on the battlefield to the corridors of Washington to the shipyards of Liverpool. It encompasses deeds heroic and dastardly; passions licit and illicit; spying, assassination plotting and cynical profiteering; and the trying out of new military interventions." Publ Wkly

Followed by Heaven and hell

North and South. Harcourt Brace Jovanovich 1982 740p $24.95

ISBN 0-15-166998-8   LC 81-47898

In this first novel of a trilogy the author "introduces two families: The Main family of South Carolina, and the Hazard family of Pennsylvania. The families are basically different. The Mains from the South grow rice and represent the old ways while the Hazards of the North produce iron and are examples of the Industrial Revolution. Their paths converge however, when Orry Main meets George Hazard as the two are entering West Point in 1842. Their friendship is immediate and strong. Orry's family owns slaves, and George, while loving his friend, cannot understand it. As the years pass each grows more entrenched in his beliefs. . . . George's sister Virgilia, an avowed abolitionist, seeks to pry the friendship apart and nearly succeeds. George and Orry's struggles are representative of that which plague the nation." West Coast Rev Books

Followed by Love and war

James, Henry, 1843-1916
The ambassadors.

Available from various publishers

First published 1903 by Harper

"The central character and first 'ambassador,' Lambert Strether, is sent to Paris by Mrs. Newsome, a wealthy widow whom he plans to marry, in order to persuade her son Chad to come home. Chad is deeply involved with a charming French woman, Madame de Vionnet, and the novel deals chiefly with Strether's gradual conversion to the idea that life may hold more real meaning for Chad in Paris than in Woollett, Massachusetts. Strether comes to this conclusion in spite of his discovery that Chad and Mme de Vionnet are, in fact, more than just good friends. After the arrival of a second ambassador, Chad's sister Sarah, Strether decides to return to Woollett, urging Chad to remain in Paris. The essence of the novel is in Strether's remark, 'Live all you can; it's a mistake not to.'" Reader's Ency. 3d edition

The American.

Available from Kelley

First published 1877 by J. R. Osgood and Company

"A self-made American goes to Europe to enjoy his 'pile,' and becomes engaged to a French widow of noble family. The match is a good one for both parties, but at length the powers that rule this exclusive social world deliver their verdict: the engagement must be annulled. The American's pluck and good nature are happily contrasted with the colossal pride and essential meanness of the old noblesse." Baker. Guide to the Best Fic

"With much humour and delicacy of perception, the author depicts the reaction of different American types to the European environment." Oxford Companion to Engl Lit

The American novels and stories of Henry James; edited and with an introduction by F. O. Matthiessen. Knopf 1947 xxvi, 993p o.p.

Partially analyzed in Short story index

The Bostonians, The Europeans and Washington Square, are entered separately

This volume includes The Bostonians; the unfinished novel: The ivory tower; two novelettes: The Europeans and Washington Square and the following short stories: The story of a year; The point of view; A New England winter; Pandora; "Europe"; Julia Bride; The jolly corner; Crapy Cornelia; A round of visits

In The ivory tower, Rosanna Gaw tries to effect a reconciliation between her father and his estranged former partner, two dying millionaires. The partner has summoned his nephew, Graham Fielding, whom Rosanna loves, back from Europe to Newport to inform him that he is his heir. Cissy Foy, loved by a rejected former suitor of Rosanna has her eye on Fielding and his prospective wealth

The Aspern papers

  In James, H. The complete tales of Henry James v6

  In James, H. The Henry James reader p165-254

  In James, H. Short novels of Henry James p257-354

The author of "Beltraffio"

  In James, H. The complete tales of Henry James v5

  In James, H. The Henry James reader

The beast in the jungle

  In James, H. The complete tales of Henry James v11

  In James, H. The Henry James reader p357-400

The Bostonians. Knopf 1992 394p $17

ISBN 0-679-41750-8   LC 92-52889

Also available from Buccaneer Bks.

James, Henry, 1843-1916—*Continued*

"Everyman's library"

First published 1886 by Macmillan

In this satirical novel, "Basil Ransom, a Mississippi lawyer, comes to Boston to seek his fortune, and becomes acquainted with his cousins, the flirtatious widow, Mrs. Luna, and her neurotic sister, Olive Chancellor. He is taken by Olive, a radical feminist, to a suffragette meeting. . . . They hear an address by beautiful young Verena Tarrant, whose gift of persuasion interests Olive as an instrument for her own use. Olive removes the girl to her own luxurious home, converts her to the feminist cause, and even urges her to vow that she will never marry. Fleeing the attentions of Mrs. Luna, Ransom attempts to win Verena to his belief that her proper sphere is a home and a drawing room, not a career as lecturer for a preposterous political movement." Oxford Companion to Am Lit. 5th edition

"It was in fact one of the first American novels to deal more or less explicitly with Lesbianism." Herzberg. Reader's Ency of Am Lit

also in James, H. The American novels and stories of Henry James p424-746

The complete tales of Henry James; edited with an introduction by Leon Edel. Lippincott 1962-1965 12v o.p.

Analyzed in Short story index

Contents: v1: 1864-1868: A tragedy of errors; The story of a year; A landscape painter; A day of days; My friend Bingham; Poor Richard; The story of a masterpiece; The romance of certain old clothes; A most extraordinary case; A problem; De Grey: a romance

v2: 1868-1872: Osborne's revenge; A light man; Gabrielle de Bergerac; Travelling companions; A passionate pilgrim; At Isella; Master Eustace; Guest's confession

v3: 1873-1875: The Madonna of the future; The sweetheart of M. Briseux; The last of the Valerii; Madame de Mauves [novelette]; Adina; Professor Fargo; Eugene Pickering; Benvolio

v4: 1876-1882: Crawford's consistency; The ghostly rental; Four meetings; Rose-Agathe; Daisy Miller: a study [novelette]; Longstaff's marriage; An international episode [novelette]; The pension Beaurepas; The diary of a man of fifty; A bundle of letters; The point of view

v5: 1883-1884: The siege of London [novelette]; The impressions of a cousin; Lady Barbarina [novelette]; The author of "Beltraffio" [novelette]; Pandora

v6: 1884-1888: Georgina's reasons; A New England winter; The path of duty; Mrs. Temperly; Louisa Panant; The Aspern papers [novelette]; The liar

v7: 1888-1891: The modern warning; A London life; The lesson of the master; The Patagonia; The solution; The pupil [novelette]

v8: 1891-1892: Brooksmith; The marriages; The chaperon; Sir Edmund Orme; Nona Vincent; The private life; The real thing; Lord Beaupré; The visits; Sir Dominick Ferrand; Collaboration; Greville Fane; The wheel of time

v9: 1892-1898: Owen Wingrave; The middle years; The death of the lion; The Coxon Fund; The next time; The altar of the dead; The figure in the carpet; Glasses; The way it came (The friends of the friends); John Delavoy

v10: 1898-1899: The turn of the screw [novelette]; In the cage [novelette]; Covering end; The given case; The great condition; "Europe"; Paste; The real right thing

v11: 1900-1903: The great good place; Maud-Evelyn; Miss Gunton of Poughkeepsie; The tree of knowledge; The abasement of the Northmores; The third person; The special type; The tone of time; Broken wings; The two faces; Mrs. Medwin; The Beldonald Holbein; The story in it; Flickerbridge; The beast in the jungle [novelette]; The birthplace

v12: 1903-1910: The papers; Fordham Castle; Julia Bride; The jolly corner; The Velvet Glove; Mora Montravers; Crapy Cornelia; The bench of desolation; A round of visits

Daisy Miller

In James, H. The complete tales of Henry James v4

In James, H. Daisy Miller [and An international episode] v1

In James, H. The Henry James reader p403-61

In James, H. Short novels of Henry James p1-58

Daisy Miller [and An international episode]; illustrated from drawings by Harry W. McVickar. Harper 2v in 1 il o.p.

Daisy Miller was first published 1878; An international episode, 1879

"The book's title character is a young American woman traveling in Europe with her mother. There she is courted by Frederick Forsyth Winterbourne, an American living abroad. In her innocence, Daisy is compromised by her friendship with an Italian man. Her behavior shocks Winterbourne and the other Americans living in Italy, and they shun her. Only after she dies does Winterbourne recognize that her actions reflected her spontaneous, genuine, and unaffected nature and that his suspicions of her were unwarranted." Merriam-Webster's Ency of Lit

An international episode is about a romance between an English nobleman and a young American woman

The Europeans.

Available from Buccaneer Bks. and Queens House

First published 1878

"Two expatriates, the Baroness Muenster and her brother Felix Young, come to Boston to visit some relatives they have never seen. The baroness futilely tries to make a wealthy marriage, and Felix seeks to paint portraits of the Bostonians he meets. A contrast is drawn between the sophistication of the pair and the strict New Englanders. Felix marries one of his kinswomen, who is eager to escape from her bleak environment." Benet's Reader's Ency of Am Lit

also in James, H. The American novels and stories of Henry James p37-161

The golden bowl. Knopf 1992 596p $20

ISBN 0-679-41733-8   LC 92-52927

Also available from Kelley

"Everyman's library"

First published 1904 by Scribner

Maggie Verver, daughter of an American millionaire living in London, marries an indigent "Italian prince who has had a love affair with Maggie's closest friend, Charlotte Stant. Charlotte visits the pair and continues her intimacy. Then she marries Maggie's father. Everybody tries to keep secret from the others that he or she knows all that has happened or is happening. The complications

James, Henry, 1843-1916—*Continued*
are solved when Maggie's father goes back to America with Charlotte. James depicts with all the subtlety of his late style the cultural and moral involvements that follow on international marriage and irregular sex relationships." Benet's Reader's Ency of Am Lit

The Henry James reader; selected with a foreword and headnotes by Leon Edel. Scribner 626p $45

ISBN 0-684-14745-9
"Hudson River editions"
First published 1965 and analyzed in Short story index
Contains the short novels: Washington Square (1881); The Aspern papers (1888); The turn of the screw (1898); The beast in the jungle (1903); Daisy Miller (1878); The author of Beltraffio (1884); also the following short stories: Pandora; Owen Wingrave; The real thing; The two faces

In the cage
In James, H. The complete tales of Henry James v10
In James, H. What Maisie knew, In the cage, The pupil

An international episode
In James, H. The complete tales of Henry James v4
In James, H. Daisy Miller [and An international episode] v2

The ivory tower
In James, H. The American novels and stories of Henry James p867-993

Lady Barbarina
In James, H. The complete tales of Henry James v5

Madame de Mauves
In James, H. The complete tales of Henry James v3

The portrait of a lady. Knopf 1991 xxv, 626p $20

ISBN 0-679-40562-3   LC 91-52999
Also available from Kelley
"Everyman's library"
First published 1881 by Houghton
"This is one of the best James's early works, in which he presents various types of American character transplanted into a European environment. The story centres in Isabel Archer, the 'Lady,' an attractive American girl. Around her we have the placid old American banker, Mr. Touchett; his hard repellent wife; his ugly, invalid, witty, charming son Ralph, whom England has thoroughly assimilated; and the crude, brilliant, indomitably American journalist Henrietta Stackpole. Isabel refuses the offer of marriage of a typical English peer, the excellent Lord Warburton, and of a bulldog-like New Englander, Casper Goodwood, to fall a victim, under the influence of the slightly sinister Madame Merle (another cosmopolitan American), to a worthless and spiteful dilettante, Gilbert Osmond, who marries her for her fortune and ruins her life; but to whom she remains loyal in spite of her realization of his vileness." Oxford Companion to Engl Lit. 5th edition

The pupil
In James, H. The complete tales of Henry James v7
In James, H. Short novels of Henry James p355-405
In James, H. What Maisie knew, In the cage, The pupil

Roderick Hudson.
Available from Kelley
First published serially 1875 in The Atlantic Monthly; in book form 1876 by J. R. Osgood and Company
"The titular hero is a talented young American sculptor who goes to study in Rome at the insistance of a wealthy benefactor and becomes gradually disillusioned about his art and utterly demoralized by his experience. He neglects his New England fiancée; becomes involved in a love affair with Christina Light and finally leaps over a cliff." Univ Handbk for Readers and Writers

Short novels of Henry James; with eight full-page illustrations; introduction by E. Hudson Long. Dodd, Mead 1961 530p il o.p.

"Great illustrated classics"
Contents: Daisy Miller (1878); Washington Square (1881); The Aspern papers (1888); The pupil (1892); The turn of the screw (1898)
The first, second and the last titles are entered separately. The pupil is entered in a combined edition with: What Maisie knew, In the cage and The pupil.
"In 'The Aspern Papers,' an unnamed American editor rents a room in Venice in the home of Juliana Bordereau, the elderly mistress of Jeffrey Aspern, a deceased Romantic poet, in order to procure from her the poet's papers." Merriam-Webster's Ency of Lit

The short stories of Henry James; selected and edited with an introduction by Clifton Fadiman. Random House 1945 xx, 644p o.p.

Analyzed in Short story index
Contents: Four meetings; A bundle of letters; Louisa Pallant; The liar; The real thing; The pupil [novelette]: Booksmith; The middle years; The altar of the dead; "Europe"; The great good place; The tree of knowledge; The tone of time; Mrs. Medwin; The birthplace; The beast in the jungle [novelette]; The jolly corner

The siege of London
In James, H. The complete tales of Henry James v5

The spoils of Poynton.
Available from Amereon and Kelley
First published 1896 by Houghton
"Owen Gareth, heir to the great house at Poynton, spurns his mother's favorite, Fleda Vetch, to marry Mona Brigstock. Old Mrs. Gareth thereupon removes her art treasures from Poynton. Owen was in fact in love with Fleda, and offers her any object she may desire at Poynton, but suddenly the house is ruined by an accidental fire, which ruins the spoils that have warped so many lives." Haydn. Thesaurus of Book Dig

The turn of the screw.
Available from Amereon and Queens House

James, Henry, 1843-1916—*Continued*

First published 1898

"This framed first-person narrative is a study in ambiguity. A young governess put in sole charge of two small children, Miles and Flora, in a country house called Bly records her progressive discoveries that the children are not innocent but demonic, in communication with the ghosts of their deceased former governess, Miss Jessel, and a male servant, Peter Quint. The young governess fights for the souls of the two children against the pervasive influence of the evil dead." Benet's Reader's Ency of Am Lit

also in James, H. The complete tales of Henry James v10

also in James, H. The Henry James reader p255-356

also in James, H. Short novels of Henry James p407-530

Washington Square.

Available from Buccaneer Bks.

First published 1881 by Harper

"The novel concerns Catherine Sloper, the shy and stolid daughter of wealthy, urbane, sardonic Dr. Austin Sloper. When young Morris Townsend, who is courting Catherine for her money, learns that her father will disinherit her if she marries him, he leaves her. Renewing his courtship after Dr. Sloper dies and leaves Catherine a small fortune, Morris is rejected sadly but firmly by Catherine, who lives on at Washington Square and is by then a spinster. Thus Catherine, plain and unintelligent, nevertheless withstands the world's assaults." Benet's Reader's Ency of Am Lit

also in James, H. The American novels and stories of Henry James p162-295

also in James, H. The Henry James reader p1-163

also in James, H. Short novels of Henry James p59-256

What Maisie knew

In James, H. What Maisie knew, In the cage, The pupil

What Maisie knew, In the cage, The pupil. Scribner xxi, 576p o.p. Kelley reprint available $45 (ISBN 0-678-02811-7)

"The Novels and tales of Henry James. New York edition v11"

A combined edition of one novel and two novelettes first published 1897, 1898 and 1891 respectively

What Maisie knew concerns a twelve-year-old girl whose parents have divorced and remarried. Living alternately with each parent she learns that her stepmother and stepfather are having an adulterous affair, just as she had learned of her parents' earlier infidelities. She decides to go to live with her old governess rather than with either parent. In the cage concerns a young woman who works as a telegram dispatcher in a London grocery store. She experiences vicarious enjoyment by imagining details in the lives of her well-to-do customers and even puts off marriage to her working-class fiancé while she tries to aid in the affairs of an aristocratic lady and her lover. But when she learns the unsavory truth about

the couple from an outside source she decides to proceed with her marriage at once. The pupil deals with an American student who becomes a tutor for the sickly son of a shabby American family traveling about in Europe, develops a strong attachment to the boy, and tries to help him leave his despicable family—with tragic results

The wings of the dove. Modern Lib. 1993 711p $19

ISBN 0-679-60067-1   LC 93-15338

Also available from Kelley

First published 1902 by Scribner

"The story is set in London and Venice. Kate Croy is a Londoner who encourages her secret fiancé, Merton Densher, to woo and marry Milly Theale, a wealthy young American who is dying of a mysterious malady. This, Kate reasons, although Milly will die soon, she will at least be happily in love, Merton will inherit her fortune, and Kate and Merton can marry and be rich. Shortly after Milly learns of Merton's and Kate's motives, she dies, leaving Merton a legacy that he is too guilt-ridden to accept. Kate is unwilling to forgo the inheritance, and she and Merton part forever, their relationship destroyed by Milly's unwittingly prescient gift." Merriam-Webster's Ency of Lit

James, P. D.

The black tower. Scribner 1975 271p o.p.

"Adam Dalgleish, convalescing after a severe illness, arrives at Toynton Grange (Dorset coast), the rest home for the young disabled, just too late to find out why his old friend Father Baddeley had sent for him. The monk-robed Wilfred Anstey and his staff are an odd lot, as are the few patients, all in wheelchairs. There's already been a suspicious suicide, and Dalgleish is not satisfied that the old priest's death was caused by myocarditis alone. Handicapped by poor health, he finally manages to unearth the secret of the grange." Barzun. Cat of Crime. Rev and enl edition

also in James, P. D. Murder in triplicate v3

The children of men. Knopf 1993 c1992 241p $22

ISBN 0-679-41873-3   LC 92-54280

Also available large print edition $24 (ISBN 0-679-42210-2)

First published 1992 in the United Kingdom

In this "thriller set in 2021, the human race is dying out because men have inexplicably become infertile. Dismayed by society's descent into chaos, Oxford historian Theodore Faron—cousin of England's new dictator—finds himself drawn to a group of revolutionaries." Libr J

"In this convincingly detailed world—where kittens are (illegally) christened, sex has lost its allure and the arts have been abandoned—James concretely explores an unthinkable prospect. Readers should persevere through the slow start, for the rewards of this story, including its reminder of the transforming power of hope, are many and lasting." Publ Wkly

Cover her face

In James, P. D. Crime times three

Crime times three; three complete novels featuring Adam Dalgliesh of Scotland Yard. Scribner 1979 3v in 1 o.p.

LC 78-12790

James, P. D.—*Continued*

An omnibus edition of three titles originally published separately in the United Kingdom and first published in the United States by Scribner in 1966, 1967 and 1971 respectively

Three murder mysteries involving the poet-detective Adam Dalgliesh. In the first he investigates the murder of Sally Jupp, a servant girl in an English country family; in A mind to murder, Dalgliesh is called in on the case of a murdered administrative head of a fashionable psychiatric clinic; and in Shroud for a nightingale, the detective hunts for a murderer on the loose after two student nurses die under mysterious circumstances

Contents: Cover her face (c1962); A mind to murder (c1963); Shroud for a nightingale (c1971)

Death of an expert witness. Scribner 1977 322p o.p.

LC 77-21530

The setting of this novel is "a forensic-science laboratory in a small East Anglia village. One of the senior biologists is found murdered in his triple-locked and delicately alarm-wired office, and Commander Adam Dalgliesh of Scotland Yard . . . is assigned to the case." New Yorker

"Basically James is a novelist who happens to put her character into mystery stories. She is just as much interested in people and their relationships as she is in the conventions of the genre. And being the perceptive and sensitive writer she is, she constructs books that can be read on several levels." N Y Times Book Rev

Devices and desires. Knopf 1990 c1989 433p $19.95

ISBN 0-394-58070-2   LC 89-45305

Also available G.K. Hall large print edition

First published 1989 in the United Kingdom

"Commander Adam Dalgliesh, travels to the coastal Norfolk community of Larksoken to settle up the estate of his recently deceased aunt. Inevitably, Dalgliesh becomes embroiled in the affairs of the locals, many of them connected with the Larksoken nuclear power plant, which has brought a new economy to the area but has also stirred the juices of antinuclear protestors. Meanwhile, a mad killer called the Whistler is aprowl, savaging women with a bizarre modus operandi." Booklist

"As always with P. D. James, the whodunit element is the lagniappe, so interesting are her characters, so absorbing her depiction of time and place, so rich the texture of the tale she tells." N Y Times Book Rev

Innocent blood. Scribner 1980 311p o.p.

LC 79-28699

"What starts things moving in the tale is a young (adopted) woman's determination to find her real parents. This headstrong wish is gratified, creating social difficulties, deep changes in personal relations, the plotting of a murder, the experience of jail, and miscellaneous sexual activity. The diverse characters are admirably drawn and the author's fingerwork in tying and untying threads is as deft as her touches of sordid life and as nimble as her prose." Barzun. Cat of Crime. Rev and enl edition

A mind to murder

In James, P. D. Crime times three

Murder in triplicate; three complete novels by the queen of crime. Scribner 1980 3v in 1 o.p.

LC 80-18493

An omnibus edition of three titles originally published separately. An unsuitable job for a woman and The black tower are entered separately. Unnatural causes, first published 1973 in England, is a mystery featuring Commander Adam Dalgliesh

Contents: Unnatural causes; An unsuitable job for a woman; The black tower

Shroud for a nightingale

In James, P. D. Crime times three

The skull beneath the skin. Scribner 1982 328p o.p.

LC 82-5981

"Fading actress Clarissa Lisle has been receiving frightening notes and is terrified of failing in her comeback performance, a revival of 'The Duchess of Malfi', held on a small private island off Dorset. Her husband hires detective Cordelia Gray to stop the notes. Once on the island, Cordelia discovers that nearly everyone there has a good reason to hate Clarissa, who is soon found gruesomely battered to death. The isolated group of suspects, hidden clues, and macabre atmosphere of an island castle complete with skulls and underground passageways make a pleasant traditional mystery. But James is never superficial, and her in-depth characterizations and excellent writing reveal complex relationships, motives, and human frailties." Libr J

A taste for death. Knopf 1986 459p $18.95

ISBN 0-394-55583-X   LC 86-45273

Sir Paul Berowne, a minister of the Crown, is found with his throat cut in the vestry of St. Matthew's church in London. A tramp has also been killed. Dalgliesh and his assistant Kate Miskin seek the solution to the mystery in the victims' past. All the family members and witnesses have something to conceal

This "book is about murder and the way murder changes everything. . . . It is also about the human condition in London today, enlarged by a sense of the British past that stretches back like a rich and barely dwindling perspective." N Y Times Book Rev

Unnatural causes

In James, P. D. Murder in triplicate v1

An unsuitable job for a woman. Scribner 1973 c1972 216p o.p.

First published 1972 in the United Kingdom

"In this book James's usual investigator, Chief Superintendent Dalgleish, plays only a minor part. It is Cordelia Gray, the young, intelligent, and clear-thinking owner of an unsuccessful detective agency, who solves the case. She is hired by Sir Ronald Callender to investigate the death by suicide of his son, Mark. Miss Gray's meticulous research leads her to suspect that Mark was murdered and makes her a prime target for murder. There are suspenseful moments, close calls, and a very surprising encounter, at last, between Cordelia and Supt. Dalgleish." Shapiro. Fic for Youth. 3d edition

also in James, P. D. Murder in triplicate v2

James, Stephanie *See* Krentz, Jayne Ann

Jance, Judith A., 1944-
Lying in wait; a J.P. Beaumont mystery; by J.A. Jance. Morrow 1994 303p $17.95
ISBN 0-688-02013-5   LC 94-15565

Police detective J.P. Beaumont "tackles a case with its origins in the Nazi death camps of World War II. When not one but two grisly torture-murder victims are discovered in the Seattle area, Beau and his new partner, Sue Danielson, are called in to investigate. Much to Beau's surprise, he finds that one of the victims was married to a former high school classmate, Else Didricksen." Booklist
"Beau and Sue probe Else's high school romance, the missing accident victim and the Nazi connection before they come up with the killer in this red hot, fast-paced story." Publ Wkly

Jarman, Rosemary Hawley
The courts of illusion. Little, Brown 1983 370p o.p.
          LC 83-80792

"The chaotic years following the death of Richard III at the Battle of Bosworth Field in 1485 form the backdrop for [this novel]. . . . The tale is told by a Plantagenet loyalist, young Nicholas Archer, whose devotion to the Pretender [known in history as Perkin Warbeck] takes him on a journey that is also a search for self. The Pretender's cause fails under the Tudor ascendancy as does young Nicholas's quest for love." Publ Wkly
The author "offers the reader a vivid and expertly crafted re-creation of 15th-century England. Jarman gives us a fresh and sympathetic view of Warbeck, deftly allowing readers to form their own conclusions as to the validity of his claim." Libr J

Jeffries, Roderic, 1926-
Death takes time; an Inspector Alvarez mystery. St. Martin's Press 1994 208p $18.95
ISBN 0-312-11260-2   LC 94-32250
Also available G.K. Hall large print edition

In this mystery Inspector Alvarez of Majorca faces "three puzzling murders. An Englishwoman dies in a fall from her terrace in the south of France. The police suspect foul play, but their only evidence is a rental car from Majorca. Told to trace the car, Alvarez is diverted by the sudden death, from a heroin overdose, of an English resident of the island." Publ Wkly
Jeffries "proves that with deft plotting and a solid feel for locale, it is quite possible to take the standard British police procedural, transplant it abroad, and watch it thrive." Booklist

Jen, Gish
Typical American. Houghton Mifflin 1991 296p o.p.
          LC 90-48423

"Yefing Chang becomes Ralph Chang in America and begins a hard struggle to achieve the American dream—a career, a family and a home of his own. In poverty, he succeeds finally to win a doctoral degree, a college position, a happy marriage to Helen, two delightful daughters and a close reunion with his older sister,

Theresa. The dream becomes a nightmare when he meets Grover Ding whose corrupt influence over Ralph and Helen begins to unravel all that the Changs have managed to achieve. This is an honest novel that does not promise happy endings and recognizes the human weaknesses that can destroy a family's stability." Shapiro. Fic for Youth. 3d edition

Jenkins, Dan, 1929-
Semi-tough. Atheneum Pubs. 1972 307p o.p.

The novel takes place during "the week of the Super Bowl: the Giants, still playing in New York thanks to a new Commissioner of Football (who has foiled a plan by the Mara family to move the team to Bermuda), are about to play the dog-ass Jets for the championship. All America watches. Since the memoirs of great athletes . . . are of no small commercial value, Billy Clyde Puckett, the great Giant fullback (Jimmy Brown's ability, Tucker Frederickson's cosmetology) is tape recording his pre-game experiences for his book." N Y Times Book Rev

Jenkins, Will F., 1896-1975
Exploration team
In The Hugo winners v1 p95-142

Jennings, Gary
Aztec. Atheneum Pubs. 1980 754p o.p. Buccaneer Bks. reprint available $27.95 (ISBN 1-56849-410-6)
          LC 80-55608

"Mixtli (Dark Cloud), the book's hero, is a Mexícatl who is born on the outskirts of the capital city of Tenochtítlan a half-century before the arrival of Cortés. He becomes, in turn, a student, a scribe, a soldier, a merchant, a cultural anthropologist, an adviser to noble rulers, and finally an involuntary chronicler of his people's past for the victorious Spaniards. The book is presented as the verbatim transcript of the reminiscences of this 'elderly male Indian,' recorded at the command of Emperor Charles I, who is eager to learn more about his recently acquired colony of New Spain." N Y Times Book Rev

The journeyer. Atheneum Pubs. 1984 782p $19.95
ISBN 0-689-11403-6   LC 83-45077

This novel "is intended to evoke the personal story of Marco Polo's travels lacking from his own account. After being banished from Venice at 17 (in this story), Marco travels with his father and uncle to the Orient. The older men are extraordinary traders, but Marco is set on adventure. His experiences . . . lead him to maturity and finally to a position of importance to Kublai Khan." Libr J

Raptor. Doubleday 1992 980p o.p.
          LC 92-9433

In this "historical novel about the Gothic conquest of the Roman Empire, Thorn, the hermaphrodite hero/heroine, is seduced first by a monk and then by a nun. Evicted from a monastery and a convent, Thorn is then schooled in the ways of the world by the grumpy, blasphemous woodsman Wyrd. Rugged yet sensitive,

Jennings, Gary—*Continued*

usually dressed as a man, Thorn is raptorial (i.e., predatory) in his thirst for lovers, male and female, and for adventure. He serves as field marshal, sidekick and spy for bloody Theodoric (A.D. 454-526), king of the Ostrogoths, depicted here as a benevolent despot." Publ Wkly

"Like Michener, Jennings fills his boldly sketched historical canvas with lively action and dense, well-researched detail; in the works of both, a strong plot and interesting characters often camouflage an absence of style. But readers will enjoy this trip to an exotic world." Booklist

Jewett, Sarah Orne, 1849-1909

The best stories of Sarah Orne Jewett; selected and arranged with a preface by Willa Cather. Houghton Mifflin 1925 2v o.p. Smith, P. reprint available $16.55 (ISBN 0-8446-1248-0)

"The Mayflower edition"

Analyzed in Short story index

Volume 1 with running title: The country of the pointed firs was first published 1896; v2 contains stories published at various dates from 1886-1923

Contents: v1 Return; Mrs. Todd; Schoolhouse; At the schoolhouse window; Captain Littlepage; Waiting place; Outer island; Green island; William; Where penny-royal grew; Old singers; Strange sail; Poor Joanna; Hermitage; On Shellheap island; Great expedition; Country road; Bowden reunion; Feast's end; Along shore; Dunnett shepherdess; Queen's twin; William's wedding; Backward view

v2 A white heron; The flight of Betsy Lane; The Dulham ladies; Going to Shrewsbury; The only rose; Miss Tempy's watchers; Martha's lady; The guests of Mrs. Timms; The town poor; The Hilton's holiday; Aunt Cynthy Dallett

The country of the pointed firs. Houghton Mifflin 1896 213p o.p.

Available from Amereon

"Highly regarded for its sympathetic yet unsentimental portrayal of the town of Dunnet Landing and its residents, this episodic book is narrated by a nameless summer visitor who relates the life stories of various inhabitants, capturing the idiomatic language, customs, mannerisms, and humor peculiar to Down-Easters." Merriam-Webster's Ency of Lit

also in Jewett, S. O. The best stories of Sarah Orne Jewett v1

also in Jewett, S. O. The country of the pointed firs and other stories p1-139

The country of the pointed firs and other stories. Modern Lib. 1995 247p $13.50

ISBN 0-679-60173-2   LC 95-2831

In addition to the title story (entered separately above) this volume also includes the following: The queen's twin; A Dunnet shepherdess; The foreigner; William's wedding

Jhabvala, Ruth Prawer

Heat and dust. Harper & Row 1976 c1975 181p o.p. Smith, P. reprint available $21.50 (ISBN 0-8446-6335-2)

"A Joan Kahn book"

First published 1975 in the United Kingdom

"The juxtaposition of past and present India is explored in this novel. The 1923 storyline tells of Olivia, who, though married to a British officer stationed in India, falls madly in love with an Indian prince. It is also about Olivia's husband's granddaughter by a second marriage, who has come to India to discover the details of Olivia's life but finds that, although India and women have become modernized, she must face many of the same choices as Olivia. The intrusion of British culture on India's own traditions and values is a second theme in the novel." Shapiro. Fic for Youth. 3d edition

Out of India; selected stories. Morrow 1986 288p o.p.

LC 85-25961

Contents: My first marriage; The widow; The interview; A spiritual call; Passion; The man with the dog; An experience of India; The housewife; Rose petals; Two more under the Indian sun; Bombay; On bail; In the mountains; How I became a holy mother; Desecration

"Out of a web of subtle but not precious ironies, couched in a limpid style, arises a sense of the author's obvious love-hate attitude toward this land that is so difficult to live in, for foreigner and native alike. Jhabvala sensitively explores the tense juncture between Western and Indian cultures; plots and characters glow with realism and energy." Booklist

Poet and dancer. Doubleday 1993 199p $19.95

ISBN 0-385-46869-5   LC 92-22945

This novel is set in Manhattan. The unnamed "narrator, subjected to a mother's reminiscences about her dead daughter, Angel, reimagines the tragic pas de deux between the doomed child and her first cousin Lara (the poet and dancer, respectively, of the title). Overwhelmed as a child by Lara's vibrancy, as an adult Angel crosses the line into obssession. After Lara begins an affair with Angel's divorced father, and the two young women move in together, sisterly attention turns into a warped give-and-take." Voice Lit Suppl

"Jhabvala tells a psychologically elaborate but clearly expressed story that will draw readers closely into its heart." Booklist

Three continents. Morrow 1987 384p $18.95

ISBN 0-688-07184-8   LC 87-7880

The author "describes the emotional seduction of Harriet Wishwell by the members of a fanatic religious sect, the Fourth World Movement, as well as her physical seduction by one of its leaders. Harriet and her homosexual twin brother Michael are equally drawn to charismatic Crishi, who marries Harriet for the huge inheritance she'll receive on her 21st birthday. Crishi and his cohorts are swindlers and dope pushers, activities they hide behind the movement's pious facade." Publ Wkly

Johnson, Charles Richard, 1948-

Middle passage; [by] Charles Johnson.
Atheneum Pubs. 1990 209p $17.95

ISBN 0-689-11968-2   LC 90-32713

The protagonist of this novel, set in 1830, "is Rutherford Calhoun, a newly freed slave leading a dissolute life in New Orleans. Rutherford finds himself forced into marriage with Isadora Bailey, a proper yet severe Boston schoolteacher, and, to quickly escape both wedlock and his Louisiana debts, he stows away on the first available ship. To his shock and horror, Rutherford learns that the vessel, the Republic, is a slave ship bound for Africa. Its captain is the American soldier of fortune, Ebenezer Falcon, a buccaneer and empire-builder. . . . The Republic's mission is to transport the last survivors of a nearly legendary tribe, the Allmuseri, from their devastated homeland to the New World." Publisher's note

"Johnson's exciting sea narrative provides an unusual historical look at the horrifying Middle Passage experience. . . . Like Moby-Dick's Ahab, the captain of the Republic is on his own special quest (in this case, the capture of the African trickster god). . . . Above all, the book is valuable in offering a rare perspective of the shocking experience of the slave trade and the consequences of that event for American blacks." Choice

Johnston, Terry C., 1947-

Cry of the hawk; a novel. Bantam Bks.
1992 391p o.p.

LC 92-46

"To get out of the Union prison at Rock Island, Illinois, Confederate Jonah Hook volunteers to go West and fight Indians as a 'galvanized Yankee.' When the Civil War and his service for the hated North end, he returns home to find his family has been abducted by a roaming band of Mormon Danites. Jonah's turbulent search for them over the Western plains develops into a stunning narrative of violent life on the frontier." Libr J

Johnston, Velda

The Etruscan smile; a novel of suspense.
Dodd, Mead 1977 213p o.p.

LC 77-3727

"The plot centers around a young teacher, Samantha Develin, and her search for her missing older sister, a talented, though slightly eccentric artist. Samantha travels to the Tuscan countryside near Milan, her sister's last home. There Samantha discovers two suitors, a priceless Etruscan statue, love, danger, and, eventually, the answer to the riddle of her sister's disappearance. Colorful, breezy, well-plotted." Libr J

Jones, Diana Wynne

A sudden wild magic. Morrow 1992 412p
o.p.

LC 92-10860

"Computer expert Mark Lister, incidentally the only male member of the Inner Ring of witches in Great Britain, unexpectedly comes across evidence that Earth is being manipulated by a distant planet called Arth. This pirate world, an all-male society sworn to celibacy, is sending wars, plagues, and environmental disasters (notably global warming) to Earth and then observing and appropriating Earth's leaders' solutions. In defense, the witches' council decides to transport some attractive female recruits to Arth to sabotage the inhabitants' oaths and restore the balance of power." Booklist

"Jones's sly sense of humor and her accurate, affectionate depiction of relations between women and men give an extra kick to this effervescent tale." Publ Wkly

Jones, Douglas C., 1924-

Arrest Sitting Bull. Scribner 1977 249p
o.p.

LC 77-7645

In this second volume of a western historical trilogy, the author tells it "as it really *did* happen when the order went out: 'Arrest Sitting Bull.' We begin with the Ghost Dance, when that confusion of Indian mythology and missionary-brought Christianity has fired the Plain Indians to a belief in the coming of an Indian Messiah. Sitting Bull, already the conqueror of Custer, the veteran of Buffalo Bill's Wild West Show, is back on the reservation, but at the center of a growing revolt against the white man. . . . Jones makes us understand the torment of a minority of decent white men and women who really cared about the Indians and of the Indians, trapped between a fight to the death (the novel closes with Wounded Knee three days off), and a willingness to try to assimilate themselves to the white man's ways." Publ Wkly

Followed by A creek called Wounded Knee

The barefoot brigade. Holt, Rinehart &
Winston 1982 313p o.p.

LC 82-892

In this Civil War novel featuring members of the Hasford-Pay family, Jones writes "about a little band of country boys and men from his native Arkansas who become Confederate infantry recruits, almost without quite realizing what is happening to them. Raw, naive, most of them illiterate, they stumble into battle life true innocents. . . . Ahead of them lie Antietam, Gettysburg, the battles of The Wilderness, for many of them death and for only a few survival. . . . Jones is not concerned with the great issues of the Civil War. . . . Instead, he shows us with photographic realism and compassion just what the war meant to those who served in it, not for glory, not as officers, as just another rural 'barefoot brigade.'" Publ Wkly

Come winter. Holt & Co. 1989 418p o.p.

LC 89-1760

"A Donald Hutter book"

In this volume in the author's Hasford-Pay saga "Roman Hasford makes a fortune selling livestock in Kansas and then heads back to his small hometown in northwestern Arkansas. Out of pity, he marries a withdrawn young woman, the victim of child abuse, and builds her a house so grand the locals are appalled. Roman constructs a bank, starts up a horse farm, and throws himself wholeheartedly into politics in an attempt to find some distraction from his unhappy marriage." Booklist

"The story has all the elements of classic tragedy, leavened with a bittersweet humor and wit that is quintessentially American. . . . A master storyteller is at work here, offering a singular and knowledgeable vision of the nation's final frontier days." Publ Wkly

Jones, Douglas C., 1924——*Continued*

The court-martial of George Armstrong Custer. Scribner 1976 291p o.p.

In this novel, the first of a trilogy, history is reshuffled. "Custer survives the Little Big Horn, leaving behind 260 dead comrades. Professionally scandalized, the army under William Sherman charges Custer with insubordination although the man is a folk hero often puffed up in the papers. Marshalling evidence for the government falls to Judge Advocate General Asa Gardiner. A determined idealist, he senses that superiors deem Custer a menace, a 'Golden Cavalier' with dubious ambitions. The defense ostensibly rests on a breakdown in communication and bad field intelligence; actually the implications cut deeper: Custer knows enough to have his Civil War cronies (Schofield, Miles, Sheridan) put in the stockade." Publ Wkly

"Slowly building the cases for the prosecution and defense, Jones does well by mixing the drama of courtroom proceedings with the color of a controversial incident." Booklist

Followed by Arrest Sitting Bull

A creek called Wounded Knee. Scribner 1978 236p o.p.

LC 78-16660

In the concluding volume of the trilogy, the author "tells the story of the Wounded Knee tragedy through the eyes of the principals: the Indians, the Federal troops, and the Press. Each chapter of the novel begins with a verbatim lead from an 1890 newspaper that if not finding the war inevitable at least found it irresistible. The Press did much to make the day." Best Sellers

"We all know what will happen here, and Jones vividly dramatizes it, but, perhaps more important, he dramatizes how it had to happen. For him people create history, and their actions, beliefs, foibles, aspirations, and apprehensions combine to make his 'Wounded Knee' not a historical pageant but a very human tragedy." Libr J

Elkhorn Tavern. Holt, Rinehart & Winston 1980 311p o.p.

LC 79-27818

Chronologically the first volume about the Hasford-Pay clan. Other related titles are: The barefoot brigade; Winding stair (1979); Roman (1986); Remember Santiago; Come winter; Weedy Rough (1981)

The author "conveys the turmoil faced by a family caught in the Civil War. Ora Hasford and her two teenage children struggle to preserve the family farm, first against scavenging jayhawkers and later from the artillery launched during the Battle of Pea Ridge, which was waged in their fields and in the nearby town. Not only has Jones used actual wartime events and military figures, but also the Hasford family is itself based on the author's ancestors." Booklist

Remember Santiago. Holt & Co. 1988 354p o.p.

LC 88-10310

A Hasford-Pay novel. "Employing the divergent viewpoints and eye-witness accounts of a number of participants, Jones . . . captures the mayhem and confusion that characterized the Spanish-American War. Drawn into the senseless conflict by a combination of happenstance and ill luck, attorney Eben Pay and his faithful Osage sidekick, Joe Mountain, encounter a host of unconventional characters during the brief course of the Cuban invasion." Booklist

This novel is "unyielding in its depiction of the political machinations which marked this warfare and tied the hands of the few genuinely concerned officers in the field." Voice Youth Advocates

The search for Temperance Moon. Holt & Co. 1991 324p o.p.

LC 90-25134

Available Thorndike Press large print edition

"A Donald Hutter book"

"Oscar Schiller, cashiered U.S. deputy marshal, is summoned to Fort Smith, Arkansas' most famous bordello where the madam, Jewel Moon, asks him to solve the murder of her outlaw mother Temperance. The murder has been committed across the river in the Indian Nations, where only tribal police forces and federal courts have jurisdiction. Oscar develops a psychological portrait of Temperance from interviews and enlists the aid of several police comrades in his investigation." Libr J

"Taking obvious delight in his colorful and complex characters, Jones offers a particularly unsentimental view of the post-Civil War West." Booklist

Season of yellow leaf. Holt, Rinehart & Winston 1983 323p il o.p.

LC 83-117

"In the Texas area during the first half of the 1800s the Parry family, Welsh settlers, are eking out a living and facing the usual dangers of frontier life. Their ten-year-old daughter and her younger brother are captured in a raid by Comanche Indians led by Sanchess, son of Iron Shirt. Morfydd is taken into the tribe, since the Indians looked upon all females as potential bearers of warrior sons. She gradually becomes part of the Indian culture and is renamed Chosen. The novel portrays the precarious life of the Indians who had to worry about battles not only with the white man but also with other Indian tribes. Iron Shirt, a respected peace chief of the tribe, foresees the 'season of yellow leaf,' the eventual disappearance of the Indian as the white man moves farther into the West usurping the land and killing buffalo for hides rather than for food." Shapiro. Fic for Youth. 3d edition

Followed by Gone the dreams and dancing (1984)

This savage race. Holt & Co. 1993 401p il o.p.

LC 92-36881

Available Thorndike Press large print edition

"In 1808, Boone Fawley takes his family out of the relatively civilized city of St. Louis and enters the territory that will soon be called the Louisiana Purchase. They make a hard living near the Mississippi, mostly at the mercy of the Osage and Cherokee or the equally dangerous fur traders. Boone's son Questor exemplifies the agricultural virtues, but son John becomes a hardened wilderness man. When the earthquake of 1811 wipes out the family, they move to Arkansas, where they find that the rudimentary civilization there is even more treacherous than the wilderness." Libr J

"To watch the Fawleys take, pick up stakes, move and then take again, is to watch the American spirit as it is born, for both better and worse." N Y Times Book Rev

Jones, James, 1921-1977

From here to eternity. Scribner 1951 861p
o.p.

A story of Army life in Hawaii in the last months
before Pearl Harbor. The chief characters are two soldiers—Pfc Robert Prewitt and First Sergeant Milton
Warden—and the women they loved

"Mr. Jones has grappled with a variety of materials
and handles some of them less successfully than others.
There is a good deal of weak stuff in the two love
affairs and the characterizations of the women, and the
sorties into the field of general ideas are unimpressive.
The book as a whole, however, is a spectacular achievement; it has tremendous vitality and driving power and
graphic authenticity." Atlantic

The thin red line. Scribner 495p $45

ISBN 0-684-15555-9
"Hudson River editions"
First published 1962

"The Thin Red Line is a kind of companion piece
[to From here to eternity] which describes the Guadalcanal campaign. . . . Company C-for-Charlie is the 'hero'
of this novel which has no hero—except the collective
behavior of a wide and varied cross-section of American
military men. . . . From the abstract strategy of the
Guadalcanal campaign and the Big Brass who have come
to watch the show, down to the fighting men who carry
out the battle plans without knowing or caring about
them, [it] is a many-leveled chronicle of the whole am-
phibious military operation." N Y Times Book Rev

"This novel will surely offend some readers, lavishly
bespattered as it is with Anglo-Saxon words and physiological detail. Nevertheless, it bears the Jones stamp of
authenticity and is a major combat novel of World War
II." Ont Libr Rev

Followed by Whistle

Whistle. Delacorte Press 1978 457p o.p.
LC 77-11980

This is the final installment of Jones' war trilogy,
which also includes From here to eternity and The thin
red line. This book begins in 1943, when "four soldiers
from an infantry company in the Pacific are sent by
boat and train to an army hospital in Tennessee. . .
. These men, who have known no security except what
the company provided, are quickly unhinged by faithless
wives and intolerable families, by their rage and despair
at the human condition. . . . To stave off disintegration,
these out-of-work warriors resort to . . . drink and
brawls, politics and sex. . . . The outline for the conclusion of the book . . . has been pieced together [following
his death] from Jones's notes and conversations by his
friend and fellow writer Willie Morris." Newsweek

Jones, Stephen, 1953-

(ed) The Best horror from Fantasy Tales.
See The Best horror from Fantasy Tales

(ed) Best new horror [1]-4. See Best new
horror [1]-4

Jones, Ted, 1937-

Hard road to Gettysburg; a novel. Lyford
Bks. 1993 316p o.p.
LC 92-41960

This "Civil War novel finds identical twin brothers
pitted against each other when one brother impersonates
the other in order to spy on the Confederate army."
Booklist

"The premise and the numerous subplots may sound
somewhat preposterous, but in fact *Hard Road* has some
powerful writing . . . and manages to animate the human
aspect in the history." Publ Wkly

Jones, Thom

The pugilist at rest; stories. Little, Brown
1993 230p $18.95

ISBN 0-316-47302-2   LC 92-35762

Analyzed in Short story index
Contents: The pugilist at rest; Break on through; The
black lights; Wipeout; Mosquitoes; Unchain my heart;
"As of July 6, I am responsible for no debts other than
my own"; Silhouettes; I want to live!; A white horse;
Rocket man

"The grim locales that Jones depicts in this debut
collection include Vietnam, a mental asylum, the boxing
ring, an emergency room. Gritty, gory details are
heightened by the author's unflinching pessimism;
juxtapositions of quotes from Schopenhauer and Nietz-
sche are startingly apt. Jones is a new, irresistible voice."
Publ Wkly

Jong, Erica

Any woman's blues; a novel of obsession.
Harper & Row 1990 362p $18.95

ISBN 0-06-016272-4   LC 89-45676

The painter Leila Sand "is addicted to a younger man,
the . . . handsome narcissist, D.V. 'Dart' Donegal. . .
. Leila's efforts to free herself . . . result in a sensual
and spiritual odyssey that takes her from Alcoholics
Anonymous meetings to violent performance art in a
pitch-black East Village nightclub, from glittering parties
with SoHo celebrities, painters, art dealers, drug addicts,
and 'debutramps' to a liaison with a millionaire antique
merchant." Publisher's note

"This work begins with lots of promise, and the narrative is jazzed up with Jong's trademark raucous exploits
and on-the-mark observations; the running theme of
duality also adds interest." Libr J

Fear of flying; a novel. Holt, Rinehart &
Winston 1973 340p o.p.

Isadora Wing, the heroine "is twice-married, Barnard-
educated, under thirty, and . . . fiercely restless. . . .
In Vienna with her psychiatrist husband, she meets an
English Laingian who . . . exhorts her to cast off marital
ties and live by his self-proclaimed existentialist nonrules.
. . . After two weeks of roaring about the Continent
in a Triumph, coupling with each other and with
strangers met in roadside camps, they split: it's time for
the English existentialist to rejoin his wife and kids.
Spirits intact, Isadora hunts up her husband's holiday
digs; finding him away when she calls, she awaits his
return (on the closing page) in his tub." Atlantic

"At times, Jong gets caught in clichés about women,
men, sex, and Jewish mothers, all [of] which she could
do without. However, when she takes herself more
seriously, the language is penetrating, paying tribute to
her worth as a poet." Libr J

Followed by How to save your own life (1977) and
Parachutes and kisses (1984 paper only)

Jönsson, Reidar, 1944-

My life as a dog; translated by Eivor Martinus. Farrar, Straus & Giroux 1990 219p $17.95

ISBN 0-374-35108-2   LC 89-46390

Original Swedish edition, 1983; this translation first published 1989 in the United Kingdom

"This novel focuses on "the thirteenth and fourteenth years of a Swedish boy named Ingemar Johansson. Ingemar's mother is dying of tuberculosis, and his absentee father is away at sea. Somehow Ingemar repeatedly falls into exploits, scrapes, and disasters that, he thinks, make his mother's condition worse. Ingemar is . . . sent away to live with his uncle. . . . [His dog Sickan] is put to sleep because no one can spare the time and attention to care for it." Horn Book

"The novel's anecdotal style accommodates a boy's confabulation. Occasionally wayward and a bit too long in their descriptions, his comedic exploits cast Ingemar as schlemiel, underdog and, yes, dog. . . . It is Sickan's fate that finally helps Ingemar come to terms with his dead mother." N Y Times Book Rev

Jordan, Anne Devereaux, 1943-

(ed) The Best horror stories. See The Best horror stories

Jordan, Laura, 1948-

For works written by this author under other names see Brown, Sandra, 1948-

Jorgenson, Ivar

For works written by this author under other names see Silverberg, Robert

Joyce, James, 1882-1941

Dubliners. Knopf 1991 lv, 287p $15

ISBN 0-679-40574-7   LC 91-53001

First published 1914 in the United Kingdom; first United States edition published 1916 by Huebsch; first Modern Library edition 1926 analyzed in Short story index

Contents: The sisters; An encounter; Araby; Eveline; After the race; Two gallants; The boarding house; A little cloud; Counterparts; Clay; A painful case; Ivy day in the committee room; A mother; Grace; The dead

"This collection of 15 stories provides an introduction to the style and motifs found in Joyce's writing. The stories stand alone as individual scenes of Dublin society and are intertwined by the use of autobiography and symbolism." Shapiro. Fic for Youth. 3d edition

Finnegans wake. Viking 1939 628p o.p.

This novel is "written in a unique and extremely difficult style, making use of puns and portmanteau words, and a very wide range of allusion. The central theme of the work is a cyclical pattern of fall and resurrection. This is presented in the story of Humphrey Chimpden Earwicker, a Dublin tavern-keeper, and the book is apparently a dream-sequence representing the stream of his unconscious mind through the course of one night. Other characters are his wife Anna Livia Plurabelle, their sons Shem and Shaun, and their daughter Isabel." Oxford Companion to Engl Lit. 5th edition

A portrait of the artist as a young man. Available from various publishers

First appeared serially, 1914-1915 in the United Kingdom, first United States edition published 1916 by Huebsch

This autobiographical novel "portrays the childhood, school days, adolescence, and early manhood of Stephen Dedalus, later one of the leading characters in Ulysses. Stephen's growing self-awareness as an artist forces him to reject the whole narrow world in which he has been brought up, including family ties, nationalism, and the Catholic religion. The novel ends when, having decided to become a writer, he is about to leave Dublin for Paris. Rather than following a clear narrative progression, the book revolves around experiences that are crucial to Stephen's development as an artist; at the end of each chapter Stephen makes some assertion of identity. Through his use of the stream of consciousness technique, Joyce reveals the actual materials of his hero's world, the components of his thought processes." Reader's Ency. 3d edition

A shorter Finnegans wake; edited by Anthony Burgess. Viking 1967 c1966 xxviii, 256p il o.p.

An abridgement of the work listed above

The text of Finnegans Wake reproduced in part in this book is that of the 1958 Viking Press edition, in which Joyce's own corrections made in the finished book shortly before his death were for the first time incorporated in the text

"Burgess has reduced the text to somewhat over a third of its original length and has attempted through a bracketed running commentary to explain the [novel's] multilayered and multilingual allusions, puns, parodies, verbal music, and plot threads." Libr J

Ulysses; the corrected text prepared by Hans Walter Gabler with Wolfhard Steppe and Claus Melchior. Random House 1986 608p $29.95

ISBN 0-394-55373-X   LC 85-28279

First published 1922

"The novel is constructed as a modern parallel to Homer's Odyssey. All of the action of the novel takes place in Dublin on a single day (June 16, 1904). The three central characters—Stephen Dedalus (the hero of Joyce's earlier Portrait of the Artist as a Young Man), Leopold Bloom, a Jewish advertising canvasser, and his wife Molly Bloom—are intended to be modern counterparts of Telemachus, Ulysses, and Penelope, and the events of the novel parallel the major events in Odysseus' journey home. The main stream of Ulysses lies in its depth of character portrayal and its breadth of humor." Merriam-Webster's Ency of Lit

K

Kafka, Franz, 1883-1924

Amerika; translated by Edwin Muir; preface by Klaus Mann; afterword by Max Brod; illustrated by Emlen Etting. Schocken Bks. 1962 299p il o.p.

Original German edition, 1927; this translation first published 1938 in the United Kingdom

The narrative of this unfinished novel "concerns the efforts of young Karl Rossmann, newly arrived in America, to find his place in an enigmatic and hostile society. The account of his expulsion from his parents' household in Prague following an affair with the family cook enhibits the surreal distortion of memory that characterizes much of Kafka's best work. The narration becomes increasingly conventional, however, in the later sections recounting Karl's exploitation. The novel breaks off just as the protagonist has seemingly found his niche with the traveling Oklahoma Theater." Merriam-Webster's Ency of Lit

The castle. Knopf 1992 378p $17

ISBN 0-679-41735-4   LC 92-52904

"Everyman's library"
Original German edition, 1926

The hero, "known only as K., is constantly frustrated in his efforts to gain entrance into a mysterious castle, which is administered by an extraordinarily complicated and inaccessible bureaucratic hierarchy. The book invites allegorical interpretation; K.'s striving has been seen as the human quest for comprehension of the ways of an incomprehensible God and his frustration has been seen as symbolic of the actual human condition. But apart from any exact interpretation, the novel clearly reflects Kafka's convictions about the problematic nature of human existence, as well as his stylistic mastery and frequent ironic humor." Reader's Ency

Collected stories; edited and introduced by Gabriel Josipvici. Knopf 1993 lv, 503p $20

ISBN 0-679-42303-6   LC 93-1858

"Everyman's library"
Analyzed in Short story index

Contents: Children on a country road; Unmasking a confidence trickster; The sudden walk; Resolutions; Excursion into the mountains; Bachelor's ill luck; The tradesman; Absent-minded window-gazing; The way home; Passers-by; On the tram; Clothes; Rejection; Reflections for gentlemen-jockeys; The street window; The wish to be a red Indian; The trees; Unhappiness; The judgment; The stoker; The metamorphosis; In the penal colony; The new advocate; A country doctor; Up in the gallery; An old manuscript; Before the law; Jackals and Arabs; A visit to a mine; The next village; An imperial message; The cares of a family man; Eleven sons; A fratricide; A dream; A report to an Academy; The bucket rider; First sorrow; A little woman; A hunger artist; Josephine the singer; Description of a struggle; Wedding preparations in the country; The student; The angel; The village schoolmaster [the giant mole]; Blumfeld, an elderly bachelor; The Hunter Gracchus; The proclamation; The bridge; The Great Wall of China; The knock at the manor gate; An ancient sword; New lamps; My neighbor; A crossbreed [a sport]; A splendid beast; The watchman; A common confusion; The truth about Sancho Panza; The silence of the sirens; Prometheus; The city coat of arms; Poseidon; Fellowship; At night; The problem of

our laws; The conscription of troops; The test; The vulture; The helmsman; The top; Hands; A little fable; Isabella; Home-coming; A Chinese puzzle; The departure; Advocates; Investigations of a dog; The married couple; Give it up!; On parables; The burrow

The complete stories; edited by Nahum N. Glatzer; with a new foreword by John Updike. Centennial ed. Schocken Bks. 1983 xxi, 486p il o.p.

LC 83-3233

Analyzed in Short story index
First published 1971

The longer stories included are: Description of a struggle; Wedding preparations in the country; The judgment; The metamorphosis; In the penal colony; The village schoolmaster; Blumfeld, an elderly bachelor; A country doctor; The Hunter Gracchus; The Great Wall of China; A report to an Academy; The refusal; A hunger artist; Investigations of a dog; A little woman; The burrow; Josephine the singer

"The stories are divided into two groups—longer and shorter—and are arranged chronologically, insofar as is possible, within each group. Publishing history is given for each story." Libr J

Metamorphosis. Vanguard Press 1945 98p il o.p. Amereon reprint available $16.95 (ISBN 0-88411-450-3)

Written in 1915 this is "often regarded as Kafka's most perfect finished work. 'The Metamorphosis' begins as its hero, Gregor Samsa, awakens one morning to find himself changed into a huge insect; the story proceeds to develop the effects of this change upon Gregor's business and family life, and ends with his death. It has been read as everything from a religious allegory to a psychoanalytic case history; but its really attractive qualities are its clarity of depiction and attention to significant detail, which give its completely fantastic occurrences an aura of indisputable truth, so that no allegorical interpretaion is necessary to demonstrate its greatness." Reader's Ency. 3d edition

also in Kafka, F. Collected stories p73-128

also in Kafka, F. The complete stories

also in Kafka, F. The metamorphosis and other stories p117-92

also in Kafka, F. The penal colony: stories and short pieces

also in Kafka, F. Selected short stories of Franz Kafka

The metamorphosis and other stories; translated by Joachim Neugroschel. Scribner 1993 xxiii, 227p $25

ISBN 0-684-19426-0   LC 92-43912

Analyzed in Short story index

Contents: Conversation with the worshiper; Conversation with the drunk; Great noise; Children on the highway; Exposing a city slicker; The sudden stroll; Decisions; The outing in the mountains; The bachelor's unhappiness; The businessman; Absently gazing out; The way home; The people running by; The passenger; Frocks; The rejection; Reflections for amateur jockeys; The window facing the street; The wish to be an Indian; The trees; Unhappiness; The judgment; The stoker; The

Kafka, Franz, 1883-1924—*Continued*
metamorphosis; The new lawyer; An ancient manuscript; Jackals and Arabs; A fratricide; A dream; A report for an Academy

The penal colony: stories and short pieces; translated by Willa and Edwin Muir. Schocken Bks. 1948 320p il o.p.

Analyzed in Short story index
Stories included are: The judgment; The metamorphosis; A country doctor; In the penal colony; A hunger artist

Selected short stories of Franz Kafka; translated by Willa and Edwin Muir; introduction by Philip Rahv. Modern Lib. 1993 xxv, 346p $14.50

ISBN 0-679-60061-2   LC 93-14747

Analyzed in Short story index
First Modern Library edition published 1952
Contents: The judgment; The metamorphosis; In the penal colony; The Great Wall of China; The country doctor; Common confusion; New advocate; Old manuscripts; A fratricide; Report to an Academy; Hunter Gracchus; A hunger artist; Investigations of a dog; The burrow; Josephine the singer

The trial; translated from the German by Willa and Edwin Muir; revised, with additional notes, by E. M. Butler. Knopf 1992 299p $17

ISBN 0-679-40994-7
"Everyman's library"
Original edition, 1924; first Everyman's Library edition, 1922
"Joseph K., a respected bank assessor, is arrested and spends his remaining years fighting charges about which he has no knowledge. The helplessness of an insignificant individual within a mysterious bureaucracy where answers are never accessible is described in this provocative and disturbing book." Shapiro. Fic for Youth. 3d edition

Kallen, Lucille
C. B. Greenfield: a little madness. Random House 1986 181p o.p.

LC 85-18290

"Charlie Greenfield, suburban news editor, has solved some murders . . . [with] reporter Maggie Rome, who, though happily (or steadily) married, has for years kept her blood on the simmer by exchanging quips with her maddeningly mandarin boss. But when Greenfield drops a bomb in the form of a crush on a red-haired British violinist, Maggie's blood boils. Unbecomingly jealous, she flees—possibly through a subconscious association—to a woman's peace rally at a nearby missile base. But there her rival precedes her, and her employer follows. And when a conservative political figure disappears, personal problems are disconcertingly entangled with public ones. . . . Lucille Kallen's books have a New England braininess and suavity quite comforting to modern readers." N Y Times Book Rev

C. B. Greenfield: no lady in the house. Wyndham Bks. 1982 224p o.p.

LC 81-21839

"A rash of burglaries has hit the small town of Sloan's Ford. Finally the stereo of newspaper editor C. B. Greenfield is stolen—and the body of an immigrant cleaning woman left instead. Greenfield insists on investigating this personal outrage himself by sending reporter Maggie Rome to interview the circle of dissatisfied women who employed the dead woman." Libr J

C. B. Greenfield: the piano bird. Random House 1984 175p o.p.

LC 83-43197

This Maggie Rome-C.B. Greenfield mystery "takes the couple to an island off the Florida coast. At least, it first takes Maggie there. She is playing nurse to her mother, who is laid up with disc problems. A group of theater people is on the island. Maggie observes the tensions among them. Murder ensues, and Greenfield, who wants Maggie back at his weekly newspaper in Connecticut, arrives to solve the case." N Y Times Book Rev

C. B. Greenfield: the Tanglewood murders. Wyndham Bks. 1980 222p o.p.

LC 80-12803

"The story begins with Maggie Rome and her boss Charlie Greenfield arriving to cover the concerts at Tanglewood. During a rehearsal, violinist Noel Damaskin drops dead of poison and Charlie instantly pushes Maggie into racing around after clues involving a number of suspects with reasons to loathe Noel." Publ Wkly
"Miss Kallen has a light touch that gives her story a brittle humor and good-natured tartness. Her characters are believable and so is their speech. She writes knowledgeably about the subjects involved—music, poison and Tanglewood." Books of the Times

Kaminsky, Stuart M.
Buried caesars; a Toby Peters mystery. Mysterious Press 1989 179p o.p.

LC 88-25449

"It's September 1942, and Gen. Douglas MacArthur has hired private eye Toby Peters to recover some incriminating papers that might keep the general from going into public life after the war. The papers, and funds that could help MacArthur finance a campaign, have been stolen by a civilian aide, Andrew Lansing. Meanwhile, Peters is offered the services of another detective, former Pinkerton op Dashiell Hammett, who's hiding out from Lillian Hellman while trying to recover his health so he can enlist in the army. The chase leads the two to Angel Springs, Calif., and to the mysterious and eccentric millionaire, Mr. Pintacki, who has his own ideas about keeping America great, which don't include a general as president." Publ Wkly

A cold red sunrise; an Inspector Porfiry Rostnikov mystery. Scribner 1988 210p o.p.

LC 88-15359

"Inspector Porfiry Rostnikov of the Moscow police . . . is assigned to Tumsk in deepest Siberia. . . . Two people have died mysteriously—the young and beautiful daughter of a famed dissident father who is scheduled, in the new climate of 'glasnost,' to depart for the West, and the police Commisar from Moscow who was sent to Tumsk to investigate her death. With him on this mission is his trusted associate, Emil Karpo." West Coast Rev Books

Kaminsky, Stuart M.—*Continued*

"The author has fine-tuned Porfiry and Karpo into a delightful sleuthing team and a fascinating study in odd contrasts." Booklist

Death of a Russian priest. Fawcett Columbine 1992 223p o.p.

LC 91-58638

In this Inspector Porfiry Rostnikov mystery "two crimes need solving: the disappearance of a Syrian diplomat's daughter and the ax murder of a prominently outspoken priest. The missing girl becomes the preoccupation of Rostnikov's emotionally messed-up young assistant Sasha, while Rostnikov himself, working with the vampiric Karpo, uncovers the priest's secret life, hindered by silent friends who seem to be dying for their loyalty." Booklist

The devil met a lady. Mysterious Press 1993 194p $18.95

ISBN 0-89296-436-7   LC 92-50659

Los Angeles PI Toby Peters "is hired to protect Bette Davis by her second husband, pilot Arthur Farnsworth. Knowing that Farnsworth has access to plans for a new bombsight, Nazi agents threaten to abduct Davis and destroy her career by airing a secret recording of her tryst with Howard Hughes. The slightly goofy gang kidnaps Davis twice and Peters three times before the almost farcical climax. The plotting is as fast and intricate as the characters are colorful." Publ Wkly

Lieberman's choice; [by] Stuart Kaminsky. St. Martin's Press 1993 216p $18.95

ISBN 0-312-08836-1   LC 92-40797

"A Thomas Dunne book"

Abe Lieberman is "an aging Jewish Chicago cop who's comfortable and at ease on the street but troubled by his domestic life. He can handle the perpetrators but is puzzled by the paths that end in violence. The case here involves a cop who kills his wife and her lover and then barricades himself atop an apartment building. Political expediency clashes repeatedly with prudence as Abe struggles with the situation." Booklist

"Abe's conversation—whether with his old Jewish buddies, some small-time cons or his family—is pure pleasure, with never a false, extraneous note." Publ Wkly

Lieberman's day; [by] Stuart Kaminsky. Holt & Co. 1994 260p $19.95

ISBN 0-8050-2575-8   LC 93-22910

Chicago homicide detective Abe Lieberman's "nephew, David, and David's pregnant wife are shot in a late night mugging. David dies; his wife and unborn child survive, barely. Lieberman gets the case and in the following 24 hours deals with the grief of his brother and sister-in-law, the aftereffects of the collapse of his daughter's marriage, the desperate deal he cuts with a violent drug-dealer called El Perro to catch the killers and the busting of two con artists." Publ Wkly

The author is "extraordinarily attuned to the domestic minutiae of his detectives' lives." N Y Times Book Rev

Lieberman's folly; [by] Stuart Kaminsky. St. Martin's Press 1991 216p o.p.

LC 90-49309

"A Thomas Dunne book"

This mystery "features the partnership of Chicago cops Abe 'Rabbi' Lieberman and Bill 'Father Murphy' Hanrahan. When prostitute Estralda Valdez, a past informer, asks the pair for protection, tippler Hanrahan agrees to watch her apartment from a Chinese restaurant across the street. After Valdez is murdered during Hanrahan's watch, he and Lieberman investigate her death, despite the objections of their captain, who is unhappy about negative publicity." Publ Wkly

The man who walked like a bear; an Inspector Porfiry Rostnikov novel. Scribner 1990 261p o.p.

LC 89-29082

"Beset by the usual demons (including the plumbing in his apartment), visited by a few new ones, and still a thorn in the side of the Soviet bureaucracy, Rostnikov must deal with a host of problems: . . . a plot to kill a Politburo member, shady deals in a Moscow shoe factory, and several demented nationalists who mastermind a scheme to destroy Lenin's tomb. Then there's the inspector's sick wife to visit in the hospital and the matter of getting his son out of the military." Booklist

"Kaminsky masterfully balances stories of family life, humorous anecdotes and riveting suspense involving his distinctive characters." Publ Wkly

The melting clock. Mysterious Press 1991 198p $17.95

ISBN 0-89296-435-9   LC 91-50203

In this mystery Hollywood detective Toby Peters' services are retained by surrealist Salvador Dali. "The case begins as something of a lark, with Toby tossing wisecracks over his shoulder as he chases the thief who made off with three of Dali's paintings and three antique clocks belonging to his Russian-born wife. But when two corpses show up, along with two mutilated canvases, Dali admits that an elaborate joke, his little *chiste*, has taken a dark and dangerous turn." N Y Times Book Rev

Poor butterfly. Mysterious Press 1990 179p $17.95

ISBN 0-89296-411-1   LC 89-40524

"Leopold Stokowski's San Francisco performance of *Madame Butterfly* faces opposition from many sides. The local zealots are concerned with the pro-Japanese content of the opera (it's 1942), and more sinister trouble brews from the Phantom-like soul raising havoc from high above the stage. The maestro calls on Toby [Peters] and his band of crack operatives—assorted dwarves, dentists, and an existentialist ex-wrestler—to sort things out." Booklist

Rostnikov's vacation; an Inspector Porfiry Rostnikov novel. Scribner 1991 244p $19.95

ISBN 0-684-19022-2   LC 91-13874

Also available Thorndike Press large print edition

"While on forced vacation in Yalta, Rostnikov chances upon the murder of an acquaintance from military intelligence. He also befriends an American policeman, who points out the man tailing Rostnikov. Back in Moscow, meanwhile, Rostnikov's subordinates track a beautiful young woman and two accomplices connected with the murder of a German businessman. Kaminsky solidly and ably controls all these complications, but not without offering certain political vagaries, a cold-blooded atmosphere, and a certain dry humor." Libr J

Think fast, Mr. Peters; [by] Stuart Kaminsky. St. Martin's Press 1987 198p $15.95

ISBN 0-312-01520-8   LC 87-27616

Kaminsky, Stuart M.—*Continued*

"A Thomas Dunne book"

This mystery set in 1940s Los Angeles features detective Toby Peters. "Searching for his client's wife, who supposedly ran away with Peter Lorre, Peters soon finds himself suspect in the murder of Pete R. Lowry, a Lorre look-alike." Libr J

Kantor, MacKinlay, 1904-1977

Andersonville. World Pub. 1955 767p il o.p.

Available from Buccaneer Bks. and P. Smith

"A lovely woodland in southwestern Georgia was transformed into the Confederacy's largest prison camp administered by a senile general who derived savage satisfaction from watching Yankees die of exposure, starvation, and disease. Individual stories merge to create an indelible impression of sublimity amidst degradation within the prison, and of the shamed helplessness of cultured Southerners unable to counter the inhumanity of the dregs of their armies." Booklist

Valley Forge; a novel. Evans & Co. 1975 339p o.p.

"Kantor's panorama is a composite of glances at what went on during the famous winter at Valley Forge in the American Revolution. With a style evocative of period vernacular, the author . . . spotlights a sampling of soldiers ranging from a teenage deserter to General Washington, depicting the hardships that were encountered and some not survived." Booklist

Kanwar, Asha

(ed) The Unforgetting heart: an anthology of short stories by African American women (1859-1993). See The Unforgetting heart: an anthology of short stories by African American women (1859-1993)

Katkov, Norman

Blood & orchids. St. Martin's Press 1983 503p o.p.

LC 83-2889

"Set in Hawaii in the early '30s, [this] crime novel is based on an actual case. The story begins when a quartet of beach boys play Good Samaritan and end up accused of beating and raping the U.S. naval officer's wife they rescued, Hester Murdock. The trial brings to a boil the simmering racial tensions in the islands, and when it ends in a hung jury, vigilante justice takes over. Three of the boys are kidnapped and flogged by sailors, while the other is shot to death. A flamboyant trial lawyer named Bergman is imported from the States to defend the accused: Hester's husband, Gerald; Doris Ashby, her mother; and a hapless gob who was in the wrong place at the wrong time. As Honolulu detective Curt Maddox digs deeper into the matter, the situation is revealed to be even more sordid and scandalous than originally supposed. Studded with vivid characterizations, the story rolls inexorably to an awesome, tragic conclusion." Publ Wkly

Katzenbach, John

Just cause. Putnam 1992 431p o.p.

LC 91-15135

"Matthew Cowart is at the top of his profession—a member of the editorial page staff of a major Miami newspaper. Cowart thinks his days as a crime reporter are behind him until he receives a letter from death row inmate Robert Ferguson, who not only proclaims his innocence, but also to have learned the identity of the real murderer. Cowart, his personal life a mess, takes the bait, hits the crime beat again, and writes a series of articles that lead to Ferguson's release and win the journalist a Pulitzer Prize. But Cowart has opened a Pandora's box of events which leads to a showdown with the killer." Libr J

"Despite some extraneous subplots, the story generally proceeds at a breakneck pace, enhanced by ear-perfect dialogue and complex characterization." Publ Wkly

Kaufman, Bel

Up the down staircase. Prentice-Hall 1964 340p il o.p. Buccaneer Bks. reprint available $21.95 (ISBN 1-56849-148-4)

"Fresh from graduate study in English and crammed with pedagogy courses, young Sylvia Barrett begins her first year as a teacher in Calvin Coolidge High School. The experiences of this first year teacher, determined to remain true to her ideals despite the administrative confusion and organizational chaos of a New York City high school, form the core of Up the Down Staircase. . . . It tells its story through a series of letters, administrative memoranda, student compositions, suggestion box contributions, and intraschool communications." Best Sellers

Kaufman, Sue

Diary of a mad housewife. Random House 1967 311p o.p.

"Bettina Balser, in her mid-thirties, with a husband, two daughters ages nine and seven, and a bright apartment on Central Park West, (New York City), has arrived at a point in her life where she has completely lost her way, her purpose, her identity. She is literally terrified of so many things . . . that she is also afraid she is losing her mind. She decides to write out the things that so alarm her, as a form of therapy." Best Sellers

Kawabata, Yasunari, 1899-1972

Nobel Prize in literature, 1968

Snow country

In Kawabata, Y. Snow country, and Thousand cranes p1-175

Snow country, and Thousand cranes; the Nobel Prize edition of two novels; translated from the Japanese by Edward G. Seidensticker. Knopf 1969 2v in 1 o.p.

First United States editions published 1957 and 1959, respectively

Snow country "describes the three visits of Shimamura, a rich Tokyo dilettante, to a hotspring in the west of Japan, the snowiest region in the world. Here a young geisha, Komako, becomes his mistress and falls in love with him. . . . Komako's sparkling freshness stirs him, and he is touched by the 'irresistible sadness' she makes him feel, a sense of beauty going to waste and of immanent decay. But he cannot return her love; and their

Kawabata, Yasunari, 1899-1972—*Continued*
strange relationship, to which she gives so much, is doomed from the start." Atlantic

Thousand cranes is entered separately

The sound of the mountain; translated from the Japanese by Edward M. Seidensticker. Knopf 1970 276p o.p.

"This translation of the 1954 novel . . . is set in post-occupation Tokyo and Kamakura. An elderly businessman, nearing retirement, attempts to come to grips with the practical problems of the failing marriages of both his children and the psychological problems resulting from deaths of close friends and abortions completed or desired by his daughter-in-law and his son's mistress. Behind all is the nagging suspicion that his affection for his daughter-in-law is greater than that he has for his own daughter because the daughter-in-law resembles his early lost love, his wife's sister." Libr J

"The language is delicate, allusive, intensely Japanese; and, since plot and character development count for little, the style is all-important. We are fortunate that it should have been a writer with Mr. Seidensticker's gifts who ventured to convey [Kawabata's] rarefied novels into English." N Y Times Book Rev

Thousand cranes; translated by Edward G. Seidensticker. Knopf 1959 c1958 147p o.p.

Original Japanese edition, 1949

"This melancholy tale uses the classical tea ceremony as a background for the story of a young man's relationships to two women, his father's former mistress and her daughter. Although it has been praised for the beauty of its spare and elegant style, the novel has also been criticized for its coldness and its suggestion of nihilism." Merriam-Webster's Ency of Lit

also in Kawabata, Y. Snow country and Thousand cranes p3-147

Kay, Terry
Shadow song. Pocket Bks. 1994 388p $20
ISBN 0-671-89261-4   LC 94-15369

"Naïve and gentlemanly Madison Lee ('Bobo') Murphy is 17 when, in 1955, he leaves rural Georgia to work at a resort in the Catskills, where he experiences instant culture shock among the inn's Jewish clientele. He comes under the influence of Avrum Feldman, an elderly eccentric who has devoted his life to the memory of Amelita Galli-Curci, the legendary soprano. . . . Avrum encourages Bobo when he falls chastely in love with Amy Lourie, a rich Jewish girl from New York visiting the resort with her protective parents. . . . Now, 38 years later, Bobo has returned to the Catskills to bury Avrum—and discovers that Amy is there too." Publ Wkly

"An absolutely enchanted and lyrical testimonial to the indomitable spirit of friendship and the tenacity of true love." Booklist

Kaye, M. M. (Mary Margaret), 1908-
Death in Berlin. St. Martin's Press 1985 254p o.p.

LC 85-1733

First published 1955 with title: Death walked in Berlin
This murder mystery is "set mainly in West Berlin in 1953, before cold war preoccupations had overshadowed concern about the Nazi evil. Young Miranda Brand, its English heroine, is appealing in the innocent way fictional characters nowadays rarely are. An orphan, she is wraith-thin, lovely-looking, intelligent and compassionate. Simon Lang, the mysterious hero, can't resist her. The plot revolves around a fortune in Dutch diamonds that was stolen by the Nazis and then disappeared—along with Herr Ridder, the functionary entrusted with them, and his wife. . . . This well-paced mystery has a nicely sustained atmosphere of menace." N Y Times Book Rev

Death in Kashmir. St. Martin's Press 1984 332p o.p.

LC 84-11748

Revised version of the novel first published 1953 in the United Kingdom with title: Death walked in Kashmir
Set in Kashmir, the book "involves the efforts of an intrepid heroine to uncover the circumstances surrounding a bizarre series of murders. Young Sarah Parrish becomes unwittingly entangled in a treacherous plot that threatens the safety of the entire free world, and during the course of her investigations she stumbles onto important evidence, places her own life in grave jeopardy, and finds true love." Booklist

"The setting—Kashmir's mountains, lakes, houseboats and hotels—comes exotically, enticingly alive. And the narrative unfolds superbly." N Y Times Book Rev

Death in Kenya. St. Martin's Press 1983 308p o.p.

Revised version of the novel first published 1958 under the author's pseudonym Mollie Hamilton, with title: Later than you think

"On a vast cattle farm in Kenya's Rift Valley, a battalion of characters is assembled: Em, crusty matriarch who thinks nothing of leaping into her land rover to shoot a wild gazelle or two when her beloved dogs run out of fresh meat; Eden, her handsome son and presumptive heir; Alice, his timid, barren wife; Gilly, boozy, misplaced farm foreman who much prefers playing the piano and reciting Shakespeare sonorously to overseeing the workers; his wife Lisa, spendrift hussy lusting after Eden; high-spirited Victoria, Eden's cousin and one-time fiancée come from London to help her aging Aunt Em run the farm. A series of eerie poltergeistic happenings culminates in the murder of Alice, closely followed by the uncanny demises of Gilly and a native black farmhand." Publ Wkly

Death in the Andamans. St. Martin's Press 1986 301p o.p.

LC 86-1825

First published 1960 in the United Kingdom with title: Night on the island
This novel is "based on a trip the author made to the Andaman Islands in her youth. The tale begins with a terrifying tropical storm on Christmas Eve. Our hero, Copper, is visiting a friend on the sparsely populated islands and finds that one terror leads to another. Three gruesome murders are followed by the criminal's accidental suicide. But even after the murderer is revealed and done away with, the suspense goes on: Will Copper and the dashing but mysterious Nick get together?" Booklist

Death in Zanzibar. St. Martin's Press 1983 269p o.p.

LC 83-2946

Revised version of the novel first published 1959 with title: The house of shade
"Young Dany Ashton is invited to vacation at her stepfather's house in Zanzibar, but even before her air-

Kaye, M. M. (Mary Margaret), 1908- —
Continued

plane takes off there is a stolen passport, a midnight intruder—and murder. The house is named 'Kivulimi,' the mysterious 'House of Shade' where Captain Rory Frost of 'Trade Wind' [entered below] buried a fortune in gold a hundred years before. Dany and the rest of the houseguests learn that one of them is a desperate and ruthless murderer, determined to take for himself the hidden treasure, and the air of gaiety and nonchalance that opened the tropical house-party fades into growing terror." Publisher's note

The far pavilions. St. Martin's Press 1978 957p o.p.

LC 78-3975

This historical novel of India between the Mutiny of 1857 and the second Afghan war focuses on "the early life, loves, and military career of Ashton Pelham-Martyn, an impetuous Englishman born in mid-Victorian India, reared by a Hindu serving-woman, and educated in the stuffiest of British schools. Considered an odd duck by his fellow Englishmen for his liberal view on race, and held at arm's length by his Indian friends, Pelham-Martyn resolves undivided loyalties by serving as a secret agent for the British Guides. . . . A romantic subplot concerns his quest for an Indian princess he has loved all his life, and lost to a Rajah." Libr J
"It's a leisurely, panoramic, enjoyable tale, convincing and varied in characterization, rich in adventure, heroism, cruelty and love, rich in India." Publ Wkly

Shadow of the moon. St. Martin's Press 1979 614p o.p.

LC 79-5033

First published 1957 in the United Kingdom; an abridged version of this novel was published 1957, in the United States by Messner
The historical background of this novel "deals with the events leading up to and encompassing the Indian Mutiny of 1857, a rather haphazard rebellion by the Indian soldiers (Sepoys) against cruel and scornful British officers. . . . The novel tells the story of lovely Winter de Ballesteros, her premature engagement and marriage to the British Commissioner of Lunjore, her love for Captain Alex Randall, and her life and adventures in India. The book culminates in the bloody rebellion against the English which forces Alex and Winter, with two others, to flee into the shelter of the jungle." Best Sellers
The author exhibits "an intimate knowledge of Indian history, a deep feel for the land, unflagging vitality and an unfailing instinct for suspense. These qualities make her story delightfully readable." Publ Wkly

Trade wind. St. Martin's Press 1981 553p il o.p.

LC 80-28302

Rewritten and expanded version of a novel first published 1963 in the United Kingdom and 1964 in the United States
"Twenty-one year old Hero Athena Hollis sets out from Boston for Zanzibar to fulfill her mission in life—to stop slave trading. On the journey she is washed overboard and rescued by Rory Frost, a piratical slave trader. Stubborn, spoiled Hero clashes with equally stubborn, overconfident, wicked Rory. Disagreements come in rapid succession about her naïve assumptions, his overbearing manner, her proposed marriage, his occupa-

tion, etc. Palace intrigue, revolution, a pirate raid on the island, and a murder lead up to Rory's kidnapping of Hero." Libr J

Kaye, Mary Margaret *See* Kaye, M. M. (Mary Margaret), 1908-

Kazan, Elia

America, America; with an introduction by S. N. Behrman. Stein & Day 1962 190p o.p.

Copyright 1961 as an unpublished dramatic work with title: Hamal
"A young Greek boy, Stavros, pursues his intense desire to leave the tyranny of his land and seek a new life in America. As a means of attaining his goal, he accepts his family's offer to go to Constantinople with wealth and prized possessions where he is to establish himself in his uncle's rug business. After losing his family fortune enroute, he sinks to degradation in an effort to secure money for passage to America. After suffering incredible hardships his dream of America is realized." Wis Libr Bull
"Elia Kazan's book is a scenario, with the spareness, emphasis on the concrete, the appeal to eye and ear of the film story. It has a rugged simplicity, vividly sketched characters, and a strong story line." Libr J
Followed by The Anatolian (1982)

Kazantzakis, Nikos, 1883-1957

The last temptation of Christ; translated from the Greek by P. A. Bien. Simon & Schuster 1960 506p o.p.
"This novel is a retelling of the life story of Jesus of Nazareth as Kazantzakis imagined it might actually have happened, the human events from which the worshipful Gospel account was derived and their meaning to the people who experienced them." Atlantic
"The Christ created here by Kazantzakis is definitely not the Christ of the Gospels. . . . Far from it. Kazantzakis has composed a fictional biography of Jesus that is written with passion, a colorful, lyric testimony of his, Kazantzakis' own anguished search for God." Best Sellers

Zorba the Greek; translated by Carl Wildman. Simon & Schuster 1952 311p o.p. Buccaneer Bks. reprint available $26.95 (ISBN 1-56849-178-6)
"The spirit of Zorba, full of energy and peasant philosophy, is contrasted with that of the narrator, a learned but staid Englishman who comes to Crete for adventure. The relationship between the two men deepens despite Zorba's mismanagement of the narrator's mining business, and despite Zorba's attempts to change his friend's behavior to a more zestful one. Kazantzakis creates in Zorba a character that represents the vitality sapped by the inhibitions civilization has created." Shapiro. Fic for Youth. 3d edition

Keating, H. R. F. (Henry Reymond Fitzwalter), 1926-

The body in the billiard room. Viking 1987 247p o.p.

LC 87-40038

Keating, H. R. F. (Henry Reymond Fitz-walter), 1926- — *Continued*

"A Viking novel of mystery and suspense"
Inspector Ghote is "summoned to the hill station of Ootacamund ('Ooty') in South India, where he must locate a 'diabolically ingenious murderer.' A former ambassador, Surinder Mehta, calls upon Ghote to probe the death of Pichu, billiards marker at the genteel Ooty Club, gathering place for well-to-do Indians and English. Pichu has been found sprawled in the middle of the billiard table, stabbed in the heart; the murder weapon is missing, as are many of the club's silver trophies." Publ Wkly

Cheating death. Mysterious Press 1994 172p $18.95

ISBN 0-89296-512-6   LC 94-9502

This "Inspector Ghote novel finds the lovable Indian detective embroiled in an academic cheating scandal, under pressure from his superiors and vexed by pressing domestic business. When a final exam paper is circulated throughout Bombay's Oceanic College prior to the test, Ghote is sent to investigate, only to find his prime suspect in a coma, having tried to commit suicide (Or was it a murder attempt?)." Publ Wkly

Doing wrong; an Inspector Ghote novel. Penzler Bks. 1994 218p $20

ISBN 1-883402-80-8   LC 94-9287

"From Bombay, the exquisitely courteous, ever persistent police detective, Inspector Ghote, travels to the holy city of Banaras to find the murderer of the much loved Mrs. Popatkar, 'veteran freedom fighter, former Minister, upholder of a hundred good causes'. . . . In spite of a leisurely pace befitting a country where foot-sore pilgrims, sacred cattle and auto rickshaws clog the roads, this is an absorbing tale and an illuminating tour of Banaras." Publ Wkly

Go West, Inspector Ghote. Doubleday 1981 182p o.p.

LC 80-3008

"Published for the Crime Club"
"Ganesh Ghote is sent to California by a Bombay tycoon whose daughter has joined a dubious cult headed by a swami who may be no more than a confidence trickster. Ghote (called 'Goat' by the American private eye who helps him) gets the girl back to India, having 'exploded' the swami after some odd occurrences." Barzun. Cat of Crime. Rev and enl edition

The iciest sin. Mysterious Press 1990 183p $18.95

ISBN 0-89296-427-8   LC 90-6093

In this mystery Inspector Ghote of the Bombay police "becomes entangled in blackmail—what Rebecca West called 'the iciest sin'—and finds it everywhere, from his son's demands for a home computer to the tactics of hair-tonic advertisers." Publ Wkly

Inspector Ghote trusts the heart. Doubleday 1973 c1972 201p o.p.

"Published for the Crime Club"
First published 1972 in the United Kingdom
In this mystery "Inspector Ghote is the go-between in a kidnapping case. The child of a rich man is snatched. A mixup follows, and it is a poor man's son who is taken. The kidnappers still hold the rich man up for ransom, posing him with a terrible dilemma." N Y Times Book Rev

The author "writes with wonderful ease and energy—his understanding of the individuality of human beings is profound." New Yorker

The rich detective. Mysterious Press 1993 248p $18.95

ISBN 0-89296-506-1   LC 92-53719
Also available Thorndike Press large print edition

This mystery features "William Sylvester, a detective inspector with South Mercia CID. Often the butt of his colleague's jokes, Bill is a resolute, miserly, somewhat lonely chap. He lives for the hunt, taking the occasional break for Jude, a kindly whore, and a Spanish holiday. . . . Sylvester is convinced that antique dealer Charles Roanoke is a killer, separating several wealthy nursing-home residents from their fortunes, then mysteriously killing them off. But proving the influential Roanoke's guilt from within the force is hard." Publ Wkly

"Skillfully written, this is an intelligent detective novel with a sinister and unusual twist." Booklist

Keating, Henry Reymond Fitzwalter *See* Keating, H. R. F. (Henry Reymond Fitzwalter), 1926-

Keillor, Garrison

The book of guys; stories. Viking 1993 340p $22

ISBN 0-670-84943-X   LC 93-2168

Analyzed in Short story index
Contents: Lonesome Shorty; The Chuck show of television; The mid-life crisis of Dionysus; Buddy the leper; Mr. St. Paul; That old Picayune-Moon; Marooned; Don Giovanni; Roy Bradley, boy broadcaster; Gary Keillor; Omoo the wolf boy; The country mouse and the city mouse; Casey at the bat (road game); Herb Johnson, the god of Canton; Earl Grey; Winthrop Thorpe Tortuga; Al Denny; George Bush; Christmas in Vermont; Norman conquest; Zeus the Lutheran

"A few of the stories are flat, lacking the enhancement of the author's deadpan vocal delivery, but most are pretty funny and a few are even touching." Libr J

Happy to be here. Atheneum Pubs. 1982 210p o.p.

LC 81-66033

Analyzed in Short story index
Contents: Jack Schmidt, Arts Administrator; Don: the true story of a young person; My North Dakota railroad days; WLT (The Edgar era); The Slim Graves Show; Friendly neighbor; Attitude; Around the Horne; The new baseball; How are the legs, Sam?; U.S. still on top, says rest of world; Congress in crisis: the proximity bill; Re the tower project; How it was in America a week ago Tuesday; Shy rights: why not pretty soon; Mission to Mandalla; Nana hami ba reba; Plainfolks; The people's shopper; Your wedding and you; The lowliest bush a purple sage would be; Local family keeps son happy; Oya life these days; Your transit commission; Be careful; Ten stories for Mr. Richard Brautigan, and other stories; The drunkard's Sunday; Happy to be here; Drowning 1954

Lake Wobegon days. Viking 1985 337p o.p.

LC 85-40029

Keillor, Garrison—*Continued*

This book is the author's "history and season-by-season chronicle of his imaginary hometown, [Lake Wobegon]. . . . It's a town 'where nobody locks the doors or knows where the keys are,' where wearing black tennis shoes marks a boy for life and where it's thought that newfangled contraptions like dishwashers lead to degeneracy." Newsweek

"Much of this is satirical, but Keillor's subtle humor is gentle, rather than biting or mocking, as he exposes the foibles and faults of Lake Wobegonians with affection and sympathy." Publ Wkly

Leaving home. Viking 1987 xxiii, 244p o.p.

LC 87-40219

Analyzed in Short story index

Contents: A trip to Grand Rapids; A ten-dollar bill; Easter; Corinne; A glass of Wendy; The speeding ticket; Seeds; Chicken; How the crab apple grew; Truckstop; Dale; High rise; Collection; Life is good; Lyle's roof; Pontoon boat; State Fair; David and Agnes, a romance; The killer; Eloise; The royal family; Homecoming; Brethren; Thanksgiving; Darlene makes a move; Christmas dinner; Exiles; New Year's; Where did it go wrong?; Post office; Out in the cold; Hawaii; Hansel; Du, du liegst mir im herzen; Aprille; Goodbye to the lake

"These radio monologues [from A Prairie Home Companion] read easily, and listeners to the weekly radio show will find the flow of Keillor's distinctive flat rendition ringing in their ears." Wilson Libr Bull

WLT; a radio romance. Viking 1991 401p $21.95

ISBN 0-670-81857-7   LC 91-50160

This novel "chronicles the story of the birth (in 1926), ripening and decline of a Minneapolis radio station, the brainchild of the brothers Ray and Roy Soderbjerg. Its characters are WLT's principal staffers, both those on the mike and those behind it." N Y Times Book Rev

"Garrison Keillor's mythical America, unlike the faded and inoffensive Midwest of Sandburg, is dreamed with an unblinking eye. His characters are idiosyncratic. They are culled from who knows where—from our collective past, certainly, but also from the demotic oral tradition of a rich and very real community that is gone and now exists only in recollection." Nation

Kellerman, Faye

Day of atonement; a Peter Decker/Rina Lazarus mystery. Morrow 1991 359p o.p.

LC 90-22682

Available G.K. Hall large print edition

"When Los Angeles detective Peter Decker and new wife Rina Lazarus visit her Jewish kinfolks in Brooklyn, startling events disturb their honeymoon. Quite unexpectedly and with great antipathy, Decker—an adoptee—recognizes his natural mother at a holiday gathering. Before he can confront her, though, her troubled 14-year-old grandson goes missing and Decker, fortuitously on hand, begins the search. . . . Hard-hitting details, vignettes of Jewish life, and uncomfortably close glimpses of a cold-hearted psycho make this an entrancing page turner." Libr J

False prophet; a Peter Decker/Rina Lazarus mystery. Morrow 1992 367p $20

ISBN 0-688-10553-X   LC 91-36129

Also available G.K. Hall large print edition

"Cop Peter Decker is first on the crime scene. The victim, Lilah Brecht, is a beautiful health club owner, the daughter of a movie starlet, and a probable rape victim. But the medical details of the attack aren't crystal clear." Booklist

"Full attention to detail and characterization cap a masterful effort." Libr J

Grievous sin; a Peter Decker/Rina Lazarus mystery. Morrow 1993 368p $20

ISBN 0-688-10554-8   LC 93-12344

"Complications in the delivery room lead to major surgery for Rina Decker, who, when last seen in *False Prophet*, was pregnant with her and husband Peter Decker's first child. She is barely out of danger when an infant vanishes from the hospital's understaffed nursery, and proud father Peter, an LAPD detective sergeant, declares . . . 'I *owe* it to that little baby girl to find her.'" Publ Wkly

"While the plot comes dangerously close to being overly saccharine and annoyingly artificial, Kellerman does know how to hook her readers. First, she tantalizes them with ambiguous clues and ominous glimpses of an unbalanced villain's psyche, then she teases them with a blend of pulse-quickening suspense and heartwarming family tableaux. Only then does she deliver the shocking climax." Booklist

Milk and honey; a novel. Morrow 1990 384p o.p.

LC 89-39592

"On a summer night in a housing development near Los Angeles, police sergeant Peter Decker finds a winsome two-year-old girl playing on a swing set—and wearing blood-soaked pajamas. Unclaimed, 'Sally' is placed in a foster home while Decker and partner Marge Dunn try to learn her identity. Bee stings on her arms lead them days later to the scene of a bloody multiple murder at a honey farm. While piecing together a bizarre puzzle of betrayal and revenge . . . Peter is also investigating rape and assualt charges brought against an old army buddy from Vietnam. The pressures of the murder case and doubts about his friend's innocence compound Peter's anxiety as he waits for young Orthodox Jewish widow Rina Lazarus to decide if she will marry him." Publ Wkly

The quality of mercy; a novel. Morrow 1989 607p o.p.

LC 88-29275

"Rebecca Lopez and William Shakespeare first encounter each other in a London graveyard where she is burying her betrothed and he his mentor and best friend. Their paths cross again as they seek to avenge these untimely deaths, she joining in her family's mission to rescue fellow Jews from the Spanish Inquisition, he searching for the murderer among London's criminals. Shakespeare offers excitement and intellectual stimulation to the brilliant, adventurous Rebecca, stifled by the restricted life of an Elizabethan woman, but political and religious events overtake them and doom the relationship." Libr J

"Deft characterization and dazzling prose evoke the ambiance of the period. More than just a mystery, the novel is a spectacular epic—romantic, bawdy, witty and abounding with adventure." Publ Wkly

Sanctuary; a Peter Decker/Rina Lazarus mystery. Morrow 1994 396p $20

ISBN 0-688-04612-6   LC 94-11350

Kellerman, Faye—*Continued*

"L.A.P.D. sergeant Pete Decker and his Orthodox Jewish wife, Rina Lazarus, the parents of a baby daughter, are caught up in a case involving Rina's old school chum, Honey Klein, who comes to stay with the Deckers after leaving her diamond-merchant husband. When Honey and her children mysteriously disappear, Rina is first puzzled and then alarmed, especially considering that Pete is working on a double homicide involving another Jewish diamond merchant and his family. To solve the case, the Deckers travel to Israel and find themselves risking their lives to track down the disturbing truth." Booklist

Kellerman, Jonathan

Bad love. Bantam Bks. 1994 386p $22.95

ISBN 0-553-08919-6   LC 93-26678

Child "psychologist Alex Delaware receives a terrifying audiotape full of bloodcurdling screams and a disjointed voice chanting, 'Bad love, bad love.' Alex can't connect the tape with anything, but when he begins to get threatening phone calls, and someone brutally harpoons one of his beloved koi fish, he realizes he could be in danger. With the help of his friend, Detective Milo Sturgis, Delaware begins to unravel the complex, multilayered plot that seems to be linked to a conference he chaired 20 years ago. Delaware finally discovers he's being pursued by a tormented, relentless, deranged killer." Booklist

The author "spins a tight, complicated plot and is careful to balance his grisly murder scenes with substantive shoptalk about childhood trauma and the devastating effects of authoritarian discipline." N Y Times Book Rev

Devil's waltz. Bantam Bks. 1993 416p o.p.
     LC 92-18089

"Alex Delaware, the child psychologist and amateur sleuth . . . returns to the beleaguered Los Angeles pediatrics hospital where he was trained. Called in to consult on the baffling case of a 2-year-old girl with phantom ailments, Alex performs his clinical chores with his customary tenderness, while bearing the details of the child's extraordinary medical history. Despite Mr. Kellerman's overelaborate approach, he maintains the harrowing suspense of a medical mystery too horrid to be anything but real." N Y Times Book Rev

Over the edge. Atheneum Pubs. 1987 373p o.p.
     LC 86-47936

This novel featuring "child psychologist Alex Delaware begins with a desperate, garbled phone call from former patient Jamey Cadmus, genius of record and heir to a construction fortune. The next day, Jamey is accused of the Lavender Slashings, a series of grisly homosexual murders that have rocked Los Angeles. The teenager's lawyer asks Alex to examine Jamey's recent history with the hope that a plea of diminished capacity will protect Jamey from a prison sentence. Though soon fired, Alex continues his investigation." Publ Wkly

Private eyes. Bantam Bks. 1992 475p o.p.
     LC 91-17314

Available large print edition $25 (ISBN 0-385-42283-0)

"Harvard-bound, 18-year-old heiress Melissa Dickinson, whom child psychologist Alex Delaware had successfully treated for anxiety 10 years earlier, calls him with concerns about leaving her wealthy mother, an agoraphobe. Years before Melissa's birth, Gina Dickinson Ramp had been disfigured by acid thrown for never-revealed reasons by a former lover, now out of prison and back in town. Widowed for many years, recently remarried and making progress in her own intensive therapy with a noted husband-and-wife team of behaviorial psychologists, Gina is still fragile. When she disappears, Melissa enlists Delaware's help and that of his friend, Milo Sturgis, on leave from the LAPD. . . . Kellerman deftly handles the strings of his plot." Publ Wkly

Self-defense. Bantam Bks. 1995 390p $22.95

ISBN 0-553-08920-X   LC 94-26175

Psychologist Alex Delaware "is treating 25-year-old Lucy Lowell for a recurring nightmare that she has been having ever since serving on the hanging jury that convicted a serial killer. . . . When Lucy's terrifying dream is complicated by incidents of sleepwalking, bed-wetting, narcolepsy and a possible suicide attempt, Alex suspects a repressed childhood memory. After putting his patient through hypnotic regression, he is convinced that she witnessed a murder and he sets out to prove it. . . . An exciting story that is loaded with tension and packed with titillating insights into abnormal psychology." N Y Times Book Rev

Silent partner. Bantam Bks. 1989 404p o.p.
     LC 89-6490

"At a glitzy party, child psychologist Alex Delaware meets a woman from his past who seems troubled. When she is found dead later that night, Delaware decides to investigate. Combining a judicious use of psychological detail with suspenseful sleuthing, Kellerman's . . . novel is certain to increase the author's already substantial audience." Booklist

Time bomb; a novel. Bantam Bks. 1990 468p o.p.
     LC 90-349

Available large print edition $21.95 (ISBN 0-385-41578-8)

This novel featuring "child psychologist and private detective Alex Delaware begins when Delaware is called upon to deal with the potential trauma to elementary-school children of a sniper killed in their midst during lunch recess. He quickly learns that the sniper's target may not have been the children at all, but either a right-wing politician holding a news conference at the school or his liberal counterpart, a publicity-hungry, former 1960's radical who had appeared unexpectedly for an impromptu debate and whose bodyguard shot the sniper to death." N Y Times Book Rev

When the bough breaks. Atheneum Pubs. 1985 293p o.p.
     LC 81-16805

Psychologist Alex Delaware "turns detective when he is called upon to interview a young girl who is the only living witness to a brutal dual murder. Whatever the girl may have seen, the actual crime veils an even more horrible contemporary phenomenon: a ring of child molesters at a school in Southern California. The psychologist is soon out of his professional depth in pursuing clues and leads, but he plods onward to solve the case, nearly at the expense of the girl's and his own life. Kellerman's story is long on sensational descriptions and short on believable disclosures—too many of the good turns of fortune seem coincidentally opportune—but as a suspenseful drama, the novel does rack up its points." Booklist

Kellogg, Marjorie

Tell me that you love me, Junie Moon. Farrar, Straus & Giroux 1968 216p o.p.

"Junie Moon, in a rehabilitation center after a crazy boyfriend threw acid in her face, meets Warren, a paraplegic who has been shot in the spine on a hunting trip, and Arthur, who is slowly dying of a degenerative nerve disease. Amid the protests of the hospital staff the three decide to leave the center to set up a household. The reaction of their new neighbors is anything but encouraging, but one of them, an Italian fish merchant, befriends them and sends them on a vacation in his truck. It is a wonderful interlude until Arthur, recognizing that he is in the last stages of his illness, asks to be taken home to die." Shapiro. Fic for Youth. 3d edition

Kells, Susannah

The aristocrats. St. Martin's Press 1986 352p o.p.

LC 86-11908

First published in the United Kingdom with title: Coat of arms

"The focus of this novel is Howarth, an English stately home. The Marquess of Arlington and his wife will do nearly anything to keep it—he, because of his attachment to it, she because, as a middle-class girl, it establishes her aristocratic status. . . . He is willing to let his son make a disastrous marriage that will keep the estate in the family but finds that there are moral limits to what he will do for Howarth." Libr J

"In compact yet lyrically expressive prose, Kells portrays the materialism and pretentiousness of these allegedly genteel individuals. She also adroitly uses Howarth as an emblem of the social status without which they are merely unremarkable, even contemptible." Publ Wkly

Kelly, James Patrick

Mr. Boy

In Modern classic short novels of science fiction p561-616

Kelly, Patrick, 1917-

For works written by this author under other names see Allbeury, Ted, 1917-

Kelton, Elmer, 1926-

The far canyon. Doubleday 1994 323p $22.95

ISBN 0-385-24895-4   LC 93-44344

Also available Thorndike Press large print edition

"Ten years after the Civil War, Jeff Layne, a Confederate veteran weary of killing both men and buffalo, wends his way along dusty cattle trails toward his family ranch in Texas. When he gets to his hometown, however, he finds that the property has been stolen by the dastardly Vesper Freed, who also stole Jeff's girl, Eva, some years ago. Jeff decides to gather up some cattle and a party of companions and head to a remote canyon in north Texas to start up a new ranch. Along the way, the party encounters Crow Feather and his Comanche family, who are trying to escape from the newly formed reservation." Libr J

Slaughter. Doubleday 1992 369p o.p.

LC 92-10317

Available Thorndike Press large print edition

"Set on the Great Plains shortly after the end of the Civil War, the story focuses on the intertwining lives of a half dozen characters. Among them are Jeff Layne, a bitter, middle-aged Confederate veteran; Crow Feather, a proud Comanche warrior; Sully, a recently freed slave; and Arletta Browder, a displaced easterner who takes over her dead father's buffalo-hunting business. It is buffalo that throw them all together, the whites hoping to slaughter the great beasts for profit, the Indians hoping to preserve a way of life that requires the buffalo's survival." Booklist

"Well written and fast-paced, this powerful, moving novel proceeds inexorably toward the extinction of the great herds and of the indigenous peoples' way of life." Publ Wkly

Followed by The far canyon

Kemelman, Harry

The day the rabbi resigned. Fawcett Columbine 1992 273p o.p.

LC 91-72891

"Twenty-five years after coming to the Boston suburb of Barnard's Crossing, Rabbi David Small is considering retirement. But before he can get so much as one foot out of the pulpit, a local college professor dies in a car accident and the weary clergyman finds himself once again drawn from his own everyday concerns into more serious matters." Publ Wkly

"Mr. Kemelman's fans will be mollified by his clever resolution of Rabbi Small's career crisis, which is woven into a deft murder mystery involving several characters of different faiths." N Y Times Book Rev

Friday the rabbi slept late. Crown 1964 224p o.p.

"Rabbi Small, an unstylish young scholar, is up for contract renewal in a fashionable New England community, when a young girl's murdered body is found on the Temple grounds. Her purse is in his car. Because of his character, he is not a leading suspect and works with the Catholic police chief to find the killer." Book Week

"Here are conflict and suspense, understanding and conversation, and a remarkable Biblical explanation of the differences between priests, ministers and rabbis." Libr J

Monday the rabbi took off. Putnam 1972 316p o.p.

"The rabbi and his family set out for Israel. The action alternates between Massachusetts, where Rabbi Small may or may not be losing his congregation to the rabbi substituting for him, and Jerusalem, where he soon becomes embroiled in troubles involving a TV commentator, the commentator's son, and plotting Arab militants." Saturday Rev

"This is not so much a novel of mystery and detection as it is a beautifully conceived and executed novel of conditions in Israel and a rabbi's dilemma." Best Sellers

One fine day the rabbi bought a cross. Morrow 1987 234p o.p.

LC 86-23571

"Central to the plot is a Palestine Liberation Organization arms cache that Druse fighters would dearly love to steal. An American professor unwittingly delivers a letter with a map of the cache to a Druse agent in

Kemelman, Harry—*Continued*

Jerusalem. The American is promptly murdered. Rabbi Small is in Jerusalem and solves the case." N Y Times Book Rev

Saturday the rabbi went hungry. Crown 1966 249p o.p.

"The absent-minded knowledgeable young Rabbi, leader of a Conservative congregation, collaborates with his friend the Irish Catholic police chief in solving a mystery, this time deciding whether a death is murder or suicide and, if it is murder, who did it. The story is a good mixture of Jewish folk wisdom with modern community problems and with a murder mystery all nicely seasoned with humor." Publ Wkly

Someday the rabbi will leave. Morrow 1985 264p o.p.

LC 84-14766

"The new president of Rabbi David Small's temple is wealthy and influential Howard Magnuson, whose aim is to replace the rabbi with a man of his choice, less bound by the laws of Judaism. Small refuses to officiate at the wedding of Magnuson's daughter Laura to a gentile, John Scofield, but the rabbi has other problems more important than Magnuson's dwindling adherence to his faith. A young neighbor has been arrested for the hit-and-run killing of a local hood with ties to unscrupulous politicans. Small is convinced that the accused is innocent, and Talmudic reasoning (as well as luck) helps him to prove a case of murder and unmask the killer." Publ Wkly

Sunday the rabbi stayed home. Putnam 1969 253p o.p.

"After six years at the Temple in Barnard's Crossing, Rabbi David Small is a little weary of the politics, dissention and factionalism of his congregation, and slightly disconcerted by the idea of a 'swinging Passover Service.' The weekend visit to Massachusetts College doesn't provide the release he expects, but neither does it prepare him for dealing with the rash of modern urban problems that confront him on Sunday when the body of Moose Carter is found in the empty house on the beach after a college student cookout." Libr J

Thursday the rabbi walked out. Morrow 1978 250p o.p.

LC 78-8466

"Kemelman's famous town, Barnard's Crossing, is in a turmoil after the murder of mean, anti-Semitic Ellsworth Jordan. Again Police Chief Lanigan asks Rabbi Small for help with the case, complicated by too many suspects. Those with motive and opportunity include members of Small's flock. Maltzman, president of the Temple, is one. So are the head of the local bank and his secretary as well as the dead man's illegitimate son by a Jewish mother." Publ Wkly

Tuesday the rabbi saw red. Fields, A. 1974 c1973 276p o.p.

"The rabbi, who serves a small suburban New England congregation, takes on a new job—teaching a course in Jewish Thought at Windermere Christian College. He gets considerably more than he bargained for—students who argue every point, a faculty that occasionally patronizes him with a touch of anti-Semitism, even a bomb that goes off in the dean's office and leads to a murder. With skill, wit and courtesy he tackles everything from the generation gap between father and son to the solution to the killing." Publ Wkly

Wednesday the rabbi got wet. Morrow 1976 312p o.p.

In this story Rabbi Small "champions a young hippie, Akiva, suspected of causing a death. He has filled two prescriptions at his father's pharmacy. On the wet Wednesday, a wheeler-dealer member of Small's congregation, Safferstein, picks up the pills—a vial for his ailing wife and one for crotchety old Kestler. Kestler dies. His prescription is not what the doctor ordered. Dissension within the Temple's membership, with Small at odds with powerful men among them, adds to the excitement as the Rabbi applies Talmudic 'pilpul' (logical reasoning) to solve the problem of the switched dosage and exonerate the boy." Publ Wkly

Kenan, Randall

Let the dead bury their dead and other stories. Harcourt Brace Jovanovich 1992 334p $19.95

ISBN 0-15-149886-5   LC 91-36179

Analyzed in Short story index

Contents: Clarence and the dead; Things of this world; Foundations of the earth; The origin of whales; Cornsilk; The strange and tragic ballad of Mabel Pearsall; This far; Run, mourner, run; What are days?; Ragnarök! The day the gods die; Tell me, tell me; Let the dead bury their dead

"This collection of short fiction features residents of Tim Creek, North Carolina. Many of the pieces are fables of rural life, with dignified elders and lively young folk all wrapped in a warm blanket of shared family history and their African American heritage. . . . Possessing a tone of passionate authority, these varied stories exhibit the author's breadth and command the reader's considered attention." Booklist

Keneally, Thomas

Confederates. Harper & Row 1980 c1979 427p o.p.

LC 80-7606

First published 1979 in the United Kingdom

"Several impressionistic stories, blends of fact and fiction, are woven into [this novel] of American Civil War as seen from the Southern side. The focus is not so much on the strategy of generals or the schemes of politicians as on the lot of the white farm boys who made up the core of the Confederate armies. There is Usaph, a Shenandoah Volunteer, tortured by the thought that the beautiful wife he left behind may be unfaithful (as she is); an intrepid widow who is both a hospital matron and, from deep moral conviction, a Union spy; an English journalist who loves the widow and is himself a Union spy; and the moody and brilliant Stonewall Jackson, victor of many battles against the odds." Publ Wkly

This book "transcends historical issues of right and wrong; it is a gripping, deeply satisfying work of art." Newsweek

A family madness. Simon & Schuster 1986 336p o.p.

LC 85-26121

"Approximately half of the chapters of 'A Family Madness' are set in the present and concern a young working-class Australian, Terry Delaney, who becomes involved with a family of Byelorussian origin, the Kab-

Keneally, Thomas—*Continued*

bels (originally Kabbelski), who immigrated to Sydney in the late 1940's. The other half deals with the terrible modern history of that family, a history reaching back to the early days of World War II." N Y Times Book Rev

"Keneally brilliantly combines three diverse narrative techniques, and while the book is not light or easy reading, it is enormously rewarding." Publ Wkly

Flying hero class. Warner Bks. 1991 289p $19.95

ISBN 0-446-51582-5   LC 90-50524

Also available G.K. Hall large print edition

"A troupe of Australian aboriginal dancers is flying from New York to Frankfurt on the last leg of a world tour when their jetliner is hijacked by Palestinian terrorists, and Frank McCloud their manager is identified as an enemy of the people and sentenced to death. In . . . [an] account of the next 48 hours Keneally relates blow-by-blow the hijackers' plot to intimidate, demoralize, and manipulate the minds of a plane load of people." Libr J

This is "despite some problems, a good book. Unlike many suspense novels, it never deadens our sensibilities with predictable characters, simple-minded politics or slick prose. Mr. Keneally's people are always fascinating, and so are the ideas his plot generates, making the hijacking a metaphor for the complex relationship between the West and third world peoples deprived of land and dignity." N Y Times Book Rev

The playmaker. Simon & Schuster 1987 353p o.p.

LC 87-13127

This novel is based on an incident in Australian history. In 1789, Lieutenant Ralph Clark was "invited by the new Government to recruit a cast of convicts and put on a play—George Farquhar's Restoration comedy 'The Recruiting Officer.'" N Y Times Book Rev

The author's "sophisticated and highly self-conscious blend of fact and fiction works wonderfully to transport us back into a forgotten world and to hint at its consequences." New Statesman

Schindler's list. Simon & Schuster 1982 400p $25

ISBN 0-671-51688-4   LC 82-10489

"An actual occurrence during the Nazi regime in Germany forms the basis for this story. Oskar Schindler, a Catholic German industrialist, chose to act differently from those Germans who closed their eyes to what was happening to the Jews. By spending enormous sums on bribes to the SS and on food and drugs for the Jewish prisoners whom he housed in his own camp-factory in Cracow, he succeeded in sheltering thousands of Jews, finally transferring them to a safe place in Czechoslovakia. Fifty Schindler survivors from seven nations helped the author with information." Shapiro. Fic for Youth. 3d edition

To Asmara. Warner Bks. 1989 290p o.p.

LC 89-40035

"An Australian journalist named Darcy disappears in the remote Ethiopian province of Eritrea, where rebels are fighting a savage war of independence against the ruling Marxist regime. His legacy: a number of cassette tapes and notebooks, in which he has recorded the details of his mysteriously aborted journey. From these sources we learn that Darcy had gone to Eritrea to investigate reports of rebel attacks on UN food shipments to that famine-oppressed region. In his company were an American aide seeking the rescue of his imprisoned Somali lover, an aging English feminist bent on putting an end to the ritualized mutilation of females, and a young French girl searching for her missing photojournalist father. After touring rebel-controlled territory and surviving many close scrapes with Ethiopian forces, Darcy learns that many of his basic assumptions about the famine are in error. Spurred on by this knowledge, he commits himself to a course of action that may or may not have claimed his life." Booklist

This novel "is a rare entity in contemporary fiction, a work of advocacy and engagement that unhesitatingly takes sides in one of the world's longest-running and least understood wars." N Y Times Book Rev

Woman of the inner sea. Doubleday 1993 c1992 277p $21

ISBN 0-385-46795-8   LC 92-28554

First published 1992 in the United Kingdom

"In the Australian state of New South Wales, Kate Gaffney-Kozinski, in her early thirties, has a marriage that's unworkable, despite all outward appearances of its success. Not ordinarily the kind of person who would do so, Kate nonetheless is pushed to the limit and flees—to the outback, where she hides her identity yet, tested again, comes into her own as a person." Booklist

This novel "succeeds on many fronts. It is a picaresque and often hilarious adventure story, recounting one woman's unforgettable if improbable travels. It is a series of love stories, as Kate meets the man who is appropriate for her at each stage of her life, and it is a mystery story as well. But the novel is also very much an exploration of ethics." N Y Times Book Rev

Kennedy, Raymond A.

The bitterest age; [by] Raymond Kennedy. Ticknor & Fields 1994 218p $19.95

ISBN 0-395-61133-4   LC 93-30337

"For ten-year-old Ingeborg Maas, Potsdam in the final days of World War II holds both fear and hope. Living with her mother and younger brother, Ingeborg waits for her father's return from the Russian front. As the bombing and devastation reduce Potsdam to chaos, she holds steadfastly to her belief in her father's safety." Libr J

"An achingly beautiful and sensitively rendered portrait of the triumph of innocence and love over decadence and despair. This heartrending saga of survival will appeal to a wide spectrum of readers." Booklist

Kennedy, William, 1928-

The ink truck. Dial Press (NY) 1969 278p o.p.

The novel begins following "a year-long Guild strike at a city newspaper. . . . Bailey is a columnist, syndicated in 28 papers before the strike began. Now he is obsessed with harassing the company. . . . He devises a plan to drain the printing ink from one of the company trucks. The plan goes awry and Bailey, frustrated, burns down a store housing gypsies who work for the company. The gypsy queen dies as a result of the fire and her son, Septimo Smith, goes after Bailey. In a series of escapades . . . he is abducted and seduced, attends a burial service for a cat . . . and conducts a one-man picketing fast on the street." Book World

Kennedy, William, 1928—*Continued*

"Kennedy's style is at once profound and humorous, and intriguing blend of sarcasm and serious comtemplation. Filled with colorful characters, realistic dialogue and bizarre situations, this is a riveting read." Publ Wkly

Ironweed; a novel. Viking 1983 227p o.p.
LC 82-40370

With this "tale of skid-row life in the Depression, Kennedy adds another chapter to his 'Albany cycle'—a group of novels set in the Albany, New York, underworld from the 1920s onward. Following 'Legs' and 'Billy Phelan's Greatest Game,' 'Ironweed' tells the story of Francis Phelan, a 58-year-old bum with muscatel on his breath and hallucinations on his mind. Chief among the latter is a vision of his infant son, who died after falling out of Francis' arms. It is the desire to reconcile himself to the memory of his dead son that brings Francis home to Albany, ultimately opening the door to a possible reconciliation with his family." Booklist

"The fullblooded life in Ironweed is most copiously found in the language with which Kennedy has endowed these 'marginal' people so as to make them anything but marginal." New Repub

Quinn's book. Viking 1988 289p il o.p.
LC 86-45858

This novel is set in Albany, New York from 1849 to 1864. The narrator, "Daniel Quinn, America's foremost Civil War reporter, recalls his adolescent years . . . and his 15-year pursuit of the mysterious Maud Fallon, a theater star world-renowned for her nude interpretations of Byron and Keats." Libr J

"In the past, Kennedy has excelled at revealing the dignity hidden within mean, pinched lives. This time he gives his characters plenty of elbowroom and lets them move toward folly or heroism. But the end result is the same: a novel that is both engrossing and eerily profound." Time

Very old bones. Viking 1992 292p $22
ISBN 0-670-83457-2   LC 91-40723

The protagonist and narrator in this installment of The Albany cycle is "Orson Purcell, the bastard son of artist Peter Phelan. . . . Building his tale around a family gathering in 1958, Purcell relates his own life story as well as episodes in the history of each family member, both living and dead, who struggle to overcome their collective and individual pasts." Libr J

"Orson is wounded, pompous, a bit pedantic in his initial attempt at family history. What transpires in [the book] is the growth and increasing authenticity of his voice. . . . Beneath the mete and just end of this closely worked novel lie bitter bones of estrangement, of love hidden or misplaced, lives wasted by jealousy and fear." N Y Times Book Rev

Kenney, Susan, 1941-

Graves in academe. Viking 1985 274p o.p.
LC 85-40093

"After accepting a temporary teaching appointment, the intrepid Ms. Howard finds that she has walked into an English department under siege. Roz determines that the apparent accidents that are befalling one professor after another are in fact the work of a serial killer who is using the 'Norton Anthology of English Literature' as a how-to-manual. (One victim dies like Grendel, another like Chaucer's Pardoner, etc.)" Booklist

"A very elegant and entertaining mystery. Kenney's view of academia is authentic, and both satiric and sentimental. She has a real gift for language, too. An unusual description here, a lovely turn of phrase there, make this a novel worthy of note." Wilson Libr Bull

Kent, Alexander
See also Reeman, Douglas

Kerouac, Jack, 1922-1969

The Dharma bums. Viking 1958 244p o.p.
Available from Amereon and Buccaneer Bks.

"This novel deals with Zen Buddhism. It's about two young men who are seeking to find themselves through meditation, voluntary poverty, separation from society, and intimate contact with nature, especially the Western mountains. . . . Sometimes Kerouac seems a little foolish, often he is extreme, but he is genuine, he is alive, and he is native." Libr J

On the road. Viking 1957 310p o.p.
Available from Amereon and Buccaneer Bks.

This semi-autobiographical novel "describes the wanderings across America, casual friendships, labours, and affairs of Sal Paradise, a young writer, and his friend and hero, Dean Moriarty. Episodic, fast-moving, unstructured, it produced a mythology of its own and many imitators." Oxford Companion to Engl Lit. 5th edition

Kesey, Ken

Demon box. Viking 1986 384p o.p.
LC 85-32290

"A collection of experiences, stories, and poetry. Most of the tales concern the life and times of 'Devlin E. Deboree,' a counterculture author who serves time in Mexico on a narcotics charge and later returns to his family farm in Oregon. Though he gives himself an alias, Kesey usually identifies his friends, including Jack Kerouac, Larry McMurtry, Hunter Thompson, and a 'Rolling Stone' reporter who accompanies him to the great pyramids." Libr J

"Kesey's distinctive gift with language and tough sense of humor unify this somewhat disorganized collection, and his elegy for the passing of the mad energy of the '60s will strike a responsive chord with all those who lived through those dangerous, liberating years." Publ Wkly

One flew over the cuckoo's nest; a novel. Viking 1962 311p o.p.
Available Thorndike Press large print edition

"Life in a mental institution is predictable and suffocating under the iron rule of Nurse Ratched, who tolerates no disruption of routine on her all-male ward. Half-Indian Chief Bromden, almost invisible on the ward because he is thought to be deaf and dumb, describes the arrival of rowdy Randle Patrick McMurphy. McMurphy takes on the nurse as an adversary in his attempt to organize his fellow inmates and breathe some self-esteem and joy into their lives. The battle is vicious on the part of the nurse, who is relentless in her efforts to break McMurphy, but a spark of human will brings an element of hope to counter the despotic institutional power." Shapiro. Fic for Youth. 3d edition

Sailor song. Viking 1992 535p $23.50
ISBN 0-670-83521-8   LC 92-5406

Kesey, Ken—*Continued*

"The story, set some 30 years hence, involves Ike Sallas, a once-famous ecoterrorist now living in an Alaskan fishing village. Ike's carefully cultivated disengagement is threatened first by the arrival of a Hollywood film company, there to make a movie based on a children's book, and then by his thawing relations with Alice Carmody, a fisherman's wife whose marriage is on the rocks. When Ike discovers that the film company has a sinister motive, he tries to rally the town, yet defeat seems imminent until an environmental apocalypse throws a monkey wrench into everyone's plans." Libr J

The author "includes a great deal of purposeful foolery, flooding the narrative with farcical incongruities, crude asides, wacky in-jokes, and countless allusions to literary classics and popular culture. . . . In sum, Sailor Song is vintage Ken Kesey: not for the faint-hearted, perhaps, but certainly instructive, and never boring." New Leader

Sometimes a great notion. Viking 1964 628p o.p.

"This novel focuses on the person of Hank Stamper, raw and aggressive scion of an Oregon lumber empire. The struggle is . . . with a society unwilling to accommodate a strong individualist, but the issues are deepened and complicated by the fact that Hank's principal antagonist turns out to be his cerebral, introspective half-brother, Lee, and by Kesey's development of Lee as an equally appealing character, Kesey manipulates the clash of fraternal egos to a powerful climax, before reconciling the brothers to a tragic understanding of their own vulnerability to an indifferent fate and to a group of townspeople who have been made intolerably uncomfortable by the sight of the Stampers' strength." Ency of World Lit in the 20th Century

Kessel, John

The Franchise

In Nebula awards 29 p203-41

Kessler, Julia Braun

For works written by this author in collaboration with Gabrielle Donnelly see Barrett, Julia

Keyes, Daniel, 1927-

Flowers for Algernon. Harcourt Brace Jovanovich 1966 274p o.p. Buccaneer Bks. reprint available $18.95 (ISBN 0-89968-345-2)

"Charlie Gordon, aged thirty-two, is mentally retarded and enrolls in a class to 'become smart.' He keeps a journal of his progress after an experimental operation that increases his I.Q. Although Charlie becomes brilliant, he is unhappy because he cannot shed his former personality and is tormented by his memories. In the end he begins to lose the mental powers he has gained." Shapiro. Fic for Youth. 3d edition

Flowers for Algernon [novelette]

In The Hugo winners v1 p245-73

Kienzle, William X., 1928-

Assault with intent. Andrews & McMeel 1982 273p o.p.

LC 82-1628

"The action takes place in a seminary in Detroit and it involves an apparent plot to kill some or all of the priests in seminaries. It is a perfect setting for one of the instructors at the seminary, Father Koesler, a priest-detective. . . . The attempts at murdering the priests are continuously foiled either by circumstances or the ineptitude of the assailant. We are led from one seminary to the other as the would-be murderers change their targets. The plot attracts such media attention that a TV movie is filmed at the major seminary to document the plot against the priests. In the process of the investigation attention is focused on a group of ultraconservative Catholics and their leader, Roman Kirkus." Best Sellers

Bishop as pawn. Andrews & McMeel 1994 266p $18.95

ISBN 0-8362-6130-5   LC 93-47149

"The murder of a much-disliked bishop propels Detroit's Father Koesler [into a new case]. When auxiliary Bishop Ramon Diego is bludgeoned to death, his aide, Father Don Carleson, formerly a missionary in Central America, is arrested quickly. Even though the ruthlessly ambitious Diego had used his amiable adjunct as a mere gofer, Carleson doesn't seem the murdering type to Koesler or the rest of the city's clergy. But an ambitious prosecuting attorney and the investigating police lieutenant are pleased with the quick arrest and eager for a high-profile conviction." Publ Wkly

Body count. Andrews & McMeel 1992 266p o.p.

LC 92-3266

This mystery involves Father Koesler, "Detroit detective-priest in conflicts between old and new Catholic theology. Hitman Guido Vespa loudly confesses to Koesler that he has bumped off Father Keating, the spiritual leader of a nearby parish, and buried the body in the grave of the long-dead, much beloved Monsignor Kern. Overhearing the confession, exuberant new resident priest Nick Dunn is delighted: one of the reasons he came to St. Joseph's was to be near its sleuthing pastor. Nick's enthusiasm increases when the police ask Koesler for help with Keating's disappearance." Publ Wkly

Chameleon. Andrews & McMeel 1991 289p o.p.

LC 91-6433

Available Thorndike Press large print edition

"When a prominent nun, a diocesan bureaucrat, and a retired archbishop are targeted for murder, [Father Robert] Koesler dubiously agrees to shepherd Lieutenant Alonzo 'Zoo' Tully of the Detroit police department through the arcane intricacies of the Roman Catholic church. Father Bob and Zoo must work in concert in order to unravel a deadly game of revenge mired in the complexities of canon law. An intriguing blend of glory and gore from the master of the theological mystery." Booklist

Dead wrong. Andrews & McMeel 1992 269p o.p.

LC 92-46287

Kienzle, William X., 1928——_Continued_

In this mystery Father Koesler investigates "an unsolved 33-year-old murder case. Aging millionaire Charles Nash asks Koesler to intervene in the adulterous affair between his married son Ted, an ostentatiously pious land developer, and Koesler's foster cousin Brenda Monahan. Brenda's job in the archdiocese chancery gives her access to information profitable to the Nash empire; if the affair goes public, the company will suffer significantly. Koesler's questions lead him to the middle of everybody's family secrets, including those of his own family." Publ Wkly

Deadline for a critic. Andrews, McMeel & Parker 1987 263p o.p.

LC 86-32288

"As Catholic priest Bob Koesler says the Mass for the Dead over his longtime acquaintance, Ridley Groendal, he ruminates about the events leading up to Groendal's death. He dwells on six people whose lives were irrevocably changed by Groendal, who used his power as performing arts critic for the New York _Herald_ to destroy their careers. After moving back to the Detroit area Groendal has come in contact with all six. Now he is dead under strange circumstances." Libr J

Death wears a red hat. Andrews & McMeel 1980 304p o.p.

LC 79-28353

"Detroit is the setting of a series of baffling murders. Some puzzling motive brings the murderer to decapitate his victims and deposit the heads on church statues. Each head has the same horror stricken countenance, as if the victim was frightened to death. The police and press are baffled by the case, but Father Robert Koesler . . . suspects that there is some logic in it all. This is a swiftly paced narrative, expertly plotted to juxtapose the progress of the investigations of the police, the press and Father Koesler. Koesler's knowledge of church history, mythology, and his fellow clergymen gives him insight while the police and newsmen remain confused." Best Sellers

Deathbed. Andrews, McMeel & Parker 1986 258p o.p.

LC 86-1184

"The fate of St. Vincent's Hospital in Detroit hangs in the balance as Father Koesler investigates sinister goings-on. A fanatical volunteer prowls the hospital at night, his clumsy attempts at sabotage helped by a more accomplished and deadly presence. The suspects include Dr. John Haroldson and Sister Rosamunda, both reluctantly approaching retirement and both bitter at the chief executive officer of the hospital, Sister Eileen Monahan." Booklist

Eminence. Andrews & McMeel 1989 312p o.p.

LC 88-35007

When Father Koesler "reluctantly accepts an assignment from his cardinal to investigate the rather dubious credentials of a purported faith healer, he becomes embroiled in an ingenious scam involving intimidation, extortion, and murder. With the able assistance of Lieutenant Alonzo ('Zoo') Tully of the Detroit police . . . Father Koesler exposes a devious plot to profit at the expense of the Catholic church." Booklist

Marked for murder. Andrews, McMeel & Parker 1988 281p o.p.

LC 87-37353

"A man in clerical dress is killing, eviscerating and branding elderly prostitutes in Detroit's inner city. When priest Richard Kramer is found in circumstances that appear to be leading up to another murder, homicide lieutenant Alonzo Tully is certain he is guilty. Koesler, a friend of the priest, is not so sure and begins to investigate at the urging of Kramer's assistant, Sister Mary Therese." Publ Wkly

Masquerade. Andrews & McMeel 1990 267p o.p.

LC 89-77890

"There's a mystery writers' conference at Detroit's Marygrove College, and on the dais are various clergy—Jewish, Catholic, Episcopalian—who are accomplished practitioners of the whodunit craft. Then the guest of honor, the Reverend Klaus Krieg, a sleazy televangelist, is murdered, and the rabbi, nun, monk, and priest become the chief suspects. Koesler toughs it out in his usual self-effacing way, lending assistance to the Detroit police through his expert powers of deduction and his knowledge of things religious." Booklist

Mind over murder. Andrews & McMeel 1981 296p o.p.

LC 81-723

Father Bob Koesler becomes involved in a search for missing Monsignor "'Tommy' Thompson, head of the Roman Catholic matrimonial court in Detroit. When Tommy disappears, Joe Cox of the Detroit _News_ prints the priest's scandalous diary, and evidence of his cavalier dismissal of permission to re-marry point to several suspects with motive for murder." Publ Wkly

The rosary murders. Andrews & McMeel 1979 257p o.p.

LC 78-31833

"From Ash Wednesday, when the murderer first struck Detroit's Catholic community, the police seemed helpless to solve the string of senseless murders. The weeks that followed became a nightmare for the crack homicide team of investigators headed by Lieutenant Walter Koznicki, until Father Koesler broke the madman's code." Publisher's note

Sudden death. Andrews, McMeel & Parker 1985 257p o.p.

LC 84-28268

"When aging football star Hank 'The Hun' Hunsinger is murdered, there's a goodly supply of suspects. A dirty player on and off the field, Hunsinger was unpopular, to say the least, with the team's owner, general manager, trainer, quarterback, rookie tight end, field-goal kicker and the owner's estranged wife. Father Robert Koesler, a leader of a team Bible-study group, is once again asked to assist the Detroit police." Publ Wkly

Kijewski, Karen

Copy Kat. Doubleday 1992 261p $18.50

ISBN 0-385-42096-X   LC 92-14482

"A Perfect crime book"

"Hard-boiled female private eye Kat Colorado . . . takes on a new identity as Kate, the dyed-blonde bartender, to try to discover who murdered Diedre Durkin, the local bartender's wife. As she investigates motives, suspects, and alibis, Kat encounters blackmail and in-

Kijewski, Karen—Continued

fidelity, a deep-seated and dangerous sibling rivalry, twisted family jealousies, and a web of bitter deceit and hatred." Booklist

Kat's cradle. Doubleday 1992 244p o.p.

LC 91-32218

"A Perfect crime book"

"Narrator Kat Colorado, a socially conscious Sacramento private investigator with a Las Vegas policeman lover, accepts the challenge of finding the birth parents of an 'orphan' whose autocratic-but-rich grandmother has just died. Paige Morrell and scruffy boyfriend Paul may be more interested in proving her right to inherit; however, Kat thinks she has a right to know about her folks." Libr J

"Outstanding among today's female detectives, PI Kat Colorado exhibits conscience and compassion, muscle and wisecracking savvy in an appealing and believable combination." Publ Wkly

Wild Kat. Doubleday 1994 343p $19.95

ISBN 0-385-46851-2   LC 93-25740

Sacramento private eye Kat Colorado is drawn into a "case of corporate criminality when she is hired to protect Amanda Hudson, an accountant who has blown the whistle on a medical supplies company for manufacturing artificial hearts with defective valves." N Y Times Book Rev

The author's in "fine form here, combining her easy, breezy style and deadpan humor with a sinister, suspenseful plot that's thought-provoking, fast-paced, and entertaining." Booklist

Kincaid, Jamaica

Annie John. Farrar, Straus & Giroux 1985 148p $18.95

ISBN 0-374-10521-9   LC 84-28630

"Annie John, a young girl living in Antigua in the West Indies, describes her most intimate feelings about her parents (mixed between love and hate), her friends (loyal but changing), and her experiences in school (excellent in scholarship but not in behavior). Her emotions are recognizable for the confusion that adolescents suffer as they grow from early teens to young adulthood." Shapiro. Fic for Youth. 3d edition

Lucy. Farrar, Straus & Giroux 1990 163p $17.95

ISBN 0-374-19434-3   LC 90-83987

Also available G.K. Hall large print edition

The narrator, Lucy Potter, a nineteen year old from Antigua, tells of her experiences as an *au pair* for a wealthy family in a large North American city

"The great motifs of Western literature, like goodness and evil, innocence and experience, resonate in Kincaid's novel in a completely updated and unselfconscious way. In other hands, this story of a West Indian *au pair* would just be sociology. In Kincaid's recasting, it is both art and argument." Christ Sci Monit

King, Laurie R.

The beekeeper's apprentice; or, On the segregation of the queen. St. Martin's Press 1994 347p $21.95

ISBN 0-312-10423-5   LC 93-43522

"A Thomas Dunne book"

"In the early years of WWI, 15-year-old American Mary Russell encounters Holmes, retired in Sussex Downs where Conan Doyle left him raising bees. Mary, an orphan rebelling against her guardian aunt's strictures, impresses the sleuth with her intelligence and acumen. Holmes initiates her into the mysteries of detection, allowing her to participate in a few cases when she comes home from her studies at Oxford. The collaboration is ignited by the kidnapping in Wales of Jessica Simpson, daughter of an American senator." Publ Wkly

"A wonderfully original and entertaining story that is funny, heartwarming, and full of intrigue. . . . Holmes fans, history buffs, lovers of humor and adventure, and mystery devotees will all find King's book absorbing from beginning to end." Booklist

King, Stephen, 1947-

Apt pupil

In King, S. Different seasons p103-296

The Bachman books: four early novels by Stephen King. New Am. Lib. 1985 692p o.p.

LC 85-11411

An omnibus edition of four novels first published in paperback under the author's pseudonym Richard Bachman

Contents: Rage (1977); The long walk (1979); Roadwork (1981); The running man (1982)

"In *Rage*, a high-school student goes berserk in the classroom, killing the teacher and holding the class hostage. Set in a militaristic ultra-conservative America, *The Long Walk* pits 100 teenagers against each other in a grueling 450-mile marathon walk in which the penalty is death. *Roadwork* is a novel of societal conflict, man vs. progress. The first three thrillers, while entertaining and gripping, occasionally suffer from unfocused and uneven writing. Unresolved questions cause the books to be somewhat unsatisfying. However the fourth novel, *The Running Man* . . . is an action-packed futuristic romp. Protagonist Ben Richards bets his life on a TV show in order to win the money to save the life of his deathly ill daughter. The story combines social commentary, adventure and science fiction, set against the backdrop of a decaying society." SLJ

The body

In King, S. Different seasons p299-451

The breathing method

In King, S. Different seasons p453-518

Carrie. Doubleday 1974 199p $25

ISBN 0-385-08695-4

Also available G.K. Hall large print edition

"Carrie is 16, lonely, the butt of all her Maine classmates' tricks and jokes, an object of scorn even to her own mother, who is fanatically religious and believes anything remotely sexual is from the devil. Then one girl becomes ashamed of the cruelty being vented on Carrie and plans an act of kindness that will give her the first happiness in her young life. The only trouble is the act backfires horribly and Carrie is worse off than ever before. It is at this point, at the senior prom, that Carrie begins to put into effect her awesome telekinetic powers, powers with which she has only toyed before." Publ Wkly

King, Stephen, 1947-—*Continued*

Christine. Viking 1983 526p $25

ISBN 0-670-22026-4 LC 82-20105

"Arnie Cunningham—a teenager who has never fit in—buys a dilapidated 1958 Plymouth Fury from an equally broken-down Army veteran, Roland LeBay. But Christine—and the soon-dead LeBay—have mysterious regenerative powers; Christine's odometer runs backwards and the car repairs itself. Arnie becomes obsessed by the car and possessed by its previous owner, losing his girlfriend and his best friend as they work together to save him from Christine's clutches." Publ Wkly

"As always, there is the sense of descriptive detail that is the author's trademark. Yet the strength of King's prose is best seen here in the remarkable accuracy of language and attitude that captures the spirit of the teenage characters." Libr J

Cujo. Viking 1981 319p $27.50

ISBN 0-670-45193-2 LC 81-50265
Also available G.K. Hall large print edition

"A Saint Bernard gone berserk, Cujo is the 200-pound family pet who is bitten by a rabid bat one very hot summer in Castle Rock, Maine. Victims of his violence are two families—that of his owner, backwoods auto mechanic Joe Cambers, and of Vic Trenton, an ad man struggling to keep an important account while 'dealing with his wife's infidelity and his four year old's fears.' Counterpoint to the ad campaign's folksy slogan and the writer's lush reveries are . . . vigils in stalled Pintos where one awaits deadly assault." SLJ

"Carefully plotted, the novel throbs with the malignant evil that permeates all of King's fiction." Saturday Rev

The dark half. Viking 1989 431p $21.95

ISBN 0-670-82982-X LC 88-40628
Also available G.K. Hall large print edition

The protagonist of this novel "is literary novelist Thad Beaumont, whose greatest success has come with three gory thrillers written under the pseudonym George Stark. . . . When a blackmailer threatens to reveal Stark's identity . . . Beaumont and his literary agent decide to foil the plan and capitalize on Stark's 'demise.' But Stark, who of course was never alive, will not stay dead either. Beaumont's alter ego . . . seeks revenge against all those involved in killing him off." Publ Wkly

The author is "a very good storyteller. 'The Dark Half' mostly succeeds, as both parable and chiller, in spite of occasional clichés of thought and expression and bits of sophomoric humor." N Y Times Book Rev

The dead zone. Viking 1979 426p $27.95

ISBN 0-670-26077-0 LC 79-12785
Also available G.K. Hall large print edition

"Following a car accident, New England high school English teacher Johnny Smith is unconscious for five years only to wake a bewildered psychic in post-Watergate America. He quickly runs afoul of a national scandal sheet that wants to exploit his power to see the future. He also catches a sex murderer and eventually takes an interest in presidential politics. In the end he turns assassin to save the country from a Hitler-like congressman with White House aspirations." Libr J

Different seasons. Viking 1982 527p $29.95

ISBN 0-670-27266-3 LC 82-70145

In this collection of four short novels the first one, The body, "is semiautobiographical and might be called King's 'American Graffiti,' detailing a late summer expedition by four boys to view the dead body of one of their peers run over by a train. What starts out almost as a lark turns into a horrifying ordeal and points the way for each boy's subsequent development. 'The Body' is the earliest written story, and while totally engaging, is not as satisfyingly well written as the later 'Rita Hayworth and Shawshank Redemption,' which concerns the relationship between two convicts in a Maine prison, one of whom never lets the system beat him down, and the other who is redeemed by him. 'The Breathing Method' introduces us to an unusual men's club where the books and furnishings are subtly alien and horror stories are told around the fireplace. The horror story within the story has an unusually gruesome finale. 'Apt Pupil,' the longest story in the book, recounts to chilling effect the increasingly complex and bizarre relationship between a teenage boy and a former concentration camp commandant." Publ Wkly

Dolores Claiborne. Viking 1993 305p $23.50

ISBN 0-670-84452-7 LC 92-15467
Also available G.K. Hall large print edition

This novel unfolds in the form of a monologue "by the title character, who is suspected of murdering her loutish, insensitive husband and the difficult, rich, and senile woman for whom she has kept house for many years. As Dolores tells her story to the local authorities, the details of a life of drudgery and marital unhappiness emerge, along with the ironic truth behind the deaths." Libr J

"What drives Dolores Claiborne is a powerful characterization of the title figure, a cranky old Maine islander who takes no guff from life or death. . . . King's mimicry is startlingly good." Time

Firestarter. Viking 1980 428p $27.50

ISBN 0-670-31541-9 LC 80-14793

"Two college students sign up as paid guinea pigs for a secret and unknowingly dangerous government experiment in telekinesis. . . . When the subjects marry and have a baby, however, their child develops not only telekinesis but pyrokinesis as well; in short, the tot can not only push things with her mind, but set them ablaze as well. The government's plan to use the girl as a human weapon set [the author's] plot into action, and an extended chase ensues with expected havoc wreaked in vivid detail." Booklist

"This is your advanced post-Watergate cynical American thriller with some eerie parapsychological twists, and it's been done so distinctively well that we'd better talk about genius rather than genre." Quill Quire

Four past midnight. Viking 1990 763p $29.95

ISBN 0-670-83538-2 LC 90-50046
Also available G.K. Hall large print edition

Analyzed in Short story index
Contents: The Langoliers; Secret window, secret garden; The library policeman; The sun dog

"In 'Langoliers' a group of airline passengers . . . become stuck in time out of sync with the present at 20,000 feet. 'Secret Window, Secret Garden' finds novelist Mort Rainey confronted by an eerie character who accuses him of plagiarism, and has come to settle up. In 'Sun Dog,' Kevin Delevan gets exactly what he wanted

King, Stephen, 1947——*Continued*

for his 15th birthday, a Polaroid 'Sun 660' camera, but every picture he takes shows a salivating 'hell hound' getting closer and closer. In 'Library Policeman,' . . . Sam Peebles borrows two books from the library late one night, and the librarian warns him not to be late returning them. What Sam doesn't know is that she was a child murderer who committed suicide in 1960." SLJ

"As the poet laureate of pop, Mr. King is read by many who might otherwise never read fiction at all. He creates an immediate and familiar landscape and could form the ideal bridge from the Road Runner to Dostoyevsky's Raskolnikov. There is little here Mr. King has not done before, but once again he proves difficult to lay aside." N Y Times Book Rev

Gerald's game. Viking 1992 332p $23.50

ISBN 0-670-84650-3   LC 91-47628

"Jessie and Gerald Burlingame have been married for 20 years. Kinky sex is Gerald's game; lately he has taken to handcuffing his wife to the bedposts. During one such session, via a series of bizarre circumstances, Jessie accidentally kills her husband, and for the next 28 hours she is trapped." Publ Wkly

Even after escaping, Jessie "still has to deal with the corpse-like figure she thinks invaded the cabin just as she freed herself and that pursued her to her car and has haunted her during her convalescence. Was—is—it real? Somewhat like King's earlier naturalistic shocker, *Misery*, this book is grim and nasty. Unlike *Misery*, it's not semiconsciously misogynistic. Quite the reverse: it seems to say that virtually no man and no men's institution can treat a woman decently. A very disturbing stylistic tour de force, this may be King's darkest book." Booklist

Insomnia. Viking 1994 787p $27.95

ISBN 0-670-85503-0   LC 94-784

Also available G.K. Hall large print edition

"On one of the long, exhausting walks old Ralph Roberts starts taking as a brain tumor slowly kills his wife, he witnesses a friendly young neighbor, Ed Deepneau, behaving totally out of character—indeed, like someone possessed. About a year later and after his wife's death, Ralph begins waking early and then earlier and earlier. He also starts seeing things—intense colors streaming off people and animals. Meanwhile, Ed has turned into an antiabortion fanatic and wife-beater. Ralph intervenes to help Helen Deepneau escape from Ed, for which Ed threatens him. Or is it Ed? Ralph senses that someone or something else is in control of the troubled man. Ralph's right, of course. Ed has been involuntarily recruited on one side, and, it develops, Ralph and his also-widowed neighbor, Lois Chasse, on the other, of a supercosmic struggle the import of which King reveals with deliciously tantalizing gradualness." Booklist

It. Viking 1986 1138p $27

ISBN 0-670-81302-8   LC 85-41062

"Six adults, living separately in a blessed fog of forgetfulness, are summoned back to their hometown to complete the destruction of a horrific, shape-changing entity who breakfasts on the city's children. This same group first encountered the menace more than a quarter century before, as schoolchildren in the 1950s. Their quest breeds some riveting chase scenes as adults and children alike flee from an assortment of menacing humans and slavering monsters—most of which are manifestations of an evil so vile its true nature can never be known.

King's considerable talent for grounding this supernatural stuff in the minutiae of everyday life is evident." Booklist

The Langoliers

In King, S. Four past midnight p1-246

The library policeman

In King, S. Four past midnight p401-604

The long walk

In King, S. The Bachman books: four early novels by Stephen King

Misery. Viking 1987 310p $21.95

ISBN 0-670-81364-8   LC 86-40504

"Paul Sheldon is a serious novelist plagued by the commercial success of his 'Misery Chastain' romance series. He fictionally kills off his irritating heroine and finally writes his great American novel, celebrating with a drunken drive through a rural Colorado blizzard; but he learns what real misery means when he wrecks his car and awakens as the crippled prisoner/patient of a psychotic ex-nurse named Annie Wilkes—Misery's biggest, and angriest, fan. In a graphically gruesome story, Paul must bring Misery back to life just for Annie; but will this new novel buy his freedom, or is he only prolonging his physical and mental torture?" Libr J

"Even if 'Misery' is less terrifying than his usual work—no demons, no witchcraft, no nether-world horrors—it creates strengths out of its realities. Its excitements are more subtle. And, as such, it is an intriguing work." N Y Times Book Rev

Needful things. Viking 1991 690p $24.95

ISBN 0-670-83953-1   LC 91-50148

Also available G.K. Hall large print edition

A mysterious merchant named Leland Gaunt arrives in Castle Rock, Maine, and sets up an old curiosity shop. Calling his shop "Needful Things", Gaunt "sells objects that revive his customers' deepest and most selfish desires—things they must have at any cost. As part of the bargain, he requires that his purchasers carry out various 'pranks' on each other. One thing leads to another and an eventual bloodbath." Times Lit Suppl

"As the dreams of each strikingly memorable character, major and minor, inexorably turn to nightmare, individuals and soon the community are overwhelmed, while the precise nature of Gaunt's evil thrillingly stays just out of focus. King, like Leland Gaunt, knows just what his customers want." Publ Wkly

Night shift. Doubleday 1978 xxii, 336p $25

ISBN 0-385-12991-2   LC 77-75146

Analyzed in Short story index

Contents: Jerusalem's Lot; Graveyard shift; Night surf; I am the doorway; The mangler; The boogeyman; Gray matter; Battleground; Trucks; Sometimes they come back; Strawberry spring; The ledge; The lawnmower man; Quitters, Inc.; I know what you need; Children of the corn; The last rung on the ladder; The man who loved flowers; One for the road; The woman in the room

Nightmares & dreamscapes. Viking 1993 816p $27.50

ISBN 0-670-85108-6   LC 92-46881

Also available G.K. Hall large print edition

King, Stephen, 1947- —*Continued*

Analyzed in Short story index

Includes the following stories: Dolan's Cadillac; The end of the whole mess; Suffer the little children; The Night Flier; Popsy; It grows on you; Chattery teeth; Dedication; The moving finger; Sneakers; You know they got a hell of a band; Home delivery; Rainy season; My pretty pony; The ten o'clock people; Crouch End; The house on Maple Street; The fifth quarter; The doctor's case; Umney's last case

"There's certainly nothing skimpy about this collection of large, leisurely short stories. . . . Fans of Mr. King's work will find here his usual menu: wild conspiracies; repellent, zestful monsters; scenes speckled and splashed with gore." N Y Times Book Rev

Pet sematary. Doubleday 1983 373p $25

ISBN 0-385-18244-9   LC 82-45360

Also available from Buccaneer Bks.

"For Dr. Louis Creed and his family, their new house is perfection, with a fairyland forest within walking distance. But the woods contain a bizarre pet cemetery tended by local children, and eventually the Creeds discover its secret—an ancient burial ground with the power to raise the dead." Libr J

"King's characters are so solid and next-door neighborly that we are drawn quite naturally and trustingly into their lives. And then, a single note at a time, the eerie music begins and we are entranced." Best Sellers

Rage

In King, S. The Bachman books: four early novels by Stephen King

Rita Hayworth and Shawshank redemption

In King, S. Different seasons p1-101

Roadwork

In King, S. The Bachman books: four early novels by Stephen King

The running man

In King, S. The Bachman books: four early novels by Stephen King

Salem's Lot. Doubleday 1975 439p $25

ISBN 0-385-00751-5

Also available G.K. Hall large print edition

"The small Maine town of Jerusalem's Lot, or Salem's Lot as the natives call it, has become what appears to be a ghost town. Its streets, however, are deserted only in the daylight hours, for the villagers have turned into vampires." Booklist

"It is to Stephen King's credit as a stylist that he has charmed us into such familiar territory. Sparing the endless atmospheric creaks and cobwebs and cupolas of this New England landscape, he thrusts us into the private terror of his characters." Best Sellers

Secret window, secret garden

In King, S. Four past midnight p247-399

The shining. Doubleday 1977 447p $25

ISBN 0-385-12167-9   LC 76-24212

Also available G.K. Hall large print edition

"The Overlook Hotel, high in the mountains of Colorado, has in the past played host to a colorful selection of visitors, from gangsters to presidents. But a few even more extraordinary guests are in residence when Jack Torrance comes to the Overlook with his wife, Wendy, and son, Danny, to be winter caretaker. Danny is precognitive and telepathic, a condition that allows him to outmaneuver the hotel's spirits of the dead that attempt to lay claim to the entire Torrance family." Booklist

"In a fast-paced and gory denouement, the terror comes to a violent end. King is a masterful technician of suspense whose readers as well as characters are the victims of his relentless heightening of horror." Libr J

Skeleton crew. Putnam 1985 512p o.p.

LC 84-15947

Analyzed in Short story index

Contents: The mist; Here there be tygers; The monkey; Cain rose up; Mrs. Todd's shortcut; The jaunt; The wedding gig; Paranoid: A chant; The raft; Word processor of the gods; The man who would not shake hands; Beachworld; The reaper's image; Nona; For Owen; Survivor type; Uncle Otto's truck; Morning deliveries (Milkman #1); Big wheels: a tale of the laundry game (Milkman #2); Gramma; The ballad of the flexible bullet; The reach

This "collection of King's shorter work is a hefty sampler from all stages of his career, and demonstrates the range of his abilities." Publ Wkly

The stand. Doubleday 1978 823p $18.95

ISBN 0-385-12168-7   LC 77-16928

Also available in a complete and uncut version $34.95 (ISBN 0-385-19957-0)

"A flu-like plague escapes from an experimental lab. Within days it devastates the country, leaving only a few thousand immune people. Besides their immunity, the survivors have in common a terrible dream pitting a faceless man of evil against a woman of goodness. The survivors make their choices and head west, gathering for the confrontation between the satanic Randall Flagg and the God-anointed Mother Abigail." Libr J

"Stephen King takes liberties permitted in science fiction and thrillers (the good guys share clairvoyant powers, and the plot often turns on lucky coincidences), but he grounds his apocalyptic fantasy in a detailed vision of the blighted American vista, and he avoids the formulas of less talented popular novelists." New Yorker

The sun dog

In King, S. Four past midnight p605-763

The talisman; [by] Stephen King, Peter Straub. Viking 1984 644p o.p.

LC 83-40677

"As lung cancer consumes his mother, Jack is sent on a mystic quest through a parallel country called the Territories. He must obtain the talisman which can save his mother's life and that of her 'Twinner,' the queen of the Territories. But evil forces crave the talisman for their own use; Jack must dodge and fight his way across a continent." Libr J

"This is 'The Wizard of Oz' written as a boy's adventure, with spacey adumbrations on the theme of good and evil and their symmetry in the universe." N Y Times Book Rev

Thinner; [by] Richard Bachman. New Am. Lib. 1984 309p o.p.

LC 84-11462

King, Stephen, 1947——Continued

"While driving, Billy Halleck is distracted by his wife and accidentally strikes and kills an old gypsy woman. After he's acquitted through the aid of two influential friends, all three are cursed by the gypsy leader. Halleck begins to lose weight rapidly, and must race with death to try to have the curse removed." Libr J

"Bachman blends extraordinary events so cleanly and credibly into the fabric of his characters' lives that we are compelled to read on to the story's chilling conclusion. A superbly crafted drama." Booklist

The Tommyknockers. Putnam 1987 558p o.p.

LC 87-16845

"A weird metal object—an ancient flying saucer, perhaps?—lies buried in the Maine woods, and the local people and animals start acting strange as a neurotic young woman begins to unearth the monolith in an ambitious dig." Booklist

"There can be few human dreads more horrible and more basic than that of having one's mind and body controlled by an outside source, and King draws all too clear a picture of that dread become reality." West Coast Rev Books

Kingsolver, Barbara

Animal dreams; a novel. HarperCollins Pubs. 1990 342p o.p.

LC 89-46571

Available G.K. Hall large print edition

This novel is set in Grace, Arizona. The narrator is Cosima (Codi) Noline, who returns home after abandoning a career in medicine. Codi looks after her aging father, the local doctor, and teaches high school biology. Her sister Halimeda (Hallie) is an agronomist helping the Sandinistas in Nicaragua. In Grace, Codi becomes involved with a former boyfriend, Loyd Peregrina, a Native American. She struggles to come to terms with her past and works to save the town from an impending ecological disaster

"Like all good novels, Animal Dreams is a web of interlacing news. It is dense and vivid, and makes ever tighter circles around the question of what it means to be alive." Nation

The bean trees; a novel. Harper & Row 1988 232p o.p.

LC 87-45633

In this novel, "Taylor Greer, a poor, young woman, flees her Kentucky home and heads west. . . . While passing through Oklahoma, she becomes responsible for a two-year-old Cherokee girl. The two continue on the road. When they roll off the highway in Tucson, Taylor and the child, whom she has named Turtle, . . . meet Mattie, a widow who runs Jesus Is Lord Used Tires and is active in the sanctuary movement on the side." Ms

This book "gives readers something that's increasingly hard to find today—a character to believe in and laugh with and admire." Christ Sci Monit

Followed by Pigs in heaven

Pigs in heaven; a novel. HarperCollins Pubs. 1993 343p o.p.

LC 92-54739

Available G.K. Hall large print edition

In this sequel to the title entered above, Taylor Greer and her adopted Cherokee Indian daughter Turtle "are on a trip to the Hoover Dam, where Turtle is the only person to see a man fall over the side. . . . The rescue makes Turtle a heroine. But becoming a heroine, which culminates in an appearance on 'Oprah,' engenders a new disaster. Annawake Fourkiller, an Indian-rights lawyer, sees the white mother with her Cherokee daughter on TV and decides the child must be returned to the Cherokee Nation. . . . But Taylor isn't about to let go of the little girl. . . . They pack up and run." Newsweek

"Possessed of an extravagantly gifted narrative voice, [Kingsolver] blends a fierce and abiding moral vision with benevolent, concise humor." N Y Times Book Rev

Kingston, Maxine Hong

Tripmaster Monkey; his fake book. Knopf 1989 340p $19.95

ISBN 0-394-56831-1   LC 88-45762

"After graduating from Berkeley in English Literature, Wittman Ah Sing searches for his niche in the Bay Area of the 1960s. He is a typical product of this time—pot-smoking, free-loving, draft-dodging, unemployed, anti-big business, long-haired, and sandal-shod. But he is also a Chinese-American fighting Chinese stereotypes." Libr J

"Kingston's exploration of racial memories and stereotypes serves to help undermine the idealistic notion of assimilation into American society. The final scene culminates in a wild moment of rage—a stunning theatrical vignette of personal vindication and catharsis." Booklist

Kinsella, W. P.

Box socials; a novel. Ballantine Bks. 1992 225p o.p.

LC 91-58628

"The narrator keeps promising he will tell us about the day Truckbox Al McClintock got to play against Bob Feller of the Cleveland Indians. He keeps on promising this from time to time, but first he has to tell us all about the residents of the Six Towns area of Alberta during those depression and World War II days." Libr J

"With humor and tenderness Kinsella evokes the social rites of the Norwegian-, German-, Ukrainian- and English-speaking hillbillies, their courtships and heartbreaks, fistfights and philanderings, through a series of weddings, dances, whist drives and box socials. Jamie's teenage memories poke gentle fun at small-town society and at adulthood itself while still celebrating his coming-of-age—the real story here, despite Truckbox McClintock's brush with athletic fame." Publ Wkly

The further adventures of Slugger McBatt; baseball stories. Houghton Mifflin 1988 179p o.p.

LC 87-37824

Analyzed in Short story index

Contents: Distances; Reports concerning the death of the Seattle Albatross are somewhat exaggerated; The further adventures of Slugger McBatt; Frank Pierce, Iowa; K Mart; The Valley of the Schmoon; Punchlines; The Eddie Scissons syndrome; Diehard; Searching for Freddy

"Kinsella's baseball fiction combines myth, fantasy, irony, parody, and a delightfully quirky sense of character. He's at the top of his form in these short stories." Booklist

Kinsella, W. P.—*Continued*

Red wolf, red wolf. Southern Methodist Univ. Press 1990 182p $17.50

ISBN 0-87074-319-8   LC 90-52661

Analyzed in Short story index

Contents: Red wolf, red wolf; Something to think about; Lieberman in love; Driving patterns; Elvis bound; Oh, Marley; Truth and history; Evangeline's mother; Billy in Trinidad; Apartheid; Butterfly winter; For Zoltan, who sings; Mother Tucker's Yellow Duck

"Dense with meaning, engagingly readable and with a universal truth at their core, these stories have the impact of well-wrought poetry. . . . The stories' themes and characters are often fanciful, sometimes verging on the bizarre . . . but in Kinsella's hands they become poignantly credible." Publ Wkly

Kinsolving, William

Bred to win; a novel. Doubleday 1990 612p o.p.

LC 89-23600

"Saving the life of a racehorse owned by the handsome and wealthy Sam Cumberlands is fifteen-year-old Annie Grebauer's entrée into the exciting and often precarious world of thoroughbred horse racing. Through sheer determination and will, this child/woman, bred in a shack in the hills of Kentucky, becomes a force to be reckoned with, whether fighting for the man she loves or outsmarting a gangster with a vendetta." Libr J

"The briskly paced action culminates in an explosively violent climax that will not disappoint expectant readers. Superb entertainment heightened by the author's extensive knowledge of the glamorous thoroughbred business." Booklist

Kipling, Rudyard, 1865-1936

Nobel Prize in literature, 1907

The best short stories of Rudyard Kipling; edited by Randall Jarrell. Hanover House 1961 o.p.

Analyzed in Short story index

Contents: Lispeth; At the pit's mouth; A wayside comedy; The story of Muhammad Din; A bank fraud; At the end of the passage; Without benefit of clergy; Jews in Sushan; The return of Imray; The phantom 'rickshaw; Moti Guj—mutineer; The drums of the fore and aft; On Greenhow Hill; The man who would be king; Baa baa black sheep; In the rukh; A matter of fact; The disturber of traffic; "The finest story in the world"; "Brugglesmith"; The Children of the Zodiac; The Maltese Cat; The miracle of Purun Bhagat; The undertakers; Kaa's hunting; The King's ankus; Red Dog; A Centurion of the Thirtieth; On the Great Wall; The Winged Hats; Marklake witches; "Wireless"; A Sahib's war; As easy as A.B.C.; "They"; An habitation enforced; The village that voted the earth was flat; Regulus; The propagation of knowledge; "My son's wife"; Friendly Brook; Mary Postgate; "In the interests of the brethren"; A madonna of the trenches; Dayspring mishandled; The Janeites; The Wish House; The manner of men; Unprofessionl; The Eye of Allah

Collected stories; selected and introduced by Robert Gottlieb. Knopf 1994 xxxvii, 911p $20

ISBN 0-679-43592-1   LC 94-5854

"Everyman's library"

Analyzed in Short story index

Contents: In the house of Suddhoo; Beyond the pale; A bank fraud; Pig; On Greenhow Hill; "Love-o'-women"; The drums of the fore and aft; Dray wara yow dee; "The City of Dreadful Night"; Without benefit of clergy; The head of the district; Jews in Shushan; The man who would be king; "The finest story in the world"; The mark of the beast; The strange ride of Morrowbie Jukes; The disturber of traffic; Mrs. Hauksbee sits out [play]; A wayside comedy; Baa baa, black sheep; The bridge-builders; The maltese cat; "In ambush"; A sahibs' war; "Wireless"; Mrs. Bathurst; "Swept and garnished"; Mary Postgate; "Dymchurch flit"; With the night mail; The house surgeon; The wish house; The Janeites; The bull that thought; A madonna of the trenches; The eye of Allah; The gardener; Dayspring mishandled; The church that was at Antioch; The manner of men

The light that failed.

Available from Amereon and Buccaneer Bks.

First published 1890

"Through his experiences as an illustrator in the Sudan, the hero, Dick Heldar, wins both professional success and a firm friend in the war correspondent Torpenhow. He is in love with his foster sister Maisie, now also an artist, but Maisie is shallow and selfish and does not appreciate his devotion. Dick gradually goes blind from a sword cut received in the Sudan, working courageously against time on his painting, 'Melancholia.' Although Maisie is summoned by Torpenhow, she heartlessly leaves Dick to his fate, and he carries out his plan of dying at the front." Reader's Ency

Kirkwood, James, 1930-1989

Some kind of hero; a novel. Crowell 1975 399p o.p.

"Eddie Keller's four years as a POW in Vietnam are climaxed by the senseless death of his buddy just days before their release. Eddie returns to the U.S. to find his marriage ruined, his mother paralyzed, and his father crassly selfish. Eddie takes arms against his cruel fate, heists some negotiable securities and sells them to the Mafia. Then he retires to Martha's Vineyard to become a writer." Libr J

This novel "combines several elements, effectively and dramatically; both funny and sad, it winds up in an exciting crime caper and chase, and it treats bisexuality openly as something to be accepted as perfectly normal." Publ Wkly

Kirst, Hans Hellmut, 1914-1989

Forward, Gunner Asch!; translated from the German by Robert Kee. Little, Brown 1956 368p o.p.

Sequel to The revolt of Gunner Asch

Original German edition, 1954; published in the United Kingdom as part two of the trilogy: Zero eight fifteen, with title: Gunner Asch goes to war

"The action of the book alternates between a sector of the Russian front in late winter of 1941-2, and a base depot somewhere in Germany. Gunner Asch and his companions, whom we met in the first volume training at home, have now gone to war. . . . The characters move like Breughel peasants against a bleak winter landscape; unshaven, filthy, swaddled in greatcoats and sacking, their minds set only on self-preservation, food, and, where possible, women." New Statesman

Followed by The return of Gunner Asch

Kirst, Hans Hellmut, 1914-1989—*Continued*

The night of the generals; a novel; translated from the German by J. Maxwell Brownjohn. Harper & Row 1963 319p o.p.

Original German edition, 1962

"A crime novel in which a German counter-espionage officer and later a Sureté official attempt to solve the three similar sex murders of prostitutes in Warsaw during 1942, Paris in 1944, and Dresden in 1956. There are three suspects, all German generals: . . . an old-school corps commander, his chief of staff, who questions German militarism in general and the War in particular, and the commander of an elite division, a hero of almost legendary proportions. The 'Night of the Generals,' an attempted army coup against Hitler in July 1944, plays a large part in the plot." Libr J

The nights of the long knives; translated by J. Maxwell Brownjohn. Coward, McCann & Geoghegan 1976 279p o.p.

Original German edition, 1975

"In Lugano, in Italian Switzerland, a German is found shot with an unusual weapon. His memoirs, hidden in a bank, reveal him to have been an unreconstructed Nazi, a dedicated charter member of the SS in a group specially trained for murder, and unquestioning obedience to higher authority, in this case, a supremely sinister aristocrat, and ultimately to Hitler himself. The group is meticulously schooled in things such as pistol shooting, gymnastics, destroying evidence, and advanced anti-Semitism." Libr J

"Kirst expertly knits together the suspense of murder investigation with the brutal tone of the Nazi era into a forceful story." Booklist

The return of Gunner Asch; translated from the German by Robert Kee. Little, Brown 1957 310p o.p.

Sequel to Forward, Gunner Asch!

Original German edition, 1955; published in the United Kingdom as third part of the trilogy: Zero eight fifteen

The third volume in the author's series about the adventures of a German army sergeant in World War II describes "the disintegration of the front-line units of the German Army as the Allies advanced in the closing days of combat in Europe in 1945. Asch becomes involved in an effort to track down two officers who left their men to needless slaughter to catch up with a black-market cache." Booklist

Followed by What became of Gunner Asch (1964)

The revolt of Gunner Asch; translated from the German by Robert Kee. Little, Brown 1955 311p o.p.

First in a series of four novels about Gunner Asch

Original German edition, 1954; published in the United Kingdom as part of the trilogy Zero eight fifteen, with title: The strange mutiny of Gunner Asch

This is "a German novel poking fun at the more idiotic aspects of Army discipline. Set in a garrison town just before the last war, it tells of a one-man battle fought by Gunner Asch, a nice young man with a capacity for indignation, against the bullying N.C.O.'s of his company." Manchester Guardian

"A tale in which elements of drama and suspense are skillfully fused with high comedy—a tale which the author brings to a startling and altogether delightful conclusion. . . . Kirst has succeeded in distilling robust fun out of brutal realities without ever suggesting that the realities were other than brutal." Atlantic

Followed by Forward, Gunner Asch!

Kittredge, Mary, 1949-

Poison pen. Walker & Co. 1990 182p $18.95

ISBN 0-8027-5768-5   LC 90-35481

Charlotte Kent, "now living in New Haven, Connecticut, and working as editor of *Pen and Pencil,* walks into her office to find Wesley Bell, a prominent novelist and her most valuable contributor, dead in her desk chair. After the lurking murderer knocks her out with ether, Charlotte recovers to find that her novelist friend Owen Strathmore, the lover of Bell's wife, has been accused of the murder. Convinced that Owen isn't a killer, Charlotte begins snooping around in literary circles and quickly turns up a plethora of suspects." Booklist

Rigor mortis; an Edwina Crusoe mystery. St. Martin's Press 1991 201p o.p.

LC 90-49295

Available Thorndike Press large print edition

"Millionaire Edwina Crusoe is a private nurse whose practice is limited to 'consultation.' Her business card, she thinks, might just as well have read 'Professional Snoop—Medical/Health Matters Only.' The formidable heroine is working at Chelsea Memorial Hospital in New Haven, Conn., when a third patient of nurse Jillian Nash dies. After the patient's niece accuses Jillian of murder, Jillian's father hires Edwina to investigate." Publ Wkly

Klein, Norma, 1938-1989

Sunshine; a novel. Holt, Rinehart & Winston 1975 c1974 218p o.p.

Originally published 1974 in paperback by Avon Books

Based on a true story, this novel "is 19-year-old Kate's journal about being a young wife and mother; being in love with her husband and baby girl; and coming to grips with her own imminent death. After she learns she has cancer in her knee, Kate refuses to have her leg amputated and become a cripple, unable to raise her small daughter. Subsequently, when the cancer spreads, she first refuses radiation treatments and then medication because of their physical and mental effects. When it becomes too difficult for her to write her diary, she makes tapes—her legacy to Jill—so her daughter can know the kind of person her mother was." SLJ

Kluger, Richard

The Sheriff of Nottingham. Viking 1992 485p $19.95

ISBN 0-670-84022-X   LC 91-50240

"Kluger's revisionist novel portrays the infamous Sheriff of Nottingham of Robin Hood fame as a scrupulously upright man fighting to retain his integrity in a vicious world, and his loyalty to a king whose cruelty and capricious temperament are legendary." Libr J

The author "approaches this novelistic portrait of medieval England with the eye of a social historian guided by moral concerns. His carefully rendered characters span the social classes, and his portrayal of the degradation and exploitation suffered by medieval women, regardless of their status, is sensitive and affecting." N Y Times Book Rev

Knebel, Fletcher, 1911-1993
Seven days in May; by Fletcher Knebel and Charles W. Bailey II. Harper & Row 1962 341p o.p.

"The story set against a . . . political Washington background, is about a military plot to take over the government. Its hero is a President of the U.S. in the 1970's, who with six men he trusts, sets out to prove the plot exists and to foil it." Publ Wkly

Knight, Damon Francis, 1922-
The best of Damon Knight; with an introduction by Barry N. Malzberg. Taplinger 1978 c1976 307p o.p.

Analyzed in Short story index
First published 1976 in paperback by Pocket Books
Contents: Not with a bang; To serve man; Cabin boy; The analogues; Babel II; Special delivery; Thing of beauty; Anachron; Extempore; Backward, O time; The last word; Man in the jar; The enemy; Eripmav; A likely story; Time enough; Mary; The handler; The big pat boom; Semper fi; Masks; Down there

"A writer of estimable talent, as these twenty-two stories from 1948-73 prove. Knight's motifs are common—time travel, after-the-holocaust, cyborgs, alien visitors to earth—but the wit, penetrating social satire, and quick narrative twists are distinctly his own." Booklist

Knopf, Marcy, 1969-
(ed) The Sleeper wakes. See The Sleeper wakes

Knowles, John, 1926-
Indian summer. Random House 1966 242p o.p.

A "study of a lifelong friendship that has an unrecognized source of tragedy. Cleet Kinsolving's idealization of the friendship is destroyed when he realizes that Neil Reardon is disguising envy by using his wealth to turn Cleet into a hanger-on. Cleet breaks off the association and starts his life over with the knowledge that his revenge, an attack on Neil's wife, is animalistic and reveals his own weaknesses." Booklist

"The theme of individualism is explored with great energy and charm; and the commentaries on the rich, the poor, success, failure, and politics are dipped in truth and rolled in humor." Libr J

Peace breaks out. Holt, Rinehart & Winston 1981 193p o.p.

LC 80-19678

Set in the Devon School in New Hampshire, scene of A separate peace, this novel takes place during the 1945-46 term. "Pete Hallam—Class of '37—returning . . . as a teacher, hopes to recover there from wartime traumas. But the boys in the class of '46 are an edgy bunch, frustrated and guilty because they won't be graduating from the prep school to the armed forces like the classes before them. There's a simmering air of violence among them during the long winter as Pete in his low-keyed way tries to help them across the threshold to adulthood." Publ Wkly

A separate peace; a novel. Macmillan 1960 c1959 186p $40

ISBN 0-02-564850-0
Also available G.K. Hall large print edition
First published 1959 in the United Kingdom
"Gene Forrester looks back on his school days, spent in a New England town just before World War II. He both admires and envies his close friend and roommate, Finny, who is a natural athlete, in contrast to Gene's special competence as a scholar. When Finny suffers a crippling accident, Gene must face his own involvement in it." Shapiro. Fic for Youth. 3d edition

Koen, Karleen
Through a glass darkly. Random House 1986 743p o.p.

LC 86-422

Set in early eighteenth century England and France, this novel "tells the story of Barbara Alderley, who is fifteen when the story begins, and about to be bartered in marriage to the middle-aged but gorgeous Roger Montgeoffry. The barterer is her own mother, [Diana]. . . . Barbara is in love with Roger, Roger is in love with Bentwoodes, the family seat that is to be her dowry, and Diana is in love with money and power." N Y Times Book Rev

"Expertly paced, the novel blends quaint historical romance with a sharp-edged, contemporary psychodramatic style. Its characters are memorable and full-bodied, maturing through a series of rapidly escalating tragedies that bring the sweetly naive heroine into full womanhood and force her to make a decision that will forever change her life. A sophisticated, atmospheric work." Booklist

Koestler, Arthur, 1905-1983
Darkness at noon; translated by Daphne Hardy. Macmillan 1987 267p $35

ISBN 0-02-565210-9   LC 86-31273
"A Macmillan Hudson River edition"
First published 1940 in the United Kingdom; this is a reissue of the 1941 edition
This novel "deals with the arrest, imprisonment, trial, and execution of N. S. Rubashov in an unnamed dictatorship over which 'No. 1' presides. Koestler describes Rubashov as 'a synthesis of the lives of a number of men who were victims of the so-called Moscow trials,' and the novel did much to draw attention to the nature of Stalin's regime." Oxford Companion to Engl Lit. 5th edition

Koontz, Dean R. (Dean Ray), 1945-
The bad place. Putnam 1990 382p o.p.

LC 89-10861
Available Thorndike Press large print edition
"Married detectives Julie and Bobby Dakota agree to help frightened amnesiac Frank Pollard figure out what he does when he's asleep. . . . In due course, Frank and the Dakotas join forces against murderer Candy Pollard and his weird sisters, who want to kill Frank—evidently the sole human in the monstrous family. Candy extends psychic feelers toward potential victims, emanations that are sensed by Julie's younger brother Thomas. A Down's syndrome child, Thomas is telepathically gifted and able to warn Bobby of the demons who threaten Julie." Publ Wkly

Koontz, Dean R. (Dean Ray), 1945- —
Continued

Cold fire. Putnam 1991 382p o.p.

LC 90-46806

Available Thorndike Press large print edition

Teacher Jim Ironheart "is sent by forces unknown to save chosen people in life-threatening situations. By chance, [Holly Thorne], a young but jaded reporter stumbles onto his missions, and joins him to investigate who is controlling him and why. Shared nightmares begin to point to an extraterrestrial influence, and the pair are forced to confront Ironheart's forgotten past for answers." Libr J

"Koontz is perhaps the least given to verbal pyrotechnics of the current horror masters. His work displays a subdued prose style; cultural sidebars are kept to a minimum; and blood spills are few and far between. But he also knows how to generate genuine terror without gore." Booklist

Dark rivers of the heart; a novel; [by] Dean Koontz. Knopf 1994 487p $24

ISBN 0-679-42524-1   LC 94-12090

"Spencer Grant is on the run from a nameless, violent government agency. His goal is to keep away from his pursuers long enough to find the woman he met the night before, who appears to be their real target. Spencer has no idea why they want to kill Valerie Keene, but his brief acquaintance with her has convinced him that the killers have no good reason for wanting her dead. With his . . . dog, Rocky, Spencer leads the killers on a frustrating chase." Libr J

"Koontz has succeeded where many genre writers have failed: he has switched gears, put the zombies and creepy crawlers aside, and written a believable high-tech thriller." N Y Times Book Rev

Dragon tears; [by] Dean Koontz. Putnam 1993 377p o.p.

LC 92-28854

Available Thorndike Press large print edition

"In southern California, police detective Harry Lyon and his partner, Connie Guliver, find themselves hounded by a golem who appears in the shape of a towering vagrant. Called Ticktock because he grants his victims only hours to live, the vagrant has tremendous physical power, a taste for gruesomely described violence and the ability to stop time and rearrange reality. Koontz romps playfully and skillfully through this grown-up enchantment." Publ Wkly

The face of fear

In Koontz, D. R. Three complete novels p323-510

Hideaway. Putnam 1992 384p o.p.

LC 91-29786

Available Thorndike Press large print edition

"When Californians Hatch and Lindsey Harrison are run off a mountain road, Hatch drowns. A helicopter lifts him to an Orange County state-of-the-art hospital, however, and after being dead for 80 minutes Hatch is resuscitated. Weeks later, impelled by newfound joy in life, Hatch and Lindsey adopt bright, crippled 10-year-old Regina. The only clouds in their delight are visions that Hatch seems to share with a deranged killer." Publ Wkly

Lightning. Putnam 1988 351p o.p.

LC 87-21649

"On the night of Laura Shane's birth, a stranger appears from the lightning to prevent her delivery's being botched by an alcoholic physician. Throughout Laura's childhood the stranger reappears at times of danger. He protects rather than threatens, yet menace seems to follow him. Thirty years later another storm flashes and the stranger collapses, shot, at Laura's door. Now Laura protects her erst-while guardian from mysterious hunters. He reveals that he and the hunters are time travelers. Laura, quick-witted and brave, leads the way to a bloody showdown." Libr J

The author "quickly grabs the reader's attention. But then he kicks in with his usual stop-start suspense rhythm, giving rise to a certain impatience with the heroine's roller-coaster perils. Nonetheless, there are enough imaginative twists here, along with likable characters . . . to win him new fans and please old ones." N Y Times Book Rev

also in Koontz, D. R. Three complete novels p9-321

Midnight. Putnam 1989 383p o.p.

LC 88-22830

Available Thorndike Press large print edition

"A set of mysterious disappearances and suspicious deaths in the northern California town of Moonlight Cove brings together an undercover F.B.I. agent named Sam Booker and Tessa Lockland, a documentary film producer who suspects that the local police report of her sister's suicide has been falsified. They discover that someone has been turning the town's citizens into humanoids." N Y Times Book Rev

Mr. Murder; [by] Dean Koontz. Putnam 1993 415p $23.95

ISBN 0-399-13874-9   LC 93-19368

Also available Thorndike Press large print edition

This novel concerns "mystery novelist Martin Stillwater and his wife and two young daughters. Mr. Murder is the name bestowed on Martin by *People* magazine; his wife, Paige, is a wonderful woman, and their little girls are, of course, adorable. Unfortunately, into this idyllic world comes a superhuman hit man who coincidentally happens to look just like Martin and who's decided he wants the family for his very own and will kill Martin to get them." Booklist

"Playing on every emotion and keeping the story racing along, Koontz masterfully escalates the tension. He closes the narrative with the most ingenious twist ending of his career." Publ Wkly

Night chills. Atheneum Pubs. 1976 334p o.p.

"It all begins with a plausible network of self-serving types—a scientist peddling a chemical formula, a businessman mindful of profits, a Pentagon superpatriot. All three see a chance for millions by injecting potable water with a drug that causes people to heed subliminal suggestions transmitted personally or through the media. Taking over an Arab emirate saturated with petro-resources is a possibility, but first comes the trial run and this involves the New England township of Black River in a grizzly shakedown exercise. Villagers act like zombies, ignoring the murder of a child, the son of a tourist, just as long as code phrases prompt Pavlovian responses. Yet the boy's father Paul Annendale undercuts mass manipulation by exploiting a trauma buried with scientist Paul Salsbury's perverse psyche." Publ Wkly

Koontz, Dean R. (Dean Ray), 1945- —
Continued

Strangers. Putnam 1986 526p o.p.

LC 85-25677

"Eight characters—all strangers to each other—form the core of the novel. Each is plagued by suspiciously similar fears and anxieties. Ernie Block, who runs a Nevada motel, fears the dark. Ginger Weiss, a Boston cardiology resident, suffers from panic attacks. Southern California horror novelist Dom Corvaisis is vexed with somnambulism. These and other seemingly disparate characters share only one link aside from their bewildering array of related symptoms—all had spent three days during the previous July at Block's motel, not far from a secret military depository." Booklist

Three complete novels; [by] Dean Koontz. Putnam 1993 704p $11.98

ISBN 0-399-13843-9   LC 92-35322

An omnibus edition of three suspense novels. Lightning is entered separately. The face of fear (1977) was published under the author's pseudonym Brian Coffey and is about a man and woman trapped on the fortieth floor of a deserted office building by a psychopath. The vision (1977) is about a woman being stalked by a mysterious, knife-wielding killer

The vision

In Koontz, D. R. Three complete novels p511-704

Watchers. Putnam 1987 352p o.p.

LC 86-22687

Available Thorndike Press large print edition

"When the Russians sabotage a genetic research project in California, two mutated creatures escape from the lab. One is a golden retriever with high enough intelligence to think and communicate with humans; the other is the Outsider, a vicious monster created from a baboon and bred to kill. Both the man who befriends and adopts the dog and his new bride find themselves stalked by government agents anxious to find the dog, a particularly repulsive Mafia hit man intent on stealing him, and the Outsider, with whom the dog is linked telepathically." Libr J

"Despite some pedestrian writing, the suspense holds to the end. Displaying a little more depth and a lot more humor than Stephen King, Dean R. Koontz has really hit his stride." N Y Times Book Rev

Korda, Michael, 1933-

Curtain; a novel. Summit Bks. 1991 378p o.p.

LC 90-23198

"Robert Vance is a superb Shakespearean actor. He falls in love with an actress, Felicia Lisle, whose fastidious beauty conceals fierce passion. Unable to escape their marriages, they become Britain's favorite adulterous celebrity couple, playing the role of lovers both on stage and in private. Korda opens this pageturner with a prologue set 40 years in the future and hinting at dark, long-hidden secrets. He then flashes back to the 1940s when Vance and Felicia are stranded in Hollywood, broke after a disastrous attempt at taking *Romeo and Juliet* on the road in the U.S. Felicia, drinking and pill-popping, is on the verge of a breakdown, and Robby is anxious to return to London and

serve in the RAF. . . . Having set his novel on stage, Korda can pull out all the stops—nothing is too theatrical. And it's a hit." Booklist

The fortune. Summit Bks. 1989 481p o.p.

LC 88-37980

"The wealthy, snobbish Bannerman family is a fictional hybrid of the Rockefellers and the Binghams. It's bad enough that Arthur Bannerman has the poor taste to die in the bed of an attractive young woman. But when she declares herself his widow and delivers a will giving her control of the family fortune, his son Robert and the redoubtable matriarch Eleanor haul out the heavy artillery. Korda has a wonderful ear for bitchy, brittle society chatter, and he takes satirical swipes in every direction." Publ Wkly

The immortals; a novel. Poseidon Press 1992 559p $20

ISBN 0-671-74526-3   LC 92-22265

A "novel about the love affair between John F. Kennedy and Marilyn Monroe. The theme it rests on is this: as JFK's star ascended, MM's descended, and as their stars crossed, heat was definitely generated. Korda understands politics as well as fatal attraction, so his fiction is several notches above your basic steamy romance." Booklist

Worldly goods. Random House 1982 353p o.p.

LC 81-40213

A saga about a "Hungarian family torn apart by various fortunes, a terrible betrayal back in Nazi days (there are flashbacks to Hitler, Himmler, and the Holocaust), and insatiable lust for money, power, and vengeance now. Paul Foster (née Grunwald) survived Auschwitz and has at last amassed the worldy wherewithal to avenge his father, all unbeknownst to his betraying uncle and cousin. Foster is a cold fish (though there's a heroine to adhere to him), but he only wants to take enough fortune away from his uncle to make him cry 'uncle.'" Saturday Rev

"At once a Holocaust novel from a new point of view, and a look at love, hate, power, and sex in the stratosphere of the modern corporation, this book is tightly constructed." Libr J

Kornbluth, C. M. (Cyril M.), 1923-1958

(jt. auth) Pohl, F. The space merchants

Kornbluth, Cyril M. *See* Kornbluth, C. M. (Cyril M.), 1923-1958

Kosinski, Jerzy N., 1933-1991

Being there; [by] Jerzy Kosinski. Harcourt Brace Jovanovich 1971 c1970 142p o.p.

"An illiterate gardener, Chance, knows the world only through his gardening and by watching television, to which he is addicted. Without education or any identifiable background, he is evicted into the outside world when his employer dies. He makes horticultural analogies to current events, which give him a reputation for wisdom that he really does not have, and which catapult him into national prominence. Chance's simple statements are interpreted by his listeners to be profound observations, and we see him being considered for positions of great importance. This is a satire on human

Kosinski, Jerzy N., 1933-1991—*Continued*
behavior in the worlds of power, government, and the
media." Shapiro. Fic for Youth. 3d edition

Blind date; [by] Jerzy Kosinski. Houghton
Mifflin 1977 236p o.p.

LC 77-21968

The author "depicts the complex inner and outer lives
of George Levanter, once a student in Moscow, now a
rich and mysterious dabbler in death, sex, the manipulation of those weaker than he. Levanter has his quixotic
moments when those he kills or brings to ruin are themselves evil people responsible for torturing others. Yet
as he whirls from one 'blind date' with fate to another
he is often as perverted and brutal as those he condemns. He begins with boyhood incest with his mother.
In his teens in Communist Russia he commits a particularly savage rape (recounted in minute detail). Later
in life, having escaped to the West, he survives by outwitting the rich and foolish and becomes a lover extraordinaire." Publ Wkly

This is "a disturbing examination of the alienation and
rootlessness which characterize the modern world, often
erupting into mindless brutality." West Coast Rev Books

The devil tree; [by] Jerzy Kosinski.
Harcourt Brace Jovanovich 1973 208p o.p.

This novel "confronts the disintegration of the American dream as seen through the eyes of Jonathan James
Whalen, the man-who-has-everything. For Whalen and
many of the people who surround him, the American
dream has become the American nightmare. Their efforts
to escape their roots become a frenetic search to find
their roots, until, like the devil tree, they get turned
upside down and confirm the fact of their own extinction. Jonathan Whalen is as empty as the life he leads,
although on the surface he is a man who can be and
do anything he wants." Publ Wkly

The hermit of 69th Street; the working
papers of Norbert Kosky; [by] Jerzy
Kosinski. Seaver Bks. 1988 529p o.p.

LC 87-10924

"Tantric Jew, macho enigma, and first-rate second-rate
novelist, Norbert Kosky chronicles the composition of
his ninth book, an 'autofictional' account of a burned-out
writer who bears an uncanny resemblance to Kosinski.
The huge punning text—edited by J.K., or Jay Kay—is
accompanied by an equally huge collection of scholarly
footnotes, evidencing a lifelong obsession with the
Holocaust, cabala, contemporary literary theory, and girlie
magazines." Libr J

"The outlines of the story may seem familiar to
readers who know the author's work, but the narrative
technique charts new ground, knocking down the barrier
between erudition and pretension with a complex and
rather tricky canvas intended to capture an artist's intimate self-portrait." Booklist

The painted bird; [by] Jerzy Kosinski. 2nd
Modern Library ed. Modern Lib. 1983
c1965 234p $6.95

ISBN 0-394-60433-4   LC 82-42869

First published 1965 by Houghton Mifflin

"In Eastern Europe during World War II a ten-year-old
boy is separated from his parents and struggles to survive in primitive villages where he is viewed as an unwanted outsider. Dark-haired and dark-eyed, he is unlike
the Polish villagers among whom he tries to find refuge.
He is the gypsy, the 'painted bird,' and savage abuse

is heaped upon him time after time. He has, nevertheless, the will to transcend the sadism and superstition
of these ignorant people." Shapiro. Fic for Youth. 3d
edition

Passion play; [by] Jerzy Kosinski. St.
Martin's Press 1979 271p o.p.

LC 79-5035

"Fabian, the protagonist, is a peripatetic polo-player
who travels in an hermetic recreational vehicle, his Van-
Home. He is past his prime, obsessed with aging and
poverty, stricken from the ranks of 'good team players,'
seeking financial support through odd jobs and friendships on the playing fields of the idle rich and by one-
on-one polo jousts. This latter-day Knight of the Sad
Countenance is also obsessed with sexual dominance,
proving his mastery with a string of underage Dulcineas."
West Coast Rev Books

The author's "descriptions of equestrian combat belong
on the same shelf with Hemingway and Tolstoy. His
accounts of a South American republic where the main
sources of power are the ox and the jet are masterpieces
of irony and pure narrative. He tirelessly examines what
he terms 'the regency of pain.' Like Dostoyevsky's,
Kosinski's characters explore their own souls, always
reaching for limits." Time

Kotzwinkle, William

E.T.; the extra-terrestrial; a novel. Putnam
1982 246p o.p.

LC 82-9078

"Based on a screenplay by Melissa Mathison." Title
page

"A ten million year old alien botanist is accidentally
marooned on Earth. He is befriended by three children
and in particular by Elliott, whose bedroom closet
becomes his hideout. With their help he learns something
of our planet's bewildering ways, puts together a beacon
to call for rescue and thrives on a diet of M&Ms, Oreos
and, even more important, the children's love. Of course,
the government suspects his presence and is hunting him,
but after he is captured Elliott helps him escape in time
to rendezvous with his ship." Publ Wkly

"Kotzwinkle's many gifts, particularly for realistic detail
and black humor, make this a book capable of standing
on its own merits apart from the motion picture." Booklist

The Game of Thirty. Houghton Mifflin;
Lawrence, S. 1994 262p $21.95

ISBN 0-395-53270-1   LC 94-9503

This novel "introduces Jimmy McShane, who is hired
to solve the grisly murder of a shady dealer in rare
antiquities. Pitted against a killer whose methods include
cobra venom and disembowelment, McShane is joined
by Dr. Ann Henderson, a chiropractor and aspiring
sleuth. It turns out that the deceased was killed while
playing the Game of Thirty, an ancient Egyptian board
game, and that the killer is playing the game with Jimmy, using all of New York City as the board." Booklist

"The author's literate, fluid prose, which sparkles with
le mot juste, thus reveals an admirable hero, solid plot,
and Egyptian cachet as well as the author's versatility."
Libr J

Krantz, Judith

I'll take Manhattan. Crown 1986 437p o.p.

LC 85-22403

Krantz, Judith—*Continued*

"The magazine empire of the late Zachary Amberville is being pulled to pieces by his envious younger brother, Cutter, whose first official act after marrying his sister-in-law is to ax four periodicals. Within a year, he expects to sell those remaining at a huge profit. But Cutter hasn't reckoned on his fiesty niece, Maxi, who, at 29, has been a mother once, a divorcée three times, and a spendthrift all her life. Sailing into battle with aid from her brother Justin, a photographer with a past of his own, and her macho first husband, Rocco, Maxi turns a dying magazine into a wild success. Light sparring between the formerly-marrieds keeps the book humming along, although the scuffle with Cutter is abruptly dropped when the extent of his duplicity becomes known. Weak subplots are easily glossed over by punchy dialogue and an amusing, likable cast." Publ Wkly

Mistral's daughter. Crown 1983 c1982 531p o.p.

LC 82-17966

"Three generations of Lunel women are intimately involved with Julien Mistral, France's greatest artist. Maggy is his model, the inspiration for a series of remarkable nude paintings in 1925, and he is her first lover. Years later Teddy, star of her mother Maggy's New York modeling agency, meets Mistral on assignment and lightening strikes; she becomes his mistress and the mother of Fauve. And Mistral's daughter Fauve, though an 'enfante adulterine,' has some of his talent and brightens his life before their estrangement." Libr J

The author "possesses an undeniable talent for plot-weaving and descriptive detail." Best Sellers

Till we meet again. Crown 1988 534p o.p.

LC 88-11857

This novel features "three heroines with whirlwind life-styles: Eve, the vicomtesse Paul-Sebastian de Lancel, and her daughters Danielle and Freddy, a movie star and an aviator. Eve's story begins in 1910 when an affair with a music-hall singer shames her family and momentarily takes her life in a different direction from her upper-middle-class roots. By the time her daughters are born, Eve is the wife of a diplomat, but Danielle and Freddy both possess their mother's restless genes." Booklist

Krentz, Jayne Ann

Grand passion. Pocket Bks. 1994 309p $22

ISBN 0-671-77870-6   LC 93-10345

Also available Thorndike Press large print edition

"Max Fortune arrives at Cleo Robbins' inn on a quest for five priceless paintings left to him in his employer's will. Cleo has never seen the paintings, and as Max continues to stay at Robbins' Nest Inn to search for his inheritance, he becomes part of Cleo's eccentric family and grows increasingly closer to Cleo herself. When Cleo is threatened by a mysterious stalker who objects to an erotic novel she wrote, Max steps in to protect her and to discover who is threatening her life." Booklist

Kress, Nancy

And wild for to hold

In Modern classic short novels of science fiction p617-57

Beggars & choosers. TOR Bks. 1994 315p $22.95

ISBN 0-312-85749-7   LC 94-21753

"A Tom Doherty Associates book"

Sequel to Beggars in Spain

"As a byproduct of their genetic mental enhancements, the Sleepless neither sleep nor age. For those reasons, they are reviled by the unmodified majority of humans. Yet in a world of overpopulation, chronic joblessness, environmental depletion, and uncontrolled plagues of nanotechnological origin, the Sleepless may hold the key to humanity's salvation—if only they can be persuaded to come out of their self-imposed hiding." Libr J

"Kress's work remains strongly character driven, an approach that in her hands raises social-speculation sf to about as high a level as one can reasonably expect." Booklist

Beggars in Spain. Morrow 1993 438p $23

ISBN 0-688-12189-6   LC 92-25070

"An AvoNova book"

Based on a novella of the same title

In this novel, "genetic enhancements have placed Leisha Camden and a few other individuals in a category of their own. Smarter and healthier than normal humans, born without the need to sleep, the 'Sleepless'—as they are called—grow up in a world that turns increasingly hostile toward the super-achievers in their midst." Libr J

"This book is an intellectual roller-coaster ride, supplying no simple conclusions about right and wrong, and racing along with its brisk prose, stimulating ideas, and a variety of challenging characters." SLJ

Followed by Beggars & choosers

Kundera, Milan

The book of laughter and forgetting; translated from the Czech by Michael Henry Heim. Knopf 1980 228p o.p.

LC 80-7657

First published 1979 in France

"The novel is written in seven parts with an interwoven structure that the author likened to polyphonic music. The repetition of incidents, characters, and themes provides *The Book of Laughter and Forgetting* with its formal shape. Memories, which the characters want to keep or to forget, are a recurring subject, as is laughter, which is as often ironic as joyous." Merriam-Webster's Ency of Lit

Immortality; translated from the Czech by Peter Kussi. Grove Weidenfeld 1991 345p o.p.

LC 90-28628

"Kundera, himself a prominent character in the circular narrative, here contrasts the troubled, comic relationships among Goethe; his wife, Christiane; and Goethe's much younger friend Bettina von Arnim to the modern-day triangle of three imaginary Parisians: Paul; his wife, Agnes; and Agnes's sister Laura." Publ Wkly

"Immortality swings easily, almost imperceptibly, from narrative to rumination and back again, collapsing the distinction between action and concepts. . . . Out of a story about contemporary neuroses, Kundera has fabricated a context in which everything, literally, can be claimed to matter. What is more, the author indulges this obsessiveness without ever droning or turning out a dull page. In its inventiveness and its dazzling display

Kundera, Milan—*Continued*
of what written words can convey, Immortality gives
fiction back its good name." Time

The joke. definitive version, fully revised
by the author. HarperCollins Pubs. 1992
317p o.p.

LC 91-58349

Original Czech edition, 1967; first English translation
published 1969 by Coward, McCann
In this novel "a young communist intellectual, Ludvik,
is imprisoned, then stigmatized for life for having written
an irreverent postcard to a girlfriend ('Optimism is the
opium of the people! . . . Long live Trotsky!'). Years
later he seeks revenge in another 'joke'; he will cold-
bloodedly seduce the wife, Helena, of the party leader
who denounced him." Newsweek
"Kundera's brilliance resides in his ability to strip
away the lies and disguises which Ludvik and the others
need to survive, and which their society has
institutionalized and sanctified." New Repub

Laughable loves; translated from the
Czech by Suzanne Rappaport. Knopf 1974
242p o.p.
Analyzed in Short story index
Original Czech edition, 1970
Contents: The hitchhiking game; Let the old dead
make room for the young dead; Nobody will laugh; The
golden apple of eternal desire; Symposium; Dr. Havel
after ten years; Edward and God
"The stories in [this volume] are buoyantly energetic
and virtuosic. . . . The politics here is sexual: male
dominance and impotence, role-playing and fantasizing
detonate with startling effect." Newsweek

The unbearable lightness of being; translated from the Czech by Michael Henry
Heim. Harper & Row 1984 314p o.p.

LC 83-48363

"Set against the background of Czechoslovakia in the
1960s, the novel concerns a young Czech physician who
substitutes a series of erotic adventures over which he
thinks he can maintain control for becoming involved
in his country's politics, where he feels he can have no
power or freedom. Inevitably, he is drawn into Czechoslovakia's political unrest. In a parallel vein, he is forced
to choose among the women with whom he is involved."
Merriam-Webster's Ency of Lit

Kunetka, James W., 1944-
(jt. auth) Strieber, W. Warday

Kuniczak, W. S., 1930-
The thousand hour day. Dial Press (NY)
1967 c1966 628p o.p.
First volume of a trilogy that includes The march
(1979) and Valedictory (1983)
"The time of this novel is 1939; the setting, Poland.
Mr. Kuniczak covers the first 1000 hours of World War
II when the small, ill-equipped Polish army made a
magnificent holding action before the final surrender to
the attacking Germans. Against the speeding background
of the war evolves the story of General January Prus,
a gentle man of strong character, and his influence on
his government and on the men and women around
him." Libr J

The story "usually sustains its interest. The few flat
scenes are more than overbalanced by compelling
episodes. . . . There are the vivid battle scenes. . . .
We also see a good deal of the countryside, with its
peasants and hunters and wandering armies." Saturday
Rev

Kurtén, Björn
Dance of the tiger; a novel of the ice age;
introduction by Stephen Jay Gould.
Pantheon Bks. 1980 255p il o.p.

LC 80-7724

Original Swedish edition, 1978
The author sets "his novel in the Scandinavia of
35,000 years ago, when Cro-Magnon man was moving
into Neandertal territory. He attempts an imaginative
reconstruction of the meeting of Neandertal and Cro-
Magnon and the mysterious disappearance of Neandertal
man, who vanished while Cro-Magnon prospered. Tiger,
a . . . Cro-Magnon, is separated from his people in a
raid. He learns to live with the Neandertals, but is plotting . . . revenge on Shelk, the Neandertal leader of
the raid who killed Tiger's father." Libr J
The author, "who is an unquestioned giant of paleon-
tology, proves with this exciting, lyrical and often moving
novel that there is nothing paradoxical about a scientist's
creating first-rate fiction." N Y Times Book Rev

Kurtz, Katherine
The harrowing of Gwynedd. Ballantine
Bks. 1989 384p (Heirs of Saint Camber, v1)
o.p.

LC 88-7414

"A Del Rey book"
This is the first volume of The heirs of Saint Camber
trilogy; other titles are: King Javan's year (1992) and The
bastard prince (1994). An earlier Deryni tale: The quest
for Saint Camber, is entered below
This is a "tale of the events immediately after Saint
Camber's death. The persecution of the Deryni is
widespread and brutal, their own leadership is beginning
to descend from the high culture of Camber's time to
the petty politics of a later era, and Camber's daughter
must face death to continue her father's work. Kurtz also
manages to be sufficiently graphic about the violence
without being gratuitous, and in short has added another
well-told tale to the Deryni canon." Booklist

The quest for Saint Camber. Ballantine
Bks. 1986 xxvi, 435p (Histories of King
Kelson, v3) $16.95
ISBN 0-345-31826-9   LC 86-8249
"A Del Rey book"
Earlier titles in the King Kelson series are The
bishop's heir (1984) and The King's justice (1985)
"The reported death of King Kelson on a quest for
the tomb of the Deryni Saint Camber throws the Kingdom of Gwynedd into turmoil. As Kelson's friends set
out to search for the truth, a power struggle at court
brings deceit and murder in its wake. [This installment
in the author's] Deryni series . . . skillfully combines
magic with the medieval in a novel that will appeal to
fantasy readers and medievalists alike." Libr J

Kuznetŝov, Anatolii Vasil'evich *See* Anatoli,
A., 1929-

L

La Farge, Oliver, 1901-1963

Laughing Boy. Houghton Mifflin 1929 302p o.p. Buccaneer Bks. reprint available $24.95 (ISBN 0-89960-367-2)

"This novel takes place in the early years of the twentieth century in Navajo country in the American Southwest. It is the story of the ill-fated love of Laughing Boy, worker in silver and maker of songs, and Slim Girl, whose education in American schools has embittered her. The reader is immersed in their tender romance but also learns a great deal about the culture and philosophical outlook of the Native American." Shapiro. Fic for Youth. 3d edition

Lackey, Mercedes

Winds of change. DAW Bks. 1992 449p il (Mage winds, bk 2) $20

ISBN 0-88677-534-5

This second volume in the Mage Winds trilogy "continues the adventures of Elspeth and Skif among the Hawkbrothers. . . . At the end of the previous book, Falconsbane the villain had escaped, so the main thrust of the follow-up is the joint effort by the whole series cast to bring him down." Booklist

Followed by Winds of fury

Winds of fate. DAW Bks. 1991 385p il (Mage winds, bk 1) o.p.

This first volume of a trilogy is set in the "imperiled land of Valdemar, encountered earlier in Lackey's Heralds of Valdemar series. The heir to the throne, Herald Elspeth, sets out with Gwena, her Companion (a Guardian Spirit embodied as a horse), to find an Adept who can teach her people both to use and to deflect the power of magic. . . . Lackey's delightful world of magic is inhabited by strong and believable men, women and creatures." Publ Wkly

Followed by Winds of change

Winds of fury. DAW Bks. 1993 387p il (Mage winds, bk3) $20

ISBN 0-88677-562-0　　　　　　LC 93-219013

"In this concluding book of the Mage Winds trilogy . . . Elspeth returns home via the Forest of Sorrows where the manifest spirit of Vanyel and his lover, the bard Stefan, pull her from her intended destination to explain the now diminished shields against magic and the interlocking mind-web he once placed on Valdemar and how Elspeth must prepare to fight the evil and voracious Ancar of Hardorn." Voice Youth Advocates

(jt. auth) Norton, A. The elvenbane

(jt. auth) Norton, A. Elvenblood

Lagerkvist, Pär, 1891-1974

Nobel Prize in literature, 1951

Barabbas; translated by Alan Blair; with a preface by Lucien Maury and a letter by André Gide. Random House 1951 180p o.p.

Original Swedish edition, 1950

This "is a psychological study of the spiritual journey of Barabbas, the criminal in the New Testament who was offered to the mob in place of Jesus but was spared from execution. The widely translated work was noted for its economical writing style, and it brought Lagerkvist international fame." Merriam-Webster's Ency of Lit

Laker, Rosalind, 1925-

Banners of silk. Doubleday 1981 469p o.p.

LC 80-1453

"A historical romance portraying the rags-to-riches climb of two likable and hard-working couturiers in the nineteenth-century Parisian fashion world. Fate brings Charles Worth and Louise Vernet together when they are young and poor. Although they separate and lose touch, they again meet as colleagues after both have gained reputations as innovative dress designers." Booklist

Circle of pearls. Doubleday 1990 519p o.p.

LC 89-29458

Available G.K. Hall large print edition

A historical romance set in 17th century England. "As the reader follows the maturation of Julia Pallister, a young girl whose family members are staunch royalists, the political, social, and religious conflicts between upper and middle class, Puritan and 'Papist,' Roundhead and Cavalier unfold. Julia is a plucky, brave, and captivating heroine; an interesting mélange of characters, both historical and fictional, march through her life." Booklist

The golden tulip. Doubleday 1991 585p o.p.

LC 90-27591

This novel "follows the exploits of Francesca Visser and her family during late seventeenth-century Holland, as they move in the circles of Rembrandt, Vermeer, and William of Orange. Francesca's dream to become a master artist threatens to be thwarted by the devious Ludolf van Deventer, who manipulates her heavily indebted father into signing a marriage contract for her. Only her own determination and the constant support of Pieter van Doorne—the tulip grower who loves her selflessly—and her sisters guide Francesca toward her goal." Booklist

"The suspense rarely slackens, for Francesca's spirited younger sisters, Aletta and Sybylla, enter into highly entertaining and surprising romances of their own. Laker's . . . tightly woven novel, swift-moving and filled with lusty characters, is weakened only by a convoluted, lengthy cloak-and-dagger finale." Publ Wkly

Jewelled path. Doubleday 1983 378p o.p.

LC 82-45264

"Set at the turn of the century, [this] romance deals with the luxurious world of famous jewelers and their wealthy clients. Her heroine, Irene, the daughter of a prominent London jeweler, has artistic talent and is determined to carve out a career as a jeweler herself. In this she succeeds, despite a broken love affair and strong opposition from her father, who considers her unstable but refuses to explain why. A reunion with her mysterious maternal grandmother (the cause of her father's unease) moves the scene to Paris and then to Monte Carlo, where Irene realizes her dream of success. Additional plot complications are provided by Irene's reluctant love for a married man." Libr J

The silver touch. Doubleday 1987 356p o.p.

LC 86-24199

"Based on the true story of Hester Bateman, an indomitable 18th century English silversmith, this novel . . . chronicles her life from age 12 to 83, as well as the triumphs and catastrophes befalling her six children."

Laker, Rosalind, 1925-—*Continued*

Publ Wkly

The author "concocts a stirring family drama as Hester bears six children, becomes a silversmith herself, and eventually establishes her own reputation as one of the finest artisans in London. Plenty of intriguing romantic quandaries beset Hester and her children as they pursue the family business. Certain to captivate Laker's many readers." Booklist

The sugar pavilion. Doubleday 1994 c1993 370p $22.50

ISBN 0-385-46826-1   LC 93-13713

Also available Thorndike Press large print edition

First published 1993 in the United Kingdom

Sophie Delcourt "flees revolutionary France with her aristocratic employer's young son, Antoine, and settles in Brighton, newly made fashionable by the Prince of Wales. Her goal is to become a confectioner, but no job is beneath her. She begins by waiting tables and becoming a cook at a large Brighton restaurant, and later working at Prinny's Marine Pavilion as a linen maid until her confectionary business succeeds. She is torn by her quiet affection for Rory Morgan, the brave excise officer who patrols the coast at Brighton for smugglers, and her attraction for the dashing, mysterious Tom Foxhill, who knows too much about smuggling for Sophie's peace of mind." Libr J

"With her sharp characterizations and deft ability to slip in historical gossip, Laker transports the reader straight into the inns, shops, bathing machines, and Royal Pavilion of eighteenth-century Brighton." Booklist

This shining land. Doubleday 1985 374p o.p.

LC 84-25894

This novel is "about Johanna Ryen and Steffen Larsen, two young Norwegians who meet and fall in love during the German occupation of Norway between 1940 and 1945. Steffen becomes a leader among the Norwegian resistance, and Johanna, too, is intimately involved in resistance efforts. The young couple's love is tried through separation, conflict and the ravages of war." Best Sellers

To dance with kings. Doubleday 1988 564p o.p.

LC 88-3698

"Set during the reigns of Louis XIV and Louis XVI, the sweeping saga takes place mainly in the Chateau of Versailles and the surrounding town from which the magnificent edifice took its name. . . . Spanning four generations, the protagonists are the women of one family, named, in turn, Marguerite, Jasmin, Violette and Rose, all of whose destinies are entwined with those of their monarchs as well as the dashing men who bring them love and heartache." Publ Wkly

The Venetian mask. Doubleday 1993 422p o.p.

LC 92-12488

Available Thorndike Press large print edition

This historical romance "recounts the enduring friendship of three girls who meet in an 18th-century Venetian music conservatory for orphans. Adrianna happily abandons her opera career for marriage, but blonde Elena and dark-haired Marietta aren't so lucky; they're married to men who are sworn enemies." Libr J

"Laker has a marvelous gift for evoking atmosphere with assiduously researched, intriguing details which she places throughout a genuinely exciting narrative." Publ Wkly

L'Amour, Louis, 1908-1988

Bendigo Shafter. Dutton 1979 324p o.p.

LC 78-15280

"This book's hero is 18-year-old Bendigo Shafter. He is part of a small band of migrants that breaks off its westward trek and builds a small community. The group increases with the coming of other members. It has to fight off the dangers of the frontier both within and outside its confines. Among the main influences on Ben's life are the Widow Macken, who inspires him to read Locke, Rousseau, and Blackstone; Uruwishi, an old Indian brave; and Ethan Sackett, woodsman nonpareil. There are heroes and villains, both white and red, and shooting from the hip in old Western style as Ben demonstrates all the traditional values of courage, honesty, loyalty, and stamina." Shapiro. Fic for Youth. 3d edition

The Californios. Saturday Review Press 1974 188p o.p.

"Eileen Mulkerin is about to lose her ranch because of debts but an ancient Indian, survivor of the Old Ones, leads her to a hidden cache of gold while her son fights off the killers sent to do them in." Booklist

"An expert blend of the fascinating settling of California in the 1840's; strong, self-reliant characters . . . and a plot of evil doings but triumphant good. The theme of mysticism and the legends of The Old Ones is what lifts this book above the typical western. Intriguing even for those who aren't westerns fans." Libr J

The Cherokee Trail. Bantam Bks. 1982 179p o.p.

LC 82-90288

"The leading character [of this novel] is a woman, Southern born and bred, who is left a widow with a small girl in Colorado of the 1860's. She is a tough lady who believes anything a man can do, she can do, and does. As the only woman operator of a station on the Cherokee Trail, Mary Breydon battles enemies with her guns, brains, and supportive friends, male and female. . . . As always, L'Amour respects the history and nature of the West: His characters and language are representative; his details of life on a station are accurate." Libr J

The daybreakers

In L'Amour, L. The Sacketts: beginnings of a dynasty

Four complete novels; The tall stranger; Kilkenny; Hondo; Showdown at Yellow Butte. Avenel Bks. 1980 490p o.p.

LC 80-17734

Omnibus edition of four titles originally published in 1957, 1954, 1953 and 1953 respectively

In The tall stranger a wagon train is headed West when they discover their guide is a killer. Kilkenny is the story of a man who always seems to find himself involved with violence, thieving, and death. In Showdown at Yellow Butte, Tom Kendrick is hired by the townspeople to infiltrate and contain a band of murderers. Hondo is the story of a man who was captured by the Apache Indians

L'Amour, Louis, 1908-1988—*Continued*

The haunted mesa. Bantam Bks. 1987 357p $18.95

ISBN 0-553-05182-2   LC 86-47576

This novel is a "combination of western and occult adventure, with the former given a decided edge. Mike Raglan, the hero, is an investigator of occult phenomena, but he is also a tough loner who knows how to use a six-gun. When he travels to a remote Southwest mesa to investigate the mystery of the Anasazi—a race of vanished cliff-dwellers—he manages to cross over to the Other Side, a fourth dimension that turns out to be very much another western frontier, replete with hidden gold, treacherous landscapes and plenty of Indians to shoot down." N Y Times Book Rev

"Although L'Amour's didactic approach and his needless repetition of details get in the way, this curious hybrid should satisfy fans of both genres." Booklist

Hondo

In L'Amour, L. Four complete novels p221-364

Jubal Sackett. Bantam Bks. 1985 375p o.p.
                 LC 84-91724

This installment of the Sackett saga "features Jubal Sackett, a wily, homespun seventeenth-century hero who sets off to traverse the vast, unexplored North American hinterland. As he ranges through and beyond the mountains, Jubal befriends Keokotah, a fiercely proud Kickapoo brave, and together they help shield an astonishingly beautiful Natchez princess from a vengeful renegade Indian and an unscrupulous Spanish soldier." Booklist

"An absorbing story filled with adventure, romance, a hint of the occult, and information about Indian tribes and life in the mountains in the 17th century." Libr J

Kilkenny

In L'Amour, L. Four complete novels p97-220

Lando

In L'Amour, L. The Sacketts: beginnings of a dynasty

Last of the breed. Bantam Bks. 1986 358p o.p.

                 LC 86-3622

The setting "is modern-day Siberia; the main character [is] Maj. Joe Makatozi, a part Sioux, part Cheyenne Air Force pilot who has been forced down over the Soviet Union and imprisoned in a desolate region roughly equidistant from Moscow and the western tip of Alaska. . . . The athletically inclined 'Joe Mack' slips out of his cell, pole-vaults over the wall and begins heading east with the Russians, and most particularly a hulking Yakut named Alekhin, in hot pursuit." Newsweek

"Joe Mack is a classic American hero, thrown back into the wilderness and forced to rely on his wits and his ancestral skills to survive the deadly cold and elude his Soviet pursuers, including his nemesis, a Siberian tracker. L'Amour brings the same colorful realism to this sweeping adventure that has made his Westerns so beloved." Publ Wkly

The lonesome gods. Bantam Bks. 1983 450p o.p.

                 LC 82-45945

"In the early 1840s six-year-old Johannes Verne survives abandonment in the desert to spend his growing years dreaming of vengeance for the murder of his father and defending himself against enemies, including his grandfather, who are determined to kill him. The pace is almost leisurely, and the book is filled with splendid descriptions of the desert country, historical facts, and nature lore. An absorbing story of the early years of California with plenty of action, gun play, heroes, and villains." Libr J

The man from the broken hills. Large print ed. Hall, G.K. & Co. 1976 c1975 433p o.p.

First published 1975 in paperback by Bantam Books

Set in the Old West this is the story of Milo Talon, an outlaw, who is seeking revenge against a man who betrayed his family

Other titles about the Talons are: Rivers West (1975) and Milo Talon (1981)

The outlaws of Mesquite; frontier stories. Bantam Bks. 1990 199p il o.p.

                 LC 89-18254

Available large print edition $21.95 (ISBN 0-385-41542-7)

Analyzed in Short story index

Contents: The outlaws of Mesquite; Love and the Cactus Kid; The Ghost Maker; The drift; No rest for the wicked; That Packsaddle affair; Showdown on the Tumbling T; The sixth shotgun

Over on the dry side. Saturday Review Press 1975 184p o.p.

"Why was Clive Chantry, 'a silent mysterious man,' foully murdered on his [Colorado] homestead in the Western hills? His brother Owen, the fastest draw west of the Rockies, aims to find out. . . . [The story involves] 15 outlaws and a beautiful in-law, who have different designs on Chantry, and . . . the hardworking father and son who are squatters on the deceased Chantry's premises." N Y Times Book Rev

Other titles about the Chantrys are: North to the Rails (1971); The Ferguson rifle (1973); Borden Chantry (1978); Fair blows the wind (1978)

The riders of High Rock; a Hopalong Cassidy novel. Bantam Bks. 1993 271p o.p.

                 LC 92-37034

First published 1951 with title: Hopalong Cassidy and the riders of High Rock, by the author writing as Tex Burns

This Hopalong Cassidy adventure pits him against a gang of frontier cattle rustlers

The rustlers of West Fork; a Hopalong Cassidy novel; afterword by Beau L'Amour. Bantam Bks. 1991 259p $18

ISBN 0-553-07325-7   LC 91-1969

Also available large print edition $22 (ISBN 0-385-41996-1)

First published 1951 with title: Hopalong Cassidy and the rustlers of West Fork, by the author writing as Tex Burns

In this western, Hopalong Cassidy "heads west to deliver a fortune in bank notes to his old friend, Dick Jordan. He soon learns that Jordan and his daughter, Pam, are being held prisoners on their Circle J ranch by a desperate, trigger-happy band of outlaws, led by the cunning, ruthless Avery Sparr and his partner, smooth-talking and double-crossing Arnold Soper. Even

L'Amour, Louis, 1908-1988—*Continued*
if Hopalong can free his friends, he must guide them
through rough and untamed Apache country while being
constantly stalked by men who have vowed to shoot him
down." Publisher's note

Sackett

In L'Amour, L. The Sacketts: beginnings
of a dynasty

The Sacketts: beginnings of a dynasty.
Saturday Review Press 1976 3v in 1 o.p.
Contains The daybreakers, Sackett, and Lando, originally published by Bantam Books in 1960, 1961 and 1962
respectively. The three novels included in this omnibus
edition all concern members of the Sackett family during
the great frontier heyday of the 1850s and 1860s
"The first tale takes Tyrel and Orrin from the Tennessee hills to Santa Fe. The second adventure is told by
William Tell Sackett, the third by Lando. All are well-
drawn portraits of a unique period, unmistakably
L'Amour, unmistakably among his best." Booklist
Other titles about the Sacketts are: Mojave crossing
(1964); Sackett brand (1965); Mustang man (1966); The
lonely man (1966); The sky-liners (1967); Galloway
(1970); Treasure Mountain (1972); Ride the dark trail
(1972); Sackett's land, entered separately; To the far blue
mountains, entered separately; The warrior's path (1980);
Lonely on the mountain (1980); Ride the river (1983);
and Jubal Sackett, entered separately

Sackett's land. Saturday Review Press
1974 198p o.p.
Chronologically the first of the author's Sackett novels.
Barnabas Sackett "is a small landowner of Cambridge-
shire, but he has noble forebears and is skilled with the
sword. A run-in with an arrogant aristocrat sends him
fleeing to London, where he relaxes at the Globe Theatre
between bouts of swordsplay. He falls in with some
seafarers, sails for America, trades (and fights) with the
Indians, and makes it back to England with a load of
furs. But his destiny lies in America, and he's heading
back there at story's end." Publ Wkly

Showdown at Yellow Butte

In L'Amour, L. Four complete novels
p365-490

The tall stranger

In L'Amour, L. Four complete novels
p1-95

To the far blue mountains. Saturday
Review Press 1976 287p o.p.
In this Sackett novel Barnabas returns from America
with a cargo of goods. He "is in Lincolnshire on business
when he learns that there is a queen's warrant out for
him because he is suspected of stealing the crown jewels.
He is thrown in prison but manages to escape and make
his way to Bristol and a ship back to Raleigh's Land.
In Virginia, he recruits a band of brave settlers and
strong women and they take boats up the James River
in the direction of the blue mountains until they find
rich land to farm. There Barnabas's children are born
and the community flourishes even though there is ever-
present danger from hostile Indians. This tale is much
more leisurely and nonviolent than the usual L'Amour
story, but it has its share of suspense and gives us a
different kind of look at colonial America." Publ Wkly

The trail to Seven Pines; a Hopalong Cassidy novel. Bantam Bks. 1992 244p o.p.
LC 91-43760
Available large print edition $24 (ISBN 0-385-42369-1)
First published 1951 with title: Hopalong Cassidy and
the trail to Seven Pines, by the author writing as Tex
Burns
"Hopalong was headed northeast toward open country
when he crossed the path of six suspicious-looking men
wearing silver-plated Colts. By the time he heard the
gunshots, he was too far up the trail to do anything—
riding back in time to find a robbed stagecoach and two
bodies lying sprawled and bloody in the dust. The shipment of gold was the fourth to be hijacked in only three
months, and appeared to be connected to the range war
exploding around the Rocking R Ranch in the nearby
town of Seven Pines. Hiring on at the Rocking R,
Hopalong organizes a rough and ragtag outfit to save
the ranch, only to find himself accused of murder and
the target of a ruthless gunman." Publisher's note

Trouble shooter; a Hopalong Cassidy
novel. Bantam Bks. 1994 254p o.p.
LC 93-37947
First published 1952 with title: Hopalong Cassidy, trouble shooter, by the author writing as Tex Burns
In this novel Bill "Hopalong" Cassidy "comes to New
Mexico to help an old friend, Pete Melford, but by the
time Hoppy arrives, Melford is dead, and all traces of
his ranch have vanished. Also looking for the ranch are
Melford's niece, Cindy Blair, and her friend, Rig Taylor.
Standing in their way is Colonel Treadway, owner of
the huge Box T spread and the most powerful individual
in the region. . . . This isn't just a rediscovered
curiosity; it's a pretty good western in its own right."
Booklist

The walking drum. Bantam Bks. 1984
423p o.p.
LC 83-25703
"In 12th century Brittany, young Mathurin Ker-
bouchard, escaping from the evil baron who has slain
Mathurin's mother and plundered their estate, is forced
into galley slavery. He gains control of the boat and
lands in Moorish Spain, where he quickly makes powerful friends and enemies. Mathurin's quest is to rescue
his corsair father, prisoner in the Persian stronghold of
the Assassins. On the way the youth becomes a famed
scholar . . . warrior, merchant, doctor and lover." Publ
Wkly

Lampedusa, Giuseppe Tomasi di *See* Tomasi
di Lampedusa, Giuseppe, 1896-1957

Landrum, Graham, 1922-
The famous DAR murder mystery. St.
Martin's Press 1992 198p $18.95
ISBN 0-312-06968-5   LC 91-33458
Also available G.K. Hall large print edition
"A Thomas Dunne book"
"Several Daughters of the American Revolution (DAR)
ladies relate their roles in solving a murder. When four
members of the Old Orchard Fort chapter (Borderville,
Virginia) of the NSDAR visit an unfrequented graveyard
in search of a patriot's grave, they find a battered body
behind a tombstone. Ascertaining that the sheriff will
give the killing of an apparent vagrant low priority,
Helen Delaporte, regent for the chapter and wife of a

Landrum, Graham, 1922—— *Continued*

lawyer, spearheads an investigation that uses genealogical know-how, gossipy information from lively oldsters, and shrewd common sense. Solid, wholesome, and lively." Libr J

Langton, Jane

The Dante game; illustrations by the author; blackboard sketches by Giovanni Zibo. Viking 1991 325p il o.p.

LC 90-50427

This "Homer Kelly mystery unfolds in Italy, where he joins the faculty of the newly formed American School of Florentine Studies. As students and professors read their way through Dante's *Divine Comedy*, they and the author draw parallels to modern-day Florence, where a bank official (and secret heroin smuggler) plots to assassinate the anti-drug-crusading Pope, using a Beatrice-like student as hostage. After three murders at the school, Homer and a friend investigate." Libr J

"A little pixilated, perhaps, by the richness of her setting, Ms. Langton stuffs too many criminal plots into her busy story, which features the Pope himself in its teeming cast. But her descriptions of the city's visual delights are as voluptuously detailed as any armchair traveler might desire." N Y Times Book Rev

Divine inspiration; a Homer Kelly mystery. Viking 1993 406p il $20

ISBN 0-670-84709-7   LC 93-1693

Homer Kelly "investigates a puzzling set of events involving the First Church of the Commonwealth in Boston. A fire has destroyed the church's organ and left its sexton dead. Now that the glorious new organ is being installed, strange things are happening: an apparently abandoned baby crawls into the church, inexplicable accidents keep delaying the organ's installation, a former musical genius reappears in a homeless shelter, and the church is literally coming apart at the seams. Langton has a knack for weaving dozens of seemingly unrelated plot threads together to form a satisfying and entertaining mystery." Booklist

Emily Dickinson is dead; a novel of suspense; illustrations by the author. St. Martin's Press 1984 247p il o.p.

LC 83-24451

"A Joan Kahn book"

"In a mystery that pokes fun at the behavior of professors in the academic world, a famous poet is chosen as a theme for a literary conference. Stemming from a photograph that an undistinguished professor from a small midwestern college claims is an authentic photo of Emily Dickinson, the faculty of an elite university begin to fight among themselves—sometimes even physically—about who will star at the conference. Entangled in that is Winifred Gaw, an overweight graduate student, and the professor whom she worships, as well as beautiful Allison Groves who becomes the object of Winifred's jealousy and hatred. Emily Dickinson, quietly dead for so many years, becomes a motivation for arson, forgery, and murder." Shapiro. Fic for Youth. 3d edition

God in Concord; illustrations by the author. Viking 1992 338p il $19

ISBN 0-670-84260-5   LC 91-42940

Also available Thorndike Press large print edition

As Homer Kelley, the "transcendentalist detective and his tiny band of partisans stand by fuming, a rapacious Boston developer swoops down on Concord to poison 'the sacred water' of Walden Pond with commercial real estate complexes. Transfixed by the dragon's enticements of new sewage plants and an enriched tax base, the simpleton townsfolk don't even notice when the elderly residents of a choicely situated trailer camp begin to die mysterious deaths." N Y Times Book Rev

Good and dead. St. Martin's Press 1986 244p il o.p.

LC 86-13802

"A Joan Kahn book"

"This is the story of twelve funerals. And a church in Nashoba, Massachusetts, and the presiding officer of the Parish Committee, a virtuous man named Edward Bell. And Homer Kelly, . . . who was once a detective and who was as puzzled as most of the parishioners by the amazing number of local deaths. *What* or who was responsible, if someone or something was, for it all? Was there a pattern? Was the sickness connected with the church?" Publisher's note

The author, "who shows a deep love of New England and its history, has peopled her fictional village with a memorable gallery of sunny, sensible parishioners who, far from being models of rectitude, try gamely to cope with their lust, greed and jealousy." Publ Wkly

Murder at the Gardner; a novel of suspense; illustrations by the author. St. Martin's Press 1988 353p il o.p.

LC 87-27452

"A Joan Kahn book"

"Within the palatial walls of Boston's Gardner Museum, paintings by Botticelli and Titian shed artistic light on a hodgepodge of lesser collectibles, all forever fixed in place as decreed by the inflexible terms of Isabella Stewart Gardner's will, which demands that the whole collection be auctioned off should any changes or unwelcome disturbances occur. The museum's very boyish director, Titus Moon, turns a blind eye to such pranks as tadpoles in the courtyard fountain and ghostly music in the galleries, but even he is appalled when a particularly awful benefactor meets an untimely end." Publ Wkly

Natural enemy; illustrations by the author. Ticknor & Fields 1982 282p il o.p.

LC 81-16618

"A Joan Kahn book"

"Young John Hand, amateur spider expert, has a summer job as live-in-handyman for Barbara and Virginia Heron, whose father has just died. But their pushy neighbor Buddy Whipple moves in too and begins to manipulate everything—including Virginia—in a sinister way. John, whose schoolboy crush on Virginia has not abated, calls on his uncle Homer Kelly to help." Libr J

Lapierre, Dominique

(jt. auth) Collins, L. The fifth horseman

Lardner, Ring, 1885-1933

The best short stories of Ring Lardner. Scribner 1957 346p $40

ISBN 0-684-14743-2

Lardner, Ring, 1885-1933—*Continued*
Analyzed in Short story index
Contents: The Maysville minstrel; I can't breathe; Haircut; Alibi Ike; Liberty Hall; Zone of quiet; Mr. Frisbie; Hurry Kane; Champion; A day with Conrad Green; Old folks' Christmas Harmony; The love nest; Ex parte; The golden honeymoon; Horseshoes; There are smiles; Anniversary; Reunion; Travelogue; Who dealt; My roomy; Some like them cold; A caddy's diary; Mr. & Mrs. Fix-it

Ring around the bases; the complete baseball stories of Ring Lardner; edited and with an introduction by Matthew J. Bruccoli; foreword by Ring Lardner, Jr. Scribner 1992 609p il $35

ISBN 0-684-19374-4   LC 91-38363

Partially analyzed in Short story index
This volume contains You know me Al, entered separately and Lose with a smile, originally published 1933. Also included are two articles and the following stories that have not appeared in any Lardner volume: The busher reenlists; The battle of Texas; The busher pulls a Mays; Sick 'em; Back to Baltimore; The poor simp; Where do you get that noise?; Good for the soul; The crook; The hold-out; The yellow kid; Take a walk

You know me, Al; a busher's letters; by Ring W. Lardner. Doran, G.H. 1916 247p o.p.
Available from Amereon and Buccaneer Bks.
Experiences of a professional baseball player told in his humorously illiterate letters to a "pal"
"Modern baseball players may be more educated and sophisticated than Jack Keefe, but Jack, the cocksure, gullible, naïve pitcher was essentially 'a human being . . . more meaningful than any type could be.'" Libr J

also in Lardner, R. Ring around the bases

Larsen, Jeanne
Silk road; a novel of 8th century China. Holt & Co. 1989 434p il o.p.
LC 88-27286

The author has "several ideas going in this novel set in eighth-century China and seen through the eyes of a young girl transformed into a beautiful woman and eventually a wandering warrior. First, there's a romantic tale of how a heroine, snatched as a child from her parents, is sold into slavery and trained as a concubine. Second, there's a story of mystical revenge, with the girl seeking justice for the mother she barely knew. Superimposed on these stories are the details of Chinese history and culture." Booklist
This novel "maintains a wonderfully mellow tone, perhaps so even a tone as to subvert intensity. But it accommodates much merriment, and moments of sadness and joy, as this feminist fable of mother- and sister-bonding draws together." N Y Times Book Rev

Lathen, Emma
By hook or by crook. Simon & Schuster 1975 223p o.p.
"A Simon and Schuster novel of suspense"
A "mystery involving Wall Street's Sloan Guaranty Trust and its executives, notably John Putnam Thatcher, senior vice-president and a most sophisticated detective

on the side. A colorful and highly emotional Armenian family, whose wealth comes from the Oriental rug business, locks into a violent family feud, the fires fed by a greedy WASP woman who has married into the clan. An aged aunt suddenly emerges out of the Soviet Union. The shares she holds in Parajians, Inc. (which the Sloan has been holding in trust for her) can tip the balance one way or the other. Right on her way to get the whole thing settled she drops dead in the lobby of the Sloan and her death is no accident." Publ Wkly
"The 'large family' theme is intertwined with the 'possible impostor' theme and a neat turning of the tables closes a tale in which Thatcher comes to a conclusion late but on good evidence." Barzun. Cat of Crime. Rev and enl edition

Death shall overcome. Macmillan 1966 190p o.p.
"A Cock Robin mystery"
"The use made here of the civil rights movement, with its attendant sing-ins and sit-ins, is masterly, and one can forgive the authors' playing down of mystery and detection in favor of social comment and superb characterization." Barzun. Cat of Crime. Rev and enl edition

Double, double, oil and trouble. Simon & Schuster 1978 255p o.p.
LC 78-5151
Available G.K. Hall large print edition
"A negotiation vital to construction in the North Sea oil fields is interrupted when an executive is kidnapped. A large ransom is paid and the British government awards the contract to the victim's firm, unfairly in the view of the competition. Matters become complicated when the victim is killed in a car bombing in Houston, and personal rather than business considerations become paramount." Libr J
"The scene shifts from London to Istanbul and Houston to Switzerland, in a story that wouldn't work in the hands of a less skilled writer. Lathen knows how to keep her novels from becoming bogged down by excess verbiage and unnecessary violence." Booklist

East is east. Simon & Schuster 1991 268p o.p.
LC 91-32789
Available Thorndike Press large print edition
This John Putnam Thatcher adventure "takes the senior banking executive from the Sloan Guaranty Trust building in Manhattan on evenly paced travels to Japan, Alaska and England. Lackawanna Electric Industries, rebounding from bankruptcy under the forceful leadership of Carl Kruger, is about to pull off a distribution coup with Yonezawa Trading, one of Japan's largest corporations. Thatcher is present at the Tokyo signing, which is delayed by the discovery of a murdered accountant in Japan's Ministry of International Trade and Investment and a note suggesting a $1-million bribe." Publ Wkly
Ms. Lathen "has a wonderful knack for turning the driest, most complicated corporate maneuvers into high drama, and occasionally burlesque." N Y Times Book Rev

Going for the gold. Simon & Schuster 1981 251p o.p.
"Unprecedented banking demands in Lake Placid during the Winter Olympics have caused the Sloan to open a branch. But the man in charge is not what he seems and his doings are followed by two murders and

Lathen, Emma—*Continued*

a blizzard. Thatcher and Co. have 48 hours to straighten out the mess. As usual, the background—here athletic—is worked into the plot without seeming forced or padded." Barzun. Cat of Crime. Rev and enl edition

Green grow the dollars. Simon & Schuster 1982 249p o.p.

LC 81-18395

In this novel banker detective John "Thatcher has to determine whether a new strain of tomato, a genetic miracle, has been developed by the long-established Vandam Nursery or a competitor, Wisconsin Seedsmen. Scott Wenzel, Wisconsin's belligerent botanist, claims credit for the hybrid tomato and Wisconsin files suit against Vandam, freezing their deposits in Thatcher's bank. He soon realizes that he must look for a murderer, presumably a patent thief, when someone kills a Wisconsin employee and attempts to kill another. At stake are professional reputations and high profits and the suspects are many in this exciting tale." Publ Wkly

Murder makes the wheels go 'round. Macmillan 1966 183p o.p.

"A Cock Robin mystery"

The author "gives John Putnam Thatcher, that pillar of Wall Street, a chance to exercise his unique skill in unravelling the economics of murder, and to show how fiscal improprieties on a corporate scale add up to death, as he investigates Michigan Motors as a potential investment for the Sloan Guaranty Trust." Libr J

Pick up sticks. Simon & Schuster 1970 224p o.p.

Available G.K. Hall large print edition

"An Inner sanctum mystery"

"Most of the action in this one takes place away from the offices of the Sloan Guaranty Trust, the Wall Street banking firm involved in each of the Lathen mysteries. John Putnam Thatcher, Sloan vice-president and a non-banking friend are walking the Appalachian trail when they become embroiled in a murder stemming out of two real estate entrepreneur's attempts to hardsell a vacation colony in New Hampshire." Publ Wkly

Right on the money; a John Putnam Thatcher mystery. Simon & Schuster 1993 256p $20

ISBN 0-671-73708-2   LC 92-35673

A "Wall Street mystery featuring banker John Thatcher of Sloan Guaranty Trust. When a Princeton manufacturing firm represented by a sister bank targets a Sloan family-owned business client for takeover, Thatcher monitors the ensuing negotiations. Friction erupts into fracas, however, when rumors fly, financial records burn, and possible industrial sabotage culminates in murder." Libr J

Something in the air. Simon & Schuster 1988 270p o.p.

LC 88-4491

This mystery featuring "John Thatcher of New York's Sloan Guaranty Trust is set mainly in Boston, headquarters of the commuter airline Sparrow Flyways. A product of airline deregulation, Sparrow is a nonunion operation surviving on horizontal management and project development teams. Mitchell Scovil, CEO and guiding figure of the founders, dreams of expansion, but a group of lower-level employees (and shareholders) is worried about their investment. When their arrogant spokesperson is murdered, the Sloan, holding 20% of unsalable Sparrow stock in a trust, becomes involved." Publ Wkly

A stitch in time. Macmillan 1968 185p o.p.

"A Cock Robin mystery"

John Putnam Thatcher, bank vice-president "has problems in settling the estate of the late Pemberton Freebody because Atlantic Mutual Insurance says Freebody was a suicide, and therefore refuses to pay the $100,000 policy on his life to Hanover University. The university takes the case to court, and the trial of the century begins when the company calls Dr. Wendell Martin of Southport Memorial Hospital to the stand." Libr J

Latsis, Mary J.

For works written by this author in collaboration with Martha Hennissart see Lathen, Emma

Latt, Mimi Lavenda

Powers of attorney. Simon & Schuster 1993 506p $23

ISBN 0-671-78708-X   LC 93-16281

The protagonist of this novel is "Kate Alexander, a criminal lawyer with a top Los Angeles firm. Kate is up for a partnership and has fierce competition, but she also has a powerful mentor and grand ambition—she intends to run for District Attorney. When a power broker who is ready to support her is murdered and his widow arrested, it is Kate for the defense." N Y Times Book Rev

"Stereotypical figures . . . slightly detract from a generally high level of intrigue but do serve to keep the action moving towards a surprising and satisfying happy ending." Publ Wkly

Lawless, Anthony *See* MacDonald, Philip, 1899-1981

Lawrence, D. H. (David Herbert), 1885-1930

Collected stories; with an introduction by Craig Raine. Knopf 1994 xxxv, 1397p $25

ISBN 0-679-43135-7   LC 94-2493

"Everyman's library"

Analyzed in Short story index

Contents: A modern lover; The old Adam; Her turn; Strike-pay; The witch à la mode; New Eve and old Adam; A prelude; Love among the haystacks; A chapel and a hay hut among the mountains; Once; A fly in the ointment; Lessford's rabbits; A lesson on a tortoise; The Prussian officer; The thorn in the flesh; Daughters of the vicar; A fragment of stained glass; The shades of spring; Second best; The shadow in the rose garden; Goose fair; The white stocking; A sick collier; The christening; Odour of chrysanthemums; England, my England; Tickets, please; The blind man; Monkey nuts; Wintry peacock; You touched me; Samson and Delilah; The thimble; The mortal coil; The primrose path; The horse dealer's daughter; Delilah and Mr. Bircumshaw; Fanny and Annie; The ladybird; The fox; The captain's doll; St. Mawr; The princess; Two blue birds; Sun; The woman who rode away; Smile; The border line; Jimmy and the desperate woman; The last laugh; In love; Glad

Lawrence, D. H. (David Herbert), 1885-1930—*Continued*

ghosts; None of that; The man who loved islands; The lovely lady; Rawdon's roof; The rocking-horse winner; Mother and daughter; The blue moccasins; Things; The virgin and the gipsy; The man who died

Lady Chatterley's lover; the historic unexpurgated Grove Press edition; with Archibald MacLeish's letter to Barney Rosset, an introduction by Mark Schorer, and Judge Bryan's decision in the obscenity case. Modern Lib. 1993 liii, 491p $16.50

ISBN 0-679-60065-5   LC 93-15337

Also available Cambridge University Press edition

First published 1928 in a limited edition in Florence

A novel "presenting the author's mystical theories of sex in the story of Constance, or Connie, the wife of an English aristocrat who runs away with her gamekeeper. Her husband, Sir Clifford, has been rendered impotent by a war wound and is also an emotional cripple. The gamekeeper, Mellors, is a forthright individualistic man, uncontaminated by industrial society. Because of the frank language and detailed descriptions of love-making, the book was banned in England and the U.S. as obscene. After historic court cases the ban was lifted in the U.S. in 1959 and in England in 1960." Reader's Ency. 3d edition

The plumed serpent (Quetzalcoatl); edited by L. D. Clark. Cambridge Univ. Press 1987 xlvii, 569p il $110

ISBN 0-521-22262-1   LC 86-32674

"Cambridge edition of the works and letters of D. H. Lawrence"

First published 1926

This novel is "a powerful, vivid evocation of Mexico and its ancient Aztec religion. Kate Leslie, an Irish visitor to Mexico, goes to a bullfight and is horrified by the vulgar cruelty of modern Mexico. But then she meets Don Ramón, a scholar and political leader, and General Cipriano, a military leader, and becomes involved in their resurrection of the ancient Mexican religion. For Lawrence, this religion is characterized by 'blood consciousness,' emotional and symbolic depth, and sex awareness. It is marked by dominance of the male over the female and the political leader over the masses, a Nietzschean type of superman. Don Ramón, the sexual, political, and religious hero of the book, is regarded as the reincarnated Quetzalcoatl, the Plumed Serpent that the Aztecs used to worship. He rises to lead the people, drawing them away from 'outworn' Christianity toward the Aztec religion. Eventually the cult spreads over the whole of Mexico and Kate, too, comes under its spell." Reader's Ency. 3d edition

The rainbow; with an introduction by Barbara Hardy. Knopf 1993 xxxv, 460p $20

ISBN 0-679-42305-2   LC 93-1860

Also available from Buccaneer Bks.

"Everyman's library"

First published 1915

"The story line traces three generations of the Brangwen family in the Midlands of England from 1840 to 1905. The marriage of farmer Tom Brangwen and foreigner Lydia Lensky eventually breaks down. Likewise, the marriage of Lydia's daughter Anna to Tom's nephew Will gradually fails. The novel is largely devoted to Will and Anna's oldest child, the schoolteacher Ursula, who stops short of marriage when she is unsatisfied by her love affair with the conventional soldier Anton Skrebensky. The appearance of a rainbow at the end of the novel is a sign of hope for Ursula, whose story is continued in Lawrence's *Women in Love*." Merriam-Webster's Ency of Lit

Sons and lovers.

Available from various publishers

First published 1913

"Paul Morel, adored youngest son of a middle-class mother who feels that her coal-miner husband was unworthy of her, has difficulty in breaking away from her. Mrs. Morel has given her son all her warmth and love for so long a time that Paul finds it impossible to establish a relationship with another woman. Miriam is supportive and understanding of his artistic nature but appeals mainly to his higher nature; Clara Dawes becomes his mistress but she is married, and will not divorce her husband. After the death of his mother, Paul arranges a reconciliation between Clara and her husband and, after months of grieving for his mother, at last finds the strength to strike out on his own." Shapiro. Fic for Youth. 3d edition

The white peacock. o.p.

First published 1911

"A story of rural England, its characters being farmers and sons of farmers, and its scenes all enacted in the midst of crops and harvests, woods and country lanes. Everywhere we come in close contact with the life of the open, free out-of-doors; everywhere we get the scent of the soil. The tragedy of a rabbit mangled by the steel teeth of a trap, a nest of field-mice dug up and crushed remorselessly, one by one; the sordid wretchedness of a hovel swarming with dirty, quarreling, half-clad children, mismanaged by a slatternly, overworked drudge of a woman who occasionally relieves her feelings by hitting them over the head with a battered saucepan—such scenes as these are done with relentless skill that makes them actually hurt as you read them." Bookman's Manual

Women in love. Knopf 1992 475p $20

ISBN 0-679-40995-5   LC 91-53191

Also available from Amereon and Buccaneer Bks.

"Everyman's library"

Sequel to The rainbow

First published 1920

This novel "examines the ill effects of industrialization on the human psyche, resolving that individual and collective rebirth is possible only through human intensity and passion. *Women in Love* contrasts the love affair of Rupert Birkin and Ursula Brangwen with that of Gudrun, Ursula's artistic sister, and Gerald Crich, a domineering industrialist. Birkin, an introspective misanthrope, struggles to reconcile his metaphysical drive for self-fulfillment with Ursula's practical view of sentimental passion. Their love affair and eventual marriage are set as a positive antithesis to the destructive relationship of Gudrun and Crich." Merriam-Webster's Ency of Lit

Lawrence, David Herbert *See* Lawrence, D. H. (David Herbert), 1885-1930

Le Carré, John, 1931-

The honourable schoolboy. Knopf 1977 533p $24.95

ISBN 0-394-41645-7   LC 77-75001

Le Carré, John, 1931-—*Continued*

Jerry Westerby is the honorable schoolboy of the title. He works with George Smiley of the British Secret Service, described by the author as The Circus, to discover why the Russian Secret Service is paying $25,000 a month into the bank account of the prosperous Hong Kong business man, Drake Ko. The action takes place in London and Southeast Asia. The story opens in the Hong Kong press club

This "is superbly well-organized, combining a grandiose sweep with an intricate pattern. It has hard-edged reality instead of fuzzy near-fantasy, a host of sharply etched characters instead of a few eccentric caricatures, and a style which, subtle and flexible . . . never obtrudes, yet never goes unnoticed." Times Lit Suppl

also in Le Carré, J. The quest for Karla p253-678

The little drummer girl. Knopf 1983 429p $24.95

ISBN 0-394-53015-2 LC 82-48733

"A series of bomb-attacks upon Israeli officials throughout Europe is investigated by Kurtz and his assistant Litvak . . . who plan not merely to track down the terrorists but to infiltrate the core of the illicit Palestinian organisation and explode it from within. Charlie, a footloose actress with radical affinities, is taken up by a . . . stranger who gradually introduces her into a network of political altruism. She is schooled to succumb to the charms of a Palestinian guerrilla yet at a deeper level to be still working for the Israelis." New Statesman

"Mr. le Carré's novel is certainly the most mature, inventive and powerful book about terrorists-come-to-life this reader has experienced. It transcends the genre." NY Times Book Rev

The looking glass war. Coward-McCann 1965 320p o.p.

This spy story "concerns a former military espionage department in London (small, left over from the . . . days of World War II) and its struggle to train one of its former agents for a mission into East Germany." NY Times Book Rev

"A bitter, cruel, dispassionate—yet passionate—study of an unimportant piece of espionage and the unimportant little men who are involved in it." Book Week

The night manager; a novel. Knopf 1993 429p $24

ISBN 0-679-42513-6 LC 92-55070

"Jonathan Pine, hotel night manager and volunteer spy, [sets] out to avenge the death of Sophie, a high-class Egyptian prostitute whom he loved and betrayed. . . . With the help of a maverick branch of British Intelligence determined to wrest operational control from the latter-day cold warriors, Pine sets out to trap Dicky Roper, the man responsible for Sophie's death, a world-class arms dealer about to embark on a massive drugs-for-guns deal." Booklist

Le Carré "brings to the world of the drug wars the same skilled characterization, perceptive detail, and dramatic storytelling that made him the undisputed master of the Cold War spy novel. This novel is precisely what we have come to expect from him: a work of high literary merit that's also great entertainment." Libr J

A perfect spy. Knopf 1986 475p $18.95

ISBN 0-394-55141-9 LC 85-45587

"The protagonist of the story, Magnus Pym, aged 53, is . . . a senior partner in 'the firm' of British intelligence, working out of the British Embassy in Vienna. He is a man respected and admired for his intelligence and common sense. He is also a man of mystery . . . [His disappearance] sets the plot in motion. Friends, colleagues, and family haven't a clue to his whereabouts. His superiors fear that 'the perfect spy' has defected and that British agents in Czechoslovakia, a group supervised by Pym, may be targeted. Jack Brotherhood, Pym's agency superior, begins an investigation." West Coast Rev Books

"Not a spy novel in the usual sense . . . but a skillfully manipulated, complex, and probingly written study spiced with lively anecdotes. To be savored." Libr J

The quest for Karla. Knopf 1982 952p $13.95

ISBN 0-394-52848-4 LC 82-47961

An omnibus edition of three titles first published 1974, 1977 and 1979 respectively and entered separately

Contents: Tinker, tailor, soldier, spy; The honourable schoolboy; Smiley's people

The Russia house. Knopf 1989 353p $19.95

ISBN 0-394-57789-2 LC 88-46159

Also available G.K. Hall large print edition

"A mysterious manuscript purporting to prove the Soviet defense system is unworkable is smuggled out of Moscow. It was intended for a flaky English publisher, a womanizing saxophone-playing boozer, but the smuggler has turned it over to British intelligence. In order to prove its authenticity, they recruit the publisher as an amateur spy and send him to Moscow to reestablish contact with the author. But the 'truth' Barley Blair finds there is love and a purpose for his shambles of a life." Libr J

"With scarcely an intimation of sex, no violence and not a side arm visible, Le Carre has again managed to construct a plot of commanding suspense. . . . The Russia House is both afire and thought provoking, a thriller that demands a second reading as a treatise on our time." Time

The secret pilgrim. Knopf 1990 335p $21.95

ISBN 0-394-58842-8 LC 90-52944

This novel "takes the form of a reverie-memoir, a series of reflections on a long life in the espionage business recalled by a surnameless man called Ned. . . . Now on the verge of retirement, Ned is running Sarratt, the training school for new recruits to British intelligence. He invites the legendary George Smiley to address the impending graduates and, after dinner, the night is whiled away as the next generation of spies picks the brains of a past master. As Smiley responds to their questions, allusions and remarks that he makes trigger Ned's recollections about his own past." N Y Times Book Rev

"There's always been a didatic quality to le Carré's work that has been part of his novels' charm, but in no other book has he said so much about the ravages that the spying profession works upon the agent." Newsweek

Le Carré, John, 1931——*Continued*

A small town in Germany. Coward-McCann 1968 383p o.p.

"Alan Turner arrives from London to investigate a breach in security [of the British Embassy at Bonn]. A temporary employee, Leo Harting, has apparently absconded with the crucial Green File and a mass of other secret papers. Turner's job: find them. The permanent staff, an encyclopedia of the English class system, dislikes Turner, the angriest of young men, and tries to keep him at arm's length. Turner stops at nothing." Newsweek

"The plot is ingeniously constructed with ever-mounting suspense and it is related with the deftness of a writer who possesses an enviable command of description and narration." Best Sellers

Smiley's people. Knopf 1980 c1979 374p $25

ISBN 0-394-50843-2   LC 79-2299

First published 1979 in the United Kingdom

"George Smiley, who retired as master of the British secret service known as the Circus when the Cold War was supplanted by détente, is . . . recalled to duty when one of his former 'people,' a brilliant anti-Soviet Estonian emigré called the General, is murdered on Hampstead Heath. The General, as Smiley patiently works it out, had been trying to reach him with what was understood to be documentary evidence that could destroy the infamous Russian spymaster Karla." New Yorker

This novel "is a complete winner, exciting, well-paced, and convincing. . . . There is a lot of the Le Carré gloom, but now it seems almost elegiac and touching. Absolutely not to be missed." Libr J

also in Le Carré, J. The quest for Karla p679-952

The spy who came in from the cold. Coward-McCann 1964 c1963 256p o.p.

First published 1963 in the United Kingdom

"The story of Alec Leamas, 50-year-old professional who has grown stale in espionage, who longs to 'come in from the cold'—and how he undertakes one last assignment before that hoped-for retirement. Over the years Leamas has grown unsure where his workday carapace ends and his real self begins. . . . Recalled from Berlin after the death of his last East German contact at the Wall, Leamas lets himself be seduced into a pretended defection—thereby providing the East Germans with data from which they can deduce that the head of their own spy apparatus is a double agent." NY Times Book Rev

"The setting, the job itself as it unrolls, are grim, grim, grim, and breathlessly exciting; the tone is as terse and as merciless as the Service itself." Harpers

Tinker, tailor, soldier, spy. Knopf 1974 355p $24.50

ISBN 0-394-49219-6

The novel's protagonist, British agent George Smiley, "is asked to come out of retirement and root out as unobtrusively as possible the 'mole,' or Russian agent, that has burrowed his way to the center of England's secret intelligence organization, the Circus. Smiley is feeling glum. His wife has left him and his retirement was forced upon him the year before when power was reshuffled at the Circus. It is clear, too, that the mole must be one of Smiley's old colleagues." Newsweek

Smiley "instinctively realises from the outset who the traitor is but refuses to confront the embarrassing truth. A perceptive reader will sense the secret too, but one goes on reading entranced not so much by the ramifications of the plot, beautifully engineered though it is, as by concern for the characters, a rare thing in thrillers." New Statesman

also in Le Carré, J. The quest for Karla p1-252

Le Guin, Ursula K., 1929-

Always coming home; composer: Todd Barton; artist: Margaret Chodos; George Hersh, geomancer; maps drawn by the author. Harper & Row 1985 523p il o.p.

LC 85-880

With this novel "Le Guin achieved a synthesis of her several themes in a futuristic Earth setting. In this large collection of the stories, poetry, myths, and legends—and even music—of the Kesh, she developed, by gradual accretion of detail, a powerful demonstration of how a world torn apart by 'civilization' may be rebuilt with timeless archetypal ritual." New Ency of Sci Fic

The beginning place. Harper & Row 1980 183p o.p.

LC 79-2653

"For Hugh, on the run from the demands of his domineering mother and from the dullness of his job as a checkout boy at a local market . . . and for Irene, fearful of sexual harrassment at the hands of her stepfather and other men, [a fantastical] world becomes a refuge. Then an unknown evil begins to pervade their paradise and they are chosen to face the 'fear.' Irene, jealous of newcomer Hugh's acceptance into the world she has been visiting for so long, reluctantly acts as guide for Hugh who, as sword-wielder, is to be the savior. Having finally slain a monster, Irene and Hugh seek to escape Eden turned nightmare." SLJ

"The style is fluent, concise and elegant, and the story that is told is easily understood by anyone who has ever found himself at a loss to deal with the realities of modern life." Best Sellers

City of illusions. Harper & Row 1978 c1967 199p o.p.

First published 1967 in paperback by Ace Books

This novel "chronicles the search for identity by a man without a past, named Falk, as he wanders through a world where scientists and shamans live in separate societies. In the city of Shing, a city of illusion and trickery, Falk regains his memory and becomes a threat to the ruling Shing. Standard adventure fare raised from the ordinary by Le Guin's richly drawn background of Earth taken over by aliens." Booklist

The dispossessed; an ambiguous Utopia. Harper & Row 1974 341p il o.p.

"Shevek, a brilliant physicist, is caught between the prejudices and hatreds of two worlds. His quest to bridge the gap between Ararres, an anarchist, egalitarian society, and Varas, a structured, capitalistic world, unleashes a storm of intrigue and drama. The two distinct cultures provide insights into the role of women in society, the issue of free will versus obligation to the state, human rights, and ecomonic systems." Shapiro. Fic for Youth. 3d edition

Le Guin, Ursula K., 1929-——*Continued*
The eye of the heron. Harper & Row 1983 c1978 179p o.p.

LC 82-48146

Originally published 1978 in anthology: Millennial women, edited by Virginia Kidd

"Two communities that have been exiled from Earth and are living on another planet represent the forces of War and Peace. The City Dwellers with their comfortable and protected lives are the Bosses; the inhabitants of Shantih (Shanty-Town) are the peace-seekers and the laborers for the City. The novel is a parable of the confrontation of two philosophies—violence and non-violence. Lev is the spokesperson for the Shanty-Towners, the seekers of peaceful solutions. Luz is the daughter of the top Boss of the City who, in spite of her background, sees the evil in the methods of her father and his chief aide, Herman Macmillan. Le Guin portrays a conflict that not only is reminiscent of the outrages suffered by the victims of the Nazi regime but is also illustrative of the problems of the nuclear age." Shapiro. Fic for Youth. 3d edition

A fisherman of the inland sea; science fiction stories. HarperPrism 1994 191p il $19.99

ISBN 0-06-105200-0   LC 94-5397

Analyzed in Short story index

Contents: The first contact with the Gorgonids; Newton's sleep; The ascent of the north face; The rock that changed things; The kerastion; The Shobie's story; Dancing to Ganam; Another story; or, A fisherman of the inland sea

"Le Guin demonstrates her storytelling virtuosity in each of these diverse tales." Voice Youth Advocates

The lathe of heaven. Scribner 1971 184p o.p. Bentley reprint available $14 (ISBN 0-8376-0464-8)

"A psychiatrist sets out to use a patient whose dreams can alter reality to create utopia, but in usurping this power he is gradually delivered into madness." Anatomy of Wonder 4

"The author has done some profound research in psychology, cerebro-physiology and biochemistry. . . . In addition, her perceptions of such matters as geopolitics, race, socialized medicine and the patient/shrink relationship are razor-sharp and more than a little cutting." Natl Rev

The left hand of darkness; with a new afterword and appendixes by the author. 25th Anniversary ed. Walker & Co. 1994 345p $27.50

ISBN 0-8027-1302-5   LC 94-27147

A reissue of the title first published 1969 by Walker & Company

"This is a tale of political intrigue and danger on the world of Gethen, the Winter planet. Genly Ai, high official of the Eukeman—the commonwealth of worlds—is on Gethen to convince the royalty to join the Federation. He soon becomes a pawn in Gethen's power struggles, set against the elaborate mores of the Gethenians, a unisex hermaphroditic people whose intricate sexual physiology plays a key role in the conflict. Allied with Estraven, fallen lord, Genly is forced to cross the savage and impassable Gobrin Ice." Shapiro. Fic for Youth. 3d edition

Malafrena. Putnam 1979 369p o.p.

LC 79-11042

"Sorde is the heir of a well-to-do landowner in Malafrena. He goes off to college and finds that he does have something to live for—his concept of freedom. His fight for that freedom leads him to publish revolutionary tracts, spend two years in prison, and then lead a short-lived insurrection." Best Sellers

Set in "the 19th Century in an imaginary European country. . . . Le Guin portrays Sorde's coming of age—and how he and those who love him discover their life's work and personal strengths—with a Tolstoyesque flavor and grandeur. A book about freedom and commitment that should win a grateful, enthusiastic audience." Libr J

(ed) The Norton book of science fiction. See The Norton book of science fiction

Orsinian tales. Harper & Row 1976 179p o.p. Ultramarine reprint available $25 (ISBN 0-06-012561-6)

Analyzed in Short story index

Contents: The fountains; The barrow; Ile Forest; Conversations at night; The road east; Brothers and sisters; A week in the country; An die Musik; The house; The lady of Moge; Imaginary countries

This is a cycle of interrelated short stories. "Set in a vaguely Middle-European country, Le Guin's tales deal with love, freedom, and tyranny in a society which over a series of historical periods appears to be perpetually in the last stages preceding cataclysm." Booklist

Planet of exile. Harper & Row 1978 c1966 140p o.p.

LC 77-3794

First published 1966 in paperback by Ace Books

"On the planet Eltanin, the natives live in distrust of the small colony of 'farborns'—humans—and will not join them to fight the threat of the years-long winter or the marauding nomads, the Gaals. Rolery, a local girl, and Jakob, a farborn, become lovers, increasing the mutual distrust. But when the Gaals destroy the native village and besiege the farborn city, both sides are forced to unify—and the farborns discover that they are no longer quite human." Publ Wkly

This novel "has all the essentials of a fine science-fiction adventure story—romance, intrigue, suspense, heroism, strange creatures, and new worlds." Best Sellers

Rocannon's world. Harper & Row 1977 c1966 136p o.p. Ultramarine reprint available $25 (ISBN 0-06-012568-3)

First published 1966 in paperback by Ace Books

A "story about Rocannon, a Terran scientist sent to survey the culture on Fomalhaut II just as it comes under attack from a vicious race of aliens. The sole survivor of his team, Rocannon rallies the humanoids of Fomalhaut II and, drawing on their innate courage and love of freedom, preserves the planet from subjugation. The main interest here is in Le Guin's early attempt at creating life in a truly alien environment and the introduction of the Hainish culture." Booklist

Searoad; chronicles of Klatsand. HarperCollins Pubs. 1991 193p o.p.

LC 91-55160

Analyzed in Short story index

Includes the following stories: Bill Weisler; Crosswords; Foam women, rain women; Geezers; Hand, cup, shell; Hernes; In and out; Quoits; The Ship Ahoy; Sleep-

Le Guin, Ursula K., 1929-—Continued

walkers; Texts; True love

"In these stories, connected loosely but powerfully by their rugged Pacific Northwest setting, LeGuin portrays residents of a small Oregon shore town with sympathy and no sentiment. Many of the tales center around women drawn together in threes—mother, daughter, grandmother—by illness or death. Passionate, independent and questioning, these characters generally choose, sooner or later, personal freedom over convention, but not without pain." Publ Wkly

The word for world is forest. Berkley 1976 c1972 189p o.p.

Originally published 1972 in the anthology: Again, dangerous visions, edited by Harlan Ellison

"Human colonists on an alien world cause untold damage to the innocent natives and their environment. A harsh comment on the ethics and politics of colonialism, making good use of anthropological perspectives." Anatomy of Wonder 4

also in The Hugo winners v3 p225-327

Lear, Peter *See* Lovesey, Peter

Leavitt, David, 1961-

The lost language of cranes. Knopf 1986 319p o.p.

LC 86-45277

"The story focuses on Philip Benjamin, a 25-year-old New Yorker, . . . gay, who is involved in his first 'serious' romance. This situation is complicated by the struggle of Philip's father to deal more openly with his own long-standing, but thus far closeted, homosexual inclinations. With Philip's coming out, father is thrown into even greater turmoil, mother begins to realize the complete truth, and all are forced to reexamine the ties that bind them." Libr J

"Mr Leavitt's sense of pacing, his graceful sentences and his storytelling ability dovetail nicely. On the other hand, the book feels young—experientially thin, intellectually timid, contrived, erratic and, understandably, not yet wise. . . . 'The Lost Language of Cranes' lingers in the mind, greater than the sum of its problematic parts." N Y Times Book Rev

(ed) Penguin book of gay short fiction. See Penguin book of gay short fiction

While England sleeps. Viking 1993 304p $22

ISBN 0-670-83349-5   LC 92-45878

This novel is narrated by "English public school boy Brian Botsford. During a promiscous post-university period in the 1930s, Brian dallies with both leftist political interests and the affections of a working-class Underground ticket taker, Edward Phelan, in a highly charged sexual affair. He also convinces himself that he is in love with a young woman of his own class, Philippa Archibald, with whom he has a sexual liaison. Having discovered Brian's affair with Philippa, Edward flees to Spain to join the International Brigade. Risking prison, he later deserts, and Brian rushes to Spain to help." Libr J

"A narrative that for the most part rings true, though in a curiously mannered way. The reader ends up with a feeling of respect for the assiduous research that has been undertaken, rather than with any sense of deep involvement with the characters." N Y Times Book Rev

Lederer, William J., 1912-

The ugly American; [by] William J. Lederer and Eugene Burdick. Norton 1958 285p o.p.

Analyzed in Short story index

Contents: Lucky, Lucky Lou #1; Lucky, Lucky Lou #2; Nine friends; Everybody loves Joe Bing; Confidential and personal; Employment opportunities abroad; The girl who got recruited; The ambassador and the working press; Everyone has ears; The ragtime kid; The iron of war; The lessons of war; What would you do if you were President; How to buy an American junior grade; The six-foot swami from Savannah; Captain Boning, USN; The ugly American; The ugly American and the ugly Sarkhanese; The bent backs of Chang 'Dong; Senator, Sir; The sum of tiny things

Lee, C. Y., 1917-

The flower drum song. Farrar, Straus & Cudahy 1957 244p o.p.

A story of family life in San Francisco's Chinatown. The principal characters are the elderly Mr. Wang and his oldest son, Wang Ta, torn between Chinese tradition and western custom

"A first novel that is always fascinating, and by turns amusing and pathetic—a novel written with grace and decorum in the even, unimpassioned narrative style that is characteristic of classical Chinese fiction." Chicago Sunday Trib

Gate of rage; a novel of one family trapped by the events at Tiananmen Square. Morrow 1991 309p $20

ISBN 0-688-09764-2   LC 90-28490

"This novel examines China's so-called thaw and the attempt to woo foreign investors in the early 1980s. Lee creates an involved family situation in which each member acts out a different facet of political awareness. Jimmy is a moderate college professor; his wife, Do Do, is a radical reporter for Radio Beijing. Jimmy's father, Charles Hong, Hong Kong hotel tycoon who fled the country in 1948, reappears, heartened by the new China and eager to build a hotel chain." Booklist

Lee, Gentry

(jt. auth) Clarke, A. C. Cradle
(jt. auth) Clarke, A. C. The Garden of Rama
(jt. auth) Clarke, A. C. Rama II
(jt. auth) Clarke, A. C. Rama revealed

Lee, Gus

China boy. Dutton 1991 322p $19.95

ISBN 0-525-24994-X   LC 90-21687

"The rough-and-tumble tale of Kai Ting, the only son of an aristocratic Shanghai couple whose escape from the Communists landed them in San Francisco's tough, predominantly black, Panhandle district. When Kai Ting's mother dies, his father marries a white woman who tries

Lee, Gus—*Continued*

to eradicate her stepchildren's Chinese heritage. She sends the skinny, sheltered, and bewildered boy out into the neighborhood, where he becomes everyone's favorite punching bag." Am Libr

"Based on events in his own childhood, Mr. Lee's depiction of Kai's efforts to reconcile his Chinese heritage with the several equally bewildering worlds of American culture he is simultaneously exposed to . . . is vivid and moving. More broadly, 'China Boy' is a fascinating, evocative portrait of the Chinese community in California in the 1950's, caught between two complex, demanding cultures, fighting to adapt to the new world without sacrificing the nourishing traditions and intense family loyalties of the old." N Y Times Book Rev

Followed by Honor & duty

Honor & duty. Knopf 1994 425p $24

ISBN 0-679-41258-1   LC 92-42711

This novel "continues the saga of Kai Ting's struggle to become an American without abandoning Chinese cultural values. Now, Kai faces the challenge of West Point. Having survived his brutal stepmother and life on San Francisco's mean streets, first-year hazing seems insignificant, but other problems arise. Kai is required to pass engineering courses with no math ability; he is an Asian in the military at a time when America's involvement in Vietnam is deepening; and he is a man of honor faced with a cheating scandal." Libr J

"Although his plot becomes maudlin at times, Lee fashions a generally convincing first-person narrative in Kai's voice, skillfully drawing the reader into each of his young narrator's painful dilemmas." Publ Wkly

Lee, Harper, 1926-

To kill a mockingbird. 35th anniversary ed. HarperCollins Pubs. 1995 323p $17

ISBN 0-06-017322-X

A reissue with a new foreword by the author of the title first published 1960 by Lippincott

"Scout, as Jean Louise is called, is a precocious child. She relates her impressions of the time when her lawyer father, Atticus Finch, is defending a black man accused of raping a white woman in a small Alabama town during the 1930's. Atticus's courageous act brings the violence and injustice that exists in their world sharply into focus as it intrudes into the lighthearted life that Scout and her brother Jem have enjoyed until that time." Shapiro. Fic for Youth. 3d edition

Lee, Lilian *See* Li, Pi-hua

Lee, Manfred, 1905-1971

For works written by this author in collaboration with Frederic Dannay see Queen, Ellery

Leffland, Ella

The knight, death, and the devil. Morrow 1990 718p il o.p.

LC 89-33836

This historical novel presents a "depiction of Hermann Göring, head of the Luftwaffe and backbone of the Nazi party. Göring was a man both pitiable and conniving; loving toward his children yet an able assassin; unparalleled as an art thief; decadent to the point of effeminacy in his plush robes; drug-addicted; suspicious of Himmler and Goebbels; and in need of his Führer's favor and of his country's triumph, yet perhaps not defeated without them." Libr J

The author "goes a large distance in giving us the resonance of the Göring life. Those who have spent either much or little time looking at this era will be fascinated by the richness of the pictures and the authenticity of this massive work." N Y Times Book Rev

Rumors of peace. Harper & Row 1979 389p o.p.

LC 78-20209

"Suse Hansen, living in a small town near San Francisco, is a young tomboyish girl with vivid imagination and strong opinions on many subjects. Her unblinking look at the atrocities caused by war leads her to become obsessive about the possibility that she and her family could be destroyed in the war initiated when the Japanese attack Pearl Harbor. Through her relationships with her teachers, her school friends—especially Peggy Hatton—and her family, we watch Suse develop into a young woman whose mind is being sharpened by a respect for knowledge. The series of crushes Suse feels for various men—a normal burgeoning of sexuality—culminates in an intense feeling for Egon, a young graduate student and German-Jewish refugee whose influence we feel will be a lasting one." Shapiro. Fic for Youth. 3d edition

Legal fictions; short stories about lawyers and the law; edited by Jay Wishingrad. Overlook Press 1992 402p o.p.

LC 91-46664

Analyzed in Short story index

Contents: The tender offer, by L. Auchincloss; About Boston, by W. Just; The balloon of William Fuerst, by L. B. Komie; The contract, by H. Jacobs; Still life, by M. Thurm; After you've gone, by A. Adams; Weight, by M. Atwood; Puttermesser: her work history, her ancestry, her afterlife, by C. Ozick; Centaurs, by J. S. Marcus; Discipline, by L. Brown; Witness, by M. S. Bell; Earthly justice, by E. S. Goldman; The most outrageous consequences, by J. R. Parker; The colonel's foundation, by L. Auchincloss; Justice is blind, by T. Wolfe; Triumph of justice, by I. Shaw; The paradise of bachelors, by H. Melville; The web of circumstance, by C. W. Chesnutt; Bartleby, the scrivener, by H. Melville; Congress in crisis: the proximity bill, by G. Keillor; Szyrk v. Village of Tatamount et al., in the United States District Court, Southern District of Virginia, No. 105-87, by W. Gaddis; Coyote v. Acme, by I. Frazier; Before the law, by F. Kafka; The litigants, by I. B. Singer; Crimes of conscience, by N. Gordimer; A few selected sentences, by B. S. Johnson; Heart of a judge, by R. S. Easmon; Joy and the law, by G. Di Lampedusa; The condemned man's last night, by B. Peret; Legal aid, by F. O'Connor; General bellomo, by P. West; The Clairvoyant, by K. Čapek; The case for the defence, by G. Greene; Rumpole for the prosecution, by J. Mortimer; The judge's wife, by I. Allende

LeGuin, Ursula *See* Le Guin, Ursula K., 1929-

Lehrer, Jim

Kick the can. Putnam 1988 253p o.p.

LC 87-19192

"After he loses his left eye in a freakish kick-the-can mishap, an endearing young man designating himself the One-Eyed Mack embarks upon a deliciously wacky ramble across the Southwest. During the course of his exuberant expedition, Mack encounters all manners of offbeat personalities, serving as a microcosm of uniquely American eccentrics, idols, and heroes. An irresistibly original adventure fraught with warmth, humor, and humanity." Booklist

Leiber, Fritz, 1910-1992

Gonna roll the bones

In The Best of the Nebulas p211-27

In The Hugo winners v2 p460-83

Ill met in Lankhmar

In The Hugo winners v3 p55-115

Ship of shadows

In The Hugo winners v3 p5-50

The Wanderer. Walker & Co. 1970 c1964 318p o.p. Buccaneer Bks. reprint available $18.95 (ISBN 0-89968-349-5)

First published 1964 in paperback by Ballantine Books
"The passage of a strange world through the Solar System causes havoc to the Earth and the Moon; the story alternates between the experiences of various people amid the resulting riots, pillage, earthquakes, etc." Ency of Sci Fiction and Fantasy v1

Leinster, Murray *See* Jenkins, Will F., 1896-1975

Leithauser, Brad

(ed) The Norton book of ghost stories. See The Norton book of ghost stories

Lem, Stanisław

Eden; translated by Marc E. Heine. Harcourt Brace Jovanovich 1989 262p o.p.

LC 89-1963

"A Helen and Kurt Wolff book"
This novel "details the adventures of the crew of a crash-landed spaceship on an alien planet. The crew, composed of Captain, Engineer, Physicist, Cyberneticist, Doctor and Chemist, and remaining mostly nameless . . . sets about repairing the ship and exploring the beautiful, unmapped planet. They encounter increasingly exotic creatures and phenomena which they assume they understand, but all-too-human errors lead them to misinterpret nearly everything. Finally, when a communication of sorts is initiated with one of the planet's natives, the crew learns the full extent of their illusions." Publ Wkly
"No one writes sf more intellectually challenging or of greater literary distinction than Lem." Booklist

Fiasco; translated from the Polish by Michael Kandel. Harcourt Brace Jovanovich 1987 322p $17.95

ISBN 0-15-130640-0   LC 86-31816

"A Helen and Kurt Wolff book"
Original Polish edition, 1986
The author "imagines a time when Earth has found evidence of life on the planet Quinta and has sent a spaceship, the Hermes, to open communications with its inhabitants. For reasons impossible to know, Quinta is a silent planet; the goal of the expedition is to make it speak. The Hermes is manned with specialists in logic, game theory and 'exobiology,' as well as a Dominican monk called Arago (after the 19th-century French physicist) and a master computer whimsically named DEUS." N Y Times Book Rev
"The crew's dense, challenging discussions—of physics, philosophy, military tactics, morality, cybernetics, psychology, game theory, etc.—are punctuated by bursts of action whose initial release only serves to increase the tension, as new data disproves old theses and one fiasco follows another. Brilliant and demanding, this is one of Lem's best novels, putting the reader through an intellectual and emotional wringer." Publ Wkly

His Master's Voice; translated from the Polish by Michael Kandel. Harcourt Brace Jovanovich 1983 c1968 199p o.p.

LC 82-15765

"A Helen and Kurt Wolff book"
Original Polish edition, 1968
"A stream of 'signals' from outer space is the subject of various attempted decodings and an excuse for all kinds of wild hypotheses about who might have sent the message and why, in which are reflected various human hopes and fears. Good satire." Anatomy of Wonder 4

Memoirs of a space traveler; further reminiscences of Ijon Tichy; drawings by the author; translated by Joel Stern and Maria Swiecicka-Zirmionek. Harcourt Brace Jovanovich 1982 153p il o.p.

LC 81-47310

"A Helen and Kurt Wolff book"
Analyzed in Short story index
Contents: The eighteenth voyage; The twenty-fourth voyage; Further reminiscences of Ijon Tichy; Doctor Diagoras; Let us save the universe
"These stories of Ijon Tichy appeared in the original 1971 Polish edition of 'The Star Diaries' but were omitted from the English language editions of 1976. Some of these space age tall tales are funny, some are serious, but all are pointed. The targets range from SF itself to politics and commercialism." Publ Wkly

Lemarchand, Elizabeth

Alibi for a corpse. Walker & Co. 1986 190p $14.95

ISBN 0-8027-5638-7   LC 85-26395

First published 1985 in the United Kingdom
This "Inspector Pollard mystery summons the Scotland Yard detective and his sidekick Sergeant Toye to the tiny English village of Twiggadon after local constables declare themselves stumped by an unidentifiable skeleton found in the trunk of a car. . . . Lemarchand's usual brooding moorlands setting provides the proper atmosphere for an intricately plotted murder story." Booklist

Death of an old girl. Walker & Co. 1985 c1967 255p o.p.

LC 84-26948

Lemarchand, Elizabeth—*Continued*

First published 1967 in the United Kingdom

"At the annual meeting of the Old Meldonian Society, the alumnae of an English girls' school gather to greet old friends and note the institution's new directions. Beatrice Baynes, a pestilent, relentless snoop and the aging leader of a disgruntled clique of old girls, loudly criticizes the innovative young art teacher. When Miss Bayne's corpse is discovered in the art studio two days later, chief detective-inspector Pollard and sergeant Toye of Scotland Yard are summoned to sift through a group of suspects that includes the deceased's feckless grand-nephew, her tyrannized god-daughter, a shell-shocked caretaker and the overly suave owner of an art gallery." Publ Wkly

The Glade Manor murder. Walker & Co. 1989 c1988 176p $17.95

ISBN 0-8027-5741-3   LC 89-32449

First published 1988 in the United Kingdom

"Nanky Gover, nanny and then housekeeper to the Morley family, has lived happily at Glade Manor for 30 years. After returning from a distant wedding, however, John Morley and son Richard, antiquarian book restorers, discover her body at the bottom of the quarry. Scotland Yard's Tom Pollard investigates, suspecting at first John's adopted son, but soon getting on to the real motive and killer." Libr J

Nothing to do with the case. Walker & Co. 1981 187p il o.p.

LC 81-51975

The protagonist in this novel is "Virginia Gould, the 26-year-old niece by marriage of wealthy old Walter Kerslake. When he dies in an accident and leaves Virginia his mansion and its furnishings, his nephew by blood, Nigel, spreads gossip suggesting Virginia has killed Walter. Cleared of the charges, she leaves the town, to settle in a far northern English village, Marleigh, but bad-penny Nigel turns up there as well. Someone torches a manor house . . . and Virginia comes to the attention of the local police as well as Scotland Yard when details of Walter's death are aired. A stolen Cellini medallion, rumors of a bastard son never acknowledged by the owner of the torched mansion and Virginia's reputation combine to give the investigators [Pollard and Toye] a hard time and the reader a good one." Publ Wkly

Who goes home? Walker & Co. 1987 c1986 186p $15.95

ISBN 0-8027-5675-1   LC 87-6181

First published 1986 in the United Kingdom

"What begins with the deliberate torching of a desolate farmhouse becomes a complex case for Pollard and Toye of New Scotland Yard. . . . The burned shell of Anstey Farm holds two surprises for the police—a skeleton hidden behind a wall and traces of heroin. . . . The investigation focuses on Paul and Hugh, the sons of old John Anstey. . . . After building a business in London and being victimized by an earlier 'accidental' fire, Paul inherits the farm when his father dies. Lemarchand's short novel sacrifices full-bodied characterization in order to develop a twisting, carefully structured plot with a clever solution." Booklist

L'Engle, Madeleine, 1918-

Certain women. Farrar, Straus & Giroux 1992 351p $21

ISBN 0-374-12025-0   LC 91-34048

In this novel, "terminally ill David Wheaton, a prominent and much-married American actor, obsessively recalls an unfinished play about King David, a role he coveted. L'Engle explores Christian faith, love, and the nature of God by framing the delayed-maturation story of Emma, Wheaton's daughter, within three subplots: the Wheaton family saga, the story of King David, and the history of the play's development. The characterizations of both Davids are compelling, but the primary interest here is the community of women which surrounds each man. L'Engle describes complex truths very simply. . . . Because she also details the emotional cost of discovering and accepting such concepts, many readers will find these observations memorable but never simplistic." Libr J

The love letters. Farrar, Straus & Giroux 1966 365p o.p.

A "counterpoint tale of two young women, three centuries apart in time, tormented by their experience of love, each needing to understand love in its deepest sense for her salvation. One is Mariana, long-ago Portuguese nun, won from her vow and soon deserted by a French soldier. The other is Charlotte Napier whose disintegrating marriage, built on an emotionally insecure childhood, has sent her in flight to Beja, Portugal. Learning about Mariana, lingering over her published letters, and pondering her fate, Charlotte comes to understand what love demands of her." Booklist

The other side of the sun. Farrar, Straus & Giroux 1971 344p o.p.

Available Thorndike Press large print edition

"Set in the post-bellum era, [this Gothic novel] chronicles the experiences of a 19-year-old English girl, Stella, who shortly after her marriage is sent alone to the South while her husband embarks on a secret . . . mission to Africa. . . . Through a brace of aging, eccentric relatives and some violent encounters with the blacks who inhabit the nearby scrub, she comes to know something of the Renier family. Her curiosity grows until it plunges her into a cauldron of racial strife. . . . [Woven into the plot are] richly drawn characters, the scars and guilt of the Civil War, and scattered bits of brilliant insight into the human condition." Libr J

A severed wasp. Farrar, Straus & Giroux 1982 388p o.p.

LC 82-15694

In this sequel to The small rain, "international pianist Katherine Vigneras settles into her comfortable brownstone on Greenwich Village's 10th Street . . . [expecting] a music-dominated retirement, peaceful and restorative. Instead, she becomes involved, through friendship with one of her tenents, a Jewish doctor stationed at nearby St. Vincent's Hospital, with the Episcopal community of the great Cathedral of St. John the Divine. . . . At the cathedral she finds connections with her own tortuous past through her music, her friendship with a retired bishop and with the young family of the cathedral's present dean." Publ Wkly

The small rain. Farrar, Straus & Giroux 1984 c1945 371p $14.95

ISBN 0-374-26637-9   LC 84-47839

L'Engle, Madeleine, 1918——*Continued*
A reissue of the title first published 1945 by Vanguard Press

The story of Katherine Forrester from the age of ten to twenty. The daughter of musicians, Katherine is to become a pianist but before she can begin her career she must pass thru the heartaches and joys and disappointments of adolescence, school days and early love affairs

Followed by A severed wasp

Leonard, Elmore, 1925-
Bandits. Arbor House 1987 345p o.p.
LC 86-14104

Available G.K. Hall large print edition

"Ex-con Jack Delaney, a former hotel burglar turned mortician's assistant, finds his 'window of opportunity' in the form of a Calvin Klein-clad ex-nun, Lucy Nichols, who enlists his help in a plot to steal five million dollars from Colonel Dagoberto Godoy, a Nicaraguan contra visiting New Orleans to raise money. Jack, Lucy, and two other ex-cons form a motley crew of bandits, each with a different set of motives and illusions." Booklist

"At its heart, the novel is about taking sides, the politically charged background of Contra aid used as one more tool to pull the reader in and out of the moral quicksand. Leonard is no Graham Greene, but the ethical issues called into play here give the novel depth and immediacy. This, then, is not just another gritty adventure novel; it's a top-notch thriller with a real moral resonance." Publ Wkly

Cat chaser. Arbor House 1982 283p o.p.
LC 81-71687

"Ex-Marine George Moran intends to lead a quiet life at his Florida motel, but then he falls in love with the American wife of exiled Dominican General Andres de Boya. After a visit to the Dominican Republic, he's pestered by con men and private eyes, getting caught in the crossfire between them and de Boya, and it's hard to tell which is more dangerous." Libr J

This "is a tidy little thriller with sufficient twists and turns (not to mention sex and violence) to keep you intrigued and entertained. The characters are well drawn, the plotting is complicated but clear, and the suspense is strong without being too painful." Best Sellers

City primeval

In Leonard, E. Elmore Leonard's double Dutch treat: three novels

Elmore Leonard's double Dutch treat: three novels; introduction by Bob Greene. Arbor House 1986 594p o.p.
LC 85-26774

Contents: City primeval (1980); The moonshine war (1969); Gold Coast (1980)

This companion volume to the title entered below reprints "three more novels in the author's extensive canon of tough talk, mean streets, and violent action. *The Moonshine War* charts the exploits of Son Martin, a hell-raising Kentucky moonshiner, *Gold Coast* tells the tale of a Mafia don's widow, whose inheritance is contingent on her never touching another man for the rest of her life; and *City Primeval* portrays an angry Detroit cop in search of a particularly demented killer. Recommended for all Leonard fans, whether they've read them before or not." Booklist

Elmore Leonard's Dutch treat: 3 novels; introduction by George F. Will. Arbor House 1985 568p o.p.
LC 85-11246

An omnibus edition of three of the author's mid-1970s novels

Contents: Mr. Majestyk (1974); Swag (1976); The hunted (1977)

In "*Mr. Majestyk*, a California melon grower, is set upon by professional killers but manages to turn his predators into prey. In *Swag*, originally called *Ryan's Rules*, two small-time Detroit thieves prosper until they go for bigger loot. Riveting though these two tales are, they will strike readers as mere curtain raisers for *The Hunted*. Set in Israel, it focuses on the perilous state of Al Rosen, an American who receives large sums of money regularly from his lawyer in Detroit. When news of Rosen's whereabouts gets back to his home city, a gang of paid hoods jets to Tel Aviv and goes gunning for him. Sgt. Davis of the U.S. Marines, perceiving their lethal intentions, drives Rosen to a desolate spot in hopes of getting the drop on the pursuers. The climax to this story is a stunning, unforgettable surprise." Publ Wkly

Freaky Deaky. Arbor House 1988 341p o.p.
LC 87-19466

"Soon after Chris Mankowski—lately transferred from the bomb squad to sex crimes—visits rich, mindless alcoholic Woody Ricks on a rape complaint, someone blows up Woody's limousine—along with Woody's brother Mark. Ghosts from their student activist past have returned to haunt them. One ex-Panther even now takes care of Woody, and two ex-demonstrators hope to extort cash." Libr J

Leonard "excels here with his trademark menace and his deadpan, throwaway humor. His superlative ear for the vernacular makes all the characters spring to life; Woody, 'always in low with his dims on,' is a brilliant creation." Publ Wkly

Get Shorty. Delacorte Press 1990 292p o.p.
LC 89-25816

Available G.K. Hall large print edition

When Chili Palmer, a Miami extortionist, "agrees to help a fellow mobster track down a movie producer trying to evade his Las Vagas debts, a new world of opportunities opens up before him." Quill Quire

"Leonard's strongest books make you stand up and sit down a lot during their tight moments, but 'Get Shorty,' despite its occasional white-knuckle passages, belongs to that vast vinegary canon known as the Hollywood novel. . . . Best of all is the portrait Leonard gives us of a seven-million-dollar-a-picture star named Michael Weir." New Yorker

Glitz. Arbor House 1985 228p o.p.
LC 84-16794

This novel is "set in the high-roller world of casino gambling, alternating between Puerto Rico and Atlantic City. Miami cop Vincent Mora is on medical leave in San Juan when two seemingly unrelated events conspire to end his vacation: a paroled rapist who Mora arrested turns up bent on revenge, and a Puerto Rican girl employed by an Atlantic City casino owner turns up dead." Booklist

Leonard, Elmore, 1925-—_Continued_

"There is a steady flow of intrigue and action set just outside the law in a world both dirty and glamorous. Several characters develop into complex personalities, but Mora is never quite clear." Libr J

Gold Coast

_In_ Leonard, E. Elmore Leonard's double Dutch treat: three novels

The hunted

_In_ Leonard, E. Elmore Leonard's Dutch treat: 3 novels

Killshot. Arbor House 1989 287p o.p.

LC 88-31532

Available G.K. Hall large print edition

"When a professional hit man gets in on a shakedown planned by a psychotic killer, the luck that's kept him alive for 50 years starts running out. Trying to make the score, they run into not the realtor they'd targeted, but Carmen Colson and her ironworker husband, Wayne, who rough them up and run them off. The thugs decide to kill the couple, but that's not easily done. Electing protection by the Federal Witness Security Program, the Colsons have no picnic, either. The cops treat them like dirt, the home they're given by the program is a dump, and the deputy marshal guarding them puts the make on Carmen." Booklist

"Mr. Leonard has either done his homework or he's been there—up on the high beams in Detroit, on the Mississippi towing barges from Baton Rouge to Hickman, Ky., looking into the flat stare of an irritated cop, and somehow, improbably, inside the head of a woman who has had it with being treated like 'the wife.' 'Killshot' is pure, distilled, vintage Leonard." N Y Times Book Rev

LaBrava. Arbor House 1983 283p o.p.

LC 83-72676

"The time is now; the scene, Miami's South Beach area. Joe LaBrava is a former Secret Service agent turned freelance photographer. A friend of his has been taking care of Jean Shaw, a middle-aged beauty who was once a movie actress. LaBrava fell in love with Jean's image when he was 12. She played the spider-woman role: she enticed second leads to their deaths and never married the hero. Now in real life the predator may be cast as the victim: a psychotic extortionist and his creepy Cuban sidekick are looking for her. Jean receives a crudely typed note demanding that she pay $600,000 for the privilege of remaining alive." Newsweek

"What makes the author's work memorable is his uncompromisingly direct prose, his affectionately crafted yet very real characters, and, of course, the fact that Leonard knows that providing entertainment is the novelist's first commandment. Nobody brings the illogic of crime and criminals to life better." Christ Sci Monit

Maximum Bob. Delacorte Press 1991 295p o.p.

LC 91-6539

Available G.K. Hall large print edition

"Maximum Bob is a Florida judge famous for his tough sentencing and, among women who have to work with him, as a fairly crude lecher. Parole officer Kathy Diaz Baker is the book's protagonist, though. For a slight violation, her parolee Dale Crowe Junior gets one of Bob's stiff sentences, by which he's not too pleased. Moreover, Dale's uncle Elvin, just out after doing 10 years from Bob on a murder conviction, conceivably could be nursing a grudge. What's more, Elvin hooks up with rich Dr. Tommy Vasco, who's under house arrest for illegal drugs—a sentence given him by guess who. When a live and lively alligator shows up in the judge's backyard, swallowing his wife's dog and scaring its owner clean out of town, and then when shots are fired through hizzoner's windows, Kathy gets suspicious and suspiciouser. Leonard's trademark toughness, grit, and sleaze are on every page." Booklist

The moonshine war

_In_ Leonard, E. Elmore Leonard's double Dutch treat: three novels

Mr. Majestyk

_In_ Leonard, E. Elmore Leonard's Dutch treat: 3 novels

Pronto. Delacorte Press 1993 265p $21.95

ISBN 0-385-30846-9   LC 93-2999

Also available large print edition $27.95 (ISBN 0-385-31087-0)

This novel "tracks the misadventures of Harry Arno, a small-time operator who runs a sports book for the Miami syndicate. Federal investigators try to pressure him to rat on his boss, Jimmy Cap, by planting a rumor that he is skimming. As, of course, he is. Squeezed by both sides, Harry takes his nest egg and flees to Rapallo, a harbor town on the Italian Riviera." N Y Times Book Rev

"Leonard's spare language and propulsive plotting still leave room for expositions of Sicilian slang, gamblers' lingo and Ezra Pound's private life. His colorful characters work together splendidly." Publ Wkly

Rum punch. Delacorte Press 1992 297p $21

ISBN 0-385-30143-X   LC 91-38738

Also available large print edition $25 (ISBN 0-385-30765-9)

"A combination of coincidence and choice connects the fates of Jackie Burke, a 44-year-old, thrice-married stewardess, bail bondsman Max Cherry, overweight and in his 50s, and brash young gun dealer Ordell Robbie, in Miami. When Jackie is caught bringing cash into the U.S. from the Bahamas for Ordell, she agrees to cooperate with federal and state agents to catch him in a sting operation. Max, who has posted Jackie's bond and is drawn to her, becomes her sounding board as she contemplates a sting of her own." Publ Wkly

"Mr. Leonard never tells you; he shows you. The story is all action, a scam within a scam. . . . His style is the absence of style, stripped of fancy baggage . . . the absence, as far as it's possible, of an authorial ego." NY Times Book Rev

Split images. Arbor House 1982 282p o.p.

LC 81-67524

"When millionaire Robbie Daniels hires a trigger-happy cop as bodyguard, reporter Angela Nolan, who's been doing a story on Daniels, becomes worried. Daniels has killed people—supposedly by accident and in self-defense— and seems to be getting a taste for it. She and policeman Bryan Hurd find themselves in a deadly race to thwart Daniels' plans, which include video taping his killings. This is a fast-paced suspense novel with interesting characters and a warm-hearted romance between Hurd and Nolan." Libr J

Stick. Arbor House 1983 304p o.p.

LC 82-72073

Leonard, Elmore, 1925-—*Continued*

"After seven years in a Michigan prison for armed robbery, Ernest Stickley, Jr. heads for Florida and gets together with a friend who served a three-four year sentence at the same prison for possession with intent to deliver. Stick is soon in the center of Miami's underworld of big money and illegal drugs. He barely escapes from the scene of a slaying, which is more of a human sacrifice than a murder. Soon a couple of drug-pushing czars and their goons are on his trail. But Stick is not exactly hiding, and his trail leads across yachts, through mansions, and to a country club gala." Best Sellers

"Despite his violence, Stick is likeable, and the scam he pulls on the drug dealers has the reader firmly on his side. Escapist but not shallow." Libr J

Swag

In Leonard, E. Elmore Leonard's Dutch treat: 3 novels

Touch. Arbor House 1987 245p o.p.

LC 87-12624

"Charlie Lawson once served as Brother Juvenal in a Catholic order; now he cares for alcoholics in a Detroit hospice. Charlie/Juvenal cures those he touches through miracles manifested by the Stigmata, the wounds of Christ that appear on Charlie's body. The phenomenon lures a flashy promoter, Bill Hill, aiming to get rich by exploiting the reclusive, gentle man who is also the intended prey of rabid right-winger August Murray." Publ Wkly

"The hard-as-nails-and-twice-as-real dialogue and sharp characterizations make this weird nonviolent thriller . . . as absorbing as Leonard's usual, more menacing fare." Booklist

Lescroart, John T.

The 13th juror; a novel. Fine, D.I. 1994 484p $22.95

ISBN 1-55611-402-8   LC 93-74487

Also available G.K. Hall large print edition

"Jennifer's fairytale life as the wife of Dr. Larry Witt seems perfect. When Larry and their seven-year-old son are murdered while Jennifer is out jogging, the newspapers have a field day weeping with the photogenic young widow. After she is arrested for the crime, a full-fledged tabloid feeding frenzy erupts. Into this fray steps Dismas Hardy, a fortysomething former district attorney's office hotshot and an ex-bartender who is 43 days into his new job with a prestigious law firm." Libr J

"The story gets off to a slow start, and sometimes Lescroart belabors the obvious. . . . Despite these flaws, however, an intricate story and satisfying courtroom scenes carry the day." Publ Wkly

Hard evidence. Fine, D.I. 1993 478p $21.95

ISBN 1-55611-344-7   LC 92-54457

"Dismas Hardy, the grief-stricken former district attorney turned bartender who first appeared in *The Vig* (1991) and *Dead Irish* (1990), returns with a new wife, a child, and his old job with the prosecutor's office. Pushing 40, Dis thought he'd paid his dues during his previous stint as a D.A., but now he's back at the low end of the totem pole, prosecuting small-time drug dealers, hookers, and other losers. He needs a case, a real case, to relaunch his career. It comes in the form of a hand in a dead shark's stomach. The hand is soon connected (figuratively, of course) to a recently murdered silicon-chip king." Booklist

"Lescroart blends an intricate plot, a great locale, wonderfully colorful characters, and taut courtroom drama to create a book that will leave readers eager for more." Libr J

Leslie, Josephine Aimee Campbell, 1898-1979

The ghost and Mrs. Muir. Ziff-Davis 1945 174p o.p. Buccaneer Bks. reprint available $21.95 (ISBN 0-89968-395-9)

"When Lucy Muir, a pretty young widow, bent on living her own life at long last, flees from her domineering inlaws, she falls in love with Gull Cottage in an English coast town and rents the place, thus inheriting a ghost who has made things so disagreeable for previous tenants that none of them would stay in the haunted house. Though no one she has ever met has been on intimate terms with a ghost, Lucy soon finds herself hobnobbing with the gruff old sea captain and comes to depend on the old fellow in all the crises, emotional and financial, in her life." Bookmark

Lessing, Doris May, 1919-

African stories; [by] Doris Lessing. Simon & Schuster 1965 636p o.p.

Analyzed in Short story index

Contents: The black Madonna; The trinket box; The pig; Traitors; The old Chief Mshlanga; A sunrise on the veld; No witchcraft for sale; The second hut; The nuisance; The De Wets come to Kloof Grange; Little Tembi; Old John's place; "Leopard" George; Winter in July; A home for the highland cattle; Eldorado; The antheap; Hunger; The words he said; Lucy Grange; A mild attack of locusts; Flavours of exile; Getting off the altitude; A road to the big city; Flight; Plants and girls; The sun between their feet; A letter from home; The new man; The story of two dogs

Briefing for a descent into Hell; [by] Doris Lessing. Knopf 1971 308p o.p.

"Charles Watkins, a classics professor, is found wandering and incoherent. Gradually, through shock and drug therapy, his other 'existences' (including a stint as a guerilla fighter in World War II and hallucinatory stay on a desert island) overwhelm his mundane life, but finally he is restored to 'normality.' A difficult and searing book, this novel explores . . . the narrow demarcation between sanity and insanity, between social reality and psychic disturbance." Choice

Children of violence; [by] Doris Lessing. v1-5 o.p.

v1-4 published by Simon & Schuster; v5 published 1969 by Knopf with title: The four-gated city

Contents: v1 Martha Quest (1964; United Kingdom edition 1952); v2 A proper marriage (1964; United Kingdom edition 1954); v3 A ripple from the storm (1966; United Kingdom edition 1958); v4 Landlocked (1966; United Kingdom edition 1965); v5 The four-gated city (1969)

This "is an account of the life of Martha Quest and of her search for self-definition, which for her is to be achieved through total commitment to a person or a cause. We follow her from her beginnings as a wayward but intelligent child on a Rhodesian farm, through two unsuccessful marriages and active involvement in the

Lessing, Doris May, 1919—*Continued*

Communist party in Salisbury during World War II. After the war Martha goes to London and becomes an increasingly disenchanted observer of London life and behavior in the 1950s; the last volume of the sequence anticipates an apocalyptic, science-fiction future, as Martha dies in a devastated, radioactive world at the end of the twentieth century." Wakeman. World Authors, 1950-1970

The fifth child; [by] Doris Lessing. Knopf 1988 133p $16.95

ISBN 0-394-57105-3   LC 88-2680

"Mildly eccentric English couple Harriet and David Lovatt are the contented parents of four healthy children. Suddenly, their peace is forever shattered by their fifth child, Ben, a fiercely malevolent goblin-child with a penchant for violence. . . . Only Harriet tries to civilize the boy, and he gradually learns to function on a primitive level and even collects a band of similar outcasts about him. Unwanted, they leave their homes to wander England." Libr J

"Acting as a social moralist, Lessing exposes the division between the warm and comfortable domestic scene and the harsh reality of the outside world, piercing the boundary between the two as human desires clash with a more brutal vision of existence. A psychologically probing and emotionally powerful performance." Booklist

The four-gated city

In Lessing, D. M. Children of violence v5

The golden notebook; [by] Doris Lessing. Simon & Schuster 1962 567p o.p.

"A lengthy and ambitious novel which was hailed as a landmark by the Women's Movement: sections of conventional narrative ironically entitled 'Free Women' enclose and intersperse the four experimental notebooks of writer Anna Wulf who is struggling with crises in her domestic and political life, and with a writer's block. In each notebook she approaches experience from a different angle (through fiction, parody, political documentation, realistic recording of daily events), a method that reflects her sense of fragmentation and need to keep aspects of life in separate compartments. The novel ends, after a period of breakdown, with release, union, and renewed creativity." Oxford Companion to Engl Lit. 5th edition

The good terrorist; [by] Doris Lessing. Knopf 1985 375p o.p.

LC 85-40214

"Alice Mellings is the 'good' terrorist, a sort of house mother for a group of London radicals who take over an abandoned and badly vandalized house as communal home and headquarters. Picketing with trade unionists and spray-painting bridges with slogans protesting vivisection, chemicals in food, Trident, and sexism, these small-time revolutionaries get involved in something big, and very dangerous, as the story progresses. Alice, whose contempt for her mother's middle-class values informs her rebellion, winds up just like her mother, decorating the squatters' squalid home and cooking for her comrades. [This is] a novel about home, family, and revolt." Libr J

"Unsparingly, fiercely, often satirically, Lessing is writing a narrative about death: the death of the heart when ideology tyrannizes over just, kindly human relations, abstractions over common sense." Ms

The grass is singing; [by] Doris Lessing. Crowell 1950 245p o.p.

The novel begins with the newspaper notice of the death of Mary Turner, wife of an unsuccessful South African farmer. There seems to be some reluctance among the other whites about discussing the case. The author then turns back to the story of Mary Turner's life, showing her gradual disintegration as a person, and ending with her murder by a Kaffir houseboy

This novel "besides being very well-written is an extremely mature psychological study. It is full of those terrifying touches of truth, seldom mentioned but instantly recognized. By any standards, this book shows remarkable powers and imagination." New Statesman

Landlocked

In Lessing, D. M. Children of violence v4

Martha Quest

In Lessing, D. M. Children of violence v1

The memoirs of a survivor; [by] Doris Lessing. Knopf 1975 c1974 213p o.p.

First published 1974 in the United Kingdom

This "novel is a projection into the near future when technological structures have broken down and society is forging new patterns among the chaos. [The] speaker, never named, lives through progressive disorientation in an English city, (also never named) where bands of children terrorize those people who haven't left yet. As her everyday life becomes more and more survival-bound, she fashions an imaginary world beyond her living room wall. When [Emily], a young girl, comes into her care, she is forced to see her emerging strength and womanhood as the hope of an uncertain future." Libr J

This is "an extraordinary and compelling meditation about the enduring need for loyalty, love and responsibility in an unprecedented time that places unbearable demands upon people." Time

The other woman

In Lessing, D. M. Stories p157-211

A proper marriage

In Lessing, D. M. Children of violence v2

The real thing; stories and sketches; [by] Doris Lessing. HarperCollins Pubs. 1992 214p o.p.

LC 91-59932

Analyzed in Short story index

Published in the United Kingdom with title: London observed

Contents: Debbie and Julie; Sparrows; The mother of the child in question; Pleasures of the park; Womb ward; Principles; D.H.S.S.; Casualty; In defence of the underground; The new café; Romance 1988; What price the truth?; Among the roses; Storms; Her; The pit; Two old women and a young one; The real thing

In this "sharply observed collection of short works, Lessing offers a rich portrait of life and love in contemporary London." N Y Times Book Rev

A ripple from the storm

In Lessing, D. M. Children of violence v3

Lessing, Doris May, 1919-—*Continued*

Shikasta; re: colonised planet 5; personal, psychological, historical documents relating to visit by Johor (George Sherban) emissary (grade 9) 87th of the period of the last days; [by] Doris Lessing. Knopf 1979 364p (Canopus in Argos: archives) o.p.

LC 79-11295

"First of the Canopus in Argos: Archives five-volume series. Shikasta is Earth, whose history—extending over millions of years—is here put into the cosmic perspective, observed by Canopeans who seem to be in charge of galactic history although responsible to some higher, impersonal authority. The sequels follow the exploits of various human cultures whose affairs are subtly influenced by the Canopeans; all share the remotely detached perspective that transforms the way in which individual endeavors are seen. Thoughtful and painstaking." Anatomy of Wonder 4

Followed by The marriages between zones three, four, and five (1980); The Sirian experiments (1981); The making of the representative for Planet 8 (1982); Documents relating to the sentimental agents in the Volyen Empire (1983)

Stories; [by] Doris Lessing. Knopf 1978 625p o.p.

LC 77-20709

Analyzed in Short story index

Contents: The habit of loving; The woman; Through the tunnel; Pleasure; The witness; The day Stalin died; Wine; He; The eye of God in Paradise; The other woman; One off the short list; A woman on a roof; How I finally lost my heart; A man and two women; A room; England versus England; Two potters; Between men; Our friend Judith; Each other; Homage for Isaac Babel; Outside the ministry; Dialogue; Notes for a case history; To room nineteen; An old woman and her cat; Side benefits of an honourable profession; A year in Regent's Park; Report on the threatened city; Mrs. Fortescue; An unposted love letter; Lions, leaves, roses; Not a very nice story; The other garden; The temptation of Jack Orkney

"All of Lessing's non-African stories are brought together from three of her previous collections: 'The habit of Loving,' 'A Man and Two Women,' and 'The Temptation of Jack Orkney and other Stories'. In addition, 'The Other Woman,' a short novel, previously published only in Great Britain, is also included." Booklist

The summer before the dark; [by] Doris Lessing. Knopf 1973 273p o.p.

"Kate Brown is ejected for a summer from the life into which she has fitted herself for 25 years—the pleasant, efficient, compassionate Mrs. Brown, wife and mother of four; and she reassesses her memories and her relationships with her family, trying to find her real self. A highly paid job with a global foods conference in Turkey is followed by an unsatisfactory affair with a younger man in Spain, illness in a London hotel, and convalescence in a flat with a young hippie girl, Maureen, who is undergoing her own agonizing decisions about what to do with her life." Choice

"Despite its downbeat and perhaps portentous ending, Mrs Lessing's book is not the moan of growing old, of unfulfilled potentialities. This is why, despite an obvious message about the desperation of the female role our society has created, this is neither a depressing nor a tiresomely polemical book." Times Lit Suppl

Lester, Julius

And all our wounds forgiven. Arcade Pub. 1994 228p $19.95

ISBN 1-55970-258-3   LC 93-50049

A novel about Harvard-educated John Calvin Marshall, "a famous slain civil rights leader. From the grave, Cal shares his thoughts, as do his wife, Andrea; his mistress, Elizabeth, who is a blue-eyed blond from a privileged white family; and Card, a veteran of civil rights work in Mississippi. The novel teeters back and forth, from the present at Andrea's deathbed to the tempestuous 1960s, examining the personal, political, and social impact of the past on the present and future. Lester captures well the essence of a leader struggling with immense responsibility and his own human nature." Libr J

Do Lord remember me; a novel. Holt & Co. 1985 c1984 210p o.p.

LC 84-3845

"The final day of Rev. Joshua Smith's earthly existence is a reminiscence: of his turn-of-the-century boyhood in a hardscrabble county in Mississippi as the son of sharecroppers; of his gift as the 'singing preacher' for churches all over the segregated South; of his disappointment at never leading a big church in Detroit or Chicago; of his love for his fair-skinned wife and the trouble her appearance caused them." Publ Wkly

"Smith's memories link with those of older people in his past, whose stories take him back to slavery times. What emerges is a picture of black experience covering more than 150 years, with memory and storytelling providing continuity between present and past. A rich and moving reading experience." Booklist

Levenkron, Steven, 1941-

The best little girl in the world. Contemporary Bks. 1978 196p o.p.

LC 78-9063

"Francesca is 15, an excellent student, a docile girl at home in her affluent parents' Manhattan apartment. But Francesca sets about killing her 'fat' self to become imaginary Kessa—slim and firm. Within weeks she starves herself, so that she drops from 98 to an alarming 84 pounds and is hospitalized, another young victim of anorexia nervosa. The reader is drawn into the arena where dedicated professionals battle to save Francesca's life and the lives of others like her. This book, fiction in name only, proves what an impassioned and skillful author can do to make a novel more powerful than dry facts." Publ Wkly

Leventhal, Alice Walker *See* Walker, Alice, 1944-

Levi, Primo, 1919-1987

If not now, when?; translated from the Italian by William Weaver; introduction by Irving Howe. Summit Bks. 1985 c1982 349p o.p.

LC 85-2526

Levi, Primo, 1919-1987—*Continued*

Original Italian edition, 1982

"The author, himself a victim of Nazi atrocities, has based his novel on true events. A band of Jewish partisans makes its way from Russia to Italy waging their personal war against the Nazis. They blow up trains, rescue concentration camp inmates, and face incredible dangers in their efforts to strike back against a ruthless, seemingly invincible enemy. The story is a testament to human endurance and courage." Shapiro. Fic for Youth. 3d edition

The monkey's wrench; translated from the Italian by William Weaver. Summit Bks. 1986 171p o.p.

LC 86-5803

Original Italian edition, 1978

"In this tale of two lonely and quite different men, a steel rigger entertains a chemist with memories of his world travels." Booklist

"Among other things, The Monkey's Wrench is a model of the interplay between storytellers and listeners. For their part, readers can envy Levi's sixth sense about building bridges between what can be seen and what must be imagined." Time

The sixth day, and other tales; translated by Raymond Rosenthal. Summit Bks. 1990 222p o.p.

LC 90-9734

Analyzed in Short story index

Contents: The mnemogogues; Angelic butterfly; Order on the cheap; Man's friend; Some applications of the Mimer; Versamina; The sleeping beauty in the fridge: a winter's tale; The measure of beauty; Full employment; The sixth day; Retirement fund; Westward; Seen from afar; The hard-sellers; Small red lights; For a good purpose; Psychophant; Recuenco: the nurse; Recuenco: the rafter; His own blacksmith: to Italo Calvino; The servant; Mutiny: to Mario Rigoni Stern; Excellent is the water

"These bizarre stories from master storyteller Levi are full of shadowed meanings, conveying truths about our technological society and how our scientific appetites have outstripped our moral capacities." Libr J

Levin, Ira

The boys from Brazil; a novel. Random House 1976 312p o.p.

"Ninety-four potential Hitlers are created through the technique of cloning by Dr. Mengele, infamous doctor of Auschwitz. Striving to re-create the early environment of the original Hitler, Mengele plots the murder of the fathers of these ninety-four children. Yakov Liebermann, a pursuer of Nazis, tries to stop the murders at the cost of great, almost mortal, danger to himself." Shapiro. Fic for Youth. 3d edition

A kiss before dying. Simon & Schuster 1953 244p o.p.

"An Inner sanctum mystery"

"The plot has to do with a remarkably ingenious, subtle, and relentless murderer, who does away with a pregnant college girl, goes on from there to kill her sister and a more or less innocent bystander, and is cheated of the fortune that has driven him to these desperate measures only by a couple of tiny oversights that might easily have escaped Sherlock Holmes. The book is a succession of solid and quite legitimate surprises, the suspense is admirably sustained, the detail is thorough

and convincing, and the writing is considerably above the level usually associated with fictional crime and passion." New Yorker

Rosemary's baby. Armchair Detective Lib. 1991 245p $18.95

ISBN 0-922890-84-6   LC 90-23997

A reissue with a new introduction by the author of the title first published 1967 by Random House

"Guy and Rosemary Woodhouse dismiss the warnings of friends and move into a luxurious Manhattan apartment building where, supposedly, rites of witchcraft and suicides have occurred. Rosemary's instincts warn her to beware of their neighbors, the Castevets, but her husband is not convinced and they become a dominant influence on Guy when Rosemary becomes pregnant. She is alone in her fear and becomes a helpless victim." Shapiro. Fic for Youth. 3d edition

Sliver; a novel. Bantam Bks. 1991 190p o.p.

LC 90-46204

Available large print edition $21.95 (ISBN 0-385-41826-4)

The author sets this "novel in a gleaming, modern 'Sliver' of an apartment house that seems to stab ominously into the New York City sky. When a book editor named Kay Norris moves into this eerie high-rise, which has been the scene of several recent murders, the building's owner immediately begins electronic surveillance of her. On this intricately suspenseful foundation, Mr. Levin constructs an edifice of terror. Even the concrete, it turns out, contains a terrible secret." N Y Times Book Rev

The Stepford wives. Random House 1972 145p o.p.

"Attractive, talented Joanna moves with her husband and kids to a suburb, where she comes to suspect that the village housewives have all been murdered and replaced by robots, the suspected villain being a chauvinistic Men's Association . . . and so Joanna begins to fear for her life." Libr J

"There is a broad current of humor beneath the horrific surface of this little ambush of Women's Lib, life and the pursuit of happiness." N Y Times Book Rev

Levin, Meyer, 1905-1981

Compulsion. Simon & Schuster 1956 495p o.p.

Using fictionalized names and probing deeply into the psychological aspects of the crime, this is a retelling of the Loeb-Leopold murder case

"The writing shows the hand of a master. Despite the fact that the reader who is familiar with the history of the case knows the outcome, Mr. Levin manages to fill this book with sustained suspense." N Y Times Book Rev

Lewin, Michael Z.

And baby will fall. Morrow 1988 261p o.p.

LC 88-1089

A mystery introducing social worker/detective Adele Buffington. "Working late one evening, Buffington is pushed around by an intruder who only wants information from the social agency files. When a former colleague is apparently murdered soon thereafter, Detective Sergeant Homer Proffitt of the Indianapolis P. D. in-

Lewin, Michael Z.—*Continued*

vestigates. He and Buffington unearth a seamy ring of baby brokers who deal in illegal adoptions. . . . Wonderful entertainment from an underappreciated master." Booklist

Late payments. Morrow 1986 216p o.p.

LC 85-25927

A mystery about "police lieutenant Leroy Powder, who is in charge of the missing persons office. . . . 'Late Payments' has several strands. One has to do with Powder's relation to his son, who has been sent to jail by Powder himself on a drug charge. One has to do with a boy whose father is missing. One has to do with the request of a family to find a relative who disappeared 17 years ago. And a computer expert in the department is collating information that suggests a mass murderer in Indiana." N Y Times Book Rev

Lewis, C. S. (Clive Staples), 1898-1963

The dark tower and other stories; edited by Walter Hooper. Harcourt Brace Jovanovich 1977 158p o.p.

Analyzed in Short story index

Contents: The dark tower; The man born blind; The shoddy lands; Ministering angels; Forms of things unknown; After ten years

Out of the silent planet. Macmillan 1990 174p $45

ISBN 0-02-570795-7　　　　　　　LC 89-13969

Also available from Buccaneer Bks.

First volume of trilogy about the adventures of Dr. Ransom

First published 1938 in the United Kingdom; first Macmillan edition published 1943

"A philologist, kidnapped by a physicist and a promoter is taken via space-ship from England to Malacandra (Mars). There he escapes and goes on the run. Philological, philosophical, social and religious overtones, plus human-interest detail on the Malacandrians make this a credible and stimulating 'tour de force.'" Libr J

Followed by Perelandra

Perelandra; a novel. Macmillan 222p $40

ISBN 0-02-570845-7

Also available from Amereon

"Hudson River editions"

First published 1944

In the second volume of the fantasy trilogy Dr. Ransom "is ordered to Perelandra (Venus) by the supreme being and finds there a paradise threatened by the villainous scientist Weston, who becomes the devil incarnate." Booklist

Followed by That hideous strength

That hideous strength; a modern fairy-tale for grown-ups. Macmillan 382p $60

ISBN 0-02-571255-1

First published 1946

In the final volume of the fantasy trilogy Ransom and Weston again represent the struggle between good and evil, this time in a college community on Earth. Mark Studdock learns the error of his attempts to play faculty politics, and his wife discovers the footlessness of modern theories of love and life

Till we have faces; a myth retold. Harcourt Brace & Co. 1957 c1956 313p il o.p.

First published 1956 in the United Kingdom

"Introducing his own version of the myth of Psyche and Cupid the author weaves it into a fantasy in which he gives expression to some of his persisting ideas on the forces at work in the soul of man. Orual, queen of a fictional kingdom of the Near East in ancient times, tells the story." Booklist

"The religious allegory is plain to read. In Mr. Lewis's sensitive hands the ancient myth retains its fascination, while being endowed with new meanings, new depths, new terrors." Saturday Rev

Lewis, Clive Staples *See* Lewis, C. S. (Clive Staples), 1898-1963

Lewis, Hilda Winifred, 1896-1974

I am Mary Tudor; [by] Hilda Lewis. McKay, D. 1972 c1971 422p o.p.

First published 1971 in the United Kingdom

The author "traces the life of Mary Tudor, daughter of King Henry VIII and his queen, Catherine of Aragon, from her birth in 1516 to her accession. Mary was at first favored and treated royally but, by the age of nine, she began to suffer the disfavor of her father. Henry's great desire for a male heir, plus his later passion for Anne Boleyn, made him take the matters of marriage and religion into his own hands. Through Mary's eyes, readers watch Henry declare himself head of the Church of England; declare Mary a bastard; and marry, one after the other, five unlucky women. With her half-sister, Elizabeth, and half-brother, Edward, Mary waited upon the father she both loved and hated until she finally ascended the throne." Libr J

Lewis, Sinclair, 1885-1951

Nobel Prize in literature, 1930

Arrowsmith. Harcourt Brace & Co. 1925 448p $15.95

ISBN 0-15-168216-2

Also available from Amereon and Buccaneer Bks.

"Although he is most interested in bacteriology and research, Martin Arrowsmith turns from that area to general medicine and then to public health. He is unable, however, to deal with the political aspects of the public health field and returns to laboratory work and research. Martin develops an antitoxin that he believes will be effective against bubonic plague, but when he gets the chance to test the serum during an epidemic in the West Indies, he invalidates the results by not adhering to a control situation. Returning to the States, he feels that he is a failure and refuses the offer of a prestigious position in order to join an old friend at a rural laboratory in a search for a cure for pneumonia." Shapiro. Fic for Youth. 3d edition

Babbitt.

Available from various publishers

First published 1922 by Harcourt, Brace

Satire on American middle-class life in a good-sized city. George F. Babbitt is a successful real estate man, a regular fellow, booster, Rotarian, Elk, Republican, who uses all the current catchwords, molds his opinions on those of the Zenith Advocate-Times and believes in "a sound business administration in Washington"

Lewis, Sinclair, 1885-1951—*Continued*

"The novel's scathing indictment of middle-class American values made Babbittry a synonym for adherence to a conformist, materialistic, anti-intellectual way of life." Merriam-Webster's Ency of Lit

Cass Timberlane; a novel of husbands and wives. Random House 1945 390p o.p.
Available from Amereon and Buccaneer Bks.

Cass Timberlane at forty-one was sober, thoughtful, and respected by the Minnesota town in which he was a judge. This story of Cass's second marriage to a girl in her early twenties is punctuated by stories of the married lives of many of his friends

Dodsworth; a novel. Harcourt Brace & Co. 1929 377p o.p. Amereon reprint available $24.95 (ISBN 0-8488-0565-8)
"The book's protagonist, Sam Dodsworth, is an American automobile manufacturer who sells his company and takes an extended European vacation with his wife, Fran. *Dodsworth* recounts their reactions to Europeans and European values, their various relationships with others, their estrangement, and their brief reconciliation." Merriam-Webster's Ency of Lit

Elmer Gantry. Harcourt Brace & Co. 1927 432p o.p. Amereon reprint available $21.95 (ISBN 0-8488-0827-4)
This novel "deals with a brazen ex-football player who enters the ministry and, through his half-plagiarized sermons, his physical attractiveness, and his unerring instinct for promotion, becomes a successful evangelist and later the leader of a large Middle Western church. Carefully researched, the novel was realistic enough to shock both the faithful and unfaithful." Reader's Ency. 3d edition

It can't happen here; a novel. Doubleday, Doran 1935 458p o.p. AMS Press reprint available $38 (ISBN 0-404-20158-X)
"Doremus Jessup, editor of a small New England newspaper, follows the rise to the presidency of the United States of a fascist demagogue, Berzelius Windrip. Doremus and his friends publish an underground newspaper that tells the truth about what is happening. Doremus is imprisoned, escapes to Canada, and joins the underground movement, which is headed by the man who had opposed Windrip in the election. The novel inveighs against some aspects of capitalism as well as fascism, and communists come in for their share of criticism also." Shapiro. Fic for Youth. 3d edition

Kingsblood royal. Random House 1947 348p o.p.
This look at racial prejudice focuses on a Midwestern banker who discovers he has some black blood
"Lewis is savagely satiric in his depiction of types in an average American community viewing the advocates of race prejudice as not only wicked but appallingly dull." Benet's Reader's Ency of Am Lit

Main Street. Harcourt Brace & Co. 451p $15.95
ISBN 0-15-155547-8
Also available from Amereon and Buccaneer Bks.
First published 1920
"Carol Milford, a girl of quick intelligence but no particular talent, after graduation from college meets and marries Will Kennicott, a sober, kindly, unimaginative physician of Gopher Prairie, Minn., who tells her that the town needs her abilities. She finds the village to be a smug, intolerant, unimaginatively standardized place, where the people will not accept her efforts to create more sightly homes, organize a dramatic association, and otherwise improve the village life." Oxford Companion to Am Lit. 5th edition

Li, Pi-hua

Farewell to my concubine; [by] Lilian Lee; translated by Andrea Lingenfelter. Morrow 1993 255p $18
ISBN 0-688-12020-2   LC 93-16777

The author "sets an intricate love triangle against the backdrop of China during the warlord period, the Japanese occupation, the Communist victory, and the Cultural Revolution. Singers Duan Xialou and Cheng Dieyi grow up together and come to play leading roles at the Peking Opera; their bravura performance is *Farewell to My Concubine*, in which the devoted mistress of a general kills herself rather than face her man's defeat. Cheng incarnates female roles so totally that he falls passionately in love with Duan, who feels only brotherly affection for his stage partner and marries a beautiful courtesan. The obsessive Cheng tries repeatedly to undermine the marriage. Unlike most Chinese fiction, this novel seamlessly integrates the personal and the social; its riveting drama of a *menage à trois* also reveals the burden of recent Chinese history." Libr J

Lightman, Alan P., 1948-

Einstein's dreams; [by] Alan Lightman. Pantheon Bks. 1993 179p il $17
ISBN 0-679-41646-3   LC 92-50465

"In 1905, while working as an examiner at the Swiss Patent Office in Bern, Einstein published three important papers in Annals of Physics. Here Lightman re-creates the dreams that allegedly culminated in the famous essay on the relativity of time." Libr J
"Lightman starts out with commonplaces, neurological conditions or abstractions of our personal experience of time. Then, with one or two exceptions, he embodies the concept in brilliant, folkloric tales with extraordinary assurance." New Statesman Soc

Lin, Yutang, 1895-1976

Moment in Peking; a novel of contemporary Chinese life. Day 1939 815p o.p.
A story of family life among the upper middle class of China, covering forty years from the time of the Boxer Rebellion to the Japanese invasion
"There are many scenes and passages of great beauty in the book, excerpts from the classics, poetry and philosophy. There are also incidents of humor, delicate and subtle. Equally skillful is the author in depicting scenes of dramatic intensity, stark tragedy of war and acts of heroism" Springfield Repub

Lindsey, David L.

An absence of light. Doubleday 1994 519p $23
ISBN 0-385-42311-X   LC 93-35730

Lindsey, David L.—*Continued*

"When a member of Houston's Police Intelligence Division turns up an apparent suicide, a chilling chain of events is triggered, unveiling the compromise of highly sensitive data, a sophisticated drug smuggling scam, and the relocation of vast sums of money. To avoid publicity and scandal, Capt. Marcus Garver hires an old friend in the 'intelligence-for-profit business' to assist him and a tight crew from the force in the pursuit of the wily kingpin of the enterprise." Libr J

"Along with deft plotting and abundant surprises, . . . Lindsey offers suspense shrewdly balanced by a number of thoughtful meditations on the nature of betrayal and deceit." Publ Wkly

Mercy; a novel. Doubleday 1990 513p o.p.
LC 89-38623

The author has constructed a "psychological thriller around a gruesome subject: a series of brutally sadistic murders among the lesbian demimonde of monied Houston. The victims are found nude, beaten, bitten, slashed—and perfumed and flawlessly made-up, but with their eyelids expertly sliced from their eyes. Lindsey's likable heroine, recently divorced detective Carmen Palma, frantically tries to discover the murderer before another strike, battling both male chauvinism within the department and a growing discomfort with her task." Publ Wkly

"A relentless researcher, Lindsey never wallows in sexual psychobabble; his world is full of pitch-black souls, hidden societies, pasts full of pain, and stillborn futures. A spine-tingling novel that exerts a subversive pull on even the most wary reader." Booklist

Linebarger, Paul M. A., 1913-1966

For works written by this author under other names see Smith, Cordwainer, 1913-1966

Linington, Elizabeth, 1921-

For works written by this author under other names see Shannon, Dell, 1921-

Skeletons in the closet. Doubleday 1982 178p o.p.
LC 82-45075

"Published for the Crime Club"

"This police procedural featuring Ivor and Sue Maddox deals with the discovery of some very old bodies inside a house being demolished, plus the usual murders, burglaries, holdups, and hit-and-runs. Typical of Linington, this is neatly done, a balance between intriguing mystery and the humdrum of routine police work." Libr J

Lipman, Elinor

The way men act; a novel. Pocket Bks. 1992 305p o.p.
LC 91-31878

"At 30, Melinda LeBlanc, without any marital prospects, higher education or a career of her own, has come back to live with her mother in the snobby college town of Harrow in Massachusetts. She arranges flowers for Forget-Me-Not, a shop owned by her cousin Roger and his wife, Robin. . . . Melinda renews old friendships, gossips incessantly and chases the limited supply of available men in an attempt both to resuscitate and to erase her earlier successes." N Y Times Book Rev

"Putting a wicked 1990s spin on the game of courtship, Lipman comes up with a winner—a wry, witty, fond look at decent people attempting to make connections with each other." Libr J

A **Literary** Christmas; great contemporary Christmas stories; edited and with an introduction by Lilly Golden. Atlantic Monthly Press 1992 321p $20
ISBN 0-87113-490-X   LC 92-10703

Analyzed in Short story index

Contents: Christmas morning, by F. O'Connor; Auggie Wren's Christmas story, by P. Auster; Champagne, by T. Wolff; The birds for Christmas, by M. Richard; Christmas for Sassafrass, Cypress & Indigo, by N. Shange; A Christmas conspiracy tale, by I. Klíma; Two of a kind, by S. O'Faolain; Jesu, Joy of Man's Desiring, by M. Tournier; The frozen fields, by P. Bowles; The world in a bowl of soup: a Christmas story, by A. Dillard; Xmas, by T. M. Disch; The centerpiece, by P. Matthiessen; Santa's children, by I. Calvino; A clock ticks at Christmas, by P. Highsmith; Christmas, by H. Lee; The loudest voice, by G. Paley; The doll, by E. O'Brien; Drawing names, by B. A. Mason; Where you'll find me, by A. Beattie; Put yourself in my shoes, by R. Carver; The night of the Magi, by L. Rosten; A Christmas carillon, by H. Calisher; Long distance, by J. Smiley; And there was the evening and the morning. . . ., by H. Böll; Christmas Eve at Johnson's Drugs N Goods, by T. C. Bambara; Bless me, Father, for I have sinned, by R. Bradbury; The H Street sledding record, by R. Carlson

"It is their distinctively modern mien that truly unites these 27 stories. . . . Noël as seen here may not always be joyous, but is certainly sophisticated." Publ Wkly

The **Literary** ghost; great contemporary ghost stories; edited and with an introduction by Larry Dark. Atlantic Monthly Press 1991 369p o.p.
LC 91-15052

Analyzed in Short story index

Contents: The lost, strayed, stolen, by M. F. K. Fisher; The Portobello Road, by M. Spark; The ghost who vanished by degrees, by R. Davies; The others, by J. C. Oates; A story of Don Juan, by V. S. Pritchett; Up north, by M. Gallant; The warden, by J. Gardner; The death of Edward Lear, by D. Barthelme; The circular valley, by P. Bowles; The third voice, by W. Ferguson; Marmilion, by P. McGrath; Spirit seizures, by M. Pritchard; Revenant as typewriter, by P. Lively; Ghostly populations, by J. Matthews; The ghost soldiers, by T. O'Brien; Family, by L. Olsen; Letter from a dogfighter's aunt, deceased, by P. Powell; The ghost, by A. Sexton; Angel, all innocence, by F. Weldon; Jack's girl, by C. Kadohata; The next room, by A. S. Byatt; Grass, by B. Yourgrau; Eisenheim the illusionist, by S. Millhauser; Ghost and flesh, water and dirt, by W. Goyen; Letter from his father, by N. Gordimer; Old man of the temple, by R. K. Narayan; A little place off the Edgware Road, by G. Greene; A crown of feathers, by I. B. Singer

The **Literary** traveler; an anthology of contemporary short fiction; edited and with an introduction by Larry Dark. Viking 1994 354p $22.95

ISBN 0-670-84578-7 LC 94-8796

Analyzed in Short story index

Includes the following stories: The gardens of Mont-Saint-Michel, by W. Maxwell; Great Barrier Reef, by D. Johnson; I'm worried about you, by W. S. Just; Travel, by S. Miller; Delirium eclipse, by J. Lasdun; Wasted lives, by F. Weldon; In Isfahan, by W. Trevor; American express, by J. Salter; The fellow passenger, by E. Jolley; The sepia postcard, by S. Millhauser; Portrait of a lady, by P. Theroux; You have left your lotus pods on the bus, by P. Bowles; Summer opportunity, by M. Thomas; Cruise, by J. Updike; Hold me fast, don't let me pass, by A. Munro; Which is more than I can say about some people, by L. Moore; Virgin of tenderness, by K. Braverman; Succor, by A. Barnett; Verona: a young woman speaks, by H. Brodkey

Littell, Robert, 1935-

The revolutionist. Bantam Bks. 1988 467p $18.95

ISBN 0-553-05260-8 LC 87-27072

"In 1917 Alexander Til, his stepbrother, Leon, and Atticus Tuohy leave New York City and the grinding life of the working-class poor for a better life: Til and Tuohy for the revolution in Russia, Leon for Palestine. Some 35 years later they meet again at Stalin's death. In the intervening years Til and Tuohy have fought and followed first Trotsky, then Lenin, and finally Stalin. Gradually Til's youthful vigor and passion yield to despair as his friends, his great love, his family, and his belief are destroyed by the party leadership." Libr J

"A clever mix of history and fiction, carefully researched and vigorously written." Publ Wkly

Lively, Penelope, 1933-

City of the mind; a novel. HarperCollins Pubs. 1991 231p o.p.

LC 90-56365

"Architect Matthew Halland is tuned into the physical world. London's night sky asks him unanswerable questions about time and space. The dilapidated old buildings and blackened brick walls resound with human experience. Everything Matthew knows of London pulls him out of its present and into its past, leaving him spellbound by the realization that some things will never change for its inhabitants. . . . Like countless Londoners before him, he is tested by the pressures of city life, and his knowledge of the past sustains him until a chance meeting with Sarah Bridges focuses his sights on the future." Libr J

"This book is largely a meditation on time and the individual experience. . . . The 'allusions' in the novel are to figures, major or minor, from London's past, recent or remote. . . . Penelope Lively evokes these personalities and their stories with great power and charm." London Rev Books

Cleopatra's sister. HarperCollins Pubs. 1993 281p o.p.

LC 92-54424

In alternating chapters, the author "depicts the lives of paleontologist Howard Beamish and crusading journalist Lucy Faulkner, both successful in their careers but unfulfilled because they have not established enduring relationships. They meet when the plane they are taking to Cairo makes a forced landing in Callimbia, a fictional country in the throes of a bloody revolution led by a lunatic dictator. Lively's . . . construction of Callimbia's history ranges from its establishment by Cleopatra's sister Berenice through the rise of the 'moral renegade' who orders the plane's British passengers taken hostage. Through the eyes of Howard and Lucy, and in counterpoint to their growing love for each other, Lively depicts the passengers' responses to their plight." Publ Wkly

Moon tiger. Grove Press 1988 c1987 208p o.p.

LC 87-23798

Available G.K. Hall large print edition

First published 1987 in the United Kingdom

"The heroine is Claudia Hampton, an unconventional historian and former war correspondent who lies in a hospital bed dying of cancer. Forced inward, Claudia moves randomly across time and place to reconstruct the strata of her life." Libr J

"Moon Tiger is an extremely accomplished novel which tells an interesting story with an impressive variety of fictional techniques." Quill Quire

Pack of cards and other stories. Grove Press 1989 c1986 323p $19.95

ISBN 0-8021-1156-4 LC 89-1851

Analyzed in Short story index

First published 1986 in the United Kingdom with title: Pack of cards: stories, 1978-1986

Contents: Nothing missing but the samovar; The voice of God in Adelaide Terrace; Interpreting the past; Servants talk about people: gentlefolk discuss things; Help; Miss Carlton and the pop concert; Revenant as typewriter; Next term, we'll mash you; At the Pitt-Rivers; Nice people; A world of her own; Presents of fish and game; A clean death; Party; Corruption; Venice, now and then; Grow old along with me, the best is yet to be; The darkness out there; The pill-box; Customers; Yellow trains; The ghost of a flea; The art of biography; What the eye doesn't see; The emasculation of Ted Roper; A long night at Abu Simbel; Bus-stop; Clara's day; The French exchange; The dream merchant; Pack of cards; The Crimean hotel; A dream of fair women; Black dog

"These witty, profoundly civilized stories display Lively's compassion, intelligence, and versatility." Libr J

Passing on. Grove Weidenfeld 1990 c1989 210p o.p.

LC 89-7459

First published 1989 in the United Kingdom

This novel describes the reactions of Helen and Edward Glover to the death of their mother Dorothy. "Long years in Greystones, the family nest in a pleasant Cotswold village, have all but atrophied their desire to make lives of their own, free of their widowed mother's commanding presence; both have remained unmarried. . . . Opening the novel with Dorothy's funeral, Lively traces the events of the months that follow and poses the question whether real change is possible in the lives of such repressed and gentle characters." Times Lit Suppl

"Penelope Lively is blessed with the gift of being able to render matters of great import with a breath, a barely audible sigh, a touch. The result is wonderful writing, and a marvelous book." N Y Times Book Rev

Lively, Penelope, 1933—*Continued*
The road to Lichfield. Grove Weidenfeld
1991 215p o.p.

LC 90-47673

Available G.K. Hall large print edition
First published 1977 in the United Kingdom
This novel "centers around British housewife Anne,
whose father is dying in a nursing home. Anne goes to
see him, in Lichfield, and in the process of cleaning out
his house discovers that her father was someone she
hadn't known well at all. 'I knew my father in one
dimension only,' she realizes. Her relationships with her
husband, brother, and lover might be similarly described.
Lively's prose is clean and readable." Libr J

Livingston, Nancy
Mayhem in Parva. St. Martin's Press 1991
192p o.p.

LC 91-20911

First published 1990 in the United Kingdom
This "mystery featuring G. D. H. Pringle has the
sprightly, retired tax inspector looking for his roots in
the quaint village of Parva, undergoing the rigors of a
local flower festival coupled with the restoration of ancient wall paintings in the village church—all accompanied by the rivalry between local matrons fighting to
the death for social leadership." Booklist
"For all the amusement she takes in the eccentric
customs of the country, Ms. Livingston does not neglect
craft for charm. There's ingenuity in this pretty puzzle,
and Mr. Pringle unravels the well-knotted plot with as
much intellignece as humor." N Y Times Book Rev

Llewellyn, Richard, 1906-1983
Green, green, my valley now. Doubleday
1975 236p o.p.

In this concluding novel about the Morgan family,
"Huw with his wife Sus, returns to Wales from his self-
imposed exile in Patagonia. He's rich now, and prepares
to retire in comfort after spending a great deal of time
and money in renovating an ancient house in a small
village. Then his wife dies suddenly, and he finds himself
innocently mixed up with some fanatical IRA members
who have represented themselves as his relatives, and
who hope to use his land as a front and a base for
their illegal activities. . . . The plotters are discovered
and arrested, and the book ends with Huw's remarriage."
Libr J
"Llewellyn's belief in the value of life is strong enough
to carry his hero through the vicissitudes of great wealth,
on the wings of prose that is nearly poetic." N Y Times
Book Rev

How green was my valley. Macmillan
1940 495p $40

ISBN 0-02-573420-2
Also available from Amereon
First novel about the Morgan family. Other titles are:
Up, into the singing mountain (1960); And I shall sleep
. . . down where the moon is small (1966); Green, green
my valley now, entered above
In this "novel of the Welsh mining country the story
is told by Huw Morgan, youngest son of a miner's
family. In his boyhood, in the '80's, the valley was green
and beautiful, the people were prosperous and law
abiding; gradually the countryside was changed to a place
of desolation as slag-heaps of mine refuse covered the

mountain slopes; hard times, with strikes and layoffs,
brought suffering, and a wholesome way of life was
destroyed." Booklist
"A remarkably beautiful novel of Wales. And although
it follows stirringly in the romantic traditions, there is
the resonance of a profound and noble realism in its
evocation, its intensity and reach of truth." N Y Times
Book Rev

None but the lonely heart. Macmillan
1969 518p o.p.

"First published in 1943, this novel of London low-life
has been revised and finished—author Llewellyn was
called into the armed services before the work was completed." Best Sellers
This is an intimate character study of a young
Cockney, Ernie Mott, living in the London slums. Ernie's
father, who had been an artist, was killed at Verdun;
his mother ran a second hand shop. Ernie himself
worked with a firm of commercial artists, and it was
when he lost his job and was faced with the bitterness
of telling Ma, that he met Henry Twite, an elderly eccentric Robin Hood, and began his career of crime
The "additional chapters make it a stronger book. For
the first time the career and character of Ernie Verdun
Mott are rounded out and the Cockney adolescent
becomes a man." Libr J

Llosa, Mario Vargas *See* Vargas Llosa,
Mario, 1936-

Lloyd, Levanah, 1935-
*For works written by this author under
other names see* Black, Veronica, 1935-

Llywelyn, Morgan
Bard; the odyssey of the Irish. Houghton
Mifflin 1984 466p o.p.

LC 84-6645

"At the center of the narrative is Amergin, a fourth-
century Celtic bard who existed in fact and is given
vitality as a complex visionary who inspired his warrior
clan, the Gaels, to cross the sea from the Iberian
Peninsula to Ierne (present-day Ireland). The conquering
tribe, driven by rivalry among themselves, attempts to
take Ierne by sword, rejecting the welcome offered by
the gentle, mystical Tuatha De Danann, the little people
of Irish legend." Booklist
"The author has deftly combined history and legend
with family saga and turned it into a compelling epic."
Libr J

Druids. Morrow 1991 456p o.p.

LC 90-44292

"Caesar's Gallic Wars are recounted from the viewpoint of the losers in this . . . evocation of the culture
of the European Celts. Ainvar of the Carnutes, a young
orphan druid-in-training, receives instruction for the
'manmaking' rituals with prince Vercingetorix of the Ar-
verni, forging a bond that will later unite them in an
effort to free Celtic Gaul from Roman domination." Publ
Wkly
"Llywelyn's skill at making ancient history come alive
for a modern audience without sacrificing authenticity of
fact or detail is nothing short of brilliant. A richly atmospheric tale filled with subtle flashes of humor,
perceptive characterizations, and heart-stopping suspense."
Booklist

Llywelyn, Morgan—*Continued*

The elementals. TOR Bks. 1993 303p $21.95

ISBN 0-312-85568-0   LC 93-12760

"Remnants of humanity escape the great flood and make their way to safety in prehistoric Ireland. A singer and his companions survive the volcanic eruption that destroys the palace of Minos in Crete. A farmer's wife in 19th-century New Hampshire discovers the secrets of a sacred stone, and in the 21st century, George Burning Feather seeks the wisdom of the past to combat the ultimate natural disaster—the death of the air. . . . Though the connections among the four stories comprising this volume emerge only in the final story, each tale bears its own compelling message." Libr J

Finn Mac Cool. Forge 1994 400p $23.95

ISBN 0-312-85476-5   LC 94-4043

"Finn MacCool is a warrior/poet, a leader of the *Fianna*, the first Irish army, in third-century Ireland. Separated from his parents after a battle with their ancient enemies, the clan of Morna, Finn is brought up in primitive circumstances. After learning of his heritage, he determines to become the strongest man in Ireland so that he will never have to run away from anything again." Publ Wkly

"In addition to being fast paced and full of action, this novel is witty in its descriptions of how Finn's legends were seeded." Booklist

The horse goddess. Houghton Mifflin 1982 417p o.p.

    LC 82-6234

"The Celts of 700 B.C. were a variety of tribes spread over Central Europe. Epona, a teenage Celt has just been initiated into womanhood when four strange horsemen visit her community. She is drawn to the leader, Kazhak, and leaves with the Scythians to escape the lecherous Druid priest. Epona's affinity for animals is held in awe by her new tribe, as is her boldness in a world where women are seen in veils only and never heard. Epona is eventually forced to flee the Russian steppes and returns to her old home, where her acquired wisdom helps her become the new Druid priestess." Libr J

"The author emphasizes the independent status of Celtic women, a proto-feminist characteristic that should heighten the appeal of the book." Publ Wkly

The last prince of Ireland. Morrow 1992 368p o.p.

    LC 91-42516

Published in the United Kingdom with title: O'Sullivan's march

This "novel takes place in 17th-century Ireland as Queen Elizabeth I of England seeks to obliterate 2000 years of Celtic tradition and religion. It begins on December 30, 1602, soon after the Battle of Kinsale sounded the death knell for Irish independence. Fugitive nobleman Donal Cam O'Sullivan, the 'prince' of the title, denounces the queen and seeks to march 1000 followers to safety across wintry, dangerous terrain. Death, desertion, and near-constant fighting with the enemy, both English and Irish, reduce his band to a starving and exhausted group of 35 survivors." Libr J

"This tale of courage, love, cruelty and treachery, one of the great legends of Ireland, receives vivid, evocative treatment here." Publ Wkly

Red Branch. Morrow 1989 558p o.p.

    LC 88-13508

In this novel the author has created a legendary world "based on disparate tales of Ireland's mythical warrior-hero Cuchulain. . . . The story begins with a boy, Setanta, born in mysterious circumstances to Dectera, the King's half sister. Either Dectera's husband, the King, or a god is Setanta's father. But the truth is concealed from him, and in a land where status and privilege derive from birthright, his uncertain paternity is a painful mark of difference. Though still a youth, Setanta's ferocity while in combat with a monstrous wolfhound owned by a blacksmith, Cullen, earns him the name Cuchulain, or hound of Cullen. Soon after, he enters a warrior clan, the 'Red Branch' of the book's title." NY Times Book Rev

"Llywelyn works a massive canvas, peopling it with larger-than-life characters, yet shaping them with intimate insights." Publ Wkly

Lockridge, Ross, 1914-1948

Raintree County. Houghton Mifflin 1948 1066p il o.p. Buccaneer Bks. reprint available $49.95 (ISBN 0-89966-865-8)

An epic novel describing a day, the Fourth of July of 1892, in the life of school teacher Johnny Shawnessy in which he participates in the holiday ceremonies of his small Indiana town and meets two old boyhood friends. These events set off a series of flashbacks in his mind and he relives his schooldays, his Civil war experiences, his brief political life, his two marriages, and a love affair that ends badly

"The book is full-blooded, it has gusto, ribaldry, vision, beauty, and narrative skill. It is also repetitious, overly 'organized,' reminiscent of a variety of predecessors, 'literary' in the wrong sense, and too dependent upon source material. But the breath of life sweeps through its voluminous pages." Saturday Rev

Lofts, Norah, 1904-1983

Bless this house. Doubleday 1954 235p o.p.

Available from Amereon and Queens House

The chronicle of a house and its inmates over a period of more than three hundred and fifty years. The house was called Merravay, a handsome E-shaped building, which was erected in East Anglia in 1577 and went through many hands until 1953 when it came back to the Rowhedges

"To span four centuries in a normal-sized book requires some fast footwork on the part of the writer. Miss Lofts covers the distance by weaving together eight separate episodes, each of a different generation. . . . The individual episodes are uneven in quality, but all are enveloped in a rosy romanticism." N Y Times Book Rev

The claw. Doubleday 1982 c1981 186p o.p.

    LC 81-43635

First published 1981 in the United Kingdom

A "character study of a contemporary small town in England which is shaken out of apathy into terror by the attack of a rapist-murderer." Libr J

"What is pleasing in this story is that it does not seem to be sensationalized. If the action were to have taken place, it would have been quite believable as described. The novel is full of sufficient suspense and is engaging enough to enable the reader to understand each charac-

Lofts, Norah, 1904-1983—*Continued*

ter's role in the community, as well as in the attempt to unravel the mystery of 'Terror.'" Best Sellers

The day of the butterfly. Doubleday 1980 c1979 328p o.p.

LC 79-7566

First published 1979 in the United Kingdom

"A lovely and spirited young innocent, Daisy Holt, loses her nursemaid position and takes refuge in a high-class brothel where, instead of becoming a prostitute, she dances in the concert room for the clients. Thereafter the vicissitudes of her life include an adored artist-lover, who leaves her pregnant; her baby, whom she is not allowed to keep; and a wealthy older husband, whom she deserts for a rogue." Booklist

"Lofts's storytelling conveys the claustrophobic, male-dominated atmosphere in which Regency women lived, and the special poignancy of a woman who was beautiful but poor." Publ Wkly

Gad's Hall. Doubleday 1978 c1977 282p o.p.

LC 77-92220

First published 1977 in the United Kingdom

"Dismissing Mrs. Spender's claims that Gad's Hall is haunted, her son Bob and daughter-in-law Jill buy the grand English country estate. . . . With this setup, Lofts deserts her modern family to describe the lives of the Thorleys who founded Gad's Hall in the 1800s. The widowed Mrs. Thorley of that era exerts firm control over the affairs of her children and stepchildren. When unwed Lavinia becomes pregnant, Mrs. Thorley hides the girl until the baby is born. The tragedy that results creates the ghosts that haunt the manor, to affect the Spenders, more than 100 years later." Publ Wkly

Followed by The haunting of Gad's Hall

The haunting of Gad's Hall. Doubleday 1979 c1978 281p o.p.

LC 78-62603

First published 1978 in the United Kingdom with title: Haunted house

The author "continues to relate the problematic history of the Thorleys as each of the daughters marries well but meets various troubles to do with love and money. Their final years are . . . summed up so that the plot may return to the present-day inhabitants whose discovery of the source of the evil that haunts a locked attic room finally results in its exorcism and the restoration of earlier harmony." Booklist

"The chief attraction here is Lofts' spotlight on the effects of manners and mores on females in 19th-century England." Publ Wkly

The homecoming. Doubleday 1976 c1975 282p o.p.

Sequel to Knight's Acre

First published 1975 in the United Kingdom

"Set in the 15th century East Anglia. Sir Godfrey Tallboys, knight errant, returns from Spain to his accommodating wife, bringing with him the seductive Moorish girl who has saved him from slavery and is pregnant with his child. The ensuing domestic complications are cut short when the restless and somewhat muddlepated Sir Godfrey involves himself in the War of the Roses and there finds a not altogether unwelcome death. . . . It's a muted story, on the whole, memorable not so much for its action or its characterization as for its smooth and convincing portraiture of English country

society in the late Middle Ages." Publ Wkly

Followed by The lonely furrow (1977)

The house at Old Vine. Doubleday 1961 408p o.p.

Available from Amereon and Queens House

Sequel to The town house

"The house at Old Vine is the backdrop for a pageant extending over nearly two centuries, from 1496 until the latter part of the seventeenth century. It is made up of the linked stories of four women and two men who called it home at some time in those years and had ties through marriage or, sometimes unknowingly, blood. The period covers the history of England from feudalism to the rise of the middle class, centuries riven by the violence of religious and political strife." N Y Her Trib Books

"The story flows smoothly and irresistibly from one generation to another and there is thoroughly satisfying cause-and-effect relationship between the major characters and the often tragic events and their lives." Libr J

Followed by The house at sunset

The house at sunset. Doubleday 1962 370p o.p. Amereon reprint available $24.95 (ISBN 0-89190-227-9)

"The last part of the trilogy which began with 'Town house' and 'The house at Old Vine' relates episodes from the lives of the people who lived in an English mansion from the eighteenth century to the present." Chicago. Public Libr

"The trilogy, scanning nearly five centuries of English social history, will appeal mostly to historically minded readers." Booklist

Knight's Acre. Doubleday 1975 253p o.p.

"Sir Godfrey Tallboys, widely known in his trade of warfare, is fortunate in his wife Sybilla who competently maintains a settled home in England. Offered a large sum to appear in tourneys, Sir Godfrey departs for Spain. Once there, his small contingent of English knights is sacrificed in a hopeless battle against the Moors. He himself is enslaved, but is able to escape with Tana, a fugitive from Selim's harem. There are melodramatic touches in Lofts' latest novel; however, they do not detract from the fine characterizations of the remarkable detail given of the Europe of the 1450's." Libr J

Followed by The homecoming

The lost queen. Doubleday 1969 302p o.p.

A novel about "the life of Princess Caroline Matilda, sister of George III, who left England at age fifteen to become the bride of King Christian of Denmark. Unhappy in her marriage to the mentally unbalanced King Christian, Caroline was led into an affair with the politically liberal court physician. Her lover was executed but Caroline was accused of treason and exiled to an unhappy life in Hanover." Booklist

"The book is rich in the atmosphere of the 18th century. Both extremes of the economic scale are revealed and the great social cruelties and injustices of the time come to light in the author's skillful weaving of the plot. The characters are vividly drawn and Mrs. Lofts is extremely sympathetic to her heroine." Best Sellers

Nethergate. Doubleday 1973 278p o.p.

In this story set in 18th century England, Isabella de Savigny, a penniless French aristocrat, escapes the Reign of Terror and flees to Nethergate, her cousin's country estate. There she is made a servant, has an ill-fated love affair and is forced into a brutal marriage. Later, she

Lofts, Norah, 1904-1983—*Continued*
struggles to find a place for her daughter in French
emigré society but finally retreats into a dream world

The old priory. Doubleday 1982 c1981
231p o.p.

LC 81-43066

First published 1981 in the United Kingdom
This novel "concerns three generations of a family
inhabiting a once-ruined and supposedly cursed priory
in 17th century Suffolk, England. First acquired and
restored by Arthur Tresize with money he has earned
by obliging an anonymous lady in need of an heir, the
priory elicits strong loyalty from its owners, while challenging them with unusual difficulties. . . . The flavor
of Elizabethan England enriches the novel, with details
from sweatshops and taverns to the balls and charities
of the rich." Publ Wkly

Pargeters. Doubleday 1986 c1984 333p
o.p.

LC 85-12904

First published 1984 in the United Kingdom
"This historical narrative . . . begins in 17th century
England when Adam Woodley, a skilled pargeter
(plasterer), has a house named in honor of his craft. His
one-sided marriage to the daughter of Pargeter's owner
begins the line of men and women who, through the
Civil War between Royalists and Roundheads, tried to
hold on to the beloved property. It is Adam's daughter
Sarah who ultimately survives, enduring a loveless marriage to save her heritage when it is sequestered in the
postwar spoils." Publ Wkly

A rose for virtue; the very private life of
Hortense, stepdaughter of Napoleon I,
mother of Napoleon III. Doubleday 1971
348p o.p.
"The story is told by Hortense de Beauharnais, stepdaughter of Napoleon and daughter of Josephine, and
destined to become the mother of Napoleon III. The
events of the Napoleonic era are familiar, but Hortense
tells them from her own point of view, focusing on her
unhappy marriage, forced on her by her stepfather, her
secret love affair with a young cavalry officer, and her
final decision to put family allegiance above all." Publ
Wkly
"The author has re-created many famous historical
characters in this story. The devotion of Napoleon and
Josephine is made vivid, yet the determination of the
Little Colonel to have a son for an heir betrays his
incompassionate temperament. The entire Bonaparte clan,
their share in their brother-dictator's victories, and their
alienation toward the Beauharnais family is skillfully portrayed." Best Sellers

The town house; the building of the
house. Doubleday 1959 403p o.p. Amereon
reprint available $25.95 (ISBN
0-89190-230-9)
First volume of trilogy following the fortunes of the
inhabitants of a house in Suffolk, England
"This is the story of Martin Reed, who rises from
serfdom to become a wealthy merchant, and of his
family, children, and grandchildren—his lovely wife,
Kate; the gypsy girl, Magda; his strange and gifted child,
Richard; and his grandchild, Maude. This story is given
a rich background of 15th century England, not of historical events but rather personal and everyday things: food,
houses, dress, and travel." Wis Libr Bull

"A novel related by five persons speaking in turn
spans the lifetime of the first speaker, Martin Reed. .
. . A richly mounted tale, plentifully endowed with vivid
pictures of the period." Booklist
Followed by The house at Old Vine

London, Jack, 1876-1916
The call of the wild.
Available from various publishers
First published 1903 by Macmillan
"Buck, half-St. Bernard, half-Scottish sheepdog, is stolen
from his comfortable home in California and pressed
into service as a sledge dog in the Klondike. At first
he is abused by both man and dog, but he learns to
fight ruthlessly. He becomes lead dog on a sledge team,
after bettering Spitz, the vicious old leader, in a brutal
fight to the death. In John Thornton, he finally finds
a master whom he can respect and love. When Thornton
is killed by Indians, Buck breaks away to the wilds and
becomes the leader of a wolf pack, returning each year
to the site of Thornton's death." Reader's Ency. 3d edition

The complete short stories of Jack Lon-
don; edited by Earle Labor, Robert C. Leitz,
III, and I. Milo Shepard. Stanford Univ.
Press 1993 3v $180

ISBN 0-8047-2058-4   LC 92-44856

Analyzed in Short story index
"The London scholar and enthusiast will find this
collection of Jack London's short fiction invaluable for
the 5 previously unpublished stories it contains and for
the 28 others it collects for the first time since their
original publication in magazines." Choice

Martin Eden. Macmillan 1909 411p o.p.
A semi-autobiographical novel. "Eden has had a knock-
about life as a sailor, and falling in love with a girl
used to middle-class refinement and luxuries, tries to
write. He is rejected by editors, and the girl jilts him.
The abysmal contrast between the genius of this man,
his vital ideals and the big realities of life, and on the
other hand, the narrow, unintelligent mediocrity of the
'cultured classes' is brought out with characteristic force."
Baker. Guide to Hist Fic

The Sea-Wolf; with illustrations by W.J.
Aylward. Macmillan 1904 366p o.p.
"Wolf Larsen, ruthless captain of the tramp steamer
'Ghost,' receives an unexpected passenger on the high
seas, Humphrey Van Weyden, a wealthy ne'er-do-well.
In spite of his selfish brutality, Larsen becomes an
instrument for good. The treatment he gives to the dilettante Van Weyden teaches the latter to stand on his
own legs. He and the poet Maude Brewster, whom the
'Sea-Wolf' loves also, escape to an island as the 'Ghost'
sinks and Larsen, mortally sick, is deserted. The lovers
later return to civilization." Haydn. Thesaurus of Book
Dig

Short stories of Jack London; authorized
one-volume edition; edited by Earle Labor,
Robert C. Leitz III, I. Milo Shepard.
Macmillan 1990 xli, 738p $35

ISBN 0-02-567180-4   LC 90-6175

Contents: Story of a typhoon off the coast of Japan;
The white silence; To the man on trail; In a far country;
An odyssey of the north; Semper idem; The law of life;
A relic of the pliocene; Nam-Bok the unveracious; The

London, Jack, 1876-1916—*Continued*

one thousand dozen; To build a fire (1902); Moon-face; Bâtard; The story of Jees Uck; The league of the old men; Love of life; The sun-dog trail; All gold canyon; A day's lodging; The apostate; The wit of Porportuk; The unparalleled invasion; To build a fire (1908); The house of pride; The house of Mapuhi; The Chinago; Lost face; Koolau the leper; Chun Ah Chun; The heathen; Mauki; The strength of the strong; South of the Slot; Samuel; A piece of steak; The madness of John Harned; The night-born; War; Told in the drooling ward; The Mexican; The pearls of Parlay; Wonder of woman; The red one; On the Makaloa mat; The tears of Ah Kim; Shin bones; When Alice told her soul; Like Argus of the ancient times; The princess; The water baby

South Sea tales. Macmillan 1911 327p o.p.

Analyzed in Short story index
Contents: The house of Mapuki; The whale tooth; Mauki; "Yah! Yah! Yah"; The heathen; The terrible Solomons; The inevitable white man; The seed of McCoy

The star rover. Macmillan 1915 329p o.p. Amereon reprint available $21.95 (ISBN 0-8488-1082-1)

In this science fiction novel about transmigration of the soul, Darrell Standing is condemned to solitary confinement in a corrupt prison. He discovers how to free his soul from his body and escapes through time and space to relive the experiences of his past lives, which include being a caveman, a Danish soldier in the Roman legions, a French swordsman, and an American pioneer boy

Stories of Hawaii; edited by A. Grove Day. Appleton-Century 1965 282p o.p.

Analyzed in Short story index
Contents: The house of pride; Koolau the leper; Good-by, Jack; Aloha oe; Chun Ah Chun; The sheriff of Kona; On the makaloa mat; The bones of Kahekili; When Alice told her soul; Shin bones; The water baby; The tears of Ah Kim; The Kanarka surf; A royal sport: Surfing at Waikiki; From "My Hawaiian aloha"

"These are stories written when London was living in Hawaii. . . . With a wide range of themes he covers many superstitions, beliefs, problems, and pleasures of those glamorous and fascinating islands and captures the flavor of the life there at the turn of the century." Libr J

White Fang.
Available from various publishers
First published 1906

White Fang "is about a dog, a cross-breed, sold to Beauty Smith. This owner tortures the dog to increase his ferocity and value as a fighter. A new owner Weedom Scott, brings the dog to California, and, by kind treatment, domesticates him. White Fang later sacrifices his life to save Scott." Haydn. Thesaurus of Book Dig

Longyear, Barry B.

Enemy mine
In The Hugo winners v5 p5-67

Looking for a rain god: an anthology of contemporary African short stories; edited by Nadežda Obradović. Simon & Schuster 1990 284p o.p.

LC 89-48685

Analyzed in Short story index
Contents: The madman, by C. Achebe; Maruma, by I. N. C. Aniebo; In the cutting of a drink, by A. A. Aidoo; Heart of a judge, by R. S. Easmon; Emente, by O. O. Enekwe; Noorjehan, by A. Essop; Blankets, by A. La Guma; Looking for a rain god, by B. Head; A man can try, by E. D. Jones; The winner, by B. Kimenye; Black skin what mask, by D. Marechera; The criminals, by S. Mpofu; Some kinds of wounds, by C. Mungoshi; A different time, by C. Nkosi; The doum tree of Wad Hamid, by T. Salih; Thoughts in a train, by M. Tshabangu; The soldier without an ear, by P. Zaleza; The spider's web, by L. Kibera; Call me not a man, by M. Matshoba; The spearmen of Malama, by K. Mubitana; A present for my wife, M. Mzamane; The rain came, by G. Ogot; The will of Allah, by D. Owoyele; The nightmare, by W. Saidi; The return, by Ngugi wa Thiong'o; The point of no return, by M. M. Tlali

Lopez, Steve

Third and Indiana; a novel. Viking 1994 305p $21.95

ISBN 0-670-85676-2   LC 93-49815

"Ofelia Santoro is determined to save her runaway son, Gabriel, from the drug dealers whose turf is Philadelphia's Badlands. . . . Fourteen-year-old Gabriel would like nothing better than to go home to his mother, but he's in too deep. . . . Lopez's Philadelphia is a marvel, its ruined streets and decaying infrastructure drawn with a delicate precision." Booklist

Lord, Bette Bao

Spring Moon; a novel of China. Harper & Row 1981 464p o.p.

LC 78-20210

This novel "follows the history of a Mandarin Chinese family from 1892 until 1927, with an epilogue that updates the story to 1972. Through the eyes of Spring Moon, a lively and intelligent daughter of the house of Chang, we see the beauty of the inner courtyard society and observe its respect for family, order and harmony, scholarship and poetry. But we see, too, how Chinese society's rigid etiquette hobbles the lives of its women as surely as their bound feet. Unlike most women of her class and time, Spring Moon learns to read and write. The two men she loves, her eldest uncle and her husband, have both studied in America and have modern ideas. But her husband is killed in the Boxer Rebellion, and Spring Moon herself is forced into hiding for her role in the assassination of a Manchu official. She gives birth to a son she can't acknowledge and sees her daughter become a Communist revolutionary." Saturday Rev

Lovecraft, H. P. (Howard Phillips), 1890-1937

At the mountains of madness, and other novels; selected by August Derleth; with texts edited by S.T. Joshi and introduction by James Turner. Arkham House Pubs. 1985 c1964 458p $19.95

ISBN 0-87054-038-6   LC 85-1254

A reissue of the title first published 1964 and analyzed in Short story index

Contents: At the mountains of madness; The case of Charles Dexter Ward; The shunned house; The dreams in the witchhouse; The statement of Randolph Carter; The dream-quest of unknown Kadath; The silver key; Through the gates of the silver key

The Dunwich horror, and others; selected by August Derleth, with texts edited by S.T. Joshi and an introduction by Robert Block. Arkham House Pubs. 1985 c1963 433p $19.95

ISBN 0-87054-037-8

A reissue of the title first published 1963 and analyzed in Short story index

Contents: In the vault; Pickman's model; The rats in the walls; The outsider; The colour out of space; The music of Erich Zann; The haunter of the dark; The picture in the house; The call of Cthulhu; The Dunwich horror; Cool air; The whisper in darkness; The terrible old man; The thing on the doorstep; The shadow over Innsmouth; The shadow out of time

The horror in the museum, and other revisions; with texts edited by S. T. Joshi, and an introduction by August Derleth. Arkham House Pubs. 1989 450p $19.95

ISBN 0-87054-040-8   LC 88-7921

Analyzed in Short story index

Contents: The green meadow; The crawling chaos; The last test; The electric executioner; The curse of Yig; The mound [novelette]; Medusa's coil; The man of stone; The horror in the museum; Winged death; Out of the aeons; The horror in the burying-ground; The diary of Alonzo Typer; The horror at Martin's Beach; Ashes; The ghost-eater; The loved dead; Deaf, dumb, and blind; Two black bottles; The trap; The tree on the hill; The disinterment; 'Till a' the seas'; The night ocean

"The volume is divided into 'Primary Revisions,' those stories that are all Lovecraft but for an idea, and 'Secondary Revisions,' clients' manuscripts heavily edited and revised." Publ Wkly

The mound

In Lovecraft, H. P. The horror in the museum, and other revisions p96-163

Lovecraft, Howard Phillips *See* Lovecraft, H. P. (Howard Phillips), 1890-1937

Lovecraft's legacy; edited by Robert E. Weinberg [and] Martin H. Greenberg. TOR Bks. 1990 334p o.p.

Analyzed in Short story index

Contents: A secret of the heart, by M. Castle; The other man, by R. Garton; Will, by G. Masterton; Big "C", by B. Lumley; Ugly, by G. Brandner; The blade and the claw, by H. B. Cave; Soul keeper, by J. A. Citro; From the papers of Helmut Hecker, by C. Williamson; Meryphillia, by B. McNaughton; Lord of the land, by G. Wolfe; H. P. L., by G. Wilson; The order of things unknown, by E. Gorman; The Barrens, by F. P. Wilson

Lovesey, Peter

Bertie and the seven bodies. Mysterious Press 1990 196p $16.95

ISBN 0-89296-399-9   LC 89-12405

Also available Thorndike Press large print edition

In this mystery "Albert Edward, the Prince of Wales—Bertie to the ladies—sallies forth on an elaborate hunt in Buckinghamshire and bags a murderer along with the other game." N Y Times Book Rev

"Narrated by Bertie himself, the voice here is perfectly accurate; Lovesey gives his main character just the right tone of sophistication, charm, anti-intellectualism, and savoir faire—mixed in with ennui. A wonderfully put together puzzle." Booklist

Bertie and the Tinman. Mysterious Press 1987 212p $15.95

ISBN 0-89296-196-1   LC 87-40426

Prince Albert is shocked to learn of the apparent suicide of his friend Fred Archer, known as the Tinman and as England's greatest jockey. When the inquest presents discrepancies known only to Bertie, he begins sleuthing in London's underworld

"Mr. Lovesey is a specialist in the Victorian crime novel, and in 'Tinman' he has done his usual impeccable research. . . . The racetrack scenes and backgrounds crackle with authenticity. There is a great deal of humor in the book, even a strong dash of P.G. Wodehouse." N Y Times Book Rev

The detective wore silk drawers. Dodd, Mead 1971 188p o.p.

Available G.K. Hall large print edition

"A Red badge novel of suspense"

"Three London detectives of the 1880s, all boxing fans, uncover a clandestine center of the sport while investigating several headless corpses." Booklist

"Although the mystery is nothing special, it suffices, and the kicks come from the 19th century atmosphere of Victorian sex and mild sadism." Publ Wkly

Diamond solitaire. Mysterious Press 1993 c1992 343p $18.95

ISBN 0-89296-535-5   LC 92-50660

Also available Thorndike Press large print edition

First published 1992 in the United Kingdom

"Peter Diamond is plagued by bad karma. Formerly detective superintendent of police in Bath, he's sunk to being a security guard at Harrod's—until a small Asian child is found in the area of the store Peter patrols. Out of a job once again (security breaches are no laughing matter at terrorist-obsessed Harrod's), Diamond becomes intrigued by the Asian child, who is autistic and who remains unclaimed despite massive publicity. What starts out as a kindly effort to restore the child

Lovesey, Peter—*Continued*

to her parents turns into an international adventure as Diamond travels from London to New York to Japan and confronts millionaire sumo wrestlers, unethical drug researchers, and corrupt businessmen." Booklist

The false Inspector Dew. Pantheon Bks. 1982 251p o.p.

LC 81-18706

"This bizarre case revolves around a murder staged by dentist Walter Baranov and his mistress, Alma Webster, who do in Baranov's wife. The couple then flees to America aboard the 'Mauretania.' Baranov, who imitated the murderer Dr. Crippen, now assumes the name of Scotland Yard Inspector Walter Dew, the detective who solved the Crippen case. Baranov must confront the consequences of his choice, however, when a murder is committed on board and he, as Inspector Dew, is asked to solve it." Booklist

"After a slow beginning, in which the many characters are introduced with leisurely background detail, the book turns into a delightfully comic story with countless twists and turns of plot." Libr J

The last detective. Doubleday 1991 331p o.p.

LC 91-11859

Available Thorndike Press large print edition

"A Perfect crime book"

"Irascible, corpulent, cynical Chief Superintendent Peter Diamond of the Avon and Somerset murder squad attributes Britain's decline as a world power to the abolition of capital punishment in 1964. Spurning computer gadgetry, he sticks to common sense, index cards and gumshoeing: 'Knocking on doors. That's how we get results.' The almost clueless case of the naked woman's body found floating in Chew Valley Lake poses a supreme challenge for the detective, who is anxious to clear his name of recent charges of brutality." Publ Wkly

"An intricate, many-tiered examination of police work, especially modern forensic technology, complete with computers and genetic fingerprinting. Everything meshes perfectly in this airtight tale." Booklist

On the edge. Mysterious Press 1989 204p $16.95

ISBN 0-89296-363-8   LC 88-13549

Also available G.K. Hall large print edition

"Set in Britain immediately after World War II, this is a novel that balances wit and wickedness, ambitions and just desserts. Rosie married badly—to a penniless philanderer. Antonia married well—to a wealthy man—but her lover is going to the U.S. and she wants to join him there. Rosie and Antonia meet by chance, talk, and a plan is gradually hatched. With a helpful shove from Antonia, Rosie's hubby comes to a bad end beneath a tube train. The second half of the deal becomes more convoluted, as Antonia's past (she having murdered her husband's first wife) and several secret agendas throw a wrench in the works." Booklist

"Told mostly in racy, ear-perfect dialogue that magnifies the impact of events, the story dodges from one unguessable outcome to the next." Publ Wkly

Rough cider. Mysterious Press 1986 216p o.p.

LC 86-18212

"A tightly knit tale that has its roots in the hanging for murder in England of an American G.I. Twenty years later his daughter, who lives in the U.S., attempts to exonerate his name by enlisting the aid of an English

professor whose childhood was marked by the crime. Readers incidentally learn about cider making and discover some grisly evidence of murder and guilt in the course of the demonstration." Barzun. Cat of Crime. Rev and enl edition

Waxwork. Pantheon Bks. 1978 239p o.p.

LC 77-90420

"There is certainly enough here to warrant the praise given this tale by more than one highly regarded colleague in crime. Set in the London and Kew of 1888, a case of KCN poisoning following upon blackmail taxes the abilities of the police, but in the end Sgt. Cribb really does distinguish himself. The title alludes to Tussaud's Waxwork Exhibition." Barzun. Cat of Crime. Rev and enl edition

Lowry, Malcolm, 1909-1957

Under the volcano. Reynal & Hitchcock 1947 375p o.p.

This novel "presents in detail the events of [a] single day in a single place—the Day of the Dead in a town in Mexico, with Popocatepetl and Ixtaccihuatl looking down. It is the last day on earth of the British Consul, Geoffrey Firmin, and he is dying of alcoholism. Like any tragic hero, he is fully aware of the choice he has made: he clings to his sloth, he needs salvation through love but will not utter the word which will bring it, he lets his morbid lust for drink drag him from bar to bar. In other words, he has made a deliberate choice of damnation. . . . We don't despise or even dislike Firmin, despite his weaknesses and his self-destructive urge. As with all tragic heroes (and this novel is a genuine tragedy) he sums up the flaws which are latent or actual in all of us." Burgess. 99 Novels

Ludlum, Robert, 1927-

The Aquitaine progression. Random House 1984 647p $17.95

ISBN 0-394-53674-6   LC 83-19078

This novel "features five present or former generals from five different countries who mean to take over the world. They have decided to put an end to the quagmire of Western politics and set up a super-fascist state with themselves in control. The hub of this enterprise is Gen. George Marcus Delavane, a fanatic who makes Genghis Khan look like a Peace Corps volunteer. Joel Converse, an international lawyer, has reason to know and hate Delavane. It was Delavane who insisted on an Air Force mission in Vietnam that resulted in Converse's capture and subsequent agonies at the hands of the enemy. While in Geneva working on a case for his New York law firm, Converse is contacted by one A. Preston Halliday, who gives him information he finds hard to believe. But there follows a series of entanglements and murders that clearly prove Halliday's assertions." N Y Times Book Rev

The Bourne identity. Marek, R. 1980 523p o.p.

LC 79-23638

"Jason Bourne is shot and left for dead. He survives, but without a memory. Slowly, painstakingly, he retraces his past, only to find himself hunted by assassins of several governments, including his own. He fights against seemingly insurmountable odds—especially his very limited knowledge of his past—to discover his identity

Ludlum, Robert, 1927-—*Continued*

and stop his enemies before it is too late." Libr J

Followed by The Bourne supremacy

also in Ludlum, R. The Ludlum triad
p757-1149

The Bourne supremacy. Random House
1986 597p o.p.

LC 85-18318

"In this sequel to The Bourne Identity David Webb,
still suffering flashbacks to his Jason Bourne persona, is
forced to undertake a final, possibly fatal mission after
his wife is kidnapped. He must find and capture an
assassin who is posing as Bourne in Hong Kong. By
so doing he'll foil a plot that could plunge the Far East
and then the world into war." Libr J

"Every chapter ends with a cliff-hanger; the story brims
with assassination, torture, hand-to-hand combat, sudden
surprise and intrigue within intrigue. It's a sure-fire bestseller." Publ Wkly

Followed by The Bourne ultimatum

The Bourne ultimatum. Random House
1990 611p $21.95

ISBN 0-394-58408-2   LC 89-43201

Also available large print edition $24.45 (ISBN
0-679-40043-5)

"When the international terrorist known as Carlos the
Jackal penetrates his civilian identity, Webb must again
assume the Bourne persona to protect his wife and small
children. In their renewed struggle, the two master assassins uncover the revived existence of Medusa, the sinister
alliance that originally led to the establishment of the
Bourne identity." Publ Wkly

The Chancellor manuscript. Dial Press
(NY) 1977 448p o.p.

In this novel "J. Edgar Hoover does not die naturally
in his sleep, but is assassinated. Why? To keep him from
revealing the contents of his secret files which, according
to this novel, contain enough damaging information to
ruin the lives of every man, woman and child in the
nation. Five prominent personages who make up a secret
group of self-appointed world savers are determined to
get the files, ostensibly to save humanity. But they find
half the files already stolen. Their hired killer, Varek,
whose cover is the National Security Council, 'programs'
the hero, Peter Chancellor, a writer. Peter is to be the
decoy who will lead the group to the mysterious
somebody who got to the files first." Christ Sci Monit

The Gemini contenders. Dial Press (NY)
1976 402p o.p.

"The twin sons of a former Italian government official
search for a mysterious document he was forced to leave
behind when fleeing his fascist-dominated homeland in
1939." Smith. Cloak and Dagger Fic

Ludlum is "at the top of his form here as he tells
a suspenseful story that gives fresh slants to old themes."
Publ Wkly

The Holcroft covenant. Marek, R. 1978
542p o.p.

LC 77-95295

"Thirty years after Hitler, Noel Holcroft sees an astounding document, drawn up by three supposedly con-
trite Nazis (all now dead), one of them his own father.
If he signs it and collects signatures from the sons of
the other two men, the Holocaust victims' heirs should
become the beneficiaries of a gigantic fund. The fund's

'real' purpose is to establish the Fourth Reich, not atone
for the Third, but Holcroft doesn't realize this as he
flings around the world in search of those signatures,
precipitating . . . ruthless clashes between secret Nazi
and anti-Nazi organizations." Publ Wkly

also in Ludlum, R. The Ludlum triad
p1-357

The Icarus agenda. Random House 1988
677p $19.95

ISBN 0-394-54397-1

Evan Kendrick "the young Colorado Congressman,
rescues an American embassy under seige by terrorist
fanatics in Masqat, an Arab city. On condition that the
CIA not reveal his identity, he agrees to this secret mission. But when he becomes a candidate for the Vice
Presidency, his identity is revealed and he too is a target
for the Arab terrorists whom he has tricked." West Coast
Rev Books

Mix "violence, bloody deaths, and double dealings, as
well as a touch of romance, and what you have is a
vintage Ludlum novel certain to delight his legion of
readers." Booklist

The Ludlum triad. Random House 1989
1149p $16.95

ISBN 0-394-57610-1   LC 89-8472

An omnibus edition of three titles published 1978,
1979 and 1980 respectively and entered separately

Contents: The Holcroft covenant; The Matarese circle;
The Bourne identity

The Matarese Circle. Marek, R. 1979 601p
o.p.

LC 78-31673

This novel of international intrigue "features the
world's top secret agents: Scofield, American, and
Taleniekov, Russian. They have sworn to kill each
other—Scofield was responsible for the death of
Taleniekov's brother, Taleniekov for that of Scofield's
wife—yet they have much in common besides their brilliance: both are semiretired, held in suspicion by their
respective governments and encumbered (occasionally) by
the humane streak in their characters. And now they are
drawn into cooperation, as the only men capable of
destroying an international circle of killers, The Matarese,
originally Corsican, which is dedicated to reducing the
world to chaos via assassination and terror." Publ Wkly

also in Ludlum, R. The Ludlum triad
p359-756

The Matlock paper. Dial Press (NY) 1973
312p o.p.

"James Matlock, instructor in Elizabethan literature at
Carlyle University in Connecticut, formerly an Army officer in Vietnam, is drawn into the most personally
dangerous and violent struggle of his life when he is
requested to cooperate with a government narcotic agent
in exploring Carlyle's connection with the expanding drug
traffic in New England." Publ Wkly

The Parsifal mosaic. Random House 1982
630p $15.95

ISBN 0-394-52111-0   LC 84-8925

The novel "centers around the background figure of
superstar Secretary of State Anthony Matthias, whose unhinged brilliance nearly leads to nuclear disaster. In the
foreground is accomplished and durable U.S. deep-cover

Ludlum, Robert, 1927-—*Continued*

agent Michael Havelock (nee Mikhail Havlíček), protégé and surrogate son of fellow Czech Matthias. Forced to order the execution of the woman he loves, believing her to be an agent of the Soviet terrorist group VKR, Havelock leaves espionage service. But when he spots her alive in Rome he's back in, on a convoluted trial of international intrigue that leads to the highest levels of government." Libr J

"The tale has all the hallmarks of vintage Ludlum: non-stop action, precisely timed curtain-raisers, the darksome deeds of agent and double agent, a deadly secret ultimately revealed and an underlying theme of the whole world jeopardized by a few fanatics." Publ Wkly

The Rhinemann exchange. Dial Press (NY) 1974 460p o.p. Buccaneer Bks. reprint available $31.95 (ISBN 0-89966-778-3)

"A World War II espionage novel detailing an attempted treasonous exchange between the Germans and the Americans—the technological secret of a gyroscopic guidance system in return for industrial diamonds. This is to be brought off by a disenfranchised German Jew in Buenos Aires, tracked by an American agent not quite in the know and thus in jeopardy." Booklist

The road to Omaha. Random House 1992 487p $23.95

ISBN 0-394-57329-3   LC 91-23214

Also available large print edition $26 (ISBN 0-679-41016-3)

This novel features General MacKenzie Lochinvar Hawkins and legal wizard Sam Devereaux from The road to Gandolfo

In this episode "Gen. MacKenzie Hawkins uncovers loopholes in a century-old treaty that should restore valuable land taken from the Wopotami Indian tribe by the United States Government. It just so happens that this Nebraska territory includes the headquarters of the Strategic Air Command, so the Hawk's quest to return it quickly becomes a cause célèbre." N Y Times Book Rev

The Scarlatti inheritance. Armchair Detective Lib. 1990 358p $19.95

ISBN 0-922890-45-5   LC 90-38021

A reissue of the title first published 1970 by World Pub.

When American intelligence officer Matthew Canfield is hired "to find out what is happening to the Scarlatti fortunes and especially to find out whether Ulster Scarlett is dead or alive, he finds that the erstwhile playboy has become an embezzler of note and has disappeared. The ramifications of the trail become most interesting when they lead to an international group of business men who are backing the nascent Nazi party in Germany. Ulster's mother, aging but indomitable and still devotedly retaining the name of Scarlatti, determines to ruin the movement even at the expense of ruining her own family fortune. Her harassed trip to Zurich with Canfield as bodyguard is about as adventurous a journey as anyone could want." Best Sellers

The scorpio illusion. Bantam Bks. 1993 534p $23.95

ISBN 0-553-09441-6   LC 93-9272

Also available large print edition $29.95 (ISBN 0-385-47039-8)

In this thriller, "the beautiful, anarchistic Basque terrorist Amaya Bajaratt . . . modestly sets out to eliminate the leaders of the United States, Britain, France and Israel. The only person able to stop her and thus save civilization as we know it is Tyrell Nathaniel Hawthorne 3d, a disillusioned former United States Naval Intelligence officer, now going to seed in the Caribbean. The two adversaries circle warily, each desperate to eliminate the other, neither able to strike the fatal blow." N Y Times Book Rev

Lurie, Alison

Foreign affairs. Random House 1984 291p $15.95

ISBN 0-394-54076-X   LC 84-42657

This novel follows "the actions and reactions of two English professors, both Americans, both from the same university, who are on leave in London to do research: Virginia Miner, 54, unmarried, happy to be back in the city she adores, and Fred Turner, 28, separated from his wife and depressed over being more or less in exile. Both Vinnie and Fred indulge in, while there, affairs with unlikely persons, with the result that they learn more about themselves from the experiences." Booklist

"Lurie portrays these entanglements with her customary astute wit and deft characterization, but also with unexpected warmth and generosity. A wry, wonderful book." Libr J

The nowhere city. Coward-McCann 1966 c1965 276p o.p.

First published 1965 in the United Kingdom

"Paul Cattleman, a young Harvard historian, goes West to spend a year writing the history of the Nutting Electronics Corporation; he is unwillingly followed by his wife Katherine. . . . He takes to transplantation . . . [but] his wife doesn't until she falls in with an ex-Mittel-Europa analyst." New Statesman

The author describes the Los Angeles "scene with such a cool and penetrating eye, such total disbelief in its existence, that she is able to portray it with a pristine freshness. . . . Transformed by her wicked wit, the most exhausted clichés come alive, galvanized into original revelation." Newsweek

Only children. Random House 1979 259p o.p.

LC 78-21994

"The novel spans the Fourth of July weekend [of 1935]. Bill and Honey Hubbard and their eight-year-old daughter Mary Ann, and Dan and Celia Zimmern and their daughter Lolly (and Dan's sullen adolescent son from a previous marriage) abandon New York City and its suburb, Larchmont, for the Catskill farm owned by Anna King, headmistress of the progressive school the two girls attend. This innocent outing doesn't turn out to be a relaxing weekend. . . . Instead the grownups start romping in an unseemly way and end up fighting while the two little girls look on, bewildered." New Repub

"Lurie has a sharp, ironic eye for the man-woman game and a dramatic deftness for setting the scene. Her rendering of the children is particularly effective." Libr J

(ed) The Oxford book of modern fairy tales. See The Oxford book of modern fairy tales

Lurie, Alison—*Continued*

The war between the Tates. Random House 1974 372p $16.95

ISBN 0-394-46201-7

The setting of the novel is the community of Corinth, New York during late 1969 and early 1970. "Brian Tate, a university professor, complete with neuroses, approaching 50, and not nearly so successful as he had hoped to be, becomes entangled with Wendy Gahaghan, a graduate student, who, unlike Erica Tate, gives of herself so freely that Brian consents to attempt to alleviate her infatuation. Wendy slowly moves into what little there is of the Tate's family life so that she can tell Erica everything. The personality and sexual problems of these characters, compounded by the rebelliousness of the obnoxious and beautifully drawn Tate children, are intriguingly set off against recurring metaphors which are tied to the Vietnamese war." Choice

"An outline of the plot does scant justice to the substance and wit of Lurie's novel. What makes the lines sing is her skill in catching the idiosyncracies of the mind and the tongue, the twists and turns of sophisticated sensibilities trapped in absurd situations." America

Women and ghosts. Talese 1994 179p $21

ISBN 0-385-47392-3   LC 93-46332

Analyzed in Short story index

Contents: Ilse's house; The pool people; The highboy; Counting sheep; In the shadow; Waiting for baby; Fat people; Another Halloween; The double poet

"In each tale Lurie pits a female protagonist against an apparition of varied, often comical, spectral persuasions. . . . These entertaining and enchanting tales deliver far more than one might bargain for, with afterimages that reverberate long after the initial delight with Lurie's dexterous prose has worn off." Booklist

Lustbader, Eric Van, 1946-

Angel eyes. Fawcett Columbine 1991 520p o.p.

LC 90-82331

"Tori Nunn, the beautiful heroine . . . and a friend infiltrate a Medellín drug compound that produces a cocaine so deadly it kills the user in one month. Add to this a secret nationalist organization in the Soviet Union called White Star, which is developing a weapon capable of destroying just about everything." Booklist

"The book has all the elements of a bestseller—travel, romance, violence, conspiracy and betrayal in high places—and Lustbader's attentions to martial arts and Zen teachings again spice the mix." Publ Wkly

Black Blade; [by] Eric Lustbader. Fawcett Columbine 1993 518p $22

ISBN 0-449-90600-0   LC 91-72890

New York homicide cop "Wolf Matheson is assigned to investigate a chain of murders perpetrated by the furtive Black Blade Society. That's a nationalistic, militaristic, but intellectual cabal that, for centries, has been nurturing the 'Oracle,' an enhanced mental state in which practitioners are able to predict the future and attain long lifespans. Alas, the Black Blade is bent on world domination and has been maneuvering events in both the U.S. and Japan toward world war. Wolf, with his sexy-but-clairvoyant Japanese girl friend, Chika, at his side, is equal to the task of saving the world, but he wouldn't be if it weren't for his Shoshone childhood,

where shamans knew the same kind of stuff the Black Blade know." Booklist

Floating city; a Nicholas Linnear novel; by Eric Lustbader. Pocket Bks. 1994 404p $22

ISBN 0-671-86808-X   LC 93-49360

"Nicholas Linnear and his private-eye buddy, Lew Croaker, dash around the globe attempting to thwart the murder of the Yakuza boss of bosses and stop the development of a terrible new weapon and a supercartel bent on world domination." Booklist

French kiss. Fawcett Columbine 1989 c1988 501p o.p.

LC 88-24336

"New York trial lawyer Chris Haye is called to France to bring home the beheaded body of his brother Terry. Almost simultaneously, NYPD detective Steve Guarda's brother, a priest, is beheaded in Connecticut. Guarda's trail leads to France also; there Chris has learned that Terry was involved in running drugs from Indochina. Tied to both murders is an elegant Frenchman, M. Milhaud, who is determined to obtain a legendary Indochinese totem, a trio of weapons called the Forest of Swords, that would give him power over the drug lords in Cambodia, Burma and Thailand." Publ Wkly

Jian. Villard Bks. 1985 448p o.p.

LC 85-40184

This "tale pits American superspy Jake Maroc and his cohorts in the Quarry (U.S. intelligence) against the formidable Japanese KGB agent Nichiren and a web of Oriental double-dealings and counter-allegiances, all of which are metaphorically played out as 'wei qi,' the ancient Chinese game of military strategy. Brutal killings, deadly females, and an acceptably diverting amount of steamy erotica are the hallmarks of Lustbader's story, which, considering its imposing use of italicized Japanese terms, may put off all but his most rabid fans." Booklist

The Kaisho; a Nicholas Linnear novel; by Eric Lustbader. Pocket Bks. 1993 482p $22

ISBN 0-671-86806-3   LC 93-17584

In this novel Nicholas Linnear "finds himself allied to Mikio Okami, the Kaisho, or Godfather of the Yakuza, the Japanese Mafia. Linnear's mission is to protect the Kaisho from a Vietnamese assassin who has already eliminated one of Okami's allies, an American mafioso supposedly hidden under the U.S. Witness Protection Program." Publ Wkly

"What's good about this novel are the glamorous settings, the psychologically flawed characters (all of them), and the fascinating flashbacks into Vietnam circa 1965 and Japan circa 1947." Booklist

Shan. Random House 1987 c1986 503p o.p.

LC 86-10027

This novel "follows the spectacular career of a former U.S. intelligence agent, the half-Chinese Jake Maroc. Jake's Chinese father (the subject of Lustbader's 'Jian') was the guiding light behind the Cultural Revolution. Following in his father's footsteps, Jake becomes the 'zhuan,' the instrument through which the Jian's vision is to come to fruition, with China asserting itself as a world economic power. The gateway to this power is Hong Kong. Within a world of cutthroat diplomacy and espionage, Jake rises to the summit, helped by Bliss, the beautiful and dangerous woman he loves." Booklist

Lustbader, Eric Van, 1946-—*Continued*
White Ninja; [by] Eric V. Lustbader. Fawcett Columbine 1990 518p o.p.

LC 89-92008

This novel is the "third in a series that began with *The Ninja* (1985) and continued with *The Miko* [1984]. The trilogy centers on the adventures of Nicholas Linnear—the ninja—whose mother was Japanese and whose father was a British officer. As this book opens, Linnear is having marital problems, and his best friend, chairman of a large corporation, is fighting off a computer virus and pressure from a Japanese business coalition. But an even bigger crisis exists: though Linnear has become 'shiro' (white) ninja, 'an enemy has seeped into his soul,' leaving him helpless and weak." Booklist

"A distinctly good time for the unabashed thriller-reader, particularly those with a taste for the mystical, exotic and sexually kinky." Publ Wkly

Lutz, John, 1939-
Dancing with the dead. St. Martin's Press 1992 208p o.p.

LC 92-2997

"A Thomas Dunne book"

"St. Louis realtor Mary Arlington, whose mother is alcoholic and whose lover is physically abusive, lives for her mambo, cha-cha and tango lessons with Mel Holt at the Romance Studio. After kicking her lover out of her life and checking her mother into a detox center, Mary agrees to dance with Mel in the Ohio Star Ball, a major competition. Meanwhile in Seattle and New Orleans, women dancers resembling Mary are murdered. Rene Verlane, the husband of the New Orleans victim, insists the crime is related to his wife's dancing. Mary follows the case on TV and one night calls Verlane to offer her help in finding the killer." Publ Wkly

Hot. Holt & Co. 1992 273p $18.95

ISBN 0-8050-1584-1   LC 91-3153

"Fred Carver, an Orlando private eye who normally thrives in soaring temperatures, takes on a dull surveillance job for a retired cop named Henry Tiller who lives on Key Montaigne . . . where he keeps an eye peeled on the neighbors. The old man's suspicion that 'one of them neighbors ain't right' takes on ominous weight when Tiller is struck by a hit-and-run driver, leaving Carver to sweat out the watch for whatever mischief the guy next door is up to." N Y Times Book Rev

"Lutz creates terrific characters in this concise, crisply told escapade. . . . Carver remains one of the genre's most credible protagonists." Publ Wkly

Lytton, Edward Bulwer Lytton, Baron, 1803-1873
The last days of Pompeii. Harper 1834 2v o.p. Buccaneer Bks. reprint available $29.95 (ISBN 0-89966-309-5)

The setting is Pompeii just before and during the famous eruption of Vesuvius, A.D. 79. "The simple story relates principally to two young people of Grecian origin, Glaucus and Ione, who are deeply attached to each other. The former is a handsome young Athenian, impetuous, high-minded, and brilliant, while Ione is a pure and lofty-minded woman. Arbaces, her guardian, the villain of the story, under a cloak of sanctity and religion, indulges in low and criminal designs. His character is strongly drawn; and his passion for Ione, and the struggle

between him and Glaucus, form the chief part of the plot. . . . The book, full of learning and spirit, is not only a charming novel, but contains many minute and interesting descriptions of ancient customs; among which, those relating to the gladiatorial combat, the banquet, the bath, are most noteworthy." Keller. Reader's Dig of Books

M

Maalouf, Amin
The rock of Tanios; translated by Dorothy S. Blair. Braziller 1994 275p $18.50

ISBN 0-8076-1365-7   LC 94-37546

This novel "depicts the lives of Sheikh Francis, a Christian Arab who rules a Levantine satrapy named Klaryabda circa 1840, and the boy Tanios, the shiekh's illegitimate offspring. . . . Tanios' life is buffeted by politics, but it is the sheikh's secret paternity, rumored in the village, that controls Tanios' life. This 'secret' paternity sets in motion a crazy course of intrigue, exile, English intervention, and violence, culminating in Tanios' elevation by acclamation to the sheikhship." Booklist

"Using a refreshing, nearly folkloric style that turns his protagonist, Tanios, into a classic hero, Maalouf details the shifting alliances and international power struggles that follow the murder of a patriarch. As a result, the reader is propelled into the world of myth yet gains a very real sympathy for the vivid characters." Libr J

Maas, Peter, 1929-
China white. Simon & Schuster 1994 270p $23

ISBN 0-671-69417-0   LC 94-20327

"An influential Chinese business tycoon plots to transfer the assets of the Hong Kong crime syndicate to the United States in a single huge shipment of high-grade heroin. With the guidance of a law firm populated by former CIA operatives, he sets about relocating his businesses in New York's Chinatown. His counsel, Tom MacLean, is a new recruit from the U.S. attorney's office, hired by the firm specifically for his father's CIA connections. From the outset, young MacLean is caught in the crossfire between Chinese and Mafia warlords, the New York crime syndicate, and the Chinatown gangs." Libr J

"In presenting a picture of these gangs working together, Mr. Maas pulls no punches; like many political thrillers, 'China White' not only refuses to bow to political correctness, it slaps it in the face." N Y Times Book Rev

Father and son; a novel. Simon & Schuster 1989 316p o.p.

LC 88-13865

Available G.K. Hall large print edition

"Widower Michael McGuire is a New York ad exec with dwindling emotional ties to his Irish heritage, but his young son Jamie (with some indoctrination from his grandfather) becomes an outspoken supporter of the IRA at an early age. At 19, he attends Harvard but moonlights as a coffeehouse balladeer whose songs about 'the Troubles' capture the attention of a gunrunning network

Maas, Peter, 1929-——*Continued*

that decides to use him as a pawn. In alternate chapters, the author probes Michael and Jamie's relationship and strips away the layers of an IRA network that, in his portrayal, extends through every level of American government." Publ Wkly

This "novel is a thriller that brings the reader face to face with political violence, showing how the tortured intricacies of the Irish struggle can create the awful tragedies that mar its history." N Y Times Book Rev

Macdonald, Filip *See* MacDonald, Philip, 1899-1981

MacDonald, John D. (John Dann), 1916-1986

Barrier Island. Knopf 1986 229p o.p.

LC 85-45998

"In West Bay, Mississippi, Tuck Loomis fraudulently acquires Barrier Island, planning to turn the ecologically important land and waters into a posh recreation area. Loomis is accepted by the good ol' boys, wheeler-dealers who prosper from local developments, but not by real-estate agent Wade Rowley. Suspicious of Loomis, Rowley . . . learns that Loomis has bribed a representative of the U.S. Prosecutor's office to influence a hearing on Barrier Island." Publ Wkly

"The portrait of Tuck is complex and convincing. . . . Mr. MacDonald writes with passion against corruption and the despoiling of communities." N Y Times Book Rev

Bright orange for the shroud. Lippincott 1972 c1965 253p o.p.

First published in a paperback edition 1965

Travis McGee, the detective, has never met an underdog quite like Arthur Wilkinson. Arthur has apparently been tricked into marriage by a sweet young woman who turns out to be not so young and not at all sweet

Cinnamon skin; the twentieth adventure of Travis McGee. Harper & Row 1982 275p o.p.

LC 81-48159

"Travis McGee and his friend Meyer search for Meyer's niece's new husband, who has killed his wife and faked his own death in an explosion. The search is plodding and long, but MacDonald makes it interesting through the diverse and lively characters involved. The showdown, on Mexico's Yucatán Peninsula, is a bit slow but colorful and original." Libr J

A deadly shade of gold. Lippincott 1974 c1965 336p o.p.

"The Travis McGee series"

First published 1965 in paperback by Fawcett Books

An old friend of Travis McGee's is found dead, and an Aztec idol worth more than its weight in gold disappears. McGee's search for the perpetrator (or perpetrators) leads him to Florida, New York, California and Mexico

The deep blue good-by. Lippincott 1975 c1964 200p o.p.

"The Travis McGee series"

First published 1964 in paperback by Fawcett Books

"Travis McGee, as usual helping out a damsel in distress, encounters a psycho ladykiller who makes most of the women he fancies soon wish they were dead.

Plenty of action on the 'Busted Flush,' McGee's houseboat and on the deep seas off the Florida coast, but the deep blue of the title is that of a stolen sapphire. McGee's probings go back to the fly-boys of World War II, including some who came home from the China run with more gold than good conduct medals." Booklist

The dreadful lemon sky. Lippincott 1975 c1974 228p o.p.

"The Travis McGee series"

"After successfully smuggling a huge quantity of Jamaican marijuana into Florida in a plane and boat operation, a team of felons fall victim to greed and treachery among themselves. A member of the team, a girl who had once been Travis's lover, entrusts him with her share of the loot for safekeeping (not specifying its origin, of course). Then she's murdered. As Travis investigates this death, with the aid of his philosophical friend Meyer, he finds himself investigating a whole series of related deaths, none of them accidental." Publ Wkly

Dress her in indigo. Lippincott 1971 c1969 255p o.p.

"The Travis McGee series"

First published 1969 in a paperback edition

"Travis McGee and friend Meyer [go] to the Mexican village of Oaxaca, among the gay, the depraved, [the drug addicted] and the violent, to find out about the kind of life Bix Bowie led there before her tragic death." Libr J

The empty copper sea. Lippincott 1978 239p o.p. Amereon reprint available $19.95 (ISBN 0-89190-778-5)

LC 78-17868

This episode finds McGee "in his familiar Florida Gulf Coast territory. A friend and former alcoholic has been boat skipper for an enterprising young land developer. Unfortunately, his boss disappears in the murky sea, and is presumed drowned after the friend passes out on the bridge while apparently drunk. He loses his license, reputation and his livelihood and comes to McGee for help." Best Sellers

Free fall in crimson. Harper & Row 1981 246p o.p.

LC 80-7871

"The Travis McGee series"

"A jig-saw trail takes Trav to a small Iowa town where Peter Kesner is making 'Free Fall' a movie about balloon racing he hopes will salvage his career after several flops. Financing the current flick is Josie Laurant, Kesner's lover. She has inherited a fortune from her former husband and daughter, both victims of unsolved murders McGee is investigating. Adding to the bank roll are porn flicks made by Desmin Grizzel, a real-life biker Kesner had featured in a film about motorcycle gangs. Grizzel has seduced local minors and forced them to take part in the scabrous movies, outraging the citizens. A mob attacks the film crew and a pitched battle leaves scores dead and injured." Publ Wkly

The green ripper. Lippincott 1979 221p o.p. Amereon reprint available $19.95 (ISBN 0-89190-779-3)

LC 79-12063

MacDonald, John D. (John Dann), 1916-1986—*Continued*

"Gretel, Trav's fiancée, mentions the suspicious, secret visit of a leader in the Church of Apocrypha to a posh local resort. Soon after, Gretel dies, supposedly of a mysterious virus. But Trav's grief is increased by instincts that tell him his love was murdered. He leaves Florida on the trail of the cult members." Publ Wkly

"MacDonald is unsurpassed at showing the American brand of loneliness. He catches foibles in a phrase and gives us many-sided, wounded but courageous, characters." Booklist

The lonely silver rain. Knopf 1985 c1984 232p o.p.

LC 84-23373

"The Travis McGee series"

"Travis McGee is growing older, and here he has good reason to feel his age. Besides combating a drug-smuggling potentate out to kill him, he finds himself the father of a young woman, all of which make the sleuth-philosopher reflect even more somberly on his life, his friends, his lonely job. One of the last MacDonald stories, it is also one of the best." Barzun. Cat of Crime. Rev and enl edition

The long lavender look. Lippincott 1972 c1970 264p o.p.

"The Travis McGee series"

First published in paperback 1970 by Fawcett Books

When McGee avoids running his Rolls Royce into a young girl, he finds himself embroiled in intrigue

Nightmare in pink. Lippincott 1976 c1964 191p o.p.

"The Travis McGee series"

First published 1964 in paperback by Fawcett Books

"Travis McGee, whose moral and social creed in the tradition of Chandler's Marlowe is given on p. 21, leaves his beach bum's paradise in Florida to solve in New York City the murder of the man who was to marry Travis' war buddy's sister. The suspense is expertly done as usual, the sex is explicit but poeticized, the evil of riches and cities is virtually out of the Bible, and the hanky-panky of the sanatorium, though outré, is scientifically sound." Barzun. Cat of Crime. Rev and enl edition

One fearful yellow eye. Lippincott 1978 c1966 286p o.p.

LC 77-24165

"The Travis McGee series"

First published 1966 in paperback by Fawcett Books

Travis McGee "answers an SOS from Glory Geis. She tells him that her late husband had secretly disposed of a fortune in cash before his death, money Geis's other heirs accuse the widow of stealing. Smelling blackmail, McGee digs into the dead man's past and finds evidence of a venomous plot. A gang of Nazi criminals, passing for respectable citizens, had extorted Geis's money by threatening the lives of his wife and children." Publ Wkly

One more Sunday. Knopf 1984 311p o.p.

LC 83-48858

"John Tinker Meadows and his sister Mary Margaret head the Eternal Church of the Believer, a fundamentalist sect headquartered in the South. From a small country church, ECB has grown into a huge conglomerate, exuding power and wealth, masking a variety of sins—lust, greed, corruption, and murder." Libr J

The author "is far too wise to fall into any simplistic traps, nor does he dismiss all of the religious work as worthless. His descriptions of the church's organization and its power over ordinary mortals are brilliantly done, and the questions of conscience come vividly to life." N Y Times Book Rev

A purple place for dying. Lippincott 1976 c1964 204p o.p.

"The Travis McGee series"

First published 1964 in paperback by Fawcett Books

"Travis McGee is pondering whether to take on the beautiful Mona Yeoman as a client when someone decides for him by shooting her in the back and hiding the body. Mona's husband soon dies of poison, and the killers might have been in the clear if they had not tried to add McGee (and one of those lovely women he always attracts) to their list. The usual literate and fast-paced stuff expected from MacDonald." Booklist

The quick red fox. Lippincott 1974 c1964 206p o.p.

"The Travis McGee series"

First published 1964 in paperback by Fawcett Books

"A Travis McGee story that allows him to philosophize in an antisocial way about the evil world, because it brings him in contact with a ruthless female movie star, assorted playboys and their victims, and a thoroughly good and attractive woman, who leaves him from sheer goodness. McGee's object has been to secure or suppress damaging photos of the movie star. He succeeds thanks to good reasoning and a strong use of brass." Barzun. Cat of Crime. Rev and enl edition

The scarlet ruse. Lippincott 1980 c1973 262p o.p.

LC 79-24843

"The Travis McGee series"

First published 1973 in paperback by Fawcett Books

Private detective Travis McGee, "who lives on a houseboat, is told that the owner is planning on cleaning up the waterfront so he's going to lose his mooring place. McGee is bothered by this but to take his mind off this impending disaster, he takes on a case wherein a dealer of rare stamps is being made the victim of a stamp collector who is substituting 'junk' stamps—worthless stamps for valuable one-of-a-kind stamps. MacDonald keeps the pot boiling as McGee conducts his investigation and, as tradition would have it, runs into all kinds of unforeseen difficulties in settling this case, up to and including murder." West Coast Rev Books

Slam the big door. Mysterious Press 1987 c1960 212p o.p.

LC 86-40562

First published 1960 in paperback by Fawcett Books

40-ish widower Mike Rodenska attempts to save his war-buddy Troy Jamison from losing his second wife and real-estate business by another alcoholic downslide, but finds himself battling Troy's unpleasant, opportunistic stepdaughter

A tan and sandy silence. Lippincott 1979 c1971 261p o.p.

LC 78-24110

"The Travis McGee series"

First published 1972 in paperback by Fawcett Books

"Travis McGee's curiosity and love of women lure him to look for an old lady friend he suspects is in trouble as a result of her husband's greed. The search takes him to Granada, where bright sandy beaches and deadly

MacDonald, John D. (John Dann), 1916-1986—*Continued*
games mingle with a nightmarish regularity." Barzun. Cat of Crime. Rev and enl edition

The turquoise lament. Lippincott 1973 287p o.p.
"The Travis McGee series"
McGee goes to the rescue of the daughter of a man who saved his life
"One of the best McGee adventures." Publ Wkly

Macdonald, Malcolm *See* Ross-Macdonald, Malcolm

Macdonald, Malcolm Ross- *See* Ross-Macdonald, Malcolm

MacDonald, Philip, 1899-1981
The list of Adrian Messenger. Doubleday 1959 224p o.p.
Available from Amereon and Buccaneer Bks.
"Published for the Crime Club"
"A piece of paper listing ten men, six of them died 'accidentally,' sends Anthony Gethryn on a desperate man hunt for a diabolical killer." Publ Wkly
"If some readers find Mr. MacDonald's style a bit stiff and old-fashioned, they will also find that he provides such other old-fashioned elements as honest clues, characters who stick in the mind from page to page, an original idea, and, in Anthony Gethryn, a detective who inspires utter confidence." New Yorker

Macdonald, Ross, 1915-1983
Archer at large; with a foreword by the author. Knopf 1970 626p o.p.
An omnibus volume of three titles published separately in 1959, 1964 and 1966, respectively
Contents: The Galton case; The chill; Black money
All three novels are set in Southern California and feature private detective Lew Archer. In The Galton case, Archer, in search of a missing heir, uncovers a twenty-two-year-old murder. In The chill, Archer searches for a beautiful young woman who runs away from her new husband. Black money finds Archer uncovering corruption on a college campus

Archer in Hollywood; with a foreword by the author. Knopf 1967 528p o.p.
A combination of three titles published separately 1949, 1951, and 1956 respectively, starring Lew Archer, private detective
"Three exciting novels: The moving target, The way some people die [and] The barbarous coast." Title page

Archer in jeopardy; with a foreword by the author. Knopf 1979 757p $24.95
ISBN 0-394-50804-1   LC 79-63807
An omnibus volume of three titles published separately 1958, 1962 and 1968 respectively
Contents: The doomsters; The zebra-striped hearse; The instant enemy
Three mysteries featuring Lew Archer. In The doomsters the activities of an unscrupulous doctor occupy the sleuth; in The zebra-striped hearse the detective becomes involved in an ice pick murder, and in The instant enemy it is the high school runaway that is the focus of Archer's attention

"Three classic Lew Archer mysteries. . . . This stunning trilogy is a must for all mystery enthusiasts." Booklist

The barbarous coast
In Macdonald, R. Archer in Hollywood p171-346

Black money
In Macdonald, R. Archer at large

The blue hammer. Knopf 1976 270p o.p. Amereon reprint available $21.95 (ISBN 0-89190-095-0)
Detective Lew Archer "is hired to find a stolen painting, and then to locate the runaway daughter of the millionaire who has lost the art work. The painter himself vanished years ago. . . . Archer works through a maze of past histories and present wraths to find what happened." Booklist
"The plot is an ingenious one. If the solution strains credibility somewhat, Macdonald can be forgiven. He is such a master of cynicism that he can make any degree of guilt and willful ignorance seem plausible." Atlantic

The chill
In Macdonald, R. Archer at large

The doomsters
In Macdonald, R. Archer in jeopardy

The drowning pool. Knopf 1950 244p o.p.
"Admirers of the later Ross Macdonald will detect in this early book the capacities subsequently so well exploited. Lew Archer started as he continued: tough and straight; clever and informed, but not omniscient; full of love and hostility toward Southern California. This story, of a woman who has made a bad marriage to a mother-dominated husband of ambivalent sexual character, has a bit too much violence, but the character-drawing shows a sure hand, and the tangle is so capably manipulated that it does not annoy." Barzun. Cat of Crime. Rev and enl edition

The Galton case
In Macdonald, R. Archer at large

The goodbye look. Knopf 1969 243p o.p.
Private detective Lew Archer is brought "into the affairs of the Chalmers family because their lawyer thinks they are worried about a theft from their safe. But the Chalmers have other problems, and Lew becomes involved with murders old and new." Libr J

The instant enemy
In Macdonald, R. Archer in jeopardy

The moving target
In Macdonald, R. Archer in Hollywood p3-169

Ross Macdonald's Lew Archer, private investigator. Mysterious Press 1977 245p o.p.
LC 77-81870
Analyzed in Short story index
Contents: Find the woman; Gone girl; The bearded lady; The suicide; Guilt-edged blonde; The sinister habit; Wild goose chase; Midnight blue; Sleeping dog

Macdonald, Ross, 1915-1983—*Continued*

Sleeping beauty. Knopf 1973 271p o.p. Amereon reprint available $21.95 (ISBN 0-89190-096-9)

The scene "is California and the concern is with what power and money can do to wreck a family. Lew [Archer] befriends a lost lady who is running away from fears and responsibilities and from her young husband. Before very long word comes that the girl has been kidnapped and a ransom is demanded of her oil rich family. Bit by bit, as Archer probes deeper into the family relationships, he begins to see that nothing is what it seems and the key to the present lies deep in the past." Publ Wkly

The underground man. Knopf 1971 272p o.p.

"With his customary skill and economy of means, the author gets us, through Archer, into a tangle of passions about runaway spouses, disaffected and drug-taking children, amateur blackmail, and, of course, murder." Barzun. Cat of Crime. Rev and enl edition

The way some people die

In Macdonald, R. Archer in Hollywood p347-528

The zebra-striped hearse

In Macdonald, R. Archer in jeopardy

MacInnes, Helen, 1907-1985

Above suspicion. Harcourt Brace & Co. 1954 333p $24.95

ISBN 0-15-102707-2

A reprint of the title first published 1941 by Little, Brown

"An Oxford don and his pretty wife are chosen to perform a secret mission to Germany in late 1939. While using their vacation as a cover, they are to locate the whereabouts of an anti-Nazi agent. The plan seems foolproof—until someone betrays it and them." Smith. Cloak and Dagger Fic

Agent in place. Harcourt Brace Jovanovich 1976 339p o.p. Amereon reprint available $23.95 (ISBN 0-89190-106-X)

"The agent in place is Alexis—'a mole that stays underground and works out of sight'—a Soviet spy in New York who obtains and photographs the so-called NATO Memorandum. The document contains facts and figures about NATO's defense capability and dispositions, and details of the strength of the Warsaw Treaty Organization. More importantly, sources of the information are revealed." Booklist

Assignment in Brittany. Harcourt Brace Jovanovich 1971 373p $24.95

ISBN 0-15-109620-1

A reprint of the title first published 1942 by Little, Brown

"A young British officer is sent to France after the debacle of Dunkirk, in the guise of a wounded French soldier, to find out what the Nazis planned to do with the coast of France. His dangerous mission became nerve-racking in the extreme when he discovered, almost too late, that there has been important omissions in his information." Ont Libr Rev

Cloak of darkness. Harcourt Brace Jovanovich 1982 342p o.p.

LC 82-47667

"Bob Renwick, head of an independent intelligence force focusing on terrorism, finds himself marked for murder by a firm that sells illegal arms and helps train the buyers in their use. Trying to keep one step ahead of the assassin, locating an escaped terrorist, and finding the list of those who've helped the illegal arms sales keep Renwick and his associate on the move from Djibouti to New York to Chamonix." Libr J

"The story is perfectly paced, never slackening its speed but never rushing the reader beyond full comprehension of the dangers and the stakes of the game." Best Sellers

Decision at Delphi. Harcourt Brace & Co. 1960 434p $24.95

ISBN 0-15-124221-6

"Kenneth Strang and his Greek-American friend Steve Kladas are to meet in Greece for a magazine assignment, but Steve disappears en route, leaving clues that point to his family's activities in World War II. Cecilia Hillard is sent to take Steve's place, and fortunately proves to be as resourceful as she is charming, for she promptly gets involved in Kenneth's dangerous hunt for Steve." Booklist

The double image. Harcourt, Brace & World 1966 309p il o.p. Amereon reprint available $22.95 (ISBN 0-89190-105-1)

"John Craig stopped in Paris to see his sister before he went to the Mediterranean to research his projected book on trade routes as motives for war. Before he could meet her, he ran into an old friend, Dr. Sussman, and learned of his fear of Heinrich Berg, a Nazi war criminal, alive in Paris, not resting quietly in his Berlin grave. John, too, saw Berg, and after Sussman's suicide, was the only person who could identify him. Security forces felt that an intelligent amateur with good cover and essential information was invaluable, so John became part of the mixed crew of agents, double agents, and innocent bystanders who were involved in Operation Pear Tree on the Greek island of Mykonos." Libr J

Friends and lovers. Little, Brown 1947 367p o.p.

A love story in which the localities are Scotland, London, and Oxford; and the chief characters are a poor young Oxford scholar, and a wellbred young woman from a conventional family

The hidden target. Harcourt Brace Jovanovich 1980 405p o.p.

LC 80-7953

"Robert Renwick of NATO's undercover counterterrorist organization is reunited briefly in Amsterdam with Nina O'Connell, whom he hasn't seen for years. Before they can become reacquainted, Nina is off on a tour by camper with a group of students who, Renwick suspects, are not what they seem. Nina is the daughter of a U.S. government official and, she learns in Bombay, a pawn of the tourists' leaders, veteran terrorists. She runs away but is caught, then rescued by Renwick and allies who have been trailing the camper discreetly." Publ Wkly

MacInnes, Helen, 1907-1985—*Continued*

Message from Málaga. Harcourt Brace Jovanovich 1971 367p o.p.

Spain is the setting for this novel of intrigue. "C.I.A. agent Jeff Reid is killed helping his friend Tavita, a fiery flamenco dancer, smuggle a refugee from Cuba, and Jeff's friend Ian Ferrier, on vacation from the U.S. Space Agency, finds himself involved in the affair. The prospective defector is a member of the Soviet Intelligence's highly secret assassination branch, and the Americans race against time to spirit him against his will to the U.S. before the other side catches up with him." Booklist

North from Rome. Harcourt Brace & Co. 1958 307p $24.95

ISBN 0-15-167001-3

"In Rome to try to persuade his former fiancée to resume their engagement, American playwright Bill Lamiter goes to the rescue of an Italian girl who is being abducted and straightaway finds himself embroiled in intrigue and violence centering in a narcotics ring set up by Moscow with political ends in view. A pursuit leading north out of Rome, the rescue of Bill's Eleanor, who is innocently involved, and the break-up of the ring are recounted." Booklist

Prelude to terror. Harcourt Brace Jovanovich 1978 368p o.p.

"Colin Grant, art consultant, is asked by a wealthy art collector to purchase a specific seventeenth-century painting at an art auction in Vienna. The owner of the painting needs money to escape from Hungary, and the transaction must be kept secret. When Colin arrives in Vienna, he finds that the auction conceals a conspiracy for laundering money that is used to buy weapons for terrorist groups. In spite of great personal danger Colin searches for the key piece of information that will stop this source of financing." Shapiro. Fic for Youth. 2d edition

Ride a pale horse. Harcourt Brace Jovanovich 1984 355p $15.95

ISBN 0-15-177268-1   LC 84-9037

"Karen Cornell, journalist for an American world affairs magazine, is about to leave a peace convention in Prague disgruntled by her treatment and the lack of material when she is approached by a Czech intelligence officer who is about to defect. The papers he gives her to relay to a CIA expert on 'disinformation' start her on a harrowing course from Prague to Vienna, Rome, and Washington." Libr J

"The device of dual protagonists moves the plot along smartly, and the demonstration of the insidious uses of disinformation could hardly be more timely." Booklist

The Salzburg connection. Harcourt, Brace & World 1968 406p o.p.

Available Thorndike Press large print edition

"Close to the end of World War II the Nazis buried in a lake in the Austrian Alps a sealed chest that contained a list of men who had aided Hitler's cause and, if identified, might be blackmailed into doing it again. Twenty years later Bill Mathieson, an attorney investigating a routine matter for a publishing firm, becomes involved in an intricate scheme to recover the chest. The Communists, the Americans, the Nazis, and others are all desperately trying to reach the goal first." Shapiro. Fic for Youth. 2d edition

The snare of the hunter. Harcourt Brace Jovanovich 1974 306p o.p. Amereon reprint available $22.95 (ISBN 0-89190-103-5)

This novel of international intrigue revolves around Irina Kusak's flight from Czechoslovakia in search of her missing father, a Nobel Prize nominee in hiding

"As in so many MacInnes books, there is the amateur drawn into the perils of espionage. . . . As in all MacInnes books, there is the conflict between good and evil. Good is America and democracy. Evil is Russia and communism. And, as in all MacInnes books there is romance. . . . Fun and games." N Y Times Book Rev

The Venetian affair. Harcourt, Brace & World 1963 405p o.p.

This "suspense novel is set in Paris and Venice in 1961. An American newspaperman on vacation picks up the wrong raincoat on arrival at Orly airport, and finds himself involved in a communist plot to assassinate De Gaulle and implicate the United States. American agents enlist his help to thwart the plotters and to unmask the mysterious and ruthless spymaster." Publ Wkly

Mackin, Edward, 1929-

For works written by this author under other names see McInerny, Ralph M., 1929-; Quill, Monica, 1929-

Mackintosh, Elizabeth *See* Tey, Josephine, 1896-1952

MacLean, Alistair, 1922-1987

Breakheart Pass. Doubleday 1974 178p o.p.

Available G.K. Hall large print edition

The setting for his novel "is the era just after the Civil War. An Army relief train is proceeding to a fort in Indian territory, which is reportedly suffering from an epidemic of cholera. The chief characters are the Governor of Nevada, a U.S. Marshall, a major who was a renowned Civil War hero, the Governor's niece, and John Deakin, a prisoner of the marshall's wanted for atrocious crimes, including murder. As the train proceeds various mysterious accidents happen [and] . . . Deakin is revealed as a Secret Service agent." Best Sellers

Caravan to Vaccares. Doubleday 1970 259p o.p.

"The background is picturesque—the annual gypsy pilgrimage to the south of France—gypsy caravans traveling here from many countries in Europe. But some, from Iron Curtain countries, are on a special mission. It is up to secret agent Bowman to stop the ruthless gypsy leaders, who do not balk at murder and torture, from carrying out their plans." Publ Wkly

Floodgate. Doubleday 1984 c1983 369p o.p.

LC 83-45013

First published 1983 in the United Kingdom

"The novel is set in and around Amsterdam, where a band of canny, sophisticated terrorists are threatening to flood the Netherlands by blowing up dikes and exploding offshore nuclear devices. The terrorists demand that Holland must negotiate with Great Britain for the withdrawal of all British troops from Northern Ireland.

MacLean, Alistair, 1922-1987—*Continued*
Peter van Effen, senior detective and explosives expert, eventually saves the nation, a task he carries out with cool, dispassionate efficiency." Booklist

"Readers accustomed to thrillers of a more lurid hue may well appreciate MacLean's stylistic restraint, neat plotting and attention to characterization." Publ Wkly

Force 10 from Navarone. Doubleday 1968 274p o.p.

The three heroes of The guns of Navarone, Mallory, Miller and Stavros are assigned a new mission during World War II. "They are dropped into Yugoslavia to join the Partisans, prevent a German attack, blow up a dam, and provide a diversion to draw German troops out of Italy." Publ Wkly

The guns of Navarone. Doubleday 1957 320p o.p. Buccaneer Bks. reprint available $27.95 (ISBN 1-56849-306-1)

"World War II is being fought, and the Germans control the island that guards the approaches to the eastern Mediterranean with big guns. After all other attempts have failed, a five-man British army team is chosen to silence the guns of Navarone. They land on the island, elude the Nazis, and scale a seemingly unclimbable cliff." Shapiro. Fic for Youth. 3d edition

Followed by Force 10 from Navarone

H.M.S. Ulysses. Doubleday 1956 c1955 316p il o.p.

First published 1955 in the United Kingdom

"The murderous and tragic World War II sea route to Murmansk, in Arctic Russia, is the subject of [this] novel. . . . A blend of naval tactics and high powered dramatics 'HMS Ulysses' tells of the week-long disintegration of a British light cruiser and its overworked 'zombie' crew while shepherding a convoy in gale-lashed Arctic waters between Iceland and Sweden's North Cape." San Francisco Chron

Ice Station Zebra. Doubleday 1963 276p o.p.

A novel of suspense and intrigue that begins on "a bitter-cold morning in Holy Loch, Scotland, when a British doctor with top-level endorsements from the American and British military forces seeks admission to an American nuclear submarine. The submarine is slated for a perilous trip to rescue the starving, freezing British crew of a meteorological station situated on an ice floe in the Arctic." Publ Wkly

Night without end. Doubleday 1960 287p o.p. Amereon reprint available $19.95 (ISBN 0-89190-174-4)

"An airliner crash lands on the Greenland icecap near a small I.G.Y. observation station. It soon becomes clear that the landing was planned and certain of the passengers and crew murdered for reasons unknown, while at least eight of the 10 survivors were drugged into insensibility—the other two of course, being the killers. But which two? . . . A sometimes barely credible, but always absorbing, thriller that combines elements of the espionage story and murder mystery with those of the 'castaway' adventure tale." Libr J

When eight bells toll. Doubleday 1966 288p o.p.

"Sure and deadly with guns and knives, an expert at underwater work, Philip Calvert, British secret service agent, polishes his skills to a high gloss in this tense adventure story set in the western Scottish Highlands. Calvert and his friends oppose a gang of killers who operate at sea and in harbors. What the killers are doing, why they are busy in this cold, rainy, windy part of Scotland, and whether Calvert will survive his fight against them are questions that provide suspense." Publ Wkly

Where eagles dare. Doubleday 1967 312p o.p.

"Secrecy and stealth are essential to the mission of an assorted crew from MI 6 who must rescue an American general, the coordinator of Overlord, from Schloss Adler, a castle built by a mad Bavarian prince, which is the combined HQ of the German Secret Service and the Gestapo of South Germany in the bitter winter of 1943-44. And if that isn't enough, there is Major Smith's second assignment to bring out the pyrotechnic display of excitement and suspense." Libr J

MacLeod, Charlotte

(comp) Christmas stalkings. See Christmas stalkings

The corpse in Oozak's Pond. Mysterious Press 1987 213p o.p.

LC 86-62775

"History eerily repeats itself in this . . . mystery set on the rustic campus of an agricultural college in Balaclava Junction, Mass. When a corpse is found floating in Oozak's Pond dressed in turn-of-the-century costume, outfitted with a false beard, stabbed through the neck with an ice pick and weighted down with rocks, it is almost an exact reenactment of the 1905 demise of Augustus Buggins, grandson of the college's founder Balaclava Buggins, to whom the unidentified corpse bears a startling resemblance. When the bodies of the aging but still sprightly couple Trevelyan and Beatrice Buggins are discovered the same day, it is clear to Peter Shandy, professor of agronomy at the college, that a conspiracy is afoot." Publ Wkly

The Gladstone bag. Mysterious Press 1990 218p $16.95

ISBN 0-89296-370-0   LC 89-43143

Also available Thorndike Press large print edition

"Six feisty and contentious characters with inventive names surround aging-but-active Emma Kelling during her stay at a friend's Maine retreat. Strange events, attempted theft, and a sodden body propel her to consult niece and nephew-in-law/detectives Sarah and Max Bittersohn . . . , as well as cousin-in-law Theonie. Tongue-in-cheek eccentricities, the usual casual but astute deductions, and a certain luxuriousness of language make this a most welcome addition to the MacLeod canon." Libr J

An owl too many. Warner Bks. 1991 310p $17.95

ISBN 0-89296-431-6   LC 90-41227

Also available G.K. Hall large print edition

MacLeod, Charlotte—*Continued*

"A Mysterious Press book"

A mystery about the "doings at Balaclava Agricultural College. During the annual owl count, a murder occurs, and Professor Shandy is appointed to solve the mystery. He is aided by fellow avian researcher and local millionairess Winifred Binks. Binks, recently appointed associate professor and chair of Local Flora, becomes the target of an unscrupulous gang that want to kidnap her." Booklist

The recycled citizen. Mysterious Press 1988 199p o.p.

LC 87-7846

Available G.K. Hall large print edition

In this mystery featuring Sarah Kelling and husband Max Bittersohn, "Sarah's Brahmin but rather improper Bostonian kin, the Kellings, ask for the couple's help when Dolph and Mary Kelling's Senior Citizens' Recycling Center is in danger." Publ Wkly

Rest you merry. Penzler Bks. 1993 222p $22

ISBN 1-562-87052-1 LC 93-32744

"The Armchair Detective Library"

A reissue of the title first published 1978 by Doubleday

"Christmas time at Balaclava Agricultural College is the background for this academic mystery tale. Professor Peter Shandy capitulates to the badgering of a resident busy-body Jemima Ames and shows his Christmas spirit—by decorating his house with plastic reindeer, flashing lights, and leering Santas. . . . He then flees, but driven back by his conscience, he returns to find the body of Jemima in his living room. Helen Marsh, the new librarian, joins the professor in the investigation of the murder." Publisher's note

The resurrection man; a Sarah Kelling and Max Bittersohn mystery. Mysterious Press 1992 250p $17.95

ISBN 0-89296-443-X LC 91-58024

Also available Thorndike Press large print edition

"Initial suspicions about Bartolo Arbalest, the 'resurrection man' who has suddenly appeared in Boston, concern his business of art and furniture restoration, his secretive nature, and his insistence on his helpers all living with him in seclusion. He does fine work, commands high fees, employs a bodyguard, and cooks sumptuous dinners for his chosen acolytes, a rum bunch of dubious ne'erdo-wells and Beantown society types down on their luck. To Max and Sarah, the whole enterprise fairly screams of illegality. Then events grow more labyrinthine, as works recently restored start to vanish, and owners meet bad ends." Booklist

"MacLeod's sure touch with the cheerily eccentric and her keen eye for the often strange social habits of apparently staid society make this another delight." Publ Wkly

The Silver Ghost; a Sarah Kelling mystery. Mysterious Press 1988 213p o.p.

LC 87-35027

Sarah and her husband Max are hired by cousin Bill "to find out who stole his vintage 1927 Phantom Rolls Royce. Since Bill suspects that someone close to him may be responsible, he invites Max and Sarah to do their sleuthing at his annual Renaissance Revel. All the possible culprits are gathered. . . . But before the two can form any theories, another of Bill's classic Rolls Royces, the Silver Ghost, disappears. The gateman who

was guarding it is found murdered. And Sarah's Aunt Boadicea, last seen heading out to the garage, is nowhere to be found." West Coast Rev Books

Something in the water. Mysterious Press 1994 262p $18.95

ISBN 0-89296-430-8 LC 93-32779

Also available Thorndike Press large print edition

"Professor Peter Shandy, a botanist par excellence, witnesses the sudden death of a diner in a landmark Maine restaurant. No one believes that the despised man died naturally, but did he commit suicide to spite his wife or die by another's hand?" Libr J

Something the cat dragged in. Doubleday 1983 185p o.p.

"Published for the Crime Club"

"Balaclava Agricultural College is the scene for [this] story, which features Professor Peter Shandy. A former faculty member, Professor Ungley, is found dead behind the Club House of the notorious Balaclavian Society, a secretive and odd group of Balaclava Junction residents. Four file drawers of papers are also missing from Professor Ungley's apartment. Before long Ms. Ruth Smith . . . is found strangled to death on the college campus." Best Sellers

Vane pursuit; a Peter Shandy mystery. Mysterious Press 1989 185p o.p.

LC 88-25595

"Detective Peter Shandy, and his redoubtable wife, Helen the librarian, are swept up in the diabolical theft of antique weather vanes by crooks who use arson as their *mode d'accomplis*. . . . Endless puns punctuate MacLeod's delightfully absurd tale, which, beneath all the frivolity, is masterfully executed." Booklist

The withdrawing room. Doubleday 1980 186p o.p.

"Published for the Crime Club"

"Widowed Sarah Kelling takes boarders into her stately home on Boston's Beacon Hill to pay the heavy mortgage, a move that means trouble. Mr. Quiffen, who settles into the former 'withdrawing room,' is killed and so is Mr. Hartler, who rents the vacated premises. Sarah appeals to her brainy, attractive friend Max Bittersohn for help but begins to investigate her guests personally, afraid that one may be the murderer." Publ Wkly

The wrong rite; [by] Charlotte MacLeod writing as Alisa Craig. Morrow 1992 284p $19

ISBN 0-688-08643-8 LC 91-30374

When Canadian Mounted Police inspector Madoc Rhys and his wife Janet visit the Rhys ancestral home in Wales for a family reunion "dark deeds . . . commence: Janet spots a ghost; Madoc finds the local crows feasting on a slaughtered sheep and spots a badly bruised shepherd resting nearby. Then table conversation leads to fertility dances and leaping through fires. Later, a distant cousin makes the fatal fiery jump." Booklist

"If the investigation lacks thrills, the portrayal of old Welsh customs and engaging family eccentrics is delightful." Publ Wkly

MacNeil, Robert, 1931-

Burden of desire. Doubleday 1992 466p o.p.

LC 91-28919

MacNeil, Robert, 1931-—*Continued*

"The story begins with a bang—literally, as a munitions ship blows up in Halifax, Nova Scotia, in 1917 in what will be the biggest, most destructive man-made explosion until the atomic bomb. Picking up the pieces in the well-evoked ruined city are young parson Peter Wentworth, an ambitious man in an unhappy marriage, and Stewart MacPherson, a psychiatrist just beginning to treat shell-shocked returning soldiers. The two read a diary accidentally lost in the wreckage, belonging to Julia Robertson, a young, unconventional woman whose beauty and self-acknowledged sensuality ensnares each of them in turn." Publ Wkly

This novel "is at once a wonderful romance involving one of the more appealing triangles in recent fiction and a thoughtful dissection of the glacial pace of social change." N Y Times Book Rev

Mahfouz, Naguib *See* Maḥfūz, Najīb, 1912-

Maḥfūz, Najīb, 1912-

Nobel Prize in literature, 1988

Adrift on the Nile; [by] Naguib Mahfouz; translated by Frances Liardet. Doubleday 1993 167p $21

ISBN 0-385-42322-5   LC 92-20977

Original Arabic edition, 1966

A houseboat on the Nile "is a nightly diversion for a small circle of friends. Careers in the arts, business, law, and civil service are forgotten as the waterpipe makes its rounds, the intoxicating kif erasing all sense of responsibility. Anis, the 'master of ceremonies,' tends the pipe and drifts in his narcotic dreams while the others extol the absurdity of addiction. Their tranquility ends, however, when Samara, a young journalist, comes to study the group. She is the grain of seriousness that irritates their escapist shell, and around her swirls a nightly dispute over purpose, duty, love, and morality." Libr J

Mahfouz "writes hypnotic prose, by turns romantically lyrical and tartly astringent, spiced with ironical allusions to ancient Egypt and classical history, whose grandeur highlights by contrast the rootlessness of modern Egypt's secularized, cosmopolitan middle class." Publ Wkly

Arabian nights and days; [by] Naguib Mahfouz; translated by Denys Johnson-Davies. Doubleday 1995 227p $22.95

ISBN 0-385-46888-1   LC 94-6457

Original Arabic edition, 1979

In this modern reworking of The thousand and one nights, Mahfouz "introduces us to the denizens of an unnamed urban center in the Islamic world centuries ago and follows their fortunes. It's the dawn of a new day in this city, the sultan having ceased his bloodletting, for he is marrying the storytelling Shahrzad; and from there, we encounter all sorts of people from all walks of life, including the adventure-loving Sinbad. One character's experiences lead into another's, as Mahfouz unfolds a vibrant pageant of colorful lives." Booklist

"With his usual psychological acuity and a keen sense of social and political realities, Mahfouz delivers a revised classic that skewers hypocrisy, greed and corruption, especially of those in power." Publ Wkly

Autumn quail; [by] Naguib Mahfouz; translated by Roger Allen; revised by John Rodenbeck. Doubleday 1990 172p o.p.

LC 89-48671

Originally published in Arabic; this translation first published 1985 in Egypt

This novel "tells the story of Isa, a young government bureaucrat who loses his position in the political aftermath of the revolution. Fired from his job, he leaves Cairo for Alexandria, both to rethink his career and to avoid his cousin, whose own fortunes have prospered. Even Isa's hopes for a good marriage are dashed by his new situation as he tries to come to terms with his country's past and his own future." Booklist

The beginning and the end; [by] Naguib Mahfouz; translated by Ramses Awad; edited by Mason Rossiter Smith. Doubleday 1989 c1985 412p o.p.

LC 89-33116

Originally published in Arabic; this translation first published 1985 in Egypt

The author "traces the vicissitudes of one middle-class family as it tries in vain and against all odds to live out the ideal of a 'struggling but united family,' believing fervently that its attempts to shape reality into an idealized mold will eventually restore the secure fabric of life that began to unravel with the father's sudden death. . . . The tone is not moralistic; Mr. Mahfouz does not pass judgment on Hassan, the black sheep of the family, or on sister Nefisa for her emotional or sexual transgressions, not even on the ambitious brother Hassanein for his blatant narcissism and cruelty. Instead, Mr. Mahfouz poignantly, and with great sympathy and pathos, captures the family's tragic circumstances." N Y Times Book Rev

The harafish; [by] Naguib Mahfouz; translated by Catherine Cobham. Doubleday 1994 406p $22.95

ISBN 0-385-42324-1   LC 93-7782

Original Arabic edition, 1977

"The al-Nagi family's history through ten generations in their Cairo alley is 'nothing more than a succession of deviations, disasters, lessons not learned.' Ashur, the clan chief and ruler of the community, returns after the plague years to find the neighborhood deserted. Appropriating all the wealth and property, he distributes it to the impoverished (the harafish), creating the Covenant of Ashur. His legend is badly served, however, when succeeding generations succumb to the family curse." Libr J

"It is not an easy task to maintain a balanced sweep through the ages while also fashioning numerous distinct characters, but Mahfouz does it dexterously. He is an outstanding fiction writer, and further proof is offered here." Booklist

Midaq Alley; [by] Naguib Mahfouz; translated by Trevor Le Gassick. Anchor Bks. (NY) 1992 286p $21.50

ISBN 0-385-26475-5   LC 91-27459

"Written in the 1940s, this novel . . . deals with the plight of impoverished classes in an old quarter of Cairo. The lives and situations depicted create an atmosphere of sadness and tragic realism. Indeed, few of the characters are happy or successful. Protagonist Hamida, an orphan raised by a foster mother, is drawn into prostitu-

Mahfūz, Najīb, 1912-—*Continued*

tion. Kirsha, the owner of a café in the alley, is a drug addict and a lustful homosexual. Zaita makes a living by disfiguring people so that they can become successful beggars. Transcending time and place, the social issues treated here are relevant to many Arab countries today." Libr J

Palace of desire; translated by William M. Hutchins and Olive E. Kenny. Doubleday 1991 422p $22.95

ISBN 0-385-26467-4   LC 90-3753

Original Arabic edition, 1957

"Al-Sayyid Ahmad is mellowing as he leaves middle age. As this second novel of 'The Cairo Trilogy' opens, he is ending his self-imposed abstention from liquor and women, begun five years earlier upon the death of his son, Fahmy. . . . Meanwhile, his children are struggling with life beyond their father's domination. Yasin is twice divorced and incapable of resisting any woman. The two married daughters are split by an open feud. And Kamal, the intellectual center of this novel, enters college [and grapples with] . . . religion, science, and romance." Libr J

"Mr. Mahfouz excels at fusing deep emotion and soap opera. Fortunately, the translators . . . are equal to the task of animating rather than embalming Mr. Mahfouz's elegant and often explosive text." N Y Times Book Rev

Followed by Sugar Street

Palace walk; [by] Naguib Mahfouz; translated from the Arabic by William M. Hutchins with Olive E. Kenny. Doubleday 1990 c1989 498p $22.95

ISBN 0-385-26465-8   LC 89-23348

Originally published in Arabic

This is the first volume in the author's trilogy "dealing with three generations of a Cairo family in the first half of the twentieth century. The emotional and physical struggles of these middle-class people are depicted with a great deal of sympathy and honesty, from the torments of adolescent love through the banked passions of an established marriage. The novel begins with a series of domestic scenes featuring the five children of a merchant and his wife; later, the setting shifts to Cairo nightclubs, coffee shops, and stores as Mahfouz re-creates the everyday existence of his characters in almost Dickensian detail." Booklist

Followed by Palace of desire

Sugar Street; [by] Naguib Mahfouz; translated by William Maynard Hutchins and Angele Botros Samaan. Doubleday 1992 308p $22.50

ISBN 0-385-26469-0   LC 91-12938

Original Arabic edition, 1957

This is the concluding volume of the author's Cairo trilogy. "The novel opens in 1935 as Egypt smolders under British occupation, and it extends through the war. Kamal, son of the gaunt, wasted patriarch, is a grade-school teacher and philosopher who veers between lusty debauches and reading Spinoza. One of his nephews, Abd Al-Muni'm, becomes a Muslim fundamentalist; another nephew, Ahmad, takes Marx as his prophet. These two diametrically opposed brothers will share the same fate—a jail cell. The inadvertent cause of their undoing may be another scion of the patriarch, young Ridwan, a closet homosexual whose liaison with a prominent politician apparently backfires." Publ Wkly

"The ordinary nature of Mr. Mahfouz's world, with its willingness to confront the complexities of human intentions, makes it an extraordinary exception in a marketplace of manufactured ideas and is, for that, all the more admirable." N Y Times Book Rev

The thief and the dogs; [by] Naguib Mahfouz; translated by Trevor Le Gassick, M. M. Badawi; revised by John Rodenbeck. Doubleday 1989 c1984 158p o.p.

LC 89-7892

Originally published in Arabic; this translation first published 1984 in Egypt

"A stream-of-consciousness work about an ex-convict who attempts to return to his former place in society but fails with humiliating consequences. The disappointment of his early efforts and the violence of his ultimate failures make for an unusual portrait of self-destruction." Booklist

The time and the place and other stories; [by] Naguib Mahfouz; selected and translated by Denys Johnson-Davies. Doubleday 1991 174p o.p.

LC 90-20194

Analyzed in Short story index

Contents: Zaabalawi; The conjurer made off with the dish; The answer is no; The time and the place; Blessed night; The ditch; Half a day; The Tavern of the Black Cat; The lawsuit; The empty café; A day for saying goodbye; By a person unknown; The man and the other man; The wasteland; The Norwegian rat; His majesty; Fear; At the bus stop; A fugitive from justice; A long-term plan

This collection of stories details "life of Cairo residents as they try to survive poverty, brood over death, and endure outmoded tradition. . . . Mahfouz is a somber writer, but his subtle narrative technique and stately prose give one much to ponder." Libr J

Wedding song; [by] Naguib Mahfouz; translated from Arabic by Olive E. Kenny; edited and revised by Mursi Saad El Din and John Rodenbeck; introduction by Mursi Saad El Din. Doubleday 1989 c1984 174p o.p.

LC 89-7893

Originally published in Arabic; this translation first published 1984 in Egypt

"The novel opens with actor Tariq Ramadan denouncing his company's latest choice of play as clear evidence that the young playwright, Abbas Karam Younis, has killed his wife—former lover of Ramadan. As the novel progresses, the events depicted in the play are recounted from different angles by Ramadan, Younis's father Karam, his mother Halima al-Kabsh, and, finally Younis himself, and the truth slowly emerges. When Younis observes, 'Which—what I'd imagined or what actually happened—was theatrically stronger? What I'd imagined, unquestionably,' we realize that the novel is a meditation on Mahfouz's own experience as a writer." Libr J

Mailer, Norman

Ancient evenings. Little, Brown 1983 709p o.p.

LC 82-22839

Mailer, Norman—*Continued*

"Set in the span between the reigns of Ramses II and Ramses IX, Mailer's . . . novel is narrated by the remnant spirits of Menenhetet I and his great-grandson as they join mutuality to survive the land of the Dead and to ascend to Ra. The story is largely the account of Menenhetet's first life (he has had four) as he rises from peasant stock to become first charioteer to Ramses II, then general, then overseer of the harem." Libr J

"This novel is perhaps the best reconstruction of the far past since Flaubert's 'Salammbo,' but Mailer's eye is on the modern age, especially the psychic problems of America. These problems may find a solution through an understanding of the repressed areas of human sexuality, with the reality of magic. Our own rationality has failed. Here, he seems to say, is a complex civilization of high achievement based on the irrational, on the radial power of magic whose centre is both decay and resurrection. This is a different book, on whose writing and research Mailer spent over ten years, but it is not only about magic, it is magical in itself." Burgess. 99 Novels

The executioner's song. Modern Lib. 1993 1002p $20

ISBN 0-679-42471-7   LC 92-51066

A reissue of the title first published 1979 by Little, Brown

A "documentary narrative of 'the activities of Gary Gilmore and the men and women associated with him' between his release from prison in April 1976 and his execution for murder in early 1977. . . . The first half of the book, called 'Western Voices,' is the story of Gilmore's . . . attempt to fit in between the time he is released from prison and the time he is arrested, tried, and found guilty of two murders on two successive nights. But the second half, 'Eastern Voices,' is really the story of the marketing of Gilmore as he awaits—and demands—death in the Utah state prison." New Repub

"In this study of a condemned murderer Mailer not only vividly portrays the character in a real-life drama but also invokes the whole history of westward migration of the Mormons of Utah." Reader's Ency. 3d edition

Harlot's ghost. Random House 1991 1310p $30

ISBN 0-394-58832-0   LC 90-53152

"Harry Hubbard is a bright young man whose father and whose mentor, Hugh Montague (also known as Harlot), are both senior CIA figures and induct him into the Agency. Most of the book . . . is one long flashback, Harry's autobiographical account of his early career—partly in his own words, partly in an exchange of letters with Harlot's beautiful, brilliant wife, Kittredge, whom Harry admires from afar and will one day steal." Publ Wkly

"An immensely long but never laborious book, one where Mailer works compelling variations on his quintessential themes." Libr J

The naked and the dead. Holt & Co. 1948 721p o.p. Buccaneer Bks. reprint available $27.95 (ISBN 1-56849-421-1)

"In 1944 an American platoon takes part in the invasion and occupation of a Japanese-held island. The action is divided into three parts: the landing on the island, the counter-attack by night, and a daring patrol by the platoon behind enemy lines. The style is simple realism and therefore the language is rough, in keeping with the army setting." Shapiro. Fic for Youth. 3d edition

"The book is encyclopedic yet particular, both realistic and symbolic. It is one of the best novels by an American about World War II." Benet's Reader's Ency of Am Lit

Tough guys don't dance. Random House 1984 229p $16.95

ISBN 0-394-53786-6   LC 84-42514

"Tim Madden is a writer who lives in Provincetown, where the action takes place one dreary November. . . . . After a night of monumental drinking, Madden awakens with a mysterious tatoo on his arm, blood all over the passenger seat of his Porsche, and no memory of his actions. Later he discovers one, then another decapitated head buried with his stash of marijuana. Madden is obviously the prime suspect in the murders, and his task is to find which of the many unsavory characters of his acquaintance is responsible." Publ Wkly

"This genre is not exactly Mailer's forte, but the nononsense prose and the hard-as-nails style . . . may attract readers." Booklist

Mainwaring, Marion

See Wharton, E. The buccaneers, completed by Marion Mainwaring

Maitland, Sara, 1950-

Ancestral truths. Holt & Co. 1994 c1993 295p $22.50

ISBN 0-8050-2536-7   LC 93-30707

"A John Macrae book"

First published 1993 in the United Kingdom with title: Home truths

"As the book opens, Clara Kerslake has just returned to her home in Scotland from Zimbabwe, where she went with her egotistical lover David. She has been found there alone on a mountainside, her right hand mangled; incoherent, she tells her rescuers that she has killed David, yet later has no recollection of the murder. After Clara recuperates and obtains a prosthetic hand, she joins her family at a country retreat where her memory is jogged by various symbolic incidents." Publ Wkly

"There's no doubt that Maitland's written a powerful, provocative, fascinating tale that explores more than just the mystery surrounding David's death." Booklist

Major, Clarence

(ed) Calling the wind. See Calling the wind

Malamud, Bernard, 1914-1986

The assistant; a novel. Farrar, Straus & Giroux 1957 246p o.p.

"His poverty is further aggravated when Morris Bober, a Jewish grocer, is robbed and beaten in his store. Frank Alpine, a drifter, appears on the scene ostensibly to help Bober in his struggle to make a living but actually to seek forgiveness for his participation in the attack. Although Frank aspires to achieve Bober's goodness and the love of Helen, Bober's daughter, he cannot break his pattern of antisocial behavior. Frank's punishment is complete when he is driven to assault both daughter and father, thus alienating both the people for whom

Malamud, Bernard, 1914-1986—*Continued*
he cares." Shapiro. Fic for Youth. 3d edition

also in Malamud, B. A Malamud reader p75-305

Dubin's lives. Farrar, Straus & Giroux 1979 361p o.p.

LC 78-23897

"William B. Dubin is one of America's foremost writers. His biographies of Lincoln, Mark Twain, and Thoreau have won universal praise and a presidential medal; now, after several years of research, he is about to begin a life of D. H. Lawrence. Dubin lives with his wife of more than 25 years in a small town in upstate New York near the Vermont border. . . . The main action of the novel is Dubin's on-again, off-again love affair with Fanny Bick, a 22-year-old college dropout whom his wife first hires as a part-time cleaning lady." Saturday Rev

"Seldom have the travails of advancing age—of late middle-age constantly haunted by thoughts of lost youth and coming old age—been captured so tellingly, so movingly. In Dubin's lives the reader is likely to recognize, alas, all too much of his/her own." Choice

The fixer. Farrar, Straus & Giroux 1966 335p o.p.

"Yakov Bok, a handyman, is arrested and charged with the killing of a Christian boy. Innocent of the crime, he is only guilty of being a Jew in Czarist Russia. In jail he is mentally and physically tortured as a scapegoat for a crime he insists he did not commit. Although his suffering and degradation are unrelenting, Bok emerges a hero as he maintains his innocence. Malamud has fashioned a powerful story of injustice and endurance based on a true incident." Shapiro. Fic for Youth. 3d edition

A Malamud reader. Farrar, Straus & Giroux 1967 528p o.p.

Analyzed in Short story index
Contains ten short stories from: Idiots first, and The magic barrel, and selections from the novels: A new life, The natural, and The fixer. This book also includes the complete text of The assistant
Short stories included: The mourners; Idiots first; The first seven years; Take pity; The maid's shoes; Black is my favorite color; The Jewbird; The magic barrel; The German refugee; The last Mohican

The natural. Harcourt Brace & Co. 1952 237p o.p.

"The fanaticism and seriousness of baseball to both players and fans are vividly pictured in this novel about a man whose sole ambition was to be 'the greatest ever.' Roy Hobbs, who has made his own bat, Wonderboy, starts off at nineteen years of age to a possible spot on a big team. That promising beginning is blasted when he has an encounter with an erratic, seductive woman. When we next meet Roy fifteen years later, he is trying again to realize his dream as the best baseball player. His wrong-headed decisions and the exciting descriptions of the games played by his team, The Knights, make this a tense story up to the last out." Shapiro. Fic for Youth. 3d edition

The stories of Bernard Malamud. Farrar, Straus & Giroux 1983 250p $17.95

ISBN 0-374-27037-6   LC 83-14100

Analyzed in Short story index
Contents: Take pity; The first seven years; The mourners; Idiots first; The last Mohican; Black is my favorite color; My son the murderer; The German refugee; The maid's shoes; The magic barrel; The Jewbird; The letter; In retirement; The loan; The cost of living; Man in the drawer; The death of me; The bill; God's wrath; Rembrandt's hat; Angel Levine; Life is better than death; The model; The silver crown; Talking horse

The tenants. Farrar, Straus & Giroux 1971 230p o.p.

A novel "about Harry Lesser, a Jewish writer whose third novel is not completed after nearly ten years of incessant work. Lesser lives alone, the last occupant of an apartment building located in a dying neighborhood. The clash between Lesser and Willie Spearmint, an aspiring but as yet unpublished black writer who takes over one of the empty apartments, serves as the focus of the novel." Libr J

"A magnificent story is told with grieving insight into some of life's more damaging conflicts and betrayals." Saturday Rev

Malcolm, John, 1936-
The Gwen John sculpture. Scribner 1986 c1985 199p o.p.

LC 85-22255

First published 1985 in the United Kingdom
"The hero is Tim Simpson, the tough young art expert with an easily kindled temper. He had started an art investment fund for a merchant bank. As this story opens, there has been a palace revolution in the bank, and Simpson has been promoted. But he retains control over his fund, and off to France he goes to look for a hitherto unknown Rodin sculpture." N Y Times Book Rev

"A wonderful read, with much information entertainingly served on London banking, the art game, Rodin, and the Hundred Years' War." Booklist

Malone, Michael
Uncivil seasons. Delacorte Press 1983 274p o.p.

LC 83-5166

"The slow moving southern town of Hillston, North Carolina, is in the midst of a rare snow storm when murder strikes down one of its wealthiest citizens. Cloris, wife of state senator Rowell Dollard, has been found in her bedroom, skull crushed, the apparent victim of a robbery. Justin Saville, her nephew, homicide detective, and a member of the Dollard clan, is determined to find the killer even if it means uncovering family secrets and sorrows." Best Sellers

"Interest is held by Malone's brilliant manipulation of suspense and the creation of a range of memorably realized characters. The North Carolina Piedmont town where the story takes place is fleshed out down to the last detail, and a rich seasoning of humor adds zest to the recipe. A first-rate page-turner." Booklist

Malouf, David, 1934-
Remembering Babylon. Pantheon Bks. 1993 200p $20

ISBN 0-679-42724-4   LC 93-7888

Malouf, David, 1934—*Continued*

This novel tells the story of Gemmy Fairley, "an English cabin-boy washed up on the Queensland coast in the 1840s, who is found there by Aboriginals. . . . [Sixteen years later] he is 'found' by some white children. . . . The book tells of the reactions to him of the particular family who take him in, . . . and of those of the school teacher, the minister, and the others he has joined. Amid this, Malouf recalls, in separate chapters, something of the past lives of each of the main characters, in Scotland or England, including that of the white 'native' himself." Times Lit Suppl

"The book is more reflective than polemic. Without excusing the actions of the townsfolk, . . . Malouf shows how difficult original thought is for members of a community that perceives itself as surrounded by danger. The book is a joy to read: richly layered, complex, and dense." Christ Sci Monit

Malraux, André, 1901-1976

Man's fate (La condition humaine); translated by Haakon M. Chevalier. Smith & Hass 1934 360p o.p.

Original French edition, 1933; published in the United Kingdom with title: Storm in Shanghai

"The time is 1927, during the unsuccessful Communist uprising in China. The author focuses on three types of revolutionaries. Ch'en, a Chinese terrorist, believes that Chiang Kai-shek must be killed to start a revolution and is willing to sacrifice himself to bring this about. Kyo, half-French, half-Japanese, is drawn to the revolution because of his belief in human dignity. He finds it difficult to reconcile the idealistic theories of Marx with the political realities of the revolution. Katov, a Russian who has had experience in the revolution in his own country, feels there is strength in the solidarity of his comrades. Though their attempts at revolution fail, each man dies feeling he has given meaning to his life trying to bring change to China." Shapiro. Fic for Youth. 3d edition

Man's hope; translated from the French by Stuart Gilbert and Alastair Macdonald. Random House 1938 511p o.p.

Original French edition, 1937; published in the United Kingdom with title: Days of hope

The story of the first eight months of the Civil War in Spain based on the author's experiences as commander of the Loyalist government's international air force

"Vividly realistic as it is, the book is remarkably free from the senseless dwelling upon physical injuries which often weakens the effect of war novels. M. Malraux has concentrated upon the essential rather than the incidental horrors of war, of civil war in particular." Manchester Guardian

Malraux, Georges André *See* Malraux, André, 1901-1976

Mann, Paul

Season of the monsoon; a novel. Fawcett Columbine 1993 339p $20

ISBN 0-449-90768-6   LC 92-54998

"Handsome, careworn Detective Georgt Sansi is chosen to investigate the discovery of a hideously mutilated corpse on the grounds of Film City, India's answer to Hollywood. Sansi's discoveries lead him into both India's past and present-day England in an effort to catch a copycat killer whose sadistic appetite is easily satisfied in India, where most everything—including the police—is for sale. Mann's characters are invigoratingly fresh . . . and his insights into Indian religious and social history bring the tale to stunning, thought-provoking life." Booklist

Mann, Thomas, 1875-1955

Nobel Prize in literature, 1929

The black swan; translated from the German by Willard R. Trask. Knopf 1954 141p o.p. University of Calif. Press reprint available $24.50 (ISBN 0-520-07008-9)

LC 90-38617

Original German edition, 1953; this is a reissue of the 1954 Knopf edition

"A short novel about the infatuation of a middle-aged widow in Düsseldorf for the young American tutor of her son. Frau Rosalie von Tümmler had always worshipped nature; when she suddenly returned to the sexual vigor of her youth in the middle of her menopause she thanked nature for this miracle, and set about to consummate her affair. It was never to take place, for in a few weeks Frau Rosalie lay dead from cancer of the uterus." Booklist

"None of the characters is developed with enough amplitude to make them very interesting, and Mann lavishes all his attention on the invention of symbolic detail. What determines the pattern of symbolism, of course, is the special quality of Rosalie's experience—the deceptive flowering of life and joy from death and corruption." New Repub

Buddenbrooks; the decline of a family; translated from the German by John E. Woods. Knopf 1993 648p $35

ISBN 0-679-41994-2   LC 92-18990

Also available Everyman's library edition

Original German edition, 1901. First United States edition translated by H. T. Lowe-Potter published 1924 in two volumes

"Mann's first novel, it expressed the ambivalence of his feelings about the value of the life of the artist as opposed to ordinary, bourgeois life. The novel is the saga of the fall of the Buddenbrooks, a family of merchants, from the pinnacle of their material wealth in 1835 to their extinction in 1877." Merriam-Webster's Ency of Lit

Confessions of Felix Krull, confidence man; the early years; translated from the German by Denver Lindley. Knopf 1955 384p o.p. Smith, P. reprint available $21 (ISBN 0-8446-6715-3)

Originally written as a short story in 1921; this novel was first published 1954 in Germany

"Krull, a charming young man with absolutely no moral awareness, avoids military service and takes a job in a hotel. This begins a series of erotic and criminal escapades that eventually lead the young man to prison, from where he purportedly writes his confessions. Like many of Mann's characters, Krull represents the artist, and his profession indicates the symbolic connection in Mann's mind between the artist and the actor, or charlatan." Reader's Ency. 3d edition

Mann, Thomas, 1875-1955—*Continued*
Death in Venice

In Mann, T. Death in Venice and seven other stories p3-84

In Mann, T. Stories of three decades

Death in Venice and seven other stories; translated by H. T. Lowe-Porter. Modern Lib. 1992 461p $15.50

ISBN 0-679-60040-X   LC 92-25325

Analyzed in Short story index

A reissue of the edition first published 1954 by Vintage Books

Contents: Death in Venice; Tonio Kröger; Mario and the magician; Disorder and early sorrow; A man and his dog; The blood of the Walsungs; Tristan; Felix Krull

Death in Venice is a "symbol-laden story of aestheticism and decadence. . . . As in his other major works, Mann explores the role of the artist in society. The cerebral Aschenbach summons extraordinary discipline and endurance in his literary work, but his private desires overwhelm him." Merriam-Webster's Ency of Lit

Joseph and his brothers; translated from the German by H. T. Lowe-Porter; with a new introduction by the author. Knopf 1948 xxi, 1207p $65

ISBN 0-394-43132-4

An omnibus edition of the author's tetralogy based on the Biblical story of Joseph

Contents: The tales of Jacob; Young Joseph; Joseph in Egypt; Joseph the provider

The tales of Jacob (1933; first United States edition 1934 with title: Joseph and his brothers) is mainly the story of Jacob. It describes his long service with Laban, the deception by which Leah was palmed off on Jacob in place of Rachel, the birth of Leah's sons and of Rachael's Joseph, and Rachel's death in childbirth

Young Joseph (1934; first United States edition 1935) centers on adolescent Joseph, his father's favorite and the object of his brother's mounting jealousy. After he describes his arrogant dreams and flaunts his beautiful "picture robe," his brothers sell him to an Ishmaelite trader

In Joseph in Egypt (1936; first United States edition 1938 in 2 volumes) Joseph is now owned by Potiphar and eventually becomes the household steward. He rejects the advances made by Potiphar's wife who throws him into prison for revenge

Joseph the provider (1943; first United States edition 1944) describes Joseph's imprisonment, rise to power, life in Pharaoh's court, reunion with his brothers and father, settlement in Egypt and death

In these tales "Mann has expanded the original story tremendously, but most of the added episodes contribute not so much to the tale itself as to the characters' depth and symbolic significance. In its over-all attitude, the 'Joseph' tetralogy is neither ambiguous like 'The Magic Mountain' nor tragic like 'Doktor Faustus,' but unqualifiedly redemptive." Reader's Ency. 3d edition

Joseph in Egypt

In Mann, T. Joseph and his brothers p447-840

Joseph the provider

In Mann, T. Joseph and his brothers p843-1207

The magic mountain

Some editions are:

Knopf $35 translated from the German by John E. Woods (ISBN 0-679-44183-2)

Modern Lib. $19 translated by H. T. Lowe-Porter (ISBN 0-679-60041-8)

Original German edition, 1924

This novel "tells the story of Hans Castorp, a young German engineer, who goes to visit a cousin in a tuberculosis sanatorium in the mountains of Davos, Switz. Castorp discovers that he has symptoms of the disease and remains at the sanatorium for seven years, until the outbreak of World War I. During this time, he abandons his normal life to submit to the rich seductions of disease, introspection, and death. Through talking with other patients, he gradually becomes aware of and absorbs the predominant political, cultural, and scientific ideas of 20th-century Europe. The sanatorium comes to be the spiritual reflection of the possibilities and dangers of the actual world away from the magic mountain." Merriam-Webster's Ency of Lit

Stories of three decades; translated from the German by H. T. Lowe-Porter. Modern Lib. 1961 c1936 567p o.p.

First published 1936 by Knopf and analyzed in Short story index

This volume contains 21 short stories and three novellas: Tonio Kröger, Tristan, and Death in Venice

Short stories included are: Little Herr Friedemann; Disillusionment; Dilettante; Tobias Mindernickel; Little Lizzy; Wardrobe; Way to the churchyard; Hungry; Infant prodigy; Gladius Dei; Fiorenza; Gleam; At the prophet's; Weary hour; Blood of the Walsungs; Railway accident; Fight between Jappe and Do Escobar; Felix Krull; Man and his dog; Disorder and early sorrow; Mario and the magician

The novellas are psychological studies. Tonio Kröger is concerned with the struggle between the artist and normal citizen. Tristan's concern deals with music's irrational and frequently destructive powers. Death in Venice is entered separately

The tales of Jacob

In Mann, T. Joseph and his brothers p3-258

Tonio Kröger

In Mann, T. Stories of three decades

Tristan

In Mann, T. Stories of three decades

Young Joseph

In Mann, T. Joseph and his brothers p261-444

Mansfield, Katherine, 1888-1923

The garden party and other stories. Knopf 1991 xxxv, 267p $15

ISBN 0-679-40539-9   LC 91-53004

"Everyman's library"

Contents: The tiredness of Rosabel; Frau Brechenmacher attends a wedding; The swing of the pendulum; A birthday; Millie; The woman at the store; Bains Turcs;

Mansfield, Katherine, 1888-1923—*Continued*
An indiscreet journey; The little governess; Prelude; Bliss; A married man's story; Carnation; This flower; The man without a temperament; The daughters of the late colonel; Her first ball; The voyage; At the bay; The garden party; Honeymoon

The short stories of Katherine Mansfield. Knopf 1937 688p o.p.

Analyzed in Short story index

Contents: The tiredness of Rosabel; How Pearl Button was kidnapped; The journey to Bruges; A truthful adventure; New dresses; Germans at meat; The baron; The sister of the baroness; Frau Fischer; Frau Brechenmacher attends a funeral; The modern soul; At Lehmann's; The Luft bad; A birthday; The child-who-was-tired; The advanced lady; The swing of the pendulum; A blaze; The woman at the store; Ole Underwood; The little girl; Millie; Pension Séguin; Violet; Bains turcs; Something childish but very natural; An indiscreet journey; Spring pictures; The little governess; The wind blows; Prelude; At the bay; Late at night; Two tuppenny ones, please; The black cap; A suburban fairy tale; Psychology; Carnation; Feuille d'album; A dill pickle; Bliss; Je ne parle pas Francais; Sun and moon; Mr. Reginald Peacock's day; Pictures; See-saw; This flower; The wrong house; The man without a temperament; Revelations; The escape; Bank holiday; The young girl; The stranger; The lady's maid; The daughters of the late colonel; The life of Ma Parker; The singing lesson; Mr. and Mrs. Dove; An ideal family; Her first ball; Sixpence; The voyage; The garden-party; Miss Brill; Marriage à la mode; Poison; The doll's house; Honeymoon; A cup of tea; Taking the veil; The fly; The canary; A married man's story; The dove's nest; Six years after; Daphne; Father and the girls; All serene; A bad idea; A man and his dog; Such a sweet old lady; Honesty; Susannah; Second violin; Mr. and Mrs. Williams; Weak heart; Widowed

Mansfield, Kathleen Beauchamp *See* Mansfield, Katherine, 1888-1923

Mapson, Jo-Ann
Hank and Chloe; a novel. HarperCollins Pubs. 1993 310p o.p.

LC 92-53377

"Chloe Morgan lives for horses and her dog, Hannah. To earn a slight living and keep bill collectors satisfied, she waits tables at a greasy spoon and teaches horseback riding on the side. Home is a cabin in the backwoods minus electricity or running water. She meets Hank, a college professor, and both find magic where neither expected it." Libr J

"The setting is a small town in Southern California, populated with cowboy types like Wes, the owner of Wes's Feed and Tack, where Chloe pawned her prize saddle; and Hugh Nichols, the owner of the ranch where Chloe's shack stands. . . . First novelist Mapson lines her unsentimental tale of the modern West with real people and an especially strong sense of place." Booklist

March, William, 1893-1954
The bad seed. Rinehart 1954 247p o.p. Buccaneer Bks. reprint available $21.95 (ISBN 1-56849-107-7)

"Rhoda Penmark at 8 years of age had a mind of her own and a will to match. Aged people doted on her splendid manners, but rogues knew her as one of themselves while older children were afraid of her. Christine, her mother suddenly discovers her daughter's horrible tendencies and also finds out that she is the murderess of two people who stood in her way. Christine resolves to check back and finds that she had been adopted and that the mother she had never known had also been a successful killer. Christine tries to stop the pattern in her daughter, but in the process dies herself." Libr J

Marius, Richard C.
After the war; [by] Richard Marius. Knopf 1992 621p $24.50

ISBN 0-394-58322-1 LC 91-23212

"Paul Alexander is running from his past: his Greek heritage, his father's crimes, but mostly, the loss of his two friends, Guy and Bernal, in World War I. Paul leaves Europe and accepts a job in Bourbonville, Tennessee, planning to return to Greece when he has fully recovered from his war wounds, but he soon finds himself enmeshed in the lives and stories of the small town's inhabitants, including the ongoing struggle between the Klan and the town's black residents. Nor is he able to escape the past; Guy and Bernal, ghosts now, are with him always, urging him to not forget them." Booklist

"A wondrous odyssey, this moving novel is a deep meditation on whether our lives are shaped by destiny or a chain of accidents." Publ Wkly

Markandaya, Kamala, 1924-
A handful of rice; a novel. Crowell 1966 297p o.p.

"A John Day book"

"Ravi, the young man, has run away from his village home [in India] to escape its poverty and the lack of opportunity. In the city he first finds outlet for his ambitions and rebelliousness with a gang of street thieves but then is sucked into the poverty mill when he falls in love with a pretty girl and becomes assistant to her father, a poor tailor with an innate dignity but a long heritage of servility." Booklist

"There are curious echoes of Western proletarian novels here, without the revolutionary hope which relieved their somber gloom. . . . Recommended as a depressing but honest portrayal of a culture with too many people and scarcely the material means to satisfy their barest needs." Libr J

Shalimar. Harper & Row 1983 c1982 341p o.p.

LC 82-48838

"A Cornelia & Michael Bessie book"

First published 1982 in the United Kingdom with title: Pleasure city

"The Shalimar of the title is a 20th-century pleasure resort being built on the Indian coast by AIDCORP, a huge, multinational conglomerate. Markandaya tells the story of the people involved in and affected by it: Tully, descended from the consuls who once ruled India, now

Markandaya, Kamala, 1924———*Continued*
on the board of AIDCORP, who is also rebuilding his family castle nearby; Rikki, a 15-year-old native fisher boy taught by British missionaries; Zavera, the ebullient wife of an Indian director; Heblekar, the liaison officer who sometimes wonders about this intrusion into his country; Corinna, Tully's restless and dissatisfied wife; Mrs. Pearl, a dowager who comes to Shalimar as a guest and decides to stay on." Libr J

The author's "novelistic gifts are marked by delicate perception, a sharp ironic sense of human foibles and subtle insights into the strange encounters of diverse cultures radically separated by a common history and language." Publ Wkly

Marlowe, Hugh, 1929- *See* Higgins, Jack, 1929-

Maron, Margaret •
Bootlegger's daughter. Mysterious Press 1992 261p $18.95

ISBN 0-89296-445-6   LC 91-58021

This mystery takes place in "Cotton Grove, N.C., a close-knit rural community on the outskirts of Raleigh, and introduces savvy Deborah Knott, a lawyer whose singular upbringing as a child of a bootlegging power broker has prepared her well for the county race for district court judge. But just as she begins her campaign . . . Deborah is asked to turn over the dead leaves of an 18-year-old murder case. It seems that the daughter of an old flame can't start her life until she finds out who killed her mother as she watched with uncomprehending infant eyes." N Y Times Book Rev

Shooting at loons. Mysterious Press 1994 229p $18.95

ISBN 0-89296-447-2   LC 93-47141

"District Court Judge Deborah Knott, a native North Carolinian, looks forward to filling in for a sick colleague at the Harker's Island courthouse. But on her first fishing trip after arriving on the island, she discovers the body of an old fisherman known to her since childhood. . . . The down-home prose flows well, spiced by Judge Knott's wit, charm, and extended family as well as by references to the local food and drink." Libr J

Southern discomfort. Mysterious Press 1993 241p $17.95

ISBN 0-89296-446-4   LC 92-56770

Newly appointed judge Deborah Knott, "threads her way through the intricacies of district court in a small North Carolina town where familial connections abound. Murder rears its ugly head only after shared family stories and relationships establish a stylistic context. Employing her intimate knowledge of the place, Knott discovers who assaulted her teenaged niece and killed a randy building inspector inside an unfinished WomenAid house." Libr J

"Maron's written a thriller that simply oozes southern charm and atmosphere. The clever plot is full of surprises—a good blend of menace, poignancy, and humor. But perhaps Maron's real strength is her refreshing heroine, who doesn't mind admitting she wears a size fourteen dress and who approaches life with humor, determination, and good sense." Booklist

Marquand, John P. (John Phillips), 1893-1960
H. M. Pulham, esquire. Little, Brown 1941 431p o.p.

"Harry Pulham, a Back Bay Bostonian born in 1892, went to the right school, the right college, and knew only the right people. He recalls it all as he prepares to write a record for the twenty-fifth reunion of Our Class at Harvard. It is apparent that his only touches with actual life had been the World war and his love for a New York advertising girl. After this brief interlude he returned to Boston, married the proper girl, and his life went on as usual. . . . The treatment is sympathetic in spite of the satire." Booklist

The late George Apley; a novel in the form of a memoir. Little, Brown 1937 354p $18.95

ISBN 0-685-03075-X
Also available from Buccaneer Bks.

"George Apley, the epitome of the proper Bostonian, has his life reviewed here by another Bostonian, Mr. Willing. The supposed author, also Marquand's creation, is so stuffy himself that the narration has an element of humor that neither man would have been able to recognize. Although Apley was indeed an upright citizen, this narration, however unwittingly, points out the numerous times that he almost fell from grace and the mixed feelings he had when his own children managed to escape from the 'net' of proper Boston society." Shapiro. Fic for Youth. 3d edition

Point of no return. Little, Brown 1949 559p o.p.

This novel describes some decisive days in the life of Charles Gray. At the end of the week he expects to learn if he is to be promoted to the vice-presidency of his New York bank; but in the meantime business takes him to his home town in Massachusetts where he reviews his past life

"Here is the delicate dissection, the evocation of aura, the alert, unfailing eye for the idiosyncrasy which has become an integral part of the individual, which has marked Marquand's best work. . . . His quiet irony plays over this novel constantly, clarifying the quiet, occasionally melancholy passages of the sections which recreate Charles Gray's youth, and sharpening, pointing delicately and clearly the tensions and the desperately followed formulae of the man he has become." Saturday Rev

Márquez, Gabriel García *See* García Márquez, Gabriel, 1928-

Marsh, Jean, 1934-
The House of Eliott. St. Martin's Press 1994 c1993 265p $20.95

ISBN 0-312-10996-2   LC 94-2671
Also available Thorndike Press large print edition
First published 1993 in the United Kingdom

"The Eliotts are Beatrice and Evangeline, a pair of sisters in 1920s London who discover that their father's death has left them too little to survive on in genteel leisure. Their decision to open a dressmaking salon gives their close relatives apoplexy, but the young women are determined, and they are aided by several charming men who support their enterprise and fall in love with them

Marsh, Jean, 1934-—*Continued*

to boot. There's plenty of period detail in this involving story, particularly regarding the issues of poverty, unemployment, and class discrimination." Booklist

Marsh, Dame Ngaio, 1899-1982

Black as he's painted. Little, Brown 1974 260p o.p. Buccaneer Bks. reprint available $27.95 (ISBN 1-56849-307-X)

Also available G.K. Hall large print edition

The novel's protagonist, Superintendent Alleyn of Scotland Yard, is a former classmate of the "President of the African nation called Ng'ombwana, who plans a state visit to London but is impatient of security precautions. . . . An attempt is made on [President] Bartholomew Opala's life . . . but the Ng'ombwanan Ambassador is killed instead, and the murder is done in the Ng'ombwanan Embassy, which makes things difficult for both the Special Branch and for Scotland Yard." Best Sellers

Clutch of Constables. Little, Brown 1969 244p o.p.

Available from Amereon and Buccaneer Bks.

First published 1968 in the United Kingdom

"An adroitly designed tale in which Alleyn in two places and his wife alone on a short Thames cruise dovetail information leading to the capture of a picturesque gang. Motives, murders, and suspense quite freshly invented and depicted." Barzun. Cat of Crime. Rev and enl edition

Colour scheme. Little, Brown 1943 314p o.p. Amereon reprint available $22.95 (ISBN 0-88411-474-0)

Inspector Roderick Alleyn of Scotland Yard appears two thirds of the way through this tale of mystery and international espionage. "Colonel and Mrs. Claire run a modest spa in northern New Zealand. The inmates are an odd lot, including a down-at-the-heels drunkard, a businessman who is a bounder, a Shakespearean actor, and the actor's secretary. One of the guests is murdered in a boiling mud pool which was originally used for health purposes." New Yorker

Dead water. Little, Brown 1963 244p o.p. Amereon reprint available $21.95 (ISBN 0-88411-475-)

Scotland Yard's Superintendent "Roderick Alleyn finds himself involved unofficially in magic and faith healing when his former French teacher, now a formidable lady of 80, inherits an island off the coast of Cornwall which has, as its chief claim to fame and source of income, a Pixie Well supposed to cure warts, asthma and other ills. . . . Skillful writing, convincing atmosphere, and sharply etched characterization will please Ngaio Marsh fans, but the plot is less complex than some of her others." Publ Wkly

False scent. Little, Brown 1959 273p o.p. Amereon reprint available $21.95 (ISBN 0-88411-484-8)

This mystery "takes place in the opulent London home of a famous—and temperamental—actress on her 50th birthday anniversary. The flamboyant people surrounding Mary Bellamy are properly subdued only when the polished Roderick Alleyn of Scotland Yard and his capable assistant, Inspector Fox, enter the scene and uncover the ugly secrets that led to murder." Libr J

Grave mistake. Little, Brown 1978 252p o.p. Amereon reprint available $20.95 (ISBN 0-8488-0577-1)

LC 78-16910

"When a rich eccentric old lady in a rest home suddenly dies, friends and the police suspect murder. [Inspector] Alleyn's trail leads him to the old lady's daughter, her fiance, his father, a close friend, and a few assorted others including a Scots gardener—named Gardener! When a will turns up leaving all her money to the doctor who runs the rest home, the supposed case of suicide really becomes murder." West Coast Rev Books

Last ditch. Little, Brown 1977 265p o.p.

LC 76-52287

The novel takes place on one of the Channel Islands, to which Ricky, Superintendent Roderick Alleyn's son, "has come during the Easter vacation to write a novel. Here he meets Jasper and Julia Pharamond, friends of his parents, and falls in love with the magnolia-skinned Julia. . . . A riding expedition ends in a fatal accident, attended by suspicious circumstances; at the same time Ricky stumbles, he thinks, across the tracks of a gang of drug smugglers. But Scotland Yard's attention has already been called to the island, and Chief Superintendent Alleyn and Inspector Fox are soon on their way there." Times Lit Suppl

Light thickens. Little, Brown 1982 232p o.p. Amereon reprint available $19.95 (ISBN 0-8488-0579-8)

LC 82-13085

"A production of *Macbeth*, directed by Peregrine Jay at the Dolphin Theatre, is beset with macabre incidents. During rehearsals, realistic-looking dummy heads turn up in dark corners and on banquet trays, and a rat's head is found in the witch's effects. But the incidents cease, and reviews call the production 'the flawless *Macbeth*'—until the night when the actor playing Macbeth is decapitated during the play. Roderick Alleyn is, of course, in the audience." Libr J

Photo finish. Little, Brown 1980 252p o.p. Amereon reprint available $19.95 (ISBN 0-8488-0580-1)

LC 80-16697

"A temperamental and stupid diva is pursued by a spiteful 'paparazzo' who specializes in unflattering pictures. Alleyn is seconded by Scotland Yard to go to New Zealand at the request of the singer's friend, a dubious magnate, and is accompanied by Troy, Alleyn's painter-wife. They arrive for the premiere of a bad opera, the work of the singer's latest protégé, a handsome, stupid young man. All the guests are gathered at a lonely lodge, isolated by a storm. The singer is killed, and Alleyn investigates as whiffs of Sicilian vendetta seep out." Libr J

Singing in the shrouds. Little, Brown 1958 272p o.p. Amereon reprint available $21.95 (ISBN 0-88411-494-5)

Seeking the killer of a girl delivering flowers to a departing freighter-cruise ship, Inspector Alleyn of Scotland Yard boards the ship as it leaves London. His first problem is to discover whether the murderer is actually on board but there are no clues, though each of his oddly assorted shipmates seems suspect. To solve

Marsh, Dame Ngaio, 1899-1982 — *Continued*
the mystery, Alleyn sets the stage for the slayer to kill again

When in Rome. Little, Brown 1971 260p o.p. Amereon reprint available $21.95 (ISBN 0-88411-498-8)

Available G.K. Hall large print edition

First published 1970 in the United Kingdom

Set in Italy, "much of the action takes place in an ancient church which reproduces three levels of civilization. . . . The mystery centers on a sinister blackmailing tour entrepreneur who gathers together a motley group of people, some innocent, some with good reason to want him out of the way. Drugs, sex orgies, even more delicate scandals are all grist to his mill and when he meets a very nasty demise the field of suspects is wide open. Not the least of the pleasures here is a charming love affair, and the slightly comic opera encounters between English Inspector Roderick Alleyn and the Rome police." Publ Wkly

Marshall, Catherine, 1914-1983
Christy. McGraw-Hill 1967 496p il o.p. Buccaneer Bks. reprint available $27.95 (ISBN 1-56849-309-6)

This novel is based on the life of the author's "mother, Christy, who at 19 in 1912 joined an interdenominational mission in Cutter Gap, Ky. The transition from a genteel home to rugged life in the Kentucky backwoods is major, but Christy meets it with courage and enthusiasm. In her first year of teaching in a makeshift school she learns much about herself, and even more about the feuding, primitive, clannish folk she ministers to." Publ Wkly

Julie. McGraw-Hill 1984 364p o.p.
LC 84-4448

"Julie Wallace is a fetching, exuberant 18-year-old whose father has given up a post as a minister in Alabama (supposedly due to ill health) and purchased a smalltown newspaper in Pennsylvania. . . . The community and newspaper work give the lively teenager the opportunity to pursue her writing ambitions and also lead to some chaste romantic entanglements. Her father receives renewed faith and self-confidence from his work and from a showdown with the steel magnate." Booklist

"Readers will be moved by the Wallace family's triumphs, through hard work and unstoppable faith, during a critical time in America's history." N Y Times Book Rev

Marshall, Paule, 1929-
Daughters. Atheneum Pubs. 1991 408p $19.95

ISBN 0-689-12139-3   LC 91-8219

This novel deals with "the culture of blacks in the United States and in the West Indies. The book . . . shifts back and forth between New York City, home of Ursa Beatrice Mackenzie, and the Caribbean island Triunion, Ursa's birthplace and home of her father, a political reformer known simply as the PM, and her American-born mother Estelle. When the story opens, Ursa has just had an abortion and is about to end a stagnant relationship with her long-time boyfriend. She is called to Triunion by Estelle in an attempt to deter

the PM from making a deal that could ruin his career." Libr J

This novel "attempts to look at black experience in our hemisphere, to praise what progress has been made and to point to what yet needs to be done. In its willingness to take real stock, to find true answers to complex questions, it is a brave, intelligent and ambitious work." N Y Times Book Rev

Praisesong for the widow. Putnam 1983 256p o.p.
LC 82-13215

This novel "tells of a sixtyish widow, Avey Johnson, refined, well-to-do, and complacent. Troubled by strange dreams and symptoms, she cuts short her annual Caribbean cruise and disembarks on a small island. An old man recognizes her as one of the 'people who can't call their nation,' and persuades her to join him and others on their yearly ritual visit to a neighboring island they call home. There, purged of her old self, Avey rediscovers her roots." Libr J

Marshall, Sarah Catherine Wood *See* Marshall, Catherine, 1914-1983

Marsten, Richard, 1926-
For works written by this author under other names see Hunter, Evan, 1926-; McBain, Ed, 1926-

Martha, Henry *See* Harris, Mark, 1922-

Martin, George R. R.
Sandkings
In The Best of the Nebulas p547-76
In The Hugo winners v5 p70-132
A song for Lya
In The Hugo winners v3 p483-544

Martin, Malachi
King of kings; a novel. Simon & Schuster 1981 c1980 480p o.p.
LC 80-23950

The author "manipulates almost a surfeit of material— David's endless bloody battles, his perplexing relationship with Adonai in the midst of other gods, his loves and lovers, his friends, his extended family—into a fiery mosaic of a God-haunted man who forged the settlement of Zion." Publ Wkly

"A colorful reworking and elaboration of the biblical story of King David. The great scenes from David's life . . . are played out in heroic terms as Martin paints an epic portrayal that owes more to the cinematic style of Cecil B. DeMille than it does to either the religious or literary elements of the original story." Booklist

Vatican; a novel. Harper & Row 1986 657p o.p.
LC 85-42645

The author "compresses the history of the modern Roman Catholic church into . . . the 40 years since World War II. Its focus is the highly secret inner workings of the Vatican State in Rome, a religious and political bureaucracy that affects not only its members but

Martin, Malachi—*Continued*

also individuals and events around the world. The novel opens with the arrival in Rome of Richard Lansing, who at age 24 is the youngest ranking monsignor in the powerful archdiocese of Chicago. We watch as he develops from a politically naive but dedicated religious into a papal emissary and eventually into the highest ranking leader of the Catholic church. . . . This authentic depiction of the world's richest, most powerful religion will stun readers with its revelations and intrigue them with its multitextured plot." Booklist

Martin, Valerie

The great divorce. Talese 1994 340p $22.50

ISBN 0-385-42125-7　　　　LC 93-5227

This novel, set in New Orleans, interweaves the stories of three women. "Ellen, a zoo veterinarian, is trying to cope with a mysterious outbreak of illness among the animals and the knowledge that Paul, her historian husband, has fallen in love with a younger woman. Elisabeth, the subject of Paul's researches, is the legendary 'cat woman' of Louisiana, who became a leopard and murdered her abusive husband. Camille, with a seemingly tenuous grasp on reality, has frightening fantasies that she is becoming one of the great cats she works with at the zoo." Libr J

The author's gaze "is fixed on a tougher reality than a melodramatist's: she looks at a family that isn't dysfunctional, at two people who are neither bored with each other nor with their lives, who still love each other deeply, and sees that divorce can nonetheless happen. And in comprehending how that can be, she leads her reader to comprehend the complex tragedy of it." N Y Times Book Rev

Mary Reilly. Doubleday 1990 263p $18.95

ISBN 0-385-24968-3　　　　LC 89-38313
Also available Thorndike Press large print edition

In this retelling of Robert Louis Stevenson's Dr. Jekyll and Mr. Hyde, "Mary Reilly, a loyal, trusted servant in the household of Dr. Jekyll records in her diary the mysterious circumstances which lead to her Master's tragic fate." Libr J

"Whereas the atmosphere of Robert Louis Stevenson's tale was all foggy nights and sinister uncertainties, Mary Reilly weaves a somewhat more ambiguous but equally gripping web of mystery around the same riveting events. In both cases the end product is a fascinating story." Quill Quire

Martin, William, 1950-

Cape Cod. Warner Bks. 1991 652p $21.95

ISBN 0-446-51510-8　　　　LC 90-50534

In this historical saga the author "follows two intertwined yet bitterly antagonistic families from their Pilgrim origins to the present day." Publ Wkly

"Martin embraces the entire sweep of American history with unflagging relish for authentic detail and private moments. He creates generation after generation of feisty Hilyards and cruel Bigelows, pitting them against one another in religious and political skirmishes and joining them in risky love. They endure hardships and shipwrecks, scandal and imprisonment, shame and anger, and contribute their bit to the making of America." Booklist

Martini, Steven Paul

Compelling evidence; [by] Steve Martini. Putnam 1992 379p o.p.

　　　　LC 91-30253
Available G.K. Hall large print edition

"Ben Potter, successful lawyer and possible U.S. Supreme Court nominee, is found dead in his office—suicide or murder? All of the police evidence points to foul play, and his beautiful young wife, Talia, stands trial for a crime she claims she didn't commit—or did she? Paul Madriani defends Talia, but, in doing so, exposes a part of his own life that he would like to forget." SLJ

"Besides giving us the scoop on ballistics analysis and post-mortem blood distribution, the author answers just about every cynical question you've ever had about the games lawyers play." N Y Times Book Rev

Prime witness; [by] Steve Martini. Putnam 1993 384p $21.95

ISBN 0-399-13802-1　　　　LC 93-16908
Also available G.K. Hall large print edition

"When attorney Paul Madriani offers to assist a friend—the county's ailing district attorney, who subsequently dies—in investigating six brutal killings, he becomes entangled in a series of machinations that threaten his career and even his private life." Publ Wkly

"The novel effectively relays the great demands of being a district attorney and also depicts the behind-the-scenes maneuverings of a trial." Booklist

Undue influence; [by] Steve Martini. Putnam 1994 462p $22.95

ISBN 0-399-13932-X　　　　LC 94-10144
Also available G.K. Hall large print edition

"Recently widowered lawyer Paul Madriani has problems with his sister-in-law Laurel. She is involved in a nasty custody trial, and then she is arrested for the murder of her ex-husband's new wife. After Paul agrees to represent her, he gets sucked into a vipers' tangle involving Laurel, her two children, her ex-husband, a beautiful attorney, a bombing, and mistaken identities." Libr J

"The action builds to a rousing climax through a brilliant series of trial scenes with several surprises. The characters are sharply drawn, the facts of the case are presented simply and the courtroom psychology is laid out vividly." Publ Wkly

Marut, Ret *See* Traven, B.

Mason, Bobbie Ann

Feather crowns. HarperCollins Pubs. 1993 454p o.p.

　　　　LC 92-56227

This novel "tells the story of Chrissie Wheeler, a tobacco farmer's wife in Hopewell, Kentucky, who, in 1900, gives birth to America's first recorded quintuplets. Curiosity seekers pass in a steady stream through the Wheeler's small farmhouse. When the babies take ill and die, Chrissie and her husband are persuaded to go on tour, displaying the grotesquely painted bodies of the dead infants to the idly curious." Libr J

"Mason's triumph here is to make her uneducated, bewildered heroine as vivid as the country life she describes." Publ Wkly

Mason, Bobbie Ann—*Continued*

In country; a novel. Harper & Row 1985 247p o.p.

LC 85-42579

"Sam, 17, is obsessed with the Vietnam War and the effect it has had on her life—losing a father she never knew and now living with Uncle Emmett, who seems to be suffering from the effects of Agent Orange. In her own forthright way, she tries to sort out why and how Vietnam has altered the lives of the vets of Hopewell, Kentucky." SLJ

This novel is "written with disarming simplicity not because its author lacks linguistic resources but because she knows intimately the prosaic character of small-town life in her corner of the South. She also knows exactly what she wants to say, whether about the difficult process of growing up, the daily routines of country people or the larger national dramas that unite all sorts of people." N Y Times Book Rev

Love life; stories. Harper & Row 1989 241p o.p.

LC 88-45535

Analyzed in Short story index
Contents: Love life; Midnight magic; Hunktown; Marita; The secret of the Pyramids; Piano fingers; Bumblebees; Big Bertha stories; State champions; Private lies; Coyotes; Airwaves; Sorghum; Memphis; Wish

"Moments of insight emerge in Mason's stories as her Kentuckian characters encounter life's twists and turns. . . . The immediacy of these stories comes not just from Mason's frequent use of the present tense, or her often-criticized references to Wal-Mart and MTV, but, most of all, from her impressive ability to cut to the innermost emotions of a wide range of characters." SLJ

Shiloh and other stories. Harper & Row 1982 247p o.p.

LC 82-47541

Analyzed in Short story index
Contents: Shiloh; The rookers; Detroit Skyline, 1949; Offerings; Still life with watermelon; Old things; Drawing names; The climber; Residents and transients; The retreat; The ocean; Graveyard day; Nancy Culpepper; Lying doggo; A new-wave format; Third Monday

"Capturing in vivid detail the emotional frustrations of her characters and the unsettling ambience of her small-town Kentucky settings, Mason portrays the uneasy feelings of people who don't know what they want out of life but who do know that what they have isn't it." Booklist

Spence + Lila; illustrations by La Nelle Mason. Harper & Row 1988 176p il o.p.

LC 87-46155

"The Harper short novel series"
"This novel begins with a journey to a hospital and ends in a vegetable garden. In between, Mason contrasts the cold, clinical procedures of high-tech medicine with the simple but satisfying rituals of rural life. Lila's cancer temporarily separates her from her husband Spence, but as the book's title suggests, their love is abiding. Both rely on fond memories of their shared past to allay fears about the future." Libr J

"There are real strengths displayed in this novel. A particular kind of warmth presses through from time to time. Miss Mason's superb ear for dialogue is evident." N Y Times Book Rev

Mason, Richard, 1919-

The world of Suzie Wong. World Pub. 1957 344p o.p.

Available from Amereon and Buccaneer Bks.

The love story of an impecunious English painter and a charming Chinese prostitute. Robert, not understanding Chinese, takes a room in a Hong Kong hotel thinking he has found a cheap boarding house. When it becomes apparent to him that it is a house of prostitution he stays on, partly to paint the girls, and partly because he cannot afford anything better. It is here he meets Suzie

"Though the book may be a little distasteful to some readers it is never sordid or unwholesome. Suzie and the other girls have a high moral code— in their fashion." Libr J

Massie, Allan, 1938-

Caesar. Carroll & Graf Pubs. 1994 c1993 228p $20

ISBN 0-7867-0121-8   LC 94-26430

This is the third in the author's projected quartet of novels set in ancient Rome, begun with Let the emperor speak (1987) and Tiberius (1993)

First published 1993 in the United Kingdom

"Decimus Junius Brutus, a Roman general and one of Julius Caesar's closest friends, was one of the conspirators who killed Caesar on the Ides of March in 44 B.C. In this fictional memoir written while awaiting his death in Gaul, Brutus (cousin to the better known Marcus Junius Brutus) attempts to justify the murder by recounting Caesar's ever-growing lust for total power and his unbecoming desire to outshine Alexander the Great. Brutus and his friends believe that Caesar's megalomania has led him to betray the Roman Senate and destroy the Republic." Libr J

This work "offers an evocative portrait of ancient Rome as well as a gripping and suspenseful analysis of the most intriguing conspiracy of all time. Superb historical fiction." Booklist

Masters, John, 1914-1983

Bhowani Junction; a novel. Viking 1954 394p o.p.

A novel of modern India just prior to independence, in which the heroine is Victoria Jones, a young Anglo-Indian, who is confused by her racial status

"Skillful portrayal of character, racial animosities and Indian life, and full of exciting incident. Some scathing pictures of British Army officers." Libr J

Matera, Lia

Prior convictions. Simon & Schuster 1991 204p o.p.

LC 90-25203

"Lawyer Willa Jansson finishes a miserable, lonely year with an L.A. law firm and, to the delight of her hippie parents, moves back to San Francisco to accept a clerkship with liberal federal court judge Michael J. Shanna. Willa is asked by a former boyfriend to find out for Rita Delacort the intentions of her estranged husband, Phil, should she decide to seek a divorce. After Willa talks to Phil, Judge Shanna disqualifies himself from a securities-fraud case in which Phil is an attorney, on the pretext that Willa's conversation might prejudice the case.

Matera, Lia—*Continued*

Willa is confused at first, but later feels used." Publ Wkly

Matthiessen, Peter

Far Tortuga. Random House 1975 408p il o.p.

"Far Tortuga is the name given by West Indian turtle-fishing men to a remote inlet south of Cuba that is not found on modern charts. . . . To hunt the last turtles of the season Capt. Raib Avers sails from Grand Cayman island with a ragged crew in an even more ragged boat, the [Lillias] Eden. . . . The boat tacks about the cays and reefs off the coast of Nicaragua. It is too late to find more than a few turtles. As discord and desperation mount, the crew talks about better days: the folklore of hurricanes and pirate captains, of shipwrecks, ghosts and 'wild niggers' smuggled into Florida. . . . Avers, as a last gamble, strikes out for Far Tortuga." Newsweek

"Almost casually, we have been given a full measure of suspense, adventure, and first-rate descriptive writing; and along with and underneath these things, a group of characters who come fully alive with a complexity and even depth that the usual, traditional story of men at sea never gives us." Choice

Killing Mister Watson. Random House 1990 372p $21.95

ISBN 0-394-55400-0   LC 89-43424

Also available Thorndike Press large print edition

This historical novel "traces the growth of the legend of Edgar J. Watson, a famed outlaw in the Florida Everglades of a hundred years ago." Voice Lit Suppl

"By the time he was murdered, Watson was one of the most successful sugar-cane farmers between Tampa and Key West. Everyone liked and admired him, but no one trusted him. Proof was always scant but people wound up dead when Watson was around. . . . Matthiessen tells his story through the voice of Watson's family and neighbors in a series of oral histories, diary entries and old newspaper accounts, all of it fiction. By turns droll, rambunctious, foolish and wise, this collective narration mounts into a carefully orchestrated cacophony of contradictory testimony in which suspicion and mistrust are gradually revealed as the base elements of mystery." Newsweek

On the river Styx and other stories. Random House 1989 208p $17.95

ISBN 0-394-55399-3   LC 86-3206

Analyzed in Short story index

Six of the stories included in this collection originally appeared in book form in Midnight turning gray, published 1984 in paperback by Ampersand Press

Contents: Sadie; The fifth day; The centerpiece; Late in the season; Travelin man; The wolves of Aguila; Horse latitudes; Midnight turning gray; On the River Styx; Lumumba lives

Matthiessen's "stories delve into brutal facets of humankind and show the often hapless responses of well-intentioned individuals. Bitter scenes of racism are portrayed in several stories, including the title piece, in which a white couple on an innocuous fishing vacation sparks a violent racial backlash." Booklist

Maugham, Somerset *See* Maugham, W. Somerset (William Somerset), 1874-1965

Maugham, W. Somerset (William Somerset), 1874-1965

The best short stories of W. Somerset Maugham; selected, and with an introduction by John Beecroft. Modern Lib. 1957 489p o.p.

Analyzed in Short story index

Contents: The letter; The verger; The vessel of wrath; The hairless Mexican; Mr. Harrington's washing; Red; Mr. Know-All; The alien corn; The bookbag; The round dozen; The voice of the turtle; The facts of life; Lord Mountdrago; The colonel's lady; The treasure; Rain; P. & O.

Cakes and ale; or, The skeleton in the cupboard. Doubleday, Doran 1930 308p o.p.

This novel, Maugham's "most genial book, is a comedy about the good-natured Rosie Driffield, the wife of a Grand Old Man of Letters; whom most took to be based on Hardy; Alroy Kear, a self-promoting writer, was recognized as Hugh Walpole." Oxford Companion to Engl Lit. 5th edition

Complete short stories. Doubleday 1952 2v o.p.

Analyzed in Short story index

Ninety-one stories are included in this collection. The first volume includes all those previously published in "East and West." The second volume, "The World Over," contains the rest of Maugham's short stories

Contents: v 1: Rain; Fall of Edward Barnard; Mackintosh; Red; Honolulu; The pool; The letter; Before the party; Force of circumstance; The outstation; Yellow streak; P. & O.; Jane Round dozen; Creative impulse; Miss King; Hairless Mexican; Giulia Lazzari; The traitor; His Excellency; Mr. Harrington's washing; Footprints in the jungle; Human element; Virtue; Alien corn; The book-bag; Vessel of wrath; Door of opportunity; Back of beyond; Neil MacAdam

v2: Woman of fifty; Man with the scar; The bum; Closed shop; Official position; Man with a conscience; French Joe; German Harry; Four Dutchmen; End of the flight; Flotsam and Jetsam; Casual affair; Mr. Know-All; Straight flush; Portrait of a gentleman; Raw material; Friend in need; The dream; The taipan; The consul; Mirage; Mabel Masterson; Marriage of convenience; Princess September; In a strange land; Lotus eater; Salvatore; Washtub; Mayhew; Happy man; Point of honour; The mother; Romantic young lady; The poet; Man from Glasgow; Lion's skin, Three fat women of Antibes; Happy couple; Voice of the turtle; Facts of life; Gigolo and gigolette; Appearance and reality; The luncheon; The unconquered; Ant and the grasshopper; Home; The escape; Judgment seat; Sanatorium; Louise; Lord Mountdrago; String of beads; The promise; The verger; Social sense; Colonel's lady; Episode; The kite; The treasure; Winter cruise

East and West

In Maugham, W. S. Complete short stories v1

The moon and sixpence. Doran, G.H. 1919 314p o.p.

"Based closely on the life of Paul Gauguin it tells of Charles Strickland, a conventional London stockbroker, who in middle life suddenly decides to desert his wife, family, and business in order to become a painter. He

Maugham, W. Somerset (William Somerset), 1874-1965—*Continued*

goes to paint in Tahiti, where he takes a native mistress. Eventually Strickland dies of leprosy." Reader's Ency. 3d edition

Of human bondage.
Available from various publishers

First published 1915

This novel's "hero is Philip Carey, a sensitive, talented, club-footed orphan who is brought up by an unsympathetic aunt and uncle. It is a study of his struggle for independence, his intellectual development, and his attempt to become an artist. Philip gets entangled and obsessed by his love affair with Mildred, a waitress. After years of struggle as a medical student, he marries a nice woman, gives up his aspirations, and becomes a country doctor. The first part of the novel is partly autobiographical, and the book is regarded as Maugham's best work." Reader's Ency. 3d edition

The razor's edge; a novel. Doubleday, Doran 1944 343p o.p.
"The novel is concerned in large part with the search for the meaning of life and with the dichotomy between materialism and spirituality. The main focus of the story is on Larry Darrell, who has returned from service as an aviator in World War I utterly rejecting his prewar values. He is concerned chiefly with discovering the meaning of human existence and eliminating evil in the world. To that end, he spends five years in India seeking—but not finding—answers." Merriam-Webster's Ency of Lit

World over
In Maugham, W. S. Complete short stories v2

Maugham, William Somerset *See* Maugham, W. Somerset (William Somerset), 1874-1965

Maupassant, Guy de, 1850-1893

The collected stories of Guy de Maupassant. Avenel Bks. 1985 10v in 1 1003p o.p.
LC 84-20316

Analyzed in Short story index

A reissue of the 1903 edition published by Walter Black, Inc. with title: The complete short stories of Guy de Maupassant

The dark side of Guy de Maupassant; a selection and translation by Arnold Kellett with introduction and notes; foreword by Ramsey Campbell. Carroll & Graf Pubs. 1989 252p o.p.
LC 89-511

Analyzed in Short story index

Contents: The Horla; The Devil; Two friends; Fear; The hand; Coco; The mannerism; The madwoman; Mohammed-Fripouille; The blind man; At sea; Apparition; Saint-Antoine; The wolf; Terror; The diary of a madman; A vendetta; The smile of Schopenhauer; On the river; He?; Old Milon; The head of hair; The inn; Mother Savage; Was he mad?; The dead girl; Mademoiselle Cocotte; A night in Paris; The case of Louise Roque; The drowned man; Who knows?

Maupin, Armistead

Maybe the moon; a novel. HarperCollins Pubs. 1992 307p o.p.
LC 92-52596

The heroine of this novel is Cadence Roth. "All of 31 inches tall, Cady played Mr. Woods, an E.T.-like character, in a hit movie a decade ago. Now 30 years old, she performs at birthday parties and bat mitzvahs, on the fringe of an industry that doesn't have much need for chubby dwarfs. . . . Cady records daily life with her dizzy, star-struck roommate Renee, the physical challenge of turning on a shower, discrimination by people, and harassment by dogs. She begins a . . . romance with a tall, handsome pianist and then, with her best friend, Jeff—a writer active in gay politics—she plots her comeback." Libr J

"Maupin has created a funny, memorable character in Cadence Roth. Fiercely independent, unapologetic about her pint size and gallons of desire, combative, quick-witted, she is a person readers will recall long after all the topical references in this novel have faded." Times Lit Suppl

Maurois, André, 1885-1967

The collected stories of André Maurois; translated by Adrienne Foulke. Washington Sq. Press 1967 396p o.p.
Analyzed in Short story index

Contents: Reality transposed; Darling, good evening; Lord of the shadows; Ariane, my sister . . . ; Home port; Myrrhine; Biography; Thanatos Palace Hotel; Friends; Dinner under the chestnut trees; Bodies and souls; The curse of gold; For piano alone; The departure; The fault of M. Balzac; Love in exile; Wednesday's violets; A career; Ten years later; Tidal wave; Transference; Flowers in season; The will; The campaign; The life of man; The Corinthian porch; The Cathedral; The ants; The postcard; Poor Maman; The green belt; The Neuilly Fair; The birth of a master; Black masks; Irene; The letters; The cuckoo; The house

Maxwell, Patricia, 1942-

For works written by this author under other names see Blake, Jennifer, 1942-

Maxwell, William, 1908-

All the days and nights; the collected stories of William Maxwell. Knopf 1995 415p $25
ISBN 0-679-43829-7   LC 94-27509

Analyzed in Short story index

Contents: Over by the river; The Trojan women; The pilgrimage; The patterns of love; What every boy should know; A game of chess; The French scarecrow; Young Francis Whitehead; A final report; Haller's second home; The gardens of Mont-Saint-Michel; The value of money; The thistles in Sweden; The poor orphan girl; The lily-white boys; Billie Dyer; Love; The man in the moon; With reference to an incident at a bridge; My father's friends; The front and the back parts of the house; The holy terror; What he was like; A love story; The industrious tailor; The country where nobody ever grew old and died; The fisherman who had nobody to go out in his boat with him; The two women friends; The carpenter; The man who had no friends and didn't want any; A fable begotten of an echo of a line of verse by

Maxwell, William, 1908——_Continued_

W.B. Yeats; The blue finch of Arabia; The sound of waves; The woman who never drew breath except to complain; The masks; The man who lost his father; The old woman whose house was beside a running stream; The pessimistic fortune-teller; The printing office; The lamplighter; The kingdom where straightforward, logical thinking was admired over every other kind; The old man at the railroad crossing; A mean and spiteful toad; All the days and nights

This "volume is conclusive evidence that Maxwell stands at the pinnacle of American letters." Publ Wkly

May, Julian, 1931-

The adversary. Houghton Mifflin 1984 xxxviii, 470p il (Saga of Pliocene exile, v4) o.p.

LC 83-49065

"In this concluding volume of the quartet, King Aiken and the children of the telepathic rebels, exiled from the future Milieu, must fight against Marc Remillard and his allies, the Firvulag. This book will be barely intelligible to those unfamiliar with the rest of the saga—despite May's extensive synopsis—but it should keep the author's regular readers turning pages." Booklist

Blood Trillium. Bantam Bks. 1992 391p o.p.

LC 92-2888

Second in a fantasy series that started with Black Trillium by Marion Zimmer Bradley, Julian May, and Andre Norton

"The kingdom of Laboruwenda finds itself on the verge of war as a sorcerer thought to be dead returns to reclaim the three talismans of power held by Queen Anigel and her sisters, Kadiya and Haramis." Libr J

"A superior tale, giving life, character and emotion to the three Petals of the Living Trillium as they continue their adventures." Publ Wkly

Followed by Golden Trillium by Andre Norton

Diamond mask; a novel. Knopf 1994 461p $22

ISBN 0-679-43310-4   LC 93-37802

The second book in the Galactic Milieu trilogy is "set in the year 2113 and told through the memoirs of Rogatien Remillard, the story looks back on events that took place half a century earlier, when humanity became part of a vast galactic civilization. Remillard's family, virtually immortal and psychically gifted, has become Earth's most powerful force. On the death of the evil Victor Remillard in 2040, an insane metapsychic creature known as Fury comes into being." Publ Wkly

The author "maintains a personal focus on her luminary characters, opening their private lives to intense scrutiny while at the same time expanding the boundaries of an imaginative future world. Rich in intrigue and vibrating with creative energy, this is a superb addition to sf collections." Libr J

The golden torc. Houghton Mifflin 1982 xxv, 381p il (Saga of Pliocene exile, v2) o.p.

LC 81-4126

"In this second volume of the saga, May continues the story of the diverse group of time-exiles we met in the first book and shows how they help to bring about the overthrow of the Tanu and the closing of the time gate. . . . May develops her premises seriously and gives

her large cast of characters a surprising amount of life." Publ Wkly

Followed by The nonborn king

Intervention; a root tale to the Galactic milieu and a vinculum between it and the Saga of Pliocene exile. Houghton Mifflin 1987 546p o.p.

LC 87-4021

"As a follow-up to her popular four-volume Saga of Pliocene Exile, May offers this linking novel to a new trilogy, The Galactic Milieu. Here, covering the years from 1945 to 2013, she parallels the accelerating arms race with the all-too-slow development of humanity's extrasensory powers. Only the latter will allow Earth to ask for the intervention of the Galactic Milieu, the occupants of whose observation vessels have watched events with dismay." Publ Wkly

"May's novel is characterized by passages of enormous power and brilliance alternating with irritating lapses of tone. Its shortcomings aside, this effort promises well for the trilogy and is certain to have a large audience." Booklist

Jack the bodiless; a novel. Knopf 1992 463p o.p.

LC 91-53176

This is the first volume of the projected Galactic Milieu trilogy describing events that precipitated the action of the author's Saga of Pliocene exile tetralogy. "As a consortium of five alien races stands ready to accept Earth as a full partner in the Galactic Milieu, the birth of a very special child heralds a new stage in human evolution. . . . May combines a compelling vision of humanity's future with the drama and political intrigue surrounding the Remillard family, whose metapsychic powers and personal ambitions shape the destiny of the world." Libr J

Followed by Diamond mask

The many-colored land. Houghton Mifflin 1981 415p (Saga of Pliocene exile, v1) o.p.

In this first volume of a four part saga "a one-way, fixed-focus time portal to Europe in the Pliocene epoch allows the prehistoric past to become a last frontier and a refuge for misfits fed up with the well-ordered world of the 22nd century. This novel follows the adventures of a group newly arrived in Exile. They are prepared for almost anything but what they actually find, a world ruled by humanoid aliens who can control them with artificially augmented psionic powers. The arrogant, beautiful Tanu are opposed, however, by the ugly, outcast Firvulag. Allied with them the humans may hope to overthrow the Tanu and win the freedom they came for. Deftly combining SF and the Celtic myths of the Tuatha de Danaan, Julian May has made a most enjoyable entertainment that will have readers eagerly turning pages." Publ Wkly

Followed by The golden torc

The nonborn king. Houghton Mifflin 1983 xli, 394p il (Saga of Pliocene exile, v3) o.p.

LC 82-11950

"There is a new balance of power among the 22nd century's voluntary exiles to the Europe of 6-million years ago and the two factions of aliens (Tanu and Firvulag) they found waiting for them there. The humans are no longer slaves, and one of them, a trickster upstart named Aiken Drum, becomes the Tanu king. A new element is introduced in the form of yet another group

May, Julian, 1931-—*Continued*
of (involuntary) exiles, the remnants of the Metapsychic Rebellion of 2083. Beams of mental force clash spectacularly as Aiken seeks their help against Felice, the mad psychic prodigy, and in defending his throne against Tanu traditionalists." Publ Wkly

Followed by The adversary

(jt. auth) Bradley, M. Z. Black Trillium

Mayle, Peter
Hotel Pastis; a novel of Provence. Knopf 1993 389p $23

ISBN 0-679-40229-2   LC 93-14641

Also available Thorndike Press large print edition

"Encouraged by a sprightly young Frenchwoman, burned-out advertising executive Simon Shaw buys the local gendarmerie in Luberon, France and turns it into a hotel. Unfortunately, the visitors who crowd the town once the hotel opens include an escaped thief intent on a bank robbery." Libr J

The author "displays his satiric eye for social foibles by skewering advertising execs in England and the U.S.; he is equally adept at evoking typical Provencal villagers. Wickedly sharp and sympathetic at the same time, his characterizations are accurate down to nuances of class differences, voice, accent and vocabulary." Publ Wkly

Mayo, Jim, 1908-1988
For works written by this author under other names see L'Amour, Louis, 1908-1988

Mazursky, Paul
(jt. auth) Greenfeld, J. Harry and Tonto

McAuley, Paul J.
Red dust. Morrow 1994 c1993 392p $22

ISBN 0-688-13793-8   LC 95-100132

"An AvoNova book"

First published 1993 in the United Kingdom

In this science fiction novel "after centuries of stifled terraformation efforts, the Martian landscape is reverting to its native red dust, and many of its citizens are voluntarily relinquishing their bodies to merge with a ubiquitous computer mainframe. While contemplating his own future, agronomy technician Wei Lee becomes caught in the cross fire of warring political factions when he rescues a captured female soldier from the enemy asteroid belt. As the devious agenda of his government is exposed, Wei Lee becomes a linchpin in changing the planet's ultimate destiny. McAuley's far-reaching vision comfortably brings together such diverse elements as cloning, nanotechnology, cyberspace, and novel political ideologies." Booklist

McBain, Ed, 1926-
For works written by this author under other names see Hunter, Evan, 1926-

Another part of the city; a novel. Mysterious Press 1986 c1985 230p o.p.

LC 85-43170

"Uptown Manhattan is where Olivia Kidd forces her brother Sarge to sell his beloved collection of paintings as ordered by their father, a Texas trillionaire. Downtown, Detective Reardon seeks for clues to the gunmen who have shot Ralph D'Annunzio dead in his restaurant. Robbery isn't the motive; there seems to be none, nor can Reardon make a connection between D'Annunzio and a second murder victim, a lawyer killed after leaving a stock broker's office. By diligently investigating the dead men's last days, however, the detective begins to put together bits of a puzzle with appalling implications. . . . McBain's practiced skills rivet one to the story of human vultures and their prey." Publ Wkly

Blood relatives; an 87th Precinct mystery. Random House 1975 178p o.p.

"The story opens with a young girl, Patricia Lowery, running hysterically into the station house with bloody palms and face. Her murdered companion, Muriel Stark, is found almost simultaneously by another detective from the 87th, Steve Carella. Miss Lowery's initial story of what happened contains the specification of some 'perfect stranger' as the culprit. Soon thereafter, however, she changes her story and identifies her brother Andy as the murderer. You may or may not be ahead of Detective Carella when he finally pieces together what really occurred." Best Sellers

Cinderella. Holt & Co. 1986 262p o.p.

LC 85-24766

"This Cinderella is a hooker, who, finding herself down and out in Miami Beach and Lauderdale, decides to abscond with a drug magnate's secret cache of cocaine. Hoods of all sorts set out to find her, and our hero, the engaging lawyer Mr. Hope, becomes involved in this seedy, sleazy slice of underworld life." Best Sellers

Death of a nurse. Penzler Bks. 1994 184p $22

ISBN 1-56287-061-0   LC 93-49477

First published 1955 in paperback under pseudonym Richard Marsten, with title: Murder in the navy

A navy nurse is "found strangled in the radar shack of the *U.S.S. Sykes*. When a yeoman suspected of the crime takes a fatal nosedive from the fantail, the naval brass, eager to close the case, feels that justice has been served. Lieutenant Chuck Masters thinks the suicide may have tied up the loose ends a bit too quickly. . . . Alone, Masters must follow his instincts and track down a ruthless killer." Publisher's note

Downtown; a novel. Morrow 1991 301p $20

ISBN 0-688-08736-1   LC 89-32521

"The protagonist, Michael J. Barnes, is an orange grower from Florida, in New York City on business with his ad agency, and with a couple of hours to kill before catching his plane. Fat chance. In short order his wallet and credit cards are stolen, his car is stolen and he is framed for murder. In attempting to clear his name, get some money and get out of town, though not necessarily in that order, Michael finds himself teamed up with Connie Kee, a beautiful Chinese woman on the trail of killers and dope dealers." N Y Times Book Rev

"As a tour de force of kinetic plotting, *Downtown* is pretty much in a class of its own, but McBain tops off the whole weird concoction with giddy layers of stop-start dialogue, an inflamed level of sexual awareness, and oodles of film lore." Booklist

Eight black horses; an 87th Precinct novel. Arbor House 1985 250p il o.p.

LC 85-7348

McBain, Ed, 1926-—*Continued*

"The Deaf Man, scourge of McBain's famed 87th precinct, returns to plot his biggest coup in this . . . thriller. While Carella, Hawes, Brown, Kling and the other detectives investigate the murder of a woman bank teller, their legendary adversary sends them clues to his operation. . . . By switching the narrative from activities at the precinct to a description of the psychotic's fail-safe plan, the author keeps the tension at white heat from the first word to the shattering conclusion of the drama." Publ Wkly

Fuzz; an 87th Precinct mystery. Doubleday 1968 240p o.p.

A mystery novel involving Detective Steve Carella and the Deaf Man. An extortionist threatens assassination of important city officials, and despite all precautions the first murder "is carried out on schedule. As the importance of the official increases, so does the amount of money demanded. The blazing climax rises above the long arm of coincidence that pulls it together." Libr J

Ghosts; an 87th Precinct novel. Viking 1980 212p o.p.

LC 79-26557

Detectives "Steve Carella and Cotton Hawes are assigned to track down the murderer of a woman stabbed outside her apartment house. Later, they get a call reporting the killing of author Gregory Craig in the same building. Craig's lover, Hillary Scott, claims her psychic powers can help solve the cases. She persuades Carella to take her to the colonial house in Massachusetts where Craig had written his bestseller, 'Deadly Shades.'" Publ Wkly

Goldilocks. Arbor House 1978 c1977 233p o.p.

LC 77-80173

"Jamie Purchase's first wife dubbed the intruder into their marriage 'Goldilocks.' When the second Mrs. Purchase and her two daughters are brutally murdered, Jamie divulges the tawdry details of his current affair. There is sharp irony here for Matthew Hope, Jamie's lawyer, who is himself involved in an extramarital relationship. Hope's guilt runs like a leitmotif through the search for the murderer." Publ Wkly

Heat; an 87th Precinct novel. Viking 1981 227p o.p.

LC 81-65263

"Jeremiah Newman's death was almost definitely suicide, but certain details—for instance, the air conditioning was off on a 99 degree day—bother Detective Steve Carella. His partner, Bert Kling, has other problems—his wife may be cheating on him and someone's taking shots at him." Libr J

Ice; a major new novel about the world of the 87th Precinct. Arbor House 1983 317p o.p.

LC 82-74061

"A dancer in a hit musical, a cocaine-pushing punk, and a middle-aged diamond merchant have all been 'iced' the same gruesome way, with the same weapon. Searching for the missing links, the cops fan out through a variety of urban enclaves, from the ghetto to the theater district, from high-rent high-rises to 'Ramsey University.'" Newsweek

A "vivid, often brutal, description of life in the ghetto with its subculture of hookers, pushers, addicts, burglars, muggers, rapists and even savage killers. Yet despite this, it is not without its moments of humor, tenderness, compassion and occasional optimism." Best Sellers

Jack and the beanstalk. Holt, Rinehart & Winston 1984 250p o.p.

LC 83-12928

"A young ne'er-do-well, Jack McKinney, wants [lawyer Matthew] Hope to handle the purchase of a seemingly doomed, 15-acre snap-bean farm. Three days later, McKinney is dead from multiple stab wounds. Hope then becomes entangled in the events surrounding a cattle ranch owned by McKinney's strangely ungrieving mother." Booklist

"Mastery of dialogue, local color, well-drawn minor characters, and an intricate but believable story line make this memorable." Libr J

Jigsaw; an 87th Precinct mystery. Doubleday 1970 161p il o.p.

"A band of robbers leaves pieces of a photograph of the location of stolen money to scattered persons whose lives are put in jeopardy by the inheritance. Detectives of the New York 87th precinct put the pieces of both picture and crime together." Booklist

Kiss; a novel of the 87th Precinct. Morrow 1991 351p o.p.

LC 91-15908

Available G.K. Hall large print edition

"Detective Steven Carella must investigate the attempted murder of beautiful Emma Bowles while his father's murderer is tried in the city's courts. Emma's wealthy, handsome stockbroker husband imports a bodyguard for her from Chicago, who stays on the job even after the man who twice tried to kill Emma is found shot *and* hung. Carella and partner Meyer Meyer know something's not right, and doggedly keep investigating. Stoically, Carella also sits in court wondering if his father's killer will be convicted." Booklist

"With its interwoven threads of violence, tenderness and world-weary ruminations on the breakdown of urban life, this is hardboiled mystery in the tradition of Chandler and Hammett. And the ending features the best kind of twist: it's both surprising and satisfying." Publ Wkly

Lightning; an 87th Precinct novel. Arbor House 1984 304p o.p.

LC 84-3030

"A grotesque series of crimes confronts the officers of the 87th Precinct. First, two women college track stars are found hanging, lynch-mob style, from the lampposts of brilliantly lit city streets; and then a rapist who harbors wild psycho-sexual/religious hang-ups stalks an ever-increasing number of victims, torturing them through repeated attacks. A key role in catching the maniac is played by gutsy Eileen Burke, an undercover officer in Special Forces whose aggressive work puts her own life in peril. Filled with realistic police procedure, cop humor, and eerie action." Booklist

Lullaby; an 87th Precinct novel. Morrow 1989 350p o.p.

LC 88-13709

"Returning from a party, a couple find their adopted baby and her teenaged sitter murdered. There are so many ramifications, including the later death of the biological mother, that the case seems hopelessly muddled. But Carella and Meyer, outraged by the crime, stick to

McBain, Ed, 1926——*Continued*

the wearying routine and finally bring the guilty to book. . . . McBain's staccato dialogue and authentic characters, as always, make . . . [this] a page turner." Publ Wkly

Mary, Mary. Warner Bks. 1992 372p $19.95

ISBN 0-446-51738-0   LC 92-50569

A "Matthew Hope courtroom drama. Contrary Mary is crusty former schoolteacher Mary Barton, who may be the crazed murderer and mutilator of three young girls. Hope, a lawyer who defends only those he genuinely believes are innocent, makes that judgment about Mary on the basis of the elaborate garden she has grown. As the trial proceeds, Hope's belief in Mary's innocence looks dumber and dumber." Booklist

"Although the macabre explanation for Mary's behavior is too much of a psychological stretch, it doesn't detract from Mr. McBain's neck-snapping dialogue, his dynamic court scenes or his vigorous character study of a woman with the brains and nerve to teach 'Women in Love' to 12-year-old girls." N Y Times Book Rev

Mischief; a novel of the 87th Precinct. Morrow 1993 346p $20

ISBN 0-688-10221-2   LC 93-10404

"The Deaf Man, nemesis of the beleaguered 87th Precinct, is back, and he's scattering cryptic clues all over town, which only serves to multiply the frustrations of Detective Steve Carella and his coworkers. Not that their usual potpourri of crime doesn't offer its own fair share of frustration: graffiti writers are turning up dead in a series of seemingly random killings; mentally impaired senior citizens are being 'dumped' on local hospitals; and, in a city on the edge of racial violence, a free outdoor concert is expected to attract a quarter-million rap fans. . . . McBain tackles social issues . . . tells a good joke, reveals small details of his regular characters' personalities, and provides subplots that add depth and humanity to all the crime in the foreground." Booklist

The mugger. Armchair Detective Lib. 1990 150p $17.95

ISBN 0-922890-29-3   LC 90-32352

First published 1956 in paperback

In this 87th Precinct mystery the police "must contend with a plethora of eccentric criminals, including a guy who steals household cats and a mugger who attacks women, then bows debonairly and offers a polite fairwell. . . . McBain fans will instantly recognize the crisp dialogue that the series would soon become famous for: a hypnotic mix of terse truths, perpetual perplexities, and crude coptalk." Booklist

Poison; an 87th Precinct novel. Arbor House 1987 264p o.p.

LC 86-17342

"Detectives Steve Carella and Hal Wallis interrogate beautiful, wealthy Marilyn Hollis when one of her swains dies of poison, possibly a suicide. Marilyn becomes a murder suspect later, as two more men she has been socially and sexually involved with are killed in a development that creates a serious problem for the investigators. Wallis is now the woman's lover, living with her despite Carella's protest. Both detectives continue to track Marilyn's former male companions, looking for a jealous killer. But Wallis, heartsick, begins to believe that Marilyn is guilty. The taut, gripping story closes with a knockout surprise." Publ Wkly

Puss in boots. Holt & Co. 1987 248p o.p.

LC 86-22887

"Pornography, religious fanaticism, and lust for money combine for brutal doings in Calusa, Florida, where McBain's hero, lawyer Matthew Hope, is involved in his first big criminal trial. Hope's attempt to exonerate a man accused of viciously murdering his wife appears thwarted at every turn, until it is revealed that the dead woman, a talented director of commercials and award-winning documentaries, had completed work on an X-rated film with local talent and a potential for earning millions. The forces of greed collide with the outrage of the husband of the film's leading lady, who spouts quotations from Scripture while carving up human flesh." Booklist

Sadie when she died; an 87th Precinct mystery. Doubleday 1972 180p o.p.

"A woman, stabbed to death is found by her husband. He promptly calls the police. In the course of routine questioning, he somewhat ungallantly remarks, 'I'm delighted someone killed her.' Never one to let sleeping remarks lie, Detective Carella stalks the husband, who eventually leads him to the killer." Saturday Rev

Snow White and Rose Red. Holt, Rinehart & Winston 1985 248p o.p.

LC 84-19263

This mystery is "narrated by Matthew Hope, the divorced lawyer based in a Florida Town. Hope's weakness for lovely women creates a horrifying crisis, jeopardizing the life of a person dear to him. The lawyer is besotted by beautiful, brainy Sarah Whittaker, who is confined illegally, she claims, in a mental institution. Hope believes Sarah is sane, the victim of her widowed mother, who has had her daughter committed in order to control the fortune left by Sarah's father. Too late, the lawyer realizes the connection between his client and a murder under investigation by the local homicide squad." Publ Wkly

"For readers who are intrigued by the fine line that exists between sanity and insanity, this mystery will be impossible to put down." Booklist

There was a little girl. Warner Bks. 1994 323p $21.95

ISBN 0-446-51739-9   LC 94-29145

Also available G.K. Hall large print edition

In this Matthew Hope novel "the hero spends most of his time in a semi-coma after being shot outside a bar on the seedy side of Calusa, Fla. . . . Meanwhile, Hope's PI pals Warren Chambers and Toots Kiley, as well as police detective Morris Bloom, try to reconstruct Hope's previous week, probings that are intercut with flashbacks to Hope's own investigation of the years-old suicide of a circus star. What emerges is an intricate, lurid tale of sex, blackmail and murder fueled by greed." Publ Wkly

Three blind mice; a novel. Arcade Pub. 1990 293p $18.95

ISBN 1-55970-080-7   LC 89-18543

Also available G.K. Hall large print edition

In this Matthew Hope mystery "the Calusa, Fla., lawyer takes on a 'hopeless case,' defending Stephen Leeds, arrested for murder. The victims were three Vietnamese tried but found not guilty of raping Leeds's wife, Jessie. Every bit of evidence ties the crimes to Leeds, who had publicly sworn to avenge his wife's abuse, but Hope

McBain, Ed, 1926-—*Continued*
believes in his client and works diligently to free him."
Publ Wkly

"Mr. McBain's square-jawed dialogue and stout grip on detection procedures give his narrative the muscularity characteristic of the whole Hope series. But the real strength to flex those muscles comes from the perfectly constructed plot." N Y Times Book Rev

Tricks; an 87th Precinct novel. Arbor House 1987 247p o.p.

LC 87-11350

Available G.K. Hall large print edition

This novel "begins on a Halloween eve, and with the most unlikely of events. Four kids, wearing costumes and garish masks, hold up a series of liquor stores and kill the proprietors before escaping with their plunder. Detectives Brown and Genero make a grisly discovery in a garbage can—a headless torso. A professional magician, Sebastian the Great, puts on a disappearing act that confounds his attractive wife. She appeals to the police for help. Meanwhile, Detective First Class Eileen Burke draws the unenviable assignment of playing a hooker who is heavily armed and has a fondness for ladies of the evening." West Coast Rev Books

Vespers; a novel of the 87th Precinct. Morrow 1990 331p o.p.

LC 89-13124

"A priest is killed in his church, which is the scene of a standoff between a drug dealer and his assailants. Meanwhile, four blocks away, devil worshippers hold their own religious meetings. The men of the precinct must find the killer, extract the truth from myriad conflicting accounts, and explore the link with the demonic church." Booklist

Widows; a novel. Morrow 1991 332p o.p.

LC 90-49861

Available G.K. Hall large print edition

A novel of the 87th Precinct

"On the same summer night that a young blond woman, the mistress of a wealthy, older, married man, is stabbed to death, detective Steve Carella's father is killed in his bakery by two thieves. Distracted by grief, Carella, with colleague Arthur Brown, investigates the woman's murder, which is followed by the wealthy man's death and those of his first and second wives." Publ Wkly

McCabe, Patrick, 1955-
The butcher boy. Fromm Int. 1993 c1992 215p $19.95

ISBN 0-88064-147-9   LC 93-2831

First published 1992 in the United Kingdom

"Young Francie is a have-not—poor, ignorant, Catholic—in a small Irish town, but he is savvy enough to size up those who do enjoy privilege. His envy is turned up a notch after the deaths of his alcoholic father and emotionally disturbed mother. Francie then engages in increasingly desperate acts, leading to a harrowing depiction of events that are alluded to on the book's first page." Publ Wkly

"'The Butcher Boy' is the side of the murder story never revealed in the newspapers: a map of a murderer's mind, a revelation of a murderer's reason. It is the story of the heritage of madness and loneliness, a stunning picture of the desperation of the unloved." N Y Times Book Rev

McCaffrey, Anne
All the Weyrs of Pern. Ballantine Bks. 1991 404p $20

ISBN 0-345-36892-4   LC 91-91910

"A Del Rey book"

"The dream of generations of Dragonriders draws within reach as, with the aid of an intelligent computer, the possibility of destroying the devastating phenomenon known as 'Thread' becomes a reality." Libr J

"This is an exciting, full-bodied, richly detailed . . . chapter in the Pern chronicle as the knowledge of the first settlers is united with the wisdom of the descendants. . . . Once again McCaffrey's narrative flows smoothly, maintaining the world and characters she has so lovingly created and setting new challenges for them to meet." Booklist

The chronicles of Pern; first fall. Ballantine Bks. 1993 306p $22

ISBN 0-345-36898-3   LC 93-10079

"A Del Rey book"

Analyzed in Short story index

Includes the following stories: The survey: P.E.R.N.; The dolphins' bell; The ford of Red Hanrahan; The second weyr; Rescue run

"These five original stories . . . offer a glimpse into the early history of the world of 'thread' and Dragonriders. McCaffrey's unadorned prose allows characters and plot to take center stage." Libr J

The city who fought; [by] Anne McCaffrey, S.M. Stirling. Baen Pub. Enterprises 1993 435p $19

ISBN 0-671-72166-6   LC 93-2651

Previous titles in this series published in paperback are: The ship who sang (1969); Partnership (1992); and The ship who searched (1992)

"Space Station SSS-900C, a profitable but out-of-the-way trading and mining center, is attacked by Kolnari, pirates from a planet of sociopathic exiles. While awaiting the arrival of the Central Worlds' Navy, the inhabitants play for time with a major deception planned by Simeon, the shellperson operating the station." Publ Wkly

"Within the fabric of McCaffrey's universe, she and Stirling merge seamlessly, sporting wit, action galore, superior characterization, and plausible hardware." Booklist

Followed by The ship who won

Crystal line. Ballantine Bks. 1992 294p o.p.

LC 92-53219

"A Del Rey book"

Sequel to Killashandra

In this conclusion of the trilogy, "crystal singer of the Heptite Guild, Killashandra Ree enjoys the benefits of increased longevity and the status of an elite artisan at a terrible price: the slow erosion of her memory. When the Guild faces a crisis that could result in its demise, Killashandra faces a battle to overcome her own fears and learn to trust in someone other than herself." Libr J

Crystal singer. Ballantine Bks. 1982 311p o.p.

LC 82-4009

McCaffrey, Anne—*Continued*
"A Del Rey book"

In this first volume of a trilogy "Killashandra Ree learns she has failed her final audition despite ten years of all-consuming preparation for a career as a vocal concert soloist. By coincidence that day she meets a vacationing crystal singer, joins him for the remainder of his holiday and becomes acquainted with the side effects and risks of crystal singing. . . . The story ends as she accomplishes a difficult job, cutting and placing black crystal on four remote planets so they may have instant interstellar communication." SLJ

"This is a well-constructed story with a strong-willed and courageous young heroine who finds her niche in the workplace." Voice Youth Advocates

Followed by Killashandra

Damia. Putnam 1992 336p o.p.

LC 91-12416

"An Ace/Putnam book"

Some of the initial events in this novel "overlap with those that conclude *The Rowan* however, they are seen from a different perspective—that of Afra, whose strong mental Talent leads to his becoming second in command to the Rowan. Here, the Rowan remains a secondary character; center stage is held not only by Afra, but also by the Rowan's tempestuous and strong-willed daughter, Damia, who inherits much of her mother's stormy nature and grows up to surpass her parents in telepathic powers." Booklist

"McCaffrey interweaves an engrossing romance with a coming-of-age story as she examines the issue of responsibility in a society where survival depends on the abilities of a gifted few." Publ Wkly

Followed by Damia's children

Damia's children. Putnam 1993 272p $22.95

ISBN 0-399-13817-X   LC 92-31601

"An Ace/Putnam book"

This novel in the author's series about the Talented center's on "Damia and Afra's children. . . . Over three generations, the Talent has increased and broadened, giving Damia's children a combined power greater than any before. And now with the Mrdini discovery of the possible route to the Hive Home System, a new era begins and three of Damia's children become intimately involved in the chase." Booklist

Followed by Lyon's pride

The dolphins of Pern. Ballantine Bks. 1994 340p $22

ISBN 0-345-36894-0   LC 94-15570

"A Del Rey book"

"As the inhabitants of Pern finally near their longtime goal of ridding their world of the hazard of Thread, they regain contact with the *shipfish*, the dolphins that accompanied the earliest human settlers on the planet Tlion, a young dragonrider, and Readis, a boy from a fishing village , are instrumental in rebuilding the ancient partnership between humans and dolphins in preparation for the spread of humanity over the remaining wildernesses of Pern." Booklist

"Though the story reads smoothly and easily, it takes for granted a foreknowledge of Pern that would frustrate newcomers to McCaffrey's world." Voice Youth Advocates

Dragonflight; volume 1 of "The Dragonriders of Pern". Ballantine Bks. 1978 337p il $8.95

ISBN 0-345-27749-X   LC 78-16707

"A Del Rey book"

First published 1968 in paperback. Based on two award winning stories entitled: Weyr search and Dragonrider

The planet Pern, originally colonized from Earth but long out of contact with it, has been periodically threatened by the deadly silver Threads which fall from the wandering Red Star. To combat them a life form on the planet was developed into winged, fire-breathing dragons. Humans with a high degree of empathy and telepathic power are needed to train and preserve these creatures. As the story begins, Pern has fallen into decay, the threat of the Red Star has been forgotten, the Dragonriders and dragons are reduced in number and in disrepute, and the evil Lord Fax has begun conquering neighboring holds

Followed by Dragonquest

Dragonquest; volume 2 of "The Dragonriders of Pern". Ballantine Bks. 1979 351p il $8.95

ISBN 0-345-28030-X   LC 78-19721

"A Del Rey book"

Sequel to Dragonflight

First published 1971 in paperback

The inhabitants of Pern begin to resent the attitudes of the oldtime Dragonriders who were brought forward in time to aid their modern counterparts in defeating the deadly Thread from the Red Star and now feel that their new world owes them a living. The Weyrleader F'lar and his consort Lessa try to mediate between the Dragonriders and the landbound people they had protected, but new forces upset Pern's delicate social structure and threaten to destroy not only the unique privileges of the Dragonriders, but their very reason for existence

Followed by The white dragon

Dragonrider

In The Best of the Nebulas p229-313

Dragonsdawn. Ballantine Bks. 1988 431p o.p. Ultramarine reprint available $25 (ISBN 0-89366-213-5)

LC 88-9307

"A Del Rey book"

Chronologically the first novel in the Dragonriders of Pern series "it tells of the colonizing of the uninhabited planet Pern by a few thousand carefully selected humans, of the colonists' first encounter with the life-threatening spores known as Thread and of the creation (by genetic engineering) of the winged, telepathic, fire-breathing 'dragons' who become the colonists' first line of defense against the periodic falls of Thread." Booklist

The girl who heard dragons. TOR Bks. 1994 352p il $22.95

ISBN 0-312-93173-5   LC 94-118

"A Tom Doherty Associates book"

Analyzed in Short story index

Contents: The girl who heard dragons [novelette]; Velvet fields; Euterpe on a fling; Duty calls; A Sleeping Humpty Dumpty Beauty; The Mandalay cure; A flock of geese; The greatest love [novelette]; A quiet one; If Madam likes you; Zulei, Grace, Nimshi, and the damnyankees; Cinderella switch; Habit is an old horse; Lady-

McCaffrey, Anne—*Continued*
in-waiting; The bones do lie

This is a "diverse assortment of 15 short fiction pieces never before gathered in one volume. The heroine of the engaging title story, a new Pern novella and the only Pern tale in the collection, is somewhat akin to Menolly in *Dragonsong* in that she, too, eventually rises above her birthright to follow the destiny that her particular talent dictates. Perhaps the strongest inclusion here is 'The Greatest Love,' also a novella, which predicted in 1977 (when McCaffrey wrote it) the extrauterine fertilization of a human ovum to produce a healthy baby. . . . Other stories focus on everything from spaceship adventure, shifting time-storms, and the unwitting near-destruction of sentient life-forms by human colonists on a distant planet (and the fitting, if gruesome consequences)—to ghosts and romance." Booklist

The girl who heard dragons [novelette]

In McCaffrey, A. The girl who heard dragons p21-64

The greatest love [novelette]

In McCaffrey, A. The girl who heard dragons p169-225

Killashandra. Ballantine Bks. 1985 303p o.p.

LC 85-6193

"A Del Rey book"

In this second volume of the trilogy "crystal singer Killashandra Ree is desperate to get off the crystal-mining planet of Ballybran, so she takes what at first sounds like a routine assignment replacing a shattered crystal in the main Sensory Organ on planet Optheria. While she is there she is also to find out why Optherians never leave the planet. She is kidnapped and marooned on an isolated island, but escapes, only to encounter her handsome kidnapper Lars Dahl, with whom she eventually falls in love." SLJ

"This suspenseful and romantic story exhibits McCaffrey's usual verve in building convincing societies, developing vital characters, and sustaining mood." Booklist

Followed by Crystal line

The lady. Ballantine Bks. 1987 461p o.p. Ultramarine reprint available $25 (ISBN 0-89366-214-3)

LC 86-92092

This is the "romantic story of a girl and her horse. The novel chronicles a few months in the life of 13-year-old Catriona, in which her enthusiasm for and empathy with horses is seen as the constant against which her family's drama is played out: her mother's death, a new love in the life of her long-widowed aunt Eithne, Catriona's 'adoption' by surrogate mother Selina Healey, her American cousin Pat's summer visit, etc. Sentimentality runs rampant here, but McCaffrey devotees should enjoy it thoroughly." Publ Wkly

Lyon's pride. Putnam 1994 272p $22.95

ISBN 0-399-13907-9   LC 93-33863

"An Ace/Putnam book"

In this installment in the series about the Talented "the human-Mrdini Alliance is still pursuing Hive spheres, hoping to learn more about the combative creatures that, in a search for new planets to settle, destroy the indigenous life forms on any planet they select. McCaffrey is a master at creating aliens that are distinctive and believable and in faithfully maintaining their identities throughout; her human characters, particularly the Talents who are the focus, are equally well developed; and the alien-human interactions, both friendly and hostile, are convincing." Booklist

Pegasus in flight. Ballantine Bks. 1990 290p o.p.

LC 90-92901

"A Del Rey book"

Previous volumes in the Talented series first published in paperback are: To ride Pegasus (1973) and Get off the unicorn (1977)

"As director of the Jerhatten Center for Parapsychic Talents, telepath Rhyssa Owen struggles to protect her psychically gifted people—called 'Talents'—from a world that both fears and wants to exploit their abilities." Libr J

Followed by The Rowan

Power lines; [by] Anne McCaffrey, Elizabeth Ann Scarborough. Ballantine Bks. 1994 313p $20

ISBN 0-345-38174-2   LC 94-6631

"A Del Rey book"

In this sequel to Powers that be, "the sentient planet Petaybee becomes an active force in its inhabitants' battle to prevent the ruling Intergal Company's rape of the planet in search of minerals. When a Petaybean delegation tries to inform Intergal's board of directors of the planet's sentience, the group is accused of being under 'some sort of massively induced hypnotic illusion,' and an official inquiry is set in motion. One of the two investigators, an unsavory and manipulative board member, sets out at once to turn events to his advantage; the other gets to know and works with the people, eventually siding with them." Booklist

The authors "collaborate seamlessly to tell a first-rate sf adventure with strong male and female protagonists and a life-affirming theme." Libr J

Powers that be; [by] Anne McCaffrey and Elizabeth Ann Scarborough. Ballantine Bks. 1993 311p $20

ISBN 0-345-38173-4   LC 92-54992

"A Del Rey book"

"Forced by her ruined lungs to resign from active service with the Company, Major Yanaba Maddock 'retires' to the icebound planet of Petaybee with an order to mingle with the colonists and discover the source of certain anomalies on the planet. What she finds is both a new way of life and a challenge to all the loyalties she has ever known." Libr J

"Infused with an overriding sense of Inuit and Celtic lore, the story is an engrossing one in which characterizations are well defined and suspense is sustained till the planet's secret is revealed." Booklist

Followed by Power lines

The renegades of Pern. Ballantine Bks. 1989 384p il $19.95

ISBN 0-345-34096-5   LC 89-6694

"A Del Rey book"

This title in the author's Dragonriders of Pern series "is a parallel novel, set during the time of her original trilogy and telling about new events that we didn't know were happening, as well as old events through new eyes." Voice Youth Advocates

This tale "begins during the time of *Dragonquest* and continues beyond the closing of *The White Dragon*, focusing on some of the commoners, and how they cope

McCaffrey, Anne—*Continued*

with the return of the life-consuming Thread. A number of lives intertwine, such as that of the trader boy Jayge Lilcamp, whose family is almost destroyed when his father refuses to believe the first Thread warning." Publ Wkly

The Rowan. Putnam 1990 335p o.p.

LC 90-35865

This novel begins a multivolume family saga within the Talented series. "Rowan, a telepathic, telekinetic three-year-old, is the sole survivor of a mining disaster on a frontier planet. As she matures, her powers grow until she becomes one of a handful of 'Primes' with the Federal Telepath & Teleport network, the organization responsible for telecommunications and shipping of cargo throughout the galaxy. Rowan finds herself alienated from humanity and her coworkers due to her unique talents and tremendous responsibilities until she senses Jeff Raven, a fellow talent, on the fringes of explored space. . . . McCaffrey weaves believable characters with a well-written story to produce this entertaining science fiction romance." SLJ

Followed by Damia

The ship who won; [by] Anne McCaffrey, Jody Lynn Nye. Baen Pub. Enterprises 1994 330p $21

ISBN 0-671-87595-7   LC 93-43510

In this episode in the series "the brainship Carialle and her brawn, Keff, find a habitable planet inhabited by an apparent mix of races and cultures and dominated by an elite of apparent magicians. Appearances are deceiving, however, and by the time the explorers have discovered the planet's secrets—not to mention other intelligent races—they find themselves in a desperate battle to save it. . . . [The authors] blend their skills effectively to produce a brisk, well-told, often amusing tale that does not strive to do more than entertain but does so admirably." Booklist

Wehr search

In The Hugo winners v2 p329-87

The white dragon; volume 3 of "The Dragonriders of Pern". Ballantine Bks. 1978 497p il o.p.

LC 77-18913

"A Del Rey book"

Sequel to Dragonquest

"A prologue summarizes the first two volumes of the saga. . . . Young Jaxom and his white dragon Ruth (a male), previously encountered, mature, fight the deadly Threads from the Red Planet, help open the largely unexplored continent and discover in an ancient spaceship a map, key to major changes for Pern. Once all the necessary background is assimilated, it's a rousing adventure and colorful portrayal of a unique and carefully-worked-out culture." Publ Wkly

McCammon, Robert R.

Boy's life. Pocket Bks. 1991 440p o.p.

LC 91-2813

Available Thorndike Press large print edition

"In 1964, 12-year-old Cory Mackenson lives with his parents in Zephyr, Alabama. It is a sleepy, comfortable town. Cory is helping with his father's milk route one morning when a car plunges into the lake before their

eyes. His father dives in after the car and finds a dead man handcuffed to the steering wheel. Their world no longer seems so innocent: a vicious killer hides among apparently friendly neighbors." Libr J

"McCammon is both a precise and lush writer, and thus the trail Cory takes to deciphering the puzzle the dead man represents quickly firms up into a compelling, even haunting yarn of adult demons being faced and fathomed by the young. This look at life's blacker sides is neither cloying nor jejune." Booklist

Gone south. Pocket Bks. 1992 359p o.p.

LC 92-28062

"Dan, dogged by depression and Agent Orange-induced leukemia, has accidentally killed a man. On the run, he meets Arden, a disfigured woman abandoned at a truck stop. He reluctantly agrees to help her on her journey to the Louisiana swamps where, she believes, the legendary Bright Girl will heal her. Meanwhile, an unlikely pair of bounty hunters is on Dan's trail: Flint began life as a carnival freak, with his Siamese twin's tiny arm and half-formed face protuding from his chest; he is saddled with training Cecil, a self-deprecating and pathetically friendly Elvis impersonator. These four misfits collide and, finally, arrive where the Bright Girl may actually live." Libr J

"The plot flows well and quickly. The extreme characters only point up McCammon's theme: everybody has a hidden deformity and can only become free and happy by facing it. An engrossing read." Booklist

Mine. Pocket Bks. 1990 442p o.p.

LC 90-7090

"When her newborn son is kidnapped by a former Sixties radical with a violent, tumultuous past (her nickname is 'Mary Terror'), thirtysomething yuppie Laura Clayborne takes matters into her own hands and pursues Mary across the country." Libr J

"McCammon undercuts his story by portraying all his left-wing characters as motivated by adolescent rebellion, rather than by radical politics. That aside, however, he delivers an expertly constructed novel of suspense and horror." Publ Wkly

McCarry, Charles

The bride of the wilderness; a novel. New Am. Lib. 1988 438p o.p.

LC 87-31535

Set in early 18th century London and the New World. "The central character is the enterprising Fanny, half-English, half-French, who, after various vicissitudes in London, accompanies her godfather, Oliver, when he goes to Connecticut to claim his inheritance. There she is abducted by Indians, taken to Canada and finally rescued by her French lover." Publ Wkly

"Readers will be held spellbound by this indescribably funny, inventive, and most unforgettable caper. Marvelous entertainment." Booklist

McCarthy, Cormac, 1933-

All the pretty horses. Knopf 1992 301p $21

ISBN 0-394-57474-5   LC 91-58560

First volume in the author's projected Border trilogy

In the spring of 1950, after the death of his grandfather, sixteen-year-old John Grady Cole "is evicted from the Texas ranch where he grew up. He and another boy, Lacey Rawlins, head for Mexico on horseback, riding

McCarthy, Cormac, 1933-—*Continued*

south until they finally turn up at a vast ranch in mountainous Coahuila, the Hacienda de la Purísima, where they sign on as vaqueros. . . . John Grady's unusual talent for breaking, training and understanding horses becomes crucial to the *hacendado* Don Héctor's ambitious breeding program. For John Grady, La Purísima is a paradise, complete with its Eve, Don Héctor's daughter, Alejandra." N Y Times Book Rev

"Though some readers may grow impatient with the wild prairie rhythms of McCarthy's language, others will find his voice completely transporting." Publ Wkly

Followed by The crossing

The crossing. Knopf 1994 425p $23

ISBN 0-394-57475-3   LC 94-4281

Also available large print edition $22 (ISBN 0-679-75434-2)

In this second title in the author's Border trilogy "sixteen-year-old Billy Parham is obsessed with trapping a renegade wolf that has crossed the border from Mexico to raid his father's cattle ranch. By the time he finally succeeds, Billy has formed such a close bond with his prey that he decides to return the wolf to its home, and the two head off into the mountains. Billy returns months later to find that his parents have been murdered by horse thieves. He abducts his kid brother from a foster home, and they ride into Mexico to retrieve their property, encountering gypsies, desperadoes, and itinerant philosophers along the way." Libr J

"Mr. McCarthy is a great and inventive storyteller, and he writes brilliantly and knowledgeably about animals and landscapes—but finally the power and delight of the book derive from the fact that he seems incapable of writing a boring sentence. Reading him, one is very much in the hands of a stylist. His basic mode in this book . . . is a version of high modernist spareness and declarative force." N Y Times Book Rev

McCarthy, Mary, 1912-1989

Birds of America. Harcourt Brace Jovanovich 1971 344p o.p. Buccaneer Bks. reprint available $24.95 (ISBN 1-56849-426-2)

The main character is "Peter Levi, a young American who spends his junior year at the Sorbonne at the time of the bombing of Hanoi and who is much preoccupied with Kant's categorical imperative and the Destruction of Art and the Death of Nature. The Death of Nature, in fact, is the central theme. . . . The final scene, in which Peter develops a near-fatal infection after a swan attack and is visited by Kant in a vision, powerfully resolves the author's theme." Libr J

"Miss McCarthy is astringent and sharp in all the right places, gentle where she should be. What she has written is an honest and appropriate love letter to an essentially decent young American." Publ Wkly

Cannibals and missionaries. Harcourt Brace Jovanovich 1979 369p $10.95

ISBN 0-15-115387-6   LC 79-4869

"The action of the novel begins when a plane carrying Americans bound for Iran is hijacked by terrorists. Some passengers are rich art collectors; others are politicians and activists planning to investigate allegations that Savak, the shah's secret police, is using torture against political dissidents. At first the terrorists intend to use the politicians and activists as hostages, but they soon realize that masterworks of art are of more value than any human being and decide to trade the art collectors for their artworks." Merriam-Webster's Ency of Lit

A charmed life. Harcourt Brace & Co. 1955 313p $15.95

ISBN 0-15-116907-1

"John and Martha Sinnott encounter an amazing assortment of would-be bohemians when, in the hope of gaining a new lease on their marriage, they move to the artistic community of New Leeds. They long for privacy but cocktail parties, drama groups, and Martha's first husband Miles keep breaking in. Even Martha's pregnancy brings unforeseen problems for due to one after-the-party interlude the question of fatherhood broadens to two possibilities: John or Miles. The author is at her brilliant best in this comic tragedy of modern man's dilemma: the fluctuation between belief and unbelief, courage and despair." Booklist

The group. Harcourt Brace & Co. 1963 378p $15.95

ISBN 0-15-137281-0

Also available from Buccaneer Bks.

The Group is made of "eight Vassar girls of the class of '33 who had lived together during their upperclass years, in the South Tower of Main. We see them first at the wedding of Kay Strong to Harald Petersen a week after Commencement. . . . We see them last at Kay's funeral seven years later." N Y Times Book Rev

"It is perhaps as social history that the novel will chiefly be remembered; but over and above its sensitive observations it has a quality that one has not come to expect from this particular author, and that is compassion." Saturday Rev

The groves of Academe. Harcourt Brace & Co. 1952 302p o.p.

"An intelligent and sophisticated dissection of faculty life at Jocelyn, a small progressive college in Pennsylvania. The impending dismissal of self-styled liberal, Henry Mulcahy, Joycean scholar and instructor in literature, and the spring Poetry Conference are the main incidents in the narrative; but woven around them and even tying them together quite neatly is the probing, satirical and often deadly accurate account of college administration and personalities. A few of America's leading poets seem to appear pseudonymously during the conference." Libr J

McCauley, Stephen

The easy way out. Simon & Schuster 1992 298p o.p.

LC 91-43832

"Narrator Patrick, a Cambridge, Mass., travel agent in his early 30s, lives with Arthur, an immigration lawyer; but for a long time, Patrick has been sleeping on an air mattress on the floor of their bedroom. His younger brother, Tony, plans to marry his high school sweetheart but is having an affair that is far more satisfying than his relationship with his fiancée. Their older brother, Ryan, is divorced, living at home and working at his parents' hopelessly unprofitable men's clothing store. And McCauley soon makes achingly clear that the parents' marriage is far from happy." Publ Wkly

A "knack for detail, and the way it's applied to the self-delusion of an engaging cast of characters, is what makes 'The Easy Way Out' so satisfying." N Y Times Book Rev

McClure, James, 1939-

The steam pig. Harper & Row 1972 c1971 247p o.p.

Available Thorndike Press large print edition

"A Joan Kahn-Harper novel of suspense"

First published 1971 in the United Kingdom

White Lieutenant Kramer and his Zulu sergeant Zondi investigate the grisly murder of a beautiful white girl in a small South African town

"An absolutely scathing look at contemporary South Africa is provided in [this] . . . novel that is uncanny in its multi-leveled perceptions. It is a grostesquely vivid picture of life under apartheid. But it is also a first-rate mystery with a solution that is a shocker." Saturday Rev

McCorkle, Jill, 1958-

Crash diet; stories. Algonquin Bks. 1992 253p $16.95

ISBN 0-945575-75-0   LC 91-34313

Analyzed in Short story index

Contents: Crash diet; Man watcher; Gold mine; First union blues; Departures; Comparison shopping; Migration of the love bugs; Waiting for hard times to end; Words gone bad; Sleeping Beauty, revised; Carnival lights

"Widows, recent divorcées, teenage girls, retired women, and single mothers populate [this collection]. Each woman imparts to McCorkle's fortunate readers a touching, downright bone-tickling account of her individual struggle in the New South." Libr J

Ferris Beach; a novel. Algonquin Bks. 1990 343p $18.95

ISBN 0-945575-39-4   LC 90-37089

The protagonist and narrator, Katie Burns, tells of growing up in a small town in the South during the 1960s and '70s. "Ferris Beach is where excitement and glamour start—at least that's what Kate thinks as she hears about her cousin Angela who lives there. Kate has had a humdrum, 'normal' childhood; her conservative mother and humorous father have brought her up 'properly,' while Angela has had freedom and romance. But even freedom has its dark side, as Kate finds out." SLJ

"The central metaphor is the place that gives the novel its name—a place associated with ideas of sex, freedom, and broken dreams. . . . Here, Katie will get a powerful dose of reality and suffering rendered so wistfully and obliquely, with multiple forewarnings designed to heighten the sense of foreboding, and a commendable balance of tragedy and mirth, that the full texture of a child's wonder and terror is preserved." Booklist

Tending to Virginia; a novel. Algonquin Bks. 1987 312p $15.95

ISBN 0-912697-65-2   LC 87-1481

Also available G.K. Hall large print edition

"Fears and insecurities about her future and a sense of detachment from her present life drive young, married, pregnant Virginia Sue Turner Ballard to the people and places most familiar to her. Threatened by toxemia, Virginia stays at her grandmother's house for several weeks, surrounded by the women of her family." Libr J

"Characterization is the high mark, with the point of view occasionally shifting among well-defined family members. A quality performance from a talented, potentially prolific young writer." Booklist

McCrumb, Sharyn

The hangman's beautiful daughter. Scribner 1992 306p $19

ISBN 0-684-19407-4   LC 91-46057

"Revisiting some of the characters from If Ever I Return, Pretty Peggy-O . . . McCrumb weaves Appalachian folklore and death, in natural and unnatural forms, into a story that meanders like a mountain stream through the hills of east Tennessee. . . . Wake County Sheriff Spencer Arrowood asks Laura Bruce, wife of the local Baptist minister, who is now an Army chaplain stationed overseas, to comfort the bereaved at the scene of a bloody murder. Ret. Maj. Paul Underhill, his wife and two of his four children are dead, shot apparently by one of the sons, who took his own life after killing the others. Laura serves as advocate for the surviving children. . . . But when deputy Joe LeDonne discovers that the two have disinterred their father's body from its grave, he wants to know what really happened on the night of the shooting." Publ Wkly

If ever I return, pretty Peggy-O. Scribner 1990 312p $17.95

ISBN 0-684-19104-0   LC 89-24337

"Two events cause palpitations for the gentle folk of Hamelin, Tennessee. A high school reunion is planned, fanning old jealousies, and Peggy Muryan, a famous 1960s folkie—whose one-time lover and singing partner was reported MIA 20 years before—arrives in town, fixing to stay. Soon threatening letters begin arriving, animals are ritualistically slaughtered, and a local girl bearing a striking similarity to the younger Peggy is pulled from a nearby river. Local policeman Spencer Arrowood must find the killer, deal with the upcoming reunion, and grapple with the volatile collapse of his marriage." Booklist

The author's "strongly individualized characters give serious and intelligent thought to the ghosts raised by the reunion—including the tangible spector of a murderer." N Y Times Book Rev

MacPherson's lament; an Elizabeth MacPherson mystery. Ballantine Bks. 1992 260p o.p.

LC 92-52661

In this mystery Elizabeth MacPherson's "brother, Bill, a new lawyer, sets up shop in Danville, Va., with Amy Powell (A.P.) Hill, descendant of the southern general known by the same initials. The firm's first few cases aren't auspicious. . . . The pace picks up when the body of a young woman is found in the trunk of A.P.'s client's car and a wealthy businessman from New York wants to buy the house very quickly. Elizabeth, who has been represented in letters sent from Scotland, finally flies home to help the fledgling attorneys. Interspersed is the tale of Civil War soldier Gabriel Hawks, who with a friend confiscates a part of the Confederate treasury." Publ Wkly

A "witty story that will beguile both mystery buffs and Civil War enthusiasts." Booklist

Missing Susan; an Elizabeth MacPherson mystery. Ballantine Bks. 1991 295p o.p.

LC 91-91887

Available G.K. Hall large print edition

McCrumb, Sharyn—*Continued*

Elizabeth MacPherson, "an American forensic anthropologist with an interest in historical true-crime cases, takes a busman's holiday: an organized tour of England's most notorious murder sites. Looking forward to a little shoptalk . . . the quick-witted heroine is disappointed to find the obnoxiously eccentric tour guide, Rowan Rover, so guarded and, well, so very nervous about having a chat. Elizabeth attributes Rover's manner to 'a natural shyness on his part,' not knowing that, on an earlier tour of Jack the Ripper's killing ground, the financially strapped guide accepted a murder commission from an American tourist." N Y Times Book Rev

The author "spins the British cozy formula on its ear, slipping in the expected sly one-liner or two and driving her plot so far up a narrative one-way street that only a writer with her nerve and ever-ready wit would have a snowball's chance in hell of pulling the whole tricky caper off." Booklist

She walks these hills. Scribner 1994 336p $21

ISBN 0-684-19556-9   LC 94-9458

"In 1779, Katie Wyler, 18, was captured by the Shawnee in North Carolina. The story of her escape and arduous journey home through hundreds of miles of Appalachian wilderness is the topic of ethno-historian Jeremy Cobb's thesis. . . . As Cobb begins to retrace Katie's return journey, 63-year-old convicted murderer Hiram (Harm) Sorley escapes from a nearby prison. Suffering from Korsakoff's syndrome, he has no recent memory. . . . Hamelin, Tenn., police dispatcher Martha Ayers uses the opportunity to convince the sheriff to assign her as a deputy. . . . Deftly building suspense, McCrumb weaves these colorful elements into her satisfying conclusion." Publ Wkly

The Windsor knot; an Elizabeth MacPherson mystery. Ballantine Bks. 1990 281p o.p.
LC 90-34168

"Back in Chandler Grove for her nuptials, forensic anthropologist Elizabeth MacPherson finds herself involved in a local police investigation when she is called upon to identify some cremated remains." Booklist

"Elizabeth is less centrally involved in the crime and detection than usual, but this doesn't diminish the appeal of McCrumb's sparkling spoof." Publ Wkly

McCullers, Carson, 1917-1967

The ballad of the sad café [novelette]

In McCullers, C. The ballad of the sad café: the novels and stories of Carson McCullers

In McCullers, C. Collected stories p195-253

The ballad of the sad café: the novels and stories of Carson McCullers. Houghton Mifflin 1951 791p o.p.

Partially analyzed in Short story index

This volume contains three novels: The heart is a lonely hunter, The member of the wedding and Reflections in a golden eye (all three entered separately). In addition to the title novella the following short stories are also included: Wunderkind; The jockey; Madame Zilensky and the King of Finland; The sojourner; A domestic dilemma; A tree, a rock, a cloud

In the title novella "Amelia Evans, a tall and lonely woman, falls passionately in love with her cousin Lymon, a malevolent dwarf. Amelia opens a café that serves as a much-needed social outlet for their tiny Southern town. Lymon falls in love with Amelia's estranged husband, Marvin Macy, who has just been released from prison. Lymon and Macy overpower Amelia physically and wreck her café, after which they disappear together, leaving Amelia and the townspeople without hope." Merriam-Webster's Ency of Lit

Clock without hands. Houghton Mifflin 1961 241p o.p.

"Treating the disintegration of individual human lives and of the way of life in the Old South, the story occurs during the final 15 months of a small-town Georgia druggist, dying of leukemia. J.T. Malone's last days are linked with the life of Judge Clane, a former congressman, fat and fatuous in his hope of reviving the antebellum society, and yet sentimentally kind in his attachment to his grandson and to another orphan, a black named Sherman Pew. The tragic pasts of these two young men, themselves involved in ambivalent emotional relations, are intertwined because the white boy's late father, a lawyer, had unsuccessfully defended the black boy's father, unjustly accused of murdering the white husband of Old Pew's white mistress. As the clock of Malone's life ticks toward a stop, the town erupts into violence." Oxford Companion to Am Lit. 5th edition

Collected stories; including The member of the wedding and The ballad of the sad café; introduction by Virginia Spencer Carr. Houghton Mifflin 1987 392p o.p.
LC 87-3944

Analyzed in Short story index

Contents: Sucker; Court in the west eighties; Poldi; Breath from the sky; The orphanage; Instant of the hour after; Like that; Wunderkind; The aliens; Untitled piece; The jockey; Madame Zilensky and the King of Finland; Correspondence; A tree. A rock. A cloud; Art and Mr. Mahoney; The sojourner; A domestic dilemma; The haunted boy; Who has seen the wind?; The ballad of the sad café; The member of the wedding

"McCullers often wrote about grotesques, people afflicted physically and emotionally. Her themes include loneliness and the mental anguish that stems from love gone awry. Her style is unadorned, quietly rigorous. She's both charming and disquieting—an absorbing challenge to readers of serious fiction." Booklist

The heart is a lonely hunter. Modern Lib. 1993 430p $15.50

ISBN 0-679-42474-1   LC 92-51062

A reissue of the title first published 1940 by Houghton Mifflin

"After his friend is committed to a hospital for the insane, John Singer, a deaf mute, finds himself alone. He becomes the pivotal figure in a strange circle of four other lonely individuals: Biff Brannon, the owner of a cafe; Mick Kelly, a young girl; Jake Blount, a radical; and Benedict Copeland, the town's black doctor. Although Singer provides companionship for others, he remains outside the warmth of close relationships." Shapiro. Fic for Youth. 3d edition

also in McCullers, C. The ballad of the sad café: the novels and stories of Carson McCullers p141-498

McCullers, Carson, 1917-1967—*Continued*

The member of the wedding. Houghton Mifflin 1946 195p o.p.

"Twelve-year-old Frankie is experiencing a boring summer until news arrives that her older brother will soon be returning to Georgia from his Alaska home in order to marry. Plotting to accompany the newlyweds on their honeymoon occupies much of Frankie's waking hours, while at the same time she is coping with the pressures of puberty and its effects on her body and mind. Particularly revealing are her conversations with her six-year-old cousin and the nurturing black family cook, Bernice." Shapiro. Fic for Youth. 3d edition

"Finely portrays the emotional anxieties and conflicts endured by an imaginative adolescent as she tries to come to terms with her maturing self." Penguin Companion to Am Lit

also in McCullers, C. The ballad of the sad café: the novels and stories of Carson McCullers p595-791

also in McCullers, C. Collected stories p255-392

Reflections in a golden eye. Houghton Mifflin 1941 182p o.p.

"Set in the 1930s on a Southern army base, the novel concerns the relationships between self-destructive misfits whose lives end in tragedy and murder. The cast of characters includes Captain Penderton, a sado-masochistic, latent homosexual officer; his wife, who is having an affair with Major Langdon; the major's wife, who responds to the trauma of her son's death with self-mutilation; Anacleto, a homosexual servant who is befriended by the major's wife, and an army private who engages in voyeurism." Merriam-Webster's Ency of Lit

also in McCullers, C. The ballad of the sad café: the novels and stories of Carson McCullers p499-567

McCullough, Colleen, 1937-

The first man in Rome. Morrow 1990 896p il o.p.

LC 90-37080

"The first installment in a projected series outlining the demise of the Roman republic and tracing the origins of the Roman Empire, this volume commences in 110 B.C.E. and revolves around the smoldering political ambitions of two seemingly unsuitable statesmen. Lacking the requisite patrician pedigree, stolid and wealthy Gaius Marius, a brilliant general, acquires respectability by marrying into the irreproachable Julian dynasty. Deprived of his noble birthright by a dissolute and profligate father, the impoverished and curiously amoral Lucius Cornelius Sulla resorts to murder in order to claim an inheritance and purchase his way into the senate. Branded as outsiders, Marius and Sulla forge a formidable alliance, culminating in a succession of unparalled military and political triumphs." Booklist

Followed by The grass crown

Fortune's favorites. Morrow 1993 878p il $25

ISBN 0-688-09370-1   LC 93-534

The third novel in the Ancient Rome series "begins in the year 83 B.C. and runs through 69 B.C., a violent and volatile era that brought the rise and bloody rule of the maniacal, disease-ridden dictator Sulla; the career of the cocky if dense 'Magnus' Pompey; and the youth and education of Julius Caesar." Booklist

"Painstakingly researched, McCullough's Roman saga is like a trip through time. Her characters come to life as do their surroundings. While giving us rollicking good fiction, McCullough has also made clear the bribery and chicanery that made up Roman politics. She has given us clear insight into how Rome found itself changing from a republic to an empire." Libr J

The grass crown. Morrow 1991 894p il o.p.

LC 91-17009

In the second novel in the author's series about the Roman Empire "the action hinges on the rivalry between arrogant, paunchy general Marius, eager to fulfill a prophecy and become consul of Rome for a seventh time, and Sulla, a monster who has turned to warmaking out of either sexual frustration or boredom. . . . In recreating the Social War between Rome and the rebellious Italian nations (90-88 B.C.), Sulla's crushing of King Mithridates of Pontus and the ensuing bloody Roman civil war, McCullough sustains a keen sense of urgency, framing precarious personal lives against an empire in flux. A quietly magnificent tour de force." Publ Wkly

Followed by Fortune's favorites

An indecent obsession. Harper & Row 1981 317p o.p.

LC 81-47547

This novel is "set in the psychiatric ward of a small military hospital in the South Pacific soon after the end of the Second World War. A novel about duty (the 'indecent obsession'), it has the prescribed mix of bestselling ingredients, romance, sex, violence and paranoia." Oxford Companion to Australian Lit

The ladies of Missalonghi; illustrations by Peter Chapman. Harper & Row 1987 189p il o.p.

LC 86-46084

"The Harper short novel series"

"Set in the early 1900s in the tiny town of Byron, nestled in the Australia's Blue Mountains, this novel tells of the blossoming of Missy Wright, 33-year-old spinster and poor relation of the town's ruling family, the Hurlingfords. Missy, her widowed mother and crippled aunt live in genteel poverty, victims of the Hurlingford inheritance policy that gives riches and power to the male members of the family, who heartlessly abuse the women they dominate. Plain, painfully thin and doomed to dress always in serviceable brown, shockingly dark-haired in a clan of luminous blondes, Missy seems fated for a dreary future until a distant cousin, a divorcée, arrives from Sydney. Under her tutelage, Missy acquires spunk, hope and the means to a happy ending." Publ Wkly

The thorn birds. Harper & Row 1977 533p o.p.

"A multigenerational saga of life, love, and death on an Australian sheep ranch." Reader's Ency. 3d edition

"The backdrop to this congested, sensational and often bizarre plot, is the Australian outback, with its dramatic landscapes, vast distances, isolation, bush camaraderie, and natural hazards. The novel aroused lively literary controversy. It was labelled by its critics as a 'potboiler':

McCullough, Colleen, 1937-—*Continued*

crudely crafted, sensationally exaggerated, devised to cater to the florid expectations of the mass of undiscriminating readers of modern popular fiction. Its supporters see it as a vigorously-written and racy narrative." Oxford Companion to Australian Lit

McCutchan, Philip, 1920-

Cameron's crossing. St. Martin's Press 1993 171p $17.95

ISBN 0-312-09762-X   LC 93-24284

The author "uses the Battle of the Atlantic (1940-44) as the setting for [this] . . . Donald Cameron adventure. Commander Cameron along with a small crew of enlisted men take passage on the escort carrier HMS *Charger*, which is sailing from Belfast to Norfolk, Virginia, for an overhaul. On passage across the Atlantic HMS *Charger* is beset by a severe North Atlantic storm that not only damages her beyond recovery but reveals the inadequacy of the commanding officer, Captain Mason-Goodson. Cameron takes command in an effort to save both ship and crew from a watery grave." Libr J

"As usual, the stolid, intrepid Cameron soldiers along very ably, while McCutchan's spare prose smartly recreates the lore and real lives of the British navy." Publ Wkly

Convoy homeward. St. Martin's Press 1992 182p $17.95

ISBN 0-312-08168-5   LC 92-1584

In this novel Commodore John Mason Kemp embarks on "a treacherous journey from India to Scotland. His convoy of supply and war ships is further burdened with some unwelcome passengers: German POWs, British expatriates, and one slightly demented brigadier. All add to the commodore's worries." Booklist

"The climactic battle with a Nazi surface raider in the South Atlantic is terrific, and ends the novel with a satisfying, surprising bang." Publ Wkly

Convoy north. St. Martin's Press 1988 c1987 177p o.p.

LC 87-27102

First published 1987 in the United Kingdom

"As commodore in charge of a large troop convoy from Australia to America in 1942, John Mason Kemp . . . must not only shepherd men and ships halfway around the world but also safeguard a mysterious canvas bag holding top-secret intelligence for the Pentagon. . . . When a Nazi raider and a U-boat pack appear, Kemp realizes there may be a high-level intelligence leak. The climax comes when a U-boat boarding party tries to get the canvas bag." Publ Wkly

Convoy of fear. St. Martin's Press 1990 190p o.p.

LC 90-37304

This "World War II adventure starring Commodore Kemp finds the convoy in his charge crossing the Mediterranean through the Suez Canal and on to Trincomalee, Ceylon. Kemp battles more than Axis weaponry; an epidemic of cholera and a typhoon take as many of his crew members as the German surface raiders. The novelist adds further excitement to his war story with the inclusion of Wrens (WRNS, navy nurses) aboard ship. Predictable but well-written." Booklist

Convoy south. St. Martin's Press 1988 187p o.p.

LC 88-14782

Available G.K. Hall large print edition

In this World War II adventure Commodore John Kemp is placed in charge of a convoy of ships carrying Australian soldiers to the U.S. When an Australian civilian official interrogates Kemp about a bundle of top-secret data on Japanese activity in the nearby oceans, he realizes that it is not only the Nazis who wish to sabotage this troop movement." Booklist

"Commodore Kemp is blessed with the stiffest upper lip since Captain Ahab's. And the story of how he and his fellow seamen struggle against the salty odds makes a nautical war buff's feast." N Y Times Book Rev

Halfhyde and the fleet review. St. Martin's Press 1992 c1991 216p o.p.

LC 91-33835

First published 1991 in the United Kingdom

"Merchant mariner St. Vincent Halfhyde's freighter has been ordered by the admiralty to attend the fleet review for Victoria's jubilee at Cowes to curb the overbearing impulses of popinjay Watkiss, Chilian admiral and possible target of an assassination plot." Publ Wkly

"As a writer of suspenseful fiction, McCutchan has a ways to go, but the farcical elements here will definitely amuse Halfhyde fans." Booklist

The last farewell; a novel. St. Martin's Press 1991 308p $17.95

ISBN 0-312-05458-0   LC 90-49227

"McCutchan weaves a tapestry of stories about the passengers and crew aboard the *Laurentia* as it makes its final voyage from New York to England in 1915. Without a protective escort, Captain Pacey must guide his ship through waters and times more treacherous than he can possibly believe. The U-boat commander has his problems, too, as the action moves from the liner to the submarine to the offices of the British ministers, who, in noncommittal ways, have sentenced the *Laurentia* to its dismal fate. A mesmerizing tale of the sea and the men who pit their lives against nature and politics." Booklist

McDermott, Alice

At weddings and wakes. Farrar, Straus & Giroux 1992 213p $19

ISBN 0-374-10674-6   LC 91-42070

Also available G.K. Hall large print edition

Set in Brooklyn during the sixties, this novel "tells the story of an extended Irish-American family observed primarily through the eyes of the children, son and two daughters. Time circles backwards and forwards around a variety of family rituals: holiday meals, vacations at the shore, the wedding of a favorite aunt. The poignant middle-aged romance that develops between the aunt, a former nun, and her suitor, a shy mailman, exacerbates already pronounced family tensions. As they listen to oft-repeated stories about poverty, disease, and early deaths, the children are solemn witnesses to the Irish immigrant experience in America." Libr J

That night. Farrar, Straus & Giroux 1987 183p o.p.

LC 84-45765

McDermott, Alice—*Continued*

The novel's "narrator reflects on an incident that shattered the serenity and naïveté of her suburban world of the early 1960s, when she was 10 years old. . . . An opening scene of violence played out under a 'bright navy sky' on a soft midsummer night 'when Venus was bright', captures the tone and focus of the novel, which recalls the doomed love affair of teenagers Sheryl and Rick." Publ Wkly

"In spite of its brevity, 'That Night' is a wonderfully unfettered, ample novel, one that celebrates voice, personality and feeling when so much fiction avoids those rewarding characteristics. Ms. McDermott has invested her novel with a strong sense of historical authority, rendering with sure clarity a time and place marked by both a cultural innocence and the premonition of its inevitable loss." N Y Times Book Rev

Mcdonald, Gregory, 1937-

Carioca Fletch

In Mcdonald, G. The Fletch chronicles: [two]

Confess, Fletch

In Mcdonald, G. The Fletch chronicles: [two]

Fletch. Bobbs-Merrill 1974 179p o.p.

"A rich young California industrialist, Stanwyck, who is apparently dying of cancer, offers someone he takes to be a beach bum a rich reward if he'll murder him on a particular date. The 'bum' chosen is Fletch, ace journalist, ace philanderer, who accepts the proposition. However, Fletch, who is already investigating the beach drug scene for his newspaper, now investigates Stanwyck—his marital and extramarital life, his relationship with his parents, his obsession with piloting experimental planes. The two strands of the story come together in one deft twist as Fletch . . . both gets the drop on the doublecrossing Stanwyck and uncovers the source of the beach's drugs." Publ Wkly

also in Mcdonald, G. The Fletch chronicles: [two]

Fletch and the man who

In Mcdonald, G. The Fletch chronicles: three

Fletch and the Widow Bradley

In Mcdonald, G. The Fletch chronicles: one

The Fletch chronicles. Hill & Co. Pubs. 1987-1988 3v o.p.

LC 87-8742

"Rediscovery books"

A three-volume omnibus collection of nine award-winning Fletch novels, some of which first appeared in paperback

Contents: one: Fletch won (c1985) entered separately; Fletch, too (c1986) entered separately; Fletch and the Widow Bradley (c1981)

[two]: Fletch (c1974) entered separately; Carioca Fletch (c1984); Confess, Fletch (c1976)

three: Fletch's fortune (c1978); Fletch's moxie (c1982); Fletch and the man who (c1983)

Fletch reflected. Putnam 1994 222p $21.95

ISBN 0-399-13983-4   LC 94-16640

Fletch's son Jack "heads to the huge Georgia estate of billionaire inventor Chester Radleigh at the request of Shana Steufel, an old, but memorable, one-night stand of Jack's. Shana, who is engaged to one of Radleigh's sons, believes her future father-in-law's life is in danger." Publ Wkly

"The Fletch novels have always offered a unique mix of suspense and cartoonish characterizations. The son of Fletch continues the family tradition." Booklist

Fletch, too. Warner Bks. 1986 249p o.p.

LC 85-41001

Available Thorndike Press large print edition

In this novel Fletch "finds true love and marries ever-patient Barbara; he finds his long-lost father (who then proceeds to get lost); and he seeks both a murderer and a lost Roman civilization." Booklist

also in Mcdonald, G. The Fletch chronicles: one

Fletch won. Warner Bks. 1985 265p o.p.

LC 85-40009

Available Thorndike Press large print edition

"Bucking for meaty assignments as a fledgling newspaper reporter, Fletch seizes the chance to get out of the society pages when Donald Habek is shot dead. Instead of writing his assigned piece on Habek's offer to donate a fortune to the art museum, Fletch sees himself with bylines on the front pages if he can beat Biff Wilson, the crime reporter, in the race to investigate the dead man's background." Publ Wkly

also in Mcdonald, G. The Fletch chronicles: one

Fletch's fortune

In Mcdonald, G. The Fletch chronicles: three

Fletch's moxie

In Mcdonald, G. The Fletch chronicles: three

Son of Fletch. Putnam 1993 236p $19.95

ISBN 0-399-13831-5   LC 93-684

Also available Thorndike Press large print edition

"Good-natured hero Irwin Maurice ('Fletch') Fletcher discovers he has a heretofore unknown son from a friendly one-night stand 20 years earlier. Somehow son Jack has become involved with a bunch of neo-Nazi thugs fresh out of prison, but Fletch has trouble believing that the fruit of his loins could really be a bad guy at heart. . . . Good pacing, good humor, and good writing make Mcdonald's latest another fan pleaser in a predictable but comfortable series." Booklist

McElroy, Lee, 1926-

For works written by this author under other names see Kelton, Elmer, 1926-

McEwan, Ian

Black dogs. Doubleday 1992 xxii, 149p o.p.

LC 92-7418

"The narrator of this taut, questioning tale is an orphan relentlessly drawn to other people's parents. This habit of attraction and need takes full form when Jeremy becomes intrigued with his in-laws. June is spiritual,

McEwan, Ian—*Continued*

reclusive, and fatally ill; Bernard is active, pragmatic, and political. They fell in love during the grieving yet determined days following World War II, united by an ardent and idealistic faith in communism and a bold sexual passion. But their bliss was short-lived. The source of the philosophical chasm that quickly opened between them, June's epiphanic confrontation with two black dogs in rural France, is alluded to often but not fully explained until that last chapter." Booklist

This novel is "compassionate without resorting to sentimentality, clever without ever losing its honesty, an undisguised novel of ideas which is also Ian McEwan's most human work." Times Lit Suppl

The innocent. Doubleday 1990 270p o.p.

LC 89-25669

Available Thorndike Press large print edition

"Basing his story on an actual (but little known) incident, McEwan tells of the secret tunnel under the Soviet sector which the British and Americans built in 1954 to gain access to the Russians' communication system. The protagonist, Leonard Marnham, is a 25-year-old, naïve, unsophisticated English post office technician who is astonished and alarmed to find himself involved in a top-secret operation. At the same time that he loses his political innocence, Leonard experiences his sexual initiation in a clandestine affair with a German divorcée five years his senior. As his two secret worlds come together, events develop into a gruesome nightmare." Publ Wkly

"There is . . . a point to all this, which is to display the astonishing deeds that human beings can perpetrate and yet retain a measure of innocence. . . . In spite of what has happened, Leonard is able to live with himself. This is far and away Ian McEwan's most mature work." New Statesman Soc

McFarland, Dennis

The music room. Houghton Mifflin 1990 275p o.p.

LC 89-71721

Available G.K. Hall large print edition

"Marty Lambert, a San Francisco record company executive, is facing an impending divorce when his younger brother Perry, a talented composer, commits suicide in New York. Mystified by his brother's death, Marty goes to New York to seek an explanation, following an elusive trail of clues that leads from his brother's friends to the troubled history of his wealthy Virginia family. In the end he learns as much about himself as Perry, coming to terms with a legacy of alcoholism." Libr J

"In one startling realistic scene after another, with evocative description and a fluid, natural language, 'The Music Room' itself builds to a comprehensive vision, remarkable from its beginning to its surprising, satisfying end." N Y Times Book Rev

School for the blind. Houghton Mifflin 1994 287p $21.95

ISBN 0-395-64497-6   LC 93-49831

This novel "chronicles the waning years of two elderly siblings, Francis and Muriel Brimm, as they reluctantly come to grips with the past and learn to accept their gradual decline. . . . Walking on the golf course near the Florida town where Muriel has spent her life and to which retired photojournalist Frank has returned, they

discover the bones of two students from the nearby school for the blind. The search for the killer's identity forces Frank and Muriel to abandon their own willed 'blindness' and to retrieve memories of their childhood with a mean, alcoholic father and a stern, cold mother." Publ Wkly

"Readers of 'School for the Blind' may find their attention held less by the plot than by everything that supports it. This is an inversion of expectations, but not finally a disappointing one." N Y Times Book Rev

McGahern, John, 1934-

The collected stories. Knopf 1993 c1992 408p $24

ISBN 0-679-41913-6   LC 92-54448

Analyzed in Short story index

First published 1992 in the United Kingdom

Contents: Wheels; Why we're here; Coming into his kingdom; Christmas; Hearts of oak and bellies of brass; Strandhill, the sea; The key; Korea; Lavin; My love, my umbrella; Peaches; The recruiting officer; The beginning of an idea; A slip-up; All sorts of impossible things; Faith, hope and charity; The stoat; Doorways; The wine breath; Along the edges; Swallows; Gold watch; Parachutes; A ballad; Oldfashioned; Like all other men; Eddie Mac; Crossing the line; High ground; Sierra Leone; The conversion of William Kirkwood; Bank holiday; The creamery manager; The country funeral

"These stories, by a master of clean, powerful description that conveys the immaterial significance in material things, offer a vision in which love is not an end but a means of gaining the world." N Y Times Book Rev

McGarrity, Mark, 1943- *See* Gill, Bartholomew, 1943-

McGown, Jill

Murder at the old vicarage. St. Martin's Press 1989 c1988 256p o.p.

LC 88-30603

Available G.K. Hall large print edition

"A Thomas Dunne book"

First published 1988 in the United Kingdom with title: Redemption

"While snow blankets the small village of Byford, the vicar, George Wheeler, is in a hopeless muddle. . . . He finds himself attracted to a young widow—a fact that has not escaped his wife's notice. In addition, his daughter has moved back to the vicarage in order to escape an abusive husband. When the husband is discovered dead, the three members of the Wheeler family are the prime suspects. What appears to be a simple case of domestic murder to Chief Inspector Lloyd and Sergeant Judy instead becomes a complicated plot to love and revenge." Booklist

"McGown's complex plot is masterful and her sleuths and their predicament are enthralling." Publ Wkly

The other woman. St. Martin's Press 1993 c1992 236p $17.95

ISBN 0-312-08868-X   LC 92-41160

"A Thomas Dunne book"

First published 1992 in the United Kingdom

"London Det. Chief Inspector Lloyd and his colleague and lover, Judy Hill, . . . are caught up, and nearly strangled, in a convoluted plot in which they, the murder victim and the suspects are knotted together in a series

McGown, Jill—*Continued*

of unraveling, interwoven relationships. . . . McGown rescues her story from its elliptical, intricate beginning to produce a bravura finish." Publ Wkly

The stalking horse. St. Martin's Press 1988 186p o.p.

LC 88-15834

"A Thomas Dunne book"

"Businessman Bill Holt fails to convince anyone that he did not commit the two murders of which he is accused: that of his lifelong friend, Alison Bryant, and of a private detective he never even met, Michael Allsopp, who had been assigned to trail Alison. Holt spends 16 years in prison pondering the link between the crimes and becomes obsessed with discovering the identity of the murderer, belatedly realizing that it had to be one of his acquaintances. When he is paroled, he returns home to the English countryside in quest of the truth and the person who framed him." Publ Wkly

"McGown has constructed a taut, enthralling mystery, borrowing from the hard-boiled and the British procedural styles to write in a way all her own." Booklist

McGuane, Thomas, 1939-

The bushwhacked piano. Simon & Schuster 1971 220p o.p.

"The hilarious misadventures of Nicholas Payne are sketched in a slapstick style supported by pithy dialog and descriptions. In headlong pursuit of his native dreams, Nicholas thrusts himself into the real-life roles of bemused suitor, wayward son, accomodating friend, bronc buster, hospital patient, 'foreman of a pest control project' (con man on bat tower construction), and unwitting subject of a photographic exhibition." Booklist

Nobody's angel. Random House 1981 227p $14.50

ISBN 0-394-52264-8   LC 81-13885

At 36 melancholy, ex-juvenile delinquent, ex-prep school student, ex-Army captain, Patrick Fitzpatrick "returns to his family's Montana ranch . . . tends his grandfather, a dotty cowpoke, and his loony sister [Mary], and feels exhausted, depleted, bewildered. . . . At a party he meets Claire, a young Oklahoma woman who's beautiful, oil-rich and married. The action moves between Patrick's attempts to keep his family and ranch shipshape and his struggle to . . . woo and conquer Claire." Newsweek

"What stamps this as a McGuane novel are the bizarre episodes he invents for his character and the wit with which he reports them; what is new . . . is a depth of feeling." N Y Times Book Rev

Nothing but blue skies. Houghton Mifflin; Lawrence, S. 1992 349p $21.95

ISBN 0-395-54540-4   LC 92-23623

"Frank Copenhaver is a mix of modern businessman and old-style rancher. . . . As the novel begins, his wife, Gracie, leaves him, and his domestic upheaval signals a succession of setbacks in his business life. Copenhaver's downward spiral gathers speed as he engages in a series of fleeting sexual liaisons, lands in jail after a bar fight, demolishes the pick-up truck of a fling's jealous cowboy boyfriend, and almost destroys his Montana business empire." Times Lit Suppl

"The author's underlying theme is the unimportance of money by comparison with love, an old point that he makes with novel means and without sentimental sugar." Christ Sci Monit

To skin a cat; stories. Dutton; Lawrence, S. 1986 212p o.p.

LC 86-8916

Analyzed in Short story index

Contents: The millionaire; A man in Louisiana; Like a leaf; Dogs; A skirmish; Two hours to kill; The rescue; Sportsmen; Little extras; Partners; The road atlas; Flight; To skin a cat

The "stories collected here aptly display McGuane's particular gifts for precise description, understated humor, and offbeat characterizations." Booklist

McInerney, Jay

Brightness Falls. Knopf 1992 416p $23

ISBN 0-679-40219-5   LC 91-58562

"Russell Calloway, an editor for a major publishing house, and his stockbroker wife Corrine appear to be the perfect New York couple. Dissatisfied with the management of his publishing company, Russell organizes a hostile takeover bid and embarks on an affair with Trina, his investment banker. But he loses his shirt in the 1987 stock market crash, Corrine leaves him, and his best friend commits suicide." Libr J

"Mr. McInerney is disarmingly openhanded. In 'Brightness Falls,' the paste and the gems are offered with the same generosity. Jay McInerney's delight in telling a story, even a story you've heard before, is contagious." N Y Times Book Rev

McInerny, Ralph M., 1929-

For works written by this author under other names see Quill, Monica, 1929-

The basket case; a Father Dowling mystery; [by] Ralph McInerny. St. Martin's Press 1987 182p o.p.

LC 87-16313

"When Constance Farley Rush leaves her infant son in a basket at Fr. Dowling's church, she means to accuse her ex-husband, Peter Rush, of plotting to kidnap the baby. But . . . someone kills Rush, presenting the priest and his pal, Lt. Keegan of the Fox River, Ill., police, with a knotty case of murder." Publ Wkly

Bishop as pawn; a Father Dowling mystery; [by] Ralph McInerny. Vanguard Press 1978 219p o.p.

LC 78-54978

"Father Dowling's housekeeper's husband returns after a desertion of 15 years, only to be killed. Involved in this odd collection of bits and pieces is a good Catholic girl who wants to marry an irreligous man, leading to a singularly bleak affair, a young undogmatic and fundamentalist priest much disliked by Father Dowling, and an incomprehensible kidnapping of the remarkably smooth bishop." Libr J

Body and soil; an Andrew Broom mystery; [by] Ralph McInerny. Atheneum Pubs. 1989 245p o.p.

LC 88-38209

McInerny, Ralph M., 1929-—*Continued*

In this mystery Indiana attorney Andrew Broom, "represents some very unpopular clients, including a strange young man who has confessed to the murder of a local boy. In the midst of that trial, the town's wealthiest couple brawls in public, loudly insists on a divorce, and hires Broom and his partner/nephew as opposing attorneys. Then murder interrupts the proceedings. In a departure from the traditional whodunit, McInerny offers readers front-row seats to observe the villain's activities." Booklist

A cardinal offense; [by] Ralph McInerny. St. Martin's Press 1994 372p $21.95

ISBN 0-312-11283-1   LC 94-3481

"A Father Dowling mystery"

"A man, pursuing an annulment, and his wife, who is opposed, meet separately with Fr. Dowling in St. Hilary's rectory on the same day that the priest receives two surprise tickets to the next Notre Dame-Southern California football game. The husband says his wife was never really a Catholic; she insists that the 30-year marriage and the couple's grown children remain valid. After the man is murdered, Dowling and his cop friend Phil Keegan consider possible suspects." Publ Wkly

The dead weight lifter

In McInerny, R. Four on the floor p115-156

Desert sinner; [by] Ralph McInerny. St. Martin's Press 1992 182p $16.95

ISBN 0-312-08177-4   LC 92-25161

"A Father Dowling mystery"

"After Stacey Wilson, a former Las Vegas showgirl who steadfastly maintains her innocence, is tried and convicted of slaying her millionaire husband, Captain Phil Keegan of the Fox River Police Department gratefully closes the book on the scandalous case. When Elaine McCorkle, Keegan's homely secretary and an active member of St. Hilary's Catholic Church, is romanced by a handsome stranger with an inordinate interest in all the particulars of the notorious homicide, Father Dowling's insatiable curiosity is aroused." Booklist

The dutiful son

In McInerny, R. Four on the floor p157-199

Easeful death. Atheneum Pubs. 1991 261p $19.95

ISBN 0-689-12131-8   LC 91-9962

Also available Thorndike Press large print edition

"As this novel opens, a retired poet sits brooding on his Wisconsin farm; by novel's end, he has died twice. In the first instance, Howard Webster allows authorities to believe the body of a tramp found immolated on the farm is Webster himself. He then jumps on a freighter and pursues anonymity until the publication of a prose manuscript, supposedly written in the poet's final days, suddenly achieves all the fame Webster could ever have desired. The mystery of the authorship of this book is complicated by the battle over the poet's suddenly valuable estate between Webster's third wife, his greedy son-in-law, his long-neglected daughter, and various conniving legal and literary persons." Booklist

The ferocious father

In McInerny, R. Four on the floor p1-61

Four on the floor; a Father Dowling mystery quartet; [by] Ralph McInerny. St. Martin's Press 1989 199p o.p.

LC 89-30512

Analyzed in Short story index

Contents: The ferocious father; Heart of gold; The dead weight lifter; The dutiful son

"These four Father Dowling novellas are tales of murder set in or near the priest's parish, St. Hilary's. McInerny draws on the parish senior center for setting, color, and even villains. The solutions to each are uncovered by Father Dowling, with the assistance of his close friend Captain Phil Keegan of the Fox River Police." Booklist

Frigor mortis; [by] Ralph McInerny. Atheneum Pubs. 1989 245p o.p.

LC 89-31485

"The whole town of Fairland, Minnesota, is buzzing about the death of lumber magnate George Arthur. Arthur is murdered by his wife and her lover, who hope to acquire his prosperous business and a safe-deposit box filled with unreported income. However, the box is empty, and the business has been drained by a series of loans." Booklist

The grass widow; a Father Dowling mystery; [by] Ralph McInerny. Vanguard Press 1983 185p o.p.

LC 82-24775

"Clare O'Leary tells [Father] Dowling she's hiding from her husband, who, she claims, has a contract out on her life. The next day, Clare is found dead in her motel room. As Dowling investigates, the mystery surrounding the victim deepens and blurs, fanning out into a drug ring and more murder." Booklist

Heart of gold

In McInerny, R. Four on the floor p63-113

Judas Priest; a Father Dowling mystery; [by] Ralph McInerny. St. Martin's Press 1991 184p $17.95

ISBN 0-312-06375-X   LC 91-21819

Also available Thorndike Press large print edition

"A seminary friend of Dowling's, former priest Chris Bourke, and his ex-nun wife now promote sexual liberation as televangelists of Enlightened Hedonism (EH). Meeting Dowling one day after Mass, Bourke asks the parish priest to talk about the hard facts of religious life with his daughter, Sonya, who wants to enter the convent. Before Dowling can do that, Sonya is reported kidnapped and then found stabbed to death. . . . Dowling, worldly-wise and armed with ready references to St. Paul and other Church fathers, is at his vintage best." Publ Wkly

Leave of absence; [by] Ralph McInerny. Atheneum Pubs. 1986 210p o.p.

LC 85-48150

McInerny, Ralph M., 1929-—Continued*
"Vera and Andrea, friends from girlhood . . . as young women, each chose a path applauded by a more traditional church. Andrea became a Franciscan nun, Sister Duns Scotus. Vera fell in love with a Catholic dentist, married and hoped for children. But in the disarray following the Second Vatican Council, . . . her marriage to Edward, which looks on the surface like yuppie paradise—they have Jaguars and a 23-foot sloop named Dental Flaws—has foundered on a painful childlessness, on her husband's materialistic search for more 'happiness' ('Happy, unhappy—what did that have to do with marriage? Marriage was forever. They were Catholics') and most dramatically on the news that her friend Andrea has slipped not only out of her habit but into Edward's bed." N Y Times Book Rev
"These characters are ordinary, recognizable people to whom faith and religion are living, vital matters. Readers will be moved by their struggles to adjust to the profound changes in their tradition." Publ Wkly

Mom and dead; an Andrew Broom mystery. Atheneum Pubs. 1994 215p $20
ISBN 0-689-12181-4   LC 93-13444
Also available Thorndike Press large print edition
Indiana lawyer Andrew Broom's "interests are piqued when his longstanding rival begins negotiations for an unnamed client who wants to buy up riverside property. At the same time, Jack Parry, mechanic, local lothario and drug go-between, learns from his neighbor Louise that his young son, who lives nearby with his ex-wife, has found a human skull buried in the riverbank. . . . When farmer Jerome Blatz is arrested for murdering the meddlesome Louise (the murder weapon, a bloody shovel, is found in his truck), Broom agrees to defend him." Publ Wkly

The priest; [by] Ralph McInerny. Harper & Row 1973 531p o.p.
"The time is 1968, when Paul VI's encyclical on contraception polarized certain elements in the Roman Catholic church. The protagonist is a young priest just back from theological studies in Rome. Some of his classmates from the seminary have become arch-conservatives; others are contemplating marriage and one has simply gone mad. McInerny is extremely good at describing the numerous pressures on the religious and laymen in this second half of the 20th century, and perhaps this is a more interesting or accurate novel because he never makes it particularly clear precisely where he himself stands." Choice

Savings and loam; an Andrew Broom mystery. Atheneum Pubs. 1990 215p o.p.
LC 89-29079
Available Thorndike Press large print edition
"Small-town lawyer Andrew Broom sorts through a suspenseful tangle of murder, blackmail, and mistaken identity when the owner of a neighboring farmhouse is shot for the sake of a buried fortune in old German bonds." Booklist

The search committee. Atheneum Pubs. 1991 243p o.p.
LC 90-45053
"The Fort Elbow campus of the University of Ohio is in an uproar. Chancellor Herbert Laplace, a champion of MADD, has been picked up for drunk driving after speeding away from a massage parlor. Although state senator Rod Bellini had appointed the school's chancellors in the past, the faculty appoints a search committee

to name an appropriate successor to Laplace. After Bellini announces his choice without consulting the committee, the candidate is found in his car—poisoned. Soon afterward, the alternate candidate also is poisoned." Publ Wkly

Second vespers; a Father Dowling mystery; [by] Ralph McInerny. Vanguard Press 1980 224p o.p.
LC 79-56379
Father Dowling "moves in on the criminals uncovering their various attempts to cheat collectors of O'Rourke memorabilia. Among the characters are two people who have a bookshop located in the old O'Rourke mansion, the local librarian who has a collection of letters, and another who is trying to get his hands on all the available O'Rourke papers. When a body is discovered, it throws doubt on the state of the 'estate' and also on the murder of O'Rourke." West Coast Rev Books

Seed of doubt; [by] Ralph McInerny. St. Martin's Press 1993 346p $19.95
ISBN 0-312-09381-0   LC 93-556
"A Father Dowling mystery"
"The questionable death of a wealthy nonagenarian matriarch, two hitherto unknown portraits by a renowned landscape artist, and a great-granddaughter's search for self form the core of [this] Father Roger Dowling mystery." Booklist
"McInerny delivers a comfy unreality in this genteel whodunit, graced with the trappings of a traditional Catholicism." Publ Wkly

Thicker than water; a Father Dowling mystery; [by] Ralph McInerny. Vanguard Press 1981 255p o.p.
LC 81-10432
This "Father Dowling mystery takes off from a couple of petty crimes . . . to a series of bizarre murders. Father Dowling . . . discovers a dead body in a pickup truck parked in front of the rectory. Murders start piling up around the quiet little town." Booklist

McIntosh, K. H. (Kinn Hamilton)
For works written by this author under other names see Aird, Catherine

McIntyre, Vonda N.
The crystal star. Bantam Bks. 1994 309p (Star wars) $21.95
ISBN 0-553-08929-3   LC 94-28939
In this episode of the Star wars series "the abduction of her children sends Princess Leia across the galaxy in pursuit of the kidnappers, unaware that her search will coincide with Han and Luke's attempts to uncover a rumored enclave of Jedi Knights on the fringes of former imperial territory." Libr J
"Star Wars fans will certainly enjoy the book, but McIntyre's superlative storytelling gives it much broader appeal." Booklist

Dreamsnake. Houghton Mifflin 1978 313p o.p.
LC 77-18891
"This is based on McIntyre's Nebula Award-winning novelette, 'Of Mist, and Grass, and Sand,' which is also the first chapter of the book. Snake, the healer, and her three healing serpents attend a young boy ill with a

McIntyre, Vonda N.—*Continued*

tumor. His fearful parents kill Grass, the dreamsnake, who can ease the dying by removing their pain. Without Grass, Snake is incomplete as a healer, and since the dreamsnakes come from off-world, she cannot get a replacement. To atone for her carelessness in losing Grass, Snake sets off for the city where off-worlders trade, hoping to get more dreamsnakes. She has many heart-stopping adventures, and the reader is engrossed every step of the way." Libr J

Of mist, and grass, and sand

In The Best of the Nebulas p478-93

McKenna, Richard

The Sand Pebbles; with an introduction by Robert Shenk. Naval Inst. Press 1984 c1962 xxii, 597p $32.95

ISBN 0-87021-592-2   LC 83-27007

Also available from Buccaneer Bks.

"Classics of naval literature series"

A reissue of the title first published 1962 by Harper & Row

A "novel with two main, intertwined threads: the titanic struggle of a man trying to find himself and the Chinese rebellion of the 1920's. The man is Jake Holman, machinist assigned to the U.S. gunboat 'San Pablo,' patrolling Chinese waters. Misanthropic with good reason and a determined nonconformist, Jake is beginning to resolve some of his perplexities and rebellions when China erupts. Ordered to refrain from battle for diplomatic reasons 'San Pablo' remains passive under fire and insult until the crew's morale is shattered and the shamed captain takes rash, fatal action. Life in engine room, forecastle, and brothel is re-created forthrightly, and the characters, including missionaries and coolies as well as sailors, are individuals to be remembered." Booklist

McKillip, Patricia A., 1948-

The Cygnet and the firebird. Ace Bks. 1993 233p $17.95

ISBN 0-441-12628-6   LC 92-21149

"This sequel to *The Sorceress and the Cygnet* continues the adventures of Nyx Ro and her cousin Meguet Vervaine. This time their opponents include a sorcerer who is looking for an ancient key, an amnesiac firebird, and a city of dragons. . . . McKillip's writing again has the same cool elegance that makes it a pleasure to read." Booklist

The sorceress and the Cygnet. Ace Bks. 1991 231p o.p.

LC 90-44103

"More than 1000 years ago the Gold King, Dancer, Blind Lady and Warlock fought the Cygnet, lost and were banished. Commoners put their story in the constellations to remember it. Ro Holding has the sign of the Cygnet and rules the other Holds, which have the other signs. But now the Gold King, seeing a way to reestablish the alliance, sets up an elaborate plot to trick Nyx Ro, daughter of the ruling family and a powerful Sorceress, and Corleu, a peasant of the Wayfolk, into releasing the vanquished and helping them find the Heart of the Cygnet." Publ Wkly

This fantasy "features imaginative worldbuilding, strong male and female characters, and an intense (though sometimes esoteric) style." Libr J

Followed by The Cygnet and the firebird

McKnight, Reginald, 1956-

The kind of light that shines on Texas; stories. Little, Brown 1992 194p o.p.

LC 91-19487

Analyzed in Short story index

Contents: The homunculus: a novel in one chapter; The kind of light that shines on Texas; Roscoe in Hell; Peacetime; Into night; Quitting smoking; Soul food

"Filled with sharp humor and pitch-perfect dialogue, these seven stories explore African American experience with telegraphic urgency. . . . A master of narrative pacing, novelist McKnight evokes a quicksand world where survival is a victory." Publ Wkly

McLaglen, John J., 1938-

For works written by this author under other names see Harvey, John, 1938-

McMillan, Terry

Disappearing acts. Viking 1989 384p $22

ISBN 0-670-82461-5   LC 88-40412

"Franklin is an on-again off-again construction worker trying to get his life on a firmer foundation. Zora is a music teacher and would-be singer. They meet and start a relationship that initially seems ideal. Soon, however, problems emerge. Franklin's ego has never recovered from his destructive mother's abuse, and the repeated blows the oppressive white society dishes out make him increasingly depressed and hostile. The relationship begins to fall apart. Zora and Franklin have to grow a long way alone before they can come back together." Libr J

"What raises this work above a mere sentimental love story is the finely tuned humor, which McMillan uses effectively to subtly alter the meaning of a scene or to draw the reader into her circle of characters." Booklist

Waiting to exhale. Viking 1992 409p $22

ISBN 0-670-83980-9   LC 91-46564

Also available G.K. Hall large print edition

This novel "tells the stories of four 30ish black women bound together in warm, supportive friendship and in their dwindling hopes of finding Mr. Right. Savannah, Bernadine, Robin and Gloria are successful professionals or self-employed women living in Phoenix. All are independent, upwardly mobile and 'waiting to exhale'—to stop holding their breaths waiting for the proper mate to come along." Publ Wkly

"Terry McMillan's heroines are so well drawn that by the end of the novel, the reader is completely at home with the four of them. They observe men—and contemporary America—with bawdy humor, occasional melancholy and great affection. But the novel is about more than four lives; the bonds among the women are so alive and so appealing they almost seem a character in their own right." N Y Times Book Rev

McMullen, Mary, 1920-

A grave without flowers. Doubleday 1983 181p o.p.

LC 83-7209

McMullen, Mary, 1920——*Continued*

"Published for the Crime Club"

"Wealthy Flora Wallace has invited a younger friend, recently divorced and grieving Emily Denver, on an auto tour of the English countryside while they are on vacation, away from home in New York. Emily is startled when her ex-husband Robert joins them. . . . He has arranged the meeting in hopes of winning Emily back. The romantic atmosphere is clouded by an ex-convict, John Tickell, on the trail of Flora's chauffeur, Denis Taunton. A murderer, Tickell kills the girl Taunton had lived with and will kill again to get the map to a sunken hoard of gold, now in the chauffeur's possession." Publ Wkly

McMurtry, Larry

Anything for Billy. Simon & Schuster 1988 382p o.p.

LC 88-22732

This novel is based on the legend of Billy the Kid (William Bonney), here named Billy Bone. The story is "told by Ben Sippy, a dime novelist from Philadelphia who went west in 1878 in search of the real life he'd made up stories about. There he befriended a likable, bucktoothed 17-year-old who already had a reputation as a killer, and he later wrote a novelette about Billy Bone that gave him his legendary name. . . . The 'real story' is . . . recounted by Sippy in old age." Newsweek

"McMurtry's prose is as readable as ever, served up in short, episodic chapters that effectively capture time and place, conjure up authentic images of pathetic heroes and villains, and yet pull the reins in on action. The tale's strength lies in Sippy's commanding first-person delivery and the less-than-admirable profile of the title character." Booklist

Buffalo girls; a novel. Simon & Schuster 1990 351p o.p.

LC 90-42486

Available G.K. Hall large print edition

"This is a nostalgic, funny, and sad novel about the Old West when cowboys and Buffalo girls whooped it up. Their behavior was amoral rather than immoral, and they lived by their own special code of behavior. Friendship was often life-saving as well as comforting, and the women of the bawdy houses called their clients 'sweethearts' even if their encounter was only for one night. Jim Ragg and Bartle Bone had become almost a dying breed and Custer, in their opinion, was a stupid old man at Little Big Horn to think that he could fight 3,000 Indians with 200 of his men. Highlights of the book are Bill Cody's (Buffalo Bill's) Wild West show and Calamity Jane's (whose drunkenness was calamitous) letters to a daughter. Fact and fiction are entwined in an enjoyable story that is mythic and memorable." Shapiro. Fic for Youth. 3d edition

Cadillac Jack; a novel. Simon & Schuster 1982 395p o.p.

LC 82-5962

"Jack was a rodeo bulldogger before he graduated to roaming America 'in a pearl-colored Cadillac with peach velour interior,' scouting for antiques he can resell to collectors. . . . But now Jack is undergoing a midlife crisis, juggling old wives and new girl friends as he flounders in the amiable venality and lechery of Washington, D.C." Libr J

"The sheer exuberance of McMurtry's imagination makes this book well worth reading." West Coast Rev Books

The desert rose; a novel. Simon & Schuster 1983 254p o.p.

LC 83-4687

Available from Amereon

"A topless dancer in a casino, Harmony 'had been said by some to have the best legs in Las Vegas and maybe the best bust too.' But now Harmony is approaching her 39th birthday, and her teenage daughter Pepper has become a contender for those honors. . . . [The] novel charts good-natured Harmony's sudden decline and Pepper's . . . well, peppery rise." Libr J

The evening star. Simon & Schuster 1992 637p o.p.

LC 92-2596

Available G.K. Hall large print edition

Sequel to Terms of endearment

Aurora Greenway's "aging boyfriend, the general, has lost some of his zest, and her new lover is the psychoanalyst she's gone to with her troubles. Those troubles include her grandchildren—Tommy, who's in jail for shooting his girlfriend; brilliant Teddy, who met *his* girlfriend on a visit to *his* therapist; and pregnant, overweight Melanie, who has picked up yet another hapless boyfriend and is heading for California." Libr J

"The success of a book like this one depends on the tone the author manages to muster up. Mr. McMurtry's is sentimentality laced with comic irony, and it works very well. . . . And if, in the end, Aurora Greenway and her extended and highly dysfunctional family turn out to be more entertaining than genuinely moving, it's reassuring to know that they—and the reader—are in the hands of a real pro." N Y Times Book Rev

Lonesome dove; a novel. Simon & Schuster 1985 843p $25

ISBN 0-671-50420-7   LC 85-2192

"Two former Texas Rangers have been running a ramshackle stock operation near the Mexican border with a lot of work and not much success. When they hear rumors of freewheeling opportunities in the newly opened territory, they decide to break camp, pull up stakes, and head north. Their dusty trek is filled with troubles, violence, and unfulfilled yearning." Booklist

"'Lonesome Dove' shows, early on, just about every symptom of American Epic except pretentiousness. McMurtry has laconic Texas talk and leathery, slimhipped machismo down pat, and he's able to refresh heroic clichés with exact observations about cowboy prudery, ignorance and fear of losing face. . . . [The author] keeps dozens of characters in motion in far-flung locales without confusion or tedium. The whole book moves with joyous energy." Newsweek

Followed by Streets of Laredo

Pretty Boy Floyd; a novel; [by] Larry McMurtry and Diana Ossana. Simon & Schuster 1994 444p $24

ISBN 0-671-89165-0   LC 94-18863

Outlaw Charles Arthur "Pretty Boy" Floyd "pulls his first job in 1925 but gets busted and serves a short stint in the pen. Nevertheless, Charley soon improves his techniques with help from various bandits he meets along the way, and with the new mix of experience and finesse, he becomes an unstoppable and admired criminal.

McMurtry, Larry—*Continued*

Things start to turn nasty, though, when murder becomes commonplace; after Dillinger is finally gunned down, the feds dub Charley public enemy number one." Booklist

"Told in homely prose that's perfectly wedded to its subject, this engaging tragicomic novel is as much a study of quiet desperation as of crime and punishment." Publ Wkly

Some can whistle; a novel. Simon & Schuster 1989 348p o.p.

LC 89-21665

Available G.K. Hall large print edition

"Deck, at 51, is fat, lonely and rich, the latter thanks to his number one-rated TV sitcom. He is an emotional and physical recluse living in west Texas, playing perennial host to gay retired classics professor, druggie and nudist Godwin Lloyd-Jon, and communicating with a network of former lovers via answering machine. After he is contacted by his 22-year-old daughter, T.R., who he last saw on the night of her birth, Deck begins his slow progress (impeded by frequent migraines) from solitude toward a 'reconnection' with reality." Publ Wkly

"Danny Deck is exasperating and entirely believable. Well-formed fictional characters always inspire *something* in us, and Danny, virtuoso of the missed opportunity, is inspirational in his failure." N Y Times Book Rev

Somebody's darling. Simon & Schuster 1978 347p o.p.

LC 78-16781

"The story of a 37-year-old woman who has won acclaim for her modest first picture (called 'Womanly Ways!'), her life and involvement with two later films, and her relationships with two men—her friend, a 63-year-old self-professed hack who writes a 'harmless kind of garbage,' mostly for TV, and her lover, a loutish, would-be producer, a former All-American football player and tractor salesman. Each of them narrates a section." Libr J

"Mr. McMurtry's prose has life and immediacy and he is a very funny writer." N Y Times Book Rev

Streets of Laredo; a novel. Simon & Schuster 1993 589p $25

ISBN 0-671-79281-4   LC 93-19279

Also available G.K. Hall large print edition

This sequel to Lonesome Dove "takes place 20 years after the death of Gus McCrae. In this novel, Captain Woodrow Call, McCrae's old partner, tracks a young Mexican train robber, Joe Garza, with the help of a railroad accountant named Brookshire, a Texas deputy named Ted Plunkett and Pea Eye Parker, who is trying to build a family life with his wife Lorena and their children. Across the Texas Panhandle and into northern Mexico, Call pursues his prey." America

"As in some great 19th-century saga, the story has more than its share of improbable coincidences—but these seem only mild contrivances to shape a story packed with action, terror, humor and pathos. *Laredo* is a fitting conclusion to a remarkable feat of reconstruction and sheer storytelling genius." Publ Wkly

Terms of endearment; a novel. Simon & Schuster 1975 410p o.p.

"Houstonian Aurora Greenway, a transplanted New Englander, is a well-to-do widow trying to settle her own life and at the same time to dominate and control the lives of those around her—Emma, her married daughter; Rosie, her long-suffering maid; an array of suitors that includes a retired Patton-style general, an aging yachts-man, a broken-down opera singer, a bank vice president and a truly eccentric Texas millionaire. . . . Aurora alternately delights and infuriates those around her." Libr J

"Suddenly, just when we are enjoying ourselves the most, McMurtry changes his style, and we are plunged into a moving but agonizing realistic account of daughter Emma's death from cancer at 37 and the way in which her family and old friends react. . . . The shift of pace may throw some readers off stride badly. McMurtry certainly remains, however, one of our most exciting novelists." Publ Wkly

Followed by The evening star

Texasville; a novel. Simon & Schuster 1987 542p o.p.

LC 86-31520

"McMurtry returns to the town of Thalia, Texas, site of the 'The last picture show' (1966). The backwater town of the 1950s has experienced the oil boom and is now enduring the oil glut. Although some of the characters from the previous novel make appearances, McMurtry focuses on oilman Duane Moore—dynamic, yearning, caught up in the maelstrom of times. Duane is struggling with a twelve-million-dollar debt and is further bewildered by the manic behavior of his wife, his children, and other citizens of Thalia, all of whom seem to be reacting to hard times by going slightly berserk." Booklist

"What's funniest, and most lifelike, about McMurtry's . . . book is that his people, having enjoyed a brief but exhilarating run of American abundance (both financial and sexual), don't mind indulging in a little harmless romanticizing of their frontier history, but they're not about to give up what they've got and go back to their arid, windswept beginnings without some kicking and screaming. . . . In its affable, offhand way, McMurtry's novel, which ends with a joke about repetition . . . really is about history, at least as Americans live it." New Yorker

McNaught, Judith

Paradise. Pocket Bks. 1991 489p o.p.

LC 91-12897

Available Thorndike Press large print edition

"Heiress to a famous department store fortune, Meredith Bancroft chafes under the strict supervision of her interfering father. When she meets ambitious, handsome steelworker Matt Farrell, Meredith is ripe for the picking, and trouble brews on both sides of the tracks when she becomes pregnant at 18. Mcnaught's skillful treatment of Meredith, the self-styled ugly duckling and poor little rich girl, will pique readers' interest and engage their sympathy." Libr J

Perfect. Pocket Bks. 1993 516p o.p.

LC 93-83306

Available Thorndike Press large print edition

"A real gun substituted for a prop on the set of director Zack Benedict's latest movie results in his adulterous wife's murder, for which he's convicted. Escape from prison . . . throws Zack into the life of Julie Mathison, whose Blazer he highjacks to a remote Colorado hideout. Once the outcome of an escape attempt convinces Julie that Zack is no murderer, their affair is a foregone conclusion. . . . Despite an abundance of clichés, this expert genre foray works, thanks to involving characterizations and convincingly drawn action." Publ Wkly

McPherson, Jessamyn West *See* West, Jessamyn, d. 1984

Mehta, Gita

Raj; a novel. Simon & Schuster 1989 479p o.p.

LC 88-38504

An "historical novel that traces the life of an Indian princess from her birth during the year of Queen Victoria's Diamond Jubilee in 1897 until India wins its independence from the empire in the mid-twentieth century. Princess Jaya treads a path that leads from the ancient traditions of the maharajas—in which the woman was subjugated to the man—through the days in which India was held and exploited as a British possession; she becomes in the end a woman who has achieved her own independence and identity along with her country." Booklist

"Grounded in details of ancient royal tradition and Hindu ritual, Jaya's story counterpoints a vanished way of life against the complex political realities involved in the passing of the Raj and the birth of the modern nations of India and Pakistan." Publ Wkly

A river Sutra. Doubleday 1993 291p $20

ISBN 0-385-47007-X   LC 92-35779

"The narrator has left his high-ranking government job and the bustling life of the city for the tranquility of the country. He manages a rest house along the banks of the sacred Narmada River, devoting quiet hours to contemplation of the river's might, mystery, and beauty. But this seemingly peaceful realm is actually electric with the passion and tragedy of human existence as pilgrims from all walks of life make their way to the holy river. As our innkeeper converses with these troubled travelers, he becomes immersed in their startling stories." Booklist

"This is an idealized India, free of political and religious violence. 'A River Sutra' takes place in a fabled land of the romantic imagination, drawing on timeless literary traditions. Told with skill and sensitivity, Gita Mehta's tales are a delight to read, bringing to Western readers the mystery and drama of a rich cultural heritage." N Y Times Book Rev

Melville, Herman, 1819-1891

Billy Budd, sailor.

Available from Amereon

Written in 1891 but in a still "Unfinished" manuscript stage when Melville died. First publication 1924 in the United Kingdom, as part of the Standard edition of Melville's complete works. Variant title: Billy Budd, foretopman

"Narrates the hatred of petty officer Claggart by Billy, handsome Spanish sailor. Billy strikes and kills Claggart, and is condemned by Captain Vere even though the latter senses Billy's spiritual innocence." Haydn. Thesaurus of Book Dig

The confidence-man: his masquerade.

Available from various publishers

First published 1857

"The scene is a Mississippi River boat, ironically named the 'Fidele.' A plotless satire taking place on April Fool's Day, the book is filled with characters difficult to distinguish from one another; most of them are different manifestations of the confidence man. A sign hanging on the door of the 'Fidele's' barbershop expresses the theme: 'No Trust.' The confidence man, king of

a world without principle, succeeds in gulling men by capitalizing on false hopes and offering false pity. At the end of the book, the flickering light hanging above the table where an old man reads the Bible goes out completely." Reader's Ency. 3d edition

Mardi: and a voyager thither

In Melville, H. Typee; Omoo; Mardi

Moby-Dick; or, The whale.

Available from various publishers

First published 1851

"Moby Dick is a ferocious white whale, who was known to whalers as Mocha Dick. He is pursued in a fury of revenge by Captain Ahab, whose leg he has bitten off; and under Melville's handling the chase takes on a significance beyond mere externals. Moby Dick becomes a symbol of the terrific forces of the natural universe, and Captain Ahab is doomed to disaster, even though Moby Dick is killed at last." Univ Handbk for Readers and Writers

"'Moby-Dick' had some initial critical appreciation, particularly in Britain, but only since the 1920s has it been recognized as a masterpiece, an epic tragedy of tremendous dramatic power and narrative drive." Oxford Companion to Engl Lit. 5th edition

Omoo: a narrative of adventures in the South Seas.

Available from various publishers

First published 1847 by Harper

"Based on Melville's own experiences in the South Pacific, this episodic novel, in a more comical vein than that of *Typee*, tells of the narrator's participation in a mutiny on a whale ship and his subsequent wanderings in Tahiti with the former doctor of the ship." Merriam-Webster's Ency of Lit

also in Melville, H. Typee; Omoo; Mardi

Typee: a peep at Polynesian life. Northwestern Univ. Press 1968 374p il $49.95

ISBN 0-8101-0161-0

Also available from Amereon and Buccaneer Bks.

"The Writings of Herman Melville"

First published 1846

"Based on Melville's own experiences, the story tells of the hero and his friend Toby, who jump ship in the Marquesas Islands and wander mistakenly into the valley of Typee, which is inhabited by cannibals. The Typees become their benevolent captors, refusing to allow them to leave. Toby escapes, while the hero, suffering from a leg wound, remains to be nursed by the lovely Fayaway. Tempted to enjoy a somnolent, vegetative existence, the moral American chooses, with regret, to return to civilization." Reader's Ency. 3d edition

also in Melville, H. Typee; Omoo; Mardi

Typee: a peep at Polynesian life; Omoo: a narrative of adventures in the South Seas; Mardi: and a voyager thither. Library of Am. 1982 1333p $29.95

ISBN 0-940450-00-3   LC 81-18600

Omnibus edition of the author's first three novels. The first two titles are entered separately. In Mardi, first published 1849, Melville "entertained questions of ethics and metaphysics, politics and culture, sin and guilt, in-

Melville, Herman, 1819-1891—*Continued*
nocence and experience. The complexity of the novel's content, in fact, destroys all pretensions to literary form. Originally a narrative of adventure, 'Mardi' became an allegory of mind." Benet's Reader's Ency of Am Lit

Melville, James, 1931-
The bogus Buddha; a Superintendent Otani mystery. Scribner 1991 180p o.p.
LC 90-48629
"While en route to Anraku-in temple to investigate suspicious happenings at an international gathering of academics, Superintendent Otani accidentally uncovers a clandestine meeting of Japanese Mafia leaders involved in a complex real estate swindle. Both situations become clouded by murder, and Otani activates the full resources of his department to unravel the apparently disparate events. Readers able to deal with coincidence served up in a Zenlike manner should have a pleasant read." Booklist

The chrysanthemum chain. St. Martin's Press 1982 181p o.p.
LC 82-5546
"An English subject living in Japan is murdered and the British consul and the local police want to know why. David Murrow was a distinguished educator but he moved in a rather peculiar, though prominent, circle of friends, which included many political luminaries. There is great concern among them about the case and its possible effect on the out-come of an impending election. . . . Although Melville keeps the action moving in this fast paced novel, he still pays close attention to characterization and background." Best Sellers

Death of a daimyo. St. Martin's Press 1984 145p o.p.
LC 84-11749
"Following the death of Osaka's most powerful gangster, an underworld struggle for power threatens massive bloodshed unless acting police chief Kimura can intercede. Meanwhile, Superintendent Otani, vacationing in England, witnesses the murder of a Japanese businessman and is unwillingly drawn into the case. The action in this narrative shifts from Japan to England, as Otani's Old World grace is contrasted with Kimura's earnest attempts at Westernization." Booklist

A haiku for Hanae. Scribner 1989 195p o.p.
LC 89-10559
"The year is 1968, and the scene is the remote Awaji Island, where a young Mormon missionary (with an eye for the ladies) has been found murdered close to a Shinto shrine. . . . In attempting to solve the case, Otani must link Japanese spirit worship with the large number of sensual, susceptible women who were easy prey for the errant missionary." Booklist

The ninth netsuke. St. Martin's Press 1982 151p o.p.
LC 82-16782
"When Superintendent Otani takes his wife to one of the most notorious hotels in Kobe and asks for the Sweet Harmony Room, eyebrows are raised. . . . The interest Otani has in it, is that it was the recent scene of a murder. His unwilling wife is a cover, but as in previous Otani novels, she manages to locate clues overlooked by the police. In this case it is a netsuke, a small

ivory figurine in the shape of a woman, which has been hidden in the drapes. It turns out to be part of a valuable set of ten figures missing from a museum. This discovery leads Otani into far deeper hot water than he had planned, and also places his wife in great danger. The trail leads him into the field of organized crime before the final solution." West Coast Rev Books

Melville, Jennie *See* Butler, Gwendoline

Meredith, George, 1828-1909
The ordeal of Richard Feverel. o.p.
First published 1859
This novel is representative of Meredith's "best work, full of allusion and metaphor, lyrical prose and witty dialogue, with a deep exploration of the psychology of motive and rationalization. The novel's subject is the relationship between a cruelly manipulative father and a son who loves a girl of a lower social class. Both men are self-deluded and proud, and the story's ending is tragic." Merriam-Webster's Ency of Lit

Mérimée, Prosper, 1803-1870
Carmen; translated from the French and illustrated by Edmund H. Garrett, with a memoir of the author by Louise Imogen Guiney. Little, Brown 1896 xxx, 117p il o.p.
Original French edition, 1845
"Georges Bizet's opera *Carmen* is based on the story. As a hot-blooded young corporal in the Spanish cavalry stationed near Seville, Don José is ordered to arrest Carmen, a young, flirtatious Gypsy woman, for assaulting a coworker. Greatly charmed by her, José allows her to escape. He deserts the army, kills two men on Carmen's account, and takes up a life as a robber and smuggler. He is insanely jealous of Carmen, who is unfaithful to him, and when she refuses to change on his behalf, he kills her and surrenders himself to the authorities." Merriam-Webster's Ency of Lit

Mertz, Barbara, 1927-
For works written by this author under other names see Michaels, Barbara, 1927-; Peters, Elizabeth, 1927-

Meyer, Nicholas
The seven-per-cent solution; being a reprint from the reminiscences of John H. Watson, M.D., as edited by Nicholas Meyer. Dutton 1974 253p o.p.
"In this final memoir, dictated from a nursing home in 1939, Watson [the biographer of the famous detective Sherlock Holmes] confesses that the events he recounted in 'The Final Problem' are a total fabrication. . . . Watson observes that Holmes's agitation over Moriarty's evil doings occurs only when he has been taking cocaine. Fearing that Holmes is destroying himself, Watson tricks him into a trip to Vienna, where he turns him over to Sigmund Freud. . . . Freud cures Holmes of his addiction, and Holmes lingers on to observe that the schizophrenia of one of Freud's patients results from a criminal conspiracy as yet unsuspected by anyone." Newsweek

Meyer, Nicholas—*Continued*

"In a field replete with pastiche Meyer succeeds because of a superior ear for Conan Doyle's style, a gentle sense of fun, and a talent for plot that few of the imitators have possessed." Libr J

The West End horror; a posthumous memoir of John H. Watson, M.D., as edited by Nicholas Meyer. Dutton 1976 222p o.p.

This novel "is set in London's theatre district in 1895. A much disliked theatre critic has been murdered, and Sherlock Holmes is engaged to find the murderer. His client is another critic of the day whose years of fame are ahead of him: George Bernard Shaw. Inspector Lestrade, Holmes's old foil, is on the scene, but, as always, his efforts are misdirected and before long he has managed to incarcerate an obvious innocent. Clues abound and so too do real but suspicious characters." Best Sellers

Michael, Judith

Deceptions. Pocket Bks. 1982 472p o.p.

"A Poseidon Press book"

"When twin sisters, who have been mistaken for each other all their lives, are on vacation together in China, they decide on a whim to switch roles for a week, thus beginning a deception that has far-reaching effects. The aristocratic Lady Sabrina, assuming the suburban housewife's duties of her sister Stephanie Anderson, is surprised to find she scarcely misses her former high life, reveling instead in the acceptance and security of being part of a family. Stephanie, leaving her humdrum life behind to assume Sabrina's jet-set life of partying and dealing in antiques, so much enjoys her liberation that she is reluctant to come home. Sabrina has fallen in love with Stephanie's husband; she postpones ending the deception until a freak accident leaves her unsure of her identity at all." Publ Wkly

Followed by A tangled web

Inheritance; a novel. Poseidon Press 1988 607p o.p.

LC 87-35945

"The tale stars petty thief Laura Fairchild, who comes to Owen Salinger's house to rob him but instead becomes his heir. . . . But once ensconced in the Salinger house, Laura discovers that she wants no trouble, since most of the family is so good to her. A necklace is stolen, however, and years later, after inheriting much of the Salinger hotel empire, Laura's past is disclosed, leading the family to shut her out as emphatically as they once embraced her." Booklist

"Intrigue, twists and turns, love, hate, loyalty and betrayal naturally abound. Although the plot is on the preposterous side and relies heavily on coincidence, the writing is impeccable." N Y Times Book Rev

Pot of gold; a novel. Poseidon Press 1993 460p $23

ISBN 0-671-70704-3   LC 93-14336

"Claire Goddard is a hard-working, 35-year-old divorcée who has a close and loving relationship with her 17-year-old daughter Emma. When Claire wins $60 million in the lottery, they set out on their new life with sybaritic abandon: Claire quits her job, hires a money manager and begins buying luxury goods. But if they now have leisure and power, Claire and Emma also have too many choices. While on a cruise that is emblematic of their emotional displacement, the vulnerable women fall under the spell of an unscrupulous duo: Quentin Eiger, director of Eiger Cosmetics, and his son Brix." Publ Wkly

A ruling passion; a novel. Poseidon Press 1990 574p o.p.

LC 89-25484

Available G.K. Hall large print edition

"Privileged and beautiful Valerie Sterling arrives at Stanford, and ignores fellow student Sybille, daughter of her mother's dressmaker, to dabble in acting and dally with Nick, an impoverished student who loves her. Two bad marriages later, Valerie loses a cheating husband and a fortune in a mysterious plane crash, but finds her courage. Sybille, meantime, marries and divorces Nick, then scrambles to the top of the heap in network news. Her envy and hatred of Valerie snowball when Valerie becomes an investigative reporter at the cable network Nick owns and digs up dirt on a televangelist show Sybille has launched." Publ Wkly

Sleeping beauty; a novel. Poseidon Press 1991 539p o.p.

LC 91-31298

Available G.K. Hall large print edition

"The wealthy, influential Chatham family, founders of a Chicago-based realty empire, present a wholesome image to the outside world. But 30-year-old financial whiz Vince Chatham has raped his 13-year-old niece, Anne, and continues to abuse her sexually. When Anne overcomes her fear and guilt to accuse Vince at a family gathering, she is met with skepticism from her relatives and denial from Vince. After Anne runs away from home, however, Vince is stripped of his position at the corporation; enraged, he vows to destroy the rest of the Chatham clan." Publ Wkly

"Michael does this sort of thing much better than most of the competition: the characters, naturally larger than life, are still believable." Booklist

A tangled web; a novel. Simon & Schuster 1994 476p $23

ISBN 0-671-79879-0   LC 94-20114

"Michael further entangles the plot begun in her novel *Deceptions*. . . . Here, Stephanie's reported death in a yacht sinking leaves Sabrina caught up in her role. . . . This . . . novel has a dual setting: Sabrina's contented home life in Evanston . . . and a small town in France, where Stephanie is gradually regaining her memory and living with her 'husband' Max, a counterfeiter and smuggler. This plot is tangled, indeed. But the suspense of how these sisters and their loved ones can possibly emerge unscathed from such a fine mess is tightly drawn." Booklist

Michaels, Barbara, 1927-

For works written by this author under other names see Peters, Elizabeth, 1927-

The dark on the other side. Dodd, Mead 1970 250p o.p.

"Werewolf folklore permeates this taut contemporary Gothic novel set in the northeastern U.S. Commissioned to do a magazine story about the wealthy and handsome Gordon Randolph, Michael Collins is drawn to Gordon's lovely wife, Linda, who obviously fears her husband. As Michael delves into Gordon's past he discovers that those persons closest to Gordon have suffered mental breakdown or death, and it appears that Linda is presently in danger." Booklist

Michaels, Barbara, 1927-—*Continued*

Greygallows. Dodd, Mead 1972 279p o.p.

This Gothic novel is set in England during the early 1840s. "In London with her aunt, orphaned heiress Lucy Cartwright relishes the social whirl but is discomforted when Jonathan Scott, the family lawyer's young assistant, tries to open her eyes to the suffering of the poor. Then against her will she is married to the handsome, cold Baron Clare who takes her to his family's estate in Yorkshire, where her puzzlement over her husband's contradictory behavior turns to fear, and Jonathan's arrival on business brings matters to a head." Booklist

Houses of stone. Simon & Schuster 1993 334p $21

ISBN 0-671-68949-5   LC 93-27926
Also available Thorndike Press large print edition

"Michaels sets her heroine, Professor Karen Holloway, to the task of discovering the provenance of a remnant from an old manuscript. Holloway is convinced that it is a thinly disguised autobiographical novel by an obscure feminist poet whose verses have already helped Holloway carve a niche in the cutthroat business of academia. The professor's archenemies, two fellow literature experts, are equally convinced of the work's value and attempt desperate measures to gain access of the manuscript. Michaels has composed a mystery that is brimming with suspense yet revolves around authorial research rather than money and multiple murders." Booklist

Into the darkness. Simon & Schuster 1990 348p o.p.

LC 90-32412
Available G.K. Hall large print edition

"Meg Venturi is drawn back to the small New England town of her childhood when her beloved grandfather dies. She returns reluctantly, for she is haunted by family tragedies that are slowly unveiled throughout the story. Her grandfather's will leaves her half ownership of his world-famous antique jewelry store; the other half is left to a mysterious stranger—a skilled goldsmith whom her grandfather had employed. Meg is reluctant to accept her grandfather's bequest until hints of foul play and threatening missives rouse her curiosity and feistiness." Booklist

"Memorable characters and complex mystery make this one of the Michaels's best novels of romantic suspense." Publ Wkly

Search the shadows. Atheneum Pubs. 1987 358p $17.95

ISBN 0-689-11906-2   LC 87-11565

"Haskell Maloney, born in 1965, pursues her late mother's academic tradition by taking up Egyptology at the University of Chicago. But Haskell is seeking more than work experience or a degree; she is also looking for answers to her mother's untimely death and the true identity of her father." Booklist

Shattered silk. Atheneum Pubs. 1986 369p o.p.

LC 86-47658

Karen Nevitt "begins a new life in Georgetown after her unhappy marriage crumbles. She plans to open an antique-clothing shop with the encouragement of old and new friends. But a series of seemingly unrelated yet terrifying events begins to unfold, and Karen is caught up in a web of deadly suspense." Libr J

Smoke and mirrors. Simon & Schuster 1989 348p $17.95

ISBN 0-671-67037-9   LC 88-26493

"Erin Hartsock is hired as a poorly paid member of the campaign staff of Rosemary Marshall, candidate for the U.S. Senate. As the daughter of an old acquaintance of the candidate and one of the few paid staff members, Erin feels a bit of jealousy from her peers. When mysterious fires and threatening messages start appearing, Erin is under more serious suspicion. With the help of a coworker, an incredibly handsome, dedicated young man named Nick, Erin ferrets out the saboteur. The novel moves a bit slowly, suggesting that Michaels is less intent here on generating suspense than on revealing the underside of a campaign. Still, her fans will relish the way she unveils and manipulates each character's dark secrets." Booklist

Vanish with the rose. Simon & Schuster 1992 348p $20

ISBN 0-671-68948-7   LC 92-6852
Also available G.K. Hall large print edition

"In a desperate attempt to locate her missing brother, Diana Reed goes to work as a landscape architect at the last place he was seen. Unqualified for the job, she lives with fear of discovery—which, of course, eventually transpires, prompting her boss and coworkers to try and assist her search. Sinister events make murder seem the most likely explanation for her brother's disappearance." Libr J

"A cleverly spun mystery, complicated by haunting visions and music from the mansion's past." Booklist

Michener, James A. (James Albert), 1907-

Alaska. Random House 1988 868p $22

ISBN 0-394-55154-0   LC 87-43232

This novel begins with the prehistory of Alaska before concentrating on the history of the region since the 18th century

"Besides multiple heroes and heroines, there are knaves and opportunists who have depleted Alaska's resources and contributed to the high rates of alcoholism and suicide. One of Michener's favorite words is *noble*, but after mushing through his Arctic saga of persistence and greed, one is not surprised that he uses it mainly to describe grizzly bears, salmon and whales." Time

The bridges at Toko-ri. Random House 1953 146p $16.95

ISBN 0-394-41780-1

"In this hard-hitting novel of the Korean conflict, Admiral George Tarrant commands the Naval Task Force, whose carrier-based jets are to knock out strategic points throughout Korea. The focal point of the novel is Harry Brubaker, a lawyer who goes reluctantly to war after being called up as a jet pilot. The reader will remember also Beer Barrel, the landing officer who can get the jets back on the carrier's decks, no matter how rough the seas; and Mike Forney, helicopter rescue pilot who gets pilots out of the freezing waters if they are downed." Shapiro. Fic for Youth. 3d edition

Caravans; a novel. Random House 1963 341p $29.95

ISBN 0-394-41849-2

The story, set in Afghanistan in the year 1946, "focuses on Ellen Jasper, an American bored with her native land, who flees to Afghanistan to become the second wife of a man named Nazrullah. Her parents

Michener, James A. (James Albert), 1907-
—*Continued*

haven't heard from her in 13 months and Mark Miller, of the U.S. Embassy in that country, is sent to investigate. The search takes Miller into unknown territory. He joins a nomad tribe and experiences a love affair of rare beauty with Mira, daughter of the Great Zulfiqar, chieftain of all the nomadic peoples scattered around Afghanistan. [The novel describes] Ellen's degeneration into a sensualist, [and] the encounter of Miller (a Jew) with an ex-Nazi who tortured Jews." America

Caribbean. Random House 1989 672p $22.95

ISBN 0-394-56561-4   LC 89-42785

A novel about the "Caribbean islands from the days when the peace-loving Arawak Indians were overpowered by cannibalistic Caribs, to a ship's tour of today's still lush, but troubled, paradise. Sir Francis Drake, pirate Henry Morgan, Horatio Nelson, Haitian General Toussaint L'Ouverture, Fidel Castro march across the pages, and while the pace is sometimes achingly slow, the dialogue stilted and the characterization skimpy, Michener laces the whole with fiery Caribbean drama." Publ Wkly

Centennial. Random House 1974 909p $40.50

ISBN 0-394-47970-X

"Written to celebrate the United States centennial, the book centers on a fictional town in Colorado. It begins with an examination of the geological formation of the land and a discussion of the first animals to live there. It continues with the arrival of the Indians, the coming of the first settlers, the traders, the search for gold, the building of the railroads, and the start of cattle ranching—virtually all the activities that made this country develop as it did. The conclusion brings us to the social and ecological problems of the 1970s." Shapiro. Fic for Youth. 3d edition

Chesapeake. Random House 1978 865p $45

ISBN 0-394-50079-2   LC 78-2892

"Through the interwoven stories of three families and the Indians, Blacks, and Irish immigrants with whom they interact, Michener chronicles four centuries of life on Maryland's Eastern Shore. . . . Michener elaborates . . . variations on his themes of personal accountability for social change, man's self-expulsion from paradise, and the interrelated ecological network of all things." Libr J

The covenant. Random House 1980 887p $39.95

ISBN 0-394-50505-0   LC 80-5315

This novel spans 500 years of South African history. Three families mingle "with the outstanding historic figures of their times. They are the Nxumalos, the Van Doorns, and the Saltwoods, representing respectively the African, Afrikaans, and English. . . . Over several hundred years their descendants make contact, and thrive through the contact, only to become adversaries as contact subsequently gives way to conflict. Finally they find themselves irretrievably stuck in the hard concrete of South Africa's racial policies." Christ Sci Monit

Creatures of the kingdom; stories of animals and nature; illustrations by Karen Jacobsen. Random House 1993 281p il $22

ISBN 0-679-41367-7   LC 92-46075

Analyzed in Short story index

Contents: From the boundless deep; The birth of the Rockies; Diplodocus, the dinosaur; A miracle of evolution; The mastodon; Matriarch, the woolly mammoth; Portrait of Rufous; The beaver; The eagle and the snake; The hyena; Nerka the salmon; Onk-or; The invaders; Jimmy the crab; Lucifer and Hey-You; The Colonel and Genghis Khan

"Gathered in this delightful 'anthology' . . . are sections from Michener's novels that deal with animals and other less animate aspects of the natural world. . . . These selections represent nature writing as its most fluid and involving." Booklist

The drifters; a novel. Random House 1971 751p $29.95

ISBN 0-394-46200-9

This novel, "narrated by a 60-year-old American financier who roams Europe and Africa in search of good investments, follows six young adults as they travel in search of something else. . . . Each young person has a special set of circumstances with which to contend." N Y Times Book Rev

"The Drifters is something of a guidebook loosely dressed up as fiction; a guide to quaint and colorful places, especially on the Iberian peninsula, and to the life-styles of the rebellious young." Saturday Rev

The eagle and the raven; drawings by Charles Shaw. State House Press 1990 214p il $19.95

ISBN 0-938349-57-0   LC 90-9684

"This novel is actually a previously unpublished excerpt from Michener's *Texas* . . . . A fictional account of the lives of Sam Houston and Santa Anna, the book moves relentlessly to the adversaries' historic encounter at the battle of San Jacinto, which resulted, eventually, in the U.S. annexation of Texas." Booklist

"Michener makes history come alive in this engaging slice of Americana and Texas lore, a compelling testament to the precept that character is destiny." Publ Wkly

Hawaii. Random House 1959 937p $45

ISBN 0-394-42797-1

A "novel in which the racial origins of Hawaii are traced through several narrative strands that merge in contemporary history. The original Tahitian colonizers welcome the white missionaries who bring in Chinese and Japanese laborers, and all together make up the present-day 'golden' Hawaiian." Wis Libr Bull

"High-domed, long-haired *littérateurs* may argue that Michener's characters are often as paper-thin as the colored image in which Hawaii is held by mainland tourists, but 'Hawaii,' is still a masterful job of research, an absorbing performance of storytelling, and a monumental account of the islands from geologic birth to sociological emergence as the newest, and perhaps the most interesting of the United States." Saturday Rev

Journey; by James Michener. Random House 1989 244p $25

ISBN 0-394-57826-0   LC 88-43224

Also available Thorndike Press large print edition

Michener, James A. (James Albert), 1907-
—*Continued*

"In July 1897, following the discovery of Klondike gold, four British aristocrats and their Irish servant set out from London to attempt the trek into the gold fields by an exclusively Canadian route. Twenty-three months later, after testing the limits of human endurance, only two men reach their goal. . . . This episode was edited out of *Alaska* but Michener, wanting to recount the Canadian role, resurrected it and fleshed it out." Libr J

"The story is affecting enough, its historical milieu sufficiently engrossing, to overcome Michener's bland descriptive prose and perfunctory dialogue." Booklist

Mexico. Random House 1992 625p $25
ISBN 0-679-41649-8   LC 92-50151
Also available large print edition $25 (ISBN 0-679-74329-4)

In this novel set in Mexico City, "Mexico-born Norman Clay, a journalist for a New York publication, returns to his natal city to report on the bullfights that highlight its annual festival. This year two matadors are joined in a rivalry that could end in death." Libr J
"There are splendid and authentic scenes in the *plaza de toros* that are as dramatic as any written by Ernest Hemingway or Barnaby Conrad, and one chapter, where the bulls' horns are shaved by the father of a torero, is James Michener the storyteller and parabolist at his finest." N Y Times Book Rev

The novel. Random House 1991 446p $22.50
ISBN 0-679-40133-4   LC 90-53489
Also available large print edition $25 (ISBN 0-679-40348-5)

"'The novel' is divided into four parts, each told from a different point of view. The first is that of the novelist, Lukas, a plain, clean-living but big-bucks author in his late 60's whose most recent work, 'Stone Walls,' is the final work in the Grenzler Octet, an opus set in the Pennsylvania Dutch country, where he was born and raised. The second voice is that of Yvonne Marmelle, née Shirley Marmelstein, his editor. The third is that of the literary critic Karl Streibert, Lukas's fellow Pennsylvania Dutchman. And the fourth is that of a reader, Jane Garland, grand dame and philanthropist who is also Lukas's friend." N Y Times Book Rev
"To his credit, Michener tries to be fair to both sides of the literary vs. popular fiction debate. The elitist Streibert is presented as an honest, well-intentioned man who genuinely loves literature and worries about the dangers of commercialism. The position Michener seems to be advocating in 'The Novel' is that experimental, elitist fiction and old-fashioned storytelling are both legitimate forms for the novel." Christ Sci Monit

Poland. Random House 1983 556p $35
ISBN 0-394-53189-2   LC 83-4477

"Centering on the fictional village of Bukowo on the Vistula River, the novel's action occurs as a series of vignettes of Polish life from the 1200s to the 1980s. Each chapter tells the story of a different generation of three families of Bukowo—the wealthy magnate counts Lubonski, the minor nobles Bukowski, and peasants Buk." Libr J
"The author's description of the devastating invasions of Poland by Tartars, Germans, Swedes, Turks, Russians and Soviets is historically accurate as well as highly vivid. . . . But the most unforgettable and deeply

moving pages of the book are those in which Michener narrates the horrid experiences of the inmates of the Polish concentration camp of Majdanek, where 140,000 Jewish and 220,000 Christian prisoners died. . . . Michener's Poland is an engrossing and fast moving novel by a superb storyteller." America

Recessional. Random House 1994 484p $25
ISBN 0-679-43612-X   LC 94-17414
Also available large print edition $24 (ISBN 0-879-75691-4)

"Opening with obstetrician Andy Zorn taking a job as manager of one of the nation's poshest retirement and final-care facilities, the novel weaves through the challenges Zorn faces and the experiences of many of the residents of the Palms in Florida. . . . The fine line between euthanasia and the excessive use of mechanical life supports is drawn with poignant scenes of aging and AIDS patients. Despite the dreary subject, this novel is full of life and romance." Booklist

Sayonara. Random House 1954 243p o.p.

The love story of an American Air Corps major and a beautiful Japanese girl. When Major Gruver sets up housekeeping with Hanaogi there is consternation among the Americans, for Gruver is engaged to an American general's daughter. Contrary to the course of Madam Butterfly, in this instance it is the Japanese girl who says Sayonara (farewell) to the American

Space. Random House 1982 622p $17.95
ISBN 0-394-50555-7   LC 82-40127

This novel "begins at the time of World War II and features characters who eventually find themselves, in one capacity or another, involved with the space program. Some are engineers; some are politicians; some are astronauts." Libr J
"Michener has caught the essence of what motivated and then enfeebled our space program. . . . As usual, Michener has done his homework, this time with affection and excitement as well—his pro-space enthusiasm is the book's driving force, and he has deftly woven an incredible amount of information into the tale." Natl Rev

Tales of the South Pacific. Macmillan 1947 326p o.p.
Analyzed in Short story index
Contents: South Pacific; Coral Sea; Mutiny; Officer and a gentleman; The cave; Milk run; Alligator; Our heroine; Dry rot; Fo'dolla; Passion; Boar's tooth; Wine for the mess at Segi; Airstrip at Konora; Those who fraternize; The strike; Frisco Landing on Kuralei; Cemetery at Hoga Point
Describes "the strain and the boredom, the careful planning and heroic action, the color and beauty of the islands, and all that made up life during the critical days to the war in the Pacific." Wis Libr Bull

Texas. Random House 1985 1096p o.p.
LC 85-8248

This novel covers Texas history from 1527 to the present. "Texas then and now is, in a sense, all here: the Spanish missions; the early settlers; fights with the Comanches and Apaches; the Battle of the Alamo, won by the flamboyant and wily Mexican general Santa Anna . . . Sam Houston's heroic victory at San Jacinto; the birth of the Lone Star Republic—and so on." Publ Wkly

Michener, James A. (James Albert), 1907-
—Continued
"As a novel, this book is remarkably good. . . . Michener, however, has given us here something even more: a marvelous and sympathetic analysis of historical and social relations." Best Sellers

Millar, Kenneth *See* Macdonald, Ross, 1915-1983

Miller, Henry, 1891-1980
Tropic of Cancer; with a preface by Anais Nin. Modern Lib. 1983 c1961 321p o.p.
LC 82-42868
First published 1934 in France; first United States edition published 1961 by Grove Press
"An autobiographical first novel recounting the experiences, sensations, thoughts of Miller, a penniless American in the Paris of the early thirties. It is not so much a novel as an intense journal, written daily about what was happening to him daily . . . as he scrounged for food, devoured books, conversed volubly, and flung himself into numerous beds." New Repub
Miller "uses themes—cadging for food, shelter, and sex; attacks on such bourgeois values as work and marriage; denunciations of traditional art and literature—and imagery—wild, exuberant, often shockingly frank—that together represent a savage, nihilistic (and at times enormously funny) revulsion against a world of stupidity and ugliness." Ency of World Lit in the 20th Century
Followed by Tropic of Capricorn

Tropic of Capricorn. Grove Press 1962 c1961 348p o.p.
First published 1939 in France
"In a form like that of *Tropic of Cancer* the autobiographical account describes the writer's boyhood in Brooklyn, his quest to discover himself by sexual experiences and by other means, and his fury at the faults he finds in many of the values and ways of life in the U.S." Oxford Companion to Am Lit. 5th edition

Miller, Sue
Family pictures; a novel. Harper & Row 1990 389p o.p.
LC 89-46109
This novel chronicles "forty years in the lives of the Eberhardts, a Chicago family. David and Lainey's third child, Randall, is autistic. 'According to the experts of the '50s, the fault is Lainey's for unconsciously rejecting her infant son; David—himself a psychiatrist—agrees with them. A few decades later science will absolve her, but the shock and pain of her husband's betrayal throw a curse on their relationship that is never quite dispelled." Newsweek
"'Family Pictures' is a novel that might have intrigued and startled Woolf—profoundly honest, shapely, ambitious, engrossing, original and true, an important example of a new American tradition that explores what it means, not to light out for the territories but to make a home, live at home and learn what home is." N Y Times Book Rev

For love. HarperCollins Pubs. 1993 301p o.p.
LC 92-54422
Available G.K. Hall large print edition

"Fortyish freelance writer Lottie leaves her new husband in Chicago to spend part of the summer in Cambridge, Massachusetts, getting the family house ready to sell now that her brother Cameron has placed their alcoholic mother in a nursing home. While she and her son Ryan paint and clean, Lottie examines the concept of love in an article she is writing, studying her own troubled marriage and Cameron's resumption of a love affair with childhood sweetheart Elizabeth. For Elizabeth, who is staying with her mother after leaving her philandering husband, this romance is just a fling. But Cameron's obsessive love for the golden girl of his youth leads to [an accident]." Libr J
Miller "maps emotional terrain carefully, precisely, graphically, with a grit and grace that at first invite the reader's appreciation—and then, before we know it, have us involved." N Y Times Book Rev

The good mother. Harper & Row 1986 310p o.p.
LC 85-45475
In this novel "Anna Dunlap, newly divorced, is shaping a life centered around her three-year-old daughter, Molly. Then Leo Cutter sparks a sexual responsiveness new to Anna . . . Molly and Leo like each other, too, and Anna sees them as a loving family unit—until her ex-husband sues for custody, citing sexual activities that put his child at risk. The love affair is irrevocably changed, as Anna opens her life to a court-appointed psychiatrist and bends the truth to her lawyer's strategy." Libr J
"The fulcrum on which the novel's plot pivots is the allegation by Anna's ex-husband that Anna's lover has molested Molly, and the ensuing custody trial. Miller's treatment of this high point of tension in the novel is dramatic, discreet, compassionate. Each development in the legal process increases the tension. The drama heightens, the suspense builds, character is further developed, and the latitude for choice logically narrowed. Like a final judgment, the custody decision breaks over reader and character alike." Christ Sci Monit

Inventing the Abbotts and other stories. Harper & Row 1987 180p o.p.
LC 86-46089
Analyzed in Short story index
Contents: Inventing the Abbotts; Tyler and Brina; Appropriate affect; Slides; What Ernest says; Travel; Leaving home; Calling; Expensive gifts; The birds and the bees; The quality of life
"These stories report from a frontier, from the discontented and guilty world of divorce and the single parent, of marriage as a threatened institution, and if the landscape is a bleak and dispiriting one, that is not the author's fault; she is merely giving evidence. As stories they vary—some effective, others less so—but as testimonies of our times they seem highly apposite." NY Times Book Rev

Miller, Walter M., 1923-
A canticle for Leibowitz; a novel by Walter M. Miller, Jr. Lippincott 1960 c1959 320p o.p. Buccaneer Bks. reprint available $18.95 (ISBN 0-89968-353-3)
"Here is science fiction of the highest literary excellence and thematic intelligence. A monastery founded by the scientist Leibowitz is discovered decades after an atomic war. In the first part of the book a young novice in the monastery is the protagonist; in the second part

Miller, Walter M., 1923-—*Continued*
we see scholars in a new period of enlightenment; and
in the final section we observe man's proclivity for
repeating mistakes and the apparent inevitability of
history's repeating itself." Shapiro. Fic for Youth. 3d
edition

The darfsteller

In The Hugo winners v1 p5-71

Miłosz, Czesław
Nobel Prize in literature, 1980
The seizure of power; translated by Celina
Wieniewska. Farrar, Straus & Giroux 1982
245p o.p.

LC 82-9297

Original Polish edition, 1953; this translation first
published 1955 by Criterion Books
"The novel is set in summer 1944 as the Poles are
set to exchange one army of occupation, the Germans,
for another, the Russians. In Warsaw, a doomed rising
against the Nazis is under way; in the East, the Red
Army is preparing to push across the Vistula into Warsaw and is establishing a provisional Communist government. Milosz catalogues the reactions of a broad swath
of Poles to these two foreign conquerors, showing first
the splintered resistance to the Nazis and then the round
of compromises and killing that arrives with the Russians. This historical novel was based on actual characters of the period." Publ Wkly

Minot, Susan
Folly. Houghton Mifflin; Lawrence, S.
1992 278p $19.95

ISBN 0-395-60339-0   LC 92-21035

This novel opens in the aftermath of America's entry
into the First World War. "Lilian Eliot is the product
of Brahmin Boston, whose traditions and socially correct
attitudes have been instilled in her. She has been cast
in the mold. Yet at times she longs to break free, to
be someone different. Lilian sees that her choice of a
husband will determine her future, but she finds herself
most comfortable with what is familiar and marries accordingly. Later in life she is again faced with the
choice—to break free or stay. In making her choice,
Lilian finally discovers herself." Libr J
The author's "carefully thought out depiction of
Lilian's inner world and of the difficulty of finding an
accommodation between desire and reality, silence and
self-expression, has a universal resonance." Christ Sci
Monit

Lust & other stories. Houghton Mifflin;
Lawrence, S. 1989 147p o.p.

LC 89-1677

Analyzed in Short story index
Contents: Lust; Sparks; Blow; City night; Lunch with
Harry; The break-up; The swan in the garden; The
feather in the toque; The knot; A thrilling life; Ile Sèche;
The man who would not go away
"Men remain emotionally distant and unwilling to
commit throughout these 12 short stories, while women
attempt to hold back. Alas, love insinuates itself and
the man disappears. Minot's writing is sparse and poetic,
painfully close to the surface." Libr J

Monkeys. Dutton; Lawrence, S. 1986 159p
o.p.

LC 85-30775

Interconnected episodes "trace the fortunes of a large
boisterous New England family. Arranged into rough
chronological order, the stories dramatize the growing up
of the seven Vincent siblings. Their everyday world of
family gatherings, teenage parties, and vacations seems
frivolous on the surface but is underlaid with tension
and ultimately leads to tragedy. The episodic nature of
the book leaves a few questions unanswered about the
engaging clan, while occasionally some events are
reiterated. Yet there is a wonderful sense of slipping into
the private, important moments of the Vincents, sharing
their fun and their sadness." Booklist

Mishima, Yukio, 1925-1970
Acts of worship; seven stories; translated
by John Bester. Kodansha Int./USA 1989
205p $17.95

ISBN 0-87011-937-0   LC 89-45171

Analyzed in Short story index
Contents: Fountains in the rain; Raisin bread; Sword;
Sea and sunset; Cigarette; Martyrdom; Act of worship
"Above all, these stories demonstrate Mishima's ability
to render atmosphere and theme through a complex yet
orderly mixture of sharply observed physical details and
introspective musings." N Y Times Book Rev

The decay of the angel; translated from
the Japanese by Edward G. Seidensticker.
Knopf 1974 236p (Sea of fertility) o.p.
Original Japanese edition, 1971
This final novel in the series "treats the themes of
purity, beauty, evil and death. . . . [Judge Honda] is
now near death, while that spirit of tragic purity which
in the earlier stories was respectively incarnate in
Kiyoaki, Isao and Ying Chan is found here in Toru,
an evil teenaged orphan, Toru is employed, symbolically
enough, as a ship watcher when Honda, seeing him as
both evil like himself and marked for an early death,
adopts him as his son in order to thwart that destiny.
Over several years Honda proves no more of a match
for Toru than does the bride he chooses for him, but
neither man is to escape an eerie doom." Publ Wkly
"The novel concludes with a superbly written scene
that casts doubt on the reality of the events described
in the four volumes. In the end we discover that the
'sea of fertility' may be as arid as the region of that
name on the moon, although it seems to suggest infinite
richness." Ency of World Lit in the 20th Century

Forbidden colors; translated from the
Japanese by Alfred H. Marks. Knopf 1968
403p o.p.
Original Japanese edition, 1951
An elderly novelist "Shunsuke, who has been embittered by his experiences with women, is attracted to
Yuichi. Because of Yuichi's great beauty and his inability
to love a woman, Shunsuke suggests a plan to avenge
the wrongs which he feels he himself has experienced.
Three of the women in Shunsuke's past are introduced
to Yuichi and led into relationships which cause them
much difficulty. At the same time Mishima analyzes and
describes the relationships which Yuichi develops with
a number of male companions in his attempt to satisfy
his own needs for love and affection." Libr J

Mishima, Yukio, 1925-1970—*Continued*

Runaway horses; translated from the Japanese by Michael Gallagher. Knopf 1973 421p (Sea of fertility) o.p.

Original Japanese edition, 1969

In the second volume of the Sea of fertility cycle "the political and economic upheaval of the 1930's is seen primarily through the eyes of a young zealot intent upon an imperial restoration through assassination of key industrialists and then his own ritual suicide. The secondary strand involves a middle-aged judge whose carefully constructed rational and legalistic life crumbles when exposed to the younger man's idealism." Choice

"Mishima uses the same literary artistry in this novel as in the first but changes the gently romantic tone to one of martial ideology with a weirdly beautiful emphasis on ritual suicide. In the interplay of entanglements between the two novels, each self-contained, the author experiments with the Buddhist doctrine of reincarnation." Booklist

Followed by The Temple of Dawn

The sound of waves; translated by Meredith Weatherby; drawings by Yoshinori Kinoshita. Knopf 1956 182p il o.p.

"Returning to his village after a day on the fishing boats, Shinji, 18 years old, comes upon a beautiful stranger, Hatsue, who is the daughter of the wealthiest man in the village. After several unplanned encounters the two realize that they are in love, but many obstacles must be overcome before they can be married." Shapiro. Fic for Youth. 3d edition

Spring snow; translated from the Japanese by Michael Gallagher. Knopf 1972 389p (Sea of fertility) o.p.

"UNESCO collection of representative works: Japanese series"

Original Japanese edition, 1968

The first volume in the author's Sea of fertility tetralogy

"Kiyoaki Matsugae, a young Japanese, comes from a wealthy family whose attention to the most formal aspects of Japanese life has changed because of their attraction to Western culture. His best friend, Shigekuna Honda, is not so handsome or affluent but is a more serious scholar. The story emphasizes the difference in the character of the two young men as the plot describes the passionate, although ambivalent, love that Kiyoaki feels for the beautiful Satoko. When she concludes that Kiyoaki does not return her love, despite the fact that their affair has been serious and intimate, she allows herself to be betrothed to someone else. As always, what is forbidden becomes more desirable and Kiyoaki tries desperately to regain his loved one. Japanese customs and rituals intervene to bring a tragic ending to this love story." Shapiro. Fic for Youth. 3d edition

Followed by Runaway horses

The Temple of Dawn; translated from the Japanese by E. Dale Saunders and Cecilia Segawa Seigle. Knopf 1973 334p (Sea of fertility) o.p.

Original Japanese edition, 1970

The third volume in the Sea of fertility series is "divided into two parts: the first is set in southeast Asia, where we first see the Thai princess who is the reincarnation of Isao; the second takes place in Japan after World War II, when the old values of society have been corrupted." Ency of World Lit in the 20th Century

Followed by The decay of the angel

The temple of the golden pavilion; translated by Ivan Morris; introduction by Nancy Wilson Ross; drawings by Fumi Komatsu. Knopf 1959 262p il o.p.

"Based on an actual incident in 1950, when a Zen Buddhist acolyte burned down a temple which was a national shrine. Like the real arsonist, the fictional Mizoguchi is ugly and a pathological stutterer, and long before his hostility becomes overt, has developed a compulsion to destroy whatever is morally or physically beautiful. As told by the young acolyte, this is a masterly description of the growth of an obsession and an acute interpretation of the deliberate symbolism underlying Mizoguchi's irrational, perverse behavior." Booklist

Miss Read *See* Read, Miss, 1913-

Mitchell, Margaret, 1900-1949

Gone with the wind. Macmillan 1936 1037p $21.95

ISBN 0-02-585390-2

Also available G.K. Hall large print edition

This novel "shows both considerable literary skill and social insight. The heroine, Scarlett O'Hara, is an embodiment of the indomitable spirit of the South. She wants to marry Ashley Wilkes, but he marries Melanie Hamilton instead, and in a pique Scarlett marries Charles Hamilton. Later she marries another man for his money, and then finally marries Rhett Butler, a dashing and outspoken Byronic hero. Around her surges the tumult of the Civil War, the despair of Reconstruction days, and the collapse of the old social order. Scarlett's dogged determination to restore Tara, the family estate, after Sherman destroys Atlanta, attains its goal, but the cost of the realization that she has sacrificed everything else for money and security." Benet's Reader's Ency of Am Lit

Mitchell, Mark

(ed) Penguin book of gay short fiction. See Penguin book of gay short fiction

Mitford, Nancy, 1904-1973

Love in a cold climate

In Mitford, N. The pursuit of love & Love in a cold climate p285-617

The pursuit of love

In Mitford, N. The pursuit of love & Love in a cold climate p[1]-283

The pursuit of love & Love in a cold climate; two novels. Modern Lib. 1994 617p $17.50

ISBN 0-679-60090-6   LC 93-43632

A combined edition of two titles about the Radlett family originally published 1945 and 1949 respectively. Subsequent works about the family and its associates are The blessing (1951) and Don't tell Alfred (1960)

These quasi-autobiographical novels take a satiric look at the various social and amatory trials and triumphs

Mitford, Nancy, 1904-1973—*Continued*
of an eccentric upper-class English family following
World War I

Moberg, Carl Artur Vilhelm *See* Moberg,
Vilhelm, 1898-1973

Moberg, Vilhelm, 1898-1973

The emigrants; a novel; translated from
the Swedish by Gustaf Lannestock. Simon
& Schuster 1951 366p o.p. Buccaneer Bks.
reprint available $29.95 (ISBN
1-56849-312-6)

Original Swedish edition, 1949

This is the first volume of a cycle which tells the
story of a band of Swedish emigrants to the United
States. This volume tells the story in particular of one
family, Karl Oskar Nilsson, his wife and children, and
his young brother Robert; of their life in Sweden; and
of the long, arduous journey across the Atlantic in the
summer of 1850

"A novel of peasant life, drawn to the last homely
and superstitious detail. It is a story of poverty and
heartbreak over which human faith has its will. And it
is filled with an earthly humor, the unpredictable flash
of human malice and emotion which bring Mr. Moberg's
characters sharply into focus." N Y Times Book Rev

Followed by Unto a good land

The last letter home; a novel; translated
from the Swedish by Gustaf Lannestock.
Simon & Schuster 1961 383p o.p.

Originally published in Sweden 1956 and 1959. Parts
3 and 4 of the author's cycle, the first of which is The
emigrants and the second, Unto a good land

This volume follows a family of Swedish immigrants
as they cope with change in 19th century Minnesota

"It is solemn, rather slow and quietly moving. Mr.
Moberg is at least as much concerned with the thoughts
and emotions of his stolid characters as with the historical events of their time." Publ Wkly

Unto a good land; a novel; translated
from the Swedish by Gustaf Lannestock.
Simon & Schuster 1954 371p o.p. Buccaneer
Bks. reprint available $29.95 (ISBN
1-56849-313-4)

Sequel to The emigrants

Original Swedish edition, 1952

The book "tells how farmer Karl Oskar Nilsson, his
wife and children, and ten other peasants from his own
parish in the province of Smaland, sailed in the brig
Charlotta in the spring of 1850 to North America, landing ten weeks later at the East River Pier in New York
on a sweltering June day and how, by river-boat and
steam-wagon, on foot and in an ox-drawn cart, Karl
Oskar and his family reach at last the shore of the
Minnesota lake where out of the great trees he finds
there he hews himself a home." N Y Her Trib Books

Followed by The last letter home

Modern classic short novels of science
fiction; edited by Gardner Dozois. St.
Martin's Press 1994 657p $27.95

ISBN 0-312-10504-5   LC 93-42049

Analyzed in Short story index

Contents: The miracle workers, by J. Vance; The
longest voyage, by P. Anderson; On the storm planet,
by C. Smith; The star pit, by S. R. Delany; Total
environment, by B. W. Aldiss; The merchants of Venus,
by F. Pohl; The death of Doctor Island, by G. Wolfe;
Where late the sweet birds sang, by K. Wilhelm; Souls,
by J. Russ; A traveler's tale, by L. Shepard; Sailing to
Byzantium, by R. Silverberg; Mr. Boy, by J. P. Kelly;
And wild for to hold, by N. Kress

Modern classics of science fiction; edited by
Gardner Dozois. St. Martin's Press 1992
672p $27.50

ISBN 0-312-07238-4   LC 91-40412

Analyzed in Short story index

Contents: The country of the kind, by D. Knight;
Aristotle and the gun, by L. S. de Camp; The other
Celia, by T. Sturgeon; Casey Agonistes, by R. McKenna;
Mother Hitton's littul kittons, by C. Smith; The moon
moth, by J. Vance; The golden horn, by E. Pangborn;
The Lady Margaret, by K. Roberts; This moment of the
storm, by R. Zelazny; Narrow Valley, by R. A. Lafferty;
Driftglass, by S. R. Delany; The worm that flies, by B.
W. Aldiss; The fifth head of Cerberus, by G. Wolfe;
Nobody's home, by J. Russ; Her smoke rose up forever,
by J. Tiptree; The barrow, by U. K. Le Guin; Particle
theory, by E. Bryant; The ugly chickens, by H. Waldrop;
Going under, by J. Dann; Salvador, by L. Shepard; Pret-
ty Boy crossover, by P. Cadigan; The pure product, by
J. Kessel; The winter market, by W. Gibson; Chance,
by C. Willis; The edge of the world, by M. Swanwick;
Dori Bangs, by B. Sterling

Momaday, N. Scott

The ancient child; a novel. Doubleday
1989 313p $18.95

ISBN 0-385-27972-8   LC 89-31304

"Locke Setman, a highly successful Bay Area painter,
fears that he has lost touch with his 'inner child' in
the process of making it big. Then, during a brief trip
to Oklahoma, he meets a beautiful American Indian
woman named Grey who dresses in beaded buckskin,
speaks Kiowa and Nanajo like one of the elders, and
has elaborate visionary conversations with the ghost of
Billy the Kid. Armed with a medicine bundle and a bag
of peyote buttons, Grey slowly draws Setman into a
magical world of ritual that both revitalizes and transforms him. . . . A fascinating and hypnotically beautiful
book that belongs in every collection of Western
Americana." Libr J

House made of dawn. Harper & Row
1968 212p o.p. Borgo Press reprint available
$29 (ISBN 0-8095-9141-3)

"Abel, a young American Indian, lives with his grandfather, observing Indian customs, until he is drafted into
the army. The story covers the years 1945 to 1952,
during which time Abel seems unable to find his place
either in the white world, where he is driven to violence,
or on the Indian reservation where he was born. The
pain of being caught between two cultures is keenly felt
and can be comprehended as a problem that has affected
other ethnic groups." Shapiro. Fic for Youth. 3d edition

Monette, Paul

Afterlife. Crown 1990 278p $19.95

ISBN 0-517-57339-3   LC 89-48754

In this novel about AIDS "three men whose lovers all died in the same hospital during the same week decide how to live as they await their own illnesses." Booklist

"Despite its comic flourishes, this is a tough, painful book about gay sex and love, pursued in the valley of the shadow of AIDS. And its unrelenting descriptions of the ravages of the disease, along with its sexual details and 'talking dirty,' are surely going to make some readers uncomfortable." N Y Times Book Rev

Monsarrat, Nicholas, 1910-

The cruel sea. Knopf 1951 509p $25

ISBN 0-394-42090-X

"The *Compass Rose* is a British corvette commissioned to convoy duty and to the hunting of German U-boats during World War II. First Mate Lockhart and Skipper Erikson develop a close relationship. When their ship is sunk and few of the crew survive, Lockhart and Erikson team up again on a new ship, undaunted by the experiences visited upon them by the cruel sea." Shapiro. Fic for Youth. 3d edition

The kappillan of Malta. Morrow 1974 c1973 503p il o.p.

First published 1973 in the United Kingdom

Set against the background of the German-Italian siege of Malta from 1940-42, the story centers around a young priest. "During six days of bombardment, the kappillan, or priest, Father Salvatore, a deeply religious man, finds that his years of faith and service have been suddenly placed in jeopardy. Secluding himself in a monastery for 30 years, the priest remains a beloved hero to his parishioners." Booklist

Moorcock, Michael, 1939-

An alien heat; volume one of a trilogy "The dancers at the end of time". Harper & Row 1973 c1972 158p o.p.

First published 1972 in the United Kingdom

This novel "is set near the end of the world, when Earth is populated by hedonistic immortals who restructure continents and their own bodies at whim. A young man named Jhereck becomes unfashionably obsessed with Mrs. Amelia Underwood, a time traveler from the 19th century, his favorite period. He follows her to London of 1896, where he is tried for murder and hanged, which somehow returns him to the future, sans Amelia but with insights into love and the true human condition. This tale could be called an Art Nouveau morality play or a science fiction comedy of manners. The humor is genuine, the style lush but controlled." Libr J

Followed by The hollow lands

Behold the man

In The Best of the Nebulas p163-202

The end of all songs; volume three of a trilogy "The dancers at the end of time". Harper & Row 1976 271p o.p.

"Moorcock wraps up his Dancers at the End of Time trilogy with a volume that . . . brings together the two central characters—Jhereck Carnelian, one of the hedonistic immortals who dwell at the End of Time, and Mrs. Amelia Underwood, a reluctant time traveler from

Victorian England. Although their reunion is a cause for celebration, the fabric of time has been ruptured, threatening to plunge all into disordered chronological gulfs. Even the inhabitants at the End of Time—an amoral, whimsical, all-but-thoughtless, utterly powerful, and thoroughly likable lot—know concern for the first time in their immortal lives." Booklist

The hollow lands; volume two of a trilogy "The dancers at the end of time". Harper & Row 1974 182p o.p.

In this volume "jaded Jhereck Carnelian is back in his futuristic world after narrowly escaping being hanged in 1896 London while on a time trip with Mrs. Amelia Underwood. He's bored with his life of instant gratification and wants to return to his Victorian lady, but he can't find a working time machine anywhere. Until he falls into a pit full of never-aging children and a robot nurse shoots him back to 1896. Lost in London, he luckily stumbles on Frank Harris and H. G. Wells at the Cafe Royale, and they help reunite him with Amelia." Publ Wkly

Followed by The end of all songs

The revenge of the rose. Ace Bks. 1991 244p o.p.

LC 90-27350

"Moorcock returns to his most popular sword-and-sorcery series with a vengeance as he fills in the blank spaces in the life of Elric, the albino sorcerer and doomed 'Eternal Champion.' Elric's quest—to rescue the soul of his long-dead father by cheating the Lords of Chaos—leads him across time and space through the many worlds of the multiverse as diverse forces oppose him at every step. Moorcock's strength as a writer lies in his bold imagery and cosmic vision as well as in his ability to depict characters that are both larger than life and genuinely appealing." Libr J

Moore, Brian, 1921-

Black robe; a novel. Dutton 1985 246p o.p.

LC 84-21222

"A William Abrahams book"

This is a novel about a French priest in Canada in the 17th century, "Father Laforgue, who must journey from Quebec to a remote village to find out what happened to two other priests. Through snowstorms and along rivers, amid the majestic grandeur of the forests and brushes with sex and death, Laforgue comes to doubt the depth and meaning of his faith." Libr J

"Each culture is seen whole, with intelligence and sympathy, and considering the clichés that prevail about both Indians and priests, that alone makes 'Black Robe' special." N Y Times Book Rev

Catholics; a novel. Holt, Rinehart & Winston 1973 c1972 107p o.p.

A "story of a confrontation in the ecumenical world of the future between a representative of the new religion and some isolated Irish monks who have kept to their old faith." Saturday Rev

"The story is told in an objective style. That is, there is no clue to whether the author believes in the miracles of the Mass or, indeed, in God. He does not seem to be offering support to the disobedient monks or to their superiors, but rather to be issuing a speculative prophecy about the possible results of reformation in the Roman Church. . . . He stands at such a distance from his

Moore, Brian, 1921- —Continued

characters that we admire his guesswork about their mental processes, rather than applaud his insights." Times Lit Suppl

Cold heaven; a novel. Holt, Rinehart & Winston 1983 265p o.p.

LC 82-18720

"A William Abrahams book"

"Alex and Marie, two Americans on vacation, are pedal-boating in the Baie-des-Anges. Alex dives into the water to swim alongside the little boat. He is hit by an out-of-control motor boat and pronounced dead. But at the hospital, his corpse disappears. Later, returning to their hotel room, Marie finds Alex's wallet, flight tickets and travel checks missing. Throughout, Marie has the feeling that an omnipotent power is controlling her life. She is haunted by a miraculous vision." Libr J

"What begins as an extravagant thriller becomes a metaphysical story of a woman's struggle to regain control of her life. . . . The religious view that Moore expresses here is rarely found in fiction; it has the same kind of freshness that Aláric brought to Rome. 'Cold Heaven's' spell derives from its author's skill at preparing a most meticulously realistic field in which he plants two uncanny seeds—just to see what the effect will be." Newsweek

The color of blood; a novel. Dutton 1987 182p o.p.

LC 87-6695

"A William Abrahams book"

This is the story of Stephen Cardinal Bem, "the Roman Catholic cardinal-primate in an unnamed Soviet-bloc country and the precarious balance he must manage in his renderings to Caesar and to God." Commonweal

The author "invites us to consider the philosophical rather than the personal implications of political action. The thriller format becomes a vehicle to explore . . . the relationship between Church and State, the validity of 'liberation theology', the meaning of 'freedom' and 'responsibility' under a totalitarian régime. . . . Always the consummate craftsman, Moore never allows the tension to slacken." Times Lit Suppl

The doctor's wife. Farrar, Straus & Giroux 1976 277p o.p.

This is the story of "an educated, 37-year-old woman, who visits the Riviera, awaiting her all-too-busy surgeon husband to arrive from Belfast and spend a holiday with her. She meets instead a 26-year-old American and falls into a love affair that ends in an inexplicable denial of both past and future, husband and lover." Choice

"The situation is not uncommon in fiction. What is original in this novel is the manner in which the moral dimension of the situation is treated. . . . Sheila's agonies are real, and the paradox of her seeming to be, for the first time in her life, in a state of grace when she is technically sinning has a poignancy which the cool, simple, objective prose does not seek to poeticise." Burgess. 99 Novels

The emperor of ice-cream; a novel. Viking 1965 250p o.p.

At odds with both his Catholic family and Protestant Belfast, unsuccessful in his college entrance examinations, Gavin Burke considers himself a failure at seventeen. Then with the outbreak of World War II, he joins the Air Raid Precautions, and new encounters change Gavin's relationships with both his family and his girl

"By being very Irish and very individual 'The Emperor of Ice-Cream' succeeds in touching on Everyman's youth. And it does so in a most welcome manner: no sentimentality, much wit and an astringent charm on every page." N Y Times Book Rev

I am Mary Dunne; a novel. Viking 1968 217p o.p.

A portrait of a sexually emancipated modern woman. "Mary Dunne, twice-divorced, three times married, Canadian-Irish Catholic by birth, is, on the surface, a sophisticated, even glamorous, New Yorker. In the course of the one day in which her story unfolds, however . . . we catch her at her most vulnerable, tormented by premenstrual tension, brought face to face with truths about herself and the men in her life." Publ Wkly

"The sexual passages are frankly erotic but honestly related to the narrative; only the prudish would find them offensive. Mary Dunne can take her place beside Judith Hearne as one of Brian Moore's marvelously human and perceptive character studies." Libr J

Lies of silence. Doubleday 1990 197p o.p.

LC 90-30681

"Michael Dillon, manager of a hotel in the conflicted area of Ireland, has decided to leave his wife and his country to go to London with the young woman whom he loves. His decision to embark on this new life comes to a shattering stop when he is forced to participate in a terrorist attack by masked men who invade his home. His wife's safety is the leverage used to compel his compliance. The tension is high and the issues faced are moral and political. We are brought close to the danger that is part of everyday life in Northern Ireland." Shapiro. Fic for Youth. 3d edition

The lonely passion of Judith Hearne. Little, Brown 1956 c1955 223p o.p.

"An Atlantic Monthly Press book"

First published 1955 in the United Kingdom with title: Judith Hearne

"Judith Hearne is a middle-aged spinster whose plain looks and loneliness make her depressed and increasingly isolated from any social contact. The other renters in her Belfast boarding house disdain her. Only Mrs. O'Neill, an old school friend, treats her kindly. When her landlady's brother, Jim Madden, returns from America, he pays some attention to Judith, thinking she has money. Jim's bad character is revealed in many ways, including a sexual attack on a young housemaid, and Judith finds more and more solace in drinking. Her pathetic world falls apart completely when even her religious faith deserts her. This sad novel presents a portrait of despair that is almost unbearable." Shapiro. Fic for Youth. 3d edition

Moravia, Alberto, 1907-1990

Two women; translated from the Italian by Angus Davidson. Farrar, Straus & Giroux 1958 339p o.p.

"The disintegrating effects of war upon the personalities of an Italian mother and her 17-year-old daughter who are evacuated to the country in 1943. Cesira and Rosetta struggle to resist the corruption and dishonor which surround their countrymen but they are defeated by lust and by greed." Publ Wkly

Moravia, Alberto, 1907-1990—*Continued*

"Through his description of the brutal, dehumanizing forces of war we see Moravia's belief that man is man because he suffers most cogently illustrated. This novel is also probably the most poignant expression of Moravia's view of the human condition." Ency of World Lit in the 20th century

Morice, Anne

Design for dying. St. Martin's Press 1988 192p o.p.

LC 88-1004

When, after a 20 year absence from her Sussex home, Christine Marsh "arrives, attended by both her current and her former husbands, consternation increases. Billy Jones, the architect supervising the conversion of her house, is a former flame she callously discarded. She further exacerbates the simmering criticism by accusing the workmen of stealing and crushes the hopeful Dolly [her mother], ignored for 17 years, by telling her there is no way she'll share in the grand new house. Then Christine's husband, wealthy Derek Marsh, is found murdered. . . . Morice is her usual savagely witty self, and this solid mystery is social comedy as well." Publ Wkly

Morrell, David, 1943-

Assumed identity. Warner Bks. 1993 469p $21.95

ISBN 0-446-51669-4   LC 92-51040

"Undercover agent Brendan Buchanan has spent eight years under 200 assumed identities. He is bereft when his cover is blown on his latest mission. His bosses refuse to give him another role, wanting him to train other agents. Discouraged, he quits the agency when he receives a coded plea for help from Juana Mendez, a past love. With Holly McCoy, a tenacious reporter, he begins to search for Juana. On their way they battle old enemies and former associates." Libr J

"With all the action of a James Bond adventure and just a dash of the melancholy of John le Carré, this is a terrific suspense thriller." Publ Wkly

The brotherhood of the rose; a novel. St. Martin's Press 1984 353p o.p.

LC 83-21324

"Agent-assassins Chris and Saul are orphans who were raised as brothers by enigmatic Eliot, a veteran C.I.A. operative . . . Eliot trained the two to become master killers, and when he mysteriously turns against them, they band together to destroy him." N Y Times Book Rev

"Though Morrell's tale is thoroughly incredible, its engaging protagonists, whirlwind pace, and heartstopping action scenes make it an adventure of great cinematic appeal." Booklist

The covenant of the flame. Warner Bks. 1991 452p $19.95

ISBN 0-446-51563-9   LC 90-49445

"Environmental writer Tess Drake is chasing both a story on fatal attacks on polluters around the world and a strange man named Joseph. Aided by NYPD Lt. Craig, Tess discovers that Joseph has been burned to death; in his apartment she and Craig find strange artifacts that point to Albigensian heretics, worshippers of ancient god Mithras. After suggesting that the followers of Mithras

and agents of the (still vital) Inquisition remain in lethal combat, Morrell sets the Mithras baddies against Tess." Publ Wkly

Desperate measures. Warner Bks. 1994 408p $22.95

ISBN 0-446-51791-7   LC 94-279

"Burned-out and grief-stricken after the death of his son, journalist Matthew Pittman is sitting in his bathtub with a loaded revolver pointed at the roof of his mouth when the telephone rings. His suicide interrupted, Matthew is assigned to write an obituary for the dying Jonathan Millgate, an 80-year-old member of a prestigious group that advises U.S. presidents. Soon however, Millgate is kidnapped from his deathbed and killed, and Pittman is accused of the murder. . . . The in-depth characterization, believable and unpredictable plot developments, and psychological depths of this thriller will draw all readers." Libr J

The fifth profession. Warner Bks. 1990 448p $19.95

ISBN 0-446-51562-0   LC 89-40461

"Hired by wealthy and powerful clients as an executive protector, Savage is assigned to rescue Rachel Stone from her sadistic husband on the Greek island of Mykonos. Joined by Akira, his Japanese counterpart, Savage discovers this case extends far beyond merely protecting and safely delivering a client. Pursued by unknown outside forces, the threesome struggle to stay alive and solve a mystery that spans continents and brings horrifying memories to the surface." SLJ

Morris, Mary, 1947-

A mother's love. Talese 1993 287p $17.50

ISBN 0-385-42409-4   LC 92-25031

"Morris tells the story of a young, single mother struggling to raise her baby in New York. Jewelry designer Ivy Slovak decides to have her son, Bobby, even though her boyfriend cannot commit to marriage or fatherhood. Meanwhile, Ivy's past haunts her present emotional life. She finds it difficult to relate to Bobby, as she herself has never been the object of maternal love; her mother deserted her when she was seven years old, taking Ivy's younger sister with her." Libr J

"Moving between Ivy's day-to-day coping with being a single parent and her memories of a bizarre childhood, Morris delves into the ordeal of motherhood and penetrates its mysteries. On view here is the mastery of a writer in her prime, revealed in the palpable restraint of the writing and the hypnotic tempo of a commanding story." Booklist

Morris, Mary McGarry

A dangerous woman. Viking 1991 358p $19.95

ISBN 0-670-83699-0   LC 90-50405

"Martha Horgan, the emotionally disabled protagonist, was gang-raped as a teenager; now, 15 years later, her life is finally flowing smoothly. She has moved away from her cold, domineering aunt and has a job at the cleaners, a room in a boarding house, even a worshipful admirer in Wesley Mount, the town mortician. But someone has been stealing from the till and 'Marthorgan' as her taunters call her, gets canned. Back at her aunt's place she is seduced by the caretaker, a frustrated,

Morris, Mary McGarry—*Continued*

manipulative writer, and then must suffer through his affair with her aunt." Libr J

"Morris performs one of the most difficult writing tasks, creating a character crazy enough to be interesting but sane enough to describe her own dilemma." Time

Morris, Wright, 1910-

Collected stories, 1948-1986. Harper & Row 1986 274p o.p.

LC 86-45334

Analyzed in Short story index

Contents: The ram in the thicket; The sound tape; The character of the lover; The safe place; The cat in the picture; Since when do they charge admission?; Drrdla; Green grass, blue sky, white house; A fight between a white boy and a black boy in the dusk of a fall afternoon in Omaha, Nebraska; Fiona; Magic; Here is Einbaum; In another country; Real losses, imaginary gains; The cat's meow; The lover and the beloved; The customs of the country; Victrola; Glimpse into another country; Going into exile; To Calabria; Fellow creatures; Wishing you and your loved ones every happiness; Country music; Things that matter; The origin of sadness

"Spanning close to 40 years of Morris's work and ranging in settings throughout the U.S. and in many cities abroad, this collection deals with wartime experiences, race relations in the South and displacement, both cultural and temporal. Through his eyes we glimpse the mysteries of life and the small epiphanies that render them a little more comprehensible." Publ Wkly

Morrison, Toni, 1931-

Nobel Prize in literature, 1993

Beloved; a novel. Knopf 1987 275p $27.50

ISBN 0-394-53597-9

LC 86-46157

"Sethe had endured slavery on a Kentucky plantation, and the author depicts that slavery, its degradation, and its cruelty in unforgettable detail. When Sethe flees the horror of that life to try to find freedom in Ohio, she sacrifices a child to save her from the terrible life she herself has suffered as a slave. In a supernatural aspect of the novel the child's spirit invades Sethe's home and family; and, there then appears a real manifestation of the ghost in the person of Beloved. It is likely that no one who has not had direct experience of slavery can truly grasp its monstrousness, but this powerful novel will help." Shapiro. Fic for Youth. 3d edition

The bluest eye; with a new afterword by the author. Knopf 1993 215p $22

ISBN 0-679-43373-2

LC 93-43124

A reissue of the title first published 1970 by Holt, Rinehart & Winston

"This tragic study of a black adolescent girl's struggle to achieve white ideals of beauty and her consequent descent into madness was acclaimed as an eloquent indictment of some of the more subtle forms of racism in American society. Pecola Breedlove longs to have 'the bluest eye' and thus to be acceptable to her family, schoolmates, and neighbors, all of whom have convinced her that she is ugly." Merriam-Webster's Ency of Lit

Jazz. Knopf 1992 229p $21

ISBN 0-679-41167-4

LC 91-58555

Also available G.K. Hall large print edition

This novel "tells the story of Violet and Joe Trace, married for over 20 years, residents of Harlem in 1926. . . . Violet works as an unlicensed hairdresser, doing ladies hair in their own homes, and Joe sells Cleopatra cosmetics door to door. . . . When the novel opens, Joe has shot his 18-year-old lover, Dorcas, and Violet has disfigured the dead girl's body at her funeral in a fit of rage. Joe, who was not caught, is in mourning, crying all day in his darkened apartment, and Violet has taken on the task of finding out whatever she can about Dorcas." Voice Lit Suppl

"As the story unfolds, we come to understand, if not excuse, what happened. The characters themselves cannot excuse their own behavior, which baffles them. Violet is obsessed by the memory of the dead girl whose face she slashed: What was it about her that Joe found so special? She is driven to visit the girl's aunt Alice, who is understandably frightened. . . . Some of the most interesting scenes in the book are the subsequent meetings of these two very different women who come to respect each other, even before they learn to understand each other." Christ Sci Monit

Song of Solomon. Knopf 1977 337p $25

ISBN 0-394-49784-8

LC 77-874

Also available Everyman's library edition

"Chaos marked the world into which Macon (known as Milkman) Dead was born. Each member of his family was haunted by some wild obsession—his father's desire for money, land, and social status, his mother's need for love, his sisters' silence, and his Aunt Pilate's madness. To these was added Macon's desire to unearth the family's buried past. This is a novel of mystery and revelation as it unfolds the lives of four generations of blacks in America." Shapiro. Fic for Youth. 3d edition

Sula. Knopf 1974 c1973 174p $23

ISBN 0-394-48044-9

This "is the story of two black women friends and of their community of Medallion, Ohio. The community has been stunted and turned inward by the racism of the larger society. The rage and disordered lives of the townspeople are seen as a reaction to their stifled hopes. The novel follows the lives of Sula and Nel from childhood to maturity to death." Merriam-Webster's Ency of Lit

Tar baby. Knopf 1981 305p $25

ISBN 0-394-42329-1

LC 80-22821

"Retired on the Isle des Chevaliers in the Caribbean, rich Philadelphia businessman Valerian Street and his wife Margaret await the arrival of their estranged son for Christmas; and an already restless household is sharply disrupted when Margaret discovers a primitive black man hiding in her closet. The intruder, called Son, is a fugitive American on the run whose presence alters the lives of the Streets; their devoted black retainers Sydney and Ondine; the Sydney's niece Jade, an educated Paris model with whom Son falls in love." Libr J

"Each of the characters in Toni Morrison's Tar Baby comes with a history, quite a complete history that is given to us in a series of stunning performances." New Repub

Morrow, James

City of Truth

In Nebula awards 28 p228-317

Morse, Anne Christensen *See* Head, Ann

Mortimer, John Clifford, 1923-

Dunster; [by] John Mortimer. Viking 1992 296p $21

ISBN 0-670-84059-9   LC 92-31451

Also available G.K. Hall large print edition

"Philip Progmire, an Oxford-educated accountant with thespian dreams, has engaged in lifelong skirmishes with journalist Dick Dunster, one of these men whose stock-in-trade is scorn and who disbelieve everything on principle. When Dunster digs up what he believes is the dirt on Philip's employer and friend—a hideous legacy of WW II—Progmire is forced to make some terrible choices among truths, loyalties and responsibilities." Publ Wkly

"What Americans miss by having no tradition of novels that aspire to be both literary and conventional, as 'Dunster' does, is the pleasure of watching an experienced author play with conventional form. . . . This pleasure Mr. Mortimer offers in full measure." N Y Times Book Rev

Paradise postponed; [by] John Mortimer. Viking 1986 c1985 373p o.p.

     LC 85-40712

First published 1985 in the United Kingdom

"A realistic novel of manners in the grand nineteenth-century British tradition, this sweeping look at postwar England focuses on a group of villagers from the London suburb of Rapstone Fanner. From the upwardly mobile conservative politician through the activist vicar to the jazz-playing country doctor, these characters reflect the comic follies of the modern age as they try to come to grips with an overwhelming sense of expectations unfulfilled." Am Libr

Rumpole à la carte; [by] John Mortimer. Viking 1990 245p o.p.

     LC 91-161338

Analyzed in Short story index

Contents: Rumpole à la carte; Rumpole and the summer of discontent; Rumpole and the right to silence; Rumpole at sea; Rumpole and the quacks; Rumpole for the prosecution

Rumpole and the golden thread

In Mortimer, J. C. The second Rumpole omnibus p193-442

Rumpole for the defence

In Mortimer, J. C. The second Rumpole omnibus p11-192

Rumpole on trial; [by] John Mortimer. Viking 1992 243p o.p.

Available Thorndike Press large print edition

Analyzed in Short story index

Contents: Rumpole and the children of the devil; Rumpole and the eternal triangle; Rumpole and the miscarriage of justice; Rumpole and the family pride; Rumpole and the soothsayer; Rumpole and the reform of Joby Jonson; Rumpole on trial

Rumpole's last case

In Mortimer, J. C. The second Rumpole omnibus p443-667

Rumpole's return; [by] John Mortimer. Armchair Detective Lib. 1992 c1980 159p $19.95

ISBN 1-56287-037-8   LC 91-29415

Also available from Amereon

First published 1980 in paperback in the United Kingdom

"After losing in Judge Bullingham's court for the tenth straight time, Rumpole finds the beaches of Florida a welcome change from the dampness of home. Basking in the sun, he comes across an account of the Notting Hill Gate murder in a back copy of *The Times* which sparks a nerve. This is the sort of case he enjoyed. The evidence is stacked against the accused. . . . Rumpole's uncanny assessment of the situation is that the facts are out of synch." Publisher's note

The second Rumpole omnibus; [by] John Mortimer. Viking 1987 667p o.p.

Companion volume to The first Rumpole omnibus (1983)

Analyzed in Short story index

Contents: Rumpole for the defence (c1981) [variant title: Regina v. Rumpole]; Rumpole and the golden thread (c1983); Rumpole's last case (c1987)

Rumpole for the defence: Rumpole and the confession of guilt; Rumpole and the gentle art of blackmail; Rumpole and the dear departed; Rumpole and the rotten apple; Rumpole and the expert witness; Rumpole and the spirit of Christmas; Rumpole and the boat people

Rumpole and the golden thread: Rumpole and the genuine article; Rumpole and the golden thread; Rumpole and the old boy net; Rumpole and the female of the species; Rumpole and the sporting life; Rumpole and the last resort

Rumpole's last case: Rumpole and the blind tasting; Rumpole and the old, old story; Rumpole and the official secret; Rumpole and the judge's elbow; Rumpole and the bright seraphim; Rumpole and the winter break; Rumpole's last case

Summer's lease. Viking 1988 288p o.p.

"The advertisement that Molly Pargenter answered made the Tuscany villa to let sound like the ideal place—suspiciously too ideal—for her family to spend its summer vacation. Arriving in Italy with her husband, three daughters, and father, she finds an unusual assortment of locals and English expatriates for neighbors, as well as detailed notes on the proper use of the house left by her absentee landlord, one S. Kettering. Molly's obsession with learning as much as possible about the Kettering household leads her to some ominous conclusions." Libr J

"Mortimer puts in a graceful performance as he untangles a whole bundle of liaisons and portrays a whole array of human emotions with skill and subtlety." Booklist

Mortman, Doris

True colors; a novel. Crown 1995 c1994 553p $24

ISBN 0-517-59262-2   LC 94-13068

"The internationally renowned artist Isabelle de Luna, born into the aristocracy of Barcelona, Spain, lost a life of privilege when her mother was brutally raped and murdered. For Isabelle's protection she is sent to New Mexico to live with the Durans, friends of the family who raise her together with their adopted daughter, Nina.

Mortman, Doris—*Continued*

As adults, the two young women become successful but lose their bonds of sisterhood." Libr J

"Mortman sets out quite a feast: alluring and sophisticated characters, steamy sex, and a captivating plot involving murder, great wealth and power, international intrigue, art, ambition, and redemption." Booklist

Mosley, Walter

Black Betty. Norton 1994 255p $19.95

ISBN 0-393-03644-8   LC 94-6839

Also available Thorndike Press large print edition

"Mosley's distinctive black investigator, Easy Rawlins, has moved from Watts to West L.A. with his two adopted children, but trouble still follows him. Hired to locate a sultry female acquaintance from his early days in Houston, Easy searches for her gambler brother and questions her Beverly Hills employer, unwittingly provoking racist police harassment. Meanwhile, friend Raymond ('Mouse') has been released from prison and vows revenge on the snitch who put him there." Libr J

"Mosley gives us a recognizable moment in American history viewed through the eyes of a single black man. This perspective, rare in crime fiction, vivifies not only the black experience but the larger event as well. Here we feel the hot winds that would eventually ignite the Watts riots not as abstract issues in race relations, but as emotions in the hearts of individuals we have come to know and care about." Booklist

Devil in a blue dress. Norton 1990 219p $19.95

ISBN 0-393-02854-2   LC 89-25503

Also available Thorndike Press large print edition

In this novel "Ezekiel 'Easy' Rawlins, a young, tough black veteran living in 1948 Los Angeles, only wants respect and enough money to pay his mortgage. When fired from his factory job, however, he undertakes some paid errands for a shady white mobster who wishes to locate a light-haired, blue-eyed beauty. As Easy plumbs his usual hangouts for clues, he relays information to the mobster, runs afoul of the police, meets the mysterious woman, discovers a murder, then investigates in self-defense." Libr J

"Mosley's prose is a little stiff and his plot is far too complicated. But he has a keen eye for period details. . . . And his lowdown humor never deserts him." Newsweek

A red death. Norton 1991 284p $19.95

ISBN 0-393-02998-0   LC 90-23660

Also available Thorndike Press large print edition

"In this second installment in the series, the calendar has moved ahead to the early 1950s, and the good-natured (and aptly named) Easy is in a pickle. The IRS is after him for hiding income from the apartment buildings he secretly owns; a Red-hating FBI agent strong-arms him into investigating a labor agitator; and the local police suspect him in two murders." Booklist

White butterfly. Norton 1992 272p $19.95

ISBN 0-393-03366-X   LC 91-44700

Also available Thorndike Press large print edition

"Black detective Easy Rawlins aids his dangerous-but-loyal friend Mouse, accused of killing several bar girls in 1958 Los Angeles." Libr J

"Standard stuff, to be sure—the makings of your typical made-for-television movie. But what elevates it is the character. It is not just that Rawlins is such an engaging fellow. He is a man who both ages and evolves." N Y Times Book Rev

Mowat, Farley

The Snow Walker. Little, Brown 1975 222p o.p.

"An Atlantic Monthly Press book"

Analyzed in Short story index

Stories included are: The blinding of André Maloche; Stranger in Taransay; The iron men; Two who were one; The blood in their veins; The woman and the wolf; The Snow Walker; Walk well, my brother; The white canoe; Dark odyssey of Soosie

The stories range "from the ancient to the overwhelmingly modern. . . . There are tales of starvation, cannibalism out of love, the giving of one body to another with the poignancy of the Eucharist. There are tales so simple and strong you read them again to make sure you haven't been tricked into feeling a story in your stomach for a change." N Y Times Book Rev

Mowry, Jess, 1960-

Six out seven. Farrar, Straus & Giroux 1993 501p $22

ISBN 0-374-22083-2   LC 93-15676

In this novel, "a young Mississippi boy encounters the harsh realities of the ghetto. . . . When a gun accident kills a white landowner while Corbitt Wainwright and his friends are fishing on the old man's property, the young boy runs away, fearing he will be implicated. Fleeing to Oakland, where he expects better things, he instead finds a community riven by poverty, drugs, and gangs." Libr J

"Mowry has an unerring ear for gritty street talk, a graphic sense of place and an unflinching view of American urban life. Influenced by rap music, gangster movies, street slang and the ghosts and magic of a distant African past, he synthesizes a dazzling new sort of literary adventure fiction." Publ Wkly

Moyes, Patricia

Dead men don't ski

In Moyes, P. Murder by 3's p3-288

Down among the dead

In Moyes, P. Murder by 3's p289-540

Falling star

In Moyes, P. Murder by 3's p542-789

Murder by 3's; including Dead men don't ski, Down among the dead men, and Falling star; with an introduction by Anthony Boucher. Holt, Rinehart & Winston 1965 789p o.p.

"A Rinehart suspense novel"

Omnibus edition of three titles first published separately in 1960, 1961 and 1964 respectively

In the first story, Scotland Yard Inspector Henry Tibbett on vacation at a ski resort tries to prove it is a drug smugglers station. In the second story, the Inspector's sailing holiday is upset by an "accidental" drowning.

Moyes, Patricia—*Continued*

In the last story, Inspector Tibbett tackles one of his toughest cases when an aging British film star falls under the wheels of a train

Twice in a blue moon. Holt & Co. 1993 181p $19.95

ISBN 0-8050-2823-4   LC 93-9531

Also available Thorndike Press large print edition

"Londoner Susan Gardiner unexpectedly inherits the Blue Moon, an old unused inn in Essex. . . . Susan decides to turn the inn into a fashionable restaurant—despite the animosity of a rival inn owner and local rumors that her great-aunt Margaret's drowning in a nearby river 20 years earlier was actually murder. Three months after the restaurant's successful opening, a customer dies of mushroom poisoning, bringing Chief Superintendent Tibbett on the scene. . . . For die-hard fans, Moyes may not provide enough of Henry and his perceptive wife Emmy in this tightly woven cozy, but game Susan and the rest of the cast are entertaining company." Publ Wkly

Who is Simon Warwick? Holt, Rinehart & Winston 1979 c1978 168p o.p.

LC 78-53951

"A Rinehart suspense novel"

In this mystery involving Scotland Yard's Inspector Henry Tibbett, "a peer dies, leaving a fortune to an unknown nephew. Two claimants show up, one from England and one from Virginia; one is killed in the solicitor's office, and the question of the inheritance becomes even more complicated." Libr J

Mukherjee, Bharati

The holder of the world. Knopf 1993 285p $22

ISBN 0-394-58846-0   LC 93-22066

"Beigh is a contemporary New England woman of Indian heritage, who is in love with technocrat Venn from India. Beigh is obsessed with antiquities. The graduate work she was doing on the subject of the Puritans had led her to the discovery of one of her ancestors, a Hannah Easton, who traveled from her home in New England all the way to India with her trader husband. The author has woven together Hannah's story with Beigh's search for ancient jewels and legends." Libr J

The author is a "wonderful storyteller whose 17th-century Salem and India seem more real than the pale glimpses we have of contemporary America. She is always showing us coincidences and connections." New Statesman

Jasmine. Grove Weidenfeld 1989 241p o.p.

LC 89-7611

"Jasmine was born in a small Indian village, witnessed her young husband's assassination there, came to the U.S., and now lives with a middle-aged banker in a small Iowa town. Try as she might, Jasmine can't quite shrug off all the traditions and memories of her past, even though she exhibits a formidable resilience in her adjustment to the middle-class heartland. The context of this incomplete transformation is further focused and aggravated by the young Vietnamese boy who is her stepson and whose identity crisis exacerbates Jasmine's own." Booklist

"On the one hand, [this] is a tale of an individual's exile, alienness, transformations, and reckless hopes. On the other, it is an evocation of a country's transformation from pastoral innocence to perversion." Quill Quire

The middleman and other stories. Grove Press 1988 197p o.p.

LC 87-35048

Analyzed in Short story index

Contents: The middleman; A wife's story; Loose ends; Orbiting; Fighting for the rebound; The tenant; Fathering; Jasmine; Danny's girls; Buried lives; The management of grief

Muller, Marcia

Beyond the grave; [by] Marcia Muller and Bill Pronzini. Walker & Co. 1986 236p $15.95

ISBN 0-8027-5651-4   LC 86-7808

"Elena Oliverez, the young director of the Santa Barbara Museum of Mexican Arts, combines her amateur sleuth capabilities with nineteenth-century San Francisco detective John Quincannon's in their search for lost artifacts from one of 'Los ranchos grandes' of Southern California. Quincannon has been dead for many years when Elena discovers by accident, hidden in a marriage coffer she buys for the museum, the first part of his investigative report on his original search for the artifacts. As she follows clues and discovers other parts of the report the mystery heightens in both the past and the present. Quincannon and Elena both encounter murder and deceit on the trail of the artifacts, as well as their own personal problems." Best Sellers

The cavalier in white. St. Martin's Press 1986 207p o.p.

LC 86-3663

This mystery features a "woman detective named Joanna Stark, who is a widow, and ex-security consultant to art galleries and museums, and now lives in the small, wine-country town of Sonoma in northern California. Making a desultory no-go of starting her own art gallery, and feeling bored and restless after the death of her husband, Stark is visited by her ex-partner, who brings news of the theft of a Frans Hals painting, 'The Cavalier in White,' from a San Francisco museum. Stark is lured back into the detecting business and finds that all clues lead to embarrassing and potentially tragic repercussions that will affect people she cares for. Murder further complicates the investigation. A cozy tale in which plot twists well suit the rich atmosphere." Booklist

Dark star. St. Martin's Press 1989 212p o.p.

LC 89-4114

"Set in San Francisco and the wine country around Sonoma, California, this [work features] . . . intrepid sleuth Joanna Stark. From her house full of valuable paintings a worthless but quite significant one is stolen; what this tells Joanna is that her onetime lover and current enemy, the art dealer and thief Anthony Parducci, is not dead, as she had hoped. Rather, the fascinating but plainly psychotic Parducci is poised to reenter Joanna's life—an event rife with dangerous consequences. . . . Though this isn't her best effort, Muller is a reliable mystery writer who knows all the tricks of the genre." Booklist

Muller, Marcia—*Continued*

Pennies on a dead woman's eyes; a Sharon McCone mystery. Mysterious Press 1992 297p $18.95

ISBN 0-89296-454-5 LC 91-58025

Sharon McCone is "repelled by the gruesome details of a 1956 murder case that her San Francisco law firm plans to argue in a mock trial before the city's Historical Tribunal. 'There's too much emotion swirling around' for her liking, and no new evidence to vindicate the woman, recently released from prison, who was convicted of killing her husband's young mistress. Sharon, who acknowledges herself to be 'a demonic researcher,' overcomes her revulsion when she finds some loopholes in the prosecution's case." N Y Times Book Rev

"Muller is perhaps the least showy crime author around. Her protagonist, driven always into dangerous and emotional culs-de-sac, emerges as a pleasing composite of toughness and vulnerability without seeming to be either overstated or overwritten." Booklist

The shape of dread. Mysterious Press 1989 218p $16.95

ISBN 0-89296-271-2 LC 89-42606

Sharon McCone "is on the long cold trail of a missing comedian, presumed dead. A young parking valet at the club has been convicted of the 'no-body' crime, and his appeal falls into the sensitive lap of the legal co-op that offers low-paid employment to the spirited McCone." Booklist

"Solid plots, sound procedures and enlightening views of San Francisco's diversified neighborhoods are characteristic of the author's sensible style, which makes up in technical skill what it lacks in esthetics." N Y Times Book Rev

There's something in a Sunday; a Sharon McCone mystery. Mysterious Press 1989 213p $15.95

ISBN 0-89296-270-4 LC 88-22005

"San Francisco investigator Sharon McCone is hired to watch a man on his day off as he drives from flower garden to flower shop. Then the shirtmaker who has employed her is murdered, the man she follows disappears, a Mission District bum goes into hiding . . . and dark deeds are uncovered at the ranch where the missing man works." Booklist

"This is a provocative work, infused with compassion and sensitivity, that explores the complexities of human relationships and the plight of the homeless." Publ Wkly

Till the butchers cut him down; a Sharon McCone mystery. Mysterious Press 1994 339p $18.95

ISBN 0-89296-455-3 LC 93-42306

Sharon "McCone has just left the All-Souls Legal Cooperative and opened her own business when an eccentric friend from her UC-Berkeley days, who now specializes in rescuing failing corporations, asks her to find out who is sabotaging his efforts to save a San Francisco shipping firm and threatening his life." Publ Wkly

Trophies and dead things. Mysterious Press 1990 266p $16.95

ISBN 0-89296-417-0 LC 90-33448

Also available G.K. Hall large print edition

"San Francisco detective Sharon McCone . . . uncovers murderous passions still simmering from the Vietnam anti-war movement when she undertakes an investigation into why a sniper victim changed his will to disinherit his children and leave more than $1 million to four strangers." Publ Wkly

"Like her heroine, Ms. Muller works in a style more admirable for its clarity and efficiency than for boldness or brilliance. Her dense plots are models of construction, and if her characters lack spark, they are observed in a manner both sensible and rational." N Y Times Book Rev

Where echoes live. Mysterious Press 1991 326p $17.95

ISBN 0-89296-418-9 LC 90-84898

"Private eye Sharon McCone is on the ecological beat, as a renovated gold mine that could lead to environment destruction also leads to several deaths. A good mystery as fresh as today's headlines." Booklist

Wolf in the shadows. Mysterious Press 1993 356p $18.95

ISBN 0-89296-525-8 LC 92-50536

"San Francisco private eye Sharon McCone is understandably concerned about the disappearance of her mysterious lover, Hy Ripinsky. When she finds out that he had gone to Mexico to deliver $2 million in ransom, she *really* gets worried." Libr J

Munro, Alice

Friend of my youth; stories. Knopf 1990 273p $18.95

ISBN 0-394-58442-2 LC 89-43295

Analyzed in Short story index

Contents: Friend of my youth; Five points; Meneseteung; Hold me fast, don't let me pass; Oranges and apples; Pictures of the ice; Goodness and mercy; Oh, what avails; Differently; Wigtime

"Ms. Munro, who has deepened the channels of realism, is a writer of extraordinarily rich texture; her imagery stuns or wounds and her sentences stick to the rough surfaces of our world." N Y Times Book Rev

Lives of girls & women. McGraw-Hill 1971 250p o.p.

"Although the locale is Canada, Del Jordan's story could take place in the United States as well. She lives among hard-working, lower-middle-class people in a family that includes her parents and a brother, Owen. The mother seeks independence from the traditional role of women and even goes 'out on the road,' as her disapproving sisters-in-law term it, to sell encyclopedias. For Del's mother the pursuit of knowledge is an ideal. For Del and her best friend Naomi more interest lies in their maturing and curiosity about sex as a vital part of growing up. There is humor and recognizable adolescent self-questioning. While sexual scenes are explicit, they are also sensitive and real and avoid both vulgarity and titillation. In spite of the experiences that Naomi and Del have, it becomes clear that the paths they will follow will diverge greatly." Shapiro. Fic for Youth. 3d edition

The moons of Jupiter; stories. Knopf 1983 c1982 233p $13.95

ISBN 0-394-52952-9 LC 82-48734

Munro, Alice—*Continued*

Analyzed in Short story index

First published 1982 in Canada

Contents: Chaddeleys and Flemings: I Connection; Chaddeleys and Flemings: II The stone in the field; Dulse; The turkey season; Accident; Bardon bus; Prue; Labor Day dinner; Mrs. Cross and Mrs. Kidd; Hard-luck stories; Visitors; The moons of Jupiter

"These stories expose the conundrums of love and mortality. At the least they are engaging, and at their luminous best, reveal precision as the highest wisdom." Saturday Rev

Open secrets; stories. Knopf 1994 293p $23

ISBN 0-679-43575-1   LC 94-2099

Analyzed in Short story index

Contents: Carried away; A real life; The Albanian virgin; Open secrets; The Jack Randa Hotel; A wilderness station; Spaceships have landed; Vandals

The author "peoples these exquisite tales with sad, lonely eccentrics leading lives of quiet self-deception. Her heroines are often troubled souls with the unforgiving task of fitting into the rigorously confining community that spawned them. . . . Munro expertly captures the vagaries of history and geography in this satisfying and immensely pleasurable collection." Booklist

Munro, H. H. (Hector Hugh) *See* Saki, 1870-1916

Murasaki Shikibu, b. 978?

The tale of Genji; translated and with an introduction by Arthur Waley. Modern Lib. 1993 xxii, 1327p $22

ISBN 0-679-42467-9   LC 92-51068

First Modern Library edition published 1960

"A Japanese novel of the Heian period. This vast chronicle of court life centers on the career of Prince Genji and the women with whom he was associated. Its style is highly ornate and the work is rich in poetry and elaborate wordplay. Reflecting pure Japanese tradition, it has had a tremendous influence on subsequent literature and is regarded unreservedly as the greatest single work in Japanese literature." Reader's Ency. 3d edition

Murdoch, Iris

An accidental man. Viking 1971 442p o.p.

"The central figure of this novel is one of those accident-prone figures whose . . . misfortune becomes a substitute source of strength. . . . Ever since his brother injured his hand in a childhood incident, the world owes Austin a blank cheque to cover subsequent reverses—which do not fail to arrive. But someone is always sorry for him, always getting him out of trouble even at the price of their own. His self-pity destroys others in accordance with what Miss Murdoch . . . calls 'whatever deep mythological forces control the destinies of men.'" New Statesman

The bell; a novel. Viking 1958 342p o.p.

"The setting is an Anglican lay community attached to an abbey on one of the great estates of England. . . . The members of this community and its temporary residents are on the whole an odd, and certainly an oddly assorted, bunch. And their high-minded leader is a homosexual who was once involved in a scandal that ended his plans for entering the church. The story concerns itself with the relationships between various members of this hothouse world, with the arrival of a new bell for the abbey and the simultaneous discovery in the lake of the lost fourteenth-century bell about which there is a sinister legend. The climax is an eruption of scandal and disaster." Atlantic

The black prince. Viking 1973 366p o.p.

"The events in this story occurred in Bradley Pearson's '58th year, when he retired as inspector for the Inland Revenue Service to devote full time to writing. . . . Instead of being allowed to get on with the novel, he is besieged by frantic callers at his London flat. . . . As these people make their hectic, unsettling claims on the self-absorbed Bradley, the relationship of his life and art becomes hopelessly tangled." N Y Times Book Rev

"A searching, provocative tragi-comedy, the deliberate unfurling of a complicated, ambiguous man, the shapes and shadows of his life. . . . Rich in idea, association, perception and character." Publ Wkly

The book and the brotherhood. Viking 1988 c1987 607p o.p.

LC 87-40294

First published 1987 in the United Kingdom

This novel is set in England in the 1980s. "A group of idealistic men and women, who met as students [at Oxford], later formed a society to support one of their number, a brilliant radical named David Crimond, in his efforts to write a major work tackling the big questions of history, politics, philosophy, art, and ethics. As the story opens, the group members, now middle-aged, are having qualms about Crimond and the enterprise they once agreed to fund." Christ Sci Monit

"Despite its excessive length and passages that can seem almost as self-indulgent as the characters they represent, The Book and The Brotherhood demonstrates again and again that Iris Murdoch is among the most gifted descriptive and narrative writers in English—and certainly one of the most consistently entertaining." NY Rev Books

A fairly honourable defeat. Viking 1970 436p o.p.

This is a "treatment of a homosexual menage which, when the chips are down, turns out to be more stable and durable than the happy heterosexual marriage which is subject to the same malicious interference by a cruel manipulator." Publ Wkly

"As is usual with a Murdoch novel, the action in summary seems preposterous. But given her inventiveness, her Gothic imagination, her gift for melodrama and suspense, she creates a world that becomes an effective vehicle for her moral vision." Choice

The good apprentice. Viking 1986 522p o.p.

LC 85-40635

This "novel is organized thematically around sets of opposing characters and structurally around a dramatic string of reversals. Harry Cuno is a monster of will, 'a disappointed spoilt child.' His son Stuart is a monster of will-lessness. Stuart avoids life's complications, while his stepbrother Edward, having precipitated a friend's suicide, is agonizingly caught up in them. Edward seeks absolution from his 'real' father Jesse, a legendary painter and Lear-like figure imprisoned in a decaying 'enchanter's palace' by the sea." Libr J

Murdoch, Iris—*Continued*

"The esthetic puzzle is whether the comic story and the spiritual kernel can be held together by Miss Murdoch's archaic stance as an authorial will. And yet no other contemporary British novelist seems to me of her eminence." N Y Times Book Rev

The green knight. Viking 1994 c1993 472p $23.95

ISBN 0-670-85229-5   LC 93-30618

First published 1993 in the United Kingdom

"Peter Mir, the 'Green Knight' of [this novel's] title, is nearly killed when he intervenes to protect Clement Graffe from being murdered by Graffe's half-brother, Lucas. Mir mysteriously reappears and demands reparation from Lucas, provoking various responses from the two brothers and their circle of friends: Harvey Blacket; Bellamy Jones; the three Anderson sisters, Aleph, Sefton, and Moy; and their mother, Louise." Libr J

"That a cold, dark, evil act should open up a gap through which warmth and light can flood into the world is a paradox characteristic of Iris Murdoch's deeply meditated insight into the nature of the good." London Rev Books

Henry and Cato. Viking 1977 c1976 375p o.p.

First published 1976 in the United Kingdom

"After spending nine years in America, Henry Marshalson decides to go home to England when he learns of his brother Sandy's death. He becomes reacquainted with childhood friends: Cato Forbes (a priest now), Cato's sister Colette, and a woman he mistakenly believes was Sandy's mistress. Henry feels that in order to be free and happy he must rid himself of the family estate and money no matter how others may be hurt by this action." Libr J

The message to the planet. Viking 1990 563p o.p.

LC 89-40352

This novel's central character "is a philosopher who is believed by his admirers to have a message for the planet. . . . Marcus Vallar is mainly benign. He is a mathematician-turned-philosopher who veers off in a mystical direction after he raises a man from the dead. . . . Vallar's chief disciple is pleased by this apparent miracle but horrified by its implications. He fears Vallar has 'given up philosophy for holiness'. He longs for his master to come up with a message for the planet but rules out as unthinkable a message that will cause atheists to doubt their lack of faith. Vallar is undeterred." Economist

"One of Murdoch's great strengths is her ability to make us undergo the emotional, spiritual, and intellectual experiences of her characters." Christ Sci Monit

The nice and the good. Viking 1968 378p o.p.

The action "begins with a violent death in the chambers of Whitehall faintly suggestive of a Le Carré thriller. . . . At times hilariously funny, slightly shivery (intimations of blackmail, suicide, dabblings in black magic) 'The Nice and the Good' is first and foremost a delightful love story. The friends, relatives, hanger-ons, whose lives revolve around the happily married Octavian and Kate Gray are all seeking after love in their own ways. They find it, too, and sometimes in the most amazing places. The characterizations are superb, the mood that of a happy fairy tale crossed with highly sophisticated sexual comedy." Publ Wkly

Nuns and soldiers. Viking 1981 c1980 505p o.p.

LC 80-16935

First published 1980 in the United Kingdom

This novel explores the tangled lives of recently widowed Gertrude; Tim, a painter; Anne, a former nun; and "Count" Peter who is in love with Gertrude

"The glory of Iris Murdoch at her best—as she almost always is in Nuns and Soldiers—is that she can convey with total respect the awareness, readjusting and hunger, and at the same time 'place' it, with a severe but not savage irony, in a world which hints at quite different forces and priorities." New Statesman

The philosopher's pupil. Viking 1983 576p o.p.

LC 82-45901

At the heart of this novel are "aging philosopher John Robert Rozanov and his former (and rejected) pupil George McCaffrey. The scene is English spa Ennistone, George's home and Rozanov's birthplace. While the desperately bitter George hopes that Rozanov's unexpected reappearance in Ennistone heralds a reconciliation, it becomes apparent that Rozanov has returned instead to settle the future of his orphaned granddaughter. This he accomplishes, setting in motion a chain of events both farcical and tragic." Libr J

This "collaboration between Murdoch and her imagination is both challenging and irresistible: a combination of gossip and profundity, modern times and ancient edicts." Time

The sacred and profane love machine. Viking 1974 374p o.p.

"The book opens with two houses on the suburban fringe between Buckinghamshire and northwest London: Hood House and Locketts, divided from each other by a box hedge and an ambiguous and disputed orchard. The Gavenders live in Hood House, the perfect family of three. Blaise is a psychoanalyst, Harriet is a large serene matron; their child David is a grave, sage adolescent. Beyond the orchard, at Locketts, lives Montague Small . . . creator of the fictional detective Milo Fane and involuntarily haunted in nightmares by the image of his dead wife, Sophie. . . . The novel opens out to reveal a further world, another mysterious double: for Blaise has a secret life in Putney, south of the river." Encounter

"Murdoch toys with dual imagery in a novel whose surfaces and interior meanings deliberately collide." Booklist

The sea, the sea. Viking 1978 502p o.p.

LC 78-13516

The narrator of this "novel is Charles Arrowby, a former actor and director who has retired from the theater to take up solitary residence in a remote house on a northern coast. His tale begins as a mixture of diary and memoir: alternately he records his first impressions of his new home and reviews his past life as though the better to understand the man he has become. . . . His recollections largely concern a succession of love-affairs with actresses; but before all these, and dwarfing them in its importance to his development, was an unconsummated but passionate childhood relationship with a girl named Hartley, who disappeared abruptly and woundingly from his life before he was twenty and married another man." Times Lit Suppl

Musil, Robert, 1880-1942

The man without qualities; translated from the German by Sophie Wilkins; editorial consultant, Burton Pike. Knopf 1995 2v set $60

ISBN 0-394-51052-6   LC 92-37943

"The first two volumes of this monumental work were published in 1930 and 1932; a fragmentary third was published posthumously in 1942, and in 1952 the novel appeared, with additional chapters, in one volume. Apart from providing a brilliant, existential portrait of Ulrich, the scholarly, purposeless 'man without qualities,' the book is a vivid depiction of Austrian decadence before the outbreak of World War I. This single remarkable work established Musil as one of the most influential German-language novelists in the first half of the 20th century." Reader's Ency. 3d edition

Myles, Symon, 1949-

For works written by this author under other names see Follett, Ken, 1949-

Myrer, Anton

A green desire; a novel. Putnam 1982 511p o.p.

LC 81-15690

"Chapin and Tipton Ames are two brothers of old New England stock whose lives span the first half of the twentieth century. Chapin, the elder, has been 'rescued' from his poverty-stricken and abandoned mother at an early age by a wealthy aunt who rears him in Boston and spoils him with all the advantages money can provide. Tipton remains at home to support his mother and to make his own way in the world. As time goes on, both brothers fall in love with the same girl, Josefina Gaspa, the beautiful, passionate, and unpredictable granddaughter of a proud Portuguese sailor. This love triangle serves as the focal point for a wide-ranging novel which deals with practically all the major historical events of the present century from America's involvement in World War I, through the roaring twenties and the great depression, to World War II and its immediate aftermath." Best Sellers

The last convertible; a novel. Putnam 1978 526p o.p. Buccaneer Bks. reprint available $26.95 (ISBN 1-56849-240-5)

LC 77-15557

In this novel "we follow five disparate Harvard classmates, the 'Fusiliers,' from high-spirited undergraduate days in 1938, when they share a remarkable convertible called The Empress, through war, marriage and parenthood, to the present." N Y Times Book Rev

"Myrer unashamedly strikes all the major social chords of the last three decades: on one level this is life as Life magazine might have seen it. But that's its very strength as a popular novel. . . . If the characters are predictable, they are still compelling, and Myrer chronicles their loss of illusions with feeling, style and a lack of sensationalism." Newsweek

Mysterious cat stories; edited by John Richard Stephens and Kim Smith. Carroll & Graf Pubs. 1993 303p $19.95

ISBN 0-88184-948-0   LC 93-7981

Analyzed in Short story index

Contents: Beware the cat, by J. R. Stephens; The empty sleeve, by A. Blackwood; King Arthur versus the great cat, by J. Wilde; Don Quixote and the cat demons, by Cervantes; Balu, by A. Derleth; The Black Cat Club, by J. D. Corrothers; Whittington's cat, by E. Smith; The last temptation of Tony the C., by C. Fahy; The man who turned into a cat, J. W. Day; How Diana made the stars and the rain, by C. G. Leland; The great god Mau, by S. Whitelaw; The tail, by M. J. Engh; Weekend of the big puddle, by L. J. Braun; The cats of Ulthar, by H. P. Lovecraft; Catnip, by R. Bloch; Cat in glass, by N. Etchemendy; The jewel of seven stars, by B. Stoker; The yellow cat, by W. D. Steele; Ancient gods, by K. Smith; Tobermory, by Saki

"The supernatural is central to this collection of 26 cat tales, gathered from the 13th century to the present. Rarely warm or cuddly creatures, the cats met here speak to humankind's deep-seated fears and misgivings about the feline. . . . This is a thoughtfully chosen and engaging collection." Publ Wkly

The Mysterious West; edited by Tony Hillerman. HarperCollins Pubs. 1994 392p $23

ISBN 0-06-017785-3   LC 94-25842

Analyzed in Short story index

Includes the following stories: Forbidden things, by M. Muller; New moon and rattlesnakes, by W. Hornsby; Coyote peyote, by C. N. Douglas; Nooses give, by D. Stabenow; Who killed Cock Rogers? by B. Crider; Caring for Uncle Henry, by R. W. Campbell; Death of a snowbird, by J. A. Jance; With flowers in her hair, by M. D. Lake; The lost boys, by W. J. Reynolds; Tule fog, by K. Kijewski; The river mouth, by L. Matera; No better than her father, by L. Grant; Dust Devil, by R. Burns; A woman's place, by D. R. Meredith; Postage due, by S. Dunlap; The beast in the woods, by E. Gorman; Blowout in Little Man Flats, by S. M. Kaminsky; Small town murder, by H. Adams; Bingo, by J. Lutz; Engines, by B. Pronzini

"This stunning collection . . . offers readers some wonderful choices in fiction. Each story is strikingly different in tempo, plot, and setting, yet each is part of and contributes to the diversified world of the mysterious West." SLJ

N

Nabb, Magdalen, 1947-

Death in autumn. Scribner 1985 c1984 158p o.p.

LC 85-1695

"Two Swedish tourists in Florence spot a corpse under the pilings of the Ponte Vecchio. Marshal Guarnaccia, the brilliant Florentine cop who makes solving murder as exquisitely detailed as a Florentine fresco, takes on the investigation, finding that the body belonged to an inexplicably fearful, middle-aged German woman. The murder ties in with drug deaths, blackmail, and jewel theft. Nabb dresses her sensationalistic plot with dignity and offers a delicately wrought police procedural." Booklist

Nabb, Magdalen, 1947--—*Continued*

The marshal and the madwoman; a Marshal Guarnaccia mystery. Scribner 1988 192p o.p.

LC 88-9636

"While trying to teach his wife to drive, Guarnaccia, a marshal in the Carabinieri, happens upon a disturbance in a middle-class Florentine neighborhood: Clementina, a local madwoman, has the neighbors in an uproar. Tempers eventually cool down and the marshal leaves. Several weeks later, Clementina is found murdered. The crime is puzzling—the victim had no money or valuables—and the mystery deepens when it is discovered that on the day of her death Clementina tried to get in touch with Guarnaccia." Booklist

The marshal and the murderer; a Marshal Guarnaccia mystery. Scribner 1987 196p o.p.

LC 87-16092

"Marshal Guarnaccia of the Florence Carabinieri is called to a small village known for its pottery to investigate the disappearance of an attractive young Swiss woman. Monica Heer had been working on her potting and painting techniques among the craftsmen there when she vanished. Guarnaccia's investigation, aided by a local officer, a jolly steamroller of a policeman named Niccolini, soon involves murder. . . . A sad, satisfying mystery." Wilson Libr Bull

The Marshal's own case; a Marshal Guarnaccia mystery. Scribner 1990 175p o.p.

LC 90-8093

Marshal Guarnaccia "finds himself saddled with the case of a beautiful (until murdered and dismembered) transsexual prostitute. At first embarrassed and dismayed, the marshal nonetheless plods into the nether world of Florence to question Lulu's many enemies. His search finally centers on a mysterious 'patron' of Lulu, nicknamed Nanny. Back home, meanwhile, troubles brew with the marshal's two young sons." Libr J

The "author writes compassionately on the subject of alienated parents and children and reveals yet another facet of her complex hero." N Y Times Book Rev

Nabokov, Vladimir Vladimirovich, 1899-1977

Ada; or, Ardor: a family chronicle; [by] Vladimir Nabokov. McGraw-Hill 1969 589p o.p.

"In its prodigious length and with the family tree on its frontispiece the book recalls the great 19th-century novels of the author's native Russia, but *Ada* boldly turns its predecessors on their heads. For his rich, sweeping saga of the Veen-Durmanov clan, Nabokov invented an incestuous pair of 'cousins' (actually siblings, Van and Ada), a hybrid country (Amerussia), a familiar but strange planet (Antiterra), and a dimension of malleable time. The novel follows the lovers from their childhood idylls through impassioned estrangements and reunions to a tenderly shared old age. The work's rich narrative style incorporates untranslated foreign phrases, esoteric data, and countless literary allusions." Merriam-Webster's Ency of Lit

King, queen, knave; a novel; [by] Vladimir Nabokov; translated by Dmitri Nabokov in collaboration with the author. McGraw-Hill 1968 272p o.p.

Original Russian edition, 1928

"The image of a deck of playing cards is used throughout the novel. Franz, an unsophisticated young man, works in the department store of his rich uncle Dreyer. Out of boredom Martha, the uncle's young wife, seduces Franz. The lovers subsequently plot to drown Dreyer and marry each other. Martha changes her mind abruptly when she learns that an invention by Dreyer stands to increase his wealth, but she then dies suddenly from pneumonia. Her husband never discovers his wife's duplicity." Merriam-Webster's Ency of Lit

Lolita; [by] Vladimir Nabokov. Knopf 1992 c1955 335p $17

ISBN 0-679-41043-0   LC 92-52931

Also available from Buccaneer Bks.

"Everyman's library"

First published 1955 in France

"Humbert Humbert is a middle-aged intellectual who has a passion for girls between the ages of nine and fourteen. He falls in love with the twelve-year-old Dolores Haze, whom he calls Lolita. In his plot to seduce her, he marries Dolores's mother, whose accidental death then allows Lolita and Humbert to take off on an odyssey across the U.S. Humbert is surprised when, contrary to his schemes, Lolita seduces him and again when she leaves him and marries Clare Quilty, whom Humbert is forced to murder. The book presents a quest for eternal innocence, albeit in satirical terms. . . . It combines parody, fanciful imaginative flights, literary puzzles, and a brilliant satirical overview of American culture." Reader's Ency. 3d edition

Look at the harlequins!; [by] Vladimir Nabokov. McGraw-Hill 1974 253p o.p.

In this pseudo-autobiographical novel, the narrator, a Russian émigré novelist and college professor who has lived in London, Paris and the United States, recalls his life, loves (including four marriages) and work in a manner which often parodies Nabokov's own life and writings

This is a book "to enchant Nabokov fans and irritate everybody else. . . . [It] is part roman a clef, part fantasy, a tale of 'wives and books interlaced monogrammatically.' It is full of erudite allusions, Russian words in various stages of translation and absurd mistranslation, puns, anagrams, acronyms. Also opinions. . . . Comic, polished, international, [Nabokov] offers sophisticated entertainment, a concoction of romantic and literary matters." Christ Sci Monit

Nabokov's dozen; a collection of thirteen stories; [by] Vladimir Nabokov. Doubleday 1958 214p o.p. Ayer reprint available $16.50 (ISBN 0-8369-3078-9)

Analyzed in Short story index

Contents: Spring in Fialta; A forgotten poet; First love; Signs and symbols; The assistant producer; The Aurelian; Cloud, castle, lake; Conversation piece, 1945; "That in Aleppo once . . ."; Time and ebb; Scenes from the life of a double monster; Mademoiselle O; Lance

Nabokov, Vladimir Vladimirovich, 1899-1977—*Continued*

Pale fire; a novel; [by] Vladimir Nabokov. Putnam 1962 315p o.p.

This novel is "both pedantry and a satire on pedantry. The core of the novel is a 999-line poem by an American author, John Shade—a sort of Robert Frost—which consists mainly of a rather moving meditation on the tragic end of the poet's daughter. After Shade's death, a foolish scholar named Kinbote—an exile from the mythical country of Zembla and a visiting professor of Zemblan at Wordsmith College, New Wye, Appalachia—edits this work, providing a preface and a detailed corpus of notes. But Kinbote has an 'idée fixe'—the history of his own country—and he believes that Shade's poem is an allegory of this history, with Kinbote himself—fantasized into the deposed King Charles Xavier II—as the hero. The humour—and Nabokov's humour is subtle as well as occasionally brutal—lies in the disparity between the simple truth of the poem and the gross self-exalting hallucinations of its editor." Burgess. 99 Novels

Pnin; [by] Vladimir Nabokov. Doubleday 1957 191p o.p. Bentley reprint available $16 (ISBN 0-8376-0465-6)

"Not a novel, not really a collection of short stories, but rather a series of sketches, all of them dealing with Timofey Pnin, professor of Russian in a small American university. Each one finds Pnin valiantly trying to cope with the daily crises of American society—Pnin on the wrong train, Pnin learning to drive, Pnin giving a party, Pnin and the washing machine. They are all gently amusing, affectionate portraits of a Russian expatriate of the old school caught up in the inexplicable complexities of daily life." Libr J

Naipaul, V. S. (Vidiadhar Surajprasad), 1932-

A bend in the river. Knopf 1979 278p o.p. Smith, P. reprint available $21 (ISBN 0-8446-6631-9)

LC 78-21591

"Salim, an East African of East Indian descent . . . buys a general store in a large town in the interior of an unnamed African country. A man without any 'home ground' to stand on, Salim builds his business out of the rubble left by one post-independence revolution. He discovers a great deal about his own mundane existence and about that of his circle of bewildered young Africans, bedraggled European ex-patriates, and displaced East Indians, as the town (and the country) lurches toward yet another cataclysmic revolt." Saturday Rev

"This is a beautifully composed book, with an almost Conradian power of description. Aesthetically most satisfying, it is also profoundly depressing. But depression is sometimes a stone on the road to literary exaltation." Burgess. 99 Novels

The enigma of arrival; a novel. Knopf 1987 354p o.p.

LC 86-46149

"At the midpoint of the century, the narrator leaves the British colony of Trinidad and comes to the ancient countryside of England. . . . Cut off from his 'first' life in Trinidad, he enters a 'second childhood of seeing and learning.' Twenty years after his first arrival, he settles in a cottage outside Salisbury, on the grounds of an Edwardian estate whose derelict condition makes it an oddity among the other, well maintained estates in the valley." Publisher's note

This is "one of those books, not too rare, which irritates, tires and confuses while also exciting, informing and satisfying. The defects are almost as important as the excellences because what is valuable here is the inside story of the development of an exceptional writer. It is also often funny, bizarre, perceptive and poetic." New Statesman

Guerrillas. Knopf 1975 248p o.p.

The action of this novel "takes place on a troubled Caribbean island, inhabited by Asians, Africans, Americans and British colonials. Corruption and poverty are everywhere. . . . The homes of the well-to-do lie hidden in the hills. The poor are angry, the rich are panicked. . . . At the center of the brewing storm are Peter Roche, a white South African and lapsed revolutionary working for an island business; Jane, his British mistress, in confused search of adventure and challenge; and Jimmy Ahmed, a half-Chinese, half-black politician who has set up an agricultural commune that may be giving shelter to the guerrillas. Roche, cynical and self-absorbed, is employed by his firm to control Jimmy. Jimmy is obsessed with visions of personal glory, rape and mystical manhood. Jane, careless and quixotic, becomes the mistress of both men." Newsweek

"This is a novel without a villain, and there is not a character for whom the reader does not at some point feel deep sympathy and keen understanding, no matter how villainous or futile he may seem." N Y Times Book Rev

A house for Mr. Biswas; with an introduction by Karl Miller. Knopf 1995 xxi, 564p $20

ISBN 0-679-44458-0

"Everyman's library"

A reissue of the title first published 1961 by McGraw-Hill

"Trinidad, West Indies, is the setting for the story of lonely Mr. Mohun Biswas, a Hindu of high caste but low economic status. Throughout the book he longs for independence from his wife's large family and a house of his own. In a portrait that is both funny and compassionate, West Indian life is vividly described, especially the relationships among members of Mr. Biswas's family." Shapiro. Fic for Youth. 3d edition

A way in the world; a novel. Knopf 1994 380p $23

ISBN 0-394-56478-2   LC 93-44680

In this autobiographical fiction, Naipaul examines "feelings of rootlessness, the realities of the colonial experience, the impact of cultural displacement, and our need to belong. He does so through a series of linked historical narratives. Among them is an imagined vision of Raleigh's desperate but futile search for El Dorado. We are also introduced to Francisco de Miranda, one of the precursors to Bolivar's revolution. We are witness to the irony inherent in the life of Lebrun, a Trinidadian/Panamanian Communist of the 1930s. And then there is Blair, a former co-worker of the narrator in Trinidad, whose African roots prove no help when he becomes an adviser to an East African despot. These are tales of lost souls desperate to find a place at the table but who never quite succeed, leaving them doomed to remain on the fringes of history." Libr J

Naipaul, Vidiadhar Surajprasad *See* Naipaul, V. S. (Vidiadhar Surajprasad), 1932-

Narayan, R. K., 1906-
The grandmother's tale and selected stories. Viking 1994 312p $24.95

ISBN 0-670-85220-1   LC 94-4581

Analyzed in Short story index
Contents: The grandmother's tale; Guru; Salt and sawdust; Judge; Emden; An astrologer's day; The blind dog; Second opinion; A horse and two goats; Annamalai; Lawley Road; A breath of Lucifer; Under the banyan tree; Another community; The shelter; Seventh house; Cat within; The edge; Uncle
"Set in India, these 19 stories, some previously published, emphasize perceptively drawn characters and situations rather than their colorful foreign backdrops. All the tales display a wry, gentle humor." Publ Wkly

Malgudi days. Viking 1982 246p o.p.

LC 81-52204

Analyzed in Short story index
Contents: An astrologer's day; The missing mail; The doctor's word; Gateman's gift; The blind dog; Fellow-feeling; The tiger's claw; Iswaran; Such perfection; Father's help; The snake-song; Engine trouble; Forty-five a month; Out of business; Attila; The axe; Lawley Road; Trail of the green blazer; The martyr's corner; Wife's holiday; A shadow; A willing slave; Leela's friend; Mother and son; Naga; Selvi; Second opinion; Cat within; The edge; God and the cobbler; Hungry child; Emden
"This selection distills, magically, Malgudi's vibrancy, its mythological-animistic throb, the large and small corruptions of its citizens—from bureaucrats to back-street people—and the reassuring backdrop of its cyclical rhythms. Distinguished writing; rewarding reading." Booklist

Under the banyan tree and other stories. Viking 1985 193p o.p.

LC 85-3234

"An Elisabeth Sifton book"
Analyzed in Short story index
Contents: Nitya; House opposite; A horse and two goats; The Roman image; The watchman; A career; Old man of the temple; A hero; Dodu; Another community; Like the sun; Chippy; Uncle's letters; All avoidable talk; A snake in the grass; The evening gift; A breath of Lucifer; Annamalai; The shelter; The mute companions; At the portal; Four rupees; Flavour of coconut; Fruition at forty; Crime and punishment; Half a rupee worth; The antidote; Under the banyan tree
"Narayan's clarity, his mastery of technique, his respect for the spectrum of human predicament, his absence of malice and his freedom from a single philosophy that explains everything away put him in the unique position of being able to turn a teeming cultural life into lucid and enjoyable stories." New Statesman

The world of Nagaraj. Viking 1990 186p o.p.

LC 89-40662

Set in the imaginary town Malgudi, this novel concerns "fifty-year-old Nagaraj, who peacefully lives and acts inside his thoughts and whose associations with his family and friends are usually peripheral. Nagaraj perpetually dreams of writing the definitive treatise on the Sanskrit sage, Narada, yet he never studies Sanskrit." Libr J
"Narayan's genius, which plays gently over this novel, lies in his persuading us that the lives and characters of Malgudi represent substantial human nature, that what happens in India happens in Malgudi and what happens in Malgudi happens everywhere." Times Lit Suppl

Nathan, Robert, 1894-1985
Portrait of Jennie. Knopf 1940 212p $19.95
ISBN 0-394-44093-5
"Eban Adams, a struggling artist who is unable to sell his art work, meets an unusual child named Jennie in the park and immediately begins to prosper. He knows little about her except that she belongs in the past and that every few months, when their paths cross, she has aged by years. His finest painting is a portrait of her, a token of his love, which ends in predestined tragedy." Shapiro. Fic for Youth. 3d edition

Nathanson, E. M., 1928-
The dirty dozen. Random House 1965 498p o.p.
"Project Amnesty was a plan to drop 12 viciously trained American soldier-prisoners (murderers, rapists, thieves, all doomed to either execution or lengthy prison terms) behind the German lines in France just before D-Day. Their trainer-warden, 30-year-old Captain John Reisman resents the assignment." Book Week
This "is not an ordinary war book. The fight here is not so much against the Wehrmacht as it is against self, society, and 'the system.' . . . If the situation seems impossible, if Reisman seems a superman, no matter, for the insights into good and evil are richly rewarding in this exciting and highly compelling novel." Libr J

Naylor, Gloria
Bailey's Café. Harcourt Brace Jovanovich 1992 229p $19.95
ISBN 0-15-110450-6   LC 91-42089
Bailey's Cafe is the setting in which the book's characters "tell stories from their lives. . . . Bailey's and the nearby boarding house (which some call a bordello) offer respite for those who have been battered in the outside world." Libr J
The author "takes us many keys down, and sometimes back up, in this virtuoso orchestration of survival, suffering, courage and humor, sounding through the stories of these lives." N Y Times Book Rev

Linden Hills. Ticknor & Fields 1985 304p o.p.

LC 84-16222

The author "sketches the development of the community of Linden Hills through its founder, Luther Nedeed, and successive generations of Nedeeds, showing in the decline of the family the corrosive effect of ambition, arrogance and the abuse of power. The residents of Linden Hills are similarly subverted by the accommodations, sacrifices and perversions of soul blacks must endure to live in an affluent community, even, as in this case, an all-black one." Publ Wkly
"Its flaws notwithstanding, the novel's ominous atmosphere and inspired set pieces—such as the minister's drunken fundamentalist sermon before an incredulous Hills congregation—make it a fascinating departure for

Naylor, Gloria—*Continued*

Miss Naylor, as well as a provocative, iconoclastic novel about a seldom-addressed subject." N Y Times Book Rev

Mama Day. Ticknor & Fields 1988 311p o.p.

LC 87-18157

"Willow Springs is a sparsely populated sea island just off America's southeastern coast whose small black community is dominated by the elderly matriarch, Miranda 'Mama' Day. When Mama Day's greatniece, Cocoa, marries, she returns to Willow Springs with her husband for an extended visit. Once there, strange forces—both natural and supernatural—work to separate the couple." Libr J

"When she is not didactically fostering our spiritual instruction, Gloria Naylor serves another worthy purpose beautifully: she invites us to imagine the lives of complex characters at work and play, and gives us a faithfully rendered community in all its seasons." Ms

The women of Brewster Place. Viking 1982 192p o.p.

LC 81-69969

This "novel is set, as the title indicates, in Brewster Place, a block-long dead-end street of run-down apartment buildings in a northern city. In an interrelated series of vignettes, Naylor focuses on seven black women, residents of Brewster Place. She is concerned with the distance between their dreams and realities, problems and solutions; these women are of different ages, come from different backgrounds, react differently to their blackness and to men, and have different notions of personal accomplishment, but all are burdened by being both black and female. Naylor is not angry; she writes with conviction and beautiful language, but spares the reader any bitterness. Characters are not puppets but exist and function as well-rounded personalities." Booklist

Nebula awards [1]-29. Harcourt Brace & Co. 1965-1995 29v v1-27 o.p.; v28 $24.95; v29 $25

ISSN 0741-5567

Partially analyzed in Short story index

Editors: 1965 [v1] Damon Knight; v2 Brian W. Aldiss and Harry Harrison; v3 Roger Zelazny; v4 Poul Anderson; v5 James Blish; v6 Clifford D. Simak; v7 Lloyd Biggle, Jr; v8 Isaac Asimov; v9 Kate Wilhelm; v10 James Gunn; v11 Ursula K. Le Guin; v12 Gordon R. Dickson; v13 Samuel R. Delaney; v14 Frederick Pohl; v15 Frank Herbert; v16 Jerry Pournelle; v17 Joe Haldeman; v18 Robert Silverberg; v19 Marta Randall; v20-22 George Zebrowski; v23-25 Michael Bishop; v26-28 James Morrow; v29 Pamela Sargent

Volumes 1-6 published by Doubleday; volumes 7-15 published by Harper & Row; volumes 16-17 published by Holt, Rinehart & Winston; volumes 18-19 published by Arbor House. Volumes 1-11 and 16-17 have title: Nebula award stories; volumes 12-15 have title: Nebula winners; volumes 20-24 have subtitle: SWFA's choices for the best science fiction and fantasy

Contents: v28 includes the novella City of Truth, by J. Morrow; two novelettes: Danny goes to Mars, by P. Sargent; and Matter's end, by G. Benford; and six short stories: Even the queen, by C. Willis; The July ward, by S. N. Dyer; Lennon spex, by P. Di Filippo; The mountain to Mohammed, by N. Kress; Vinland the

dream, by K. S. Robinson; Life regarded as a jigsaw puzzle of highly lustrous cats, by M. Bishop

v29 includes the novella The night we buried Road Dog, by J. Cady; four novelettes: Georgia on my mind, by C. Sheffield; Death on the Nile, by C. Willis; England underway, by T. Bisson; and The Franchise, by J. Kessel; and three short stories: The man who rowed Christopher Columbus ashore, by H. Ellison; Graves, by J. Haldeman; and Alfred, by Lisa Goldstein

Neville, Katherine, 1945-

The eight; a novel. Ballantine Bks. 1989 c1988 550p o.p.

LC 87-91363

This "novel is in and of itself a complex conundrum featuring two completely interdependent plots. As the action races back and forth between the era of the French Revolution and contemporary America and Algeria, both the historical and modern characters serve as pawns in an intricately executed game of chess. Players compete to unravel the sinister secret and curse of the mythical Montglane Service, an ornate chess set custom designed for Charlemagne, possessing certain mystical powers and endowed with an almost unlimited capacity for good or evil." Booklist

"Involving Napoleon, Talleyrand, Casanova, Voltaire, Rousseau, Robespierre and Catherine the Great in the quest, Neville has great fun rewriting history and making it all ring true." Publ Wkly

The **New** treasury of great racing stories; Dick Francis and John Welcome, editors. Norton 1992 c1991 211p $19.95

ISBN 0-393-03102-0   LC 92-9647

Companion volume to The Dick Francis treasury of great horseracing stories

Analyzed in Short story index

First published 1991 in the United Kingdom with title: Classic lines: more great racing stories

Contents: Spring fever, by D. Francis; My first winter, by J. Welcome; The man who shot the 'Favourite', by E. Wallace; Pick the winner, by D. Runyon; A night at the Old Bergen County race-track, by G. Grand; Blister, by J. T. Foote; The dead cert, by J. C. Squire; The inside view, by C. C. L. Browne; The tale of the gypsy horse, by D. Byrne; Pullinstown, by M. Keane; Occasional licenses, by Somerville & Ross; The good thing, by C. Davy; The losers, by M. Gee; The oracle, by A. B. Paterson

Newman, Kim

Anno-Dracula. Carroll & Graf Pubs. 1993 359p $21

ISBN 0-88184-967-7   LC 93-21934

"In a London where Count Dracula shares the throne with Queen Victoria and it's becoming fashionable to be one of the 'undead,' an ancient vampiress and a wily human investigator trail Jack the Ripper." Booklist

"The fin-de-siècle corruption is vividly portrayed, as is the strange mixture of sexuality and vampirism. In a society where people can avoid death by casting off a few moral principles along with their warm blood, class warfare intensifies, with the privileged few literally feeding off the lower classes. This is literate, powerful, and ugly." Libr J

Nexø, Martin Andersen *See* Andersen Nexø, Martin, 1869-1954

Ng, Fae Myenne, 1956-
Bone. Hyperion 1993 193p $19.95

ISBN 1-56282-944-0 LC 92-6028

The novel concerns "two generations of Chinese Americans in San Francisco's Chinatown. Mah, who has worked hard all her life in garment sweatshops, finally is able to own her baby-clothing store. Her husband, Leon, who used to be a merchant seaman, worked two shifts in ships' laundry rooms to provide for his family. Nevertheless, the family is torn apart after Ona, the middle daughter, jumps from the tallest building in Chinatown. . . . Nina, the youngest daughter, leaves Chinatown for New York City and then Leila, the oldest, marries and moves out to the suburbs. Leon, the 'paper son' to old Leung, fails to keep his promise to take Leung's bones back to China." Libr J

"Ng is a master storyteller. Her gift for observation and language make Bone truly extraordinary." Women's Rev Books

Nichols, John Treadwell, 1940-
The Milagro beanfield war; by John Nichols; illustrations by Rini Templeton. facsimile anniversary ed. Holt & Co. 1994 456p il $27.50

ISBN 0-8050-2805-6 LC 93-11937

A reissue of the title first published 1974 by Holt, Rinehart & Winston

"Joe Mondragon, a very small time troublemaker in the sleepy Chicano town of Milagro, irrigates a little field he owns in order to grow some beans. He is violating the local water laws but the rich and powerful are afraid to take action for fear of arousing Joe's friends and neighbors. (There's a big-money, Milagro-exploiting land development in the offing; they don't want to make waves.) Actually Joe's neighbors are generally resentful of his troublemaking, or are afraid to support him. But they eventually rally to the cause, having been pushed around too long, and the resulting interaction is touching and hilarious by turns." Publ Wkly

The sterile cuckoo; by John Nichols. McKay, D. 1965 210p o.p.

When the heroine, Pookie Adams "first stumbles on the hero, Jerry Payne, waiting at a cross-country bus stop, he sees only a skinny, scrubby-haired girl, balancing a toothpick on her tongue. Then she bursts into speech and Jerry . . . remains bewitched until the last syllable. Her pursuit of Jerry is launched with . . . determination. . . . When fate places the couple at neighboring Eastern colleges, Jerry succumbs to his first frantic affair. . . . As their romance plunges into its second year, they make a final attempt to slow to a more normal pace, but on a New York weekend, somewhat the worse for an over indulgence in Tiki Puka Pukas, their affair staggers to a close." Publisher's note

Nichols, Leigh, 1945-
For works written by this author under other names see Koontz, Dean R. (Dean Ray), 1945-

Nicholson, Margaret Beda *See* Yorke, Margaret

Nin, Anaïs, 1903-1977
Children of the albatross

In Nin, A. Cities of the interior p128-238

Cities of the interior; introduction by Sharon Spencer. Swallow Press 1974 xx, 589p o.p.

First one-volume version published 1959 by the author. Although intended as a connected work exploring the lives of women, it was originally published as five separate novelettes. This edition contains the expanded and retitled version of the fifth novelette

In Ladders to fire (1946), which concerns a largely American group of characters in Paris, Lillian's hunger for life and love leave her unsatisfied with her seemingly changeless marriage to Larry. She develops an increasingly possessive relationship with Djuna, whose inner clarity and control, concealed beneath a delicate feminine exterior, offer a comforting contrast to her own emotional turbulence. Lillian's love affair with the painter Jay is complicated by the love-hate relationship which they both establish with Sabina

Children of the albatross (1947) focuses on Djuna, who achieved a sense of liberation through dancing after an unhappy childhood in an orphan asylum. It deals with her youthful love for Michael, who fled to a homosexual lover after his jealousy drove them apart, her relationship with the joyful painter Lawrence and the youth Paul who seeks shelter and love from her after fleeing his parent's stifling home, and the relationships of Jay to her, Lillian and Sabina

In The four-chambered heart (1950), Djuna and the Guatemalan guitarist Rango become lovers and Djuna takes up residence on a houseboat in the Seine. Rango's supposedly invalid wife pretends to accept and even welcome the situation, but her feigning of illness and increasingly apparent insanity nearly wreck Djuna's life

In A spy in the house of love (1954), set in and around New York City, Sabina acts out relationships with her husband and lovers who include the opera singer Philip, the African drummer Mambo, and the painter Jay. She explores her longing for freedom and guilty feelings about the lies her many loves seem to make necessary

In Seduction of the Minotaur (1961; an expanded version of Solar barque), Lillian seeks a liberating escape from her past in a Mexican town. Discovering that she is reenacting old relationships with her new acquaintances, she realizes she can transcend her past only by understanding rather than evading it and that her quest for freedom cannot take place apart from her husband, whose changelessness is a necessary complement to her own mutability

The four-chambered heart

In Nin, A. Cities of the interior p239-358

Ladders to fire

In Nin, A. Cities of the interior p1-127

Seduction of the Minotaur

In Nin, A. Cities of the interior p463-589

Nin, Anaïs, 1903-1977—*Continued*

A spy in the house of love

In Nin, A. Cities of the interior p360-462

Niven, Larry

The integral trees. Ballantine Bks. 1984 c1983 240p o.p.

LC 83-15870

"A Del Rey book"

"The descendants of humans shipwrecked in an alien solar system eke out a difficult living in a bizarre world-less ecosystem. One group, forced into exile, undergoes a series of adventures culminating in their meeting with a strange spacefarer. The plot is mainly a vehicle to display the intricately worked out environment." Anatomy of Wonder 4

Followed by The smoke ring

Lucifer's hammer; by Larry Niven & Jerry Pournelle. Playboy Press 1977 494p o.p.

LC 77-8074

"The hammer of the title is an eons-old comet that strikes earth with devastating physical and psychological consequences that are meticulously dramatized in the lives of dozens of major and minor characters. The second and more powerful part details the immense task of rebuilding civilization or preserving what remains of it. The authors excel in their suspenseful and thought-provoking hypothesis about the nature of civilized man and the ethics of survival when the future of their fragile community is at stake." Booklist

The Mote in God's Eye; by Larry Niven & Jerry Pournelle. Simon & Schuster 1974 537p o.p.

"Superior space opera in which Earth's interstellar navy contacts and does battle with an enormously hostile alien race. The scenes of space warfare are well handled, and the alien Moties are fascinating." Anatomy of Wonder 4

Followed by The gripping hand (1993)

Ringworld; a novel. Holt, Rinehart & Winston 1977 c1970 342p o.p.

LC 76-45284

First published 1970 in paperback by Ballantine Books

"The Ringworld, a world shaped like a wheel so huge that it surrounds a sun, is almost too fantastic to conceive of. With a radius of 90 million miles and a length of 600 million miles, the Ringworld's mystery is compounded by the discovery that it is artificial. What phenomenal intelligence can be behind such a creation? Four unlikely explorers, two humans and two aliens, set out for the Ringworld, bound by mutual distrust and unsure of each other's motives." Shapiro. Fic for Youth. 3d edition

Followed by The Ringworld engineers

The Ringworld engineers. Holt, Rinehart & Winston 1980 357p o.p.

LC 79-18992

"Twenty-three years after their original journey, Louis Wu and Speaker-to-Animals once more find themselves kidnapped companions of a mad Puppeteer who returns with them to Ringworld to steal a transmutation device. The Puppeteer encounters unexpected obstacles to this goal, however: Louis has become a wirehead addicted to the electric current fed almost constantly to his brain; Speaker-to-Animals is now a kzinti Patriarch and resents his enforced participation in the venture; the Ringworld has developed an unstable orbit and is about to disintegrate into its sun." SLJ

"This is a good example of the kind of novel where the basic idea—the Ringworld itself—is the true 'hero.'" Booklist

The smoke ring. Ballantine Bks. 1987 362p o.p.

LC 86-26579

"A Del Rey book"

Sequel to The integral trees

This novel "follows the adventures of the descendants of a handful of space mutineers who have created a complex civilization within the ring of breathable atmosphere around a neutron star. New complications include the discovery of the Admiralty, a large society living in 'free-fall.' Niven's engaging heroes, Jeffer and Gavving, and their families return in this saga, and the appearance of the Admiralty offers a new feast for lovers of the author's uniquely zany touch with his characters." Booklist

A world out of time; a novel. Holt, Rinehart & Winston 1976 243p o.p.

"Jaybee Corbell, who had himself cryogenically frozen in 1970, awakens in the 22nd century and finds that his mind had been transfused to the body of a brain-washed criminal, and the dictatorial State is going to send him on a biological seeding mission in a 'rammer' spaceship. On the trip out, he gains control of the human-minded computer that runs the ship and sets course for a suicidal jump to the center of the galaxy. Time gets warped during a passage through a black hole, and when Jaybee gets back to the solar system, three million years of earth-time have elapsed. On an unrecognizable Earth, he meets two weird survivors—a perpetual Boy, and an ageless lady retread, and with the aid of his orbiting rammer-computer he mediates the future of Earth." Publ Wkly

Nordan, Lewis

Wolf whistle; a novel. Algonquin Bks. 1993 290p $16.95

ISBN 1-56512-028-0   LC 93-1011

"The wolf whistle of the title comes from Bobo, a black teenager from Chicago visiting in Arrow Catcher, Mississippi. Directed at the wife of the town's most prominent white resident, this whistle soon leads to Bobo's murder. Based on the Emmett Till lynching, . . . [this novel] examines the intertwined fates of blacks and poor whites in the Mississippi delta." Libr J

"Propelled by Nordan's musical prose, much of this narrative soars above the commonplace into the realm of myth." Publ Wkly

Nordhoff, Charles, 1887-1947

Botany Bay; by Charles Nordhoff and James Norman Hall. Little, Brown 1941 374p o.p.

"The story of the Australian penal colony at Botany Bay, and especially of Hugh Tallant, an American, who had been stranded in England, turned highwayman, and was one of the first criminals shipped to Botany Bay, where life was bitterly hard and adventurous." Ont Libr Rev

Nordhoff, Charles, 1887-1947—*Continued*

The Bounty trilogy; by Charles Nordhoff and James Norman Hall; illustrations by N. C. Wyeth. Little, Brown 1936 903p il o.p.

"An Atlantic Monthly Press book"

"Comprising the three volumes: Mutiny on the Bounty, Men against the sea & Pitcairn's Island." Title page

The hurricane; by Charles Nordhoff and James Norman Hall. Little, Brown 1936 257p o.p. Amereon reprint available $20.95 (ISBN 0-88411-541-1)

"On a South Sea island live some hundred and fifty souls in amiable community. There is a priest who has labored lovingly there for fifty years, a French administrator, and his sympathetic wife. And Terangi, a superb native who, because he could not endure the jail to which a saloon brawl had sent him, becomes a fugitive from justice, a murderer with a price on his head. It takes a hurricane to solve Terangi's problem, a hurricane that wipes out the smiling island and most of the inhabitants." New Yorker

"The convincing tale depicts the life of the native and the several white inhabitants, and both the beauty and desolation of their surroundings." N Y Libr

Men against the sea; by Charles Nordhoff and James Norman Hall. Little, Brown 1934 251p o.p. Amereon reprint available $18.95 (ISBN 0-89190-564-2)

Sequel to Mutiny on the Bounty

This volume tells the story of Captain Bligh and the eighteen loyal men, who under his leadership sailed in an open boat thirty-six hundred miles from the Friendly Islands in the South Pacific to the Dutch colony of Timor in the East Indies. The story is told as if by Ledward, the surgeon, but the events, the wind and the weather of the narrative are those recorded in Captain Bligh's log

Followed by Pitcairn's Island

also in Nordhoff, C. The Bounty trilogy

Mutiny on the Bounty; by Charles Nordhoff and James Norman Hall. Little, Brown 1932 396p $27.95

ISBN 0-316-61157-3

Also available from Amereon

"This vivid narrative is based on the famous mutiny which members of the crew of the 'Bounty', a British war vessel, carried out in 1787 against their cruel commander, Captain William Bligh. The authors kept the actual historical characters and background, using as narrator an elderly man Captain Roger Byam, who had been a midshipman on the 'Bounty.' The story tells how the mate of the ship, Fletcher Christian, and a number of the crew rebel and set Captain Bligh adrift in an open boat with the loyal members of the crew." Reader's Ency. 3d edition

Followed by Men against the sea

also in Nordhoff, C. The Bounty trilogy

Pitcairn's Island; by Charles Nordhoff and James Norman Hall. Little, Brown 1934 333p o.p.

Sequel to Men against the sea

"This final volume [of the trilogy] is the history of those mutineers who, with eighteen Polynesian men and women, reached Pitcairn's Island and there destroyed the 'Bounty.' Unvisited for eighteen years, the community fought over women and possession, and all but one of the men died violent deaths. A blood-curdling story, not for the squeamish reader." Booklist

also in Nordhoff, C. The Bounty trilogy

Norman, Howard

The bird artist. Farrar, Straus & Giroux 1994 289p $20

ISBN 0-374-11330-0   LC 94-70542

"Fabian, son of Alaric and Orkney Vas, has spent his entire life in remote Witless Bay, Newfoundland. Looking back on his life, he decides that he has distinguished himself in only two ways: as a modestly successful artist whose illustrations graced the covers of *Bird Lore* magazine and as the murderer of the local lighthouse keeper, Botho August. The murder was the result of excessive coffee consumption combined with the stress brought on by his parents' plan to force him into an arranged marriage with a cousin he had never seen; this in turn would keep him from his hard-drinking girlfriend." Libr J

This work evokes "a way of life, a distinctive community and a fatalistic view of human behavior. The novel sings with tension and sparkles with antic humor." Publ Wkly

Norris, Benjamin Franklin *See* Norris, Frank, 1870-1902

Norris, Frank, 1870-1902

McTeague; a story of San Francisco. Available from various publishers

First published 1899 by Doubleday

"A prime example of the American naturalistic novel, *McTeague* treats the gradual degeneration of a stupid, but initially harmless, giant of a man whose instincts are nearer brute than human. McTeague practices dentistry without a license in a poor section of San Francisco's Polk Street and marries Trina, who has just won $5,000 in a lottery. He soon loses his job and takes to drink. Trina becomes a miser, and McTeague murders her in a fit of rage and steals her money but is tracked down and killed by her cousin." Benet's Reader's Ency of Am Lit

The octopus; a story of California. Doubleday 1901 652p o.p. Buccaneer Bks. reprint available $25.95 (ISBN 0-89968-070-4)

First volume of an unfinished trilogy The epic of wheat

"The battle waged between the wheat growers and the railroad men in California is the theme of this novel. Concerned with social injustice, man's inhumanity to man, and the relentlessness of power struggles, Norris is able to combine these themes with a love interest." Shapiro. Fic for Youth. 3d edition

Followed by The pit

The pit; a story of Chicago. Doubleday 1903 o.p.

Available from Bentley and Buccaneer Bks.

The second volume of the author's unfinished The epic of wheat trilogy "is a story of manipulations in the Chicago Exchange. Curtis Jadwin, a stock speculator, is so absorbed in making money that he neglects his

Norris, Frank, 1870-1902—*Continued*
emotionally starved wife Laura. Into this situation steps
Sheldon Corthell, dilettante artist, to console her. Laura
loves her husband, and postpones for awhile going away
with the aesthete. Meanwhile, Jadwin engages in a struggle with the Crookes gang of speculators. He beats them,
but is crushed by fluctuations in wheat production. He
and Laura effect a reconciliation." Haydn. Thesaurus of
Book Dig

Norton, Alice Mary *See* Norton, Andre,
1912-

Norton, Andre, 1912-
The elvenbane; an epic high fantasy of the
Halfblood chronicles; [by] Andre Norton,
Mercedes Lackey. Doherty Assocs. 1991
390p $19.95
ISBN 0-312-85106-5   LC 91-21177
"A TOR book"
"In a world ruled by some of the most brutal and
tyrannical elves ever encountered, the most persecuted
are the part-human, part-elven halfbloods. After her
human mother is cast into the desert, [Shana] the bastard
daughter of the powerful Lord Dyran survives and is
raised by dragons to seek her destiny as the Elvenbane."
Booklist
Followed by Elvenblood

Elvenblood; an epic high fantasy; [by]
Andre Norton and Mercedes Lackey.
Doherty Assocs. 1995 348p $22.95
ISBN 0-312-85548-6   LC 95-5797
"A TOR book"
"Following rumors of the existence of a tribe of
humans immune to the enslaving magics of the land's
elven overlords, halfelven rebel Shana and her dragon
companion encounter unexpected complications in their
struggle for freedom. The talents of collaborators Norton
and Lackey blend seamlessly as they expand the background to their epic fantasy to include an exotic desert
culture, which provides a rich contrast to the stifling
atmosphere of elven society." Libr J

Empire of the eagle; [by] Andre Norton
and Susan Shwartz. TOR Bks. 1993 416p
$22.95
ISBN 0-312-85169-3   LC 93-26551
"The story opens with the defeat and capture of a
legion of Roman soldiers at the hands of the Parthians,
an ancient Asian society. Although the Romans' lives are
spared, their honor is destroyed at the loss of their standard, the eagle, and their sale into slavery to the Ch'in
emperor. But the gods are watching over this band, particularly over their tribune, Quintus, who is guided by
a talisman of Krishna, a sensuous sybil called Draupadi,
and the emerging memories of his past life. As the legion
is transported by their captors along the Silk Road, they
battle desert storms and black magic to reclaim freedom
and honor. A fast-paced mix of history and fantasy for
adventure seekers." Booklist

Firehand; [by] Andre Norton & P.M. Griffin. TOR Bks. 1994 220p $19.95
ISBN 0-312-85313-0   LC 94-604

"A Tom Doherty Associates book"
In this "return to Norton's Time Trader world, a
young man finds himself as he teaches guerrilla warfare
to a feudal, nonterrestrial offshoot of humanity in order
to prepare them properly for a future in which space-
and time-traveling humans are battling for survival
against murderous aliens. Ross Murdock, a young
criminal recruited as a Time Agent for his survival skills,
is sent to the Dominion of Virgin, which had abruptly
turned from a populous planet to a burned cinder as
a result of time-travel by the Baldies, as the aliens are
known." Publ Wkly

Golden Trillium. Bantam Bks. 1993 296p
o.p.
                                      LC 92-43875
Third in the fantasy series that includes Black Trillium
by Marion Zimmer Bradley, Julian May, and Andre
Norton, and Blood Trillium by Julian May
"Having aided her sisters in establishing peace in the
land of Ruwenda, the warrior-maiden Kadiya journeys
through the swamps to return the Three-Orbed Sword
to the place of its origin only to find that her fight
against evil is not yet done. The grande dame of sf and
fantasy returns to a favorite theme—the discovery of an
ancient and highly advanced lost civilization—in this
heroic adventure." Libr J

The hands of Lyr. Morrow 1994 388p $22
ISBN 0-380-77097-0   LC 93-45829
This "is a quest tale: a young warrior and an equally
young priestess must find the hands (or at least the 10
fingers) of Lyr, which is something between an elemental
force and an outright god. To do so, is the only way
to restore life to a wasted land." Booklist
"Norton once again creates a mystical yet credible
world, inhabited by engaging protagonists, dastardly villains and fetching creatures." Publ Wkly

The mark of the cat. Ace Bks. 1992 248p
il o.p.
                                      LC 91-38700
"Inspired by Karen Kuykendall's famous book of paintings, *The Cat People,* and her equally famous tarot cards,
Norton has evoked a richly drawn world of five queen-
doms where domestic cats are revered, hugh rats hunt
in vicious packs, and young humans are abandoned miles
from home in a coming-of-age rite called the Solo. Hynk-
kel, the younger son of a high-ranking official, is
ostracized by his family because he's more comfortable
with animals than practicing warfare." Booklist
"Norton's distinctive style . . . transcends the limitations of the 'rite-of-passage' fantasy as characters and
cultures come to life under her expert guidance." Libr
J

Redline the stars; [by] Andre Norton,
P.M. Griffin. TOR Bks. 1993 304p $19.95
ISBN 0-312-85314-9   LC 92-43708
"A Tom Doherty Associates book"
The authors "recreate the flavor of Norton's four *Solar
Queen* books (published almost 40 years ago) while up-
dating some concepts and quite a bit of technology. The
crew of the Free Trader vessel *Solar Queen,* flying under
Capt. Míceál Jellico, has mixed reactions to new crew-
mate Rael Cofort, who is plying the space lanes as a
jack-of-all-trades despite her position as a physician and
status as sister of the successful rival Free Trader,
Teague Cofort. Upon arriving at Canuche of Halio, the
most advanced planet of the sector, the *Queen's* crew

Norton, Andre, 1912-—*Continued*
is endangered when Rael picks up the odor of man-eating rodents used in a gruesome gem-stealing scheme." Publ Wkly

Sneeze on Sunday; [by] Andre Norton and Grace Allen Hogarth. TOR Bks. 1992 249p o.p.

LC 91-36103

"A Tom Doherty Associates book"
A "mystery set in New England during the early 1950's. . . . Librarian Fredericka Wing takes a summer job minding a bookstore in South Sutton, Mass., a college town founded by a family whose reduced financial circumstances are now being ameliorated by the nationally known herb farm run by matriarch Margaret Sutton and her niece, Phillippine, a chemist rescued from a German concentration camp. Returning from a church bazaar, Fredericka finds the body of Catherine Clay, née Sutton, in the bookstore's hammock. . . . This leisurely period piece will attract readers seeking an alternative to breakneck, often brutal suspense fiction." Publ Wkly

(ed) Tales of the Witch World [1]-3. See Tales of the Witch World [1]-3

(jt. auth) Bradley, M. Z. Black Trillium

The **Norton** book of ghost stories; edited by Brad Leithauser. Norton 1994 430p $25

ISBN 0-393-03564-6   LC 94-17383

Analyzed in Short story index
Contents: The romance of certain old clothes; The friends of the friends; Maud-Evelyn; Sir Edmund Orme, by H. James; Casting the runes; "Oh, whistle, and I'll come to you, my lad"; Mr. Humphreys and his inheritance; Count Magnus, by M. R. James; Miss Mary Pask; The looking glass, by E. Wharton; Poor girl, by E. Taylor; The beckoning fair one, by O. Onions; The open window, by "Saki"; Hand in glove; The demon lover; The cat jumps, by E. Bowen; The clock, by W. F. Harvey; The tooth, by S. Jackson; A story of Don Juan, by V. S. Pritchett; The Portobello Road, by M. Spark; Three miles up, by E. J. Howard; The tower, by M. Laski; The Buick saloon, by A. Bridge; The axe, by P. Fitzgerald; Torch song; The music teacher, by J. Cheever; The July ghost, by A. S. Byatt; Ancient music, by P. Graham

The **Norton** book of science fiction; North American science fiction, 1960-1990; edited by Ursula K. Le Guin and Brian Attebery; Karen Joy Fowler, consultant. Norton 1993 869p $27.50

ISBN 0-393-03546-8   LC 93-16130

Analyzed in Short story index
Contents: The handler, by D. F. Knight; Alpha Ralpha Boulevard, by C. Smith; Tandy's story, by T. Sturgeon; 2064, or thereabouts, by D. R. Bunch; Balanced ecology, by J. H. Schmitz; The house the Blakeneys built, by A. Davidson; Over the river and through the woods, by C. D. Simak; How beautiful with banners, by J. Blish; Nine hundred grandmothers, by R. A. Lafferty; When I was Miss Dow, by S. Dorman; Comes now the power, by R. Zelazny; Day million, by F. Pohl; The winter flies, by F. Leiber; High weir, by S. R. Delany; Kyrie, by P. Anderson; For the sake of Grace, by S. H. Elgin; As simple as that, by Z. Henderson; Good news from

the Vatican, by R. Silverberg; Gather blue roses, by P. Sargent; The women men don't see, by J. Tiptree; Feather tigers, by G. Wolfe; The mountains of sunset, the mountains of dawn, by V. N. McIntyre; The private war of Private Jacob, by J. W. Haldeman; The warlord of Saturn's moons, by E. Arnason; Making it all the way into the future on Gaxton Falls of the red planet, by B. N. Malzberg; The new Atlantis, by U. K. Le Guin; A few things I know about Whileaway, by J. Russ; Strange wine, by H. Ellison; Lollipop and the tar baby, by J. Varley; Night-rise, by K. MacLean; Frozen journey, by P. K. Dick; Precession, by E. Bryant; Elbow room, by M. Z. Bradley; Tauf aleph, by P. Gotlieb; Exposures, by G. Benford; The Gernsback continuum, by W. Gibson; The start of the end of the world, by C. Emshwiller; Schrödinger's plague, by G. Bear; ". . . the world as we know 't", by H. Waldrop; The Byrds, by M. Coney; Speech sounds, by O. E. Butler; Distant signals, by A. Weiner; The lucky strike, by K. S. Robinson; The life of anybody, by R. Sheckley; Interlocking pieces, by M. Gloss; The war at home, by L. Shiner; The lake was full of artificial things, by K. J. Fowler; Snow, by J. Crowley; After the days of Dead-Eye 'Dee, by P. Cadigan; The Bob Dylan Tambourine Software & Satori Support Services Consortium, Ltd., by M. Bishop; His vegetable wife, by P. Murphy; The brains of rats, by M. Blumlein; Out of all them bright stars, by N. Kress; Rat, by J. P. Kelly; America, by O. S. Card; Schwarzschild radius, by C. Willis; Stable strategies for middle management, by E. Gunn; Kirinyaga, by M. Resnick; A midwinter's tale, by M. Swanwick; (Learning about) machine sex, by C. J. Dorsey; We see things differently, by B. Sterling; Half-life, by P. Preuss; Homelanding, by M. Atwood; And the angels sing, by K. Wilhelm; Aunt Parnetta's electric blisters, by D. Glancy; Midnight news, by L. Goldstein; Invaders, by J. Kessel

Nye, Jody Lynn, 1957-
(jt. auth) McCaffrey, A. The ship who won

O

The **O.** Henry awards. See Prize stories, 1919-1995: The O. Henry awards

Oates, Joyce Carol, 1938-
American appetites. Dutton 1989 340p o.p.

LC 88-18904

"A William Abrahams book"
"Ian McCullough, 50 years old, is editor of a prestigious journal and a research fellow. His wife, Glynnis, writes cookbooks. Their marriage is not perfect but far from unfulfilling. Then an incident from the past—Ian loaned money to a friend of Glynnis' for an abortion—resurfaces and provokes a horrible row between husband and wife. Glynnis ends up falling through a pane of glass and being killed." Booklist
"A zippy story about successful lives dramatically altered by one sudden and inexplicable lapse of judgment." Publ Wkly

Oates, Joyce Carol, 1938-—*Continued*

Because it is bitter, and because it is my heart. Dutton 1990 405p o.p.

LC 89-25965

"A William Abrahams book"
This novel "is set in a small town in western New York from the early 1950s to the early 1960s, and follows the . . . fortunes of two families, one white (the Courtneys) and one black (the Fairchilds). When Jinx Fairchild, at 16, gets in a fight with a white kid who has menaced Iris Courtney, 14, and ends up killing him, the secret they share is . . . both a bond and a barrier between the two." Nation
"At its best, the novel awakens the reader to something like the unexpected new comprehensions of the universe that Iris experiences." N Y Rev Books

Bellefleur. Dutton 1980 558p o.p.

LC 79-28193

"A Henry Robbins book"
"In this Gothic novel, Oates weaves a shimmering tapestry made of odd and contradictory threads: a hermaphroditic birth, a vulture that devours an infant, a dwarf with 'powers,' a vampire, a cannibal, religious mystics and clairvoyants. Such are the Gothic trappings of this epic about the Bellefleurs, an old and powerful American family whose estate is located in the Adirondacks and whose history is an interpretation of American history from pioneer days to the present." Benet's Reader's Ency of Am Lit

Black water. Dutton 1992 154p $17

ISBN 0-525-93455-3   LC 91-40463

"A William Abrahams book"
"A 26-year-old woman drowns when a senator's car goes off a bridge; but the point of view in this . . . novel belongs to the victim." N Y Times Book Rev
"Those who remember Chappaquiddick can predict Kelly's ultimate fate, but certainly not the horrors she must have suffered strapped to the seat of a car that would become an aqueous death chamber. Immense courage shines through the tangled streams of her thoughts, memories, and hallucinations. As witnesses to her plight, we can only keep vigil as she drifts in and out of consciousness, waiting for the reprieve that surely must be hers. Oates brilliantly redefines the meanings of guilt and innocence, vengeance and reward in this thought-provoking allegory of our life and times." Libr J

A Bloodsmoor romance. Dutton 1982 615p o.p.

LC 82-2416

The novel "details the bizarre goings-on in a 19th-century inventor's family. One daughter becomes a medium, another an actress and Mark Twain's mistress, a third runs away on her wedding night. Even Octavia, the perfect wife, is secretly subversive. . . . The narrator misunderstands and misinterprets much that happens; the reader, therefore, enters into collusion with the characters who use the period's conventions to subvert prescribed female roles." Libr J

Expensive people. Vanguard Press 1968 308p o.p.

"The journal of a self-styled 18-year-old madman, looking back at his childhood in one affluent American suburb after another, always precociously aware of what his parents demanded of him and how cruelly they misunderstood his needs. Father is a philistine with a talent for making money and a longing for a son who will play in the Little League. Mother, perhaps the most fascinating character in the novel, is a writer whose work appears in 'little magazines' and who is periodically driven to desert her family and babbitry for a life of sexual and artistic freedom. . . . It is the narrator-son's desperate oedipal love for his mother that precipitates a final crisis of horror, of the 'nice boy suddenly runs amok' variety." Publ Wkly

Foxfire; confessions of a girl gang. Dutton 1993 328p $21

ISBN 0-525-93632-7   LC 92-43858

"The leader of Foxfire, a flamboyant girl gang, is Legs Sadovsky, a tall, angular blond with enough attitude to turn her upstate New York hometown on its ear. It's 1955 and Legs, Lana, Rita, Goldie, and Maddy, the gentle narrator, are almost 16 and most certainly not sweet. These gals live on the wrong side of the tracks; their parents are deceased or alcoholic, their home lives depressing and loveless. They form Foxfire for the same reason kids always form gangs: for mutual support and protection, to demand respect, and acquire power." Booklist
"Legs Sadovsky is a brilliant creation—wholly heroic, wholly convincing, racing for her tragic consummation impelled by a finer sensibility and a more thoughtful daring than is usually granted to the tragic male outlaws we love and need. . . . 'Foxfire' burns brightly; it is completely assured and occasionally exhilarating." N Y Times Book Rev

A garden of earthly delights. Vanguard Press 1967 440p o.p.

The book describes the early life of Clara Walpole, the daughter of a migrant farm worker; her life after she leaves her father; her romance with a rum-runner; and her marriage to a rich man, whom she convinces is the father of her illegitimate baby. The final part of the novel deals with the childhood and adolescence of Swan, the son
"The book has much to say of society's indifference to the plight of the disadvantaged, and of the shallowness of a way of life based entirely on getting and spending." Libr J

Haunted; tales of the grotesque. Dutton 1994 310p $21.95

ISBN 0-525-93655-6   LC 93-25223

"A William Abrahams book"
Analyzed in Short story index
Contents: Haunted; The doll; The bingo master; The white cat; The model [novella]; Extenuating circumstances; Don't you trust me?; The guilty party; The premonition; Phase change; Poor Bibi; Thanksgiving; Blind; The radio astronomer; Accursed inhabitants of the House of Bly; Martyrdom
"All the pieces here have a redeeming literary bent, although some are transparent in their motives. Undoubtedly a master of this form, Oates plies her craft like a skilled seducer, setting the mood and moving in for the conquest night after night after night." Publ Wkly

Heat, and other stories. Dutton 1991 397p $21.95

ISBN 0-525-93330-1   LC 91-8007

"A William Abrahams book"
Analyzed on Short story index
Contents: House hunting; The knife; The hair; Shopping; The boyfriend; Passion; Morning; Naked; Heat; The buck; Yarrow; Sundays in summer; Leila Lee; The swim-

Oates, Joyce Carol, 1938-—*Continued*

mers; Getting to know all about you; Capital punishment; Hostage; Craps; Death valley; White trash; Twins; The crying baby; Why don't you come live with me it's time; Ladies and gentlemen; Family

I lock my door upon myself. Ecco Press 1990 98p $15.95

ISBN 0-88001-260-9   LC 90-31878

"In turn-of-the-century rural America, willful and elusive Calla, muzzled by an enforced marriage, church, and kin she no longer cares about, chooses a life of inertia and indifference until the arrival of roving black water dowser Tyrell Thompson." Libr J

Is this "all a parable of the artist's position as an observer and interpreter of society? Is it an illustration of how a writer constructs a coherent story out of disjointed events? Either way, it provokes thought." Atlantic

Marriages and infidelities; short stories. Vanguard Press 1972 497p o.p.

Analyzed in Short story index

Contents: The sacred marriage; Puzzle; Love and death; 29 inventions; Problems of adjustment in survivors of natural/unnatural disasters; By the river; Extraordinary popular delusions; Stalking; Scenes of passion and despair; Plot; The children; Happy onion; Normal love; Stray children; Wednesday's child; Loving, losing, loving a man; Did you ever slip on red blood?; The metamorphosis; Where I lived, and what I lived for; The lady with the pet dog; The spiral; The turn of the screw; The dead; Nightmusic

Marya; a life. Dutton 1986 310p o.p.

LC 85-16283

"A William Abrahams book"

In this novel, which begins in "a mining town near the Erie Canal, eight-year-old Marya Knauer's father is bludgeoned to death. Her mother walks away from Marya and her infant brothers. Raised by her uncle's family, and sexually abused by her cousin, Marya develops a shell: she's quick-witted, sarcastic and . . . friendless because she's so hard, so bright. She discovers that her reputation for brillance serves as 'a sort of glass barrier that would keep other people at a distance.' Driven by work, Marya presses through graduate school, becomes a tenured professor at a college much like Dartmouth, then quits to become a lioness in the New York literary world." Newsweek

"Marya's development and her innermost fears and insecurities are revealed in a very personal, almost autobiographical manner. A major work by an important writer." Libr J

The model

In Oates, J. C. Haunted p99-144

Nemesis; [by] Rosamond Smith. Dutton 1990 276p o.p.

LC 89-71533

"A William Abrahams book"

"The rape of a male graduate student by Rolf Christensen, a famous composer and faculty member, follows a cocktail party given by Maggie Blackburn, director of graduate music education at Curtis Institute of Music in Forest Park, Connecticut. When Brendan Bauer brings charges against Christensen, the less-than-courageous ethics committee generates a cover-up. Someone is out to get Christensen, however, and Bauer seems to be the only suspect. Then Maggie begins an investigation of her own." Libr J

This novel is "mesmerizing. Joyce Carol Oates in her mystery mode manages to dangle, withdraw and reintroduce clues so deftly that following her trail of suspicion is like trying to catch a firefly." N Y Times Book Rev

(ed) The Oxford book of American short stories. See The Oxford book of American short stories

The rise of life on earth. New Directions 1991 135p $16.95

ISBN 0-8112-1171-1   LC 90-48706

"A concentrated, single-minded, compact novel that explores the life and consciousness of an abused little girl who grows up to become a hospital worker bent on secret deadly acts." N Y Times Book Rev

Snake eyes; [by] Rosamond Smith. Dutton 1992 280p $20

ISBN 0-525-93404-9   LC 91-25843

"A William Abrahams book"

"Michael O'Meara is an East Coast lawyer who likes to get involved; and he gets involved in the case of Lee Roy Sears, convicted murderer. Michael helps in getting Lee Roy's death sentence commuted to life imprisonment; then he helps Lee Roy get paroled and employed in a job in the O'Meara's hometown. Well, has Michael opened a Pandora's box of evil or what, letting this man into his life?" Booklist

"The tightly crafted plot hurtles to an inevitable battery of brutal events that both shock and satisfy. The author treats current issues—the sentimentality of liberals toward criminals, 'obscene' art and censorship—with biting wit." Publ Wkly

Solstice. Dutton 1985 243p o.p.

LC 84-18710

"A William Abrahams book"

This novel "concerns recently divorced Monica Jensen, who takes a job teaching at a private boys' school in Pennsylvania. She is determined to throw herself into her work and to do the best she can, but she doesn't reckon on becoming acquainted with the local famous artist, one Shelia Trask, an ironically distant but absorbing personality, a disturbing presence and a dominating force. Their new friendship quickly intensifies, then breaks off, and Monica tries to believe it is for the best, that she's back in full control of her life. That does not last long, though; the friendship blossoms again, and this time their parasitical relationship is finally ruinous." Booklist

"*Solstice* goes well beyond technique; as an investigation of friendship and art it is provocative, relentless and splendid." Publ Wkly

Them. Vanguard Press 1969 508p o.p.

"Violent and explosive in both incident and tone, the work is set in urban Detroit from 1937 to 1967 and chronicles the efforts of the Wendell family to break away from their destructive, crime-ridden background. Critics praised the novel for its detailed social observation and its bitter indictment of American society." Merriam-Webster's Ency of Lit

Unholy loves; a novel. Vanguard Press 1979 335p o.p.

LC 79-64396

Oates, Joyce Carol, 1938-—*Continued*

This novel, organized around a series of faculty parties at a prestigious college in upstate New York, "focuses on novelist Brigit Stott, struggling with feelings of failure as an artist and woman, and draws on the lives of several of her colleagues in the English Department at Woodslee University as they react to the presence of a distinguished visiting poet from England. Lost in the self-absorption of old age, the poet muddles through his visit, which begins and ends rather shockingly, while rivalries rage about him and he inadvertently inspires a love affair between divorced Brigit and a possibly bisexual musician, Alepis Kessler." Libr J

"Characters are shown struggling with the dawning facts of their inconsequence as scholars, as husbands or wives, as lovers, or as administrators. . . . A convincing, mocking, sympathetic, acerbic, forgiving, prodigious, and supremely confident novel." Booklist

What I lived for. Dutton 1994 608p $23.95

ISBN 0-525-93836-2   LC 94-549

"A William Abrahams book"

This "novel is set in Union City, a fictional place on the New York shores of Lake Erie, something like Buffalo. It tells the story of Jerome (Corky) Corcoran, a two-bit politician and businessman. Though the book opens with the murder of Corky's father in 1959, the bulk of the action takes place over one long weekend in 1992. A lost weekend, it begins when Corky learns that his lover, Christina Kavanaugh, has been conducting their affair with the permission of her crippled husband, a discovery that shatters Corky's ego and sets him ricocheting all over the city, from one reversal to another, following a zigzag course through layers of social class, racial division, political machination and economic distress." N Y Times Book Rev

Where are you going, where have you been?; selected early stories. Ontario Review Press 1993 522p $24.95

ISBN 0-86538-077-5   LC 92-44899

Analyzed in Short story index

This retrospective collection includes stories from By the north gate (1963); Upon the sweeping flood (1966); The wheel of love (1970); Marriages and infidelities (1972); The goddess and other women (1974); and Nightside (1977)

Contents: Edge of the world; The fine white mist of winter; First views of the enemy; At the seminary; What death with love should have to do; Upon the sweeping flood; In the region of ice; Where are you going, where have you been?; Unmailed, unwritten letters; Accomplished desires; How I contemplated the world from the Detroit House of Correction and began my life over again; Four summers; Love and death; By the river; Did you ever slip on red blood?; The lady with the pet dog; The turn of the screw; The dead; Concerning the case of Bobby T.; In the warehouse; Small avalanches; The widows; The translation; Bloodstains; Daisy; The molesters; Silkie

Where is here?; stories. Ecco Press 1992 193p $18.95

ISBN 0-88001-283-8   LC 92-3634

Analyzed in Short story index

Contents: Lethal; Area man found crucified; Imperial presidency; Bare legs; Turquoise; Biopsy; The date; Angry; The ice pick; The mother; Sweet!; Forgive me!; Transfigured night; Actress; The false mirror; From the life of. . .; The heir; "Shot"; Letter, lover; My madman; Cuckold; The escape; Murder; Insomnia; Love, forever; Old dog; The artist; The wig; The maker of parables; Embrace; Beauty salon; Abandoned; Running; Pain; Where is here?

You must remember this. Dutton 1987 436p o.p.

LC 86-24337

"A William Abrahams book"

"Young Enid Maria Stevik and her Uncle Felix—uncle by blood—can't keep from getting entangled. . . . In a jarring, staccato, stream-of-consciousness voice, Oates tells the tale of the unfortunate Enid, centering it within the whole family's travails and within the national and world events of the not-so-placid 1950s." Booklist

"Ms. Oates is relying much less on the kind of violence that saturated early novels. . . . The violence is now carried inward, where it has a chance of being countered by other psychic forces. The resulting prose is more complex and more tolerant of ambiguities, though the contest between tragic and redemptive forces has not yet been fought with the decisiveness that the highest art demands." N Y Times Book Rev

Obradovi′c, Nadežda

(ed) Looking for a rain god: an anthology of contemporary African short stories. See Looking for a rain god: an anthology of contemporary African short stories

O'Brian, Patrick

The golden ocean. Norton 1994 285p $22.50

ISBN 0-393-03630-8   LC 94-11966

A reissue of the title first published 1956 in the United Kingdom; 1957 in the United States by J. Day Co.

"This novel is based on the exploits of Commodore George Anson, who set out in 1740 with five men-of-war to circle the globe and returned four years later with one ship and a small but very wealthy crew. The expedition is seen through the eyes of Peter Palafox, a young midshipman who blossoms into an able-bodied seaman. . . . As always, the author's erudition and humor are on display. . . . The attention to period speech and detail is uncompromising, and while the cascades of nautical lore can be dizzying, both aficionados and newcomers will be swept up by the richness of Mr. O'Brian's prodigious imagination." N Y Times Book Rev

The wine-dark sea. Norton 1993 261p $22.50

ISBN 0-393-03558-1   LC 93-1521

One of a series of novels set during the Napoleonic Wars and featuring Jack Aubrey, a "Royal Navy captain, and his friend Stephen Maturin, who sails with him as ship's surgeon and undercover intelligence agent. . . . On this occasion, duty takes them to the South Pacific. Here, Aubrey is to harry enemy shipping and—the true purpose of the voyage—to land Maturin in Peru to foment the independence movement against Spain." Times Lit Suppl

"The naval actions are bang-on and bang-up—fast, furious and bloody—and the Andean milieu is as vivid as the shipboard scenes." Publ Wkly

O'Brien, Edna

The country girls

In O'Brien, E. The country girls trilogy and epilogue p3-175

The country girls trilogy and epilogue. Farrar, Straus & Giroux 1986 531p $18.95

ISBN 0-374-13027-2   LC 85-32113

Omnibus edition of three titles originally published separately in 1960, 1962 and 1964 respectively, with an epilogue added by the author

Contents: The country girls (c1960); The lonely girl (c1962) [variant title: Girl with the green eyes (1964)]; Girls in their married bliss (c1964; first United States edition 1968)

The country girls portrays two friends, Kate and Baba, growing up in Ireland. They are sent to a convent school they despise and they contrive to get expelled and move to Dublin. In The lonely girl, Kate, now 21, becomes involved first with an older married man, then with a filmmaker. Eugene encourages and pampers her, but she is unresponsive. The relationship disintegrates and she moves to London. In Girls in their married bliss, Kate has married Eugene and has a son, but the marriage is destroyed when Eugene's indifference pushes Kate into a love affair. Meanwhile, Baba settles into marriage and financial security with an architect, and pulls through the crisis of a pregnancy brought on by a one-night stand. The Epilogue contains Baba's reflections, twenty years later

"O'Brien's particular appeal is that she can be tender yet merciless, romantic yet grittily sexual. She resides admirably where quality and popular writing intersect." Booklist

A fanatic heart; selected stories of Edna O'Brien. Farrar, Straus & Giroux 1984 461p $17.95

ISBN 0-374-15342-6   LC 84-13762

Analyzed in Short stories index

Contents: The Connor girls; My mother's mother; Tough men; The doll; The bachelor; Savages; Courtship; Ghosts; Sister Imelda; The love object; The mouth of the cave; Irish revel; The rug; Paradise; A scandalous woman; Over; The creature; The house of my dreams; Number 10; Baby blue; The small-town lovers; Christmas roses; Ways; A rose in the heart of New York; Mrs. Reinhardt; Violets; The call; The plan; The return

"Each story is superbly written and, despite the overall seriousness, graced by humor." Publ Wkly

Girls in their married bliss

In O'Brien, E. The country girls trilogy and epilogue p381-508

House of splendid isolation. Farrar, Straus & Giroux 1994 232p $21

ISBN 0-374-17309-5   LC 93-42602

Also available G.K. Hall large print edition

"The story centers on a tormented encounter between young IRA fugitive/killer McGreevy and his hostage—rich, reclusive, middle-aged Josie O'Meara. Both have been widowed by the protracted 'troubles.' Josie, a former barmaid, who once did a stint as a domestic in Brooklyn, reminisces before and during her 'captivity' on her advantageous but flawed marriage." Publ Wkly

The author "manages to sum up a century of Irish sorrow in this taut, lyrical novel, filled with scenes so vividly rendered they seem captured in a flash of lightning. Not the least of O'Brien's accomplishments is her ability to present both sides of the Irish problem in all their complexity without settling heavily on either side." Libr J

Lantern slides; stories. Farrar, Straus & Giroux 1990 223p $18.95

ISBN 0-374-18332-5   LC 90-33594

Analyzed in Short story index

Contents: "Oft in the stilly night"; Brother; The widow; Epitaph; What a sky; Storm; Another time; A demon; Dramas; Long distance; A little holiday; Lantern slides

"O'Brien's short stories expand on the anguish and brutality endemic to modern Irish lives, and her characters have more than their own secret problems to brood and moon about. . . . O'Brien mines her home territory to splendid effect with her glinting looks at what the Irish have made of their struggle and what Ireland has made of their unhappy lives." Booklist

The lonely girl

In O'Brien, E. The country girls trilogy and epilogue p179-377

Time and tide. Farrar, Straus & Giroux 1992 325p $21

ISBN 0-374-27776-1   LC 92-3962

"Nell is a devoted young wife, but she is also a rebel against tyranny, be it from husband or parents. Inevitably, her two sons, Paddy and Tristan, become pawns in the lengthy . . . battle that her separation from her husband involves. Nell adores her sons, yet at the same time she is . . . searching for love and adventure. Her restlessness, her dabbling with drugs and bohemia, take her to the brink and back, but not before she has lost house and home." Publisher's note

This novel is O'Brien's "harshest yet most beautiful work. She has a touchy, rich theme: the sexuality of the bond between mothers and sons. . . . O'Brien brings together the earthy and the delicately poetic: she has the soul of Molly Bloom and the skills of Virginia Woolf." Newsweek

O'Brien, Tim, 1946-

Going after Cacciato; a novel. Delacorte Press; Lawrence, S. 1978 338p o.p.

LC 77-11723

"Paul Berlin's squad is sent to retrieve Cacciato, a young deserter from the Vietnam War. Fantasy colors the progress of the squad as a dream of peace and the possibility of forsaking war follow them through many adventures. The horror and destruction of war is vividly conveyed and the language is rough, as would be expected. Cacciato becomes a kind of symbol for resisting bureaucratic militarism and an enviable model for Berlin himself." Shapiro. Fic for Youth. 3d edition

In the Lake of the Woods. Houghton Mifflin; Lawrence, S. 1994 306p $21.95

ISBN 0-395-48889-3   LC 94-5395

The protagonist of this novel "is a politician whose promising career has been destroyed by the revelation of his misconduct in Vietnam. His wife, well aware that Vietnam torments his dreams, had known nothing of the

O'Brien, Tim, 1946-—*Continued*

[My Lai] murder and massacre underlying the nightmares. The husband is equally ignorant of her opinions on several important matters. When the two retreat to a cabin in the wilds of Minnesota to recover from the shock of a disastrous election, their partnership explodes." Atl Mon

"What O'Brien really offers is a portrait of one man and woman at the most critical juncture of their relationship. It's a dark portrait, taking issue with a stock notion of commercial fiction: that after suffering comes redemption. Maybe not. Maybe there's only oblivion. A beautifully written, haunting novel that evokes lives in deep crisis." Booklist

The things they carried; a work of fiction. Houghton Mifflin 1990 273p o.p.

LC 89-39871

Analyzed in Short story index

Includes the following stories: Ambush; Church; The dentist; Enemies; Field trip; Friends; The ghost soldiers; Good form; How to tell a true war story; In the field; The lives of the dead; Love; The man I killed; Night life; Notes; On the rainy river; Speaking of courage; Spin; Stockings; Style; Sweetheart of the Song Tra Bong; The things they carried

"This collection of interrelated and coherent stories about Vietnam belongs high on the list of best fiction about any war. The narration passes through the stories from character to character, including one named Tim O'Brien. They contradict one another about incidents, undermine one another's versions. Thus Mr. O'Brien gets beyond literal descriptions of what these men went through." N Y Times Book Rev

O'Connell, Carol

Mallory's oracle. Putnam 1994 286p $21.95

ISBN 0-399-13975-3   LC 94-2234

"The investigation of a series of murders of wealthy, elderly women from the Gramercy Park area intensifies when Louis Markowitz, the head of the NYPD Special Crimes Section, is found dead with the third victim. Kathleen Mallory, his adopted daughter and a policewoman assigned to office duty, is beautiful, intelligent, fiercely independent, and obsessed with finding the killer. Mallory's computer skills supplement the street-survival savvy she learned before her adoption and the 'wall' of clues and case details left by Markowitz." Libr J

The author's "writing is stunning in its luminosity, originality, simplicity, and power. Her plot is ingenious, inventive, and enigmatic, and her characters sparkle with originality and charm." Booklist

O'Connor, Edwin, 1918-1968

All in the family. Little, Brown 1966 434p o.p.

"An Atlantic Monthly Press book"

"The Kinsellas are a wealthy, Irish Massachusetts family, dominated—at first—by the father, who insists that his sons enter politics to clean up a thoroughly corrupt political situation. One son is elected Governor, but political power subtly affects him, ethical problems evoke sharp differences and cause the eventual breakup of the family." Libr J

"The plot though rather melodramatic is outweighed by the felicitous childhood recollections of Jack, the authenticity of dialog, and the skillful establishment of political atmosphere." Booklist

The last hurrah. Little, Brown 1956 427p o.p.

"Typical of the old style political boss Frank Skeffington had kept his power as mayor of a large eastern U.S. city for almost 40 years. During the course of his last campaign . . . he is seen not only as the corrupt grafter ruthless with his enemies but also as a man of infinite charm who truly loved his city." Booklist

"A revealing study of a benevolent dictator at work. More, it is a genuine portrait of all the ebullience and rascality, loyalty and duplicity that enliven the typical Irish-American community." Christ Sci Monit

O'Connor, Flannery

Collected works. Library of Am. 1988 1281p $35

ISBN 0-940450-37-2   LC 87-37829

Partially analyzed in Short story index

This volume contains the author's two novels: Wise blood, and The violent bear it away; two short story collections: A good man is hard to find, and Everything that rises must converge [all entered separately]; miscellaneous stories, essays about writing, and correspondence

Short stories included are: The geranium; The barber; Wildcat; The crop; The turkey; The train

The complete stories. Farrar, Straus & Giroux 1971 555p $35

ISBN 0-374-12752-2

Analyzed in Short story index

Contents: The geranium; The barber; Wildcat; The crop; The turkey; The train; The peeler; The heart of the park; A stroke of good fortune; Enoch and the gorilla; A good man is hard to find; A late encounter with the enemy; The life you save may be your own; The river; The circle in the fire; The displaced person; A temple of the Holy Ghost; The artificial nigger; Good country people; You can't be any poorer than dead; Greenleaf; A view of the woods; The enduring chill; The comforts of home; Everything that rises must converge; The Partridge festival; The lame shall enter first; Why do the heathen rage?; Revelation; Parker's back; Judgement Day

Everything that rises must converge. Farrar, Straus & Giroux 1965 xxxiv, 269p o.p.

Analyzed in Short story index

Contents: Everything that rises must converge; Greenleaf; A view of the woods; The enduring chill; The comforts of home; The lame shall enter first; Revelation; Parker's back; Judgement Day

also in O'Connor, F. Collected works p481-696

A good man is hard to find and other stories. Harcourt Brace & Co. 1955 251p o.p.

Analyzed in Short story index

Contents: A good man is hard to find; The river; The life you save may be your own; A stroke of good fortune; A temple of the Holy Ghost; The artificial nigger; A circle in the fire; A late encounter with the enemy;

O'Connor, Flannery—*Continued*
Good country people; The displaced person

also in O'Connor, F. Collected works p133-328

The violent bear it away. Farrar, Straus & Cudahy 1960 243p o.p.
"A macabre tale set in the backwoods of Georgia and presenting the fanatical mission of a boy intent on baptizing a still younger boy." Oxford Companion to Am Lit. 5th edition

also in O'Connor, F. Collected works p329-480

Wise blood. Harcourt Brace & Co. 1952 232p o.p.
This novel "centers on Hazel Motes, a discharged serviceman who abandons his fundamentalist faith to become a preacher of anti-religion in a Tennessee city, establishing the 'Church Without Christ.' Motes is a ludicrous and tragic hero who meets a collection of equally grotesque characters. One of his young followers, Enoch Emery, worships a museum mummy. Hoover Shoats is a competing evangelist who creates the 'Holy Church of Christ Without Christ.' Asa Hawks is an itinerant preacher who pretends to have blinded himself to show his faith in redemption." Merriam-Webster's Ency of Lit

also in O'Connor, F. Collected works p1-132

O'Connor, Frank, 1903-1966
Collected stories; introduction by Richard Ellman. Knopf 1981 701p $20
ISBN 0-394-51602-8   LC 81-1253
Analyzed in Short story index
Contents: Guests of the nation; The late Henry Conran; The bridal night; The Grand Vizier's daughters; Song without words; The shepherds; The long road to Ummera; The cheapjack; The Luceys; Uprooted; The mad Lomasneys; News for the church; Judas; The babes in the wood; The frying-pan; The miracle; Don Juan's temptation; First confession; The man of the house; The drunkard; Christmas morning; My first Protestant; Legal aid; The masculine principle; The sentry; The lady of the sagas; Darcy in the Land of Youth; My Oedipus complex; The pretender; Freedom; Peasants; The majesty of the law; Eternal triangle; Masculine protests; The sorcerer's apprentice; Counsel for Oedipus; The old faith; Unapproved route; The study of history; Expectation of life; The ugly duckling; Fish for Friday; A set of variations on a borrowed theme; The American wife; The impossible marriage; The cheat; The weeping children; An out-and-out free gift; The Corkerys; A story by Maupassant; A great man; Androcles and the army; Public opinion; Achilles' heel; The wreath; The teacher's mass; The martyr; Requiem; An act of charity; The Mass Island; There is a lone house; The story teller; Last post; The cornet player who betrayed Ireland; Ghosts

O'Connor, Mary Flannery *See* O'Connor, Flannery

O'Connor, Robert, 1959-
Buffalo soldiers. Knopf 1993 323p $22
ISBN 0-679-41508-4   LC 92-54278
"The hero of this novel is Ray Elwood, a soldier stationed at a United States Army base in present-day Germany. Elwood is a battalion clerk, a wily factotum to a buffoonish colonel whose vanity and ineptitude provide Elwood with the opportunity—and the cover—to pursue his real vocations, which are to deal drugs to his fellow G.I.'s, to get high and to survive." N Y Times Book Rev
"O'Connor writes bitter, funny prose and creates bureaucratic snafus of the first order. Alternating scenes of Army idiocy and clinically realistic drug addiction are far more compelling than O'Connor's attempt to attribute his hero's bracing nihilism to his tragic past. Toward its end the book falters, as Elwood flirts with maudlin self-pity. But O'Connor misfires now and then only because he aims high." Publ Wkly

O'Donnell, Lillian
Cop without a shield. Putnam 1983 233p o.p.
LC 83-11114
"Sgt. Norah Mulcahaney, NYPD, is shattered when her husband, Capt. Joe Capretto, is killed in the line of duty. Dejected, Norah takes a leave she means to be permanent and goes to York Crossing, Pa., a small town far from New York's crime and violence. One evening she spots two men apparently abducting a young woman. Reluctant to get involved, Norah finally reports what she's seen, but little attention is paid to her account. But when a young woman's body is discovered in a snow-filled ditch, Norah identifies it as that of the abducted woman and begins her own investigation." Publ Wkly

Dial 577 R-A-P-E. Putnam 1974 182p o.p.
"Red mask mystery"
This police story involves Detective Norah Mulcahaney of the New York Police Department. "When her beautiful young Puerto Rican neighbor is brutally raped on the eve of her marriage, Norah transfers to the Rape Analysis Bureau. But finding the culprit, one Dana, and getting the girl to testify are not the end of the business—far from it. The maneuvers of Dana's protector, which include the hiring of a clever lawyer, see to that. To bring her man to book, Norah relentlessly probes his past, uncovering both a series of rapes and a murder, then comes uncomfortably close to becoming his latest victim." Publ Wkly

A good night to kill. Putnam 1988 240p o.p.
LC 88-11552
Two murders take place "in Manhattan on the night of a major snowstorm. In one case, a young woman, taunted by a ski-masked man on the stoop of her apartment building, shoots him and his companion. In the other, the lovely young wife of a Mafia leader is drowned in her penthouse swimming pool. Norah Mulcahaney, the head of the local homicide division, is put in charge of both cases . . . but she is distracted by the romantic attentions of a handsome TV news broadcaster." Publ Wkly

Lockout. Putnam 1994 239p $19.95
ISBN 0-399-13921-4   LC 93-42289
Also available Thorndike Press large print edition

O'Donnell, Lillian—*Continued*

"Lt. Norah Mulcahaney looks for the murderer of a rock musician while herself undergoing investigation for shooting an unarmed mugger. Another great New York City police procedural." Libr J

No business being a cop. Putnam 1979 255p o.p.

LC 78-18341

Available Thorndike Press large print edition

"Detective Norah Mulcahaney has been newly promoted to Detective Sergeant and put in charge of a rash of murders of police women, with the murderer resolved to kill all the female police on the force! One after another they are killed off while Norah hunts exasperatedly for the killer. Finally, she herself becomes a potential victim, thus forcing the killer to reveal himself and his motives." West Coast Rev Books

The other side of the door. Putnam 1987 256p o.p.

LC 87-21013

In this police procedural Norah Mulcahaney "plays a bit part, advising Detective Gary Reissig, her partner from *Ladykiller* (1984), on a muddled case. Reissig tries but fails to protect Alyssa Hanriot from further attacks by a man of unknown identity, who beats her badly in the dark and threatens to kill her." Publ Wkly

A private crime. Putnam 1991 239p o.p.

LC 90-39153

Available G.K. Hall large print edition

"When a sniper firing into a crowded East Side flea market kills a teenage mother and a baby, Norah [Mulcahaney of the NYPD] and her homicide team are assigned to the case, which has sparked public outrage." Publ Wkly

Pushover. Putnam 1992 239p $19.95

ISBN 0-399-13674-6   LC 91-30205

Also available Thorndike Press large print edition

Norah Mulcahaney "is called in to investigate the murder of an aging screen star, only to find, in addition, that the woman's grandson is missing. While sorting through suspects and evidence for a kidnapping charge, Norah is also asked to assist the New York City transit authority police in finding the 'perp' who pushes young women to their deaths from subway platforms. O'Donnell's snappy style sets the pace here, as Mulcahaney races to solve the mysteries before another death occurs." Booklist

Used to kill. Putnam 1993 240p $19.95

ISBN 0-399-13782-3   LC 92-29821

Also available Thorndike Press large print edition

This mystery features New York PI Gwenn Ramadge "Emma Trent, a dance teacher and young widow now married to older executive Douglas Trent, returns home one night to find her husband bludgeoned to death in an apparent burglary. . . . Then Adam McClure, one of Emma's young male students, kills himself after police find the baseball bats he and his friend Paulie Kellen used to commit the murder; Adam leaves a note incriminating Emma, who hires Gwenn to clear her name. . . . The kind-hearted, tough female PI resolves the tale with a neat twist." Publ Wkly

A wreath for the bride. Putnam 1990 239p o.p.

LC 89-10245

Available Thorndike Press large print edition

"On a honeymoon cruise a new bride falls to her death from the deck of the ship. Previously, a car bomb claimed one of the bridesmaids. Private investigator Gwenn Ramadge has no difficulty believing the girl's husband to be responsible. She once dated the dissipated Lothario. Trouble is, he has an alibi, even if it is an adulterous one, and several days later another new bride dies. . . . Taking her time getting to the dirty deeds, she begins by carefully exploring the characters of the dead girls and their less-than-charming spouses." Booklist

O'Donovan, Michael *See* O'Connor, Frank, 1903-1966

Ōe, Kenzaburō

Nobel Prize in literature, 1994

Nip the buds, shoot the kids; translated and introduced by Paul St. John Mackintosh and Maki Sugiyama. Boyars, M. 1995 189p $22.95

ISBN 0-7145-2997-4   LC 94-40897

Original Japanese edition, 1958

"In the waning days of WW II, a group of Japanese reformschool boys are evacuated to a remote village in a densely wooded valley. The villagers treat the teenagers horribly, making them bury a mountain of animal corpses, locking them into a shed for the night and feeding them raw potatoes. The unnamed narrator—one of the group's leaders—discovers that a plague is ravaging the valley. When a couple of people are infected by the disease, the villagers panic. Believing the boys to be infected, the villagers remove themselves to the other side of the valley and block the only road out of town. At first, the boys can think only of escape, but then . . . they start to make the village their own. . . . But each pleasant turn, every apparently liberating step away from unremitting brutality, serves to make the characters' inevitable future suffering even more painful." Publ Wkly

The pinch runner memorandum; translated by Michiko N. Wilson and Michael K. Wilson. Sharpe, M.E. 1994 251p $39.95

ISBN 1-56324-183-8   LC 93-26114

"An East Gate book"

Original Japanese edition, 1976

"Based on the metaphor of a sandlot baseball pinch runner, the novel centers around the exchange of identities of a father and a son who venture out together to confront the kingpin of the political underworld. Ōe unfolds the adventure through the complex narrative structure of the protagonist's words, which sometimes resonate and sometimes clash with the narrative voice of his ghost-writer, who initiates the tale. These two layers of the text are further enriched by a third voice, that of the idiot son Mori who speaks to his 'switched-over' father through the conduit of their clasped hands. Simultaneously, the reader is treated to a smorgasbord of satire, black humor, *manga*-like slapstick, Mikhail Bakhtin's grotesque realism, and various socio-political phenomena such as marginalization, factionalism, and terrorism." Introduction

The silent cry; translated by John Bester. Kodansha Int./USA 1974 274p $25

ISBN 4-7700-0450-8

Ōe, Kenzaburō—Continued
Original Japanese edition, 1967

"Set in the 1960s, the primary story is about the relationship between two brothers. The elder, Mitsu, is a reclusive scholar; the younger, Takashi, is drawn to political activism. They return to their ancestral village, where Takashi attempts to stage a protest against the nouveau riche Korean who is taking over the village. As the last descendant of an old and honorable family, he considers this a significant gesture. Takashi becomes increasingly violent and eventually murders a young woman. In disgrace he reveals the guilt of his past to Mitsu and commits suicide." Merriam-Webster's Ency of Lit

O'Faoláin, Seán, 1900-1991
The collected stories of Sean O'Faolain. Little, Brown 1983 1304p il o.p.

LC 83-205346

"An Atlantic Monthly Press book"
Analyzed in Short story index
Contents: Midsummer night madness and other stories: Midsummer night madness; Lilliput; Fugue; The small lady; The bombshop; The death of Stevey Long; The patriot

A purse of coppers: A broken world; The old master; Sinners; Admiring the scenery; Egotists; Kitty the wren; My son Austin; A born genius; Sullivan's trousers; A meeting; Discord; The confessional; Mother Matilda's book; There's a birdie in the cage

Teresa and other stories: Teresa; The man who invented sin; Unholy living and half dying; The silence of the valley; Innocence; The trout; Shades of the prison house; The end of a good man; Passion; A letter; Vive la France; The woman who married Clark Gable; Lady Lucifer

From the finest stories of Sean O'Faolain: Childybawn; Lovers of the lake; The fur coat; Up the bare stairs; One true friend; Persecution mania; The Judas touch; The end of the record; Lord and master; An enduring friendship

I remember! I remember!: I remember! I remember!; The sugawn chain; A shadow, silent as a cloud; A touch of autumn in the air; The younger generation; Love's young dream; Two of a kind; Angels and ministers of grace; One night in Turin; Miracles don't happen twice; No country for old men

The heat of the sun: In the bosom of the country; Dividends; The heat of the sun; The human thing; One man, one boat, one girl; Charlie's Greek; Billy Billee; Before the daystar; £1000 for Rosebud; A sweet colleen

The talking trees and other stories: The planets of the years; A dead cert; Hymeneal; The talking trees; The time of their lives; Feed my lambs; Our fearful innocence; Brainsy; Thieves; Of sanctity and whiskey; The kitchen

Foreign affairs and other stories: The faithless wife; Something, everything, anything, nothing; An inside outside complex; Murder at Cobbler's Hulk; Foreign affairs; Falling rocks, narrowing road, cul-de-sac stop; How to write a short story; Liberty

Unpublished stories: Marmalade; From Huesca with love and kisses; The wings of the dove—a modern sequel; The unlit lamp; One fair daughter and no more; A present from Clonmacnois

Foreign affairs and other stories
In O'Faolain, S. The collected stories of Sean O'Faolain p1061-1226

The heat of the sun
In O'Faolain, S. The collected stories of Sean O'Faolain p700-886

I remember! I remember!
In O'Faolain, S. The collected stories of Sean O'Faolain p544-699

Midsummer night madness and other stories
In O'Faolain, S. The collected stories of Sean O'Faolain p9-162

A purse of coppers
In O'Faolain, S. The collected stories of Sean O'Faolain p163-319

The talking trees and other stories
In O'Faolain, S. The collected stories of Sean O'Faolain p889-1060

Teresa and other stories
In O'Faolain, S. The collected stories of Sean O'Faolain p320-445

O'Flaherty, Liam, 1896-1984
The informer. Knopf 1925 312p o.p.

"During the strife caused by the Irish Civil War in the 1920s, Gypo Nolan, who is very poor, accepts reward money from the police to reveal the whereabouts of a comrade. He foolishly squanders the money in public houses, thus betraying his act because he can only have gotten that amount of money by being an informer. He is caught and tried by the revolutionary organization under the leadership of Dan Gallagher, an egotistical commander." Shapiro. Fic for Youth. 3d edition

Ogilvie, Elisabeth, 1917-
Jennie Glenroy. Down East Bks. 1993 511p $24.95

ISBN 0-89272-326-2   LC 93-12684

This novel continues the story of Jennie Hawthorne begun in Jennie about to be (1984) and The world of Jenny G. (1986)

"Alick Glenroy, an American shipbuilder, and his wife, Jennie, are raising a brood of five audacious children on a farm in Maine, 50 years after the Declaration of Independence was signed. . . . There is plenty of adventure, brought about by the frolicsome children and the politics of the times." Booklist

"Ogilvie's style is gentle and episodic; she describes the Glenroys' lives over one year. Readers of the two Jennie novels will rejoice at the return of these characters, but this book stands on its own." Libr J

When the music stopped. McGraw-Hill 1989 326p o.p.

LC 88-28636

Available Thorndike Press large print edition

"Author Eden Winters, finds herself in the midst of local scandal and terrifying deaths. Set in a small town along the Maine coast, the plot turns on the return to town of two aging sisters who had left on the wings of scandal decades earlier. While there are plenty of people with reason to despise the returning ladies—who audaciously take up residence in the area's most elegant

Ogilvie, Elisabeth, 1917-—_Continued_

house—there are just as many people, such as Eden and her family, who are delighted to see them. When the women are found brutally murdered, suspects abound, including a stranger who alternately captures Eden's suspicions and heart. Well-crafted fiction that holds the reader's attention and avoids contrivance." Booklist

O'Hara, John, 1905-1970

Appointment in Samarra. Modern Lib. 1994 c1934 xxi, 269p $13.50

ISBN 0-679-60110-4 LC 94-4340

A reissue of the title first published 1934 by Harcourt Brace

"Julian English is not a bad man, only a very weak one. He is popular with the country-club set, has the right connections with the local bootlegger, and has an attractive wife. He succeeds in offending the man who holds the mortgage on his car dealership and the bootlegger whose girl he pays too much attention to when he has again had too much to drink. When his wife announces her intention to divorce him, Julian feels that there is nothing left for him in life." Shapiro. Fic for Youth. 3d edition

"The novel is written episodically, but achieves integration by its hard-boiled theme of the destructive effects of fast living." Haydn. Thesaurus of Book Dig

Butterfield 8; a novel. Harcourt Brace & Co. 1935 310p o.p.

Available from Amereon and Buccaneer Bks.

"A novelization of the sensational lives of the night-club set involved in an actual New York murder case. Young Gloria Wandrous is found drowned on a beach near New York. The problem is to find the murderer and his motive. The investigation, described in machine-gun reportage, reveals that Gloria had had a good education, but owing to an adolescent sexual experience had become a 'party girl' in the unsavory life of New York speakeasies and luxurious Long Island clubs. Under the sleekness of Park Avenue sophistication, O'Hara reveals New York's hard soullessness." Haydn. Thesaurus of Book Dig

Collected stories of John O'Hara; selected and with an introduction by Frank Mac-Shane. Random House 1984 414p $19.95

ISBN 0-394-54083-2 LC 84-42661

Analyzed in Short story index

Contents: The doctor's son; It must have been spring; Over the river and through the woods; Price's always open; Are we leaving tomorrow; Pal Joey; The gentleman in the tan suit; Good-by, Herman; Olive; Do you like it here; Now we know; Free; Too young; Bread alone; Graven image; Common-sense should tell you; Drawing room B; The pretty daughters; The moccasins; Imagine kissing Pete; The girl from California; In the silence; Exactly eight thousand dollars exactly; Winter dance; The flatted saxophone; The friends of Miss Julia; How can I tell you?; Ninety minutes away; Our friend the sea; Can I stay here?; The hardware man; The pig; Zero; Fatimas and kisses; Natica Jackson; We'll have fun

From the terrace; a novel. Random House 1958 897p o.p.

"Alfred Eaton, the younger son of Samuel Eaton, steel magnate of Port Johnson, Pennsylvania, had a tolerably happy childhood until the death of his older brother William, when Alfred was twelve. After the death of his

favorite son, Samuel Eaton retreated into an obsessive grief. Alfred's mother, neglected, turned elsewhere for affection and Alfred was left to grow up as best as he could, closer to the servants than to his parents. The rest of his life though rewarded with business success and filled with a variety of amorous adventures, was basically barren and loveless." Booklist

The novel describes "the ways of Social Register families on the Pennsylvania-New York axis—especially in sexual encounters and marriage—in what may be described as morbidly fascinating detail. Indeed the novel's central achievement is surely the impression it conveys of the morality—or amorality, of immorality—of this class." N Y Her Trib Books

Ten North Frederick. Random House 1955 408p o.p.

A character study of one of the 'first citizens' of a Pennsylvania town, Gibbsville. "In the first quarter of a crowded, eventful narrative, Joe Chapin is seen only through the eyes of some of those at [his] funeral. Then [O'Hara] . . . switches back to Joe's parents, who established the home at Ten North Frederick Street, where Joe lived all his life. He tells Joe's story from the beginning, and the stories of those whose lives have touched Joe's at some significant point." N Y Times Book Rev

Oldenbourg, Zoé

The heirs of the kingdom; translated from the French by Anne Carter. Pantheon Bks. 1971 563p o.p.

Original French edition, 1970

A novel about the "lives of humble weavers from Arras who join the First Crusade. Marie and Jacques, a young couple deeply in love, hear Peter the Hermit preach; subsequently they join the thousands who are making the arduous pilgrimage to Jerusalem." Libr J

"A historical novel is the art of persuading one's contemporaries to believe in a time and a place and a girl at several centuries removed. Zoé Oldenbourg is a French master of this genre who has assimilated the Middle Ages so thoroughly that one follows the large tapestry of her narratives with credulity." Atlantic

Olsen, Tillie

Tell me a riddle; a collection. Lippincott 1961 156p o.p. Smith, P. reprint available $21 (ISBN 0-8446-6090-6)

Analyzed in Short story index

Contents: I stand here ironing; Hey sailor, what ship; O yes; Tell me a riddle

"In writing which is individualized but not eccentric, experimental but not obscure, Mrs. Olsen has created imagined experience which has the authenticity of autobiography or memoir. With a faultless accuracy, her stories treat the very young, the mature, the dying—poor people without the means to buy or invent lies about their situations—and yet her writing never succumbs to mere naturalism." Commonweal

Olsen, Tillie—*Continued*

Yonnondio: from the thirties. Delacorte Press/Seymour Lawrence 1974 196p o.p. Smith, P. reprint available $21 (ISBN 0-8446-6089-2)

This unfinished work was written between 1932 and 1937. Set in the 1920's, it is the story of the Holbrook family who try to make a "living at mining in Wyoming, tenant farming in South Dakota, and finally at urban scrounging in Chicago." Libr J

The author "evokes the very feel of poverty, not in the sharp-focused naturalistic detail of the muckrakers, but in broad powerful strokes of which the paint is emotion, sensation, apprehension. . . . It is remarkable that [Olsen], who already knew profoundly as a young writer what a great weight poor women carry, had also a deep sympathy for the restlessness and degraded pride of the men. And throughout . . . her portrayal of faltering, caring, motherhood and fatherhood against the most overwhelming of odds is tremendously moving." N Y Times Book Rev

O'Marie, Carol Anne

The missing Madonna. Delacorte Press 1988 253p $15.95

ISBN 0-440-50040-0   LC 88-15349

Also available G.K. Hall large print edition

In this novel "the gregarious Sister Mary Helen investigates the disappearance of an old college chum by enlisting the aid of her San Francisco chapter of OWL's (Older Women's League), a feisty bunch of busybodies who shame and nag the police into doing their duty." N Y Times Book Rev

Murder in ordinary time. Delacorte Press 1991 245p $18

ISBN 0-385-30226-6   LC 91-20455

Also available G.K. Hall large print edition

"Sister Mary Helen, the spry, elderly amateur detective . . . finds herself caught up in her third murder investigation. She doesn't even try to hide her interest or her snooping—er . . . sleuthing. After all, the victim could just as easily have been Sister Mary Helen herself because she was on the television news set when gorgeous investigative reporter Christina Kelly bit the poisoned cookie. . . . Sister Mary Helen tracks down the culprit by using both her wiles and ker kitchenside manners. Neatly plotted, entertaining mystery fare." Booklist

Ondaatje, Michael, 1943-

The English patient; a novel. Knopf 1992 307p $22

ISBN 0-679-41678-1   LC 92-53089

"Four diverse people who suffer from the physical and emotional damages of WW II meet in a deserted Tuscan villa. The badly burned English patient will die without revealing his identity, his young nurse will begin to recover her will to live, the maimed thief will watch over her and the Anglo-Indian bomb-defusing specialist will learn to exist in the atomic age." Publ Wkly

"This is a poetic and solemn narrative of the horrible process of war, the discipline, displacement, loss, and sudden, desperate love. Ondaatje seems to whisper, even confess each scene to his readers, handling them gingerly like shards of shattered glass." Booklist

In the skin of a lion; a novel. Knopf 1987 243p o.p.

LC 87-45340

The main character in this novel "is Patrick Lewis, who grows up in Canadian logging country and in 1923, at the age of twenty-one, arrives in Toronto 'as if it were land after years at sea'. He becomes one of an army of searchers for Ambrose Small, millionaire personification of 'bare-knuckle capitalism', who has vanished. Lewis's success in the search brings him into contact with Small's lover Clara Dickens and then into a deepening relationship with Clara's intimate friend Alice Gull, an actress and political activist." Times Lit Suppl

Ondaatje is a "beautiful writer. What he writes about most beautifully is *work*. Mr. Ondaatje is passionate about process, the way work, particularly construction of all kinds, is done and how it feels to do it. This is, of course, a rarity in fiction at any time, and one can only be grateful for a man who is not focused on the classroom, the bedroom and the bar." N Y Times Book Rev

O'Neal, Kathleen M.

See also Gear, Kathleen O'Neal

O'Neill, Egan, 1921-

For works written by this author under other names see Linington, Elizabeth, 1921-; Shannon, Dell, 1921-

Orczy, Emmuska, Baroness, 1865-1947

Adventures of the Scarlet Pimpernel. Doubleday, Doran 1929 302p o.p. Buccaneer Bks. reprint available $24.95 (ISBN 0-89966-459-8)

Further "exploits of the Scarlet Pimpernel, Sir Percy Blakeney, the daring Englishman, who, with his loyal friends and helpers, rescues aristocrats from the guillotine during the French Revolution. Each chapter records a separate adventure." Cleveland Public Libr

The elusive Pimpernel. Dodd, Mead 1908 344p o.p. Buccaneer Bks. reprint available $24.95 (ISBN 0-89966-488-1)

Another chapter in the adventurous life of The Scarlet Pimpernel, that thorn in the side of the terrorists of the French Revolution, and a delivering angel to condemned aristocrats. In an increasingly tense situation, this languid, Englishman deliberately enters the French trap in an attempt to rescue his wife, the beautiful Marguerite Blakeney

The Scarlet Pimpernel. Putnam 1905 312p o.p.

Available from Amereon and Buccaneer Bks.

"An adventure story of the French Revolution. The apparently foppish young Englishman, Sir Percy Blakeney, is found to be the daring Scarlet Pimpernel, rescuer of distressed aristocrats." Reader's Ency. 3d edition

Orde, Lewis

Dreams of gold; a novel. Zebra Bks. 1993 524p $20

ISBN 0-8217-4015-6

Orde, Lewis—*Continued*

A "family saga that spans two continents and over 60 years. Orphans Nathan and Leonora escape their stingy, tyrannical uncle and emigrate from London to New Orleans. The way to prosperity is not easy, however. Hopes of a future filled with love and wealth are ended by a typhoid epidemic and then by the Civil War. Still, Nathan and Leonora persevere and triumph. Interesting characters (both likable and despicable), odd twists of plot, and the setting—a fascinating period of American history—recommend this book." Libr J

Orwell, George, 1903-1950

Animal farm.

Available from various publishers

First published 1945 in the United Kingdom; first United States edition 1946 by Harcourt Brace & Company

"The animals on Farmer Jones's farm revolt in a move led by the pigs, and drive out the humans. The pigs become the leaders, in spite of the fact that their government was meant to be 'classless.' The other animals soon find that they are suffering varying degrees of slavery. A totalitarian state slowly evolves in which 'all animals are equal but some animals are more equal than others.' This is a biting satire aimed at communism." Shapiro. Fic for Youth. 3d edition

Keep the aspidistra flying. Harcourt Brace & Co. 1956 248p o.p. Amereon reprint available $20.95 (ISBN 0-8488-0603-4)

First published 1936 in the United Kingdom

"The leading character Gordon Comstock, a writer, rebels against middle-class interest in money and single-minded aspirations for a 'good' job and respectability, symbolized for him by the aspidistra growing tenaciously in every parlor." Booklist

"Not pretty, but powerful, accurate, and fair. This book projects as do few others the desperate expedients and blind rage of the educated moneyless. And Orwell's power is wielded responsibly. Neither the rebels nor the hucksters are romanticized, nor is life—which wins in the end." Chicago Sunday Trib

Nineteen eighty-four.

Available from various publishers

First published 1949 by Harcourt, Brace

"A nightmare story of totalitarianism of the future and one man's hopeless struggle against it and final defeat by acceptance. Winston Smith, the hero, has no heroic qualities, only a wistful longing for truth and decency. But in a social system where there is no privacy and to have unorthodox ideas incurs the death penalty he knows that there is no hope for him. His brief love affair ends in arrest by the Thought Police, and when, after months of torture and brainwashing, he is released, he makes his final submission of his own accord." Oxford Companion to Engl Lit. 5th edition

Osborne, David

For works written by this author under other names see Silverberg, Robert

Ossana, Diana

(jt. auth) McMurtry, L. Pretty Boy Floyd

Otto, Whitney

How to make an American quilt. Villard Bks. 1991 179p $18

ISBN 0-679-40070-2   LC 90-48233

Also available G.K. Hall large print edition

This novel "set in the small central California town of Grasse, chronicles the local quilting circle and its eight members. The stories of these women's lives are framed by a ninth one, that of the narrator, Finn Bennett-Dodd (granddaughter of one of the members), an about-to-be-married eavesdropper who is collecting advice. As she prepares for her own adult life, Finn has a wide array of stories and lessons to sort through." N Y Times Book Rev

"Otto has tremendous insight and compassion, understanding the rareness of a perfect marriage, the anger of thwarted lives, and the vagaries of love and motherhood." Booklist

Øvstedal, Barbara, 1925-

For works written by this author under other names see Laker, Rosalind, 1925-

The Oxford book of American short stories; edited by Joyce Carol Oates. Oxford Univ. Press 1992 768p $25

ISBN 0-19-507065-8   LC 92-1353

Analzyed in Short story index

Contents: Rip Van Winkle, by W. Irving; Peter Rugg, the missing man, by W. Austin; The wives of the dead, by N. Hawthorne; The paradise of bachelors, by H. Melville; The tartarus of maids, by H. Melville; The tell-tale heart, by E. A. Poe; The ghost in the mill, by H. B. Stowe; Cannibalism in the cars, by S. Clemens; A white heron, by S. O. Jewett; The storm, by K. Chopin; The sheriff's children, by C. Chesnutt; The yellow wallpaper, by C. P. Gilman; The middle years, by H. James; In a far country, by J. London; Old Woman Magoun, by M. E. W. Freeman; The little regiment, by S. Crane; A journey, by E. Wharton; The strength of God, by S. Anderson; A death in the desert, by W. Cather; Blood-burning moon, by J. Toomer; A clean, well-lighted place, by E. Hemingway; An alcoholic case, by F. S. Fitzgerald; The girl with a pimply face, by W. C. Williams; He, by K. A. Porter; That evening sun, by W. Faulkner; Sweat, by Z. N. Hurston; Red-headed baby, by L. Hughes; The man who was almost a man, by R. Wright; A distant episode, by P. Bowles; A late encounter with the enemy, by F. O'Connor; Sonny's blues, by J. Baldwin; Battle royal, by R. Ellison; There will come soft rains, by R. Bradbury; Rain in the heart, by P. Taylor; Where is the voice coming from?, by E. Welty; The lecture, by I. B. Singer; My son the murderer, by B. Malamud; Something to remember me by, by S. Bellow; The death of Justina, by J. Cheever; Texts, by U. K. Le Guin; The school, by D. Barthelme; The persistence of desire, by J. Updike; Alaska, by A. Adams; Are these actual miles?, by R. Carver; Yellow Woman, by L. M. Silko; The shawl, by C. Ozick; Heat, by J. C. Oates; Hunters in the snow, by T. Wolff; The things they carried, by T. O'Brien; Big Bertha stories, by B. A. Mason; Fever, by J. E. Wideman; The management of grief, by B. Mukherjee; Two kinds, by A. Tan; Fleur, by L. Erdrich; Gravity, by D. Leavitt; The house on Mango Street, by S. Cisneros; Town smokes, by P. Benedict

The **Oxford** book of English ghost stories; chosen by Michael Cox and R. A. Gilbert. Oxford Univ. Press 1987 c1986 504p $25

ISBN 0-19-214163-5   LC 86-8690

Analyzed in Short story index
First published 1986 in the United Kingdom
Contents: The tapestried chamber, by W. Scott; The phantom coach, by A. B. Edwards; Squire Toby's will, by J. S. Le Fanu; The shadow in the corner, by M. E. Braddon; The upper berth, by F. M. Crawford; A wicked voice, by V. Lee; The judge's house, by B. Stoker; Man-size in marble, by E. Nesbit; The roll-call of the reef, by A. Quiller-Couch; The friends of the friends, by H. James; The red room, by H. G. Wells; The monkey's paw, by W. W. Jacobs; The lost ghost, by M. E. Wilkins; Oh, whistle, and I'll come to you, my lad, by M. R. James; The empty house, by A. Blackwood; The cigarette case, by O. Onions; Rose Rose, by B. Pain; The confession of Charles Linkworth, by E. F. Benson; On the Brighton Road, by R. Middleton; Bone to his bone, by E. G. Swain; The true history of Anthony Ffryar, by A. Gray; The taipan, by W. S. Maugham; The victim, by M. Sinclair; A visitor from down under, by L. P. Hartley; Fullcircle, by J. Buchan; The clock, by W. F. Harvey; Old man's beard, by H. R. Wakefield; Mr. Jones, by E. Wharton; Smee, by A. M. Burrage; The little ghost, by H. Walpole; Ahoy, sailor boy, by A. E. Coppard; The hollow man, by T. Burke; Et in sempiternum pereant, by C. Williams; Bosworth summit pound, by L. T. C. Rolt; An encounter in the mist, by A. N. L. Munby; Hand in glove, by E. Bowen; A story of Don Juan, by V. S. Pritchett; Cushi, by C. Woodforde; Bad company, by W. De La Mare; The bottle of 1912, by S. Raven; The Cicerones, by R. Aickman; Soft voices at Passenham, by T. H. White

The **Oxford** book of gothic tales; edited by Chris Baldick. Oxford Univ. Press 1992 xxiii, 533p $29.95

ISBN 0-19-214194-5   LC 91-27290

Analyzed in Short story index
Contents: Sir Bertrand: a fragment, by A. L. Aikin; The poisoner of Montremos, by R. Cumberland; The friar's tale; Ramond: a fragment, by 'Juvenis'; The parricide punished; The ruins of the Abbey of Fitz-Martin; The vindictive monk, by I. Crookenden; The astrologer's prediction; Andreas Vesalius the anatomist, by P. Borel; Lady Eltringham, by J. Wadham; The fall of the House of Usher, by E. A. Poe; A chapter in the history of a Tyrone family, by S. Le Fanu; Rappaccini's daughter, by N. Hawthorne; Selina Sedilia, by B. Harte; Jean-ah Poquelin, by G. W. Cable; Olalla, by R. L. Stevenson; Barbara of the House of Grebe, by T. Hardy; Bloody Blanche, by M. Schwob; The yellow wall-paper, by C. P. Stetson; The adventure of the speckled band, by A. C. Doyle; Hurst of Hurstcote, by E. Nesbit; A vine on a house, by A. Bierce; Jordan's end, by E. Glasgow; The outsider, by H. P. Lovecraft; A rose for Emily, by W. Faulkner; A rendezvous in Averoigne, by C. A. Smith; The monkey, by I. Dinesen; Miss de Mannering of Asham, by F. M. Mayor; The vampire of Kaldenstein, by F. Cowles; Clytie, by E. Welty; Sardonicus, by R. Russell; The bloody countess, by A. Pizarnik; The Gospel according to Mark, by J. L. Borges; The lady of the house of love, by A. Carter; Secret observations on the goat-girl, by J. C. Oates; Blood disease, by P. McGrath; If you touched my heart, by I. Allende

The **Oxford** book of Irish short stories; edited by William Trevor. Oxford Univ. Press 1989 567p $30

ISBN 0-19-214180-5   LC 88-28147

Analyzed in Short story index
Contents: Adventures of a strolling player, by O. Goldsmith; The limerick gloves, by M. Edgeworth; The death of a devotee, by W. Carleton; The Brown Man, by G. Griffin; Green tea, by S. Le Fanu; Albert Nobbs, by G. Moore; The Sphinx without a secret, by O. Wilde; Philippa's fox-hunt, by E. C. Somerville; The priest, by D. Corkery; The weaver's grave, by S. O'Kelly; The dead, by J. Joyce; My little black ass, by P. O. Conaire; The triangle, by J. Stephens; Bush River, by J. Cary; The pedlar's revenge, by L. O'Flaherty; The fanatic, by L. O'Flaherty; Her table spread, by E. Bowen; The faithless wife, by S. O'Faolain; The sugawn chair, by S. O'Faolain; Guests of the nation, by F. O'Connor; The majesty of the law, by F. O'Connor; Pastorale, by P. Boyle; The hare-lip, by M. O. Cadhain; The poteen maker, by M. McLaverty; The ring, by B. MacMahon; Sarah, by M. Lavin; Desert island, by T. De V. White; The pilgrims, by B. Kiely; Weep for our pride, by J. Plunkett; Loser, by V. Mulkerns; The bird I fancied, by A. Higgins; Death in Jerusalem, by W. Trevor; The diviner, by B. Friel; An occasion of sin, by J. Montague; Irish revel, by E. O'Brien; First conjugation, by J. O'Faolain; The beginning of an idea, by J. McGahern; Life drawing, by B. MacLaverty; The airedale, by D. Hogan

The **Oxford** book of modern fairy tales; edited by Alison Lurie. Oxford Univ. Press 1993 455p $25

ISBN 0-19-214218-6   LC 92-28007

Analyzed in Short story index
Contents: Uncle David's nonsensical story about giants and fairies, by C. Sinclair; Feathertop, by N. Hawthorne; The King of the Golden River, by J. Ruskin; The story of Fairyfoot, by F. Browne; The light princess, by G. MacDonald; The magic fishbone, by C. Dickens; A toy princess, by M. De Morgan; The new mother, by L. L. Clifford; Good luck is better than gold, by J. H. Ewing; The apple of contentment, by H. Pyle; The griffin and the minor canon, by F. Stockton; The selfish giant, by O. Wilde; The rooted lover, by L. Housman; The song of the morrow, by R. L. Stevenson; The reluctant dragon, by K. Grahame; The book of beasts, by E. Nesbit; The queen of Quok, by L. F. Baum; The magic shop, by H. G. Wells; The kith of the elf-folk, by Lord Dunsany; The story of Blixie Bimber and the power of the gold buckskin whincher, by C. Sandburg; The lovely Myfanwy, by W. De la Mare; The troll, by T. H. White; Gertrude's child, by R. Hughes; The unicorn in the garden, by J. Thurber; Bluebeard's daughter, by S. T. Warner; The chaser, by J. Collier; The King of the Elves, by P. K. Dick; In the family, by N. Mitchison; The Jewbird, by B. Malamud; Menaseh's dream, by I. B. Singer; The glass mountain, by D. Barthelme; Prince Amilec, by T. Lee; Petronella, by J. Williams; The man who had seen the rope trick, by J. Aiken; The courtship of Mr. Lyon, by A. Carter; The princess who stood on her own two feet, by J. Desy; The wife's story, by U. Le Guin; The river maid, by J. Yolen; The porcelain man, by R. Kennedy; Old man Potchikoo, by L. Erdrich

The **Oxford** book of science fiction stories; edited by Tom Shippey. Oxford Univ. Press 1992 xxvi, 587p $25

ISBN 0-19-214204-6   LC 92-9512

Analyzed in Short story index
Contents: The land ironclads, by H. G. Wells; Finis, by F. L. Pollack; As easy as ABC, by R. Kipling; The metal man, by J. Williamson; A Martian odyssey, by S. G. Weinbaum; Night, by J. W. Campbell; Desertion, by C. D. Simak; The piper's son, by L. Padgett; The monster, by A. E. van Vogt; The second night of summer, by J. H. Schmitz; Second dawn, by A. C. Clarke; Crucifixus etiam, by W. M. Miller; The tunnel under the world, by F. Pohl; Who can replace a man?, by B. Aldiss; Billennium, by J. G. Ballard; The ballad of lost C'mell, by C. Smith; Semley's necklace, by U. K. Le Guin; How beautiful with banners, by J. Blish; A criminal act, by H. Harrison; Problems of creativeness, by T. M. Disch; How the whip came back, by G. Wolfe; Cloak of anarchy, by L. Niven; A thing of beauty, by N. Spinrad; The screwfly solution, by R. Sheldon; The way of cross and dragon, by G. R. R. Martin; Swarm, by B. Sterling; Burning chrome, by W. Gibson; Silicon muse, by H. Schenck; Karl and the ogre, by P. J. McAuley, Piecework, by D. Brin

The **Oxford** book of short stories; chosen by V. S. Pritchett. Oxford Univ. Press 1981 547p $29.95

ISBN 0-19-214116-3   LC 81-156872

Analyzed in Short story index
Contents: The two drovers, by Sir W. Scott; The birth-mark, by N. Hawthorne; The fall of the House of Usher, by E. A. Poe; The celebrated jumping frog of Calaveras County, by M. Twain; The Iliad of Sandy Bar, by B. Harte; The coup de grâce, by A. Bierce; Paste, by H. James; Thrawn Janet, by R. L. Stevenson; The secret sharer, by J. Conrad; The record of Badalia Herodsfoot, by R. Kipling; Telemachus, friend, by O. Henry; Sredni Vashtar, by H. H. Munro; The open boat, by S. Crane; An ideal craftsman, by W. De La Mare; An official position, by W. S. Maugham; I want to know why, by S. Anderson; The field of mustard, by A. E. Coppard; Grace, by J. Joyce; The rocking-horse winner, by D. H. Lawrence; Who dealt, by R. Lardner; The woman at the store, by K. Mansfield; Flowering Judas, by K. A. Porter; The tent, by L. O'Flaherty; Dry September, by W. Faulkner; Hills like white elephants, by E. Hemingway; The demon lover, by E. Bowen; Many are disappointed, by V. S. Pritchett; Sinners, by S. O'Faolain; Guests of the nation, by F. O'Connor; The runaway, by M. Callaghan; Never, by H. E. Bates; A horse and two goats, by R. K. Narayan; A visit of charity, by E. Welty; Various temptations, by W. Sansom; My vocation, by M. Lavin; Five-twenty, by P. White; Goodbye, my brother, by J. Cheever; Mrs. Fortescue, by D. Lessing; Parker's back, by F. O'Connor; Going home, by W. Trevor; Lifeguard, by J. Updike

Oz, Amos

Fima; translated from the Hebrew by Nicholas de Lange. Harcourt Brace & Co. 1993 322p o.p.

                 LC 92-44200

"A Helen and Kurt Wolff book"
Original Hebrew edition, 1991
"Efraim 'Fima' Nisan, sometime poet, sometime journalist, full-time dreamer, polemicist, philosopher and receptionist at a Jerusalem gynecological clinic, has made a mess of what was once a promising life. Twice divorced, supported mainly by gifts from his loving father, he bumbles through his days in an absentminded fog interrupted by long interior monologues and obsessive verbal diatribes in which he rails against the corruption of Israeli values." Publ Wkly
"Not only does Mr. Oz strive toward a Chekhovian compassion for his characters, but his novel depends . . . on making us believe in the possibility of last-minute grace. When tragedy strikes, we watch Fima rise to the occasion and begin to tap his own resources of generosity, humility, common sense, and his sense of purpose." N Y Times Book Rev

To know a woman; translated from the Hebrew by Nicholas de Lange. Harcourt Brace Jovanovich 1991 262p $19.95

ISBN 0-15-190449-5   LC 90-5196

Original Hebrew edition, 1989
A Helen and Kurt Wolff book
"Yoel Ravid has recently experienced two of life's most stressful events, the death of a spouse and retirement (in this case, from the Israeli secret service). With his daughter, mother, and mother-in-law, he moves to a Tel Aviv suburb to search for 'signs of life.' But Yoel is in no hurry. He is a man adrift, spending his days shopping, puttering around the house, watching TV until the screen goes blank. Everyone is concerned, urging him to recommit, but he resists. At last he gives in to his friend Arik and begins to volunteer at a local hospital." Libr J
"In the hands of a lesser writer, the tedium of Yoel's grieving introspection might have seriously undermined the novel's more ambitious symbolic subtext. But Oz is an old hand at using mundane material to evoke the dark recesses of Israel's collective unconscious." New Statesman Soc

Ozick, Cynthia

The cannibal galaxy. Knopf 1983 161p o.p.

                 LC 82-48719

"Joseph Brill, who prefers to be called Principal Brill, teaches a dual curriculum of European scholarship and Judaic literature in his school. An escapee from the Holocaust which killed most of his family, Brill searches for the bright pupils who will add luster to his mediocre school in Middle America. When Hester Lilt enrolls her daughter Beulah, he has great hopes because of the mother's intellect. He fails to perceive the potential spark of genius in the daughter and is thrown into confusion when Beulah achieves fame in her adult years." Shapiro. Fic for Youth. 3d edition

The Messiah of Stockholm; a novel. Knopf 1987 141p $15.95

ISBN 0-394-54701-2   LC 86-46014

"The protagonist, Lars Andemening, a book reviewer for a Stockholm newspaper, is obsessed with Bruno Schulz, a Polish Jewish writer murdered by the Nazis. Lars, an orphan, believes that he is Schulz's son. His dream is to find his father's lost manuscript, 'The Messiah.' When a manuscript bearing that name turns up,

Ozick, Cynthia—*Continued*

Lars's determination to know the truth about its provenance leads him to increasingly dark waters." Christ Sci Monit

This "novel is a complex and fascinating meditation on the nature of writing and the responsibilities of those who choose to create—or judge—tales. Yet on a purely realistic level, it manages to capture the atmosphere of Stockholm and to be, at times, very funny indeed about the daily operations of one of the city's newspapers and Lars's peculiar detachment from everyday work and life." N Y Times Book Rev

Rosa

In Ozick, C. The shawl

The shawl. Knopf 1989 69p $12.95

ISBN 0-394-57976-3   LC 89-2652

"This volume comprises a five-page short story entitled 'The Shawl' and a novella entitled 'Rosa.' Both first appeared in The New Yorker, the first in 1981, the second in 1984. 'The Shawl' focuses on an . . . incident in a Nazi concentration camp where Rosa Lubin, Polish Jew, has hidden her fifteen-month-old baby, Magda, in a shawl. . . . Rosa's fourteen-year-old niece, Stella, steals the shawl; subsequently, in the search for it, Magda is killed by a camp guard, who flings the baby against an electrified fence. . . . 'Rosa' opens three decades later in Miami, where Rosa, now a fifty-eight-year old, resides in the 'dark hole' of a single room at a hotel for elderly retirees. . . . She is being begrudgingly subsidized by her forty-nine-year-old niece, Stella, who appeared in 'The Shawl.'" Commonweal

"Rosa is brilliantly realized. Her dark night of the soul is lit by flashes of insight about memory, culture, old age, a welcome meditation on the euphemistic inadequacy of the word 'survivor.'" N Y Times Book Rev

P

Page, Emma

Final moments. Doubleday 1987 179p o.p.
LC 86-24090

"Published for the Crime Club"

First published 1986 in the United Kingdom

"Venetia Frankin is divorced from her husband (who wants to drastically reduce alimony payments) and enamored of a shiftless, married man who is tied to a social-climbing wife. When Venetia is found strangled, Chief Inspector Kelsey's investigation overturns many village secrets, rankling rivalries, and devious plots. More killings occur, as Kelsey struggles to beat the killer's timetable." Booklist

"Step by step, readers are led along the path of Kelsey's investigation, privy to no more information than he has. Reading this tightly crafted mystery is very like working on a complicated jigsaw puzzle." Publ Wkly

Page, Katherine Hall

The body in the basement. St. Martin's Press 1994 289p $20.95

ISBN 0-312-11470-2   LC 94-25764

"A Thomas Dunne book"

This Faith Fairchild mystery "centers around the Massachusetts housewife and caterer's next-door neighbor, occasional employee and friend, Pix Miller. Early in the

summer on Sanpere Island, Maine, Pix and her daughter check the construction work on the Fairchilds' summer cottage and discover a quilt-wrapped body buried where the foundation will soon be poured. Dead is Mitchell Pierce, an antiques seller and house restorer with a host of enemies on the island. . . . Pix begins asking questions and, although she often calls Faith with progress reports, ends up solving that murder and one that follows. This leisurely tale, with recipes for fish chowder, corn bread and blueberry tart, nicely frames the down-to-earth, eminently likable Pix, who proves an enjoyable stand-in for Faith." Publ Wkly

The body in the bouillon. St. Martin's Press 1991 210p il $17.95

ISBN 0-312-06309-1   LC 91-21704

"A Thomas Dunne book"

"Faith Fairchild, former New York City caterer, investigates a suspect retirement home in the small New England town where she now lives." Libr J

The body in the cast. St. Martin's Press 1993 276p il $19.95

ISBN 0-312-09755-7   LC 93-24389

"A Thomas Dunne book"

Since Manhattan caterer Faith Fairchild has "reestablished her business in Aleford, Massachusetts (whence cometh minister/husband Tom), she divides her time between food preparation, family, and sometime sleuthing. As location caterer for a famous film director, Faith experiences arson, food poisoning, and murder until the not-too-obvious culprit goofs. Page provides an abundance of aromatically and vividly detailed food, a veritable host of characters, and just a bit of froth." Libr J

The body in the vestibule. St. Martin's Press 1992 211p $17.95

ISBN 0-312-08148-0   LC 92-18455

"A Thomas Dunne book"

This Faith Fairchild mystery is "set in Lyons, France. Faith, four months pregnant, her husband Tom, a minister who is finishing research for his dissertation, and their three-year-old Ben live in a huge fifth-floor apartment. Taking out the garbage one evening, Faith finds the body of a homeless man from the neighborhood in the trash bin. When the police arrive, however, the body is gone and Faith's credibility is in question. At a party she meets Chief Inspector Michel Ravier, who asks about the body and tells her to call if she witnesses anything else unusual. . . . With beautifully detailed descriptions of Lyons added to Faith's intelligent observations, Page . . . continues to hit the mark with this charming series." Publ Wkly

Paley, Grace

The collected stories. Farrar Straus Giroux 1994 386p $27.50

ISBN 0-374-12636-4   LC 93-42230

Analyzed in Short story index

This volume includes stories from three previously published collections

Contents: The little disturbances of man: Goodbye and good luck; A woman, young and old; The pale pink roast; The loudest voice; The contest; An interest in life; An irrevocable diameter; The used-boy raisers; A subject of childhood; In time which made a monkey of us all; The floating truth

Paley, Grace—*Continued*

Enormous changes at the last minute: Wants; Debts; Distance; Faith in the afternoon; Gloomy tune; Living; Come on, ye sons of art; Faith in a tree; Samuel; The burdened man; Enormous changes at the last minute; Politics; Northeast playground; The little girl; A conversation with my father; The immigrant story; The long-distance runner

Later the same day: Love; Dreamer in a dead language; In the garden; Somewhere else; Lavinia: an old story; Friends; At that time; Anxiety; In this country, but in another language, my aunt refuses to marry the men everyone wants her to; Mother; Ruthy and Edie; A man told me the story of his life; The story hearer; This is a story about my friend George, the toy inventor; Zagrowsky tells; The expensvie moment; Listening

Enormous changes at the last minute

In Paley, G. The collected stories p129-256

Later the same day

In Paley, G. The collected stories p261-386

The little disturbances of man

In Paley, G. The collected stories p3-126

Palliser, Charles

The quincunx. Ballantine Bks. 1990 c1989 788p o.p.

LC 89-91787

"Set in England during the 1820s and '30s, the novel is chiefly narrated by a character who first appears as a young boy named John Mellamphy. He lives with his mother in a small village; he has no knowledge of his father, nor does he realize that Mellamphy is not his real surname. Gradually, he comes to understand that his mother possesses something that a number of other people desperately want. It is the codicil to an old, disputed will concerning the immense Huffam estate. The present holder of that property, Sir Perceval Mompesson, wants to obtain the codicil so he can destroy it." Time

"This is not an ironic parody à la Barth, not an echo of Eco, but a genuine reproduction of a full-bodied 19th-century page-turner of a novel, set in late Regency England, thick with characters of all classes, with plots, counterplots, fore-bodings, reversals and interpolated tales. . . . Mr. Palliser's re-creation of this period is absolutely convincing, his dialogue never jars, his command of details never falters." N Y Times Book Rev

Palmer, Michael, 1942-

Natural causes. Bantam Bks. 1994 389p $21.95

ISBN 0-553-09553-6   LC 93-26832

"Sarah Baldwin lived in Thailand for several years and acquired both an understanding and a practical knowledge of acupuncture and herbal medicine. Now an obstetric resident at the Medical Center of Boston, she becomes involved with a mysterious disease, a nascent diet-treatment empire, and unmitigated greed. When the wealthy father of one of the disease's victims sues Sarah for malpractice, the story starts moving on several fronts." Booklist

"Palmer uses medical dialog to submerge readers in the race to save other pregnant women still at risk and to combat the greed of treacherous medical killers. Surprises and action make for an excellent read; the climax is both plausible and frightening. The characters are all pleasingly real." Libr J

Paravisini-Gebert, Lizabeth

(ed) Green cane and juicy flotsam. See Green cane and juicy flotsam

Paretsky, Sara

Bitter medicine. Morrow 1987 321p o.p.

LC 86-33238

"A young Hispanic woman and her premature infant die in a wealthy suburban hospital. Her doctor is found beaten to death the next day. As a favor to Lottie Herschel, her long-time friend and mentor, Chicago private investigator and lawyer V. I. Warshawski agrees to look into the case. Abortion and medical ethics are the backdrop for this powerful and moving novel." Libr J

Blood shot; a novel. Delacorte Press 1988 328p o.p.

LC 88-3861

Available G.K. Hall large print edition

"Blood Shot takes [the detective-heroine V.I. Warshawski] back to the working-class Chicago neighbourhoods of her youth, where a callous industrialist lurks at the centre of a deadly web of violence and intrigue." Quill Quire

Burn marks. Delacorte Press 1990 340p o.p.

LC 89-23418

Available G.K. Hall large print edition

This "adventure of Chicago private eye Victoria Iphenigia Warshawski begins with arson and proceeds to homicide as the intrepid V.I. contends with ambitious politicians, a construction-business scam, a corrupt cop and the best intentions of her closest family friends." Publ Wkly

"The 'whydunit' in Ms. Paretsky's books is often embedded in the fabric of problems that confront us all— the poisoned environment, for example, or urban blight. This extra dimension adds an immediacy to 'Burn Marks' that is not found in many private-eye novels." N Y Times Book Rev

Deadlock; a V.I. Warshawski mystery. Dial Press (NY) 1984 252p o.p.

LC 83-14324

Available G.K. Hall large print edition

In this novel V. I. Warshawski "becomes involved in a case after her cousin, a former ice hockey star now working for a grain company, is killed on the waterfront. The police list the death as an accident. Warshawski starts poking around and kicks over the inevitable can of worms." N Y Times Book Rev

Guardian angel. Delacorte Press 1992 370p $20

ISBN 0-385-29931-1   LC 91-24976

Also available G.K. Hall large print edition

While investigating a local manufacturer Chicago private eye V.I. Warshawski uncovers a bond-parking scheme that reaches into her ex-husband's law firm and ties into the bizarre behavior of her neighbors

Paretsky, Sara—*Continued*

"The plot serves nicely to bring V.I. into contact with tough, down-and-out types, whom Ms. Paretsky draws extremely well. . . . Bits and pieces of V.I.'s background are worked into the narrative unobtrusively, so that we come to know her as the story progresses, the way we come to know people in real life." N Y Times Book Rev

Indemnity only; a novel. Dial Press (NY) 1982 244p o.p.

LC 81-5452

Available G.K. Hall large print edition

"Chicago private eye V. I. Warshawski is hired to locate a young woman and instead comes across the body of her boyfriend, a crooked union, and an insurance scam. Thugs beat V. I. up, and another man is murdered. This is all standard hard-boiled detective stuff, except that V. I. is a woman—tough, independent, good looking, and believable. Paretsky has done an excellent job of presenting a real female private eye, without falling into parody." Libr J

Killing orders. Morrow 1985 288p o.p.

LC 84-27270

Available Thorndike Press large print edition

V. I. Warshawski's "75-year-old aunt, a harridan and religious hypocrite, calls on V.I. for help. There is no love lost between the two, but family is family. The aunt is involved with fake securities found in the safe of the church for which she is the treasurer. Nobody really believes she forged the stock certificates. But who did? V.I. sets out to solve the mystery." N Y Times Book Rev

Tunnel vision. Delacorte Press 1994 432p $21.95

ISBN 0-385-29932-X   LC 94-6050

Chicago private detective V.I. Warshawski uncovers a "cynical swindle when she tries to help a wretched family she finds living in the basement of her office building. After getting the bum's rush from an advocacy group for the homeless and from feminist friends protecting their own grants, V.I. sticks out her jaw and goes it alone on this dirty, complicated fraud case. Mustn't feel sorry for V.I., though, because her outrage gives her the strength to take on the whole corrupt establishment. This principled private eye intimidates people because she doesn't know the meaning of compromise and won't tolerate moral slackers." N Y Times Book Rev

(ed) A Woman's eye. See A Woman's eye

Pargeter, Edith, 1913-1995

For works written by this author under other names see Peters, Ellis, 1913-1995

The green branch

In Pargeter, E. The heaven trilogy

The heaven tree

In Pargeter, E. The heaven tree trilogy

The heaven tree trilogy. Warner Bks. 1993 899p $24.95

ISBN 0-446-51708-9   LC 92-51033

Also available Thorndike Press large print edition

This omnibus edition contains three novels: The heaven tree (1960), The green branch (1962), and The scarlet seed (1963); the latter appearing for the first time in the U.S.

This trilogy "traces the life of a thirteenth-century British family of master artisans, the Talvaces, whose passion is stone carving. Harry Talvace is apprenticed to a wealthy benefactor, Lord Isambard, whose dream is to build a majestic cathedral. Harry uses his skills to design and build the church but becomes embroiled in the passions, ruthlessness, and power struggles of the Isambards. Harry is eventually murdered, and his young son, also a stone carver, returns to war-torn Wales to avenge his father's death." Booklist

"Pargeter's characters and her settings are vividly etched into the reader's mind. Writing feelingly about the creative genius of the artist and the complex bonds of loyalty that bound medieval men and women, Pargeter illumines a world distant in time and in outlook but makes that world immediate and unforgettable." Libr J

The scarlet seed

In Pargeter, E. The heaven trilogy

Parker, Dorothy, 1893-1967

Here lies; the collected stories of Dorothy Parker. Viking 1939 362p o.p.

The stories in this collection are included in the Modern Library volume: The poetry and short stories of Dorothy Parker $15.50 (ISBN 0-679-60132-5)

Analyzed in Short story index

Contents: Arrangement in black and white; Sexes; Wonderful old gentleman; Telephone call; Here we are; Lady with a lamp; Too bad; Mr. Durant; Just a little one; Horsie; Clothe the naked; Waltz; Little Curtis; Little hours; Big blonde; From the diary of a New York lady; Soldiers of the republic; Dusk before fireworks; New York to Detroit; Glory in the daytime; Last tea; Sentiment; You were perfectly fine; Custard heart

Parker, Gwendolyn M.

These same long bones. Houghton Mifflin 1994 260p $21.95

ISBN 0-395-67172-8   LC 94-754

This novel is set in the Hay-Ti section of Durham, North Carolina, "on the eve of integration. Sirus McDougald is a family man, bank president, and pillar of a small, middle-class black community. When he loses his beloved daughter, he is forced to come to terms with several uncomfortable aspects of his life: the deterioration of his marriage, the uneasy coexistence of the black and white communities in Durham, and changes in several longtime friendships. Besieged by grief and self-doubt, Sirus must somehow find the strength to protect his close-knit community from opportunistic white investors." Libr J

Parker's "is a closely controlled narrative voice, almost old-fashioned in the restraint and economy with which it lays out events but countered by profuse metaphor and description—an unusual combination that suits exactly the dignified but spirited town of Hay-Ti." N Y Times Book Rev

Parker, Robert B., 1932-

All our yesterdays. Delacorte Press 1994 401p $22.95

ISBN 0-385-30437-4   LC 94-2583

Also available large print edition $27.95 (ISBN 0-385-31374-8)

Parker, Robert B., 1932-—*Continued*

This "is a multigenerational saga that spans 1920s Ireland to 1990s Boston. It's the tale of three men, Conn, Gus, and Chris Sheridan, whose lives are shadowed by IRA captain Conn's love-affair-gone-wrong with American Hadley Winslow during the Irish 'troubles' of the 1920s. A terrible legacy of revenge, blackmail, deceit, and anger is passed on to Conn's son, Gus, a Boston cop, and to Gus' son, Chris, a Harvard criminology professor. . . . The surprise-a-minute plot is Parker at his best, and readers will find themselves quite taken with the three main characters." Booklist

A Catskill eagle; a Spenser novel. Delacorte Press/Seymour Lawrence 1985 311p o.p.

LC 84-28617

After Spenser "receives a plea for help from true love Susan Silverman (who is being restrained by the son of a shadowy armaments manufacturer), Spenser travels from Boston to California to Chicago to Connecticut to Idaho, taking Hawk, his favorite colleague, with him on the rescue quest. All this is mainly an excuse for derring-do and violence. At one point the FBI and CIA contract with Spenser to kill the armaments manufacturer. The plot may be ridiculous, but the dialogue is snappy as usual, and the characters are fascinating." Libr J

Ceremony; a Spenser novel. Delacorte Press/Seymour Lawrence 1982 182p o.p.

LC 81-15106

"Spenser is called upon to rescue a young girl who's fallen into prostitution in Boston's Combat Zone, an urban disaster area and human wasteland of crime and pain. Not the least of April Kyle's problems is that she doesn't want to be rescued. She is as elusive as the ruthless men who exploit her. Spenser has to dig deep. And what he comes up with is knowledge and evidence of a prostitution ring that reaches the top levels of the state government. Spenser blows the whistle, and these fine gentlemen are exposed for what they are." Best Sellers

Crimson joy. Delacorte Press 1988 211p o.p.

LC 87-33043

"When Police Lieutenant Marty Quirk is faced with an insane serial killer, who threatens to ignite all of Boston into a racial bonfire, he turns to Spenser for help. There aren't many clues to point the way, until the killer makes it personal by first going after Spenser and then his lady, psychologist Susan Silverman. Never one to take such an affront lightly, Spenser and his pal Hawk set out to put an end to these brutal murders." West Coast Rev Books

"Parker skillfully weaves Susan's objective theorizing, Spenser's *mot juste* narrative, and the killer's subjective emotions into fascinating psychological interplay." Libr J

Double Deuce. Putnam 1992 224p o.p.

LC 91-29594

Available G.K. Hall large print edition

In this novel Spenser "finds himself, at the behest of his pal Hawk, defending the residents of a gang-terrorized Boston housing project known as Double Deuce. The drive-by shooting of a teenage mother and her child brings the duo into a confrontation with gangleader Major Johnson and his posse." Publ Wkly

Early autumn; a Spenser novel. Delacorte Press/Seymour Lawrence 1981 212p o.p.

LC 80-17736

Available Thorndike Press large print edition

"Private detective Spenser is hired to find the teen-age son of a divorced couple. The father's underworld connections make it a dangerous job, but when Spenser realizes the emotionally starved boy is being used as a pawn by his parents, he takes the boy to the Maine woods to build up his self-confidence, then digs up enough dirt on the parents to blackmail them into supporting the boy financially but leaving him alone. Lots of witty writing, some tough-guy action, a little sex, and a layer of philosophy of life give this book something for everyone. And it hangs together quite well if you don't mind the concoction." Libr J

Looking for Rachel Wallace; a Spenser novel. Delacorte Press/Seymour Lawrence 1980 219p o.p.

LC 79-20776

Available Thorndike Press large print edition

Spenser's assignment is "to serve as bodyguard to Rachel Wallace, best-selling writer of books supporting feminism and lesbianism. Spenser and Wallace find the promotional tour truly perilous; Wallace is barred from a speaking enagagement, has a pie thrown at her at an autographing session, and is kidnapped by an ultra-right-wing group." Booklist

Mortal stakes. Houghton Mifflin 1975 172p o.p. Buccaneer Bks. reprint available $20.95 (ISBN 1-56054-314-0)

Also available Thorndike Press large print edition

"Midnight novel of suspense"

"Marty Raab is a pitcher for the Boston Red Sox. . . . His whole life, all his interests revolve around baseball. Yet tiny rumors have reached management's ears that Raab is throwing games or shaving runs. To forestall the possibility of a major scandal, Spenser, a private investigator, is called in by management." Best Sellers

Pale kings and princes; a Spenser novel. Delacorte Press 1987 256p o.p.

LC 86-29125

"Wheaton, Massachusetts has become the cocaine capital of the Northeast. A young investigative reporter looking for a story is murdered there and his boss hires Boston-based private eye Spenser . . . to find the killer. No one talks; but by his presence and contacts with townspeople Spenser upsets the drug lord and things begin to erupt." Libr J

Paper doll. Putnam 1993 223p o.p.

LC 92-30528

Available Thorndike Press large print edition

In this novel, Spenser is hired by "Louden Tripp to investigate the murder of his wife. Olivia Tripp was bludgeoned to death, the apparent victim of random street crime. Tripp feels the Boston PD glossed over the case. Spenser . . . decides to check Olivia's background. That thread takes him to Alton, South Carolina." Booklist

"Mr. Parker has trimmed his language and characterizations right down to the knuckle to tell this poignant story about the false fronts that people put up to shield themselves from shame. There's no flab on Spenser, either." N Y Times Book Rev

Parker, Robert B., 1932-—_Continued_
Pastime. Putnam 1991 223p o.p.

LC 91-8745

Available G.K. Hall large print edition

Boston PI Spenser "searches for the mother of Paul Giacomin, the young man saved by the burly sleuth 10 years earlier in _Early Autumn_. Spenser, now 'middle class and uptown,' is given to drinking Scotch at the Ritz with Susan Silverman, his self-possessed psychiatrist lover, and talking to their dog as if it were a child. But he still works out at the gym with his black friend Hawk, and can stand up to crime boss Joe Broz while trailing Paul's mother to the hideaway of her gangster boyfriend, who has recently stolen a million dollars from the mob." Publ Wkly

"Spenser's sagas are less tales of ratiocination than fables of exemplary conduct; the occasional violence or dubiety of the hero's actions is redeemed by the justice of his judgment, the righteousness of his character." NY Times Book Rev

Perchance to dream; Robert B. Parker's sequel to Raymond Chandler's The big sleep. Putnam 1991 271p o.p.

LC 90-47004

Available Thorndike Press large print edition

"Private eye Philip Marlowe spins a yarn of greed, madness and death with the cool-eyed cynicism (and good-guy core) that made him the classic hardboiled dick. The era is post-WWII . . . possibly early '50s . . . the L.A. dream beginning to sour. Psychotic Carmen Sternwood is missing from an expensive sanatorium. After sultry Vivian has enlisted suave gangster Eddie Mars to locate her sister, the family butler, Norris, hires Marlowe for the same purpose." Publ Wkly

"Parker plots with little more scope and linear logic than Chandler ever managed, and he fires off enough smart-ass one-liners to keep most readers happy. It's true, he never ventures near the subterranean emotional depths that Chandler would occasionally explore, but, after all, sequels—even when, they're written by the same person—rarely match the originals." Booklist

Playmates. Putnam 1989 222p o.p.

LC 88-23824

Available Thorndike Press large print edition

This mystery has Boston private detective Spenser "investigating rumors of point shaving by members of a nationally ranked college basketball team in the Boston area. Suspicion focuses on the team's star performer, an all-American power forward named Dwayne Woodcock, and soon Spenser in his peculiar way finds himself seeking at once to resolve the mystery and protect the culprit." N Y Times Book Rev

Promised land. Houghton Mifflin 1976 182p o.p.

Available Thorndike Press large print edition

"A compulsive husband, Harvey Shephard loves his wife so much, so often, that she literally runs screaming from their picket-fenced suburban home. This brings the wily detective named Spenser . . . onto the scene. Locating the runaway in a Cape Cod resort is simple enough. Deciding how to handle Pam's mood-swings, however, gets progressively sticky because Shephard himself never comes clean." Publ Wkly

A savage place; a Spenser novel. Delacorte Press/Seymour Lawrence 1981 184p o.p.

LC 80-29370

Spenser "flies to Hollywood to act as bodyguard to Candy Sloan, a TV reporter investigating the mob's takeover of Summit Films. Hired enforcers beat Candy and warn her she will die if she doesn't quit 'snooping,' but she doesn't give in. Spenser is at her side while she meets with Roger Hammond of Summit and, later, with Peter Brewster, president of the Conglomerate that owns the studio. Denials and threats of libel suits are the lofty executives' responses, followed by murders to show they mean business." Publ Wkly

Stardust. Putnam 1990 256p o.p.

LC 90-8140

Available Thorndike Press large print edition

Private detective "Spenser is hired to guard Jill Joyce, television's top star, while her show is shooting on location near Boston Common." N Y Times Book Rev

"There is no denying the efficient economy with which Stardust proceeds to its surprisingly unforeseeable conclusion. This is first-rate literary candy." Quill Quire

Taming a sea-horse; a Spenser novel. Delacorte Press/Seymour Lawrence 1986 250p o.p.

LC 85-29297

Spenser is "in grave danger on an all but unpaid quest to avenge the deaths of a prostitute he met briefly and a pimp he disliked. He confronts slick mob bosses, two-bit thugs and corrupt financiers, relying on his wits but not fearing to apply a little muscle." Time

Valediction; a Spenser novel. Delacorte Press/Seymour Lawrence 1984 228p o.p.

LC 83-15197

"A cultish religious group appears to be laundering money for a drug cartel. Spenser is hired by a dance teacher to find his girlfriend, presumably kept by the cult against her will." Best Sellers

The author "has a lot to say about the damaging effects of love in this novel. Especially about the ways people betray themselves and each other when under the influence." Wilson Libr Bull

Walking shadow. Putnam 1994 270p $19.95

ISBN 0-399-13920-6   LC 94-5127

Boston PI Spenser "encounters danger, venality and plenty of comic material in this . . . tale spanning the worlds of experimental theater and illegal immigration. While he'd rather be at work renovating the old farmhouse that he and his lover, psychiatrist Susan, have bought in nearby Concord, Spenser agrees to find out who is following the Artistic Director of the Port City Theater Company, on whose board of directors Susan sits." Publ Wkly

The widening gyre; a Spenser novel. Delacorte Press/Seymour Lawrence 1983 183p o.p.

LC 82-22083

"Spenser is security officer for Meade Alexander, running for the U.S. Senate. The candidate has received tapes of his wife Ronnie engaged in sex with an unrecognizable male. The anonymous donor threatens to make the tape public unless Meade drops out of the race. Suspecting mobster Joe Broz, said to have Alexander's opponent in his pocket, the detective follows trails to Broz's college-student son, Gerry. The result is that Spenser gets proof that Gerry is blackmailing Meade and others, as well as dealing in drugs, to make himself 'a

Parker, Robert B., 1932——*Continued*
man of respect' like his father. The detective knows his life is on the line when he gives the facts to Joe." Publ Wkly

See Chandler, R. Poodle Springs

Parker, T. Jefferson
Laguna heat. St. Martin's Press 1985 342p o.p.

LC 85-10055

"The hero is Tom Shephard, 'the new and sole member of the Laguna Beach Police Homicide Division.' Normally, one man would be all that is needed; there are not many homicides in Laguna Beach. But suddenly a sadistic murderer is loose, burning bodies after mutilating them. Shephard, an experienced cop, gets a lead very fast, is attacked and hurt, finds his home vandalized and goes through other harrowing experiences, many psychological." N Y Times Book Rev

"Parker's narrative is a bit heavy-handed, but his ultimately satisfying novel delivers deep and sensitive characterizations." Booklist

Little Saigon. St. Martin's Press 1988 354p o.p.

LC 88-11586

"Chuck Frye, a surf bum who has recently failed at journalism, business and marriage, lives in the shadow of his war-hero brother Bennett, and their father, a wealthy real-estate tycoon. Bennett's Vietnamese wife is a singer whose protest music has made her a heroine among anticommunists and Asian expatriates. When she is kidnapped during a performance, Chuck joins the search for her, hoping to end his estrangement from the Frye clan. But the more he learns about the crime's motive—politics, gang warfare or revenge are all possibilities—the more intently his family tries to shut him out of the investigation." Publ Wkly

Pacific beat. St. Martin's Press 1991 364p o.p.

LC 90-27411

"John Weir, an ex-sheriff's department employee, and brother-in-law Raymond battle corrupt police, development-at-all-cost advocates, and a known sex offender when they try to find the murderer of John's beloved sister. Splayed against the coastal community of Newport Beach, California, where oldtime residents hope to elect a 'slow-growth' candidate, their investigation reveals ever-deeper layers of deception. This exciting, multidimensional plot should grab even the most demanding mystery reader." Libr J

Summer of fear. St. Martin's Press 1993 359p $19.95

ISBN 0-312-09396-9   LC 93-15064

"When reporter/crime writer Russell Monroe finds his former lover brutally slain in an apparently ritual style, he suspects a connection to other recent murders in the county. Somehow, the case never appears on the police blotter—although Russell saw his former colleague, homicide chief Marty Parish, leaving the scene of the crime—and soon all evidence of the death disappears. Meanwhile, a string of killings continues in the same gruesome style, and Russell becomes the contact of the deranged man responsible. As the writer gets dangerouly entangled in this deadly intrigue, his wife Isabella fights a terminal brain tumor." Publ Wkly

The author "draws a striking parallel between two remarkably similar evils: one, his wife's cancer, inexplicably arising within her; the other, the serial killer's rampage, developing from within a sick society. An unforgettable novel." Booklist

Parkinson, C. Northcote (Cyril Northcote), 1909-1993
Jeeves: a gentleman's personal gentleman. St. Martin's Press 1981 c1979 191p o.p.

LC 80-29160

First published 1979 in the United Kingdom

"Readers of Parkinson's make-believe biography of Reginald Jeeves will have the high old time that the author clearly enjoyed while researching the life of the definitive valet. Jeeves's acumen, we find, is responsible for his rise from lowly pageboy to stardom in the late P.G. Wodehouse's classics. Gaining experience with every post, he comes into the orbit of Bunter, gentleman to Lord Peter Wimsey. In Monte Carlo, Jeeves consults with Father Brown who gives him the clue that solves a crime that has stumped the brilliant, titled detective and Hercule Poirot as well. . . . A tall tale that provides further hilarities about fumbling Bertie Wooster and his formidably funny kin." Publ Wkly

Parkinson, Cyril Northcote See **Parkinson, C. Northcote (Cyril Northcote), 1909-1993**

Parks, Gordon
The learning tree. Harper & Row 1963 303p o.p.

"At 12 years of age Newt is awakening to the world around him in his small town of Cherokee Flats, Kansas, in the 1920s. There is the impact of a first sexual experience and a first love, and because he is a Negro, special responsibility of behavior when one individual may represent an entire group in the eyes of the community." Shapiro. Fic for Youth. 3d edition

Pasternak, Boris Leonidovich, 1890-1960
Nobel Prize in literature, 1958

Doctor Zhivago; [by] Boris Pasternak. Pantheon Bks. 1958 558p o.p. Buccaneer Bks. reprint available $36.95 (ISBN 0-89966-839-9)

First published 1957 in Italy

Translated from the Russian by Max Hayward and Manya Harari

"The account of the life of a Russian intellectual, Yurii Zhivago, a doctor and a poet, during the first three decades of the 20th c. A broad epic picture of Russia is developed as the background to Zhivago's family life, his creative ecstasies, his love for Lara (another man's wife), his emotional upheavals, wanderings, and moments of happiness. Though the novel ends with Zhivago's decline and death as a result of what the author saw as the dehumanization of life that prevailed in the postrevolution years, the epilogue is full of expectations of the freedom that is to come." Ency of World Lit in the 20th Century

Paton, Alan

Ah, but your land is beautiful. Scribner 1982 c1981 271p o.p.

LC 81-13547

First published 1981 in the United Kingdom

This novel on racial unrest in South Africa covers the years 1952 to 1958 "and charts the response of the newly formed Liberal Party to the Suppression of Communism Act, the dispossession of black farmers, the destruction of Sophiatown, the disenfranchisement of Coloured voters, the influence of the Broederbond within the Nationalist Party and the rise to power of their premier, 'Dr. Hendrik'. . . . The parts played by Trevor Huddleston, Patrick Duncan, Geoffrey Clayton, Helen Joseph and . . . other historic figures, living and dead, are interspersed with the imagined destinies of representatives from different sections of the community." New Statesman

"Alan Paton's considerable practical life in South Africa aside, his place in the literature of social protest has been secured by his steady devotion to the ideal of the empathetic imagination in fiction." N Y Times Book Rev

Cry, the beloved country.

Available from various publishers

First published 1948 by Scribner

"The Revd Stephen Kumalo sets off from his impoverished homeland at Ndotasheni, Natal, for Johannesburg, in search of his sister Gertrude and his son Absalom. He finds Gertrude has turned to prostitution, and Absalom has murdered the son of a white farmer, James Jarvis. Absalom is convicted and condemned to death, and Kumalo returns home with Gertrude's son and Absalom's pregnant wife. The novel ends with the reconciliation of Jarvis and Kumalo, and Jarvis's determination to rise above tragedy by helping the poor black community. The book is a moving plea for racial understanding and co-operation." Oxford Companion to Engl Lit. 5th edition

Tales from a troubled land. Scribner 128p $20

ISBN 0-684-15135-9

"Hudson River editions"

First published 1961 and analyzed in Short story index

Contents: Life for a life; Sponono; Ha'penny; The wasteland; The worst thing of his life; The elephant shooter; Debbie go home; Death of a tsotsi; The divided house; A drink in the passage

"Most of the tales are told from the point of view of a compassionate white director of a boy's reformatory; however, one of the most moving concerns a native shepherd who, though innocent, becomes a victim when his employer is robbed." Booklist

Too late the phalarope. Scribner 1953 276p o.p. Amereon reprint available $21.95 (ISBN 0-89190-392-5)

"The story is basically that of a well loved white police lieutenant who in his need turns to a native girl. He is betrayed, reported and thus brings shame on himself and his family. The narrator of the story is an aunt who fills in the entire picture of family pride, righteous disdain, unbending adherence to an imposed restriction, and the falsity of many basic customs in parts of South Africa." Libr J

"The book is written with superb simplicity. It is cadenced but unaffected; it will inevitably be called Biblical and yet there is no conscious parodying of scriptual prose. It flows relentlessly to its crisis, and sometimes we cry out at its power. The people are all clear and real, the South African backgrounds are colorfully and deeply etched. The conflicts are diverse but they all contribute to the basic struggle; father and son, races, languages, prejudices." Christ Sci Monit

Patrick, Maxine, 1942-

For works written by this author under other names see Blake, Jennifer, 1942-

Patterson, Harry, 1929- *See* Higgins, Jack, 1929-

Patterson, Henry, 1929- *See* Higgins, Jack, 1929-

Patterson, James B. *See* Patterson, Jim

Patterson, Jim

Along came a spider; a novel; [by] James Patterson. Little, Brown 1993 435p $21.95

ISBN 0-316-69364-2   LC 92-24581

Also available G.K. Hall large print edition

"Alex Cross, a black Washington, D.C., police detective with a Ph.D. in psychology, and Jezzie Flanagan, a white motorcycling Secret Service agent, become lovers as they work together to apprehend a chilling psychopath who has kidnapped two children from a posh private school. . . . Patterson's storytelling talent is in top form in this grisly escapist yarn." Libr J

Kiss the girls; a novel; by James Patterson. Little, Brown 1995 451p $22.95

ISBN 0-316-69370-7   LC 94-14177

"'Casanova' works the East Coast, 'The Gentleman Caller' works the West Coast, and these two serial killers might just be working together. Washed-up Washington, D.C., police detective Alex Cross gets involved when his niece is abducted." Libr J

Patterson, Richard North

Degree of guilt. Knopf 1993 547p $23

ISBN 0-679-42064-9   LC 92-54446

"TV journalist Mary Carelli shoots and kills famous writer Mark Ransom in his hotel room, claiming that Ransom tried to rape her. The man she asks to defend her is Christopher Paget, with whom she has had a complicated relationship: Paget is the father of Mary's son, who lives with Paget and whom Mary has not seen for eight years. Paget agrees to defend Mary to protect his son." Libr J

"For those not put off by the sudsy plotting and the People magazine cast, the legal machinations are satisfactorily intricate." Time

Eyes of a child. Knopf 1995 593p $24

ISBN 0-679-42988-3   LC 94-28630

Also available large print edition $24 (ISBN 0-679-76031-8)

Patterson, Richard North—*Continued*

"The plot concerns the death of ne'er-do-well Ricardo Arias, who may or may not have committed suicide. Because of the widely publicized custody battle waged with Arias by his ex-wife and her lover, Christopher Paget (hero of *Degree of Guilt*), both are investigated and Paget indicted." Libr J

"Local San Francisco politics and an accusation of child molestation against Paget's teenage son contribute to this complex brew, in which . . . narrative skill and legal know-how take precedence over characterization and credibility." Publ Wkly

Patton, Frances Gray

Good morning, Miss Dove; illustrated by Garrett Price. Dodd, Mead 1954 218p o.p. Amereon reprint available $19.95 (ISBN 0-88411-879-7)

Miss Dove had taught geography in the same school for thirty-five years; some people in town thought that was too long. Miss Dove was a stern disciplinarian with old-fashioned ideas and ideals, but on the April day when she was stricken in the classroom the whole town came to realize how much Miss Dove had meant in their lives

"Leavened with wit and sound common sense, written with an unerring rightness of touch, the whole book rings with the truth about human nature in its nicer aspects." N Y Her Trib Books

Paul, Barbara, 1925-

For works written by this author under other names see Laker, Rosalind, 1925-

Paul, Barbara, 1931-

The apostrophe thief; a mystery with Marian Larch. Scribner 1993 247p $20

ISBN 0-684-19553-4   LC 93-16109

"NYPD officer Mariah Larch, fed up with police work and on the verge of resigning from the force, receives a call from her friend, actress Kelly Ingram, when the theater where Kelly is working is burglarized and a valuable coat that formerly belonged to theater legend Sarah Bernhardt is stolen. Larch agrees to help and, in spite of her bad case of career burnout, becomes engrossed in the case. . . . A nice blend of humor, romance, and suspense." Booklist

He huffed and he puffed. Scribner 1989 219p o.p.

LC 88-26375

"Determined to destroy an industrial competitor, wily millionaire businessman A. J. Strode gathers evidence implicating three of the firm's major stockholders in violent crimes. When they all refuse to succumb to blackmail, Strode lures his less-than-innocent victims to his luxurious home for a psychologically terrifying weekend. Artfully pitted against one another, Strode's desperate enemies join forces in a unified attempt to outwit their mutual nemesis. The resultant murder provides the mystery anticipated by the suspenseful premise. Paul continues to improve with every performance." Booklist

You have the right to remain silent; a mystery with Marian Larch. Scribner 1992 249p $20

ISBN 0-684-19380-9   LC 91-5040

This "NYPD procedural follows Sgt. Marian Larch as she heads up an investigation and tries to salvage her faltering love life. One day, while Larch is on duty in Manhattan's Lower East Side, four top-level employees of a laser technology firm—all with some level of government security clearance—are found murdered, handcuffed together and shot through the eye. Everyone agrees that their deaths are meant as a warning, but to whom or about what neither the company's president nor anyone else can fathom. . . . Readers should sympathize with Larch, who is besieged on both personal and professional levels." Publ Wkly

Payne, David

Ruin Creek. Doubleday 1993 373p $22.50

ISBN 0-385-26418-6   LC 92-42476

Also available G.K. Hall large print edition

This novel focuses on "May Tilley and Jimmy Madden's marriage. When they eloped in 1954, the popular daughter of the owner of a bustling tobacco warehouse in Kildeer, North Carolina, and the basketball-star son of the high school principal were certainly in love. But May was pregnant, and marriage and the first of their two sons ended both Jimmy's dutiful plans for medical school and his English-major dreams of acting or writing. A dozen years later, May and Jimmy chime in with memories as 11-year-old Joey puzzles out his family's past and future and allocates credit and blame for its impending collapse." Booklist

The author "knows the hopes, fears and habits of his characters, and weaves a powerful, lyrical story for them that is a joy to read." N Y Times Book Rev

Pearce, Mary Emily, 1932-

Apple tree lean down; [by] Mary E. Pearce. St. Martin's Press 1976 494p o.p.

This volume contains Apple tree lean down, Jack Mercybright and The sorrowing wind, originally published separately in the United Kingdom in 1973, 1974 and 1975 respectively

The combined stories provide a chronicle of three "earthy families inhabiting the rural Midlands during the late 18th and early 19th century. Beth Tewke forsakes easy living when she estranges her prosperous grandfather by marrying poor Jesse Izzard. Betony, their eldest child, is sharp and ambitious. In her teens she goes to London to establish a career as a teacher but becomes disillusioned with the hypocrisy and ill-treatment of the poor in the city. . . . Giving up the chances of an advantageous marriage, she devotes herself to the local school and to the care of invalid soldiers quartered nearby, to the general welfare of her community." Publ Wkly

"Many novels have depicted the upper classes of this era; few have delved so deeply into the lives of the common laborers and the lower middle class." Libr J

Followed by The land endures

Apple tree lean down [novel]

In Pearce, M. E. Apple tree lean down [omnibus volume]

Pearce, Mary Emily, 1932-—*Continued*

Cast a long shadow; [by] Mary E. Pearce. St. Martin's Press 1983 c1977 246p o.p.

LC 83-2953

First published 1977 in the United Kingdom

"The blissful early years of Richard Lancy and Ellen Wainwright's marriage in the small English village of Dingham are shattered after Richard is accidentally trapped in the cellar of a burned-out mill for 16 days. Richard's horrifying experience distorts his entire life and disrupts his family as well. After throwing his wife and son out of their house (and forcing them to find refuge with the compassionate village blacksmith), the disturbed Richard lurks about as a specter. His haunting presence torments Ellen and John and threatens the new lives they try to forge for themselves in this closed, watchful English village." Booklist

"Old-fashioned story-telling, people one cares about and low-key charm add up to solid reading pleasure." Publ Wkly

Jack Merrybright

In Pearce, M. E. Apple tree lean down [omnibus volume] p203-332

The land endures; [by] Mary E. Pearce. St. Martin's Press 1981 248p o.p.

LC 80-28953

Sequel to Apple tree lean down
First published 1978 in the United Kingdom

"After World War I, Stephen and Gwen Wayman, with their four children, buy Holland Farm [in the English countryside] and are making a go of the big gamble when Gwen dies in a freak accident. The family bears that blow and begins to recover but only after Stephen's idiosyncratic, loving cousin 'Aunt Doe' arrives and takes over the household." Publ Wkly

This is "an old-fashioned and deeply human family novel. The characters and their experiences come beautifully to life, and we really care about them." Libr J

Followed by Seedtime and harvest (1982)

The old house at Railes; [by] Mary E. Pearce. St. Martin's Press 1994 c1993 410p $23.95

ISBN 0-312-10514-2   LC 93-40364

Also available G.K. Hall large print edition

First published 1993 in the United Kingdom

"The Newton Railes manor house, built by the Tarrant family in 1565, is the most important landmark in the Cullen Valley in Gloucestershire in Pearce's mid-nineteenth-century tale. She tells of the waning fortunes of the Tarrants and the family catastrophes that beset them, finally placing the house in the hands of a local quarryman's son. Martin Cox, raised in a shack on his father's quarry, had the good fortune to be educated in the house at Railes by the family's eldest daughter when her father could not pay a debt to Martin's father. The intertwining of Martin's rising fortunes with the Tarrant's falling ones is predictably but neatly spun." Booklist

The sorrowing wind

In Pearce, M. E. Apple tree lean down [omnibus volume] p333-494

Pearson, Diane

Csardas. Lippincott 1975 576p o.p.

This "historical novel set in Hungary tells the story of the aristocratic, half-Jewish Ferenc family, who are as enslaved to their social class as are their peasants. The two glamorous Ferenc sisters, pampered darlings, watch helplessly as their fortunes crumble before world wars and revolution—inevitably, Communism claims not only their nation but their children. Symbolic of a changing society is the character Jonas, a peasant boy who rises well above his class and eventually marries into the Ferenc family." Libr J

The summer of the Barshinskeys. Crown 1984 465p o.p.

LC 84-4954

"The year is 1902, and Sophie and Edwin Willoughby, age 11 and 13, respectively, are still young enough to feel the pull of their childhood yearnings for mystery and adventure. Suddenly, with the arrival of an exotic Russian cowman named Barshinskey and his ill-matched family—son Ivan and daughters Daisy May and Galina—the respectable Willoughby children are transported into a disturbing yet hypnotic world beyond imagining. . . . In part one, Sophie discloses just what went on during the summer of the Barshinskeys, whose odd gypsy ways and violent passions frighten her into a sexual awakening. Part two tells the now-grown Edwin's tragic tale of love for Galina Barshinskey, the sensuous gypsy daughter. In the concluding section, Sophie ruminates on the meaning of all these events as well as coping with the romance of her elder sister, Lillian, and Ivan Barshinskey." Booklist

Voices of summer; a novel. Crown 1992 272p $20

ISBN 0-517-59192-8   LC 92-17427

This novel focuses on the "offstage dramas involving the members of a minor Austrian Operetta company. . . . Soprano Therese Aschmann seeks to resume a career interrupted by scandal 18 years ago. Now overweight and insecure, she still possesses a golden voice, lyrical and powerful enough to enchant the company's charming, aging director, Franz Busacher. Nevertheless, Busacher fears that Therese is too vulnerable to be paired with Karl Gesner, an arrogant bullying tenor infamous for malicious onstage tricks." Publ Wkly

"The plot is cleverly woven of spun-sugar threads twisted and arranged to support such familiar confectionary elements as the professional resuscitation of a faded soprano and the personal humiliation of a caddish tenor." N Y Times Book Rev

Pearson, Ridley

The angel maker; a novel. Delacorte Press 1993 341p o.p.

LC 92-36573

Available Thorndike Press large print edition

In this crime thriller someone is "running around with a scalpel removing a kidney here, a lung there, then selling the organs to desperate patients willing to pay upward of $15,000. This grisly brand of 'harvesting' comes to light in Seattle when victims begin turning up minus a part or two. It's the job of a police psychologist named Daphne Matthews, aided by her piano-playing ex-lover, Lou Boldt, to try to bring the perpetrator of these ghastly crimes to justice." N Y Times Book Rev

Pearson, Ridley—*Continued*

"Pearson's engaging forensic detail . . . and brisk prose will have readers racing to the cliffhanger climax." Publ Wkly

Hard fall. Delacorte Press 1992 403p o.p.

LC 91-15484

Available Thorndike Press large print edition

"Pearson pits FBI agent Cameron Daggett, obsessed with capturing the terrorist responsible for the Lockerbie-style plane bombing that killed his parents and paralyzed his son, against German terrorist Anthony Kort, a member of the radical environmental vigilante group Der Grund." Publ Wkly

"Pearson skillfully alternates point of view from Kort to Daggett, allowing us to see inside both men's heads and to realize how similar they are. . . . Remarkably, we find ourselves sympathizing completely with both hunter and hunted, anticipating moves and countermoves and dreading the inevitable confrontation." Booklist

No witnesses; a novel. Hyperion 1994 365p $22.95

ISBN 0-7868-6066-9   LC 94-11158

Also available Thorndike Press large print edition

"Wealthy food industry mogul Owen Adler receives a series of FAXes demanding that he liquidate his business and commit suicide within a month. The alternative is that consumers of Adler Foods will begin to die. After the deadline passes and two children are hospitalized with a mysterious infection, Adler lets his girlfriend, Seattle forensic psychologist Daphne Matthews, contact detective Lou Boldt. Boldt's empathy for the rising number of victims compels him to put his life at risk as he coordinates an extended investigation while trying to prevent mass panic." Libr J

Probable cause. St. Martin's Press 1990 275p o.p.

LC 89-24127

"Forensic investigator James Dewitt takes a new job, as a police sergeant in Carmel, California, hoping to put his past behind him—a past that includes his shooting to death the man who murdered his wife and permanently disabled one of his daughters. But after little more than two months, he fears he has a serial killer on his hands, a *trapper*—someone who slyly sets out traps, baits them, and then draws his victims in. The rapid twists and turns in the plot soon establish Dewitt as a suspect, even while his daughters' lives, and his, are in jeopardy. . . . This is fiction for true true-crime buffs, filled with clues, both planted and missed, fancy forensic footwork, and intriguing snares." Booklist

Undercurrents. St. Martin's Press 1988 386p o.p.

LC 88-1014

"A killer is on the loose—a brutal, terrifying murderer who was himself supposed to be dead. Seattle Police Sergeant Lou Boldt, haunted by the deaths of the man he believed to have been the Cross Killer (so called because of the crosses he slashes onto his victims) and of the real criminal's new victims, is in charge of the case and determined to solve it. . . . *Undercurrents* is not for the squeamish; it is grittily detailed and no punches pulled. But Pearson clearly understands what makes a good mystery move, and this one sprints breathlessly along, taking the reader with it to a surprising, and satisfying, conclusion." West Coast Rev Books

Pearson, T. R., 1956-

Cry me a river; a novel. Holt & Co. 1993 258p $22

ISBN 0-8050-2200-7   LC 92-13860

"A police officer is found brutally murdered in a small southern town, his head so disfigured by bullet wounds that he can only be identified by the distinctive smell of his hair tonic. A fellow officer vows to find the killer. Accompanied by a whiskey-addled sidekick who functions as a backwoods Dr. Watson, the investigator assembles clues, interviews suspects, proposes and discards theories, and in the process paints the portrait of an entire community." Libr J

A short history of a small place; a novel. Linden Press/Simon & Schuster 1985 381p o.p.

LC 84-29720

"Narrated by young Louis Benfield [this] is the story of Miss Myra Angelique Pettigrew, sister of the late mayor of a small Southern town, who is elegant and beautiful and has gone quite mad. After many years of seclusion, she finally emerges from her home to jump to her death from the water tower. In the process of telling his tale, Louis offers vignettes about other residents of Neely, N.C., and their strange habits and activities." Publ Wkly

"Pearson handles the interlinked strands of these stories with a truly wonderful offhand comic style that doesn't dismiss the reality of his characters' lives." Booklist

Peck, Robert Newton, 1928-

A day no pigs would die. Knopf 1973 c1972 150p $20

ISBN 0-394-48235-2

Also available Cornerstone Books large print edition

"Rob lives a rigorous life on a Shaker farm in Vermont in the 1920s. Since farm life is earthy, this book is filled with Yankee humor and explicit descriptions of animals mating. A painful incident that involves the slaughter of Rob's beloved pet pig is instrumental in urging him toward adulthood. The death of his father completes the process of his accepting responsibility." Shapiro. Fic for Youth. 3d edition

Penguin book of gay short fiction; edited by David Leavitt and Mark Mitchell; introduction by David Leavitt. Viking 1994 655p $27.50

ISBN 0-670-85468-9   LC 93-1390

Analyzed in Short story index

Contents: A poem of friendship, by D. H. Lawrence; Arthur Snatchfold, by E. M. Forster; Sally Bowles, by C. Isherwood; Me and the girls, by N. Coward; My father and myself, by J. R. Ackerley; May we borrow your husband? by G. Greene; Hands, by S. Anderson; The teacher of American business English, by J. Kirkup; Falconer, by J. Cheever; The folded leaf, by W. Maxwell; Servants with torches, by D. Windham; Jimmy, by D. Hogan; Torridge, by W. Trevor; Some of these days, by J. Purdy; A glass of blessings, by B. Pym; Reprise, by E. White; Dramas, by E. O'Brien; "Mrs. Tefillin", by L. Kramer; Spunk, by P. Bailey; The times as it knows us, by A. Barnett; The princess from Africa, by D. Plante; Adult art, by A. Gurganus; The Cinderella waltz, by A. Beattie; Good with words, by S. Greco; Nothing to

Penguin book of gay short fiction — *Continued*
ask for, by D. McFarland; Ignorant armies, by M. Cunningham; Run, mourner, run, by R. Kenan; Six fables, by B. Cooper; Perrin and the fallen angel, by P. Wells; My mother's clothes: the school of beauty and shame, by R. McCann; A place I've never been, by D. Leavitt; Notes towards a performance of Jean Racine's tragedy Athalie, by N. Bartlett; Buried treasure, by G. Glickman; Self-portrait in twenty-three rounds, by D. Wojnarowicz; Jump or dive, by P. Cameron; Gentlemen can wash their hands in the gents', by C. Coe; The dancing lesson, by G. Albarelli; A real doll, by A. M. Homes; The whiz kids, by A. M. Homes

The **Penguin** book of lesbian short stories; edited by Margaret Reynolds. Viking 1994 c1993 429p $27.50

ISBN 0-670-85425-5   LC 93-34061

Analyzed in Short story index
First published 1993 in the United Kingdom
Includes the following stories: Martha's lady, by S. O. Jewett; Prince Charming, by R. Vivien; Leves amores, by K. Mansfield; The wise Sappho, by H.D.; Miss Furr and Miss Skeene, by G. Stein; Ladies almanack, by D. Barnes; Miss Ogilvy finds herself, by R. Hall; Nuits blanches, by Colette; Olivia, by D. Strachey; The blank page, by I. Dinesen; Cities of the interior, by A. Nin; I am a woman, by A. Bannon; Les guérillès, by M. Wittig; These our mothers, by N. Brossard; Sweethearts, by J. A. Phillips; Esther's story, by J. Nestle; How to engage in courting rituals 1950s butch-style in the bar, by M. Mushroom; Bread, by R. Brown; His nor hers, by J. Rule; 5½ Charlotte Mews, by A. Livia; Lullaby for my dyke and her car, by S. Maitland; Don't explain, by J. Gomez; A lesbian appetite, by D. Allison; The vampire, by P. Califia; The secret of Sorrerby Rise, by F. Gapper; City of boys, by B. Nugent; Cold-blooded, by M. Atwood; Words for things, by E. Donoghue; The language of the body, by K. Acker; The poetics of sex, by J. Winterson

Penman, Sharon Kay
Falls the shadow. Holt & Co. 1988 580p $19.95

ISBN 0-8050-0300-2   LC 87-32255

In this second volume of her trilogy "Penman focuses on the mid-13th-century reign of England's Henry III and stories of those who opposed that inept king. A main detractor is French-born Simon de Montfort, Earl of Leicester, who leads the fight for parliamentary restrictions on the monarch, and later becomes Henry's brother-in-law through marriage to Eleanor, Countess of Pembroke. She emerges as a major figure, as does a distant relative by marriage, Llewelyn ap Gruffydd, who fights for supremacy in Wales." Libr J
Followed by The reckoning

Here be dragons. Holt, Rinehart & Winston 1985 704p o.p.

LC 84-23480

This first title in the author's historical trilogy about 13th century England "is the story of one man, a Welsh prince called Llewelyn the Great, who dares to dream of peace and who will spend a lifetime trying to wrest his country away from feudal England. Standing in his way is King John, who marries his daughter, Joanna,

to Llewelyn in hopes of taming the rebellious prince. Penman focuses her novel on the tempestuous emotional and political battles that Joanna is forced to endure as both the daughter and wife of warring kings." Booklist
Followed by Falls the shadow

The reckoning. Holt & Co. 1991 592p $24.95

ISBN 0-8050-1014-9   LC 90-27099

Set in 13th-century Wales and England, this concluding volume in the author's trilogy "continues the saga of three royal families, those of swashbuckling Llewelyn ap Gruffydd, prince of Wales, and his fractious, treasonous brothers; the children of heroic Lord Simon de Montfort . . . and the ruling house of England, now headed by wily Edward I." Publ Wkly
"The action involves religious and political intrigue, battles and plots. The players include well-researched historical personages and fictional characters. As with Penman's other historical novels, this one is both informative and enjoyable. Settings, events, and individuals are well drawn." Libr J

The sunne in splendour. Holt, Rinehart & Winston 1982 936p o.p.

LC 81-20149

"Today most historians agree that England's Richard III has been unjustly maligned. Penman's novel tells of a devoted brother who, as Duke of Gloucester, faithfully served his brother King Edward IV and earned a reputation for personal integrity. Richard's own tragedy begins with the death of Edward, when political circumstances force him to claim the crown for himself and declare his brother's children illegitimate. Did Richard murder the young princes as Tudor chroniclers claim? No, says Penman, and she gives a plausible account as to what might have happened." Libr J
"The novel covers a great deal of ground, tracing the shifting alliances and the battles between the noble houses of York and Lancaster from 1459, when Richard was seven to 1492, seven years after his death on Bosworth Field. . . . A historical novel of the first rank." Publ Wkly

Pentecost, Hugh, 1903-1989
Kill and kill again; a Julian Quist mystery novel. Dodd, Mead 1987 163p o.p.

LC 87-452

A "Julian Quist mystery set in upstate Bridgetown, N.Y. When the body of Martha Best, secretary to the president of the Manchester Arms Corp. is discovered in the trunk of her yellow Mercedes, the police treat the homicide as the work of a deranged transient and after a few desultory inquiries, are ready to shelve the investigation. But Martha was the sister of Wally Best, a Bridgetown boy who has risen to rock stardom, and who is convinced that Martha was murdered by executives of the multinational armaments company." Publ Wkly

Percy, Walker, 1916-1990
The last gentleman. Farrar, Straus & Giroux 1966 409p $17.95

ISBN 0-374-18372-4

Percy, Walker, 1916-1990—*Continued*

The hero, 25-year-old Williston Bibb Barrett, "returns to the South without identity, suffering from periodic amnesia and spells of 'déjà vu', with their telescoping of ancestral past and personal present. He hires on as tutor-companion to Jamie, a dying boy, son of 'Poppy' Vaught, a rich Alabama auto dealer, brother of Kitty, the displaced Southern belle Barrett loved at first sight—through his telescope up North in Central Park. . . . What Barrett seeks is some clue as to how to live." Newsweek

"The plot is less important than the delineation of character, the preoccupation with the way people speak and define themselves geographically and historically . . . and the rendering of a composite South." Burgess. 99 Novels

Followed by The second coming

The moviegoer. Knopf 1961 241p o.p.

"A philosophical exploration of the problem of personal identity, the story is narrated by Binx Bolling, a successful but alienated businessman. Bolling undertakes a search for meaning in his life, first through an obsession with the movies and later through an affair." Merriam-Webster's Ency of Lit

The second coming. Farrar, Straus & Giroux 1980 359p o.p.

LC 80-12899

In this sequel to The last gentleman, Will Barrett "has become a widowed, middle-aged millionaire. He didn't marry Kitty, who he loved in the earlier book, but a crippled heiress. He has had an unforeseen success as a Wall Street lawyer, fathered a [daughter] . . . and now, retired, suffers undiagnosed fall-downs on the golf course. Released from the amnesia that used to afflict him, he remembers . . . his suicidal father's attempt to kill him before taking his own life. Will meets and falls in love with a schizophrenic girl escaped from an asylum, who speaks in rhymes and is gradually revealed to be Kitty's daughter." Newsweek

"A beautiful . . . exploration of Percy's recurrent theme—an individual man's search for the hand of God in the meaningless muddle of contemporary life." Booklist

The thanatos syndrome. Farrar, Straus & Giroux 1987 372p $17.95

ISBN 0-374-27354-5   LC 86-29409

This work's central character, Dr. Thomas More, a psychiatrist, last appeared in Love in the Ruins (1971). After having been released from prison (he sold amphetamines to truck drivers), he returns to his Feliciana (Louisiana) practice to find his patients behaving strangely. With the help of his cousin Lucy Lipscomb, an epidemiologist, he discovers that his medical colleagues have been secretly adding heavy sodium to the water supply in an experiment intended to control antisocial behavior. Psychiatric symptoms disappear, but human beings regress to pre-primate stage

"All of Percy's fiction revolves around a central question: can humane, civilized life survive this murderous, mechanized century? . . . But Percy has done more here than simply repeat himself. The theme may be familiar, but the variations decidedly are not. For one thing, this novel embodies Percy's most detailed, explicit attack on contemporary materialism and science. For another, the philosophical warfare has been artfully disguised as a thriller." Time

Pérez Galdós, Benito, 1843-1920

Doña Perfecta; translated by Mary J. Serrano; introduction by William Dean Howells. Harper & Row 1896 319p o.p.

Original Spanish edition, 1876

"The social problem which engrosses so much of the author's interest, the struggle between scientific and social enlightenment and the tyrannous obscurantism of the church, is here set forth in the domestic conflict of a group of characters and the political strife agitating a provincial town. Dona Perfecta is a devout lady whose daughter is sought by a promising young man, a representative of modernism. A wily priest is her chief ally, and eventually the rival intrigues drag in a host of forces on either side." Baker. Guide to the Best Fic

Torquemada; translated from the Spanish by Frances M. López-Morillas. Columbia Univ. Press 1986 569p $40.50

ISBN 0-231-06228-1   LC 85-19560

Omnibus edition of the author's Torquemada tetralogy portraying middle-class Madrid society, and focusing on the miserly Francisco de Torquemada from the time he is 50 years old to his deathbed ten years later. The novels were originally published separately in the late nineteenth century

Contents: Torquemada at the stake; Torquemada on the cross; Torquemada in Purgatory; Torquemada and Saint Peter

Torquemada and Saint Peter

In Pérez Galdós, B. Torquemada p405-569

Torquemada at the stake

In Pérez Galdós, B. Torquemada p1-60

Torquemada in Purgatory

In Pérez Galdós, B. Torquemada p221-404

Torquemada on the cross

In Pérez Galdós, B. Torquemada p61-220

Perry, Anne, 1938-

Belgrave Square. Fawcett Columbine 1992 361p o.p.

LC 91-73144

"While investigating the murder of back-street usurer William Weems, killed when one of his own gold coins is fired from a gun [Inspector Thomas] Pitt learns that the victim had been blackmailing members of London's high social circles." Publ Wkly

The author "paints handsome portraits of . . . [Victorian] aristocratic society and provides luxurious details of the gala balls and garden parties, the fashionable outings at Covent Garden and the Royal Academy of Arts, where they congregate to preen themselves. But it isn't all done for show. The author has the eyes of a hawk for character nuance and her claws out for signs of the criminal injustices rampant among the privileged classes during this gilded historical period." N Y Times Book Rev

Perry, Anne, 1938-—*Continued*
Bethlehem Road. St. Martin's Press 1990 309p o.p.

LC 89-78014

"Three Members of Parliament have had their throats slit while crossing the Westminster Bridge. All three voted against female suffrage. As Pitt investigates, his suspicions fall on a vocal and much-wronged suffragette; other unlikely candidates include anarchists and madmen. As usual, Pitt's wife, Charlotte, and her delightful Great Aunt Vespasia play sleuths as well." Libr J

"The author's concern with presenting an unassailable argument for her feminist cause tends to drag the pace and dull the action. But her finely drawn characters couldn't be more comfortable within the customs and sensibility of their historical period." N Y Times Book Rev

Bluegate Fields. St. Martin's Press 1984 308p o.p.

LC 84-11769

"Inspector Pitt and his splendid wife, Charlotte, pursue [a] murder investigation that takes them from the squalor of the slums to the hypocrisy of high-society drawing rooms in Victorian London. Pitt is uncomfortable with a case built against a humorless tutor by a zealous young policeman who possesses a potentially obstructive reverence for the upper class. However the witnesses appear irrefutable . . . and Pitt's superior is adamant about not reopening so embarrassing a case—a teenager from a wealthy family was murdered in a bathtub and shoved down a London sewer. Charlotte, impelled by the tutor's wife, launches her own campaign to prove that the wrong man has been arrested." Booklist

Cardington Crescent. St. Martin's Press 1987 314p o.p.

LC 86-27942

A Victorian "mystery featuring the stalwart Inspector Thomas Pitt of Scotland Yard and his inquisitive wife, Charlotte. When Charlotte's beloved sister is suspected of poisoning her philandering husband, the Pitts undertake the investigation of the unfortunate victim's seemingly irreproachable, upper-crust family. Amid the luxurious splendor of an elegant town house and the hideous squalor of a London slum, they uncover a scandalous web of depravity and corruption that has inevitably culminated in the murder. A detailed period puzzler suffused with atmosphere, emotion, and suspense." Booklist

A dangerous mourning. Fawcett Columbine 1991 330p o.p.

LC 91-70655

"Murder in an aristocratic London household pits Inspector William Monk . . . against the Victorian sense of propriety, a bootlicking superior officer and a family's fierce determination to protect its reputation. Octavia Haslett, widowed daughter of Sir Basil Moidore, is found stabbed to death in her bedroom dressed only in night-clothes; when Monk proves no outsider could have entered the house that night, the family and servants remain sole suspects. As tension mounts in the household and a handsome and disliked footman becomes a scapegoat, Monk covertly arranges to introduce Hester Latterly, who served with Florence Nightingale in the Crimea and has helped Monk before, as a nurse in the Moidore home." Publ Wkly

Defend and betray. Fawcett Columbine 1992 385p o.p.

LC 92-52665

Available Thorndike Press large print edition

In Victorian London a "proud nurse and a brilliant lawyer team up with former policeman William Monk to defend a sympathetic upper-class woman who confesses to murdering her much-respected husband in a fit of jealousy." Libr J

"The climactic trial, and its ugly disclosures, are well wrought. . . . Throughout, the plight of the intelligent, educated woman who is not rich—her need for a meaningful independence, her culture's resistance to her fulfillment—is, while not deeply explored, frequently touched upon." N Y Times Book Rev

The face of a stranger. Fawcett Columbine 1990 328p o.p.

LC 90-34169

Available Thorndike Press large print edition

"William Monk, attached to the police in 1856 London, returns to work with amnesia after otherwise recovering from a nasty accident. Assigned to solve the murder of an aristocrat wounded in the Crimean War, he discovers, while hiding his memory loss from others, that he abhors his own character." Libr J

The author "understands her amnesiac sleuth so intimately that she knows he can rediscover himself only in moments of inspiration along the trail of his quarry. This, and the fact that Monk has more to learn about himself even as the story concludes, are brilliant touches that effectively blend contemporary understanding of character with a Victorian sensibility." N Y Times Book Rev

Farriers' Lane. Fawcett Columbine 1993 374p $20

ISBN 0-449-90569-1   LC 92-54390

Also available Thorndike Press large print edition

"In the wave of anti-Semitic hysteria in 1884 that follows the crucifixion of an English gentleman, a young Jewish actor is hastily tried and executed for the crime. Five years later, a justice of the appeals court is murdered when he attempts to reopen the sensational case. Only a man of discretion, intelligence and integrity—a man like Inspector Thomas Pitt of the Bow Street police division—can solve the devious affair of passion and political intrigue in Victorian London." NY Times Book Rev

Highgate rise. Fawcett Columbine 1991 330p o.p.

LC 90-85131

"Inspector Thomas Pitt, is appalled by the callousness of an arsonist who torches a physician's town house, burning his wife to death. Pitt's highborn wife, Charlotte, shares his horror when she learns that the dead woman was a quiet crusader on behalf of poor slum tenants. . . . Ms. Perry gives Pitt a breather from his customary gutter research by confining his investigation to the victim's upper-class social circle. Following her own conscience, Charlotte insinuates her way into elegant drawing rooms where the author's satirical wit is free to spread its rather showy skirts." N Y Times Book Rev

The Hyde Park headsman. Fawcett Columbine 1994 392p $21

ISBN 0-449-90636-1   LC 93-22124

Also available Thorndike Press large print edition

Perry, Anne, 1938-—*Continued*

Inspector Thomas Pitt "struggles to solve the brutal and confounding murder of Captain the Honorable Oakley Winthrop, R.N., who's been found beheaded in Hyde Park. Pitt suspects the victim knew his killer, but it's only after three more deadly murders take place that enough evidence can be mustered to accuse the real killer." Booklist

Paragon Walk. St. Martin's Press 1981 204p o.p.

"A psychopathic killer stalks the fashionable London neighborhood called Paragon Walk—the rapist's atrocities are as incredible, and terrifying to the Paragon Walk aristocrats as a sudden outbreak of the bubonic plague. Inspector Pitt's investigation of one brutal slaying, that of 17-year-old Fanny Nash, leads him to his own family—and himself." Booklist

Resurrection row. St. Martin's Press 1981 204p o.p.

LC 81-8846

"For no discernible reason, someone digs up the corpses of recently buried citizens and sets them up in public places. With these crimes demanding Pitt's concentration, he also has to investigate the murder of Godolphin Jones—an artist, pornographer and blackmailer. The detective's efforts to gather evidence against Jones's clients, obvious suspects, are fruitless until (as always) his quick-witted wife Charlotte drops a startling hint." Publ Wkly

Silence in Hanover Close. St. Martin's Press 1988 384p o.p.

LC 87-38253

When the Victorian Inspector Pitt is handcuffed by his superiors in investigating a diplomatic murder, he sends his wife "Charlotte's recently widowed sister undercover, posing as a lady's maid in a household where another young widow languishes until her husband's murderer can be found." N Y Times Book Rev

The sins of the wolf. Fawcett Columbine 1994 374p $21.50

ISBN 0-449-90638-8   LC 94-12099

Also available Thorndike Press large print edition

"Nurse Hester Latterly, who served courageously in the Crimean War and has assisted former policeman William Monk in many of his investigations . . . is charged with murdering a patient for personal gain. Hester hires on to accompany aging but lively Mary Farraline by train from Edinburgh to London and to administer the proper dose of heart medication. But Mary dies enroute—and her pearl brooch is discovered in Hester's bag. The dead woman's family, the police and most of Edinburgh are convinced that Hester killed her to obtain the pin. Coming to her aid are former policeman Monk, barrister Oliver Rathbone and Lady Callandra Daviot." Publ Wkly

A sudden, fearful death. Fawcett Columbine 1993 383p $20

ISBN 0-449-90637-X   LC 93-214115

Also available Thorndike Press large print edition

Victorian sleuth William Monk is "summoned to investigate the rape of a respectable young woman in her family's backyard. With little legwork or concrete evidence, Monk solves the case summarily. The remainder of the novel concerns the mystery of the fatal strangling of an educated and ambitious nurse who had served with Florence Nightingale in the Crimea." N Y Times Book Rev

Perry, Thomas

The butcher's boy. Scribner 1982 313p o.p.

LC 82-653

"A nameless hit man known as 'the Butcher's Boy' completes two killings, one of a U.S. senator, for Fieldstone Co. But when he tries to collect his $200,000 payoff, he finds that the unknown Mafia figure behind Fieldstone is out to get him and everyone who's had contact with him. Meanwhile Justice Department agent Elizabeth Waring is drawn in to investigate Fieldstone. She comes close to psyching out the true story, but it's the Butcher's Boy who becomes the hero by setting up for the Feds the Mafia chieftain at the heart of the evil doings." Libr J

Metzger's dog. Scribner 1983 314p o.p.

LC 83-9080

"Soldier of fortune Chinese Gordon and his three inept friends steal $1 million in cocaine from a university that was going to use it for experimental purposes. Gordon then inadvertently latches onto secret papers revealing American connivance in Latin America and decides to blackmail the CIA, whereupon the agency sends their top operative to recover the documents." Booklist

"Smoothly styled and humorous, the incredible story line exterminates the bungling creeps and prospers the ne'er-do-wells; but Gordon's cohorts never hurt anyone and they seem to have a great time. No deep characterization, philosophizing, or seriousness, just fast fun for the reader." Libr J

Sleeping dogs. Random House 1992 337p $22

ISBN 0-679-41064-3   LC 91-27137

This novel "brings Charles Ackerman—a.k.a., the Butcher's Boy, a killing-machine-for-hire—out of retirement in England and back to the United States to silence those people he mistakenly thinks have discovered his whereabouts. The story follows Ackerman as he travels coast to coast slaughtering one crime family's head honchos. Perry's book is well written, moves rapidly, and thankfully keeps the gore minimal." Libr J

Vanishing act. Random House 1995 289p $23

ISBN 0-679-43536-0   LC 94-17413

"Jane Whitefield is a Seneca Indian from upstate New York who has set herself up as a one-woman underground railroad to help worthy fugitives disappear. . . . A desperate man like John Felker is right up her alley. A burned-out cop who quit the job to become an accountant, Felker was set up on an embezzlement rap. But he grabbed the dough anyway, and now he has a contract on his head. Drawing on her clan contacts, Jane guides Felker on a trip into oblivion, via a rugged route across the Canadian border. This is all very satisfying and quite scenic—until certain deadly reversals tip off Jane that her operation has been compromised." N Y Times Book Rev

Peshkov, Aleksei Maksimovich *See* Gorky, Maksim, 1868-1936

Peters, Elizabeth, 1927-

For works written by this author under other names see Michaels, Barbara, 1927-

The deeds of the disturber; an Amelia Peabody mystery. Atheneum Pubs. 1988 289p o.p.

LC 87-33457

"Determined Victorian feminist Peabody refuses to be intimidated by a phenomenon reported at the British Museum, where a *sem* priest is supposedly working a curse in revenge for the desecration of an ancient mummy. The priest's supernatural figure is momentarily glimpsed at the exhibit, before a murderer strikes. Disobeying Emerson, of course, Peabody lays her life on the line and unmasks the decidedly human villain." Publ Wkly

Die for love. Congdon & Weed 1984 274p o.p. Severn House reprint available $20 (ISBN 0-7278-4491-1)

LC 83-26133

"When Jacqueline Kirby . . . decides to attend a meeting of the Historical Romance Writers of the World . . . she has no idea that she's leaving the groves of Academe for the graves of Manhattan. For amid the pink hearts, white lace and red and purple balloons of the conference, a murderer is at large." N Y Times Book Rev

The author's "romp through the world of romantic-fiction publishing satirizes both the mystery and romance genres while displaying perfect mastery of each." Booklist

The last camel died at noon. Warner Bks. 1991 352p il $18.95

ISBN 0-446-51483-7   LC 90-26759

Also available Thorndike Press large print edition

In this mystery archaeologist Amelia Peabody, "her handsome, fearless husband, Radcliffe, and their precocious 11-year-old son, Ramses, are in the Sudan, searching for archeologist Willoughby Forth, who disappeared 14 years earlier with his new wife. Rescued in the desert after every camel in their caravan dies, the Emersons are taken to a lost city where ancient Egyptian customs have been carried into modern times. There, entangled in two half-brothers' battle for the throne, Amelia and family fight for the freedom of the slave class while ferreting out the fate of Forth and his bride." Publ Wkly

"The Emersons are decidedly unstodgy Victorians—feminist, democratic, egalitarian, respectful of other cultures—and charming, witty, entertaining sleuths." Booklist

Legend in green velvet. Dodd, Mead 1976 241p o.p.

"Susan, a U.S. college student, is involved in her first exploration of an archaeological site. Susan's primary interests lie in Scottish history. . . . The plot develops as Susan is sightseeing in her Scottish dreamland. She meets a young Scotsman and together they stumble upon a murder. . . . The couple is pursued by the police and by the real murderers. As they elude the pursuers by hiding in forests and caves, they discover the answers to the reason for the murder frame-up." Best Sellers

Lion in the valley; an Amelia Peabody mystery. Atheneum Pubs. 1986 291p o.p.

LC 85-48126

"The stouthearted Victorian Englishwoman, Amelia Peabody Emerson, and her lusty, irascible husband are back in Egypt (with their precocious eight-year-old son, Ramses in tow). . . . The master criminal whom they

thwarted but did not bring to justice in 'The Mummy Case' is once again up to nefarious deeds, which include kidnapping Amelia in order to woo her. Murder, mayhem . . . and a pair of distressed young lovers, not to mention a modicum of archaeological pursuits, round out a decided treat for fans of the indomitable duo—or, perhaps, with Ramses, it is now a trio." Booklist

The mummy case. Congdon & Weed 1985 313p o.p.

LC 84-21500

"Victorian Amelia Peabody with her virile husband Emerson and precocious son Ramses embarks on a . . . archaeological dig in Egypt—but not before the death of a dealer in stolen antiquities. A disappearing mummy case and missing Coptic Papyri are the clues in this slapstick comedy-mystery. The ample archaeological detail is vivid, albeit a bit confusing. The irresistable attraction of this story: the heroine's droll tone and intrepid spirit." Libr J

The murders of Richard III. Dodd, Mead 1974 244p o.p.

This novel is "set in an English country mansion where a weekend meeting is being held by an eccentric group devoted to proving the innocence of King Richard III in the murders of the princes in the Tower of London. Although the weekend's highlight is to be the public unveiling of a document clearing Richard, the group prepares for the momentous occasion by dressing and acting as persons in King Richard's life in a charade that turns to the macabre as a malicious practical joker begins re-creating some of the killings attributed to Richard." Booklist

Naked once more. Warner Bks. 1989 296p o.p.

LC 89-40033

Available G.K. Hall large print edition

"Jacqueline Kirby, spirited librarian-turned-romance writer . . . wins a competition to write the sequel for a major bestseller whose author, Kathleen Darcy, has been declared legally dead seven years after disappearing in the Appalachian hills near her home. But soon Jacqueline, ensconced with her word processor in Kathleen's home town, begins to have accidents paralleling those that once befell Kathleen." Publ Wkly

Night train to Memphis. Warner Bks. 1994 353p $21.95

ISBN 0-446-51586-8   LC 94-3967

Vicky Bliss, "a curator at Munich's National Museum, is asked to go undercover on a cruise down the Nile. Her mission: to spot who among her fellow passengers might be the master criminal about to carry out a major theft of valuable antiquities. Vicky has a sneaking suspicion that the thief the police are after is the mysterious man she knows as John, who's perfectly capable of illegal activities and who's been both her sworn enemy and her sometime lover. When John shows up on the cruise and a crew member is murdered, Vicky begins to fear her suspicions are correct—but she doesn't have enough evidence to rule out the other passengers. This one is vintage Peters at her entertaining best." Booklist

The seventh sinner. Dodd, Mead 1972 243p o.p.

This is a "thriller about seven fashionably disheveled young scholars in Rome in the spring. They get involved in the particularly nasty murder of another scholar, an unattractive outsider, and are rescued by Jacqueline [Kir-

Peters, Elizabeth, 1927-—*Continued*

by], an older librarian. She is a felicitous creation, as tart and brisk as Mary Poppins, and a woman of sense and imagination. The novel is rather more endearing than mysterious, a pleasant entertainment." Libr J

Silhouette in scarlet. Congdon & Weed 1983 216p o.p.

LC 82-22174

"A rose, a cryptic note, and a plane ticket to Stockholm (one way, economy) lure Vicky [Bliss] to another rendezvous with art thief John Smythe and land her in the clutches of a more dangerous gang of thieves on an island in a wooded lake in Sweden." Libr J

The snake, the crocodile, and the dog. Warner Bks. 1992 340p $19.95

ISBN 0-446-51585-X   LC 92-54096

Also available G.K. Hall large print edition

In this mystery novel, archaeologist Amelia Peabody Emerson and her husband leave their son Ramses in England to excavate in Egypt. "Amelia anticipates time alone with Emerson, but the Master Criminal devises otherwise: In his quest for directions to the . . . Lost Oasis, he attempts abduction, subterfuge, and espionage." Libr J

Trojan gold; a Vicky Bliss mystery. Atheneum Pubs. 1987 o.p.

LC 86-26486

Art historian Vicky Bliss "receives a photograph of a modern woman dressed in the gold jewelry that Schliemann discovered in his archaeological excavation of Troy. The gold has been missing since the night the Soviet Army marched into Munich in 1945. The usual assortment of male admirers gather round, all trying to out-maneuver Vicky; but she manages to side-step nicely and come out the winner in this scintillating, captivating tale." Libr J

Peters, Ellis, 1913-1995

For works written by this author under other names see Pargeter, Edith, 1913-1995

The benediction of Brother Cadfael. Mysterious Press 1992 348p il maps $35

ISBN 0-89296-449-9   LC 91-50965

A combined edition of A morbid taste for bones and One corpse too many, both entered separately. This volume also includes a description of Cadfael country by Rob Talbot and Robin Whiteman

Brother Cadfael's penance; the twentieth chronicle of Brother Cadfael. Mysterious Press 1994 292p $18.95

ISBN 0-89296-599-1   LC 94-27140

Also available G.K. Hall large print edition

This Brother Cadfael mystery "has the gentle monk leaving his cloister on a journey that will prove both dangerous and wrenching. In twelfth-century Britain, a rebellion has arisen, with factional fighting between the knights supporting Empress Maud and those swearing allegiance to her cousin Stephen. Philip FitzRobert, a traitor to the empress, has taken 30 hostages, among them a young man named Olivier de Bretagne, who is Cadfael's son from a chance encounter years earlier. Although Cadfael has lost tract of the boy's mother, he's never forgotten his son, and once he finds out that

Olivier has been spirited away and imprisoned, nothing . . . can keep him from setting out to find the young man who has never known his true father." Booklist

City of gold and shadows. Morrow 1974 c1973 223p o.p.

"Detective Chief Inspector George Felse . . . [is] a minor but somewhat pivotal character in a light romantic mystery with interesting but not exhaustively detailed archaeological background. Disturbed by the disappearance of her great-uncle, Charlotte Rossignol visits the ruins of a second-century Roman city where the world-renowned archaeologist was last seen. There she meets and is drawn to Gus Hambro, whose interest in the site and in Charlotte has puzzling implications. Before the case is closed two dead bodies turn up, Gus almost becomes a third corpse, and a plot to illegally dispose of treasures from the site is uncovered." Booklist

The confession of Brother Haluin. Mysterious Press 1989 164p $15.95

ISBN 0-89296-349-2   LC 88-15141

Also available G.K. Hall large print edition

"On his deathbed, Brother Haluin confesses to the abbot and Brother Cadfael that 18 years previously he had fallen in love with Bertrade de Clary, whose mother had forbidden their marriage. The girl had later died as a result of herbs he had given her mother, Adelais de Clary, to abort their baby. Haluin unexpectedly recovers from his fall, however, and he now is determined to make a pilgrimage to the girl's tomb. . . . The two monks find more than the tomb there, and on their homeward journey through Staffordshire they encounter forbidden love, a hastily arranged marriage, violent emotions and murder." Publ Wkly

Dead man's ransom; the ninth chronicle of Brother Cadfael. Morrow 1985 189p o.p.

LC 84-22668

First published 1984 in the United Kingdom

This "novel focuses on the brutality of civil war between England and Wales in the early twelfth century, as the Benedictine monk is pulled into a hostage drama that turns into a politically repercussive murder. A young Welshman is exchanged for the sheriff of Shropshire and taken to Cadfael's abbey, where he falls in love with the sheriff's daughter. The sheriff's subsequent murder leaves rampant speculation that the young lovers are the perpetrators of the crime. Cadfael, as ever, is patient and insightful. A wonderfully atmospheric whodunit." Booklist

Death to the landlords! Morrow 1972 221p o.p.

The setting is "southern India, and the landlords are wealthy landholders who are the objectives of a terrorist murder gang. Dominic Felse . . . is at the center of the action, touring with a casual American acquaintance. The two young men meet up again and again with some of the same people as they travel India's Cape Comorin, among them a very intense English girl and a shy Indian nurse. Although the setting seems idyllic and the young people most attractive there is an undercurrent of brutal violence that hits home hard. The deaths are achieved by bombing. . . . Most effective of all is the interesting, perceptive, intuitive portrait of . . . problem-ridden India that emerges." Publ Wkly

Peters, Ellis, 1913-1995—*Continued*

The devil's novice; the eighth chronicle of Brother Cadfael. Morrow 1984 c1983 191p o.p.

LC 83-63300

First published 1983 in the United Kingdom
Brother Cadfael investigates the disappearance of a prominent young cleric
"The vocabulary and setting carry an English atmosphere. Cadfael's detective work is the focal point, but interesting characters, unfolding events and the local descriptions make this a tight, pleasing mystery." Best Sellers

An excellent mystery; the eleventh chronicle of Brother Cadfael. Morrow 1985 190p $15.95

ISBN 0-688-06250-4   LC 86-60042

This mystery featuring Benedictine monk Cadfael "concerns the appearance at the monastery of Brother Humilis and Brother Fidelis. The former had entered the cloister years earlier as a result of injuries he sustained in the Crusades. His appropriately named younger companion is mute but is unstinting in devotion to Humilis. . . . Later in the story . . . a former squire of Humilis from his days in the Crusades arrives with an unusual request: that he be allowed to seek the hand of the child to whom Humilis had been betrothed before he sustained the injury that caused him to enter the monastery. Just what became of that child and who may have murdered her are the central questions in this work." Best Sellers

Fallen into the pit. Mysterious Press; Warner Bks. 1994 c1951 324p $17.95

ISBN 0-89296-519-3   LC 92-50656

First published 1951 in the United Kingdom
"This mystery launched Peters's Inspector Felse series. Set in Britain just after WW II, the main sleuth here is not actually George Felse but his 13-year-old son Dominic. He and his best friend, Pussy Hart, are playing when Dom finds the body of Helmut Schauffler, an ex-P.O.W. who had stayed on after the war in the Comerford area. An autopsy indicates that Schauffler's skull was fractured by blows that were 'precise, neat and of murderous intention.' Helmut, a loathsome blend of cruelty, cowardice and anti-Semitism, is hardly mourned, but his death so rends the village's social fabric that solving the case is imperative. In his first murder investigation, George has difficulty viewing his neighbors as suspects." Publ Wkly

Flight of a witch. Mysterious Press 1991 c1964 232p $16.95

ISBN 0-89296-404-9   LC 90-84895
Also available G.K. Hall large print edition

First published 1964 in the United Kingdom
This "mystery revolves around the sheer beauty of 18-year-old Annet Beck, whom no one . . . knows very well. The story is told in the third person, primarily from the vantage point of Tom Kenyon, new sixth-form mathematics teacher in a small Shropshire village, who becomes a boarder at Annet's house and, like virtually every other man who comes in contact with her, falls in love with her at first sight. Did Annet indeed have a Rip van Winkle experience at the mysterious Hallowmount, where, it is said, a witch coven used to meet, or was her five-day absence a cover-up for something else? That's what Inspector George Felse would like to know when Annet is identified as being near the scene of a robbery-murder in Birmingham." Booklist

The heretic's apprentice. Mysterious Press 1990 c1989 186p $16.95

ISBN 0-89296-381-6   LC 89-34989

First published 1989 in the United Kingdom
"Accused of heresy and murder, Elave, a young clerk to a benefactor of the Abbey of Shrewsbury, seeks the aid of the medieval sleuth Brother Cadfael in a puzzling tale of politics, theology, and a priceless illuminated manuscript." Booklist

The hermit of Eyton Forest. Mysterious Press 1988 224p $15.95

ISBN 0-89296-290-9   LC 87-40398
Also available G.K. Hall large print edition

"A 10-year-old boy in school at the abbey suddenly finds himself Lord of Eaton when his father dies. His grandmother has plans for him; she wants him to marry a neighboring heiress. The abbot refuses to let him go. The grandmother takes steps to get him back. During all this, a mysterious monk living as a hermit and an equally mysterious young man who runs errands for him make their presence strongly felt. A nobleman is murdered, and the sharp eyes of Brother Cadfael notice things that are not apparent to all." N Y Times Book Rev

The holy thief. Mysterious Press 1992 246p $17.95

ISBN 0-89296-524-X   LC 92-50451

"The Benedictine monks at the Abbey of St. Peter and Paul in Shrewsbury are devastated by the inexplicable disappearance of their holiest and most revered relic, the remains of their patroness and guardian, Saint Winifred. Much to Brother Cadfael's consternation, the theft of the sacred casket could lead to the exposure of his own benign transgression. Years earlier, in compliance with the saint's final wish, he secretly exhumed her bones and buried them in her native Wales. Now Cadfael must recover the reliquary and solve a murder in order to protect himself and to exonerate a young monk accused of the crime." Booklist
"Twelfth-century Shropshire comes vividly alive when peopled with Peter's aristocratic ladies, sturdy lawmen, eager squires and, above all, devout—and devious—monks." Publ Wkly

The leper of St. Giles; the fifth chronicle of Brother Cadfael. Morrow 1982 223p il o.p.

LC 82-2101

"Brother Cadfael is faced with the dilemma of whether to help a pair of young lovers—handsome squire Joscelin Lucy and Iveta de Massard, who is being married against her will to Joscelin's middle-aged master. Their cause seems even more hopeless when Joscelin is dismissed, a valuable necklace is found in his baggage, and after he flees, his master is found murdered. Help comes from the mysterious leper of Saint Giles." Libr J

Monk's-hood; the third chronicle of Brother Cadfael. Morrow 1981 c1980 223p il o.p.

LC 80-26326

First published 1980 in United Kingdom
In this novel Brother "Cadfael investigates the murder by monkshood of Gervase Bonel, a wealthy man who was about to donate his lands to the monastery. Along

Peters, Ellis, 1913-1995—*Continued*
the way, Cadfael becomes swept up in the monastery's internecine power plays. Peters' language has a full, rich cadence, and her story is wonderfully vivid." Booklist

A morbid taste for bones. Morrow 1978 c1977 191p o.p.

First published 1977 in the United Kingdom
"When the cold and ambitious prior of the Benedictine monastery of Shrewsbury hears about the supposed miraculous powers attached to the bones of a long-dead obscure Welsh saint, he covets them for his abbey. The fact that the local Welsh villagers and their lord love their little saint and want to keep her with them is to be overruled by power and might. Sent to accompany the saint's remains back to Shrewsbury is Brother Cadfael, a most endearing detective. Come late to the cloister, after life as a warrior, he understands fully the needs of the flesh as well as those of the spirit. When two murders occur before the bones can be removed, it is Cadfael who will solve the mystery, sort out two pairs of lovers and in a most ingenious final ploy even make happy little Saint Winifred whose bones are at stake. The medieval background is portrayed very charmingly." Publ Wkly

also in Peters, E. The benediction of Brother Cadfael p3-129

One corpse too many; a medieval novel of suspense. Morrow 1980 c1979 191p il o.p.

LC 80-176

First published 1979 in the United Kingdom
This novel about monk-detective, Brother Cadfael, "takes us back to the world of 12th-century England as Stephen and Empress Maud are feuding for the throne. The castle at Shrewsbury falls in battle to Stephen, and he orders the mass execution of the 94 dissidents. Cadfael is sent to assure the dead are given a decent Christian burial. He finds one corpse too many—a victim, not of battle or execution, but of willful murder." Book World

also in Peters, E. The benediction of Brother Cadfael p211-348

The pilgrim of hate; the tenth chronicle of Brother Cadfael. Morrow 1985 c1984 190p o.p.

LC 85-62509

First published 1984 in the United Kingdom
"It is A.D. 1141, a year that brings a tide of pilgrims to the Benedictine Abbey at Shrewsbury. The occasion is a joyous one—a celebration in honor of St. Winifred, whose sacred relics were transferred to the abbey from Wales four years earlier. . . . Meanwhile, far away in embattled Winchester, a knight, supporter of the Empress Maud (who is campaigning against Stephen for the throne of England), is mysteriously murdered. But this seemingly disparate event, Cadfael begins to suspect, may be connected to the arrival at the shrine of a pair of pilgrims." Publisher's note

The potter's field; the seventeenth chronicle of Brother Cadfael, of the Benedictine Abbey of Saint Peter and Saint Paul, at Shrewsbury. Mysterious Press 1990 230p $16.95

ISBN 0-89296-419-7   LC 90-6340
Also available G.K. Hall large print edition
"After the body of a woman is found buried in a Benedictine Abbey field, Brother Cadfael tries to discover the woman's identity and locate the person responsible for her unlawful burial." Booklist
"In place of the pretty romances with which the author often lightens her historically plausible fictions, Ms. Peters provides darker characters and a more somber view of Shrewsbury life. More than the brilliant detection of a crime, the true subject of her wintry tale is human misery, as it extends from the meanest peasant cottage to the grandest manor house." N Y Times Book Rev

Rainbow's end. Morrow 1979 c1978 190p o.p.

LC 79-87538

First published 1978 in the United Kingdom
"An elegant and wealthy antiques dealer has become over night the local 'squire' in the Middlehope valley of the West Country. Despite his beautiful manor house, his attractive wife and his determination to do all the right things, Rainbow antagonizes the locals enough to make one of them toss him out of a church spire. Felse, intelligent, compassionate, perceptive, realizes early on that some rambunctious choir boys have it in for the victim and that his lovely wife has her real interests elsewhere. Pulling it all together involves old manuscripts, a ruined abbey, nighttime boyish pranks and adult sexuality. Very entertaining all the way." Publ Wkly

A rare Benedictine. Mysterious Press 1989 c1988 118p il $19.95

ISBN 0-89296-397-2   LC 89-42603
Analyzed in Short story index
First published 1988 in the United Kingdom
Contents: A light on the road to Woodstock; The price of light; Eye witness
The author "reveals for the first time how her medieval sleuth, Brother Cadfael, came to his calling at Shrewsbury Abbey. . . . For all his spirituality, mild Brother Cadfael once again impresses us with his practical grasp of the criminal side of human nature." N Y Times Book Rev

The raven in the foregate; the twelfth chronicle of Brother Cadfael. Morrow 1986 201p o.p.

LC 86-17946

"On Christmas morn A.D. 1141, the body of Father Ailnoth is found in the River Severn and again Brother Cadfael is called upon to solve a perplexing puzzle. The usual cast of characters is gathered at the monastery and vivid descriptions of 12th-century life in Shrewsbury add to the gently told tale." Libr J

The rose rent; the thirteenth chronicle of Brother Cadfael. Morrow 1986 190p $15.95

ISBN 0-688-06982-7   LC 87-5733
"When Judith Perle, a most generous benefactor of the abbey, vanishes without a trace, Cadfael immediately connects her disappearance with the vicious murder of a pious young monk and the seemingly senseless destruc-

Peters, Ellis, 1913-1995—*Continued*
tion of a rose bush. An accomplished whodunit
meticulously wrought with a wealth of medieval detail."
Booklist

Saint Peter's Fair; the fourth chronicle of
Brother Cadfael. Morrow 1981 219p il o.p.
LC 81-11020

Brother Cadfael, "who led an adventurous life in the
world before becoming a monk, is on the side of young
love, honor and truth as he investigates deaths taking
place while a local fair is in full swing. A well-respected
merchant is found murdered, and his lovely daughter
takes it upon herself to keep secrets so she involves two
young men, both of whom fancy her. Another death
occurs. Peters has an authentic eye and ear for her 12th
century way of life and death, and engages our interest
all the way." Publ Wkly

The sanctuary sparrow; the seventh
chronicle of Brother Cadfael. Morrow 1983
221p o.p.

LC 83-5389

Brother Cadfael "undertakes the problems of young
Liliwin, a juggler and acrobat of Shrewsbury who stands
accused of pilfering the valuables of one Master Walter
Aurifaber, the townships's goldsmith, while Liliwin was
amusing Aurifaber and the assembled patrons who were
at the wedding feast of Aurifaber's son, Daniel." West
Coast Rev Books

The summer of the Danes. Mysterious
Press 1991 251p $16.95

ISBN 0-89296-448-0   LC 91-11621

In this novel Brother Cadfael "must pilgrimage deep
into Wales on an errand of Church diplomacy. He is
accompanied by young Brother Mark and the passionate
Heledd, a young woman fleeing an arranged marriage.
The three become pawns in the battle between two
Welsh princes and the mercenary Danes whom one
prince has hired to help vanquish his brother. There is
a murder to be considered when Bledri ap Rhys—who
has offended everyone from Heledd's father, Canon
Meirion, to countless common soldiers—is found in his
bed, stabbed through the heart." Publ Wkly

The virgin in the ice; the sixth chronicle
of Brother Cadfael. Morrow 1983 c1982
220p il o.p.

LC 82-14500

First published 1982 in the United Kingdom
"The setting is England during the winter of 1139,
A.D. Brother Cadfael, who has taken a vow against war
and arms, finds himself in a country torn by civil war.
Brother Elyas, a fellow monk of a nearby town, is sent
to deliver two orphans, Ermina and Yves Hugonin, and
their chaperone Sister Hilaria, to Laurence d'Angers, the
childrens' uncle. During the journey Ermina sees her
chance to escape and marry her lover. . . . Brother Elyas
is attacked by a brutal band of marauders and left for
dead. Brother Cadfael, sent on a medical errand to look
after Brother Elyas, takes over his responsibility to bring
the three safely to Laurence d'Angers. During his journey,
Brother Cadfael discovers a murder and feels morally
obliged to solve it." Best Sellers

Peters, Maureen, 1935-
*For works written by this author under
other names see* Black, Veronica, 1935-

Petry, Ann Lane
The street; [by] Ann Petry. Houghton
Mifflin 1946 435p o.p.
"Set in Long Island, New York, in suburban Connecticut, and in Harlem, *The Street* is the story of intelligent,
ambitious Lutie Johnson, who strives to make a better
life for herself and her son despite a constant struggle
with sexual brutality and racism." Merriam-Webster's
Ency of Lit

Philips, Judson Pentecost *See* Pentecost,
Hugh, 1903-1989

Phillips, Caryl
Cambridge; a novel. Knopf 1992 c1991
183p $19
ISBN 0-679-40532-1   LC 91-53127
First published 1991 in the United Kingdom
A nineteenth-century "Englishwoman, Emily Cartwright,
is despatched by her father, an absentee plantation-owner,
to visit his sugar estate in the West Indies. Most of
the novel (following a third-person prologue signalling her
departure) consists of Emily's journal, in which her
impressions of the voyage and plantation life are
described. . . . Elements of gothic mystery unfold
through her eyes, around the puzzling presence in the
Great House of a slave woman, Christiana, who dabbles
in *obeah*, and the repeated chastisement of Cambridge,
a literate, Christian slave, by the enigmatic overseer, Mr.
Brown." Times Lit Suppl
"In 'Cambridge' there is action aplenty—sex, violence,
beatings, madness, murder—as, separately and equally,
the Englishwoman and the displaced African find their
sad endings. Events and ideas matter in this fictional
world, but not as much as the humanity, with all its
depths and nuances, of the characters. Mr. Phillips's artistry and integrity overwhelm all stereotypes." N Y
Times Book Rev

Crossing the river. Knopf 1994 c1993
237p $22
ISBN 0-679-40533-X   LC 93-35933
First published 1993 in the United Kingdom
This novel "begins in 18th-century Africa as three children—Nash, Martha and Travis—are sold into slavery.
What follows are 'their' life stories along with excerpts
from the logbook of the slave ship's captain. Nash
returns to Africa as a Christian missionary in the 1830s.
Martha is a former slave whom we meet as she lays
dying in Denver, having failed to reach California and
find her only child, taken from her years before. Travis
is reincarnated as an American GI stationed in England
in 1943; his story is . . . told by the British woman
he marries." Libr J
"One of the values of fiction is that it can tell the
story anew, can go back and include a neglected truth.
'Crossing the River' does this and is therefore a book
with an agenda. Mr. Phillips proposes that the diaspora
is permanent, and that blacks throughout the world who
look to Africa as a benevolent fatherland tell themselves
a stunted story. They need not to trace but to put down

Phillips, Caryl—*Continued*

roots. The message, however, is neither simply nor stridently conveyed." N Y Times Book Rev

Phillips, Jayne Anne, 1952-

Machine dreams. Dutton; Lawrence, S. 1984 331p o.p.

LC 84-4129

This "postmodernist saga takes an American family from the Depression to the Vietnam War in a series of portraits and scenes that captures the transformations undergone both by individuals and by society as a whole in the twentieth century." Booklist

"The story slows at a few points; at times the detailed, meticulous writing fails to achieve any sort of lift-off. But in the end, it amounts to a patchwork quilt of American voices." N Y Times Book Rev

Shelter. Houghton Mifflin; Lawrence, S. 1994 279p $21.95

ISBN 0-395-48890-7   LC 94-8391

The setting of this novel is a "forested mountain summer camp for girls in West Virginia during the early 1960s. Classic coming-of-age stirrings in camper sisters Lenny and Alma mingle with the frightening family secrets of Buddy, a young boy who hangs around the camp. Meanwhile, a young man named Parsons who knew Buddy's stepfather in prison, hides in an abandoned shack in the forest and watches the man he believes is the devil. The brutality the stepfather inflicts on Buddy and his 'Mam,' the camp cook, sets the stage for the terrifying drama that propels this novel. Powerful and riveting." Libr J

Pickard, Nancy

The 27 ingredient chili con carne murders. Delacorte Press 1993 296p o.p.

LC 92-17498

Available Thorndike Press large print edition

The author completes a "story begun by Virginia Rich, a onetime food writer and, at the time of her death in 1984, the author of three . . . culinary mysteries." N Y Times Book Rev

"In her home in New England, the widowed Mrs. Potter receives a call from Ricardo Ortega, manager of her Arizona ranch, who hints at trouble. Alarmed, she flies out to find that Ricardo and his granddaughter have disappeared. As neighboring ranchers and friends conduct a search, Mrs. Potter tries to determine the cause of Ricardo's unease. . . . Suspense with dollops of romance and gossip makes this offering irresistible." Publ Wkly

Bum steer; a Jenny Cain mystery. Pocket Bks. 1990 240p o.p.

LC 89-49198

Available Thorndike Press large print edition

This novel takes "Jenny Cain, director of the Port Frederick Civic Foundation, to Kansas City, where she hopes to discover why a dying millionaire has willed a vast cattle ranch to her little-known foundation. Thwarted upon arrival by the man's murder, she visits the ranch, fraternizes with two transplanted cowboys, searches out three ex-wives, and takes on a troubled teenager—all in hopes of finding the murderer." Libr J

"Although Jenny gets perkier, her companions more eccentric and their adventures more hair-raising as the hunt goes on, Ms. Pickard maintains her control over the derring-do and delivers an exciting climax." N Y Times Book Rev

But I wouldn't want to die there; a Jenny Cain mystery. Pocket Bks. 1993 243p o.p.

LC 93-15772

Available Thorndike Press large print edition

"When a colleague . . . in New York is stabbed to death in a street mugging, Jenny does the generous, if unlikely, thing: she moves into her friend's still-warm apartment, temporarily takes over her job and sets out to find her killer." NY Times Book Rev

"Pickard's in fine form here, combining a wonderfully acerbic, wickedly humorous commentary on the 'joys' of big-city life with a keep-'em-guessing plot and a smart, sexy, sensible . . . heroine." Booklist

Confession; a Jenny Cain mystery. Pocket Bks. 1994 307p $20

ISBN 0-671-78261-4   LC 93-87794

Also available Thorndike Press large print edition

"One steaming August day, Jenny, recently resigned as director of a foundation, and her police lieutenant husband, Geof Bushfield, are visited at home by angry 17-year-old David Mayer, who announces that he is Geof's illegitimate son by Judy Mayer, a high school classmate of Geof's. The winter before, Judy, an invalid, had been killed by her husband Ron, who then committed suicide. David, foulmouthed and hateful, demands that Geof reopen the case and prove the deaths were murders." Publ Wkly

"Fortunately, Geof and Jenny have a strong sense of humor, a sturdy marriage, plenty of common sense, and enough love to get them through one of the toughest tests they've faced together. Fine reading from an outstanding mystery writer." Booklist

Dead crazy; a Jenny Cain mystery. Scribner 1988 276p o.p.

LC 88-15324

"As director of a charity foundation in a small Massachusetts town, Jenny runs into community opposition—and two nasty murders—when she tries to purchase an abandoned church for restoration as a recreation center for the mentally disabled." N Y Times Book Rev

"Pickard nicely balances Jenny's wit and likability against her tough-minded, realistic examination of mental illness and its treatment. An outstanding mystery series." Booklist

Generous death. Dark Harvest 1993 c1984 239p $21.95

ISBN 0-913165-67-0

First published 1984 in paperback

This is the "first Jenny Cain story that Pickard wrote and serves as an introduction to the attractive and vivacious director of the Port Frederick Civic Foundation as well as to other characters who figure prominently in the series. The plot concerns the murders of several wealthy donors to the foundation. If the nasty little poems left with each of the bodies are any indication, Jenny herself may be the next victim." Booklist

I.O.U. Pocket Bks. 1991 234p o.p.

LC 90-15483

Pickard, Nancy—*Continued*

"Sobered by the death of her mother, a longtime coma patient in a psychiatric hospital, Jenny resolves to determine both the cause of her mother's mental illness and the full story behind the collapse of the family business." N Y Times Book Rev

"Pickard masterfully resolves both plot lines in this affecting, provocative novel centering around the mystery at the heart of mother-daughter relationships." Publ Wkly

Marriage is murder; a Jenny Cain mystery. Scribner 1987 210p o.p.

LC 87-4911

"Three homicides in two weeks: each victim the husband of a battered wife, each family beset by drinking problems, poverty, and too many children to feed. Either the wives are fighting back with a vengeance, or someone is doing their fighting for them. This is Pickard's fourth mystery starring wealthy young philanthropist Jenny Cain and her lover, policeman Geof Bushfield." Booklist

"An energetic array of Jenny's friends and co-workers keep this novel—a fine mix of romance, violence, and sleuthing—moving at a fast clip." Publ Wkly

No body; a Jenny Cain mystery. Scribner 1986 227p o.p.

LC 86-13118

Jenny Cain, "serving as the head of the Port Frederick Civic Foundation, relates events that stun the population in her New England town when a mud slide reveals the disappearance of 133 bodies, supposedly interred during the 19th century in the old cemetery. At the same time, the corpse of Sylvia Davis is found in the casket with John Rudolph just before he's due to be buried in the new cemetery. The next day, Rudolph's widow is murdered, and Jenny sets out to gather evidence on possible killers." Publ Wkly

Piercy, Marge

Braided lives; a novel. Summit Bks. 1982 443p $15.50

ISBN 0-671-43834-4   LC 81-16695

This novel concerns the lives of two women who were girls during the 1950's. Parents, friends, lovers appear as the story "follows its narrator-heroine, Jill Stuart, now 40 and an established writer who claims that her 'idea of hell is to be young again,' from her 1950's adolescence in working-class Detroit to the university in Ann Arbor, and on to New York. Jill writes, loves, suffers, commits herself to radical politics and reproductive rights, and survives. Throughout, her emotional anchor is her . . . friendship with Donna, her cousin and college roommate." Libr J

"As with most of Piercy's work, this is very political, and a major theme here is abortion—the dire need for safe, legal abortion. But while abortion is the visible theme, what lies beneath it is a rich, complex and thoroughly satisfying examination of life." Publ Wkly

Gone to soldiers; a novel. Summit Bks. 1987 703p o.p.

LC 86-30118

This is an "episodic story of World War II both at home and abroad. The turmoil of these years is shown through the lives of the numerous characters, from the female French Jewish Resistance fighter; to the Jewish factory worker/college student from Detroit and the U.S. ferry pilot, both women taking on men's roles, and the latter not wanting to give them up; to the cryptanalyst in Washington, D.C., escaping from the narrow life of his family; to the 'women's magazine' writer finally able to cover the war." Libr J

"In many male war novels character development is sacrificed; the 'woman's touch' here is excellent. The battlefront is not all blood and guts—there is also the grief of separation from family and the mitigating solace of friendship. On the home front there are race riots as well as ration books, and the heartbreak of shattered families." N Y Times Book Rev

He, she and it; a novel. Knopf 1991 446p $22

ISBN 0-679-40408-2   LC 91-52726

"Scarred by a painful divorce and custody fight, Shira Shipman leaves her 21st-century urban, male-dominated corporation and returns to the egalitarian Jewish enclave of Tikva, where she takes part in the programming of a revolutionary and illegal new cyborg named Yod. As part of Yod's education, Shira's grandmother narrates the story of the 17th-century Prague golem; the lives of the two artificial beings have obvious connections." Anatomy of Wonder 4

"Piercy's wordplay sings and entrances; the plots transcend the mere human-versus-machine theme to reach age-old philosophical issues with a touch of feminism." Booklist

The longings of women; a novel. Fawcett Columbine 1994 455p $22

ISBN 0-449-90907-7   LC 93-34125

Also available G.K. Hall large print edition

"The three heroines are Leila, a middle-aged Boston college professor and writer; her long-suffering and secretly homeless 60-ish housekeeper Mary; and Becky, an ambitious young wife accused of murdering her husband and who is the subject of Leila's new book. All three face problems typical of women ill-used by men and by society." Publ Wkly

"As Piercy draws us into the alarming predicaments of each of these women, she traces the progress of their struggles to earn respect and love with unerring accuracy and discernment. Magnetic from start to finish." Booklist

Small changes. Doubleday 1973 562p o.p.

"A chronicle novel that takes two women through perhaps a decade: Miriam, a sensual intellectual who abandons her complex relationships with two men to marry a third and bear him children; and Beth, who we first see as a mechanic's fragile bride and who over the years evolves into a radical lesbian. Beth finds herself as an activist while Miriam disintegrates." Libr J

"Avoiding both flights into political rhetoric and deterioration into soap opera, the novel depicts a new reality. If it is flawed, it lies perhaps in oversimplification, in her suggestion that Beth has found a 'solution' with another woman. . . . Nevertheless most of the book rings true." New Repub

Summer people; a novel. Summit Bks. 1989 380p o.p.

LC 89-30007

"After 11 years, the ménage à trois of Dinah Adler and Willie and Susan DeWitt is a strong family unit, accepted in its Cape Cod community. Dinah is a respected composer, devoted to her music, and Willie is a sculptor and carpenter happy with his life (and the envy of the local men). But Susan's growing discontent—with

Piercy, Marge—*Continued*
her work as a fabric designer and her role as unofficial gofer and hostess for summer people—ruptures the relationship and leads to tragedy." Libr J

"Piercy eschews sensationalism in portraying her unorthodox trio; her characterizations are solid and believable. Some readers may find the story's pace too deliberate, but those who like to ponder the ways in which character influences fate will welcome this solidly satisfying novel." Publ Wkly

Vida. Summit Bks. 1979 412p o.p.
LC 79-19298

"Wanted for a 1970 bombing which stemmed from her radical antiwar activism, Vida has been a fugitive and underground revolutionary for nine years. Shifting the narrative back and forth between the present and the years from 1967 to 1974. Piercy traces the evolution of a political movement through Vida's perceptions and her relationships with a small band of fellow adherents." Libr J

This novel "is not 'simply' a novel but a political brief. I have my differences with 'Vida,' but I think they are substantive rather than literary. It is an interesting—and challenging—book. . . . Marge Piercy has written about movement people before but never, I think, as lovingly as here." N Y Times Book Rev

Woman on the edge of time. Knopf 1976 369p o.p.

"A Hispanic-American mother undergoes experimental psychosurgery. She makes psychic contact with the 22nd-century world that has resulted from a feminist revolution whose success may depend on the subversion of the experiments in which she is involved. Outstanding for the elaborate description of the future utopia and the graphic representation of the inhumanity inherent in the way that contemporary people can and do treat one another." Anatomy of Wonder 4

Piesman, Marissa
Heading uptown; a Nina Fischman mystery. Delacorte Press 1993 247p o.p.
LC 92-30726

New York Jewish lawyer Nina Fischman "executrix of an acquaintance's will, investigates the man's 'accidental' death at the request of his teenage daughter." Libr J

"The minimalist plot does its modest job of supporting Nina's outrageous character assassinations of suburbanites who live it up in narcissistic, consumer-driven style. Acutely self-conscious about her own branded identity—the smart, independent, liberal, single Jewish woman—Nina uses her compulsive articulateness as her ultimate survival weapon." N Y Times Book Rev

Pike, Christopher
The season of passage. Doherty Assocs. 1992 344p o.p.
LC 91-37547

"A TOR book"
"The year is 2004 and, détente in place, the U.S. has sent a manned mission to Mars to find out what happened to and perhaps rescue the Russian cosmonauts who landed there two years earlier and have not been heard from since. Lauren Wagner, chief medical officer on the U.S. unit *Nova*, suspects alien infection killed the crew of the *Lenin* and worries that the same may happen to those on her ship. Little does she know that they face a fate far worse: there are vampires on Mars!" Publ Wkly

Pilcher, Rosamunde, 1924-
Flowers in the rain & other stories. St. Martin's Press 1991 277p o.p.
LC 91-18237

Available G.K. Hall large print edition
"A Thomas Dunne book"
Analyzed in Short story index
Stories included are: The doll's house; Endings and beginnings; Flowers in the rain; Playing a round with love; Christabel; The blackberry day; The red dress; A girl I used to know; The watershed; Marigold garden; Weekend; A walk in the snow; Cousin Dorothy; Whistle for the wind; Last morning; Skates

"Throughout this collection of stories, Pilcher maintains a pervasive gentility along with an abiding wisdom. Filled with poignant scenes, romantic and bittersweet, these stories, many written earlier in the author's career, will appeal to readers of Pilcher's very successful novels." Booklist

September. St. Martin's Press 1990 536p $22.95
ISBN 0-312-04419-4   LC 89-70340

"A Thomas Dunne book"
"A lavish coming-out party for the daughter of one of the leading families of a town in the Scottish Highlands brings together characters whose lives change in various ways during the novel's four-month span. The Airds and the Balmerinos of Strathcroy and their friends and relatives in London, Majorca and the States are the focal point of the love affairs, domestic complications, estrangements, reconciliations and other gently momentous events." Publ Wkly

"Character is at the heart of a story, and this fine tale has plenty of that." N Y Times Book Rev

The shell seekers. St. Martin's Press 1987 530p $21.95
ISBN 0-312-01058-3   LC 87-28345

"A Thomas Dunne book"
"Set in England's Cotswolds, the novel begins with a crisis: the mother has signed herself out of the hospital against doctor's orders and is determined to resume her independent life. This introduces the two daughters and one son who must deal not only with their mother and with each other, but also with the relationships they have established for better or worse in their own lives." Booklist

"It is a measure of this story's strength and success that a reader can be carried for more than 500 pages in total involvement with Penelope, her children, her past and the painting that hangs in her country cottage. 'The Shell Seekers' is a deeply satisfying story, written with love and confidence." N Y Times Book Rev

Voices in summer. St. Martin's Press 1984 215p o.p.
LC 83-22998

Available Thorndike Press large print edition
"Laura, married to Alec, an older divorcé, feels alienated from the people and events of her husband's past, especially his daughter and longtime friends. A recuperative stay with Alec's aunt and uncle in a lovely Cornwall mansion finally forces these and many other issues into the open." Booklist

Pilcher, Rosamunde, 1924—*Continued*

The author "evokes the sense of contentment that flows from affection grounded in a comfortable lifestyle, all of which makes for gently entertaining reading." Publ Wkly

Pincherle, Alberto *See* Moravia, Alberto, 1907-1990

Pinckney, Darryl, 1953-

High cotton. Farrar, Straus & Giroux 1992 309p $21

ISBN 0-374-16998-5   LC 91-23158

In this "novel about growing up as a 'nice Negro' in conservative Indianapolis, Ind. . . . Pinckney conveys the dedication, pride and hypocrisy that formed the society of 'upper shadies' in the 1950s and '60s. The nameless narrator demonstrates extraordinary powers of observation and expression throughout this memoir-like work, which takes him from youth to the present." Publ Wkly

"At a time in our history when a puerile 'political correctness' imposes hypocrisy on most writers dealing with sensitive topics, Darryl Pinckney has dared to treat his theme with excruciating honesty and the total freedom from restraint that Schiller said we find nowhere else but in authentic works of art." N Y Times Book Rev

Pirandello, Luigi, 1867-1936

Nobel Prize in literature, 1934

The outcast; authorized translation from the Italian by Leo Ongley. Dutton 1925 334p o.p.

Condemned and cast out by husband and father for a crime she has not committed, Marta makes a brave attempt to build life over again. She goes with her mother and sister to a town where she is unknown and there supports them by teaching. After a time happiness comes back to the three. Then the man for whose sake Marta was persecuted comes to their village. He finds Marta lovelier and more desirable than ever. The result is inevitable. The outcry against her breaks forth afresh, and she is forced into the situation she has tried to escape. Too late her chastened husband sues for forgiveness. This drama of Italian life draws to a close in a moving scene of reconciliation

The novel is "significant thematically for its unconventional treatment of adultery and historically for its subtle undermining of the assumptions of naturalism on which it appears to be based." Ency of World Lit in the 20th Century

Short stories; selected, translated and introduced by Frederick May. Oxford Univ. Press 1965 xxxvi, 260p o.p.

"Oxford library of Italian classics"

Analyzed in Short story index

Contents: The little hut; The cooper's cockerels; A dream of Christmas; Twelve letters; Fear; The best of friends; Bitter waters; The jar; The tragedy of a character; A call to duty; In the abyss; The black kid; Signora Frola and her son-in-law, Signor Ponza; The man with the flower in his mouth; Destruction of the man; Puberty; Cinci; All passion spent; The visit; The tortoise; A day goes by

Pirsig, Robert M.

Lila; an inquiry into morals; [by] Robert Pirsig. Bantam Bks. 1991 409p o.p.

LC 91-16417

Fictional sequel to the author's book of popular philosophy Zen and the art of motorcycle maintenance (1974)

This novel's narrator and protagonist, Phaedrus, "is a writer grappling with his latest treatise, the 'metaphysics of Quality.' Lila, his aging and desperate wharf-bar pickup, provides the right amount of antagonism and criticism to hone his ruminations of life and civilization to something understandable and real." Libr J

"'Lila' is a marvelous improvisation on a most improbable quartet: sailing, philosophy, sex and madness." N Y Times Book Rev

Plaidy, Jean, 1906-1993

For works written by this author under other names see Carr, Philippa, 1906-1993; Holt, Victoria, 1906-1993

The captive Queen of Scots. Putnam 1970 c1963 410p o.p.

Sequel to Royal road to Fotheringay (1968)

First published 1963 in the United Kingdom

"The story of the last 18 years of Queen Mary's life, during which she was first a prisoner of her Scottish enemies and later, after a dramatic escape and flight to England, the captive of her archenemy, Queen Elizabeth. Treated with at least some respect due a queen, Mary is pictured with her retinue of loyal friends and servants, living in varying degrees of discomfort and confinement as she moved from one castle to another at the whim of Elizabeth. She emerges as a generous, overly trustful, emotional victim, attractive even as she grew older though not wise, who met her tragic fate because she could not cope with the treachery and intrigue of both friends and enemies." Booklist

Murder most royal. Putnam 1972 542p o.p.

First published 1949 in the United Kingdom

"Concentrating on Anne Boleyn and her younger cousin Catherine Howard, the author follows the two from childhood to death on the block, with her usual thoroughness, sentimentality, and overdramatization, sparing the reader few details of torture, violence, intrigue, or thwarted love affairs." Booklist

The pleasures of love; the story of Catherine of Braganza. Putnam 1992 c1991 329p o.p.

LC 91-34593

First published 1991 in the United Kingdom

When Catherine, daughter of King John IV of Portugal, finally married Charles II her "happiness as the new Queen of England was short-lived. The Merry Monarch's notorious affairs amused the public but devastated Catherine, who longed for the love only a husband and children could provide. When it became clear that Catherine was barren, the people verged on rebellion and court intimates intrigued against her, hoping that Charles would divorce his queen, marry one of his mistresses, and beget an heir. But while Charles would never be faithful to Catherine, he loved her and was her fiercest protector. And in the end, their struggle against their enemies only drew the king and queen closer together." Publisher's note

Plaidy, Jean, 1906-1993—*Continued*

The reluctant queen; the story of Anne of York. Putnam 1991 c1990 299p o.p.

LC 90-48299

Available G.K. Hall large print edition

First published 1990 in the United Kingdom

"When King Edward IV married for love and his new Queen set out to destroy the Nevilles, disaster followed. Longtime allies suddenly became enemies, enemies became fellow conspirators, and Anne became the bargaining chip in her father's battle to choose the next king and remain the Kingmaker. Refusing to accept the future being forced upon her, Anne married her longtime friend Richard, the king's younger brother, not dreaming one day soon Richard would crown himself. Their marriage thrusts them both back into the political maelstrom that will change their lives forever." Publisher's note

The rose without a thorn. Putnam 1994 c1993 255p $22.95

ISBN 0-399-13930-3   LC 93-34598

First published 1993 in the United Kingdom

Young Katherine Howard is "given the chance to go to the Royal Court as a lady-in-waiting to the queen, Anne of Cleaves—enabling her to be near her handsome cousin, Thomas Culpepper. But when she catches the eye of the unhappily married king, Henry VIII, she is compelled to abandon her plans for a life with Thomas and eventually agrees to marry the king. Overwhelmed by the change in her fortunes, bewildered and flattered by the adoration of her husband, Katherine settles down to enjoy her life as queen. Such bliss is short-lived as Katherine's promiscuous ways come back to haunt her." Publisher's note

The scarlet cloak. Putnam 1992 c1985 335p o.p.

LC 92-8516

Available G.K. Hall large print edition

First published 1957 in the United Kingdom under the pseudonym Ellalice Tata

"In the years 1572-1578, when the faith and fanaticism of one man—King Philip II of Spain—trouble the whole of Europe, His Most Catholic Majesty's plans against accused heretics meet with stubborn, angry resistance. Dashing Blasco Carramadino and his devout older brother, Domingo, live in the quiet province of Andalusia, where the king's fanaticism is rarely felt. But soon they will be caught in a web of intrigue, as Philip plots the overthrow of England and its return to the one true faith." Publisher's note

The sixth wife. Putnam 1969 c1953 252p o.p.

First published 1953 in the United Kingdom

Henry VIII chooses Catharine Parr, fiancee of his brother-in-law, to become his sixth wife after he has condemned Catharine Howard to death. This novel tells Catharine Parr's story from the time she becomes queen until her death

"All the figures of history are here: Mary Tudor and Elizabeth, the young frail Edward VI, Lady Jane Grey, the Herberts and the Suffolks and the Seymours, the Tower of London, the torture chambers, the heretics and heretic-baiting—all the persons and the panoply and the cruelty of the Tudor era—and the story of Catherine Parr appears to be authentic. If this seems to lack the intensity, the roar and gusto that properly belongs to this period in history, it is an entertaining and even absorbing novel." Best Sellers

William's wife. Putnam 1993 276p $22.95

ISBN 0-399-13807-2   LC 92-32588

In this historical novel about the "struggle for power between Catholic and Protestant, England's heir to the throne, the lovely and bright Princess Mary, is forced to marry William of Orange in order to prevent the kingdom from falling under Catholic rule. Despite Mary's attempts to win her husband's love, the dour, power-hungry William won't even feign affection for her; instead, he continues a blatant affair with Elizabeth Villiers. As the inevitable power struggle ensues between her husband and her father, James II, Mary finds herself torn between marital and filial loyalties. But with the crown of England the ultimate prize, Mary discovers that while she is James's daughter, she is first and foremost William's wife." Publisher's note

Plain, Belva

Blessings. Delacorte Press 1989 340p $19.95

ISBN 0-385-29754-8   LC 89-1565
Also available large print edition $21.95 (ISBN 0-385-29756-4)

"The entanglements of a teenage romance surface more than a decade later to disrupt the life of a successful attorney. Jennie Rakowski finally has her life together. She provides legal counsel for poor, battered women and is on the verge of marrying a charming, widowed corporate attorney with three small children. Suddenly, Jill, the daughter Jennie gave up for adoption 19 years earlier, appears at Jennie's door; even worse, Jill brings along the man who fathered her then disappeared from Jennie's life." Booklist

"The author stretches an awkward subplot concerning mob-connected real estate developers far too thin, but her mixture of romance, suspense, and deeply felt familial conflicts should leave her fans well entertained." Publ Wkly

Crescent City; a novel. Delacorte Press 1984 429p $16.95

ISBN 0-385-29354-2   LC 84-5045

A novel "set against the backdrop of America's South during the Civil War. At the story's center is Miriam Raphael, a European Jew transplanted as a child to New Orleans, the 'Crescent City' nestled at the mouth of the Mississippi. Both she and her older brother, David, must adjust to what seems a bright, promising new land filled with languid days and lavish feasts. But all too quickly their eyes are opened to the grimmer features of their landscape—the slaves whom David vows to set free and the southern tradition of youthful marriage, which Miriam, herself no better off than a slave, must gracefully endure." Booklist

Daybreak. Delacorte Press 1994 360p $22.95

ISBN 0-385-31104-4   LC 93-43915

This "novel considers the emotional mayhem that ensues when two newborns are switched in a hospital nursery. One infant grows to hearty manhood in a home that melds Southern grace with rabid bigotry; the other, afflicted with cystic fibrosis, is given to a Jewish couple in a nearby town. When the first child dies of his disease at 18, his stunned parents learn the truth and come looking for their biological son, only to find that he has become a disciple of a rabble-rousing senatorial

Plain, Belva—*Continued*

candidate—and is less than thrilled to discover the truth of his ancestry." N Y Times Book Rev

Eden burning. Delacorte Press 1982 451p o.p.

LC 82-1452

"The Eden of the title is St. Felice, an island in the Caribbean. The story chronicles the lives of Teresa Francis and her two sons, Patrick Courzon, conceived when Teresa was raped by a young black man, and Francis Luther, the son born of her later marriage. The young men are brought up in different environments but . . . they meet when Francis comes to the island to run his mother's old estate. Patrick and Francis become friends and then enemies as the island explodes in revolution." Libr J

Evergreen; a novel. Delacorte Press 1978 593p $19.95

ISBN 0-385-28299-0   LC 77-20778
Also available from Buccaneer Bks.

"The young orphan Anna shows her spunk by leaving Poland to make a way for herself in the turn-of-the-century U.S.A. Opting for domestic service rather than the sweatshops of lower Manhattan, she becomes infatuated with the master's son, Paul Werner. His marriage to another woman puts a damper on Anna's longing, and she settles for poor but loyal Joseph Friedman. Joseph is hard working and has a vision of fulfilling the American Dream. He persuades his wife to borrow some money from the Werners, and Anna finds herself asking Paul for the money. He gladly obliges, but the old flame is fanned into heedless passion and Anna leaves with the money and a secret she will carry with her for the rest of her life." Best Sellers

"This warm and sympathetic family saga gives life and meaning to the commonplace events of unspectacular lives." Publ Wkly
Followed by The golden cup

The golden cup. Doubleday 1986 399p $17.95

ISBN 0-385-29508-1   LC 86-8851
Evergreen, "told the story of immigrant Anna Friedman and her love for Paul Werner. Here the focus shifts to Paul's aunt, Hennie DeRivera, from age 18 in 1891 through World War I. As a volunteer, Hennie teaches English at a settlement house where she meets Daniel Roth. Their relationship is frowned upon by her family, but they marry when she becomes pregnant. Her uncertainty over whether Dan would have married her otherwise is aggravated by his roving eye. The grown-up Paul, Hennie's son Fred, and Leah, an orphan she raises, are also featured." Libr J

The author "invests her story with dignity and historical relevance while insightfully depicting the class consciousness of Progressive Era Americans." Publ Wkly
Followed by Tapestry

Harvest. Delacorte Press 1990 409p $21.95
ISBN 0-385-29926-5   LC 90-34417
Also available large print edition $24.95 (ISBN 0-385-30236-3)

This novel continues the "saga of the Werners and their extended clan as they reaffirm their Jewish heritage during the stormy 1960s. Dark, sensitive Iris, daughter of the glowing, russet-haired Anna (by urbane banker Paul Werner—unbeknownst to Iris) is married to wealthy, improvident Dr. Theo Stern, whose European

glamour excites other women. Iris's jealousy goads her to play at her own romance with a sinister partner. Her four children are growing up, but rebel Steve balks at his bar mitzvah, already anticipating the anarchist/bomb expert he will be at college, radicalized by cynical professor Tim Powers, whom he doesn't know is his distant cousin. When Paul's wife dies and his mistress leaves to fulfill her mission as a doctor in Israel, Paul hovers protectively over Iris's, troubled family." Publ Wkly

Random winds. Delacorte Press 1980 496p o.p.

LC 79-26845

"Three generations of doctors in the Farrell family span the gamut from a dedicated general practitioner in the Adirondack Mountains of New York to a world-renowned but troubled brain surgeon and on to a budding feminist medical student with a career/marriage conflict. This is a dynamic record of domestic tragedies to be endured, bitter arguments to be fought, and agonizing choices to be made as the Farrells sort out lives, loves, and hopes and set forth to challenge medical traditions and forbidden passions." Booklist

The author "knows how to sweep from one dramatic scene to another, often evoking poignancy, and the irony underlying Martin's daughter's romance with Fern's stepson produces a bittersweet ending." Publ Wkly

Tapestry. Delacorte Press 1988 440p o.p.
LC 87-22346

"Paul Werner, the key figure of a powerful New York banking family, is the protagonist in this saga of one man's concerns with the impending doom of World War II and the plight of his German-Jewish relatives and friends. Paul is caught in a passionless, childless marriage, and he struggles for years with the memory and reality of his first love and subsequent affairs of the heart." Libr J
Followed by Harvest

Treasures. Delacorte Press 1992 418p $21
ISBN 0-385-29927-3   LC 91-32590
"Set primarily in the 1980's, the story involves three siblings from Ohio—Lara, Connie and Eddy Osborne. As adult children of a now-deceased alcoholic father, they each exhibit traits typical of such families, especially the need for control. Lara remains behind in Ohio to tend to her own family as Eddy and Connie seek opportunities elsewhere: he becomes a whiz on Wall Steet, while she moves to Texas and then New York, specializing in attracting wealthy men. In the fast-paced world of leveraged buyouts, junk bonds and social climbing, Eddy and Connie's appetites run wild." N Y Times Book Rev

Whispers. Delacorte Press 1993 331p $22.95
ISBN 0-385-29928-1   LC 92-36572
Also available G.K. Hall large print edition
"The Fergusons seem to have it all. Lynn runs their comfortable home in an affluent Connecticut suburb, her husband Robert is headed for a major position with his corporation and their eldest daughter Emily has been accepted at Yale. But it's a facade. Robert's inexplicable rages lead him to physically abuse Lynn; at times he is cruelly dictatorial with Emily and her troubled younger sister Annie." Publ Wkly

"Plain's purposes in rehearsing this scenario . . . are to illustrate what an abusive relationship is, to inculcate that it can afflict women in even the best strata of society, to sympathetically model getting out of such a

Plain, Belva—*Continued*

situation, and to stress how difficult getting out can be even—perhaps especially—for a good, smart, talented woman. She succeeds admirably and affectingly." Booklist

Plante, David

Annunciation. Ticknor & Fields 1994 346p $21.95

ISBN 0-395-68091-3   LC 93-44724

"Claire O'Connel is an American art historian in London researching a thesis on Renaissance artist Pietro Testa. When her 16-year-old daughter Rachel is raped and impregnated, Claire acquiesces to the girl's decision to bear the child and rededicates herself to bolstering Rachel's will to live. This goal becomes intertwined with her search for an undocumented Testa painting of the Annunciation, which takes the two women to Lucca, Italy. Claude Ricard, an art book editor for a Manhattan publisher, is saddened by death in his extended family and disillusioned after an ill-fated affair. He accepts a transfer to London, where he finds a new companion, Maurice, an elderly man born in prerevolutionary Russia. These two eventually meet Claire and Rachel and are drawn into their search for the Testa Annunciation, which takes them all to Moscow." Publ Wkly

"An intense and significant blend of theology and drama, this is a book with lasting impact." Booklist

Plath, Sylvia

The bell jar; biographical note by Lois Ames; drawings by Sylvia Plath. Harper & Row 1971 296p il o.p. Buccaneer Bks. reprint available $25.95 (ISBN 0-89966-815-1)

First published 1963 in the United Kingdom

"Esther Greenwood, having spent what should have been a glorious summer as guest editor for a young woman's magazine, came home from New York, had a nervous breakdown, and tried to commit suicide. Through months of therapy, Esther kept her rationality, if not her sanity. In telling the story of Esther, Plath thinly disguised her own experience with attempted suicide and time spent in an institution. Like Esther, she was rehabilitated and finished college. She went to London, married poet Ted Hughes, had three children and published some poetry and this novel. When she felt the world slipping away from her again, she did commit suicide." Shapiro. Fic for Youth. 3d edition

Poe, Edgar Allan, 1809-1849

The collected tales and poems of Edgar Allan Poe. Modern Lib. 1992 1026p $20

ISBN 0-679-60007-8   LC 92-50231

Partially analyzed in Short story index

First published 1938 with title: The complete tales and poems of Edgar Allan Poe

Stories included are: Unparalleled adventure of one Hans Pfaall; The gold-bug; The balloon-hoax; Von Kempelen and his discovery; Mesmeric revelations; Facts in the case of M. Valdemar; Thousand-and-second tale of Scheherazade; Ms. found in a bottle; Descent into the maelström; Murders in the Rue Morgue; Mystery of Marie Rogêt; Purloined letter; The black cat; Fall of the House of Usher; Pit and the pendulum; Premature burial; Masque of the Red Death; Cask of Amontillado; Imp of the perverse; Island of the fay; Oval portrait; The

assignation; Tell-tale heart; System of Doctor Tarr and Professor Fether; Literary life of Thingum Bob, Esq.; How to write a Blackwood article; A predicament; Mystification; X-ing a paragrab; Diddling; Angel of the odd; Mellonta Tauta; Loss of breath; Man that was used up; The business man; Maelzel's chessplayer; Power of words; Colloquy of Monos and Una; Conversation of Eiros and Charmion; Shadow—a parable; Silence—a fable; Philosophy of furniture; Tale of Jerusalem; The sphinx; Man of the crowd; Never bet the devil your head; "Thou art the man"; Hop-Frog; Four beasts in one: The homo-cameleopard; Why the little French-man wears his hand in a sling; Bon-bon; Some words with a mummy; Magazine-writing—Peter Snook; The quacks of Helicon—a satire; Astoria; Domain of Arnheim; Landor's cottage; William Wilson; Berenice; Eleonora; Ligeia; Morella; Metzengerstein; Tale of the ragged mountains; The spectacles; Duc de l'Omelette; Oblong box; King Pest; Three Sundays in a week; Devil in the belfry; Lionizing; Narrative of A. Gordon Pym (novelette entered separately)

Complete stories and poems of Edgar Allan Poe. Doubleday 1966 819p $19.95

ISBN 0-385-07407-7

Partially analyzed in Short story index

This volume contains five sections: Tales of mystery and horror; Humor and satire; Flights and fantasies; The narrative of A. Gordon Pym of Nantucket (entered separately) and The poems

Short stories included are: The murders in the Rue Morgue; The mystery of Marie Rogêt; The black cat; The gold-bug; Ligeia; A descent into the maelstrom; The tell-tale heart; The purloined letter; The assignation; Ms. found in a bottle; William Wilson; Berenice; The fall of the House of Usher; The cask of Amontillado; The pit and the pendulum; A tale of the ragged mountains; The man of the crowd; Morella; "Thou art the man"; The oblong box; The conversation of Eiros and Charmion; Metzengerstein; The masque of the Red Death; The premature burial; The imp of the perverse; The facts in the case of M. Valdemar; Hop-Frog; The system of Doctor Tarr and Professor Fether; The literary life of Thingum Bob, Esq.; How to write a Blackwood article; A predicament; Mystification; Loss of breath; The man that was used up; Diddling; The angel of the odd; Mellonta Tauta; The thousand-and-second tale of Scheherazade; X-ing a paragrab; The business man; A tale of Jerusalem; The sphinx; Why the little Frenchman wears his hand in a sling; Bon-bon; The Duc de l'Omelette; Three Sundays in a week; The devil in the belfry; Lionizing; Some words with a mummy; The spectacles; Four beasts in one; Never bet the devil your head; The balloon-hoax; Mesmeric revelation; Eleanora; The island of the fay; The oval portrait; The domain of Arnheim; Landor's cottage; The power of words; The colloquy of Monos and Una; Von Kempelen and his discovery

The imaginary voyages: The narrative of Arthur Gordon Pym; The unparalleled adventure of one Hans Pfaall; The journal of Julius Rodman. Twayne Pubs. 1981 667p o.p.

LC 81-2915

"Collected writings of Edgar Allan Poe"

Omnibus edition of three titles, the first of which is entered separately under variant form: The narrative of Arthur Gordon Pym of Nantucket, The unparalleled

Poe, Edgar Allan, 1809-1849—*Continued*
adventure of one Hans Pfaall, first published 1835
describes a voyage to the moon and The journal of
Julius Rodman, an unfinished novel first published
anonymously in 1840 deals with exploration of the Missouri River Basin

The journal of Julius Rodman

In Poe, E. A. The imaginary voyages
p508-653

The narrative of Arthur Gordon Pym of
Nantucket. Harper 1838 201p o.p.
"Comprising the details of a mutiny and atrocious but-
chery on board the American brig Grampus, on her way
to the South seas. . . . With an account of the recapture
of the vessel by the survivors; their shipwreck and subsequent horrible sufferings from famine . . ." Title page
"A New England boy stows away on a whaler, surviving mutiny, savagery, cannibalism, and wild pursuit.
At the end of the story, the hero drifts toward the South
Pole in a canoe; before him, out of the mist, rises a
great white figure. There is some confusion in detail,
because Poe, serializing the story, often did not pick up
the loose ends. Based on the factual travels of J. N.
Reynolds, whose book Poe had reviewed." Reader's Ency.
3d edition

also in Poe, E. A. The collected tales
and poems of Edgar Allan Poe

also in Poe, E. A. Complete stories and
poems of Edgar Allan Poe p617-736

also in Poe, E. A. The imaginary
voyages p4-365

The purloined letter [and] The murders in
the Rue Morgue; illustrated by Rick
Schreiter. Watts 1966 85p il o.p.
These two stories feature Monsieur C. Auguste Dupin.
In "The murders in the Rue Morgue," a mother and
daughter are the victims of a grisly murder that baffles
the police. "The purloined letter" poses the problem of
a woman of royal rank who is being blackmailed by
a government official on the basis of a compromising
letter. The police fail in the search, but Dupin is able
to locate the missive

The unparalleled adventure of one Hans
Pfaall

In Poe, E. A. The imaginary voyages
p366-506

Poey, Delia
(ed) Iguana dreams. See Iguana dreams

Pogue, John Wilbur, 1909-
(jt. auth) Bova, B. The Trikon deception

Pohl, Frederik, 1919-
The annals of the Heechee. Ballantine
Bks. 1987 388p o.p.

LC 86-26584

"A Del Rey book"
Sequel to Heechee rendezvous
In this episode "the human-Heechee cooperation that
first materialized in 'Heechee Rendezvous' has solidified

as the two races unite against a common enemy. Once
again Robinette Broadhead—alive after death as a
machine-stored personality, compliments of Heechee technology—is called upon to face a dangerous challenge. He
is the only one able to meet eyeball to eyeball with the
deadly Foe, aliens determined to mold the universe to
their own needs. . . . The novel is gripping, both in
story line and in the colorful depiction of the alien
Heechee." Booklist

Beyond the blue event horizon. Ballantine
Bks. 1980 327p o.p.

LC 79-21757

"A Del Rey book"
Sequel to Gateway
"Multimillionaire Robinette Broadhead, still mourning
the loss of his great love from the first book, backs an
expedition to investigate one of the alien Heechee's 'food
factories.' Earth is overpopulated, and the ship's resources
are desperately needed to prevent mass starvation. The
members of the expedition are all from the same family:
Lurvey, a veteran space pilot and her engineer husband;
Lurvey's money hungry father, and her precocious 14-
year-old sister. Despite the tensions which surface during
their three and a half year voyage, the family manages
to successfully make contact with the factory and its
innocent, human occupant. They begin to explore the
marvels of the alien technology, but events on Earth and
the inhabitants of another Heechee spaceship threatens
to end the expedition in disaster." Voice Youth Advocates
Followed by Heechee rendezvous

Chernobyl; a novel. Bantam Bks. 1987
355p o.p.

LC 86-47896

The author "re-creates in fiction the massive 1986
Ukrainian nuclear power plant disaster. The book opens
during normal days just before the accident; suspense
builds, as the reader expects the worst. Characters that
would actually have been on the scene are seen being
overwhelmed by berserk technology, their lives shattered.
The tale is gripping, and the locale well established."
Libr J

The day the Martians came. St. Martin's
Press 1988 248p o.p.

LC 88-14780

"A Thomas Dunne book"
In this quasi-novel of connected stories "life on Mars
exists, and the world prepares—in typical human
fashion—for the arrival of its first aliens. UFO cultists,
hucksters, politicians, and scientists fall prey to Pohl's
acerbic talent." Libr J

Gateway. St. Martin's Press 1977 313p
o.p.
First volume in the author's Heechee saga
"The novel's protagonist, Robinette Broadhead, suffers
from tremendous feelings of guilt: for the death of his
parents, for his wealth (a stroke of luck he feels he does
not deserve), and for the living death of his girl friend
and fellow crew members. Gateway presents Broadhead's
story in chapters that alternately describe his life before
the novel opens and record present conversations between Broadhead and his computer psychiatrist, Sigfrid
von Shrink. With a sensitive mixture of humor and
sympathy, Pohl explores Broadhead's condition and ends
with one of the finest affirmations of humanity in any
literary work." New Ency of Sci Fic
Followed by Beyond the blue event horizon

Pohl, Frederik, 1919——*Continued*

The gateway trip; tales and vignettes of the Heechee; illustrated by Frank Kelly Freas. Ballantine Bks. 1990 241p il o.p.

LC 90-555

"A Del Rey book"

Analyzed in Short story index

Contents: The visit; The merchants of Venus [novella]; The Gateway asteroid; The starseekers; The home planet; Other worlds; Heechee treasures; Looking for company; The age of gold; In the core

"The discovery on Venus of artifacts created by an ancient alien race prompts a galaxy-wide search for more intriguing remnants of the vanished 'Heechee' culture and gives rise to the Gateway Corporation as a means of encouraging exploration by bold and sometimes foolhardy explorers. This collection of short tales serves as a tantalizing companion piece to Pohl's other Heechee volumes." Libr J

Heechee rendezvous; a novel. Ballantine Bks. 1984 311p o.p.

LC 83-15637

"A Del Rey book"

Sequel to Beyond the blue event horizon

In this novel "the elusive, benevolent aliens called Heechee are forced to come out of hiding because the future not only of humankind but of the universe itself is at stake. Compelled by personal reasons, tycoon Robinette Broadhead takes part in another dangerous venture into space, moving inexorably toward his surprising yet fitting destiny." Booklist

Followed by The annals of the Heechee

Homegoing. Ballantine Bks. 1989 279p o.p.

LC 88-7413

"A Del Rey book"

"An alien spaceship lands on Earth for a double purpose: to give the people of Earth the benefit of their advanced technology and to return to them a human rescued in infancy and raised by the kangaroo-like Hakh'hli to be as 'human' as possible—under the circumstances. Pohl's unerring gift for satire delivers a splendidly skewed alien-eye-view of human culture while spinning a touching, slightly quirky story of a young man's coming of age." Libr J

Land's end; [by] Frederik Pohl and Jack Williamson. Doherty Assocs. 1988 369p o.p.

LC 87-51406

"A TOR book"

"A cosmic disaster destroys the surface of the earth and awakens a sleeping alien menace whose purpose is to assimilate all surviving life into itself. Two veteran sf authors combine their storytelling abilities to create a sprawling, complicated sf story." Libr J

Man Plus. Random House 1976 215p o.p.

"The novel describes the transformation of a human astronaut into a cyborg capable of living on Mars and confronts the question of human dignity: as the central character, Roger Torraway, becomes less 'human,' the people who were once so important to him are unable to cope with what he is, and Roger must also learn to handle the new thing he has become. Moreover, Roger's reflections on his growing inability to control his own life parallel the thoughts of people throughout the country who believe the world has gone out of control. The result is a remarkably readable novel that succeeds in presenting a fully rounded character in an SF setting." New Ency of Sci Fic

Mars Plus; [by] Frederik Pohl, Thomas T. Thomas. Baen Pub. Enterprises 1994 342p $20

ISBN 0-671-87605-8   LC 93-44782

"Fifty years after the events in Man Plus, 'man is, or seems to be, on Mars to stay, but things have become . . . strange, even compared to the population of cyborgs, half-cyborgs and just plain humans who now occupy the Red Planet. The computer net on which all Martian life depends has long seemed to have 'a mind of its own,' and now that mind seems to be in a very bad mood.'" Publisher's note

The merchants of Venus

In Modern classic short novels of science fiction p260-320

In Pohl, F. The gateway trip p12-128

The merchants' war. St. Martin's Press 1984 209p o.p.

LC 84-18394

Sequel to The space merchants

"Powerful advertising agencies dominate the political, economic and social life of a future Earth, whose disaffected have fled to a harsh, spartan existence on Venus. Temporarily assigned to Venus, adman Tennison Tarb gets caught up in the ongoing struggle by each planet's government to subvert the beliefs and practises of the other's inhabitants. Tarb becomes the victim of his own profession on his return to Earth when unethical advertising addicts him to a narcotic drink. What ensues is a journey through the maze of a society warped by consumerism." Publ Wkly

"At his engagingly hilarious best . . . Pohl launches satiric barbs at his favorite target—mass advertising—consistently hitting the mark." Libr J

Mining the oort. Ballantine Bks. 1992 264p o.p.

LC 91-58639

"A Del Rey book"

This is the "story of a naive young man who learns better through involvement in evil intrigues. In this case, the young man, born and raised in a Mars settlement, wants to become one of the elite who mine comets for ice to provide the arid planet with water and, eventually, air. Unfortunately, he has to go to Earth, where there is massive hostility to Martians, and stumbles into a key role in foiling a plot to use one of those comets to wipe out Japan, whose new orbiting farm habitats threaten the economy of the rest of Earth, which has invested heavily in the Mars project. Pohl handles his variation on an old theme well." Booklist

The space merchants; by Frederik Pohl and C. M. Kornbluth. Ballantine Bks. 1953 179p o.p.

"Control of the Venus economy and market is the sought-after plum of mega-advertising agencies. Mitchell Courtenay must persuade colonists to go there, but he is thwarted by the despised conservationists. Sabotage, warfare, and the degradation of the life of a consumer pervade this attack on modern consumer society." Shapiro. Fic for Youth. 3d edition

Pohl, Frederik, 1919——*Continued*

"Kornbluth later stated that he and Pohl packed into this story everything they hated about advertising, and it came out with Swiftian savagery. One of the first novels by writers with primary roots in the pulps to make an impact in mainstream circles." Anatomy of Wonder 4

Followed by The merchants' war

The world at the end of time. Ballantine Bks. 1990 393p o.p.

LC 89-18462

"A Del Rey book"

"As vast intelligences play deadly power games using stars for pawns, the fledgling colonists on the planet Home fight to maintain their existence while 'unknown forces' wreak havoc with the laws of physics and the universe. Pohl's sparkling wit attaches itself to macro- and microcosmic themes in a novel which pits a luckless human hero against a childlike being of inordinate power and extraordinary paranoia. Grand in scope, poignant in delivery." Libr J

Porlock, Martin *See* MacDonald, Philip, 1899-1981

Porter, Connie Rose

All-Bright Court; [by] Connie Porter. Houghton Mifflin 1991 224p o.p.

LC 91-8105

"All-Bright Court is a colorfully painted but crumbling housing project outside Buffalo, New York, and home to black families who migrated north in the 1950s. Porter's . . . episodic novel tells the tales of serveral All-Bright Court families over two decades. The major events of the times work their way into each household's routines, fears, and dreams, dramatizing the differences between races and generations." Am Libr

"Writing about a place its inhabitants dream of escaping would seem to be an exercise in despair, but All-Bright Court is a novel surprisingly filled with light. . . . The key to Porter's success is in her love of her characters, which shines through on every page." Women's Rev Books

Porter, Katherine Anne, 1890-1980

The collected stories of Katherine Anne Porter. Harcourt, Brace & World 1965 495p o.p.

Analyzed in Short story index

Contains three collections which are also entered separately: Flowering Judas, and other stories (1935); The leaning tower, and other stories (1944); Pale horse, pale rider (1939). Also included are four short stories which did not appear in the author's previous collections: Virgin Violeta; The martyr; The fig tree; and Holiday

Flowering Judas, and other stories. Harcourt Brace Jovanovich 1935 285p $15.95

ISBN 0-15-131811-5

"Harbrace modern classics"

Analyzed in Short story index

First published 1930. This edition adds four additional stories

Contents: María Concepción; Magic; Rope; He; Theft; That tree; The jilting of Granny Weatherall; Flowering Judas; The cracked looking-glass; Hacienda

also in Porter, K. A. The collected stories of Katherine Anne Porter p3-170

The leaning tower, and other stories. Harcourt Brace & Co. 1944 246p o.p.

Analyzed in Short story index

Contents: The source; The witness; The circus; The old order; The last leaf; The grave; The downward path to wisdom; A day's work; The leaning tower

also in Porter, K. A. The collected stories of Katherine Anne Porter p321-495

Noon wine

In Porter, K. A. The collected stories of Katherine Anne Porter p222-68

In Porter, K. A. Pale horse, pale rider: three short novels p93-176

Old mortality

In Porter, K. A. The collected stories of Katherine Anne Porter p173-221

In Porter, K. A. Pale horse, pale rider: three short novels p3-89

Pale horse, pale rider [novelette]

In Porter, K. A. The collected stories of Katherine Anne Porter p269-317

In Porter, K. A. Pale horse, pale rider: three short novels p179-264

Pale horse, pale rider: three short novels. Harcourt Brace Jovanovich 1985 c1939 264p $15.95

ISBN 0-15-170755-3   LC 85-17646

"Harbrace modern classics"

A reissue of the title first published 1939

Contents: Old mortality; Noon wine; Pale horse, pale rider

In the title story "Miranda, a young journalist, is caught in a personal dilemma. She must choose between a career and a commitment to Adam, a soldier on leave during World War I. Porter's simple tale becomes more complex as Miranda's anxieties and fears about war, death, and personal loss are revealed. She hovers close to death during the terrbile flu epidemic of 1918. Miranda survives and the war ends, but it brings her no happiness because the epidemic has claimed Adam as a victim." Shapiro. Fic for Youth. 3d edition

also in Porter, K. A. The collected stories of Katherine Anne Porter p173-317

Ship of fools. Little, Brown 1962 497p o.p. Amereon reprint available $29.50 (ISBN 0-8488-1129-1)

"An Atlantic Monthly Press book"

"A satire in which the world is likened to a ship whose passengers, fools and deranged people all, are sailing toward eternity. Porter's novel is set in 1931 aboard a German passenger ship returning to Bremerhaven, Germany, from Veracruz, Mexico. The ship carries a microcosm of peoples, including Germans, Ameri-

Porter, Katherine Anne, 1890-1980 — *Continued*

cans, Spaniards, Gypsies, and Mexicans, Jews, anti-Semites, political reactionaries, revolutionaries, and neutrals coexist aboard ship, at the same time that jealousy, cruelty and duplicity pervade their lives."
Merriam-Webster's Ency of Lit

Porter, William Sydney *See* Henry, O., 1862-1910

Portis, Charles

Gringos; a novel. Simon & Schuster 1991 269p o.p.

LC 90-42476

This novel "features Jimmy Burns, an idler from Louisiana transplanted to Mexico, where he ekes out a living finding missing persons and doing odd jobs. Equally odd are the other motley expatriates. Ninety-pound Louise Kurle, who's writing a book about benign space dwarfs, suspects her missing husband, Rudy, was abducted by UFOs. Big Dan, a paunchy ex-con guru/white supremacist/kidnapper, poses to his band of deranged hippies as El Mago, the wizard whom the Mayas predict will appear at the end of time. Murder, adventure and Indian lure animate a Mexico aswarm with New Age mystics, kooks, skinheads, graduate students, maverick archeologists and looters of shrines." Publ Wkly

"'Gringos,' by far, is Portis's most inward-turning book, a story of a grownup trying to grow up, to keep it together with some dignity. Watching him pull it off is one of the finest pleasures afforded by any novel in a long time." Newsweek

True grit; a novel. Simon & Schuster 1968 215p o.p.

"Mattie Ross, a fourteen-year-old living in Yell County, Arkansas, is determined to get justice when her father is killed by a hired hand. She is joined in her quest by Rooster Cogburn, a U.S. marshal, and by a Texas Ranger. This strange trio faces a series of perilous encounters requiring true grit to confront them." Shapiro. Fic for Youth. 3d edition

Potok, Chaim, 1929-

The book of lights. Knopf 1981 369p $19.95

ISBN 0-394-52031-9   LC 81-47505

A novel about "two rabbinical seminarians who seek self-understanding in the army chaplaincy in postwar Korea. Gershon Loran, devoutly Orthodox product of a decaying Brooklyn neighborhood, is an emotional drifter who prefers study to action and frequently has visions (or perhaps hallucinations). His roommate, Arthur Leiden, is an upper-crust Harvard graduate condemned to perpetual atonement for his father's involvement with the invention of the atomic bomb. Only Arthur's accidental death finally moves Gershon to take decisive actions to direct his future." Libr J

"Potok knows that personal illuminations, like those of physics, are transitory. . . . They must be discovered again and again generation after generation. Ironically, it is that sense of impermanence that grants the novel its sense of durability." Time

The chosen; a novel; with a foreword by the author. 25th anniversary ed. Knopf 1992 c1967 295p $30

ISBN 0-679-40222-5   LC 91-58551

A reissue of the title first published 1967 by Simon & Schuster

"Living only five blocks apart in the Williamsburg section of Brooklyn, New York, Danny and Reuven meet as opponents in a softball game. Out of this encounter evolves a strong bond of friendship between a brilliant Hasidic Jew and a scholar who is Orthodox in his religious thinking. During the course of their relationship Reuven becomes the means by which Danny's father, a rabbi, can communicate with his son, who has been reared under a code of silence." Shapiro. Fic for Youth. 2d edition

Followed by The promise

Davita's harp. Knopf 1985 371p $16.95

ISBN 0-394-54290-8   LC 84-48526

In this novel, a "child of mixed marriage and of parents committed to the Communist cause, [Ilana Davita Chandal] seeks her own truth (much to her parents' chagrin) in both the local synagogue and her aunt's Christian mission. After her father, a journalist, is killed in Guernica while covering the Spanish Civil War, the world she has come to know is turned upside down. Her mother remarries and turns to Orthodoxy, and Ilana enrolls in a yeshiva where she earns the highest honors, only to be deprived of them because she is a girl." Libr J

The people the author "depicts live in a community held together by ancient laws. Those people nourish each other in the worst of times. In doing so, they nourish Mr. Potok's readers too." N Y Times Book Rev

The gift of Asher Lev. Knopf 1990 369p $19.95

ISBN 0-394-57212-2   LC 89-43401

Sequel to My name is Asher Lev

"Following the death of his beloved uncle, Asher, who is now middle-aged and settled in France, finds he must return with his family to the Brooklyn Hasidic Jewish community from which he has been exiled 20 years. Greeted there with suspicion and anger by many who still insist that his art is anathema to Hasidim—a sentiment that continues to haunt his relationship with his father, a tireless, well-respected ambassador for the religious community's Rebbe—Asher finds himself struggling once again to balance art and faith, this time in a difficult emotional coming-to-terms that involves the future of his five-year-old son, Avrumel." Booklist

I am the clay. Knopf 1992 211p $20

ISBN 0-679-41195-X   LC 91-58550

This novel follows "the agonizing trek of an old Korean peasant couple as they leave their village in flight from the Chinese and 'the fiends from the North' during the Korean conflict. In a drainage ditch on the side of the road, they find a seriously wounded boy. Although the old man tells his wife, 'I have no wish for this child,' she will not abandon the youngster. Slowly, as they nurse him back to health, he is able to return the favor: protecting them from a pack of wild dogs, finding fish to eat, acquiring an ox. A deep believer in spirits and the good or bad fortune they bequeath according to whim, the old man gradually comes to accept this boy who has been so lucky for them. . . . This deeply

Potok, Chaim, 1929-—*Continued*
felt book leaves no doubt that even in the blighted landscape of war there is always room for luck, and love."
Publ Wkly

In the beginning. Knopf 1975 454p o.p.

The novel, set in the Bronx, New York, concerns a
gifted Jewish boy who becomes a Biblical scholar. "From
shortly after birth, in the nineteen-twenties, David Lurie
is plagued by chronic sinus illnesses that prove to be
emblematic of his growing up. He is bullied by bigger
boys, haunted by the 'accidents' that he brings upon
others, safe only within his pious home. David's inner
life, tortured with fears and bad dreams is followed
through the Depression, which nearly ruins his family;
through the late thirties and forties, as the news from
Europe grows more and more dreadful; and into his
budding years as a scholar." New Yorker

This novel "as its title suggests, is a recapitulation of
the book of Genesis from the Creation to the Flood.
. . . The style is occasionally awkward, particularly when
sentences are inverted to suggest a Yiddish accent. . .
. But the book's structure is a technical accomplishment."
N Y Times Book Rev

My name is Asher Lev. Knopf 1972 369p $25

ISBN 0-394-46137-1

"Young Asher Lev is an obedient son of strict Jewish
parents. When his artistic endeavors are discovered, he
is sent to a religious leader for consultation because artists are not viewed favorably by the Hasidim. Asher's
struggle for fulfillment and his ultimate rejection by his
parents are poignantly drawn." Shapiro. Fic for Youth.
3d edition

Followed by The gift of Asher Lev

The promise. Knopf 1969 358p o.p.

Sequel to The chosen

"Reuven Malter and Danny Saunders, two Jewish
friends living in Brooklyn, choose to alter the destinies
chosen for them by their fathers. Reuven, studying to
be a rabbi, finds his vocation blocked by a challenge
to his scholarship and his father's book. Danny, who
is studying clinical psychology, risks his career by a decision, based on intuition, that he feels can save a young
boy's sanity." Shapiro. Fic for Youth. 3d edition

Pournelle, Jerry, 1933-
(jt. auth) Niven, L. Lucifer's hammer
(jt. auth) Niven, L. The Mote in God's
Eye

Powell, Anthony, 1905-
The acceptance world
> *In* Powell, A. A dance to the music of
> time [v1]

At Lady Molly's
> *In* Powell, A. A dance to the music of
> time [v1]

Books do furnish a room
> *In* Powell, A. A dance to the music of
> time [v4]

A buyer's market
> *In* Powell, A. A dance to the music of
> time [v1]

Casanova's Chinese restaurant
> *In* Powell, A. A dance to the music of
> time [v2]

A dance to the music of time. University of Chicago Press 1995 12v in 4 pa set $72.80

ISBN 0-226-67719-2   LC 94-47228

The four volumes are also available separately

An omnibus reissue of the twelve titles comprising The
Music of time series, which were originally published
separately

Contents: [v1] First movement: A question of upbringing (1951); A buyer's market (1952); The acceptance
world (1955)

[v2] Second movement: At Lady Molly's (1957);
Casanova's Chinese restaurant (1960); The kindly ones
(1962)

[v3] Third movement: The valley of bones (1964); The
soldier's art (1966); The military philosophers (1968)

[v4] Fourth movement: Books do furnish a room
(1971); Temporary kings (1973); Hearing secret harmonies
(1975)

"The novels, spanning a period of over fifty years,
from the early 1920s, describe the school days, youth,
and maturity of the narrator-hero, Nicholas Jenkins, and
his upper-class cohorts, especially the egregious Widmer-
pool. Though primarily satiric in tone, they express an
underlying melancholy about life and time reminiscent
of Marcel Proust." Reader's Ency. 3d edition

Hearing secret harmonies
> *In* Powell, A. A dance to the music of
> time [v4]

The kindly ones
> *In* Powell, A. A dance to the music of
> time [v2]

The military philosophers
> *In* Powell, A. A dance to the music of
> time [v3]

A question of upbringing
> *In* Powell, A. A dance to the music of
> time [v1]

The soldier's art
> *In* Powell, A. A dance to the music of
> time [v3]

Temporary kings
> *In* Powell, A. A dance to the music of
> time [v4]

The valley of bones
> *In* Powell, A. A dance to the music of
> time [v3]

Power, Susan, 1961-
The grass dancer. Putnam 1994 300p $22.95

ISBN 0-399-13911-7   LC 93-47199

Power, Susan, 1961-—*Continued*

"Set on a North Dakota reservation, 'The Grass Dancer' tells the story of Harley Wind Soldier, a young Sioux trying to understand his place among people whose intertwined lives and shared heritage move backward in time in the narrative from the 1980's to the middle of the last century." N Y Times Book Rev

"Power weaves historical events—the Apollo Moon landing; the 19th-century Great Plains drought—into her narrative, reinforcing the seamless coexistence of the real and spirit realm. A consummate storyteller whose graceful prose is plangent with lyrical metaphor and sensuous detail, she deftly uses suspense, humor, irony and the gradual revelation of dramatic disclosures to compose a tapestry of human life." Publ Wkly

Powers, J. F. (James Farl), 1917-

Morte d'Urban. Doubleday 1962 336p o.p.

"Father Urban, member of a Catholic order that is financially impoverished, spends his time in two worlds, the religious and the secular. He must try to gain friends and funds for the Clementine order and yet make decisions that may cost him the friendship of his wealthy benefactors, among them eccentric and willful Billy Cosgrove and Mrs. Thwaites. The wide cast of characters within the church and the world outside makes for both a sad and amusing portrait." Shapiro. Fic for Youth. 3d edition

Wheat that springeth green. Knopf 1988 335p $18.95

ISBN 0-394-49609-4   LC 87-46104

This novel "illuminates the world of the Catholic parish. Set in the turbulent months of the late 1960s, it gently and satirically probes the inner mysteries of a younger and perhaps wiser Catholic Church. Its focus is Father Joe Hackett, a tenacious rebel of the faith in his mid-40s who has tested himself on women and drink in his youth and now seems on the verge of religious suicide." Libr J

"The beauty of Mr. Powers's writing lies in its art's being almost invisible. The craft and balance of the novel's literary achievement are discernible in every sentence, but only on second thought, so thoroughly has the author subordinated form to function." N Y Times Book Rev

Powers, James Farl *See* Powers, J. F. (James Farl), 1917-

Powers, John R.

Do black patent-leather shoes really reflect up?; a fictionalized memoir. Regnery Bks. 1975 227p o.p.

Sequel to The last Catholic in America

"In this free-wheeling fictionalized memoir . . . [the author] is as funny as a good stand-up comedian. His out-landish description of his four years at St. Patrick Bremmer High may sometimes leave the reader punch-line drunk. . . . He remembers a not-too-bright teacher, who played 'straight man to 40 comedians,' and Brother Sofeck, whose suggestion to burn oneself with a match when temptation was too great demonstrated 'that the tactics of the Mafia and the Catholic Church were so alike.' Black patent shoes, Catholic girls were warned, enabled boys to see up their dresses." Publ Wkly

The junk-drawer corner-store front-porch blues. Dutton 1992 209p $19

ISBN 0-525-93405-7   LC 91-26025

"The story follows comedy writer Donald Cooper as he returns to his family home and confronts the grief he has carried for 20 years. Cooper's memories of growing up in a Chicago neighborhood, Saturday baseball, evenings on the porch, and unfinished lives are counterpoised with the complexities of his present relationships." Libr J

"Powers exalts in descriptions of Chicago's cozy neighborhoods and their loving, straight-ahead inhabitants, giving us a wise and vibrantly funny affirmation of the absurdities and wonders of life." Booklist

The last Catholic in America; a fictionalized memoir. Saturday Review Press 1973 228p o.p. Bentley reprint available $18 (ISBN 0-8376-0439-7)

"Eddie Ryan, salesman, pauses during a business trip to visit the haunts of a South Side Chicago neighborhood where, in the 1950's, he spent his youth. The scene triggers . . . memories of his Catholic upbringing in St. Bastion's parish, where sin was clearly defined, and punishment and reward handily dispensed." Libr J

"Bittersweet variations on the familiar U.S. literary theme of growing up Catholic . . . strike funny, trite, sometimes overlong, and inevitably sensitive chords. The nostalgic entertainment, occasionally bordering on the mawkish, rings true with seriocomic overtones and honest dialog." Booklist

Followed by Do black patent-leather shoes really reflect up?

Poyer, David

The circle. St. Martin's Press 1992 432p o.p.

LC 92-2980

The author "gives us an ensign fresh out of Annapolis, assigned to a destroyer in the North Atlantic. His ship is an obsolete bucket of plates and bolts held together by mucilage. The ship is undermanned and has a resentful crew. The executive officer is a sadistic right-wing bully. Ship and crew battle furious storms. They are ordered to join the North Atlantic fleet for exercises, and something terrible occurs that results in a court-martial. The young ensign undergoes a trial by fire." NY Times Book Rev

"The individual events convincingly present the gritty details of life aboard a pre-computer-age destroyer, and Poyer provides a compelling sense of the Cold War Navy's operational dynamics." Publ Wkly

The gulf. St. Martin's Press 1990 xx, 442p o.p.

LC 90-36140

"Dan Lenson, is the executive officer on a frigate in the Persian Gulf, assigned to convoy a succession of oil tankers through perilous waters. Lenson's shipmates include hard-living helicopter pilots, minor crooks, and idealistic young officers. Not far away, a group of divers, naval reservists, must battle the hostility of 'real' sailors as they undertake a dangerous mission of their own. Lenson's physical and mental courage are sorely tried in the climactic scenes, where he battles enemies and the ocean itself." Libr J

Poyer, David—*Continued*

"As in so many Big Books, we learn more than we want to know about the heroes' emotional hang-ups and other problems. It so happens, however, that Mr. Poyer has a more delicate touch in these matters than most of his colleagues. . . . 'The Gulf' is, on the whole, a neat and well-constructed piece of work." N Y Times Book Rev

Price, Eugenia

Beauty from ashes. Doubleday 1995 627p $23.50

ISBN 0-385-26703-7   LC 94-38912

This concluding volume of the Georgia trilogy focuses on "the life of Anne Couper Fraser six years after the death of her beloved husband, John. In this time, she has lost two daughters and her mother, and she still misses John unbearably. As she struggles to rebuild her family, the South is falling apart around her as war looms on the horizon. Her only son and grandson fight for the Confederacy even as Anne and her daughter Pete support the Union. . . . Price's meticulous research, evident throughout the book, pays off in the recreation of the lives of families on St. Simon's Island, Georgia." Booklist

Before the darkness falls. Doubleday 1987 455p $17.95

ISBN 0-385-23068-0   LC 87-556

The third volume in the author's Savannah quartet

This novel "takes place in turbulent antebellum Georgia. The story revolves around the continuing hardships and joys of the McKay, Browning, and Stiles families—real people from Georgia's past. And they *seem* very real, with richly defined characters: Natalie Browning Burke, the young Savannah society belle who chooses life and love on the rough Georgia frontier; W. H. Stiles, agonizing between the political career he craves and the wife and family he adores; and Eliza McKay, wise matriarch of all three families on whom everyone depends." Libr J

Followed by Stranger in Savannah

The beloved invader. Lippincott 1965 284p o.p.

Available Thorndike Press large print edition

First published volume of a trilogy about St. Simons Island, Georgia. Chronologically follows Lighthouse and New moon rising

"A fictionalized account of the life's work of Anson Dodge, an actual person, in rebuilding a St Simons Island church that had been vandalized during the Civil War. The narrative begins with young Dodge, a Northerner, coming to the Georgia island to help look after his wealthy family's business and his discovery of the neglected church that aroused his compassion." Booklist

Bright captivity. Doubleday 1991 631p $20

ISBN 0-385-26701-0   LC 90-21819

Also available large print edition $25 (ISBN 0-385-41823-X)

This first volume of the Georgia trilogy is set on St. Simons Island "where Anne Couper, daughter in a notable island family, finds love with British lieutenant John Fraser early in the nineteenth century. The melodramatic action takes place on both sides of the Atlantic. With writing shorn of metaphor and symbol, with every bit of psychology aired like laundry rather

than left to implication, Price's novel is diversion at its sublimest." Booklist

Followed by Where shadows go

Lighthouse. Lippincott 1971 342p o.p.

Available Thorndike Press large print edition

The final volume, but chronologically the earliest, in a trilogy about St. Simons Island, Georgia

Restless James Gould leaves his Massachusetts home in 1791 and eventually ends up in Boston where he encounters Captain James Budge who owns a lumber company in Bangor and offers him a job. James has his first opportunity as a builder erecting a new house for Mrs. Budge. He falls in love with Jesse Davidson, loses her to his brother, and moves on after completing a house for his family. A job, surveying timber needed by the new American navy brings him to St. Simons Island, Georgia, where he is befriended by a plantation owner. Later he leases land in the wild Georgia Indian Country and after falling in love and marrying during a business trip to Savannah, lives a dangerous life there with his wife, children and slaves until an Indian attack forces them to flee. He learns that a builder is being sought to erect a lighthouse on St. Simons Island and returns there to realize an old dream

Margaret's story; a novel. Lippincott 1980 394p o.p.

LC 80-7870

Available Thorndike Press large print edition

This concluding volume of the author's Florida trilogy begun with Don Juan McQueen (1974) and Maria (1977) "focuses on the life of Margaret Seton Fleming whose island home was the plantation Hibernia, on the St. Johns River in northern Florida. Margaret raised a large family there and turned the 'Fleming place' into a favored stop for travelers on the St. Johns. The Civil War ravaged her family—sons fought on both sides—and virtually destroyed the big house but not the indomitable spirit of the widow, who restored it and built a small chapel where hers was the first burial, in 1878. The rich history of the Florida-Georgia coastline in the 19th century is personalized in this story of one founding family." Publ Wkly

New moon rising. Lippincott 1969 281p o.p.

Available Thorndike Press large print edition

The second volume in a trilogy about St. Simons Island, Georgia. Set chronologically prior to events in The beloved invader

"The central character is Horace Bunch Gould. His story starts, amusingly enough, when he is dismissed from Yale in [1830] for his part in a student rebellion. He returns to St. Simon's during the uneasy days of Nat Turner's uprising. Before Horace eventually goes off to war, he works the family plantation, marries, produces nine children, and develops a troubled conscience about slavery." Publ Wkly

Savannah. Doubleday 1983 595p $19.95

ISBN 0-385-15274-4   LC 82-45572

The first volume in the author's Savannah quartet

This "novel tells the story of a handsome young Yankee, Mark Browning, who finds a secure place for himself in the gracious society of Savannah, Georgia, in the early 19th century. Browning, befriended by a merchant named Robert Mackay, is taken into the man's mercantile firm, and soon finds himself in love with Mackay's virtuous wife. The situation is further complicated by Mark's growing attraction to his first cousin,

Price, Eugenia—*Continued*

Caroline Cameron, and his relationship with a blackguard uncle, Osmund Kott, who may or may not be on the edge of true repentance and conversion to Christianity." Publ Wkly

Followed by To see your face again

Stranger in Savannah. Doubleday 1989 755p $19.95

ISBN 0-385-23069-9   LC 88-33546

The final volume in the author's Savannah quartet chronicles the "lives of the members of the Brownings, the Mackays, and the Stileses, three prominent nineteenth-century families. Price tells their story against the backdrop of the Civil War era. The novel opens in 1854 as the first rumblings of secession can be heard throughout the South, tensions heighten, conflict becomes inevitable, and political and historical events come between friends and relatives." Booklist

The author "gives her characters a well-documented historical background. In addition to her fictional characters, she has 'borrowed' actual residents of the city to populate her book. . . . It isn't necessary to read the first three parts of the Savannah Quartet to enjoy and understand this one; but together they compose a uniquely American family drama." N Y Times Book Rev

To see your face again; a novel. Doubleday 1985 546p $21.95

ISBN 0-385-15275-2   LC 85-4434

The second volume in the author's Savannah quartet This novel "focuses on coquettish, headstrong Natalie Browning. In 1838, 16-year-old Natalie is aboard the steam packet 'Pulaski' when it explodes, killing many passengers including Natalie's great-uncle and her companion Virginia Mackay. Natalie and charismatic Burke Latimer survive five grueling days in the water, and adversity fosters their romance." Publ Wkly

"Price has a whole new cast of characters to populate her atmospheric re-creation of the antebellum South. Fortunately, the author also preserves her villain, the sinister Osmund Kott, to add a healthy dose of evil and to confound romantic liaisons that would otherwise run too smoothly." Booklist

Followed by Before the darkness falls

Where shadows go. Doubleday 1993 646p $22.50

ISBN 0-385-26702-9   LC 92-38400

Also available large print edition $26 (ISBN 0-385-42313-6)

"The second book in the Georgia Trilogy that began with *Bright Captivity* follows the nearly charmed life of John and Anne Couper Fraser from 1825, when the couple leaves London to return to Anne's (and Price's) home on Georgia's St. Simons Island, to 1839. Surrounded by the natural beauty of the family's coastal plantation, John overcomes his abhorrence of slavery to become a respected planter. He and Anne adore each other, raise their children and ponder the problems that seem to plague everyone but them. Late in the tale, friendship with the English actress/abolitionist Fanny Kemble Butler causes Anne to consider for the first time the moral implications of her lifestyle." Publ Wkly

Followed by Beauty from ashes

Price, Nancy, 1925-

Night woman. Pocket Bks. 1992 314p o.p.

LC 92-50164

Available Thorndike Press large print edition

"Mary Eliot leads a puzzling double life: her interior world of great creativity and strength somehow survives the constant abuse of her exterior existence. Her husband is insane, a professor of literature who poses as the family breadwinner and successful novelist while Mary is, in fact, the actual author. When he dies, she feels gloriously free until she finds herself overwhelmed by a second possessive and abusive male with murderous intent." Booklist

"Gritty, wry characterization, chilling images of insanity, and a long, ultimately satisfying tease which ends with Mary at last getting her due will keep readers flipping pages." Publ Wkly

Sleeping with the enemy. Simon & Schuster 1987 c1986 332p o.p.

LC 86-29778

"Battered women don't usually have the courage of Sara Burney. Desperate and bruised physically and emotionally, she evolves a plan to flee her obsessive husband. She knows he will come after her and kill her eventually, so that mere flight will offer only temporary reprieve. So she decides to 'get lost.' She assumes a new identity, a new look, and seeks respite and a new life hundreds of miles from their home in Massachusetts. . . . Price has written an absorbing tale and her language has a sensual quality that transports the reader into her panoramas that affect all the senses." West Coast Rev Books

Price, Reynolds, 1933-

Blue Calhoun. Atheneum Pubs. 1992 373p $23

ISBN 0-689-12146-6   LC 91-22877

This novel depicts circumstances in the life of "Blue (short for Bluford) Calhoun, a 65-year-old salesman in a music store in Raleigh. . . . The tale that Blue has to tell takes the form of a lengthy epistle addressed to his teen-age granddaughter, who blames him for failing to prevent the suicide of her father. In his attempt to win her understanding and 'mercy,' Blue ranges over the main events in his life since 1956, the year when, at the age of 35, he falls in love with a 16-year-old girl named Luna Absher." N Y Times Book Rev

"Price is in top form here, forcing us to wrestle with Blue even as he wrestles with himself, portraying his anguish in painfully clear, clean prose that captures perfectly the rhythms of the South and of the human heart." Libr J

The collected stories. Atheneum Pubs. 1993 625p $25

ISBN 0-689-12147-4   LC 92-36807

Analyzed in Short story index

Contents: Full day; The Warrior Princess Ozimba; The enormous door; A told secret; Watching her die; Serious need; The company of the dead; A sign of blood; Rapid eye movements; Twice; Washed feet; Sleeping and waking; Morning places; Michael Egerton; The last news; The anniversary; Invitation; My parents, winter 1926; The knowledge of my mother's coming death; Life for life; Design for a tomb; Endless mountains; Long night; A new stretch of woods; The last of a long correspondence; Deeds of light; Walking lessons; His final mother;

Price, Reynolds, 1933- — *Continued*

This wait; The happiness of others; A dog's death; Scars; Waiting at Dachau; The golden child; Truth and lies; Breath; Toward home; The names and faces of heroes; Nine hours alone; Night and silence; Summer games; A chain of love; Two useful visits; A final account; Uncle Grant; Troubled sleep; Good night; An evening meal; Bess Waters; An early Christmas

"Many of the characters in these magical, quietly revelatory, death-obsessed tales are transformed by chance encounters, in settings that include Price's native south but also range throughout the world." Publ Wkly

The foreseeable future. Atheneum Pubs. 1991 253p $21.95

ISBN 0-689-12110-5　　　　　LC 90-45463

Analyzed in Short story index

Contents: The fare to the moon; The foreseeable future; Back before day

"In his eloquent and distinctive voice, Price reveals in each of these stories how love and memory, loss and redemption, and essential human goodness 'prop' us up and allow us to move forward into an uncertain future." Libr J

Kate Vaiden. Atheneum Pubs. 1986 306p o.p.

　　　　　　　　　　　　　LC 85-48143

In this novel, Kate Vaiden tells her own story "to justify herself to a son she abandoned as a baby and hasn't seen in 40 years. The decisive event in Kate's life occurred in 1938, when she was 11. Her father inexplicably murdered her mother and killed himself, leaving a letter that Kate doesn't read until many years later. . . . [Kate] is lovingly raised by a taciturn aunt and uncle with a secret sorrow she gradually learns: their homosexual son, Walter, ran off 12 years earlier with another local boy. When Walter comes home on a visit, he befriends Kate, who later runs off to live with him and has a child by his lover." Newsweek

"Mr. Price's successful creation of a female voice may be a tour de force, but it never feels like a showy ventriloquial act. Instead, Kate is a wholly convincing girl and a not improbable woman." N Y Times Book Rev

The promise of rest. Scribner 1995 353p $24

ISBN 0-684-80149-3　　　　　LC 94-48086

In the conclusion of the author's Mayfield family trilogy "Wade Mayfield, great-grandson of the woman whose runaway marriage in 1903 set the family's tragic 20th-century history in motion, is dying of AIDS. Long estranged from his parents (his black lover, Wyatt Bondurant, hated them as complicit beneficiaries of the South's racist past), Wade comes home to North Carolina in April 1993, after Wyatt's death. His mother, Ann, has left his father, Hutchins, claiming that her husband has shut her out of his life for years. Meanwhile, Hutchins's lifelong friend and onetime lover, Strawson Stuart, makes his own reproaches about Hutchins's inability to fully accept love. Extended family and friends gather around the dying Wade, grappling with matters as general as America's poisoned racial heritage and as intimate as the Mayfield legacy." Publ Wkly

The source of light. Atheneum Pubs. 1981 318p o.p.

　　　　　　　　　　　　　LC 80-69650

This second volume in a trilogy begun with The surface of earth (1975) "focuses on a Southern family in 1955 and 1956. There is a core of melodrama: Rob Mayfield, dying of lung cancer, allows his son Hutchins to go off to Oxford to study without knowing of his father's malady. The centers of action are the two men's emotional and sexual lives, and there are moving portraits of the women who haplessly love both men." Libr J

"An absorbing novel surprising in plot, rich in character and meaning and in the resonance of memory. The story, which details the difficulties and the joys humans encounter as they seek to find themselves in one another and in their work, shows too, how decisions are colored by pulls of place and family and the way things were or might have been." Publ Wkly

Followed by The promise of rest

The tongues of angels. Atheneum Pubs. 1990 192p $17.95

ISBN 0-689-12093-1　　　　　LC 89-37427

Also available Thorndike Press large print edition

This novel focuses on "Bridge Boatner, a famous painter who looks back at the summer of 1954, when he was a counselor at a camp in North Carolina; and Raphael Noren, a prematurely wise, otherworldly 14-year-old who was a camper there that summer. . . . [The two] had come to the camp to find a way to cope with the sudden death of a parent. . . . Boatner finds himself as an artist that summer, producing a painting that stands the test of time." Time

"As much prey to mutual irritation as to esteem, they worry and argue their way—the 14-year-old boy and the 21-year-old man—through the 10-week intimacy of the camp, cut of from so-called civilization and therefore free, in terms they hold in common, to aim beyond the commonplace: into myth, art, ritual and pain." N Y Times Book Rev

Price, Richard, 1949-

Clockers. Houghton Mifflin 1992 599p $22.95

ISBN 0-395-53761-4　　　　　LC 91-43318

The author "divides his narrative between two main characters: Strike (a k a Ronald Dunham), the black crew leader of a small-time group of cocaine dealers—the 'clockers' of the title—in the slums of northern New Jersey, and Rocco Klein, an experienced but disillusioned white homicide detective who's about to take early retirement. The stories of Rocco and Strike are pulled together when Strike's by-all-accounts paragon brother, Victor, confesses to an apparently routine drug murder and Rocco, refusing to believe Victor guilty, becomes convinced that he's taking the heat for his brother." N Y Times Book Rev

This is "an incredible course in urban street life, particularly the crack culture." Booklist

The wanderers; a novel. Houghton Mifflin 1974 239p o.p.

"Set in the Bronx in the early 1960s, this novel looks at the brutalized lives of some Italian-American teenagers. The small gang of Wanderers are lambs compared to the Fordham Baldies, the diminutive Irish Ducky Boys armed with razors and car aerials, and the many black gangs." Publ Wkly

Price, Richard, 1949- —*Continued*

This "is an outstanding work of art because Price never imposes himself on the reader. His dialogue is musically true and emotionally correct." N Y Times Book Rev

Priestley, J. B. (John Boynton), 1894-1984
The good companions. Harper 1929 640p o.p.

"Three people set forth to solitary high adventure; Oakroyd, a Yorkshire factory hand with a nagging wife; the gentle lady of a Cotswold manor, with a small legacy in hand and thirty-seven monotonous years behind her, and Inigo Jollifant, a Cambridge man with a distaste for teaching small boys and a talent for airy improvisation on the piano. These amateur vagabonds unite in taking over a traveling dramatic company which has gone on the rocks." Cleveland Public Libr

This is "a robust and diverting tale, told in meandering fashion, lit by rich humor and warm sentiment and centered about a group of perennially engaging characters." Outlook

Priestley, John Boynton *See* Priestley, J. B. (John Boynton), 1894-1984

Prince Charming
See also Thomas, Rosanne Daryl

Pritchett, V. S. (Victor Sawdon), 1900-
Complete collected stories. Random House 1991 c1990 1219p o.p.

LC 90-47478

Analyzed in Short story index
First published 1990 in the United Kingdom
Contents: Sense of humour; A spring morning; Main road; The evils of Spain; Handsome is as handsome does; The aristocrat; The two brothers; X-ray; The scapegoat; Eleven o'clock; The upright man; Page and monarch; Miss Baker; You make your own life; The sailor; The lion's den; The saint; It may never happen; Pocock passes; The Oedipus complex; The voice; Aunt Gertrude; Many are disappointed; The chestnut tree; The ape; The clerk's tale; The fly in the ointment; The night worker; Double divan; The landlord; Passing the ball; A story of Don Juan; The ladder; The satisfactory; Things as they are; The sniff; The collection; The wheelbarrow; The fall; When my girl comes home; The necklace; Just a little more; The snag; On the scent; Citizen; The key to my heart; Noisy flushes the birds; Noisy in the doghouse; Blind love; The nest builder; A debt of honour; The cage birds; The skeleton; The speech; The liars; Our oldest friend; The honeymoon; The chainsmoker; The last throw; The Camberwell beauty; The diver; Did you invite me?; The rescue; The marvellous girl; The spree; Our wife; The lady from Guatemala; On the edge of the cliff; A family man; The Spanish bed; The wedding; The worshippers; The vice-consul; The accompanist; Tea with Mrs. Bittell; The fig tree; A careless widow; Cocky Olly; A trip to the seaside; Things; A change of policy; The image trade

(comp) The Oxford book of short stories. See The Oxford book of short stories

Pritchett, Victor Sawdon *See* Pritchett, V. S. (Victor Sawdon), 1900-

Prize stories, 1919-1995: The O. Henry awards. Doubleday 1920-1995 75v 1919-1994 o.p.; 1995 $25

ISSN 0079-5453

Analyzed in Short story index
Editors: 1919-1932, Blanche C. Williams; 1933-1940, Harry Hansen; 1941-1951, Herschel Brickell; 1954-1956, Paul Engle and Hansford Martin; 1957, Paul Engle assisted by Constance Urdang; 1958, Paul Engle assisted by Curt Harnack; 1959, Paul Engle assisted by Curt Harnack and Constance Urdang; 1961-1964, Richard Poirier; 1965-1966, Richard Poirier and William Abrahams; 1967-1995, William Abrahams
Volumes for 1919-1946 published under title: O. Henry Memorial Award prize stories
No volumes issued for 1952-1953
Contents 1995: The women come and go, by C. Nixon; Talking to Charlie, by J. J. Clayton; Shot: a New York story, by E. Hardwick; Trick or treat, by P. Powell; The haunted beach, by A. Adams; Cantor Pepper, by E. Krieger; Departing, by P. Cameron; Sarah, by A. Goodman; The stucco house, by E. Gilchrist; You petted me, and I followed you home, by J. C. Oates; Settled on the cranberry coast, by M. Byers; The intruder, by D. Gates; Across the lake, by D. Eisenberg; Truth serum, by B. Cooper; The drowning, by E. J. Delaney; Loving Wanda Beaver, by A. Baker; The black room, by J. Updike; Star box, by A. W. Pierce; Kiss away, by C. Baxter; If this letter were a beaded object, by R. Bradford; City sidewalks, by P. Klass

Pronzini, Bill
Bones. St. Martin's Press 1985 196p o.p.

LC 85-1708

"The 'Nameless Detective' is hired by Michael Kiskadon to find out why his father, pulp writer Harmon Crane, committed suicide 35 years ago. This proves to be a locked room puzzle. The twisting plot eventually turns up three murders. This is a crisply written mystery with perfect pacing; new clues are cunningly placed so that reader interest is constantly piqued." Libr J

Deadfall. St. Martin's Press 1986 212p o.p.

LC 86-3669

In this 'Nameless Detective' novel, the "San Francisco private eye is on a stakeout on a quiet residential street, waiting to repossess a deadbeat's car. He hears a gunshot coming from one of the houses on the street, goes in, and finds a mortally wounded man crawling from room to room. Lawyer Leonard Purcell's dying word is 'deadfall.' Does his death have any connection with the death of his wheeler-dealer brother six months before? No one is better at finding links between tricky homicides than 'Nameless,' and no one is more poetic in relating the details of a case: his crisp language renders a bloodspattered room almost beautiful." Booklist

Quarry; a "Nameless Detective" mystery. Delacorte Press 1992 216p o.p.

LC 91-15284

Pronzini, Bill—*Continued*

In this novel the "Nameless Detective hunts for a methodical, brutal stranger who is pursuing withdrawn Grady Haas, 31, daughter of rancher Arlo Haas, the detective's old friend. Secretive Grady won't tell why she has suddenly left her job as an insurance adjuster specializing in marine claims and returned to the Salinas Valley. Nameless finds that her San Francisco apartment has been thoroughly tossed. All he has to go on are the three claims Grady had been investigating and her ex-boyfriend's savage beating by a stranger seeking Grady's whereabouts." Publ Wkly

"Pronzini can get a shade overwrought . . . but his detective is a welcome journey into yesterday, where a shamus could bend the law and not have to agonize about it for too long afterwards." Booklist

(jt. auth) Muller, M. Beyond the grave

Prose, Francine, 1947-

Bigfoot dreams. Pantheon Bks. 1986 280p o.p.

LC 85-43454

"About to be fired from her job as a writer for a sleazy tabloid, Vera can't stop thinking of her life in terms of the outrageous headlines and invented stories that have been her stock-in-trade. Her moods swing from finding something reassuring and hopeful in bizarre tales of benign Bigfoots and 91-year-old first-time mothers to morbid depression when one of her invented stories uncannily appears to be true. As Vera reviews her roles as mother, daughter, writer, lover, wife, and friend, she finally emerges as an individual with too much common sense to believe in what she writes or to accept the tabloid's air of futility in her own life. Reflective yet amusing fiction." Booklist

Household saints. St. Martin's Press 1981 227p o.p.

LC 80-29116

"When Joseph Santangelo, the sausagemaker, wins the bride, Catherine, in a pinochle game, he sets in motion a pattern of events laced with ancient Mediterranean customs, superstition and religion that affect the women in his life. In addition to Catherine, there is his mother, a nonstop oracle of doom, and his Americanized daughter who seeks and perhaps finds Jesus in obsessive domesticity. A skillful fabulist, [the author] . . . not only captures the domestic scenes and smells of Little Italy but allows her 'naifs' to unfold in recognizable earthiness and warmth as they confront life's mysteries." Publ Wkly

Hungry hearts. Pantheon Bks. 1983 213p o.p.

LC 82-12568

"A young actress in the ever-so-serious Yiddish Art Theater of the 1920s, playing the girl possessed by her dead lover's spirit in 'The Dybbuk,' finds herself possessed by a real-life dybbuk in mid-performance on tour in Buenos Aires. It turns out that her recent life eerily parallels that of a young Jewish prostitute in the audience whose lover had recently died. How to get rid of this Spanish-speaking dybbuk, which not only threatens her sanity but jeopardizes the rest of the tour? By an exorcism, naturally, performed in a kosher slaughterhouse by a Hungarian-Uruguayan Hasidic rabbi with all the magical powers of the standard zaddik plus a few uniquely his own. This is merely the skeleton of a wildly comic, richly evocative story. Prose . . . recalls to life here the spirit of a whole departed world." Booklist

Primitive people. Farrar, Straus & Giroux 1992 227p $20

ISBN 0-374-23722-0   LC 91-28692

"Simone is an illegal immigrant from Haiti, working as an au pair for a family in upstate New York. There, she learns about American life from the shallow, self-centered 'primitive people' around her: her employer Rosemary, who is camping out with her withdrawn children in the ancestral home of her estranged husband; Rosemary's brittle and caustic best friend Shelly, an interior decorator; and Shelly's narcissistic, sexually ambiguous boyfriend Kenny, who owns a children's hair salon." Libr J

This "comedy of manners has a serious purpose but it is never earnest and provides a lot of shrewd and malicious fun. . . . The author finds it hard to write a dull sentence. Her gargoyles are sometimes gruesome. They are also witty and she has a perfect ear for the chatter of this particular set of rich Americans." Economist

Proulx, Annie

Postcards; by E. Annie Proulx. Scribner 1992 308p il $22.95

ISBN 0-684-18718-3   LC 91-25089

"Postcards are the only communication between Loyal Blood and the poor, hardworking farm family he leaves behind in Vermont. The secret Loyal carries with him—the accidental killing of his girlfriend, Billy—is revealed in the first pages, and, thereafter, as he prospects for uranium, traps coyotes, or digs for dinosaur bones, his messages continue to arrive home from across the U.S., long after his father has died and his brother, sister, and mother have moved away." Booklist

"Ms. Proulx's expansion of the concept of postcards is what transforms a rambling tale into a minimalist saga. . . . Story makes this novel compelling; technique makes it beautiful. What makes 'Postcards' significant is that Ms. Proulx uses both story and technique to make real the history of post-World War II America." N Y Times Book Rev

The shipping news. Scribner 1993 337p $20

ISBN 0-684-19337-X   LC 92-30315

The author tells "the story of a washed-up newspaperman who decides to resettle in the Newfoundland town of his ancestors—bringing with him an elderly aunt and two young daughters." Libr J

The author "blends Newfoundland argot, savage history, impressively diverse characters, fine descriptions of weather and scenery, and comic horseplay without ever lessening the reader's interest in Quoyle's progress from bumbling outsider to capable journalist." Atlantic

Proust, Marcel, 1871-1922

The captive

In Proust, M. The captive [and] The fugitive

In Proust, M. Remembrance of things past v3 p1-422

Proust, Marcel, 1871-1922—*Continued*

The captive [and] The fugitive; translated by C.K. Scott Moncrieff & Terence Kilmartin; revised by D.J. Enright. Modern Lib. 1993 957p (In search of lost time, v5) $19.50

ISBN 0-679-42477-6   LC 93-15168

Sequel to Sodom and Gomorrah

Original French edition, 1923

In The captive "Albertine is living in the narrator's Paris home, where he attempts to keep complete watch on her activities. The Verdurins provoke a scandalous rupture between Morel and Charlus. Albertine suddenly flees, just as the narrator is ready to dismiss her. [In the fugitive] the narrator seeks the return of Albertine, but after her death he observes the gradual encroachment of oblivion on grief until, on a trip to Venice, he finds his pain completely cured. Gilberte has become the social-climbing Mlle de Forcheville; she marries Saint-Loup, who is now Morel's lover." Merriam-Webster's Ency of Lit

Followed by Time regained

Cities of the plain [variant title: Sodom and Gomorrah]

In Proust, M. Remembrance of things past v2 p623-1169

The fugitive [variant title: The sweet cheat gone]

In Proust, M. The captive [and] The fugitive

In Proust, M. Remembrance of things past v3 p425-706

The Guermantes way; translated by C.K. Scott Moncrieff and Terence Kilmartin; revised by D.J. Enright. Modern Lib. 1993 834p (In search of lost time, v3) $18.50

ISBN 0-679-60028-0   LC 92-33975

Sequel to Within a budding grove

Original French edition published 1920-1921

The third book in the series "deals exhaustively with personalities, places, balls, dinners, and entertainments, gossip and conversation, family history, jealousies and animosities, social and political intrigue, duplicity, adultery, and sexual inversion in the aristocratic circle of the de Guermantes family. . . . The title, 'The Guermantes Way,' refers to one of the two paths usually taken by the narrator Marcel during childhood walks at 'Combray'—the one which led past the Guermantes property." Reader's Ency

Followed by Sodom and Gomorrah

also in Proust, M. Remembrance of things past v2 p3-620

Jean Santeuil; translated by Gerald Hopkins; with a preface by André Maurois. Simon & Schuster 1956 c1955 xxiv, 744p o.p.

Original French edition published posthumously in 1952; this translation first published 1955 in the United Kingdom

"An unrevised unfinished work discovered after World War II that tells of Jean Santeuil's development from youth to maturity in the turn-of-the-century period. The reader is confronted by the Proustian phenomenon of total recall and the probing introspection that recreates the essence of an experience. The autobiographical element, the alternating moods of happiness and despair, the magic evoked by the long, leisurely spun out sentences are all foreshadowings of the more mature genius of 'Remembrance of things past.'" Booklist

Remembrance of things past. Random House 1981 3v o.p.

LC 79-5542

Includes the seven volumes, published separately and entered in this catalog. Volume one and two translated by C. K. Scott Moncrieff and Terence Kilmartin; volume three by C. K. Scott Moncrieff, Terence Kilmartin and Andreas Mayor

Contents: v1: Swann's way; Within a budding grove; v2: The Guermantes way; Cities of the plain; v3: The captive; The fugitive (variant title: The sweet cheat gone); Time regained (variant title: The past recaptured)

This "is the first complete English version of Proust's masterpiece, translated from the definitive 1954 Pléiade edition, Terence Kilmartin has checked the Scott Moncrieff translation (which comprised the first 11 volumes of the English language version and was made from the uneven first French edition) against the impeccable Clarac-Ferre Pléiade edition. The 12th volume, Andreas Mayor's 1970 translation of 'Time Regained' was the only English translation based on the Pléiade edition prior to this one and has been incorporated into it with only minor changes." Libr J

Sodom and Gomorrah; translated by C.K. Scott Moncrieff and Terence Kilmartin; revised by D.J. Enright. Modern Lib. 1993 747p (In search of lost time, v4) $18.50

ISBN 0-679-60029-9   LC 92-27272

Sequel to The Guermantes way

Original French edition published 1921-1922. Variant title: Cities of the plain

"Marcel again meets Swann at a reception given by the Princesse de Guermantes, a cousin of the Duchesse. Swann is now suffering from a deadly ailment. He is an ardent adherent of Alfred Dreyfus. Swann urges Marcel to write to Gilberte, since she speaks of him frequently. But Gilberte, no longer has any enchantment for Marcel; Albertine again holds his affections. She offers herself to him, but distracted by physical attachments for other owmen, he desires her company only at intervals to titillate his jaded senses. Eventually he is drawn closer to her, but now his suspicion that she is a Lesbian causes him jealousy and endless torment." Haydn. Thesaurus of Book Dig

Followed by The captive

Swann's way; translated by C.K. Scott Moncrieff and Terence Kilmartin; revised by D.J. Enright. Modern Lib. 1992 xx, 615p (In search of lost time, v1) $17.50

ISBN 0-679-60005-1   LC 92-25657

Original French edition, 1913

The first volume of the In search of lost time series "describes in an involved parenthetical style, with a multitude of details, the brilliant society in which the author moved. The 'Marcel' of the story is Proust's own counterpart, and it is through his hypersensitive and critical eye that we examine the tastes, feelings, motives and actions of the characters, most of whom can be iden-

Proust, Marcel, 1871-1922—*Continued*
tified as real people." Enoch Pratt Free Libr
Followed by Within a budding grove

also in Proust, M. Remembrance of
things past v1 p3-462

Time regained; translated by Andreas
Mayor and Terence Kilmartin; revised by
D.J. Enright. Modern Lib. 1993 749p (In
search of lost time, v6) $18.50

ISBN 0-679-42476-8   LC 93-3628

Sequel to The fugitive
Original French edition, 1927
In this final volume of the series "World War I ac-
celerates the kaleidoscopic changes in society. The narrator attends a reception of the new princesse de Guermantes, actually the former Mme Verdurin, and finds
most of his acquaintances almost unrecognizable. He has
enjoyed three 'privileged moments' of memory, and in
contemplating them discovers that his vocation is to be
the shaping of his experiences into a literary work of
art." Reader's Ency. 3d edition

also in Proust, M. Remembrance of
things past v3 p709-1107

Within a budding grove; translated by
C.K. Scott Moncrieff and Terence Kilmartin;
revised by D.J. Enright. Modern Lib. 1992
749p (In search of lost time, v2) $18.50

ISBN 0-679-60006-X   LC 92-25656

Sequel to Swann's way
Original French edition, 1918
"As he grows up, Marcel falls in love with Swann's
daughter, Gilberte. It is a deep and poetic attachment,
but she gradually tires of him; his ardent nature and
his attentions begin to irritate her. Out of wounded pride
he avoids her, although he continues his friendly relations with the Swanns. Two years later he feels he is
thoroughly cured of his hopeless passion, when he
becomes involved with Albertine, a beautiful brunette he
meets in Balbec. But he eventually discovers that she
is interested only in platonic relations with men, and
so he suffers another disappointment." Haydn. Thesaurus
of Book Dig
Followed by The Guermantes way

also in Proust, M. Remembrance of
things past v1 p465-1018

Puig, Manuel
Eternal curse on the reader of these pages.
Random House 1982 232p o.p.

LC 81-51034

Original Spanish edition, 1980
"With the exception of the letters that form the
epilogue, the novel consists entirely of dialogue between
two men in New York City—an elderly Argentine invalid
and the young American who cares for him. Their relationship is revealed through a dense, sometimes confusing
narrative that blends reality and fantasy." Merriam-
Webster's Ency of Lit

Kiss of the spider woman; translated from
the Spanish by Thomas Colchie. Knopf 1979
281p o.p. Amereon reprint available $21.95
(ISBN 0-8488-0614-X)

LC 78-14307

Original Spanish edition, 1976
"Mostly consisting of dialogue between two men in an
Argentine jail cell, the novel traces the development of
their unlikely friendship. Molina is a middle-aged
homosexual who passes the long hours in prison by acting out scenes from his favorite movies. Valentín is a
young socialist revolutionary, who initially berates Molina
for his effeminacy and his lack of political conviction.
Sharing the hardships of a six-month prison term, the
two eventually forge a strong relationship that becomes
sexual. In an ironic role reversal at the end of the novel,
Molina dies as a result of his involvement in politics
while Valentín escapes the pain of torture by retreating
into a dream world." Merriam-Webster's Ency of Lit

Tropical night falling; translated by
Suzanne Jill Levine. Simon & Schuster 1991
189p o.p.

LC 91-20668

Original Spanish edition, 1988
This story, told entirely through dialog, letters, and
police reports, tells of two elderly Argentine sisters, Luci
and Nidia, who are living in self-imposed exile in Rio
de Janeiro. The sisters "share aloud not only their
memories but lengthily circumstantial gossip concerning
the romantic doings of a forty-six-year-old psychologist,
Silvia Bernabeu, who has been confiding in the younger
sister, Luci." New Yorker
"The ability to compress so much plot into such a
short book offers one virtue to balance the risks in
Puig's elliptical, often cinematographic storytelling
method. Another is that it allows him to do what he
likes best: concentrate on voices." N Y Times Book Rev

Pushkin, Aleksandr Sergeevich, 1799-1837
Alexander Pushkin: complete prose fiction;
translated with an introduction and notes,
by Paul Debreczeny; verse passages translated by Walter Arndt. Stanford Univ. Press
1983 545p $52.50

ISBN 0-8047-1142-9   LC 81-85450

Partially analyzed in Short story index
Included in this volume are the following titles: The
blackamoor of Peter the Great; A novel in letters; The
tales of the late Ivan Petrovich Belkin; A history of the
village of Goriukhino; Roslavlev; Dubrovskii; The Queen
of Spades; Kirdzhali; Egyptian nights; and the novel: The
captain's daughter
Also included are the following unfinished fictional
fragments: The guests were arriving at the dacha; In the
corner of a small square; A tale of Roman life; We were
spending the evening at Princess D's dacha; Maria
Schoning
This collection also contains the non-fictional History
of Pugachev (which furnishes historical background for
The captain's daughter) and Appendices which contain
minor fictional fragments and outlines
"The translations are accurate and graceful and well
supported by an ample array of footnotes." Libr J

Pushkin, Aleksandr Sergeevich, 1799-1837
—*Continued*
The captain's daughter

In Pushkin, A. S. Alexander Pushkin: complete prose fiction p266-357

Puzo, Mario, 1920-
The fourth K. Random House 1991 479p o.p.

LC 90-9130

Available Thorndike Press large print edition

"A pope's assassination, the kidnapping and subsequent murder of the daughter of a U.S. president (who happens to be a Kennedy), and the explosion of a nuclear device in Manhattan are but a few of the elements in [this novel]." Booklist

"Astute characterizations, vivid drama and Puzo's shrewd analyses of the paradoxes of evil detonate a top-notch thriller." Publ Wkly

The godfather. Putnam 1969 446p $24.95

ISBN 0-399-10342-2

This novel focuses on "Vito (Don) Corleone, boss of an important New York City Mafia family. Names, places, crimes have been changed, but the Mafia world remains true to fact. Here is Cosa Nostra: the wars of the competing families; their changing 'business enterprises'; their struggle for power and money; their weapons—graft, guns, spies, violence, murder. A wide variety of characters are colorfully drawn. The Don comes though as a person you will remember." Libr J

The Sicilian. Linden Press; Simon & Schuster 1984 410p o.p.

LC 84-17087

This novel "follows the wayward career of one handsome, charismatic renegade, Salvatore (Turi) Guilliano, who creates and works at enhancing his romantic hero image. While the peasants of postwar Sicily adore Turi, the Mafia leaders resent his territorial infringements. . . . After seven years of increasing difficulties, Turi can do no more: with the help of the exiled Michael Corleone (son of the Godfather), he attempts to escape to America." Libr J

"Perhaps only an American writer with deep Sicilian roots and passions could have succeeded as Mr. Puzo has in symbolizing a desperate society through the deeds of a desperado, and in revealing how thin is the line that often separates a freedom-fighter from a terrorist." N Y Times Book Rev

Pym, Barbara
An academic question. Dutton 1986 182p o.p.

LC 86-4509

Set in an English provincial university, the story is narrated by Caro Grimstone, the bored young wife of an anthropology professor. Caro "finds a cure for her tedium at a local old-people's home, where she reads to the elderly and becomes a party to her husband's purloining of an important manuscript. This little theft sparks a sequence of rivalries both academic and amorous, and the manuscript itself falls victim to a mini student riot." Publisher's note

"Assembled by Pym's literary executor from two separate, discarded drafts, this tale . . . is slightly more acid than Pym's usual work but bears her characteristic wit." Newsweek

Civil to strangers

In Pym, B. Civil to strangers and other writings p7-170

Civil to strangers and other writings. Dutton 1988 c1987 388p o.p.

LC 87-30341

First published 1987 in the United Kingdom

This is a final volume of selections from Pym's unpublished writings. It contains a complete novel, Civil to strangers, written in 1936, sections of three others: Gervase and Flora, Home front novel, and So very secret, written between 1937 and 1941, four short stories (So, some tempestuous morn; Goodbye Balkan capital; The Christmas visit; Across a crowded room) and a radio talk

"We are not often given the chance to witness a writer's struggle to find a voice. But this 'last sheaf,' blemishes and all, shows us how very hard Barbara Pym worked for the voice she eventually found." N Y Times Book Rev

Excellent women. Dutton 1978 c1952 256p o.p.

LC 78-19877

First published 1952 in the United Kingdom

"Mildred Lathbury, 30ish, a spinster, a clergyman's daughter, is an excellent woman, one who, with no life of her own to speak of, finds herself somewhat unwillingly a part of the lives of others. Her days are made up of small things—church, flowers, dinner with the bachelor vicar and his sister, brief encounters with neighbors. . . . Pym's singular world is a lonely, bittersweet familiar place. She travels it with rueful wit, views the human landscape with a wise, sharp, compassionate eye." Publ Wkly

A few green leaves. Dutton 1980 250p o.p.

LC 80-18905

This novel is set in an "Oxfordshire village. The cast of characters includes Emma Howick, an anthropologist who records her observations of the behavior of the local inhabitants; Thomas Dagnall, a clergyman more interested in researching past burial customs than in attending to the welfare of his flock; and Miss Lickerish, an elderly eccentric who shares her cottage with hedgehogs." Libr J

"All the people in A Few Green Leaves are completely realistic: the sort of people we meet every day of our lives and never particularly notice. . . . Miss Pym's art endows them with a significance which they could never possess in life." Times Lit Suppl

A glass of blessings. Dutton 1980 c1958 256p o.p.

LC 79-56384

First published 1958 in the United Kingdom

This "novel, set in London in the Fifties . . . records the doings of an eccentric well-off Anglo-Catholic parish, seen through the eyes of a well-off young married woman who drifts into it looking for some kind of antidote to her too-easy life. None of her conventional expectations are met, but she finds herself drawn, half unwillingly, into the lives of [others.]" Libr J

Pym, Barbara—*Continued*

"A splendid blend of humor and compassion—a comedy of manners, but written with deep empathy for human foibles." Booklist

Jane and Prudence. Dutton 1981 222p o.p.

LC 81-68399

First published 1953 in the United Kingdom

"Jane is the somewhat scatterbrained wife of a country vicar; Prudence, once her student at Oxford, works at a 'vague cultural organization' in London, where she alternately revels in and despairs over her unrequited passion for the rather dreary little man who is her employer. As she goes about doing 'those tasks in the parish that seem within her powers,' Jane knows she really is unsuited to be a clergyman's wife—she somehow never seems to have the right money for the collection plate—but she does love Nicholas. And in her goodhearted, if usually ineffectual, way she tries to look after Prudence too, hoping to supply a suitable man for her younger friend." Libr J

Less than angels. Vanguard Press 1957 256p o.p.

LC 80-69788

First published 1955 in the United Kingdom

In this book "a gaggle of anthropologists are observed in their natural habitat, a London research center where their idiosyncratic tribal rites of mating and manipulating provoke amusement and wonder." Publ Wkly

No fond return of love. Dutton 1982 c1961 254p o.p.

LC 82-50933

First published 1961 in the United Kingdom

"Not quite ready to be 'relegated to the shelf and good works,' Dulcie Mainwaring attends a learned conference in an effort to recover from a broken heart. There she meets Viola Dace, who also works 'on the dustier fringes of the academic world,' and hears the attractive Aylwin Forbes deliver a lecture on the problems of an editor. After the conference, she finds herself responsible not only for a niece who has come up to London for her first job but also for Viola, who has lost her lodgings through a disagreement with her landlady. Dulcie herself becomes fascinated with Aylwin Forbes, eventually going to stay at the ramshackle seaside hotel his eccentric mother runs." Libr J

Quartet in autumn. Dutton 1978 c1977 218p o.p.

LC 78-58498

First published 1977 in the United Kingdom

This novel "follows the lives and thoughts of four elderly single people on the verge of retirement, in a society that has no time for them but relegates them to the impersonal care of the Welfare State. Here Pym achieves something of a tour de force, showing, with wit and compassion, how ordinary quirky acts of impulsive kindness and human feeling make the difference between despair and hope." Libr J

Some tame gazelle. Dutton 1983 252p o.p.

LC 83-71092

First published 1950 in the United Kingdom

"The story introduces the first of Pym's village spinsters, sisters Belinda and Harriet Bede. Since her university days 30 years before, Belinda has loved Henry Hoccleve, now the local vicar. Hoccleve, spoiled and smug . . . is to married to a woman whom generous Belinda tries her best to believe is a good wife. Harriet,

the younger and slightly more adventurous sister, is courted by an Italian count, but makes a kind of hobby out of adopting young curates, making them jellies and knitting them socks." Libr J

The sweet dove died. Dutton 1979 c1978 208p o.p.

LC 78-74024

First published 1978 in the United Kingdom

"Leonora Eyre is single, beautiful, fastidious, slightly affected, more than slightly vain. Approaching 50, she attracts a widowed antique dealer, Humphrey, whom she decides to bypass for his 24-year-old nephew, James. . . . . Leonora asks, she thinks, no more than the pleasure of James's company, but [then tries] . . . to eliminate her rivals, first a feckless young woman named Phoebe, then a more formidable foe, an American homosexual who plays power games more openly and ruthlessly than Leonora can." Newsweek

"Pym's extraordinary vision of an ordinary world wherein she details the intricacies of loneliness, the ditherings of hesitating souls, the comedies of errors, sexual and asexual makes this a little masterpiece." Publ Wkly

An unsuitable attachment. Dutton 1982 256p o.p.

LC 82-70741

"The world of which Pym writes is the Anglican parish with its attractive young vicar; his wife, overly devoted to her cat; the unmarried sister-in-law and her garish dress; the veterinarian and his sister; the shy anthropologist. 'An unsuitable attachment' refers to that formed between John, a young, sometime actor, and Ianthe, an older librarian." Libr J

"The bygone mysteries of the Church of England and the lost snobberies of empire return as ghostly and gently comic echoes of themselves in the habits and pretensions of Barbara Pym's people, who, like the good antiques that furnish their rented bed-sitters . . . are no longer quite appropriate to the present day." N Y Times Book Rev

Pynchon, Thomas

The crying of lot 49. Lippincott 1966 183p o.p. Buccaneer Bks. reprint available $32.95 (ISBN 1-56849-320-7)

"Oedipa Maas becomes a coexecutor of the estate of her former multi-millionaire lover, Pierce Inverarity. She becomes involved in tracking down the significance of a geometric symbol that appears to have some connection with the existence of an ancient, revolutionary mail service. In this search, she meets a strange assortment of characters, loses her husband, her psychiatrist (named Hilarious!), and her lover. The author aims his arrows at many of those phenomena that have turned people into things. Among his targets are rock 'n' roll (a group called 'The Paranoids'), right-wing extremists, and a strange group called Inamorati Anonymous." Shapiro. Fic for Youth. 3d edition

Gravity's rainbow. Viking 1973 760p o.p.

The antihero of this novel "is Tyrone Slothrop, an American lieutenant stationed in London during the Blitz. . . . The Lieutenant becomes the equipment of PISCES (Psychological Intelligence Schemes for Expediting Surrender) when his bizarre gift is discovered: Slothrop erections anticipate German rocket launchings. . . . In his

Pynchon, Thomas—*Continued*

desperate attempts to avoid being taken over as a pure instrument, Slothrop runs for it, from London to the Riviera to Berlin, pursued by Furles disguised as Baggypants comedians." Atlantic

"Fiction allows at last what was forbidden to the original suffering poets and novelists of 1914-18—the utmost in obscene description, the limit of masochistic pornography. If 'Gravity's Rainbow' is often nauseating it is in a good cause. This is the war book to end them all." Burgess. 99 Novels

Slow learner; early stories. Little, Brown 1984 193p o.p.

LC 84-934

Analyzed in Short story index
Contents: The small rain; Low-lands; Entropy; Under the rose; The secret integration
"Readers who discovered Pynchon's stories in little magazines in the late 1950s would have seen in them an adroit young talent that might bear watching. Readers who discover them now will find an exhilarating spectacle of greatness discovering its powers." New Repub

V.; a novel. Lippincott 1963 492p o.p. Buccaneer Bks. reprint available $39.95 (ISBN 1-56849-321-5)

This novel is a "parody of the 'Black Humor' techniques it employs. The multiple plots involve the *schlemiel* Benny Profane, a hunter of alligators in New York's sewers, and Herbert Stencil, who becomes obsessed by his pursuit of V., an initial he found in his dead father's notebooks. V.'s various manifestations include a femme fatale, a spy, and a hag who happened to be present at every significant event in Europe from 1890 to World War II." Reader's Ency. 3d edition

Vineland. Little, Brown 1990 385p o.p.

LC 89-13025

"Vineland, a zone of blessed anarchy in northern California, is the last refuge of hippiedom, a culture devasted by the sobriety epidemic, Reaganomics, and the Tube. Here, in an Orwellian 1984, Zoyd Wheeler and his daughter Prairie search for Prairie's long-lost mother, a Sixties radical who ran off with a narc." Libr J

This is "manifestly the work of a man of quick intelligence and quirky invention. Many of its episodes flicker with an appealingly far-flung humor. And Pynchon displays throughout Vineland what might be called an internal loyalty: he keeps the faith with the generally feckless and almost invariably inarticulate misfits he assembles, tracking their looping thoughts and indecisive actions with a patience that seems grounded in affection." N Y Rev Books

Q

Queen, Ellery

The best of Ellery Queen; four decades of stories from The mystery masters; edited by Francis M. Nevins, Jr. and Martin H. Greenberg. Beaufort Bks. 1985 238p o.p.

LC 84-21572

Analyzed in Short story index
Contents: The glass-domed clock; The bearded lady; The mad tea-party; Man bites dog; Mind over matter; The inner circle; The Dauphin's doll; The three widows;

Snowball in July; My queer Dean!; GI story; Miracles do happen; Last man to die; Abraham Lincoln's clue; Wedding anniversary

A fine and private place. World Pub. 1971 214p o.p.

"The 'padrone,' Nino Importuna, heads a huge conglomerate. He catches one of his executives embezzling, and as the price of freedom, demands that he hand over his young daughter as the aging Nino's bride. Of course, this is the perfect setup for murder. First Nino's two brothers, who share in the conglomerate, die, then Nino himself. For the solution, Ellery Queen returns to his (their) original style of detection—a stream of bizarre clues that confuse the detective Queen no end." Publ Wkly

The house of brass. New Am. Lib. 1968 210p o.p.

"Insp. Richard Queen has just returned from his honeymoon with his pleasant middle-aged second wife, formerly a nurse, when she receives an invitation (loaded with cash) to visit an old eccentric near Tarrytown, N.Y. Five other people (all told seven, counting spouses) have been gathered in order to enable the old man to choose his heirs—all prospects being offspring of persons who helped him at bad times in his career. The expected (or unexpected) happens and after too many ups and downs Ellery arrives to 'help his Dad' straighten things out." Barzun. Cat of Crime. Rev and enl edition

The Roman hat mystery; a problem in deduction. Stokes, F.A. 1929 325p o.p. Penzler Bks. reprint available $35 (ISBN 1-883402-19-0)

"Inspector Richard Queen and his son Ellery tackle a puzzling murder with immense thoroughness and almost fatiguing pertinacity. Though the egregious bonhomie of the Queens and Ellery's pseudo bookishness occasionally irritate, the neatness of the plot involving a missing hat in a theater murder cannot be denied. But the police procedure is not what it would be now, and the criminal's luck in carrying out his complex plan strains the believables." Barzun. Cat of Crime. Rev and enl edition

The tragedy of X

In Queen, E. The XYZ murders p7-216

The tragedy of Y

In Queen, E. The XYZ murders p217-419

The tragedy of Z

In Queen, E. The XYZ murders p421-575

The XYZ murders; three mysteries in one volume complete and unabridged: The tragedy of X; The tragedy of Y; The tragedy of Z. Lippincott 1961 575p o.p.

These books were originally published under the name of Barnaby Ross in 1932, 1932 and 1933 respectively

Drury Lane, retired Shakespearean actor and brilliant connoisseur of crime, helps New York City's District Attorney Bruno and Inspector Thumm solve the mysteries

Quick, Amanda

Deception. Bantam Bks. 1993 342p o.p.

LC 93-3108

Available Thorndike Press large print edition

A "romance set in England in the early part of the nineteenth century. The hero is dashing Jared Ryder, viscount Chillinghurst, descendant of the notorious pirate Captain Jack. The heroine is Olympia Wingfield, a spirited and unconventional young woman whose passion is researching the customs and legends of foreign lands. These two are brought together when Olympia's uncle Artemis engages Jared to deliver to Olympia some goods picked up in the course of his travels. . . . Despite some inconsistent characterizations and contrived plotting, this is an engaging story, with a touch of humor and colorful period details." Booklist

Mistress. Bantam Bks. 1994 342p $19.95

ISBN 0-553-09352-5   LC 94-1244

"Learning that her aunt is being blackmailed, school mistress Iphiginia Bright boldly palms herself off as the mistress of the Earl of Masters, whom she believes dead by the hand of the same blackmailer. She succeeds admirably—until Marcus Valerius Cloud, the dead earl, suddenly walks into the room and throws her plans, and her life, into passionate chaos." Libr J

"Quick's characters are clever and her plot much superior to the usual Regency." Booklist

Quill, Monica, 1929-

For works written by this author under other names see McInerny, Ralph M., 1929-

Nun of the above; a Sister Mary Teresa mystery. Vanguard Press 1985 186p o.p.

LC 85-617

"Still acutely perceptive in her late 70s, Emtee [Sister Mary Teresa] is the bane of the Chicago police force's Detective Moriarity, brother of one of the two sisters who manage the home where the nun magisterially presides. Emtee 'helps' Moriarity solve crimes again, disregarding protests, in this witty, circuitous mystery. It jets off with the arrival of two men with strange reports about Sarah Pinking, a former student of Emtee. Shortly afterwards, Sarah is murdered and later both men are also slain. On overwhelming evidence, the detective arrests Ernesto Flavio, a porn king, presumed Sarah's lover. But Emtee's cunning investigation of others puts her one up on Moriarity again and delivers a neat surprise ending." Publ Wkly

Nun plussed; a Sister Mary Teresa mystery. St. Martin's Press 1993 216p $18.95

ISBN 0-312-09890-1   LC 93-25418

In this mystery Sister Mary Teresa "Emtee" Dempsey "investigates the murder of a divorced former student who was stabbed to death in her Chicago home. The woman's ex-husband, an antiquarian book dealer who also restores rare manuscripts, confesses to the crime, although Emtee and her right-hand nun, Sister Kim, believe he is trying to protect someone else." Publ Wkly

Sine qua nun; a Sister Mary Teresa mystery. Vanguard Press 1986 182p o.p.

LC 86-19107

"A guest on a Chicago TV talkshow, Emtee debates pseudonymous Geoffrey Chaser, whose porn novels vilify thinly disguised versions of public figures. Chaser insults the host, wheelchair-bound Basil Murphy, and that makes the TV personality a suspect when the writer is later strangled. But Murphy is then killed in the same way, and Emtee declares she knows who the murderer is. . . . This Nun's Tale ends with Emtee triumphant and her fans hugely entertained again." Publ Wkly

Sister Hood. St. Martin's Press 1991 218p o.p.

LC 90-27694

A mystery "featuring the three remaining sisters in the Chicago Order of Martha and Mary. Subpoenaed to testify before a grand jury in Chicago concerning her notorious late father, Carmelite nun Mary Magdalene (the former Donna Moran) takes shelter with the three M & M's. But when their guest goes missing after Mass and her body is later found in a bathtub, the trio feels morally obligated to find out what happened and why. Sister Mary Teresa Dempsey, aka Emtee Dempsey . . . spearheads the nuns' investigation." Publ Wkly

The veil of ignorance. St. Martin's Press 1988 200p o.p.

LC 88-16886

"Sister Mary Teresa Dempsey of the sadly diminished order of Martha and Mary takes on . . . [a] seemingly hopeless case. Lydia Hopkins, convicted of killing her husband and young daughter, is released from prison on a technicality but remains guilty in the eyes of the newspapers and the prosecutor's office. Sister Emtee, as she is known, is determined to prove Lydia's innocence with the aid of her reluctant henchwomen, Sisters Kim and Joyce, the only remaining members of the order." Publ Wkly

Quindlen, Anna

Object lessons. Random House 1991 262p $19

ISBN 0-394-56965-2   LC 90-48656

Also available Thorndike Press large print edition

This novel describes a summer in the life of an Irish American family in suburban New York in the 1960s. The central figure is twelve-year-old Maggie, daughter of Tommy Scanlan and Connie, an Italian American whose father is a cemetery caretaker in the Bronx. Tommy's father John, who made a fortune in religious goods and construction, is dying after a stroke, but still seeks to control the lives of his children and grandchildren, especially Tommy, the rebel

"Quindlen's social antennae are acute: she conveys the fierce ethnic pride that distinguishes Irish and Italian communities, their rivalry and mutual disdain. Her character portrayal is empathetic and beautifully dimensional, not only of Maggie but of her mother, who experiences her own wrenching rite of passage." Publ Wkly

One true thing. Random House 1994 289p $22

ISBN 0-679-40712-X   LC 94-22238

This novel "follows the psychological travails of Ellen Gulden, who against all personal inclinations returns home to care for her dying mother, Kate, and eventually finds herself accused of mercy-killing. Ellen, an intelligent though not particularly warm person, has spent her life

Quindlen, Anna—*Continued*

earning her professor father's approval. After achieving high school valedictorian and Harvard honors, she aspires to advance her New York career. At her father's insistence, however, she leaves her job and takes on the role of nurse and homemaker. Through long hours as companion to Kate, she discovers the real value of her mother's life." Libr J

"Quindlen's story sustains an emotional momentum, and she addresses difficult issues with compassion." Publ Wkly

Quinn, Sally

Happy endings. Simon & Schuster 1991 566p o.p.

LC 91-33141

Sequel to Regrets only (1986)

"Sadie Gray is the beautiful widow of the recently assassinated U.S. president; Allison Sterling, a formidable news reporter, is the new national affairs editor for the *Washington Daily*. These women are adversarially linked through their love of the same man, Desmond Shaw, another powerful media type. The story wends its way through Washington and beyond, finding another love interest in the form of the handsome but inaccessible Dr. Michael Lanzer, head of the National Cancer Institute, who has discovered a new AIDS treatment drug." Libr J

"If Ms. Quinn's characters do not always seem real, their loneliness and longings do. . . . The reader feels safe in Sally Quinn's cozy fiction, willing to suspend disbelief as she takes us on a twisting ride through misfortune and reversal among the well known and successful, content to breathe a sigh of relief when everything comes out happily in the end." N Y Times Book Rev

Quoirez, Françoise *See* Sagan, Françoise, 1935-

R

Rabinowitz, Sholem Yakov *See* Sholem Aleichem, 1859-1916

Radley, Sheila

Cross my heart and hope to die; an Inspector Quantrill mystery. Scribner 1992 223p $19

ISBN 0-684-19410-4   LC 91-46979

This "mystery dwells on the psychological motivation of a major suspect in the disappearance of two elderly village inhabitants. As Quantrill and Sergeant Hilary Lloyd reconstruct the last days of the pensioners, they question various locals, but the bulk of what they learn comes from a neighbor's revelatory autobiography." Libr J

"Boldly stretching the genre formula, Ms. Radley makes this revealing autobiographical narrative the centerpiece of her mystery, which the detectives solve in a wink after having one last heart-to-heart with the postmistress. This is not only the author's most ingenious novel, it is also her most moving." N Y Times Book Rev

Fate worse than death. Scribner 1986 c1985 222p o.p.

LC 85-30457

First published 1985 in the United Kingdom

"When a nubile young woman is kidnapped and murdered, all of the eccentric male inhabitants of Fodderstone Greene, a quaint Suffolk hamlet, are suspect. The crusty Quantrill and his insufferably priggish sidekick, Inspector Martin Tait, must contend with a clannish, conspiratorial population in order to solve the murder and uncover a highly unusual gambling ring. Radley's decided flair for drawing amusingly offbeat characterizations has never been more evident. A top-notch teaser." Booklist

This way out. Scribner 1989 221p o.p.

LC 89-10176

"Derek Cartwright and Hugh Packer share a similar dilemma: both are saddled with elderly in-laws whose presence seems to be ruining their lives. . . . Packer quickly realizes the possibilities and involves Cartwright—against his will—in a murderous plot in which each will kill the other's resident in-law. When Inspector Douglas Quantrill enters the case, his canny knowledge of human nature escalates the tension." Publ Wkly

Rae, Hugh C.

See also Stirling, Jessica

Ragen, Naomi

Sotah. Crown 1992 457p $22

ISBN 0-517-58977-X   LC 92-1144

"Young Dina Reich is a member of Jerusalem's ultra-orthodox community, where tradition and observance take precedence over need and desire. Unlike her sister, Dina has barely strained at the restrictions her life imposes. But her mother's death and a failed match with a man she feels she could really love combine to unleash the restless yearnings that have swirled beneath the surface. Although her arranged marriage has brought Dina a kind husband and a child, frustration eventually leads her into a relationship with a married man. When the transgression is discovered by the Moral Patrol, a group of community vigilantes, Dina is forced to leave her home and family and work as a maid in New York. . . . Ragen uses religion as an interesting backdrop for what is essentially a romance." Booklist

Rampling, Anne *See* Rice, Anne, 1941-

Rand, Ayn, 1905-1982

Anthem. Caxton Ptrs. 1953 105p o.p.

First published in 1946 by Pamphleteers

"A short novel about a heroic dissenter in a future monolithic and collectivized state." Oxford Companion to Am Lit. 5th edition

Atlas shrugged. 35th anniversary ed. Dutton 1992 1168p $32.50

ISBN 0-525-93418-9   LC 91-36842

A reissue of the title first published 1957 by Random House

"In a technological civilization Rand's characters remain insecure and look to the government for protection. In exchange they sacrifice their creativity and independence. The heroes, a copper tycoon and an inven-

Rand, Ayn, 1905-1982—*Continued*
tor, reject this philosophy and fight for the individualist."
Shapiro. Fic for Youth. 3d edition

The fountainhead. Macmillan 1943 754p
$40

ISBN 0-02-600910-2

First published by Bobbs-Merrill

This novel "celebrates the achievements of an architect (presumably suggested by Frank Lloyd Wright) who is fiercely independent in pursuing his own ideas of design and who is therefore an example of the author's concept of Objectivism, which lauds individualism and 'rational self-interest." Oxford Companion to Am Lit. 5th edition

We the living. Random House 1959 433p
o.p.

Originally published in 1936 by Macmillan, this edition of Rand's first novel contains a foreword describing the plight of the individual in the Soviet Union since then. It is the story of post-revolutionary Russia, and of a woman torn between two men who love her, one a Communist, the other an aristocrat

Randall, Robert
For works written by this author under other names see Silverberg, Robert

Rankin, Ian
The black book; an Inspector Rebus novel. Penzler Bks. 1994 c1993 278p $21

ISBN 1-883402-77-8   LC 94-8929

Frist published 1993 in the United Kingdom

In this mystery novel, Inspector Rebus of Edinburgh "has alienated his girlfriend, his ne'er-do-well brother has deposited himself in Rebus' apartment with every appearance of staying for good, his promising new sergeant has been mugged, and his most unfavorite colleague is again out to discredit Rebus. But Rebus' personal troubles pale when a local butcher is stabbed, and the investigation leads Rebus to conclude that the attack is somehow connected to a years-old unsolved arson-homicide case. . . . Rankin's compelling and original plot is *almost* as intriguing as the gruff, tough, rebellious Rebus, whose rough exterior hides a charming, funny, tenderhearted human being we'd all like to know." Booklist

Rattray, Simon, 1920-1995
For works written by this author under other names see Hall, Adam, 1920-1995; Trevor, Elleston, 1920-1995

Raucher, Herman
Summer of '42. Putnam 1971 251p o.p.
Available from Amereon and Buccaneer Bks.

This is a novel "describing with great accuracy what it was like to be a 15-year-old boy just entering the obsessed-with-sex stage of life in the wartime summer of 1942. Hermie and Oscy and Benji are three tough, foul-mouthed but innocent Brooklyn boys spending the summer on Packett Island off the coast of Maine. The central story revolves around Hermie's tender and believable relationship with a war widow who initiates him into sex at the end of the novel." Publ Wkly

"There is hilarity here and vulgarity, warmth and humanity—and so much detail and nostalgia that the work seems almost like a historical novel." Libr J

Ravenel, Shannon
(comp) The Best American short stories of the eighties. See The Best American short stories of the eighties

Rawlings, Marjorie Kinnan, 1896-1953
The Marjorie Rawlings reader; selected and edited with an introduction by Julia Scribner Bigham. Scribner 1956 504p o.p.

"Selections from Marjorie Rawlings' writings of the Florida Big Scrub region and its people. . . . There are pieces from the autobiographical narrative 'Cross Creek.'" Publ Wkly

Includes the novel: South moon under, entered separately; selections from: Cross Creek, The yearling and When the Whippoorwill; and the following short stories: Jessamine Springs; The Pelican's shadow; The shell

Short stories; edited by Rodger L. Tarr. University Press of Fla. 1994 376p $44.95

ISBN 0-8130-1252-X   LC 93-30649

Analyzed in Short story index

Contents: Cracker chidlings; Jacob's ladder; Lord Bill of the Suwannee River; A plumb clare conscience; A crop of beans; Gal young un; Alligators; Benny and the bird dogs; The pardon; Varmints; A mother in Mannville; Cocks must crow; Fish fry and fireworks; The pelican's shadow; The enemy; In the heart; Jessamine Springs; The provider; The shell; Black secret; Miriam's houses; Miss Moffatt steps out; The friendship

The sojourner. Scribner 1953 327p o.p. Amereon reprint available $22.95 (ISBN 0-87797-228-1)

"Here is the story of Asahel Linden, a simple [New York farmer] and good man who, in his inarticulate fashion, loved his family and his land. He was betrayed by his wastrel brother and by his unnatural mother. Nor was he fortunate in his children whose moral fibre was so inferior to his own. The character who prevents the tale from being gloomy is Asa's wholesome and cheerful wife, Nellie, who makes his lonely life a joy. The changing seasons and the satisfaction of farming are enjoyable aspects of a novel deeply rooted in the land." Ont Libr Rev

South moon under. Scribner 1933 334p o.p. Amereon reprint available $23.95 (ISBN 0-89190-773-4)

This novel, set in the pine woods of Florida, "is the story of Lantry, who found a refuge in the scrub, of his daughter Piety, who learned to love it, and of her son, Lant, born in the scrub and as much at home in it as the wild creatures." Booklist

"The scene and the characters are drawn with a richness and vigor which makes them wholly alive." Saturday Rev

also in Rawlings, M. K. The Marjorie Rawlings reader p3-270

Read, Miss, 1913-

Affairs at Thrush Green; illustrations by J. S. Goodall. Houghton Mifflin 1984 c1983 256p il o.p.

LC 84-6702

First published 1983 in the United Kingdom
"The catastrophic fire that destroyed Thrush Green rectory in *Gossip from Thrush Green*, has caused Charles Henstock and his wife, Dimity, to move into the luxurious, large rectory in Lulling, thus drawing the adventures of the residents of these two towns even closer. . . . Henstock tends to his new duties with gracious vigor despite his own doubts and those expressed by several parishioners." Booklist

At home in Thrush Green; illustrated by J.S. Goodall. Houghton Mifflin 1986 c1985 261p il o.p.

LC 86-20864

First published 1985 in the United Kingdom
The author describes "a year of bustling and visiting at Thrush Green. The creation of eight homes for elderly residents on the site of the old vicarage takes up much of the novel's action, absorbing the interests of the villagers as the recipients must be decided upon and settled in. School life under the stern Miss Watson and the more amiable Miss Fogarty also receives a share of attention. Readers familiar with Thrush Green's inhabitants will be delighted to note the changes in the lives of their favorite characters and will be pleased as always by the book's emphasis on familiar annual patterns." Booklist

Battles at Thrush Green; illustrated by J.S. Goodall. Houghton Mifflin 1976 c1975 239p il o.p.

First published 1975 in the United Kingdom
"Here's another delightful and unpretentious saga of the ups and downs of the quiet life in Thrush Green. Miss Read's characters are always charmers and she writes about them with unabashed affection and humor as she puts them through their paces in her engaging picture postcard English village." Publ Wkly

Celebrations at Thrush Green; illustrations by John S. Goodall. Houghton Mifflin 1993 c1992 151p il o.p.

LC 93-22983

First published 1992 in the United kingdom
"One hundred years have passed in Thrush Green since its village school was founded, so the residents are keen to celebrate. Then local author Harold Shoosmith discovers that also in 1892 a mission school was founded in Africa by Nathaniel Patten from Thrush Green. A newly discovered bundle of letters and a diary spell out how Nathaniel was guided by Thrush Green Vicar Octavius Fennel. So, a grand church-school centenary is launched. Read's cheery account of the arrangements reintroduce several old-favorite characters and bring back many memories from her previous books." Booklist

Changes at Fairacre; illustrations by John S. Goodall. Houghton Mifflin 1992 c1991 250p il o.p.

LC 92-13179

First published 1991 in the United Kingdom
"Miss Read inherits Dolly Clare's little cottage at Thrush Green, her grief at the death of her old friend and mentor somewhat assuaged by the security of home ownership; the declining enrollment at Fairacre School, where Miss Read teaches, may lead to its closing. . . . The novel's slight plot sometimes gets in the way of Read's wonderful descriptive abilities, but her characters, as always, fairly leap off the pages." Publ Wkly

Chronicles of Fairacre; comprising: Village school, Village diary and Storm in the village; illustrated by J. S. Goodall. Houghton Mifflin 1977 c1964 534p il o.p.

First published 1964 in the United Kingdom. A combined edition of three titles first published separately in 1956 (1955 in the United Kingdom), 1957, and 1959 (1958 in the United Kingdom) respectively

Village school describes one year in the life of an English schoolmistress in a two-room church-governed school in the rural English village of Fairacre. Through her eyes we see the whole of village life with its fetes, sales, outings, festivals, quarrels and friendships. Village diary continues the account of school and village life. When a retired male school teacher settles in the village, the villagers hope for a romance for their schoolmistress until a wife appears. In Storm in the village, the "storm" is caused by fear that the British Atomic Research Authority is going to take over Harold Miller's "Hundred Acre Field" to make room for a new housing development and that the village school will be closed

Farewell to Fairacre; illustrations by John S. Goodall. Houghton Mifflin 1994 213p il $19.95

ISBN 0-395-68994-5   LC 94-25628
Also available Thorndike Press large print edition

"With an influx of new students, Miss Read's worries about the future of her beloved school can finally be set aside. In their wake, however, come concerns about the head mistress' own health. Two small strokes spur her decision to retire, and she spends her final months in her usual busy fashion, tending to her students at Fairacre, fending off the surprising attentions of two suitors, and becoming ever more comfortable with thoughts of a new life ahead. Nostalgic without being sentimental, this is a fitting conclusion to a delightful series, recalling old friends and pleasant times in a tranquil English village." Booklist

Friends at Thrush Green; illustrations by John S. Goodall. Houghton Mifflin 1991 c1990 244p il $19.95

ISBN 0-395-57381-5   LC 91-10857
Also available Thorndike Press large print edition
First published 1990 in the United Kingdom
In this novel "we meet a crazy-quilt collection of delightfully eccentric characters who eagerly await and gossip endlessly about their old friends' return visit. The town's attention is also riveted to the pending sale of the much-loved residence abutting the schoolhouse at Thrush Green, speculation about which gives rise to a cornucopia of interesting tales and rumors surrounding various townspeople. While some readers might deem Miss Read's novel sluggish for its seeming uneventfulness, many others will be drawn to this throwback to an easier, slower-paced life." Booklist

Gossip from Thrush Green; illustrated by J.S. Goodall. Houghton Mifflin 1982 c1981 246p il o.p.

LC 82-11718

Read, Miss, 1913——*Continued*

First published 1981 in the United Kingdom

The residents of Thrush Green and the surrounding villages of Nidden, Lulling, and Lulling Woods "are kept occupied by a variety of local dramas including a catastrophic fire at the rectory, the midnight practices of a quartet of rock musicians renting one of the villager's homes, the closing of a tea shop, the serious illness of an eccentric animal lover, and the birth of a new resident." Booklist

Mrs. Pringle; illustrations by John S. Goodall. Houghton Mifflin 1990 c1989 165p il o.p.

LC 90-4669

First published 1989 in the United Kingdom

This novel focuses on the exploits of Mrs. Pringle, the custodian of the school in the rural English village of Fairacre

Return to Thrush Green; illustrated by J.S. Goodall. Houghton Mifflin 1979 255p il o.p.

LC 79-858

First published 1978 in the United Kingdom

In this chronicle of Thrush Green "Albert Piggott, the sexton, is his usual irascible self despite the efforts of his wandering wife and his loyal daughter. On the other hand, the return of Joan Young's ailing father works out much better than expected. Miss Fogarty handles the school crises capably and finds that some clouds do have silver linings. As flowers bloom and birds do nest, neighbors chat away as usual, and Dotty Harmer cares for her stray animals and offers acorn coffee to friends. Best of all is the village's newest romance, one that takes just about everyone by surprise." Publ Wkly

The school at Thrush Green; illustrations by John S. Goodall. Houghton Mifflin 1988 c1987 244p il o.p.

LC 88-9329

First published 1987 in the United Kingdom

Thrush Green's "beloved school teachers, Miss Dorothy and Miss Agnes, have decided to retire. The townspeople are aflutter musing about the teachers' replacements and seeking an appropriate farewell gift. After neatly setting up the requisite number of potential troubles and perplexing quandaries, the novelist then allows her familiar characters to resolve each other's difficulties as the story ambles to a pleasant close." Booklist

Storm in the village

In Read, Miss Chronicles of Fairacre p361-534

Thrush Green; illustrated by J.S. Goodall. Houghton Mifflin 1960 c1959 226p il o.p. Buccaneer Bks. reprint available $21.95 (ISBN 0-89966-435-0)

First published 1959 in the United Kingdom

"Confined to the events of May 1, the day when Mrs. Curdle's traveling carnival brings its special magic to Thrush Green, the story tells what takes place in the lives of a small boy, a lonely girl, an elderly doctor and his young assistant, and various other people, including the redoubtable Mrs. Curdle herself." Booklist

Village diary

In Read, Miss Chronicles of Fairacre p177-360

The village school

In Read, Miss Chronicles of Fairacre p9-176

Winter in Thrush Green; illustrated by J.S. Goodall. Houghton Mifflin 1962 c1961 226p il o.p. Amereon reprint available $18.95 (ISBN 0-8488-1456-8)

First published 1961 in the United Kingdom

This novel continues the story of some of the villagers: the widowed rector, Miss Ella and Miss Dimity, Dr. Lovell and Ruth (now expecting a baby). The arrival of elderly bachelor Harold Shoosmith, a newcomer, brightens many a spinster's hopes

"'Miss Read' unquestionably is a romantic, but, thankfully, she is not a sentimentalist. . . . Her humor is kindly rather than acid. It is a genuine humor and it is delightful." Chicago Sunday Trib

Read, Piers Paul, 1941-

The free Frenchman. Random House 1986 586p o.p.

LC 86-20419

"Bertrand de Roujay is a loyal Frenchman invariably unlucky in love. Women to whom he offers his name seem fated to betray him, while others whom he would not marry remain steadfast. After the Nazi invasion of France Bertrand flees to join the Free French under De Gaulle in London. He leaves behind his daughter, whose mother was a Communist, and his brother, a supporter of Pétain and collaborator with the conquering Germans. This family represents the elements that tore apart France at a time when it was in danger of losing national identity." Libr J

A season in the West. Random House 1989 238p o.p.

LC 88-29682

"Defecting from Czechoslovakia, writer Josef Birek is taken under the wing of Laura Morton, the wife of a wealthy banker, who works part-time as a translator at a foundation for dissident émigrés. Shallow, discontented Laura sees her opportunity: she introduces the naïve, idealistic Birek to her friends and literary contacts, invites him to move into her home and eventually begins an affair with the overwhelmed young man. Lionized by London's sophisticated social set, Birek finds himself financially and spiritually enslaved, while Laura becomes obsessed by the liaison." Publ Wkly

"Read engages his audience with biting pictures of British publishing and banking circles, while the romance is played up for all its blazing erotic qualities. Witty commentary on sedate lives moved by unruly passions." Booklist

Rebeta-Burditt, Joyce, 1938-

The cracker factory. Macmillan 1977 312p o.p.

"Cassie Barrett has gone crackers. Her marriage is on the rocks and the pint bottle she keeps hidden in the basement doesn't last through the day. Depressed and unable to handle her growing dependence on alcohol,

Rebeta-Burditt, Joyce, 1938—*Continued*

Cassie signs herself into the psychiatric ward of Cleveland General Hospital. The ward is no cuckoo's nest and Cassie is treated with respect and concern. At first, she is uncooperative and contemptuous of staff and patients, but she rallies after attending her first AA meeting." Libr J

The author writes "with freshness and humor that is an absolute delight. . . . Treated without sentiment or idealism, the passages dealing with [Alcoholics Anonymous] are perhaps the most real and powerful of the book." West Coast Rev Books

Redfield, James

The celestine prophecy; an adventure. Warner Bks. 1994 246p $17.95

ISBN 0-446-51862-X   LC 93-61754

"The saga begins when the unnamed middle-aged male narrator whimsically quits his nondescript life to track down an ancient Peruvian manuscript (pretentiously called the Manuscript) containing nine Insights that supposedly prophesy the modern emergence of New Age spirituality. South of the border, he encounters resistance from the Peruvian government and church authorities, who believe the document will undermine traditional family values. While dodging evil soldiers, paranoid priests and pseudoscientific researchers, our hero sequentially discovers all nine Insights during a series of chance encounters. Redfield has a real talent for page-turning action." Publ Wkly

Reed, Barry, 1939-

The choice. Crown 1991 358p $20

ISBN 0-517-58124-8   LC 90-48217

"Frank Galvin is at the peak of his legal career with a blue-chip Boston law firm. As chronicled in *The Verdict* [1980] he has risen to the height of Boston's legal set through a brilliant performance in a highly publicized hospital case. When he is approached by a young and inexperienced attorney with evidence that a highly touted new wonder drug may cause birth defects, he sees it as an opportunity to exert his firm's sense of humanity. However, the firm is the principal legal counsel for the drug's manufacturer. What seems at first to be a simple matter of potential conflict of interest rapidly escalates into an intricate web of intrigue involving both U.S. and British law as well as medical ethics." Libr J

The indictment. Crown 1994 370p $22

ISBN 0-517-59433-1   LC 94-8346

This novel concerns "a possible grand jury indictment against a prominent doctor suspected of murdering a young woman. When Boston attorney Dan Sheridan agrees to defend Dr. Christopher Dillard, he pits himself against a DA with an eye on a U.S. Senate seat and a shady Irish kingmaker who wants the entire case buried. Sheridan also becomes an unwitting target of an FBI sting operation against local lawyers suspected of criminal ties, even as he becomes romantically involved with the agent who is working undercover as one of his secretaries." Publ Wkly

"Reed surrounds the mystery plot with an intriguing, behind-the-scenes look at the historically fascinating sociopolitical world of Boston, and he offers plenty of detail on the decision-making, strategy, and processes that go into preparing a criminal case." Booklist

Reed, Ishmael, 1938-

Japanese by spring. Atheneum Pubs. 1993 225p $20

ISBN 0-689-12072-9   LC 92-36280

A "satiric thrust at university life in America. Ambitious black professor Chappie Puttbutt wants to rise at predominantly white Jack London University, but he gets more than he bargained for when his serene tutor in Japanese—actually leader of a filthy-rich group of Asians—suddenly buys the university and threatens to take over the American West." Libr J

"Borrowing from vivid African-American slang and turning academic jargon inside out, Mr. Reed constructs brilliant verbal fusillades that reduce his targets to their most ridiculous components." N Y Times Book Rev

The last days of Louisiana Red. Random House 1974 179p o.p.

"Louisiana Red, an international organization of bad guys is trying to take over the manufacture of 'gumbo,' a mysterious product with healing properties developed through black magic and voodoo. To defeat the Red Menace and its militants, the Moochers, the Solid Gumbo Works Corporation brings in renowned occult detective Papa LaBas." Libr J

"Reed ignores long-established trends in black writing, using satire instead of rage, fantasy instead of realism, to make telling points about life in a white man's society. . . . The comic cast sorts things out in grand style, with Reed at his bravura best in the use of language and parody." Publ Wkly

The terrible threes. Atheneum Pubs. 1989 180p $16.95

ISBN 0-689-11893-7   LC 89-166

Sequel to The terrible twos

The author "imagines a period between Thanksgiving and Christmas in the late 1990's, as President Dean Clift has been removed from the White House as a consequence of scandal. In his place rules Jesse Hatch, whose kitchen cabinet of advisers includes a televangelist and a former TV producer." Booklist

"Reed's uproarious, wisecracking, deadly serious farce swings between the inspired and the heavy-handed, but when he is on target, which is much of the time, he is one of the sharpest socio-political satirists around." Publ Wkly

The terrible twos. St. Martin's Press 1982 178p o.p.

         LC 81-21504

This satirical novel "first visits Christmastime in New York as the world ushers in the age of Reagan. Then it moves to Christmastime 1990. Exclusive rights to Santa Claus are owned by one company; the President of the U.S. is a former fashion model who is controlled by a group of four 'advisers' that includes an evangelist, an admiral, a beer king and a media expert; a cult that worships Saint Nicholas plans to kidnap the commercial Santa Claus and spoil Christmas for the merchants." Publ Wkly

"Reed's mastery of crosscutting techniques and his extravagant inventiveness keep the madness on the boil and help disguise this novel's essential commitment to savage social criticism." Saturday Rev

Followed by The terrible threes

Reed, Kit, 1932-
Gone; [by] Kit Craig. Little, Brown 1992
278p o.p.

LC 91-37566

"Clary Hale's husband Tom, a navy captain, was lost
at sea four years ago. When Clary disappears, her three
children—Teah, Mike, and Tommy (aged 16, 15, and
four)—believe she's gone on a secret mission to find
their father. But as time passes, they realized she's been
kidnapped by Cleve Morrow, a charismatic madman
from her past. They trail the pair from Connecticut to
the jungles of Florida, where a tense cat-and-mouse game
is played to the death." Libr J

"Despite a few lapses, Ms. Craig manages to build and
sustain the novel's tension. Her story contains just the
right mix of diverse characters, suspense and unpredictable twists." N Y Times Book Rev

Reed, Lillian Craig *See* Reed, Kit, 1932-

Reeman, Douglas
A ship must die. Morrow 1979 284p o.p.

LC 79-66009

"In January 1944 Captain Richard Blake, Royal Navy,
is preparing to hand over his battle-scarred cruiser 'Andromeda' to the Australian navy. Before he can do so,
a German commerce raider appears in the Indian Ocean,
and Blake is ordered to destroy him." Libr J

"Reeman gives dimension to his characters and imparts
his usual sense of realism in vivid scenes of battle action." Booklist

Reid Banks, Lynne, 1929-
The L shaped room. Simon & Schuster
1961 320p o.p.

First published 1960 in the United Kingdom

Unmarried and pregnant, Jane Graham goes to live
in a dingy London boarding house and is befriended by
the other roomers

"Love is the book's theme, developed in bright, warm
prose, through the diverse and interesting characters. .
. . So deep is the author's sense of compassion and
gentleness, and so vividly drawn are her scenes and
characters, that it is perhaps petty to suggest that the
story is also somewhat romantic. Not many girls in
Jane's situation find these friends." N Y Times Book
Rev

Followed by The backward shadow (1970) and Two
is lonely (1974)

The warning bell. St. Martin's Press 1987
c1984 344p o.p.

LC 86-25971

First published 1984 in the United Kingdom

"Maggie Robertson's desire to escape her puritanical
Scottish home and become a stage actress leads her to
marriage and motherhood in Africa, alienation from her
family, and a long struggle to regain her dream after
divorce and more family conflicts and personal heartaches. The 'warning bells' marked turning points in Maggie's life, but she often ignored them, and learned to
have no regrets in her quest for personal and professional happiness and satisfaction." Libr J

The author has a "knack for painting characters with
swift, sure strokes. She has created a strong cast of
touching, courageous and decisive characters to prop up
the flimsiness of the show's star." N Y Times Book Rev

Remarque, Erich Maria, 1898-1970
All quiet on the western front; translated
from the German by A. W. Wheen. Little,
Brown 1929 291p $19.95

ISBN 0-316-73992-8

Also available from Amereon and Buccaneer Bks.

"Four German youths are pulled abruptly from school
to serve at the front as soldiers in World War I. Only
Paul survives, and he contemplates the needless violation
of the human body by weapons of war. No longer innocent or lighthearted, he is repelled by the slaughter of
soldiers and questions the usefulness of war as a means
of adjudication. Although the young men in this novel
are German, the message is universal in its delineation
of the feelings of the common soldier." Shapiro. Fic for
Youth. 3d edition

Followed by The road back

Arch of triumph; translated from the German by Walter Sorell and Denver Lindley.
Appleton-Century 1945 455p o.p.

"A story of Paris in the period preceding the [Second
World] war. The central character is a German doctor
who, having escaped from the Nazis, is living illegally
in France, subject to deportation if the police discover
his presence. Without a passport and identification papers
he is not allowed to practice, but in secret performs
difficult operations for a well-known society doctor. Other
refugees, figures from the underworld, outcasts and
derelicts are the characters in a book which pictures a
society nearing its doom." Wis Libr Bull

The night in Lisbon; translated by Ralph
Manheim. Harcourt, Brace & World 1964
244p o.p.

Original German edition, 1962

"One night in Lisbon in 1942 a German refugee offers
passage to the U.S. and his passport to another refugee
on condition that he be kept company through the night
and that he be permitted to tell his story. The narration
reveals the first refugee's flight from Germany in the
1930's, his hazardous return after five years to see his
wife, his second escape in which his wife joins him, and
their subsequent flight from place to place in Europe
during which, in spite of dangers, they achieved moments
of intense happiness because of their mutual love and
understanding." Booklist

The road back; translated from the German by A. W. Wheen. Little, Brown 1931
343p o.p.

Sequel to All quiet on the western front

Containing some of the characters of All quiet on the
western front, this story is about a "little group of war-
weary, disillusioned German soldiers [who] return to their
homes and find that adjustment to peace in a Fatherland
which is a rioting, cynical republic is impossible."
Cleveland Public Libr

"A profoundly moving, a painfully moving, document.
Unlike tragedy, it has no katharsis, but, like a tragedy,
it has to be looked at open-eyed, honestly, courageously."
Spectator

Remarque, Erich Maria, 1898-1970 — *Continued*

Three comrades; translated from the German by A. W. Wheen. Little, Brown 1937 479p o.p.

"During the days of pre-Hitler Germany, three wartime comrades continue their bonds of friendship in an automobile repair shop where they work together and finally fail in their attempts to earn a living. The tender but unconventional love of Patricia Hollmann and Bobby, the youngest of the three, furnishes the romantic and pathetic element of the book." Booklist

"The story throughout is admirably written: the situations are convincingly contrived; a world, even though it be a world dominated by ruthless cruelty, is created with authentic power." Manchester Guardian

A time to love and a time to die; translated from the German by Denver Lindley. Harcourt Brace & Co. 1954 378p o.p.

"Ernst, a young German soldier, gets a furlough in the closing days of World War II. He marries Elizabeth, a neighbor girl, who grew up while he was away. Their brief but touching honeymoon helps them to discover love and each other—a time to love. Upon his return from a furlough, Ernst is sent to guard four Russian prisoners. In a generous gesture, he releases them, but one of them, turns on him and kills him—a time to die." Wis Libr Bull

"The whole story is told with great restraint, with little sentimentality for those in misery and with little open rage at those who caused it." Chicago Sunday Trib

Renault, Mary, 1905-1983

The bull from the sea. Pantheon Bks. 1962 343p o.p.

"A sequel to *The King Must Die*, this mythological novel begins with Theseus, King of Athens, returning in triumph from Crete, where he has killed the Minotaur. On a subsequent adventure he captures and falls in love with the warrior princess, Hippolyta. Although married to Phaedra of Crete, Theseus continues his relationship with Hippolyta and both women bear him sons. Tragedy occurs when Phaedra is attracted to and spurned by Hippolyta's youthful son." Shapiro. Fic for Youth. 3d edition

The charioteer. Pantheon Bks. 1959 346p o.p.

"A modern-day allegorical story of a young Englishman whose inclination toward homosexuality reaches a critical point when he is wounded at Dunkirk and under treatment in a military hospital in England during World War II." Publ Wkly

"This unusual novel, told with artistry and skill, is compelling and haunting. Slowly the life of these men who love men emerges into reality—a life of sordidness, greatness, pain and joy." Wis Libr Bull

Fire from heaven. Pantheon Bks. 1969 375p o.p.

"This is the story of Alexander the Great from his earliest childhood until the death of his father, Philip of Macedonia. . . . We meet everyone who ever influenced the young Alexander—Aristotle, his teacher; Hephaiston, his friend and lover; Olympias, his strange priestess mother; and scores of others. This was a time of ritual feasts and bacchanalian orgies, of unbashed sexual freedom, of bloody wars and insidious plottings, of pageantry and splendor, myths and mysteries." Publ Wkly

Followed by The Persian boy

Funeral games. Pantheon Bks. 1981 335p o.p.

LC 81-47273

This concludes the story of Alexander the Great that began in Fire from heaven and The Persian boy. "At 32 Alexander is dying in Babylon. The generals, two pregnant wives and a covey of conspirators keep a jackal-like vigil, anticipating the fight for possession of the empire, extending from Europe to India, that will break out when the godlike leader dies. At his death, the murderous power struggle ensues—Alexander's mother and his brain-injured half-brother, Philip, vie with the Regent and other extrafamilial seekers of the throne." Publ Wkly

"Miss Renault's main problem has been to make these monsters and monomaniacs believable, and this, at times with disconcerting insight, she does. . . . It might be argued that Funeral Games lacks a dominant central character. In fact the true center is the empty throne, and it is Alexander himself who, in death as in life, commands the scene absolutely." N Y Rev Books

The king must die. Pantheon Bks. 1958 338p o.p.

"Theseus, the hero king of Athens and son of Aegeus, is the central figure and narrator of this tale based on Greek mythology. A handsome and adventuresome youth, he is constantly challenged by both humans and gods. Renault describes his battles with the sons of Pallas, his conquest of the Marathonian bull, and his valiant rescue of seven youths and seven maidens from the Minotaur." Shapiro. Fic for Youth. 3d edition

Followed by The bull from the sea

The last of the wine. Pantheon Bks. 1956 389p o.p.

"This is a fictionalized account of Athens during the years of the Peloponnesian War told by Alexias, a young Athenian of good family background. We learn the details of daily life within the Greek city state, including the literary, cultural, recreational, and political texture of the time. One very memorable account is that of a wrestling match at the Isthmian Games." Shapiro. Fic for Youth. 3d edition

The mask of Apollo. Pantheon Bks. 1966 371p o.p.

A novel set in Syracuse and Athens in the fourth century B.C. which concerns Nikeratos, the actor, who carries an antique mask of Apollo with him on his travels. The mask becomes by degrees his artistic conscience. Niko narrates the struggle for power between Dion, philosopher and soldier, the friend of Plato, and the tyrant Dionysios the Younger

The Persian boy. Pantheon Bks. 1972 432p o.p.

This sequel to Fire from heaven continues the "story of Alexander the Great, focusing upon his momentous expedition into Asia. This time we observe events through the eyes of Bagoas, a beautiful Persian eunuch who was loved by King Darius and then by Alexander himself. The multiple facets of Renault's art, familiar to a host of admirer's, are once again apparent: a particularly sensitive depiction of boyhood and youth; an astounding grasp of the facts and the spirit of the ancient world; an unerring sense of the dramatic which, along with her

Renault, Mary, 1905-1983—*Continued*
superb descriptive powers, brings to life a great historical period." Libr J
Followed by Funeral games

Rendell, Ruth, 1930-
See also Vine, Barbara, 1930-

The bridesmaid. Mysterious Press 1989 259p $17.95
ISBN 0-89296-388-3   LC 88-43471
Also available Thorndike Press large print edition

"Londoner Philip Wardman falls for a beautiful, enigmatic woman he meets at his sister's wedding. Wardman abhors any depiction of violent death, but Senta believes they should each kill someone to prove their love for each other. He fantasizes a murder, while she, an actress and perhaps just a little mad, tells a quite convincing story of murdering one of his enemies. What he discovers about her tale leads to grief and horror." Libr J

"Ms. Rendell is a diabolically subtle writer. For much of this claustrophobic study of mutual obsession, she has us peering into Senta's mind through Philip's eyes, suspiciously analyzing her bizarre statements and mysterious behavior. But, like a cunning old spider, the author has caught two flies in her web; and in the end, Philip proves the more interesting study, with his phobia about violence and his fanaticism for propriety." N Y Times Book Rev

Collected stories. Pantheon Bks. 1988 c1987 536p o.p.
LC 87-35949
This volume includes four of the author's previously published collections: The fallen curtain and other stories (1976); Means of evil (1980 c1979); The fever tree and other stories (1983 c1982); and The new girl friend and other stories of suspense (1986 c1985)

Analyzed in Short story index
First published 1987 in the United Kingdom
The fallen curtain and other stories contains the following stories: The fallen curtain; People don't do such things; A bad heart; You can't be too careful; The double; The venus fly trap; The clinging woman; The vinegar mother; The fall of a coin; Almost human; Divided we stand
Means of evil contains the following stories: Means of evil; Old wives' tales; Ginger and the Kingsmarkham chalk circle; Achilles heel; When the wedding was over
The fever tree and other stories contains the following stories: The fever tree; The dreadful day of judgement; A glowing future; An outside interest; A case of coincidence; Thornapple; May and June; A needle for the devil; Front seat; Paintbox place; The wrong category
The new girl friend and other stories of suspense contains the following stories: The new girl friend; A dark blue perfume; The orchard walls; Hare's house; Bribery and corruption; The whistler; The convolvulus clock; Loopy; Fen Hall; Father's Day; The green road to Quephanda

The crocodile bird. Crown 1993 361p $20
ISBN 0-517-59576-1   LC 93-14734
Also available Thorndike Press large print edition

"After the police question her mother, Eve, about the death of Jonathan Tobias, the owner of Shrove House, 16-year-old Liza runs away with Sean, the young garden hand at the remote English manor. It is to him, over the course of 101 nights, that Liza gradually reveals her strange upbringing, living alone with Eve in the gatehouse of the Tobias estate." Publ Wkly

"A kind of fairy-tale unreality informs this narrative, for all its present-day accoutrements; it is written in careful, straightforward, almost childlike prose; and it keeps you on tenterhooks, once you've surrendered to the atmosphere." Times Lit Suppl

Death notes. Pantheon Bks. 1981 207p o.p.
LC 81-47211

"When the banns are read for aging, world-renowned musician Manual Carmague and a woman many years his junior, it signals the reappearance of Carmague's long-lost daughter, Natalie. Carmague is found drowned before his wedding day and after confiding to his fiancée that he believes 'Natalie' to be an imposter. Obsessed with the desire to solve the mystery, [Chief Inspector] Wexford, 'on holiday in the States,' seeks information concerning Natalie's past and coincidentally provides the reader with a delightfully dry British point of view concerning Americans." Libr J

The face of trespass. Doubleday 1974 184p o.p.
"Published for the Crime Club"

"Gray Lanceton, depressed, impoverished and struggling with a serious writing block, holes up in the 'hovel,' a shabby cottage deep in the English woods. He is in flight from himself and the world. Gradually we learn what has brought him to this pass—a feverish sexual obsession with a willful married woman who is always promising to come away with him forever—if only her tiresome husband can be gotten out of the way." Publ Wkly

The author "conveys the derelict half-dream, half-nightmare life Gray is leading in an Essex hovel far better than a crime-writer need, and through this . . . makes credible the blindness that allows him to be led to total disaster." Times Lit Suppl

The fallen curtain and other stories
In Rendell, R. Collected stories p1-135

The fever tree and other stories
In Rendell, R. Collected stories p265-406

Going wrong. Mysterious Press 1990 260p $18.95
ISBN 0-89296-389-1   LC 90-40421
"Guy Curran—remarkably handsome, rich, the product of London's underworld, at once ill educated and quite bright—is obsessed with Leonora Chisholm, a childhood sweetheart who has drawn away from him, indeed plans to marry another man, but who oddly and somewhat irresolutely continues to have a rital lunch with Curran every Saturday. Curran repeatedly convinces himself that she is still in love with him but has been turned away by a college roommate, or her mother, stepfather or some other evil figure." N Y Times Book Rev

"Rendell is a master of depicting the long, slow slide into madness, making each tiny step toward the abyss resound with chilling logic." Publ Wkly

Heartstones; illustrations by George Underwood. Harper & Row 1987 80p il o.p.
LC 86-46098

Rendell, Ruth, 1930——*Continued*
"The Harper short novel series"

"Adolescent Elvira is in intense spiritual communion with her father; she plans to devote all the rest of her life to him. Elvira's mother is dead, and her sister is outside the orbit that Elvira and her father have created for themselves. This arrangement works fine, as long as it lasts, but trouble arrives in the form of a woman Elvira's father wants to marry. Elvira is determined the marriage will not take place. And, alas, the fiancée dies—violently!" Booklist

"Such is Rendell's mastery of psychological suspense that throughout we remain unsure of the seriousness of Elvira's intentions." Libr J

A judgment in stone. Doubleday 1978 c1977 188p o.p. Amereon reprint available $19.95 (ISBN 0-89190-888-9)

LC 77-76961

"Despite our knowing on p.2 who will die, and at whose hand, we are carried along by the powerful suspense of events in one upper-middle-class English family. The sense of impending doom amply takes the place of detective work, of which there is a little in the last three short chapters. The depiction of the 'perfect servant' is masterly and the whole thing a tour de force." Barzun. Cat of Crime. Rev and enl edition

The killing doll. Pantheon Bks. 1984 258p o.p.

LC 83-43255

"Madness and black magic pervade this psychological thriller. Two stories intertwine: that of the Yearman family—an emotionally distant father, his younger second wife, his disfigured daughter and occultist son—and that of Diarmit Bawne, a shell-shocked paranoid who slips back and forth between sanity and murderous fantasy." Libr J

Kissing the gunner's daughter. Mysterious Press 1992 378p $19.95

ISBN 0-89296-390-5   LC 91-50615

"Chief Inspector Reginald Wexford investigates his first case in four years, conducting us to stately Tancred House, where celebrity writer Davina Flory and her family have been murdered. The only survivor is granddaughter Daisy, who is pointedly contrasted with Wexford's own rebellious daughter." Libr J

This is an "intricate story that hinges on vanity and self-deception, a story in which the most minor and seemingly innocent relationships are charged with meaning and malice." N Y Times Book Rev

The lake of darkness. Doubleday 1980 210p o.p.

LC 79-6087

"Published for the Crime Club"

"Martin is a stiff, pompous young man and when he wins the British football pools he never lets on to the friend who actually filled in the coupon for him. Instead he embarks on a grandiose scheme to give away half his winnings to 'deserving' people, one of them his mother's cleaning woman, Lena. Tim, the pal, is bitter and sets up a savage revenge scheme designed to get some of that money for himself. But Tim's machinations are as nothing compared to what Lena's psychotic killer son has in mind in the guise of doing Martin 'a favor' as he construes it." Publ Wkly

Live flesh. Pantheon Bks. 1986 272p o.p.

LC 86-4922

"The main character of [this novel] is a mentally disturbed young man. Driven by an uncontrollable panic, Victor Jenner has committed several rapes. He shoots a promising young police officer in the back, confining David Fleetwood to a wheelchair for the rest of his life. Victor is sent to prison for 14 years. After he is released he befriends David and his girlfriend Clare, with disastrous results." Christ Sci Monit

"The obvious way to write this novel would have been to tell it through the eyes of the crippled policeman; Rendell takes the bolder path of getting inside the mind of Jenner. . . . [This] is a frightening, resonant novel—an extraordinary achievement." New Statesman

Make death love me. Doubleday 1979 246p o.p.

LC 78-22621

"Alan Groombridge, the manager of a small English village bank, [is] bound to a daily grind. . . . But Groombridge is a romantic; he longs to break away from his non-existence to a real life. Fate, in the form of two teenage bank robbers, gives Groombridge his chance. Rendell splices two stories throughout this thriller: the story of Groombridge's assistant, Joyce, held captive by the bank robbers, and that of Groombridge himself, freed from his old life, but still trapped by a lack of identity." Booklist

Master of the moor. Pantheon Bks. 1982 218p o.p.

LC 82-47871

"On one of his solitary walks on the moor, Stephen Walby finds the body of a young woman, shorn of her blonde hair. A very strange character, Stephen seems a likely suspect in the killing until evidence found with a second body points away from him. But Stephen discovers the killer's lair in an abandoned mine on the moor and feels a kinship with him, eventually killing another blonde woman and disposing of the body in imitation of him." Libr J

Means of evil, five mystery stories

In Rendell, R. Collected stories p137-262

Murder being once done. Doubleday 1972 201p o.p. Amereon reprint available $19.95 (ISBN 0-89190-372-0)
"Published for the Crime Club"

Chief Inspector Wexford "recovering from an ailment is staying with his nephew, a highly placed policeman in London. A particularly sordid murder takes place in a cemetery and the nephew is placed in charge of the case. The old man, shrewd and afraid of being in the way, takes a hand in investigating the singularly squalid background of the crime." Libr J

The new girl friend and other stories of suspense

In Rendell, R. Collected stories p409-536

A sleeping life. Doubleday 1978 180p o.p.

LC 77-27716

When Chief Inspector Wexford is "called in to investigate the murder of one Rhoda Comfrey he is baffled to be unable to learn anything at all about her private life, friends, or means of supporting herself. His only

Rendell, Ruth, 1930——*Continued*

clue, an expensive leather wallet, leads him up and down blind alleys until a chance remark by his own daughter, whose marriage is in jeopardy, leads him to Webster's International Dictionary and a brilliant deduction about the motive of the murderer." Shapiro. Fic for Youth. 3d edition

Speaker of Mandarin; a new Inspector Wexford mystery. Pantheon Bks. 1983 223p o.p.

LC 83-47745

This "Inspector Wexford novel finds the generally sensible, self-reliant country cop experiencing hallucinations and paranoid fantasies—and finally doubting his own sanity. Wexford takes a police junket to China, where he plunges into a world of recurring nightmares and the certainty that he's being followed. Back home in Kingmarkham, Wexford is called in to investigate the slaying of elderly Adela Knighton, one of the 10 British tourists he met in China. Fascinating psychological probe from a suspense specialist." Booklist

Talking to strange men. Pantheon Bks. 1987 280p o.p.

LC 87-43062

"Subtle interweaving of the adult and adolescent worlds is this author's specialty. A lonely man grieving over his unfaithful wife imaginatively interprets some coded messages that he discovers taped to the support of an automobile overpass (in Britain, a flyover). Unknown to him, the schoolboys who leave the messages are pretend-spies doing battle with their counterparts at a rival school. The consequences of multiple mix-ups, though hardly logical, are suspenseful and occasionally humorous." Barzun. Cat of Crime. Rev and enl edition

The tree of hands. Pantheon Bks. 1985 c1984 271p o.p.

LC 84-19002

First published 1984 in the United Kingdom

"Benet, successful author and unwed mother, is visited by her mentally unstable mother, Mopsa. When the baby dies, Mopsa snatches another child to give to Benet. Substitute-baby Jason is the offspring of child abuser, larcenous Carol. The child's putative father is a gigolo intent on defrauding his current patroness. The story explores spectrum of parental feeling against a background of pervasive anxiety and impending doom. This is not a mystery, really, but rather an engrossing psychological thriller." Libr J

An unkindness of ravens; a new Inspector Wexford mystery. Pantheon Bks. 1985 245p o.p.

LC 84-26624

This novel "concerns a missing husband who months later is found murdered. Investigation reveals some unpleasant things about his marital arrangments and sexual preferences. Wexford also has to deal with a society of young women who draw ravens with a woman's face on their arms." N Y Times Book Rev

"Rendell, always with a keen eye toward social observation, offers sharp insights into feminism, pregnancy, and the mother-child relationship, while providing a thought-provoking mystery." Libr J

The veiled one. Pantheon Bks. 1988 277p o.p.

LC 88-9926

Available G.K. Hall large print edition

"A seemingly modest, unassuming, middle-aged housewife is found garroted to death in an underground parking lot in Wexford's small English hometown. But the inspector is distracted by problems of his own: a bomb is planted in his daughter's car, and it almost claims him as the victim. The investigation into the murder centers on the odd son of the woman who discovered the body." Booklist

This novel "reminds us that, without exaggeration or soap opera or running gags, Ruth Rendell has created, in canny Wexford and naïve Burden, one of the genre's most durable, complex and affectingly human misalliances." N Y Times Book Rev

Reynolds, Margaret

(ed) The Penguin book of lesbian short stories. See The Penguin book of lesbian short stories

Rhodes, Jewell Parker

Voodoo dreams; a novel of Marie Laveau. St. Martin's Press 1993 436p $22.95

ISBN 0-312-09869-3   LC 93-24283

This novel is about "Marie Laveau, New Orleans' legendary nineteenth-century voodoo queen. Although few biographical facts are known about Marie, Rhodes has parlayed them into a character of vast dimension and feminine power. Like her grandmother and mother before her, Marie is a *voodooienne,* a woman visited and possessed by the African god Damballah, and the third Marie Laveau to suffer the consequences of this terrifying blessing in a world poisoned by the sin of slavery. As Rhodes imagines Marie's strange and painful life, from her protected childhood deep in the bayou to her reign as healer in New Orleans, she evokes all the lust, tumult, and cruelty of that race-obsessed city." Booklist

Rhys, Jean

After leaving Mr. Mackenzie. Knopf 1931 227p o.p.

This "work is a study of the gradual breakdown of a kept woman who is no longer kept. The parting from Mr. Mackenzie marks the downward turning point in Julia's life, a bleak one at best, though one with a few illusions. It is the loss of these that Julia is not able to face. Spiritually isolated and lacking a means of support, Julia attempts to return to her sister and invalid mother. After a devastatingly bleak encounter, the sisters remain as morally and spiritually isolated from each other as their mother, the victim of a stroke, remains from them." Libr J

"The 'feeling of foreboding, of anxiety, as if her heart were being squeezed' that afflicts Julia Martin afflicts the reader so freshly that a catastrophic final crash would come as a relief. Jean Rhys refuses us that. Her special subject is the longevity of fecklessness. We read her with apprehension—fascinated, embarrassed. She is an extraordinary artist." Newsweek

The collected short stories; introduction by Diana Athill. Norton 1987 403p o.p.

LC 88-138678

Rhys, Jean—*Continued*

Analyzed in Short story index

Contents: Illusion; A spiritualist; From a French prison; In a café; Tout Montparnasse and a lady; Mannequin; In the Luxemburg Gardens; Tea with an artist; Trio; Mixing cocktails; Again the Antilles; Hunger; Discourse of a lady standing a dinner to a down-and-out friend; A night; In the Rue de l'Arrivée; Learning to be a mother; The blue bird; The grey day; The Sidi; At the Villa d'Or; La grosse Fifi; Vienne; Till September Petronella; The day they burned the books; Let them call it jazz; Tigers are better-looking; Outside the machine; The lotus; A solid house; The sound of the river; I spy a stranger; Temps perdi; Pioneers, oh, pioneers; Good-bye Marcus, good-bye Rose; The Bishop's feast; Heat; Fishy waters; Overture and beginners please; Before the deluge; On not shooting sitting birds; Kikimora; Night out 1925; The Chevalier of the Place Blanche; The insect world; Rapunzel, Rapunzel; Who knows what's up in the attic; Sleep it off lady; I used to live here once; Kismet; The whistling bird; Invitation to the dance

Good morning, midnight. Harper & Row 1970 c1939 189p o.p.

First published 1939 in the United Kingdom

The story, "told in the first person, of middle-aged Sasha Jensen, lonely and adrift in Paris, with a dead marriage and a dead baby behind her, seeking ambiguous consolation in a relationship with a gigolo." Oxford Companion to Engl Lit. 5th edition

Quartet. Simon & Schuster 1929 228p o.p.

First published 1928 in the United Kingdom with title Postures

"The ingredients: an English girl in Paris, married to a Polish adventurer, who is imprisoned for theft and leaves her penniless, a stranger except for casual acquaintances in the foreign colony, to become the guest of an English couple, a man who desires her and can arouse her passion, and his wife, who keeps the girl in the home where she has her always under observation, always at a disadvantage, until she can finally crush her. The attitudes of the three are exposed with pitiless precision—the utter helplessness of the victim, the diabolic ingenuity of the wife, the social cowardice of the husband which makes a peculiarly disgusting setting for his lust. The background of Paris, in its cold hostility, with its tedious round of mechanical pleasures, throws the episode into harsh relief." Bookman

Voyage in the dark. Morrow 1935 266p o.p.

First published 1934 in the United Kingdom

Set in 1914. "19-year-old Anna Morgan, daughter of not-so-prosperous West Indian colonials, has emigrated to England and is making her way as a member of a third-rate theatrical touring company. Despondent and lonely, she loses her virginity to Walter Jeffries, a middle-aged and kindly, but essentially unconcerned, London man-about-town. When he leaves her, after a short and happy affair, Anna becomes depressed and aimlessly drifts from place to place, man to man, finally aborting a child." Publ Wkly

"Rhys' writing, particularly in this . . . book, is well adapted to her subject matter, simple in style, pared to the bone, free of undue sentimentality, yet admirably expressing the poignancy and instability of the situation in which she places her heroines." Saturday Rev

Wide Sargasso Sea; introduction by Francis Wyndham. Norton 1967 c1966 189p o.p.

Available Thorndike Press large print edition

First published 1966 in the United Kingdom

This novel, "set in Dominica and Jamaica during the 1830s, presents the life of the mad Mrs. Rochester from 'Jane Eyre,' a Creole heiress here called Antoinette Cosway; in the brief last section she is imprisoned in the attic in Thornfield Hall." Oxford Companion to Engl Lit. 5th edition

Ribakov, Anatoliï *See* Rybakov, Anatoliï Naumovich

Riboud, Barbara Chase- *See* Chase-Riboud, Barbara, 1939-

Rice, Anne, 1941-

Cry to heaven. Knopf 1982 533p $25

ISBN 0-394-52351-2   LC 81-19368

This novel, "written in a classical literary style, deals with castrated male sopranos—those somewhat freakish creatures whose voices enraptured music lovers across Europe during the 18th century. The principal character is one Tonio Treschi, a Venetian prince on the verge of manhood who is kidnapped, castrated, and turned over to a 'maestro' to be trained for an eventual debut in Rome. The boy not unnaturally is more interested in gaining revenge than in studying music, but eventually he is caught up in musical ecstasy. The narrative includes . . . accounts of Tonio's passionately romantic affairs with characters of both sexes." Publ Wkly

"A strong element of suspense keeps the complex plot moving. Rice displays a sure hand for details of time and place, but her most successful creations are the characters—deeply felt, richly imagined, they compel attention and sympathy." Libr J

The Feast of All Saints. Simon & Schuster 1979 571p o.p.

LC 79-16680

"The world of the Free People of Color (the 'gens de couleur libre') in antebellum New Orleans (the old French city) is the background for this romantic historical novel that brings to life an era and a place. . . . Quadroon Marcel Ste. Maria and his lovely sister Marie, children of a white plantation owner, and the lovely Cecile, his dusky mistress, grow up in the demimonde, housed and supported and educated as gentility by their father, but destined to be separated from his world by virtue of their mixed blood. . . . [The story] pits passion and principle and love against the hard realities of class and color in old New Orleans." Publ Wkly

Interview with the vampire; a novel. Knopf 1976 371p $23

ISBN 0-394-49821-6   LC 75-36792

First volume of the author's series about vampires

"In contemporary New Orleans a young reporter listens as Louis, a vampire, unfolds his tale. His story spans several hundred years . . . of a Faustian search for some meaning to his life-in-death existence, an existence complicated by his relationship to three other vampires. Lestat, the vampire who made him, is hated by Claudia, the five-year-old extraordinarily beautiful child-vampire

Rice, Anne, 1941----*Continued*

Louis loves. . . . After Claudia attempts to kill Lestat she and Louis go to Europe in search of other vampires. In Paris they find Armand, Master Vampire, and he and Louis fall in love, remaining together for a time after Claudia's death in a state of meaningless immortality." Libr J

The author "strikes and sustains a tone of deadly quiet that rises when need be to a pitch of ecstatic voluptuousness. . . . Though it has its blood-and-thunder satisfactions [the novel] is a prolonged meditation on the gradual loss of human feeling and the inconveniences of immortality." Newsweek

Followed by The vampire Lestat

Lasher; a novel. Knopf 1993 577p $25

ISBN 0-679-41295-6   LC 93-12246

"Returning to the Mayfair clan she introduced in *The Witching Hour* Rice offers another vast, transcontinental saga of witchcraft and demonism in the tradition of Gothic melodrama. . . . Embedded in this antique demonism is a contemporary tale of incest and family abuse that achieves resonance. It is maintained through the character of Lasher, both child and man at the same time, who manipulates his victims with his own pain. At their best, Rice's characters rise above the more wooden plot machinations with an ironic and modern complexity." Publ Wkly

Followed by Taltos

The queen of the damned; the third book in the vampire chronicles. Knopf 1988 448p $25

ISBN 0-394-55823-5   LC 88-45311

In this third volume in the Vampire chronicles "the plot revolves around an internecine struggle in vampiredom. On one side is 6000-year-old Akasha, who has concluded that the world would be a safer, more peaceful and equitable place if women ran it. Her plan is to set herself up as the reigning Goddess of Earth; then to kill off all human males except a few breeders, until such time when female values are firmly in place and males can be allowed to flourish again. Her opponents argue that you can't make a peaceful world through violence." Ms

"Don't let the title or the subject matter fool you; this is quality fiction written with care and intelligence. There are no false steps or wasted words in the multilayered plot, and the many characters each have a distinct voice. It's not absolutely necessary to have read the other 'Chronicles' to understand this one, but it would add greatly to the richness of the whole." Libr J

Followed by The tale of the body thief

The tale of the body thief. Knopf 1992 430p $24

ISBN 0-679-40528-3   LC 92-53085

In this fourth novel in the Vampire chronicles Lestat encounters Raglan James, "a mortal con man whose extraordinary psychic powers let him cheat the vampire out of his demonic, enormously powerful body. . . . Lestat, in a male human body, charges about the world with his mortal friend David Talbot, trying to reclaim his vampire body." Time

"Readers who crave a happy ending, a justice and a moral coherence that transcend the muddle they really live in, may feel [the author] has broken faith with them. After all, isn't that what escapist fiction is supposed to provide? Grown-ups, on the other hand, will be intelli-

gently entertained, and no more disquieted than usual." Newsweek

Taltos; lives of the Mayfair witches. Knopf 1994 467p $25

ISBN 0-679-42573-X   LC 93-35693

"This third book in the Mayfair Witches series tells the story of Ash, a centuries-old Taltos who resides in New york City. The Taltos grow to a height of seven feet, carry an extra set of chromosomes, and have a superior intelligence that enables them to digest dictionaries and encyclopedias in moments. There is something rotten in the state of the Talamasca, an order of scholars who study the supernatural and keep records of the Mayfair witches. When one such scholar is murdered, Rowan Mayfair, the mother of the two late Taltos in *Lasher*, and husband Michael Curry investigate. . . . Although this novel is a suspenseful and sometimes thought-provoking page-turner, it does not stand on its own; the first two books in the series must be read first." Libr J

The vampire Lestat; the second book in the chronicles of the vampires. Knopf 1985 481p $25

ISBN 0-394-53443-3   LC 85-40123

In this second volume of the Vampire chronicles Lestat "isn't dead, but has been alive, well, and resting in his New Orleans crypt since 1929. The chance to become the lead singer with a satanic heavy metal rock band is just enough to wrest him from his unquiet grave, however, and Lestat's desires to become a celebrity and to set the world straight on vampires prompt him to recount his life." Booklist

This novel "is ornate and pungently witty. In the classic tradition of Gothic fiction, it teases and tantalizes us into accepting its kaleidoscopic world. Even when they annoy us or tell us more than we want to know, its undead characters are utterly alive. Their adventures and frustrations are funny, frightening and surprising at once." N Y Times Book Rev

Followed by The queen of the damned

The witching hour; a novel. Knopf 1990 965p $22.95

ISBN 0-394-58786-3   LC 90-53103

Rice "tells the story of the prominent and wealthy Mayfair family who, for five centuries, has cavorted with a supernatural entity that has brought them both great bounty as well as abject misery. Neurosurgeon Rowan Mayfair inherits the family fortune, along with the sinister attentions of this entity. When Rowan saves the life of Michael Curry their fates become entwined, and together they seek to understand and destroy the terrible force that holds her family in its power. Helping them in this dangerous task is occult investigator Aaron Lightner. . . . Although a bit long-winded at times, this is still a compelling novel." Libr J

Followed by Lasher

Rice, Luanne

Blue moon. Viking 1993 305p $21

ISBN 0-670-84301-6   LC 92-50732

Also available Thorndike Press large print edition

This novel focuses on "four generations of a Rhode Island resort-town fishing family. The action focuses primarily on the grand-daughters of the family founders (and mainly on the youngest, Cass), who are helping

Rice, Luanne—*Continued*

their parents run the family's waterfront restaurant. . . . Dad is thinking of retiring and selling off the waterfront property to developers, Cass's teenage son can't believe how incredibly dense his parents are, and Billy, Cass's husband, is nearly lost at sea." Libr J

"Such a rare combination of realism and romance comes along well, once in a blue moon. You don't have to be a sucker for happy endings to love this book, but it helps." N Y Times Book Rev

Stone heart. Viking 1990 322p o.p.

LC 89-40641

"When archaeologist Maria Dark returns to her small, close-knit New England community after years of living abroad, she sees her family with new eyes. There are subtle signs of abuse and fear in her sister Sophie and in Sophie's children, yet everyone else denies noticing anything wrong." Libr J

"Given its sensational climax, 'Stone Heart,' . . . is a remarkably understated account of domestic violence and of the equivocation, the suddenly slowed motion, that can overtake the members of a family who are brought, reluctantly, to bear witness to it." N Y Times Book Rev

Rich, Meredith

Tender offerings. Simon & Schuster 1994 347p $22

ISBN 0-671-78883-3 LC 93-42074

"Sheila Lockwood, owner of the image-building company V.I.P., gets more than she bargained for when her brother-in-law arranges for her to pitch to lucrative Covington International. What begins as the answer to her financial problems quickly becomes a political and personal mess when corporate raiders R.C. Diamond and Edgar Schultz go after Covington in separate takeover attempts. . . . Sheila unsuccessfully tries to juggle her work in Atlanta and her home life in Los Angeles, where her boyfriend soon tires of a commuting relationship. Then handsome actor Yale Hollander, the unknowing father of Sheila's daughter, becomes a spokesperson for Covington. An entertaining novel with some surprises." Libr J

Rich, Virginia

The baked bean supper murders. Dutton 1983 267p o.p.

LC 83-70156

"Eugenia Potter arrives at her sometime home in Northcutt Harbor, Me., just in time for the annual baked-bean dinner. She is also just in time to see her dearest friends carried off, first by accident and then by natural causes. She begins to feel uneasy, and when her beloved weimaraner is electrocuted in an accident that saves her own life, she takes another look at the earlier deaths. While Mrs. Potter goes about discovering who is responsible for what she determines to be murder, we get to sample Maine cooking, complete with recipes." Publ Wkly

"Colorful and chatty, with a fleet of diverse, realistic characters, this novel presents the rich tapestry of small-town life." Libr J

The cooking school murders. Dutton 1982 207p o.p.

LC 81-22162

"Harrington, Iowa, has its own 'beautiful people' and 12 of them gather for the first session of a gourmet cooking class. James Redmond, chef 'extraordinaire,' instructs his students in the versatility of a thin, sharp boning knife. The next day, the enrollment is minus three. One lies dead, stabbed with a boning knife. One is an apparent suicide and murderer. One is drowned accidentally. Eugenia Potter, home on a visit, knows the town and suspects that not all is what it seems." Publ Wkly

The Nantucket diet murders. Delacorte Press 1985 276p o.p.

LC 84-21501

"It is the middle of winter in Nantucket, and a group of year-round residents, more or less well-to-do widows who call themselves 'Les Girls,' gather to welcome home an old friend, Eugenia Potter, an erstwhile member of the group who now resides in Arizona and Maine. Their latest subject for talk is the arrival of a charismatic diet doctor, the mysterious Count Tony Ferencz, who has Les Girls all in a flutter and looking better than they have in years. No sooner has Eugenia arrived however, than strange events begin to occur. . . . Eugenia finally manages to find the answers in a dangerous and suspense-filled conclusion. Fans of Nantucket and haute cuisine will find and enjoy both in this somewhat overlong, but well-written book." Publ Wkly

Richardson, Samuel, 1689-1761

Clarissa; or, The history of a young lady. o.p.

First published 1749

This novel "is constructed as a series of letters to Clarissa's friend, Miss Howe. To avoid a marriage to which her heart cannot consent, but to which she is urged by her parents, Clarissa casts herself on the protection of a lover, named Lovelace, who abuses the confidence reposed on him. He afterwards proposes marriage; but she refuses his proposal, and retires to a solitary dwelling, where she pines to death with grief and shame." Reader's Ency

Pamela. o.p.

First published 1740-1741

"On the death of Pamela Andrews' mistress, her mistress's son, Mr. B, begins a series of mild stratagems designed to end in Pamela's seduction. These failing, he abducts her and renews his siege in earnest. Pamela spurns his advances, and halfway through the novel Mr. B offers marriage. In the second half of the novel, Pamela wins over those who had disapproved of the misalliance." Merriam-Webster's Ency of Lit

Richler, Mordecai, 1931-

Joshua then and now; a novel. Knopf 1980 435p o.p.

LC 79-3489

The hero of this novel is a Canadian Jew whose "mother was a stripper, his father a third rate boxer who ended up being an 'enforcer' for a local gangster. Joshua works out of it all, makes it on his own as a journalist and TV commentator with a huge following. But Joshua can never, never forget what it was really like 'then' in Montreal, being Jewish, any more than he can deny what it is like now, married to a social, gentile wife who has her own terrible doubts. At the heart of his story is the working out of the marriage, the coming

Richler, Mordecai, 1931—— *Continued*
to terms with the past, including dreams of glory and sacrifice in Republican Spain fighting Franco, the contacts with the old-line Jewish Montrealers who were his father's contemporaries and are now dying out." Publ Wkly

The author "incorporates gags, social satire, suspense, stinging dialogue, sports and political trivia, and flashbacks to Joshua's boyhood . . . [but] never permits his comic shticks to run away with his story." Books of the Times

Solomon Gursky was here; a novel. Knopf 1990 413p $19.95

ISBN 0-394-53995-8   LC 89-43393

This is a "reworking of Canadian history that chronicles the fortunes of the mythical Gursky family. . . . From patriarch Ephraim, a con man who arrived with a doomed British Arctic exploration team, through his bootlegger grandsons Bernard, Solomon, and Morrie, who parlayed prohibition into a distillery fortune, the Gurskys' penchant for grand and petty larceny is played off against upper-crust-Canadian and English society, torn between greed and anti-Semitism. Moses Berger, Solomon's appropriately alcoholic biographer, assembles the pieces of Gursky history in a hilarious narrative that jumps back and forth from Victorian England to modern Montreal and all points in between." Libr J

Richler is a "ringmaster, making his performers do dazzling backflips without missing a beat. At the same time he is a moralist, recoiling from those who would sentimentalize the Holocaust or make power a sacrament." Time

Richter, Conrad, 1890-1968

The awakening land. Knopf 1966 3v in 1 $29.95

ISBN 0-394-41703-8

Omnibus edition of the author's trilogy about the American frontier, all three titles are entered separately

Contents: The trees; The fields; The town

The fields. Knopf 1946 288p o.p.

Sequel to The trees

This sequel to The trees continues the family chronicle set in "southern Ohio in the early 19th century. How Sayward, unlettered but 'cam,' steady and independent, undertakes, with the help of her grist of children, the back-breaking job of making a farm out of her clearing in the endless wilderness, is instrumental in bringing a church and a school to the scattered settlement and refuses, in spite of her lawyer-husband's desire to leave, to run away and be licked by the encroaching trees, is related in the vigorous speech of the period." Bookmark

Followed by The town

also in Richter, C. The awakening land p169-329

The grandfathers. Knopf 1964 179p o.p.

The author portrays a "small backwoods community in Maryland seen through the eyes of a 16-year-old girl, the oldest of several children. The mother is reticent as to their paternity, and Chariter draws her own conclusions as to which of the community's older men could be her grandfather. This and her courtship by an apprentice undertaker bring her to independence and maturity." Libr J

"As usual, the author writes his story in the simple, colloquial, and idiomatic tone that attracts and beguiles the reader. Not only is there broad comedy here, but there is poignancy too, the poignancy of place and innocence." Saturday Rev

The lady. Knopf 1957 191p o.p. Amereon reprint available $18.95 (ISBN 0-89190-332-1)

Northern New Mexico in the 1880's is the scene of this tale of violence and revenge. The lady is Ellen Sessions, wife of a district judge and a member of a wealthy English-Spanish family. The narrator is the boy Jud, a relative of Judge Sessions, who went to live with The Lady and her husband, after the death of his own father. When the feud between The Lady and her sister's wicked husband finally culminated in the latter's death, Jud is all the man Ellen has left, for her husband and son had vanished mysteriously

"This short novel is bathed in the light and the legends of territorial New Mexico. Doña Ellen is the only fully developed character, but she is enough. With her vitality, her charm, her sparkling spirit, and her power of endurance, she easily dominates this story of malice and retribution." Saturday Rev

The light in the forest. Knopf 1953 179p $23

ISBN 0-394-43314-9

Also available from Amereon and Buccaneer Bks.

Companion volume to A country of strangers (1966)

"John Butler is kidnapped at the age of four and raised by Delaware Indians. Eleven years later, under a truce agreement between the Indians and the colonials, he is forcibly returned to his family. Irrevocably divided in his heart, he escapes and goes back to the Indians but is sent away after the failure of an Indian ambush." Shapiro. Fic for Youth. 3d edition

The sea of grass. Knopf 1937 149p $13.95

ISBN 0-394-44397-7

"Set in New Mexico in the late 19th century, the novel concerns the often violent clashes between the pioneering ranchers, whose cattle range freely through the vast sea of grass, and the farmers, or 'nesters,' who build fences and turn the sod. Against this background is set the triangle of rancher Colonel Jim Brewton, his unstable Eastern wife Lutie, and the ambitious Brice Chamberlain. Richter casts the story in Homeric terms, with the children caught up in the conflicts of their parents." Merriam-Webster's Ency of Lit

A simple honorable man. Knopf 1962 309p o.p.

This novel tells the story of Harry Donner, the father of the hero of The Waters of Kronos (1960). The day-to-day activities of the kindly storekeeper turned Lutheran preacher in rural early twentieth century Pennsylvania are depicted. He is seen as son, husband, father, friend, and counselor in an age when home and family exerted moral conviction and social authority

"A quiet, slow-moving story that has a fine regional feeling for the Pennsylvania farming and mining country, some wonderful, sturdy, likable characters and a strong theme of integrity and human sympathy." Publ Wkly

Richter, Conrad, 1890-1968—*Continued*

The town. Knopf 1950 433p o.p. Buccaneer Bks. reprint available $17.95 (ISBN 0-89967-048-2)

Sequel to The fields

In this concluding volume of the trilogy the town grows and even changes its name. Sayward Wheeler and her husband move from the old cabin into a mansion, and one by one the children set up their own homes. Chancey, the youngest, delicate and spoiled by his mother, is one of the central characters. The book closes with Sayward's death

"Even in its drier passages The Town is always readable, full of a sweet nostalgia that only occasionally spills over into sentimentality. . . . A good bit of fictional Americana." Time

also in Richter, C. The awakening land
p331-630

The trees. Knopf 1940 302p $18.95

ISBN 0-394-44951-7

The first volume of a trilogy depicting a pioneer family over the years

"In the lonely American wilderness north of the Ohio river, the pioneer Luckett family face isolation, the hardships of primitive living, privation and sorrow. It is through the mind of Sayward, the oldest daughter and the staunchest of them all, that the events are viewed, from the death of the mother overcome by her horror of the trees to Sayward's own revolt against them." Bookmark

"Just as the spare, lyric style of the whole book takes its quality from the simple language of the people, the details of that primitive existence emerge unobtrusively from a background of simple necessity." New Repub

Followed by The fields

also in Richter, C. The awakening land
p1-167

Riley, Judith Merkle

In pursuit of the green lion. Delacorte Press 1990 440p o.p.

LC 90-32498

"This novel continues the story of spunky Margaret [begun in A vision of light] widowed once again and married to acerbic scholar Gregory who rescues her from her former husband's rapacious relatives only to plunge her into the midst of his own family's greedy machination to control her wealth. The eternal wars of the 14th century beckon, however, and Gregory, now a knight in the Duke of Lancaster's forces in France, is captured. Margaret, accompanied by wise Mother Hilde and alchemist Brother Malachi journeys to the stronghold of the sinister Count of St. Medard, where once again her unusual powers and quick wit overcome the forces of evil." Libr J

"In this non-stop picaresque adventure quips fly as thickly as a barrage of arrows; a steady stream of drunken noblemen, corrupt priests, scheming ladies and truculent ghosts keep the action white-hot." Booklist

The oracle glass. Viking 1994 510p $22.95

ISBN 0-670-85054-3　　　　　　　LC 93-4665

In this novel set in 17th century France, "Genevieve Pasquier, the ugly, scholarly daughter of a financier who fell along with Nicholas Fouquet, is beloved by her father but no one else; when he dies she is imprisoned by selfish relatives convinced that she has access to a secret fortune. Escaping, she is saved from suicide by a notorious occultist and her secret organization. They transform her into the Marquise de Morville, whose mystery and fortune-telling gifts capture the attention of members of the Sun King's court. Based on a real-life scandal known as the 'Affaire des Poisons,' this tale is riveting from start to finish." Libr J

A vision of light. Delacorte Press 1989 442p o.p.

LC 88-17514

"14th century Englishwoman Margaret of Ashbury heeds a 'voice' commanding her to compose her life story. Her kindly old husband Roger Kendall pays for her to dictate her memoirs to unfrocked Brother Gregory. . . . First married at 14 to a sadistic fur merchant—reputed to be the Devil—who leaves her for dead during the Plague, Margaret survives to become apprenticed to the herbalist Mother Hilde. In trances of divine light Margaret gains the healing gift, and envisions a forged, steel-fingered weapon for the soldierly work of midwifery. But these forceps and Margaret's powers stir the envy of priests and male doctors, and she is forced to clear herself of witchcraft." Publ Wkly

This "is a chronicle rich with the ambience and flavor of the Middle Ages, but it is a 14th-century story told with a 20th-century sensibility." N Y Times Book Rev

Followed by In pursuit of the green lion

Rilke, Rainer Maria, 1875-1926

The notebooks of Malte Laurids Brigge; translated by Stephen Mitchell. Random House 1983 277p o.p.

LC 83-3432

Original German edition, 1910. First English translation by John Linton published 1930 in the United Kingdom; United States edition of that translation published by Norton with title: Journal of my other self

"The hero is a young Danish poet of noble birth who comes to Paris, where he lives in poverty. The novel is written as if it were a collection of diary entries, in which observations on the suffering and squalor of his immediate experience, reminiscences of his youth, and speculations on life and art are seemingly indiscriminately mixed. The book's overall structure, which emerges only gradually, is a symbolic repetition of the story of the 'Prodigal Son.'" Reader's Ency. 3d edition

Rinehart, Mary Roberts, 1876-1958

The case of Jennie Brice

In Rinehart, M. R. Mary Roberts Rinehart's mystery book p349-442

The circular staircase; with illustrations by Lester Ralph. Bobbs-Merrill 1908 362p il o.p. Buccaneer Bks. reprint available $19.95 (ISBN 0-89968-181-6)

Featuring the detective talents of Mr. Jamieson, this novel concerns a maiden aunt and her nephew and niece who take a country house for the summer and are plunged into a series of mysterious crimes

also in Rinehart, M. R. Mary Roberts Rinehart's mystery book p3-178

Rinehart, Mary Roberts, 1876-1958 — *Continued*

Haunted lady

In Rinehart, M. R. Miss Pinkerton: adventures of a nurse detective p249-403

The man in lower ten

In Rinehart, M. R. Mary Roberts Rinehart's mystery book p181-345

Mary Roberts Rinehart's mystery book; The circular staircase, The man in lower ten [and] The case of Jennie Brice. Rinehart 1947 442p o.p.

An omnibus volume of the titles first published 1908, 1909, and 1913 respectively. The circular staircase is entered separately

In The man in lower ten "The Washington Flier is wrecked, just after a murder has been commited as a result of a tangle of forgery and blackmail." Barzun. Cat of Crime

The case of Jennie Brice is about a reporter on the lookout for a sensational story who arranges a disappearance, but it turns to murder

Miss Pinkerton [novel]

In Rinehart, M. R. Miss Pinkerton: adventures of a nurse detective p95-245

Miss Pinkerton: adventures of a nurse detective. Rinehart 1959 403p o.p. Amereon reprint available $22.95 (ISBN 0-89190-327-5)

Two short stories and two novels in which "Nurse Pinkerton," that is, Hilda Adams, figures

Contents: The buckled bag; Locked doors; Miss Pinkerton (1932); Haunted lady (1942)

Ripley, Alexandra

Scarlett; the sequel to Margaret Mitchell's Gone with the wind. Warner Bks. 1991 823p $24.95

ISBN 0-446-51507-8   LC 91-50272

Also available G.K. Hall large print edition

This follow-up to Gone With The Wind is an account of Rhett Butler and Scarlett O'Hara's lives during Reconstruction. The novel, which begins in 1873, is first set in Atlanta, Savannah, and Charleston, where Scarlett encounters Rhett again. In the book's second half Scarlett travels to Ireland to find her O'Hara roots

"*GWTW* fans might enjoy sampling this, as Ripley does her darnedest to capture the flavor of the original." Booklist

Robards, Karen

Maggy's child. Delacorte Press 1994 344p $19.95

ISBN 0-385-31205-9   LC 93-23792

"Magdalena Garcia married wealthy Lyle Forrest so that she could escape the harsh life of the projects in Louisville, Kentucky. Twelve years later, Maggy suffers physical abuse at the hands of her blue-blood husband, who emotionally manipulates her 11-year-old son David

as the means of keeping her in the marriage. Then Nick King, Maggy's childhood protector and later her lover, reappears, swearing he never stopped loving her, a declaration which elicits dangerous reactions from Lyle and leaves her torn between the love of her life and her son." Libr J

Nobody's angel. Delacorte Press 1992 324p o.p.

LC 91-39753

Available Thorndike Press large print edition

"Set in the Carolinas during the colonial period, this . . . Cinderella story concerns the unexpected seduction of a Methodist minister's plain and practical daughter. Susannah Redmond . . . buys an indentured prisoner named Ian to help with the heavy chores. When Ian washes and shaves his beard, Susannah finds (to her horror) that he's the devilishly handsome prince of her dreams. Though she fears he will seduce her innocent sisters, she is the one who loses her virginity and her heart to him. It turns out, of course, that Ian is actually the wealthy Marquis of Derne. When he returns to England to right the wrong done to him and recoup his title and riches, he takes the incredulous Susannah with him against her will. Amidst the glamour of London's high society, she realizes she has given her heart and her body to a man whose social standing is far above hers." Publ Wkly

One summer. Delacorte Press 1993 345p o.p.

LC 92-30725

In this "tale of romantic suspense, Johnny Harris returns to the small Kentucky town of Tylerville after serving ten years in prison for the murder of his high school girlfriend. His former teacher, Rachel Grant, the only person to believe in his innocence, barely recognizes the angry, embittered man her old student has become. The two are nonetheless strongly attracted to each other and begin an affair that scandalizes an already hostile town. When a woman is brutally murdered in circumstances pointing to Johnny as the killer, Rachel provides him with an alibi that few people believe." Libr J

Robb, Candace M.

The Lady Chapel; an Owen Archer mystery; [by] Candace Robb. St. Martin's Press 1994 287p $20.95

ISBN 0-312-11409-5   LC 94-25779

"In the summer of 1365, gentle Will Crounce, who portrayed Jesus in the Mercers' Guild Corpus Christi play, is brutally slain and his severed hand left in a friend's room. . . . The Archbishop of York orders Captain Owen Archer to investigate this and subsequent murders." Publ Wkly

"Rich in authentic historical detail, this taut thriller will appeal to the growing legion of medieval mystery fans." Booklist

Robbins, Tom

Half asleep in frog pajamas. Bantam Bks. 1994 386p $23.95

ISBN 0-553-07625-6   LC 94-11549

Robbins, Tom—*Continued*

In this novel "Gwen, an endangered stockbroker, is involved with straitlaced Belford and his born-again monkey. When she is attracted to Larry—who has cancer and is currently between trips to Timbuktu—she must choose among the American dream, the Timbuktu alternate, and something else." Libr J

"The yarn has a genuineness, a warmth, a humor, and an incredibly compelling plot, which hold our attention to the end." Booklist

Jitterbug perfume. Bantam Bks. 1984 342p $15.95

ISBN 0-553-05068-0   LC 84-45233

"Priscilla Partido, a Seattle member of Daughters of the Daily Special (waitresses with college degrees), gets a beet tossed in her window; Madame Devalier and V'lu Jackson, New Orleans purveyors of fine perfume, get a beet too; so do the owners of LeFever Odeurs in Paris. What does it all mean? . . . The real theme here is immortality, in the person of Alobar, a 1000-year-old Nordic imp who sports across the globe (ending up as Einstein's janitor) with the secrets to olfactory wisdom and eternal life and love. Also at large is a Leary-esque philanderer, Wiggs Dannyboy, who as founder of an immortalist sect, the Last Laugh Foundation, accompanies Priscilla on her quest for happiness and the perfect (beet-based) scent. Robbins is still in top form, still mixing the lunatic and the thoughtful—or rather, doing a literary watusi up every page and jitterbugging back down." Publ Wkly

Skinny legs and all. Bantam Bks. 1990 422p il o.p.

LC 89-18309

"A painter's struggle with her art, a restaurant opened as an experiment in brotherhood, the journey of several inanimate objects to Jerusalem, a preacher's scheme to hasten Armageddon, and a performance of a legendary dance: these are the diverse elements around which Robbins has built this wild, controversial novel. Ellen Cherry Charles, one of the 'Daughters of the Daily Special' in *Jitterbug Perfume*, takes center stage. She has married Boomer Petway and moved to New York, hoping to make it as a painter. Instead, she winds up a waitress at the Isaac and Ishmael, a restaurant co-owned by an Arab and a Jew. . . . Few contemporary novelists mix tomfoolery and philosophy so well." Libr J

Roberts, Kenneth Lewis, 1885-1957

Arundel; by Kenneth Roberts. Doubleday, Doran 1930 618p o.p.

"Being the recollections of Steven Nason of Arundel, in the province of Maine, attached to the secret expedition led by Colonel Benedict Arnold against Quebec and later a captain in the Continental army serving at Valcour island, Bemis heights, and Yorktown." Title page

An historical novel of the Revolutionary period, the setting of which is the garrison house at Arundel in southern Maine. Steven Nason, the hero of the story, goes with his friend Benedict Arnold on a hazardous expedition against Quebec. Young Nason has a very personal interest in the success of the enterprise, since Mary Mallinson, the girl he loves, has been taken by the Indians and is a captive in Quebec. Steven's recollections of the hardship and dangers of the expedition, and its blunders and failure in spite of individual acts of heroism, make up the bulk of the narrative

Followed by Rabble in arms

Lydia Bailey; by Kenneth Roberts. Doubleday 1947 488p o.p.

"A susceptible young Maine lawyer who has fallen in love with the portrait of a girl he believes to be in Haiti reaches the island just as Napoleon's attempt to take over the government sets off the bloody . . . uprising under Toussaint. The hero finds the girl, and from that point the extremely elaborate plot carries them through an encounter with Tobias Lear, the pig-headed evil genius of Jefferson's State Department; spirited engagements against the French; capture by Barbary pirates and slavery in Tripoli; and, finally, the Tripolitan War and its intrigues and political jealousies." New Yorker

Northwest Passage; by Kenneth Roberts. Doubleday, Doran 1937 709p o.p.

"This sprawling novel describes Major Robert Rogers' expedition in 1759 to destroy the Indian town of St. Francis and then his idea of finding an overland route to the Northwest. . . . Roberts, in preparing his novel, made extensive research, unearthed documents that historians had believed were lost. The book is one of Roberts' best works." Benet's Reader's Ency of Am Lit

Oliver Wiswell; [by] Kenneth Roberts. Doubleday, Doran 1940 836p o.p.

"The American revolution as seen by Oliver Wiswell, a young American who remained loyal to the English government, and was therefore the victim of fanatics, bent not only on fighting for liberty but also on destroying the liberty of others. Hounded out of his home in Milton, he fled to Boston with his father and a constantly devoted friend. He experienced there the privations of war and observed the tactical stupidities of the English. Then on to Halifax, England, France and finally back to America, where he fought with the Loyalists. The war over, Oliver found again his childhood sweetheart and turned with new hope to Nova Scotia." Booklist

Rabble in arms; a chronicle of Arundel and the Burgoyne invasion; by Kenneth Roberts. Doubleday, Doran 1933 870p o.p.

Sequel to Arundel

The principal villain of this realistic, unromantic tale of the American Revolution is the American Congress, the real hero is Benedict Arnold. The story relates the adventures of a group of men from Arundel, Maine, who fight with the American forces in the campaign ending with the battle of Saratoga. Men and events, politics and battles are seen through the eyes of one Peter Merrill, mariner, who tells the story

Followed by The Lively Lady (1931) and Captain Caution (1934)

Roberts, Nora, 1950-

Hidden riches. Putnam 1994 395p $21.95

ISBN 0-399-13948-6   LC 93-37425

Also available Thorndike Press large print edition

"At an auction in Virginia, antiques dealer Dora Conroy purchases a mismatched box of porcelain figurines and an abstract painting on a whim. Across the country, a man opens his expected shipment to discover the items he received are not the ones he arranged to have shipped. A search begins immediately for the lost shipment; it's a search that brings a murderer closer and closer to Dora Conroy. With the help of her tenant, ex-cop Jed Skimmerhorn, Dora unravels the nature of the violence that has trailed the auction items." Booklist

Roberts, Nora, 1950-—*Continued*
Honest illusions. Putnam 1992 383p o.p.

LC 92-277

"Max Nouvelle is the patriarch of a family of magicians and jewel thieves made up of Lily, his partner in love; Roxanne, his headstrong, beautiful daughter; and Luke, the abused runaway Max had taken in years ago, now a charming young man. They join Max in elaborate performances onstage and in equally elaborate robberies. For years Roxanne and Luke battle constantly, but as young adults they finally realize they are deeply in love. Luke, haunted by the fear that his past will hurt his adopted family, is the target of coldblooded Sam Wyatt, driven by a vow of revenge on the Nouvelles." Publ Wkly

Private scandals. Putnam 1993 384p $19.95

ISBN 0-399-13828-5   LC 92-39607
Also available Thorndike Press large print edition

This romantic thriller "concerns the rise of hot new talk-show host Deanna Reynolds. Deanna, a sincere and dedicated one-time local reporter in Chicago, has moved to New York, determined to be number one in the field. This pits her against her former mentor, the high strung and manipulative current talk-show queen, Angela Perkins. Angela doesn't take well to the competition and resorts to stealing guests, blackmail and crossing boundaries of good journalism in her effort to fight Deanna's increasing popularity. Deanna's romance with the handsome and much lauded reporter Finn Riley, Angela's former love interest, only increases the tension. But the novel's main question is who will do in Deanna first, the obsessed fan who seems to know her every move, or Angela. . . . The novel is a fun read with a good pace." Publ Wkly

Robertson, Don
Praise the human season. Fields, A. 1974 495p o.p.

"Amberson is 74, his wife 72, when he begins to keep his journal, 'an attempt to sort out confusions.' Both are dying, both want to know what it has all 'meant.' After 50 years of marriage, they set off on a motor trip to they know not where. When half of the $2000 he is taking runs out, they will turn back. Robertson alternates between excerpts from the journal, with its record of the past, and what takes place in the present as they seek to come to grips with the past." Publ Wkly
"The book is a remarkably perceptive intrusion into two ordinary lives made rich and tragically meaningful by a skillful and sensitive artist." Best Sellers

Robinson, Kim Stanley
Green Mars. Bantam Bks. 1994 535p il $22.95

ISBN 0-553-09640-0   LC 93-39516

This second novel in the trilogy "details an early 22nd-century Mars controlled by Earth's metanationals, gigantic corporations intent on exploiting Mars. Debate among the settlers—some native-born, some the surviving members of the First Hundred—is divided between the minimalist areoformists, who have come to love Mars in all its harshness, and the terraformists, who want to replicate Earth." Publ Wkly

"Grounded in current and projected technology, yet relying on human drama to propel the story forward, Robinson's latest novel is solidly written and powerfully explicated." Libr J

Red Mars. Bantam Bks. 1993 519p il $22.95

ISBN 0-553-09204-9   LC 92-21607

This novel, the first in a projected trilogy "concerns the first permanent settlement on Mars, a multinational band of 100 hardy experts, and their mission—to begin making Mars habitable for humans by releasing underground water and oxygen into the atmosphere. Unfortunately, they are divided over whether this is a desirable step in human evolution or an ecological crime." Booklist
"A novel fully inhabited both by detailed technical processes and by people whose careers those processes are; it is also a novel with a complex sense of political reality. . . . This is one of the finest works of American SF because it is one of the few that aspire to the dignity of the genuinely tragic." Times Lit Suppl
Followed by Green Mars

Robinson, Sheila
For works written by this author under other names see Radley, Sheila

Robinson, Spider
By any other name
In The Hugo winners v4 p141-97

Stardance [novelette]
In The Hugo winners v4 p327-88

Rod Serling's Night gallery reader; edited by Carol Serling, Charles G. Waugh, & Martin H. Greenberg. Dembner Bks. 1987 326p o.p.

LC 87-14360

Analyzed in Short story index
Original versions of stories later adapted for the television series, Night gallery
Contents: The escape route, by R. Serling; The dead man, by F. Leiber; The little black bag, by C. M. Kornbluth; The house, by A. Maurois; The boy who predicted earthquakes, by M. St. Clair; The academy, by D. Ely; The devil is not mocked, by M. W. Wellman; Brenda, by M. St. Clair; Big surprise, by R. Matheson; House—with ghost, by A. Derleth; The dark boy, by A. Derleth; Pickman's model, by H. P. Lovecraft; Cool air, by H. P. Lovecraft; Sorworth place, by R. Kirk; The return of the sorcerer, by C. A. Smith; The girl with the hungry eyes, by F. Leiber; The horsehair trunk, by D. Grubb; The ring with the velvet ropes, by E. D. Hoch

Rodriguez, Abraham, 1961-
Spidertown; a novel; by Abraham Rodriguez, Jr. Hyperion 1993 323p $19.95

ISBN 1-56282-845-2   LC 92-34088

This "novel tells the story of Miguel, a 16-year-old Puerto Rican American crack runner in the South Bronx. He falls in love with Cristalena, whose disapproval of what crack has done to her neighborhood forces him

Rodriguez, Abraham, 1961-—*Continued*

to look at this life with a different perspective. His struggle to hang onto Cristalena puts him in conflict with the world of the streets." Libr J

"'Spidertown' takes us beyond the easy idea that life is merely cheap. To be sure, Mr. Rodriguez's characters act like thugs, but beneath the bravado lie desperate dreams. . . . Mr. Rodriguez has given us a redemptive and absorbing work." N Y Times Book Rev

Roger Caras' Treasury of great cat stories. Dutton 1987 495p o.p.

LC 86-2200

"A Truman Talley book"

Analyzed in Short story index

Contents: The cat that walked by himself, by R. Kipling; The cat by the fire, by L. Hunt; The white cat, by W. W. Jacobs; The black cat, by E. A. Poe; Cats, by P. G. Hamerton; The Cat, by M. E. W. Freeman; Calvin, the cat, by C. D. Warner; Ye marvelous legend of Tom Connor's cat, by S. Lover; Dick Baker's cat, by M. Twain; The conscientious cat, by A. A. Sandham; He wrote to the rats, by J. Ralph; The philanthropist and the happy cat, by Saki; Tobermory, by Saki; Midshipman, the cat, by J. C. Adams; A black affair, by W. W. Jacobs; When in doubt—wash, by P. Gallico; Jennie's lessons to Peter on how to behave like a cat, by P. Gallico; The witch's cat, by M. W. Wellman; A feline felony, by L. J. Littke; The Cyprian cat, by D. L. Sayers; Novice, by J. H. Schmitz; The fat cat, by Q. Patrick; My father, the cat, by H. Slesar; The sin of Madame Phloi, by L. J. Braun; The King of Cats, by S. V. Benét; The game of rat and dragon, by C. Smith; Podolo, by L. P. Hartley; Space-time for springers, by F. Leiber; Spooner, by E. Farjeon; The story of Webster, by P. G. Wodehouse; Out of place, by P. Sargent; Cat nipped, by J. Schaefer; The cat who lived in a drainpipe, by J. Aiken; Some are born cats, by T. Carr; Autumn: the garden of stubborn cats, by I. Calvino

Roger Caras' Treasury of great dog stories. Dutton 1987 497p o.p.

LC 86-6264

"A Truman Talley book"

Analyzed in Short story index

Contents: For the love of man, by J. London; A dog's tale, by M. Twain; An adventure with a dog, by J. Muir; A dark-brown dog, by S. Crane; Mumú, by I. Turgenev; Memoirs of a yellow dog, by O. Henry; Getting rid of Fluff, by E. P. Butler; The tailless tyke at bay, by A. Ollivant; That Spot, by J. London; The coming of Lad, by A. P. Terhune; Gun-shy, by E. Fenton; The grudge, by A. P. Terhune; The voice of Bugle Ann, by M. Kantor; Mister Dog, by M. Ellis; Slipstream, by C. Ford; Brag dog, by V. Bell; The test, by D. Henderson; Broken treaty, by D. Henderson; Moses, by W. D. Edmonds; Don, by Z. Grey; Rex, by D. H. Lawrence; Blue milk, by B. Tarkington; The faithful, by L. Del Rey; Blood will tell, by D. Marquis; Lassie come-home, by E. Knight; Rabchik, a Jewish dog, by Sholem Aleichem; The emissary, by R. Bradbury; The blind dog, by R. K. Narayan; Attila, by R. K. Narayan; Dog Star, by A. C. Clarke; A dog's night, by F. Sagan

Roiphe, Anne Richardson, 1935-

If you knew me; a novel. Little, Brown 1993 212p $19.95

ISBN 0-316-75430-7   LC 92-38200

Also available Thorndike Press large print edition

"Microbiologist Leah Rose has retreated to her childhood summer home, the fictitious West Pine, Long Island (the Hamptons), to await scientific inspiration. Alone there, as in the city, lonely, though loathe to admit it, she moves slowly into a relationship with Ollie Marcus, a local high school teacher burdened with the care of his retarded sister. Their dance toward intimacy is fraught with memories of the past—hers of her suicidal mother, Ollie's of being a 'peculiar' child, shy, an outsider—and the realities of the present." Libr J

"In her own quiet way, Anne Roiphe wields some of the outrageous lyric power of Kathy Acker or John Hawkes. It lets us gaze into the honest lives of people caught together as if in the unforgettable, poignant yet almost meaningless arrangements of shell and sea-wrack we find on the beach after a storm we missed." N Y Times Book Rev

Lovingkindness; a novel; by Anne Roiphe. Summit Bks. 1987 279p o.p.

LC 87-6448

"Annie Johnson, widowed before the birth of her daughter Andrea, is a modern, successful, professional woman. Her relations with Andrea has been marked with alienation on her daughter's part, as she appears to be intent on destroying her life as a drop-out from schools, an abuser of drugs, and a young woman who has already experienced three abortions. Annie Johnson seeks psychiatric help for Andrea with no success. It is not until Andrea, finding herself a visitor in Israel, is taken into a yeshiva community that some change in her behavior comes about. The rigorous, although warm, Jewish orthodox discipline appears to change Andrea into a submissive young woman living a life completely foreign to anything her mother understands. The destruction inherent in some parent-child conflicts is painfully described here." Shapiro. Fic for Youth. 3d edition

Up the sandbox! Simon & Schuster 1970 155p o.p.

"The story alternates the inner musings of Margaret Reynolds—a young, sensitive mother, as she watches over her two small children, at a playground along Manhattan's upper Broadway—and Margaret Reynolds, a creator of outrageous dream episodes [such as] . . . blowing up the George Washington Bridge with a team of black militants." New Repub

"Margaret's inner scene will be recognized and applauded by young mothers everywhere who, like Margaret, are 'too old for an identity crisis and yet not past the age of uncertainty.' If the author's insights are at times more precious than rare, her message is not." Time

Rölvaag, Ole Edvart, 1876-1931

Giants in the earth; a saga of the prairie; by O. E. Rölvaag; translated from the Norwegian. Harper 1927 465p o.p.

This novel "chronicles the struggles of Norwegian immigrant settlers in the Dakota territory in the 1870s. . . . The book's indomitable protagonist, Per Hansa, his wife Beret, their children, and three other Norwegian immigrant families settle at Spring Creek, living in makeshift sod huts. Surviving the winters' fierce bliz-

Rölvaag, Ole Edvart, 1876-1931—Continued
zards, they see their crops destroyed by locusts in summer. They nonetheless persist; new settlers arrive, and the community grows." Merriam-Webster's Ency of Lit
Followed by Peder Victorious

Peder Victorious; a novel; by O. E. Rölvaag; translated from the Norwegian; English text by Nora O. Solum and the author. Harper 1929 350p o.p. Greenwood Press reprint available $57.50 (ISBN 0-8371-7067-2)

"Carries on the characters of 'Giants in the earth,' the interest centering in Peder Victorious and Beret, the boy's mother, against the background of a community no longer intensely struggling with the soil, but adapting itself to the ways of the new country, or resisting adaptation as Beret continues to do. The boy Peder, with his changing ideas and his ardent pursuit of girls is a foil for the character of Beret, perhaps the most finely conceived personality in the book." N Y Libr
Followed by Their father's God (1931)

Roosevelt, Elliott, 1910-1990

A first class murder. St. Martin's Press 1991 261p $17.95

ISBN 0-312-05527-7   LC 90-48994
Also available G.K. Hall large print edition

"An Eleanor Roosevelt mystery"

"When First Lady of mystery Eleanor Roosevelt boards the *Normandie* to return to America, she is pleased to learn that Henry Luce, Charles Lindbergh, Jack Benny, Josephine Baker, and the young John F. Kennedy are among her traveling companions. She is not so pleased when the Russian ambassador, also on board, dies of strychnine poisoning, but she sets about to solve the mystery anyway." Publ Wkly

The Hyde Park murder. St. Martin's Press 1985 231p o.p.

LC 85-1752

"A stock swindle threatens to keep two young lovers apart. Bob Hannah is the son of the indicted financier, and his fiancée's father wants no part of a family marked by scandal. Mrs. Roosevelt's matchmaking for the two sweethearts is further complicated when the elder Hannah dies in what is claimed to be a suicide. Bob Hannah and Eleanor suspect murder." Wilson Libr Bull

"The author's fascinating glimpses into history, into the Roosevelts at home, and into corrupt politics are delivered in a measured and surefooted manner." Booklist

Murder and the First Lady. St. Martin's Press 1984 227p o.p.

LC 83-24659

"This historical mystery is set just before World War II, when international tensions are at a peak. Philip Garber, a lowly bookkeeper and assistant to the chief usher at the White House, is found murdered. Eleanor Roosevelt turns sleuth when it's discovered that Garber was found dead in the room of her British secretary, Pamela Rush-Hodgeborne." Booklist

Murder at Hobcaw Barony. St. Martin's Press 1986 233p o.p.

LC 86-3807

"Eleanor Roosevelt, a guest at the South Carolina estate of Bernard Baruch, socializes with some Hollywood types including Bogart, Crawford, Zanuck, and Tallulah Bankhead. After movie producer Ben Partridge is blown to bits in his bedroom, Mrs. R. finds that most of the guests had reasons for murder." Libr J

Murder at the palace. St. Martin's Press 1987 232p o.p.

LC 87-27961
Available G.K. Hall large print edition
"A Thomas Dunne book"

This novel "is set at Buckingham Palace in wartime London. On a visit to British and American troops (including son Elliott), Mrs. Roosevelt greets the king and queen, princesses Margaret and Elizabeth, and Sir Alan Burton. . . . When Burton becomes a suspect in a top-secret and terribly embarrassing murder case, Mrs. Roosevelt comes to his aid." Booklist

Murder in the Blue Room. St. Martin's Press 1990 215p o.p.

LC 89-77677
Available G.K. Hall large print edition
"A Thomas Dunne book"

"Set in 1942 during Soviet Foreign Minister Molotov's secret visit to FDR, [this] mystery . . . finds the author's mother, Eleanor Roosevelt, solving a double murder and combating racial discrimination in the armed forces. A droll, yet affectionate, portrait that is standard but intriguing fare." Booklist

Murder in the East Room. St. Martin's Press 1993 201p $18.95

ISBN 0-312-09878-2   LC 93-26590
"A Thomas Dunne book"

This mystery is "set in the early 1940s as FDR contemplates a third term and Germany is about to invade France. The plot involves the murder of a controversial senator during a state dinner at the White House. Since the D.C. cops seem flummoxed by the situation, Mrs. Roosevelt agrees to lend her considerable sleuthing skills to the case. . . . Roosevelt again conveys a wonderfully intimate and authentic picture of the FDR White House and its inhabitants. His story is well plotted, entertaining, and full of ambience." Booklist

Murder in the Oval Office; an Eleanor Roosevelt mystery. St. Martin's Press 1989 247p o.p.

LC 88-18848
Available G.K. Hall large print edition
"A Thomas Dunne book"

"Her sense of justice (not to mention her curiosity) sparked by the murder of a Southern Congressman during a White House soiree, the resourceful First Lady shows spunk and wit, and also considerable charm, in her investigation of the locked room puzzle." N Y Times Book Rev

Murder in the Red Room. St. Martin's Press 1992 249p $18.95

ISBN 0-312-07637-1   LC 92-4212
"A Thomas Dunne book"

This novel "is set in early 1937, just as FDR is making his attempt to 'enlarge' . . . the U.S. Supreme Court. Two days before the planned announcement of that campaign, a small-time hoodlum from Cleveland is murdered in the Red Room while the Roosevelts host guests—including seven Supreme Court justices—in the State Dining Room next door. Mrs. Roosevelt joins

Roosevelt, Elliott, 1910-1990—*Continued*

Secret Service agent Stan Szczygiel and Washington, D.C., police lieutenant Ed Kennelly in scrutinizing the motley crew of suspects for this and a later murder." Booklist

Murder in the Rose Garden. St. Martin's Press 1989 232p o.p.

LC 89-35326

Available G.K. Hall large print edition

"A Thomas Dunne book"

"During the summer of 1936, popular Washington hostess Vivian Taliafero is strangled in the White House Rose Garden. . . . The First Lady helps the Secret Service and the D.C. police gather information about the murdered woman who was, it turns out, an extortionist. . . . Vivian's partner in blackmail, photographer Joe Bob Skaggs, is killed, as is one of their victims, while Mrs. Roosevelt strives to solve the mystery." Publ Wkly

Murder in the west wing; an Eleanor Roosevelt mystery. St. Martin's Press 1992 247p $18.95

ISBN 0-312-08144-8   LC 92-26155

"A Thomas Dunne book"

"President Roosevelt's special assistant has been murdered, and it certainly looks as if Therese did it— given how she was quick to rinse out his cyanide-laced glass of bourbon. But Eleanor Roosevelt thinks otherwise, and she sets out to prove it." Libr J

New deal for death; a "Blackjack" Endicott novel. St. Martin's Press 1993 251p $18.95

ISBN 0-312-09267-9   LC 93-7434

"A Thomas Dunne book"

This novel features "Boston bon vivant 'Blackjack' Endicott, who serves as friend and protector to Franklin D. Roosevelt. . . . Endicott, a yachtsman, race car driver, flier, lover and crack shot, must travel to Hollywood to foil an unholy alliance of film producers and crooked union leaders out to stop the newly nominated FDR from carrying out labor reform." Publ Wkly

"Although the book gets off to a slow start . . . once it gets rolling, there's plenty of action, a heart-stopping climax, and a fascinating blend of nostalgia and glitzy glamour." Booklist

The President's man; a Blackjack Endicott novel. St. Martin's Press 1991 245p o.p.

LC 91-20625

"A Thomas Dunne book"

"When a Tammany Hall politician tells FDR of a death threat, the New York governor asks his millionaire sportsman friend Jack Endicott to investigate. Mobsters grown powerful during Prohibition fear FDR will favor repeal and undercut their influence. Through a bootlegger connection, Endicott tries to convince such gang leaders as Lucky Luciano, Dutch Schultz and the imprisoned but still formidable Al Capone, that nothing would be gained by killing FDR. . . . A lively yarn that succeeds despite occasional naïve or infelicitous turns of phrase." Publ Wkly

A royal murder. St. Martin's Press 1994 234p $19.95

ISBN 0-312-10970-9   LC 94-7143

"A Thomas Dunne book"

"FDR sends the indefatigable First Lady to the Bahamas, where she simultaneously manages to accomplish a delicate diplomatic mission and quash a flourishing espionage ring. While trying to discourage the recently exiled Duke and Duchess of Windsor from touring the U.S. in order to broadcast their decidedly pro-German point of view, Mrs. Roosevelt becomes involved in a baffling murder case. During the course of her investigation, she exposes an insidious nest of Nazi spies, who have successfully infiltrated both the Bahamian government and the business community. A pleasantly entertaining blend of history and mystery." Booklist

The White House pantry murder; an Eleanor Roosevelt mystery. St. Martin's Press 1987 231p o.p.

LC 86-26249

"A Thomas Dunne book"

"It is December, 1941, and Winston Churchill is a guest at the White House. The body of an unidentified man is found in the White House freezer. When weapons are found in a storm sewer leading to the White House, espionage or an assassination attempt is suspected. Mrs. Roosevelt, ably assisted by Secret Service agent Deconcini and British Lieutenant-Commander Leach, must find the person responsible before something terrible happens." Libr J

Roquelaure, A. N. *See* Rice, Anne, 1941-

Rosenberg, Nancy Taylor

First offense. Dutton 1994 338p $22.95

ISBN 0-525-93853-2   LC 94-550

"Probation officer Ann Carlisle's husband, a highway patrolman, disappeared mysteriously four years ago, and it's been tough for Ann and her 12-year-old son to put their lives back together. A new love interest plus a heavy caseload at work are just beginning to help heal Ann's wounds when she becomes involved in a narcotics trial that will unravel her life all over again." Booklist

"Just when readers will have figured all the angles, savvy Rosenberg unveils the villain and flips the plot into an exciting manhunt, with Ann as bait." Publ Wkly

Interest of justice; a novel. Dutton 1993 368p $21

ISBN 0-525-93680-7   LC 93-13005

"Lara Sanderstone, a California judge, finds her life turned upside down when her house is burglarized, her sister and brother-in-law are brutally murdered, and she's left with a sullen 14-year-old nephew to care for. With the help of police sergeant Ted Rickerson, Lara tries to determine if the crimes were the random work of some sicko or if one of the deadbeats she's sent to prison is out for revenge." Booklist

"Lara Sanderstone is such an intelligent, finely detailed character that even the unlikeliest plot twists work in this absorbing legal thriller." Publ Wkly

Mitigating circumstances. Dutton 1993 362p $21

ISBN 0-525-93587-8   LC 92-23035

In this novel "Lily Forrester, a district attorney in Southern California, is an ambitious woman with a deteriorating marriage. Her life becomes a nightmare when both she and her daughter are brutally attacked. Recognizing their attacker, but unwilling to submit her child to the abuse of the legal system, Forrester moves to deal out justice herself." Libr J

Rosenberg, Nancy Taylor—*Continued*

"For all the adrenaline that the author pumps into her story, her writing is far more persuasive when it isn't so feverish—during intimate mother-daughter exchanges, for example, and in the realistically mundane procedures of ordinary, hard-working cops and lawyers." N Y Times Book Rev

Ross, Jonathan, 1916-

A rattling of old bones. Scribner 1982 c1979 187p o.p.

LC 81-14478

First published 1979 in the United Kingdom

In this mystery, Supt. George Rogers "faces, in a closet, the shriveled corpse of a woman who disappeared five years earlier. The technical difficulties are obvious, though the local pathologist Dr. Briget Hunter, who is the inspector's unofficial lover, does her best as usual and adds the fact that the woman was three months pregnant. The author's imagination about details comes in brilliantly and leads to a powerful and legitimate surprise ending." Barzun. Cat of Crime. Rev and enl edition

Ross, Leonard Q. *See* Rosten, Leo Calvin, 1908-

Ross, Malcolm *See* Ross-Macdonald, Malcolm

Ross-Macdonald, Malcolm

All desires known; [by] Malcolm Macdonald. St. Martin's Press 1994 c1993 346p $21.95

ISBN 0-312-10415-4   LC 93-35853

First published 1993 in the United Kingdom

In this "tale of Victorian Ireland, Dr. Michael Raven and his wife, Lucy, popular leaders of Dublin society, are deeply in debt, the cost of maintaining their social status being considerably higher than Dr. Raven's income. Thus the pair jump at the chance for Michael to run an exclusive clinic in the country, safely away from expensive social 'obligations.' Meanwhile, Ebenezer O'Dea, the moneylender behind this scheme, has his own reasons for enticing the Ravens away from Dublin. The clinic's architect is a childhood playmate of Lucy's who has always loved her, and the matron whom O'Dea hires is an old flame of Michael's with a secret of her own." Libr J

The author "combines strong characters and brisk narrative full of trenchant observations about life, love and the eternal communication problems between sexes." Publ Wkly

Dancing on snowflakes; [by] Malcolm Macdonald. St. Martin's Press 1994 384p $21.95

ISBN 0-312-11256-4   LC 94-26106

"Katy O'Barry, née Katarina Oberg, is banished from her parents' Dublin home in 1897 when she falls madly in love with the wrong person during her social season. She's to stay with her strict, straight-laced aunt and uncle in Stockholm. With the help of male and female acquaintances, some more bizarre than others, Katy manages to go out on her own, maintain her integrity

as a Victorian maiden, learn about growing up, and fall in love with the proper person." Libr J

"Macdonald has chosen a glorious setting, nineteenth-century Stockholm on the brink of the International Exhibition, for some convention-defying fiction." Booklist

For they shall inherit; a novel; [by] Malcolm Macdonald. St. Martin's Press 1985 c1984 591p o.p.

LC 84-52352

First published 1984 in the United Kingdom with title: In love and war

This "novel is set in 19th century England and centers on a dynamic friendship, cemented in boyhood, between clever, ambitious, working-class Freddy and aristocratic Clive, son of the wealthy industrialist who is Freddy's first employer. The fireworks begin when they fall in love with the same woman and Freddy finds himself the legal father of his friend's child. Thereupon they embark on careers that feature exotic adventures in South Africa, South America, the Middle East and elsewhere, accompanied by Freddy's relentless rise to power and wealth, finally at Clive's expense, and the inextricable social and genetic intertwining of their two families." Publ Wkly

"MacDonald skillfully depicts the English class system and the struggles inherent in it. The characters are multifaceted and solidly drawn, and the writing is smooth. An absorbing portrayal of human emotion and an individual's will to prevail." Libr J

Hell hath no fury; [by] Malcolm Macdonald. St. Martin's Press 1992 374p o.p.

LC 91-41090

"The year is 1885, and the place is Dublin. The unsinkable Daisy O'Lindon, faced with a life of genteel poverty under her father's roof, sets out to make her own way in the world. Her first job is as an artist's model. From there, her fortunes steadily improve through shrewd moves and hard work. But throughout the years, there remains the nagging suspicion that revenge, rather than security, may be her greatest motivation. Beautifully written." Booklist

An innocent woman. St. Martin's Press 1991 c1989 378p o.p.

LC 90-15545

First published 1989 in the United Kingdom

"Upon the death of his wife in late 1859, Wilfred Hervey, in an attempt to maintain his daughter's innocence until she is wed, moves himself and 19-year-old Jane to Cornwall. Thinking Jane will be safe there, not only from the facts of life but from the realities of her mother's past and a few of his own dark secrets, Wilfred has, instead, unknowingly brought her right to the heart of her mother's disgrace. As Jane unravels the secrets of life, she stumbles onto the clues to her ancestry and draws quite a few of the neighbors—and her chaperone—into the growing-up process with her." Booklist

The author "pens a delicate, almost dreamy, tale of a woman who is determined to find her own way while still maintaining an accepted place in a society that keeps 'respectable' women under a tight rein." Publ Wkly

The rich are with you always. Knopf 1976 483p o.p.

"In this sequel to 'The World From Rough Stones' Macdonald continues the interlocking family dramas of John and Nora Stevenson, born dirt poor, driving hard for money and power in Victorian England, and Walter and Arabella Thornton, aristocratic, unhappy, the

Ross-Macdonald, Malcolm—*Continued*

Stevensons' opposites in every way. It is Nora and John who dominate this part of the saga in the fierce get-rich-quick era of railroad schemes and bonanzas and bankruptcies." Publ Wkly

Followed by Sons of fortune (1978)

To the end of her days; [by] Malcolm Macdonald. St. Martin's Press 1994 407p il $23.95

  ISBN 0-312-11080-4   LC 94-6397

This "historical romance is set in a Cornish town during the 1920s, following the death of Jessica Lanyon's husband, Ian, from war injuries. Only 30 and with three children to support, Jessica faces an uncertain future. Lorna Sancreed, whose fiancé served with Ian and died on the same day as he, shows up after the funeral to change Jessica's life forever. Though only in her early 20s, Lorna serves as a catalyst to shake up the lives around her and to force alterations in relationships, both personal and business." Libr J

A woman alone; [by] Malcolm Macdonald. St. Martin's Press 1991 c1990 377p o.p.
                              LC 90-28635

First published 1990 in the United Kingdom

"As the result of a joke, headstrong Roseanne Kitto attends the local Ram-Buck fair with Stephen Morvah, the squire's son, in this romance set in 19th-century Cornwall. While Stephen and Roseanne find themselves happily surprised by their easy affection, Annette, Stephen's young, ambitious sister, and Mark Bodilly, Roseanne's erstwhile boyfriend, are not. . . . [A] robust romance, which handily evokes the natural landscape of Cornwall and the dialect and class distinctions of its inhabitants." Publ Wkly

A woman possessed; [by] Malcolm Macdonald. St. Martin's Press 1993 c1992 375p $21.95

  ISBN 0-312-09416-7   LC 93-15061

First published 1992 in the United Kingdom

The settled routine of Cornwall residents "Giles and Laura Curnow is severely disrupted by the return from South Africa of Maurice Petifer, Laura's once penniless first love who is now a millionaire. After Maurice buys the property adjoining the Curnows', Giles, a well-to-do merchant who has prided himself on treating Laura as an equal, finds himself consumed with primitive jealousy, while Laura, the mother of five, feels ambivalent and restless." Publ Wkly

A woman scorned; [by] Malcolm Macdonald. St. Martin's Press 1992 422p $22.95

  ISBN 0-312-08341-6   LC 92-27470

"The Bellinghams of Castle Moore become engaged in the primitive business of ancient blood feuds when most of their number are brutally murdered in their summer pavilion during a birthday celebration. Years later, one of the survivors, Judith Carty, returns to her home near the castle with two things on her mind: solving the mystery of the Castle Moore murders and coming to terms with the question of marriage." Publisher's note

"This lively account of life among the Anglo-Irish aristocracy combines absorbing historical background, a pleasing romance and colorful characters." Publ Wkly

The world from rough stones. Knopf 1975 535p il o.p.

"Within a year, in the early 1840s, John Stevenson, with Nora at his side, rises from the ranks of railroad construction laborer to the position of a respected and influential contractor. Nora, the ragged and starving teenage girl who had come to John out of the night, becomes his wife. . . . The minor characters, Walter and Arabella Thornton, are middleclass English who are swept along by the tumultuous Stevensons. Walter driven by his sexual fantasies and urges, and Arabella, the pious and good but frigid wife." Best Sellers

"This saga of England in 1839-40 and the start of a great railroad building dynasty opens fast and never once lets up its pace and drama. Above all, its people are believable human beings, caught up in the tumultuous movement of beginning social change." Publ Wkly

Followed by The rich are with you always

Rossiter, John *See* Ross, Jonathan, 1916-

Rossner, Judith

August. Houghton Mifflin 1983 376p o.p.
                          LC 83-6191

"'August,' when analysts vacation, is the tale of an analysis, with parallel story-lines for patient and doctor. Teenaged golden girl Dawn Henley has a bizarre background: orphaned as an infant, she was raised by a beloved lesbian aunt and her lover, whose 'divorce' sent Dawn to an analyst. Fortyish Dr. Lulu Shinefeld is twice divorced with a grown daughter from whom she's estranged. So Dawn becomes Dr. Shinefeld's 'analytic daughter.'" Libr J

"Rossner writes about the technical side of analysis and simultaneously shows it at work. In spite of a few awkward passages that tell rather than show how analysis works and an unavoidable lack of completeness resulting from the nature of her topic, Rossner has written a fascinating study of the human mind growing." Best Sellers

Emmeline. Simon & Schuster 1980 331p o.p.
                          LC 80-15553

The novel concerns Emmeline Mosher who "was 13 years old in 1839 when she was sent from her family's farm in Maine to earn 55 cents a week in the cotton mills of Lowell, Mass. There she was seduced by an overseer, gave birth to a child at the home of an aunt before her fifteenth birthday and returned to her parents without telling them her secret. Her venture into the world had saved her family from destitution. In her 30s, having resigned herself to a single life, she made a happy marriage, which ended in calamity. She lived another 40 years as an outcast. . . . Her story is true, according to [the author]." Newsweek

The author "handles her material so meticulously that she inspires a renewed respect for the complexities of skillful story-telling. Instead of propagandizing, she evinces complete respect for the period and setting of her story." Books of the Times

His little women; a novel. Summit Bks. 1990 367p o.p.
                          LC 89-26128

Rossner, Judith—*Continued*

A "novel about movie mogul Sam Pearlstein and his four daughters from three marriages. Writer Louisa Abrahams and lawyer Nell Berman, from marriages one and two, are drawn together by their adoration for Daddy (who can be a charmer), by the libel suit brought against Louisa's novel about a Hollywood producer and his daughters, and by the search for truth as each sees it. Nell, whose story this is, ponders the line between fiction and truth, a legal and personal question for her and a potential focus for this book, which dwells on Sam and his womanizing." Libr J

"In the age of the minimalist novel, pared down to the point where it frequently disappears, Ms. Rossner is refreshing. She doesn't shrink from narrative complexity. Obsessions fascinate her, as do the extremes of behavior. She loves scenes full of high drama." N Y Times Book Rev

Looking for Mr. Goodbar. Simon & Schuster 1975 284p o.p.

This novel opens with the police transcript of a murderer's confession. The novel "is based loosely on the actual case of Roseann Quinn, a quiet, rigidly brought-up Catholic schoolteacher, who was wholly unremarkable except that she sought out her sexual partners in New York singles bars. The last of them bashed in her skull on New Year's Day, 1973. The question the author asks as she tours the life of Theresa Dunn, the Roseann Quinn-like character of the book, is 'What's a nice girl like you doing in a place like this?'" N Y Times Book Rev

"The tale is stark, capably told, believable; Rossner's prose is a delight, and her sense of the inner life of her characters, all tortured, is deft and sure. This is a very good novel." Booklist

Olivia; or, The weight of the past. Crown 1994 334p $23

ISBN 0-517-59720-9   LC 93-50211

"Caroline finds success as a television chef in New York after her marriage fails. Daughter Olivia, Roman Catholic by virtue of her father, has been left behind in Rome. But Caroline's life goes into a tailspin when Olivia opts to join her mother in Manhattan, while seizing upon her perceived abandonment as reason for discord in their tenuous relationship." Booklist

"Rossner takes some risks here in debating Jewish/Catholic attitudes toward abortion, but as both Cara and Livvy probe their uncertain ways to identify as mothers and as independent women, the novel ends on a satisfying, if realistically ambiguous, note. Anyone who likes to eat, cook or read about food will savor Rossner's descriptions of tasty dishes and culinary lore, conveyed with gusto and sensuous detail." Publ Wkly

Rosten, Leo Calvin, 1908-

Captain Newman, M.D. Harper 1962 c1961 331p o.p.

First published 1961 in the United Kingdom

"Describes life in a hospital at an Air Force base in the Southwest during the war. Captain Newman, chief of the psychiatric ward, is a warm, kindly person, the antithesis of the military man, and it is around him that the story revolves. The action is made up of a series of episodes." Libr J

"A book of great insight, warmth and humor. . . . It is a tremendously impressive piece of verbal tight-rope walking. There are the expected flashes of GI humor, the much-documented war of rank, there are also moments of great tenderness and understanding in this chronicle of that most delicate of explorations, the exploration into the shattered minds that are the common responsibilities of all of us." N Y Her Trib Books

Roth, Henry, 1906-1995

Call it sleep; with an introduction by Alfred Kazin and an afterword by Hana Wirth-Nesher. Farrar, Straus & Giroux 1991 xx, 9-462p $30

ISBN 0-374-11819-1   LC 91-21130

A reissue of the title first published 1934 by R.O. Ballou

"The years between the sixth and ninth birthdays of a young boy are described in this vivid, sensitive portrayal of a Jewish childhood in the ghettos of Brownsville, and the Lower East Side in New York. Because David's father is a violent and bitter man, the child always turns to his mother, with whom he is very close. Her love protects him from the terrors of street gangs, poverty, the sexual conflicts between his parents, and his own initiation into sex by a lame girl. A literary technique that distinguishes between the language used by members of this family when they are speaking their native tongue (Yiddish) and when they speak broken English they have learned as immigrants in the United States is an unusual feature in this remarkable book." Shapiro. Fic for Youth. 3d edition

A diving rock on the Hudson. St. Martin's Press 1995 418p (Mercy of a rude stream, v2) $23.95

ISBN 0-312-11777-9

This second volume of the author's autobiographical cycle "continues the saga of Ira Stigman, teenage son of Orthodox Jewish immigrant parents, as he struggles to find his way in the larger world. Narrated by the now elderly Ira, it effectively evokes both life in 1920s New York and the angst of adolescent existence. In Ira's case, this angst results not only from the growing distance that separates his and his parents' views of the world but from uncontrollable urges that drive him to violate one of society's strongest taboos."

"Simultaneously, we are inside the mind of a troubled adolescent and that of an aged but still mentally vital man, a man engaged with words, with concepts, obsessively reconsidering the role of the artist and in particular his own responsibility in portraying events truthfully." Booklist

A star shines over Mt. Morris Park. St. Martin's Press 1994 290p (Mercy of a rude stream, v1) $23

ISBN 0-312-10499-5   LC 93-37270

This is the first volume of a projected six part series

Ira Stigman, the hero of this novel "narrates both as a boy, in the past, and in the present, as a philosophical and pain-wracked octogenarian. Young Ira's tale begins in 1914, when he and his parents move from the East Side's cozy Jewish enclave to Harlem, then primarily Irish. This dislocation, which makes Ira despise his Jewishness, coincides with the arrival of his mother's parents and siblings, fresh off the boat from Austria-

Roth, Henry, 1906-1995—*Continued*

Hungary. As Ira copes with all these changes, he takes comfort in books. . . . As he navigates the rough course of his impoverished life from ages 8 to 15, he reports on the absurdities and abusiveness of family life, school, and various jobs as well as the shadow of war, the many hues of anti-Semitism and racism, and the shock of sexuality." Booklist

"Mr. Roth remains an admirable craftsman, and the scenes of immigrant life in the second decade of the century are evoked with persuasive concreteness." N Y Times Book Rev

Followed by A diving rock on the Hudson

Roth, Philip

The anatomy lesson. Farrar, Straus & Giroux 1983 291p o.p.

LC 83-11645

"Roth's novelist/hero in The Ghost Writer and Zuckerman Unbound, Nathan Zuckerman at 40 can no longer write: he has lost his subject ('as a medium for his books he had ceased to be') and is losing his hair. Severely incapacitated by chronic pain . . . and addicted to painkillers, Zuckerman decides to become a doctor, one who deals not in words but in real 'stuff,' 'the lowest of genres—life itself.' He ends up in a hospital rather than medical school when a disastrously euphoric return to Chicago, scene of his first literary triumph, results in a drug-induced breakdown." Libr J

"A ferocious, heartfelt book. . . . One might venture to say that, like a goodly number of Roth's previous works, 'The Anatomy Lesson' revolves around the paradox of incarnation—the astonishing coexistence in one life of infantilism and intelligence, of selfishness and altruism, of sexual appetite and social conscience—and has the form and manner of a monologue conducted under psychoanalysis." New Yorker

also in Roth, P. Zuckerman bound: a trilogy and epilogue

The counterlife. Farrar, Straus & Giroux 1986 324p il $18.95

ISBN 0-374-13026-4 LC 86-18296

"Returning here, and writing his own (post-humous) story, is Nathan Zuckerman, who was supposed to have been all wrapped up in the trilogy-plus-novella 'Zuckerman Bound.' Zuckerman, himself a creator of Rothian characters, is really the creation of Peter Tarnopol, the novelist in 'My Life as a Man,' we are assured. Are we to believe it? There are twists and turns in 'The Counterlife' that disabuse us of easy belief; down its byways we hear all of Mr. Roth's fictions whispering to one another. His old themes and concerns are here, but now we understand them differently. But do we? Mr. Roth's sport with the nature of reality becomes an exhilarating contest for his reader." N Y Times Book Rev

Deception; a novel. Simon & Schuster 1990 208p $18.95

ISBN 0-671-70374-9 LC 89-49207

"Philip, a successful, middle-aged, and highly opinionated Jewish-American novelist, moves to a small flat in London to work on his new book. He begins seeing a married Englishwoman in his spare time, and soon he has filled a notebook with their pre-and post-coital conversations. When he publishes this document

as a novel, his indignant mistress accuses him of deceiving both her and his public." Libr J

Roth "does give, through the novel's voices, a tender and vivid sense of the artificial, pleasurable, short-lived enclosedness of a secret affair in a single room. . . . Still, it's not adultery as sexual or social plot that he is primarily intrigued by, it's adultery as the occasion for authorial deception." New Repub

The ghost writer. Farrar, Straus & Giroux 1979 179p o.p.

LC 79-13146

"A brief but intricate tale about a young writer [Nathan Zuckerman] who, when accused of travestying his fellow Jews, seeks counsel from a respected older Jewish author and finds this distinguished figure ambiguously involved with a girl whom the young writer fantasizes to be Anne Frank." Oxford Companion to Am Lit. 5th edition

Followed by Zuckerman unbound

also in Roth, P. Zuckerman bound: a trilogy and epilogue

Goodbye, Columbus, and five short stories. Modern Library ed. Modern Lib. 1995 298p $13.50

ISBN 0-679-60159-7 LC 94-44528

Also available from Amereon and Buccaneer Bks.

A reissue of the title first published 1959 by Houghton Mifflin and analyzed in Short story index

Contents: Goodbye, Columbus; The conversion of the Jews; Defender of the faith; You can't tell a man by the song he sings; Eli, the fanatic

"In the featured story Neil Klugman and Brenda Patimkin are involved in a summer love affair that lacks the substance necessary to sustain a lasting relationship. In another story, 'The Conversion of the Jews,' Ozzie Freedman is a disruptive element in his Hebrew school. Sgt. Nathan Marx finds himself the 'defender of the faith' when he becomes the First Sergeant of a training company that includes Grossbart, an exploiter of people and situations. Trouble brews for Epstein when he begins to emulate the romantic behavior of the young people in his house. In 'You Can't Tell a Man by the Song He Sings,' a young student learns an early lesson about believing everything he is told. In the last story, Eli becomes a fanatic who assumes the guilt for the Jews in his community in his last law case." Shapiro. Fic for Youth. 3d edition

The great American novel. Holt, Rinehart & Winston 1973 382p o.p.

"Sportswriter 'Word' Smith narrates the chaotic history of a forgotten ('suppressed,' he claims) third major league and its bungling nemeses the Ruppert Mundays, a team of neurotic misfit leftovers. In 1943, war has decimated the league; the Mundays are cast out from their stadium (which is needed for wartime priorities) on 'an endless road trip,' to wander the circuit and suffer." Libr J

This novel is "at once a burlesque and an allegory, its telling of the downfall of a great baseball team serving as a satirical parallel to contemporary American political and social events." Oxford Companion to Am Lit. 5th edition

Letting go. Random House 1962 630p $12.50

ISBN 0-394-43305-X

Roth, Philip—_Continued_

Gabe Wallach is "a young university instructor who is literally unable to let go in his personal relationships. This is true with his father, a well-to-do Jewish dentist who suffers because his wife is dead and his only child lives in Chicago instead of New York; with Martha Reganhart, a divorcée, mother of two small children, a woman Gabe loves enough to make his mistress but not his wife; and with Paul and Libby Herz, a young couple suffering the difficulties arising from a mixed marriage, no money, inability to have children, and a host of other problems real and imagined." Libr J

My life as a man. Holt, Rinehart & Winston 1974 330p o.p.

The "novel consists of three stories: a long autobiographical narrative told by the novelist Peter Tarnopol, preceded by two of Peter's stories, 'useful fictions' in which elements of his 'true story' are metamorphosed. Peter's alter ego, Nathan Zuckerman, is, like his author, a highly self-conscious intellectual urban Jew, adept at eliciting astonishing sexual performances from teen-age girls, but fatally drawn into a disastrous marriage with an older, damaged woman who is incapable of sexual response." Newsweek

Operation Shylock; a confession. Simon & Schuster 1993 398p $23

ISBN 0-671-70376-5   LC 92-41959

This novel chronicles the "emotional and moral crises in the life of a Jewish American writer named Philip Roth. Roth has just barely recovered from a Halcion-induced breakdown when he finds out that a man claiming to be Philip Roth is in Jerusalem promoting a bizarrely perverse movement to return Israeli Jews of European descent to Europe." Booklist

"The increasingly frenzied and farcical minuet between the two Philips takes place against a complex background of contemporary scenes and questions. . . . Nearly everyone the narrator meets has fallen prey to an obsession of one sort or another—he is in the Middle East, after all—and during the course of the novel, so does he. They are preoccupied by history, he by himself. The peculiar genius of Operation Shylock is to portray how such dementias can be fatal but rarely serious." Time

Portnoy's complaint. Random House 1969 274p o.p. Buccaneer Bks. reprint available $32.95 (ISBN 1-56849-324-X)

"An irreverently funny account of a modern man torn between the repressive, traditional values embodied by his Jewish mother, his passion for WASP women, and his desperate desire to be released from the past to create himself as a human being out of his own nothingness." Reader's Ency. 3d edition

"Roth has the courage to wish to show things as he has experienced them, but the exaggerations of _Portnoy's Complaint_ have a shrillness which could be considered unwholesome if the book were not so funny. It is very funny." Burgess. 99 Novels

The Prague orgy

_In_ Roth, P. Zuckerman bound: a trilogy and epilogue

The professor of desire. Farrar, Straus & Giroux 1977 263p o.p.

LC 77-24032

This novel concerns "David Kepesh, professor of comparative literature. . . . Kepesh becomes involved with a series of women: the coeds at Syracuse University, whom he affronts with his outrageous candor; two Swedish girls in London, who join him, one with self-loathing and the other with zest, in various sexual adventures; a disorganized California beauty, with whom he takes up at the end of his graduate studies at Stanford University; and a well-organized New York beauty, who rescues him from the wreckage of his marriage to the Californian." New Yorker

"Like most writers who prove they have enough talent for the long haul of a career, Roth has found the story he will tell until either he or it is exhausted. It is a good story and, as The Professor of Desire proves, it gets better with each telling." Time

When she was good. Random House 1967 306p o.p.

This is "a story of a girl obsessed with her own criteria of what a man should be. Set in a Midwestern town the novel is concerned with Lucy Nelson, who disappointed with a feckless father, fights him and scorns her mother for her love of him. Having wreaked havoc in her parents' marriage, she applies the same steely demands to a husband who has been either the seduced or the seducer depending on whose view is accepted. She destroys the marriage and herself in a final abandonment to her compulsion." Booklist

"Roth knows exactly what he's doing. With unerring fidelity, he records the flat surface of provincial American life, the look and feel and sound of it—and then penetrates it to the cesspool of its invisible dynamisms. Beneath the 'good,' and impelling it, he says, lies the horrid." Newsweek

Zuckerman bound: a trilogy and epilogue. Farrar, Straus & Giroux 1985 784p $22.50

ISBN 0-374-29943-9   LC 84-23265

An omnibus edition of the author's Zuckerman novels: The ghost writer, Zuckerman unbound and The anatomy lesson, all entered separately together with a new novella, The Prague orgy

In The Prague orgy "Zuckerman pays a calamitous visit to Czechoslovakia on an Aspern Papers mission to rescue the unpublished manuscript of a great martyred Yiddish writer. The young Zuckerman once spun a feverish fantasy in which he appeased his disapproving Jewish parents by bringing Anne Frank home to Newark as his bride. His heroic Prague quest is no more successful. It ends sardonically, with Zuckerman forced to listen to a cultural commissar extol the great American writer Betty MacDonald." Newsweek

Zuckerman unbound. Farrar, Straus & Giroux 1981 225p o.p.

LC 81-4640

"After three marriages and a respected body of fiction, Nathan Zuckerman has suddenly struck free with the scandalous and subversive success of a book about a Portnoyish complainer called Carnovsky. The promising apprentice of The Ghost Writer who engaged in biographical fantasy, has himself become a creature of public fantasy who cannot cope comfortably even with material success. The consequences range from bizarre comedy (the plague of a ruined quiz show contestant who claims his life has been plagiarized) to the distortion of family relations." Libr J

Followed by The anatomy lesson

Roth, Philip—*Continued*
also in Roth, P. Zuckerman bound: a trilogy and epilogue

Rothman, Judith, 1935-
For works written by this author under other names see Black, Veronica, 1935-

Rowan, Hester
For works written by this author under other names see Radley, Sheila

Ruark, Robert
Something of value; drawings by Daniel Schwartz. Doubleday 1955 566p il o.p. Buccaneer Bks. reprint available $36.95 (ISBN 0-89966-816-X)

This novel is set in "the British East African colony of Kenya. The hero is Peter McKenzie, left motherless on a farm and reared by the senior wife of a Kikuyu headman. Peter and the man's first-born son, Kimani, thereby become virtual brothers. The book then traces their careers from a companionable boyhood through diverging maturities until the climax brings Kimani to violent death at Peter's hands." Publisher's note

Uhuru; a novel of Africa today. McGraw-Hill 1962 555p o.p. Buccaneer Bks. reprint available $36.95 (ISBN 1-56849-025-9)

This novel "tells of the Kenya of 1960—eight years after the Mau-Mau rebellion—a Kenya where native Africans are heard in the House of Parliament and the UN, where modern-day sophistication is blended with ancient tribal customs to produce a new form of cannibalism, where one nauseating throat-cutting ceremony follows another nauseating betrayal of ethics and morals." Libr J

Rubens, Bernice
A solitary grief. Sinclair-Stevenson 1991 240p o.p.
LC 92-143819

"Dr. Alistair Crown, a psychiatrist, is the sort of man who brings his wife flowers stolen from a cemetery to celebrate the birth of their first child. When he learns the child is a girl, he prepares cunning ways to express his displeasure—and when told his daughter has Down syndrome, he assumes a manner of complete avoidance. . . . In an odd way, this deeply disturbed character exerts a curious hold on the reader. Finally, the only way to gain knowledge of his twisted psyche is to continue turning the pages. The conclusion delivers a veritable blow and also reveals the author's level of excellence at her craft." Booklist

Rule, Ann
Possession; a novel. Norton 1983 348p o.p.
LC 82-14377

This is a "tale of a psychotic killer stalking a deputy sheriff and his wife as they backpack in the Washington wilderness. The woman, insecure and dependent despite her beauty, and then with her mind unhinged by her husband's death, transfers her allegiance to the stranger, who says he will lead her to safety. Her subsequent rape, the sexual relationship she develops with the rapist, and his lurid fantasies are distasteful, but the parallel story of her husband's partner's search for the pair, his gathering of evidence, and his defense in the murder investigation brought against him exemplifies highly competent crime writing." Libr J

Runyon, Alfred Damon *See* Runyon, Damon, 1880-1946

Runyon, Damon, 1880-1946
Best of Runyon; E. C. Bentley selected these stories; Nicolas Bentley drew the pictures. Stokes, F. A. 1938 xxv, 318p il o.p.
Analyzed in Short story index
Contents: Breach of promise; Romance in the roaring forties; Dream Street Rose; Old doll's house; Blood pressure; Bloodhounds of Broadway; Tobias the terrible; Snatching of Bookie Bob; Lily of St. Pierre; Hold 'em Yale; Earthquake; "Gentlemen, the King!"; Nice price; Broadway financier; Brian goes home

Blue plate special
In Runyon, D. Guys and dolls [omnibus volume] p345-505

Guys and dolls. Lippincott 1950 505p o.p. Amereon reprint available $18.95 (ISBN 0-89190-438-7)

An omnibus volume of three titles first published by F.A. Stokes in 1931, 1935 and 1934 respectively and analyzed in Short story index
Contents: Guys and dolls: Bloodhounds of Broadway; Social error; Lily of St. Pierre; Butch minds the baby; Lillian; Romance in the roaring forties; Very honorable guy; Madame La Gimp; Dark Dolores; "Gentlemen, the King!"; Hottest guy in the world; Brain goes home; Blood pressure
Money from home: Earthquake; Bred for battle; Breach of promise; Story goes with it; Sense of humor; Broadway financier; Broadway complex; It comes up mud; Nice price; Pick the winner; Undertaker song; Tobias the terrible
Blue plate special: Hold 'em Yale!; That ever-loving wife of Hymie's; What, no butler?; Brakeman's daughter; Snatching of Bookie Bob; Dream Street Rose; Little Miss Marker; Dancing Dan's Christmas; Old doll's house; Lemon drop kid; Three wise guys; Princess O'Hara; For a pal

Money from home
In Runyon, D. Guys and dolls [omnibus volume] p167-337

Rusch, Kristine Kathryn
(ed) The Best from Fantasy & Science Fiction: a 45th anniversary anthology. See The Best from Fantasy & Science Fiction: a 45th anniversary anthology

Rush, Norman
Mating. Knopf 1991 480p $22.95
ISBN 0-394-54472-2   LC 90-25752

Rush, Norman—*Continued*

The author "relates the tale of an American female anthropologist in Africa, whose thesis research (on fertility) has already gone dead when she falls for a man who is in Africa running a utopian community for unfortunate women." Booklist

"Mr. Rush has created one of the wiser and wittier fictive meditations on the subject of mating. His novel illuminates why we yield when we don't have to. It seeks to illuminate the nature of true intimacy—how to define it, how to know when one has achieved it. And few books evoke so eloquently that state of love at its apogee." N Y Times Book Rev

Rushdie, Salman

East, west; stories. Pantheon Bks. 1995 c1994 214p $21

ISBN 0-679-43965-X   LC 94-28277

Analyzed in Short story index
First publishd 1994 in the United Kingdom
Contents: Good advice is rarer than rubies; The free radio; The prophet's hair; At the auction of the ruby slippers; Christopher Columbus and Queen Isabella of Spain consummate their relationship (Santa Fé, AD 1492); The harmony of the spheres; Chekov and Zulu; The courter

"Rushdie's brilliant style reinforces his stories' marvelous combination of dignity and poignancy. Though these stories were originally published in such periodicals as the *New Yorker* and the *Atlantic,* the collection will serve for many readers as an introduction to Rushdie's talent in the short story form." Booklist

Haroun and the sea of stories. Viking 1990 219p $18.95

ISBN 0-670-83804-7   LC 90-45496

"This delightful fantasy is filled with adventures, amusing characters with names like Iff and Butt, and villains to fight against and defeat. Rushdie's puns and rhymes will be enjoyed by young and old—the catchy tunes by the younger readers and the political allegory by the adults. Rashid is a professional story-teller whose son, Haroun, delights in hearing them. When Rashid's source of stories seems to have disappeared Haroun faces many dangerous opponents to help his father regain his Gift of Gab." Shapiro. Fic for Youth. 3d edition

Midnight's children; with an introduction by Anita Desai. Knopf 1995 xxxi, 589p $20

ISBN 0-679-44462-9   LC 90-38447

"Everyman's library"
A reissue of the title first published 1980 in the United Kingdom; 1981 in the United States

"The novel is about Shiva and Saleem, two of the 1,001 babies born in the hour following [Indian] independence at midnight on August 15, 1947. It is notable as much for its portrayal of contemporary politics in India as for the brilliance of its style and insights into human nature and mind." Reader's Ency. 3d edition

The satanic verses. Viking 1989 546p $19.95

ISBN 0-670-82537-9   LC 88-40266

"When a terrorist's bomb destroys a jumbo jet high above the English Channel, two passengers fall safely to earth: Gibreel [Farishta], an Indian movie actor, and Saladin [Chamcha], star of the controversial British television program, The Alien Show. The near-death ex-perience changes them into living symbols of good and evil—Saladin grows horns, Gibreel a halo." Libr J

"As a display of narrative energy and wealth of invention, 'The Satanic Verses' is impressive. As a sustained exploration of the human condition, it flies apart into delirium." N Y Times Book Rev

Shame. Knopf 1983 319p o.p.

LC 83-48103

"Omar Khayyam Shakil is an improbable hero, lugging his great bulk through the turbulence of modern Pakistan on two very tired feet. He is a reluctant hero as well, preferring sensual delight to the dictates of inexorable fate. But Omar Khayyam is a man of destiny, drawn into the political power struggle between Raza Hyder and Iskander Harappa, and doomed by his love for Sufiya Zinobia, Hyder's retarded daughter." Libr J

"This novel of crossed family destinies in contemporary Pakistan teems with interesting characters, dramatic events, and marvellous verbal inventions. . . . It recreates an exotic but thoroughly believable world that is a delight to experience." Quill Quire

Rushing, Jane Gilmore, 1925-

Mary Dove; a love story. Doubleday 1974 209p o.p.

"The setting is West Texas in the late 19th century, as the first settlers were moving onto the land. Mary Dove has been raised in isolation by her white father, who wished to protect her from the prejudice her Negro blood would provoke. The father dies, and the girl and her cowboy fall in love—a love seen against the background of approaching 'civilization' with its ingrained powers and prejudices." Libr J

Russ, Joanna, 1937-

Souls

In Modern classic short novels of science fiction p415-58

Russell, Paul

Sea of tranquillity. Dutton 1994 402p $21.95

ISBN 0-525-93895-8   LC 94-6474

"In 1970, astronaut Allen Cloud is about to begin training for an Apollo moon mission when his personal life crumbles. He separates from his wife, Joan, and discovers that his mercurial son Jonathan is gay. Joan and Jonathan depart Houston for Tennessee, where Jonathan meets Stayton Voegli, a shy preacher's son who becomes his lover. Events then shift to 1990 when Allen's life has soured as a result of a bad business deal and Jonathan is dying of AIDS." Libr J

"Russell leaves us contemplating the paradox of how some endeavors, even an event as radical as walking on the moon, seem to evaporate with hardly a trace, while others, far more natural and spontaneous, prove fatal." Booklist

Russo, Richard, 1949-

Nobody's fool. Random House 1993 549p $23

ISBN 0-394-57778-7   LC 92-56844

Russo, Richard, 1949-—*Continued*

"Sixty-year-old Sully is *nobody's fool*, except maybe his own. Out of work (undeclared-income work is what he does, when he can), down to his last few bucks, hampered by an arthritic broken knee, Sully is worried that he's started on a run of bad luck. And he has. The banker son of his octogenarian landlady wants him evicted; Sully's estranged son comes home for Thanksgiving only to have his wife split; Sully's own high-strung ex-wife seems headed for a nervous breakdown; and his longtime lover is blaming him for her daughter's winding up in the hospital with a busted jaw. But Sully's biggest problem is the memory of his own abusive father." Libr J

"A grand read sparkling with witty dialogue and memorable characters, Russo's novel is a rollicking tale of a born loser on a downward slide. An economically depressed upper New York State community is the setting, and its lower-middle-class and blue-collar inhabitants are portrayed with empathy and a shrewd understanding of human nature." Publ Wkly

The risk pool. Random House 1988 479p o.p.

LC 88-42666

"A story on not-so-successful folk in a decaying town in New York as seen through the eyes of Ned Hall, better known as 'Sam's son.' Sam was once an average citizen who grew up, married, and went off to fight in World War II but returned a drifter. Leaving his wife and small son at home, he would haunt the bars and pool halls and hobnob with his cronies. Now and then he'd appear from nowhere to take Ned with him. When Ned's mother, Jenny, trips over the edge, Ned goes to live with Sam in a delapidated loft above the town's one department store and share his father's roguish life." Libr J

"A superbly original, maliciously funny book, peopled by characters that most of us would back away from plenty fast if they ever lurched toward our barstool. It is Mr. Russo's brilliant, deadpan writing that gives their wasted lives and miserable little town such haunting power and insidious charm." N Y Times Book Rev

Rutherfurd, Edward

Russka; the novel of Russia. Crown 1991 760p $25

ISBN 0-517-58048-9   LC 90-34457

"Tells the story of a Ukrainian village . . . and some of the families who lived there from A.D. 180 to the 1917 Revolution and, anecdotally, almost to the present." N Y Times Book Rev

The book "does provide a sweeping overview of the land whose very vastness and complexity make it overwhelming and fascinating." Christ Sci Monit

Sarum; the novel of England. Crown 1987 897p o.p. Buccaneer Bks. reprint available $45.95 (ISBN 1-56849-114-X)

LC 87-6710

This novel, set in Salisbury, England, aims to trace English history from the last Ice Age to the present through the lives of five fictional families

"Rutherfurd is strong on the explication of trends and the narration of events. But he relies heavily on the repetition of character types. Nevertheless, 'Sarum' is fascinating and will appeal to Anglophiles, history buffs, and fans of epic-style novels." Christ Sci Monit

Ryan, Rachel, 1948-

For works written by this author under other names see Brown, Sandra, 1948-

Rybakov, Anatolii Naumovich

Children of the Arbat; translated by Harold Shukman. Little, Brown 1988 685p $19.95

ISBN 0-316-76372-1   LC 87-33918

Original Russian edition, 1987

This autobiographical novel "of Soviet life in the 1930s concerns the unjust arrest of the loyal young student Sasha Pankratov, his confinement in prison, and his subsequent exile to Siberia . . . juxtaposed against Stalin's obsession with power." Libr J

"The length and depth of the novel is never intimidating, for it moves nimbly; besides being an important historical document, shedding light on a consequential period, it is personal, sensitive, and subtle in its detail as well as overwhelming in its impact." Booklist

S

Saavedra, Miguel de Cervantes *See* Cervantes Saavedra, Miguel de, 1547-1616

Sabatini, Rafael, 1875-1950

Captain Blood; his odyssey. Houghton Mifflin 1922 356p o.p. Buccaneer Bks. reprint available $21.95 (ISBN 0-89968-546-3)

"Peter Blood was many things in his time—soldier, country doctor, slave, pirate, and finally Governor of Jamaica. Incidentally, he was an Irishman. Round his humorous-heroic figure Mr. Sabatini has written an exciting romance of the Spanish Main, the facts of which he alleges to have been found in the diary and log books of one Jeremiah Pitt, a follower of Monmouth in 1685 and Blood's faithful companion in adventure." Times Lit Suppl

Scaramouche; a romance of the French revolution. Houghton Mifflin 1921 392p o.p.

Available from Amereon and Buccaneer Bks. Large print edition available from Thorndike Press

"The story, primarily of love and adventure, is woven around a hero who devoted himself to furthering the republican cause during the first years of the French Revolution (1788-1792). The title character, successively a lawyer, politician, swordsman, and buffoon, crosses paths repeatedly with his sworn enemy, in the end attaining love and happiness." Lenrow. Reader's Guide to Prose Fic

Followed by Scaramouche, the king-maker (1931)

The Sea-hawk. Lippincott 1915 362p o.p. Buccaneer Bks. reprint available $21.95 (ISBN 1-56849-483-1)

"Elemental in its record of unrepressed loves and hates is the story of how Sir Oliver Tressilian, Cornish gentleman and sometime commander of one of her majesty's ships which dispersed the Spanish Armada, became a follower of Mahmud—and a Barbary-corsair, winning for

Sabatini, Rafael, 1875-1950—*Continued*
himself the title of Sakr-el-Bahr—Hawk of the sea."
Boston Transcr

Saberhagen, Fred, 1930-
The first book of lost swords: Wound-healer's story. Doherty Assocs. 1986 281p o.p.

LC 86-50319

"A TOR book"
This book begins a new sequence in the author's fantasy series about mythical swords
"Hoping to find a cure for the mysterious illness that has cursed his son since birth, Prince Mark makes a pilgrimage to the shrine of the legendary sword Wound-healer only to find that his enemies have preceded him." Libr J
A "pleasant adventure that benefits greatly from Saberhagen's narrative gifts as the various strands leapfrog forward, keeping the reader off balance but constantly intrigued." Publ Wkly

The second book of lost swords: Sightblinder's story. Doherty Assocs. 1987 248p o.p.
LC 87-50477

"A TOR book"
"The present story limits itself to a single locale, the island castle of the wizard Honan-Fu, where Prince Mark is imprisoned in ice alongside the wizard by the usurper called the Ancient One. Mark's friends find themselves the temporary allies of Honan-Fu's traitorous daughter, Ninazu, and of the magician emperor, currently incognito with a traveling show. . . . An entertainment of high order." Publ Wkly

The third book of lost swords: Stonecutter's story. Doherty Assocs. 1988 247p o.p.
LC 87-51397

"A TOR book"
This novel "deals with the search of Prince al-Farabi and Magistrate Wen Chang for the lost sword Stonecutter. The book's virtues include a cast of well-drawn characters and some vividly realized societies, as well as Saberhagen's usual spare prose and sound narrative technique." Booklist

The fourth book of lost swords: Far-slayer's story. Doherty Assocs. 1989 252p o.p.
LC 89-11638

"A TOR book"
"Two rival families wage a war of attrition and vengeance for possession of 'Farslayer,' one of the 12 Lost Swords made by the gods and imbued with unearthly powers. A grim sense of fatality underlies the deceptive simplicity of the author's style." Libr J

The fifth book of lost swords: Coinspinner's story. Doherty Assocs. 1989 244p o.p.
LC 89-39878

"A TOR book"
"When the legendary sword Woundheale disappears from its resting place in the White Temple of Sarykam, investigations reveal that the Sword of Chance, Coinspinner, is once again loose in the world." Libr J

The sixth book of lost swords: Mindsword's story. TOR Bks. 1990 250p o.p.
LC 90-38899

"A Tom Doherty Associates book"
"Intended as a peace offering from Prince Murat to the Princess Kristin, the Mindsword—one of the legendary weapons used in the war that brought about the death of the gods—plunges two countries into near-war as the well-meaning Murat falls victim to the sword's seductive powers. Saberhagen treads a fine line between fantasy and moral fable in his latest addition to a popular series." Libr J

The seventh book of lost swords: Wayfinder's story. TOR Bks. 1992 251p o.p.
LC 92-858

"A Tom Doherty Associates book"
"One of 12 magical swords forged by the Gods, Wayfinder has the power to guide its possessor to whatever the seeker wants. Chance brings Wayfinder to Ben of Purkinje, who uses it to find Woundhealer, the sword with powers to cure the injured wife of Prince Mar of Sarykam. The evil magician Wood also wants the swords; his attack on Ben brings Mark, and even more swords, into the fray. . . . Saberhagen keeps the plot moving, providing a pleasurable light reading experience." Publ Wkly

The last book of swords: Shieldbreaker's story. TOR Bks. 1994 255p $20.95
ISBN 0-312-85001-8   LC 93-43232

"A Tom Doherty associates book"
In this concluding book of the saga, "battle extends from palace to peasant hut—indeed, all the way to the moon—and is loaded with remnants of premagical technology as well as the secret of why the Old World fell and magic came to rule. Key to the battle against Vikata the Dark King is Prince Mark's second son, Prince Stephen, who turns out to be a formidable wielder of swords. By the time journeys and battles are done, the only one of the twelve swords that survives is Woundhealer, for even the terrifying Shieldbreaker has perished." Booklist

Sackville-West, V. (Victoria), 1892-1962
All passion spent. Doubleday, Doran 1931 294p o.p. Buccaneer Bks. reprint available $29.95 (ISBN 0-89966-745-7)
"When Lady Slane, after the death of her famous husband, shocks her family by going to live by herself in a little house in Hempstead, she is for the first time in her eighty-eight years asserting her right to live her own life. The year of quiet reminiscences there is not without exciting moments, for a man who has loved her silently for sixty years renews his friendship, tells her of his love, then suddenly dies, and leaves her his enormous fortune. What she does with this fortune is another instance of her self-assertion. Gentle, charming Lady Slane, her family, and her friends, drawn with wit and skill in this tale of graceful old age, create an impression of subtlety and beauty." Booklist

The Edwardians. Doubleday, Doran 1930 314p o.p.
Available from Amereon and Buccaneer Bks.
The setting of this story of Edwardian England is the beautiful old manor-house of Chevron. The characters are grouped about Sebastian, the young heir to the dukedom, and his mother, a famous hostess of the day. Individuals count for less in the novel—a decadent but decorative society. The close of the story, marked by

Sackville-West, V. (Victoria), 1892-1962 — *Continued*

King George's coronation, finds the young duke breaking with the traditions that have bound him, not unwillingly, and starting a new era for himself

"'The Edwardians' is of undoubted excellence from two points of view. First, it is a magnificent portrait of a class and an era. Secondly, it is remarkable for its excellent prose style." Springfield Repub

Sackville-West, Victoria *See* Sackville-West, V. (Victoria), 1892-1962

Safire, William

Freedom. Doubleday 1987 1,125p o.p.

LC 86-29254

This novel spans the first twenty months of the Civil War. It covers the period "between Lincoln's suspension of habeas corpus and his signing of the Emancipation Proclamation." Libr J

"The book is a triumph of historical imagination. . . . Safire uses the trained eye of a Washington insider to show us the characters' tentative political and military gropings based on limited information and sketchy precedents. . . . Our scribe tells this monumental and heartbreaking tale in a way one won't soon forget." Christ Sci Monit

Full disclosure; a novel. Doubleday 1977 525p o.p.

LC 76-18365

This novel begins "in Yalta with the Soviet Foreign Minister engineering a plot to assassinate the Soviet Premier and the US President, who are riding together in a helicopter. The Premier dies and the President is blinded. The rest of the book concerns the President's efforts to keep from being declared disabled and removed from office under the 25th Amendment." New Repub

"Safire keeps the suspense going while giving his characters true validity—and their own unique personalities. Even the President's seeing eye dog has a definite character of his own. Safire's people are real, imbued with feelings with which the reader empathizes." West Coast Rev Books

Sagan, Carl, 1934-

Contact; a novel. Simon & Schuster 1985 432p o.p.

LC 85-14645

"Ellie Arroway, working with a huge array of radio telescopes in the New Mexico desert, discovers a signal from the star Vega. The message has several levels, one of which contains instructions for building a faster-than-light spacecraft. A debate ensues between scientists and religious leaders as to whether or not such a machine should be built; the scientists win, and finally the long-sought 'contact' is established." Booklist

"A serious blend of science fact and speculation with a fast-paced and well-crafted story . . . suggesting that Sagan is more interested in illustrating human relations and human response than depicting alien creatures. . . . Sagan has provided a novel of ideas, and finds drama in how people interact with them in a situation of challenge and discovery." Christ Sci Monit

Sagan, Françoise, 1935-

Bonjour tristesse; translated from the French by Irene Ash. Dutton 1955 128p o.p.

Original French edition, 1954

"The story of a jealous, sophisticated 17-year-old girl whose meddling in her father's impending remarriage leads to tragic consequences, it was written with 'classical' restraint and a tone of cynical disillusionment. The book showed the persistence of traditional form during a period of experimentation in French fiction." Merriam-Webster's Ency of Lit

The painted lady; translated by Lee Fahnestock. Dutton 1983 c1981 468p o.p.

LC 82-17810

Original French edition, 1981

"A group of wealthy music lovers embark upon a ten-day tour of the Mediterranean. Among the passengers on board the 'Narcissus' are the world's greatest conductor and pianist, a diva, a sugar baron, a Hollywood producer with a starlet, an art forger, and the publisher of a leftist newspaper with his wife Clarisse, a steelworks heiress. Clarisse has been traumatized by her husband and has become an alcoholic who hides her feelings under grotesquely thick make-up. The art forger falls in love with her and persuades this 'Painted Lady' to remove her make-up to reveal her beauty. He then proceeds to woo her away from her husband." Libr J

This book "is more than entertaining; its verve and humor disguise a serious work." Time

A reluctant hero; translated by Christine Donougher. Dutton 1987 191p o.p.

LC 87-6699

Original French edition, 1985; published in the United Kingdom with title: Engagements of the heart

"In the summer of 1942 Alice and Jerome, two members of the French Resistance, arrive at the home of Jerome's friend Charles, an apolitical industrialist in Vichy, France. Their goal is to convince Charles to make his factory a haven for political refugees from occupied France. In the process of seducing Charles to the cause, Alice falls in love with him, thus jeopardizing their operation and wounding Jerome, who loves her." Libr J

"On the surface, this is a novel of intrigue; but, at its heart, it is also a novel of psychology, of the senses, and ultimately, of love." Booklist

Saint, Dora Jessie *See* Read, Miss, 1913-

Saint, H. F. (Harry F.)

Memoirs of an invisible man. Atheneum Pubs. 1987 396p o.p.

LC 85-48144

"A clash between a scientist and an antinuclear demonstrator at a nuclear energy plant catalyzes an explosion that renders Nick Halloway, a securities analyst, invisible. Realizing that he will become a caged, scrutinized guinea pig if he surrenders to federal intelligence agents, Nick makes a run for his freedom. . . . Nick displays the distinct sensibilities of a fugitive and a Wall Street smart guy as he invisibly fends for himself in the jungles he knows best—the East Side of Manhattan and the trader's desk." Publ Wkly

Saint, H. F. (Harry F.)—*Continued*

"The CIA agents, always just one step behind, are deliciously funny Keystone Cops, ridiculous in their attempts to capture a non-entity. This delightful first novel updates a common childhood fantasy with the excitement of a spy story and a hilarious adult portrayal of life and love under the most peculiar conditions." Libr J

Saint, Harry F. *See* Saint, H. F. (Harry F.)

Saint-Aubin, Horace de *See* Balzac, Honoré de, 1799-1850

Saint-Exupéry, Antoine de, 1900-1944

The little prince; written and drawn by Antoine de Saint Exupéry; translated from the French by Katherine Woods. Harcourt Brace Jovanovich 1943 91p il $14

ISBN 0-15-246503-0
Also available from Amereon
First published by Reynal & Hitchcock
"This many-dimensional fable of an airplane pilot who has crashed in the desert is for readers of all ages. The pilot comes upon the little prince soon after the crash. The prince tells of his adventures on different planets and on Earth as he attempts to learn about the universe in order to live peacefully on his own small planet. A spiritual quality enhances the seemingly simple observations of the little prince." Shapiro. Fic for Youth. 3d edition

Night flight; preface by André Gide; translated by Stuart Gilbert. Century 1932 198p o.p.

"In a story that captures the adventures of early aviation, Rivière, chief of the airport at Buenos Aires, supervises the night flights of airmail in South America. He challenges his crew to meet any and all obstacles. When one of his three mail planes crashes over the Andes, he dispatches the European mail plane on schedule anyway." Shapiro. Fic for Youth. 3d edition

Saki, 1870-1916

The short stories of Saki; complete, with an introduction by Christopher Morley. Viking 1930 718p o.p.

Analyzed in Short story index
Contents: Reginald; Reginald on Christmas presents; Reginald on the academy; Reginald at the theatre; Reginald's peace poem; Reginald's choir treat; Reginald on worries; Reginald on house-parties; Reginald at the Carlton; Reginald on besetting sins; Reginald's drama; Reginald on tariffs; Reginald's Christmas revel; Reginald's Rubaiyat; Innocence of Reginald; Reginald in Russia; Reticence of Lady Anne; Lost Sanjak; Sex that doesn't shop; Blood-feud of Toad-water; Young Turkish catastrophe; Judkin of the parcels; Gabriel-Ernest; Saint and the goblin; Soul of Laploshka; Bag; Strategist; Cross currents; Baker's dozen; Mouse; Esmé; Match-maker; Tobermory; Mrs. Packletide's tiger; Stampeding of Lady Bastable; Background; Hermann the Irascible—a story of the great weep; Unrest-cure; Jesting of Arlington Stringham; Sredni Vashtar; Adrian; Chaplet; Quest; Wratislav; Easter egg; Filboid Studge, the story of a mouse that helped; Music on the hill; Story of St. Vespaluus; Way to the dairy; Peace offering; Peace of Mowsle Barton; Talking-out of Tarrington; Hounds of fate; Recessional; Matter of sentiment; Secret sin of Septimus Brope; "Ministers of grace"; Remoulding of Groby Lington; She-wolf; Laura; Boar-pig; Brogue; Hen; Open window; Treasureship; Cobweb; Lull; Unkindest blow; Romancers; Schwartz-Metterklume method; Seventh pullet; Blind spot; Dusk; Touch of realism; Cousin Teresa; Yarkand manner; Byzantine omelette; Feast of Nemesis; Dreamer; Quince tree; Forbidden buzzards; Stake; Clovis on parental responsibilities; Holiday task; Stalled ox; Storyteller; Defensive diamond; Elk; "Down pens"; Nameday; Lumberroom; Fur; Philanthropist and the happy cat; On approval; Toys of peace; Louise; Tea; Disappearance of Crispina Umberleigh; Wolves of Cernogratz; Louis; Guests; Penance; Phantom luncheon; Bread and butter miss; Bertie's Christmas; Forewarned; Interlopers; Quail seed; Canossa; Threat; Excepting Mrs. Pentherby; Mark; Hedgehog; Mappined life; Fate; Bull; Morivera; Shock tactics; Seven cream jugs; Occasional garden; Sheep; Oversight; Hyacinth; Image of the lost soul; Purple of the Balkan kings; Cupboard of the yesterdays; For the duration of the war; Square eggsf business; Comments of Moung Ka

Salinger, J. D. (Jerome David), 1919-

The catcher in the rye. Little, Brown 1951 277p $22.95

ISBN 0-316-76953-3
Also available from Buccaneer Bks.
"The story of adolescent Holden Caulfield who runs away from boarding-school in Pennsylvania to New York where he preserves his innocence despite various attempts to lose it. The colloquial, lively, first-person narration, with its attacks on the 'phoniness' of the adult world and its clinging to family sentiment in the form of Holden's affection for his sister Phoebe, made the novel accessible to and popular with a wide readership, particularly with the young." Oxford Companion to Engl Lit. 5th edition

Franny and Zooey. Little, Brown 1961 201p $22.95

ISBN 0-316-76954-1
"At 20, Franny Glass is experiencing desperate dissatisfaction with her life and seems to be looking for help via a religious awakening. Her brother Zooey tries to help her out of this depression. He recalls the influence on their growth and development of their appearance as young radio performers on a network program called 'It's a Wise Child.' An older brother, Buddy, is also an important component of the interrelationships in the Glass family." Shapiro. Fic for Youth. 3d edition

Nine stories. Little, Brown 1953 302p $22.95

ISBN 0-316-76956-8
Analyzed in Short story index
Published in the United Kingdom with title: For Esmé; with love and squalor
Contents: A perfect day for bananafish; Uncle Wiggily in Connecticut; Just before the war with the Eskimos; The laughing man; Down at the dinghy; For Esmé—with love and squalor; Pretty mouth and green my eyes; De Daumier-Smith's blue period; Teddy
This collection "introduced various members of the Glass family who would dominate the remainder of Salinger's work. Critical response divided itself between high praise and cult worship. Most of the stories deal with precocious, troubled children, whose religious yearn-

Salinger, J. D. (Jerome David), 1919- —
Continued

ings—often tilting toward the East—are in vivid contrast to the materialistic and spiritually empty world of their parents. The result was a perfect literary formula for the 1950s." Benet's Reader's Ency of Am Lit

Raise high the roof beam, carpenters, and Seymour: an introduction. Little, Brown 1963 248p $21.95

ISBN 0-316-76957-6

This volume "reprints stories from *The New Yorker* (1955, 1959), in which Buddy Glass tells, first, of his return to New York during the war to attend his brother Seymour's wedding and of Seymour's jilting of the bride and then of their later elopement; and, second, after Seymour's suicide, of Buddy's own brooding, to the point of breakdown, upon Seymour's virtues, human and literary." Oxford Companion to Am Lit. 5th edition

Seymour: an introduction

In Salinger, J. D. Raise high the roof beam, carpenters, and Seymour: an introduction p1

Zooey

In Salinger, J. D. Franny and Zooey

Salinger, Jerome David *See* Salinger, J. D. (Jerome David), 1919-

Sams, Ferrol, 1922-
When all the world was young. Longstreet Press 1991 610p $23.95

ISBN 1-56352-001-X   LC 91-61938

Concluding volume in trilogy begun with Run with the horsemen (1982) and The whisper of the river (1984)

"Sams here continues the saga of Porter Osborne Jr., a likable Georgia farmboy. In the beginning of this . . . novel, set during World War II, Porter is a medical student. He deliberately flunks out so that he can join the war effort and is sent to Normandy as a medical assistant. Porter and his friends deal with the same issues found in any coming-of-age novel—family, religion, personal identity, and relations with the opposite sex. Porter, however, has an edge. He has strong ties to his Baptist family and to the rich soil that is their livelihood and a head full of poetry that becomes his solace and inspiration." Libr J

Sand, George, 1804-1876
Lélia; translated, with an introduction by Maria Espinosa. Indiana Univ. Press 1978 xxi, 234p o.p.

LC 77-23639

Original French edition, 1833

"The highly romantic tale describes the tragically misdirected feelings of love that motivate the various characters. These include Lélia, the lovely heroine; her sister Pulcherie, a prostitute; Stenio, an idealistic young poet; and Magnus, a priest who becomes insane." Reader's Ency

Marianne; edited and translated by Siân Miles. Carroll & Graf Pubs. 1988 171p $14.95

ISBN 0-88184-415-2   LC 88-7308

Original French edition, 1876

"Marianne Chevreuse, the 25-year-old heroine of this romantic tale set in 1825 . . . is independent yet intensely female, and she breaks many conventions of society while living by her own deeply held moral beliefs. Pierre André is an older man who has known her since her childhood. When asked to introduce her to a prospective suitor, he discovers his own love for Marianne. The plot twists and turns until the unsuitable Philippe Gaucher—who is indeed gauche—is sent packing and Pierre and Marianne are betrothed. While very much a period piece, this last scrap of Sand's tremendous oeuvre is a charming bit of entertainment." Publ Wkly

Sandburg, Carl, 1878-1967
Remembrance Rock. Harcourt Brace & Co. 1948 1067p o.p.

"Sandburg's only novel, the work is a massive chronicle that uses historical facts and both historical and fictional characters to depict American history from 1607 to 1945 in a mythic, passionate tribute to the American people." Merriam-Webster's Ency of Lit

Sanders, Lawrence, 1920-
The eighth commandment. Putnam 1986 381p o.p.

LC 85-25642

"Six-foot-two and every inch of her honest, Mary Lou 'Dunk' Bateson is a coin appraiser at a New York auction house. She is forced to become an amateur detective when a prized Greek coin disappears from a collection that has been transferred to her company for auction. First treated as a prime suspect, Dunk determines to clear her name by ferreting out the real thief. In the process, she finds two interesting suitors in the cop and the insurance investigator who are assigned to the case, as well as encountering the bizarre family of Archibald Havistock, owner of the purloined coin." Publ Wkly

The first deadly sin. Putnam 1973 566p o.p. Buccaneer Bks. reprint available $29.95 (ISBN 1-56849-330-4)

This novel "pits a psychopathic killer loose in New York against a tough, dedicated police officer who is not without his own hangups. Telling his story alternately from the psychopath's point of view and that of the detective, Mr. Sanders draws the two men closer and closer together on an inevitable collision course. Probing the dark side of the killer's mind, his sexual conflicts and involvement with a strange trio of brother, sister and valet who are as kinky as they come, he shows the man's accelerating descent into total madness. Meanwhile, Captain Edward X. Delaney, in whose upper East Side precinct a series of random murders is taking place, accepts an undercover assignment to track down the man responsible." Publ Wkly

The fourth deadly sin. Putnam 1985 380p o.p.

LC 84-24789

Sanders, Lawrence, 1920-—_Continued_

"When psychiatrist Dr. Ellerbee is beaten to death with a ball-peen hammer, retired detective Edward X. Delaney agrees to supplement the police investigation. The victim's beautiful wife provides a list of potentially violent patients for Delaney and his team to question." Libr J

"Delaney displays that combination of computerlike efficiency and human touch that make him such an appealing detective. It's a masterly performace, not only chilling, but thought-provoking and often touching." Publ Wkly

McNally's caper. Putnam 1994 319p $22.95

ISBN 0-399-13919-2   LC 93-23581
Also available G.K. Hall large print edition

Palm Beach sleuth Archy McNally investigates theft, scandal and murder involving a prominent local family. "Called in by patriarch Griswold Forsythe II—a client of Archy's father, who even the closemouthed senior McNally admits is pretty dull—our happy-go-lucky sleuth commences a covert search to discover which intimate relative is lifting the family valuables piece by piece." Publisher's note

McNally's luck. Putnam 1992 319p o.p.
LC 92-1394

"Hot on the trail of a stolen cat on behalf of a client of his family's law firm, McNally and Son, Archy enters Palm Beach's seamy nether-world of psychics, charlatans, and thieves. His seemingly innocuous search for the missing cat leads him to the heart of a grisly and intricate plot. As the body count climbs, Archy must resolve the links between several violent local murders and the disappearance of the ill-tempered feline." Publisher's note

McNally's risk. Putnam 1993 319p o.p.
LC 92-39270

This mystery features playboy sleuth Archy McNally the head of the Department of Discreet Inquiries in his father's Palm Beach law firm. In this outing Archy investigates a seeming golddigger accused of murder

McNally's secret. Putnam 1992 317p o.p.
LC 91-9803

Available G.K. Hall large print edition

"Four priceless U.S. airmail stamps issued in 1918 and known as 'inverted Jennies' have been stolen from a wealthy matron's mansion in Palm Beach. . . . McNally's task is to find the thief 'without the barest hint of scandal coming to light.' There are lots of suspects, a couple of deaths, and a fine romance." Booklist

The second deadly sin. Putnam 1977 412p o.p.
LC 77-3652

A "police procedural in which Edward X. Delaney, recently retired as Manhattan's chief of detectives, returns by invitation of the department to work on the mystery-murder of a thoroughly unlikable genius, painter Victor Maitland. Delaney, a curious mixture of force and sensitivity, is teamed with a young sergeant, whose drinking has brought him to the edge of dismissal. The two, with an accidentally added starter, Jason T. Jason (black, smart, and very big), by a combination of hard work, intuition, and some luck finally track down the killer." Booklist

The seventh commandment. Putnam 1991 351p o.p.
LC 90-43225

Available G.K. Hall large print edition

"Insurance agent Dora Conti falls for a cop when she starts investigating the violent murder of a jewelry magnate whose family seems bent on breaking _all_ the commandments." Libr J

The sixth commandment; a novel. Putnam 1979 350p o.p.
LC 78-13158

When the investigator for a philanthropic group arrives in a small upstate New York town to research the application for a grant made by a former Nobel laureate in medicine, "the town's leading citizen, no suspicions are aroused. Yet, a few interviews reveal that the town is shielding some damaging secret about the famous man. When the sleuth penetrates the screen he finds a sordid love affair, but also the shocking revelation that the doctor is using human subjects in his experiments to achieve immortality." Libr J

"This gloomy escapade about a hard-drinking, chain-smoking, world-pitying investigator . . . is brimful of juice and excitement, with some insight and much foolishness—a genuinely riveting diversion." New Yorker

Sullivan's sting. Putnam 1990 348p o.p.
LC 89-70046

Available G.K. Hall large print edition

This novel "profiles the slimy underbelly of south Florida, where con men posing as financial wizards bilk greedy, unsuspecting investors out of their money (aging widows are a prime mark). The main player here is sexy David Rathbone, a man who apparently could sell igloos to Eskimos. Equally sexy undercover cop Rita Angela Sullivan is on a mission from the SEC to 'sting' Rathbone. She traps her prey, starts to play house, and moves in for the kill—then finds herself falling in love with the guy." Booklist

The tangent factor. Putnam 1978 308p o.p.
LC 77-21173

Sequel to The tangent objective (1976)

"A year after Obiri Anokye, the Napoleonic 'Little Captain,' seizes power in oil-rich Asante on the African coast, he sets his sights on conquering the poor, but strategically important neighboring countries as the first step in a plan to unite all of Africa under his rule. Peter Tangent, American oil company official, is convinced this courageous and cunning black leader has the vision needed to bring Africa into the 20th century, and devotes himself to Anokye's cause. The gamble for enormous stakes draws in the forces of the oil corporation for which Tangent works as well as the CIA." Publ Wkly

The tenth commandment; a novel. Putnam 1980 385p o.p.
LC 80-13002

"Joshua Bigg (he's 5' 3½), chief investigator for a New York law firm, gets two tough assignments from his bosses. One is a missing person case: a crotchety professor whose family wants an estate settlement. The other is an apparent suicide: an aging textile manufacturer whose merry young widow has suddenly become religiously attracted to a churchless clergyman. Bigg plows his way through mountains of clues, allies himself with a black police detective and unearths evidence to indicate

Sanders, Lawrence, 1920-—*Continued*

that the suicide was murder and that the missing man is dead." Publ Wkly

The third deadly sin. Putnam 1981 444p o.p.

LC 80-26325

"Sergeant Boone of Manhattan's Homicide Squad persuades former Chief of Detectives Delaney to help find what police fear most, a random killer. The two men . . . begin the slow, almost hopeless, scrupulously painstaking chore of tracking down and piecing together the tiniest clues. The detecting account alternates with vivid, step-by-step descriptions of drab Zoe Kohler, who tarts herself up periodically and ritually murders men she picks up in convention-crowded hotels. In the telling, Sander's characters discuss facets of feminism and crime provocatively, and not at all simplistically, adding to the dimensions of a superior mystery." Publ Wkly

The Timothy files. Putnam 1987 380p o.p.

LC 86-25496

Three novella-length episodes "feature Timothy Cone, 'the Wall Street dick,' who works for an investigative agency. . . . The files deal respectively with a murderous real-estate conglomerate, a fertility clinic devoted to considerably more than 'original biotechnological research' and an investment house involved in drugs—though only detective work of the highest caliber can discover the seamy details." Publ Wkly

Timothy's game. Putnam 1988 382p o.p.

LC 87-29073

This novel is "set on Wall Street, where clever detective Timothy Cone dresses in Salvation Army chic, chain-smokes Camels, and drinks too much. Cone has a cat named Cleo who eats ham hocks, potato salad, and garlic salami, and a girlfriend named Samantha who sports long, auburn hair. Throw in a foul-mouthed woman who owns a garbage-hauling firm controlled by the mob, an insider-trading leak, murder, and a tong war in Chinatown, and you have the usual brand of Sanders' readable fiction." Booklist

Sandford, John, 1944-

Eyes of prey. Putnam 1991 318p o.p.

LC 90-25333

"Operating on the buddy system, a disfigured actor murders the wife of a forensic pathologist he meets in a bar, a favor repaid when the drug-crazed doctor dispatches a theater director who intended to fire the actor. But the slaughter doesn't stop with this initial business transaction. Obsessed with the idea that his victims are staring at him from beyond the grave, 'Dr. Death' goads his deranged accomplice into a killing spree that has the celebrity cop Lucas Davenport stripping the gears of his Porsche in vexation." N Y Times Book Rev

Night prey. Putnam 1994 336p $22.95

ISBN 0-399-13914-1 LC 94-7564

"Minneapolis deputy police chief Lucas Davenport is on the trail of a serial killer—this time a particularly nasty specimen with a yen for disemboweling his victims. Meagan Connell, an investigator from a state agency, plays the . . . role of Davenport's feisty, determined female assistant. Davenport is also peripherally involved in a case that appears to involve the Seeds, a loosely organized group of white supremacists." Booklist

"Despite its length, *Night Prey* is a tight, fast-moving thriller with appealing good guys and a suitably evil villain. Especially fascinating among the characters is Policewoman Connell." Libr J

Rules of prey. Putnam 1989 316p o.p.

LC 89-4040

"A killer who calls himself the 'maddog' has been murdering Minneapolis women, seemingly without pattern or motive. The crimes are linked only by their brutality and by the slayer's 'signature': at each scene, he leaves a written rule of crime, such as 'Never kill anyone you know,' or, 'Never carry a weapon after it has been used.' Into the case comes Lucas Davenport, a policeman with five kills in the line of duty, a surefire sense of how to handle the thirsty media and strong instincts about the killer's psyche." Publ Wkly

Shadow prey. Putnam 1990 318p o.p.

LC 89-70233

"When an Indian-gouging slumlord and an Indian-hating parole officer turn up dead from the same gory M.O.—throats slit by obsidian knives—Minneapolis police figure it's more than coincidental. When, soon after, a New York City welfare commissioner who has urged making short shrift of such permanent deadbeats as Indians is similarly offed, they *know* something big's going down. Thanks to intelligence unit detective Lucas Davenport, a killer is nailed, but not before Davenport is briefly taken hostage—a situation from which he's saved by Lily Rothenburg, a Big Apple cop also working on the case." Booklist

Silent prey. Putnam 1992 320p o.p.

LC 91-43696

"Mad pathologist Bekker's face is battered and broken after his encounter with unorthodox Minneapolis cop Lucas Davenport in *Eyes of Prey*. Now Bekker's on the loose again, having escaped during his trial and landed in New York City. Even more nutso than ever, he's determined to exact revenge on Lucas and to continue his evil experiments, in which he searches the eyes of his victims in the few, pain-creased seconds before death." Booklist

Winter prey. Putnam 1993 336p $21.95

ISBN 0-399-13815-3 LC 92-42072

Also available G.K. Hall large print edition

"In a rural area of northern Wisconsin, a family of three is savagely wiped out by the Iceman, who then torches their house. In pursuit of a damaging photograph—a snapshot of him in a sexual situation with a local boy—this fiend puts no value on human life. Enter Davenport, the laconic, slightly cynical ex-cop from Minneapolis, who uncovers several disturbing truths before determining the Iceman's identity." Publ Wkly

"Davenport, a cool, cynical man of action, is entirely in his element in this harsh terrain—so bitter that it turns animals against men, so brutal that it turns men into beasts." N Y Times Book Rev

Santayana, George, 1863-1952

The last Puritan; a memoir in the form of a novel. Scribner 602p $60

ISBN 0-684-16833-2

"Hudson River editions"

First published 1936

"The book is a study of Oliver Alden, descendant of an old and wealthy New England family, who comprises in himself the Puritan characteristics of austerity, single-mindedness, gravity, and conscientious, scrupulous devo-

Santayana, George, 1863-1952—*Continued*
tion to purpose. He is out of place in the civilization of the 20th century. In style, subject matter, and approach, *The Last Puritan* recalls the novels of Henry James." Reader's Ency. 3d edition

Santmyer, Helen Hooven, 1895-1986

"—and ladies of the club". Ohio State Univ. Press 1982 1344p $62.50

ISBN 0-8142-0323-X   LC 81-22401

"In 1868 in a small town in southwestern Ohio, a group of women form a literary club. Through the personal, political, and social upheavals of the next 64 years the club remains the one constant factor in the lives of these diverse women and their descendants." Libr J

The author's "perceptive saga is steeped not just in the changing political, religious, and social mores of the period covered, but also in the personal joys, sorrows, and scandals that beat the cadence of life in a midwestern town. This novel has an old-fashioned dignity and seriousness that will win some readers and lose others, and although its girth is perhaps its most notable quality, its literary scope and depth of feeling are equally impressive." Booklist

Sargent, Pamela

Danny goes to Mars

In Nebula awards 28 p27-51

(ed) Nebula awards [1]-29. See Nebula awards [1]-29

Saroyan, William, 1908-1981

The human comedy; illustrated by Don Freeman. Harcourt Brace Jovanovich 1989 c1943 242p il $15.95

ISBN 0-15-142301-6   LC 89-32785

"An HBJ modern classic"

A reissue of the title first published 1944

"Homer, the narrator, identifies himself in this novel as a night messenger for the Postal Telegraph office. He creates a view of family life in the 1940s in a small town in California. His mother, Ma Macauley, presides over the family and takes care of four children after her husband dies. Besides Homer, there is Marcus, the oldest, who is in the army; Bess; and Ulysses, the youngest, who describes the world from his perspective as a solemn four-year-old." Shapiro. Fic for Youth. 3d edition

Sarton, May, 1912-1995

Anger; a novel. Norton 1982 223p $12.95

ISBN 0-393-01643-9   LC 82-7843

"Successful Boston banker Ned Fraser finds himself captivated by an unexpected encounter with mezzo-soprano Anna Lindstrom. He pursues the gifted, determined-to-be-famous performer without success until, at a chance meeting, he wins her—somewhat to the surprise of them both. They marry within a short time, no starry-eyed youngsters, but two mature adults. Both are settled in their emotional patterns: she given to outspoken and tempestuous outbursts of joy and despair, he to internalizing his feelings and maintaining the proper facade. This results in a lack of communication that threatens their marriage until Anna penetrates Ned's reserve. A romantic, yet realistic portrait." Libr J

As we are now; a novel. Norton 1973 133p $10.95

ISBN 0-393-08372-1

This book is "a novel in the form of a diary, written by a retired schoolteacher. Mentally tough but not quite physically able to care for herself, she is deposited by relatives in an old people's home. Subjected to subtle humiliations, petty and almost unthinking cruelties, deprived of all mental stimulus, she fights a tough battle to preserve first her dignity, then her sanity." Christ Sci Monit

"It is a bitter book, more a tract than a novel, and an utterly desolating experience, as it is meant to be. There are complexities that unwind themselves now and then, which preserve the concerns of the novel; but on the whole, the work is a piece of rhetoric, and very good rhetoric, too. . . . For the book satisfies in the way that cold anger can when it is pure, despairing, and written with no aim but the impulse to record the way things are." Saturday Rev/World

The education of Harriet Hatfield; a novel. Norton 1989 320p o.p.

LC 88-38042

"Released from a confining lesbian relationship by the death of her lover, Harriet at 60 fulfills her dream of opening a bookstore for women in a Boston working-class neighborhood. Vandalism and threats lead to a news article that forces Harriet to re-evaluate her life and face its impact on others." Libr J

"Although the crises presented here are decidedly soft-edged—with a gentler outcome almost guaranteed from the start—Harriet's story is an affirming look at the possibilities of independence, freedom, and self-acceptance at any age." Booklist

The fur person; illustrated by David Canright. Norton 1978 106p il o.p.

LC 78-8240

"A novelette based on the history of the author's cat relates the adventures of a characterful feline, one Tom Jones. Tiring of his vagabond existence, Tom decided to settle down and search systematically until he found not one but two ideal housekeepers—old maids in possession of a small house with attic, cellar, and garden, but no children. A humorous, unsentimental tale for cat lovers." Booklist

Joanna and Ulysses; a tale; illustrated by James J. Spanfeller. Norton 1963 127p il o.p.

A "story about an idyllic holiday on a Greek island. The heroine, Joanna, a good-looking 30-year-old, is taking her first holiday in ten years after a harrowing decade of family troubles. Her companion, whom she rescues from ill treatment, is a little gray donkey named Ulysses. It is a wonderful escape for Joanna, who enjoys nursing Ulysses back to health and loves plunging into the painting that has been her dream of a life work." Publ Wkly

Kinds of love; a novel. Norton 1970 464p o.p.

The novel "is set in a small New Hampshire town much visited over the years by summer people. Christina and Cornelius Chapman, elderly and long-standing summer people, have retreated to Williard following Cornelius's partly crippling stroke and have resolved to win-

Sarton, May, 1912-1995—*Continued*

ter there for the first time. Around them and around their house swirl the events of the story." N Y Times Book Rev

"The touching friendship of two elderly women, the love/hate relationship of the permanent residents and the summer people, and a young girl's discovery of the magic and the pain of love are some of the threads in this quiet tale." Booklist

The magnificent spinster; a novel. Norton 1985 379p $16.95

ISBN 0-393-02220-X   LC 85-4893

"Cam, the 70-year-old narrator and a historian by trade, is writing a novel about a beloved, recently dead old friend, Jane Reid. It is an attempt to capture the special quality of the woman's life and the relationship that began years ago when they met at a progressive Cambridge day school, where Jane taught history and Cam was one of her adoring students. Early on, Jane's loving admiration for another woman is rebuffed, and she remains ever after romantically and sexually unattached, devoting herself to a wide circle of people and causes. Cam, meanwhile, spends two decades in a union with another woman in an era when such liaisons are not openly acknowledged." Publ Wkly

Mrs. Stevens hears the mermaids singing; a novel. Norton 1965 220p o.p.

"In the course of a day in which she prepares herself for an interview by two young representatives from a national magazine and during the interview itself, Hilary Stevens, a seventy-year-old poet, brings her life into focus. Her musings recollect a happy marriage to an uncomplicated man during which her muse remains quiescent and Lesbian experiences which brings her poetic powers to life. A well-written character study of a poet obsessed by her craft in the pursuit of which she transforms her husband's death and her less regular loves into material for her pen." Booklist

"The plot of this short novel is deceptively simple, the mood subtle, the feeling intense. And the music of Miss Sarton's prose leaves compelling echoes in one's mind." N Y Times Book Rev

A reckoning; a novel. Norton 1978 254p $11.95

ISBN 0-393-08828-6   LC 78-9691

"Laura Spelman, genteel Boston widow, has just learned that she is dying of cancer. Determined to take a candid look at herself as a means of tying up loose ends, she is surprised to find her thoughts turning mostly to women. Confiding in strangers, avoiding her family, Laura speaks of discovering herself as a woman. In particular, she examines her relationships with her domineering mother and with a dearly loved friend, the two people who, she feels, have shaped her life most profoundly. Ironically, as her body becomes increasingly unfamiliar, her old, unexamined passions begin to resolve themselves." Atlantic

"Sarton incorporates . . . the issues of mother/daughter relationships, what it is to be a woman (and a man), and the conflict of art and life." Libr J

A small room; a novel. Norton 1961 249p o.p.

"Lucy Winter, professor and seeker of refuge in the kingdom of a progressive [New England] women's college, becomes involved when a top student is caught in a case of plagiarism, and peace dissolves. The faculty must face the guilt of having pushed for intellectual attainment with inadequate knowledge and consideration for emotional factors, i.e. the crime of not teaching 'the whole child.' Each person reacts to crisis differently—sometimes disastrously, but all can meet finally in the small room to evaluate the past and to agree on the college's proposed plan for the future." Libr J

Sarton "presents her cast of faculty types with scrupulous respect. There is no villain among them. . . . The essence of this novel is not so much in the conflict of characters as in the conflict in ideas—and ideas about teaching." N Y Her Trib Books

Sartre, Jean Paul, 1905-1980

Nobel Prize in literature, 1964

The age of reason; translated from the French by Eric Sutton. Knopf 1947 397p (Roads to freedom, 1) o.p.

Original French edition, 1945

First of a series of three novels by the French philosopher, exponent of existentialism. The scene of this novel is Paris in 1938. A fourth title was never completed

"The central character is Mathieu, a professor of philosophy who writes one short story a year. . . . The problem that obsesses Mathieu, that of freedom, how to remain free, is worked out in the story and exemplified in the lives of the characters. . . . Mathieu differs from your ordinary character of fiction in that he is motivated by this abstract ethical ideal to keep his freedom. It is assailed as soon as the novel opens, for he learns that his mistress is pregnant; the action consists largely of his attempts to raise by borrowing—in the end, by stealing—the five thousand francs required to procure an abortion; unnecessarily, as it turns out, for Marcelle decides to marry someone else and have the child." Spectator

Followed by The reprieve

Intimacy, and other stories; translated by Lloyd Alexander. New Directions 1952 c1948 270p o.p.

Analyzed in Short story index

First published 1948 in a limited edition with title: The wall, and other stories

Contents: The wall; The room; Erostratus; Intimacy; The childhood of a leader

"The most impressive thing about the book, rising from it like a stench, is a disgust for life, a sense of universal defilement. The insistence on the physical in the stories is indistinguishable from an aversion to it." New Repub

Nausea; translated from the French by Lloyd Alexander. New Directions 1949 238p o.p. Bentley reprint available $14 (ISBN 0-8376-0443-5)

Original French edition, 1938

"*Nausea* is written in the form of a diary that narrates the recurring feelings of revulsion that overcome Roquentin, a young historian, as he comes to realize the banality and emptiness of existence. As the attacks of nausea occur more frequently, Roquentin abandons his

Sartre, Jean Paul, 1905-1980—*Continued*

research and loses his few friends. In an indifferent world, without work, love, or friendship to sustain him, he must discover value and meaning within himself." Merriam-Webster's Ency of Lit

The reprieve; translated from the French by Eric Sutton. Knopf 1947 445p (Roads to freedom, 2) o.p.

Original French edition, 1945

This sequel to The age of reason "confines itself to the eight frenetic days that led to the Munich Pact and the rape of Czechoslovakia. The original characters reappear merging now with many others as a shocked France mobilizes for war. Sartre, the leading exponent of Existentialism manages in this kaleidoscope novel to re-create the confusion, even the odor of the fear that gripped Europe in September, 1938." Libr J

Followed by Troubled sleep

Troubled sleep; translated from the French by Gerald Hopkins. Knopf 1950 421p (Roads to freedom, 3) o.p.

Sequel to The reprieve

Original French edition, 1949; published in the United Kingdom with title: Iron in the soul

"A story of the French people after the fall of Paris in World War II, of many individuals of different walks of life and their reactions to defeat." Publ Wkly

"No other book gives such insight into the anguished feelings of the French as they passed from apathy to consciousness of their dignity as men revolting against fate, accepting their solidarity with other men—wretched, but lucid and free fighters." Saturday Rev

Saul, John

Creature. Bantam Bks. 1989 329p o.p.
LC 88-7770

"When his family moves to idyllic Silverlake, Colorado, made over into a company town by his father Blake's high-tech employer, Mark Tanner is a puny 16-year-old stunted by a childhood illness. The town hosts an experimental sports center that amazingly converts weaklings into hulking jocks, and what's more, the company pushes its execs to get their boys into the program. Blake's dreams for Mark are within reach. Of course, there are some risks: a few athletes have gone berserk and, after attacking their parents, have had to be locked up. Despite his wife's misgivings—she thinks the whole town's fishy—Blake signs Mark up, and risk becomes reality." Booklist

Darkness. Bantam Bks. 1991 341p o.p.
LC 90-25842

This is the "tale of a little town in the Florida swamps where a lot of old guys are remarkably youthful and a lot of kids rather soulless. 'Dead in the eyes' is how folks see these children, a new one of whom, Kelly Anderson, has just come to town with her adoptive parents. She hooks up with another teenager, also an adoptee, Michael Sheffield. Together they find out about, and are irresistibly drawn to, a mysterious circle of children controlled by the Dark Man that meets deep in the swamp." Booklist

Guardian. Fawcett Columbine 1993 390p $21.50

ISBN 0-449-90862-3   LC 93-19002

"Mary Anne Carpenter, trying to cope with the return of the loutish husband who earlier deserted the family, heads off to Idaho with her 13-year-old daughter and 10-year-old son in order to comfort her recently orphaned godson. Joey Wilkenson's parents have died in mysterious accidents and his mother, MaryAnne's best friend, had named her Joey's guardian. Joey seems an average 13-year-old, if given to understandable bouts of moody withdrawal. But the apparently peaceful mountain valley becomes menacing when a camper is brutally killed, perhaps by an animal, and MaryAnne feels increasingly isolated as winter approaches." Publ Wkly

The homing. Fawcett Columbine 1994 389p $21.50

ISBN 0-449-90863-1   LC 93-50606

"Karen Spellman and her daughters Julie, 16, and Molly, 9, move from L.A. back to the bucolic community in which Karen grew up. For with the girls' father years dead, Karen has remet and decided to marry farmer Russell Owen. Things start going awry right away: at Karen and Russell's home wedding, Molly is stung by a bee, and although it's happened before with no untoward results, this time she nearly dies. More accidents with bees and other insects occur—not least to Julie—and while local entomologist Carl Henderson, who works for the agricultural branch of a huge chemical company, is able to provide seemingly effective antivenins when folks react badly to bites, he also occasionally behaves most peculiarly." Booklist

The author provides "splendidly creepy bug-infested house of horrors and a fitting revenge for the villain." Libr J

Second child. Bantam Bks. 1990 341p o.p.
LC 89-77149

Melissa "doesn't fit into the snooty social life of the exclusive East Coast beach community of Secret Cove, and her cruel mother hates her for this failing. The arrival of Melissa's beautiful half-sister, Teri, exacerbates the situation. Melissa escapes her mother's punishments by entering a trance state where her imaginary friend D'Arcy protects her. And who is D'Arcy? Apparently, the ghost of a spurned servant girl who returned an engagement ring still attached to her severed hand. Murderous Teri tries to manipulate Melissa's apparent psychosis, but D'Arcy intercedes. Mother and half-sister are evil incarnate." Booklist

Shadows. Bantam Bks. 1992 390p o.p.
LC 92-1317

"Ten-year-old genius Josh MacCallum is bored, lonely and almost always angry at his older, teasing classmates. After he attempts suicide, his frantic single mother jumps at the chance to enroll him in the Academy, a school for very gifted kids in Northern California. Run by aloof Dr. Engersol and matronly housemother Hildie, the school, which occupies an old mansion, offers Josh a friend in another genius, Amy Carlson. . . . Engersol and Hildie are revealed as nasty and the mad-scientist plot hurtles to a violent conclusion featuring dueling brains connected to a mainframe computer." Publ Wkly

Savery, Constance

See Brontë, C. Emma

Sawyer, Corinne Holt

Murder has no calories. Fine, D.I. 1994 216p $19.95

ISBN 1-55611-412-5   LC 94-71106

"Sleuths Angela Benbow and Caledonia Wingate, adventurous seniors, infiltrate an exclusive, weight-watching health spa in order to investigate the murder of a beautiful young employee." Libr J

Sayers, Dorothy L. (Dorothy Leigh), 1893-1957

Busman's honeymoon; a love story with detective interruptions. Harcourt Brace & Co. 1937 381p o.p.

"Not near the top of her form, but remarkable as a treatment of the newly wedded and bedded pair of eccentrics, Peter Wimsey and Harriet Vane, with Bunter in the offing and three local characters, chiefly comic. Peter's mother—dowager duchess of Denver—Peter's sister, John Donne, a case of vintage port, and the handling of 'corroded sut' provide plenty of garnishing for an indifferent murder, even if we weren't also given an idea of Lord Peter's sexual tastes and powers under trying circumstances." Barzun. Cat of Crime. Rev and enl edition

Clouds of witnesses. Dial Press (NY) 1927 288p o.p.

Variant title: Clouds of witness

The unpleasant duty of clearing his brother, the Duke of Denver, of a murder charge devolves upon Lord Peter Wimsey. Even when his only sister is involved—the dead man was her unregretted fiancé—Lord Peter does not lose his head

The Dawson pedigree. Dial Press (NY) 1928 c1927 299p o.p.

First published 1927 in the United Kingdom; reissued 1987 by Harper & Row with title: Unnatural death

A chance remark overheard in a restaurant starts a long inquiry and an apparently natural death is proved to have been a murder. But Lord Peter Wimsey, aided by his friends, Parker from Headquarters, and that garrulous and delightful maiden lady, Miss Climpson, has a very difficult time to catch the murderer

The documents in the case; [by] Dorothy L. Sayers and Robert Eustace. Harper & Row 1987 c1930 285p $17.95

ISBN 0-06-055034-1   LC 86-45690

Also available Thorndike Press large print edition

A reissue of the title first published 1930 by Brewer & Warren

An "account, largely in letter form, of a case of poisoning by synthetic muscarine alkaloid made to look like mushroom poisoning. Evidence of optical activity and what it means beautifully handled, although the authors are said to have made a mistake in their choice of the particular mushroom to which the 'accidental' death should be attributed. Characters outstanding." Barzun. Cat of Crime. Rev and enl edition

The five red herrings; (Suspicious characters). Harper & Row 1958 c1931 306p il o.p. Buccaneer Bks. reprint available $32.95 (ISBN 1-56849-332-0)

First published 1931. Variant title: Suspicious characters

Lord Peter Wimsey had always found himself welcome in the proud Scottish village of Kirkcudbright, although the villagers were not ordinarily tolerant of outsiders. But one day the body of an artist was found on the pointed rocks. The artist might have fallen, but there were too many suspicious elements in his death, especially when six suspects had wished him dead. Lord Peter uses all his ingenuity to unravel the tangles of this crime

"A work that grows on rereading and remains in the mind as one of the richest, most colorful of her group studies. The Scottish setting, the artists in the colony, the train-ticket puzzle, and the final chase place this triumph among the four or five chefs d'oeuvre from her hand." Barzun. Cat of Crime. Rev and enl edition

Gaudy Night. Harcourt Brace & Co. 1936 469p o.p.

First published 1935 in the United Kingdom

Harriet's return to Oxford for the Gaudy Dinner is welcomed by poison-pen letters and attempted blackmail. Lord Peter, of course, summons all his skill to detect the blackmailer and win Harriet

"Harriet Vance and the grown-up nephew of Lord Peter help give variety, and the college scene justifies good intellectual talk. The motive is magnificently orated on by the culprit, a scene that in itself is a unique bit of work. And though the don-esses are sometimes hard to keep apart, the architecture is very good." Barzun. Cat of Crime. Rev and enl edition

Hangman's holiday. Harcourt Brace & Co. 1933 282p o.p.

Analyzed in Short story index

Short stories included are: The image in the mirror; The incredible elopement of Lord Peter Wimsey; The queen's square; The necklace of pearls; The poisoned Dow '08; Sleuths on the scent; Murder in the morning; One too many; Murder at Pentecost; Maher-shalal-hashbaz; The man who knew how; The fountain plays

Have his carcase. Brewer, Warren & Putnam 1932 448p o.p.

Harriet Vane finds a body on the beach and Lord Peter Wimsey has a case to solve. Other ingredients of the mystery are an ivory-handled razor, three hundred pounds in gold coins and a coded message

"A great achievement, despite some critics' carping. The people, the motive, the cipher, and the detection are all topnotch. Here, too, is the first (and definitive) use of hemophilia as a misleading fact. And surely the son, the mother, and her self-deluded gigolo are definitive types." Barzun. Cat of Crime. Rev and enl edition

In the teeth of the evidence and other stories. Harcourt Brace & Co. 1940 311p o.p.

Available G.K. Hall large print edition

Analyzed in Short story index

First published 1939 in the United Kingdom

Short stories included are: Absolutely elsewhere: a Lord Peter Wimsey story; Arrow o'er the house; Bitter almonds: a Montague Egg story; Blood sacrifice; My best thriller; Dilemma; Dirt cheap: a Montague Egg story; False weight: a Montague Egg story; In the teeth of the evidence; Inspiration of Mr. Budd; Leopard lady; The

Sayers, Dorothy L. (Dorothy Leigh), 1893-1957—*Continued*
milk-bottles; Nebuchadnezzar; Professor's manuscript: a Montague Egg story; Scrawns; Shot at goal: a Montague Egg story; Suspicion

Lord Peter; a collection of all the Lord Peter Wimsey stories; compiled and with an introduction by James Sandoe; coda by Carolyn Heilburn; codetta by E.C. Bentley. Harper & Row 1972 464p o.p.
Available from Amereon and Borgo Press
Analyzed in Short story index
Contents: The abominable history of the man with copper fingers; The entertaining episode problem of Uncle Meleager's will; The fantastic horror of the cat in the bag; The unprincipled affair of the practical joker; The undignified melodrama of the bone of contention; The vindictive story of the footsteps that ran; The bibulous business of a matter of taste; The learned adventure of the Dragon's Head; The piscatorial farce of the stolen stomach; The unsolved puzzle of the man with no face; The adventurous exploit of the cave of Ali Baba; The image in the mirror; The incredible elopement of Lord Peter Wimsey; The queen's square; The necklace of pearls; In the teeth of the evidence; Absolutely elsewhere; Striding folly; The haunted policeman

Murder must advertise; a detective story. Harcourt Brace & Co. 1933 344p o.p.
Lord Peter Wimsey, less whimsical and more interesting than usual, enters the advertising profession in order to solve the possible murder by catapult of an advertising copywriter
"A superb example of Sayers' ability to set a group of people going. The advertising agency is inimitable, and hence better than the De Momerie crowd that goes with it." Barzun. Cat of Crime. Rev and enl edition

The nine tailors. Harcourt Brace Jovanovich 1989 c1934 397p il $15.95
ISBN 0-15-165897-8   LC 89-38102
"An HBJ modern classic"
A reissue of the title first published 1934
"One New Year's Eve, Lord Peter Wimsey, driving through a snowstorm, goes off the road near Fenchurch, St Paul, and is the chance guest of the rector. A providential visit all around, for Peter, acquainted with the ancient art of bellringing, acts that night as a substitute, but further than that, he finds use for his versatile mind later, upon the shocking discovery of a mutilated corpse in another man's grave. The unusual plot is developed with dexterity and ingenuity." N Y Libr

Strong poison. Brewer & Warren 1930 344p o.p. Amereon reprint available $18.95 (ISBN 0-8488-1154-2)
Because Harriet Vane's lover died of arsenic poisoning, and because Harriet was writing a book on the subject of poisons, everybody—except Lord Peter Wimsey—was convinced of her guilt. Lord Peter, with the aid of the inimitable Miss Climpson, gets to work on the business of clearing Harriet

The unpleasantness at the Bellona Club. Payson & Clarke 1928 345p o.p.
Lord Peter Wimsey investigates the murder of an elderly member of a staid men's club

Whose body? Boni & Liveright 1923 278p o.p.
When a nude corpse, wearing a golden pince-nez only, is found in the bathtub of the flat of a timid little architect, and the discovery coincides with the disappearance of a wealthy financier, Sir Reuben Levy, whom the body resembled, Sir Peter's sporting blood is aroused. Together with a friend from Scotland Yard he unofficially, playfully, as it were, conducts a roundabout inquiry under the jealous eye of the bungling official Scotland Yard investigators and finally tracks down the murderer

Scarborough, Elizabeth Ann
(jt. auth) McCaffrey, A. Power lines
(jt. auth) McCaffrey, A. Powers that be

Schaefer, Jack Warner, 1907-1991
The collected stories of Jack Schaefer; with an introduction by Winfield Townley Scott. Houghton Mifflin 1966 520p o.p.
Analyzed in Short story index
Contents: Major Burl; Miley Bennett; Emmet Dutrow; Sergeant Houck; Jeremy Rodock; Cooter James; Kittura Remsberg; General Pingley; Elvie Burdette; Josiah Willett; Something lost; Leander Frailey; Jacob; My town; Old Anse; That Mark horse; Ghost town; Takes a real man; Out of the past; Hugo Kertchak, builder; Prudence by name; Harvey Kendall; Cat nipped; Stalemate; Nate Bartlett's store; Salt of the earth; One man's honor. The old man; The coup of Long Lance; Enos Carr; The fifth man; Stubby Pringle's Christmas
"The author's mastery of narrative technique, his excellent character development, and his consistently concise description combine in avoiding the unfortunate aspects of typical 'Western' fiction and melodrama." Libr J

Monte Walsh. Houghton Mifflin 1963 501p o.p. Buccaneer Bks. reprint available $21.95 (ISBN 1-56849-042-9)
This novel of the old West follows Monte from runaway boy to trail hand, to topnotch cowhand and bronc buster, to aging saddle bum and encompasses the rise, the peak and the eventual collapse of the open range
"His characters seem real, and, according to the author, the characters and the episodes are based upon historical accounts. This is not just another 'Western.' It is worthy of a place alongside the writing of Will James and Eugene Manlove Rhodes." Libr J

Shane; [by] Jack Schaefer; illustrated by John McCormack. Houghton Mifflin 1954 214p il $15.95
ISBN 0-395-07090-2
Also available from Buccaneer Bks.
An illustrated edition of the title first published 1949
"Wyoming in 1889 is the scene of conflict between cattlemen and homesteaders when Shane mysteriously appears. He works hard as a hired hand for the Starrett family, and young Bob Starrett grows to love him, unaware that he is a feared gunfighter escaping his past." Shapiro. Fic for Youth. 3d edition

Schofield, Susan Clark, 1958-

Telluride; a novel. Algonquin Bks. 1993 328p $18.95

ISBN 0-945575-96-3   LC 93-1072

Also available Thorndike Press large print edition

"In the fall of 1892, 14 years after leaving his family in Telluride, Colo., retired gunslinger Zachary Coleman (known as Cole) returns to investigate his father's mysterious death. He gets scant welcome from his fiercely independent sister Gretel, who feels he abandoned her, and has a painful reunion with his former lover Catharine, who now shares a loveless marriage with the enigmatic and sinister Heinrich Braunn. Johnny Torres, foreman of Braunn's silver mine, tries to help, but Cole is entrapped by the erotic games Catharine and her husband play. . . . Historical accuracy and splendidly rich detail make this a winner in any genre." Publ Wkly

Schulberg, Budd

The disenchanted. Random House 1950 388p o.p.

"Manley Halliday, has-been literary genius of the 20's is given a last chance by Hollywood: to co-author a college musical. A trip East to pick up atmosphere serves as catalyst to bring about Halliday's complete physical and spiritual disintegration. As Fitzgeraldian as Fitzgerald, Halliday is the very essence of 'the lost generation,' and the novel contrasts effectively the manners and ideology of that period with our own." Libr J

Waterfront; a novel. Random House 1955 320p o.p. Bentley reprint available $20 (ISBN 0-8376-0434-6)

"The prize-winning screen play 'On the waterfront' has been expanded into a novel which differs on several counts from the film. It remains an angry indictment of racketeering in the labor unions along the New Jersey waterfront, but the happy ending of the screen play has been supplanted by a tragic one, in which the hero Terry Malloy is murdered by the henchmen of Johnny Friendly, the labor racketeer, and the terrorism along the waterfront continues. The more leisurely framework of the novel form permits the author to document to the full the abuses in longshoremen's unions, without sacrificing the explosive force of the film." Booklist

What makes Sammy run? Modern Lib. 1941 303p o.p.

Available from Bentley and Buccaneer Bks.

"The hero, Sammy Glick, is a tough New York youth who works his way into a position of power in the motion-picture industry, where his harshness and crude manners are not out of place. The novel is filled with much realistic detail of life in the movie colony." Reader's Ency. 3d edition

Schwartz, Lynne Sharon

Disturbances in the field. Harper & Row 1983 371p o.p.

LC 83-47555

"Lydia is a chamber musician . . . Victor is an artist, and their life in Manhattan is at last coming together. Lydia revels in the individual personalities of her four children and of her best women friends from college (Barnard) with whom, as in the old days, she argues philosophy in the most sincere, least highbrow manner possible. But her two youngest children are killed in a bus crash, a tragedy so profound she doesn't know how to react. . . . Then Victor moves out to live with another woman, although neither he nor Lydia can totally divorce themselves from all they have shared together." Publ Wkly

"There are weighty passages and themes here, not for the casual reader. However, the journey from resignation to a grudging reaffirmation of living, of returning to the field, disturbs the reader's own field with its unmistakable ring of truth." Libr J

Schwarz-Bart, André, 1928-

The last of the just; translated from the French by Stephen Becker. Atheneum Pubs. 1960 374p o.p. Bentley reprint available $22 (ISBN 0-8376-0456-7)

Original French edition, 1959

This novel "traces the martyrdom of the Jews through thirty-six generations of the Levy family, culminating with the death of Ernie in the Auschwitz concentration camp." Reader's Ency. 3d edition

"The thread that runs through the narration is the ancient Jewish tradition of the Lamed-Vov, according to which the world reposes upon 36 Just Men, who often are not aware themselves of the position they hold. . . . Harrowing as the book is, it is a valuable addition to the titles on the Holocaust, lest we forget how inhumane man can be." Shapiro. Fic for Youth. 3d edition

Scoppettone, Sandra, 1936-

Everything you have is mine. Little, Brown 1991 261p $19.95

ISBN 0-316-77646-7   LC 90-48889

"Lauren Laurano, a bighearted, wisecracking lesbian who makes her debut here as a Manhattan private eye, brings cunning as well as caring to her investigation of the murder of a young rape victim who might have met her killer by hooking into a dating service on her personal computer." N Y Times Book Rev

I'll be leaving you always. Little, Brown 1993 251p $19.95

ISBN 0-316-77647-5   LC 92-5096

Private investigator Lauren Laurano's friend Megan "is murdered in her Greenwich Village jewelry shop. Three more bodies follow . . . as Lauren learns that upstairs neighbor William, last to see Megan alive, was trying to score some coke from her at the time although he protests he's not an addict and Megan wasn't a dealer." Booklist

My sweet untraceable you. Little, Brown 1994 275p $19.95

ISBN 0-316-77648-3   LC 93-47426

"NYC lesbian private eye Lauren Laurano agrees to search for the truth about an ex-con's mother who has been presumed dead for 38 years." Libr J

"Scoppettone is a highly entertaining writer with her fingers on current political and commercial pulses. So she ably transmits the modish urban-grit feel of Laurano's encounters with Manhattan's winos, weirdos, and wise guys as she counterpoints the complex case her sleuth is solving with the deterioration from AIDS of the brother of Laurano's lesbian partner of 14 years." Booklist

Scott, Justin

The nine dragons; a novel of Hong Kong, 1997. Bantam Bks. 1991 457p o.p.

LC 90-25090

"When Duncan Mackintosh, the head of an illustrious, private Hong Kong trading company, is murdered at sea, his 32-year-old daughter, Victoria, takes over. She immediately faces a beleaguered reign as taipan, and her toughest adversary is her father's former mistress and 'right hand,' Vivian Loh. When Vicky falls in love with the Eurasian son of her father's suspected killer and Hong Kong's richest resident, Two-Way Wong, it's all but certain that Vicky will be toppled—or worse—from her lofty perch. . . . Fresh writing, memorable characters, an exotic locale, and a surprise ending make this saga a satisfying read." Booklist

Scott, Paul, 1920-1978

The day of the scorpion; a novel. Morrow 1968 483p o.p.

This second volume of the Raj quartet tells the lives of Sarah and Susan Layton, Lady Manners and Parvati; Kasim and his two sons and Captain Merrick, all caught up in the violence and strife that engulfed India when the Congress Party adopted a resolution calling for a nation-wide insurrection

The author's "ability in characterization and in realization of the love-hate relationship of Indian and Englishman are again amply demonstrated in a poignant story constantly interest-holding." Booklist

Followed by The towers of silence

also in Scott, P. The Raj quartet

A division of the spoils; a novel. Morrow 1975 597p o.p.

In this concluding volume of The Raj quartet, the end of the British rule in India is viewed primarily through the eyes of Guy Perron, a young historian serving as a sergeant in an army intelligence unit. The novel "spans the pivotal years 1945-1947 just before India and Pakistan gained independence. Central to the plot is Ronald Merrick, wounded, enigmatic colonel of the police whose interference in the lives of members of the British Raj . . . leads to cruelties as well as to revelations of individual responsibilities." Booklist

"Scott makes nothing simple; thus his work bears a disturbing resemblance to life. He mixes up lovers, friends, enemies, families, servants, strangers, soldiers, businessmen, murders, suicides, illnesses in five or six interrelated stories. . . . And all have one focus: corrupted British morality in India." N Y Times Book Rev

also in Scott, P. The Raj quartet

The jewel in the crown; a novel. Morrow 1966 462p o.p.

This is the first volume of The Raj quartet

"Around a central incident of the rape of a young Englishwoman in an Indian garden in August, 1942, the author has woven a . . . picture of India before independence. The two main threads of plot are the stages of the raped girl and the tragic end of an elderly English school-teacher who is a very brave woman. There are other stories within the story. . . . This is a masterly narrative, a leisurely and skillful depiction of a wide Indian landscape and a large canvas showing people who are made very real. It is also a dissection of Anglo-British animosities." Publ Wkly

Followed by The day of the scorpion

also in Scott, P. The Raj quartet

The Raj quartet. Morrow 1976 4v in 1 o.p.

An omnibus edition of the four quartet titles, all entered separately

Contents: The jewel in the crown; The day of the scorpion; The towers of silence; A division of the spoils

Staying on; a novel. Morrow 1977 215p o.p.

LC 77-1491

"After India succeeds in obtaining independence from Britain, Tusker and Lucy Smalley, part of the British colonial army, stay on in the country where almost all their married life has been spent. The book describes their relationships with the Indians who, at this point, constitute all of their daily and social contacts. . . . There is humor in the informative portrayals of the relationships between the British and the Indians, and the final scene is as simple and moving a description of loss as has ever been written." Shapiro. Fic for Youth. 3d edition

The towers of silence; a novel. Morrow 1972 c1971 392p o.p.

First published 1971 in the United Kingdom

In the third volume of the Raj quartet "attention focuses on Barbara Batchelor, the retired mission-school teacher, and many, but not all, of the events are seen through her eyes. This time the Manners case and Congress leader Mohammed Ali Kasim are relegated to the background, but the earlier reported activities of Mildred Layton and her daughters, Teddie Bingham, Captain Merrick, and others are repeated." Libr J

"This elegy on the decline and fall of the Indian empire sounds harsh notes, but is moving as well. Mr. Scott has the trick of being sympathetic without ever losing his clear sightedness." Times Lit Suppl

Followed by A division of the spoils

also in Scott, P. The Raj quartet

Scott, Sir Walter, 1771-1832

The bride of Lammermoor. o.p.

First published 1819

"The most tragic of Scott's romances, on which Donizetti's opera 'Lucia di Lammermoor' is based. The last scion of a ruined family and the daughter of his ancestral enemy in possession of the estates fall in love. For a while there is a glimpse of hope and happiness; but the ambitious mother opposes the match, prophecies and apparitions prognosticate tragedy, and the romance closes in death and sorrow. . . . Caleb Balderstone, the faithful retainer, is one of Scott's humorous creations, whose obstinate care for his unhappy master relieves the overpowering tragedy." Baker. Guide to the Best Fic

Ivanhoe.

Available from Amereon and Buccaneer Bks.

First published 1819

"A tale of the period following the Norman Conquest. The titular hero is Wilfred, knight of Ivanhoe, the son of Cedric the Saxon, in love with his father's ward Rowena. Cedric, however, wishes her to marry Athelstane, who is descended from the Saxon royal line and may restore the Saxon supremacy. The real heroine is Rebecca the Jewess, daughter of the wealthy Isaac of York and a person of much more character and charm

Scott, Sir Walter, 1771-1832—*Continued*

than the mild Rowena. Richard the Lion-heart in the guise of the Black Knight and Robin Hood as Locksley play prominent roles." Reader's Ency. 3d edition

Kenilworth. o.p.

First published 1821

A novel "famous for its portrayal of Queen Elizabeth and her court. The other principal characters are Robert Dudley, the earl of Leicester, who entertains ambitions of becoming king-consort, and his beautiful, unhappy wife, Amy Robsart. She suffers neglect, insult and finally death at his hands." Reader's Ency. 3d edition

Quentin Durward. o.p.

First published 1823

"The novel is set in 15th-century France, where the title character saves the life of Louis XI, protects and falls in love with Countess Isabelle de Croye (a Burgundian heiress), helps defeat the king's brutal enemy, and wins Isabelle's hand in marriage." Merriam-Webster's Ency of Lit

Rob Roy; with an introduction by Eric Anderson. Knopf 1995 xliii, 494p $18

ISBN 0-679-44362-2

"Everyman's library"

First published 1817; first Everyman's library edition 1906

"Full of intrigue with political overtones, it is set in northern England just before the Jacobite rebellion of 1715, and it is considered one of the author's masterpieces. Francis Obaldistone, the novel's hero, contends with his jealous, unscrupulous cousin Rashleigh for the hand of the beautiful Diana Vernon. Aided by the Scottish outlaw Rob Roy (based on a historical Jacobite outlaw), Francis succeeds in exposing Rashleigh's villainy." Merriam-Webster's Ency of Lit

The talisman. o.p.

First published 1825

A historical novel "relating the adventures of Sir Kenneth, prince royal of Scotland, as a knight in disguise in the Holy Land under Richard I. Richard and his noble enemy Saladin are leading characters. The talisman is an amulet of singular healing powers with which Saladin effects the cure of Richard's sickness." Reader's Ency. 3d edition

Waverly; or, 'Tis sixty years since. o.p.

First published 1814

"This celebrated romance of the '45 [Jacobite] Rebellion depicts more especially its earlier stages . . . the later period of the Derby retreat being rapidly sketched, while the disaster of Culloden is introduced only in the shape of news. The book, even apart from its own special merits, must always hold a position of great importance as being Scott's first venture in fiction." Nield. Guide to the Best Hist Novels & Tales

Scott, Warwick, 1920-1995

For works written by this author under other names see Hall, Adam, 1920-1995; Trevor, Elleston, 1920-1995

Sebastian, Lee

For works written by this author under other names see Silverberg, Robert

Segal, Erich, 1937-

Acts of faith. Bantam Bks. 1992 529p o.p.

LC 91-24206

"Daniel Luria is the heir apparent to the Brooklyn-based Silczer dynasty of rabbis. After Timothy Hogan (an 'orphan' with two living parents) breaks the Lurias' window, Rabbi Luria hires him to turn out the lights on Sabbath nights. When the rabbi sees his daughter Deborah and Timothy poised for a forbidden embrace, he banishes Deborah to Jerusalem. Timothy, a rising star en route to Catholic priesthood, eventually encounters Deborah on her kibbutz; they consummate their relationship, despite Timothy's vows of celibacy. Meanwhile, in rabbinical school, Daniel finds doubt as well as lust in his heart." Publ Wkly

Segal "sticks closely to formula, but any reader even remotely opinionated regarding religion will find themselves thinking." Booklist

Doctors. Bantam Bks. 1988 679p o.p.

LC 88-14547

This novel "follows four doctors from their training at Harvard Medical School through internship, residency, and life in something that looks vaguely like the real world." Booklist

"With his usual facility, Segal spins a highly readable story that addresses the gravest, most pressing issues facing doctors today." Publ Wkly

Love story. Harper & Row 1970 131p o.p. Buccaneer Bks. reprint available $27.95 (ISBN 1-56849-334-7)

"Oliver is Harvard, rich, a big campus athlete. Jenny is a Radcliffe scholarship student in music from a poor Italian Catholic background. They meet, fall in love, and marry, even though the boy's father wants him to go to law school first. Jenny gives up a chance to study in Paris and works to put her young husband through law school—and they win out to the beginnings of a great life and promising career for him. Then tragedy steps in." Publ Wkly

"A very professionally crafted short first novel. The author makes no great claims of insight for his work. Indeed, the story is all on the surface. But it is funny and sad and generally recommended." Libr J

Followed by Oliver's story (1977)

Selinko, Annemarie

Désirée. Morrow 1953 594p o.p. Buccaneer Bks. reprint available $27.95 (ISBN 1-56849-548-X)

"Eugénie Désirée Clary, the daughter of a rich silk merchant of Marseille, records in her diary the history of her two love affairs, the first with Napoleon Bonaparte, who jilted her to marry Josephine, and the second with General Bernadotte, who married her and ended his career as the first of a new line of Swedish kings. Since Eugénie's two loves happen to be famous in history, the diary Miss Selinko has written for her naturally reads like a chronicle of the period between 1794 and 1829." New Yorker

Serling, Carol

(ed) Rod Serling's Night gallery reader. See Rod Serling's Night gallery reader

Serling, Rod, 1924-1975

Rod Serling's Night gallery reader. See Rod Serling's Night gallery reader

Seth, Vikram, 1952-

A suitable boy; a novel. HarperCollins Pubs. 1993 1349p o.p.

LC 92-54744

"Set in the post-colonial India of the 1950s, this sprawling saga involves four families—the Mehras, the Kapoors, the Chatterjis and the Khans—whose domestic crises illuminate the historical and social events of the era. Like an old-fashioned soap opera (or a Bombay talkie), the multi-charactered plot pits mothers against daughters, fathers against sons, Hindus against Muslims and small farmers against greedy landowners facing government-ordered dispossession." Publ Wkly

This novel is, "at its heart an elegy as well as a comedy of manners, about a traditional society in a time of change, and about a leisurely world of graces giving way to a new, more democratic time." Times Lit Suppl

Seton, Anya, d. 1990

Avalon. Houghton Mifflin 1965 440p o.p.

"The romance is a deep lifelong attachment between a wandering French prince, an idealistic, poetic man, and a Cornish girl of peasant and Viking blood. The story opens in a courtly, gentle mood which changes to fury, lust and murderous greed when the scene shifts to the English court, and to adventure and exploration when the girl is captured by her father's people and the Vikings take the center of the stage." Publ Wkly

"Late tenth- and early eleventh-century life in England and in the lands colonized by the Norsemen [i.e. Iceland] is re-created from early Anglo-Saxon chronicles, French manuscripts, and secondary sources. . . . The action and milieu are vivid and though the characterization is not strong the psychological and historical motivations are believable. An honest historical novel for enthusiasts of the genre." Booklist

Dragonwyck. Houghton Mifflin 1944 336p o.p. Buccaneer Bks. reprint available $29.95 (ISBN 1-56849-484-X)

An American "Gothic" novel. The time is the 1830's and 1840's; the place, New York City and the great Van Ryn estate, Dragonwyck, on the Hudson. A young farm girl, a distant cousin of the Van Ryn's goes to live at Dragonwyck as governess to the Van Ryns' small daughter. At the death of the child's mother, Miranda becomes the second Mrs. Van Ryn. The story of Miranda's gradual horrified awakening follows

"For all its trappings and devices—and they are good, spine-chilling trappings, handled with considerable skill—the novel manages to have life and substance." N Y Her Trib Books

Green darkness. Houghton Mifflin 1973 c1972 591p o.p.

Available from Amereon and Buccaneer Bks.

First published 1972 in the United Kingdom

"Reincarnation is the theme of [this] . . . novel. A 16th-century Benedictine monk, Stephen Marsdon, falls prey to a consuming passion for alluring Celia de Bohun and forsakes his vows. The tragic end of the lovers, involving murder and suicide, brings, nearly 400 years later, madness and near death to their reincarnations, newlyweds Celia and Richard Marsdon. Fortunately, a Hindu doctor (himself a reincarnated Italian physician in Tudor England who longed for warmer climates) hovers nearby to monitor the proceedings and brings the souls to rest." Libr J

Katherine. Houghton Mifflin 1954 588p o.p.

Available from Amereon and Buccaneer Bks.

Historical romance about the life of Katherine Swynford, sister-in-law of Geoffrey Chaucer, and mistress and later wife of John Gaunt

"It is a story that demands no intellectual or emotional effort from the reader. . . . But Miss Seton presents her facts accurately. Her research extends as far as visiting what remains of any of John of Gaunt's 30 castles and her zest for her subject communicates itself to the reader." San Francisco Chron

The Winthrop woman. Houghton Mifflin 1958 586p o.p.

In this biographical novel the author rallies to the defense of a maligned historical figure. "The young widow Elizabeth Winthrop was perhaps the most unwilling Puritan who ever came to New England, for she detested and feared Governor John Winthrop, who was her uncle as well as her father-in-law. A second marriage to Robert Feake, the governor's choice, dragged through years of Robert's increasing insanity; when he deserted her Elizabeth secured a divorce in New Amsterdam, contracted a common-law marriage with virile William Hallet, and found with him a love that was adequate recompense for exile and persecution." Booklist

"The novel is noteworthy for its insights into the Puritan 'Bible Commonwealth.'" Saturday Rev

Settle, Mary Lee

Celebration. Farrar, Straus & Giroux 1986 355p o.p.

LC 86-12100

In 1960s London widow Teresa Cerrutti "meets geologist Ewen McLeod in the British Museum. Together they enter not only a romance but a joint exorcism of accumulated pain. Their friends . . . include a gigantic African Jesuit, a tormented homosexual, an eager young woman from Turkey, and a rigid CIA spy. As these lonely people unite in tentative friendship and communality, the novel reaches a powerful and painful conclusion." Libr J

Charley Bland. Farrar, Straus & Giroux 1989 207p o.p.

"Having fled the suffocating small-town environment of her West Virginia home and re-created herself as a writer in postwar Paris, the heroine of this condensed, lyric novel returns to discover that having dreams come true is sometimes disastrous. For there she again meets Charley Bland, the golden boy she worshiped as a child, now the town's most eligible—and elusive—bachelor. . . . The affair they begin quickly demolishes everything this woman had made of herself in the years she had been away." Libr J

Settle, Mary Lee—*Continued*

This novel's "precision and emotional power urge one to listen ferociously for the hidden melodies that reveal the history underneath the social plottings, the story not just of people but of a world." N Y Times Book Rev

The killing ground. Farrar, Straus & Giroux 1982 385p o.p.

LC 82-2477

"In this novel, the last of the Beulah Quintet, Settle describes the various homecomings of Hannah McKarkle, a woman from an affluent West Virginia coal-mining family who has pursued a writing career in New York. In 1960, Hannah returns to find that her brother Johnny has been killed by a man who turns out to be a poor distant relative. The brother's death, the intricate interplay among classes in the closed rural society of West Virginia, and the inevitable pull of one's native home on the heart and soul are central to her subsequent visits in 1978 and 1980." Libr J

O Beulah Land; a novel. Viking 1956 368p o.p.

First published volume of the author's Beulah Quintet, set in rural West Virginia. Chronologically follows Prisons (1973). Subsequent titles in the series: Know nothing (1960); The scapegoat (1980) and The killing ground (entered above)

Historical novel of the Virginia frontier from 1754 to 1775. "Jonathan Lacey is a strong man, as only a gentleman is strong. And he is a gentleman, by the standards of the Virginia wilderness country in the years preceding the American Revolution. After his service at the Battle of Little Meadows in 1775, Johnny scouts and surveys far into the mountains, and leads a heterogeneous group of early Americans westward with him, to claim and clear his bounty land in the undefended King's Part of the colony, beyond the Proclamation Line. It is on this land, called Beulah by Jeremiah the New Light preacher, that Johnny proves his strength." N Y Times Book Rev

Shaara, Michael, 1929-1988

The killer angels; a novel. McKay, D. 1974 374p $19.95

ISBN 0-679-50466-4

Also available Thorndike Press large print edition

This is a fictionalized account of four days in July, 1863 at the Battle of Gettysburg. The point of view of the Southern forces is represented by Generals Robert E. Lee and James Longstreet, while Colonel Joshua Chamberlain and General John Buford are the focus for the North

"Shaara's version of private reflections and conversations are based on his reading of documents and letters. Although some of his judgments are not necessarily substantiated by historians, he demonstrates a knowledge of both the battle and the area. The writing is vivid and fast moving." Libr J

Shacochis, Bob

Swimming in the volcano; a novel. Scribner 1993 519p $22

ISBN 0-684-19260-8

LC 92-37116

"In 1976, Mitchell Wilson signs on as an agricultural economist on St. Catherine, a fictional island in the Lesser Antilles. Just as he has settled into a routine and a circle of expatriate and native friends, his life is disrupted by the appearance of his first love, the volatile Johanna. Equally unsteady is the island's ruling coalition, which is coming apart under threat from a counter-revolutionary menace fabricated by discontented members." Publ Wkly

"This may sound like a fast-paced thriller, but though there's a mystery to crack at the heart of this richly detailed novel, Shacochis in fact offers a chilling evocation of the misunderstandings that arise between feckless Americans and struggling islanders for whom St. Catherine's is no paradise." Libr J

Shagan, Steve

A cast of thousands. Pocket Bks. 1993 358p o.p.

LC 92-32118

In this "novel the major executive players of Gemstone Pictures set up a bogus studio takeover plot in order to make a killing on their stock holding. To ensure the success of this scam, they greenlight a doomed-to-fail David Lean-type expensive epic about the Spanish Civil War, to be made on location by a cast and crew of emotional misfits." Libr J

"Real and fictitious movies—starring real and fictitious luminaries—add considerable punch, as do such vividly evoked locations as New York, Beverly Hills, Rome, Jamaica, Madrid and St. Moritz. While many of these elements are *de rigueur* for Hollywood sagas, and the plot is reminiscent of the film *The Producers,* Shagan always manages a fillip that lifts his elements above the madding crowd." Publ Wkly

Shange, Ntozake

Betsey Brown; a novel. St. Martin's Press 1985 207p o.p.

LC 85-2663

The novelist presents "the life of a prosperous black family in St. Louis during 1957, the year of school desegregation. The story focuses on three generations of women, 13-year-old Betsey Brown and her mother and grandmother." Libr J

"Miss Shange is a superb storyteller who keeps her eye on what brings her characters together rather than what separates them: courage and love, innocence and the loss of it, home and homelessness. Miss Shange understands backyards, houses, schools and churches. [This novel] rejoices in—but never sentimentalizes—those places on earth where you are accepted, where you are comfortable with yourself." N Y Times Book Rev

Liliane; resurrection of the daughter. St. Martin's Press 1994 288p $18.95

ISBN 0-312-11310-2

LC 94-26107

"Liliane epitomizes Shange's ideal black woman—a profoundly sensual and artistic renegade haunted by the suffering of people of color and her lost loved ones. The daughter of an ambitious, domineering father and a beautiful, selfish mother, Liliane grew up politicized as well as deeply attuned to beauty, eroticism, and the sharp pleasure of living a self-directed life. Shange conducts a rough-and-ready little chorus of friends, cousins, and lovers to tell Liliane's complex and emblematic story. Several chapters are narrated by one of Liliane's more alluring and amusing lovers, Victor-Jésus María,

Shange, Ntožake—*Continued*

while other sections document Liliane's sessions with her analyst. This is a novel with personality: it's moody, inconsistent, and frustrating." Booklist

Sassafrass, Cypress & Indigo; a novel. St. Martin's Press 1982 224p o.p.

LC 82-5565

This novel "tells of three sisters from Charleston, South Carolina. Indigo, the youngest, is full of magic and has trouble reconciling her inner worlds and reality. She bridges the gap with her poetry and her violin playing; both reveal an idiosyncratic style. Sassafrass, the oldest, writes and weaves, lives in Los Angeles with a man who seems a sometime thing, and tries to make sense of life, its connections and memories. Cypress is a dancer living in New York: 'when she danced, she was alive; when she danced, she was free.'" Publ Wkly

"Poetry, magical spells, recipes, and choreographs are woven into the narrative providing a vital interplay between the sisters and their creations. The setting of much of the story, Charleston, South Carolina, becomes a place of magic and joy for the reader." Libr J

Shannon, Dell, 1921-

For works written by this author under other names see Linington, Elizabeth, 1921-

Appearances of death. Morrow 1977 226p o.p.

LC 77-5709

"Luis Mendoza, LAPD's somewhat quirky chief crime fighter, is at the top of his super-meticulous form. . . . His robbery-homicide squad is pitted against a series of bizarre cases, involving a stickup artist with a stammer, a rapist, and an abducted nurse, and only Mendoza can pull them together into a cohesive crime-fighting unit." Booklist

Blood count. Morrow 1986 227p o.p.

LC 86-12466

Lt. Luis Mendoza and his staff at L.A.P.D. have a number of cases to investigate. "A woman visiting L.A. from Indianapolis is found murdered in her car, a well-manicured derelict's corpse turns up and an old man is discovered lying dead amongst his scattered furniture. Most upsetting are the crimes against children: the rape of a 12-year-old girl, the murder of an infant and the suicide of a youngster egged on by her fanatical father. . . . The cases, with their sudden mysteries, keep the plot moving quickly." Publ Wkly

Chaos of crime. Morrow 1985 190p o.p.

LC 84-22624

"A maniac is loose on the streets of Los Angeles, tying prostitutes to their beds, beheading them, disemboweling them, and then surgically dissecting them like laboratory animals. Detective Luis Mendoza and the Los Angeles Police Department are sufficiently stumped in trying to locate this madman who never leaves a clue—until finally the discovery of a rare French wristwatch helps to reveal a seemingly unlikely killer." Booklist

Destiny of death. Morrow 1984 227p o.p.

LC 84-60090

"Luis Mendoza and the cops in Robbery-Homicide are faced with a bewildering glut of cases while their personal lives present a series of crises." Booklist

Exploit of death. Morrow 1983 215p o.p.

LC 82-21649

"While struggling to solve everyday holdups, muggings, stabbings, and assorted urban atrocities, members of the Robbery-Homicide Division of the LAPD focus on one particularly hideous or outlandish murder. In this case, a young French woman, Juliette Martin, whom Mendoza and his wife recently met on a transcontinental flight, is found dead in L.A., seemingly from a self-inflicted drug overdose. Mendoza investigates, sure that what appears to be suicide is actually a very clever murder." Booklist

Felony file. Morrow 1980 249p o.p.

LC 79-22033

Luis Mendoza and the Los Angeles precinct detectives "work doggedly with faint clues to track and collar felons, while concurrently trying to find why the corpse of a respectable, middle-aged woman has been dumped in a city park. Other cases include the repeated robbing of a posh department store, the killing of an old couple . . . the rape-murder of a small child and more." Publ Wkly

The Manson curse. Morrow 1990 262p o.p.

LC 90-36989

An American reporter based in London visits his novelist friend in Cornwall and becomes curious about the writer's obsession with the occult

Murder by the tale. Morrow 1987 226p o.p.

LC 87-15419

Analyzed in Short story index

Contents: The clue; The cat; The ring; Accident; The motive; The long chance; The bronze cat; Novelties; Happy release; Rannysore; They will call it insane; Conundrum; Need-fire; The practical joke; Flash attachment

This "collection of short stories . . . runs the gamut of crime fiction, from realistic procedurals to macabre tales of the supernatural. Surprisingly, the eight stories featuring Lieutenant Luis Mendoza are less effective than the supernatural pieces. Shannon's realistic writing in the shorter form is soft on characterization and too reliant on unlikely solutions. Still, the best of these short pieces vividly celebrate the subtle twist that converts the apparently normal to the criminal or the bizarre." Booklist

Murder most strange. Morrow 1981 228p o.p.

LC 80-24573

In this novel Mendoza and the LAPD Murder and Homicide Division "track down a rapist-murderer, check on the unexplained disappearance of a young girl, find the reason behind a double homicide/suicide, look into the implausible 'natural' death of a senator, and solve other baffling mysteries." West Coast Rev Books

Shannon, Doris

See also Giroux, E. X.

Sharp, Margery, 1905-1991

Cluny Brown. Little, Brown 1944 270p o.p.

Cluny (short for Clover) Brown was a plumber's niece given to exploring by-paths beyond her own station in life. Her poor uncle, nonplussed by Cluny's behavior, shipped her off to Devonshire to service as parlor-maid in a great house. There Cluny's behavior was unconven-

Sharp, Margery, 1905-1991—*Continued*
tional although not too startling until the end when she
eloped with one of the guests, a very important Polish
literary light

Shaw, Felicity *See* Morice, Anne

Shaw, Irwin, 1913-1984
Acceptable losses; a novel. Arbor House
1982 303p o.p.

LC 82-72056

"Confronted with a stranger's threatening phone calls,
Roger Damon, New York literary agent, faces one of
the realities of modern life: the 'random evil spirit'
which can claim anyone as a victim. Requested by the
police to list possible enemies, he dredges up aspects of
his past which can only be rationalized as 'acceptable
losses': former lovers, a failed first marriage, professional
enemies. Damon's present life is a happy one, yet the
insoluble puzzle takes a toll on his health, and he nearly
dies from complications of ulcers." Libr J

Beggarman, thief. Delacorte Press 1977
436p o.p.

LC 77-24523

Sequel to Rich man, poor man
"Wayward brother Tom Jordache has been murdered,
leaving his son Wesley with a legacy of violence and
revenge that is echoed in his nephew Billy, who becomes
involved in a terrorist group in Brussels while serving
in the U.S. Army. The story does not focus entirely on
the second generation—the tangled lives of the older
Jordaches are also featured. . . . Scenes from the earlier
novel are interwoven allowing the unfamiliar reader to
complete enjoyment and understanding." Booklist

Bread upon the waters. Delacorte Press
1981 438p o.p.

LC 81-3106

This novel "concerns the effects of misdirected philanthropy on a middle-class New York family—the Strands.
Allen Strand is a history teacher at a public (state)
school. His wife Leslie gives piano lessons to bring in
extra money. Jimmy, their son, has ambitions to be a
rock singer. The elder daughter, Eleanor, is an executive
in a large corporation, and the younger daughter,
Caroline is a sporty schoolgirl. One night Caroline . .
. saves a millionaire called Russell Hazen from attack
by a gang of muggers. She takes him home to have a
wound dressed and Hazen is swiftly entranced by the
warmth and harmony of the Strand family. His gratitude
prompts him to set about making their dreams come
true." Times Lit Suppl

Evening in Byzantium. Delacorte Press
1973 368p o.p.
The author writes of "a once-famous Hollywood
producer, now 48, something of a has-been, who is
reliving the past and preparing a final conquest of the
future at the Cannes Film Festival. Jesse Craig is in
trouble and he knows it. His marriage has been a failure,
he is desperately fond of his daughter but cannot help
her at a crisis moment in her own life, his attractive
mistress is making demands he no longer cares to meet,
and a shrewd, tough-minded young woman interviewer
has him just where she wants him." Publ Wkly

Nightwork. Delacorte Press 1975 344p o.p.

"In the room of a seedy hotel in New York where
he works as a night clerk, Grimes stumbles on the nude
corpse of a guest—and a cardboard tube stuffed with
$100,000. . . . Grimes takes the money and runs to
Switzerland where he falls in with a suave Lothario and
gambler named Fabian. . . . They set about increasing
their ill-gotten gain by investing in everything from race
horses to pornographic films." Newsweek
This "is an easy, enjoyable book to read and was, I
suspect, an easy and enjoyable book to write. Its serious
moments are there to be found—most occur when Shaw
takes time out to show how the American Way of Life
screws Americans—but he is wise enough to curtail them
before they slow the pace of his largely good-tempered
narrative." New Statesman

Rich man, poor man. Delacorte Press
1970 723p o.p.
"A family chronicle which tells the story of the three
children of Axel Jordache, a baker in a small town on
the Hudson River. Thomas becomes a prizefighter,
Rudolph a successful business man, and Gretchen eventually achieves a theatrical career after being seduced by
the local mill-owner. . . . This is the dawn-to-dusk,
1940's-to-1970's, success-to-failure, poor-to-rich spectrum."
N Y Times Book Rev
"Each member of the clan is doomed in one way or
another. They fight, love, live hard and their fortunes
are inevitably intertwined. Mr. Shaw has juxtaposed their
rise and fall against a panoramic picture of the times.
. . . This may not be great literature but it certainly
has popular appeal." Publ Wkly
Followed by Beggarman, thief

Short stories: five decades. Delacorte Press
1978 756p o.p.

LC 78-16020

Analyzed in Short story index
Contents: The eighty-yard run; Borough of cemeteries;
Main currents of American thought; Second mortgage;
Sailor off the Bremen; Strawberry ice cream soda; Wel-
come to the city; The girls in their summer dresses;
Search through the streets of the city; The monument;
I stand by Dempsey; God on Friday night; Return to
Kansas City; Triumph of justice; No jury would convict;
The lament of Madame Rechevsky; The deputy sheriff;
Stop pushing, Rocky; "March, march on down the field";
Free conscience, void of offense; Weep in years to come;
The city was in total darkness; Night, birth and opinion;
Preach on the dusty roads; Hamlets of the world; Medal
from Jerusalem; Walking wounded; Night in Algiers;
Gunners' passage; Retreat; Act of faith; The man with
one arm; The passion of Lance Corporal Hawkins; The
dry rock; Noises in the city; The Indian in depth of
night; Material witness; Little Henry Irving; The house
of pain; A year to learn the language; The Greek general;
The green nude; The climate of insomnia; Goldilocks at
graveside; Mixed doubles; A wicked story; Age of reason;
Peter Two; The sunny banks of the river Lethe; The
man who married a French wife; Voyage out, voyage
home; Tip on a dead jockey; The inhabitants of Venus;
In the French style; Then we were three; God was here
but he left early; Love on a dark street; Small Saturday;
Pattern of love; Whispers in bedlam; Where all things
wise and fair descend; Full many a flower; Circle of light

Shaw, Irwin, 1913-1984—*Continued*

The young lions. Random House 1948 689p o.p.

"World War II changes the lives of Christian, ex-Communist and Nazi; Michael, a Broadway stage manager; and Noah, an American Jew married to a Christian woman. We follow their lives during the years 1938 to 1945 as they experience frustrations, hardships, and the dangers of the war. The three fight, and two are killed." Shapiro. Fic for Youth. 3d edition

Sheckley, Robert, 1928-

(jt. auth) Zelazny, R. Bring me the head of Prince Charming

Sheed, Wilfrid

The boys of winter; a novel. Knopf 1987 280p $17.95

ISBN 0-394-55874-X   LC 86-46319

"Jonathan Ogelthorpe, the overworked editor of a 'quality' publishing company, weekends in the Hamptons, where most of his authors also reside. Waldo Spinks, a not-so-young literary hotshot whose best work is behind him, has recently completed a novel that's been turned down by his longtime publisher. Jonathan, who desperately wants Spinks' book to beef up his spring list, regards the author with a mixture of envy and admiration. Meanwhile, Jonathan is secretly writing a thinly fictionalized version of life in the Hamptons with Spinks as the leading villain. When he discovers that Spinks' novel is also set in the Hamptons—with an evil editor as the main character—the plot thickens." Booklist

This novel "brings Grub Street to contemporary times and the exurbs—and it's funny. Finally it does the satirist's good work of demolition, but it also, alas, tells much of the truth about literary politicking. And for watchful readers, it tells some of the truth about politicking in general." N Y Times Book Rev

Sheffield, Charles

Georgia on my mind

In Nebula awards 29 p95-136

Sheldon, Alice Hastings Bradley *See* Tiptree, James, 1916-1987

Sheldon, Raccoona, 1916-1987

See also Tiptree, James, 1916-1987

Sheldon, Sidney, 1917-

The doomsday conspiracy. Morrow 1991 412p $22

ISBN 0-688-08489-3   LC 91-12109

Also available large print edition $25 (ISBN 0-688-10444-4)

"Navy Commander Robert Bellamy is assigned to investigate the crash of a weather balloon in the Swiss Alps. All witnesses to the accident must be found and questioned. However, for Bellamy it is the beginning of a journey of terror into the incomprehensible. From Washington to London, Zurich, Rome, and Paris the story unfolds to reveal Bellamy's past—why the woman he loves most cannot return his love, why his friends

become his deadly enemies, and why the world must never learn an incredible secret shielded by an unknown lethal force." Publisher's note

Master of the game. Morrow 1982 495p o.p.

LC 82-60920

"Kate Blackwell, born of a loveless marriage, striving through will, intelligence, and charm to control one of the richest conglomerates in the world, uses her power in wonderfully fiendish ways, which almost result in the destruction of those she loves most. The South African diamond mines provide vivid adventure; when the scene shifts to the United States, we encounter the more political maneuverings of business, but the pace never slackens." Libr J

Nothing lasts forever. Morrow 1994 398p $23

ISBN 0-688-08491-5   LC 94-5437

This novel "begins with the trial of a San Francisco doctor, Paige Taylor, who in 1995 is accused of killing a patient to gain access to a large inheritance. The narrative then backs up to 1990 and chronicles the journeys of Taylor, Honey Taft, and Kat Hunter, the only three females in a group of new residents at Embarcadero County Hospital. The women, who quickly become roommates and friends, face long hours, a frenetic work pace, and unwanted advances from male colleagues. Kat becomes involved in unsavory underworld activities. Honey's questionable medical skills are overlooked by the male administrators, who value her other services. Paige tries to forget a lost love. This readable and entertaining story ends with a dramatic . . . flourish." Libr J

Rage of angels. Morrow 1980 504p $18.95

ISBN 0-688-03687-2   LC 80-13328

"Young lawyer Jennifer Parker makes an incredible blunder in her first day as assistant D.A. Fired and in disgrace, she is reduced to serving writs to earn a living. Smart and stubborn, she perseveres, taking on unpromising clients. By inspired strategies of courtroom drama, she wins a few spectacular cases. Soon the world is taking notice, especially the Mafia. Their attractive offers are refused, but one day Parker must ask them for help in a desperate situation. In return, she becomes a Mafia mouthpiece, tempered somewhat by her love affair with the Mafioso." Libr J

The sands of time. Morrow 1988 412p $22.95

ISBN 0-688-06571-6   LC 88-25916

This novel "stars a leader of the ETA, the Basque Nationalist guerrilla organization. Jaime Miró is a 'legend, a hero to the Basque people and anathema to Spanish government.' His capture and death is the obsession of Colonel Acoca, a ruthless Spanish officer funded and directed by a powerful cabal (OPUS MUNDO) and charged with hunting Basque terrorists. Acoca's first attack is upon a Cistercian convent whose reclusive residents are suspected of having harbored Miró. After Acoca's attack, four surviving sisters are teamed with Miró's band and readily fall prey to worldly ways." Booklist

"Not a breath of subtlety touches these pages, but goodwill and lively subplots move the book along at a spirited pace." Publ Wkly

Sheldon, Sidney, 1917-—*Continued*

The stars shine down. Morrow 1992 400p $23

ISBN 0-688-08490-7   LC 92-25280

Also available large print edition $27 (ISBN 0-688-12100-4)

This is the "story of real-estate tycoon Lara Cameron as she claws her way to the top. Fleeing Nova Scotia and the memories of her lowly roots and drunken father, Lara builds an empire in Chicago and New York that is based on snap decisions and gutsy gambles. But with only the platonic friendship of her financial adviser and a passionate but shallow liaison with a married Mafia boss, it's lonely in the penthouse until Lara meets concert pianist Philip Adler. As Lara's love life takes off, however, her career starts being sabotaged. Setting them in just enough romantic locales, Sheldon weaves just enough of the details of power-brokering and the lives of the rich and famous into the tight plot to ground but not slow the action." Booklist

Windmills of the gods. Morrow 1987 384p $22.95

ISBN 0-688-06570-8   LC 86-23593

The heroine of this novel is a "college lecturer from Kansas elevated to the politically volatile position of ambassador to Romania. Mary Ashley is plunged unaware into a cauldron of intrigue. Her surprise appointment, coming after the mysterious death of her husband, is the first stage in a newly elected president's plans to cement East-West relations. Up against Mary and the president are a secret alliance of political extremists and a ruthless international assassin known as Angel." Booklist

"The story speeds along and the epilogue is a chiller." Libr J

Shelley, Mary Wollstonecraft, 1797-1851

Frankenstein; or, The modern Prometheus.
Available from various publishers

First published 1818

"The tale relates the exploits of Frankenstein, an idealistic Genevan student of natural philosophy, who discovers at the university of Ingolstadt the secret of imparting life to inanimate matter. Collecting bones from charnel-houses, he constructs the semblance of a human being and gives it life. The creature, endowed with supernatural strength and size and terrible in appearance, inspires loathing in whoever sees it." Oxford Companion to Engl Lit. 5th edition

Shepard, Jim

(ed) You've got to read this. See You've got to read this

Shepard, Lucius

A traveler's tale

In Modern classic short novels of science fiction p459-503

Sherwood, Frances, 1940-

Vindication. Farrar, Straus & Giroux 1993 435p $22

ISBN 0-374-28390-7   LC 92-41934

This biographical novel focuses on the life of Mary Wollstonecraft, "the author in 1792 of *A Vindication of the Rights of Woman*; the wife of William Godwin; and a mother who died giving birth to Mary Wollstonecraft Godwin (later Shelley), author of *Frankenstein*. Sherwood portrays her as a remarkable woman who transcends her era. To escape an abusive home, Wollstonecraft became a seamstress and governess and ran a girls' school before finding a home, salon, and work as a writer at Joseph Johnson's *Analytical Review*. Driven to attempted suicide by unhappy relationships with married and otherwise unavailable men . . . she finally married the reformer Godwin, then died, at 37, of childbed fever, after bearing their famous daughter." Booklist

In Sherwood's "episodic narrative of the stormy life of the most famous female writer of her times, droll and witty portraits of Tom Paine, Henry Fuseli, William Blake and others punctuate a darkly ironic tale that conveys the torments of a brilliant mind struggling against hypocritical and stifling social conventions." Publ Wkly

Sherwood, John, 1913-

A botanist at bay; a Celia Grant mystery. Scribner 1985 175p o.p.

LC 85-14519

In this mystery botanist Celia Grant tracks "a murder (and some interesting botanical specimens) through the New Zealand bush. Traveling to New Zealand for the imminent birth of a grandchild, Grant is asked by a duchess friend to look up her 'Uncle Bertie,' Lord Albert Merton, who is suspected of running off with a shameless redhead. Grant finds herself in the thick of a conservationist battle over a proposed dam that would endanger rare wild plants, and at the center of a murder investigation. Extraordinary, well-detailed settings, a nicely contrived political atmosphere, and gutsy characterization." Booklist

The hanging garden. Scribner 1992 189p $20

ISBN 0-684-19429-5   LC 92-18511

Also available G.K. Hall large print edition

This Celia Grant novel is set in Madeira. "After being appointed executrix of a relative's estate, the petite horticulturist must clear up all sorts of mysteries. Was Antonia Hanbury murdered, and why is her aging father's young companion Maria acting so suspiciously? Feuding neighbors, a bevy of the dead woman's lovers, and an ex-convict/ex-husband serve to complicate matters." Booklist

"Mr. Sherwood's various plots and subplots ensnare the characters in acts of political terrorism, kidnapping and blackmail, not to mention botanical theft." N Y Times Book Rev

The mantrap garden. Scribner 1986 186p o.p.

LC 86-11818

Available Thorndike Press large print edition

"Celia Grant, horticulturist and amateur sleuth . . . is elected to the board of trustees at the famous English gardens at Monk's Mead, where she finds the gardens rundown and vandalized and a family split by years of feuding and bitterness. Anthony, a poet and soldier, died during World War II, and his homosexuality and acts of treason were a family secret. Julian (who emerges as the real traitor) had been Anthony's secret lover before he married into the family to cover his past. When

Sherwood, John, 1913—*Continued*
Julian tries to stop the blackmail payments, the precious gardens are ruined, and an innocent tourist is murdered on the grounds." Booklist

Shields, Carol
The republic of love. Viking 1992 366p $22

ISBN 0-670-83875-6   LC 91-16154

"Fay McLeod and Tom Avery are likable souls: kind to their parents, close to friends and co-workers, dedicated to their professions (she's a folklorist, he's a radio talk show host). But thus far both have been unlucky in love. Fay has never married; Tom has married and divorced rather too often. Participating on the periphery of lives of married friends has begun to pall. They finally meet, and it is a *coup de foudre* for both, but Fay is leaving that night for a month of mermaid research in Europe. Even when she returns, their affair is jeopardized by upheavals in others' lives." Libr J

"Not only are Fay and Tom exceptionally likable and capable of arresting insights, their worlds are complete and organic. Secondary characters are respectfully but economically drawn via short monologues, and the city of Winnipeg bustles in the background." Publ Wkly

The stone diaries. Viking 1994 361p il $21.95

ISBN 0-670-85309-7   LC 93-30239

This "novel provides, glancingly, a panorama of 20th-century life in North America. Written in a diary format, it traces the life of one seemingly unremarkable woman: Daisy Goodwill Flett, who is born in 1905 and lives into the 1990's." N Y Times Book Rev

This book is a "miraculous meeting of intellectual rigour and imaginative flow. On the one hand, it's a sharp-as-tacks investigation into the limits of the autobiographical form; on the other, a novel of effortless pleasure and sensuality. Daisy Goodwill . . . attempts intermittently to tell the story of a life remarkable only in its large tracts of ordinariness." New Statesman

Shields, David
Dead languages; a novel. Knopf 1989 245p $18.95

ISBN 0-394-57388-9   LC 88-13444

This "coming-of-age novel, set in California, tells the . . . story of Jeremy Zorn, whose 1960s childhood is centered on one problem: his stuttering. Jeremy's highly literate parents, both journalists, use language to earn their living: 'My family was living in language whereas I was dying in it.' Jeremy's goal is to rid himself of the prison that words have made for him. Many of his cures are amusing (learning Latin, no need to articulate) or sad (love affairs with insensitive and inappropriate girls)." Booklist

"As touching and funny a rendering of adolescence as *The Catcher in the Rye*. Those recently emerged from adolescence will readily see its truth; the well read will delight at Shields's ability with narrative. But *Dead Languages* speaks to everyone who has ever struggled to articulate an emotion and failed to find the words." Libr J

Shikibu, Murasaki *See* Murasaki Shikibu, b. 978?

Shippey, T. A. (Tom A.)
(ed) The Oxford book of science fiction stories. See The Oxford book of science fiction stories

Shippey, Tom A. *See* Shippey, T. A. (Tom A.)

Shoemaker, Bill, 1931-
Stalking horse. Fawcett Columbine 1994 311p $21.95

ISBN 0-449-90595-0   LC 93-22125

Ex-jockey Coley Killebrew is enlisted by Raymond Starbuck, "the man who ruined his career to help stop an underworld takeover of one of the nation's great tracks. The assignment takes him to Louisiana's Magnolia Park, where he insinuates himself into a milieu of fast horses, even faster women, and a dangerous array of unsavory characters presided over by corrupt aristocrat Remy Courville." Booklist

"The plot is big, complicated and thoroughbred-fast as Coley's hard-boiled, first-person chapters alternate with a third-person focus on Starbuck. Shoemaker's characters provide the most fun." Publ Wkly

Shoemaker, Willie *See* Shoemaker, Bill, 1931-

Sholem Aleichem, 1859-1916
The adventures of Menaham-Mendl; translated from the Yiddish by Tamara Kahana. Putnam 1969 222p o.p.

Original Yiddish edition published 1909 in Russia

This book "consists of an exchange of letters between the hero and his . . . wife Sheineh-Sheindl, whom he has left behind looking after the children in their . . . native town of Kasrilevka while he tries to make his fortune in the big city—first Odessa, then Kiev. Menaham-Mendl is . . . [an] over-optimistic schemer who somehow contrives to make a living out of thin air; at one moment he is a currency speculator . . . then next a dabbler in commodities, after that a would-be broker, a journalist, a matchmaker, an insurance agent." N Y Rev of Books

The adventures of Mottel, the cantor's son; translated by Tamara Kahana; illustrated by Ilya Schor. Abelard-Schuman 1953 342p il o.p.

Translated from the Yiddish

"The lighthearted humor of young Mottel, the narrator, adds a touch of pathos to the stories of an impoverished Jewish family in a European village, its wanderings in Europe en route to America, and finally its arrival and settlement in the U.S." Booklist

The best of Sholom Aleichem; edited by Irving Howe and Ruth R. Wisse. New Republic Bks. 1979 276p o.p.

Analyzed in Short story index
Translated from the Yiddish
Contents: The haunted tailor; A Yom Kippur scandal; Eternal life; Station Baranovich; The pot; The clock that struck thirteen; Home for Passover; On account of a hat; Dreyfus in Kasrilevke; Two anti-semites; A Passover

Sholem Aleichem, 1859-1916—*Continued*

expropriation; If I were Rothschild; Tevye strikes it rich; The bubble bursts; Chava; Get thee out; From Mottel the cantor's son; Bandits; The guest; The Krushniker delegation; One in a million; Once there were four

The bloody hoax; by Sholom Aleichem; translated by Aliza Shevrin; introduction by Maurice Friedberg. Indiana Univ. Press 1991 373p $29.95

ISBN 0-253-30401-6 LC 91-11717

"Jewish literature and culture"

Original Yiddish edition published 1923 in Poland

"The plot is modeled on the 1911 Beiliss blood libel case in Kiev, in which a Jew was tried for murdering a Gentile boy in order to obtain Christian blood to bake matzos for Passover. Two high school friends, a Jew, Hersh Rabinovitch, and a Russian, Grigori Popov, decide after graduation to trade places for a year so that Grigori can learn first hand what it is like to be a Jew in Tsarist Russia, and Hersh can enter university unimpeded by quotas. When Grigori, now Hersh, is accused of the blood libel, the plot becomes three dimensional—a Christian posing as a Jew is now subject to the prejudice and groundless fears his own family helped perpetrate." Libr J

The nightingale; or, The Saga of Yosele Solovey the cantor; translated by Aliza Shevrin. Putnam 1985 240p o.p.

LC 85-12073

Originally written in Yiddish and copyrighted 1917

"The cantor's son, Yosele Solovey, has a voice so lovely that he is called 'The Nightingale.' He is a timid lad, living in a small town (shtetl) that is peopled with earthy as well as flighty types. Innocently, he is introduced to nefarious pursuits like gambling and womanizing by a famous cantor who is a wheeler-dealer and whose influence creates havoc in Yosele's life and in the shtetl's, as well." West Coast Rev Books

This "is more than a popular novel; it is a social document, a study of a failed artist and, in its way, an early feminist work." N Y Times Book Rev

Tevye the dairyman and The railroad stories; translated from the Yiddish and with an introduction by Hillel Halkin. Schocken Bks. 1987 xli, 309p o.p.

LC 86-24835

"Library of Yiddish classics"

Contents: Tevye the dairyman: Tevye strikes it rich; Tevye blows a small fortune; Today's children; Hodl; Chava; Shprintze; Tevye leaves for the land of Israel; Lekh-Lekho

The railroad stories: To the reader; Competitors; The happiest man in all Kodny; Baranovich Station; Eighteen from Pereshchepena; The man from Buenos Aires; Elul; The slowpoke express; The miracle of Hoshana Rabbah; The wedding that came without its band; The tallis koton; A game of sixty-six; High school; The automatic exemption; It doesn't pay to be good; Burned out; Hard luck; Fated for misfortune; Go climb a tree if you don't like it; The tenth man; Third class

"These portraits of eastern European shtetl life, of Jews coping with the persecution of czarist Russia, provide a compelling, vital study of the era. Beyond their historical significance, they are phenomenally entertaining as fiction." Booklist

Tevye's daughters; translated by Frances Butwin. Crown 1949 302p o.p.

Analyzed in Short story index

Contents: Bubble bursts; If I were Rothschild; Modern children; Competitors; Another page from The Song of Songs; Hodel; Happiest man in Kodno; Wedding without musicians; What will become of me; Chava; Joys of parenthood; Littlest of kings; Man from Buenos Aires; May God have mercy; Schprintze; The merrymakers; Easy fast; Little pot; Two shalachmones; Tevye goes to Palestine; Gymana-sia; Purim feast; From Passover to Succos; Get thee out; Passover expropriation; The German; Third class

Translated from the Yiddish, many of these stories are "about the seven daughters of Tevye the Dairyman and the life each chooses as she comes of age in Russia during the years preceding the first World War." Publ Wkly

Sholokhov, Mikhail Aleksandrovich, 1905-1984

Nobel Prize in literature, 1965

And quiet flows the Don; [by] Mikhail Sholokhov; translated from the Russian by Stephen Garry. Knopf 1934 755p o.p.

"Set in the Don River basin of southwestern Russia at the end of the czarist period, the novel traces the progress of the Cossack Gregor Melekhov from youthful lover to Red Army soldier and finally to Cossack nationalist. War—in the form of both international conflict and civil revolution—provides the epic backdrop for the narrative and determines its tone of moral ambiguity." Merriam-Webster's Ency of Lit

Followed by The Don flows home to the sea

The Don flows home to the sea; [by] Mikhail Sholokhov; translated from the Russian by Stephen Garry. Knopf 1941 777p o.p.

This translation first published 1940 in the United Kingdom

This sequel to the title entered above covers the period following the Revolution of 1917 to the end of the civil war in 1921. The narrative traces the fortunes of a group of Cossacks as they fight alternately with the Reds and the Whites

"It is a tale of misfortunes multiplied, yet a broad and earthy humor and the hearty Cossack gaiety break continuously over the grim surface. At the end the Cossack, with his intense individualism, his passionate love of the land, and his primitive pride, stands revealed." Nation

Followed by Seeds of tomorrow (1959)

Shreve, Anita

Eden Close; a novel. Harcourt Brace Jovanovich 1989 265p $17.95

ISBN 0-15-127582-3 LC 89-34712

Also available Thorndike Press large print edition

"As next-door neighbors, 'best buddies,' and then awkward adolescents, Eden and Andy find solace in each other's company until a tragic event occurs as Andy prepares to leave their small home town and heads off to college. The awful accident drives them apart, but then inadvertently draws them together again some 15 years later. Their relationship is rekindled when Andy returns home to attend his mother's funeral." Libr J

Shreve, Anita—*Continued*

"'Eden Close' is not a novel of suspense but one of sensibility. Its insights are keen, its language measured and haunting. In it, a sense of loss and then of rupture is everywhere." N Y Times Book Rev

Strange fits of passion; a novel. Harcourt Brace Jovanovich 1991 336p $18.95

ISBN 0-15-185760-1   LC 90-23874

This novel opens "with oblique hints of a violent event—here a murder committed by a woman in response to domestic abuse—then segues to flashbacks that slowly reveal the circumstances leading up to it. A reporter who wrote a book about the crime shares her notes, presented in alternating versions and voices. Most affecting is the voice of the accused woman, who flees Manhattan with her six-month-old daughter to seek sanctuary in a coastal Maine village where she is protected by the clannish but sympathetic townspeople. She finds temporary solace in an affair with a sensitive lobsterman, but is betrayed to her husband by another man out of jealousy." Publ Wkly

Where or when; a novel. Harcourt Brace & Co. 1993 240p $19.95

ISBN 0-15-131461-6   LC 92-39392

"When 44-year-old real estate insurance salesman Charles Callahan sees a photograph of poet Siăn Richards, he recognizes her as the young woman he met three decades earlier at a Catholic camp for teenagers. Impulsively, he writes Siăn, and sets in motion the love affair they were destined to have. Though both are married and have children, each is unfulfilled, craving true partnership." Publ Wkly

The "two main characters are not presented in isolation, enveloped by a cloud of concupiscence. Instead, they are placed against a richly drawn background that encompasses everything from the grim reality of a deteriorating economy to the thin black dirt of the Richards farm." N Y Times Book Rev

Shreve, Susan Richards

A country of strangers. Simon & Schuster 1989 239p o.p.

LC 88-28735

"Outside of Washington, D.C., in the midst of World War II, Charley Fletcher strives to create a perfect community for himself and his family. He purchases a large rural estate, but, in doing so, has to confront the Bellows, the black tenants who have moved into the empty residence from their shacks on the property. Fletcher's awkward, friendly overtures are met with bewilderment and hostility, though his step-daughter, Kate, finally finds some success when she forms a deep alliance with Prudential Bellows, 13 years old and awaiting the birth of a child." Booklist

This is an "ambitious novel that attempts to create a parable of how racial harmony may be achieved. And, because of their youthful exuberance and quirkiness, Prudential and Kate are finally memorable characters." N Y Times Book Rev

Daughters of the new world. Doubleday 1992 471p o.p.

LC 91-8146

This "novel chronicles the lives of a remarkable family of women. The story begins with passionate Anna, a servant who marries the master's son; scandal drives the couple west. Daughter Amanda grows up with the Chip-

pewe Indians and then, disguising herself as a man, becomes a photographer in France during World War I. Her daughter Sara, Sara's youngest daughter Eleanor, and Eleanor's two young daughters bring the novel into the present." Libr J

"As the novel unfolds and daughters become mothers, mothers grandmothers, grandmothers great-grandmothers, Shreve explores the wonder of personalities and genetics, the astonishing accommodation and resiliency of women, the courage and dignity of true love, and the surge of change that has driven this unlikely century. An enveloping, rewarding, and heroic tale told with great skill and much heart." Booklist

Shulman, Alix Kates

Memoirs of an ex-prom queen; a novel. Knopf 1972 274p o.p.

"In the third grade, tomboy Sasha realizes that 'there's only one thing worth bothering about: becoming beautiful,' and begins to apply herself to that end. At 15 she has succeeded: she is elected queen of the high school prom and loses her virginity the same evening, an occurrence not at all coincidental, since she measures beauty in terms of sex appeal. By her 25th birthday, she's had 25 lovers. Although she's intelligent (a Columbia Ph.D. candidate) and ambitious, she is unable to escape the trap she has set for herself. Her identity is determined only in terms of her femininity and her relationships with men. Her ideas and ambitions must be sacrificed to theirs, if necessary, and it always seems to 'be' necessary. Her decline from potential philosopher to typical housewife appears completed by the birth of her children, but age and fading looks finally prove to be her salvation." Publ Wkly

Shulman, Max, 1919-1988

The many loves of Dobie Gillis; eleven campus stories. Doubleday 1951 223p o.p. Amereon reprint available $19.95 (ISBN 0-89190-982-6)

Analyzed in Short story index

Contents: Unlucky winner; She shall have music; Love is a fallacy; Sugar bowl; Everybody loves my baby; Love of two chemists; Face is familiar but—; Mock governor; Boy bites man; King's English; You think you got trouble

"Here are 11 short stories dealing with Dobie Gillis, of the crew cut set, and his adventures and misadventures on the Golden Gopher's campus. The stories appeared individually in the Saturday Evening Post, American Magazine and other periodicals. Most of the time Dobie is becoming infatuated or disinfatuated with one fair coed or another, and the woes and worries which these damsels bring with them supply obstacles for the nimble-witted freckled Casanova." San Francisco Chron

Rally round the flag, boys! Doubleday 1957 278p o.p. Buccaneer Bks. reprint available $21.95 (ISBN 1-56849-139-5)

"The setting is a small Connecticut town where three ethnic groups struggle for dominance—the Commuters, the Italians, and the Yankee Natives. The establishment of a Nike base in the town leads to no end of hilarious complications." Libr J

"A bit of lusty fun at the expense of commuters, exurbian manners and mores, teen-age cults, Army red tape, progressive education, and whatever else catches the author's satiric eye." Booklist

Shute, Nevil, 1899-1960

The legacy; a novel. Morrow 1950 308p
o.p.

Published in the United Kingdom with title: A town
like Alice

A novel about a young British "girl who returns to
the Far East to follow up people who had shared her
horrible experiences as a Japanese prisoner. In so doing,
she finds love and helps to rehabilitate an Australian
ghost town." Libr J

On the beach. Morrow 1957 320p $22.95

ISBN 0-688-02223-5

"A nuclear war annihilates the world's Northern Her-
misphere, and as atomic wastes are spreading southward,
residents of Australia try to come to grips with their
mortality. In spite of the inevitability of death, these
people face their end with courage and live from day
to day. They even plant trees they may never see mature." Shapiro. Fic for Youth. 3d edition

Shwartz, Susan

(jt. auth) Norton, A. Empire of the eagle

Sibley, Celestine

Ah, sweet mystery. HarperCollins Pubs.
1991 217p o.p.

LC 90-55970

This mystery introduces "reporter Kate Mulcay, resident of northern Fulton County, where new mansions
supplant the old settlers. When someone murders the
local developer and police blame a dear old lady/
neighbor, Kate takes steps to 'save' the feisty woman.
Kate's friends on the police force actually do most of
the work behind the scenes, while she covers the human
angles. The charm of this book lies in deftly handled
details of place and character, which compensate for the
rather abrupt ending." Libr J

Siddons, Anne Rivers

Colony; a novel. HarperCollins Pubs. 1992
466p o.p.

LC 91-58357

Available G.K. Hall large print edition

"Muskrattish Maude Gascoigne, raised in the swamps,
discovers the outer world on the fateful night her older
brother brings home a Princeton buddy, Bostonian Peter
Chambliss, to escort her to the traditional St. Cecilia's
coming-out ball in Charleston. Instant and deep, her love
for Peter catapults her into the highly structured world
of the summering place called 'Retreat.' This saga of
three generations of Chamblisses culminates in Maude's
desperate struggle to protect and pass the legacy on to
her granddaughter before the place is destroyed." Booklist

"Ms. Siddons portrays children paying for the mistakes
of their parents, and sees patterns of behavior being
passed from one generation to the next. Most of all,
she explores the complex, often unpredictable, nature of
love. To her credit, these themes are never presented
in a heavy-handed fashion; they never interfere with the
enjoyment of a well-told story." N Y Times Book Rev

Downtown; a novel. HarperCollins Pubs.
1994 374p $24

ISBN 0-06-017934-1   LC 94-9202

Also available G.K. Hall large print edition

"Protagonist Maureen 'Smoky' O'Donnell emerges from
the Savannah docks to write for Atlanta's award-winning
Downtown magazine. Mentored by the charismatic editor-
in-chief, Smoky gets awards for covering the city's war
on poverty. As the novel gains momentum, she dumps
wealthy Brad to find adventure with Freedom Summer
veteran Lucas—only to lose him to the war in Vietnam."
Libr J

"What's intriguing about Siddons is how much she
transcends the usual parameters of fluff fiction, both in
terms of literary finesse and penetrating intelligence."
Booklist

Heartbreak Hotel. Simon & Schuster 1976
252p o.p.

"Maggie Deloach, a Southern beauty of the 50s, seems
well on the way to success Dixie-style. Sorority girl, wellborn, a leader, she is pinned to Boots Claiborne, scion
of an old land-owning Delta family. It would seem that
marriage and a happy-ever-after life are ahead of her.
But Randolph University exposes her to more that frat
parties and frivolity. A professor, a reporter and a student from New Jersey sow the seeds of questions. A
visit to Boot's family and an ugly incident there make
Maggie's questions more insistent and, for her, unnerving
since they not only challenge her carefully planned future,
but reveal stirring in the South she had never anticipated." Publ Wkly

Hill towns; a novel. HarperCollins Pubs.
1993 356p $22

ISBN 0-06-017935-X   LC 92-54720

Also available G.K. Hall large print edition

"An American couple reassess their marriage as they
travel from the 'hilltowns' of North Carolina to the 'hilltowns' of Italy. While college professor Hays Bennett
seemed dashing stateside, wife Cat finds that he suddenly
pales in comparison with a sexy painter they meet." Libr
J

This novel features the "heady atmospheres of Rome,
Venice, and the hill towns of Tuscany. Siddons is keenly
attuned to the power of these fabled locales and brilliantly describes them as bewitched and perversely saturated
with both beauty and death." Booklist

Homeplace; a novel. Harper & Row 1987
330p o.p.

LC 86-46099

"Micah Winship is a successful journalist living in New
York City, a troubled childhood in small-town Georgia
far behind her. Her father's illness, however, brings her
back to the home she had fled in fury and disgrace 20
years earlier in the wake of a family storm concerning
Micah's growing interest in the Civil Rights Movement.
Now, in this hot summer visit, the past encroaches on
the present, and Micah is drawn back into the family
politics and sexual drama of her adolescence." Libr J

"About love and death, greed and passion, the pull
of family and the push of self, *Homeplace* is a deeply
moving story of a fierce and necessary forgiveness." Publ
Wkly

King's oak; a novel. Harper & Row 1990
623p o.p.

LC 89-46116

Available Thorndike Press large print edition

"Moving with her daughter to elite Georgia hunt country, Andy Calhoun is drawn . . . to Tom Dabney, a
'crazy' man passionately committed to the primeval
woods where he lives. Finally succumbing to her attrac-

Siddons, Anne Rivers—*Continued*

tion to Tom, she becomes involved with his efforts to save the woods from the nuclear wastes emanating from the Big Silver nuclear weapons plant." Libr J

The author "does know how to endow a story with undeniable narrative drive." N Y Times Book Rev

Outer banks; a novel. HarperCollins Pubs. 1991 400p o.p.

LC 90-56370

Available Thorndike Press large print edition

"Kate Abrams hasn't spoken to three of her sorority sisters for 28 years. But now Ginger, the eager rich girl who stole and married Kate's brilliant boyfriend, is hosting a reunion at her home in Nags Head, N.C. And Cecie, the orphan whose wit and cynical reserve attracted Kate, and Fig Newton, the unsightly and bumbling outcast, will both attend. . . . The narrative flows smoothly, journeying seamlessly between places and eras. While the pseudo-thriller ending seems pat, Siddons displays real strength in her subtle characterizations and delineation of emotional nuances." Publ Wkly

Peachtree Road; a novel. Harper & Row 1988 566p o.p.

LC 88-45060

Available G.K. Hall large print edition

"Sheppard Gibbs Bondurant 3d, the benumbed, reclusive son of an aristocratic Georgia family, narrates the tale, which spans some 40-odd years of life on Peachtree Road, the axis of Atlanta's exclusive Buckhead section. Baroque rituals precisely dictate the pattern of Buckhead's social fabric, and Shep devotes his life to protecting his beloved cousin Lucy from these censorious standards." N Y Times Book Rev

"An ambitious and masterful work with a sharp vision." Booklist

Sienkiewicz, Henryk, 1846-1916

Nobel Prize in literature, 1905

The deluge; in modern translation by W. S. Kuniczak. Copernicus Soc. of Am. 1991 2v o.p.

LC 91-5047

Available from AMS Press and Scholarly Press

Original Polish edition, 1886

In this second volume of the trilogy "a mere five years have passed since the knights of the Polish-Lithuanian Commonwealth threw back the Cossack invasion from the East, yet a new and far more dangerous threat appears: Swedish troops are pouring across the Northern border. . . . Central to the story is Andrei Kmita, a young Lithuanian noble whose ruthlessness obscures his military sagacity and bravery, branding him an outlaw. But for the love of the beautiful Olenka, he undertakes to reshape his character in the forge of battle, and in so doing helps save king, country, and church from the heretic invaders." Libr J

Followed by Fire in the steppe

Fire in the steppe; translated by W. S. Kuniczak. Copernicus Soc. of Am. 1992 717p $24.95

ISBN 0-7818-0025-0

Original Polish edition, 1887

"The Polish people's struggle against Cossacks, Tartars and Turks in the 1670s prefigures modern Poland's quest for nationhood in this [final] installment of the rousing epic of love, war, adventure and madness. Basia, the

gutsy, bright, determind heroine, who chases bandits on horseback, riding a man's saddle, almost steals the show from her Hamlet-like husband, Col. Pan Volodyovski." Publ Wkly

This "is an unabashed, extravagant celebration of romance and patriotism, but with a difference: the novel ends with wrenching scenes of Polish nobility, courage and hope in the face of defeat—showing why Sienkiewicz's trilogy is so beloved in his native country." N Y Times Book Rev

Quo vadis; in modern translation by W. S. Kuniczak. Macmillan 1993 579p $25

ISBN 0-02-566855-2   LC 92-46251

Also available Amereon reprint of Little, Brown edition translated by Jeremiah Curtin

First published 1896 by Little, Brown

"Set in ancient Rome during the reign of the emperor Nero, *Quo Vadis?* tells the story of the love that develops between a young Christian woman and a Roman officer who, after meeting her fellow Christians, converts to her religion. Underlying their relationship is the contrast between the worldly opulence of the Roman aristocracy and the poverty, simplicity, and spiritual power of the Christians. The novel has as a subtext the persecution and political subjugation of Poland by Russia." Merriam-Webster's Ency of Lit

With fire and sword; in modern translation by W.S. Kuniczak; foreword by James A. Michener. Copernicus Soc. of Am. 1991 1135p o.p.

LC 91-161

Original Polish edition, 1883

"The first book in a trilogy covering Polish history from 1648 to 1673. The novel's main stage is occupied by the Ukrainian cossacks' rebellion against the Poles. Yan Skshetuski, a Polish lieutenant dispatched to gather information about the rebellion, is taken prisoner by the cossacks. After numerous battles, retreats, and betrayals on both sides, the revolt culminates in the cossacks' siege of the city of Zbaraz." Booklist

This novel "should have taken place in the general literary repertory long ago, alongside the works of the elder Dumas, Walter Scott, Margaret Mitchell." N Y Times Book Rev

Followed by The deluge

Sillitoe, Alan

The loneliness of the long-distance runner. Knopf 1960 c1959 176p o.p.

Analyzed in Short story index

First published 1959 in the United Kingdom

Contents: The loneliness of the long-distance runner; Uncle Ernest; Mr. Raynor the schoolteacher; The fishing-boat picture; Noah's ark; On Saturday afternoon; The match; The disgrace of Jim Scarfedale; The decline and fall of Frankie Buller

"This collection of short stories portrays life from the point of view of the English working class. The unnamed narrator in the title story, which is probably the best known in the book, is a roguish young man who has been in trouble with authority all his life. He is told by the head of a Borstal institution where he is an inmate that he can reform himself by training to be a long-distance runner. He enters into training, and during practice runs, his thoughts go back to the circumstances that led to his detention. The climax of the story is in a track meet between his penal institution and a

Sillitoe, Alan—*Continued*

private school. The boy easily outruns his competitors but pulls up at the finish line and refuses to cross it, thus revenging himself against the head of the institution and spoiling the victory of the other school." Shapiro. Fic for Youth. 3d edition

Saturday night and Sunday morning. Knopf 1959 c1958 239p $16.95

ISBN 0-394-44377-2

First published 1958 in the United Kingdom

"Arthur Seton, the hero, is a rebellious young loner whose weekdays are spent working at a dull job in a foul-smelling factory. Although he doesn't particularly mind his work, he treats it with an intentional indifference, because if he were to work hard, his labors would only reward the managerial class for whom he harbors considerable contempt. His Saturday nights are devoted to boozing, brawling, and promiscuity; on Sunday mornings he nurses his hangover at a peaceful fishing spot in the country. He eventually succumbs to the almost-secure life of marriage with a nice, very ordinary woman. Sillitoe's realistic, unsentimental characterization of working-class life in this novel led to his public identification with the 'Angry Young Men'." Reader's Ency. 3d edition

Silone, Ignazio, 1900-1978

Bread and wine; a new version translated from the Italian by Harvey Fergusson II; with a new preface by the author. Atheneum Pubs. 1962 331p o.p.

First published 1937 in the United States by Harper

"Translated from the edition revised by the author to modify the political concepts of the original." Publ Wkly

"The hero, Pietro Spina, returns to his native Abruzzi after fifteen years of exile to continue his antifascist agitation. As he travels through the country, disguised as a priest, he sees the inroads made upon the Italian character by Mussolini's rule. Finding that the underground movement is in chaos and doubting the validity of his old revolutionary slogans, he eventually flees to avoid certain arrest." Reader's Ency. 3d edition

Followed by The seed beneath the snow (1942)

Silverberg, Robert

At winter's end. Warner Bks. 1988 404p o.p.

LC 87-40416

A "tribe of 60 has lived in its cocoon underground, safe from the ravages of the death stars that destroyed the Earth's surface and caused the 700,000 year Long Winter. But now it is the Time of Coming Forth, the long-awaited springtime, and Koshmar as chieftain leads her people to the fabled city of the lost sapphire-eyes folk where the Chronicles have foretold that humans will find machines to help them rule the Great World once again. Once outside, others in the tribe are seeking to establish their own identities, and the once-solid group finds itself torn apart and beset by enemies." Voice Youth Advocates

Followed by The new springtime

The collected stories of Robert Silverberg. v1: Secret sharers. Bantam Bks. 1992 546p o.p.

LC 92-9958

Analyzed in Short story index

Contents: Homefaring; Basileus; Dancers in the time-flux; Gate of horn, gate of ivory; Amanda and the alien; Snake and ocean, ocean and snake; Tourist trade; Multiples; Against Babylon; Symbiont; Sailing to Byzantium; Sunrise on Pluto; Hardware; Hannibal's elephants; The pardoner's tale; The iron star; The secret sharer; House of bones; The dead man's eyes; Chip runner; To the promised land; The Asenion solution; A sleep and a forgetting; Enter a soldier. Later: enter another

Downward to the Earth

In Silverberg, R. A Robert Silverberg omnibus

The Face of the Waters. Bantam Bks. 1991 353p o.p.

LC 91-13530

"On the planet Hydros, the human settlers are forced out of their precarious home on floating islands by the hostility of the native Hydrans. The humans face a long and perilous journey across the watery face of the planet to the legendary safe place, the Face of the Waters." Booklist

Silverberg "pays tribute to humanity's endless fascination with the sea—as adversary, savior, and source of life—in a novel that works on many levels. Stock characters . . . transcend their stereotypes in this story of survival and salvation by one of sf's most lyrical storytellers." Libr J

Gilgamesh the king. Arbor House 1984 320p o.p.

LC 84-12434

"Fantasy, myth, and ancient history interweave seamlessly in this powerful retelling of the epic of Gilgamesh, the Sumerian god-king who sought eternal life and found instead the bitter wisdom of mortality. Silverberg extends his mastery of the fantasy genre to the re-creation of the magic and mystery of ancient Sumer, uncovering the deep human truths that lie beneath the legend. Elegantly written." Libr J

(ed) The Horror hall of fame. See The Horror hall of fame

Hot sky at midnight. Bantam Bks. 1994 327p o.p.

LC 93-29755

"While Japanese-owned megacorporations search for new technologies that will allow humankind to adapt to a dying environment or seek out new habitats, a few individuals fight their own war to preserve their humanity in the face of increasingly unacceptable odds. Silverberg's 'dark future' contains few incorruptible protagonists. Instead, he offers a cast of characters whose only choices involve degrees of compromise. Cynical, grim, and superbly told . . . [this novel] doubles as technothriller and cautionary tale." Libr J

Kingdoms of the Wall. Bantam Bks. 1993 307p o.p.

LC 92-34862

In this novel, the people of the village of Jespodar live "at the foot of a mountain so steep and so tall that it is known as the Wall. Their myths tell of a . . . First Climber who ascended the Wall and brought back useful knowledge from the gods who live at the summit. In honor of this First Climber, the people periodically choose 40 of their best and brightest as Pil-

Silverberg, Robert—*Continued*

grims, who try to climb the Wall and parley with the gods. Most fail to return; those who do are invariably mad." N Y Times Book Rev

Lord Valentine's castle. Harper & Row 1980 449p o.p.

LC 79-2658

"Majipoor is an enormous planet inhabited by intelligent beings and ruled by a benevolent lord. . . . The story begins as Valentine, a young amnesiac, wanders into the city of Pidruid in time for a festival celebrating a once-in-a-lifetime visit of another Valentine, Lord Valentine, the supreme ruler of the planet. Early in the book readers know what Valentine is slow to understand; he is the real Lord Valentine and the one in power is an imposter. On a coming-of-age journey to Lord Valentine's Castle, gathering friends, supporters, and ultimately troops en route, Valentine discovers his true identity and gains a better understanding of the people and place he is destined to rule. A good story, inventively told, which abounds with adventure and curious characters." SLJ
Followed by Majipoor chronicles

Majipoor chronicles; a novel. Arbor House 1982 314p il o.p.

LC 81-67589

The protagonist is "a bored teenage clerk in the House of Records who risks his job and more by delving into forbidden records of the Registry of Souls. This Registry holds every minute, every experience of billions of inhabitants of Majipoor since it was colonized thousands of years ago. By calling up a record, he is given the opportunity to live episodes from the lives of famous and ordinary people of both sexes." SLJ
"Majipoor is probably the finest creation of Silverberg's powerful imagination and certainly one of the most fully realized worlds in modern sf." Booklist
Followed by Valentine Pontifex

The man in the maze

In Silverberg, R. A Robert Silverberg omnibus

The new springtime. Warner Bks. 1990 358p $19.95

ISBN 0-446-51442-X

LC 89-29846

This sequel to At winter's end "continues the tale of a far-future Earth recovering from a massive ecological catastrophe. Two city-states have become bitter rivals, each has its own internal divisions, and an insectoid species threatens both. A sprawling story, but one full of ingenious pieces of characterization and world building." Booklist

Nightwings. Walker & Co. 1970 c1969 190p o.p.

First published 1969 in paperback
An expanded version of the novella of the same title
A novel "in which a decadent Earth is taken over by aliens who have old scores to settle, but who might offer humankind a path to salvation too. Lushly romantic and elegiac far-future fantasy." Anatomy of Wonder 4

also in Silverberg, R. A Robert Silverberg omnibus

Nightwings [novelette]

In The Hugo winners v2 p503-57

A Robert Silverberg omnibus; The man in the maze; Nightwings; Downward to the Earth. Harper & Row 1981 544p o.p.

LC 80-8232

An omnibus edition of three titles first published separately 1969, 1969, and 1970 respectively
Nightwings is entered separately. The man in the maze dramatizes aspects of alienation and Downward to the Earth employs religious imagery in a story of repentence and rebirth
All three novels in this collection "feature strong but psychologically wounded male protagonists, descriptions of bizarre beings and far-away worlds and imaginative, if sometimes unrealistic plots. . . . For readers who appreciate swiftly-paced action." Voice Youth Advocates

Sailing to Byzantium

In Modern classic short novels of science fiction p504-60

Valentine Pontifex. Arbor House 1983 347p o.p.

LC 83-45526

"A complicated sequel, this follows 'Lord Valentine's Castle' in action and 'The Majipoor Chronicles' in setting. Silverberg now explores Valentine as a maturing politician and statesman seeking a way to communicate with the Metamorph adversaries who are destroying Majipoor with famines." Libr J

(jt. auth) Asimov, I. Nightfall
(jt. auth) Asimov, I. The positronic man

Simak, Clifford D., 1904-1988

The big front yard

In The Hugo winners v1 p171-226

Simenon, Georges, 1903-1989

Across the street; translated from the French by John Petrie. Harcourt Brace & Co. 1992 188p $18.95

ISBN 0-15-103266-1

LC 92-7218

"A Helen and Kurt Wolff book"
Original French edition, 1945; this translation first published 1964 in the United Kingdom
This is "the claustrophobic tale of a solitary, unbalanced Parisian woman who lives vicariously through her neighbors, on whom she spies obsessively. Dominique watches through the shutters as one sick neighbor dies just after his wife is late in giving him medicine. Dominique weaves fantasies around the widow, her domineering mother-in-law and her secret mulatto lover, sending her anonymous notes. . . . Simenon invests Dominique with an unshakable dignity even as he probes her existential failure as one for whom the past and her fantasy life count at least as much as the present." Publ Wkly

Five times Maigret. Harcourt, Brace & World 1964 525p o.p.

Originally published 1962 in the United Kingdom
Contents: Maigret right and wrong (Maigret in Montmartre & Maigret's mistake); Maigret has scruples; Maigret and the reluctant witnesses; Maigret goes to school. English translations first published separately in the United Kingdom 1954, 1958, 1959 and 1957 respectively

Simenon, Georges, 1903-1989—_Continued_

Maigret and the apparition; translated by Eileen Ellenbogen. Harcourt Brace Jovanovich 1976 159p o.p.

"A Helen and Kurt Wolff book"

Original French edition, 1964; published in the United Kingdom with title: Maigret and the ghost

The book "begins with the shooting of a policeman who has been dogged by bad luck all his career. This time, however, as Maigret investigates, he discovers that the badly wounded Lognon was actually on the trail of a major conspiracy involving the art world and French, British, American participants. Also at the heart of the case is an old man's helpless love for a feckless young wife." Publ Wkly

Maigret and the black sheep; translated from the French by Helen Thomson. Harcourt Brace Jovanovich 1976 158p o.p.

"A Helen and Kurt Wolff book"

Original French edition, 1972

"The victim is a retired carton manufacturer who has been shot, without apparent motive, while sitting at home in his favorite armchair. To [Chief Inspector Maigret's] chagrin, he can find no crack or crevice in the utter respectability of the dead man's life. . . . The season is the end of summer. Parisians are drifting back to the city from their vacations, there is a nip in the air. . . . Maigret sips his beer in several cafés, confers with his faithful colleague Lapointe, and ponders the many facts of this . . . case." New Yorker

Maigret and the burglar's wife; translated by J. Maclaren-Ross. Harcourt Brace Jovanovich 1989 167p $18.95

ISBN 0-15-155572-9   LC 89-15625

Also available Thorndike Press large print edition

"A Helen and Kurt Wolff book"

Original French edition, 1951

"Inspector Maigret responds to a call for help from a respectable housewife, remembering her as a cheeky hooker called Lofty. Her husband, 'Sad Freddie,' an inept safecracker, has fled their home in Paris after seeing a dead woman in a residence he planned to rob. Assuring the detective that her husband is a simple burglar, incapable of murder, Lofty convinces Maigret and his men to investigate." Publ Wkly

Maigret and the fortune-teller; translated by Geoffrey Sainsbury. Harcourt Brace Jovanovich 1989 140p $16.95

ISBN 0-15-155571-0   LC 88-16301

"A Helen and Kurt Wolff book"

Original French edition, 1944

Maigret "is forewarned of a murder but fails to prevent it. He tracks down the villain by exercising his famous 'capacity for putting himself in other people's shoes.' In this case, the shoes belong to a woebegone old man, apparently senile, who was found at the scene of the crime. Obviously more terrified of his wife and daughter than he is of the thunderous Maigret, the old man piques the policeman's interest and so leads him to the solution." Booklist

Maigret and the gangsters; translated from the French by Louise Varèse. 4th ed. Harcourt Brace Jovanovich 1986 168p $14.95

ISBN 0-15-155565-6   LC 86-294

"A Helen and Kurt Wolff book"

Original French edition, 1952; first United States edition published 1954 by Doubleday with title: Inspector Maigret and the killers

"Inspector Lognon, widely known as 'the most dismal man in the Paris police,' is always trying to solve some spectacular case that will land him with Maigret's Crime Squad on the Quai des Orfevres. Lognon's latest exploit involves a drug stakeout during which he sees a car pull up to the curb and a body dumped out on the pavement. By the time Lognon makes his call, another car has pulled up to retrieve the corpse. Maigret joins Lognon in finding the disappearing body, while events become more outlandish and dangerous. The witty pace featuring kidnappings and shootings, is effectively sustained throughout." Booklist

Maigret and the Hotel Majestic; translated from the French by Caroline Hiller. Harcourt Brace Jovanovich 1978 c1977 174p o.p.

LC 77-84398

"A Helen and Kurt Wolff book"

Original French edition, 1942; this translation first published 1977 in the United Kingdom

Maigret faces "the murder of Emilienne Clark, a sophisticated French woman married to a wealthy American. The setting in a Parisian luxury hotel with a dozen possible suspects ranging from a mysterious and elegant guest to an insignificant and humble breakfast cook." Best Sellers

Maigret and the loner; translated from the French by Eileen Ellenbogen. Harcourt Brace Jovanovich 1975 161p o.p. Amereon reprint available $16.95 (ISBN 0-89190-429-8)

"A Helen and Kurt Wolff book"

Original French edition, 1971

"In hot summer, Maigret tackles the case of an elderly recluse found murdered in a condemned and abandoned house where he had apparently holed up for some time." Barzun. Cat of Crime. Rev and enl edition

Maigret and the madwoman; translated from the French by Eileen Ellenbogen. Harcourt Brace Jovanovich 1972 176p o.p.

"A Helen and Kurt Wolff book"

Original French edition, 1970

"Maigret exerts himself to make up for his failure to prevent the murder of a nice old lady who had told him of her fears. He goes to Toulon to interview a suspect and generally behaves as a chief superintendent should. Madame Maigret plays a larger part than usual." Barzun. Cat of Crime. Rev and enl edition

Maigret and the man on the bench; translated from the French by Eileen Ellenbogen. Harcourt Brace Jovanovich 1975 180p o.p.

"A Helen and Kurt Wolff book"

Original French edition, 1953

"A man is found murdered in an alley, Maigret begins the case with some disinterest but soon becomes intensely concerned about the pattern of facts about the

Simenon, Georges, 1903-1989—*Continued*
slain man which point to a crime with implications beyond the original assumption of a drunken brawl." Best Sellers

Maigret and the Nahour case; translated by Alastair Hamilton. Harcourt Brace Jovanovich 1982 c1967 160p o.p.

LC 82-47661

Available G.K. Hall large print edition
"A Helen and Kurt Wolff book"
Original French edition, 1967
"When the young woman turned up at the doctor's office for treatment of a bullet wound, the doctor did not know that the young man with her was her lover or that the body of her husband was about to be discovered. As . . . Inspector Maigret probes into the matter, his investigation leads to an intriguing array of characters and to a pack of lies that almost prevents him from getting to the bottom of it all." Publ Wkly

Maigret and the old lady
In Simenon, G. Maigret cinq p203-307

Maigret and the reluctant witnesses
In Simenon, G. Five times Maigret p323-421

Maigret and the Saturday caller; translated by Tony White. Harcourt Brace Jovanovich 1991 124p o.p.

LC 90-46032

"A Helen and Kurt Wolff book"
Original French edition, 1962
"Maigret is visited by a harelipped man who confesses that he wants to murder his wife and her lover but hasn't yet done so. Needless to say, Maigret cannot dismiss the man's plans as the fantasy of a harmless lunatic and begins to probe around the edges, irritated by the handicaps imposed by the public prosecutor's recent restrictions on police powers." Booklist

Maigret and the spinster; translated from the French by Eileen Ellenbogen. Harcourt Brace Jovanovich 1977 155p o.p.

LC 76-27416

"A Helen and Kurt Wolff book"
Original French edition, 1942
"A pathetic old maid who has been haunting Maigret's office with vague tales of midnight prowlers comes with a real tale of terror, but Maigret neglects to see her. When the woman's elderly, miserly aunt is found murdered, and the spinster turns up strangled in a broom closet at police headquarters, Maigret feels both personal guilt and a supreme challenge. His investigation involves all the other tenants in the building where the two murdered women lived." Publ Wkly

Maigret and the toy village; translated by Eileen Ellenbogen. Harcourt Brace Jovanovich 1979 139p o.p.

LC 79-1843

"A Helen and Kurt Wolff book"
Original French edition, 1944
In this novel "Maigret, the solemn, slow-moving, yet brilliant Chief Superintendent of the Police Judiciare, is entangled in the most exasperating murder case of his career. A man is slain in a new suburban housing development (the 'toy village' of the title). The prime suspect is his housekeeper, a young woman who has the motive for murder (she stands to inherit the old man's money), plenty of opportunities to execute the crime, and a maddening propensity for keeping Maigret at bay." Booklist

Maigret and the wine merchants; translated from the French by Eileen Ellenbogen. Harcourt Brace Jovanovich 1971 187p o.p.

"A Helen and Kurt Wolff book"
Original French edition, 1970
"A wealthy wine merchant [in Paris] is shot down. His wife takes the news with complete unsurprise and a shrug of the shoulders. His business associates discuss him as some sort of artifact coolly, unemotionally. His mistresses neither liked nor disliked him. Eventually the murderer comes into Maigret's sight." N Y Times Book Rev

Maigret and the young girl
In Simenon, G. Maigret cinq p7-105

Maigret at the Gai-Moulin; translated by Geoffrey Sainsbury. 2nd ed. Harcourt Brace Jovanovich 1991 166p $17.95

ISBN 0-15-155568-0   LC 91-7774

"A Helen and Kurt Wolff book"
Original French edition, 1931; first English translation with title: At the Gai-Moulin, published 1940 in the collection Maigret abroad
"Two Belgian teenage boys hide out in the Gai-Moulin, a nightclub, after closing time in order to steal from the till. Sneaking up to the bar, however, they see the body of a man on the floor and flee in panic. The next day, the body is found in a wicker basket on the lawn of the zoo. The dead man, a rich Greek, had hired Maigret to follow and protect him, but then eluded the inspector. The police arrest one of the boys while the other hides. Puzzled about why the victim had been in Belgium, Maigret helps the Liège Sûreté unravel a deeper plot." Publ Wkly

Maigret bides his time; translated by Alastair Hamilton. Harcourt Brace Jovanovich 1985 c1966 165p o.p.

LC 84-25134

Available Thorndike Press large print edition
"A Helen and Kurt Wolff book"
Original French edition, 1965; this translation first published 1966 in the United Kingdom
This novel "combines a delight in the sensual world with an exploration of the horrors of human cruelty. The plot revolves around the murder of master jewel thief and gang leader Manuel Palmari, a criminal Maigret has known for many years and whose death he half-guiltily mourns. The chief suspect is Palmari's young mistress, though Maigret finds many more suspects and motives crowded into the deceased man's life. Maigret's investigation does not end until a welter of vice has been uncovered—and more murder is committed. Vintage Simenon." Booklist

Maigret cinq. Harcourt, Brace & World 1965 523p o.p.

A Helen and Kurt Wolff book
First published in 1964 in the United Kingdom with title: The second Maigret omnibus
Five cases featuring Chief Inspector Maigret of the Paris police
Contents: Maigret and the young girl (1951); Maigret's little joke (1955); Maigret and the old lady (1957); Maigret's first case (1958); Maigret takes a room (1960)

Simenon, Georges, 1903-1989—*Continued*

Maigret goes home; translated by Robert Baldick. Harcourt Brace Jovanovich 1989 139p $16.95

ISBN 0-15-155150-2   LC 89-2011

Also available Thorndike Press large print edition

"A Helen and Kurt Wolff book"

Original French edition, 1931; this translation first published 1940 in the United Kingdom

"The countess of the estate where Maigret grew up drops dead during early mass on All Souls' Day, shocked to death by a fake newspaper report falsely reporting the suicide of her son. Although the estate had been heavily mortgaged to pay for the son's debts and the countess' young lovers, the inheritance is still not inconsiderable, and, of course, there are at least three likely suspects." Booklist

Maigret goes to school

In Simenon, G. Five times Maigret p425-525

Maigret has scruples

In Simenon, G. Five times Maigret p223-320

Maigret in court; translated from the French by Robert Brain. Harcourt Brace Jovanovich 1983 c1961 147p o.p.

LC 83-4341

"A Helen and Kurt Wolff book"

Original French edition, 1961

"In this story Gaston Meurant is accused of having killed his aunt Léontine and a young child for whom she was caring. Maigret, convinced of Meurant's innocence, introduces testimony relating to the infidelity of Gaston's wife, Givette. The suspense and mystery deepen when Gaston is acquitted and begins a search for one of the men linked to Givette. The emphasis is on a study of character rather than the usual violence and gore." Shapiro. Fic for Youth. 3d edition

Maigret in exile; translated by Eileen Ellenbogen. Harcourt Brace Jovanovich 1979 c1978 162p o.p.

LC 78-13771

"A Helen and Kurt Wolff book"

Original French edition, 1942; this translation first published 1978 in the United Kingdom

"Having fallen from grace in his department in Paris, Maigret has been sent to the Northern Provinces for a cooling off period. He is bored and depressed, an outsider in the small fishing villages of the area, until murder rears its ugly head. When an unknown corpse appears in the home of a retired judge, all changes for Maigret, and everyone becomes his friend and wants to help." West Coast Rev Books

Maigret in Holland; translated by Geoffrey Sainsbury. 2nd ed. Harcourt Brace & Co. 1993 165p $18.95

ISBN 0-15-155159-6   LC 92-30504

"A Helen and Kurt Wolff Book"

Original French edition, 1931; first English translation with title Crime in Holland, published 1940 in the collection Maigret abroad

"Although Maigret speaks no Dutch, he is called to Holland to assist a compatriot, Jean Duclos. Unfortunately, Duclos was present when Conrad Popinga, a former captain in the merchant marine, was murdered, and the Dutch police think Duclos, along with Popinga's wife and sister-in-law, a young sailor, and a local farm girl, is a prime suspect. Once the capable but long-suffering Maigret arrives, he methodically reviews the evidence and questions suspects. . . . Readers will marvel at the inspector's brilliant logic." Booklist

Maigret in Montmartre

In Simenon, G. Five times Maigret p9-116

Maigret on the defensive; translated from the French by Alastair Hamilton. Harcourt Brace Jovanovich 1981 c1966 148p o.p.

LC 81-47576

"A Helen and Kurt Wolff book"

Original French edition, 1964; this translation first published 1966 in the United Kingdom

"Maigret is preemptorily summoned to the Chief Commissioner's office. What he is told there is more than enough to destroy his career and reputation. A young woman, daughter of a man of standing and influence, has filed a complaint: According to her, Maigret picked her up in a bar, got her drunk, and took her to a shady hotel and undressed her. A highly unlikely story for anyone who knows Maigret, but hard to disprove. And the Commissioner chooses to believe it." Publisher's note

Maigret on the Riviera; translated by Geoffrey Sainsbury. Harcourt Brace Jovanovich 1988 c1940 137p $14.95

ISBN 0-15-155149-9   LC 87-26866

"A Helen and Kurt Wolff book"

Original French edition, 1932; first published 1940 in the United Kingdom with title: Liberty Bar

"When wealthy businessman and influential government official William Brown is murdered on the Riviera, . . . Maigret is called in to conduct a discreet investigation." Libr J

Maigret takes a room

In Simenon, G. Maigret cinq p421-523

Maigret's first case

In Simenon, G. Maigret cinq p309-419

Maigret's little joke

In Simenon, G. Maigret cinq p107-202

Maigret's memoirs; translated from the French by Jean Stewart. Harcourt Brace Jovanovich 1985 c1963 134p $13.95

ISBN 0-15-155148-0   LC 85-8591

"A Helen and Kurt Wolff book"

Original French edition, 1951; this translation first published 1963 in the United Kingdom

"Inspector Maigret, upset by writer Georges Simenon's 'caricature' of him, decides to correct the world's misconception of his personality and his cases by writing his memoirs. . . . Maigret outlines a few criminal cases, digresses about the Parisian weather, explains his dislike for Simenon, and presents his views on the criminal mind and on life in general in this odd but marvelous 'autobiographical' account." Booklist

Maigret's mistake

In Simenon, G. Five times Maigret p117-219

Simenon, Georges, 1903-1989—*Continued*

Maigret's pickpocket; translated from the French by Nigel Ryan. Harcourt, Brace & World 1968 151p o.p.

"A Helen and Kurt Wolff book"

Original French edition, 1967

"The story begins when Maigret, to his chagrin, has his wallet lifted while riding on a Paris bus. It is promptly returned, however, as a direct lead-in to the murder case." Publ Wkly

Maigret's revolver; translated from the French by Nigel Ryan. Harcourt Brace Jovanovich 1984 c1952 167p $12.95

ISBN 0-15-155562-1   LC 84-4634

Also available G.K. Hall large print edition

"A Helen and Kurt Wolff book"

Original French edition, 1952; this translation first published 1956 in the United Kingdom

In this novel "the inspector's cherished weapon—a gift from the F.B.I.—is stolen from his home by a young man who snatches it from a mantelpiece while Mme Maigret's back is turned. Supposedly, the young man is waiting to talk to the Inspector when he returned from police headquarters. Thus begins a tangled tale of a psychotic man who commits a gruesome murder and a reluctant trip by Maigret to London in order to track down the young man with the gun." West Coast Rev Books

"Here, Simenon devotes himself almost exclusively to the workings of the intricate plot, rather than (as in so many other Maigrets) to the inner workings of the detective himself." Booklist

Maigret's rival; translated by Helen Thomson. Harcourt Brace Jovanovich 1980 c1979 176p o.p.

LC 79-3362

"A Helen and Kurt Wolff book"

Original French edition, 1944; this translation first published 1979 in the United Kingdom

"Maigret has been sent by a friend to the man's relatives in the country, to investigate a case of slander. When he arrives at the house where he is to begin his investigation, he discovers a former police rival who is now a private investigator also on the scene, being very mysterious. His host and the family also seem to be extremely nervous at Maigret's presence, and not overly anxious to be of help." West Coast Rev Books

Maigret's war of nerves; translated by Geoffrey Sainsbury. Harcourt Brace Jovanovich 1986 c1940 151p $13.95

ISBN 0-15-155570-2   LC 85-24749

"A Helen and Kurt Wolff book"

Original French edition, 1931; first United States edition published 1940 with title: The patience of Maigret

Maigret is convinced that Heurtin, a condemned prisoner is innocent. The Inspector persuades officials to allow Heurtin to escape hoping that he will lead Maigret to the real killer

The murderer; translated from the French by Geoffrey Sainsbury. Harcourt Brace Jovanovich 1986 c1937 138p $15.95

ISBN 0-15-163270-7   LC 86-269

"A Helen and Kurt Wolff book"

Original French edition, 1937

The murderer of title is "Dr. Hans Kuperus of Sneek, a small town in Friesland. After killing his wife and her lover, Herr Schutter, Kuperus escapes suspicion and the townspeople sympathize with the widower for a time. Then he begins behaving extravagantly, flaunting his affair with his housekeeper and scandalizing the crabbed, insular community in other ways. Finally, the doctor has no practice, no friends; he and the housekeeper are prisoners in his house. Faithfully translated by Sainsbury, the narrative hauntingly describes the disintegration of human beings, damned by weaknesses that Simenon compels the reader to recognize and pity." Publ Wkly

The old man dies; translated from the French by Bernard Frechtman. Harcourt, Brace & World 1967 152p o.p.

"A Helen and Kurt Wolff book"

Original French edition, 1966

"Les Halles, that wonderful market in Paris where tourists go for onion soup at 4 a.m., is the setting for one of Simenon's superb character studies. The old man who dies is a restaurant owner whose life-long goal has been his estate. What happens to the legacy is less vital than what happens to his children." Cincinnati Public Libr

The rules of the game; translated by Howard Curtis. Harcourt Brace Jovanovich 1988 154p $18.95

ISBN 0-15-169475-3   LC 88-2279

"A Helen and Kurt Wolff book"

Original French edition, 1955

This novel focuses on the "manager of the local supermarket, Walter Higgins. A caring husband and father, proud of his family and the status he has achieved after a deprived childhood in a New Jersey slum, Higgins happily anticipates joining the country club. When the committee blackballs him, the snub is a terrible blow. Higgins's wife and their children give him loving support but he becomes obsessed by thoughts of revenge against those who play a game with secret rules against those who 'don't count.'" Publ Wkly

The truth about Bébé Donge; translated from the French by Louise Varèse. 2nd ed. Harcourt Brace Jovanovich 1992 170p $18.95

ISBN 0-15-191319-6   LC 91-27983

"A Helen and Kurt Wolff book"

Original French edition, 1942; first English translation with title: I take this woman published 1953 in the collection Satan's children

"When wealthy merchant François Donge is poisoned with arsenic, police arrest his wife, Bébé. Throughout the ensuing investigation and trial, she keeps her composure and her own counsel while the other characters offer a *Rashomon*-like diversity of views about her." Publ Wkly

Simpson, Dorothy, 1933-

Dead by morning. Scribner 1989 277p o.p.

LC 89-6270

"Inspector Thanet is faced with a murder at a luxurious English country inn and an overzealous superintendent who is busily reorganizing with all the annoying haste of the newly promoted." Booklist

Simpson, Dorothy, 1933——_Continued_

Dead on arrival. Scribner 1987 c1986 242p o.p.

LC 86-10243

First published 1986 in the United Kingdom

This novel "about the admirable British Inspector Luke Thanet involves the murder of Steven Long, possibly by Harry Carpenter, whose wife and child have died after Steve caused their car to crash. But the detective's methodical habits lead him to question others with reasons to hate the murder victim: his former wife and her new lover and Steve's younger brothers. Only his twin, Geoffrey, has a kind word for the deceased trouble-maker." Publ Wkly

"To fiddle with identical twins in crime fiction is very dangerous, but our author meets the menace head-on and escapes disaster by a daring twist that deserves applause." Barzun. Cat of Crime. Rev and enl edition

Doomed to die. Scribner 1991 245p $19.95

ISBN 0-684-19381-7   LC 91-4185

Also available Thorndike Press large print edition

"Inspector Thanet's mother-in-law has had a heart attack; Sergeant Lineham's wife is clinically depressed; and Superintendent Draco has just learned that his beloved wife, Angharad, has leukemia. Among the civilian populace of this suddenly blighted Kentish town, a young nanny is stricken with a ruptured appendix, and the woman who takes her place, a tormented artist with an abusive husband and a dying mother, is found murdered." N Y Times Book Rev

"Confirmed clue-sniffers should be ready for a surprise here: both the solution and the sinner are shockers, though eminently fair ones." Booklist

Element of doubt. Scribner 1988 c1987 265p o.p.

LC 87-26308

First published 1987 in the United Kingdom

"This mild and methodical mystery unfolds in a picturesque English village where gentlemanly detective-inspector Luke Thanet is hard-pressed to discover who pushed beautiful but unpleasant Nerine Tarrant over the second-story balcony of her manor 'High Gables' to her death below. There is no lack of suspects, and Thanet, with stolid, respectable Sgt. Lineham at his side, is kept busy interviewing them." Publ Wkly

Last seen alive; a Luke Thanet mystery. Scribner 1985 220p o.p.

LC 85-14530

The author "invites us to reflect on the murder by strangling of a lovely woman, widowed, who is spending one night only in a small Kentish village, ostensibly to hear a violin recital. What could possibly account for a killing under such conditions? The congenial pair of Thanet and Lineham uncovers several 'pasts,' 20 years distant, when all parties were teen-agers in school. Dramatic surprises punctuate a piece of detection in which the ratiocination is neither static nor obvious." Barzun. Cat of Crime. Rev and enl edition

No laughing matter. Scribner 1993 262p $20

ISBN 0-684-19626-3   LC 93-19799

Scotland Yard's Inspector Luke Thanet investigates the murder of a "vintner who went through the laboratory window of his prosperous family-owned vineyard in the Kentish countryside." N Y Times Book Rev

"Simpson turns out her usual high-caliber tale and gives the reader more to ponder than a simple mystery. Her shrewd understanding of what makes humans tick results in a story that is both entertaining and thought-provoking." Booklist

Suspicious death; a Luke Thanet mystery. Scribner 1988 247p o.p.

LC 88-22507

"Detective Inspector Luke Thanet, who keeps the peace in the Kent countryside . . . [is] a man of gentle mien, he is inclined to use psychology and tact, rather than showboat heroics, when pursuing his murder inquiries. Here that fastidious demeanor allows the detective to worm his way into the village of Telford Green, where the mistress of the local manor has been done in. It's plod, plod, plod all the way, as Thanet painstakingly dissects the victim's unlovable character and reconstructs her intriguingly complex relationships with the villagers. Like Inspector Thanet, the reader leaves Telford Green footsore but satisfied." N Y Times Book Rev

Wake the dead. Scribner 1992 250p $19

ISBN 0-684-19507-0   LC 92-19962

Also available Thorndike Press large print edition

"Inspector Luke Thanet investigates the murder of Isobel Fairleigh, a rich, ruthless, manipulative old woman who stopped at nothing to further the political career of her son, Hugo. Thanet has to decide who among Isobel's acquaintances and relatives might have hated the old woman enough to smother her while she lay half-conscious following a stroke." Booklist

Simpson, Mona

Anywhere but here. Knopf 1987 c1986 406p $18.95

ISBN 0-394-55283-0   LC 86-45282

The "novel opens with its two heroines, Adele and her daughter Ann, fleeing their provincial home-town in Wisconsin for a fresh start in California. . . . Adele is both protector and manipulator, encouraging Ann's success as a child star but also displaying her own unrealistic expectations and selfish motives. Ann tolerates her mother's lying and eccentricity, but she longs for a rootedness her mother cannot give her. The . . . flashbacks to stories told by Adele's Wisconsin relatives give us a sense of the home they have left behind, and the disparity between it and their new home." Libr J

"Any single episode could stand on its own, but Simpson keeps piling them on, building with strength and grace." Booklist

Sinclair, April

Coffee will make you black. Hyperion 1994 239p $19.95

ISBN 1-56282-796-0   LC 93-13271

This novel's protagonist "is Jean ('Stevie') Stevenson, a spunky 11-year-old when the story begins; a high-school student when it concludes. The setting is Chicago, circa 1965-70. . . . Raised by a strict, if well-meaning, mother and an affectionate, if vague, father, Stevie soon finds herself caught up in one of the many riddles of youth: to be cool or to be square. Before she can sort it all out, she has her first period, a less than thrilling event, and, after experiencing her first flirtatious taunts from men on the street, decides that 'breasts might be more trouble than they're worth.' Meanwhile, she is listening

Sinclair, April—*Continued*

to Dr. Martin Luther King and Malcolm X and liberating herself from the confines of her upbringing and her fear of being 'different.'" Booklist

"Sinclair gives a realistic portrayal of personal awakening during a politically tumultuous time." Publ Wkly

Sinclair, Upton, 1878-1968

Between two worlds

In Sinclair, U. [Lanny Budd series]

Boston; a novel. Boni, A.C. 1928 2v o.p.

Available from Bentley and Scholarly Press

"An elderly woman, one of the Boston 'Brahmins', suffers pangs of social conscience and goes to work in a factory, where she becomes acquainted with Sacco and Vanzetti. As the battle between industry and labor increases in intensity, she observes at close range the world-shaking events following the arrest of the two men for murder and their trial, appeal, and execution. The book, which partially follows the trail transcript, seethes with indignation." Benet's Reader's Ency of Am Lit

Dragon harvest

In Sinclair, U. [Lanny Budd series]

Dragon's teeth

In Sinclair, U. [Lanny Budd series]

The jungle.

Available from various publishers

First published 1906 by Doubleday, Page

"Jurgis Rudkus, an immigrant from Lithuania, arrives in Chicago with his father, his fiancée, and her family. He is determined to make a life for his bride in the new country. The deplorable conditions in the stockyards and the harrowing experiences of impoverished workers are vividly described by the author." Shapiro. Fic for Youth. 3d edition

[Lanny Budd series]. o.p.

Contents, chronologically: World's end (1940); Between two worlds (1941); Dragon's teeth (1942); Pulitzer Prize (1943); Wide is the gate (1943); Presidential agent (1944); Dragon harvest (1945); A world to win (1946); Presidential mission (1947); One clear call (1948); O shepherd, speak! (1949); The return of Lanny Budd (1953)

A series of novels ranging from World War I through World War II, in which the author uses the device of a single protagonist, Lanny Budd. "Budd becomes a latter day 'questing spirit' who, in the course of the novels, becomes intimate with many of the world's most prominent figures and witnesses many of modern history's most important events. Through Budd, Sinclair voices his convictions concerning modern political and social developments." Benet's Reader's Ency of Am Lit

O shepherd, speak!

In Sinclair, U. [Lanny Budd series]

One clear call

In Sinclair, U. [Lanny Budd series]

Presidential agent

In Sinclair, U. [Lanny Budd series]

Presidential mission

In Sinclair, U. [Lanny Budd series]

The return of Lanny Budd

In Sinclair, U. [Lanny Budd series]

Wide is the gate

In Sinclair, U. [Lanny Budd series]

A world to win

In Sinclair, U. [Lanny Budd series]

World's end

In Sinclair, U. [Lanny Budd series]

Singer, Isaac Bashevis, 1904-1991

Nobel Prize in literature, 1978

The certificate; translated by Leonard Wolf. Farrar, Straus & Giroux 1992 231p $22

ISBN 0-374-12029-3

Originally serialized 1967 in Yiddish newspaper

"David Bendiger, an Orthodox rabbi's son intent on becoming a writer, returns to Warsaw in the early 1920s after several years' absence. . . . Bendiger looks up Sonya, a childhood friend, and rents a tiny room from Edusha, a Communist intellectual, and her sister Minna. But instead of settling down to work on his study of Spinoza and the Cabala, Bendiger quickly finds himself romantically involved with all three women." Libr J

"Singer is the most magical of writers, transforming reality into art with seemingly effortless sleight of hand. His deceptively spare prose has a pristine clarity that is stunning in its impact." N Y Times Book Rev

The collected stories of Isaac Bashevis Singer. Farrar, Straus & Giroux 1982 610p o.p.

LC 81-12436

Analyzed in Short story index

This is a selection of forty-seven stories chosen by the author from eight prior collections

Contents: Gimpel the fool; The gentleman from Cracow; Joy; The little shoemakers; The unseen; The Spinoza of Market Street; The destruction of Kreshev; Taibele and her demon; Alone; Yentl the yeshiva boy; Zeidlus the Pope; The last demon; Short Friday; The séance; The slaughterer; The dead fiddler; Henne Fire; The letter writer; A friend of Kafka; The cafeteria; The joke; Powers; Something is there; A crown of feathers; A day in Coney Island; The cabalist of East Broadway; A quotation from Klopstock; A dance and a hop; Grandfather and grandson; Old love; The admirer; The yearning heifer; A tale of two sisters; Three encounters; Passions; Brother Beetle; The betrayer of Israel; The psychic journey; The manuscript; The power of darkness; The bus; A night in the poorhouse; Escape from civilization; Vanvild Kava; The reencounter; Neighbors; Moon and madness

The death of Methuselah and other stories. Farrar, Straus & Giroux 1988 244p $17.95

ISBN 0-374-13563-0   LC 87-21238

Analyzed in Short story index

Contents: The Jew from Babylon; The house friend; Burial at sea; The recluse; Disguised; The accuser and the accused; The trap; The smuggler; A peephole in the gate; The bitter truth; The impresario; Logarithms; Gifts; Runners to nowhere; The missing line; The hotel; Dazzled; Sabbath in Gehenna; The last gaze; The death of Methuselah

Singer, Isaac Bashevis, 1904-1991 — Continued

Enemies, a love story. Farrar, Straus & Giroux 1972 280p o.p.

Originally written in Yiddish, 1966

This novel is "about a Polish Jew who, out of gratitude, marries the girl who helped him escape the Nazis after he believes his wife is dead, takes a mistress whom he bigamously weds when she becomes pregnant, and then discovers that his first wife has also escaped from Poland to New York." Oxford Companion to Am Lit. 5th edition

"The book has the surface gaiety, ribaldry and surprise of a medieval fabliau. Yet the New York subways, telephone calls, Bronx Zoo, bus trip to the Adirondacks are solidly, meticulously real. Herman's three women expand into mythic dimension. . . . Whether or not you accept its ending, [this] is a brilliant, unsettling novel." Newsweek

The estate. Farrar, Straus & Giroux 1969 374p o.p.

Sequel to The manor

This novel covers the last years of the nineteenth century. It explores the lives of a Polish Jewish family who have emerged from the ghettos to seek a new life in a country that is itself struggling to emerge from a feudal past.

"Even in their manner of dying, Singer's characters seem to be literally swept away by storms of passion. Indeed, the only thing that keeps the book from disintegrating into an anthology of melodramatic episodes is Singer's unfaltering stylistic control." N Y Times Book Rev

The family Moskat; translated from the Yiddish by A.H. Gross. Knopf 1950 611p o.p.

"Panoramic in sweep, the novel follows many characters and story lines in depicting Jewish life in Warsaw from 1911 to the late 1930s. Singer examines Hasidism, Orthodoxy, the rise of secularism, the breakdown of 19th-century traditions, assimilation, Marxism, and Zionism." Merriam-Webster's Ency of Lit

Gimpel the fool, and other stories. Farrar, Straus & Giroux 205p o.p.

First published 1955 by Noonday and analyzed in Short story index

Translated from the Yiddish by Saul Bellow, Elaine Gottlieb, and others

Contains the following stories: By the light of memorial candles; Fire; From the diary of one not born; Gentleman from Cracow; Gimpel the fool; Joy; Little shoemakers; The mirror; Old man; The unseen; Wife killer

An Isaac Bashevis Singer reader. Farrar, Straus & Giroux 1971 560p o.p.

Partially analyzed in Short story index

This collection contains 15 short stories, the complete novel, The magician of Lublin (entered separately) and stories from five collections

Short stories included are: Gimpel the fool; The mirror; The unseen; The Spinoza of Market Street; The black wedding; The man who came back; Short Friday; Yentl the yeshiva boy; Blood; The fast; The séance; The slaughterer; The lecture; Getzel the monkey; A friend of Kafka

The king of the fields. Farrar, Straus & Giroux 1988 244p $18.95

ISBN 0-374-18128-4   LC 88-81548

"Long ago in the valley of the Vistula, the fierce but agrarian Poles brutally subjugate the Lesniks, a tribe of peace-loving hunters. Still, it is the Lesnik Cybula who eventually becomes 'The King of the Fields.'" Libr J

"A bilingual reader will enjoy the book most, greeting with laughter Mr. Singer's deliberately infantile excursions into folklore, linguistics and etymology. . . . A playground of kulaks, krols and the devil, prehistoric Poland in 'The King of the Fields' represents the opposite of a paradise lost, the usual goal for a return to one's origins." N Y Times Book Rev

The magician of Lublin. Farrar, Straus & Giroux 246p o.p. Buccaneer Bks. reprint available $14.95 (ISBN 0-89966-156-4)

Originally serialized 1959 in Yiddish newspaper; first published in book form 1960 by Noonday

Translated from the Yiddish by Elaine Gottlieb and Joseph Singer

"The novel is set in late 19th-century Poland. It concerns Yasha Mazur, an itinerant professional conjurer, tightrope walker, and hypnotist. He loves five women, including his barren and pious wife. To support himself, his assorted women, and his future plans to escape to Italy, he attempts a robbery and fails. Yasha has a crisis of conscience and returns to his wife, becoming a recluse. People begin to refer to him as Jacob the Penitent, and they flock to him as if to a holy man." Merriam-Webster's Ency of Lit

also in Singer, I. B. An Isaac Bashevis Singer reader p317-560

The manor. Farrar, Straus & Giroux 1967 442p o.p.

"This volume, although it stands as an independent story, constitutes Part One of the complete saga of 'The Manor.'" Author's note

"The action of this novel occurs in the period between the Polish insurrection of 1863 and the end of the nineteenth century. The manor is the estate of Count Jambloski, appropriated by the Russians and leased to Calman, a religious Jewish grain merchant. The novel relates the financial success story of Calman against a background of family life and changing times that draw his children away from traditional ways." Shapiro. Fic for Youth. 3d edition

Followed by The estate

Meshugah; translated by the author and Nili Wachtel. Farrar, Straus & Giroux 1994 232p $22

ISBN 0-374-20847-6   LC 93-42785

Originally serialized in Yiddish newspaper as Lost souls

In this novel, "Singer explores the complications and contradictions that arise when a young Holocaust survivor named Miriam falls simultaneously in love with two older men: Aaron, a 47-year-old writer for the *Forward* who is seemingly patterned after Singer himself, and Max, a 67-year-old bon vivant speculator who goes bust, both financially and physically. That Max and Miriam are both married to others adds yet another twist to the situation, as does the truth about the way in which Miriam managed her survival. Ever the consummate storyteller, Singer understands that there is a bit of God and the devil in everyone and that passion cannot be explained." Libr J

Singer, Isaac Bashevis, 1904-1991 —
Continued

The penitent. Farrar, Straus & Giroux
1983 169p $13.95

ISBN 0-374-23064-1   LC 83-8977

Originally written in Yiddish, 1974

"Joseph Shapiro, a wealthy businessman, stretched thin between the demands of wife, mistress, and job, one day feels such total disgust for his lifestyle that he abandons everything and flies to Israel, where he assumes the role of a baal-tshuvah, a penitent. Divorcing the 'wanton,' he marries the rabbi's daughter and devotes himself to prayer and study." Libr J

"As in the past, Singer fuses two styles: the fabulist confined to his shtetl and the modernist who regards the universe as a stark and enigmatic combat zone. If Joseph Shapiro is disagreeable, he is never less than credible." Time

Reaches of heaven; a story of the Baal Shem Tov; with twenty-four original etchings by Ira Moskowitz. Farrar, Straus & Giroux 1980 95p il o.p.

     LC 80-36672

"A beautifully woven biographical tale about an orphaned Jewish lad, Israel ben Eliezer, whose diligent studies and visionary gifts made him a beloved leader of the Jews in eighteenth-century Poland. In his brief introduction Singer states that 'this work is nothing more than the writer's expressions or fantasies of Rabbi Israel's way of thinking, his emotions, his spiritual achievements and disappointments.' This modest summary tells of the content but neglects the eloquence with which the novelist brings to life this powerful religious figure and the people who surround him and sought his aid." Booklist

Satan in Goray. Farrar, Straus & Giroux 239p o.p.

First published 1955 by Noonday

Translated from the Yiddish by Jacob Sloan

"This black-mirror narrative of miracles and cabala, of a hamlet in seventeenth-century Poland and a false Messiah, is in the tradition of such classics as 'The Dybbuk' and 'The Golem.' Poetically conceived, it captures the fever of longing, the folk-frenzy for salvation, that possessed the Jewish population of central Europe after the dark decade of the Chmielnicki massacres, three centuries before Hitler." N Y Times Book Rev

Scum; translated from Yiddish by Rosaline Dukalsky Schwartz. Farrar, Straus & Giroux 1991 217p $19.95

ISBN 0-374-25511-3   LC 90-85276

"Max Barabander is a secularized Jew living in Buenos Aires in the early part of the century. In his prime, rich, and in love with his dynamic wife, Rochelle, he's satisfied with life until their only child, a 17-year-old boy, dies unexpectedly. Rochelle withdraws into her grief, leaving Max impotent, frustrated, and desperate. After consulting unsuccessfully with doctors, he decides that a trip back to his native Poland will refresh him. But his past was a seedy one, and Max reverts immediately to his old 'underworld mentality.' He charms one woman after another, seeking a cure. He's out of control, one minute proposing marriage to a rabbi's daughter, the next agreeing to procure girls for prostitution in Argentina. He goes from shul to séance, from guilt to justification, he

adrift in moral turpitude like flotsam in a fouled sea." Booklist

"In Max Barabander, the reader is offered a chilling character for whom other lives have no real meaning, a character perhaps bereft of the moral certainties offered by the soon-to-vanish world of the rabbis of the *shtetl*." N Y Times Book Rev

Shosha. Farrar, Straus & Giroux 1978 277p o.p.

Originally serialized 1974 in the Yiddish newspaper

"Against the tragic backdrop of war clouds about to break and wash Warsaw into World War II, Singer sets his despairing protagonist, Aaron Greidinger. The young writer, caught between ambitious dreams and a Poland gone mad, between his youthful religion and the passionless cynicism of his present, escapes political confrontations by involving himself with women: a devout Communist; a peasant maid; his friend's wife; a visiting American actress, for whom he writes an unsuccessful play; and his still childlike early love, Shosha. It is Shosha he chooses to marry, an act seemingly devoid of hope but which Aaron sees as penitence for self-betrayal and one which sets a pattern for his deliverance." Booklist

"Why do people write so rarely about how funny Singer can be? Without ever resorting to parody, he has a wonderful gift for having his characters discuss great issues—the meaning of life, good versus evil, the plight of modern man, death and immortality—and making the reader chuckle only when the author wants him to." Newsweek

The slave; a novel; translated from the Yiddish by the author and Cecil Hemley. Farrar, Straus & Giroux 1962 311p o.p.

"The setting of the story is seventeenth-century Poland. . . . Jacob, a saintly young Jew, driven from his native town by a Cossack raid, has become a slave of a Polish peasant. He loves, and is loved by, the peasant's daughter, Wanda. Polish and Jewish law forbid their marriage on pain of death, and the couple become wanderers, outcasts from both worlds. Yet, through the sufferings of their love they learn great wisdom and faith." Atlantic

"A brilliant portrayal of a tumultuous society and a poignant account of a man who in wrestling with God found his soul." Saturday Rev

Singer, Israel Joshua, 1893-1944

The brothers Ashkenazi; [by] I. J. Singer; translated from the Yiddish by Maurice Samuel. Knopf 1936 642p o.p.

"Deals with the rise and decay of the textile city of Lodz, Poland, and with the fortunes of the Polish-Jewish brothers, Max and Jacob Ashkenazi, whose personalities gradually come to dominate the life of the town. . . . What gives the book its significance is not the picture of nineteenth-century Jewish family life, and not the characterizations of the two brothers, but the clear exposition of the class struggle of which Max and Jacob form unconscious parts." New Yorker

Sjöwall, Maj, 1935-

Cop killer; the story of a crime; [by] Maj Sjöwall and Per Wahlöö; translated from the Swedish by Thomas Teal. Pantheon Bks. 1975 296p o.p. Amereon reprint available $21.95 (ISBN 0-89190-377-1)

Original Swedish edition, 1974

"A divorced woman is murdered, has 'disappeared,' but Martin Beck, Chief Detective Inspector, is called in from Stockholm to investigate. Prime suspect is a former convict who lived near the victim, Sigbrit; and her ex-husband, ex-ship captain, may also be guilty. It takes a midnight shoot-out between three cops and two teenagers to help speed the identification of the real killer." Best Sellers

The laughing policeman; [by] Maj Sjöwall and Per Wahlöö; translated from the Swedish by Alan Blair. Pantheon Bks. 1970 211p o.p.

Available G.K. Hall large print edition

Original Swedish edition, 1968

"A Stockholm bus is found on a rainy night with all the passengers and the driver shot dead. One of the dead men, a young police detective, had been working on his own time to investigate a sex crime that was declared unsolvable years before. Martin Beck, police detective assigned to the bus killings, gains information from the girlfriend of the dead detective that helps Beck retrace the steps that led to the deaths. The careful unraveling of the mystery as the lives of all the people involved are researched is the hallmark of the writing of this Swedish duo." Shapiro. Fic for Youth. 2d edition

The locked room; [by] Maj Sjöwall and Per Wahlöö: translated from the Swedish by Paul Britten Austin. Pantheon Bks. 1973 311p o.p.

Original Swedish edition, 1972

"A man commits suicide or is murdered in a completely locked room [in Stockholm]. He is shot but there is no weapon. Martin Beck rises from his sick bed to handle this situation." Best Sellers

The man on the balcony; the story of a crime; [by] Maj Sjöwall and Per Wahlöö; translated from the Swedish by Alan Blair. Pantheon Bks. 1968 180p o.p.

Original Swedish edition, 1967

"The chief problem is child murder in Stockholm, and it is a macabre race with death when the only clues are disturbing and intangible for Beck and for the 75-man force assigned to help him." Libr J

Murder at the Savoy; [by] Maj Sjöwall and Per Wahlöö; translated from the Swedish by Amy and Ken Knoespel. Pantheon Bks. 1971 216p o.p.

Original Swedish edition, 1970

"In the dining room of the posh Savoy hotel in Malmö, Viktor Palmgren's address is interrupted when a killer guns him down, then escapes through a window. Was the wealthy industrialist murdered for personal reasons—or for political motives related to his arms shipments to Africa? Once again Chief Inspector Martin Beck of Swedish National Police goes into action." Saturday Rev

Skimin, Robert

Apache autumn; a novel of the Apache Nation. St. Martin's Press 1993 426p $22.95

ISBN 0-312-08697-0   LC 92-34387

This novel "covers 70 years of Chihenne Apache history through the lives of Lazaro, an Apache chief, and Carlota, the beautiful Mexican girl who becomes his obsession. The novel opens in 1821 as Lazaro becomes a stepson of the chief and is thus destined to take his place as leader of the Chihenne. Captured and unwillingly made Lazaro's wife, Carlota bears him a son, Andres, but she does not accept her new life and escapes back to New Mexico with Andres. It is through their lives that we see the history of the Chihenne, a once proud and independent people who are finally forced onto reservations." Libr J

The author "depicts Apache society and culture with understanding and empathy, and resists sentimentalism in chronicling the tribe's demise." Publ Wkly

Skinner, B. F. (Burrhus Frederic), 1904-1990

Walden two. Macmillan 1948 266p o.p.

"Unlike most post-World War II science fiction, which considered social control by psychological conditioning to be a form of hell on Earth, Skinner presented it grandly as utopian. The structure of the story (which, as a story, doesn't amount to much) is a debate between an advocate of human free choice and a champion of behavioral manipulation, which is offered as the answer to all of society's ills." Anatomy of Wonder 4

Skinner, Burrhus Frederic *See* Skinner, B. F. (Burrhus Frederic), 1904-1990

Škvorecký, Josef

The engineer of human souls; an entertainment on the old themes of life, women, fate, dreams, the working class, secret agents, love and death; translated from the Czech by Paul Wilson. Knopf 1984 c1977 571p $17.95

ISBN 0-394-50500-X   LC 83-48888

Original Czech edition published 1977 in Canada

In this novel "narrator Danny Smiricky (a Czech writer teaching at a Toronto university) observes his fellow émigrés, argues with his students and colleagues about politics and literature, and recalls the last years of the World War II and the Communist takeover of Czechoslovakia. Poignant letters from his boyhood friends, back at home and on other continents, complete the picture of a generation deeply affected by two repressive ideologies." Libr J

"This beautiful, moving novel is both a concrete evocation of the plight of political exiles and a general examination of the perilous business of being human in an age warped by ideologies." Publ Wkly

The **Sleeper** wakes; Harlem Renaissance stories by women; edited and with an introduction by Marcy Knopf; foreword by Nellie Y. McKay. Rutgers Univ. Press 1993 xxxix, 277p $40

ISBN 0-8135-1944-6   LC 92-30446

The Sleeper wakes—*Continued*

Analyzed in Short story index

Contents: The sleeper wakes; Double trouble [and] Mary Elizabeth, by J. R. Fauset; Wedding day, by G. Bennett; Free, by G. D. Johnson; Funeral; The typewriter [and] Prologue to a life, by D. West; One boy's story; Drab rambles [and] Nothing new, by M. Bonner; The closing door, by A. W. Grimké; Bathesda of Sinners Run, by M. I. Owens; The foolish and the wise: Sallie Runner is introduced to Socrates and Sanctum 777 N.S.D.C.O.U. meets Cleopatra, by L. A. Pendleton; Cross crossings cautiously [and] Three dogs and a rabbit, by A. S. Coleman; Blue aloes [and] To a wild rose, by O. B. Graham; His great career [and] Summer session, by A. Dunbar-Nelson; Masks [and] Mademoiselle 'Tasie, by E. B. Thompson; John Redding goes to sea [and] The bone of contention, by Z. N. Hurston; Sanctuary; The wrong man [and] Freedom, by N. Larsen

"This anthology rescues short stories written by the women writers of the Harlem Renaissance from archival obscurity. . . . While these writers share some common themes . . . each has her own distinctive voice, and none sacrifices the art of storytelling for polemics. A passionate, dynamic, and invaluable collection." Booklist

Smiley, Jane, 1949-

The age of grief; a novella and stories. Knopf 1987 213p $15.95

ISBN 0-394-55848-0   LC 87-45120

Analyzed in Short story index

Contents: The pleasure of her company; Lily; Jeffrey, believe me; Long distance; Dynamite; The age of grief

"These short pieces are about male-female relations—the high points and the pitfalls (more of the latter than the former). Smiley knows her characters inside out and lets the reader in on everything she knows." Booklist

The age of grief [novelette]

In Smiley, J. The age of grief p119-213

Good will

In Smiley, J. Ordinary love & Good will

The Greenlanders. Knopf 1988 555p $19.95

ISBN 0-394-55120-6   LC 88-2758

An "historical novel based on the tenth-century settlement of Greenland by Norseman Erik the Red and a band of Norse colonists. After flourishing in Greenland for centuries, the colonists disappeared, leaving behind only their buildings and artifacts." Booklist

"Vivid, even stunning descriptions of the land and customs of these 'lost settlements' are the book's strong points. Characterizations are less successful; many personalities remain wooden throughout the lengthy action. Nevertheless, the exotic subject matter will appeal to historical novel fans." Libr J

Ordinary love

In Smiley, J. Ordinary love & Good will

Ordinary love & Good will; two novellas. Knopf 1989 197p $17.95

ISBN 0-394-57772-8   LC 89-45284

"In 'Ordinary Love,' a mother [Rachel Kinsella] explores her tentative relationship with her five grown children on the return of one of her twin boys from two years in India. After she reveals to them information about the brief affair that caused the collapse of her marriage to their father 20 years earlier, and her loss of custody, they tell heartbreaking details of their years without her. [In] 'Good Will', . . . the careful, totally 'organic' lifestyle of a rural couple disintegrates before their eyes when their seven-year-old son confronts the 'real world' at school, with anguishing results." Libr J

"Jane Smiley's stories are shaped with a constant, overseeing intelligence, with full sympathy for humanity's tendency to destroy its own best visions." N Y Times Book Rev

A thousand acres. Knopf 1991 371p $25

ISBN 0-394-57773-6   LC 91-52720

Also available Thorndike Press large print edition

The author "creates an idyllic world of family farm life in Iowa in 1979: the neat yard, freshly painted house, clean clothes on the line, and fertile, well-tended fields. The owner of these well-managed acres is Larry Cook, who abruptly decides to turn the farm over to his two eldest daughters and their husbands. Ginny and Ty are hard-working farmers who try to placate her ornery father, while sister Rose and hard-drinking Pete try to stand up to him. Dark secrets surface after the property transfer and the family's careful world unravels with a grim inevitability." Libr J

"What makes this novel such a triumph is Smiley's brilliant twist on the Lear story: she tells it not from Larry's point of view but from his eldest daughter's. . . . In the end Smiley does what Shakespeare himself never did: she creates a female heroine who grows through her own anguish until she towers over the hero and conquers him." Newsweek

Smith, April, 1949-

North of Montana; a novel. Knopf 1994 295p $23

ISBN 0-679-43197-7   LC 94-12311

As this mystery opens, "success-hungry L.A.-based FBI agent Ana Grey is just waiting for the case that will catapault her from the humdrum Bank Robbery Squad into the exalted Kidnapping and Extortion Division. The hoped-for promotion is Ana's first step to her ultimate goal: a plum job as Special Agent in Charge. But department politics, a jealous supervisor, and Ana's abrasive impatience detour her to a case that's a real hot potato. Glamorous movie star Jayne Mason, past her prime but still adored by her fans, claims a local M.D. hooked her on painkillers. She wants his head on a platter courtesy of the FBI, even though the doctor appears to be clean as a whistle." Booklist

This is "an LA novel in the tradition of some of the best writers of detective fiction. . . . There are swift, vivid portraits of scene and characters." Times Lit Suppl

Smith, Betty, 1896-1972

Joy in the morning. Harper & Row 1963 308p o.p. Buccaneer Bks. reprint available $21.95 (ISBN 1-56849-169-7)

"When their families find out that Annie McGairy and Carl Brown have married, the two are cut off without a cent. Carl, a law student, takes a full-time job and goes to law school at night. Annie, who had dropped out of school to help her family, longs to be at college.

Smith, Betty, 1896-1972—*Continued*

She is given a chance to audit a course in literature because of her abiding interest in it. Her pregnancy, however, increases the pressure on their lives, and only their deep love sees them through their difficulties." Shapiro. Fic for Youth. 3d edition

Maggie-Now. Harper & Row 1958 437p o.p.

"Maggie-Now, though she never left Brooklyn, was worldly with stability and understanding. This is the story of her life as she became a mother to her baby brother, a housekeeper to her father and a faithful wife to a man who left her restlessly each spring and returned each fall." Publ Wkly

"On the whole Maggie-Now's life was an uneventful one; her book a quiet book. It is not story-suspense, which gives this novel its very special quality. That lies rather in the almost seeable, feelable fabric of Williamsburg as Miss Smith presents it." N Y Her Trib Books

A tree grows in Brooklyn; a novel. Harper & Brothers 1943 443p o.p. Buccaneer Bks. reprint available $27.95 (ISBN 0-89966-303-6)

Also available G.K. Hall large print edition

"Life in the Williamsburg section of Brooklyn during the early 1900s is rough, but the childhood and youth of Francie Nolan is far from somber. Nurtured by a loving mother, Francie blossoms and reaches out for happiness despite poverty and the alcoholism of a father whose weakness is somewhat compensated for by his lovable disposition." Shapiro. Fic for Youth. 3d edition

Smith, Caesar, 1920-1995

For works written by this author under other names see Hall, Adam, 1920-1995; Trevor, Elleston, 1920-1995

Smith, Charles Merrill, d. 1985

Reverend Randollph and the Splendid Samaritan. Putnam 1986 223p o.p.

LC 85-30132

"When a member of Randollph's flock is murdered, the minister helps his friend detective Casey to investigate. The victim, James Trent, was called the Splendid Samaritan because of his excess altruism. Randollph, however, had suspected the financier as a whited sepulchre. . . . Randollph's keen perceptions solve the case and end the witty, cunningly plotted mystery." Publ Wkly

Reverend Randollph and the unholy Bible. Putnam 1983 221p o.p.

LC 82-18125

"Football player-turned-minister Con Randollph discovers the body of one of his parishioners, reclusive Johannes Humbrecht, in his decaying mansion. Kidnapped by thugs who believe he's murdered Humbrecht, Randollph learns that the old man owned a Gutenberg Bible, which is now missing." Libr J

Reverend Randollph and the wages of sin. Putnam 1974 254p o.p.

The Reverend Cesare Paul Randollph "is temporarily placed in a prosperous Chicago parish, and it soon develops that there is some kind of financial chicanery going on involving what seems to be a conspiracy between a member of the staff and an unusually louche board of trustees. In due course, a member of the choir, the wife of a trustee, is murdered." Libr J

Reverend Randollph gently investigates "suspects among his congregation, playing upon their psychological quirks to ferret out the culprit. Much of this is formula whodunit material, but the humor, the characterization, the rendering of ecclesiastical politics—these make for an amiably different mystery." Publ Wkly

Smith, Cordwainer, 1913-1966

On the storm planet

In Modern classic short novels of science fiction p94-163

Smith, Evelyn E.

Miss Melville rides a tiger. Fine, D.I. 1991 217p $18.95

ISBN 1-55611-219-X   LC 90-55016

Also available G.K. Hall large print edition

"Freelance assassin and socialite artist Susan Melville here takes on an international drug cartel. The head of a secret government organization needs a female hitperson to eliminate the reclusive Begum of Gandistan, mother of the ruling sultan. After initially declining the job, Miss Melville changes her mind when she comes face to face with the Begum and recognizes the haughty woman as her old enemy Berengaria 'Berry' Rundle. . . . As in her previous books, Smith aims pithy barbs at fashionable New York society and those who take it seriously." Publ Wkly

Smith, Janet L.

A vintage murder. Fawcett Columbine 1994 228p $20

ISBN 0-449-90871-2   LC 94-15130

"An Annie MacPherson mystery"

"Annie MacPherson has let her old friendship with Taylor North lapse because she couldn't stand Taylor's loud-mouthed, aggressive husband, Steven Vick. But now that Taylor's been accused of Steven's murder, Annie makes the trip to Washington's scenic wine country to try to save her friend from a first-degree murder conviction. Annie simply can't believe Taylor would have killed the man she loved, but as Annie investigates, she finds Taylor is guarding some nasty secrets." Booklist

Smith, Julie, 1944-

The Axeman's jazz. St. Martin's Press 1991 341p o.p.

LC 91-19064

"A Thomas Dunne book"

In this mystery featuring New Orleans homicide detective Skip Langdon, "the killer, who calls himself the Axeman after an infamous murderer who terrorized New Orleans in the early 1900's, preys on the most vulnerable souls who frequent the city's many 12-step programs. .

Smith, Julie, 1944——*Continued*

. . Thwarted by the anonymity given their members by these groups, the murder task force goes undercover at meetings, posing as alcoholics, drug addicts and co-dependents." N Y Times Book Rev

"With an acute ear for New Orleans speech and a sharp eye for the city's social stratification, Smith keeps the reader's heart palpitating to the end of this mystery of unusual depth, which leaves Skip in love, confident she's a good cop and triumphant over social-climbing, tradition-bound parents." Publ Wkly

Jazz funeral; a Skip Langdon novel. Fawcett Columbine 1993 365p $18

ISBN 0-449-90742-2   LC 92-54997

This mystery featuring New Orleans cop Skip Langdon is "about the murder of a local jazz entrepreneur and the disappearance of his 16-year-old sister. . . . Even though she wears her badge like a piece of jewelry, Skip has the social skills to pump information from her up-town friends, and her amateur detection methods pay off with solid insights into an emotionally bankrupt family. Ms. Smith takes special pains to be gentle with a musically gifted teen-ager who runs away from the horrors of home to join a family band very much like the Neville Brothers. The kid is a bit of a brat, but the portrayal has such integrity that it makes up for Skip's lax procedures." N Y Times Book Rev

New Orleans beat; a Skip Langdon novel. Fawcett Columbine 1994 359p $21.50

ISBN 0-449-90743-0   LC 93-46506

New Orleans detective Skip Langdon "investigates the suspicious death of a man who was involved with an electronic bulletin board community." Libr J

"Smith is a skilled writer who can evoke the steamy, mysterious ambience of New Orleans while simultaneously proving that computer jargon can be comprehensible even to the 'computer-challenged.' This is a humorous, suspenseful mystery." Booklist

Smith, Kim

(ed) Mysterious cat stories. See Mysterious cat stories

Smith, Lee, 1944-

Cakewalk. Putnam 1981 256p o.p.

LC 81-8501

Analyzed in Short story index

Contents: Between the lines; Georgia Rose; All the days of our lives; The seven deadly sins; Gulfport; Artists; Heat lightning; Dear Phil Donahue; Mrs. Darcy meets the blue-eyed stranger at the beach; Not pictured; Saint Paul; Horses; The French Revolution: a love story; Cakewalk

"The stories are gentle, dealing with subtleties of personality and involving no outlandish characters. Small-town southern ambience is strong-flavored throughout the collection. Smith has a perfect voice, incorporating hints of both refinement and shabbiness. Quite simply, excellent writing." Booklist

The devil's dream. Putnam 1992 315p o.p.

LC 92-1027

Available Thorndike Press large print edition

The author traces the history of country music "through several generations of the Bailey family of Grassy Springs, Virginia. Starting in 1833 with the marriage of Moses Bailey, a preacher's son who thinks fiddle music is the voice of the Devil laughing, to Kate Malone who comes from a fiddle-playing family, the Baileys are torn between their love of God and their love of music. Plain Baptist hymns and haunting Appalachian ballads shape the lives of the early generations. Grandsons R.C. and Durwood marry Lucie and Tampa, who, as the Grassy Branch Girls, take part in the early 'hillbilly recordings' of the 1920s. Rose Annie and Blackjack Johnny Raines are the 'King and Queen of Country Music' in the Rockabilly 1950s until Rose Annie shoots Johnny after he's cheated on her once too often. Cousin Katie Crocker abandons the bland Nashville sound of the 1960s when she cuts a traditional record with her family at the Opryland Hotel." Libr J

"It is ultimately the writer's sensibility that gives 'The Devil's Dream' its charm and power. If there's weeping to be done, Ms. Smith allows her reader to weep, but she never descends to sentimentality." N Y Times Book Rev

Fair and tender ladies. Putnam 1988 316p o.p.

LC 88-10915

This novel of life in the Appalachians "unfolds through a series of letters written by Ivy Rowe, a Virginia mountain girl. Ivy, born with the century, begins her letter writing when she is about 10 years old; the letters continue for nearly 65 years." N Y Times Book Rev

An "exquisite novel. . . . Through Ivy's curiously spelled and situated letters, we see the growth not only of her own family, but also of wider Appalachia." Christ Sci Monit

Family linen. Putnam 1985 272p o.p.

LC 85-3664

"The Hess clan gather in their hometown of Booker Creek, Virginia, upon the death of their matriarch, Miss Elizabeth. There are some serious skeletons in the family closet—sexual abuse, an illegitimate child, a murder. The family history is recounted in turn by relatives spanning four generations, and their narratives reveal both comical attempts to seek solace and bewilderment at the complexity of their lives." Booklist

"This is a companionable, chatty book populated by people who tell us about themselves in a rambling style and with good humor." N Y Times Book Rev

Me and my baby view the eclipse; stories. Putnam 1990 206p o.p.

LC 89-27377

Analyzed in Short story index

Contents: Bob, a dog; Mom; Life on the moon; Tongues of fire; Dreamers; The interpretation of dreams; Desire on Domino Island; Intensive care; Me and my baby view the eclipse

"Tiny explosions, little surprises, minor epihanies pepper the lives of Smith's characters. . . . Revelatory writing from a master storyteller." Libr J

Oral history. Putnam 1983 286p o.p.

LC 82-18081

This "is the tale of the working out of a family curse, the revenge of a red-haired witch spurned by one Almarine Cantrell. Almarine (b.1876), is a subsistence farmer, the owner of all of Hoot Owl Holler in the western corner of Virginia, husband of two women, father of

Smith, Lee, 1944—*Continued*

seven, stepfather of one, grandfather of at least five and a regional figure to reckon with. The story is told in a series of voices and includes mountain neighbors and citizens of nearby Tug and Black Rock." Nation

"Smith is excellent at making the separate voices distinctive. . . . Serious fiction readers will be interested in Smith's techniques and will appreciate her decision to utilize this 'oral history' format to best achieve her intentions." Booklist

Smith, Lillian Eugenia, 1897-1966

Strange fruit; a novel; [by] Lillian Smith. Harcourt Brace & Co. 1944 371p $12.95 o.p.

ISBN 0-15-185769-5

Originally published by Reynal & Hitchcock

This novel, set in a small town in Georgia, is about the love of an educated black girl for a white man. The reaction to this affair results in murder and a lynching

This is a "regional novel, in the finest sense. As such, it offers a magnificently detailed picture of the small-town South, lashed by an urge for self-destruction as old as time. The author has suggested no cure for that urge: you will find no black messiahs here, no white devils." N Y Times Book Rev

Smith, Martin Cruz

Gorky Park. Random House 1981 365p $13.95

ISBN 0-394-51748-2 LC 80-6022

"Chief Investigator Renko of the Moscow police is determined to solve the mystery of the three mutilated bodies in Gorky Park, despite obstruction by other officials. His main help comes from New York police Lt. William Kirwin, in Moscow to find his brother, who turns out to be one of the Gorky Park victims. Renko falls in love with Irina, the major witness in the affair, and is brought with her to New York by agents of both nations to defuse what's become a serious situation." Libr J

The author "has succeeded in rendering very believable, realistic, and gripping portrayals of certain segments of Soviet society and of one man's search for meaning." Christ Sci Monit

Polar Star. Random House 1989 386p il o.p.

LC 88-43232

Available Thorndike Press large print edition

This mystery "finds former Moscow investigator Arkady Renko toiling as a second-class seaman on a Russian factory ship, the *Polar Star*, which is part of a joint U.S.-Soviet fishing venture in the Bering Sea. Labeled 'politically unreliable' after the events of *Gorky Park*, Renko has spent years dodging the KGB in Siberia—hence, his ignominious station on the ship's 'slime line,' gutting and chopping fish. Things change when the body of a Russian girl, who worked in the ship's galley, turns up in a fish net. At first unwillingly, Renko becomes swept up in the investigation, which leads to cocaine trafficking, elaborate espionage plots, and a grisly climax on the ice-covered sea." Booklist

"Rich in humor, generous in spirit, endlessly entertaining and deeply serious, 'Polar Star' is not merely the work of our best writer of suspense, but of one of our best writers, period." N Y Times Book Rev

Red Square. Random House 1992 418p o.p.

LC 92-50166

Available Thorndike Press large print edition

"Just prior to the 1991 attempted coup, [Arkady Renko] finds himself reestablished as an investigator with the Moscow police and struggling to contain a flourishing underworld in the newly democratic Soviet Union. . . . A seemingly straightforward murder investigation leads Arkady first to corruption in high places, then to official censure, and finally to Munich, where he is reunited with Irina, the lover who got him in . . . trouble back in the early 1980s." Booklist

Stallion Gate. Random House 1986 321p $17.95

ISBN 0-394-53006-3 LC 85-24444

"In a New Mexico blizzard, four men cross a barbed-wire fence at Stallion Gate to select the test site for the first atomic weapon. They are Oppenheimer, the physicist; Groves, the general; Fuchs, the spy. The fourth man is Sergeant Joe Peña, a hero, informer, fighter, musician, Indian. Oppenheimer and Groves have hidden Los Alamos on a mesa surrounded by vast Indian reservations. . . . To it come soldiers, roughnecks and scientists, including Anna Weiss, a mathematician and refugee from the Holocaust with whom Joe falls in love." Publisher's note

"Obviously Stallion Gate is not meant to be taken too literally. There is a touch of the folk hero about Peña as he moves across the New Mexican landscape. A conscious stylist, Smith relies strongly on emotional echoes and calibrated suspense." Time

Smith, Robert Kimmel, 1930-

Jane's house. Morrow 1982 344p o.p.

LC 82-2277

"This book is about how one family deals with the loss of a parent. Paul Klein's wife of 18 years, Jane, died suddenly, leaving him to raise their two children, Hilary and Bobby. The first part of the book deals with Paul's slow adjustment to single parenthood, emphasizing the day-to-day problems. Then he meets Ruth, a lively and intelligent advertising woman. They fall in love and marry. The second part of the story is seen mostly through Ruth's eyes, as she tries to gain the children's friendship." Libr J

Sadie Shapiro's knitting book; a novel. Simon & Schuster 1973 190p o.p.

"Sadie, quite possibly the best knitter in the world, sends off some of her patterns to a third-rate male-dominated, publishing house. Inevitably, a 'craftsy book' falls to the lot of the one down-trodden woman editor. She and Sadie and other friends of Sadie at the Mount Eden Citizens Hotel whip up a phenomenal package, a book that triumphs over all odds to become a best seller. Naturally, Sadie being Sadie, there is a fair amount of Jewish mother muddling in other people's lives, but it all works." Publ Wkly

Smith, Rosamond, 1938-
See also Oates, Joyce Carol, 1938-

Smith, Scott B.
A simple plan; a novel. Knopf 1993 335p
$21

ISBN 0-679-41985-3   LC 92-42478

"When Hank Mitchell, his obese, feckless brother Jacob
and Jacob's smarmy friend Lou accidentally find a
wrecked small plane and its dead pilot in the woods
near their small Ohio town, they decide not to tell the
authorities about the $4.4 million stuffed into a duffel
bag. Instead, they agree to hide the money and later
divide it among themselves. The 'simple plan' sets in
motion a spiral of blackmail, betrayal and multiple
murder." Publ Wkly
This novel is so "cunningly imagined that for the most
part Mr. Smith drags us willingly through what in less
deft hands could be a morally repugnant story." N Y
Times Book Rev

Smith, Wilbur A.
The angels weep; [by] Wilbur Smith.
Doubleday 1983 c1982 468p o.p. Trafalgar
Sq. reprint available $29.95 (ISBN
0-434-71414-3)

LC 82-45885

First published 1982 in the United Kingdom
The the third volume in the saga of the Ballantyne
family in Rhodesia. "Part I, which starts in 1895, centers
on the complex relations among various Ballantynes—
preeminently pioneer settler Zouga, his missionary-doctor
sister Robyn and his gold-prospecting son Ralph—and
the diamond-hungry, empire-building Cecil Rhodes. But
it also covers (from an inside perspective) a bloody and
abortive Matabele rebellion and the skulduggery in high
places that precipitated the Boer War. Part II, which is
set in 1977 and might have been called 'African
Revenge,' features the gory transition from Rhodesia to
Zimbabwe and the end of the Ballantynes' 'great African
adventure.'" Publ Wkly
Followed by The leopard hunts in darkness

The burning shore; [by] Wilbur Smith.
Doubleday 1985 420p o.p.

LC 85-4479

"Young Centaine de Thiry falls in love with Michael
Courtney, a South African ace flying for the British in
World War I. Only after she has buried her lover, fallen
in combat, does Centaine discover she will bear his
child. His family generously arranges passage for her to
Cape Town, but a U-boat torpedoes the hospital ship
on which she is journeying. Surviving a desperate struggle
with a man-eating shark, Centaine is washed ashore on
Africa's Skeleton Coast, on the fringe of the Kalahari
Desert. Weak, frightened, and thirst-crazed, she is rescued
by two nomadic aborigines who lead her across the barren sands to a secret paradise where she bears her child."
Publ Wkly
Followed by Power of the sword

The Courtneys; [by] Wilbur Smith. Little,
Brown 1988 c1987 938p $29.95

ISBN 0-316-80182-8   LC 87-83450

An omnibus edition of three titles originally published
separately in the United Kingdom and first published
in the United States in 1964, 1966, and 1978 respectively. This combined edition first published 1987 in the
United Kingdom
Contents: When the lion feeds (c1964); The sound of
thunder (c1966; U.S. title: The roar of thunder); A sparrow falls (c1977)
The hero of these three novels, set in South Africa,
is Sean Courtney. "In *When the Lion Feeds*, Sean's farming days are halted by the threat of Zulu spears, and
he throws himself into a life crowded with passion and
violence. The *Sound of Thunder* sees Sean returning to
civilization a rich man, only to lose his wagon, his gold,
and the girl he loves. When he tries to rebuild his life
in peace, inveterate family hatred and jealousy bring him
conflict more bitter than any he had known in war. .
. . Together these three novels trace the turbulence of
South Africa's formative years through the life of one
powerful and dominant man." Publisher's note

Cry wolf; [by] Wilbur Smith. Doubleday
1977 c1976 401p o.p.

LC 76-50791

First published 1976 in the United Kingdom
"British neer-do-well Gareth Swales and a Texas
mechanic named Jack Barton settle on an arrangement
of self-interests. The year is 1935, the place Tanganyika,
their goal, delivering to Ethiopia armed personnel carriers—for a swollen profit, of course. Amid bantering
dialogue which reveals Gareth to be a delicious character
indeed, the pair plunge northward towards an amorous
intrigue and invading Italians." Publ Wkly

Elephant song; [by] Wilbur Smith.
Random House 1992 c1991 498p il $23

ISBN 0-679-40899-1   LC 91-53113

First published 1991 in the United Kingdom
"Acclaimed documentary filmmaker and African
ecologist Daniel Armstrong vows revenge after a gang
of poachers steals a huge cache of South African
government-protected ivory, in the process brutally killing
Chief Warden Johnny Nzou, Armstrong's childhood
friend, and his family. Tracing the smuggling operation
to its highest source, Armstrong comes up against a
sadistic Chinese diplomat and his profoundly wealthy
clan, an unscrupulous entrepreneur expatriate from India,
a knighted British tycoon, assorted thugs and a torture-
crazed leopard guarding a warehouse." Publ Wkly

Flight of the falcon; [by] Wilbur Smith.
Doubleday 1982 c1980 545p o.p.

LC 81-43328

First published 1980 in the United Kingdom
The first of the author's Ballantyne novels. "In 1854
no medical school in England would enroll a woman
student. Yet, Robyn Ballantyne masqueraded as a male
and obtained her medical degree. With this same determined willfulness Robyn persuades her brother to return
to Africa with her to seek their long-lost missionary
father. Although each pursues a separate goal, they both
find themselves enmeshed in the greed, danger, and
human misery of the African slave trade. Robyn's burning hatred of the slavers also leads her to two men,
though her heart's choice conflicts with her head's
choice." Libr J
Followed by Men of men

Smith, Wilbur A.—*Continued*

Golden fox; [by] Wilbur Smith. Random House 1991 c1990 433p $22

ISBN 0-394-58971-8   LC 90-39062

First published 1990 in the United Kingdom

This novel in the Courtney family series is set in 1969. "Ramón de Santiago y Machado is a fallen Spanish marques working for the KGB and involved with Cuban guerrillas fighting in Africa. He sets his sights on Isabella Courtney, daughter of South African industrialist Shasa Courtney, woos her, and impregnates her, with the hollow promise that he will make things legit as soon as his divorce comes through. It's all a ruse, of course. Ramon's intentions are dastardly, and his superiors abduct the child that is born and blackmail Isabella into helping them sabotage the political and military plans of the white South African government." Booklist

"Smith excels at creating finely drawn characters; descriptive settings in London, Europe, and Africa; and a masterful development of an action-packed thriller that gets better as each new predicament unfolds." SLJ

Hungry as the sea; [by] Wilbur Smith. Doubleday 1980 c1978 395p o.p.

LC 78-22368

First published 1978 in the United Kingdom

"Toppled from his position as chairman of Christy Marine, a worldwide shipping consortium, and losing his wife and son to its new chairman, Nicholas Berg is left with a struggling towing and salvage company." Libr J

"A story of rescue and salvage that keeps the reader prisoner of a narrative told by one who has mastered the arts of pace, description and suspense." Best Sellers

The leopard hunts in darkness; [by] Wilbur Smith. Doubleday 1984 423p o.p. Trafalgar Sq. reprint available $27.50 (ISBN 0-434-71415-1)

LC 84-4078

This volume in the author's Ballantyne saga focuses on "best-selling author Craig Mellow [who] decides to return to his native land for several reasons. He knows a poaching ring is operating to destroy the wildlife that is an African treasure; he suspects this ring is protected by someone high in the government of Zimbabwe. He's been hired by the World Bank to investigate these activities along with reports of a pending Russian-supported coup. He wants to see how his homeland has fared since the Ian Smith regime. Most of all, he is seeking his roots—the links with the past that have provided the raw material for his successful writing." Libr J

Men of men; [by] Wilbur Smith. Doubleday 1983 c1981 578p o.p.

LC 82-45566

First published 1981 in the United Kingdom

This second title in the author's series about the Ballantyne family is set in Southern Africa of the late 19th century and examines how the family is drawn into the empire-building schemes of Cecil Rhodes

"The author's intricately plotted, fast-paced novel describes without prejudice the dreams of the men and women, both European and African, to whom [Africa] was home. The reader comes to know each one and feels the pain of the inevitable conflict." Libr J

Followed by The angels weep

Power of the sword; [by] Wilbur Smith. Little, Brown 1986 618p $19.95

ISBN 0-316-80171-2   LC 86-10279

"The central characters in this robust tale of politics, adventure and romance set in South Africa are stepbrothers Manfred and Shasa, sons of Centaine Courtney (from 'The Burning Shore'), owner of a diamond mine. As representatives, respectively, of the Afrikaner cause and that of the more liberal, English-speaking whites, headed in the early days by Jan Smuts, they are, however, destined to be enemies. . . . What Smith may lack in subtlety, he makes up for in raw vigor." Publ Wkly

Followed by Rage

Rage; by Wilbur Smith. Little, Brown 1987 627p $19.95

ISBN 0-316-80179-8   LC 87-3078

This novel in the Courtney family saga is set in post-World War II South Africa. "Shasa Courtney is a wealthy United Party minister to the South African Parliament. A moderate of English heritage, he is often opposed to the Nationalist Party's Manfred De La Rey, an Afrikaner. Their mother, the matriarchal Centaine Courtney-Malcomess, is able to mediate their conflicts but not to control Shasa's wife, Tara, who . . . falls in love with the black Moses Gama, an advocate of violent opposition to apartheid." Publ Wkly

"The interlocking stories of these and many others, set against the authentic African historical and cultural background that Smith so effectively provides, produces both a compelling tale and some real insights into South Africa." Libr J

Followed by A time to die

River god; [by] Wilbur Smith. St. Martin's Press 1994 c1993 530p $24.95

ISBN 0-312-10612-2   LC 93-45249

"A Thomas Dunne book"

First published 1993 in the United Kingdom

This novel, set in Egypt ca.1780 B.C., "tells the story of Taita the eunuch, slave to a noble's daughter. Taita narrates the dramatic events of which he was either witness or participant as his mistress receives the dubious honor of marriage to the pharaoh. The brutality of life in ancient times is everywhere evident in Taita's tale, which involves fatal intrigue at every turn. It's clear Smith knows his subject: his graphic depiction of lust, bloodletting, politics, and, in Taita's case, honor is firmly grounded in rich details that evoke the period." Booklist

The sound of thunder

In Smith, W. A. The Courtneys p[297]-601

A sparrow falls

In Smith, W. A. The Courtneys p[603]-938

A time to die; [by] Wilbur Smith. Random House 1990 c1989 448p $19.95

ISBN 0-394-58475-9   LC 89-27360

First published 1989 in the United Kingdom

This novel in the Courtney family saga, focuses on "Sean Courtney, Rhodesian African Rifles officer turned big-game hunter. Leading a safari on his licensed land in Africa, Courtney is lured over the Mozambique border in pursuit of a long-sought elephant trophy, for which his client promises him half a million dollars. Courtney

Smith, Wilbur A.—*Continued*
turns into the quarry, however, when a Mozambiquan guerrilla leader kidnaps the client's daughter, Claudia, and forces Courtney into abetting the rebel cause. A few stolen American-made missiles and the devastation of a Soviet-equipped helicopter base later, Courtney and Claudia are fleeing for their lives through the African wilderness." Booklist

Followed by Golden fox

When the lion feeds

In Smith, W. A. The Courtneys p[5]-295

Smollett, Tobias George, 1721-1771
Humphry Clinker; an authoritative text, contemporary responses, criticism; edited by James L. Thorson. Norton 1983 xxi, 436p o.p.

LC 81-18724

First published 1771 with title: The expedition of Humphry Clinker

In this epistolary novel "the letters are written by Matthew Bramble, his sister Tabitha, their niece, their nephew, and their maid, Winifred Jenkins. Each correspondent has a highly individual style and caricatures himself unwittingly. The titular hero of this comic masterpiece, who plays a lesser role than the Brambles, is a workhouse lad who enters into their service by chance and who later becomes a Methodist preacher. He falls in love with Winifred, and is eventually found to be the natural son of Mr. Bramble. The 'expedition' of the title is a family tour through England and Scotland, during which the correspondents express surprisingly varied reactions to the same events. Of particular note is the picture of Hot Wells (a sobriquet for the city of Bath), a fashionable watering place." Reader's Ency. 3d edition

Sneider, Vern, 1916-1981
The Teahouse of the August Moon. Putnam 1951 282p o.p.

This "novel centers around Captain Fisby, member of a Government Team in Okinawa, his colonel, and Plan B for the welfare of the natives. The plan would have gone according to schedule if Fisby hadn't received a gift of two geishas, and if Miss Higa Jiga and other maiden ladies hadn't felt they must compete on an equitable basis with the geishas. The chicanery of the ladies, and Fisby's coping with the situation make this a wonderfully humorous and satirical story." Libr J

Snow, C. P. (Charles Percy), 1905-1980
The affair. Scribner 1960 374p (Strangers and brothers) o.p.

One of the Strangers and brothers series of eleven novels set in England during the first half of the the 20th century. The series is "a sequence of novels comprising the life story of the narrator Lewis Eliot and alternating between his direct and observed experience." Publisher's note

"A novel set in one of England's important universities, the central situation is the dismissal of a young scientist accused of fraud. A re-opening of his case splits the university wide open, both for moral and for political reasons." Publ Wkly

A coat of varnish. Scribner 1979 328p $10.95

ISBN 0-684-16315-2   LC 79-16221

A Scotland yard detective investigates a murder in 1976 London. "The fashionable setting and all but one of the characters serve the author's purpose of social criticism and also generate dramatic tension." Barzun. Cat of Crime. Rev and enl edition

The conscience of the rich. Scribner 1958 342p (Strangers and brothers) o.p.

"As a result of his friendship with Charles March, Lewis Eliot is taken into the private world of one of England's wealthiest and most influential Jewish families and through his eyes the March drama is slowly unfolded; the close bond between Charles, his father, and his sister, Charles's marriage to a gentle Communist, and the ensuing political scandal which estranges father and son, brother and sister. . . . Set in London during the late 1920's and the 1930's." Booklist

Corridors of power. Scribner 1964 403p (Strangers and brothers) o.p.

"The workings of inner power in the British government—with key administrators, politicians, and the wealthy manipulators, male and female—[are] traced in a novel of the period 1955-1958. . . . Since the power in this fictional case is concerned with the use of nuclear arms, the fate of the world can easily hang on the fate of one minister, Roger Quaife." Publ Wkly

"We see the corridors of political power illuminated with a fine and discriminating light." Libr J

Death under sail. Doubleday 1932 307p o.p.

"Six close friends of Dr. Roger Mills join him on his yacht for two weeks of sailing and partying. But on the morning of the first day's sailing Roger is found shot to death. . . . Arriving on the scene . . . is Finbow, a civil servant from Hong Kong, who . . . methodically eliminates one suspect after another. But as he nears the identification of the murderer, there are new twists." Best Sellers

Homecoming. Scribner 1956 399p (Strangers and brothers) o.p.

"An introspective, subtly shaded novel which again stars Lewis Eliot. . . . Eliot's unhappy marriage to a neurotic woman, her death, and his affair with and eventual marriage to a woman more worthy of his love comprise the chief incidents in a story that accents not the events themselves but their psychological effect upon the persons involved. Crisp, carefully fashioned prose; for the discriminating." Booklist

Last things. Scribner 1970 435p (Strangers and brothers) o.p.

"Student protest, Lewis Eliot's decision on whether or not to enter the Labor government's ministry, his serious eye operation during which a cardiac arrest brings him near to death—these are some of the essential plot elements [of this novel]." Publ Wkly

The light and the dark. Scribner 406p (Strangers and brothers) $22.25

ISBN 0-684-14841-2

"Hudson River editions"

First published 1947 in the United Kingdom; first Scribner edition published 1961

Cambridge University is the scene of the greater part

Snow, C. P. (Charles Percy), 1905-1980—
Continued

of this character study of a young Cambridge don. In an attempt to curb his dark moods Roy tries promiscuity, drink, concentration on his studies, and religion. With the out-break of the war he joins the RAF and is killed in action

"A painstaking and readable account of university life seen from high table." Times Lit Suppl

The malcontents. Scribner 1972 277p o.p.

"Seven youthful, intelligent, deeply committed political activists—'malcontents' who call their secret society the 'core'—intrigue to embarrass the English political establishment by exposing institutional racism. Their plans fail. They are compromised politically and betrayed from within. Who among the trusted cell is guilty?" Choice

The author "examines the motives of social revolt amongst the young . . . sympathetically, but perhaps with a certain complacency." Christ Sci Monit

The masters. Scribner 374p (Strangers and brothers) $20

ISBN 0-684-14744-0
"Hudson River editions"
First published 1951

"Lewis Eliot, a Cambridge Fellow, tells about the election of a new Master of his college, and uses the rivalry and jealousy attendant on the election to illuminate the lives and hearts of the candidates and their friends and enemies. The book begins with notice of the impending death of the old Master, Vernon Royce, continues at a leisurely rate as Royce waits to die and finally dies, and ends with the election of the new Master." New Yorker

"For a quiet novel of subtle characterization this one contains a surprising element of suspense." Ont Libr Rev

The new men. Scribner 1954 311p (Strangers and brothers) o.p.

The novel describes a group of nuclear scientists and high government officials working together in England during the war. As usual Lewis Eliot is the narrator

The author "handles a fateful new theme with challenging insight and impressive moral sensitivity. . . . [This is a] novel which searchingly explores the moral dilemmas created by the atom bomb." Atlantic

The sleep of reason. Scribner 1969 c1968 483p (Strangers and brothers) o.p.

The book "brings back Sir Lewis Eliot, now retired, 58, living in London. In the nearby university town of his birth, in the midst of his own personal crises of health and family, the concentric circles of his life—past, present, and future—merge to thrust upon him a new and problematical responsibility, one that he finds revolts, horrifies, and fascinates him. The lesbian niece of an old friend is on trial with her lover for the grisly abduction, torture and murder of an eight-year-old boy. Sir Lewis attends the trial at his friend's request, and the trial, the peak of the book, throws into relief some specific and general problems of our age. The two murderesses are seen as miniscule reincarnations of what went on at Auschwitz. Snow ponders the whys, hows, wherefores of such inhuman behavior, and the roles of the courts, medicine, psychiatry, law, the non-participating onlookers." Publ Wkly

Strangers and brothers. Scribner 309p (Strangers and brothers) $39

ISBN 0-684-15367-X

"Hudson River editions"
First published 1940 in the United Kingdom; first Scribner edition published 1960

This is also the title of the three volume omnibus edition of the series published 1972 by Scribner. In the collected edition this volume was renamed George Passant

George Passant, a solicitor in an English provincial town, exerts a crucial influence on his group of young protegés, Lewis Eliot among them. An idealist, courageous and high-principled Passant seems destined for great things yet the story ends in his trial for fraud. The reasons for this are revealed

"Essentially the tragedy of a good man defeated by the mediocrity of his world, the story of George Passant is completed in the novel 'Homecoming.' . . . Like all the novels in the series, 'Strangers and Brothers' is distinguished by virtue of its analysis of motive and character and its anatomization of a world in which a smooth mediocrity is the greatest virtue." Libr J

Time of hope. Scribner 408p (Strangers and brothers) $22.25

ISBN 0-684-15315-7
"Hudson River editions"
First published 1950 by Macmillan; first Scribner edition published 1961

"Here, as in *Light and the Dark* (1948) Lewis Eliot is the main character that typifies middle class English life, and as in the earlier work, Mr. Snow shows the impact of spiritual values on individuals. The 1930s are the background here and the years are brilliantly drawn. Moral problems are vivid and the characters are varied in their reactions." Libr J

Snow, Charles Percy *See* Snow, C. P. (Charles Percy), 1905-1980

Snow white, blood red; edited by Ellen Datlow & Terri Windling. Morrow 1992 411p $22

ISBN 0-688-10913-6   LC 92-24899

"An AvoNova book"
Analyzed in Short story index

Contents: Like a red, red rose, by S. Wade; The moon is drowning while I sleep, by C. de Lint; The frog prince, by G. Wilson; Stalking beans, by N. Kress; Snowdrop, by T. Lee; Little red, by W. Wheeler; I shall do thee mischief in the wood, by K. Koja; The root of the matter, by G. Frost; The princess in the tower, by E. A. Lynn; Persimmon, by H. Jacobs; Little Poucet, by S. R. Tem; The changelings, by M. Tem; The Springfield swans, by C. Stevermer; Troll bridge, by N. Gaiman; A sound, like angels singing, by L. Rysdyk; Puss, by E. M. Friesner; The glass casket, by J. Dann; Knives, by J. Yolen; The snow queen, by P. A. McKillip; Breadcrumbs and stones, by L. Goldstein

"The dark and shadowed aspects of well-known folk stories and fairy tales are explored in updated retellings. . . . Some of these tales are enchanting; some are horrifying; most, like the originals, offer insight into human nature." Publ Wkly

Solomita, Stephen

Force of nature. Putnam 1989 282p il o.p.
LC 89-30949

Solomita, Stephen—*Continued*

"Long-time New York City police detective Stanley Moodrow 'selects' a suitable partner to succeed him as he nears retirement. He and Jim Tilley, only 27 and an ex-boxer, search their precinct for crack-crazy Levander 'Kubla Khan' Greenwood, inveterate drug dealer, wife-abuser, thief, and cop-killer. As the two proceed, Moodrow teaches Tilley how he operates so successfully, Tilley falls for Greenwood's beautiful wife, and the intricate plan to trap Greenwood evolves. . . . Graphic, wisely observant, violent, and totally absorbing." Libr J

A good day to die. Penzler Bks. 1993 297p $21

ISBN 1-883402-03-4   LC 93-19400
Also available G.K. Hall large print edition

"Roland Means, a chronic maverick in the NYPD, is pulled from cop purgatory—ballistics duty—to go after 'King Thong,' the supposed serial killer responsible for the murder of seven male prostitutes in New York City. Vanessa Bouton, a black cop, hates Means's guts but needs his streetwise methods to help prove her hunch that only one killing was prompted by a motive, which the other six are meant to mask." Publ Wkly

"As Means researches the profiled backgrounds of serial killers, he recognizes his own abused childhood; his search for the killer becomes a search for himself. This multiethnic thriller vividly depicts the gritty streets of the city, the dark and feral forest, and the danger lurking in both." Libr J

Last chance for glory. Penzler Bks. 1994 310p $21

ISBN 1-883402-27-1   LC 93-38616

"Marty Blake, an out-of-work private investigator, is hired to help clear the name of a slightly retarded young man wrongly convicted of murder. To aid in the investigation, Marty contacts Sgt. Bela Kosinski, the original arresting officer, who is now retired from the NYPD and drinking himself to death. As this unlikely pair reinvestigate the murder, they find it easy to prove the young man's innocence, but they also discover a murder cover-up that extends into the highest echelons of the police force and New York City government." Libr J

"Blake and Kosinski initially form an uneasy alliance that inevitably turns to friendship, but it happens easily and believably. It's the old mismatched-partner plot, but seldom has it been handled better." Booklist

A piece of the action. Putnam 1992 271p o.p.

LC 91-43155

"It's 1957, and after winning a boxing match at which he represents the police department, beat cop Moodrow is rewarded with a promotion to the rank of detective. His 'rabbi,' or mentor, is inspector Pat Cohan, a proud Irish cop who has been on the take for years—a fact Moodrow is unaware of. Cohan allows Moodrow to court his daughter, Kathleen, and the young cop couldn't be happier—until a neighbor asks him to inquire about a homicide that the police don't seem interested in solving. . . . Solomita offers a well-plotted narrative and nicely evokes New York City a generation ago. This is hard-boiled police fiction at its best." Publ Wkly

A twist of the knife. Putnam 1988 288p o.p.

LC 88-9769

"As Detective Sgt. Stanley Moodrow tracks the killers of his girlfriend throughout Manhattan, vowing revenge, members of the American Red Army, a politically motivated terrorist group, design ruthless, random attacks that leave the police at loose ends." Libr J

The author's "quirkily matter-of-fact style captures perfectly the resignation and even acceptance that true New Yorkers use to describe a place that makes the Inferno seem like a day at the beach." Booklist

Solzhenitsyn, Aleksandr, 1918-

Nobel Prize in literature, 1970

August 1914; translated by Harry T. Willets. Farrar, Straus & Giroux 1989 854p (Red wheel/knot 1) o.p.

LC 88-30966

Original Russian edition published 1971 in France; this is an expanded and newly translated version of the title first published 1972 in the United States

Set at the outbreak of the First World War, this novel, the first in a projected series, explores the responsibility for Russia's defeat in the Battle of Tannenberg

"For at least 20 years Mr. Solzhenitsyn has been working on a vast cycle of novels called 'The Red Wheel,' which he envisages as a panorama of modern Russia, but still more as a corrective to what he regards as the distortions of Russian history by writers contaminated with liberal and radical ideas. . . . The book forms the opening volume of 'The Red Wheel,' which is structured as a series of what the author calls 'knots,' or renderings of crucial historical moments that have determined the course of Russian, perhaps all of modern, history." NY Times Book Rev

Cancer ward; translated by Nicholas Bethell and David Burg. Modern Lib. 1984 c1969 560p $20

ISBN 0-394-60499-7   LC 83-42701

This translation first published 1969 by Farrar, Straus & Giroux

"Set mostly in a provincial cancer ward, the novel traces the ways in which a number of moribund patients come to terms with their death, centering on an investigation of the moral and psychological development of the exiled hero, Kostoglotov. This novel, in which the cancer ward has been widely interpreted as symbolizing the Soviet state, was typeset for publication in the Soviet Union but never published there." Reader's Ency. 3d edition

The first circle; translated from the Russian by Thomas P. Whitney. Harper & Row 1968 580p o.p. Borgo Press reprint available $41 (ISBN 0-8095-9000-X)

This novel "depicts life in a *sharashka*, i.e., a prison for educated people who carry on scientific research while serving long terms. Encompassing a span of only three days, this long novel both traces the ineluctable apprehension of Innokenty Artemyevich Vologin, a state counselor in the Ministry of Foreign Affairs, and recreates, in an integrated web of short chapters, the daily routine and moral condition of the highly educated inmates of the *sharashka*. The experiences of the hero, Nerzhin, parallel those of the author, while the character of Lev Rubin, the longtime Party member who maintains his faith in the Communist ideal despite the injustices done to him and his fellows, is modeled on Lev

Solzhenitsyn, Aleksandr, 1918-——*Continued*
Kopelev, a central figure in the civil rights movement
of the 1960s and 1970s." Reader's Ency. 3d edition

One day in the life of Ivan Denisovich;
translated from the Russian by H. T. Willets; with an introduction by John Bayley.
Knopf 1995 xxvii, 159p $15

ISBN 0-679-44464-5
"Everyman's library"
Original Russian edition, 1962; this is a reissue of the
translation published 1991 by Farrar, Straus, Giroux
"Drawing on his own experiences, the author writes
of one day, from reveille to lights-out, in the prison
existence of Ivan Denisovich Shukhov. Innocent of any
crime, he has been convicted of treason and sentenced
to ten years in one of Stalin's notorious slave-labor com-
pounds. The protagonist is a simple man trying to survive the brutality of a totalitarian system." Shapiro. Fic
for Youth. 3d edition

Somers, Jane *See* Lessing, Doris May, 1919-

Somtow, S. P.
Jasmine nights. St. Martin's Press 1995
379p $23.95

ISBN 0-312-11834-1   LC 94-33715
"A Wyatt book"
This is the "story of a precocious Thai growing up
in 1963 on an isolated estate with three eccentric, strict
aunts. The 12-year-old narrator, a cunning if naïve
recluse named Justin, learns the art of adaptation, a skill
he will sorely need, from his pet chameleon, Homer. His
parents absent for many years, may be CIA agents in
Vietnam; his senile great-grandmother enacts scenes from
Hitchcock's *Psycho*; and each of his aunts is secretly
bedding the rakish family doctor. Meanwhile, Justin's
treehouse playmate, Virgil, a black American from Georgia, oscillates between vernacular 'Black English' and
WASP-like diction, puncturing the racial stereotypes and
prejudices of his and Justin's two comrades—one
Afrikaner, one white American—and of Justin's aunts.
. . . Even if the satire wears thin as incongruities pile
up, Somtow's manic comic energy and gift for human
drama power a novel of abundant riches." Publ Wkly

Sontag, Susan, 1933-
The volcano lover; a romance. Farrar,
Straus & Giroux 1992 419p il $22

ISBN 0-374-28516-0   LC 92-71738
"The 'volcano lover' of the title is Sir William Hamilton, the British diplomat and antiquary who is best
remembered as the complaisant husband of Emma
Hamilton, notorious mistress of Admiral Nelson. The
book is set for the most part in Naples, where, from
1764 until his recall under a cloud in 1800, Sir William
was the British envoy to the court of the egregious Bourbon monarch Ferdinand IV, later to become Ferdinand
I, King of the Two Sicilies. . . . The novel is a kind
of triptych, divided among Hamilton, his wife and Lord
Nelson." N Y Times Book Rev
Sontag's "narrative deftly blends the magnetism of personality and the suspense of event with shrewd commentary and sly mockery as she contrasts the habits of
thought in that age with ours and reflects on the
meaning of mercy and vengeance, self-invention and

praise, love and obsession. In all, a memorable group
portrait and a brilliant, fresh improvisation on classically
grand themes." Booklist

Spark, Muriel
The Abbess of Crewe. Viking 1974 116p
o.p.
Set in the convent of Crewe in England, this novel
traces the efforts of Sister Alexandra to win the elective
position of abbess. "The problem is Sister Felicity, who
has a following amongst the nuns. But Felicity has committed certain indiscretions, and Alexandra and her supporters are able to discredit her." Christ Sci Monit
"The Abbess of Crewe has the closely woven texture
and the structural coherence of good poetry: it is executed with a subtlety and intelligence that safeguard
against the tones of complacent moralizing that might
very easily have spoiled the articulation of the book's
themes." Saturday Rev/World

The ballad of Peckham Rye. Lippincott
1960 160p o.p.
"Young Dougal Douglas, the Devil in contemporary
clothing, has quite an impact on an industrial town adjacent to London since, among other things, he is
responsible for a groom leaving his bride-to-be at the
altar and the nervous breakdown of a veteran employee
in one of the local factories." Booklist
"A fresh comic style does not appear every day, and
that is what Muriel Spark has developed in this expert
fantasy. . . . The wackiness is cumulative, the style deadpan and blow-by-blow, and above all no overt attempt
is ever made to get a laugh." N Y Times Book Rev

also in Spark, M. A Muriel Spark trio
p233-386

The comforters
In Spark, M. A Muriel Spark trio
p13-228

The driver's seat. Knopf 1970 117p o.p.
Originally published in the New Yorker, this is the
story of "Lise, a fascinatingly eccentric, pent-up creature
whose vacation in the South of Europe turns into a
macabre disaster, one she herself helps to bring about."
Choice
"The author's perspective is cosmically cool and fantastic: she knows no more about her protagonist, Lise,
than does the reader. . . . She follows this woman,
another of her slightly bizarre lunatics, through a day's
grotesque project, narrating only its circumstances, leaving
all motive, all emotion, all inner plan to be inferred.
The result is a long, elusive joke that casts as deep an
irony on life's arbitrariness as do the more 'compassionate' ironies of, say, E. M. Forster." Nation

A far cry from Kensington. Houghton
Mifflin 1988 189p o.p.
LC 88-5904
"The narrator, Mrs. Hawkins, remembers back to 1954
when she was a young war widow living in furnished
rooms in a boarding house in South Kensington, London.
Mrs. Hawkins was the unwitting confidante of her fellow
boarders and coworkers—she was an editor but lost two
jobs because of standing up against a writer she believed
was a hack. This same man intruded into her private
life as well." Booklist

Spark, Muriel—*Continued*

"Spark balances devastatingly eccentric characters and funny situations with darker elements, even pathos. Her well-constructed novel has no loose ends and few contrived situations." Libr J

The girls of slender means. Knopf 1963 176p o.p.

"The novel, set primarily in London during World War II, focuses on the inhabitants of a residential club for unmarried women and on the friendship of several of them with a young man named Nicholas Farringdon. When tragedy strikes and 13 of the women are killed, Nicholas realizes that there is no safety anywhere, especially for those on whom fortune had once seemed to smile. This epiphany stimulates his conversion to Roman Catholicism. Years later, he dies in Haiti, where he has gone as a missionary." Merriam-Webster's Ency of Lit

The go-away bird

In Spark, M. The stories of Muriel Spark p221-62

Memento mori. Lippincott 1959 c1958 224p o.p.

"Several elderly London friends receive anonymous telephone calls with a single message: 'Remember you must die.' Each hears and interprets the words differently. Old rivalries and romances still color the friends' relations, and Spark makes clear that their personalities in old age are but a continuation of their earlier lives." Merriam-Webster's Ency of Lit

also in Spark, M. A Muriel Spark trio p393-608

A Muriel Spark trio; The comforters; The ballad of Peckham Rye; Memento mori. Lippincott 1962 608p o.p.

The three complete novels reprinted here were first published 1957, 1960 and 1959 respectively. The first title is a novel in experimental form. It is a book within a book, in which many of the characters are neurotics or oddities of some sort. The most normal character is Louisa Jepp, aged seventy-eight, whose experiments with smuggling diamonds provide much of the action. The scene is England, and Roman Catholic life is part of the background

The second and third titles are entered separately

The prime of Miss Jean Brodie. Lippincott 1962 c1961 187p o.p.

First published 1961 in the United Kingdom

"Miss Jean Brodie, teacher at the Marcia Blaine School for Girls in Edinburgh in the 1930s, gathers around herself a group of young girls who are set apart from other students as the Brodie set: Monica Douglas, who will be famous for her mathematical ability; Rose Stanley, who will be famous for her sex appeal; Eunice Gardiner, of great swimming and gymnastic ability; Sandy Stranger, of the small eyes and outstanding vowel sounds; and Mary MacGregor, who is considered a silent lump. Miss Brodie will make these girls the 'crème de la crème,' especially if they will follow her advice to recognize their prime. Her teaching is unorthodox and her relationship with the students most informal, so that they are privy to her affair with the school's music teacher. We get glimpses into the future of these young girls and are made aware that students are capable of treachery as well as teacher-worship." Shapiro. Fic for Youth. 3d edition

The stories of Muriel Spark. Dutton 1985 314p o.p.

LC 85-10355

Analyzed in Short story index

"The present volume combines the stories from three previous collections (Collected Stories I (1968); The Go-Away Bird (1961), Voices at Play (1962) with others, more recent, which have so far appeared only in The New Yorker or Mademoiselle." New Repub

Contents: The Portobello Road; The curtain blown by the breeze; The Black Madonna; Bang-bang you're dead; The Seraph and the Zambesi; The twins; The Playhouse called Remarkable; The pawnbroker's wife; Miss Pinkerton's apocalypse; A sad tale's best for winter; The leaf-sweeper; Daisy Overend; You should have seen the mess; Come along, Marjorie; The ormolu clock; The dark glasses; A member of the family; The house of the famous poet; The father's daughters; Alice Long's dachshunds; The go-away bird; The first year of my life; The Gentile Jewesses; The executor; The fortune-teller; Another pair of hands; The Dragon

Spellman, Cathy Cash

Paint the wind. Delacorte Press 1990 713p o.p.

LC 89-35050

"The tale opens with Fancy Deverell, a little Louisiana girl of genteel heritage, losing her parents to the carnage resulting from the Confederacy's fall to Union forces. As the nation puts its life back together, so does Fancy gather and repair the fragments of her own. Joining a circus train, she proceeds westward, eventually meeting up with the brothers McAllister, who were raised in a cabin in Kansas and driven by frontier urges to make good. Married life for Fancy brings fortune, then ruination; in the final act, she finds peace of soul and heart." Booklist

The author "blends New Age mysticism with the roaring Wild West of saloons, whorehouses and noble Indians in a vibrantly colored yarn that is good entertainment." Publ Wkly

Spencer, Elizabeth

Knights and dragons

In Spencer, E. The stories of Elizabeth Spencer p127-218

The light in the piazza. McGraw-Hill 1960 110p o.p.

"Clara, a young woman in her twenties, has the mentality of a child as the result of an accident. Her mother is delighted when Fabrizio, a young Italian, begins to court Clara, and she rationalizes that the marriage will be a successful one in spite of Clara's handicap. The union is arranged with Fabrizio's father—at a price." Shapiro. Fic for Youth. 3d edition

"This is a very-well-told story, very lucid and very smooth; although slight in treatment it has a good deal of substance to it." New Statesman

The stories of Elizabeth Spencer; with a foreword by Eudora Welty. Doubleday 1981 429p o.p.

LC 79-6601

Spencer, Elizabeth—*Continued*

Analyzed in Short story index

The stories included in this collection were written between 1944 and 1977 and were originally published in various periodicals. The novelette Knights & dragons was published separately in 1965 by McGraw-Hill. It concerns an American divorcee living in Rome. Other stories in the collection are: The little brown child; The eclipse; First dark; A southern landscape; Moon rocket; The white azalea; The visit; Ship Island; The fishing lake; The adult holiday; The Pincian gate; The absence; The day before; The Bufords; Judith Kane; Wisteria; A bad cold; Presents; On the Gulf; Sharon; The finder; Instrument of destruction; Go South in the winter; A kiss at the door; A Christian education; Mr. McMillan; I, Maureen; Prelude to a parking lot; Indian summer; The search; Port of embarkation: The girl who loved horses

Spencer, LaVyrle

Bitter sweet. Putnam 1990 382p o.p.

LC 89-38089

"The untimely death of her husband leaves Maggie Pearson wealthy but emotionally bereft. Two decades after she has left home, Maggie returns to Wisconsin to fortify her spirits and decides to open a bed-and-breakfast despite dire warnings from her tight-lipped mother and the hurt fury of her college-age daughter. Her first love, Eric Severson, is also back in town, running a family-owned charter fishing boat to the great displeasure of his beautiful, ambitious wife." Publ Wkly

"Readers who can accept the plausibility of Maggie's original separation from Eric will enjoy following her journey of self-discovery and reawakening." Booklist

Family blessings. Putnam 1994 384p $22.95

ISBN 0-399-13906-0   LC 93-32685

"Lee Reston answers her front door and learns that her son, Greg, has been killed in an accident. Chris Lallek, Greg's roommate and fellow police officer, brings the news and grieves with the Reston family. Lee, a widow who has already lost one son, tries to be strong for her remaining children and for Chris. Chris refuses to let her shoulder her grief alone, and through shared memories, the two are drawn closer together, first as friends and then as lovers. . . . Spencer delivers a moving novel, which revives memories of the loss of loved ones and allows a resolution of feelings and a sense of peace." Booklist

Forgiving. Putnam 1991 382p o.p.

LC 90-42821

Available G.K. Hall large print edition

"Sarah Merritt arrives in Deadwood, Dakota territory, in 1876 with her father's printing press and two ambitions—to find her sister Addie and to establish a local newspaper. In a town of mining bachelors, Sarah quickly becomes the center of attention in more ways than one, particularly when she knocks heads with marshal Noah Campbell, her soon-to-be romantic interest. Sarah finds Addie working in a local brothel and commences a long struggle to win back her affection and her soul." Publ Wkly

"Bowing to the formulaic demands of historical romance without descending into parody or cliché, Spencer gives us an interesting, titillating story peopled by intriguingly human characters." Booklist

Home song. Putnam 1995 366p $23.95

ISBN 0-399-14014-X   LC 94-24852

Also available G.K. Hall large print edition

"When transfer student Kent Arens enrolls at Tom's suburban St. Paul school, Tom realizes that Kent's mother, Monica, is the college acquaintance he took to bed the night of his bachelor party in a brief rebellion against having to marry his pregnant girlfriend, Claire; Kent is the son the principal didn't know he had. Tom delays telling English teacher Claire and children Robby, a senior, and Chelsea, a junior, this secret, until Kent and Chelsea appear to be attracted to one another." Booklist

Spencer, Scott

Endless love. Knopf 1979 417p o.p.

LC 79-2089

"A 17-year-old boy, David Axelrod, forbidden to see his girl friend, Jade Butterfield, for 30 days because their love affair has become too intense, sets fire to the Butterfield house on an impulse. That act changes everyone's life: the Butterfield family is scattered, and David is sent to a mental institution and forbidden ever to contact them. This novel is a record of the subsequent ten years of David's life, and his one goal of being reunited with Jade." Libr J

The author "has achieved something quite remarkable in this unabashedly romantic and often harrowing novel. He has created an adolescent love that is believably endless. . . . Mr. Spencer has an acute grasp of character and situation. He gives us details that make these often tormented people uncommonly convincing." N Y Times Book Rev

Men in black; a novel. Knopf 1995 321p $23

ISBN 0-679-43452-6   LC 95-2669

"Sam Holland's life is mired in failure. Constantly aware of his inadequacies as a son, husband, father, and writer, he is made even more uneasy by a quirky success. His book on UFOs, written for quick money, suddenly propels him onto the best-sellers lists. Ironically, the status he has longed for is now an embarrassment. As he is pulled into a semicelebrity world of book tours and publicity, his family comes apart. His runaway son winds up cavorting with petty criminals, his wife suffers from her own estrangements, and his former lover is pregnant." Libr J

"In other hands, this could be a trite story, but Spencer's wry take on moral values, midlife crisis and family relationships shows a mature and thoughtful writer at work." Publ Wkly

Spielberg, Steven, 1947-

Close encounters of the third kind; a novel. Delacorte Press 1977 256p o.p.

LC 77-12922

Novelization of Spielberg's motion picture

Roy Neary, a young engineer, finds his whole life altered on the night of a strange local blackout. His investigations of the mysterious forces behind the power failure lead him far and wide until finally one day on a high mountain in Wyoming he witnesses the strangest sight

Spurlock, Clark *See* Stuart, Colin

St. Claire, Erin, 1948-
For works written by this author under other names see Brown, Sandra, 1948-

Stafford, Jean, 1915-1979
The collected stories of Jean Stafford. Farrar, Straus & Giroux 1969 463p $30

ISBN 0-374-12632-1
Analyzed in Short story index
Contents: Maggie Meriwether's rich experience; The children's game; The echo and the nemesis; The maiden; A modest proposal; Caveat emptor; Life is no abyss; The hope chest; Polite conversation; A country love story; The bleeding heart; The lippia lawn; The interior castle; The healthiest girl in town; The tea time of stouthearted ladies; The mountain day; The darkening moon; Bad characters; In the zoo; The liberation; A reading problem; A summer day; The philosophy lesson; Children are bored on Sunday; Beatrice Trueblood's story; Between the porch and the altar; I love someone; Cops and robbers; The captain's gift; The end of a career

Stark, Richard
For works written by this author under other names see Westlake, Donald E.

Stavans, Ilan
(ed) Growing up Latino. See Growing up Latino

Stead, Christina, 1902-1983
The little hotel; a novel. Holt, Rinehart & Winston 1975 c1973 191p o.p.

First published 1973 in the United Kingdom
This novel is set in "the late 1940s in Montreux, Switzerland. Its characters are obscure, forgotten folk, ailing or in hiding within the genteel but thin walls of a cheap pension-hotel called the Swiss Touring. While the men worry the bank clerks over falling exchange rates, the women eat, shop and gossip with the proprietress, Selda Bonnard, who becomes the novel's narrator by virtue of listening to their stories." Nation
Stead "is above all else an enthusiast for living, monstrous and ridiculous as human vanity may make it, and she refuses to let her characters admit defeat. . . . The Little Hotel will do as well as any of her books to remind the public that Miss Stead is a magnificent and truly original novelist." Times Lit Suppl

The man who loved children; with an introduction by Doris Lessing. Knopf 1995 xxxvii, 529p $22

ISBN 0-679-44364-9
"Everyman's library"
A reissue of the title first published 1940 by Simon & Schuster
"Unfolding a harrowing portrait of a disintegrating family, Stead examines the hostility between a husband and wife: Sam Pollit, revealed to be a tyrannical crank far removed from the civilized man he thinks he is, whose claim to love his children lends the ironic title; and Henny, who has become a bitter virago." Merriam-Webster's Ency of Lit

Stearn, Jess
(jt. auth) Caldwell, T. I, Judas

Steel, Danielle
Accident. Delacorte Press 1994 305p $23.95

ISBN 0-385-30602-4   LC 93-31272
Also available large print edition $28.95 (ISBN 0-385-31116-8)
This novel is set in "California's plush Marin County. Page Clarke, devoted wife of Brad and mother of Allyson and Andy, finds her golden life shattered when 15-year-old Allyson sneaks off with friend Chloe to meet two boys. In a subsequent head-on collision, one boy is killed, Chloe is seriously injured and Allyson lapses into a coma. Page can't reach Brad, who confesses when he comes home that he is having an affair. Stunned and hurt, Page keeps a vigil at Allyson's bedside while also coping with needy seven-year-old Andy and an ambivalent husband who can't decide whether to stay or leave. Her only support comes from Chloe's father, Trygve Thorensen." Publ Wkly
"A touching, satisfying romance sung, for the most part, in perfect tune." Booklist

The gift. Delacorte Press 1994 216p $15
ISBN 0-385-31292-X   LC 94-439
"It's 1952, and the Whittakers are the perfect happy family. But when five-year-old Annie dies of meningitis the day after Christmas, their lives fall apart. Teenager Tommy begins frequenting a diner where he meets 16-year-old waitress Maribeth Robertson, who's pregnant and has been thrown out of her home. The two lonely adolescents slowly fall in love." Publ Wkly
"Clichéd, sentimental? Maybe, but Steel *believes* in the goodness of her characters and here, more than ever before, shows absolute faith in a simple tale of rewarded virtue. This is the author at her best: mature, to the point, refreshed by the tale of her young lovers." Booklist

Heartbeat. Delacorte Press 1991 358p $21.95

ISBN 0-385-29908-7   LC 90-3044
Also available large print edition $24.95 (ISBN 0-385-30320-3)
Divorced television writer and producer Bill Thigpen is "living in Hollywood [and] life is sweet: a top-rated show, casual affairs, warm, happy, vacations with his two sons. His life is in perfect balance. Adrian Townsend thought she had everything. A job she liked, as production assistant for a network TV news show, and a husband she loved, who was a rising star in his own field. An enviable life that they had both worked hard to achieve—The American Dream. Until she got pregnant. Suddenly all she had was chaos. Adrian's life collides with Bill Thigpen's when they both buy groceries at midnight. And the very sight of her suddenly makes him want more in his life." Publisher's note

Jewels. Delacorte Press 1991 471p $23
ISBN 0-385-30490-0   LC 91-8672
Also available large print edition $25 (ISBN 0-385-30515-X)
"The duchess of Whitfield reflects upon her past on the occasion of her seventy-fifth birthday. She recalls her first marriage to a cad and her second and far more successful marriage to William, which brought her a chateau in France, buckets of jewels, and five children.

Steel, Danielle—*Continued*

. . . There is also space devoted to the development of Whitfield's Jewels—exclusive shops that evolved from the benevolent post—World War II purchases of jewelry by the duke and duchess from locals in France who needed money to migrate or simply survive." Booklist

Mixed blessings. Delacorte Press 1992 369p $23.50

ISBN 0-385-29910-9   LC 91-43224
Also available large print edition $28 (ISBN 0-385-29910-9)

"Three California couples are married on the same day; none of the women proves able to conceive. The couples never meet, but Steel tracks their common fate with a vigor that rivals her characters' quest for children. Various partners consult fertility experts, and ultimately every conceivable aspect of reproductive medicine, including surrogate motherhood, is given its due. Steel explores the emotional strain on the couples. . . . Marriages founder, but conventionally good characters find their way to happy endings." Publ Wkly

No greater love. Delacorte Press 1991 392p $23

ISBN 0-385-29909-5   LC 90-29106
Also available large print edition $27.50 (ISBN 0-385-30509-5)

As this novel "opens, the boisterous Winfield family is boarding the ill-fated ocean liner *Titanic* for their return to America from England. Kate Winfield, mistress of the perfect family, nobly stays behind with her beloved husband and thrusts her children into the lifeboats under the care of 20-year-old daughter Edwina. After the disaster, Edwina takes seriously her mother's entreaty to care for her five siblings, who range in age from 2 to 16. For the next 12 years, Edwina, aided by a substantial inheritance, dutifully cares for the kids, even to the point of pursuing her runaway teenage sister back to England (by boat) and wresting her out of the arms of a cad. Steel's tale eventually takes an interesting turn into the early days of Hollywood." Booklist

Vanished. Delacorte Press 1993 304p $23.95

ISBN 0-385-30603-2   LC 92-37118
Also available large print edition $28 (ISBN 0-385-31043-9)

"When Marielle Delauney marries New York steel magnate Malcolm Patterson in 1939, she does not tell him of her tragic past—neither the drowning accident that claimed her first child, nor the subsequent beating by her husband Charles that caused her to miscarry. . . . When they have their own child, Teddy, Malcolm, to all appearances, is an adoring father. The still-vulnerable Marielle begins to gain self-confidence, even though she endures daily confrontations with a hostile and even sinister household staff. Then the day after Marielle has a chance meeting with Charles, who drunkenly makes vague threats against Teddy, the four-year-old is snatched from his room." Publ Wkly

"The questions Steel raises about the tug-of-wars between guilt and responsibility, independence and security, sexual freedom and the web of relationships that form society and the family are anything but simple." Booklist

Wings. Delacorte Press 1994 400p $23.95

ISBN 0-385-30605-9   LC 93-51253
Also available large print edition $28.95 (0-385-31295-4)

"Although Cassie O'Malley, 17, knows more about planes than her father, Pat, who runs a small private airport outside Chicago, he refuses to let her fly. So Nick Gavin, Pat's WW I protégé and new employee, teaches Cassie in secret, and soon she can pilot like an ace. After Pat grudgingly gives Cassie a job at the airport, she takes several medals at a local air show and captures the attention of Desmond Williams, a young tycoon who offers her the chance to test planes and set world records. Nick encourages Cassie to take the offer, despite his heartbreak. . . . After a slow start that's bogged down by excess background information, the narrative takes off, with a mix of colorful characters bringing the heady early days of aviation to life." Publ Wkly

Stegner, Wallace Earle, 1909-1993

All the little live things. Viking 1967 345p o.p.

"When Joseph Allston, 64, and his wife, Ruth, move West to their 'Prospero's island' (rural California, near San Francisco), the retirement days 'drip away like honey off a spoon.' They live quietly without involvement . . . hoping to erase scars caused by the death of their rebellious son. The press of life first intrudes on them when young Jim Peck, a bearded free-thinker, camps on their property. . . . Then a young married couple, Marian and John Caitlin, arrive in the neighborhood, and the Allstons find themselves exposed to a depth of emotional involvement with others they had not wanted to experience ever again." Publ Wkly

"Mr. Stegner's narrative skill and his talent for imaginative recreation is evident throughout the book. His choice of words, the turn of a phrase, evoking a scene, an emotion, or a personality are to be savored. His writing, leisurely as it may appear, can be dramatic and moving." Best Sellers

Followed by The spectator bird

Angle of repose; [by] Wallace Stegner. Doubleday 1971 569p o.p.

This novel "is set mainly in the West in the late 1800's; but the central characters cannot be confined to the West nor to the 19th Century. They have a healing effect on the narrator, their grandson and biographer. . . . The beautiful, talented, charming Susan and her inarticulate engineer husband Oliver Ward rough it in mining camps and desolate, unfinished irrigation project camps. Their lives are hard and their marriage is strained past redemption. Yet their suffering and their strength do redeem." Libr J

The Big Rock Candy Mountain; [by] Wallace Stegner. Duell, Sloan & Pearce 1943 515p o.p.

This novel is set in far western states and Saskatchewan from about 1906 to 1942. The "principal characters are Bo Mason, his wife Elsa, and their two boys. Life is an almost continuous moving day because the next town, county, or state persistently beckons to Bo as the place where he will make his fortune." Libr J

"A well-written study of the footloose family. . . . The life of the household is a misery of continual cruelty and often crushing poverty, alternating with occasional scenes of simple family happiness which stand out beautifully and unforgettably." New Yorker

Collected stories of Wallace Stegner. Random House 1990 525p $21.95

ISBN 0-394-58409-0   LC 89-37342

Stegner, Wallace Earle, 1909-1993 — Continued

Analyzed in Short story index

Contents: The traveler; Buglesong; Beyond the glass mountain; The berry patch; The women on the wall; Balance his, swing yours; Saw gang; Goin' to town; The view from the balcony; Volcano; Two rivers; Hostage; In the twilight; Butcher bird; The double corner; The colt; The Chink; Chip off the old block; The sweetness of the twisted apples; The blue-winged teal; Pop goes the alley cat; Maiden in a tower; Impasse; The volunteer; A field guide to the western birds; Something spurious from the Mindanao deep; Genesis; The wolfer; Carrion spring; He who spits at the sky; The city of the living

"This retrospective . . . exhibits a mastery of the effortlessly beautiful metaphor, an abiding interest in the American West, and an ability to create quick but complete portraits and concise but fully engrossing narratives." Booklist

Crossing to safety; [by] Wallace Stegner. Random House 1987 277p $25

ISBN 0-394-56200-3   LC 87-20482

"The Langs and the Morgans, young couples who meet when their husbands begin teaching at a Wisconsin university, forge bonds of wonderful, lasting friendship. Charity Lang and Sally Morgan are unlike in personality but see each other through devastating crises because of that friendship. Sid Lang is a frustrated poet whose life is over-directed by his wife; Larry Morgan, much less financially secure than Sid, realizes a slow but successful climb to a position of noted writer. This novel has no violence, explicit sex or ugliness. Instead it is a hymn to solid marriages and loyalty in friendship. The dramatic events are those that occur in the lives of ordinary people." Shapiro. Fic for Youth. 3d edition

The spectator bird; [by] Wallace Stegner. Doubleday 1976 214p o.p. Smith, P. reprint available $20.50 (ISBN 0-8446-6607-6)

Retired literary agent Joseph Allston, who "moved west with his wife Ruth in Stegner's novel 'All the Little Live Things' is still waging his gentle battles with age (he's nearly seventy now), the younger generation, and guilt about his son's accidental death years ago. A post card from Countess Astrid Wredel-Krarup, with whom the Allstons stayed on a trip to [Denmark] in 1954, revives Joe's interest in an old journal which tells an intriguing story about the Countess and adds dimension to Joe's character and the Allston's marriage." Libr J

"Since Mr. Stegner is not one to beat his reader over the head with a moral, the tale can be interpreted in several ways, but regardless of interpretation, it is consistently elegant and entertaining reading." Atlantic

Stein, Gertrude, 1874-1946

Three lives; stories of the good Anna, Melanctha, and the gentle Lena. Grafton Press 1909 279p o.p.

"Written in a clear and masterly style, free from any of its author's later stylistic mannerisms, this book consists of three character studies of women. 'The Good Anna' deals with a kindly but domineering German servingwoman; 'Melanctha' is concerned with an uneducated but sensitive black girl; and 'The Gentle Lena' is about a pathetically feebleminded young German maid." Reader's Ency. 3d edition

Steinbeck, John, 1902-1968

Nobel Prize in literature, 1962

Cannery Row. Viking 1945 208p o.p.

"In this episodic work Steinbeck returned to the manner of Tortilla Flat (1935) and produced a rambling account of the adventures and misadventures of workers in a California cannery and their friends." Benet's Reader's Ency of Am Lit

Followed by Sweet Thursday

East of Eden. Viking 1986 c1952 778p $24.95

ISBN 0-670-28738-5   LC 86-1526

A reissue of the title first published 1952

"The saga of more than half a century in the lives of two American families—the Trasks, a mixture of gentleness and brutality doled out in unequal measure and the Hamiltons, Steinbeck's own forebears, a well adjusted, lovable group who provide a tranquil background for the turbulent careers of the Trasks. The scene is chiefly Salinas, California from the turn of the century through the first World War, and thanks to a great wealth of fascinating detail woven through the plot, we are given a complete and unforgettable picture of country and small town life during the period." Libr J

Steinbeck's "most ambitious post-war novel is . . . a parable of the fall of man, of Cain and Abel, and of human possibility, showing many of the virtues of his best books, but touched with sentimentality, melodrama and intrusive commentary." Penguin Companion to Am Lit

The grapes of wrath; introduction by Studs Terkel. Viking 1989 xx, 619p $25

ISBN 0-670-82638-3   LC 88-40296

Also available Everyman's library edition

A reissue of the title first published 1939

"Awarded the Pulitzer Prize in 1940, this moving and highly successful proletarian novel tells of the hardships of the Joad family. 'Okie' farmers forced out of their home in the Oklahoma dustbowl region by economic desperation, they drive to California in search of work as migrant fruit-pickers. The grandparents die on the way; on their arrival the others are harassed by the police and participate in strike violence, during which Tom, the Joad son, kills a man. At the conclusion of the novel, throughout which descriptive and philosophical passages alternate with narrative portions, the family is defeated but still resolute." Reader's Ency. 3d edition

In dubious battle. Covici-Friede 1936 349p o.p.

"One of the more important books to come out of the proletarian movement. This was Steinbeck's first successful novel. 'In Dubious Battle' deals with a fruit strike in a California valley and the attempts of the radical leaders to organize, lead, and provide for the striking pickers. Perhaps the most important, although not the central, character is Doc Burton, who helps the strikers and is concerned with seeing things as they exist, without labels of good and bad attached. The strike fails, and Jim, one of the two leaders, is senselessly killed." Benet's Reader's Ency of Am Lit

The long valley. Viking 1938 304p o.p.

Analyzed in Short story index

Contents: Chrysanthemums; White quail; Flight; Snake; Breakfast; Raid; Harness; Vigilante; Johnny Bear; Murder; St. Katy the virgin; Red pony; Leader of the people

This volume "includes the four magnificent 'Red Pony' stories, and could serve as an admirable introduction to

Steinbeck, John, 1902-1968—*Continued*

Steinbeck, showing his characteristic interests—the tensions of the town and country, of past and present, of labour and ownership, as well as the objectivity of biological observation and a sort of Lawrencean mystic concept of personal power." Penguin Companion to Am Lit

The moon is down; a novel. Viking 1942 188p o.p.

This novel describes the occupation of a small mining town, presumably in Norway, by an unidentified army, evidently German. The villagers resort to sabotage and completely ignore the invaders whenever possible. In the end the courageous village mayor is shot to bring the people to terms. The mayor goes to his death reciting Socrates's dying message, knowing full well that his people will understand his death, and will continue their resistance

Of mice and men. Viking 1986 107p $19.95

ISBN 0-670-52071-3   LC 86-1300
Also available G.K. Hall large print edition
First published 1937 by Covici-Friede
"Two uneducated laborers dream of a time when they can share the ownership of a rabbit farm in California. George is a plotter and a schemer, while Lennie is a mentally deficient hulk of a man who has no concept of his physical strength. As a team they are not particularly successful, but their friendship is enduring." Shapiro. Fic for Youth. 3d edition

also in Steinbeck, J. The portable Steinbeck p225-323

The pearl; with drawings by José Clemente Orozco. Viking 1947 122p il o.p.

"Kino, a poor pearl-fisher, lives a happy albeit spartan life with his wife and their child. When he finds a magnificent pearl, the Pearl of the World, he is besieged by dishonest pearl merchants and envious neighbors. Even a greedy doctor ties his professional treatment of their baby when it is bitten by a scorpion to the possible acquisition of the pearl. After a series of disasters, Kino throws the pearl away since it has brought him only unhappiness." Shapiro. Fic for Youth. 3d edition

The portable Steinbeck; revised, selected, and introduced by Pascal Covici, Jr. Viking 1971 xlii, 692p o.p.

"Viking portable library"
Partially analyzed in Short story index
First published 1943 with title: Steinbeck
This volume contains the complete texts of the short novels Of mice and men and The red pony; selections from the novels The pastures of heaven, Tortilla Flat, In dubious battle, The grapes of wrath, and Cannery Row; four short stories from The long valley; and excerpts from a travel book, Sea of Cortez, and a memorial to a friend, "About Ed Ricketts"
Short stories included are: Flight; The snake; The harness; The chrysanthemums; The affair at 7, rue de M—; How Mr. Hogan robbed a bank

The red pony

In Steinbeck, J. The long valley

In Steinbeck, J. The portable Steinbeck p325-415

The short reign of Pippin IV; a fabrication; drawings by William Péne du Bois. Viking 1957 188p il o.p.

A satire on French politics. Having run out of governments the French decide to revive the monarchy and settle on Pippin, a quiet amateur astronomer who happens to be a descendant of Charlemagne. Bored with the whole situation Pippin is instrumental in starting a revolution, and finally wanders off home

Sweet Thursday. Viking 1954 273p o.p.

Sequel to Cannery Row
After World War II the "Palace Flophouse passed into new hands, the Bear Flag Café got a new madam named Fauna (nee Flora), and Doc lost his old pleasure in women, liturgical music, and the Western Biological Laboratories. Then Suzy came to Cannery Row . . . [and] egged on by the others, she brought Doc back to his prewar contentment." Booklist

Tortilla Flat; illustrated by Ruth Gannett. Covici-Friede 1935 316p o.p.

Available G.K. Hall large print edition
"This episodic tale concerns the poor but carefree 'paisano' Danny and his friends Pillon, Pablo, Big Joe Portagee, Jesus Maria Corcoran, and the old Pirate, all of whom gather in Danny's house, which Steinbeck tells us 'was not unlike the Round Table.' The novel (accepted after nine publishers had turned it down) contrasts the complexities of modern civilization with the simple life of the 'paisanos.'" Benet's Reader's Ency of Am Lit

The wayward bus. Viking 1947 312p o.p.

"A novel in which the passengers on a stranded bus in California become a microcosm of contemporary American frustrations." Camb Guide to Lit in Engl

The winter of our discontent. Viking 1961 311p o.p.

Ethan Allen Hawley, the impoverished heir to an upright New England tradition is the focus of this story. Ethan, under pressure from his restless wife and discontented children who want more of this world's goods than his grocery store job provides, decides to take a holiday from his scrupulous standards to achieve wealth and success. What happens as he compromises with his integrity makes up this story
In this novel Steinbeck "continues his exploration of the moral dilemmas involved in being fully human, this time in contemporary America, where choices between genteel poverty and corrupt comfort press in upon the protagonist with a force and reality that suggest no easy resolution." Ency of World Lit in the 20th Century

Stemple, Jane H. Yolen *See* Yolen, Jane

Stendhal, 1783-1842

The charterhouse of Parma; translated from the French by C. K. Scott Moncrieff. Knopf 1992 521p $20

ISBN 0-679-41743-5   LC 92-52908
"Everyman's library"
Original French edition, 1839. Variant title: The chartreuse of Parma
"The scene is a little Italian Court, whither the young adventurer Fabrice has found his way, and in dramatic importance plays second fiddle to the fascinating Duchess Sanseverina and her jealous lover, the astute minister, Count Mosca. The book opens with a famous narrative

Stendhal, 1783-1842—*Continued*
of the battle of Waterloo. It is a novel that set a standard of flawless technique, of the lucid unfolding of character and motive, of accurate comprehension of the inherent disorder of life, that has rarely been approached in dramatic narration." Baker. Guide to the Best Fic

The red and the black; translated by C. K. Scott Moncrieff. Modern Lib. 1995 639p $18.50

ISBN 0-679-60162-7   LC 95-11613
Also available Everyman's library edition with title: Scarlet and black
Original French edition, 1830; first United States edition published 1898 by G.H. Richmond
"The author's most celebrated work, it is equally acclaimed for its psychological study of its protagonist—the provincial young romantic Julien Sorel—and as a satiric analysis of the French social order under the Bourbon restoration. Its intensely dramatic plot is purposively romantic in nature, while Stendhal's careful portraiture of Sorel's inner states is the work of a master realist, foreshadowing new developments in the form of the novel." Reader's Ency. 3d edition

Stephens, Eve *See* Anthony, Evelyn, 1928-

Stephens, John Richard
(ed) Mysterious cat stories. See Mysterious cat stories

Stephenson, Neal
The diamond age; or, Young lady's illustrated primer. Bantam Bks. 1995 455p $22.95

ISBN 0-553-09609-5   LC 94-30486
"In the 22d century, nation-states have withered away, to be replaced by 'phyles,' groups of people united by self-defined interests. . . . The action in 'The Diamond Age' centers on the neo-victorians, who share an admiration for the social discipline of 19th-century England, and a group of Chinese who are trying to erect a neo-Confucian phyle in the power vacuum left by the collapse of the 'Mao Dynasty.' On his own initiative, a neo-Victorian Equity Lord orders a 'bespoke engineer' named John Percival Hackworth to fashion an interactive primer that will teach young people a genuinely subversive lesson: that only by questioning everything they are taught about their world can they hope to become truly useful members of their phyle. When the primer falls into the hands of Nell, a child of the despised underclass, the repercussions are global." N Y Times Book Rev
"With breathtaking vision and insight, Stephenson establishes himself as not only a major voice in contemporary sf but also a prophet of technology's future." Booklist

Sterne, Laurence, 1713-1768
The life and opinions of Tristram Shandy, gentleman
In Sterne, L. The life and opinions of Tristram Shandy, gentleman and A

sentimental journey through France and Italy p1-689

The life and opinions of Tristram Shandy, gentleman and A sentimental journey through France and Italy. Modern Lib. 1995 832p $19.50

ISBN 0-679-60091-4
A combined edition of two titles first published 1759-67 and 1768 respectively
The life and opinions of Tristram Shandy, gentleman is the "chaotic account by Tristram of his life from the time of his conception to the present. . . . In between are sandwiched his 'opinions,' long-winded and philosophical reflections on everything under the sun, including his novel, and accounts of the lives of 'Yorick'; his father, Walter Shandy; his mother; and his 'Uncle Toby.' The form of the book is in fact the character of Tristram himself, doomed by improbably fantastic fatalities to write a hodgepodge instead of a history." Reader's Ency. 3d edition
A sentimental journey is a "combination of autobiography, fiction, and observations made by Sterne on his own travels, chronicles the journey through France of a charming and sensitive young man named Yorick and his servant LaFleur. (Though the title mentions Italy, the book ends before they reach that country.)" Merriam-Webster's Ency of Lit

A sentimental journey through France and Italy
In Sterne, L. The life and opinions of Tristram Shandy, gentleman and A sentimental journey through France and Italy p691-832

Stevenson, D. E. (Dorothy Emily), 1892-1973
Celia's house. Farrar & Rinehart 1943 307p o.p.
"At Dunnian, the Scottish border country estate, generations of the Dunne family live, love and die. From 1905 on we follow the fortunes of Humphrey Dunne, Celia's heir and grand-nephew, and his five lively children through 40 years of attachment to Dunnian. How the big house eventually passes to the latest generation makes a captivating tale told with astringent charm, full of warmth, good feeling and appreciation for family roots." Publ Wkly

Stevenson, Dorothy Emily *See* Stevenson, D. E. (Dorothy Emily), 1892-1973

Stevenson, Robert Louis, 1850-1894
The beach of Falesá
In Stevenson, R. L. The complete short stories v2 p307-71
In Stevenson, R. L. The complete short stories of Robert Louis Stevenson
In Stevenson, R. L. The strange case of Dr. Jekyll and Mr. Hyde, and other famous tales

Stevenson, Robert Louis, 1850-1894 — *Continued*

The complete short stories; edited and introduced by Ian Bell. Centenary ed. Holt & Co. 1994 2v set $50

ISBN 0-8050-3203-7   LC 93-79628

Contents: v1 The Plague-Cellar; When the devil was well; Edifying letters of the Rutherford family; An old song; A lodging for the night; Will o' the Mill; The Sire de Malétroit's door; The Suicide Club: Story of the young man with the cream tarts; Story of the physician and the Saratoga trunk; The adventure of the hansom cabs; The Rajah's diamond: Story of the bandbox; Story of the young man in holy orders; Story of the house with the green blinds; The adventure of Prince Florizel and a detective; Providence and the guitar; The pavilion on the links; The story of a lie [novelette]; Thrawn Janet; The body snatcher; The Merry Men [novelette]

v2 The treasure of Franchard; Diogenes; Zero's tale of the explosive bomb; Markheim; Dr Jekyll and Mr Hyde [novelette]; The misadventures of John Nicholson [novelette]; Olalla; The enchantress; The bottle imp; The beach of Falesá [novelette]; The Isle of Voices; The waif woman; Fables

The complete short stories of Robert Louis Stevenson; with a selection of the best novels; edited and with an introduction by Charles Neider. Doubleday 1969 xxx, 678p o.p.

Analyzed in Short story index

Contents: A lodging for the night; Story of the young man with the cream tarts; Story of the physician and the Saratoga trunk; The adventure of the hansom cab; Story of the bandbox; Story of the young man in holy orders; Story of the house with green blinds; The adventure of Prince Florizel and a detective; Providence and the guitar; The Sire de Maletroit's door; Will o' the mill; The story of a lie [novelette]; Thrawn Janet; The merry men [novelette]; The body snatcher; Markheim; Strange case of Dr. Jekyll and Mr. Hyde [novelette]; The bottle imp; The beach of Falesá [novelette]; The isle of voices

The strange case of Dr. Jekyll and Mr. Hyde is entered separately. In The story of a lie (first published 1879 in New Quarterly magazine, 1882 in book form) Dick Naseby, a young Englishman, becomes estranged from his father due to a misunderstanding and from the girl he loves due to his concealment of the true character of her father—an untalented, parasitical but likable painter, whom the girl hasn't seen since childhood and romantically idolizes. The Merry Men (1887) is set on an island off the coast of Scotland. It deals with a man of dour religious temperament who kills the survivor of a shipwreck in a fit of drunken madness and is driven to death by his guilt after another shipwreck. The beach of Falesá (first published 1893 in Island nights' entertainments) concerns a trader on a South Seas island whose marriage to a native woman is promoted by a business rival who knows that she is the object of a native taboo which will pass on to her husband

Dr. Jekyll and Mr. Hyde [variant title: The strange case of Dr. Jekyll and Mr. Hyde]

In Stevenson, R. L. The complete short stories v2 p102-64

The master of Ballantrae; a winter's tale. o.p.

Available from Amereon

First published 1889

"The novel is an example of the moral ambiguity Stevenson had explored earlier in *Dr. Jekyll and Mr. Hyde.* Ballantrae is bold and unscrupulous; his younger brother Henry is plodding, good-natured, and honest. While Ballantrae joins the fight to restore the Stuarts to the English throne during the 1745 rebellion, his brother stays behind as a supporter of King George. Ballantrae is believed dead but returns to find Henry in charge of the estate, married to Ballantrae's love. The elder brother begins to persecute the younger, in Scotland and then America; both eventually die in the Adirondacks." Merriam-Webster's Ency of Lit

The Merry Men

In Stevenson, R. L. The complete short stories v1 p436-77

In Stevenson, R. L. The complete short stories of Robert Louis Stevenson

The misadventures of John Nicholson

In Stevenson, R. L. The complete short stories v2 p165-222

The story of a lie

In Stevenson, R. L. The complete short stories v1 p361-408

In Stevenson, R. L. The complete short stories of Robert Louis Stevenson

The strange case of Dr. Jekyll and Mr. Hyde; wood engravings by Barry Moser; foreword by Joyce Carol Oates. University of Neb. Press 1990 157p il $15

ISBN 0-8032-4212-3   LC 90-30544

Also available from Buccaneer Bks.

First published 1886. Variant title: Dr. Jekyll and Mr. Hyde

"The work is known for its vivid portrayal of the psychopathology of a 'split personality.' The calm, respectable Dr. Jekyll develops a potion that will allow him to separate his good and evil aspects for scientific study. At first Jekyll has no difficulty abandoning the drug induced persona of the repulsive Mr. Hyde, but as the experiments continue the evil personality wrests control from Jekyll and commits murder. Afraid of being discovered, he takes his life; Hyde's body is found, together with a confession written in Jekyll's hand." Merriam-Webster's Ency of Lit

also in Stevenson, R. L. The complete short stories of Robert Louis Stevenson

also in Stevenson, R. L. The strange case of Dr. Jekyll and Mr. Hyde, and other famous tales p1-69

Stevenson, Robert Louis, 1850-1894 — *Continued*

The strange case of Dr. Jekyll and Mr. Hyde, and other famous tales; with photographs of the author and his environment as well as illustrations from early editions of the stories, together with an introduction by W. M. Hills. Dodd, Mead 1961 339p il o.p.

"Great illustrated classics"

Analyzed in Short story index

Contents: The strange case of Dr. Jekyll and Mr. Hyde [novelette]; The pavilion on the links; A lodging for the night; Markheim; The Sire de Malétroit's door; The beach of Falesá [novelette]; The suicide club; Story of the young man with the cream tarts; Story of the physician and the Saratoga trunk; The adventures of the hansom cab

The title novelette is entered separately, and the novelette: The beach of Falesá is described under: The complete short stories of Robert Louis Stevenson. The three-part story: The suicide club, which originally appeared in The New Arabian Nights (1882) is a partly satirical fantasy-adventure story about a sinister London club which exploits the nihilistic tendencies of its members, and the mysterious Prince Florizel who opposes it

Stewart, Edward, 1938-

Deadly rich. Delacorte Press 1991 566p o.p.

LC 91-17638

A "thriller about a serial murderer who calls himself 'Society Son of Sam.' His first victim is a wealthy socialite found unpleasantly done in on a dressing room floor of an exclusive department store, and after a few more high society types are similarly dispatched, Lieutenant Vince Cardozo of the NYPD finds himself deeply involved in Yuppie scandal." Libr J

Mortal grace. Delacorte Press 1994 490p $21.95

ISBN 0-385-31132-X   LC 94-1280

In this mystery NYPD Lieutenant Vince Cardozo investigates "the brutal murders of several homeless teenagers. The first body is found dismembered and lodged in a Styrofoam carton in a city park. When the pieces of the body are autopsied, a Communion wafer is discovered under the corpse's tongue. More gruesome killings follow, all connected by the wafer clue. . . . Stewart has written a cleverly plotted (if lengthy) story with psychologically complex characters, a provocative, multilayered plot, and a series of perplexing clues that will baffle the most astute armchair detectives." Booklist

Stewart, Fred Mustard, 1932-

Ellis Island; a novel. Morrow 1983 396p o.p.

LC 82-14301

"In 1907 five young immigrants arrive at the legendary Ellis Island, the gateway to the American Dream. There's Jacob Rubenstein, fortunate to escape the pogrom that destroyed his family; Tom Banicek, who fled conscription into the Austro-Hungarian Army; Marco Santorelli, possessed of magnificent looks and driving ambition; and the beautiful O'Donnell sisters, escaping the Irish troubles." Libr J

"Stewart is a wonderful storyteller, and his novel—sentimental and even corny in spots—is nevertheless thoroughly satisfying." Publ Wkly

The glitter and the gold. New Am. Lib. 1989 452p o.p.

LC 89-33620

The "story of the Collingwoods of California—offspring of a German Jewish bourgeoise and a farmer-turned-bank robber, whom we meet at the center of the nineteenth century. Immigrating to California in the wake of the Gold Rush, Emma de Meyer takes over her husband's store after his death and prospers enough to bankroll escaped con Archer Collingwood all the way to the U.S. Senate. The generations roll down to the present day, when Claudia Collingwood is fighting off a rapacious, murderous, Anglo-Chinese businessman who wants the family ranch." Booklist

Pomp and circumstance; a novel. Dutton 1991 416p o.p.

LC 90-24602

Available G.K. Hall large print edition

"In the Victorian countryside, irresistible Lizzie, daughter of a sin-obsessed vicar, and Adam, the poor but nobly connected local 'hunk,' consummate their love. Despite Lizzie's pregnancy and a favorable upturn in Adam's fortunes, circumstances drive the two apart into liaisons with others and heroic adventures on several continents—adventures which underscore the great events and issues of the 1850s and 1860s. Backdrops include British stately homes, Napoleon III's Paris, antebellum Virginia, Civil War battlefields, and New York's worlds of theater and high finance." Libr J

"Although the dialogue is sometimes anachronistic and Stewart's use of stereotypical dialect for the black characters seems gratuitous, overall this is an entertaining read in the freewheeling, romantic tradition." Publ Wkly

Stewart, J. I. M. (John Innes Mackintosh), 1906-1994

For works written by this author under other names see Innes, Michael, 1906-1994

Stewart, Mary, 1916-

Airs above the ground. Mill, M.S. 1965 286p o.p.

Vanessa, a young English veterinarian, "after inadvertently discovering that her husband is not just a traveling salesman but doubles as a secret agent, helps him solve a case involving the Lipizzan horses, a medieval Austrian castle, a circus, a murder, and a narcotics ring." Booklist

The crystal cave. Morrow 1970 521p o.p.

First title in the author's Merlin trilogy. "Presumed to be the offspring of the daughter of the King of Wales and the devil himself, Merlin spends a difficult childhood in the court of the king. He learns much that is mystical under the tutelage of a learned wizard and gains a knowledge of several languages. Escaping to 'Less Britain,' Merlin becomes an important element in the struggle to unite all Britain. The book is rich in descriptions of fifth-century Britain and Brittany, the Druids and their fearful rites, and the superstitions surrounding pagan worship." Shapiro. Fic for Youth. 3d edition

Followed by The hollow hills

also in Stewart, M. Mary Stewart's Merlin trilogy

Stewart, Mary, 1916——*Continued*

The Gabriel hounds. Morrow 1967 320p o.p.

"This story is freely based on the accounts of the life of the Lady Hester Stanhope." Author's note

"Traveling in the Middle East Christy Mansel runs into her second cousin Charles in Damascus and the pair decide to visit their great aunt, an eccentric recluse who lives in a crumbling palace in Lebanon. Odd even for their aunt's household the situation at the castle arouses the cousins' suspicions, and their investigation turns up a startling secret in the underground passages." Booklist

The hollow hills. Morrow 1973 499p o.p. Buccaneer Bks. reprint available $28.95 (ISBN 0-89966-855-0)

This second novel in the author's Merlin trilogy begins with "Merlin's dismissal by Uther, Arthur's father, who has nonetheless promised to deliver the babe, when born, to Merlin's care. The book traces Merlin's travels to the east, during which time he monitors, through his second sight, Arthur's growth in Brittany and in England. Merlin returns to finish Arthur's education, and the book concludes with Arthur being proclaimed king. With this Merlin epic Mary Stewart has rightly won an honorable place among the modern writers of Arthurian legend." Tymn. Fantasy Lit

Followed by The last enchantment

also in Stewart, M. Mary Stewart's Merlin trilogy

The ivy tree. Mill, M.S. 1961 320p o.p.

A Canadian girl visiting England is mistaken for a missing and supposedly dead heiress to an estate "by handsome Connor Winslow, a cousin of the runaway, and now manager of Whitescar. Finally convinced that she is Mary Grey, he and his dour sister Lisa persuade her to masquerade as the long-gone Annabel, promising her the opportunity to claim the considerable legacy left to Annabel by her mother on condition that she surrender her share in Whitescar to Connor upon the death of Uncle Matthew. Reluctantly, Mary enters into the scheme, but soon repents but finds herself too deeply involved." Best Sellers

The last enchantment. Morrow 1979 538p o.p.

LC 79-12937

This is the concluding volume of a trilogy about "Merlin the Enchanter, set amidst the turbulent events of fifth-century Britain when Arthur became High King. . . . This novel tells of the early years of Arthur's reign: the battles with the Saxons, building of Camelot, marriages with two successive Guiniveres, and birth of Mordred" Libr J

also in Stewart, M. Mary Stewart's Merlin trilogy

Mary Stewart's Merlin trilogy. Morrow 1980 919p il $19.95

ISBN 0-688-00347-8   LC 80-21019

This omnibus edition includes The crystal cave, The hollow hills and The last enchantment, all three titles are entered separately

The moon-spinners. Mill, M.S. 1963 c1962 303p o.p.

First published 1962 in the United Kingdom

"Nicola Ferris, an English girl on vacation in Crete, decides to walk the last mile over a rough track to the tiny village where she is expected the next day. She walks into a mystery. She stumbles upon a shepherd's hut guarded by a Greek who threatens to kill her if she makes a sound. Inside the hut, she finds a young Englishman seriously wounded and much upset by her intrusion. In her determination to help him, she is drawn into his dangerous situation." Horn Book

My brother Michael. Mill, M.S. 1960 313p o.p.

This suspense story has "a modern Greek setting enriched by classical antiquities and haunted by the shades of Hellenic tragedy. Camilla Haven, the heroine-narrator, is on her way to Delphi when she encounters Simon Lester, an English schoolmaster who has come to investigate the death of his brother Michael, supposedly killed fighting during World War II. A strange letter written just before his death leads Camilla, along with Simon, through a terrifying maze of danger and violence to an amazing discovery on the slopes of Mount Parnassus." Booklist

Nine coaches waiting. Mill, M.S. 1959 c1958 342p o.p.

First published 1958 in the United Kingdom

"Intelligent, spirited Linda Martin comes to Valmy, an isolated château in the French Alps, as English governess to nine-year-old Philippe, the orphaned Comte de Valmy. After several frightening 'accidents' Linda discovers that her pupil is the object of a murder plot which apparently involves his crippled uncle and the latter's handsome son Raoul, with whom she is in love." Booklist

The stormy petrel. Morrow 1991 189p o.p.
LC 91-14509

Available Thorndike Press large print edition

The title "refers to both a little seabird and a boat piloted by one of the two young men who intrude upon young professor Rose Fenemore's country-cottage holiday on one of the smaller Hebrides. Unfortunately, the Petrel pilot, although he's the handsomer, turns out to be a dicey character. It's the other gent, helming another boat, who's steadier, though plainer." Booklist

"The visitors are jumpy, evasive and mutually antagonistic, and Rose's suspicions are aroused. The mystery of their relationship and real purpose, never menacing, is quickly solved, and takes second place to Stewart's vivid rendering of Moila's lochs, glens and wild birds, especially the graceful stormy petrels who nest there." Publ Wkly

This rough magic. Mill, M.S. 1964 336p o.p.

Available Thorndike Press large print edition

"Lucy Waring, a young English actress, comes to spend a vacation with her married sister on the Greek island of Corfu, which is reputed to be the scene of Shakespeare's 'The tempest.' There she meets Sir Julian Gale, a retired Shakespearean actor, his blunt composer son Max, and a deceptively pleasant writer, Godfrey Manning. During subsequent events involving a friendly dolphin, the legends surrounding a local saint, and a cold-blooded smuggling plot, Lucy experiences more than her share of offstage drama, romance, and danger." Booklist

Stewart, Mary, 1916-—*Continued*

Thornyhold. Morrow 1988 207p il o.p.

LC 88-13194

"Early in the 1950's Gilly Ramsey, daughter of a pedestrian vicar, inherits the Wiltshire home of her godmother, Cousin Geillis. Exploring Thornyhold, the haven she has always dreamed of, Gilly confirms her childhood impression that her cousin was, if not a witch at least a 'wise woman,' and that she herself has inherited those gifts. While there is danger from sinister Agnes Trapp, eager to get her hands on Cousin Geillis's book of old fashioned herbal recipes, whatever evil lurks in the woods is no match for a nature that loves the light." Publ Wkly

"Stewart doesn't always tie up the ends of the narrative too neatly—some readers may suspect that these loose threads are blind trails intended to mislead anyway—but her incomparable blend of mystery and love story should quicken the pulse and stir the heartstrings of her devoted audience." Booklist

Thunder on the right. Mill, M.S. 1958 c1957 284p o.p.

First published 1957 in the United Kingdom

"Jennifer answers her cousin Gillian's plea to visit a French convent in the Pyrenees where Gillian hopes to become a nun. On her arrival from England, Jennifer discovers that her cousin has supposedly died after a mysterious auto accident. She does some sleuthing and unveils smuggling and murder. All the ingredients for a mystery-love story with authentic background." Libr J

Touch not the cat. Morrow 1976 336p o.p.

A "tale set on a family estate in England. Garbled words of warning uttered by her dying father lead Bryony Ashley into danger as she investigates the intricacies of past and present intrigues within the Ashley family. Bryony's inherited extrasensory abilities add to the suspenseful story." Booklist

The wicked day. Morrow 1983 453p o.p.

LC 83-12091

The author "returns to the Arthurian world she portrayed . . . in her Merlin trilogy. The principal character is Mordred, born of the incestuous liaison between Arthur the High King and his half-sister, the evil sorceress and northern queen Morgause. Mordred is summoned to Camelot by the formidable warrior king, along with Morgause and her four legitimate but ungovernable sons, and told of his true parentage. After growing to manhood in Arthur's court . . . Mordred is left in charge of the kingdom, and of Queen Guinevere, while Arthur is off fighting the Romans in Brittany. Reported dead, the king returns to Britain and there ensues the fulfillment of the 'wicked day' that has been prophesied by Merlin." Publ Wkly

Wildfire at midnight. Appleton-Century-Crofts 1956 214p o.p.

Gianetta Brooke comes to the Isle of Skye to forget the husband she has painfully divorced and finds herself in danger as a series of murders takes place

Stirling, Jessica

Lantern for the dark. St. Martin's Press 1992 377p o.p.

LC 92-3601

"Set in eighteenth-century Scotland, this tale opens with Clare Kelso, an accused murderer, meeting her new legal representative, Cameron Adams. Adams is convinced of Kelso's innocence on the charge of infanticide, but her reluctance to disclose her secrets leaves him powerless to save her from hanging. His persuasive powers must first be tested in the jail cell before he can even begin to work on the judiciary." Booklist

The author "deploys fully realized characters against the background of a greedy and corrupt society operating under a thin veneer of respectability. This richly detailed morality tale features a taut trial scene and a cache of surprising secrets that will keep readers totally involved." Publ Wkly

Followed by Shadows on the shore

Shadows on the shore. St. Martin's Press 1994 c1993 346p $21.95

ISBN 0-312-10546-0 LC 93-42102

Also available Thorndike Press large print edition

Sequel to Lantern for the dark

First published 1993 in the United Kingdom

Once under suspicion for the murder of her infant son, Clare Kelso Quinn "is now a prosperous salt dealer and a widow with an eight-year-old daughter. Quinn's placid life is altered when Frederick Striker reappears, counting on his charm to once again seduce a docile Clare. It seems he is effective, for she plans to marry him, a move that would place all of her late husband's inheritance into Striker's hands. But Clare is a far stronger, cleverer woman than she once was, and she also wants vengeance." Booklist

"The narrative keeps the reader guessing; flashes of dry wit and humorous characterizations . . . again indicate that Stirling is a deft practitioner of the genre." Publ Wkly

Stirling, S. M.

(jt. auth) McCaffrey, A. The city who fought

Stoker, Bram, 1847-1912

The Bram Stoker bedside companion; 10 stories by the author of Dracula; edited and with an introduction by Charles Osborne. Taplinger 1973 224p o.p.

Partially analyzed in Short story index

Contents: The secret of the growing gold; Dracula's guest; The invisible giant; The Judge's House; The burial of the rats; A star trap; The squaw; Grooken sands; The combeen man (from The snake's pass); The Watter's Mou'

Dracula.

Available from various publishers

First published 1897

"Count Dracula, an 'undead' villain from Transylvania, uses his supernatural powers to lure and prey upon innocent victims from whom he gains the blood on which he lives. The novel is written chiefly in the form of journals kept by the principal characters—Jonathan Harker, who contacts the vampire in his Transylvanian castle; Harker's fiancée (later his wife), Mina, adored by the Count; the well-meaning Dr. Seward; and Lucy Westenra, a victim who herself becomes a vampire. The doctor and friends destroy Dracula in the end, but only after they drive a stake through Lucy's heart to save her soul." Merriam-Webster's Ency of Lit

Stoker, Bram, 1847-1912—*Continued*

Midnight tales; edited and with an introduction by Peter Haining. Owen, P. distributed by Dufour Eds. 1990 182p il $30

ISBN 0-7206-0777-9

Analyzed in Short story index

Contents: The dream in the dead house; The spectre of doom; The dualitists; Death in the wings; The Gombeen man; The squaw; A deed of vengeance; The man from Shorrox'; The Red Stockade; Midnight tales; A criminal star; The bridal of death

Stone, Irving, 1903-1989

The agony and the ecstasy; a novel of Michelangelo. Doubleday 1961 664p $19.95

ISBN 0-385-01092-3

Also available from Buccaneer Bks.

"Michelangelo's career is traced from his promising boyhood apprenticeships to the painted Ghirlandajo and the sculptor Bertoldo thru all the many years of his flowering genius. . . . Florence and Rome are the principal cities which serve as background for the development of the artist's life and work." Chicago Sunday Trib

"Stone's Michelangelo is an idealized version, purged not only of ambisexuality, but of the egotism, faultfinding, harsh irony, and ill temper that we know were characteristic of Michelangelo." Saturday Rev

The Greek treasure; a biographical novel of Henry and Sophia Schliemann. Doubleday 1975 479p il $12.95

ISBN 0-385-07309-7

In this "fictionalized biography the hero is the indomitable Henry Schliemann, excavator with his young Greek wife, Sophia, of Homer's fabled city of Troy. . . . [The] narrative parallels treatment of archaeological discoveries and their attendant controversies with a . . . recreation of the personalities of the pioneers whose contribution to studies of Greek antiquities is the central theme of this tribute." Booklist

"Stone's archaeology and history are accurate. He also had access to the Schliemann archives at the American School of Classical Studies in Athens. He was even able to see most of the unpublished correspondence between Schliemann and Sophia." Time

Immortal wife; the biographical novel of Jessie Benton Fremont. Doubleday 1944 456p $24.95

ISBN 0-385-04219-1

A biography "in fiction form, of an ambitious woman who had a hand in the making of history in the West. At sixteen, Jessie Benton fell in love with the explorer, John Charles Fremont, and for the rest of her life her energy and ability were focused on promoting her husband's tempestuous career as soldier, explorer, and politician. He was one of the most spectacular men in America, was twice court-martialed, was nominated for president, and made and lost a fortune." Booklist

"Altogether, this book—more biography than novel, but a good blend of the two—is to be commended to all who like authentic history vigorously and interestingly presented." N Y Times Book Rev

Love is eternal; a novel about Mary Todd and Abraham Lincoln. Doubleday 1954 468p $24.95

ISBN 0-385-02040-6

Also available from Buccaneer Bks.

This novel presents a sympathetic portrait of Mary Todd Lincoln. The author absolves her from the shrewishness with which many historians have clothed her and pictures her marriage to Abraham Lincoln as a great love story

"Recommended in spite of the controversial nature of its interpretation of Mary Todd Lincoln." Booklist

Lust for life; a novel of Vincent van Gogh; illustrated with 150 reproductions of Vincent van Gogh's pictures arranged by J. B. Neumann. Twentieth anniversary ed. Doubleday 1954 507p il $17.95

ISBN 0-385-04270-1

Also available from Amereon and Buccaneer Bks.

First published 1934 by Longmans, Green and Co.

"Vincent Van Gogh lived a turbulent life but throughout it he was loved and supported by his brother, Theo. Sons of a Dutch Protestant minister, Vincent and Theo were raised rather strictly, but Vincent's love of color and movement led him into the life of an artist. He always felt challenged to fill a blank canvas with light and color. Vincent's search for meaning and fulfillment in his life took him over Europe but only toward the end of his life did he meet other artists who shared his artistic views, and it was not until after his death that his work began to be appreciated." Shapiro. Fic for Youth. 3d edition

The passions of the mind; a novel of Sigmund Freud. Doubleday 1971 808, xxxiip o.p. Buccaneer Bks. reprint available $35.95 (ISBN 1-56849-564-1)

In this novel the author "takes Freud from his 26th year, when he was still involved in physiology research and smitten with his wife-to-be (Martha Bernays), through over half-a-century in Vienna. He leaves him as the great man arrives in England, bedevilled by cancer and shattered by the ugly political realities of Hitler." Publ Wkly

The President's lady; a novel about Rachel and Andrew Jackson. Doubleday 1951 338p $24.95

ISBN 0-385-04362-7

A biographical novel based on the lives of Andrew and Rachel Jackson. "The story is told without fireworks or melodrama. Mr. Stone could have wrecked the emotions, could have let himself go on local color, but he chose a gentler flow of narration that is steadily engrossing. The reasonableness and restraint of the treatment make his Rachel and Andrew Jackson seem the real ones." Christ Sci Monit

Those who love; a biographical novel of Abigail and John Adams. Doubleday 1965 662p $19.95

ISBN 0-385-00157-6

"This warm love story of Abigail Smith and John Adams is unfolded against the panorama of our country's struggle for independence." Chicago. Public Libr

Stone, Katherine

Happy endings. Kensington Pub. Corp. 1994 362p $15.95

ISBN 0-8217-4646-4

"Raven Winter is the best entertainment attorney in the business. She is handling the reclusive, best-selling author Holly, who fears that Jason Cole, an Academy Award-winning filmmaker, is going to change the happy ending in the film version of her book. Nick is introduced to this group when Raven distractedly jogs in front of his nursery truck. . . . Most romance readers expect a happy ending, but the pleasure comes in the journey to reach it, and Stone does not disappoint." Libr J

Rainbows. Zebra Bks. 1992 381p $20

ISBN 0-8217-3590-X   LC 91-062183

"Alexa Taylor is a wildly successful but sweetly humble actress, star of the hit series *Pennsylvania Avenue.* Her sister Catherine is an insecure but extraordinarily beautiful concert pianist. The plot concentrates on their relationships with the men in their lives . . . and how they earn the right to their soulmates." Libr J

"Maneuvering the lives of the rich and royal, Stone keeps the reader pleasantly off guard, and her finale is a veritable torrent of cataclysms and revelations." Publ Wkly

Stone, Robert, 1937-

Children of light. Knopf 1986 258p $17.95

ISBN 0-394-52573-6   LC 85-45602

"Gordon Walker, sometime actor and successful screenwriter, is on an alcohol-cocaine binge after playing King Lear on stage and being deserted by his wife. He's drawn to a former lover, actress Lee Verger, who's on location filming his screenplay of Kate Chopin's 'The Awakening.' Lee is insane; Gordon becomes her helpless accomplice. The claustrophobic, high-tension world of the set, located on the eerie, primeval coast of Mexico, crackles with conflict, intrigue, and malice." Booklist

"A fine, complex, often funny tale, full of lights and shadows, with great dialogue and a sharp sense of character and place. It has some problems . . . but they measure the daring of trying something new, and the risk proves well worth taking." N Y Times Book Rev

Dog soldiers; a novel. Houghton Mifflin 1974 342p o.p.

This novel "chronicles the nightmarish misadventure of Converse, Marge, and Hicks, who smuggle a bundle of Vietnamese heroin into the U.S. only to be pursued and 'ripped off' by a corrupt narcotic agent." Libr J

"Part melodrama, part morality play, 'Dog Soldiers' offers a vision of a predatory, insensate society from which all moral authority has fled. It is a world in which innocence or vestigial remnants of decent behavior prove fatal to their owners; Hicks . . . is nearly violent enough to survive, but he is done in by his own loyalty to Marge. All of this corruption and vulnerability, this savagery and stoned withdrawal, this combination of passion and cynicism works convincingly, for Stone is a very good storyteller indeed." Newsweek

A flag for sunrise; a novel. Knopf 1981 439p $15.95

ISBN 0-394-40757-1   LC 81-47507

"A dramatic tale with political and philosophic views of a Latin American country undergoing revolution in the post-Vietnam era." Oxford Companion to Am Lit. 5th edition

This "book is at once a high-tension adventure tale, a densely plotted political novel and, at its heart, a meditation on the inavailability of God. Stone writes as if announcements of the death of the novel had not reached him: 'A Flag for Sunrise' shows narrative confidence, criss-crossed motives, a moral sense and sustained inventiveness of an amplitude we have almost given up expecting from fiction." Newsweek

Outerbridge Reach. Ticknor & Fields 1992 409p $21.95

ISBN 0-395-58781-6   LC 91-34875

Also available Thorndike Press large print edition

This novel concerns Owen Browne, an ex-navy man who has become a successful sailboat salesperson. "Avid for honor and glory, he enters a highly publicized, round-the world, singlehanded sailboat race. As the loneliness and exertion of his voyage tests Browne, so the attention of a shallow filmmaker test Anne, Browne's wife. Both learn truths about themselves and one another which destroy one spouse but which compel the other to further trials of strength and will." Libr J

"Robert Stone's blend of heroic aspiration and mordantly deflationary irony results in something like tragicomedy. . . . But whatever you call it, 'Outerbridge Reach' seems to me a triumph—a beautifully and painstakingly composed piece of literary art." N Y Times Book Rev

Stone, Zachary, 1949-

For works written by this author under other names see Follett, Ken, 1949-

Stories not for the nervous. See Alfred Hitchcock presents: Stories not for the nervous

Stout, Rex, 1886-1975

All aces; A Nero Wolfe omnibus. Viking 1958 442p o.p.

Contents: Some buried Caesar (1939); Too many women (1947); and, Trouble in triplicate (1949) which consists of three short stories: Before I die; Help wanted, male; Instead of evidence

In Some buried Caesar, Nero Wolfe leaves his New York kitchen and orchid conservatory to solve a mystery in an upstate community of wealthy cattle breeders. Too many women has Mr. Wolfe and Archie, his roving reporter disguised as a personnel expert, delving into the conflicts, personalities and activities of an engineering supply company involved in murder

Blood will tell

In Stout, R. Trio for blunt instruments p169-247

The cop-killer

In Stout, R. Kings full of aces p369-420

Stout, Rex, 1886-1975—*Continued*

Death of a doxy; a Nero Wolfe novel.
Viking 1966 186p o.p.

The problem of money and the possibility of divided
loyalty concerns both Nero Wolfe and Archie as they
seek to clear their sometime assistant, Orrie Cather, of
a murder charge

"First-rate Stout done at the age of eighty. The tight-
ness of the plot, the wit, and the people are done with
sureness and speed, so that the book, though short, gives
one the sense of having lived through a long stretch of
tense expectation." Barzun. Cat of Crime. Rev and enl
edition

Die like a dog

In Stout, R. Royal flush p431-74

Door to death

In Stout, R. Five of a kind p399-441

The doorbell rang; a Nero Wolfe novel.
Viking 1965 186p o.p.

"Nero Wolfe tangles with the FBI, on behalf of a
wealthy woman who has sent as gifts to prominent
people 10,000 copies of Fred Cook's book criticizing the
FBI. . . . She is being shadowed and spied on by the
FBI. To the surprise of Wolfe and of Archie Goodwin,
they have the good will of the New York Police Department. The New York Police believe that FBI agents have
murdered a magazine writer who was doing an article
on the FBI. The police are powerless to prove anything
or to prosecute. Clever and ingenious, this ranks among
the best Rex Stout mysteries." Publ Wkly

A family affair; a Nero Wolfe novel.
Viking 1975 152p o.p.

Nero Wolfe discovers why "a frightened waiter given
sanctuary in Wolfe's guest room is murdered by an infer-
nal machine, an industrialist is found shot to death in
a stolen car, a young woman is gunned down on West
Fifty-fourth Street [and] a man is blown to pieces on
Wolfe's doorstep." New Yorker

The father hunt; a Nero Wolfe novel.
Viking 1968 183p o.p.

"Mysteries in which the detectives have no clues at
all to work on are the best; this situation is exactly what
is presented to Nero Wolfe and Archie Goodwin when
a young girl asks them to find her father whom she
has never known. Amy Denovo's mother, who never
revealed the father's identity, has just been killed by a
hit-and-run driver. She blotted out her past up to Amy's
birth. It is fascinating to watch Nero and Archie dig
out the facts on a case which may be a murder case."
Publ Wkly

Fer-de-lance; a Nero Wolfe mystery. Farrar
& Rinehart 1934 313p o.p.

The first "of the Nero Wolfe stories, in which all the
familiar characters and their habits get established. The
murder is done by means of a golf club—the implement,
not the membership—and it entangles a college president,
a baby, some Italian nondescripts, and much
philosophizing by Wolfe and futilizing by the police."
Barzun. Cat of Crime. Rev and enl edition

also in Stout, R. Royal flush p1-180

The final deduction

In Stout, R. Three aces

Five of a kind; the third Nero Wolfe omnibus. Viking 1961 441p o.p. Ayer reprint
available $29.95 (ISBN 0-8369-4136-5)

Partially analyzed in Short story index

Contains the complete text of: The rubber band, first
published 1936 by Farrar & Rinehart; In the best
families, and Three doors to death, both originally
published 1950 by Viking. Included in the latter title
are these three novelettes: Man alive; Omit flowers; and
Door to death

Gambit; a Nero Wolfe novel. Viking 1962
188p o.p.

"Nero Wolfe, with his usual witty, urbane, conver-
sational approach, looks into a case of arsenic poisoning
in a Manhattan chess club." Publ Wkly

"There is more detection in this story than in any
other of the mulling-and-quizzing sort; here we really see
N.W.'s thoughts whirring. Moreover, Archie is in excellent form, and although a chess tournament is a feature,
the game itself is not. The great scene is that in which
Nero reads and burns the pages of Webster's Dictionary,
Third Edition." Barzun. Cat of Crime. Rev and enl edition

Home to roost

In Stout, R. Kings full of aces p325-68

In the best families

In Stout, R. Five of a kind p155-303

Kill now—pay later

In Stout, R. Trio for blunt instruments
p1-87

Kings full of aces; a Nero Wolfe omnibus.
Viking 1969 472p o.p.

Partially analyzed in Short story index

Contains three separately published titles: Too many
cooks (1938), Plot it yourself (1959) and Triple jeopardy
(1952). The latter contains three novelettes: Home to
roost, The cop-killer, and The squirt and the monkey

Man alive

In Stout, R. Five of a kind p307-55

Might as well be dead

In Stout, R. Three aces

Murder by the book

In Stout, R. Royal flush p181-333

Murder is corny

In Stout, R. Trio for blunt instruments
p89-167

The next witness

In Stout, R. Royal flush p337-84

Omit flowers

In Stout, R. Five of a kind p356-98

Plot it yourself

In Stout, R. Kings full of aces p189-322

Stout, Rex, 1886-1975—*Continued*

Royal flush; the fourth Nero Wolfe omnibus. Viking 1965 474p o.p.

Contains the complete text of: Fer-de-lance, which is entered separately; Murder by the book, and Three witnesses both published by Viking in 1951 and 1956, respectively. The latter title includes the three novelettes: The next witness; When a man murders and Die like a dog

The rubber band

In Stout, R. Five of a kind p1-153

Some buried Caesar

In Stout, R. All aces p1-153

The squirt and the monkey

In Stout, R. Kings full of aces p421-72

Three aces; a Nero Wolfe omnibus. Viking 1971 473p o.p.

Contents: Too many clients (1960); Might as well be dead (1956); The final deduction (1961)

Three doors to death

In Stout, R. Five of a kind p307-441

Three witnesses

In Stout, R. Royal flush p335-474

Too many clients

In Stout, R. Three aces

Too many cooks

In Stout, R. Kings full of aces p1-187

Too many women

In Stout, R. All aces p155-302

Trio for blunt instruments; a Nero Wolfe threesome. Viking 1964 247p o.p.

Contents: Kill now—pay later; Murder is corny; Blood will tell

"Three stories featuring Nero Wolfe and Archie Goodwin. They concern the defenestration of a businessman, the murder of a deliveryman, and a bloodstained tie sent to Archie from Greenwich Village." Publ Wkly

Triple jeopardy

In Stout, R. Kings full of aces p325-472

Trouble in triplicate

In Stout, R. All aces p303-442

When a man murders

In Stout, R. Royal flush p385-430

Stowe, Harriet Beecher, 1811-1896

The minister's wooing

In Stowe, H. B. Uncle Tom's cabin; The minister's wooing; Oldtown Folks p521-876

Oldtown folks

In Stowe, H. B. Uncle Tom's cabin; The minister's wooing; Oldtown Folks p877-1468

Uncle Tom's cabin; with an introduction by Alfred Kazin. Knopf 1995 xxix, 494p $20

ISBN 0-679-44365-7

Also available from Modern Library

"Everyman's library"

"The book relates the trials, suffering, and human dignity of Uncle Tom, an old black slave. Cruelly treated by a Yankee plantation owner, Simon Legree, Tom dies as the result of a beating. Uncle Tom is devoted to Little Eva, the daughter of his white owner, Augustine St. Clare. Other important characters are the mulatto girl Eliza; the impish black child Topsy; Miss Ophelia St. Clare, a New England spinster; and Marks, the slave catcher. The setting is Kentucky and Louisiana." Reader's Ency. 3d edition

also in Stowe, H. B. Uncle Tom's cabin; The minister's wooing; Oldtown Folks p1-519

Uncle Tom's cabin: or, Life among the lowly; The minister's wooing; Oldtown folks. Library of Am. 1982 1477p il $27.50

ISBN 0-940450-01-1   LC 81-18629

Omnibus edition of three titles first published 1852, 1859 and 1869 respectively; the first is entered separately

In the minister's wooing, a young woman rejects her suitor because he has no religious faith. Oldtown folks concerns the everyday life of a small Massachusetts town

Straight, Susan

Blacker than a thousand midnights. Hyperion 1994 388p $21.95

ISBN 0-7868-6003-0   LC 93-30432

This sequel to the title entered below is set "in Rio Seco, a poor, hard-bitten suburb in East L.A. to which Marietta moved to be near her grown twin sons, both of whom play professional football. Marietta and her male friend, Roscoe, a poetically minded gardener, are part of an intensely realized, racially mixed American community in which the struggles of one young couple, Darnell and Brenda Tucker, figure most prominently. Darnell, but 20 years old, has a love of fires—he works part-time fighting the drought-induced conflagrations that race across the parched hillsides outside of L.A." Publ Wkly

I been in sorrow's kitchen and licked out all the pots; a novel. Hyperion 1992 355p o.p.

LC 92-3566

"Self-conscious and restless around people, Marietta is happiest alone in the woods behind her tiny coastal community of old slave cabins in South Carolina. Even though it's the late 1950s, life there has a distinctly antebellum flavor. Her father died before she drew breath, so when her mother dies, Marietta, only 15, takes off on her own to Charleston. Her size and blue-black skin amaze and intimidate people, but she finds work and works hard, ever-watchful and courageous. When she becomes pregnant, she goes home to have her twins, two strapping boys, and finds work on the abandoned plantation that is being restored to attract tourists. In a distressing sort of déjà vu, Marietta finds herself reenacting the lives of her ancestors, an impossible, even dangerous situation as the fight for civil rights ignites across the South." Booklist

Straight, Susan—*Continued*

"Time and place . . . are evoked with stirring accuracy. But it is Marietta's intricate constitution, and the Gullah rhythms streaming through her mind, that give the novel its special edge and distinction." N Y Times Book Rev

Followed by Blacker than a thousand midnights

Straub, Peter

The buffalo hunter

In Straub, P. Houses without doors p109-207

Ghost story. Coward, McCann & Geoghegan 1979 483p o.p.

LC 78-27120

"Set largely in a snow-bound village in present-day upstate New York, this . . . tale of supernatural menace pits two elderly lawyers, a novelist, and a teenager against a life-form that thrives on one's memories and with time on one's blood." Libr J

"With considerable technical skill, Peter Straub has constructed an extravagant entertainment which, though flawed, achieves in its second half some awesome effects." Newsweek

Houses without doors. Dutton 1990 358p o.p.

LC 90-2902

Analyzed in Short story index

Contents: Blue rose; The juniper tree; A short guide to the city; The buffalo hunter [novella]; Something about a death, something about a fire; Mrs. God [novella]

"'The Buffalo Hunter' fastidiously chronicles the fixations of a 35-year-old who numbs his fear of women by sucking his coffee and cognac from baby bottles. In the ambitious gothic thriller/academic spoof 'Mrs. God,' a fatuous professor is lured to a creepy English mansion crammed with grisly secrets to research the papers of his poet ancestress; dead babies provide a subtheme. . . In addition to having popular allure, Straub's fictions are playfully postmodern, resonating with insights on genre, craft and process." Publ Wkly

Koko. Dutton 1988 562p o.p.

LC 88-3864

In this first volume of the author's Blue rose trilogy "innocent people are suddenly murdered in Singapore. Each mutilated victim is found with a playing card in his mouth, the mysterious word 'Koko' written on it in blood. Four Vietnam vets who used to do the same thing with some of the enemy they killed during the war, realize the killings are being done by a member of their own platoon and fly to Singapore to stop him." West Coast Rev Books

"The characters are realistic and complex, and the story continues to resonate in the mind long after the final page is turned." Publ Wkly

Mrs. God

In Straub, P. Houses without doors p223-352

Mystery. Dutton 1990 548p il o.p.

LC 89-7734

Second title in the author's Blue rose trilogy. "When a traffic accident nearly ends his young life, Tom Pasmore experiences all the usual near-death sensations: warm lights at the end of tunnels and friendly faces beckoning him onward. But by cheating death, his life is forever changed. Tom becomes obsessed with murder, with detection, and especially with a recent killing on Mill Walk, the fictional Caribbean island where his family lives. Tom's sleuthing mania is fed by an eccentric neighbor, Lamont von Heilitz, a famous retired detective. . . . The remarkable depth of characterization make apparent the fact that *Mystery* is meant to be much more than a conventional shocker. For the most part, Straub delivers the goods." Booklist

The throat. Dutton 1993 689p $24

ISBN 0-525-93503-7   LC 92-36604

In this conclusion to the author's trilogy "the citizens of Millhaven, Ill., thought they had overcome the unsolved serial murders that plagued the town in the 1940s—the killer had scrawled the words 'Blue Rose' near the bodies—but another resident has just fallen prey to a new Blue Rose. The victim's husband, John Ransom, enlists the aid of Tim Underhill, a high school buddy and fellow Vietnam vet who has written a book about the murders. Although Tim thinks of his hometown as 'oddly interchangeable' with Vietnam, he returns to join forces with famed local sleuth Tom Pasmore to solve both the earlier and the later murders. . . . Painted from a darkly colorful palette, Straub's characters inhabit a razor-edged world of unremitting suspense." Publ Wkly

(jt. auth) King, S. The talisman

Streeter, Edward, 1891-1976

Father of the bride; illustrated by Gluyas Williams. Simon & Schuster 1949 244p il o.p. Buccaneer Bks. reprint available $21.95 (ISBN 1-56849-136-0)

"From the day of her engagement to the end of the wedding day, the bride and her trousseau, her plans and her wedding, the in-laws and the guests, and especially the effect on his home life and his bank account are seen through the eyes of the Father of the Bride." Wis Libr Bull

"To be the father of the bride is to play a painful role as Mr. Stanley Banks discovers when preparations are launched for the big event of his one and only. The very good fun of this warmly human tale is pointed up with touches of pathos." Ont Libr Rev

Streshinsky, Shirley

Hers the kingdom. Putnam 1982 c1981 371p o.p.

LC 81-13763

"An engrossing first person narrative from Lena Kerr, a valiant, compassionate and rather modest woman, afflicted with congenital dislocation of the hip. Her life at first seems destined to be lived in the shadow of her feisty and adventuresome sister, Willa. Early into the story, Willa marries Owen Reade, a Princeton graduate with a fortune of three million. . . . Owen proves to be not such a good husband as he is entrepreneur, and it is the drive of Willa, especially after the death of her husband, which develops, protects and extends his fortune. But it is sister Lena whose own romantic in-

Streshinsky, Shirley—*Continued*

volvement with Eurasian Wing Soong enlarges the scope of the novel and makes Lena's story equally, if not more, interesting than Willa's." Best Sellers

Strieber, Whitley

Billy. Putnam's 1990 317p o.p.

LC 90-37404

"Fat, 40-ish Barton Royal, kiddy-clown in an L.A. bookstore, is obsessed with pubescent boys. He wants to be their 'father' but when they turn against him he has a 'black room' for their punishment. Seeing 12-year-old Billy Neary in an Iowa shopping mall, Barton is smitten. He follows the boy home, craftily and boldly abducts him and begins a nonstop drive to L.A. The book alternates scenes of the devastation wrought on Billy's family, a national manhunt, Billy's growing awareness of his peril and Barton's violent mood swings." Publ Wkly

"This is naturalistic horror fiction at its best." Booklist

The forbidden zone. Dutton 1993 309p $21

ISBN 0-525-93683-1   LC 93-6726

"Not long after physicist Brian Kelly and his pregnant wife hear human screams coming from within a dirt mound, inhabitants of their upstate New York town are attacked by wasp-like fireflies, women transformed into grub-like creatures are dug from the earth and an otherworldly being terrorizes motorists from its Dodge Viper. Brian theorizes that somehow the space-time fabric has been breached, and before long he and a few companions are engaged in a classic battle with an army of ancient demons." Publ Wkly

"The action and danger in this novel are exciting, and while the physics and the explanation for the horrific events are rather muddy, the story works well as a Lovecraft-style tale brought into modern times." Libr J

Majestic. Putnam 1989 317p o.p.

LC 89-8495

The author "combines fictitious confessions and military documents with genuine newspaper reports to depict a reputed encounter with alien beings near New Mexico's Roswell Army Air Field in 1947. What appears to be a disabled U.F.O. is discovered, and a paranoid military appoints a man named Will Stone to direct the investigation—and to conceal the incident in an operation code named Majestic. Forty years later, Stone reveals the cover-up to a shocked reporter, Nicholas Duke, who narrates the tale." N Y Times Book Rev

"Strieber has managed to weave two major themes in ufology (crashes and abductions) into an intriguing and unconventional tale that has both the dialogue and flavor of postwar America as well as the surrealistic aura of contemporary fiction." Booklist

Warday; and the journey onward; [by] Whitley Strieber and James W. Kunetka. Holt, Rinehart & Winston 1984 374p o.p.

LC 83-18678

"On Oct. 28, 1988, the Soviet Union launches a surprise attack on the United States. Ten-megaton atomic bombs detonate over Washington, San Antonio and the eastern edge of Queens. Smaller bombs strike the Minuteman and MX missile fields spread out across the northern plains. Washington and San Antonio are 'instantly vaporized.' Manhattan escapes destruction but is abandoned. Five years later, two writers brave the hazards of post-Warday travel to report back to us on how surviving America 'feels and tastes and smells.'" NY Times Book Rev

The Wolfen. Morrow 1978 252p o.p.

LC 78-7482

"Two cops are brutally killed and their guts are devoured by what appears to be a pack of wild animals. The police in charge, a middle-aged slob and a newly fledged woman detective, bicker endlessly through the killings of a blind man, a couple of junkies, and more, while the pack, mutant wolves, kill for food and to keep their secret from being discovered. This is a very specialized form of animal disaster novel, but much more suspenseful and imaginative than most. The windup is total thrill." Libr J

Strindberg, August, 1849-1912

By the open sea; introduced and translated from the Swedish by Mary Sandbach. University of Ga. Press 1985 c1984 192p o.p.

LC 85-8433

Original Swedish edition, 1890. First English translation by Ellie Schleussner published 1913; another English translation by Elizabeth Clarke Westergren published 1913 with title: On the seaboard. Present translation first published 1984 in the United Kingdom

A story of the East Skerry Islands where Axel Borg, a man of vast scientific learning, is sent by the Academy of Agriculture to make an investigation of the stromling fisheries. He lives there as an outsider among the people who cannot understand him. He falls in love with someone he feels to be his inferior. He could neither lift her up to his level nor sink himself to hers. The story ends when, in a mad frenzy, he sails out to sea in an open boat, to be heard of no more

The scapegoat; translated from the Swedish by Arvid Paulson; introduction by Richard B. Vowles. Eriksson 1967 175p o.p.

Original Swedish edition, 1906

"Strindberg's scapegoat is Edward Libotz, a struggling young lawyer who tries to find a life for himself in a bourgeois Swedish mountain village. Haunted by a family background that plagues him wherever he goes, and scorned by people who make his life almost unbearable, he still manages to triumph over stupidity and bigotry and becomes a quiet hero." Libr J

Struther, Jan, 1901-1953

Mrs. Miniver. Harcourt Brace & Co. 1942 298p o.p. Amereon reprint available $21.95 (ISBN 0-88411-677-8)

Analyzed in Short story index

First published 1939 in the United Kingdom; first United States edition published 1940. This 1942 edition adds a story: Mrs. Miniver makes a list

A succession of episodes relating the daily occurrences over a period of two years in the life of the humorous, perceptive, contented Mrs. Miniver

Contents: Mrs. Miniver comes home; New car; Guy Fawkes' day; Eve of the shoot; Christmas shopping; Three stockings; New engagement book; Last day of the holidays; In search of a charwoman; First day of spring; On Hampstead Heath; Country house visit; Mrs. Downce; Married couples; Drive to Scotland; Twelfth of August; At the games; Autumn flit; Gas masks; "Back

Struther, Jan, 1901-1953—*Continued*
to normal"; Badger and the echidna; Wild day; New
Year's Eve; Choosing a doll; At the dentist's; Pocketful
of pebbles; Brambles and apple-trees; Khelim rug; On
the river; Left and right; "Doing a mole"; New dimension; London in August; Back from abroad; At the hop-
picking; "From needing danger . . ."; Mrs. Miniver
makes a list

Stuart, Colin
Walks Far Woman. Dial Press 1976 342p
o.p.
"Walks Far Woman, a 90-year-old Blackfoot Indian,
recounts her adventures to her grandson and his white
fiancée (a device which permits the author to insert
numerous explanations of obscure customs or more).
Stuart's tale is an embellishment of stories told him by
two Montana Indian women, and he depicts actual historical characters and events such as the Battle of Little
Big Horn, as well as the most intimate details of Indian
life." Booklist

Stuart, Ian, 1922-1987 *See* MacLean,
Alistair, 1922-1987

Stubbs, Jean, 1926-
Family games. St. Martin's Press 1994
294p $21.95
ISBN 0-312-10437-5   LC 93-44054
Also available Thorndike Press large print edition
The Malpas family assembles for Christmas at their
Cornwall farmhouse: "headstrong daughter Blanche, an
unwed mother, brings her infant son and temporarily
abandons her feud with her father, the brilliant and
irascible Anthony; recently separated son Edward, still
reeling from his wife's departure, arrives with his two
children; and beautiful, dependent daughter Lydia surprises the others by bringing a likable woman friend
instead of another one of a parade of 'moneyed and
moronic' male beaux. At the close of the Malpases' impromptu Christmas Eve open house, three unexpected
visitors appear, Magi-like, at the door. One is Natalie,
Anthony's imperious twin sister; another is Katrina, Edward's estranged wife; the third is Daniel Kidd, the
father of Blanche's child." Publ Wkly
"The writer appears fully in control of this entertaining
romp concerning one very dysfunctional, if provocative,
family." Booklist

Kelly Park. St. Martin's Press 1992 310p
$19.95
ISBN 0-312-07850-1   LC 92-944
"Almost 40, divorced, Flavia Polland is forced to
choose a new direction for her life after her lover and
partner in their popular London bistro abandons both
her and the business in 1978. . . . Flavia rethinks her
options at Parc Celli . . . the venerable but faded Cornwall estate of old friend and man-about-town Humphrey
Jarvis. Quickly grasping the possibilities inherent in the
old manor house, she suggests turning it into a first-rate
inn. . . . Humphrey is ambivalent, but agrees and
promises cash. The clannish townspeople, wary at first,
warm to Flavia as they recognize the prospect of steady
employment. And Humphrey's old friend, roguish Tom
Faull, shows up to organize a colorful workforce of
idiosyncratic villagers." Publ Wkly

Light in summer. St. Martin's Press 1991
c1990 292p o.p.
LC 90-49228
First published 1990 in the United Kingdom
"From the outset of this novel, Marina is bereft, utterly dismantled by the long illness and death of her nine-
year-old daughter, Sarah, her unquestioned favorite of the
twins. Left to grapple with her strange and silent husband, Giles, and her bumbling son, Joshua, who preserves the memory of his departed sister as an imaginary
twin, Marina is without solace. But this is only the
beginning of her journey through grief to discovery and
acceptance, of her search for life amid the rubble." Booklist
The author "guides her convincingly delineated characters through some intriguingly complicated relationships."
Publ Wkly

Like we used to be. St. Martin's Press
1990 c1989 387p o.p.
LC 89-27133
First published 1989 in the United Kingdom
"This is the story of Leila and Zoe Gideon, sisters
who are in every way different, yet who love each other
and their marvelous British family unreservedly. The
story begins with Zoe's wedding and Leila's first love
affair in the summer of 1953, and spans the next 15
years. Zoe struggles to create a loving home with her
difficult husband, Matthew. Leila, the rebellious sister,
makes an independent life for herself as an artist in
London. Told alternately by Leila and Zoe, the book
has leisurely pace filled with emotional detail. This will
appeal to lovers of old-fashioned family novels." Libr
J
"Social ferment and family history are vigorously blended in a dramatic style characteristic of a master storyteller." Publ Wkly

Sturgeon, Theodore, 1918-1985
Slow sculpture
In The Best of the Nebulas p403-18

Styron, William, 1925-
The confessions of Nat Turner. Modern
Lib. 1994 xliv, 428p $15.50
ISBN 0-679-60101-5   LC 94-9393
Also available from Buccaneer Bks.
A reissue of the title first published 1967 by Random
House
This "account of an actual person and event is based
on the brief contemporary pamphlet of the same title
presented to a trial court as evidence and published in
Virginia a year after the revolt of fellow slaves led by
Turner in 1831. Imagining much of Turner's youth and
early manhood before the rebellion that he headed at
the age of 31, Styron in frequently rhetorical and pseudo-
Biblical style has Turner recall his religious faith and
his power of preaching to other slaves." Oxford Companion to Am Lit. 5th edition

Lie down in darkness; a novel. Random
House 1979 400p $24.95
ISBN 0-394-50659-6   LC 79-12859

Styron, William, 1925-—*Continued*

First published 1951 by Bobbs-Merrill; this is a reissue of the 1957 Viking edition

"Mr. Styron takes a marriage for the framework of his story, the journey of a hearse to the cemetery for his action, and the suicide of a young woman for his impetus, his mood, and his climax. The marriage is that of Milton and Helen Loftis, a Virginia couple, and the hearse, which they follow in separate limousines, carries the remains of their daughter Peyton, who is in death, as she was in life, only a symbol of her parents' mutual hatred, their despair, and their overpowering self-pity." New Yorker

"The book is not bleakly written. On the contrary, it is richly and even (in the best sense) poetically written. . . . If the parts seem to succeed each other with no apparent logic or dialectic, each part is brilliantly made and lovingly accomplished." Atlantic

The long march. Random House 1968 c1952 120p o.p.

Originally appeared 1952 in periodical; first paperback edition 1956

"The story of a forced 36-mile march at a Marine base in the Carolinas, it is essentially a treatment of contrasts: the placid tenor of civilian life against the brash authoritarianism and occasional idiocy of the military; Captain Al Mannix, the eternal rebel, against Colonel 'Old Rocky' Templeton—both seen through the eyes of Lieutenant Tom Culver, fledgling lawyer, husband, father, and unwilling soldier. Though these contrasts are pronounced, they are the more disturbing because they are not simply black against white but, as it were, a struggle of grays." Libr J

Set this house on fire. Random House 1960 507p $15

ISBN 0-394-44482-5

"The narrator, Peter Leverett, a government employee returning to the U.S., stops in the little Italian village of Sambuco to see his old schoolmate Mason Flagg. The next morning the satyrical Flagg is found dead at the base of a cliff, a peasant girl has been raped and beaten until she dies, and Cass Kinsolving, a drunken, psychoneurotic American painter and the butt of Flagg's devilish humor, has temporarily disappeared. Though the case is written off as one of murder and suicide, the remainder of the novel probes minutely the past lives of the main characters, focusing through Peter's concern and his desire to know the whole truth. A large part of the action takes place in the Mediterranean village, but the novel is also one of contemporary America and Americans; of a world of conflict, too much wealth, too much sex and commercialism, too prevalent shallowness and lack of values." Libr J

Sophie's choice. Random House 1979 515p $29.95

ISBN 0-394-46109-6   LC 78-21835

Also available G.K. Hall large print edition

"Sophie Zawistowska is a Polish Catholic who has somehow survived Auschwitz and resettled in America after the war. Here, in a Jewish boarding house in Flatbush, she meets two men—Nathan Landau, a brilliant but dangerously unstable Jew who becomes her lover; and Stingo, a young Southern writer (and autobiographical simulacrum of Styron himself). The novel traces Stingo's intense involvement with the lovers—their euphoric highs as well as their cataclysmic descents into

psychopathy—and his growing fascination with the horror of Sophie's past." Libr J

"It was a daring act for Styron, whose sensibilities are wholly Southern, to venture into the territory of the American Jew, to say nothing of his plunge into European history. The book is powerfully moving, despite the Southern tendency to grandiloquence, the decking of his prose with magnolia blossoms where starkness was more in order." Burgess. 99 Novels

A Tidewater morning: three tales from youth. Random House 1993 142p $17

ISBN 0-679-42742-2   LC 93-3639

Analyzed in Short story index

"Three long short stories (each previously published in *Esquire*) form a triptych capturing as if in amber a trio of moments in Paul Whitehurst's youth and early manhood. In 'Love Day,' he's a Marine preparing to participate in the assault on Okinawa in the last days of World War II. . . . 'Shadrach' features a younger Paul's reactions (he's 10 that summer) to an ancient black man who returns to the local plantation where he was born in slavery, to die and be buried. . . . The triptych's final panel, 'A Tidewater Morning,' is actually situated chronologically between its predecessors, and it's the most affecting of the three. With a pungency that keenly pierces the reader's heart by use of a blade devoid of sentimentality, Paul recalls his father's disgust with a God that would take in such an excruciating manner the life of his wife, Paul's mother." Booklist

Suarez, Virgil, 1962-

(ed) Iguana dreams. See Iguana dreams

Sullivan, Eleanor

(ed) Fifty years of the best from Ellery Queen's Mystery Magazine. See Fifty years of the best from Ellery Queen's Mystery Magazine

Süskind, Patrick

Perfume: the story of a murderer; translated from the German by John E. Woods. Knopf 1986 255p $16.95

ISBN 0-394-55084-6   LC 86-45419

Original German edition, 1985

Set in eighteenth-century France, Perfume relates the "tale of Jean-Baptiste Grenouille, a person as gifted as he was abominable. Born without a smell of his own but endowed with an extraordinary sense of smell, Grenouille becomes obsessed with procuring the perfect scent that will make him fully human." Libr J

"Those readers who feel they are wasting their time with novels unless they are picking up facts will welcome Süskind's encyclopedic overview of the methods of making perfume. Like the best scents, there is something fundamentally formulaic about this novel, but its effects will linger long after it has been stoppered." Time

Sutcliff, Rosemary, 1920-1992
Sword at sunset. Coward-McCann 1963 495p o.p.

A novel based on historical facts about the legendary Arthur. "The time is the century after the last Roman legions leave Britain, and Arthur is desperately striving to hold Britain against the Saxons, Picts, and other invading savage tribes. [This is] the story of his tragic fate, his good times and bad." Publ Wkly

Sutton, David, 1944-
(ed) The Best horror from Fantasy Tales. See The Best horror from Fantasy Tales

Swarthout, Glendon Fred
Bless the beasts and children; [by] Glendon Swarthout. Doubleday 1970 205p o.p.

"Six rich teenagers, rejected by their parents and avoided by their peers, group together at Box Canyon Summer Boys' Camp. Fragile egos and self-destructive personalities begin to heal under the leadership of Cotton, who gently pokes fun at their soft spots while building up their self-esteem. An effort on the part of the group to stop the wanton slaughter of buffalo provides a high point of suspense." Shapiro. Fic for Youth. 3d edition

The homesman; [by] Glendon Swarthout. Weidenfeld & Nicolson 1988 239p o.p.

LC 88-10102

"After venturing west of the Missouri to stake claims in uncharted territory, a number of settlers find the earth fallow and the desolate, lonely winters unbearable. When four of the wives go mad, the local minister entrusts a prim, strong-willed young schoolmarm, Mary Bee Cuddy, to transport them back to Iowa by covered wagon. With her, virtually against his will, is Briggs, a dishonest, foul-mouthed land-grabber (he steals other peoples' claims) whom Mary Bee saved from a lynching in exchange for his help." Publ Wkly

"Swarthout captures both the adventurous spirit and the sometimes abysmal realities of frontier life." Booklist

The shootist; [by] Glendon Swarthout. Doubleday 1975 186p o.p.

"J. B. Books, last of the West's big-time gunfighters and stoic sufferer of terminal cancer, plays out his death rites. Ensconced in a boarding house in El Paso, Books is approached by a host of exploiters who desire to use his impending death to enhance their own reputations and monetary status; the shootist, however, plans otherwise. He maneuvers his adversaries' self-aggrandizing behavior to his advantage, engineering them to carry out his desire; a quick and respectable death by bullet." Booklist

"This is definitely more than a Western; the characterization is flawless, the plot absorbing and convincing." Libr J

Swift, Jonathan, 1667-1745
Gulliver's travels.
Available from various publishers
First published 1726

"In the account of his four wonder-countries Swift satirizes contemporary manners and morals, art and politics—in fact the whole social scheme—from four different points of view. The huge Brobdingnagians reduce man to his natural insignificance, the little people of Lilliput parody Europe and its petty broils, in Laputa philosophers are ridiculed, and finally all Swift's hatred and contempt find their satisfaction in degrading humanity to a bestial condition." Baker. Guide to the Best Fic

Swift, Margaret *See* Drabble, Margaret, 1939-

Swindells, Madge
Summer harvest. Doubleday 1984 c1983 470p o.p.

LC 83-45373

First published 1983 in the United Kingdom

"This is a character study of a self-willed woman who, after being disinherited by her wealthy family for marrying a poor wheat farmer in South Africa, sets her mind to becoming rich again. So single-minded is she that she is unable to understand or love her husband, her children, or anyone else. But there is another side to her personality; she has great moral integrity. She saves the life of her husband's illegitimate daughter and then rears her as the twin of her own son, sharing her secret with no one. Twenty years later, after she has become a millionaire, political opponents pick at the old rumor and expose the truth." Libr J

"This is a lushly textured family saga brimming with romance, power, scandal and destruction. . . . The narrative is a compelling one." Publ Wkly

Symons, Julian, 1912-1994
The Blackheath poisonings; a Victorian murder mystery. Harper & Row 1978 302p o.p.

LC 78-4745

"A Joan Kahn book"

"In two architecturally outrageous mansions built by an eccentric toy manufacturer live the builder's descendants, related by marriage—and very soon linked by murder. What a pompous doctor dismisses as death from a gastric upset is followed by another very similar demise. Poison is suspected, a body is exhumed and a tangle of family greed, adultery and secret sexual aberrations is brought into the open. Much of the story is seen through the eyes of a stepson whose teenage devotion to a young married woman almost brings her down to destruction. . . . The inquisitive stepson turns sleuth and untangles the mystery." Publ Wkly

"Knowing this able writer, one is not surprised that his first attempt at a period piece (1890) should be faithful in manners and language." Barzun. Cat of Crime. Rev and enl edition

Death's darkest face. Viking 1990 272p o.p.

LC 90-50049

Available G.K. Hall large print edition

Symons "introduces the novel by explaining that what we are about to receive is a manuscript that came into his hands by chance. Symons warns that we should not take every detail at face value. The 'author' of the manuscript is Geoffrey Elder, an actor who died at the end of the seventies. The story he tells tracks back and forth through his life from the thirties to the sixties, in an attempt to get to the bottom of a mystery that

Symons, Julian, 1912-1994—*Continued*

has always perplexed him: what really happened to the scurrilous modernist poet Hugo Headley, who disappeared in mysterious circumstances in 1936?" New Statesman Soc

"Mr. Symons could remove all the mystery elements of this story and still have a wonderful novel, but as we near the end, we are happier for the challenge of solving the crime." N Y Times Book Rev

The Kentish manor murders. Viking 1988 191p o.p.

LC 87-40460

"A Viking novel of mystery and suspense"

"The detective in this book is an actor famous for his Sherlock Holmes readings. A reclusive billionaire engages him for a private reading. It seems that the man is a Conan Doyle enthusiast and a collector of Holmesiana. It seems also that an unknown Sherlock Holmes story has just turned up and the actor is asked to be a go-between in a sale to the billionaire. But is he really the billionaire? Or is he an impersonator? Fun and games, in Mr. Symons' best style." N Y Times Book Rev

Playing happy families. Mysterious Press 1995 308p $19.95

ISBN 0-89296-578-9   LC 94-15119

Also available Thorndike Press large print edition

"The adult children of John and Eleanor Midway gather for their parents 30th wedding anniversary. Champagne is poured; good food is served. But a crisis changes the lives of the Midways, or perhaps it renders visible aspects of their lives formerly hidden. Their firebrand daughter Jenny vanishes one afternoon; she is revealed as wild and promiscuous. In grief, John falls into the arms of his secretary, while Eleanor becomes an unlikely restaurant mogul. Eleanor's son Eversley, visiting from America, negotiates the sale of a priceless work of art with the gallery where Jenny worked. That odd coincidence sets Detective Superintendent Hilary Catchpole on a hunt for a killer." Publ Wkly

Something like a love affair. Mysterious Press 1992 199p $17.95

ISBN 0-89296-495-2   LC 92-5980

"Judith is in bad shape long before she finds out the sordid truth about her husband, a successful architect of perfectionist temperament. Bored to distraction by her doll-like existence in a Sussex suburb . . . she has been writing herself passionate love letters cribbed from historical romances. When that mute cry for attention goes unnoticed, Judith throws herself into an obsessive affair with the loutish youth who has been giving her driving lessons. The next step is murder." N Y Times Book Rev

"Symons' tale is chillingly and compellingly told. Exploring the dark underside of the human spirit, it's story of a desperate woman who can no longer cope." Booklist

A three-pipe problem. Harper & Row 1975 216p o.p.

"A Joan Kahn book"

Symons "a successful TV actor who plays Sherlock Holmes becomes convinced that he can solve the crimes which have heretofore baffled the police, and to this end he enlists a Watson and a group of Baker Street Irregulars. . . . Symons is eminently professional in a highly literate way, and excitement is maintained right up to the astonishing denouement." Libr J

Szeman, Sherri

The Kommandant's mistress; a novel. HarperCollins Pubs. 1993 273p o.p.

LC 92-54714

"This story of the relationship between a young Jewish death-camp inmate and the brutal commander of the camp is told from both of their perspectives." Booklist

This novel "is remarkable for the controlled passion with which it sustains its fierce moral focus, its bleak rage seething and rolling just beneath the surface but always held tight, always at the service of the work." N Y Times Book Rev

T

Tait, Dorothy *See* Fairbairn, Ann, 1901 or 2-1972

Tales of the Witch World [1]-3; created by Andre Norton. Doherty Assocs. 1987-1990 3v o.p.

LC 87-50473

"A TOR book"

Analyzed in Short story index

Contents: v1: Of the shaping of Ulm's heir, by A. Norton; Heir apparent, by R. Bloch; Fenneca, by W. S. Belden; Bloodspell, by A. C. Crispin; The white road, by C. de Lint; Cat and the Other, by M. Dunn; Oathbound, by P. Griffin; Of ancient swords and evil mist, by J. R. Heidbrink; Nine words in winter, by C. Inks; Were-hunter, by M. Lackey; Neither rest nor refuge, by A. Mayhar; To rebuild the Eyrie, by S. Miller; Milk from a maiden's breast, by E. Scarborough; Night hound's moon, by M. H. Schaub; Isle of illusion, by C. Severance; Green in High Hallack, by K. Stuart; The Road of Dreams and death, by R. E. Vardeman

v2: The hunting of Lord Etsalian's daughter, by C. Bell; Sea-serpents of Domnudale, by G. S. Curry; Old toad, by G. Gravel; The judgement of Neave, by S. N. Lewitt; Through the moon gate, by J. Lichtenberg; Dream pirates' jewel, by B. and C. Linaweaver; La verdad: the magic sword, by A. R. Major; Darkness over Mirhold, by P. S. Mathews; Peacock eyes, by S. Meier; The salt garden, by S. Miesel; The stones of Sharnon, by A. Miller; Heroes, by D. L. Paxson; Rite of failure, by S. Shwartz; Futures yet unseen, by M. M. Snodgrass; S'olcarias's sons, by L. Swallow; The sentinel at the edge of the world, by D. Wind; Tall dames go walking, by R. Wolf

v3: Voice of memory, by M. E. Allen; Plumduff Potato-Eye, by J. Carr; The scent of magic, by J. Coulson; Heartspell, by A. C. Crispin; The weavers, by E. M. Friesner; The root of all evil, by S. Green; Knowledge, by P. M. Griffin; The circle of sleep, by C. Inks; Falcon's chick, by P. S. Mathews; Fortune's children, by P. A. McKillip; Godron's daughter, by A. Miller and K. E. Rigley; A question of magic, by M. Randall; Strait of storms, by K. L. Roberts; Candletrap, by M. H. Schaub; Whispering cane, by C. Severance; Gunnora's gift, by E. Waters; Wolfhead, by M. D. Winkle; Wereflight, by L. Woodworth; The sword-seller, by P. C. Wrede

Tallent, Elizabeth, 1954-

Honey; stories. Knopf 1993 207p $22

ISBN 0-394-58304-3   LC 93-18235

Analyzed in Short story index
Contents: Prowler; Black dress; Ciudad Juárez; Earth to Molly; Honey; Get it back for me; Kid gentle; The minute I saw you; James was here
"Situated mainly in the states of New Mexico and California, the narratives capture moments of obsession in the lives of characters who have been hovering on the edge of heartbreak. . . . All nine pieces in this collection chart memorably the often wayward course of contemporary marriage in America." Libr J

Tan, Amy

The Joy Luck Club. Putnam 1989 288p $18.95

ISBN 0-399-13420-4   LC 88-26492

"Four aging Chinese women who knew life in China before 1949 and now live in San Francisco meet regularly to play mah-jongg and share thoughts about their American-born children. In alternating sections we learn about the cultural differences between the elderly 'aunties' and the younger generation. When one of the older women dies, her daughter is pressed to take her place in the Joy Luck Club. Her feeling of being out of place gradually gives way to an understanding of the need to retain cultural continuity and an appreciation for the strength and endurance of the older women." Shapiro. Fic for Youth. 3d edition

The kitchen god's wife. Putnam 1991 415p o.p.

LC 91-7828

Available Thorndike Press large print edition
"Pressed to tell her American-born daughter the truth about her life in China, Winnie unburdens herself of old angers and fears, recounting her violent, war-wrenched youth and the barbaric tyranny of her arranged marriage." Am Libr
"Within the peculiar construction of Amy Tan's second novel is a harrowing, compelling and at times bitterly humorous tale in which an entire world unfolds in a Tolstoyan tide of event and detail." N Y Times Book Rev

Tanenbaum, Robert

Immoral certainty; [by] Robert K. Tanenbaum. Dutton 1991 282p o.p.

LC 90-13841

"The action is set mainly in the wilds of New York City's East Village, where a serial killer who brutalizes children is on the rampage. There's also a messy Mob hit in Little Italy to complicate the lives of no-nonsense D.A. Butch Karp and his colleague and 'occasional main squeeze,' Marlene. Are the cases related? And just how involved is one Felix Tighe, an ambitious yet minor-league criminal with a major-league mother fixation. The novel boasts a wealth of well-developed characters (the principals as well as the minor players); a slew of gallows humor; and a visceral prose style ideally suited to dealing with the sickening brutality of child abuse." Booklist

Reversible error; [by] Robert K. Tanenbaum. Dutton 1992 294p $20

ISBN 0-525-93423-5   LC 91-34464

New York "assistant D.A. Butch Karp faces a dilemma. A rogue cop is on the streets, taking out drug dealers, but Karp's investigation is brought to a halt when he is asked to suppress evidence. Sharing center stage with Karp's case is that of the D.A.'s colleague and lover, Marlene, who is on the trail of a rapist who wraps a pair of panty hose around each victim. With some unexpected help, Marlene spots a similarity in the victims. . . . With twin plots sizzling and exploding, the novel takes us inside the psyches of its characters, revealing the crime fighters' dark humor, rigid notions of right and wrong, and righteous anger." Booklist

Tapply, William G.

Client privilege. Delacorte Press 1990 260p o.p.

LC 89-23729

"Acting on behalf of his client and best friend, Judge Popowski (Pops) [Boston attorney] Coyne meets a TV reporter, Wayne Churchill, who threatens the judge's virtually certain appointment to the federal courts. Implicitly trusting the judge's statement that the newsman has no real grounds for blackmail, Coyne refuses Churchill's demand of $10,000 for his silence. The reporter's murder that same night brings the police to question the attorney, who, standing on client privilege, withholds Pops's name and therefore risks his own arrest as the killer. The circumstances force Coyne to search for the guilty party in order to clear himself." Publ Wkly

Dead meat; a Brady Coyne mystery. Scribner 1987 213p o.p.

LC 86-26143

"Heeding the call of one of his eccentric, well-to-do clients, Brady packs rod and reel and journeys to Raven Lake Lodge in the wilds of Maine, where his friend Tiny Wheeler, the lodge's owner, is trying to cope with the disappearance of a guest and a takeover bid by a group of Indian activists, who contend that the lodge is situated on sacred tribal ground. It doesn't take Brady long to realize that the situations are inextricably linked in a web of intrigue that points toward organized crime." Booklist

Dead winter; a Brady Coyne novel. Delacorte Press 1989 230p $16.95

ISBN 0-385-29711-4   LC 88-13867

Also available G.K. Hall large print edition
"A friend's daughter-in-law has been murdered on board the family yacht and Brady Coyne, the attorney-turned-sleuth, is called in when all fingers point to the victim's husband. This is the first in a trio of murders in which Brady becomes involved. A mysterious bald man is murdered in a nearby town and a young waitress with a brutal husband is slain locally. Yet only Brady sees the connections and starts a search to find out not only who-dun-it, but how these three unrelated murders are connected." West Coast Rev Books
"The plot takes some gothic turns—bastardy, incest, and earlier violent death—but Tapply never neglects his nicely defined characterizations or loses his cool control over narrative tension in this very satisfying caper." Publ Wkly

The seventh enemy. Penzler Bks. 1995 234p $21

ISBN 1-883402-99-9   LC 94-29386

Tapply, William G.—*Continued*

Boston lawyer Brady Coyne lends a "hand to Walt Kinnick, an old fishing buddy who has become a well-known outdoorsman and staunch conservationist. Kinnick enrages a rabid group of hunters called SAFE ('Second Amendment For Ever') when he switches his position on gun control and publicly supports a ban on semiautomatic weapons. Before you can say 'Uzi, Beretta AR-70, AK-47, Valmet, FNC Paratrooper, Galil 223-AR,' Kinnick takes a gut shot from an assassin. As his lawyer, Coyne is assigned the seventh slot on SAFE's enemies list and starts getting threats." N Y Times Book Rev

The author "fluidly incorporates both sides of the volatile gun-control issue into an entertaining and satisfying suspense novel." Booklist

The snake eater. Penzler Bks. 1993 273p o.p.

LC 93-19362

Boston lawyer-sleuth Brady Coyne "represents Daniel McCloud, a reclusive Vietnam veteran and Agent Orange victim accused of trafficking in marijuana (which he requires as a medicine). The state drops the case without explanation, but Coyne becomes friendly with McCloud, who then asks him to get his book published. After the book disappears and someone murders Daniel, Brady hastens to uncover what damning knowledge the man possessed." Libr J

The author "is such an old hand that there's never a break in that practiced, flowing style he has mastered over a dozen books. But this time his theme of friendship has jagged edges of anger and pain that cut through Coyne's reserve and draw blood." N Y Times Book Rev

Tight lines; a Brady Coyne novel. Delacorte Press 1992 277p o.p.

LC 91-31880

Brady Coyne, "a Boston lawyer whose client base is profoundly rich if not famous, is called to the side of Susan Ames, a wealthy widow dying of cancer. Using the pretense of establishing ground rules for the disposition of the historically significant family estate, she asks Brady to find the daughter she hasn't seen in 11 years." Booklist

A void in hearts; a Brady Coyne mystery. Scribner 1988 198p o.p.

LC 88-12203

Available G.K. Hall large print edition

"A marginally unscrupulous private eye, Les Katz, gets himself killed after blackmailing a client. Brady is called to the sleuth's deathbed but arrives too late, leaving him no choice but to figure out what happened." Booklist

Tarkington, Booth, 1869-1946

Alice Adams; illustrated by Arthur William Brown. Doubleday, Page 1921 434p il o.p. Amereon reprint available $26.95 (ISBN 0-89190-737-8)

"A social climber, the title character is ashamed of her unsuccessful family. Hoping to attract a wealthy husband, she lies about her background, but she is found out and is shunned by those whom she sought to attract. At the novel's end, she knows her chances for happiness and a successful marriage are bleak, but she remains unbowed." Merriam-Webster's Ency of Lit

The gentleman from Indiana.
Available from AMS Press and Scholarly Press

First published 1899 by Doubleday & McClure

Tarkington "tells the story of John Harkless, a promising young college graduate who buys and edits a newspaper in a small Hoosier town. Harkless discovers many things that are wrong, especially in local politics, and he attacks with particular vigor a gang of 'White Caps.' They assault him, and his disappearance leads to the belief that he has been murdered. The girl he has fallen in love with takes over his paper and carries it on with equal vigor. Young John returns, secures a nomination to the House of Representatives, and is elected. He sees his enemies punished and the community purified." Benet's Reader's Ency of Am Lit

The magnificent Ambersons.
Available from various publishers

First published 1918 by Doubleday, Page

"The novel traces the growth of the United States through the decline of the once-powerful, socially prominent Amberson family. Their fall is contrasted with the rise of new industrial tycoons and land developers, whose power comes not through family connections but through financial dealings and modern manufacturing." Merriam-Webster's Ency of Lit

Monsieur Beaucaire. Doubleday 1900 115p o.p. Amereon reprint available $16.95 (ISBN 0-88411-703-0)

"The scene is laid in 18th-century Bath, and the hero is a cousin of Louis XV, Louis Philippe de Valois. Disguised as a barber, on adventure bent, he falls in love with Lady Mary Carlisle and forces his rival, the Duke of Winterset, whom he has caught cheating at cards, to present him as the Duke de Chateaurien. All goes well with his suit until Winterset announces that he is a mere barber, whereupon Lady Mary treats him with the utmost scorn. Shortly after, on an occasion of state, he is greeted as the Duke of Orleans, but her regret is of no avail." Reader's Ency

Seventeen. Grosset & Dunlap 1916 249p o.p.
Available from Amereon and Buccaneer Bks.

The novel's "hero is William Sylvanus Baxter, Silly Billy, an adolescent in the throes of his first love affair. The object of his attention is Lola Pratt, whose chief occupation is lavishing baby talk on her pet dog Flopit and on her numerous admirers." Reader's Ency. 3d edition

"This story of the first love experience of William Sylvanus Baxter shows an almost uncanny insight into the emotions and mental processes of the adolescent boy. It is full of humor and gentle sarcasm, but also understanding and sympathy for the tragedies and absurdities of youth." Wis Libr Bull

Tarr, Judith

A fall of princes. Doherty Assocs. 1988 401p (Avaryan rising, v3) o.p.

LC 87-51392

"A TOR book"

In the concluding volume of the trilogy "two princes of mutually hostile lands find themselves thrown together in a battle for survival that forges an unlikely bond between them that could save—or destroy—both their kingdoms." Libr J

"Tarr's background in medieval history sustains her excellent world building, and the intrigue here is abundant and detailed." Booklist

Tarr, Judith—*Continued*

The golden horn. Bluejay Bks. 1985 262p (Hound and the falcon trilogy, v2) o.p.

LC 85-15741

"The second volume of Tarr's trilogy takes Alfred of St. Ruan's to Constantinople during the Fourth Crusade. He is befriended by a Greek family but loses his ally, Thea, when Crusaders sack the city. Torn between his magical powers and his religious conscience, Alfred finds that his judgment becomes dangerously impaired." Booklist

Followed by The Hounds of God

The hall of the mountain king. Doherty Assocs. 1986 278p (Avaryan rising, v1) o.p.

"A TOR book"

"In the kingdom of Ianon, Mirain is heir to the realm of his father, the Sun God. This tale concerns itself primarily with Mirain's successful defense of his claim against the treacheries of his mortal relatives. Occasional lapses in narrative technique only slightly detract from Tarr's characterizations and obvious command of language." Booklist

Followed by The lady of Han-Gilen

The Hounds of God. Bluejay Bks. 1986 344p (Hound and the falcon trilogy, v3) o.p.

In the concluding volume of the trilogy "ex-monk Alfred is now reconciled to his magical powers and is not only Chancellor of the Kingdom of Rhiyana but about to become a father. When the kingdom is attacked by the hounds of God (modeled after the Dominicans of the early Inquisition), the king's son is slain, Alfred's lover Thea and their newborn twins are carried off to Rome, and Alfred must follow them to confront the pope himself." Booklist

The isle of glass. Bluejay Bks. 1985 276p (Hound and the falcon trilogy, v1) o.p.

LC 85-1295

This first volume of the author's fantasy trilogy featuring Alfred of St. Ruan's is set "during the reign of Richard the Lionheart, a time of legends and magic beliefs. Alfred's appearances and abilities are qualities that are usually associated with the Fair Folk. Alfred is content to spend his life in the abbey, but one night the elf-king's ambassador comes seeking Alfred's help . . . and Alfred must go into the world to carry Alun's message to King Richard. Some of the people are aware of Alfred's background or guess at it, and this causes problems, good and bad, and adds a great deal of suspense to the novel." Voice Youth Advocates

Followed by The golden horn

The lady of Han-Gilen. Doherty Assocs. 1987 310p il (Avaryan rising, v2) o.p.

LC 87-205780

"A TOR book"

In this second volume of the trilogy, "Elian, the Lady of Han-Gilen, is beautiful, intelligent, stubborn and hot-tempered. Through her own insistence, she is skilled in martial as well as courtly arts, a horsewoman, hawker, linguist, musician, etc. When nobles ask for her hand, she bests them in their special talents and sends them packing. Her search for an equal or better leads her to a choice between handsome, witty High Prince Ziad-Ilarios, heir to the sophisticated Asanion empire, and her childhood companion Mirain, son of a priestess and a god, a barbarian conqueror who is building his own empire." Publ Wkly

Followed by The fall of princes

Tarrant, John, 1927-

For works written by this author under other names see Egleton, Clive, 1927-

Tate, Ellalice, 1906-1993

For works written by this author under other names see Carr, Philippa, 1906-1993; Holt, Victoria, 1906-1993; Plaidy, Jean, 1906-1993

Tax, Meredith

Rivington Street. Morrow 1982 431p o.p.

LC 81-22587

"This is the story of Russian immigrant men and women caught up in the social upheavals at the beginning of this century. Set on the Lower East Side of New York, the book concerns strong-willed Hannah Levy, her daughters, Sarah, a social activist, and Ruby, a creative designer of clothes, and their beautiful and romantic friend, Rachel Cohen. It is the women who dominate this book. Their struggle to survive the terrible working conditions and low pay of jobs in the garment industry and the violence that comes when they demand a better life make an absorbing story. Tax has used real incidents—the fire at the Triangle Waist factory, a strike of garment workers, and the jailing of suffragists—to add color and authenticity to the story." Libr J

Followed by Union Square

Union Square. Morrow 1988 437p o.p.

LC 88-9075

This sequel to Rivington Street focuses on a "mostly Russian-born family of socialist workers and confirmed Marxists, forced by pogroms to flee to America's Lower East Side, where their political divisiveness continues. . . . The focus is on Hannah and Moyshe Levy and their daughter Sarah, who has married Marxist apologist Avi Spector. The ideological rift between the Levys and the Spectors widens when, at the onset of the Depression, Moyshe sides with the Bundists while Avi supports the Stalinists. As Sarah campaigns for unions and women's right to decent pay, her sister Ruby, married to Ben Berliner, becomes a force in the fashion industry." Publ Wkly

"The point of Meredith Tax's novels isn't the quality of her prose. She is telling gritty, satisfying stories." NY Times Book Rev

Taylor, Elizabeth, 1912-1975

Mrs. Palfrey at the Claremont. Viking 1971 178p o.p.

A "tale about an elderly British widow who takes up residence in one of those shabby, genteel hotels along London's Cromwell Road. She is at a desperate loss for what to do with herself to fill in the time and try to make her fellow lodgers believe she still has some semblance of a personal life. The portraits of the elderly and crotchety residents are drawn with a pen only lightly tipped in acid, and Mrs. Palfrey herself is very human and endearing. She finds her real hope for the future in pretending that a rather callow but not unkind casual acquaintance is really her grandson." Publ Wkly

Taylor, Elizabeth Atwood

The cable car murder. St. Martin's Press 1981 246p o.p.

LC 81-5809

"Maggie Elliott—gamely fighting back against depression and alcoholism—receives a double blow when her rich half-sister is killed in a suspicious cable-car accident and soon afterward her niece dies in a plane crash. When she meets ex-cop Richard Patrick O'Reagan, witness to the cable car accident, they pool their suspicions and information to investigate." Libr J

"The characters are believable and Maggie's feelings about her alcoholism are insightful and interesting. Taylor gives us a humdinger of a final scene filled with dire threats and spectacular action." Publ Wkly

Murder at Vassar. St. Martin's Press 1987 257p o.p.

LC 86-27946

Maggie Elliott is "a full-fledged private investigator operating out of the Bay Area with her partner, Richard Patrick O'Reagan. Maggie thinks she has come east to attend her fifteenth college reunion . . . [but] two murders rock the peace of Vassar's campus when a rich old woman and a poor young coed are murdered as the alumnae gather. Maggie is hired to look into matters when Pudgie Warren Brown is charged with the murder of her aunt. Operating under the assumption that the crimes must have something to do with old Mrs. Warren's vast wealth, Maggie starts digging." Wilson Libr Bull

The northwest murders. St. Martin's Press 1992 278p $18.95

ISBN 0-312-07753-X   LC 92-4255

"To recover from a long bout with chronic fatigue syndrome, environmentally conscious, politically correct PI Maggie Elliott leaves San Francisco . . . for a cabin her partner recently inherited near the California-Oregon border. She arrives two days after a young hiker was murdered and mutilated, and his girlfriend raped and nearly killed as well. . . . Regional rituals and history, including 50-year-old-diaries and a legend of lost gold nuggets, flavor this entertaining escapade." Publ Wkly

Taylor, Jane See Krentz, Jayne Ann

Taylor, Kamala Purnaiya See Markandaya, Kamala, 1924-

Taylor, Peter Hillsman, 1917-1994

A summons to Memphis; [by] Peter Taylor. Knopf 1986 209p $15.95

ISBN 0-394-41062-9   LC 86-45417

"A son, now a grown man, recounts the family's subservience to a strong-willed father. Against a background of Southern manners in Memphis and Nashville, the Carver daughters and sons experience frustration of their hopes to marry and enjoy family lives of their own. The mother, soon after her marriage to George Carver, withdraws from resisting his authority. The daughters never find suitors who suit their father. One brother, escaping to war, is killed and the narrator, Philip, a bachelor still at 49, is summoned home by his sisters to prevent their father, at 81, from remarrying. The seemingly selfless

care given by the daughters might stem from self-interest rather than filial devotion." Shapiro. Fic for Youth. 3d edition

Taylor, Robert Lewis

The travels of Jaimie McPheeters. Doubleday 1958 544p o.p.

Available from Amereon and Buccaneer Bks.

"Fourteen-year old Jaimie McPheeters, the son of Sardius McPheeters, an unsuccessful, windy-minded doctor who is given to gambling and drink, sets out with his father from their Louisville home in the spring of 1849 for the California gold fields, and in the course of the next three years or so is kidnapped by outlaws; is captured by Indians; witnesses a lot of brutality, including a duel, fires, killings, and some startling Indian cruelty; suffers semi-starvation and degradation; and in the end, after his father's death, becomes part owner of a handsome California ranch, where he settles with his mother, his sisters, and his Indian sweetheart." New Yorker

"The piquant combination of solid historical content, satisfying adventure, good literary style, sophisticated wit and humor will give this book wide appeal." Libr J

Tennant, Emma, 1937-

Pemberley; or Pride and prejudice continued. St. Martin's Press 1993 184p $18.95

ISBN 0-312-10793-5   LC 94-171082

"It is the Christmas season, and Elizabeth Darcy (Elizabeth Bennet of Pride and Prejudice) now the uneasy mistress of the great estate of Pemberley, anticipates the holidays with growing trepidation. Her foolish widowed mother and two of her sisters, flighty Kitty and pedantic Mary, are soon to descend upon the household. Adding to the guest list, as well as the complications, are her husband's formidable aunt, Lady Catherine de Bourgh, and the Wickhams (the cad who eloped with Elizabeth's sister after his unsuccessful attempt to run off with her sister-in-law). Sweet-tempered Jane will also be present, but her imminent confinement is a constant reminder to Elizabeth of her own barrenness." Libr J

The author's "narrative is made uncomfortably compelling by her utter mastery of Austen's style. In its pace and sensibility, the text virtually breathes Jane Austen; the malaise that Ms. Tennant so powerfully exploits is solidly rooted in her model." N Y Times Book Rev

Followed by An unequal marriage

An unequal marriage; or, Pride and prejudice twenty years later. St. Martin's Press 1994 186p $18.95

ISBN 0-312-11533-4   LC 94-26108

"In this sequel-to-the-sequel, [Elizabeth and Darcy] experience the mixed blessings children can bring. At 17, Miranda is lovely, competent, and her father's pride and joy, but heir-apparent Edward, a student at Eton, has long been a problem. As guests gather for the wedding of close friend Colonel Fitzwilliam, reports come that Edward has fallen under bad influences in London and gambled away part of the family estate. Cold disciplinarian Darcy acts, while compassionate chatelaine Elizabeth is distraught and susceptible to the admiring glances of handsome Mr. Gresham." Libr J

Tennenbaum, Silvia, 1928-

Yesterday's streets. Random House 1981 528p o.p.

LC 81-1119

This novel "traces the fortunes of a prosperous German-Jewish family from the turn of the century to the end of the Second World War, when the survivors are dispersed to Palestine, Zurich, or New York. The prosperity of the Wertheim clan is based solidly on the wholesale woollens business of Papa Moritz, which supports not only the sons who enter the business, but also the one intellectual, who becomes a bookseller, and the black sheep, Gottfried, who is sent off to America. The next generation branches out even further; the two emancipated daughters, Lene and Emma, both make disastrous marriages with goyim; one of the sons becomes an ardent Zionist and the other is openly homosexual. . . . Lene's daughter Clara, who is seventeen in 1945, is the author herself, and the novel her offering to the ghosts of her Jewish past." Times Lit Suppl

Tepper, Sheri S.

The gate to Women's Country. Doubleday 1988 278p o.p.

LC 88-387

"A Foundation book"
"A feminist fable set somewhere in the Pacific Northwest 300 years after a nuclear holocaust. Men and women now live in separate but adjacent communities. Although the men are organized into military garrisons, the women appear to have the upper hand in government, deciding matters of trade and law and, most important, reproduction. . . . The elaborate society that the author takes such pains to describe is based on a big lie; the story she tells is part of the deception. Some will find this narrative strategy as distasteful as the secret it conceals. But Ms. Tepper is not afraid to ask hard questions, beginning with this: If biology is destiny, how can society hope to control its self-destructive tendencies without controlling biology as well?" N Y Times Book Rev

Grass. Doubleday 1989 426p o.p.

LC 89-30105

"A Foundation book"
In this first volume of a trilogy "diplomats are dispatched to the planet Grass in search of the cure for a deadly disease that is spreading throughout inhabited space. The human settlers, xenophobic and conservative landed gentry, lead an existence tightly structured around the Hunt, a complex and violent ritual involving the use of alien mounts that seem nearly demonic in their malevolence. The presence of a number of not particularly sympathetic religious groups adds complexity to the situation. This is a beautifully written novel with well-developed characters and a number of very interesting aliens." Anatomy of Wonder 4
Followed by Raising the stones

Northshore. Doherty Assocs. 1987 248p (Awakeners, v1) o.p.

LC 86-50961

"A TOR book"
"The World River flows west; to travel east—on water or land—is to risk the wrath of the Awakeners, the feared keepers of the secrets of the dead. Brought together by a miracle, Thrasne, a Boatman with a gift for carving wood and asking questions, and Pamra Don,

an Awakener disillusioned by the 'truths' of her religion, challenge the teachings of centuries in an attempt to discover the hidden secrets of their world." Libr J
"The interwoven stories of love and politics, the painstakingly developed characters and customs, all pale beside a world so vividly created that the book seems to be illustrated." Voice Youth Advocates
Followed by Southshore

A plague of angels. Bantam Bks. 1993 423p o.p.

LC 93-158

"A young woman named Orphan leaves her archetypal village in pursuit of a prophecy, while a farm boy named Abasio travels to the gang-infested city in search of adventure. Together, Abasio and Orphan become the catalysts that enable the land of Artemisia to discover the secrets left to them by their ancestors, who abandoned their world for the stars." Libr J
"If the fantasy and SF elements don't always merge seamlessly, the setting is well-realized. . . . Tepper's prose is colorful and, while occasionally strident, tempered with wry wit and astute observations about human nature." Publ Wkly

Raising the stones. Doubleday 1990 453p o.p.

LC 90-30191

"A Foundation book"
In this second volume of the trilogy set in a far away galaxy "a community of good people (who live in peace and harmony under the subtle mind control of an alien intelligence they refer to as 'the God') are threatened by a sect of religious fanatics (whose megalomaniacal creed not only permits the enslavement of unbelievers but 'insists' on it)." N Y Times Book Rev
This is a "complicated, exciting narrative that explores central questions of religion and faith, and of the dangers and usefulness of technology." Women's Rev Books
Followed by Sideshow

Shadow's end; a novel. Bantam Bks. 1994 388p $22.95

ISBN 0-553-09514-5   LC 94-6611

"A band of reluctant heroes, assembled by fate on the planet Dinadh, scramble to identify and defeat a force that is systematically wiping out the populations of neighboring worlds." Booklist
"Strong characters with personal dilemmas—whose resolutions have far-reaching consequences—add depth and immediacy to the story." Libr J

Sideshow. Bantam Bks. 1992 467p o.p.

LC 91-40420

In this concluding volume of the trilogy begun with Grass, "a sentient fungus has infested most of the galaxy, reworking the life forms it inhabits to enhance their physical and spiritual comfort. The people of the planet Elsewhere, however, see the fungus's contented hosts as slaves; to preserve free will on Elsewhere, the rulers have imposed absolute cultural relativity within which pleasant and unsavory societies coexist, their integrity rigidly maintained by Enforcers. But powers have arisen to challenge the status quo." Publ Wkly
"Tepper's imaginative vision holds forth and delivers one of her most challenging works." Libr J

Southshore. Doherty Assocs. 1987 250p (Awakeners, v2) o.p.

LC 86-51487

Tepper, Sheri S.—*Continued*

"A TOR book"

The second volume of the author's science fiction diptych. "While ex-Awakener Pamra Don—now truly awakened—leads a crusade against the evil done in the name of religion, the Boatman Thrasne embarks on a voyage across the World River to search for a land of safety on the legendary 'Southshore.'" Libr J

The author "continues her gradual, teasing revelations about the planet's history, particularly in the wonderful story of Tharius Don, who became a cleric to get at the books that would answer his youthful questions. As before, this clever, intricately constructed world is appropriately distant and cool." Publ Wkly

Tevis, Walter S., 1928-1984

The queen's gambit; [by] Walter Tevis. Random House 1983 243p o.p.

LC 82-15058

This "is the story of an orphan girl who is taught to play chess by the janitor of her orphanage. Beth Harmon has genius; she wins her first tournament when she is 14, becomes American champion at 18 and starts the international circuit. She may well be the second best player in the world. Only the world champion, a Russian . . . is stronger than she, and she is scared to death of him. The climax of the book comes when they meet over the board in a Moscow tournament." N Y Times Book Rev

"Familiarity with chess is not needed in order to enjoy this book though aficionados will delight in its evocation of their esoteric freemasonry." Times Lit Suppl

Tey, Josephine, 1896-1952

Brat Farrar. Macmillan 1950 c1949 219p o.p. Bentley reprint available $16 (ISBN 0-8376-0445-1)

Also available G.K. Hall large print edition

First published 1949 in the United Kingdom

"The scene is an English country home owned by the orphaned Ashby children and managed for them by their aunt, who has made a success of the horses she bred and exhibited. Simon, charming and spoiled, is about to take over as he comes of age, when a well-coached imposter arrives and claims to be the elder brother who had disappeared eight years before, leaving a suicide note." Booklist

also in Tey, J. Three by Tey v3

The daughter of time. Macmillan 1952 c1951 204p o.p. Buccaneer Bks. reprint available $23.95 (ISBN 0-89966-184-X)

First published 1951 in the United Kingdom

"Alan Grant, injured policeman hospitalized and bored, is diverted by a photograph of Richard III, commonly conceded murderer of the princes in the Tower. With the invaluable assistance of a research student, Grant's convalescence becomes a lively pursuit of the truth as shown by records in Richard's time." Libr J

The author "not only reconstructs the probably historical truth, she re-creates the intense dramatic excitement of the scholarly research necessary to unveil it." N Y Times Book Rev

also in Tey, J. Four, five and six by Tey v3

Four, five and six by Tey. Macmillan 1958 3v in 1 o.p.

"Murder revisited series"

An omnibus edition of three complete Scotland Yard mysteries in which Inspector Alan Grant solves the crimes. Includes The singing sands (1952) and The daughter of time (1951) both entered separately, and A shilling for candles (1936), about a film star whose death by strangulation is the focus of Grant's investigation

The Franchise affair. Macmillan 1948 238p o.p. Bentley reprint available $16 (ISBN 0-8376-0446-X)

Also available Thorndike Press large print edition

"A lawyer in an English country town answers an appeal for help from two women who, having only recently inherited a home, were still outsiders to the townspeople and, being independent, reserved, and unusual, were called witches. When a girl in another town accused them of imprisoning, starving, and beating her in their attic, they were helpless, for the circumstantial evidence seemed indisputable. Good characterization, good writing, and to the lawyer's surprise, an emotional involvement for him." Booklist

also in Tey, J. Three by Tey v2

The man in the queue. Macmillan 1953 213p o.p. Bentley reprint available $16 (ISBN 0-8376-0450-8)

First published 1929 by Dutton under the pseudonym Gordon Daviot

A man is stabbed to death waiting in the ticket line of a popular London musical, and Inspector Grant of the C.I.D. is assigned to the case

"Every detail of the discovery of first the identity and then the murderer of the knifed man is admirably invented, and the story, at first sight a simple build-up . . . turns out to be a serious inductive exercise." Springfield Repub

Miss Pym disposes. Macmillan 1948 213p o.p. Bentley reprint available $16 (ISBN 0-8376-0447-8)

First published 1946 in the United Kingdom

An English woman psychologist delivers a lecture at a physical training college and decides to stay a little longer. She becomes very friendly with some of the seniors, and eventually finds herself involved in an "accident" which turns out to be a murder

also in Tey, J. Three by Tey v1

A shilling for candles

In Tey, J. Four, five and six by Tey v1

The singing sands. Macmillan 1953 c1952 221p o.p.

First published 1952 in the United Kindgom. Variant title: Grant's last case

A cryptic fragment of verse, found near a dead man on a train en route to Scotland is Inspector Grant's only clue to the identity of the man's murderer

also in Tey, J. Four, five and six by Tey v2

Tey, Josephine, 1896-1952—*Continued*

Three by Tey; Miss Pym disposes; The Franchise affair [and] Brat Farrar; with an introduction by James Sandoe. Macmillan 1954 3v in 1 o.p.

"Murder revisited series. A Cock Robin mystery"

An omnibus edition of three titles entered separately

To love and be wise. Macmillan 1951 c1950 210p o.p.

Available G.K. Hall large print edition

First published 1950 in the United Kindgom

"Leslie Searle, a too-handsome too-charming American photographer, wangles an invitation to the country, sets an artistic colony by the ears, and appears to be winning nice Liz Garrowby from her tiresome fiancé, Walter Whitcomb. When Leslie disappears, Walter is a likely murder suspect, but some intelligent police work [by Inspector Alan Grant] discovers what really happened and why." Booklist

Thackeray, William Makepeace, 1811-1863

The history of Henry Esmond, esquire. o.p.

First published 1852; first United States edition published 1879 by Harper with title: Henry Esmond

"The story, narrated by Esmond, begins in 1691 when he is 12 and ends in 1718. Its complexity of incident is given unity by Esmond and his second cousin Beatrix, who stand out against a background of London society and the political life of the time. Beatrix dominates the book. One of Thackeray's great creations, she is a heroine of a new type, emotionally complex and compelling, but not a pattern of virtue." Merriam-Webster's Ency of Lit

Followed by The Virginians

Vanity fair; a novel without a hero. Knopf 1991 xliv, 878p il $20

ISBN 0-679-40566-6   LC 91-52983

Also available from Buccaneer Bks.

"Everyman's library"

First published 1848

"The book is a densely populated, multi-layered panorama of manners and human frailties. . . . The novel deals mainly with the interwoven fortunes of two women, the wellborn, passive Amelia Sedley and the ambitious, essentially amoral Becky Sharp, the latter perhaps the most memorable character Thackeray created. The adventuress Becky is the character around whom all the men play their parts." Merriam-Webster's Ency of Lit

The Virginians. o.p.

First published 1857; first United States edition published 1869 by Fields, Osgood & Co.

"A sequel to 'Henry Esmond', it relates the story of George and Harry Warrington, the twin grandsons of Colonel Henry Esmond. The novel takes the two brothers, of differing tastes and temperaments, through boyhood in America, through various experiences in England, where they are favorites of their wicked old aunt, Baroness Bernstein (the Beatrix of *Henry Esmond*), and through the American Revolution, in which George fights on the British side and Harry on the side of his friend George Washington." Reader's Ency. 3d edition

Thane, Elswyth, 1900-

Dawn's early light. Duell, Sloan & Pearce 1943 317p o.p.

Available from Amereon and Buccaneer Bks.

The first volume in the author's series of historical novels about a Williamsburg, Virginia family

"When, in May 1774, young fatherless Julian Day arrives in Virginia from London, he is uncertain of his next step, but the friendliness of St. John Sprague impels him to stay on in Williamsburg as a teacher, and soon Julian, the Loyalist, is strangely interested in the activities of the Colonial government and in the personalities of men like Washington and Jefferson. His championship of the abused 11-year-old twin, Tibby Mawes, who displays an unusual bent for learning, wins him a place in the Southern community, while he is temporarily ensnared by Sprague's beautiful and flirtatious lady-love, Regina Gildersleeves." Bookmark

Followed by Yankee stranger

Ever after. Duell, Sloan & Pearce 1945 334p o.p.

Available from Amereon and Buccaneer Bks.

Continuing the chronicles of the Day/Murray/Sprague family of Williamsburg, Virginia one generation further, this novel centers on journalist Bracken Murray who finds romance in England in the year of Queen Victoria's Jubilee (1897) and, along with his cousin, cub-reporter Fitz Sprague, covers the Spanish-American War in Cuba for the New York Star

Followed by The light heart

Homing. Duell, Sloan & Pearce 1957 272p o.p.

Available from Amereon and Buccaneer Bks.

This novel "continues the lives of the Sprague-Day family. . . . Romantic interest centers on Jeff Day, now working as a foreign correspondent in London, who is the image of his eighteenth-century Grandfather Julian, and on his distant English cousin Mab, who seems the reincarnation of Julian's wife Tibby." Booklist

Kissing kin. Duell, Sloan & Pearce 1948 374p o.p.

Available from Amereon and Buccaneer Bks.

"The fifth of a series of novels about a Williamsburg family. Camilla and Calvert the twins, start out in 1917 to take part in the war, Calvert on a gun crew and Camilla to serve as a nurses' aid in her cousin's hospital in England. A Christmas party at the cousin's ancestral home sets several love affairs in motion and complicates the lives of several characters throughout the book." Ont Libr Rev

Followed by This was tomorrow

The light heart. Duell, Sloan & Pearce 1947 341p o.p.

Available from Amereon and Buccaneer Bks.

The fourth volume in the author's series of historical novels about the Spragues and the Days of Williamsburg, Virginia. The heroine this time is Phoebe Sprague, who became engaged to her cousin Miles just before her departure for England to attend the coronation of Edward VII. There she met the man she really loved. The book closes after a raid on London during World War I

Followed by Kissing kin

This was tomorrow. Duell, Sloan & Pearce 1951 319p o.p.

Available from Amereon and Buccaneer Bks.

Thane, Elswyth, 1900—*Continued*

The sixth volume of the author's series about a Williamsburg family is about the romance of two pairs of cousins. Two of the cousins who are dancers, take a show to London where they meet their English counterparts. The time is just before the Second World War, 1934-1938

Followed by Homing

Yankee stranger. Duell, Sloan & Pearce 1944 306p o.p.

Available from Amereon and Buccaneer Bks.

Second title in the author's series about a Virginia family. "In Williamsburg one gusty, stormy day just before the Civil War, [Cabot Murray], a handsome, tall young Northerner, a newspaper correspondent, runs bang into lovely, 17-year-old Eden Day [great-granddaughter of Julian and Tibby Day] and, as suddenly, invades her heart. How Eden's remarkable 'Gran,' a beautiful old lady of 95 who had herself long ago fallen in love at first sight, aids and abets the lovers during the following terrible years is related in an attractive historical romance . . . [in] a deftly contrived plot." Bookmark

Followed by Ever after

Thayer, Nancy, 1943-

Everlasting. Viking 1991 322p o.p.

LC 90-50462

Available. Thorndike Press large print edition

"Catherine Eliot, at 18, is aimless until she falls into a job in a flower shop and realizes that this is the business she was born for. Though her social register family has cut her off, she uses her own social connections to build her business into a giant. This rejected daughter does all she can to rescue her family from financial and emotional distress. Though her help is neither understood nor appreciated, Catherine eventually finds contentment in herself, her marriage, and her business. An absorbing story and heroine." Libr J

Family secrets. Viking 1993 338p $21

ISBN 0-670-84439-X   LC 92-50746

Also available Thorndike Press large print edition

At the center of this novel is "Diane, driven, successful, and suffering the disillusionment of mid-life crisis. The FBI contacts her in an attempt to locate her recently widowed mother, who they believe possesses top-secret information. At the same time, Julia, her unhappily college-bound daughter who's desperately in love with the boy next door and more desperately in need of breaking away from her mother's expectations, runs off to be married. Meanwhile, Diane's mother, Jean, captures the foregone dream of her youth: traveling through Europe with no itinerary, enjoying only quiet, anonymous days of her very own. Gradually, gently, the lives of these women unfold before us and Jean's mysterious secret is revealed." Booklist

My dearest friend. Scribner 1989 342p o.p.

LC 89-6276

Available Thorndike Press large print edition

"Divorcée Daphne Miller is the mother of a 16-year-old daughter who takes off abruptly for California to live with a father she has not heard from for 14 years. Deprived of child support payments, Daphne moves into a country shack. Once a college professor like her ex-husband and two married swains, she is now a lowly but plucky department secretary. Flashbacks reveal her best friend's betrayal and its impact on Daphne's marriage, and counterpoint her slow recovery during which Daphne again allows friends to play key roles in her life." Publ Wkly

Thayer, Steve

The weatherman; a novel. Viking 1995 452p $21.95

ISBN 0-670-84958-8   LC 94-20142

"Dixon Bell is a television meteorologist with an eerie gift for reading the weather. Rick Beanblossom is a news producer who hides his disfigured face behind a mask. Andrea Labore is the beautiful cop turned reporter whom they both love. Meanwhile, the Calendar Killer is strangling a woman each season during a significant weather event. When Bell is arrested and accused of the murders, Beanblossom and Labore join forces to prove his innocence. The novel's characters are deeply developed, and the riveting plot is cloaked in descriptive episodes of weather. Additionally, readers will receive a fascinating view of the intense machinations of television news productions." Libr J

Theroux, Paul

Doctor DeMarr

In Theroux, P. Half Moon Street

Doctor Slaughter

In Theroux, P. Half Moon Street

Half Moon Street; two short novels. Houghton Mifflin 1984 219p o.p.

LC 84-10495

This work "contains two novellas on a single theme: the terrors of leading a double life. In 'Doctor DeMarr,' the shorter work, a man who believes his twin brother to be dead steps into his brother's life. . . . [In 'Doctor Slaughter,' an] American woman on a study grant in London finds nothing working well for her until she sells her talents to an 'escort service.'" Newsweek

"Theroux endows these two cautionary tales with a palpable sense of danger and a trenchant wit that are both disturbing and enticing." Booklist

Millroy the Magician. Random House 1994 437p $24

ISBN 0-679-40247-0   LC 93-25046

"This novel 'links Jilly Farina,' a teenaged runaway, with a mysterious magician named Millroy. After meeting at a county fair, the two join forces to proclaim Millroy's gospel of good nutrition. Their first venue is a children's television show; Millroy routs his opponents with feats of prestidigitation. . . . After he opens a chain of vegetarian diners and becomes famous throughout the country, all those jealous of or threatened by his success join forces to destroy him." Libr J

"Mr. Theroux has written a wicked, and often disgusting, satire of American obsessions—self-serving evangelism, the need to be 'regular', the role of television in society and so on." Economist

The Mosquito Coast; a novel; with woodcuts by David Frampton. Houghton Mifflin 1982 374p o.p. Buccaneer Bks. reprint available $32.95 (ISBN 1-56849-348-7)

LC 81-6787

Theroux, Paul—*Continued*

"Allie Fox, a cantankerous Yankee inventor fed up with an America gone soft, pursues his obsession with total self-sufficiency to the wild coast of Honduras, dragging his devoted but uneasy family behind. His aim is to make a 'slightly better job than God' of this poisoned world, as far from cheeseburgers and drive-in churches as possible. And his ingenious pioneer Eden actually works, until his swelling egomania finally topples it." Libr J

"The physical impact of the style, the exact observation, the occasional intrusion of the hallucinatory make this a remarkable work of art; its philosophical content is profound." Burgess. 99 Novels

My secret history. Putnam 1989 511p o.p.

LC 88-32182

"From an early adolescence torn between a call to the priesthood and the call of the flesh, through late-adolescent sexual initiation and a young adult's escapades as a teacher in Africa, to a grown man's crisis in marriage, Theroux recounts the 'secret history' of Andy Parent, a writer suspiciously resembling Theroux himself." Libr J

"'My secret history' is about the permanence of marriage in the face of mistrust and infidelity; it's about the wisdom of women and the foolishness of men; and it's about mature love as the necessary and sometimes successful antidote to youthful selfishness." N Y Times Book Rev

Picture palace; a novel. Houghton Mifflin 1978 359p o.p.

LC 77-18725

"At seventy, Maude Pratt is a world famous photographer. . . . As the book opens, a young man is sifting through her photographs to prepare a retrospective of her work. The images bring up buried memories of her photographic adventures, her incestuous longings for her brother, and the many self-deceptions that marked her life." Saturday Rev

Picture palace "is an elaborate visual conceit, a sublime meditation on seeing and knowing. Confident and commanding, the author displays his narrative gifts which range from the laconic to the lyrical, the telescopic to the microscopic. This is a novel which, like a photograph, one will return to again and again." Christ Sci Monit

World's end and other stories. Houghton Mifflin 1980 211p o.p.

LC 80-12207

Analyzed in Short story index

Contents: World's end; Zombies; The imperial icehouse; Yard sale; Algebra; The English adventure; After the war; Words are deeds; White lies; Clapham Junction; The odd-job man; Portrait of a lady; Volunteer speaker; The greenest island; Acknowledgments

Theroux "displays a hilarious callousness and a pleasure in showing up a particular world—diplomatic literary, commercial—in all its fraudulence." New Statesman

Thoene, Bodie, 1951-

The twilight of courage; a novel; [by] Bodie and Brock Thoene. Nelson, T. 1994 614p $19.99

ISBN 0-7852-8196-7

LC 94-26088

"A Jan Dennis book"

"Chronicling the events of World War II from the occupation of Poland to the battle of Dunkirk, the novel follows the lives of a wide range of characters as they attempt to come to terms, both morally and spiritually, with the crisis of war. For example, in a story fashioned after the Moses story of the Old Testament, a German soldier hides a Jewish baby and passes the baby into the hands of an American woman journalist." Libr J

Thoene, Brock, 1952-

(jt. auth) Thoene, B. The twilight of courage

Thom, James Alexander

The children of first man. Ballantine Bks. 1994 547p $23

ISBN 0-345-37005-8

LC 93-42240

"Eight centuries ago, Madoc, an illegitimate son of a mediocre Welsh king, may have led ten boatloads of his countrymen across the Atlantic and settled them in the Tennessee and Ohio River valleys. Thom's multigenerational historical novel . . . enlarges the scant evidence for this legend. Madoc's Welsh build a benevolent colony (complete with castles), die by hubris, and repeat their history." Libr J

"There are epic battles among the Welsh and the Native Americans and between the tribes themselves, as well as hurricanes, tornadoes, floods, and diseases; the sex is bawdy and the violence is unrelentingly bloody, but the individual human spirit shines through. . . . A terrifically entertaining novel, particularly in dealing with the advance of white society from the Native American viewpoint." Booklist

Panther in the sky. Ballantine Bks. 1989 655p il o.p.

LC 88-48012

The "portrait of Tecumseh, the renowned Shawnee chief and warrior who established a confederacy of tribes in order to resist U.S. encroachment into the Ohio valley, is suitably suffused with fascinating elements of native American lore, legend, and culture. . . . Action and reflection are juxtaposed in a riveting narrative that animates a remarkable cast of celebrated characters and vivifies recorded events. This respectful version of the life of a heroic and courageous native American represents historical fiction at its finest." Booklist

Thomas, Craig, 1942-

Firefox. Holt, Rinehart & Winston 1977 288p o.p.

LC 77-71356

"When intelligence leaks out that the Soviets have developed an incredibly sophisticated warplane codenamed Firefox, with a speed of Mach 5, the Western allies, who couldn't match it in years, decide to 'steal' the plane during its first test flight. The CIA and Britain's SIS join forces, and they pick Vietnam vet Mitchell Gant—emotionally unstable, but a superb pilot—to nab Firefox." Publ Wkly

"Suspenseful to the end, the psychological ups and downs are well handled, as are the flight sequences." Booklist

Followed by Firefox down

Thomas, Craig, 1942-—*Continued*
Firefox down. Bantam Bks. 1983 340p
o.p.

LC 83-90654

"This sequel to 'Firefox' picks up the story of the stolen MIG-31 as it leaves Soviet airspace with Mitchell Gant attempting to fly the plane to Britain. A fuel leak causes an emergency landing on a Finnish lake and the pilot escapes before the plane sinks. The story of the British-American effort to recover the plane and locate Gant parallels Russian efforts to the same end and both are hampered by awful weather and political setbacks." Libr J

A hooded crow. HarperCollins Pubs. 1992 423p o.p.

LC 91-50437

Master spy Sir Kenneth Aubrey's "mission is to track down certain devious enemies of democracy and stop them from smuggling the secrets of Western high-tech military hardware to the Russians. Aubrey, along with good guys Patrick Hyde and Tony Godwin, begin their quest in Africa, where they will once again confront the nefarious South African businessman Paulus Malan and his brutal henchman Blantyre." Booklist

"Though often difficult to follow, Thomas's novel offers action and intrigue in full measure." Publ Wkly

Playing with cobras. HarperCollins Pubs. 1993 319p o.p.

LC 92-54723

Available Thorndike Press large print edition

In this thriller British agent Patrick Hyde is "called out of retirement by Peter Shelley, the new Director General of the Secret Intelligence Service, to run an errand in India. One of Shelley's operatives, Philip Cass, is accused of murdering his lover, the wife of V. K. Sharmar, a government minister who is next in line to be prime minister of India. . . . Cass has become an embarrassment to the British government and Hyde is ordered to eliminate the problem." Publ Wkly

"Thomas writes lyrically and with a seemingly personal knowledge of the back streets of Delhi, of the workings of the Indian government, and of the great natural beauty of India; each of his characters springs vividly to life." Booklist

Thomas, D. M.
Flying in to love. Scribner 1992 242p $20

ISBN 0-684-19510-0   LC 92-16895

"A Robert Stewart book"

This is a fictional re-creation of the events leading up to and surrounding the death of John Fitzgerald Kennedy

"Thomas's interest . . . goes far beyond the mere facts to an exploration of the creation of myth and its impact on individual lives. . . . The portraits that emerge are vivid and intensely human." Libr J

Pictures at an exhibition. Scribner 1993 278p $22

ISBN 0-684-19586-0   LC 93-2412

This novel opens in "Auschwitz, as Dr. Galewski, a young Jewish inmate, analyzes Dr. Lorenz, a Nazi who suffers from headaches and nightmares. . . . The setting then changes to London 50 years later and revolves around elderly Jewish psychoanalyst Oscar Jacobson and his wife, Myra, an Auschwitz survivor." Libr J

"Thomas employs letters, historical documents, and the odd, one-sided discourse of therapy sessions to relate the histories and troubles of his burdened characters. . . . A troubling book that reminds us how deeply the world has been scarred by the evil and tragedy of the Holocaust." Booklist

The white hotel. Viking 1981 274p o.p.

LC 80-52004

This novel "tells the story of 'Anna G.,' a fictitious patient of Freud's. Anna, an intelligent and sensitive musician, suffers from recurring pains in her left breast and ovary, with no organic cause. The 'white hotel' is the setting of Anna's vivid sexual fantasies and visions of death. Anna's poetry and journal, as well as Freud's covering letters and his case history of her analysis, are followed by a narrative history of Elisabeth Erdman ('Anna G.')." Libr J

"Repetition, stunningly enacted in imagery that continually circles in on itself, is the method by which Thomas binds us to his prose. The white hotel is the leitmotif. . . . The richness of this book is reminiscent of a painstakingly woven tapestry; one can focus on the details but must be absorbed by the whole." New Repub

Thomas, Dylan, 1914-1953
The collected stories. New Directions 1984 362p o.p.

LC 84-6822

Analyzed in Short story index

Contents: After the fair; The tree; The true story; The enemies; The dress; The visitor; The vest; The burning baby; The orchards; The end of the river; The lemon; The horse's ha; The school for witches; The mouse and the woman; A prospect of the sea; The holy six; Prologue to an adventure; The map of love; In the direction of the beginning; An adventure from a work in progress

Portrait of the artist as a young dog: The peaches; A visit to grandpa's; Patricia, Edith, and Arnold; The fight; Extraordinary little cough; Just like little dogs; Where Tawe flows; Who do you wish was with us; Old Garbo; One warm Saturday

A fine beginning; Plenty of furniture; Four lost souls; Quite early one morning; A child's Christmas in Wales; Holiday memory; The crumbs of one man's year; Return journey; The followers; A story; Brember; Jarley's; In the garden; Gasper, Melchior, Balthasar

Portrait of the artist as a young dog

In Thomas, D. The collected stories p122-238

Thomas, Elizabeth Marshall, 1931-
The animal wife. Houghton Mifflin 1990 289p $19.95

ISBN 0-395-52453-9   LC 90-4485

"A Peter Davison book"

This novel "is set in Siberia 20,000 years ago. . . . While out hunting, Kori captures a woman from another tribe whom he names Muskrat. Their evolving relationship and the interactions among the family tribe members as they move from their summer grounds to their winter grounds in the constant search for food form the heart of the novel." Libr J

Thomas, Elizabeth Marshall, 1931- — *Continued*

The author "has created a novel of rare beauty and depth. . . . In Ms. Thomas's spare, evocative prose is much wisdom about men and women and the limits of our understanding of each other." N Y Times Book Rev

Reindeer Moon. Houghton Mifflin 1987 338p o.p.

LC 86-18530

"A Peter Davison book"

"We meet the protagonist, Yanan, as a young girl, living with her family in what is now Siberia. Just a few chapters into the narrative, she dies and becomes a spirit who must serve the members of her lodge by finding food for them, often by taking on the form and behavioral characteristics of animals or birds. The story proceeds in flashback as Yanan relates the memories of her youth." Publ Wkly

"What makes the reader care for this young girl so far removed from us by time and distance is that in telling her story the author conveys sentiments and feelings not remote from our own today." N Y Times Book Rev

Thomas, Michael M.

Black money. Crown 1994 309p $22

ISBN 0-517-59523-0   LC 93-33813

This novel "tracks a criminal scam from its detection in a small California mall through its connections to South American drug cartels, the Mafia, and the highest reaches of the U.S. government. A middle-level federal bureaucrat and the socially well-connected editor of a muckraking magazine join forces to expose an enormously complicated scheme for laundering drug money." Booklist

Thomas "writes a very exciting and almost-too-believable tale of power politics and international crime." Libr J

Hanover Place. Warner Bks. 1990 479p $19.45

ISBN 0-446-51330-X   LC 89-40038

"Hanover Place, in 1924, is the site of a moderately successful brokerage house owned by the Warringtons. Thomas' novel charts the triumphs, losses, and peccadilloes of the Warringtons and their kind, also serving up a portrait of the world of high finance, from the rudimentary days of stocks (and the Depression) to the modern age of junk bonds, forced mergers, unfriendly takeovers, and so on. One prominent theme here is anti-Semitism, symbolized by a bright young Jewish clerk who is upgraded into the partners' circle, yet must endure the bigotry of the WASPish men and women who dominate high-level New York society. Later, financial revenge is wrought. A big tale of Americans and their money certain to entertain." Booklist

Thomas, Rosanne Daryl

The angel carver. Random House 1993 260p $20

ISBN 0-679-42363-X   LC 92-37032

A novel "about a Marilyn Monroe look-alike and two artists, one who carves her likeness in wood and the other who imagines how she might be perfected with surgery." N Y Times Book Rev

"This very modern fairy tale, in which such timeless evils as envy, greed and cruelty are abetted by the latest advances in computer graphics technology, has the spare impact of both its literary antecedents and television cartoons." Publ Wkly

Thomas, Rosie

All my sins remembered. Bantam Bks. 1992 c1991 548p o.p.

LC 92-8547

First published 1991 in the United Kingdom

This "tale revolves around interviews biographer Elizabeth Ainger records with her grandmother's elderly cousin, Clio, an accomplished novelist. Once three generations of family history are reconstructed, Elizabeth's project has revealed much more than girlish crushes and failed love affairs. This rousing, thoroughly engaging read moves from Victorian drawing rooms to bohemian Bloomsbury and Nazi Germany, with painful secrets and bittersweet betrayals revealed at every turn." Booklist

Bad girls, good women. Bantam Bks. 1989 664p o.p.

LC 88-7922

"This is the story of Julia and Mattie, two vivacious English girls who run away to London in 1955. Recklessly rebellious Mattie, escaping childhood poverty and sexual abuse, wants to be an actress. Julia, stylish and smart, just knows she must get away from her repressive parents. The girls' hunger for life sets the tone for the novel, as we follow them through the sleaziest and most glamorous parts of London; through three decades of relationships, marriages, career struggles, mother-daughter conflicts, and a friendship that wavers but never dies." Libr J

The author "paints an engaging portrait of 60's England, especially the musty provincial theaters, the carefree Soho clubs and the trendy shops around the King's Road in London." N Y Times Book Rev

Other people's marriages. Morrow 1994 c1993 425p $21

ISBN 0-688-12962-5   LC 93-8885

Also available Thorndike Press large print edition

First published 1993 in the United Kingdom

"Within a few weeks of her arrival in the London suburb of Grafton, a young widow begins an affair with a married man. The affair is soon discovered, however, and it sets off a chain reaction of infidelities through five married couples." N Y Times Book Rev

"Effective, precise details vivify physical settings (various homes are as acutely rendered as the cathedral, the novel's central symbol), and the characters, some unappealing but all understandable, are well drawn." Libr J

A woman of our times. Bantam Bks. 1990 500p o.p.

LC 90-470

"Harriet Trott is foundering in a dead-end retailing career and an equally moribund marriage when she goes in search of the father she never knew—and is given not a new name but a new game. After a few false starts . . . Harriet parlays that game into a successful company, setting the London business world on its ear." N Y Times Book Rev

Thomas, Rosie—*Continued*

"The novel rises above its hackneyed 'having it all' theme thanks to sensitive characterizations. Although Thomas gets off to a slow start and provides too many descriptions of elegant clothing and food, she is skillful at building suspense. In its best moments, the book's dialog crackles." Libr J

Thomas, Ross, 1926-1995

Ah, treachery! Mysterious Press 1994 274p $21.95

ISBN 0-89296-452-9   LC 94-15118

Also available Thorndike Press large print edition

"In 1989, army major Edd 'Twodees' Partain took part in an illegal operation in El Salvador that his former comrades now want expunged from the record. Meanwhile, top political fund-raiser Millicent Altford needs to recover $1.2 million in stolen under-the-table contributions. These two scenarios dovetail as Altford engineers to have Partain, who was drummed out of the service for assaulting a superior officer, fired from his job in a Wyoming gun store in order to hire him to 'ride shotgun' as she goes after the loot. . . . Thomas's yarn reaffirms his expertise at the black-humored political thriller." Publ Wkly

Briarpatch. Simon & Schuster 1984 332p o.p.

LC 84-13883

This novel "begins with the car-bombing death of Felicity Dill, superb young detective on the police force of her hometown somewhere in the Southwest. Her brother Benjamin, 10 years her senior and the one who raised her, works in Washington, D.C., as investigator for a Senate subcommittee. Dill's trip home for his sister's funeral is financed by the subcommittee, which coincidentally has unfinished business there with fugitive Jake Spivey, Dill's boyhood best friend. On arrival Dill is informed that he's the beneficiary of Felicity's quarter-million-dollar insurance policy. . . . The police imply she was on the take, but Dill won't believe it. Meanwhile his official business is with Jake, an ex-CIA agent who'd gotten rich as an arms dealer in Vietnam. Ultimately, in a tough, suspense-filled and ambiguous climax, the two cases come together." Publ Wkly

Chinaman's chance; a novel. Simon & Schuster 1978 383p o.p.

LC 77-25326

"Billionaire Randall Piers hires [Artie Wu and Quincy Durant] to find Silk, sister of his beloved wife Lace, who is emotionally ill from worry about the missing girl. Silk hides out after the death of her lover, a congressman, and his wife. The case has been judged a murder-suicide. But Silk knows it was a double murder. The minions of mobster Imperlino have also hired Wu and Durant to find Silk and shut her mouth for good. The congressman and his wife were killed because they knew of the mob's plans, backed by bribed authorities, to take over a California town." Publ Wkly

The fourth Durango. Mysterious Press 1989 312p o.p.

LC 89-3091

Available Thorndike Press large print edition

Durango, California is "the ideal hideout for a man with a price on his life. For a fee, the shrewd mayor and her loyal chief of police offer sanctuary to a judge who has just done time on a cooked-up bribery charge.

The judge and his son-in-law, a disbarred lawyer, move into 'the only money-losing Holiday Inn west of Beirut' and devise a plan for smoking out the person with the vendetta against the judge. For an even bigger fee, the mayor and her top cop are game to conspire in the scheme—until an extremely ugly man comes to town and starts shooting up the citizenry." N Y Times Book Rev

Missionary stew. Simon & Schuster 1983 300p o.p.

LC 83-13610

"Morgan Citron is a world-weary journalist recently escaped from the clutches of an African despot with a taste for human flesh ('missionary stew'). In a sequence of seemingly random events, Citron stumbles on to information concerning a CIA-instigated plot to use drug smuggling as a way of financing a right-wing Central American government." Booklist

"This is an intricately plotted, entertaining literary romp, replete with unpredictable developments, witty dialogue, credible characters with incredible names, unconventional situations, and the eye for detail and sparse description that is the hallmark of Thomas' works." Libr J

Voodoo, Ltd. Mysterious Press 1992 282p $19.95

ISBN 0-89296-451-0   LC 91-51185

Also available G.K. Hall large print edition

"Ione Gamble, an actress 'with a face known throughout the world,' is in a real jam. The police think she murdered her former lover, Billy Rice, a dissolute publishing heir and independent movie producer, at his Malibu beach house. Gamble isn't so sure about that, since she was blind drunk at the time. Desperate, she hires Enno Glimm, who will spare no expense in recruiting a discreet hypnotist to probe her alcoholic blackout for the truth without concurrently selling her story to the tabloids. Glimm's company, based in Germany, is a sort of global office-temp agency that fills unusual short-term employment requirements." N Y Times Book Rev

Thomas, Thomas T.

(jt. auth) Pohl, F. Mars Plus

Tilly, Meg

Singing songs. Dutton 1994 242p $19.95

ISBN 0-525-93778-1   LC 93-43203

"Anna lives with her large family in a variety of squalid locations, finally settling on an island in the Northwest. Her Radcliffe-educated mother, deserted by her well-to-do husband, has become a careless slut; she has married an older man who turns out to be a 'layabout,' a child-beater and -molester. Anna's many siblings, blood and step, try to make it against these terrible odds, while Anna herself struggles unsuccessfully to cushion them from her stepfather's brutality and lechery, fiercely tries to protect herself from a number of sexual assaults and attempts to wrest some comfort from her overwrought mother." Publ Wkly

"All of the virtues of 'Singing Songs' arise out of the remarkable coherence and clarity of Anna's voice. The brief chapters—some no longer than a page or two—correspond precisely to the short attention span and episodic perspective of a child." N Y Times Book Rev

Tiptree, James, 1916-1987

Houston, Houston, do you read?

In The Best of the Nebulas p420-60

In The Hugo winners v4 p200-56

Tolkien, J. R. R. (John Ronald Reuel), 1892-1973

After the king. See After the king

The book of lost tales; part I-II; edited by Christopher Tolkien. Houghton Mifflin 1984 2v (History of Middle Earth) o.p.
LC 83-12782

Part one first published 1983 in the United Kingdom
Contents: pt. 1 The cottage of lost play; The music of the Ainur; The coming of the Valar and the building of Valinor; The chaining of Melko; The coming of the Elves and the making of Kôr; The theft of Melko and the darkening of Valinor; The flight of the Noldoli; The tale of the Sun and Moon; The hiding of Valinor; Gilfanon's tale: the travail of the Noldoli and the coming of Mankind

pt. II: The tale of Tinúviel; Turambar and the Foalókë; The fall of Gondolin; The Nauglafring; The tale of Eärendel; The history of Eriol; AElfwine of England
"These fascinating stories of fairies and elves battling evil creatures shed considerable light on the evolution of Tolkien's elaborate fictional world." Booklist

The fellowship of the ring; being the first part of The lord of the rings. 2nd ed. Houghton Mifflin 1986 c1965 423p il $19.95
ISBN 0-395-48931-8   LC 88-120282

First published 1954
"Frodo, a home-loving young hobbit, inherits the magic ring which his uncle Bilbo brought back from the adventures described in the juvenile fantasy 'The hobbit'. This sequel, expressly addressed to adults, is the first of a three-part saga that tells of Frodo's valiant journey undertaken to prevent the ring from falling into the hands of the powers of darkness. Elves, dwarfs, hobbits, men, and sundry evil beings, each as real as the other, populate an allegorical tale that shows how power corrupts." Booklist

Followed by The two towers

also in Tolkien, J. R. R. The lord of the rings v1

The hobbit; or, There and back again; illustrated by Michael Hague. Houghton Mifflin 1984 290p il $24.95
ISBN 0-395-36290-3   LC 84-9023

First published 1937 in the United Kingdom; first United States edition 1938
"This fantasy features the adventures of hobbit Bilbo Baggins, who joins a band of dwarves led by Gandalf the Wizard. Together they seek to recover the stolen treasure that is hidden in Lonely Mountain and guarded by Smaug the Dragon. This book precedes the *Lord of the Rings* trilogy." Shapiro. Fic for Youth. 3d edition
"It must be understood that this is a children's book only in the sense that the first of many readings can be undertaken in the nursery. . . . [The hobbit] will be funniest to its youngest readers, and only years later, at a tenth or twentieth reading, will they begin to realize

what deft scholarship and profound reflection have gone to make everything in it so ripe, so friendly, and in its own way so true." Times Lit Suppl

The lord of the rings. 2nd ed. Houghton Mifflin 1986 c1965 3v set $55
ISBN 0-395-48932-6   LC 88-122831

The trilogy was first published 1954-55 in the United Kingdom. The revised edition was published 1966 in the United Kingdom. Each title is entered separately
Contents: v1 The fellowship of the ring; v2 The two towers; v3 The return of the king

The return of the king; being the third part of The lord of the rings. 2nd ed. Houghton Mifflin 1986 c1965 440p $19.95
ISBN 0-395-48930-X   LC 88-195987

First published 1955 in the United Kingdom
In the concluding volume of the trilogy "The dark lord of evil is overthrown, the rightful king comes into his own, and the Age of Men begins." Booklist

also in Tolkien, J. R. R. The lord of the rings v3

The Silmarillion; edited by Christopher Tolkien. Houghton Mifflin 1977 365p o.p.
LC 77-8025

Partially analyzed in Short story index
"J.R.R. Tolkien Quenta Silmarillion; (The history of the Silmarils) together with Ainudalë (The music of the Ainur) and Valaquenta; (Account of the Valar) To which is appended Akallabéth (The downfall of Númenor) and of the Rings of Power and the Third age." Facing title page
"Tolkien began writing these introductory legends in 1917 and, sporadically throughout his life, continued adding to them; his son Christopher has edited and compiled the various versions into a single cohesive work. Two brief tales, which outline the origin of the world and describe the gods who create and rule, precede the title story about the Silmarils—three brilliant, jewel-like creatures who are desired and fought over, setting up a clash between good and evil." Booklist

The two towers; being the second part of The lord of the rings. 2nd ed. Houghton Mifflin 1986 c1965 352p $19.95
ISBN 0-395-48933-4   LC 88-195969

First published 1954
"Here the Companions of the Ring, separated, meet Saruman the wizard, cross the Dead Marshes, and prepare for the Great War in which the power of the Ring will be undone." Libr J
Followed by The return of the king

also in Tolkien, J. R. R. The lord of the rings v2

Unfinished tales of Númenor and Middle-earth; edited with introduction, commentary, index, and maps by Christopher Tolkien. Houghton Mifflin 1980 472p o.p.
LC 80-83072

Analyzed in Short story index
Contents: Of Tuor and his coming to Gondolin; The childhood of Túrin; The words of Húrin and Morgoth; The departure of Túrin; Túrin in Duriath; Túrin among the outlaws; Of Mim the dwarf; The return of Túrin to Dorlómin; The coming of Túrin into Brethil; The

Tolkien, J. R. R. (John Ronald Reuel), 1892-1973—*Continued*

journey of Morwen and Nienor to Nargothrond; Nienor in Brethil; The coming of Glaurung; The death of Glaurung; The death of Túrin; A description of the Island of Númenor; Aldarion and Erendis; The disaster of the Gladden Fields; The Northmen and the Wainriders; The ride of Eorl; Cirion and Eorl; The tradition of Isildur; The quest of Erebor; Of the journey of the Black Riders according to the account that Gandalf gave to Frodo; Concerning Gandalf, Saruman and the Shire; The battles of the Fords of Isen; The Drúedain; The Istari; The Palantiri

"This book was not planned by Tolkien and is a disparate collection held together by the continuing editorial presence of his son Christopher." Publ Wkly

Tolkien, John Ronald Reuel *See* Tolkien, J. R. R. (John Ronald Reuel), 1892-1973

Tolstoy, Leo, graf, 1828-1910

Anna Karenina

Some editions are:

Knopf (Everyman's lib) $20 Translated by Louise and Aylmer Maude (ISBN 0-679-41000-7)

Modern Lib. $20 Translated by Constance Garnett (ISBN 0-679-60084-1)

Written in 1873-1876

This novel is "the story of a tragic, adulterous love. Anna meets and falls in love with Aleksei Vronski, a handsome young officer. She abandons her child and husband in order to be with Vronski. When she thinks Vronski has tired of her, she kills herself by leaping under a train. The idea for the story reputedly came to Tolstoy after he had viewed the body of a young woman who committed a similar suicide. A subplot concerns the contrasting happy marriage of Konstantin Levin and his young wife Kitty. Levin's search for meaning in his life and his love for a natural, simple existence on his estate are reflections of Tolstoy's own moods and thoughts of the time." Readers's Ency. 3d edition

Childhood, Boyhood and Youth; translated from the Russian by C. J. Hogarth. Knopf 1991 314p $17

ISBN 0-679-40578-X   LC 91-52984

"Everyman's library"

Originally published separately, 1852, 1854 and 1857 respectively; this edition first published 1912

"An autobiographical trilogy. 'Childhood' was the first of Tolstoi's works to receive wide attention. The description of life on a provincial estate are among the best depictions of nature in Russian literature." Reader's Ency

The Cossacks

In Tolstoy, L. The short novels of Tolstoy

The death of Iván Ilyitch

In Tolstoy, L. The short novels of Tolstoy

The death of Ivan Ilyitch, and other stories; a new translation from the Russian by Constance Garnett. Dodd, Mead 1927 362p o.p. Buccaneer Bks. reprint available $20.95 (ISBN 0-89966-611-6)

Analyzed in Short story index

Contents: The death of Ivan Ilyitch; Family happiness; Polikushka; Two hussars; The snowstorm; Three deaths

The Devil

In Tolstoy, L. The Kreutzer sonata, The Devil, and other tales

In Tolstoy, L. The short novels of Tolstoy

Family happiness

In Tolstoy, L. The Kreutzer sonata, The Devil, and other tales

In Tolstoy, L. The short novels of Tolstoy

Father Sergius

In Tolstoy, L. The Kreutzer sonata, The Devil, and other tales

Hadji Murád

In Tolstoy, L. The short novels of Tolstoy

The Kreutzer sonata

In Tolstoy, L. The portable Tolstoy p523-601

The Kreutzer sonata, The Devil, and other tales; translation of Family happiness, by J. D. Duff, and of other stories by Aylmer Maude; with an introduction by Aylmer Maude. Oxford Univ. Press 1957 xxi, 375p o.p.

Contents: Family happiness; The Kreutzer sonata; The Devil; Father Sergius; François; The porcelain doll

Master and man

In Tolstoy, L. The portable Tolstoy p602-52

In Tolstoy, L. The short novels of Tolstoy

Polikúshka

In Tolstoy, L. The short novels of Tolstoy

The portable Tolstoy; selected and with a critical introduction, biographical summary, and bibliography by John Bayley. Viking 1978 888p o.p.

LC 78-6784

"The Viking portable library"

Partially analyzed in Short story index

Short stories included are: The raid; The woodfelling; Sevastopol; Strider; God sees the truth, but waits; What men live by; How much land does a man need?

This volume contains short stories, episodes from Childhood, Boyhood and Youth, excerpts from The Cossacks and selections from the author's philosophical,

Tolstoy, Leo, graf, 1828-1910—*Continued*
critical and social writing. The play The power of darkness is also included as well as the three short novels: Two hussars; The Kreutzer sonata, and Master and man

Resurrection. o.p.
Original Russian edition, 1899
"The story deals with the spiritual regeneration of a young nobleman, Prince Nekhlyudov. In his earlier years, he seduced a young girl, Katyusha Maslova. She became a prostitute and later became involved with a man she is accused of poisoning. Nekhlyudov, serving on the jury, recognizes her and decides that he is morally guilty for her predicament. He decides to marry her, and when she is convicted he follows her to Siberia to accomplish his aim. Maslova is repelled by his reforming zeal. She marries another prisoner, but is finally convinced of Nekhlyudov's sincerity and accepts his friendship." Reader's Ency. 3d edition

The short novels of Tolstoy; selected with an introduction by Philip Rahv; translated by Aylmer Maude. Dial Press 1946 xx, 716p o.p.
Contents: Two hussars; Family happiness; The Cossacks; Polikúshka; The death of Iván Ilyitch; The Devil; Master and man; Hadji Murád

Short stories; selected and introduced by Ernest J. Simmons. Modern Lib. 1964-1965 2v o.p.
Analyzed in Short story index
Contents: v 1: A history of yesterday; The raid; A billiard-markers' notes; The wood-felling; Sevastopol in December 1854; Sevastopol in May 1855; Sevastopol in August 1855; Meeting a Moscow acquaintance in the detachment; The snow storm; Lucerne; Albert; Three deaths; Strider; The porcelain doll
v2: God sees the truth, but waits; A prisoner in the Caucasus; The bearhunt; What men live by; A spark neglected burns the house; Two old men; Where love is, God is; Evil allures, but good endures; Little girls wiser than men; Elias; The story of Iván, the Fool; The repentant sinner; The three hermits; The imp and the crust; How much land does a man need; A grain as big as a hen's egg; The godson; The empty drum; Esarhaddon, King of Assyria; Work, death and sickness; Three questions; The memoirs of a madman; After the ball; Fëdor Kuzmich; Alyósha

Two hussars
In Tolstoy, L. The portable Tolstoy p294-357

In Tolstoy, L. The short novels of Tolstoy

War and peace
Some editions are:
Knopf 3v set $40 Translated by Louise and Aylmer Maude (ISBN 0-679-40573-9)
Modern Lib. $22 Translated by Constance Garnett (ISBN 0-679-60084-1)
Original Russian edition, 1864-1869
"The story covers roughly the years between 1805 and 1820, centering on the invasion of Russia by Napoleon's army in 1812 and the Russian resistance to the invader. Over five hundred characters, all carefully rendered, populate the pages of the novel. Every social level, from Napoleon himself to the peasant Platon Karatayev, is represented. Interwoven with the story of the war are narrations of the lives of several main characters, especially those of Natasha *Rostova*, Prince Andrey *Bolkonsky*, and Pierre *Bezukhov*. These people are shown as they progress from youthful uncertainties and searchings toward a more mature understanding of life." Reader's Ency. 3d edition

Tomasi di Lampedusa, Giuseppe, 1896-1957
The leopard; translated from the Italian by Archibald Colquhoun. Knopf 1991 300p $15
ISBN 0-679-40757-X　　　　　　LC 91-52980
Also available from P. Smith
Original Italian edition, 1958; this translation first published 1960 by Pantheon Books
This historical novel "describes the impact of Garibaldi's invasion of Sicily and the subsequent unification of Italy on an aristocratic Sicilian family who had flourished under the Bourbon kings. The novel's depiction of the failure of the 'Risorgimento' created heated political debates when it was first published. However, the controversy subsided and the book was widely recognized as a penetrating psychological study of an age, written in a highly symbolic and richly poetic style." Reader's Ency. 3d edition

Toole, John Kennedy, 1937-1969
A confederacy of dunces; foreword by Walker Percy. Louisiana State Univ. Press 1980 338p $22.95
ISBN 0-8071-0657-7　　　　　　LC 79-20190
Also available from Amereon
The protagonist of this novel set in New Orleans is Ignatius J. Reilly, "a medievalist whose fortunes take a downward turn when he is nearly arrested for being a 'suspicious character.' Things only get worse when he and his mother (leaving the Night of Joy bar, where they've gone to soothe their nerves after the near-arrest) run their car into a building, and Ignatius is forced to find a job to pay for the damages." Christ Sci Monit
"At the heart of this splendid mock-heroic with its blundering and canniness, its falstaffian excesses and 'Alice in Wonderland' wit, lies a profound sense of solitude. Like everything else in Ignatuis J. Reilly's world, the absence of love is larger than life." Newsweek

Torsvan, Traven *See* Traven, B.

Townsend, Sue
The Adrian Mole diaries. Grove Press 1986 c1985 342p o.p.
　　　　　　　　　　　　　　LC 86-226
First published 1985 in the United Kingdom
A combined edition of two titles: The secret diary of Adrian Mole, age 13 ¾ (1982); and Growing pains (1984)
"The messy, inconsistent world of adulthood is seen through the eyes of a 14-year-old aspiring intellectual and poet. Adrian Mole begins his diary when spots appear on his face and his parents' marriage dissolves. By the diary's end he has been in love, become helpmate to a feisty 89-year-old, and held his mother's hand during the birth of his sister. Adrian's pithy commentary records the ludicrousness of school and state bureaucracy and the aberrations of the nuclear age." Booklist
Followed by Adrian Mole: the lost years

Townsend, Sue—*Continued*
Adrian Mole: the lost years. Soho Press
1994 309p $22

ISBN 1-56947-014-6   LC 94-11276

"Portions of this text appeared in *The True Confessions of Adrian Albert Mole*, while 'Adrian Mole and the Small Amphibians' appeared in *Adrian Mole, From Minor to Major*. *Adrian Mole, The Wilderness Years* appears in its entirety. All were first published in Great Britain." Verso of title page

"Adrian's latest diaries chronicle his mighty struggle to survive the adolescent and postpubescent years. His outrageous clothes and strong views about everything from the government to unwed mothers can't disguise the angst he suffers: he's still trying to find a niche for his unrecognized genius. . . . Townsend is a satirist of the first order, offering brilliantly witty humor peppered with sobering insights into the troubles and traumas of working-class Brits." Booklist

Growing pains
In Townsend, S. The Adrian Mole
diaries

The secret diary of Adrian Mole, age 13¾
In Townsend, S. The Adrian Mole
diaries

Trafzer, Clifford E.
(ed) Earth song, sky spirit. See Earth song, sky spirit

Traven, B.
The treasure of the Sierra Madre. Knopf
1935 366p o.p.

Available from Amereon and Bentley. Large print edition available from Thorndike Press

Original German edition, 1927

This novel analyzes the "psychology of greed in telling of three Americans searching for a lost gold mine in Mexican mountains." Oxford Companion to Am Lit. 5th edition

Traver, Robert, 1903-1991
Anatomy of a murder. St. Martin's Press
1958 437p o.p.

Available from Amereon and Buccaneer Bks.

"Not the usual murder mystery but a review by the lawyer for the defense from the time he takes the case of an army lieutenant who admits to having killed the man who raped his wife, until the end of the trial. Much attention is given to establishing the fact of rape. Although the recital is wordy it maintains suspense in showing the legal and personal resources the lawyer calls on to build his defense and the way that rivalry between prosecution and defense shapes the trial." Booklist

Tremain, Rose
Sacred country. Atheneum Pubs. 1993
c1992 323p $21

ISBN 0-689-12170-9   LC 92-21457

First published 1992 in the United Kingdom

"At the age of six, Mary Ward, standing with her family in a wintry Suffolk field to observe a two-minute silence in honor of the death of King George VI, comes to the realization that she was meant to be a boy. From this beginning in 1952 until 1980, Tremain tells the evocative tale of Mary's lonely quest to transform herself into Martin. Emotionally abandoned by her parents, Mary finds refuge first with her grandfather, Cord, and later with her schoolteacher, Miss McRae." Libr J

The author "gives us a precisely imagined landscape and a complicated group of characters that we come to care deeply about." N Y Times Book Rev

Tremaine, Jennie *See* Chesney, Marion

Trenhaile, John
The gates of exquisite view. Dutton 1988
374p o.p.

LC 87-13630

"Saga of English capitalist Simon Young, his Hong Kong enterprise, and the secrets in his supercomputer." Smith. Cloak and Dagger Fic

"Trenhaile craftily weaves a portentous web of political intrigue, masking until the final pages the exact nature of his characters' intentions and loyalties. . . . Neatly paced suspense from a master of the genre." Booklist

Trevanian
The Eiger sanction. Crown 1972 316p o.p.

"American art professor-mountain climber Dr. Jonathan Hemlock moonlights as an assassin in the employ of the Search and Sanction Division of the mythical counter-assassination bureau known as C-11. In his last mission before retirement, he is sent along on a top-flight mountain climbing expedition in Switzerland with orders to liquidate one of three companions known to have killed an unlucky C-11 agent in Montreal. Not knowing the identity of the assassin Hemlock ruthlessly plans to bump off all three." Smith. Cloak and Dagger Fic

Shibumi. Crown 1979 374p o.p.

LC 78-20950

This novel relates the "feats of Hel, the world's highest-paid assassin. Hel guns down political terrorists of the CIA, PLO, and various other organizations, then takes on the superpower of espionage agencies, the Mother Company." Publ Wkly

The summer of Katya. Crown 1983 242p
o.p.

LC 83-1790

"The time is 1914 and the story takes place in a small French Basque village. Dr. Jean-Marc Montjean, young and newly graduated from medical school, meets and falls in love with Katya, a beautiful young girl. Their encounter comes by way of an accident that befalls Katya's brother Paul, to whom she is very attached. Jean-Marc becomes involved with their family and begins to pay court to Katya. He is warned that any romantic attachment is out of the question because of her delicate health. A mystery in the background of the family hangs over all their relationships, and in a final meeting there is a shocking climax that leaves the reader stunned." Shapiro. Fic for Youth. 3d edition

Trevor, Elleston, 1920-1995

For works written by this author under other names see Hall, Adam, 1920-1995

The flight of the Phoenix. Harper & Row 1964 242p o.p.

A "story of survival in a desert. Fourteen men in a plane from an oil town crash-land in the Sahara, position unknown, radio out, almost no food, a meager supply of water. The clash of personalities, the increasing desperation of the situation, the triumph of brains and ingenuity that gives them a chance for survival make [up the story]." Publ Wkly

"Drama, psychological conflict, and sustained suspense mark a first-rate tale of engineering ingenuity and desert survival." Booklist

Trevor, William, 1928-

The collected stories. Viking 1992 1261p $35

ISBN 0-670-84129-3   LC 92-54071

Analyzed in Short story index

This volume includes short stories from Trevor's "seven previous books, as well as four stories that have never appeared in book form in America." Publisher's note

Contents: A meeting in middle age; Access to the children; The general's day; Memories of Youghal; The table; A school story; The penthouse apartment; In at the birth; The introspections of J. P. Powers; The day we got drunk on cake; Miss Smith; The Hotel of the Idle Moon; Nice day at school; The original sins of Edward Tripp; The forty-seventh Saturday; The ballroom of romance; A happy family; The grass widows; The Mark-2 wife; An evening with John Joe Dempsey; Kinkies; Going home; A choice of butchers; O fat white woman; Raymond Bamber and Mrs. Fitch; The distant past; In Isfahan; Angels at the Ritz; The death of Peggy Meehan; Mrs. Silly; A complicated nature; Teresa's wedding; Office romances; Mr. McNamara; Afternoon dancing; Last wishes; Mrs. Acland's ghosts; Another Christmas; Broken homes; Matilda's England; Torridge; Death in Jerusalem; Lovers of their time; The raising of Elvira Tremlett; Flights of fancy; Attracta; A dream of butterflies; The bedroom eyes of Mrs. Vansittart; Downstairs at Fitzgerald's; Mulvihill's memorial; Beyond the pale; The blue dress; The teddy-bears' picnic; The time of year; Being stolen from; Mr. Tennyson; Autumn sunshine; Sunday drinks; The Paradise Lounge; Mags; The news from Ireland; On the Zattere; The wedding in the garden; Lunch in winter; The property of Colette Nervi; Running away; Cocktails at Doney's; Her mother's daughter; Bodily secrets; Two more gallants; The smoke trees of San Pietro; Virgins; Music; Events at Drimaghleen; Family sins; A trinity; The third party; Honeymoon in Tramore; The printmaker; In love with Ariadne; A husband's return; Coffee with Oliver; August Saturday; Children of the headmaster; Kathleen's field

Felicia's journey. Viking 1995 c1994 212p $21.95

ISBN 0-670-85745-9   LC 94-32413

First published 1994 in the United Kingdom

"When handsome Johnny Lysaght, home from England to visit his mother, first catches sight of Felicia, she is standing outside Hickey's Hotel in a bridesmaid's dress. When the famously fat and affable Mr. Hilditch first catches sight of her, a few months later, she is pregnant and desperate, asking for directions outside a Midlands factory, with her grandmother's stolen pension money stuffed in her plastic carrier bag. Hilditch can tell at a glance that the Irish girl needs a special friend. . . . The insignificance of Felicia's ever-narrowing life is challenged by our terror that she will lose it." New Yorker

"Trevor is chilling and precise in his evocation of the loss of innocence, loss of heart, while he highlights the dismal features of contemporary society. Felicia's journey proceeds in an inimical atmosphere in which disquiet and corruption are the order of the day." New Statesman Soc

My house in Umbria

In Trevor, W. Two lives: Reading Turgenev and My house in Umbria p225-375

(ed) The Oxford book of Irish short stories. See The Oxford book of Irish short stories

Reading Turgenev

In Trevor, W. Two lives: Reading Turgenev and My house in Umbria p1-222

The silence in the garden. Viking 1988 204p o.p.

LC 87-40662

"Told in an elliptical, slow-moving narrative is this tale of the Rolleston family, a once vital aristocratic Irish family who peters away into seemingly inexplicable hopelessness. The elder sons remain bachelors. . . . The beautiful daughter withers, as she tosses away one fiancé and, in her mid-30s, chooses a man too old for her and incapable of siring children. As poor relation Sarah discovers at last, this is voluntary self-punishment for a shared act of cruelty that had violent repercussions." Libr J

"While the subject might seem common, Trevor's treatment is a dazzling tour de force of epigrammatic detail and psychological insinuation as the writer reconstructs whole lives through the telling deployment of a single episode. Moreover, there is a tissue of lies, secrets, and deceptions that is gradually revealed in the progress of these people's stories. Trevor captures the contradictions and subtle ironies brilliantly." Booklist

Two lives: Reading Turgenev and My house in Umbria. Viking 1991 375p $21.95

ISBN 0-670-83933-7   LC 91-50137

This volume consists of a "pair of mirroring narratives. The first novella, 'Reading Turgenev,' is the story of a woman who, denied love in her marriage, turns to a half-imaginary romance with a cousin who reads Turgenev to her in a cemetery; later, she desolately retreats into the shadowy world of her memories and desires. 'My House in Umbria' is a first-person narrative about an aging writer of romances with a mysterious past whose fiction exhibits resolution and a kind of tranquility. A passenger on a train attacked by terrorists, the writer takes in a group of fellow survivors of the blast. Their healing becomes cathartic for her, bringing elements of her past to the surface." Publ Wkly

Trevor, William, 1928-—*Continued*

"William Trevor is considered a traditionalist, an almost nonliterary writer, yet at a deep level Two Lives is a radical, perhaps even subversive, criticism of the art of fiction." N Y Times Book Rev

Trimble, Barbara Margaret *See* Gill, B. M.

Trocheck, Kathy Hogan, 1954-
Every crooked nanny. HarperCollins Pubs. 1992 286p o.p.

LC 91-58359

This novel introduces "J. Callahan Garrity, a former cop and failed gumshoe who now runs a cleaning service in Atlanta, Ga. While cleaning the home of snooty society lady Lilah Rose Beemish, Callahan is hired to trace Kristee, the family's Mormon nanny, who has absconded with furs, jewels and, Callahan learns, incriminating business secrets gleaned from Lilah's husband Bo during their affair." Publ Wkly

"This quick-paced thriller provides an intriguing introduction to a delightfully down-to-earth sleuth." Booklist

Trollope, Anthony, 1815-1882
Barchester Towers. Knopf 1992 xxxiii, 277p $20

ISBN 0-679-40587-9　　　　　LC 91-53197

First published 1857. Second of the Chronicles of Barsetshire

"Continues the picture of clerical society with its peculiar humors and foibles. The chief incidents are connected with the appointment of a new bishop, the troubles and disappointments this involves, and the intrigues and jealousies of the clergy: the henpecked bishop, the ambitious archdeacon, and the dean, canons, and others, with their wives. The picture of the eccentric Stanhope family is particularly delicious." Lenrow. Reader's Guide to Prose Fic

Followed by Doctor Thorne

Can you forgive her?; with an introduction by A.O.J. Cockshut. Knopf 1994 xxxiii, 447p $23

ISBN 0-679-43595-6　　　　　LC 94-6553

"Everyman's library"

First published 1864-65

This first of the Palliser novels "tells the interwoven stories of two women, Alice Vavasor and Lady Glencora M'Cluskie, who struggle to come to terms with the choices available to them concerning marriage." Merriam-Webster's Ency of Lit

Can you forgive her? [abridged]
In Trollope, A. The Pallisers p11-115

The complete shorter fiction; edited by Julian Thompson. Carroll & Graf Pubs. 1992 959p $38

ISBN 0-88184-854-9

Analyzed in Short story index

Includes the following stories: Relics of General Chassé, a tale of Antwerp; The courtship of Susan Bell; The O'Conors of Castle Conor, County Mayo; La Mère Bauche; An unprotected female at the pyramids; The chateau of Prince Polignac; Miss Sarah Jack of Spanish Town, Jamaica; John Bull on the Guadalquivir; A ride across Palestine; Mrs. General Talboys; The parson's daughter of Oxney Colne; Returning home; The man who kept his money in a box; Aaron Trow; The House of Heine Brothers in Munich; George Walker at Suez; The mistletoe bough; The journey to Panama; The widow's mite; The two generals; Miss Ophelia Gledd; Malachi's Cove; Father Giles of Ballymoy; The geltle Euphemia; Lotta Schmidt; The adventures of Fred Pickering; The last Austrian who left Venice; The Turkish bath; Mary Gresley; Josephine de Montmorenci; The Panjandrum; The spotted dog; Mrs. Brumby; Christmas day at Kirkby Cottage; Christmas at Thompson Hall; Why Frau Frohmann raised her prices; The telegraph girl; The lady of Launay; Alice Dugdale; Catherine Carmichael; or, Three years running; The two heroines of Plumplington; Not if I know it

Doctor Thorne; with an introduction by N. John Hall. Knopf 1993 xxxi, 319p $20

ISBN 0-679-42304-4　　　　　LC 93-1853

Also available Oxford University Press edition

"Everyman's library"

First published 1858. Third of the Chronicles of Barsetshire

"A story of quiet country life; and the interest of the book lies in the character studies rather than in the plot. The scene is laid in the west of England about 1854. The heroine, Mary Thorne, is a sweet, modest girl, living with her kind uncle Doctor Thorne, in the village of Greshambury, where Frank Gresham, the young heir of Greshambury Park, falls in love with her." Keller. Reader's Dig of Books

Followed by Framley parsonage

The Duke's children [abridged]
In Trollope, A. The Pallisers p387-437

The Eustace diamonds.
Available from various publishers

First published 1872

The third Palliser novel. "The story follows two contrasting women and their courtships. Lizzie Eustace and Lucy Morris are both hampered in their love affairs by their lack of money. Lizzie's trickery and deceit, however, contrast with Lucy's constancy. Trollope was understood to be commenting on the malaise in Victorian England that allowed a character like Lizzie, who marries for money, steals the family diamonds, and behaves despicably throughout, to rise unscathed in society." Merriam-Webster's Ency of Lit

The Eustace diamonds [abridged]
In Trollope, A. The Pallisers p189-264

Framley parsonage; with an introduction by Graham Handley. Knopf 1994 xxxi, 587p $20

ISBN 0-679-43133-0

"Everyman's library"

First published 1861. Fourth of the Chronicles of Barsetshire

"The vicar of Framley, a weak but honest young man, is led astray and into debt by a spendthrift M. P., and finds himself in a false position. The other branch of the story deals with his sister's chequered love affair and marriage to young Lord Lufton. A great crowd of characters are engaged in the social functions, the intrigues and the match making, the general effect of which is comic, though graver interest is never far off, and there are

Trollope, Anthony, 1815-1882—*Continued*
situations of deepest pathos." Baker. Guide to the Best
Fic
Followed by The small house at Allington

The last chronicle of Barset; with an introduction by Graham Handley. Knopf 1995 xxix, 983p $24

ISBN 0-679-44366-5   LC 95-75205
"Everyman's library"
First published 1867. Sixth in the Chronicles of Barsetshire
"The ecclesiastical society of 'The Warden,' Mr.
Harding, Mrs. Proudie, and the rest make their last appearance. The dominant situation is one of intense
anguish. A poor country clergyman, proud, learned, sternly conscientious is accused of a felony, and the pressure
of family want makes his guilt seem only too probable."
Baker. Guide to the Best Fic

The Pallisers; abridged and introduced by Michael Hardwick. Coward, McCann & Geoghegan 1975 c1974 436p o.p.

One volume abridgment of six "parliamentary novels"
Can you forgive her?, The Eustace diamonds and The
prime minister are entered separately
Contents: Can you forgive her; Phineas Finn; The
Eustace diamonds; Phineas Redux; The prime minister;
The Duke's children

Phineas Finn [abridged]

In Trollope, A. The Pallisers p117-88

Phineas Redux [abridged]

In Trollope, A. The Pallisers p265-323

The prime minister. o.p.

First published 1876
"Considered by modern critics to represent the apex
of the 'Palliser novels', it is the fifth in the series and
sustains two plot lines. One records the clash between
the Duke of Omnium, now prime minister of a coalition
government, and his high-spirited wife, Lady Glencora,
whose drive to become the most brilliant hostess in
society causes embarrassment for her husband and eventually contributes to his downfall. The second plot
reveals the machinations of Ferdinand Lopez, an ambitious social climber who wins the support of Lady
Glencora—but not her husband—for an election campaign. The novel brilliantly dissects the politics of both
marriage and government." Merriam-Webster's Ency of
Lit

The prime minister [abridged]

In Trollope, A. The Pallisers p325-85

The small house at Allington. o.p.

First published 1864. Fifth of the Chronicles of Barsetshire
"Country life, its quiet, its pleasures and troubles,
monotony and dullness, and with digressions into
boardinghouse life in London and into high society.
Many old friends appear in the usual concourse of
characters, among whom stand out Mr. Crosbie, a snobbish and cowardly trifler. . . . Lily Dale, the jilted
maiden, amiable and weak Johnny Eames, and the
aristocratic doll, Lady Dumbello; all closely copied from
life." Baker. Guide to the Best Fic
Followed by The last chronicle of Barset

The warden. Knopf 1991 xxxiii, 203p $15

ISBN 0-679-40551-8   LC 91-52985

"Everyman's library"
First published 1855. First of the Chronicles of Barsetshire
"The Reverend Septimus Harding, the conscientious
warden of a charitable retirement home for men, resigns
after being accused of making too much profit from the
sinecure." Merriam-Webster's Ency of Lit
Followed by Barchester Towers

The way we live now. o.p.

First published 1875
"The novel chronicles the fleeting fame of Augustus
Melmotte, a villainous financier of obscure origins who
briefly captivates the aristocratic society of London with
his image as a man of wealth and prestige. Lady Matilda
Carbury, mother of the incompetent Felix, is a novelist
who prefers popularity to critical acclaim. Marie Melmotte, Hetta Carbury, and Georgiana Longstaffe struggle to
negotiate the mutable marketplace of marriage. Some
critics view the virtuous and nostalgic Roger Carbury as
Trollope's mouthpiece, voicing concern over the selfishness of other characters." Merriam-Webster's Ency of Lit

Trollope, Joanna

The men and the girls. Random House 1993 c1992 248p $20

ISBN 0-679-42587-X   LC 93-18421
Also available Thorndike Press large print edition
First published 1992 in the United Kingdom
Oxford is the setting for a "story of the intimate and
suddenly volatile relationships of two former school
friends, now past 60 years of age. James lives with Kate
(who is thirtysomething), her teenage daughter (nose ear-
ring, shorn head, black boots, etc.), and crochety Uncle
Leonard. Hugh's wife, Julia, also thirtyish, is the mother
of young twins. Into the very settled lives of these two
households comes Beatrice, an elderly spinster, knocked
off her bicycle by James' car." Booklist
"One of the pleasures in good contemporary British
fiction like 'The Men and the Girls' is the writing itself—deft, fluid, perceptive and concise. Another is the
wonderfully wry humor, particularly when its objects are
sacred cows. Like Muriel Spark, Joanna Trollope is
hilarious about old people, for instance." N Y Times
Book Rev

The rector's wife. Random House 1994 287p $21

ISBN 0-679-43702-9   LC 94-20625
First published 1991 in the United Kingdom
The provincial English "rector in *The Rector's Wife*,
Peter Bouverie, has spent his life and defined his
ministry according to what other people think, and he
expects his family to do the same. . . . The turning
point comes early in the story, when Peter is passed
over for a much hoped-for appointment to the position
of archdeacon. When his career hits dead end, it
becomes bitterly clear that he has no inner resources or
satisfying relationships to fall back on. In his marriage
and ministry, Peter has dried up. Anna, too, is on the
verge of either drying up or going mad. As her frustration deepens over Peter's disappointment and the
estrangement between them, she decides to change her
life. She begins to carve out small spaces of independence from the parish by transferring their daughter to
a Catholic school, taking a job at a local supermarket
and, finally, seeking the love absent in her marriage with
the brother of the new archdeacon." Christ Century

Truman, Margaret, 1924-

Murder at the FBI. Arbor House 1985 256p o.p.

LC 85-7345

This mystery "begins with the corpse of an FBI agent falling onto the firing range during a public tour. Native American special agent Christine Saksis and her lover Ross Lizenby are assigned to the investigating team. Lizenby very soon begins to act suspiciously and the FBI higher-ups seem to be suppressing information." Libr J

Murder at the Kennedy Center. Random House 1989 310p $17.95

ISBN 0-394-57602-0   LC 88-43204

Also available Thorndike Press large print edition

The story "opens with a grand performance at the Kennedy Center honoring Senator Ewald, favored to win his party's nomination for president. But hopes dim after the extravaganza when Professor Mackensie (Mac) Smith finds an Ewald campaign worker, Andrea Feldman, shot dead behind the Center. The senator's son Paul, who has been sexually involved with Andrea, is arrested for the murder whereupon his wife, Janet, disappears. As a professor of law and Ewald's friend, Mac uses his skills to investigate those in Ewald's orbit." Publ Wkly

Murder at the National Cathedral. Random House 1990 293p $18.95

ISBN 0-394-57603-9   LC 89-43433

Also available large print edition $21.95 (ISBN 0-679-40044-3)

Sleuth Mackensie Smith "and his lover, Annabel Reed, have just been married. Then the Episcopal priest who performed the service is murdered, and criminal law professor Smith launches his investigation. . . . Links between a world peace organization, federal and international spy networks, scorned lovers, activist priests, and distraught choir boys are . . . interwoven into the plot." Booklist

Murder at the Pentagon. Random House 1992 291p $21

ISBN 0-394-57604-7   LC 91-51023

Also available large print edition $22.95 (ISBN 0-679-41357-X)

"Air Force helicopter pilot and lawyer Major Margit Falk is assigned the defense of Robert Cobol, a CIA officer charged with the murder of Dr. Richard Joycelen. The victim, deputy director of a defense research project devoted to small nuclear devices, was shot inside the Pentagon, purportedly the most secure building in the world. While Margit works up Cobol's defense with the help of mentor Mackensie Smith . . . world powers adjust to the nuclear capability recently exhibited by a small Arab nation." Publ Wkly

Murder in Georgetown. Arbor House 1986 267p o.p.

LC 86-8047

"Investigating murderous doings in the nation's capital, 'Washington Post' crime reporter Jo Potamos is assigned to probe the slaying of the daughter of a prominent U.S. senator. Potamos is pulled off the case at the insistence of an influential syndicated columnist, who feels that the journalist is uncovering information that is better left undetected. Enlisting the aid of a group of precocious Georgetown University J-school students, Potamos unravels the intricate threads of the case on his own time.

. . . If nothing else, the author effectively portrays the geographic parameters of the Washington scene." Booklist

Murder in the CIA. Random House 1987 371p o.p.

LC 87-42654

"A literary agent who happens to be a CIA courier is murdered in London's Heathrow airport. Collette Cahill, member of the CIA unit in Budapest, wants to know why her friend died. As she travels from Europe to Washington, D.C. and the British Virgin Islands she makes a few startling discoveries about herself and the organization for which she works." Libr J

Truman "can juggle false leads with the best of them. And of course she has one thing that her colleagues do not—an unparalleled insider's knowledge about the workings of Washington." N Y Times Book Rev

Murder in the Smithsonian; a novel. Arbor House 1983 298p o.p.

LC 83-70479

"Historian Lewis Tunney is murdered in the National Museum of American History—stabbed with Thomas Jefferson's sword—and a jewel-covered medal is missing. Captain MacHanrahan's investigation is both helped and complicated by the appearance of Tunney's Scottish fiancée Heather McBean." Libr J

Murder in the Supreme Court; a novel. Arbor House 1982 284p o.p.

LC 81-71678

"When the Chief Clerk of the Chief Justice is shot and killed in the Chief Justice's chair on the bench in the Supreme Court, even the Chief Justice himself becomes a suspect, and the two investigators, one a woman lawyer from the Justice Dept. and the other a lieutenant of the Washington Police dept., find themselves deeply involved in political and romantic intrigue. The inside look into the public and private lives of the Supreme Court Justices, their families and their working staffs create situations most unusual and unexpected among the high and mighty." West Coast Rev Books

Murder in the White House; a novel. Arbor House 1980 235p o.p.

LC 79-54004

"When Secretary of State Blaine is murdered in the Lincoln Sitting Room of the White House, President Webster orders Special Counsel Fairchild to coordinate efforts to solve the case with the authorities. The lawyer turned detective begins investigating everyone with access to the White House, including Webster, the First Lady and her daughter Lynne." Publ Wkly

Murder on Capitol Hill; a novel. Arbor House 1981 255p o.p.

LC 80-70223

"Lawyer Lydia James agrees to the request of Veronica Caldwell to act as counsel for the senatorial committee investigating the killing of her husband, Senate Majority leader Cale Caldwell. He has been stabbed at a reception honoring him, where his black-sheep son Mark, member of a fanatical cult, is among the 200 or more guests. Mark is arrested for the murder, and also on suspicion of having killed Jimmye, Veronica's niece, years earlier, an unsolved crime. His mother and brother, Cale Jr., sorrowfully agree that Mark is guilty, but Lydia believes the charges are trumped up. She gets herself into dicey situations, chasing clues." Publ Wkly

Truman, Margaret, 1924-—*Continued*
Murder on Embassy Row; a novel. Arbor House 1984 316p o.p.

LC 84-9209

"The British Ambassador is poisoned, his valet-chauffeur disappears, and high American and British officials put the brakes on a Washington captain of detectives who starts getting close to the truth. A major cover-up is in the making. So the captain decides to go it on his own, aided by his girlfriend in the Police Department." N Y Times Book Rev

"The characters, plot, and dialogue are believable; the settings in Washington, London, and Copenhagen are most appealing." Libr J

Murder on the Potomac. Random House 1994 290p $21

ISBN 0-679-43309-0   LC 93-44746
Also available large print edition $20 (ISBN 0-679-75387-7)

"When the body pf Pauline Juris, personal secretary of wealthy developer Wendell Tierney, is found in the Potomac River, Tierney calls former attorney, now law professor, [Mac] Smith for advice. Mac, whose beloved wife Annabel wants him to stop dabbling in detection, agrees to see Wendell. . . . Both Mac and Annabel are drawn into the case." Publ Wkly

"The plot's pretty standard, and the writing's just okay, but Truman's quirky characters are amusing, and her insights into the lives of the rich and famous are heady and fascinating." Booklist

Trumbo, Dalton, 1905-1976
Johnny got his gun. Lippincott 1939 309p o.p.

"Far more than an antiwar polemic, this compassionate description of the effects of war on one soldier is a poignant tribute to the human instinct to survive. Badly mutilated, blind, and deaf, Johnny fights to communicate with an uncomprehending medical world debating his fate." Shapiro. Fic for Youth. 3d edition

Truscott, Lucian K., 1947-
Dress gray; [by] Lucian K. Truscott IV. Doubleday 1979 c1978 489p o.p.

LC 78-1250

A West Point "plebe is found drowned; information, quickly suppressed, indicates he was murdered; a cadet, one Rysam Parker Slaight III, gets wind of the coverup and finds himself in trouble with the coverup authorities, a group of West Point officers and some powerful cronies at the Pentagon." New Yorker

Tryon, Thomas
Crowned heads. Knopf 1976 399p o.p.

"The interlocking destinies of four fictionalized movie stars' lives are related in a somewhat breathless narrative which pays as much attention to the myths of Hollywood as to the effect these legends have on the characters themselves. Starring in Tryon's full-length feature are a once beautiful silent-screen actress with a mysterious past, a blonde former starlet now suffering from depression, a child actor unaccountably still telling his fantastic stories, and a debonair matinee idol whose memorabilia-filled mansion is invaded by Manson-type youths." Booklist

Harvest home. Knopf 1973 401p o.p.

"A contemporary ex-urbanite man faces the unknown practices of the rural community where he has moved to escape the evils of the city. Ted Constantine and his wife and daughter come to Cornwall Coombe, a New England spot so untouched it still celebrates a medieval mystery play once a year. . . . There is a great deal more to the play than appears, and the terror and mystery for the outsiders grows into a kind of primeval nightmare." Libr J

"This potent horror story opens quietly and builds to a climactic frenzy. . . . Mr. Tryon has his own kind of terror to inflict on his spellbound readers." Publ Wkly

In the fire of spring. Knopf 1991 609p o.p.

LC 91-414

In this sequel to The wings of the morning "a runaway slave, Rose Mills, is helped to safety by the abolitionist Appleton Talcott and two of his daughters as they return home to Pequot Landing. . . . The Talcotts and the slave-owning Grimes family are still feuding, but it's now 1841, and fuel has been added to the fire. First of all, the Talcotts open a school for young black women, which gives the Grimeses something new to holler about. Second, Appleton's wife, Mabel Talcott, is secretly dying. As she ponders her mortality and worries about her children, her dying wish is granted: daughter Aurora, abroad for years with husband and child, returns home. Mab's heart breaks as she learns of her daughter's travails and of her undying love for the true father of her child—none other than the swashbuckling, lady-killing Sinjin Grimes." Booklist

The other. Knopf 1971 280p o.p.
Buccaneer Bks. reprint available $18.95 (ISBN 0-89968-443-2)

"Bizarre events occur in and around the once-prosperous Perry family in Connecticut during the 1930s. The men have all died mysteriously and brutally. Niles and Holland, 12-year-old twins, seem to be linked to the ghastly deaths and disasters. A compassionate Russian grandmother plays along with Niles's deception and tries to protect him." Shapiro. Fic for Youth. 3d edition

The wings of the morning. Knopf 1990 567p o.p.

LC 89-39513

"Set in the 1820s and 1830s in the small Connecticut town of Pequot Landing, the novel tells of the feud between the town's two first families—the Talcotts and the Grimeses. The link between the two families is the miller's daughter, Georgie Ross—childhood friend to the rakish Sinjin Grimes and former servant and close friend to the Talcotts. Georgie is a levelheaded, independent heroine and her experiences highlight the conditions of women in that time." Libr J

"Unalloyed pleasure for fans of this genre, Tryon's literate 19th-century soap opera is steeped in the rhythms of Trollope and Scott." Publ Wkly
Followed by In the fire of the spring

Ts'ao, Chan *See* Ts'ao, Hsüeh-ch'in, ca. 1717-1763

Ts'ao, Hsüeh-ch'in, ca. 1717-1763

The dream of the red chamber; (Hung lou mêng); a Chinese novel of the early Ching period; English translation by Florence and Isabel McHugh. Pantheon Bks. 1958 xxi, 582p il o.p. Greenwood Press reprint available $37.50 (ISBN 0-8371-8113-5)

This autobiographical "novel depicts the decline in the fortunes of the large, aristocratic Chia family. It is written with great psychological insight and is unique among Chinese novels for the depth and subtlety of its characterization." Reader's Ency. 3d edition

Turgenev, Ivan Sergeevich, 1818-1883

Fathers and sons; a new translation by Michael R. Katz. Norton 1994 157p $25

ISBN 0-393-03559-X   LC 92-40010

Also available Everyman's library edition translated by Avril Pyman

Original Russian edition, 1862. Variant title: Fathers and children

This novel "concerns the inevitable conflict between generations and between the values of traditionalists and intellectuals. The physician Bazarov, the novel's protagonist, is the most powerful of Turgenev's creations. He is a nihilist, denying the validity of all laws save those of the natural sciences. Uncouth and forthright in his opinions, he is nonetheless susceptible to love and by that fact doomed to unhappiness. In sociopolitical terms he represents the victory of the revolutionary nongentry intelligentsia over the gentry intelligentsia to which Turgenev belonged." Merriam-Webster's Ency of Lit

First love; translated from the Russian by Isaiah Berlin and introduced by Lord David Cecil [and] A fire at sea; translated from the French and introduced by Isaiah Berlin. Viking 1983 150p o.p. Amereon reprint available $14.95 (ISBN 0-88411-445-7)

     LC 82-50888

The short novel First love was originally published 1860 in Russian. This translation was first published in 1950. The autobiographical story A fire at sea was published in French in 1883

In First love "a boy of sixteen falls desperately in love with Zinaida, a mysterious, enchanting girl a few years older than himself, who, surrounded by a doubtful and mixed circle of people, has come with her mother to stay for the holidays in a house next to that of his parents. Gradually he finds out that she is carrying on an intrigue with his aloof, formidable and fascinating father." Introduction

The torrents of spring.
Available from Ayer

Original Russian edition, 1875

This classic Russian novel "is a love story beautifully and simply told: a young Russian nobleman, Dimitry Sanin, falls in love with a pure and sweet girl, Gemma, but through unforeseen circumstances and his own weakness he forsakes her for a sensual woman of the world, Maria Nikolayevna, for whom men are mere playthings of the moment. He does so in spite of being fully aware that this liaison will bring him nothing but ruin and humiliation. . . . This short novel has no political over-

tones and deals only with the emotional experiences of the characters." Libr J

Turow, Scott

The burden of proof. Farrar, Straus & Giroux 1990 515p $22.95

ISBN 0-374-11734-9   LC 90-33593

Also available G.K. Hall large print edition

Lawyer Sandy Stern featured in Presumed innocent "returns home to find his wife has committed suicide. Stern is currently involved in the defense of his brother-in-law, Dixon, who is accused of shady doings on the commodities market; also involved are Stern's daughter and her husband." Libr J

"The plotting is clear and clean, spun out with Greek inevitability and the niceties of law and finance are lucidly, smoothly, explained. Stern's complex character is well-drawn . . . and the members of his family are individualized and believable. The Federal judges and prosecutors have unique backgrounds and prejudices. Even the minor characters are given faces and personalities." America

Pleading guilty. Farrar, Straus & Giroux 1993 386p $24

ISBN 0-374-23457-4   LC 93-70819

Also available G.K. Hall large print edition

This novel is narrated by Mack Mallone, a former policeman and now a partner in the law firm of Gage & Griswell. "The firm's senior partners offered him an ultimatum: find the associate who has been embezzling millions of dollars from the firm's lifeblood client, or it's adios. As Mack searches, he encounters his former partner from the police force, nicknamed Pigeyes, who, because Mack testified against him on charges of pocketing cash during busts, is now a private investigator." Booklist

Turow is "genuinely interested in showing what makes his characters behave the way they do. . . . Pleading Guilty is both an irresistible tale and a dark, moral thriller." Time

Presumed innocent. Farrar, Straus & Giroux 1987 431p $22.95

ISBN 0-374-23713-1   LC 87-368

Rusty Sabich, the chief deputy prosecuting attorney assigned to investigate the murder of his co-worker and former lover, Carolyn Polhemus, is the narrator who draws us into the world of big-city crime and law enforcement as seen through a lawyer's eyes. Because his boss, Raymond Horgan, the Prosecuting Attorney in this unnamed Midwestern city, is up for re-election, Carolyn's murder has become a political issue, and the heat is on Rusty to bring in the killer as soon as he can." NY Times Book Rev

This novel contains "high drama and suspense, as scenes in and out of the courtroom crackle with the amazing interactions of complex, fascinating characters. This is a great book." Libr J

Twain, Mark, 1835-1910

The adventures of Huckleberry Finn.
Available from various publishers

First published 1885. This is a companion volume to The adventures of Tom Sawyer

This novel "begins with Huck's escape from his drunken, brutal father to the river, where he meets up with Jim, a runaway slave. The story of their journey

Twain, Mark, 1835-1910—*Continued*

downstream, with occasional forays into the society along the banks, is an American classic that captures the smells, rhythms, and sounds, the variety of dialects and the human activity of life on the great river. It is also a penetrating social commentary that reveals corruption, moral decay, and intellectual impoverishment through Huck and Jim's encounters with traveling actors and con men, lynch mobs, thieves, and southern gentility. Through Jim, and through his own observations and experiences, Huck learns about the dignity and worth of human life. By the end, when Jim is recaptured, Huck is able to help Jim escape. Thus Mark Twain repudiates the moral blindness of the respectable slave-holding society whose decaying social order is portrayed so vividly throughout the novel. Huck Finn remains one of the greatest creations in American fiction." Reader's Ency. 3d edition

also in Twain, M. The complete novels of Mark Twain v1 p731-969

The adventures of Tom Sawyer.
Available from various publishers

First published 1876. This is a companion volume to The adventures of Huckleberry Finn

"Tom, a shrewd and adventurous boy, is at home in the respectable world of his Aunt Polly, as well as in the self-reliant, parentless world of Huck Finn. The two friends, out in the cemetery under a full moon, attempt to cure warts with a dead cat. They accidentally witness a murder, of which Muff Potter is later wrongly accused. Knowing that the true murderer is Injun Joe, the boys are helpless with fear; they decide to run away to Jackson's Island. After a few pleasant days of smoking and swearing, they realize that the townspeople believe them dead. Returning in time to hear their funeral eulogies, they become town heroes. At the trial of Muff Potter, Tom, unable to let an innocent person be condemned, reveals his knowledge. Injun Joe flees. Later Tom and his sweetheart, Becky Thatcher, get lost in the cave in which the murderer is hiding. They escape, and Tom and Huck return to find the treasure Joe has buried." Reader's Ency. 3d edition

also in Twain, M. The adventures of Tom Sawyer, Tom Sawyer abroad, Tom Sawyer, detective p31-236

also in Twain, M. The complete novels of Mark Twain v1 p385-556

The adventures of Tom Sawyer, Tom Sawyer abroad, Tom Sawyer, detective; edited by John C. Gerber, Paul Baender, and Terry Firkins. University of Calif. Press 1980 717p il $45
ISBN 0-520-03353-1   LC 76-47974

A combined edition of three Tom Sawyer titles first published 1876, 1894 and 1896, respectively. The adventures of Tom Sawyer is entered separately and the other two titles are listed under The complete novels of Mark Twain

The American claimant
In Twain, M. The complete novels of Mark Twain v1 p263-416

The complete novels of Mark Twain; edited with an introduction by Charles Neider. Doubleday 1964 2v o.p.
Contents: v1: The gilded age (1873); The adventures of Tom Sawyer (1876); The prince and the pauper (1881); Adventures of Huckleberry Finn (1881)
v2: A Connecticut Yankee in King Arthur's court (1889); The American claimant (1892); Tom Sawyer abroad (1894); Pudd'nhead Wilson (1894); Those extraordinary twins (1894); Personal recollections of Joan of Arc (1896); Tom Sawyer, detective (1896)

The complete short stories; now collected for the first time; edited and with an introduction by Charles Neider. Doubleday 1957 xxiv, 676p o.p.
Available from Amereon and Buccaneer Bks.

Contents: The notorious jumping frog of Calaveras County; The story of the bad little boy; Cannibalism in the cars; A day at Niagara; Legend of the Capitoline Venus; Journalism in Tennessee; A curious dream; The facts in the great beef contract; How I edited an agricultural paper; A medieval romance; My watch; Political economy; Science vs. luck; The story of the good little boy; Buck Fanshaw's funeral; The story of the Old Ram; Tom Quartz; A trial; The trials of Simon Erickson; A true story; Experience of the McWilliamses with membranous croup; Some learned fables for good old boys and girls; The canvasser's tale; The loves of Alonzo Fitz Clarence and Rosannah Ethelton; Edward Mills and George Benton: a tale; The man who put up at Gadsby's; Mrs. McWilliams and the lightning; What stumped the Bluejays; A curious experience; The invalid's story; The McWilliamses and the burglar alarm; The stolen white elephant; A burning brand; A dying man's confession; The professor's yarn; A ghost story; Luck; Playing courier; The Californian's tale; The diary of Adam and Eve; The Esquimau maiden's romance; Is he living or is he dead?; The £1,000,000 bank-note; Cecil Rhodes and the shark; The joke that made Ed's fortune; A story without an end; The man that corrupted Hadleyburg; The death disk; Two little tales; The belated Russian passport; A double-barreled detective story; The five boons of life; Was it Heaven? or Hell?; A dog's tale; The $30,000 bequest; A horse's tale; Hunting the deceitful turkey; Extract from Captain Stormfield's visit to Heaven; A fable; The mysterious stranger

A Connecticut Yankee in King Arthur's court.
Available from various publishers

First published 1889; published in the United Kingdom with title: Yankee at the court of King Arthur

This satiric novel is a "tale of a commonsensical Yankee who is carried back in time to Britain in the Dark Ages, and it celebrates homespun ingenuity and democratic values in contrast to the superstitious ineptitude of a feudal monarchy." Merriam-Webster's Ency of Lit

also in Twain, M. The complete novels of Mark Twain v2 p1-262

The gilded age; [by] Mark Twain and C. D. Warner. o.p.
First published 1873

"Mark Twain and Dudley Warner were neighbours at Hartford, Conn., when they collaborated in this portrayal of their times; the bitter account of the Easterners is

Twain, Mark, 1835-1910—*Continued*

Warner's; the humorist drew the Westerners, scoffed at Washington and Congress, and created the mighty optimist Colonel Sellers." Baker. Guide to the Best Fic

also in Twain, M. The complete novels of Mark Twain v1 p1-383

The man that corrupted Hadleyburg, and other stories and essays. Harper 1900 364p o.p.

Partially analyzed in Short story index

Contents: The man that corrupted Hadleyburg; My début as a literary person; £1,000,000 bank-note; Esquimau maiden's romance; My first lie, and how I got out of it; Belated Russian passport; Two little tales; About play-acting; Diplomatic pay and clothes; Is he living or is he dead?; My boyhood dreams; Austrian Edison keeping school again; Death disk; Double-barreled detective story; Petition to the Queen of England

Mysterious stranger, and other stories. Harper 1922 324p il o.p. Amereon reprint available $20.95 (ISBN 0-8488-0652-2)

Analyzed in Short story index

Contents: Mysterious stranger; Horse's tale; Extract from Captain Stormfield's visit to Heaven; Fable; My platonic sweetheart; Hunting the deceitful turkey; McWilliamses and the burglar alarm

Personal recollections of Joan of Arc; by the Sieur Louis de Conte (her page and secretary); illustrated by G. B. Cutts. Harper 1926 596p il o.p.

First published 1896

"De Conte, who tells the story in the first person, has been reared in the same village with its subject, has been her daily playmate there, and has followed her fortunes in later life, serving her to the end, his being the friendly hand that she touches last. After her death, he comes to understand her greatness; he calls hers 'the most noble life that was ever born into this world save only One.' Beginning with a scene in her childhood that shows her innate sense of justice, goodness of heart, and unselfishness, the story follows her throughout her stormy career. We have her audiences with the king; her marches with her army; her entry into Orleans; her fighting; her trial; her execution; all simply and naturally and yet vividly told. The historical facts are closely followed." Keller. Reader's Dig of Books

also in Twain, M. The complete novels of Mark Twain v2 p661-998

The prince and the pauper

In Twain, M. The complete novels of Mark Twain v1 p559-730

Pudd'nhead Wilson.

Available from Amereon and Buccaneer Bks.

First published 1894 with title: The tragedy of Pudd'nhead Wilson

"David Wilson is called 'Pudd'nhead' by the townspeople, who fail to understand his combination of wisdom and eccentricity. He redeems himself by simultaneously solving a murder mystery and a case of transposed identities. The mystery revolves around two children, a white boy and a mulatto, who are born on the same day. . . . The book is an implicit condemnation of a society that allows slavery. It also includes a series of brilliant

epigrams, each the headpiece of a chapter, which are distillations of Twain's wit and wisdom." Reader's Ency. 3d edition

also in Twain, M. The complete novels of Mark Twain v2 p491-608

Those extraordinary twins

In Twain, M. The complete novels of Mark Twain v2 p609-60

Tom Sawyer abroad

In Twain, M. The adventures of Tom Sawyer; Tom Sawyer abroad; Tom Sawyer, detective p251-341

In Twain, M. The complete novels of Mark Twain v2 p417-90

Tom Sawyer abroad, and other stories. Grosset & Dunlap 1924 217p o.p.

Contents: Tom Sawyer abroad; The great revolution in Pitcairn; The canvasser's tale; An encounter with an interview; Paris notes; Legend of Sagenfeld, in Germany; Speech on the weather; Concerning the American language; Rogers; The loves of Alonzo Fitz Clarence and Rosannah Ethelton

Tom Sawyer, detective

In Twain, M. The adventures of Tom Sawyer; Tom Sawyer abroad; Tom Sawyer, detective p357-415

In Twain, M. The complete novels of Mark Twain v2 p999-1048

Tweedsmuir, John Buchan, Baron *See* Buchan, John, 1875-1940

Two hundred years of great American short stories. See 200 years of great American short stories

Tyers, Kathy, 1952-

The truce at Bakura. Bantam Bks. 1994 311p (Star wars) $21.95

ISBN 0-553-09541-2   LC 93-11388

"Hard on the heels of the emperor's death, the Alliance receives word of an outpost planet beseiged by a new alien invader, a lizardlike race of creatures bent on conquest of the galaxy. Flushed with their recent victory and stunned by the revelation of their parentage, Luke and Leia travel to the edge of the Empire to join forces with their erstwhile enemies to combat an even deadlier foe. Set prior to the events of Timothy Zahn's 'Star Wars' cycle, Tyers's first foray into the Star Wars universe captures the feel of space opera while attempting a three-dimensional portrayal of the forces of a decaying empire." Libr J

Tyler, Anne, 1941-

The accidental tourist. Knopf 1985 355p $25

ISBN 0-394-54689-X   LC 85-40161

Tyler, Anne, 1941——*Continued*

"After 20 years of marriage, Macon and Sarah separate. Thus, a man used to intense order in his life finds his existence thrown into disorder; forced to create a new life for himself, Macon must overcome numerous obstacles—particularly his inability to communicate, to relate to other people's needs and problems." Booklist

"Thanks to her inimitable mix of an extraordinary inventiveness with characters and a profound humanity, Tyler makes this book a joy to read." Wilson Libr Bull

Breathing lessons. Knopf 1988 327p $25

ISBN 0-394-57234-3   LC 88-45260

Also available Thorndike Press large print edition

"Maggie and Ira Moran, late middle-aged, travel from their home in Baltimore to a friend's funeral in Pennsylvania. The expedition precipitates an introspective journey into their individual and collective pasts and presents and futures." Booklist

This novel has "irresistibly funny passages you want to read out loud and poignant insights that illuminate the serious business of sharing lives in an unsettling world." Publ Wkly

Celestial navigation. Knopf 1974 273p o.p.

Set in Baltimore, this novel tells of artist Jeremy Pauling's attempts to overcome his comfortable isolation and make contact with others

The author "is especially gifted in the art of freeing her characters and then keeping track of them as they move in their unique and often solitary orbits. . . . She has a way of transcribing their peculiarities with such loving wholeness that when we examine them we keep finding more and more pieces of ourselves." N Y Times Book Rev

The clock winder. Knopf 1972 312p o.p.

"It all starts when Elizabeth Abbott agrees to become Mrs. Emerson's handyman for the summer. Before it's over, one of the Emersons (Timothy) kills himself, another (Andrew) shoots Elizabeth, and Mrs. Emerson has a stroke. The 'handyman' finds herself holding the family together and ultimately stays on to become an Emerson herself by marrying Matthew." Libr J

The author has a "remarkable understanding of the intricacies of family life, a sympathy for odd-ball characters who never become merely southern grotesques . . . but are observed so gently that the term 'neurotic' seems equally inappropriate for them." New Repub

Dinner at the Homesick Restaurant. Knopf 1982 303p $25

ISBN 0-394-52381-4   LC 81-13694

"Pearl Tull, an angry woman who vacillates between excesses of maternal energy and spurts of terrifying rage, has been deserted by her husband and has brought up her three children alone. Cody, the eldest, is handsome, wild, and in a lifelong battle of jealousy with his young brother, the sweet-tempered and patient Ezra. Their sister Jenny tries, through three marriages, to find a stability which was never present in Pearl's home. Ezra also tries to achieve a permanence through his homey Homesick Restaurant in Baltimore, but he is cruelly tricked by his brother and is unable to establish any unity in the family." Shapiro. Fic for Youth. 3d edition

Earthly possessions. Knopf 1977 197p o.p.

LC 76-41222

This "novel concerns Charlotte Emory, a 35-year-old woman who goes to her bank in Clarion, Md., one morning to withdraw enough cash to leave her husband. Instead, she is hustled off as hostage to a bank robber and peripatetic demolition-derby rider named Jake Simms. Simms needs funds to get to Florida and take his girlfriend out of a home for unwed mothers. All that he and Charlotte share, apart from the stolen car they are riding in, is a distrust of 'closed-in spaces'—for him, the prison he has just escaped; for her, a household that includes a gaunt preacher husband, two children, three brothers-in-law and a procession of itinerant sinners, soldiers and salesmen." Newsweek

"The book is contrapuntal, alternating chapters of the present action with chapters of first-person flashback. . . . The dialogue has perfect pitch, the visual detail seems astonishing yet apt." New Repub

Morgan's passing. Knopf 1980 311p $13.95

ISBN 0-394-50958-7   LC 79-20272

"A young girl-wife goes into labor while she and her boy-husband are putting on a puppet-show of Cinderella at a church fair in Baltimore in 1967. Her baby is delivered en route to the hospital by a member of the audience who claims to be a doctor. . . . The fake doctor—who lives in a tumultuous . . . cluttered house with an imperturbable wife, seven daughters, his half-senile mother, and crackpot sister—attaches himself to the young couple and their child, following them, popping up at odd moments. Later, after they have all become friends, this attachment, narrows, focusing upon the young wife, with unsettling consequences for everyone." New Repub

Saint maybe. Knopf 1991 337p $22

ISBN 0-679-40361-2   LC 91-52704

Also available large print edition $24.50 (ISBN 0-679-40771-5)

"The Bedloe family living in Baltimore in the 1960s is an ideal family. That pleasant domestic scene changes when Danny, after a very brief courtship, marries Lucy, a divorcee with two children. Ian, Danny's younger brother, in a careless remark casting suspicion on Lucy's behavior, brings destruction upon Danny and his family. When Ian becomes involved with the Church of the Second Chance, he decides that he must atone for his guilt by accepting responsibility for the children Danny has left behind. The story describes both the trials and satisfactions of Ian's experience as a parent for all the years until the children are adults. The ending brings special happiness to Ian when he himself finds fulfillment in marriage." Shapiro. Fic for Youth. 3d edition

Searching for Caleb. Knopf 1976 c1975 309p o.p.

"The Pecks of Baltimore are wealthy, stand-offish, stolidly self-satisfied. In their suburban enclave . . . four generations have lived quietly together . . . [presided over by the] grandfather, Daniel. Only two have rebelled: Caleb, Daniel's dreamy, cello-playing brother who disappeared without a trace 60 years ago, and Duncan, Daniel's grandson. . . . When Duncan marries his cousin Justine, hitherto an ardent Peck, she begins to discover her own thirst for adventure. . . . And so, when Daniel decides to find his lost brother, Justine is the one who joins him." N Y Times Book Rev

Tyler, Anne, 1941——*Continued*

"Anne Tyler's tone is understated, ironic, and elliptical, which suits her characters well. Searching for Caleb rarely gives us heights and depths of emotion or the excitement of discovery, but it does offer the very welcome old-fashioned virtues of a patient, thoughtful chronicle." Saturday Rev

A slipping-down life. Knopf 1970 214p o.p.

"Evie Decker, unattractive and unpopular, and Drumsticks Casey, an unknown rock musician, are misfits living in a small Southern town. They are drawn together in a union which is more bizarre than romantic. It is a union, however, that seems to fulfill the needs of each and makes for a marriage that is marked by quiet desperation." Shapiro. Fic for Youth. 3d edition

The tin can tree. Knopf 1965 273p o.p.

"Six-year-old Janie Rose Pike was killed in a fall from a tractor, an accident which shook but does not really change the little world in which she lived. Mrs. Pike, left stunned and silent by her daughter's death, is too apathetic to pay attention to her 10-year-old son, Simon. Her grown-up niece, who lives with the family, tries to take care of Simon and at the same time to cope with her own problems. It is Simon himself . . . who finally awakens his mother to the need for life to continue." Libr J

U

Uhnak, Dorothy

False witness; a novel. Simon & Schuster 1981 314p o.p.

LC 81-1591

"An ambitious bureau chief for the New York district attorney finds she has a racist, sexist, and political bombshell on her hands when a beautiful black talk-show host is brutally raped and disfigured in a vicious attack. But the attorney also finds that this case can propel her right into the D.A.'s office itself, if she plays her cards right, which may or may not involve prosecuting the man actually responsible for the crime. These career plans, however, raise conflicts in the lawyer's private life as legal aspirations slam up against an increasingly recalcitrant and questioning lover." Booklist

"This is a very tough-minded book. It works in terms of making us believe that this is the way in which this attempted murder might have happened. It works very well." Publ Wkly

The investigation; a novel. Simon & Schuster 1977 344p o.p.

LC 77-7981

Sgt. Joe Peters is "a detective on the Queens County district attorney's squad. He accompanies his partner one morning on a house call involving two missing children. The distraught parents are George and Kitty Keeler. George is 'an obese, balding, sloppy middle-aged man' who owns a bar. Kitty, more than twenty years his junior, is a 'very beautiful kid' who manages a health spa owned by a small-time gangster. The Keeler marriage is shaky, and Kitty accuses George of having taken the boys. But when their bodies are found in a nearby park and Kitty's account of her actions begins to sound suspi-

cious, she is indicted for murder. . . . Out of curiosity and an attraction to Kitty, [Peters] sets out to investigate on his own." Newsweek

Law and order; a novel. Simon & Schuster 1973 512p o.p.

"The scene is New York City from 1937 to the 1970s, the leading characters three generations of Irish-American policemen, their families, the women they love and hate, the friends with whom they are linked in fierce loyalty, the enemies they will ruthlessly destroy no matter how much they have to bend or break the law to do it." Publ Wkly

The Ryer Avenue story. St. Martin's Press 1993 406p $22.95

ISBN 0-312-08888-4   LC 92-43655

"On a winter's night in 1935, six Bronx children flee from the body of a local drunk and child molester felled by blows from his shovel. Later, the miscreant father of one of the children confesses and is executed for the crime; the children swear never to speak of what they believe really happened. Years pass, and the now-adult survivors are summoned together to confront the event again. Lives, careers, families, and more are in grave jeopardy as one of their own plots revenge." Libr J

The author provides "just enough detail, complexity and old-fashioned storytelling verve to keep the plot purring along." N Y Times Book Rev

Victims; a novel. Simon & Schuster 1986 c1985 316p o.p.

LC 85-26246

"Young nurse Anna Grace is stabbed to death on a street in Queens in full view of scores of apartment dwellers who decide not to get involved. Tough, good-looking NYPD detective Miranda Torres investigates the crime in association with bigshot newspaper columnist Mike Stein, whose only goal is to show the insensitivities of modern society without caring who the criminal is or why poor Anna was his victim. Miranda stays honest in trying to do her job, but finds that the well-spring of corruption in law enforcement is so powerful that it even touches her friends in the highest levels of government." Booklist

The witness. Simon & Schuster 1969 222p o.p.

This novel is about the murder of a young black law student who is active in "civil-liberties demonstrations. A New York cop finds the gun in his hand. The city, especially the black population, cries for revenge. But one person saw the gun shoved into his hand—Christie Opara, a detective. . . . The Mayor and the Chief of Detectives toil to avert the consequences of a 'long hot summer.'" Best Sellers

"This is a sober story, told with warmth and understanding, and conveying no little of the sometimes painfully ambiguous role of a woman detective." N Y Times Book Rev

Ullman, James Ramsey, 1907-1971

The White Tower; [by] James R. Ullman. Lippincott 1945 479p o.p.

When Martin Ordway's plane crashed over Switzerland, he came down into a little valley in the Alps which he had known years before the war. Overshadowing the valley is the Weisstrum (White Tower) a high peak never climbed from that side. While he is waiting for an opportunity to get back home Martin succumbs to a long

Ullman, James Ramsey, 1907-1971 — *Continued*

felt desire to try the climb and with five others he makes the attempt. The story combines the account of the adventure of climbing with the meditations and reminiscences of the various members of the group

Underwood, Michael, 1916-

A dangerous business. St. Martin's Press 1991 191p $15.95

ISBN 0-312-05842-X　　　　　LC 90-29880

In this "Rosa Epton mystery, the barrister and her lover, Peter Chen, become involved with Britain's Security Service. Rosa sees former client Eddie Ruding in Amsterdam when he is supposed to be in an English prison after a burglary conviction. Shortly thereafter, an attempt is made on her life and Ruding is found murdered outside a prison, but not the one in which he had been incarcerated." Publ Wkly

The uninvited corpse. St. Martin's Press 1987 173p o.p.

LC 87-4435

"When lawyer Rosa Epton appears on the TV program *Legal Aid*, Vernon Gray, a wealthy old eccentric, decides to hire her to oversee the drafting of his will. But when Gray disappears with a housekeeper that Rosa herself helped him select, and when the police discover an unidentified corpse in his apartment, Rosa finds herself embroiled in both the search for Gray and for the identity of the uninvited corpse." Publ Wkly

Undset, Sigrid, 1882-1949

Nobel Prize in literature, 1928

The axe

In Undset, S. The master of Hestviken v1

The bridal wreath

In Undset, S. Kristin Lavransdatter v1

The cross

In Undset, S. Kristin Lavransdatter v3

In the wilderness

In Undset, S. The master of Hestviken v3

Kristin Lavransdatter; translated from the Norwegian. Knopf 1935 3v in 1 $40

ISBN 0-394-43262-2

Contains three novels originally published separately in Norway in 1920, 1921, and 1922 respectively; first United States publication with titles: The bridal wreath (1923); The mistress of Husaby (1925); The cross (1927)

Although the "action takes place in the fourteenth century, the lives of the characters are marked by almost the same problems depicted in modern novels: passion, adultery, premarital pregnancy, ambition, conflict. Kristin, daughter of Lavrans and Ragnfrid, is betrothed to Simon Andressön but falls in love with Erlend Nikulassön and finally wins her father's approval to marry him. Her father realizes on their wedding night that they are already lovers. The book follows Kristin's life as she tries to manage her estate and as her husband loses his lands and leaves her after a bitter quarrel. After several attempts at reconciliation, Erlend returns, only to be killed

in a fight. The six sons of Kristin follow different paths. Two die during the Black Plague, which was so dreadful a scourge in that era. The portrayal of this Norwegian woman is vivid and human." Shapiro. Fic for Youth. 3d edition

The master of Hestviken; translated from the Norwegian by Arthur G. Chater. Knopf 1952 4v in 1 o.p.

Four volumes originally published 1925-1927 in Norway. First United States editions published separately as follows: The axe, 1928; The snake pit, 1929; In the wilderness, 1929; and The son avenger, 1930

"It is a rich picture of Norwegian life in the Middle Ages, and resembles the 'Kristin Lavransdatter' trilogy in that it is concerned with the secret sin of a pair of young lovers, their suffering and final atonement." Cleveland Public Libr

The mistress of Husaby

In Undset, S. Kristin Lavransdatter v2

The snake pit

In Undset, S. The master of Hestviken v2

The son avenger

In Undset, S. The master of Hestviken v4

The **Unforgetting** heart: an anthology of short stories by African American women (1859-1993); edited by Asha Kanwar. Aunt Lute Bks. 1993 xxi, 292p $20.95

ISBN 1-879960-31-1　　　　　LC 93-3240

Analyzed in short story index

Contents: The two offers, by F. E. W. Harper; Aunt Lindy: a story founded on real life, by V. E. Matthews; Tony's wife, by A. Dunbar; A dash for liberty, by P. E. Hopkins; The octoroon's revenge, by R. D. Todd; After many days: a Christmas story, by F. B. Williams; The preacher at Hill Station, by K. D. C. Tillman; Guests unexpected: a Thanksgiving story, by M. K. Griffin; The judgment of Roxenie, by E. W. Smith; Breaking the color-line, by A. McCary; Mammy: a story, by A. F. Ries; Mary Elizabeth: a story, by J. Fauset; Goldie, by A. W. Grimké; Isis, by Z. N. Hurston; Sanctuary, by N. Larsen; Doby's gone, by A. Petry; In the laundry room, by A. Childress; Brooklyn, by P. Marshall; The funeral, by A. A. Shockley; A happening in Barbados, by L. M. Meriwether; Mom Luby and the social worker, by K. Hunter; The library, by N. Giovanni; After Saturday night comes Sunday, by S. Sanchez; Nineteen fifty-five, by A. Walker; The lesson, by T. C. Bambara; Kiswana Browne, by G. Naylor; Johnnieruth, by B. Birtha; Fifth Sunday, by R. Dove; The life you live (may not be your own), by J. C. Cooper; Ma'Dear, by T. McMillan; Emerald City: Third & Pike, by C. W. Sherman; Croon, by W. Coleman

Unsworth, Barry, 1930-

Morality play. Talese 1995 192p $22.50

ISBN 0-385-47953-0　　　　　LC 95-4106

This novel, set in 14th century England, is narrated by "Nicholas Barber, a young monk who has forsaken his calling and joined an itinerant troupe of players that gets caught up in the real-life drama of a small-town

Unsworth, Barry, 1930-—*Continued*

murder. The crime presents Barber and his fellows with an opportunity to attract a larger-than-usual audience, and they turn sleuths, weaving the bits of information yielded by their investigation into an improvised play that eventually reveals the surprising, sordid truth. Rich in historical detail, Unsworth's well-told tale explores some timeless moral dilemmas and reads like a modern page-turner." Libr J

Sacred hunger. Doubleday 1992 629p o.p.

LC 91-33237

A novel about the 18th century slave trade. "William Kemp hopes to recoup his losses in cotton speculation by entering the Triangular Trade. As ship's doctor, his nephew Matthew experiences firsthand the horrors of shipboard life, ultimately leading a revolt that lands the crew and remaining slaves on the southeastern coast of Florida. Here they try to establish 'a paradise place'." Libr J

"Deftly utilizing a flood of period detail, Unsworth has written a book whose stately pace, like the scope of its meditations, seems accurately to evoke the age. Tackling here a central perversity of our history—the keeping of slaves in a land where 'all men are created equal'— Unsworth illuminates the barbaric cruelty of slavery, as well as the subtler habits of politics and character that it creates." Publ Wkly

Updike, John

The afterlife and other stories. Knopf 1994 316p $24

ISBN 0-679-43583-2   LC 94-9818

Analyzed in Short story index

Contents: The afterlife; Wildlife; Brother grasshopper; Conjunction; The journey to the dead; The man who became a soprano; Short Easter; A sandstone farmhouse; The other side of the street; Tristan and Iseult; George and Vivian: Aperto, Chiuso, Bluebeard in Ireland; Farrell's caddie; The rumor; Falling asleep up North; The brown chest; His mother inside him; Baby's first step; Playing with dynamite; The black room; Cruise; Grandparenting

"In these mellow, reflective stories, where parents die and grandchildren are born, Updike's heroes are acutely aware of lost glory yet discover the strength to persevere." Libr J

Bech: a book. Knopf 1970 206p o.p.

Analyzed in Short story index

Contents: Bech in Russia; Bech in Rumania; The Bulgarian poetess; Bech takes pot luck; Bech panics; Bech swings; Bech enters Heaven

"In seven episodes presented in the guise of lectures with a spurious bibliography, the work reveals the literary and personal life of Henry Bech, a distinguished Jewish author of New York. Revelatory incidents include Bech's travels in the 1960s as a kind of cultural ambassador in Russia and Eastern Europe, his visit as a lecturer to adulatory pupils at a girls' school, his diverse romantic affairs, his difficulties in writing as he ages, and his ultimate enshrinement as a major American author." Oxford Companion to Am Lit. 5th edition

Followed by Bech is back

Bech is back. Knopf 1982 195p $25

ISBN 0-394-52806-9   LC 82-161

Analyzed in Short story index

Contents: Three illuminations in the life of an American author; Bech third-worlds it; Australia and Canada; The Holy Land; Macbech; Bech wed; White on white

"Updike's Jewish-American writer, the 'exquisitely unprolific' Henry Bech of 'Bech: a book' [is featured in these stories]. . . . The novella-length 'Bech Wed' finds him married to suburban Bea who provides three teenagers, a dog, and a house in Ossining where Bech finally finishes his fourth novel, 'Think Big,' which is hyped and heralded after his 15-year silence: 'The squalid book we all deserve,' said Alfred Kazin in the 'New York Times Book Review.' In the other stories . . . Bech tours Third-World countries; writes his name 28,500 times for a new signed edition of an old novel; is interviewed in Canada and Australia; and visits Israel with his Episcopalian bride. An atmospheric travelogue and funny satire of the literary scene." Libr J

Brazil. Knopf 1994 260p $23

ISBN 0-679-43071-7   LC 93-28632

"Tristão Raposo, a nineteen-year-old black child of the Rio slums, and Isabel Leme, an eighteen-year-old upper-class white girl, meet on Copacabana Beach; their flight into marriage takes them to the farthest reaches of Brazil's wild west. Privation, violence, captivity, and reversals of fortune afflict them; his mother curses them, her father harries them with hirelings, and neither lover is absolutely faithful. Yet Tristão and Isabel hold to the faith that each is the other's fate for life." Publisher's note

This novel, "for all its political incorrectness, seems good-natured and bent on self-parody. . . . If the book's surface is sometimes a little sticky, its allegorical underpinnings are graceful and firm." N Y Times Book Rev

The centaur. Knopf 1963 302p $24.95

ISBN 0-394-41881-6

"Utilizing a contemporay setting in Olinger, Pennsylvania, Updike attempts to retell the myth of Chiron, wisest of the centaurs, a creature who gave up his immortality on behalf of Prometheus. In this modern version, Chiron is a high-school science teacher, George Caldwell, and Prometheus is his 15-year-old son, Peter. The story revolves around three critical days in their lives." Shapiro. Fic for Youth. 3d edition

The coup. Knopf 1978 298p $27.50

ISBN 0-394-50268-X   LC 78-55399

A fictional "account of political and social upheavals in a mythical African nation called Kush. . . . Colonel Hakim Felix Ellelloû, the narrator, is a U.S.-educated (and -hating) nationalist who derives power from a king whom he personally executes, only to yield it up for exile in France. First-person occasionally gives way to third-person as Ellelloû watches his own activities with a bemused objectivity. Updike's prose is as rich as ever." Choice

Memories of the Ford Administration; a novel. Knopf 1992 371p $23

ISBN 0-679-41681-1   LC 92-52955

Professor Alfred Clayton "has received a request from the Northern New England Association of American Historians for his memories and impressions of the Gerald Ford Administration (1974-77). 'Alf' obliges with his memories of a turbulent period in his personal history, as well as pages of an unpublished book he was writing at the time, on the life of James Buchanan, the fifteenth President of the United States (1857-61)." Publisher's note

Updike, John—*Continued*

"Updike's elegant, yet slangy portrait of the Ford era demonstrates considerable finesse. Even more impressive is his authentic, yet unstilted, evocation of Buchanan's era." Christ Sci Monit

Of the farm. Knopf 1965 173p $17.95

ISBN 0-394-43898-1

In this novel "a man of thirty-five takes his second wife and her eleven-year-old son to visit his widowed mother on her farm in Pennsylvania. . . . Nothing dramatic happens except that the mother has a seizure— what she calls a 'spell'—after church on Sunday. The four characters talk, and as they talk, the reader becomes aware of the complicated relationships that exist between mother and son, man and wife, wife and mother-in-law, stepfather and stepson, and so on in all possible combinations. . . . When the book ends, conflicts have been clarified but not resolved." Saturday Rev

Pigeon feathers, and other stories. Knopf 1962 278p $19.95

ISBN 0-394-44056-0

Analyzed in Short story index

Contents: Walter Briggs; The persistence of desire; Still life; Flight; Should Wizard hit Mommy; A sense of shelter; Dear Alexandros; Wife-wooing; Pigeon feathers; Home; Archangel; You'll never know, dear, how much I love you; The astronomer; A & P; The doctor's wife; Lifeguard; The crow in the woods; The blessed man of Boston, my grandmother's thimble, and Fanning Island: Packed dirt, churchgoing, a dying cat, a traded car

"This is a collection of 19 stories, most of which deal with memories and the way they tie our lives together." Shapiro. Fic for Youth. 3d edition

The poorhouse fair; with an introduction by the author. Knopf 1977 xx, 185p $25

ISBN 0-394-41050-5   LC 76-21156

A reissue with a new introduction of the title first published 1959

This novel concerns the lives of a handful of marvelously eccentric and understandable people in a poorhouse on the undulating plains of central New Jersey. It begins on the morning of the annual Fair, an innovation of Conner, the new and very ambitious prefect. Conner's struggle to institutionalize old age inevitably meets the stiff opposition of those who want to individualize it

"This is a wise book with much to say on individualism and conformity, mechanization and craftsmanship, the 'welfare state' and the 'old days'—and, foremost, on 'death' as it is looked upon by the aged and the young. Updike's old people are memorable." Libr J

Rabbit at rest. Knopf 1990 512p $21.95

ISBN 0-394-58815-0   LC 90-52953

Also available large print edition $24.95 (ISBN 0-394-58936-X)

Sequel to Rabbit is rich

"In John Updike's fourth and final novel about ex-basketball player Harry 'Rabbit' Angstrom, the hero has acquired heart trouble, a Florida condo, and a second grandchild. His son, Nelson, is behaving erratically; his daughter-in-law, Pru, is sending out mixed signals; and his wife, Janice, decides in midlife to become a working girl." Publisher's note

"The being that most illuminates the Rabbit quartet is not finally Harry Angstrom himself but the world through which he moves in his slow downward slide, meticulously recorded by one of our most gifted American realists." N Y Times Book Rev

Rabbit is rich. Knopf 1981 467p $30

ISBN 0-394-52087-4   LC 81-1287

Sequel to Rabbit redux

"Rabbit and Janice have now inherited a half interest in his late father-in-law's business and, having found a kind of place in society, he is a member of the local country club. He is resigned to good relations with Stavros, and he sees Ruth to determine if a chance acquaintance is their daughter. Rabbit finds that the girl is not his daughter, but he does become involved in paternal problems with his son Nelson, now in college, who has gotten his girl friend pregnant." Oxford Companion to Am Lit. 5th edition

"A superlative comic novel that is also an American romance." Time

Followed by Rabbit at rest

Rabbit redux. Knopf 1971 406p $27.50

ISBN 0-394-47273-X

Sequel to Rabbit, run

"Updike profiles Harry (Rabbit) Angstrom, 10 years after his first appearance, as a conservative suburbanite no longer running away from responsibilities but unable to resolve the anxieties that are brought to him from outside. His wife takes a lover and, after decrying Rabbit's lack of will to keep her, leaves their home. Rabbit and his thirteen-year-old son Nelson become involved with Jill Pendleton, a young hippie girl whom Rabbit takes into his house; to him she is a sometimes baffling sexual partner, to Nelson an older sister. Jill's friend Skeeter then arrives, a black man of devastating wit and antic humor who initiates Rabbit to marijuana and encourages him to read black history." Booklist

"There are some structural faults, and moments when characters don't ring true. But I can think of no stronger vindication of the claims of essentially realistic fiction than this extraordinary synthesis of the disparate elements of contemporary experience." N Y Times Book Rev

Followed by Rabbit is rich

Rabbit, run. Knopf 1960 307p $25

ISBN 0-394-44206-7

"Contemporary in setting and tone, and brilliant in its evocation of everyday life in America, the novel is about Harry Angstrom ('Rabbit'), a salesman who, on an impulse, leaves home, his alcoholic wife, Janice, and his child, Nelson, to find freedom. After several escapades and a liaison with an ex-prostitute, he returns to his wife and child and attempts to settle down again. In this novel, Updike conveys the longings and frustrations of family life. Rabbit's malaise is not so much a yearning for freedom as, perhaps, a yearning for guiding spiritual values and meaning. At the end, still dissatisfied and guilt-ridden because of the responsibility he feels for the death of his second child, he begins running again." Reader's Ency. 3d edition

Followed by Rabbit redux

Roger's version. Knopf 1986 328p $17.95

ISBN 0-394-55435-3   LC 86-45298

"Divinity professor Roger Lambert is visited by Dale Kohler, an earnest young student who wants a grant to prove the existence of God by computer. The visit disrupts Roger's ordinary existence, bringing him into con-

Updike, John—*Continued*

tact with . . . Verna (his half-sister's daughter), and leading to his wife's affair with Dale." Libr J

This novel "succeeds in spite of its symbolic structure. Its power and charm lie in the terrific appeal it makes to our capacity for intellectual wonderment. It's rather thrilling to watch Updike assimilate the new vocabularies of particle physics and computer technology—and then fuse them with the ancient vocabulary of religious belief." Newsweek

S. Knopf 1988 279p $17.95

ISBN 0-394-56835-4   LC 87-40496

This novel "concerns Sarah Worth, a latter-day Hester Prynne who has become enamored of a Hindu religious leader called the Arhat. A New Englander, she goes west to join his commune in Arizona, and there mingles with the other sannyasins (pilgrims) in the . . . attempt to subdue ego and achieve moksha (salvation, release from illusion)." Publisher's note

This "is an acid comedy of illusions and delusions told entirely in the words of a woman who is both deceived and deceiver." Atlantic

Trust me; short stories. Knopf 1987 302p $17.95

ISBN 0-394-55833-2   LC 86-46018

Analyzed in Short story index

Contents: Trust me; Killing; Still of some use; The city; The lovely troubled daughters of our old crowd; Unstuck; A constellation of events; Deaths of distant friends; Pygmalion; More stately mansions; Learn a trade; The ideal village; One more interview; The other; Slippage; Poker night; Made in heaven; Getting into the set; The wallet; Leaf season; Beautiful husbands; The other woman

The witches of Eastwick. Knopf 1984 307p $25

ISBN 0-394-53760-2   LC 83-49048

"A novel about three Rhode Island women whose marriages have collapsed and who turn to devil worship and witchcraft." Reader's Ency. 3d edition

"While not a typical Updike narrative, the author's glittering wit, pungent observations, and fabled legerdemain at tabulating mundane particulars reach their peaks in the first half of the novel. Only in the last sections does the reader's attention flag." Booklist

Uris, Leon, 1924-

Armageddon; a novel of Berlin. Doubleday 1964 632p o.p.

Berlin from the close of World War II to the end of the airlift is the setting of this novel. Sean O'Sullivan, an American captain responsible for the military government of the city of Rombaden, nurses a fierce hatred of the Germans, and is faced with a dilemma when he falls in love with a German girl

The author "provides a broad and moving panorama of the rebuilding of post-war Germany at the time when the Allies and the Russians first came to clash over Berlin and its routes of access." Atlantic

Battle cry. Putnam 1953 505p o.p.

"Taking an average group of American boys from their home environment through the ordeal of boot camp, to the battlefields of Guadalcanal, Tarawa, and Saipan, the author fills in a detailed picture of Marine training and traditions." Booklist

Exodus. Doubleday 1958 626p il $21.95

ISBN 0-385-05082-8

Also available from Buccaneer Bks.

"Following World War II the British forbade immigration of the Jews to Israel. European Jewish underground groups, aided by Palestinian agent Ari Ben Canaan, made every effort to aid these unfortunate victims of Nazi persecution. The novel provides insight into the heritage of the Jews and understanding of the danger involved in helping them reach a safe haven. It also includes the warm love story of Ari and a gentile nurse, Kitty Fremont, who cared very much for the welfare of the Jewish children caught in this nightmare." Shapiro. Fic for Youth. 3d edition

Mila 18. Doubleday 1961 539p o.p.

"Mila 18 was the actual command post of the resistance movement organized by the Warsaw Jews. . . . [This is the story] of the handful of men and women who, knowing they had to die, defied the whole German Army with their homemade weapons, and won the respect of the world." N Y Times Book Rev

"Uris' major talent is that he is a master storyteller. And in 'Mila 18' he uses this talent fully and unhampered, in a straight narrative that generates an almost unbelievable dramatic intensity." San Francisco Chron

Mitla Pass. Doubleday 1988 435p o.p.

       LC 88-14008

Available G. K. Hall large print edition

"Against the backdrop of the 1956 Sinai War, Uris provides a . . . portrait (possibly autobiographical) of a man caught in personal crisis. Gideon Zadok, best-selling novelist and successful Hollywood screenwriter, has come to Israel with his family to research a new novel and to shore up a crumbling marriage. But he jeopardizes that by starting a passionate affair with a beautiful Auschwitz survivor. Zadok is a man wavering on the edge of a breakdown. As the political crisis escalates, and his family is evacuated, Zadok asks to accompany Israeli paratroopers on a desperate mission to seal off the strategic Mitla Pass." Libr J

This is a "vital story that brings the complexities of modern Near East history and politics down to understandable human terms." Booklist

QB VII. Doubleday 1970 504p o.p. Buccaneer Bks. reprint available $29.95 (ISBN 1-56849-563-3)

This novel is "about the trial of an American novelist in Queen's Bench 7 for libeling a Polish surgeon by contending he performed experimental sterilizations of Jews in a concentration camp." Oxford Companion to Am Lit. 5th edition

"Two thirds of this jumbo novel are concerned with the trial, Kelna versus Cady. The judge allows this and overrules that. Dramatic, impassioned confrontations before the Queen's Bench alternate with contributory scenes: the two principals surrounded by worried families, mistresses and friends, the police pressing their search for missing witnesses, the speculation about who's guilty and who's innocent." N Y Times Book Rev

Topaz; a novel. McGraw-Hill 1967 341p o.p.

A Russian defector tells about Topaz, an espionage network operating inside the French government for the Soviet Union, and the existence of "Soviet offensive weapons in Cuba. The problem is to get the U.S. and France to believe what would rather not be believed, particularly by France. In the middle sits André

Uris, Leon, 1924— —*Continued*

Devereaux, a high-echelon French intrigue-diplomat loyal to America, but in love with France. The novel chronicles the attempt to get the French to believe in the existence of Topaz whose principal 'raison d'etre' is to discredit the Americans in the eyes of the rest of the world by supplying 'disinformation.'" Best Sellers

Trinity. Doubleday 1976 751p il $21.95

ISBN 0-385-03458-X

This novel is set in Ireland between the 1840's and 1916. "The trinity includes the Larkin clan of Ballyutogue, Catholic hill-farmers who have eked out a bare subsistence in County Donegal for generations; the powerful Hubble dynasty, British aristocracy which has dominated the area for three centuries; and the MacLeods of Belfast, shipyard workers whose Scottish Presbyterian forebears were planted there by the British to solidify the power of the Crown." Christ Sci Monit

"The story has a kind of relentless power, based on the real tragedy of Ireland, and Uris's achievement is that he has neither cheapened nor trivialized that tragedy." N Y Times Book Rev

Urquhart, Jane, 1949-

Away; a novel. Viking 1994 c1993 356p $21.95

ISBN 0-670-85504-9   LC 94-178660

The "saga of a family who must leave Ireland for Canada during the potato famine of the 1840's. As a young girl in Ireland, Mary is taken 'away' to the faeries after a young sailor (a faerie-daemon) whom she rescued dies in her arms. Although she does eventually marry, have a family, and start a new life in the Canadian wilderness, Mary still hears the call of her sailor and finally leaves her family to live the rest of her life alone by a lake. Her daughter Eileen, in turn, falls in love with an Irish nationalist whose passion is only for his cause; she spends the rest of her life 'away' in thoughts of him." Libr J

"Urquhart's blending of the spiritual and political sides of the Irish makes an amazing story told in a language that is melodious and laden with complex imagery." Booklist

V

Vachss, Andrew H.

Down in the zero; a novel; by Andrew Vachss. Knopf 1994 259p $21

ISBN 0-679-43328-7   LC 94-12312

In this mystery Burke is "confronted with young adult suicides and sexual blackmail in an affluent Connecticut suburb. Hired to watch the young son of a former lover, Burke is drawn into a bizarre situation populated by characters almost as strange as his friends. The suicides and the sadomasochistic sex, which are weirdly connected, force Burke to enlist his usual cohorts. Fans will want this crisply written work." Libr J

Hard candy; a novel; by Andrew Vachss. Knopf 1989 241p $17.95

ISBN 0-394-57791-4   LC 89-45272

Also available from Buccaneer Bks.

In this "novel featuring unlicensed New York private eye Burke, word is out that the ex-con PI has become a gun-for-hire. Besides coping with this crazy rumor, Burke contends with two figures from his youth who suddenly turn up. One of them, Candy, now a miniskirted call girl fond of whips and leashes, wants Burke to rescue her teenaged daughter from a cult in Brooklyn; the other, Wesley, an Uzi-toting hit man, already has the cult's leader, Train, in his sights. When Burke learns that the cult safehouse is a baby-breeding operation, vigilante-style justice ensues." Publ Wkly

Sacrifice; a novel. Knopf 1991 271p o.p.

LC 90-53582

"Super-tough Manhattan maverick PI Burke works both sides of the law to save Luke, an eight-year-old suspect in a series of baby murders." Publ Wkly

"Vachss' clipped, blunt, ocassionally overly melodramatic sentences may, in some way, be ripe for parody (à la Mickey Spillane), but they also convey the frightening impact of the somber, shocking, emotionally deadening hellholes that Burke, breaking every civilized rule, battles gamely through." Booklist

Valin, Jonathan

Day of wrath. Congdon & Lattes 1982 244p o.p.

LC 82-1432

"Harry Stoner, private eye, . . . must trace an adolescent girl who has run away from her upper-middle-class family in Cincinnati to join a commune headed by an unscrupulous villain. The violence in the last chapter provides a true *Dies Irae*, but nowhere is there real detection." Barzun. Cat of Crime. Rev and enl edition

Dead letter. Dodd, Mead 1981 248p o.p.

LC 81-3112

"Physics professor Daryl Lovingwell asks Stoner to retrieve some explosive government documents about nuclear power which his Marxist daughter Sarah has stolen. Stoner becomes engulfed in family and Marxist politics, Lovingwell is found shot to death, and Sarah confesses to a family struggle that would make a gothic novel look tame." Booklist

Extenuating circumstances; a novel. Delacorte Press 1989 234p $15.95

ISBN 0-440-50110-5   LC 88-29933

"When an upstanding Cincinnati businessman and philanthropist, Ira Lessing, turns up missing, Stoner is hired to find him. Before he can begin to look, though, Lessing's blood-soaked BMW is discovered, followed shortly by his savagely beaten body. It seems that Lessing was heavily into S&M, which brought him into contact with two male prostitutes." Booklist

"The story stands as a 'mainstream' novel as well as a fine mystery." Publ Wkly

The music lovers; a Harry Stoner mystery. Delacorte Press 1993 233p $19.95

ISBN 0-385-29965-6   LC 92-31323

Though Cincinnati PI Harry Stoner "usually works his city's mean streets, this case has its beginnings in a cozier milieu. Mild, middle-aged Leon Tubin is missing some prized and valuable LPs. He's convinced that his fellow stereophile club member and all-around bigot Sherwood Leoffler is responsible and hires Stoner to prove it. . . . Rooting his story in crimes of the past,

Valin, Jonathan—*Continued*

Valin calls on hard-hitting plotting and plenty of audio lore to yield a powerful conclusion that satisfyingly caps the story's gentler start." Publ Wkly

Second chance; a Harry Stoner novel. Delacorte Press 1991 278p o.p.

LC 90-23259

"Cincinnati private eye Harry Stoner is summoned to the home of wealthy psychiatrist Phil Pearson, whose daughter, a student at the University of Chicago, has disappeared. Stoner soon realizes she's joined forces with her emotionally disturbed brother on a mission of vengeance. It seems they both believe their mother was murdered, and her killer, imprisoned for an unrelated act, has just been paroled." Booklist

"Mr. Valin is very good at turning the screws on a tense situation like this one. A writer who knows and respects proper investigative procedures, he sends his hard-boiled detective on the requisite blind-alley interviews and wild-goose paper chases that draw him closer to a dirty family secret but complicate his exhausting search." N Y Times Book Rev

Van de Wetering, Janwillem, 1931-

The blond baboon; a novel. Houghton Mifflin 1978 194p o.p.

LC 77-17338

"Elaine Carnet, one-time chanteuse, is found by her daughter at the bottom of the stairs leading to the garden. Elaine, retired from the cabaret world, has run a profitable furniture business for some years now. It is not clear who might wish her dead, if anyone did. But . . . [detectives Grijpstra and de Gier] feel Carnet's daughter and her explanation of the events don't ring true." Publ Wkly

The corpse on the dike. Houghton Mifflin 1976 182p o.p.

Grijpstra and De Gier, "Amsterdam municipal policemen, while staking out a petty criminal, run across the corpse of a sad, well-brought-up young man in a shack on a dike. A sharpshooting lesbian is arrested but the uncertainty of the policemen results in further investigation, which uncovers . . . the entire criminal population of the dike." Libr J

The Japanese corpse; a novel. Houghton Mifflin 1977 280p o.p.

"A waitress in a Japanese restaurant reports her fiancé's disappearance. . . . She is afraid he has been killed by agents of the yakuza, a Japanese version of the Mafia, which employed him to sell works of art stolen from Japanese temples to European collectors. By the time his corpse is found detectives de Gier and Grijpstra have learned that the restaurant is a yakuza headquarters for smuggling heroin as well as works of art." Publisher's note

Just a corpse at twilight. Soho Press 1994 265p $17.95

ISBN 1-56947-016-2   LC 94-9499

"Responding to de Gier's trans-Atlantic call for help, Grijpstra leaves the cozy embrace of his mistress, Nellie, for a daunting journey to a small coastal island in Maine where his former partner has gone to seek solitude and wisdom . . . and is being blackmailed for having pushed a local woman, his sometime lover, over a cliff to her death. . . . More than one drug-running operation, a

money-making scam of lesser proportion, gratuitous cruelty, venality, a Papuan rite of revenge and intelligent, unpredictable humor wrap up this narrative delight." Publ Wkly

The Maine massacre. Houghton Mifflin 1979 250p o.p.

LC 78-10185

"Amsterdam Sergeant de Gier is sent on a fact-finding junket to Maine and ends up confronting a series of murders masquerading as accidents and a complicated tangle of thwarted emotions." Booklist

"Local color is genuine and the plot is respectable." Barzun. Cat of Crime. Rev and enl edition

Outsider in Amsterdam. Houghton Mifflin 1975 245p o.p.

"Grijpstra and de Gier . . . have a tricky case on their hands when they find the corpse of the owner of a mystical commune-cum-restaurant hanging from a beam. Suspects include the victim's mad mother, his beautiful wife, an almost full-blooded Papuan, who is a relic of Dutch colonialism and the most interesting character in the story, and some dope pushers who had been using the society as a front. On foot or in their battered VW, the detectives hunt for clues among the city's ancient alleyways, and a steadily suspenseful narrative climaxes in some brisk action." Publ Wkly

The streetbird. Putnam 1983 286p o.p.

LC 82-21488

"'The Streetbird' is titled after a vulture De Gier sees at the scene of a crime in the red light district. There should be no vultures in Amsterdam, but neither should there be murders. This particular murder victim was a pimp—unmourned by his ladies, feared by his rivals and despised by the authorities—and now only a police matter to be disposed of with typical Dutch tidiness. Reluctantly, Rinus de Gier, still looking for love, Grijpstra (whose awful wife has at last left him) and the arthritic and wise Commissaris try to unravel a particularly unsavory business." Publisher's note

"Van de Wetering's night-watch tale of this bizarre, seamy city within a city is full of life, death, intrigue and a shadowy magic. Top drawer." Publ Wkly

Tumbleweed. Houghton Mifflin 1976 180p o.p.

In this mystery novel featuring the Dutch policemen De Gier and Grijpstra, "a sexy young woman from Curaçao is found stabbed in a houseboat on an Amsterdam canal. Her three regular lovers, a Belgian diplomat, an American NATO colonel, and a Dutch tycoon, are automatic suspects, but the murder is complicated by the discovery of henbane and mandrake root on the premises. The commissioner of police goes to Curaçao, a nice change from damp Holland, to investigate suspicions of witchcraft." Libr J

Van Gulik, Robert *See* Gulik, Robert Hans van, 1910-1967

Van Slyke, Helen, 1919-1979

A necessary woman. Doubleday 1979 425p o.p.

LC 78-62606

Van Slyke, Helen, 1919-1979—*Continued*

This novel "charts the course of a cruise to the South Pacific and follows the fortunes of two women on board. . . . Mary Morgan seems to have it all. At 39, she's been married 15 years, is a successful radio personality in San Francisco. She runs things at home and wishes she didn't. The long trip is to help her make a decision about continuing her marriage to her devoted but spineless mate. Her companion on the voyage is her youthful niece, Jayne, who is recovering from an unfortunate love affair. What happens to each as the duo sails into love and new dreams and then returns home to face the music makes for [an] . . . old-fashioned romantic yarn." Publ Wkly

No love lost. Lippincott & Crowell 1980 414p o.p.

LC 79-26056

This "is a bifocal look at four generations of women of the same family with concentration on the third generation. Each woman in her own way, tempered somewhat by the mores of her generation, struggles to maintain her individuality and her independence. The men married to the Thresher women are domineering and ambitious and emerge financially powerful through the years of the 1930's Great Depression, the Prohibition Era, and the War Years. . . . The book is primarily Lindsay Thresher's story. Wealthy and beautiful, imperious and impervious from birth, at age fifty she learns to love and to look forward optimistically to a new life." Best Sellers

Public smiles, private tears; [by] Helen Van Slyke with James Elward. Harper & Row 1982 o.p.

LC 81-47794

"Beverly Thyson Richmond is an ambitious career woman in the 1940s and 1950s, a time when most women were homemakers and those with careers were viewed skeptically. Beverly chooses to work in a large department store rather than attend college. With the assistance of her mentor, Beverly develops a retailing career that eventually dominates her life." Libr J

"On her death in 1979 Van Slyke . . . left the uncompleted first half of a novel that has now been completed by Elward, a playwright and author of three pseudonymous novels. The result is an expert combination; one cannot tell where the splice occurs, and the spirit and tone are consistent." Publ Wkly

Vance, Jack, 1916-

The last castle

In The Hugo winners v2 p245-305

The miracle workers

In Modern classic short novels of science fiction p1-64

When the five moons rise. Underwood/Miller 1992 252p $29.95

ISBN 0-88733-145-9   LC 92-18617

Analyzed in short story index

Contents: Noise; Dust of far suns; When the five moons rise; The new prime; Men of the ten books; The masquerade on Dicantropus; Where Hesperus falls; Telek; Ullward's retreat; Dodkin's job; The Devil on Salvation Bluff; Ecological onslaught

"On remote planets in the distant future, Vance's heroes battle aliens, illusions, and conformity. Ironic quirks, quick plots, and good characterization make these stories as fresh and viable as when they first appeared more than 30 years ago." Booklist

Vance, John Holbrook *See* Vance, Jack, 1916-

Vargas Llosa, Mario, 1936-

Aunt Julia and the scriptwriter; translated by Helen R. Lane. Farrar, Straus & Giroux 1982 374p o.p.

LC 82-5159

Original Spanish edition, 1977

In this novel Vargas Llosa "draws on memories of his youth during the mid-1950s, namely his marriage to an aunt despite strong family opposition, and the action-packed soap operas penned by a mad colleague at a Lima radio station where Vargas Llosa was employed. The work's overriding irony stems from the juxtaposition of the two plot lines, the first based on fact and the second on imaginary events. The end result is a kind of metanovel in which the author sees the objective account of his courtship and marriage gradually assume the characteristics of melodrama." Ency of World Lit in the 20th Century

Captain Pantoja and the Special Service; translated from the Spanish by Gregory Kolovakos and Ronald Christ. Harper & Row 1978 244p o.p.

LC 76-26280

Original Spanish edition, 1973

"Pantoja is a diligent young army officer who is sent to the Peruvian tropics to organize a squadron of prostitutes and thus make life more bearable for lonely soldiers stationed in remote out-posts. Because of his puritanical nature and zealously analytical approach to his assignment, Pantoja elicits the reader's guffaws from the beginning, but ultimately he comes to typify the absurd hero who continues to struggle against overwhelming odds. The theme of absurdity is underscored, moreover, by the hilarious parodies of military procedures, the clashing montage of incompatible episodes, and generous doses of irony and the grotesque." Ency of World Lit in the 20th Century

The storyteller; translated by Helen Lane. Farrar, Straus & Giroux 1989 245p $17.95

ISBN 0-374-27085-6   LC 89-7452

"In alternating chapters, the author tells the story of Saul Zuratas, a Peruvian Jew who becomes an *habladore* (storyteller) to the Machiguengas—a tribe still wandering the Amazon jungle—and the stories themselves of the tribe." Libr J

"The author, in a masterly interweaving of actual myth and novelistic imagination, takes us directly into the Machiguenga world, yet never presumes to speak as one of them. There is no observer and observed here, only participation—which is what storytelling is all about." N Y Times Book Rev

The war of the end of the world; translated by Helen R. Lane. Farrar, Straus & Giroux 1984 568p $18.95

ISBN 0-374-28651-5   LC 84-10187

Vargas Llosa, Mario, 1936-—_Continued_
Original Spanish edition, 1981
"A historical novel about the popular rebellion in the impoverished northeast of Brazil against the military government and the eventual crushing of the rebels by the army." Reader's Ency. 3d edition
"The story [is told] with minute novelistic detail, fashioning a brilliant panorama of the forces great and small which fuel a revolution. Modern-day parallels with the situations in the Middle East and Central America easily offer themselves to the reader." Libr J

Varley, John, 1947-
Demon. Putnam 1984 464p o.p.
LC 84-4814

The author "concludes his trilogy about Gaea, the sentient asteroid circling Titan. Cirocco Jones and her allies, including various Titanides and a Terran bodybuilder, struggle to provide the last refuge for fugitives from an Earth devastated by nuclear war." Booklist

The persistence of vision

_In_ The Best of the Nebulas p495-529

_In_ The Hugo winners v4 p459-507

Titan; illustrated by Freff. Berkley Pub. Corp. 1979 302p il o.p.
LC 78-23865

The first volume of a trilogy that includes Wizard and Demon
"The heroine finds an artificial world among the satellites of Saturn and becomes an agent of its resident intelligence, the godlike Gaea, before being forced to turn against 'her.' Conscientiously nonsexist action-adventure SF." Anatomy of Wonder. 3d edition
Followed by Wizard

Wizard; illustrated by Freff. Berkley Pub. Corp. 1980 354p il o.p.
LC 79-24871

"In this sequel to . . . 'Titan,' Varley continues his exploration of the sentient, wheel-shaped world called Gaea. Twenty years have passed, and now that Earth is aware of her, Gaea has tried to protect herself by becoming valuable to humanity—offering us 'miracles' based on her immense scientific knowledge. Two supplicants for such boons are the central characters: Chris, a man from Earth, and Robin, a woman from the Coven, an all-female orbital colony. To earn their miracles, Gaea requires them to become heroes. To achieve this, they accompany Rocky and Gaby (heroines of the first book, back in supporting roles) on a dangerous odyssey through Gaea's rebellious regions and learn that Gaea herself is the real enemy." Publ Wkly
Followed by Demon

Verne, Jules, 1828-1905
Around the world in eighty days.
Available from various publishers
Original French edition, 1873
"The hero, Phileas Fogg, undertakes his hasty world tour as the result of a bet made at his London club. He and his French valet Passepartout meet with some fantastic adventures, but these are overcome by the loyal servant, and the endlessly inventive Fogg. The feat they perform is incredible for its day: Fogg wins his bet, having circled the world in only 80 days." Reader's Ency. 3d edition

Five weeks in a balloon; or, Journeys and discoveries in Africa, by three Englishmen; compiled in French by J. Verne, from the original notes of Dr. Ferguson, and done into English by W. Lackland. Appleton, D. & Co. 1869 345p o.p. Amereon reprint available $24.95 (ISBN 0-88411-907-6)
Original French edition, 1863
A description of five weeks of balloon travel, exploring the heart of Africa, visiting such places as the Cape, Zanzibar, The Nile and Timbuctoo

From the earth to the moon, and Round the moon. o.p.
The two books comprising this volume were first published 1865 and 1872 respectively
This book is a "striking example of early hard SF, detailing with great precision the preparations and scientific premises (still mostly correct, apart from the deadly effect of acceleration on the passengers) for a voyage to the moon." New Ency of Sci Fic

A journey to the centre of the earth.
Available from Amereon
Original French edition, 1864. Variant title: A trip to the center of the earth
"More than half the book is given to the preliminaries before the actual descent begins, the first two chapters relying on a standard point of departure, the discovery of a manuscript giving the location of the caverns in Iceland. The narrative shows Verne's intense care in presenting the latest scientific thought of his age, while the sighting of the plesiosaurus and the giant humanoid shepherding mammoths indicates how well he incorporated lengthy imaginary episodes to flesh out the factual report." Anatomy of Wonder 4

The mysterious island; pictures by N. C. Wyeth. Scribner 1988 c1918 493p il $25.95
ISBN 0-684-18957-7
LC 88-3167

Sequel to Twenty thousand leagues under the sea
Original French edition, 1874; first United States edition published 1883 by J. W. Lovell; this is a reissue of the 1918 edition
A story of adventure in three parts: Dropped from the clouds; Abandoned; and The secret of the island
"Five men and a dog are carried out to sea in a balloon and drop from the clouds on the mysterious island. Their Crusoe-like resourcefulness and adventures are the theme of the book." Toronto Public Libr

Round the moon

_In_ Verne, J. From the earth to the moon, and round the moon

Twenty thousand leagues under the sea.
Available from various publishers
Original French edition, 1870
"The voyage of the _Nautilus_ permitted Verne to describe the wonders of an undersea world almost totally unknown to the general public of the period. Indebted to literary tradition for his Atlantis, he made his major innovation in having the submarine completely powered by electricity, although the interest in electrical forces goes back to Poe and Shelley. So far as the enigmatic ending is concerned, his readers had to wait for the three-part The Mysterious Island (1874-1875) to learn that Nemo had been the Indian warrior-prince Dakkar, who had been involved in the Sepoy Mutiny of 1857." Anatomy of Wonder 4

Veryan, Patricia, 1923-

Ask me no questions. St. Martin's Press 1993 340p $21.95

ISBN 0-312-08699-7   LC 92-41836

Third title in the author's Tales of the Jewelled Men series

This romance follows the "fate of a genteel, penniless, widowed young artist, Ruth Allington. Little knowing that her family's financial demise and the death of her brother and father were abetted by the highly secret society of traitors known, to few, as the Jewelled Men, Ruth must find some profitable turn for her talents to support her brother's orphaned twins. A position restoring a fresco opens in a gracious mansion along the Dover coast, but duplicity is needed—first, to obtain the job, then to keep the boys hidden." Booklist

Followed by A shadow's bliss

Had we never loved. St. Martin's Press 1992 310p $19.95

ISBN 0-312-07769-6   LC 92-1010

Second title in the author's Tales of the Jewelled Men series

"Just as Lord Horatio Glendenning's family becomes the target of the League of Jewelled Men, a secret society that aims to overthrow the monarchy and establish a republic, a beautiful and spirited gypsy named Amy Consett steals his purse at a fair. Class conflicts and much sparring constitute their courtship. But the Jewelled Men are scheming to use Glendenning's treasonous Jacobite activities and his stepbrother's propensity for gambling to frame his family and seize their estate." Publ Wkly

Followed by Ask me no questions

Never doubt I love. St. Martin's Press 1995 352p $21.95

ISBN 0-312-11864-3   LC 94-42079

Fifth title in the author's Tales of the Jewelled Men series

In this episode of the series "a gentleman and a lady tumble quite unwittingly into the midst of the evil doings of the nefarious League. The dubious pair of Lieutenant Peregrine Cranford and Miss Zoe Grainger must ally themselves to protect the League's next target, Zoe's brother. Unfortunately, the sinister arm of the League reaches further into their lives than they ever guessed." Publisher's note

A shadow's bliss. St. Martin's Press 1994 324p $21.95

ISBN 0-312-10543-6   LC 93-44038

Also available G.K. Hall large print edition

Fourth title in the author's Tales of the Jewelled Men series

This episode is set in a "village in Cornwall. Here Jonathan, perceived as the village idiot for his refusal to raise a hand in self-defense and his spells of forgetfulness that impel him into manic activity, falls madly in love with the schoolmarm, who happens to be the lady from the castle. August Falcon and Lieutenant Morris arrive on the scene in pursuit of the Jewelled Men. . . . Jonathan is called upon to help track down evidence and in doing so regains his identity, for, it seems, he was also a victim of these evil conspirators." Booklist

Followed by Never doubt I love

Time's fool. St. Martin's Press 1991 375p o.p.

LC 90-27673

First title in the author's Tales of the Jewelled Men series

"Back from the Low Countries and the horrors of war, Captain Gideon Rossiter finds his betrothed, Lady Naomi Lutonville, has not only grown up, but has also grown cool towards him. Their feelings for one another, however, heat up again as they find themselves working together to uncover the plot that has brought financial ruin to Gideon's father and threatens the very security of England itself. Love proves to be anything but time's fool in this dashing Georgian romance." Booklist

Followed by Had we never loved

Vida, Nina

Goodbye, Saigon; a novel. Crown 1994 281p $20

ISBN 0-517-59908-2   LC 94-8384

This novel "depicts the lives of Vietnamese immigrants in the violent, gang-ridden Little Saigon of Westminster, California, in the 1990s. The novel's central character, Ahn, comes to the United States with her extended family as a refugee of the Vietnam War. The devastating events of Ahn's life, from her early years in Vietnam to her arrival and adjustment to American life, are slowly revealed through short flashbacks. . . . The plot revolves around Ahn's business partnership with Jana, a white American woman. Ironically, they have led and continue to lead parallel lives despite their vastly different cultures and upbringings." Libr J

The author "delivers a superb range of minor characters, terrific set pieces . . . moments of glorious high comedy and dialogue filled with wit and wonder." NY Times Book Rev

Vidal, Gore, 1925-

1876; a novel. Random House 1976 364p $19.95

ISBN 0-394-49750-3

A volume in the author's American chronicle series

"As in 'Burr,' Charles Schuyler, hinted-at as the illegitimate son of Aaron Burr, again narrates. Now a respected and popular journalist-historian, Schuyler at 63 has returned, after years abroad, to the U.S. in the company of his widowed daughter, the Princess d'Agrigente, who is in need of a well-connected husband—thereby giving Vidal another occasion to crash society's party as he follows Schuyler on his journalistic assignments through New York, the city of Washington, later to Philadelphia for the Centennial, then Cincinnati for the Republican Convention." Publ Wkly

Burr; a novel. Random House 1973 430p o.p.

A volume in the author's American chronicle series

"Burr is a novel in the form of a memoir told in part by Burr and in part by the young journalist Charles Schuyler, a fictional creation and Vidal's strongest character." Choice

Creation; a novel. Random House 1981 510p il o.p.

LC 79-5528

Vidal, Gore, 1925—— *Continued*

"The narrator, old and blind and finishing out his days as Persian ambassador to Pericles' Athens, is recounting his life's experiences, mostly as acquired in the service of Darius the Great and his son Xerxes. . . . In particular, he describes his special missions to India, where, as well as meeting a variety of world princes, he converses with the Buddha, and to what is now China, where he becomes a friend and admirer of Confucius." Publ Wkly

Empire; a novel. Random House 1987 486p o.p.

LC 86-29782

A volume in the author's American chronicle series

"The core of Vidal's story is the inexorable march of one Caroline Sanford, newspaper owner, into the inner circle of the Washington, D.C., power elite." Booklist

"Interesting and well-developed real-life characters abound, including, most memorably, Secretary of State and Lincoln's old friend John Hay. Intermixed with the well-researched backdrop of historical characters and events is Caroline's personal story." Libr J

Hollywood. Random House 1990 437p $19.95

ISBN 0-394-57659-4   LC 89-42834

A volume in the author's American chronicle series

The main characters, newspaper publishers Blaise and Caroline Stanford, first appeared in Washington, D.C. "Assigned to travel to Hollywood [in 1917] to help pull the infant 'photo play' industry behind the war effort, Caroline discovers that, at the age of 40, she has the looks and potential to become a film star. Sold to a world-wide audience as 'Emma Traxler', she begins to understand that cinema has the power to re-shape the world. . . . [Meanwhile], President Wilson is struggling to win support for his vision of a League of Nations. When he fails, the way is open for the Republican Warren Harding to assume power. The ensuing corruption scandals culminate in the Tea Pot Dome affair." New Statesman Soc

Vidal's "highly polished prose style, in part the fruit of his classical training, is a constant delight." N Y Times Book Rev

Julian. Little, Brown 1964 503p o.p.

A novel about Julian the Apostate who was brought up as a Christian but who tried to restore the old gods of Hellenism after he became emperor of Rome in 361 A.D. The author "imagines a correspondence between the great pagan orator Libanius and the philosopher Priscus, both of whom were old friends of Julian. Libanius, long after Julian's death, is proposing to write the life of his old friend, and Priscus fortunately has by him a journal written by Julian himself during the Persia campaign in which he lost his life. He sends this journal to Libanius together with his own comments." Book Week

The author displays "an easy and fluent gift for narrative; a theatrical sense of scene and dramatic occasion; and a revealing eye and ear for character delineation—to say nothing of wide reading." Newsweek

Lincoln. Modern Lib. 1993 712p $19

ISBN 0-679-60048-5   LC 92-27273

A volume in the author's American chronicle series

A reissue of the title first published 1984 by Random House

"In the atmosphere of intrigue that permanently settled over Washington City during the Civil War, the initially unpromising Lincoln, an unlikely hero, rises to greatness; despite almost insurmountable troubles that deteriorate his physical and mental well-being, Lincoln shows his true mastery of crisis leadership, necessary not only to save the Union but to refashion it." Booklist

This novel "is not so much an imaginative reconstruction of an era as an intelligent, lucid and highly informative transcript of it, never less than workmanlike in its blocking out of scenes and often extremely compelling." N Y Times Book Rev

Live from Golgotha; a novel. Random House 1992 232p $22

ISBN 0-679-41611-0   LC 92-9260

In this satirical novel "Saint Paul is a tap-dancing homosexual and Saint Timothy, the narrator, is his well-endowed but reluctant bedmate. . . . NBC-TV goes back in time to film the Crucifixion, and chooses Timothy to anchor the broadcast. Meanwhile, a computer virus is retroactively altering the Gospels. Only Timothy's writings will be immune, and he must tell the true story of Jesus in order to save Christianity as Judgment Day nears." Newsweek

"Although Vidal offers a fiendish gospel—a counter-gospel—he must be taken seriously. He is, after all, asking basic epistemological questions. . . . I suggest that Vidal's provocative, distasteful novel is, perhaps, one of his most sustained meditations on the nature of things." Commonweal

Myra Breckinridge

In Vidal, G. Myra Breckinridge [and] Myron p1-213

Myra Breckinridge [and] Myron. Random House 1986 417p $19.95

ISBN 0-394-55376-4   LC 86-11423

Combined edition of two titles first published 1968 and 1974 respectively

In the first novel, Myra who was once Myron seduces both Rusty Godowsky and his girlfriend Mary-Ann Pringle. The sequel is set in 1973. Myron Breckinridge, the alter ego of the transsexual heroine, is pushed through his television screen and onto the set of a 1948 film "Siren of Babylon" starring Maria Montez. He has difficulty in getting out. Myra periodically takes command of Myron's body. She attempts to save the world from overpopulation by altering the male sex

Myron

In Vidal, G. Myra Breckinridge [and] Myron p217-417

Washington, D.C.; a novel. Little, Brown 1967 377p o.p.

A volume in the author's American chronicle series

Set from the New Deal to the McCarthy years this "political novel features the ambitions of both a senator and his young secretary for the Presidency. The senator loses his chance for the Democratic nomination when Roosevelt decides to run for a third term. The secretary, mapping his course to the top, with the help of a journalist invents a non-happening which makes him a national hero. He then blackmails the senator into withdrawing from the race and wins the senatorial seat for himself." Booklist

Viertel, Joseph, 1915-

Life lines; a novel. Simon & Schuster 1982 526p o.p.

LC 82-673

This "story encompasses 100 years of Jewish experience and probes the meaning of Jewishness in several national contexts. In the process it highlights the triumph of Jewish family and ethnic identity in the face of forbidding odds. The chief character is Yuri Karpeyko, distinguished Minsk physician, Soviet patriot and war hero, and the son of an old Bolshevik, who, after falling victim to government-backed anti-Semitism, gradually and reluctantly reaches out to long-forgotten relatives in America and Israel for help. . . . Set in Russia, America and Israel, the story mingles exciting present action with epistolary records of Tsarist pogroms, the Holocaust and other events of the past, and ends with the heroic attempt by Yuri's relatives to smuggle him and his family out of Russia." Publ Wkly

Villars, Elizabeth, 1941-

Lipstick on his collar. Warner Bks. 1990 342p $18.95

ISBN 0-446-51512-4   LC 89-40459

Also available Thorndike Press large print edition

"Successful and respected New York publisher Hallie Porter has just made the cover of *Time* magazine. The thrill of her career achievement is suddenly squelched, however, when she discovers that her husband, Jake Fox, is having an affair with her good friend and colleague, Olivia Collins. So begins this novel of interpersonal relations, power struggles, and corporate game-playing in the fast lane." Libr J

The Normandie affair. Doubleday 1982 319p o.p.

LC 81-43727

This novel is "set aboard an opulent cruise liner, the 'Normandie,' in the days when luxury and sumptuousness were taken for granted. Villars' story covers six days of irrevocable change in the lives of several passengers crossing from New York to France in 1936. At the center of this drama is mysterious Anson Sherwood, a wealthy Bostonian with a passion for and inordinate knowledge of the 'Normandie.' Sherwood turns out to be a dedicated meddler who interferes in the lives of his fellow passengers, involving himself in both romantic entanglements and political intrigues, usually with fortuitous results. Neatly bundling drama and romance, Villars has captured the dichotomous nature of shipboard life." Booklist

Too close for comfort; [by] Ellen Feldman. Delacorte Press 1994 305p $19.95

ISBN 0-385-30912-0   LC 93-48439

"When Isobel married Pete, she knew that his in-home psychiatric office was off-limits to her. Staying out of the kitchen during office hours proves difficult, however, even though she must cross the waiting room to get there. When Isobel starts getting strange phone calls and threatening letters, she and Pete blame each other, and their marriage starts to suffer. Trying to discover who is stalking her, Isobel must also convince Pete that the danger is real and not just her paranoia." Libr J

"Ms. Feldman, who is too clever to make any of her characters entirely likable, potently suggests the tangible rhythms of being stalked." N Y Times Book Rev

Wars of the heart. Doubleday 1987 346p $16.95

ISBN 0-385-19569-9   LC 86-13529

"On December 7, 1941, the lives of all Americans changed. Men prepared to serve their country, leaving women at home to cope as best they could. . . . Villars tells of three of these women. Isabelle is a poor little rich girl searching for her reason for being, who finds her niche as a radio reporter. Eliza turns from a stay-at-home wife and mother into an advertising executive. When Lily's father throws her out, she goes to Hollywood, is discovered, and becomes a movie star. Thrown together by the war, they support each other. Each worries about her man but succumbs to the charms of another." Libr J

Vine, Barbara, 1930-

See also Rendell, Ruth, 1930-

Anna's book; [by] Ruth Rendell writing as Barbara Vine. Harmony Bks. 1993 394p $22

ISBN 0-517-58796-3   LC 92-34309

Published in the United Kingdom with title: Asta's book

This "tale of psychological suspense revolves around a woman's discovery that the published memoirs of her deceased grandmother hid evidence of an elderly woman's murder and the disappearance of a little girl." Libr J

"Vine's story is utterly riveting, rich and multifaceted in its complexity. Her characters are wonderfully real and fascinatingly unconventional." Booklist

A dark-adapted eye. Bantam Bks. 1986 264p o.p.

LC 85-48231

"A crime writer decides to reopen the case of Vera Hillyard, hanged for murder 30 years before. Hillyard's family is still shattered by events of the past, and her niece Faith Severn decides to protect the series of secrets that enshrouds the family by doing some investigating of her own. This novel proceeds by dark hints, building to an all-eclipsing climax." Booklist

A fatal inversion. Bantam Bks. 1987 268p o.p.

LC 87-47556

Ecalpemos, "the inversion of the title, is the utopian 'someplace' where Adam (now a computer executive), Rufus (now a prosperous doctor) and a handful of others set up an impromptu commune on a landed estate that Adam unexpectedly inherited in 1976. That experiment ended in disaster. Now, 10 years later, someone has finally dug up some incriminating evidence: human bones in a pet cemetery." Newsweek

In this novel "people are barely able to establish links with each other—love and affection are turned inwards. Therein lies the novel's only weakness: there's little of the compassion so important for a humanist like Rendell. . . . [Her eye is] so focused on gloom that she sees little else. That's no condemnation: crime fiction demands such morbidity." New Statesman

Gallowglass. Harmony Bks. 1990 272p $19.95

ISBN 0-517-57744-5   LC 89-29026

Vine, Barbara, 1930-—*Continued*

In this novel the "reader comes to know the perversities of lamebrain Joe and his malicious friend, Sandor, who concoct—Sandor actually drawing up the plans, Joe just following along out of dumb adoration—a scheme to kidnap a wealthy woman. Events transpiring in the woman's household—particularly, her relations with and the backgrounds of the people in her domestic employ—add double and triple layers to the conflict." Booklist

"Miss Vine's most penetrating foray yet into the dark mysteries of the heart's obsessions, this haunting novel examines love in many guises—romantic, parental, idolatrous, possessive, selfless, erotic, platonic and sick. The scope of observation is dazzling; the tone, remarkably nonjudgmental." N Y Times Book Rev

The house of stairs; [by] Ruth Rendell writing as Barbara Vine. Harmony Bks. 1989 c1988 277p o.p.

LC 88-38303

First published 1988 in the United Kingdom

"Elizabeth Vetch, a writer, recalls her adolescence and young womanhood living with her cousin Cosette in a big, eccentric house in the Notting Hill section of London. Lots of people besides Elizabeth and Cosette lived in the House of Stairs, though; it was nest to many of their friends as well. Cosette is intent on recovering her lost youth, and because of her vulnerability in that direction, two residents conspire against her to gain her money. The consequence is violent death, with Elizabeth losing the one person she truly loved. A complex, eloquent novel—sure to retain Vine's large readership and undoubtedly gain her even more followers." Booklist

King Solomon's carpet. Harmony Bks. 1992 c1991 355p $19

ISBN 0-517-58795-5   LC 91-43668

First published 1991 in the United Kingdom

"Tom, a brain-damaged flutist who plays aviary music in the London Underground, is obsessed with Alice, a violinist obsessed with Axel, whose own obsession is with bombs and death. Along with Jed, who loves no one but his pet hawk, and Jasper, a 9-year-old boy who rides the tops of subway cars and loves the danger, they all live in a rotting old Victorian mansion owned by Jarvis Stringer, who has the most interesting obsession of all: the master study he is compiling on the world's subway systems." N Y Times Book Rev

The author "displays her remarkable ability to spot and dissect the terrifying beneath the ordinary, to imbue a setting with its own, almost palpable terror, and to construct in the process a narrative maze filled with constant, fearful surprise." Booklist

No night is too long. Harmony Bks. 1995 c1994 315p $23

ISBN 0-517-79964-2   LC 94-13064

First published 1994 in the United Kingdom

The narrator of this novel, Tim Cornish, a student of creative writing at an English university, is "filled with remorse. . . . Friendless, indifferent to his future, he lives alone in the rotting old house where he grew up, conjuring up the ghost of [Dr Ivo Steadman], the lover he knocked unconscious and left for dead on a desert island. His only correspondent is a mysterious letter writer who taunts him with true stories of castaways who survived." New Statesman Soc

"This is a novel about the effects of passion in which the mood is as bleak as the cold North Sea; a murder mystery in which the crucial killing is imaginary, and the actual killing arbitrary. . . . Nevertheless—the novel does grip and its scheme is impressive; it is hard to withhold applause from an author so lavishly endowed with the capacity to invent interlocking segments of plot." Times Lit Suppl

Vinge, Joan D., 1948-

Catspaw. Warner Bks. 1988 392p o.p.

LC 88-40082

"Hired by the powerful taMing dynasty to protect its Security Council candidate from assassination, a half-human telepath known as 'Cat' uncovers a larger conspiracy that threatens to destroy the remnants of individual freedom in a world controlled by interstellar corporations. Political intrigue, shifting loyalties, and fully realized characters add uncommon depth to this sequel." Libr J

This book is "essentially an adult sequel to Vinge's young adult novel Psion [1987]." Booklist

The Snow Queen. Dial Press (NY) 1980 536p o.p.

LC 79-20555

"A Quantum novel"

"An amalgam of SF and heroic fantasy borrowing the structure of Hans Christian Andersen's famous story, set on a barbarian world exploited by technologically superior outworlders, against the background of a fallen galactic empire." Anatomy of Wonder 4

Followed by World's end

The Summer Queen. Warner Bks. 1991 670p $21.95

ISBN 0-446-51397-0   LC 90-50521

Sequel to World's end

"As the Summer Star ascends in the skies above the planet Tiamat, marking the end of more than a century of exploitation by the technologically advanced Hegemony, Moon Dawntreader—the Summer Queen appointed to lead her people back to their traditional ways—breaks with ancient custom, choosing instead to prepare to meet the Hegemony's inevitable return on equal terms." Libr J

"Plots and subplots proliferate, and although the prose is sometimes florid and the romance and sex scenes overly sentimental, the book is so full of drama, conflict and tragedy that it justifies its length." Publ Wkly

World's end. Bluejay Bks. 1984 230p o.p. Ultramarine reprint available $25 (ISBN 0-89366-141-4)

LC 83-21374

In this novel "BZ Gundhalinu, a police inspector who played a minor role in . . . [The Snow Queen] is the central character. Having left Carbuncle at the time of the Change he has traveled to World's End in search of his two irresponsible older brothers. World's End, a barely habitable frontier planet, is center of a 'Company' mining operation but also contains Fire Lake, an unexplained anomaly that appears to drive those who approach it insane." Voice Youth Advocates

Followed by The Summer Queen

Vinge, Vernor

A fire upon the deep. TOR Bks. 1992 391p $21.95

    ISBN 0-312-85182-0   LC 91-39020

"A Tom Doherty Associates book"

"Fleeing a menace of galactic proportions, a spaceship crashes on an unfamiliar world, leaving the survivors—a pair of children—to the not-so-tender mercies of a medieval, lupine race. Responding to the crippled ship's distress signal, a rescue mission races against time to retrieve the children and recover the weapon they need to prevent the universe from being forever changed." Libr J

"Thoughtful space opera at its best, this book delivers everything it promises in terms of galactic scope, audacious concepts and believable characters both human and nonhuman." N Y Times Book Rev

Viorst, Judith

Murdering Mr. Monti; a merry little tale of sex and violence. Simon & Schuster 1994 254p $21

    ISBN 0-671-76074-2   LC 93-37919

Also available Thorndike Press large print edition

This novel's "heroine is Brenda Kovner, a middle-aged advice columnist whose overwhelming desire for control drives her family crazy. Her dedicated mothering leads her to plot the death of Mr. Monti, her son's future father-in-law—and, by the way, one of the three men Brenda slept with in a 24-hour quest to broaden her horizons." Libr J

"Sticklers for credibility and common sense won't buy Brenda's motives for wanting to murder Mr. Monti, but they will like all the noise she makes trying. . . . 'Murdering Mr. Monti' has an endearing tendency to look over its own shoulder, to worry, to take its own pulse—to chart a romp with Jewish guilt." N Y Times Book Rev

The **Virago** book of ghost stories; edited by Richard Dalby; with an introduction by Jennifer Uglow. McGraw-Hill 1989 c1987 331p o.p.

    LC 88-13341

Analyzed in Short story index

First published 1987 in the United Kingdom

Contents: The eyes, by E. Wharton; The violet car, by E. Nesbit; The crimson blind, by H. D. Everett; The token, by M. Sinclair; The shadowy third, by E. Glasgow; The return, by M. E. Lambe; The haunted saucepan, by M. Lawrence; Mr. Tallent's ghost, by M. Webb; The amorous ghost, by E. Bagnold; The accident and a persistent woman, by M. Bowen; The waiting-room, by P. Bottome; The ghost, by C. Wells; Will ye no' come back again, by E. Scott; Sophy Mason comes back, by E. M. Delafield; The doll's house, by H. Gorst; The night nurse's story, by E. Olivier; The voice of God, by W. Holtby; The follower, by C. Asquith; Miss De Mannering of Asham, by F. M. Mayor; Roaring tower, by S. Gibbons; Juggernaut, by D. K. Broster; The happy autumn fields, by E. Bowen; The empty schoolroom, by P. H. Johnson; Three miles up, by E. J. Howard; Whitewash, by R. Macaulay; Poor girl, by E. Taylor; On no account, my love, by E. Jenkins; The mistress in black, by R. Timperley; A curious experience, by N.

Lofts; Breakages, by F. Weldon; Dual control, by E. Walter; Lady with unicorn, by S. Maitland; Diamond Jim, by L. St Aubin de Terán; Ashputtle, by A. Carter

Voelker, John Donaldson *See* Traver, Robert, 1903-1991

Voigt, Cynthia

Glass mountain; a novel. Harcourt Brace Jovanovich 1991 288p $19.95

    ISBN 0-15-135825-7   LC 91-16247

Also available Thorndike Press large print edition

"Gregor, the seemingly fortune-hunting butler of playboy Theo, meets and courts shy, diffident, wealthy Alexis secretly. Theo's parents and Alexis's parents are setting up a match between those two. Gregor doesn't realize that Alexis is Theo's intended. Also, Theo has a yen for someone else. Then there is Theo's sister Sara and her woes with Brad." Libr J

"This sophisticated comedy of errors, set in Manhattan, lacks only the background music of Porter or Gershwin. Light romance at its best." Booklist

Voltaire, 1694-1778

Candide.

Available from Amereon

Original French edition, 1759

"In this philosophical fantasy, naive Candide sees and suffers such misfortune that he ultimately rejects the philosopy of his tutor Doctor Pangloss, who claims that 'all is for the best in this best of all possible worlds.' Candide and his companions—Pangloss, his beloved Cunegonde, and his servant Cacambo—display an instinct for suvival that provides them hope in an otherwise somber setting. When they all retire together to a simple life on a small farm, they discover that the secret of happiness is 'to cultivate one's garden,' a practical philosophy that excludes escessive idealism and nebulous metaphysics." Merriam-Webster's Ency of Lit

> *also in* Voltaire. Candide and other stories
>
> *also in* Voltaire. Voltaire's Candide, Zadig, and selected stories p3-101

Candide and other stories; translated from the French, with an introduction and notes, by Roger Pearson. Knopf 1992 307p $17

    ISBN 0-679-41746-X

"Everyman's library"

Contents: Candide; Micromegas; Zadig; The ingenu; The white bull

Voltaire's Candide, Zadig, and selected stories; translated with an introduction by Donald M. Frame. Candide illustratins by Paul Klee. Indiana Univ. Press 1961 351p il o.p.

Analyzed in Short story index

Contains 14 satiric tales in addition to Candide (1759) and Zadig (1748)

Contents: Candide; Zadig; Micromegas; The world as it is; Memnon; Bababec and the fakirs; History of Scarmentado's travels; Plato's dream; Account of the sickness, confession, death, and apparition of the Jesuit Berthier; Story of a good Brahman; Jeannot and Colin; An Indian

Voltaire, 1694-1778—*Continued*

adventure; Ingenuous; The one-eyed porter; Memory's adventure; Court Chesterfield's ears and Chaplain Goudman

Zadig

In Voltaire. Candide and other stories

In Voltaire. Voltaire's Candide, Zadig, and selected stories p102-72

Von Goethe, Johann Wolfgang *See* Goethe, Johann Wolfgang von, 1749-1832

Vonnegut, Kurt, 1922-

Breakfast of champions; or, Goodbye blue Monday!; by Kurt Vonnegut, Jr; with drawings by the author. Delacorte Press 1973 295p il o.p. Buccaneer Bks. reprint available $35.95 (ISBN 1-56849-354-1)

"In this novel Pontiac dealer Dwayne Hoover, science fiction writer Kilgore Trout, artist Rabo Karabekian and others play out a drama that runs the gamut from race tensions and sexual fantasies to pollution, the power 'bad chemicals' can exert over a human being, the sheer insanity of trying to prove you are a human being when you suspect you are just another machine in a machine-mad world." Publ Wkly

"In this novel Vonnegut is . . . clearing his head by throwing out acquired ideas, and also liberating some of the characters from his previous books. . . . This explosive meditation ranks with Vonnegut's best." N Y Times Book Rev

Cat's cradle; by Kurt Vonnegut, Jr. Holt, Rinehart & Winston 1963 233p o.p.

"In this mordant satire on religion, research, government, and human nature, a free-lance writer becomes the catalyst in a chain of events that unearths the secret of ice-nine. This is an element potentially more lethal than that produced by nuclear fission. The search leads to a mythical island, San Lorenzo, where the writer also discovers the leader of a new religion, Bokonon." Shapiro. Fic for Youth. 3d edition

Deadeye Dick. Delacorte Press 1982 240p o.p.

LC 82-13024

"In Midland City, Ohio, the [Waltz] family is isolated and scorned by the community for patriarch Otto's ersatz career as an artist and his strident support for Nazi policies. Their wealth and what's left of their social position is decimated when younger son Rudy (Deadeye Dick) accidently shoots a pregnant woman. Father pleads guilty to the crime, Rudy becomes a night-shift pharmacist, author of the prize-winning but unsuccessful play 'Katmandu' and cook and maid for his useless mother. Brother Felix becomes the president of NBC, and mother dies of radiation emitted from the fireplace of their 'shit-box' home. The entire populace is eventually exterminated . . . by the inadvertent dropping of a neutron bomb." SLJ

Galápagos; a novel. Delacorte Press/Seymour Lawrence 1985 295p o.p.

LC 85-4581

"A group of tourists on a cruise survive the end of the world, settling on a small Galapagos Island and beginning a new evolutionary sequence. The ghostly narrator looks back on things from a perspective one million years later." Anatomy of Wonder 4

God bless you, Mr. Rosewater; or, Pearls before swine; by Kurt Vonnegut, Jr. Holt, Rinehart & Winston 1965 217p o.p.

"With a satirist's eye for the meanness of man, especially his greed, Vonnegut tells the story of Eliot Rosewater, president of the Rosewater Foundation, who uses his position to help all petitioners. Discovering a plot to remove him from authority Rosewater gives all his money to over 50 children he is falsely accused of fathering." Booklist

Hocus pocus. Putnam 1990 302p o.p.

LC 90-34535

This novel is set in an America of the future. The story is told by Eugene Debs Hartke, a West Point graduate and Vietnam veteran, as he awaits trial for complicity in a mass escape from a black prison where he has been teaching inmates to read. It is 2001: "most of the United States has been sold to foreigners, and what is left is broken down and depleted. Black markets, race war, martial law, tuberculosis and AIDS are all somewhere between endemic and epidemic." N Y Times Book Rev

"Vonnegut remains an effectual stylist, combining deadpan irony and *faux naïveté*. As usual, his central narrative winds through a mosaic of aphorisms, verbal tics, digressions, homilies, obscure facts. . . . This compendium of devices and concerns may have hardened into a formula, but it has not yet ceased to be a diverting one." Times Lit Suppl

Jailbird; a novel; by Kurt Vonnegut, Jr. Delacorte Press/Seymour Lawrence 1979 246p o.p.

LC 79-12881

This novel "opens with Walter F. Starbuck, a 64-year-old victim of Watergate, about to be released from a Georgia prison for white-collar workers. Bereft of fortune and family (his wife is dead, his son is ungrateful) Starbuck retreats to the past via flashbacks of World War II, old love affairs, and past occupations. Eventually he regains respectability in the ubiquitous RAMJAC Corporation . . . which owns 19% of America and continues to swallow every major enterprise in its path." Libr J

Mother night; by Kurt Vonnegut, Jr. Harper & Row 1966 202p o.p.

This novel consists of the diary written in jail in Israel by a former Nazi radio broadcaster who is awaiting trial as a war criminal. It "presents Howard W. Campbell, Jr., 'a man who served evil too openly, and good too secretly, the crime of his times.' American by birth, Nazi by reputation, and former U.S. counter-intelligence agent, he was recruited in 1938 in a Berlin park by the man he called his blue fairy godmother." Libr J

"The plot gives free play to sardonic humor at the expense of the Nazis, the Russians, and American reactionary fringe movements." Publ Wkly

Player piano; by Kurt Vonnegut, Jr. Scribner 1952 295p o.p.

"Paul Proteus, engineer, leads revolt against machine-computer conformist civilization, only to find that when it succeeds, people wish for the machines again. In order or in chaos, mob psychology is stupid. Modern civiliza-

Vonnegut, Kurt, 1922-—*Continued*

tion has hate-love affinity for machines. Incisive satire; a classic modern dystopia." Anatomy of Wonder. 3d edition

The sirens of Titan; by Kurt Vonnegut, Jr. Houghton Mifflin 1961 c1959 319p o.p.

First published 1959 in paperback by Dell

This novel "attacks the concept of causality and the confusion of luck with God's will, reveals human history as a trivial incident manipulated by the alien Tralfamadorians to further an equally trivial scheme." New Ency of Sci Fic

Slapstick; or, Lonesome no more! a novel. Delacorte Press/Seymour Lawrence 1976 243p o.p.

In this satirical fantasy, President of the United States Dr. Wilbur Daffodil-11 Swain sits in the ruins of Manhattan's Skyscraper National Park writing his memoirs. As deformed children, he and his twin sister were separately regarded as idiots but discovered that together they were super-intelligent and went on to write a best-selling child-rearing manual. As president, Wilbur instituted a program to combat loneliness by forming artificial extended families

"Slapstick is a deceptively short and simple book. Its readability should not distract one from the fact that Vonnegut has found a fictional situation which considers serious human problems." New Repub

Slaughterhouse-five; or, The children's crusade: a duty-dance with death. 25th anniversary ed. Delacorte Press; Lawrence, S. 1994 205p il $22.50

ISBN 0-385-31208-3   LC 94-171120

A reissue of the title first published 1969

This novel "mixes a fictionalized account of the author's experience of the fire bombing of Dresden with a compensatory fantasy of the planet Tralfamadore, the science-fiction element is progressively dominated by the overall concerns of satire, black humor, and absurdism." Reader's Ency. 3d edition

"A masterpiece, in which Vonnegut penetrated to the heart of the issues developed in his earlier absurdist fabulations. A key work of modern SF." Anatomy of Wonder 4

Welcome to the monkey house; a collection of short works; by Kurt Vonnegut, Jr. Delacorte Press 1968 298p o.p.

"A Seymour Lawrence book"

Analyzed in Short story index

Contents: Where I live; Harrison Bergeron; Who am I this time?; Welcome to the monkey house; Long walk to forever; The Foster portfolio; Miss Temptation; All the king's horses; Tom Edison's shaggy dog; New dictionary; Next door; More stately mansions; The Hyannis Port story; D.P.; Report on the Barnhouse Effect; The euphio question; Go back to your precious wife and son; Deer in the works; The lie; Unready to wear; The kid nobody could handle; The manned missiles; EPICAC; Adam; Tomorrow and tomorrow and tomorrow

W

Wahlöö, Maj Sjöwall *See* Sjöwall, Maj, 1935-

Wahlöö, Per, 1926-1975

(jt. auth) Sjöwall, M. Cop killer

(jt. auth) Sjöwall, M. The laughing policeman

(jt. auth) Sjöwall, M. The locked room

(jt. auth) Sjöwall, M. Murder at the Savoy

Wakefield, Dan

Starting over. Delacorte Press/Seymour Lawrence 1973 290p o.p.

"Phil Potter, this book's hero, is 34, a failed actor who has become a successful New York public-relations executive. His four-year marriage to Jessica, a lovely model and closet alcoholic, has ended in divorce, and everyone tells him how lucky he is. Lucky? Being alone, he discovers, can be as bad as a homicidal marriage. So Potter decides to fashion a new life. He moves to Boston, takes a job teaching 'Communications' at Gilpen Junior College and prescribes sexual encounters with every available New England divorcee and matron as the perfect anodyne to his painful isolation." Newsweek

"A powerful, naturalistic depiction of the agony suffered by a man whose affluence merely conceals an utter absence of value and direction." Libr J

Walker, Alice, 1944-

The color purple. 10th anniversary ed. Harcourt Brace Jovanovich 1992 290p il $19.95

ISBN 0-15-119154-9   LC 91-47202

A reissue of the title first published 1982

"A feminist novel about an abused and uneducated black woman's struggle for empowerment, the novel was praised for the depth of its female characters and for its eloquent use of black English vernacular." Merriam-Webster's Ency of Lit

Possessing the secret of joy. Harcourt Brace Jovanovich 1992 286p $19.95

ISBN 0-15-173152-7   LC 92-6883

"Walker details the life of Tashi, a woman who grew up in the Olinka tribe in Africa but spent most of her adult life in the U.S. As a child, when the custom of circumcision is ordinarily carried out among Olinka females, Tashi was spared; later, though, her muddled need to reidentify with her origins causes her to submit to the tribal circumciser's blade. Rather than reknitting her soul to that of her people, the episode and its disastrous consequences alienate her body from sexuality and her mind from reality." Booklist

"The people in Ms. Walker's book are archetypes rather than characters as we have come to expect them in the 20th-century novel, and this is by defiant intention. . . . When the novel is operating genuinely on this archetypal level, it has a mythic strength. Its many voices are not rendered as stream-of-consciousness monologues, nor are they made to belong to distinct individuals. Instead, they are highly stylized, operatic, prophetic—and powerfully poetic." N Y Times Book Rev

Walker, Alice, 1944-—*Continued*
The temple of my familiar. Harcourt Brace Jovanovich 1989 416p $19.95

ISBN 0-15-188533-8   LC 88-7995

"Time and place range from precolonial Africa to post-slavery North Carolina to modern-day San Francisco; and the characters themselves change and evolve as their stories are told, their myriad histories revealed. Most often present are Miss Lissie, an old woman with a fascinating host of former lives; her companion, the gentle Mr. Hal; Arveyda, a soul-searching musician; his wife Carlotta, who was born in the South American jungle; Fanny, a young woman who has a tendency to fall in love with spirits; and her husband Suwelo, who tries hard but simply does not understand her." Libr J

This is a "novel only in a loose sense. Rather, it is a mixture of mythic fantasy, revisionary history, exemplary biography and sermon. It is short on narrative tension, long on inspirational message." N Y Times Book Rev

You can't keep a good woman down; stories. Harcourt Brace Jovanovich 1981 167p o.p.

LC 80-8761

Analyzed in Short story index

Contents: Nineteen fifty-five; How did I get away with killing one of the biggest lawyers in the States? It was easy; Elethia; The lover; Petunias; Coming apart Fame; The abortion; Porn; Advancing Luna—and Ida B. Wells; Laurel; A letter of the times; or, Should this sadomasochism be saved; A sudden trip home in the spring; Source

Walker, Margaret, 1915-
Jubilee. Houghton Mifflin 1966 497p o.p.

"Vyry was a slave and the daughter of a slave. She suffered slavery's tribulations and looked forward to the time of freedom to bring her a home of her own and provide an education for her children. The Civil War and the Reconstruction period brought the possibility of that day of jubilation, but the attainment of her two desires still seemed remote. The author gives a clear picture of the everyday life of slaves, their modes of behavior, and the patterns and rhythms of their speech." Shapiro. Fic for Youth. 3d edition

Wallace, Irving, 1916-1990
The man; a novel. Simon & Schuster 1964 766p o.p.

This is the story of a black Senator who becomes the first black President of the United States after the deaths, in rapid succession, of first the Vice President and then both the President and the Speaker of the House

The portrayal of the "President as a man, an able, intelligent, politically moderate man who has never been to the fore but must take responsibility overnight, is excellent. With a huge cast of characters and one crisis after another in the plot, this makes an absorbing story." Publ Wkly

The prize. Simon & Schuster 1962 768p o.p.

This novel is an "inquiry into the private lives of a batch of Nobel Prize winners. . . . The prize winners are . . . a French husband-and-wife team of chemists whose marriage is collapsing, a neurotic American heart surgeon broodingly resentful that he must share the award in medicine with an Italian doctor, a gentle German-born physicist from Atlanta who is being wooed by the Communists of East Germany, and an American novelist who is just coming out of a long alcoholic trance. Wallace . . . assembles them all in Stockholm and embarks them on the frenzied series of public and private events that surround Nobel award weeks in the Swedish capital." N Y Her Trib Books

Wallace, Lew, 1827-1905
Ben-Hur; a tale of the Christ. Harper 1880 552p o.p. Buccaneer Bks. reprint available $27.95 (ISBN 0-89966-289-7)

First published 1880

This novel "depicts the oppressive Roman occupation of ancient Palestine and the origins of Christianity. The Jew Judah Ben-Hur is wrongly accused by his former friend, the Roman Messala, of attempting to kill a Roman official. He is sent to be a slave and his mother and sister are imprisoned. Years later he returns, wins a chariot race against Messala, and is reunited with his now leprous mother and sister. Mother and daughter are cured on the day of the Crucifixion, and the family is converted to Christianity." Merriam-Webster's Ency of Lit

Wallant, Edward Lewis, 1926-1962
The pawnbroker; [by] Edward L. Wallant. Harcourt, Brace & World 1961 279p o.p. Buccaneer Bks. reprint available $16.95 (ISBN 0-686-92468-1)

"Sol Nazerman is a survivor of the Holocaust. In the past he had been a university teacher in Poland; now he runs a pawnshop in Harlem in which Murillio, a ruthless racketeer, has a financial interest. Into Nazerman's shop come people who are sad, sick, or criminal. He also meets Marilyn Birchfield, a friendly social worker who tries to get past the frozen outward indifference of the pawnbroker. In flashbacks that describe the horror and torture suffered by Nazerman and his family, the reader begins to understand his withdrawal from humanity. The relationship between him and his young, ambitious, and confused assistant, Jesus Ortiz, provides the novel's shattering climax." Shapiro. Fic for Youth. 3d edition

Waller, Robert James, 1939-
Border music. Warner Bks. 1995 248p $17.95

ISBN 0-446-51858-1   LC 94-29350

This is the "story of an archetypal loser/loner/Vietnam vet named Texas Jack Carmine. In Chapter 1 he rescues an exotic dancer named Linda Lobo from some drunk who has ripped off her G-string and they set off in his pickup truck, on the road again. After stopping at several motels they end up a Jack's ranch in west Texas and try to make a go of it." N Y Times Book Rev

"Scores of writers handle Vietnam more astutely . . . . but it won't do simply to dismiss Waller as formulaic. To write forthrightly of love between a man and a woman is not only shrewd, it's bold." Booklist

The bridges of Madison County. Warner Bks. 1992 171p il $17.95

ISBN 0-446-51652-X   LC 91-50416

Also available Thorndike Press large print edition

Waller, Robert James, 1939——*Continued*

"This is the story of four days that change forever the lives of two lonely people. Robert Kincaid is a roving photographer for *National Geographic* and Francesca Johnson is a housewife whose marriage suffers from a lack of romance. Francesca's family is out of town when Kincaid arrives on the scene, and the pair are instantly attracted. They soon become lovers, and Kincaid asks Francesca to run away with him, but she refuses. Francesca stays loyal to her family, and memories of Kincaid are all that remain." Libr J

"An erotic, bittersweet tale of lingering memories and forsaken possibilities." Publ Wkly

Slow waltz in Cedar Bend. Warner Bks. 1993 197p $16.95

ISBN 0-446-51653-8   LC 93-15246

Also available Thorndike Press large print edition

"Michael Tillman, a tenured economics professor enjoying his role of academic maverick, feels an immediate attraction to Jellie Braden when she walks into a dean's reception with her husband. Their common past experiences in India provide a basis for friendship, which develops into a spiritual link; Michael realizes that he has waited a lifetime to meet Jellie. Within a year, their love intensifies, and the affair is consummated. Yet there is much Michael doesn't know about Jellie, and her sudden, unannounced visit to India prompts his quest for the secret of her past." Libr J

This is a "formula romance, but Waller delivers it in sophisticated fashion, with a sustained, gentle satire of academia and an entertaining trek through India. His send-up of campus sexual politics is quite amusing." Booklist

Waltari, Mika, 1908-1979

The Egyptian; a novel; translated by Naomi Walford. Putnam 1949 503p o.p. Buccaneer Bks. reprint available $35.95 (ISBN 0-89966-863-1)

This is the first volume of the author's trilogy which includes the Etruscan and The Roman

Original Finnish edition, 1945

"The novel is set in Egypt during the 18th dynasty when Akhnaton, who ruled from 1353 to 1336 BC, established a new monotheistic cult. Narrated by its protagonist, a physician named Sinuhe who is in contact with both rich and poor, the novel describes the daily life, religion, and politics of the era. His travels take him as far away as Syria and Crete. A confidante of pharaohs, he eventually lives in permanent exile." Merriam-Webster's Ency of Lit

The Etruscan; translated by Lily Leino. Putnam 1956 381p o.p. Buccaneer Bks. reprint available $29.95 (ISBN 0-56849-485-8)

This is the second volume of the author's trilogy, the first and third being The Egyptian and The Roman

Original Finnish edition, 1955

Set in the ancient Mediterranean world, this novel recounts "the life story of a wealthy Etruscan who, after a great many fantastic adventures, dies in the year 500 B.C. believing himself to be immortal. . . . Its plot [is filled] with narrow escapes, blighted love affairs and supernatural events." Publ Wkly

"'The Etruscan' is truly a remarkable novel, whether viewed as sheer adventure, or as mysticism with occult meaning." N Y Her Trib Books

The Roman; The memoirs of Minutus Launsus Manilianus, who has won the Insignia of a Triumph, who has the rank of consul, who is chairman of the Priests' Collegium of the god Vespasian and a member of the Roman Senate; English version by Joan Tate. Putnam 1966 637p o.p. Buccaneer Bks. reprint available $29.95 (ISBN 1-56849-486-6)

This is the final volume of the trilogy, the first being The Egyptian, and the second, The Etruscan

Original Finnish edition, 1964

The story is set in the first century A.D. during the reigns of Claudius and Nero. Minutus is born in Antioch, comes to Rome at the age of fifteen, visits Jerusalem and Britain with the army, and wins honors and power and has several love affairs. He becomes intimate with Nero and helps him persecute the Christians

"Though Minutus is somewhat wooden, his adventures are astonishing. Waltari shuttles his hero around the empire, from Britain to Ephesus, in order to describe the growing decadence of Rome, the rise of Christianity, and the existence of other religions. Waltari's sense of humor and irony points up his pageant of Roman life." Publ Wkly

Walters, Minette

The sculptress. St. Martin's Press 1993 308p $21.95

ISBN 0-312-09909-6   LC 93-21527

"Roz Leigh, an author embittered by the tragic death of a child and a split from her husband, agrees to write the story of Olive Martin, a grossly fat, untidy woman serving a long prison sentence for the particularly grisly murder of her mother and sister. Visiting Olive in jail, Roz finds herself drawn to the woman, and despite the fact that 'the sculptress' readily confessed to the crime, she begins to find odd discrepancies in the evidence against her." Publ Wkly

"Walters mesmerizes her readers with a sleek, exciting tale whose slick veneer disguises a sinister, menacing evil." Booklist

Wambaugh, Joseph

The black marble. Delacorte Press 1978 354p o.p.

LC 77-14262

"Veteran Los Angeles detective Valnikov is on the bottle and subject to nightmares now that his wife has left him and his close colleague has died. His reluctant partner Natalie thinks he's gone crazy and plans to report his behavior. However, when a top-flight dog handler named Philo, under pressure from loan sharks, 'dognaps' a prize schnauzer from a seemingly wealthy (actually quite poor) Pasadena society woman, Valnikov and Natalie get drawn into the case—and toward each other." Publ Wkly

"The unusual plot is laced with facetiousness that culminates as the bumbling dognapper—a lascivious old trainer who gets stoned at a dog show and comments acridly on the whole ordeal—and the police detective meet for a showdown, locked in a dog cage. A novel of surprises without the grimness of his earlier work." Booklist

Wambaugh, Joseph—*Continued*

The blue knight. Little, Brown 1972 338p o.p.

"An Atlantic Monthly Press book"

A novel about "Bumper Morgan, a fat Irish cop at 50, dyspeptic, lusty, tough, egotistic, with only two days to go before his planned retirement from the Los Angeles police department." Libr J

"The caricature is deliberate; the author means to endow a stereotype with complexity and sentiment. Bumper has his own street ethics. . . . The book tends to be a bit ostentatious in such honesties, as if they established Bumper's credibility. In the end, Wambaugh sentimentalizes Bumper as a sort of repellently lovable super-cop who, whenever he is not strongarming 'pukepots,' is bantering in Yiddish, Spanish or Arabic with the ethnics on the beat." Time

The Delta Star. Morrow 1983 276p o.p.

LC 82-21638

"A Perigord Press book"

The plot of this police novel concerns "a scam to divert the Nobel Prize in Chemistry from one professor to another less deserving. It involves two murders, the Russians, sexual blackmail, the chemistry faculty at Caltech and a . . . police detective." Newsweek

"Perhaps better than any other contemporary writer, Wambaugh is able to convey just what it is that makes cops different from the rest of us and, more important, why. In this latest novel . . . the reader meets an array of Wambaugh's finest, from Rumpled Ronald, who is merely trying to stay alive to collect his pension, to the Bad Czech, who helps solve a double murder all because of a chopstick in his shoe." Libr J

Finnegan's week. Morrow 1993 348p $22

ISBN 0-688-12801-7   LC 93-24890

Also available Thorndike Press large print edition

"The owner of a waste-hauling firm shaves costs by mislabeling drums of highly toxic pesticide and dumping them illegally. When two deaths result, Fin Finnegan teams up with civilian and Navy investigators to solve the series of related crimes." SLJ

"There is a boyish excessiveness to Mr. Wambaugh's writing that produces an odd synergy with his carefully constructed plots and his colorful characters." N Y Times Book Rev

Fugitive nights. Morrow 1992 336p $22

ISBN 0-688-11128-9   LC 91-17114

Also available Thorndike Press large print edition

This novel "focuses on Palm Springs PD detective Lynn Cutter, who's awaiting his pension after blowing out a knee while serving as Mayor Sonny Bono's bodyguard. Penniless from Charles Keating's Lincoln Savings scam, Lynn housesits for absent millionaires, sometimes eats dogfood, and always drinks cheap scotch. He needs a job but all he knows is police work; doing anything physically active could threaten his pension. Enter beautiful private eye Breda Burroughs and diminutive patrolman Nelson ('Half Nelson') Hareem, who engage him on separate-but-intersecting quirky quests that range from the desert to Bob Hope's neighbor's house." Booklist

"'Fugitive Nights' is a psychological novel that is topical in its approach. Jesse Jackson, Iraq, Sinead O'Connor, the recession and George Bush are to be found in its pages. Lynn Cutter gives a running, cynical account of what's wrong with the world." N Y Times Book Rev

The Glitter Dome. Morrow 1981 299p o.p.

"A Perigord Press book"

"Two very human detectives, Martin Welborn and Aloysius Mackey, specialized in converting obvious homicides (unsolved) into official suicides (solved). Their current assignment is the murder of Nigel St. Clair, the president of a film company. For allies, the duo depends upon Weasel and Ferret, a wry team of Narcs." Publ Wkly

"Wambaugh utilizes a brash and earthy style to maximum effect, sketching a grimy, unglamorous landscape of rough action, tough language, and gruesome detail. Artful characterization and occasional humor enliven the whole, and prevent the problems associated with police work (alcoholism, divorce, suicide) from becoming overly depressing." Libr J

The Golden Orange. Morrow 1990 317p $19.95

ISBN 0-688-09408-2   LC 89-13430

"A Perigord Press book"

This novel is "about a drunken ex-cop who comes to the attention of an Orange County grass widow who wonders why the inheritance from her father isn't bigger than it apparently is. Eventually, gal gets gold with the help, only half-witting, of our sodden hero, who concludes he's been flimflammed." Booklist

Wambaugh "combines page-turning entertainment, black humor, and fascinating technical detail with his own recurrent themes and settings." Choice

The new centurions. Little, Brown 1971 c1970 376p o.p.

"An Atlantic Monthly Press book"

The author "shows us the excitement, danger and sordidness found in the daily work of three young Los Angeles policemen. From the police academy to the first foot patrol, from the first patrol-car duty to the first promotion, Wambaugh follows his three main characters in their professional and personal lives, and shows us that police work, like the ministry, medicine or the military, is a profession demanding 24-hour dedication, determination, discipline and often a frustrating acceptance of defeat." Natl Rev

"As a novel the book has lapses, it wears its exposition on its sleeve—necessarily, perhaps, in view of what it's trying to do—and the three protagonists, though very different in type, are perhaps not sufficiently different in sensibility. . . . But never mind that. What he knows Wambaugh tells truly, perceptively, and well." Book World

The secrets of Harry Bright. Morrow 1985 345p o.p.

LC 85-10453

"A Perigord Press book"

"Victor Watson, a millionaire California businessman, wants to know how his paragon of a son could have been murdered in the depths of a desert canyon frequented by motorcycle gangs, drug dealers and lizards. Sidney Blackpool, a Los Angeles homicide detective who suffers from acute lack of ambition, aggravated cynicism and terminal weariness, agrees to investigate on a freelance basis." N Y Times Book Rev

Ward, Mary Jane, 1905-

The snake pit. Random House 1946 278p
o.p.

Available from Amereon and Buccaneer Bks.

Related in the first person, this tells of the experiences
undergone by the patient, Virginia Cunningham, in a
state mental hospital. It follows the course of her
insanity from her commitment to her final release. It
also takes the reader through mental hospital routine in
all its reality

"Chronicled so quietly and unemphatically, the horrors
of asylum life become infinitely more poignant than they
appear in the hands of grimmer writers who are out
to shock. Obviously an incomplete picture, but an extraordinarily moving one." New Yorker

Warner, Charles Dudley, 1829-1900

(jt. auth) Twain, M. The gilded age

Warner, Sylvia Ashton- See Ashton-Warner,
Sylvia, 1908-1984

Warren, Robert Penn, 1905-1989

All the king's men. Harcourt Brace & Co.
1946 464p o.p.

Available from various publishers

"In the South during the 1920s a young journalist,
Jack Burden, becomes involved in the drive for political
power by soon-to-be governor Willie Stark. The journey
is a rocky, disillusioning one, and involves exploitation,
deceit, and violence. When asked by Stark to uncover
a scandal in the past of Judge Irwin, Jack must weigh
the many consequences of such action." Shapiro. Fic for
Youth. 3d edition

Band of angels. Random House 1955 375p
o.p.

"Amantha Starr, reared as a white girl on her father's
Kentucky plantation and sent to Oberlin at nine for her
education, is called home at sixteen by her father's sudden death. At his funeral she is seized by the sheriff
who informs her that because her mother whom she
never knew was a slave, she is to be sold to a slave
dealer to satisfy her father's creditors. As she is swept
helplessly into slavery, she is haunted by both resentment
and guilty memories of her own part in the thoughtless
cruelties of the slave system." Booklist

The cave. Random House 1959 403p o.p.

This "novel concerns a Tennessee mountain boy,
trapped in a cave, who becomes a national celebrity
because of the news of the attempts made to rescue him.
Another young man tries to capitalize on the rescue
attempts as the newspapers and TV news reporters
swarm around his land, on which the cave is located."
Publ Wkly

A place to come to; a novel. Random
House 1977 401p $12.95

ISBN 0-394-41064-5   LC 76-50129

"Jediah Tewksbury, a poor white from rural Alabama,
grows into the complex, 60-year-old classic scholar who
looks back and constructs his life, and this novel. The
structure of both is determined by the deaths of people
crucial to that growth: primarily his father; then his mentor Stahlmann; a Nazi officer, a classical scholar too,
whom he murders; his wife, of cancer; the first husband

of his mistress, which haunts his affair; and lastly his
mother, which brings him home to the novel's title.
Nashville, Chicago, and Europe are important places, too,
and it all moves to the subtle variations of Time—in
it, through it, outside of it, always measured by it. .
. . An altogether masterful performance." Libr J

World enough and time; a romantic novel.
Random House 1950 512p o.p.

"A Kentucky murder and trial of the 1820's that attracted wide attention are the basis for the novel. Interest
is directed here to the murderer, Jeremiah Beaumont,
to the personal involvements and train of thought and
emotion that led to the murder, his justification, and
his repentance. Second in importance is his wife Rachel,
whom he began to love out of a feeling of outrage when
he learned that his old friend and benefactor, Colonel
Fort, had seduced her. . . . The turbulent politics of
the period also enter the story and many tales of frontier
characters . . . add to the background and atmosphere
and make a full-bodied period novel of emotion and
violence." Booklist

Washington, Alex See Harris, Mark, 1922-

Waugh, Charles G. (Charles Gordon), 1943-

(ed) Rod Serling's Night gallery reader.
See Rod Serling's Night gallery reader

Waugh, Evelyn, 1903-1966

Brideshead revisited; with an introduction
by Frank Kermode. Knopf 1993 xxxvii,
315p $17

ISBN 0-679-42300-1   LC 93-1854

"Everyman's library"
A reissue of the title first published 1945 by Little,
Brown

"Narrated by Charles Ryder, it describes his emotional
involvement with an ancient aristocratic Roman Catholic
family, which grows from his meeting as an undergraduate at Oxford the handsome, whimsical younger
son, Sebastian Flyte, already an incipient alcoholic.
Through Sebastian Charles meets his mother, the devout
Lady Marchmain, who . . . attempts to enlist Charles's
support in preventing Sebastian's drinking, but Sebastian
finally escapes to North Africa, where, after his mother's
death, he becomes some kind of saintly down-and-out.
Meanwhile Charles, now an unhappily married but
successful artist, falls in love with Julia, also unhappily
married; they both plan to divorce and begin a new life;
but the power of the Church reclaims Julia, and they
part forever. The narrative is set in a war-time
framework of prologue and epilogue, in which Charles
is billeted in Brideshead, the great country house which
had once dominated his imagination." Oxford Companion to Engl Lit. 5th edition

Charles Ryder's schooldays and other
stories. Little, Brown 1982 292p o.p.

LC 82-214221

Analyzed in Short story index
The "discovery of a fragment possibly intended as the
first chapter of a novel on the public school career of
the narrator of 'Brideshead Revisited' apparently prompted this collection of 12 stories. Apart from the title story
. . . this is essentially a reissue of the 1936 collection
'Mr. Loveday's Little Outing,' published in the U.S. in

Waugh, Evelyn, 1903-1966—*Continued*

a limited edition of 750 copies." Libr J

Contents: Mr. Loveday's little outing; By special request; Cruise; Period piece; On guard; Incident in Azania; Out of depth; Excursion in reality; Love in the slump; Bella Fleace gave a party; Winner takes all; Charles Ryder's schooldays

Decline and fall; illustrated by the author. Little, Brown 1977 c1928 293p il $15.45

ISBN 0-316-92619-1 LC 77-88222

Also available Everyman's library edition

First published 1928 in the United Kingdom; first United States edition published 1929 by Doubleday, Doran

This novel "recounts the chequered career of Paul Pennyfeather, sent down from Scone College, Oxford, for 'indecent behaviour', as the innocent victim of a drunken orgy. Thus forced to abandon a career in the church, he becomes a schoolmaster at Llanabba Castle, where he encounters headmaster Fagan and his daughters, the dubious, bigamous, and reappearing Captain Grimes, and young Beste-Chetwynde, whose glamorous mother Margot carries him off to the dangerous delight of high society. They are about to be married when Paul is arrested at the Ritz and subsequently imprisoned for Margot's activities in the white slave trade." Oxford Companion to Engl Lit. 5th edition

The end of the battle. Little, Brown 1962 c1961 319p o.p.

Sequel to Officers and gentlemen

First published 1961 in the United Kingdom with title: Unconditional surrender

In this final volume of the trilogy "Guy volunteers for service in Italy with the military government, and he eventually goes to Yugoslavia as a liaison officer with the Partisans. Virginia gives birth to a son (not Guy's) and is killed in an air raid. At the end of the book Guy has again asserted himself, in the rescue of a group of Jewish refugees, and realizes what kind of man he used to be: one who believed that his private honour would be satisfied by war. In an Epilogue we learn that he has remarried and surrounded himself with a family." Camb Guide to Lit in Engl

The loved one; an Anglo-American tragedy. Little, Brown 1948 164p o.p.

"Depicting romance in a mortuary could be gruesome but the author succeeds both in poking satirical fun at the maudlin pretentiousness of the funeral industry and in delighting the reader with a hilarious love story." Shapiro. Fic for Youth. 3d edition

Men at arms. Little, Brown 1952 o.p.

This is the first volume of the trilogy that includes Officers and gentlemen and The end of the battle

This novel "introduces 35-year-old divorced Catholic Guy Crouchback, who after much effort succeeds in enlisting in the Royal Corps of Halberdiers just after the outbreak of the Second World War. Much of the plot revolves around his eccentric fellow-officer Apthorpe, an old Africa hand who suffers repeatedly from 'Bechuana tummy', is deeply devoted to his 'thunder box' (or chemical closet), and dies in West Africa at the end of the novel of some unspecified tropical disease, aggravated by Guy's thoughtful gift of a bottle of whisky. Other characters include Guy's ex-wife, the beautiful socialite Virginia Troy, her second (but not her final) husband, Tommy Blackhouse, and the ferocious one-eyed Brigadier Ritchie-

Hook, who involves Guy in a near-disastrous escapade." Oxford Companion to Engl Lit. 5th edition

Followed by Officers and gentlemen

Officers and gentlemen. Little, Brown 1955 339p o.p.

Sequel to Men at arms

This novel "continues Waugh's semi-satiric, semi-emotional portrayal of civilian and military life with an account of Guy's training on the Hebridean island of Mugg with a Commando unit, and of the exploits of ex-hairdresser Trimmer, now Captain McTavish, which include an affair with Virginia and the blowing up of a French railway; the action moves to Alexandria, then to the withdrawal from Crete, with all but four of 'Hookforce' taken prisoner." Oxford Companion to Engl Lit. 5th edition

Followed by The end of the battle

Put out more flags. Little, Brown 1942 286p o.p.

A satirical story of the opening days of World War II as they affected certain members of the English upper classes. Basil Seal, the idol of three women—his mother, his sister, and his mistress—has his own way of meeting the responsibilities devolving upon him

"Each prim recital of military behaviour, from battalion exercise to death in action, emphasizes again what we already knew: that Mr. Waugh has a unique gift for pinning down the occasionally memorable astonishment of plain truth." New Statesman

Vile bodies. Little, Brown 1930 321p o.p.

"Set in England between the wars, the novel examines the frenetic but empty lives of the Bright Young Things, young people who indulge in constant party-going, heavy drinking, and promiscuous sex. At the novel's end, the realities of the world intrude, with Adam Fenwick-Symes, the protagonist, serving on a battlefield at the onset of another world war." Merriam-Webster's Ency of Lit

Waugh, Hillary, 1920-

A death in town. Carroll & Graf Pubs. 1990 244p o.p.

LC 89-10041

"When pretty Sally Anders is raped and bludgeoned to death with a hammer in the very upscale Connecticut town of Crockford, all of the residents find it convenient to believe that the suspicious-looking stranger who had been in town on the day of the murder must be the guilty one. When it turns out that this likely suspect was actually in jail in a nearby town at the time of the murder, the uncomfortable idea that perhaps a local resident might be a murderer gradually takes hold, with sometimes devastating results." Booklist

Webb, James H.

A sense of honor. Prentice-Hall 1981 308p o.p.

LC 80-25852

"Plebe life at Annapolis in 1968 proceeds as normal while the specter of Vietnam haunts the routine of midshipmen and the careers of recent graduates. Traditional military ways begin to yield to changing times and altered perceptions; on a personal level this conflict is captured in the relationship between a fourth-year student and a plebe who questions the rigid code of honor and unblinking acceptance of the hazing ritual." Booklist

Webb, James H.—*Continued*

"In this powerful novel, Webb . . . a graduate of the Academy, pulls the reader right into the caldron of Annapolis for a vivid picture of heroes and martinets living according to their various interpretations of 'honor'; and he illuminates the mystique that makes men voluntarily stay in such a meat grinder." Publ Wkly

Weidman, Jerome, 1913-

I can get it for you wholesale. Simon & Schuster 1937 370p o.p.

"This novel, a realistic satire, tells the story of an ambitious and unscrupulous young Jew named Harry Bogen, who begins as a shipping clerk in the New York garment center and rapidly becomes a successful dress manufacturer with money to burn. In this process he double-crosses every friend he has, except the chorus girl whose sex appeal is his stimulus. A few compunctions, raised by associations with his mother and a childhood sweetheart, he stifles with a little vague discomfort. His only standard is to be smarter than the other fellow." Saturday Rev

Weinberg, Robert E.

(ed) Lovecraft's legacy. See Lovecraft's legacy

Welch, James, 1940-

The Indian lawyer. Norton 1990 349p o.p.
LC 90-6894

"Sylvester Yellow Calf, the hero of this novel, has fought his way, despite the odds, to a top post in a prestigious Montana law firm and now is being wooed as a candidate for Congress by political power brokers. Sylvester, ex-basketball star and Stanford Law School graduate, recognizes that such a move could put him in a position to help his fellow Native Americans and at the same time to work for the preservation of the environment. While his responsibilities are all too clear to him, Yellow Calf hesitates, and, as he ponders his decision, he is drawn by a convict into a web that nearly strangles him." Choice

"The novel contains good, fast-paced action with succinct insight into our ordinary dilemmas." Nation

Welcome, John, 1914-

(ed) The Dick Francis treasury of great racing stories. See The Dick Francis treasury of great racing stories

(ed) The New treasury of great racing stories. See The New treasury of great racing stories

Weldon, Fay

The cloning of Joanna May. Viking 1989 265p o.p.
LC 89-40429

"Joanna May is the childless, sixtyish, spurned former wife of Carl May, an old-style baron of a new-style industry, nuclear power, a man who had the misfortune to spend a good deal of his childhood chained in a dog kennel. While she's recovering from the divorce, Joanna discovers that, as an experiment in another kind of power, Carl secretly had her cloned 30 years before. Somewhere she has four unknown sisters/daughters/twins." N Y Times Book Rev

"Joanna May's is the dominant voice—lyrical, disbelieving, despairing. . . . As for the clones, each has enough of a background sketched in to deserve a novel in her own right, leaving just enough symmetry to meet the demands of the story with comfort. Beautifully rhythmic sentences, a sarcastic environmentalism and a constant clever needling awareness stamp this novel as one of Fay Weldon's best." New Statesman Soc

Darcy's utopia. Viking 1991 c1990 235p $18.95

ISBN 0-670-83645-1   LC 90-50463

First published 1990 in the United Kingdom

This novel tells "the story of Eleanor Darcy, the enigmatic wife of a notorious monetary economist, now in prison, and two journalists, Valerie and Hugo, who separately conduct interviews with Eleanor for their publications but who together conduct an impetuous and passionate affair in a Holiday Inn. Eleanor tells her interviewers the story of her life and interweaves it with her utopian vision of the future." Quill Quire

"The novel is full of utopias of every stripe—social, political, erotic. . . . While the book's last twist of plot may tax the credulity of even the most indulgent readers, Ms. Weldon tosses it off with such aplomb that we find ourselves accepting it." N Y Times Book Rev

The heart of the country. Viking 1988 201p o.p.
LC 88-40062

Natalie and Sonia live not far from Galstonbury, England. "As the story opens, Natalie's husband, Harry Harris, has absconded to Spain with his secretary and the wages from his bankrupt computer firm, leaving Natalie with guests for dinner, two frozen chickens, half a tankful of petrol in the Volvo, the children, and nothing in the bank. . . . Sonia, for her part, has faced the situation of abandoned wife for some years. . . . Convicted of manslaughter and arson after setting fire to a carnival float, she is . . . telling Natalie's story as a therapeutic exercise from the psychiatric institution to which she has been confined." Times Lit Suppl

"In some of Ms. Weldon's other novels, her characters' naivete, her love of the offbeat, occasionally become a test of her readers' credulity. But in this book there's hardly a moment that doesn't ring perfectly true." N Y Times Book Rev

The hearts and lives of men. Viking 1988 c1987 357p $18.95

ISBN 0-670-82098-9   LC 87-40303

First published 1987 in the United Kingdom

"Dashing but self-centered Clifford, rising star of Leonardo's art auction house, marries pretty Helen, poor daughter of gifted but undiscovered artist John Lally. Their union produces poor little Nell, soon lost to both in a custody fight, then left to wander the world 20 years while her parents divorce, remarry, re-divorce, etc." Libr J

The novel "takes an arch, Jane Austen-ish approach to some rather messy sexual relationships and makes a highly enjoyable diversion out of some standard fictional fare." Quill Quire

Leader of the band. Viking 1989 196p o.p.
LC 88-40402

Weldon, Fay—*Continued*

"Starlady Sandra is an astronomer fed up with her proper life. She takes up with a saxophonist named Mad Jack, then decides to join him on his European tour. In so doing, she also joins the motley family of Mad Jack's band, including assorted wives, lovers, and troubled musicians. The discovery of Sandra's fame (she is well known for her serious late-night television show and as the discoverer of a planet) unsettles her lover and irritates the others. Left in solitude, Sandra broods about her family origins. There is plenty to ponder since she is the daughter of a Gypsy impregnated by an SS officer in a concentration camp." Booklist

"The novel, to which three short stories written by Sandra are appended, is, like its protagonist, a little scattered, but is vintage Weldon nonetheless—a wickedly delightful explication of those female truths she bares so well." Publ Wkly

The life and loves of a she-devil. Pantheon Bks. 1984 c1983 241p o.p.

LC 84-7070

First published 1983 in the United Kingdom

This is "the story of the vengeful path taken by a betrayed wife. An ugly, hulking, yet diligent and virtuous soul, Ruth has tolerated Bobbo's infidelity for years, but his infatuation with wealthy romantic novelist, Mary Fisher, threatens to destroy their family life totally. The break comes suddenly when Bobbo declares that he is leaving, calling Ruth a 'she-devil.' This epithet ringing in her ears, Ruth devises a master plan for revenge and justice." Booklist

This novel "is devilishly delightful. It affords a scintillating, mind-boggling, vicarious thrill for any reader who has ever fantasized dishing out retribution for one wrong or another." N Y Times Book Rev

Life force; a novel. Viking 1992 222p $22

ISBN 0-670-84146-3　　　　LC 91-26870

"The center of the tale is one Leslie Beck, famous among his circle for the formidable size of his male member. His charm, arrogance, and manipulativeness correspond accordingly. Over the years, Beck, now in his sixties, has had two wives and at least four lovers, all of whom are, or were, close friends. Three of these women were married and two managed to bring Beck's children into the world under their husband's name and care. The fourth remained single and, under mysterious circumstances, became a savvy, well-off gallery owner. His second wife's death brings Beck and his 'life force' back into the lives of his former lovers, inspiring one of them, Nora, to record their tangled and shameless escapades." Booklist

"Nora is, in the end, more than a recorder; she's a creator, making herself the collective voice of the women, and so she is their authority, their author, just as Leslie Beck is the author (the progenitor) of the illegitimate children he fathers. In this way, for all its social barbs and dry humor, 'Life Force' is less a comedy of manners than it is a parable about the act of creativity itself." N Y Times Book Rev

Puffball; a novel. Summit Bks. 1980 248p o.p.

LC 80-14585

"Liffey and Richard Lee-Fox's move to the country is not the idyll Liffey expected; Richard decides to commute, living in London during the week, and Liffey learns that she's pregnant. Neighbor Mabs, a witch who dabbles in herbal formulas, believes that her husband Tucker is the father of Liffey's baby (as well he might be) and maliciously schemes against Liffey while irresponsible Richard acquires three mistresses in London." Libr J

The author "knows how to take motherhood and other things we revere and don't question and make mincemeat of them. . . . The portrait of the naive Liffey as she is forced, quite against her will, to come of age, is sharp, funny and enormously entertaining. Weldon has a wonderfully wicked way of shattering illusions, and of pitting cherished dreams against realities." Publ Wkly

Trouble. Viking 1993 228p $21

ISBN 0-670-84148-X　　　　LC 93-254

Published in the United Kingdom with title: Affliction

Annette "has been happily married for ten years to Spicer, a wine merchant. She is pregnant with their first child and also about to deliver her first novel when the trouble commences. Influenced by a New Age astrologist/psychiatrist he once would have scorned, Spicer becomes increasingly abusive toward his wife. Annette is transformed into a type of woman . . . so intensely focused on maintaining even a bad relationship that she is unable to see the harm she is inflicting on herself." Libr J

"Weldon's satiric wit and devilish view of sexual politics are in full force in this brutally funny and wildly exaggerated novel, which consists almost entirely of dialogue, giving it the vitality and immediacy of theater." Booklist

Wellesley, Charles *See* Brontë, Charlotte, 1816-1855

Wells, H. G. (Herbert George), 1866-1946

The complete short stories of H. G. Wells. St. Martin's Press 1987 c1927 1038p $19.95

ISBN 0-317-15855-6　　　　LC 87-27478

Analyzed in Short story index

First published 1927 in the United Kingdom with title: The short stories of H. G. Wells

A collection of 62 short stories and the complete text of The time machine

Short stories included are: The empire of the ants; A vision of judgment; The land ironclads; The beautiful suit; The door in the wall; The pearl of love; The country of the blind; The stolen bacillus; The flowering of the strange orchid; In the Avu observatory; The triumphs of a taxidermist; A deal in ostriches; Through a window; The temptation of Harringay; The flying man; The diamond maker; Æpyornis Island; The remarkable case of Davidson's eyes; The Lord of the Dynamos; The Hammerpond Park burglary; The moth; The treasure in the forest; The Plattner story; The Argonauts of the air; The story of the late Mr. Elvesham; In the abyss; The apple; Under the knife; The sea raiders; Pollock and the Porroh man; The red doom; The cone; The purple pileus; The jilting of Jane; In the modern vein; A catastrophe; The lost inheritance; The sad story of a dramatic critic; A slip under the microscope; The reconciliation; My first aeroplane; Little mother up the Morderberg; The story of the last trump; The grizzly folk; The crystal egg; The star; The story of the stone age; A story of the days to come; The man who could work miracles; Filmer; The magic shop; The valley of spiders; The truth about Pyecraft; Mr. Skelmersdale in

Wells, H. G. (Herbert George), 1866-1946
—Continued
Fairyland; The inexperienced ghost; Jimmy Goggles the god; The new accelerator; Mr. Ledbetter's vacation; The stolen body; Mr. Brisher's treasure; Miss Winchelsea's heart; A dream of Armageddon

The first men in the moon
In Wells, H. G. Seven famous novels

The food of the gods
In Wells, H. G. Seven famous novels

In the days of the comet
In Wells, H. G. Seven famous novels

The invisible man.
Available from Amereon and Buccaneer Bks.

First published 1897
"The story concerns the life and death of a scientist named Griffin who has gone mad. Having learned how to make himself invisible, Griffin begins to use his invisibility for nefarious purposes, including murder. When he is finally killed, his body becomes visible again." Merriam-Webster's Ency of Lit

also in Wells, H. G. Seven famous novels

The island of Doctor Moreau.
Available from Buccaneer Bks.

First published 1896
This is "an evolutionary fantasy about a shipwrecked naturalist who becomes involved in an experiment to 'humanize' animals by surgery." Oxford Companion to Engl Lit. 5th edition

also in Wells, H. G. Seven famous novels

Seven famous novels; with a preface by the author. Knopf 1934 860p o.p.
The first four titles in this omnibus edition are entered separately
Contents: The time machine; The island of Dr. Moreau; The invisible man; The war of the worlds; The first men in the moon (1901); The food of the gods (1904); In the days of the comet (1906)

The time machine.
Available from Amereon and Bentley

First published 1895
"Wells advanced his social and political ideas in this narrative of a nameless Time Traveller who is hurtled into the year 802,701 by his elaborate ivory, crystal, and brass contraption. The world he finds is peopled by two races: the decadent Eloi, fluttery and useless, are dependent for food, clothing, and shelter on the simian subterranean Morlocks, who prey on them. The two races—whose names are borrowed from the Biblical Eli and Moloch—symbolize Wells's vision of the eventual result of unchecked capitalism: a neurasthenic upper class that would eventually be devoured by a proletariat driven to the depths." Merriam-Webster's Ency of Lit

also in Wells, H. G. The complete short stories of H. G. Wells

also in Wells, H. G. Seven famous novels

Tono-Bungay.
Available from Amereon and Buccaneer Bks.

First published 1908
"The narrator is George Ponderevo, son of the housekeeper on a large estate, who is apprenticed to his uncle, Edward Ponderevo, a small-town druggist. His fantastic uncle soon moves to London and makes a fortune from his quack medicine Tono-Bungay. George helps his uncle, ironically observes his rise in the world, and uses some of his money to set himself up as an airplane designer. George resembles H. G. Wells himself—the son of a housekeeper, apprenticed to a druggist, a socialist, and a man with a vision of progress through properly used science." Reader's Ency. 3d edition

The war of the worlds.
Available from Amereon and Buccaneer Bks.

First published 1898
"The inhabitants of Mars, a loathsome though highly organized race, invade England, and by their command of superior weapons subdue and prey on the people." Baker. Guide to the Best Fic
In this novel the author "introduced the 'Alien' being into the role which became a cliché—a monstrous invader of Earth, a competitor in a cosmic struggle for existence. Though the Martians were a ruthless and terrible enemy, HGW was careful to point out that Man had driven many animal species to extinction, and that human invaders of Tasmania had behaved no less callously in exterminating their cousins." Sci Fic Ency

also in Wells, H. G. Seven famous novels

Wells, Herbert George *See* Wells, H. G. (Herbert George), 1866-1946

Welty, Eudora, 1909-
The bride of Innisfallen and other stories
In Welty, E. The collected stories of Eudora Welty

The collected stories of Eudora Welty. Harcourt Brace Jovanovich 1980 622p $29.95
ISBN 0-15-118994-3
Analyzed in Short story index
This volume contains four previously published collections: A curtain of green (1941); The wide net and other stories (1943); The golden apples (entered separately); and The bride of Innisfallen and other stories (1955). Also included in this volume are two uncollected pieces: Where is the voice coming from? and The demonstrators
Contents of A curtain of green: Clytie; A curtain of green; Death of a travelling salesman; Flowers for Marjorie; The hitchhikers; Keela, the outcast Indian maiden; The key; Lily Daw and the three ladies; A memory; Old Mr. Marblehall; Petrified man; Piece of news; Powerhouse; Visit of charity; The whistle; Why I live at the P.O.; Worn path
The wide net and other stories: The wide net; First love; A still moment; Asphodel; The winds; The purple hat; Livvie; At the landing
The bride of the Innisfallen, and other stories: No place for you, my love; The burning; The bride of the Innisfallen; Ladies in spring; Circe; Kin; Going to Naples

A curtain of green
In Welty, E. The collected stories of Eudora Welty p1-149

Welty, Eudora, 1909-—*Continued*

Delta wedding; a novel. Harcourt Brace & Co. 1946 247p o.p. Amereon reprint available $20.95 (ISBN 0-89190-516-2)

A "portrait of a Southern plantation family in 1923. Set in the context of the wedding of one of the daughters, the novel explores the relationships among members of the Fairchild family, most of whom have been sheltered from any contact with the world outside the Mississippi Delta. Although they quarrel among themselves, they also unite against any threats to the family's status, honoring the belief in the family as a sacred and unchanging entity." Merriam-Webster's Ency of Lit

The golden apples. Harcourt Brace & Co. 1949 244p o.p.

Analyzed in Short story index
Contents: Shower of gold; June recital; Sir Rabbit; Moon Lake; Whole wide world knows; Music from Spain; The wanderers

also in Welty, E. The collected stories of Eudora Welty

Losing battles. Random House 1970 436p il o.p.

"At a large family gathering in Banner, Mississippi, the Renfro and Beecham families have assembled to celebrate Granny's ninetieth birthday. They are also celebrating Jack Renfro's return from the prison farm. As one might expect, the day is made up of reminiscences and recountings of earlier events, so that the novel actually spans many years. One of the key figures is Gloria, an orphan. She is frequently teased about being the daughter of another orphan, Rachel Sojourner, and of one of the Beecham boys who died in World War I. Gloria, who had married Jack just prior to his imprisonment, feels that they must get away from the clan, all of whom seem proud of their ignorance in spite of Miss Julia Mortimer's lifelong struggle to teach them something. It was a losing battle, probably even for Gloria." Shapiro. Fic for Youth. 3d edition

The optimist's daughter. Random House 1972 180p o.p. Amereon reprint available $18.95 (ISBN 0-8488-0660-3)

"This novel is considered the high point of Welty's lengthy career. The strong character study examines 45-year-old Laurel McKelva Hand, who returns from Chicago to Mississippi, where her father is dying. She is forced to consider her complex and ambiguous emotions about her powerful and dynamic father, the impact of this relationship on her life, and her puzzlement at his late marriage to a coarse and shallow woman who is Laurel's own age." Shapiro. Fic for Youth. 3d edition

The Ponder heart; drawings by Joe Krush. Harcourt Brace & Co. 1954 156p il o.p. Amereon reprint available $16.95 (ISBN 0-8488-0661-1)

"Cast as a monologue, [this comic novella] is rich with colloquial speech and descriptive imagery. The narrator of the story is Miss Edna Earle Ponder, one of the last living members of a once-prominent family, who manages the Beulah Hotel in Clay, Miss. She tells a traveling salesman the history of her family and fellow townsfolk." Merriam-Webster's Ency of Lit

The robber bridegroom; designed and illustrated by Barry Moser. Harcourt Brace Jovanovich 1987 c1942 134p il $19.95

ISBN 0-15-178318-7   LC 87-21195

A reissue of the title first published 1942 by Doubleday

"A novelette combining fairy tale and ballad form, telling of the wooing of Rosamond, the daughter of a Mississippi planter, by a bandit chief." Oxford Companion to Am Lit. 5th edition

"Miss Welty uses the magic of metaphor and simile like a lyric poet, and writes with a limpid purity, and exquisite sense of descriptive coloring that gives a warm glow of beauty to a fantastic, and unfortunately sometimes tiresome story." Springfield Repub

The wide net and other stories

In Welty, E. The collected stories of Eudora Welty

Werfel, Franz

The forty days of Musa Dagh. Viking 1934 824p o.p.

Available from Amereon and Buccaneer Bks.

Original German edition, 1933; published in the United Kingdom with title: The forty days

"Gabriel Bagradian returns to his ancestral village in Syria, where he learns that the Turks are disarming the Armenians and sending them into exile. Gabriel plans the resistance to the Turks and directs the fortification of the mountain Musa Dagh. The Turks are successfully repulsed a number of times but at great cost in lives to the Armenians on the mountain. On the fortieth day the remnant of the Armenian force is rescued by the French." Shapiro. Fic for Youth. 3d edition

The song of Bernadette; translated by Ludwig Lewisohn. Viking 1942 575p o.p.

Available from Amereon and Buccaneer Bks.

Original German edition, 1941

A slightly fictionalized version of "the life of Saint Bernadette of Lourdes. While it is not exactly a religious work, it is truly reverent in its approach to the inscrutable, the unfathomable, the divine. There is an engrossing picture of emperor, bishops, priests, nuns, merchants and artisans. A living pageant of the second Empire in France." Ont Libr Rev

Wesley, Mary

A dubious legacy. Viking 1992 271p $21

ISBN 0-670-84672-4   LC 92-6168

"In 1944, Henry Tillotson brings his bride Margaret to his country house, where she takes to her bed and remains in self-indulgent isolation. Ten years later, two younger friends of Henry bring their girlfriends for the weekend. In the years that follow, the two couples marry and return regularly, their mundane lives punctuated by Margaret's eccentric boudoir conversations or scandalous ventures into their company." Libr J

"Margaret Tillotson is a character so wonderfully warped that she proves irresistible—to readers as well as to the members of her firmly rebuffed husband's makeshift social set. Margaret can always be counted on to be wildly inconsiderate, often deliciously rude, and as she lurks in her constantly redecorated, mirror-bedecked boudoir, leafing through mail-order catalogues

Wesley, Mary—*Continued*

and inventing ever-more-elaborate sexual slurs against Henry, she provides vast stretches of high-class low comedy." N Y Times Book Rev

West, Dorothy, 1909-

The wedding. Doubleday 1995 240p $20

ISBN 0-385-47143-2   LC 94-27285

This novel is "set on Martha's Vineyard during the 1950s and focuses on the black bourgeois community known as the Oval. Dr. Clark Coles and his wife, Corinne, highly respected Ovalites, are preparing for the wedding of their youngest daughter, Shelby, who, much to their consternation, is marrying a white jazz musician. Lute McNeil, a compulsive womanizer who has recently made a fortune in the furniture business, is determined to stop Shelby's wedding; he is confident that he can convince Shelby to marry him, which would bring him the social acceptance he has always craved." Booklist

"Through the ancestral histories of the Coles family, West . . . subtly reveals the ways in which color can burden and codify behavior. The author makes her points with a delicate hand, maneuvering with confidence and ease through a sometimes incendiary subject." Publ Wkly

West, Jessamyn, d. 1984

Collected stories of Jessamyn West. Harcourt Brace Jovanovich 1986 480p o.p.

LC 86-12031

Analyzed in Short story index

Contents: Probably Shakespeare; A time of learning; The mysteries of life in an orderly manner; Love, death, and the ladies' drill team; Homecoming; The battle of the suits; Tom Wolfe's my name; Learn to say good-bye; A little collar for the monkey; Public-address system; Foot-shaped shoes; Horace Chooney, M.D.; The linden trees; Breach of promise; The singing lesson; The Calla Lilly Cleaners & Dyers; The wake; Grand opening; Aloha, farewell to thee; Reverdy; Up a tree; There ought to be a judge; Gallup Poll; Alive and real; I'll ask him to come sooner; Hunting for hoot owls; Crimson Ramblers of the world, farewell; Night piece for Julia; Live life deeply; Mother's Day; The heavy stone; 99.6; The day of the hawk; Like visitant of air; The condemned librarian; Child of the century; Flow gently, sweet aspirin; The second (or perhaps third) time round

Cress Delahanty; drawings by Joe Krush. Harcourt Brace & Co. 1953 311p il o.p.

"In story-sketches that reveal with touching humor an adolescent's real problems from her 12th to her 16th year, likable Cress grows up on a California ranch, making her mark at school, exploring the strange ways of 'boys,' and being always loved and cherished by her often bewildered parents." Bookmark

"Anyone who knows adolescence, and especially that of young girls, will love this book. It is beautifully written, with the most extraordinary insight and delicacy." Commonweal

Except for me and thee; a companion to The friendly persuasion. Harcourt, Brace & World 1969 309p o.p.

"Episodes in the Birdwell family chronicle which round out their story as related in 'The friendly persuasion'. Jess's courting of Eliza, their migration from Ohio to southern Indiana, the building of the new home, and growth of the children to maturity supply material for a low-keyed nostalgic narrative interrupted occasionally by excitement and sorrow, as when Jess becomes a conductor on the Underground Railway and Quaker principles are abandoned by the younger generation during the Civil War and Reconstruction." Booklist

This book "has all the warmth, the sturdy affection, and the quiet humor of its predecessor. . . . In part the charm of the novel owes to the vibrant authenticity of its characters; in great part it is due to the practiced ease and resilience of style." Saturday Rev

The friendly persuasion. Harcourt Brace & Co. 1945 214p o.p.

Available from Amereon and Buccaneer Bks.

"The Birdwell family of Indiana led a quiet life until the Civil War came into their lives. They were Quakers and tried to live according to the teachings of William Penn. Jess Birdwell, a nurseryman, loved a fast horse as well as his trees and the people he knew. Eliza, his wife, was a Quaker minister and a gentle, albeit strict, soul. When the war reached Indiana, Josh, the oldest son, was torn between his Quaker upbringing and his belief in the rightness of the Union cause; Mattie was at that difficult age between childhood and womanhood; and Little Jess, the youngest, ran into trouble with Eliza's geese. This is a wonderful family chronicle, with the laughter, tears, and tenderness that can be found in many families." Shapiro. Fic for Youth. 3d edition

Followed by Except for me and thee

The massacre at Fall Creek. Harcourt Brace Jovanovich 1975 373p o.p.

"Fictional treatment of the historic slaughter of nine Indians (mostly women and children) by white settlers on the Indiana frontier in 1824 and the trial for murder which resulted in the killers' deaths by hanging. An eminently readable book. Lovers of American history will find the circumstances well researched; the long-ago time and its people vividly brought to life with terse and witty dialogue and much authentic detail of frontier domesticity. The sub-plots are West's own. These involve a preacher of the old-time religion; his red-haired tomboy daughter, avidly pursued and finally won; lone hunters and their near-savage ways . . . and Indians, whose attitudes and philosophies are presented with sympathy." Choice

The state of Stony Lonesome. Harcourt Brace Jovanovich 1984 184p o.p.

LC 84-12882

This "book is set in 1919 California and introduces the reader to the Chalmers clan: spunky, adventurous Ginerva, her strong-minded yet whimsical mother Birdeen, taciturn brother Neddie, and womanizing Uncle Zen. As Ginerva reminisces with an ailing Uncle Zen, she recalls her growing up, her perplexed attempts to make sense of adult behavior, and her sometimes romantic, always loving relationship with Zen. It is Zen who has been fleeing the 'state' of the novel's title: 'I've spent my life trying to avoid it. Sweethearts, wives, liquor, automobiles. . . .' How he did the avoiding and what

West, Jessamyn, d. 1984—*Continued*

Ginerva learns from him create an appealing story." Libr J

West, Morris L., 1916-

The clowns of God; a novel; by Morris West. Morrow 1981 370p o.p.

LC 80-27153

This second novel in the author's Vatican trilogy takes place in the last decade of the 20th century. As the story opens, "Jean Marie Barette, lately Pope, has been forced into abdication because the cardinals don't know how else to cope with his apocalyptic vision of the approaching end of the world and the second coming of Jesus Christ. What follows [concerns his efforts] . . . to find a way to proclaim his vision without sending his cherished world into a tailspin of chaos and hysteria." Christ Sci Monit

"The fugitive ex-pope posits all the fearful questions about life that have perplexed us since Hiroshima. West's ultimate answers will disturb some and be dismissed by others, but no one will be left unmoved. The sheer power of his prose and his keen understanding of human nature make this novel a stunning accomplishment." Libr J

Followed by Lazarus

The devil's advocate. Morrow 1959 319p $17.95

ISBN 0-688-01453-4

In this novel "the plot concerns a British Monsignor who investigates the petition for canonization of a man who died before a partisan firing squad in Calabria during World War II. As the investigation progresses, he learns a great deal about the man, his family, the village in which he lived and, especially, about himself." Publ Wkly

"The characters all are firmly, brightly established. The writing, without fanciness or flourish, goes along with a fine, steady drive. There are no profound insights, no remarkable illuminations. But there is an engrossing story, expertly told, about a set of fascinating people whose lives are viewed as meaningful." Chicago Sunday Trib

Lazarus; [by] Morris West. St. Martin's Press 1990 293p $19.95

ISBN 0-312-04339-2   LC 89-77919

"Pope Leo XIV faces death from heart disease as the novel opens and is targeted for assassination by a fundamentalist group, but he realizes a need for tolerance and begins to undo the very policies that have made him a reactionary." Smith. Cloak and Dagger Fic

"A tense and exciting thriller, Lazarus also explores world crises and theological politics quite as fascinating to non-Catholics as to Catholics. . . . While the book can be read as a complement to the other two novels, it stands alone as a superb, absorbing novel." Libr J

Masterclass; [by] Morris West. St. Martin's Press 1991 330p o.p.

LC 90-28090

Available G.K. Hall large print edition

Max Mather "served as the paleographer (manuscript archivist) for a well-known Italian family. But when he comes into possession of two Raphael originals, Max becomes incredibly wily, both about the effect his discovery will have on the international art world and about his prospects for cashing in. Big-time collectors,

dealers, and auctioneers are drawn into Mather's game, with the players flitting easily from New York to Zurich to Florence to Amsterdam and back again. Amid all the artsy oneupmanship, West gives us a subplot involving the murder of a Manhattan painter whose brilliance extended from her way with palette and brush to kinky, omnivorous sex. Solid plotting and interesting characters make this flashy novel of intrigue fully enjoyable." Booklist

The shoes of the fisherman; a novel. Morrow 1963 374p o.p. Buccaneer Bks. reprint available $21.95 (ISBN 1-56849-146-8)

Also available G.K. Hall large print edition

In this first title in the author's Vatican trilogy, "a humble Ukrainian pope finds himself the central negotiator in an attempt to prevent the United States and the Soviet Union from starting World War III. During the negotiations, the pope must confront the Russian who once tortured him. The work, a popular and critical success, demonstrates West's concern with modern man's inability to communicate with his brother." McCormick and Fletcher. Spy Fic

Followed by The clowns of God

West, Nathanael, 1903-1940

The complete works of Nathanael West. Farrar, Straus & Cuhady 1957 421p o.p.

"Included here are 'The Dream Life of Balso Snell' 1931, a surrealist sexual nightmare in prose, 'Miss Lonelyhearts,' 1933, [entered separately] a biting satire on modern man and his aspirations, 'A Cool Million,' 1934, melodramatic satire on the American dream of success, and 'The Day of the Locust,' 1939, a bitter tale of Hollywood and its hangers-on." Libr J

A cool million

In West, N. The complete works of Nathanael West p143-256

The day of the locust

In West, N. The complete works of Nathanael West p259-421

The dream life of Balso Snell

In West, N. The complete works of Nathanael West p3-62

Miss Lonelyhearts. Liveright 1933 213p o.p.

"The story of a man who writes an 'advice to the lovelorn' column, the theme of the book is the loneliness of the individual in modern society. The hero tries to live the role of omniscient counselor he has assumed for the paper, but his attempts to reach out to suffering humanity are twisted by circumstances, and he is finally murdered by a man he has tried to help." Reader's Ency. 3d edition

also in West, N. The complete works of Nathanael West p65-140

West, Paul, 1930-

Love's mansion. Random House 1992 339p $22

ISBN 0-394-58734-0   LC 92-6804

West, Paul, 1930-—*Continued*

"Set in England, the story moves from the late Victorian era to mid-century, telling the story of two lovers, Harry and Hilly, whose lives are irrevocably changed by World War I. Tantalizingly, the novel's point of view is that of the couple's son, who must look back in time, guessing at motives, imagining dialog, intuiting emotions." Libr J

"As Mr. West has made vividly clear, we have much to learn from the Moxons and their changing world. It is perhaps unfashionable to write about the pain and transformations that characterize the love of a long-married couple, but Mr. West is concerned with something much more personal than literary fashion. At times the astounding 'diligence of human memory' takes off in his book and produces passages that are close to poetry, almost always when his style is at its least extended and inclusive." N Y Times Book Rev

The women of Whitechapel and Jack the Ripper. Random House 1991 420p $22

    ISBN 0-394-58733-2   LC 90-9046

"Painter Walter Sickert, fascinated by the dark side of life in Victorian London, introduces Princess Alexandra's son to the prostitute/models at Cleveland Street. An unwanted pregnancy follows, word of which the royal family desperately attempts to suppress, inadvertently setting off a chain of events which lead to [murder]." Libr J

"The late Victorian period, with all its charm and filth and wretchedness, is delivered up in dazzling set pieces—from frolics with a bathing machine at Yarmouth to a plague of flies descending on London—that never interfere with the story's grimly steady momentum. Mr. West's lyrical, clever prose, now and then too ostentatiously paraded in his previous novels, remains under shrewd control here." N Y Times Book Rev

West, Dame Rebecca, 1892-1983

Cousin Rosamund; with an afterword by Victoria Glendinning. Viking 1986 c1985 294p o.p.

                    LC 85-40780

First published 1985 in the United Kingdom

In the last book of the author's trilogy about the Aubrey family, "Rose, Mary, and Rosamund come to maturity. . . . It is a maturity that Rose and Mary do not entirely choose for themselves, one they are forced into when Rosamund marries a man of dubious morals and unfathomable vulgarity—a man they can only despise. No longer guided by Rosamund's radiance, Mary and Rose must find their own light. Unable to look beyond the magic circle of their childhood, they retreat to an inn on the Thames, where, with Mr. Morpurgo, Queenie, and Nancy—friends they have known all their lives—they find a haven of security." Publisher's note

In this novel "West's signature talents are again displayed: meticulous rendering of period details, evocation of the spirit of an age through outspoken views on its music, art, fashion, politics and social mores." Publ Wkly

The fountain overflows; a novel. Viking 1956 435p o.p.

This first novel in the author's trilogy "spans the 10 years in which the Aubreys formed one of the most unusual households in Edwardian London. Rose, the most discerning of the four children, paints a vivid picture of Papa, a pamphleteer, political reformer, and gambler whose wife declared that he was in love with poverty and disgrace, and of Mamma, a gifted musician with a plain face and a charming personality." Booklist

"All of the best qualities of the superb writer are gathered together in this novel. . . . Wit, subtlety, and humour with a realistic approach to the problems of a family." Libr J

Followed by This real night

Sunflower; with an afterword by Victoria Glendinning. Viking 1987 c1986 276p o.p.

                    LC 86-40262

First published 1986 in the United Kingdom

"Sunflower is Sybil Fassendyll, a beautiful, 30 year old actress at the peak of her career. For the past ten years, she has been the mistress of the brilliant but moody and domineering Lord Essington. When she meets American millionaire politician Francis Pitt in London, she soon leaves Essington and becomes involved with Pitt to the point of obsession. Though outwardly a powerfully public woman, Sunflower secretly yearns for marriage and family, home and security." Publisher's note

This "tantalizingly unfinished novel . . . though incomplete, is a finished work of art in its emotional intensity, its analytical force, and its intricately wrought design of tiny, jewel-like details reflecting and amplifying the flash of its major themes." Christ Sci Monit

This real night. Viking 1985 c1984 265p o.p.

                    LC 84-40467

First published 1984 in the United Kingdom

The second novel about the Aubreys "is set in the few years immediately prior to World War I. The family's unreliable father has now abandoned them, and Mother has to provide. School for the children is over, and they are beginning to take personal lessons in the vicissitudes of adult life. (The narrator, Rose, is embarking, with one of her sisters, on a career as a professional pianist.)" Booklist

"A fascinating glimpse into a superb stylist's workshop, and one hopes that newcomers to West will be intrigued rather than distracted. Fans of the first volume are sure to enjoy following young Rose Aubrey as she continues to narrate the fates of her family and friends through the shattering events of World War I." Libr J

Followed by Cousin Rosamund

West, V. Sackville- *See* Sackville-West, V. (Victoria), 1892-1962

Westheimer, David

My sweet Charlie. Doubleday 1965 255p o.p.

"When her father learns that Marlene Chambers, a seventeen-year-old poor white girl, is pregnant, she is forced to leave home. Charles Roberts, a black lawyer, is a fugitive from the South because he killed a white man during the turmoil of a protest march. He shares a refuge with Marlene in a deserted summer cottage for several weeks, and their hostility and suspicion turn to understanding and trust." Shapiro. Fic for Youth. 2d edition

Westheimer, David—*Continued*

Von Ryan's Express. Doubleday 1964 327p o.p.

"Colonel Joseph Ryan is shot down over Italy and is sent to a prisoner-of-war camp, where he imposes military discipline upon the other prisoners. After Italy's surrender, when the prisoners are put on a train for Germany, Ryan plans a daring takeover of the train and gets the men to Switzerland." Shapiro. Fic for Youth. 2d edition

Followed by Von Ryan's return (1980)

Westlake, Donald E.

After I'm gone

In Westlake, D. E. Levine p151-82

Baby, would I lie?; a romance of the Ozarks. Mysterious Press 1994 291p $19.95

ISBN 0-89296-532-0   LC 93-40485

Also available Thorndike Press large print edition

This comic mystery, featuring characters from the author's Trust me on this, "is set in 'the new Nashville': Branson, Missouri. Singer Ray Jones is accused of one murder and then of a second. Out on bail, he continues to entertain in this theater. Meanwhile, an army of troops from the sleazy tabloid *Weekly Galaxy* descends to bug offices, lie, infiltrate, and do anything else necessary to get some sort of story on the upcoming trial. Also arriving are reporters Sara and Jack, lovers and representatives of a trendy New York magazine called *Trend: The Magazine for the Way We Live This Instant.* The action is jet-fast, and the satiric commentary on country western stars and fans is wonderfully wicked." Libr J

Bank shot. Simon & Schuster 1972 224p o.p.

In this novel "criminal mastermind Dortmunder . . . plans to rob a Long Island suburban bank by stealing the whole bank—a mobile trailer home being used temporarily while the new bank building is under construction. Dortmunder's cohorts include Victor, a former FBI agent ousted because he thought the FBI ought to have a secret hand-shake; Herman X, a black militant lock expert; and a female cab driver who wears a neck brace while trying to collect a phoney insurance claim." Booklist

It is Westlake's "triumph that whereas on one hand the reader knows he simply can't take the characters and situations seriously, those characters are so deftly drawn that they are eminently believable." N Y Times Book Rev

The best-friend murder

In Westlake, D. E. Levine p3-31

Come back, come back

In Westlake, D. E. Levine p35-59

Cops and robbers. Evans & Co. 1972 286p o.p.

"Two New York City policemen plot to steal two million dollars. Unable to pull off a heist that large on their own, they offer their services to the Mafia." Chicago. Public Libr

Westlake's "strongest qualities remain his wild but seamless plotting and his tape-recorder ears, but this time his characterizations are more dimensional and compassionate. . . . The exciting ending is a jewel of complexity." Libr J

The death of a bum

In Westlake, D. E. Levine p121-50

Don't ask. Mysterious Press 1993 327p $18.95

ISBN 0-89296-469-3   LC 92-53721

In this novel John Dormunder "and his cohorts agree to steal a religious relic, the femur of a thirteenth-century saint, that is a bone of contention between two fledgling Eastern European countries. Possession of the bone will lead to a seat in the United Nations." Booklist

"If the plot is of no great concern, it is the effortlessness, wit, and sheer good-heartedness of the telling that make 'Don't Ask' such a consistent delight." N Y Times Book Rev

Drowned hopes. Mysterious Press 1990 422p $18.95

ISBN 0-89296-178-3   LC 89-35859

In this "comedy-mystery, ex-con John Dortmunder and his benevolent criminal cohorts are continuously frustrated in their attempts to recover $700,000 in stolen money from a 50-foot-deep reservoir in upper New York State." Booklist

"In 'Drowned Hopes,' Donald Westlake's lean prose and deadpan delivery are engaging, as always. His psychology is sharp and his characters colorful." N Y Times Book Rev

The feel of the trigger

In Westlake, D. E. Levine p61-87

Good behavior. Mysterious Press 1985 244p o.p.

LC 85-43178

"John Archibald Dortmunder runs across several Manhattan rooftops after trying to pull a break-in. He ends up on the roof of a building in a newly trendy but unsettled neighborhood, then falls through a skylight into a covey of cloistered nuns, who see the thief as an answer to their prayers." Booklist

The author "manages to create characters who are a curious mixture of stereotypes and archetypes. If he is a master of the comic crime caper, and he is, he also does what the best comic writers throughout history have done—make a comment on society." N Y Times Book Rev

The hot rock. Simon & Schuster 1970 249p o.p.

"The hot rock is the Balambo Emerald, part of an African exhibit at the New York Coliseum, owned by Akinzi, and coveted by the breakaway state of Talabwo. Major Iko of Talabwo selects John Dortmunder as the mastermind for the heist. But lifting the stone from the Coliseum is only the first caper for Dortmunder's carefully chosen crew." Libr J

This novel "comes awesomely close to the ultimate in comic, big-caper novels; it's . . . filled with mocking style and action and imagination." N Y Times Book Rev

Humans. Mysterious Press 1992 355p $18.95

ISBN 0-89296-468-5   LC 91-52864

Westlake, Donald E.—*Continued*

"God is fed up with humanity and has concluded it's time for the world to end. He dispatches an angel to trick a few carefully chosen humans into engineering Armageddon, but the devil has other ideas. He'd like to save the world. As the gods struggle, a few straggling humans—including a Russian fireman dying from nuclear exposure at Chernobyl, a once-famous singer now a lonely activist, an AIDS-infected African whore, and a habitual criminal looking for the big score—just might have some small say in our destiny." Booklist

"Westlake evokes—both humorously and bitterly—the loneliness and hopelessness that color the human condition, posing the age-old question of what makes life worth living despite so much evil. Though he treats this issue only shallowly, Westlake . . . lifts his tale with snappy prose and sympathetic characters." Publ Wkly

Levine. Mysterious Press 1984 182p $14.95

ISBN 0-89296-063-9   LC 83-63034

Analyzed in Short story index

"Six novellas featuring Abe Levine, the 53-year-old Brooklyn detective with the irregular heartbeat. . . . In 'The Best-Friend Murder,' Levine and his partner, Jack Crawley, contend with a college youth who insists he poisoned his best friend, although his motive seems spurious. In 'Come Back, Come Back,' the problem is a successful businessman who looks down from the ledge of a tall building and threatens to jump to his death. . . . 'The Sound of Murder' concerns a ten-year-old girl who could have been the inspiration for 'The Bad Seed,' 'The Death of a Bum' is a psychological piece that Westlake had some difficulty in selling. The final story, 'After I'm Gone,' is a pure action piece that somehow doesn't seem to fit the mold of the other Levine stories, but its interest never flags." West Coast Rev Books

Sacred monster. Mysterious Press 1989 231p o.p.

LC 88-28888

In this novel "Westlake limns the life of Jack Pine, fabulously wealthy but drug-hazed and slightly mad movie star. As the plot progresses (depending on the current clarity or cloudiness of his mind), Jack delivers a series of carefully orchestrated flashbacks to an interviewer revelatory of his acting career, ex-wives, paternity suits, and ubiquitous best friend/sponge Buddy Pal. The scenes twist bitterly into the present, and the true reasons for the drugs and the interview become clear." Libr J

This novel's "full of pungent, right-on-the-money, satirical asides on today's Hollywood." N Y Times Book Rev

The sound of murder

In Westlake, D. E. Levine p89-120

The spy in the ointment. Random House 1966 200p o.p.

Pacifist Gene Raxford is mistakenly invited to a meeting of a terrorist group run by his girlfriend's Communist brother. The FBI persuades Gene to infiltrate the group, leading the pacifist gunman into danger and wild adventures

Trust me on this. Mysterious Press 1988 293p o.p.

LC 87-22098

Available G.K. Hall large print edition

"As a young and comely reporter is driving down that highway on route to reporting for her new job at the 'Weekly [Galaxy]' she finds a bloody corpse hanging half-out of a Buick Riviera. When she is assigned to her new editor, a driven personality, as are all who are employed at this paper, she tells him about the corpse on the road thinking he will assign her to the story. But this kind of story is not what interests that kind of paper—the corpse is probably a nobody, the car he was in was surely a nothing. But Sara Joslyn is haunted by what she saw even though she hasn't the time or freedom to look into the matter further." West Coast Rev Books

"In between stories about space battles, 100-year-old twins, dead country music stars and bizarre medical happenings, Mr. Westlake has sandwiched a nice romance and a fairish murder mystery." N Y Times Book Rev

Why me? Viking 1983 191p o.p.

LC 82-10921

"Unlucky burglar John A. Dortmunder has made the biggest haul of his life—and he doesn't want it. An enormous ruby ring called the Byzantine Fire has been stolen en route from the United States to Turkey and hidden in the little jewelry store Dortmunder robs. Every cop in New York City, the FBI, several foreign intelligence agencies, a terrorist group or two, and (because they're tired of being hassled by the police) the city's entire criminal population are all after the ring and poor Dortmunder. Westlake's comic talents are well used here." Libr J

Wetering, Janwillem van de *See* Van de Wetering, Janwillem, 1931-

Wharton, Edith, 1862-1937

The age of innocence; introduction by R. W. B. Lewis. Scribner 361p $40

ISBN 0-684-14659-2

Also available G.K. Hall large print edition

"Hudson River editions"

First published 1920 by D. Appleton & Co.; first Scribner edition, 1968

"New York City in the 1920s was a place of tight social stratification with rituals for everything from romance to etiquette at the opera. The young attorney Newland Archer was engaged to lovely, socially acceptable May Welland. He faced the power of family and social mores when he became attracted to May's bohemian cousin, Ellen." Shapiro. Fic for Youth. 3d edition

The buccaneers

In Wharton, E. Fast and loose and The buccaneers p119-479

The buccaneers, completed by Marion Mainwaring. Viking 1993 406p $22

ISBN 0-670-85219-8   LC 93-13901

"When Wharton died in 1937, she left unfinished a novel about fresh young Americans in class-bound England that *Time* declared would have been her masterpiece. Now Wharton scholar Mainwaring has polished up the rough draft and interpolated a few passages. . . . When the St. George girls and their friend Lizzy Elmsworth aren't accepted in New York society because their bloodlines just don't go back far enough, no matter how

Wharton, Edith, 1862-1937—*Continued*

rich they are, the St. George governess recommends that they go to England." Libr J

"Ms. Mainwaring has produced a commendably brave pastiche. Throughout the added sections, she turns shadowy walk-ons into full-blown protagonists, twists half-started subplots into integral parts of the story, concocts symbolic names as shamelessly heavy-handed as those of her model, and injects descriptions with a venom that would have made Wharton smile. This new 'Buccaneers' may not be the novel Wharton herself would have written, but it is certainly a lively, engaging piece of fiction." N Y Times Book Rev

Certain people

In Wharton, E. The collected short stories of Edith Wharton v2

The children. Scribner 282p $25

ISBN 0-684-18453-2

First published 1928 by D. Appleton & Co.

Standing at the rail of the liner, Martin Boyne surveyed his fellow-passengers in the act of coming aboard. 'Not a soul I shall want to speak to—as usual!' was his comment. Then he saw Judy Wheater carrying a fat, rosy baby up the gang plank and he changed his mind. Judy was only sixteen, but there was nothing inexperienced in the way she herded her troupe of brothers and sisters and 'steps' over to Europe while her father and mother played at divorce and remarriage. For a whole summer, Martin, old bachelor that he was, joined forces with Judy in her gallant attempt to keep her flock together

The collected short stories of Edith Wharton; edited and with an introduction by R. W. B. Lewis. Scribner 1987-1989 2v ea $50

ISBN 0-02-570600-4 (v1); 0-02-626161-8 (v2)

LC 87-14446

"A Scribners/Macmillan Hudson River edition"

A reissue of the title first published 1968 by Scribner and partially analyzed in Short story index

Contains ten collections of stories: The greater inclination (1899); Crucial instances (1901); The descent of man (1904); The hermit and the wild woman (1908); Tales of men and ghosts (1910); Xingu (1916); Here and beyond (1926); Certain people (1930); Human nature (1933); The world over (1936). Also included are thirteen miscellaneous stories, two dramatic sketches and some articles about the short story and ghost stories

Contents for the short stories included in the volumes are as follows:

The greater inclination: The muse's tragedy; A journey; The pelican; Souls belated: A coward; A cup of cold water; The portrait

Crucial instances: The Duchess at prayer; The angel at the grave; The recovery; The Rembrandt; The moving finger; The confessional

The descent of man: The descent of man; The mission of Jane; The other two; The quicksand; The dilettante; The reckoning; Expiation; The lady's maid's bell; A Venetian night's entertainment

The hermit and the wild woman: The hermit and the wild woman; The last asset; In trust; The pretext; The verdict; The potboiler; The best man

Tales of men and ghosts: The bolted door; His father's son; The Daunt Diana; The debt; Full circle; The legend; The eyes; The blond beast; Afterward; The letters

Xingu: Xingu; Coming home; Autres temps . . .; Kerfol; The long run; The triumph of night; The choice

Here and beyond: Miss Mary Pask; The young gentlemen; Bewitched; The seed of the faith; The temperate zone; Velvet ear pads

Certain people: Atrophy; A bottle of Perrier; After Holbein; Dieu d'amour; The refugees; Mr. Jones

Human nature: Her son; The day of the funeral; A glimpse; Joy in the house; Diagnosis

The world over: Charm incorporated; Pomegranate seed; Permanent wave; Confession: Roman fever; The looking glass; Duration

Miscellaneous short stories: Mrs. Manstey's views; The fullness of life; That good may come; The lamp of phyche; April showers; Friends; The line of least resistance; The letter; The House of the Dead Hand; The introducers; Les metteurs en scène; Writing a war story; All Souls'

Crucial instances

In Wharton, E. The collected short stories of Edith Wharton v1

The custom of the country. Scribner 594p $55

ISBN 0-684-14655-X

Also available from Everyman's library

"Hudson River editions"

First published 1913

"The story of Undine Spragg, a young woman with social aspirations who convinces her nouveau riche parents to leave the Midwest and settle in New York. There she captures and marries a young man from New York's high society. This and each subsequent relationship she engineers prove unsatisfactory, chiefly because of her greed and great ambition." Merriam-Webster's Ency of Lit

The descent of man

In Wharton, E. The collected short stories of Edith Wharton v1

Ethan Frome; with an introduction by Mrs. Wharton. Scribner 181p $30

ISBN 0-684-15326-2

Also available from Amereon

"Hudson River editions"

First published 1911

This is "an ironic tragedy of love, frustration, jealousy, and sacrifice. The scene is a New England village, where Ethan barely makes a living out of a stony farm and is at odds with his wife Zeena (short for Zenobia), a whining hypochondriac. Mattie, a cousin of Zeena's comes to live with them, and love develops between her and Ethan. They try to end their impossible lives by steering a bobsled into a tree; instead ending up crippled and tied for the rest of their unhappy time on earth to Zeena and the barren farm. Zeena, however, is transformed into a devoted nurse and Mattie becomes the nagging invalid." Benet's Reader's Ency of Am Lit

False dawn

In Wharton, E. Old New York

Fast and loose

In Wharton, E. Fast and loose and The buccaneers p1-111

Wharton, Edith, 1862-1937—*Continued*

Fast and loose and The buccaneers; edited and with an introduction by Viola Hopkins Winner. University Press of Va. 1993 xxviii, 514p il $49.50

ISBN 0-8139-1482-5   LC 93-11207

A combined edition of Wharton's first and last novels. Fast and loose was begun when the author was fourteen and first published in 1977 by the University Press of Virginia with author's pseudonym David Olivieri on title page. The buccaneers, left unfinished at the author's death, first published 1938 by D. Appleton & Co.

"The connections between the two novels go beyond the similarities in names—Georgie Rivers and Guy Hastings in the former; Nan St. George and Guy Thwarte in the latter. In both, the women are trapped by social convention and fateful forces into stultifying, destructive marriages." Publisher's note

The greater inclination

In Wharton, E. The collected short stories of Edith Wharton v1

Here and beyond

In Wharton, E. The collected short stories of Edith Wharton v2

The hermit and the wild woman

In Wharton, E. The collected short stories of Edith Wharton v1

The house of mirth. Scribner 329p $50

ISBN 0-684-14658-4

Also available from Everyman's library

"Hudson River editions"

First published 1905

"The story concerns the tragic fate of the beautiful and well-connected but penniless Lily Bart, who at age 29 lacks a husband to secure her position in society. Maneuvering to correct this situation, she encounters both Simon Rosedale, a rich man outside her class, and Lawrence Selden, who is personally appealing and socially acceptable but not wealthy. She becomes indebted to an unscrupulous man, has her reputation sullied by a promiscuous acquaintance, and slides into genteel poverty. Unable or unwilling to ally herself with either Rosedale or Selden, she finally despairs and takes an overdose of pills." Merriam-Webster's Ency of Lit

Human nature

In Wharton, E. The collected short stories of Edith Wharton v2

New Year's Day

In Wharton, E. Old New York

The old maid

In Wharton, E. Old New York

Old New York. Appleton, D. & Co. 1924 4v o.p.

Contents: False dawn; The old maid; The spark; New Year's Day

Four stories of four successive decades in New York social life which together form an authentic social history of Old New York in the middle years of the last century. 'False dawn' is a picture of the city in the 'fabulous forties.' 'The old maid' is an intense drama throbbing under the smooth surface of the complacent fifties—a story of mother-love revolving about the unacknowledged

parentage of Tina Lovell. 'The spark' tells the story of Hayley Delane, apparently acquiescent to his frivolous wife and the petty social round in which he moves. 'New Year's Day' is the story of Lizzie Hazeldean—another poignant tragedy unsuspected under the conventional surface of the seventies

The reef. Scribner 367p $20

ISBN 0-684-15557-5

"Hudson River editions"

First published 1912 by D. Appleton & Co.; first Scribner edition, 1965

In this novel the "action is confined almost exclusively to a chateau in France and the issue narrowed to a psychological struggle in the mind of the heroine, Anna Leath, who discovers that the man she has agreed to marry has had an affair with the young woman who is about to marry her step-son." Ref Guide to Am Lit. 2d edition

The selected short stories of Edith Wharton; introduced and edited by R.W.B. Lewis. Scribner 1991 xxi, 390p $24.95

ISBN 0-684-19304-3   LC 91-11433

Analyzed in Short story index

Contents: A journey; The pelican; Souls belated; The descent of man; The mission of Jane; The other two; The dilettante; The lady's maid's bell; The legend; The eyes; Xingu; Autres temps; Kerfol; The long run; A bottle of Perrier; After Holbein; Mr. Jones; Pomegranate seed; Roman fever; Duration; All Souls'

The spark

In Wharton, E. Old New York

The stories of Edith Wharton; selected and introduced by Anita Brookner. Carroll & Graf Pubs. 1990 2v ea $18.95

ISBN 0-88184-620-1 (v1); 0-88184-637-6 (v2)

Analyzed in Short story index

Contents: v1 The pelican; The other two; The mission of Jane; The reckoning; The last asset; The letters; Autres temps . . . ; The long run; After Holbein; Atrophy; Pomegranate seed; Her son; Charm incorporated; All Souls'

v2 The lamp of psyche; A journey; The line of least resistance; The moving finger; Expiation; *Les metteurs en scène*; Full circle; The daunt Diana; Afterward; The bolted door; The temperate zone; Diagnosis; The day of the funeral; Confession

Tales of men and ghosts

In Wharton, E. The collected short stories of Edith Wharton v2

The world over

In Wharton, E. The collected short stories of Edith Wharton v2

Xingu

In Wharton, E. The collected short stories of Edith Wharton v2

Wharton, William

Birdy. Knopf 1979 c1978 309p o.p.

LC 77-28023

Wharton, William—_Continued_

"At the close of World War II, in the mental ward of a veteran's hospital, there is a patient whose behavior quite baffles the psychiatrists. The patient's only childhood friend, another soldier who has a severe facial wound, is transferred to the hospital in the hope he may be of help. The friend instantly recognizes that the patient is behaving exactly like a bird. (The keeping of birds had always been an obsession of the patient throughout his adolescence.)" Choice

"Only the most rigorous imagination can make a story of this sort work for a reader who is generally indifferent to birds. Wharton has just such an imagination." Newsweek

Dad; a novel. Knopf 1981 449p o.p.

LC 80-2725

"Jack Tremont is a fifty-two year old American artist who lives in Paris. He is called home to care for his parents, both of whom have recently become ill. His nineteen year old son shows up also, since his grandparent's home is so convenient to the California State University that he has just left. We meet father and son after they leave California and begin a cross country drive. We move back and forth from past to present, comparing and contrasting the perceptions, concerns, and needs of three generations in one family. Each chapter presents a different character's point of view." Best Sellers

"It's an old story, this man-in-the-middle business, but fresh in Wharton's telling because he lets experience—lunch, a crisis, baseball on TV—accumulate as naturally and surely as aging itself." Saturday Rev

Wheeler, Harvey, 1918-

(jt. auth) Burdick, E. Fail-safe

Whitaker, Rodney See Trevanian

Whitby, Sharon, 1935-

For works written by this author under other names see Black, Veronica, 1935-

White, Edmund, 1940-

The beautiful room is empty. Knopf 1988 227p $17.95

ISBN 0-394-56444-8   LC 87-40495

In this sequel to A boy's own story, the author "follows our nameless hero from his final year at prep school in the mid-1950s through his cruisy but self-deprecating college years to the 'turning point' in his life—the famous Stonewall uprising of 1969 in which the clients of a New York gay bar stood up to the policemen trying to close it down. What emerges is the picture of a young man desperately struggling to come to terms with himself, a struggle that is a universal even if the context for every individual is different. Artfully constructed, this work clearly transcends its 'gay' theme." Libr J

A boy's own story. Dutton 1982 217p o.p.

LC 82-9536

A nameless narrator reminisces about his homosexual childhood and his conflicting emotions in coming of age during the 1950s. At fifteen years of age, the boy hopes that "he is just passing through a homosexual 'stage.'

At prep school he goes to a . . . psychiatrist who pops pills and talks of his own problems—and with no help from this man he begins slowly to see the real dimensions of his own life." Newsweek

This first-person novel is "written with the flourish of a master stylist. . . . It is an endearing portrait of a child's longing to be charming, popular, powerful, and loved, and of his struggles with adults . . . [told with] sensitivity and elegance." Harpers

Followed by The beautiful room is empty

(ed) The Faber book of gay short fiction. See The Faber book of gay short fiction

White, Patrick, 1912-1990

Nobel Prize in literature, 1973

The eye of the storm. Viking 1974 c1973 608p o.p.

First published 1973 in the United Kingdom

"Elizabeth Hunter, once a brilliant socialite and a rich, sensual, materialistic woman, now into her eighties, is dying in her Sydney mansion, perceived as a house-shrine by the nurses and servants who devotedly revolve around her. Mrs. Hunter's crucial experience, during the eye of a cyclone, of harmony between her inner, essential self and the outer void has determined the rest of her life, especially the act of dying. Flawed as she is, her strength and intense authenticity of being is communicated in varying degrees to her servants, her lawyer and to her two inauthentic children, the Princess de Lascabanes and Sir Basil Hunter. The comic brilliance of White's conception of Sir Basil, the weary actor for whom life and acting are perpetually fused, is one of the novel's highlights." Oxford Companion to Australian Lit

The tree of man; a novel. Viking 1955 499p o.p.

"Epic and even biblical in tone, [this novel] narrates the lives of a pioneering couple, Stan and Amy Parker, from youth to old age. White has said that he tried to suggest in this novel 'every possible aspect of life, through the lives of an ordinary man and woman. But at the same time . . . to discover the extraordinary behind the ordinary, the mystery and poetry which alone could make bearable the lives of such people.' The novel includes a representation of rural life as a felt actuality, but Stan and Amy's inner lives and especially the increasing conflict between Stan's intuitions of meaning and the outer confusion are the centre of interest. The vision that is granted to him before his death comprehends both the unity of being and the inevitable isolation of the self." Oxford Companion to Australian Lit

The vivisector. Viking 1970 567p o.p.

In this novel "White treats a difficult and complex subject, the act of creation and its costs as realized from within the artist's consciousness. Hurtle Duffield, the artist-protagonist, is the vivisector who cuts up living experiences and relationships for the purposes of his art. But Hurtle also comprehends art as an avenue to a realization of the Divine Vivisector, God, and both the successive women in his life and his paintings represent stages in his quest for a perception of pure being. The quest culminates in his final attempt, disrupted by his last stroke, to paint God. As a background to Hurtle's experiences, described with uncompromising honesty, is White's most comprehensive and intimately realized picture of the changing Australian social milieu." Oxford Companion to Australian Lit

White, Phyllis Dorothy James *See* James, P. D.

White, T. H. (Terence Hanbury), 1906-1964

The book of Merlyn; the unpublished conclusion to The once and future king; prologue by Sylvia Townsend Warner; illustrated by Trevor Stubley. University of Tex. Press 1977 xx, 137p il o.p.

LC 77-3454

Sequel to The once and future king
"White, who believed that the central theme of Malory's 'Morte d'Arthur' was to find an antidote to war, pursues that theme here, going to the animals for his answer. Old and defeated King Arthur is led by magician Merlyn into a badger's sett where a group of animals are discussing people. It's Merlyn, however, who becomes chief orator. Publ Wkly
"Writing during World War II, White vented his feelings about the futility of war with a fierceness that sometimes overwhelms the intriguing mixture of fantasy, humor, and rationality which pervaded the tetralogy." Booklist

The candle in the wind

In White, T. H. The once and future king p545-677

The ill-made knight

In White, T. H. The once and future king p325-544

The once and future king. Putnam 1958 677p $22.95

ISBN 0-399-10597-2
"An omnibus edition of four novels; The sword in the stone (1939), The witch in the wood (1939, now called The Queen of Air and Darkness) and The ill-made Knight (1940) [the first two titles are entered separately]. A number of alterations have been made in the earlier books. Previously unpublished, The candle in the wind 'deals with the plotting of Mordred and his kinsmen of the house of Orkney, and their undying enmity to King Arthur." Times Lit Suppl
"White's contemporary retelling of Malory's *LeMorte d'Arthur* is romantic and exciting." Shapiro. Fic for Youth. 3d edition
Followed by The book of Merlyn

The Queen of Air and Darkness [variant title: The witch in the wood]

In White, T. H. The once and future king p215-323

The sword in the stone; with decorations by the author and end papers by Robert Lawson. Putnam 1939 311p il o.p.
First published 1938 in the United Kingdom
An "account of everyday life in a great medieval manor, with two boys, Kay and Wart (who turns out to be King Arthur) learning the code of being a gentleman, busy with hawking, jousting, sword play, and hunting. The whole trend of the story is how the boy Wart was made worthy to become a king." Ont Libr Rev

"Delightful, fantastic, satirical nonsense, for the reader with a background of Arthurian legend." Wis Libr Bull
Followed by The witch in the wood

also in White, T. H. The once and future king p1-213

The witch in the wood; with decorations by the author. Putnam 1939 269p il o.p.
Sequel to The sword in the stone
The boy, Wart, is now a mature King Arthur fighting against other kings for recognition. Merlin and other characters reappear in the fantasy but it is mainly the story of Queen Morguase (the witch in the wood) and her four sons. Set in the Land of Lothian and Orkney
Followed by The ill-made knight (1940)

White, Terence Hanbury *See* White, T. H. (Terence Hanbury), 1906-1964

White, William Anthony Parker *See* Boucher, Anthony, 1911-1968

Whitney, Phyllis A., 1903-

Black amber. Appleton-Century 1964 284p o.p.
A "suspense story in a Turkish setting, a villa on the water near Istanbul. The 23-year-old [American] heroine has come in the disguise of a secretary-researcher for an artist, to try to find out how her stepsister, the artist's wife, had died. She enters a mysterious household, full of rivalries and hatreds." Publ Wkly
"Tracy learns too much for her own safety about Anabel's connection with an international opium smuggling operation. Setting and atmosphere are prime ingredients in a competently written romantic suspense novel." Booklist

Columbella. Doubleday 1966 306p o.p.
A mystery-romance set in St. Thomas, Virgin Islands. A young teacher, Jessica Abbott, is hired to tutor the 14-year-old daughter of a wealthy family. She is both drawn to and repelled by the girl's father. But when the mother, a spoiled willful woman, who engages in reckless affairs with young men, is murdered and suspicion falls on the husband, Jessica becomes convinced of the latter's innocence and sets out to discover the real murderer

Daughter of the stars. Crown 1994 286p $20

ISBN 0-517-59929-5   LC 94-25532
Also available Random House large print edition
This "novel takes place in Harper's Ferry, where a young woman discovers a family her mother has kept secret throughout her life. Lacy Elliot reads a letter addressed to her mother in order to protect her during convalescence, only to discover a family she has never known. The letter is a plea for help, and Lacy responds by showing up in Harper's Ferry in her mother's stead. She falls in love with a writer whom she meets on the ferry and is introduced to an aunt, her great-grandmother, and cousins, while learning of her father's unsolved murder. The tension from that long-ago incident is revived by the reappearance of the major suspect, her grandfather." Booklist

Domino. Doubleday 1979 351p o.p.

LC 79-7331

Whitney, Phyllis A., 1903-—*Continued*

"Domino is a ghost town, an abandoned silver mine camp in the Colorado Rockies that holds the secret to young Laurie Morgan's psychic wound. During the 20 years since she left her grandmother's mansion, she has endured nightmarish recollections of a peripheral role in her father's shooting. Now Laurie is summoned to the bedside of that imperious old woman, who needs the assistance of a blood relative if the Morgan territory is to resist the overtures of opportunist land developers." Publ Wkly

Dream of orchids. Doubleday 1985 303p o.p.

LC 84-8014

"Life on Long Island no longer satisfies Laurel York. Her mother has just died, and running her bookstore is too comfortably safe. Ripe for diversion, she heads for Key West and her father (now a famous novelist) who abandoned her when she was a child. Her reunion fantasies are met by a distracted man mourning his second wife's death and a household shivering in fear of some eerie secret. Two half-sisters introduce Laurel to the family passion—a green-house of beautiful orchids, the very place of the mother's 'accidental' death. . . . Though the suspense mounts slowly and relies on characters stereotyped by their roles, the result is a tension-charged mystery skillfully played against a colorful backdrop of libertines and literati, gold-seekers and sun-worshipers." Publ Wkly

The ebony swan. Doubleday 1992 269p o.p.

LC 92-4384

Available G.K. Hall large print edition

"Susan Prentice comes home to the Virginia she left at age six, after her mother's death. She is greeted by her grandmother, suspicious neighbors, a childhood friend, and an aura of foreboding." Booklist

"The suspense never falters, and Whitney wonderfully enriches her storytelling with the lush background of Tidewater Virginia and well-integrated historical commentary." Publ Wkly

Emerald. Doubleday 1983 307p o.p.

LC 82-45369

"Carol Hamilton, fleeing from a powerful and abusive ex-husband who is trying again to kidnap their child, seeks shelter with a distant relative, Monica Arlen, former movie star. Carol finds no sanctuary there, for her ex-husband tracks her down, but she does find a mystery: why did Monica Arlen so suddenly abandon her screen career and her romance with her screen lover, Saxon Scott? This secret leads to murder. While solving the mystery, Carol solves her own personal problems." Libr J

Feather on the moon. Doubleday 1988 280p o.p.

LC 87-6692

Available G.K. Hall large print edition

"The kidnapping of her daughter, Deborah, from a supermarket in Connecticut eventually leads Jennifer Blake to a stately home in Victoria, British Columbia, where she has reason to believe her daughter is living. It has been four years since Jennifer has seen Deborah, and she has doubts that the girl she encounters in Victoria, a willful seven year old named Alice, could possibly be hers. Summoned to Canada by a wealthy older woman who also has doubts about the girl's identity, Jennifer finds that every member of the household, from the chauffeur to the old woman's physician, harbors troublesome secrets." Booklist

Flaming Tree. Doubleday 1986 c1985 278p o.p.

LC 85-1601

"Although Jody Hammond and his mother Ruth have survived a terrible fall off the ocean cliffs at Carmel, Calif., Jody can't speak or recognize anyone, and his tyrannical father, Tyler, gives up hope for his recovery. In the Hammond household at La Casa de la Sombra, life has never seemed hopeful anyway, troubled as it is with dark secrets from the past. Meanwhile, Kelsey Stewart, struggling to forget the death of her own small son, has arrived in Carmel to stay with her aunt, the owner of a local inn. A therapist for brain-damaged children, Kelsey offers to help Jody, but her efforts seem blocked by mysterious forces." Publ Wkly

The glass flame. Doubleday 1978 276p o.p.

A "suspense-romance set in the Great Smoky Mountains of Tennessee. Karen Hamilton has just been widowed. Her husband, David, an arson expert, had been asked by his architect brother, Trevor, to investigate some fires set in a new and beautiful housing development that Trevor has designed. David dies, victim of a devastating blaze in one of the nearly completed homes. His last letter to Karen, though full of marital recriminations, says that if he loses his life in this latest assignment, it will not be an accident. Karen feels obligated to solve the mystery of David's death and goes to Tennessee to do so. She stays with Trevor and his family in a beautiful mountain-top home and begins her search." Publ Wkly

The golden unicorn. Doubleday 1976 279p o.p. Amereon reprint available $21.95 (ISBN 0-89190-535-9)

"After losing her adoptive parents, [journalist] Courtney Marsh becomes determined to find her natural mother and father. Clues lead to East Hampton, the home of the Rhodes family. They are an exasperating lot, prone to violent outbursts and guilty secrets. Courtney's investigative skills uncover the secret of her birth and involve her in a family scandal that almost causes her death." Libr J

Hunter's green. Doubleday 1968 252p o.p.

This story is "set in present-day England. Eve, young American wife of Justin North and narrator of the story, returns to her husband's English estate after a three-year separation from Justin who has now decided to divorce her and remarry. Eve determines to win back her husband's love, but a sinister turn of events seems to mark Eve for violent death." Booklist

Poinciana. Doubleday 1980 345p o.p.

LC 80-949

"Poinciana is the exquisite Palm Beach estate to which young and naive Sharon comes as chatelaine. Married at a vulnerable period in her life to Ross Logan, 60-year-old robber baron, she becomes another of his possessions, a beautiful object like the netsuke collection in his museum-home. There are counterforces in ex-wives, a senile mother, a scheming daughter and Logan's death before Sharon develops her own resources." Publ Wkly

Whitney, Phyllis A., 1903——*Continued*

Rainbow in the mist. Doubleday 1989 309p o.p.

LC 88-18099

Available Thorndike Press large print edition

"Christy Loren has inherited psychic powers from her mother, a renowned psychic. Haunted by the images of murder victims she has helped to find, she flees to her aunt in Virginia, only to find that here, too, her powers are needed to solve a possible murder and the disappearance of a strange young woman. Fearing the evil she senses, and attracted to the husband of the missing woman, Christy only reluctantly investigates. In solving the puzzle, she comes to terms with her gift." Libr J

Sea Jade. Appleton-Century 1965 c1964 277p o.p.

Set in New England during the last days of the clipper ships, this novel is about Miranda Heath, a young girl who has been tricked into a loveless marriage. Danger surrounds her when she attempts to solve the mystery of an old murder on one of the local ships

Silverhill. Doubleday 1967 244p o.p.

Malinda Rice, a young woman, accompanies her mother's body to New Hampshire for burial. At Silverhill, her mother's ancestral home, she meets her grandmother Julia Gorham who has dominated the family. Malinda attempts to deliver her mother's dying message to her half-demented Aunt Arvilla and uncovers old hatreds and fears when she begins probing into family secrets

The singing stones. Doubleday 1990 507p o.p.

LC 89-37137

Available Thorndike Press large print edition

Lynn McLeod "is an ombudsman for terminally ill children who is suddenly summoned to assist the daughter of her first husband. But the child is not physically ill. She is haunted by the near-fatal accident that crippled her father and the threatening presence of her wicked stepmother (whom everyone believes to be the epitome of quiet kindness). Lynn enters the complicated family situation with great reluctance, bewitched by the spiritualist philosophies of one character yet driven by her own sympathy for a child in distress. A terrific work of romantic suspense in a contemporary setting." Booklist

Snowfire. Doubleday 1973 319p o.p.

"A skiing resort in the Poconos owned by the McCabe family is the setting. Everybody skis, from Julian McCabe himself, whose athletic career had been ruined by an automobile accident, to his younger daughter Adria. Julian's wife, Margot, who had also been injured in the same auto accident, has recently been killed when her wheel-chair had sped down its ramp and off a cliff. Stuart Parrish, whom Julian had been grooming as an Olympic skier, has been arrested on suspicion of murder. Linda Earle, who no one knows is Stuart's stepsister, is employed as companion to Adria, secretly determined to clear her brother's name and find the real murderer." Publ Wkly

Spindrift. Doubleday 1975 301p o.p.

This novel is set in Newport, Rhode Island. "Christy Moreland, having recovered from a breakdown after the apparent suicide of her father, newspaperman Adam Keene, arrives at 'Spindrift,' her domineering mother-in-law's estate. Theo [her mother-in-law] is set on keeping young Peter, son of Christy and her passive husband,

Joel. Christy is equally determined to get the boy back and to prove her father was murdered. She suspects Theo and others in the lush company, except strong, personable Bruce Perry. With her marriage failing, Christy turns to Bruce who she hopes will help her and with whom she feels she's falling in love." Publ Wkly

Star flight. Crown 1993 286p $20

ISBN 0-517-59499-4   LC 93-8728

This "tale of murder and romance is haunted by an adulterous affair between two Hollywood stars of the 1930s. Lauren Castle, granddaughter of this liaison, visits the North Carolina site of her mother's supposed suicide after Lauren's husband dies in a mysterious accident while filming at this haunted location. . . . The villainess is not terribly surprising, but the suspense is well plotted." Booklist

The stone bull. Doubleday 1977 304p o.p. Amereon reprint available $22.95 (ISBN 0-89190-536-7)

LC 76-50802

"Jenny Vaughn, Cinderella sister of Ariel Vaughn, one of the world's most accomplished dancers, believes she shares in the guilt for Ariel's suicide. Her distress increases when she discovers that her new husband, a member of the family that owns the [Catskill resort] hotel, once loved Ariel. And Ariel has been blamed for an unusual murder the family wants to cover up. A stone bull, a dark tower and a murky vault play roles in Jenny's search for her identity and the identity of the real murderer." Publ Wkly

The trembling hills. Appleton-Century-Crofts 1956 344p o.p.

"The unfolding of a skeleton-in-the-closet family history, several romances, and a young girl's emergence from adolescence to maturity provide the stock-in-trade elements of a novel set in San Francisco in the period of the 1906 earthquake." Booklist

The turquoise mask. Doubleday 1974 323p o.p.

"Amanda Austin has lived with her widowed father from the time she was five years old. She was brought up in New England and in ignorance of her mother's death 'from a fall.' Her grandfather, Juan Cordova, lives near Santa Fe and has written to her asking her to come there to visit him before he dies. She finds the Cordova hacienda surrounded by adobe walls and full of a bewildering tension and of relatives—her mother was Dorotea Cordova—who all want her to leave as soon as possible. The Cordovas also own a large store, Cordova, in Santa Fe, which is almost half museum for the artifacts which Juan Cordova collects and Gavin Bran, his son-in-law, manages. Amanda is terrified but resolute in her determination to remain even in a hostile atmosphere until she can clear up the cause of her mother's death." Best Sellers

Window on the square. Appleton-Century-Crofts 1962 313p o.p. Amereon reprint available $21.95 (ISBN 0-8488-0085-0)

"When Meegan Kincaid is summoned to the Washington Square home of rich Mr. Brandon Reid, she discovers that the Reids are not looking for a seamstress but want her to see what she can do with Jeremy, a difficult, moody boy of nine. Meegan senses the unhappiness that pervades the house and slowly discovers some

Whitney, Phyllis A., 1903——*Continued*
of the reasons for it. Jeremy is supposed to have willfully shot his father and, after a surprisingly short interval, his mother had married the dead husband's brother. Further to complicate matters, Meegan falls in love with Brandon Reid and makes an implacable enemy of Mrs. Reid's old servant." SLJ

Woman without a past. Doubleday 1991 302p o.p.

LC 90-3860

Available G.K. Hall large print edition

Molly Hunt "is a budding young star in the world of suspense fiction, yet her psyche is still wounded from the sudden, violent death of her husband. A chance meeting in her publisher's office is the incident that sweeps Molly physically into the Old South ambience of Charleston, South Carolina, and emotionally onto a trail that leads to the discovery of the truth about her parentage and her place within the Mountfort family." Booklist

The author "combines a dynamic, likable heroine with eccentric characters, romantic entanglements, family ghosts and a charming setting." Publ Wkly

Wibberley, Leonard, 1915-1983

The mouse that roared. Little, Brown 1955 279p o.p.

Available from Amereon and Buccaneer Bks.

"The 'Tiny Twenty' overtake the major powers of the world after plotting a bold maneuver to steal the atomic secrets of the United States. Centuries of industrialization and sophistication separate the tiny European nation from the enraged larger countries, who must acquiesce to the will of the former. Underneath this lighthearted tale is a serious warning about the dangers of nuclear power." Shapiro. Fic for Youth. 3d edition

Wideman, John Edgar

Philadelphia fire; a novel. Holt & Co. 1990 199p o.p.

LC 90-30590

This novel "is, as the title reflects, centered on the 1985 destruction of the Philadelphia headquarters of an organization called MOVE. The narrator is a black American who has removed himself from his homeland and taken refuge from the cares of life on an easygoing island in the Aegean. Nevertheless, when news of the MOVE incident reaches him, he becomes obsessed with its meaning—to him personally, to black Americans in general." Booklist

"Wideman is best when he is most personal. . . . By turns brilliant and murky, seamless and ragged, Philadelphia Fire is on to something big. Wideman's vision of racism in the U.S. suggests nothing less than a genetic disorder present at the birth of the nation." Time

The stories of John Edgar Wideman. Pantheon Bks. 1992 432p $25

ISBN 0-679-40719-7   LC 91-50839

Analyzed in Short story index

Contents: All stories are true; Casa Grande; Backseat; Loon man; Everybody knew Bubba Riff; Signs; What he saw; A voice foretold; Newborn thrown in trash and dies; Welcome; Doc's story; The Statue of Liberty; Valaida; Hostages; Surfiction; Rock River; When it's time to go; Concert; Presents; The tambourine lady; Little Brother; Fever; Damballah; Daddy Garbage; Lizabeth: the

caterpillar story; Hazel; The Chinaman; The watermelon story; The songs of Reba Love Jackson; Across the wide Missouri; Rashad; Tommy; Solitary; The beginning of Homewood

"The 25 stories pulled together here demonstrate [the author's] eloquence in picturing various elements in the constant friction between black and white societies in the U.S. Family and place are, thus, two prominent themes. He writes lushly, beautifully, yet loudly as well; his voice is deep, rich, booming." Booklist

Wiesel, Elie, 1928-

The accident

In Wiesel, E. Night, Dawn, The accident: three tales p205-318

A beggar in Jerusalem; a novel; translated from the French by Lily Edelman and the author. Random House 1970 211p o.p.

Original French edition, 1969

"This novel consists of the stories of the characters who have gathered at the Wailing Wall in Jerusalem. A 'beggar' named David loiters and waits, in the aftermath of the Six-Day War, in the company of . . . [a] crew of 'beggars.' . . . He is waiting—or passively searching—for his friend Katriel, who has died in the fighting, and for Katriel's widow, Malka. At the same time the 'beggar' is certainly no beggar; his name may not be David. . . . The war is not only the Six-Day War—it is every action in which the Jews have been threatened with destruction. And Katriel may not be dead at all." Book World

"Reading Elie Wiesel is not an easy experience. It is certainly by no means an act of escape, the traditional function of literary entertainment. His works touch all of one's fibers. . . . After we have listened to what Wiesel has to say, other literature seems meaningless." Saturday Rev

Dawn; translated from the French by Frances Frenaye. Hill & Wang 1961 89p o.p.

Original French edition, 1960

"Elisha, a young Jewish terrorist fighting for the creation of Israel in the 1940s, is faced with an agonizing moral dilemma. He is to be the executioner of a British officer in reprisal for the hanging of a captured terrorist. A survivor of the concentration camps and a victim all of his life, Elisha considers whether he is any different from his oppressors if he can execute a helpless prisoner in cold blood." Shapiro. Fic for Youth. 3d edition

also in Wiesel, E. Night, Dawn, The accident: three tales p121-204

The fifth son; a novel; translated from the French by Marion Wiesel. Summit Bks. 1985 220p o.p.

LC 84-24071

Original French edition, 1983

"The protagonist (and first-person narrator) is tormented by his father's silence about the past. From his father's friend, he discovers a terrible secret: he had an older brother who was brutally murdered by the Germans, and his father participated in the assassination of the 'Angel of Davarowsk,' the German officer who oversaw the destruction of their village. When it is revealed that the attempt failed and the man is now a respected

Wiesel, Elie, 1928——*Continued*
industrialist, the younger Tamiroff vows to complete the job." Libr J

"Wiesel, who remains a most eloquent spokesman for the strength of human beings in the midst of tragedy, has written a powerful and poetic novel." Booklist

The forgotten; translated by Stephen Becker. Summit Bks. 1992 237p o.p.

LC 91-46826

Original French edition, 1989

Holocaust "survivor Elhanan Rosenbaum, now living in New York and a distinguished professor with a psychiatric practice, is tragically losing his prodigious memory. While he can still remember, he creates a 'backup' by bequeathing to his son, Malkiel, his stories of the martyred death of his father in his Carpathian village (for whom his son is named); his teenage stint in the army and his return to a ghetto empty of Jews; his adventures in the underground partisan movement; and his love of Talia, the extraordinary woman who rescued him and who died giving birth to his only son." Libr J

"Mr. Wiesel is a writer of contention and his characters, even when affectionate, speak with a bitter music. The most loving—and the saddest—of these sounds occur in the dark duets between father and son, especially as Elhanan admits to Malkiel that he 'cannot recall the essential thing that I want so much to pass on to you.' Elhanan's faith, his temptation to faith . . . is as stunning as the loss he confronts." N Y Times Book Rev

The gates of the forest; translated from the French by Frances Frenaye. Holt, Rinehart & Winston 1966 226p o.p.

Original French edition, 1964

Gregor "a Jewish boy of seventeen survives, alone of his family, in a cave in Hungary. Briefly he takes refuge in a peasant village, then joins the partisans in the forest, and ultimately finds safety, but not peace in the United States. All the while he seeks, and discovers, himself." Atlantic

"A poetically written allegory about the abrasion of a man's innocence and integrity by fear, horror and forced compromise, and his despair of God's existence." Publ Wkly

The Golem; the story of a legend; as told by Elie Wiesel and illustrated by Mark Podwal; translated by Anne Borchardt. Summit Bks. 1983 105p il o.p.

LC 83-9304

"The Golem exists only to save his people, the Jews of sixteenth century Prague in this case, from the heinous, antisemitic acts of the gentile population. Mute, made of clay, and given life through the faith of Rabbi Yehuda Loew, the Golem goes about Prague in secret, uncovering the trumped up charges of the gentiles against individual members of the local community. Eventually, at the behest of the Rabbi, the Golem leaves. The narrator asks for his return, knowing the Golem's work is not done." Best Sellers

"This fable is eloquently presented through the combination of Wiesel's facile storytelling skills and Mark Podwal's evocative line drawings." Booklist

Night, Dawn, The accident: three tales. Hill & Wang 1972 318p o.p.

Originally published separately in French, 1958, 1960 and 1961 respectively; in English 1960, 1961 and 1962 respectively

The first three works of Elie Wiesel are brought together in this volume. Dawn is entered separately. Night is a memoir. The accident concerns a survivor of Auschwitz who, recovering from a near-fatal accident, questions the meaning of man's existence and purpose, and death

The oath; translated from the French by Marion Wiesel. Random House 1973 283p o.p.

"Azriel meets a young man attempting to commit suicide. Azriel tries to take the man's mind off his plight by interesting him in a story. It is the story of Kolvillag, where all Jews (but one) were killed on the merest pretext by those whose excuse was the charge of Christ-killers. All of the Jews, however, had taken an oath (of the title) never to tell how they suffered—a kind of weapon of silence against their persecutors. Azriel is now faced with breaking that vow to help save the would-be suicide's life. He tells the tale." America

A "powerful novel, interwoven with threads of Hasidic tales, cabalistic mysticism, Talmudic sayings, and pietistic folklore." Libr J

The testament; a novel; translated from the French by Marion Wiesel. Summit Bks. 1981 346p o.p.

LC 80-27251

Original French edition, 1980

"In modern-day Israel, awaiting his mother's arrival on a plane filled with Russian immigrants, [Grisha] reflects on his childhood and youth and rereads the 'testament of Paltiel Kossover,' a confession/autobiography written by his father in prison shortly before his execution in 1947. The manuscript (which was smuggled out by a stenographer) reveals an idealist dedicated to perfecting humanity, an innocent victim of the machinations of the Soviet regime." Libr J

"In none of Wiesel's earlier novels are the characters so earthy, so real, so finely chiseled, as in this one. Women advance more fully to center stage and play more dominant roles. . . . The almost photographic realism of the narrative gives it a cumulative power that is overwhelming." Christ Century

The town beyond the wall; translated from the French by Stephen Becker. New ed. Holt, Rinehart & Winston 1967 c1964 179p o.p.

Original French edition, 1962; this translation first published 1964 by Atheneum

"In his mid-thirties, Michael is a survivor of the concentration camp where his family perished. . . . Through the years a face has haunted Michael, an impassive face that merely looked on while the Jews in the town square were herded off to camp. Indifference is an attitude incomprehensible to Michael, and he is set upon returning to his birthplace in Hungary, an undertaking of considerable risk, to confront this man and humiliate him. With the aid of a friend he manages to return and find him; but Michael is then captured by the Russians and mistakenly accused as an agent. It is while resisting a torture which with perverse irony is called 'The Prayer' that Michael's past unfolds in episodic scenes." Saturday Rev

Wiesel, Elie, 1928-—_Continued_

"God-tormented, God-intoxicated, 'The Town beyond the Wall' is a fiction which refuses to be a novel in any usual sense. It is an exemplary tale such as people may in terror and hope tell one another. It is a legend—archaic, modern, timeless; a legend of an ascent from purgatory to possibility." Newsweek

Twilight; translated from the French by Marion Wiesel. Summit Bks. 1988 217p o.p.

LC 88-2634

Original French edition, 1987

"Raphael is a professor on sabbatical studying at an exclusive upstate New York asylum (the Mountain Clinic, which caters to patients whose 'schizophrenia is linked to Ancient History, to Biblical times'). Wiesel's portraits of these descendants of Adam (one actually believes himself to be Adam) bring a dark humor to this otherwise somber story. Raphael studies not only the patients and staff, but also his own past, reliving the effect of the Holocaust on his family, his own escape, and the loss of his savior, Pedro. . . . Raphael's guilt at having survived has begun to smother him, yet it is his struggle that prompts him to ask such probing questions about God, life, and death." Booklist

"Despite the Holocaust and its atrocities, so specially devised to destroy human life and dignity, we experience in Mr. Wiesel's novel how good the family is, how good people are. Utterly without sentimentality, he gives us a small but real measure of what the world's loss has been." N Y Times Book Rev

Wiggen, Henry W. _See_ Harris, Mark, 1922-

Wiggins, Marianne

John Dollar. Harper & Row 1989 214p o.p.

LC 88-45538

"Just after World War I, Charlotte Lewes, a 25-year-old schoolteacher raised on Kipling, is sent to Rangoon to instill British values in the children of English colonists. During a festive sailing expedition, a tidal wave strands her and seaman John Dollar on an island with eight schoolgirls." Libr J

"Writing with an impressive degree of control and sophistication, Marianne Wiggins investigates the ghastly processes which crush the marooned children. . . . The phenomenon that particularly fascinates Wiggins in the spiritual disintegration she depicts as the consequence of this spectacle is the growth of a parodic religion." London Rev Books

Wilcox, Collin

Dead center. Holt & Co. 1992 262p o.p.

LC 91-31076

In this Frank Hastings mystery "a series of powerful and wealthy men are shot to death on the street, the weapon the .22 favored by professional hitmen. The cops finally connect the victims as rather nasty members of the ultra-exclusive Rabelais Club. . . . Old scandals (a hooker's death covered up, a notorious high-stakes poker circle), heavy political and media pressure and glimpses (for us) of the killer's mind-set lead up to Hastings's harrowing, climactic confrontation with the murderer." Publ Wkly

A death before dying. Holt & Co. 1989 231p o.p.

LC 89-11213

"Sex as a near-death experience, performed in front of a video camera for the viewing pleasure of her lover, may provide Meredith Powell with a silver Mercedes and a Nob Hill condo, but it also has her afraid for her life. After confiding her fears to a childhood pal, San Francisco cop Frank Hastings, Meredith turns up dead, strangled and abandoned in the nighttime cold of Golden Gate Park." Booklist

Wilcox "creates suspense through a tightly knit narrative format that confines the novel's action to an 18-day span and flashes short scenes before the reader much like a film montage. This is a smooth performance by a real professional." Publ Wkly

Except for the bones. Doherty Assocs. 1991 282p o.p.

LC 91-21579

"A TOR book"

"Detective Alan Bernhardt looks into the suspicious death of a New York real estate tycoon's latest girlfriend—a death secretly witnessed by the man's estranged stepdaughter in Cape Cod." Libr J

"Wilcox delivers a taut, suspenseful mystery with credible dialogue and good local color." Publ Wkly

Find her a grave. Forge 1993 288p $19.95

ISBN 0-312-85244-4   LC 93-26557

"A Tom Doherty Associates book"

"Alan Bernhardt is a San Francisco stage director who moonlights as a private eye. He's hired to help the illegitimate daughter of a late Mafia chieftain collect her inheritance, which is buried by the headstone of her mother's grave." Booklist

The author "gradually establishes an authentic mobster milieu, offering the required mix of brutality and honor." Publ Wkly

Hire a hangman. Holt & Co. 1991 248p o.p.

LC 90-40317

"Within the first 12 hours after three slugs ruin the arrogant features of ace surgeon Brice Hanchett, the list of suspects is long enough to stretch all the way up the steep hills from Fisherman's Wharf to the swank Russian Hill abode where the shooting occurred. San Francisco cop Frank Hastings scrapes away the surface glamour—the Jaguars and the wood-panelled interiors—and quickly gets to the dirt. . . . Wilcox gets compared with Hammett a lot—and deservedly so. He mines the noir angles of the city with the same restless eye, and his skin-tight plots make the same sudden jumps from the gutter to the high hills and back again." Booklist

Switchback. Holt & Co. 1993 256p $19.95

ISBN 0-8050-2104-3   LC 93-18197

San Francisco's Lt. Frank Hastings "pursues the murderer of a beautiful but selfish young woman who revelled in controlling others. Hastings questions both Haight-Ashbury acquaintances and Nob Hill lovers; meanwhile, constant erotic tension flows from the mutual attraction between Hastings (who lives with divorcée Ann) and bunco squad cop Janet. Wilcox's practiced hand lends a deft descriptive touch, whether to setting, plot or character: add this to the better police procedurals list." Libr J

Wilde, Oscar, 1854-1900

The picture of Dorian Gray. Modern Lib. 1985 248p $9.95

ISBN 0-394-60514-4 LC 84-25541

Also available from Buccaneer Bks.

First published 1891 in the United Kingdom; first United States edition published 1895 by G. Munro's Sons

"An archetypal tale of a young man who purchases eternal youth at the expense of his soul, the novel was a romantic exposition of Wilde's Aestheticism. Dorian Gray is a wealthy Englishman who gradually sinks into a life of dissipation and crime. Despite his unhealthy behavior, his physical appearance remains youthful and unmarked by dissolution. Instead, a portrait of himself catalogues every evil deed by turning his once handsome features into a hideous mask." Merriam-Webster's Ency of Lit

Wilder, Thornton, 1897-1975

The bridge of San Luis Rey; illustrated by Amy Drevenstedt. Boni, A.C. 1967 c1927 235p il o.p. Buccaneer Bks. reprint available $22.95 (ISBN 0-89966-853-4)

"On Friday, July 20, 1714, high in the Andes of Peru, the famous bridge of San Luis Rey collapsed, killing the five people who were crossing it. A priest who was witness to the event decided that the tragedy provided the chance to prove the wisdom of God in that instance, and thereafter spent years investigating the lives of the people who had been killed." Shapiro. Fic for Youth. 3d edition

The eighth day. Harper & Row 1967 435p o.p. Amereon reprint available $24.95 (ISBN 0-8488-0669-7)

"A chronicle of two early 20th-century Midwestern families and their involvement in a murder case raising serious questions about human nature." Oxford Companion to Am Lit. 5th edition

Wilder "offers the reader no certainty, but he does inspire a beautiful sense of human possibilities. He does not deny the existence of evil . . . but he believes that for some people in some places in some times life can be satisfying." Saturday Rev

The ides of March. Harper 1948 246p o.p. Buccaneer Bks. reprint available $24.95 (ISBN 1-56849-445-9)

This novel offers "divergent views of Caesar's last months seen through letters and documents." Oxford Companion to Am Lit. 5th edition

Theophilus North. Harper & Row 1973 374p o.p.

"A Cass Canfield book"

"In the summer of 1926, a 30-year-old teacher named Theophilus North comes to Newport, R.I., to tutor the children of the fashionably rich and to read out loud. . . . In Newport he discovers nine separate cities differing in age and social class. In these stories of which this novel is composed, North marches through them all—careers and cities—healing the sick, repairing marriages, rescuing a damsel from injustice, restoring life and health to the old and frail, and freedom to the confined." Newsweek

Wilhelm, Kate

And the angels sing; stories. St. Martin's Press 1992 260p o.p.

LC 91-39003

Analyzed in Short story index

Contents: The look alike; O homo; O femina; O tempora; The chosen; On the road to Honeyville; The great doors of silence; The day of the sharks; The loiterer; The scream; Strangeness, charm and spin; The dragon seed; Forever yours, Anna; And the angels sing

"Positioned on the border between fantasy and mainstream fiction, these 12 stories provide pleasure and provoke thought by undermining the reader's expectations at every turn." N Y Times Book Rev

The best defense. St. Martin's Press 1994 342p $21.95

ISBN 0-312-10937-7 LC 94-2039

"Attorney Barbara Holloway, introduced in Death Qualified, here defends Paula Kennerman, a battered wife accused of killing her daughter and burning down the safe house in which they had been sheltered. . . . The Holloways' crack team of private investigators assures that important clues are developed in time to use as evidence as Barbara skillfully conducts the defense in a suspenseful trial. The ambitious plot-subplot net threads together abortion rights, antifeminist backlash, and the inequities of legal aid for rich and poor." Libr J

Crazy time. St. Martin's Press 1988 248p o.p.

LC 87-27480

This "novel revolves around Lauren Steele, a Seattle psychologist beset by feelings of inadequacy. When a spectacular laser weapon is tested nearby, Lauren's worries begin to seem insignificant in the face of some far more baffling and profound concerns. First a man beside her suddenly is engulfed by a glowing blue aura and disappears. Then, even more mysteriously, this stranger reappears and attempts to communicate with Lauren. Soon the bewildered psychologist finds herself accused of being a spy by a neurotic colonel who is in charge of testing the laser weapon." Booklist

The dark door. St. Martin's Press 1988 248p o.p.

LC 88-14777

"A private investigator follows the trail of a serial arsonist only to find himself allied with his prey in an effort to destroy an unearthly device that spreads insanity in its wake." Libr J

"Wilhelm is in top form as the thriller plot races along while characters teeter over an abyss of insanity and loss." Publ Wkly

Death qualified; a mystery of chaos. St. Martin's Press 1991 438p o.p.

LC 90-27504

"Nell Kendricks is charged with murdering her estranged husband, Lucas, who disappeared years ago while working on a top-secret experiment attempting to use chaos theory to change the observer's perception of the universe. Now it appears that Lucas had spent the intervening years drugged and amnesiac, a handyman at the university where the studies had taken place. Attorney Barbara Holloway, who is 'death qualified' (i.e., legally permitted to act in capital cases), agrees to defend Nell, despite having left the profession, disillusioned by its practices." Publ Wkly

Wilhelm, Kate—*Continued*

"It is difficult to describe the novel's many dimensions, ranging from tense courtroom scenes to the almost fantastic descriptions of the scientific study. Most astonishing is the author's ability to peel off one layer after another, revealing new ways of looking at the same facts." Libr J

The Hamlet trap. St. Martin's Press 1987 234p o.p.

LC 87-16368

"Ashland, Oregon, home of the Oregon Shakespearean Festival, provides the setting for this [mystery]. . . . The action centers on the fictional Harley Theatre, a repertory group coexisting in Ashland with the more famous Shakespeare company. When a new director arrives on the scene and selects a controversial winner in a new-playwright's contest, trouble brews. Soon corpses dot the tranquil southern Oregon community, and the niece of the theater's owner is about to be indicted for murder. To the rescue comes an engaging pair of sleuths—ex-cop Charlie Meiklejohn and his psychologist wife Constance Leidl." Booklist

This "is a psychological mystery, and a classic murder puzzle as well. Constance and Charlie are a loving couple and skillful detectives; good company for one another and for the reader." Wilson Libr Bull

Juniper time; a novel. Harper & Row 1979 280p o.p.

LC 78-2247

"The world of the near future is on the brink of war because of worldwide drought and depression, and a message that may be from aliens offers the only hope. . . . Cluny has devoted his life to reviving the space station project which had been killed by the depression. Jean blamed the station for her father's death and made linguistics her career. But destiny reunites these former childhood friends when Cluny asks Jean's help in authenticating an apparently alien scroll found in orbit near the station, and Jean decides to take responsibility for shaping history with her conclusions. This is a SF novel of rare depth." Publ Wkly

Justice for some. St. Martin's Press 1993 260p $18.95

ISBN 0-312-09319-5   LC 93-15046

"Heading for a family gathering at her father's home/water garden business in rural California, widowed Sarah Drexler anticipates a respite from her work as an Oregon state judge. Instead she finds her deductive skills challenged and the lives of those dearest to her threatened. Joining the tense family dinner is Fran Donatio, a woman whose presence Sarah's father Ralph does not explain. The next morning, after Ralph's body is pulled from a lily pond, police Lt. Arthur Fernandez arrives with questions on another matter. . . . This tale . . . offers a bonus in Fernandez who, running his own, equally intelligent investigation in the background, provides a welcome change from the expected solitary-sleuth plot structure." Publ Wkly

Sweet, sweet poison. St. Martin's Press 1990 262p o.p.

LC 89-77847

The first victim in this "mystery is a watchdog named Sadie, owned by Al and Sylvie Zukal, two likable, spectacularly vulgar *kvetches* from the Bronx who invested some recent lottery winnings in a rural estate in Spen-

der's Ferry, N.Y. After the Zukals' young friend David dies, the well-oiled, older detective team of Charlie Meiklejohn and Constance Leidl . . . begins to question the conclusions of the local sheriff, who labels these and additional inventive killings—by poison, drugs, bees and gas—accident or suicide." Publ Wkly

Wilhelm "offers studied prose, an almost too heavy dose of local color, and tightly knit plotting in a novel that isn't like most mysteries. Here, hidden fantasies emerge from the subtext, and narrative detours that would lose most crime writers are handled adroitly." Booklist

Welcome, chaos. Houghton Mifflin 1983 285p o.p.

LC 83-6181

An expanded version of the author's novella The winter beach, published 1981 in the collection Listen, listen

"A serum that immunizes against all disease and stops aging is kept secret by a group of scientists because many people cannot survive the initial administration. Their hopes of increasing its success rate and overcoming the sterility that is its main side effect are dashed when the world comes to the brink of nuclear war because the Soviet government apparently has the secret, and they must decide whether to make public what they know. A gripping account of individuals wrestling with a novel moral dilemma; excellent characterization." Anatomy of Wonder 4

Where late the sweet birds sang. Harper & Row 1976 251p o.p.

"Pollution and pestilence are the consequences of a war that destroys most of the earth and its inhabitants. The elder Sumners have created a scientific research center whose goal is to perfect a technique for cloning since, among the other results of the world disaster, men and women have become sterile. The younger Sumners are victimized by these clones, who perpetuate the form of humans but have no humaneness or humanity." Shapiro. Fic for Youth. 3d edition

also in Modern classic short novels of science fiction p373-414

Williams, Ben Ames, 1889-1953

House divided. Houghton Mifflin 1947 1514p o.p.

"A long narrative about the American Civil War and its effect on the Currain family. As an old Virginia family with plantations in Virgina, and North and South Carolina, and houses in Richmond, the Currains were loyal to the Confederate cause and felt the full impact of the war. General James Longstreet is introduced as a friend of the Currains and his activities and the battles in which he took part are followed in considerable detail. An alleged relationship between the Currains and Abraham Lincoln adds . . . to a story that, in spite of its length, does not flag in interest." Booklist

Followed by The unconquered

Leave her to heaven. Houghton Mifflin 1944 429p o.p. Buccaneer Bks. reprint available $27.95 (ISBN 0-89966-257-9)

A psychological novel in which the character of a despicable woman is the motivating force. Ellen Berent began her psychopathic possessiveness while she was still a baby. The object of her affection was her father. After his death she successfully pursued a man who resembled

Williams, Ben Ames, 1889-1953—*Continued*
her father, married him, and proceeded to ruin his life.
Even after her suicide, which she arranged to resemble
a murder, her evil influence was still felt

The unconquered. Houghton Mifflin 1953
689p o.p.

This continuation of House divided "apportions interest
between the affairs of the Currain family after the Civil
War and a picture of Reconstruction in Louisiana from
1965 through 1874. Trav Currain is forced out of his
beloved eastern plantations and joins in a cottonseed oil
enterprise in New Orleans. Here the family is caught
up in the political and social strife of Reconstruction
that is only in small part alleviated by the temperance
and constructiveness of men like Trav Currain, General
Longstreet, and the Yankee from Maine who marries
Lucy Currain." Booklist

Williams, John Alfred, 1925-
The man who cried I am; a novel; by
John A. Williams. Little, Brown 1967 403p
o.p.

This novel consists of the "autobiographical recollections of a dying black author in the U.S. and Europe."
Oxford Companion to Am Lit. 5th edition

Williams, Tennessee, 1911-1983
Collected stories; with an introduction by
Gore Vidal. New Directions 1985 xxv, 574p
o.p.

LC 85-10642

Analyzed in Short story index
Contents: The angel in the alcove; Chronicle of a
demise; Completed; Desire and the black masseur; Field
of blue children; "Grand"; Happy August the Tenth; The
important thing; The inventory at Fontana Bella; The
killer chicken and the closet queen; The kingdom of
earth; The knightly quest; The malediction; Mama's old
stucco house; Man bring this up road; The mattress by
the tomato patch; Miss Coynte of Greene; The mysteries
of the Joy Rio; The night of the Iguana; One arm;
Oriflamme; The poet; Portrait of a girl in glass; Resemblance between a violin case and a coffin; Sabbatha and
solitude; Three players of a summer game; Two on a
party; The vengence of Nitocris; The vine; The yellow
bird; A lady's beaded bag; Something by Tolstoi; Big
Black; A Mississippi idyll; The accent of a coming foot;
Twenty-seven wagons full of cotton; Sand; Ten minute
stop; Gift of an apple; In memory of an aristocrat; The
dark room; The interval; Tent worms; Something about
him; Rubio y Morena; The coming of something to
Widow Holly; Hard candy; A recluse and his guest; Das
Wasser ist Kalt; Mother Yaws

The Roman spring of Mrs. Stone. New
Directions 1950 148p o.p. Buccaneer Bks.
reprint available $27.95 (ISBN
1-56849-360-6)

A wealthy widowed American ex-actress is the heroine
of this short novel. At fifty Mrs. Stone is losing her
beauty, her stage career is ended, and she finds herself
just 'drifting' through an aimless existence in Rome.
When an unscrupulous countess introduces a handsome
young gigolo to Mrs. Stone it is the beginning of the
end

"There are many superb moments, scenes which move
with a dramatist's ease. There is a hard candor about
Mrs. Stone, about all people who fail at real living and
attempt a life of fantasy and fail at that, leaving them
vulnerable to annihilation. . . . This different version
of Mr. Williams' repeated theme has resulted in a sharp,
witty and moving novel." Chicago Sunday Trib

Williams, Thomas Lanier *See* Williams, Tennessee, 1911-1983

Williamson, Jack, 1908-
(jt. auth) Pohl, F. Land's end

Willis, Connie
Death on the Nile
In Nebula awards 29 p142-66

Willocks, Tim
Green river rising; a novel. Morrow 1994
359p $23

ISBN 0-688-13571-4   LC 94-8730

This novel focuses on "an uprising at a state penitentiary in Texas. . . . [The warden] Hobbes plants the
seeds for the uprising by manipulating existing racial and
sexual tensions and then ordering a total lockdown of
the cellblocks." Libr J
"The story is violent, horrifying, and gut-wrenching,
describing a prison riot that's part Dante's Inferno, part
Stephen King horror novel. . . . This book is not for
the squeamish, the sensitive, or those who are easily
offended by four-letter words." Booklist

Wilson, A. N. (Andrew Norman), 1950-
Love unknown. Viking 1987 c1986 202p
o.p.

LC 86-40511

First published 1986 in the United Kingdom
A novel about "three women and one man whose lives
intersect at several points in the past and present. The
three women, who shared a flat in their younger days,
have pursued distinct paths in careers and marriages but
have also kept in touch with one another sporadically.
When two of the group embark on a tour of Fontainebleau, they unexpectedly run into the husband of
the third woman, but he is caught in the company of
a fourth, much younger woman. The stage is set for
Wilson's examination of human wiles and follies." Booklist
"Mr. Wilson's title vibrates with irony. Most of his
characters don't know the dimensions of love while
imagining themselves at the center of it. . . . When we
love, says A. N. Wilson, we love in ignorance. We cannot control love. We endure it. Bitter news, if news it
is, but brilliantly delivered in 'Love Unknown.'" N Y
Times Book Rev

The vicar of sorrows. Norton 1994 c1993
391p $23

ISBN 0-393-03610-3   LC 93-11538

First published 1993 in the United Kingdom
"The longtime vicar of Ditcham, Francis Kreer, has
a nervous breakdown after the death of his mother, who,
without explanation, has left half of his rightful in-

Wilson, A. N. (Andrew Norman), 1950-—
Continued

heritance to her former lover, whom Francis has never met. In a rapid descent into despair, Francis falls in love with a beautiful young vagabond, devastating his dimwitted wife and adolescent daughter. What's more, a sexually frustrated member of his congregation accuses Francis of poking her lasciviously with a broom, among other prurient offenses." N Y Times Book Rev

"Mr. Wilson is a brilliantly mordant observer of human types, of which this book offers a merciless catalogue." Natl Rev

Wilson, Andrew Norman *See* Wilson, A. N. (Andrew Norman), 1950-

Wilson, F. Paul (Francis Paul)
The select. Morrow 1994 333p $22

ISBN 0-688-04618-5   LC 93-22923

The select "are the 50 students who will be granted admission to the Ingraham College of Medicine, which is entirely funded by the Kleederman Foundation and completely subsidizes the lucky 50. . . . One of this year's finest prospects is Tim Brown, an aviator shades-wearing party animal who uses his eidetic memory to count cards at the blackjack table when he is not acing medical school exams. Tim helps the beautiful Quinn Cleary gain admittance by a small scam—it seems Ingraham isn't all that keen on women doctors. Together they discover that all is not what it seems in this '24-karat medical school.'" Libr J

Wilson, Francis Paul *See* Wilson, F. Paul (Francis Paul)

Wilson, John Anthony Burgess *See* Burgess, Anthony, 1917-1993

Wilson, Sloan, 1920-
The man in the gray flannel suit. Simon & Schuster 1955 304p o.p.

Available from Amereon and Buccaneer Bks.

The man of the title is the ordinary, upper middle class New York business employee, who at five o'clock heads for his home, wife, and children in Connecticut. Thomas Rath is his name in this book. Tom joins a large corporation, does an honest job, and is evidently headed for bigger money. As an undercurrent to his daily life Tom remembers his war service, the girl he met in Rome, and his illegitimate son

"Thoughtful, searching novel. . . . Sloan Wilson manages to hold the reader's interest and at the same time to solve Rath's problems without distorting his character." N Y Her Trib Books

Windling, Terri
(ed) Black thorn, white rose. See Black thorn, white rose

(ed) Snow white, blood red. See Snow white, blood red

(ed) The Year's best fantasy and horror. See The Year's best fantasy and horror

Winterson, Jeanette, 1959-
Written on the body. Knopf 1993 c1992 190p $20

ISBN 0-679-42117-X   LC 92-54475

First published 1992 in the United Kingdom

In this novel the "narrator, unnamed, sex undeclared, chronicles the arc of an affair with a married woman named Louise." N Y Times Book Rev

"The fascination is the lush, plush language and the way two aspects of the physical—passion and bodily decay—are delicately interwoven. Not to everyone's taste, but serious readers and sensualists will enjoy." Libr J

Winton, Tim
The riders. Scribner 1995 377p $23

ISBN 0-684-80296-1   LC 94-45375

"Fred Scully has gone to Ireland, where he is restoring a dilapidated cottage and waiting for Jennifer, his wife, and their seven-year-old daughter, Billie, to arrive from Australia. But on the appointed day, Billie arrives without her mother, too traumatized to explain what happened during their last stop at Heathrow. Thus begins a mad search through Greece, Italy, France, and Holland, always just missing the elusive Jennifer." Libr J

"Winton is a mesmerizing raconteur, and he infuses the narrative with throbbing energy and lyrically charged prose." Publ Wkly

Wishingrad, Jay
(ed) Legal fictions. See Legal fictions

Wodehouse, P. G. (Pelham Grenville), 1881-1975
The code of the Woosters. Doubleday, Doran 1938 298p o.p. Amereon reprint available $19.95 (ISBN 0-89190-291-0)

"It was only the fact that Jeeves belonged to an exclusive club of gentlemen's personal gentlemen, where all the secrets in the lives of employers were filed for reference, that saved Bertie Wooster when the disappearance of an eighteenth-century silver cows-creamer threatened to land him in jail. Two rival collectors who coveted the piece of silver, and two pairs of bickering lovers, made Bertie's life a burden until Jeeves unearthed evidence that was a weapon." Booklist

How right you are, Jeeves. Simon & Schuster 1960 183p o.p.

Available from Amereon and Buccaneer Bks.

"Foolishly accepting his Aunt Dahlia's invitation to a house party at her country place while the indispensable Jeeves is off on vacation, Bertie Wooster gets himself embroiled as usual. His entanglements, involving a former headmaster, an old school chum, an American heiress, and a masquerading psychiatrist, among others, have become positively labyrinthine before Jeeves rushes to the rescue." Booklist

The inimitable Jeeves. Autograph ed. British Bk. Centre 1956 192p o.p. Amereon reprint available $19.95 (ISBN 0-8488-0676-X)

First published 1923 in the United Kingdom

The resourceful valet again takes command of a typical Wodehouse situation

Wodehouse, P. G. (Pelham Grenville), 1881-1975—Continued

Jeeves and the tie that binds. Simon & Schuster 1971 189p o.p. Amereon reprint available $18.95 (ISBN 0-8488-0674-3)

"Bertie Wooster's reputation as a kleptomaniac, developed in previous adventures, appears confirmed as he seeks to aid an old pal who is standing for Parliament in Market Snodsbury. Aunt Dahlia, the good aunt, is there, and so is Bertie's former fiancée, Madeline Bassett, who thinks that 'the stars are God's daisy chain and that every time a fairy blows it's wee nose a baby is born.' A loutish lord and a renegade valet play the heavies." Newsweek

Tales from the Drones Club. International Polygonics 1991 352p $21.95

ISBN 1-55882-088-4 LC 91-8386

Analyzed in Short story index
First published 1982 in the United Kingdom
Contents: Fate; Tried in the furnace; Trouble down at Tudsleigh; The amazing hat mystery; Goodbye to all cats; The luck of the Stiffhams; Noblesse oblige; Uncle Fred flits by; The masked troubadour; All's well with Bingo; Bingo and the Peke crisis; The editor regrets; Sonny boy; The shadow passes; Bramley is so bracing; The fat of the land; The word in season; Leave it to Algy; Oofy, Freddie and the beef trust; Bingo bans the bomb; Stylish stouts

A Wodehouse bestiary; edited and with a preface by D.R. Bensen; foreword by Howard Phipps, Jr. Ticknor & Fields 1985 329p o.p.

LC 85-7999

Analyzed in Short story index
Contents: Unpleasantness at Bludleigh Court; Sir Roderick comes to lunch; Something squishy; Pig-Hoo-o-o-o-ey; Comrade Bingo; Monkey business; Jeeves and the impending doom; Open house; Ukridge's dog college; The story of Webster; The go-getter; Jeeves and the old school chum; Uncle Fred flits by; The mixer

"An anthology of tales featuring animals of all sorts wreaking havoc in the lives of Bertie Wooster, the indomitable Jeeves, Mr. Muliner's various relations, and other familiar characters from the madcap Wodehousian world. The numerous mishaps, involving snakes, pigs, gorillas, swans, dogs, and cats, prove as amusing as ever." Booklist

The world of Jeeves. Harper & Row 1988 c1967 654p o.p.

LC 88-45072

Analyzed in Short story index
First published 1967 in the United Kingdom
Contents: Jeeves takes charge; Jeeves in the springtime; Scoring off Jeeves; Sir Roderick comes to lunch; Aunt Agatha takes the count; The artistic career of Corky; Jeeves and Chump Cyril; Jeeves and the unbidden guest; Jeeves and the hard-boiled egg; The aunt and the sluggard; Comrade Bingo; The great sermon handicap; The purity of the turf; The metropolitan touch; The delayed exit of Claude and Eustace; Bingo and the little woman; The rummy affair of Old Biffy; Without the option; Fixing it for Freddie; Clustering round young Bingo; Jeeves and the impending doom; The inferiority complex of Old Sippy; Jeeves and the Yule-tide spirit; Jeeves and the song of songs; Episode of the dog Mcintosh; The spot of art; Jeeves and the kid Clementina; The love

that purifies; Jeeves and the old school chum; Indian summer of an uncle; The ordeal of young Tuppy; Bertie changes his mind; Jeeves makes an omelette; Jeeves and the greasy bird

Wodehouse, Pelham Grenville See Wodehouse, P. G. (Pelham Grenville), 1881-1975

Woiwode, Larry

Indian affairs; a novel. Atheneum Pubs. 1992 290p $20

ISBN 0-689-12155-5 LC 91-30540

Sequel to What I'm going to do, I think
This novel set in Michigan is, "in part, an anatomy of a marriage strained by the death of a baby and racial differences: Chris is a native American and Ellen a white Christian Scientist. They have returned to their home turf to stay in Ellen's grandparents' cabin so Chris can work on his dissertation about the Michigan poet Roethke in peace and quiet, but they get very little of either. . . . Both Chris and Ellen fall into depression. Chris is suffering an identity crisis over the conflict between his native American heritage and his academic pursuits, while Ellen decides to write about her grief over being childless." Booklist

"'Indian Affairs' is an intelligent, psychologically harrowing book." N Y Times Book Rev

What I'm going to do, I think; [by] L. Woiwode. Farrar, Straus & Giroux 1969 309p o.p.

"Ellen is beautiful and frightened; Chris is bright, nervous, alienated, and on the make. They meet at a campus party, have an on-again, off-again relationship that culminates after three years in Ellen's pregnancy and their decision to marry. Most of the story takes place during their honeymoon, during which they discover that their need to love each other is just not strong enough to forge the blissful union that they, in an uncompromising young way, have envisaged." Publ Wkly

Woiwode "has written a touching, sometimes deeply moving novel about youth growing up to the pain of loss, the puzzle of love, and the sense of despair lying near the surface of modern consciousness." N Y Times Book Rev

Followed by Indian affairs

Wolf, Christa

What remains

In Wolf, C. What remains and other stories

What remains and other stories; translated by Heike Schwarzbauer and Rick Takvorian. Farrar, Straus & Giroux 1993 295p $25

ISBN 0-374-28888-7 LC 92-27906

Analyzed in Short story index
Contents: Exchanging glances; Tuesday, September 27; June afternoon; Unter en Linden; The new life and opinions of a tomcat; A little outing to H.; Self-experiment; What remains [novella]

The title novella "takes place in Berlin, where the author lives, but because of its totalitarian framework, the time could be either the Nazi or the Communist

Wolf, Christa—*Continued*

era. It is a Kafkaesque tale, complete with a character called 'Colleague K.,' about a woman who is being watched by the police (now in synthetic parkas rather than leather coats) and how they, even without speaking to her, eventually unhinge her mind." N Y Times Book Rev

"Wolf dissects German society with a deadly blend of skilled accuracy, sure drama, and stinging humor." Booklist

Wolfe, Gene

Caldé of the long sun. TOR Bks. 1994 381p $22.95

ISBN 0-312-85583-4   LC 94-12915

"A Tom Doherty Associates book"
Sequel to Nightside the long sun (1993) and Lake of the long sun (1994)
The long sun volumes are "set on a vast spaceship known as the Whorl. The inhabitants, having forgotten their origins, think that the Whorl is the universe. Their lives are governed by a religion that deifies the creators of the spaceship, who have immortalized themselves as programs within the Whorl's main computer. In the first two volumes of the series, a young priest of this religion, Patera Silk, learns the truth about the Whorl, but he also has a vision of a god known as the Outsider who seems to transcend the Whorl itself. In the third volume, Silk and his allies confront the corrupt government of the city of Viron; drawn into the battle are some of the gods themselves." N Y Times Book Rev

"The author continues to prove himself one of the genre's most literate writers and luminescent thinkers." Libr J

Castleview. Doherty Assocs. 1990 278p o.p.

     LC 89-25712

"A TOR book"
"The inhabitants of the small town of Castleview, in a 'forgotten and countrified corner of upstate Illinois,' have grown accustomed to glimpsing a 'mirage' that resembles a medieval castle suspended in air. With the arrival in town of Will E. Shields, who has just bought a local automobile dealership, mysteries multiply like goose bumps. The town's hospital and funeral home fill with the victims of peculiar accidents, unsavory strangers knock on doors or peer through windows or suddenly appear on rainy highways riding horses with too many legs—and you just know Castleview is in for a major crisis." N Y Times Book Rev

Wolfe's "deceptively simple prose masks a wealth of complexity." Libr J

The Citadel of the Autarch. Timescape Bks. 1983 317p (Book of the new Sun, v4) $40

ISBN 0-671-45251-7   LC 82-5964

In this concluding volume of the tetralogy "Severian, the exiled torturer . . . attains the destiny hinted at since the first book and becomes the Autarch, 'who in one body is a thousand,' ruler of the Commonwealth and potential saviour of a dying Earth waiting for its reddened sun to go out." Publ Wkly

"Wolfe plays with the language like a master wordsmith, yet never loses control of the multi-layered story he's weaving. His style is paradoxically both baroque and simple—the lush beauty of the words never renders the tale impenetrable." Best Sellers

The claw of the conciliator. Timescape Bks. 1981 303p (Book of the new Sun, v2) o.p.

     LC 80-20569

In this second volume of the series "Severian, a journeyman torturer, struggles to return the magical Claw of the Conciliator to its guardians. His quest is delayed when men under the leadership of the bandit Vodalus capture him to prevent the execution of a comrade. Severian and his companion Jonas win their freedom by agreeing to carry a message to an agent of Vodalus' at the Castle Absolute, seat of power for the ruling Autarch. Severian has no intention of carrying the promise through, in spite of his admiration for Vodalus. His intention to find his lover and continue his personal quest suffers a temporary setback at the hands of Castle guards." West Coast Rev Books

Followed by The sword of the Lictor

The death of Doctor Island

In Modern classic short novels of science fiction p321-72

The shadow of the torturer. Simon & Schuster 1980 303p (Book of the new Sun, v1) o.p.

     LC 79-22371

"A TOR book"
A novel about "the experiences of Severian, a young man apprenticed to a legally sanctioned guild of torturers. . . . When Severian breaks the rules of the guild by allowing a 'client' to commit suicide, he is sent from his strange home, the only place he has known, on a journey through an inhospitable and dangerous world." Libr J

"The book combines elements of fantasy and sf, and the slow pacing is balanced by the excellent characterization and the richly detailed, thoroughly compelling future world." Booklist

Followed by The claw of the conciliator

The sword of the Lictor. Timescape Bks. 1981 302p (Book of the new Sun, v3) o.p.
     LC 81-9427

In this third volume of the series "Severian, the torturer demoted to executioner, has reached Thrax, city of his exile, only to find that he can no longer do his work. He lets a prisoner escape rather than kill her (his original crime was to offer a prisoner the escape of death) and flees to the mountains. He meets the Alzabo, a terrifying creature in whom those eaten seem to live on, adopts a son and loses him, fights a revivified tyrant of the past and wins, helps the people of the floating islands, meets aliens and learns something of their true nature. The magical jewel called the Claw of the Conciliator is smashed, but Severian finds its essential heart, which is indeed a claw." Publ Wkly

Followed by The Citadel of the Autarch

The Urth of the new sun. Doherty Assocs. 1987 372p o.p.

     LC 87-50478

"A TOR book"
This sequel to the four-volume Book of the New Sun continues "the story of Severian, a one-time torturers' apprentice who becomes Autarch and then leaves Urth to find the 'new sun' that alone can rejuvenate an exhausted humanity." N Y Times Book Rev

Wolfe, Gene—*Continued*

For all its obvious unity, the book also has a strongly picaresque quality, with many episodes and characters developed as lovingly and skillfully as Wolfe can manage—which is very well indeed." Booklist

Wolfe, Thomas, 1900-1938

The complete short stories of Thomas Wolfe; edited by Francis E. Skipp; foreword by James Dickey. Scribner 1987 xxix, 621p $27.50

ISBN 0-684-18743-4   LC 86-13782

Analyzed in Short story index

Contents: An angel on the porch; The train and the city; Death the proud brother; No door; The four lost men; Boom town; The sun and the rain; The house of the far and lost; Dark in the forest, strange as time; For professional appearance; The names of the nation; One of the girls in our party; Circus at dawn; His father's earth; Old Catawba; Arnold Pentland; The face of the war; Gulliver, the story of a tall man; In the park; Only the dead know Brooklyn; Polyphemus; The far and the near; The bums at sunset; The bell remembered; Fame and the poet; Return; Mr. Malone; Oktoberfest; 'E, a recollection; April, late April; The child by tiger; Katamoto; The lost boy; Chickamauga; The company; A prologue to America; Portrait of a literary critic; The birthday; A note on experts: Dexter Vespasian Joyner; Three o'clock; The winter of our discontent; The dark Messiah; The hollyhock sowers; Nebraska Crane; So this is man; The promise of America; The hollow men; The anatomy of loneliness; The lion at morning; The plumed knight; The newspaper; No cure for it; On leprechauns; The return of the prodigal; Old Man Rivers; Justice is blind; No more rivers; The Spanish letter

The good child's river; edited and with an introduction by Suzanne Stutman. University of N.C. Press 1991 292p $24.95

ISBN 0-8078-2002-4   LC 91-2946

"This book, a collection of chapters and fragments of an incomplete novel, was written during the last years of Wolfe's life. The central character, Esther Jack, is based on the life of Wolfe's lover, Aline Bernstein, a Jewish costume and set designer for the New York stage. Wolfe expands his focus to include stories about her family and friends." Libr J

"This rescued novel is a torrent of words, a whitewater ride through a magnificent canyon alternately sundazzled and cloud-shadowed. Wolfe has a mighty, exalted, and incantatory voice that seems to reach us from a much earlier, more potent time, an era long before our digital, humdrum, and packaged days. His stereotyping and excess may be offensive, but his genius for evocation cannot be denied." Booklist

"I have a thing to tell you"

In Wolfe, T. The short novels of Thomas Wolfe p236-78

Look homeward, angel; a story of the buried life; with an introduction by Maxwell E. Perkins. Scribner 563p $45

ISBN 0-684-15158-8

Also available from Buccaneer Bks.

First published 1929

This novel, autobiographical in character, "describes the childhood and youth of Eugene Gant in the town of Altamont, state of Catawba (said to be Asheville, North Carolina), as he grows up, becomes aware of the relations among his family, meets the eccentric people of the town, goes to college, discovers literature and ideas, has his first love affairs, and at last sets out alone on a mystic and romantic 'pilgrimage.'" Reader's Ency. 3d edition

Followed by Of time and the river

The lost boy; a novella; edited and with an introduction by James W. Clark, Jr.; illustrations by Ed Lindolf. University of N.C. Press 1992 81p il $19.95

ISBN 0-8078-2063-6   LC 92-53704

"A Chapel Hill book"

First published in abridged form 1937 in Redbook magazine

This "autobiographical novella explores the themes of time and remembrance that Wolfe later amplified in Look Homeward, Angel. . . . In part one, we visit a small North Carolina town through the account of young Grover. His mother, Eliza, narrates part two, describing her ill-fated son's behavior during a train trip to the St. Louis World's Fair. In the third section, a sister recalls the day when Grover contracted typhoid fever. Next, Grover's younger brother (the Wolfe character), fully grown, visits his childhood home. . . . *The Lost Boy* is a moving valediction and a sure-footed example of Wolfe's stylistic power." Publ Wkly

No door

In Wolfe, T. The short novels of Thomas Wolfe p158-231

Of time and the river; a legend of man's hunger in his youth. Scribner 912p $35

ISBN 0-684-14739-4

First published 1935

In this sequel to Look homeward, angel, "Eugene Gant, the hero, spends two years as a graduate student at Harvard, returns home for the dramatic death of his father, and teaches literature in New York City at the 'School for Utility Culture' (New York University). Eventually he tours France, returning home financially and emotionally exhausted." Reader's Ency. 3d edition

The party at Jack's

In Wolfe, T. The short novels of Thomas Wolfe p282-323

The portable Thomas Wolfe; edited by Maxwell Geismar. Viking 1946 712p o.p.

"Viking portable library"

Partially analyzed in Short story index

Contains episodes from four novels: Look homeward, angel; Of time and the river; The web and the rock; You can't go home again. Also six short stories: Face of the war; Only the dead know Brooklyn; Dark in the forest, strange as time; Circus at dawn; In the park; Chickamauga. Also includes the complete work, Story of a novel

A portrait of Bascom Hawke

In Wolfe, T. The short novels of Thomas Wolfe p4-71

Wolfe, Thomas, 1900-1938—*Continued*

The short novels of Thomas Wolfe; edited with an introduction and notes by C. Hugh Holman. Scribner xx, 323p $40

ISBN 0-684-14554-5
"Hudson River editions"
First published 1961
"Five short novels—'A Portrait of Bascom Hawke,' 'The Web of Earth,' 'No Door,' 'I Have a Thing to Tell You' and 'The Party at Jack's'—originally published in magazines [between 1932 and 1939], with an introduction and notes by the editor. Several of these were modified later and woven in Wolfe's long novels." N Y Her Trib Books

The web and the rock. Harper 1939 695p o.p.

This "is an autobiographical account of a successful young writer from North Carolina living in New York City in the early 20th century. The main character, George Webber, bears many similarities to Eugene Gant, the soul-searching protagonist of Wolfe's earlier novels." Merriam-Webster's Ency of Lit

"Wolfe's large scheme has the scope, massive detail and sense of space and time of an epic structure, but also the redundancy of its cyclic conception. The interest lies with the accurate dialogues, realistic descriptions and passages of poetic rhetoric sometimes of considerable power." Penguin Companion to Am Lit
Followed by You can't go home again

The web of earth

In Wolfe, T. The short novels of Thomas Wolfe p76-154

You can't go home again. Harper 1940 743p o.p.

Available from Amereon and Buccaneer Bks.

"In this sequel to 'The web and the rock,' George Webber, having returned from Europe, resumes his affair with Esther Jack and becomes a successful writer. He revisits his hometown and is disillusioned by what he sees, an episode said to parallel Wolfe's own experience in Asheville, North Carolina." Reader's Ency. 3d edition

Wolfe, Tom

The bonfire of the vanities. Farrar, Straus & Giroux 1987 659p $19.95

ISBN 0-374-11534-6   LC 87-17691

"The novel relates the fall of Sherman McCoy, an investment banker making a million a year who seems blind to everything except appearances, sex and money. He lives in the middle of New York City without knowing New York City. He seems barely to know his decorative wife, his decorative daughter or his libidinous mistress, to say nothing of himself. He's all surface is Sherman, and when he blunders off the expressway into the welfare jungle of the South Bronx in his $48,000 Mercedes, into the biggest trouble of his heretofore charmed life, he is without reserves of experience, imagination or moral awareness with which to guide himself." N Y Times Book Rev

"Erupting from the first line with noise, color, tension and immediacy, this immensely entertaining novel accurately mirrors a system that has broken down: from the social code of basic good manners to the fair practices of the law." Publ Wkly

Wolitzer, Hilma

Hearts. Farrar, Straus & Giroux 1980 342p o.p.

LC 80-18556

"Widowed at 26 after six weeks of marriage, Linda Reismann finds herself pregnant and saddled with her husband's 13-year-old daughter, whom she hardly knows. Robin, a perpetually sullen and hostile child who already looks like a woman, is her stepmother's natural antagonist. . . . Taking only what she can stow in the trunk of her car, Linda drives Robin west from New Jersey. She has three items on her agenda: an abortion, the surrender of Robin to her grandfather in Iowa, and her own new life in California. . . . Robin has her own agenda: to find and take revenge on her mother, who ran out on her when she was 5." Newsweek

"This is a comedy about the heart-wrenching process of growth; it is written with great skill and no condescension. Few readers will fail to be moved." New Repub

Tunnel of love. HarperCollins Pubs. 1994 376p $20

ISBN 0-06-118007-6   LC 93-51064

"Michael di Capua books"
"Linda Reismann is a 24-year-old widow, saddled with an unborn child and teenage Robin, the daughter of her former husband. She travels from Newark to Los Angeles looking for a new start. An aging liquor-store owner hires her, proposes marriage, then is shot by a robber. A Latino dance instructor helps her get work at an upscale aerobic salon, but he turns out to be married. Cynthia Sterling, a wealthy soap-opera producer, hires her as a personal trainer; she supplies incredible medical care and moral support in the aftermath of a terrible car accident (caused by Robin), then files suit for custody of Linda's baby, calling her an unfit mother." Booklist

"The reader is shocked at first by the similarities between this novel and an earlier one, 'Hearts.' . . . In fiction, however, as in nature, God resides in the details. Besides which, while Robin is almost a butterfly in parts of 'Hearts,' here she has advanced backward to become a great fat caterpillar, a gorgeous carbuncle on a solid and good-hearted novel." N Y Times Book Rev

Wolitzer, Meg, 1959-

Friends for life; a novel. Crown 1994 213p $20

ISBN 0-517-59586-9   LC 93-32353

"Three young girls innocently vow to stay friends forever, unaware of how difficult that vow is to keep. As they approach 'thirtysomething,' discontent over their lives—especially their love lives—grows. Meredith, the beautiful one, is having an affair with a married man. Lisa, the nice one, is a good doctor but a confused wife and mother. Ann, the smart one, becomes an enthusiastic lesbian. When their friendship is temporarily shattered, each woman has time to reflect on her emotional needs." Libr J

"While this plot is little more than adequate, Wolitzer repeatedly rises above predictability, crafting scenes that sparkle with wit and glow with the relief of being able to laugh at the ridiculousness of life." Booklist

Wolverton, Dave

The courtship of Princess Leia. Bantam Bks. 1994 327p (Star wars) $21.95

ISBN 0-553-08928-5   LC 93-20977

"Still at war with the Empire, the fledgling New Republic receives an offer of alliance with the 63 worlds of the Hapes Consortium, provided that Princess Leia will marry its heir, Prince Isolder. As Gen. Han Solo and Isolder fight a cosmic battle for Leia's heart, the discovery of a conspiracy of dark-force wielders lures Luke, Han, Leia, and Isolder to a rendezvous with danger on the mysterious planet Dathomir. Wolverton . . . is a vivid scene builder, capturing the cinematic flavor of the Star Wars universe while expanding on the outer reaches of the galaxy." Libr J

A Woman's eye; edited by Sara Paretsky. Delacorte Press 1991 448p o.p.

LC 90-28102

Available G.K. Hall large print edition

Analyzed in Short story index

Stories included are: Lucky dip, by L. Cody; Murder without a text, by A. Cross; The puppet, by D. S. Davis; Death and diamonds, by S. Dunlap; Getting to know you, by A. Fraser; Full circle, by S. Grafton; Her good name, by C. G. Hart; That summer at Quichiquois, by D. B. Hughes; Discards, by F. Kellerman; Deborah's judgement, by M. Maron; Benny's space, by M. Muller; Where are you, Monica?, by M. A. Oliver; Settled score, by S. Paretsky; The scar, by N. Pickard; A man's home, by S. Singer; Looking for Thelma, by G. Slovo; A match made in hell, by J. Smith; The cutting edge, by M. Wallace; Ghost station, by C. Wheat; Theft of the poet, by B. Wilson; Kill the man for me, by M. Wings

Wood, Barbara, 1947-

See also Harvey, Kathryn, 1947-

The dreaming; a novel of Australia. Random House 1991 453p $19.50

ISBN 0-394-56592-4   LC 90-52883

"After her parents tragic deaths in 1871, Joanna Drury leaves her native India for Australia, to unlock the secret past that haunted her mother, Lady Emily, and led to her mysterious, sudden death at age 40. In Melbourne, Joanna meets dashing and sensitive frontiersman Hugh Westbrook, and together they build Hugh's sheep station into a thriving enterprise, all the while looking for the source of the 'curse' on Joanna's family that took hold in an ancient time the aborigines call 'the dreaming.' . . . Wood's soft-edged prose, likable characters, and period details are always a big hit with her many fans." Booklist

Green City in the sun. Random House 1988 699p o.p.

LC 87-26527

This "saga takes readers into colorful turn-of-the-century Nairobi, the capital of Kenya and the 'Green City' of the book's title. The story opens in the present, with Dr. Deborah Treverton's return to her native Kenya at the behest of a dying African medicine woman whose curse on the Treverton family caused Deborah to leave Africa 15 years earlier. Now 33, Deborah has come back to learn the truth of her ancestry and to find the man she once planned to marry. Through flash-backs, we learn how Deborah's family came to live in East Africa; about her Aunt Grace's establishment of a medical mission in Kenya 68 years earlier; and about her father's sexual indiscretions and the resultant possibility that Deborah might be part black as well as the half-sister of her former lover." Booklist

"The author has obviously done extensive research into the history of Africa. The cultures, lifestyles and differing ideologies are portrayed with stark reality and a feeling of immediacy." West Coast Rev Books

Soul flame. Random House 1987 372p o.p.

LC 86-3893

"Selene, abandoned at birth in order to save her life and raised by a 'healer-woman,' follows her adoptive mother's craft and adds to it through run-ins with other healers throughout the first-century Roman world. Her other tutor is Andreas, a cynical, handsome Greek surgeon with whom she falls in love only to be separated from him and sent on years of travels." Booklist

The author "enriches this dramatic, unpredictable narrative with intriguing material about history, spirituality and the medical practices of antiquity." Publ Wkly

Virgins of paradise. Random House 1993 521p $22

ISBN 0-679-41579-3   LC 92-37356

"As young girls from the upper-class Rasheed family in Cairo, Jasmine and Camelia are carefully schooled in Egyptian ritual by their enigmatic grandmother. As they mature and break away from strict Muslim custom, their lives catapult them into irregular directions. To the family's horror Camelia becomes an exotic dancer. At the age of 16, Jasmine is married off to her cousin, who abuses her physically and psychologically. When he divorces her due to a rape scandal, Jasmine is banished and forced to leave her children behind. She pursues her dream of becoming a doctor and only returns to Cairo when mysteriously summoned by her grandmother." Libr J

"Lush and lavish fiction underscored by a fascinating history of contemporary Egypt." Booklist

Vital signs. Doubleday 1985 326p o.p.

LC 84-13639

"Three women share an apartment and their dreams in medical school in the late 1960s, each of them driven: Sondra by her suspected black ancestry, Ruth by the father she could never please, Mickey by the birthmark that scarred her psyche more than her face. Each has professional success and personal heartache in the 18-year span of the novel, Sondra working at a medical mission in Kenya, Ruth with a fertility clinic and a large family to juggle, and Mickey, her own scar eradicated, as a plastic surgeon to the rich and famous." Libr J

"Wood's expert knowledge of medicine and her deft interplay of plot and character make this a richly textured and quite credible story that is delightfully unpredictable from the first page through the last." Booklist

Wood, Ted

On the inside; a Reid Bennett mystery. Scribner 1990 277p o.p.

LC 89-70146

Wood, Ted—*Continued*

"Policeman Reid Bennett takes a job as constable in Elliot, a mining town in Ontario, in order to investigate allegations of police corruption there. Soon framed for theft and attempt[ed] murder, Bennett nevertheless bounces back to become sergeant when his accuser supposedly commits suicide." Libr J

Woods, Sara

Away with them to prison. St. Martin's Press 1985 222p o.p.

LC 85-1744

"The somewhat renegade British barrister Antony Maitland uses his dangerous dash to help his uncle, Sir Nicholas, solve an especially tricky mystery. A London news agent who failed to pay protection money is murdered, and the two investigating police officers are charged with covering up the evidence. The case turns into a legal snarl, with scared witnesses recanting their testimony. Woods' characteristic flair for combining the vagaries of English trial law with detective-story excitement is well in evidence here." Booklist

The lie direct. St. Martin's Press 1983 191p o.p.

LC 83-2982

London barrister/detective "Maitland agrees to defend John Ryder, on trial for treason, in spite of the overwhelming evidence against him. Dr. Boris Gollnow defects from Russia and identifies Ryder as the man who has been selling secrets to the Soviets. Winifred Paull, who claims Ryder has married her in a bigamous ceremony, confirms the identification and so do others. Only the accused's legal wife, Carol, and Antony believe in him. Maitland . . . turns detective and searches for proof of perjury by the witnesses for the prosecution. When Winifred is murdered and Carol is charged with that crime, the lawyer's problems magnify." Publ Wkly

Naked villainy. St. Martin's Press 1987 269p o.p.

LC 86-27925

This case featuring barrister-sleuth Antony Maitland, "begins with one of Maitland's friends telling him about cosmetics king Georges Letendre, who, while visiting her sister in London, found a photograph of her naked on an altar at the climactic moment of a Black Mass. Letendre is subsequently murdered, and Maitland is asked to defend the chief suspect, the dead man's son. Maitland delves deeply into the occult and financial chicanery before putting together a brilliant Old Bailey performance." Booklist

Woods, Stuart

Chiefs. Norton 1981 427p $14.95

ISBN 0-393-01461-4   LC 80-27350

"Set in the small town of Delano, Ga., the novel tells of three Delano police chiefs—a farmer, a sadistic racist and a black—who must deal with the same case: the disappearances and murders of a number of white, teenaged boys over the course of 40 years. The mystery—readers will discern the killer's identity quite early—is played against the South in transition as local politics acquire national prominence when the son of the first chief becomes a candidate for governor and is eyed by the JFK White House as a potential running mate in the reelection campaign." Publ Wkly

Dead eyes. HarperCollins Pubs. 1994 303p $22.95

ISBN 0-06-017715-2   LC 93-14221

Also available Thorndike Press large print edition

"Young Hollywood actress Chris Callaway is poised at the brink of stardom when her world collapses. Shortly after she begins receiving disquieting letters signed 'Admirer,' she is nearly blinded in a fall at the construction site of her new Malibu home. As Admirer becomes a menacing stalker, sending gifts and a gruesome photo and calling on the phone, Chris is stoutly guarded by her best friend and confidant, hairdresser Danny Devere. Also on duty is Beverly Hills police detective and stalker expert Jon Larsen. . . . Woods's style is lean and staccato, if unsubtle, and he's a pro at turning up the suspense." Publ Wkly

Grass roots; a novel. Simon & Schuster 1989 459p o.p.

LC 89-32198

Available G.K. Hall large print edition

"After years as chief of staff for a venerable Georgia senator, Will Lee decides to run for the seat himself when a stroke cripples his mentor. Standing in his way are an ambitious governor in the Democratic primary and, possibly, a far-right fundamentalist in the general election. In addition, Will must interrupt his campaign to serve as the defense lawyer in a controversial race-murder trial, while elsewhere, a dedicated ex-cop pursues the head of a Klan-like vigilante group that's been carrying out gangland-style killings." Publ Wkly

"A consummate storyteller, Woods . . . demonstrates his narrative ability by intertwining contemporary southern politics and the murder trial into a most satisfying tale." Libr J

Heat. HarperCollins Pubs. 1994 346p $23

ISBN 0-06-017776-4   LC 94-4175

Also available Thorndike Press large print edition

"Unjustly imprisoned, bereft of wife and daughter, ex-DEA agent Jesse Warden is offered a daring gamble: if he can infiltrate and destroy a heavily armed religious cult, he can win his freedom." Libr J

"Despite a few momentary lapses into banal predictability, Woods has concocted a high-octane story filled with nail-biting suspense and enough unusual twists to keep even experienced puzzle-solvers guessing." Booklist

Imperfect strangers. HarperCollins Pubs. 1995 269p $23

ISBN 0-06-017775-6   LC 94-34506

"Woods' 'imperfect' strangers meet on an airplane. Sandy Kinsolving is an attractive, well-dressed man of means. He's flying from London to New York because his father-in-law, who's bankrolled his lucrative wine-selling business, has just had a stroke. Sandy and his wife are far from close, and he's concerned that his father-in-law's death will have unpleasant financial consequences. His seatmate, Peter Martindale, also a well-dressed man of means, is a gallery owner based in San Francisco. It seems that he and his wife are also on the outs, and he, too, stands to lose his livelihood. . . . Peter proposes that they murder each other's wives. The trick here is to complicate matters, and Woods succeeds admirably." Booklist

L.A. Times; a novel. HarperCollins Pubs. 1993 329p $21

ISBN 0-06-017714-4   LC 92-54724

Also available Thorndike Press large print edition

Woods, Stuart—*Continued*

"Vincente Michaele Callabrese works as a shakedown artist for the mob in New York City's Little Italy, but moviegoing is his passion. Early in the story, he changes his name to Michael Vincent and makes a break for L.A., where with the help of powerful studio head Leo Goldman he fulfills his dream of becoming a big-time producer. Vincent's *cosa nostra* connections keep in touch, particularly old pal Tommy Provenzano whose rise to power in New York parallels Vincent's in Hollywood. Eventually, Vincent's desire to bring a gentle turn-of-the-century novel to the screen leads him to employ the sorts of techniques and friends that served him in his mafia days." Publ Wkly

New York dead. HarperCollins Pubs. 1991 303p o.p.

LC 90-56374

A mystery "set in Manhattan's Upper East Side, the stomping ground of Stone Barrington, a well-bred but unpretentious detective. . . . Late one evening, as Stone trudges home from Elaine's Restaurant, popular TV newscaster Sasha Nijinsky plummets 12 stories from her terrace and lands on a heap of dirt 20 yards away from him—remarkably, still alive. Stone fails to apprehend the person who flees Sasha's penthouse and, after the ambulance carrying her collides with a fire truck, Sasha herself disappears. Despite the fact that no corpse is in evidence, the baffled NYPD eagerly pins a murder rap on Sasha's distraught lesbian lover. Stone refuses to accept his colleagues' pat solution." Publ Wkly

Palindrome. Harper & Row 1991 344p o.p.

LC 90-55587

"When Liz Barwick is beaten nearly to death by her steroid-crazed husband, Baker Ramsey, a star NFL running back, she quickly divorces him, takes a large cash settlement and disappears from public view. Liz, whose book of sports photographs has just been released, takes advantage of her publisher's offer to live in his cottage on an isolated private island off the Georgia coast. But when Ramsey goes on a murderous rampage, Liz's lawyer and publisher and his wife are among his victims. Meanwhile other events are unfolding on Cumberland Island, where Liz becomes involved with the Drummond family." Publ Wkly

Santa Fe rules. HarperCollins Pubs. 1992 303p o.p.

LC 91-58476

Available Thorndike Press large print edition

"You're a rich, successful Hollywood producer who awakens the morning before Thanksgiving in your Santa Fe home with no memory of the previous night. Ignoring your dog's attempts to get you to visit the guest wing of the house, you leave and fly your private plane to Los Angeles. But you never get there: a breakdown forces you to spend the holiday isolated in a small airport town. When you finally see the newspaper the next day, you read that the bodies of your wife, your business partner and a third man—assumed to be you—have been found in the guest room of the Santa Fe residence. . . Wolf Willett decides to stay 'dead' for a while and finish work on his new film, then hires a top defense attorney and turns himself in." Publ Wkly

Under the lake. Simon & Schuster 1987 301p o.p.

LC 86-31632

"Years ago, in a deceptively quiet Southern town, a wealthy industrialist arranged for the construction of a man-made lake. . . . Now, though, things are stirring in Sutherland's lake; and with the arrival of two strangers, much that has been hidden from the light of day will be revealed. These out-of-towners are John Howell, whose career as an investigative journalist has degenerated so badly that he has accepted a job as a ghost-writer for a fried-chicken mogul, and Heather ('Scotty') MacDonald, an enthusiastic young reporter who has arrived undercover to investigate reports of police corruption." West Coast Rev Books

"Woods' straightforward recounting of the couple's eerie discoveries and dangerous exploits results in a gripping, plausible mystery/ghost story that concludes with suitably ironic twists." Booklist

Woodson, Jacqueline

Autobiography of a family photo; a novel. Dutton 1995 113p $17.95

ISBN 0-525-93721-8

LC 94-3639

Set in Brooklyn, Woodson's "novel is a coming-of-age story set in the Vietnam era, when the picture-perfect Brady Bunch set a national standard for the ideal family. Her heroine-narrator, a little African American girl, has another kind of family. She has an older brother who's a drag queen. Her younger, half-white half-brother is an endless reminder to her father of her mother's infidelity. Mother, who presses dolls on the less than enthusiastic narrator, plays Al Green records over and over and slowly waltzes with the broom, encased in her own world, wearing panties on her head when she can't find a scarf. Woodson brings the narrator to her mid-teens, poised on the brink of an awakening, struggling to come to terms with her sexuality, and literally screaming to leave her earlier life behind." Booklist

The novel "brims with complicated emotion and nuanced social observation; its prose percolates with rage and tenderness and lyricism." N Y Times Book Rev

Woolf, Virginia, 1882-1941

Between the acts. Harcourt Brace & Co. 1941 219p o.p.

This novel "describes a pageant on English history, written and directed by Miss La Trobe, and its effects on the people who watch it. Most of the audience misunderstand it in various ways; a clergyman reduces its vision to a sermon. But, for a moment, Woolf implies, the pageant—or art—has imposed order on the chaos of human life" Reader's Ency. 3d edition

The complete shorter fiction of Virginia Woolf; edited by Susan Dick. Harcourt Brace Jovanovich 1985 313p o.p.

Analyzed in Short story index

Contents: Phyllis and Rosamond; The mysterious case of Miss V.; The journal of Mistress Joan Martyn; Memoirs of a novelist; The mark on the wall; Kew Gardens; The evening party; Solid objects; Sympathy; An unwritten novel; A haunted house; A society; Monday or Tuesday; The string quartet; Blue & green; A woman's college from outside; In the orchard: Mrs. Dalloway in Bond Street; Nurse Lugton's curtain; The widow and the parrot: a true story; The new dress; Happiness; Ancestors; The introduction; Together and apart; The man who loved his kind; A simple melody; A summing up; Moments of being: 'Slater's pins have no points'; The lady in the looking-glass: a reflection; The fascination of the

Woolf, Virginia, 1882-1941—*Continued*

pool; Three pictures; Scenes from the life of a British naval officer; Miss Pryme; Ode written partly in prose on seeing the name of Cutbush above a butcher's shop in Pentonville; Portraits; Uncle Vanya; The Duchess and the jeweller; The shooting party; Lappin and Lapinova; The searchlight; Gipsy, the mongrel; The legacy; The symbol; The watering place

"Woolf's 46 short stories demonstrate her fondness for experimenting with narrative forms and voices. Arranged chronologically, the pieces range from tales with traditional plot lines to denser interior monologues, and enable the reader to appreciate Woolf's development as a writer of fiction." Publ Wkly

Jacob's room. Harcourt Brace & Co. 1923 303p o.p.

First published 1922 in the United Kingdom

"The life story, character, and friends of Jacob Flanders are presented in a series of separate scenes and moments. The story of this sensitive, promising young man carries him from his childhood, through college at Cambridge, love affairs in London, and travels in Greece, to his death in the war. At the end, instead of describing his death, Virginia Woolf describes his empty room." Reader's Ency. 3d edition

Mrs. Dalloway. Knopf 1993 xxviii, 219p $15

ISBN 0-679-42042-8   LC 92-54300

"Everyman's library"

A reissue of the title first published 1925 by Harcourt Brace & Co.

"In this stream-of-consciousness novel all action takes place on a single day. By probing the thoughts and memories of various characters, the author has encompassed several people's lives. Clarissa has a party planned for the evening and is thinking of her daughter's involvement with a religious fanatic. Also in her thoughts are old friends like Sally Seton, who drops by at the party, and Clarissa's former lover, Peter Walsh, who is drawn to Sally, much to Clarissa's chagrin. When a noted psychiatrist arrives late at the party because one of his patients, Septimus Smith, has committed suicide, Clarissa is affected, not because she knew the victim, but because suicide is tantamount to wastefulness." Shapiro. Fic for Youth. 3d edition

Orlando; a biography. Harcourt Brace & Co. 1928 333p il o.p.

"Orlando begins as a young Elizabethan nobleman and ends, three hundred years later, as a contemporary young woman, based on the author's friend Victoria Sackville-West. The novel contains a great deal of literary history and brilliant, ironic insights into the social history of the ages through which Orlando lives. Orlando starts life as a male poet and ends as an equally intense and able woman poet, in order to emphasize the author's belief that women are intellectually men's equals." Reader's Ency. 3d edition

To the lighthouse. Harcourt Brace & Co. 1927 310p

Available from various publishers

Arranged in three parts, the first "called 'The window,' describes a day during Mr. and Mrs. Ramsay's house party at their country home by the sea. Mr. Ramsay is a distinguished scholar . . . whose mind works rationally, heroically and rather icily. . . . The Ramsays have arranged to take a boat out to the lighthouse, the next morning, and their little son James is bitterly disap-

pointed when a change in weather makes it impossible. The second section, called 'Time passes' describes the seasons and the house, unused and decaying, in the years after Mrs. Ramsay's death. In the third section, The 'Lighthouse,' Mr. Ramsay and his freinds are back at the house. He takes the postponed trip to the lighthouse with his now 16-year-old son, who is at last able to communicate silently with him and forgive him for being different from his mother." Reader's Ency. 3d edition

The voyage out. Harcourt Brace & Co. 1920 375p o.p.

First published 1915 in the United Kingdom

"The story concerns a young woman of 24, Rachel Vinrace, an innocent, 'unlicked' girl who voyages to South America on board her father's ship, the *Euphrosyne*. Accompanying her are her aunt, Helen Ambrose, and uncle Ridley, together with an assortment of English characters whose social interaction is delicately observed. In South America Rachel meets a young Englishman, Terence Hewet, an aspiring writer working on his first novel. . . . He and Rachel fall in love and become engaged, determined to establish their future marriage on a new basis of equality. However, during an expedition Rachel contracts an unspecified disease and is confined to her bed with a fever. After a fortnight's illness she dies." Camb Guide to Lit in Engl

The waves. Harcourt Brace & Co. 1931 297p o.p. Smith, P. reprint available $19.75 (ISBN 0-8446-6078-7)

"Highly original, unconventional, and poetic, it describes the characters, lives, and relationships of six persons living in England. The book is composed of interior monologues, spoken by the six characters in rotation, and of interludes describing the ascent and descent of the sun, the rise and fall of the waves, and the passing of the seasons. These natural cycles symbolize the progress of time, which carries the individual from birth to death." Reader's Ency. 3d edition

The years. Harcourt Brace & Co. 1937 435p o.p.

This novel "traces the history of a family, opening in 1880 as the children of Colonel and Mrs. Pargiter, living together in a large Victorian London house (later described by one of them as 'Hell') wait for their mother's death and the freedom it will bring; it takes them through several carefully dated and documented sections to the 'Present Day' of 1936, and a large family reunion, where two generations gather." Oxford Companion to Engl Lit

Worboys, Anne

China silk. St. Martin's Press 1992 c1991 375p $21.95

ISBN 0-312-08156-1   LC 92-28380

First published 1991 in the United Kingdom

"Hellen North, a village-born girl, falls in love with dashing Oliver Marathon, whose position in the colonial government of Hong Kong beckons Hellen to leave her London home and journey east. Oliver's powerful uncle, the governor, who opposes the marriage, and the manipulative, self-serving George Curtain, who has other plans for Hellen, and the unlucky chain of events that follows all place nearly insurmountable obstacles in the path of the star-crossed lovers." Booklist

Worboys, Anne—*Continued*

"While Hellen is naive and immature and her impulsive behavior is the cause of many of the adventures that befall her, her character is well drawn, as are those of others she meets. The book is a page-turner." Libr J

Wouk, Herman, 1915-

The Caine mutiny; a novel of World War II. Doubleday 1951 494p $27.50

ISBN 0-385-04053-9

Also available from Buccaneer Bks.

"The old American mine sweeper 'Caine' patrols the Pacific during World War II. The action shifts from the bridge of the ship to the wardroom, and from scenes of petty tyranny on the part of the skipper to incidents of fierce action and heroism on the part of the men. Ensign Willie Keith is assigned to the ship and leads a mutiny against paranoid Captain Queeg, who is eventually brought to trial in a scene that poses the difficulty of weighing evidence to prove that the takeover by the men was justifiable." Shapiro. Fic for Youth. 3d edition

The city boy, the adventures of Herbie Bookbinder and his cousin Cliff; a novel. Simon & Schuster 1948 306p o.p.

"This somewhat autobiographical story recounts the adventures of an eleven-year-old boy from the Bronx named Herbie—small, fat, and likable—as he bounds through New York City public schools and summer camp in the Coolidge era. The author describes Herbie's campaigns against the adults in his life in a style that reviewers have called a mixture of Booth Tarkington and Sinclair Lewis." Shapiro. Fic for Youth. 3d edition

The hope; a novel. Little, Brown 1993 693p $24.95

ISBN 0-316-95519-1   LC 93-4427

This "novel covers Israel's history from the new state's first battle for survival in 1948 through its . . . victory in the Six-Day War of 1967." Libr J

"Readers familiar with Wouk's historical novels of World War II . . . will recognize many of the same techniques at work here: solid historical research; a large canvas where fictional characters of Wouk's own invention rub shoulders with real-life historical figures, . . . and straightforward, old-fashioned story-telling that makes it easy to follow the complicated maneuverings of soldiers, statesmen, diplomats, and other key players on the stage of history." Christ Sci Monit

Inside, outside; a novel. Little, Brown 1985 644p o.p.

LC 84-26087

This work focuses on "the Jewish-American experience through the life of one man. The story starts in Watergate-era Washington, where narrator I. David Goodkind, tax lawyer and former scriptwriter, is serving as a consultant to President Nixon. To fill the long hours in which he has nothing to do, Goodkind is scribing the story of his life and times. . . . [Through Goodkind's] eyes, we see his immigrant parents and their Russian origins, the Bronx neighborhoods where he grew up, and the assimilated Jews he met at Columbia." Libr J

"With great skill, Wouk moves between past and present, as he narrates. . . . The scenes in Israel with Goodkind as an unofficial White House emissary, and his meetings with Golda Meir, have an authenticity that

will be recognized by readers of Wouk's memorable World War II novels. Throughout these pages, one can see Wouk's mastery of the novelist's supreme art, the ability to relate social history to individual destiny." Natl Rev

Marjorie Morningstar. Doubleday 1955 565p o.p. Buccaneer Bks. reprint available $27.95 (ISBN 1-56849-559-5)

"The story of a middle-class Jewish girl who temporarily rejects her upbringing in her infatuation with the world of show business." Reader's Ency. 3d edition

War and remembrance; a novel. Little, Brown 1978 1042p $19.95

ISBN 0-316-95501-9   LC 78-17746

Sequel to The winds of war

This book "covers the events of 1941-1945. particularly as experienced by the fictional Henry family, Captain Victor ('Pug') Henry, continuing his remarkable naval career which brings him into contact with President Roosevelt and other historical luminaries, ends up an admiral. His marriage to Rhoda, however, finally comes undone for good and their oldest son, Warren, is killed at Midway. Byron, the Henrys' other son, eventually commands a submarine in the Pacific, but his Jewish wife, Natalie, their infant son, and her famous uncle, Aaron Jastow, are irresistibly sucked into the clutches of the Nazis." Libr J

Wouk's "work is a journey of extraordinary emotional riches. Quantity in time becomes quality, movement becomes scope, and history becomes human yearning." N Y Times Book Rev

The winds of war; a novel. Little, Brown 1971 885p $24.95

ISBN 0-316-95500-0

"On the broadest of tapestries, Wouk weaves the effect of the preparation and the actual outbreak of World War II upon the family of Commander 'Pug' Henry. The affairs of the Henry family became intertwined with those of others, in such varying scenes as Washington, Berlin, Rome, London, and Moscow. In Henry's progress toward a command of his own, he performs special missions for the President that bring about dramatic encounters with Hitler and Göring. But the great scenes of the novel are with F.D.R.. . . . Despite the novel's breadth, the development of Henry's character as the middle-class military leader America needed in the 1940's is surprisingly credible. And Wouk's development of such sensitive subjects as Roosevelt's maneuvering of American public opinion in preparation for the inevitable conflict displays great scholarship and perception." Choice

Followed by War and remembrance

Youngblood Hawke; a novel. Doubleday 1962 783p $21.95

ISBN 0-385-02974-8

A "story about an aspiring novelist named Arthur Youngblood Hawke. Hawke hails from the small coal-mining town of Hovey, Kentucky. From the age of 11, he has dreamed of the time when he will make his mark as a literary great. Upon leaving the Seabees, Hawke hikes to New York City with a completed war novel ready for market. The book is accepted by a successful publishing firm, and thus Artie Hawke's literary career pushes off to a fast start. It also marks the beginning of a lengthy passionate love affair with a wealthy mother of four children; a series of involved legal entanglements

Wouk, Herman, 1915——*Continued*

as a result of Hawke's obsession with money; and an unfulfilled romance with a pretty and intelligent young girl who edits Hawke's novels." Libr J

Wozencraft, Kim

Notes from the country club. Houghton Mifflin 1993 205p $19.95

ISBN 0-395-62892-X   LC 93-13007

"The 'country club' is actually a federal psychiatric prison for women. Cynthia Mitchell is being held there while doctors determine whether or not she's sane enough to stand trial for the murder of her husband. Cynthia was a successful public relations free-lancer living in New York when she met Daniel, a commercial pilot. He wooed her tenderly, installed her in his Texas home, and shattered her life. We learn the sickening particulars of his habitual beatings, rapes, and death threats in flashbacks, even as we see Cynthia learning to cope with her shock, fear, and grief, and figuring out how to survive in this weird little locked-up world of rules and restrictions." Booklist

Wren, P. C. (Percival Christopher), 1885-1941

Beau Geste. Lippincott 1927 579p o.p. Buccaneer Bks. reprint available $21.95 (ISBN 0-89966-489-X)

"A foreign-legion column comes upon a desert fortress manned entirely by dead men. One of the corpses, a sergeant, has apparently been bayoneted by one of his own men. A flashback unravels the mystery of the three English Geste brothers. They confess to jewel theft and enlist in the French Foreign Legion, which sends them to North Africa, where they encounter the tyrannical sergeant." Shapiro. Fic for Youth. 3d edition

Wren, Percival Christopher *See* Wren, P. C. (Percival Christopher), 1885-1941

Wright, Eric, 1929-

A body surrounded by water; an Inspector Charlie Salter mystery. Scribner 1987 166p o.p.

LC 87-20675

"Charlie is vacationing with his wife, Annie, and son, Angus, on Prince Edward Island, but things aren't going well: Charlie's inlaws live nearby; two of Annie's college friends are staying with them; Angus has a crush on one of them; and Charlie is getting crotchety without any crimes to solve. Happily, things brighten up when several break-ins occur on the waterfront property, and a local historian is murdered. Charlie has a busman's holiday sorting it all out." Booklist

Death in the old country; an Inspector Charlie Salter mystery. Scribner 1985 175p o.p.

LC 85-2395

"Wright mixes appropriate amounts of decent curiosity and quiet authority in the character of Insp. Charlie Salter, when the Canadian policeman and his wife vacation in an English village and encounter murder. While Annie takes in the tourist sites, Salter acts as visiting consultant to the local police. The banter between offi-

cials of the two countries adds entertainment to a well-executed plot." Barzun. Cat of Crime. Rev and enl edition

The man who changed his name; an Inspector Charlie Salter mystery. Scribner 1986 212p o.p.

LC 85-25080

"A former wife re-enters the Canadian Insp. Charlie Salter's life, bringing her old antagonisms against men in general and the police in particular. She demands that Charlie find out who killed a young acquaintance of hers, a social worker. The tale is perhaps too much a study in human relations to be a good piece of crime fiction, but the author's talents are in evidence as before." Barzun. Cat of Crime. Rev and enl edition

A question of murder. Scribner 1988 200p o.p.

LC 88-11380

Inspector Charlie Salter of the Toronto police "investigates a bombing that occurred within yards of the path of a visiting English princess. Was it a terrorist attempt, a drug-related killing, or a by-product of the friction between street peddlers and the now-upscale shops of Yorkville? Salter sorts it all out in this well-paced and admirably plotted novel. A surefire hit with Salter fans and an excellent recommendation for procedural buffs." Booklist

Wright, Jack R. *See* Harris, Mark, 1922-

Wright, Richard, 1908-1960

Eight men. World Pub. 1961 250p o.p.

Analyzed in Short story index

Contents: The man who was almost a man; The man who lived underground; Big black good man; The man who saw the flood; Man, God ain't like that . . .; The man who killed a shadow; The man who went to Chicago

Lawd today!

In Wright, R. Works

Native son. Harper & Brothers 1940 359p o.p.

Available G.K. Hall large print edition

"Bigger Thomas is black. He is driven by anger, hate, and frustration, which are born out of the poverty that has dominated his life. When he gets a job with the Daltons, a white family, he is confused by their behavior and misinterprets their patronizing friendship. Tragedy follows when he accidentally kills Mary Dalton and escalates when Bigger murders his black girlfriend, Bessie." Shapiro. Fic for Youth. 3d edition

also in Wright, R. Works

The outsider. Harper & Row 1953 440p o.p.

"Cross Damon, a black man who works in the Chicago post office, is caught in a subway accident but escapes without serious injury, though because of a mistaken identity his death is announced. He decides to take advantage of this error to start life anew and thus free himself of his entanglements with women and debts. He goes to New York to live under an assumed name and before long becomes enmeshed in the Communist party. By it he is used as a murderer, until he is himself killed

Wright, Richard, 1908-1960—*Continued*
by a Party member." Oxford Companion to Am Lit. 5th edition

also in Wright, R. Works

Uncle Tom's children. Harper & Row 1938 215p o.p. Borgo Press reprint available $23 (ISBN 0-8095-9070-0)

Analyzed in Short story index
Contents: The ethics of living Jim Crow; Big Boy leaves home; Down by the riverside; Long black song; Fire and cloud; Bright and morning star

also in Wright, R. Works

Works. Library of Am. 1991 2v set $70

ISBN 0-940450-75-5   LC 91-60540

This set contains the complete novels: Native son and The outsider; the story collection Uncle Tom's children (all entered separately); Wright's first novel Lawd today! published posthumously in 1963; and the memoir Black boy (American hunger)

Lawd today! recounts one day in the life of a black postal clerk in Depression era Chicago

Wurts, Janny
(jt. auth) Feist, R. E. Mistress of the empire
(jt. auth) Feist, R. E. Servant of the empire

Wylie, Philip, 1902-1971
(jt. auth) Balmer, E. When worlds collide

Y

Yarbro, Chelsea Quinn, 1942-
A candle for D'Artagnan; an historical horror novel, third in the Atta Olivia Clemens series. TOR Bks. 1989 485p $22.95

ISBN 0-312-93202-2   LC 89-5109

"A Tom Doherty Associates book"
Sequel to Crusader's torch
"This third and concluding volume of Yarbro's Atta Olivia Clemens series finishes the female vampire's career. It is set in seventeenth-century France, where Olivia arrives as part of the suite of Cardinal Mazarin. There she becomes involved in political intrigue (frequently bloody) and finds both the love of her life, the historical D'Artagnan, and a final release from her near-immortal vampire existence. The realism never becomes gratuitous, and there is a well-constructed (if sometimes slow-paced) story." Booklist

Crusader's torch. Doherty Assocs. 1988 459p o.p.

LC 88-4806

"A TOR horror book"
Sequel to A flame of Byzantium (1987)
Vampire Olivia Clemens is a "capable modern woman whose longevity beyond her own enlightened Roman era makes her a kind of time traveler. Her efforts here to return to Rome from Tyre (in what is now Lebanon) becomes an epic of frustration as bureaucrats and a rigid patriarchal society are complicated by the Third Crusade and the plague of the late 12th century. While she searches for a kindred sensibility to relieve her loneliness, Olivia must cope with a time of almost willful ignorance, when bathing is considered both unhealthy and unholy. Another of Yarbro's slowly revealed but rewarding historical tapestries." Publ Wkly

Followed by A candle for D'Artagnan

The **Year's** best fantasy. See The Year's best fantasy and horror

The **Year's** best fantasy and horror; 1st-8th annual collections; edited by Ellen Datlow and Terri Windling. St. Martin's Press 1988-1995 8v 1-3 o.p.; 4-6 ea $27.95; 7-8 ea $26.95

Partially analyzed in Short story index
First two annual compilations published with title: The Year's best fantasy
Each annual collection includes short stories, poems, and essays. The nonfiction sections cover such topics as trends in fantasy and horror publishing; fantasy and horror films, television and comics; nonprint media; and obituaries. Over the years contributors of stories have included Charles De Lint, Steve Rasnic Tem, Garry Kilworth, Angela Carter, Karel Capek, Isabel Allende, Terry Bisson, Jane Yolen, Thomas Ligotti and Clive Barker

The **Year's** best science fiction; 1st-12th annual collections; Gardner Dozois, editor. St. Martin's Press 1984-1995 12v 1-10 o.p.; 11 $26.95; 12 $27.95

Analyzed in Short story index
First three annual compilations published by Bluejay Bks.
Contents: 11th annual collection includes the following stories: Papa, by I. MacLeod; Sacred cow, by B. Sterling; Dancing on air, by N. Kress; A visit to the farside, by D. Webb; Alien bootlegger, by R. Ore; Death on the Nile, by C. Willis; Friendship bridge, by B. W. Aldiss; Into the Miranda Rift, by G. D. Nordley; Mwalimu in the squared circle, by M. Resnick; Guest of honor, by R. Reed; Love toys of the gods, by P. Cadigan; Chaff, by G. Egan; Georgia on my mind, by C. Sheffield; Cush by N. Barrett; On the collection of humans, by M. Rich; There and then, by S. Utley; The night we buried Road Dog, by J. Cady; Feedback, by J. W. Haldeman; Lieserl, by S. Baxter; Flashback, by D. Simmons; A child's Christmas in Florida, by W. B. Spencer; Whispers, by M. F. McHugh; Wall, stone, craft, by W. J. Williams
12th annual collection includes Forgiveness day, by U. K. Le Guin; The Remoras, by R. Reed; Nekropolis, by M. F. McHugh; Margin of error, by N. Kress; Cilia-of-Gold, by S. Baxter; Going after Old Man Alabama, by W. Sanders; Melodies of the heart, by M. F. Flynn; The hole in the Hole, by T. Bisson; Paris in June, by P. Cadigan; Flowering mandrake, by G. Turner; None so blind, by J. W. Haldeman; Cocoon, by G. Egan; Seven views of Olduvai Gorge, by M. Resnick; Dead space for the unexpected, by G. Ryman; Cri de coeur, by M. Bishop; The Sawing Boys, by H. Waldrop; The matter of Seggri, by U. K. Le Guin; Ylem, by E. Fintushel; Asylum, by K. Kerr; Red Elvis, by W. J. Williams; California dreamer, by M. Rosenblum; Split light, by L. Goldstein; Les fleurs du mal, by B. Stableford

Yolen, Jane

Briar Rose. Doherty Assocs. 1992 190p o.p.

LC 92-25456

"Fairy tale series"

"Yolen takes the story of Briar Rose (commonly known as Sleeping Beauty) and links it to the Holocaust. . . . Rebecca Berlin, a young woman who has grown up hearing her grandmother Gemma tell an unusual and frightening version of the Sleeping Beauty legend, realizes when Gemma dies that the fairy tale offers one of the very few clues she has to her grandmother's past. To discover the facts behind Gemma's story, Rebecca travels to Poland." Publ Wkly

"Both heartbreaking and heartwarming, Yolen's novel is a compelling reminder of the Holocaust as well as a contemporary tale of secrets and romance." Booklist

Sister Light, Sister Dark. Doherty Assocs. 1988 244p o.p.

LC 88-12177

"A TOR book"

"Set in the future, this fantasy is the first part of an account of events that ended a culture, spawned legends, and eventually inspired scholarship. The tale begins with the prophecy of the White Babe, then continues with what really happens to Jo-an-enna, an orphaned girl brought up in a mountain Sisterhood. An unusual, intellectually challenging fantasy." Booklist

Followed by White Jenna

White Jenna. Doherty Assocs. 1989 265p o.p.

LC 90-104805

"A TOR book"

Sequel to Sister Light, Sister Dark

This fantasy "deals with an event in the history of Yolen's world known as the Gender Wars. Legendary and mythical accounts are presented, complete with poetry and songs, as the warrior Jenna and her friends complete their quest. A quietly successful novel." Booklist

Yorke, Margaret

Admit to murder. Viking 1990 267p o.p.

LC 90-50054

"The disappearance of their daughter 12 years earlier still haunts George and Susan Vaughan, who now live with housekeeper/friend Norah in reduced circumstances due to the profligacy of their adopted son. Detective Marsh, recently returned to the English village of Feringham, stirs up trouble when he once again looks into the case. . . . Yorke carefully establishes a comfortable but changing English community, sets a leisurely pace, and then revs up, as overheated emotions lead to violence and an ultimate irony." Libr J

Crime in question. Viking 1989 234p o.p.

LC 88-40631

"A young man escapes from his parents and quickly falls into a life of petty crime. When he teams up with a hardened criminal, the stakes escalate and a simple breaking-and-entering leads to the murder of a woman. Meanwhile, another criminal escapes from the nearby open prison to visit his estranged wife. His escape is badly timed, and he is blamed for the murder. Unfortunately, the novel's predictability robs it of the psychological edge that often distinguishes Yorke's work. Still, there are compensations. Yorke offers a series of astute character studies and an incisive look at the hard realities of working-class British life, where violence is an everyday occurrence." Booklist

Criminal damage. Mysterious Press 1992 248p $17.95

ISBN 0-89296-499-5   LC 91-51182

"Mrs. Newton, a widow, enjoys a quiet and determinedly tidy life in the picturesque English village of Middle Bardolph, but storms are brewing that seem likely to unsettle it. Geoffrey, her boring and not very pleasant son, thinks his mother should underwrite the larger home his ambitious wife demands. Temperamental daughter Jennifer is increasingly obsessed with her former lover and his new fiancée and seems bent on disrupting their lives. . . . Yorke . . . mixes this deftly drawn, untrustworthy cast with robbery, violence and a hidden past, keeping readers guessing about what will be done and who will do it." Publ Wkly

Dangerous to know. Mysterious Press 1994 c1993 268p $17.95

ISBN 0-89296-500-2   LC 92-51042

First published 1993 in the United Kingdom

A "portrait of a marriage gone horribly wrong. Walter is tyrannical and unreasonable; Hermione, his emotionally battered wife, is a virtual slave to his every whim. Walter's ever-present rage is stoked when Hermione begins to show signs of change. A new friend, a part-time job—what will be next? Will Hermione find the courage to leave Walter before he explodes in truly murderous rage? As suspense builds, the reader roots for Hermione to make her bid for freedom before it's too late. Exciting to the end." Libr J

Evidence to destroy. Viking 1987 239p o.p.

LC 87-40028

"Flighty Thelma Hallows returns home to rural Milton St. Gabriel after her latest failed affair, bringing young Edward Fletcher, whom she picks up on the way. Thelma's widowed mother reluctantly accepts the two, despite her disapproval. With the passing days, Thelma attracts elderly Arthur Morrison who hires her as his housekeeper. When Arthur is killed, the police search for Edward, the obvious suspect as an ex-convict and presumably Thelma's rejected lover. But the situation, deftly built by the author to a tragic climax, reveals a stronger motive for murder." Publ Wkly

Find me a villain. St. Martin's Press 1983 184p o.p.

LC 83-9754

"Nina Crowther, torn apart by her husband's infidelity and by the breakup of their 24-year marriage, takes a job house-sitting an isolated old mansion. Nina starts getting weird phone calls, and begins to fear for her life when a young woman's body is found in a copse nearby." Booklist

"Vividly portrayed secondary characters add interest to this novel of suspense centering on a rather ordinary woman who plucks up the courage to conquer her own problems while caring for others." Libr J

Intimate kill. St. Martin's Press 1985 215p o.p.

LC 85-1754

Yorke, Margaret—*Continued*

"Stephen Dawes, convicted of killing his wife 10 years previously, has just been released from prison and is seeking his ex-mistress and their daughter. In his search, he finds out that his lover doesn't want to be found and that the circumstances surrounding his wife's death have extended unresolved into the present. As always, Yorke brilliantly builds suspense and presents, in exquisite detail, insightful views of complex people. This thriller gets better with every page." Booklist

Safely to the grave. St. Martin's Press 1986 240p o.p.

LC 86-1821

The author "shows how ordinary lives can be marred or utterly destroyed by evil. Cruel circumstances bring a handful of gentle villagers in touch with Mick Harvey, a delivery man who personifies evil. Harvey scares his child and beats his wife. But now his job leads him to two women whom he tried to force off the road the previous week. Mick is angry, feeling victimized, and murder follows. This intense psychological study builds slowly and effectively to a wrenching climax." Booklist

A small deceit. Viking 1991 200p $18.95

ISBN 0-670-83977-9   LC 91-50147

Also available Thorndike Press large print edition

"A dullish, obsessive-compulsive judge and his timid, unassuming wife become the objects of a newly released rapist's harassment; however, the rapist's continuing life of mail fraud, opportunism, and violence toward women causes the judge and his wife to examine their relationship." Libr J

"Only a writer with Margaret Yorke's smooth cunning and deceptively simplistic narrative technique could whip a taut climax and a cathartic emotional release out of this disciplined, metronomic tale. She isn't showy, or graphic, or gothic. She just instinctively knows her British characters." Booklist

The smooth face of evil. St. Martin's Press 1984 208p o.p.

LC 84-2077

"Terry Brett, a personable con artist, pegs elderly Alice Armitage as a likely patsy for his financial scams. But having inveigled himself into Alice's affections, Terry sights richer victims for the fleecing. Alice is a lonely widow whose daughter-in-law Helen has shunted her off into a mean, comfortless apartment on the plush estate Alice had helped her son Giles to buy. Sue Norris and Jonathan Cooper, an unmarried couple, occupy the estate's lodge. When Sue and Terry meet, they become lovers and plot to dispose of Jonathan so that Sue is free to seduce Giles and make off with the Armitage fortune. Inevitably, murders result, but not in ways that the reader would suspect. Yorke's restrained style and skillfully created characters strengthen the effects of this spellbinder." Publ Wkly

Speak for the dead. Viking 1988 207p o.p.

LC 87-40626

"In London, Gordon Matthews is freed after serving a minimum sentence for murdering his wife. Meeting pretty, seemingly innocent Carrie Foster, he tells her he is divorced, and she marries him. It's the case of a trickster tricked, for Carrie doesn't reveal her life as a prostitute. The couple settles down in suburbia where Carrie soon tires of her whining, jobless husband and goes back 'on the game.' While traveling to London by train, she attracts Nicholas Fitzmaurice, a young student who becomes obsessed by her." Publ Wkly

Yoshimoto, Banana, 1964-

Kitchen; translated from the Japanese by Megan Backus. Grove Press 1993 152p o.p.

LC 92-12871

Original Japanese edition, 1987

The volume comprises two works of fiction, the title novella and a short story. "Both 'Kitchen' and 'Moonlight Shadow,' each narrated by young women, are about loss. In the longer story, Mikage, the female narrator, moves into the house of Yuichi and his mother/father [a transexual] after the death of her grandmother; in the second, the girl has lost a boyfriend in a car crash, and is granted a vision of her beloved by a mysterious lady on a bridge." Times Lit Suppl

"In supple, precise prose Yoshimoto conveys her protagonists' emotional states by according them unusual sensitivity to the natural world; they share an enhanced vision that makes things shine with luminous clarity or emanate the gloom of mortality." Publ Wkly

Kitchen [novella]

In Yoshimoto, B. Kitchen

Young, Carrie

The wedding dress; stories from the Dakota Plains. University of Iowa Press 1992 126p $16.95

ISBN 0-87745-386-1   LC 92-6522

Also available Thorndike Press large print edition

Contents: The wedding dress; Bank night; The skaters; The nights of Ragna Rundhaug; The sins of the fathers; Blue horses; Twilight and June

"Set in the Dakota Plains of the 1930s, [these stories] map the emotional lives and day-to-day struggles of the Norwegian American settlers of that harsh land. Rural in subject matter, yet warm, compassionate, and timeless in theme, Young's stories capture the slow unfolding of the seasons: seasons of marrying, childbearing, romance, unrequited love, and unexpected turns of fate and the human heart." Libr J

Yourcenar, Marguerite

Memoirs of Hadrian, and reflections on the composition of Memoirs of Hadrian; translated from the French by Grace Frick in collaboration with the author. Farrar, Straus 1963 347p $22.95

ISBN 0-374-20728-3

Also available Modern Library edition

Memoirs of Hadrian first published 1951 in France; this edition first published 1963 by Farrar, Straus

"The memoirs portray the emperor on the eve of his death and describe his reflections as he gazes out upon the city that seemed to him indestructible and that he now fears will fall. As with most of her work, the book is a minutely researched reconstruction of actual events in the distant past through which she develops penetrating and fully credible portraits of the people she describes." Reader's Ency. 3d edition

You've got to read this; contemporary American writers introduce stories that held them in awe; edited by Ron Hansen and Jim Shepard. HarperPerennial 1994 630p o.p.

LC 94-14460

Analyzed in Short story index
Contents: A mother's tale, by J. Agee; Guy de Maupassant, by I. Babel; Sonny's blues, by J. Baldwin; The school, by D. Barthelme; The aleph, by J. L. Borges; A day in the open, by J. Bowles; A distant episode, by P. Bowles; The star café, by M. Caponegro; Reflections, by A. Carter; Cathedral, by R. Carver; Goodbye, my brother, by J. Cheever; Gooseberries, by A. Chekhov; A Christmas carol, by C. Dickens; Pie dance, by M. Giles; Greatness strikes where it pleases, by L. Gustafsson; The interview, by R. P. Jhabvala; The dead, by J. Joyce; In the penal colony, by F. Kafka; Girl, by J. Kincaid; The smallest woman in the world, by C. Lispector; The daughters of the late colonel, by K. Mansfield; Labor Day dinner, by A. Munro; Spring in Fialta, by V. Nabokov; The things they carried, by T. O'Brien; A good man is hard to find, by F. O'Connor; I stand here ironing, by T. Olsen; Wants, by G. Paley; In dreams begin responsibilities, by D. Schwartz; The man to send rain clouds, by L. M. Silko; Helping, by R. Stone; Master and man, by L. Tolstoy; Packed dirt, church-going, a dying cat, a traded car, by J. Updike; The flowers, by A. Walker; No place for you, my love, by E. Welty; Paper garden, by J. Wilson

Z

Zahn, Timothy

Dark force rising. Bantam Bks. 1992 376p (Star wars, v2) $18.50

ISBN 0-553-08574-3   LC 92-743

Sequel to Heir to the empire (1991)
A sci-fi adventure based on characters from the Star wars movies. "Political infighting threatens the fragile, victorious Rebel Alliance in its ongoing struggle against the empire. . . . Luke, Leia, and Han face separate challenges from a mad Jedi, an Imperial Grand Admiral, and a smuggler with a dangerous secret, and the fate of the alliance hangs on the outcome of their missions." Libr J
"Zahn has a real flair for endowing Lucas' characters and universe with acceptable sf underpinnings." Booklist
Followed by The last command

The last command. Bantam Bks. 1993 407p (Star wars, v3) o.p.

LC 92-43876

In this concluding volume of the Star wars trilogy "Thrawn mounts a final siege against the Republic. While Han and Chewbacca struggle to form a wary alliance of smugglers in a last-ditch attack against the Empire, Leia keeps the Alliance together and prepares for the birth of her Jedi twins. But the Empire has too many ships and too many clones to combat. The Republic's only hope lies in sending a small force, led by Luke, into the very stronghold that houses Thrawn's terrible cloning machines." Publisher's note

Zaroulis, N. L.

Call the darkness light; [by] Nancy Zaroulis. Doubleday 1979 560p o.p.

LC 78-74714

"Orphaned at an early age, Sabra enters the household of a cotton mill manager, but is turned away, unfairly, as a bad influence on one of his daughters. She marries, but is deserted by her husband; goes to work in the mill, but is dismissed for associating with an agitator. The nadir of her fortunes finds her living with the despised immigrant Irish and soliciting in the streets to keep herself and her child alive." Publ Wkly
"Nancy Zaroulis has given a comprehensive account of industrialization and immigration in the early nineteenth century and the ideologies characterizing the period. Her detailed examination of various aspects and social strata of the age is impressive." Best Sellers

The last waltz; [by] Nancy Zaroulis. Doubleday 1984 398p o.p.

LC 81-43547

This novel is "set in Boston around the end of the nineteenth century. The story centers around Isabel January and Marian Childs. Isabel is the pampered darling of the Januarys whose wealth had come from decades of Boston merchant shipping. They take in Marian as a very young woman. Her family has culture, but very little money. Yet her mother pushes her into a position as companion of sorts to various members of the January family. After inheriting January money from a potty old uncle, Marian takes her place in Boston society, and it is she who tells this story." Best Sellers

Massachusetts; a novel; by Nancy Zaroulis. Fawcett Columbine 1991 709p il o.p.

LC 90-82332

The author "tells the story of a single family, the Revells, and through them the history of Massachusetts from the arrival of the *Mayflower* to the present. A Revell or a relative is present at the first Thanksgiving, the Salem witch trials, and the Boston tea party. Revells are shown helping to start the China trade, founding the American factory system and the Boston Symphony, agitating for abolitionism, women's suffrage, or to save Sacco and Vanzetti." Libr J
"Using well-researched background material that takes Bay State history through the 1960s, Zaroulis weaves a fictional tapestry rich with details of real and imaginary characters." Publ Wkly

Zelazny, Roger

Blood of Amber. Arbor House 1986 215p o.p.

LC 86-3530

"A Del Rey book"
Sequel to Trumps of doom
In this seventh installment in the author's Amber fantasy series "the sorcerer Merlin of Amber—aka Merle Corey of San Francisco—learns the identities of two would-be assassins but makes a truce with one to pursue the greater, more dangerous power beyond them. Once again, the limited plot is enlivened by Zelazny's irony, his bravura sequences . . . and his laconic sense of the incongruous." Publ Wkly
Followed by Sign of chaos

Zelazny, Roger—*Continued*

Bring me the head of Prince Charming; [by] Roger Zelazny and Robert Sheckley. Bantam Bks. 1991 279p il $22

ISBN 0-553-07678-7   LC 91-18153

"Frankenstein meets Sleeping Beauty at the end of the millennium as the forces of Good and Evil vie for dominance over the next thousand years of history in this comic effort by two veteran sf/fantasy authors. The plot—in which an ambitious devil attempts to prove that fairy tales don't always have happy endings . . . [serves] as an excuse for jibes against bureaucracy (the real hell), Santa Claus, and the civilized world." Libr J

The courts of chaos. Doubleday 1978 183p o.p.

LC 78-3263

Sequel to The hand of Oberon

This fifth title in the author's "Amber fantasy series answers many of the questions central to previous installments; the nature of the magical kingdom of Amber and the tangents it sometimes forms with the real world; the mystery behind the disappearance of Oberon the King— which forms the plot of the stories—and the machinations of Corwin, Prince of Amber, and his siblings, who thrive on intrigue." Booklist

Followed by Trumps of doom

The doors of his face, the lamps of his mouth

In The Best of the Nebulas p35-61

Eye of cat. Timescape Bks. 1982 217p o.p. Ultramarine reprint available $25 (ISBN 0-671-25519-3)

LC 82-10433

"An escaped alien pursues a blood feud against the human who captured it; he takes refuge in the homeland of his Navajo ancestors, throwing himself into a shamanic trance in order to confuse his telpathic tracker. Human telepaths try to help out, but can only delay the inevitable confrontation. A chase thriller whose use of the mythological themes that dominated Zelazny's earlier work recalls a little of their brilliance." Anatomy of Wonder. 3d edition

The guns of Avalon. Doubleday 1972 180p o.p.

Sequel to Nine princes in Amber

In this second volume of the author's Amber series Corwin "again walks the shadow worlds in search of his stolen birthright and encounters dreaded forces of evil conjured up by his own terrible curse." Booklist

Followed by Sign of the unicorn

The hand of Oberon. Doubleday 1976 181p o.p.

"The fourth title in Zelazny's epic fantasy of the world called Amber picks up in mid-dialogue form the conclusion of the previous novel 'Sign of the Unicorn.'" Booklist

"Oberon, the royal leader of the land of Amber, is unexpectedly missing, and his large family of sons and daughters is engaged in searching for him, or else trying to keep him missing." Publ Wkly

Followed by The courts of chaos

He who shapes

In The Best of the Nebulas p73-141

Home is the hangman

In The Hugo winners v4 p5-67

Knight of shadows. Morrow 1989 251p o.p.

LC 89-34658

Sequel to Sign of chaos

"The ninth book in Zelazny's Amber sagas. . . . Merlin, son of Corwin, escapes at the last minute from the Citadel of the FourWorlds. He is immediately plunged into intrigue and adventure. By book's end, it is apparent that his travels are not yet complete. Zelazny's pacing and the ingenious games he plays with magic continue to be rewarding." Booklist

Followed by Prince of chaos

Lord of light. Doubleday 1967 257p o.p.

This novel "describes a planet colonized by refugees from India who are tyrannized by a few of their fellow citizens who have assumed the guise and powers of the Hindu gods. Instead of easing his readers into the strange setting and unfamiliar mythology, Zelazny began the story in the middle, centuries after the initial landing; that the reader can absorb—and care to absorb—the complexities of the plot and setting is a tribute to the author's storytelling ability." New Ency of Sci Fic

A night in the lonesome October; illustrations by Gahan Wilson. Morrow 1993 280p il $20

ISBN 0-688-12508-5   LC 93-18414

"An AvoNova book"

"Jack the Ripper meets Dracula, Dr. Frankenstein, Sherlock Holmes, and a few other choice individuals in this romp through the annals of literary horror and mystery. Seen through the eyes of Jack's dog, Dracula's pet bat, and other animal companions, the machinations of those who traffic with powers supernatural take on a distinctly skewed perspective. Zelazny's quirky humor and Wilson's appropriately creepy drawings complement each other in grand style." Libr J

Nine princes in Amber. Doubleday 1970 188p o.p.

This tale, the first in the author's Amber series, is a fantasy and adventure story about Corwin, who, following an attack of amnesia, realizes that he is one of nine princes in the kingdom of Amber. Each one of the nine princes and four princesses wants the throne, and war breaks out between the brothers

Followed by The guns of Avalon

Prince of chaos. Morrow 1991 225p o.p.

LC 91-17296

Sequel to Knight of shadows

The tenth book in the Amber sagas "takes Merlin Corey to the actual Courts of Chaos, which have figured as offstage presences in the series beginning with *Trumps of Doom*. We now see the Courts from the inside, and a certain amount of the mystery about Corey's world and future is dispelled, although not without the usual quota of intrigues and dangers. The finer nuances of the series are becoming a little hard to appreciate without having followed it from the beginning. The vivid imagination and high command of language, however, can still be enjoyed on a volume-by-volume basis." Booklist

Zelazny, Roger—*Continued*

Sign of chaos. Arbor House 1987 214p o.p.

LC 87-14509

Sequel to Blood of Amber

In the eighth volume of the author's Amber fantasy series "Merlin Corey follows a confused trail to the Keep of Four Worlds, where he learns the secret of the involvement of the Courts of Chaos in all the intrigues and wars to which he is heir." Booklist

Followed by Knight of shadows

Sign of the unicorn. Doubleday 1975 186p o.p.

Sequel to The guns of Avalon

"Third in a series of science fiction-fantasy adventures featuring Corwin, Prince of Amber. . . . Court intrigue is rampant among the surviving princes and princesses of Amber, all of whom weave in and out of Shadow, a multi-dimensional world they can manipulate, and unite to rescue a brother imprisoned by evil beings threatening the kingdom. This, though action packed, does not advance the fortunes of Corwin to any extent but does fill in background." Booklist

Followed by The hand of Oberon

Trumps of doom. Arbor House 1985 183p o.p.

LC 84-299

Sequel to The courts of chaos

"A new sequence [in the Amber fantasy series] begins in this sixth volume centering on Corwin's son Merlin, a sorcerer who has followed the father he barely knew from their powerful realm of Amber to an Earth that is one of Amber's many shadowy alternate worlds. Attempts on Merlin's life force him to return to Amber, where he becomes embroiled once more in family quarrels and finally confronts the man who has been stalking him. This fast-paced, colorful tale is enriched by Zelazny's literary analogs of his alternate worlds as he flips from one frame of reference to another (tarot, computers, lawyerly logic) and from one voice to another (hardboiled detective, classical allusions, high fantasy)." Publ Wkly

Followed by Blood of Amber

Zola, Émile, 1840-1902

Germinal; translated from the French by Leonard Tanock. Knopf 1991 xxxi, 498p $17

ISBN 0-679-40556-9   LC 91-52987

"Everyman's library"

Original French edition, 1885, one of the Rougon-Macquart series

"A study of life in the mines. The illegitimate son of Gervaise, Étienne Lanier, a socialist, is forced to work in the mines. Low wages and fines cause a strike, of which Lanier is one of the leaders. He counsels moderation; but hunger drives the miners to desperation, and force is met by force. Several are killed, Lanier is deported, and the miners fall back into their old slavery." Keller. Reader's Dig of Books

Nana. o.p.

Original French edition, 1880, one of the Rougon-Macquart series

"A study of the life of a courtesan and actress. Nana is the daughter of Gervaise and the drunkard Coupeau. She grows up in the streets and disreputable haunts until she comes under the notice of a theatre manager. Her great physical beauty attracts men of all classes, and none resist her. . . . The greatest fortunes are dissipated by her and yet at her door is heard the continual ring of the creditor. She contracts the black smallpox, and dies deserted and wretched." Keller. Reader's Dig of Books

Three faces of love; especially translated for this volume by Roland Gant. Vanguard Press 1969 c1968 151p o.p.

Analyzed in Short story index

These three early Zola stories explore different kinds of love. In For One Night of Love "Zola tells of a dullard whose passion leads to suicide through his having been accessory in the murder of his rival, killed by the girl, a marquise. 'Round Trip' is a lyric of youthful sensuality triumphing over middle-aged insensitivity. In 'Winkles for M. Chabre' Zola deals with a triangle (aging husband, young wife, young man); the husband has been told to expect a child if he follows a diet of shellfish; he gets the child, unaware that it is not because of winkles. Slight things, these stories, but welcome additions to the austere works usually associated with Zola." Libr J

TITLE AND SUBJECT INDEX

This index to the books listed in part 1 includes title and subject entries, arranged in one alphabet. A shortened form of the author's name is the key to the location of the book in part 1, where full information for each book will be found.

Title entries. Title entries are given for all works entered in part 1. For novels published in omnibus editions and for novelettes, *In* or *also in* designations are included and page numbers are usually provided

Subject entries. Subject headings are printed in capital letters. The listing of a work under a subject indicates that a major portion of the work is about that subject.

3 by Irving. Irving, J.
3: This gun for hire, The confidential agent, The ministry of fear. Greene, G.
The **4:50** from Paddington. See Christie, A. What Mrs. McGillicuddy saw!
The **13th** juror. Lescroart, J. T.
The **13th** valley. Del Vecchio, J. M.
The **14** sisters of Emilio Montez O'Brien. See Hijuelos, O. The fourteen sisters of Emilio Montez O'Brien
18mm blues. Browne, G. A.
19 Purchase Street. Browne, G. A.
22 stories. Gilliatt, P.
27. Diehl, W.
The **27** ingredient chili con carne murders. Pickard, N.
The **42nd** parallel. Dos Passos, J.
   also in Dos Passos, J. U.S.A. v1
50. Corman, A.
The **158-pound** marriage. Irving, J.
   In Irving, J. 3 by Irving p561-718
200 years of great American short stories. Entered in Part I under title
1876. Vidal, G.
1919. Dos Passos, J.
   also in Dos Passos, J. U.S.A v2
1959. Davis, T.
1984. See Orwell, G. Nineteen eighty-four
2001: a space odyssey. Clarke, A. C.
2010: odyssey two. Clarke, A. C.
2061: odyssey three. Clarke, A. C.

A

The **A.B.C.** murders. Christie, A.
"A" is for alibi. Grafton, S.

ABANDONED CHILDREN
   See also Orphans

ABANDONED TOWNS *See* Extinct cities

ABANDONMENT OF FAMILY *See* Desertion and nonsupport

The **Abbess** of Crewe. Spark, M.

ABBESSES *See* Nuns

ABBEYS
   See also Cathedrals; Churches; Convent life; Monasticism and religious orders
   Austen, J. Northanger Abbey

The **abbott's** ghost. Alcott, L. M.
   In Alcott, L. M. Behind a mask: the unknown thrillers of Louisa May Alcott p209-77

ABDUCTION *See* Kidnapping

ABNORMALITIES AND DEFORMITIES *See* Deformities; Dwarfs; Face—Abnormalities and deformities; Monsters

ABOLITIONISTS
   See also Slavery; Underground railroad
   Stowe, H. B. Uncle Tom's cabin
   Tryon, T. In the fire of spring

ABORIGINES, AUSTRALIAN *See* Australian aborigines

ABORTION
   Fast, H. The trial of Abigail Goodman
   Goldreich, G. Four days
   Irving, J. The cider house rules
   Piercy, M. Braided lives
Above suspicion. MacInnes, H.
Absalom, Absalom! Faulkner, W.
An **absence** of light. Lindsey, D. L.
Absolute truths. Howatch, S.

ABUSE OF CHILDREN *See* Child abuse

ABUSED WIVES *See* Wife abuse

ABYSSINIA *See* Ethiopia
An **academic** question. Pym, B.

ACADIANS
            Louisiana
   See Cajuns
Acceptable losses. Shaw, I.
The **acceptance** world. Powell, A.
   In Powell, A. A dance to the music of time [v1]
Accident. Steel, D.
The **accident.** Wiesel, E.
   In Wiesel, E. Night, Dawn, The accident: three tales p205-318

ACCIDENTAL DEATH *See* Accidents
An **accidental** man. Murdoch, I.
The **accidental** tourist. Tyler, A.

ACCIDENTS
   See also Airplane accidents; Drowning; Fires; Industrial accidents; Shipwrecks and castaways; Traffic accidents
   Brown, R. Tender mercies
   Horgan, P. Whitewater
   Oates, J. C. American appetites
   Proulx, A. Postcards
   Trollope, J. The men and the girls
   Vonnegut, K. Deadeye Dick

ACCIDENTS, INDUSTRIAL *See* Industrial accidents

ACCOUNTANTS
   Mortimer, J. C. Dunster

ACCULTURATION
    See also Americanization
    Momaday, N. S. House made of dawn
Across the board. Francis, D.
Across the bridge. Gallant, M.
Across the river and into the trees. Hemingway, E.
Across the street. Simenon, G.
An **act** of terror. Brink, A. P.
Act of will. Bradford, B. T.
Active service. Crane, S.
    In Crane, S. The complete novels of Stephen Crane
      p429-592
ACTORS
    See also Motion picture actors and actresses; Strolling players; Theater life
    Baldwin, J. Tell me how long the train's been gone
    Carroll, J. Fault lines
    Davies, R. World of wonders
    Dickinson, P. Perfect gallows
    Diehl, W. 27
    Irving, J. A son of the circus
    Isaacs, S. Almost paradise
    Korda, M. Curtain
    L'Engle, M. Certain women
    Leonard, E. Get Shorty
    Mahfūz, N. Wedding song
    Miller, W. M. The darfsteller
    Renault, M. The mask of Apollo
    Stewart, M. This rough magic
    Tryon, T. Crowned heads
    West, N. The day of the locust
    Westlake, D. E. Sacred monster
ACTRESSES
    See also Motion picture actors and actresses; Strolling players; Theater life
    Alcott, L. M. Behind a mask [novelette]
    Baldwin, J. Tell me how long the train's been gone
    Blatty, W. P. The exorcist
    Bradford, B. T. Voice of the heart
    Briskin, J. Dreams are not enough
    Clark, M. H. Weep no more, my lady
    Colette. Chance acquaintances
    Crispin, E. Sudden vengeance
    Dailey, J. Aspen gold
    Dart, I. R. I'll be there
    Didion, J. Play it as it lays
    Dunne, J. G. Playland
    Goldsmith, O. Flavor of the month
    Goudge, E. Such devoted sisters
    Hodge, J. A. Escapade
    Kennedy, W. Quinn's book
    Korda, M. Curtain
    Krantz, J. Till we meet again
    Leonard, E. LaBrava
    Maupin, A. Maybe the moon
    Price, E. Where shadows go
    Prose, F. Hungry hearts
    Stewart, M. This rough magic
    Stone, K. Rainbows
    Stone, R. Children of light
    Tey, J. A shilling for candles
    Thomas, R. Voodoo, Ltd
    Tryon, T. Crowned heads
    West, N. The day of the locust
    West, Dame R. Sunflower
    Whitney, P. A. Emerald
    Williams, T. The Roman spring of Mrs. Stone
Acts of faith. Segal, E.
Acts of worship. Mishima, Y.
Ada. Nabokov, V. V.
Adam Bede. Eliot, G.
ADAMS, ABIGAIL, 1744-1818
    Stone, I. Those who love
ADAMS, JOHN, 1735-1826
    Stone, I. Those who love

Addie Pray. Brown, J. D.
ADIRONDACK MOUNTAINS (N.Y.)
    Doctorow, E. L. Loon Lake
Admiral Hornblower in the West Indies. Forester, C. S.
Admit to murder. Yorke, M.
ADOLESCENCE
    See also Boys; Girls; Youth
    Bassani, G. The garden of the Finzi-Continis
    Boswell, R. Mystery ride
    Bowen, E. The death of the heart
    Burns, O. A. Cold Sassy tree
    Capote, T. Other voices, other rooms
    Colette. Claudine at school
    Colette. Gigi
    Colette. The tender shoot
    Dart, I. R. I'll be there
    Davis, T. 1959
    Doctorow, E. L. Billy Bathgate
    Doig, I. English Creek
    Duras, M. The lover
    Duras, M. The North China lover
    Estleman, L. D. Sudden country
    Eugenides, J. The virgin suicides
    Fast, H. April morning
    Fitzgerald, F. S. The Basil and Josephine stories
    Fitzgerald, F. S. This side of paradise
    Freedman, J. F. The obstacle course
    Godwin, G. The finishing school
    Gold, H. A girl of forty
    Grass, G. Cat and mouse
    Guest, J. Second heaven
    Guy, R. Ruby
    Hamner, E. The homecoming
    Hamner, E. Spencer's Mountain
    Hemingway, E. The Nick Adams stories
    Hesse, H. Demian
    Hoeg, P. Borderliners
    Horgan, P. Whitewater
    Humphreys, J. Rich in love
    Irving, J. Setting free the bears
    Jönsson, R. My life as a dog
    Joyce, J. A portrait of the artist as a young man
    Kennedy, W. Quinn's book
    Kincaid, J. Annie John
    King, S. Carrie
    King, S. Christine
    Kinsella, W. P. Box socials
    Knowles, J. Peace breaks out
    Knowles, J. A separate peace
    Lee, G. China boy
    Lee, H. To kill a mockingbird
    Leffland, E. Rumors of peace
    L'Engle, M. The small rain
    Lessing, D. M. Martha Quest
    Levenkron, S. The best little girl in the world
    Lopez, S. Third and Indiana
    Mason, B. A. In country
    McCaffrey, A. The lady
    McCammon, R. R. Boy's life
    McCarthy, C. All the pretty horses
    McCarthy, C. The crossing
    McCorkle, J. Ferris Beach
    McCullers, C. Clock without hands
    McDermott, A. That night
    Meredith, G. The ordeal of Richard Feverel
    Mowry, J. Six out seven
    Munro, A. Lives of girls & women
    Oates, J. C. Foxfire
    O'Brien, E. The country girls
    Palliser, C. The quincunx
    Parks, G. The learning tree
    Phillips, J. A. Shelter
    Potok, C. Davita's harp
    Powers, J. R. Do black patent-leather shoes really reflect up?
    Price, R. The tongues of angels
    Price, R. The wanderers
    Quindlen, A. Object lessons

ADOLESCENCE—*Continued*

Raucher, H. Summer of '42
Richter, C. The grandfathers
Rölvaag, O. E. Peder Victorious
Rosenberg, N. T. Interest of justice
Roth, H. A diving rock on the Hudson
Roth, H. A star shines over Mt. Morris Park
Salinger, J. D. The catcher in the rye
Shange, N. Betsey Brown
Shields, D. Dead languages
Sinclair, A. Coffee will make you black
Smith, B. A tree grows in Brooklyn
Somtow, S. P. Jasmine nights
Spencer, L. Home song
Steel, D. The gift
Swarthout, G. F. Bless the beasts and children
Tarkington, B. Seventeen
Townsend, S. The Adrian Mole diaries
West, J. Cress Delahanty
West, J. The state of Stony Lonesome
White, E. A boy's own story
Wolitzer, H. Hearts
Woodson, J. Autobiography of a family photo
Wouk, H. The city boy, the adventures of Herbie Bookbinder and his cousin Cliff

ADOLESCENTS *See* Adolescence

ADOPTED CHILDREN *See* Adoption; Foster children

ADOPTION

See also Foster children
Busch, F. Long way from home
Dart, I. R. The Stork Club
Goldsmith, O. Fashionably late
Greenberg, J. Age of consent
Harris, M. Lost and found
James, P. D. Innocent blood
Kingsolver, B. Pigs in heaven
Mishima, Y. The decay of the angel
Mortman, D. True colors
Tevis, W. S. The queen's gambit
Whitney, P. A. The golden unicorn
The **Adrian** Mole diaries. Townsend, S.
Adrian Mole: the lost years. Townsend, S.
Adrift just off the Islets of Langerhans: latitude 38° 54′ N, longitude 77° 00′ 13 W. Ellison, H.
In The Hugo winners v3 p547-81
Adrift on the Nile. Maḥfūẓ, N.

ADULTERY *See* Marriage problems
Adulthood rites. Butler, O. E.

ADVENTURE

See also Buried treasure; Escapes; International intrigue; Manhunts; Picaresque novels; Pirates; Science fiction; Sea stories; Soldiers of fortune; Spies; Voyages and travels; Western stories
Allen, H. Anthony Adverse
Bagley, D. Night of error
Bainbridge, B. The birthday boys
Bates, H. E. Fair stood the wind for France
Benchley, P. Beast
Benchley, P. Jaws
Berger, T. Little Big Man
Bosse, M. J. Mister Touch
Brent, M. Golden urchin
Brown, D. Chains of command
Brown, S. Where there's smoke
Buchan, J. The thirty-nine steps
Butler, O. E. Parable of the sower
Caputo, P. Horn of Africa
Cervantes Saavedra, M. de. Don Quixote de la Mancha
Clancy, T. Without remorse
Clavell, J. Gai-Jin
Clavell, J. Shogun
Clavell, J. Tai-Pan
Clavell, J. Whirlwind
Cleary, J. The faraway drums
Cleary, J. High road to China
Cody, L. Rift

Conrad, J. The Nigger of the Narcissus
Conrad, J. Nostromo
Cooper, J. F. The Deerslayer
Cooper, J. F. The last of the Mohicans
Cooper, J. F. The Leatherstocking tales
Cooper, J. F. The Pathfinder
Cooper, J. F. The prairie
Cornwell, B. Sharpe's company
Cornwell, B. Sharpe's devil
Cornwell, B. Sharpe's eagle
Cornwell, B. Sharpe's enemy
Cornwell, B. Sharpe's gold
Cornwell, B. Sharpe's honour
Cornwell, B. Sharpe's regiment
Cornwell, B. Sharpe's revenge
Cornwell, B. Sharpe's rifles
Cornwell, B. Sharpe's siege
Cornwell, B. Sharpe's sword
Cornwell, B. Sharpe's Waterloo
Costain, T. B. The black rose
Crichton, M. Sphere
Cussler, C. Dragon
Cussler, C. Inca gold
Cussler, C. Night probe!
Cussler, C. Sahara
Cussler, C. Treasure
Cussler, C. Vixen 03
De Hartog, J. The centurion
De Hartog, J. The Commodore
De Hartog, J. The outer buoy
Dickey, J. Deliverance
Dickson, G. R. Wolf and iron
DiMercurio, M. Attack of the Seawolf
Doig, I. The sea runners
Doyle, Sir A. C. The lost world
Du Maurier, Dame D. Jamaica Inn
Dumas, A. The Count of Monte Cristo
Dumas, A. The three musketeers
Dunnett, D. Checkmate
Dunnett, D. Pawn in frankincense
Dunnett, D. The ringed castle
Dunnett, D. Scales of gold
Dunnett, D. The unicorn hunt
Elegant, R. S. Manchu
Forester, C. S. Admiral Hornblower in the West Indies
Forester, C. S. The African Queen
Forester, C. S. Beat to quarters
Forester, C. S. Commodore Hornblower
Forester, C. S. Flying colours
Forester, C. S. Hornblower and the Atropos
Forester, C. S. Hornblower and the Hotspur
Forester, C. S. Hornblower during the crisis, and two stories: Hornblower's temptation and The last encounter
Forester, C. S. The last nine days of the Bismarck
Forester, C. S. Lieutenant Hornblower
Forester, C. S. Lord Hornblower
Forester, C. S. Ship of the line
Forester, C. S. To the Indies
Forsyth, F. The day of the jackal
Gann, E. K. The aviator
Gardner, J. E. Maestro
Gardner, J. E. The secret families
Gardner, J. E. The secret generations
Gardner, J. E. The secret houses
Gilman, D. The amazing Mrs. Pollifax
Gilman, D. Caravan
Gilman, D. The elusive Mrs. Pollifax
Gilman, D. Incident at Badamya
Gilman, D. Mrs. Pollifax and the Hong Kong Buddha
Gilman, D. Mrs. Pollifax on safari
Gilman, D. A palm for Mrs. Pollifax
Gilman, D. The unexpected Mrs. Pollifax
Graham, W. The twisted sword
Greene, G. Our man in Havana
Greene, G. Travels with my aunt
Haasse, H. S. The scarlet city
Haggard, H. R. King Solomon's mines

ADVENTURE—*Continued*

Haggard, H. R. She
Harrison, H. The Stainless Steel Rat sings the blues
Heaven, C. The wind from the sea
Hesse, H. Narcissus and Goldmund
Higgins, J. Storm warning
Hilton, J. Lost horizon
Hoagland, E. Seven rivers west
Hodge, J. A. The winding stair
Holland, C. The firedrake
Hope, A. The prisoner of Zenda
Horgan, P. A distant trumpet
Household, G. Rogue male
Innes, H. High stand
Innes, H. Isvik
Innes, H. Medusa
Innes, H. The wreck of the Mary Deare
Jakes, J. California gold
Jennings, G. The journeyer
Jennings, G. Raptor
Johnston, T. C. Cry of the hawk
Jones, D. C. This savage race
Kaye, M. M. Trade wind
Keneally, T. To Asmara
L'Amour, L. Last of the breed
L'Amour, L. Sackett's land
L'Amour, L. The walking drum
Le Guin, U. K. Rocannon's world
Llywelyn, M. Druids
Llywelyn, M. Finn Mac Cool
Llywelyn, M. The last prince of Ireland
Llywelyn, M. Red Branch
London, J. The Sea-Wolf
Ludlum, R. The Bourne identity
Ludlum, R. The Bourne supremacy
Ludlum, R. The Bourne ultimatum
Ludlum, R. The Chancellor manuscript
Lustbader, E. V. Floating city
Lustbader, E. V. French kiss
Lustbader, E. V. The Kaisho
Lustbader, E. V. White Ninja
MacInnes, H. Above suspicion
MacInnes, H. Decision at Delphi
MacInnes, H. The hidden target
MacInnes, H. The Venetian affair
MacLean, A. Force 10 from Navarone
MacLean, A. The guns of Navarone
MacLean, A. Ice Station Zebra
MacLean, A. Night without end
MacLean, A. When eight bells toll
Martin, W. Cape Cod
McCammon, R. R. Gone south
McCarthy, C. The crossing
McCutchan, P. Cameron's crossing
McCutchan, P. Convoy homeward
McCutchan, P. Convoy north
McCutchan, P. Convoy of fear
McCutchan, P. Convoy south
McCutchan, P. The last farewell
McMurtry, L. Lonesome dove
McMurtry, L. Streets of Laredo
Michener, J. A. Alaska
Michener, J. A. Caravans
Michener, J. A. Caribbean
Michener, J. A. The drifters
Michener, J. A. Hawaii
Michener, J. A. Journey
Morrell, D. Assumed identity
Nordhoff, C. Botany Bay
Nordhoff, C. The hurricane
Nordhoff, C. Pitcairn's Island
Norton, A. Empire of the eagle
O'Brian, P. The golden ocean
O'Brian, P. The wine-dark sea
Orczy, E., Baroness. Adventures of the Scarlet Pimpernel
Orczy, E., Baroness. The elusive Pimpernel
Orczy, E., Baroness. The Scarlet Pimpernel

Poe, E. A. The narrative of Arthur Gordon Pym of Nantucket
Poyer, D. The circle
Poyer, D. The gulf
Redfield, J. The celestine prophecy
Reed, K. Gone
Riley, J. M. In pursuit of the green lion
Roberts, K. L. Lydia Bailey
Roberts, K. L. Rabble in arms
Sabatini, R. Captain Blood
Sabatini, R. Scaramouche
Sabatini, R. The Sea-hawk
Scott, Sir W. Quentin Durward
Scott, Sir W. Rob Roy
Scott, Sir W. The talisman
Scott, Sir W. Waverly
Seton, A. Avalon
Shaw, I. Nightwork
Sienkiewicz, H. The deluge
Sienkiewicz, H. Fire in the steppe
Sienkiewicz, H. With fire and sword
Silverberg, R. Lord Valentine's castle
Silverberg, R. Majipoor chronicles
Silverberg, R. Valentine Pontifex
Smith, W. A. The burning shore
Smith, W. A. Elephant song
Smith, W. A. Flight of the falcon
Smith, W. A. Golden fox
Smith, W. A. The leopard hunts in darkness
Smith, W. A. Men of men
Smith, W. A. Power of the sword
Smith, W. A. River god
Smith, W. A. A time to die
Stendhal. The charterhouse of Parma
Stevenson, R. L. The master of Ballantrae
Stevenson, R. L. The misadventures of John Nicholson
Stewart, F. M. Pomp and circumstance
Stewart, M. The Gabriel hounds
Stewart, M. The ivy tree
Stewart, M. This rough magic
Stone, R. Dog soldiers
Swarthout, G. F. Bless the beasts and children
Taylor, R. L. The travels of Jaimie McPheeters
Traven, B. The treasure of the Sierra Madre
Trevanian. Shibumi
Twain, M. Tom Sawyer abroad
Tyers, K. The truce at Bakura
Ullman, J. R. The White Tower
Uris, L. Mitla Pass
Varley, J. Titan
Varley, J. Wizard
Verne, J. Around the world in eighty days
Verne, J. Five weeks in a balloon
Verne, J. A journey to the centre of the earth
Verne, J. The mysterious island
Verne, J. Twenty thousand leagues under the sea
Waltari, M. The Etruscan
Westheimer, D. Von Ryan's Express
Westlake, D. E. The spy in the ointment
Wolverton, D. The courtship of Princess Leia
Wren, P. C. Beau Geste
Zahn, T. Dark force rising
Zahn, T. The last command
The **adventures** of Augie March. Bellow, S.
The **adventures** of Don Quixote. See Cervantes Saavedra, M. de. Don Quixote de la Mancha
The **adventures** of Huckleberry Finn. Twain, M.
 also in Twain, M. The complete novels of Mark Twain v1 p731-969
The **adventures** of Joseph Andrews. See Fielding, H. Joseph Andrews
The **adventures** of Menahem-Mendl. Sholem Aleichem
The **adventures** of Mottel, the cantor's son. Sholem Aleichem
The **adventures** of Oliver Twist. See Dickens, C. Oliver Twist

Adventures of Sherlock Holmes. Doyle, Sir A. C.
  also in Doyle, Sir A. C. The complete Sherlock Holmes
Adventures of the Scarlet Pimpernel. Orczy, E., Baroness
The **adventures** of Tom Sawyer. Twain, M.
  also in Twain, M. The adventures of Tom Sawyer, Tom Sawyer abroad, Tom Sawyer, detective p31-236
  also in Twain, M. The complete novels of Mark Twain v1 p385-556
The **adventures** of Tom Sawyer, Tom Sawyer abroad, Tom Sawyer, detective. Twain, M.
The **adversary**. May, J.

ADVERTISING
  Beauvoir, S. de. Les belles images
  Pohl, F. The merchants' war
  Pohl, F. The space merchants
  Wells, H. G. Tono-Bungay
Advise and consent. Drury, A.
The **advocate's** devil. Dershowitz, A. M.

AERONAUTICS
  See also Air pilots; Flight
  Faulkner, W. Pylon
  Michener, J. A. Space

Flights
  See Air travel

AERONAUTICS, COMMERCIAL *See* Commercial aeronautics
AERONAUTICS, MILITARY *See* Military aeronautics
The **affair**. Snow, C. P.
Affairs at Thrush Green. Read, Miss
Affliction. Banks, R.
Affliction. See Weldon, F. Trouble

AFGHANISTAN
  Bradshaw, G. Horses of heaven

19th century
  Fraser, G. M. Flashman

20th century
  Michener, J. A. Caravans

Russian Invasion, 1979
  Follett, K. Lie down with lions

AFRICA
  See also Central Africa; Libyan Desert; Southern Africa; West Africa
  Conrad, J. Heart of darkness
  Lessing, D. M. African stories
  Looking for a rain god: an anthology of contemporary African short stories

15th century
  Dunnett, D. Scales of gold

19th century
  Haggard, H. R. King Solomon's mines
  Haggard, H. R. She
  Phillips, C. Crossing the river
  Smith, W. A. Flight of the falcon
  Smith, W. A. Men of men

20th century
  Boyd, W. Brazzaville Beach
  Caputo, P. Horn of Africa
  Cussler, C. Sahara
  Greene, G. A burnt-out case
  Lessing, D. M. The golden notebook
  Naipaul, V. S. A bend in the river
  Smith, W. A. Elephant song
  Updike, J. The coup

Kings and rulers
  Updike, J. The coup

Native peoples
  See also Zulus (African people)
  Bellow, S. Henderson the rain king
  Hulme, K. The nun's story

  Ruark, R. Something of value
  Ruark, R. Uhuru
  Smith, W. A. Men of men

Politics
  See Politics—Africa

Race relations
  Gordimer, N. A guest of honor

AFRICA, CENTRAL *See* Central Africa
AFRICA, SOUTH *See* South Africa
AFRICA, SOUTHERN *See* Southern Africa
AFRICA, WEST *See* West Africa

AFRICAN AMERICANS
  See also Blacks; Mulattoes; Slavery
  Baldwin, J. Going to meet the man
  Baldwin, J. Just above my head
  Bambara, T. C. Gorilla, my love
  Barrett, W. E. The lilies of the field
  Bradley, D. The Chaneysville incident
  Calling the wind
  Campbell, B. M. Brothers and sisters
  Campbell, B. M. Your blues ain't like mine
  Conrad, J. The Nigger of the Narcissus
  Dawson, C. Body of knowledge
  Doctorow, E. L. Ragtime
  Dove, R. Through the ivory gate
  Fairbairn, A. Five smooth stones
  Fast, H. Freedom road
  Faulkner, W. The reivers
  Gaines, E. J. The autobiography of Miss Jane Pittman
  Harris, M. Bang the drum slowly, by Henry W. Wiggen
  Himes, C. The collected stories of Chester Himes
  Hughes, L. Laughing to keep from crying
  Hughes, L. Not without laughter
  Hughes, L. Simple speaks his mind
  Hughes, L. Simple stakes a claim
  Hughes, L. Simple takes a wife
  Hughes, L. Simple's Uncle Sam
  Hurston, Z. N. The complete stories
  Lee, H. To kill a mockingbird
  Lewis, S. Kingsblood royal
  Marshall, P. Daughters
  Marshall, P. Praisesong for the widow
  McCullers, C. Clock without hands
  McCullers, C. The member of the wedding
  McKnight, R. The kind of light that shines on Texas
  McMillan, T. Waiting to exhale
  Morrison, T. Beloved
  Morrison, T. Jazz
  Morrison, T. Song of Solomon
  Morrison, T. Tar baby
  Mowry, J. Six out seven
  Naylor, G. Bailey's Café
  Naylor, G. Linden Hills
  Naylor, G. Mama Day
  Naylor, G. The women of Brewster Place
  Parks, G. The learning tree
  Petry, A. L. The street
  Phillips, C. Crossing the river
  Price, R. Clockers
  Reed, I. Japanese by spring
  Reed, I. The last days of Louisiana Red
  Shange, N. Liliane
  Shange, N. Sassafrass, Cypress & Indigo
  The Sleeper wakes
  Smith, L. E. Strange fruit
  Somtow, S. P. Jasmine nights
  Stowe, H. B. Uncle Tom's cabin
  Styron, W. The confessions of Nat Turner
  The Unforgetting heart: an anthology of short stories by African American women (1859-1993)
  Unsworth, B. Sacred hunger
  Updike, J. Rabbit redux
  Walker, A. Possessing the secret of joy
  Walker, A. The temple of my familiar
  Walker, A. You can't keep a good woman down

AFRICAN AMERICANS—Continued
Walker, M. Jubilee
Wallace, I. The man
Westheimer, D. My sweet Charlie
Wideman, J. E. Philadelphia fire
Wideman, J. E. The stories of John Edgar Wideman
Williams, J. A. The man who cried I am
Wright, R. Eight men
Wright, R. Native son
Wright, R. The outsider
Wright, R. Uncle Tom's children
Wright, R. Works

Civil rights
Brown, R. Civil wars
Davis, T. 1959
Fairbairn, A. Five smooth stones
Lester, J. And all our wounds forgiven
Straight, S. I been in sorrow's kitchen and licked out all the pots

Relations with Jews
Malamud, B. The tenants

California
Holland, C. Pacific Street
Straight, S. Blacker than a thousand midnights

Chicago (Ill.)
Sinclair, A. Coffee will make you black

Connecticut
Tryon, T. In the fire of spring

Georgia
Bambara, T. C. The salt eaters
Woods, S. Chiefs

Indiana
Pinckney, D. High cotton

Kansas
Clair, M. Rattlebone

Louisiana
Gaines, E. J. The gathering of old men
Gaines, E. J. In my father's house
Gaines, E. J. A lesson before dying
Rhodes, J. P. Voodoo dreams

Massachusetts
West, D. The wedding

Michigan
Estleman, L. D. King of the corner

Mississippi
Faulkner, W. Absalom, Absalom!
Faulkner, W. Intruder in the dust
Faulkner, W. Light in August
Faulkner, W. Requiem for a nun
Faulkner, W. The sound and the fury
French, A. Billy
Grisham, J. A time to kill
Nordan, L. Wolf whistle
Shange, N. Liliane

Missouri
Shange, N. Betsey Brown

New York (N.Y.)
Baker, D. Young man with a horn
Baldwin, J. Another country
Baldwin, J. Go tell it on the mountain
Baldwin, J. If Beale Street could talk
Baldwin, J. Tell me how long the train's been gone
Childress, A. A short walk
Denker, H. Mrs. Washington and Horowitz, too
Ellison, R. Invisible man
Guy, R. A measure of time
Guy, R. Ruby
McMillan, T. Disappearing acts
Woodson, J. Autobiography of a family photo

New York (State)
Oates, J. C. I lock my door upon myself

Porter, C. R. All-Bright Court

North Carolina
Kenan, R. Let the dead bury their dead and other stories
Parker, G. M. These same long bones

Ohio
Morrison, T. The bluest eye
Morrison, T. Sula

South Carolina
Childress, A. A short walk

Southern States
Grau, S. A. Roadwalkers
Heidish, M. A woman called Moses
Lester, J. Do Lord remember me
Walker, A. The color purple

Tennessee
Marius, R. C. After the war

Texas
Brandon, J. Rules of evidence

Virginia
Davis, T. 1959
Shreve, S. R. A country of strangers
The **African** Queen. Forester, C. S.
African stories. Lessing, D. M.
AFRICAN TRIBES See Africa—Native peoples

AFRIKANERS
Brink, A. P. A chain of voices
Michener, J. A. The covenant
Smith, W. A. Power of the sword
Smith, W. A. Rage

AFRO-AMERICANS See African Americans
After all these years. Isaacs, S.
After I'm gone. Westlake, D. E.
   In Westlake, D. E. Levine p151-82
After leaving Mr. Mackenzie. Rhys, J.
After many a summer dies the swan. Huxley, A.
After the king. Entered in Part I under title
After the war. Marius, R. C.
After worlds collide. Balmer, E.
   In Balmer, E. When worlds collide
After you've gone. Adams, A.
Afterlife. Monette, P.
The **afterlife** and other stories. Updike, J.
Agatha Christie: five complete novels of murder and detection. Christie, A.
Agatha Raisin and the potted gardener. Beaton, M. C.
Agatha Raisin and the quiche of death. Beaton, M. C.
Age of consent. Greenberg, J.
The **age** of discretion. Beauvoir, S. de
   In Beauvoir, S. de. The woman destroyed p9-85
The **age** of grief. Smiley, J.
The **age** of grief [novelette]. Smiley, J.
   In Smiley, J. The age of grief p119-213
The **age** of innocence. Wharton, E.
Age of iron. Coetzee, J. M.
The **age** of reason. Sartre, J. P.
The **age** of wonders. Appelfeld, A.

AGED See Old age
Agent in place. MacInnes, H.

AGENTS, SECRET See Spies

AGNOSTICISM
Joyce, J. A portrait of the artist as a young man
The **agony** and the ecstasy. Stone, I.
Ah, but your land is beautiful. Paton, A.
Ah, sweet mystery. Sibley, C.
Ah, sweet mystery of life. Dahl, R.
Ah, treachery! Thomas, R.

AIDS (DISEASE)
Hoffman, A. At risk
Monette, P. Afterlife
Price, R. The promise of rest
Quinn, S. Happy endings

AIDS (DISEASE)—*Continued*
Russell, P. Sea of tranquillity

AIR CRASHES *See* Airplane accidents

AIR FORCE OFFICERS *See* Argentina—Air Force—Officers; United States. Air Force—Officers

AIR MAIL SERVICE
Saint-Exupéry, A. de. Night flight

AIR PILOTS
See also Women air pilots
Bates, H. E. Fair stood the wind for France
Brown, D. Chains of command
Buffett, J. Where is Joe Merchant?
Coonts, S. Final flight
Coonts, S. Flight of the Intruder
Coonts, S. The Intruders
Coonts, S. The minotaur
Francis, D. Rat race
Gann, E. K. The aviator
Gann, E. K. The high and the mighty
Gann, E. K. In the company of eagles
Griffin, W. E. B. The aviators
Heller, J. Catch-22
L'Amour, L. Last of the breed
Michener, J. A. The bridges at Toko-ri
Michener, J. A. Sayonara
Saint-Exupéry, A. de. The little prince
Saint-Exupéry, A. de. Night flight
Shaw, I. Nightwork
Thomas, C. Firefox
Thomas, C. Firefox down

AIR TRAVEL
Cleary, J. High road to China
Follett, K. Night over water
Gann, E. K. The high and the mighty

AIR WARFARE *See* Military aeronautics; World War, 1914-1918—Aerial operations; World War, 1939-1945—Aerial operations

AIRCRAFT CARRIERS
Michener, J. A. The bridges at Toko-ri

AIRLINES
See also Airports

Flight attendants
See Flight attendants

AIRMEN *See* Air pilots

AIRPLANE ACCIDENTS
Gann, E. K. The aviator
Trevor, E. The flight of the Phoenix

AIRPLANE CARRIERS *See* Aircraft carriers

AIRPLANES
See also Transport planes
Follett, K. Night over water
Thomas, C. Firefox
Thomas, C. Firefox down

Accidents
See Airplane accidents

Pilots
See Air pilots
Airport. Hailey, A.

AIRPORTS
Hailey, A. Airport
Airs above the ground. Stewart, M.

ALABAMA
Capote, T. A Christmas memory
Capote, T. The Thanksgiving visitor
Childress, M. Crazy in Alabama
Flagg, F. Fried green tomatoes at the Whistle-Stop Cafe
Lee, H. To kill a mockingbird
McCammon, R. R. Boy's life

Montgomery
Brown, R. M. Southern discomfort
Alas, Babylon. Frank, P.

ALASKA
Ferber, E. Ice Palace
Kesey, K. Sailor song
Michener, J. A. Alaska

Frontier and pioneer life
See Frontier and pioneer life—Alaska

Politics
See Politics—Alaska
Alaska. Michener, J. A.

ALBANIA
Gilman, D. The unexpected Mrs. Pollifax

ALBANY (N.Y.) *See* New York (State)—Albany
Albatross. Anthony, E.

ALBERTA *See* Canada—Alberta

ALCOHOLICS *See* Alcoholism

ALCOHOLISM
Allison, D. Bastard out of Carolina
Amis, K. The old devils
Banks, R. Affliction
Bradbury, R. Green shadows, white whale
Breslin, J. Table money
Brontë, A. The tenant of Wildfell Hall
Coetzee, J. M. Age of iron
Coughlin, W. J. Shadow of a doubt
Del Vecchio, J. M. Carry me home
Francis, D. Knockdown
Golding, W. The paper men
Harrison, J. The seven-ounce man
Hassler, J. North of hope
Hemingway, E. Islands in the stream
Hemingway, E. The torrents of spring
Jackson, C. The lost weekend
Jong, E. Any woman's blues
Korda, M. Curtain
Lowry, M. Under the volcano
MacDonald, J. D. Slam the big door
McFarland, D. The music room
McMillan, T. Disappearing acts
McMurtry, L. Buffalo girls
Minot, S. Monkeys
Oates, J. C. What I lived for
O'Hara, J. Appointment in Samarra
Rebeta-Burditt, J. The cracker factory
Richler, M. Solomon Gursky was here
Russell, P. Sea of tranquillity
Schulberg, B. The disenchanted
Siddons, A. R. Peachtree Road
Stone, R. Children of light
Styron, W. Set this house on fire
Wambaugh, J. The Golden Orange

ALEXANDER, THE GREAT, 356-323 B.C.
Bova, B. Orion and the conqueror
Renault, M. Fire from heaven
Renault, M. Funeral games
Renault, M. The Persian boy
Alexander Pushkin: complete prose fiction. Pushkin, A. S.

ALEXANDRIA (EGYPT) *See* Egypt—Alexandria
The Alexandria quartet: Justine; Balthazar; Mountolive [and] Clea. Durrell, L.
Alfred Hitchcock presents: Stories not for the nervous. Entered in Part I under title

ALGERIA
Camus, A. The first man
Camus, A. A happy death

Oran
Camus, A. The plague

ALGONQUIAN INDIANS
See also Shawnee Indians
Alibi for a corpse. Lemarchand, E.
Alice Adams. Tarkington, B.
An **alien** heat. Moorcock, M.
ALIENATION (SOCIAL PSYCHOLOGY)
See also Social isolation
Camus, A. The first man
Heinemann, L. Paco's story
Hoeg, P. Borderliners
Lessing, D. M. The fifth child
Strindberg, A. By the open sea
Trevor, W. Felicia's journey
Wideman, J. E. Philadelphia fire
The **alienist**. Carr, C.
ALIENS, ILLEGAL See Undocumented aliens
ALIENS, UNDOCUMENTED See Undocumented aliens
All aces. Stout, R.
All around the town. Clark, M. H.
All-Bright Court. Porter, C. R.
All desires known. Ross-Macdonald, M.
All in the family. O'Connor, E.
All my sins remembered. Thomas, R.
All our yesterdays. Parker, R. B.
All passion spent. Sackville-West, V.
All quiet on the western front. Remarque, E. M.
All souls' rising. Bell, M. S.
All that remains. Cornwell, P. D.
All the days and nights. Maxwell, W.
All the king's men. Warren, R. P.
All the little live things. Stegner, W. E.
All the pretty horses. McCarthy, C.
All the Weyrs of Pern. McCaffrey, A.
All this, and heaven too. Field, R.
ALLEGORIES
See also Fables; Fantasies; Good and evil;
Parables; Symbolism
Abe, K. The box man
Abe, K. The woman in the dunes
Adams, R. Watership Down
Anderson, P. Goat song
Appelfeld, A. Unto the soul
Atwood, M. The handmaid's tale
Auster, P. In the country of last things
Auster, P. Leviathan
Auster, P. Mr. Vertigo
Ballard, J. G. The unlimited dream company
Barth, J. Giles goat-boy
Beagle, P. S. The last unicorn
Bradley, M. Z. The firebrand
Brooks, T. The sword of Shannara
Bunyan, J. The Pilgrim's progress
Cabell, J. B. Jurgen: a comedy of justice
Caldwell, T. Ceremony of the innocent
Calvino, I. Mr. Palomar
Camus, A. The fall
Cheever, J. Oh, what a paradise it seems
Chesterton, G. K. The man who was Thursday
Coetzee, J. M. Life & times of Michael K.
Donoso, J. A house in the country
Ellison, H. The deathbird
Faulkner, W. A fable
Fuentes, C. Terra nostra
García Márquez, G. The autumn of the patriarch
García Márquez, G. One hundred years of solitude
Gardner, J. Grendel
Gardner, J. The sunlight dialogues
Golding, W. Darkness visible
Golding, W. The inheritors
Golding, W. Lord of the Flies
Golding, W. The scorpion god: three short novels
Golding, W. The spire
Grass, G. Cat and mouse
Grass, G. The flounder
Guy, R. My love, my love
Hawthorne, N. The marble faun
Hesse, H. Narcissus and Goldmund

Hesse, H. Siddhartha
Hoban, R. Pilgermann
Hoban, R. Riddley Walker
Hoban, R. Turtle diary
Irving, J. A prayer for Owen Meany
James, P. D. The children of men
Kafka, F. The castle
Kafka, F. The trial
King, S. The stand
Le Guin, U. K. The beginning place
Lessing, D. M. Shikasta
Lewis, C. S. Out of the silent planet
Lewis, C. S. Perelandra
Lewis, C. S. That hideous strength
Lewis, C. S. Till we have faces
Malamud, B. Dubin's lives
Malamud, B. The natural
Martin, V. Mary Reilly
Melville, H. Mardi: and a voyager thither
Murdoch, I. The green knight
Oates, J. C. Black water
O'Connor, F. The violent bear it away
Ôe, K. Nip the buds, shoot the kids
Orwell, G. Animal farm
Oz, A. To know a woman
Ozick, C. The Messiah of Stockholm
Porter, K. A. Ship of fools
Robbins, T. Jitterbug perfume
Rushdie, S. Haroun and the sea of stories
Rushdie, S. Midnight's children
Rushdie, S. Shame
Saint-Exupéry, A. de. The little prince
Singer, I. B. The king of the fields
Stevenson, R. L. The strange case of Dr. Jekyll and
Mr. Hyde
Tepper, S. S. A plague of angels
Theroux, P. The Mosquito Coast
Thomas, R. D. The angel carver
Tolkien, J. R. R. The fellowship of the ring
Tolkien, J. R. R. The hobbit
Tolkien, J. R. R. The lord of the rings
Tolkien, J. R. R. The return of the king
Tolkien, J. R. R. The Silmarillion
Tolkien, J. R. R. The two towers
Updike, J. Brazil
Updike, J. The witches of Eastwick
Vargas Llosa, M. The storyteller
Wiggins, M. John Dollar
Wilde, O. The picture of Dorian Gray
Almayer's folly. Conrad, J.
In Conrad, J. Tales of the East and West p1-128
Almost paradise. Isaacs, S.
Almost perfect. Adams, A.
Along came a spider. Patterson, J.
ALPS
MacInnes, H. The Salzburg connection
Mann, T. The magic mountain
Ullman, J. R. The White Tower
Altered states. Chayefsky, P.
ALUMNI, COLLEGE See College alumni
Alvin Journeyman. Card, O. S.
Always and forever. Freeman, C.
Always coming home. Le Guin, U. K.
The **amazing** Mrs. Pollifax. Gilman, D.
AMAZON RIVER VALLEY
Cussler, C. Inca gold
Vargas Llosa, M. The storyteller
AMBASSADORS See Diplomatic life
The **ambassadors**. James, H.
The **ambassador's** women. Gaskin, C.
Amber [series]
Zelazny, R. Blood of Amber
Zelazny, R. The courts of chaos
Zelazny, R. The guns of Avalon
Zelazny, R. The hand of Oberon

Amber—[series]—*Continued*
Zelazny, R. Knight of shadows
Zelazny, R. Nine princes in Amber
Zelazny, R. Prince of chaos
Zelazny, R. Sign of chaos
Zelazny, R. Sign of the unicorn
Zelazny, R. Trumps of doom

AMBITION
See also Self-made men
Archer, J. As the crow flies
Archer, J. First among equals
Archer, J. Kane & Abel
Archer, J. The prodigal daughter
Auchincloss, L. The dark lady
Auchincloss, L. The lady of situations
Birmingham, S. The Rothman scandal
Bradford, B. T. Hold the dream
Bradford, B. T. To be the best
Bradford, B. T. A woman of substance
Burgess, A. Hun
Caldwell, T. Captains and kings
Crichton, R. The Camerons
Daley, R. Wall of brass
Delderfield, R. F. God is an Englishman
Dexter, P. The paperboy
Dunne, D. The two Mrs. Grenvilles
Fuentes, C. The death of Artemio Cruz
Greeley, A. M. Thy brother's wife
Jakes, J. California gold
Kinsolving, W. Bred to win
Laker, R. Banners of silk
Marsh, J. The House of Eliott
Michael, J. A ruling passion
Rand, A. The fountainhead
Reid Banks, L. The warning bell
Rich, M. Tender offerings
Ross-Macdonald, M. Hell hath no fury
Ross-Macdonald, M. The rich are with you always
Ross-Macdonald, M. The world from rough stones
Schulberg, B. What makes Sammy run?
Spellman, C. C. Paint the wind
Stendhal. The red and the black
Trollope, A. The Eustace diamonds
Uhnak, D. False witness
Vidal, G. Washington, D.C.
Warren, R. P. All the king's men
Weidman, J. I can get it for you wholesale
West, N. A cool million
Woods, S. L.A. Times

AMERGIN (LEGENDARY CHARACTER)
Llywelyn, M. Bard

AMERICA
See also Central America; South America

Discovery and exploration
Forester, C. S. To the Indies
Thom, J. A. The children of first man
America, America. Kazan, E.
The **American**. James, H.
American appetites. Oates, J. C.

American chronicle [series]
Vidal, G. 1876
Vidal, G. Burr
Vidal, G. Empire
Vidal, G. Hollywood
Vidal, G. Washington, D.C.

AMERICAN CIVIL WAR, 1861-1865 *See* United
States—Civil War, 1861-1865
The **American** claimant. Twain, M.
In Twain, M. The complete novels of Mark Twain
v1 p263-416
The **American** heiress. Eden, D.

AMERICAN INDIAN DIALECT *See* Dialect stories—
American Indian

AMERICAN LOYALISTS
Cooper, J. F. The spy
Roberts, K. L. Oliver Wiswell
The **American** novels and stories of Henry James. James,
H.
AMERICAN REVOLUTION, 1775-1783 *See* United
States—Revolution, 1775-1783
AMERICAN SOLDIERS *See* Soldiers—United States
AMERICAN SPANISH WAR, 1898 *See* United States—
War of 1898
An **American** tragedy. Dreiser, T.
American voices. Entered in Part I under title

AMERICANIZATION
Alvarez, J. How the Garcia girls lost their accents
Bojer, J. The emigrants
Cather, W. My Ántonia
Cather, W. O pioneers!
Jen, G. Typical American
Rölvaag, O. E. Peder Victorious

AMERICANS
Afghanistan
Michener, J. A. Caravans

Africa
Bellow, S. Henderson the rain king
Rush, N. Mating

Australia
Nordhoff, C. Botany Bay

Austria
MacInnes, H. The Salzburg connection

Belgium
Benedict, E. Safe conduct

Cambodia
Del Vecchio, J. M. For the sake of all living things

Canada
Freedman, B. Mrs. Mike

Caribbean region
Marshall, P. Praisesong for the widow

Central America
Didion, J. A book of common prayer
Stone, R. A flag for sunrise

China
Barrett, W. E. The left hand of God
Buck, P. S. East wind: west wind
Hersey, J. A single pebble

Czech Republic
Roth, P. The Prague orgy

Denmark
Stegner, W. E. The spectator bird

England
Bradford, B. T. Everything to gain
Coulter, C. The valentine legacy
Coulter, C. The Wyndham legacy
Dickinson, P. Perfect gallows
Donleavy, J. P. The ginger man
Du Maurier, Dame D. The house on the strand
Eden, D. The American heiress
Galsworthy, J. Maid in waiting
Gaskin, C. The ambassador's women
Godwin, G. Mr. Bedford
Harper, K. Circle of gold
Higgins, J. The eagle has landed
James, H. The golden bowl
Lurie, A. Foreign affairs
McMullen, M. A grave without flowers
McMurtry, L. Buffalo girls
Murdoch, I. An accidental man
Robards, K. Nobody's angel
Straub, P. Mrs. God
Thane, E. Kissing kin
Thane, E. The light heart

AMERICANS—England—_Continued_
Thane, E. This was tomorrow
Theroux, P. Doctor Slaughter
Wharton, E. The buccaneers
Wharton, E. The buccaneers, completed by Marion Mainwaring

Europe
Blake, J. Wildest dreams
Cather, W. One of ours
Folsom, A. R. The day after tomorrow
Hemingway, E. The sun also rises
Highsmith, P. The boy who followed Ripley
Hunter, E. Lizzie
James, H. The portrait of a lady
James, H. The wings of the dove
Lewis, S. Dodsworth
Maugham, W. S. The razor's edge
McCarthy, M. Birds of America
Plante, D. Annunciation
Price, R. The source of light
Pynchon, T. Gravity's rainbow
Thoene, B. The twilight of courage
Wharton, E. The children
Wolfe, T. Of time and the river
Wolfe, T. The web and the rock
Wolfe, T. You can't go home again

France
Baldwin, J. Giovanni's room
Elkin, S. Van Gogh's room at Arles
Fitzgerald, F. S. Tender is the night
James, H. The ambassadors
James, H. The American
Krantz, J. Mistral's daughter
MacInnes, H. The double image
Miller, H. Tropic of Cancer
Moore, B. The doctor's wife
Nin, A. Children of the albatross
Nin, A. The four-chambered heart
Nin, A. Ladders to fire
Shaw, I. Evening in Byzantium
Wharton, E. The reef

Germany
Berger, T. Crazy in Berlin
Carroll, J. Family trade
Isaacs, S. Shining through
O'Connor, R. Buffalo soldiers
Uris, L. Armageddon
Vonnegut, K. Slaughterhouse-five
Wiesel, E. The fifth son

Guatemala
Goldman, F. The long night of white chickens

Honduras
Theroux, P. The Mosquito Coast

India
Bromfield, L. The rains came
Mukherjee, B. The holder of the world
Waller, R. J. Slow waltz in Cedar Bend

Ireland
Binchy, M. Firefly summer
Donleavy, J. P. The ginger man
Greeley, A. M. Irish gold
Ripley, A. Scarlett

Islands of the Pacific
Melville, H. Omoo: a narrative of adventures in the South Seas

Israel
Leonard, E. The hunted
Singer, I. B. The penitent
Uris, L. Exodus

Italy
Anthony, E. Mission to Malaspiga
Hawthorne, N. The marble faun
Hemingway, E. Across the river and into the trees

Hemingway, E. A farewell to arms
James, H. The Aspern papers
James, H. Roderick Hudson
Leonard, E. Pronto
MacInnes, H. North from Rome
Martin, M. Vatican
Siddons, A. R. Hill towns
Spencer, E. Knights and dragons
Spencer, E. The light in the piazza
Styron, W. Set this house on fire
Williams, T. The Roman spring of Mrs. Stone

Japan
Dickey, J. To the white sea

Marquesas Islands
Melville, H. Typee: a peep at Polynesian life

Mexico
Doerr, H. Consider this, señora
Doerr, H. Stones for Ibarra
Fuentes, C. Apollo and the whores
Fuentes, C. The old gringo
McCarthy, C. The crossing
Michener, J. A. Mexico
Morrell, D. Assumed identity
Nin, A. Seduction of the Minotaur
Portis, C. Gringos
Traven, B. The treasure of the Sierra Madre

Netherlands
Williams, J. A. The man who cried I am

North Africa
Bowles, P. The sheltering sky

Okinawa
Sneider, V. The Teahouse of the August Moon

Portugal
L'Engle, M. The love letters

Romania
Wiesel, E. The forgotten

Russia
DeMille, N. The charm school
Freemantle, B. The button man
Gray, F. du P. World without end
L'Amour, L. Last of the breed
Littell, R. The revolutionist

Scotland
Peters, E. Legend in green velvet

Sicily
Hersey, J. A bell for Adano

Singapore
Clavell, J. King Rat

Southeast Asia
Lederer, W. J. The ugly American

Spain
Hemingway, E. For whom the bell tolls

Thailand
Somtow, S. P. Jasmine nights

Turkey
Whitney, P. A. Black amber

Vietnam
Greene, G. The quiet American

West Indies
Shacochis, B. Swimming in the volcano

Zaire
Griffin, W. E. B. The new breed
Amerika. Kafka, F.

AMNESIA
Adler, E. The secret of the Villa Mimosa
Barnard, R. Out of the blackout
Bawden, N. Family money
Dailey, J. Masquerade

AMNESIA—*Continued*
De Hartog, J. The lamb's war
Fielding, J. See Jane run
Greene, G. The ministry of fear
Hilton, J. Random harvest
Lessing, D. M. Briefing for a descent into Hell
Ludlum, R. The Bourne identity
Michael, J. A tangled web
Veryan, P. A shadow's bliss

AMSTERDAM (NETHERLANDS) *See* Netherlands—Amsterdam

AMUSEMENT PARKS
Bradbury, R. Something wicked this way comes

ANALYSTS *See* Psychoanalysts

ANARCHISM AND ANARCHISTS
Chesterton, G. K. The man who was Thursday
Follett, K. The man from St. Petersburg
Sinclair, U. Boston

ANARCHISTS *See* Anarchism and anarchists
The **Anastasia** syndrome. Clark, M. H.
In Clark, M. H. The Anastasia syndrome and other stories p9-157
The **Anastasia** syndrome and other stories. Clark, M. H.
The **anatomy** lesson. Roth, P.
also in Roth, P. Zuckerman bound: a trilogy and epilogue
Anatomy of a murder. Traver, R.
Ancestral truths. Maitland, S.
The **ancient** child. Momaday, N. S.
Ancient evenings. Mailer, N.
And all our wounds forgiven. Lester, J.
And baby will fall. Lewin, M. Z.
And eternity. Anthony, P.
"**—and** ladies of the club". Santmyer, H. H.
And quiet flows the Don. Sholokhov, M. A.
And the angels sing. Wilhelm, K.
And then there were none. Christie, A.
And where were you, Adam? Böll, H.
In Böll, H. The stories of Heinrich Böll p34-152
And wild for to hold. Kress, N.
In Modern classic short novels of science fiction p617-57
Andersonville. Kantor, M.

ANDERSONVILLE PRISON
Kantor, M. Andersonville
The **Andromeda** strain. Crichton, M.
Angel. Bradford, B. T.
The **angel** carver. Thomas, R. D.
Angel eyes. Lustbader, E. V.
The **angel** maker. Pearson, R.
The **angelic** avengers. Dinesen, I.

ANGELS
Westlake, D. E. Humans
Angels and insects. Byatt, A. S.
Angels of September. Greeley, A. M.
The **angels** weep. Smith, W. A.
Anger. Sarton, M.
Angle of repose. Stegner, W. E.

ANGLICAN AND EPISCOPAL BISHOPS
Trollope, A. Barchester Towers
Trollope, A. The warden

ANGLICAN AND EPISCOPAL CLERGY
Auchincloss, L. The Rector of Justin
Austen, J. Mansfield Park
Austen, J. Pride and prejudice
Brontë, C. Jane Eyre
Brontë, C. Shirley
Butler, S. The way of all flesh
Craven, M. I heard the owl call my name
Eliot, G. Middlemarch
Godwin, G. Father Melancholy's daughter
Goldsmith, O. The Vicar of Wakefield
Goudge, E. A city of bells
Goudge, E. The dean's watch
Howatch, S. Absolute truths
Howatch, S. Glamorous powers
Howatch, S. Glittering images
Howatch, S. Mystical paths
Howatch, S. Scandalous risks
Howatch, S. Ultimate prizes
L'Engle, M. A severed wasp
MacNeil, R. Burden of desire
Maitland, S. Ancestral truths
Paton, A. Cry, the beloved country
Pym, B. A few green leaves
Pym, B. Some tame gazelle
Pym, B. An unsuitable attachment
Trollope, A. Barchester Towers
Trollope, A. Framley parsonage
Trollope, A. The last chronicle of Barset
Trollope, A. The warden
Trollope, J. The rector's wife
Wilson, A. N. The vicar of sorrows

ANGLO-SAXONS
Gardner, J. Grendel
Sutcliff, R. Sword at sunset
The **angry** tide. Graham, W.
Animal dreams. Kingsolver, B.
Animal farm. Orwell, G.
The **animal** wife. Thomas, E. M.

ANIMALS
See also names of individual animals
Burnford, S. Bel Ria
Burnford, S. The incredible journey
Gallico, P. Three legends: The snow goose; The small miracle; Ludmila
Goethe, J. W. von. Novella
Irving, J. Setting free the bears
Michener, J. A. Creatures of the kingdom
Orwell, G. Animal farm
Wells, H. G. The island of Doctor Moreau
White, T. H. The book of Merlyn
Wodehouse, P. G. A Wodehouse bestiary
Anna Karenina. Tolstoy, L., graf
The **Anna** papers. Gilchrist, E.
The **annals** of the Heechee. Pohl, F.
Anna's book. Vine, B.

ANNE, OF AUSTRIA, 1601-1666 *See* Anne, Queen, consort of Louis XIII, King of France, 1601-1666

ANNE, QUEEN, CONSORT OF LOUIS XIII, KING OF FRANCE, 1601-1666
Anthony, E. The Cardinal and the Queen
Dumas, A. The three musketeers
Dumas, A. Twenty years after

ANNE, QUEEN, CONSORT OF RICHARD III, KING OF ENGLAND, 1456-1485
Plaidy, J. The reluctant queen

ANNE BOLEYN, QUEEN, CONSORT OF HENRY VIII, KING OF ENGLAND, 1507-1536
Anthony, E. Anne Boleyn
Kress, N. And wild for to hold
Plaidy, J. Murder most royal
Anne Boleyn. Anthony, E.
Annie John. Kincaid, J.
Anno-Dracula. Newman, K.
Annunciation. Plante, D.
The **Anodyne** Necklace. Grimes, M.

ANOREXIA NERVOSA
Levenkron, S. The best little girl in the world
Another country. Baldwin, J.
Another part of the city. McBain, E.

ANSON, GEORGE ANSON, BARON, 1697-1762
O'Brian, P. The golden ocean
Answer as a man. Caldwell, T.
Answer came there none. Ferrars, E. X.
Answered prayers. Capote, T.

ANTARCTIC REGIONS
See also Arctic regions
Bainbridge, B. The birthday boys
Innes, H. Isvik

Anthem. Rand, A.

Anthills of the Savannah. Achebe, C.

Anthony Adverse. Allen, H.

ANTHROPOLOGISTS
Jackson, S. The haunting of Hill House
Pym, B. An academic question
Pym, B. A few green leaves
Pym, B. Less than angels
Pym, B. An unsuitable attachment
Vargas Llosa, M. The storyteller

Antic hay. Huxley, A.

ANTIGUA AND BARBUDA
Kincaid, J. Annie John

ANTIOCH (TURKEY) *See* Turkey—Antioch

ANTIQUE DEALERS
See also Art dealers
Gash, J. The Vatican rip
McMurtry, L. Cadillac Jack
Pym, B. The sweet dove died
Roberts, N. Hidden riches

ANTIQUES
See also Antiquities
Neville, K. The eight

ANTIQUITIES
See also Archeology
Hoving, T. Discovery

ANTISEMITISM
See also Holocaust, Jewish (1933-1945); Jews—Persecutions
Appelfeld, A. The age of wonders
Appelfeld, A. Katerina
Bassani, G. The garden of the Finzi-Continis
Follett, K. A dangerous fortune
Greenberg, J. I never promised you a rose garden
Hobson, L. K. Z. Gentleman's agreement
Malamud, B. The fixer
Richler, M. Solomon Gursky was here
Schwarz-Bart, A. The last of the just
Sholem Aleichem. The bloody hoax
Thomas, M. M. Hanover Place
Viertel, J. Life lines

Anton Chekhov's short stories. Chekhov, A. P.

Antonietta. Hersey, J.

ANTS
Byatt, A. S. Morpho Eugenia

Anvil of stars. Bear, G.

ANXIETY *See* Fear

Any old iron. Burgess, A.

Any woman's blues. Jong, E.

Anything for Billy. McMurtry, L.

Anywhere but here. Simpson, M.

Apache autumn. Skimin, R.

APACHE INDIANS
Gipson, F. B. Savage Sam
L'Amour, L. Hondo
Skimin, R. Apache autumn

Wars, 1883-1886
Horgan, P. A distant trumpet

APARTHEID *See* South Africa—Race relations

APARTMENT HOUSES
Levin, I. Sliver
Malamud, B. The tenants

APARTMENTS *See* Apartment houses

Ape and essence. Huxley, A.

APES
Boulle, P. Planet of the Apes

Apollo and the whores. Fuentes, C.
In Fuentes, C. The orange tree p148-204

The Apostle. Asch, S.

APOSTLES
Costain, T. B. The silver chalice

The **apostrophe** thief. Paul, B.

APOTHECARIES *See* Pharmacists

APPALACHIAN MOUNTAINS
See also Blue Ridge Mountains
McCrumb, S. The hangman's beautiful daughter
McCrumb, S. She walks these hills
Phillips, J. A. Shelter

APPALACHIAN REGION
Giardina, D. The unquiet earth
Marshall, C. Christy
Smith, L. Fair and tender ladies
Smith, L. Oral history

Appearances of death. Shannon, D.

Apple tree lean down. [omnibus volume] Pearce, M. E.

Apple tree lean down [novel]. Pearce, M. E.
In Pearce, M. E. Apple tree lean down [omnibus volume]

Appleby and Honeybath. Innes, M.

Appleby and the Ospreys. Innes, M.

Appleby's end. Innes, M.

Appointment in Samarra. O'Hara, J.

Apprentice Adept [series]
Anthony, P. Blue Adept
Anthony, P. Juxtaposition
Anthony, P. Out of Phaze
Anthony, P. Phaze doubt
Anthony, P. Robot Adept
Anthony, P. Split infinity
Anthony, P. Unicorn point

APPRENTICES
Andersen Nexø, M. Pelle the conqueror: v2 Apprenticeship

April morning. Fast, H.

The **April** Rainers. Fraser, A.

Apt pupil. King, S.
In King, S. Different seasons p103-296

The **Aquitaine** progression. Ludlum, R.

ARAB-JEWISH RELATIONS *See* Jewish-Arab relations

ARABIAN NIGHTS
Parodies, travesties, etc.
Maḥfūz, N. Arabian nights and days

Arabian nights and days. Maḥfūz, N.

ARABS
See also Jewish-Arab relations; Moors; Palestinian Arabs
Maḥfūz, N. Arabian nights and days

Borneo
Conrad, J. Almayer's folly

Arch of triumph. Remarque, E. M.

ARCHEOLOGICAL SPECIMENS *See* Antiquities

ARCHEOLOGISTS
See also Women archeologists
Drabble, M. The realms of gold
Galsworthy, J. Maid in waiting
Michael, J. Sleeping beauty
Rice, L. Stone heart
Stone, I. The Greek treasure

ARCHEOLOGY
See also Antiquities; Prehistoric man; Stone Age
Cussler, C. Inca gold
Drabble, M. The realms of gold
Peters, E. Legend in green velvet
Stone, I. The Greek treasure

Archer at large. Macdonald, R.

Archer in Hollywood. Macdonald, R.

Archer in jeopardy. Macdonald, R.

ARCHITECTS
See also Building
Böll, H. Billiards at half-past nine
Colegate, I. The summer of the royal visit
Dickens, C. Martin Chuzzlewit
Ferber, E. So Big

ARCHITECTS—*Continued*
Galsworthy, J. The man of property
Greene, G. A burnt-out case
Lively, P. City of the mind
MacInnes, H. Decision at Delphi
Rand, A. The fountainhead

ARCTIC REGIONS
    See also Alaska; Antarctic regions; Greenland
MacLean, A. Ice Station Zebra
Michener, J. A. Journey
Mowat, F. The Snow Walker
Arfive. Guthrie, A. B.

ARGENTINA

        19th century
Fuentes, C. The campaign

        20th century
Griffin, W. E. B. Honor bound

        Air Force—Officers
Higgins, J. Exocet

        Prisoners and prisons
    See Prisoners and prisons—Argentina

        Rural life
Greene, G. The honorary consul

        Buenos Aires
Cortázar, J. Hopscotch
Puig, M. Kiss of the spider woman
Saint-Exupéry, A. de. Night flight

ARGENTINE INVASION OF THE FALKLAND IS-LANDS, 1982 *See* Falkland Islands War, 1982

ARGENTINE REPUBLIC *See* Argentina

ARGENTINES

        Brazil
Puig, M. Tropical night falling

        Europe
Blasco Ibáñez, V. The four horsemen of the Apocalypse

        France
Cortázar, J. Hopscotch

        United States
Puig, M. Eternal curse on the reader of these pages

ARGENTINIANS *See* Argentines

ARGONAUTS (GREEK MYTHOLOGY)
    See also Jason (Greek mythology)
Graves, R. Hercules, my shipmate

ARISTOCRACY
    See also Courts and courtiers; Society novels

        England
Barnard, R. Corpse in a gilded cage
Belle, P. Treason's gift
Chesney, M. Back in society
Chesney, M. Colonel Sandhurst to the rescue
Chesney, M. Lady Fortescue steps out
Chesney, M. Miss Tonks turns to crime
Chesney, M. Mrs. Budley falls from grace
Chesney, M. Sir Philip's folly
Colegate, I. The shooting party
Dickinson, P. The last houseparty
Eden, D. The Salamanca drum
Gaskin, C. The ambassador's women
Hardwick, M. The Duchess of Duke Street
Harper, K. Circle of gold
Heyer, G. Lady of quality
Kells, S. The aristocrats
Laker, R. The sugar pavilion
Lofts, N. The homecoming
Lofts, N. Knight's Acre
Plaidy, J. The rose without a thorn
Quick, A. Mistress
Sackville-West, V. The Edwardians
Tarkington, B. Monsieur Beaucaire

Thackeray, W. M. The history of Henry Esmond, esquire
Wodehouse, P. G. The code of the Woosters
Wodehouse, P. G. Tales from the Drones Club

        France
Dickens, C. A tale of two cities
Du Maurier, Dame D. The scapegoat
Haasse, H. S. In a dark wood wandering
Holt, V. The Devil on horseback
James, H. The American
Laker, R. To dance with kings
Orczy, E., Baroness. Adventures of the Scarlet Pimpernel
Orczy, E., Baroness. The elusive Pimpernel
Orczy, E., Baroness. The Scarlet Pimpernel
Proust, M. The Guermantes way
Proust, M. Sodom and Gomorrah
Riley, J. M. The oracle glass
Stendhal. The red and the black
Tarkington, B. Monsieur Beaucaire

        Hungary
Pearson, D. Csardas

        Ireland
Ross-Macdonald, M. A woman scorned

        Italy
Bassani, G. The garden of the Finzi-Continis
Stendhal. The charterhouse of Parma

        Japan
Mishima, Y. Spring snow

        Sicily
Tomasi di Lampedusa, G. The leopard
The **aristocrats**. Kells, S.

ARIZONA
    See also Tonto Basin (Ariz.)

        19th century
Henry, W. Mackenna's gold
Horgan, P. A distant trumpet

        20th century
Harrison, J. The beige dolorosa
Kingsolver, B. Animal dreams
Kingsolver, B. The bean trees
Kingsolver, B. Pigs in heaven

        Phoenix
McMillan, T. Waiting to exhale

        Tucson
Kingsolver, B. Pigs in heaven
The **Arizona** clan. Grey, Z.

ARKANSAS
        19th century
Jones, D. C. Come winter
Jones, D. C. Elkhorn Tavern
Jones, D. C. The search for Temperance Moon
Jones, D. C. This savage race

        Farm life
    See Farm life—Arkansas

        Frontier and pioneer life
    See Frontier and pioneer life—Arkansas

ARLES (FRANCE) *See* France—Arles
Armageddon. Uris, L.

ARMAMENTS
    See also Munitions

ARMED FORCES

        United States
    See United States—Armed forces

ARMENIAN GENOCIDE, 1915-1923 *See* Armenian massacres, 1915-1923

ARMENIAN MASSACRES, 1915-1923
Edgarian, C. Rise the Euphrates

ARMENIAN MASSACRES, 1915-1923—_Continued_
Werfel, F. The forty days of Musa Dagh

ARMENIANS

Syria
Werfel, F. The forty days of Musa Dagh

United States
Edgarian, C. Rise the Euphrates

ARMISTICE DAY _See_ Veterans Day

ARMS AND ARMOR
See also Munitions

ARMY AIR FORCES (U.S.) _See_ United States. Army Air Forces

ARMY HOSPITALS _See_ Hospitals and sanatoriums

ARMY OFFICERS _See_ France—Army—Officers; Germany—Army—Officers; Great Britain. Army—Officers; Peru—Army—Officers; Poland—Army—Officers; Russia—Army—Officers; United States. Army—Officers; Vietnam—Army—Officers

ARNOLD, BENEDICT, 1741-1801
Roberts, K. L. Arundel
Roberts, K. L. Rabble in arms
Around the world in eighty days. Verne, J.
Arrest Sitting Bull. Jones, D. C.
Arrow to the heart. Blake, J.
Arrowsmith. Lewis, S.

ARSON
Barnard, R. A city of strangers
Mishima, Y. The temple of the golden pavilion
Smiley, J. Good will
Spencer, S. Endless love
Whitney, P. A. The glass flame

ART
McCarthy, M. Cannibals and missionaries
Stone, I. The agony and the ecstasy

ART COLLECTORS
Davies, R. What's bred in the bone
Hoving, T. Discovery
Hoving, T. Masterpiece
Krentz, J. A. Grand passion
McCarthy, M. Cannibals and missionaries
Wharton, E. False dawn

ART CRITICS
Farmer, P. J. Riders of the purple wage
Morrow, J. City of Truth

ART DEALERS
See also Antique dealers
Banks, O. T. The Rembrandt panel
MacInnes, H. Prelude to terror
West, M. L. Masterclass
Woods, S. Imperfect strangers

ART FORGERIES _See_ Forgery of works of art

ART GALLERIES AND MUSEUMS
Brown, R. M. Venus envy

ART OBJECTS
See also Antiques
Archer, J. A matter of honor
James, H. The spoils of Poynton
Johnston, V. The Etruscan smile

ARTAGNAN, CHARLES DE BATZ-CASTELMORE, COMTE D', 1613?-1673
Dumas, A. The iron mask
Dumas, A. The three musketeers
Dumas, A. Twenty years after
Artemia. Hill, P.

ARTHUR, KING
Berger, T. Arthur Rex
Bradley, M. Z. The mists of Avalon
Stewart, M. The wicked day
Sutcliff, R. Sword at sunset
Twain, M. A Connecticut Yankee in King Arthur's court
White, T. H. The book of Merlyn
White, T. H. The once and future king
White, T. H. The sword in the stone
White, T. H. The witch in the wood
Arthur Rex. Berger, T.

ARTIFICIAL LIFE
Heinlein, R. A. Friday

ARTIST COLONIES
McCarthy, M. A charmed life

ARTIST LIFE
Crane, S. The third violet
Laker, R. The golden tulip
Mann, T. Tonio Kröger
McCarthy, M. A charmed life
Sanders, L. The second deadly sin
Tyler, A. Celestial navigation
An **artist** of the floating world. Ishiguro, K.

ARTISTS
See also Artist life; Illustrators; Painters; Sculptors; Women artists
Adams, A. Almost perfect
Allen, C. V. Painted lives
Jong, E. Any woman's blues
Kay, T. Shadow song
Kincaid, J. Lucy
Oates, J. C. The model
Price, R. The tongues of angels
Stubbs, J. Like we used to be
Arundel. Roberts, K. L.
As I lay dying. Faulkner, W.
As the crow flies. Archer, J.
As we are now. Sarton, M.
Ascent into hell. Greeley, A. M.

ASCETICISM
Gide, A. Strait is the gate (La porte étroite)

ASEXUAL REPRODUCTION
See also Fertilization in vitro
Brin, D. Glory season
Crichton, M. Jurassic Park
Tiptree, J. Houston, Houston, do you read?
Vinge, J. D. The Snow Queen
Weldon, F. The cloning of Joanna May
Wilhelm, K. Where late the sweet birds sang

ASIA
See also East Asia; Southeast Asia
Bosse, M. J. Fire in heaven

Communism
See Communism—Asia

ASIA, SOUTHEASTERN _See_ Southeast Asia

ASIA MINOR
See also Troy (Ancient city)
Renault, M. The Persian boy
Ask me no questions. Veryan, P.
Aspen gold. Dailey, J.
The **Aspern** papers. James, H.
_In_ James, H. The complete tales of Henry James v6
_In_ James, H. The Henry James reader p165-254
_In_ James, H. Short novels of Henry James p257-354
The **asphalt** jungle. Burnett, W. R.
The **assassin** in the greenwood. Doherty, P. C.

ASSASSINATION
Anthony, E. The Doll's House
Anthony, E. The Janus imperative
Batchelor, J. C. Father's day
Brink, A. P. An act of terror
Buckley, W. F. Mongoose, R.I.P
Buckley, W. F. A very private plot
Carr, P. The black swan
Cleary, J. The faraway drums
Coonts, S. Under siege
Egleton, C. Hostile intent
Fallaci, O. A man
Finney, P. Firedrake's eye
Fleming, I. For your eyes only

ASSASSINATION—*Continued*
Follett, K. The man from St. Petersburg
Folsom, A. R. The day after tomorrow
Forsyth, F. The day of the jackal
Forsyth, F. The dogs of war
Greenberg, J. Age of consent
Grisham, J. The pelican brief
Higgins, J. The eagle has flown
Higgins, J. Eye of the storm
Higgins, J. Touch the devil
Ludlum, R. The Chancellor manuscript
Ludlum, R. The scorpio illusion
Lustbader, E. V. The Kaisho
McCutchan, P. Halfhyde and the fleet review
Mishima, Y. Runaway horses
Morrell, D. The brotherhood of the rose
Perry, T. The butcher's boy
Perry, T. Sleeping dogs
Puzo, M. The fourth K
Safire, W. Full disclosure
Trevanian. The Eiger sanction
Trevanian. Shibumi
Assault with intent. Kienzle, W. X.

ASSES AND MULES
Gallico, P. The small miracle
Sarton, M. Joanna and Ulysses
Assignment in Brittany. MacInnes, H.
ASSISI (ITALY) *See* Italy—Assisi
The **assistant**. Malamud, B.
also in Malamud, B. A Malamud reader p75-305
Assumed identity. Morrell, D.
Asta's book. See Vine, B. Anna's book

ASTEROIDS
Pohl, F. Beyond the blue event horizon
Pohl, F. Gateway
Pohl, F. Heechee rendezvous

ASTRONAUTS
Michener, J. A. Space
Russell, P. Sea of tranquillity
Tiptree, J. Houston, Houston, do you read?

ASTRONOMERS
Hazzard, S. The transit of Venus

ASTRONOMY
See also Outer space; Stars; names of individual planets
At Bertram's Hotel. Christie, A.
At death's door. Barnard, R.
At home in Thrush Green. Read, Miss
At Lady Molly's. Powell, A.
In Powell, A. A dance to the music of time [v1]
At risk. Hoffman, A.
At the Gai-Moulin. See Simenon, G. Maigret at the Gai-Moulin
At the mountains of madness, and other novels. Lovecraft, H. P.
At the sign of the Cat and Racket. Balzac, H. de
In Balzac, H. de. The short novels of Balzac
At weddings and wakes. McDermott, A.
At winter's end. Silverberg, R.
ATHENS (GREECE) *See* Greece—Athens

ATHLETES
See also Women athletes
Bass, R. Field events
Dershowitz, A. M. The advocate's devil
Jenkins, D. Semi-tough
ATLANTA (GA.) *See* Georgia—Atlanta
ATLANTIC CITY (N.J.) *See* New Jersey—Atlantic City

ATLANTIC OCEAN

World War, 1939-1945
See World War, 1939-1945—Atlantic Ocean
Atlas shrugged. Rand, A.

ATOMIC BOMB
Burdick, E. Fail-safe

Clancy, T. The sum of all fears
Collins, L. The fifth horseman
Cussler, C. Dragon
Fleming, I. Thunderball
Follett, K. Triple
Golding, W. Lord of the Flies
Smith, M. C. Stallion Gate
Snow, C. P. The new men
Strieber, W. Warday
Vonnegut, K. Cat's cradle
Wibberley, L. The mouse that roared
ATOMIC ENERGY *See* Nuclear energy
ATOMIC SUBMARINES *See* Nuclear submarines
ATOMIC WARFARE *See* Nuclear warfare

ATONEMENT
Greene, G. Brighton rock
ATROCITIES
See also Holocaust, Jewish (1933-1945); Jews—Persecutions; Massacres; World War, 1939-1945—Atrocities
Attack of the Seawolf. DiMercurio, M.
ATTEMPTED MURDER *See* Murder stories
ATTEMPTED SUICIDE *See* Suicide
ATTILA, KING OF THE HUNS, d. 453
Burgess, A. Hun

ATTITUDE (PSYCHOLOGY)
See also Prejudices
ATTORNEYS *See* Law and lawyers

AU PAIRS
Bellow, S. A theft
Kincaid, J. Lucy
Prose, F. Primitive people
Audrey Rose. De Felitta, F.
The **Auerbach** will. Birmingham, S.
August. Rossner, J.
August 1914. Solzhenitsyn, A.
AUGUSTUS, EMPEROR OF ROME, 63 B.C.-14 A.D.
Graves, R. I, Claudius
Aunt Julia and the scriptwriter. Vargas Llosa, M.
Auntie Mame. Dennis, P.

AUNTS
See also Nieces
Brookner, A. Dolly
Childress, M. Crazy in Alabama
Dennis, P. Auntie Mame
Dickens, C. David Copperfield
Goudge, E. Such devoted sisters
Greene, G. Travels with my aunt
Heyer, G. Cousin Kate
McDermott, A. At weddings and wakes
Pérez Galdós, B. Doña Perfecta
Proulx, A. The shipping news
Somtow, S. P. Jasmine nights
Vargas Llosa, M. Aunt Julia and the scriptwriter
Whitney, P. A. The trembling hills

AUSTEN, JANE, 1775-1817
Parodies, travesties, etc.
Aiken, J. Eliza's daughter
Aiken, J. Jane Fairfax
Aiken, J. Mansfield revisited
Barrett, J. Presumption
Tennant, E. Pemberley
Tennant, E. An unequal marriage

AUSTRALIA
19th century
Eden, D. The vines of Yarrabee
Franklin, M. The end of my career
Franklin, M. My brilliant career
Holt, V. The black opal
Holt, V. The road to Paradise Island
Keneally, T. The playmaker
Malouf, D. Remembering Babylon
Wood, B. The dreaming

AUSTRALIA—*Continued*

20th century

Battle, L. The past is another country
Cleary, J. The sundowners
Keneally, T. A family madness
Keneally, T. Woman of the inner sea
McCullough, C. The ladies of Missalonghi
McCullough, C. The thorn birds
White, P. The eye of the storm
White, P. The tree of man
White, P. The vivisector

Farm life

See Farm life—Australia

Frontier and pioneer life

See Frontier and pioneer life—Australia

Native peoples

See Australian aborigines

Rural life

Cleary, J. The sundowners
Franklin, M. The end of my career
Franklin, M. My brilliant career
Holt, V. The pride of the peacock

Melbourne

Shute, N. On the beach

New South Wales

Eden, D. The vines of Yarrabee
Nordhoff, C. Botany Bay

Queensland

Shute, N. The legacy

AUSTRALIAN ABORIGINES

Keneally, T. Flying hero class
Malouf, D. Remembering Babylon
Wood, B. The dreaming

AUSTRALIAN SOLDIERS *See* Soldiers—Australia

AUSTRALIANS

England

Cleary, J. Spearfield's daughter
Francis, D. For kicks
Hazzard, S. The transit of Venus

Ethiopia

Keneally, T. To Asmara

Europe

Winton, T. The riders

United States

Battle, L. War brides
Cleary, J. Spearfield's daughter

AUSTRIA

20th century

Appelfeld, A. The age of wonders
Appelfeld, A. Badenheim 1939
MacInnes, H. The Salzburg connection
Pearson, D. Voices of summer

Rural life

Stewart, M. Airs above the ground

Salzburg

MacInnes, H. The Salzburg connection

Vienna

Irving, J. Setting free the bears
Lightman, A. P. Einstein's dreams
MacInnes, H. Prelude to terror
Musil, R. The man without qualities
Stone, I. The passions of the mind

AUSTRIAN ALPS *See* Alps

AUSTRIAN REFUGEES

Goudge, E. The heart of the family

AUSTRIAN SOLDIERS *See* Soldiers—Austria

AUSTRIANS

England

Goudge, E. The heart of the family
The **author** of "Beltraffio". James, H.
   In James, H. The complete tales of Henry James
    v5
   In James, H. The Henry James reader

AUTHORITARIANISM *See* Totalitarianism

AUTHORS

   See also Art critics; Dramatists; Poets; Women
   authors; names of individual authors, dramatists,
   poets, etc.
Auster, P. Leviathan
Ballard, J. G. The kindness of women
Barth, J. The last voyage of somebody the sailor
Barth, J. The Tidewater tales
Bellow, S. Humboldt's gift
Bellow, S. What kind of day did you have?
Berger, T. Being invisible
Boyle, T. C. East is East
Bradbury, R. Green shadows, white whale
Brown, S. Charade
Bulgakov, M. A. The master and Margarita
Burgess, A. Earthly powers
Campbell, R. Needing ghosts
Capote, T. Answered prayers
Clark, M. H. The Anastasia syndrome
Coetzee, J. M. The master of Petersburg
Colette. Claudine married
Cook, T. H. Evidence of blood
Davies, R. What's bred in the bone
Dickinson, P. Hindsight
Doctorow, E. L. Lives of the poets [novelette]
Drabble, M. The gates of ivory
Dunne, J. G. Playland
Dunne, J. G. The red, white, and blue
Durrell, L. Balthazar
Durrell, L. Clea
Durrell, L. Constance
Durrell, L. Livia
Durrell, L. Quinx
Endō, S. Scandal
Estleman, L. D. Sudden country
Fast, H. Citizen Tom Paine
Fowles, J. Daniel Martin
Freeman, C. The last princess
Frost, M. The list of 7
Gaddis, W. A frolic of his own
Gide, A. The counterfeiters (Les faux-monnayeurs)
Godwin, G. The good husband
Godwin, G. Mr. Bedford
Golding, W. The paper men
Goudge, E. Blessing in disguise
Greene, G. The end of the affair
Greene, G. The honorary consul
Hammett, D. Tulip
Hamsun, K. Hunger
Heller, J. Good as Gold
Helprin, M. Ellis Island
Irving, J. The world according to Garp
James, H. The Aspern papers
King, S. The dark half
King, S. Misery
King, S. Salem's Lot
Koontz, D. R. Mr. Murder
Kosinski, J. N. The hermit of 69th Street
Leavitt, D. While England sleeps
London, J. Martin Eden
Ludlum, R. The Chancellor manuscript
Mailer, N. Tough guys don't dance
Malamud, B. Dubin's lives
Malamud, B. The tenants
Mann, T. Death in Venice
Maugham, W. S. Cakes and ale
Michaels, B. The dark on the other side
Michener, J. A. The novel

AUTHORS—*Continued*

Murdoch, I. The black prince
Murdoch, I. The book and the brotherhood
Nabokov, V. V. Look at the harlequins!
Naipaul, V. S. The enigma of arrival
Naipaul, V. S. A way in the world
Pirsig, R. M. Lila
Powell, A. Books do furnish a room
Powers, J. R. The junk-drawer corner-store front-porch blues
Price, N. Night woman
Price, R. The source of light
Read, P. P. A season in the West
Roth, P. The anatomy lesson
Roth, P. The counterlife
Roth, P. Deception
Roth, P. The ghost writer
Roth, P. My life as a man
Roth, P. Operation Shylock
Roth, P. Zuckerman bound: a trilogy and epilogue
Roth, P. Zuckerman unbound
Schulberg, B. The disenchanted
Sheed, W. The boys of winter
Singer, I. B. Meshugah
Singer, I. B. Shosha
Smith, W. A. The leopard hunts in darkness
Spencer, S. Men in black
Stone, K. Happy endings
Stone, R. Children of light
Strieber, W. Warday
Styron, W. Sophie's choice
Theroux, P. My secret history
Tyler, A. The accidental tourist
Updike, J. Bech: a book
Updike, J. Bech is back
Uris, L. Mitla Pass
Uris, L. QB VII
Vargas Llosa, M. Aunt Julia and the scriptwriter
Vidal, G. Burr
Vonnegut, K. Breakfast of champions
Wallace, I. The prize
Whitney, P. A. Dream of orchids
Wolfe, T. Of time and the river
Wolfe, T. The web and the rock
Wolfe, T. You can't go home again
Wouk, H. Youngblood Hawke

AUTHORSHIP
See also Authors

AUTISTIC CHILDREN
Miller, S. Family pictures

AUTOBIOGRAPHICAL STORIES
Anderson, S. Tar: a midwest childhood
Baldwin, J. Go tell it on the mountain
Ballard, J. G. Empire of the Sun
Ballard, J. G. The kindness of women
Beauvoir, S. de. The woman destroyed [novelette]
Beckett, S. Dream of fair to middling women
Bradbury, R. Green shadows, white whale
Brontë, C. Villette
Brown, C. Down all the days
Butler, S. The way of all flesh
Camus, A. The first man
Capote, T. Answered prayers
Capote, T. A Christmas memory
Capote, T. The Thanksgiving visitor
Colette. The complete Claudine
Colette. Music-hall sidelights
Demetz, H. The journey from Prague Street
Dennis, P. Auntie Mame
Dickens, C. David Copperfield
Dostoyevsky, F. The gambler
Dostoyevsky, F. The house of the dead
Eliot, G. Middlemarch
Goethe, J. W. von. The sorrows of young Werther
Gold, H. Fathers
Halter, M. The book of Abraham
Hamsun, K. Hunger

Hardwick, E. Sleepless nights
Hawthorne, N. The Blithedale romance
Hemingway, E. The garden of Eden
Huxley, A. Eyeless in Gaza
Joyce, J. A portrait of the artist as a young man
Kazantzakis, N. Zorba the Greek
Kerouac, J. On the road
Kosinski, J. N. The hermit of 69th Street
Kundera, M. The book of laughter and forgetting
Lee, G. China boy
Lee, G. Honor & duty
London, J. Martin Eden
Malraux, A. Man's hope
Maugham, W. S. Of human bondage
Melville, H. Omoo: a narrative of adventures in the South Seas
Melville, H. Typee: a peep at Polynesian life
Miller, H. Tropic of Cancer
Miller, H. Tropic of Capricorn
Mitford, N. Love in a cold climate
Mitford, N. The pursuit of love
Nabokov, V. V. Look at the harlequins!
Naipaul, V. S. The enigma of arrival
Naipaul, V. S. A way in the world
Peck, R. N. A day no pigs would die
Pinckney, D. High cotton
Plath, S. The bell jar
Powell, A. A dance to the music of time
Powers, J. R. Do black patent-leather shoes really reflect up?
Powers, J. R. The last Catholic in America
Proust, M. The captive
Proust, M. The fugitive
Proust, M. The Guermantes way
Proust, M. Jean Santeuil
Proust, M. Remembrance of things past
Proust, M. Sodom and Gomorrah
Proust, M. Swann's way
Proust, M. Time regained
Proust, M. Within a budding grove
Rilke, R. M. The notebooks of Malte Laurids Brigge
Roth, H. A diving rock on the Hudson
Roth, H. A star shines over Mt. Morris Park
Roth, P. The anatomy lesson
Roth, P. The counterlife
Roth, P. The ghost writer
Roth, P. My life as a man
Roth, P. Operation Shylock
Roth, P. Zuckerman bound: a trilogy and epilogue
Roth, P. Zuckerman unbound
Rybakov, A. N. Children of the Arbat
Sand, G. Lélia
Singer, I. B. Meshugah
Škvorecký, J. The engineer of human souls
Sterne, L. The life and opinions of Tristram Shandy, gentleman
Sterne, L. A sentimental journey through France and Italy
Strindberg, A. The scapegoat
Styron, W. Sophie's choice
Theroux, P. My secret history
Thomas, D. Portrait of the artist as a young dog
Tolstoy, L., graf. Childhood, Boyhood and Youth
Ts'ao, H.-C. The dream of the red chamber
Vonnegut, K. Slaughterhouse-five
Ward, M. J. The snake pit
West, Dame R. Sunflower
Williams, J. A. The man who cried I am
Wolfe, T. Look homeward, angel
Wolfe, T. The lost boy
Wolfe, T. Of time and the river
Wolfe, T. The web and the rock

Autobiography of a family photo. Woodson, J.

The **autobiography** of Miss Jane Pittman. Gaines, E. J.

AUTOMATA *See* Robots

AUTOMATION
Vonnegut, K. Player piano

AUTOMOBILE ACCIDENTS *See* Traffic accidents

AUTOMOBILE DRIVERS
See also Chauffeurs

AUTOMOBILE RACES
Remarque, E. M. Three comrades

AUTOMOBILES
Cady, J. The night we buried Road Dog
King, S. Christine

Accidents
See Traffic accidents

Repairing
Remarque, E. M. Three comrades

Touring
McMurtry, L. Cadillac Jack
Robertson, D. Praise the human season
The **autumn** of the patriarch. García Márquez, G.
Autumn quail. Maḥfūẓ, N.
Avalon. Seton, A.

AVANT GARDE STORIES *See* Experimental stories

AVARICE
See also Misers
Dickens, C. Our mutual friend
Follett, K. A dangerous fortune
Gage, E. The master stroke
Garwood, J. Prince Charming
Jen, G. Typical American
Kells, S. The aristocrats
Maḥfūẓ, N. The harafish
McInerny, R. M. Easeful death
Michael, J. A ruling passion
Palmer, M. Natural causes
Pérez Galdós, B. Torquemada
Plain, B. Treasures
Richler, M. Solomon Gursky was here
Robbins, T. Half asleep in frog pajamas
Sanders, L. The seventh commandment
Simenon, G. The old man dies
Smith, S. B. A simple plan
Thomas, M. M. Black money
Unsworth, B. Sacred hunger

Avaryan rising [series]
Tarr, J. A fall of princes
Tarr, J. The hall of the mountain king
Tarr, J. The lady of Han-Gilen
The **avenue** of the dead. Anthony, E.

AVIATION *See* Aeronautics
The **aviator.** Gann, E. K.

AVIATORS *See* Air pilots
The **aviators.** Griffin, W. E. B.

AVIGNON (FRANCE) *See* France—Avignon
Avignon quintet
Durrell, L. Constance
Durrell, L. Livia
Durrell, L. Monsieur
Durrell, L. Quinx
Durrell, L. Sebastian

Awakeners [series]
Tepper, S. S. Northshore
Tepper, S. S. Southshore
The **awakening** land. Richter, C.
Away. Urquhart, J.
Away with them to prison. Woods, S.
The **axe.** Undset, S.
In Undset, S. The master of Hestviken v1
The **Axeman's** jazz. Smith, J.
Aztec. Jennings, G.

AZTECS
Fuentes, C. The two shores
Jennings, G. Aztec

B

"B" is for burglar. Grafton, S.
BA'AL SHEM ṬOV, ca. 1700-1760
Singer, I. B. Reaches of heaven
Babbitt. Lewis, S.
Babel's children. Barker, C.
In Barker, C. In the flesh
Babi Yar. Anatoli, A.

BABI YAR MASSACRE, 1941
Anatoli, A. Babi Yar
Baby, would I lie? Westlake, D. E.
Babylon revisited, and other stories. Fitzgerald, F. S.
Babylon South. Cleary, J.

BACHELORS *See* Single men
The **Bachman** books: four early novels by Stephen King.
King, S.
Back in society. Chesney, M.
Backhand. Cody, L.
Bad girls, good women. Thomas, R.
Bad intent. Hornsby, W.
Bad love. Kellerman, J.
The **bad** place. Koontz, D. R.
The **bad** seed. March, W.
Badenheim 1939. Appelfeld, A.

Badge of honor [series]
Griffin, W. E. B. The murderers

BAG LADIES *See* Homeless persons
BAHIA (BRAZIL) *See* Brazil—Bahia

BAIL
Leonard, E. Rum punch
Bailey's Café. Naylor, G.

BAJA CALIFORNIA (MEXICO: PENINSULA) *See*
Mexico—Baja California
The **baked** bean supper murders. Rich, V.

BALL GAMES
See also Baseball; Football; Softball; Tennis
The **ballad** of Peckham Rye. Spark, M.
also in Spark, M. A Muriel Spark trio p233-386
The **ballad** of the sad café [novelette]. McCullers, C.
In McCullers, C. The ballad of the sad café: the
novels and stories of Carson McCullers
In McCullers, C. Collected stories p195-253
The **ballad** of the sad café: the novels and stories of
Carson McCullers. McCullers, C.

BALLET
See also Dancers
Godden, R. Pippa passes
Godden, R. Thursday's children

BALLOONS
Twain, M. Tom Sawyer abroad
Verne, J. Five weeks in a balloon

BALLS (PARTIES) *See* Parties
BALSAMO, GUISEPPE *See* Cagliostro, Alessandro,
conte di, 1743-1795
Balthazar. Durrell, L.
also in Durrell, L. The Alexandria quartet p205-390
BALTIMORE (MD.) *See* Maryland—Baltimore
Band of angels. Warren, R. P.

BANDITS *See* Brigands and robbers
Bandits. Leonard, E.
Bang the drum slowly, by Henry W. Wiggen. Harris,
M.

BANGKOK (THAILAND) *See* Thailand—Bangkok
BANK CLERKS *See* Clerks

BANK ROBBERS
Higgins, G. V. The friends of Eddie Coyle
McMurtry, L. Pretty Boy Floyd
Rendell, R. Make death love me
Tyler, A. Earthly possessions
Westlake, D. E. Bank shot

Bank shot. Westlake, D. E.

Banker. Francis, D.

BANKERS

    Auchincloss, L. The stoic

    Dickens, C. Hard times

    Francis, D. Banker

    Higgins, G. V. The Mandeville talent

    Howatch, S. Sins of the fathers

    Marquand, J. P. Point of no return

    Parker, G. M. These same long bones

    Plain, B. Tapestry

    Rendell, R. Make death love me

    Sarton, M. Anger

    Wolfe, T. The bonfire of the vanities

BANKS

    See also Bankers

    Campbell, B. M. Brothers and sisters

    Dickens, C. Hard times

    Follett, K. A dangerous fortune

Banners of silk. Laker, R.

BAPTISTS

    Edgerton, C. Killer diller

BARABBAS (BIBLICAL FIGURE)

    Lagerkvist, P. Barabbas

Barabbas. Lagerkvist, P.

BARBADOS

    Anthony, E. The tamarind seed

The **barbarous** coast. Macdonald, R.

    In Macdonald, R. Archer in Hollywood p171-346

BARCELONA (SPAIN) *See* Spain—Barcelona

Barchester Towers. Trollope, A.

Bard. Llywelyn, M.

The **barefoot** brigade. Jones, D. C.

BARKENTINES *See* Sailing vessels

Barking man and other stories. Bell, M. S.

Barnaby Rudge. Dickens, C.

BARONS *See* Aristocracy

BARQUENTINES *See* Sailing vessels

Barren ground. Glasgow, E.

Barrier Island. MacDonald, J. D.

BARRISTERS *See* Law and lawyers

BARS *See* Hotels, taverns, etc.

BARTER

    Simak, C. D. The big front yard

BASEBALL

    See also Softball

    Duncan, D. J. The brothers K

    Harris, M. Bang the drum slowly, by Henry W. Wiggen

    Kessel, J. The Franchise

    Kinsella, W. P. Box socials

    Kinsella, W. P. The further adventures of Slugger McBatt

    Lardner, R. Ring around the bases

    Lardner, R. You know me, Al

    Malamud, B. The natural

    Roth, P. The great American novel

The **Basil** and Josephine stories. Fitzgerald, F. S.

The **basket** case. McInerny, R. M.

Bastard out of Carolina. Allison, D.

BASTARDY *See* Illegitimacy

BATAVIA (N.Y.) *See* New York (State)—Batavia

BATEMAN, HESTER, 1709-1794

    Laker, R. The silver touch

BATH (ENGLAND) *See* England—Bath

Bath tangle. Heyer, G.

BATTERED WIVES *See* Wife abuse

BATTLE CREEK (MICH.) *See* Michigan—Battle Creek

Battle cry. Uris, L.

The **battle** of the Villa Fiorita. Godden, R.

Battleground. Griffin, W. E. B.

BATTLES

    See also names of individual battles

    Caputo, P. Horn of Africa

    Cornwell, B. Copperhead

    Cornwell, B. Rebel

    Cornwell, B. Sharpe's company

    Cornwell, B. Sharpe's devil

    Cornwell, B. Sharpe's eagle

    Cornwell, B. Sharpe's enemy

    Cornwell, B. Sharpe's honour

    Cornwell, B. Sharpe's regiment

    Cornwell, B. Sharpe's revenge

    Cornwell, B. Sharpe's rifles

    Cornwell, B. Sharpe's siege

    Cornwell, B. Sharpe's sword

    Cornwell, B. Sharpe's Waterloo

    Del Vecchio, J. M. The 13th valley

    Griffin, W. E. B. Line of fire

    Jennings, G. Raptor

    Jones, D. C. The barefoot brigade

    Kuniczak, W. S. The thousand hour day

    Llywelyn, M. Druids

    Llywelyn, M. The last prince of Ireland

    Sienkiewicz, H. The deluge

    Sienkiewicz, H. Fire in the steppe

    Sienkiewicz, H. With fire and sword

    Tolstoy, L., graf. War and peace

Battles at Thrush Green. Read, Miss

BATTLESHIPS *See* Warships

BATZ-CASTELMORE, CHARLES, COMTE D'ARTAGNAN *See* Artagnan, Charles de Batz-Castelmore, comte d', 1613?-1673

Baumgartner's Bombay. Desai, A.

BAVARIA (GERMANY) *See* Germany—Bavaria

The **beach** of Falesá. Stevenson, R. L.

    In Stevenson, R. L. The complete short stories v2 p307-71

    In Stevenson, R. L. The complete short stories of Robert Louis Stevenson

    In Stevenson, R. L. The strange case of Dr. Jekyll and Mr. Hyde, and other famous tales

The **bean** trees. Kingsolver, B.

The **Beans** of Egypt, Maine. Chute, C.

The **Bear** Flag. Holland, C.

BEAR FLAG REVOLT, 1846

    Holland, C. The Bear Flag

BEARE, DONAL CAM O'SULLIVAN *See* O'Sullivan Beare, Donal Cam, 1560-1618

Bearing an hourglass. Anthony, P.

The **bearkeeper's** daughter. Bradshaw, G.

BEARS

    Jenkins, W. F. Exploration team

Beast. Benchley, P.

The **beast** in the jungle. James, H.

    In James, H. The complete tales of Henry James v11

    In James, H. The Henry James reader p357-400

BEAT GENERATION *See* Bohemianism
Beat to quarters. Forester, C. S.
BEATNIKS *See* Bohemianism
Beau Geste. Wren, P. C.
The **beautiful** and damned. Fitzgerald, F. S.
A **beautiful** death. Haymon, S. T.
Beautiful girl. Adams, A.
The **beautiful** room is empty. White, E.
Beauty from ashes. Price, E.
Because it is bitter, and because it is my heart. Oates, J. C.
Bech: a book. Updike, J.
Bech is back. Updike, J.
The **beekeeper's** apprentice. King, L. R.
The **Beet** Queen. Erdrich, L.
Before and after. Brown, R.
Before the darkness falls. Price, E.
A **beggar** in Jerusalem. Wiesel, E.
Beggarman, thief. Shaw, I.
Beggars & choosers. Kress, N.
Beggars in Spain. Kress, N.
The **beginning** and the end. Maḥfūẓ, N.
The **beginning** place. Le Guin, U. K.

BEHAVIOR MODIFICATION
    See also Brainwashing
    Cussler, C. Deep six
    Koontz, D. R. Night chills
Behind a mask [novelette]. Alcott, L. M.
    In Alcott, L. M. Behind a mask: the unknown thrillers of Louisa May Alcott p1-104
Behind a mask: the unknown thrillers of Louisa May Alcott. Alcott, L. M.
Behold the man. Moorcock, M.
    In The Best of the Nebulas p163-202
The **beige** dolorosa. Harrison, J.
    In Harrison, J. Julip p185-275
Being a green mother. Anthony, P.
Being invisible. Berger, T.
Being there. Kosinski, J. N.
Bel Ria. Burnford, S.

BELFAST (NORTHERN IRELAND) *See* Northern Ireland—Belfast
Belgarath the sorcerer. Eddings, D.

BELGIAN CONGO *See* Zaire

BELGIUM

19th century
    Stone, I. Lust for life

Brussels
    Benedict, E. Safe conduct
    Brontë, C. The professor
    Brontë, C. Villette

Flanders
    Dunnett, D. Niccolò rising
Belgrave Square. Perry, A.
BELL, ELLIS *See* Brontë, Emily, 1818-1848
The **bell.** Murdoch, I.
A **bell** for Adano. Hersey, J.
The **bell** jar. Plath, S.

BELL-RINGERS *See* Bells and bell ringers
Bella. See Eden, D. Ravenscroft
The **Bellarosa** connection. Bellow, S.
    also in Bellow, S. Something to remember me by p[1]-89
Bellefleur. Oates, J. C.

BELLEROPHON (GREEK MYTHOLOGY)
    Barth, J. Bellerophoniad
Bellerophoniad. Barth, J.
    In Barth, J. Chimera p135-308
Les **belles** images. Beauvoir, S. de

BELLS AND BELL RINGERS
    Hersey, J. A bell for Adano
    Hugo, V. The hunchback of Notre Dame

Beloved. Morrison, T.
The **beloved** invader. Price, E.
The **belt** of gold. Holland, C.
Ben-Hur. Wallace, L.
BENARES (INDIA) *See* India—Benares
A **bend** in the river. Naipaul, V. S.
Bendigo Shafter. L'Amour, L.
The **benediction** of Brother Cadfael. Peters, E.
BENSON, ARTHUR CHRISTOPHER, 1862-1925
    Aiken, J. The haunting of Lamb House
BEOWULF
    Gardner, J. Grendel

BEREAVEMENT
    Banks, R. The sweet hereafter
    Bradford, B. T. Everything to gain
    Monette, P. Afterlife
    Ozick, C. Rosa
    Parker, G. M. These same long bones
    Spencer, L. Family blessings
    Stubbs, J. Light in summer
    Yoshimoto, B. Kitchen

BERLIN (GERMANY) *See* Germany—Berlin
Berlin game. Deighton, L.
    also in Deighton, L. Game, set & match
The **Berlin** memorandum. See Hall, A. The Quiller memorandum
The **Berlin** stories. Isherwood, C.

BERMUDA
    Benchley, P. Beast
BERNADETTE, SAINT, 1844-1879
    Werfel, F. The song of Bernadette
Bertie and the seven bodies. Lovesey, P.
Bertie and the Tinman. Lovesey, P.

The **Best** American short stories, 1915-1995. Entered in Part I under title
The **Best** American short stories of the eighties. Entered in Part I under title
The **best** defense. Wilhelm, K.
The **best-friend** murder. Westlake, D. E.
    In Westlake, D. E. Levine p3-31
The **Best** from Fantasy & Science Fiction. Entered in Part I under title
The **Best** from Fantasy & Science Fiction: a 40th anniversary anthology. Entered in Part I under title
The **Best** from Fantasy & Science Fiction: a 45th anniversary anthology. Entered in Part I under title
The **Best** from Fantasy and Science Fiction: a special 25th anniversary anthology. Entered in Part I under title
The **Best** horror from Fantasy Tales. Entered in Part I under title
The **Best** horror stories. Entered in Part I under title
The **best** known works of Anton Chekhov. Chekhov, A. P.
The **best** little girl in the world. Levenkron, S.
Best new horror [1]-4. Entered in Part I under title
The **best** of Damon Knight. Knight, D. F.
The **best** of Ellery Queen. Queen, E.
The **best** of H. E. Bates. Bates, H. E.
The **best** of Marion Zimmer Bradley. Bradley, M. Z.
Best of Runyon. Runyon, D.
The **best** of Sholom Aleichem. Sholem Aleichem
Best of the Best American short stories, 1915-1950. Entered in Part I under title
The **Best** of the Nebulas. Entered in Part I under title
The **best** science fiction of Arthur Conan Doyle. Doyle, Sir A. C.
The **best** science fiction of Isaac Asimov. Asimov, I.
Best SF: 1968-1975. Entered in Part I under title
Best SF stories of Brian W. Aldiss. See Aldiss, B. W. Man in his time

The **best** short stories of Bret Harte. Harte, B.
The **best** short stories of Dostoevsky. Dostoyevsky, F.
The **best** short stories of J. G. Ballard. Ballard, J. G.
The **best** short stories of O. Henry. Henry, O.
The **best** short stories of Ring Lardner. Lardner, R.
The **best** short stories of Rudyard Kipling. Kipling, R.
The **best** short stories of W. Somerset Maugham.
  Maugham, W. S.
The **best** stories of Sarah Orne Jewett. Jewett, S. O.
Best western stories, Max Brand's. Brand, M.
The **best** western stories of John Jakes. Jakes, J.
Bethlehem Road. Perry, A.

BETROTHALS
  Balzac, H. de. Eugénie Grandet
  Elkin, S. Town Crier exclusive, Confessions of a
    Princess manqué
  Hardy, T. Under the greenwood tree
  Veryan, P. Time's fool
Betsey Brown. Shange, N.
BETTING *See* Gambling
Between the acts. Woolf, V.
Between two worlds. Sinclair, U.
  In Sinclair, U. [Lanny Budd series]
Beulah Land. Coleman, L.
Beware of the dog. Ferrars, E. X.
Beyond the blue event horizon. Pohl, F.
Beyond the curve. Abe, K.
Beyond the fall of night. Clarke, A. C.
Beyond the grave. Muller, M.
Bhowani Junction. Masters, J.

BIBLICAL STORIES
  Asch, S. The Apostle
  Asch, S. Mary
  Asch, S. Moses
  Asch, S. The Nazarene
  Asch, S. The prophet
  Caldwell, T. Dear and glorious physician
  Caldwell, T. Great lion of God
  Caldwell, T. I, Judas
  Costain, T. B. The silver chalice
  Douglas, L. C. The Big Fisherman
  Douglas, L. C. The robe
  Holmes, M. The Messiah
  Holmes, M. Three from Galilee
  Kazantzakis, N. The last temptation of Christ
  Lagerkvist, P. Barabbas
  Mann, T. Joseph and his brothers
  Martin, M. King of kings
  Wallace, L. Ben-Hur
The **Bicentennial** Man. Asimov, I.
  In Asimov, I. The complete robot
  In Asimov, I. The complete stories v2
  In The Hugo winners v4 p259-99

BIERCE, AMBROSE, 1842-1914?
  Fuentes, C. The old gringo
The **big** clock. Fearing, K.
The **Big** Fisherman. Douglas, L. C.
The **big** front yard. Simak, C. D.
  In The Hugo winners v1 p171-226
The **big** knockover. Hammett, D.
Big Mama's funeral. García Márquez, G.
  In García Márquez, G. Collected stories p97-200
  In García Márquez, G. No one writes to the colonel,
    and other stories p65-170
The **big** money. Dos Passos, J.
  In Dos Passos, J. U.S.A. v3
The **Big** Rock Candy Mountain. Stegner, W. E.
The **big** sky. Guthrie, A. B.
The **big** sleep. Chandler, R.
  also in Chandler, R. Stories and early novels p587-
    764
A **big** storm knocked it over. Colwin, L.

BIGAMY
  Alcott, L. M. A long fatal love chase
  Alcott, L. M. The mysterious key and what it opened

Bigfoot dreams. Prose, F.
BIGOTRY *See* Prejudices
BILL, BUFFALO *See* Buffalo Bill, 1846-1917
Billiards at half-past nine. Böll, H.
BILLY, THE KID
  McMurtry, L. Anything for Billy
  Momaday, N. S. The ancient child
Billy. French, A.
Billy. Strieber, W.
Billy Bathgate. Doctorow, E. L.
Billy Budd, sailor. Melville, H.
The **bingo** palace. Erdrich, L.

BIOCHEMISTS
  Du Maurier, Dame D. The house on the strand
BIOGRAPHERS *See* Authors

BIOLOGISTS
  Herbert, F. The white plague
  Steinbeck, J. Cannery Row
  Steinbeck, J. Sweet Thursday

BIONICS
  Piercy, M. He, she and it
  Pohl, F. Man Plus
  Pohl, F. Mars Plus
The **bird** artist. Norman, H.
The **bird** in the tree. Goudge, E.

BIRDS
  See also Parrots
  Wharton, W. Birdy
The **bird's** nest. Jackson, S.
Birds of America. McCarthy, M.
Birdy. Wharton, W.

BIRTH CONTROL
  See also Abortion
The **birthday** boys. Bainbridge, B.

BIRTHDAY PARTIES *See* Birthdays

BIRTHDAYS
  Welty, E. Losing battles

BISEXUALITY
  See also Homosexuality
  Baldwin, J. Giovanni's room
  Barker, P. The eye in the door
  Greeley, A. M. Fall from grace
  Piercy, M. Summer people
Bishop as pawn. Kienzle, W. X.
Bishop as pawn. McInerny, R. M.

BISHOPS, ANGLICAN AND EPISCOPAL *See* Anglican
  and Episcopal bishops

BISHOPS, CATHOLIC *See* Catholic bishops

BISMARCK, OTTO, FÜRST VON, 1815-1898
  Fraser, G. M. Royal Flash

BISMARCK (BATTLESHIP)
  Forester, C. S. The last nine days of the Bismarck

BISON
  Kelton, E. Slaughter
Bitter medicine. Paretsky, S.
Bitter sweet. Spencer, L.
The **bitterest** age. Kennedy, R. A.
Black amber. Whitney, P. A.
Black as he's painted. Marsh, Dame N.
Black Betty. Mosley, W.
Black Blade. Lustbader, E. V.
The **black** book. Rankin, I.
Black cherry blues. Burke, J. L.
Black cipher. Harrison, P.
Black cross. Iles, G.
The **black** dahlia. Ellroy, J.
Black dogs. McEwan, I.

BLACK ENGLISH DIALECT *See* Dialect stories—Black
  English

BLACK HUMOR *See* Humor; Satire

The **black** ice. Connelly, M.

BLACK-JEWISH RELATIONS *See* African Americans—Relations with Jews

BLACK MAGIC *See* Witchcraft

The **black** marble. Wambaugh, J.

BLACK MARKETS
Clavell, J. King Rat
Black money. Macdonald, R.
In Macdonald, R. Archer at large
Black money. Thomas, M. M.
The **black** moon. Graham, W.
Black Narcissus. Godden, R.
The **black** opal. Holt, V.
The **black** prince. Murdoch, I.
Black robe. Moore, B.
The **black** rose. Costain, T. B.
Black sand. Caunitz, W. J.
The **black** seraphim. Gilbert, M.
Black Sunday. Harris, T.
The **black** swan. Carr, P.
The **black** swan. Mann, T.
Black thorn, white rose. Entered in Part I under title
The **black** tower. James, P. D.
also in James, P. D. Murder in triplicate v3
Black Trillium. Bradley, M. Z.
The **black** unicorn. Brooks, T.
The **black** velvet gown. Cookson, C.
Black water. Oates, J. C.
The **blackboard** jungle. Hunter, E.
Blacker than a thousand midnights. Straight, S.

BLACKFOOT INDIANS *See* Siksika Indians

The **Blackheath** poisonings. Symons, J.

BLACKMAIL
See also Extortion
Carr, P. A time for silence
Follett, K. A dangerous fortune
Greene, G. The heart of the matter
Hill, S. Mrs. de Winter
Parker, R. B. All our yesterdays
Quick, A. Mistress
Roberts, N. Honest illusions

BLACKS
See also African Americans
Bell, M. S. All souls' rising
Condé, M. I, Tituba, black witch of Salem
Conrad, J. The Nigger of the Narcissus
Phillips, C. Cambridge

BLACKSMITHS
Pearce, M. E. Cast a long shadow
Bleak House. Dickens, C.
Bleak spring. Cleary, J.
Bleeding hearts. Haddam, J.
Bless the beasts and children. Swarthout, G. F.
Bless this house. Lofts, N.
Blessed assurance: a moral tale. Gurganus, A.
In Gurganus, A. White people p192-252

BLESSED VIRGIN MARY, SAINT *See* Mary, Blessed Virgin, Saint

Blessing in disguise. Goudge, E.
The **blessing** way. Hillerman, T.
also in Hillerman, T. The Joe Leaphorn mysteries
Blessings. Plain, B.

BLIGH, WILLIAM, 1754-1817
Nordhoff, C. The Bounty trilogy
Nordhoff, C. Men against the sea
Nordhoff, C. Mutiny on the Bounty

BLIND
Brontë, C. Jane Eyre
Greenberg, J. Of such small differences
Humphrey, W. The Ordways
Kipling, R. The light that failed
London, J. The Sea-Wolf
Safire, W. Full disclosure
Shreve, A. Eden Close

Varley, J. The persistence of vision
West, P. Love's mansion
Woods, S. Dead eyes
Blind date. Kosinski, J. N.
Blindsight. Cook, R.
The **Blithedale** romance. Hawthorne, N.
also in Hawthorne, N. The complete novels and selected tales of Nathaniel Hawthorne

BLIZZARDS *See* Storms

The **blond** baboon. Van de Wetering, J.
The **blonde** in lower six. Gardner, E. S.
The **blonde** in lower six [novelette]. Gardner, E. S.
In Gardner, E. S. The blonde in lower six p7-144
Blood & orchids. Katkov, N.
Blood and sand. Blasco Ibáñez, V.
Blood count. Shannon, D.
Blood flies upward. Ferrars, E. X.
Blood of Amber. Zelazny, R.
Blood relatives. McBain, E.
Blood shot. Paretsky, S.
Blood sport. Francis, D.
In Francis, D. Across the board p253-493
Blood sympathy. Hill, R.
Blood Trillium. May, J.
Blood type. Greenleaf, S.
Blood will tell. Stout, R.
In Stout, R. Trio for blunt instruments p169-247
Blood will tell. See Christie, A. Mrs. McGinty's dead
The **bloodied** ivy. Goldsborough, R.
A **Bloodsmoor** romance. Oates, J. C.
The **bloody** hoax. Sholem Aleichem
Bloody season. Estleman, L. D.
Blue Adept. Anthony, P.
Blue Calhoun. Price, R.
Blue eyes, black hair. Duras, M.
The **blue** hammer. Macdonald, R.
The **blue** knight. Wambaugh, J.
Blue moon. Rice, L.
Blue plate special. Runyon, D.
In Runyon, D. Guys and dolls [omnibus volume] p345-505

BLUE RIDGE MOUNTAINS
Hamner, E. The homecoming
Hamner, E. Spencer's Mountain
Blue voyage. Aiken, C.
In Aiken, C. The collected novels of Conrad Aiken p15-166
Bluebeard's egg and other stories. Atwood, M.
Bluegate Fields. Perry, A.
The **bluest** eye. Morrison, T.

BOARDERS *See* Boarding houses

BOARDING HOUSES
Balzac, H. de. Old Goriot
Bausch, R. Rebel powers
Naylor, G. Bailey's Café
Reid Banks, L. The L shaped room
Spark, M. A far cry from Kensington
Tyler, A. Celestial navigation

BOARDING SCHOOLS *See* School life

The **boat.** Buchheim, L.-G.

BOATS AND BOATING
See also Sailing vessels; Tugboats
Barth, J. The Tidewater tales
Bodies. Barnard, R.
Bodily harm. Atwood, M.
The **body.** King, S.
In King, S. Different seasons p299-451

Body & soul. Conroy, F.

Body and soil. McInerny, R. M.

Body count. Kienzle, W. X.

The body farm. Cornwell, P. D.

The body in Blackwater Bay. Gosling, P.

The body in the basement. Page, K. H.

The body in the billiard room. Keating, H. R. F.

The body in the bouillon. Page, K. H.

The body in the cast. Page, K. H.

The body in the cornflakes. Beck, K. K.

The body in the library. Christie, A.
>   *also in* Christie, A. Five complete Miss Marple
>   novels p555-650

The body in the vestibule. Page, K. H.

Body of evidence. Cornwell, P. D.

Body of knowledge. Dawson, C.

A body surrounded by water. Wright, E.

BOER WAR, 1899-1902 *See* South African War, 1899-
1902

BOERS *See* Afrikaners

The bogus Buddha. Melville, J.

BOHEMIANISM
>   Kerouac, J. The Dharma bums
>   Kerouac, J. On the road
>   Maugham, W. S. Of human bondage
>   McCarthy, M. A charmed life
>   Powell, A. Casanova's Chinese restaurant
>   Powell, A. Hearing secret harmonies

BOHEMIANS

United States
>   *See* Czechs—United States

BOLEYN, ANNE *See* Anne Boleyn, Queen, consort of
Henry VIII, King of England, 1507-1536

BOLÍVAR, SIMÓN, 1783-1830
>   García Márquez, G. The general and his labyrinth

BOLSHEVISM *See* Communism

Bolt. Francis, D.

BOMBAY (INDIA) *See* India—Bombay

Bomber's law. Higgins, G. V.

BOMBING MISSIONS *See* World War, 1914-1918—
Aerial operations; World War, 1939-1945—Aerial
operations

BOMBS
>   *See also* Atomic bomb
>   Grisham, J. The chamber

Bon voyage. Coward, N.
>   *In* Coward, N. The collected stories of Noël Coward
>   p562-630

BONAPARTE, JOSÉPHINE *See* Josephine, Empress,
consort of Napoleon I, Emperor of the French, 1763-
1814

BONAPARTE, LOUIS *See* Louis, King of Holland,
1778-1846

BONAPARTE, LOUIS-NAPOLÉON *See* Napoleon III,
Emperor of the French, 1808-1873

BONAPARTE, NAPOLEON *See* Napoleon I, Emperor
of the French, 1769-1821

Bonded Fleming. Fleming, I.

Bone. Ng, F. M.

The bone people. Hulme, K.

Bonecrack. Francis, D.

Bones. Pronzini, B.

Bones and silence. Hill, R.

Boneyards. Campbell, R. W.

The bonfire of the vanities. Wolfe, T.

Bonjour tristesse. Sagan, F.

BONN (GERMANY) *See* Germany—Bonn

BONNEY, WILLIAM H. *See* Billy, the Kid

The book and the brotherhood. Murdoch, I.

The book class. Auchincloss, L. *See* Arabian nights

The book of Abraham. Halter, M.

A book of common prayer. Didion, J.

The book of Daniel. Doctorow, E. L.

The book of evidence. Banville, J.

The book of guys. Keillor, G.

The book of laughter and forgetting. Kundera, M.

The book of lights. Potok, C.

The book of lost tales. Tolkien, J. R. R.

The book of Merlyn. White, T. H.

The book of sand. Borges, J. L.

Book of the new Sun [series]
>   Wolfe, G. The Citadel of the Autarch
>   Wolfe, G. The claw of the conciliator
>   Wolfe, G. The shadow of the torturer
>   Wolfe, G. The sword of the Lictor
>   Wolfe, G. The Urth of the new sun

BOOK SHOPS *See* Booksellers and bookselling

Booked to die. Dunning, J.

BOOKS
>   *See also* Manuscripts
>   Books do furnish a room. Powell, A.
>   *In* Powell, A. A dance to the music of time [v4]

The books of blood. Barker, C.

Books of blood v4. See Barker, C. The inhuman condition

Books of blood v5. See Barker, C. In the flesh

The books of Rachel. Gross, J.

BOOKSELLERS AND BOOKSELLING
>   Goudge, E. A city of bells
>   Orwell, G. Keep the aspidistra flying
>   Sarton, M. The education of Harriet Hatfield

The boomerang clue. Christie, A.
>   *In* Christie, A. Five classic murder mysteries p305-
>   442

Bootlegger's daughter. Maron, M.

BOOTLEGGING *See* Liquor traffic

BORDEN, LIZZIE, 1860-1927
>   Hunter, E. Lizzie

Border music. Waller, R. J.

Borderliners. Hoeg, P.

BORMANN, MARTIN, 1900-1945
>   Higgins, J. The Valhalla exchange

BORNEO
>   Conrad, J. Almayer's folly

BOSNIA AND HERCEGOVINA
>   Andrić, I. The bridge on the Drina

BOSTON (MASS.) *See* Massachusetts—Boston

Boston. Sinclair, U.

The Bostonians. James, H.
>   *also in* James, H. The American novels and stories
>   of Henry James p424-746

A botanist at bay. Sherwood, J.

BOTANISTS
>   Bellow, S. More die of heartbreak

Botany Bay. Nordhoff, C.

BOTSWANA
>   Rush, N. Mating

BOUNTY (SHIP)
>   Nordhoff, C. The Bounty trilogy

BOUNTY (SHIP)—*Continued*
Nordhoff, C. Mutiny on the Bounty
The **Bounty** trilogy. Nordhoff, C.

BOURGEOISIE *See* Middle classes
The **Bourne** identity. Ludlum, R.
  also in Ludlum, R. The Ludlum triad p757-1149
The **Bourne** supremacy. Ludlum, R.
The **Bourne** ultimatum. Ludlum, R.
The **box** man. Abe, K.
Box socials. Kinsella, W. P.

BOXING
Dexter, P. Brotherly love
Lee, G. China boy
Lovesey, P. The detective wore silk drawers
A **boy** and his dog. Ellison, H.
  In The Best of the Nebulas p359-89
The **boy** who followed Ripley. Highsmith, P.

BOYS
  See also Adolescence; Children; Youth
Ballard, J. G. Empire of the Sun
Bradbury, R. Dandelion wine
Bradbury, R. Something wicked this way comes
Camus, A. The first man
Capote, T. The Thanksgiving visitor
Card, O. S. Lost boys
Childress, M. Crazy in Alabama
Conroy, P. The lords of discipline
Dickens, C. David Copperfield
Dickens, C. Dombey and Son
Dickens, C. Oliver Twist
Doyle, R. Paddy Clarke, ha ha ha
Faulkner, W. The reivers
Freedman, J. F. The obstacle course
French, A. Billy
Gallico, P. The small miracle
Gipson, F. B. Old Yeller
Gipson, F. B. Savage Sam
Golding, W. Lord of the Flies
Grisham, J. The client
Hemingway, E. The old man and the sea
Hilton, J. Good-bye Mr. Chips
Hughes, L. Not without laughter
King, S. Apt pupil
King, S. The body
Knowles, J. Peace breaks out
Knowles, J. A separate peace
Kosinski, J. N. The painted bird
Kotzwinkle, W. E.T.
McCabe, P. The butcher boy
Ōe, K. Nip the buds, shoot the kids
Payne, D. Ruin Creek
Potok, C. I am the clay
Powers, J. R. The last Catholic in America
Price, R. The tongues of angels
Raucher, H. Summer of '42
Rendell, R. Talking to strange men
Richter, C. The light in the forest
Roth, H. Call it sleep
Roth, H. A star shines over Mt. Morris Park
Saroyan, W. The human comedy
Saul, J. Shadows
Smiley, J. Good will
Steinbeck, J. The red pony
Swarthout, G. F. Bless the beasts and children
Townsend, S. The Adrian Mole diaries
Twain, M. The adventures of Huckleberry Finn
Twain, M. The adventures of Tom Sawyer
White, E. A boy's own story
Wolfe, T. The lost boy
Woolf, V. Jacob's room
Wouk, H. The city boy, the adventures of Herbie Bookbinder and his cousin Cliff

The **boys** from Brazil. Levin, I.
Boy's life. McCammon, R. R.
The **boys** of winter. Sheed, W.
A **boy's** own story. White, E.
Braided lives. Piercy, M.
Brain. Cook, R.

BRAINWASHING
Higgins, J. Day of judgment
Koontz, D. R. Strangers
The **Bram** Stoker bedside companion. Stoker, B.
Brat Farrar. Tey, J.
  also in Tey, J. Three by Tey v3
Brave new world. Huxley, A.

BRAZIL

19th century
Vargas Llosa, M. The war of the end of the world

Conselheiro insurrection, 1897
Vargas Llosa, M. The war of the end of the world

20th century
Amado, J. Dona Flor and her two husbands
Amado, J. Gabriela, clove and cinnamon
Amado, J. The war of the saints
Levin, I. The boys from Brazil
Updike, J. Brazil

Politics
  See Politics—Brazil

Bahia
Amado, J. Dona Flor and her two husbands
Amado, J. Gabriela, clove and cinnamon
Vargas Llosa, M. The war of the end of the world

Rio de Janeiro
Puig, M. Tropical night falling
Brazil. Updike, J.
Brazzaville Beach. Boyd, W.
Bread and wine. Silone, I.
Bread upon the waters. Shaw, I.
Break in. Francis, D.
Breakfast at Tiffany's. Capote, T.
Breakfast at Tiffany's [novelette]. Capote, T.
  In Capote, T. Breakfast at Tiffany's
Breakfast of champions. Vonnegut, K.
Breakheart Pass. MacLean, A.
Breathing lessons. Tyler, A.
The **breathing** method. King, S.
  In King, S. Different seasons p453-518
Bred to win. Kinsolving, W.

BRIAN, BOROIMHE, KING OF IRELAND, 926-1014
Holland, C. The kings in winter

BRIAN BORU *See* Brian, Boroimhe, King of Ireland, 926-1014
Briar Rose. Yolen, J.
Briarpatch. Thomas, R.

BRIBERY
Higgins, G. V. Defending Billy Ryan
The **bridal** canopy. Agnon, S. Y.
The **bridal** wreath. Undset, S.
  In Undset, S. Kristin Lavransdatter v1
The **bride** of Innisfallen and other stories. Welty, E.
  In Welty, E. The collected stories of Eudora Welty
The **bride** of Lammermoor. Scott, Sir W.
The **bride** of Newgate. Carr, J. D.
Bride of Pendorric. Holt, V.
The **bride** of the wilderness. McCarry, C.
Brideshead revisited. Waugh, E.
The **bridesmaid**. Rendell, R.
The **bridge** of San Luis Rey. Wilder, T.
The **bridge** on the Drina. Andrić, I.
The **bridge** over the River Kwai. Boulle, P.

BRIDGEPORT (CONN.) *See* Connecticut—Bridgeport

BRIDGES
Andrić, I. The bridge on the Drina
Boulle, P. The bridge over the River Kwai

The **bridges** at Toko-ri. Michener, J. A.
The **bridges** of Madison County. Waller, R. J.
Brief lives. Brookner, A.
Briefing for a descent into Hell. Lessing, D. M.

BRIGANDS AND ROBBERS
See also Outlaws; Robbery
Blackmore, R. D. Lorna Doone
Puzo, M. The Sicilian
Bright captivity. Price, E.
Bright orange for the shroud. MacDonald, J. D.
Bright star. Coyle, H. W.
Brightness Falls. McInerney, J.

BRIGHTON (ENGLAND) *See* England—Brighton
Brighton rock. Greene, G.
Bring me the head of Prince Charming. Zelazny, R.

BRITISH

Afghanistan
Brent, M. Stormswift
Fraser, G. M. Flashman

Africa
Boyd, W. Brazzaville Beach
Conrad, J. Heart of darkness
Gordimer, N. A guest of honor
Ruark, R. Something of value
Ruark, R. Uhuru
Smith, W. A. Flight of the falcon
Smith, W. A. The leopard hunts in darkness
Smith, W. A. Men of men

Argentina
Greene, G. The honorary consul

Australia
Eden, D. The vines of Yarrabee
Shute, N. The legacy

Austria
Stewart, M. Airs above the ground

Canada
Michener, J. A. Journey

China
Ballard, J. G. Empire of the Sun
Brent, M. Moonraker's bride
Elegant, R. S. Manchu

Corfu
Stewart, M. This rough magic

Crete
Stewart, M. The moon-spinners

Egypt
Deighton, L. City of gold
Durrell, L. Mountolive

France
Bates, H. E. Fair stood the wind for France
Dinesen, I. The angelic avengers
Du Maurier, Dame D. The scapegoat
Durrell, L. Constance
Durrell, L. Livia
Godden, R. The greengage summer
Hemingway, E. The sun also rises
Holt, V. The Devil on horseback
Laker, R. Banners of silk
Mayle, P. Hotel Pastis
Orczy, E., Baroness. Adventures of the Scarlet Pimpernel
Orczy, E., Baroness. The elusive Pimpernel
Orczy, E., Baroness. The Scarlet Pimpernel
Rhys, J. Good morning, midnight
Rhys, J. Quartet
Stewart, M. Nine coaches waiting
Stewart, M. Thunder on the right

Germany
Fraser, G. M. Royal Flash
Hall, A. The Quiller memorandum
Isherwood, C. The last of Mr. Norris

Le Carré, J. A small town in Germany
Le Carré, J. The spy who came in from the cold
MacLean, A. Where eagles dare

Greece
Fowles, J. The magus
Hodge, J. A. Strangers in company
Stewart, M. My brother Michael

Hong Kong
Clavell, J. Tai-Pan
Mason, R. The world of Suzie Wong
Worboys, A. China silk

India
Cleary, J. The faraway drums
Forster, E. M. A passage to India
Fraser, G. M. Flashman
Fraser, G. M. Flashman and the mountain of light
Godden, R. Black Narcissus
Holt, V. The India fan
Jhabvala, R. P. Heat and dust
Kaye, M. M. Death in Kashmir
Kaye, M. M. The far pavilions
Kaye, M. M. Shadow of the moon
Markandaya, K. Shalimar
Masters, J. Bhowani Junction
Scott, P. The day of the scorpion
Scott, P. A division of the spoils
Scott, P. The jewel in the crown
Scott, P. The Raj quartet
Scott, P. Staying on
Scott, P. The towers of silence
Stewart, F. M. Pomp and circumstance

Ireland
Uris, L. Trinity

Italy
Forster, E. M. A room with a view
Gash, J. The Vatican rip
Godden, R. The battle of the Villa Fiorita
Godden, R. Pippa passes
Mortimer, J. C. Summer's lease
Powell, A. Temporary kings
West, M. L. The devil's advocate

Japan
Clavell, J. Gai-Jin
Clavell, J. Shogun

Kenya
Kaye, M. M. Death in Kenya
Wood, B. Green City in the sun

Lebanon
Stewart, M. The Gabriel hounds

Mexico
Lowry, M. Under the volcano

New Zealand
Eden, D. An important family

Norway
Francis, D. Slayride

Palestine
Wiesel, E. Dawn

Russia
Egleton, C. A killing in Moscow
Francis, D. Trial run

Sicily
Hodge, J. A. Escapade

South Africa
Francis, D. Smokescreen
Lessing, D. M. Children of violence
Michener, J. A. The covenant
Spark, M. The go-away bird

Spain
Hemingway, E. The sun also rises
Lofts, N. Knight's Acre

BRITISH—*Continued*
Switzerland
Brookner, A. Hotel du Lac

Tahiti
Maugham, W. S. The moon and sixpence

Turkey
Holt, V. The captive
Holt, V. Secret for a nightingale

Uganda
Hill, R. Dream of darkness

United States
Bristow, G. Celia Garth
Dickens, C. Martin Chuzzlewit
Fast, H. Seven days in June
Garwood, J. Prince Charming
Harper, K. Circle of gold
L'Amour, L. Sackett's land
L'Engle, M. The other side of the sun
Twain, M. The American claimant
Waugh, E. The loved one

Vietnam
Greene, G. The quiet American

West Africa
Forester, C. S. The African Queen
Greene, G. The heart of the matter

West Indies
Naipaul, V. S. Guerrillas
Phillips, C. Cambridge

Yugoslavia
MacLean, A. Force 10 from Navarone

Zanzibar
Kaye, M. M. Death in Zanzibar

BRITISH ANTARCTIC ("TERRA NOVA") EXPEDITION (1910-1913)
Bainbridge, B. The birthday boys

BRITISH ARISTOCRACY *See* Aristocracy—England

BRITISH COLUMBIA *See* Canada—British Columbia

BRITISH SOLDIERS *See* Soldiers—Great Britain

BRITISH WEST INDIES *See* West Indies

BRITTANY (FRANCE) *See* France—Brittany

Brokenclaw. Gardner, J. E.

BRONTË, EMILY, 1818-1848
Manuscripts
Barnard, R. The case of the missing Brontë

BRONX (NEW YORK, N.Y.) *See* New York (N.Y.)—Bronx

BROOKLYN (NEW YORK, N.Y.) *See* New York (N.Y.)—Brooklyn

BROTHELS *See* Prostitution

Brother Cadfael's penance. Peters, E.

Brother Wind. Harrison, S.

The **brotherhood** of the rose. Morrell, D.

Brotherhood of the tomb. Easterman, D.

Brotherhood of war [series]
Griffin, W. E. B. The aviators
Griffin, W. E. B. The new breed

Brotherly love. Dexter, P.

BROTHERS
See also Brothers and sisters; Half-brothers; Twins
Bagley, D. Night of error
Baldwin, J. Just above my head
Baldwin, J. Tell me how long the train's been gone
Banks, R. Affliction
Briskin, J. Paloverde
Caldwell, T. Testimony of two men
Carroll, J. The city below
De la Roche, M. Jalna
Dexter, P. Brotherly love
Dexter, P. The paperboy
Dostoyevsky, F. The brothers Karamazov

Du Maurier, Dame D. The flight of the falcon
Duncan, D. J. The brothers K
Dunne, J. G. True confessions
Ford, F. M. The last post
Francis, D. Knockdown
Francis, D. Twice shy
Greeley, A. M. Thy brother's wife
Grisham, J. The client
Hijuelos, O. The Mambo Kings play songs of love
Jones, T. Hard road to Gettysburg
Mann, T. Young Joseph
McCarthy, C. The crossing
McCauley, S. The easy way out
McFarland, D. The music room
Murdoch, I. The green knight
Myrer, A. A green desire
Ôe, K. The silent cry
Plaidy, J. The scarlet cloak
Price, R. Clockers
Simenon, G. The old man dies
Singer, I. J. The brothers Ashkenazi
Stevenson, R. L. The master of Ballantrae
Wren, P. C. Beau Geste

BROTHERS AND SISTERS
See also Twins
Alther, L. Original sins
Appelfeld, A. Unto the soul
Barth, J. The sot-weed factor
Bradford, B. T. Angel
Colette. Julie de Carneilhan
Conroy, P. The prince of tides
Coscarelli, K. Heir apparent
Del Vecchio, J. M. For the sake of all living things
Doctorow, E. L. The book of Daniel
Durrell, L. Constance
Durrell, L. Monsieur
Eliot, G. The mill on the Floss
Erdrich, L. The Beet Queen
Galsworthy, J. Maid in waiting
Gardner, J. October light
Godden, R. Thursday's children
Greenberg, J. Age of consent
Han, S. The enchantress
Harrison, J. Julip
Hawthorne, N. The House of the Seven Gables
Heaven, C. The wind from the sea
Holland, C. The Sea Beggars
Howatch, S. The shrouded walls
James, H. The Europeans
Jen, G. Typical American
Jhabvala, R. P. Three continents
Lively, P. Passing on
Lively, P. The road to Lichfield
McFarland, D. School for the blind
Miller, S. For love
Nabokov, V. V. Ada
Oates, J. C. Them
Phillips, J. A. Machine dreams
Plain, B. Treasures
Reed, K. Gone
Rice, A. The Feast of All Saints
Roiphe, A. R. If you knew me
Salinger, J. D. Franny and Zooey
Segal, E. Acts of faith
Settle, M. L. The killing ground
Smith, W. A. Flight of the falcon
Steel, D. No greater love
Theroux, P. Picture palace
Thomas, R. Briarpatch
Trevanian. The summer of Katya
Vonnegut, K. Slapstick
Brothers and sisters. Campbell, B. M.
The **brothers** Ashkenazi. Singer, I. J.

BROTHERS-IN-LAW
Bonner, C. Looking after Lily

The **brothers** K. Duncan, D. J.
The **brothers** Karamazov. Dostoyevsky, F.
Brules. Combs, H.
BRUSSELS (BELGIUM) *See* Belgium—Brussels
BRUTALITY *See* Cruelty; Violence
BRUTUS, LUCIUS JUNIUS
    Massie, A. Caesar
BUBONIC PLAGUE *See* Plague
The **buccaneers.** Wharton, E.
    In Wharton, E. Fast and loose and The buccaneers
        p119-479
The **buccaneers,** completed by Marion Mainwaring. Wharton, E.
BUCHANAN, JAMES, 1791-1868
    Updike, J. Memories of the Ford Administration
BUCHAREST (ROMANIA) *See* Romania—Bucharest
Bucket nut. Cody, L.
Buddenbrooks. Mann, T.
BUDDHA, GAUTAMA *See* Gautama Buddha
BUDDHISM
    See also Zen Buddhism
    Bradshaw, G. Horses of heaven
    Hesse, H. Siddhartha
    Mishima, Y. The Temple of Dawn
    Mishima, Y. The temple of the golden pavilion
    Zelazny, R. Lord of light
BUENOS AIRES (ARGENTINA) *See* Argentina—Buenos Aires
BUFFALO, AMERICAN *See* Bison
BUFFALO BILL, 1846-1917
    McMurtry, L. Buffalo girls
Buffalo girls. McMurtry, L.
The **buffalo** hunter. Straub, P.
    In Straub, P. Houses without doors p109-207
Buffalo soldiers. O'Connor, R.
BUILDING
    Follett, K. Pillars of the earth
    Hodgins, E. Mr. Blandings builds his dream house
The **building** of Jalna. De la Roche, M.
BULGARIA

                Sofia
    Gilman, D. The elusive Mrs. Pollifax
The **bull** from the sea. Renault, M.
BULL RUN, 1ST BATTLE, 1861
    Cornwell, B. Rebel
Bullet Park. Cheever, J.
BULLFIGHTERS AND BULLFIGHTING
    Blasco Ibáñez, V. Blood and sand
    Hemingway, E. The sun also rises
    Michener, J. A. Mexico
BULLFIGHTING *See* Bullfighters and bullfighting
Bum steer. Pickard, N.
Bump in the night. Holland, I.
BUNKER HILL, BATTLE OF, 1775
    Fast, H. Seven days in June
BUONARROTI, MICHEL ANGELO *See* Michelangelo Buonarroti, 1475-1564
Burden of desire. MacNeil, R.
The **burden** of proof. Turow, S.
BUREAUCRACY
    See also Civil service
    Bulgakov, M. A. The master and Margarita
    Frayn, M. A landing on the sun

Burger's daughter. Gordimer, N.
The **burglar** in the closet. Block, L.
The **burglar** who liked to quote Kipling. Block, L.
The **burglar** who painted like Mondrian. Block, L.
The **burglar** who studied Spinoza. Block, L.
The **burglar** who traded Ted Williams. Block, L.
BURGLARS *See* Thieves
BURIAL *See* Funeral rites and ceremonies
Buried alive. See Dostoyevsky, F. The house of the dead
Buried caesars. Kaminsky, S. M.
BURIED TREASURE
    Bagley, D. Night of error
    Brent, M. Moonraker's bride
    Conrad, J. Nostromo
    Coulter, C. The Nightingale legacy
    Coulter, C. The valentine legacy
    Coulter, C. The Wyndham legacy
    Cussler, C. Inca gold
    Cussler, C. Treasure
    Durrell, L. Quinx
    Forester, C. S. Hornblower and the Atropos
    Pohl, F. The merchants of Venus
    Quick, A. Deception
BURMA
    Gilman, D. Incident at Badamya
Burn marks. Paretsky, S.
The **burning** house. Beattie, A.
The **burning** shore. Smith, W. A.
A **burnt-out** case. Greene, G.
BURR, AARON, 1756-1836
    Vidal, G. Burr
Burr. Vidal, G.
BURYING GROUNDS *See* Cemeteries
BUSES
    Steinbeck, J. The wayward bus

                Accidents
    See Traffic accidents
BUSH, GEORGE, 1924-
    Kessel, J. The Franchise
The **bushwhacked** piano. McGuane, T.
BUSINESS
    See also Advertising; Department stores; Merchants
    Birmingham, S. The Auerbach will
    Birmingham, S. The LeBaron secret
    Gaddis, W. J R
    Howells, W. D. The rise of Silas Lapham
    Myrer, A. A green desire
    Norris, F. The pit
    O'Hara, J. From the terrace
    Tarkington, B. The magnificent Ambersons
    Vonnegut, K. Jailbird
    Wilson, S. The man in the gray flannel suit

              Unscrupulous methods
    Bellow, S. More die of heartbreak
    Birmingham, S. Carriage trade
    Browne, G. A. Hot Siberian
    Clavell, J. Noble house
    Crichton, M. Disclosure
    Crichton, M. Rising sun
    Dailey, J. Masquerade
    Dunne, D. An inconvenient woman
    Gage, E. The master stroke
    Goldsmith, O. Fashionably late
    Hailey, A. Strong medicine
    Norris, F. The octopus
    Shaw, I. Nightwork
    Sheldon, S. The stars shine down
    Wells, H. G. Tono-Bungay
BUSINESS DEPRESSION, 1929
    Algren, N. A walk on the wild side
    Brown, J. D. Addie Pray
    Doctorow, E. L. Loon Lake
    Hamner, E. The homecoming

BUSINESS DEPRESSION, 1929—*Continued*
Kennedy, W. Ironweed
Marshall, C. Julie
Olsen, T. Yonnondio: from the thirties

BUSINESSMEN
Birmingham, S. Carriage trade
Bradford, B. T. The women in his life
Crichton, M. Disclosure
Delderfield, R. F. God is an Englishman
Korda, M. Worldly goods
Lewis, S. Babbitt
McGuane, T. Nothing but blue skies
Percy, W. The moviegoer

BUSINESSWOMEN
Allen, C. V. Leftover dreams
Archer, J. The prodigal daughter
Beauvoir, S. de. Les belles images
Birmingham, S. The Rothman scandal
Bradford, B. T. Hold the dream
Bradford, B. T. To be the best
Bradford, B. T. A woman of substance
Brown, S. French Silk
Campbell, B. M. Brothers and sisters
Coscarelli, K. Heir apparent
Crichton, M. Disclosure
Gage, E. The master stroke
Gage, E. Pandora's box
Goldsmith, O. Fashionably late
Hailey, A. Strong medicine
Harvey, K. Stars
Marsh, J. The House of Eliott
McNaught, J. Paradise
Rich, M. Tender offerings
Scott, J. The nine dragons
Sheldon, S. Master of the game
Sheldon, S. The stars shine down
Swindells, M. Summer harvest
Thayer, N. Everlasting
Thomas, R. A woman of our times
Van Slyke, H. Public smiles, private tears
Vidal, G. Empire
Villars, E. Lipstick on his collar
Busman's honeymoon. Sayers, D. L.
But I wouldn't want to die there. Pickard, N.
The butcher boy. McCabe, P.
The butcher's boy. Perry, T.

BUTLERS
Ishiguro, K. The remains of the day
Voigt, C. Glass mountain
Wodehouse, P. G. The world of Jeeves
Butterfield 8. O'Hara, J.
The button man. Freemantle, B.
A buyer's market. Powell, A.
  In Powell, A. A dance to the music of time [v1]
By any other name. Robinson, S.
  In The Hugo winners v4 p141-97
By hook or by crook. Lathen, E.
By love possessed. Cozzens, J. G.
By the open sea. Strindberg, A.
By the pricking of my thumbs. Christie, A.

BYZANTINE EMPIRE
Bradshaw, G. The bearkeeper's daughter
Bradshaw, G. Imperial purple
Holland, C. The belt of gold
Tarr, J. The golden horn

Courts and courtiers
See Courts and courtiers—Byzantine Empire

C

C. B. Greenfield: a little madness. Kallen, L.
C. B. Greenfield: no lady in the house. Kallen, L.
C. B. Greenfield: the piano bird. Kallen, L.
C. B. Greenfield: the Tanglewood murders. Kallen, L.
"C" is for corpse. Grafton, S.
Cabal. Barker, C.
Cabal [novelette]. Barker, C.
  In Barker, C. Cabal
Cabbages and kings. Henry, O.
  In Henry, O. The complete works of O. Henry p551-679
The cable car murder. Taylor, E. A.
Cadillac Jack. McMurtry, L.

CAESAR, JULIUS, 100-44 B.C.
McCullough, C. Fortune's favorites
Wilder, T. The ides of March
Caesar. Massie, A.
CAFÉS *See* Restaurants, lunchrooms, etc.

CAGLIOSTRO, ALESSANDRO, CONTE DI, 1743-1795
Dumas, A. The Queen's necklace
Cain x 3. Cain, J. M.
The Caine mutiny. Wouk, H.
CAIRO (EGYPT) *See* Egypt—Cairo

CAJUNS
Gaines, E. J. The gathering of old men
Grau, S. A. The condor passes
Grau, S. A. The hard blue sky
Cakes and ale. Maugham, W. S.
Cakewalk. Smith, L.

CALABRIA (ITALY) *See* Italy—Calabria

CALAMITY JANE, 1852-1903
McMurtry, L. Buffalo girls
Caldé of the long sun. Wolfe, G.
Calico Palace. Bristow, G.

CALIFORNIA
Butler, O. E. Parable of the sower
Gibson, W. Virtual light
Jakes, J. California gold

19th century
Briskin, J. Paloverde
Bristow, G. Jubilee Trail
De Blasis, C. The proud breed
Holland, C. The Bear Flag
L'Amour, L. The Californios
L'Amour, L. The lonesome gods
Stewart, F. M. The glitter and the gold

1846-1900
Bristow, G. Calico Palace
Holland, C. Pacific Street
Norris, F. The octopus
Steinbeck, J. East of Eden
Streshinsky, S. Hers the kingdom

20th century
Adams, A. Families and survivors
Dailey, J. Tangled vines
Dart, I. R. The Stork Club
Del Vecchio, J. M. Carry me home
Fast, H. The immigrant's daughter
Fast, H. Second generation
Ferrigno, R. The Horse Latitudes
Gold, H. A girl of forty
Hailey, E. F. Home free
Huxley, A. After many a summer dies the swan
Krantz, J. Till we meet again
Lee, C. Y. The flower drum song
Leffland, E. Rumors of peace

CALIFORNIA—20th century—*Continued*
Leonard, E. Mr. Majestyk
Mapson, J.-A. Hank and Chloe
Otto, W. How to make an American quilt
Parker, T. J. Little Saigon
Pynchon, T. The crying of lot 49
Pynchon, T. Vineland
Rosenberg, N. T. Interest of justice
Rosenberg, N. T. Mitigating circumstances
Saroyan, W. The human comedy
Saul, J. The homing
Steel, D. Mixed blessings
Stegner, W. E. All the little live things
Steinbeck, J. East of Eden
Steinbeck, J. The grapes of wrath
Steinbeck, J. In dubious battle
Steinbeck, J. The long valley
Steinbeck, J. Of mice and men
Steinbeck, J. The wayward bus
Stewart, F. M. The glitter and the gold
Thomas, R. Chinaman's chance
Thomas, R. The fourth Durango
Wambaugh, J. The Golden Orange
West, J. Cress Delahanty
West, J. The state of Stony Lonesome
Whitney, P. A. Flaming Tree
Woods, S. Dead eyes

Farm life
See Farm life—California

Frontier and pioneer life
See Frontier and pioneer life—California

Gold discoveries
See California—1846-1900

Hollywood
Bradbury, R. A graveyard for lunatics
Briskin, J. Dreams are not enough
Dart, I. R. I'll be there
Didion, J. Play it as it lays
Dunne, D. An inconvenient woman
Dunne, J. G. Playland
Fitzgerald, F. S. The last tycoon
Goldsmith, O. Flavor of the month
Goudge, E. Such devoted sisters
Korda, M. Curtain
Leonard, E. Get Shorty
Maupin, A. Maybe the moon
McMurtry, L. Somebody's darling
Rossner, J. His little women
Schulberg, B. The disenchanted
Schulberg, B. What makes Sammy run?
Shagan, S. A cast of thousands
Steel, D. Heartbeat
Steel, D. No greater love
Stone, K. Happy endings
Tryon, T. Crowned heads
Vidal, G. Hollywood
Vidal, G. Myra Breckinridge [and] Myron
Wambaugh, J. The Glitter Dome
Waugh, E. The loved one
West, N. The day of the locust
Westlake, D. E. Sacred monster
Woods, S. L.A. Times

Los Angeles
Allende, I. The infinite plan
Briskin, J. Paloverde
Campbell, B. M. Brothers and sisters
Crichton, M. Rising sun
Dunne, J. G. True confessions
Ellroy, J. The black dahlia
Ellroy, J. Dick Contino's blues
Ellroy, J. L.A. confidential
Ellroy, J. White jazz
Huxley, A. Ape and essence
Latt, M. L. Powers of attorney
Lurie, A. The nowhere city

Monette, P. Afterlife
Perry, T. Metzger's dog
Rich, M. Tender offerings
Simpson, M. Anywhere but here
Straight, S. Blacker than a thousand midnights
Thomas, R. Voodoo, Ltd
Vida, N. Goodbye, Saigon
Wambaugh, J. The blue knight
Wambaugh, J. The Delta Star
Wambaugh, J. The new centurions
Wolitzer, H. Tunnel of love

Malibu
Streshinsky, S. Hers the kingdom

Monterey
Steinbeck, J. Cannery Row
Steinbeck, J. Sweet Thursday
Steinbeck, J. Tortilla Flat

Oakland
Mowry, J. Six out seven

Palm Springs
Harvey, K. Stars
Wambaugh, J. Fugitive nights
Whitney, P. A. Emerald

San Diego
Wambaugh, J. Finnegan's week

San Francisco
Adams, A. Almost perfect
Adams, A. Caroline's daughters
Adler, E. Fortune is a woman
Adler, E. The secret of the Villa Mimosa
Bristow, G. Calico Palace
Fast, H. The establishment
Fast, H. The immigrants
Freeman, C. Fairytales
Holland, C. Pacific Street
Kingston, M. H. Tripmaster Monkey
Lee, C. Y. The flower drum song
Lee, G. China boy
Lescroart, J. T. Hard evidence
Ng, F. M. Bone
Norris, F. McTeague
Patterson, R. N. Degree of guilt
Patterson, R. N. Eyes of a child
Sheldon, S. Nothing lasts forever
Tan, A. The Joy Luck Club
Whitney, P. A. The trembling hills
California gold. Jakes, J.
The **Californios**. L'Amour, L.

CALIGULA, EMPEROR OF ROME, 12-41
Douglas, L. C. The robe
Call it sleep. Roth, H.
The **call** of earth. Card, O. S.
The **call** of the toad. Grass, G.
The **call** of the wild. London, J.
Call the darkness light. Zaroulis, N. L.
Calling the wind. Entered in Part I under title

CALVINISTS
Holland, C. The Sea Beggars

CAMBODIA
Del Vecchio, J. M. For the sake of all living things
Drabble, M. The gates of ivory
Hall, A. Quiller Salamander

Politics
See Politics—Cambodia

CAMBRIDGE (MASS.) *See* Massachusetts—Cambridge
Cambridge. Phillips, C.

CAMBRIDGE UNIVERSITY *See* University of Cambridge
The **camelia-lady**. See Dumas, A. Camille

The **Camerons**. Crichton, R.
Cameron's crossing. McCutchan, P.
Camille. Dumas, A.
The **campaign**. Fuentes, C.
CAMPAIGNS, PRESIDENTIAL

United States
See Presidents—United States—Election
CAMPING
See also Wilderness survival
CAMPS, SUMMER *See* Summer camps
CAMPUS LIFE *See* College life
Can you forgive her? Trollope, A.
Can you forgive her? [abridged]. Trollope, A.
In Trollope, A. The Pallisers p11-115
CANADA

To 1763 (New France)
Cather, W. Shadows on the rock
Moore, B. Black robe

19th century
Brand, M. The Stingaree
Urquhart, J. Away

20th century
Atwood, M. Wilderness tips
Davies, R. Fifth business
Davies, R. The manticore
Davies, R. Murther & walking spirits
Davies, R. What's bred in the bone
Munro, A. Friend of my youth
Munro, A. The moons of Jupiter
Munro, A. Open secrets
Ondaatje, M. In the skin of a lion
Shields, C. The stone diaries
Urquhart, J. Away

College life
See College life—Canada

Frontier and pioneer life
See Frontier and pioneer life—Canada

Rural life
Davies, R. World of wonders
Kinsella, W. P. Box socials
Munro, A. Lives of girls & women

Alberta
Kinsella, W. P. Box socials

British Columbia
Craven, M. I heard the owl call my name
Whitney, P. A. Feather on the moon

Montreal
Richler, M. Joshua then and now
Richler, M. Solomon Gursky was here

Newfoundland
Norman, H. The bird artist
Proulx, A. The shipping news

Northwest Territories
Freedman, B. Mrs. Mike

Nova Scotia
MacNeil, R. Burden of desire

Ontario
Burnford, S. The incredible journey
Davies, R. Fifth business
De la Roche, M. The building of Jalna
De la Roche, M. Centenary at Jalna
De la Roche, M. Jalna
De Lint, C. Memory and dream

Québec (Province)
Atwood, M. Surfacing

Québec (Québec)
Cather, W. Shadows on the rock

Saskatchewan
Stegner, W. E. The Big Rock Candy Mountain

Toronto
Allen, C. V. Leftover dreams
Atwood, M. Cat's eye
Atwood, M. Life before man
Atwood, M. The robber bride
Davies, R. The lyre of Orpheus
Davies, R. The rebel angels
Škvorecký, J. The engineer of human souls

Winnipeg
Shields, C. The republic of love

Yukon Territory
Innes, H. High stand
London, J. The call of the wild
London, J. White Fang
Michener, J. A. Journey

CANADA. ROYAL CANADIAN MOUNTED POLICE
See Royal Canadian Mounted Police

CANADIAN INVASION, 1775-1776
Roberts, K. L. Arundel

CANADIAN SOLDIERS *See* Soldiers—Canada

CANADIANS

England
Allen, C. V. Leftover dreams

Italy
Ondaatje, M. The English patient

West Indies
Atwood, M. Bodily harm

CANCER
Coetzee, J. M. Age of iron
Gilchrist, E. The Anna papers
Godwin, G. The good husband
Klein, N. Sunshine
Lively, P. Moon tiger
Mann, T. The black swan
Mason, B. A. Spence + Lila
Price, R. The source of light
Quindlen, A. One true thing
Robbins, T. Half asleep in frog pajamas
Sarton, M. A reckoning
Siddons, A. R. Outer banks
Solzhenitsyn, A. Cancer ward
Sturgeon, T. Slow sculpture
Swarthout, G. F. The shootist
West, M. L. The devil's advocate
Winterson, J. Written on the body
Cancer ward. Solzhenitsyn, A.
Candide. Voltaire
also in Voltaire. Candide and other stories
also in Voltaire. Voltaire's Candide, Zadig, and selected stories p3-101
Candide and other stories. Voltaire
A **candle** for D'Artagnan. Yarbro, C. Q.
The **candle** in the wind. White, T. H.
In White, T. H. The once and future king p545-677
Cannery Row. Steinbeck, J.
CANNES (FRANCE) *See* France—Cannes
The **cannibal** galaxy. Ozick, C.

CANNIBALISM
Anderson, P. The sharing of flesh
Wiggins, M. John Dollar

CANNIBALS
Melville, H. Omoo: a narrative of adventures in the South Seas
Melville, H. Typee: a peep at Polynesian life
Cannibals and missionaries. McCarthy, M.

CANOES AND CANOEING
Dickey, J. Deliverance
Doig, I. The sea runners

Canopus in Argos: archives [series]
Lessing, D. M. Shikasta

A **canticle** for Leibowitz. Miller, W. M.

CANTON (CHINA) *See* China—Guangzhou

CAPE COD (MASS.) *See* Massachusetts—Cape Cod
Cape Cod. Martin, W.

CAPITAL PUNISHMENT
Dreiser, T. An American tragedy
Gaines, E. J. A lesson before dying
Grisham, J. The chamber
Irving, C. Final argument
Mailer, N. The executioner's song

CAPITALISTS AND FINANCIERS
    See also Bankers; Millionaires; Wealth
Archer, J. Kane & Abel
Baum, V. Grand Hotel
Bromfield, L. Mrs. Parkington
Clancy, T. Debt of honor
Clavell, J. Noble house
Crichton, M. Rising sun
Dickens, C. Dombey and Son
Doctorow, E. L. Loon Lake
Durrell, L. Justine
Fast, H. The immigrants
Ferber, E. Saratoga trunk
Fuentes, C. The death of Artemio Cruz
Gordimer, N. The conservationist
Norris, F. The pit
Ondaatje, M. In the skin of a lion
Rand, A. Atlas shrugged
Scott, J. The nine dragons
Singer, I. J. The brothers Ashkenazi
Smith, W. A. Hungry as the sea
Thomas, M. M. Hanover Place
Trenhaile, J. The gates of exquisite view
The **captain**. De Hartog, J.
The **captain** and the enemy. Greene, G.
Captain Blood. Sabatini, R.
Captain Newman, M.D. Rosten, L. C.
Captain Pantoja and the Special Service. Vargas Llosa, M.
Captains and kings. Caldwell, T.
The **captain's** daughter. Pushkin, A. S.
    In Pushkin, A. S. Alexander Pushkin: complete prose fiction p266-357
CAPTAINS OF SHIPS *See* Shipmasters
The **captive**. Holt, V.
The **captive**. Proust, M.
    In Proust, M. The captive [and] The fugitive
    In Proust, M. Remembrance of things past v3 p1-422
The **captive** [and] The fugitive. Proust, M.
The **captive** Queen of Scots. Plaidy, J.
The **Caravaggio** obsession. Banks, O. T.
Caravan. Gilman, D.
Caravan to Vaccares. MacLean, A.
Caravans. Michener, J. A.
The **Cardinal** and the Queen. Anthony, E.
The **Cardinal** of the Kremlin. Clancy, T.
A **cardinal** offense. McInerny, R. M.
The **cardinal** virtues. Greeley, A. M.

CARDINALS
Moore, B. The color of blood
Cardington Crescent. Perry, A.

CARGO PLANES *See* Transport planes
Caribbean. Michener, J. A.

CARIBBEAN ISLANDS *See* West Indies
A **Caribbean** mystery. Christie, A.
    In Christie, A. Five complete Miss Marple novels p149-262

CARIBBEAN REGION
    See also Spanish Main
Abrahams, P. Lights out
Buffett, J. Where is Joe Merchant?
Coulter, C. Impulse

Green cane and juicy flotsam
Hemingway, E. Islands in the stream
Marshall, P. Daughters
Matthiessen, P. Far Tortuga
Michener, J. A. Caribbean
Vonnegut, K. Cat's cradle
Carioca Fletch. Mcdonald, G.
    In Mcdonald, G. The Fletch chronicles: [two]
Carmen. Mérimée, P.

CARNIVALS (CIRCUS) *See* Amusement parks

CAROLINE MATHILDE, QUEEN OF DENMARK AND NORWAY, 1751-1775
Lofts, N. The lost queen
Caroline's daughters. Adams, A.

CARPATHIAN MOUNTAINS
Wiesel, E. The oath

CARPENTERS
Eliot, G. Adam Bede
Carriage trade. Birmingham, S.
Carrie. King, S.

CARRIERS, AIRCRAFT *See* Aircraft carriers
Carry me home. Del Vecchio, J. M.

CARS (AUTOMOBILES) *See* Automobiles
Casanova's Chinese restaurant. Powell, A.
    In Powell, A. A dance to the music of time [v2]
The **case** book of Sherlock Holmes. Doyle, Sir A. C.
    In Doyle, Sir A. C. The complete Sherlock Holmes
The **case** of Jennie Brice. Rinehart, M. R.
    In Rinehart, M. R. Mary Roberts Rinehart's mystery book p349-442
A **case** of need. Crichton, M.
The **case** of the missing Brontë. Barnard, R.
The **case** of the postponed murder. Gardner, E. S.
The **case** of the sulky girl. Gardner, E. S.
The **case** of the worried waitress. Gardner, E. S.
Cashelmara. Howatch, S.
Casino Royale. Fleming, I.
Cass Timberlane. Lewis, S.

CASSANDRA (GREEK MYTHOLOGY)
Bradley, M. Z. The firebrand
Cast a long shadow. Pearce, M. E.
A **cast** of thousands. Shagan, S.

CASTELMORE, CHARLES BATZ-, COMTE D'AR-TAGNAN *See* Artagnan, Charles de Batz-Castelmore, comte d', 1613?-1673
The **castle**. Kafka, F.

CASTLES
Holt, V. Bride of Pendorric
Stewart, M. Nine coaches waiting
Castleview. Wolfe, G.

CASTRATI *See* Eunuchs

CASTRO, FIDEL, 1927-
Kessel, J. The Franchise
Cat and mouse. Grass, G.
    also in Grass, G. The Danzig trilogy
Cat chaser. Leonard, E.
The **cat** who ate Danish modern. Braun, L. J.
The **cat** who came to breakfast. Braun, L. J.
The **cat** who knew a cardinal. Braun, L. J.
The **cat** who lived high. Braun, L. J.
The **cat** who moved a mountain. Braun, L. J.
The **cat** who sniffed glue. Braun, L. J.
The **cat** who talked to ghosts. Braun, L. J.
The **cat** who walks through walls. Heinlein, R. A.
The **cat** who wasn't there. Braun, L. J.
The **cat** who went into the closet. Braun, L. J.
The **cat** who went underground. Braun, L. J.
The **cat-woman**. Gardner, E. S.
    In Gardner, E. S. Dead men's letters p105-46

CATASTROPHES See Disasters

Catch-22. Heller, J.

The **catcher** in the rye. Salinger, J. D.

CATHARINE HOWARD, QUEEN, CONSORT OF HENRY VIII, KING OF ENGLAND, d. 1542
Plaidy, J. Murder most royal
Plaidy, J. The rose without a thorn

CATHARINE PARR, QUEEN, CONSORT OF HENRY VIII, KING OF ENGLAND, 1512-1548
Plaidy, J. The sixth wife

Cathedral. Carver, R.

CATHEDRAL LIFE
Dickens, C. The mystery of Edwin Drood
Dickens, C. The mystery of Edwin Drood, concluded by Leon Garfield
Golding, W. The spire
Goudge, E. A city of bells
Goudge, E. The dean's watch
Hugo, V. The hunchback of Notre Dame
L'Engle, M. A severed wasp
Trollope, A. Barchester Towers
Trollope, A. The warden

CATHEDRAL TOWNS
See also Cathedral life

CATHEDRALS
Dickens, C. The mystery of Edwin Drood
Dickens, C. The mystery of Edwin Drood, concluded by Leon Garfield
Follett, K. Pillars of the earth
L'Engle, M. A severed wasp
Pargeter, E. The heaven tree

CATHERINE, OF BRAGANZA, QUEEN, CONSORT OF CHARLES II, KING OF ENGLAND, 1638-1705
Plaidy, J. The pleasures of love

CATHERINE HOWARD See Catharine Howard, Queen, consort of Henry VIII, King of England, d. 1542

CATHERINE PARR See Catharine Parr, Queen, consort of Henry VIII, King of England, 1512-1548

CATHOLIC BISHOPS
Cather, W. Death comes for the archbishop
Cather, W. Shadows on the rock

CATHOLIC CHURCH See Catholic faith

CATHOLIC CLERGY See Catholic priests

CATHOLIC FAITH
See also Cardinals; Catholic bishops; Catholic priests; Convent life; Inquisition; Monasticism and religious orders
Barrett, W. E. The left hand of God
Barrett, W. E. The lilies of the field
Battle, L. The past is another country
Böll, H. The clown
Butler, R. O. They whisper
Caldwell, T. Answer as a man
Campbell, R. W. Boneyards
Carroll, J. The city below
Carroll, J. Prince of peace
Cather, W. Death comes for the archbishop
Cather, W. Shadows on the rock
Cronin, A. J. A pocketful of rye
Cronin, A. J. A song of sixpence
Dunne, J. G. The red, white, and blue
Eco, U. The name of the rose
Endō, S. The samurai
Finney, P. Firedrake's eye
Girzone, J. F. The shepherd
Godden, R. In this house of Brede
Gordon, M. The company of women
Gordon, M. Final payments
Gordon, M. The other side
Grass, G. Cat and mouse
Greeley, A. M. Angels of September
Greeley, A. M. Ascent into hell
Greeley, A. M. The cardinal virtues

Greeley, A. M. Fall from grace
Greeley, A. M. Lord of the dance
Greeley, A. M. An occasion of sin
Greeley, A. M. Patience of a saint
Greeley, A. M. Thy brother's wife
Greene, G. Brighton rock
Greene, G. The end of the affair
Greene, G. The heart of the matter
Greene, G. Monsignor Quixote
Greene, G. The power and the glory
Hassler, J. North of hope
Hulme, K. The nun's story
Martin, M. Vatican
McDermott, A. At weddings and wakes
McInerny, R. M. Leave of absence
McInerny, R. M. The priest
Moore, B. Black robe
Moore, B. Catholics
Moore, B. Cold heaven
Moore, B. The color of blood
Percy, W. The thanatos syndrome
Plaidy, J. The scarlet cloak
Plante, D. Annunciation
Powers, J. F. Morte d'Urban
Powers, J. F. Wheat that springeth green
Powers, J. R. Do black patent-leather shoes really reflect up?
Powers, J. R. The last Catholic in America
Prose, F. Household saints
Quindlen, A. Object lessons
Rossner, J. Olivia
Segal, E. Acts of faith
Spark, M. The comforters
Stendhal. The red and the black
Waugh, E. Brideshead revisited
Waugh, E. The end of the battle
Werfel, F. The song of Bernadette
West, M. L. The clowns of God
West, M. L. Lazarus
West, M. L. The shoes of the fisherman

CATHOLIC PRIESTS
See also Cardinals; Catholic bishops; Catholic faith; Ex-priests
Blatty, W. P. The exorcist
Camus, A. The plague
Carroll, J. Prince of peace
Cather, W. Death comes for the archbishop
Cronin, A. J. The keys of the kingdom
Dunne, J. G. True confessions
Eliot, G. Romola
Endō, S. Silence
Gallico, P. The small miracle
Gordon, M. The company of women
Gordon, M. Immaculate man
Greeley, A. M. The cardinal virtues
Greeley, A. M. Fall from grace
Greeley, A. M. An occasion of sin
Greeley, A. M. Thy brother's wife
Greene, G. A burnt-out case
Greene, G. The honorary consul
Greene, G. Monsignor Quixote
Greene, G. The power and the glory
Guareschi, G. Don Camillo and his flock
Guareschi, G. The little world of Don Camillo
Hassler, J. North of hope
Higgins, J. Confessional
Kienzle, W. X. Assault with intent
Kienzle, W. X. Bishop as pawn
Kienzle, W. X. Body count
Kienzle, W. X. Chameleon
Kienzle, W. X. Dead wrong
Kienzle, W. X. Deadline for a critic
Kienzle, W. X. Death wears a red hat
Kienzle, W. X. Deathbed
Kienzle, W. X. Eminence
Kienzle, W. X. Marked for murder
Kienzle, W. X. Masquerade
Kienzle, W. X. Mind over murder

CATHOLIC PRIESTS—*Continued*
Kienzle, W. X. The rosary murders
Kienzle, W. X. Sudden death
McCullough, C. The thorn birds
McInerny, R. M. The priest
Monsarrat, N. The kappillan of Malta
Moore, B. Black robe
Murdoch, I. Henry and Cato
Powers, J. F. Morte d'Urban
Powers, J. F. Wheat that springeth green
Pym, B. A glass of blessings
Schulberg, B. Waterfront
Segal, E. Acts of faith
West, M. L. The devil's advocate
Wilder, T. The bridge of San Luis Rey

CATHOLIC RELIGION *See* Catholic faith

CATHOLICS *See* Catholic faith

Catholics. Moore, B.

Catnap. Douglas, C. N.

CATS
Burnford, S. The incredible journey
Greenfeld, J. Harry and Tonto
Mysterious cat stories
Roger Caras' Treasury of great cat stories
Sarton, M. The fur person

Cat's cradle. Vonnegut, K.

Cat's eye. Atwood, M.

The **cat's meow**. Campbell, R. W.

A **Catskill eagle**. Parker, R. B.

CATSKILL MOUNTAINS (N.Y.)
Gardner, J. Nickel mountain
Kay, T. Shadow song
Lurie, A. Only children
Whitney, P. A. The stone bull

Catspaw. Vinge, J. D.

CATTLE
Gallico, P. Ludmila
Grey, Z. Knights of the range

CATTLE DRIVERS
McMurtry, L. Lonesome dove

The **cavalier case**. Fraser, A.

The **cavalier in white**. Muller, M.

CAVALRY (U.S.) *See* United States. Army. Cavalry

The **cave**. Warren, R. P.

CAVES
Warren, R. P. The cave

The **caves of steel**. Asimov, I.
In Asimov, I. The rest of the robots p165-362

Celebration. Settle, M. L.

Celebrations at Thrush Green. Read, Miss

Celestial navigation. Tyler, A.

The **celestial omnibus**. See Forster, E. M. The collected tales of E. M. Forster

The **celestine prophecy**. Redfield, J.

Celia Garth. Bristow, G.

Celia's house. Stevenson, D. E.

CELTIC BRITAIN *See* England—To 55 B.C.

CELTS
Llywelyn, M. Bard
Llywelyn, M. Druids
Llywelyn, M. The horse goddess

CEMETERIES
Appelfeld, A. Unto the soul
Beagle, P. S. A fine and private place
King, S. Pet sematary

The **centaur**. Updike, J.

Centenary at Jalna. De la Roche, M.

Centennial. Michener, J. A.

CENTRAL AFRICA
Verne, J. Five weeks in a balloon

CENTRAL AMERICA
Forester, C. S. Beat to quarters
Stone, R. A flag for sunrise

Thomas, R. Missionary stew

Politics

See Politics—Central America

CENTRAL EUROPE
Korda, M. Worldly goods

CENTRAL INTELLIGENCE AGENCY (U.S.) *See* United States. Central Intelligence Agency

The **centurion**. De Hartog, J.

CEPHALONIA ISLAND (GREECE)
De Bernières, L. Corelli's mandolin

CEREBRAL PALSY
Brown, C. Down all the days

CEREMONIES *See* Rites and ceremonies

Ceremony. Parker, R. B.

Ceremony of innocence. Dean, S. F. X.

Ceremony of the innocent. Caldwell, T.

Certain people. Wharton, E.
In Wharton, E. The collected short stories of Edith Wharton v2

Certain things last. Anderson, S.

Certain women. L'Engle, M.

The **certificate**. Singer, I. B.

CERVANTES SAAVEDRA, MIGUEL DE, 1547-1616
Parodies, Travesties, etc.
Greene, G. Monsignor Quixote

Chad Hanna. Edmonds, W. D.

A **chain of voices**. Brink, A. P.

Chains of command. Brown, D.

Challenges. Bova, B.

The **chamber**. Grisham, J.

Chamber music. Grumbach, D.

Chameleon. Kienzle, W. X.

Chance acquaintances. Colette
In Colette. Gigi. Julie de Carneilhan. Chance acquaintances p225-315

The **Chancellor manuscript**. Ludlum, R.

CHANCELLORSVILLE, BATTLE OF, 1863
Crane, S. The red badge of courage

CHANDLER, RAYMOND, 1888-1959
Parodies, travesties, etc.
Parker, R. B. Perchance to dream

The **Chaneysville incident**. Bradley, D.

Changes at Fairacre. Read, Miss

CHANNEL ISLANDS
Goudge, E. Green Dolphin Street

Chanur's Legacy. Cherryh, C. J.

Chaos mode. Anthony, P.

Chaos of crime. Shannon, D.

Chapterhouse: Dune. Herbert, F.

Charade. Brown, S.

The **charioteer**. Renault, M.

CHARITIES *See* Endowments

CHARLES II, KING OF GREAT BRITAIN, 1630-1685
Goudge, E. The child from the sea
Plaidy, J. The pleasures of love

CHARLES XIV JOHN, KING OF SWEDEN AND NORWAY, 1763-1844
Selinko, A. Désirée

CHARLES, D'ORLÉANS, 1394-1465
Haasse, H. S. In a dark wood wandering

CHARLES, DUKE OF BURGUNDY, 1433-1477
Scott, Sir W. Quentin Durward

CHARLES, THE BOLD *See* Charles, Duke of Burgundy, 1433-1477

A **Charles** Dickens Christmas. Dickens, C.
Charles Ryder's schooldays and other stories. Waugh, E.
CHARLESTON (S.C.) *See* South Carolina—Charleston
Charley Bland. Settle, M. L.
Charlie's apprentice. Freemantle, B.
The **Charlotte** Armstrong reader. Armstrong, C.
The **Charlotte** Perkins Gilman reader. Gilman, C. P.
The **charm** school. DeMille, N.
The **charmed** circle. Gaskin, C.
A **charmed** life. McCarthy, M.
Charms for the easy life. Gibbons, K.
The **charterhouse** of Parma. Stendhal
The **chartreuse** of Parma. See Stendhal. The charterhouse of Parma

CHARWOMEN
    Gallico, P. Mrs. 'Arris goes to Paris

CHASIDISM *See* Hasidism

CHATEAUX *See* Castles

CHAUFFEURS
    Grau, S. A. The condor passes
Cheating death. Keating, H. R. F.
Checkmate. Dunnett, D.

CHEERFUL STORIES
    Aldrich, B. S. A lantern in her hand
    Austen, J. Emma
    Benson, E. F. Make way for Lucia
    Chesney, M. Deborah goes to Dover
    Colwin, L. Happy all the time
    Davies, V. Miracle on 34th Street
    Gallico, P. Mrs. 'Arris goes to Paris
    Goudge, E. A city of bells
    Goudge, E. The dean's watch
    Goudge, E. Pilgrim's inn
    Heyer, G. Bath tangle
    Heyer, G. The grand Sophy
    Heyer, G. Lady of quality
    Keillor, G. The book of guys
    Keillor, G. Lake Wobegon days
    Leslie, J. A. C. The ghost and Mrs. Muir
    Parkinson, C. N. Jeeves: a gentleman's personal gentleman
    Powers, J. R. Do black patent-leather shoes really reflect up?
    Powers, J. R. The last Catholic in America
    Priestley, J. B. The good companions
    Read, Miss. Affairs at Thrush Green
    Read, Miss. At home in Thrush Green
    Read, Miss. Battles at Thrush Green
    Read, Miss. Celebrations at Thrush Green
    Read, Miss. Changes at Fairacre
    Read, Miss. Chronicles of Fairacre
    Read, Miss. Farewell to Fairacre
    Read, Miss. Friends at Thrush Green
    Read, Miss. Gossip from Thrush Green
    Read, Miss. Mrs. Pringle
    Read, Miss. Return to Thrush Green
    Read, Miss. The school at Thrush Green
    Read, Miss. Thrush Green
    Read, Miss. Winter in Thrush Green
    Sarton, M. The fur person
    Sharp, M. Cluny Brown
    Streeter, E. Father of the bride
    Tarkington, B. Seventeen
    Voigt, C. Glass mountain
    West, J. Except for me and thee
    West, J. The friendly persuasion
    Wodehouse, P. G. The code of the Woosters
    Wodehouse, P. G. How right you are, Jeeves
    Wodehouse, P. G. The inimitable Jeeves
    Wodehouse, P. G. Jeeves and the tie that binds
    Wodehouse, P. G. Tales from the Drones Club
    Wodehouse, P. G. A Wodehouse bestiary
    Wodehouse, P. G. The world of Jeeves

Chekhov: the early stories, 1883-1888. Chekhov, A. P.

CHEMISTS
    See also Medicines, Patent, proprietary, etc.
    Deighton, L. Funeral in Berlin
    Levi, P. The monkey's wrench
    Wallace, I. The prize
Chéri. Colette
    In Colette. Six novels p411-534
Chernevog. Cherryh, C. J.
Chernobyl. Pohl, F.

CHERNOBYL NUCLEAR ACCIDENT, CHERNOBYL, UKRAINE, 1986
    Pohl, F. Chernobyl

CHEROKEE INDIANS
    Brown, D. A. Creek Mary's blood
    Conley, R. J. Mountain windsong
    Dailey, J. The proud and the free
    Kingsolver, B. Pigs in heaven
The **Cherokee** Trail. L'Amour, L.
The **cherry** blossom corpse. Barnard, R.
Chesapeake. Michener, J. A.

CHESAPEAKE BAY (MD. AND VA.)
    Barth, J. The Tidewater tales
    Michener, J. A. Chesapeake
The **Cheshire** moon. Ferrigno, R.

CHESS
    Dunnett, D. Pawn in frankincense
    Neville, K. The eight
    Tevis, W. S. The queen's gambit

CHEYENNE INDIANS
    Berger, T. Little Big Man
    Brand, M. Fugitives' fire

CHICAGO (ILL.) *See* Illinois—Chicago

CHICANOS *See* Mexican Americans
Chiefs. Woods, S.

CHILD ABUSE
    Allison, D. Bastard out of Carolina
    Brownmiller, S. Waverly Place
    Busch, F. Closing arguments
    Clark, M. H. All around the town
    Guest, J. Second heaven
    McFarland, D. School for the blind
    Oates, J. C. The rise of life on earth
    Phillips, J. A. Shelter
    Rice, L. Stone heart
    Tanenbaum, R. Immoral certainty
    Tilly, M. Singing songs

CHILD AND PARENT *See* Parent and child
The **child** from the sea. Goudge, E.

CHILD LABOR
    Dickens, C. Oliver Twist

CHILD MOLESTING *See* Child sexual abuse

CHILD SEXUAL ABUSE
    Greeley, A. M. Fall from grace
    Patterson, R. N. Eyes of a child
    Tilly, M. Singing songs

CHILDHOOD *See* Boys; Children; Girls
Childhood, Boyhood and Youth. Tolstoy, L., graf
Childhood's end. Clarke, A. C.

CHILDLESS MARRIAGE
    Steel, D. Mixed blessings
    Tennant, E. Pemberley

CHILDLESSNESS
    See also Childless marriage
    Cook, R. Vital signs
    Oates, J. C. I lock my door upon myself
    Woiwode, L. Indian affairs

CHILDREN
    See also Adolescence; Boys; Emotionally disturbed children; Foster children; Girls; Mentally handicapped children; Orphans
    Anderson, S. Tar: a midwest childhood

CHILDREN—*Continued*
Ashton-Warner, S. Spinster
Dickinson, P. Play dead
Godden, R. The battle of the Villa Fiorita
Godden, R. An episode of sparrows
Godden, R. The greengage summer
Goudge, E. The bird in the tree
Goudge, E. A city of bells
Goudge, E. The dean's watch
Goudge, E. Pilgrim's inn
James, H. The turn of the screw
Lee, H. To kill a mockingbird
McCullers, C. The member of the wedding
McDermott, A. At weddings and wakes
Patton, F. G. Good morning, Miss Dove
Roth, H. Call it sleep

Adoption
See Adoption

CHILDREN, ADOPTED *See* Adoption
CHILDREN, AUTISTIC *See* Autistic children
CHILDREN, CRUELTY TO *See* Child abuse
CHILDREN, GIFTED *See* Gifted children
CHILDREN, SICK *See* Sick children
The **children**. Wharton, E.
CHILDREN AS SLAVES *See* Slavery
The **children** in the woods. Busch, F.
Children of Dune. Herbert, F.
The **children** of first man. Thom, J. A.
Children of light. Stone, R.
The **children** of men. James, P. D.
Children of the albatross. Nin, A.
In Nin, A. Cities of the interior p128-238
Children of the Arbat. Rybakov, A. N.
Children of the sea. See Conrad, J. The Nigger of the Narcissus
Children of violence. Lessing, D. M.
Child's play. Hill, R.

CHILE
19th century
Cornwell, B. Sharpe's devil

20th century
Allende, I. The house of the spirits
Donoso, J. A house in the country

Politics
See Politics—Chile
The **chill**. Macdonald, R.
In Macdonald, R. Archer at large
Chilly scenes of winter. Beattie, A.
Chimera. Barth, J.
The **chimes**. Dickens, C.
In Dickens, C. A Charles Dickens Christmas p101-202
In Dickens, C. Christmas tales

CHINA
See also Yangtze River (China)
To 1643
Costain, T. B. The black rose
Larsen, J. Silk road

17th century
Elegant, R. S. Manchu

18th century
Han, S. The enchantress
Ts'ao, H.-C. The dream of the red chamber

19th century
See also Taiping Rebellion, 1850-1864
Buck, P. S. Imperial woman
Elegant, R. S. Mandarin
Lord, B. B. Spring Moon

War of 1840-1842
Clavell, J. Tai-Pan

20th century
Li, P.-H. Farewell to my concubine
Tan, A. The Joy Luck Club

1900-1949
Barrett, W. E. The left hand of God
Bosse, M. J. Fire in heaven
Bosse, M. J. The warlord
Brent, M. Moonraker's bride
Buck, P. S. Dragon seed
Buck, P. S. East wind: west wind
Buck, P. S. The good earth
Buck, P. S. A house divided
Buck, P. S. Pavilion of women
Buck, P. S. Sons
Cronin, A. J. The keys of the kingdom
Elegant, R. S. Dynasty
Han, S. Till morning comes
Hersey, J. A single pebble
Lin, Y. Moment in Peking
Lord, B. B. Spring Moon
Malraux, A. Man's fate (La condition humaine)
McKenna, R. The Sand Pebbles
Tan, A. The kitchen god's wife

1949-
Elegant, R. S. Dynasty
Gilman, D. Mrs. Pollifax on the China station
Han, S. Till morning comes
Lee, C. Y. Gate of rage

Communism
See Communism—China

Courts and courtiers
See Courts and courtiers—China

Farm life
See Farm life—China

Kings and rulers
Buck, P. S. Imperial woman

Peasant life
See Peasant life—China

Politics
See Politics—China

Guangzhou
Clavell, J. Tai-Pan

Hong Kong
See Hong Kong

Shanghai
Ballard, J. G. Empire of the Sun
Malraux, A. Man's fate (La condition humaine)

Tibet
Hilton, J. Lost horizon

CHINA. ARMY *See* China. People's Liberation Army
CHINA. PEOPLE'S LIBERATION ARMY
Bosse, M. J. The warlord
China boy. Lee, G.
China Court. Godden, R.
The **China** governess. Allingham, M.
China silk. Worboys, A.
China white. Maas, P.
Chinaman's chance. Thomas, R.

CHINATOWN (NEW YORK, N.Y.) *See* New York (N.Y.)—Chinatown

CHINESE
Hawaii
Michener, J. A. Hawaii

Indochina
Duras, M. The lover
Duras, M. The North China lover

United States
Buck, P. S. A house divided

CHINESE—United States—*Continued*
Dillard, A. The living
Fast, H. The immigrants
Lee, C. Y. The flower drum song
Steinbeck, J. Cannery Row

CHINESE AMERICANS
Jen, G. Typical American
Kingston, M. H. Tripmaster Monkey
Lee, G. China boy
Lee, G. Honor & duty
Ng, F. M. Bone
Tan, A. The Joy Luck Club
Tan, A. The kitchen god's wife
The **Chinese** bell murders. Gulik, R. H. van

CHINESE PEOPLE'S LIBERATION ARMY *See* China.
People's Liberation Army

CHINESE SOLDIERS *See* Soldiers—China

CHIPPEWA INDIANS
Erdrich, L. The bingo palace
Erdrich, L. Love medicine
Erdrich, L. Tracks
Hassler, J. North of hope
The **Chisholms.** Hunter, E.

CHIVALRY
See also Knights and knighthood; Middle Ages
Cervantes Saavedra, M. de. Don Quixote de la Mancha
Doyle, Sir A. C. The White Company
Scott, Sir W. The talisman
Twain, M. A Connecticut Yankee in King Arthur's court
White, T. H. The once and future king
The **choice.** Reed, B.
The **chosen.** Potok, C.

CHRIST *See* Jesus Christ

CHRISTIAN VII, KING OF DENMARK AND NORWAY, 1749-1808
Lofts, N. The lost queen

CHRISTIAN LIFE
Bunyan, J. The Pilgrim's progress
Douglas, L. C. Magnificent obsession
Girzone, J. F. Joshua and the children
Girzone, J. F. Joshua in the Holy Land
Girzone, J. F. The shepherd
Tyler, A. Saint maybe

CHRISTIANITY
See also Apostles; Catholic faith; names of Christian churches or sects
Asch, S. The Apostle
Asch, S. Mary
Asch, S. The Nazarene
Caldwell, T. Dear and glorious physician
Caldwell, T. Great lion of God
Caldwell, T. I, Judas
Costain, T. B. The silver chalice
Easterman, D. Brotherhood of the tomb
Endō, S. The samurai
Endō, S. Silence
L'Engle, M. Certain women
Sienkiewicz, H. Quo vadis
Vidal, G. Julian
Vidal, G. Live from Golgotha

CHRISTIANS, EARLY *See* Early Christians
Christine. King, S.
A **Christmas** carol. Dickens, C.
also in Dickens, C. A Charles Dickens Christmas p3-98
also in Dickens, C. Christmas tales p11-77
also in Dickens, C. The complete ghost stories of Charles Dickens p89-151
A **Christmas** memory. Capote, T.
also in Capote, T. Breakfast at Tiffany's

Christmas stalkings. Entered in Part I under title

CHRISTMAS STORIES
Capote, T. A Christmas memory
Christmas stalkings
Davies, V. Miracle on 34th Street
Dickens, C. A Charles Dickens Christmas
Dickens, C. A Christmas carol
Dickens, C. Christmas stories
Dickens, C. Christmas tales
Dickens, C. The cricket on the hearth
Hamner, E. The homecoming
A Literary Christmas
Reed, I. The terrible twos
Stubbs, J. Family games
Christmas stories. Dickens, C.
Christmas tales. Dickens, C.
Christy. Marshall, C.
Chronicle of a death foretold. García Márquez, G.
also in García Márquez, G. Collected novellas p167-249

Chronicles of Barsetshire [series]
Trollope, A. Barchester Towers
Trollope, A. Doctor Thorne
Trollope, A. Framley parsonage
Trollope, A. The last chronicle of Barset
Trollope, A. The small house at Allington
Trollope, A. The warden

Chronicles of Fairacre. Read, Miss
The **chronicles** of Pern. McCaffrey, A.

Chronicles of Thomas Covenant, the Unbeliever [series]
Donaldson, S. R. The Illearth war
Donaldson, S. R. Lord Foul's bane
Donaldson, S. R. The One Tree
Donaldson, S. R. The power that preserves
Donaldson, S. R. White gold wielder
Donaldson, S. R. The wounded Land

The **chrysanthemum** chain. Melville, J.

CHURCH AND STATE

Eastern Europe
Moore, B. The color of blood

CHURCH HISTORY

Primitive and early church
Caldwell, T. Dear and glorious physician
Caldwell, T. Great lion of God
Caldwell, T. I, Judas
Sienkiewicz, H. Quo vadis
Waltari, M. The Roman

CHURCH OF ENGLAND
Howatch, S. Absolute truths
Howatch, S. Glamorous powers
Howatch, S. Glittering images
Howatch, S. Mystical paths
Howatch, S. Scandalous risks
Howatch, S. Ultimate prizes

CHURCH SCHOOLS
Powers, J. R. Do black patent-leather shoes really reflect up?
Powers, J. R. The last Catholic in America

CHURCHES
See also Cathedrals
Barrett, W. E. The lilies of the field
Price, E. The beloved invader

CI XI *See* Tz'u-hsi, Empress dowager of China, 1835-1908

CIA *See* United States. Central Intelligence Agency
The **cider** house rules. Irving, J.
Cimarron. Ferber, E.
Cinderella. McBain, E.
Cinnamon skin. MacDonald, J. D.
The **circle**. Poyer, D.
Circle of friends. Binchy, M.
Circle of gold. Harper, K.
Circle of pearls. Laker, R.
The **circular** staircase. Rinehart, M. R.
    also in Rinehart, M. R. Mary Roberts Rinehart's
    mystery book p3-178

CIRCUS
    Edmonds, W. D. Chad Hanna
    Irving, J. A son of the circus
    Singer, I. B. The magician of Lublin
    Stewart, M. Airs above the ground
The **citadel**. Cronin, A. J.
The **Citadel** of the Autarch. Wolfe, G.

CITIES AND TOWNS
    See also Extinct cities; Imaginary cities

CITIES AND TOWNS, RUINED, EXTINCT, ETC. *See*
    Extinct cities
Cities of the interior. Nin, A.
Cities of the plain [variant title: Sodom and Gomorrah].
    Proust, M.
    In Proust, M. Remembrance of things past v2 p623-
    1169
Citizen of the galaxy. Heinlein, R. A.
Citizen Tom Paine. Fast, H.
The **city** and the stars. Clarke, A. C.
The **city** below. Carroll, J.
The **city** boy, the adventures of Herbie Bookbinder and
    his cousin Cliff. Wouk, H.
A **city** of bells. Goudge, E.
City of gold. Deighton, L.
City of gold and shadows. Peters, E.
City of illusions. Le Guin, U. K.
A **city** of strangers. Barnard, R.
City of the mind. Lively, P.
City of Truth. Morrow, J.
    In Nebula awards 28 p228-317
City of widows. Estleman, L. D.
City primeval. Leonard, E.
    In Leonard, E. Elmore Leonard's double Dutch treat:
    three novels
The **city** who fought. McCaffrey, A.

CIVIL RIGHTS DEMONSTRATIONS *See* African
    Americans—Civil rights

CIVIL SERVICE
    Dickens, C. Little Dorrit
    Frayn, M. A landing on the sun
    Greene, G. The heart of the matter
    Snow, C. P. Homecoming
Civil to strangers. Pym, B.
    In Pym, B. Civil to strangers and other writings
    p7-170
Civil to strangers and other writings. Pym, B.

CIVIL WAR

England
    See England—17th century

Spain
    See Spain—Civil War, 1936-1939

United States
    See United States—Civil War, 1861-1865
Civil wars. Brown, R.

CIVILIZATION *See* Social problems

CIVILIZATION AND TECHNOLOGY *See* Technology
    and civilization
CIXI *See* Tz'u-hsi, Empress dowager of China, 1835-1908

CLAIRVOYANCE
    Conrad, J. Secret agent
    Garcia, C. Dreaming in Cuban

    Gaskin, C. Fiona
    McCrumb, S. The hangman's beautiful daughter
The **Clan** of the Cave Bear. Auel, J. M.

CLANS
    See also Tribes
    Holland, C. The kings in winter
    Scott, Sir W. Waverly
Clarissa. Richardson, S.
Clarissa Harlowe. See Richardson, S. Clarissa

CLARK, RALPH, D. 1794
    Keneally, T. The playmaker

CLASS DISTINCTION
    See also Middle classes; Social classes
    Brown, R. M. Southern discomfort
    Crane, S. Active service
    Crane, S. The third violet
    Dreiser, T. An American tragedy
    Dunne, D. People like us
    Forster, E. M. A room with a view
    Greene, G. The tenth man
    Harper, K. Circle of gold
    Holt, V. The Devil on horseback
    Holt, V. The legend of the seventh virgin
    Ishiguro, K. The remains of the day
    James, H. The American
    Leavitt, D. While England sleeps
    McNaught, J. Paradise
    Pearce, M. E. The old house at Railes
    Rice, A. The Feast of All Saints
    Richler, M. Solomon Gursky was here
    Robards, K. Nobody's angel
    Ross-Macdonald, M. A woman alone
    Siddons, A. R. Colony
    Simenon, G. The rules of the game
    Tarkington, B. Alice Adams
    Trollope, A. The way we live now
    Wharton, E. The buccaneers
    Wharton, E. The buccaneers, completed by Marion
    Mainwaring
    Wharton, E. Fast and loose
Class reunion. Jaffe, R.

CLASS STRUGGLE
    Crichton, R. The Camerons
    Singer, I. J. The brothers Ashkenazi
Classic lines: more great racing stories. See The New
    treasury of great racing stories
The **classic** Philip José Farmer, 1952-1964–1964-1973.
    Farmer, P. J.
Classics of the macabre, Daphne du Maurier's. Du
    Maurier, Dame D.
Claudine and Annie. Colette
    In Colette. The complete Claudine p516-632
Claudine at school. Colette
    In Colette. The complete Claudine p1-206
    In Colette. Six novels p1-234
Claudine in Paris. Colette
    In Colette. The complete Claudine p209-364
Claudine married. Colette
    In Colette. The complete Claudine p367-510

CLAUDIUS, EMPEROR OF ROME, 10 B.C.-54
    Graves, R. Claudius, the god and his wife Messalina
    Graves, R. I, Claudius
Claudius, the god and his wife Messalina. Graves, R.
The **claw**. Lofts, N.
The **claw** of the conciliator. Wolfe, G.
Clea. Durrell, L.
    also in Durrell, L. The Alexandria quartet p653-884

CLEANING WOMEN
    See also Charwomen; Maids (Servants)
Clear and present danger. Clancy, T.
Clear light of day. Desai, A.
Cleopatra Gold. Caunitz, W. J.
Cleopatra's sister. Lively, P.

CLERGY
    See also Evangelists; Rabbis; Women clergy
    Baldwin, J. Go tell it on the mountain

CLERGY—*Continued*
Barrie, J. M. The little minister
Colegate, I. The summer of the royal visit
Field, R. All this, and heaven too
Gaines, E. J. In my father's house
Hawthorne, N. The scarlet letter
Heinlein, R. A. Job: a comedy of justice
Lewis, S. Elmer Gantry
MacDonald, J. D. One more Sunday
Price, E. The beloved invader
Richter, C. A simple honorable man

CLERGY, ANGLICAN AND EPISCOPAL *See* Anglican and Episcopal clergy

CLERGY, CATHOLIC *See* Catholic priests

CLERGY, ITINERANT *See* Itinerant clergy

CLERKS
See also Civil service
Kafka, F. The trial
Pym, B. Quartet in autumn

CLEVELAND (OHIO) *See* Ohio—Cleveland
The **client**. Grisham, J.
Client privilege. Tapply, W. G.

CLIPPER SHIPS *See* Sailing vessels
The **cloak** and the staff. Dickson, G. R.
In The Hugo winners v5 p209-43
Cloak of darkness. MacInnes, H.
The **clock** winder. Tyler, A.
Clock without hands. McCullers, C.
Clockers. Price, R.

CLOCKS AND WATCHES
Goudge, E. The dean's watch
A **clockwork** orange. Burgess, A.

CLONES *See* Asexual reproduction
The **cloning** of Joanna May. Weldon, F.
Clonk clonk. Golding, W.
In Golding, W. The scorpion god: three short novels p63-114

CLONTARF, BATTLE OF, 1014
Holland, C. The kings in winter
Close combat. Griffin, W. E. B.
Close encounters of the third kind. Spielberg, S.
Close quarters. Golding, W.
Close relations. Isaacs, S.
A **closed** eye. Brookner, A.
Closing arguments. Busch, F.
Closing time. Heller, J.

CLOTHING INDUSTRY
Laker, R. Banners of silk
Tax, M. Rivington Street
Tax, M. Union Square
Weidman, J. I can get it for you wholesale

CLOTHING WORKERS *See* Clothing industry
Clouds of witness. See Sayers, D. L. Clouds of witnesses
Clouds of witnesses. Sayers, D. L.
The **clown**. Böll, H.

CLOWNS
Böll, H. The clown
Hamsun, K. Mysteries
The **clowns** of God. West, M. L.
A **clubbable** woman. Hill, R.

CLUBS
Auchincloss, L. The book class
Dickens, C. The posthumous papers of the Pickwick Club
King, S. The breathing method
Santmyer, H. H. "—and ladies of the club"
Spark, M. The girls of slender means
Tan, A. The Joy Luck Club
Wodehouse, P. G. Tales from the Drones Club

Cluny Brown. Sharp, M.
Clutch of Constables. Marsh, Dame N.

COAL MINERS *See* Coal mines and mining

COAL MINES AND MINING

France
Zola, É. Germinal

Pennsylvania
Richter, C. A simple honorable man

Scotland
Crichton, R. The Camerons

Wales
Llewellyn, R. How green was my valley

West Virginia
Giardina, D. The unquiet earth

Wyoming
Olsen, T. Yonnondio: from the thirties

COAL TOWNS *See* Coal mines and mining
Coat of arms. See Kells, S. The aristocrats
A **coat** of varnish. Snow, C. P.

COCAINE
See also Crack (Drug)
Cook, R. Blindsight
Daley, R. A faint cold fear
Dart, I. R. I'll be there
Perry, T. Metzger's dog
Price, R. Clockers
Stone, R. Children of light

COCKNEY DIALECT *See* Dialect stories—English—Cockney

COCKTAIL PARTIES *See* Parties
Code of honor. Coyle, H. W.
The **code** of the Woosters. Wodehouse, P. G.

CODY, WILLIAM FREDERICK *See* Buffalo Bill, 1846-1917

Coffee will make you black. Sinclair, A.
Coffin and the Paper Man. Butler, G.
A **coffin** for Charley. Butler, G.
Coffin in the Museum of Crime. Butler, G.
Coffin on Murder Street. Butler, G.

COINS
Sanders, L. The eighth commandment
Coinspinner's story. See Saberhagen, F. The fifth book of lost swords: Coinspinner's story
Cold fire. Koontz, D. R.
Cold Harbour. Higgins, J.
Cold heaven. Moore, B.
Cold light. Harvey, J.
A **cold** red sunrise. Kaminsky, S. M.
Cold Sassy tree. Burns, O. A.

COLLABORATIONISTS *See* World War, 1939-1945—Collaborationists
Collected novellas. García Márquez, G.
The **collected** novels of Conrad Aiken. Aiken, C.
Collected short fiction, 1892-1912, Willa Cather's. Cather, W.

Collected short stories. Graves, R.
Collected short stories. Huxley, A.
The collected short stories. Rhys, J.
The collected short stories of Edith Wharton. Wharton, E.
The collected stories. Babel', I.
Collected stories. García Márquez, G.
Collected stories. Greene, G.
Collected stories. Kafka, F.
Collected stories. Kipling, R.
Collected stories. Lawrence, D. H.
Collected stories. McCullers, C.
The collected stories. McGahern, J.
Collected stories. O'Connor, F.
The collected stories. Paley, G.
The collected stories. Price, R.
Collected stories. Rendell, R.
The collected stories. Thomas, D.
The collected stories. Trevor, W.
Collected stories. Williams, T.
Collected stories, 1939-1976. Bowles, P.
Collected stories, 1948-1986. Morris, W.
The collected stories of André Maurois. Maurois, A.
The collected stories of Chester Himes. Himes, C.
The collected stories of Colette. Colette
The collected stories of Elizabeth Bowen. Bowen, E.
The collected stories of Eudora Welty. Welty, E.
The collected stories of Guy de Maupassant. Maupassant, G. de
The collected stories of Hortense Calisher. Calisher, H.
The collected stories of Isaac Bashevis Singer. Singer, I. B.
The collected stories of Jack Schaefer. Schaefer, J. W.
The collected stories of Jean Stafford. Stafford, J.
Collected stories of Jessamyn West. West, J.
Collected stories of John O'Hara. O'Hara, J.
The collected stories of Katherine Anne Porter. Porter, K. A.
The collected stories of Louis Auchincloss. Auchincloss, L.
The collected stories of Max Brand. Brand, M.
The collected stories of Noël Coward. Coward, N.
The collected stories of Philip K. Dick. Dick, P. K.
The collected stories of Robert Silverberg. Silverberg, R.
The collected stories of Sean O'Faolain. O'Faoláin, S.
Collected stories of Wallace Stegner. Stegner, W. E.
Collected stories of William Faulkner. Faulkner, W.
The collected stories of William Humphrey. Humphrey, W.
Collected tales. De la Mare, W.
The collected tales and poems of Edgar Allan Poe. Poe, E. A.
The collected tales of E. M. Forster. Forster, E. M.
Collected works. O'Connor, F.

COLLECTIVE SETTLEMENTS
United States
Piercy, M. Small changes
Updike, J. S
Varley, J. The persistence of vision
The collector. Fowles, J.

COLLECTORS AND COLLECTING
Chatwin, B. Utz

COLLEGE ALUMNI
Jaffe, R. Class reunion
Myrer, A. The last convertible

COLLEGE LIFE
See also School life; Students; Teachers
Barth, J. Giles goat-boy
Canada
Davies, R. The lyre of Orpheus
Davies, R. The rebel angels
England
Amis, K. Lucky Jim
Lewis, C. S. That hideous strength
Pym, B. An academic question

Snow, C. P. The masters
Snow, C. P. The sleep of reason
France
McCarthy, M. Birds of America
Ireland
Binchy, M. Circle of friends
Italy
Du Maurier, Dame D. The flight of the falcon
United States
Barth, J. The end of the road
Corman, A. Prized possessions
Fitzgerald, F. S. This side of paradise
Galbraith, J. K. A tenured professor
Godwin, G. The good husband
Hawthorne, N. Fanshawe
Jaffe, R. Class reunion
Kemelman, H. Tuesday the rabbi saw red
McCarthy, M. The groves of Academe
McInerny, R. M. The search committee
Nabokov, V. V. Pnin
Nichols, J. T. The sterile cuckoo
Oates, J. C. Nemesis
Oates, J. C. Unholy loves
Reed, I. Japanese by spring
Roth, P. Letting go
Salinger, J. D. Franny and Zooey
Sarton, M. A small room
Segal, E. Doctors
Shulman, M. The many loves of Dobie Gillis
Smith, B. Joy in the morning
Updike, J. Memories of the Ford Administration
Waller, R. J. Slow waltz in Cedar Bend
Wolfe, T. Of time and the river

COLLEGE STUDENTS
See also College life

COLLEGE TEACHERS See Teachers
The colloquy of the dogs. Cervantes Saavedra, M. de
    In Cervantes Saavedra, M. de. Three exemplary novels p125-217

COLOMBIA
Coyle, H. W. Code of honor
García Márquez, G. The general and his labyrinth
20th century
Daley, R. A faint cold fear
Rural life
García Márquez, G. Chronicle of a death foretold
García Márquez, G. Collected novellas
García Márquez, G. In evil hour
García Márquez, G. Leaf storm, and other stories
García Márquez, G. No one writes to the colonel, and other stories
García Márquez, G. One hundred years of solitude

COLOMBO, CRISTOFORO See Columbus, Christopher
Colonel Chabert. Balzac, H. de
    In Balzac, H. de. The short novels of Balzac
Colonel Sandhurst to the rescue. Chesney, M.

COLONIAL UNITED STATES See United States—To 1776

COLONIALISM See Imperialism

COLONIES
Great Britain
See Great Britain—Colonies

COLONIES, ARTIST See Artist colonies
Colony. Siddons, A. R.
The color of blood. Moore, B.
The color purple. Walker, A.

COLORADO
Michener, J. A. Centennial
19th century
L'Amour, L. Over on the dry side
Schofield, S. C. Telluride

COLORADO—*Continued*

20th century

Borland, H. When the legends die
Cather, W. The song of the lark
Dailey, J. Aspen gold
Greenberg, J. The far side of victory
Greenberg, J. No reck'ning made
Greenberg, J. Simple gifts
Grey, Z. The vanishing American
King, S. The shining
Whitney, P. A. Domino

Frontier and pioneer life

See Frontier and pioneer life—Colorado
Colour scheme. Marsh, Dame N.
Columbella. Whitney, P. A.

COLUMBUS, CHRISTOPHER

Dorris, M. The crown of Columbus
Forester, C. S. To the Indies
Fuentes, C. The two Americas

COLUMNISTS *See* Journalists
Coma. Cook, R.

COMANCHE INDIANS

Combs, H. Brules
Jones, D. C. Season of yellow leaf
Kelton, E. The far canyon
Kelton, E. Slaughter
Come along with me. Jackson, S.
Come and get it. Gardner, E. S.
In Gardner, E. S. Dead men's letters p189-227
Come back, come back. Westlake, D. E.
In Westlake, D. E. Levine p35-59
Come pour the wine. Freeman, C.
Come to me. Bloom, A.
Come winter. Jones, D. C.
Comeback. Francis, D.
The comedians. Greene, G.

COMETS

Niven, L. Lucifer's hammer
The comforters. Spark, M.
In Spark, M. A Muriel Spark trio p13-228
Coming attractions. Flagg, F.

COMING OF AGE STORIES *See* Adolescence; Youth

COMMANCHE INDIANS *See* Comanche Indians

COMMERCIAL AERONAUTICS

See also Air mail service; Transport planes
Francis, D. Rat race
Saint-Exupéry, A. de. Night flight
Steel, D. Wings

COMMERCIAL AVIATION *See* Commercial aeronautics
A commission in lunacy. Balzac, H. de
In Balzac, H. de. The short novels of Balzac
The Commodore. De Hartog, J.
Commodore Hornblower. Forester, C. S.

COMMUNES *See* Collective settlements

COMMUNICATION

Lem, S. Fiasco
Pynchon, T. The crying of lot 49

COMMUNISM

See also Totalitarianism
Greene, G. Monsignor Quixote
McEwan, I. Black dogs
Wright, R. The outsider

Asia

Bosse, M. J. Fire in heaven

China

Han, S. Till morning comes
Li, P.-H. Farewell to my concubine

Cuba

Uris, L. Topaz

Czechoslovakia

Kundera, M. The joke

Eastern Europe

Moore, B. The color of blood

England

Lessing, D. M. The golden notebook
Snow, C. P. The conscience of the rich

Germany

Higgins, J. Day of judgment

Ireland

O'Flaherty, L. The informer

Italy

Guareschi, G. Don Camillo and his flock
Guareschi, G. The little world of Don Camillo
MacInnes, H. North from Rome

Russia

Koestler, A. Darkness at noon
Littell, R. The revolutionist
Pasternak, B. L. Doctor Zhivago
Rand, A. We the living
Sholokhov, M. A. And quiet flows the Don
Sholokhov, M. A. The Don flows home to the sea
Solzhenitsyn, A. Cancer ward
Wiesel, E. The testament

South Africa

Lessing, D. M. Landlocked
Lessing, D. M. A ripple from the storm

United States

Doctorow, E. L. The book of Daniel

Vietnam

Greene, G. The quiet American

COMMUNISTS *See* Communism

COMMUNITY LIFE

Parker, G. M. These same long bones

COMPANIONS

Eden, D. An important family
Hodge, J. A. Strangers in company
The company of saints. Anthony, E.
The company of women. Gordon, M.
Compelling evidence. Martini, S. P.
The compleat werewolf. Boucher, A.
In Boucher, A. The compleat werewolf and other stories of fantasy and science fiction p7-62
The compleat werewolf and other stories of fantasy and science fiction. Boucher, A.
The complete Claudine. Colette
Complete collected stories. Pritchett, V. S.
The complete ghost stories of Charles Dickens. Dickens, C.
The complete novels and selected tales of Nathaniel Hawthorne. Hawthorne, N.
The complete novels of Jane Austen. Austen, J.
The complete novels of Mark Twain. Twain, M.
The complete novels of Stephen Crane. Crane, S.
The complete robot. Asimov, I.
The complete Sherlock Holmes. Doyle, Sir A. C.
The complete short fiction of Joseph Conrad. Conrad, J.
Complete short stories. Maugham, W. S.
The complete short stories. Stevenson, R. L.
The complete short stories. Twain, M.
The complete short stories & sketches of Stephen Crane. Crane, S.
The complete short stories of Ambrose Bierce. Bierce, A.
The complete short stories of Ernest Hemingway. Hemingway, E.
The complete short stories of Guy de Maupassant. See Maupassant, G. de. The collected stories of Guy de Maupassant

The **complete** short stories of H. G. Wells. Wells, H. G.

The **complete** short stories of Jack London. London, J.

Complete short stories of Nathaniel Hawthorne. Hawthorne, N.

The **complete** short stories of Robert Louis Stevenson. Stevenson, R. L.

The **complete** short stories of Thomas Wolfe. Wolfe, T.

The **complete** shorter fiction. Trollope, A.

The **complete** shorter fiction of Virginia Woolf. Woolf, V.

The **complete** stories. Asimov, I.

The **complete** stories. Hurston, Z. N.

The **complete** stories. Kafka, F.

The **complete** stories. O'Connor, F.

Complete stories and poems of Edgar Allan Poe. Poe, E. A.

Complete stories of Erskine Caldwell. Caldwell, E.

The **complete** tales of Henry James. James, H.

The **complete** tales of Washington Irving. Irving, W.

The **complete** works of Nathanael West. West, N.

The **complete** works of O. Henry. Henry, O.

COMPOSERS
Aiken, J. Morningquest
Conroy, F. Body & soul
Grumbach, D. Chamber music
Hesse, H. Gertrude
Piercy, M. Summer people
Compromising positions. Isaacs, S.
Compulsion. Levin, M.

COMPULSORY MILITARY SERVICE *See* Draft

COMPUTER SIMULATION *See* Virtual reality

COMPUTERS
Anderson, P. Goat song
Brunner, J. Stand on Zanzibar
Card, O. S. The call of earth
Card, O. S. Earthborn
Card, O. S. Earthfall
Card, O. S. The memory of earth
Card, O. S. The ships of earth
Crichton, M. Disclosure
Crichton, M. The terminal man
Francis, D. Twice shy
Gage, E. The master stroke
Heinlein, R. A. The moon is a harsh mistress
Lustbader, E. V. White Ninja
Saul, J. Shadows
Sheffield, C. Georgia on my mind
Thomas, M. M. Black money
Trenhaile, J. The gates of exquisite view
Updike, J. Roger's version
Wilhelm, K. Death qualified
Comrade Charlie. Freemantle, B.

CON MEN *See* Swindlers and swindling
Conan Doyle's tales of medical humanism and values: Round the red lamp. Doyle, Sir A. C.

CONCENTRATION CAMPS
See also Political prisoners; World War, 1939-1945—Prisoners and prisons
De Hartog, J. The lamb's war
Iles, G. Black cross
Styron, W. Sophie's choice
Szeman, S. The Kommandant's mistress
Thomas, D. M. Pictures at an exhibition
The **concrete** blonde. Connelly, M.
The **condor** passes. Grau, S. A.

CONDUCT OF LIFE *See* Ethics

CONDUCTORS (MUSIC)
Gardner, J. E. Maestro
A **confederacy** of dunces. Toole, J. K.

CONFEDERATE AGENTS *See* Spies

CONFEDERATE STATES OF AMERICA. ARMY
Brown, R. M. High hearts
Cornwell, B. Copperhead
Cornwell, B. Rebel

Jones, D. C. The barefoot brigade
Jones, D. C. Elkhorn Tavern
Jones, T. Hard road to Gettysburg
Kantor, M. Andersonville
Keneally, T. Confederates
Shaara, M. The killer angels
Confederates. Keneally, T.
Confess, Fletch. Mcdonald, G.
In Mcdonald, G. The Fletch chronicles: [two]

CONFESSION
Banville, J. The book of evidence
Confession. Pickard, N.
The **confession** of Brother Haluin. Peters, E.
Confessional. Higgins, J.
Confessions of Felix Krull, confidence man. Mann, T.
The **confessions** of Nat Turner. Styron, W.
The **confidence-man:** his masquerade. Melville, H.
The **confidential** agent. Greene, G.
In Greene, G. 3: This gun for hire, The confidential agent, The ministry of fear

CONFLICT OF GENERATIONS
Berger, T. Vital parts
Greenberg, J. A season of delight
Lee, C. Y. The flower drum song
Lurie, A. The war between the Tates
Snow, C. P. The sleep of reason
Stegner, W. E. All the little live things
Thayer, N. Family secrets
Trollope, J. The men and the girls
Turgenev, I. S. Fathers and sons
Tyler, A. A slipping-down life
West, D. The wedding
Wharton, W. Dad

CONFORMITY
See also Individualism
Berger, T. Neighbors
Hoeg, P. Borderliners
Lewis, S. Babbitt
Marquand, J. P. H. M. Pulham, esquire
Trollope, J. The rector's wife
Wilson, S. The man in the gray flannel suit
Confusion. Howard, E. J.

CONGO (DEMOCRATIC REPUBLIC) *See* Zaire
The **conjugial** angel. Byatt, A. S.
In Byatt, A. S. Angels and insects

CONNECTICUT
19th century
Tryon, T. In the fire of spring
Tryon, T. The wings of the morning

20th century
Allen, C. V. Dreaming in color
Beattie, A. Falling in place
De Vries, P. Reuben, Reuben
Fast, H. The outsider
Hobson, L. K. Z. Gentleman's agreement
Hodgins, E. Mr. Blandings builds his dream house
Knowles, J. Indian summer
Plain, B. Whispers
Rice, L. Stone heart
Shulman, M. Rally round the flag, boys!
Simenon, G. The rules of the game
Tryon, T. The other

Bridgeport
Howard, M. Natural history
A **Connecticut** Yankee in King Arthur's court. Twain, M.
also in Twain, M. The complete novels of Mark Twain v2 p1-262

CONSCIENCE
See also Ethics; Guilt
Conrad, J. Lord Jim
Dostoyevsky, F. Crime and punishment
Hawthorne, N. The marble faun
Hawthorne, N. The scarlet letter

The **conscience** of the rich. Snow, C. P.

CONSCIENTIOUS OBJECTORS
Barker, P. The eye in the door
Renault, M. The charioteer
Westlake, D. E. The spy in the ointment

CONSELHEIRO, ANTONIO *See* Maciel, Antônio Vicente Mendes, 1828-1897

CONSELHEIRO INSURRECTION, 1897 *See* Brazil—Conselheiro insurrection, 1897
Consenting adult. Hobson, L. K. Z.
Consenting adults. De Vries, P.

CONSERVATION OF NATURE *See* Nature conservation
The **conservationist**. Gordimer, N.

CONSERVATIONISTS
Cheever, J. Oh, what a paradise it seems
Consider this, señora. Doerr, H.

CONSPIRACIES
Abrahams, P. Hard rain
Archer, J. Honor among thieves
Barker, C. Babel's children
Bradshaw, G. Imperial purple
Brink, A. P. An act of terror
Cook, R. Harmful intent
Cook, R. Mortal fear
Cook, R. Outbreak
Cook, R. Vital signs
Cussler, C. Dragon
Cussler, C. Sahara
DeLillo, D. Libra
Diehl, W. 27
Easterman, D. Brotherhood of the tomb
Eco, U. Foucault's pendulum
Egleton, C. A killing in Moscow
Finder, J. The Moscow Club
Folsom, A. R. The day after tomorrow
Forsyth, F. The negotiator
Harris, R. Fatherland
Higgins, J. The eagle has flown
Hoeg, P. Smilla's sense of snow
Hoving, T. Masterpiece
Jarman, R. H. The courts of illusion
Koontz, D. R. Dark rivers of the heart
Ludlum, R. The Aquitaine progression
Ludlum, R. The Holcroft covenant
Lustbader, E. V. Black Blade
Lustbader, E. V. The Kaisho
Massie, A. Caesar
Morrell, D. Desperate measures
Palmer, M. Natural causes
Reed, B. The indictment
Sheldon, S. The doomsday conspiracy
Sheldon, S. Windmills of the gods
Smith, W. A. Elephant song
Thomas, M. M. Black money
Veryan, P. Ask me no questions
Veryan, P. Had we never loved
Veryan, P. Never doubt I love
Veryan, P. A shadow's bliss
Veryan, P. Time's fool
West, M. L. Masterclass
Constance. Durrell, L.
Constancia, and other stories for virgins. Fuentes, C.
CONSTANTINOPLE *See* Turkey—Istanbul

CONSTRUCTION INDUSTRY
Markandaya, K. Shalimar
Ondaatje, M. In the skin of a lion
CONSULS *See* Diplomatic life
Contact. Sagan, C.
Contents under pressure. Buchanan, E.
Continental drift. Banks, R.
The **Continental** Op. Hammett, D.
CONTINO, DICK
Ellroy, J. Dick Contino's blues

CONVENT LIFE
See also Abbeys; Nuns
Godden, R. Black Narcissus
Godden, R. In this house of Brede
Grau, S. A. Roadwalkers
Gregory, P. The wise woman
Hulme, K. The nun's story
L'Engle, M. The love letters
Spark, M. The Abbess of Crewe
Stewart, M. Thunder on the right
Westlake, D. E. Good behavior
CONVENTS *See* Convent life
CONVENTS AND NUNNERIES *See* Convent life

CONVERSATION
Gaddis, W. J R
Huxley, A. Crome Yellow
Murdoch, I. A fairly honourable defeat
Puig, M. Eternal curse on the reader of these pages
Roth, P. Deception
Segal, E. Love story
Conversation. Aiken, C.
In Aiken, C. The collected novels of Conrad Aiken p473-575

CONVERSION
Baldwin, J. Go tell it on the mountain
Galsworthy, J. Flowering wilderness
CONVICTS *See* Crime and criminals; Ex-convicts; Prisoners and prisons
CONVICTS, ESCAPED *See* Escaped convicts
Convoy homeward. McCutchan, P.
Convoy north. McCutchan, P.
Convoy of fear. McCutchan, P.
Convoy south. McCutchan, P.

COOKERY
Berger, T. Reinhart's women
Esquivel, L. Like water for chocolate
The **cooking** school murders. Rich, V.

COOKS
Faulkner, W. The sound and the fury
Hardwick, M. The Duchess of Duke Street
Laker, R. The sugar pavilion
McCullers, C. The member of the wedding
Rossner, J. Olivia
Stubbs, J. Kelly Park
A **cool** million. West, N.
In West, N. The complete works of Nathanael West p143-256
Cool repentance. Fraser, A.

COOPERATIVE SOCIETIES
Hawthorne, N. The Blithedale romance
COOPERSTOWN (N.Y.) *See* New York (State)—Cooperstown
Cop killer. Sjöwall, M.
The **cop-killer**. Stout, R.
In Stout, R. Kings full of aces p369-420
Cop without a shield. O'Donnell, L.
The **copper** beech. Binchy, M.

COPPER MINES AND MINING
Du Maurier, Dame D. Hungry Hill
Copperhead. Cornwell, B.
Cops and robbers. Westlake, D. E.
Copy Kat. Kijewski, K.
Corelli's mandolin. De Bernières, L.

CORFU ISLAND (GREECE)
Stewart, M. This rough magic
CORINTH (N.Y.) *See* New York (State)—Corinth
CORK (IRELAND: COUNTY) *See* Ireland—Cork (County)
CORNWALL (ENGLAND) *See* England—Cornwall
CORNWALL DIALECT *See* Dialect stories—English—Cornwall

Corporate bodies. Brett, S.

CORPORATIONS *See* Business

Corps [series]
    Griffin, W. E. B. Battleground
    Griffin, W. E. B. Close combat
    Griffin, W. E. B. Counterattack
    Griffin, W. E. B. Line of fire

Corpse in a gilded cage. Barnard, R.
The **corpse** in Oozak's Pond. MacLeod, C.
The **corpse** on the dike. Van de Wetering, J.

CORPULENCE *See* Obesity

Corridors of power. Snow, C. P.

CORRUPTION (IN POLITICS)
    See also Bribery; Political ethics
    Adams, H. Democracy
    Atwood, M. Bodily harm
    Barnard, R. A scandal in Belgravia
    Battle, L. Storyville
    Campbell, R. W. Boneyards
    Daley, R. Man with a gun
    Estleman, L. D. Motown
    Greeley, A. M. Patience of a saint
    Grisham, J. The pelican brief
    Hiaasen, C. Strip tease
    Higgins, G. V. Defending Billy Ryan
    Koontz, D. R. Dark rivers of the heart
    Ludlum, R. The Chancellor manuscript
    Morrell, D. The fifth profession
    Oates, J. C. What I lived for
    Patterson, R. N. Eyes of a child
    Puzo, M. The godfather
    Reed, B. The indictment
    Tanenbaum, R. Reversible error
    Tarkington, B. The gentleman from Indiana
    Thomas, R. Ah, treachery!
    Thomas, R. Briarpatch
    Thomas, R. The fourth Durango
    Thomas, R. Missionary stew
    Turow, S. Presumed innocent
    Twain, M. The gilded age
    Uhnak, D. False witness
    Vidal, G. Hollywood
    Vonnegut, K. Jailbird
    Wambaugh, J. Fugitive nights
    Warren, R. P. All the king's men

CORSAIRS *See* Pirates

CORTEZ, HERNÁN TORRES *See* Torres Cortez, Hernán

COSA NOSTRA *See* Mafia

COSMETICS INDUSTRY
    Michael, J. Pot of gold
Cosmicomics. Calvino, I.

COSSACKS
    Babel', I. Red cavalry
    Pushkin, A. S. The captain's daughter
    Sholokhov, M. A. And quiet flows the Don
    Sholokhov, M. A. The Don flows home to the sea
    Sienkiewicz, H. With fire and sword
    Tolstoy, L., graf. The Cossacks
The **Cossacks.** Tolstoy, L., graf
    In Tolstoy, L. The short novels of Tolstoy

COSTUME PARTIES *See* Parties

COTSWOLDS (ENGLAND)
    Lively, P. Passing on
    Pilcher, R. The shell seekers
The **Count** of Eleven. Campbell, R.
The **Count** of Monte Cristo. Dumas, A.

COUNTER CULTURE
    Abrahams, P. Hard rain
    Duncan, D. J. The brothers K
    Lessing, D. M. The good terrorist
    Pynchon, T. Vineland

COUNTER-REFORMATION *See* Reformation

Counterattack. Griffin, W. E. B.

COUNTERESPIONAGE *See* International intrigue; Spies

The **counterfeiters** (Les faux-monnayeurs). Gide, A.
The **counterlife.** Roth, P.
The **country** doctor. Balzac, H. de
The **country** girls. O'Brien, E.
    In O'Brien, E. The country girls trilogy and epilogue p3-175
The **country** girls trilogy and epilogue. O'Brien, E.

COUNTRY LIFE
    See also Farm life; Mountain life; Plantation life; Ranch life; Small town life
    Allison, D. Bastard out of Carolina
    Smiley, J. Good will

COUNTRY MUSIC
    Smith, L. The devil's dream
    Westlake, D. E. Baby, would I lie?
A **country** of old men. Hansen, J.
A **country** of strangers. Shreve, S. R.
The **country** of the pointed firs. Jewett, S. O.
    also in Jewett, S. O. The best stories of Sarah Orne Jewett v1
    also in Jewett, S. O. The country of the pointed firs and other stories p1-139
The **country** of the pointed firs and other stories. Jewett, S. O.
The **coup.** Updike, J.

COUPS D'ÉTAT
    Forsyth, F. The dogs of war
    Knebel, F. Seven days in May
    Updike, J. The coup

COURAGE
    See also Heroism
    Forester, C. S. The last nine days of the Bismarck
    Hemingway, E. The old man and the sea
    Hersey, J. The wall
    Holland, C. The Sea Beggars
    Nordhoff, C. Men against the sea
    Saint-Exupéry, A. de. Night flight
    Uris, L. Mila 18

COURT LIFE *See* Courts and courtiers
The **court-martial** of George Armstrong Custer. Jones, D. C.

COURTESANS
    See also Prostitutes
    Dumas, A. Camille
    Li, P.-H. Farewell to my concubine
The **Courtneys.** Smith, W. A.

COURTROOM SCENES *See* Trials

COURTS AND COURTIERS
    See also names of individual kings, queens, and rulers; also subdivision Kings and rulers under names of countries
    Bradshaw, G. Horses of heaven
    Hope, A. The prisoner of Zenda

    Byzantine Empire
    Bradshaw, G. The bearkeeper's daughter
    Holland, C. The belt of gold

    China
    Buck, P. S. Imperial woman

    Denmark
    Lofts, N. The lost queen

    Egypt
    Smith, W. A. River god

    England
    Anthony, E. Anne Boleyn
    George, M. Mary Queen of Scotland and the Isles
    Holland, C. The earl
    Holt, V. My enemy the Queen
    Jarman, R. H. The courts of illusion
    Lewis, H. W. I am Mary Tudor
    Penman, S. K. Falls the shadow

COURTS AND COURTIERS—England—*Continued*
Penman, S. K. Here be dragons
Penman, S. K. The reckoning
Penman, S. K. The sunne in splendour
Plaidy, J. The captive Queen of Scots
Plaidy, J. Murder most royal
Plaidy, J. The pleasures of love
Plaidy, J. The reluctant queen
Plaidy, J. The rose without a thorn
Plaidy, J. The sixth wife
Plaidy, J. William's wife
Seton, A. Katherine

France
Anthony, E. The Cardinal and the Queen
Dumas, A. The iron mask
Dumas, A. The three musketeers
Haasse, H. S. In a dark wood wandering
Laker, R. To dance with kings
Riley, J. M. The oracle glass
Selinko, A. Désirée
Twain, M. The prince and the pauper

Italy
Sontag, S. The volcano lover
Stendhal. The charterhouse of Parma
Tomasi di Lampedusa, G. The leopard

Japan
Mishima, Y. Spring snow
Murasaki Shikibu. The tale of Genji

Scotland
Hill, P. The sword and the flame

COURTS-MARTIAL
DeMille, N. Word of honor
Jones, D. C. The court-martial of George Armstrong
  Custer
Nordhoff, C. Mutiny on the Bounty
Poyer, D. The circle
The **courts** of chaos. Zelazny, R.
The **courts** of illusion. Jarman, R. H.

COURTSHIP
Burns, O. A. Leaving Cold Sassy
Colette. Claudine in Paris
Colette. Gigi
Colwin, L. Happy all the time
Hawthorne, N. Fanshawe
James, H. Washington Square
Stowe, H. B. The minister's wooing
Tarkington, B. Monsieur Beaucaire
The **courtship** of Princess Leia. Wolverton, D.
Cousin Bette. Balzac, H. de
Cousin Kate. Heyer, G.
Cousin Pons. Balzac, H. de
Cousin Rosamund. West, Dame R.

COUSINS
Balzac, H. de. Cousin Bette
Briskin, J. The other side of love
Capote, T. A Christmas memory
Capote, T. The Thanksgiving visitor
Colwin, L. Happy all the time
Coulter, C. The Wyndham legacy
Davenport, K. Shark dialogues
Du Maurier, Dame D. My cousin Rachel
Faulkner, W. The mansion
Giardina, D. The unquiet earth
Gide, A. Strait is the gate (La porte étroite)
James, H. The Europeans
Jhabvala, R. P. Poet and dancer
Maḥfūz, N. Autumn quail
Maitland, S. Ancestral truths
McCorkle, J. Ferris Beach
Mitford, N. Love in a cold climate
Mitford, N. The pursuit of love
Orde, L. Dreams of gold
Pearce, M. E. The land endures
Seton, A. Dragonwyck
Siddons, A. R. Peachtree Road

Stewart, M. The Gabriel hounds
Thomas, R. All my sins remembered
Trevor, W. Reading Turgenev
The **covenant**. Michener, J. A.
The **covenant** of the flame. Morrell, D.
Cover her face. James, P. D.
  In James, P. D. Crime times three

COWARDICE
Conrad, J. Lord Jim
Crane, S. The red badge of courage
Fleming, T. J. Time and tide
Warren, R. P. The cave

COWBOYS
Clark, W. V. T. The Ox-bow incident
Estleman, L. D. Bloody season
Houston, P. Cowboys are my weakness
L'Amour, L. The man from the broken hills
McCarthy, C. All the pretty horses
Schaefer, J. W. Monte Walsh
Cowboys are my weakness. Houston, P.

COWHANDS *See* Cowboys

COWS *See* Cattle

Coyote. Barnes, L.
Coyote waits. Hillerman, T.

CRACK (DRUG)
Rodriguez, A. Spidertown
The **cracker** factory. Rebeta-Burditt, J.
Cracking open a coffin. Butler, G.
Cradle. Clarke, A. C.
The **cradle** will fall. Clark, M. H.
Crash diet. McCorkle, J.
Crazy in Alabama. Childress, M.
Crazy in Berlin. Berger, T.
Crazy time. Wilhelm, K.

CREATION (LITERARY, ARTISTIC, ETC.)
Ishiguro, K. The unconsoled
Creation. Vidal, G.
Creature. Saul, J.
Creatures of the kingdom. Michener, J. A.

CREDIBILITY *See* Truthfulness and falsehood
A **creek** called Wounded Knee. Jones, D. C.
Creek Mary's blood. Brown, D. A.
Crescent City. Plain, B.
Cress Delahanty. West, J.

CRETE
Kazantzakis, N. Zorba the Greek
Renault, M. The king must die
Stewart, M. The moon-spinners
The **cricket** on the hearth. Dickens, C.
  also in Dickens, C. A Charles Dickens Christmas
    p205-308
  also in Dickens, C. Christmas tales p147-215

CRICKETS
Dickens, C. The cricket on the hearth

CRIME AND CRIMINALS
  See also Arson; Bank robbers; Brigands and rob-
    bers; Child abuse; Escaped convicts; Extortion;
    Gangs; Gangsters; Hostages; Juvenile delinquency;
    Kidnapping; Mafia; Murder stories; Rape; Smug-
    gling; Swindlers and swindling; Thieves; Under-
    world; War criminals; Wife abuse
Abrahams, P. Lights out
Barker, C. In the flesh [novelette]
Bawden, N. Family money
Berger, T. Who is Teddy Villanova?
Bosse, M. J. The vast memory of love
Breslin, J. The gang that couldn't shoot straight
Brett, S. Dead romantic
Brett, S. A shock to the system
Browne, G. A. 19 Purchase Street
Buckley, C. T. Wet work
Burnett, W. R. The asphalt jungle
Camus, A. The plague
Carroll, J. The city below

CRIME AND CRIMINALS—*Continued*
Caunitz, W. J. Black sand
Cheever, J. Falconer
Clark, M. H. The cradle will fall
Condon, R. Prizzi's family
Condon, R. Prizzi's glory
Condon, R. Prizzi's honor
Condon, R. Prizzi's money
Cook, R. Blindsight
Crichton, M. The great train robbery
Defoe, D. Moll Flanders
Delany, S. R. Time considered as a helix of semi-
  precious stones
Dickens, C. Great expectations
Dickens, C. Oliver Twist
Dostoyevsky, F. Crime and punishment
Dostoyevsky, F. The house of the dead
Dreiser, T. An American tragedy
Durham, M. The man who loved Cat Dancing
Ellroy, J. L.A. confidential
Ellroy, J. White jazz
Estleman, L. D. Kill zone
Estleman, L. D. King of the corner
Estleman, L. D. Motown
Estleman, L. D. Whiskey River
Faulkner, W. Intruder in the dust
Follett, K. Paper money
Forsyth, F. The day of the jackal
Francis, D. Forfeit
Francis, D. Knockdown
Francis, D. Twice shy
Genet, J. Our Lady of the Flowers
Gill, B. M. Time and time again
Godey, J. The taking of Pelham one two three
Graham, W. The walking stick
Greene, G. Brighton rock
Guest, J. Killing time in St. Cloud
Guy, R. A measure of time
Hemingway, E. To have and have not
Hiaasen, C. Native tongue
Hiaasen, C. Skin tight
Hiaasen, C. Strip tease
Higgins, G. V. Bomber's law
Higgins, G. V. The friends of Eddie Coyle
Higgins, G. V. The patriot game
Highsmith, P. The boy who followed Ripley
Highsmith, P. Ripley's game
Hugo, V. Les misérables
Hunter, S. Dirty white boys
Irving, C. Final argument
James, P. D. Innocent blood
Katkov, N. Blood & orchids
Katzenbach, J. Just cause
Leiber, F. Ill met in Lankhmar
Leonard, E. Freaky Deaky
Leonard, E. Get Shorty
Leonard, E. Killshot
Leonard, E. Maximum Bob
Leonard, E. The moonshine war
Leonard, E. Mr. Majestyk
Leonard, E. Pronto
Leonard, E. Rum punch
Leonard, E. Split images
Leonard, E. Stick
Levin, M. Compulsion
Llewellyn, R. None but the lonely heart
Ludlum, R. The Matlock paper
Maas, P. China white
Mailer, N. The executioner's song
Mann, P. Season of the monsoon
Markandaya, K. A handful of rice
Mayle, P. Hotel Pastis
McBain, E. Downtown
McMurtry, L. Pretty Boy Floyd
Patterson, J. Along came a spider
Perry, T. Metzger's dog
Perry, T. Vanishing act
Price, R. Clockers

Puzo, M. The godfather
Reed, B. The indictment
Rendell, R. Going wrong
Rendell, R. A judgment in stone
Rendell, R. Make death love me
Rosenberg, N. T. First offense
Rosenberg, N. T. Mitigating circumstances
Sanders, L. Sullivan's sting
Sheldon, S. Nothing lasts forever
Sheldon, S. Rage of angels
Singer, I. B. Scum
Tanenbaum, R. Immoral certainty
Tanenbaum, R. Reversible error
Thomas, M. M. Black money
Thomas, R. Chinaman's chance
Thomas, R. Voodoo, Ltd
Tolstoy, L., graf. Resurrection
Uhnak, D. Victims
Vine, B. A dark-adapted eye
Wambaugh, J. The blue knight
Wambaugh, J. The Delta Star
Wambaugh, J. Finnegan's week
Wambaugh, J. The Glitter Dome
Wambaugh, J. The new centurions
Westlake, D. E. Bank shot
Westlake, D. E. Cops and robbers
Westlake, D. E. Don't ask
Westlake, D. E. Drowned hopes
Westlake, D. E. Good behavior
Westlake, D. E. The hot rock
Westlake, D. E. Why me?
Willocks, T. Green river rising
Woods, S. Grass roots
Yorke, M. Crime in question
Crime and Mr. Campion. Allingham, M.
Crime and punishment. Dostoyevsky, F.
Crime in Holland. *See* Simenon, G. Maigret in Holland
Crime in question. Yorke, M.
CRIME PASSIONEL *See* Crimes of passion
Crime times three. James, P. D.
CRIMES OF PASSION
  See also Murder stories
  Tolstoy, L., graf. The Kreutzer sonata
Criminal conversation. Hunter, E.
Criminal damage. Yorke, M.
CRIMINALLY INSANE *See* Insane, Criminal and
  dangerous
CRIMINALS *See* Crime and criminals
Crimson joy. Parker, R. B.
CRO-MAGNON MAN *See* Prehistoric man
The **crocodile** bird. Rendell, R.
Crome Yellow. Huxley, A.
The **cross**. Undset, S.
  In Undset, S. Kristin Lavransdatter v3
Cross my heart and hope to die. Radley, S.
The **crossing**. McCarthy, C.
Crossing by night. Aaron, D.
Crossing the river. Phillips, C.
Crossing to safety. Stegner, W. E.
The **crown** of Columbus. Dorris, M.
Crowned heads. Tryon, T.
Crucial instances. Wharton, E.
  In Wharton, E. The collected short stories of Edith
    Wharton v1
The **crucible** of time. Brunner, J.
Cruel & unusual. Cornwell, P. D.
The **cruel** sea. Monsarrat, N.
CRUELTY
  See also Violence
  Banks, R. Continental drift
  Conroy, P. The lords of discipline
  Kantor, M. Andersonville
  Kosinski, J. N. The painted bird
  Ōe, K. Nip the buds, shoot the kids

CRUELTY TO CHILDREN *See* Child abuse
Crusader's torch. Yarbro, C. Q.
CRUSADES
   See also Knights and knighthood

First, 1096-1099
   Hoban, R. Pilgermann
   Oldenbourg, Z. The heirs of the kingdom

Third, 1189-1192
   Scott, Sir W. The talisman
A **cry** in the night. Clark, M. H.
Cry me a river. Pearson, T. R.
Cry of the hawk. Johnston, T. C.
Cry, the beloved country. Paton, A.
Cry to heaven. Rice, A.
Cry wolf. Smith, W. A.
The **crying** of lot 49. Pynchon, T.
CRYONICS
   Berger, T. Vital parts
   Niven, L. A world out of time
The **crystal** cave. Stewart, M.
   also in Stewart, M. Mary Stewart's Merlin trilogy
Crystal line. McCaffrey, A.
Crystal singer. McCaffrey, A.
The **crystal** star. McIntyre, V. N.
Csardas. Pearson, D.

CUBA

19th century
   Jones, D. C. Remember Santiago
   Thane, E. Ever after

20th century
   Hemingway, E. Islands in the stream
   Hemingway, E. To have and have not

Communism
   See Communism—Cuba

Havana
   Garcia, C. Dreaming in Cuban
   Greene, G. Our man in Havana
   Hemingway, E. The old man and the sea
   Uris, L. Topaz

CUBAN AMERICANS
   Hijuelos, O. The fourteen sisters of Emilio Montez
   O'Brien

CUBAN REFUGEES
   Bell, C. The Perez family

CUBANS

Africa
   Smith, W. A. Golden fox

United States
   Bell, C. The Perez family
   Garcia, C. Dreaming in Cuban
   Hijuelos, O. The Mambo Kings play songs of love

CUCHULAIN (LEGENDARY CHARACTER)
   Llywelyn, M. Red Branch
Cujo. King, S.

CULTS
   Campbell, R. The Nameless
   Durrell, L. Sebastian
   Jhabvala, R. P. Three continents
   Woods, S. Heat

CULTURE CONFLICT
   See also East and West
   Alvarez, J. How the Garcia girls lost their accents
   Banks, R. Continental drift
   Condé, M. I, Tituba, black witch of Salem
   Doerr, H. Consider this, señora
   Doerr, H. Stones for Ibarra
   Erdrich, L. Love medicine
   Erdrich, L. Tracks
   Garcia, C. Dreaming in Cuban
   Growing up Latino

   Han, S. Till morning comes
   Ishiguro, K. An artist of the floating world
   Jennings, G. Aztec
   Kingsolver, B. Pigs in heaven
   Kingston, M. H. Tripmaster Monkey
   Lee, C. Y. The flower drum song
   Lee, G. China boy
   Lee, G. Honor & duty
   Lord, B. B. Spring Moon
   Malouf, D. Remembering Babylon
   Markandaya, K. Shalimar
   Michener, J. A. Caribbean
   Momaday, N. S. House made of dawn
   Moore, B. Black robe
   Mukherjee, B. The holder of the world
   Mukherjee, B. Jasmine
   Naipaul, V. S. A way in the world
   Ng, F. M. Bone
   Power, S. The grass dancer
   Richter, C. The light in the forest
   Shacochis, B. Swimming in the volcano
   Singer, I. B. The manor
   Skimin, R. Apache autumn
   Škvorecký, J. The engineer of human souls
   Tan, A. The Joy Luck Club
   Wood, B. Green City in the sun

CULTURE CONTACT *See* Acculturation

CURSES
   King, S. Thinner
   Maḥfūẓ, N. The harafish

CURSES, FAMILY *See* Family curses
Curses!. Elkins, A. J.
Curtain. Christie, A.
Curtain. Korda, M.
A **curtain** of green. Welty, E.
   In Welty, E. The collected stories of Eudora Welty
   p1-149

CUSTER, GEORGE ARMSTRONG, 1839-1876
   Jones, D. C. The court-martial of George Armstrong
   Custer

CUSTODY OF CHILDREN
   Miller, S. The good mother
   Patterson, R. N. Eyes of a child
The **custom** of the country. Wharton, E.
Cyberbooks. Bova, B.

CYBERNETICS
   See also Bionics

CYBORGS *See* Bionics
Cyclops. Cussler, C.
The **Cygnet** and the firebird. McKillip, P. A.

CYPRUS
   Dunnett, D. Race of scorpions

CYRUS, KING OF PERSIA, D. 529 B.C.
   Asch, S. The prophet

CYSTIC FIBROSIS
   Plain, B. Daybreak

CZECH REFUGEES
   Read, P. P. A season in the West

CZECH REPUBLIC
   See also Czechoslovakia

CZECHOSLOVAKIA
   See also Czech Republic
   Chatwin, B. Utz
   Demetz, H. The house on Prague Street
   Kundera, M. The book of laughter and forgetting
   Kundera, M. The joke
   Kundera, M. Laughable loves
   Kundera, M. The unbearable lightness of being
   Roth, P. The Prague orgy

CZECHS

Austria
MacInnes, H. The snare of the hunter

Canada
Škvorecký, J. The engineer of human souls

England
Read, P. P. A season in the West

United States
Cather, W. My Ántonia
Cather, W. O pioneers!
Demetz, H. The journey from Prague Street
Kafka, F. Amerika

D

"D" is for deadbeat. Grafton, S.
Dad. Wharton, W.
The Dain curse. Hammett, D.
In Hammett, D. The novels of Dashiell Hammett
p143-292
The Daisy Ducks. Boyer, R.
Daisy Miller. James, H.
In James, H. The complete tales of Henry James
v4
In James, H. Daisy Miller [and An international
episode] v1
In James, H. The Henry James reader p403-61
In James, H. Short novels of Henry James p1-58
Daisy Miller [and An international episode]. James, H.

DAKOTA INDIANS
Brown, D. A. Killdeer Mountain
Hill, R. B. Hanta yo
Jones, D. C. Arrest Sitting Bull
Power, S. The grass dancer

DALÍ, SALVADOR, 1904-1989
Kaminsky, S. M. The melting clock
Damage. Hart, J.
Damia. McCaffrey, A.
Damia's children. McCaffrey, A.
The damnation game. Barker, C.
A dance at the slaughterhouse. Block, L.
Dance hall of the dead. Hillerman, T.
also in Hillerman, T. The Joe Leaphorn mysteries
Dance of the tiger. Kurtén, B.
A dance to the music of time. Powell, A.

DANCERS
Baum, V. Grand Hotel
Durrell, L. Justine
Godden, R. Thursday's children
Hiaasen, C. Strip tease
Jhabvala, R. P. Poet and dancer
Lutz, J. Dancing with the dead
MacInnes, H. Message from Málaga
McMurtry, L. The desert rose
Nin, A. Children of the albatross
Robinson, S. Stardance [novelette]
Dancers at the end of time [series]
Moorcock, M. An alien heat
Moorcock, M. The end of all songs
Moorcock, M. The hollow lands
Dancers in mourning. Allingham, M.
In Allingham, M. Crime and Mr. Campion p363-575
Dancing at the Rascal Fair. Doig, I.
Dancing girls and other stories. Atwood, M.
Dancing on snowflakes. Ross-Macdonald, M.
Dancing with the dead. Lutz, J.
Dandelion wine. Bradbury, R.

DANES
See also Vikings

France
Dinesen, I. The angelic avengers

The danger. Francis, D.
Danger from the dead. Ferrars, E. X.
A dangerous business. Underwood, M.
A dangerous fortune. Follett, K.
A dangerous mourning. Perry, A.
Dangerous to know. Yorke, M.
Dangerous visions. Entered in Part I under title
A dangerous woman. Morris, M. M.
Dangling man. Bellow, S.
Daniel Martin. Fowles, J.
Danny goes to Mars. Sargent, P.
In Nebula awards 28 p27-51
The Dante game. Langton, J.
DANZIG (POLAND) *See* Poland—Gdansk
The Danzig trilogy. Grass, G.
Daphne du Maurier's classics of the macabre. Du
Maurier, Dame D.
DAR *See* Daughters of the American Revolution
Darcy's utopia. Weldon, F.
The darfsteller. Miller, W. M.
In The Hugo winners v1 p5-71
A dark-adapted eye. Vine, B.
DARK AGES *See* Europe—392-814; Middle Ages
The dark design. Farmer, P. J.
The dark door. Wilhelm, K.
Dark force rising. Zahn, T.
The dark half. King, S.
The dark lady. Auchincloss, L.
Dark mirror. Duane, D.
The dark on the other side. Michaels, B.
Dark rivers of the heart. Koontz, D. R.
Dark Rosaleen. Brand, M.
In Brand, M. Max Brand's best western stories v2
The dark side of Guy de Maupassant. Maupassant, G.
de
Dark star. Muller, M.
Dark summer. Cleary, J.
The dark tower and other stories. Lewis, C. S.
The dark wind. Hillerman, T.
also in Hillerman, T. The Jim Chee mysteries
Darkness. Saul, J.
Darkness at noon. Koestler, A.
Darkness visible. Golding, W.
D'ARTAGNAN, CHARLES DE BATZ-CASTELMORE,
COMTE *See* Artagnan, Charles de Batz-Castelmore,
comte d', 1613?-1673
DATING (SOCIAL CUSTOMS)
Clark, M. H. Loves music, loves to dance
Daughter of deceit. Holt, V.
Daughter of the stars. Whitney, P. A.
The daughter of time. Tey, J.
also in Tey, J. Four, five and six by Tey v3
DAUGHTERS *See* Fathers and daughters; Mothers and
daughters; Stepdaughters
Daughters. Marshall, P.
DAUGHTERS-IN-LAW
Friedman, P. Reasonable doubt
DAUGHTERS OF THE AMERICAN REVOLUTION
Landrum, G. The famous DAR murder mystery
Daughters of the new world. Shreve, S. R.
DAVID, KING OF ISRAEL
L'Engle, M. Certain women
Martin, M. King of kings
David Copperfield. Dickens, C.
Davita's harp. Potok, C.
Dawn. Butler, O. E.
Dawn. Wiesel, E.
also in Wiesel, E. Night, Dawn, The accident: three
tales p121-204

Dawn's early light. Thane, E.

The **Dawson** pedigree. [variant title: Unnatural death] Sayers, D. L.

The **day** after tomorrow. Folsom, A. R.

A **day** no pigs would die. Peck, R. N.

Day of atonement. Kellerman, F.

Day of judgment. Higgins, J.

The **day** of the butterfly. Lofts, N.

The **day** of the jackal. Forsyth, F.

   also in Forsyth, F. Forsyth's three

The **day** of the locust. West, N.

   In West, N. The complete works of Nathanael West p259-421

The **day** of the scorpion. Scott, P.

   also in Scott, P. The Raj quartet

Day of wrath. Valin, J.

The **day** the Martians came. Pohl, F.

The **day** the rabbi resigned. Kemelman, H.

Daybreak. Plain, B.

The **daybreakers**. L'Amour, L.

   In L'Amour, L. The Sacketts: beginnings of a dynasty

Days of hope. See Malraux, A. Man's hope

Dayworld. Farmer, P. J.

Dayworld breakup. Farmer, P. J.

Dayworld rebel. Farmer, P. J.

DE GAULLE, CHARLES *See* Gaulle, Charles de, 1890-1970

DE MIRANDA, FRANCISCO *See* Miranda, Francisco de, 1750-1816

DE MONTFORT, SIMON *See* Montfort, Simon de, Earl of Leicester, 1208?-1265

DE SANTA ANNA, ANTONIO LÓPEZ *See* Santa Anna, Antonio López de, 1794?-1876

DEAD

   See also Funeral rites and ceremonies

   Barker, C. Cabal [novelette]

   King, S. The dark half

   King, S. Pet sematary

Dead by morning. Simpson, D.

Dead center. Wilcox, C.

Dead cert. Francis, D.

   In Francis, D. Three to show p3-216

Dead crazy. Pickard, N.

Dead eyes. Woods, S.

Dead giveaway. Brett, S.

Dead languages. Shields, D.

Dead letter. Valin, J.

A **dead** liberty. Aird, C.

Dead man's island. Hart, C. G.

Dead man's ransom. Peters, E.

Dead meat. Tapply, W. G.

Dead men don't ski. Moyes, P.

   In Moyes, P. Murder by 3's p3-288

Dead men's hearts. Elkins, A. J.

Dead men's letters. Gardner, E. S.

Dead men's letters [novelette]. Gardner, E. S.

   In Gardner, E. S. Dead men's letters p1-47

Dead on arrival. Simpson, D.

Dead romantic. Brett, S.

The **dead** side of the mike. Brett, S.

Dead water. Marsh, Dame N.

The **dead** weight lifter. McInerny, R. M.

   In McInerny, R. Four on the floor p115-156

Dead winter. Tapply, W. G.

Dead wrong. Kienzle, W. X.

The **dead** zone. King, S.

Deadeye Dick. Vonnegut, K.

Deadfall. Pronzini, B.

Deadheads. Hill, R.

Deadline for a critic. Kienzle, W. X.

Deadlock. Paretsky, S.

Deadly rich. Stewart, E.

A **deadly** shade of gold. MacDonald, J. D.

Deadwood. Dexter, P.

DEAF

   Greenberg, J. In this sign

   Greenberg, J. Of such small differences

   McCullers, C. The heart is a lonely hunter

DEAFNESS *See* Deaf

Dealings with the firm of Dombey and Son. See Dickens, C. Dombey and Son

DEANS (CATHEDRAL AND COLLEGIATE) *See* Anglican and Episcopal clergy

The **dean's** December. Bellow, S.

The **dean's** watch. Goudge, E.

Dear and glorious physician. Caldwell, T.

DEATH

   See also Bereavement; Dead

   Agee, J. A death in the family

   Allen, C. V. Leftover dreams

   Anthony, P. On a pale horse

   Banks, R. The sweet hereafter

   Bellow, S. The dean's December

   Camus, A. A happy death

   Cather, W. Lucy Gayheart

   Coetzee, J. M. Age of iron

   Craven, M. I heard the owl call my name

   DeLillo, D. White noise

   Dew, R. F. Fortunate lives

   Dexter, P. Brotherly love

   Dillard, A. The living

   Fleming, T. J. Over there

   Godwin, G. The good husband

   Hart, J. Damage

   Hoffman, A. At risk

   Jönsson, R. My life as a dog

   Kawabata, Y. The sound of the mountain

   King, S. The body

   King, S. The long walk

   Lively, P. Moon tiger

   Lively, P. Passing on

   Mann, T. Death in Venice

   Mason, B. A. Feather crowns

   McDermott, A. At weddings and wakes

   McFarland, D. School for the blind

   McInerny, R. M. Easeful death

   Monette, P. Afterlife

   Parker, G. M. These same long bones

   Price, R. The promise of rest

   Sarton, M. A reckoning

   Settle, M. L. The killing ground

   Spark, M. Memento mori

   Steel, D. The gift

   Stubbs, J. Light in summer

   Tolstoy, L., graf. Master and man

   Trevor, W. Reading Turgenev

   Tyler, A. Saint maybe

   Tyler, A. The tin can tree

   Varley, J. The persistence of vision

   Willis, C. Death on the Nile

   Wolfe, T. The lost boy

   Yoshimoto, B. Kitchen

Death and taxes. Dunlap, S.

Death and the chaste apprentice. Barnard, R.

Death and the lover. See Hesse, H. Narcissus and Goldmund

Death and the mad heroine. Dean, S. F. X.

Death and the Princess. Barnard, R.

A death at St. Anselm's. Holland, I.

A death before dying. Wilcox, C.

Death by sheer torture. Barnard, R.

Death by the light of the moon. Hess, J.

Death comes as the end. Christie, A.
  In Christie, A. Five classic murder mysteries p545-671

Death comes for the archbishop. Cather, W.
  also in Cather, W. Willa Cather, later novels

Death dream. Bova, B.

A death for a dancer. Giroux, E. X.

Death for a dancing doll. Giroux, E. X.

Death for a dietitian. Giroux, E. X.

A death for a dodo. Giroux, E. X.

A death for a double. Giroux, E. X.

Death ground. Gorman, E.
  In Great stories of the American West p197-287

Death in a cold climate. Barnard, R.

Death in a tenured position. Cross, A.

Death in autumn. Nabb, M.

Death in Berlin. Kaye, M. M.

Death in disguise. Graham, C.

Death in Kashmir. Kaye, M. M.

Death in Kenya. Kaye, M. M.

Death in purple prose. See Barnard, R. The cherry blossom corpse

Death in the Andamans. Kaye, M. M.

A death in the family. Agee, J.

Death in the old country. Wright, E.

A death in town. Waugh, H.

Death in Venice. Mann, T.
  In Mann, T. Death in Venice and seven other stories p3-84
  In Mann, T. Stories of three decades

Death in Venice and seven other stories. Mann, T.

Death in Zanzibar. Kaye, M. M.

Death is a lonely business. Bradbury, R.

Death is forever. Gardner, J. E.

Death lives next door. Butler, G.

Death notes. Rendell, R.

The death of a bum. Westlake, D. E.
  In Westlake, D. E. Levine p121-50

Death of a charming man. Beaton, M. C.

Death of a daimyo. Melville, J.

Death of a doxy. Stout, R.

Death of a ghost. Allingham, M.
  In Allingham, M. Crime and Mr. Campion p7-175

Death of a glutton. Beaton, M. C.

Death of a god. Haymon, S. T.

Death of a hussy. Beaton, M. C.

The death of a Joyce scholar. Gill, B.

Death of a literary widow. Barnard, R.

Death of a minor character. Ferrars, E. X.

Death of a nurse. McBain, E.

Death of a perfect mother. Barnard, R.

Death of a Russian priest. Kaminsky, S. M.

Death of a salesperson, and other untimely exits. Barnard, R.

Death of a snob. Beaton, M. C.

Death of a travelling man. Beaton, M. C.

Death of a unicorn. Dickinson, P.

Death of a warrior queen. Haymon, S. T.

Death of an expert witness. James, P. D.

Death of an old girl. Lemarchand, E.

The death of Artemio Cruz. Fuentes, C.

The death of Doctor Island. Wolfe, G.
  In Modern classic short novels of science fiction p321-72

The death of Iván Ilyitch. Tolstoy, L., graf
  In Tolstoy, L. The short novels of Tolstoy

The death of Ivan Ilyitch, and other stories. Tolstoy, L., graf

The death of love. Gill, B.

The death of Methuselah and other stories. Singer, I. B.

The death of the heart. Bowen, E.

Death on a cold, wild river. Gill, B.

Death on the Nile. Christie, A.

Death on the Nile. Willis, C.
  In Nebula awards 29 p142-66

Death penalty. Coughlin, W. J.

Death qualified. Wilhelm, K.

Death shall overcome. Lathen, E.

Death speaks softly. Fraser, A.

Death takes time. Jeffries, R.

Death to go. Harrod-Eagles, C.

Death to the landlords! Peters, E.

Death under sail. Snow, C. P.

Death walked in Berlin. See Kaye, M. M. Death in Berlin

Death walked in Kashmir. See Kaye, M. M. Death in Kashmir

Death watch. Harrod-Eagles, C.

Death wears a red hat. Kienzle, W. X.

Deathbed. Kienzle, W. X.

DEATHBED SCENES
  Fuentes, C. The death of Artemio Cruz
  Grau, S. A. The condor passes
  White, P. The eye of the storm

The deathbird. Ellison, H.
  In The Hugo winners v3 p437-68

Death's darkest face. Symons, J.

Deborah goes to Dover. Chesney, M.

Debt of honor. Clancy, T.

DECADENCE *See* Degeneration

The decay of the angel. Mishima, Y.

The deceiver. Forsyth, F.

Deception. Quick, A.

Deception. Roth, P.

Deceptions. Michael, J.

Decider. Francis, D.

Decision at Delphi. MacInnes, H.

Decked. Clark, C. H.

Decline and fall. Waugh, E.

The deeds of the disturber. Peters, E.

The deep blue good-by. MacDonald, J. D.

Deep purple. Allbeury, T.

Deep six. Cussler, C.

Deep sleep. Fyfield, F.

Deep summer. Bristow, G.
  In Bristow, G. Gwen Bristow's Plantation trilogy p1-258

The Deer Leap. Grimes, M.

The Deerslayer. Cooper, J. F.
  also in Cooper, J. F. The Leatherstocking tales v2 p483-1030

DEFECTORS
  Allbeury, T. Deep purple
  Anthony, E. The tamarind seed
  Clancy, T. The hunt for Red October
  Deighton, L. Mexico set
  Egleton, C. Hostile intent

Defend and betray. Perry, A.

Defending Billy Ryan. Higgins, G. V.

DEFOE, DANIEL, 1661?-1731
Robinson Crusoe
  Coetzee, J. M. Foe

DEFORMITIES
  See also Face—Abnormalities and deformities; Monsters
  Golding, W. Darkness visible
  Grass, G. Cat and mouse
  McCammon, R. R. Gone south

DEGENERACY *See* Degeneration

DEGENERATION
  Algren, N. A walk on the wild side

DEGENERATION—*Continued*
Butler, O. E. Parable of the sower
Caldwell, E. Tobacco road
Capote, T. Answered prayers
Chute, C. The Beans of Egypt, Maine
Dickey, J. Deliverance
Faulkner, W. Absalom, Absalom!
Faulkner, W. As I lay dying
Faulkner, W. The hamlet
Faulkner, W. Sanctuary
Faulkner, W. The sound and the fury
Gide, A. The immoralist
Herlihy, J. L. Midnight cowboy
Huxley, A. Antic hay
James, H. Roderick Hudson
Kennedy, W. Ironweed
Kosinski, J. N. The devil tree
Norris, F. McTeague
Proulx, A. Postcards
Rossner, J. Looking for Mr. Goodbar
Styron, W. Lie down in darkness
Wilde, O. The picture of Dorian Gray
Zola, É. Nana
Degree of guilt. Patterson, R. N.

DELAWARE INDIANS
Richter, C. The light in the forest

DELHI (INDIA) *See* India—Delhi
Deliverance. Dickey, J.

DELPHI (GREECE) *See* Greece—Delphi
The **Delta** Star. Wambaugh, J.
Delta wedding. Welty, E.
The **deluge.** Sienkiewicz, H.
Demian. Hesse, H.
Democracy. Adams, H.
Democracy. Didion, J.
Demon. Varley, J.
Demon box. Kesey, K.
Demon lord of Karanda. Eddings, D.

DEMONIAC POSSESSION
See also Exorcism
Prose, F. Hungry hearts
Seton, A. Green darkness

DEMONOLOGY
See also Demoniac possession; Satanism; Witchcraft
Vance, J. The miracle workers
Demons. Dostoyevsky, F.

DENMARK

18th century
Lofts, N. The lost queen

19th century
Andersen Nexø, M. Pelle the conqueror: v1 Childhood
Andersen Nexø, M. Pelle the conqueror: v2 Apprenticeship
Dinesen, I. Winter's tales

20th century
Hoeg, P. Borderliners

Courts and courtiers
See Courts and courtiers—Denmark

Copenhagen
Hoeg, P. Smilla's sense of snow

DENTISTS
Grass, G. Local anaesthetic
Norris, F. McTeague
Smiley, J. The age of grief [novelette]

DEPARTMENT STORES
Archer, J. As the crow flies
Birmingham, S. Carriage trade
Bradford, B. T. Hold the dream
Bradford, B. T. To be the best
Bradford, B. T. A woman of substance
Davies, V. Miracle on 34th Street
McNaught, J. Paradise

DEPRESSION, 1929 *See* Business depression, 1929
DEPRESSIONS, BUSINESS *See* Business depression, 1929

DERBYSHIRE (ENGLAND) *See* England—Derbyshire
DERBYSHIRE DIALECT *See* Dialect stories—English—Derbyshire

DERELICTS
Innes, H. The wreck of the Mary Deare
The **descent** of man. Wharton, E.
In Wharton, E. The collected short stories of Edith Wharton v1
The **desert** rose. McMurtry, L.
Desert sinner. McInerny, R. M.

DESERTION, MILITARY *See* Military desertion

DESERTION AND NONSUPPORT
Gaines, E. J. In my father's house

DESERTS
See also Libyan Desert; Sahara
Caputo, P. Horn of Africa
Herbert, F. Children of Dune

DESIDERIA *See* Désirée, Queen, consort of Charles XIV John, King of Sweden and Norway, 1777-1860
Design for dying. Morice, A.

DÉSIRÉE, QUEEN, CONSORT OF CHARLES XIV JOHN, KING OF SWEDEN AND NORWAY, 1777-1860
Selinko, A. Désirée
Désirée. Selinko, A.
Desperate measures. Morrell, D.

DESTINY *See* Fate and fatalism
Destiny of death. Shannon, D.

DESTRUCTION OF EARTH *See* Earth, Destruction of
DESTRUCTION OF THE JEWS *See* Holocaust, Jewish (1933-1945)

DETECTIVE AND MYSTERY STORIES *See* Mystery and detective stories
The **detective** wore silk drawers. Lovesey, P.

DETECTIVES
Adams, Doc. See stories by Boyer, R.
Adams, Hilda. See stories by Rinehart, M. R.
Aldington, Claire. See stories by Holland, I.
Alleyn, Superintendent Roderick. See stories by Marsh, Dame N.
Alvarez, Inspector. See stories by Jeffries, R.
Appleby, Sir John. See stories by Innes, M.
Archer, Lew. See stories by Macdonald, R.
Archer, Owen. See stories by Robb, C. M.
Bailey, Chief Superintendent Geoffrey. See stories by Fyfield, F.
Baley, Elijah. See stories by Asimov, I.
Balzic, Mario. See stories by Constantine, K. C.
Barnaby, Chief Inspector. See stories by Graham, C.
Basnett, Andrew. See stories by Ferrars, E. X.
Battle, Superintendent. See stories by Christie, A.
Bear, Goldy. See stories by Davidson, D. M.
Beaumont, J. P. See stories by Jance, J. A.
Beaumont, Ned. See stories by Hammett, D.
Beck, Inspector Martin. See stories by Sjöwall, M.
Benbow, Angela. See stories by Sawyer, C. H.
Bennett, Reid. See stories by Wood, T.
Beresford, Tommy. See stories by Christie, A.
Beresford, Tuppence. See stories by Christie, A.
Bernhardt, Alan. See stories by Wilcox, C.
Bittersohn, Max. See stories by MacLeod, C.
Bliss, Vicky. See stories by Peters, E.
Bond, James. See stories by Fleming, I.
Bond, James. See stories by Gardner, J. E.
Bosch, Hieronymous. See stories by Connelly, M.
Bradshaw, Charlie. See stories by Dobyns, S.
Brandstetter, Dave. See stories by Hansen, J.
Broom, Andrew. See stories by McInerny, R. M.
Brown, Father. See stories by Chesterton, G. K.
Burke. See stories by Vachss, A. H.
Cadfael, Brother. See stories by Peters, E.

DETECTIVES—*Continued*

Cain, Jenny. See stories by Pickard, N.

Calder, Keith. See stories by Hammond, G.

Campion, Albert. See stories by Allingham, M.

Cardozo, Lieutenant Vincent. See stories by Stewart, E.

Carella, Lieutenant Steve. See stories by McBain, E.

Carlyle, Carlotta. See stories by Barnes, L.

Carver, Fred. See stories by Lutz, J.

Castang, Henri. See stories by Freeling, N.

Charles, Nick. See stories by Hammett, D.

Charles, Nora. See stories by Hammett, D.

Chee, Jim. See stories by Hillerman, T.

Coffin, John. See stories by Butler, G.

Colorado, Kat. See stories by Kijewski, K.

Cone, Timothy. See stories by Sanders, L.

Continental Op. See stories by Hammett, D.

Corbett, Hugh. See stories by Doherty, P. C.

Corning, Ken. See stories by Gardner, E. S.

Coyne, Brady. See stories by Tapply, W. G.

Cribb, Detective-Sergeant. See stories by Lovesey, P.

Crow, Inspector Angus. See stories by Gardner, J. E.

Crusoe, Edwina. See stories by Kittredge, M.

Cuddy, John. See stories by Healy, J. F.

Dalgliesh, Commander Adam. See stories by James, P. D.

Dalziel, Inspector. See stories by Hill, R.

Darling, Annie. See stories by Hart, C. G.

Darling, Max. See stories by Hart, C. G.

Davenport, Lucas. See stories by Sandford, J.

De Gier, Detective-Sergeant. See stories by Van de Wetering, J.

Decker, Peter. See stories by Kellerman, F.

Dee, Judge. See stories by Gulik, R. H. van

Delaney, Chief Edward X. See stories by Sanders, L.

Delaware, Alex. See stories by Kellerman, J.

Delphick, Superintendent. See stories by Carvic, H.

Demarkian, Gregor. See stories by Haddam, J.

Dew, Inspector Walter. See stories by Lovesey, P.

Diamond, Peter. See stories by Lovesey, P.

Dowling, Father. See stories by McInerny, R. M.

Drake, Paul. See stories by Gardner, E. S.

Dupin, C. Auguste. See stories by Poe, E. A.

Edward VII, King of Great Britain. See stories by Lovesey, P.

Elliott, Maggie. See stories by Taylor, E. A.

Endicott, Jack. See stories by Roosevelt, E.

Epton, Rosa. See stories by Underwood, M.

Fairchild, Faith. See stories by Page, K. H.

Fairweather, Doran. See stories by Hardwick, M.

Falco, Marcus Didius. See stories by Davis, L.

Fansler, Kate. See stories by Cross, A.

Felse, Dominic. See stories by Peters, E.

Felse, Superintendent George. See stories by Peters, E.

Fen, Professor Gervase. See stories by Crispin, E.

Fielding, Kit. See stories by Francis, D.

Fischman, Nina. See stories by Piesman, M.

Fitzgerald, Fiona. See stories by Adler, W.

Flannery, Jimmy. See stories by Campbell, R. W.

Fletch. See stories by Mcdonald, G.

Flynn, Terry. See stories by Granger, B.

Forsythe, Robert. See stories by Giroux, E. X.

Freer, Felix. See stories by Ferrars, E. X.

Freer, Virginia. See stories by Ferrars, E. X.

Gabriel, Matt. See stories by Gosling, P.

Garrity, Callahan. See stories by Trocheck, K. H.

Gently, Dirk. See stories by Adams, D.

Gethryn, Anthony. See stories by MacDonald, P.

Ghote, Inspector Ganesh. See stories by Keating, H. R. F.

Goodwin, Archie. See stories by Goldsborough, R.

Goodwin, Archie. See stories by Stout, R.

Grant, Celia. See stories by Sherwood, J.

Grant, Inspector Alan. See stories by Tey, J.

Gray, Cordelia. See stories by James, P. D.

Greenfield, C. B. See stories by Kallen, L.

Grijpstra, Adjutant-Detective. See stories by Van de Wetering, J.

Guarnaccia, Marshal. See stories by Nabb, M.

Hanks, Arly. See stories by Hess, J.

Haristeen, Mary Minor "Harry". See stories by Brown, R. M.

Haskell, Ellie. See stories by Cannell, D.

Hastings, Frank. See stories by Wilcox, C.

Hatcher, Amos. See stories by Banks, O. T.

Havers, Barbara. See stories by George, E.

Hayes, Julie. See stories by Davis, D. S.

Helen, Sister Mary. See stories by O'Marie, C. A.

Henrie O. See stories by Hart, C. G.

Hill, Inspector Judy. See stories by McGown, J.

Holmes, Sherlock. See stories by Doyle, Sir A. C.

Holmes, Sherlock. See stories by King, L. R.

Holmes, Sherlock. See stories by Meyer, N.

Honeybath, Charles. See stories by Innes, M.

Hope, Matthew. See stories by McBain, E.

Howard, Roz. See stories by Kenney, S.

Jago, Constable Henry. See stories by Lovesey, P.

Jamieson, Mr. See stories by Rinehart, M. R.

Janek, Lieutenant Frank. See stories by Bayer, W.

Janeway, Cliff. See stories by Dunning, J.

Jansson, Willa. See stories by Matera, L.

Jenkins, Ed. See stories by Gardner, E. S.

Joan, Sister. See stories by Black, V.

Jurnet, Detective-Inspector Benjamin. See stories by Haymon, S. T.

Jury, Inspector Richard. See stories by Grimes, M.

Karpo, Emil. See stories by Kaminsky, S. M.

Kelley, Homer. See stories by Langton, J.

Kelling, Emma. See stories by MacLeod, C.

Kelling, Sarah. See stories by MacLeod, C.

Kelly, Homer. See stories by Langton, J.

Kelly, Neil. See stories by Dean, S. F. X.

Kelsey, Detective Inspector. See stories by Page, E.

Kent, Charlotte. See stories by Kittredge, M.

Kenworthy, Superintendent. See stories by Hilton, J. B.

Kimura, Inspector Jiro. See stories by Melville, J.

Kirby, Jacqueline. See stories by Peters, E.

Kling, Detective Bert. See stories by McBain, E.

Knott, Deborah. See stories by Maron, M.

Koesler, Father. See stories by Kienzle, W. X.

Kramer, Lieutenant Tromp. See stories by McClure, J.

Lane, Drury. See stories by Queen, E.

Langdon, Skip. See stories by Smith, J.

Larch, Detective Marian. See stories by Paul, B.

Laurano, Lauren. See stories by Scoppettone, S.

Lazarus, Rina. See stories by Kellerman, F.

Leaphorn, Lieutenant Joe. See stories by Hillerman, T.

Lee, Anna. See stories by Cody, L.

Leidl, Constance. See stories by Wilhelm, K.

Levine, Detective Abraham. See stories by Westlake, D. E.

Lewis, Sergeant. See stories by Dexter, C.

Lieberman, Abe. See stories by Kaminsky, S. M.

Lineham, Sergeant Mike. See stories by Simpson, D.

Lloyd, Chief Inspector. See stories by McGown, J.

Lovejoy. See stories by Gash, J.

Luke, Superintendent. See stories by Allingham, M.

Lynley, Detective Inspector Thomas. See stories by George, E.

MacBeth, Hamish. See stories by Beaton, M. C.

MacPherson, Annie. See stories by Smith, J. L.

MacPherson, Elizabeth. See stories by McCrumb, S.

Maddox, Detective Sue. See stories by Linington, E.

Maddox, Sergeant Ivor. See stories by Linington, E.

Maigret, Chief Inspector. See stories by Simenon, G.

Maitland, Antony. See stories by Woods, S.

Malloy, Claire. See stories by Hess, J.

Malone, Scobie. See stories by Cleary, J.

Malory, Sheila. See stories by Holt, H.

Marlowe, Philip. See stories by Chandler, R.

Marlowe, Philip. See stories by Parker, R. B.

DETECTIVES—*Continued*

Marple, Miss Jane. See stories by Christie, A.
Marsala, Cat. See stories by D'Amato, B.
Marsh, Detective Inspector. See stories by Yorke, M.
Mary Teresa, Sister. See stories by Quill, M.
Mason, Perry. See stories by Gardner, E. S.
Maybridge, Chief Inspector Tom. See stories by Gill, B. M.
McCone, Sharon. See stories by Muller, M.
McGarr, Chief Inspector Peter. See stories by Gill, B.
McGee, Travis. See stories by MacDonald, J. D.
McGowan, Maggie. See stories by Hornsby, W.
McKee, Bergen. See stories by Hillerman, T.
McNally, Archy. See stories by Sanders, L.
Meiklejohn, Charlie. See stories by Wilhelm, K.
Melville, Miss Susan. See stories by Smith, E. E.
Mendoza, Lieutenant Luis. See stories by Shannon, D.
Millhone, Kinsey. See stories by Grafton, S.
Monk, Inspector William. See stories by Perry, A.
Montero, Britt. See stories by Buchanan, E.
Moodrow, Stanley. See stories by Solomita, S.
Morse, Inspector. See stories by Dexter, C.
Mulcahaney, Lieutenant Norah. See stories by O'Donnell, L.
Mulcay, Kate. See stories by Sibley, C.
Neill, Henry F. See stories by Hammett, D.
Norgren, Chris. See stories by Elkins, A. J.
Oliver, Gideon. See stories by Elkins, A. J.
Oliverez, Elena. See stories by Muller, M.
Opara, Christie. See stories by Uhnak, D.
O'Shaughnessy, Kiernan. See stories by Dunlap, S.
Otani, Superintendent Tetsuo. See stories by Melville, J.
Pamplemousse, Monsieur. See stories by Bond, M.
Pargeter, Mrs. Melita. See stories by Brett, S.
Paris, Charles. See stories by Brett, S.
Parrish, Inspector George. See stories by Barnard, R.
Pascoe, Inspector. See stories by Hill, R.
Peabody, Amelia. See stories by Peters, E.
Peace, Charlie. See stories by Barnard, R.
Pel, Inspector Evariste Cloris Désiré. See stories by Hebden, M.
Peters, Sergeant Joe. See stories by Uhnak, D.
Peters, Toby. See stories by Kaminsky, S. M.
Pibble, Superintendent Jimmy. See stories by Dickinson, P.
Pinkerton, Nurse. See stories by Rinehart, M. R.
Pitt, Inspector. See stories by Perry, A.
Poirot, Hercule. See stories by Christie, A.
Pollard, Detective-Chief Superintendent Tom. See stories by Lemarchand, E.
Pollifax, Mrs. Emily. See stories by Gilman, D.
Potter, Eugenia. See stories by Pickard, N.
Potter, Eugenia. See stories by Rich, V.
Powder, Lieutenant Leroy. See stories by Lewin, M. Z.
Pringle, G. D. H. See stories by Livingston, N.
Pyne, Parker. See stories by Christie, A.
Quantrill, Chief Inspector Douglas. See stories by Radley, S.
Queen, Ellery. See stories by Queen, E.
Queen, Inspector Richard. See stories by Queen, E.
Quincannon, John. See stories by Muller, M.
Quist, Julian. See stories by Pentecost, H.
Qwilleran, Jim. See stories by Braun, L. J.
Raisin, Agatha. See stories by Beaton, M. C.
Ramadge, Gwenn. See stories by O'Donnell, L.
Randollph, Reverend. See stories by Smith, C. M.
Rawlins, Easy. See stories by Mosley, W.
Rebus, Inspector. See stories by Rankin, I.
Reilly, Regan. See stories by Clark, C. H.
Reissig, Detective Gary. See stories by O'Donnell, L.
Renko, Arkady. See stories by Smith, M. C.
Resnick, Inspector Charlie. See stories by Harvey, J.
Rhodenbarr, Bernie. See stories by Block, L.
Rhys, Madoc. See stories by MacLeod, C.
Robicheaux, Dave. See stories by Burke, J. L.

Rogers, Detective Superintendent George. See stories by Ross, J.
Rome, Maggie. See stories by Kallen, L.
Roosevelt, Eleanor. See stories by Roosevelt, E.
Rostnikov, Inspector Porfiry. See stories by Kaminsky, S. M.
Ryan, Blackie. See stories by Greeley, A. M.
Salter, Inspector Charlie. See stories by Wright, E.
Scarpetta, Kay. See stories by Cornwell, P. D.
Scudder, Matthew. See stories by Block, L.
Seeton, Miss Emily. See stories by Carvic, H.
Shandy, Peter. See stories by MacLeod, C.
Shore, Jemima. See stories by Fraser, A.
Simpson, Tim. See stories by Malcolm, J.
Slider, Inspector Bill. See stories by Harrod-Eagles, C.
Sloan, Inspector. See stories by Aird, C.
Small, Rabbi David. See stories by Kemelman, H.
Smith, Jill. See stories by Dunlap, S.
Smith, Mac. See stories by Truman, M.
Spade, Sam. See stories by Hammett, D.
Spenser. See stories by Parker, R. B.
Stark, Joanna. See stories by Muller, M.
Stoner, Harry. See stories by Valin, J.
Tait, Detective Inspector Martin. See stories by Radley, S.
Tanner, John Marshall. See stories by Greenleaf, S.
Thackeray, Detective-Constable Edward. See stories by Lovesey, P.
Thanet, Detective Inspector Luke. See stories by Simpson, D.
Thatcher, John Putnam. See stories by Lathen, E.
Tibbett, Inspector Henry. See stories by Moyes, P.
Tibbs, Virgil. See stories by Ball, J. D.
Toye, Inspector Gregory. See stories by Lemarchand, E.
Trethowan, Superintendent Perry. See stories by Barnard, R.
Van der Valk, Arlette. See stories by Freeling, N.
Van der Valk, Inspector. See stories by Freeling, N.
Vane, Harriet. See stories by Sayers, D. L.
Walker, Amos. See stories by Estleman, L. D.
Warshawski, V. I. See stories by Paretsky, S.
Watson, Dr. John H. See stories by Doyle, Sir A. C.
Webb, Chief Inspector David. See stories by Fraser, A.
West, Helen. See stories by Fyfield, F.
Wexford, Chief Inspector. See stories by Rendell, R.
Whistler. See stories by Campbell, R. W.
Wimsey, Lord Peter. See stories by Sayers, D. L.
Wingate, Caledonia. See stories by Sawyer, C. H.
Wiseman, Detective Chief Superintendent. See stories by Morice, A.
Wolfe, Nero. See stories by Goldsborough, R.
Wolfe, Nero. See stories by Stout, R.
Wycliffe, Superintendent. See stories by Burley, W. J.
Zondi, Detective Sergeant Mickey. See stories by McClure, J.

DETECTIVES, PRIVATE
Berger, T. Who is Teddy Villanova?
Hill, R. Blood sympathy
Koontz, D. R. The bad place
Pronzini, B. Bones
Pronzini, B. Deadfall
Pronzini, B. Quarry
Straub, P. The throat
Wambaugh, J. Fugitive nights

DETROIT (MICH.) *See* Michigan—Detroit
Devices and desires. James, P. D.

DEVIL
Benét, S. V. The Devil and Daniel Webster
Bulgakov, M. A. The master and Margarita
Spark, M. The ballad of Peckham Rye
Westlake, D. E. Humans
The Devil. Tolstoy, L., graf
  In Tolstoy, L. The Kreutzer sonata, The Devil, and other tales

The Devil. Tolstoy, L., graf—*Continued*
  In Tolstoy, L. The short novels of Tolstoy
The Devil and Daniel Webster. Benét, S. V.
  also in Benét, S. V. Selected works. Volume two: Prose
Devil in a blue dress. Mosley, W.
The **devil** knows you're dead. Block, L.
The **devil** met a lady. Kaminsky, S. M.
The **Devil** on horseback. Holt, V.
The **devil** tree. Kosinski, J. N.

DEVIL WORSHIP *See* Satanism
The **devils.** See Dostoyevsky, F. Demons
The **devil's** advocate. West, M. L.
The **devil's** alternative. Forsyth, F.
The **devil's** dream. Smith, L.
The **devil's** mode. Burgess, A.
The **devil's** novice. Peters, E.
Devil's waltz. Kellerman, J.

DEVON (ENGLAND) *See* England—Devon
Dewey decimated. Goodrum, C. A.

DHARMA
Kerouac, J. The Dharma bums
The **Dharma** bums. Kerouac, J.
Dial 577 R-A-P-E. O'Donnell, L.

DIALECT STORIES

American Indian
Hill, R. B. Hanta yo

Black English
Gaines, E. J. The autobiography of Miss Jane Pittman
Hughes, L. Not without laughter
Hughes, L. Simple speaks his mind
Hughes, L. Simple stakes a claim
Hughes, L. Simple takes a wife
Hughes, L. Simple's Uncle Sam
Shange, N. Sassafrass, Cypress & Indigo
Stowe, H. B. Uncle Tom's cabin
Straight, S. I been in sorrow's kitchen and licked out all the pots
Twain, M. Pudd'nhead Wilson
Walker, A. The color purple
Walker, M. Jubilee

English—Cockney
Forester, C. S. The African Queen
Gallico, P. Mrs. 'Arris goes to Paris
Llewellyn, R. None but the lonely heart

English—Cornwall
Holt, V. The legend of the seventh virgin

English—Derbyshire
Lawrence, D. H. Lady Chatterley's lover

English—Staffordshire
Eliot, G. Adam Bede

New England
Wharton, E. Ethan Frome

Scottish
Barrie, J. M. The little minister
Sayers, D. L. The five red herrings

Southern States
Arnow, H. L. S. The dollmaker
Burns, O. A. Cold Sassy tree
Burns, O. A. Leaving Cold Sassy
Hyman, M. No time for sergeants
O'Connor, F. The violent bear it away
O'Connor, F. Wise blood
Rawlings, M. K. The Marjorie Rawlings reader
Rawlings, M. K. South moon under
Stowe, H. B. Uncle Tom's cabin
Walker, M. Jubilee

Swedish
Cather, W. O pioneers!

DIALOGUE *See* Conversation
The **diamond** age. Stephenson, N.
Diamond mask. May, J.

DIAMOND MINES AND MINING
Sheldon, S. Master of the game
Smith, W. A. Men of men
Diamond solitaire. Lovesey, P.
The **diamond** throne. Eddings, D.

DIAMONDS
  See also Diamond mines and mining
Browne, G. A. Hot Siberian
Fleming, I. Diamonds are forever
Gross, J. The books of Rachel
Haggard, H. R. King Solomon's mines
Spark, M. The comforters
Trollope, A. The Eustace diamonds
Diamonds are forever. Fleming, I.
  In Fleming, I. More gilt-edged Bonds p443-661

DIARIES (STORIES ABOUT)
Goudge, E. The scent of water
Greeley, A. M. Irish gold
MacNeil, R. Burden of desire

DIARIES (STORIES IN DIARY FORM)
  See also Letters (Stories in letter form)
Aiken, J. The haunting of Lamb House
Beauvoir, S. de. The woman destroyed [novelette]
Bellow, S. Dangling man
Bosse, M. J. The vast memory of love
Bowen, E. The death of the heart
Brontë, A. The tenant of Wildfell Hall
Butler, O. E. Parable of the sower
Cheever, J. The Wapshot chronicle
Collins, W. The woman in white
Flagg, F. Coming attractions
Fowles, J. The collector
Golding, W. Close quarters
Golding, W. Fire down below
Golding, W. Rites of passage
Hailey, E. F. Joanna's husband and David's wife
Hersey, J. The wall
Hoban, R. Turtle diary
James, P. D. The children of men
Kaufman, S. Diary of a mad housewife
Keyes, D. Flowers for Algernon
Klein, N. Sunshine
Lessing, D. M. The golden notebook
Maupin, A. Maybe the moon
Oates, J. C. Expensive people
Phillips, C. Cambridge
Read, Miss. Village diary
Rilke, R. M. The notebooks of Malte Laurids Brigge
Robertson, D. Praise the human season
Robinson, S. By any other name
Sarton, M. As we are now
Selinko, A. Désirée
Shields, C. The stone diaries
Townsend, S. The Adrian Mole diaries
Townsend, S. Adrian Mole: the lost years
Vidal, G. Julian
Vine, B. Anna's book
Vonnegut, K. Mother night
Diary of a mad housewife. Kaufman, S.
Dick Contino's blues. Ellroy, J.
  In Ellroy, J. Hollywood nocturnes p13-91
The **Dick** Francis treasury of great racing stories. Entered in Part I under title

DICTATORS
  See also Fascism; Totalitarianism
García Márquez, G. The autumn of the patriarch
Greene, G. The comedians
Lewis, S. It can't happen here
Orwell, G. Animal farm
Steinbeck, J. The moon is down
Updike, J. The coup

DICTATORSHIP *See* Dictators
Die for love. Peters, E.
Die like a dog. Stout, R.
    In Stout, R. Royal flush p431-74
A **diet** to die for. Hess, J.
DIETING *See* Reducing
Different seasons. King, S.
Dinner at the Homesick Restaurant. Tyler, A.

DINOSAURS
    Crichton, M. Jurassic Park

DION, TYRANT OF SYRACUSE, 408-353 B.C.
    Renault, M. The mask of Apollo

DIPLOMATIC LIFE
    Durrell, L. Monsieur
    Durrell, L. Mountolive
    Greene, G. The honorary consul
    Le Carré, J. A small town in Germany
    Michener, J. A. Caravans
    Sheldon, S. Windmills of the gods
    Sontag, S. The volcano lover
    Wouk, H. The winds of war
DIPLOMATS *See* Diplomatic life
DIRECTORS, MOTION PICTURE *See* Motion picture producers and directors
Dirk Gently's Holistic Detective Agency. Adams, D.
The **dirty** dozen. Nathanson, E. M.
The **dirty** duck. Grimes, M.
Dirty white boys. Hunter, S.
DISAPPEARANCES *See* Missing persons
Disappearing acts. McMillan, T.

DISASTERS
    See also Earthquakes; Epidemics; Famines; Floods; Industrial accidents; Shipwrecks and castaways
    Bromfield, L. The rains came
    Leiber, F. The Wanderer
    Lessing, D. M. The memoirs of a survivor
    MacNeil, R. Burden of desire
    White, P. The tree of man
Disclosure. Crichton, M.
Discovery. Hoving, T.

DISEASES
    See also AIDS (Disease); Tuberculosis
    Cussler, C. Sahara
The **disenchanted**. Schulberg, B.
DISGUISES *See* Impersonations
DISORDERS OF PERSONALITY *See* Personality disorders
Displaced person. Hilton, J. B.
Disposal of the living. See Barnard, R. Fête fatale
The **dispossessed**. Le Guin, U. K.

DISSENTERS
    Anthony, E. The relic
    Hall, A. Quiller bamboo
DISSIDENTS *See* Dissenters
A **distant** trumpet. Horgan, P.
DISTILLING, ILLICIT *See* Moonshiners
DISTRICT OF COLUMBIA *See* Washington (D.C.)
Disturbances in the field. Schwartz, L. S.
Divine inspiration. Langton, J.
A **diving** rock on the Hudson. Roth, H.
A **division** of the spoils. Scott, P.
    also in Scott, P. The Raj quartet

DIVORCE
    See also Desertion and nonsupport; Divorced persons; Marriage problems
    Banks, R. Affliction
    Bellow, S. What kind of day did you have?
    Colette. Julie de Carneilhan
    Corman, A. Kramer versus Kramer
    Drabble, M. The needle's eye
    Galsworthy, J. In chancery
    Galsworthy, J. Over the river
    Godden, R. The battle of the Villa Fiorita

    Guest, J. Second heaven
    Isaacs, S. Close relations
    Martin, V. The great divorce
    Michaels, B. Shattered silk
    Miller, S. The good mother
    Reid Banks, L. The warning bell
    Rossner, J. Olivia
    Smiley, J. Ordinary love
    Wakefield, D. Starting over
    Wharton, E. The custom of the country

DIVORCED PERSONS
    Allende, I. The infinite plan
    Bausch, R. Rebel powers
    Beattie, A. Picturing Will
    Boswell, R. Mystery ride
    Fielding, J. Good intentions
    Goldsmith, O. The First Wives Club
    Gordon, M. Immaculate man
    Hailey, E. F. Home free
    Hiaasen, C. Strip tease
    Hoffman, A. Second nature
    Hoffman, A. Seventh heaven
    Hoffman, A. Turtle Moon
    Michael, J. Pot of gold
    O'Brien, E. Time and tide
    Shields, C. The republic of love
    Spencer, E. Knights and dragons
    Steel, D. Accident
    Weldon, F. The cloning of Joanna May
    Wood, B. Virgins of paradise
    Woods, S. Palindrome
DIVORCÉES *See* Divorced persons
DIVORCÉS *See* Divorced persons
Dixie City jam. Burke, J. L.
Do black patent-leather shoes really reflect up? Powers, J. R.
Do Lord remember me. Lester, J.
DOCK HANDS *See* Longshore workers
Doctor DeMarr. Theroux, P.
    In Theroux, P. Half Moon Street
Doctor Grimshawe's secret. Hawthorne, N.
Doctor Martino, and other stories. See Faulkner, W. Collected stories of William Faulkner
Doctor No. Fleming, I.
Doctor Slaughter. Theroux, P.
    In Theroux, P. Half Moon Street
Doctor Thorne. Trollope, A.
Doctor Zhivago. Pasternak, B. L.
DOCTORS *See* Physicians; Surgeons; Women physicians
Doctors. Segal, E.
The **doctor's** wife. Moore, B.
DOCUMENTS *See* Manuscripts
The **documents** in the case. Sayers, D. L.
DODGE, ANSON
    Price, E. The beloved invader
Dodsworth. Lewis, S.
DOG SLED RACING *See* Sled dog racing
Dog soldiers. Stone, R.
Dog years. Grass, G.
    also in Grass, G. The Danzig trilogy

DOGS
    Burnford, S. Bel Ria
    Burnford, S. The incredible journey
    Ellison, H. A boy and his dog
    Gipson, F. B. Old Yeller
    Gipson, F. B. Savage Sam
    King, S. Cujo
    Koontz, D. R. Watchers
    London, J. The call of the wild
    London, J. White Fang
    Roger Caras' Treasury of great dog stories
    Wambaugh, J. The black marble
The **dogs** of war. Forsyth, F.
    also in Forsyth, F. Forsyth's three

Doing wrong. Keating, H. R. F.
Dolley. Brown, R. M.
The **dollmaker.** Arnow, H. L. S.
The **Doll's** House. Anthony, E.
Dolly. Brookner, A.
Dolores Claiborne. King, S.

DOLPHINS
  McCaffrey, A. The dolphins of Pern
The **dolphins** of Pern. McCaffrey, A.
Dombey and Son. Dickens, C.
Domes of fire. Eddings, D.

DOMESTIC RELATIONS *See* Family life

DOMINICAN AMERICANS
  Alvarez, J. How the Garcia girls lost their accents

DOMINICAN REPUBLIC
  Alvarez, J. In the time of the butterflies
Domino. Whitney, P. A.
Don Camillo and his flock. Guareschi, G.
The **Don** flows home to the sea. Sholokhov, M. A.
Don Quixote de la Mancha. Cervantes Saavedra, M. de
Dona Flor and her two husbands. Amado, J.
Doña Perfecta. Pérez Galdós, B.

DONKEYS *See* Asses and mules
DONS *See* Teachers
Don't ask. Westlake, D. E.
Don't look now. Du Maurier, Dame D.
Doomed to die. Simpson, D.
The **doomsday** conspiracy. Sheldon, S.
The **doomsters.** Macdonald, R.
  In Macdonald, R. Archer in jeopardy
Door to death. Stout, R.
  In Stout, R. Five of a kind p399-441
The **doorbell** rang. Stout, R.
The **doors** of his face, the lamps of his mouth. Zelazny,
  R.
  In The Best of the Nebulas p35-61

DORSET (ENGLAND) *See* England—Dorset

DOSTOEVSKIĬ, FEDOR MIKHAĬLOVICH *See*
  Dostoyevsky, Fyodor, 1821-1881

DOSTOYEVSKY, FYODOR, 1821-1881
  Coetzee, J. M. The master of Petersburg
The **double.** Dostoyevsky, F.
  In Dostoyevsky, F. The short novels of Dostoevsky
  p475-615
A **double** deception. Egleton, C.
Double Deuce. Parker, R. B.
Double, double, oil and trouble. Lathen, E.
Double Dutch treat: three novels, Elmore Leonard's.
  Leonard, E.
The **double** image. MacInnes, H.
Double indemnity. Cain, J. M.
  In Cain, J. M. Cain x 3 p363-465
Double star. Heinlein, R. A.
Down all the days. Brown, C.
Down among the dead. Moyes, P.
  In Moyes, P. Murder by 3's p289-540
Down in the zero. Vachss, A. H.
Downriver. Estleman, L. D.

DOWN'S SYNDROME
  Rubens, B. A solitary grief
Downtown. McBain, E.
Downtown. Siddons, A. R.
Downward to the Earth. Silverberg, R.
  In Silverberg, R. A Robert Silverberg omnibus

DOWRY *See* Marriage customs

DOYLE, SIR ARTHUR CONAN, 1859-1930
  Frost, M. The list of 7
              Parodies, travesties, etc.
  Gardner, J. E. The return of Moriarty
  Gardner, J. E. The revenge of Moriarty
  King, L. R. The beekeeper's apprentice
  Meyer, N. The seven-per-cent solution
  Meyer, N. The West End horror
  Symons, J. A three-pipe problem

DOYLE, CONAN *See* Doyle, Sir Arthur Conan, 1859-
  1930
Dr. Jekyll and Mr. Hyde. See Stevenson, R. L. The
  strange case of Dr. Jekyll and Mr. Hyde
Dr. Jekyll and Mr. Hyde [variant title: The strange case
  of Dr. Jekyll and Mr. Hyde]. Stevenson, R. L.
  In Stevenson, R. L. The complete short stories v2
  p102-64
Dracula. Stoker, B.

DRAFT
  Bellow, S. Dangling man
  Carroll, J. Fault lines
  Carroll, J. Memorial bridge

DRAFT, MILITARY *See* Draft
DRAFT RESISTERS *See* Draft
Dragon. Cussler, C.

Dragon [series]
  Dickson, G. R. The dragon at war
  Dickson, G. R. The dragon knight
  Dickson, G. R. The dragon on the border
  Dickson, G. R. The dragon, the Earl, and the troll

The **dragon** at war. Dickson, G. R.
Dragon harvest. Sinclair, U.
  In Sinclair, U. [Lanny Budd series]
The **dragon** knight. Dickson, G. R.
The **dragon** on the border. Dickson, G. R.
Dragon seed. Buck, P. S.
Dragon tears. Koontz, D. R.
The **dragon,** the Earl, and the troll. Dickson, G. R.
Dragonflight. McCaffrey, A.
Dragonquest. McCaffrey, A.
Dragonrider. McCaffrey, A.
  In The Best of the Nebulas p229-313

Dragonriders of Pern [series]
  McCaffrey, A. All the Weyrs of Pern
  McCaffrey, A. The dolphins of Pern
  McCaffrey, A. Dragonflight
  McCaffrey, A. Dragonquest
  McCaffrey, A. Dragonsdawn
  McCaffrey, A. The renegades of Pern
  McCaffrey, A. The white dragon

DRAGONS
  McCaffrey, A. All the Weyrs of Pern
  McCaffrey, A. Dragonflight
  McCaffrey, A. Dragonquest
  McCaffrey, A. Dragonrider
  McCaffrey, A. Dragonsdawn
  McCaffrey, A. The girl who heard dragons
  McCaffrey, A. The renegades of Pern
  McCaffrey, A. Wehr search
  McCaffrey, A. The white dragon
  Norton, A. The elvenbane
  Norton, A. Elvenblood
Dragon's teeth. Sinclair, U.
  In Sinclair, U. [Lanny Budd series]
Dragonsdawn. McCaffrey, A.
Dragonwyck. Seton, A.
A **dram** of poison. Armstrong, C.
  In Armstrong, C. The Charlotte Armstrong reader
  p185-341

DRAMATISTS
  Hailey, E. F. Joanna's husband and David's wife
  Hazzard, S. The transit of Venus
  Mahfūz, N. Wedding song
  Murdoch, I. The sea, the sea
The **dreadful** lemon sky. MacDonald, J. D.
The **dream** life of Balso Snell. West, N.
  In West, N. The complete works of Nathanael West
  p3-62

Dream of darkness. Hill, R.
Dream of fair to middling women. Beckett, S.
Dream of orchids. Whitney, P. A.
The **dream** of the red chamber. Ts'ao, H.-C.
Dream train. Allen, C. V.
The **dreaming**. Wood, B.
The **dreaming** damozel. Hardwick, M.
Dreaming in color. Allen, C. V.
Dreaming in Cuban. Garcia, C.

DREAMS
Ballard, J. G. The unlimited dream company
Hill, R. Dream of darkness
Le Guin, U. K. The lathe of heaven
O'Brien, T. Going after Cacciato
West, N. The dream life of Balso Snell
Dreams are not enough. Briskin, J.
Dreams of gold. Orde, L.
Dreamsnake. McIntyre, V. N.
DRESDEN (GERMANY) See Germany—Dresden
Dress gray. Truscott, L. K.
Dress her in indigo. MacDonald, J. D.

DRESSMAKERS
Bristow, G. Celia Garth
The **drifters**. Michener, J. A.
The **driver's** seat. Spark, M.
Driving force. Francis, D.
Droll stories. Balzac, H. de
Drowned hopes. Westlake, D. E.

DROWNING
Bass, R. Mahatma Joe
Hamilton, J. A map of the world
Oates, J. C. Black water
The **drowning** pool. Macdonald, R.

DRUG ABUSE
See also Drugs
Del Vecchio, J. M. Carry me home
Westlake, D. E. Sacred monster

DRUG ADDICTION
Cheever, J. Falconer
Childress, M. Tender
Dickens, C. The mystery of Edwin Drood, concluded by Leon Garfield
Mahfūz, N. Adrift on the Nile
Mahfūz, N. Midaq Alley
Meyer, N. The seven-per-cent solution
O'Connor, R. Buffalo soldiers

DRUG INDUSTRY See Pharmaceutical industry

DRUG TRAFFIC
Abrahams, P. Lights out
Anthony, E. Mission to Malaspiga
Brown, D. Hammerheads
Buckley, C. T. Wet work
Clancy, T. Clear and present danger
Clancy, T. Without remorse
Coonts, S. Under siege
Daley, R. A faint cold fear
Ferrigno, R. The Horse Latitudes
Fleming, I. Risico
Francis, D. Driving force
Graham, W. Stephanie
Grant, M. Officer down
Higgins, J. A season in hell
Le Carré, J. The night manager
Leonard, E. Rum punch
Leonard, E. Stick
Lopez, S. Third and Indiana
Ludlum, R. The Matlock paper
Lustbader, E. V. Angel eyes
Lustbader, E. V. French kiss
Maas, P. China white
MacInnes, H. North from Rome
McBain, E. Downtown
Price, R. Clockers
Stewart, M. Airs above the ground
Stone, R. Dog soldiers

Thomas, M. M. Black money
Whitney, P. A. Black amber
DRUGGISTS See Pharmacists
DRUGS
See also Drug addiction; Drug traffic
Bradley, M. Z. The house between the worlds
Du Maurier, Dame D. The house on the strand
Koontz, D. R. Night chills
Mowry, J. Six out seven
DRUGSTORES See Pharmacists
The **druid** of Shannara. Brooks, T.
Druids. Llywelyn, M.

DRUIDS AND DRUIDISM
Bradley, M. Z. The forest house
Llywelyn, M. Druids
Drums along the Mohawk. Edmonds, W. D.

DRUNKARDS
See also Alcoholism

DU MAURIER, DAME DAPHNE, 1907-1989
Parodies, travesties, etc.
Hill, S. Mrs. de Winter

DUAL PERSONALITY
This subject is used for novels and stories describing a condition in which one individual shows in alternation two very different characters. For tales dealing with individuals who assume or act the character of another, see the subject: Impersonations
See also Multiple personality; Personality disorders
Atwood, M. Lady Oracle
Campbell, R. The Count of Eleven
Hesse, H. Steppenwolf
Martin, V. Mary Reilly
Stevenson, R. L. The strange case of Dr. Jekyll and Mr. Hyde
Dubin's lives. Malamud, B.
A **dubious** legacy. Wesley, M.

DUBLIN (IRELAND) See Ireland—Dublin
Dublin 4. Binchy, M.
In Binchy, M. The lilac bus: stories p165-327
Dubliners. Joyce, J.
The **Duchess** of Duke Street. Hardwick, M.

DUDLEY, AMY ROBSART, LADY, 1532?-1560
Scott, Sir W. Kenilworth

DUDLEY, ROBERT See Leicester, Robert Dudley, Earl of, 1532?-1588
The **duel**. Conrad, J.
In Conrad, J. Tales of land and sea p441-504

DUELING
Conrad, J. The duel
DUELS See Dueling
The **Duke's** children [abridged]. Trollope, A.
In Trollope, A. The Pallisers p387-437
Dune. Herbert, F.

Dune [series]
Herbert, F. Chapterhouse: Dune
Herbert, F. Children of Dune
Herbert, F. Dune
Herbert, F. Dune messiah
Herbert, F. God Emperor of Dune
Herbert, F. Heretics of Dune
Dune messiah. Herbert, F.

DUNKIRK, BATTLE OF, 1940
Gallico, P. The snow goose
Dunster. Mortimer, J. C.
The **Dunwich** horror, and others. Lovecraft, H. P.
Dunyazadiad. Barth, J.
In Barth, J. Chimera p1-56

DURHAM (N.C.) *See* North Carolina—Durham
During the reign of the Queen of Persia. Chase, J.
DÜSSELDORF (GERMANY) *See* Germany—Düsseldorf
Dust across the range. Brand, M.
    In Brand, M. Max Brand's best western stories v1

DUTCH

Borneo
    Conrad, J. Almayer's folly
Dutch treat: 3 novels, Elmore Leonard's. Leonard, E.
Dutch uncle. Durham, M.
The **dutiful** son. McInerny, R. M.
    In McInerny, R. Four on the floor p157-199

DWARFS
    Dickens, C. The old curiosity shop
    Grass, G. The tin drum
    Hamsun, K. Mysteries
    Maupin, A. Maybe the moon
    Swift, J. Gulliver's travels
Dynasty. Elegant, R. S.

E

"E" is for evidence. Grafton, S.
E.T. Kotzwinkle, W.
The **eagle** and the raven. Michener, J. A.
The **eagle** has flown. Higgins, J.
The **eagle** has landed. Higgins, J.
The **earl.** Holland, C.
Early autumn. Parker, R. B.

EARLY CHRISTIANS
    See also Church history—Primitive and early
        church
    Asch, S. The Apostle
    Asch, S. Mary
    Asch, S. The Nazarene
    Costain, T. B. The silver chalice
    Holmes, M. The Messiah
    Lagerkvist, P. Barabbas
    Sienkiewicz, H. Quo vadis
    Waltari, M. The Roman
Early graves. Hansen, J.
Early novels and stories. Cather, W.

EARTH, DESTRUCTION OF
    Bear, G. Anvil of stars
    Bear, G. The forge of God
    Hoban, R. Riddley Walker
    Niven, L. Lucifer's hammer
    Pohl, F. Land's end
Earth. Brin, D.
Earth song, sky spirit. Entered in Part I under title
Earthborn. Card, O. S.
Earthfall. Card, O. S.
Earthlight. Clarke, A. C.
Earthly possessions. Tyler, A.
Earthly powers. Burgess, A.

EARTHQUAKES
    See also Disasters
    Jones, D. C. This savage race
    Whitney, P. A. The trembling hills
Earth's children [series]
    Auel, J. M. The Clan of the Cave Bear
    Auel, J. M. The Mammoth Hunters
    Auel, J. M. The plains of passage
    Auel, J. M. The Valley of Horses
Easeful death. McInerny, R. M.
EAST (FAR EAST) *See* East Asia

EAST AND WEST
    See also Acculturation
    Buck, P. S. East and West
    Buck, P. S. East wind: west wind
    Buck, P. S. A house divided

    Clavell, J. Gai-Jin
    Clavell, J. Noble house
    Clavell, J. Shogun
    Elegant, R. S. Dynasty
    Endō, S. The samurai
    Endō, S. Silence
    Forster, E. M. A passage to India
    Han, S. Till morning comes
    Hersey, J. A single pebble
    Kingston, M. H. Tripmaster Monkey
    Lustbader, E. V. Shan
    Scott, P. The day of the scorpion
    Scott, P. The jewel in the crown
    Somtow, S. P. Jasmine nights
    Tan, A. The Joy Luck Club
East and West. Buck, P. S.
East and West. Maugham, W. S.
    In Maugham, W. S. Complete short stories v1
EAST ANGLIA (ENGLAND) *See* England—East Anglia

EAST ASIA
    Jennings, G. The journeyer

EAST INDIANS

Africa
    Naipaul, V. S. A bend in the river

England
    Seton, A. Green darkness

Italy
    Ondaatje, M. The English patient

Trinidad and Tobago
    Naipaul, V. S. A house for Mr. Biswas

United States
    Mukherjee, B. The holder of the world
    Mukherjee, B. Jasmine
East is East. Boyle, T. C.
East is east. Lathen, E.
East of Eden. Steinbeck, J.
EAST SIDE, LOWER (NEW YORK, N.Y.) *See* New
    York (N.Y.)—Lower East Side
East, west. Rushdie, S.
East wind: west wind. Buck, P. S.
EASTER REBELLION, 1916 *See* Ireland—Sinn Fein
    Rebellion, 1916

EASTERN EUROPE
    Appelfeld, A. Unto the soul
    Moore, B. The color of blood

Communism
    See Communism—Eastern Europe
Easy to kill. Christie, A.
    In Christie, A. Agatha Christie: five complete novels
        of murder and detection
The **easy** way out. McCauley, S.
The **ebony** swan. Whitney, P. A.

ECCENTRICS AND ECCENTRICITIES
    See also Recluses
    Aiken, J. Morningquest
    Auster, P. Mr. Vertigo
    Boyle, T. C. East is East
    Boyle, T. C. Road to Wellville
    Buffett, J. Where is Joe Merchant?
    Childress, M. Crazy in Alabama
    Dennis, P. Auntie Mame
    Edgerton, C. Killer diller
    Erdrich, L. The Beet Queen
    Gardner, J. October light
    Harrison, J. The seven-ounce man
    Irving, J. A son of the circus
    Kay, T. Shadow song
    Lehrer, J. Kick the can
    Leonard, E. Maximum Bob
    McMurtry, L. Some can whistle
    Mitford, N. Love in a cold climate
    Mitford, N. The pursuit of love
    Pearson, T. R. A short history of a small place

ECCENTRICS AND ECCENTRICITIES—*Continued*

Portis, C. Gringos
Somtow, S. P. Jasmine nights
Spark, M. A far cry from Kensington
Theroux, P. Millroy the Magician
Toole, J. K. A confederacy of dunces
Tyler, A. Morgan's passing
Vine, B. King Solomon's carpet
Wolfe, T. The good child's river
Echoes. Binchy, M.

ECOLOGY

Llywelyn, M. The elementals
MacDonald, J. D. Barrier Island
Michener, J. A. Chesapeake
Silverberg, R. Hot sky at midnight

ECONOMISTS

Galbraith, J. K. A tenured professor

ECUADOR

See also Galapagos Islands
Eden. Lem, S.
Eden burning. Plain, B.
Eden Close. Shreve, A.
The **edge.** Francis, D.

EDINBURGH (SCOTLAND) *See* Scotland—Edinburgh

EDITORS

See also Journalists; Women editors
Hailey, E. F. Life sentences
McInerney, J. Brightness Falls
Plante, D. Annunciation
Siddons, A. R. Downtown

EDUCATION

See also Teachers
Dickens, C. Hard times
Meredith, G. The ordeal of Richard Feverel
The **education** of Harriet Hatfield. Sarton, M.

EDUCATORS *See* Teachers

EDWARD I, KING OF ENGLAND, 1239-1307

Penman, S. K. The reckoning

EDWARD IV, KING OF ENGLAND, 1442-1483

Penman, S. K. The sunne in splendour

EDWARD VI, KING OF ENGLAND, 1537-1553

Twain, M. The prince and the pauper

EDWARD VII, KING OF GREAT BRITAIN, 1841-1910

Hardwick, M. The Duchess of Duke Street
Lovesey, P. Bertie and the Tinman

EDWARD, PRINCE OF WALES, 1330-1376

Doyle, Sir A. C. The White Company

EDWARD, THE BLACK PRINCE *See* Edward, Prince of Wales, 1330-1376

The **Edwardians.** Sackville-West, V.
Edwin Drood. See Dickens, C. The mystery of Edwin Drood

EGOISM

Hardy, T. The Mayor of Casterbridge
Meredith, G. The ordeal of Richard Feverel
Wilde, O. The picture of Dorian Gray

EGYPT

Willis, C. Death on the Nile

To 640

Asch, S. Moses
Christie, A. Death comes as the end
Golding, W. The scorpion god
Mailer, N. Ancient evenings
Mann, T. Joseph in Egypt
Mann, T. Joseph the provider
Smith, W. A. River god
Waltari, M. The Egyptian

19th century

Kipling, R. The light that failed

20th century

Durrell, L. Constance
Durrell, L. Monsieur

Follett, K. Triple
Maḥfūẓ, N. Autumn quail
Maḥfūẓ, N. The time and the place and other stories

Courts and courtiers

See Courts and courtiers—Egypt

Politics

See Politics—Egypt

Alexandria

Caldwell, T. Dear and glorious physician
Durrell, L. The Alexandria quartet: Justine; Balthazar; Mountolive [and] Clea
Durrell, L. Balthazar
Durrell, L. Clea
Durrell, L. Justine
Durrell, L. Mountolive

Cairo

Deighton, L. City of gold
Follett, K. The key to Rebecca
Maḥfūẓ, N. Adrift on the Nile
Maḥfūẓ, N. The beginning and the end
Maḥfūẓ, N. The harafish
Maḥfūẓ, N. Midaq Alley
Maḥfūẓ, N. Palace of desire
Maḥfūẓ, N. Palace walk
Maḥfūẓ, N. Sugar Street
Wood, B. Virgins of paradise
The **Egyptian.** Waltari, M.

EGYPTIANS

Switzerland

Durrell, L. Sebastian
The **Eiger** sanction. Trevanian
The **eight.** Neville, K.
Eight black horses. McBain, E.
Eight men. Wright, R.
Eight million ways to die. Block, L.
Eighteen hundred seventy six. See Vidal, G. 1876
Eighteen millimeter blues. See Browne, G. A. 18mm blues
The **eighth** commandment. Sanders, L.
The **eighth** day. Wilder, T.

EINSTEIN, ALBERT, 1879-1955

Lightman, A. P. Einstein's dreams
Einstein's dreams. Lightman, A. P.
The **el** murders. Granger, B.

ELDERLY

See also Old age

ELECTIONS

See also Presidents—Election; Presidents—United States—Election
Higgins, G. V. Victories
O'Connor, E. The last hurrah
Vidal, G. 1876

ELECTRONIC COMPUTERS *See* Computers

Element of doubt. Simpson, D.
The **elementals.** Llywelyn, M.
Elenium [series]

Eddings, D. The diamond throne
Eddings, D. The ruby knight
Eddings, D. The sapphire rose

Elephant song. Smith, W. A.
The **elfqueen** of Shannara. Brooks, T.
The **Elfstones** of Shannara. Brooks, T.

ELIZABETH I, QUEEN OF ENGLAND, 1533-1603

Finney, P. Firedrake's eye
Holt, V. My enemy the Queen
Plaidy, J. The captive Queen of Scots
Scott, Sir W. Kenilworth
Eliza's daughter. Aiken, J.
Elkhorn Tavern. Jones, D. C.
Ellen Foster. Gibbons, K.
Ellis Island. Helprin, M.
In Helprin, M. Ellis Island & other stories p128-96

Ellis Island. Stewart, F. M.
Ellis Island & other stories. Helprin, M.
Elmer Gantry. Lewis, S.
Elmore Leonard's double Dutch treat: three novels. Leonard, E.
Elmore Leonard's Dutch treat: 3 novels. Leonard, E.
The elusive Mrs. Pollifax. Gilman, D.
The elusive Pimpernel. Orczy, E., Baroness
The elvenbane. Norton, A.
Elvenblood. Norton, A.

EMBEZZLEMENT
Ludlum, R. The Scarlatti inheritance
Emerald. Whitney, P. A.

EMERALDS
Westlake, D. E. The hot rock
The emigrants. Bojer, J.
The emigrants. Moberg, V.
EMIGRÉS See Refugees
Emily Dickinson is dead. Langton, J.
Eminence. Kienzle, W. X.
Emma. Austen, J.
    also in Austen, J. The complete novels of Jane Austen
Emma. Brontë, C.
Emmeline. Rossner, J.

EMOTIONALLY DISTURBED CHILDREN
Guest, J. Second heaven
Levenkron, S. The best little girl in the world
Potok, C. The promise
The emperor of ice-cream. Moore, B.
Empire. Vidal, G.
Empire of the eagle. Norton, A.
Empire of the Sun. Ballard, J. G.
The empty copper sea. MacDonald, J. D.
The empty house. Gilbert, M.
The enchantress. Han, S.
The end of all songs. Moorcock, M.
The end of my career. Franklin, M.
The end of the affair. Greene, G.
The end of the battle. Waugh, E.
End of the chapter. Galsworthy, J.
The end of the hunt. Flanagan, T.
The end of the pier. Grimes, M.
The end of the road. Barth, J.
The end of the tether. Conrad, J.
    In Conrad, J. Tales of land and sea p505-610
END OF THE WORLD
    See also Earth, Destruction of
Balmer, E. When worlds collide
Benford, G. Matter's end
Butler, O. E. Adulthood rites
Butler, O. E. Dawn
Butler, O. E. Imago
Ellison, H. The deathbird
Shute, N. On the beach
West, M. L. The clowns of God
Ender Wiggin [series]
Card, O. S. Ender's game
Card, O. S. Speaker for the Dead
Card, O. S. Xenocide
Ender's game. Card, O. S.
Endless love. Spencer, S.
Endless night. Christie, A.

ENDOWMENTS
Vonnegut, K. God bless you, Mr. Rosewater
The enduring hills. Giles, J. H.
Enemies, a love story. Singer, I. B.
Enemy mine. Longyear, B. B.
    In The Hugo winners v5 p5-67
ENGAGEMENTS See Betrothals
Engagements of the heart. See Sagan, F. A reluctant hero
The engineer of human souls. Škvorecký, J.

ENGINEERS
Hersey, J. A single pebble

Levi, P. The monkey's wrench
Vonnegut, K. Player piano
ENGLAND
    See also Cotswolds (England); Stonehenge (England)
Lessing, D. M. The memoirs of a survivor
Rutherfurd, E. Sarum
Woolf, V. Orlando

To 55 B.C.
Holland, C. Pillar of the Sky

Roman period, 55 B.C.-449 A.D.
Bradley, M. Z. The forest house
De Hartog, J. The centurion
Graves, R. Claudius, the god and his wife Messalina

Anglo-Saxon period, 449-1066
Berger, T. Arthur Rex
Bradley, M. Z. The mists of Avalon
Seton, A. Avalon
Stewart, M. The crystal cave
Stewart, M. The hollow hills
Stewart, M. The last enchantment
Stewart, M. Mary Stewart's Merlin trilogy
Stewart, M. The wicked day
Sutcliff, R. Sword at sunset
Twain, M. A Connecticut Yankee in King Arthur's court

12th century
Follett, K. Pillars of the earth
Holland, C. The earl
Scott, Sir W. Ivanhoe

13th century
Costain, T. B. The black rose
Garwood, J. Saving grace
Kluger, R. The Sheriff of Nottingham
Pargeter, E. The green branch
Pargeter, E. The heaven tree
Pargeter, E. The heaven tree trilogy
Pargeter, E. The scarlet seed
Penman, S. K. Falls the shadow
Penman, S. K. Here be dragons
Penman, S. K. The reckoning
White, T. H. The once and future king
White, T. H. The sword in the stone
White, T. H. The witch in the wood

14th century
Lofts, N. The town house
Riley, J. M. In pursuit of the green lion
Riley, J. M. A vision of light
Seton, A. Katherine
Unsworth, B. Morality play

15th century
Jarman, R. H. The courts of illusion
Lofts, N. The homecoming
Lofts, N. Knight's Acre
Lofts, N. The town house
Penman, S. K. The sunne in splendour
Plaidy, J. The reluctant queen

16th century
Anthony, E. Anne Boleyn
Dunnett, D. The ringed castle
George, M. Mary Queen of Scotland and the Isles
Gregory, P. The wise woman
Holt, V. My enemy the Queen
L'Amour, L. Sackett's land
L'Amour, L. To the far blue mountains
Lewis, H. W. I am Mary Tudor
Lofts, N. The house at Old Vine
Plaidy, J. The captive Queen of Scots
Plaidy, J. Murder most royal
Plaidy, J. The rose without a thorn
Plaidy, J. The scarlet cloak
Plaidy, J. The sixth wife
Scott, Sir W. Kenilworth
Seton, A. Green darkness
Twain, M. The prince and the pauper

ENGLAND—*Continued*

17th century

Barth, J. The sot-weed factor
Belle, P. Treason's gift
Blackmore, R. D. Lorna Doone
Defoe, D. Moll Flanders
Du Maurier, Dame D. Frenchman's Creek
Du Maurier, Dame D. The King's general
Dumas, A. Twenty years after
Goudge, E. The child from the sea
Laker, R. Circle of pearls
Lofts, N. The house at Old Vine
Lofts, N. The old priory
Lofts, N. Pargeters
Plaidy, J. The pleasures of love
Plaidy, J. William's wife

18th century

Brontë, C. Emma
Carr, P. Voices in a haunted room
Collins, W. The rationalist
Fielding, H. The history of Tom Jones, a foundling
Fielding, H. Joseph Andrews
Fowles, J. A maggot
Goldsmith, O. The Vicar of Wakefield
Graham, W. The angry tide
Graham, W. The black moon
Graham, W. The four swans
Gregory, P. Meridon
Heaven, C. The wind from the sea
Hodge, J. A. Windover
Holt, V. The Devil on horseback
Koen, K. Through a glass darkly
Laker, R. The sugar pavilion
Lofts, N. The house at sunset
Lofts, N. Nethergate
Richardson, S. Pamela
Sherwood, F. Vindication
Smollett, T. G. Humphry Clinker
Tarkington, B. Monsieur Beaucaire
Thackeray, W. M. The history of Henry Esmond, esquire
Thackeray, W. M. The Virginians
Veryan, P. Ask me no questions
Veryan, P. Had we never loved
Veryan, P. Never doubt I love
Veryan, P. A shadow's bliss
Veryan, P. Time's fool

19th century

Aiken, J. Eliza's daughter
Aiken, J. Jane Fairfax
Aiken, J. Mansfield revisited
Alcott, L. M. A long fatal love chase
Austen, J. The complete novels of Jane Austen
Austen, J. Emma
Austen, J. Lady Susan
Austen, J. Mansfield Park
Austen, J. Northanger Abbey
Austen, J. Persuasion
Austen, J. Pride and prejudice
Barrett, J. Presumption
Brontë, C. Shirley
Byatt, A. S. Angels and insects
Colegate, I. The summer of the royal visit
Cookson, C. The black velvet gown
Coulter, C. The Nightingale legacy
Coulter, C. The valentine legacy
Coulter, C. The Wyndham legacy
Delderfield, R. F. Give us this day
Delderfield, R. F. God is an Englishman
Delderfield, R. F. Theirs was the kingdom
Dickens, C. Barnaby Rudge
Dickens, C. Bleak House
Dickens, C. A Charles Dickens Christmas
Dickens, C. A Christmas carol
Dickens, C. The cricket on the hearth
Dickens, C. David Copperfield
Dickens, C. Dombey and Son

Dickens, C. Great expectations
Dickens, C. Hard times
Dickens, C. Little Dorrit
Dickens, C. Nicholas Nickleby
Dickens, C. The old curiosity shop
Dickens, C. The posthumous papers of the Pickwick Club
Dickens, C. Sketches by Boz
Eden, D. Ravenscroft
Eden, D. The Salamanca drum
Eliot, G. Adam Bede
Eliot, G. Middlemarch
Eliot, G. The mill on the Floss
Follett, K. A dangerous fortune
Forester, C. S. Commodore Hornblower
Forester, C. S. Lord Hornblower
Fowles, J. The French lieutenant's woman
Fraser, G. M. Flashman
Goudge, E. The dean's watch
Graham, W. The loving cup
Graham, W. The miller's dance
Graham, W. The stranger from the sea
Graham, W. The twisted sword
Hardy, T. Under the greenwood tree
Hawthorne, N. Doctor Grimshawe's secret
Heyer, G. Bath tangle
Heyer, G. Cousin Kate
Heyer, G. The grand Sophy
Heyer, G. Lady of quality
Hill, P. Artemia
Hill, P. Vollands
Holt, V. The black opal
Holt, V. The India fan
Holt, V. Mistress of Mellyn
Holt, V. The road to Paradise Island
Holt, V. Secret for a nightingale
James, H. The spoils of Poynton
James, H. The turn of the screw
Lofts, N. The day of the butterfly
Lofts, N. Gad's Hall
Lofts, N. The haunting of Gad's Hall
Lofts, N. The house at sunset
Lofts, N. Nethergate
McCutchan, P. Halfhyde and the fleet review
Michaels, B. Greygallows
Pearce, M. E. Cast a long shadow
Pearce, M. E. The old house at Railes
Quick, A. Deception
Quick, A. Mistress
Richler, M. Solomon Gursky was here
Ross-Macdonald, M. For they shall inherit
Ross-Macdonald, M. An innocent woman
Ross-Macdonald, M. The rich are with you always
Ross-Macdonald, M. A woman alone
Ross-Macdonald, M. A woman possessed
Ross-Macdonald, M. The world from rough stones
Stewart, F. M. Pomp and circumstance
Tennant, E. Pemberley
Tennant, E. An unequal marriage
Thackeray, W. M. The history of Henry Esmond, esquire
Thackeray, W. M. Vanity fair
Trollope, A. Barchester Towers
Trollope, A. Doctor Thorne
Trollope, A. The Eustace diamonds
Trollope, A. Framley parsonage
Trollope, A. The last chronicle of Barset
Trollope, A. The Pallisers
Trollope, A. The prime minister
Trollope, A. The small house at Allington
Trollope, A. The warden
Trollope, A. The way we live now
Wells, H. G. Tono-Bungay
Woolf, V. The years

20th century

Aiken, J. Morningquest
Allbeury, T. Deep purple
Amis, K. The folks that live on the hill

ENGLAND—20th century—*Continued*

Anthony, E. The house of Vandekar
Archer, J. As the crow flies
Benson, E. F. Make way for Lucia
Binchy, M. Silver wedding
Bradford, B. T. Act of will
Bradford, B. T. Hold the dream
Bradford, B. T. To be the best
Bradford, B. T. A woman of substance
Burgess, A. The pianoplayers
Campbell, R. The Count of Eleven
Campbell, R. The long lost
Campbell, R. The Nameless
Carr, P. A time for silence
Chesney, M. Deborah goes to Dover
Christie, A. The boomerang clue
Colegate, I. The shooting party
Delderfield, R. F. Give us this day
Delderfield, R. F. The green gauntlet
Delderfield, R. F. A horseman riding by
Dickinson, P. Hindsight
Dickinson, P. The last houseparty
Dickinson, P. Perfect gallows
Drabble, M. The ice age
Drabble, M. A natural curiosity
Drabble, M. The radiant way
Drabble, M. The realms of gold
Eden, D. The American heiress
Eden, D. The Salamanca drum
Edwards, A. Wallis
Ford, F. M. The last post
Forster, E. M. Maurice
Forster, E. M. A room with a view
Fowles, J. The collector
Francis, D. Forfeit
Francis, D. High stakes
Francis, D. Twice shy
Frayn, M. A landing on the sun
Galsworthy, J. End of the chapter
Gardner, J. E. The secret generations
Gaskin, C. The charmed circle
Glendinning, V. The grown-ups
Godden, R. In this house of Brede
Graham, W. Stephanie
Hart, J. Damage
Hart, J. Sin
Howard, E. J. Confusion
Howard, E. J. The light years
Howard, E. J. Marking time
Howatch, S. Absolute truths
Howatch, S. Glamorous powers
Howatch, S. Glittering images
Howatch, S. Mystical paths
Howatch, S. Scandalous risks
Howatch, S. Ultimate prizes
Huxley, A. Antic hay
James, P. D. Innocent blood
Leslie, J. A. C. The ghost and Mrs. Muir
Lessing, D. M. Briefing for a descent into Hell
Lessing, D. M. The fifth child
Lively, P. Moon tiger
Lively, P. Passing on
MacInnes, H. Friends and lovers
Mitford, N. Love in a cold climate
Mitford, N. The pursuit of love
Mortimer, J. C. Dunster
Mortimer, J. C. Paradise postponed
Murdoch, I. The book and the brotherhood
Murdoch, I. Henry and Cato
Murdoch, I. The message to the planet
Pearce, M. E. Apple tree lean down
Pearce, M. E. The land endures
Powell, A. Books do furnish a room
Powell, A. A dance to the music of time
Powell, A. Hearing secret harmonies
Powell, A. The soldier's art
Pym, B. Quartet in autumn
Read, P. P. The free Frenchman

Renault, M. The charioteer
Rendell, R. The crocodile bird
Rendell, R. The killing doll
Seton, A. Green darkness
Sillitoe, A. The loneliness of the long-distance runner
Sillitoe, A. Saturday night and Sunday morning
Snow, C. P. Corridors of power
Snow, C. P. Last things
Snow, C. P. The new men
Snow, C. P. Time of hope
Spark, M. The comforters
Spark, M. Memento mori
Stewart, M. Thornyhold
Stubbs, J. Like we used to be
Thane, E. Homing
Thomas, R. Other people's marriages
Townsend, S. The Adrian Mole diaries
Townsend, S. Adrian Mole: the lost years
Tremain, R. Sacred country
Trevor, W. Felicia's journey
Uris, L. QB VII
Walters, M. The sculptress
Waugh, E. Brideshead revisited
Waugh, E. Decline and fall
Weldon, F. Life force
Wells, H. G. Tono-Bungay
Wesley, M. A dubious legacy
West, Dame R. Sunflower
Whitney, P. A. Hunter's green
Wilson, A. N. The vicar of sorrows
Wodehouse, P. G. The code of the Woosters
Wodehouse, P. G. The inimitable Jeeves
Wodehouse, P. G. Jeeves and the tie that binds
Wodehouse, P. G. Tales from the Drones Club
Woolf, V. Jacob's room
Woolf, V. The years
Yorke, M. Crime in question
Yorke, M. Dangerous to know

Aristocracy
See Aristocracy—England

Civil War
See England—17th century

College life
See College life—England

Communism
See Communism—England

Courts and courtiers
See Courts and courtiers—England

Farm life
See Farm life—England

Kings and rulers
Elkin, S. Town Crier exclusive, Confessions of a Princess manqué

Politics
See Politics—England

Prisoners and prisons
See Prisoners and prisons—England

Rural life
Aiken, J. The haunting of Lamb House
Aiken, J. Jane Fairfax
Aiken, J. Mansfield revisited
Austen, J. Emma
Austen, J. Mansfield Park
Austen, J. Persuasion
Austen, J. Pride and prejudice
Austen, J. Sense and sensibility
Benson, E. F. Make way for Lucia
Blackmore, R. D. Lorna Doone
Brent, M. Stormswift
Brent, M. Tregaron's daughter
Butler, S. The way of all flesh

ENGLAND—Rural life—*Continued*
Collins, W. The rationalist
Cookson, C. The Maltese Angel
Dahl, R. Ah, sweet mystery of life
Delderfield, R. F. The green gauntlet
Delderfield, R. F. A horseman riding by
Delderfield, R. F. To serve them all my days
Eden, D. Ravenscroft
Eliot, G. Adam Bede
Eliot, G. The mill on the Floss
Ferrars, E. X. Trial by fury
Forster, E. M. Howards End
Francis, D. Bonecrack
Golding, W. Darkness visible
Golding, W. The spire
Goldsmith, O. The Vicar of Wakefield
Goudge, E. A city of bells
Goudge, E. The dean's watch
Harper, K. Circle of gold
Heyer, G. Cousin Kate
Hoban, R. Riddley Walker
Holt, V. The pride of the peacock
Holt, V. Seven for a secret
Ishiguro, K. The remains of the day
Kells, S. The aristocrats
Lawrence, D. H. Sons and lovers
Lawrence, D. H. The white peacock
Lively, P. The road to Lichfield
Lofts, N. Gad's Hall
Lofts, N. Nethergate
McMullen, M. A grave without flowers
Mortimer, J. C. Paradise postponed
Murdoch, I. The bell
Murdoch, I. The philosopher's pupil
Murdoch, I. The sea, the sea
Pearce, M. E. Apple tree lean down
Pearce, M. E. Cast a long shadow
Pearce, M. E. The land endures
Pearson, D. The summer of the Barshinskeys
Peters, E. The murders of Richard III
Pilcher, R. The shell seekers
Pilcher, R. Voices in summer
Priestley, J. B. The good companions
Pym, B. An academic question
Pym, B. Civil to strangers
Pym, B. Jane and Prudence
Pym, B. Some tame gazelle
Read, Miss. Affairs at Thrush Green
Read, Miss. At home in Thrush Green
Read, Miss. Battles at Thrush Green
Read, Miss. Celebrations at Thrush Green
Read, Miss. Changes at Fairacre
Read, Miss. Chronicles of Fairacre
Read, Miss. Farewell to Fairacre
Read, Miss. Friends at Thrush Green
Read, Miss. Gossip from Thrush Green
Read, Miss. Mrs. Pringle
Read, Miss. Return to Thrush Green
Read, Miss. The school at Thrush Green
Read, Miss. Thrush Green
Read, Miss. Winter in Thrush Green
Sackville-West, V. The Edwardians
Sharp, M. Cluny Brown
Snow, C. P. The sleep of reason
Snow, C. P. Strangers and brothers
Struther, J. Mrs. Miniver
Trollope, A. Phineas Redux
Trollope, J. The rector's wife
Weldon, F. The heart of the country
Weldon, F. Puffball
West, P. Love's mansion
Wodehouse, P. G. How right you are, Jeeves
Woolf, V. Between the acts
Yorke, M. Find me a villain
Yorke, M. The smooth face of evil

World War, 1914-1918
See World War, 1914-1918—England

World War, 1939-1945
See World War, 1939-1945—England

Bath
Colegate, I. The summer of the royal visit
Heyer, G. Bath tangle
Heyer, G. Lady of quality
Tarkington, B. Monsieur Beaucaire

Brighton
Greene, G. Brighton rock
Laker, R. The sugar pavilion

Channel Islands
See Channel Islands

Cornwall
Brent, M. Tregaron's daughter
Carr, P. The black swan
Carr, P. A time for silence
Carr, P. We'll meet again
Du Maurier, Dame D. Frenchman's Creek
Du Maurier, Dame D. The house on the strand
Du Maurier, Dame D. Jamaica Inn
Du Maurier, Dame D. The King's general
Du Maurier, Dame D. My cousin Rachel
Du Maurier, Dame D. Rebecca
Godden, R. China Court
Graham, W. The angry tide
Graham, W. The black moon
Graham, W. The four swans
Graham, W. The loving cup
Graham, W. The miller's dance
Graham, W. The stranger from the sea
Graham, W. The twisted sword
Heyer, G. Penhallow
Hill, S. Mrs. de Winter
Holt, V. Bride of Pendorric
Holt, V. The captive
Holt, V. The legend of the seventh virgin
Holt, V. Menfreya in the morning
Holt, V. Mistress of Mellyn
Howatch, S. Penmarric
Pilcher, R. Voices in summer
Ross-Macdonald, M. An innocent woman
Ross-Macdonald, M. To the end of her days
Ross-Macdonald, M. A woman alone
Ross-Macdonald, M. A woman possessed
Shannon, D. The Manson curse
Stubbs, J. Family games
Stubbs, J. Kelly Park
Stubbs, J. Light in summer
Veryan, P. A shadow's bliss

Cotswold Hills
See Cotswolds (England)

Derbyshire
Lawrence, D. H. Lady Chatterley's lover

Devon
Blackmore, R. D. Lorna Doone
Delderfield, R. F. The green gauntlet
Delderfield, R. F. A horseman riding by
Delderfield, R. F. To serve them all my days
Du Maurier, Dame D. The King's general
Sharp, M. Cluny Brown

Dorset
Fowles, J. The French lieutenant's woman
Hardy, T. Far from the madding crowd
Hardy, T. Jude the obscure
Hardy, T. The Mayor of Casterbridge
Hardy, T. The return of the native
Hardy, T. Tess of the D'Urbervilles
Hardy, T. Under the greenwood tree
Hardy, T. Wessex tales
Murdoch, I. The nice and the good

ENGLAND—*Continued*

East Anglia
Lofts, N. The homecoming

Gloucestershire
Pearce, M. E. The old house at Railes

Hampshire
Goudge, E. The bird in the tree
Goudge, E. The heart of the family
Goudge, E. Pilgrim's inn

Hertfordshire
Amis, K. The Green Man

Kent
Dickens, C. The mystery of Edwin Drood
Dickens, C. The mystery of Edwin Drood, concluded
  by Leon Garfield
Godden, J. In her garden
Pearson, D. The summer of the Barshinskeys

Lancashire
De Hartog, J. The peaceable kingdom

London—16th century
Finney, P. Firedrake's eye
Kellerman, F. The quality of mercy

London—Plague, 1665
Defoe, D. A journal of the plague year

London—18th century
Bosse, M. J. The vast memory of love
Dickens, C. A tale of two cities
Laker, R. The silver touch
McCarry, C. The bride of the wilderness
Richardson, S. Clarissa
Robards, K. Nobody's angel
Roberts, K. L. Northwest Passage

London—19th century
Austen, J. Sense and sensibility
Carr, J. D. The bride of Newgate
Chesney, M. Back in society
Chesney, M. Colonel Sandhurst to the rescue
Chesney, M. Lady Fortescue steps out
Chesney, M. Miss Tonks turns to crime
Chesney, M. Mrs. Budley falls from grace
Chesney, M. Sir Philip's folly
Crichton, M. The great train robbery
Dickens, C. Little Dorrit
Dickens, C. Martin Chuzzlewit
Dickens, C. Oliver Twist
Dickens, C. Our mutual friend
Eden, D. The millionaire's daughter
Galsworthy, J. The Indian summer of a Forsyte
Galsworthy, J. The man of property
Gardner, J. E. The return of Moriarty
Gardner, J. E. The revenge of Moriarty
Heyer, G. The grand Sophy
Holt, V. Daughter of deceit
Holt, V. The silk vendetta
James, H. The golden bowl
Martin, V. Mary Reilly
Moorcock, M. An alien heat
Moorcock, M. The hollow lands
Newman, K. Anno-Dracula
Palliser, C. The quincunx
Stevenson, R. L. The strange case of Dr. Jekyll and
  Mr. Hyde
Trollope, A. Phineas Finn
West, P. The women of Whitechapel and Jack the
  Ripper
Wharton, E. The buccaneers
Wharton, E. Fast and loose
Wilde, O. The picture of Dorian Gray

London—20th century
Ackroyd, P. English music
Allen, C. V. Leftover dreams
Amis, K. The Russian girl
Amis, M. London fields

Archer, J. First among equals
Barnard, R. Out of the blackout
Bawden, N. Family money
Beckett, S. Murphy
Binchy, M. Light a penny candle
Bowen, E. The death of the heart
Bowen, E. The heat of the day
Brett, S. A shock to the system
Brookner, A. A closed eye
Brookner, A. Dolly
Brookner, A. Family and friends
Brookner, A. A private view
Byatt, A. S. Possession
Carter, A. Wise children
Cary, J. The horse's mouth
Chesterton, G. K. The man who was Thursday
Clark, M. H. The Anastasia syndrome
Cronin, A. J. The citadel
Deighton, L. SS-GB: Nazi-occupied Britain 1941
Dickinson, P. Play dead
Donleavy, J. P. The ginger man
Drabble, M. The gates of ivory
Drabble, M. Jerusalem the golden
Drabble, M. The middle ground
Drabble, M. The needle's eye
Drabble, M. The waterfall
Follett, K. The man from St. Petersburg
Follett, K. Paper money
Ford, F. M. A man could stand up
Gallico, P. Mrs. 'Arris goes to Paris
Galsworthy, J. End of the chapter
Galsworthy, J. A modern comedy
Galsworthy, J. To let
Godden, R. An episode of sparrows
Godden, R. Thursday's children
Godwin, G. Mr. Bedford
Gordon, M. Living at home
Graham, W. The walking stick
Greene, G. The end of the affair
Greene, G. The human factor
Greene, G. The ministry of fear
Hambly, B. Those who hunt the night
Hardwick, M. The Duchess of Duke Street
Hilton, J. Random harvest
Hoban, R. Turtle diary
Huxley, A. Point counter point
Jhabvala, R. P. Three continents
Korda, M. Curtain
Le Carré, J. The looking glass war
Leavitt, D. While England sleeps
Lessing, D. M. The four-gated city
Lessing, D. M. The good terrorist
Lessing, D. M. The real thing
Lessing, D. M. The summer before the dark
Lively, P. City of the mind
Llewellyn, R. None but the lonely heart
Lovesey, P. On the edge
Lurie, A. Foreign affairs
Marsh, J. The House of Eliott
Maugham, W. S. Of human bondage
Moorcock, M. The end of all songs
Murdoch, I. An accidental man
Murdoch, I. The black prince
Murdoch, I. A fairly honourable defeat
Murdoch, I. The green knight
Murdoch, I. The nice and the good
Murdoch, I. Nuns and soldiers
O'Brien, E. Girls in their married bliss
O'Brien, E. Time and tide
Orwell, G. Keep the aspidistra flying
Powell, A. At Lady Molly's
Powell, A. The military philosophers
Pym, B. Excellent women
Pym, B. A glass of blessings
Pym, B. Less than angels
Pym, B. No fond return of love
Pym, B. The sweet dove died
Pym, B. An unsuitable attachment

ENGLAND—London—20th century—*Continued*
Pynchon, T. Gravity's rainbow
Read, P. P. A season in the West
Reid Banks, L. The L shaped room
Rendell, R. The bridesmaid
Rendell, R. Going wrong
Rendell, R. Talking to strange men
Rendell, R. The tree of hands
Rhys, J. After leaving Mr. Mackenzie
Rhys, J. Voyage in the dark
Rubens, B. A solitary grief
Sackville-West, V. All passion spent
Settle, M. L. Celebration
Snow, C. P. A coat of varnish
Snow, C. P. The conscience of the rich
Snow, C. P. Homecoming
Snow, C. P. The malcontents
Spark, M. The ballad of Peckham Rye
Spark, M. A far cry from Kensington
Spark, M. The girls of slender means
Taylor, E. Mrs. Palfrey at the Claremont
Thane, E. Kissing kin
Thane, E. The light heart
Thane, E. This was tomorrow
Theroux, P. Doctor Slaughter
Thomas, R. All my sins remembered
Thomas, R. Bad girls, good women
Thomas, R. A woman of our times
Van Slyke, H. No love lost
Vine, B. Anna's book
Vine, B. The house of stairs
Vine, B. King Solomon's carpet
Waugh, E. Put out more flags
Waugh, E. Vile bodies
Weldon, F. Trouble
West, Dame R. Cousin Rosamund
West, Dame R. The fountain overflows
West, Dame R. This real night
Wharton, E. The buccaneers, completed by Marion Mainwaring
Wilson, A. N. Love unknown
Woolf, V. Mrs. Dalloway

Northumberland
Cookson, C. The black velvet gown
Stewart, M. The ivy tree

Nottingham
Sillitoe, A. Saturday night and Sunday morning

Nottinghamshire
Lawrence, D. H. The rainbow
Lawrence, D. H. Women in love

Oxford
Fowles, J. Daniel Martin
Goudge, E. The scent of water
Trollope, J. The men and the girls

Oxfordshire
Colegate, I. The shooting party
Galsworthy, J. Maid in waiting
Pym, B. A few green leaves

Somerset
Blackmore, R. D. Lorna Doone
Fielding, H. Joseph Andrews
Trollope, A. Barchester Towers
Trollope, A. Doctor Thorne
Trollope, A. Framley parsonage
Trollope, A. The last chronicle of Barset
Trollope, A. The small house at Allington
Trollope, A. The warden

Suffolk
Lofts, N. Bless this house
Lofts, N. The claw
Lofts, N. The house at Old Vine
Lofts, N. The old priory
Rendell, R. Make death love me

Surrey
Forster, E. M. A room with a view

Sussex
Howatch, S. The shrouded walls
Symons, J. Something like a love affair

Warwickshire
Eliot, G. Middlemarch
Eliot, G. Silas Marner

Wiltshire
Belle, P. Treason's gift
Dickens, C. Martin Chuzzlewit
Naipaul, V. S. The enigma of arrival

Worcestershire
Pearce, M. E. Cast a long shadow
Pearce, M. E. The land endures

Yorkshire
Brontë, A. The tenant of Wildfell Hall
Brontë, C. Jane Eyre
Brontë, C. Shirley
Brontë, E. Wuthering Heights
Holt, V. Kirkland Revels
Michaels, B. Greygallows
England underway. Bisson, T.
    In Nebula awards 29 p181-202

ENGLISH CIVIL WAR *See* England—17th century
English Creek. Doig, I.

ENGLISH DIALECT *See* Dialect stories—English
English music. Ackroyd, P.
The **English** patient. Ondaatje, M.

ENGLISH PEOPLE *See* British
The **enigma** of arrival. Naipaul, V. S.
Enormous changes at the last minute. Paley, G.
    In Paley, G. The collected stories p129-256
Enquiry. Francis, D.
    also in Francis, D. Across the board p499-715

ENTERTAINERS
    See also Actors; Actresses; Clowns; Ventriloquists
Carter, A. Wise children
Colette. Mitsou
McMurtry, L. Buffalo girls
Singer, I. B. The magician of Lublin
Tyler, A. A slipping-down life

ENTERTAINING *See* Parties

ENTOMOLOGISTS
Abe, K. The woman in the dunes
Byatt, A. S. Morpho Eugenia
Saul, J. The homing

ENVIRONMENTALISTS
Hiaasen, C. Native tongue
Morrell, D. The covenant of the flame
Siddons, A. R. King's oak
Envoy extraordinary. Golding, W.
    In Golding, W. The scorpion god: three short novels p115-78

ENVY *See* Jealousy
The **epicurean.** Auchincloss, L.
    In Auchincloss, L. Three lives

EPIDEMICS
    See also Plague
Cook, R. Outbreak
King, S. The stand

EPILEPTICS
Crichton, M. The terminal man
Dostoyevsky, F. The idiot

EPISCOPAL CLERGY *See* Anglican and Episcopal clergy
An **episode** of sparrows. Godden, R.

EPISODIC NOVELS
Munro, A. Lives of girls & women
Oates, J. C. Bellefleur
Porter, C. R. All-Bright Court

EPLF *See* Eritrean People's Liberation Front

ERIE CANAL (N.Y.)
Edmonds, W. D. Chad Hanna

ERITREA (ETHIOPIA)
Keneally, T. To Asmara

ERITREAN PEOPLE'S LIBERATION FRONT
Keneally, T. To Asmara

EROTICISM *See* Sex

Escapade. Hodge, J. A.

ESCAPED CONVICTS
Hunter, S. Dirty white boys
McCrumb, S. She walks these hills
McNaught, J. Perfect

ESCAPES
Bates, H. E. Fair stood the wind for France
Dumas, A. The Count of Monte Cristo
Forester, C. S. Flying colours
Forester, C. S. Hornblower and the Atropos
Gilman, D. Incident at Badamya
Hersey, J. The wall
Higgins, J. The Valhalla exchange
King, S. Rita Hayworth and Shawshank redemption
MacInnes, H. The snare of the hunter
Westheimer, D. Von Ryan's Express

ESKIMOS *See* Inuit

ESP *See* Extrasensory perception

ESPIONAGE *See* International intrigue; Spies

The establishment. Fast, H.

The estate. Singer, I. B.

ESTATES *See* Houses

Eternal curse on the reader of these pages. Puig, M.

The eternal husband. Dostoevsky, F.
In Dostoyevsky, F. The short novels of Dostoevsky
p343-473

The eternal moment. See Forster, E. M. The collected
tales of E. M. Forster

Ethan Frome. Wharton, E.

ETHICS
See also Conscience; Medical ethics; Political
ethics; Sin; Truthfulness and falsehood;
Utilitarianism
Caputo, P. Horn of Africa
Coughlin, W. J. Death penalty
Coughlin, W. J. Shadow of a doubt
Dershowitz, A. M. The advocate's devil
Dexter, P. The paperboy
Goldreich, G. Four days
Higgins, G. V. Victories
Reed, B. The choice
Santayana, G. The last Puritan
Shreve, A. Strange fits of passion
Snow, C. P. The affair
Snow, C. P. The new men
Steinbeck, J. The winter of our discontent

ETHIOPIA
Cody, L. Rift
Keneally, T. To Asmara
Smith, W. A. Cry wolf

Politics
See Politics—Ethiopia

ETHNOLOGISTS
Lovecraft, H. P. The mound

ETRURIANS *See* Etruscans

The Etruscan. Waltari, M.

The Etruscan smile. Johnston, V.

ETRUSCANS
Waltari, M. The Etruscan

Eugénie Grandet. Balzac, H. de

EUNUCHS
Rice, A. Cry to heaven
Smith, W. A. River god

EURASIANS
Bosse, M. J. Fire in heaven

EUROPE
See also Central Europe; Eastern Europe

To 476
Burgess, A. Hun
Llywelyn, M. The horse goddess

392-814
Jennings, G. Raptor

11th century
Dunnett, D. King hereafter
Holland, C. The firedrake

12th century
L'Amour, L. The walking drum

15th century
Dunnett, D. Niccolò rising
Dunnett, D. Race of scorpions
Dunnett, D. Scales of gold
Dunnett, D. The spring of the ram
Dunnett, D. The unicorn hunt

16th century
Dunnett, D. Checkmate

18th century
Allen, H. Anthony Adverse

19th century
Alcott, L. M. A long fatal love chase
Cornwell, B. Sharpe's company
Cornwell, B. Sharpe's eagle
Cornwell, B. Sharpe's enemy
Cornwell, B. Sharpe's gold
Cornwell, B. Sharpe's honour
Cornwell, B. Sharpe's regiment
Cornwell, B. Sharpe's revenge
Cornwell, B. Sharpe's rifles
Hodge, J. A. Escapade
James, H. The portrait of a lady
Laker, R. Jewelled path

20th century
Archer, J. A matter of honor
Camus, A. A happy death
Greene, G. Orient Express
Ishiguro, K. The unconsoled
Pearson, D. Csardas
Pynchon, T. Gravity's rainbow
Sartre, J. P. The reprieve
Sinclair, U. [Lanny Budd series]
Steel, D. Jewels
Wiesel, E. The oath
Winton, T. The riders

Politics
See Politics—Europe

EUROPE, CENTRAL *See* Central Europe

EUROPE, EASTERN *See* Eastern Europe

EUROPEANS

Africa
Forsyth, F. The dogs of war

China
Elegant, R. S. Mandarin

India
Bromfield, L. The rains came

The Europeans. James, H.
also in James, H. The American novels and stories
of Henry James p37-161

The Eustace diamonds. Trollope, A.

The Eustace diamonds [abridged]. Trollope, A.
In Trollope, A. The Pallisers p189-264

EUTHANASIA
Quindlen, A. One true thing

Eva Luna. Allende, I.
Eva Trout. Bowen, E.

EVANGELISTS
Bass, R. Mahatma Joe
Brown, S. French Silk
Leonard, E. Touch
Lester, J. Do Lord remember me
Lewis, S. Elmer Gantry
MacDonald, J. D. One more Sunday
Evening in Byzantium. Shaw, I.
The evening star. McMurtry, L.
The evening wolves. Chase, J.
Ever after. Thane, E.
Evergreen. Plain, B.
Everlasting. Thayer, N.
Everville. Barker, C.
Every brilliant eye. Estleman, L. D.
Every crooked nanny. Trocheck, K. H.
Everything that rises must converge. O'Connor, F.
  also in O'Connor, F. Collected works p481-696
Everything to gain. Bradford, B. T.
Everything you have is mine. Scoppettone, S.
Evidence of blood. Cook, T. H.
Evidence to destroy. Yorke, M.
EVIL *See* Good and evil
Evil under the sun. Christie, A.
  also in Christie, A. Agatha Christie: five complete novels of murder and detection

EVOLUTION
Vonnegut, K. Galápagos

EX-CONVICTS
Abrahams, P. Lights out
Durham, M. The man who loved Cat Dancing
Estleman, L. D. King of the corner
Gill, B. M. Time and time again
Heinlein, R. A. The moon is a harsh mistress
James, P. D. Innocent blood
Leonard, E. Glitz
Leonard, E. Rum punch
Leonard, E. Stick
Maḥfūẓ, N. The thief and the dogs
Oates, J. C. Snake eyes
Phillips, J. A. Shelter
Robards, K. One summer

EX-HUSBANDS *See* Divorced persons

EX-NAZIS *See* National socialism

EX-NUNS
Carroll, J. Prince of peace
Greeley, A. M. Ascent into hell
Leonard, E. Bandits
McInerny, R. M. Leave of absence
Murdoch, I. Nuns and soldiers

EX-PRIESTS
Greeley, A. M. Ascent into hell
An excellent mystery. Peters, E.
Excellent women. Pym, B.
Except for me and thee. West, J.
Except for the bones. Wilcox, C.
The executioner's song. Mailer, N.

EXECUTIONS AND EXECUTIONERS
Doctorow, E. L. The book of Daniel
French, A. Billy
Mailer, N. The executioner's song
Wiesel, E. Dawn
Exile and the kingdom. Camus, A.

EXILES
  See also Refugees
Anthony, E. The relic
Cortázar, J. Hopscotch
Hale, E. E. The man without a country
Puig, M. Eternal curse on the reader of these pages

EXISTENTIALISM
Banville, J. The book of evidence
Barth, J. The end of the road

Beauvoir, S. de. The mandarins
Camus, A. The fall
Maḥfūẓ, N. Adrift on the Nile
Sartre, J. P. The age of reason
Sartre, J. P. Nausea
Sartre, J. P. The reprieve
Sartre, J. P. Troubled sleep
Exit lines. Hill, R.
Exocet. Higgins, J.
Exodus. Uris, L.

EXORCISM
  See also Demoniac possession
Blatty, W. P. The exorcist
The exorcist. Blatty, W. P.

EXPATRIATES *See* Exiles
The expedition of Humphry Clinker. See Smollett, T. G. Humphry Clinker
Expensive habits. Howard, M.
Expensive people. Oates, J. C.

EXPERIMENTAL DRUGS *See* Drugs

EXPERIMENTAL MEDICINE *See* Medicine—Research

EXPERIMENTAL STORIES
  See also Surrealism
Amis, M. Time's arrow
Barnes, J. A history of the world in 10½ chapters
Barth, J. The last voyage of somebody the sailor
Beckett, S. Dream of fair to middling women
Calvino, I. If on a winter's night a traveler
Cortázar, J. Hopscotch
Dixon, S. Interstate
Fuentes, C. Terra nostra
Gaddis, W. A frolic of his own
Gaddis, W. J R
Gaddis, W. The recognitions
García Márquez, G. The autumn of the patriarch
Handke, P. The left-handed woman
Howard, M. Natural history
Joyce, J. Finnegans wake
Joyce, J. A shorter Finnegans wake
Joyce, J. Ulysses
Kesey, K. Sailor song
Kosinski, J. N. The hermit of 69th Street
Naipaul, V. S. A way in the world
Ōe, K. The pinch runner memorandum
Puig, M. Tropical night falling
Pynchon, T. Gravity's rainbow
Walker, A. The temple of my familiar
Wideman, J. E. Philadelphia fire
Wright, R. Lawd today!

EXPERIMENTS, SCIENTIFIC *See* Scientific experiments
Exploit of death. Shannon, D.
Exploration team. Jenkins, W. F.
  In The Hugo winners v1 p95-142

EXPLORERS
Bainbridge, B. The birthday boys
Boyle, T. C. Water music
Forester, C. S. To the Indies
Gilman, C. P. Herland
Poe, E. A. The journal of Julius Rodman
Thom, J. A. The children of first man
Verne, J. Five weeks in a balloon
Exposure. Anthony, E.
Extenuating circumstances. Valin, J.

EXTERMINATION, JEWISH *See* Holocaust, Jewish (1933-1945)

EXTINCT CITIES
  See also Pompeii (Ancient city); Troy (Ancient city)
Whitney, P. A. Domino

EXTORTION
Armstrong, C. The gift shop
Colette. Julie de Carneilhan
Dickens, C. Our mutual friend
Ferrigno, R. The Horse Latitudes

EXTORTION—*Continued*
Gardner, J. E. License renewed
Godey, J. The taking of Pelham one two three
Leonard, E. Freaky Deaky
Leonard, E. LaBrava
Wambaugh, J. The black marble

EXTRASENSORY PERCEPTION
See also Clairvoyance; Telepathy
Anderson, P. The Saturn game
Bradley, M. Z. The house between the worlds
King, S. The dead zone
King, S. The shining
Koontz, D. R. The bad place
Le Guin, U. K. The left hand of darkness
Lessing, D. M. The four-gated city
Lustbader, E. V. Black Blade
May, J. Intervention
Stewart, M. Touch not the cat
Whitney, P. A. Rainbow in the mist
Woods, S. Under the lake
The **eye** in the door. Barker, P.
Eye of cat. Zelazny, R.
The **eye** of the heron. Le Guin, U. K.
Eye of the needle. Follett, K.
Eye of the storm. Higgins, J.
The **eye** of the storm. White, P.
Eyeless in Gaza. Huxley, A.
Eyes of a child. Patterson, R. N.
Eyes of prey. Sandford, J.

EYEWITNESSES *See* Witnesses

F

"**F**" is for fugitive. Grafton, S.
The **Faber** book of gay short fiction. Entered in Part I under title
A **fable**. Faulkner, W.

FABLES
See also Allegories
Maḥfūẓ, N. The harafish
Rushdie, S. Haroun and the sea of stories
The **fabulous** riverboat. Farmer, P. J.

FACE

Abnormalities and deformities
Kellogg, M. Tell me that you love me, Junie Moon
The **face** of a stranger. Perry, A.
The **face** of fear. Koontz, D. R.
In Koontz, D. R. Three complete novels p323-510
The **Face** of the Waters. Silverberg, R.
The **face** of trespass. Rendell, R.

FACTORIES
See also Clothing industry; Labor and laboring classes
Zaroulis, N. L. Call the darkness light

FACULTY (EDUCATION) *See* Teachers
Fahrenheit 451. Bradbury, R.
Fahrenheit 451 [novelette]. Bradbury, R.
In Bradbury, R. Fahrenheit 451 p19-150
Fail-safe. Burdick, E.
A **faint** cold fear. Daley, R.
Fair and tender ladies. Smith, L.
Fair land, fair land. Guthrie, A. B.
Fair stood the wind for France. Bates, H. E.
A **fairly** honourable defeat. Murdoch, I.

FAIRS
Read, Miss. Thrush Green
Updike, J. The poorhouse fair

FAIRY TALES *See* Fantasies
Fairytales. Freeman, C.

FAITH
Butler, R. O. They whisper
Howatch, S. Absolute truths
Howatch, S. Glamorous powers
Howatch, S. Mystical paths
Howatch, S. Scandalous risks
Howatch, S. Ultimate prizes
L'Engle, M. Certain women
Plante, D. Annunciation
Potok, C. I am the clay
Thoene, B. The twilight of courage
Wilson, A. N. The vicar of sorrows
Faith. Deighton, L.

FAITH CURE
Bambara, T. C. The salt eaters
Leonard, E. Touch

FAITH HEALERS *See* Faith cure
A **falcon** flies. See Smith, W. A. Flight of the falcon
A **falcon** for a queen. Gaskin, C.
Falconer. Cheever, J.

FALKLAND ISLANDS WAR, 1982
Higgins, J. Exocet
The **fall**. Camus, A.

FALL CREEK (IND.)

Massacre, 1824
West, J. The massacre at Fall Creek
Fall from grace. Greeley, A. M.
A **fall** of moondust. Clarke, A. C.
A **fall** of princes. Tarr, J.
The **fallen** curtain and other stories. Rendell, R.
In Rendell, R. Collected stories p1-135
Fallen into the pit. Peters, E.
Falling in place. Beattie, A.
Falling star. Moyes, P.
In Moyes, P. Murder by 3's p542-789
Falls the shadow. Penman, S. K.

FALSE ACCUSATION
Abrahams, P. Lights out
Baldwin, J. If Beale Street could talk
Eliot, G. Silas Marner
Freedman, J. F. The obstacle course
Gaines, E. J. A lesson before dying
Greenberg, J. No reck'ning made
Hamilton, J. A map of the world
Holt, V. The black opal
Katkov, N. Blood & orchids
Lee, H. To kill a mockingbird
Malamud, B. The fixer
Robards, K. One summer
Sholem Aleichem. The bloody hoax
Snow, C. P. The affair
Tey, J. The Franchise affair
Wilder, T. The eighth day
False conception. Greenleaf, S.
False dawn. Wharton, E.
In Wharton, E. Old New York
The **false** Inspector Dew. Lovesey, P.
False prophet. Kellerman, F.
False scent. Marsh, Dame N.
False witness. Uhnak, D.

FAME
Childress, M. Tender
Families and survivors. Adams, A.
Family. Gold, H.
A **family** affair. Stout, R.
Family and friends. Brookner, A.
Family blessings. Spencer, L.

FAMILY CHRONICLES
See also Family life
Adams, A. Caroline's daughters
Adler, E. Legacy of secrets
Aldrich, B. S. A lantern in her hand
Allende, I. The house of the spirits
Anthony, E. The house of Vandekar
Archer, J. As the crow flies
Auchincloss, L. Portrait in brownstone
Baldwin, J. Go tell it on the mountain
Battle, L. Southern women

FAMILY CHRONICLES—*Continued*

Birmingham, S. The Auerbach will
Birmingham, S. Carriage trade
Birmingham, S. The LeBaron secret
Blasco Ibáñez, V. The four horsemen of the Apocalypse
Böll, H. Billiards at half-past nine
Boyle, T. C. World's end
Bradford, B. T. Act of will
Breslin, J. Table money
Bromfield, L. Mrs. Parkington
Brown, D. A. Creek Mary's blood
Burgess, A. Any old iron
Butler, S. The way of all flesh
Carr, R. Woman's own
Carter, A. Wise children
Chase, J. During the reign of the Queen of Persia
Cheever, J. The Wapshot chronicle
Cheever, J. The Wapshot scandal
Coleman, L. Beulah Land
Coleman, L. The legacy of Beulah Land
Coleman, L. Look away, Beulah Land
Cookson, C. The Maltese Angel
Davenport, K. Shark dialogues
Davies, R. The manticore
Davies, R. Murther & walking spirits
Dawson, C. Body of knowledge
De Blasis, C. The proud breed
De Blasis, C. A season for Swans
De Blasis, C. Swan's chance
De la Roche, M. The building of Jalna
De la Roche, M. Centenary at Jalna
De la Roche, M. Jalna
Delderfield, R. F. Give us this day
Delderfield, R. F. God is an Englishman
Delderfield, R. F. The green gauntlet
Delderfield, R. F. A horseman riding by
Delderfield, R. F. Theirs was the kingdom
Dorris, M. A yellow raft in blue water
Du Maurier, Dame D. Hungry Hill
Dunne, D. A season in purgatory
Dunnett, D. Niccolò rising
Dunnett, D. Race of scorpions
Dunnett, D. The spring of the ram
Eden, D. The Salamanca drum
Edgarian, C. Rise the Euphrates
Elegant, R. S. Dynasty
Elegant, R. S. Mandarin
Fairbairns, Z. Stand we at last
Fast, H. The establishment
Fast, H. The immigrants
Fast, H. The immigrant's daughter
Fast, H. The legacy
Fast, H. Second generation
Faulkner, W. Flags in the dust
Faulkner, W. Sartoris
Ferber, E. Ice Palace
Ferber, E. Show boat
Follett, K. A dangerous fortune
Freeman, C. No time for tears
Galsworthy, J. End of the chapter
Galsworthy, J. The Forsyte saga
Galsworthy, J. The man of property
Galsworthy, J. A modern comedy
Garcia, C. Dreaming in Cuban
García Márquez, G. One hundred years of solitude
Gardner, J. E. The secret families
Gardner, J. E. The secret generations
Gardner, J. E. The secret houses
Gaskin, C. The charmed circle
Gibbons, K. Charms for the easy life
Glasgow, E. Vein of iron
Godden, R. China Court
Goldreich, G. Leah's children
Graham, W. The angry tide
Graham, W. The four swans
Graham, W. The loving cup
Graham, W. The miller's dance

Graham, W. The stranger from the sea
Graham, W. The twisted sword
Grau, S. A. The condor passes
Grau, S. A. The keepers of the house
Greeley, A. M. Lord of the dance
Gross, J. The books of Rachel
Halter, M. The book of Abraham
Hawthorne, N. The House of the Seven Gables
Hijuelos, O. The fourteen sisters of Emilio Montez O'Brien
Hill, R. B. Hanta yo
Howard, E. J. Confusion
Howard, E. J. The light years
Howard, E. J. Marking time
Howard, M. Natural history
Howatch, S. Cashelmara
Howatch, S. Penmarric
Howatch, S. The wheel of fortune
Humphrey, W. The Ordways
Hunter, E. The Chisholms
Isaacs, S. Almost paradise
Jakes, J. Heaven and hell
Jakes, J. Homeland
Jakes, J. Love and war
Jakes, J. North and South
Jennings, G. Aztec
Kells, S. The aristocrats
Kennedy, W. Very old bones
Kesey, K. Sometimes a great notion
Krantz, J. Mistral's daughter
Krantz, J. Till we meet again
Laker, R. To dance with kings
L'Amour, L. The Sacketts: beginnings of a dynasty
Lawrence, D. H. The rainbow
L'Engle, M. Certain women
Lofts, N. Bless this house
Lofts, N. The haunting of Gad's Hall
Lofts, N. The house at Old Vine
Lofts, N. The old priory
Lofts, N. The town house
Lord, B. B. Spring Moon
Mahfūz, N. The harafish
Mahfūz, N. Palace of desire
Mahfūz, N. Palace walk
Mahfūz, N. Sugar Street
Mann, T. Buddenbrooks
Marquand, J. P. The late George Apley
Martin, W. Cape Cod
McCorkle, J. Tending to Virginia
McCullough, C. The thorn birds
Michener, J. A. Chesapeake
Michener, J. A. Mexico
Michener, J. A. Poland
Miller, S. Family pictures
Morrison, T. Song of Solomon
Nabokov, V. V. Ada
Naylor, G. Linden Hills
Ng, F. M. Bone
Oates, J. C. Bellefleur
Orde, L. Dreams of gold
Parker, R. B. All our yesterdays
Pearce, M. E. Apple tree lean down
Pearce, M. E. The old house at Railes
Pearson, D. Csardas
Pilcher, R. September
Pilcher, R. The shell seekers
Plain, B. Evergreen
Plain, B. The golden cup
Plain, B. Harvest
Plain, B. Random winds
Plain, B. Tapestry
Porter, C. R. All-Bright Court
Price, E. Before the darkness falls
Price, E. Savannah
Price, E. Stranger in Savannah
Price, E. To see your face again
Rawlings, M. K. The sojourner
Richler, M. Solomon Gursky was here

FAMILY CHRONICLES—*Continued*

Ross-Macdonald, M. For they shall inherit
Ross-Macdonald, M. The rich are with you always
Ross-Macdonald, M. A woman scorned
Ross-Macdonald, M. The world from rough stones
Rushdie, S. Shame
Rutherfurd, E. Russka
Rutherfurd, E. Sarum
Scott, Sir W. The bride of Lammermoor
Seth, V. A suitable boy
Shange, N. Betsey Brown
Shaw, I. Beggarman, thief
Shaw, I. Rich man, poor man
Sheldon, S. Master of the game
Shreve, S. R. Daughters of the new world
Siddons, A. R. Colony
Simpson, M. Anywhere but here
Singer, I. B. The family Moskat
Smith, L. The devil's dream
Smith, L. Family linen
Smith, L. Oral history
Smith, W. A. The angels weep
Stegner, W. E. Angle of repose
Steinbeck, J. East of Eden
Stevenson, D. E. Celia's house
Stevenson, R. L. The master of Ballantrae
Stewart, F. M. The glitter and the gold
Streshinsky, S. Hers the kingdom
Swindells, M. Summer harvest
Tarkington, B. The magnificent Ambersons
Tennenbaum, S. Yesterday's streets
Thackeray, W. M. The Virginians
Thane, E. Dawn's early light
Thane, E. Ever after
Thane, E. Homing
Thane, E. Kissing kin
Thane, E. The light heart
Thane, E. This was tomorrow
Thane, E. Yankee stranger
Thomas, M. M. Hanover Place
Tryon, T. In the fire of spring
Tryon, T. The wings of the morning
Tyler, A. Dinner at the Homesick Restaurant
Tyler, A. Searching for Caleb
Uhnak, D. Law and order
Undset, S. Kristin Lavransdatter
Undset, S. The master of Hestviken
Uris, L. Trinity
Urquhart, J. Away
Van Slyke, H. No love lost
Viertel, J. Life lines
Welty, E. Losing battles
West, D. The wedding
Wood, B. Green City in the sun
Woolf, V. The years
Zaroulis, N. L. Massachusetts

FAMILY CURSES

Caldwell, T. Captains and kings
Hawthorne, N. The House of the Seven Gables
Holt, V. Bride of Pendorric
Smith, L. Oral history
Wood, B. The dreaming
Family games. Stubbs, J.
Family happiness. Colwin, L.
Family happiness. Tolstoy, L., graf
In Tolstoy, L. The Kreutzer sonata, The Devil, and other tales
In Tolstoy, L. The short novels of Tolstoy

FAMILY LIFE

See also Aunts; Brothers; Brothers and sisters; Family chronicles; Fathers; Fathers and sons; Grandchildren; Granddaughters; Grandfathers; Grandmothers; Half-brothers; Half-sisters; Marriage; Marriage problems; Mothers and daughters; Mothers and sons; Mothers-in-law; Nephews; Nieces; Parent and child; Sisters; Stepchildren; Stepdaughters; Stepfathers; Stepmothers; Stepsons; Twins; Uncles

Agee, J. A death in the family

Aiken, J. Morningquest
Aldrich, B. S. A lantern in her hand
Allende, I. The house of the spirits
Allison, D. Bastard out of Carolina
Alvarez, J. How the Garcia girls lost their accents
Amis, K. The folks that live on the hill
Anderson, S. Tar: a midwest childhood
Appelfeld, A. The age of wonders
Archer, J. The prodigal daughter
Auchincloss, L. Honorable men
Auchincloss, L. Portrait in brownstone
Austen, J. Emma
Austen, J. Mansfield Park
Austen, J. Northanger Abbey
Austen, J. Sense and sensibility
Baldwin, J. Just above my head
Balzac, H. de. Cousin Bette
Bassani, G. The garden of the Finzi-Continis
Bausch, R. Rare & endangered species
Bausch, R. Rebel powers
Beattie, A. Falling in place
Beauvoir, S. de. Les belles images
Bellow, S. Henderson the rain king
Bellow, S. Mr. Sammler's planet
Berger, T. The feud
Berger, T. The houseguest
Berger, T. Reinhart's women
Berger, T. Vital parts
Bermant, C. The patriarch
Binchy, M. Firefly summer
Binchy, M. Silver wedding
Boswell, R. Mystery ride
Bowen, E. The death of the heart
Bradbury, R. Dandelion wine
Bradford, B. T. Hold the dream
Bradford, B. T. To be the best
Bradford, R. Red sky at morning
Briskin, J. Dreams are not enough
Briskin, J. Paloverde
Bromfield, L. Mrs. Parkington
Brookner, A. Family and friends
Brown, C. Down all the days
Brown, R. Before and after
Brown, R. Civil wars
Buck, P. S. Dragon seed
Buck, P. S. The good earth
Buck, P. S. Pavilion of women
Buck, P. S. Sons
Busch, F. Closing arguments
Caldwell, T. Captains and kings
Card, O. S. Lost boys
Casey, J. Spartina
Chase, J. During the reign of the Queen of Persia
Chase, J. The evening wolves
Cheever, J. Bullet Park
Chute, C. The Beans of Egypt, Maine
Cleary, J. The sundowners
Colwin, L. A big storm knocked it over
Colwin, L. Family happiness
Connell, E. S. Mr. Bridge
Connell, E. S. Mrs. Bridge
Conroy, P. The prince of tides
Corman, A. Prized possessions
Crichton, R. The Camerons
Cronin, A. J. A song of sixpence
De la Roche, M. The building of Jalna
De la Roche, M. Centenary at Jalna
De la Roche, M. Jalna
Delderfield, R. F. Give us this day
Delderfield, R. F. God is an Englishman
Delderfield, R. F. The green gauntlet
Delderfield, R. F. A horseman riding by
Delderfield, R. F. Theirs was the kingdom
DeLillo, D. White noise
Demetz, H. The house on Prague Street
Desai, A. Clear light of day
Dew, R. F. Fortunate lives
Doig, I. Dancing at the Rascal Fair

FAMILY LIFE—*Continued*

Doig, I. English Creek
Donoso, J. A house in the country
Doyle, R. Paddy Clarke, ha ha ha
Drabble, M. The realms of gold
Du Maurier, Dame D. The scapegoat
Duncan, D. J. The brothers K
Eden, D. The vines of Yarrabee
Eliot, G. The mill on the Floss
Fast, H. April morning
Faulkner, W. As I lay dying
Faulkner, W. Flags in the dust
Faulkner, W. The mansion
Faulkner, W. Sartoris
Faulkner, W. The sound and the fury
Faulkner, W. The town
Ferber, E. So Big
Forster, E. M. Howards End
Fox, P. A servant's tale
Freeman, C. The last princess
Galsworthy, J. The Forsyte saga
Gardner, J. October light
Gaskin, C. The ambassador's women
Glasgow, E. In this our life
Glasgow, E. Vein of iron
Godwin, G. A mother and two daughters
Godwin, G. A Southern family
Gold, H. Family
Gold, H. Fathers
Goldreich, G. Four days
Goldreich, G. Leah's journey
Goldreich, G. That year of our war
Goldsmith, O. The Vicar of Wakefield
Gordon, M. The other side
Goudge, E. Blessing in disguise
Goudge, E. The bird in the tree
Goudge, E. The heart of the family
Goudge, E. Pilgrim's inn
Greenberg, J. In this sign
Greenberg, J. A season of delight
Greenberg, J. Simple gifts
Guest, J. Ordinary people
Hailey, E. F. Home free
Hailey, E. F. Joanna's husband and David's wife
Hailey, E. F. A woman of independent means
Hamilton, J. A map of the world
Hamner, E. The homecoming
Hamner, E. Spencer's Mountain
Head, A. Mr. & Mrs. Bo Jo Jones
Heller, J. Good as Gold
Heller, J. Something happened
Hill, P. Vollands
Hilton, J. Random harvest
Hoffman, A. At risk
Hoffman, A. Second nature
Hood, A. Places to stay the night
Horowitz, E. Plain Jane
Howatch, S. Sins of the fathers
Hughes, L. Not without laughter
Humphreys, J. Rich in love
Irving, J. The Hotel New Hampshire
Irving, J. The world according to Garp
Jewett, S. O. The country of the pointed firs
Jones, D. C. Elkhorn Tavern
Jones, D. C. This savage race
Kafka, F. Metamorphosis
Kaufman, S. Diary of a mad housewife
King, S. Pet sematary
Krantz, J. I'll take Manhattan
Laker, R. The silver touch
Lawrence, D. H. The white peacock
Leavitt, D. The lost language of cranes
Lee, C. Y. The flower drum song
Lee, G. Honor & duty
L'Engle, M. The other side of the sun
Lessing, D. M. The four-gated city
Lin, Y. Moment in Peking
Llewellyn, R. How green was my valley

Maḥfūz, N. The beginning and the end
Maitland, S. Ancestral truths
Marquand, J. P. H. M. Pulham, esquire
Marshall, C. Julie
Mason, B. A. Feather crowns
Mason, B. A. In country
McCabe, P. The butcher boy
McCauley, S. The easy way out
McCorkle, J. Ferris Beach
McCullers, C. The member of the wedding
McCullough, C. The thorn birds
McDermott, A. At weddings and wakes
McFarland, D. The music room
Meredith, G. The ordeal of Richard Feverel
Michael, J. Sleeping beauty
Minot, S. Folly
Minot, S. Monkeys
Mitford, N. Love in a cold climate
Mitford, N. The pursuit of love
Moberg, V. The emigrants
Moberg, V. The last letter home
Moberg, V. Unto a good land
Morrison, T. Song of Solomon
Mortimer, J. C. Paradise postponed
Mortimer, J. C. Summer's lease
Murdoch, I. A fairly honourable defeat
Naipaul, V. S. A house for Mr. Biswas
Oates, J. C. A Bloodsmoor romance
Oates, J. C. Expensive people
Oates, J. C. Them
Oates, J. C. You must remember this
O'Connor, E. All in the family
Ogilvie, E. Jennie Glenroy
O'Hara, J. Ten North Frederick
Olsen, T. Yonnondio: from the thirties
Paton, A. Too late the phalarope
Payne, D. Ruin Creek
Pearce, M. E. The land endures
Pearson, D. The summer of the Barshinskeys
Peck, R. N. A day no pigs would die
Phillips, J. A. Machine dreams
Pilcher, R. Voices in summer
Plain, B. Evergreen
Plain, B. Harvest
Plain, B. Tapestry
Plain, B. Whispers
Potok, C. Davita's harp
Potok, C. In the beginning
Potok, C. My name is Asher Lev
Powers, J. R. The junk-drawer corner-store front-porch blues
Price, E. Beauty from ashes
Price, E. Before the darkness falls
Price, E. Margaret's story
Price, E. Stranger in Savannah
Price, E. Where shadows go
Price, R. The promise of rest
Prose, F. Household saints
Proulx, A. Postcards
Quindlen, A. Object lessons
Rawlings, M. K. The sojourner
Reid Banks, L. The warning bell
Rice, L. Blue moon
Richter, C. The awakening land
Richter, C. The fields
Richter, C. The grandfathers
Richter, C. The town
Roiphe, A. R. Up the sandbox!
Rölvaag, O. E. Giants in the earth
Rölvaag, O. E. Peder Victorious
Rossner, J. Emmeline
Roth, H. Call it sleep
Roth, H. A star shines over Mt. Morris Park
Russell, P. Sea of tranquillity
Russo, R. Nobody's fool
Salinger, J. D. Franny and Zooey
Salinger, J. D. Raise high the roof beam, carpenters, and Seymour: an introduction

FAMILY LIFE—*Continued*
Saroyan, W. The human comedy
Schwartz, L. S. Disturbances in the field
Settle, M. L. Charley Bland
Shaw, I. Bread upon the waters
Shields, D. Dead languages
Siddons, A. R. Peachtree Road
Sinclair, A. Coffee will make you black
Singer, I. B. The estate
Singer, I. B. The family Moskat
Singer, I. B. The manor
Smiley, J. A thousand acres
Smith, B. Maggie-Now
Smith, B. A tree grows in Brooklyn
Smith, R. K. Jane's house
Snow, C. P. The conscience of the rich
Snow, C. P. Last things
Snow, C. P. Time of hope
Spencer, L. Family blessings
Spencer, L. Home song
Spencer, S. Endless love
Stead, C. The man who loved children
Steel, D. Accident
Steel, D. The gift
Stegner, W. E. The Big Rock Candy Mountain
Steinbeck, J. The grapes of wrath
Stevenson, D. E. Celia's house
Stone, I. Those who love
Straight, S. Blacker than a thousand midnights
Struther, J. Mrs. Miniver
Stubbs, J. Family games
Stubbs, J. Like we used to be
Styron, W. Lie down in darkness
Tarkington, B. Alice Adams
Tarkington, B. Seventeen
Taylor, P. H. A summons to Memphis
Tennant, E. An unequal marriage
Tilly, M. Singing songs
Townsend, S. The Adrian Mole diaries
Trevor, W. The silence in the garden
Trollope, A. The Duke's children
Trollope, A. Phineas Redux
Trollope, J. The men and the girls
Trollope, J. The rector's wife
Tryon, T. The other
Turow, S. The burden of proof
Twain, M. The adventures of Tom Sawyer
Tyler, A. Breathing lessons
Tyler, A. The clock winder
Tyler, A. Dinner at the Homesick Restaurant
Tyler, A. Earthly possessions
Tyler, A. Morgan's passing
Tyler, A. Saint maybe
Tyler, A. The tin can tree
Updike, J. Of the farm
Updike, J. Rabbit at rest
Updike, J. Rabbit is rich
Vida, N. Goodbye, Saigon
Weidman, J. I can get it for you wholesale
Welty, E. Delta wedding
Welty, E. Losing battles
Welty, E. The optimist's daughter
West, J. Cress Delahanty
West, J. Except for me and thee
West, J. The friendly persuasion
West, J. The state of Stony Lonesome
West, Dame R. The fountain overflows
Wharton, E. The children
White, P. The tree of man
Whitney, P. A. The trembling hills
Wilder, T. The eighth day
Williams, B. A. House divided
Williams, B. A. The unconquered
Wolfe, T. Look homeward, angel
Woodson, J. Autobiography of a family photo
Woolf, V. To the lighthouse
Wouk, H. Inside, outside
Wouk, H. Marjorie Morningstar

Family linen. Smith, L.
A family madness. Keneally, T.
Family money. Bawden, N.
The family Moskat. Singer, I. B.
Family pictures. Miller, S.

FAMILY REUNIONS
Stubbs, J. Family games
A family romance. See Brookner, A. Dolly
Family secrets. Thayer, N.
Family trade. Carroll, J.

FAMINES
Buck, P. S. The good earth
The famous DAR murder mystery. Landrum, G.

Famous ghost stories. Entered in Part I under title
Famous tales of Sherlock Holmes. Doyle, Sir A. C.
A fanatic heart. O'Brien, E.

FANATICISM
Boyle, T. C. Road to Wellville
DeLillo, D. Libra
Finney, P. Firedrake's eye
Heinlein, R. A. Job: a comedy of justice
King, S. Insomnia
Plaidy, J. The scarlet cloak

FANATICS See Fanaticism
Fanshawe. Hawthorne, N.
  In Hawthorne, N. The complete novels and selected
    tales of Nathaniel Hawthorne

FANTASIES
  See also Allegories; End of the world; Experimental
    stories; Future; Science fiction; Utopias
Adams, R. Watership Down
After the king
Anthony, P. And eternity
Anthony, P. Bearing an hourglass
Anthony, P. Being a green mother
Anthony, P. Blue Adept
Anthony, P. Chaos mode
Anthony, P. For love of evil
Anthony, P. Fractal mode
Anthony, P. Juxtaposition
Anthony, P. Killobyte
Anthony, P. On a pale horse
Anthony, P. Out of Phaze
Anthony, P. Phaze doubt
Anthony, P. Robot Adept
Anthony, P. Split infinity
Anthony, P. Unicorn point
Anthony, P. Virtual mode
Anthony, P. Wielding a red sword
Anthony, P. With a tangled skein
Ballard, J. G. The unlimited dream company
Barker, C. Everville
Barker, C. The great and secret show
Barker, C. Imajica
Barker, C. Weaveworld
Barth, J. The last voyage of somebody the sailor
Beagle, P. S. A fine and private place
Beagle, P. S. The innkeeper's song
Beagle, P. S. The last unicorn
Berger, T. Being invisible
The Best from Fantasy & Science Fiction: a 40th
    anniversary anthology
The Best from Fantasy & Science Fiction: a 45th
    anniversary anthology
The Best from Fantasy and Science Fiction: a special
    25th anniversary anthology
Black thorn, white rose
Boucher, A. The compleat werewolf and other stories
    of fantasy and science fiction
Bradbury, R. Something wicked this way comes
Bradley, M. Z. Black Trillium
Bradley, M. Z. The forest house
Bradley, M. Z. The house between the worlds
Bradley, M. Z. The mists of Avalon
Brooks, T. The black unicorn
Brooks, T. The druid of Shannara

FANTASIES—*Continued*

Brooks, T. The elfqueen of Shannara
Brooks, T. The Elfstones of Shannara
Brooks, T. Magic kingdom for sale—sold!
Brooks, T. The scions of Shannara
Brooks, T. The sword of Shannara
Brooks, T. The talismans of Shannara
Brooks, T. The Tangle Box
Brooks, T. The wishsong of Shannara
Brooks, T. Wizard at large
Cabell, J. B. Jurgen: a comedy of justice
Calvino, I. Cosmicomics
Calvino, I. Invisible cities
Capote, T. The grass harp
Card, O. S. Alvin Journeyman
Card, O. S. Prentice Alvin
Card, O. S. Red prophet
Card, O. S. Seventh son
Chayefsky, P. Altered states
Cherryh, C. J. Chernevog
Cherryh, C. J. Yvgenie
Chesterton, G. K. The man who was Thursday
Davies, R. Murther & walking spirits
Davies, V. Miracle on 34th Street
De Lint, C. Memory and dream
Dickens, C. The cricket on the hearth
Dickson, G. R. The dragon at war
Dickson, G. R. The dragon knight
Dickson, G. R. The dragon on the border
Dickson, G. R. The dragon, the Earl, and the troll
Donaldson, S. R. The Illearth war
Donaldson, S. R. Lord Foul's bane
Donaldson, S. R. The One Tree
Donaldson, S. R. The power that preserves
Donaldson, S. R. White gold wielder
Donaldson, S. R. The wounded Land
Eddings, D. Belgarath the sorcerer
Eddings, D. Demon lord of Karanda
Eddings, D. The diamond throne
Eddings, D. Domes of fire
Eddings, D. Guardians of the west
Eddings, D. The hidden city
Eddings, D. King of the Murgos
Eddings, D. The ruby knight
Eddings, D. The sapphire rose
Eddings, D. The seeress of Kell
Eddings, D. The shining ones
Eddings, D. Sorceress of Darshiva
Ellison, H. Adrift just off the Islets of Langerhans:
  latitude 38° 54' N, longitude 77° 00' 13 W
Feist, R. E. Mistress of the empire
Feist, R. E. Servant of the empire
Feist, R. E. Shadow of a dark queen
Genet, J. Our Lady of the Flowers
Gilman, C. P. Herland
Golding, W. The scorpion god
Goldman, W. The princess bride
Grass, G. The flounder
Haggard, H. R. She
Helprin, M. Winter's tale
Hesse, H. The glass bead game (Magister Ludi)
Hilton, J. Lost horizon
Hoban, R. Turtle diary
Hudson, W. H. Green mansions
Huxley, A. Island
Jones, D. W. A sudden wild magic
Kafka, F. Amerika
King, S. The stand
King, S. The talisman
Kurtz, K. The harrowing of Gwynedd
Kurtz, K. The quest for Saint Camber
Lackey, M. Winds of change
Lackey, M. Winds of fate
Lackey, M. Winds of fury
Larsen, J. Silk road
Le Guin, U. K. The beginning place
Le Guin, U. K. Orsinian tales
Leiber, F. Gonna roll the bones

Leslie, J. A. C. The ghost and Mrs. Muir
Levin, I. The Stepford wives
Lewis, C. S. Out of the silent planet
Lewis, C. S. Perelandra
Lewis, C. S. That hideous strength
Llywelyn, M. The elementals
Llywelyn, M. Red Branch
Mahfūz, N. Arabian nights and days
May, J. The adversary
May, J. Blood Trillium
May, J. The golden torc
May, J. The many-colored land
May, J. The nonborn king
McCaffrey, A. All the Weyrs of Pern
McCaffrey, A. The chronicles of Pern
McCaffrey, A. Crystal line
McCaffrey, A. Crystal singer
McCaffrey, A. The dolphins of Pern
McCaffrey, A. Dragonflight
McCaffrey, A. Dragonquest
McCaffrey, A. Dragonrider
McCaffrey, A. Dragonsdawn
McCaffrey, A. The girl who heard dragons
McCaffrey, A. Killashandra
McCaffrey, A. The renegades of Pern
McCaffrey, A. The white dragon
McIntyre, V. N. Of mist, and grass, and sand
McKillip, P. A. The Cygnet and the firebird
McKillip, P. A. The sorceress and the Cygnet
Miller, W. M. A canticle for Leibowitz
Moorcock, M. An alien heat
Moorcock, M. The end of all songs
Moorcock, M. The hollow lands
Moorcock, M. The revenge of the rose
Nabokov, V. V. Pale fire
Nathan, R. Portrait of Jennie
Norton, A. The elvenbane
Norton, A. Elvenblood
Norton, A. Empire of the eagle
Norton, A. Golden Trillium
Norton, A. The hands of Lyr
Norton, A. The mark of the cat
Orwell, G. Animal farm
The Oxford book of modern fairy tales
Piercy, M. Woman on the edge of time
Prose, F. Bigfoot dreams
Rand, A. Atlas shrugged
Robbins, T. Jitterbug perfume
Rushdie, S. The satanic verses
Saberhagen, F. The first book of lost swords: Wound-
  healer's story
Saberhagen, F. The second book of lost swords: Sight-
  blinder's story
Saberhagen, F. The third book of lost swords:
  Stonecutter's story
Saberhagen, F. The fourth book of lost swords: Fars-
  layer's story
Saberhagen, F. The fifth book of lost swords:
  Coinspinner's story
Saberhagen, F. The sixth book of lost swords: Mind-
  sword's story
Saberhagen, F. The seventh book of lost swords: Way-
  finder's story
Saberhagen, F. The last book of swords: Shield-
  breaker's story
Saint, H. F. Memoirs of an invisible man
Saint-Exupéry, A. de. The little prince
Silverberg, R. Gilgamesh the king
Silverberg, R. Lord Valentine's castle
Silverberg, R. Majipoor chronicles
Silverberg, R. Valentine Pontifex
Snow white, blood red
Spark, M. The ballad of Peckham Rye
Steinbeck, J. The short reign of Pippin IV
Swift, J. Gulliver's travels
Tales of the Witch World [1]-3
Tarr, J. A fall of princes
Tarr, J. The golden horn

FANTASIES—*Continued*

Tarr, J. The hall of the mountain king
Tarr, J. The Hounds of God
Tarr, J. The isle of glass
Tarr, J. The lady of Han-Gilen
Tepper, S. S. A plague of angels
Tolkien, J. R. R. The book of lost tales
Tolkien, J. R. R. The fellowship of the ring
Tolkien, J. R. R. The hobbit
Tolkien, J. R. R. The lord of the rings
Tolkien, J. R. R. The return of the king
Tolkien, J. R. R. The Silmarillion
Tolkien, J. R. R. The two towers
Tolkien, J. R. R. Unfinished tales of Númenor and Middle-earth
Twain, M. A Connecticut Yankee in King Arthur's court
Vinge, J. D. The Snow Queen
Vinge, J. D. The Summer Queen
Vonnegut, K. Cat's cradle
Vonnegut, K. Slapstick
Welty, E. The robber bridegroom
Westlake, D. E. Humans
White, T. H. The book of Merlyn
White, T. H. The once and future king
White, T. H. The sword in the stone
White, T. H. The witch in the wood
Wibberley, L. The mouse that roared
Wilhelm, K. And the angels sing
Wolfe, G. Castleview
Wolfe, G. The Citadel of the Autarch
Wolfe, G. The claw of the conciliator
Wolfe, G. The shadow of the torturer
Wolfe, G. The sword of the Lictor
Wolfe, G. The Urth of the new sun
Woolf, V. Orlando
Yarbro, C. Q. A candle for D'Artagnan
Yarbro, C. Q. Crusader's torch
The Year's best fantasy and horror
Yolen, J. Briar Rose
Yolen, J. Sister Light, Sister Dark
Yolen, J. White Jenna
Zelazny, R. Blood of Amber
Zelazny, R. Bring me the head of Prince Charming
Zelazny, R. The courts of chaos
Zelazny, R. The guns of Avalon
Zelazny, R. The hand of Oberon
Zelazny, R. Knight of shadows
Zelazny, R. A night in the lonesome October
Zelazny, R. Nine princes in Amber
Zelazny, R. Prince of chaos
Zelazny, R. Sign of chaos
Zelazny, R. Sign of the unicorn
Zelazny, R. Trumps of doom

FANTASTIC FICTION *See* Fantasies; Science fiction
Fantastic voyage. Asimov, I.
Fantastic voyage II. Asimov, I.
The **far** canyon. Kelton, E.
A **far** cry from Kensington. Spark, M.
FAR EAST *See* East Asia
Far from the madding crowd. Hardy, T.
The **far** pavilions. Kaye, M. M.
The **far** side of victory. Greenberg, J.
Far Tortuga. Matthiessen, P.
The **faraway** drums. Cleary, J.
Farewell, my lovely. Chandler, R.
  In Chandler, R. Stories and early novels p765-984
A **farewell** to arms. Hemingway, E.
Farewell to Fairacre. Read, Miss
Farewell to my concubine. Li, P.-H.

FARM LIFE
  See also Peasant life; Women in agriculture
Arkansas
Jones, D. C. Elkhorn Tavern
Australia
White, P. The tree of man

California
Norris, F. The octopus
China
Buck, P. S. Dragon seed
Buck, P. S. The good earth
Denmark
Andersen Nexø, M. Pelle the conqueror: v1 Childhood
England
Hardy, T. Far from the madding crowd
Lawrence, D. H. The white peacock
Pearce, M. E. Apple tree lean down
Pearce, M. E. The land endures
Illinois
Ferber, E. So Big
Iowa
Boswell, R. Mystery ride
Smiley, J. A thousand acres
Waller, R. J. The bridges of Madison County
Kentucky
Mason, B. A. Feather crowns
Mason, B. A. Spence + Lila
Kenya
Ruark, R. Something of value
Minnesota
Clark, M. H. A cry in the night
Nebraska
Cather, W. O pioneers!
Cather, W. One of ours
New England
Wharton, E. Ethan Frome
New Hampshire
Benét, S. V. The Devil and Daniel Webster
New York (State)
Rawlings, M. K. The sojourner
North Dakota
Bojer, J. The emigrants
Norway
Undset, S. Kristin Lavransdatter
Undset, S. The master of Hestviken
Ohio
Chase, J. During the reign of the Queen of Persia
Pennsylvania
Updike, J. Of the farm
South Africa
Lessing, D. M. The grass is singing
South Dakota
Rölvaag, O. E. Giants in the earth
Rölvaag, O. E. Peder Victorious
Sweden
Moberg, V. The emigrants
Vermont
Gardner, J. October light
Peck, R. N. A day no pigs would die
Proulx, A. Postcards
Virginia
Glasgow, E. Barren ground
Shreve, S. R. A country of strangers
Wales
Llewellyn, R. Green, green, my valley now
Western States
Stegner, W. E. The Big Rock Candy Mountain
Wisconsin
Hamilton, J. A map of the world

FARM TENANCY *See* Tenant farming

FARMERS *See* Farm life

Farriers' Lane. Perry, A.

Farslayer's story. See Saberhagen, F. The fourth book of lost swords: Farslayer's story

FASCISM

    See also Communism; Dictators; National socialism; Totalitarianism

    De Bernières, L. Corelli's mandolin

Italy

Bassani, G. The garden of the Finzi-Continis

Silone, I. Bread and wine

United States

Lewis, S. It can't happen here

The fashion in shrouds. Allingham, M.

    In Allingham, M. Three cases for Mr. Campion p9-255

FASHION INDUSTRY AND TRADE

    Freeman, C. Always and forever

    Goldsmith, O. Fashionably late

    Laker, R. Banners of silk

    Marsh, J. The House of Eliott

FASHION MODELS

    Brown, S. French Silk

Fashionably late. Goldsmith, O.

Fast and loose. Wharton, E.

    In Wharton, E. Fast and loose and The buccaneers p1-111

Fast and loose and The buccaneers. Wharton, E.

A fatal advent. Holland, I.

A fatal attachment. Barnard, R.

Fatal cure. Cook, R.

A fatal inversion. Vine, B.

FATE AND FATALISM

    Anthony, P. With a tangled skein

    García Márquez, G. Chronicle of a death foretold

    Ôe, K. The silent cry

    Wilder, T. The bridge of San Luis Rey

Fate worse than death. Radley, S.

Father Abraham. Faulkner, W.

Father and son. Maas, P.

Father Brown mystery stories. Chesterton, G. K.

The Father Brown omnibus. Chesterton, G. K.

The father hunt. Stout, R.

Father Melancholy's daughter. Godwin, G.

Father of the bride. Streeter, E.

Father Sergius. Tolstoy, L., graf

    In Tolstoy, L. The Kreutzer sonata, The Devil, and other tales

Fatherland. Harris, R.

FATHERS

    See also Fathers and daughters; Fathers and sons; Stepfathers

    Banks, R. Affliction

    Dickens, C. Hard times

    Glasgow, E. In this our life

Fathers. Gold, H.

Fathers and children. See Turgenev, I. S. Fathers and sons

FATHERS AND DAUGHTERS

    See also Fathers and sons; Parent and child

    Atwood, M. Surfacing

    Balzac, H. de. Eugénie Grandet

    Balzac, H. de. Old Goriot

    Bellow, S. Mr. Sammler's planet

    Boswell, R. Mystery ride

    Brown, J. D. Addie Pray

    Burgess, A. The pianoplayers

    Carr, P. The black swan

    Chase, J. The evening wolves

    Clark, M. H. I'll be seeing you

    Conrad, J. Almayer's folly

    Cookson, C. The Maltese Angel

    Coulter, C. Impulse

    Davis, T. 1959

De Bernières, L. Corelli's mandolin

Dickens, C. Dombey and Son

Dixon, S. Interstate

Doig, I. Ride with me, Mariah Montana

Follett, K. The man from St. Petersburg

Galsworthy, J. The silver spoon

Galsworthy, J. Swan song

Godwin, G. Father Melancholy's daughter

Gordimer, N. Burger's daughter

Gordon, M. Final payments

Goudge, E. Blessing in disguise

Graham, W. Stephanie

Guy, R. Ruby

Ishiguro, K. An artist of the floating world

James, H. The golden bowl

James, H. Washington Square

Kennedy, R. A. The bitterest age

Kingsolver, B. Animal dreams

L'Engle, M. Certain women

Lively, P. The road to Lichfield

McInerny, R. M. Easeful death

McMurtry, L. Some can whistle

McNaught, J. Paradise

Oates, J. C. The model

Oz, A. To know a woman

Proulx, A. The shipping news

Rendell, R. Heartstones

Rossner, J. His little women

Sagan, F. Bonjour tristesse

Segal, E. Love story

Siddons, A. R. Homeplace

Smiley, J. A thousand acres

Streeter, E. Father of the bride

Thomas, R. A woman of our times

Undset, S. The bridal wreath

Undset, S. The mistress of Husaby

Vidal, G. 1876

Whitney, P. A. Dream of orchids

Winton, T. The riders

FATHERS AND SONS

    See also Fathers and daughters; Parent and child

    Ackroyd, P. English music

    Allende, I. The infinite plan

    Andersen Nexø, M. Pelle the conqueror: v1 Childhood

    Carroll, J. Memorial bridge

    Coetzee, J. M. The master of Petersburg

    Corman, A. Kramer versus Kramer

    Dexter, P. The paperboy

    Dickens, C. Dombey and Son

    Dostoyevsky, F. The brothers Karamazov

    Fuentes, C. Sons of the Conquistador

    Gaines, E. J. In my father's house

    Gold, H. Fathers

    Gordimer, N. The conservationist

    Gordimer, N. My son's story

    Griffin, W. E. B. Honor bound

    Hart, J. Damage

    Hemingway, E. Islands in the stream

    Kennedy, W. Very old bones

    Lee, C. Y. The flower drum song

    Lee, C. Y. Gate of rage

    Maalouf, A. The rock of Tanios

    Maas, P. Father and son

    Meredith, G. The ordeal of Richard Feverel

    Murdoch, I. The good apprentice

    Ôe, K. The pinch runner memorandum

    Parker, R. B. All our yesterdays

    Peck, R. N. A day no pigs would die

    Potok, C. The chosen

    Potok, C. My name is Asher Lev

    Potok, C. The promise

    Price, R. The promise of rest

    Price, R. The source of light

    Richter, C. The sea of grass

    Roth, H. Call it sleep

    Roth, P. Portnoy's complaint

    Russo, R. Nobody's fool

    Russo, R. The risk pool

FATHERS AND SONS—*Continued*
Segal, E. Love story
Snow, C. P. The conscience of the rich
Snow, C. P. The sleep of reason
Spencer, S. Men in black
Stevenson, R. L. The misadventures of John Nicholson
Stewart, M. The wicked day
Taylor, R. L. The travels of Jaimie McPheeters
Tolstoy, L., graf. Two hussars
Updike, J. The centaur
Wharton, W. Dad
Wiesel, E. The forgotten
Fathers and sons. Turgenev, I. S.
Father's day. Batchelor, J. C.
The **Faulkner** reader. Faulkner, W.
Fault lines. Carroll, J.
FBI *See* United States. Federal Bureau of Investigation

FEAR
Du Maurier, Dame D. Rebecca
Heller, J. Something happened
Shaw, I. Acceptable losses
Fear of flying. Jong, E.
The **Feast** of All Saints. Rice, A.
Feather crowns. Mason, B. A.
Feather on the moon. Whitney, P. A.
The **feats** and adventures of Raoul de Bragelonne. See Dumas, A. The iron mask [variant title: The man in the iron mask]
FEDERAL BUREAU OF INVESTIGATION (U.S.) *See* United States. Federal Bureau of Investigation
The **feel** of the trigger. Westlake, D. E.
In Westlake, D. E. Levine p61-87
Felicia's journey. Trevor, W.
Felix Krull. See Mann, T. Confessions of Felix Krull, confidence man
FELL, MARGARET *See* Fox, Margaret Askew Fell, 1614-1702
The **fellowship** of the ring. Tolkien, J. R. R.
also in Tolkien, J. R. R. The lord of the rings v1
Felony file. Shannon, D.

FEMINISM
Atwood, M. The robber bride
Battle, L. Storyville
Blair, L. The side of the angels
Fairbairns, Z. Stand we at last
Franklin, M. The end of my career
Franklin, M. My brilliant career
French, M. The women's room
Gilman, C. P. Herland
Godwin, G. Violet Clay
Goldreich, G. Years of dreams
Gray, F. du P. Lovers and tyrants
Irving, J. The world according to Garp
Isaacs, S. Close relations
James, H. The Bostonians
Jong, E. Fear of flying
Lessing, D. M. The golden notebook
Lessing, D. M. The summer before the dark
Piercy, M. Braided lives
Piercy, M. Small changes
Roiphe, A. R. Lovingkindness
Rush, N. Mating
Sherwood, F. Vindication
Tepper, S. S. The gate to Women's Country
Walker, A. Possessing the secret of joy
Weldon, F. The heart of the country
Weldon, F. Leader of the band
Femmes fatal. Cannell, D.
Fer-de-lance. Stout, R.
also in Stout, R. Royal flush p1-180
The **ferocious** father. McInerny, R. M.
In McInerny, R. Four on the floor p1-61

FERRARA (ITALY) *See* Italy—Ferrara
Ferris Beach. McCorkle, J.

FERTILIZATION IN VITRO
McCaffrey, A. The greatest love

FESTIVALS
Du Maurier, Dame D. The flight of the falcon
Fête fatale. Barnard, R.

FETUS
See also Pregnancy
The **feud.** Berger, T.

FEUDALISM
Clavell, J. Gai-Jin
Clavell, J. Shogun
Kluger, R. The Sheriff of Nottingham
Lofts, N. The town house

FEUDS
Berger, T. ·The feud
Dawson, C. Body of knowledge
Graham, W. The black moon
Holland, C. The kings in winter
Holt, V. The silk vendetta
Jones, D. C. Come winter
Kells, S. The aristocrats
Richter, C. The lady
Tryon, T. In the fire of spring
Tryon, T. The wings of the morning
The **fever** tree and other stories. Rendell, R.
In Rendell, R. Collected stories p265-406
A **few** dying words. Gosling, P.
A **few** green leaves. Pym, B.
Fiasco. Lem, S.
Ficciones. Borges, J. L.
FIDDLERS *See* Violinists
Fidelity. Berry, W.

FIELD, HENRIETTE
Field, R. All this, and heaven too
Field events. Bass, R.
In Bass, R. Platte River p45-95

FIELDING, HENRY, 1707-1754
Bosse, M. J. The vast memory of love
The **fields.** Richter, C.
also in Richter, C. The awakening land p169-329
The **fifth** book of lost swords: Coinspinner's story. Saberhagen, F.
Fifth business. Davies, R.

FIFTH CENTURY, B.C.
Vidal, G. Creation
The **fifth** child. Lessing, D. M.

FIFTH COLUMN *See* World War, 1939-1945—Collaborationists
The **fifth** horseman. Collins, L.
The **fifth** profession. Morrell, D.
The **fifth** son. Wiesel, E.
Fifty. See Corman, A. 50
Fifty stories. Boyle, K.
Fifty years of the best from Ellery Queen's Mystery Magazine. Entered in Part I under title

FIGURINES *See* Art objects
Fima. Oz, A.
Final argument. Irving, C.
Final curtain. Ballard, M. F.
The **final** deduction. Stout, R.
In Stout, R. Three aces
Final flight. Coonts, S.
The **final** martyrs. Endō, S.
Final moments. Page, E.
Final payments. Gordon, M.

FINANCE
See also Banks
Thomas, M. M. Hanover Place

FINANCIERS *See* Capitalists and financiers
Find her a grave. Wilcox, C.
Find me a villain. Yorke, M.
A **fine** and private place. Beagle, P. S.
A **fine** and private place. Queen, E.
Fine feathers and other stories. Benson, E. F.
The **finishing** school. Godwin, G.
Finn Mac Cool. Llywelyn, M.

FINN MACCOOL *See* Finn MacCumhaill, 3rd cent.

FINN MACCUMHAILL, 3RD CENT.
    Llywelyn, M. Finn Mac Cool
Finnegans wake. Joyce, J.
Finnegan's week. Wambaugh, J.
Fiona. Gaskin, C.
Fire down below. Golding, W.
Fire from heaven. Renault, M.
Fire in heaven. Bosse, M. J.
Fire in the steppe. Sienkiewicz, H.
Fire on the mountain. Desai, A.
A **fire** upon the deep. Vinge, V.
The **firebrand.** Bradley, M. Z.
The **firedrake.** Holland, C.
Firedrake's eye. Finney, P.

FIREFIGHTERS
    Straight, S. Blacker than a thousand midnights
Firefly summer. Binchy, M.
Firefox. Thomas, C.
Firefox down. Thomas, C.
Firehand. Norton, A.
The **fireman's** fair. Humphreys, J.

FIRES
    See also Arson; Disasters
    Wideman, J. E. Philadelphia fire
Firestarter. King, S.
The **firm.** Grisham, J.
First among equals. Archer, J.
The **first** book of lost swords: Woundhealer's story.
    Saberhagen, F.
The **first** circle. Solzhenitsyn, A.
A **first** class murder. Roosevelt, E.
The **first** deadly sin. Sanders, L.
First love. Turgenev, I. S.
The **first** man. Camus, A.
The **first** man in Rome. McCullough, C.
The **first** men in the moon. Wells, H. G.
    In Wells, H. G. Seven famous novels
First offense. Rosenberg, N. T.
The **First** Wives Club. Goldsmith, O.

FISHERIES
    Strindberg, A. By the open sea
A **fisherman** of the inland sea. Le Guin, U. K.

FISHERMEN
    See also Fishing
    Casey, J. Spartina
    Grass, G. The flounder
    Guterson, D. Snow falling on cedars
    Mishima, Y. The sound of waves
    Rice, L. Blue moon

FISHES
    Grass, G. The flounder

FISHING
    See also Fishermen; Pearl fishing
    Bass, R. Platte River
    Hemingway, E. Islands in the stream
    Hemingway, E. The old man and the sea
    Zelazny, R. The doors of his face, the lamps of his
    mouth

The **fist** of God. Forsyth, F.
The **Fitzgerald** reader. Fitzgerald, F. S.
The **five** bells and bladebone. Grimes, M.
Five classic murder mysteries. Christie, A.
Five complete Miss Marple novels. Christie, A.
Five complete novels of murder and detection. *See*
    Christie, A. Agatha Christie: five complete novels of
    murder and detection
Five of a kind. Stout, R.
The **five** red herrings. Sayers, D. L.
Five smooth stones. Fairbairn, A.
Five times Maigret. Simenon, G.
Five weeks in a balloon. Verne, J.
The **fixer.** Malamud, B.
A **flag** for sunrise. Stone, R.
Flags in the dust. Faulkner, W.

FLAMENCO DANCERS *See* Dancers
Flaming Tree. Whitney, P. A.

FLANDERS (BELGIUM) *See* Belgium—Flanders
Flanders sky. Freeling, N.

The **Flannery** O'Connor Award: selected stories. Entered
    in Part I under title

FLANNIGAN, KATHERINE MARY O'FALLON
    Freedman, B. Mrs. Mike
Flashman. Fraser, G. M.
Flashman and the mountain of light. Fraser, G. M.

FLAUBERT, GUSTAVE, 1821-1880
    Barnes, J. Flaubert's parrot
Flaubert's parrot. Barnes, J.
Flavor of the month. Goldsmith, O.

FLEMING, IAN, 1908-1964
        Parodies, travesties, etc.
    Gardner, J. E. Brokenclaw
    Gardner, J. E. Death is forever
    Gardner, J. E. License renewed
    Gardner, J. E. The man from Barbarossa
    Gardner, J. E. Seafire

FLEMING, MARGARET SETON, 1813-1878
    Price, E. Margaret's story
Fletch. Mcdonald, G.
    also in Mcdonald, G. The Fletch chronicles: [two]
Fletch and the man who. Mcdonald, G.
    In Mcdonald, G. The Fletch chronicles: three
Fletch and the Widow Bradley. Mcdonald, G.
    In Mcdonald, G. The Fletch chronicles: one
The **Fletch** chronicles. Mcdonald, G.
Fletch reflected. Mcdonald, G.
Fletch, too. Mcdonald, G.
    also in Mcdonald, G. The Fletch chronicles: one
Fletch won. Mcdonald, G.
    also in Mcdonald, G. The Fletch chronicles: one
Fletch's fortune. Mcdonald, G.
    In Mcdonald, G. The Fletch chronicles: three
Fletch's moxie. Mcdonald, G.
    In Mcdonald, G. The Fletch chronicles: three

FLIERS *See* Air pilots

FLIGHT
    Ballard, J. G. The unlimited dream company
    Steel, D. Wings

FLIGHT ATTENDANTS
    Fleming, I. Quantum of solace
    Leonard, E. Rum punch
Flight of a witch. Peters, E.
The **flight** of the falcon. Du Maurier, Dame D.
Flight of the falcon. Smith, W. A.
Flight of the Intruder. Coonts, S.
Flight of the Old Dog. Brown, D.
The **flight** of the Phoenix. Trevor, E.
Floating city. Lustbader, E. V.
The **floating** opera. Barth, J.
Floodgate. MacLean, A.

FLOODS
    See also Disasters
    Marshall, C. Julie

FLORENCE (ITALY) *See* Italy—Florence

FLORIDA

Frank, P. Alas, Babylon

18th century

Unsworth, B. Sacred hunger

19th century

Matthiessen, P. Killing Mister Watson
Price, E. Margaret's story

20th century

Banks, R. Continental drift
Buffett, J. Where is Joe Merchant?
Dexter, P. The paperboy
Fielding, J. Good intentions
Harrison, J. Julip
Hiaasen, C. Native tongue
Hiaasen, C. Skin tight
Hiaasen, C. Strip tease
Hoffman, A. Turtle Moon
Irving, C. Final argument
Leonard, E. Cat chaser
Leonard, E. LaBrava
Leonard, E. Maximum Bob
Leonard, E. Rum punch
Leonard, E. Stick
McFarland, D. School for the blind
Michener, J. A. Recessional
Rawlings, M. K. The Marjorie Rawlings reader
Rawlings, M. K. Short stories
Rawlings, M. K. South moon under
Sanders, L. Sullivan's sting
Saul, J. Darkness
Updike, J. Rabbit at rest

Key West

Hemingway, E. To have and have not
Hersey, J. Key West tales
Whitney, P. A. Dream of orchids

Miami

Bell, C. The Perez family
Cook, R. Terminal
Leonard, E. LaBrava
Leonard, E. Pronto

Miami Beach

Elkin, S. Mrs. Ted Bliss

Palm Beach

Whitney, P. A. Poinciana
The **flounder**. Grass, G.
The **flower** drum song. Lee, C. Y.
Flowering Judas, and other stories. Porter, K. A.
   also in Porter, K. A. The collected stories of
      Katherine Anne Porter p3-170
Flowering wilderness. Galsworthy, J.
   In Galsworthy, J. End of the chapter p331-592
Flowers for Algernon. Keyes, D.
Flowers for Algernon [novelette]. Keyes, D.
   In The Hugo winners v1 p245-73
Flowers for the judge. Allingham, M.
   In Allingham, M. Crime and Mr. Campion p177-362
Flowers in the rain & other stories. Pilcher, R.

FLOYD, CHARLES ARTHUR *See* Floyd, Pretty Boy,
1904-1934

FLOYD, PRETTY BOY, 1904-1934

McMurtry, L. Pretty Boy Floyd

FLUTISTS

Piercy, M. Summer people

FLYING *See* Flight
Flying colours. Forester, C. S.
Flying finish. Francis, D.
   also in Francis, D. Across the board p1-249
Flying hero class. Keneally, T.
Flying in to love. Thomas, D. M.

FLYING SAUCERS

Heinlein, R. A. The puppet masters

Spielberg, S. Close encounters of the third kind
Strieber, W. Majestic
Foe. Coetzee, J. M.
The **folks** that live on the hill. Amis, K.
Folly. Minot, S.

FOOD

Rossner, J. Olivia
Theroux, P. Millroy the Magician
The **food** of the gods. Wells, H. G.
   In Wells, H. G. Seven famous novels
A **fool** for murder. Babson, M.
The **fool's** progress. Abbey, E.

FOOTBALL

   See also Super Bowl Game (Football)
Jenkins, D. Semi-tough
For Esmé; with love and squalor. See Salinger, J. D.
   Nine stories
For **kicks**. Francis, D.
For **love**. Miller, S.
For **love** of evil. Anthony, P.
For **my** daughters. Delinsky, B.
For **the** sake of all living things. Del Vecchio, J. M.
For **the** sake of Elena. George, E.
For **they** shall inherit. Ross-Macdonald, M.
For **whom** the bell tolls. Hemingway, E.
For **your** eyes only. Fleming, I.
   In Fleming, I. Bonded Fleming p189-328
The **forbidden**. Barker, C.
   In Barker, C. In the flesh
Forbidden colors. Mishima, Y.
The **forbidden** zone. Strieber, W.
Force 10 from Navarone. MacLean, A.
Force of nature. Solomita, S.

FORCED LABOR

Solzhenitsyn, A. One day in the life of Ivan
   Denisovich

FORD, GERALD R., 1913-

Updike, J. Memories of the Ford Administration
Foreign affairs. Lurie, A.
Foreign affairs and other stories. O'Faoláin, S.
   In O'Faoláin, S. The collected stories of Sean O'Fa-
      oláin p1061-1226

FOREIGN LEGION *See* France—Army—Foreign Legion

FOREIGN SERVICE *See* Diplomatic life

Foreigner. Cherryh, C. J.
The **foreseeable** future. Price, R.
The **forest** house. Bradley, M. Z.

FORESTS AND FORESTRY

Innes, H. High stand
Le Guin, U. K. The word for world is forest
Forever. Gould, J.
The **forever** war. Haldeman, J. W.
Forfeit. Francis, D.
   also in Francis, D. Two by Francis
The **forge** of God. Bear, G.

FORGERY OF WORKS OF ART

Banks, O. T. The Rembrandt panel
Davies, R. The lyre of Orpheus
Davies, R. What's bred in the bone
Gaddis, W. The recognitions
Forgiving. Spencer, L.
The **forgotten**. Wiesel, E.
The **Forsyte** saga. Galsworthy, J.
Forsyth's three. Forsyth, F.
Fortunate lives. Dew, R. F.
The **fortune**. Korda, M.
Fortune is a woman. Adler, E.

FORTUNES *See* Wealth

The **fortunes** and misfortunes of Moll Flanders. See
   Defoe, D. Moll Flanders

Fortune's favorites. McCullough, C.
The forty days of Musa Dagh. Werfel, F.
Forward, Gunner Asch! Kirst, H. H.
Forward the Foundation. Asimov, I.

FOSSILS
 Doyle, Sir A. C. The lost world
FOSTER CHILDREN
 See also Adoption
 Austen, J. Mansfield Park
 Eliot, G. Silas Marner
 Gibbons, K. Ellen Foster
 Harris, M. Lost and found
 March, W. The bad seed
Foucault's pendulum. Eco, U.
Foundation. Asimov, I.
Foundation [series]
 Asimov, I. Forward the Foundation
 Asimov, I. Foundation
 Asimov, I. Foundation and earth
 Asimov, I. Foundation and empire
 Asimov, I. Foundation's edge
 Asimov, I. Prelude to Foundation
 Asimov, I. Second Foundation
Foundation and earth. Asimov, I.
Foundation and empire. Asimov, I.
FOUNDATIONS (ENDOWMENTS) *See* Endowments
Foundation's edge. Asimov, I.
The fountain overflows. West, Dame R.
The fountainhead. Rand, A.
The four-chambered heart. Nin, A.
 In Nin, A. Cities of the interior p239-358
Four complete novels. L'Amour, L.
Four days. Goldreich, G.
Four, five and six by Tey. Tey, J.
The four-gated city. Lessing, D. M.
 In Lessing, D. M. Children of violence v5
The four horsemen of the Apocalypse. Blasco Ibáñez, V.
The four million. Henry, O.
 In Henry, O. The complete works of O. Henry p1-108
Four on the floor. McInerny, R. M.
Four past midnight. King, S.
The four swans. Graham, W.
Foursome. Healy, J. F.
The fourteen sisters of Emilio Montez O'Brien. Hijuelos, O.
The fourth book of lost swords: Farslayer's story. Saberhagen, F.
The fourth deadly sin. Sanders, L.
The fourth Durango. Thomas, R.
The fourth K. Puzo, M.

FOURTH OF JULY
 Lockridge, R. Raintree County
 Lurie, A. Only children
The fourth protocol. Forsyth, F.
FOX, GEORGE, 1624-1691
 De Hartog, J. The peaceable kingdom
FOX, MARGARET ASKEW FELL, 1614-1702
 De Hartog, J. The peaceable kingdom
Foxfire. Oates, J. C.
Fractal mode. Anthony, P.
Framley parsonage. Trollope, A.

FRANCE

15th century
Haasse, H. S. In a dark wood wandering
Scott, Sir W. Quentin Durward
Twain, M. Personal recollections of Joan of Arc

16th century
Plaidy, J. The scarlet cloak

17th century
Anthony, E. The Cardinal and the Queen

Dumas, A. The iron mask
Dumas, A. The three musketeers
Dumas, A. Twenty years after
Laker, R. To dance with kings

18th century
Dickens, C. A tale of two cities
Doherty, P. C. The masked man
Dumas, A. The Queen's necklace
Holt, V. The Devil on horseback
Koen, K. Through a glass darkly
Laker, R. To dance with kings
Lofts, N. A rose for virtue
Selinko, A. Désirée
Sterne, L. A sentimental journey through France and Italy
Süskind, P. Perfume: the story of a murderer

1789-1799
Dickens, C. A tale of two cities
Forester, C. S. Lord Hornblower
Orczy, E., Baroness. Adventures of the Scarlet Pimpernel
Orczy, E., Baroness. The elusive Pimpernel
Orczy, E., Baroness. The Scarlet Pimpernel
Sabatini, R. Scaramouche
Sherwood, F. Vindication

1799-1815
Forester, C. S. Lord Hornblower

19th century
Colette. Claudine at school
Cornwell, B. Sharpe's siege
Flaubert, G. Sentimental education
Hugo, V. Les misérables
Lofts, N. A rose for virtue
Proust, M. Jean Santeuil
Sand, G. Lélia
Sand, G. Marianne
Selinko, A. Désirée

1815-1848
Field, R. All this, and heaven too
Stendhal. The red and the black

1848-1870
Werfel, F. The song of Bernadette

1870-1940
Céline, L.-F. Journey to the end of the night
Faulkner, W. A fable
Ford, F. M. No more parades

20th century
Adler, E. The secret of the Villa Mimosa
Cocteau, J. The impostor
Colette. The complete Claudine
Colette. Music-hall sidelights
Fleming, T. J. Over there
Gray, F. du P. Lovers and tyrants
Hemingway, E. The garden of Eden
Krantz, J. Till we meet again
Proust, M. The captive
Proust, M. The captive [and] The fugitive
Proust, M. The fugitive
Proust, M. The Guermantes way
Proust, M. Remembrance of things past
Proust, M. Sodom and Gomorrah
Proust, M. Time regained
Sartre, J. P. The reprieve
Simenon, G. The truth about Bébé Donge
Wharton, E. The reef

1940-1945
Bates, H. E. Fair stood the wind for France
Durrell, L. Constance
Francis, C. Night sky
Greene, G. The tenth man
Read, P. P. The free Frenchman
Sagan, F. A reluctant hero
Sartre, J. P. Troubled sleep

FRANCE—*Continued*

Aristocracy

See Aristocracy—France

Army

Tolstoy, L., graf. War and peace

Army—Foreign Legion

Wren, P. C. Beau Geste

Army—Officers

Conrad, J. The duel

Coal mines and mining

See Coal mines and mining—France

College life

See College life—France

Courts and courtiers

See Courts and courtiers—France

German occupation, 1940-1945

See France—1940-1945

Kings and rulers

Steinbeck, J. The short reign of Pippin IV

Politics

See Politics—France

Prisoners and prisons

See Prisoners and prisons—France

Rural life

Balzac, H. de. The country doctor
Balzac, H. de. Eugénie Grandet
Bates, H. E. Fair stood the wind for France
Du Maurier, Dame D. The scapegoat
Durrell, L. Constance
Durrell, L. Livia
Durrell, L. Monsieur
Durrell, L. Quinx
Godden, R. The greengage summer
MacLean, A. Caravan to Vaccares
Proust, M. Swann's way
Proust, M. Within a budding grove
Sartre, J. P. Nausea
Stewart, M. The crystal cave
Stewart, M. Nine coaches waiting
Stewart, M. Thunder on the right
Trevanian. The summer of Katya

World War, 1914-1918

See World War, 1914-1918—France

Arles

Elkin, S. Van Gogh's room at Arles

Avignon

Durrell, L. Constance
Durrell, L. Livia
Durrell, L. Monsieur
Durrell, L. Quinx

Brittany

MacInnes, H. Assignment in Brittany
Stewart, M. The crystal cave
Stewart, M. Mary Stewart's Merlin trilogy

Cannes

Shaw, I. Evening in Byzantium

Gascony

Dumas, A. The three musketeers

Normandy

Flaubert, G. Madame Bovary

Paris—15th century

Hugo, V. The hunchback of Notre Dame

Paris—17th century

Anthony, E. The Cardinal and the Queen
Riley, J. M. The oracle glass

Paris—18th century

Dickens, C. A tale of two cities
Sabatini, R. Scaramouche

Paris—19th century

Balzac, H. de. Cousin Bette
Balzac, H. de. Cousin Pons
Balzac, H. de. Old Goriot
Dumas, A. The Count of Monte Cristo
Graham, W. The twisted sword
James, H. The ambassadors
James, H. The American
Laker, R. Banners of silk
Zola, É. Nana

Paris—20th century

Baldwin, J. Giovanni's room
Beauvoir, S. de. Les belles images
Beauvoir, S. de. The mandarins
Colette. Chance acquaintances
Colette. Claudine in Paris
Colette. Gigi
Colette. Gigi. Julie de Carneilhan. Chance acquaintances
Colette. Julie de Carneilhan
Colette. Mitsou
Cortázar, J. Hopscotch
Dumas, A. Camille
Gallant, M. Overhead in a balloon
Gallico, P. Mrs. 'Arris goes to Paris
Genet, J. Our Lady of the Flowers
Gide, A. The counterfeiters (Les faux-monnayeurs)
Hemingway, E. The sun also rises
Krantz, J. Mistral's daughter
MacInnes, H. The Venetian affair
McCarthy, M. Birds of America
Miller, H. Tropic of Cancer
Nin, A. Children of the albatross
Nin, A. The four-chambered heart
Nin, A. Ladders to fire
Remarque, E. M. Arch of triumph
Rhys, J. Good morning, midnight
Rhys, J. Quartet
Rilke, R. M. The notebooks of Malte Laurids Brigge
Sartre, J. P. The age of reason
Simenon, G. Across the street
Simenon, G. The old man dies
Steinbeck, J. The short reign of Pippin IV
Uris, L. Topaz
Wilson, A. N. Love unknown

Provence

Mayle, P. Hotel Pastis

Versailles

Laker, R. To dance with kings
The **Franchise**. Kessel, J.
In Nebula awards 29 p203-41
The **Franchise** affair. Tey, J.
also in Tey, J. Three by Tey v2

FRANCISCANS

Endō, S. The samurai
Frankenstein. Shelley, M. W.

FRANKFURT AM MAIN (GERMANY) *See* Germany—Frankfurt am Main

Franny and Zooey. Salinger, J. D.

FRATRICIDE

Cheever, J. Falconer

Fraud. Brookner, A.
Freaky Deaky. Leonard, E.
Free fall in crimson. MacDonald, J. D.
The **free Frenchman**. Read, P. P.
FREEDOM *See* Liberty
Freedom. Safire, W.
Freedom road. Fast, H.
FREEZING OF HUMAN BODIES *See* Cryonics
FREIGHT PLANES *See* Transport planes
FRÉMONT, JESSIE BENTON, 1824-1902
Stone, I. Immortal wife
FRÉMONT, JOHN CHARLES, 1813-1890
Stone, I. Immortal wife

FRENCH

Africa
Smith, W. A. The burning shore

Algeria
Camus, A. The first man

Canada
Cather, W. Shadows on the rock

England
Du Maurier, Dame D. Frenchman's Creek
Heaven, C. The wind from the sea
Laker, R. The sugar pavilion
Lofts, N. Nethergate
Read, P. P. The free Frenchman
Tarkington, B. Monsieur Beaucaire

Indochina
Duras, M. The lover
Duras, M. The North China lover

Ireland
Flanagan, T. The year of the French

United States
Cather, W. Death comes for the archbishop
Field, R. All this, and heaven too

FRENCH AND INDIAN WAR, 1755-1763 *See* United
States—French and Indian War, 1755-1763
French kiss. Lustbader, E. V.
The **French lieutenant's woman**. Fowles, J.
FRENCH REVOLUTION *See* France—1789-1799
FRENCH RIVIERA *See* Riviera (France and Italy)
French Silk. Brown, S.
FRENCH SOLDIERS *See* Soldiers—France
Frenchman's Creek. Du Maurier, Dame D.
Frequent hearses. See Crispin, E. Sudden vengeance
FREUD, SIGMUND, 1856-1939
Meyer, N. The seven-per-cent solution
Stone, I. The passions of the mind
Thomas, D. M. The white hotel
Friday. Heinlein, R. A.
Friday the rabbi slept late. Kemelman, H.
Fried green tomatoes at the Whistle-Stop Cafe. Flagg, F.
Friend of my youth. Munro, A.
The **friend of the family**. Dostoyevsky, F.
In Dostoyevsky, F. The short novels of Dostoyevsky
p617-811
The **friendly persuasion**. West, J.
FRIENDS *See* Friendship
FRIENDS, SOCIETY OF *See* Society of Friends
Friends and lovers. MacInnes, H.
Friends at Thrush Green. Read, Miss
Friends for life. Wolitzer, M.
The **friends of Eddie Coyle**. Higgins, G. V.
FRIENDSHIP
See also Love
Adler, E. Fortune is a woman
Armstrong, C. The turret room
Atwood, M. The robber bride
Balzac, H. de. Cousin Pons
Binchy, M. Circle of friends
Binchy, M. Light a penny candle

Bradford, B. T. Voice of the heart
Brookner, A. Brief lives
Carroll, J. Prince of peace
Colwin, L. A big storm knocked it over
Doig, I. Dancing at the Rascal Fair
Erdrich, L. The Beet Queen
Gordon, M. Final payments
Gray, F. du P. World without end
Herlihy, J. L. Midnight cowboy
Highsmith, P. The boy who followed Ripley
Jakes, J. North and South
Kay, T. Shadow song
Kipling, R. The light that failed
Knowles, J. Indian summer
Knowles, J. A separate peace
Laker, R. The Venetian mask
L'Engle, M. A severed wasp
Li, P.-H. Farewell to my concubine
Longyear, B. B. Enemy mine
MacDonald, J. D. Slam the big door
McMillan, T. Waiting to exhale
Monette, P. Afterlife
Morrison, T. Sula
Mortimer, J. C. Dunster
Murdoch, I. The book and the brotherhood
Murdoch, I. Henry and Cato
Myrer, A. The last convertible
Oates, J. C. Solstice
Potok, C. The promise
Powell, A. A question of upbringing
Price, R. The tongues of angels
Puig, M. Eternal curse on the reader of these pages
Pym, B. Jane and Prudence
Reid Banks, L. The L shaped room
Remarque, E. M. Three comrades
Ross-Macdonald, M. For they shall inherit
Sarton, M. The magnificent spinster
Settle, M. L. Celebration
Siddons, A. R. Outer banks
Stegner, W. E. Crossing to safety
Steinbeck, J. Of mice and men
Steinbeck, J. Tortilla Flat
Taylor, E. Mrs. Palfrey at the Claremont
Thomas, R. Bad girls, good women
Trollope, J. The men and the girls
Weldon, F. Life force
Wharton, W. Birdy
Wilson, A. N. Love unknown
Wolitzer, M. Friends for life
Frigor mortis. McInerny, R. M.
A **frolic of his own**. Gaddis, W.
From a view to a kill. Fleming, I.
In Fleming, I. Bonded Fleming p191-213
From here to eternity. Jones, J.
From Russia, with love. Fleming, I.
From the earth to the moon, and Round the moon.
Verne, J.
From the terrace. O'Hara, J.
From time to time. Finney, J.

FRONTIER AND PIONEER LIFE
Richter, C. The light in the forest

Alaska
Ferber, E. Ice Palace

Arkansas
Jones, D. C. The search for Temperance Moon

Australia
Eden, D. The vines of Yarrabee
Malouf, D. Remembering Babylon
Nordhoff, C. Botany Bay
White, P. The tree of man

California
Bristow, G. Jubilee Trail
De Blasis, C. The proud breed
Holland, C. The Bear Flag

FRONTIER AND PIONEER LIFE—*Continued*

Canada
Freedman, B. Mrs. Mike
Urquhart, J. Away

Colorado
Michener, J. A. Centennial

Indiana
West, J. The massacre at Fall Creek

Kentucky
Giles, J. H. Hannah Fowler

Middle Western States
Cooper, J. F. The prairie

Minnesota
Moberg, V. The last letter home
Moberg, V. Unto a good land

Montana
Guthrie, A. B. Arfive

Nebraska
Aldrich, B. S. A lantern in her hand
Cather, W. My Ántonia
Cather, W. O pioneers!

New Mexico
Durham, M. Dutch uncle

New York (State)
Cooper, J. F. The Deerslayer
Cooper, J. F. The last of the Mohicans
Cooper, J. F. The Leatherstocking tales
Cooper, J. F. The Pathfinder
Cooper, J. F. The pioneers
Edmonds, W. D. Drums along the Mohawk

New Zealand
Eden, D. An important family
Goudge, E. Green Dolphin Street

North Dakota
Bojer, J. The emigrants
Young, C. The wedding dress

Ohio
Richter, C. The awakening land
Richter, C. The fields
Richter, C. The town
Richter, C. The trees

Ohio River Valley
Settle, M. L. O Beulah Land

Oklahoma
Ferber, E. Cimarron

South Africa
Smith, W. A. The Courtneys

South Dakota
Dexter, P. Deadwood
Rölvaag, O. E. Giants in the earth
Rölvaag, O. E. Peder Victorious

Southern States
Jones, D. C. This savage race

Texas
Gipson, F. B. Old Yeller
Gipson, F. B. Savage Sam
Michener, J. A. Texas

Virginia
L'Amour, L. To the far blue mountains

Washington (State)
Dillard, A. The living

Western States
Berger, T. Little Big Man
Fisher, V. Mountain man
Guthrie, A. B. The big sky
Guthrie, A. B. Fair land, fair land
Guthrie, A. B. The way West

Hunter, E. The Chisholms
Jones, D. C. Season of yellow leaf
L'Amour, L. The Cherokee Trail
L'Amour, L. Jubal Sackett
L'Amour, L. The Sacketts: beginnings of a dynasty
McMurtry, L. Buffalo girls
McMurtry, L. Lonesome dove
Portis, C. True grit
Schaefer, J. W. The collected stories of Jack Schaefer
Swarthout, G. F. The homesman
Taylor, R. L. The travels of Jaimie McPheeters

Wyoming
L'Amour, L. Bendigo Shafter

FRUIT PICKERS *See* Migrant labor

The **fugitive** [variant title: The sweet cheat gone]. Proust, M.
In Proust, M. The captive [and] The fugitive
In Proust, M. Remembrance of things past v3 p425-706

Fugitive nights. Wambaugh, J.

FUGITIVE SLAVES
Bradley, D. The Chaneysville incident
Edmonds, W. D. Chad Hanna
Tryon, T. In the fire of spring
Twain, M. The adventures of Huckleberry Finn

FUGITIVES
See also Escaped convicts; Fugitive slaves; Manhunts; Outlaws
Piercy, M. Vida
Saint, H. F. Memoirs of an invisible man
Westheimer, D. My sweet Charlie

Fugitives' fire. Brand, M.

Full disclosure. Safire, W.

Funeral games. Renault, M.

Funeral in Berlin. Deighton, L.

FUNERAL RITES AND CEREMONIES
Agee, J. A death in the family
Faulkner, W. As I lay dying
Styron, W. Lie down in darkness
Tyler, A. Breathing lessons
Waugh, E. The loved one
Welty, E. Losing battles
Welty, E. The optimist's daughter

The **fur** person. Sarton, M.

FUR TRADE
Guthrie, A. B. The big sky
L'Amour, L. Sackett's land

The **further** adventures of Slugger McBatt. Kinsella, W. P.

FUTURE
See also Science fiction
Amis, M. London fields
Anderson, P. Goat song
Anderson, P. Harvest of stars
Anderson, P. Harvest the fire
Anderson, P. Orion shall rise
Anderson, P. The stars are also fire
Asimov, I. The caves of steel
Asimov, I. Forward the Foundation
Asimov, I. Foundation
Asimov, I. Foundation and earth
Asimov, I. Foundation and empire
Asimov, I. Foundation's edge
Asimov, I. The naked sun
Asimov, I. Prelude to Foundation
Asimov, I. Robots and empire
Asimov, I. The robots of dawn
Asimov, I. Second Foundation
Atwood, M. The handmaid's tale
Auster, P. In the country of last things
Batchelor, J. C. Father's day
Bear, G. Anvil of stars
Bear, G. The forge of God
Bear, G. Moving Mars
Benford, G. Timescape

FUTURE—*Continued*

Bosse, M. J. Mister Touch
Bova, B. Millennium
Bova, B. The Trikon deception
Brin, D. Earth
Brin, D. The postman
Brown, D. Chains of command
Brown, D. Flight of the Old Dog
Brown, D. Night of the hawk
Brown, D. Sky masters
Brunner, J. Stand on Zanzibar
Burgess, A. A clockwork orange
Butler, O. E. Parable of the sower
Cherryh, C. J. Foreigner
Clancy, T. Debt of honor
Clancy, T. Red Storm rising
Clancy, T. The sum of all fears
Clarke, A. C. Beyond the fall of night
Clarke, A. C. The city and the stars
Clarke, A. C. Imperial Earth
Coyle, H. W. Bright star
Coyle, H. W. Code of honor
Delany, S. R. Stars in my pocket like grains of sand
Delany, S. R. Time considered as a helix of semi-precious stones
Dickson, G. R. Wolf and iron
DiMercurio, M. Attack of the Seawolf
Donaldson, S. R. The gap into madness: chaos and order
Ellison, H. A boy and his dog
Farmer, P. J. Dayworld
Farmer, P. J. Dayworld breakup
Farmer, P. J. Dayworld rebel
Farmer, P. J. Riders of the purple wage
Gibson, W. Virtual light
Greenberg, J. With the Snow Queen
Haldeman, J. W. Mindbridge
Harrison, P. Storming Intrepid
Heinlein, R. A. Friday
Heinlein, R. A. The moon is a harsh mistress
Helprin, M. Winter's tale
Herbert, F. Children of Dune
Herbert, F. Dune
Herbert, F. Dune messiah
Herbert, F. God Emperor of Dune
Herbert, F. Heretics of Dune
Hesse, H. The glass bead game (Magister Ludi)
Hoban, R. Riddley Walker
Huxley, A. Ape and essence
Huxley, A. Brave new world
James, P. D. The children of men
Kesey, K. Sailor song
King, S. The long walk
King, S. The running man
Knebel, F. Seven days in May
Koontz, D. R. Night chills
Kress, N. And wild for to hold
Lessing, D. M. The memoirs of a survivor
Lessing, D. M. Shikasta
May, J. Intervention
McAuley, P. J. Red dust
Miller, W. M. A canticle for Leibowitz
Miller, W. M. The darfsteller
Moore, B. Catholics
Niven, L. The Mote in God's Eye
Orwell, G. Nineteen eighty-four
Piercy, M. He, she and it
Pike, C. The season of passage
Pohl, F. The annals of the Heechee
Pohl, F. Beyond the blue event horizon
Pohl, F. Gateway
Pohl, F. Heechee rendezvous
Pohl, F. Land's end
Pohl, F. Man Plus
Pohl, F. Mars Plus
Pohl, F. The merchants' war
Pohl, F. The space merchants
Reed, I. The terrible threes

Reed, I. The terrible twos
Robinson, S. By any other name
Robinson, S. Stardance [novelette]
Sagan, C. Contact
Scott, J. The nine dragons
Silverberg, R. At winter's end
Silverberg, R. Hot sky at midnight
Silverberg, R. The new springtime
Silverberg, R. Nightwings
Silverberg, R. Nightwings [novelette]
Stephenson, N. The diamond age
Tepper, S. S. The gate to Women's Country
Trenhaile, J. The gates of exquisite view
Varley, J. The persistence of vision
Vidal, G. Live from Golgotha
Vonnegut, K. Cat's cradle
Vonnegut, K. Galápagos
Vonnegut, K. Hocus pocus
West, M. L. Lazarus
Wilhelm, K. Juniper time
Wilhelm, K. Where late the sweet birds sang
Wolfe, G. The Citadel of the Autarch
Wolfe, G. The claw of the conciliator
Wolfe, G. The shadow of the torturer
Wolfe, G. The sword of the Lictor
Wolfe, G. The Urth of the new sun
Yolen, J. Sister Light, Sister Dark
Yolen, J. White Jenna
Zelazny, R. He who shapes
Zelazny, R. Lord of light
Fuzz. McBain, E.

G

"G" is for gumshoe. Grafton, S.
The **Gabriel** hounds. Stewart, M.
Gabriela, clove and cinnamon. Amado, J.
Gad's Hall. Lofts, N.
Gai-Jin. Clavell, J.
GAIUS CAESAR *See* Caligula, Emperor of Rome, 12-41
Galápagos. Vonnegut, K.

GALAPAGOS ISLANDS
Vonnegut, K. Galápagos

GALATIANS *See* Celts

GALES *See* Storms

GALICIA (POLAND AND UKRAINE)
Agnon, S. Y. The bridal canopy
Gallowglass. Vine, B.
The **Galsworthy** reader. Galsworthy, J.
The **Galton** case. Macdonald, R.
In Macdonald, R. Archer at large
Gambit. Stout, R.
The **gambler**. Dostoyevsky, F.
also in Dostoyevsky, F. The gambler, and other stories
also in Dostoyevsky, F. The short novels of Dostoevsky p1-126
The **gambler**, and other stories. Dostoyevsky, F.

GAMBLERS *See* Gambling

GAMBLING
Amado, J. Dona Flor and her two husbands
Dickens, C. The old curiosity shop
Dostoyevsky, F. The gambler
Ferber, E. Show boat
Fleming, I. Casino Royale
Francis, D. Forfeit
Francis, D. Twice shy
Kells, S. The aristocrats
Leiber, F. Gonna roll the bones
Shaw, I. Nightwork

The **Game** of Thirty. Kotzwinkle, W.
Game, set & match. Deighton, L.
GAMES
 See also Sports
 Thomas, R. A woman of our times
The **gang** that couldn't shoot straight. Breslin, J.
GANGS
 See also Juvenile delinquency
 Mowry, J. Six out seven
 Oates, J. C. Foxfire
GANGSTERS
 See also Mafia
 Auster, P. Mr. Vertigo
 Bradford, B. T. Angel
 Burnett, W. R. The asphalt jungle
 Condon, R. Prizzi's family
 Condon, R. Prizzi's glory
 Condon, R. Prizzi's honor
 Condon, R. Prizzi's money
 Coulter, C. Impulse
 Doctorow, E. L. Billy Bathgate
 Dunne, D. An inconvenient woman
 Dunne, J. G. Playland
 Estleman, L. D. Motown
 Kinsolving, W. Bred to win
 Leonard, E. Get Shorty
The **gap** into madness: chaos and order. Donaldson, S. R.
A **garden** of earthly delights. Oates, J. C.
The **garden** of Eden. Hemingway, E.
Garden of lies. Goudge, E.
The **Garden** of Rama. Clarke, A. C.
The **garden** of the Finzi-Continis. Bassani, G.
GARDEN PARTIES *See* Parties
The **garden** party and other stories. Mansfield, K.
GARDENERS
 Coetzee, J. M. Life & times of Michael K.
 Godden, J. In her garden
 Kosinski, J. N. Being there
 Laker, R. The golden tulip
GARDENING *See* Gardens
GARDENS
 Godden, R. An episode of sparrows
GARMENT WORKERS *See* Clothing industry
GASCONY (FRANCE) *See* France—Gascony
Gate of rage. Lee, C. Y.
The **gate** to Women's Country. Tepper, S. S.
The **gates** of exquisite view. Trenhaile, J.
The **gates** of ivory. Drabble, M.
The **gates** of the forest. Wiesel, E.
Gateway. Pohl, F.
The **gateway** trip. Pohl, F.
The **gathering** of old men. Gaines, E. J.
Gaudy Night. Sayers, D. L.
GAUGUIN, PAUL, 1848-1903
 Maugham, W. S. The moon and sixpence
GAUL
 Llywelyn, M. Druids
GAULLE, CHARLES DE, 1890-1970
 Forsyth, F. The day of the jackal
GAULS *See* Celts
GAUTAMA BUDDHA
 Hesse, H. Siddhartha
 Mishima, Y. The Temple of Dawn
 Mishima, Y. The temple of the golden pavilion
GAY MEN *See* Homosexuality
GAY WOMEN *See* Lesbianism
GDANSK (POLAND) *See* Poland—Gdansk
GEESE
 Gallico, P. The snow goose
GEISHAS
 Kawabata, Y. Snow country

The **Gemini** contenders. Ludlum, R.
GEMS *See* Diamonds; Emeralds; Rubies
GENEALOGY
 Halter, M. The book of Abraham
The **general** and his labyrinth. García Márquez, G.
General murders. Estleman, L. D.
GENERALS
 Fleming, T. J. Over there
 Massie, A. Caesar
The **general's** daughter. DeMille, N.
GENERATION GAP *See* Conflict of generations
Generous death. Pickard, N.
GENETIC EXPERIMENTATION *See* Genetics
GENETIC RESEARCH *See* Genetics
GENETICS
 Cook, R. Mortal fear
 Cook, R. Mutation
 Crichton, M. Jurassic Park
 Herbert, F. Dune
 Herbert, F. Dune messiah
 Herbert, F. Heretics of Dune
 Herbert, F. The white plague
 Koontz, D. R. Watchers
 Kress, N. Beggars & choosers
 Kress, N. Beggars in Spain
 Saul, J. Guardian
GENEVA (SWITZERLAND) *See* Switzerland—Geneva
GENIUS
 See also Gifted children
 Conroy, F. Body & soul
 Ozick, C. The cannibal galaxy
 Rand, A. The fountainhead
 Saul, J. Shadows
The **gentle** desperado. Brand, M.
The **gentle** grafter. Henry, O.
 In Henry, O. The complete works of O. Henry p267-354
The **gentleman** from Indiana. Tarkington, B.
Gentleman's agreement. Hobson, L. K. Z.
Geodyssey [series]
 Anthony, P. Isle of woman
 Anthony, P. Shame of man
GEOLOGISTS
 Hoeg, P. Smilla's sense of snow
 Verne, J. A journey to the centre of the earth
GEORGE IV, KING OF GREAT BRITAIN, 1762-1830
 Laker, R. The sugar pavilion
George Passant. *See* Snow, C. P. Strangers and brothers
George's mother. Crane, S.
 In Crane, S. The complete novels of Stephen Crane p301-47
 In Crane, S. The portable Stephen Crane p89-146
GEORGETOWN (WASHINGTON, D.C.) *See* Washington (D.C.)—Georgetown
GEORGIA
 See also Saint Simons Island (Ga.)

    19th century
 Coleman, L. Beulah Land
 Coleman, L. The legacy of Beulah Land
 Coleman, L. Look away, Beulah Land
 Price, E. Beauty from ashes
 Price, E. Before the darkness falls
 Price, E. Bright captivity
 Price, E. Lighthouse
 Price, E. Savannah
 Price, E. Stranger in Savannah
 Price, E. To see your face again
 Price, E. Where shadows go

    20th century
 Bambara, T. C. The salt eaters
 Burns, O. A. Cold Sassy tree
 Burns, O. A. Leaving Cold Sassy

GEORGIA—20th century—*Continued*
Caldwell, E. God's little acre
Caldwell, E. Tobacco road
Cook, T. H. Evidence of blood
Dexter, P. Paris Trout
Faulkner, W. Soldiers' pay
Goudge, E. Blessing in disguise
Hyman, M. No time for sergeants
McCullers, C. The member of the wedding
Siddons, A. R. Heartbreak Hotel
Siddons, A. R. Homeplace
Siddons, A. R. King's oak
Smith, L. E. Strange fruit
Woods, S. Grass roots
Woods, S. Palindrome
Woods, S. Under the lake

Atlanta
Rich, M. Tender offerings
Siddons, A. R. Downtown
Siddons, A. R. Peachtree Road

Savannah
Battle, L. Southern women
Price, E. Savannah
Georgia on my mind. Sheffield, C.
In Nebula awards 29 p95-136
Gerald's game. King, S.

GERMAN AMERICANS
Jakes, J. Homeland

GERMAN REFUGEES
Desai, A. Baumgartner's Bombay
Remarque, E. M. Arch of triumph
Remarque, E. M. The night in Lisbon

GERMAN SOLDIERS *See* Soldiers—Germany

GERMANS
Brazil
Levin, I. The boys from Brazil

Czechoslovakia
Demetz, H. The house on Prague Street

Egypt
Follett, K. The key to Rebecca

England
Deighton, L. SS-GB: Nazi-occupied Britain 1941
Follett, K. Eye of the needle
Higgins, J. The eagle has landed

France
MacInnes, H. Assignment in Brittany
Remarque, E. M. All quiet on the western front
Remarque, E. M. Arch of triumph

India
Desai, A. Baumgartner's Bombay

Islands of the Pacific
Conrad, J. Victory

Norway
Steinbeck, J. The moon is down

Poland
Hersey, J. The wall
Miłosz, C. The seizure of power
Uris, L. Mila 18

Russia
Anatoli, A. Babi Yar
Kirst, H. H. Forward, Gunner Asch!

United States
Dreiser, T. Jennie Gerhardt
Smith, B. Maggie-Now

GERMANY
Hesse, H. Narcissus and Goldmund

19th century
Böll, H. Billiards at half-past nine
Fraser, G. M. Royal Flash

Mann, T. Buddenbrooks

20th century
Böll, H. Billiards at half-past nine
Böll, H. The clown
Böll, H. Group portrait with lady
Böll, H. The lost honor of Katharina Blum
Grass, G. Dog years
Grass, G. The tin drum
Handke, P. The left-handed woman
Hesse, H. Steppenwolf
Le Carré, J. A small town in Germany
Pearson, R. Hard fall
Remarque, E. M. The night in Lisbon
Remarque, E. M. The road back
Remarque, E. M. Three comrades
Remarque, E. M. A time to love and a time to die
Tennenbaum, S. Yesterday's streets

1918-1945
Böll, H. A soldier's legacy
Grass, G. Dog years
Grass, G. The tin drum
Isherwood, C. The Berlin stories
Kirst, H. H. The nights of the long knives
Leffland, E. The knight, death, and the devil
Remarque, E. M. The night in Lisbon
Remarque, E. M. The road back
Remarque, E. M. Three comrades
Remarque, E. M. A time to love and a time to die

1945-
Anthony, E. The Janus imperative
Forsyth, F. The Odessa file
Grass, G. The call of the toad
Grass, G. Dog years
Grass, G. Local anaesthetic
Handke, P. The left-handed woman
Harris, R. Fatherland
Higgins, J. Day of judgment
Kaye, M. M. Death in Berlin
Uris, L. Armageddon

American occupation, 1945-1955
See Germany—1945-

Army
Anatoli, A. Babi Yar
Kirst, H. H. Forward, Gunner Asch!
Remarque, E. M. All quiet on the western front
Solzhenitsyn, A. August 1914

Army—Officers
Kirst, H. H. The night of the generals
Kirst, H. H. The return of Gunner Asch

Communism
See Communism—Germany

Navy
Buchheim, L.-G. The boat

World War, 1939-1945
See World War, 1939-1945—Germany

Bavaria
MacLean, A. Where eagles dare

Berlin
Abbott, M. The last innocent hour
Baum, V. Grand Hotel
Berger, T. Crazy in Berlin
Carroll, J. Family trade
Deighton, L. Berlin game
Deighton, L. Funeral in Berlin
Deighton, L. London match
Isherwood, C. The Berlin stories
Kaye, M. M. Death in Berlin
McEwan, I. The innocent
Nabokov, V. V. King, queen, knave
Uris, L. Armageddon
Wolf, C. What remains

GERMANY—*Continued*

Bonn

Böll, H. The clown

Le Carré, J. A small town in Germany

Cologne

Böll, H. The silent angel

Dresden

Vonnegut, K. Slaughterhouse-five

Düsseldorf

Mann, T. The black swan

Frankfurt am Main

Tennenbaum, S. Yesterday's streets

Potsdam

Kennedy, R. A. The bitterest age

Germinal. Zola, É.

GERMS *See* Microorganisms

GERONTOLOGISTS *See* Physicians

Gertrude. Hesse, H.

GESTAPO *See* National socialism

Get Shorty. Leonard, E.

GETTYSBURG, BATTLE OF, 1863

Shaara, M. The killer angels

GHETTOS *See* Jews—Segregation

The **ghost** and Mrs. Muir. Leslie, J. A. C.

GHOST STORIES

See also Gothic romances; Horror stories; Supernatural phenomena

Aiken, J. The haunting of Lamb House

Alcott, L. M. The abbott's ghost

Amis, K. The Green Man

Barker, C. In the flesh [novelette]

Beagle, P. S. A fine and private place

Black, V. My name is Polly Winter

Byatt, A. S. The conjugial angel

Cady, J. The night we buried Road Dog

Davies, R. Murther & walking spirits

Dickens, C. A Christmas carol

Dickens, C. The complete ghost stories of Charles Dickens

Famous ghost stories

Jackson, S. The haunting of Hill House

James, H. The turn of the screw

Leslie, J. A. C. The ghost and Mrs. Muir

The Literary ghost

Lofts, N. Gad's Hall

Lofts, N. The haunting of Gad's Hall

Lovecraft, H. P. The mound

Lurie, A. Women and ghosts

Marius, R. C. After the war

The Norton book of ghost stories

The Oxford book of English ghost stories

Saul, J. Second child

Straub, P. Ghost story

Straub, P. Mrs. God

The Virago book of ghost stories

Woods, S. Under the lake

Ghost story. Straub, P.

GHOST TOWNS *See* Extinct cities

The **ghost** writer. Roth, P.

also in Roth, P. Zuckerman bound: a trilogy and epilogue

GHOSTS *See* Ghost stories

Ghosts. McBain, E.

The **ghostway**. Hillerman, T.

also in Hillerman, T. The Jim Chee mysteries

Giant. Ferber, E.

GIANTS

Swift, J. Gulliver's travels

Wells, H. G. The food of the gods

Giants in the earth. Rölvaag, O. E.

The **gift**. Steel, D.

The **gift** of Asher Lev. Potok, C.

The **gift** shop. Armstrong, C.

GIFTED CHILDREN

Delany, S. R. The star pit

Gaddis, W. J R

Potok, C. My name is Asher Lev

Gigi. Colette

In Colette. Gigi. Julie de Carneilhan. Chance acquaintances p9-74

In Colette. Six novels p649-97

Gigi. Julie de Carneilhan. Chance acquaintances. Colette

The **gilded** age. Twain, M.

also in Twain, M. The complete novels of Mark Twain v1 p1-383

Giles goat-boy. Barth, J.

Gilgamesh the king. Silverberg, R.

GILMORE, GARY

Mailer, N. The executioner's song

Gimpel the fool, and other stories. Singer, I. B.

The **ginger** man. Donleavy, J. P.

Giovanni's room. Baldwin, J.

GIPSIES *See* Gypsies

A **girl** of forty. Gold, H.

The **girl** who heard dragons. McCaffrey, A.

The **girl** who heard dragons [novelette]. McCaffrey, A.

In McCaffrey, A. The girl who heard dragons p21-64

Girl with the green eyes. See O'Brien, E. The lonely girl

GIRLS

See also Adolescence; Children; Youth

Allison, D. Bastard out of Carolina

Binchy, M. Light a penny candle

Brontë, C. Emma

Cisneros, S. The house on Mango Street

Davis, T. 1959

Dickens, C. The old curiosity shop

Flagg, F. Coming attractions

Gibbons, K. Ellen Foster

Gill, B. M. Nursery crimes

Goldreich, G. That year of our war

Hoffman, A. Illumination night

Kennedy, R. A. The bitterest age

Leffland, E. Rumors of peace

Lurie, A. Only children

March, W. The bad seed

McCaffrey, A. The girl who heard dragons

McCorkle, J. Ferris Beach

Morrison, T. The bluest eye

Oates, J. C. Foxfire

Phillips, J. A. Shelter

Sinclair, A. Coffee will make you black

Spark, M. The prime of Miss Jean Brodie

Tarkington, B. Alice Adams

Tilly, M. Singing songs

West, J. Cress Delahanty

Whitney, P. A. The singing stones

Woodson, J. Autobiography of a family photo

Girls at war, and other stories. Achebe, C.

Girls in their married bliss. O'Brien, E.

In O'Brien, E. The country girls trilogy and epilogue p381-508

The **girls** of slender means. Spark, M.

Give us this day. Delderfield, R. F.

The **Glade** Manor murder. Lemarchand, E.

GLADIATORS

Lytton, E. B. L., Baron. The last days of Pompeii

Sienkiewicz, H. Quo vadis

The **Gladstone** bag. MacLeod, C.
Glamorous powers. Howatch, S.
A **glancing** light. Elkins, A. J.
GLASGOW (SCOTLAND) See Scotland—Glasgow
The **glass** bead game (Magister Ludi). Hesse, H.
The **glass** flame. Whitney, P. A.
The **glass** key. Hammett, D.
   also in Hammett, D. The novels of Dashiell Hammett p441-588
Glass mountain. Voigt, C.
A **glass** of blessings. Pym, B.
The **glass-sided** ants' nest. Dickinson, P.
The **Glendower** legacy. Gifford, T.
The **glitter** and the gold. Stewart, F. M.
The **Glitter** Dome. Wambaugh, J.
Glittering images. Howatch, S.
Glitz. Leonard, E.
Glory season. Brin, D.
GLOUCESTERSHIRE (ENGLAND) See England—Gloucestershire

GNOSTICISM
   Durrell, L. Monsieur
The **go-away** bird. Spark, M.
   In Spark, M. The stories of Muriel Spark p221-62
Go down, Moses. Faulkner, W.
Go tell it on the mountain. Baldwin, J.
Go West, Inspector Ghote. Keating, H. R. F.
Goat song. Anderson, P.
   In The Hugo winners v3 p330-64
Gobseck. Balzac, H. de
   In Balzac, H. de. The short novels of Balzac

GOD
   Updike, J. Roger's version
   Wiesel, E. The gates of the forest
God bless you, Mr. Rosewater. Vonnegut, K.
God Emperor of Dune. Herbert, F.
God in Concord. Langton, J.
God is an Englishman. Delderfield, R. F.
The **godfather**. Puzo, M.
Godplayer. Cook, R.
God's little acre. Caldwell, E.
Gods of Riverworld. Farmer, P. J.
The **gods** themselves. Asimov, I.
GOERING, HERMANN See Göring, Hermann, 1893-1946

GOGH, VINCENT VAN, 1853-1890
   Stone, I. Lust for life
Going after Cacciato. O'Brien, T.
Going for the gold. Lathen, E.
Going to meet the man. Baldwin, J.
Going wrong. Rendell, R.

GOLD
   Cornwell, B. Sharpe's gold
   Dunnett, D. Scales of gold
   Estleman, L. D. Sudden country
   Fleming, I. Goldfinger
   L'Amour, L. The Californios
   Michener, J. A. Journey
The **Gold** Coast. DeMille, N.
Gold Coast. Leonard, E.
   In Leonard, E. Elmore Leonard's double Dutch treat: three novels

GOLD MINES AND MINING
   Henry, W. Mackenna's gold
   Traven, B. The treasure of the Sierra Madre

GOLD RUSH See California—1846-1900
The **golden** apples. Welty, E.
   also in Welty, E. The collected stories of Eudora Welty

The **golden** apples of the sun. Bradbury, R.
The **golden** bowl. James, H.
The **golden** cup. Plain, B.
GOLDEN FLEECE See Argonauts (Greek mythology)
Golden fox. Smith, W. A.
The **golden** horn. Tarr, J.
The **golden** notebook. Lessing, D. M.
The **golden** ocean. O'Brian, P.
The **Golden** Orange. Wambaugh, J.
The **golden** torc. May, J.
Golden Trillium. Norton, A.
The **golden** tulip. Laker, R.
The **golden** unicorn. Whitney, P. A.
Golden urchin. Brent, M.
The **golden** years. See Hardwick, M. The Duchess of Duke Street
Goldfinger. Fleming, I.
Goldilocks. McBain, E.
Goldmund. See Hesse, H. Narcissus and Goldmund

GOLEM
   Wiesel, E. The Golem
The **Golem**. Wiesel, E.
Gone. Reed, K.
Gone south. McCammon, R. R.
Gone to soldiers. Piercy, M.
Gone with the wind. Mitchell, M.
Gonna roll the bones. Leiber, F.
   In The Best of the Nebulas p211-27
   In The Hugo winners v2 p460-83
Good and dead. Langton, J.

GOOD AND EVIL
   See also Sin; Suffering
   Anthony, P. And eternity
   Anthony, P. Bearing an hourglass
   Anthony, P. Being a green mother
   Anthony, P. For love of evil
   Anthony, P. On a pale horse
   Anthony, P. Wielding a red sword
   Anthony, P. With a tangled skein
   Barker, C. Everville
   Barker, C. The great and secret show
   Barker, C. Imajica
   Barker, C. Weaveworld
   Brooks, T. The druid of Shannara
   Brooks, T. The elfqueen of Shannara
   Brooks, T. The Elfstones of Shannara
   Brooks, T. The scions of Shannara
   Brooks, T. The sword of Shannara
   Brooks, T. The talismans of Shannara
   Brooks, T. The wishsong of Shannara
   Bulgakov, M. A. The master and Margarita
   Dickey, J. Deliverance
   Doctorow, E. L. Welcome to Hard Times
   Eddings, D. Belgarath the sorcerer
   Eddings, D. Demon lord of Karanda
   Eddings, D. Guardians of the west
   Eddings, D. King of the Murgos
   Eddings, D. The seeress of Kell
   Eddings, D. Sorceress of Darshiva
   Endō, S. Scandal
   García Márquez, G. In evil hour
   Greene, G. The captain and the enemy
   James, H. The turn of the screw
   King, S. Apt pupil
   King, S. The dark half
   King, S. Insomnia
   King, S. The stand
   King, S. The talisman
   Koontz, D. R. Cold fire
   Lewis, C. S. Out of the silent planet
   Lewis, C. S. Perelandra
   Lewis, C. S. That hideous strength
   Lewis, C. S. Till we have faces
   McCammon, R. R. Boy's life
   McEwan, I. Black dogs
   Melville, H. Billy Budd, sailor
   Morrell, D. The covenant of the flame

GOOD AND EVIL—*Continued*

Mortimer, J. C. Dunster
Murdoch, I. The green knight
Murdoch, I. The nice and the good
Phillips, J. A. Shelter
Rawlings, M. K. The sojourner
Rice, A. Lasher
Rice, A. Taltos
Rice, A. The witching hour
Rushdie, S. The satanic verses
Russ, J. Souls
Saul, J. Second child
Steinbeck, J. East of Eden
Straub, P. Ghost story
Styron, W. Set this house on fire
Weldon, F. Puffball
Westlake, D. E. Humans
Wright, R. The outsider
Zelazny, R. Bring me the head of Prince Charming
The **good** apprentice. Murdoch, I.
Good as Gold. Heller, J.
Good behavior. Westlake, D. E.
Good-bye Mr. Chips. Hilton, J.
The **good** child's river. Wolfe, T.
The **good** companions. Priestley, J. B.
A **good** day to die. Solomita, S.
The **good** earth. Buck, P. S.
The **good** husband. Godwin, G.
Good intentions. Fielding, J.
A **good** man is hard to find and other stories. O'Connor, F.
> *also in* O'Connor, F. Collected works p133-328

Good morning, midnight. Rhys, J.
Good morning, Miss Dove. Patton, F. G.
The **good** mother. Miller, S.
A **good** night to kill. O'Donnell, L.
The **good** soldier Svejk. Hašek, J.
The **good** terrorist. Lessing, D. M.
Good will. Smiley, J.
> *In* Smiley, J. Ordinary love & Good will

Goodbye, Columbus, and five short stories. Roth, P.
The **goodbye** look. Macdonald, R.
Goodbye, Saigon. Vida, N.
Goodbye to Berlin. Isherwood, C.
> *In* Isherwood, C. The Berlin stories v2

Goodbye without leaving. Colwin, L.

GORDON RIOTS, 1870

Dickens, C. Barnaby Rudge
Gorilla, my love. Bambara, T. C.

GÖRING, HERMANN, 1893-1946

Leffland, E. The knight, death, and the devil
Gorky Park. Smith, M. C.
Gossip from Thrush Green. Read, Miss

GOTHIC ROMANCES

> *See also* Horror stories

Alcott, L. M. Behind a mask: the unknown thrillers of Louisa May Alcott
Austen, J. Northanger Abbey
Blake, J. Arrow to the heart
Brent, M. Moonraker's bride
Brent, M. Stormswift
Brent, M. Tregaron's daughter
Brontë, C. Emma
Brontë, C. Jane Eyre
Brontë, E. Wuthering Heights
Carr, P. Voices in a haunted room
Carr, P. We'll meet again
Clark, M. H. A cry in the night
Gaskin, C. A falcon for a queen
Gaskin, C. Fiona
Gregory, P. Meridon
Heaven, C. The wind from the sea
Heyer, G. Cousin Kate
Hill, P. Vollands
Hodge, J. A. The winding stair
Holt, V. The black opal
Holt, V. Bride of Pendorric

Holt, V. The captive
Holt, V. Daughter of deceit
Holt, V. The Devil on horseback
Holt, V. The India fan
Holt, V. The Judas kiss
Holt, V. Kirkland Revels
Holt, V. The legend of the seventh virgin
Holt, V. The mask of the enchantress
Holt, V. Menfreya in the morning
Holt, V. Mistress of Mellyn
Holt, V. The pride of the peacock
Holt, V. The road to Paradise Island
Holt, V. Secret for a nightingale
Holt, V. Seven for a secret
Holt, V. The silk vendetta
Howatch, S. The shrouded walls
Johnston, V. The Etruscan smile
Kaye, M. M. Death in Kashmir
Kaye, M. M. Death in Kenya
Kaye, M. M. Death in Zanzibar
L'Engle, M. The other side of the sun
Michaels, B. The dark on the other side
Michaels, B. Greygallows
Michaels, B. Into the darkness
Michaels, B. Search the shadows
Michaels, B. Shattered silk
Michaels, B. Smoke and mirrors
Michaels, B. Vanish with the rose
Ogilvie, E. When the music stopped
The Oxford book of gothic tales
Peters, E. Legend in green velvet
Seton, A. Dragonwyck
Shelley, M. W. Frankenstein
Stewart, M. The Gabriel hounds
Stewart, M. The ivy tree
Stewart, M. Nine coaches waiting
Stewart, M. Thornyhold
Stewart, M. Thunder on the right
Stewart, M. Touch not the cat
Stewart, M. Wildfire at midnight
Stoker, B. Dracula
Trevanian. The summer of Katya
Whitney, P. A. Black amber
Whitney, P. A. Columbella
Whitney, P. A. Daughter of the stars
Whitney, P. A. Dream of orchids
Whitney, P. A. The ebony swan
Whitney, P. A. Flaming Tree
Whitney, P. A. The glass flame
Whitney, P. A. Hunter's green
Whitney, P. A. Poinciana
Whitney, P. A. Rainbow in the mist
Whitney, P. A. Sea Jade
Whitney, P. A. Silverhill
Whitney, P. A. The singing stones
Whitney, P. A. Snowfire
Whitney, P. A. Spindrift
Whitney, P. A. Star flight
Whitney, P. A. The stone bull
Whitney, P. A. The turquoise mask
Whitney, P. A. Window on the square
Whitney, P. A. Woman without a past
Wood, B. The dreaming

GOTHIC STORIES *See* Gothic romances

GOULD, HORACE BUNCH, 1812-1881

Price, E. New moon rising

GOULD, JAMES

Price, E. Lighthouse

GOVERNESSES

> *See also* Housekeepers

Alcott, L. M. Behind a mask [novelette]
Allingham, M. The China governess
Brontë, C. Jane Eyre
Coulter, C. The valentine legacy
Field, R. All this, and heaven too
Gaskin, C. Fiona
Holt, V. The captive

GOVERNESSES—*Continued*
Holt, V. Menfreya in the morning
Holt, V. Mistress of Mellyn
James, H. The turn of the screw
Seton, A. Dragonwyck
Stewart, M. Nine coaches waiting
Wharton, E. The reef
Whitney, P. A. Window on the square

GOVERNMENT, RESISTANCE TO *See* Resistance to government

GOVERNMENTAL INVESTIGATIONS
United States
Strieber, W. Majestic

GRAIL
Costain, T. B. The silver chalice

GRANADA (SPAIN) *See* Spain—Granada
Grand Hotel. Baum, V.
Grand passion. Krentz, J. A.
The **grand** Sophy. Heyer, G.

GRANDCHILDREN
See also Granddaughters
Bradford, B. T. Hold the dream
Bradford, B. T. To be the best
García Márquez, G. The incredible and sad tale of innocent Eréndira and her heartless grandmother
McMurtry, L. The evening star
Siddons, A. R. Colony

GRANDDAUGHTERS
Davenport, K. Shark dialogues

GRANDFATHERS
Burns, O. A. Cold Sassy tree
Dickens, C. Martin Chuzzlewit
Dickens, C. The old curiosity shop
Farmer, P. J. Riders of the purple wage
Ferber, E. Ice Palace
Gaskin, C. A falcon for a queen
Grisham, J. The chamber
Gurganus, A. A hog loves its life: something about my grandfather
Humphrey, W. The Ordways
McGuane, T. Nobody's angel
Whitney, P. A. The turquoise mask
The **grandfathers**. Richter, C.

GRANDMOTHERS
Blair, L. The side of the angels
Bromfield, L. Mrs. Parkington
Colette. Gigi
De la Roche, M. Jalna
Desai, A. Fire on the mountain
Dickinson, P. Play dead
Edgarian, C. Rise the Euphrates
García Márquez, G. The incredible and sad tale of innocent Eréndira and her heartless grandmother
Glasgow, E. Vein of iron
Goudge, E. The bird in the tree
Goudge, E. Pilgrim's inn
Hodge, J. A. The winding stair
Jhabvala, R. P. Heat and dust
Read, Miss. Thrush Green
Tryon, T. The other
Whitney, P. A. Domino
Whitney, P. A. Silverhill
Wood, B. Virgins of paradise
Yolen, J. Briar Rose
The **grandmother's** tale and selected stories. Narayan, R. K.

Grant's last case. See Tey, J. The singing sands

The **grapes** of wrath. Steinbeck, J.
Grass. Tepper, S. S.
The **grass** crown. McCullough, C.
The **grass** dancer. Power, S.
The **grass** harp. Capote, T.
The **grass** is singing. Lessing, D. M.
Grass roots. Woods, S.
The **grass** widow. McInerny, R. M.
A **grave** matter. Davies, L. P.
Grave mistake. Marsh, Dame N.
A **grave** without flowers. McMullen, M.
Gravedigger. Hansen, J.
Graves in academe. Kenney, S.
A **graveyard** for lunatics. Bradbury, R.

GRAVEYARDS *See* Cemeteries
Gravity's rainbow. Pynchon, T.
The **great** American novel. Roth, P.
The **great** and secret show. Barker, C.

GREAT AUNTS *See* Aunts

GREAT BRITAIN
See also England; Northern Ireland; Scotland; Wales

Colonies
Clavell, J. Tai-Pan

Kings and rulers
Dickinson, P. Skeleton-in-waiting
GREAT BRITAIN. ARMY
Boulle, P. The bridge over the River Kwai
Cornwell, B. Redcoat
Kaye, M. M. The far pavilions
Kaye, M. M. Shadow of the moon
Llewellyn, R. None but the lonely heart
Waugh, E. Men at arms
Waugh, E. Officers and gentlemen
Officers
Cornwell, B. Sharpe's company
Cornwell, B. Sharpe's eagle
Cornwell, B. Sharpe's enemy
Cornwell, B. Sharpe's gold
Cornwell, B. Sharpe's honour
Cornwell, B. Sharpe's regiment
Cornwell, B. Sharpe's revenge
Cornwell, B. Sharpe's rifles
Cornwell, B. Sharpe's siege
Cornwell, B. Sharpe's sword
Fast, H. Seven days in June
Forester, C. S. Hornblower and the Atropos
Forester, C. S. Ship of the line
Waugh, E. The end of the battle

GREAT BRITAIN. NAVY *See* Great Britain. Royal Navy

GREAT BRITAIN. PARLIAMENT
Archer, J. First among equals

GREAT BRITAIN. ROYAL NAVY
Forester, C. S. Admiral Hornblower in the West Indies
Forester, C. S. Beat to quarters
Forester, C. S. Flying colours
Forester, C. S. Mr. Midshipman Hornblower
McCutchan, P. Halfhyde and the fleet review
Melville, H. Billy Budd, sailor
Monsarrat, N. The cruel sea
Nordhoff, C. The Bounty trilogy
McCutchan, P. Cameron's crossing
Officers
Forester, C. S. Hornblower and the Hotspur
Forester, C. S. Hornblower during the crisis, and two stories: Hornblower's temptation and The last encounter
Forester, C. S. Lieutenant Hornblower
MacLean, A. H.M.S. Ulysses
McCutchan, P. Convoy homeward
McCutchan, P. Convoy north
McCutchan, P. Convoy of fear
McCutchan, P. Convoy south
O'Brian, P. The wine-dark sea

GREAT BRITAIN. ROYAL NAVY — Officers — *Continued*
Reeman, D. A ship must die
Great circle. Aiken, C.
In Aiken, C. The collected novels of Conrad Aiken p167-295
A **great** deliverance. George, E.
The **great** divorce. Martin, V.
Great expectations. Dickens, C.
The **Great** Gatsby. Fitzgerald, F. S.
also in Fitzgerald, F. S. The Fitzgerald reader p105-238
also in Fitzgerald, F. S. The portable F. Scott Fitzgerald p1-168
Great lion of God. Caldwell, T.
Great racing stories. See The Dick Francis treasury of great racing stories
Great short works of Joseph Conrad. Conrad, J.
GREAT SMOKY MOUNTAINS (N.C. AND TENN.)
Whitney, P. A. The glass flame
Great stories of the American West. Entered in Part I under title
The **great** train robbery. Crichton, M.
The **greater** inclination. Wharton, E.
In Wharton, E. The collected short stories of Edith Wharton v1
The **greatest** love [novelette]. McCaffrey, A.
In McCaffrey, A. The girl who heard dragons p169-225
GREECE
See also Corfu Island (Greece); Mykonos Island (Greece)
Bova, B. Orion and the conqueror
Bradley, M. Z. The firebrand
Crane, S. Active service
Graves, R. Hercules, my shipmate
Renault, M. The bull from the sea
Renault, M. Fire from heaven
Renault, M. Funeral games
Renault, M. The king must die
Renault, M. The last of the wine
Renault, M. The mask of Apollo

20th century
Fallaci, O. A man
Fowles, J. The magus
Hodge, J. A. Strangers in company
MacInnes, H. Decision at Delphi
Sarton, M. Joanna and Ulysses
Stewart, M. My brother Michael

Politics
See Politics—Greece

Athens
Douglas, L. C. The robe
Renault, M. The last of the wine
Vidal, G. Creation

Delphi
Stewart, M. My brother Michael
GREED *See* Avarice
GREEK CIVIL WAR, 1944-1949 *See* Greece—20th century
The **Greek** treasure. Stone, I.
GREEKS

Turkey
Kazan, E. America, America

United States
Caunitz, W. J. Black sand
Marius, R. C. After the war
GREEN BERETS *See* United States. Army. Special Forces
The **green** branch. Pargeter, E.
In Pargeter, E. The heaven trilogy
Green cane and juicy flotsam. Entered in Part I under title

Green City in the sun. Wood, B.
Green darkness. Seton, A.
A **green** desire. Myrer, A.
Green Dolphin country. See Goudge, E. Green Dolphin Street
Green Dolphin Street. Goudge, E.
The **green** gauntlet. Delderfield, R. F.
Green, green, my valley now. Llewellyn, R.
Green grow the dollars. Lathen, E.
The **green** knight. Murdoch, I.
The **Green** Man. Amis, K.
Green mansions. Hudson, W. H.
Green Mars. Robinson, K. S.
The **green** ripper. MacDonald, J. D.
Green river rising. Willocks, T.
Green shadows, white whale. Bradbury, R.
The **greengage** summer. Godden, R.
GREENLAND
MacLean, A. Night without end
Smiley, J. The Greenlanders
The **Greenlanders.** Smiley, J.
GREENWICH VILLAGE (NEW YORK, N.Y.) *See* New York (N.Y.)—Greenwich Village
Grendel. Gardner, J.
GRENVILLE, SIR RICHARD, 1600-1658
Du Maurier, Dame D. The King's general
Greygallows. Michaels, B.
GRIEF *See* Bereavement
Grievous sin. Kellerman, F.
Gringos. Portis, C.
Grinning gods. Gardner, E. S.
In Gardner, E. S. The blonde in lower six p189-227
GROCERS
Malamud, B. The assistant
Steinbeck, J. The winter of our discontent
The **group.** McCarthy, M.
Group portrait with lady. Böll, H.
The **groves** of Academe. McCarthy, M.
Growing pains. Townsend, S.
In Townsend, S. The Adrian Mole diaries
Growing up Latino. Entered in Part I under title
The **grown-ups.** Glendinning, V.
GUADALCANAL CAMPAIGN *See* World War, 1939-1945—Solomon Islands
GUANAJA ISLAND (HONDURAS)
Shepard, L. A traveler's tale
GUANGZHOU (CHINA) *See* China—Guangzhou
Guardian. Saul, J.
GUARDIAN AND WARD
See also Adoption
Edgerton, C. Walking across Egypt
Kingsolver, B. The bean trees
Guardian angel. Paretsky, S.
Guardians of the west. Eddings, D.
GUATEMALA
Goldman, F. The long night of white chickens

Politics
See Politics—Guatemala
GUATEMALANS

France
Nin, A. The four-chambered heart
GUENEVERE, QUEEN (LEGENDARY CHARACTER)
White, T. H. The candle in the wind
The **Guermantes** way. Proust, M.
also in Proust, M. Remembrance of things past v2 p3-620
GUERRILLAS
See also World War, 1939-1945—Underground movements
Ambler, E. The Levanter
Hemingway, E. For whom the bell tolls
Levi, P. If not now, when?

GUERRILLAS—*Continued*
MacLean, A. Force 10 from Navarone
Naipaul, V. S. Guerrillas
Nathanson, E. M. The dirty dozen
Smith, W. A. A time to die
Guerrillas. Naipaul, V. S.
A **guest** of honor. Gordimer, N.

GUIDED MISSILE BASES
Shulman, M. Rally round the flag, boys!

GUILT
See also Sin
Appelfeld, A. Unto the soul
Armstrong, C. The unsuspected
Bausch, R. Violence
Begley, L. Wartime lies
Berger, T. Crazy in Berlin
Brink, A. P. An act of terror
Camus, A. The fall
Carroll, J. Fault lines
Endō, S. The sea and poison
Follett, K. A dangerous fortune
Gordon, M. The rest of life
Greene, G. The tenth man
Hamilton, J. A map of the world
Hart, J. Damage
Highsmith, P. The boy who followed Ripley
Kennedy, W. Ironweed
McEwan, I. The innocent
Miller, S. Family pictures
Morrison, T. Jazz
Nordan, L. Wolf whistle
Ōe, K. The silent cry
Roiphe, A. R. If you knew me
Rossner, J. Looking for Mr. Goodbar
Smiley, J. Ordinary love
Smith, S. B. A simple plan
Styron, W. Sophie's choice
Trevor, W. The silence in the garden
Tyler, A. Saint maybe
Uhnak, D. The Ryer Avenue story
Vine, B. A fatal inversion
Wiesel, E. Twilight

GUINEVERE, QUEEN (LEGENDARY CHARACTER)
See Guenevere, Queen (Legendary character)
The **gulf.** Poyer, D.

GULF STREAM
Hemingway, E. The old man and the sea

GULF WAR, 1991 *See* Persian Gulf War, 1991
Gulliver's travels. Swift, J.

GUNBOATS *See* Warships
Gunner Asch goes to war. See Kirst, H. H. Forward,
Gunner Asch!
The **guns** of Avalon. Zelazny, R.
The **guns** of Navarone. MacLean, A.
Guys and dolls. Runyon, D.
Gwen Bristow's Plantation trilogy. Bristow, G.
The **Gwen** John sculpture. Malcolm, J.

GYPSIES
Barrie, J. M. The little minister
Hugo, V. The hunchback of Notre Dame
King, S. Thinner
Lofts, N. The town house
MacLean, A. Caravan to Vaccares
Mérimée, P. Carmen
The **Gyrth** chalice mystery. Allingham, M.
In Allingham, M. Three cases for Mr. Campion
p421-604

H

"**H**" is for homicide. Grafton, S.
H. M. Pulham, esquire. Marquand, J. P.
H.M.S. Ulysses. MacLean, A.
Had we never loved. Veryan, P.
Hadji Murád. Tolstoy, L., graf
In Tolstoy, L. The short novels of Tolstoy
HADRIAN, EMPEROR OF ROME, 76-138
Yourcenar, M. Memoirs of Hadrian, and reflections
on the composition of Memoirs of Hadrian
A **haiku** for Hanae. Melville, J.

HAITI
Revolution, 1791-1804
Bell, M. S. All souls' rising
Roberts, K. L. Lydia Bailey

20th century
Greene, G. The comedians

Port-au-Prince
Greene, G. The comedians

HAITIAN REFUGEES
Banks, R. Continental drift

HAITIANS
United States
Prose, F. Primitive people
Half asleep in frog pajamas. Robbins, T.

HALF-BROTHERS
Kesey, K. Sometimes a great notion
Murdoch, I. The good apprentice
Plain, B. Eden burning
Smith, W. A. Power of the sword
Smith, W. A. Rage

HALF-CASTES *See* Mixed bloods
Half Moon Street. Theroux, P.

HALF-SISTERS
Dailey, J. Heiress
Harris, R. Love and money
Holt, V. The mask of the enchantress
Whitney, P. A. Dream of orchids

Halfblood chronicles
Norton, A. The elvenbane
Norton, A. Elvenblood

Halfhyde and the fleet review. McCutchan, P.
The **hall** of the mountain king. Tarr, J.
**HALLET, ELIZABETH FONES WINTHROP FEAKE,
B. 1610**
Seton, A. The Winthrop woman

HALLUCINATIONS AND ILLUSIONS
See also Personality disorders
Goldman, W. Magic

HAMILTON, LADY EMMA, 1761?-1815
Sontag, S. The volcano lover

HAMILTON, SIR WILLIAM, 1730-1803
Sontag, S. The volcano lover
The **hamlet.** Faulkner, W.
also in Faulkner, W. Snopes p1-349
The **Hamlet** trap. Wilhelm, K.
The **hammer** of God. Clarke, A. C.
Hammerheads. Brown, D.

HAMPSHIRE (ENGLAND) *See* England—Hampshire
The **hand** of Oberon. Zelazny, R.

HAND-TO-HAND FIGHTING
See also Boxing; Wrestling
A **handful** of rice. Markandaya, K.
The **handmaid's** tale. Atwood, M.
Hands of a stranger. Daley, R.
The **hands** of Lyr. Norton, A.
The **handsome** road. Bristow, G.
In Bristow, G. Gwen Bristow's Plantation trilogy
p263-530

HANDYMEN *See* Hired men

HANDYWOMEN *See* Hired women

The **hanging** garden. Sherwood, J.

The **hangman's** beautiful daughter. McCrumb, S.

Hangman's holiday. Sayers, D. L.

Hank and Chloe. Mapson, J.-A.

Hannah Fowler. Giles, J. H.

Hanover Place. Thomas, M. M.

Hanta yo. Hill, R. B.

Happy all the time. Colwin, L.

Happy are those who thirst for justice. Greeley, A. M.

A **happy** death. Camus, A.

Happy endings. Quinn, S.

Happy endings. Stone, K.

Happy to be here. Keillor, G.

The **harafish**. Mahfūz, N.

HARASSMENT, SEXUAL *See* Sexual harassment

The **hard** blue sky. Grau, S. A.

Hard candy. Vachss, A. H.

Hard case. D'Amato, B.

Hard evidence. Lescroart, J. T.

Hard fall. Pearson, R.

Hard luck. D'Amato, B.

Hard rain. Abrahams, P.

Hard road to Gettysburg. Jones, T.

Hard times. Dickens, C.

Hard times for these times. See Dickens, C. Hard times

Hard women. D'Amato, B.

HARELIP *See* Face—Abnormalities and deformities

HARLEM (NEW YORK, N.Y.) *See* New York (N.Y.)—Harlem

Harlot's ghost. Mailer, N.

Harmful intent. Cook, R.

Haroun and the sea of stories. Rushdie, S.

The **harrowing** of Gwynedd. Kurtz, K.

Harry and Tonto. Greenfeld, J.

HARVARD UNIVERSITY
  Cross, A. Death in a tenured position
  Wolfe, T. Of time and the river

Harvest. Plain, B.

Harvest home. Tryon, T.

Harvest of stars. Anderson, P.

Harvest the fire. Anderson, P.

HASEKURA, TSUNENAGA, 1571-1622
  Endō, S. The samurai

HASIDISM
  Agnon, S. Y. The bridal canopy
  Potok, C. The chosen
  Potok, C. The gift of Asher Lev
  Potok, C. My name is Asher Lev
  Potok, C. The promise
  Singer, I. B. Reaches of heaven

Hatter Fox. Harris, M.

Haunted. Oates, J. C.

Haunted house. See Lofts, N. The haunting of Gad's Hall

HAUNTED HOUSES *See* Ghost stories

Haunted lady. Rinehart, M. R.
  In Rinehart, M. R. Miss Pinkerton: adventures of a nurse detective p249-403

The **haunted** man [variant title: The haunted man and the ghost's bargain]. Dickens, C.
  In Dickens, C. Christmas tales

The **haunted** mesa. L'Amour, L.

The **haunted** monastery. Gulik, R. H. van

The **haunting** of Gad's Hall. Lofts, N.

The **haunting** of Hill House. Jackson, S.

The **haunting** of Lamb House. Aiken, J.

HAVANA (CUBA) *See* Cuba—Havana

Have his carcase. Sayers, D. L.

HAWAII
  Davenport, K. Shark dialogues
  Jones, J. From here to eternity
  Katkov, N. Blood & orchids
  London, J. Stories of Hawaii

  Michener, J. A. Hawaii

Politics
  See Politics—Hawaii

Race relations
  Katkov, N. Blood & orchids

Hawaii. Michener, J. A.

HAWAIIAN ISLANDS *See* Hawaii

He huffed and he puffed. Paul, B.

He, she and it. Piercy, M.

He who shapes. Zelazny, R.
  In The Best of the Nebulas p73-141

Head case. Cody, L.

Heading uptown. Piesman, M.

HEADMASTERS *See* School superintendents and principals; Teachers

HEADMISTRESSES *See* School superintendents and principals; Teachers

HEALTH RESORTS
  See also Summer resorts
  Boyle, T. C. Road to Wellville
  Clark, M. H. Weep no more, my lady
  Murdoch, I. The philosopher's pupil

Hearing secret harmonies. Powell, A.
  In Powell, A. A dance to the music of time [v4]

HEART

Diseases
  Aiken, J. Voices in an empty house
  Howard, M. Expensive habits

A **heart** for the gods of Mexico. Aiken, C.
  In Aiken, C. The collected novels of Conrad Aiken p415-72

The **heart** is a lonely hunter. McCullers, C.
  also in McCullers, C. The ballad of the sad café: the novels and stories of Carson McCullers p141-498

Heart of darkness. Conrad, J.
  also in Conrad, J. Great short works of Joseph Conrad p175-256
  also in Conrad, J. The portable Conrad p490-603
  also in Conrad, J. Tales of land and sea p33-104

Heart of gold. McInerny, R. M.
  In McInerny, R. Four on the floor p63-113

The **heart** of the country. Weldon, F.

The **heart** of the family. Goudge, E.

The **heart** of the matter. Greene, G.

Heart of the West. Henry, O.
  In Henry, O. The complete works of O. Henry p109-266

Heartbeat. Steel, D.

Heartbreak Hotel. Siddons, A. R.

Heartburn. Ephron, N.

Hearts. Wolitzer, H.

The **hearts** and lives of men. Weldon, F.

Heartstones. Rendell, R.

Heat. McBain, E.

Heat. Woods, S.

Heat and dust. Jhabvala, R. P.

Heat, and other stories. Oates, J. C.

The **heat** of the day. Bowen, E.

The **heat** of the sun. O'Faoláin, S.
  In O'Faoláin, S. The collected stories of Sean O'Faoláin p700-886

HEAVEN
  See also Angels
  Heinlein, R. A. Job: a comedy of justice

Heaven and hell. Jakes, J.

The **heaven** tree. Pargeter, E.
  In Pargeter, E. The heaven tree trilogy

The **heaven** tree trilogy. Pargeter, E.

Heaven's prisoners. Burke, J. L.

Heavy time. Cherryh, C. J.

HEBRIDES (SCOTLAND)
  See also Skye (Scotland)
  Stewart, M. The stormy petrel
  Woolf, V. To the lighthouse

HEDONISM
Colette. Claudine married
Kazantzakis, N. Zorba the Greek
Heechee rendezvous. Pohl, F.
Heir apparent. Coscarelli, K.
Heiress. Dailey, J.

HEIRESSES *See* Inheritance and succession; Wealth

HEIRS *See* Inheritance and succession; Wealth
The **heirs** of the kingdom. Oldenbourg, Z.
Hell hath no fury. Ross-Macdonald, M.
Hellburner. Cherryh, C. J.
Helliconia spring. Aldiss, B. W.
Helliconia summer. Aldiss, B. W.
Helliconia winter. Aldiss, B. W.
Help the poor struggler. Grimes, M.

HEMINGS, HARRIET, 1801-1876
Chase-Riboud, B. The President's daughter

HEMINGS, SALLY, 1773-1835
Chase-Riboud, B. Sally Hemings
The **Hemingway** reader. Hemingway, E.
Henderson the rain king. Bellow, S.
also in Bellow, S. The portable Saul Bellow
Henrietta who? Aird, C.

HENRY II, KING OF ENGLAND, 1133-1189
Holland, C. The earl

HENRY III, KING OF ENGLAND, 1207-1272
Penman, S. K. Falls the shadow

HENRY VII, KING OF ENGLAND, 1457-1509
Jarman, R. H. The courts of illusion

HENRY VIII, KING OF ENGLAND, 1491-1547
Anthony, E. Anne Boleyn
Lewis, H. W. I am Mary Tudor
Plaidy, J. Murder most royal
Plaidy, J. The rose without a thorn
Plaidy, J. The sixth wife
Henry and Cato. Murdoch, I.
Henry Esmond. See Thackeray, W. M. The history of Henry Esmond, esquire
The **Henry** James reader. James, H.
Her mother's daughter. French, M.
Her sense of timing. Elkin, S.
In Elkin, S. Van Gogh's room at Arles: three novellas p1-109

HERACLES (LEGENDARY CHARACTER) *See* Hercules (Legendary character)
The **Herb** of Grace. See Goudge, E. Pilgrim's inn

HERCEGOVINA *See* Bosnia and Hercegovina
Hercule Poirot's casebook. Christie, A.

HERCULES (LEGENDARY CHARACTER)
Graves, R. Hercules, my shipmate
Hercules, my shipmate. Graves, R.
Here and beyond. Wharton, E.
In Wharton, E. The collected short stories of Edith Wharton v2
Here be dragons. Penman, S. K.
Here lies. Parker, D.
The **heretic's** apprentice. Peters, E.
Heretics of Dune. Herbert, F.
Heritage of Shannara [series]
Brooks, T. The druid of Shannara
Brooks, T. The elfqueen of Shannara
Brooks, T. The scions of Shannara
Brooks, T. The talismans of Shannara
Herland. Gilman, C. P.

HERMAPHRODITISM
Jennings, G. Raptor
The **hermit** and the wild woman. Wharton, E.
In Wharton, E. The collected short stories of Edith Wharton v1

The **hermit** of 69th Street. Kosinski, J. N.
The **hermit** of Eyton Forest. Peters, E.

HERMITS
See also Recluses

HEROES
See also Heroism
Llywelyn, M. Finn Mac Cool
Norton, A. Empire of the eagle

HEROISM
See also Courage; Heroes
Brown, D. A. Killdeer Mountain
Glasgow, E. Vein of iron
Keneally, T. Flying hero class
Hers the kingdom. Streshinsky, S.

HERTFORDSHIRE (ENGLAND) *See* England—Hertfordshire
Herzog. Bellow, S.

HICKOCK, MARTHA JANE CANARY *See* Calamity Jane, 1852-1903

HICKOK, WILD BILL, 1837-1876
Dexter, P. Deadwood
The **hidden** city. Eddings, D.
Hidden riches. Roberts, N.
The **hidden** target. MacInnes, H.
Hideaway. Koontz, D. R.
The **high** and the mighty. Gann, E. K.
The **High** Commissioner. Cleary, J.
High cotton. Pinckney, D.
High fall. Dunlap, S.
High hearts. Brown, R. M.
High road to China. Cleary, J.

HIGH SCHOOLS *See* School life
High stakes. Francis, D.
High stand. Innes, H.
The **high** window. Chandler, R.
also in Chandler, R. Stories and early novels p985-1177
Highgate rise. Perry, A.

HIJACKING OF AIRPLANES
Keneally, T. Flying hero class
McCarthy, M. Cannibals and missionaries
Puzo, M. The fourth K

HIJACKING OF SHIPS
Follett, K. Triple
MacLean, A. When eight bells toll

HIJACKING OF SUBWAYS
Godey, J. The taking of Pelham one two three
The **Hildebrand** rarity. Fleming, I.
In Fleming, I. Bonded Fleming p298-328
Hill towns. Siddons, A. R.
Him with his foot in his mouth and other stories. Bellow, S.

HIMALAYA MOUNTAINS
Godden, R. Black Narcissus
Hindsight. Dickinson, P.

HINDUS
Kaye, M. M. The far pavilions
Seth, V. A suitable boy

England
See also East Indians—England

HIPPIES
See also Bohemianism; Collective settlements
Kingston, M. H. Tripmaster Monkey
Powell, A. Hearing secret harmonies
Hire a hangman. Wilcox, C.

HIRED KILLERS
Estleman, L. D. Kill zone
Perry, T. The butcher's boy
Perry, T. Sleeping dogs

HIRED MEN
Malamud, B. The fixer

HIRED WOMEN
Tyler, A. The clock winder
His last bow. Doyle, Sir A. C.
In Doyle, Sir A. C. The complete Sherlock Holmes
His little women. Rossner, J.
His Master's Voice. Lem, S.

HISPANIC AMERICANS
Allende, I. The infinite plan
Growing up Latino
Iguana dreams

HISTORIANS
Bradley, D. The Chaneysville incident
Gifford, T. The Glendower legacy
Lurie, A. The nowhere city
The **history** of Henry Esmond, esquire. Thackeray, W. M.
A **history** of the world in 10½ chapters. Barnes, J.
The **history** of Tom Jones, a foundling. Fielding, H.
The **Hitchhiker's** Guide to the Galaxy. Adams, D.
also in Adams, D. The hitchhiker's quartet
The **hitchhiker's** quartet. Adams, D.

HITLER, ADOLF, 1889-1945
Harris, R. Fatherland

HO CHI MINH CITY (VIETNAM) *See* Vietnam—Ho Chi Minh City

HOAXES
Poe, E. A. The unparalleled adventure of one Hans Pfaall
Pynchon, T. The crying of lot 49
Sholem Aleichem. The bloody hoax
The **hobbit.** Tolkien, J. R. R.
Hocus pocus. Vonnegut, K.

HODGKIN'S DISEASE
Harris, M. Bang the drum slowly, by Henry W. Wiggen

HOFFMANN, E. T. A. (ERNST THEODOR AMADEUS), 1776-1822
Davies, R. The lyre of Orpheus

HOFFMANN, ERNST THEODOR AMADEUS *See* Hoffmann, E. T. A. (Ernst Theodor Amadeus), 1776-1822
A **hog** loves its life: something about my grandfather. Gurganus, A.
In Gurganus, A. White people p139-80
The **Holcroft** covenant. Ludlum, R.
also in Ludlum, R. The Ludlum triad p1-357
Hold the dream. Bradford, B. T.
The **holder** of the world. Mukherjee, B.

HOLDUPS *See* Robbery

HOLIDAYS
See also Christmas stories; Fourth of July; Thanksgiving Day; Vacations; Veterans Day

HOLLAND *See* Netherlands
The **Hollow.** Christie, A.
The **hollow** hills. Stewart, M.
also in Stewart, M. Mary Stewart's Merlin trilogy
The **hollow** lands. Moorcock, M.

HOLLYWOOD (CALIF.) *See* California—Hollywood
Hollywood. Vidal, G.
Hollywood nocturnes. Ellroy, J.

HOLOCAUST, JEWISH (1933-1945)
See also Jews—Persecutions
Amis, M. Time's arrow
Appelfeld, A. The age of wonders
Appelfeld, A. Badenheim 1939
Appelfeld, A. Tzili, the story of a life
Begley, L. Wartime lies
Bellow, S. The Bellarosa connection
Demetz, H. The house on Prague Street
Goldreich, G. That year of our war
Harris, R. Fatherland
Hersey, J. The wall
Iles, G. Black cross
Keneally, T. Schindler's list

Korda, M. Worldly goods
Ozick, C. The Messiah of Stockholm
Ozick, C. Rosa
Ozick, C. The shawl
Singer, I. B. Meshugah
Szeman, S. The Kommandant's mistress
Thomas, D. M. Pictures at an exhibition
Uris, L. Mila 18
Wiesel, E. The fifth son
Wiesel, E. The forgotten
Wiesel, E. The town beyond the wall
Wiesel, E. Twilight
Yolen, J. Briar Rose

HOLOCAUST SURVIVORS
Appelfeld, A. The age of wonders
Appelfeld, A. Tzili, the story of a life
Begley, L. Wartime lies
Bellow, S. Mr. Sammler's planet
Chatwin, B. Utz
De Hartog, J. The inspector
Demetz, H. The house on Prague Street
Demetz, H. The journey from Prague Street
Goldreich, G. Four days
Ozick, C. The shawl
Singer, I. B. Meshugah
Thomas, D. M. Pictures at an exhibition
Wallant, E. L. The pawnbroker
Wiesel, E. The accident
Wiesel, E. The fifth son
Wiesel, E. The forgotten
Wiesel, E. The town beyond the wall
Wiesel, E. Twilight

HOLY COAT
Douglas, L. C. The robe
Holy disorders. Crispin, E.

HOLY GRAIL *See* Grail
The **holy** thief. Peters, E.

HOLY WEEK
Faulkner, W. A fable
Home free. Hailey, E. F.
Home is the hangman. Zelazny, R.
In The Hugo winners v4 p5-67
Home song. Spencer, L.
Home to roost. Stout, R.
In Stout, R. Kings full of aces p325-68
Home truths. See Maitland, S. Ancestral truths
The **homecoming.** Hamner, E.
The **homecoming.** Lofts, N.
Homecoming. Snow, C. P.

Homecoming [series]
Card, O. S. The call of earth
Card, O. S. Earthborn
Card, O. S. Earthfall
Card, O. S. The memory of earth
Card, O. S. The ships of earth

HOMECOMINGS
Faulkner, W. Soldiers' pay
Fowles, J. Daniel Martin
Settle, M. L. The killing ground
Homegoing. Pohl, F.
Homeland. Jakes, J.

HOMELESS PERSONS
Auster, P. In the country of last things
Coetzee, J. M. Age of iron
Grau, S. A. Roadwalkers
Hailey, E. F. Home free
Kennedy, W. Ironweed
Piercy, M. The longings of women

Homeplace. Siddons, A. R.

HOMES See Houses

HOMES FOR THE ELDERLY See Old age homes

The **homesman**. Swarthout, G. F.

HOMESTEADING

    See also Frontier and pioneer life

    Aldrich, B. S. A lantern in her hand

    Bojer, J. The emigrants

    Doig, I. Dancing at the Rascal Fair

    Stegner, W. E. The Big Rock Candy Mountain

The **homing**. Saul, J.

Homing. Thane, E.

HOMOSEXUALITY

    See also Bisexuality; Lesbianism

    Baldwin, J. Just above my head

    Baldwin, J. Tell me how long the train's been gone

    Barker, P. The eye in the door

    Burgess, A. Earthly powers

    Capote, T. Answered prayers

    Dart, I. R. The Stork Club

    Durrell, L. Clea

    Durrell, L. Monsieur

    Eden, D. The millionaire's daughter

    The Faber book of gay short fiction

    Forster, E. M. Maurice

    Genet, J. Our Lady of the Flowers

    Gide, A. The counterfeiters (Les faux-monnayeurs)

    Gide, A. The immoralist

    Grumbach, D. Chamber music

    Hobson, L. K. Z. Consenting adult

    Kirkwood, J. Some kind of hero

    Leavitt, D. The lost language of cranes

    Leavitt, D. While England sleeps

    Lessing, D. M. The good terrorist

    Maitland, S. Ancestral truths

    Mann, T. Death in Venice

    Maupin, A. Maybe the moon

    McCauley, S. The easy way out

    Mishima, Y. Forbidden colors

    Monette, P. Afterlife

    Murdoch, I. The bell

    Murdoch, I. A fairly honourable defeat

    Oates, J. C. Nemesis

    Penguin book of gay short fiction

    Price, R. Kate Vaiden

    Price, R. The promise of rest

    Puig, M. Kiss of the spider woman

    Pym, B. The sweet dove died

    Renault, M. The charioteer

    Renault, M. The mask of Apollo

    Renault, M. The Persian boy

    Russell, P. Sea of tranquillity

    Vidal, G. Live from Golgotha

    Vine, B. No night is too long

    White, E. The beautiful room is empty

    White, E. A boy's own story

HOMOSEXUALS See Homosexuality; Lesbianism

Hondo. L'Amour, L.

    In L'Amour, L. Four complete novels p221-364

HONDURAS

    See also Guanaja Island (Honduras)

    Theroux, P. The Mosquito Coast

Honest illusions. Roberts, N.

Honest money, and other short novels. Gardner, E. S.

HONESTY

    See also Truthfulness and falsehood

Honey. Tallent, E.

HONG KONG

    Adler, E. Fortune is a woman

    Clavell, J. Noble house

    Clavell, J. Tai-Pan

    Elegant, R. S. Dynasty

    Gilman, D. Mrs. Pollifax and the Hong Kong Buddha

    Maas, P. China white

    Mason, R. The world of Suzie Wong

    Scott, J. The nine dragons

    Trenhaile, J. The gates of exquisite view

    Worboys, A. China silk

HONGKONG See Hong Kong

Honor & duty. Lee, G.

Honor among thieves. Archer, J.

Honor bound. Griffin, W. E. B.

Honorable men. Auchincloss, L.

The **honorary** consul. Greene, G.

The **honourable** schoolboy. Le Carré, J.

    also in Le Carré, J. The quest for Karla p253-678

A **hooded** crow. Thomas, C.

HOOVER, J. EDGAR (JOHN EDGAR), 1895-1972

    Ludlum, R. The Chancellor manuscript

HOOVER, JOHN EDGAR See Hoover, J. Edgar (John Edgar), 1895-1972

Hopalong Cassidy and the riders of High Rock. See L'Amour, L. The riders of High Rock

Hopalong Cassidy and the rustlers of West Fork. See L'Amour, L. The rustlers of West Fork

Hopalong Cassidy and the trail to Seven Pines. See L'Amour, L. The trail to Seven Pines

Hopalong Cassidy, trouble shooter. See L'Amour, L. Trouble shooter

The **hope**. Wouk, H.

A **hopeless** case. Beck, K. K.

Hopscotch. Cortázar, J.

Hopscotch. Garfield, B.

Horn of Africa. Caputo, P.

Hornblower and the Atropos. Forester, C. S.

Hornblower and the Hotspur. Forester, C. S.

Hornblower during the crisis, and two stories: Hornblower's temptation and The last encounter. Forester, C. S.

The **Horror** hall of fame. Entered in Part I under title

The **horror** in the museum, and other revisions. Lovecraft, H. P.

HORROR STORIES

    See also Ghost stories; Gothic romances; Murder stories; Supernatural phenomena; Vampires; Werewolves

    Aiken, C. King Coffin

    Alfred Hitchcock presents: Stories not for the nervous

    Barker, C. The books of blood

    Barker, C. Cabal

    Barker, C. The damnation game

    Barker, C. Everville

    Barker, C. The great and secret show

    Barker, C. In the flesh

    Barker, C. The inhuman condition

    Berger, T. The houseguest

    The Best horror from Fantasy Tales

    The Best horror stories

    Best new horror [1]-4

    Bloch, R. Psycho house

    Bradbury, R. A graveyard for lunatics

    Bradbury, R. Something wicked this way comes

    Campbell, R. The Count of Eleven

    Campbell, R. The long lost

    Campbell, R. The Nameless

    Campbell, R. Needing ghosts

    Campbell, R. Strange things and stranger places

    Card, O. S. Lost boys

    Clark, M. H. A cry in the night

    Davies, L. P. A grave matter

    De Felitta, F. Audrey Rose

    Dinesen, I. The angelic avengers

    Doyle, Sir A. C. Tales of terror and mystery

    Du Maurier, Dame D. Daphne du Maurier's classics of the macabre

    Fowles, J. The collector

    Goldman, W. Magic

    Hambly, B. Those who hunt the night

    The Horror hall of fame

    Jackson, S. The haunting of Hill House

    Jackson, S. We have always lived in the castle

    James, H. The turn of the screw

    King, S. The breathing method

HORROR STORIES—*Continued*
King, S. Carrie
King, S. Christine
King, S. Cujo
King, S. The dark half
King, S. Firestarter
King, S. Four past midnight
King, S. Gerald's game
King, S. Insomnia
King, S. It
King, S. Needful things
King, S. Night shift
King, S. Pet sematary
King, S. Salem's Lot
King, S. The shining
King, S. Skeleton crew
King, S. The stand
King, S. Thinner
King, S. The Tommyknockers
Koontz, D. R. The bad place
Koontz, D. R. Cold fire
Koontz, D. R. Hideaway
Koontz, D. R. Midnight
Koontz, D. R. Strangers
Koontz, D. R. Watchers
Levin, I. Rosemary's baby
Levin, I. The Stepford wives
Lovecraft, H. P. The horror in the museum, and other revisions
Lovecraft's legacy
March, W. The bad seed
Martin, V. Mary Reilly
Maupassant, G. de. The dark side of Guy de Maupassant
McCammon, R. R. Boy's life
McCammon, R. R. Mine
Michaels, B. The dark on the other side
Newman, K. Anno-Dracula
O'Connor, F. The violent bear it away
The Oxford book of gothic tales
Rice, A. Interview with the vampire
Rice, A. Lasher
Rice, A. The queen of the damned
Rice, A. The tale of the body thief
Rice, A. Taltos
Rice, A. The vampire Lestat
Rice, A. The witching hour
Rod Serling's Night gallery reader
Saul, J. Creature
Saul, J. Darkness
Saul, J. Guardian
Saul, J. The homing
Saul, J. Second child
Saul, J. Shadows
Shelley, M. W. Frankenstein
Stevenson, R. L. The strange case of Dr. Jekyll and Mr. Hyde
Stoker, B. The Bram Stoker bedside companion
Stoker, B. Dracula
Stoker, B. Midnight tales
Straub, P. The buffalo hunter
Straub, P. Ghost story
Strieber, W. Billy
Strieber, W. The forbidden zone
Strieber, W. The Wolfen
Tryon, T. Harvest home
Tryon, T. The other
Woods, S. Under the lake
Yarbro, C. Q. A candle for D'Artagnan
Yarbro, C. Q. Crusader's torch
The Year's best fantasy and horror

HORSE BREEDING
De Blasis, C. A season for Swans
The **horse** goddess. Llywelyn, M.
The **Horse** Latitudes. Ferrigno, R.

HORSE RACING
See also Jockeys
The Dick Francis treasury of great racing stories

Francis, D. Bolt
Francis, D. Bonecrack
Francis, D. Break in
Francis, D. Comeback
Francis, D. The danger
Francis, D. Decider
Francis, D. Driving force
Francis, D. The edge
Francis, D. Enquiry
Francis, D. For kicks
Francis, D. Forfeit
Francis, D. High stakes
Francis, D. Hot money
Francis, D. Longshot
Francis, D. Nerve
Francis, D. Rat race
Francis, D. Reflex
Francis, D. Risk
Francis, D. Slayride
Francis, D. Smokescreen
Francis, D. Three to show
Francis, D. Twice shy
Francis, D. Two by Francis
Francis, D. Whip hand
Francis, D. Wild horses
Kinsolving, W. Bred to win
The New treasury of great racing stories
Shoemaker, B. Stalking horse

HORSE TRADING
Faulkner, W. Father Abraham
The **Horse** You Came In On. Grimes, M.
A **horseman** riding by. Delderfield, R. F.

HORSEMANSHIP
Kosinski, J. N. Passion play

HORSES
See also Lippizaner horses
Brand, M. Dark Rosaleen
Francis, D. Banker
Francis, D. Blood sport
Francis, D. Flying finish
Francis, D. Knockdown
Hawkes, J. Sweet William
McCaffrey, A. The lady
McCarthy, C. All the pretty horses
Steinbeck, J. The red pony
The **horse's** mouth. Cary, J.
Horses of heaven. Bradshaw, G.

HORTENSE, CONSORT OF LOUIS, KING OF HOLLAND, 1783-1837
Lofts, N. A rose for virtue

HOSPITALS AND SANATORIUMS
Barker, P. The eye in the door
Barker, P. Regeneration
Clark, M. H. The cradle will fall
Cook, R. Brain
Cook, R. Coma
Cook, R. Fatal cure
Cook, R. Godplayer
Cook, R. Harmful intent
Cook, R. Terminal
Crichton, M. A case of need
Crichton, M. The terminal man
Cronin, A. J. A pocketful of rye
Douglas, L. C. Magnificent obsession
Endō, S. The sea and poison
Greene, G. A burnt-out case
Hemingway, E. A farewell to arms
Hooker, R. MASH
Hulme, K. The nun's story
Jackson, C. The lost weekend
Jones, J. Whistle
Kesey, K. One flew over the cuckoo's nest
Mann, T. The magic mountain
Mason, B. A. Spence + Lila
McCullough, C. An indecent obsession
Palmer, M. Natural causes

HOSPITALS AND SANATORIUMS—*Continued*
Renault, M. The charioteer
Ross-Macdonald, M. All desires known
Rosten, L. C. Captain Newman, M.D.
Sanders, L. The sixth commandment
Sheldon, S. Nothing lasts forever
Solzhenitsyn, A. Cancer ward
Steel, D. Accident
Wharton, W. Birdy
Wilson, F. P. The select
Wood, B. Soul flame

HOSTAGES
Greene, G. The tenth man
King, S. Misery
Lively, P. Cleopatra's sister
O'Brien, E. House of splendid isolation
Rule, A. Possession
Tyler, A. Earthly possessions
Wiesel, E. Dawn
Hostile intent. Egleton, C.
Hot. Lutz, J.
Hot money. Francis, D.
The hot rock. Westlake, D. E.
Hot Siberian. Browne, G. A.
Hot sky at midnight. Silverberg, R.
Hotel. Hailey, A.
Hotel du Lac. Brookner, A.
The Hotel New Hampshire. Irving, J.
Hotel Pastis. Mayle, P.

HOTELS, TAVERNS, ETC.
Amado, J. Gabriela, clove and cinnamon
Amis, K. The Green Man
Baum, V. Grand Hotel
Brookner, A. Hotel du Lac
Caldwell, T. Answer as a man
Chesney, M. Back in society
Chesney, M. Colonel Sandhurst to the rescue
Chesney, M. Lady Fortescue steps out
Chesney, M. Miss Tonks turns to crime
Chesney, M. Mrs. Budley falls from grace
Chesney, M. Sir Philip's folly
Conrad, J. Victory
Du Maurier, Dame D. Jamaica Inn
Estleman, L. D. City of widows
Gilman, D. A palm for Mrs. Pollifax
Godden, R. The greengage summer
Goudge, E. Pilgrim's inn
Greenberg, J. Simple gifts
Hailey, A. Hotel
Hardwick, M. The Duchess of Duke Street
Harvey, K. Stars
Holland, C. Pacific Street
Irving, J. The Hotel New Hampshire
King, S. The shining
Krentz, J. A. Grand passion
Markandaya, K. Shalimar
Mayle, P. Hotel Pastis
Mehta, G. A river Sutra
Michael, J. Inheritance
Moore, B. Lies of silence
Stead, C. The little hotel
Taylor, E. Mrs. Palfrey at the Claremont
The hound of the Baskervilles. Doyle, Sir A. C.
    also in Doyle, Sir A. C. The complete Sherlock
        Holmes

The Hounds of God. Tarr, J.
The house at Old Vine. Lofts, N.
The house at sunset. Lofts, N.
The house between the worlds. Bradley, M. Z.
A house divided. Buck, P. S.
House divided. Williams, B. A.
A house for Mr. Biswas. Naipaul, V. S.
A house in the country. Donoso, J.
House made of dawn. Momaday, N. S.
The house of brass. Queen, E.
The House of Eliott. Marsh, J.
The house of mirth. Wharton, E.
House of Niccolò [series]
    Dunnett, D. Niccolò rising
    Dunnett, D. Race of scorpions
    Dunnett, D. Scales of gold
    Dunnett, D. The spring of the ram
    Dunnett, D. The unicorn hunt
The house of shade. See Kaye, M. M. Death in Zanzibar
House of splendid isolation. O'Brien, E.
The house of stairs. Vine, B.
The house of the dead. Dostoyevsky, F.
The House of the Seven Gables. Hawthorne, N.
    also in Hawthorne, N. The complete novels and
        selected tales of Nathaniel Hawthorne
The house of the spirits. Allende, I.
The house of Vandekar. Anthony, E.
The house on Mango Street. Cisneros, S.
The house on Prague Street. Demetz, H.
The house on the strand. Du Maurier, Dame D.
The houseguest. Berger, T.

HOUSEHOLD EMPLOYEES
    See also Au pairs; Butlers; Charwomen; Cooks;
    Hired men; Hired women; Housekeepers; Maids
    (Servants); Nursemaids; Valets
Bellow, S. A theft
Household saints. Prose, F.

HOUSEKEEPERS
Appelfeld, A. Katerina
Dawson, C. Body of knowledge
Eden, D. The vines of Yarrabee
Ferrars, E. X. Trial by fury
McFarland, D. School for the blind
Piercy, M. The longings of women
Stein, G. Three lives

HOUSEMAIDS *See* Maids (Servants)

HOUSES
    See also Apartment houses
De la Roche, M. The building of Jalna
De la Roche, M. Centenary at Jalna
De la Roche, M. Jalna
Du Maurier, Dame D. The house on the strand
Forster, E. M. Howards End
Godden, R. China Court
Hawthorne, N. The House of the Seven Gables
Hodgins, E. Mr. Blandings builds his dream house
Holt, V. The legend of the seventh virgin
Holt, V. Menfreya in the morning
Howatch, S. Cashelmara
Howatch, S. Penmarric
Howatch, S. The wheel of fortune
James, H. The spoils of Poynton
Kells, S. The aristocrats
Lofts, N. Bless this house
Lofts, N. Gad's Hall
Lofts, N. The haunting of Gad's Hall
Lofts, N. The house at Old Vine
Lofts, N. The house at sunset
Lofts, N. Nethergate
Lofts, N. The old priory
Lofts, N. Pargeters
Naipaul, V. S. A house for Mr. Biswas
Pearce, M. E. The old house at Railes
Stevenson, D. E. Celia's house
Stewart, M. Touch not the cat

HOUSES—*Continued*
Vine, B. A fatal inversion
Whitney, P. A. Silverhill
Yorke, M. Find me a villain
Houses of stone. Michaels, B.
Houses without doors. Straub, P.

HOUSING PROJECTS *See* Public housing

HOUSTON, SAMUEL, 1793-1863
Michener, J. A. The eagle and the raven

HOUSTON (TEX.) *See* Texas—Houston

Houston, Houston, do you read? Tiptree, J.
In The Best of the Nebulas p420-60
In The Hugo winners v4 p200-56

A **hovering** of vultures. Barnard, R.

How green was my valley. Llewellyn, R.

How right you are, Jeeves. Wodehouse, P. G.

How the Garcia girls lost their accents. Alvarez, J.

How to make an American quilt. Otto, W.

How to murder your mother-in-law. Cannell, D.

How violence develops and where it can lead. See Böll,
H. The lost honor of Katharina Blum

Howards End. Forster, E. M.
also in Forster, E. M. A room with a view and
Howards End

Huckleberry Finn. See Twain, M. The adventures of
Huckleberry Finn

The **Hugo** winners. Entered in Part I under title

The **human** comedy. Saroyan, W.

The **human** factor. Greene, G.

Human nature. Wharton, E.
In Wharton, E. The collected short stories of Edith
Wharton v2

Humans. Westlake, D. E.

Humboldt's gift. Bellow, S.

HUMOR
See also Cheerful stories; Parodies; Satire
Adams, D. The Hitchhiker's Guide to the Galaxy
Adams, D. The hitchhiker's quartet
Adams, D. Life, the universe, and everything
Adams, D. The restaurant at the end of the universe
Adams, D. So long, and thanks for all the fish
Alvarez, J. How the Garcia girls lost their accents
Amis, K. Lucky Jim
Balzac, H. de. Droll stories
Bell, C. The Perez family
Bellow, S. Henderson the rain king
Bellow, S. Mr. Sammler's planet
Berger, T. The feud
Berger, T. Little Big Man
Berger, T. Reinhart's women
Berger, T. Sneaky people
Berger, T. Who is Teddy Villanova?
Boyle, T. C. Water music
Bradford, R. Red sky at morning
Breslin, J. The gang that couldn't shoot straight
Brown, R. M. Six of one
Brown, R. M. Venus envy
Capote, T. The grass harp
Carter, A. Wise children
Cary, J. The horse's mouth
Cheever, J. The Wapshot chronicle
Cheever, J. The Wapshot scandal
Crichton, R. The secret of Santa Vittoria
Davies, V. Miracle on 34th Street
De Vries, P. Consenting adults
De Vries, P. Slouching towards Kalamazoo
Dennis, P. Auntie Mame
Dickens, C. The posthumous papers of the Pickwick
Club
Duncan, D. J. The brothers K
Ephron, N. Heartburn
Faulkner, W. The reivers
Flagg, F. Fried green tomatoes at the Whistle-Stop
Cafe
Fraser, G. M. Flashman
Fraser, G. M. Flashman and the mountain of light
Fraser, G. M. Royal Flash

Greene, G. Monsignor Quixote
Greene, G. Travels with my aunt
Guareschi, G. Don Camillo and his flock
Guareschi, G. The little world of Don Camillo
Hašek, J. The good soldier Svejk
Heller, J. Catch-22
Helprin, M. Ellis Island
Hemingway, E. The torrents of spring
Hodgins, E. Mr. Blandings builds his dream house
Hooker, R. MASH
Hughes, L. Simple speaks his mind
Hughes, L. Simple stakes a claim
Hughes, L. Simple takes a wife
Hughes, L. Simple's Uncle Sam
Hyman, M. No time for sergeants
Irving, J. The Hotel New Hampshire
Irving, J. The water-method man
Kafka, F. Amerika
Keillor, G. The book of guys
Keillor, G. Lake Wobegon days
Keillor, G. WLT
Kingsolver, B. The bean trees
Kinsella, W. P. Box socials
Kundera, M. The book of laughter and forgetting
Lardner, R. You know me, Al
Lehrer, J. Kick the can
Leslie, J. A. C. The ghost and Mrs. Muir
Levi, P. The monkey's wrench
Lipman, E. The way men act
Lurie, A. Only children
McBain, E. Downtown
McMurtry, L. Cadillac Jack
McMurtry, L. The evening star
McMurtry, L. Terms of endearment
McMurtry, L. Texasville
Murdoch, I. The nice and the good
Nabokov, V. V. Pnin
Narayan, R. K. The world of Nagaraj
Parkinson, C. N. Jeeves: a gentleman's personal gen-
tleman
Pearson, T. R. A short history of a small place
Portis, C. Gringos
Portis, C. True grit
Powers, J. R. The junk-drawer corner-store front-porch
blues
Prose, F. Hungry hearts
Pym, B. A glass of blessings
Pym, B. Jane and Prudence
Richter, C. The grandfathers
Roth, P. My life as a man
Roth, P. Portnoy's complaint
Runyon, D. Best of Runyon
Runyon, D. Guys and dolls
Rushdie, S. Midnight's children
Rushdie, S. Shame
Saint, H. F. Memoirs of an invisible man
Sarton, M. The fur person
Sholem Aleichem. The adventures of Menaham-Mendl
Sholem Aleichem. The adventures of Mottel, the can-
tor's son
Shulman, M. The many loves of Dobie Gillis
Shulman, M. Rally round the flag, boys!
Smith, R. K. Sadie Shapiro's knitting book
Smollett, T. G. Humphry Clinker
Sneider, V. The Teahouse of the August Moon
Spark, M. The comforters
Spark, M. The prime of Miss Jean Brodie
Steinbeck, J. Cannery Row
Steinbeck, J. Sweet Thursday
Stevenson, R. L. The misadventures of John
Nicholson
Streeter, E. Father of the bride
Struther, J. Mrs. Miniver
Swarthout, G. F. Bless the beasts and children
Tarkington, B. Seventeen
Taylor, R. L. The travels of Jaimie McPheeters
Toole, J. K. A confederacy of dunces
Townsend, S. The Adrian Mole diaries

HUMOR—*Continued*
Townsend, S. Adrian Mole: the lost years
Trollope, A. The Duke's children
Twain, M. The adventures of Huckleberry Finn
Twain, M. The adventures of Tom Sawyer
Twain, M. Those extraordinary twins
Viorst, J. Murdering Mr. Monti
Voigt, C. Glass mountain
Waugh, E. Decline and fall
Waugh, E. The loved one
Waugh, E. Men at arms
Waugh, E. Officers and gentlemen
Welty, E. The Ponder heart
West, J. Cress Delahanty
West, J. Except for me and thee
West, J. The friendly persuasion
Westlake, D. E. Bank shot
Westlake, D. E. Don't ask
Westlake, D. E. Drowned hopes
Westlake, D. E. Good behavior
Westlake, D. E. The hot rock
Westlake, D. E. The spy in the ointment
Westlake, D. E. Why me?
Wibberley, L. The mouse that roared
Wodehouse, P. G. The code of the Woosters
Wodehouse, P. G. How right you are, Jeeves
Wodehouse, P. G. The inimitable Jeeves
Wodehouse, P. G. Jeeves and the tie that binds
Wodehouse, P. G. Tales from the Drones Club
Wodehouse, P. G. A Wodehouse bestiary
Zelazny, R. Bring me the head of Prince Charming

HUMOROUS STORIES *See* Humor
Humphry Clinker. Smollett, T. G.
Hun. Burgess, A.
   In Burgess, A. The devil's mode p152-269
The **hunchback** of Notre Dame. Hugo, V.

HUNCHBACKS
Hugo, V. The hunchback of Notre Dame
McCullers, C. The ballad of the sad café [novelette]

HUNDRED YEARS' WAR, 1339-1453
Doyle, Sir A. C. The White Company
Haasse, H. S. In a dark wood wandering

HUNGARY
Pearson, D. Csardas
Wiesel, E. The town beyond the wall

        Aristocracy
   See Aristocracy—Hungary

      World War, 1939-1945
   See World War, 1939-1945—Hungary

HUNGER
   See also Starvation
Hunger. Hamsun, K.
Hungry as the sea. Smith, W. A.
Hungry hearts. Prose, F.
Hungry Hill. Du Maurier, Dame D.
The **hunt** for Red October. Clancy, T.
The **hunted.** Leonard, E.
   In Leonard, E. Elmore Leonard's Dutch treat: 3 novels

HUNTERS *See* Hunting
Hunter's green. Whitney, P. A.
Hunter's moon. Anderson, P.
   In The Hugo winners v4 p510-50

HUNTING
   See also Trappers and trapping; Whaling
Colegate, I. The shooting party
Cooper, J. F. The pioneers
Golding, W. Clonk clonk
Guthrie, A. B. The big sky
Rawlings, M. K. South moon under
Thomas, E. M. The animal wife
Thomas, E. M. Reindeer Moon

         Africa
Gilman, D. Mrs. Pollifax on safari

Ruark, R. Something of value
Smith, W. A. A time to die
The **hurricane.** Nordhoff, C.

HURRICANES
Nordhoff, C. The hurricane

HUSBAND AND WIFE
   See also Desertion and nonsupport; Marriage
Lewis, S. Cass Timberlane
Lewis, S. Dodsworth
Mason, B. A. Spence + Lila
Oates, J. C. American appetites

HUSTON, JOHN, 1906-1987
Bradbury, R. Green shadows, white whale
The **Hyde** Park headsman. Perry, A.
The **Hyde** Park murder. Roosevelt, E.
The **Hydra** head. Fuentes, C.

HYDROGEN BOMB *See* Atomic bomb

HYDROPHOBIA *See* Rabies

HYPNOSIS *See* Hypnotism

HYPNOTISM
Stoker, B. Dracula
Thomas, R. Voodoo, Ltd

HYPOCRISY
Dickens, C. Martin Chuzzlewit

I

I am Mary Dunne. Moore, B.
I am Mary Tudor. Lewis, H. W.
I am the clay. Potok, C.
I am the only running footman. Grimes, M.
I been in sorrow's kitchen and licked out all the pots. Straight, S.
I can get it for you wholesale. Weidman, J.
I, Claudius. Graves, R.
"I have a thing to tell you". Wolfe, T.
   In Wolfe, T. The short novels of Thomas Wolfe p236-78
I heard the owl call my name. Craven, M.
"I" is for innocent. Grafton, S.
I, Judas. Caldwell, T.
I lock my door upon myself. Oates, J. C.
I never promised you a rose garden. Greenberg, J.
I.O.U. Pickard, N.
I remember! I remember! O'Faoláin, S.
   In O'Faolain, S. The collected stories of Sean O'Faolain p544-699
I, robot. Asimov, I.
I sing the Body Electric! Bradbury, R.
I take this woman. See Simenon, G. The truth about Bébé Donge
I, Tituba, black witch of Salem. Condé, M.
The **Icarus** agenda. Ludlum, R.
Ice. McBain, E.

ICE AGE *See* Prehistoric times
The **ice** age. Drabble, M.
Ice Palace. Ferber, E.
Ice Station Zebra. MacLean, A.
Iced. Clark, C. H.

ICELAND

         10th century
Seton, A. Avalon
The **iciest** sin. Keating, H. R. F.
Icy clutches. Elkins, A. J.

IDAHO
Saul, J. Guardian
Woods, S. Heat

IDENTITY *See* Personality
The **ides** of March. Wilder, T.
The **idiot**. Dostoyevsky, F.
If Beale Street could talk. Baldwin, J.
If ever I return, pretty Peggy-O. McCrumb, S.
If not now, when? Levi, P.
If on a winter's night a traveler. Calvino, I.
If the river was whiskey. Boyle, T. C.
If you knew me. Roiphe, A. R.
Iguana dreams. Entered in Part I under title
I'll be leaving you always. Scoppettone, S.
I'll be seeing you. Clark, M. H.
I'll be there. Dart, I. R.
The **ill-made** knight. White, T. H.
    In White, T. H. The once and future king p325-544
Ill met in Lankhmar. Leiber, F.
    In The Hugo winners v3 p55-115
I'll take Manhattan. Krantz, J.
The **Illearth** war. Donaldson, S. R.
ILLEGAL ALIENS *See* Undocumented aliens
ILLEGITIMACY
    See also Unmarried mothers
    Aiken, J. Eliza's daughter
    Allen, H. Anthony Adverse
    Allison, D. Bastard out of Carolina
    Archer, J. Kane & Abel
    Bradshaw, G. The bearkeeper's daughter
    Carter, A. Wise children
    Cheever, J. Bullet Park
    Coulter, C. The Wyndham legacy
    Dickens, C. Bleak House
    Dreiser, T. Jennie Gerhardt
    Dunnett, D. Pawn in frankincense
    Eden, D. The American heiress
    Faulkner, W. The sound and the fury
    Fielding, H. The history of Tom Jones, a foundling
    Gaines, E. J. In my father's house
    Gardner, J. Nickel mountain
    Haasse, H. S. The scarlet city
    Harris, R. Love and money
    Hawthorne, N. The scarlet letter
    Hill, P. Vollands
    Holt, V. Daughter of deceit
    Holt, V. The mask of the enchantress
    Howatch, S. Penmarric
    Howatch, S. The shrouded walls
    Kennedy, W. Very old bones
    Krantz, J. Mistral's daughter
    Lofts, N. Gad's Hall
    Maalouf, A. The rock of Tanios
    Oates, J. C. A garden of earthly delights
    Plain, B. Blessings
    Rossner, J. Emmeline
    Spencer, L. Home song
    Stubbs, J. Family games
    Swindells, M. Summer harvest
    Tryon, T. In the fire of spring
    Vine, B. Anna's book
    Wharton, E. The old maid

ILLINOIS
        19th century
- Dickens, C. Martin Chuzzlewit

        20th century
    Bradbury, R. Dandelion wine
    Steel, D. The gift
    Straub, P. The throat
    Wilder, T. The eighth day

        Farm life
    See Farm life—Illinois

        Chicago
    Algren, N. The man with the golden arm
    Bellow, S. The adventures of Augie March
    Bellow, S. Dangling man
    Bellow, S. The dean's December
    Bellow, S. Humboldt's gift

    Bellow, S. What kind of day did you have?
    Birmingham, S. The Auerbach will
    Campbell, B. M. Your blues ain't like mine
    Campbell, R. W. Boneyards
    Cisneros, S. The house on Mango Street
    Diehl, W. Primal fear
    Dreiser, T. Jennie Gerhardt
    Dreiser, T. Sister Carrie
    Fielding, J. Tell me no secrets
    Greeley, A. M. Ascent into hell
    Greeley, A. M. Fall from grace
    Greeley, A. M. Lord of the dance
    Greeley, A. M. Patience of a saint
    Greeley, A. M. Thy brother's wife
    Hailey, A. Airport
    Jakes, J. Homeland
    Miller, S. Family pictures
    Norris, F. The pit
    Olsen, T. Yonnondio: from the thirties
    Powers, J. R. The junk-drawer corner-store front-porch blues
    Sinclair, A. Coffee will make you black
    Sinclair, U. The jungle
    Spencer, S. Endless love
    Wright, R. Lawd today!
    Wright, R. Native son
    Wright, R. The outsider

ILLNESS
    See also Invalids; Mental illness; Terminal illness
    James, H. The wings of the dove
    Sarton, M. A reckoning
Illumination night. Hoffman, A.
ILLUSIONS *See* Hallucinations and illusions
The **illustrated** man. Bradbury, R.
ILLUSTRATORS
    Godwin, G. Violet Clay
    Norman, H. The bird artist

IMAGINARY CITIES
    Calvino, I. Invisible cities
    Le Guin, U. K. City of illusions
    Le Guin, U. K. The eye of the heron

IMAGINARY KINGDOMS
    Anthony, P. Blue Adept
    Anthony, P. Juxtaposition
    Anthony, P. Out of Phaze
    Anthony, P. Phaze doubt
    Anthony, P. Robot Adept
    Anthony, P. Split infinity
    Anthony, P. Unicorn point
    Barker, C. Weaveworld
    Brooks, T. The black unicorn
    Brooks, T. The druid of Shannara
    Brooks, T. The elfqueen of Shannara
    Brooks, T. The Elfstones of Shannara
    Brooks, T. Magic kingdom for sale—sold!
    Brooks, T. The scions of Shannara
    Brooks, T. The sword of Shannara
    Brooks, T. The talismans of Shannara
    Brooks, T. The Tangle Box
    Brooks, T. The wishsong of Shannara
    Brooks, T. Wizard at large
    Cabell, J. B. Jurgen: a comedy of justice
    Eddings, D. Belgarath the sorcerer
    Eddings, D. Demon lord of Karanda
    Eddings, D. The diamond throne
    Eddings, D. Domes of fire
    Eddings, D. Guardians of the west
    Eddings, D. The hidden city
    Eddings, D. King of the Murgos
    Eddings, D. The ruby knight
    Eddings, D. The sapphire rose
    Eddings, D. The seeress of Kell
    Eddings, D. The shining ones
    Eddings, D. Sorceress of Darshiva
    Hope, A. The prisoner of Zenda
    Pohl, F. Beyond the blue event horizon

IMAGINARY KINGDOMS—*Continued*

Silverberg, R. Lord Valentine's castle
Silverberg, R. Majipoor chronicles
Silverberg, R. Valentine Pontifex
Swift, J. Gulliver's travels
Tarr, J. The Hounds of God
Tolkien, J. R. R. The hobbit
Tolkien, J. R. R. The lord of the rings
Tolkien, J. R. R. The return of the king
Tolkien, J. R. R. The Silmarillion
Tolkien, J. R. R. The two towers
Tolkien, J. R. R. Unfinished tales of Númenor and Middle-earth
Vinge, J. D. The Snow Queen
Vinge, J. D. The Summer Queen
Vinge, J. D. World's end
The **imaginary** voyages: The narrative of Arthur Gordon Pym; The unparalleled adventure of one Hans Pfaall; The journal of Julius Rodman. Poe, E. A.

IMAGINARY WARS AND BATTLES

Norton, A. Firehand
Vance, J. The last castle
Imago. Butler, O. E.
Imajica. Barker, C.
Immaculate man. Gordon, M.
In Gordon, M. The rest of life: three novellas

IMMIGRANTS

Bojer, J. The emigrants
Cather, W. My Ántonia
Doctorow, E. L. Ragtime
Fox, P. A servant's tale
Helprin, M. Ellis Island
Jakes, J. Homeland
Jen, G. Typical American
Mukherjee, B. Jasmine
Roth, H. A star shines over Mt. Morris Park
Sinclair, U. The jungle
Škvorecký, J. The engineer of human souls
Stewart, F. M. Ellis Island
Stewart, F. M. The glitter and the gold
The **immigrants.** Fast, H.
The **immigrant's** daughter. Fast, H.
Immoral certainty. Tanenbaum, R.
The **immoralist.** Gide, A.
Immortal wife. Stone, I.

IMMORTALITY

Kelly, J. P. Mr. Boy
Kundera, M. Immortality
Robbins, T. Jitterbug perfume
Silverberg, R. Sailing to Byzantium
Wilhelm, K. Welcome, chaos
Immortality. Kundera, M.
The **immortals.** Korda, M.
An **imperfect** spy. Cross, A.
Imperfect strangers. Woods, S.
Imperial Earth. Clarke, A. C.
Imperial purple. Bradshaw, G.
Imperial woman. Buck, P. S.

IMPERIALISM

Fuentes, C. The campaign
Naipaul, V. S. A way in the world
Scott, P. The day of the scorpion
Scott, P. The jewel in the crown

IMPERSONATIONS

This subject is used for stories dealing with individuals who assume or act the character of another. For tales describing a condition in which one individual shows in alternation two very different characters see subject: Dual personality
See also Impostors; Mistaken identity
Alcott, L. M. Behind a mask [novelette]
Barrett, W. E. The left hand of God
Barrie, J. M. The little minister
Brown, D. A. Killdeer Mountain
Brown, R. M. High hearts
DeMille, N. The charm school

Dickens, C. Our mutual friend
Dickens, C. A tale of two cities
Du Maurier, Dame D. The scapegoat
Dumas, A. The Queen's necklace
Eden, D. The American heiress
Greene, G. The tenth man
Heinlein, R. A. Double star
Helprin, M. Ellis Island
Higgins, J. Night of the fox
Holt, V. The mask of the enchantress
Hope, A. The prisoner of Zenda
Jones, T. Hard road to Gettysburg
Lovesey, P. The false Inspector Dew
Michael, J. Deceptions
Michael, J. A tangled web
Roth, P. Operation Shylock
Stewart, M. The ivy tree
Tarkington, B. Monsieur Beaucaire
Tey, J. Brat Farrar
Twain, M. The American claimant
Twain, M. The prince and the pauper
Twain, M. Pudd'nhead Wilson
Whitney, P. A. Emerald
An **important** family. Eden, D.
The **impostor.** Cocteau, J.

IMPOSTORS

See also Impersonations
Dickinson, P. Perfect gallows

IMPROBABLE STORIES

See also Fantasies
Impulse. Coulter, C.
In a dark wood wandering. Haasse, H. S.
In chancery. Galsworthy, J.
In Galsworthy, J. The Forsyte saga p363-639
In country. Mason, B. A.
In dubious battle. Steinbeck, J.
In evil hour. García Márquez, G.
In full of account. Gardner, E. S.
In Gardner, E. S. Dead men's letters p229-75
In her garden. Godden, J.
In La-La Land we trust. Campbell, R. W.
In love and war. See Ross-Macdonald, M. For they shall inherit
In my father's house. Gaines, E. J.
In our time. Hemingway, E.
In pursuit of the green lion. Riley, J. M.
In search of lost time [series]
Proust, M. The captive [and] The fugitive
Proust, M. The Guermantes way
Proust, M. Sodom and Gomorrah
Proust, M. Swann's way
Proust, M. Time regained [variant title: The past recaptured]
Proust, M. Within a budding grove
In the beginning. Potok, C.
In the best families. Stout, R.
In Stout, R. Five of a kind p155-303
In the cage. James, H.
In James, H. The complete tales of Henry James v10
In James, H. What Maisie knew, In the cage, The pupil
In the company of eagles. Gann, E. K.
In the country of last things. Auster, P.
In the days of the comet. Wells, H. G.
In Wells, H. G. Seven famous novels
In the electric mist with Confederate dead. Burke, J. L.
In the fire of spring. Tryon, T.
In the flesh. Barker, C.
In the flesh [novelette]. Barker, C.
In Barker, C. In the flesh

In the frame. Francis, D.
In the heat of the night. Ball, J. D.
In the Lake of the Woods. O'Brien, T.
In the presence of enemies. Coughlin, W. J.
In the skin of a lion. Ondaatje, M.
In the teeth of the evidence and other stories. Sayers, D. L.
In the time of the butterflies. Alvarez, J.
In the wilderness. Undset, S.
   In Undset, S. The master of Hestviken v3
In this house of Brede. Godden, R.
In this our life. Glasgow, E.
In this sign. Greenberg, J.
In transit. Gallant, M.
Inadmissable evidence. Friedman, P.
Inca gold. Cussler, C.
Incarnations of immortality [series]
   Anthony, P. And eternity
   Anthony, P. Bearing an hourglass
   Anthony, P. Being a green mother
   Anthony, P. For love of evil
   Anthony, P. On a pale horse
   Anthony, P. Wielding a red sword
   Anthony, P. With a tangled skein

INCAS
   Cussler, C. Inca gold

INCEST
   Appelfeld, A. Unto the soul
   Chute, C. The Beans of Egypt, Maine
   Gage, E. The master stroke
   King, S. Gerald's game
   Korda, M. Curtain
   Michael, J. Sleeping beauty
   Oates, J. C. You must remember this
   Rice, A. Lasher
   Rossner, J. Emmeline
   Roth, H. A diving rock on the Hudson
   Theroux, P. Picture palace
   Tilly, M. Singing songs
Incident at Badamya. Gilman, D.
An **inconvenient** woman. Dunne, D.
The **incredible** and sad tale of innocent Eréndira and her heartless grandmother. García Márquez, G.
   In García Márquez, G. Collected stories p262-311
   In García Márquez, G. Innocent Eréndira, and other stories p1-59
The **incredible** journey. Burnford, S.
The **incredulity** of Father Brown. Chesterton, G. K.
   In Chesterton, G. K. The Father Brown omnibus p433-630
An **indecent** obsession. McCullough, C.
Indemnity only. Paretsky, S.

INDENTURED SERVANTS
   Doig, I. The sea runners

INDEPENDENCE DAY (UNITED STATES) *See* Fourth of July

INDIA
   Aldiss, B. W. Total environment
   Benford, G. Matter's end
   Hesse, H. Siddhartha
   Mehta, G. A river Sutra
   Zelazny, R. Lord of light

17th century
   Mukherjee, B. The holder of the world

British occupation, 1765-1947
   Cleary, J. The faraway drums
   Forster, E. M. A passage to India
   Fraser, G. M. Flashman
   Fraser, G. M. Flashman and the mountain of light
   Holt, V. The India fan
   Jhabvala, R. P. Heat and dust
   Kaye, M. M. The far pavilions
   Kaye, M. M. Shadow of the moon

Mehta, G. Raj
Scott, P. The day of the scorpion
Scott, P. A division of the spoils
Scott, P. The jewel in the crown
Scott, P. The Raj quartet
Scott, P. The towers of silence
Stewart, F. M. Pomp and circumstance

20th century
Bromfield, L. The rains came
Godden, R. Black Narcissus

1947-
Desai, A. Clear light of day
Desai, A. Fire on the mountain
Jhabvala, R. P. Out of India
Jhabvala, R. P. Three continents
Markandaya, K. A handful of rice
Masters, J. Bhowani Junction
Narayan, R. K. Under the banyan tree and other stories
Rushdie, S. Midnight's children
Scott, P. Staying on
Seth, V. A suitable boy
Waller, R. J. Slow waltz in Cedar Bend

Politics
   See Politics—India

Race relations
Forster, E. M. A passage to India
Masters, J. Bhowani Junction

Rural life
Jhabvala, R. P. Heat and dust
Markandaya, K. Shalimar
Narayan, R. K. The grandmother's tale and selected stories
Narayan, R. K. Malgudi days
Narayan, R. K. The world of Nagaraj

Benares
Mishima, Y. The Temple of Dawn

Bombay
Desai, A. Baumgartner's Bombay
Irving, J. A son of the circus
Mann, P. Season of the monsoon
Rushdie, S. Midnight's children

Delhi
Desai, A. Clear light of day
Thomas, C. Playing with cobras
The **India** fan. Holt, V.
Indian affairs. Woiwode, L.
The **Indian** lawyer. Welch, J.
INDIAN OCEAN *See* World War, 1939-1945—Indian Ocean
Indian summer. Knowles, J.
The **Indian** summer of a Forsyte. Galsworthy, J.
   In Galsworthy, J. The Forsyte saga p313-59
   In Galsworthy, J. The Galsworthy reader p543-86
INDIANA
   See also Fall Creek (Ind.)

19th century
Lockridge, R. Raintree County
Tarkington, B. The gentleman from Indiana
Tarkington, B. The magnificent Ambersons
West, J. Except for me and thee
West, J. The friendly persuasion
West, J. The massacre at Fall Creek

20th century
Tarkington, B. Alice Adams
Vonnegut, K. God bless you, Mr. Rosewater

INDIANA—*Continued*

Frontier and pioneer life
See Frontier and pioneer life—Indiana

Politics
See Politics—Indiana

Indianapolis
Pinckney, D. High cotton

INDIANAPOLIS (IND.) *See* Indiana—Indianapolis

INDIANS OF MEXICO
See also Aztecs; Incas

INDIANS OF NORTH AMERICA
See also names of specific tribes or nations
Brown, D. A. Creek Mary's blood
Cooper, J. F. The Leatherstocking tales
Cooper, J. F. The pioneers
De Hartog, J. The peculiar people
Dillard, A. The living
Dorris, M. The crown of Columbus
Earth song, sky spirit
Fisher, V. Mountain man
Gear, K. O. People of the lakes
Gear, K. O. People of the lightning
Gear, W. M. People of the river
Gear, W. M. People of the sea
Grey, Z. The vanishing American
Guthrie, A. B. The big sky
Guthrie, A. B. Fair land, fair land
Guthrie, A. B. The way West
Harrison, S. Brother Wind
Harrison, S. Mother earth, father sky
Harrison, S. My sister the moon
Hill, R. B. Hanta yo
Jones, D. C. This savage race
Kingsolver, B. Animal dreams
L'Amour, L. The haunted mesa
L'Amour, L. Jubal Sackett
L'Amour, L. Last of the breed
Ludlum, R. The road to Omaha
McMurtry, L. Buffalo girls
Michener, J. A. Centennial
Momaday, N. S. House made of dawn
Moore, B. Black robe
Perry, T. Vanishing act
Roberts, K. L. Northwest Passage
Smith, M. C. Stallion Gate
Spellman, C. C. Paint the wind
Welch, J. The Indian lawyer
West, J. The massacre at Fall Creek
Woiwode, L. Indian affairs

Captivities
Berger, T. Little Big Man
Giles, J. H. Hannah Fowler
McCrumb, S. She walks these hills
Richter, C. The light in the forest

Wars
See also United States—French and Indian War, 1755-1763
Cooper, J. F. The Deerslayer
Cooper, J. F. The last of the Mohicans
Cooper, J. F. The Pathfinder
Cooper, J. F. The prairie
Edmonds, W. D. Drums along the Mohawk

California
L'Amour, L. The Californios

Montana
Dorris, M. A yellow raft in blue water
Stuart, C. Walks Far Woman

New Mexico
Cather, W. Death comes for the archbishop

North Dakota
Erdrich, L. The bingo palace
Erdrich, L. Love medicine
Erdrich, L. Tracks

Power, S. The grass dancer

INDIANS OF SOUTH AMERICA
Hudson, W. H. Green mansions
Vargas Llosa, M. The storyteller
The **indictment**. Reed, B.

INDIVIDUALISM
Knowles, J. Indian summer
Orwell, G. Nineteen eighty-four
Pasternak, B. L. Doctor Zhivago
Rand, A. Anthem
Rand, A. Atlas shrugged

INDOCHINA
Duras, M. The lover
Duras, M. The North China lover
Lustbader, E. V. French kiss

INDOCTRINATION, FORCED *See* Brainwashing
The **indulgent** husband. See Colette. Claudine married

INDUSTRIAL ACCIDENTS
Cussler, C. Sahara
DeLillo, D. White noise

INDUSTRIAL CONDITIONS
Dickens, C. Hard times
Singer, I. J. The brothers Ashkenazi
Zaroulis, N. L. Call the darkness light

INDUSTRIALISTS *See* Capitalists and financiers

INDUSTRIALIZATION *See* Industrial conditions

INFANTICIDE
Appelfeld, A. Katerina
Stirling, J. Lantern for the dark
The **infinite** plan. Allende, I.
The **informer**. O'Flaherty, L.

INFORMERS
See also Treason
O'Flaherty, L. The informer
The **ingenious** gentleman, Don Quixote de la Mancha.
See Cervantes Saavedra, M. de. Don Quixote de la Mancha
Inheritance. Michael, J.

INHERITANCE AND SUCCESSION
See also Wills
Aiken, J. Voices in an empty house
Alcott, L. M. The mysterious key and what it opened
Brent, M. Golden urchin
Brent, M. Stormswift
Brent, M. Tregaron's daughter
Cheever, J. The Wapshot chronicle
Coscarelli, K. Heir apparent
Coughlin, W. J. In the presence of enemies
Coulter, C. The Wyndham legacy
Dailey, J. Heiress
Dickens, C. Bleak House
Dickens, C. Great expectations
Dickens, C. Our mutual friend
Francis, D. Decider
Francis, D. Straight
Fuentes, C. Sons of the Conquistador
Gregory, P. Meridon
Gross, J. The books of Rachel
Hawthorne, N. Doctor Grimshawe's secret
Holt, V. Kirkland Revels
Howatch, S. The shrouded walls
James, H. The ivory tower
James, H. Washington Square
James, H. The wings of the dove
Kells, S. The aristocrats
Korda, M. The fortune
Leonard, E. Gold Coast
Michael, J. Inheritance
Michaels, B. Into the darkness
Murdoch, I. Henry and Cato
Palliser, C. The quincunx
Renault, M. Funeral games
Robards, K. Nobody's angel
Ross-Macdonald, M. An innocent woman

INHERITANCE AND SUCCESSION—*Continued*
Simenon, G. The old man dies
Stewart, M. The ivy tree
Thackeray, W. M. The history of Henry Esmond, esquire
Thayer, N. Everlasting
Twain, M. The American claimant
Voigt, C. Glass mountain
White, P. The eye of the storm
Woods, S. Imperfect strangers
The **inheritors**. Golding, W.
The **inhuman** condition. Barker, C.
The **inimitable** Jeeves. Wodehouse, P. G.
The **ink** truck. Kennedy, W.
The **inland** sea. See Cooper, J. F. The Pathfinder
INNKEEPERS *See* Hotels, taverns, etc.
The **innkeeper's** song. Beagle, P. S.
The **innocence** of Father Brown. Chesterton, G. K.
   also in Chesterton, G. K. The Father Brown omnibus p1-226
The **innocent**. McEwan, I.
Innocent blood. James, P. D.
Innocent Eréndira, and other stories. García Márquez, G.
The **innocent** wife. See Colette. Claudine and Annie
An **innocent** woman. Ross-Macdonald, M.
INNS *See* Hotels, taverns, etc.
INQUISITION
Holland, C. The Sea Beggars
Plaidy, J. The scarlet cloak
INSANE, CRIMINAL AND DANGEROUS
   See also Insanity; Mentally ill
Clark, M. H. A cry in the night
Clark, M. H. A stranger is watching
Harris, T. Red Dragon
Harris, T. The silence of the lambs
Katzenbach, J. Just cause
King, S. Misery
King, S. Rage
Koontz, D. R. The face of fear
Koontz, D. R. Hideaway
Koontz, D. R. Mr. Murder
Leonard, E. City primeval
Leonard, E. Glitz
Lutz, J. Dancing with the dead
Oates, J. C. Snake eyes
Patterson, J. Along came a spider
Patterson, J. Kiss the girls
Reed, K. Gone
Rendell, R. Live flesh
Rule, A. Possession
Strieber, W. Billy
INSANE ASYLUMS *See* Mentally ill—Care and treatment
INSANITY
   See also Insane, Criminal and dangerous; Mental illness; Personality disorders
Armstrong, C. The turret room
Brontë, C. Jane Eyre
Cheever, J. Bullet Park
Faulkner, W. The sound and the fury
Galsworthy, J. Maid in waiting
Jackson, S. We have always lived in the castle
Keneally, T. A family madness
King, S. Roadwork
Nin, A. The four-chambered heart
Oates, J. C. Expensive people
Stevenson, R. L. The Merry Men
Ward, M. J. The snake pit
West, M. L. The clowns of God
Wiesel, E. Twilight
INSECTS
Kafka, F. Metamorphosis
Saul, J. The homing

Inside, outside. Wouk, H.
Insomnia. King, S.
The **inspector.** De Hartog, J.
Inspector Ghote trusts the heart. Keating, H. R. F.
Inspector Maigret and the killers. See Simenon, G. Maigret and the gangsters
INSPIRATION *See* Creation (Literary, artistic, etc.)
The **instant** enemy. Macdonald, R.
   In Macdonald, R. Archer in jeopardy
INSTRUCTORS *See* Teachers
INSURANCE BROKERS
Cain, J. M. Double indemnity
Gurganus, A. Blessed assurance: a moral tale
Shreve, A. Where or when
The **integral** trees. Niven, L.
INTELLECTUALS
   See also Scholars
Oz, A. Fima
INTELLIGENCE AGENTS *See* Secret service
INTER-RACIAL MARRIAGE *See* Interracial marriage
Interest of justice. Rosenberg, N. T.
INTERFAITH MARRIAGE
Freeman, C. The last princess
Richler, M. Joshua then and now
Roth, P. Letting go
Singer, I. B. The slave
An **international** episode. James, H.
   In James, H. The complete tales of Henry James v4
   In James, H. Daisy Miller [and An international episode] v2
INTERNATIONAL INTRIGUE
   See also Adventure; Secret service; Spies
Allbeury, T. Deep purple
Allbeury, T. The Judas factor
Ambler, E. The Levanter
Anthony, E. Albatross
Anthony, E. The avenue of the dead
Anthony, E. The company of saints
Anthony, E. Exposure
Anthony, E. The Janus imperative
Anthony, E. The tamarind seed
Archer, J. Honor among thieves
Archer, J. A matter of honor
Bova, B. Voyagers
Brown, D. Chains of command
Browne, G. A. Hot Siberian
Buchan, J. The thirty-nine steps
Buckley, W. F. Mongoose, R.I.P
Buckley, W. F. Tucker's last stand
Buckley, W. F. A very private plot
Carroll, J. Family trade
Clancy, T. The Cardinal of the Kremlin
Clancy, T. Clear and present danger
Clancy, T. Debt of honor
Clancy, T. The hunt for Red October
Clancy, T. Patriot games
Clancy, T. Red Storm rising
Clancy, T. The sum of all fears
Clavell, J. Noble house
Collins, L. The fifth horseman
Coonts, S. The minotaur
Coonts, S. The red horseman
Coyle, H. W. Bright star
Cussler, C. Cyclops
Cussler, C. Deep six
Cussler, C. Dragon
Cussler, C. Night probe!
Cussler, C. Raise the Titanic!
Cussler, C. Sahara
Cussler, C. Treasure
Cussler, C. Vixen 03
Deighton, L. Berlin game
Deighton, L. Faith
Deighton, L. Funeral in Berlin
Deighton, L. Game, set & match

INTERNATIONAL INTRIGUE—*Continued*

Deighton, L. The Ipcress file
Deighton, L. London match
Deighton, L. Mexico set
Deighton, L. Spy hook
Deighton, L. Spy line
Deighton, L. Spy sinker
Deighton, L. XPD
DiMercurio, M. Attack of the Seawolf
Durrell, L. Mountolive
Egleton, C. Hostile intent
Finder, J. The Moscow Club
Fleming, I. Bonded Fleming
Fleming, I. Casino Royale
Fleming, I. Doctor No
Fleming, I. From Russia, with love
Fleming, I. Goldfinger
Fleming, I. The man with the golden gun
Fleming, I. More gilt-edged Bonds
Fleming, I. On Her Majesty's Secret Service
Fleming, I. You only live twice
Follett, K. Lie down with lions
Follett, K. Triple
Folsom, A. R. The day after tomorrow
Forsyth, F. The day of the jackal
Forsyth, F. The deceiver
Forsyth, F. The devil's alternative
Forsyth, F. The dogs of war
Forsyth, F. The fist of God
Forsyth, F. The fourth protocol
Forsyth, F. The negotiator
Francis, C. Wolf winter
Fraser, G. M. Royal Flash
Freemantle, B. Charlie's apprentice
Freemantle, B. Comrade Charlie
Fuentes, C. The Hydra head
Gardner, J. E. Brokenclaw
Gardner, J. E. Death is forever
Gardner, J. E. License renewed
Gardner, J. E. Maestro
Gardner, J. E. The man from Barbarossa
Gardner, J. E. Never send flowers
Gardner, J. E. Seafire
Gardner, J. E. The secret families
Gardner, J. E. The secret generations
Gardner, J. E. The secret houses
Garfield, B. Hopscotch
Gifford, T. The Glendower legacy
Gilman, D. The amazing Mrs. Pollifax
Gilman, D. The elusive Mrs. Pollifax
Gilman, D. Mrs. Pollifax and the Hong Kong Buddha
Gilman, D. Mrs. Pollifax on safari
Gilman, D. Mrs. Pollifax on the China station
Gilman, D. A palm for Mrs. Pollifax
Gilman, D. The unexpected Mrs. Pollifax
Goldman, W. Marathon man
Grady, J. Six days of the condor
Greene, G. 3: This gun for hire, The confidential agent, The ministry of fear
Greene, G. The captain and the enemy
Greene, G. The ministry of fear
Greene, G. Our man in Havana
Greene, G. The quiet American
Greene, G. Travels with my aunt
Hall, A. Quiller bamboo
Hall, A. Quiller barracuda
Hall, A. The Quiller memorandum
Hall, A. Quiller meridian
Hall, A. Quiller Salamander
Hall, A. Quiller solitaire
Harris, R. Fatherland
Harris, T. Black Sunday
Harrison, P. Black cipher
Harrison, P. Storming Intrepid
Higgins, J. Day of judgment
Higgins, J. The eagle has flown
Higgins, J. The eagle has landed
Higgins, J. Exocet

Higgins, J. Eye of the storm
Higgins, J. On dangerous ground
Higgins, J. Touch the devil
Hoving, T. Masterpiece
Le Carré, J. The honourable schoolboy
Le Carré, J. The little drummer girl
Le Carré, J. The looking glass war
Le Carré, J. The night manager
Le Carré, J. A perfect spy
Le Carré, J. The quest for Karla
Le Carré, J. The Russia house
Le Carré, J. The secret pilgrim
Le Carré, J. A small town in Germany
Le Carré, J. Smiley's people
Le Carré, J. The spy who came in from the cold
Le Carré, J. Tinker, tailor, soldier, spy
Ludlum, R. The Aquitaine progression
Ludlum, R. The Bourne identity
Ludlum, R. The Bourne supremacy
Ludlum, R. The Bourne ultimatum
Ludlum, R. The Gemini contenders
Ludlum, R. The Holcroft covenant
Ludlum, R. The Icarus agenda
Ludlum, R. The Matarese Circle
Ludlum, R. The Parsifal mosaic
Ludlum, R. The Rhinemann exchange
Ludlum, R. The Scarlatti inheritance
Ludlum, R. The scorpio illusion
Lustbader, E. V. Angel eyes
Lustbader, E. V. Floating city
Lustbader, E. V. Jian
Lustbader, E. V. Shan
MacInnes, H. Agent in place
MacInnes, H. Cloak of darkness
MacInnes, H. Decision at Delphi
MacInnes, H. The double image
MacInnes, H. The hidden target
MacInnes, H. Message from Málaga
MacInnes, H. North from Rome
MacInnes, H. Prelude to terror
MacInnes, H. Ride a pale horse
MacInnes, H. The Salzburg connection
MacInnes, H. The snare of the hunter
MacInnes, H. The Venetian affair
MacLean, A. Caravan to Vaccares
MacLean, A. Ice Station Zebra
MacLean, A. Where eagles dare
Mailer, N. Harlot's ghost
McCutchan, P. Convoy north
Morrell, D. The brotherhood of the rose
Morrell, D. The fifth profession
Neville, K. The eight
Sanders, L. The tangent factor
Sheldon, S. Windmills of the gods
Smith, W. A. The leopard hunts in darkness
Thomas, C. Firefox
Thomas, C. Firefox down
Thomas, C. A hooded crow
Trenhaile, J. The gates of exquisite view
Uris, L. Topaz

INTERNATIONAL MARRIAGES
Bosse, M. J. Fire in heaven
Drabble, M. The needle's eye
James, H. The golden bowl
Stevenson, R. L. The beach of Falesá

INTERPLANETARY COMMUNICATION *See* Interstellar communication

INTERPLANETARY TRAVEL *See* Interplanetary voyages

INTERPLANETARY VISITORS
See also Martians
Anderson, P. The longest voyage
Anthony, P. Chaos mode
Anthony, P. Fractal mode
Anthony, P. Virtual mode
Bear, G. Anvil of stars
Bear, G. The forge of God

INTERPLANETARY VISITORS—*Continued*
Campbell, R. Medusa
Clarke, A. C. Cradle
Clarke, A. C. Imperial Earth
Clarke, A. C. Rama II
Clarke, A. C. Rendezvous with Rama
Dickson, G. R. The cloak and the staff
King, S. The Tommyknockers
Kotzwinkle, W. E.T.
Le Guin, U. K. City of illusions
Pohl, F. The day the Martians came
Robinson, S. Stardance [novelette]
Russ, J. Souls
Saint-Exupéry, A. de. The little prince
Sargent, P. Danny goes to Mars
Sheldon, S. The doomsday conspiracy
Shepard, L. A traveler's tale
Silverberg, R. Nightwings [novelette]
Simak, C. D. The big front yard
Spielberg, S. Close encounters of the third kind
Vance, J. The last castle
Wells, H. G. The war of the worlds

INTERPLANETARY VOYAGES
See also Science fiction; Space flight
Adams, D. The Hitchhiker's Guide to the Galaxy
Adams, D. The hitchhiker's quartet
Adams, D. Life, the universe, and everything
Adams, D. The restaurant at the end of the universe
Adams, D. So long, and thanks for all the fish
Balmer, E. When worlds collide
Clarke, A. C. 2001: a space odyssey
Clarke, A. C. 2010: odyssey two
Clarke, A. C. 2061: odyssey three
Heinlein, R. A. Citizen of the galaxy
Heinlein, R. A. Double star
Lewis, C. S. Out of the silent planet
Lewis, C. S. Perelandra
Niven, L. A world out of time
Verne, J. From the earth to the moon, and Round the moon
Vonnegut, K. The sirens of Titan

INTERPLANETARY WARS
Butler, O. E. Survivor
Card, O. S. Ender's game
Card, O. S. Xenocide
Clarke, A. C. Earthlight
Haldeman, J. W. The forever war
Le Guin, U. K. Rocannon's world
Longyear, B. B. Enemy mine
Pohl, F. The annals of the Heechee
Vance, J. The miracle workers
Wells, H. G. The war of the worlds

INTERRACIAL MARRIAGE
Buck, P. S. East wind: west wind
Conrad, J. Almayer's folly
Grau, S. A. The keepers of the house
Greene, G. The human factor
Han, S. Till morning comes
Mason, R. The world of Suzie Wong
Michener, J. A. Sayonara
Rushing, J. G. Mary Dove
Warren, R. P. Band of angels
West, D. The wedding
Williams, J. A. The man who cried I am
Woiwode, L. Indian affairs
Interstate. Dixon, S.

INTERSTELLAR COLONIES *See* Space colonies

INTERSTELLAR COMMUNICATION
Haldeman, J. W. Mindbridge
Lem, S. His Master's Voice
Sagan, C. Contact

Intervention. May, J.
Interview with the vampire. Rice, A.
Intimacy, and other stories. Sartre, J. P.
Intimate kill. Yorke, M.
Into the darkness. Michaels, B.
INTROSPECTIVE NOVELS *See* Psychological novels
Intruder in the dust. Faulkner, W.
The **Intruders.** Coonts, S.

INUIT
Mowat, F. The Snow Walker

INVALIDS
See also Paraplegics
Allen, C. V. Dreaming in color
Cather, W. Sapphira and the slave girl
Dickens, C. Dombey and Son
Nin, A. The four-chambered heart
Wharton, E. Ethan Frome
Inventing the Abbotts and other stories. Miller, S.

INVENTORS
Anderson, S. Poor white
Francis, D. High stakes
Golding, W. Envoy extraordinary
Sturgeon, T. Slow sculpture
Theroux, P. The Mosquito Coast
The **investigation.** Uhnak, D.

INVISIBILITY
Berger, T. Being invisible
Saint, H. F. Memoirs of an invisible man
Invisible cities. Calvino, I.
Invisible man. Ellison, R.
The **invisible** man. Wells, H. G.
also in Wells, H. G. Seven famous novels

IOWA
Boswell, R. Mystery ride
Smiley, J. A thousand acres
Waller, R. J. The bridges of Madison County
Waller, R. J. Slow waltz in Cedar Bend

      Farm life
See Farm life—Iowa
The **Ipcress** file. Deighton, L.
IRA *See* Irish Republican Army

IRAN

      To 640 A.D.
Vidal, G. Creation

      20th century
Clavell, J. Whirlwind

IRAQ
Forsyth, F. The fist of God

IRELAND
See also Northern Ireland
Crane, S. The O'Ruddy
O'Faoláin, S. The collected stories of Sean O'Faolain
The Oxford book of Irish short stories

      To 1172
Holland, C. The kings in winter
Llywelyn, M. Bard
Llywelyn, M. Finn Mac Cool
Llywelyn, M. Red Branch

      17th century
Llywelyn, M. The last prince of Ireland

      French invasion, 1798
Flanagan, T. The year of the French

      19th century
Du Maurier, Dame D. Hungry Hill
Flanagan, T. The tenants of time
Howatch, S. Cashelmara
Ripley, A. Scarlett
Ross-Macdonald, M. All desires known
Ross-Macdonald, M. A woman scorned
Uris, L. Trinity

IRELAND—*Continued*

20th century

Adler, E. Legacy of secrets
Banville, J. The book of evidence
Binchy, M. Circle of friends
Binchy, M. The copper beech
Binchy, M. Firefly summer
Binchy, M. Light a penny candle
Bradbury, R. Green shadows, white whale
Collins, M. The man who dreamt of lobsters
Flanagan, T. The end of the hunt
Greeley, A. M. Irish gold
Herbert, F. The white plague
Higgins, J. Confessional
Joyce, J. Dubliners
Joyce, J. Finnegans wake
Joyce, J. A shorter Finnegans wake
Joyce, J. Ulysses
O'Brien, E. House of splendid isolation
O'Brien, E. Lantern slides
O'Connor, F. Collected stories
Parker, R. B. All our yesterdays
Powell, A. The valley of bones
Uris, L. Trinity

Sinn Fein Rebellion, 1916

O'Flaherty, L. The informer

Aristocracy

See Aristocracy—Ireland

College life

See College life—Ireland

Communism

See Communism—Ireland

Peasant life

See Peasant life—Ireland

Politics

See Politics—Ireland

Rural life

Binchy, M. Echoes
McCabe, P. The butcher boy
O'Brien, E. The country girls
Trevor, W. Reading Turgenev

Cork (County)

Trevor, W. The silence in the garden

Dublin

Beckett, S. Murphy
Binchy, M. The lilac bus: stories
Brown, C. Down all the days
Donleavy, J. P. The ginger man
Doyle, R. Paddy Clarke, ha ha ha
Flanagan, T. The end of the hunt
Greeley, A. M. Irish gold
Joyce, J. Dubliners
Joyce, J. Finnegans wake
Joyce, J. A portrait of the artist as a young man
Joyce, J. A shorter Finnegans wake
Joyce, J. Ulysses
O'Brien, E. The lonely girl
O'Flaherty, L. The informer
Ross-Macdonald, M. Hell hath no fury

Mayo

Flanagan, T. The year of the French

IRENE, EMPRESS OF THE EAST, 752?-803

Holland, C. The belt of gold

IRISH

Australia

McCullough, C. The thorn birds

Canada

Urquhart, J. Away

Egypt

Durrell, L. Balthazar

Durrell, L. Justine

England

Beckett, S. Murphy
O'Brien, E. Time and tide
Trevor, W. Felicia's journey
Trollope, A. Phineas Finn
Trollope, A. Phineas Redux

France

Moore, B. The doctor's wife

Mexico

Lawrence, D. H. The plumed serpent (Quetzalcoatl)

Sweden

Ross-Macdonald, M. Dancing on snowflakes

United States

Adler, E. Legacy of secrets
Breslin, J. Table money
Caldwell, T. Answer as a man
Caldwell, T. Captains and kings
Dreiser, T. Jennie Gerhardt
Gordon, M. The other side
Higgins, G. V. The patriot game
L'Amour, L. The Californios
McDermott, A. At weddings and wakes
O'Connor, E. All in the family
O'Connor, E. The last hurrah
Smith, B. Maggie-Now
Uhnak, D. Law and order

IRISH AMERICANS

Campbell, R. W. Boneyards
Carroll, J. The city below
Dunne, D. A season in purgatory
Greeley, A. M. Irish gold
Hijuelos, O. The fourteen sisters of Emilio Montez O'Brien
Howard, M. Natural history
Oates, J. C. What I lived for
Parker, R. B. All our yesterdays
Quindlen, A. Object lessons
Reed, B. The indictment

Irish gold. Greeley, A. M.

IRISH REPUBLICAN ARMY

Higgins, G. V. The patriot game
Higgins, J. Confessional
Llewellyn, R. Green, green, my valley now
Maas, P. Father and son
O'Brien, E. House of splendid isolation

The iron hand of Mars. Davis, L.

Iron in the soul. See Sartre, J. P. Troubled sleep

The iron mask. [variant title: The man in the iron mask] Dumas, A.

Ironweed. Kennedy, W.

IRONY

See also Satire

Kundera, M. The joke

An Isaac Bashevis Singer reader. Singer, I. B.

ISAIAH (BIBLICAL FIGURE)

Asch, S. The prophet

ISLAM

See also Muslims

Maḥfūẓ, N. Arabian nights and days
Rushdie, S. The satanic verses

Island. Huxley, A.

The island of Doctor Moreau. Wells, H. G.

also in Wells, H. G. Seven famous novels

ISLANDS

See also names of individual islands and groups of islands

Defoe, D. Robinson Crusoe
Guterson, D. Snow falling on cedars
Hoffman, A. Second nature
Huxley, A. Island
MacDonald, J. D. Barrier Island
Naylor, G. Mama Day
Shacochis, B. Swimming in the volcano

ISLANDS—*Continued*
Stevenson, R. L. The Merry Men
Verne, J. The mysterious island
Wells, H. G. The island of Doctor Moreau
Wolfe, G. The death of Doctor Island
Islands in the stream. Hemingway, E.

ISLANDS OF THE PACIFIC
See also Solomon Islands
Bagley, D. Night of error
Conrad, J. Victory
Holt, V. The mask of the enchantress
Michener, J. A. Tales of the South Pacific
Nordhoff, C. The Bounty trilogy
Nordhoff, C. The hurricane
Stevenson, R. L. The beach of Falesá
The isle of glass. Tarr, J.

ISLE OF SKYE *See* Skye (Scotland)
Isle of woman. Anthony, P.

ISRAEL
See also Jerusalem; Zionism
Follett, K. Triple
Freeman, C. No time for tears
Kemelman, H. Monday the rabbi took off
Kemelman, H. One fine day the rabbi bought a cross
Leonard, E. The hunted
Oz, A. Fima
Oz, A. To know a woman
Roiphe, A. R. Lovingkindness
Roth, P. The counterlife
Roth, P. Operation Shylock
Singer, I. B. Meshugah
Singer, I. B. The penitent
Uris, L. Exodus
Uris, L. Mitla Pass
Vonnegut, K. Mother night
Wouk, H. The hope

ISRAEL-ARAB WAR, 1956 *See* Sinai Campaign, 1956

ISRAEL-ARAB WAR, 1967
Wiesel, E. A beggar in Jerusalem
Wouk, H. The hope

ISRAEL BEN ELIEZER *See* Ba'al Shem Ṭov, ca. 1700-1760

ISRAELI SOLDIERS *See* Soldiers—Israel

ISRAELIS
See also Jews

ISRAELITES *See* Jews

ISTANBUL (TURKEY) *See* Turkey—Istanbul
Isvik. Innes, H.
It. King, S.
It can't be my grave. Dean, S. F. X.
It can't happen here. Lewis, S.

ITALIAN AMERICANS
Price, R. The wanderers
Quindlen, A. Object lessons
Shulman, M. Rally round the flag, boys!

ITALIAN RIVIERA *See* Riviera (France and Italy)

ITALIANS
Greece
De Bernières, L. Corelli's mandolin
New York (N.Y.)
Condon, R. Prizzi's family
Condon, R. Prizzi's glory
Condon, R. Prizzi's honor
Condon, R. Prizzi's money
Prose, F. Household saints
Russia
Levi, P. The monkey's wrench
South America
Conrad, J. Nostromo
United States
Breslin, J. The gang that couldn't shoot straight
Fast, H. The immigrants

Malamud, B. The assistant
Puzo, M. The godfather
Waller, R. J. The bridges of Madison County

ITALY
See also Pompeii (Ancient city); Sicily
14th century
Eco, U. The name of the rose
15th century
Eliot, G. Romola
Stone, I. The agony and the ecstasy
16th century
Haasse, H. S. The scarlet city
Stone, I. The agony and the ecstasy
18th century
Rice, A. Cry to heaven
Stendhal. The charterhouse of Parma
19th century
Hawthorne, N. The marble faun
Tomasi di Lampedusa, G. The leopard
20th century
Anthony, E. Mission to Malaspiga
Bassani, G. The garden of the Finzi-Continis
Godden, R. The battle of the Villa Fiorita
Godden, R. Pippa passes
Guareschi, G. Don Camillo and his flock
Guareschi, G. The little world of Don Camillo
Heller, J. Catch-22
Helprin, M. A soldier of the great war
Hemingway, E. Across the river and into the trees
Hoving, T. Discovery
Leonard, E. Pronto
Siddons, A. R. Hill towns
Silone, I. Bread and wine

Aristocracy
See Aristocracy—Italy
College life
See College life—Italy
Communism
See Communism—Italy
Courts and courtiers
See Courts and courtiers—Italy
Fascism
See Fascism—Italy
Peasant life
See Peasant life—Italy
Politics
See Politics—Italy
Rural life
Crichton, R. The secret of Santa Vittoria
Du Maurier, Dame D. The flight of the falcon
Guareschi, G. Don Camillo and his flock
Guareschi, G. The little world of Don Camillo
Johnston, V. The Etruscan smile
MacInnes, H. North from Rome
Styron, W. Set this house on fire
Trevor, W. My house in Umbria
World War, 1939-1945
See World War, 1939-1945—Italy
Assisi
Gallico, P. The small miracle
Calabria
West, M. L. The devil's advocate
Ferrara
Bassani, G. The garden of the Finzi-Continis
Florence
Du Maurier, Dame D. My cousin Rachel

ITALY—Florence—*Continued*
Eliot, G. Romola
Forster, E. M. A room with a view
Stone, I. The agony and the ecstasy

Milan
Eco, U. Foucault's pendulum

Naples
Sontag, S. The volcano lover

Parma
Stendhal. The charterhouse of Parma

Rome
Hawthorne, N. The marble faun
Silverberg, R. Nightwings [novelette]
Stone, I. The agony and the ecstasy

Rome—13th century
Tarr, J. The Hounds of God

Rome—19th century
Hawthorne, N. The marble faun
James, H. Roderick Hudson

Rome—20th century
Gallico, P. The small miracle
Gash, J. The Vatican rip
MacInnes, H. North from Rome
Martin, M. Vatican
West, M. L. The shoes of the fisherman
Williams, T. The Roman spring of Mrs. Stone

Syracuse
Renault, M. The mask of Apollo

Turin
Gordon, M. The rest of life

Tuscany
Ondaatje, M. The English patient

Venice
Anthony, E. The company of saints
Brent, M. Tregaron's daughter
Durrell, L. Monsieur
Godden, R. Pippa passes
Hemingway, E. Across the river and into the trees
James, H. The Aspern papers
Laker, R. The Venetian mask
MacInnes, H. The Venetian affair
Mann, T. Death in Venice
Powell, A. Temporary kings
Wharton, E. The children

ITINERANT CLERGY
Eliot, G. Adam Bede
Ivanhoe. Scott, Sir W.
The **ivory** tower. James, H.
In James, H. The American novels and stories of Henry James p867-993
The **ivy** tree. Stewart, M.

J

"J" is for judgment. Grafton, S.
J R. Gaddis, W.
Jack and the beanstalk. McBain, E.
Jack Merrybright. Pearce, M. E.
In Pearce, M. E. Apple tree lean down [omnibus volume] p203-332
Jack the bodiless. May, J.
JACK THE RIPPER
Newman, K. Anno-Dracula
West, P. The women of Whitechapel and Jack the Ripper
JACKSON, ANDREW, 1767-1845
Stone, I. The President's lady

JACKSON, RACHEL DONELSON ROBARDS, 1767-1828
Stone, I. The President's lady
JACKSON, STONEWALL, 1824-1863
Keneally, T. Confederates
JACKSON, THOMAS JONATHAN *See* Jackson, Stonewall, 1824-1863
JACKSON (MISS.) *See* Mississippi—Jackson
JACOB (BIBLICAL FIGURE)
Mann, T. The tales of Jacob
JACOBITE REBELLION, 1745-1746
Scott, Sir W. Waverly
JACOBITES
Stevenson, R. L. The master of Ballantrae
Thackeray, W. M. The history of Henry Esmond, esquire
Jacob's room. Woolf, V.
Jailbird. Vonnegut, K.
Jalna. De la Roche, M.

JAMAICA
Fleming, I. The man with the golden gun
Jamaica Inn. Du Maurier, Dame D.
JAMES, HENRY, 1843-1916
Aiken, J. The haunting of Lamb House
A **James** Bond omnibus. See Fleming, I. Bonded Fleming
The **James** Joyce murder. Cross, A.
JANE, CALAMITY *See* Calamity Jane, 1852-1903
Jane and Prudence. Pym, B.
Jane Eyre. Brontë, C.
Jane Fairfax. Aiken, J.
Jane's house. Smith, R. K.
The **Janus** imperative. Anthony, E.

JAPAN

11th century
Murasaki Shikibu. The tale of Genji

17th century
Clavell, J. Shogun
Endō, S. The samurai
Endō, S. Silence

19th century
Clavell, J. Gai-Jin

1867-1945
Kawabata, Y. Snow country, and Thousand cranes
Kawabata, Y. Thousand cranes
Mishima, Y. Runaway horses
Mishima, Y. Spring snow

20th century
Dickey, J. To the white sea
Endō, S. The sea and poison
Ishiguro, K. An artist of the floating world
Mishima, Y. The sound of waves
Mishima, Y. The Temple of Dawn
Ōe, K. Nip the buds, shoot the kids

1945-
Clancy, T. Debt of honor
Endō, S. Scandal
Kawabata, Y. The sound of the mountain
Lustbader, E. V. White Ninja
Michener, J. A. Sayonara
Mishima, Y. The decay of the angel
Mishima, Y. Forbidden colors
Ōe, K. The pinch runner memorandum
Ōe, K. The silent cry
Yoshimoto, B. Kitchen

JAPAN—*Continued*

Aristocracy
See Aristocracy—Japan

Courts and courtiers
See Courts and courtiers—Japan

Rites and ceremonies
See Rites and ceremonies—Japan

Rural life
Abe, K. The woman in the dunes

Kamakura
Kawabata, Y. The sound of the mountain

Okinawa
Sneider, V. The Teahouse of the August Moon

Tokyo
Abe, K. The box man
Kawabata, Y. The sound of the mountain
Mishima, Y. Forbidden colors
Mishima, Y. Spring snow

JAPAN. ARMY
Boulle, P. The bridge over the River Kwai

JAPANESE

China
Ballard, J. G. Empire of the Sun

Hawaii
Michener, J. A. Hawaii

United States
Boyle, T. C. East is East
Crichton, M. Rising sun
Reed, I. Japanese by spring

JAPANESE AMERICANS
Guterson, D. Snow falling on cedars

Evacuation and relocation, 1942-1945
Harris, M. Lost and found
Japanese by spring. Reed, I.
The **Japanese** corpse. Van de Wetering, J.
Jasmine. Mukherjee, B.
Jasmine nights. Somtow, S. P.

JASON (GREEK MYTHOLOGY)
Graves, R. Hercules, my shipmate
Jaws. Benchley, P.
Jazz. Morrison, T.
Jazz funeral. Smith, J.

JAZZ MUSIC
Baker, D. Young man with a horn

JEALOUSY
Balzac, H. de. Cousin Bette
Bradshaw, G. Horses of heaven
Cather, W. Sapphira and the slave girl
Eliot, G. Middlemarch
Goudge, E. Such devoted sisters
Hart, J. Sin
Mann, T. Young Joseph
Michael, J. A ruling passion
Pirandello, L. The outcast
Proust, M. The captive
Proust, M. The captive [and] The fugitive
Proust, M. The fugitive
Rendell, R. Going wrong
Ross-Macdonald, M. All desires known
Ross-Macdonald, M. A woman possessed
Tolstoy, L., graf. The Kreutzer sonata
Williams, B. A. Leave her to heaven
Jean Santeuil. Proust, M.

JEANNE D'ARC, SAINT *See* Joan, of Arc, Saint, 1412-1431

Jeeves: a gentleman's personal gentleman. Parkinson, C. N.
Jeeves and the tie that binds. Wodehouse, P. G.

JEFFERSON, THOMAS, 1743-1826
Chase-Riboud, B. The President's daughter
Chase-Riboud, B. Sally Hemings
Jemima Shore at the sunny grave and other stories. Fraser, A.
Jennie Gerhardt. Dreiser, T.
Jennie Glenroy. Ogilvie, E.

JERUSALEM
Bayer, W. Pattern crimes
Bulgakov, M. A. The master and Margarita
Oz, A. Fima
Ragen, N. Sotah
Roth, P. Operation Shylock
Wiesel, E. A beggar in Jerusalem
Jerusalem Inn. Grimes, M.
Jerusalem the golden. Drabble, M.

JESUITS
Blatty, W. P. The exorcist
Higgins, J. Day of judgment

JESUS BARABBAS *See* Barabbas (Biblical figure)

JESUS CHRIST
Asch, S. Mary
Asch, S. The Nazarene
Bulgakov, M. A. The master and Margarita
Caldwell, T. I, Judas
Douglas, L. C. The Big Fisherman
Douglas, L. C. The robe
Holmes, M. The Messiah
Holmes, M. Three from Galilee
Kazantzakis, N. The last temptation of Christ
Wallace, L. Ben-Hur

Crucifixion
Moorcock, M. Behold the man
The **jewel** in the crown. Scott, P.
also in Scott, P. The Raj quartet

JEWEL ROBBERIES *See* Robbery
The **jewel** that was ours. Dexter, C.

JEWELERS
Laker, R. Jewelled path
Jewelled path. Laker, R.

JEWELRY
See also Diamonds; Emeralds; Necklaces; Pearls; Rings; Rubies
Bellow, S. A theft
Tolkien, J. R. R. The Silmarillion
Trollope, A. The Eustace diamonds
Jewels. Steel, D.

JEWISH-ARAB RELATIONS
Ambler, E. The Levanter
Girzone, J. F. Joshua in the Holy Land
Harris, T. Black Sunday

JEWISH-BLACK RELATIONS *See* African Americans—Relations with Jews

JEWISH HOLOCAUST (1933-1945) *See* Holocaust, Jewish (1933-1945)

JEWISH REFUGEES
See also Holocaust survivors
Appelfeld, A. Tzili, the story of a life
Bellow, S. Mr. Sammler's planet
De Hartog, J. Star of Peace
Uris, L. Exodus
Wiesel, E. The accident
Wiesel, E. The gates of the forest

JEWISH SECTS *See* Pharisees

JEWS
See also Antisemitism; Hasidism; Jewish-Arab relations; Judaism; World War, 1939-1945—Jews
Appelfeld, A. Unto the soul
Asch, S. Moses
Bellow, S. The Bellarosa connection
Demetz, H. The journey from Prague Street

JEWS—*Continued*

Freeman, C. The last princess
Gardner, J. E. Maestro
Goldreich, G. Leah's children
Gross, J. The books of Rachel
Halter, M. The book of Abraham
Hoban, R. Pilgermann
Oz, A. Fima
Ozick, C. The shawl
Piercy, M. He, she and it
Prose, F. Hungry hearts
Roth, P. The counterlife
Roth, P. Operation Shylock
Sholem Aleichem. The best of Sholom Aleichem
Sholem Aleichem. Tevye the dairyman and The railroad stories
Singer, I. B. The collected stories of Isaac Bashevis Singer
Singer, I. B. The death of Methuselah and other stories
Singer, I. B. The penitent
Singer, I. B. Scum
Thomas, D. M. Pictures at an exhibition
Wiesel, E. A beggar in Jerusalem
Wiesel, E. The forgotten
Wiesel, E. Night, Dawn, The accident: three tales
Wouk, H. The hope

Persecutions
See also Holocaust, Jewish (1933-1945)

Anatoli, A. Babi Yar
Appelfeld, A. Badenheim 1939
Appelfeld, A. Katerina
Appelfeld, A. Tzili, the story of a life
De Hartog, J. Star of Peace
Keneally, T. Schindler's list
Levi, P. If not now, when?
Malamud, B. The fixer
Schwarz-Bart, A. The last of the just
Szeman, S. The Kommandant's mistress
Uris, L. Exodus
Uris, L. QB VII
Viertel, J. Life lines
Wiesel, E. The oath
Wiesel, E. The testament

Relations with African Americans
See African Americans—Relations with Jews

Religion
See Judaism

Segregation
Hersey, J. The wall
Uris, L. Mila 18

Afghanistan
Michener, J. A. Caravans

Argentina
Ludlum, R. The Rhinemann exchange

Austria
Appelfeld, A. The age of wonders
Appelfeld, A. Badenheim 1939

Babylonia
Asch, S. The prophet

Canada
Richler, M. Joshua then and now
Richler, M. Solomon Gursky was here

China
Elegant, R. S. Mandarin

Czech Republic
Demetz, H. The house on Prague Street

Egypt
Asch, S. Moses
Deighton, L. City of gold
Durrell, L. Justine
Durrell, L. Mountolive

Mann, T. Joseph in Egypt
Mann, T. Joseph the provider

England
Kellerman, F. The quality of mercy
Scott, Sir W. Ivanhoe
Snow, C. P. The conscience of the rich

Europe
Wiesel, E. The oath

Germany
Grass, G. Dog years
Schwarz-Bart, A. The last of the just
Tennenbaum, S. Yesterday's streets
Wiesel, E. The accident

Hungary
Pearson, D. Csardas
Wiesel, E. The gates of the forest
Wiesel, E. The town beyond the wall

India
Desai, A. Baumgartner's Bombay

Italy
Bassani, G. The garden of the Finzi-Continis
Levi, P. If not now, when?

Miami Beach (Fla.)
Elkin, S. Mrs. Ted Bliss
Ozick, C. Rosa

Netherlands
De Hartog, J. The inspector

New York (N.Y.)
Bellow, S. Mr. Sammler's planet
Birmingham, S. Carriage trade
Colwin, L. Family happiness
Courter, G. The midwife
Courter, G. The midwife's advice
Denker, H. Mrs. Washington and Horowitz, too
Goldreich, G. That year of our war
Goldreich, G. Years of dreams
Green, G. The last angry man
Helprin, M. Ellis Island
Malamud, B. The assistant
Plain, B. The golden cup
Potok, C. The book of lights
Potok, C. The chosen
Potok, C. Davita's harp
Potok, C. The gift of Asher Lev
Potok, C. In the beginning
Potok, C. My name is Asher Lev
Potok, C. The promise
Ragen, N. Sotah
Rossner, J. Olivia
Roth, H. Call it sleep
Roth, H. A diving rock on the Hudson
Roth, H. A star shines over Mt. Morris Park
Segal, E. Acts of faith
Sholem Aleichem. The adventures of Mottel, the cantor's son
Singer, I. B. Meshugah
Smith, R. K. Sadie Shapiro's knitting book
Styron, W. Sophie's choice
Tax, M. Rivington Street
Tax, M. Union Square
Wallant, E. L. The pawnbroker
Weidman, J. I can get it for you wholesale
Wiesel, E. The accident
Wolfe, T. The good child's river
Wouk, H. Inside, outside
Wouk, H. Marjorie Morningstar

New York (State)
Kay, T. Shadow song
Wiesel, E. Twilight

Palestine
Asch, S. The Apostle
Asch, S. Mary
Caldwell, T. Great lion of God

JEWS—Palestine—*Continued*
Douglas, L. C. The robe
Mann, T. The tales of Jacob
Mann, T. Young Joseph
Wallace, L. Ben-Hur
Wiesel, E. Dawn

Poland
Agnon, S. Y. The bridal canopy
Appelfeld, A. Katerina
Begley, L. Wartime lies
Hersey, J. The wall
Ozick, C. The Messiah of Stockholm
Singer, I. B. The certificate
Singer, I. B. The estate
Singer, I. B. The family Moskat
Singer, I. B. Gimpel the fool, and other stories
Singer, I. B. The magician of Lublin
Singer, I. B. The manor
Singer, I. B. Reaches of heaven
Singer, I. B. Satan in Goray
Singer, I. B. Shosha
Singer, I. B. The slave
Singer, I. J. The brothers Ashkenazi
Uris, L. Mila 18
Yolen, J. Briar Rose

Rome
Asch, S. The Apostle

Russia
Anatoli, A. Babi Yar
Babel', I. Red cavalry
Courter, G. The midwife
Malamud, B. The fixer
Sholem Aleichem. The adventures of Menahem-Mendl
Sholem Aleichem. The bloody hoax
Sholem Aleichem. The nightingale
Sholem Aleichem. Tevye's daughters
Viertel, J. Life lines
Wiesel, E. The testament

Scotland
Bermant, C. The patriarch

South America
Vargas Llosa, M. The storyteller

United States
Auchincloss, L. The dark lady
Beagle, P. S. A fine and private place
Bellow, S. The adventures of Augie March
Bellow, S. Herzog
Bellow, S. Mr. Sammler's planet
Birmingham, S. The Auerbach will
Doctorow, E. L. The book of Daniel
Doctorow, E. L. Ragtime
Ephron, N. Heartburn
Fast, H. The immigrants
Fast, H. The outsider
Freeman, C. Come pour the wine
Freeman, C. No time for tears
Gold, H. Family
Gold, H. Fathers
Goldreich, G. Four days
Goldreich, G. Leah's journey
Greenberg, J. A season of delight
Heller, J. Good as Gold
Hobson, L. K. Z. Gentleman's agreement
Horowitz, E. Plain Jane
Malamud, B. Dubin's lives
Orde, L. Dreams of gold
Ozick, C. The cannibal galaxy
Plain, B. Crescent City
Plain, B. Daybreak
Plain, B. Evergreen
Plain, B. Harvest
Plain, B. Tapestry
Potok, C. The book of lights
Roth, P. The anatomy lesson
Roth, P. The ghost writer

Roth, P. Goodbye, Columbus, and five short stories
Roth, P. Letting go
Roth, P. My life as a man
Roth, P. Portnoy's complaint
Roth, P. The professor of desire
Roth, P. Zuckerman bound: a trilogy and epilogue
Roth, P. Zuckerman unbound
Shaw, I. The young lions
Viorst, J. Murdering Mr. Monti
Wiesel, E. The gates of the forest
Wouk, H. Inside, outside
Jian. Lustbader, E. V.
Jigsaw. McBain, E.
The **Jim** Chee mysteries. Hillerman, T.
Jitterbug perfume. Robbins, T.
JOAN, OF ARC, SAINT, 1412-1431
Twain, M. Personal recollections of Joan of Arc
Joanna and Ulysses. Sarton, M.
Joanna's husband and David's wife. Hailey, E. F.
Job: a comedy of justice. Heinlein, R. A.

JOCKEYS
Francis, D. Bolt
Francis, D. Bonecrack
Francis, D. Break in
Francis, D. The edge
Francis, D. Enquiry
Francis, D. Flying finish
Francis, D. Hot money
Francis, D. Nerve
Francis, D. Odds against
Francis, D. Rat race
Francis, D. Reflex
Francis, D. Risk
Francis, D. Slayride
Francis, D. Straight
Francis, D. Three to show
Francis, D. Whip hand
The **Joe** Leaphorn mysteries. Hillerman, T.
Joey's case. Constantine, K. C.
JOHANNESBURG (SOUTH AFRICA) *See* South
  Africa—Johannesburg
JOHN, KING OF ENGLAND, 1167-1216
Penman, S. K. Here be dragons
**JOHN, OF GAUNT, DUKE OF LANCASTER, 1340-
  1399**
Seton, A. Katherine
John Dollar. Wiggins, M.
Johnny got his gun. Trumbo, D.
The **joke**. Kundera, M.
JONES, JOHN PAUL, 1747-1792
Cooper, J. F. The pilot
JOSEPH (BIBLICAL FIGURE)
Mann, T. Joseph and his brothers
Joseph and his brothers. Mann, T.
Joseph and his brothers (Tales of Jacob). See Mann, T.
  The tales of Jacob
Joseph Andrews. Fielding, H.
Joseph in Egypt. Mann, T.
  In Mann, T. Joseph and his brothers p447-840
Joseph the provider. Mann, T.
  In Mann, T. Joseph and his brothers p843-1207
**JOSEPHINE, EMPRESS, CONSORT OF NAPOLEON
  I, EMPEROR OF THE FRENCH, 1763-1814**
Lofts, N. A rose for virtue
Joshua and the children. Girzone, J. F.
Joshua in the Holy Land. Girzone, J. F.
Joshua then and now. Richler, M.
The **journal** of Julius Rodman. Poe, E. A.
  In Poe, E. A. The imaginary voyages p508-653
Journal of my other self. See Rilke, R. M. The
  notebooks of Malte Laurids Brigge
A **journal** of the plague year. Defoe, D.

JOURNALISM
Cleary, J. Spearfield's daughter
Westlake, D. E. Trust me on this

JOURNALISTS
See also Women journalists
Allende, I. Of love and shadows
Anthony, E. The Janus imperative
Böll, H. The lost honor of Katharina Blum
Boucher, A. We print the truth
Brown, D. A. Killdeer Mountain
Buffett, J. Where is Joe Merchant?
Camus, A. The plague
Carr, C. The alienist
Dexter, P. The paperboy
Dickinson, P. Death of a unicorn
Doctorow, E. L. The waterworks
Estleman, L. D. Whiskey River
Fast, H. The trial of Abigail Goodman
Fearing, K. The big clock
Ferber, E. Cimarron
Francis, D. Forfeit
Goldman, F. The long night of white chickens
Gordon, M. Living at home
Gray, F. du P. World without end
Greeley, A. M. Patience of a saint
Greene, G. The quiet American
Grisham, J. The pelican brief
Guterson, D. Snow falling on cedars
Hobson, L. K. Z. Gentleman's agreement
Huxley, A. Island
Jones, D. C. A creek called Wounded Knee
Katzenbach, J. Just cause
Keneally, T. To Asmara
Kipling, R. The light that failed
Koontz, D. R. Cold fire
Leonard, E. Split images
MacInnes, H. The Venetian affair
Marshall, C. Julie
Michener, J. A. Mexico
Morrell, D. Desperate measures
Mortman, D. True colors
Naipaul, V. S. A house for Mr. Biswas
Ozick, C. The Messiah of Stockholm
Plath, S. The bell jar
Prose, F. Bigfoot dreams
Proulx, A. The shipping news
Richler, M. Joshua then and now
Siddons, A. R. Homeplace
Singer, I. B. Shosha
Strieber, W. Majestic
Tarkington, B. The gentleman from Indiana
Thane, E. Ever after
Thane, E. Homing
Thane, E. Yankee stranger
Thayer, S. The weatherman
Thomas, R. Missionary stew
Vidal, G. 1876
West, N. Miss Lonelyhearts
Westlake, D. E. Baby, would I lie?
Whitney, P. A. The golden unicorn
Wiesel, E. The accident

JOURNALS See Diaries (Stories about); Diaries (Stories in diary form)
Journey. Michener, J. A.
The **journey** from Prague Street. Demetz, H.
A **journey** to the centre of the earth. Verne, J.
Journey to the end of the night. Céline, L.-F.
The **journeyer.** Jennings, G.

JOURNEYS See Overland journeys; Voyages and travels
Joy in the morning. Smith, B.
The **Joy** Luck Club. Tan, A.
Juana. Balzac, H. de
In Balzac, H. de. The short novels of Balzac
Jubal Sackett. L'Amour, L.
Jubilee. Walker, M.
Jubilee Trail. Bristow, G.

JUDAH LOEW BEN BEZALEL, CA. 1525-1609
Wiesel, E. The Golem

JUDAISM
See also Hasidism; Jews; Zionism
Greenberg, J. A season of delight
Potok, C. The book of lights
Potok, C. The chosen
Potok, C. Davita's harp
Potok, C. The gift of Asher Lev
Potok, C. In the beginning
Potok, C. My name is Asher Lev
Potok, C. The promise
Ragen, N. Sotah
Roiphe, A. R. Lovingkindness
Segal, E. Acts of faith
Singer, I. B. The estate
Singer, I. B. The magician of Lublin
Singer, I. B. The manor
Singer, I. B. Reaches of heaven
Singer, I. B. The slave
Wiesel, E. The Golem
Wouk, H. Inside, outside
The **Judas** factor. Allbeury, T.

JUDAS ISCARIOT
Asch, S. The Nazarene
Caldwell, T. I, Judas
Kazantzakis, N. The last temptation of Christ
The **Judas** kiss. Holt, V.
Judas Priest. McInerny, R. M.
Jude the obscure. Hardy, T.

JUDEA See Palestine—To 70 A.D.

JUDGES
Coughlin, W. J. Death penalty
Leonard, E. Maximum Bob
Rosenberg, N. T. Interest of justice
Judgment day. Farrell, J. T.
In Farrell, J. T. Studs Lonigan
A **judgment** in stone. Rendell, R.
Judith Hearne. See Moore, B. The lonely passion of Judith Hearne

JULIA AUGUSTA See Livia Drusilla, Consort of Augustus, Emperor of Rome, 58? B.C.-29 A.D.

JULIAN, EMPEROR OF ROME, 331-363
Vidal, G. Julian
Julian. Vidal, G.

JULIANUS, APOSTATA, EMPEROR OF ROME See Julian, Emperor of Rome, 331-363
Julie. Marshall, C.
Julie de Carneilhan. Colette
In Colette. Gigi. Julie de Carneilhan. Chance acquaintances p77-222
Julip. Harrison, J.
Julip [novella]. Harrison, J.
In Harrison, J. Julip p3-82

JULY FOURTH See Fourth of July
July's people. Gordimer, N.
Jump and other stories. Gordimer, N.
The **jungle.** Sinclair, U.

JUNGLES
Conrad, J. Heart of darkness
Forester, C. S. The African Queen
Vargas Llosa, M. The storyteller
Juniper time. Wilhelm, K.
The **junk-drawer** corner-store front-porch blues. Powers, J. R.
Jurassic Park. Crichton, M.
Jurgen: a comedy of justice. Cabell, J. B.

JURY DUTY See Trials
Just a corpse at twilight. Van de Wetering, J.
Just above my head. Baldwin, J.
Just cause. Katzenbach, J.
Justice for some. Wilhelm, K.
Justine. Durrell, L.
also in Durrell, L. The Alexandria quartet p11-203

JUVENILE DELINQUENCY
Burgess, A. A clockwork orange
Edgerton, C. Walking across Egypt

JUVENILE DELINQUENCY—*Continued*
  Godden, R. An episode of sparrows
  Hunter, E. The blackboard jungle
  Levin, M. Compulsion
  Ōe, K. Nip the buds, shoot the kids
  Price, R. The wanderers
Juxtaposition. Anthony, P.

K

"K" is for killer. Grafton, S.
KAFIRS (AFRICAN PEOPLE) *See* Zulus (African people)
The **Kaisho.** Lustbader, E. V.
KAMAKURA (JAPAN) *See* Japan—Kamakura
KAMPUCHEA *See* Cambodia
Kane & Abel. Archer, J.
KANSAS
  Hughes, L. Not without laughter
  Parks, G. The learning tree

Kansas City
  Clair, M. Rattlebone

KANSAS CITY (KAN.) *See* Kansas—Kansas City
KANSAS CITY (MO.) *See* Missouri—Kansas City
The **kappillan** of Malta. Monsarrat, N.
KARL XIV JOHAN, KING OF SWEDEN AND NOR-WAY, 1763-1844 *See* Charles XIV John, King of Sweden and Norway, 1763-1844
Kate Vaiden. Price, R.
Katerina. Appelfeld, A.
KATHERINE, DUCHESS OF LANCASTER, 1350-1403
  Seton, A. Katherine
Katherine. Seton, A.
Kat's cradle. Kijewski, K.
Keep the aspidistra flying. Orwell, G.
The **keepers** of the house. Grau, S. A.
KELLOGG, JOHN HARVEY, 1852-1943
  Boyle, T. C. Road to Wellville
Kelly Park. Stubbs, J.
Kenilworth. Scott, Sir W.
KENNEDY, JOHN F. (JOHN FITZGERALD), 1917-1963
  Korda, M. The immortals
Assassination
  Buckley, W. F. Mongoose, R.I.P
  DeLillo, D. Libra
  Thomas, D. M. Flying in to love

KENT (ENGLAND) *See* England—Kent
The **Kentish** manor murders. Symons, J.

KENTUCKY
18th century
  Giles, J. H. Hannah Fowler
19th century
  Harper, K. Circle of gold
  Warren, R. P. World enough and time
20th century
  Arnow, H. L. S. The dollmaker
  Giles, J. H. The enduring hills
  Leonard, E. The moonshine war
  Mason, B. A. Feather crowns
  Mason, B. A. In country
  Mason, B. A. Spence + Lila
  Robards, K. Maggy's child
  Robards, K. One summer

Farm life
  See Farm life—Kentucky
Frontier and pioneer life
  See Frontier and pioneer life—Kentucky
Politics
  See Politics—Kentucky

KENYA
  Dinesen, I. Shadows on the grass
  Ruark, R. Something of value
  Ruark, R. Uhuru
  Wood, B. Green City in the sun
Farm life
  See Farm life—Kenya
Race relations
  Ruark, R. Something of value
The **kepi.** Colette
  In Colette. The collected stories of Colette p498-531
The **key** to Rebecca. Follett, K.
KEY WEST (FLA.) *See* Florida—Key West
Key West tales. Hersey, J.
The **keys** of the kingdom. Cronin, A. J.

KHMERS
  Del Vecchio, J. M. For the sake of all living things
Kick the can. Lehrer, J.
KID ANTRIM *See* Billy, the Kid
KIDNAPPING
  See also Hostages
  Anderson, P. The Queen of Air and Darkness
  Campbell, R. The Nameless
  Clark, M. H. All around the town
  Clark, M. H. A stranger is watching
  Clark, M. H. Where are the children?
  Cleary, J. High road to China
  Condon, R. Prizzi's money
  Durham, M. The man who loved Cat Dancing
  Forsyth, F. The negotiator
  Fowles, J. The collector
  Francis, D. Bonecrack
  Francis, D. The danger
  Francis, D. Risk
  Gardner, J. E. The man from Barbarossa
  Garwood, J. Prince Charming
  Greene, G. The honorary consul
  Hawthorne, N. Fanshawe
  Highsmith, P. The boy who followed Ripley
  Keating, H. R. F. Inspector Ghote trusts the heart
  Levin, M. Compulsion
  McCammon, R. R. Mine
  Parker, T. J. Little Saigon
  Patterson, J. Along came a spider
  Puzo, M. The fourth K
  Reed, K. Gone
  Rendell, R. The tree of hands
  Smith, W. A. Golden fox
  Smith, W. A. A time to die
  Steel, D. Vanished
  Strieber, W. Billy
  Vine, B. Gallowglass
  Whitney, P. A. Feather on the moon

KIEV (UKRAINE) *See* Ukraine—Kiev
Kilkenny. L'Amour, L.
  In L'Amour, L. Four complete novels p97-220
Kill and kill again. Pentecost, H.
Kill now—pay later. Stout, R.
  In Stout, R. Trio for blunt instruments p1-87

Kill zone. Estleman, L. D.
Killashandra. McCaffrey, A.
Killdeer Mountain. Brown, D. A.
The **killer** angels. Shaara, M.
Killer diller. Edgerton, C.
The **killing** doll. Rendell, R.
The **killing** ground. Settle, M. L.
A **killing** in Moscow. Egleton, C.
Killing Mister Watson. Matthiessen, P.
The **killing** of Katie Steelstock. Gilbert, M.
Killing orders. Paretsky, S.
Killing time in St. Cloud. Guest, J.
The **killings** at Badger's Drift. Graham, C.
Killobyte. Anthony, P.
Killshot. Leonard, E.
The **kind** of light that shines on Texas. McKnight, R.
The **kindly** ones. Powell, A.
    In Powell, A. A dance to the music of time [v2]
The **kindness** of women. Ballard, J. G.
Kinds of love. Sarton, M.
Kinflicks. Alther, L.
King Coffin. Aiken, C.
    In Aiken, C. The collected novels of Conrad Aiken
    p297-414
King hereafter. Dunnett, D.
The **king** must die. Renault, M.
King of kings. Martin, M.
King of the corner. Estleman, L. D.
The **king** of the fields. Singer, I. B.
King of the Murgos. Eddings, D.
King, queen, knave. Nabokov, V. V.
King Rat. Clavell, J.
King Solomon's carpet. Vine, B.
King Solomon's mines. Haggard, H. R.
Kingdoms of the Wall. Silverberg, R.

KINGS AND RULERS
    See also Courts and courtiers; names of kings and rulers
    Bradshaw, G. Horses of heaven
    Maalouf, A. The rock of Tanios
Kings full of aces. Stout, R.
The **King's** general. Du Maurier, Dame D.
The **kings** in winter. Holland, C.
King's oak. Siddons, A. R.
Kingsblood royal. Lewis, S.

KINSHIP
    See also Tribes

KIOWA INDIANS
    Momaday, N. S. The ancient child
Kirkland Revels. Holt, V.
Kiss. McBain, E.
A **kiss** before dying. Levin, I.
Kiss of the spider woman. Puig, M.
Kiss the girls. Patterson, J.
Kissing kin. Thane, E.
Kissing the gunner's daughter. Rendell, R.
Kitchen. Yoshimoto, B.
Kitchen [novella]. Yoshimoto, B.
    In Yoshimoto, B. Kitchen
The **kitchen** god's wife. Tan, A.
KKK *See* Ku Klux Klan
The **knight,** death, and the devil. Leffland, E.
Knight of shadows. Zelazny, R.
KNIGHTHOOD *See* Knights and knighthood
Knight's Acre. Lofts, N.
Knights and dragons. Spencer, E.
    In Spencer, E. The stories of Elizabeth Spencer p127-218

KNIGHTS AND KNIGHTHOOD
    See also Chivalry; Middle Ages
    Berger, T. Arthur Rex
    Cervantes Saavedra, M. de. Don Quixote de la Mancha
    Doyle, Sir A. C. The White Company
    Holland, C. The firedrake
    Lofts, N. The homecoming

Lofts, N. Knight's Acre
Scott, Sir W. Ivanhoe
Scott, Sir W. The talisman
White, T. H. The once and future king
Knights of the range. Grey, Z.
Knockdown. Francis, D.

KNOLLYS, LETTICE
    Holt, V. My enemy the Queen
KNOXVILLE (TENN.) *See* Tennessee—Knoxville
Koko. Straub, P.
The **Kommandant's** mistress. Szeman, S.

KOREA

Peasant life
    See Peasant life—Korea

KOREAN REFUGEES
    Potok, C. I am the clay

KOREAN WAR, 1950-1953
    Hooker, R. MASH
    Michener, J. A. The bridges at Toko-ri
    Potok, C. The book of lights
    Potok, C. I am the clay
Kramer versus Kramer. Corman, A.
The **Kreutzer** sonata. Tolstoy, L., graf
    In Tolstoy, L. The portable Tolstoy p523-601
The **Kreutzer** sonata, The Devil, and other tales. Tolstoy, L., graf

KRIS KRINGLE *See* Santa Claus
Kristin Lavransdatter. Undset, S.

KU KLUX KLAN
    Grisham, J. The chamber
    Marius, R. C. After the war

KUBLAI KHAN, 1216-1294
    Calvino, I. Invisible cities
    Jennings, G. The journeyer

KWAKIUTL INDIANS
    Craven, M. I heard the owl call my name

L

L.A. confidential. Ellroy, J.
L.A. Times. Woods, S.
The **L** shaped room. Reid Banks, L.
LA MOTTE, JEANNE DE SAINT-RÉMY DE VALOIS, COMTESSE DE, 1756-1791
    Dumas, A. The Queen's necklace

LABOR AND LABORING CLASSES
    See also Apprentices; Labor unions; Migrant labor; Proletarian novels; Strikes and lockouts

Denmark
Andersen Nexø, M. Pelle the conqueror: v2 Apprenticeship

England
Brontë, C. Shirley
Pearce, M. E. Apple tree lean down
Sillitoe, A. Saturday night and Sunday morning

France
Zola, É. Germinal

Poland
Singer, I. J. The brothers Ashkenazi

United States
Hemingway, E. The torrents of spring
Steinbeck, J. In dubious battle
Tax, M. Rivington Street
Tax, M. Union Square
Zaroulis, N. L. Call the darkness light

Wales
Llewellyn, R. How green was my valley

LABOR AND LABORING CLASSES—*Continued*
West Virginia
Giardina, D. The unquiet earth

LABOR UNIONS
See also Labor and laboring classes; Strikes and lockouts
Dexter, P. Brotherly love
Giardina, D. The unquiet earth
Kennedy, W. The ink truck
Schulberg, B. Waterfront
LaBrava. Leonard, E.
The **labyrinthine** ways. See Greene, G. The power and the glory
LACKLAND, JOHN *See* John, King of England, 1167-1216
The **lacquer** screen. Gulik, R. H. van
Ladders to fire. Nin, A.
In Nin, A. Cities of the interior p1-127
The **ladies** of Missalonghi. McCullough, C.
The **lady.** McCaffrey, A.
The **lady.** Richter, C.
Lady Barbarina. James, H.
In James, H. The complete tales of Henry James v5
The **Lady** Chapel. Robb, C. M.
Lady Chatterley's lover. Lawrence, D. H.
Lady Fortescue steps out. Chesney, M.
The **lady** in the lake. Chandler, R.
also in Chandler, R. Later novels and other writings p1-200
The **lady** of Han-Gilen. Tarr, J.
Lady of quality. Heyer, G.
The **lady** of situations. Auchincloss, L.
Lady Oracle. Atwood, M.
Lady Susan. Austen, J.
Lady with the camellias. See Dumas, A. Camille
Lady yesterday. Estleman, L. D.
The **lagoon.** Conrad, J.
In Conrad, J. Great short works of Joseph Conrad p5-17
Laguna heat. Parker, T. J.
The **lake** of darkness. Rendell, R.

LAKE ONTARIO (N.Y. AND ONT.)
Cooper, J. F. The Pathfinder
Lake Wobegon days. Keillor, G.

LAMAS
Hilton, J. Lost horizon
The **lamb's** war. De Hartog, J.

LANCASHIRE (ENGLAND) *See* England—Lancashire

LANCELOT (LEGENDARY CHARACTER)
White, T. H. The candle in the wind
The **land** endures. Pearce, M. E.

LAND REFORM *See* Land tenure

LAND SPECULATION *See* Speculation

LAND TENURE
Smith, W. A. A sparrow falls
A **landing** on the sun. Frayn, M.
Landlocked. Lessing, D. M.
In Lessing, D. M. Children of violence v4

LANDLORD AND TENANT
See also Tenant farming
Lando. L'Amour, L.
In L'Amour, L. The Sacketts: beginnings of a dynasty
Land's end. Pohl, F.
The **Langoliers.** King, S.
In King, S. Four past midnight p1-246

LANGUAGE AND LANGUAGES
Hoban, R. Riddley Walker

[**Lanny** Budd series]. Sinclair, U.
Lantern for the dark. Stirling, J.
A **lantern** in her hand. Aldrich, B. S.
Lantern slides. O'Brien, E.

LARCENY *See* Theft

LARGE PRINT BOOKS
Aaron, D. Crossing by night
Adams, A. Almost perfect
Adams, A. Caroline's daughters
Adler, E. Fortune is a woman
Adler, E. Legacy of secrets
Adler, E. The secret of the Villa Mimosa
Aiken, J. Eliza's daughter
Aiken, J. The haunting of Lamb House
Aiken, J. Jane Fairfax
Allbeury, T. A time without shadows
Allen, C. V. Painted lives
Allende, I. The stories of Eva Luna
Allingham, M. The return of Mr. Campion
Amis, K. The folks that live on the hill
Anthony, E. The Doll's House
Anthony, E. Exposure
Anthony, E. The house of Vandekar
Anthony, E. The relic
Atwood, M. Cat's eye
Atwood, M. The handmaid's tale
Auchincloss, L. Tales of yesteryear
Auel, J. M. The Clan of the Cave Bear
Auel, J. M. The Mammoth Hunters
Bainbridge, B. The birthday boys
Barnard, R. A fatal attachment
Barnard, R. A hovering of vultures
Barnard, R. The masters of the house
Barnard, R. A scandal in Belgravia
Barnes, L. Coyote
Barnes, L. The snake tattoo
Barnes, L. Snapshot
Barnes, L. Steel guitar
Barnes, L. A trouble of fools
Barrett, J. Presumption
Battle, L. The past is another country
Battle, L. Storyville
Bawden, N. Family money
Bayer, W. Pattern crimes
Benchley, P. Beast
Binchy, M. Circle of friends
Binchy, M. The copper beech
Binchy, M. Echoes
Blake, J. Wildest dreams
Block, L. The burglar who traded Ted Williams
Block, L. A walk among the tombstones
Boswell, R. Mystery ride
Bradford, B. T. Angel
Bradford, B. T. Remember
Braun, L. J. The cat who came to breakfast
Braun, L. J. The cat who knew a cardinal
Braun, L. J. The cat who lived high
Braun, L. J. The cat who moved a mountain
Braun, L. J. The cat who talked to ghosts
Braun, L. J. The cat who wasn't there
Braun, L. J. The cat who went underground
Brett, S. The dead side of the mike
Brett, S. Mrs. Pargeter's package
Brookner, A. Dolly
Brown, D. Storming heaven
Brown, R. M. Rest in pieces
Brown, R. Before and after
Brown, S. Charade
Brown, S. French Silk
Brown, S. Where there's smoke
Buchanan, E. Contents under pressure
Buchanan, E. Miami, it's murder
Buck, P. S. The good earth
Buckley, W. F. Tucker's last stand
Buckley, W. F. A very private plot
Burke, J. L. Dixie City jam
Burke, J. L. In the electric mist with Confederate dead
Burley, W. J. Wycliffe and the cycle of death

LARGE PRINT BOOKS—*Continued*

Burns, O. A. Leaving Cold Sassy
Butler, G. Cracking open a coffin
Butler, G. Death lives next door
Campbell, R. W. Boneyards
Canin, E. The palace thief
Cannell, D. Femmes fatal
Cannell, D. How to murder your mother-in-law
Carr, P. We'll meet again
Cather, W. Sapphira and the slave girl
Chandler, R. The high window
Chandler, R. The lady in the lake
Cheever, J. Bullet Park
Christie, A. The A.B.C. murders
Christie, A. At Bertram's Hotel
Christie, A. The body in the library
Christie, A. Curtain
Christie, A. Endless night
Christie, A. Evil under the sun
Christie, A. The mirror crack'd
Christie, A. Miss Marple: the complete short stories
Christie, A. Mr. Parker Pyne, detective
Christie, A. A murder is announced
Christie, A. Sleeping murder
Christie, A. Thirteen at dinner
Christie, A. Three blind mice, and other stories
Christie, A. Towards zero
Christie, A. The witness for the prosecution, and other stories
Christmas stalkings
Clancy, T. Clear and present danger
Clancy, T. Debt of honor
Clancy, T. Red Storm rising
Clancy, T. The sum of all fears
Clark, C. H. Decked
Clark, M. H. Loves music, loves to dance
Cleary, J. Bleak spring
Cleary, J. Dark summer
Colwin, L. A big storm knocked it over
Condon, R. Prizzi's money
Connelly, M. The black ice
Connelly, M. The concrete blonde
Cook, R. Blindsight
Cook, R. Fatal cure
Cook, R. Mutation
Cook, R. Terminal
Cook, T. H. Evidence of blood
Cookson, C. The Maltese Angel
Coonts, S. The minotaur
Coonts, S. Under siege
Cornwell, B. Rebel
Cornwell, B. Redcoat
Cornwell, B. Sharpe's revenge
Cornwell, B. Sharpe's rifles
Cornwell, P. D. All that remains
Cornwell, P. D. Postmortem
Coughlin, W. J. In the presence of enemies
Coughlin, W. J. Shadow of a doubt
Coulter, C. The Wyndham legacy
Crichton, M. Disclosure
Crichton, M. Jurassic Park
Crichton, M. Rising sun
Cussler, C. Dragon
Cussler, C. Inca gold
Cussler, C. Sahara
Dahl, R. Ah, sweet mystery of life
Dailey, J. Masquerade
Dailey, J. Tangled vines
Davies, R. The lyre of Orpheus
Deighton, L. City of gold
Deighton, L. Spy hook
Deighton, L. Spy line
Deighton, L. Spy sinker
DeLillo, D. Libra
Delinsky, B. For my daughters
DeMille, N. The charm school
DeMille, N. The general's daughter
Dennis, P. Auntie Mame

Dew, R. F. Fortunate lives
Dexter, C. The jewel that was ours
Dexter, C. The way through the woods
The Dick Francis treasury of great racing stories
Dickinson, P. Play dead
Dickinson, P. The yellow room conspiracy
Dillard, A. The living
Dobyns, S. Saratoga snapper
Doig, I. Ride with me, Mariah Montana
Douglas, L. C. Magnificent obsession
Dunne, D. An inconvenient woman
Dunne, D. A season in purgatory
Edgerton, C. Killer diller
Elkins, A. J. A glancing light
Evanovich, J. One for the money
Fast, H. The trial of Abigail Goodman
Ferrars, E. X. Smoke without fire
Fielding, J. See Jane run
Fitzgerald, F. S. Tender is the night
Flagg, F. Fried green tomatoes at the Whistle-Stop Cafe
Follett, K. A dangerous fortune
Follett, K. Night over water
Forester, C. S. The African Queen
Forester, C. S. Mr. Midshipman Hornblower
Forsyth, F. The negotiator
Francis, D. Comeback
Francis, D. Decider
Francis, D. Driving force
Francis, D. Enquiry
Francis, D. Flying finish
Francis, D. Forfeit
Francis, D. In the frame
Francis, D. Longshot
Francis, D. Odds against
Francis, D. Risk
Francis, D. Straight
Francis, D. Whip hand
Freeman, C. Always and forever
Freemantle, B. Charlie's apprentice
French, A. Billy
Gage, E. The master stroke
Galbraith, J. K. A tenured professor
Gardner, E. S. The case of the sulky girl
Garwood, J. Saving grace
Gash, J. The sin within her smile
George, E. For the sake of Elena
George, E. A great deliverance
George, E. Payment in blood
George, E. Playing for the Ashes
George, E. A suitable vengeance
Gibbons, K. A virtuous woman
Gilman, D. The amazing Mrs. Pollifax
Gilman, D. Caravan
Gilman, D. Mrs. Pollifax and the Golden Triangle
Gilman, D. Mrs. Pollifax and the second thief
Gilman, D. Mrs. Pollifax and the whirling dervish
Gilman, D. A palm for Mrs. Pollifax
Girzone, J. F. Joshua and the children
Girzone, J. F. Joshua in the Holy Land
Girzone, J. F. The shepherd
Godden, R. China Court
Godden, R. Pippa passes
Godden, R. Thursday's children
Godwin, G. Father Melancholy's daughter
Golding, W. The scorpion god: three short novels
Goldsborough, R. The bloodied ivy
Goldsborough, R. The missing chapter
Goldsmith, O. Fashionably late
Gordimer, N. Jump and other stories
Gordon, M. The rest of life: three novellas
Gosling, P. The body in Blackwater Bay
Gosling, P. A few dying words
Goudge, E. Blessing in disguise
Goudge, E. Such devoted sisters
Grafton, S. "G" is for gumshoe
Grafton, S. "H" is for homicide
Grafton, S. "I" is for innocent
Grafton, S. "J" is for judgment

LARGE PRINT BOOKS—*Continued*
Greeley, A. M. Fall from grace
Greeley, A. M. Irish gold
Greeley, A. M. An occasion of sin
Greeley, A. M. St. Valentine's night
Greene, G. The captain and the enemy
Greene, G. The last word and other stories
Grey, Z. Knights of the range
Grimes, M. The Horse You Came In On
Grimes, M. The Old Silent
Grisham, J. The chamber
Grisham, J. The client
Grisham, J. The firm
Grisham, J. The pelican brief
Grisham, J. A time to kill
Hailey, E. F. Home free
Hall, A. Quiller bamboo
Hall, A. Quiller meridian
Hall, A. Quiller solitaire
Hamilton, J. A map of the world
Harris, R. Fatherland
Harris, R. Love and money
Harrison, S. Mother earth, father sky
Harrod-Eagles, C. Death to go
Harrod-Eagles, C. Orchestrated death
Hart, C. G. Dead man's island
Hart, C. G. Scandal in Fair Haven
Hart, J. Sin
Harvey, K. Stars
Hawthorne, N. The House of the Seven Gables
Haymon, S. T. A beautiful death
Hemingway, E. A farewell to arms
Hemingway, E. For whom the bell tolls
Hemingway, E. The old man and the sea
Hersey, J. A bell for Adano
Hersey, J. A single pebble
Hess, J. Martians in Maggody
Heyer, G. Bath tangle
Heyer, G. The grand Sophy
Heyer, G. Penhallow
Higgins, J. Cold Harbour
Higgins, J. The eagle has flown
Higgins, J. Eye of the storm
Higgins, J. On dangerous ground
Hill, R. Recalled to life
Hill, S. Mrs. de Winter
Hillerman, T. The blessing way
Hillerman, T. Dance hall of the dead
Hillerman, T. The dark wind
Hillerman, T. The ghostway
Hillerman, T. Listening woman
Hillerman, T. People of darkness
Hillerman, T. Sacred clowns
Hillerman, T. Talking God
Hodge, J. A. Escapade
Hodge, J. A. Windover
Hoffman, A. At risk
Hoffman, A. Second nature
Hoffman, A. Seventh heaven
Hoffman, A. Turtle Moon
Holland, C. Pacific Street
Holland, I. A fatal advent
Holt, V. The captive
Holt, V. Daughter of deceit
Holt, V. The India fan
Holt, V. Seven for a secret
Howard, E. J. Confusion
Howatch, S. Mystical paths
Howatch, S. Scandalous risks
Humphreys, J. The fireman's fair
Hunter, E. Criminal conversation
Innes, M. Appleby and the Ospreys
Isaacs, S. Shining through
James, P. D. The children of men
James, P. D. Devices and desires
Jeffries, R. Death takes time
Jones, D. C. The search for Temperance Moon
Jones, D. C. This savage race
Kaminsky, S. M. Rostnikov's vacation

Keating, H. R. F. The rich detective
Kellerman, F. Day of atonement
Kellerman, F. False prophet
Kellerman, J. Private eyes
Kellerman, J. Time bomb
Kelton, E. The far canyon
Kelton, E. Slaughter
Keneally, T. Flying hero class
Kesey, K. One flew over the cuckoo's nest
Kienzle, W. X. Chameleon
Kincaid, J. Lucy
King, S. Carrie
King, S. Cujo
King, S. The dark half
King, S. The dead zone
King, S. Dolores Claiborne
King, S. Four past midnight
King, S. Insomnia
King, S. Needful things
King, S. Nightmares & dreamscapes
King, S. Salem's Lot
King, S. The shining
Kingsolver, B. Animal dreams
Kingsolver, B. Pigs in heaven
Kipling, R. The light that failed
Kittredge, M. Rigor mortis
Knowles, J. A separate peace
Koontz, D. R. The bad place
Koontz, D. R. Cold fire
Koontz, D. R. Dragon tears
Koontz, D. R. Hideaway
Koontz, D. R. Midnight
Koontz, D. R. Mr. Murder
Koontz, D. R. Watchers
Krentz, J. A. Grand passion
Laker, R. Circle of pearls
Laker, R. The sugar pavilion
Laker, R. The Venetian mask
L'Amour, L. The man from the broken hills
L'Amour, L. The outlaws of Mesquite
L'Amour, L. The rustlers of West Fork
L'Amour, L. The trail to Seven Pines
Landrum, G. The famous DAR murder mystery
Langton, J. God in Concord
Lathen, E. Double, double, oil and trouble
Lathen, E. East is east
Lathen, E. Pick up sticks
Le Carré, J. The Russia house
L'Engle, M. The other side of the sun
Leonard, E. Bandits
Leonard, E. Get Shorty
Leonard, E. Killshot
Leonard, E. Maximum Bob
Leonard, E. Pronto
Leonard, E. Rum punch
Lescroart, J. T. The 13th juror
Levin, I. Sliver
Lively, P. Moon tiger
Lively, P. The road to Lichfield
London, J. The call of the wild
Lovesey, P. Bertie and the seven bodies
Lovesey, P. The detective wore silk drawers
Lovesey, P. Diamond solitaire
Lovesey, P. The last detective
Lovesey, P. On the edge
Ludlum, R. The Bourne ultimatum
Ludlum, R. The road to Omaha
Ludlum, R. The scorpio illusion
Maas, P. Father and son
MacInnes, H. The Salzburg connection
MacLean, A. Breakheart Pass
MacLeod, C. The Gladstone bag
MacLeod, C. An owl too many
MacLeod, C. The recycled citizen
MacLeod, C. The resurrection man
MacLeod, C. Something in the water
Marsh, J. The House of Eliott
Marsh, Dame N. Black as he's painted

LARGE PRINT BOOKS—*Continued*

Marsh, Dame N. When in Rome
Martin, V. Mary Reilly
Martini, S. P. Compelling evidence
Martini, S. P. Prime witness
Martini, S. P. Undue influence
Matthiessen, P. Killing Mister Watson
Mayle, P. Hotel Pastis
McBain, E. Kiss
McBain, E. There was a little girl
McBain, E. Three blind mice
McBain, E. Tricks
McBain, E. Widows
McCammon, R. R. Boy's life
McCarthy, C. The crossing
McClure, J. The steam pig
McCorkle, J. Tending to Virginia
McCrumb, S. Missing Susan
McCutchan, P. Convoy south
McDermott, A. At weddings and wakes
Mcdonald, G. Fletch, too
Mcdonald, G. Fletch won
Mcdonald, G. Son of Fletch
McEwan, I. The innocent
McFarland, D. The music room
McGown, J. Murder at the old vicarage
McInerny, R. M. Easeful death
McInerny, R. M. Judas Priest
McInerny, R. M. Mom and dead
McInerny, R. M. Savings and loam
McMillan, T. Waiting to exhale
McMurtry, L. Buffalo girls
McMurtry, L. The evening star
McMurtry, L. Some can whistle
McMurtry, L. Streets of Laredo
McNaught, J. Paradise
McNaught, J. Perfect
Michael, J. A ruling passion
Michael, J. Sleeping beauty
Michaels, B. Houses of stone
Michaels, B. Into the darkness
Michaels, B. Vanish with the rose
Michener, J. A. Journey
Michener, J. A. Mexico
Michener, J. A. The novel
Michener, J. A. Recessional
Miller, S. For love
Mitchell, M. Gone with the wind
Morrison, T. Jazz
Mortimer, J. C. Dunster
Mortimer, J. C. Rumpole on trial
Mosley, W. Black Betty
Mosley, W. Devil in a blue dress
Mosley, W. A red death
Mosley, W. White butterfly
Moyes, P. Twice in a blue moon
Muller, M. Trophies and dead things
O'Brien, E. House of splendid isolation
O'Donnell, L. Lockout
O'Donnell, L. No business being a cop
O'Donnell, L. A private crime
O'Donnell, L. Pushover
O'Donnell, L. Used to kill
O'Donnell, L. A wreath for the bride
Ogilvie, E. When the music stopped
O'Marie, C. A. The missing Madonna
O'Marie, C. A. Murder in ordinary time
Otto, W. How to make an American quilt
Paretsky, S. Blood shot
Paretsky, S. Burn marks
Paretsky, S. Deadlock
Paretsky, S. Guardian angel
Paretsky, S. Indemnity only
Paretsky, S. Killing orders
Pargeter, E. The heaven tree trilogy
Parker, R. B. Early autumn
Parker, R. B. Looking for Rachel Wallace
Parker, R. B. Mortal stakes
Parker, R. B. Paper doll

Parker, R. B. Pastime
Parker, R. B. Perchance to dream
Parker, R. B. Playmates
Parker, R. B. Promised land
Parker, R. B. Stardust
Paton, A. Cry, the beloved country
Patterson, J. Along came a spider
Patterson, R. N. Eyes of a child
Payne, D. Ruin Creek
Pearce, M. E. The old house at Railes
Pearson, R. The angel maker
Pearson, R. Hard fall
Pearson, R. No witnesses
Peck, R. N. A day no pigs would die
Perry, A. Defend and betray
Perry, A. The face of a stranger
Perry, A. Farriers' Lane
Perry, A. The Hyde Park headsman
Perry, A. The sins of the wolf
Perry, A. A sudden, fearful death
Peters, E. The last camel died at noon
Peters, E. Naked once more
Peters, E. The snake, the crocodile, and the dog
Peters, E. Brother Cadfael's penance
Peters, E. The confession of Brother Haluin
Peters, E. Flight of a witch
Peters, E. The hermit of Eyton Forest
Peters, E. The potter's field
Pickard, N. The 27 ingredient chili con carne murders
Pickard, N. Bum steer
Pickard, N. But I wouldn't want to die there
Pickard, N. Confession
Piercy, M. The longings of women
Pilcher, R. Flowers in the rain & other stories
Pilcher, R. Voices in summer
Plaidy, J. The reluctant queen
Plaidy, J. The scarlet cloak
Plain, B. Blessings
Plain, B. Harvest
Plain, B. Whispers
Price, E. The beloved invader
Price, E. Lighthouse
Price, E. Margaret's story
Price, E. New moon rising
Price, E. Where shadows go
Price, N. Night woman
Price, R. The tongues of angels
Puzo, M. The fourth K
Quick, A. Deception
Quindlen, A. Object lessons
Read, Miss. Farewell to Fairacre
Read, Miss. Friends at Thrush Green
Rendell, R. The bridesmaid
Rendell, R. The crocodile bird
Rendell, R. The veiled one
Rhys, J. Wide Sargasso Sea
Rice, L. Blue moon
Ripley, A. Scarlett
Robards, K. Nobody's angel
Roberts, N. Hidden riches
Roberts, N. Private scandals
Roiphe, A. R. If you knew me
Roosevelt, E. A first class murder
Roosevelt, E. Murder at the palace
Roosevelt, E. Murder in the Blue Room
Roosevelt, E. Murder in the Rose Garden
Sabatini, R. Scaramouche
Sanders, L. McNally's caper
Sanders, L. McNally's secret
Sanders, L. The seventh commandment
Sanders, L. Sullivan's sting
Sandford, J. Winter prey
Sayers, D. L. The documents in the case
Sayers, D. L. In the teeth of the evidence and other stories
Schofield, S. C. Telluride
Shaara, M. The killer angels
Sheldon, S. The doomsday conspiracy

LARGE PRINT BOOKS—*Continued*

Sheldon, S. The stars shine down
Sherwood, J. The hanging garden
Sherwood, J. The mantrap garden
Shreve, A. Eden Close
Siddons, A. R. Colony
Siddons, A. R. Downtown
Siddons, A. R. Hill towns
Siddons, A. R. King's oak
Siddons, A. R. Outer banks
Siddons, A. R. Peachtree Road
Simenon, G. Maigret and the burglar's wife
Simenon, G. Maigret and the Nahour case
Simenon, G. Maigret bides his time
Simenon, G. Maigret goes home
Simenon, G. Maigret's revolver
Simpson, D. Doomed to die
Simpson, D. Wake the dead
Sjöwall, M. The laughing policeman
Smiley, J. A thousand acres
Smith, B. A tree grows in Brooklyn
Smith, E. E. Miss Melville rides a tiger
Smith, L. The devil's dream
Smith, M. C. Polar Star
Smith, M. C. Red Square
Solomita, S. A good day to die
Spark, M. A far cry from Kensington
Spencer, L. Bitter sweet
Spencer, L. Forgiving
Spencer, L. Home song
Steel, D. Accident
Steel, D. Heartbeat
Steel, D. Mixed blessings
Steel, D. No greater love
Steel, D. Vanished
Steel, D. Wings
Steinbeck, J. Of mice and men
Steinbeck, J. Tortilla Flat
Stewart, F. M. Pomp and circumstance
Stewart, M. The stormy petrel
Stewart, M. This rough magic
Stirling, J. Shadows on the shore
Stone, R. Outerbridge Reach
Stubbs, J. Family games
Styron, W. Sophie's choice
Symons, J. Death's darkest face
Tan, A. The kitchen god's wife
Tapply, W. G. Dead winter
Tapply, W. G. A void in hearts
Tey, J. Brat Farrar
Tey, J. The Franchise affair
Tey, J. To love and be wise
Thayer, N. Everlasting
Thayer, N. Family secrets
Thayer, N. My dearest friend
Thomas, C. Playing with cobras
Thomas, R. Other people's marriages
Thomas, R. Ah, treachery!
Thomas, R. The fourth Durango
Thomas, R. Voodoo, Ltd
Trollope, J. The men and the girls
Truman, M. Murder at the Kennedy Center
Truman, M. Murder at the National Cathedral
Truman, M. Murder at the Pentagon
Truman, M. Murder on the Potomac
Turow, S. The burden of proof
Turow, S. Pleading guilty
Tyler, A. Breathing lessons
Tyler, A. Saint maybe
Uris, L. Mitla Pass
Veryan, P. A shadow's bliss
Villars, E. Lipstick on his collar
Viorst, J. Murdering Mr. Monti
Voigt, C. Glass mountain
Waller, R. J. The bridges of Madison County
Waller, R. J. Slow waltz in Cedar Bend
Wambaugh, J. Finnegan's week
Wambaugh, J. Fugitive nights

West, M. L. Masterclass
West, M. L. The shoes of the fisherman
Westlake, D. E. Baby, would I lie?
Westlake, D. E. Trust me on this
Wharton, E. The age of innocence
Whitney, P. A. Daughter of the stars
Whitney, P. A. The ebony swan
Whitney, P. A. Feather on the moon
Whitney, P. A. Rainbow in the mist
Whitney, P. A. The singing stones
Whitney, P. A. Woman without a past
A Woman's eye
Woods, S. Dead eyes
Woods, S. Grass roots
Woods, S. Heat
Woods, S. L.A. Times
Woods, S. Santa Fe rules
Wright, R. Native son
Yorke, M. A small deceit
Young, C. The wedding dress

LAS VEGAS (NEV.) *See* Nevada—Las Vegas
Lasher. Rice, A.
The **last** angry man. Green, G.
The **last** book of swords: Shieldbreaker's story. Saberhagen, F.
The **last** camel died at noon. Peters, E.
The **last** castle. Vance, J.
  In The Hugo winners v2 p245-305
The **last** Catholic in America. Powers, J. R.
Last chance for glory. Solomita, S.
The **last** chronicle of Barset. Trollope, A.
The **last** command. Zahn, T.
The **last** convertible. Myrer, A.
The **last** days of Louisiana Red. Reed, I.
The **last** days of Pompeii. Lytton, E. B. L., Baron
The **last** detective. Lovesey, P.
Last ditch. Marsh, Dame N.
The **last** enchantment. Stewart, M.
  also in Stewart, M. Mary Stewart's Merlin trilogy
The **last** farewell. McCutchan, P.
The **last** gentleman. Percy, W.
The **last** houseparty. Dickinson, P.
The **last** hurrah. O'Connor, E.
The **last** innocent hour. Abbott, M.
The **last** letter home. Moberg, V.
The **last** nine days of the Bismarck. Forester, C. S.
The **last** of Chéri. Colette
  In Colette. Six novels p535-648
The **last** of Mr. Norris. Isherwood, C.
  In Isherwood, C. The Berlin stories v1
Last of the breed. L'Amour, L.
The **last** of the just. Schwarz-Bart, A.
The **last** of the Mohicans. Cooper, J. F.
  also in Cooper, J. F. The Leatherstocking tales v1 p467-878
The **last** of the wine. Renault, M.
The **last** post. Ford, F. M.
  In Ford, F. M. Parade's end
The **last** prince of Ireland. Llywelyn, M.
The **last** princess. Freeman, C.
The **last** Puritan. Santayana, G.
Last respects. Aird, C.
Last seen alive. Simpson, D.
The **last** suppers. Davidson, D. M.
Last tales. Dinesen, I.
The **last** temptation of Christ. Kazantzakis, N.
Last things. Snow, C. P.
The **last** tycoon. Fitzgerald, F. S.
The **last** unicorn. Beagle, P. S.
The **last** valley. Guthrie, A. B.
The **last** voyage of somebody the sailor. Barth, J.
The **last** waltz. Zaroulis, N. L.
The **last** word and other stories. Greene, G.
The **late** George Apley. Marquand, J. P.
Late payments. Lewin, M. Z.
Later novels and other writings. Chandler, R.
Later than you think. See Kaye, M. M. Death in Kenya

Later the same day. Paley, G.
  In Paley, G. The collected stories p261-386
The **lathe** of heaven. Le Guin, U. K.

LATIN AMERICA
  Allende, I. Eva Luna
  Allende, I. Of love and shadows
  García Márquez, G. Love in the time of cholera
  Naipaul, V. S. A way in the world

Politics
  See Politics—Latin America

LATIN AMERICANS

Europe
  García Márquez, G. Strange pilgrims
LATINOS (U.S.) *See* Hispanic Americans
Laugh that off. Gardner, E. S.
  In Gardner, E. S. Dead men's letters p49-104
Laughable loves. Kundera, M.
Laughing Boy. La Farge, O.
The **laughing** policeman. Sjöwall, M.
Laughing to keep from crying. Hughes, L.

LAVEAU, MARIE, 1794-1881
  Rhodes, J. P. Voodoo dreams

LAW AND LAWYERS
  See also Judges; Trials; Women lawyers
  Amiel, J. A question of proof
  Auchincloss, L. Honorable men
  Auchincloss, L. The realist
  Banks, R. The sweet hereafter
  Brandon, J. Rules of evidence
  Busch, F. Closing arguments
  Camus, A. The fall
  Carroll, J. Memorial bridge
  Clark, M. H. Remember me
  Connell, E. S. Mr. Bridge
  Connell, E. S. Mrs. Bridge
  Cook, R. Harmful intent
  Coughlin, W. J. Death penalty
  Coughlin, W. J. In the presence of enemies
  Coughlin, W. J. Shadow of a doubt
  Cozzens, J. G. By love possessed
  Crichton, M. Disclosure
  Davies, R. The manticore
  DeMille, N. The Gold Coast
  Dershowitz, A. M. The advocate's devil
  Dickens, C. Bleak House
  Dickens, C. The posthumous papers of the Pickwick
    Club
  Diehl, W. Primal fear
  Drabble, M. The needle's eye
  Dunne, J. G. The red, white, and blue
  Friedman, P. Inadmissible evidence
  Friedman, P. Reasonable doubt
  Gaddis, W. A frolic of his own
  Greene, G. The tenth man
  Grisham, J. The chamber
  Grisham, J. The client
  Grisham, J. The firm
  Grisham, J. The pelican brief
  Grisham, J. A time to kill
  Guest, J. Second heaven
  Higgins, G. V. Defending Billy Ryan
  Higgins, G. V. The Mandeville talent
  Humphreys, J. The fireman's fair
  Hunter, E. Criminal conversation
  Irving, C. Final argument
  Isaacs, S. Shining through
  Kaufman, S. Diary of a mad housewife
  King, S. Thinner
  Lee, H. To kill a mockingbird
  Legal fictions
  Lescroart, J. T. The 13th juror
  Lescroart, J. T. Hard evidence
  Ludlum, R. The Aquitaine progression
  Maas, P. China white
  Martini, S. P. Compelling evidence

  Martini, S. P. Prime witness
  Martini, S. P. Undue influence
  McCullers, C. Clock without hands
  Miller, S. The good mother
  Mishima, Y. The decay of the angel
  Mishima, Y. Runaway horses
  Mishima, Y. The Temple of Dawn
  Mortimer, J. C. Rumpole à la carte
  Mortimer, J. C. Rumpole on trial
  Mortimer, J. C. Rumpole's return
  Mortimer, J. C. The second Rumpole omnibus
  Oates, J. C. Snake eyes
  Palmer, M. Natural causes
  Patterson, R. N. Degree of guilt
  Patterson, R. N. Eyes of a child
  Plain, B. Blessings
  Reed, B. The choice
  Reed, B. The indictment
  Richter, C. The lady
  Roberts, K. L. Lydia Bailey
  Snow, C. P. Strangers and brothers
  Snow, C. P. Time of hope
  Strindberg, A. The scapegoat
  Tanenbaum, R. Immoral certainty
  Tanenbaum, R. Reversible error
  Tey, J. The Franchise affair
  Traver, R. Anatomy of a murder
  Turow, S. The burden of proof
  Turow, S. Pleading guilty
  Turow, S. Presumed innocent
  Uhnak, D. False witness
  Vida, N. Goodbye, Saigon
  Warren, R. P. All the king's men
  Warren, R. P. World enough and time
  Welch, J. The Indian lawyer
  Wilhelm, K. The best defense
  Woods, S. Grass roots
Law and order. Uhnak, D.
Lawd today! Wright, R.
  In Wright, R. Works

LAWSUITS *See* Law and lawyers

LAWYERS *See* Law and lawyers
Lazarus. West, M. L.
Leader of the band. Weldon, F.
Leaf storm. García Márquez, G.
  In García Márquez, G. Collected novellas p1-106
  In García Márquez, G. Leaf storm, and other stories
    p1-97
Leaf storm, and other stories. García Márquez, G.
Leah's children. Goldreich, G.
Leah's journey. Goldreich, G.
The **leaning** tower, and other stories. Porter, K. A.
  also in Porter, K. A. The collected stories of
    Katherine Anne Porter p321-495

LEARNING AND SCHOLARSHIP *See* Scholars
The **learning** tree. Parks, G.
The **Leatherstocking** saga. See Cooper, J. F. The Leather-
  stocking tales
The **Leatherstocking** tales. Cooper, J. F.
Leave her to heaven. Williams, B. A.
Leave of absence. McInerny, R. M.
Leaving Cold Sassy. Burns, O. A.
Leaving home. Keillor, G.

LEBANON
  Maalouf, A. The rock of Tanios
  Stewart, M. The Gabriel hounds

The **LeBaron** secret. Birmingham, S.
The **left** hand of darkness. Le Guin, U. K.
The **left** hand of God. Barrett, W. E.
The **left-handed** woman. Handke, P.
Leftover dreams. Allen, C. V.

LEGACIES *See* Inheritance and succession
The **legacy**. Fast, H.
The **legacy**. Shute, N.
The **legacy** of Beulah Land. Coleman, L.
Legacy of secrets. Adler, E.
Legal fictions. Entered in Part I under title
LEGAL PROFESSION *See* Law and lawyers
Legend in green velvet. Peters, E.
The **legend** of the seventh virgin. Holt, V.

LEGENDS AND FOLK TALES
  See also Grail
  Benét, S. V. The Devil and Daniel Webster
  Berger, T. Arthur Rex
  Bradley, M. Z. The forest house
  Bradley, M. Z. The mists of Avalon
  Graves, R. Hercules, my shipmate
  Lewis, C. S. Till we have faces
  Llywelyn, M. Bard
  Llywelyn, M. Finn Mac Cool
  Llywelyn, M. The horse goddess
  Lovecraft, H. P. The mound
  Mailer, N. Ancient evenings
  Mehta, G. A river Sutra
  Renault, M. The bull from the sea
  Renault, M. The king must die
  Schwarz-Bart, A. The last of the just
  Silverberg, R. Gilgamesh the king
  Steinbeck, J. The pearl
  Stewart, M. The hollow hills
  Stewart, M. The last enchantment
  Stewart, M. The wicked day
  Sutcliff, R. Sword at sunset
  Updike, J. The centaur
  Welty, E. The robber bridegroom
  White, T. H. The once and future king
  White, T. H. The sword in the stone
  White, T. H. The witch in the wood
  Wiesel, E. The Golem

LEICESTER, ROBERT DUDLEY, EARL OF, 1532?-1588
  Scott, Sir W. Kenilworth
Lélia. Sand, G.

LENINGRAD (SOVIET UNION) *See* Russia—St. Petersburg
The **leopard**. Tomasi di Lampedusa, G.
The **leopard** hunts in darkness. Smith, W. A.

LEOPOLD, NATHAN FREUNDENTHAL, 1904 OR 5-1971
  Levin, M. Compulsion
The **leper** of St. Giles. Peters, E.

LEPROSY
  Greene, G. A burnt-out case

LESBIANISM
  See also Homosexuality
  Berger, T. Reinhart's women
  Brown, R. M. Sudden death
  Brown, R. M. Venus envy
  Colette. Claudine married
  Durrell, L. Livia
  Grumbach, D. Chamber music
  Guy, R. Ruby
  Hall, R. The well of loneliness
  Hunter, E. Lizzie
  Lindsey, D. L. Mercy
  Naylor, G. The women of Brewster Place
  Nin, A. Ladders to fire
  The Penguin book of lesbian short stories
  Piercy, M. Small changes
  Sarton, M. The education of Harriet Hatfield
  Sarton, M. The magnificent spinster
  Snow, C. P. The sleep of reason

Vine, B. The house of stairs
Wolitzer, M. Friends for life
Less than angels. Pym, B.
A **lesson** before dying. Gaines, E. J.
Let the dead bury their dead and other stories. Kenan, R.

LETTERS (STORIES ABOUT)
  Bellow, S. Herzog
  Campbell, R. The Count of Eleven
  Coetzee, J. M. Age of iron
  L'Engle, M. The love letters
  Viertel, J. Life lines

LETTERS (STORIES IN LETTER FORM)
  Austen, J. Lady Susan
  Davies, R. Fifth business
  Goethe, J. W. von. The sorrows of young Werther
  Grass, G. Dog years
  Hailey, E. F. A woman of independent means
  Lardner, R. You know me, Al
  Murdoch, I. An accidental man
  Poe, E. A. The unparalleled adventure of one Hans Pfaall
  Price, R. Blue Calhoun
  Richardson, S. Clarissa
  Richardson, S. Pamela
  Sholem Aleichem. The adventures of Menahem-Mendl
  Smith, L. Fair and tender ladies
  Smollett, T. G. Humphry Clinker
  Updike, J. S
  Walker, A. The color purple
Letters from the underworld. See Dostoyevsky, F. Notes from underground
Letting go. Roth, P.

LEUKEMIA
  Doerr, H. Stones for Ibarra
  Segal, E. Love story
The **Levanter**. Ambler, E.
Leviathan. Auster, P.
Levine. Westlake, D. E.
Lew Archer, private investigator. See Macdonald, R. Ross Macdonald's Lew Archer, private investigator

LEXINGTON, BATTLE OF, 1775
  Fast, H. April morning
LEXINGTON (MASS.) *See* Massachusetts—Lexington

LIBEL
  Galsworthy, J. The silver spoon
  Rossner, J. His little women

LIBERTY
  Asimov, I. The Bicentennial Man
  Asimov, I. The positronic man
  Coetzee, J. M. Life & times of Michael K.
  Sartre, J. P. The age of reason
Liberty Bar. See Simenon, G. Maigret on the Riviera
Libra. DeLillo, D.

LIBRARIANS
  Pym, B. An unsuitable attachment
The **library** policeman. King, S.
  In King, S. Four past midnight p401-604

LIBYAN DESERT
  Trevor, E. The flight of the Phoenix
License renewed. Gardner, J. E.
The **lie** direct. Woods, S.
Lie down in darkness. Styron, W.
Lie down with lions. Follett, K.
Lieberman's choice. Kaminsky, S. M.
Lieberman's day. Kaminsky, S. M.
Lieberman's folly. Kaminsky, S. M.

LIECHTENSTEIN
  Gallico, P. Ludmila
Lies of silence. Moore, B.
Lieutenant Hornblower. Forester, C. S.
The **life** & adventures of Nicholas Nickleby. See Dickens, C. Nicholas Nickleby

Life & times of Michael K. Coetzee, J. M.

The life and adventures of Martin Chuzzlewit. See Dickens, C. Martin Chuzzlewit

The life and adventures of Robinson Crusoe. See Defoe, D. Robinson Crusoe

The life and death of the Mayor of Casterbridge. See Hardy, T. The Mayor of Casterbridge

The life and loves of a she-devil. Weldon, F.

The life and opinions of Tristram Shandy, gentleman. Sterne, L.

> In Sterne, L. The life and opinions of Tristram Shandy, gentleman and A sentimental journey through France and Italy p1-689

The life and opinions of Tristram Shandy, gentleman and A sentimental journey through France and Italy. Sterne, L.

The life and strange surprising adventures of Robinson Crusoe of York, mariner. See Defoe, D. Robinson Crusoe

Life before man. Atwood, M.

Life force. Weldon, F.

Life lines. Viertel, J.

LIFE ON OTHER PLANETS
> See also Interplanetary visitors; Interstellar communication

Aldiss, B. W. Helliconia spring

Aldiss, B. W. Helliconia summer

Aldiss, B. W. Helliconia winter

Anderson, P. Hunter's moon

Anderson, P. The Queen of Air and Darkness

Asimov, I. Nightfall

Brunner, J. The crucible of time

Burroughs, E. R. A Princess of Mars

Butler, O. E. Adulthood rites

Butler, O. E. Dawn

Butler, O. E. Imago

Butler, O. E. Survivor

Cherryh, C. J. Chanur's Legacy

Cherryh, C. J. Foreigner

Delany, S. R. The star pit

Haldeman, J. W. Mindbridge

Le Guin, U. K. Planet of exile

Lem, S. Eden

Lem, S. Fiasco

Longyear, B. B. Enemy mine

Martin, G. R. R. Sandkings

Martin, G. R. R. A song for Lya

McCaffrey, A. All the Weyrs of Pern

McCaffrey, A. Dragonflight

McCaffrey, A. Dragonquest

McCaffrey, A. Dragonsdawn

McCaffrey, A. The renegades of Pern

McCaffrey, A. The white dragon

Niven, L. The Mote in God's Eye

Robinson, K. S. Green Mars

Robinson, K. S. Red Mars

Sagan, C. Contact

Silverberg, R. Downward to the Earth

Silverberg, R. The Face of the Waters

Smith, C. On the storm planet

Tepper, S. S. Grass

Tepper, S. S. Raising the stones

Tepper, S. S. Shadow's end

Tepper, S. S. Sideshow

Varley, J. Demon

Varley, J. Titan

Vinge, V. A fire upon the deep

Life sentences. Hailey, E. F.

Life, the universe, and everything. Adams, D.
> also in Adams, D. The hitchhiker's quartet

Light a penny candle. Binchy, M.

The light and the dark. Snow, C. P.

The light heart. Thane, E.

Light in August. Faulkner, W.

Light in summer. Stubbs, J.

The light in the forest. Richter, C.

The light in the piazza. Spencer, E.

The light that failed. Kipling, R.

Light thickens. Marsh, Dame N.

The light years. Howard, E. J.

Lighthouse. Price, E.

Lightning. Koontz, D. R.
> also in Koontz, D. R. Three complete novels p9-321

Lightning. McBain, E.

Lights out. Abrahams, P.

Like water for chocolate. Esquivel, L.

Like we used to be. Stubbs, J.

Lila. Pirsig, R. M.

The lilac bus. Binchy, M.
> In Binchy, M. The lilac bus: stories p1-163

The lilac bus: stories. Binchy, M.

Liliane. Shange, N.

The lilies of the field. Barrett, W. E.

Lily. Bonner, C.

LIMA (PERU) See Peru—Lima

LINCOLN, ABRAHAM, 1809-1865
Safire, W. Freedom
Stone, I. Love is eternal
Vidal, G. Lincoln

LINCOLN, MARY TODD, 1818-1882
Stone, I. Love is eternal

Lincoln. Vidal, G.

Linden Hills. Naylor, G.

Line of fire. Griffin, W. E. B.

Lion in the valley. Peters, E.

LIPPIZANER HORSES
Stewart, M. Airs above the ground

Lipstick on his collar. Villars, E.

LIQUOR INDUSTRY See Liquor traffic

LIQUOR TRAFFIC
> See also Moonshiners

Estleman, L. D. Whiskey River
Francis, D. Proof

The list of 7. Frost, M.

The list of Adrian Messenger. MacDonald, P.

Listening woman. Hillerman, T.
> also in Hillerman, T. The Joe Leaphorn mysteries

LITERARY AGENTS
Campbell, R. The Nameless
Shaw, I. Acceptable losses

A Literary Christmas. Entered in Part I under title

The Literary ghost. Entered in Part I under title

LITERARY LIFE
> See also Authors

Boyle, T. C. East is East
Byatt, A. S. Possession
Harris, R. Modern women
McInerney, J. Brightness Falls
Michener, J. A. The novel
Sarton, M. Mrs. Stevens hears the mermaids singing
Sheed, W. The boys of winter

The Literary traveler. Entered in Part I under title

LITHUANIA
Brown, D. Night of the hawk

LITHUANIANS
United States
Sinclair, U. The jungle

Little Big Man. Berger, T.

The little disturbances of man. Paley, G.
> In Paley, G. The collected stories p3-126

The **little** dog laughed. Hansen, J.

Little Dorrit. Dickens, C.

The **little** drummer girl. Le Carré, J.

The **little** hotel. Stead, C.

A **little** local murder. Barnard, R.

The **little** minister. Barrie, J. M.

The **little** prince. Saint-Exupéry, A. de

Little Saigon. Parker, T. J.

The **little** sister. Chandler, R.
> *In* Chandler, R. Later novels and other writings p201-416
> *In* Chandler, R. The midnight Raymond Chandler p201-416

Little victims. See Barnard, R. School for murder

The **little** world of Don Camillo. Guareschi, G.

Live and let die. Fleming, I.
> *In* Fleming, I. More gilt-edged Bonds p1-218

Live flesh. Rendell, R.

Live from Golgotha. Vidal, D.

Lives of girls & women. Munro, A.

Lives of the poets. Doctorow, E. L.

Lives of the poets [novelette]. Doctorow, E. L.
> *In* Doctorow, E. L. Lives of the poets p81-145

Livia. Durrell, L.

LIVIA DRUSILLA, CONSORT OF AUGUSTUS, EMPEROR OF ROME, 58? B.C.-29 A.D.
> Graves, R. I, Claudius

The **living**. Dillard, A.

Living at home. Gordon, M.
> *In* Gordon, M. The rest of life: three novellas

Lizzie. Hunter, E.

LLEWELYN AP IORWERTH, d. 1240
> Penman, S. K. Here be dragons

LLYWELYN AP GRUFFYDD, d. 1282
> Penman, S. K. The reckoning

LOANS
> *See also* Moneylenders

Local anaesthetic. Grass, G.

The **locked** room. Sjöwall, M.

Lockout. O'Donnell, L.

LODZ (POLAND) *See* Poland—Lodz

LOEB, RICHARD A., 1905 OR 6-1936
> Levin, M. Compulsion

Lolita. Nabokov, V. V.

LONDON (ENGLAND) *See* England—London

London fields. Amis, M.

London match. Deighton, L.
> *also in* Deighton, L. Game, set & match

London observed. See Lessing, D. M. The real thing

LONDON ZOOLOGICAL GARDENS
> Hoban, R. Turtle diary

LONELINESS
> Bowen, E. The death of the heart
> Brookner, A. Fraud
> Brookner, A. A private view
> Greenberg, J. Rites of passage
> Hoban, R. Turtle diary
> Moore, B. The lonely passion of Judith Hearne
> Pym, B. Excellent women
> Pym, B. Quartet in autumn
> Pym, B. The sweet dove died
> Rossner, J. Looking for Mr. Goodbar
> Simenon, G. Across the street
> Taylor, E. Mrs. Palfrey at the Claremont
> Trevor, W. Reading Turgenev
> Tyler, A. The accidental tourist
> West, N. Miss Lonelyhearts

The **loneliness** of the long-distance runner. Sillitoe, A.

The **lonely** girl. O'Brien, E.
> *In* O'Brien, E. The country girls trilogy and epilogue p179-377

The **lonely** passion of Judith Hearne. Moore, B.

The **lonely** silver rain. MacDonald, J. D.

Lonesome dove. McMurtry, L.

The **lonesome** gods. L'Amour, L.

The **long** dark tea-time of the soul. Adams, D.

A **long** fatal love chase. Alcott, L. M.

The **long** goodbye. Chandler, R.
> *also in* Chandler, R. Later novels and other writings p417-734
> *also in* Chandler, R. The midnight Raymond Chandler p417-734

LONG ISLAND (N.Y.)
> Benchley, P. Jaws
> Berger, T. The houseguest
> DeMille, N. The Gold Coast
> Fitzgerald, F. S. The Great Gatsby
> Hoffman, A. Seventh heaven
> Isaacs, S. After all these years
> Isaacs, S. Close relations
> McDermott, A. That night
> Roiphe, A. R. If you knew me
> Steinbeck, J. The winter of our discontent
> Westlake, D. E. Bank shot
> Whitney, P. A. The golden unicorn

The **long** lavender look. MacDonald, J. D.

A **long** line of dead men. Block, L.

The **long** lost. Campbell, R.

The **long** march. Styron, W.

The **long** night of white chickens. Goldman, F.

The **long** valley. Steinbeck, J.

The **long** walk. King, S.
> *In* King, S. The Bachman books: four early novels by Stephen King

Long way from home. Busch, F.

Longer stories from the last decade. Chekhov, A. P.

The **longest** voyage. Anderson, P.
> *In* The Hugo winners v1 p279-310
> *In* Modern classic short novels of science fiction p65-93

LONGEVITY
> *See also* Rejuvenation
> Hilton, J. Lost horizon
> Huxley, A. After many a summer dies the swan
> Sanders, L. The sixth commandment

The **longings** of women. Piercy, M.

LONGSHORE WORKERS
> Schulberg, B. Waterfront

LONGSHOREMEN *See* Longshore workers

Longshot. Francis, D.

LONGSTREET, JAMES, 1821-1904
> Williams, B. A. House divided
> Williams, B. A. The unconquered

Look at the harlequins! Nabokov, V. V.

Look away, Beulah Land. Coleman, L.

Look homeward, angel. Wolfe, T.

Looking after Lily. Bonner, C.

Looking for a rain god: an anthology of contemporary African short stories. Entered in Part I under title

Looking for Mr. Goodbar. Rossner, J.

Looking for Rachel Wallace. Parker, R. B.

The **looking** glass war. Le Carré, J.

Loon Lake. Doctorow, E. L.

Lord Edgeware dies. See Christie, A. Thirteen at dinner

Lord Foul's bane. Donaldson, S. R.
Lord Hornblower. Forester, C. S.
Lord Jim. Conrad, J.
Lord of light. Zelazny, R.
Lord of the dance. Greeley, A. M.
Lord of the Flies. Golding, W.
The lord of the rings. Tolkien, J. R. R.
Lord Peter. Sayers, D. L.
Lord Valentine's castle. Silverberg, R.
The lords of discipline. Conroy, P.
Lorna Doone. Blackmore, R. D.
LOS ALAMOS (N.M.) See New Mexico—Los Alamos
LOS ANGELES (CALIF.) See California—Los Angeles
Losing battles. Welty, E.
Lost and found. Harris, M.
The lost boy. Wolfe, T.
Lost boys. Card, O. S.
Lost Dorsai. Dickson, G. R.
    In The Hugo winners v5 p137-206
The lost honor of Katharina Blum. Böll, H.
Lost horizon. Hilton, J.
Lost in the funhouse. Barth, J.
A lost lady. Cather, W.
    also in Cather, W. Willa Cather, later novels
The lost language of cranes. Leavitt, D.
The lost queen. Lofts, N.
Lost souls. See Singer, I. B. Meshugah
The lost weekend. Jackson, C.
The lost world. Doyle, Sir A. C.
The lottery; or, The adventures of James Harris. Jackson,
    S.
The lottery winner. Clark, M. H.

LOUIS XI, KING OF FRANCE, 1423-1483
    Scott, Sir W. Quentin Durward

LOUIS XIII, KING OF FRANCE, 1601-1643
    Anthony, E. The Cardinal and the Queen

LOUIS XIV, KING OF FRANCE, 1638-1715
    Dumas, A. The iron mask
    Laker, R. To dance with kings

LOUIS XV, KING OF FRANCE, 1710-1774
    Laker, R. To dance with kings

LOUIS XVI, KING OF FRANCE, 1754-1793
    Laker, R. To dance with kings

LOUIS, KING OF HOLLAND, 1778-1846
    Lofts, N. A rose for virtue
Louis Lambert. Balzac, H. de
    In Balzac, H. de. The short novels of Balzac
Louisa May Alcott: a selected fiction. Alcott, L. M.

LOUISIANA

        19th century
Blake, J. Arrow to the heart
Gaines, E. J. The autobiography of Miss Jane Pittman

        20th century
Capote, T. Other voices, other rooms
Gaines, E. J. The gathering of old men
Gaines, E. J. In my father's house
Grau, S. A. The hard blue sky
McCammon, R. R. Gone south
Percy, W. The thanatos syndrome

        Politics
See Politics—Louisiana

        New Orleans
Algren, N. A walk on the wild side
Battle, L. Storyville
Brown, S. French Silk
Dailey, J. Masquerade
Ferber, E. Saratoga trunk
Grau, S. A. The condor passes
Hailey, A. Hotel
Harris, T. Black Sunday
Martin, V. The great divorce
Orde, L. Dreams of gold
Percy, W. The moviegoer
Plain, B. Crescent City

Rhodes, J. P. Voodoo dreams
Rice, A. The Feast of All Saints
Roberts, N. Honest illusions
Toole, J. K. A confederacy of dunces
Warren, R. P. Band of angels
Williams, B. A. The unconquered

LOVE
    See also Friendship
Godden, J. In her garden
Helprin, M. A soldier of the great war
Sarton, M. Kinds of love
Wilson, A. N. Love unknown

LOVE AFFAIRS
    See also Courtship; Love stories; Lovers; Marriage
    problems
Adams, A. Almost perfect
Alvarez, J. How the Garcia girls lost their accents
Amiel, J. A question of proof
Amis, K. The Russian girl
Anthony, E. The Cardinal and the Queen
Anthony, E. The tamarind seed
Atwood, M. Life before man
Auchincloss, L. The lady of situations
Baldwin, J. Another country
Battle, L. The past is another country
Beattie, A. Love always
Bellow, S. What kind of day did you have?
Benedict, E. Safe conduct
Berger, T. Reinhart's women
Bowen, E. The heat of the day
Bradford, B. T. Voice of the heart
Bradley, D. The Chaneysville incident
Briskin, J. Too much, too soon
Brown, R. M. Southern discomfort
Brown, S. French Silk
Carr, P. A time for silence
Casey, J. Spartina
Cather, W. Lucy Gayheart
Chase-Riboud, B. Sally Hemings
Cheever, J. Oh, what a paradise it seems
Coetzee, J. M. The master of Petersburg
Colette. Chéri
Colette. The last of Chéri
Collins, W. The rationalist
Colwin, L. Family happiness
Condon, R. Prizzi's family
Condon, R. Prizzi's honor
Dickinson, P. Death of a unicorn
Dickinson, P. Play dead
Dostoyevsky, F. The gambler
Drabble, M. The ice age
Drabble, M. Jerusalem the golden
Drabble, M. The waterfall
Dunne, D. An inconvenient woman
Dunne, J. G. Playland
Duras, M. The lover
Duras, M. The North China lover
Durrell, L. Constance
Durrell, L. Livia
Fallaci, O. A man
Fielding, H. The history of Tom Jones, a foundling
Fleming, I. The spy who loved me
Follett, K. The man from St. Petersburg
Freeman, C. Always and forever
French, M. The women's room
Gage, E. The master stroke
Glendinning, V. The grown-ups
Gold, H. A girl of forty
Gordimer, N. The conservationist
Gordimer, N. A guest of honor
Gordimer, N. My son's story
Gordon, M. The company of women
Gordon, M. Final payments
Gordon, M. Immaculate man
Gordon, M. Living at home
Goudge, E. Blessing in disguise
Graham, W. Stephanie
Greene, G. The end of the affair

LOVE AFFAIRS—*Continued*

Harris, R. Love and money
Hart, J. Sin
Harvey, K. Stars
Hazzard, S. The transit of Venus
Hemingway, E. The garden of Eden
Hoving, T. Masterpiece
Howatch, S. Mystical paths
Howatch, S. Penmarric
Howatch, S. Scandalous risks
Howatch, S. Ultimate prizes
Isaacs, S. Close relations
James, H. The ambassadors
James, H. What Maisie knew
Jen, G. Typical American
Jhabvala, R. P. Heat and dust
Jones, J. From here to eternity
Jong, E. Any woman's blues
Kawabata, Y. Snow country
Kawabata, Y. Thousand cranes
Keneally, T. A family madness
Korda, M. Curtain
Korda, M. The immortals
Krantz, J. Mistral's daughter
Kundera, M. Immortality
Kundera, M. The unbearable lightness of being
Laker, R. Jewelled path
Leavitt, D. While England sleeps
Leonard, E. Cat chaser
Lester, J. And all our wounds forgiven
Lipman, E. The way men act
Lively, P. The road to Lichfield
Lofts, N. The day of the butterfly
Lurie, A. Foreign affairs
Malamud, B. Dubin's lives
Marius, R. C. After the war
Martin, V. The great divorce
Martini, S. P. Compelling evidence
Maupin, A. Maybe the moon
McCauley, S. The easy way out
McEwan, I. The innocent
McGuane, T. Nobody's angel
McGuane, T. Nothing but blue skies
McInerney, J. Brightness Falls
McMillan, T. Disappearing acts
McMillan, T. Waiting to exhale
McMurtry, L. Cadillac Jack
McMurtry, L. The evening star
McMurtry, L. Terms of endearment
McMurtry, L. Texasville
Miller, S. The good mother
Mitford, N. Love in a cold climate
Mitford, N. The pursuit of love
Moore, B. The doctor's wife
Moore, B. Lies of silence
Mukherjee, B. The holder of the world
Murdoch, I. An accidental man
Murdoch, I. The black prince
Murdoch, I. The nice and the good
Nichols, J. T. The sterile cuckoo
Nin, A. Cities of the interior
Oates, J. C. I lock my door upon myself
Oates, J. C. What I lived for
O'Brien, E. The lonely girl
O'Brien, E. Time and tide
O'Hara, J. From the terrace
Ondaatje, M. In the skin of a lion
Oz, A. Fima
Patterson, R. N. Degree of guilt
Piercy, M. Vida
Price, R. Blue Calhoun
Proust, M. The captive
Proust, M. The captive [and] The fugitive
Proust, M. The fugitive
Pym, B. Less than angels
Ragen, N. Sotah
Rendell, R. The bridesmaid
Rhys, J. Good morning, midnight

Robards, K. Maggy's child
Roberts, N. Private scandals
Rosenberg, N. T. First offense
Ross-Macdonald, M. All desires known
Ross-Macdonald, M. For they shall inherit
Rossner, J. Olivia
Roth, P. Deception
Sagan, F. The painted lady
Scott, J. The nine dragons
Settle, M. L. Charley Bland
Shacochis, B. Swimming in the volcano
Shange, N. Liliane
Sheldon, S. Nothing lasts forever
Shreve, A. Strange fits of passion
Shreve, A. Where or when
Siddons, A. R. Downtown
Siddons, A. R. Outer banks
Sillitoe, A. Saturday night and Sunday morning
Singer, I. B. The certificate
Singer, I. B. Enemies, a love story
Smith, W. A. Hungry as the sea
Smith, W. A. A sparrow falls
Sontag, S. The volcano lover
Spencer, E. Knights and dragons
Spencer, S. Men in black
Steel, D. Heartbeat
Streshinsky, S. Hers the kingdom
Stubbs, J. Light in summer
Symons, J. Something like a love affair
Thayer, N. My dearest friend
Thomas, R. Other people's marriages
Tolstoy, L., graf. Anna Karenina
Tryon, T. In the fire of spring
Uhnak, D. False witness
Uris, L. Mitla Pass
Wakefield, D. Starting over
Waller, R. J. Slow waltz in Cedar Bend
Weldon, F. Leader of the band
Weldon, F. Life force
West, M. L. Masterclass
West, Dame R. Sunflower
Westlake, D. E. Trust me on this
Wilson, A. N. The vicar of sorrows
Winterson, J. Written on the body
Wolitzer, M. Friends for life
Woods, S. Palindrome
Love always. Beattie, A.
Love and money. Harris, R.
Love and war. Jakes, J.
Love in a cold climate. Mitford, N.
  In Mitford, N. The pursuit of love & Love in a cold climate p285-617
Love in the time of cholera. García Márquez, G.
Love is eternal. Stone, I.
The **love** letters. L'Engle, M.
Love life. Mason, B. A.
Love medicine. Erdrich, L.

LOVE STORIES
  See also Courtship; Gothic romances; Love affairs; Lovers
Abbott, M. The last innocent hour
Adler, E. Fortune is a woman
Adler, E. Legacy of secrets
Adler, E. The secret of the Villa Mimosa
Aiken, J. Jane Fairfax
Aiken, J. Mansfield revisited
Alcott, L. M. A long fatal love chase
Allende, I. Eva Luna
Allende, I. Of love and shadows
Amado, J. The war of the saints
Anderson, P. The Saturn game
Anthony, E. The Doll's House
Anthony, E. Exposure
Anthony, E. The relic
Auel, J. M. The Mammoth Hunters
Auel, J. M. The Valley of Horses
Austen, J. Emma
Austen, J. Lady Susan

LOVE STORIES—*Continued*

Austen, J. Mansfield Park
Austen, J. Persuasion
Austen, J. Sense and sensibility
Baldwin, J. If Beale Street could talk
Balzac, H. de. Eugénie Grandet
Barrett, J. Presumption
Barrie, J. M. The little minister
Bass, R. Field events
Binchy, M. Echoes
Birmingham, S. The Rothman scandal
Blair, L. The side of the angels
Blake, J. Arrow to the heart
Blake, J. Wildest dreams
Böll, H. The silent angel
Bonner, C. Lily
Bonner, C. Looking after Lily
Bradford, B. T. Angel
Bradford, B. T. Everything to gain
Bradford, B. T. Remember
Bradford, B. T. The women in his life
Bradley, M. Z. The forest house
Brand, M. Dust across the range
Brent, M. Golden urchin
Briskin, J. Dreams are not enough
Briskin, J. The other side of love
Bristow, G. Calico Palace
Brontë, A. The tenant of Wildfell Hall
Brontë, C. Jane Eyre
Brontë, C. The professor
Brontë, C. Villette
Brontë, E. Wuthering Heights
Brookner, A. Brief lives
Brookner, A. A closed eye
Brown, S. Charade
Brown, S. Where there's smoke
Byatt, A. S. Possession
Carr, R. Woman's own
Chesney, M. Back in society
Chesney, M. Colonel Sandhurst to the rescue
Chesney, M. Lady Fortescue steps out
Chesney, M. Miss Tonks turns to crime
Chesney, M. Mrs. Budley falls from grace
Chesney, M. Sir Philip's folly
Colette. The kepi
Colwin, L. Happy all the time
Conley, R. J. Mountain windsong
Cookson, C. The Maltese Angel
Coulter, C. The Nightingale legacy
Coulter, C. The valentine legacy
Coulter, C. The Wyndham legacy
Coward, N. Bon voyage
Crane, S. Active service
Crane, S. The third violet
Dailey, J. Aspen gold
Dailey, J. Masquerade
Dailey, J. The proud and the free
Dailey, J. Tangled vines
De Bernières, L. Corelli's mandolin
De Blasis, C. The proud breed
De Blasis, C. Swan's chance
Del Vecchio, J. M. For the sake of all living things
DeMille, N. Spencerville
Denker, H. Mrs. Washington and Horowitz, too
Dickens, C. Barnaby Rudge
Dickens, C. Great expectations
Doig, I. Dancing at the Rascal Fair
Dorris, M. The crown of Columbus
Dostoyevsky, F. Poor people
Drabble, M. The realms of gold
Du Maurier, Dame D. Frenchman's Creek
Durham, M. The man who loved Cat Dancing
Durrell, L. Sebastian
Eden, D. The American heiress
Eden, D. An important family
Erdrich, L. The bingo palace
Esquivel, L. Like water for chocolate
Fast, H. The immigrants

Finney, J. Time and again
Follett, K. Lie down with lions
Fowles, J. Daniel Martin
Fowles, J. The French lieutenant's woman
Gage, E. Pandora's box
García Márquez, G. Love in the time of cholera
Garwood, J. Prince Charming
Garwood, J. Saving grace
Giardina, D. The unquiet earth
Gide, A. Strait is the gate (La porte étroite)
Gilman, D. Caravan
Godden, R. Pippa passes
Goethe, J. W. von. The sorrows of young Werther
Goudge, E. Garden of lies
Goudge, E. Such devoted sisters
Goudge, E. Green Dolphin Street
Graham, W. The black moon
Graham, W. The miller's dance
Grass, G. The call of the toad
Gray, F. du P. World without end
Greeley, A. M. Irish gold
Greenberg, J. Of such small differences
Guy, R. My love, my love
Harper, K. Circle of gold
Hassler, J. North of hope
Heaven, C. The wind from the sea
Helprin, M. Ellis Island
Hemingway, E. A farewell to arms
Hemingway, E. For whom the bell tolls
Heyer, G. The grand Sophy
Hill, P. Artemia
Hilton, J. Random harvest
Hodge, J. A. Escapade
Hodge, J. A. Windover
Hoffman, A. Turtle Moon
Holt, V. The black opal
Holt, V. Daughter of deceit
Holt, V. The India fan
Holt, V. Secret for a nightingale
Holt, V. Seven for a secret
Holt, V. The silk vendetta
Howatch, S. Glittering images
Howatch, S. Penmarric
Humphreys, J. The fireman's fair
Humphreys, J. Rich in love
Isaacs, S. Shining through
Jakes, J. California gold
Kay, T. Shadow song
Kaye, M. M. The far pavilions
Kaye, M. M. Shadow of the moon
Kaye, M. M. Trade wind
Kellerman, F. The quality of mercy
Kingsolver, B. Animal dreams
Kinsolving, W. Bred to win
Koen, K. Through a glass darkly
Krantz, J. I'll take Manhattan
Krentz, J. A. Grand passion
La Farge, O. Laughing Boy
Laker, R. Banners of silk
Laker, R. Circle of pearls
Laker, R. The golden tulip
Laker, R. The sugar pavilion
Laker, R. This shining land
L'Engle, M. The love letters
Lively, P. City of the mind
Lively, P. Cleopatra's sister
Lively, P. Moon tiger
Lofts, N. Pargeters
MacInnes, H. Friends and lovers
MacNeil, R. Burden of desire
Mapson, J.-A. Hank and Chloe
Marsh, J. The House of Eliott
Martin, W. Cape Cod
Mason, B. A. Spence + Lila
Mason, R. The world of Suzie Wong
McCarry, C. The bride of the wilderness
McCullough, C. An indecent obsession
McCullough, C. The ladies of Missalonghi

LOVE STORIES—*Continued*
McDermott, A. At weddings and wakes
McDermott, A. That night
McNaught, J. Paradise
McNaught, J. Perfect
Michael, J. Pot of gold
Michael, J. Sleeping beauty
Michaels, B. Search the shadows
Michener, J. A. Sayonara
Miller, S. For love
Mishima, Y. The sound of waves
Mishima, Y. Spring snow
Momaday, N. S. The ancient child
Murdoch, I. Nuns and soldiers
Murdoch, I. The sea, the sea
Myrer, A. A green desire
Nabokov, V. V. Ada
Nathan, R. Portrait of Jennie
Norman, H. The bird artist
Oates, J. C. A Bloodsmoor romance
Oates, J. C. You must remember this
Pargeter, E. The scarlet seed
Parker, R. B. All our yesterdays
Penman, S. K. Here be dragons
Percy, W. The last gentleman
Percy, W. The second coming
Piercy, M. He, she and it
Pilcher, R. September
Plain, B. Blessings
Plain, B. Random winds
Price, E. Bright captivity
Price, E. Savannah
Price, E. To see your face again
Pym, B. A few green leaves
Pym, B. A glass of blessings
Pym, B. No fond return of love
Pym, B. An unsuitable attachment
Quick, A. Deception
Quick, A. Mistress
Quinn, S. Happy endings
Rand, A. The fountainhead
Rand, A. We the living
Remarque, E. M. The night in Lisbon
Remarque, E. M. Three comrades
Remarque, E. M. A time to love and a time to die
Rich, M. Tender offerings
Richter, C. The sea of grass
Ripley, A. Scarlett
Robards, K. Nobody's angel
Robards, K. One summer
Roberts, N. Hidden riches
Roberts, N. Honest illusions
Robertson, D. Praise the human season
Rodriguez, A. Spidertown
Roiphe, A. R. If you knew me
Ross-Macdonald, M. Dancing on snowflakes
Ross-Macdonald, M. An innocent woman
Ross-Macdonald, M. To the end of her days
Ross-Macdonald, M. A woman alone
Ross-Macdonald, M. A woman possessed
Rush, N. Mating
Rushing, J. G. Mary Dove
Sagan, F. A reluctant hero
Saint, H. F. Memoirs of an invisible man
Sand, G. Marianne
Sayers, D. L. Busman's honeymoon
Schofield, S. C. Telluride
Scott, Sir W. Rob Roy
Segal, E. Acts of faith
Segal, E. Doctors
Segal, E. Love story
Settle, M. L. Celebration
Sheldon, S. The stars shine down
Shields, C. The republic of love
Sholem Aleichem. The nightingale
Shreve, A. Eden Close
Siddons, A. R. Colony
Siddons, A. R. King's oak

Sienkiewicz, H. The deluge
Singer, I. B. Meshugah
Singer, I. B. The slave
Smith, W. A. Golden fox
Spellman, C. C. Paint the wind
Spencer, E. The light in the piazza
Spencer, L. Bitter sweet
Spencer, L. Family blessings
Spencer, L. Forgiving
Spencer, S. Endless love
Steel, D. Accident
Steel, D. The gift
Steel, D. No greater love
Steel, D. Wings
Stevenson, R. L. The story of a lie
Stewart, F. M. Pomp and circumstance
Stewart, M. The stormy petrel
Stone, I. The President's lady
Stone, I. Those who love
Stone, K. Happy endings
Stone, K. Rainbows
Strindberg, A. By the open sea
Styron, W. Sophie's choice
Tennant, E. An unequal marriage
Thane, E. Yankee stranger
Thayer, N. Family secrets
Thomas, R. D. The angel carver
Thomas, R. All my sins remembered
Thomas, R. Bad girls, good women
Thomas, R. A woman of our times
Trevanian. The summer of Katya
Trevor, W. Reading Turgenev
Tryon, T. The wings of the morning
Turgenev, I. S. First love
Turgenev, I. S. The torrents of spring
Updike, J. Brazil
Urquhart, J. Away
Vargas Llosa, M. Aunt Julia and the scriptwriter
Veryan, P. Ask me no questions
Veryan, P. Had we never loved
Veryan, P. Never doubt I love
Veryan, P. A shadow's bliss
Veryan, P. Time's fool
Villars, E. The Normandie affair
Voigt, C. Glass mountain
Waller, R. J. Border music
Waller, R. J. The bridges of Madison County
West, J. The massacre at Fall Creek
Wood, B. Soul flame
Wood, B. Vital signs
Worboys, A. China silk
Love story. Segal, E.
Love unknown. Wilson, A. N.

Lovecraft's legacy. Entered in Part I under title
The **loved** one. Waugh, E.
The **lover**. Duras, M.

LOVERS
Duras, M. Blue eyes, black hair
Harrison, J. Julip
Piercy, M. Summer people
Lovers and tyrants. Gray, F. du P.
Love's mansion. West, P.
Loves music, loves to dance. Clark, M. H.
The **loving** cup. Graham, W.
Lovingkindness. Roiphe, A. R.

LOWELL (MASS.) *See* Massachusetts—Lowell

LOWER EAST SIDE (NEW YORK, N.Y.) *See* New
York (N.Y.)—Lower East Side
LOWRY, MALCOLM, 1909-1957
Aiken, C. A heart for the gods of Mexico
LOYALISTS, AMERICAN *See* American loyalists
Lucia in London. Benson, E. F.
In Benson, E. F. Make way for Lucia p179-358
LUCIANO, LUCKY, 1897-1962
Higgins, J. Luciano's luck
Luciano's luck. Higgins, J.
Lucia's progress. See Benson, E. F. The worshipful Lucia

Lucifer's hammer. Niven, L.
The Luck of Roaring Camp, and other tales. Harte, B.
Lucky Jim. Amis, K.
Lucy. Kincaid, J.
Lucy Gayheart. Cather, W.
  In Cather, W. Willa Cather, later novels
The Ludlum triad. Ludlum, R.
Ludmila. Gallico, P.
  In Gallico, P. Three legends: The snow goose; The small miracle; Ludmila p77-126
LUGANO (SWITZERLAND) *See* Switzerland—Lugano
LUKE, SAINT
  Caldwell, T. Dear and glorious physician
Lullaby. McBain, E.
Lullaby of murder. Davis, D. S.

LUMBER INDUSTRY
  Kesey, K. Sometimes a great notion
Lust & other stories. Minot, S.
Lust for life. Stone, I.

LUTHERANS
  Richter, C. A simple honorable man
Lydia Bailey. Roberts, K. L.
Lying in wait. Jance, J. A.

LYNCHING
  Clark, W. V. T. The Ox-bow incident
  Nordan, L. Wolf whistle
  Smith, L. E. Strange fruit
Lyon's pride. McCaffrey, A.
The lyre of Orpheus. Davies, R.

M

MACABRE STORIES *See* Horror stories
MACBETH, KING OF SCOTLAND, d. 1057
  Dunnett, D. King hereafter

MACEDONIA
  Bova, B. Orion and the conqueror
MACGREGOR, ROBERT *See* Rob Roy, 1671-1734
Machine dreams. Phillips, J. A.
MACHINERY AND CIVILIZATION *See* Technology and civilization
MACIEL, ANTÔNIO VICENTE MENDES, 1828-1897
  Vargas Llosa, M. The war of the end of the world
Mackenna's gold. Henry, W.
MacPherson's lament. McCrumb, S.
Madame Bovary. Flaubert, G.
Madame de Mauves. James, H.
  In James, H. The complete tales of Henry James v3

MADISON, DOLLEY, 1768-1849
  Brown, R. M. Dolley
MADISON, JAMES, 1751-1836
  Brown, R. M. Dolley
MADNESS *See* Insanity; Mental illness
Madness in Maggody. Hess, J.
MADOC *See* Madog ab Owain Gwynedd, 1150-1180?
MADOG AB OWAIN GWYNEDD, 1150-1180?
  Thom, J. A. The children of first man
The Madonna. Barker, C.
  In Barker, C. In the flesh
MADRID (SPAIN) *See* Spain—Madrid
Maestro. Gardner, J. E.
MAFIA
  See also Gangsters
  Breslin, J. The gang that couldn't shoot straight
  Condon, R. Prizzi's family
  Condon, R. Prizzi's glory
  Condon, R. Prizzi's honor
  Condon, R. Prizzi's money
  DeMille, N. The Gold Coast

  Dexter, P. Brotherly love
  Grisham, J. The client
  Grisham, J. The firm
  Higgins, G. V. Bomber's law
  Higgins, J. Luciano's luck
  Higgins, J. On dangerous ground
  Hunter, E. Criminal conversation
  Leonard, E. Gold Coast
  Leonard, E. Pronto
  Lustbader, E. V. The Kaisho
  Maas, P. China white
  Puzo, M. The godfather
  Puzo, M. The Sicilian
  Sheldon, S. Rage of angels
  Tanenbaum, R. Immoral certainty
  Thomas, R. Chinaman's chance
  Westlake, D. E. Cops and robbers
  Woods, S. L.A. Times

MAGAZINES *See* Periodicals
Mage winds [series]
  Lackey, M. Winds of change
  Lackey, M. Winds of fate
  Lackey, M. Winds of fury
Maggie: a girl of the streets (a story of New York). Crane, S.
  also in Crane, S. The complete novels of Stephen Crane p99-155
  also in Crane, S. The portable Stephen Crane p3-74
Maggie-Now. Smith, B.
Maggody in Manhattan. Hess, J.
A maggot. Fowles, J.
Maggy's child. Robards, K.
MAGIC
  See also Supernatural phenomena; Witchcraft
  Card, O. S. Alvin Journeyman
  Card, O. S. Prentice Alvin
  Card, O. S. Red prophet
  Card, O. S. Seventh son
  Esquivel, L. Like water for chocolate
  Gregory, P. The wise woman
  Mailer, N. Ancient evenings
  Nordan, L. Wolf whistle
  Norton, A. Empire of the eagle
  Tolkien, J. R. R. The fellowship of the ring
  Tolkien, J. R. R. The hobbit
  Tolkien, J. R. R. The lord of the rings
  Tolkien, J. R. R. The return of the king
  Tolkien, J. R. R. The two towers
  Updike, J. The witches of Eastwick
Magic. Goldman, W.
Magic hour. Isaacs, S.
Magic kingdom for sale—sold! Brooks, T.
Magic Kingdom of Landover [series]
  Brooks, T. The black unicorn
  Brooks, T. Magic kingdom for sale—sold!
  Brooks, T. The Tangle Box
  Brooks, T. Wizard at large
The magic labyrinth. Farmer, P. J.
The magic mountain. Mann, T.
The magician of Lublin. Singer, I. B.
  also in Singer, I. B. An Isaac Bashevis Singer reader p317-560
MAGICIANS
  Auster, P. Mr. Vertigo
  Davies, R. World of wonders
  Gardner, J. The sunlight dialogues
  Goldman, W. Magic
  Roberts, N. Honest illusions
  Stewart, M. The crystal cave
  Stewart, M. The hollow hills
  Stewart, M. The last enchantment
  Stewart, M. Mary Stewart's Merlin trilogy
  Theroux, P. Millroy the Magician
  White, T. H. The book of Merlyn

MAGICIANS—*Continued*

Magister Ludi. See Hesse, H. The glass bead game (Magister Ludi)

The **magnificent** Ambersons. Tarkington, B.

Magnificent obsession. Douglas, L. C.

The **magnificent** spinster. Sarton, M.

The **magus.** Fowles, J.

Mahatma Joe. Bass, R.

    In Bass, R. Platte River p3-42

Maid in waiting. Galsworthy, J.

    In Galsworthy, J. End of the chapter p1-330

MAIDS (SERVANTS)

    Caldwell, T. Ceremony of the innocent

    Fox, P. A servant's tale

    Richardson, S. Pamela

    Sharp, M. Cluny Brown

Maigret and the apparition. Simenon, G.

Maigret and the black sheep. Simenon, G.

Maigret and the burglar's wife. Simenon, G.

Maigret and the fortune-teller. Simenon, G.

Maigret and the gangsters. Simenon, G.

Maigret and the ghost. See Simenon, G. Maigret and the apparition

Maigret and the Hotel Majestic. Simenon, G.

Maigret and the loner. Simenon, G.

Maigret and the madwoman. Simenon, G.

Maigret and the man on the bench. Simenon, G.

Maigret and the Nahour case. Simenon, G.

Maigret and the old lady. Simenon, G.

    In Simenon, G. Maigret cinq p203-307

Maigret and the reluctant witnesses. Simenon, G.

    In Simenon, G. Five times Maigret p323-421

Maigret and the Saturday caller. Simenon, G.

Maigret and the spinster. Simenon, G.

Maigret and the toy village. Simenon, G.

Maigret and the wine merchants. Simenon, G.

Maigret and the young girl. Simenon, G.

    In Simenon, G. Maigret cinq p7-105

Maigret at the Gai-Moulin. Simenon, G.

Maigret bides his time. Simenon, G.

Maigret cinq. Simenon, G.

Maigret goes home. Simenon, G.

Maigret goes to school. Simenon, G.

    In Simenon, G. Five times Maigret p425-525

Maigret has scruples. Simenon, G.

    In Simenon, G. Five times Maigret p223-320

Maigret in court. Simenon, G.

Maigret in exile. Simenon, G.

Maigret in Holland. Simenon, G.

Maigret in Montmartre. Simenon, G.

    In Simenon, G. Five times Maigret p9-116

A **Maigret** omnibus. See Simenon, G. Five times Maigret

Maigret on the defensive. Simenon, G.

Maigret on the Riviera. Simenon, G.

Maigret takes a room. Simenon, G.

    In Simenon, G. Maigret cinq p421-523

Maigret's first case. Simenon, G.

    In Simenon, G. Maigret cinq p309-419

Maigret's little joke. Simenon, G.

    In Simenon, G. Maigret cinq p107-202

Maigret's memoirs. Simenon, G.

Maigret's mistake. Simenon, G.

    In Simenon, G. Five times Maigret p117-219

Maigret's pickpocket. Simenon, G.

Maigret's revolver. Simenon, G.

Maigret's rival. Simenon, G.

Maigret's war of nerves. Simenon, G.

Main Street. Lewis, S.

MAINE

    Jewett, S. O. The country of the pointed firs

    Jewett, S. O. The country of the pointed firs and other stories

    19th century

    Ogilvie, E. Jennie Glenroy

    Rossner, J. Emmeline

    20th century

    Carroll, J. Fault lines

    Chute, C. The Beans of Egypt, Maine

    Delinsky, B. For my daughters

    Irving, J. The cider house rules

    King, S. The body

    King, S. Carrie

    King, S. Cujo

    King, S. Dolores Claiborne

    King, S. Insomnia

    King, S. It

    King, S. Needful things

    King, S. Pet sematary

    King, S. Rita Hayworth and Shawshank redemption

    King, S. Salem's Lot

    King, S. The Tommyknockers

    Koontz, D. R. Night chills

    Ogilvie, E. When the music stopped

    Shreve, A. Strange fits of passion

    Siddons, A. R. Colony

The **Maine** massacre. Van de Wetering, J.

Maitre Cornélius. Balzac, H. de

    In Balzac, H. de. The short novels of Balzac

Majestic. Strieber, W.

Majipoor chronicles. Silverberg, R.

Make death love me. Rendell, R.

Make no bones. Elkins, A. J.

Make way for Lucia. Benson, E. F.

MALADJUSTED CHILDREN *See* Emotionally disturbed children

Malafrena. Le Guin, U. K.

MÁLAGA (SPAIN) *See* Spain—Málaga

A **Malamud** reader. Malamud, B.

MALAYA

    See also Malaysia

    Shute, N. The legacy

MALAYANS

    Conrad, J. The end of the tether

MALAYS *See* Malayans

MALAYSIA

    Conrad, J. The lagoon

    Conrad, J. Lord Jim

The **malcontents.** Snow, C. P.

The **male** impersonator. Benson, E. F.

    In Benson, E. F. Make way for Lucia p535-48

Malgudi days. Narayan, R. K.

MALIBU (CALIF.) *See* California—Malibu

Malice domestic. Hardwick, M.

Malice in Maggody. Hess, J.

Malloreon [series]

    Eddings, D. Demon lord of Karanda

    Eddings, D. Guardians of the west

    Eddings, D. King of the Murgos

    Eddings, D. The seeress of Kell

    Eddings, D. Sorceress of Darshiva

Mallory's oracle. O'Connell, C.

Malone dies. Beckett, S.

    In Beckett, S. Molloy, Malone dies, and The unnamable p241-398

MALPRACTICE

    Cook, R. Harmful intent

MALTA

    Monsarrat, N. The kappillan of Malta

The **Maltese** Angel. Cookson, C.

The **Maltese** falcon. Hammett, D.

    also in Hammett, D. The novels of Dashiell Hammett p293-440

Mama Day. Naylor, G.

The **Mambo** Kings play songs of love. Hijuelos, O.

MAMMALS, FOSSIL *See* Fossils

The **Mammoth** Hunters. Auel, J. M.

MAN, PREHISTORIC *See* Prehistoric man; Prehistoric times

A man. Fallaci, O.
The man. Wallace, I.
Man alive. Stout, R.
    In Stout, R. Five of a kind p307-55
A man could stand up. Ford, F. M.
    In Ford, F. M. Parade's end
The man from Barbarossa. Gardner, J. E.
The man from St. Petersburg. Follett, K.
The man from the broken hills. L'Amour, L.
Man in his time. Aldiss, B. W.
The man in lower ten. Rinehart, M. R.
    In Rinehart, M. R. Mary Roberts Rinehart's mystery book p181-345
The man in the gray flannel suit. Wilson, S.

MAN IN THE IRON MASK
    Doherty, P. C. The masked man
    Dumas, A. The iron mask
The man in the iron mask. See Dumas, A. The iron mask
The man in the maze. Silverberg, R.
    In Silverberg, R. A Robert Silverberg omnibus
The man in the queue. Tey, J.
Man of glass. Cervantes Saavedra, M. de
    In Cervantes Saavedra, M. de. Three exemplary novels p75-121
The man of property. Galsworthy, J.
    also in Galsworthy, J. The Forsyte saga p3-309
    also in Galsworthy, J. The Galsworthy reader p15-294
The man on the balcony. Sjöwall, M.
Man Plus. Pohl, F.
The man that corrupted Hadleyburg, and other stories and essays. Twain, M.
The man who changed his name. Wright, E.
The man who cried I am. Williams, J. A.
The man who dreamt of lobsters. Collins, M.
The man who liked slow tomatoes. Constantine, K. C.
The man who liked to look at himself. Constantine, K. C.
The man who loved Cat Dancing. Durham, M.
The man who loved children. Stead, C.
The man who walked like a bear. Kaminsky, S. M.
The man who was Thursday. Chesterton, G. K.
Man with a gun. Daley, R.
The man with a load of mischief. Grimes, M.
The man with the golden arm. Algren, N.
The man with the golden gun. Fleming, I.
The man without a country. Hale, E. E.
The man without qualities. Musil, R.

MANASSAS, BATTLES OF *See* Bull Run, 1st Battle, 1861

Manchu. Elegant, R. S.

MANCHUS
    Elegant, R. S. Manchu
    Elegant, R. S. Mandarin

MANDAN INDIANS
    Thom, J. A. The children of first man
Mandarin. Elegant, R. S.
The mandarins. Beauvoir, S. de
The Mandeville talent. Higgins, G. V.

MANHATTAN (NEW YORK, N.Y.) *See* New York (N.Y.)—Manhattan

Manhattan transfer. Dos Passos, J.

MANHUNTS
    See also Adventure
    Forsyth, F. The Odessa file
    Household, G. Rogue male
The manor. Singer, I. B.

MANORS *See* Houses

Man's fate (La condition humaine). Malraux, A.
Man's hope. Malraux, A.
Mansfield Park. Austen, J.
    also in Austen, J. The complete novels of Jane Austen

Mansfield revisited. Aiken, J.
The mansion. Faulkner, W.
    also in Faulkner, W. Snopes p673-1065

MANSIONS *See* Houses

The Manson curse. Shannon, D.
The manticore. Davies, R.
The mantrap garden. Sherwood, J.

MANUSCRIPTS
    Archer, J. A matter of honor
    Durrell, L. Balthazar
    Ludlum, R. The Gemini contenders
    Michaels, B. Houses of stone
    Ozick, C. The Messiah of Stockholm
    Redfield, J. The celestine prophecy
The many-colored land. May, J.
The many loves of Dobie Gillis. Shulman, M.

MAORIS
    Ashton-Warner, S. Spinster
    Hulme, K. The bone people
A map of the world. Hamilton, J.
Mapp and Lucia. Benson, E. F.
    In Benson, E. F. Make way for Lucia p549-762
Maps in a mirror. Card, O. S.
Marathon man. Goldman, W.
The marble faun. Hawthorne, N.
    also in Hawthorne, N. The complete novels and selected tales of Nathaniel Hawthorne
Mardi: and a voyager thither. Melville, H.
    In Melville, H. Typee; Omoo; Mardi

MARDI GRAS
    Faulkner, W. Pylon
Margaret's story. Price, E.
Marianne. Sand, G.

MARIE ANTOINETTE, QUEEN, CONSORT OF LOUIS XVI, KING OF FRANCE, 1755-1793
    Dumas, A. The Queen's necklace

MARINE CORPS (U.S.) *See* United States. Marine Corps

MARINES (U.S.) *See* United States. Marine Corps

MARIUS, GAIUS, CA. 157-86 B.C.
    McCullough, C. The first man in Rome
    McCullough, C. Fortune's favorites
    McCullough, C. The grass crown
Marjorie Morningstar. Wouk, H.
The Marjorie Rawlings reader. Rawlings, M. K.
The mark of the cat. Norton, A.
Marked for murder. Kienzle, W. X.
Marking time. Howard, E. J.

MARQUESAS ISLANDS
    Melville, H. Omoo: a narrative of adventures in the South Seas
    Melville, H. Typee: a peep at Polynesian life

MARRIAGE
    See also Childless marriage; Divorce; Family life; Husband and wife; Interfaith marriage; Interracial marriage; Marriage problems; Weddings
    Barth, J. The Tidewater tales
    Battle, L. War brides
    Byatt, A. S. Morpho Eugenia
    Carroll, J. Memorial bridge
    Colwin, L. A big storm knocked it over
    Colwin, L. Goodbye without leaving
    Colwin, L. Happy all the time
    Connell, E. S. Mr. Bridge
    Connell, E. S. Mrs. Bridge
    Doerr, H. Stones for Ibarra
    Dunne, J. G. The red, white, and blue
    Fleming, T. J. The officers' wives
    Gardner, J. Nickel mountain
    Garwood, J. Prince Charming
    Gibbons, K. A virtuous woman
    Glendinning, V. The grown-ups
    Greeley, A. M. Patience of a saint
    Hailey, E. F. Joanna's husband and David's wife
    Holt, V. The legend of the seventh virgin

MARRIAGE—*Continued*
Jaffe, R. Class reunion
James, H. The Europeans
James, H. The spoils of Poynton
James, H. The wings of the dove
Koen, K. Through a glass darkly
McEwan, I. Black dogs
Minot, S. Folly
Price, E. Where shadows go
Pym, B. An academic question
Pym, B. Civil to strangers
Rice, L. Blue moon
Ross-Macdonald, M. All desires known
Ross-Macdonald, M. A woman scorned
Sarton, M. Anger
Seth, V. A suitable boy
Siddons, A. R. Hill towns
Smiley, J. Good will
Stegner, W. E. Crossing to safety
Stegner, W. E. The spectator bird
Stone, R. Outerbridge Reach
Tallent, E. Honey
Tennant, E. An unequal marriage
Thayer, N. Family secrets
Theroux, P. My secret history
Thomas, E. M. The animal wife
Trollope, J. The men and the girls
Tyler, A. Breathing lessons
Vidal, G. 1876
Weldon, F. Puffball
Wesley, M. A dubious legacy
West, P. Love's mansion
West, Dame R. Cousin Rosamund
Wharton, E. The buccaneers
Wharton, E. The buccaneers, completed by Marion
  Mainwaring
Wharton, E. Fast and loose
Wood, B. The dreaming

MARRIAGE, CHILDLESS *See* Childless marriage

MARRIAGE, INTERFAITH *See* Interfaith marriage

MARRIAGE, INTERRACIAL *See* Interracial marriage

MARRIAGE BROKERS
Chesney, M. Deborah goes to Dover
Pym, B. Jane and Prudence

MARRIAGE COUNSELING *See* Marriage problems

MARRIAGE CUSTOMS
Agnon, S. Y. The bridal canopy
Marriage is murder. Pickard, N.

MARRIAGE PROBLEMS
  See also Divorce; Family life; Interfaith marriage;
  Love affairs
Abbott, M. The last innocent hour
Aiken, C. Conversation
Aiken, C. Great circle
Alcott, L. M. A long fatal love chase
Allison, D. Bastard out of Carolina
Amado, J. Dona Flor and her two husbands
Amis, K. The Russian girl
Anderson, S. Poor white
Atwood, M. Life before man
Auchincloss, L. Honorable men
Auchincloss, L. The stoic
Barth, J. The end of the road
Bausch, R. Violence
Beattie, A. Chilly scenes of winter
Beattie, A. Falling in place
Beauvoir, S. de. The age of discretion
Beauvoir, S. de. The mandarins
Beauvoir, S. de. The monologue
Belle, P. Treason's gift
Bellow, S. Herzog
Benedict, E. Safe conduct
Berger, T. Sneaky people
Berger, T. Vital parts
Bowles, P. The sheltering sky
Boyd, W. Brazzaville Beach

Bradford, B. T. Hold the dream
Bradshaw, G. Horses of heaven
Breslin, J. Table money
Brontë, A. The tenant of Wildfell Hall
Brown, R. M. High hearts
Brown, R. Civil wars
Brown, R. Tender mercies
Buck, P. S. Pavilion of women
Butler, R. O. They whisper
Cain, J. M. Mildred Pierce
Cain, J. M. The postman always rings twice
Carroll, J. Prince of peace
Casey, J. Spartina
Cather, W. A lost lady
Colette. Chance acquaintances
Colette. Claudine and Annie
Colette. The last of Chéri
Colwin, L. Family happiness
Corman, A. 50
Cronin, A. J. The citadel
Daley, R. Hands of a stranger
De la Roche, M. Jalna
Demetz, H. The journey from Prague Street
DeMille, N. The Gold Coast
Dickens, C. Hard times
Didion, J. Democracy
Donleavy, J. P. The ginger man
Drabble, M. Jerusalem the golden
Drabble, M. The needle's eye
Drabble, M. The realms of gold
Drabble, M. The waterfall
Dreiser, T. Sister Carrie
Du Maurier, Dame D. The house on the strand
Durrell, L. Justine
Durrell, L. Mountolive
Eliot, G. Middlemarch
Elkin, S. Her sense of timing
Ephron, N. Heartburn
Fast, H. The immigrants
Fast, H. The outsider
Ferber, E. Giant
Fielding, J. Good intentions
Fielding, J. See Jane run
Fitzgerald, F. S. The beautiful and damned
Fitzgerald, F. S. The Great Gatsby
Fitzgerald, F. S. Tender is the night
Flaubert, G. Madame Bovary
Fleming, I. Quantum of solace
Ford, F. M. No more parades
Fox, P. A servant's tale
Freeman, C. Always and forever
Freeman, C. Come pour the wine
Freeman, C. Fairytales
Freeman, C. The last princess
Freeman, C. Seasons of the heart
French, M. The women's room
Galsworthy, J. The Forsyte saga
Galsworthy, J. The man of property
Galsworthy, J. Swan song
Galsworthy, J. The white monkey
García Márquez, G. Chronicle of a death foretold
Glasgow, E. Vein of iron
Godden, R. The battle of the Villa Fiorita
Godwin, G. The good husband
Golding, W. The paper men
Gordon, M. Final payments
Grau, S. A. The keepers of the house
Greeley, A. M. Ascent into hell
Greeley, A. M. Thy brother's wife
Greene, G. The end of the affair
Greene, G. The heart of the matter
Grumbach, D. Chamber music
Hailey, E. F. Life sentences
Handke, P. The left-handed woman
Hardy, T. The return of the native
Hart, J. Damage
Hawthorne, N. The scarlet letter
Hazzard, S. The transit of Venus

MARRIAGE PROBLEMS—*Continued*

Head, A. Mr. & Mrs. Bo Jo Jones
Hemingway, E. The garden of Eden
Hoffman, A. Illumination night
Hood, A. Places to stay the night
Howatch, S. Penmarric
Hughes, L. Simple takes a wife
Hunter, E. Criminal conversation
Irving, J. The 158-pound marriage
Isaacs, S. After all these years
Isaacs, S. Almost paradise
James, H. The golden bowl
James, H. The portrait of a lady
James, H. What Maisie knew
Jones, D. C. Come winter
Katkov, N. Blood & orchids
Kaufman, S. Diary of a mad housewife
Kawabata, Y. The sound of the mountain
Kaye, M. M. Shadow of the moon
Keneally, T. Woman of the inner sea
Kirkwood, J. Some kind of hero
Lawrence, D. H. Lady Chatterley's lover
L'Engle, M. The love letters
Lessing, D. M. The grass is singing
Lessing, D. M. A proper marriage
Lewis, S. Cass Timberlane
Lewis, S. Dodsworth
Lively, P. The road to Lichfield
Lofts, N. The day of the butterfly
Lofts, N. The haunting of Gad's Hall
Lovesey, P. On the edge
Lowry, M. Under the volcano
Lurie, A. Foreign affairs
Lurie, A. The nowhere city
Lurie, A. Only children
Lurie, A. The war between the Tates
MacDonald, J. D. Slam the big door
Martin, V. The great divorce
Maugham, W. S. Cakes and ale
McCarthy, M. A charmed life
McCauley, S. The easy way out
McFarland, D. The music room
McGuane, T. Nothing but blue skies
McInerney, J. Brightness Falls
McInerny, R. M. Leave of absence
Michaels, B. Greygallows
Mishima, Y. Forbidden colors
Mitford, N. Love in a cold climate
Mitford, N. The pursuit of love
Moore, B. Cold heaven
Moore, B. The doctor's wife
Moore, B. Lies of silence
Morrison, T. Jazz
Murdoch, I. The black prince
Murdoch, I. A fairly honourable defeat
Murdoch, I. The sacred and profane love machine
Nabokov, V. V. King, queen, knave
Nin, A. Cities of the interior
Norman, H. The bird artist
Norris, F. McTeague
Norris, F. The pit
Oates, J. C. American appetites
Oates, J. C. I lock my door upon myself
O'Brien, E. Girls in their married bliss
O'Brien, T. In the Lake of the Woods
O'Hara, J. From the terrace
O'Hara, J. Ten North Frederick
Parker, G. M. These same long bones
Payne, D. Ruin Creek
Pearce, M. E. Cast a long shadow
Piercy, M. Small changes
Pirandello, L. The outcast
Plain, B. Evergreen
Plain, B. Harvest
Plain, B. Tapestry
Plain, B. Whispers
Powell, A. Casanova's Chinese restaurant
Price, N. Night woman

Price, N. Sleeping with the enemy
Price, R. Blue Calhoun
Price, R. The promise of rest
Ragen, N. Sotah
Read, P. P. A season in the West
Rebeta-Burditt, J. The cracker factory
Rhys, J. Quartet
Rice, L. Stone heart
Robards, K. Maggy's child
Roiphe, A. R. Up the sandbox!
Ross-Macdonald, M. For they shall inherit
Ross-Macdonald, M. The rich are with you always
Ross-Macdonald, M. The world from rough stones
Rossner, J. His little women
Roth, P. Deception
Roth, P. The ghost writer
Roth, P. Letting go
Roth, P. My life as a man
Roth, P. When she was good
Rubens, B. A solitary grief
Russell, P. Sea of tranquillity
Sagan, F. The painted lady
Sand, G. Lélia
Schwartz, L. S. Disturbances in the field
Seton, A. The Winthrop woman
Sholem Aleichem. The adventures of Menahem-Mendl
Sholokhov, M. A. And quiet flows the Don
Shreve, A. Where or when
Simenon, G. The truth about Bébé Donge
Singer, I. B. The estate
Singer, I. B. The manor
Smiley, J. The age of grief [novelette]
Smith, B. Joy in the morning
Smith, B. Maggie-Now
Smith, W. A. Hungry as the sea
Snow, C. P. Homecoming
Sontag, S. The volcano lover
Spencer, L. Home song
Spencer, S. Men in black
Stead, C. The man who loved children
Steel, D. Accident
Steel, D. Heartbeat
Steel, D. Mixed blessings
Stegner, W. E. Angle of repose
Stubbs, J. Family games
Stubbs, J. Light in summer
Stubbs, J. Like we used to be
Styron, W. Lie down in darkness
Swindells, M. Summer harvest
Symons, J. Something like a love affair
Tax, M. Union Square
Thayer, N. My dearest friend
Thomas, R. Other people's marriages
Tolstoy, L., graf. Anna Karenina
Tolstoy, L., graf. The Kreutzer sonata
Trevor, W. Reading Turgenev
Trollope, A. The prime minister
Trollope, J. The rector's wife
Tyler, A. The accidental tourist
Tyler, A. Earthly possessions
Tyler, A. Morgan's passing
Updike, J. Rabbit redux
Updike, J. Rabbit, run
Uris, L. Mitla Pass
Van Slyke, H. A necessary woman
Van Slyke, H. No love lost
Villars, E. Lipstick on his collar
Villars, E. Too close for comfort
Waller, R. J. The bridges of Madison County
Waller, R. J. Slow waltz in Cedar Bend
Weldon, F. The hearts and lives of men
Weldon, F. The life and loves of a she-devil
Weldon, F. Trouble
Wharton, E. The custom of the country
Wharton, E. Ethan Frome
Wharton, E. The spark
Whitney, P. A. Hunter's green
Whitney, P. A. Poinciana

MARRIAGE PROBLEMS—*Continued*
Whitney, P. A. Spindrift
Williams, B. A. Leave her to heaven
Wilson, A. N. Love unknown
Wilson, A. N. The vicar of sorrows
Woiwode, L. Indian affairs
Woiwode, L. What I'm going to do, I think
Wood, B. Vital signs
Woods, S. Imperfect strangers
Yorke, M. Dangerous to know
Marriages and infidelities. Oates, J. C.
Marrying off mother, and other stories. Durrell, G. M.

MARS (PLANET)
Bear, G. Moving Mars
Bova, B. Mars
Bradbury, R. The Martian chronicles
Burroughs, E. R. A Princess of Mars
Heinlein, R. A. Double star
Lewis, C. S. Out of the silent planet
McAuley, P. J. Red dust
Pike, C. The season of passage
Pohl, F. Man Plus
Pohl, F. Mars Plus
Robinson, K. S. Green Mars
Robinson, K. S. Red Mars
Sargent, P. Danny goes to Mars
Mars. Bova, B.
Mars Plus. Pohl, F.
The **marshal** and the madwoman. Nabb, M.
The **marshal** and the murderer. Nabb, M.
The **Marshal's** own case. Nabb, M.
Martha Quest. Lessing, D. M.
In Lessing, D. M. Children of violence v1

MARTHA'S VINEYARD (MASS.)
Hoffman, A. Illumination night
West, D. The wedding
The **Martian** chronicles. Bradbury, R.

MARTIANS
See also Interplanetary visitors; Mars (Planet)
Heinlein, R. A. Stranger in a strange land
Pohl, F. The day the Martians came
Pohl, F. Mining the oort
Martians in Maggody. Hess, J.
Martin Chuzzlewit. Dickens, C.
Martin Eden. London, J.

MARY I, QUEEN OF ENGLAND, 1516-1558
Lewis, H. W. I am Mary Tudor

MARY II, QUEEN OF GREAT BRITAIN, 1662-1694
Plaidy, J. William's wife

MARY, BLESSED VIRGIN, SAINT
Asch, S. Mary

MARY, OF GUISE *See* Mary, Queen, consort of James V, King of Scotland, 1515-1560

MARY, QUEEN, CONSORT OF JAMES V, KING OF SCOTLAND, 1515-1560
Hill, P. The sword and the flame

MARY, QUEEN OF SCOTS, 1542-1587
George, M. Mary Queen of Scotland and the Isles
Hill, P. The sword and the flame
Plaidy, J. The captive Queen of Scots
Mary. Asch, S.
Mary Dove. Rushing, J. G.

MARY MAGDALENE, SAINT
Holmes, M. Three from Galilee
Mary, Mary. McBain, E.
Mary Queen of Scotland and the Isles. George, M.
Mary Reilly. Martin, V.
Mary Roberts Rinehart's mystery book. Rinehart, M. R.
Mary Stewart's Merlin trilogy. Stewart, M.
MARY TUDOR *See* Mary I, Queen of England, 1516-1558
Marya. Oates, J. C.

MARYLAND
See also Chesapeake Bay (Md. and Va.)
Michener, J. A. Chesapeake

17th century
Barth, J. The sot-weed factor

19th century
De Blasis, C. A season for Swans
De Blasis, C. Swan's chance

20th century
Freedman, J. F. The obstacle course
Michaels, B. Vanish with the rose
Richter, C. The grandfathers
Tyler, A. Searching for Caleb

Baltimore
Tyler, A. Celestial navigation
Tyler, A. The clock winder
Tyler, A. Dinner at the Homesick Restaurant
Tyler, A. Morgan's passing
Tyler, A. Saint maybe
MASH. Hooker, R.
The **mask** of Apollo. Renault, M.
The **mask** of the enchantress. Holt, V.
The **masked** man. Doherty, P. C.
Masquerade. Dailey, J.
Masquerade. Kienzle, W. X.

MASSACHUSETTS
See also Martha's Vineyard (Mass.)
Zaroulis, N. L. Massachusetts

19th century
Hunter, E. Lizzie
Stowe, H. B. Oldtown folks
Zaroulis, N. L. Call the darkness light

20th century
Dew, R. F. Fortunate lives
Gifford, T. The Glendower legacy
Higgins, G. V. The Mandeville talent
Hood, A. Places to stay the night
Lipman, E. The way men act
Marquand, J. P. Point of no return
McCauley, S. The easy way out
Sarton, M. The education of Harriet Hatfield
Updike, J. Roger's version

Politics
See Politics—Massachusetts

Boston—17th century
Hawthorne, N. The scarlet letter

Boston—18th century
Fast, H. Seven days in June

Boston—19th century
Howells, W. D. The rise of Silas Lapham
James, H. The Bostonians
James, H. The Europeans
Marquand, J. P. The late George Apley
Zaroulis, N. L. The last waltz

Boston—20th century
Carroll, J. The city below
Cook, R. Coma
Cook, R. Godplayer
Crichton, M. A case of need
Fielding, J. See Jane run
Higgins, G. V. Bomber's law
Higgins, G. V. Defending Billy Ryan
Higgins, G. V. The friends of Eddie Coyle
Higgins, G. V. The patriot game
Marquand, J. P. H. M. Pulham, esquire
Marquand, J. P. The late George Apley
Minot, S. Folly
Myrer, A. A green desire
Palmer, M. Natural causes
Parker, R. B. All our yesterdays
Piercy, M. The longings of women
Reed, B. The choice
Reed, B. The indictment
Sarton, M. Anger
Sinclair, U. Boston
Theroux, P. Doctor DeMarr

MASSACHUSETTS—Boston—20th century—*Continued*
Wakefield, D. Starting over

Cambridge
Dershowitz, A. M. The advocate's devil
Miller, S. For love
Piercy, M. Small changes

Cape Cod
Martin, W. Cape Cod
Piercy, M. Summer people
Theroux, P. Picture palace

Lexington
Fast, H. April morning

Lowell
Rossner, J. Emmeline
Zaroulis, N. L. Call the darkness light

Provincetown
Mailer, N. Tough guys don't dance

Salem
Condé, M. I, Tituba, black witch of Salem
Hawthorne, N. The House of the Seven Gables
Mukherjee, B. The holder of the world
Massachusetts. Zaroulis, N. L.
The **massacre** at Fall Creek. West, J.

MASSACRES
> *See also* Fall Creek (Ind.)—Massacre, 1824; Armenian massacres, 1915-1923
DeMille, N. Word of honor
O'Brien, T. In the Lake of the Woods
Master and man. Tolstoy, L., graf
> *In* Tolstoy, L. The portable Tolstoy p602-52
> *In* Tolstoy, L. The short novels of Tolstoy
The **master** and Margarita. Bulgakov, M. A.
The **master** of Ballantrae. Stevenson, R. L.
The **master** of Hestviken. Undset, S.
The **master** of Petersburg. Coetzee, J. M.
Master of the game. Sheldon, S.
Master of the moor. Rendell, R.
The **master** stroke. Gage, E.
Masterclass. West, M. L.
Masterpiece. Hoving, T.
The **masters**. Snow, C. P.
The **masters** of the house. Barnard, R.

MATABELE (AFRICAN PEOPLE)
Smith, W. A. The angels weep
Smith, W. A. Men of men
The **Matarese** Circle. Ludlum, R.
> *also in* Ludlum, R. The Ludlum triad p359-756

MATCHMAKERS *See* Marriage brokers
Mating. Rush, N.
The **Matlock** paper. Ludlum, R.

MATRIARCHS *See* Mothers

MATRICIDE *See* Parricide
The **matter** is life. Cooper, J. C.
A **matter** of honor. Archer, J.
Matter's end. Benford, G.
> *In* Nebula awards 28 p52-94

MAU MAU
Ruark, R. Something of value
Ruark, R. Uhuru
Maurice. Forster, E. M.
Max Brand's best western stories. Brand, M.
Maximum Bob. Leonard, E.

MAY DAY
Read, Miss. Thrush Green
May Day. Fitzgerald, F. S.
> *In* Fitzgerald, F. S. The Fitzgerald reader p3-53
May we borrow your husband? Greene, G.
> *In* Greene, G. Collected stories p1-161

Maybe the moon. Maupin, A.
Mayhem in Parva. Livingston, N.

MAYO (IRELAND) *See* Ireland—Mayo
The **Mayor** of Casterbridge. Hardy, T.

MAYORS
Crichton, R. The secret of Santa Vittoria
Guareschi, G. Don Camillo and his flock
Guareschi, G. The little world of Don Camillo
Hardy, T. The Mayor of Casterbridge
A **maze** of stars. Brunner, J.

MCCARTY, HENRY *See* Billy, the Kid
McGarr and the legacy of a woman scorned. Gill, B.
McGarr on the Cliffs of Moher. Gill, B.
McNally's caper. Sanders, L.
McNally's luck. Sanders, L.
McNally's risk. Sanders, L.
McNally's secret. Sanders, L.
McTeague. Norris, F.
Me and my baby view the eclipse. Smith, L.
Means of evil, five mystery stories. Rendell, R.
> *In* Rendell, R. Collected stories p137-262
A **measure** of time. Guy, R.
The **meat** eaters. See Collins, M. The man who dreamt of lobsters

MEAT INDUSTRY
Sinclair, U. The jungle

MEDICAL ETHICS
Endō, S. The sea and poison
Green, G. The last angry man
Michener, J. A. Recessional

MEDICAL LIFE *See* Physicians

MEDICAL RESEARCH *See* Medicine—Research

MEDICAL STUDENTS *See* Students

MEDICINE
> *See also* Surgery
Caldwell, T. Testimony of two men
Doyle, Sir A. C. Conan Doyle's tales of medical humanism and values: Round the red lamp
Wood, B. Soul flame

Research
Cook, R. Brain
Endō, S. The sea and poison
Sanders, L. The sixth commandment
Saul, J. Shadows
Uris, L. QB VII

MEDICINE, EXPERIMENTAL *See* Medicine—Research

MEDICINE, PRACTICE OF *See* Physicians

MEDICINES, PATENT, PROPRIETARY, ETC.
Capote, T. The grass harp
Wells, H. G. Tono-Bungay

MEDIEVAL LIFE *See* Middle Ages

MEDITERRANEAN REGION
Dunnett, D. Pawn in frankincense
Innes, H. Medusa
Waltari, M. The Etruscan

MEDITERRANEAN SEA
Sagan, F. The painted lady

MEDIUMS *See* Spiritualism
Medusa. Campbell, R.
> *In* Campbell, R. Strange things and stranger places p38-91
Medusa. Innes, H.

MELANCHOLY
Snow, C. P. The light and the dark

MELBOURNE (AUSTRALIA) *See* Australia—Melbourne
The **Mellstock** quire. See Hardy, T. Under the greenwood tree

The **melting** clock. Kaminsky, S. M.
The **member** of the wedding. McCullers, C.
 also in McCullers, C. The ballad of the sad café: the novels and stories of Carson McCullers p595-791
 also in McCullers, C. Collected stories p255-392
Memento mori. Spark, M.
 also in Spark, M. A Muriel Spark trio p393-608
Memoirs from the house of the dead. See Dostoyevsky, F. The house of the dead
Memoirs from the underground. See Dostoyevsky, F. Notes from underground
Memoirs from underground. See Dostoyevsky, F. Notes from underground
Memoirs of a space traveler. Lem, S.
The **memoirs** of a survivor. Lessing, D. M.
Memoirs of an ex-prom queen. Shulman, A. K.
Memoirs of an invisible man. Saint, H. F.
Memoirs of Hadrian, and reflections on the composition of Memoirs of Hadrian. Yourcenar, M.
Memoirs of Sherlock Holmes. Doyle, Sir A. C.
 In Doyle, Sir A. C. The complete Sherlock Holmes
Memorial bridge. Carroll, J.
Memorials of a dead house. See Dostoyevsky, F. The house of the dead
Memories of the Ford Administration. Updike, J.
MEMORY
 See also Amnesia
 Abbott, M. The last innocent hour
 Appelfeld, A. Unto the soul
 Kay, T. Shadow song
 Maitland, S. Ancestral truths
 McFarland, D. School for the blind
 O'Brien, E. House of splendid isolation
 Price, R. The tongues of angels
 Smith, C. On the storm planet
 Wiesel, E. The forgotten
Memory and dream. De Lint, C.
The **memory** of earth. Card, O. S.
MEMPHIS (TENN.) *See* Tennessee—Memphis
MEN
 See also Single men
 Keillor, G. The book of guys
 Oates, J. C. What I lived for
Men against the sea. Nordhoff, C.
 also in Nordhoff, C. The Bounty trilogy
The **men** and the girls. Trollope, J.
Men at arms. Waugh, E.
Men in black. Spencer, S.
Men of men. Smith, W. A.
Men without women. Hemingway, E.
Menfreya in the morning. Holt, V.
MENORCA (SPAIN) *See* Minorca (Spain)
MENTAL DISORDERS *See* Mental illness
MENTAL HOSPITALS *See* Mentally ill—Care and treatment
MENTAL ILLNESS
 See also Dual personality; Hallucinations and illusions; Nervous breakdown; Paranoia; Personality disorders; Schizophrenia
 Adams, A. Almost perfect
 Aiken, C. King Coffin
 Banville, J. The book of evidence
 Barker, C. Babel's children
 Beattie, A. Chilly scenes of winter
 Bulgakov, M. A. The master and Margarita
 Crichton, M. The terminal man
 De Hartog, J. The lamb's war
 Didion, J. Play it as it lays
 Doctorow, E. L. The book of Daniel
 Dostoyevsky, F. The idiot
 Finney, P. Firedrake's eye
 Godwin, G. Father Melancholy's daughter
 Guest, J. Ordinary people
 Lessing, D. M. Briefing for a descent into Hell
 McCabe, P. The butcher boy

 Morris, M. M. A dangerous woman
 Percy, W. The moviegoer
 Percy, W. The second coming
 Plath, S. The bell jar
 Price, N. Night woman
 Rendell, R. Going wrong
 Rendell, R. The killing doll
 Rhys, J. Wide Sargasso Sea
 Roth, P. When she was good
 Spark, M. The driver's seat
 Stone, R. Children of light
 Straub, P. The buffalo hunter
 Villars, E. Too close for comfort
 Vonnegut, K. Breakfast of champions
 Vonnegut, K. Slaughterhouse-five
 Walker, A. Possessing the secret of joy
MENTAL TELEPATHY *See* Telepathy
MENTALLY HANDICAPPED
 See also Mentally handicapped children
 Dickens, C. Barnaby Rudge
 Faulkner, W. The sound and the fury
 Gaines, E. J. A lesson before dying
 Hunter, S. Dirty white boys
 Keyes, D. Flowers for Algernon
 Ôe, K. The pinch runner memorandum
 Roiphe, A. R. If you knew me
 Spencer, E. The light in the piazza
 Steinbeck, J. Of mice and men
 Welty, E. The Ponder heart
MENTALLY HANDICAPPED CHILDREN
 See also Autistic children
 Appelfeld, A. Tzili, the story of a life
 Heller, J. Something happened
 Ôe, K. The silent cry
 Rubens, B. A solitary grief
MENTALLY ILL
 See also Insane, Criminal and dangerous
 Swarthout, G. F. The homesman
Care and treatment
 Greenberg, J. I never promised you a rose garden
 Harris, M. Hatter Fox
 Kesey, K. One flew over the cuckoo's nest
 Lessing, D. M. Briefing for a descent into Hell
 McCullough, C. An indecent obsession
 Piercy, M. Woman on the edge of time
 Plath, S. The bell jar
 Rebeta-Burditt, J. The cracker factory
 Rosten, L. C. Captain Newman, M.D.
 Ward, M. J. The snake pit
 Wharton, W. Birdy
 Wiesel, E. Twilight
 Wolfe, G. The death of Doctor Island
MERCENARIES *See* Soldiers of fortune
MERCHANT MARINE *See* Seamen
MERCHANTS
 See also Department stores
 Clavell, J. Tai-Pan
 Delderfield, R. F. God is an Englishman
 Dunnett, D. Niccolò rising
 Dunnett, D. Race of scorpions
 Dunnett, D. The spring of the ram
 Elegant, R. S. Mandarin
 Naipaul, V. S. A bend in the river
 Orde, L. Dreams of gold
 Singer, I. B. The estate
 Singer, I. B. The manor
 Tolstoy, L., graf. Master and man
The **merchants** of Venus. Pohl, F.
 In Modern classic short novels of science fiction p260-320
 In Pohl, F. The gateway trip p12-128

The **merchants'** war. Pohl, F.
Mercy. Lindsey, D. L.
MERCY DEATH *See* Euthanasia
Mercy of a rude stream [series]
    Roth, H. A diving rock on the Hudson
    Roth, H. A star shines over Mt. Morris Park
Meridon. Gregory, P.

MERLIN (LEGENDARY CHARACTER)
    Stewart, M. The crystal cave
    Stewart, M. The hollow hills
    Stewart, M. The last enchantment
    Stewart, M. Mary Stewart's Merlin trilogy
    White, T. H. The book of Merlyn

MERMAIDS
    Shields, C. The republic of love
The **Merry** Men. Stevenson, R. L.
    In Stevenson, R. L. The complete short stories v1
        p436-77
    In Stevenson, R. L. The complete short stories of
        Robert Louis Stevenson
Meshugah. Singer, I. B.
Message from Málaga. MacInnes, H.
The **message** to the planet. Murdoch, I.
MESSALINA, VALERIA, D. 48
    Graves, R. Claudius, the god and his wife Messalina
The **Messiah**. Holmes, M.
The **Messiah** of Stockholm. Ozick, C.

METAMORPHOSIS
    Chayefsky, P. Altered states
Metamorphosis. Kafka, F.
    also in Kafka, F. Collected stories p73-128
    also in Kafka, F. The complete stories
    also in Kafka, F. The metamorphosis and other
        stories p117-92
    also in Kafka, F. The penal colony: stories and short
        pieces
    also in Kafka, F. Selected short stories of Franz
        Kafka
The **metamorphosis** and other stories. Kafka, F.
Metzger's dog. Perry, T.

MEXICAN AMERICANS
    See also Mexicans—United States
    Cisneros, S. The house on Mango Street
    Cisneros, S. Woman Hollering Creek and other stories
    Nichols, J. T. The Milagro beanfield war
    Piercy, M. Woman on the edge of time

MEXICAN REVOLUTION *See* Mexico—20th century

MEXICANS

United States
    Durham, M. Dutch uncle

MEXICO
    See also Sierra Madre Mountains (Mexico)
    Fuentes, C. Terra nostra
    Michener, J. A. Mexico

16th century
    Jennings, G. Aztec

19th century
    Fuentes, C. The death of Artemio Cruz
    Michener, J. A. The eagle and the raven

20th century
    Cussler, C. Inca gold
    Doerr, H. Consider this, señora
    Doerr, H. Stones for Ibarra
    Esquivel, L. Like water for chocolate
    Fuentes, C. The Hydra head
    Fuentes, C. The old gringo
    Greene, G. The power and the glory
    Lawrence, D. H. The plumed serpent (Quetzalcoatl)
    Lowry, M. Under the volcano
    McCarthy, C. All the pretty horses
    McCarthy, C. The crossing
    Morrell, D. Assumed identity

Nin, A. Seduction of the Minotaur
Portis, C. Gringos
Stone, R. Children of light

Acapulco
Fuentes, C. Apollo and the whores

Baja California
Steinbeck, J. The pearl

Mexico City
Gilman, D. The unexpected Mrs. Pollifax
Mexico. Michener, J. A.
MEXICO CITY (MEXICO) *See* Mexico—Mexico City
Mexico set. Deighton, L.
    also in Deighton, L. Game, set & match
MIAMI (FLA.) *See* Florida—Miami
MIAMI BEACH (FLA.) *See* Florida—Miami Beach
Miami, it's murder. Buchanan, E.
MICHELANGELO BUONARROTI, 1475-1564
    Stone, I. The agony and the ecstasy

MICHIGAN
20th century
Eugenides, J. The virgin suicides
Harrison, J. The seven-ounce man
Traver, R. Anatomy of a murder
Woiwode, L. Indian affairs
Woiwode, L. What I'm going to do, I think

Battle Creek
Boyle, T. C. Road to Wellville

Detroit
Arnow, H. L. S. The dollmaker
Douglas, L. C. Magnificent obsession
Estleman, L. D. Kill zone
Estleman, L. D. King of the corner
Estleman, L. D. Motown
Estleman, L. D. Whiskey River
Guest, J. Second heaven
Leonard, E. City primeval
Leonard, E. Freaky Deaky
Leonard, E. Swag
Oates, J. C. Them
Piercy, M. Braided lives

MICROORGANISMS
    Crichton, M. The Andromeda strain
Midaq Alley. Maḥfūz, N.

MIDDLE AGE
    Beauvoir, S. de. The woman destroyed
    Berger, T. Reinhart's women
    Berger, T. Vital parts
    Cather, W. The professor's house
    Colette. Chéri
    Connell, E. S. Mr. Bridge
    Connell, E. S. Mrs. Bridge
    Corman, A. 50
    Drabble, M. The middle ground
    Goudge, E. The scent of water
    Gray, F. du P. World without end
    Heller, J. Something happened
    Lessing, D. M. The memoirs of a survivor
    Lessing, D. M. The summer before the dark
    Lewis, S. Cass Timberlane
    Lewis, S. Dodsworth
    Mann, T. The black swan
    McMurtry, L. The desert rose
    McMurtry, L. Texasville
    Rhys, J. Good morning, midnight
    Richler, M. Joshua then and now
    Spark, M. The prime of Miss Jean Brodie
    Tyler, A. The accidental tourist
    Tyler, A. Breathing lessons
    Updike, J. Rabbit at rest
    Updike, J. Rabbit is rich
    Updike, J. Rabbit redux
    Williams, T. The Roman spring of Mrs. Stone

MIDDLE AGES

See also Europe—392-814; Chivalry; Feudalism; Knights and knighthood

Costain, T. B. The black rose
Doyle, Sir A. C. The White Company
Follett, K. Pillars of the earth
Golding, W. The spire
Haasse, H. S. In a dark wood wandering
Hesse, H. Narcissus and Goldmund
Holland, C. The earl
Holland, C. The firedrake
Lofts, N. The homecoming
Lofts, N. Knight's Acre
Lofts, N. The town house
Oldenbourg, Z. The heirs of the kingdom
Pargeter, E. The green branch
Pargeter, E. The heaven tree
Pargeter, E. The heaven tree trilogy
Pargeter, E. The scarlet seed
Riley, J. M. In pursuit of the green lion
Riley, J. M. A vision of light
Scott, Sir W. Quentin Durward
Twain, M. Personal recollections of Joan of Arc
Undset, S. Kristin Lavransdatter
Undset, S. The master of Hestviken
White, T. H. The once and future king
White, T. H. The sword in the stone

MIDDLE CLASSES

Barnard, R. A city of strangers
Beattie, A. Falling in place
Berger, T. The houseguest
Berger, T. Neighbors
Breslin, J. Table money
Cheever, J. Bullet Park
Connell, E. S. Mr. Bridge
Connell, E. S. Mrs. Bridge
Cozzens, J. G. By love possessed
Drabble, M. Jerusalem the golden
Drabble, M. The waterfall
Eliot, G. Middlemarch
Lewis, S. Babbitt
Maḥfūz, N. The beginning and the end
Marquand, J. P. Point of no return
McCauley, S. The easy way out
Orwell, G. Keep the aspidistra flying
Powell, A. A question of upbringing
Trollope, A. The way we live now
Updike, J. Rabbit is rich
Updike, J. Rabbit redux
Wilson, S. The man in the gray flannel suit
Wouk, H. Marjorie Morningstar

MIDDLE EAST

Coyle, H. W. Bright star
Girzone, J. F. Joshua in the Holy Land
Poyer, D. The gulf
Puzo, M. The fourth K
The middle ground. Drabble, M.
Middle passage. Johnson, C. R.

MIDDLE WESTERN STATES

See also Old Northwest

Berger, T. The feud
Berger, T. Sneaky people
Berger, T. Vital parts
Burnett, W. R. The asphalt jungle
De Vries, P. Consenting adults
DeLillo, D. White noise
McMurtry, L. Pretty Boy Floyd
Powers, J. F. Wheat that springeth green
Roth, P. When she was good
Simpson, M. Anywhere but here

Frontier and pioneer life

See Frontier and pioneer life—Middle Western States

The middleman and other stories. Mukherjee, B.
Middlemarch. Eliot, G.

MIDGETS See Dwarfs

Midnight. Koontz, D. R.
Midnight cowboy. Herlihy, J. L.
The midnight Raymond Chandler. Chandler, R.
Midnight tales. Stoker, B.
Midnight's children. Rushdie, S.

MIDSHIPMEN

Webb, J. H. A sense of honor
Midsummer night madness and other stories. O'Faoláin, S.

In O'Faolain, S. The collected stories of Sean O'Faolain p9-162

MIDWEST See Middle Western States
The midwife. Courter, G.
The midwife's advice. Courter, G.

MIDWIVES

Courter, G. The midwife
Courter, G. The midwife's advice
Riley, J. M. A vision of light
Might as well be dead. Stout, R.
In Stout, R. Three aces

MIGRANT LABOR

Oates, J. C. A garden of earthly delights
Steinbeck, J. The grapes of wrath
Steinbeck, J. In dubious battle
Steinbeck, J. Of mice and men
Mila 18. Uris, L.
The Milagro beanfield war. Nichols, J. T.
MILAN (ITALY) See Italy—Milan
Mildred Pierce. Cain, J. M.
In Cain, J. M. Cain x 3 p103-362

MILITARY AERONAUTICS

See also Aircraft carriers; World War, 1914-1918—Aerial operations; World War, 1939-1945—Aerial operations

Berent, M. Steel tiger
Berent, M. Storm flight
Brown, D. Hammerheads
Brown, D. Sky masters
Brown, D. Storming heaven
Coonts, S. Final flight
Coonts, S. Flight of the Intruder
Coonts, S. The Intruders
Coonts, S. The minotaur
Heller, J. Catch-22
Malraux, A. Man's hope
Thomas, C. Firefox
Thomas, C. Firefox down

MILITARY DESERTION

Hemingway, E. A farewell to arms
O'Brien, T. Going after Cacciato

MILITARY EDUCATION

Conroy, P. The lords of discipline
Webb, J. H. A sense of honor
The military philosophers. Powell, A.
In Powell, A. A dance to the music of time [v3]

MILITARY SCHOOLS See Military education

MILITARY SERVICE, COMPULSORY See Draft

MILITARY TRAINING CAMPS

Hyman, M. No time for sergeants
McCullers, C. Reflections in a golden eye
Styron, W. The long march
Milk and honey. Kellerman, F.
The mill on the Floss. Eliot, G.
Millennium. Bova, B.

MILLERS

Pearce, M. E. Cast a long shadow
The miller's dance. Graham, W.

MILLIONAIRES

See also Capitalists and financiers; Wealth
Bellow, S. Henderson the rain king

MILLIONAIRES—*Continued*
Binchy, M. Firefly summer
Fleming, I. Moonraker
Fowles, J. The magus
Huxley, A. After many a summer dies the swan
James, H. The ivory tower
Knowles, J. Indian summer
Korda, M. Worldly goods
Leonard, E. Split images
Pohl, F. The merchants of Venus
Vonnegut, K. God bless you, Mr. Rosewater
The **millionaire's** daughter. Eden, D.
Millroy the Magician. Theroux, P.

MIND CONTROL *See* Brainwashing
Mind over murder. Kienzle, W. X.

MIND READING *See* Telepathy
A **mind** to murder. James, P. D.
In James, P. D. Crime times three
Mindbend. Cook, R.
Mindbridge. Haldeman, J. W.
Mindsword's story. See Saberhagen, F. The sixth book
of lost swords: Mindsword's story
Mine. McCammon, R. R.

MINERS *See* Coal mines and mining; Copper mines and
mining; Diamond mines and mining; Gold mines
and mining; Mines and mining

MINES AND MINING
See also Coal mines and mining; Copper mines
and mining; Diamond mines and mining; Gold
mines and mining
Bagley, D. Night of error
Stegner, W. E. Angle of repose
Mining the oort. Pohl, F.

MINISTERS *See* Clergy
The **minister's** wooing. Stowe, H. B.
In Stowe, H. B. Uncle Tom's cabin; The minister's
wooing; Oldtown Folks p521-876
The **ministry** of fear. Greene, G.
also in Greene, G. 3: This gun for hire, The
confidential agent, The ministry of fear

MINNEAPOLIS (MINN.) *See* Minnesota—Minneapolis

MINNESOTA

19th century
Moberg, V. The last letter home
Moberg, V. Unto a good land

20th century
Hassler, J. North of hope
Keillor, G. Lake Wobegon days
Keillor, G. WLT
Lewis, S. Cass Timberlane
Lewis, S. Main Street
O'Brien, T. In the Lake of the Woods
Powers, J. F. Morte d'Urban
Spencer, L. Family blessings
Spencer, L. Home song

Farm life
See Farm life—Minnesota

Frontier and pioneer life
See Frontier and pioneer life—Minnesota

Minneapolis
Thayer, S. The weatherman

MINOR PLANETS *See* Asteroids

MINORCA (SPAIN)
Innes, H. Medusa
The **minotaur.** Coonts, S.

MIRABEL FAMILY
Alvarez, J. In the time of the butterflies
Miracle on 34th Street. Davies, V.
The **miracle** workers. Vance, J.
In Modern classic short novels of science fiction
p1-64

MIRACLES
Gallico, P. The small miracle
Werfel, F. The song of Bernadette

MIRANDA, FRANCISCO DE, 1750-1816
Naipaul, V. S. A way in the world
The **mirror** crack'd. Christie, A.
also in Christie, A. Five complete Miss Marple
novels p1-147
The **mirror** crack'd from side to side. See Christie, A.
The mirror crack'd
Mirror dance. Bujold, L. M.
Mirror maze. Bayer, W.
The **misadventures** of John Nicholson. Stevenson, R. L.
In Stevenson, R. L. The complete short stories v2
p165-222

MISCEGENATION
See also Interracial marriage
Brown, R. M. Southern discomfort
Chase-Riboud, B. The President's daughter
Chase-Riboud, B. Sally Hemings
Goudge, E. Blessing in disguise
Paton, A. Too late the phalarope
Mischief. McBain, E.
Mischief in Maggody. Hess, J.
Les **misérables.** Hugo, V.

MISERS
Balzac, H. de. Eugénie Grandet
Dickens, C. A Christmas carol
Eliot, G. Silas Marner
Misery. King, S.
Miss Lonelyhearts. West, N.
also in West, N. The complete works of Nathanael
West p65-140
Miss Mapp. Benson, E. F.
In Benson, E. F. Make way for Lucia p359-534
Miss Marple: the complete short stories. Christie, A.
Miss Melville rides a tiger. Smith, E. E.
Miss Pinkerton [novel]. Rinehart, M. R.
In Rinehart, M. R. Miss Pinkerton: adventures of
a nurse detective p95-245
Miss Pinkerton: adventures of a nurse detective.
Rinehart, M. R.
Miss Pym disposes. Tey, J.
also in Tey, J. Three by Tey v1
Miss Seeton draws the line. Carvic, H.
Miss Smilla's feeling for snow. See Hoeg, P. Smilla's
sense of snow
Miss Tonks turns to crime. Chesney, M.

MISSILES *See* Munitions
The **missing** chapter. Goldsborough, R.
Missing Joseph. George, E.
The **missing** Madonna. O'Marie, C. A.

MISSING PERSONS
Abrahams, P. Hard rain
Allende, I. Of love and shadows
Brookner, A. Fraud
Buffett, J. Where is Joe Merchant?
Dickens, C. The mystery of Edwin Drood
Dickens, C. The mystery of Edwin Drood, concluded
by Leon Garfield
Ferrigno, R. The Horse Latitudes
Johnston, V. The Etruscan smile
Le Carré, J. A perfect spy
MacInnes, H. Decision at Delphi
Michaels, B. Vanish with the rose
Michener, J. A. Caravans
Moore, B. Cold heaven
O'Brien, T. In the Lake of the Woods
Ondaatje, M. In the skin of a lion
Sanders, L. The tenth commandment
Tyler, A. Searching for Caleb
Winton, T. The riders
Missing Susan. McCrumb, S.
Mission to Malaspiga. Anthony, E.

MISSIONARIES
Barrett, W. E. The left hand of God

MISSIONARIES—*Continued*
Bosse, M. J. The warlord
Brent, M. Moonraker's bride
Cather, W. Death comes for the archbishop
Cronin, A. J. The keys of the kingdom
Endō, S. The samurai
Endō, S. Silence
Forester, C. S. The African Queen
Marshall, C. Christy
Melville, H. Omoo: a narrative of adventures in the South Seas
Michener, J. A. Hawaii
Phillips, C. Crossing the river
Missionary stew. Thomas, R.

MISSISSIPPI
Faulkner, W. Go down, Moses
Faulkner, W. Intruder in the dust
Faulkner, W. The portable Faulkner
Faulkner, W. Requiem for a nun
Faulkner, W. Sanctuary

19th century
Faulkner, W. Absalom, Absalom!
Faulkner, W. The unvanquished

20th century
Campbell, B. M. Your blues ain't like mine
Childress, M. Tender
Faulkner, W. Father Abraham
Faulkner, W. Flags in the dust
Faulkner, W. The hamlet
Faulkner, W. Light in August
Faulkner, W. The mansion
Faulkner, W. Sartoris
Faulkner, W. The sound and the fury
Faulkner, W. The town
Flagg, F. Coming attractions
French, A. Billy
Grisham, J. The chamber
Grisham, J. A time to kill
MacDonald, J. D. Barrier Island
Nordan, L. Wolf whistle
Spencer, E. The stories of Elizabeth Spencer
Welty, E. Delta wedding
Welty, E. The golden apples
Welty, E. Losing battles
Welty, E. The optimist's daughter
Welty, E. The Ponder heart

Jackson
Brown, R. Civil wars

MISSISSIPPI RIVER
Ferber, E. Show boat
Twain, M. The adventures of Huckleberry Finn
Twain, M. The adventures of Tom Sawyer
Welty, E. The robber bridegroom

MISSOURI
Twain, M. The adventures of Tom Sawyer
Twain, M. Pudd'nhead Wilson

Kansas City
Connell, E. S. Mr. Bridge
Connell, E. S. Mrs. Bridge

Saint Louis
Shange, N. Betsey Brown

MISSOURI RIVER
Poe, E. A. The journal of Julius Rodman

MISTAKEN IDENTITY
See also Impersonations
Collins, W. The woman in white
Delany, S. R. Time considered as a helix of semi-precious stones
MacInnes, H. North from Rome
Stewart, M. The ivy tree

Mister Roberts. Heggen, T.
Mister Touch. Bosse, M. J.
Mistral's daughter. Krantz, J.
Mistress. Quick, A.
The **mistress** of Husaby. Undset, S.
In Undset, S. Kristin Lavransdatter v2
Mistress of Mellyn. Holt, V.
Mistress of the empire. Feist, R. E.
The **mists** of Avalon. Bradley, M. Z.
MITCHELL, MARGARET, 1900-1949
Parodies, travesties, etc.
Ripley, A. Scarlett
Mitigating circumstances. Rosenberg, N. T.
Mitla Pass. Uris, L.
Mitsou. Colette
In Colette. Six novels p339-410
Mixed blessings. Steel, D.

MIXED BLOODS
See also Eurasians; Mulattoes
Erdrich, L. The Beet Queen
Masters, J. Bhowani Junction
Moby-Dick. Melville, H.

Mode series
Anthony, P. Chaos mode
Anthony, P. Fractal mode
Anthony, P. Virtual mode
The **model.** Oates, J. C.
In Oates, J. C. Haunted p99-144
A **model** world and other stories. Chabon, M.
MODELS, FASHION See Fashion models
Modern classic short novels of science fiction. Entered in Part I under title
Modern classics of science fiction. Entered in Part I under title
A **modern** comedy. Galsworthy, J.
Modern women. Harris, R.
MOHAMMEDANISM See Islam
MOHAMMEDANS See Muslims

MOHAWK VALLEY (N.Y.)
Edmonds, W. D. Chad Hanna
Edmonds, W. D. Drums along the Mohawk

MOHEGAN INDIANS
Cooper, J. F. The last of the Mohicans
MOHICAN INDIANS See Mohegan Indians
Moll Flanders. Defoe, D.
Molloy. Beckett, S.
In Beckett, S. Molloy, Malone dies, and The unnamable p2-240
Molloy, Malone dies, and The unnamable. Beckett, S.
Mom and dead. McInerny, R. M.
Moment in Peking. Lin, Y.
MONASTERIES See Monasticism and religious orders
MONASTICISM AND RELIGIOUS ORDERS
See also Abbeys; Convent life; Jesuits; Monks
Gulik, R. H. van. The haunted monastery
Miller, W. M. A canticle for Leibowitz
Moore, B. Catholics
Monday the rabbi took off. Kemelman, H.
MONEY
See also Finance
Thomas, M. M. Black money
Money from home. Runyon, D.
In Runyon, D. Guys and dolls [omnibus volume] p167-337
MONEYLENDERS
See also Pawnbrokers
Dickens, C. Nicholas Nickleby
Pérez Galdós, B. Torquemada
MONGOLISM (DISEASE) See Down's syndrome
MONGOLS
Costain, T. B. The black rose

Mongoose, R.I.P. Buckley, W. F.
Monkey planet. See Boulle, P. Planet of the Apes
Monkeys. Minot, S.
The **monkey's** wrench. Levi, P.
MONKS
    See also Monasticism and religious orders
    Eco, U. The name of the rose
    Hesse, H. Narcissus and Goldmund
    Unsworth, B. Morality play
Monk's-hood. Peters, E.
MONMOUTH'S REBELLION, 1685
    Blackmore, R. D. Lorna Doone
The **monologue.** Beauvoir, S. de
    In Beauvoir, S. de. The woman destroyed p87-120
MONROE, MARILYN, 1926-1962
    Korda, M. The immortals
Monsieur. Durrell, L.
Monsieur Beaucaire. Tarkington, B.
Monsieur Pamplemousse. Bond, M.
Monsieur Pamplemousse and the secret mission. Bond, M.
Monsieur Pamplemousse investigates. Bond, M.
Monsieur Pamplemousse rests his case. Bond, M.
Monsignor Quixote. Greene, G.
MONSTERS
    Gardner, J. Grendel
MONTAGU, JOHN *See* Sandwich, John Montagu, 4th Earl of, 1718-1792
MONTANA
             19th century
    Guthrie, A. B. Arfive
    Guthrie, A. B. These thousand hills
             20th century
    Bass, R. Mahatma Joe
    Bass, R. Platte River
    Cady, J. The night we buried Road Dog
    Doig, I. Dancing at the Rascal Fair
    Doig, I. English Creek
    Doig, I. Ride with me, Mariah Montana
    Guthrie, A. B. Arfive
    Guthrie, A. B. The last valley
    McGuane, T. Nobody's angel
    McGuane, T. Nothing but blue skies
    Welch, J. The Indian lawyer
          Frontier and pioneer life
    See Frontier and pioneer life—Montana
Monte Walsh. Schaefer, J. W.
MONTEREY (CALIF.) *See* California—Monterey
MONTEZ, LOLA, 1818-1861
    Fraser, G. M. Royal Flash
MONTFORT, SIMON DE, EARL OF LEICESTER, 1208?-1265
    Penman, S. K. Falls the shadow
MONTGOMERY (ALA.) *See* Alabama—Montgomery
MONTREAL (QUÉBEC) *See* Canada—Montreal
MOON
    See also Space flight to the moon
    Clarke, A. C. A fall of moondust
    Heinlein, R. A. The cat who walks through walls
    Heinlein, R. A. The moon is a harsh mistress
    Poe, E. A. The unparalleled adventure of one Hans Pfaall
    Verne, J. From the earth to the moon, and Round the moon
    Wells, H. G. The first men in the moon
The **moon** and sixpence. Maugham, W. S.
The **moon** is a harsh mistress. Heinlein, R. A.
The **moon** is down. Steinbeck, J.
The **moon-spinners.** Stewart, M.
Moon tiger. Lively, P.
Moonraker. Fleming, I.
    In Fleming, I. More gilt-edged Bonds p219-441

Moonraker's bride. Brent, M.
The **moons** of Jupiter. Munro, A.
The **moonshine** war. Leonard, E.
    In Leonard, E. Elmore Leonard's double Dutch treat: three novels
MOONSHINERS
    Faulkner, W. Sanctuary
    Grey, Z. The Arizona clan
    Leonard, E. The moonshine war
    Rawlings, M. K. South moon under
Moonspender. Gash, J.
The **moonstone.** Collins, W.
MOORS
    Lofts, N. The homecoming
    Lofts, N. Knight's Acre
MORALITY
    See also Ethics; Good and evil
Morality play. Unsworth, B.
A **morbid** taste for bones. Peters, E.
    also in Peters, E. The benediction of Brother Cadfael p3-129
MORDRED (LEGENDARY CHARACTER)
    Stewart, M. The wicked day
More die of heartbreak. Bellow, S.
More gilt-edged Bonds. Fleming, I.
More work for the undertaker. Allingham, M.
Morgan's passing. Tyler, A.
MORMONISM *See* Mormons and Mormonism
MORMONS AND MORMONISM
    Card, O. S. Lost boys
    Grey, Z. Riders of the purple sage
A **morning** for flamingos. Burke, J. L.
Morningquest. Aiken, J.
Morpho Eugenia. Byatt, A. S.
    In Byatt, A. S. Angels and insects
Mortal fear. Cook, R.
Mortal grace. Stewart, E.
Mortal remains in Maggody. Hess, J.
Mortal stakes. Parker, R. B.
Morte d'Urban. Powers, J. F.
MOSCOW (RUSSIA) *See* Russia—Moscow
The **Moscow** Club. Finder, J.
MOSES (BIBLICAL FIGURE)
    Asch, S. Moses
Moses. Asch, S.
The **Mosquito** Coast. Theroux, P.
Mostly harmless. Adams, D.
The **Mote** in God's Eye. Niven, L.
A **mother** and two daughters. Godwin, G.
Mother earth, father sky. Harrison, S.
Mother night. Vonnegut, K.
MOTHERHOOD *See* Mothers
MOTHERS
    See also Mothers and daughters; Mothers and sons; Mothers-in-law; Stepmothers; Surrogate mothers
    Arnow, H. L. S. The dollmaker
    Bawden, N. Family money
    Colwin, L. A big storm knocked it over
    Colwin, L. Goodbye without leaving
    Eden, D. The Salamanca drum
    Greenberg, J. A season of delight
    Morris, M. A mother's love
    Oates, J. C. Them
    Pilcher, R. The shell seekers
    Sheldon, S. Master of the game
    Smiley, J. Ordinary love
    Smith, L. Family linen
    Steel, D. Jewels
    Viorst, J. Murdering Mr. Monti
MOTHERS AND DAUGHTERS
    See also Parent and child
    Adams, A. Caroline's daughters
    Allen, C. V. Dreaming in color
    Alther, L. Kinflicks

MOTHERS AND DAUGHTERS—*Continued*

Austen, J. Lady Susan
Battle, L. Southern women
Blatty, W. P. The exorcist
Bosse, M. J. Fire in heaven
Bradford, B. T. Act of will
Brookner, A. Fraud
Busch, F. Long way from home
Cain, J. M. Mildred Pierce
Coetzee, J. M. Age of iron
Cookson, C. The black velvet gown
Delinsky, B. For my daughters
Didion, J. A book of common prayer
Doerr, H. Consider this, señora
Dorris, M. A yellow raft in blue water
Edgarian, C. Rise the Euphrates
French, M. Her mother's daughter
Garcia, C. Dreaming in Cuban
Gibbons, K. Charms for the easy life
Godwin, G. A mother and two daughters
Goudge, E. Garden of lies
Goudge, E. Such devoted sisters
Grau, S. A. Roadwalkers
James, P. D. Innocent blood
Kincaid, J. Annie John
Kingsolver, B. Pigs in heaven
Krantz, J. Mistral's daughter
Krantz, J. Till we meet again
Lipman, E. The way men act
Lively, P. Passing on
Lofts, N. Nethergate
Marshall, P. Daughters
McMurtry, L. Buffalo girls
McMurtry, L. The desert rose
McMurtry, L. Terms of endearment
Michael, J. Pot of gold
Miller, S. The good mother
Moravia, A. Two women
Morrison, T. Beloved
Oates, J. C. Marya
Ozick, C. Rosa
Plain, B. Blessings
Plante, D. Annunciation
Quindlen, A. Object lessons
Quindlen, A. One true thing
Rendell, R. The crocodile bird
Rhys, J. After leaving Mr. Mackenzie
Rice, L. Stone heart
Rich, M. Tender offerings
Roiphe, A. R. Lovingkindness
Rosenberg, N. T. Mitigating circumstances
Rossner, J. Olivia
Shange, N. Liliane
Shreve, A. Eden Close
Shreve, A. Strange fits of passion
Shreve, S. R. Daughters of the new world
Siddons, A. R. King's oak
Simpson, M. Anywhere but here
Spencer, E. The light in the piazza
Spencer, L. Bitter sweet
Stirling, J. Shadows on the shore
Tan, A. The Joy Luck Club
Tan, A. The kitchen god's wife
Thayer, N. Family secrets
Thayer, N. My dearest friend
Urquhart, J. Away
Vine, B. Anna's book
Wharton, E. The old maid
Whitney, P. A. Feather on the moon
Whitney, P. A. The trembling hills
Whitney, P. A. The turquoise mask
Wolitzer, H. Tunnel of love

MOTHERS AND SONS

See also Parent and child

Beattie, A. Chilly scenes of winter
Birmingham, S. The Rothman scandal
Coetzee, J. M. Life & times of Michael K.
Conroy, F. Body & soul

Crane, S. George's mother
Ferber, E. So Big
Fox, P. A servant's tale
Gold, H. Family
Gold, H. A girl of forty
Hobson, L. K. Z. Consenting adult
Hoffman, A. Seventh heaven
Hoffman, A. Turtle Moon
Irving, J. The world according to Garp
James, H. The spoils of Poynton
Jönsson, R. My life as a dog
Lawrence, D. H. Sons and lovers
Lively, P. Passing on
Lopez, S. Third and Indiana
McCammon, R. R. Mine
Oates, J. C. Expensive people
Oates, J. C. A garden of earthly delights
O'Brien, E. Time and tide
Price, R. Kate Vaiden
Robards, K. Maggy's child
Rölvaag, O. E. Peder Victorious
Rosenberg, N. T. First offense
Roth, H. Call it sleep
Roth, P. Portnoy's complaint
Straight, S. I been in sorrow's kitchen and licked out all the pots
Stubbs, J. Light in summer
Toole, J. K. A confederacy of dunces
Undset, S. The cross
Updike, J. Of the farm
Wolfe, T. The lost boy

Mother's boys. See Barnard, R. Death of a perfect mother

MOTHERS-IN-LAW

Dunne, D. The two Mrs. Grenvilles
Naipaul, V. S. A house for Mr. Biswas

A **mother's** love. Morris, M.

MOTION PICTURE ACTORS AND ACTRESSES

Francis, D. Smokescreen
Fuentes, C. Apollo and the whores
Whitney, P. A. Star flight
Woods, S. Dead eyes

MOTION PICTURE DIRECTORS See Motion picture producers and directors

MOTION PICTURE PRODUCERS AND DIRECTORS

Bradbury, R. Green shadows, white whale
Francis, D. Wild horses
McMurtry, L. Somebody's darling
Rossner, J. His little women
Shagan, S. A cast of thousands
Shaw, I. Evening in Byzantium
Stone, K. Happy endings
Woods, S. L.A. Times
Woods, S. Santa Fe rules

MOTION PICTURES

Bradbury, R. A graveyard for lunatics
Bradford, B. T. Angel
Briskin, J. Dreams are not enough
Crispin, E. Sudden vengeance
Dailey, J. Aspen gold
Davies, R. Murther & walking spirits
Dunne, J. G. Playland
Fitzgerald, F. S. The last tycoon
Kesey, K. Sailor song
Leonard, E. Get Shorty
McMurtry, L. Somebody's darling
Percy, W. The moviegoer
Schulberg, B. What makes Sammy run?
Shagan, S. A cast of thousands
Shaw, I. Evening in Byzantium
Stone, R. Children of light
Vidal, G. Hollywood
Vidal, G. Myra Breckinridge [and] Myron
West, N. The day of the locust

MOTOR BUSES *See* Buses

Motor City blue. Estleman, L. D.

Motown. Estleman, L. D.

The **mound**. Lovecraft, H. P.
  In Lovecraft, H. P. The horror in the museum, and other revisions p96-163

MOUND BUILDERS
  Gear, K. O. People of the lakes
  Gear, K. O. People of the lightning
  Gear, W. M. People of the river
  Gear, W. M. People of the sea

MOUNTAIN CLIMBING *See* Mountaineering

MOUNTAIN LIFE

Southern States
  Arnow, H. L. S. The dollmaker
  Caldwell, E. God's little acre
  Giles, J. H. The enduring hills
  Hamner, E. The homecoming
  Hamner, E. Spencer's Mountain
  Marshall, C. Christy
  Smith, L. Fair and tender ladies
  Smith, L. Oral history

Mountain man. Fisher, V.

Mountain windsong. Conley, R. J.

MOUNTAINEERING
  Trevanian. The Eiger sanction
  Ullman, J. R. The White Tower

MOUNTAINS
  See also Adirondack Mountains (N.Y.); Great Smoky Mountains (N.C. and Tenn.); Himalaya Mountains; Pocono Mountains (Pa.); Rocky Mountains; Sierra Madre Mountains (Mexico); Volcanoes

Mountolive. Durrell, L.
  also in Durrell, L. The Alexandria quartet p391-652

MOURNING *See* Bereavement

MOURNING CUSTOMS *See* Funeral rites and ceremonies

The **mouse** that roared. Wibberley, L.

The **mousetrap**. See Christie, A. Three blind mice

The **moviegoer**. Percy, W.

The **moving** finger. Christie, A.
  In Christie, A. Five classic murder mysteries p445-542

Moving Mars. Bear, G.

MOVING PICTURE INDUSTRY *See* Motion pictures

MOVING PICTURES *See* Motion pictures

The **moving** target. Macdonald, R.
  In Macdonald, R. Archer in Hollywood p3-169

Mr. & Mrs. Bo Jo Jones. Head, A.

Mr. Bedford. Godwin, G.
  In Godwin, G. Mr. Bedford and the muses p1-104

Mr. Bedford and the muses. Godwin, G.

Mr. Blandings builds his dream house. Hodgins, E.

Mr. Boy. Kelly, J. P.
  In Modern classic short novels of science fiction p561-616

Mr. Bridge. Connell, E. S.

Mr. Majestyk. Leonard, E.
  In Leonard, E. Elmore Leonard's Dutch treat: 3 novels

Mr. Midshipman Hornblower. Forester, C. S.

Mr. Murder. Koontz, D. R.

Mr. Norris changes trains. See Isherwood, C. The last of Mr. Norris

Mr. Palomar. Calvino, I.

Mr. Parker Pyne, detective. Christie, A.

Mr. Sammler's planet. Bellow, S.

Mr. Vertigo. Auster, P.

Mrs. 'Arris goes to Paris. Gallico, P.

Mrs. Bridge. Connell, E. S.

Mrs. Budley falls from grace. Chesney, M.

Mrs. Dalloway. Woolf, V.

Mrs. de Winter. Hill, S.

Mrs. God. Straub, P.
  In Straub, P. Houses without doors p223-352

Mrs. Malory, detective in residence. Holt, H.

Mrs. McGinty's dead. Christie, A.

Mrs. Mike. Freedman, B.

Mrs. Miniver. Struther, J.

Mrs. Palfrey at the Claremont. Taylor, E.

Mrs. Pargeter's package. Brett, S.

Mrs. Pargeter's pound of flesh. Brett, S.

Mrs. Parkington. Bromfield, L.

Mrs. Pollifax and the Golden Triangle. Gilman, D.

Mrs. Pollifax and the Hong Kong Buddha. Gilman, D.

Mrs. Pollifax and the second thief. Gilman, D.

Mrs. Pollifax and the whirling dervish. Gilman, D.

Mrs. Pollifax on safari. Gilman, D.

Mrs. Pollifax on the China station. Gilman, D.

Mrs. presumed dead. Brett, S.

Mrs. Pringle. Read, Miss

Mrs. Stevens hears the mermaids singing. Sarton, M.

Mrs. Ted Bliss. Elkin, S.

Mrs. Washington and Horowitz, too. Denker, H.

The **mugger**. McBain, E.

MULATTOES
  Cather, W. Sapphira and the slave girl
  Chase-Riboud, B. The President's daughter
  Rice, A. The Feast of All Saints
  Walker, M. Jubilee
  Warren, R. P. Band of angels

MULTIPLE PERSONALITY
  See also Dual personality; Personality disorders
  Clark, M. H. All around the town
  Jackson, S. The bird's nest

The **mummy** case. Peters, E.

MUNITIONS
  Coulter, C. Impulse
  Fleming, I. Moonraker
  Higgins, J. Exocet
  MacInnes, H. Cloak of darkness
  Smith, W. A. Cry wolf

Murder and the First Lady. Roosevelt, E.

Murder at Government House. Huxley, E.

The **murder** at Hazelmoor. Christie, A.
  In Christie, A. Agatha Christie: five complete novels of murder and detection

Murder at Hobcaw Barony. Roosevelt, E.

Murder at Monticello; or, Old sins. Brown, R. M.

Murder at the cat show. Babson, M.

Murder at the FBI. Truman, M.

Murder at the Gardner. Langton, J.

Murder at the Kennedy Center. Truman, M.

Murder at the National Cathedral. Truman, M.

Murder at the old vicarage. McGown, J.

Murder at the palace. Roosevelt, E.

Murder at the Pentagon. Truman, M.

Murder at the Savoy. Sjöwall, M.

The **murder** at the vicarage. Christie, A.

Murder at Vassar. Taylor, E. A.

Murder being once done. Rendell, R.

Murder by 3's. Moyes, P.

Murder by the book. Stout, R.
  In Stout, R. Royal flush p181-333

Murder by the tale. Shannon, D.

Murder has no calories. Sawyer, C. H.

Murder in Georgetown. Truman, M.

Murder in ordinary time. O'Marie, C. A.

Murder in the Blue Room. Roosevelt, E.

Murder in the Calais coach. [variant title: Murder on the Orient Express] Christie, A.

Murder in the CIA. Truman, M.

Murder in the East Room. Roosevelt, E.

Murder in the navy. See McBain, E. Death of a nurse

Murder in the Oval Office. Roosevelt, E.
Murder in the Red Room. Roosevelt, E.
Murder in the Rose Garden. Roosevelt, E.
Murder in the Smithsonian. Truman, M.
Murder in the Supreme Court. Truman, M.
Murder in the west wing. Roosevelt, E.
Murder in the White House. Truman, M.
Murder in triplicate. James, P. D.
Murder in waiting. Eberhart, M. G.
A **murder** is announced. Christie, A.
Murder is corny. Stout, R.
   In Stout, R. Trio for blunt instruments p89-167
Murder is easy. See Christie, A. Easy to kill
Murder makes the wheels go 'round. Lathen, E.
Murder most royal. Plaidy, J.
Murder most strange. Shannon, D.
Murder must advertise. Sayers, D. L.
The **murder** of Roger Ackroyd. Christie, A.
   also in Christie, A. Five classic murder mysteries
   p161-302
Murder on Capitol Hill. Truman, M.
Murder on Embassy Row. Truman, M.
Murder on safari. Huxley, E.
Murder on the Iditarod Trail. Henry, S.
Murder on the Orient Express. See Christie, A. Murder
   in the Calais coach
Murder on the Potomac. Truman, M.
Murder she said. See Christie, A. What Mrs. McGillicud-
   dy saw!
Murder song. Cleary, J.

MURDER STORIES
   See also Assassination; Crime and criminals;
   Fratricide; Infanticide; International intrigue;
   Murderers; Mystery and detective stories; Parricide;
   Poisons; Violence
Adler, E. Legacy of secrets
Adler, E. The secret of the Villa Mimosa
Amiel, J. A question of proof
Amis, M. London fields
Appelfeld, A. Katerina
Ballard, M. F. Final curtain
Banville, J. The book of evidence
Birmingham, S. Carriage trade
Böll, H. The lost honor of Katharina Blum
Bradford, B. T. Everything to gain
Brett, S. Dead romantic
Brett, S. A shock to the system
Brown, R. Before and after
Brown, S. French Silk
Cain, J. M. Double indemnity
Cain, J. M. The postman always rings twice
Campbell, B. M. Your blues ain't like mine
Campbell, R. The Count of Eleven
Camus, A. A happy death
Carr, C. The alienist
Carr, P. A time for silence
Childress, M. Crazy in Alabama
Christie, A. The boomerang clue
Christie, A. Death comes as the end
Clark, M. H. All around the town
Clark, M. H. The cradle will fall
Clark, M. H. Loves music, loves to dance
Cook, R. Godplayer
Cook, T. H. Evidence of blood
Cookson, C. The Maltese Angel
Coscarelli, K. Heir apparent
Coughlin, W. J. Shadow of a doubt
Coulter, C. The Nightingale legacy
Crichton, M. Rising sun
Daley, R. Wall of brass
Davies, L. P. A grave matter
Davies, R. Murther & walking spirits
DeMille, N. The general's daughter
Dickey, J. Deliverance
Dickinson, P. Death of a unicorn
Dickinson, P. Play dead
Diehl, W. Primal fear

Dostoyevsky, F. The brothers Karamazov
Dostoyevsky, F. Crime and punishment
Dreiser, T. An American tragedy
Du Maurier, Dame D. The flight of the falcon
Du Maurier, Dame D. Rebecca
Dunne, D. A season in purgatory
Dunne, D. The two Mrs. Grenvilles
Dunne, J. G. True confessions
Durrell, L. Monsieur
Easterman, D. Brotherhood of the tomb
Egleton, C. A killing in Moscow
Ellroy, J. The black dahlia
Faulkner, W. Requiem for a nun
Faulkner, W. Sanctuary
Ferrars, E. X. Trial by fury
Ferrigno, R. The Horse Latitudes
Field, R. All this, and heaven too
Folsom, A. R. The day after tomorrow
Freemantle, B. The button man
French, A. Billy
Friedman, P. Inadmissable evidence
Friedman, P. Reasonable doubt
Gaines, E. J. The gathering of old men
García Márquez, G. Chronicle of a death foretold
García Márquez, G. The incredible and sad tale of
   innocent Eréndira and her heartless grandmother
Gill, B. M. Nursery crimes
Gill, B. M. Time and time again
Goldman, F. The long night of white chickens
Gould, J. Forever
Graham, W. Stephanie
Greene, G. Brighton rock
Griffin, W. E. B. The murderers
Grisham, J. A time to kill
Guest, J. Killing time in St. Cloud
Guterson, D. Snow falling on cedars
Harris, R. Fatherland
Harris, T. Red Dragon
Harris, T. The silence of the lambs
Harvey, K. Stars
Heyer, G. Penhallow
Higgins, G. V. The Mandeville talent
Highsmith, P. Ripley's game
Hill, R. Dream of darkness
Hoeg, P. Smilla's sense of snow
Hoffman, A. Turtle Moon
Holt, V. The black opal
Holt, V. Daughter of deceit
Holt, V. The Judas kiss
Howatch, S. The shrouded walls
Hunter, E. Lizzie
Hunter, S. Dirty white boys
Isaacs, S. After all these years
Johnston, V. The Etruscan smile
Katzenbach, J. Just cause
Kaye, M. M. Death in Berlin
Kaye, M. M. Death in the Andamans
King, S. Dolores Claiborne
King, S. Misery
King, S. Rage
Kirst, H. H. The nights of the long knives
Latt, M. L. Powers of attorney
Leonard, E. City primeval
Leonard, E. Split images
Lescroart, J. T. The 13th juror
Lescroart, J. T. Hard evidence
Levin, I. A kiss before dying
Levin, I. Sliver
Lindsey, D. L. An absence of light
Lindsey, D. L. Mercy
Lofts, N. The claw
Lovesey, P. On the edge
Lustbader, E. V. Black Blade
Lustbader, E. V. Floating city
Lutz, J. Dancing with the dead
MacInnes, H. Message from Málaga
MacLean, A. Night without end
Maḥfūz, N. Wedding song

MURDER STORIES—*Continued*

Mailer, N. The executioner's song
Mailer, N. Tough guys don't dance
Mann, P. Season of the monsoon
March, W. The bad seed
Martini, S. P. Prime witness
Martini, S. P. Undue influence
Matthiessen, P. Killing Mister Watson
McBain, E. Downtown
McCabe, P. The butcher boy
McCammon, R. R. Boy's life
McCrumb, S. The hangman's beautiful daughter
McCrumb, S. If ever I return, pretty Peggy-O
McEwan, I. The innocent
McFarland, D. School for the blind
McMullen, M. A grave without flowers
Michaels, B. Into the darkness
Michaels, B. Vanish with the rose
Michener, J. A. The novel
Morrison, T. Jazz
Mortman, D. True colors
Murdoch, I. The green knight
Nabokov, V. V. King, queen, knave
Norman, H. The bird artist
Norris, F. McTeague
Oates, J. C. Because it is bitter, and because it is my heart
Oates, J. C. Expensive people
Oates, J. C. The model
Oates, J. C. Nemesis
Oates, J. C. The rise of life on earth
Oates, J. C. Snake eyes
Oates, J. C. What I lived for
Ogilvie, E. When the music stopped
O'Hara, J. Butterfield 8
Pargeter, E. The heaven tree
Patterson, J. Kiss the girls
Patterson, R. N. Degree of guilt
Patterson, R. N. Eyes of a child
Pearson, R. The angel maker
Pearson, R. No witnesses
Pearson, R. Undercurrents
Pearson, T. R. Cry me a river
Perry, T. The butcher's boy
Perry, T. Sleeping dogs
Peters, E. Legend in green velvet
Phillips, C. Cambridge
Price, R. Clockers
Reed, B. The indictment
Rendell, R. The crocodile bird
Rendell, R. The face of trespass
Rendell, R. A judgment in stone
Rendell, R. The lake of darkness
Rendell, R. Master of the moor
Rice, L. Stone heart
Robards, K. One summer
Roberts, N. Private scandals
Rosenberg, N. T. Interest of justice
Ross-Macdonald, M. A woman scorned
Rule, A. Possession
Sanders, L. The first deadly sin
Sanders, L. The second deadly sin
Sanders, L. The third deadly sin
Sandford, J. Rules of prey
Saul, J. Guardian
Saul, J. The homing
Seton, A. Dragonwyck
Shreve, A. Strange fits of passion
Simenon, G. The murderer
Smith, L. E. Strange fruit
Smith, S. B. A simple plan
Spark, M. The driver's seat
Stewart, M. Nine coaches waiting
Stewart, M. Wildfire at midnight
Stirling, J. Lantern for the dark
Straub, P. Koko
Straub, P. The throat
Styron, W. Set this house on fire

Süskind, P. Perfume: the story of a murderer
Symons, J. Something like a love affair
Thayer, S. The weatherman
Thomas, M. M. Black money
Thomas, R. Voodoo, Ltd
Traver, R. Anatomy of a murder
Uhnak, D. The Ryer Avenue story
Uhnak, D. Victims
Unsworth, B. Morality play
Vine, B. Anna's book
Vine, B. No night is too long
Viorst, J. Murdering Mr. Monti
Walters, M. The sculptress
Wambaugh, J. The Golden Orange
Warren, R. P. World enough and time
Welty, E. The Ponder heart
West, M. L. Masterclass
West, P. The women of Whitechapel and Jack the Ripper
Whitney, P. A. Columbella
Whitney, P. A. Daughter of the stars
Whitney, P. A. Domino
Whitney, P. A. Rainbow in the mist
Whitney, P. A. Sea Jade
Whitney, P. A. The singing stones
Whitney, P. A. Star flight
Wilhelm, K. Death qualified
Woods, S. Chiefs
Woods, S. Grass roots
Woods, S. Imperfect strangers
Woods, S. Palindrome
Woods, S. Santa Fe rules
Wozencraft, K. Notes from the country club
Yorke, M. Crime in question
Yorke, M. Safely to the grave
Yorke, M. The smooth face of evil

MURDER TRIALS *See* Trials
Murder unprompted. Brett, S.
Murder with mirrors. Christie, A.
The **murderer**. Simenon, G.

MURDERERS
> *See also* Murder stories

Brown, S. Charade
De Blasis, C. A season for Swans
Dexter, P. The paperboy
Irving, J. A son of the circus
L'Amour, L. The tall stranger
Martin, V. The great divorce
Piercy, M. The longings of women
Strieber, W. Billy
Trevor, W. Felicia's journey
The **murderers**. Griffin, W. E. B.
Murdering Mr. Monti. Viorst, J.
The **murders** of Richard III. Peters, E.
A **Muriel** Spark trio. Spark, M.
Murphy. Beckett, S.
Murther & walking spirits. Davies, R.

MUSEUMS
Greeley, A. M. Angels of September
Hoving, T. Masterpiece

MUSIC
Hersey, J. Antonietta
Mann, T. Tristan

MUSIC HALL ENTERTAINERS *See* Entertainers
Music-hall sidelights. Colette
> *In* Colette. Six novels p237-337

The **music** lovers. Valin, J.
The **music** room. McFarland, D.

MUSICIANS
> *See also* Conductors (Music); Flutists; Pianists; Trumpet players; Violinists

Baldwin, J. Another country
Baldwin, J. Just above my head
Balzac, H. de. Cousin Pons
Cather, W. Lucy Gayheart
Davies, R. The lyre of Orpheus

MUSICIANS—*Continued*
  Edgerton, C. Killer diller
  Ellroy, J. Dick Contino's blues
  Hesse, H. Gertrude
  Hijuelos, O. The Mambo Kings play songs of love
  L'Engle, M. A severed wasp
  L'Engle, M. The small rain
  Oates, J. C. Nemesis
  Sagan, F. The painted lady
  Sarton, M. Anger
  Smith, L. The devil's dream
  Tyler, A. Searching for Caleb
  Tyler, A. A slipping-down life
  Weldon, F. Leader of the band
  West, Dame R. Cousin Rosamund
  West, Dame R. The fountain overflows
  West, Dame R. This real night

MUSLIMS
    See also Islam
  Seth, V. A suitable boy

MUTATION (BIOLOGY)
  Anderson, P. The sharing of flesh
  Smith, C. On the storm planet
  Mutation. Cook, R.

MUTINY
  Faulkner, W. A fable
  MacLean, A. H.M.S. Ulysses
  Nordhoff, C. Mutiny on the Bounty
  Unsworth, B. Sacred hunger
  Wouk, H. The Caine mutiny
  Mutiny on the Bounty. Nordhoff, C.
    also in Nordhoff, C. The Bounty trilogy
  My Ántonia. Cather, W.
    also in Cather, W. Early novels and stories p707-938
  My brilliant career. Franklin, M.
  My brother Michael. Stewart, M.
  My career goes bung. Franklin, M.
  My cousin Rachel. Du Maurier, Dame D.
  My dearest friend. Thayer, N.
  My enemy the Queen. Holt, V.
  My house in Umbria. Trevor, W.
    In Trevor, W. Two lives: Reading Turgenev and My house in Umbria p225-375
  My life as a dog. Jönsson, R.
  My life as a man. Roth, P.
  My love, my love. Guy, R.
  My name is Asher Lev. Potok, C.
  My name is Polly Winter. Black, V.
  My secret history. Theroux, P.
  My sister the moon. Harrison, S.
  My son's story. Gordimer, N.
  My sweet Charlie. Westheimer, D.
  My sweet untraceable you. Scoppettone, S.

MYKONOS ISLAND (GREECE)
  MacInnes, H. The double image
  Myra Breckinridge. Vidal, G.
    In Vidal, G. Myra Breckinridge [and] Myron p1-213
  Myra Breckinridge [and] Myron. Vidal, G.
  Myron. Vidal, G.
    In Vidal, G. Myra Breckinridge [and] Myron p217-417
  Mysteries. Hamsun, K.
  The **mysterious** affair at Styles. Christie, A.
  Mysterious cat stories. Entered in Part I under title
  The **mysterious** island. Verne, J.
  The **mysterious** key and what it opened. Alcott, L. M.
    In Alcott, L. M. Behind a mask: the unknown thrillers of Louisa May Alcott p153-208
  Mysterious stranger, and other stories. Twain, M.
  The **Mysterious** West. Entered in Part I under title
  Mystery. Straub, P.

MYSTERY AND DETECTIVE STORIES
    See also Crime and criminals; Gothic romances; International intrigue; Murder stories
  Adams, D. Dirk Gently's Holistic Detective Agency
  Adams, D. The long dark tea-time of the soul

  Allingham, M. The return of Mr. Campion
  Armstrong, C. The gift shop
  Asimov, I. The caves of steel
  Asimov, I. The naked sun
  Asimov, I. The robots of dawn
  Christie, A. Murder in the Calais coach
  Christmas stalkings
  Clark, C. H. Decked
  Clark, C. H. Iced
  Doyle, Sir A. C. A study in scarlet
  Doyle, Sir A. C. Tales of terror and mystery
  Fifty years of the best from Ellery Queen's Mystery Magazine
  Francis, D. Across the board
  Francis, D. Two by Francis
  Hammett, D. The big knockover
  Hill, R. Recalled to life
  James, P. D. Crime times three
  James, P. D. Murder in triplicate
  Kirst, H. H. The night of the generals
  Lathen, E. Double, double, oil and trouble
  Lovesey, P. Diamond solitaire
  Lovesey, P. The false Inspector Dew
  Melville, J. Death of a daimyo
  Meyer, N. The seven-per-cent solution
  Mosley, W. White butterfly
  Neville, K. The eight
  Peters, E. City of gold and shadows
  Poe, E. A. The collected tales and poems of Edgar Allan Poe
  Poe, E. A. Complete stories and poems of Edgar Allan Poe
  Queen, E. The best of Ellery Queen
  Queen, E. The house of brass
  Queen, E. The XYZ murders
  Simenon, G. Maigret and the man on the bench
  Snow, C. P. Death under sail
  Straub, P. Mystery
  Tey, J. Miss Pym disposes
  Truman, M. Murder in the CIA
  Vine, B. A dark-adapted eye
  A Woman's eye

Africa
  Huxley, E. Murder at Government House
  Huxley, E. Murder on safari

Andaman Islands
  Kaye, M. M. Death in the Andamans

Australia
  Cleary, J. Babylon South
  Cleary, J. Bleak spring
  Cleary, J. Dark summer
  Cleary, J. Murder song
  Cleary, J. Now and then, amen
  Cleary, J. Pride's harvest
  Francis, D. In the frame

Belgium
  Simenon, G. Maigret at the Gai-Moulin

Canada
  Giroux, E. X. Death for a dancing doll
  Wood, T. On the inside
  Wright, E. A body surrounded by water
  Wright, E. The man who changed his name
  Wright, E. A question of murder

China
  Gulik, R. H. van. The Chinese bell murders
  Gulik, R. H. van. The haunted monastery
  Gulik, R. H. van. The lacquer screen
  Gulik, R. H. van. The Red Pavilion
  Gulik, R. H. van. The willow pattern

Corfu
  Brett, S. Mrs. Pargeter's package

Egypt
  Christie, A. Death on the Nile
  Peters, E. Lion in the valley

MYSTERY AND DETECTIVE STORIES — Egypt —
Continued
Peters, E. The mummy case
Peters, E. Night train to Memphis
Peters, E. The snake, the crocodile, and the dog

England
Aird, C. A dead liberty
Aird, C. Henrietta who?
Aird, C. Last respects
Aird, C. Passing strange
Aird, C. Some die eloquent
Allingham, M. The China governess
Allingham, M. Crime and Mr. Campion
Allingham, M. More work for the undertaker
Allingham, M. Three cases for Mr. Campion
Ambler, E. Waiting for orders
Babson, M. A fool for murder
Babson, M. Murder at the cat show
Babson, M. Nine lives to murder
Babson, M. Past regret
Babson, M. Shadows in their blood
Barnard, R. At death's door
Barnard, R. Bodies
Barnard, R. The case of the missing Brontë
Barnard, R. The cherry blossom corpse
Barnard, R. A city of strangers
Barnard, R. Corpse in a gilded cage
Barnard, R. Death and the chaste apprentice
Barnard, R. Death and the Princess
Barnard, R. Death by sheer torture
Barnard, R. Death of a literary widow
Barnard, R. Death of a perfect mother
Barnard, R. Death of a salesperson, and other untimely exits
Barnard, R. A fatal attachment
Barnard, R. Fête fatale
Barnard, R. A hovering of vultures
Barnard, R. A little local murder
Barnard, R. The masters of the house
Barnard, R. Out of the blackout
Barnard, R. A scandal in Belgravia
Barnard, R. School for murder
Barnard, R. The skeleton in the grass
Beaton, M. C. Agatha Raisin and the potted gardener
Beaton, M. C. Agatha Raisin and the quiche of death
Beaton, M. C. Death of a travelling man
Black, V. My name is Polly Winter
Brett, S. Corporate bodies
Brett, S. Dead giveaway
Brett, S. The dead side of the mike
Brett, S. Mrs. Pargeter's pound of flesh
Brett, S. Mrs, presumed dead
Brett, S. Murder unprompted
Brett, S. A nice class of corpse
Brett, S. A reconstructed corpse
Brett, S. What bloody man is that?
Burley, W. J. Wycliffe and the cycle of death
Burley, W. J. Wycliffe and the dead flautist
Burley, W. J. Wycliffe and the quiet virgin
Butler, G. Coffin and the Paper Man
Butler, G. A coffin for Charley
Butler, G. Coffin in the Museum of Crime
Butler, G. Coffin on Murder Street
Butler, G. Cracking open a coffin
Butler, G. Death lives next door
Cannell, D. Femmes fatal
Cannell, D. How to murder your mother-in-law
Cannell, D. The thin woman
Cannell, D. The widows club
Carr, J. D. The bride of Newgate
Carvic, H. Miss Seeton draws the line
Carvic, H. Odds on Miss Seeton
Chesterton, G. K. Father Brown mystery stories
Chesterton, G. K. The Father Brown omnibus
Chesterton, G. K. The innocence of Father Brown
Christie, A. The A.B.C. murders
Christie, A. Agatha Christie: five complete novels of murder and detection

Christie, A. And then there were none
Christie, A. At Bertram's Hotel
Christie, A. The body in the library
Christie, A. By the pricking of my thumbs
Christie, A. Curtain
Christie, A. Endless night
Christie, A. Evil under the sun
Christie, A. Five complete Miss Marple novels
Christie, A. Hercule Poirot's casebook
Christie, A. The Hollow
Christie, A. The mirror crack'd
Christie, A. Miss Marple: the complete short stories
Christie, A. The moving finger
Christie, A. Mr. Parker Pyne, detective
Christie, A. Mrs. McGinty's dead
Christie, A. The murder at the vicarage
Christie, A. A murder is announced
Christie, A. The murder of Roger Ackroyd
Christie, A. Murder with mirrors
Christie, A. The mysterious affair at Styles
Christie, A. The mystery of the blue train
Christie, A. N or M!
Christie, A. The pale horse
Christie, A. A pocket full of rye
Christie, A. Sad cypress
Christie, A. The secret adversary
Christie, A. The secret of chimneys
Christie, A. Sleeping murder
Christie, A. Thirteen at dinner
Christie, A. Three blind mice, and other stories
Christie, A. Towards zero
Christie, A. The witness for the prosecution, and other stories
Cleary, J. The High Commissioner
Cody, L. Bucket nut
Cody, L. Head case
Collins, W. The moonstone
Collins, W. The woman in white
Conrad, J. Secret agent
Crispin, E. Holy disorders
Crispin, E. Sudden vengeance
Dean, S. F. X. Ceremony of innocence
Dean, S. F. X. Death and the mad heroine
Dean, S. F. X. It can't be my grave
Dexter, C. The jewel that was ours
Dexter, C. The secret of annexe 3
Dexter, C. The way through the woods
Dexter, C. The wench is dead
Dickens, C. Bleak House
Dickens, C. The mystery of Edwin Drood
Dickens, C. The mystery of Edwin Drood, concluded by Leon Garfield
Dickinson, P. The glass-sided ants' nest
Dickinson, P. The last houseparty
Dickinson, P. Skeleton-in-waiting
Dickinson, P. The yellow room conspiracy
Doherty, P. C. The assassin in the greenwood
Doyle, Sir A. C. Adventures of Sherlock Holmes
Doyle, Sir A. C. The complete Sherlock Holmes
Doyle, Sir A. C. Famous tales of Sherlock Holmes
Doyle, Sir A. C. The hound of the Baskervilles
Doyle, Sir A. C. The return of Sherlock Holmes
Doyle, Sir A. C. The sign of four
Doyle, Sir A. C. The valley of fear
Ferrars, E. X. Answer came there none
Ferrars, E. X. Beware of the dog
Ferrars, E. X. Blood flies upward
Ferrars, E. X. Danger from the dead
Ferrars, E. X. Death of a minor character
Ferrars, E. X. Sleep of the unjust
Ferrars, E. X. Smoke without fire
Ferrars, E. X. Something wicked
Ferrars, E. X. Thy brother death
Ferrars, E. X. Woman slaughter
Francis, D. Banker
Francis, D. Bolt
Francis, D. Break in
Francis, D. Comeback

MYSTERY AND DETECTIVE STORIES—England—
Continued
Francis, D. The danger
Francis, D. Decider
Francis, D. Driving force
Francis, D. The edge
Francis, D. Enquiry
Francis, D. Hot money
Francis, D. Longshot
Francis, D. Nerve
Francis, D. Odds against
Francis, D. Proof
Francis, D. Rat race
Francis, D. Reflex
Francis, D. Risk
Francis, D. Straight
Francis, D. Three to show
Francis, D. Whip hand
Francis, D. Wild horses
Fraser, A. The April Rainers
Fraser, A. Death speaks softly
Fraser, A. Symbols at your door
Fraser, A. The cavalier case
Fraser, A. Cool repentance
Fraser, A. Jemima Shore at the sunny grave and other stories
Fraser, A. Oxford blood
Fraser, A. A splash of red
Frost, M. The list of 7
Fyfield, F. Deep sleep
Gardner, J. E. The return of Moriarty
Gardner, J. E. The revenge of Moriarty
Gash, J. Moonspender
Gash, J. Paid and loving eyes
Gash, J. The sin within her smile
Gash, J. The very last gambado
George, E. For the sake of Elena
George, E. A great deliverance
George, E. Missing Joseph
George, E. Playing for the Ashes
George, E. A suitable vengeance
George, E. Well-schooled in murder
Gilbert, M. The black seraphim
Gilbert, M. The empty house
Gilbert, M. The killing of Katie Steelstock
Gill, B. M. Seminar for murder
Gill, B. The death of a Joyce scholar
Giroux, E. X. A death for a dancer
Giroux, E. X. Death for a dietitian
Giroux, E. X. A death for a dodo
Giroux, E. X. A death for a double
Graham, C. Death in disguise
Graham, C. The killings at Badger's Drift
Grimes, M. The Anodyne Necklace
Grimes, M. The Deer Leap
Grimes, M. The dirty duck
Grimes, M. The five bells and bladebone
Grimes, M. Help the poor struggler
Grimes, M. I am the only running footman
Grimes, M. Jerusalem Inn
Grimes, M. The man with a load of mischief
Grimes, M. The Old Contemptibles
Grimes, M. The old fox deceiv'd
Grimes, M. The Old Silent
Hardwick, M. The dreaming damozel
Hardwick, M. Malice domestic
Hardwick, M. Parson's pleasure
Hardwick, M. Perish in July
Harrod-Eagles, C. Death to go
Harrod-Eagles, C. Death watch
Harrod-Eagles, C. Orchestrated death
Harvey, J. Cold light
Harvey, J. Wasted years
Haymon, S. T. Death of a god
Haymon, S. T. Death of a warrior queen
Haymon, S. T. Ritual murder
Haymon, S. T. A very particular murder
Hill, R. Blood sympathy
Hill, R. Bones and silence
Hill, R. Child's play
Hill, R. A clubbable woman
Hill, R. Deadheads
Hill, R. Exit lines
Hill, R. Pictures of perfection
Hill, R. Underworld
Innes, M. Appleby and Honeybath
Innes, M. Appleby and the Ospreys
James, P. D. The black tower
James, P. D. Devices and desires
James, P. D. The skull beneath the skin
James, P. D. A taste for death
James, P. D. An unsuitable job for a woman
Keating, H. R. F. The rich detective
King, L. R. The beekeeper's apprentice
Lemarchand, E. Alibi for a corpse
Lemarchand, E. Death of an old girl
Lemarchand, E. The Glade Manor murder
Lemarchand, E. Nothing to do with the case
Lemarchand, E. Who goes home?
Livingston, N. Mayhem in Parva
Lovesey, P. Bertie and the seven bodies
Lovesey, P. Bertie and the Tinman
Lovesey, P. The detective wore silk drawers
Lovesey, P. The last detective
Lovesey, P. Rough cider
Lovesey, P. Waxwork
MacDonald, P. The list of Adrian Messenger
Macdonald, R. The drowning pool
Marsh, Dame N. Black as he's painted
Marsh, Dame N. Clutch of Constables
Marsh, Dame N. Dead water
Marsh, Dame N. False scent
Marsh, Dame N. Grave mistake
Marsh, Dame N. Last ditch
Marsh, Dame N. Light thickens
Marsh, Dame N. Singing in the shrouds
McCrumb, S. Missing Susan
McGown, J. Murder at the old vicarage
McGown, J. The other woman
McGown, J. The stalking horse
Meyer, N. The West End horror
Morice, A. Design for dying
Moyes, P. Murder by 3's
Moyes, P. Twice in a blue moon
Moyes, P. Who is Simon Warwick?
Page, E. Final moments
Perry, A. Belgrave Square
Perry, A. Bethlehem Road
Perry, A. Bluegate Fields
Perry, A. Cardington Crescent
Perry, A. A dangerous mourning
Perry, A. Defend and betray
Perry, A. The face of a stranger
Perry, A. Farriers' Lane
Perry, A. Highgate rise
Perry, A. The Hyde Park headsman
Perry, A. Paragon Walk
Perry, A. Resurrection row
Perry, A. Silence in Hanover Close
Perry, A. The sins of the wolf
Perry, A. A sudden, fearful death
Peters, E. The deeds of the disturber
Peters, E. The last camel died at noon
Peters, E. The benediction of Brother Cadfael
Peters, E. Brother Cadfael's penance
Peters, E. The confession of Brother Haluin
Peters, E. Dead man's ransom
Peters, E. The devil's novice
Peters, E. An excellent mystery
Peters, E. Fallen into the pit
Peters, E. Flight of a witch
Peters, E. The heretic's apprentice
Peters, E. The hermit of Eyton Forest
Peters, E. The holy thief
Peters, E. The leper of St. Giles
Peters, E. Monk's-hood

MYSTERY AND DETECTIVE STORIES—England—
Continued

Peters, E. A morbid taste for bones
Peters, E. One corpse too many
Peters, E. The pilgrim of hate
Peters, E. The potter's field
Peters, E. Rainbow's end
Peters, E. A rare Benedictine
Peters, E. The raven in the foregate
Peters, E. The rose rent
Peters, E. Saint Peter's Fair
Peters, E. The sanctuary sparrow
Peters, E. The summer of the Danes
Peters, E. The virgin in the ice
Pickard, N. Bum steer
Radley, S. Cross my heart and hope to die
Radley, S. Fate worse than death
Radley, S. This way out
Rendell, R. Collected stories
Rendell, R. Death notes
Rendell, R. Kissing the gunner's daughter
Rendell, R. Master of the moor
Rendell, R. Murder being once done
Rendell, R. A sleeping life
Rendell, R. Speaker of Mandarin
Rendell, R. An unkindness of ravens
Rendell, R. The veiled one
Robb, C. M. The Lady Chapel
Ross, J. A rattling of old bones
Sayers, D. L. Busman's honeymoon
Sayers, D. L. Clouds of witnesses
Sayers, D. L. The Dawson pedigree
Sayers, D. L. The documents in the case
Sayers, D. L. Gaudy Night
Sayers, D. L. Have his carcase
Sayers, D. L. Lord Peter
Sayers, D. L. Murder must advertise
Sayers, D. L. The nine tailors
Sayers, D. L. Strong poison
Sayers, D. L. The unpleasantness at the Bellona Club
Sayers, D. L. Whose body?
Sherwood, J. The mantrap garden
Simpson, D. Dead by morning
Simpson, D. Dead on arrival
Simpson, D. Doomed to die
Simpson, D. Element of doubt
Simpson, D. Last seen alive
Simpson, D. No laughing matter
Simpson, D. Suspicious death
Simpson, D. Wake the dead
Snow, C. P. A coat of varnish
Symons, J. The Blackheath poisonings
Symons, J. Death's darkest face
Symons, J. The Kentish manor murders
Symons, J. Playing happy families
Symons, J. A three-pipe problem
Tey, J. Brat Farrar
Tey, J. The daughter of time
Tey, J. Four, five and six by Tey
Tey, J. The Franchise affair
Tey, J. The man in the queue
Tey, J. The singing sands
Tey, J. Three by Tey
Tey, J. To love and be wise
Underwood, M. A dangerous business
Underwood, M. The uninvited corpse
Woods, S. Away with them to prison
Woods, S. The lie direct
Woods, S. Naked villainy
Wright, E. Death in the old country
Yorke, M. Admit to murder
Yorke, M. Criminal damage
Yorke, M. Evidence to destroy
Yorke, M. Find me a villain
Yorke, M. Intimate kill
Yorke, M. A small deceit
Yorke, M. Speak for the dead

France

Bond, M. Monsieur Pamplemousse
Bond, M. Monsieur Pamplemousse and the secret mission
Bond, M. Monsieur Pamplemousse investigates
Bond, M. Monsieur Pamplemousse rests his case
Doherty, P. C. The masked man
Freeling, N. Flanders sky
Hebden, M. Pel and the missing persons
Hebden, M. Pel and the party spirit
Hilton, J. B. Displaced person
Page, K. H. The body in the vestibule
Poe, E. A. The purloined letter [and] The murders in the Rue Morgue
Simenon, G. Five times Maigret
Simenon, G. Maigret and the apparition
Simenon, G. Maigret and the black sheep
Simenon, G. Maigret and the burglar's wife
Simenon, G. Maigret and the fortune-teller
Simenon, G. Maigret and the gangsters
Simenon, G. Maigret and the Hotel Majestic
Simenon, G. Maigret and the loner
Simenon, G. Maigret and the madwoman
Simenon, G. Maigret and the Nahour case
Simenon, G. Maigret and the Saturday caller
Simenon, G. Maigret and the spinster
Simenon, G. Maigret and the toy village
Simenon, G. Maigret and the wine merchants
Simenon, G. Maigret bides his time
Simenon, G. Maigret cinq
Simenon, G. Maigret goes home
Simenon, G. Maigret in court
Simenon, G. Maigret in exile
Simenon, G. Maigret on the defensive
Simenon, G. Maigret on the Riviera
Simenon, G. Maigret's memoirs
Simenon, G. Maigret's pickpocket
Simenon, G. Maigret's revolver
Simenon, G. Maigret's rival
Simenon, G. Maigret's war of nerves

Germany

Kaye, M. M. Death in Berlin
Peters, E. Trojan gold

India

Kaye, M. M. Death in Kashmir
Keating, H. R. F. The body in the billiard room
Keating, H. R. F. Cheating death
Keating, H. R. F. Doing wrong
Keating, H. R. F. The iciest sin
Keating, H. R. F. Inspector Ghote trusts the heart
Peters, E. Death to the landlords!

Ireland

Gill, B. The death of love
Gill, B. Death on a cold, wild river
Gill, B. McGarr and the legacy of a woman scorned
Gill, B. McGarr on the Cliffs of Moher
Haymon, S. T. A beautiful death

Israel

Bayer, W. Pattern crimes
Kemelman, H. Monday the rabbi took off
Kemelman, H. One fine day the rabbi bought a cross

Italy

Davis, L. The iron hand of Mars
Davis, L. Venus in copper
Eco, U. Foucault's pendulum
Eco, U. The name of the rose
Gilman, D. Mrs. Pollifax and the second thief
Langton, J. The Dante game
Marsh, Dame N. When in Rome
Nabb, M. Death in autumn
Nabb, M. The marshal and the madwoman
Nabb, M. The marshal and the murderer
Nabb, M. The Marshal's own case
Peters, E. The seventh sinner

MYSTERY AND DETECTIVE STORIES—*Continued*

Japan
Lathen, E. East is east
Melville, J. The bogus Buddha
Melville, J. The chrysanthemum chain
Melville, J. A haiku for Hanae
Melville, J. The ninth netsuke
Van de Wetering, J. The Japanese corpse

Kenya
Kaye, M. M. Death in Kenya

Madeira
Sherwood, J. The hanging garden

Majorca (Spain)
Jeffries, R. Death takes time

Mexico
Elkins, A. J. Curses!
MacDonald, J. D. A deadly shade of gold
MacDonald, J. D. Dress her in indigo

Morocco
Gilman, D. Mrs. Pollifax and the whirling dervish

Netherlands
Freeling, N. Sand castles
Simenon, G. Maigret in Holland
Van de Wetering, J. The blond baboon
Van de Wetering, J. The corpse on the dike
Van de Wetering, J. The Japanese corpse
Van de Wetering, J. Outsider in Amsterdam
Van de Wetering, J. The streetbird
Van de Wetering, J. Tumbleweed

New Zealand
Marsh, Dame N. Colour scheme
Marsh, Dame N. Photo finish
Sherwood, J. A botanist at bay

North Africa
Wren, P. C. Beau Geste

Norway
Barnard, R. Death in a cold climate
Francis, D. Slayride

Russia
Francis, D. Trial run
Kaminsky, S. M. A cold red sunrise
Kaminsky, S. M. Death of a Russian priest
Kaminsky, S. M. The man who walked like a bear
Kaminsky, S. M. The melting clock
Kaminsky, S. M. Rostnikov's vacation
Smith, M. C. Gorky Park
Smith, M. C. Polar Star
Smith, M. C. Red Square

Scotland
Beaton, M. C. Death of a charming man
Beaton, M. C. Death of a glutton
Beaton, M. C. Death of a hussy
Beaton, M. C. Death of a snob
Black, V. A vow of sanctity
Braun, L. J. The cat who went into the closet
Gash, J. The tartan sell
George, E. Payment in blood
Hammond, G. Thin air
Rankin, I. The black book
Sayers, D. L. The five red herrings

South Africa
Francis, D. Smokescreen
McClure, J. The steam pig

Sweden
Peters, E. Silhouette in scarlet
Sjöwall, M. Cop killer
Sjöwall, M. The laughing policeman
Sjöwall, M. The locked room
Sjöwall, M. The man on the balcony
Sjöwall, M. Murder at the Savoy

Thailand
Gilman, D. Mrs. Pollifax and the Golden Triangle

United States
Adler, W. The ties that bind
Ball, J. D. In the heat of the night
Banks, O. T. The Caravaggio obsession
Banks, O. T. The Rembrandt panel
Barnes, L. Coyote
Barnes, L. The snake tattoo
Barnes, L. Snapshot
Barnes, L. Steel guitar
Barnes, L. A trouble of fools
Bayer, W. Mirror maze
Bayer, W. Switch
Beck, K. K. The body in the cornflakes
Beck, K. K. A hopeless case
Bloch, R. Psycho house
Block, L. The burglar in the closet
Block, L. The burglar who liked to quote Kipling
Block, L. The burglar who painted like Mondrian
Block, L. The burglar who studied Spinoza
Block, L. The burglar who traded Ted Williams
Block, L. A dance at the slaughterhouse
Block, L. The devil knows you're dead
Block, L. Eight million ways to die
Block, L. A long line of dead men
Block, L. Out on the cutting edge
Block, L. The sins of the fathers
Block, L. A ticket to the boneyard
Block, L. Time to murder and create
Block, L. A walk among the tombstones
Block, L. When the sacred ginmill closes
Boyer, R. The Daisy Ducks
Boyer, R. Yellow bird
Bradbury, R. Death is a lonely business
Bradbury, R. A graveyard for lunatics
Braun, L. J. The cat who ate Danish modern
Braun, L. J. The cat who came to breakfast
Braun, L. J. The cat who knew a cardinal
Braun, L. J. The cat who lived high
Braun, L. J. The cat who moved a mountain
Braun, L. J. The cat who sniffed glue
Braun, L. J. The cat who talked to ghosts
Braun, L. J. The cat who wasn't there
Braun, L. J. The cat who went underground
Brown, R. M. Murder at Monticello; or, Old sins
Brown, R. M. Rest in pieces
Brown, R. M. Wish you were here
Buchanan, E. Contents under pressure
Buchanan, E. Miami, it's murder
Burke, J. L. Black cherry blues
Burke, J. L. Dixie City jam
Burke, J. L. Heaven's prisoners
Burke, J. L. In the electric mist with Confederate dead
Burke, J. L. A morning for flamingos
Burke, J. L. The neon rain
Burke, J. L. A stained white radiance
Burnett, W. R. The asphalt jungle
Campbell, R. W. The cat's meow
Campbell, R. W. In La-La Land we trust
Campbell, R. W. Nibbled to death by ducks
Carr, C. The alienist
Caunitz, W. J. Cleopatra Gold
Caunitz, W. J. One Police Plaza
Caunitz, W. J. Suspects
Chandler, R. The big sleep
Chandler, R. The high window
Chandler, R. The lady in the lake
Chandler, R. Later novels and other writings
Chandler, R. The little sister
Chandler, R. The long goodbye
Chandler, R. The midnight Raymond Chandler
Chandler, R. Playback
Chandler, R. Poodle Springs
Chandler, R. Stories and early novels
Clark, C. H. Snagged
Clark, M. H. The lottery winner
Clark, M. H. Weep no more, my lady

MYSTERY AND DETECTIVE STORIES — United
States—*Continued*

Clark, M. H. While my pretty one sleeps
Cody, L. Backhand
Connelly, M. The black ice
Connelly, M. The concrete blonde
Constantine, K. C. Joey's case
Constantine, K. C. The man who liked slow tomatoes
Constantine, K. C. The man who liked to look at himself
Cornwell, P. D. All that remains
Cornwell, P. D. The body farm
Cornwell, P. D. Body of evidence
Cornwell, P. D. Cruel & unusual
Cornwell, P. D. Postmortem
Crider, B. The Texas capitol murders
Cross, A. Death in a tenured position
Cross, A. An imperfect spy
Cross, A. The James Joyce murder
Cross, A. No word from Winifred
Cross, A. The players come again
Cross, A. Sweet death, kind death
Cross, A. The Theban mysteries
Cross, A. A trap for fools
D'Amato, B. Hard case
D'Amato, B. Hard luck
D'Amato, B. Hard women
Davidson, D. M. The last suppers
Davis, D. S. Lullaby of murder
Dean, S. F. X. Nantucket soap opera
Deighton, L. Violent ward
Dobyns, S. Saratoga backtalk
Dobyns, S. Saratoga bestiary
Dobyns, S. Saratoga haunting
Dobyns, S. Saratoga headhunter
Dobyns, S. Saratoga snapper
Douglas, C. N. Catnap
Dunlap, S. Death and taxes
Dunlap, S. High fall
Dunlap, S. Too close to the edge
Dunning, J. Booked to die
Eberhart, M. G. Murder in waiting
Eberhart, M. G. Next of kin
Elkins, A. J. Dead men's hearts
Elkins, A. J. A glancing light
Elkins, A. J. Icy clutches
Elkins, A. J. Make no bones
Elkins, A. J. Old scores
Ellroy, J. Dick Contino's blues
Ellroy, J. Hollywood nocturnes
Estleman, L. D. Downriver
Estleman, L. D. Every brilliant eye
Estleman, L. D. General murders
Estleman, L. D. Lady yesterday
Estleman, L. D. Motor City blue
Estleman, L. D. Silent thunder
Estleman, L. D. Sugartown
Evanovich, J. One for the money
Fearing, K. The big clock
Ferrigno, R. The Cheshire moon
Gardner, E. S. The blonde in lower six
Gardner, E. S. The case of the postponed murder
Gardner, E. S. The case of the sulky girl
Gardner, E. S. The case of the worried waitress
Gardner, E. S. The cat-woman
Gardner, E. S. Come and get it
Gardner, E. S. Dead men's letters
Gardner, E. S. Grinning gods
Gardner, E. S. Honest money, and other short novels
Gardner, E. S. In full of account
Gardner, E. S. Laugh that off
Gardner, E. S. This way out
Gardner, E. S. The wax dragon
Gardner, E. S. Yellow shadows
Gilman, D. The tightrope walker
Goldsborough, R. The bloodied ivy
Goldsborough, R. The missing chapter
Goodrum, C. A. Dewey decimated

Gosling, P. The body in Blackwater Bay
Gosling, P. A few dying words
Grafton, S. "A" is for alibi
Grafton, S. "B" is for burglar
Grafton, S. "C" is for corpse
Grafton, S. "D" is for deadbeat
Grafton, S. "E" is for evidence
Grafton, S. "F" is for fugitive
Grafton, S. "G" is for gumshoe
Grafton, S. "H" is for homicide
Grafton, S. "I" is for innocent
Grafton, S. "J" is for judgment
Grafton, S. "K" is for killer
Granger, B. The el murders
Greeley, A. M. Happy are those who thirst for justice
Greeley, A. M. St. Valentine's night
Greenleaf, S. Blood type
Greenleaf, S. False conception
Greenleaf, S. Southern cross
Griffin, W. E. B. The murderers
Grimes, M. The end of the pier
Grimes, M. The Horse You Came In On
Haddam, J. Bleeding hearts
Hammett, D. The Continental Op
Hammett, D. The glass key
Hammett, D. The Maltese falcon
Hammett, D. The novels of Dashiell Hammett
Hammett, D. The thin man
Hammett, D. Woman in the dark
Hansen, J. A country of old men
Hansen, J. Early graves
Hansen, J. Gravedigger
Hansen, J. The little dog laughed
Hart, C. G. Dead man's island
Hart, C. G. Scandal in Fair Haven
Hart, C. G. Southern ghost
Healy, J. F. Foursome
Healy, J. F. Shallow graves
Henry, S. Murder on the Iditarod Trail
Hess, J. Death by the light of the moon
Hess, J. A diet to die for
Hess, J. Madness in Maggody
Hess, J. Maggody in Manhattan
Hess, J. Malice in Maggody
Hess, J. Martians in Maggody
Hess, J. Mischief in Maggody
Hess, J. Mortal remains in Maggody
Hess, J. O little town of Maggody
Hess, J. Poisoned pins
Hess, J. Roll over and play dead
Hess, J. Tickled to death
Hiaasen, C. Skin tight
Hillerman, T. The blessing way
Hillerman, T. Coyote waits
Hillerman, T. Dance hall of the dead
Hillerman, T. The dark wind
Hillerman, T. The ghostway
Hillerman, T. The Jim Chee mysteries
Hillerman, T. The Joe Leaphorn mysteries
Hillerman, T. Listening woman
Hillerman, T. People of darkness
Hillerman, T. Sacred clowns
Hillerman, T. Skinwalkers
Hillerman, T. Talking God
Hillerman, T. A thief of time
Holland, I. Bump in the night
Holland, I. A death at St. Anselm's
Holland, I. A fatal advent
Holt, H. Mrs. Malory, detective in residence
Hornsby, W. Bad intent
Innes, M. Appleby's end
Isaacs, S. Compromising positions
Isaacs, S. Magic hour
James, P. D. Death of an expert witness
Jance, J. A. Lying in wait
Jones, D. C. The search for Temperance Moon
Kallen, L. C. B. Greenfield: a little madness
Kallen, L. C. B. Greenfield: no lady in the house

MYSTERY AND DETECTIVE STORIES — United States—*Continued*

Kallen, L. C. B. Greenfield: the piano bird
Kallen, L. C. B. Greenfield: the Tanglewood murders
Kaminsky, S. M. Buried caesars
Kaminsky, S. M. The devil met a lady
Kaminsky, S. M. Lieberman's choice
Kaminsky, S. M. Lieberman's day
Kaminsky, S. M. Lieberman's folly
Kaminsky, S. M. Poor butterfly
Kaminsky, S. M. Think fast, Mr. Peters
Keating, H. R. F. Go West, Inspector Ghote
Kellerman, F. Day of atonement
Kellerman, F. False prophet
Kellerman, F. Grievous sin
Kellerman, F. Milk and honey
Kellerman, F. Sanctuary
Kellerman, J. Bad love
Kellerman, J. Devil's waltz
Kellerman, J. Over the edge
Kellerman, J. Private eyes
Kellerman, J. Self-defense
Kellerman, J. Silent partner
Kellerman, J. Time bomb
Kellerman, J. When the bough breaks
Kemelman, H. The day the rabbi resigned
Kemelman, H. Friday the rabbi slept late
Kemelman, H. Saturday the rabbi went hungry
Kemelman, H. Someday the rabbi will leave
Kemelman, H. Sunday the rabbi stayed home
Kemelman, H. Thursday the rabbi walked out
Kemelman, H. Tuesday the rabbi saw red
Kemelman, H. Wednesday the rabbi got wet
Kenney, S. Graves in academe
Kienzle, W. X. Assault with intent
Kienzle, W. X. Bishop as pawn
Kienzle, W. X. Body count
Kienzle, W. X. Chameleon
Kienzle, W. X. Dead wrong
Kienzle, W. X. Deadline for a critic
Kienzle, W. X. Death wears a red hat
Kienzle, W. X. Deathbed
Kienzle, W. X. Eminence
Kienzle, W. X. Marked for murder
Kienzle, W. X. Masquerade
Kienzle, W. X. Mind over murder
Kienzle, W. X. The rosary murders
Kienzle, W. X. Sudden death
Kijewski, K. Copy Kat
Kijewski, K. Kat's cradle
Kijewski, K. Wild Kat
Kittredge, M. Poison pen
Kittredge, M. Rigor mortis
Koontz, D. R. Dragon tears
Kotzwinkle, W. The Game of Thirty
Landrum, G. The famous DAR murder mystery
Langton, J. Divine inspiration
Langton, J. Emily Dickinson is dead
Langton, J. God in Concord
Langton, J. Good and dead
Langton, J. Murder at the Gardner
Langton, J. Natural enemy
Lathen, E. By hook or by crook
Lathen, E. Death shall overcome
Lathen, E. Going for the gold
Lathen, E. Green grow the dollars
Lathen, E. Murder makes the wheels go 'round
Lathen, E. Pick up sticks
Lathen, E. Right on the money
Lathen, E. Something in the air
Lathen, E. A stitch in time
Lewin, M. Z. And baby will fall
Lewin, M. Z. Late payments
Linington, E. Skeletons in the closet
Lutz, J. Hot
MacDonald, J. D. Bright orange for the shroud
MacDonald, J. D. Cinnamon skin
MacDonald, J. D. A deadly shade of gold

MacDonald, J. D. The deep blue good-by
MacDonald, J. D. The dreadful lemon sky
MacDonald, J. D. The empty copper sea
MacDonald, J. D. Free fall in crimson
MacDonald, J. D. The green ripper
MacDonald, J. D. The long lavender look
MacDonald, J. D. Nightmare in pink
MacDonald, J. D. One fearful yellow eye
MacDonald, J. D. A purple place for dying
MacDonald, J. D. The quick red fox
MacDonald, J. D. The scarlet ruse
MacDonald, J. D. A tan and sandy silence
MacDonald, J. D. The turquoise lament
Macdonald, R. Archer at large
Macdonald, R. Archer in Hollywood
Macdonald, R. Archer in jeopardy
Macdonald, R. The blue hammer
Macdonald, R. The goodbye look
Macdonald, R. Ross Macdonald's Lew Archer, private investigator
Macdonald, R. Sleeping beauty
Macdonald, R. The underground man
MacLeod, C. The corpse in Oozak's Pond
MacLeod, C. The Gladstone bag
MacLeod, C. An owl too many
MacLeod, C. The recycled citizen
MacLeod, C. Rest you merry
MacLeod, C. The resurrection man
MacLeod, C. The Silver Ghost
MacLeod, C. Something in the water
MacLeod, C. Something the cat dragged in
MacLeod, C. Vane pursuit
MacLeod, C. The withdrawing room
Malcolm, J. The Gwen John sculpture
Malone, M. Uncivil seasons
Maron, M. Bootlegger's daughter
Maron, M. Shooting at loons
Maron, M. Southern discomfort
Matera, L. Prior convictions
McBain, E. Another part of the city
McBain, E. Blood relatives
McBain, E. Cinderella
McBain, E. Death of a nurse
McBain, E. Eight black horses
McBain, E. Fuzz
McBain, E. Ghosts
McBain, E. Goldilocks
McBain, E. Heat
McBain, E. Ice
McBain, E. Jack and the beanstalk
McBain, E. Jigsaw
McBain, E. Kiss
McBain, E. Lightning
McBain, E. Lullaby
McBain, E. Mary, Mary
McBain, E. Mischief
McBain, E. The mugger
McBain, E. Poison
McBain, E. Puss in boots
McBain, E. Sadie when she died
McBain, E. Snow White and Rose Red
McBain, E. There was a little girl
McBain, E. Three blind mice
McBain, E. Tricks
McBain, E. Vespers
McBain, E. Widows
McCrumb, S. MacPherson's lament
McCrumb, S. The Windsor knot
Mcdonald, G. Fletch
Mcdonald, G. The Fletch chronicles
Mcdonald, G. Fletch reflected
Mcdonald, G. Fletch, too
Mcdonald, G. Fletch won
Mcdonald, G. Son of Fletch
McInerny, R. M. The basket case
McInerny, R. M. Bishop as pawn
McInerny, R. M. Body and soil
McInerny, R. M. A cardinal offense

MYSTERY AND DETECTIVE STORIES — United States—*Continued*

McInerny, R. M. Desert sinner
McInerny, R. M. Four on the floor
McInerny, R. M. Frigor mortis
McInerny, R. M. The grass widow
McInerny, R. M. Judas Priest
McInerny, R. M. Mom and dead
McInerny, R. M. Savings and loam
McInerny, R. M. The search committee
McInerny, R. M. Second vespers
McInerny, R. M. Seed of doubt
McInerny, R. M. Thicker than water
Mosley, W. Black Betty
Mosley, W. Devil in a blue dress
Mosley, W. A red death
Muller, M. Beyond the grave
Muller, M. The cavalier in white
Muller, M. Dark star
Muller, M. Pennies on a dead woman's eyes
Muller, M. The shape of dread
Muller, M. There's something in a Sunday
Muller, M. Till the butchers cut him down
Muller, M. Trophies and dead things
Muller, M. Where echoes live
Muller, M. Wolf in the shadows
The Mysterious West
Norton, A. Sneeze on Sunday
O'Connell, C. Mallory's oracle
O'Donnell, L. Cop without a shield
O'Donnell, L. Dial 577 R-A-P-E
O'Donnell, L. A good night to kill
O'Donnell, L. Lockout
O'Donnell, L. No business being a cop
O'Donnell, L. The other side of the door
O'Donnell, L. A private crime
O'Donnell, L. Pushover
O'Donnell, L. Used to kill
O'Donnell, L. A wreath for the bride
O'Marie, C. A. The missing Madonna
O'Marie, C. A. Murder in ordinary time
Page, K. H. The body in the basement
Page, K. H. The body in the bouillon
Page, K. H. The body in the cast
Paretsky, S. Bitter medicine
Paretsky, S. Blood shot
Paretsky, S. Burn marks
Paretsky, S. Deadlock
Paretsky, S. Guardian angel
Paretsky, S. Indemnity only
Paretsky, S. Killing orders
Paretsky, S. Tunnel vision
Parker, R. B. A Catskill eagle
Parker, R. B. Ceremony
Parker, R. B. Crimson joy
Parker, R. B. Double Deuce
Parker, R. B. Early autumn
Parker, R. B. Looking for Rachel Wallace
Parker, R. B. Mortal stakes
Parker, R. B. Pale kings and princes
Parker, R. B. Paper doll
Parker, R. B. Pastime
Parker, R. B. Perchance to dream
Parker, R. B. Playmates
Parker, R. B. Promised land
Parker, R. B. A savage place
Parker, R. B. Stardust
Parker, R. B. Taming a sea-horse
Parker, R. B. Valediction
Parker, R. B. Walking shadow
Parker, R. B. The widening gyre
Parker, T. J. Laguna heat
Parker, T. J. Pacific beat
Parker, T. J. Summer of fear
Paul, B. The apostrophe thief
Paul, B. He huffed and he puffed
Paul, B. You have the right to remain silent
Pearson, R. Probable cause

Pentecost, H. Kill and kill again
Perry, T. The butcher's boy
Perry, T. Sleeping dogs
Peters, E. Die for love
Peters, E. Naked once more
Pickard, N. The 27 ingredient chili con carne murders
Pickard, N. But I wouldn't want to die there
Pickard, N. Confession
Pickard, N. Dead crazy
Pickard, N. Generous death
Pickard, N. I.O.U
Pickard, N. Marriage is murder
Pickard, N. No body
Piesman, M. Heading uptown
Pronzini, B. Bones
Pronzini, B. Deadfall
Pronzini, B. Quarry
Queen, E. A fine and private place
Queen, E. The Roman hat mystery
Quill, M. Nun of the above
Quill, M. Nun plussed
Quill, M. Sine qua nun
Quill, M. Sister Hood
Quill, M. The veil of ignorance
Rich, V. The baked bean supper murders
Rich, V. The cooking school murders
Rich, V. The Nantucket diet murders
Rinehart, M. R. The circular staircase
Rinehart, M. R. Mary Roberts Rinehart's mystery book
Rinehart, M. R. Miss Pinkerton: adventures of a nurse detective
Roosevelt, E. A first class murder
Roosevelt, E. The Hyde Park murder
Roosevelt, E. Murder and the First Lady
Roosevelt, E. Murder at Hobcaw Barony
Roosevelt, E. Murder at the palace
Roosevelt, E. Murder in the Blue Room
Roosevelt, E. Murder in the East Room
Roosevelt, E. Murder in the Oval Office
Roosevelt, E. Murder in the Red Room
Roosevelt, E. Murder in the Rose Garden
Roosevelt, E. Murder in the west wing
Roosevelt, E. New deal for death
Roosevelt, E. The President's man
Roosevelt, E. A royal murder
Roosevelt, E. The White House pantry murder
Sanders, L. The eighth commandment
Sanders, L. The fourth deadly sin
Sanders, L. McNally's caper
Sanders, L. McNally's luck
Sanders, L. McNally's risk
Sanders, L. McNally's secret
Sanders, L. The seventh commandment
Sanders, L. The Timothy files
Sanders, L. Timothy's game
Sandford, J. Eyes of prey
Sandford, J. Night prey
Sandford, J. Shadow prey
Sandford, J. Silent prey
Sandford, J. Winter prey
Sawyer, C. H. Murder has no calories
Scoppettone, S. Everything you have is mine
Scoppettone, S. I'll be leaving you always
Scoppettone, S. My sweet untraceable you
Shannon, D. Appearances of death
Shannon, D. Blood count
Shannon, D. Chaos of crime
Shannon, D. Destiny of death
Shannon, D. Exploit of death
Shannon, D. Felony file
Shannon, D. Murder by the tale
Shannon, D. Murder most strange
Shoemaker, B. Stalking horse
Sibley, C. Ah, sweet mystery
Smith, A. North of Montana
Smith, C. M. Reverend Randollph and the Splendid Samaritan

MYSTERY AND DETECTIVE STORIES — United States—*Continued*

Smith, C. M. Reverend Randollph and the unholy Bible
Smith, C. M. Reverend Randollph and the wages of sin
Smith, E. E. Miss Melville rides a tiger
Smith, J. L. A vintage murder
Smith, J. The Axeman's jazz
Smith, J. Jazz funeral
Smith, J. New Orleans beat
Solomita, S. Force of nature
Solomita, S. A good day to die
Solomita, S. Last chance for glory
Solomita, S. A piece of the action
Solomita, S. A twist of the knife
Stewart, E. Deadly rich
Stewart, E. Mortal grace
Stout, R. All aces
Stout, R. Death of a doxy
Stout, R. The doorbell rang
Stout, R. A family affair
Stout, R. The father hunt
Stout, R. Fer-de-lance
Stout, R. Five of a kind
Stout, R. Gambit
Stout, R. Kings full of aces
Stout, R. Royal flush
Stout, R. Three aces
Stout, R. Trio for blunt instruments
Tapply, W. G. Client privilege
Tapply, W. G. Dead meat
Tapply, W. G. Dead winter
Tapply, W. G. The seventh enemy
Tapply, W. G. The snake eater
Tapply, W. G. Tight lines
Tapply, W. G. A void in hearts
Taylor, E. A. The cable car murder
Taylor, E. A. Murder at Vassar
Taylor, E. A. The northwest murders
Trocheck, K. H. Every crooked nanny
Truman, M. Murder at the FBI
Truman, M. Murder at the Kennedy Center
Truman, M. Murder at the National Cathedral
Truman, M. Murder at the Pentagon
Truman, M. Murder in Georgetown
Truman, M. Murder in the Smithsonian
Truman, M. Murder in the Supreme Court
Truman, M. Murder in the White House
Truman, M. Murder on Capitol Hill
Truman, M. Murder on Embassy Row
Truman, M. Murder on the Potomac
Truscott, L. K. Dress gray
Turow, S. Pleading guilty
Twain, M. Tom Sawyer, detective
Uhnak, D. The investigation
Uhnak, D. The witness
Vachss, A. H. Down in the zero
Vachss, A. H. Hard candy
Vachss, A. H. Sacrifice
Valin, J. Day of wrath
Valin, J. Dead letter
Valin, J. Extenuating circumstances
Valin, J. The music lovers
Valin, J. Second chance
Van de Wetering, J. Just a corpse at twilight
Van de Wetering, J. The Maine massacre
Wambaugh, J. The Delta Star
Wambaugh, J. Fugitive nights
Wambaugh, J. The Glitter Dome
Wambaugh, J. The secrets of Harry Bright
Waugh, H. A death in town
Westlake, D. E. Baby, would I lie?
Westlake, D. E. Levine
Westlake, D. E. Trust me on this
Wilcox, C. Dead center
Wilcox, C. A death before dying
Wilcox, C. Except for the bones
Wilcox, C. Find her a grave
Wilcox, C. Hire a hangman
Wilcox, C. Switchback
Wilhelm, K. The Hamlet trap
Wilhelm, K. Justice for some
Wilhelm, K. Sweet, sweet poison
Woods, S. Chiefs
Woods, S. New York dead

Wales

MacLeod, C. The wrong rite

West Indies

Christie, A. A Caribbean mystery

Zanzibar

Kaye, M. M. Death in Zanzibar
Mystery book, Mary Roberts Rinehart's. Rinehart, M. R.
The **mystery** of Edwin Drood. Dickens, C.
The **mystery** of Edwin Drood, concluded by Leon Garfield. Dickens, C.
The **mystery** of the blue train. Christie, A.
Mystery ride. Boswell, R.
Mystical paths. Howatch, S.

MYSTICISM

Hesse, H. Siddhartha
Llywelyn, M. Druids
Martin, G. R. R. A song for Lya
McEwan, I. Black dogs
Murdoch, I. The message to the planet
Wiesel, E. Twilight

MYTHICAL ANIMALS

See also Dragons; Unicorns; Vampires; Werewolves

MYTHOLOGY

See also Argonauts (Greek mythology); Cassandra (Greek mythology); Jason (Greek mythology); Theseus (Greek mythology)
Lewis, C. S. Till we have faces
Momaday, N. S. The ancient child
Murdoch, I. The green knight

N

N or M! Christie, A.
Nabokov's dozen. Nabokov, V. V.
The **naked** and the dead. Mailer, N.
Naked once more. Peters, E.
The **naked** sun. Asimov, I.
In Asimov, I. The rest of the robots
Naked villainy. Woods, S.
The **name** of the rose. Eco, U.
The **Nameless**. Campbell, R.
Nana. Zola, É.

NANNIES See Governesses; Nursemaids
The **Nantucket** diet murders. Rich, V.
Nantucket soap opera. Dean, S. F. X.

NAPLES (ITALY) See Italy—Naples

NAPOLEON I, EMPEROR OF THE FRENCH, 1769-1821

Lofts, N. A rose for virtue
Selinko, A. Désirée
Tolstoy, L., graf. War and peace

NAPOLEON III, EMPEROR OF THE FRENCH, 1808-1873

Lofts, N. A rose for virtue

NAPOLEONIC ERA See Europe—19th century

NAPOLEONIC WARS, 1800-1815

See also Peninsular War, 1807-1814; Waterloo, Battle of, 1815
O'Brian, P. The wine-dark sea

Narcissus and Goldmund. Hesse, H.

NARCOTIC HABIT *See* Drug addiction

NARCOTICS, CONTROL OF *See* Drug traffic

NARCOTICS AGENTS *See* Drug traffic

The **narrative** of Arthur Gordon Pym of Nantucket. Poe, E. A.
    also in Poe, E. A. The collected tales and poems of Edgar Allan Poe
    also in Poe, E. A. Complete stories and poems of Edgar Allan Poe p617-736
    also in Poe, E. A. The imaginary voyages p4-365

NASA *See* United States. National Aeronautics and Space Administration

NAT TURNERS' INSURRECTION *See* Southampton Insurrection, 1831

NATIONAL AERONAUTICS AND SPACE ADMINISTRATION (U.S.) *See* United States. National Aeronautics and Space Administration

NATIONAL GUARD (U.S.) *See* United States. National Guard

NATIONAL SECURITY COUNCIL (U.S.) *See* United States. National Security Council

NATIONAL SOCIALISM
    See also Germany—1918-1945
  Abbott, M. The last innocent hour
  Amis, M. Time's arrow
  Deighton, L. SS-GB: Nazi-occupied Britain 1941
  Diehl, W. 27
  Forsyth, F. The Odessa file
  Gardner, J. E. Maestro
  Grass, G. Dog years
  Griffin, W. E. B. Honor bound
  Hall, A. The Quiller memorandum
  Harris, R. Fatherland
  Higgins, J. Cold Harbour
  Higgins, J. Thunder point
  Iles, G. Black cross
  Keneally, T. Schindler's list
  King, S. Apt pupil
  Kirst, H. H. The nights of the long knives
  Korda, M. Worldly goods
  Leffland, E. The knight, death, and the devil
  Ludlum, R. The Holcroft covenant
  Ludlum, R. The Scarlatti inheritance
  MacInnes, H. Above suspicion
  Shaw, I. The young lions
  Szeman, S. The Kommandant's mistress
  Thomas, D. M. Pictures at an exhibition
  Uris, L. Mila 18
  Vonnegut, K. Mother night

NATIONALISM
  Grass, G. The call of the toad
  Werfel, F. The forty days of Musa Dagh

Native son. Wright, R.
  also in Wright, R. Works

Native tongue. Hiaasen, C.

The **natural**. Malamud, B.

Natural causes. Palmer, M.

A **natural** curiosity. Drabble, M.

Natural enemy. Langton, J.

Natural history. Howard, M.

NATURALISTS
  See also Paleontologists
  Hudson, W. H. Green mansions
  Wells, H. G. The island of Doctor Moreau

NATURE
  Goethe, J. W. von. Novella
  Hoagland, E. Seven rivers west
  McCarthy, M. Birds of America
  Rawlings, M. K. South moon under
  Thomas, E. M. Reindeer Moon

NATURE CONSERVATION
  Cheever, J. Oh, what a paradise it seems

Nausea. Sartre, J. P.

NAVAHO INDIANS *See* Navajo Indians

NAVAJO INDIANS
  Harris, M. Hatter Fox
  Hillerman, T. The blessing way
  Hillerman, T. Coyote waits
  Hillerman, T. Dance hall of the dead
  Hillerman, T. The dark wind
  Hillerman, T. The ghostway
  Hillerman, T. The Jim Chee mysteries
  Hillerman, T. The Joe Leaphorn mysteries
  Hillerman, T. Listening woman
  Hillerman, T. People of darkness
  Hillerman, T. Sacred clowns
  Hillerman, T. Skinwalkers
  Hillerman, T. Talking God
  Hillerman, T. A thief of time
  La Farge, O. Laughing Boy

NAVAL BATTLES
  See also United States—Revolution, 1775-1783—Naval operations; Sea stories; World War, 1914-1918—Naval operations; World War, 1939-1945—Naval operations
  Forester, C. S. Beat to quarters
  Forester, C. S. Commodore Hornblower
  Forester, C. S. Hornblower and the Atropos
  Forester, C. S. The last nine days of the Bismarck
  Forester, C. S. Ship of the line
  McCutchan, P. Cameron's crossing

NAVAL OFFICERS *See* Great Britain. Royal Navy—Officers; United States. Navy—Officers

The **Nazarene.** Asch, S.

NAZIS *See* National socialism

NAZISM *See* National socialism

NDEBELE (AFRICAN PEOPLE) *See* Matabele (African people)

NEANDERTHAL RACE
  See also Prehistoric man
  Golding, W. The inheritors
  Kurtén, B. Dance of the tiger

NEAR EAST *See* Middle East

NEBRASKA

          19th century
  Aldrich, B. S. A lantern in her hand
  Cather, W. My Ántonia
  Cather, W. O pioneers!

          20th century
  Cather, W. A lost lady
  Cather, W. One of ours

          Farm life
  See Farm life—Nebraska

      Frontier and pioneer life
  See Frontier and pioneer life—Nebraska

Nebula awards [1]-29. Entered in Part I under title

A **necessary** woman. Van Slyke, H.

NECKLACES
  Dumas, A. The Queen's necklace

Necrochip. See Harrod-Eagles, C. Death to go

Needful things. King, S.

Needing ghosts. Campbell, R.
  In Campbell, R. Strange things and stranger places p166-256

The **needle's** eye. Drabble, M.

The **negotiator.** Forsyth, F.

NEGROES *See* African Americans

NEIGHBORS
  Berger, T. Neighbors
  Brookner, A. A private view
  Cheever, J. Bullet Park
  Hamilton, J. A map of the world
  Hoffman, A. Illumination night

NEIGHBORS—*Continued*
Miller, S. For love
Powers, J. R. The junk-drawer corner-store front-porch blues
Puig, M. Tropical night falling
Ross-Macdonald, M. A woman possessed
Shreve, A. Eden Close
Neighbors. Berger, T.
NELSON, HORATIO NELSON, VISCOUNT, 1758-1805
Sontag, S. The volcano lover
Nemesis. Asimov, I.
Nemesis. Christie, A.
In Christie, A. Five complete Miss Marple novels p263-408
Nemesis. Oates, J. C.
The **neon** rain. Burke, J. L.

NEPHEWS
Dennis, P. Auntie Mame
Nabokov, V. V. King, queen, knave
Rosenberg, N. T. Interest of justice
NERO, EMPEROR OF ROME, 37-68
Sienkiewicz, H. Quo vadis
Nerve. Francis, D.
also in Francis, D. Three to show p219-491

NERVOUS BREAKDOWN
Wilson, A. N. The vicar of sorrows

NERVOUS SYSTEM
Diseases
Kellogg, M. Tell me that you love me, Junie Moon
Nethergate. Lofts, N.

NETHERLANDS
16th century
Holland, C. The Sea Beggars
17th century
Laker, R. The golden tulip
20th century
De Hartog, J. The captain
MacLean, A. Floodgate
Amsterdam
Camus, A. The fall
Williams, J. A. The man who cried I am
NEURASTHENIA *See* Nervous breakdown

NEUROSES
Beauvoir, S. de. The woman destroyed
Rossner, J. August
NEUROTICS *See* Neuroses

NEVADA
19th century
Clark, W. V. T. The Ox-bow incident
Las Vegas
Dunne, J. G. Playland
McMurtry, L. The desert rose
Never doubt I love. Veryan, P.
Never send flowers. Gardner, J. E.
The **new** breed. Griffin, W. E. B.
The **new** centurions. Wambaugh, J.
New deal for death. Roosevelt, E.

NEW ENGLAND
Hawthorne, N. Twice-told tales
Jewett, S. O. The best stories of Sarah Orne Jewett
Santayana, G. The last Puritan
17th century
Seton, A. The Winthrop woman
18th century
McCarry, C. The bride of the wilderness
Stone, I. Those who love
Stowe, H. B. The minister's wooing

19th century
Wharton, E. Ethan Frome
Whitney, P. A. Sea Jade
20th century
Auchincloss, L. The Rector of Justin
Brown, R. Tender mercies
Cheever, J. The Wapshot chronicle
Cheever, J. The Wapshot scandal
Cozzens, J. G. By love possessed
Jackson, S. The bird's nest
Jackson, S. We have always lived in the castle
Knowles, J. Peace breaks out
Knowles, J. A separate peace
Levin, I. The Stepford wives
McCarthy, M. A charmed life
Michaels, B. Into the darkness
Minot, S. Monkeys
Myrer, A. A green desire
Sarton, M. A small room
Theroux, P. Picture palace
Tryon, T. Harvest home
Farm life
See Farm life—New England
NEW ENGLAND DIALECT *See* Dialect stories—New England
The **new** girl friend and other stories of suspense. Rendell, R.
In Rendell, R. Collected stories p409-536

NEW GUINEA
Native peoples
Dickinson, P. The glass-sided ants' nest

NEW HAMPSHIRE
19th century
Benét, S. V. The Devil and Daniel Webster
20th century
Banks, R. Affliction
Brown, R. Before and after
Irving, J. A prayer for Owen Meany
Sarton, M. Kinds of love
Updike, J. Memories of the Ford Administration
Whitney, P. A. Silverhill
Farm life
See Farm life—New Hampshire

NEW JERSEY
20th century
Clark, M. H. The cradle will fall
Price, R. Clockers
Updike, J. The poorhouse fair
Atlantic City
Leonard, E. Glitz
The **new** men. Snow, C. P.

NEW MEXICO
Schaefer, J. W. Monte Walsh
19th century
Cather, W. Death comes for the archbishop
Cather, W. The professor's house
Durham, M. Dutch uncle
Estleman, L. D. City of widows
Richter, C. The lady
20th century
Bradford, R. Red sky at morning
Nichols, J. T. The Milagro beanfield war
Strieber, W. Majestic
Frontier and pioneer life
See Frontier and pioneer life—New Mexico
Los Alamos
Smith, M. C. Stallion Gate
Santa Fe
Mortman, D. True colors

NEW MEXICO—Santa Fe—*Continued*
Whitney, P. A. The turquoise mask
Woods, S. Santa Fe rules
New moon rising. Price, E.

NEW ORLEANS (LA.) *See* Louisiana—New Orleans
New Orleans beat. Smith, J.

NEW SOUTH WALES (AUSTRALIA) *See* Australia—New South Wales

NEW SOUTHWEST *See* Southwestern States
The new springtime. Silverberg, R.

The New treasury of great racing stories. Entered in Part I under title

New Year's Day. Wharton, E.
In Wharton, E. Old New York

NEW YORK (N.Y.)

19th century

Bromfield, L. Mrs. Parkington
Carr, C. The alienist
Crane, S. Maggie: a girl of the streets (a story of New York)
Doctorow, E. L. The waterworks
Eden, D. The millionaire's daughter
Field, R. All this, and heaven too
Finney, J. Time and again
James, H. Washington Square
Vidal, G. 1876
Wharton, E. The age of innocence
Wharton, E. The buccaneers
Wharton, E. The buccaneers, completed by Marion Mainwaring
Wharton, E. Old New York
Whitney, P. A. Window on the square

20th century

Auchincloss, L. The book class
Auchincloss, L. Honorable men
Auchincloss, L. The lady of situations
Auchincloss, L. Portrait in brownstone
Auchincloss, L. The stoic
Baker, D. Young man with a horn
Baldwin, J. Another country
Beattie, A. Falling in place
Bellow, S. Mr. Sammler's planet
Birmingham, S. The Auerbach will
Bromfield, L. Mrs. Parkington
Caldwell, T. Ceremony of the innocent
Clark, M. H. A stranger is watching
Colwin, L. A big storm knocked it over
Colwin, L. Family happiness
Condon, R. Prizzi's family
Condon, R. Prizzi's glory
Condon, R. Prizzi's honor
Condon, R. Prizzi's money
Conroy, F. Body & soul
Conroy, P. The prince of tides
Cook, R. Blindsight
Cook, R. Brain
Cook, R. Mindbend
Daley, R. Man with a gun
Daley, R. Tainted evidence
Daley, R. Wall of brass
Davies, V. Miracle on 34th Street
De Felitta, F. Audrey Rose
Denker, H. Mrs. Washington and Horowitz, too
Dos Passos, J. Manhattan transfer
Dreiser, T. Sister Carrie
Fitzgerald, F. S. The Great Gatsby
Fitzgerald, F. S. May Day
Fox, P. A servant's tale
Godey, J. The taking of Pelham one two three
Godwin, G. Violet Clay
Goldreich, G. That year of our war
Goldreich, G. Years of dreams
Goldsmith, O. Fashionably late
Goldsmith, O. The First Wives Club
Goudge, E. Garden of lies
Grant, M. Officer down

Harris, R. Modern women
Heller, J. Closing time
Helprin, M. Winter's tale
Hobson, L. K. Z. Gentleman's agreement
Howatch, S. Sins of the fathers
Hunter, E. The blackboard jungle
Hunter, E. Criminal conversation
Isaacs, S. Shining through
Jackson, C. The lost weekend
Jen, G. Typical American
Jenkins, D. Semi-tough
Jong, E. Any woman's blues
Leavitt, D. The lost language of cranes
Levin, I. Sliver
Malamud, B. The tenants
McBain, E. Downtown
McInerney, J. Brightness Falls
Miller, H. Tropic of Capricorn
Moore, B. I am Mary Dunne
Morris, M. A mother's love
Nathan, R. Portrait of Jennie
Nin, A. A spy in the house of love
O'Hara, J. Butterfield 8
Piercy, M. Braided lives
Plath, S. The bell jar
Rand, A. The fountainhead
Rossner, J. August
Rossner, J. Olivia
Roth, H. A diving rock on the Hudson
Runyon, D. Best of Runyon
Runyon, D. Guys and dolls
Saint, H. F. Memoirs of an invisible man
Salinger, J. D. The catcher in the rye
Salinger, J. D. Franny and Zooey
Salinger, J. D. Raise high the roof beam, carpenters, and Seymour: an introduction
Sanders, L. The sixth commandment
Sanders, L. The tenth commandment
Shaw, I. Bread upon the waters
Sheldon, S. Rage of angels
Singer, I. B. Enemies, a love story
Straub, P. The buffalo hunter
Tanenbaum, R. Immoral certainty
Tanenbaum, R. Reversible error
Thomas, M. M. Hanover Place
Uhnak, D. Law and order
Van Slyke, H. No love lost
Van Slyke, H. Public smiles, private tears
Villars, E. Lipstick on his collar
Voigt, C. Glass mountain
Weidman, J. I can get it for you wholesale
Westlake, D. E. Don't ask
Westlake, D. E. Good behavior
Westlake, D. E. Why me?
Wharton, E. The house of mirth
Wolfe, T. The good child's river
Wolfe, T. The web and the rock
Wolfe, T. You can't go home again
Wolfe, T. The bonfire of the vanities
Wolitzer, M. Friends for life
Wouk, H. Youngblood Hawke
Wright, R. The outsider

Bronx

Beagle, P. S. A fine and private place
Doctorow, E. L. Billy Bathgate
Potok, C. In the beginning
Price, R. The wanderers
Rodriguez, A. Spidertown
Uhnak, D. The Ryer Avenue story
Wouk, H. The city boy, the adventures of Herbie Bookbinder and his cousin Cliff
Wouk, H. Inside, outside

Brooklyn

Breslin, J. The gang that couldn't shoot straight
Garcia, C. Dreaming in Cuban
Green, G. The last angry man
Malamud, B. The assistant

NEW YORK (N.Y.)—Brooklyn—Continued
McDermott, A. At weddings and wakes
Potok, C. The chosen
Potok, C. The gift of Asher Lev
Potok, C. My name is Asher Lev
Prose, F. Bigfoot dreams
Singer, I. B. Enemies, a love story
Smith, B. Maggie-Now
Smith, B. A tree grows in Brooklyn
Styron, W. Sophie's choice
Woodson, J. Autobiography of a family photo

Chinatown
Maas, P. China white

Greenwich Village
Brownmiller, S. Waverly Place
Harris, R. Modern women
Puig, M. Eternal curse on the reader of these pages
White, E. The beautiful room is empty

Harlem
Baldwin, J. Go tell it on the mountain
Baldwin, J. If Beale Street could talk
Baldwin, J. Tell me how long the train's been gone
Childress, A. A short walk
Guy, R. A measure of time
Guy, R. Ruby
Hughes, L. Simple speaks his mind
Hughes, L. Simple stakes a claim
Hughes, L. Simple takes a wife
Hughes, L. Simple's Uncle Sam
Morrison, T. Jazz
Petry, A. L. The street
Roth, H. A star shines over Mt. Morris Park
Wallant, E. L. The pawnbroker

Lower East Side
Courter, G. The midwife
Courter, G. The midwife's advice
Crane, S. Maggie: a girl of the streets (a story of New York)
Roth, H. Call it sleep
Tax, M. Rivington Street
Tax, M. Union Square

Manhattan
Bellow, S. A theft
Berger, T. Who is Teddy Villanova?
Caunitz, W. J. Black sand
Collins, L. The fifth horseman
Colwin, L. Happy all the time
Corman, A. Kramer versus Kramer
De Felitta, F. Audrey Rose
Dennis, P. Auntie Mame
Dunne, D. People like us
Fitzgerald, F. S. The beautiful and damned
Friedman, P. Inadmissable evidence
Goldman, W. Marathon man
Goldreich, G. Four days
Goudge, E. Such devoted sisters
Heller, J. Good as Gold
Herlihy, J. L. Midnight cowboy
Hijuelos, O. The Mambo Kings play songs of love
Jhabvala, R. P. Poet and dancer
Kaufman, B. Up the down staircase
Kaufman, S. Diary of a mad housewife
Korda, M. The fortune
Krantz, J. I'll take Manhattan
L'Engle, M. A severed wasp
Levenkron, S. The best little girl in the world
Levin, I. Rosemary's baby
Malamud, B. The tenants
O'Hara, J. Butterfield 8
Percy, W. The last gentleman
Prose, F. Household saints
Robinson, S. By any other name
Roiphe, A. R. Up the sandbox!
Sanders, L. The tenth commandment
Schulberg, B. Waterfront
Schwartz, L. S. Disturbances in the field

Singer, I. B. Meshugah
Steel, D. Vanished
Strieber, W. The Wolfen
Westlake, D. E. Cops and robbers
Wouk, H. Marjorie Morningstar

Queens
Breslin, J. Table money
Gordon, M. The other side
Isaacs, S. Close relations
Shange, N. Liliane
Smith, R. K. Sadie Shapiro's knitting book

NEW YORK (STATE)
See also Adirondack Mountains (N.Y.); Erie Canal (N.Y.); Long Island (N.Y.); Mohawk Valley (N.Y.)

18th century
Cooper, J. F. The Deerslayer
Cooper, J. F. The last of the Mohicans
Cooper, J. F. The Pathfinder
Cooper, J. F. The spy

19th century
Rawlings, M. K. The sojourner
Seton, A. Dragonwyck

20th century
Banks, R. The sweet hereafter
Bass, R. Field events
Busch, F. Closing arguments
Cheever, J. Bullet Park
Dreiser, T. An American tragedy
Gardner, J. Nickel mountain
Godwin, G. The finishing school
Jhabvala, R. P. Three continents
Lurie, A. Only children
Malamud, B. Dubin's lives
Oates, J. C. Because it is bitter, and because it is my heart
Oates, J. C. Foxfire
Oates, J. C. I lock my door upon myself
Oates, J. C. Unholy loves
Oates, J. C. What I lived for
Oates, J. C. You must remember this
Perry, T. Vanishing act
Prose, F. Primitive people
Puzo, M. The godfather
Quindlen, A. Object lessons
Russo, R. Nobody's fool
Russo, R. The risk pool
Shreve, A. Eden Close
Spencer, S. Men in black
Straub, P. Ghost story
Strieber, W. The forbidden zone
Westlake, D. E. Drowned hopes
Whitney, P. A. The stone bull

Farm life
See Farm life—New York (State)

Frontier and pioneer life
See Frontier and pioneer life—New York (State)

Politics
See Politics—New York (State)

Albany
Kennedy, W. The ink truck
Kennedy, W. Ironweed
Kennedy, W. Quinn's book
Kennedy, W. Very old bones

Batavia
Gardner, J. The sunlight dialogues

Cooperstown
Cooper, J. F. The pioneers

Corinth
Lurie, A. The war between the Tates

NEW YORK (STATE)—*Continued*
New York City
See New York (N.Y.)

Saratoga Springs
Ferber, E. Saratoga trunk

Southampton
Sheed, W. The boys of winter

Westchester County
Boyle, T. C. World's end
New York dead. Woods, S.

NEW ZEALAND
Sheffield, C. Georgia on my mind

19th century
Eden, D. An important family
Goudge, E. Green Dolphin Street

20th century
Ashton-Warner, S. Spinster
Hulme, K. The bone people

Frontier and pioneer life
See Frontier and pioneer life—New Zealand

NEWFOUNDLAND *See* Canada—Newfoundland

NEWPORT (R.I.) *See* Rhode Island—Newport

NEWSPAPER PUBLISHERS *See* Publishers and publishing

NEWSPAPERMEN *See* Journalists

NEWSPAPERS
Böll, H. The lost honor of Katharina Blum
Boucher, A. We print the truth
Guthrie, A. B. The last valley
Kennedy, W. The ink truck
Marshall, C. Julie
Quinn, S. Happy endings
Rand, A. The fountainhead
Schulberg, B. What makes Sammy run?
Spencer, L. Forgiving
Vidal, G. Empire
Next of kin. Eberhart, M. G.
The next witness. Stout, R.
In Stout, R. Royal flush p337-84
Nibbled to death by ducks. Campbell, R. W.

NICARAGUANS

United States
Leonard, E. Bandits
Niccolò rising. Dunnett, D.
The nice and the good. Murdoch, I.
A nice class of corpse. Brett, S.
Nicholas Nickleby. Dickens, C.
The Nick Adams stories. Hemingway, E.
Nickel mountain. Gardner, J.

NIECES
Amado, J. The war of the saints
Beattie, A. Love always
Garwood, J. Prince Charming
Van Slyke, H. A necessary woman

NIGER RIVER
Boyle, T. C. Water music

NIGERIA
Achebe, C. Girls at war, and other stories
The Nigger of the Narcissus. Conrad, J.
also in Conrad, J. Great short works of Joseph Conrad p21-140
also in Conrad, J. The portable Conrad p292-453
also in Conrad, J. Tales of land and sea p106-210
Night chills. Koontz, D. R.

NIGHT CLUBS
Hiaasen, C. Strip tease
Night, Dawn, The accident: three tales. Wiesel, E.
Night flight. Saint-Exupéry, A. de
Night gallery reader, Rod Serling's. See Rod Serling's Night gallery reader

The night in Lisbon. Remarque, E. M.
A night in the lonesome October. Zelazny, R.
The night manager. Le Carré, J.
Night of error. Bagley, D.
Night of the fox. Higgins, J.
The night of the generals. Kirst, H. H.
Night of the hawk. Brown, D.
Night on the island. See Kaye, M. M. Death in the Andamans
Night over water. Follett, K.
Night prey. Sandford, J.
Night probe! Cussler, C.
Night shift. King, S.
Night sky. Francis, C.
Night train to Memphis. Peters, E.
The night we buried Road Dog. Cady, J.
In Nebula awards 29 p242-96
Night without end. MacLean, A.
Night woman. Price, N.
Nightfall. Asimov, I.
Nightfall, and other stories. Asimov, I.
The nightingale. Sholem Aleichem
The Nightingale legacy. Coulter, C.
Nightmare in pink. MacDonald, J. D.
Nightmares & dreamscapes. King, S.
The nights of the long knives. Kirst, H. H.
Nightwings. Silverberg, R.
also in Silverberg, R. A Robert Silverberg omnibus
Nightwings [novelette]. Silverberg, R.
In The Hugo winners v2 p503-57
Nightwork. Shaw, I.

NIHILISM
See also Anarchism and anarchists
Dostoyevsky, F. Demons
Pynchon, T. V.
Styron, W. Set this house on fire
Tolstoy, L., graf. War and peace
Turgenev, I. S. Fathers and sons
The nine billion names of God. Clarke, A. C.
Nine coaches waiting. Stewart, M.
The nine dragons. Scott, J.
Nine lives to murder. Babson, M.
Nine princes in Amber. Zelazny, R.
Nine stories. Salinger, J. D.
The nine tailors. Sayers, D. L.
Nineteen eighty-four. Orwell, G.
Nineteen fifty-nine. See Davis, T. 1959
The ninth netsuke. Melville, J.
Nip the buds, shoot the kids. Õe, K.
No body. Pickard, N.
No business being a cop. O'Donnell, L.
No door. Wolfe, T.
In Wolfe, T. The short novels of Thomas Wolfe p158-231
No fond return of love. Pym, B.
No greater love. Steel, D.
No lady in the house. See Kallen, L. C. B. Greenfield: no lady in the house
No laughing matter. Simpson, D.
No love lost. Van Slyke, H.
No more parades. Ford, F. M.
In Ford, F. M. Parade's end
No night is too long. Vine, B.
No one writes to the colonel. García Márquez, G.
In García Márquez, G. Collected novellas p107-66
In García Márquez, G. No one writes to the colonel, and other stories p3-62
No one writes to the colonel, and other stories. García Márquez, G.
No reck'ning made. Greenberg, J.
No time for sergeants. Hyman, M.
No time for tears. Freeman, C.
No witnesses. Pearson, R.
No word from Winifred. Cross, A.

NOBEL PRIZES
Wallace, I. The prize

NOBILITY See Aristocracy

Noble house. Clavell, J.

Nobody's angel. McGuane, T.

Nobody's angel. Robards, K.

Nobody's fool. Russo, R.

The **nonborn** king. May, J.

None but the lonely heart. Llewellyn, R.

None to accompany me. Gordimer, N.

Noon wine. Porter, K. A.
> In Porter, K. A. The collected stories of Katherine Anne Porter p222-68
> In Porter, K. A. Pale horse, pale rider: three short novels p93-176

NORMANDIE (STEAMSHIP)
> Villars, E. The Normandie affair

The **Normandie** affair. Villars, E.

NORMANDY (FRANCE) See France—Normandy

NORTH AFRICA
> See also Sahara

North and South. Jakes, J.

NORTH CAROLINA
> See also Great Smoky Mountains (N.C. and Tenn.)

Gurganus, A. The oldest living Confederate widow tells all

20th century
Ballard, M. F. Final curtain

Card, O. S. Lost boys

Edgerton, C. Killer diller

Edgerton, C. Walking across Egypt

Gibbons, K. Charms for the easy life

Godwin, G. A mother and two daughters

Godwin, G. A Southern family

Gurganus, A. Blessed assurance: a moral tale

Gurganus, A. A hog loves its life: something about my grandfather

Kenan, R. Let the dead bury their dead and other stories

McCorkle, J. Tending to Virginia

Payne, D. Ruin Creek

Pearson, T. R. A short history of a small place

Percy, W. The second coming

Price, R. Blue Calhoun

Price, R. Kate Vaiden

Price, R. The promise of rest

Price, R. The tongues of angels

Tyler, A. A slipping-down life

Tyler, A. The tin can tree

Whitney, P. A. Star flight

Wolfe, T. The lost boy

Wolfe, T. The web and the rock

Durham
Parker, G. M. These same long bones

The **North** China lover. Duras, M.

NORTH DAKOTA
19th century
Bojer, J. The emigrants

Jones, D. C. Arrest Sitting Bull

20th century
Erdrich, L. The Beet Queen

Erdrich, L. The bingo palace

Erdrich, L. Tracks

Power, S. The grass dancer

Farm life
> See Farm life—North Dakota

Frontier and pioneer life
> See Frontier and pioneer life—North Dakota

North from Rome. MacInnes, H.

North of hope. Hassler, J.

North of Montana. Smith, A.

Northanger Abbey. Austen, J.
> also in Austen, J. The complete novels of Jane Austen

NORTHERN IRELAND
> Maas, P. Father and son

Politics
> See Politics—Northern Ireland

Belfast
Moore, B. The doctor's wife

Moore, B. The emperor of ice-cream

Moore, B. Lies of silence

Moore, B. The lonely passion of Judith Hearne

NORTHERN RHODESIA See Zambia

NORTHMEN See Vikings

Northshore. Tepper, S. S.

NORTHUMBERLAND (ENGLAND) See England—Northumberland

NORTHWEST, OLD See Old Northwest

NORTHWEST, PACIFIC See Pacific Northwest

The **northwest** murders. Taylor, E. A.

Northwest Passage. Roberts, K. L.

NORTHWEST TERRITORIES See Canada—Northwest Territories

The **Norton** book of ghost stories. Entered in Part I under title

The **Norton** book of science fiction. Entered in Part I under title

NORWAY
To 1397
Undset, S. The axe

Undset, S. In the wilderness

Undset, S. Kristin Lavransdatter

Undset, S. The master of Hestviken

Undset, S. The snake pit

Undset, S. The son avenger

1814-1905
Hamsun, K. Hunger

Hamsun, K. Mysteries

20th century
Francis, C. Wolf winter

1940-1945
Laker, R. This shining land

Farm life
> See Farm life—Norway

Rural life
Hamsun, K. Mysteries

Undset, S. Kristin Lavransdatter

Undset, S. The master of Hestviken

NORWEGIAN AMERICANS
> Young, C. The wedding dress

NORWEGIANS
> See also Vikings

United States
Bojer, J. The emigrants

Rölvaag, O. E. Giants in the earth

Rölvaag, O. E. Peder Victorious

Nostromo. Conrad, J.

Not a penny more, not a penny less. Archer, J.

Not after midnight and other stories. See Du Maurier, Dame D. Don't look now

Not without laughter. Hughes, L.

The **notebooks** of Malte Laurids Brigge. Rilke, R. M.

Notes from the country club. Wozencraft, K.

Notes from underground. Dostoyevsky, F.
> also in Dostoyevsky, F. The best short stories of Dostoyevsky p115-260
> also in Dostoyevsky, F. The short novels of Dostoevsky p127-222

Nothing but blue skies. McGuane, T.

Nothing lasts forever. Sheldon, S.

Nothing to do with the case. Lemarchand, E.

Notre Dame de Paris. See Hugo, V. The hunchback of Notre Dame

NOTTINGHAM (ENGLAND) *See* England—Nottingham

NOTTINGHAMSHIRE (ENGLAND) *See* England—Nottinghamshire

NOVA SCOTIA *See* Canada—Nova Scotia

The **novel**. Michener, J. A.

NOVELETTES

> *See also* Short stories

Alcott, L. M. Behind a mask: the unknown thrillers of Louisa May Alcott

Aldiss, B. W. Total environment

Anderson, P. The longest voyage

Appelfeld, A. Badenheim 1939

Auchincloss, L. Three lives

Balzac, H. de. The short novels of Balzac

Barker, C. In the flesh

Barrett, W. E. The lilies of the field

Barth, J. Chimera

Bass, R. Field events

Bass, R. Mahatma Joe

Bass, R. Platte River

Bausch, R. Rare & endangered species

Beaton, M. C. Death of a snob

Beaton, M. C. Death of a travelling man

Beauvoir, S. de. The woman destroyed

Bellow, S. The Bellarosa connection

Bellow, S. Seize the day [novelette]

Bellow, S. Something to remember me by

Bellow, S. A theft

Bellow, S. What kind of day did you have?

Benét, S. V. The Devil and Daniel Webster

Benford, G. Matter's end

The Best of the Nebulas

Bisson, T. England underway

Böll, H. And where were you, Adam?

Böll, H. The lost honor of Katharina Blum

Böll, H. A soldier's legacy

Böll, H. The train was on time

Böll, H. When the war broke out

Böll, H. When the war was over

Boucher, A. The compleat werewolf

Boucher, A. We print the truth

Bradbury, R. Fahrenheit 451 [novelette]

Brand, M. Dark Rosaleen

Brand, M. Dust across the range

Brand, M. Outcasts

Byatt, A. S. Angels and insects

Cady, J. The night we buried Road Dog

Cain, J. M. Cain x 3

Calvino, I. Mr. Palomar

Campbell, R. Medusa

Campbell, R. Needing ghosts

Capote, T. Breakfast at Tiffany's

Capote, T. The Thanksgiving visitor

Cervantes Saavedra, M. de. Three exemplary novels

Cheever, J. Oh, what a paradise it seems

Chesney, M. Back in society

Chesney, M. Colonel Sandhurst to the rescue

Chesney, M. Deborah goes to Dover

Chesney, M. Lady Fortescue steps out

Chesney, M. Miss Tonks turns to crime

Chesney, M. Mrs. Budley falls from grace

Chesney, M. Sir Philip's folly

Christie, A. Three blind mice

Cisneros, S. The house on Mango Street

Clark, M. H. The Anastasia syndrome

Cocteau, J. The impostor

Colette. Gigi. Julie de Carneilhan. Chance acquaintances

Colette. The kepi

Colette. Six novels

Colette. The tender shoot

Conrad, J. Almayer's folly

Conrad, J. Heart of darkness

Conrad, J. Secret agent

Conrad, J. Tales of land and sea

Conrad, J. Youth

Coward, N. Bon voyage

Crane, S. The complete novels of Stephen Crane

Davies, V. Miracle on 34th Street

Delany, S. R. The star pit

Desai, A. Fire on the mountain

Dickens, C. A Charles Dickens Christmas

Dickens, C. A Christmas carol

Dickens, C. The cricket on the hearth

Doctorow, E. L. Lives of the poets [novelette]

Dostoyevsky, F. The gambler

Dostoyevsky, F. Notes from underground

Dostoyevsky, F. Poor people

Dostoyevsky, F. The short novels of Dostoevsky

Duras, M. Blue eyes, black hair

Duras, M. The lover

Elkin, S. Her sense of timing

Elkin, S. Town Crier exclusive, Confessions of a Princess manqué

Elkin, S. Van Gogh's room at Arles

Fitzgerald, F. S. May Day

Fitzgerald, F. S. The rich boy

Fleming, I. For your eyes only

Fleming, I. From a view to a kill

Fleming, I. The Hildebrand rarity

Fleming, I. Quantum of solace

Fleming, I. Risico

Fuentes, C. Apollo and the whores

Fuentes, C. The orange tree

Fuentes, C. Sons of the Conquistador

Fuentes, C. The two Americas

Fuentes, C. The two Numantias

Fuentes, C. The two shores

Gallico, P. The small miracle

Gallico, P. The snow goose

Gallico, P. Three legends: The snow goose; The small miracle; Ludmila

Galsworthy, J. The Indian summer of a Forsyte

García Márquez, G. Chronicle of a death foretold

García Márquez, G. Collected novellas

García Márquez, G. The incredible and sad tale of innocent Eréndira and her heartless grandmother

García Márquez, G. Leaf storm

García Márquez, G. No one writes to the colonel

Gardner, E. S. The cat-woman

Gardner, E. S. Come and get it

Gardner, E. S. Dead men's letters

Gardner, E. S. Grinning gods

Gardner, E. S. In full of account

Gardner, E. S. Laugh that off

Gardner, E. S. This way out

Gardner, E. S. The wax dragon

Gardner, E. S. Yellow shadows

Gibbons, K. Ellen Foster

Gibbons, K. A virtuous woman

Godwin, G. Mr. Bedford

Goethe, J. W. von. Novella

Golding, W. The scorpion god: three short novels

Gordon, M. Immaculate man

Gordon, M. Living at home

Gordon, M. The rest of life

Gorman, E. Death ground

Greenberg, J. With the Snow Queen

Gurganus, A. Blessed assurance: a moral tale

Gurganus, A. A hog loves its life: something about my grandfather

Hale, E. E. The man without a country

Hammett, D. Woman in the dark

Hamner, E. The homecoming

Handke, P. The left-handed woman

Harrison, J. The beige dolorosa

Harrison, J. Julip

Harrison, J. The seven-ounce man

Helprin, M. Ellis Island

Hemingway, E. The Hemingway reader

Hemingway, E. The old man and the sea

Hemingway, E. The torrents of spring

Hilton, J. Good-bye Mr. Chips

The Hugo winners

James, H. The Aspern papers

James, H. The complete tales of Henry James

NOVELETTES—*Continued*

James, H. The Henry James reader
James, H. Short novels of Henry James
James, H. What Maisie knew, In the cage, The pupil
Kafka, F. Metamorphosis
Kawabata, Y. Snow country, and Thousand cranes
Kawabata, Y. Thousand cranes
Kelly, J. P. Mr. Boy
Kessel, J. The Franchise
King, S. Different seasons
King, S. Four past midnight
Kress, N. And wild for to hold
L'Amour, L. The tall stranger
Le Guin, U. K. Planet of exile
Le Guin, U. K. The word for world is forest
Lessing, D. M. The fifth child
Lessing, D. M. The other woman
Levin, I. The Stepford wives
London, J. The call of the wild
Lovecraft, H. P. The mound
Mann, T. The black swan
Mann, T. Death in Venice
Mann, T. Tonio Kröger
Mann, T. Tristan
McCaffrey, A. The girl who heard dragons
McCaffrey, A. The greatest love
McCullers, C. The ballad of the sad café [novelette]
McEwan, I. Black dogs
McInerny, R. M. Four on the floor
Melville, H. Billy Budd, sailor
Mérimée, P. Carmen
Minot, S. Monkeys
Modern classic short novels of science fiction
Moore, B. Catholics
Morrow, J. City of Truth
Nebula awards [1]-29
Nin, A. Cities of the interior
Oates, J. C. Black water
Oates, J. C. I lock my door upon myself
Oates, J. C. The model
Oates, J. C. The rise of life on earth
Ozick, C. The Messiah of Stockholm
Ozick, C. Rosa
Poe, E. A. The imaginary voyages: The narrative of Arthur Gordon Pym; The unparalleled adventure of one Hans Pfaall; The journal of Julius Rodman
Poe, E. A. The narrative of Arthur Gordon Pym of Nantucket
Pohl, F. The merchants of Venus
Porter, K. A. Noon wine
Porter, K. A. Old mortality
Porter, K. A. Pale horse, pale rider [novelette]
Porter, K. A. Pale horse, pale rider: three short novels
Pym, B. Civil to strangers
Rand, A. Anthem
Rendell, R. Heartstones
Roth, P. The Prague orgy
Russ, J. Souls
Sagan, F. Bonjour tristesse
Salinger, J. D. Franny and Zooey
Salinger, J. D. Raise high the roof beam, carpenters, and Seymour: an introduction
Sand, G. Marianne
Sargent, P. Danny goes to Mars
Sarton, M. The fur person
Segal, E. Love story
Sheffield, C. Georgia on my mind
Shepard, L. A traveler's tale
Silverberg, R. Sailing to Byzantium
Simenon, G. Five times Maigret
Simenon, G. Maigret and the fortune-teller
Simenon, G. Maigret and the Saturday caller
Simenon, G. Maigret cinq
Simenon, G. Maigret goes home
Simenon, G. Maigret in court
Simenon, G. Maigret on the Riviera
Simenon, G. The murderer
Singer, I. B. Reaches of heaven

Smiley, J. The age of grief [novelette]
Smith, C. On the storm planet
Spark, M. The Abbess of Crewe
Spark, M. The driver's seat
Spark, M. The go-away bird
Spencer, E. Knights and dragons
Spencer, E. The light in the piazza
Steinbeck, J. Of mice and men
Steinbeck, J. The pearl
Steinbeck, J. The red pony
Stevenson, R. L. The beach of Falesá
Stevenson, R. L. The Merry Men
Stevenson, R. L. The misadventures of John Nicholson
Stevenson, R. L. The story of a lie
Stevenson, R. L. The strange case of Dr. Jekyll and Mr. Hyde
Stout, R. The cop-killer
Stout, R. Die like a dog
Stout, R. Door to death
Stout, R. Home to roost
Stout, R. Man alive
Stout, R. The next witness
Stout, R. Omit flowers
Stout, R. The squirt and the monkey
Stout, R. When a man murders
Straub, P. The buffalo hunter
Straub, P. Mrs. God
Styron, W. The long march
Theroux, P. Half Moon Street
Tolstoy, L., graf. The Kreutzer sonata
Tolstoy, L., graf. Master and man
Tolstoy, L., graf. The short novels of Tolstoy
Tolstoy, L., graf. Two hussars
Trevor, W. My house in Umbria
Trevor, W. Reading Turgenev
Turgenev, I. S. First love
Vance, J. The miracle workers
Welty, E. The Ponder heart
West, N. The dream life of Balso Snell
Westlake, D. E. Levine
Wharton, E. Fast and loose
Wharton, E. Old New York
Wiesel, E. Dawn
Wiesel, E. Night, Dawn, The accident: three tales
Wilhelm, K. Where late the sweet birds sang
Williams, T. The Roman spring of Mrs. Stone
Willis, C. Death on the Nile
Wolf, C. What remains
Wolfe, G. The death of Doctor Island
Wolfe, T. The lost boy
Wolfe, T. The short novels of Thomas Wolfe
Woodson, J. Autobiography of a family photo
Yoshimoto, B. Kitchen

NOVELISTS *See* Authors

Novella. Goethe, J. W. von
In Goethe, J. W. von. The sorrows of young Werther, and Novella p169-201

NOVELLAS *See* Novelettes

NOVELS, UNFINISHED *See* Unfinished novels
The **novels** of Dashiell Hammett. Hammett, D.
Now and then, amen. Cleary, J.
The **nowhere** city. Lurie, A.

NSC *See* United States. National Security Council

NUCLEAR BOMB *See* Atomic bomb

NUCLEAR ENERGY
Anderson, P. Orion shall rise

NUCLEAR POWER *See* Nuclear energy

NUCLEAR POWER PLANTS
Pohl, F. Chernobyl

NUCLEAR SUBMARINES
Clancy, T. The hunt for Red October
DiMercurio, M. Attack of the Seawolf
MacLean, A. Ice Station Zebra

NUCLEAR WARFARE
    See also Atomic bomb
Bova, B. Millennium
Brin, D. The postman
Burdick, E. Fail-safe
Frank, P. Alas, Babylon
Shute, N. On the beach
West, M. L. The clowns of God

NUCLEAR WEAPONS
Coonts, S. The red horseman
Forsyth, F. The fourth protocol
Nun of the above. Quill, M.
Nun plussed. Quill, M.

NUNS
    See also Ex-nuns
Barrett, W. E. The lilies of the field
Battle, L. The past is another country
Godden, R. Black Narcissus
Godden, R. In this house of Brede
Hulme, K. The nun's story
L'Engle, M. The love letters
Maitland, S. Ancestral truths
Russ, J. Souls
Sheldon, S. The sands of time
Spark, M. The Abbess of Crewe
Nuns and soldiers. Murdoch, I.
The **nun's** story. Hulme, K.

NURSEMAIDS
Dickinson, P. Play dead
Nursery crimes. Gill, B. M.

NURSES AND NURSING
Cook, R. Terminal
Denker, H. Mrs. Washington and Horowitz, too
Faulkner, W. Soldiers' pay
Fleming, T. J. Over there
Hamilton, J. A map of the world
Hemingway, E. A farewell to arms
Holt, V. Secret for a nightingale
Hulme, K. The nun's story
Kesey, K. One flew over the cuckoo's nest
McCullough, C. An indecent obsession
Oates, J. C. The rise of life on earth
Ondaatje, M. The English patient
Rinehart, M. R. Miss Pinkerton: adventures of a nurse detective
Ross-Macdonald, M. All desires known

O

O Beulah Land. Settle, M. L.
The **O.** Henry awards. See Prize stories, 1919-1995: The O. Henry awards
O little town of Maggody. Hess, J.
O pioneers!. Cather, W.
    also in Cather, W. Early novels and stories p133-290
O shepherd, speak! Sinclair, U.
    In Sinclair, U. [Lanny Budd series]

OAKLAND (CALIF.) *See* California—Oakland
The **oath.** Wiesel, E.

OBESITY
Dawson, C. Body of knowledge
Walters, M. The sculptress

      Psychological aspects
    See also Anorexia nervosa
Object lessons. Quindlen, A.
The **obstacle** course. Freedman, J. F.

OBSTETRICIANS *See* Physicians
An **occasion** of sin. Greeley, A. M.

OCCULTISM
    See also Supernatural phenomena; Superstition; Witchcraft
Eco, U. Foucault's pendulum

Frost, M. The list of 7
King, S. Firestarter
Riley, J. M. The oracle glass
Shannon, D. The Manson curse

OCEAN
Silverberg, R. The Face of the Waters
Verne, J. Twenty thousand leagues under the sea

OCEAN TRAVEL
    See also Whaling; Yachts and yachting
Aiken, C. Blue voyage
Coward, N. Bon voyage
Gallico, P. The Poseidon adventure
Golding, W. Close quarters
Golding, W. Fire down below
Golding, W. Rites of passage
McCutchan, P. The last farewell
Moberg, V. The emigrants
Porter, K. A. Ship of fools
Sagan, F. The painted lady
Van Slyke, H. A necessary woman
Villars, E. The Normandie affair
Woolf, V. The voyage out

OCEANIA *See* Islands of the Pacific

OCTAVIAN *See* Augustus, Emperor of Rome, 63 B.C.-14 A.D.

October light. Gardner, J.
The **octopus.** Norris, F.
The **odd** woman. Godwin, G.
Odds against. Francis, D.
    also in Francis, D. Three to show p495-774
Odds on Miss Seeton. Carvic, H.
The **Odessa** file. Forsyth, F.
    also in Forsyth, F. Forsyth's three
Of human bondage. Maugham, W. S.
Of love and shadows. Allende, I.
Of mice and men. Steinbeck, J.
    also in Steinbeck, J. The portable Steinbeck p225-323
Of mist, and grass, and sand. McIntyre, V. N.
    In The Best of the Nebulas p478-93
Of such small differences. Greenberg, J.
Of the farm. Updike, J.
Of time and the river. Wolfe, T.
Officer down. Grant, M.
Officers and gentlemen. Waugh, E.
The **officers'** wives. Fleming, T. J.
Oh, what a paradise it seems. Cheever, J.

OHIO
Santmyer, H. H. "—and ladies of the club"

      18th century
Richter, C. The awakening land
Richter, C. The trees

      19th century
Anderson, S. Poor white
Anderson, S. Tar: a midwest childhood
Anderson, S. Winesburg, Ohio
Richter, C. The awakening land
Richter, C. The fields
Richter, C. The town

      20th century
DeMille, N. Spencerville
Dove, R. Through the ivory gate
Gold, H. Family
Gold, H. Fathers
Morrison, T. The bluest eye
Morrison, T. Sula
Smith, S. B. A simple plan
Vonnegut, K. Deadeye Dick

      Farm life
    See Farm life—Ohio

      Frontier and pioneer life
    See Frontier and pioneer life—Ohio

      Cleveland
Horowitz, E. Plain Jane

OHIO RIVER VALLEY
Richter, C. The trees
Settle, M. L. O Beulah Land

Frontier and pioneer life

See Frontier and pioneer life—Ohio River Valley

OIL INDUSTRY *See* Petroleum industry

OIL WELLS *See* Petroleum industry

OJIBWA INDIANS *See* Chippewa Indians

OKINAWA (JAPAN) *See* Japan—Okinawa

OKLAHOMA

19th century

Ferber, E. Cimarron

20th century

Hunter, S. Dirty white boys

Frontier and pioneer life

See Frontier and pioneer life—Oklahoma

Politics

See Politics—Oklahoma

OLD AGE
Amis, K. The old devils
Bawden, N. Family money
Bradford, B. T. Hold the dream
Bromfield, L. Mrs. Parkington
Brookner, A. Fraud
Cary, J. The horse's mouth
Cheever, J. Oh, what a paradise it seems
Coetzee, J. M. Age of iron
Conrad, J. The end of the tether
De Hartog, J. The outer buoy
Denker, H. Mrs. Washington and Horowitz, too
Edgerton, C. Walking across Egypt
Elkin, S. Mrs. Ted Bliss
Galsworthy, J. The Indian summer of a Forsyte
Galsworthy, J. Swan song
García Márquez, G. No one writes to the colonel
Gardner, J. October light
Godden, J. In her garden
Gordon, M. Final payments
Greenfeld, J. Harry and Tonto
Gurganus, A. The oldest living Confederate widow
tells all
Hemingway, E. The old man and the sea
Hilton, J. Good-bye Mr. Chips
Kawabata, Y. The sound of the mountain
King, S. Insomnia
Malamud, B. Dubin's lives
McFarland, D. School for the blind
McMurtry, L. The evening star
Michener, J. A. Recessional
Puig, M. Eternal curse on the reader of these pages
Puig, M. Tropical night falling
Robertson, D. Praise the human season
Sackville-West, V. All passion spent
Sarton, M. As we are now
Sarton, M. The education of Harriet Hatfield
Sarton, M. Kinds of love
Scott, P. Staying on
Smith, R. K. Sadie Shapiro's knitting book
Spark, M. Memento mori
Stegner, W. E. The spectator bird
Taylor, E. Mrs. Palfrey at the Claremont
Trollope, J. The men and the girls
Updike, J. The poorhouse fair
Wharton, W. Dad
White, P. The eye of the storm
Wiesel, E. The forgotten

OLD AGE HOMES
See also Retirement communities
Sarton, M. As we are now
Smith, R. K. Sadie Shapiro's knitting book
Updike, J. The poorhouse fair

The **Old** Contemptibles. Grimes, M.
The **old** curiosity shop. Dickens, C.
The **old** devils. Amis, K.
The **old** fox deceiv'd. Grimes, M.
Old Goriot. Balzac, H. de
The **old** gringo. Fuentes, C.
The **old** house at Railes. Pearce, M. E.

OLD LADIES *See* Old age
The **old** maid. Wharton, E.
In Wharton, E. Old New York

OLD MAIDS *See* Single women
The **old** man and the sea. Hemingway, E.
The **old** man dies. Simenon, G.

OLD MEN *See* Old age
Old mortality. Porter, K. A.
In Porter, K. A. The collected stories of Katherine
Anne Porter p173-221
In Porter, K. A. Pale horse, pale rider: three short
novels p3-89
Old New York. Wharton, E.

OLD NORTHWEST
Roberts, K. L. Northwest Passage
The **old** priory. Lofts, N.
Old scores. Elkins, A. J.
The **Old** Silent. Grimes, M.

OLD SOUTHWEST
Richter, C. The sea of grass

OLD WOMEN *See* Old age
Old Yeller. Gipson, F. B.
The **oldest** living Confederate widow tells all. Gurganus,
A.
Oldtown folks. Stowe, H. B.
In Stowe, H. B. Uncle Tom's cabin; The minister's
wooing; Oldtown Folks p877-1468
Oliver Twist. Dickens, C.
Oliver Wiswell. Roberts, K. L.
Olivia. Rossner, J.
Omit flowers. Stout, R.
In Stout, R. Five of a kind p356-98
Omoo: a narrative of adventures in the South Seas. Mel-
ville, H.
also in Melville, H. Typee; Omoo; Mardi
On a pale horse. Anthony, P.
On dangerous ground. Higgins, J.
On Her Majesty's Secret Service. Fleming, I.
On the beach. Shute, N.
On the edge. Lovesey, P.
On the inside. Wood, T.
On the river Styx and other stories. Matthiessen, P.
On the road. Kerouac, J.
On the seaboard. See Strindberg, A. By the open sea
On the storm planet. Smith, C.
In Modern classic short novels of science fiction
p94-163
The **once** and future king. White, T. H.
One clear call. Sinclair, U.
In Sinclair, U. [Lanny Budd series]
One corpse too many. Peters, E.
also in Peters, E. The benediction of Brother Cadfael
p211-348
One day in the life of Ivan Denisovich. Solzhenitsyn,
A.
One fearful yellow eye. MacDonald, J. D.
One fine day the rabbi bought a cross. Kemelman, H.
One flew over the cuckoo's nest. Kesey, K.
One for the money. Evanovich, J.
One hundred years of solitude. García Márquez, G.
One more river. See Galsworthy, J. Over the river
One more Sunday. MacDonald, J. D.
One of ours. Cather, W.
also in Cather, W. Early novels and stories p939-
1298

One Police Plaza. Caunitz, W. J.
One summer. Robards, K.
The **One** Tree. Donaldson, S. R.
One true thing. Quindlen, A.
One very hot day. Halberstam, D.
Only children. Lurie, A.

ONTARIO *See* Canada—Ontario

OPALS
  Holt, V. The pride of the peacock
Open secrets. Munro, A.

OPERA
  Davies, R. The lyre of Orpheus
  Li, P.-H. Farewell to my concubine
  Pearson, D. Voices of summer
Operation Chaos. Anderson, P.

OPERATION DESERT STORM *See* Persian Gulf War, 1991

Operation Shylock. Roth, P.

OPERATIONS, SURGICAL *See* Surgery

OPIUM WAR, 1840-1842 *See* China—War of 1840-1842

OPPENHEIMER, J. ROBERT, 1904-1967
  Smith, M. C. Stallion Gate

OPPENHEIMER, ROBERT *See* Oppenheimer, J. Robert, 1904-1967
The **optimist's** daughter. Welty, E.
Options. Henry, O.
  In Henry, O. The complete works of O. Henry p680-810
The **oracle** glass. Riley, J. M.
Oral history. Smith, L.

ORAN (ALGERIA) *See* Algeria—Oran
The **orange** tree. Fuentes, C.
Orchestrated death. Harrod-Eagles, C.
The **ordeal** of Richard Feverel. Meredith, G.
Ordinary love. Smiley, J.
  In Smiley, J. Ordinary love & Good will
Ordinary love & Good will. Smiley, J.
Ordinary people. Guest, J.
The **Ordways.** Humphrey, W.

OREGON
  Brin, D. The postman
  Duncan, D. J. The brothers K
  Kesey, K. Sometimes a great notion

ORIENT AND OCCIDENT *See* East and West
Orient Express. Greene, G.
Original sins. Alther, L.
Orion and the conqueror. Bova, B.
Orion in the dying time. Bova, B.
Orion shall rise. Anderson, P.

ORISKANY, BATTLE OF, 1777
  Edmonds, W. D. Drums along the Mohawk
Orlando. Woolf, V.

ORLÉANS, CHARLES D' *See* Charles, d'Orléans, 1394-1465

ORPHANS
  Allende, I. Eva Luna
  Auster, P. Mr. Vertigo
  Brent, M. Moonraker's bride
  Brontë, C. Emma
  Brontë, C. Jane Eyre
  Brontë, E. Wuthering Heights
  Brown, J. D. Addie Pray
  Brown, R. Civil wars
  Capote, T. The grass harp
  Cronin, A. J. A song of sixpence
  Dickens, C. Great expectations
  Dickens, C. The old curiosity shop
  Dickens, C. Oliver Twist
  Doctorow, E. L. The book of Daniel
  Durham, M. Dutch uncle
  Edmonds, W. D. Chad Hanna
  Ferber, E. Ice Palace
  Gallico, P. The small miracle

  Gilman, D. Incident at Badamya
  Goldman, F. The long night of white chickens
  Grau, S. A. Roadwalkers
  Harris, M. Lost and found
  Hoeg, P. Borderliners
  Holt, V. The black opal
  Holt, V. The Judas kiss
  Irving, J. The cider house rules
  Michaels, B. Greygallows
  Nin, A. Children of the albatross
  Orde, L. Dreams of gold
  Ozick, C. The Messiah of Stockholm
  Sholem Aleichem. The adventures of Mottel, the cantor's son
  Spellman, C. C. Paint the wind
  Tevis, W. S. The queen's gambit
  Wood, B. The dreaming
Orsinian tales. Le Guin, U. K.
The **O'Ruddy.** Crane, S.
  In Crane, S. The complete novels of Stephen Crane p593-790

OSAGE INDIANS
  Jones, D. C. Remember Santiago

O'SULLIVAN BEARE, DONAL CAM, 1560-1618
  Llywelyn, M. The last prince of Ireland
O'Sullivan's march. See Llywelyn, M. The last prince of Ireland

OSWALD, LEE HARVEY
  DeLillo, D. Libra
The **other.** Tryon, T.
Other people's marriages. Thomas, R.
The **other** side. Gordon, M.
The **other** side of love. Briskin, J.
The **other** side of the door. O'Donnell, L.
The **other** side of the sun. L'Engle, M.
Other voices, other rooms. Capote, T.
The **other** woman. Lessing, D. M.
  In Lessing, D. M. Stories p157-211
The **other** woman. McGown, J.
Our Lady of the Flowers. Genet, J.
Our man in Havana. Greene, G.
Our mutual friend. Dickens, C.
Out of India. Jhabvala, R. P.
Out of Phaze. Anthony, P.
Out of the blackout. Barnard, R.
Out of the silent planet. Lewis, C. S.
Out on the cutting edge. Block, L.
Outbreak. Cook, R.
The **outcast.** Pirandello, L.
Outcasts. Brand, M.
  In Brand, M. Max Brand's best western stories v2

OUTDOOR LIFE
  See also Country life; Wilderness survival
Outer banks. Siddons, A. R.
The **outer** buoy. De Hartog, J.

OUTER SPACE
  See also Space flight

            Communication
  See Interstellar communication

            Exploration
  Anderson, P. The Saturn game
Outerbridge Reach. Stone, R.

OUTLAWS
  See also Brigands and robbers
  Bonner, C. Lily
  Bonner, C. Looking after Lily
  Estleman, L. D. City of widows
  Gorman, E. Death ground
  Henry, W. Mackenna's gold
  Jones, D. C. The search for Temperance Moon
  L'Amour, L. The man from the broken hills
  L'Amour, L. The outlaws of Mesquite
  L'Amour, L. Over on the dry side
  McMurtry, L. Anything for Billy
  McMurtry, L. Pretty Boy Floyd

OUTLAWS—*Continued*
McMurtry, L. Streets of Laredo
The **outlaws** of Mesquite. L'Amour, L.
The **outsider.** Fast, H.
The **outsider.** Wright, R.
   also in Wright, R. Works
The **outsider.** See Camus, A. The stranger
Outsider in Amsterdam. Van de Wetering, J.
Over on the dry side. L'Amour, L.
Over the edge. Kellerman, J.
Over the river. Galsworthy, J.
   In Galsworthy, J. End of the chapter p593-897
Over there. Fleming, T. J.
The **overcoat,** and other tales of good and evil. Gogol', N. V.
Overhead in a balloon. Gallant, M.

OVERLAND JOURNEYS
Bristow, G. Jubilee Trail
Hunter, E. The Chisholms
Wolitzer, H. Hearts

OVERLAND JOURNEYS TO THE PACIFIC
Guthrie, A. B. The way West
Taylor, R. L. The travels of Jaimie McPheeters
An **owl** too many. MacLeod, C.
The **Ox-bow** incident. Clark, W. V. T.

OXFORD (ENGLAND) *See* England—Oxford
Oxford blood. Fraser, A.

The **Oxford** book of American short stories. Entered in Part I under title

The **Oxford** book of English ghost stories. Entered in Part I under title

The **Oxford** book of gothic tales. Entered in Part I under title

The **Oxford** book of Irish short stories. Entered in Part I under title

The **Oxford** book of modern fairy tales. Entered in Part I under title

The **Oxford** book of science fiction stories. Entered in Part I under title

The **Oxford** book of short stories. Entered in Part I under title

OXFORD UNIVERSITY *See* University of Oxford

OXFORDSHIRE (ENGLAND) *See* England—Oxfordshire

P

Pacific beat. Parker, T. J.

PACIFIC NORTHWEST
Doig, I. The sea runners
Tilly, M. Singing songs

PACIFIC OCEAN

World War, 1939-1945
   See World War, 1939-1945—Pacific Ocean
Pacific Street. Holland, C.

PACIFISM *See* Conscientious objectors

PACK, ELIZABETH THORPE
Aaron, D. Crossing by night
Pack of cards and other stories. Lively, P.
Paco's story. Heinemann, L.
Paddy Clarke, ha ha ha. Doyle, R.

PAGANISM
Asch, S. The prophet
Lawrence, D. H. The plumed serpent (Quetzalcoatl)
Renault, M. The king must die
Sienkiewicz, H. Quo vadis
Vidal, G. Julian
Waltari, M. The Etruscan

PAGEANTS
Woolf, V. Between the acts

Paid and loving eyes. Gash, J.

PAIN
   See also Suffering

PAINE, THOMAS, 1737-1809
Fast, H. Citizen Tom Paine
Paint the wind. Spellman, C. C.
The **painted** bird. Kosinski, J. N.
The **painted** lady. Sagan, F.
Painted lives. Allen, C. V.

PAINTERS
Aiken, C. Conversation
Cary, J. The horse's mouth
Clark, M. H. A cry in the night
Colwin, L. Family happiness
Crane, S. The third violet
Durrell, L. Clea
Eden, D. The vines of Yarrabee
Farmer, P. J. Riders of the purple wage
Gallico, P. The snow goose
Godwin, G. Violet Clay
Graham, W. The walking stick
Gray, F. du P. World without end
Hawthorne, N. The marble faun
Hemingway, E. Islands in the stream
Ishiguro, K. An artist of the floating world
James, H. The Europeans
Kipling, R. The light that failed
Krantz, J. Mistral's daughter
Lofts, N. The day of the butterfly
Mason, R. The world of Suzie Wong
Maugham, W. S. The moon and sixpence
Momaday, N. S. The ancient child
Murdoch, I. Nuns and soldiers
Nathan, R. Portrait of Jennie
Potok, C. The gift of Asher Lev
Potok, C. My name is Asher Lev
Roberts, K. L. Northwest Passage
Sarton, M. Joanna and Ulysses
Siddons, A. R. Hill towns
Stone, I. Lust for life
Styron, W. Set this house on fire
Wharton, W. Dad
White, P. The vivisector
Whitney, P. A. The golden unicorn

PAINTINGS
Banks, O. T. The Caravaggio obsession
Plante, D. Annunciation

PAKISTAN
Rushdie, S. Shame
Palace of desire. Maḥfūz, N.
The **palace** thief. Canin, E.
Palace walk. Maḥfūz, N.
Pale fire. Nabokov, V. V.
The **pale** horse. Christie, A.
Pale horse, pale rider [novelette]. Porter, K. A.
   In Porter, K. A. The collected stories of Katherine Anne Porter p269-317
   In Porter, K. A. Pale horse, pale rider: three short novels p179-264
Pale horse, pale rider: three short novels. Porter, K. A.
   also in Porter, K. A. The collected stories of Katherine Anne Porter p173-317
Pale kings and princes. Parker, R. B.

PALEONTOLOGISTS
Lively, P. Cleopatra's sister
Vine, B. No night is too long

PALESTINE
   See also Israel; Jerusalem

To 70 A.D.
Asch, S. The Apostle
Asch, S. Mary
Asch, S. The Nazarene
Caldwell, T. Dear and glorious physician
Caldwell, T. Great lion of God
Caldwell, T. I, Judas

PALESTINE—To 70 A.D.—*Continued*
Costain, T. B. The silver chalice
Douglas, L. C. The Big Fisherman
Douglas, L. C. The robe
Holmes, M. The Messiah
Holmes, M. Three from Galilee
Martin, M. King of kings
Wallace, L. Ben-Hur

11th century
Oldenbourg, Z. The heirs of the kingdom

12th century
Scott, Sir W. The talisman

20th century
Freeman, C. No time for tears
Uris, L. Exodus
Wiesel, E. Dawn

PALESTINIAN ARABS
See also Jewish-Arab relations
Keneally, T. Flying hero class
Palindrome. Woods, S.
The **Pallisers.** Trollope, A.
PALM BEACH (FLA.) *See* Florida—Palm Beach
A **palm** for Mrs. Pollifax. Gilman, D.
PALM SPRINGS (CALIF.) *See* California—Palm Springs
Paloverde. Briskin, J.
Pamela. Richardson, S.

PANAGOULIS, ALEXANDER
Fallaci, O. A man
Pandora's box. Gage, E.
Panther in the sky. Thom, J. A.
PAPACY *See* Catholic faith; Popes
Paper doll. Parker, R. B.
The **paper** men. Golding, W.
Paper money. Follett, K.
The **paperboy.** Dexter, P.
PAPERS *See* Manuscripts
Parable of the sower. Butler, O. E.

PARABLES
See also Allegories
Appelfeld, A. Tzili, the story of a life
Butler, O. E. Parable of the sower
Girzone, J. F. Joshua and the children
Girzone, J. F. Joshua in the Holy Land
Girzone, J. F. The shepherd
Goethe, J. W. von. Novella
Grass, G. Dog years
Han, S. The enchantress
Hemingway, E. The old man and the sea
Hoban, R. Pilgermann
Kosinski, J. N. Being there
Llywelyn, M. The elementals
Oates, J. C. I lock my door upon myself
Shaw, I. Acceptable losses
Spark, M. The Abbess of Crewe
Steinbeck, J. East of Eden
Steinbeck, J. The pearl
Vonnegut, K. Deadeye Dick
Vonnegut, K. Galápagos
Weldon, F. The life and loves of a she-devil
Wiesel, E. The gates of the forest
Parade's end. Ford, F. M.
Paradise. McNaught, J.
Paradise. McNaught, J.
Paradise postponed. Mortimer, J. C.
Paragon Walk. Perry, A.

PARALYSIS
See also Paraplegics

PARANOIA
Achebe, C. Anthills of the Savannah
Pynchon, T. Vineland

PARAPLEGICS
Kellogg, M. Tell me that you love me, Junie Moon

PARENT AND CHILD
See also Conflict of generations; Fathers and daughters; Fathers and sons; Mothers and daughters; Mothers and sons
Banks, R. Affliction
Beattie, A. Picturing Will
Brookner, A. Family and friends
Brown, R. Before and after
Card, O. S. Lost boys
Carroll, J. Fault lines
Clark, M. H. Remember me
Dart, I. R. The Stork Club
Dew, R. F. Fortunate lives
Doctorow, E. L. The book of Daniel
Godden, R. The battle of the Villa Fiorita
Greene, G. The captain and the enemy
James, H. What Maisie knew
Lessing, D. M. The fifth child
Levenkron, S. The best little girl in the world
Lurie, A. Only children
Lurie, A. The war between the Tates
Miller, S. Family pictures
Plain, B. Daybreak
Price, R. Blue Calhoun
Rubens, B. A solitary grief
Russell, P. Sea of tranquillity
Smiley, J. Good will
Spencer, L. Home song
Steel, D. Accident
Straight, S. I been in sorrow's kitchen and licked out all the pots
Tarkington, B. Alice Adams
Tyler, A. The clock winder
Tyler, A. Dinner at the Homesick Restaurant
Weldon, F. The hearts and lives of men
West, P. Love's mansion
Whitney, P. A. The golden unicorn
Wolitzer, H. Hearts
Pargeters. Lofts, N.

PARIS (FRANCE) *See* France—Paris
Paris Trout. Dexter, P.

PARK, MUNGO, 1771-1806
Boyle, T. C. Water music
Parker Pyne investigates. See Christie, A. Mr. Parker Pyne, detective

PARKS
See also Amusement parks; Zoos

PARLIAMENT (GREAT BRITAIN) *See* Great Britain. Parliament

PARMA (ITALY) *See* Italy—Parma

PAROCHIAL SCHOOLS *See* Church schools

PARODIES
See also Arabian nights and names of prominent authors with the subdivision Parodies, travesties, etc.
Berger, T. Arthur Rex
Berger, T. Who is Teddy Villanova?
Fielding, H. Joseph Andrews
Hemingway, E. The torrents of spring
Nabokov, V. V. Lolita

PARR, KATHERINE *See* Catharine Parr, Queen, consort of Henry VIII, King of England, 1512-1548

PARRICIDE
Oates, J. C. Expensive people

PARROTS
Barnes, J. Flaubert's parrot
The **Parsifal** mosaic. Ludlum, R.
Parson's pleasure. Hardwick, M.

PARTIES
See also Birthdays
Dickinson, P. The last houseparty
Huxley, A. Crome Yellow
Oates, J. C. Unholy loves
Peters, E. The murders of Richard III
Pilcher, R. September

PARTISANS *See* Guerrillas
The **party** at Jack's. Wolfe, T.
  In Wolfe, T. The short novels of Thomas Wolfe p282-323
A **passage** to India. Forster, E. M.
Passing on. Lively, P.
Passing strange. Aird, C.
Passion play. Kosinski, J. N.

PASSION WEEK *See* Holy Week
The **passions** of the mind. Stone, I.
The **past** is another country. Battle, L.
Past regret. Babson, M.
Pastime. Parker, R. B.

PASTORS *See* Clergy

PATENT MEDICINES *See* Medicines, Patent, proprietary, etc.
The **Pathfinder.** Cooper, J. F.
  also in Cooper, J. F. The Leatherstocking tales v2 p1-482

PATHOLOGISTS *See* Physicians
Patience of a saint. Greeley, A. M.
The **patience** of Maigret. See Simenon, G. Maigret's war of nerves
The **patriarch.** Bermant, C.
The **patriot** game. Higgins, G. V.
Patriot games. Clancy, T.

PATRIOTISM
  Eden, D. The Salamanca drum
  Forester, C. S. The last nine days of the Bismarck
  Hale, E. E. The man without a country
  Mishima, Y. Runaway horses
Pattern crimes. Bayer, W.

PAUL, THE APOSTLE, SAINT
  Asch, S. The Apostle
  Caldwell, T. Great lion of God
Pauline's passion and punishment. Alcott, L. M.
  In Alcott, L. M. Behind a mask: the unknown thrillers of Louisa May Alcott p105-52
Pavilion of women. Buck, P. S.
Pawn in frankincense. Dunnett, D.
The **pawnbroker.** Wallant, E. L.

PAWNBROKERS
  Wallant, E. L. The pawnbroker
Payment in blood. George, E.
Paz. Balzac, H. de
  In Balzac, H. de. The short novels of Balzac

PEA RIDGE, BATTLE OF, 1862
  Jones, D. C. Elkhorn Tavern
Peace breaks out. Knowles, J.
The **peaceable** kingdom. De Hartog, J.
Peachtree Road. Siddons, A. R.
The **pearl.** Steinbeck, J.

PEARL FISHING
  Steinbeck, J. The pearl

PEARLS
  Browne, G. A. 18mm blues
  Steinbeck, J. The pearl

PEASANT LIFE
                    China
  Buck, P. S. Dragon seed
  Buck, P. S. The good earth
                   Ireland
  Uris, L. Trinity
                    Italy
  Silone, I. Bread and wine
                    Korea
  Potok, C. I am the clay
                   Russia
  Sholokhov, M. A. The Don flows home to the sea
  Tolstoy, L., graf. Master and man

                    Sicily
  Puzo, M. The Sicilian
The **peculiar** people. De Hartog, J.
Peder Victorious. Rölvaag, O. E.
Pegasus in flight. McCaffrey, A.
Pel and the missing persons. Hebden, M.
Pel and the party spirit. Hebden, M.
The **pelican** brief. Grisham, J.
Pelle the conqueror: v1 Childhood. Andersen Nexø, M.
Pelle the conqueror: v2 Apprenticeship. Andersen Nexø, M.
Pemberley. Tennant, E.
The **penal** colony: stories and short pieces. Kafka, F.
Penguin book of gay short fiction. Entered in Part I under title
The **Penguin** book of lesbian short stories. Entered in Part I under title
Penhallow. Heyer, G.

PENINSULAR WAR, 1807-1814
  Cornwell, B. Sharpe's company
  Cornwell, B. Sharpe's eagle
  Cornwell, B. Sharpe's enemy
  Cornwell, B. Sharpe's gold
  Cornwell, B. Sharpe's honour
  Cornwell, B. Sharpe's regiment
  Cornwell, B. Sharpe's revenge
  Cornwell, B. Sharpe's rifles
  Cornwell, B. Sharpe's siege
  Cornwell, B. Sharpe's sword
  Cornwell, B. Sharpe's Waterloo
  Forester, C. S. Commodore Hornblower
  Forester, C. S. Hornblower and the Hotspur
  Forester, C. S. Lieutenant Hornblower
  Forester, C. S. Ship of the line
  Graham, W. The twisted sword
The **penitent.** Singer, I. B.
Penmarric. Howatch, S.
Pennies on a dead woman's eyes. Muller, M.

PENNSYLVANIA
  See also Pocono Mountains (Pa.)
                 18th century
  De Hartog, J. The peaceable kingdom
                 19th century
  Bradley, D. The Chaneysville incident
  Jakes, J. Heaven and hell
  Jakes, J. Love and war
  Jakes, J. North and South
  O'Hara, J. Ten North Frederick
                 20th century
  Brown, R. M. Six of one
  Caldwell, T. Answer as a man
  Caldwell, T. Ceremony of the innocent
  Caldwell, T. Testimony of two men
  Del Vecchio, J. M. Carry me home
  Hijuelos, O. The fourteen sisters of Emilio Montez O'Brien
  King, S. Christine
  Marshall, C. Julie
  Michener, J. A. The novel
  Oates, J. C. Solstice
  O'Hara, J. From the terrace
  O'Hara, J. Ten North Frederick
  Richter, C. A simple honorable man
  Smiley, J. Good will
  Updike, J. The centaur
  Updike, J. Of the farm
  Updike, J. Rabbit at rest
  Updike, J. Rabbit is rich
  Updike, J. Rabbit redux
  Updike, J. Rabbit, run
  Wharton, W. Birdy

PENNSYLVANIA—*Continued*

Coal mines and mining

See Coal mines and mining—Pennsylvania

Farm life

See Farm life—Pennsylvania

Philadelphia

Amiel, J. A question of proof
Carr, R. Woman's own
Chase-Riboud, B. The President's daughter
Dexter, P. Brotherly love
Griffin, W. E. B. The murderers
Lopez, S. Third and Indiana
Roberts, N. Hidden riches
Wideman, J. E. Philadelphia fire

Valley Forge

Kantor, M. Valley Forge

PENSIONS

García Márquez, G. No one writes to the colonel
People like us. Dunne, D.
People of darkness. Hillerman, T.
also in Hillerman, T. The Jim Chee mysteries
People of the lakes. Gear, K. O.
People of the lightning. Gear, K. O.
People of the river. Gear, W. M.
People of the sea. Gear, W. M.
Perchance to dream. Parker, R. B.
Perelandra. Lewis, C. S.
The **Perez** family. Bell, C.
Perfect. McNaught, J.
Perfect gallows. Dickinson, P.
A **perfect** spy. Le Carré, J.

PERFORMERS *See* Entertainers
Perfume: the story of a murderer. Süskind, P.

PERFUMES

Blake, J. Wildest dreams
Peril at End House. Christie, A.
In Christie, A. Agatha Christie: five complete novels of murder and detection

PERIODICALS

Krantz, J. I'll take Manhattan
Siddons, A. R. Downtown
Perish in July. Hardwick, M.

PERSECUTION

See also Jews—Persecutions
Perseid. Barth, J.
In Barth, J. Chimera p57-134

PERSEUS (GREEK MYTHOLOGY)

Barth, J. Perseid

PERSIA *See* Iran
The **Persian** boy. Renault, M.

PERSIAN GULF WAR, 1991

Forsyth, F. The fist of God
The **persistence** of vision. Varley, J.
In The Best of the Nebulas p495-529
In The Hugo winners v4 p459-507

PERSONAL ADVERTISING *See* Personals
Personal recollections of Joan of Arc. Twain, M.
also in Twain, M. The complete novels of Mark Twain v2 p661-998

PERSONALITY

Ludlum, R. The Bourne identity
Ludlum, R. The Bourne supremacy
Theroux, P. Doctor DeMarr
Theroux, P. Doctor Slaughter
Tyler, A. Morgan's passing

PERSONALITY DISORDERS

See also Dual personality; Hallucinations and illusions; Insane, Criminal and dangerous; Multiple personality
Brownmiller, S. Waverly Place
Conroy, P. The prince of tides
Goldman, W. Magic

Levenkron, S. The best little girl in the world
Oates, J. C. The rise of life on earth
Thomas, D. M. The white hotel

PERSONALS

Clark, M. H. Loves music, loves to dance
Persuasion. Austen, J.
also in Austen, J. The complete novels of Jane Austen

PERU

18th century

Wilder, T. The bridge of San Luis Rey

20th century

Redfield, J. The celestine prophecy
Vargas Llosa, M. Captain Pantoja and the Special Service

Army—Officers

Vargas Llosa, M. Captain Pantoja and the Special Service

Lima

Vargas Llosa, M. Aunt Julia and the scriptwriter
Wilder, T. The bridge of San Luis Rey
Pet sematary. King, S.

PETER, THE APOSTLE, SAINT

Douglas, L. C. The Big Fisherman

PETROLEUM INDUSTRY

Ferber, E. Cimarron
Ferber, E. Giant
Fuentes, C. The Hydra head
McMurtry, L. Texasville
Sanders, L. The tangent factor

PETS

Delany, S. R. The star pit

PHARISEES

Asch, S. The Nazarene

PHARMACEUTICAL INDUSTRY

Cook, R. Mindbend
Hailey, A. Strong medicine
Reed, B. The choice
Wilson, F. P. The select

PHARMACISTS

See also Medicines, Patent, proprietary, etc.
Amado, J. Dona Flor and her two husbands
Beagle, P. S. A fine and private place
Cather, W. Shadows on the rock
McCullers, C. Clock without hands
Phaze doubt. Anthony, P.

PHILADELPHIA (PA.) *See* Pennsylvania—Philadelphia
Philadelphia fire. Wideman, J. E.

PHILANTHROPY *See* Endowments

PHILIP II, KING OF MACEDONIA, 382-336 B.C.

Renault, M. Fire from heaven

PHILOSOPHERS

Murdoch, I. The message to the planet
Murdoch, I. The philosopher's pupil
The **philosopher's** pupil. Murdoch, I.

PHILOSOPHICAL NOVELS

Ackroyd, P. English music
Amis, M. Time's arrow
Andrić, I. The bridge on the Drina
Auster, P. Leviathan
Barker, P. The eye in the door
Barker, P. Regeneration
Barnes, J. Flaubert's parrot
Barnes, J. A history of the world in 10½ chapters
Beauvoir, S. de. The mandarins
Beckett, S. Molloy, Malone dies, and The unnamable
Bellow, S. The dean's December
Bellow, S. Henderson the rain king
Bellow, S. Herzog
Bellow, S. Mr. Sammler's planet
Bellow, S. A theft

PHILOSOPHICAL NOVELS—*Continued*

Bellow, S. What kind of day did you have?
Bosse, M. J. Mister Touch
Bulgakov, M. A. The master and Margarita
Byatt, A. S. Morpho Eugenia
Calvino, I. If on a winter's night a traveler
Calvino, I. Mr. Palomar
Camus, A. The fall
Camus, A. A happy death
Cervantes Saavedra, M. de. The colloquy of the dogs
Cervantes Saavedra, M. de. Man of glass
Chesterton, G. K. The man who was Thursday
Coetzee, J. M. Age of iron
Coetzee, J. M. Foe
Coetzee, J. M. The master of Petersburg
Davies, R. The rebel angels
Doctorow, E. L. The waterworks
Dostoyevsky, F. Notes from underground
Drabble, M. The gates of ivory
Duncan, D. J. The brothers K
Durrell, L. Constance
Durrell, L. Quinx
Fowles, J. A maggot
Fuentes, C. The campaign
Gaddis, W. The recognitions
García Márquez, G. The general and his labyrinth
Gardner, J. Grendel
Gardner, J. The sunlight dialogues
Golding, W. Close quarters
Golding, W. Fire down below
Golding, W. The inheritors
Golding, W. Rites of passage
Greene, G. Monsignor Quixote
Helprin, M. A soldier of the great war
Hoban, R. Pilgermann
Hoban, R. Riddley Walker
Hoeg, P. Borderliners
Hulme, K. The bone people
Huxley, A. Eyeless in Gaza
Johnson, C. R. Middle passage
Kundera, M. Immortality
Kundera, M. The unbearable lightness of being
Le Guin, U. K. The dispossessed
Lewis, C. S. Out of the silent planet
Lewis, C. S. Perelandra
Lewis, C. S. That hideous strength
Lightman, A. P. Einstein's dreams
Lively, P. City of the mind
Maḥfūẓ, N. Adrift on the Nile
Maḥfūẓ, N. Palace of desire
Maḥfūẓ, N. Sugar Street
Maḥfūẓ, N. Wedding song
Malouf, D. Remembering Babylon
Mann, T. The magic mountain
Maugham, W. S. The razor's edge
McCarthy, C. All the pretty horses
McCarthy, M. Birds of America
McEwan, I. Black dogs
Melville, H. Mardi: and a voyager thither
Mishima, Y. The temple of the golden pavilion
Moore, B. Black robe
Murdoch, I. The book and the brotherhood
Murdoch, I. The good apprentice
Murdoch, I. The green knight
Murdoch, I. The message to the planet
Murdoch, I. The philosopher's pupil
Naylor, G. Linden Hills
Ōe, K. Nip the buds, shoot the kids
Ondaatje, M. The English patient
Oz, A. To know a woman
Ozick, C. The cannibal galaxy
Percy, W. The last gentleman
Percy, W. The moviegoer
Percy, W. The second coming
Percy, W. The thanatos syndrome
Phillips, C. Cambridge
Pirsig, R. M. Lila
Plante, D. Annunciation

Potok, C. I am the clay
Puig, M. Tropical night falling
Robbins, T. Skinny legs and all
Saint-Exupéry, A. de. The little prince
Santayana, G. The last Puritan
Sartre, J. P. Nausea
Stone, R. Outerbridge Reach
Updike, J. Roger's version
Vidal, G. Creation
Voltaire. Zadig
Vonnegut, K. Galápagos
Wiesel, E. The forgotten
Wiesel, E. Twilight
Winterson, J. Written on the body
Phineas Finn [abridged]. Trollope, A.
  In Trollope, A. The Pallisers p117-88
Phineas Redux [abridged]. Trollope, A.
  In Trollope, A. The Pallisers p265-323
PHOENIX (ARIZ.) *See* Arizona—Phoenix
Photo finish. Marsh, Dame N.

PHOTOGRAPHERS
  See also Women photographers
Allen, C. V. Dream train
Beattie, A. Picturing Will
Brink, A. P. An act of terror
Jakes, J. Homeland
McFarland, D. School for the blind
Theroux, P. Picture palace
Waller, R. J. The bridges of Madison County

PHYSICALLY HANDICAPPED
  See also Blind; Deaf; Hunchbacks; Paraplegics; Quadriplegics
Brown, C. Down all the days
Brown, R. Tender mercies
Elkin, S. Her sense of timing
Graham, W. The walking stick
Greenberg, J. Of such small differences
Maitland, S. Ancestral truths
Maugham, W. S. Of human bondage
McCullers, C. The ballad of the sad café [novelette]
Rendell, R. Live flesh
Stewart, M. Nine coaches waiting
Streshinsky, S. Hers the kingdom
Trumbo, D. Johnny got his gun

PHYSICIANS
  See also Psychiatrists; Surgeons; Veterinarians; Women physicians
Amis, K. The Green Man
Amis, M. Time's arrow
Balzac, H. de. The country doctor
Baum, V. Grand Hotel
Benford, G. Matter's end
Buck, P. S. East wind: west wind
Caldwell, T. Dear and glorious physician
Caldwell, T. Testimony of two men
Camus, A. The plague
Céline, L.-F. Journey to the end of the night
Clark, M. H. The cradle will fall
Collins, W. The rationalist
Cook, R. Brain
Cook, R. Coma
Cook, R. Fatal cure
Cook, R. Godplayer
Cook, R. Harmful intent
Cook, R. Mindbend
Cook, R. Terminal
Crichton, M. A case of need
Crichton, M. The terminal man
Cronin, A. J. The citadel
Cronin, A. J. A pocketful of rye
De Bernières, L. Corelli's mandolin
Doctorow, E. L. The waterworks
Douglas, L. C. Magnificent obsession
Durrell, L. Monsieur
Eliot, G. Middlemarch
Endō, S. The sea and poison
Fast, H. Seven days in June

PHYSICIANS—*Continued*
Flaubert, G. Madame Bovary
Fleming, I. Doctor No
Fleming, T. J. Over there
García Márquez, G. Leaf storm
Green, G. The last angry man
Greene, G. The honorary consul
Hailey, A. Strong medicine
Harris, M. Hatter Fox
Holt, V. Secret for a nightingale
Hooker, R. MASH
Huxley, A. After many a summer dies the swan
Huxley, A. Eyeless in Gaza
Iles, G. Black cross
Irving, J. The cider house rules
Irving, J. A son of the circus
Lewis, S. Arrowsmith
MacLean, A. Ice Station Zebra
Martin, V. Mary Reilly
Maugham, W. S. Of human bondage
Michener, J. A. Recessional
Pasternak, B. L. Doctor Zhivago
Plain, B. Random winds
Read, Miss. Thrush Green
Reed, B. The indictment
Remarque, E. M. Arch of triumph
Ross-Macdonald, M. All desires known
Rosten, L. C. Captain Newman, M.D.
Sabatini, R. Captain Blood
Sanders, L. The sixth commandment
Segal, E. Doctors
Stevenson, R. L. The strange case of Dr. Jekyll and Mr. Hyde
Taylor, R. L. The travels of Jaimie McPheeters
Theroux, P. Doctor DeMarr
Trevanian. The summer of Katya
Trollope, A. Doctor Thorne
Unsworth, B. Sacred hunger
Wallace, I. The prize
Waltari, M. The Egyptian
Wilson, F. P. The select

PHYSICISTS
Benford, G. Timescape
Bova, B. Voyagers
Le Guin, U. K. The dispossessed
Snow, C. P. The new men
Strieber, W. The forbidden zone
Wallace, I. The prize

PHYSIOLOGICAL PSYCHOLOGY
Keyes, D. Flowers for Algernon

PIANISTS
Burgess, A. The pianoplayers
Conroy, F. Body & soul
Goudge, E. The heart of the family
Ishiguro, K. The unconsoled
L'Engle, M. A severed wasp
L'Engle, M. The small rain
Sheldon, S. The stars shine down
Stone, K. Rainbows
The piano bird. See Kallen, L. C. B. Greenfield: the piano bird
The pianoplayers. Burgess, A.

PICARESQUE NOVELS
Abbey, E. The fool's progress
Allen, H. Anthony Adverse
Auster, P. Mr. Vertigo
Barth, J. The floating opera
Barth, J. The sot-weed factor
Bellow, S. The adventures of Augie March
Berger, T. Little Big Man
Boyle, T. C. Water music
Brown, J. D. Addie Pray
Cervantes Saavedra, M. de. Don Quixote de la Mancha
Cervantes Saavedra, M. de. Rinconete and Cortadillo
Defoe, D. Moll Flanders

Dickens, C. The posthumous papers of the Pickwick Club
Doctorow, E. L. Billy Bathgate
Doctorow, E. L. Loon Lake
Doig, I. Ride with me, Mariah Montana
Donleavy, J. P. The ginger man
Elegant, R. S. Manchu
Fielding, H. The history of Tom Jones, a foundling
Fraser, G. M. Flashman
Fraser, G. M. Flashman and the mountain of light
Fraser, G. M. Royal Flash
Holland, C. The firedrake
Jennings, G. Aztec
Jennings, G. The journeyer
Keneally, T. Woman of the inner sea
Kennedy, W. Quinn's book
Kerouac, J. On the road
Kosinski, J. N. Passion play
Lehrer, J. Kick the can
Mann, T. Confessions of Felix Krull, confidence man
McGuane, T. The bushwhacked piano
Portis, C. Gringos
Priestley, J. B. The good companions
Proulx, A. Postcards
Shaw, I. Nightwork
Stendhal. The red and the black
Toole, J. K. A confederacy of dunces
Voltaire. Candide
Pick up sticks. Lathen, E.

PICKPOCKETS *See* Thieves
Pickwick papers. See Dickens, C. The posthumous papers of the Pickwick Club
The picture of Dorian Gray. Wilde, O.
Picture palace. Theroux, P.
Pictures at an exhibition. Thomas, D. M.
Pictures of perfection. Hill, R.
Picturing Will. Beattie, A.
A piece of the action. Solomita, S.
Pigeon feathers, and other stories. Updike, J.

PIGS
Peck, R. N. A day no pigs would die
Pigs in heaven. Kingsolver, B.

PILATE, PONTIUS, 1ST CENT.
Caldwell, T. Dear and glorious physician
Pilgermann. Hoban, R.
The pilgrim of hate. Peters, E.

PILGRIMAGES *See* Pilgrims and pilgrimages

PILGRIMS AND PILGRIMAGES
Hoban, R. Pilgermann
Mehta, G. A river Sutra
Oldenbourg, Z. The heirs of the kingdom
Pilgrim's inn. Goudge, E.
The Pilgrim's progress. Bunyan, J.
Pillar of the Sky. Holland, C.
Pillars of the earth. Follett, K.
The pilot. Cooper, J. F.

PILOTS, AIRPLANE *See* Air pilots

PIMPS
See also Prostitutes
The pinch runner memorandum. Ōe, K.

PIONEER LIFE *See* Frontier and pioneer life
The pioneers. Cooper, J. F.
also in Cooper, J. F. The Leatherstocking tales v1 p1-465
Pippa passes. Godden, R.

PIRACY *See* Pirates

PIRATES
See also United States—Tripolitan War, 1801-1805
Du Maurier, Dame D. Frenchman's Creek
Holland, C. The Sea Beggars
Sabatini, R. Captain Blood
Sabatini, R. The Sea-hawk
Waltari, M. The Etruscan

The **pit**. Norris, F.

PITCAIRN ISLAND
Nordhoff, C. Pitcairn's Island
Pitcairn's Island. Nordhoff, C.
also in Nordhoff, C. The Bounty trilogy
A **place** to come to. Warren, R. P.
Places to stay the night. Hood, A.

PLAGIARISM
Sarton, M. A small room

PLAGUE
See also England—London—Plague, 1665; Disasters
Bosse, M. J. Mister Touch
Camus, A. The plague
Herbert, F. The white plague
Mann, T. Death in Venice
Ôe, K. Nip the buds, shoot the kids
Undset, S. The cross
The **plague**. Camus, A.
A **plague** of angels. Tepper, S. S.
Plain Jane. Horowitz, E.
The **plains** of passage. Auel, J. M.
Planet of exile. Le Guin, U. K.
Planet of the Apes. Boulle, P.

PLANETS, MINOR *See* Asteroids

PLANTATION LIFE
Bell, M. S. All souls' rising
Bristow, G. Gwen Bristow's Plantation trilogy
Coleman, L. Beulah Land
Coleman, L. The legacy of Beulah Land
Coleman, L. Look away, Beulah Land
Faulkner, W. Absalom, Absalom!
Gaines, E. J. The autobiography of Miss Jane Pittman
Gaskin, C. Fiona
L'Engle, M. The other side of the sun
Mitchell, M. Gone with the wind
Phillips, C. Cambridge
Price, E. Where shadows go
Spark, M. The go-away bird
Stowe, H. B. Uncle Tom's cabin
Walker, M. Jubilee
Plantion trilogy, Gwen Bristow's. Bristow, G.

PLATONIC LOVE *See* Love
Platte River. Bass, R.
Platte River [novella]. Bass, R.
In Bass, R. Platte River p99-145
Play dead. Dickinson, P.
Play it as it lays. Didion, J.
Playback. Chandler, R.
In Chandler, R. Later novels and other writings p735-871
Player piano. Vonnegut, K.
The **players** come again. Cross, A.
Playing for the Ashes. George, E.
Playing happy families. Symons, J.
Playing with cobras. Thomas, C.
Playland. Dunne, J. G.
The **playmaker**. Keneally, T.
Playmates. Parker, R. B.

PLAYWRIGHTS *See* Dramatists
Pleading guilty. Turow, S.

PLEASURE *See* Hedonism
Pleasure city. See Markandaya, K. Shalimar
The **pleasures** of love. Plaidy, J.
Plot it yourself. Stout, R.
In Stout, R. Kings full of aces p189-322
The **plumed** serpent (Quetzalcoatl). Lawrence, D. H.
Pnin. Nabokov, V. V.

POACHING
See also Hunting
A **pocket** full of rye. Christie, A.
A **pocketful** of rye. Cronin, A. J.

POCONO MOUNTAINS (PA.)
Whitney, P. A. Snowfire

Poet and dancer. Jhabvala, R. P.

POETS
See also Women poets
Barker, P. The eye in the door
Barker, P. Regeneration
Byatt, A. S. Possession
De Vries, P. Reuben, Reuben
Dorris, M. The crown of Columbus
Fallaci, O. A man
Galsworthy, J. Flowering wilderness
Haasse, H. S. In a dark wood wandering
Huxley, A. Crome Yellow
McInerny, R. M. Easeful death
Nabokov, V. V. Pale fire
Oates, J. C. Unholy loves
Orwell, G. Keep the aspidistra flying
Price, R. The promise of rest
Salinger, J. D. Raise high the roof beam, carpenters, and Seymour: an introduction
Sarton, M. Mrs. Stevens hears the mermaids singing
Spark, M. The girls of slender means
Symons, J. Death's darkest face
Waugh, E. The loved one
Wiesel, E. The testament

POGROMS *See* Jews—Persecutions
Poinciana. Whitney, P. A.
Point counter point. Huxley, A.
Point of no return. Marquand, J. P.

POISON *See* Poisons
Poison. McBain, E.
Poison pen. Kittredge, M.

POISON PEN LETTERS *See* Letters (Stories about)
Poisoned pins. Hess, J.

POISONING
See also Poisons
Pearson, R. No witnesses
Simenon, G. The truth about Bébé Donge

POISONOUS SNAKES *See* Snakes

POISONS
See also Poisoning
Armstrong, C. A dram of poison
Rendell, R. Heartstones

POLAND
See also Galicia (Poland and Ukraine)
Michener, J. A. Poland
Singer, I. B. The king of the fields

17th century
Sienkiewicz, H. The deluge
Sienkiewicz, H. Fire in the steppe
Sienkiewicz, H. With fire and sword
Singer, I. B. Satan in Goray
Singer, I. B. The slave

18th century
Singer, I. B. Reaches of heaven

19th century
Agnon, S. Y. The bridal canopy
Singer, I. B. The estate
Singer, I. B. The magician of Lublin
Singer, I. B. The manor

20th century
Appelfeld, A. Katerina
Begley, L. Wartime lies
Kosinski, J. N. The painted bird
Kuniczak, W. S. The thousand hour day
Miłosz, C. The seizure of power

Army—Officers
Kuniczak, W. S. The thousand hour day

Rural life
Singer, I. B. The estate
Singer, I. B. The manor
Singer, I. B. Satan in Goray

POLAND—*Continued*

World War, 1939-1945

See World War, 1939-1945—Poland

Gdansk

Grass, G. The call of the toad
Grass, G. Cat and mouse
Grass, G. The Danzig trilogy
Grass, G. Dog years
Grass, G. The tin drum

Lodz

Singer, I. J. The brothers Ashkenazi

Warsaw

Hersey, J. The wall
Singer, I. B. The certificate
Singer, I. B. The family Moskat
Singer, I. B. Scum
Singer, I. B. Shosha
Uris, L. Mila 18
Poland. Michener, J. A.

POLAR REGIONS *See* Antarctic regions; Arctic regions
Polar Star. Smith, M. C.

POLES

England

Murdoch, I. Nuns and soldiers

France

Rhys, J. Quartet

Italy

Mann, T. Death in Venice

United States

Archer, J. Kane & Abel
Styron, W. Sophie's choice

POLICE

Daley, R. A faint cold fear
Rendell, R. Live flesh

Boston (Mass.)

Higgins, G. V. Bomber's law
Parker, R. B. All our yesterdays

California

See also Police—Los Angeles (Calif.)
Koontz, D. R. Dragon tears
Rosenberg, N. T. Interest of justice
Wambaugh, J. Finnegan's week
Wambaugh, J. Fugitive nights
Wambaugh, J. The secrets of Harry Bright
Woods, S. Dead eyes

Chicago (Ill.)

Campbell, R. W. Boneyards

Detroit (Mich.)

Leonard, E. City primeval
Leonard, E. Freaky Deaky
Leonard, E. Split images

England

See also Police—London (England)

Florida

Hoffman, A. Turtle Moon
Leonard, E. Maximum Bob
Leonard, E. Rum punch

Georgia

Woods, S. Chiefs

Hollywood (Calif.)

See Police—Los Angeles (Calif.)

Houston (Tex.)

Lindsey, D. L. An absence of light
Lindsey, D. L. Mercy

India

Mann, P. Season of the monsoon

Jerusalem

Bayer, W. Pattern crimes

London (England)

Deighton, L. SS-GB: Nazi-occupied Britain 1941
Forsyth, F. The day of the jackal
Gilbert, M. The killing of Katie Steelstock
Snow, C. P. A coat of varnish

Los Angeles (Calif.)

Crichton, M. Rising sun
Dunne, J. G. True confessions
Ellroy, J. The black dahlia
Ellroy, J. L.A. confidential
Ellroy, J. White jazz
Linington, E. Skeletons in the closet
Shannon, D. Appearances of death
Shannon, D. Blood count
Shannon, D. Chaos of crime
Shannon, D. Destiny of death
Shannon, D. Exploit of death
Shannon, D. Felony file
Shannon, D. Murder most strange
Wambaugh, J. The black marble
Wambaugh, J. The blue knight
Wambaugh, J. The Delta Star
Wambaugh, J. The Glitter Dome
Wambaugh, J. The new centurions

Miami (Fla.)

Leonard, E. Glitz

Minnesota

Sandford, J. Rules of prey
Spencer, L. Family blessings

Netherlands

De Hartog, J. The inspector

New Jersey

Price, R. Clockers

New Orleans (La.)

Burke, J. L. The neon rain

New York (N.Y.)

Carr, C. The alienist
Caunitz, W. J. Black sand
Caunitz, W. J. Cleopatra Gold
Caunitz, W. J. One Police Plaza
Caunitz, W. J. Suspects
Daley, R. Hands of a stranger
Daley, R. Man with a gun
Daley, R. Tainted evidence
Daley, R. Wall of brass
Doctorow, E. L. The waterworks
Grant, M. Officer down
Lustbader, E. V. Black Blade
McBain, E. Another part of the city
McBain, E. Downtown
Sanders, L. The first deadly sin
Sanders, L. The second deadly sin
Sanders, L. The third deadly sin
Strieber, W. The Wolfen
Tanenbaum, R. Reversible error
Uhnak, D. False witness
Uhnak, D. The investigation
Uhnak, D. Law and order
Uhnak, D. Victims
Uhnak, D. The witness
Westlake, D. E. Cops and robbers
Westlake, D. E. Levine

New York (State)

Gardner, J. The sunlight dialogues

North Carolina

Malone, M. Uncivil seasons

Oklahoma

Hunter, S. Dirty white boys

Paris (France)

Forsyth, F. The day of the jackal

POLICE—*Continued*

Philadelphia (Pa.)
Griffin, W. E. B. The murderers

Russia
Freemantle, B. The button man

San Antonio (Tex.)
Brandon, J. Rules of evidence

San Francisco (Calif.)
Adler, E. The secret of the Villa Mimosa

South Africa
Paton, A. Too late the phalarope

Texas
See also Police—Houston (Tex.)

Virginia
Pearson, T. R. Cry me a river

Washington (State)
Pearson, R. The angel maker
Pearson, R. No witnesses
Pearson, R. Undercurrents
Rule, A. Possession
Polikúshka. Tolstoy, L., graf
In Tolstoy, L. The short novels of Tolstoy

POLISH REFUGEES
Sharp, M. Cluny Brown

POLITICAL CAMPAIGNS *See* Politics

POLITICAL CORRUPTION *See* Corruption (in politics)

POLITICAL CRIMES AND OFFENSES
See also Assassination; Political prisoners; Terrorism

POLITICAL DEFECTORS *See* Defectors

POLITICAL ETHICS
See also Power (Social sciences)
O'Connor, E. All in the family

POLITICAL INTRIGUE *See* International intrigue; Politics

POLITICAL PRISONERS
Fallaci, O. A man
Haasse, H. S. In a dark wood wandering
Higgins, J. Day of judgment
Solzhenitsyn, A. The first circle
Solzhenitsyn, A. One day in the life of Ivan Denisovich

POLITICIANS *See* Politics

POLITICS
See also Utopias; Women in politics; World politics
Bosse, M. J. Fire in heaven

Africa
Cussler, C. Vixen 03
Gordimer, N. A guest of honor
Naipaul, V. S. A bend in the river
Ruark, R. Uhuru
Smith, W. A. Golden fox
Smith, W. A. A time to die
Updike, J. The coup

Alaska
Ferber, E. Ice Palace

Brazil
Amado, J. Gabriela, clove and cinnamon

Cambodia
Del Vecchio, J. M. For the sake of all living things
Drabble, M. The gates of ivory

Central America
Didion, J. A book of common prayer
Stone, R. A flag for sunrise

Chile
Allende, I. The house of the spirits

China
Bosse, M. J. The warlord
Buck, P. S. Imperial woman
Lee, C. Y. Gate of rage
Li, P.-H. Farewell to my concubine

Egypt
Durrell, L. Mountolive

England
Anthony, E. Anne Boleyn
Archer, J. First among equals
Delderfield, R. F. A horseman riding by
Dickinson, P. Play dead
Drabble, M. The radiant way
Eden, D. Ravenscroft
Hart, J. Damage
Snow, C. P. Corridors of power
Snow, C. P. The malcontents
Thackeray, W. M. The history of Henry Esmond, esquire
Trollope, A. The Eustace diamonds
Trollope, A. Phineas Finn
Trollope, A. The prime minister

Ethiopia
Keneally, T. To Asmara

Europe
Dunnett, D. Niccolò rising
Dunnett, D. Race of scorpions
Dunnett, D. The spring of the ram
Fraser, G. M. Royal Flash
Hodge, J. A. The winding stair
Sartre, J. P. The reprieve
Sinclair, U. [Lanny Budd series]

France
Beauvoir, S. de. The mandarins
Steinbeck, J. The short reign of Pippin IV

Greece
Fallaci, O. A man

Guatemala
Goldman, F. The long night of white chickens

Hawaii
Michener, J. A. Hawaii

India
Masters, J. Bhowani Junction
Mehta, G. Raj
Scott, P. A division of the spoils

Indiana
Tarkington, B. The gentleman from Indiana

Ireland
Carr, P. The black swan
Flanagan, T. The end of the hunt
Greeley, A. M. Irish gold
Uris, L. Trinity

Italy
Silone, I. Bread and wine
Tomasi di Lampedusa, G. The leopard

Kentucky
Warren, R. P. World enough and time

Latin America
Allende, I. Eva Luna
Allende, I. Of love and shadows
García Márquez, G. The autumn of the patriarch

Louisiana
Williams, B. A. The unconquered

Massachusetts
Martin, W. Cape Cod

New York (State)
Isaacs, S. Close relations
Oates, J. C. What I lived for

POLITICS—*Continued*

Northern Ireland
Moore, B. Lies of silence

Oklahoma
Ferber, E. Cimarron

Rome
Massie, A. Caesar
McCullough, C. The first man in Rome
McCullough, C. Fortune's favorites
McCullough, C. The grass crown
Waltari, M. The Roman

Russia
Anthony, E. The relic
Koestler, A. Darkness at noon
Pasternak, B. L. Doctor Zhivago
Rybakov, A. N. Children of the Arbat

Scotland
Hill, P. The sword and the flame

South Africa
Bond, L. Vortex
Gordimer, N. Burger's daughter
Gordimer, N. My son's story
Gordimer, N. None to accompany me
Gordimer, N. A sport of nature
Paton, A. Ah, but your land is beautiful
Smith, W. A. Rage

South America
Conrad, J. Nostromo

South Carolina
Fast, H. Freedom road

Southern States
Blair, L. The side of the angels
Plain, B. Daybreak
Warren, R. P. All the king's men
Woods, S. Grass roots

Spain
Sheldon, S. The sands of time

Texas
Michener, J. A. Texas

United States
Lewis, S. It can't happen here
Sandburg, C. Remembrance Rock
Sinclair, U. [Lanny Budd series]
Vidal, G. Hollywood

United States—To 1900
Adams, H. Democracy
Brown, R. M. Dolley
Jakes, J. Heaven and hell
Jakes, J. Love and war
Lockridge, R. Raintree County
Stone, I. Love is eternal
Stone, I. The President's lady
Twain, M. The gilded age
Vidal, G. 1876
Vidal, G. Burr
Vidal, G. Empire
Vidal, G. Lincoln

United States—1900-
Batchelor, J. C. Father's day
Buckley, W. F. Tucker's last stand
Caldwell, T. Captains and kings
Carroll, J. The city below
Clark, M. H. Stillwatch
Cussler, C. Deep six
Didion, J. Democracy
Doctorow, E. L. The book of Daniel
Drury, A. Advise and consent
Drury, A. Preserve and protect
Dunne, D. A season in purgatory
Greeley, A. M. Thy brother's wife
Heller, J. Good as Gold
Higgins, G. V. Victories

Knebel, F. Seven days in May
Ludlum, R. The Icarus agenda
Michaels, B. Smoke and mirrors
O'Brien, T. In the Lake of the Woods
O'Connor, E. All in the family
O'Connor, E. The last hurrah
Puzo, M. The fourth K
Quinn, S. Happy endings
Reed, I. The terrible threes
Reed, I. The terrible twos
Safire, W. Full disclosure
Stone, I. Immortal wife
Thomas, R. Ah, treachery!
Thomas, R. Missionary stew
Vidal, G. Washington, D.C.
Vonnegut, K. Jailbird
Wallace, I. The man
West, N. A cool million

West Africa
Achebe, C. Anthills of the Savannah
Sanders, L. The tangent factor

West Indies
Atwood, M. Bodily harm
Naipaul, V. S. Guerrillas
Plain, B. Eden burning
Shacochis, B. Swimming in the volcano

Zimbabwe
Smith, W. A. The leopard hunts in darkness

POLLUTION
Benford, G. Timescape
Cussler, C. Sahara

POLO, MARCO, 1254-1323?
Calvino, I. Invisible cities
Jennings, G. The journeyer

POLO PLAYERS
Kosinski, J. N. Passion play

POLYGAMY
See also Mormons and Mormonism
Updike, J. The coup

POLYNESIA
See also Pitcairn Island

POLYNESIANS
See also Maoris
Davenport, K. Shark dialogues
Michener, J. A. Hawaii
Nordhoff, C. The hurricane
Nordhoff, C. Pitcairn's Island
Pomp and circumstance. Stewart, F. M.

POMPEII (ANCIENT CITY)
Lytton, E. B. L., Baron. The last days of Pompeii
The **Ponder** heart. Welty, E.

PONTIUS PILATE *See* Pilate, Pontius, 1st cent.
Poodle Springs. Chandler, R.

POOR *See* Poverty
Poor butterfly. Kaminsky, S. M.
Poor folk. See Dostoyevsky, F. Poor people
Poor people. Dostoyevsky, F.
In Dostoyevsky, F. The gambler, and other stories

Poor Relation [series]
Chesney, M. Back in society
Chesney, M. Colonel Sandhurst to the rescue
Chesney, M. Lady Fortescue steps out
Chesney, M. Miss Tonks turns to crime
Chesney, M. Mrs. Budley falls from grace
Chesney, M. Sir Philip's folly
Poor white. Anderson, S.
The **poorhouse** fair. Updike, J.

POPES
Burgess, A. Earthly powers
Martin, M. Vatican
West, M. L. The clowns of God

POPES—*Continued*
West, M. L. Lazarus
West, M. L. The shoes of the fisherman

POPULATION
Aldiss, B. W. Total environment

PORNOGRAPHY
Rosenberg, N. T. Interest of justice

PORT-AU-PRINCE (HAITI) *See* Haiti—Port-au-Prince
The **portable** Conrad. Conrad, J.
The **portable** F. Scott Fitzgerald. Fitzgerald, F. S.
The **portable** Faulkner. Faulkner, W.
The **portable** Hawthorne. Hawthorne, N.
The **portable** Saul Bellow. Bellow, S.
The **portable** Steinbeck. Steinbeck, J.
The **portable** Stephen Crane. Crane, S.
The **portable** Thomas Wolfe. Wolfe, T.
The **portable** Tolstoy. Tolstoy, L., graf
Portnoy's complaint. Roth, P.
Portrait in brownstone. Auchincloss, L.
The **portrait** of a lady. James, H.
A **portrait** of Bascom Hawke. Wolfe, T.
In Wolfe, T. The short novels of Thomas Wolfe p4-71
Portrait of Jennie. Nathan, R.
Portrait of the artist as a young dog. Thomas, D.
In Thomas, D. The collected stories p122-238
A **portrait** of the artist as a young man. Joyce, J.

PORTUGAL

19th century
Hodge, J. A. The winding stair

Rural life
L'Engle, M. The love letters

PORTUGUESE

Japan
Endō, S. Silence
The **Poseidon** adventure. Gallico, P.
The **positronic** man. Asimov, I.
The **possessed.** See Dostoyevsky, F. Demons
Possessing the secret of joy. Walker, A.

POSSESSION, DEMONIAC *See* Demoniac possession
Possession. Byatt, A. S.
Possession. Rule, A.

POSTAL SERVICE
See also Air mail service
Wright, R. Lawd today!
Postcards. Proulx, A.
Posthumous papers. See Barnard, R. Death of a literary widow
The **posthumous** papers of the Pickwick Club. Dickens, C.
The **postman.** Brin, D.
The **postman** always rings twice. Cain, J. M.
In Cain, J. M. Cain x 3 p1-101
Postmortem. Cornwell, P. D.
Postures. See Rhys, J. Quartet
Pot of gold. Michael, J.

POTATO FAMINE *See* Famines

POTSDAM (GERMANY) *See* Germany—Potsdam
The **potter's** field. Peters, E.

POVERTY
Allison, D. Bastard out of Carolina
Balzac, H. de. Cousin Pons
Bosse, M. J. The vast memory of love
Brown, C. Down all the days
Caldwell, E. Tobacco road
Camus, A. The first man
Chute, C. The Beans of Egypt, Maine
Cisneros, S. The house on Mango Street
Crichton, R. The Camerons
Dickens, C. Little Dorrit
Dostoyevsky, F. Poor people
García Márquez, G. No one writes to the colonel
Giardina, D. The unquiet earth

Hardy, T. Jude the obscure
Hugo, V. Les misérables
Mahfūz, N. Midaq Alley
Markandaya, K. A handful of rice
Morrison, T. The bluest eye
Morrison, T. Sula
Mowry, J. Six out seven
Norris, F. McTeague
Oates, J. C. A garden of earthly delights
Oates, J. C. Them
Olsen, T. Yonnondio: from the thirties
Richter, C. A simple honorable man
Rodriguez, A. Spidertown
Sinclair, U. The jungle
Singer, I. B. The certificate
Straight, S. I been in sorrow's kitchen and licked out all the pots
Tilly, M. Singing songs
Welty, E. Losing battles
West, Dame R. The fountain overflows
Wright, R. Native son

POWER (SOCIAL SCIENCES)
See also Political ethics
Achebe, C. Anthills of the Savannah
Archer, J. First among equals
Burgess, A. Earthly powers
Burgess, A. Hun
Clavell, J. Gai-Jin
Clavell, J. Shogun
Heinlein, R. A. Citizen of the galaxy
Holland, C. Pillar of the Sky
Howatch, S. Sins of the fathers
Martin, M. Vatican
Rand, A. Atlas shrugged
Sheldon, S. Master of the game
Spark, M. The Abbess of Crewe
Thomas, M. M. Hanover Place
Vidal, G. Empire
The **power** and the glory. Greene, G.
Power lines. McCaffrey, A.
Power of the sword. Smith, W. A.
The **power** that preserves. Donaldson, S. R.
Powers of attorney. Latt, M. L.
Powers that be. McCaffrey, A.

PRAGMATISM
See also Utilitarianism
The **Prague** orgy. Roth, P.
In Roth, P. Zuckerman bound: a trilogy and epilogue
The **prairie.** Cooper, J. F.
also in Cooper, J. F. The Leatherstocking tales v1 p879-1317

PRAIRIE LIFE
Aldrich, B. S. A lantern in her hand
Cather, W. My Ántonia
Cather, W. O pioneers!
Praise the human season. Robertson, D.
Praisesong for the widow. Marshall, P.
A **prayer** for Owen Meany. Irving, J.

PRECOGNITIONS *See* Premonitions

PREDESTINATION
Irving, J. A prayer for Owen Meany
Wilder, T. The bridge of San Luis Rey

PREDICTIONS *See* Prophecies

PREGNANCY
See also Abortion; Fertilization in vitro
Barth, J. The Tidewater tales
Cook, R. Mindbend
Goldreich, G. Four days
Steel, D. The gift
Weldon, F. Puffball
Westheimer, D. My sweet Charlie

PREHISTORIC ANIMALS *See* Fossils

PREHISTORIC MAN
See also Prehistoric times
Auel, J. M. The Clan of the Cave Bear
Auel, J. M. The Mammoth Hunters
Auel, J. M. The plains of passage
Auel, J. M. The Valley of Horses
Gear, K. O. People of the lakes
Gear, K. O. People of the lightning
Gear, W. M. People of the river
Gear, W. M. People of the sea
Golding, W. The inheritors
Harrison, S. Brother Wind
Harrison, S. Mother earth, father sky
Harrison, S. My sister the moon
Holland, C. Pillar of the Sky
Kurtén, B. Dance of the tiger
Thomas, E. M. The animal wife
Thomas, E. M. Reindeer Moon

PREHISTORIC TIMES
See also Stone Age
Auel, J. M. The Clan of the Cave Bear
Auel, J. M. The Mammoth Hunters
Auel, J. M. The plains of passage
Auel, J. M. The Valley of Horses
Golding, W. Clonk clonk
Holland, C. Pillar of the Sky
Kurtén, B. Dance of the tiger
Singer, I. B. The king of the fields
Thomas, E. M. The animal wife
Thomas, E. M. Reindeer Moon

PREJUDICES
See also Antisemitism
Brown, R. Civil wars
Dexter, P. Paris Trout
Girzone, J. F. Joshua and the children
Grau, S. A. The keepers of the house
Guterson, D. Snow falling on cedars
Lewis, S. Kingsblood royal
Morrison, T. Tar baby
Pérez Galdós, B. Doña Perfecta
Plain, B. Daybreak
Stewart, F. M. Pomp and circumstance
Vida, N. Goodbye, Saigon
West, D. The wedding
Prelude to Foundation. Asimov, I.
Prelude to terror. MacInnes, H.

PREMONITIONS
King, S. The dead zone
King, S. The shining
Prentice Alvin. Card, O. S.
Preserve and protect. Drury, A.
Presidential agent. Sinclair, U.
In Sinclair, U. [Lanny Budd series]
Presidential mission. Sinclair, U.
In Sinclair, U. [Lanny Budd series]

PRESIDENTS

Election
King, S. The dead zone

United States
Batchelor, J. C. Father's day
Burdick, E. Fail-safe
Knebel, F. Seven days in May
Puzo, M. The fourth K
Safire, W. Full disclosure
Vonnegut, K. Slapstick
Wallace, I. The man

United States—Election
Drury, A. Preserve and protect
Hall, A. Quiller barracuda

The **President's** daughter. Chase-Riboud, B.
The **President's** lady. Stone, I.
The **President's** man. Roosevelt, E.
Presumed innocent. Turow, S.
Presumption. Barrett, J.
Pretty Boy Floyd. McMurtry, L.
The **pretty** how town. See Freeling, N. Flanders sky
Pride and prejudice. Austen, J.
also in Austen, J. The complete novels of Jane Austen

PRIDE AND VANITY
Golding, W. The spire
The **pride** of the peacock. Holt, V.
Pride's harvest. Cleary, J.
The **priest**. McInerny, R. M.

PRIESTS *See* Anglican and Episcopal clergy; Catholic priests; Clergy

PRIESTS, CATHOLIC *See* Catholic priests
Primal fear. Diehl, W.
The **prime** minister. Trollope, A.
The **prime** minister [abridged]. Trollope, A.
In Trollope, A. The Pallisers p325-85
The **prime** of Miss Jean Brodie. Spark, M.
Prime witness. Martini, S. P.

PRIMITIVE CHRISTIANITY *See* Church history—Primitive and early church
Primitive people. Prose, F.

PRIMITIVE RELIGION *See* Religion

PRIMITIVE SOCIETY
Singer, I. B. The king of the fields
The **prince** and the pauper. Twain, M.
In Twain, M. The complete novels of Mark Twain v1 p559-730
Prince Charming. Garwood, J.
Prince of chaos. Zelazny, R.
Prince of peace. Carroll, J.
The **prince** of tides. Conroy, P.

PRINCES
See also Princesses
Saint-Exupéry, A. de. The little prince
The **princess** bride. Goldman, W.
A **Princess** of Mars. Burroughs, E. R.

PRINCESSES
Mehta, G. Raj
Mishima, Y. The Temple of Dawn
Prior convictions. Matera, L.

PRISON CAMPS *See* Vietnamese War, 1961-1975—Prisoners and prisons; World War, 1939-1945—Prisoners and prisons

PRISON ESCAPES *See* Escapes
Prison life in Siberia. See Dostoyevsky, F. The house of the dead
The **prisoner** of Zenda. Hope, A.

PRISONERS, POLITICAL *See* Political prisoners

PRISONERS AND PRISONS
See also Ex-convicts; Political prisoners; Prisoners of war
Baldwin, J. If Beale Street could talk
Bausch, R. Rebel powers
Cheever, J. Falconer
Gaines, E. J. A lesson before dying
Gilman, D. Incident at Badamya
Grisham, J. The chamber
Hale, E. E. The man without a country
Hope, A. The prisoner of Zenda
Kantor, M. Andersonville
Katzenbach, J. Just cause
Keneally, T. The playmaker
King, S. Rita Hayworth and Shawshank redemption
Koestler, A. Darkness at noon
London, J. The star rover
Mailer, N. The executioner's song
Quindlen, A. One true thing
Vonnegut, K. Jailbird

PRISONERS AND PRISONS—*Continued*
Willocks, T. Green river rising
Woods, S. Heat
Wozencraft, K. Notes from the country club

Argentina
Puig, M. Kiss of the spider woman

England
Defoe, D. Moll Flanders
Dickens, C. Little Dorrit
Dickens, C. The posthumous papers of the Pickwick Club
Walters, M. The sculptress

France
Dumas, A. The Count of Monte Cristo
Genet, J. Our Lady of the Flowers

Russia
See also Prisoners and prisons—Siberia (Russia)
Solzhenitsyn, A. The first circle

Siberia (Russia)
Dostoyevsky, F. The house of the dead
Solzhenitsyn, A. One day in the life of Ivan Denisovich

PRISONERS OF WAR
See also Concentration camps; World War, 1939-1945—Prisoners and prisons
Clancy, T. Without remorse
Kantor, M. Andersonville
Kirkwood, J. Some kind of hero
Shute, N. The legacy
Vonnegut, K. Slaughterhouse-five

PRISONS *See* Prisoners and prisons
A **private** crime. O'Donnell, L.

PRIVATE DETECTIVES *See* Detectives, Private

PRIVATE EYE STORIES *See* Detectives, Private; Mystery and detective stories
Private eyes. Kellerman, J.
Private scandals. Roberts, N.

PRIVATE SCHOOLS *See* School life
A **private** view. Brookner, A.
The **prize**. Wallace, I.
Prize stories, 1919-1995: The O. Henry awards. Entered in Part I under title
Prized possessions. Corman, A.
Prizzi's family. Condon, R.
Prizzi's glory. Condon, R.
Prizzi's honor. Condon, R.
Prizzi's money. Condon, R.
Probable cause. Pearson, R.

PROBATION OFFICERS
Leonard, E. Maximum Bob
Rosenberg, N. T. First offense

PROBLEM CHILDREN *See* Emotionally disturbed children
The **prodigal** daughter. Archer, J.
The **professor**. Brontë, C.
The **professor** of desire. Roth, P.

PROFESSORS *See* Teachers
The **professor's** house. Cather, W.
In Cather, W. Willa Cather, later novels

PROLETARIAN NOVELS
Nichols, J. T. The Milagro beanfield war
Steinbeck, J. The grapes of wrath
Steinbeck, J. In dubious battle
Zola, É. Germinal
The **promise**. Potok, C.
The **promise** of rest. Price, R.
Promised land. Parker, R. B.
Pronto. Leonard, E.
Proof. Francis, D.
A **proper** marriage. Lessing, D. M.
In Lessing, D. M. Children of violence v2

PROPERTY
See also Real estate

PROPHECIES
Bradley, M. Z. The firebrand
Dunnett, D. Checkmate
The **prophet**. Asch, S.

PROPHETS
Vargas Llosa, M. The war of the end of the world

PROSTITUTES
See also Courtesans
Burgess, A. The pianoplayers
Campbell, R. W. Boneyards
Clancy, T. Without remorse
Crane, S. Maggie: a girl of the streets (a story of New York)
Defoe, D. Moll Flanders
Faulkner, W. Sanctuary
Fuentes, C. Apollo and the whores
Jones, D. C. The search for Temperance Moon
Maḥfūz, N. Midaq Alley
Mason, R. The world of Suzie Wong
McMurtry, L. Buffalo girls
O'Hara, J. Butterfield 8
Spencer, L. Forgiving

PROSTITUTION
See also Prostitutes
Battle, L. Storyville
Lofts, N. The day of the butterfly
Martini, S. P. Compelling evidence
Theroux, P. Doctor Slaughter
Vargas Llosa, M. Captain Pantoja and the Special Service
Wharton, E. New Year's Day

PROTESTANT REFORMATION *See* Reformation
The **proud** and the free. Dailey, J.
The **proud** breed. De Blasis, C.

PROVENCE (FRANCE) *See* France—Provence

PROVINCETOWN (MASS.) *See* Massachusetts—Provincetown

PSYCHE (GODDESS)
Lewis, C. S. Till we have faces

PSYCHIATRISTS
See also Mentally ill—Care and treatment; Psychoanalysts
Adler, E. The secret of the Villa Mimosa
Barker, P. The eye in the door
Barker, P. Regeneration
Fitzgerald, F. S. Tender is the night
Greenberg, J. I never promised you a rose garden
Guest, J. Ordinary people
Jackson, S. The bird's nest
Jong, E. Fear of flying
Le Guin, U. K. The lathe of heaven
MacNeil, R. Burden of desire
Percy, W. The thanatos syndrome
Potok, C. The promise
Rosten, L. C. Captain Newman, M.D.
Rubens, B. A solitary grief
Villars, E. Too close for comfort
Weldon, F. Trouble

PSYCHIC PHENOMENA *See* Extrasensory perception; Occultism; Spiritualism; Supernatural phenomena
Psycho house. Bloch, R.

PSYCHOANALYSIS
Davies, R. The manticore
Rossner, J. August
Roth, P. My life as a man
Roth, P. Portnoy's complaint
Stone, I. The passions of the mind
Thomas, D. M. Pictures at an exhibition
Thomas, D. M. The white hotel

PSYCHOANALYSTS
Durrell, L. Constance
Durrell, L. Quinx

PSYCHOANALYSTS—*Continued*
Murdoch, I. The sacred and profane love machine
Rossner, J. August
Zelazny, R. He who shapes

PSYCHOKINESIS
King, S. Carrie
King, S. Firestarter

PSYCHOLOGICAL NOVELS
Abbott, M. The last innocent hour
Adams, A. Almost perfect
Aiken, C. Blue voyage
Aiken, C. Great circle
Aiken, C. King Coffin
Alcott, L. M. A long fatal love chase
Allen, C. V. Leftover dreams
Allen, C. V. Painted lives
Amis, M. Time's arrow
Appelfeld, A. Katerina
Armstrong, C. The unsuspected
Atwood, M. Cat's eye
Atwood, M. Life before man
Atwood, M. The robber bride
Atwood, M. Surfacing
Bainbridge, B. The birthday boys
Bambara, T. C. The salt eaters
Banks, R. Affliction
Barker, P. The eye in the door
Barker, P. Regeneration
Barnard, R. Out of the blackout
Bausch, R. Violence
Bawden, N. Family money
Beattie, A. Picturing Will
Bellow, S. Dangling man
Bowen, E. The death of the heart
Bowen, E. Eva Trout
Brett, S. Dead romantic
Brett, S. A shock to the system
Brink, A. P. An act of terror
Brookner, A. Brief lives
Brookner, A. A closed eye
Brookner, A. Dolly
Brookner, A. Fraud
Brookner, A. A private view
Brown, R. Before and after
Brown, R. Tender mercies
Burgess, A. Earthly powers
Busch, F. Long way from home
Butler, R. O. They whisper
Campbell, R. The long lost
Carroll, J. Fault lines
Chase, J. The evening wolves
Cheever, J. Falconer
Clark, M. H. All around the town
Clark, M. H. Remember me
Clark, W. V. T. The Ox-bow incident
Collins, W. The rationalist
Conrad, J. Lord Jim
Corman, A. 50
Crane, S. The red badge of courage
Crichton, M. The terminal man
Del Vecchio, J. M. Carry me home
Dew, R. F. Fortunate lives
Didion, J. Democracy
Diehl, W. Primal fear
Dixon, S. Interstate
Dostoyevsky, F. The brothers Karamazov
Dostoyevsky, F. Crime and punishment
Dostoyevsky, F. The idiot
Drabble, M. The gates of ivory
Drabble, M. The waterfall
Dreiser, T. An American tragedy
Endō, S. Scandal
Eugenides, J. The virgin suicides
Faulkner, W. The mansion
Fielding, J. See Jane run
Fitzgerald, F. S. Tender is the night
Flaubert, G. Madame Bovary

Forster, E. M. A passage to India
Fowles, J. The collector
Gann, E. K. The high and the mighty
García Márquez, G. Chronicle of a death foretold
García Márquez, G. The general and his labyrinth
Gide, A. The counterfeiters (Les faux-monnayeurs)
Gide, A. The immoralist
Gill, B. M. Nursery crimes
Gill, B. M. Time and time again
Godden, R. Black Narcissus
Godwin, G. The finishing school
Golding, W. Darkness visible
Goldreich, G. Four days
Gordimer, N. None to accompany me
Graham, W. The walking stick
Grass, G. The tin drum
Gray, F. du P. World without end
Greene, G. Brighton rock
Greene, G. The end of the affair
Grumbach, D. Chamber music
Hamilton, J. A map of the world
Hamsun, K. Mysteries
Handke, P. The left-handed woman
Hardy, T. Jude the obscure
Hardy, T. The return of the native
Hart, J. Sin
Hawthorne, N. The marble faun
Heller, J. Something happened
Hesse, H. Demian
Hill, R. Dream of darkness
Hoeg, P. Borderliners
Hoffman, A. Illumination night
Howatch, S. Glamorous powers
Humphreys, J. The fireman's fair
Ishiguro, K. The remains of the day
Ishiguro, K. The unconsoled
Jackson, C. The lost weekend
Jackson, S. The bird's nest
James, H. The Aspern papers
James, H. Roderick Hudson
James, H. Washington Square
James, H. The wings of the dove
Jhabvala, R. P. Poet and dancer
Jhabvala, R. P. Three continents
Jong, E. Fear of flying
Joyce, J. A portrait of the artist as a young man
Kincaid, J. Lucy
King, S. Dolores Claiborne
King, S. Gerald's game
Kingsolver, B. Animal dreams
Koontz, D. R. The vision
Kosinski, J. N. The devil tree
Lawrence, D. H. The rainbow
Lawrence, D. H. Sons and lovers
Lawrence, D. H. Women in love
Lessing, D. M. Briefing for a descent into Hell
Lessing, D. M. The fifth child
Lessing, D. M. The grass is singing
Levin, I. Sliver
Levin, M. Compulsion
Lindsey, D. L. Mercy
Lively, P. City of the mind
Lively, P. Cleopatra's sister
Lively, P. Moon tiger
Lively, P. Passing on
Lutz, J. Dancing with the dead
Maḥfūẓ, N. Autumn quail
Maḥfūẓ, N. The thief and the dogs
Maitland, S. Ancestral truths
Malraux, A. Man's fate (La condition humaine)
Mann, T. Death in Venice
Mann, T. Tonio Kröger
Mann, T. Tristan
March, W. The bad seed
Martin, V. The great divorce
Maugham, W. S. Of human bondage
McCabe, P. The butcher boy
McCammon, R. R. Mine

PSYCHOLOGICAL NOVELS—*Continued*

McCullers, C. The heart is a lonely hunter
McCullers, C. The member of the wedding
McEwan, I. The innocent
McFarland, D. The music room
McFarland, D. School for the blind
McInerny, R. M. Easeful death
McMillan, T. Disappearing acts
Meredith, G. The ordeal of Richard Feverel
Miller, S. Family pictures
Miller, S. For love
Minot, S. Folly
Mishima, Y. Spring snow
Mishima, Y. The temple of the golden pavilion
Morrison, T. Jazz
Mortimer, J. C. Dunster
Mukherjee, B. The holder of the world
Mukherjee, B. Jasmine
Murdoch, I. The bell
Murdoch, I. The black prince
Murdoch, I. The philosopher's pupil
Murdoch, I. The sea, the sea
Naipaul, V. S. Guerrillas
Nin, A. Cities of the interior
Oates, J. C. Black water
Oates, J. C. Expensive people
Oates, J. C. Snake eyes
Oates, J. C. Solstice
Oates, J. C. Them
Oates, J. C. What I lived for
O'Brien, T. In the Lake of the Woods
Ōe, K. The pinch runner memorandum
Ōe, K. The silent cry
O'Flaherty, L. The informer
O'Hara, J. Appointment in Samarra
O'Hara, J. From the terrace
Ondaatje, M. The English patient
Oz, A. Fima
Ozick, C. The cannibal galaxy
Pérez Galdós, B. Torquemada
Pohl, F. Gateway
Proust, M. The captive
Proust, M. The captive [and] The fugitive
Proust, M. The fugitive
Proust, M. The Guermantes way
Proust, M. Remembrance of things past
Proust, M. Sodom and Gomorrah
Proust, M. Swann's way
Proust, M. Time regained
Proust, M. Within a budding grove
Remarque, E. M. The road back
Rendell, R. The bridesmaid
Rendell, R. The crocodile bird
Rendell, R. The face of trespass
Rendell, R. Going wrong
Rendell, R. Heartstones
Rendell, R. A judgment in stone
Rendell, R. The killing doll
Rendell, R. Live flesh
Rendell, R. Make death love me
Rendell, R. Master of the moor
Rendell, R. The tree of hands
Rice, L. Stone heart
Rilke, R. M. The notebooks of Malte Laurids Brigge
Robards, K. Maggy's child
Roiphe, A. R. Up the sandbox!
Rölvaag, O. E. Giants in the earth
Rossner, J. August
Roth, P. When she was good
Rubens, B. A solitary grief
Rule, A. Possession
Sagan, F. A reluctant hero
Saint-Exupéry, A. de. Night flight
Salinger, J. D. The catcher in the rye
Sams, F. When all the world was young
Sanders, L. The first deadly sin
Sanders, L. The third deadly sin
Sarton, M. Mrs. Stevens hears the mermaids singing

Sarton, M. A reckoning
Shange, N. Liliane
Shaw, I. Acceptable losses
Shaw, I. Evening in Byzantium
Shreve, A. Eden Close
Simenon, G. Across the street
Simenon, G. The murderer
Simenon, G. The old man dies
Simenon, G. The rules of the game
Simenon, G. The truth about Bébé Donge
Singer, I. B. Scum
Smiley, J. Ordinary love
Snow, C. P. Homecoming
Spencer, S. Men in black
Stegner, W. E. The spectator bird
Stendhal. The red and the black
Stone, R. Outerbridge Reach
Strindberg, A. By the open sea
Strindberg, A. The scapegoat
Süskind, P. Perfume: the story of a murderer
Symons, J. Something like a love affair
Tennant, E. Pemberley
Thomas, D. M. The white hotel
Tilly, M. Singing songs
Tolstoy, L., graf. Anna Karenina
Tolstoy, L., graf. The Kreutzer sonata, The Devil, and other tales
Tremain, R. Sacred country
Trevanian. The summer of Katya
Trevor, W. My house in Umbria
Trevor, W. The silence in the garden
Tryon, T. The other
Turow, S. The burden of proof
Turow, S. Presumed innocent
Tyler, A. Breathing lessons
Tyler, A. Celestial navigation
Tyler, A. Dinner at the Homesick Restaurant
Villars, E. Too close for comfort
Vine, B. Anna's book
Vine, B. A dark-adapted eye
Vine, B. A fatal inversion
Vine, B. Gallowglass
Vine, B. The house of stairs
Vine, B. King Solomon's carpet
Vine, B. No night is too long
Walters, M. The sculptress
Wambaugh, J. Fugitive nights
Warren, R. P. The cave
Wharton, E. Ethan Frome
Whitney, P. A. The singing stones
Wiesel, E. The accident
Wiesel, E. Dawn
Wiesel, E. The fifth son
Wiesel, E. The testament
Wilhelm, K. Death qualified
Williams, B. A. Leave her to heaven
Winton, T. The riders
Woiwode, L. Indian affairs
Wolf, C. What remains
Wolfe, T. Look homeward, angel
Wolfe, T. The web and the rock
Wolfe, T. You can't go home again
Woolf, V. Between the acts
Woolf, V. Jacob's room
Woolf, V. Mrs. Dalloway
Woolf, V. To the lighthouse
Woolf, V. The voyage out
Woolf, V. The waves
Woolf, V. The years
Yorke, M. Safely to the grave

PSYCHOLOGISTS

Carr, C. The alienist
Dart, I. R. The Stork Club
Ferrigno, R. The Horse Latitudes
Wilhelm, K. Crazy time

PSYCHOLOGY, PHYSIOLOGICAL *See* Physiological psychology

PSYCHOPATHS *See* Insane, Criminal and dangerous; Personality disorders

PSYCHOTHERAPISTS *See* Psychotherapy

PSYCHOTHERAPY
Shange, N. Liliane

PUBLIC HOUSING
Porter, C. R. All-Bright Court
Read, Miss. Storm in the village

PUBLIC SCHOOLS *See* School life
Public smiles, private tears. Van Slyke, H.

PUBLISHERS AND PUBLISHING
See also Newspapers; Periodicals
Amiel, J. A question of proof
Beattie, A. Love always
Birmingham, S. The Rothman scandal
Bova, B. Cyberbooks
Colwin, L. A big storm knocked it over
Du Maurier, Dame D. The house on the strand
Eco, U. Foucault's pendulum
Krantz, J. I'll take Manhattan
McInerney, J. Brightness Falls
Michener, J. A. The novel
Powell, A. Books do furnish a room
Smith, R. K. Sadie Shapiro's knitting book
Spark, M. A far cry from Kensington
Vidal, G. Empire
Vidal, G. Washington, D.C.
Villars, E. Lipstick on his collar
Wouk, H. Youngblood Hawke

PUBS *See* Hotels, taverns, etc.
Pudd'nhead Wilson. Twain, M.
also in Twain, M. The complete novels of Mark Twain v2 p491-608

PUERTO RICANS

New York (N.Y.)
Rodriguez, A. Spidertown
Puffball. Weldon, F.

PUGILISM *See* Boxing
The **pugilist** at rest. Jones, T.

PUNS
Farmer, P. J. Riders of the purple wage
The **pupil.** James, H.
In James, H. The complete tales of Henry James v7
In James, H. Short novels of Henry James p355-405
In James, H. What Maisie knew, In the cage, The pupil
The **puppet** masters. Heinlein, R. A.

PUPPETS AND PUPPET PLAYS
Dove, R. Through the ivory gate
Tyler, A. Morgan's passing

PURITANISM
Santayana, G. The last Puritan
Seton, A. The Winthrop woman

PURITANS
See also Calvinists
Condé, M. I, Tituba, black witch of Salem
Hawthorne, N. The House of the Seven Gables
Hawthorne, N. The scarlet letter
Mukherjee, B. The holder of the world
The **purloined** letter [and] The murders in the Rue Morgue. Poe, E. A.
A **purple** place for dying. MacDonald, J. D.
A **purse** of coppers. O'Faoláin, S.
In O'Faoláin, S. The collected stories of Sean O'Faolain p163-319
The **pursuit** of love. Mitford, N.
In Mitford, N. The pursuit of love & Love in a cold climate p[1]-283

The **pursuit** of love & Love in a cold climate. Mitford, N.
Pushover. O'Donnell, L.
Puss in boots. McBain, E.
Put out more flags. Waugh, E.
Pylon. Faulkner, W.

Q

Q-squared. David, P.
QB VII. Uris, L.

QUADRIPLEGICS
Brown, R. Tender mercies

QUADROONS *See* Mulattoes
The **quality** of mercy. Kellerman, F.
Quantum of solace. Fleming, I.
In Fleming, I. Bonded Fleming p248-66

QUARRELING
Gardner, J. October light
Quarry. Pronzini, B.
Quartet. Rhys, J.
Quartet in autumn. Pym, B.

QUAYLE, DAN
Sargent, P. Danny goes to Mars

QUÉBEC (PROVINCE) *See* Canada—Québec (Province)
QUÉBEC (QUÉBEC) *See* Canada—Québec (Québec)
Queen Lucia. Benson, E. F.
In Benson, E. F. Make way for Lucia p1-178
The **Queen** of Air and Darkness. Anderson, P.
In The Hugo winners v3 p143-90
The **Queen** of Air and Darkness [variant title: The witch in the wood]. White, T. H.
In White, T. H. The once and future king p215-323
The **queen** of the damned. Rice, A.

QUEENS
See also Courts and courtiers

QUEENS (NEW YORK, N.Y.) *See* New York (N.Y.)—Queens
The **queen's** gambit. Tevis, W. S.
The **Queen's** necklace. Dumas, A.

QUEENSLAND (AUSTRALIA) *See* Australia—Queensland
Quentin Durward. Scott, Sir W.
The **quest** for Karla. Le Carré, J.
The **quest** for Saint Camber. Kurtz, K.
A **question** of murder. Wright, E.
A **question** of proof. Amiel, J.
A **question** of upbringing. Powell, A.
In Powell, A. A dance to the music of time [v1]
The **quick** red fox. MacDonald, J. D.
The **quiet** American. Greene, G.
Quiller bamboo. Hall, A.
Quiller barracuda. Hall, A.
The **Quiller** memorandum. Hall, A.
Quiller meridian. Hall, A.
Quiller Salamander. Hall, A.
Quiller solitaire. Hall, A.

QUILTS
Otto, W. How to make an American quilt
The **quincunx.** Palliser, C.
Quinn's book. Kennedy, W.

QUINTUPLETS
Mason, B. A. Feather crowns
Quinx. Durrell, L.

QUISLINGS *See* World War, 1939-1945—Collaborationists

Quo vadis. Sienkiewicz, H.

R

RABBIS
Agnon, S. Y. The bridal canopy
Fast, H. The outsider
Kemelman, H. Friday the rabbi slept late
Kemelman, H. Monday the rabbi took off
Kemelman, H. One fine day the rabbi bought a cross
Kemelman, H. Saturday the rabbi went hungry
Kemelman, H. Someday the rabbi will leave
Kemelman, H. Sunday the rabbi stayed home
Kemelman, H. Thursday the rabbi walked out
Kemelman, H. Tuesday the rabbi saw red
Kemelman, H. Wednesday the rabbi got wet
Potok, C. The book of lights
Potok, C. The promise
Rabbit at rest. Updike, J.
Rabbit is rich. Updike, J.
Rabbit redux. Updike, J.
Rabbit, run. Updike, J.

RABBITS
Adams, R. Watership Down
Rabble in arms. Roberts, K. L.

RABIES
King, S. Cujo
Race of scorpions. Dunnett, D.

RACE RELATIONS
See also African Americans; African Americans—Relations with Jews; Antisemitism; Culture conflict; Interracial marriage; Miscegenation; Prejudices

Africa
See Africa—Race relations

Hawaii
See Hawaii—Race relations

India
See India—Race relations

Kenya
See Kenya—Race relations

South Africa
See South Africa—Race relations

United States
See United States—Race relations

West Indies
See West Indies—Race relations

RACEHORSES *See* Horses
RACIAL INTERMARRIAGE *See* Interracial marriage
RACING
See also Automobile races; Horse racing
RACISM *See* Antisemitism; Prejudices
RACKETEERS *See* Crime and criminals; Gangsters; Mafia
RACKETS *See* Gambling
RADCLIFFE COLLEGE
Adams, A. Superior women
The **radiant** way. Drabble, M.

RADIATION
Physiological effect
Shute, N. On the beach

RADICALISM *See* Radicals and radicalism
RADICALS AND RADICALISM
See also Anarchism and anarchists
Leonard, E. Freaky Deaky
Lessing, D. M. The good terrorist

Piercy, M. Vida
Plain, B. Harvest

RADIO
Keillor, G. WLT
Vargas Llosa, M. Aunt Julia and the scriptwriter

RADIO BROADCASTING
Shields, C. The republic of love

RADIOACTIVITY
Physiological effect
See Radiation—Physiological effect
Rage. King, S.
In King, S. The Bachman books: four early novels by Stephen King
Rage. Smith, W. A.
Rage of angels. Sheldon, S.
Ragtime. Doctorow, E. L.
The **railroad** stories. See Sholem Aleichem. Tevye the dairyman and The railroad stories

RAILROADS
See also Subways
Cather, W. A lost lady
Ferber, E. Saratoga trunk
Norris, F. The octopus
Rand, A. Atlas shrugged
Ross-Macdonald, M. The rich are with you always
Ross-Macdonald, M. The world from rough stones

Travel
Allen, C. V. Dream train
Greene, G. Orient Express
The **rainbow**. Lawrence, D. H.
Rainbow in the mist. Whitney, P. A.
Rainbows. Stone, K.
Rainbow's end. Peters, E.
The **rains** came. Bromfield, L.
Raintree County. Lockridge, R.
Raise high the roof beam, carpenters, and Seymour: an introduction. Salinger, J. D.
Raise the Titanic! Cussler, C.
Raising the stones. Tepper, S. S.
Raj. Mehta, G.
The **Raj** quartet. Scott, P.
RALEGH, WALTER *See* Raleigh, Sir Walter, 1552?-1618
RALEIGH, SIR WALTER, 1552?-1618
Naipaul, V. S. A way in the world
Rally round the flag, boys! Shulman, M.
Rama II. Clarke, A. C.
Rama revealed. Clarke, A. C.

RANCH LIFE
See also Cowboys
Brand, M. Dust across the range
Briskin, J. Paloverde
De Blasis, C. The proud breed
Doig, I. English Creek
Ferber, E. Giant
Greenberg, J. Simple gifts
Guthrie, A. B. Arfive
Guthrie, A. B. These thousand hills
Harrison, J. The beige dolorosa
Kelton, E. The far canyon
L'Amour, L. The Californios
L'Amour, L. The man from the broken hills
McCarthy, C. All the pretty horses
McCullough, C. The thorn birds
McGuane, T. Nobody's angel
Richter, C. The lady
Richter, C. The sea of grass
Rushing, J. G. Mary Dove
Schaefer, J. W. Monte Walsh
Schaefer, J. W. Shane
Steinbeck, J. Of mice and men
Steinbeck, J. The red pony
Streshinsky, S. Hers the kingdom
Waller, R. J. Border music

Random harvest. Hilton, J.
Random winds. Plain, B.

RAPE
  Cookson, C. The Maltese Angel
  Corman, A. Prized possessions
  Daley, R. Hands of a stranger
  Dershowitz, A. M. The advocate's devil
  Fielding, J. Tell me no secrets
  Grisham, J. A time to kill
  Hailey, E. F. Life sentences
  Hill, P. Vollands
  Kosinski, J. N. Blind date
  Lofts, N. The claw
  Michael, J. Sleeping beauty
  Oates, J. C. Nemesis
  O'Donnell, L. Dial 577 R-A-P-E
  Patterson, R. N. Degree of guilt
  Plante, D. Annunciation
  Rendell, R. Live flesh
  Rosenberg, N. T. Mitigating circumstances
  Rule, A. Possession
  Scott, P. The day of the scorpion
  Scott, P. The jewel in the crown
  Szeman, S. The Kommandant's mistress
  Traver, R. Anatomy of a murder
  Uhnak, D. False witness
Raptor. Jennings, G.
Rare & endangered species. Bausch, R.
  In Bausch, R. Rare & endangered species: a novella
    & stories p155-257
Rare & endangered species: a novella & stories. Bausch,
  R.
A **rare** Benedictine. Peters, E.
Rat race. Francis, D.
The **rationalist.** Collins, W.
Rattlebone. Clair, M.
A **rattling** of old bones. Ross, J.
The **raven** in the foregate. Peters, E.
Ravenscroft. Eden, D.
The **razor's** edge. Maugham, W. S.
Re: colonized planet 5, Shikasta. Lessing, D. M.
Reaches of heaven. Singer, I. B.
Reading Turgenev. Trevor, W.
  In Trevor, W. Two lives: Reading Turgenev and My
    house in Umbria p1-222

REAL ESTATE
  See also Speculation
  Freeman, C. Seasons of the heart
  Hiaasen, C. Native tongue
  MacDonald, J. D. Barrier Island

REAL ESTATE BUSINESS
  Sheldon, S. The stars shine down

REAL PROPERTY *See* Real estate
The **real** thing. Lessing, D. M.
The **realist.** Auchincloss, L.
  In Auchincloss, L. Three lives
The **realms** of gold. Drabble, M.
Reasonable doubt. Friedman, P.
Rebecca. Du Maurier, Dame D.
Rebel. Cornwell, B.
The **rebel** angels. Davies, R.
Rebel powers. Bausch, R.
REBELLIONS *See* Revolutions
Recalled to life. Hill, R.
Recessional. Michener, J. A.
The **reckoning.** Penman, S. K.
A **reckoning.** Sarton, M.

RECLUSES
  Harvey, K. Stars
  McMurtry, L. Some can whistle
The **recognitions.** Gaddis, W.
A **reconstructed** corpse. Brett, S.

RECONSTRUCTION
  See also United States—1865-1898
  Fast, H. Freedom road
  Mitchell, M. Gone with the wind

  Ripley, A. Scarlett
  Twain, M. The gilded age
  Williams, B. A. The unconquered

RECONSTRUCTION (1939-1951)
        Sicily
  Hersey, J. A bell for Adano
The **Rector** of Justin. Auchincloss, L.

RECTORS *See* Anglican and Episcopal clergy; Catholic
  priests
The **rector's** wife. Trollope, J.
The **recycled** citizen. MacLeod, C.
The **red** and the black. Stendhal

RED ARMY (SOVIET UNION) *See* Russia—Army
The **red** badge of courage. Crane, S.
  also in Crane, S. The complete novels of Stephen
    Crane p197-299
  also in Crane, S. The portable Stephen Crane p189-
    318
  also in Crane, S. The red badge of courage, and
    other stories
The **red** badge of courage, and other stories. Crane, S.
Red Branch. Llywelyn, M.
Red cavalry. Babel', I.
  In Babel', I. The collected stories p41-200
A **red** death. Mosley, W.
Red Dragon. Harris, T.
Red dust. McAuley, P. J.
Red harvest. Hammett, D.
  In Hammett, D. The novels of Dashiell Hammett
    p1-142
The **red** horseman. Coonts, S.
Red Mars. Robinson, K. S.
The **Red** Pavilion. Gulik, R. H. van
The **red** pony. Steinbeck, J.
  In Steinbeck, J. The long valley
  In Steinbeck, J. The portable Steinbeck p325-415
Red prophet. Card, O. S.
Red sky at morning. Bradford, R.
Red Square. Smith, M. C.
Red Storm rising. Clancy, T.
Red wheel/knot 1 [series]
  Solzhenitsyn, A. August 1914
The **red,** white, and blue. Dunne, J. G.
Red wolf, red wolf. Kinsella, W. P.
Redcoat. Cornwell, B.

REDEMPTION *See* Atonement
Redemption. See McGown, J. Murder at the old vicarage
Redline the stars. Norton, A.

REDUCING
  Levenkron, S. The best little girl in the world
The **reef.** Wharton, E.
Reflections in a golden eye. McCullers, C.
  also in McCullers, C. The ballad of the sad café:
    the novels and stories of Carson McCullers
    p499-567
Reflex. Francis, D.

REFORMATION
  See also Europe—16th century
  Anthony, E. Anne Boleyn

REFORMATORIES
  Harris, M. Hatter Fox

REFORMERS
  See also Abolitionists

REFUGEES
  See also Exiles
  Bellow, S. The Bellarosa connection
  Brookner, A. Family and friends
  Kosinski, J. N. The painted bird

REFUGEES, AUSTRIAN *See* Austrian refugees

REFUGEES, CUBAN *See* Cuban refugees

REFUGEES, CZECH *See* Czech refugees

REFUGEES, GERMAN *See* German refugees

REFUGEES, HAITIAN *See* Haitian refugees

REFUGEES, JEWISH *See* Jewish refugees

REFUGEES, KOREAN *See* Korean refugees

REFUGEES, POLISH *See* Polish refugees

REFUGEES, RUSSIAN *See* Russian refugees

REFUGEES, VIETNAMESE *See* Vietnamese refugees

REGENCY ENGLAND *See* England—19th century

Regeneration. Barker, P.

Regina v. Rumpole. *See* Mortimer, J. C. Rumpole for the defence

REINCARNATION
Anthony, P. Isle of woman
Anthony, P. Shame of man
De Felitta, F. Audrey Rose
Ellison, H. The deathbird
Mailer, N. Ancient evenings
Mishima, Y. The decay of the angel
Seton, A. Green darkness
Zelazny, R. Lord of light
Reindeer Moon. Thomas, E. M.
Reinhart in love. Berger, T.
Reinhart's women. Berger, T.
The **reivers.** Faulkner, W.

REJUVENATION
Haggard, H. R. She

RELATIVES *See* Family life

RELATIVITY (PHYSICS)
See also Space and time
The **relic.** Anthony, E.

RELIGION
See also Agnosticism; Biblical stories; Buddhism; Catholic faith; Christianity; Clergy; Conversion; Faith; God; Judaism; Mormons and Mormonism; Paganism
Amado, J. The war of the saints
Asimov, I. Nightfall
Baldwin, J. Go tell it on the mountain
Barrie, J. M. The little minister
Bunyan, J. The Pilgrim's progress
Dostoyevsky, F. The brothers Karamazov
Duncan, D. J. The brothers K
Eliot, G. Romola
Golding, W. The scorpion god
Greene, G. A burnt-out case
Heinlein, R. A. Job: a comedy of justice
Herbert, F. God Emperor of Dune
Herbert, F. Heretics of Dune
Irving, J. A prayer for Owen Meany
Kafka, F. The castle
Leonard, E. Touch
Lewis, S. Elmer Gantry
MacDonald, J. D. One more Sunday
Marshall, C. Christy
Marshall, C. Julie
Martin, G. R. R. A song for Lya
Mason, B. A. Feather crowns
Mishima, Y. The temple of the golden pavilion
Murdoch, I. The bell
Murdoch, I. The green knight
O'Connor, F. Wise blood
Pérez Galdós, B. Doña Perfecta
Robbins, T. Skinny legs and all
Salinger, J. D. Franny and Zooey
Stowe, H. B. The minister's wooing
Tepper, S. S. Northshore
Tepper, S. S. Shadow's end
Tepper, S. S. Southshore
Theroux, P. Millroy the Magician
Updike, J. S
Vidal, G. Creation

West, M. L. The devil's advocate
Wiesel, E. The town beyond the wall

RELIGION, PRIMITIVE *See* Religion

RELIGIOUS LIFE *See* Convent life; Monasticism and religious orders

A **reluctant** hero. Sagan, F.

The **reluctant** queen. Plaidy, J.

The **remains** of the day. Ishiguro, K.

The **Rembrandt** panel. Banks, O. T.

Remember. Bradford, B. T.

Remember me. Clark, M. H.

Remember Santiago. Jones, D. C.

Remembering Babylon. Malouf, D.

Remembrance of things past. Proust, M.

Remembrance Rock. Sandburg, C.

RENAISSANCE
See also Italy—15th century; Italy—16th century

Rendezvous with Rama. Clarke, A. C.

The **renegades** of Pern. McCaffrey, A.

REPENTANCE
See also Sin

REPORTERS *See* Journalists

The **reprieve.** Sartre, J. P.

REPRODUCTION, ASEXUAL *See* Asexual reproduction

The **republic** of love. Shields, C.

Requiem for a nun. Faulkner, W.

RESCUE OPERATIONS *See* Search and rescue operations

RESCUES
Brown, D. Night of the hawk

RESEARCH
Michener, J. A. Space
Pym, B. Less than angels
Wilhelm, K. Where late the sweet birds sang

RESISTANCE MOVEMENTS (WORLD WAR, 1939-1945) *See* World War, 1939-1945—Underground movements

RESISTANCE TO GOVERNMENT
Alvarez, J. In the time of the butterflies

RESORTS *See* Hotels, taverns, etc. Summer resorts

Rest in pieces. Brown, R. M.

The **rest** of life. Gordon, M.
In Gordon, M. The rest of life: three novellas

The **rest** of life: three novellas. Gordon, M.

The **rest** of the robots. Asimov, I.

Rest you merry. MacLeod, C.

The **restaurant** at the end of the universe. Adams, D.
also in Adams, D. The hitchhiker's quartet

RESTAURANTS, LUNCHROOMS, ETC.
Cain, J. M. The postman always rings twice
Gardner, J. Nickel mountain
McCullers, C. The ballad of the sad café [novelette]
Naylor, G. Bailey's Café
Powell, A. Casanova's Chinese restaurant
Rice, L. Blue moon
Simenon, G. The old man dies
Steinbeck, J. Sweet Thursday
Steinbeck, J. The wayward bus
Stubbs, J. Kelly Park

RESTORATION ENGLAND *See* England—17th century

RESURRECTION
Amado, J. Dona Flor and her two husbands
Farmer, P. J. The dark design
Farmer, P. J. The fabulous riverboat
Farmer, P. J. Gods of Riverworld
Farmer, P. J. The magic labyrinth
Farmer, P. J. River of eternity
Farmer, P. J. To your scattered bodies go

Resurrection. Tolstoy, L., graf
The **resurrection** man. MacLeod, C.
Resurrection row. Perry, A.

RETIREMENT
See also Old age
Amis, K. The folks that live on the hill
Brookner, A. A private view
Goudge, E. The scent of water
Pym, B. Quartet in autumn
Stegner, W. E. All the little live things

RETIREMENT COMMUNITIES
Michener, J. A. Recessional
The **return** of Gunner Asch. Kirst, H. H.
The **return** of Lanny Budd. Sinclair, U.
In Sinclair, U. [Lanny Budd series]
The **return** of Moriarty. Gardner, J. E.
The **return** of Mr. Campion. Allingham, M.
The **return** of Sherlock Holmes. Doyle, Sir A. C.
also in Doyle, Sir A. C. The complete Sherlock Holmes
The **return** of the king. Tolkien, J. R. R.
also in Tolkien, J. R. R. The lord of the rings v3
The **return** of the native. Hardy, T.
Return to Eden. Harrison, H.
Return to Thrush Green. Read, Miss
Reuben, Reuben. De Vries, P.

REUNIONS
Bradford, B. T. Voice of the heart
Jaffe, R. Class reunion
McCrumb, S. If ever I return, pretty Peggy-O
Myrer, A. The last convertible
Siddons, A. R. Outer banks

REVENGE
Abrahams, P. Lights out
Alcott, L. M. Pauline's passion and punishment
Amis, K. The Russian girl
Anderson, P. The sharing of flesh
Archer, J. As the crow flies
Balzac, H. de. Cousin Bette
Barker, C. Cabal [novelette]
Bear, G. Anvil of stars
Brand, M. Outcasts
Briskin, J. Too much, too soon
Brontë, E. Wuthering Heights
Browne, G. A. 19 Purchase Street
Buckley, C. T. Wet work
Clancy, T. Debt of honor
Clancy, T. Without remorse
Combs, H. Brules
Conrad, J. Victory
Cookson, C. The Maltese Angel
Coulter, C. Impulse
Dickens, C. Great expectations
Dickens, C. A tale of two cities
Dumas, A. The Count of Monte Cristo
French, A. Billy
Gage, E. The master stroke
García Márquez, G. Chronicle of a death foretold
Goldsmith, O. The First Wives Club
Grisham, J. A time to kill
Herbert, F. The white plague
Higgins, J. A season in hell
Hill, P. Vollands
Hill, S. Mrs. de Winter
James, P. D. Innocent blood
Korda, M. Worldly goods
Kurtén, B. Dance of the tiger
L'Amour, L. The man from the broken hills
Le Carré, J. The night manager
Leonard, E. Glitz
Maḥfūẓ, N. The thief and the dogs
McCarthy, C. The crossing
Melville, H. Moby-Dick
Michael, J. A ruling passion
Michael, J. Sleeping beauty
Murdoch, I. The green knight

Pargeter, E. The green branch
Parker, R. B. All our yesterdays
Pearce, M. E. Cast a long shadow
Pearson, R. Hard fall
Pérez Galdós, B. Doña Perfecta
Puzo, M. The fourth K
Roberts, N. Honest illusions
Roberts, N. Private scandals
Rosenberg, N. T. Mitigating circumstances
Ross-Macdonald, M. Hell hath no fury
Shaw, I. Beggarman, thief
Simenon, G. The rules of the game
Smith, W. A. Elephant song
Stirling, J. Shadows on the shore
Uhnak, D. The Ryer Avenue story
Warren, R. P. World enough and time
Weldon, F. The life and loves of a she-devil
Wiesel, E. The fifth son
Woods, S. Palindrome
The **revenge** of Moriarty. Gardner, J. E.
The **revenge** of the rose. Moorcock, M.
Reverend Randollph and the Splendid Samaritan. Smith, C. M.
Reverend Randollph and the unholy Bible. Smith, C. M.
Reverend Randollph and the wages of sin. Smith, C. M.
Reversible error. Tanenbaum, R.
The **revolt** of Gunner Asch. Kirst, H. H.

REVOLUTION, AMERICAN, 1775-1783 *See* United States—Revolution, 1775-1783

REVOLUTIONARIES *See* Revolutionists

REVOLUTIONARY WAR, 1775-1783 *See* United States—Revolution, 1775-1783
The **revolutionist.** Littell, R.

REVOLUTIONISTS
Allende, I. Eva Luna
Alvarez, J. In the time of the butterflies
Coetzee, J. M. The master of Petersburg
Donoso, J. A house in the country
Fuentes, C. The campaign
Le Guin, U. K. Malafrena
Littell, R. The revolutionist
Naipaul, V. S. A way in the world
Puig, M. Kiss of the spider woman
Sheldon, S. The sands of time

REVOLUTIONS
See also Coups d'état; Revolutionists; Taiping Rebellion, 1850-1864
Bell, M. S. All souls' rising
Didion, J. A book of common prayer
Flanagan, T. The tenants of time
Gordimer, N. July's people
Gordimer, N. A sport of nature
Heinlein, R. A. The moon is a harsh mistress
Keneally, T. To Asmara
Plain, B. Eden burning
Sienkiewicz, H. With fire and sword
Stone, R. A flag for sunrise
The **Rhinemann** exchange. Ludlum, R.

RHODE ISLAND
Casey, J. Spartina
Rice, L. Blue moon
Shreve, A. Where or when
Updike, J. The witches of Eastwick

Newport
James, H. The ivory tower
Stowe, H. B. The minister's wooing
Whitney, P. A. Spindrift
Wilder, T. Theophilus North

RHODESIA, NORTHERN *See* Zambia

RHODESIA, SOUTHERN *See* Zimbabwe

RICH, VIRGINIA
Parodies, travesties, etc.
Pickard, N. The 27 ingredient chili con carne murders

The **rich** are with you always. Ross-Macdonald, M.
The **rich** boy. Fitzgerald, F. S.
In Fitzgerald, F. S. The Fitzgerald reader p239-75
The **rich** detective. Keating, H. R. F.
Rich in love. Humphreys, J.
Rich man, poor man. Shaw, I.
RICH PEOPLE *See* Wealth
RICHARD I, KING OF ENGLAND, 1157-1199
  Scott, Sir W. Ivanhoe
  Scott, Sir W. The talisman
  Tarr, J. The isle of glass
RICHARD III, KING OF ENGLAND, 1452-1485
  Penman, S. K. The sunne in splendour
  Peters, E. The murders of Richard III
  Plaidy, J. The reluctant queen
  Tey, J. The daughter of time
RICHARD, THE LION HEART *See* Richard I, King of England, 1157-1199
RICHELIEU, ARMAND JEAN DU PLESSIS, CARDINAL, DUC DE, 1585-1642
  Anthony, E. The Cardinal and the Queen
  Dumas, A. The three musketeers
Riddley Walker. Hoban, R.
Ride a pale horse. MacInnes, H.
Ride with me, Mariah Montana. Doig, I.
The **riders.** Winton, T.
The **riders** of High Rock. L'Amour, L.
Riders of the purple sage. Grey, Z.
Riders of the purple wage. Farmer, P. J.
  In Farmer, P. J. The classic Philip José Farmer, 1964-1973 p30-103
  In The Hugo winners v2 p388-459
Rift. Cody, L.
Right on the money. Lathen, E.
Rigor mortis. Kittredge, M.
Rimrunners. Cherryh, C. J.
Rinconete and Cortadillo. Cervantes Saavedra, M. de
  In Cervantes Saavedra, M. de. Three exemplary novels p9-71
Ring around the bases. Lardner, R.
The **ringed** castle. Dunnett, D.
RINGS
  Tolkien, J. R. R. The fellowship of the ring
  Tolkien, J. R. R. The lord of the rings
  Tolkien, J. R. R. The return of the king
  Tolkien, J. R. R. The two towers
Ringworld. Niven, L.
The **Ringworld** engineers. Niven, L.
RIO DE JANEIRO (BRAZIL) *See* Brazil—Rio de Janeiro
RIOTS
  See also Gordon Riots, 1870
  Willocks, T. Green river rising
Ripley's game. Highsmith, P.
A **ripple** from the storm. Lessing, D. M.
  In Lessing, D. M. Children of violence v3
The **rise** of life on earth. Oates, J. C.
The **rise** of Silas Lapham. Howells, W. D.
Rise the Euphrates. Edgarian, C.
Risico. Fleming, I.
  In Fleming, I. Bonded Fleming p267-97
Rising sun. Crichton, M.
Risk. Francis, D.
The **risk** pool. Russo, R.
Rita Hayworth and Shawshank redemption. King, S.
  In King, S. Different seasons p1-101
RITES AND CEREMONIES
  Tryon, T. Harvest home

Caribbean region
  Marshall, P. Praisesong for the widow

Japan
  Kawabata, Y. Thousand cranes

Rites of passage. Golding, W.
Rites of passage. Greenberg, J.
Ritual murder. Haymon, S. T.
River god. Smith, W. A.
RIVER LIFE

China
  Hersey, J. A single pebble
River of eternity. Farmer, P. J.
A **river** Sutra. Mehta, G.
RIVERBOATS *See* Steamboats
RIVERS, W. H. R. (WILLIAM HALSE RIVERS), 1864-1922
  Barker, P. The eye in the door
RIVERS, WILLIAM HALSE RIVERS *See* Rivers, W. H. R. (William Halse Rivers), 1864-1922
RIVERS
  See also Mississippi River; Missouri River; Niger River; Yangtze River (China)
Riverworld [series]
  Farmer, P. J. The dark design
  Farmer, P. J. The fabulous riverboat
  Farmer, P. J. Gods of Riverworld
  Farmer, P. J. The magic labyrinth
  Farmer, P. J. To your scattered bodies go
RIVIERA (FRANCE AND ITALY)
  Fitzgerald, F. S. Tender is the night
  MacInnes, H. Agent in place
  Sagan, F. Bonjour tristesse
Rivington Street. Tax, M.
The **road** back. Remarque, E. M.
The **road** to Lichfield. Lively, P.
The **road** to Omaha. Ludlum, R.
The **road** to Paradise Island. Holt, V.
Road to Wellville. Boyle, T. C.
Roads of destiny. Henry, O.
  In Henry, O. The complete works of O. Henry p355-550
Roads to freedom [series]
  Sartre, J. P. The age of reason
  Sartre, J. P. The reprieve
  Sartre, J. P. Troubled sleep
Roadwalkers. Grau, S. A.
Roadwork. King, S.
  In King, S. The Bachman books: four early novels by Stephen King
The **roar** of thunder. See Smith, W. A. The sound of thunder
ROB ROY, 1671-1734
  Scott, Sir W. Rob Roy
Rob Roy. Scott, Sir W.
ROBBER BARONS *See* Capitalists and financiers
The **robber** bride. Atwood, M.
The **robber** bridegroom. Welty, E.
ROBBERS *See* Brigands and robbers; Robbery
ROBBERY
  See also Bank robbers; Theft
  Browne, G. A. 19 Purchase Street
  Burnett, W. R. The asphalt jungle
  Crichton, M. The great train robbery
  Durham, M. The man who loved Cat Dancing
  Kirkwood, J. Some kind of hero
  Malamud, B. The assistant
  Roberts, N. Honest illusions
  Westlake, D. E. The hot rock
  Westlake, D. E. Why me?
The **robe.** Douglas, L. C.
A **Robert** Silverberg omnibus. Silverberg, R.
Robinson Crusoe. Defoe, D.
Robot Adept. Anthony, P.
Robot visions. Asimov, I.
ROBOTS
  Asimov, I. The Bicentennial Man

ROBOTS—*Continued*
  Asimov, I. The caves of steel
  Asimov, I. The complete robot
  Asimov, I. I, robot
  Asimov, I. The naked sun
  Asimov, I. The positronic man
  Asimov, I. The rest of the robots
  Asimov, I. Robot visions
  Asimov, I. Robots and empire
  Asimov, I. The robots of dawn
  Miller, W. M. The darfsteller
  Zelazny, R. Home is the hangman
Robots and empire. Asimov, I.
The **robots** of dawn. Asimov, I.
Rocannon's world. Le Guin, U. K.

ROCK MUSIC
  Bradford, B. T. Angel
  Buffett, J. Where is Joe Merchant?
ROCK MUSICIANS *See* Rock music
The **rock** of Tanios. Maalouf, A.

ROCKY MOUNTAINS
  Gann, E. K. The aviator
  Poe, E. A. The journal of Julius Rodman
Rod Serling's Night gallery reader. Entered in Part I
  under title

RODEOS
  Borland, H. When the legends die
Roderick Hudson. James, H.
Roger Caras' Treasury of great cat stories. Entered in
  Part I under title
Roger Caras' Treasury of great dog stories. Entered in
  Part I under title

ROGERS, ROBERT, 1731-1795
  Roberts, K. L. Northwest Passage
Roger's version. Updike, J.
Rogue male. Household, G.

ROGUES AND VAGABONDS
  Boyle, T. C. Water music
  Brown, J. D. Addie Pray
  Colette. The tender shoot
  Doctorow, E. L. Loon Lake
  Kerouac, J. The Dharma bums
  Kerouac, J. On the road
  Mann, T. Confessions of Felix Krull, confidence man
  Steinbeck, J. Cannery Row
  Steinbeck, J. Sweet Thursday
  Steinbeck, J. Tortilla Flat
Roll over and play dead. Hess, J.
Rolling stones. Henry, O.
  In Henry, O. The complete works of O. Henry p941-
  1060
The **Roman**. Waltari, M.

ROMAN CATHOLIC CHURCH *See* Catholic faith
ROMAN CATHOLIC RELIGION *See* Catholic faith
ROMAN EMPERORS *See* Rome—Kings and rulers
ROMAN EMPIRE *See* Rome
The **Roman** hat mystery. Queen, E.
ROMAN SOLDIERS *See* Soldiers—Rome
The **Roman** spring of Mrs. Stone. Williams, T.
The **romance** of Monte Beni. See Hawthorne, N. The
  marble faun

ROMANCES (GOTHIC) *See* Gothic romances
ROMANCES (LOVE STORIES) *See* Love affairs; Love
  stories

ROMANIA
  Wiesel, E. The forgotten

          Bucharest
  Bellow, S. The dean's December

ROMANIANS

          England
  Dickinson, P. Play dead

ROMANTIC SUSPENSE NOVELS *See* Gothic
  romances

ROME

          510-30 B.C.
  Fuentes, C. The two Numantias
  Massie, A. Caesar
  McCullough, C. The first man in Rome
  McCullough, C. Fortune's favorites
  McCullough, C. The grass crown
  Norton, A. Empire of the eagle
  Wilder, T. The ides of March

          30 B.C.-476 A.D.
  Asch, S. The Nazarene
  Caldwell, T. Dear and glorious physician
  Costain, T. B. The silver chalice
  Douglas, L. C. The robe
  Graves, R. Claudius, the god and his wife Messalina
  Graves, R. I, Claudius
  Lytton, E. B. L., Baron. The last days of Pompeii
  Sienkiewicz, H. Quo vadis
  Vidal, G. Julian
  Wallace, L. Ben-Hur
  Waltari, M. The Roman
  Wood, B. Soul flame
  Yourcenar, M. Memoirs of Hadrian, and reflections
  on the composition of Memoirs of Hadrian

          Kings and rulers
  Golding, W. Envoy extraordinary

          Politics
  See Politics—Rome

ROME (ITALY) *See* Italy—Rome
Romola. Eliot, G.
A **room** with a view. Forster, E. M.
  also in Forster, E. M. A room with a view and
  Howards End
A **room** with a view and Howards End. Forster, E. M.
ROOMING HOUSES *See* Boarding houses
ROOSEVELT, FRANKLIN D. (FRANKLIN DELANO),
1882-1945
  Roosevelt, E. The President's man

ROOSTERS
  García Márquez, G. No one writes to the colonel
Rosa. Ozick, C.
  In Ozick, C. The shawl
The **rosary** murders. Kienzle, W. X.
ROSE, BILLY, 1899-1966
  Bellow, S. The Bellarosa connection
A **rose** for virtue. Lofts, N.
The **rose** rent. Peters, E.
The **rose** without a thorn. Plaidy, J.
Rosemary's baby. Levin, I.
Ross Macdonald's Lew Archer, private investigator. Mac-
  donald, R.
Rostnikov's vacation. Kaminsky, S. M.
The **Rothman** scandal. Birmingham, S.
Rough cider. Lovesey, P.
Round the moon. Verne, J.
  In Verne, J. From the earth to the moon, and round
  the moon
Round the red lamp. Doyle, Sir A. C.
  In Doyle, Sir A. C. Conan Doyle's tales of medical
  humanism and values p15-302
Round up. See Lardner, R. The best short stories of Ring
  Lardner
The **Rowan.** McCaffrey, A.
ROYAL CANADIAN MOUNTED POLICE
  Freedman, B. Mrs. Mike
Royal Flash. Fraser, G. M.
Royal flush. Stout, R.
A **royal** murder. Roosevelt, E.
The **rubber** band. Stout, R.
  In Stout, R. Five of a kind p1-153

RUBIES
  Westlake, D. E. Why me?
Ruby. Guy, R.
The **ruby** knight. Eddings, D.
Ruin Creek. Payne, D.
Rules of evidence. Brandon, J.
Rules of prey. Sandford, J.
The **rules** of the game. Simenon, G.
A **ruling** passion. Michael, J.
Rum punch. Leonard, E.
RUMANIA See Romania
Rumors of peace. Leffland, E.
Rumpole à la carte. Mortimer, J. C.
Rumpole and the golden thread. Mortimer, J. C.
  In Mortimer, J. C. The second Rumpole omnibus
    p193-442
Rumpole for the defence. Mortimer, J. C.
  In Mortimer, J. C. The second Rumpole omnibus
    p11-192
Rumpole on trial. Mortimer, J. C.
Rumpole's last case. Mortimer, J. C.
  In Mortimer, J. C. The second Rumpole omnibus
    p443-667
Rumpole's return. Mortimer, J. C.
Run silent, run deep. Beach, E. L.
Runaway horses. Mishima, Y.

RUNAWAYS (CHILDREN)
  Guest, J. Second heaven

RUNAWAYS (YOUTH)
  Freedman, J. F. The obstacle course
  Lopez, S. Third and Indiana
  Mowry, J. Six out seven
  Spencer, S. Men in black
  Theroux, P. Millroy the Magician
The **running** man. King, S.
  In King, S. The Bachman books: four early novels
    by Stephen King

RURAL LIFE See Country life
RUSSIA
  See also Lithuania; Siberia (Russia); Ukraine
  Viertel, J. Life lines

16th century
Dunnett, D. The ringed castle

18th century
Pushkin, A. S. The captain's daughter

19th century
Chekhov, A. P. Anton Chekhov's short stories
Chekhov, A. P. The best known works of Anton Chekhov
Chekhov, A. P. Chekhov: the early stories, 1883-1888
Chekhov, A. P. Longer stories from the last decade
Dostoyevsky, F. The best short stories of Dostoevsky
Dostoyevsky, F. The brothers Karamazov
Dostoyevsky, F. Crime and punishment
Dostoyevsky, F. Demons
Dostoyevsky, F. The gambler
Dostoyevsky, F. The gambler, and other stories
Dostoyevsky, F. The house of the dead
Dostoyevsky, F. The idiot
Dostoyevsky, F. Notes from underground
Dostoyevsky, F. The short novels of Dostoevsky
Gogol', N. V. The overcoat, and other tales of good
  and evil
Gorky, M. Selected short stories
Pushkin, A. S. Alexander Pushkin: complete prose fiction
Sholem Aleichem. The nightingale
Tolstoy, L., graf. Anna Karenina
Tolstoy, L., graf. Childhood, Boyhood and Youth
Tolstoy, L., graf. The death of Ivan Ilyitch, and other
  stories
Tolstoy, L., graf. The Kreutzer sonata, The Devil, and
  other tales
Tolstoy, L., graf. The portable Tolstoy
Tolstoy, L., graf. Resurrection
Tolstoy, L., graf. The short novels of Tolstoy
Tolstoy, L., graf. Short stories
Tolstoy, L., graf. War and peace
Turgenev, I. S. Fathers and sons
Turgenev, I. S. First love

1900-1917
Babel', I. The collected stories
Malamud, B. The fixer
Pasternak, B. L. Doctor Zhivago
Pearson, D. The summer of the Barshinskeys
Sholem Aleichem. The adventures of Mottel, the cantor's son
Sholem Aleichem. The bloody hoax
Sholem Aleichem. Tevye's daughters

1917-1945
Anatoli, A. Babi Yar
Babel', I. The collected stories
Koestler, A. Darkness at noon
Littell, R. The revolutionist
Pasternak, B. L. Doctor Zhivago
Rand, A. We the living
Rybakov, A. N. Children of the Arbat
Sholokhov, M. A. And quiet flows the Don
Sholokhov, M. A. The Don flows home to the sea

1945-
Clancy, T. Red Storm rising
DeMille, N. The charm school
Finder, J. The Moscow Club
Pohl, F. Chernobyl
Solzhenitsyn, A. Cancer ward
Solzhenitsyn, A. The first circle
Solzhenitsyn, A. One day in the life of Ivan
  Denisovich
Thomas, C. Firefox
Thomas, C. Firefox down
Wiesel, E. The testament

Army—Officers
Solzhenitsyn, A. August 1914
Uris, L. Armageddon

Communism
See Communism—Russia

Navy
Clancy, T. The hunt for Red October

Peasant life
See Peasant life—Russia

Politics
See Politics—Russia

Prisoners and prisons
See Prisoners and prisons—Russia

Revolution of 1917
See Russia—1917-1945

Rural life
Dostoyevsky, F. Demons
Rutherfurd, E. Russka
Sholokhov, M. A. And quiet flows the Don
Sholokhov, M. A. The Don flows home to the sea
Solzhenitsyn, A. Cancer ward

Leningrad
See Russia—St. Petersburg

Moscow
Bulgakov, M. A. The master and Margarita
Egleton, C. A killing in Moscow
Freemantle, B. The button man
Tolstoy, L., graf. Childhood, Boyhood and Youth

St. Petersburg
Coetzee, J. M. The master of Petersburg
Dostoyevsky, F. Crime and punishment
Dostoyevsky, F. The idiot

The **Russia** house. Le Carré, J.
The **Russian** girl. Amis, K.

RUSSIAN REFUGEES
 Bermant, C. The patriarch
 Bosse, M. J. The warlord
 Nabokov, V. V. Look at the harlequins!
 Nabokov, V. V. Pnin

RUSSIAN REVOLUTION, 1905 *See* Russia—1900-1917

RUSSIAN REVOLUTION, 1917-1921 *See* Russia—1917-1945

RUSSIAN SECRET POLICE *See* Police—Russia

RUSSIAN SOLDIERS *See* Soldiers—Russia

RUSSIANS

   Australia
 Keneally, T. A family madness

   Belgium
 Benedict, E. Safe conduct

   England
 Amis, K. The Russian girl
 Follett, K. The man from St. Petersburg
 Pearson, D. The summer of the Barshinskeys

   Germany
 Turgenev, I. S. The torrents of spring
 Uris, L. Armageddon

   Poland
 Miłosz, C. The seizure of power

   United States
 Nabokov, V. V. Pnin
Russka. Rutherfurd, E.
The **rustlers** of West Fork. L'Amour, L.
Ryan's rules. See Leonard, E. Swag
The **Ryer** Avenue story. Uhnak, D.

S

S. Updike, J.

SAAVEDRA, MIGUEL DE CERVANTES *See* Cervantes Saavedra, Miguel de, 1547-1616

SABOTAGE
 Follett, K. Night over water
 MacLean, A. Force 10 from Navarone
 MacLean, A. The guns of Navarone
 Vonnegut, K. Player piano

SABOTEURS *See* Sabotage

SACCO, NICOLA, 1891-1927
 Sinclair, U. Boston
Sackett. L'Amour, L.
 In L'Amour, L. The Sacketts: beginnings of a dynasty
The **Sacketts:** beginnings of a dynasty. L'Amour, L.
Sackett's land. L'Amour, L.
The **sacred** and profane love machine. Murdoch, I.
Sacred clowns. Hillerman, T.
Sacred country. Tremain, R.
Sacred hunger. Unsworth, B.
Sacred monster. Westlake, D. E.
Sacrifice. Vachss, A. H.
Sad cypress. Christie, A.
Sadie Shapiro's knitting book. Smith, R. K.
Sadie when she died. McBain, E.

SADISM
 See also Cruelty
 Snow, C. P. The sleep of reason
 Thomas, D. M. Pictures at an exhibition

SAFARIS *See* Hunting—Africa
Safe conduct. Benedict, E.
Safely to the grave. Yorke, M.
Saga of Pliocene exile [series]
 May, J. The adversary

 May, J. The golden torc
 May, J. The many-colored land
 May, J. The nonborn king

SAHARA
 Bowles, P. The sheltering sky
 Cussler, C. Sahara
 Gilman, D. Caravan
Sahara. Cussler, C.

SAIGON (VIETNAM) *See* Vietnam—Ho Chi Minh City
Sailing to Byzantium. Silverberg, R.
 In Modern classic short novels of science fiction p504-60

SAILING VESSELS
 Higgins, J. Storm warning
 Pirsig, R. M. Lila
 Stone, R. Outerbridge Reach
Sailor song. Kesey, K.

SAILORS *See* Seamen

SAINT LOUIS (MO.) *See* Missouri—Saint Louis
Saint maybe. Tyler, A.
Saint Peter's Fair. Peters, E.

SAINT PETERSBURG (RUSSIA) *See* Russia—St. Petersburg

SAINT SIMONS ISLAND (GA.)
 Price, E. The beloved invader
 Price, E. Lighthouse
 Price, E. New moon rising

SAINT THOMAS (VIRGIN ISLANDS OF THE U.S.)
 Whitney, P. A. Columbella

SAINTS
 West, M. L. The devil's advocate
Saints and strangers. Carter, A.

SAKYAMUNI *See* Gautama Buddha

SALADIN, SULTAN OF EGYPT AND SYRIA, 1137-1193
 Scott, Sir W. The talisman

SALAMANCA, BATTLE OF, 1812
 Cornwell, B. Sharpe's sword
The **Salamanca** drum. Eden, D.

SALEM (MASS.) *See* Massachusetts—Salem
Salem's Lot. King, S.

SALES PERSONNEL AND SELLING
 Berger, T. Sneaky people
 Gurganus, A. Blessed assurance: a moral tale
 Kafka, F. Metamorphosis
 Updike, J. Rabbit is rich
 Vonnegut, K. Breakfast of champions

SALESMEN AND SALESMENSHIP *See* Sales personnel and selling
Sally Hemings. Chase-Riboud, B.
The **salt** eaters. Bambara, T. C.

SALVAGE
 Cussler, C. Dragon
 Cussler, C. Inca gold
 Cussler, C. Night probe!
 Cussler, C. Raise the Titanic!
 Cussler, C. Treasure
 Innes, H. The wreck of the Mary Deare

SALVATION
 See also Atonement

SALZBURG (AUSTRIA) *See* Austria—Salzburg
The **Salzburg** connection. MacInnes, H.

SAMURAI
 Clavell, J. Gai-Jin
 Clavell, J. Shogun
 Endō, S. The samurai
 Mishima, Y. Runaway horses

The **samurai**. Endō, S.

SAN ANTONIO (TEX.) *See* Texas—San Antonio

SAN FRANCISCO (CALIF.) *See* California—San Francisco

SAN JACINTO, BATTLE OF, 1836
Michener, J. A. The eagle and the raven

SANATORIUMS *See* Hospitals and sanatoriums
Sanctuary. Faulkner, W.
Sanctuary. Kellerman, F.
The **sanctuary** sparrow. Peters, E.
Sand castles. Freeling, N.
The **Sand** Pebbles. McKenna, R.
Sandkings. Martin, G. R. R.
  In The Best of the Nebulas p547-76
  In The Hugo winners v5 p70-132
The **sands** of time. Sheldon, S.

SANDSTORMS *See* Storms

SANDWICH, JOHN MONTAGU, 4TH EARL OF, 1718-1792
Bosse, M. J. The vast memory of love

SANTA ANNA, ANTONIO LÓPEZ DE, 1794?-1876
Michener, J. A. The eagle and the raven

SANTA CLAUS
Davies, V. Miracle on 34th Street

SANTA FE (N.M.) *See* New Mexico—Santa Fe
Santa Fe rules. Woods, S.

SANTA FE TRAIL
Bristow, G. Jubilee Trail

SANTIAGO CAMPAIGN, 1898
Jones, D. C. Remember Santiago
Sapphira and the slave girl. Cather, W.
  also in Cather, W. Willa Cather, later novels
The **sapphire** rose. Eddings, D.
Saratoga backtalk. Dobyns, S.
Saratoga bestiary. Dobyns, S.
Saratoga haunting. Dobyns, S.
Saratoga headhunter. Dobyns, S.
Saratoga snapper. Dobyns, S.

SARATOGA SPRINGS (N.Y.) *See* New York (State)—Saratoga Springs
Saratoga trunk. Ferber, E.
Sartoris. Faulkner, W.
Sartoris [uncut version] See Faulkner, W. Flags in the dust
Sarum. Rutherfurd, E.

SASKATCHEWAN *See* Canada—Saskatchewan
Sassafrass, Cypress & Indigo. Shange, N.

SASSOON, SIEGFRIED, 1886-1967
Barker, P. The eye in the door
Barker, P. Regeneration
Satan in Goray. Singer, I. B.
The **satanic** verses. Rushdie, S.

SATANISM
  See also Demoniac possession
Bosse, M. J. The vast memory of love
Tryon, T. Harvest home

SATIRE
  See also Humor; Irony; Parodies
Abbey, E. The fool's progress
Adams, D. The Hitchhiker's Guide to the Galaxy
Adams, D. The hitchhiker's quartet
Adams, D. Life, the universe, and everything
Adams, D. The restaurant at the end of the universe
Adams, D. So long, and thanks for all the fish
Alther, L. Original sins
Amado, J. The war of the saints
Amis, K. The folks that live on the hill
Amis, K. The Green Man
Amis, K. The old devils
Amis, K. The Russian girl
Austen, J. Northanger Abbey
Austen, J. Sense and sensibility
Barnard, R. Corpse in a gilded cage

Barth, J. Chimera
Barth, J. The end of the road
Barth, J. Giles goat-boy
Barth, J. The sot-weed factor
Beattie, A. Love always
Bellow, S. Humboldt's gift
Bellow, S. More die of heartbreak
Berger, T. Arthur Rex
Berger, T. The feud
Berger, T. The houseguest
Berger, T. Neighbors
Berger, T. Reinhart in love
Berger, T. Vital parts
Boulle, P. The bridge over the River Kwai
Boulle, P. Planet of the Apes
Bova, B. Cyberbooks
Boyle, T. C. East is East
Boyle, T. C. Road to Wellville
Buckley, C. T. Wet work
Burgess, A. A clockwork orange
Burgess, A. The pianoplayers
Butler, S. The way of all flesh
Cabell, J. B. Jurgen: a comedy of justice
Campbell, R. The Count of Eleven
Capote, T. Answered prayers
Cervantes Saavedra, M. de. Don Quixote de la Mancha
Cheever, J. The Wapshot chronicle
Cheever, J. The Wapshot scandal
Chesterton, G. K. The man who was Thursday
Connell, E. S. Mr. Bridge
Davies, R. The lyre of Orpheus
Davies, R. Murther & walking spirits
Dawson, C. Body of knowledge
De Bernières, L. Corelli's mandolin
De Vries, P. Consenting adults
De Vries, P. Reuben, Reuben
De Vries, P. Slouching towards Kalamazoo
DeLillo, D. White noise
DeMille, N. The Gold Coast
Dickens, C. Bleak House
Dickens, C. Hard times
Dickens, C. Little Dorrit
Dickens, C. Sketches by Boz
Donoso, J. A house in the country
Dos Passos, J. The 42nd parallel
Dos Passos, J. 1919
Dos Passos, J. U.S.A.
Dunne, D. People like us
Eco, U. Foucault's pendulum
Edgerton, C. Killer diller
Farmer, P. J. Riders of the purple wage
Fielding, H. The history of Tom Jones, a foundling
Fielding, H. Joseph Andrews
Flagg, F. Coming attractions
Fraser, G. M. Flashman
Fraser, G. M. Flashman and the mountain of light
Fraser, G. M. Royal Flash
Frayn, M. A landing on the sun
Gaddis, W. A frolic of his own
Gaddis, W. J R
Gaddis, W. The recognitions
Galbraith, J. K. A tenured professor
García Márquez, G. In evil hour
García Márquez, G. One hundred years of solitude
Gilman, C. P. Herland
Golding, W. The inheritors
Golding, W. The scorpion god: three short novels
Goldman, W. The princess bride
Grass, G. The call of the toad
Grass, G. Dog years
Grass, G. Local anaesthetic
Grass, G. The tin drum
Greene, G. Our man in Havana
Greenfeld, J. Harry and Tonto
Guareschi, G. Don Camillo and his flock
Guareschi, G. The little world of Don Camillo
Hašek, J. The good soldier Svejk

SATIRE—*Continued*

Heinlein, R. A. Job: a comedy of justice
Heinlein, R. A. The moon is a harsh mistress
Heinlein, R. A. Stranger in a strange land
Heller, J. Closing time
Heller, J. Good as Gold
Hemingway, E. The torrents of spring
Hesse, H. The glass bead game (Magister Ludi)
Hiaasen, C. Native tongue
Hiaasen, C. Strip tease
Hodgins, E. Mr. Blandings builds his dream house
Huxley, A. After many a summer dies the swan
Huxley, A. Antic hay
Huxley, A. Ape and essence
Huxley, A. Brave new world
Huxley, A. Crome Yellow
Huxley, A. Point counter point
Irving, J. The 158-pound marriage
Irving, J. A prayer for Owen Meany
Irving, J. The world according to Garp
Isaacs, S. After all these years
Isaacs, S. Close relations
Ishiguro, K. The remains of the day
James, H. The Bostonians
Kafka, F. Amerika
Kaufman, B. Up the down staircase
King, S. The running man
Kirst, H. H. Forward, Gunner Asch!
Kirst, H. H. The night of the generals
Kirst, H. H. The return of Gunner Asch
Kirst, H. H. The revolt of Gunner Asch
Kosinski, J. N. Being there
Kosinski, J. N. The hermit of 69th Street
Lem, S. Memoirs of a space traveler
Lewis, C. S. That hideous strength
Lewis, S. Babbitt
Lewis, S. Cass Timberlane
Lewis, S. Dodsworth
Lewis, S. Elmer Gantry
Lewis, S. It can't happen here
Lewis, S. Main Street
Ludlum, R. The road to Omaha
Lurie, A. The war between the Tates
Marquand, J. P. H. M. Pulham, esquire
Marquand, J. P. The late George Apley
Marquand, J. P. Point of no return
Maugham, W. S. Cakes and ale
Mayle, P. Hotel Pastis
McCarthy, M. Birds of America
McCarthy, M. A charmed life
McCarthy, M. The group
McCarthy, M. The groves of Academe
McGuane, T. The bushwhacked piano
McInerney, J. Brightness Falls
McMurtry, L. Some can whistle
Melville, H. The confidence-man: his masquerade
Mitford, N. Love in a cold climate
Mitford, N. The pursuit of love
Moore, B. Catholics
Mortimer, J. C. Paradise postponed
Murdoch, I. The book and the brotherhood
Murdoch, I. A fairly honourable defeat
Nabokov, V. V. Lolita
Nabokov, V. V. Pale fire
Nabokov, V. V. Pnin
Naipaul, V. S. A house for Mr. Biswas
Oates, J. C. Unholy loves
Ōe, K. The pinch runner memorandum
Orwell, G. Animal farm
Orwell, G. Keep the aspidistra flying
Orwell, G. Nineteen eighty-four
Pearson, T. R. Cry me a river
Pohl, F. The day the Martians came
Pohl, F. Homegoing
Pohl, F. The merchants' war
Pohl, F. The space merchants
Portis, C. Gringos
Powell, A. A dance to the music of time

Powers, J. F. Morte d'Urban
Powers, J. F. Wheat that springeth green
Prose, F. Household saints
Prose, F. Primitive people
Pym, B. An academic question
Pym, B. Civil to strangers
Pym, B. Less than angels
Pynchon, T. The crying of lot 49
Pynchon, T. V.
Pynchon, T. Vineland
Read, P. P. A season in the West
Reed, I. Japanese by spring
Reed, I. The last days of Louisiana Red
Reed, I. The terrible threes
Reed, I. The terrible twos
Richler, M. Joshua then and now
Richler, M. Solomon Gursky was here
Robbins, T. Half asleep in frog pajamas
Robbins, T. Jitterbug perfume
Robbins, T. Skinny legs and all
Roth, P. The great American novel
Santayana, G. The last Puritan
Shagan, S. A cast of thousands
Sheed, W. The boys of winter
Shulman, M. The many loves of Dobie Gillis
Shulman, M. Rally round the flag, boys!
Sneider, V. The Teahouse of the August Moon
Somtow, S. P. Jasmine nights
Spark, M. The ballad of Peckham Rye
Spark, M. A far cry from Kensington
Spark, M. The girls of slender means
Spark, M. Memento mori
Steinbeck, J. The short reign of Pippin IV
Sterne, L. The life and opinions of Tristram Shandy, gentleman
Swift, J. Gulliver's travels
Thackeray, W. M. Vanity fair
Theroux, P. Millroy the Magician
Tolkien, J. R. R. The fellowship of the ring
Tolkien, J. R. R. The hobbit
Tolkien, J. R. R. The lord of the rings
Tolkien, J. R. R. The return of the king
Tolkien, J. R. R. The two towers
Toole, J. K. A confederacy of dunces
Trollope, A. Phineas Redux
Trumbo, D. Johnny got his gun
Twain, M. A Connecticut Yankee in King Arthur's court
Twain, M. The gilded age
Updike, J. Bech: a book
Updike, J. Bech is back
Updike, J. The coup
Updike, J. S
Vargas Llosa, M. Captain Pantoja and the Special Service
Vidal, G. Hollywood
Vidal, G. Live from Golgotha
Vidal, G. Myra Breckinridge [and] Myron
Voltaire. Candide
Voltaire. Voltaire's Candide, Zadig, and selected stories
Vonnegut, K. Breakfast of champions
Vonnegut, K. Cat's cradle
Vonnegut, K. Deadeye Dick
Vonnegut, K. God bless you, Mr. Rosewater
Vonnegut, K. Hocus pocus
Vonnegut, K. Jailbird
Vonnegut, K. Mother night
Vonnegut, K. Player piano
Vonnegut, K. Slapstick
Waugh, E. Brideshead revisited
Waugh, E. Decline and fall
Waugh, E. The end of the battle
Waugh, E. The loved one
Waugh, E. Men at arms
Waugh, E. Officers and gentlemen
Waugh, E. Put out more flags
Waugh, E. Vile bodies
Weidman, J. I can get it for you wholesale

SATIRE—*Continued*
Weldon, F. The cloning of Joanna May
Weldon, F. Darcy's utopia
Weldon, F. The heart of the country
Weldon, F. The hearts and lives of men
Weldon, F. Leader of the band
Weldon, F. The life and loves of a she-devil
Weldon, F. Life force
Weldon, F. Trouble
Wells, H. G. Tono-Bungay
Wesley, M. A dubious legacy
West, N. The complete works of Nathanael West
West, N. Miss Lonelyhearts
Westlake, D. E. Baby, would I lie?
Westlake, D. E. Humans
Westlake, D. E. Trust me on this
White, T. H. The sword in the stone
White, T. H. The witch in the wood
Wibberley, L. The mouse that roared
Wilhelm, K. Crazy time
Wilson, A. N. The vicar of sorrows
Wolfe, T. The bonfire of the vanities
Saturday night and Sunday morning. Sillitoe, A.
Saturday the rabbi went hungry. Kemelman, H.
The **Saturn** game. Anderson, P.
In The Hugo winners v5 p269-325
A **savage** place. Parker, R. B.
Savage Sam. Gipson, F. B.
SAVANNAH (GA.) *See* Georgia—Savannah
Savannah. Price, E.
Saving grace. Garwood, J.
Savings and loam. McInerny, R. M.
SAVONAROLA, GIROLAMO, 1452-1498
Eliot, G. Romola
SAXONS *See* Anglo-Saxons
Sayonara. Michener, J. A.
Scales of gold. Dunnett, D.
Scandal. Endō, S.
A **scandal** in Belgravia. Barnard, R.
Scandal in Fair Haven. Hart, C. G.
The **scandal** of Father Brown. Chesterton, G. K.
In Chesterton, G. K. The Father Brown omnibus p815-974
Scandalous risks. Howatch, S.
SCANDINAVIA
Kurtén, B. Dance of the tiger
SCANDINAVIANS
Pacific Northwest
Doig, I. The sea runners
The **scapegoat.** Du Maurier, Dame D.
The **scapegoat.** Strindberg, A.
Scaramouche. Sabatini, R.
The **Scarlatti** inheritance. Ludlum, R.
Scarlet and black. See Stendhal. The red and the black
The **scarlet** city. Haasse, H. S.
The **scarlet** cloak. Plaidy, J.
The **scarlet** letter. Hawthorne, N.
also in Hawthorne, N. The complete novels and selected tales of Nathaniel Hawthorne
also in Hawthorne, N. The portable Hawthorne p337-546
The **Scarlet** Pimpernel. Orczy, E., Baroness
The **scarlet** ruse. MacDonald, J. D.
The **scarlet** seed. Pargeter, E.
In Pargeter, E. The heaven trilogy
Scarlett. Ripley, A.
The **scent** of water. Goudge, E.
SCHEHERAZADE (LEGENDARY CHARACTER)
Barth, J. Dunyazadiad
SCHINDLER, OSKAR, 1908-1974
Keneally, T. Schindler's list
Schindler's list. Keneally, T.
SCHIZOPHRENIA
See also Dual personality; Personality disorders
Greenberg, J. I never promised you a rose garden

SCHLESWIG-HOLSTEIN QUESTION
Fraser, G. M. Royal Flash
SCHLIEMANN, HEINRICH, 1822-1890
Stone, I. The Greek treasure
SCHLIEMANN, SOPHIA KASTROMENOS
Stone, I. The Greek treasure
SCHOLARS
See also Intellectuals
Amis, K. The Russian girl
Bellow, S. Herzog
Bellow, S. More die of heartbreak
Blair, L. The side of the angels
Bulgakov, M. A. The master and Margarita
Cather, W. The professor's house
Davies, R. The rebel angels
Dorris, M. The crown of Columbus
Eco, U. Foucault's pendulum
Hesse, H. The glass bead game (Magister Ludi)
Langton, J. Emily Dickinson is dead
MacInnes, H. The double image
MacInnes, H. Friends and lovers
Michaels, B. Houses of stone
Potok, C. In the beginning
Snow, C. P. The light and the dark
Updike, J. Roger's version
Warren, R. P. A place to come to
The **school** at Thrush Green. Read, Miss
School for murder. Barnard, R.
School for the blind. McFarland, D.
SCHOOL LIFE
Belgium
Brontë, C. The professor
Brontë, C. Villette
Denmark
Hoeg, P. Borderliners
England
Brontë, C. Emma
Delderfield, R. F. To serve them all my days
Dickens, C. David Copperfield
Dickens, C. Nicholas Nickleby
Dickinson, P. Hindsight
Hilton, J. Good-bye Mr. Chips
Read, Miss. Chronicles of Fairacre
Europe
L'Engle, M. The small rain
France
Colette. Claudine at school
Flaubert, G. Sentimental education
Germany
Grass, G. Local anaesthetic
Ireland
O'Brien, E. The country girls
Scotland
Spark, M. The prime of Miss Jean Brodie
United States
Auchincloss, L. The Rector of Justin
Conroy, P. The lords of discipline
Hunter, E. The blackboard jungle
Kaufman, B. Up the down staircase
Knowles, J. Peace breaks out
Knowles, J. A separate peace
Patton, F. G. Good morning, Miss Dove
Powers, J. R. Do black patent-leather shoes really reflect up?
Powers, J. R. The last Catholic in America
Saul, J. Shadows
Sinclair, A. Coffee will make you black
Spencer, L. Home song
SCHOOL SUPERINTENDENTS AND PRINCIPALS
Auchincloss, L. The Rector of Justin
Guthrie, A. B. Arfive
Ozick, C. The cannibal galaxy

SCHOOL SUPERINTENDENTS AND PRINCIPALS
—*Continued*
Spencer, L. Home song
SCHOOL TEACHERS *See* Teachers
SCHOOLS *See* School life
SCHULZ, BRUNO, 1892-1942
Ozick, C. The Messiah of Stockholm
SCIENCE FICTION
See also End of the world; Extrasensory perception;
Fantasies; Future; Interplanetary visitors; Inter-
planetary voyages; Interplanetary wars; Life on
other planets; Robots; Space colonies; Space flight;
Space ships; Time travel
Adams, D. Dirk Gently's Holistic Detective Agency
Adams, D. The Hitchhiker's Guide to the Galaxy
Adams, D. The hitchhiker's quartet
Adams, D. Life, the universe, and everything
Adams, D. The long dark tea-time of the soul
Adams, D. Mostly harmless
Adams, D. The restaurant at the end of the universe
Adams, D. So long, and thanks for all the fish
Aldiss, B. W. Helliconia spring
Aldiss, B. W. Helliconia summer
Aldiss, B. W. Helliconia winter
Aldiss, B. W. Man in his time
Aldiss, B. W. Total environment
Anderson, P. Harvest of stars
Anderson, P. Harvest the fire
Anderson, P. Operation Chaos
Anderson, P. Orion shall rise
Anderson, P. The shield of time
Anderson, P. Star of the sea
Anderson, P. The stars are also fire
Anderson, P. Tau Zero
Anderson, P. The Time Patrol
Anderson, P. The year of the ransom
Anthony, P. Blue Adept
Anthony, P. Chaos mode
Anthony, P. Fractal mode
Anthony, P. Isle of woman
Anthony, P. Juxtaposition
Anthony, P. Killobyte
Anthony, P. Out of Phaze
Anthony, P. Phaze doubt
Anthony, P. Robot Adept
Anthony, P. Shame of man
Anthony, P. Split infinity
Anthony, P. Unicorn point
Anthony, P. Virtual mode
Asimov, I. The best science fiction of Isaac Asimov
Asimov, I. The caves of steel
Asimov, I. The complete robot
Asimov, I. The complete stories
Asimov, I. Fantastic voyage
Asimov, I. Fantastic voyage II
Asimov, I. Forward the Foundation
Asimov, I. Foundation
Asimov, I. Foundation and earth
Asimov, I. Foundation and empire
Asimov, I. Foundation's edge
Asimov, I. The gods themselves
Asimov, I. I, robot
Asimov, I. The naked sun
Asimov, I. Nemesis
Asimov, I. Nightfall
Asimov, I. Nightfall, and other stories
Asimov, I. The positronic man
Asimov, I. Prelude to Foundation
Asimov, I. The rest of the robots
Asimov, I. Robot visions
Asimov, I. The robots of dawn
Asimov, I. Second Foundation
Ballard, J. G. The best short stories of J. G. Ballard
Balmer, E. When worlds collide
Bear, G. Moving Mars
Benford, G. Timescape
The Best from Fantasy & Science Fiction

The Best from Fantasy & Science Fiction: a 40th
anniversary anthology
The Best from Fantasy & Science Fiction: a 45th
anniversary anthology
The Best from Fantasy and Science Fiction: a special
25th anniversary anthology
The Best of the Nebulas
Best SF: 1968-1975
Bisson, T. England underway
Blish, J. The Star Trek reader [I]-IV
Boucher, A. The compleat werewolf and other stories
of fantasy and science fiction
Boulle, P. Planet of the Apes
Bova, B. Challenges
Bova, B. Cyberbooks
Bova, B. Death dream
Bova, B. Mars
Bova, B. Millennium
Bova, B. Orion and the conqueror
Bova, B. Orion in the dying time
Bova, B. To save the sun
Bova, B. Voyagers
Bradbury, R. Fahrenheit 451
Bradbury, R. I sing the Body Electric!
Bradbury, R. The illustrated man
Bradbury, R. The Martian chronicles
Bradbury, R. The stories of Ray Bradbury
Bradley, M. Z. The best of Marion Zimmer Bradley
Brin, D. Earth
Brin, D. Glory season
Brin, D. The postman
Brunner, J. The crucible of time
Brunner, J. A maze of stars
Brunner, J. Stand on Zanzibar
Bujold, L. M. Mirror dance
Butler, O. E. Adulthood rites
Butler, O. E. Dawn
Butler, O. E. Imago
Butler, O. E. Survivor
Campbell, R. Medusa
Card, O. S. The call of earth
Card, O. S. Earthborn
Card, O. S. Earthfall
Card, O. S. Ender's game
Card, O. S. The memory of earth
Card, O. S. The ships of earth
Card, O. S. Speaker for the Dead
Card, O. S. Xenocide
Chayefsky, P. Altered states
Cherryh, C. J. Chanur's Legacy
Cherryh, C. J. Foreigner
Cherryh, C. J. Heavy time
Cherryh, C. J. Hellburner
Cherryh, C. J. Rimrunners
Cherryh, C. J. Tripoint
Clarke, A. C. 2001: a space odyssey
Clarke, A. C. 2010: odyssey two
Clarke, A. C. 2061: odyssey three
Clarke, A. C. Beyond the fall of night
Clarke, A. C. Childhood's end
Clarke, A. C. The city and the stars
Clarke, A. C. Cradle
Clarke, A. C. Earthlight
Clarke, A. C. A fall of moondust
Clarke, A. C. The Garden of Rama
Clarke, A. C. The hammer of God
Clarke, A. C. Imperial Earth
Clarke, A. C. The nine billion names of God
Clarke, A. C. Rama II
Clarke, A. C. Rama revealed
Clarke, A. C. Rendezvous with Rama
Crichton, M. The Andromeda strain
Crichton, M. Jurassic Park
Crichton, M. Sphere
Crichton, M. The terminal man
Dangerous visions
David, P. Q-squared
De Hartog, J. The outer buoy

SCIENCE FICTION—_Continued_

Delany, S. R. Stars in my pocket like grains of sand
Dickson, G. R. Lost Dorsai
Dickson, G. R. Young Bleys
Donaldson, S. R. The gap into madness: chaos and order
Doyle, Sir A. C. The best science fiction of Arthur Conan Doyle
Doyle, Sir A. C. The lost world
Duane, D. Dark mirror
Farmer, P. J. The classic Philip José Farmer, 1952-1964--1964-1973
Farmer, P. J. The dark design
Farmer, P. J. Dayworld
Farmer, P. J. Dayworld breakup
Farmer, P. J. Dayworld rebel
Farmer, P. J. The fabulous riverboat
Farmer, P. J. Gods of Riverworld
Farmer, P. J. The magic labyrinth
Farmer, P. J. River of eternity
Farmer, P. J. To your scattered bodies go
Gibson, W. Virtual light
Haldeman, J. W. The forever war
Haldeman, J. W. Mindbridge
Harrison, H. Return to Eden
Harrison, H. The Stainless Steel Rat sings the blues
Harrison, H. Stainless steel visions
Harrison, H. West of Eden
Harrison, H. Winter in Eden
Heinlein, R. A. The cat who walks through walls
Heinlein, R. A. Citizen of the galaxy
Heinlein, R. A. Double star
Heinlein, R. A. Friday
Heinlein, R. A. The moon is a harsh mistress
Heinlein, R. A. The puppet masters
Heinlein, R. A. Stranger in a strange land
Heinlein, R. A. Time enough for love
Herbert, F. Chapterhouse: Dune
Herbert, F. God Emperor of Dune
The Hugo winners
James, P. D. The children of men
Jenkins, W. F. Exploration team
Kelly, J. P. Mr. Boy
Kessel, J. The Franchise
Keyes, D. Flowers for Algernon
Knight, D. F. The best of Damon Knight
Koontz, D. R. Strangers
Kotzwinkle, W. E.T.
Kress, N. Beggars & choosers
Kress, N. Beggars in Spain
Le Guin, U. K. Always coming home
Le Guin, U. K. City of illusions
Le Guin, U. K. The dispossessed
Le Guin, U. K. The eye of the heron
Le Guin, U. K. A fisherman of the inland sea
Le Guin, U. K. The lathe of heaven
Le Guin, U. K. The left hand of darkness
Le Guin, U. K. Planet of exile
Le Guin, U. K. Rocannon's world
Le Guin, U. K. The word for world is forest
Leiber, F. The Wanderer
Lem, S. Eden
Lem, S. Fiasco
Lem, S. His Master's Voice
Lem, S. Memoirs of a space traveler
Lessing, D. M. Shikasta
Levi, P. The sixth day, and other tales
Lewis, C. S. Out of the silent planet
Lewis, C. S. Perelandra
London, J. The star rover
May, J. The adversary
May, J. Diamond mask
May, J. The golden torc
May, J. Intervention
May, J. Jack the bodiless
May, J. The many-colored land
May, J. The nonborn king
McAuley, P. J. Red dust

McCaffrey, A. All the Weyrs of Pern
McCaffrey, A. The city who fought
McCaffrey, A. Damia
McCaffrey, A. Damia's children
McCaffrey, A. Dragonflight
McCaffrey, A. Dragonquest
McCaffrey, A. Dragonsdawn
McCaffrey, A. The greatest love
McCaffrey, A. Lyon's pride
McCaffrey, A. Pegasus in flight
McCaffrey, A. Power lines
McCaffrey, A. Powers that be
McCaffrey, A. The renegades of Pern
McCaffrey, A. The Rowan
McCaffrey, A. The ship who won
McCaffrey, A. The white dragon
McIntyre, V. N. The crystal star
McIntyre, V. N. Dreamsnake
Miller, W. M. A canticle for Leibowitz
Modern classic short novels of science fiction
Modern classics of science fiction
Moorcock, M. An alien heat
Moorcock, M. Behold the man
Moorcock, M. The end of all songs
Moorcock, M. The hollow lands
Morrow, J. City of Truth
Nebula awards [1]-29
Niven, L. The integral trees
Niven, L. Lucifer's hammer
Niven, L. The Mote in God's Eye
Niven, L. Ringworld
Niven, L. The Ringworld engineers
Niven, L. The smoke ring
Niven, L. A world out of time
Norton, A. Firehand
Norton, A. Redline the stars
The Norton book of science fiction
The Oxford book of science fiction stories
Piercy, M. He, she and it
Pohl, F. The annals of the Heechee
Pohl, F. Beyond the blue event horizon
Pohl, F. The day the Martians came
Pohl, F. Gateway
Pohl, F. The gateway trip
Pohl, F. Heechee rendezvous
Pohl, F. Homegoing
Pohl, F. Land's end
Pohl, F. Man Plus
Pohl, F. Mars Plus
Pohl, F. The merchants' war
Pohl, F. Mining the oort
Pohl, F. The space merchants
Pohl, F. The world at the end of time
Robinson, K. S. Green Mars
Robinson, K. S. Red Mars
Sagan, C. Contact
Sheffield, C. Georgia on my mind
Shelley, M. W. Frankenstein
Silverberg, R. At winter's end
Silverberg, R. The collected stories of Robert Silverberg
Silverberg, R. The Face of the Waters
Silverberg, R. Hot sky at midnight
Silverberg, R. Kingdoms of the Wall
Silverberg, R. Lord Valentine's castle
Silverberg, R. Majipoor chronicles
Silverberg, R. The new springtime
Silverberg, R. Nightwings
Silverberg, R. A Robert Silverberg omnibus
Silverberg, R. Valentine Pontifex
Spielberg, S. Close encounters of the third kind
Stephenson, N. The diamond age
Tepper, S. S. Grass
Tepper, S. S. Northshore
Tepper, S. S. A plague of angels
Tepper, S. S. Raising the stones
Tepper, S. S. Shadow's end
Tepper, S. S. Sideshow

SCIENCE FICTION—*Continued*
Tepper, S. S. Southshore
Tyers, K. The truce at Bakura
Vance, J. When the five moons rise
Varley, J. Demon
Varley, J. Titan
Varley, J. Wizard
Verne, J. From the earth to the moon, and Round the moon
Verne, J. A journey to the centre of the earth
Vinge, J. D. Catspaw
Vinge, J. D. The Snow Queen
Vinge, J. D. The Summer Queen
Vinge, J. D. World's end
Vinge, V. A fire upon the deep
Vonnegut, K. Breakfast of champions
Vonnegut, K. The sirens of Titan
Vonnegut, K. Slaughterhouse-five
Wells, H. G. The invisible man
Wells, H. G. Seven famous novels
Wells, H. G. The time machine
Wells, H. G. The war of the worlds
Wilhelm, K. And the angels sing
Wilhelm, K. Crazy time
Wilhelm, K. The dark door
Wilhelm, K. Death qualified
Wilhelm, K. Juniper time
Wilhelm, K. Welcome, chaos
Wilhelm, K. Where late the sweet birds sang
Willis, C. Death on the Nile
Wolfe, G. Caldé of the long sun
Wolfe, G. The death of Doctor Island
Wolverton, D. The courtship of Princess Leia
The Year's best science fiction
Zahn, T. Dark force rising
Zahn, T. The last command
Zelazny, R. Eye of cat
SCIENTIFIC EXPEDITIONS
Innes, H. Isvik
SCIENTIFIC EXPERIMENTS
Aldiss, B. W. Total environment
Benford, G. Timescape
Doctorow, E. L. The waterworks
Ellison, H. Adrift just off the Islets of Langerhans: latitude 38° 54′ N, longitude 77° 00′ 13 W
Hoeg, P. Smilla's sense of snow
Keyes, D. Flowers for Algernon [novelette]
Koontz, D. R. Midnight
Lem, S. His Master's Voice
Saul, J. Creature
Wells, H. G. The island of Doctor Moreau
Wilhelm, K. Death qualified
SCIENTIFIC RESEARCH *See* Research
SCIENTISTS
See also Anthropologists; Archeologists; Astronomers; Biochemists; Biologists; Chemists; Inventors; Paleontologists; Physicists; Women scientists
Chayefsky, P. Altered states
Cook, R. Mortal fear
Cook, R. Mutation
Crichton, M. The Andromeda strain
Crichton, M. Jurassic Park
Crichton, M. Sphere
Koontz, D. R. Night chills
Le Guin, U. K. Rocannon's world
Lem, S. His Master's Voice
Robinson, S. By any other name
Snow, C. P. The affair
Snow, C. P. The new men
The scions of Shannara. Brooks, T.
The scorpio illusion. Ludlum, R.
The scorpion god. Golding, W.
In Golding, W. The scorpion god: three short novels p9-62

The scorpion god: three short novels. Golding, W.
SCOTLAND
See also Hebrides (Scotland); Skye (Scotland)

To 1603
Dunnett, D. King hereafter
Garwood, J. Saving grace

16th century
George, M. Mary Queen of Scotland and the Isles
Hill, P. The sword and the flame
Plaidy, J. The captive Queen of Scots

18th century
Scott, Sir W. The bride of Lammermoor
Scott, Sir W. Rob Roy
Scott, Sir W. Waverly
Smollett, T. G. Humphry Clinker
Stevenson, R. L. The master of Ballantrae
Stirling, J. Shadows on the shore

19th century
Barrie, J. M. The little minister
Price, E. Bright captivity
Stevenson, R. L. The Merry Men

20th century
Cronin, A. J. The keys of the kingdom
Maitland, S. Ancestral truths
Peters, E. Legend in green velvet
Pilcher, R. September

Coal mines and mining
See Coal mines and mining—Scotland

Courts and courtiers
See Courts and courtiers—Scotland

Politics
See Politics—Scotland

Rural life
Buchan, J. The thirty-nine steps
Crichton, R. The Camerons
Cronin, A. J. A song of sixpence
Gaskin, C. A falcon for a queen
MacLean, A. When eight bells toll
Stevenson, D. E. Celia's house

Edinburgh
Spark, M. The prime of Miss Jean Brodie

Glasgow
Bermant, C. The patriarch
Stirling, J. Lantern for the dark

SCOTS

England
Dunnett, D. The ringed castle
Spark, M. The ballad of Peckham Rye

France
Scott, Sir W. Quentin Durward

Russia
Dunnett, D. The ringed castle

United States
Doig, I. Dancing at the Rascal Fair

West Indies
Gaskin, C. Fiona
SCOTT, ROBERT FALCON, 1868-1912
Bainbridge, B. The birthday boys
SCOTTISH DIALECT *See* Dialect stories—Scottish

SCOUTS AND SCOUTING
Berger, T. Little Big Man
Cooper, J. F. The Deerslayer
Cooper, J. F. The last of the Mohicans
Cooper, J. F. The Leatherstocking tales

SCRIPTWRITERS *See* Authors

SCULPTORS
Hawthorne, N. The marble faun

SCULPTORS—*Continued*
Hesse, H. Narcissus and Goldmund
James, H. Roderick Hudson
Piercy, M. Summer people
Stone, I. The agony and the ecstasy
The **sculptress**. Walters, M.

SCULPTURE
See also Wood carving
Scum. Singer, I. B.

SCYTHIANS
Llywelyn, M. The horse goddess

SEA *See* Ocean
The **sea** and poison. Endō, S.
The **Sea** Beggars. Holland, C.

SEA CAPTAINS *See* Seamen; Shipmasters
The **Sea-hawk**. Sabatini, R.
Sea Jade. Whitney, P. A.

Sea of fertility [series]
Mishima, Y. The decay of the angel
Mishima, Y. Runaway horses
Mishima, Y. Spring snow
Mishima, Y. The Temple of Dawn

The **sea** of grass. Richter, C.
Sea of tranquillity. Russell, P.
The **sea** runners. Doig, I.

SEA STORIES
See also Seamen; Whaling; names of wars with
the subdivision Naval operations
Beach, E. L. Run silent, run deep
Buchheim, L.-G. The boat
Conrad, J. The end of the tether
Conrad, J. Lord Jim
Conrad, J. The Nigger of the Narcissus
Conrad, J. Tales of land and sea
Conrad, J. Typhoon
Conrad, J. Youth
Cooper, J. F. The pilot
De Hartog, J. The captain
De Hartog, J. The Commodore
DiMercurio, M. Attack of the Seawolf
Fleming, T. J. Time and tide
Forester, C. S. Admiral Hornblower in the West Indies
Forester, C. S. Beat to quarters
Forester, C. S. Commodore Hornblower
Forester, C. S. Flying colours
Forester, C. S. Hornblower and the Atropos
Forester, C. S. Hornblower and the Hotspur
Forester, C. S. Hornblower during the crisis, and two
stories: Hornblower's temptation and The last
encounter
Forester, C. S. The last nine days of the Bismarck
Forester, C. S. Lieutenant Hornblower
Forester, C. S. Lord Hornblower
Forester, C. S. Mr. Midshipman Hornblower
Forester, C. S. Ship of the line
Graves, R. Hercules, my shipmate
Heggen, T. Mister Roberts
Higgins, J. Storm warning
Innes, H. Medusa
Innes, H. The wreck of the Mary Deare
London, J. The Sea-Wolf
MacLean, A. H.M.S. Ulysses
MacLean, A. When eight bells toll
Matthiessen, P. Far Tortuga
McCutchan, P. Cameron's crossing
McCutchan, P. Convoy homeward
McCutchan, P. Convoy north
McCutchan, P. Convoy of fear
McCutchan, P. Convoy south
McCutchan, P. The last farewell
Melville, H. Billy Budd, sailor
Melville, H. Moby-Dick
Melville, H. Omoo: a narrative of adventures in the
South Seas
Monsarrat, N. The cruel sea
Nordhoff, C. The Bounty trilogy

Nordhoff, C. Men against the sea
Nordhoff, C. Mutiny on the Bounty
Nordhoff, C. Pitcairn's Island
O'Brian, P. The golden ocean
O'Brian, P. The wine-dark sea
Poe, E. A. The narrative of Arthur Gordon Pym of
Nantucket
Poyer, D. The circle
Poyer, D. The gulf
Reeman, D. A ship must die
Sabatini, R. Captain Blood
Sabatini, R. The Sea-hawk
Smith, W. A. Hungry as the sea
Stone, R. Outerbridge Reach
Strindberg, A. By the open sea
Unsworth, B. Sacred hunger
Verne, J. The mysterious island
Verne, J. Twenty thousand leagues under the sea
The **sea**, the sea. Murdoch, I.
The **Sea-Wolf**. London, J.
Seafire. Gardner, J. E.

SEAMEN
See also Midshipmen; Sea stories; Shipmasters;
Vikings
Beach, E. L. Run silent, run deep
Conrad, J. The Nigger of the Narcissus
Cooper, J. F. The pilot
De Hartog, J. The Commodore
Forester, C. S. Ship of the line
Heggen, T. Mister Roberts
Innes, H. The wreck of the Mary Deare
London, J. The Sea-Wolf
MacLean, A. H.M.S. Ulysses
Matthiessen, P. Far Tortuga
McCutchan, P. Cameron's crossing
McCutchan, P. Convoy homeward
McCutchan, P. Convoy north
McCutchan, P. Convoy of fear
McCutchan, P. Convoy south
McCutchan, P. The last farewell
McKenna, R. The Sand Pebbles
Melville, H. Billy Budd, sailor
Melville, H. Moby-Dick
Monsarrat, N. The cruel sea
Nordhoff, C. Men against the sea
O'Brian, P. The golden ocean
O'Brian, P. The wine-dark sea
Poe, E. A. The narrative of Arthur Gordon Pym of
Nantucket
Poyer, D. The circle
Poyer, D. The gulf
Wouk, H. The Caine mutiny

SEAMSTRESSES *See* Dressmakers

SEANCES *See* Spiritualism

SEARCH AND RESCUE OPERATIONS
Atwood, M. Surfacing
Clarke, A. C. A fall of moondust
MacLean, A. Where eagles dare
The **search** committee. McInerny, R. M.
The **search** for Temperance Moon. Jones, D. C.
Search the shadows. Michaels, B.
Searching for Caleb. Tyler, A.
Searoad. Le Guin, U. K.

SEASIDE RESORTS
Duras, M. Blue eyes, black hair

A **season** for Swans. De Blasis, C.
A **season** in hell. Higgins, J.
A **season** in purgatory. Dunne, D.
A **season** in the West. Read, P. P.
A **season** of delight. Greenberg, J.
The **season** of passage. Pike, C.
Season of the monsoon. Mann, P.
Season of yellow leaf. Jones, D. C.
Seasons of the heart. Freeman, C.
SEATTLE (WASH.) *See* Washington (State)—Seattle
Sebastian. Durrell, L.

The **second** book of lost swords: Sightblinder's story.
    Saberhagen, F.

Second chance. Valin, J.
Second child. Saul, J.
The **second** coming. Percy, W.
The **second** deadly sin. Sanders, L.
Second Foundation. Asimov, I.
Second generation. Fast, H.
Second heaven. Guest, J.
The **second** Maigret omnibus. See Simenon, G. Maigret
    cinq
Second nature. Hoffman, A.
The **second** Rumpole omnibus. Mortimer, J. C.

SECOND SIGHT *See* Clairvoyance; Extrasensory percep-
    tion
Second vespers. McInerny, R. M.
The **secret** adversary. Christie, A.
    In Christie, A. Five classic murder mysteries p1-158
Secret agent. Conrad, J.
    In Conrad, J. Tales of the East and West p353-544
SECRET AGENTS *See* Secret service; Spies
The **secret** diary of Adrian Mole, age 13¾. Townsend, S.
    In Townsend, S. The Adrian Mole diaries
The **secret** families. Gardner, J. E.
Secret for a nightingale. Holt, V.
The **secret** generations. Gardner, J. E.
The **secret** houses. Gardner, J. E.
The **secret** of annexe 3. Dexter, C.
The **secret** of chimneys. Christie, A.
The **secret** of Father Brown. Chesterton, G. K.
    In Chesterton, G. K. The Father Brown omnibus
    p631-811

The **secret** of Santa Vittoria. Crichton, R.
The **secret** of the Villa Mimosa. Adler, E.
The **secret** pilgrim. Le Carré, J.
SECRET SERVICE
    See also International intrigue; World War, 1939-
    1945—Secret service
Allbeury, T. Deep purple
Allbeury, T. A time without shadows
Anthony, E. Albatross
Anthony, E. The avenue of the dead
Anthony, E. The company of saints
Anthony, E. The Janus imperative
Anthony, E. The tamarind seed
Block, L. The thief who couldn't sleep
Buchan, J. The thirty-nine steps
Clancy, T. The Cardinal of the Kremlin
Cleary, J. The faraway drums
Conrad, J. Secret agent
Deighton, L. Berlin game
Deighton, L. Faith
Deighton, L. Funeral in Berlin
Deighton, L. Game, set & match
Deighton, L. The Ipcress file
Deighton, L. London match
Deighton, L. Mexico set
Deighton, L. Spy hook
Deighton, L. Spy line
Deighton, L. Spy sinker
Deighton, L. XPD
Egleton, C. Hostile intent
Egleton, C. A killing in Moscow
Fleming, I. Bonded Fleming
Fleming, I. Casino Royale

Fleming, I. Doctor No
Fleming, I. From Russia, with love
Fleming, I. Goldfinger
Fleming, I. The man with the golden gun
Fleming, I. More gilt-edged Bonds
Fleming, I. On Her Majesty's Secret Service
Fleming, I. You only live twice
Forsyth, F. The deceiver
Forsyth, F. The fourth protocol
Forsyth, F. The Odessa file
Freemantle, B. Charlie's apprentice
Freemantle, B. Comrade Charlie
Fuentes, C. The Hydra head
Gardner, J. E. Brokenclaw
Gardner, J. E. Death is forever
Gardner, J. E. License renewed
Gardner, J. E. Never send flowers
Gardner, J. E. Seafire
Gardner, J. E. The secret families
Gardner, J. E. The secret generations
Gardner, J. E. The secret houses
Garfield, B. Hopscotch
Gifford, T. The Glendower legacy
Greene, G. The human factor
Greene, G. Our man in Havana
Hall, A. Quiller bamboo
Hall, A. Quiller barracuda
Hall, A. The Quiller memorandum
Hall, A. Quiller meridian
Hall, A. Quiller Salamander
Hall, A. Quiller solitaire
Harris, T. Black Sunday
Heinlein, R. A. Friday
Higgins, J. Confessional
Higgins, J. Day of judgment
Higgins, J. The eagle has landed
Higgins, J. Eye of the storm
Higgins, J. Night of the fox
Higgins, J. On dangerous ground
Higgins, J. Touch the devil
Le Carré, J. The honourable schoolboy
Le Carré, J. The little drummer girl
Le Carré, J. The quest for Karla
Le Carré, J. Smiley's people
Le Carré, J. The spy who came in from the cold
Le Carré, J. Tinker, tailor, soldier, spy
Ludlum, R. The Matarese Circle
Ludlum, R. The Parsifal mosaic
Ludlum, R. The Scarlatti inheritance
Lustbader, E. V. Jian
Maas, P. Father and son
MacInnes, H. Above suspicion
MacInnes, H. Assignment in Brittany
MacInnes, H. Message from Málaga
MacInnes, H. Ride a pale horse
MacInnes, H. The snare of the hunter
MacLean, A. Caravan to Vaccares
MacLean, A. When eight bells toll
Morrell, D. The brotherhood of the rose
Smith, W. A. Golden fox
Stewart, M. Airs above the ground
Thomas, C. A hooded crow
Thomas, C. Playing with cobras
Uris, L. Topaz

SECRET SOCIETIES
Hodge, J. A. The winding stair
Ludlum, R. The Matarese Circle
Neville, K. The eight
Secret window, secret garden. King, S.
    In King, S. Four past midnight p247-399

SECRETARIES
Vida, N. Goodbye, Saigon
The **secrets** of Harry Bright. Wambaugh, J.
The **secrets** of the Princess de Cadignan. Balzac, H. de
    In Balzac, H. de. The short novels of Balzac

SEDUCTION
Colette. Mitsou

SEDUCTION—*Continued*
Fraser, G. M. Flashman
Fraser, G. M. Royal Flash
Nabokov, V. V. Lolita
Tolstoy, L., graf. Resurrection
Seduction of the Minotaur. Nin, A.
In Nin, A. Cities of the interior p463-589
See Jane run. Fielding, J.
Seed of doubt. McInerny, R. M.
The **seeress** of Kell. Eddings, D.
Seize the day. Bellow, S.
Seize the day [novelette]. Bellow, S.
In Bellow, S. The portable Saul Bellow
In Bellow, S. Seize the day
The **seizure** of power. Miłosz, C.
The **select**. Wilson, F. P.
Selected short stories. Gorky, M.
The **selected** short stories of Edith Wharton. Wharton, E.
Selected short stories of Franz Kafka. Kafka, F.
Selected stories of Roald Dahl. Dahl, R.
Selected works. Volume two: Prose. Benét, S. V.
Self-defense. Kellerman, J.

SELF-MADE MEN
See also Success
Bermant, C. The patriarch
Caldwell, T. Captains and kings
Grau, S. A. The condor passes
James, H. The American
Weidman, J. I can get it for you wholesale
West, N. A cool million

SELF-SACRIFICE
De Hartog, J. The inspector
Dickens, C. A tale of two cities
French, M. Her mother's daughter
Glasgow, E. In this our life
Tolstoy, L., graf. Resurrection

SELFISHNESS
Balzac, H. de. Old Goriot
Glasgow, E. In this our life
Semi-tough. Jenkins, D.
Seminar for murder. Gill, B. M.
SENATE (U.S.) *See* United States. Congress. Senate
Sense and sensibility. Austen, J.
also in Austen, J. The complete novels of Jane Austen
A **sense** of honor. Webb, J. H.
A **sense** of reality. Greene, G.
In Greene, G. Collected stories p164-323
Sentimental education. Flaubert, G.
A **sentimental** journey through France and Italy. Sterne, L.
In Sterne, L. The life and opinions of Tristram Shandy, gentleman and A sentimental journey through France and Italy p691-832
A **separate** peace. Knowles, J.
SEPOY REBELLION *See* India—British occupation, 1765-1947
September. Pilcher, R.
September song. Humphrey, W.
SERGEANTS *See* Soldiers
Serpent war saga [series]
Feist, R. E. Shadow of a dark queen
Servant of the empire. Feist, R. E.

SERVANTS
See also Indentured servants; types of household employees
Amado, J. Gabriela, clove and cinnamon
Böll, H. The lost honor of Katharina Blum
Bosse, M. J. The vast memory of love
Cookson, C. The black velvet gown
Coulter, C. The Nightingale legacy
Dickens, C. The posthumous papers of the Pickwick Club
Faulkner, W. Requiem for a nun
Faulkner, W. The sound and the fury

Gordimer, N. July's people
Greene, G. A burnt-out case
Hemingway, E. The torrents of spring
Pushkin, A. S. The captain's daughter
Scott, Sir W. The bride of Lammermoor
Verne, J. Around the world in eighty days
A **servant's** tale. Fox, P.
Set this house on fire. Styron, W.
Setting free the bears. Irving, J.
In Irving, J. 3 by Irving p1-284
Seven by five. See Bates, H. E. The best of H. E. Bates
Seven days in June. Fast, H.
Seven days in May. Knebel, F.
Seven famous novels. Wells, H. G.
Seven for a secret. Holt, V.
Seven Gothic tales. Dinesen, I.
The **seven-ounce** man. Harrison, J.
In Harrison, J. Julip p85-182
The **seven-per-cent** solution. Meyer, N.
Seven rivers west. Hoagland, E.
Seventeen. Tarkington, B.
The **seventh** book of lost swords: Wayfinder's story. Saberhagen, F.
The **seventh** commandment. Sanders, L.
The **seventh** enemy. Tapply, W. G.
Seventh heaven. Hoffman, A.
The **seventh** sinner. Peters, E.
Seventh son. Card, O. S.
A **severed** wasp. L'Engle, M.

SEVILLE (SPAIN) *See* Spain—Seville

SEX
Amis, M. London fields
Baldwin, J. Another country
Ballard, J. G. The kindness of women
Barker, C. Imajica
Beckett, S. Dream of fair to middling women
Bellow, S. More die of heartbreak
Burgess, A. The pianoplayers
Busch, F. Closing arguments
Butler, R. O. They whisper
Capote, T. Answered prayers
Collins, W. The rationalist
Coulter, C. Impulse
Courter, G. The midwife's advice
De Vries, P. Consenting adults
Ellison, H. A boy and his dog
Eugenides, J. The virgin suicides
Gage, E. The master stroke
Gordimer, N. A sport of nature
Gould, J. Forever
Gregory, P. The wise woman
Hart, J. Damage
Herlihy, J. L. Midnight cowboy
Jennings, G. Raptor
Jong, E. Any woman's blues
Jong, E. Fear of flying
King, S. Gerald's game
Kosinski, J. N. Blind date
Kosinski, J. N. Passion play
Krantz, J. I'll take Manhattan
Lustbader, E. V. Angel eyes
Lustbader, E. V. White Ninja
MacNeil, R. Burden of desire
McMillan, T. Waiting to exhale
Michael, J. A ruling passion
Mishima, Y. The Temple of Dawn
Murdoch, I. The sacred and profane love machine
Oates, J. C. Foxfire
Patterson, J. Along came a spider
Patterson, R. N. Degree of guilt
Pirsig, R. M. Lila
Robards, K. Nobody's angel
Roberts, N. Honest illusions
Roth, P. The counterlife
Roth, P. The professor of desire
Sheed, W. The boys of winter
Shreve, A. Where or when

SEX—*Continued*
Siddons, A. R. Peachtree Road
Singer, I. B. Scum
Theroux, P. My secret history
Updike, J. Memories of the Ford Administration
Updike, J. Rabbit redux
Updike, J. Roger's version
Vidal, G. Myra Breckinridge [and] Myron
Viorst, J. Murdering Mr. Monti
Weldon, F. Life force
Winterson, J. Written on the body
Woodson, J. Autobiography of a family photo

SEX PROBLEMS
    See also Hermaphroditism; Incest; Marriage problems; Sexual perversion; Transsexuals
De Vries, P. Reuben, Reuben
Drabble, M. The waterfall
Huxley, A. Point counter point
Irving, J. The water-method man
Nabokov, V. V. Lolita
Rossner, J. Looking for Mr. Goodbar
Roth, P. My life as a man
Roth, P. Portnoy's complaint
Thomas, D. M. The white hotel
Tolstoy, L., graf. The Kreutzer sonata, The Devil, and other tales
Tremain, R. Sacred country
Woolf, V. The voyage out

SEXUAL HARASSMENT
Crichton, M. Disclosure
Sheldon, S. Nothing lasts forever

SEXUAL PERVERSION
Endō, S. Scandal
Seymour: an introduction. Salinger, J. D.
    In Salinger, J. D. Raise high the roof beam, carpenters, and Seymour: an introduction p1
Shadow of a dark queen. Feist, R. E.
Shadow of a doubt. Coughlin, W. J.
Shadow of the moon. Kaye, M. M.
The shadow of the torturer. Wolfe, G.
Shadow prey. Sandford, J.
Shadow song. Kay, T.
Shadows. Saul, J.
A shadow's bliss. Veryan, P.
Shadow's end. Tepper, S. S.
Shadows in their blood. Babson, M.
Shadows on the grass. Dinesen, I.
Shadows on the rock. Cather, W.
    also in Cather, W. Willa Cather, later novels
Shadows on the shore. Stirling, J.

SHAKERS
Harper, K. Circle of gold
Peck, R. N. A day no pigs would die

SHAKESPEARE, WILLIAM, 1564-1616
Kellerman, F. The quality of mercy
             Macbeth
Marsh, Dame N. Light thickens
Shalimar. Markandaya, K.
Shallow graves. Healy, J. F.
Shame. Rushdie, S.
Shame of man. Anthony, P.
Shan. Lustbader, E. V.
Shane. Schaefer, J. W.

SHANGHAI (CHINA) *See* China—Shanghai
The shape of dread. Muller, M.

SHARECROPPERS *See* Tenant farming
The sharing of flesh. Anderson, P.
    In The Hugo winners v2 p558-94
Shark dialogues. Davenport, K.

SHARKS
Benchley, P. Jaws

Sharpe's company. Cornwell, B.
Sharpe's devil. Cornwell, B.
Sharpe's eagle. Cornwell, B.
Sharpe's enemy. Cornwell, B.
Sharpe's gold. Cornwell, B.
Sharpe's honour. Cornwell, B.
Sharpe's regiment. Cornwell, B.
Sharpe's revenge. Cornwell, B.
Sharpe's rifles. Cornwell, B.
Sharpe's siege. Cornwell, B.
Sharpe's sword. Cornwell, B.
Sharpe's Waterloo. Cornwell, B.
Shattered silk. Michaels, B.
The shawl. Ozick, C.

SHAWNEE INDIANS
Thom, J. A. Panther in the sky
She. Haggard, H. R.
She walks these hills. McCrumb, S.

SHEEP
Cleary, J. The sundowners
Hardy, T. Far from the madding crowd

SHEEP FARMING *See* Sheep
Sheer torture. See Barnard, R. Death by sheer torture
The shell seekers. Pilcher, R.
Shelter. Phillips, J. A.
The sheltering sky. Bowles, P.
The shepherd. Girzone, J. F.

SHERIFF OF NOTTINGHAM (LEGENDARY CHARACTER)
Kluger, R. The Sheriff of Nottingham
The Sheriff of Nottingham. Kluger, R.

SHERIFFS
DeMille, N. Spencerville
Estleman, L. D. City of widows
McCrumb, S. The hangman's beautiful daughter
McCrumb, S. If ever I return, pretty Peggy-O
McCrumb, S. She walks these hills
Spencer, L. Forgiving
Shibumi. Trevanian
The shield of time. Anderson, P.
Shieldbreaker's story. See Saberhagen, F. The last book of swords: Shieldbreaker's story
Shikasta. Lessing, D. M.
A shilling for candles. Tey, J.
    In Tey, J. Four, five and six by Tey v1
Shiloh and other stories. Mason, B. A.
The shining. King, S.
The shining ones. Eddings, D.
Shining through. Isaacs, S.

SHIP CAPTAINS *See* Shipmasters

SHIP HIJACKING *See* Hijacking of ships
A ship must die. Reeman, D.
Ship of fools. Porter, K. A.
Ship of shadows. Leiber, F.
    In The Hugo winners v3 p5-50
Ship of the line. Forester, C. S.
The ship who won. McCaffrey, A.

SHIPMASTERS
Clavell, J. Shogun
Conrad, J. The end of the tether
Conrad, J. Typhoon
De Hartog, J. The captain
De Hartog, J. Star of Peace
Innes, H. The wreck of the Mary Deare
Kaye, M. M. Trade wind
McCutchan, P. Halfhyde and the fleet review
Melville, H. Billy Budd, sailor
Unsworth, B. Sacred hunger
Whitney, P. A. Sea Jade

SHIPPING
Price, E. Savannah
Smith, W. A. Hungry as the sea

The **shipping** news. Proulx, A.

SHIPS

   See also Sailing vessels; Shipping; Steamboats; Submarines; Warships

Officers

   See Shipmasters

The **ships** of earth. Card, O. S.

SHIPWRECKS AND CASTAWAYS

   See also Survival (after airplane accidents, shipwrecks, etc.)

Brent, M. Golden urchin

Clavell, J. Shogun

Conrad, J. Lord Jim

Cussler, C. Raise the Titanic!

Defoe, D. Robinson Crusoe

Gallico, P. The Poseidon adventure

Holt, V. The captive

Innes, H. The wreck of the Mary Deare

Smith, W. A. Hungry as the sea

Stevenson, R. L. The Merry Men

Wells, H. G. The island of Doctor Moreau

Shirley. Brontë, C.

A **shock** to the system. Brett, S.

The **shoes** of the fisherman. West, M. L.

Shogun. Clavell, J.

Shooting at loons. Maron, M.

The **shooting** party. Colegate, I.

The **shootist.** Swarthout, G. F.

SHOPKEEPERS *See* Merchants

SHOPPING BAG LADIES *See* Homeless persons

A **short** history of a small place. Pearson, T. R.

The **short** novels of Balzac. Balzac, H. de

The **short** novels of Dostoevsky. Dostoyevsky, F.

Short novels of Henry James. James, H.

The **short** novels of Thomas Wolfe. Wolfe, T.

The **short** novels of Tolstoy. Tolstoy, L., graf

The **short** reign of Pippin IV. Steinbeck, J.

SHORT STORIES

   See also Novelettes

200 years of great American short stories

Abe, K. Beyond the curve

Achebe, C. Girls at war, and other stories

Adams, A. After you've gone

Adams, A. Beautiful girl

After the king

Alcott, L. M. Louisa May Alcott: a selected fiction

Aldiss, B. W. Man in his time

Alfred Hitchcock presents: Stories not for the nervous

Allende, I. The stories of Eva Luna

Allingham, M. The return of Mr. Campion

Ambler, E. Waiting for orders

American voices

Anderson, P. The Time Patrol

Anderson, S. Certain things last

Anderson, S. Short stories

Anderson, S. Winesburg, Ohio

Archer, J. A twist in the tale

Asimov, I. The best science fiction of Isaac Asimov

Asimov, I. The complete robot

Asimov, I. The complete stories

Asimov, I. I, robot

Asimov, I. Nightfall, and other stories

Asimov, I. The rest of the robots

Asimov, I. Robot visions

Atwood, M. Bluebeard's egg and other stories

Atwood, M. Dancing girls and other stories

Atwood, M. Wilderness tips

Auchincloss, L. The collected stories of Louis Auchincloss

Auchincloss, L. Tales of yesteryear

Babel', I. The collected stories

Baldwin, J. Going to meet the man

Ballard, J. G. The best short stories of J. G. Ballard

Balzac, H. de. Droll stories

Bambara, T. C. Gorilla, my love

Barker, C. The books of blood

Barker, C. Cabal

Barker, C. The inhuman condition

Barnard, R. Death of a salesperson, and other untimely exits

Barth, J. Lost in the funhouse

Barthelme, D. Sixty stories

Bates, H. E. The best of H. E. Bates

Bausch, R. Rare & endangered species: a novella & stories

Beattie, A. The burning house

Beattie, A. Where you'll find me and other stories

Bell, M. S. Barking man and other stories

Bellow, S. Him with his foot in his mouth and other stories

Bellow, S. Seize the day

Bellow, S. Something to remember me by

Benson, E. F. Fine feathers and other stories

Berry, W. Fidelity

The Best American short stories, 1915-1995

The Best American short stories of the eighties

The Best from Fantasy & Science Fiction

The Best from Fantasy & Science Fiction: a 40th anniversary anthology

The Best from Fantasy & Science Fiction: a 45th anniversary anthology

The Best from Fantasy and Science Fiction: a special 25th anniversary anthology

The Best horror from Fantasy Tales

The Best horror stories

Best new horror [1]-4

Best of the Best American short stories, 1915-1950

The Best of the Nebulas

Best SF: 1968-1975

Bierce, A. The complete short stories of Ambrose Bierce

Binchy, M. The lilac bus: stories

Black thorn, white rose

Blish, J. The Star Trek reader [I]-IV

Block, L. Some days you get the bear

Bloom, A. Come to me

Böll, H. The stories of Heinrich Böll

Borges, J. L. The book of sand

Borges, J. L. Ficciones

Boucher, A. The compleat werewolf and other stories of fantasy and science fiction

Bova, B. Challenges

Bowen, E. The collected stories of Elizabeth Bowen

Bowles, P. Collected stories, 1939-1976

Boyle, K. Fifty stories

Boyle, T. C. If the river was whiskey

Boyle, T. C. Without a hero

Bradbury, R. Fahrenheit 451

Bradbury, R. The golden apples of the sun

Bradbury, R. I sing the Body Electric!

Bradbury, R. The illustrated man

Bradbury, R. The Martian chronicles

Bradbury, R. The stories of Ray Bradbury

Bradley, M. Z. The best of Marion Zimmer Bradley

Brand, M. The collected stories of Max Brand

Brand, M. Max Brand's best western stories

Brecht, B. Short stories, 1921-1946

Buck, P. S. East and West

Burgess, A. The devil's mode

Busch, F. The children in the woods

Caldwell, E. Complete stories of Erskine Caldwell

Calisher, H. The collected stories of Hortense Calisher

Calling the wind

Calvino, I. Cosmicomics

Calvino, I. Under the jaguar sun

Campbell, R. Strange things and stranger places

Camus, A. Exile and the kingdom

Canin, E. The palace thief

Capote, T. Breakfast at Tiffany's

Capote, T. A tree of night, and other stories

Card, O. S. Maps in a mirror

Carter, A. Saints and strangers

Carver, R. Cathedral

SHORT STORIES—*Continued*

Carver, R. What we talk about when we talk about love

Carver, R. Where I'm calling from

Cather, W. The troll garden

Cather, W. Willa Cather's collected short fiction, 1892-1912

Chabon, M. A model world and other stories

Chandler, R. The midnight Raymond Chandler

Chandler, R. Stories and early novels

Cheever, J. The stories of John Cheever

Cheever, J. Thirteen uncollected stories

Chekhov, A. P. Anton Chekhov's short stories

Chekhov, A. P. The best known works of Anton Chekhov

Chekhov, A. P. Chekhov: the early stories, 1883-1888

Chekhov, A. P. Longer stories from the last decade

Chesterton, G. K. Father Brown mystery stories

Chesterton, G. K. The Father Brown omnibus

Chesterton, G. K. The innocence of Father Brown

Christie, A. Hercule Poirot's casebook

Christie, A. Miss Marple: the complete short stories

Christie, A. Mr. Parker Pyne, detective

Christie, A. Three blind mice, and other stories

Christie, A. The witness for the prosecution, and other stories

Christmas stalkings

Cisneros, S. Woman Hollering Creek and other stories

Clair, M. Rattlebone

Clark, M. H. The Anastasia syndrome and other stories

Clark, M. H. The lottery winner

Clarke, A. C. The nine billion names of God

Colette. The collected stories of Colette

Collins, M. The man who dreamt of lobsters

Conrad, J. Great short works of Joseph Conrad

Conrad, J. The portable Conrad

Conrad, J. Tales of land and sea

Conrad, J. Tales of the East and West

Cooper, J. C. The matter is life

Coward, N. The collected stories of Noël Coward

Crane, S. The complete short stories & sketches of Stephen Crane

Crane, S. The portable Stephen Crane

Crane, S. The red badge of courage, and other stories

Dahl, R. Ah, sweet mystery of life

Dahl, R. Selected stories of Roald Dahl

Dangerous visions

De la Mare, W. Collected tales

The Dick Francis treasury of great racing stories

Dickens, C. Christmas stories

Dickens, C. Christmas tales

Dickens, C. The complete ghost stories of Charles Dickens

Dickens, C. Sketches by Boz

Dinesen, I. Last tales

Dinesen, I. Seven Gothic tales

Dinesen, I. Shadows on the grass

Dinesen, I. Winter's tales

Dixon, S. The stories of Stephen Dixon

Doctorow, E. L. Lives of the poets

Dorris, M. Working men

Dostoyevsky, F. The best short stories of Dostoevsky

Doyle, Sir A. C. Adventures of Sherlock Holmes

Doyle, Sir A. C. The best science fiction of Arthur Conan Doyle

Doyle, Sir A. C. The complete Sherlock Holmes

Doyle, Sir A. C. Conan Doyle's tales of medical humanism and values: Round the red lamp

Doyle, Sir A. C. Famous tales of Sherlock Holmes

Doyle, Sir A. C. The return of Sherlock Holmes

Doyle, Sir A. C. Tales of terror and mystery

Doyle, Sir A. C. Uncollected stories

Du Maurier, Dame D. Daphne du Maurier's classics of the macabre

Du Maurier, Dame D. Don't look now

Dumas, A. Short stories

Durrell, G. M. Marrying off mother, and other stories

Earth song, sky spirit

Ellroy, J. Hollywood nocturnes

Endō, S. The final martyrs

Estleman, L. D. General murders

The Faber book of gay short fiction

Famous ghost stories

Farmer, P. J. The classic Philip José Farmer, 1952-1964--1964-1973

Faulkner, W. Collected stories of William Faulkner

Faulkner, W. The Faulkner reader

Faulkner, W. Go down, Moses

Faulkner, W. The portable Faulkner

Faulkner, W. Uncollected stories of William Faulkner

Faulkner, W. The unvanquished

Fifty years of the best from Ellery Queen's Mystery Magazine

Fitzgerald, F. S. Babylon revisited, and other stories

Fitzgerald, F. S. The Basil and Josephine stories

Fitzgerald, F. S. The Fitzgerald reader

Fitzgerald, F. S. The portable F. Scott Fitzgerald

Fitzgerald, F. S. The short stories of F. Scott Fitzgerald

Fitzgerald, F. S. Six tales of the jazz age, and other stories

Fitzgerald, F. S. The stories of F. Scott Fitzgerald

The Flannery O'Connor Award: selected stories

Forester, C. S. Mr. Midshipman Hornblower

Forster, E. M. The collected tales of E. M. Forster

Fraser, A. Jemima Shore at the sunny grave and other stories

Fuentes, C. Constancia, and other stories for virgins

Gallant, M. Across the bridge

Gallant, M. In transit

Gallant, M. Overhead in a balloon

Galsworthy, J. The Galsworthy reader

García Márquez, G. Collected stories

García Márquez, G. Innocent Eréndira, and other stories

García Márquez, G. Leaf storm, and other stories

García Márquez, G. No one writes to the colonel, and other stories

García Márquez, G. Strange pilgrims

Gilliatt, P. 22 stories

Gilman, C. P. The Charlotte Perkins Gilman reader

Godwin, G. Mr. Bedford and the muses

Gogol', N. V. The overcoat, and other tales of good and evil

Gordimer, N. Jump and other stories

Gordon, M. Temporary shelter

Gorky, M. Selected short stories

Graves, R. Collected short stories

Great stories of the American West

Green cane and juicy flotsam

Greenberg, J. Rites of passage

Greenberg, J. With the Snow Queen

Greene, G. Collected stories

Greene, G. The last word and other stories

Growing up Latino

Gurganus, A. White people

Hammett, D. The big knockover

Hammett, D. The Continental Op

Hardy, T. Wessex tales

Harrison, H. Stainless steel visions

Harte, B. The best short stories of Bret Harte

Harte, B. The Luck of Roaring Camp, and other tales

Hawthorne, N. The complete novels and selected tales of Nathaniel Hawthorne

Hawthorne, N. Complete short stories of Nathaniel Hawthorne

Hawthorne, N. The portable Hawthorne

Hawthorne, N. Twice-told tales

Helprin, M. Ellis Island & other stories

Hemingway, E. The complete short stories of Ernest Hemingway

Hemingway, E. The Hemingway reader

Hemingway, E. In our time

Hemingway, E. Men without women

Hemingway, E. The Nick Adams stories

SHORT STORIES—*Continued*

Hemingway, E. The short stories of Ernest Hemingway
Hemingway, E. The snows of Kilimanjaro, and other stories
Henry, O. The best short stories of O. Henry
Henry, O. The complete works of O. Henry
Hersey, J. Key West tales
Hesse, H. Stories of five decades
Himes, C. The collected stories of Chester Himes
The Horror hall of fame
Houston, P. Cowboys are my weakness
Hughes, L. Laughing to keep from crying
Hughes, L. Simple's Uncle Sam
The Hugo winners
Humphrey, W. The collected stories of William Humphrey
Humphrey, W. September song
Hurston, Z. N. The complete stories
Huxley, A. Collected short stories
Iguana dreams
Irving, W. The complete tales of Washington Irving
Irving, W. Washington Irving's Tales of the supernatural
Isherwood, C. Goodbye to Berlin
Jackson, S. Come along with me
Jackson, S. The lottery; or, The adventures of James Harris
Jakes, J. The best western stories of John Jakes
James, H. The American novels and stories of Henry James
James, H. The complete tales of Henry James
James, H. The Henry James reader
James, H. The short stories of Henry James
Jewett, S. O. The best stories of Sarah Orne Jewett
Jewett, S. O. The country of the pointed firs and other stories
Jhabvala, R. P. Out of India
Jones, T. The pugilist at rest
Joyce, J. Dubliners
Kafka, F. Collected stories
Kafka, F. The complete stories
Kafka, F. The metamorphosis and other stories
Kafka, F. The penal colony: stories and short pieces
Kafka, F. Selected short stories of Franz Kafka
Keillor, G. The book of guys
Keillor, G. Happy to be here
Keillor, G. Leaving home
Kenan, R. Let the dead bury their dead and other stories
King, S. Night shift
King, S. Nightmares & dreamscapes
King, S. Skeleton crew
Kinsella, W. P. The further adventures of Slugger McBatt
Kinsella, W. P. Red wolf, red wolf
Kipling, R. The best short stories of Rudyard Kipling
Kipling, R. Collected stories
Knight, D. F. The best of Damon Knight
Kundera, M. Laughable loves
L'Amour, L. The outlaws of Mesquite
Lardner, R. The best short stories of Ring Lardner
Lardner, R. Ring around the bases
Lawrence, D. H. Collected stories
Le Guin, U. K. A fisherman of the inland sea
Le Guin, U. K. Orsinian tales
Le Guin, U. K. Searoad
Lederer, W. J. The ugly American
Legal fictions
Lem, S. Memoirs of a space traveler
Lessing, D. M. African stories
Lessing, D. M. The real thing
Lessing, D. M. Stories
Levi, P. The sixth day, and other tales
Lewis, C. S. The dark tower and other stories
A Literary Christmas
The Literary ghost
The Literary traveler
Lively, P. Pack of cards and other stories
London, J. The complete short stories of Jack London

London, J. Short stories of Jack London
London, J. South Sea tales
London, J. Stories of Hawaii
Looking for a rain god: an anthology of contemporary African short stories
Lovecraft, H. P. At the mountains of madness, and other novels
Lovecraft, H. P. The Dunwich horror, and others
Lovecraft, H. P. The horror in the museum, and other revisions
Lovecraft's legacy
Lurie, A. Women and ghosts
Macdonald, R. Ross Macdonald's Lew Archer, private investigator
Maḥfūz, N. The time and the place and other stories
Malamud, B. A Malamud reader
Malamud, B. The stories of Bernard Malamud
Mann, T. Death in Venice and seven other stories
Mann, T. Stories of three decades
Mansfield, K. The garden party and other stories
Mansfield, K. The short stories of Katherine Mansfield
Mason, B. A. Love life
Mason, B. A. Shiloh and other stories
Matthiessen, P. On the river Styx and other stories
Maugham, W. S. The best short stories of W. Somerset Maugham
Maugham, W. S. Complete short stories
Maupassant, G. de. The collected stories of Guy de Maupassant
Maupassant, G. de. The dark side of Guy de Maupassant
Maurois, A. The collected stories of André Maurois
Maxwell, W. All the days and nights
McCaffrey, A. The chronicles of Pern
McCaffrey, A. The girl who heard dragons
McCorkle, J. Crash diet
McCullers, C. The ballad of the sad café: the novels and stories of Carson McCullers
McCullers, C. Collected stories
McGahern, J. The collected stories
McGuane, T. To skin a cat
McKnight, R. The kind of light that shines on Texas
Michener, J. A. Creatures of the kingdom
Michener, J. A. Tales of the South Pacific
Miller, S. Inventing the Abbotts and other stories
Minot, S. Lust & other stories
Mishima, Y. Acts of worship
Modern classics of science fiction
Morris, W. Collected stories, 1948-1986
Mortimer, J. C. Rumpole à la carte
Mortimer, J. C. Rumpole on trial
Mortimer, J. C. The second Rumpole omnibus
Mowat, F. The Snow Walker
Mukherjee, B. The middleman and other stories
Munro, A. Friend of my youth
Munro, A. The moons of Jupiter
Munro, A. Open secrets
Mysterious cat stories
The Mysterious West
Nabokov, V. V. Nabokov's dozen
Narayan, R. K. The grandmother's tale and selected stories
Narayan, R. K. Malgudi days
Narayan, R. K. Under the banyan tree and other stories
Nebula awards [1]-29
The New treasury of great racing stories
The Norton book of ghost stories
The Norton book of science fiction
Oates, J. C. Haunted
Oates, J. C. Heat, and other stories
Oates, J. C. Marriages and infidelities
Oates, J. C. Where are you going, where have you been?
Oates, J. C. Where is here?
O'Brien, E. A fanatic heart
O'Brien, E. Lantern slides
O'Brien, T. The things they carried

SHORT STORIES—*Continued*

O'Connor, F. The complete stories
O'Connor, F. Everything that rises must converge
O'Connor, F. A good man is hard to find and other stories
O'Connor, F. Collected stories
O'Faoláin, S. The collected stories of Sean O'Faolain
O'Hara, J. Collected stories of John O'Hara
Olsen, T. Tell me a riddle
The Oxford book of American short stories
The Oxford book of English ghost stories
The Oxford book of gothic tales
The Oxford book of Irish short stories
The Oxford book of modern fairy tales
The Oxford book of science fiction stories
The Oxford book of short stories
Paley, G. The collected stories
Parker, D. Here lies
Paton, A. Tales from a troubled land
Penguin book of gay short fiction
The Penguin book of lesbian short stories
Peters, E. A rare Benedictine
Pilcher, R. Flowers in the rain & other stories
Pirandello, L. Short stories
Poe, E. A. The collected tales and poems of Edgar Allan Poe
Poe, E. A. Complete stories and poems of Edgar Allan Poe
Pohl, F. The gateway trip
Porter, K. A. The collected stories of Katherine Anne Porter
Porter, K. A. Flowering Judas, and other stories
Porter, K. A. The leaning tower, and other stories
Price, R. The collected stories
Price, R. The foreseeable future
Pritchett, V. S. Complete collected stories
Pushkin, A. S. Alexander Pushkin: complete prose fiction
Pym, B. Civil to strangers and other writings
Pynchon, T. Slow learner
Queen, E. The best of Ellery Queen
Rawlings, M. K. The Marjorie Rawlings reader
Rawlings, M. K. Short stories
Rendell, R. Collected stories
Rhys, J. The collected short stories
Rod Serling's Night gallery reader
Roger Caras' Treasury of great cat stories
Roger Caras' Treasury of great dog stories
Roth, P. Goodbye, Columbus, and five short stories
Runyon, D. Best of Runyon
Runyon, D. Guys and dolls
Rushdie, S. East, west
Saki. The short stories of Saki
Salinger, J. D. Nine stories
Sartre, J. P. Intimacy, and other stories
Sayers, D. L. Hangman's holiday
Sayers, D. L. In the teeth of the evidence and other stories
Sayers, D. L. Lord Peter
Schaefer, J. W. The collected stories of Jack Schaefer
Shannon, D. Murder by the tale
Shaw, I. Short stories: five decades
Sholem Aleichem. The best of Sholom Aleichem
Sholem Aleichem. Tevye the dairyman and The railroad stories
Sholem Aleichem. Tevye's daughters
Shulman, M. The many loves of Dobie Gillis
Sillitoe, A. The loneliness of the long-distance runner
Silverberg, R. The collected stories of Robert Silverberg
Singer, I. B. The collected stories of Isaac Bashevis Singer
Singer, I. B. The death of Methuselah and other stories
Singer, I. B. Gimpel the fool, and other stories
Singer, I. B. An Isaac Bashevis Singer reader
The Sleeper wakes
Smiley, J. The age of grief
Smith, L. Cakewalk

Smith, L. Me and my baby view the eclipse
Snow white, blood red
Spark, M. The stories of Muriel Spark
Spencer, E. The stories of Elizabeth Spencer
Stafford, J. The collected stories of Jean Stafford
Stegner, W. E. Collected stories of Wallace Stegner
Steinbeck, J. The long valley
Steinbeck, J. The portable Steinbeck
Stevenson, R. L. The complete short stories
Stevenson, R. L. The complete short stories of Robert Louis Stevenson
Stevenson, R. L. The strange case of Dr. Jekyll and Mr. Hyde, and other famous tales
Stoker, B. The Bram Stoker bedside companion
Stoker, B. Midnight tales
Straub, P. Houses without doors
Struther, J. Mrs. Miniver
Styron, W. A Tidewater morning: three tales from youth
Tales of the Witch World [1]-3
Tallent, E. Honey
Theroux, P. World's end and other stories
Thomas, D. The collected stories
Tolkien, J. R. R. The book of lost tales
Tolkien, J. R. R. Unfinished tales of Númenor and Middle-earth
Tolstoy, L., graf. The death of Ivan Ilyitch, and other stories
Tolstoy, L., graf. The portable Tolstoy
Tolstoy, L., graf. Short stories
Trevor, W. The collected stories
Trollope, A. The complete shorter fiction
Twain, M. The complete short stories
Twain, M. The man that corrupted Hadleyburg, and other stories and essays
Twain, M. Mysterious stranger, and other stories
Twain, M. Tom Sawyer abroad, and other stories
The Unforgetting heart: an anthology of short stories by African American women (1859-1993)
Updike, J. The afterlife and other stories
Updike, J. Bech: a book
Updike, J. Bech is back
Updike, J. Pigeon feathers, and other stories
Updike, J. Trust me
Vance, J. When the five moons rise
The Virago book of ghost stories
Voltaire. Candide and other stories
Voltaire. Voltaire's Candide, Zadig, and selected stories
Vonnegut, K. Welcome to the monkey house
Walker, A. You can't keep a good woman down
Waugh, E. Charles Ryder's schooldays and other stories
Wells, H. G. The complete short stories of H. G. Wells
Welty, E. The collected stories of Eudora Welty
Welty, E. The golden apples
West, J. Collected stories of Jessamyn West
West, J. The friendly persuasion
Wharton, E. The collected short stories of Edith Wharton
Wharton, E. The selected short stories of Edith Wharton
Wharton, E. The stories of Edith Wharton
Wideman, J. E. The stories of John Edgar Wideman
Wilhelm, K. And the angels sing
Williams, T. Collected stories
Wodehouse, P. G. Tales from the Drones Club
Wodehouse, P. G. A Wodehouse bestiary
Wodehouse, P. G. The world of Jeeves
Wolf, C. What remains and other stories
Wolfe, T. The complete short stories of Thomas Wolfe
Wolfe, T. The portable Thomas Wolfe
A Woman's eye
Woolf, V. The complete shorter fiction of Virginia Woolf
Wright, R. Eight men
Wright, R. Uncle Tom's children
The Year's best fantasy and horror

SHORT STORIES—*Continued*
The Year's best science fiction
Young, C. The wedding dress
You've got to read this
Zola, É. Three faces of love
Short stories. Anderson, S.
Short stories. Dumas, A.
Short stories. Pirandello, L.
Short stories. Rawlings, M. K.
Short stories. Tolstoy, L., graf
Short stories, 1921-1946. Brecht, B.
Short stories: five decades. Shaw, I.
The **short** stories of Ernest Hemingway. Hemingway, E.
The **short** stories of F. Scott Fitzgerald. Fitzgerald, F. S.
The **short** stories of H.G. Wells. See Wells, H. G. The complete short stories of H. G. Wells
The **short** stories of Henry James. James, H.
Short stories of Jack London. London, J.
The **short** stories of Katherine Mansfield. Mansfield, K.
The **short** stories of Saki. Saki
A **short** walk. Childress, A.
A **shorter** Finnegans wake. Joyce, J.
Shosha. Singer, I. B.
Show boat. Ferber, E.
Showdown at Yellow Butte. L'Amour, L.
In L'Amour, L. Four complete novels p365-490
Shroud for a nightingale. James, P. D.
In James, P. D. Crime times three
The **shrouded** walls. Howatch, S.

SIAMESE CATS *See* Cats

SIAMESE TWINS
McCammon, R. R. Gone south
Twain, M. Those extraordinary twins

SIBERIA (RUSSIA)
Dostoyevsky, F. The house of the dead
L'Amour, L. Last of the breed
Pasternak, B. L. Doctor Zhivago
Prisoners and prisons
See Prisoners and prisons—Siberia (Russia)
The **Sicilian.** Puzo, M.

SICILY
See also Italy—Syracuse
Hersey, J. A bell for Adano
Higgins, J. Luciano's luck
Hodge, J. A. Escapade
Pirandello, L. The outcast
Puzo, M. The Sicilian
Renault, M. The mask of Apollo
Tomasi di Lampedusa, G. The leopard
Aristocracy
See Aristocracy—Sicily
Peasant life
See Peasant life—Sicily

SICK CHILDREN
McIntyre, V. N. Of mist, and grass, and sand

SICKERT, WALTER, 1860-1942
West, P. The women of Whitechapel and Jack the Ripper

SIDDHĀRTHA *See* Gautama Buddha
Siddhartha. Hesse, H.
The **side** of the angels. Blair, L.
Sideshow. Tepper, S. S.

SIEGE OF BADAJOZ *See* Peninsular War, 1807-1814
The **siege** of London. James, H.
In James, H. The complete tales of Henry James v5

SIERRA MADRE MOUNTAINS (MEXICO)
Traven, B. The treasure of the Sierra Madre
Sightblinder's story. See Saberhagen, F. The second book of lost swords: Sightblinder's story

Sign of chaos. Zelazny, R.
The **sign** of four. Doyle, Sir A. C.
also in Doyle, Sir A. C. The complete Sherlock Holmes
also in Doyle, Sir A. C. Famous tales of Sherlock Holmes p187-311
The **sign** of the four. See Doyle, Sir A. C. The sign of four
Sign of the unicorn. Zelazny, R.

SIKSIKA INDIANS
Stuart, C. Walks Far Woman
Silas Marner. Eliot, G.
Silence. Endō, S.
Silence in Hanover Close. Perry, A.
The **silence** in the garden. Trevor, W.
The **silence** of the lambs. Harris, T.
The **silent** angel. Böll, H.
The **silent** cry. Ōe, K.
Silent partner. Kellerman, J.
Silent prey. Sandford, J.
Silent thunder. Estleman, L. D.
Silhouette in scarlet. Peters, E.

SILK INDUSTRY
Holt, V. The silk vendetta
Silk road. Larsen, J.
The **silk** vendetta. Holt, V.
The **Silmarillion.** Tolkien, J. R. R.
The **silver** chalice. Costain, T. B.
The **Silver** Ghost. MacLeod, C.

SILVER MINES AND MINING
Conrad, J. Nostromo
Schofield, S. C. Telluride
The **silver** spoon. Galsworthy, J.
In Galsworthy, J. A modern comedy
The **silver** touch. Laker, R.
Silver wedding. Binchy, M.
Silverhill. Whitney, P. A.

SILVERSMITHS
Laker, R. The silver touch
Simple gifts. Greenberg, J.
A **simple** honorable man. Richter, C.
A **simple** plan. Smith, S. B.
Simple speaks his mind. Hughes, L.
Simple stakes a claim. Hughes, L.
Simple takes a wife. Hughes, L.
Simple's Uncle Sam. Hughes, L.

SIMPSON, WALLIS WARFIELD *See* Windsor, Wallis Warfield, Duchess of, 1896-1986

SIN
See also Guilt
Greene, G. Brighton rock
Sin. Hart, J.
The **sin** within her smile. Gash, J.

SINAI CAMPAIGN, 1956
Uris, L. Mitla Pass
Wouk, H. The hope
Sine qua nun. Quill, M.

SINGAPORE
Boulle, P. The bridge over the River Kwai
Clavell, J. King Rat

SINGERS
Cather, W. The song of the lark
Childress, M. Tender
Dart, I. R. I'll be there
Hesse, H. Gertrude
Li, P.-H. Farewell to my concubine
McCrumb, S. If ever I return, pretty Peggy-O
Pearson, D. Voices of summer
Pynchon, T. The crying of lot 49
Rice, A. Cry to heaven
Sarton, M. Anger
Smith, L. The devil's dream
Thomas, D. M. The white hotel
Tyler, A. A slipping-down life

Singing in the shrouds. Marsh, Dame N.
The **singing** sands. Tey, J.
   also in Tey, J. Four, five and six by Tey v2
Singing songs. Tilly, M.
The **singing** stones. Whitney, P. A.

SINGLE MEN
See also Widowers
Barth, J. The floating opera
Brookner, A. A private view
Pym, B. Less than angels
Pym, B. Quartet in autumn
Read, Miss. Winter in Thrush Green

SINGLE-PARENT FAMILY
Corman, A. 50
Corman, A. Kramer versus Kramer
Dart, I. R. The Stork Club
Dorris, M. The crown of Columbus
Godwin, G. Father Melancholy's daughter
Gold, H. A girl of forty
Morris, M. A mother's love
Petry, A. L. The street
Smith, R. K. Jane's house
A **single** pebble. Hersey, J.

SINGLE WOMEN
See also Unmarried mothers; Widows
Ashton-Warner, S. Spinster
Balzac, H. de. Cousin Bette
Brookner, A. Fraud
Brookner, A. Hotel du Lac
Capote, T. The grass harp
Clark, M. H. The Anastasia syndrome
Faulkner, W. Intruder in the dust
Forester, C. S. The African Queen
Godwin, G. The odd woman
Godwin, G. Violet Clay
Gordon, M. Final payments
Greeley, A. M. Angels of September
Harrison, J. Julip
Heyer, G. Lady of quality
Hiaasen, C. Strip tease
Holland, C. Pacific Street
Lipman, E. The way men act
Lurie, A. Foreign affairs
McCullough, C. The ladies of Missalonghi
McFarland, D. School for the blind
Moore, B. The lonely passion of Judith Hearne
Oates, J. C. Black water
Patton, F. G. Good morning, Miss Dove
Pym, B. Excellent women
Pym, B. A few green leaves
Pym, B. Jane and Prudence
Pym, B. Less than angels
Pym, B. No fond return of love
Pym, B. Quartet in autumn
Pym, B. Some tame gazelle
Pym, B. The sweet dove died
Pym, B. An unsuitable attachment
Rhys, J. After leaving Mr. Mackenzie
Roiphe, A. R. If you knew me
Rosenberg, N. T. Interest of justice
Rossner, J. Looking for Mr. Goodbar
Sand, G. Marianne
Sarton, M. The fur person
Sarton, M. Joanna and Ulysses
Sarton, M. The magnificent spinster
Shields, C. The republic of love
Siddons, A. R. Downtown
Spark, M. The driver's seat
Steel, D. No greater love
Wharton, E. The old maid

SINN FEIN REBELLION, 1916 See Ireland—Sinn Fein
   Rebellion, 1916

The **sins** of the fathers. Block, L.
Sins of the fathers. Howatch, S.
The **sins** of the wolf. Perry, A.

SIOUX INDIANS See Dakota Indians
Sir Philip's folly. Chesney, M.
The **sirens** of Titan. Vonnegut, K.
Sister Carrie. Dreiser, T.
Sister Hood. Quill, M.
Sister Light, Sister Dark. Yolen, J.

SISTERS
See also Brothers and sisters; Half-sisters; Twins
Allen, C. V. Leftover dreams
Alvarez, J. How the Garcia girls lost their accents
Alvarez, J. In the time of the butterflies
Austen, J. Pride and prejudice
Austen, J. Sense and sensibility
Barrett, J. Presumption
Briskin, J. Too much, too soon
Brown, R. M. Six of one
Capote, T. The grass harp
Carr, P. We'll meet again
Carter, A. Wise children
Delinsky, B. For my daughters
Desai, A. Clear light of day
Eden, D. Ravenscroft
Eugenides, J. The virgin suicides
Forster, E. M. Howards End
Gilchrist, E. The Anna papers
Golding, W. Darkness visible
Goudge, E. Such devoted sisters
Goudge, E. Green Dolphin Street
Hart, J. Sin
Harvey, K. Stars
Hazzard, S. The transit of Venus
Hijuelos, O. The fourteen sisters of Emilio Montez
   O'Brien
Jackson, S. We have always lived in the castle
Johnston, V. The Etruscan smile
Lawrence, D. H. Women in love
Lin, Y. Moment in Peking
Marsh, J. The House of Eliott
Michael, J. Deceptions
Michael, J. A tangled web
Mortman, D. True colors
Ng, F. M. Bone
Oates, J. C. A Bloodsmoor romance
Pearson, D. Csardas
Phillips, J. A. Shelter
Puig, M. Tropical night falling
Pym, B. Some tame gazelle
Rhys, J. After leaving Mr. Mackenzie
Rice, L. Stone heart
Shange, N. Sassafrass, Cypress & Indigo
Smiley, J. A thousand acres
Spencer, L. Forgiving
Stone, K. Rainbows
Streshinsky, S. Hers the kingdom
Stubbs, J. Like we used to be
Walker, A. The color purple
West, Dame R. Cousin Rosamund
Whitney, P. A. The stone bull
Wood, B. Virgins of paradise

SISTERS AND BROTHERS See Brothers and sisters

SISTERS-IN-LAW
Colette. Claudine and Annie
The **Sittaford** mystery. See Christie, A. The murder at
   Hazelmoor

SITTING BULL, DAKOTA CHIEF, 1831-1890
Jones, D. C. Arrest Sitting Bull

SIX-DAY WAR *See* Israel-Arab War, 1967
Six days of the condor. Grady, J.
Six novels. Colette
Six of one. Brown, R. M.
Six out seven. Mowry, J.
Six tales of the jazz age, and other stories. Fitzgerald, F. S.
Sixes and sevens. Henry, O.
    In Henry, O. The complete works of O. Henry p811-940
The sixth book of lost swords: Mindsword's story. Saberhagen, F.
The sixth commandment. Sanders, L.
The sixth day, and other tales. Levi, P.
The sixth wife. Plaidy, J.
Sixty stories. Barthelme, D.
Skeleton crew. King, S.
The skeleton in the grass. Barnard, R.
Skeleton-in-waiting. Dickinson, P.
Skeletons in the closet. Linington, E.
Sketches by Boz. Dickens, C.
Skin tight. Hiaasen, C.
Skinny legs and all. Robbins, T.
Skinwalkers. Hillerman, T.

SKIS AND SKIING
    Whitney, P. A. Snowfire
The skull beneath the skin. James, P. D.
Sky masters. Brown, D.

SKYE (SCOTLAND)
    Stewart, M. Wildfire at midnight
Slam the big door. MacDonald, J. D.
Slapstick. Vonnegut, K.
Slaughter. Kelton, E.
Slaughterhouse-five. Vonnegut, K.
The slave. Singer, I. B.

SLAVE TRADE
    Johnson, C. R. Middle passage
    Kaye, M. M. Trade wind
    Phillips, C. Crossing the river
    Smith, W. A. Flight of the falcon
    Unsworth, B. Sacred hunger

SLAVERY
    See also Abolitionists; African Americans; Fugitive slaves; Slave trade; Underground railroad
    Bell, M. S. All souls' rising
    Bradley, D. The Chaneysville incident
    Bradshaw, G. Imperial purple
    Brink, A. P. A chain of voices
    Cather, W. Sapphira and the slave girl
    Chase-Riboud, B. The President's daughter
    Chase-Riboud, B. Sally Hemings
    Condé, M. I, Tituba, black witch of Salem
    De Hartog, J. The peculiar people
    Gaines, E. J. The autobiography of Miss Jane Pittman
    Gaskin, C. Fiona
    Heidish, M. A woman called Moses
    Heinlein, R. A. Citizen of the galaxy
    Holt, V. The captive
    L'Engle, M. The other side of the sun
    Morrison, T. Beloved
    Phillips, C. Cambridge
    Phillips, C. Crossing the river
    Plain, B. Crescent City
    Price, E. Where shadows go
    Rhodes, J. P. Voodoo dreams
    Smith, W. A. River god
    Stowe, H. B. Uncle Tom's cabin
    Styron, W. The confessions of Nat Turner
    Twain, M. Pudd'nhead Wilson
    Vance, J. The last castle
    Walker, M. Jubilee
    Warren, R. P. Band of angels

SLAVES *See* Slavery
Slayride. Francis, D.
    also in Francis, D. Two by Francis

SLED DOG RACING
    Henry, S. Murder on the Iditarod Trail

SLEEP
    Kress, N. Beggars & choosers
    Kress, N. Beggars in Spain
The sleep of reason. Snow, C. P.
Sleep of the unjust. Ferrars, E. X.
The Sleeper wakes. Entered in Part I under title
Sleeping beauty. Macdonald, R.
Sleeping beauty. Michael, J.
Sleeping dogs. Perry, T.
A sleeping life. Rendell, R.
Sleeping murder. Christie, A.
Sleeping with the enemy. Price, N.
Sleepless nights. Hardwick, E.
A slipping-down life. Tyler, A.
Sliver. Levin, I.
Slouching towards Kalamazoo. De Vries, P.
Slow learner. Pynchon, T.
Slow sculpture. Sturgeon, T.
    In The Best of the Nebulas p403-18
Slow waltz in Cedar Bend. Waller, R. J.

SLUM LIFE
    Algren, N. A walk on the wild side
    Bellow, S. The adventures of Augie March
    Brown, C. Down all the days
    Crane, S. George's mother
    Crane, S. Maggie: a girl of the streets (a story of New York)
    Dickens, C. Oliver Twist
    Godden, R. An episode of sparrows
    Green, G. The last angry man
    Llewellyn, R. None but the lonely heart
    Naylor, G. The women of Brewster Place
    Oates, J. C. Them
    Petry, A. L. The street
    Smith, B. A tree grows in Brooklyn
    Wright, R. Native son

SLUMS *See* Slum life
Small changes. Piercy, M.
A small deceit. Yorke, M.
The small house at Allington. Trollope, A.
The small miracle. Gallico, P.
    also in Gallico, P. Three legends: The snow goose; The small miracle; Ludmila p47-75
The small rain. L'Engle, M.
A small room. Sarton, M.
A small town in Germany. Le Carré, J.

SMALL TOWN LIFE
    Anderson, S. Poor white
    Anderson, S. Tar: a midwest childhood
    Anderson, S. Winesburg, Ohio
    Bambara, T. C. The salt eaters
    Banks, R. Affliction
    Banks, R. The sweet hereafter
    Berger, T. The feud
    Bradbury, R. Dandelion wine
    Brown, R. M. Six of one
    Burns, O. A. Cold Sassy tree
    Burns, O. A. Leaving Cold Sassy
    Caldwell, T. Answer as a man
    Caldwell, T. Testimony of two men
    Capote, T. The grass harp
    Cheever, J. The Wapshot chronicle
    Cheever, J. The Wapshot scandal
    Cook, T. H. Evidence of blood
    Cozzens, J. G. By love possessed
    Davis, T. 1959
    Dawson, C. Body of knowledge
    Dexter, P. Paris Trout
    Edgerton, C. Walking across Egypt
    Faulkner, W. The hamlet
    Faulkner, W. The mansion
    Faulkner, W. Soldiers' pay
    Faulkner, W. The town

SMALL TOWN LIFE—*Continued*

Flagg, F. Fried green tomatoes at the Whistle-Stop Cafe
Freedman, J. F. The obstacle course
Gardner, J. The sunlight dialogues
Greenberg, J. No reck'ning made
Guthrie, A. B. The last valley
Hailey, E. F. A woman of independent means
Hamilton, J. A map of the world
Heinemann, L. Paco's story
Higgins, G. V. The Mandeville talent
Higgins, G. V. Victories
Hoffman, A. Turtle Moon
Hood, A. Places to stay the night
Horgan, P. Whitewater
Jackson, S. We have always lived in the castle
Jewett, S. O. The country of the pointed firs
Jones, D. C. Come winter
Keillor, G. Lake Wobegon days
Keillor, G. Leaving home
King, S. Carrie
Lee, H. To kill a mockingbird
Leffland, E. Rumors of peace
Lewis, S. Main Street
Lockridge, R. Raintree County
Marius, R. C. After the war
Marquand, J. P. Point of no return
Mason, B. A. In country
McCammon, R. R. Boy's life
McCorkle, J. Ferris Beach
McCrumb, S. The hangman's beautiful daughter
McCrumb, S. If ever I return, pretty Peggy-O
McCrumb, S. She walks these hills
McCullers, C. Clock without hands
McCullers, C. The heart is a lonely hunter
McMurtry, L. Texasville
Morris, M. M. A dangerous woman
Naylor, G. Mama Day
Nichols, J. T. The Milagro beanfield war
Nordan, L. Wolf whistle
O'Hara, J. Ten North Frederick
Otto, W. How to make an American quilt
Parks, G. The learning tree
Patton, F. G. Good morning, Miss Dove
Pearson, T. R. Cry me a river
Pearson, T. R. A short history of a small place
Robards, K. One summer
Roth, P. When she was good
Russo, R. Nobody's fool
Russo, R. The risk pool
Santmyer, H. H. "—and ladies of the club"
Saroyan, W. The human comedy
Sarton, M. Kinds of love
Settle, M. L. Charley Bland
Sholem Aleichem. The nightingale
Shreve, A. Strange fits of passion
Smith, L. Family linen
Spencer, L. Bitter sweet
Spencer, L. Family blessings
Steinbeck, J. East of Eden
Stowe, H. B. Oldtown folks
Straub, P. The throat
Tarkington, B. Alice Adams
Tarkington, B. The gentleman from Indiana
Tarkington, B. Seventeen
Thomas, R. The fourth Durango
Tryon, T. In the fire of spring
Tryon, T. The wings of the morning
Twain, M. Pudd'nhead Wilson
Warren, R. P. The cave
Welty, E. The golden apples
Welty, E. Losing battles
Welty, E. The optimist's daughter
West, J. The state of Stony Lonesome
Wolfe, T. Look homeward, angel
Woods, S. Chiefs
Smiley's people. Le Carré, J.
also in Le Carré, J. The quest for Karla p679-952

Smilla's sense of snow. Hoeg, P.
Smoke and mirrors. Michaels, B.
The **smoke** ring. Niven, L.
Smoke without fire. Ferrars, E. X.
Smokescreen. Francis, D.
The **smooth** face of evil. Yorke, M.
SMUGGLERS *See* Smuggling
SMUGGLING
Cussler, C. Inca gold
Du Maurier, Dame D. Jamaica Inn
Fleming, I. Diamonds are forever
Heaven, C. The wind from the sea
Hemingway, E. To have and have not
Innes, H. High stand
Innes, H. Medusa
Johnston, V. The Etruscan smile
Laker, R. The sugar pavilion
Maas, P. Father and son
Roberts, N. Hidden riches
Spark, M. The comforters
Stewart, M. This rough magic
Stone, R. Dog soldiers
Snagged. Clark, C. H.
The **snake** eater. Tapply, W. G.
Snake eyes. Oates, J. C.
The **snake** pit. Undset, S.
In Undset, S. The master of Hestviken v2
The **snake** pit. Ward, M. J.
The **snake** tattoo. Barnes, L.
The **snake**, the crocodile, and the dog. Peters, E.
SNAKES
McIntyre, V. N. Of mist, and grass, and sand
Snapshot. Barnes, L.
The **snare** of the hunter. MacInnes, H.
Sneaky people. Berger, T.
Sneeze on Sunday. Norton, A.
Snopes. Faulkner, W.
Snow country. Kawabata, Y.
In Kawabata, Y. Snow country, and Thousand cranes p1-175
Snow country, and Thousand cranes. Kawabata, Y.
Snow falling on cedars. Guterson, D.
The **snow** goose. Gallico, P.
also in Gallico, P. Three legends: The snow goose; The small miracle; Ludmila p21-45
The **Snow** Queen. Vinge, J. D.
SNOW STORMS *See* Storms
The **Snow** Walker. Mowat, F.
Snow White and Rose Red. McBain, E.
Snow white, blood red. Entered in Part I under title
Snowfire. Whitney, P. A.
The **snows** of Kilimanjaro, and other stories. Hemingway, E.
SNOWSTORMS *See* Storms
So Big. Ferber, E.
So long, and thanks for all the fish. Adams, D.
also in Adams, D. The hitchhiker's quartet
SOCIAL CLASSES
See also Class distinction; Society novels
Bellow, S. The adventures of Augie March
Binchy, M. Echoes
Colegate, I. The shooting party
Doctorow, E. L. Ragtime
Donoso, J. A house in the country
Eden, D. The millionaire's daughter
Graham, W. The black moon
Guy, R. My love, my love
James, H. In the cage
James, H. The portrait of a lady
Oates, J. C. Because it is bitter, and because it is my heart
O'Hara, J. Ten North Frederick
Taylor, P. H. A summons to Memphis
Waugh, E. Decline and fall
Wilder, T. Theophilus North

SOCIAL CONDITIONS *See* Social problems

SOCIAL ISOLATION
Abe, K. The box man
Desai, A. Fire on the mountain
Handke, P. The left-handed woman
Silverberg, R. The man in the maze
Warren, R. P. A place to come to

SOCIAL PROBLEMS
See also Child labor; Crime and criminals; Divorce; Drug abuse; Drug addiction; Homeless persons; Juvenile delinquency; Poverty; Prejudices; Prostitution; Slum life; Suicide; Technology and civilization; Unemployed; Violence
Alther, L. Original sins
Bosse, M. J. The vast memory of love
Calvino, I. Invisible cities
Cronin, A. J. The citadel
De Hartog, J. The peaceable kingdom
Doctorow, E. L. Ragtime
Dos Passos, J. The 42nd parallel
Dos Passos, J. 1919
Dos Passos, J. Manhattan transfer
Dos Passos, J. U.S.A.
Dreiser, T. An American tragedy
Dreiser, T. Jennie Gerhardt
Fast, H. The legacy
Forster, E. M. A passage to India
Godden, R. An episode of sparrows
Green, G. The last angry man
Hugo, V. Les misérables
Kingsolver, B. Animal dreams
Llewellyn, R. None but the lonely heart
Maḥfūẓ, N. Midaq Alley
Markandaya, K. A handful of rice
Masters, J. Bhowani Junction
Momaday, N. S. House made of dawn
Morrison, T. Sula
Musil, R. The man without qualities
Rossner, J. Looking for Mr. Goodbar
Sinclair, U. The jungle
Smith, B. A tree grows in Brooklyn
Smith, L. E. Strange fruit
Steinbeck, J. The grapes of wrath
Styron, W. Set this house on fire
Tolstoy, L., graf. Childhood, Boyhood and Youth
Turgenev, I. S. Fathers and sons
Wells, H. G. Tono-Bungay
Wouk, H. Marjorie Morningstar
Wright, R. Native son
Wright, R. The outsider
Zaroulis, N. L. Call the darkness light

SOCIAL SATIRE *See* Satire

SOCIALISM
Hawthorne, N. The Blithedale romance
Tax, M. Union Square
Zola, É. Germinal

SOCIETY, PRIMITIVE *See* Primitive society

SOCIETY NOVELS
Auchincloss, L. The book class
Auchincloss, L. The dark lady
Auchincloss, L. Honorable men
Auchincloss, L. The lady of situations
Auchincloss, L. Portrait in brownstone
Beauvoir, S. de. Les belles images
Benson, E. F. Make way for Lucia
Dunne, D. An inconvenient woman
Dunne, D. People like us
Dunne, D. The two Mrs. Grenvilles
Edwards, A. Wallis
Galsworthy, J. The silver spoon
Graham, W. The twisted sword
Howells, W. D. The rise of Silas Lapham
Huxley, A. Point counter point
James, H. The Europeans
James, H. The ivory tower
James, H. The spoils of Poynton

Minot, S. Folly
Mitford, N. Love in a cold climate
Mitford, N. The pursuit of love
Musil, R. The man without qualities
Powell, A. A dance to the music of time
Proust, M. The Guermantes way
Sackville-West, V. The Edwardians
Thackeray, W. M. Vanity fair
Tolstoy, L., graf. Anna Karenina
Trollope, A. Framley parsonage
Trollope, A. The prime minister
Trollope, A. The way we live now
Vidal, G. 1876
Voigt, C. Glass mountain
Waugh, E. Brideshead revisited
Waugh, E. Vile bodies
Wesley, M. A dubious legacy
Wharton, E. The age of innocence
Wharton, E. The buccaneers
Wharton, E. The buccaneers, completed by Marion Mainwaring
Wharton, E. The children
Wharton, E. Fast and loose
Wharton, E. The house of mirth
Wharton, E. Old New York
Wolfe, T. The good child's river
Zaroulis, N. L. The last waltz

SOCIETY OF FRIENDS
De Hartog, J. The lamb's war
De Hartog, J. The peaceable kingdom
De Hartog, J. The peculiar people
Renault, M. The charioteer
West, J. Except for me and thee
West, J. The friendly persuasion

SOCRATES
Renault, M. The last of the wine
Sodom and Gomorrah. Proust, M.

SOFIA (BULGARIA) *See* Bulgaria—Sofia

SOFTBALL
Sheed, W. The boys of winter
The **sojourner**. Rawlings, M. K.
Solar barque. See Nin, A. Seduction of the Minotaur
A **soldier** of the great war. Helprin, M.

SOLDIERS
De Bernières, L. Corelli's mandolin
Dickson, G. R. Lost Dorsai
Jennings, G. Raptor

Australia
McCullough, C. An indecent obsession

Austria
Hašek, J. The good soldier Svejk

Canada
MacNeil, R. Burden of desire

China
Buck, P. S. Sons

France
Balzac, H. de. The country doctor
Colette. The kepi
Faulkner, W. A fable
Flanagan, T. The year of the French

Germany
Böll, H. The silent angel
Böll, H. A soldier's legacy
Crichton, R. The secret of Santa Vittoria
Higgins, J. The eagle has landed
Kennedy, R. A. The bitterest age
Kirst, H. H. Forward, Gunner Asch!
Kirst, H. H. The return of Gunner Asch
Kirst, H. H. The revolt of Gunner Asch
Remarque, E. M. All quiet on the western front
Remarque, E. M. A time to love and a time to die
Shaw, I. The young lions
Solzhenitsyn, A. August 1914

SOLDIERS—*Continued*

Great Britain

Barker, P. The eye in the door
Barker, P. Regeneration
Boulle, P. The bridge over the River Kwai
Cornwell, B. Sharpe's company
Cornwell, B. Sharpe's eagle
Cornwell, B. Sharpe's enemy
Cornwell, B. Sharpe's gold
Cornwell, B. Sharpe's honour
Cornwell, B. Sharpe's regiment
Cornwell, B. Sharpe's revenge
Cornwell, B. Sharpe's rifles
Cornwell, B. Sharpe's siege
Cornwell, B. Sharpe's sword
Cornwell, B. Sharpe's Waterloo
Ford, F. M. A man could stand up
Ford, F. M. No more parades
Llewellyn, R. None but the lonely heart
MacLean, A. Force 10 from Navarone
MacLean, A. The guns of Navarone
Ondaatje, M. The English patient
Price, E. Bright captivity
Scott, P. A division of the spoils
Waugh, E. Men at arms
Waugh, E. Officers and gentlemen

Israel

Wouk, H. The hope

Rome

Bradley, M. Z. The forest house
De Hartog, J. The centurion
Douglas, L. C. The robe
Llywelyn, M. Druids
Norton, A. Empire of the eagle

Russia

See also Cossacks
Solzhenitsyn, A. August 1914
Tolstoy, L., graf. Two hussars
Tolstoy, L., graf. War and peace

United States

Berent, M. Steel tiger
Berent, M. Storm flight
Bristow, G. Celia Garth
Brown, R. M. High hearts
Clavell, J. King Rat
Coyle, H. W. Code of honor
Crane, S. The red badge of courage
Del Vecchio, J. M. The 13th valley
Del Vecchio, J. M. For the sake of all living things
Fleming, T. J. Over there
Griffin, W. E. B. The aviators
Griffin, W. E. B. The new breed
Halberstam, D. One very hot day
Hersey, J. A bell for Adano
Higgins, J. Night of the fox
Hooker, R. MASH
Horgan, P. A distant trumpet
Hyman, M. No time for sergeants
Jones, D. C. The barefoot brigade
Jones, D. C. Elkhorn Tavern
Jones, D. C. Remember Santiago
Jones, J. From here to eternity
Jones, J. The thin red line
Jones, J. Whistle
Kantor, M. Valley Forge
Mailer, N. The naked and the dead
Nathanson, E. M. The dirty dozen
O'Brien, T. Going after Cacciato
Sams, F. When all the world was young
Shaw, I. The young lions
Shulman, M. Rally round the flag, boys!

Vietnam

Halberstam, D. One very hot day
The **soldier's** art. Powell, A.
In Powell, A. A dance to the music of time [v3]

A **soldier's** legacy. Böll, H.
In Böll, H. The stories of Heinrich Böll p316-81

SOLDIERS OF FORTUNE

Caputo, P. Horn of Africa
Elegant, R. S. Manchu
Forsyth, F. The dogs of war
Smith, W. A. Cry wolf
Soldiers' pay. Faulkner, W.

SOLICITORS *See* Law and lawyers
A **solitary** grief. Rubens, B.
Solomon Gursky was here. Richler, M.

SOLOMON ISLANDS

See also World War, 1939-1945—Solomon Islands
London, J. South Sea tales
Solstice. Oates, J. C.
Some buried Caesar. Stout, R.
In Stout, R. All aces p1-153
Some can whistle. McMurtry, L.
Some days you get the bear. Block, L.
Some die eloquent. Aird, C.
Some do not. Ford, F. M.
In Ford, F. M. Parade's end
Some kind of hero. Kirkwood, J.
Some tame gazelle. Pym, B.
Somebody's darling. McMurtry, L.
Someday the rabbi will leave. Kemelman, H.

SOMERSET (ENGLAND) *See* England—Somerset
Something happened. Heller, J.
Something in the air. Lathen, E.
Something in the water. MacLeod, C.
Something like a love affair. Symons, J.
Something of value. Ruark, R.
Something the cat dragged in. MacLeod, C.
Something to remember me by. Bellow, S.
Something wicked. Ferrars, E. X.
Something wicked this way comes. Bradbury, R.
Sometimes a great notion. Kesey, K.
The **son** avenger. Undset, S.
In Undset, S. The master of Hestviken v4
Son of Fletch. Mcdonald, G.
A **son** of the circus. Irving, J.
A **song** for Lya. Martin, G. R. R.
In The Hugo winners v3 p483-544
The **song** of Bernadette. Werfel, F.
A **song** of sixpence. Cronin, A. J.
Song of Solomon. Morrison, T.
The **song** of the lark. Cather, W.
also in Cather, W. Early novels and stories p291-706

SONGWRITERS *See* Composers
SONS *See* Fathers and sons; Mothers and sons; Stepsons
Sons. Buck, P. S.
Sons and lovers. Lawrence, D. H.
Sons of the Conquistador. Fuentes, C.
In Fuentes, C. The orange tree p50-100
Sophie's choice. Styron, W.
The **sorceress** and the Cygnet. McKillip, P. A.
Sorceress of Darshiva. Eddings, D.

SORCERY *See* Witchcraft
The **sorrowing** wind. Pearce, M. E.
In Pearce, M. E. Apple tree lean down [omnibus volume] p333-494
The **sorrows** of young Werther. Goethe, J. W. von
In Goethe, J. W. von. The sorrows of young Werther, and Novella p1-167
The **sorrows** of young Werther, and Novella. Goethe, J. W. von
Sorry, wrong number. Fletcher, L.
In Alfred Hitchcock presents: Stories not for the nervous
The **sot-weed** factor. Barth, J.
Sotah. Ragen, N.

SOUBIROUS, BERNADETTE *See* Bernadette, Saint, 1844-1879

SOUL

See also Transmigration

Soul flame. Wood, B.

Souls. Russ, J.

In Modern classic short novels of science fiction p415-58

The **sound** and the fury. Faulkner, W.

also in Faulkner, W. The Faulkner reader p5-251

The **sound** of murder. Westlake, D. E.

In Westlake, D. E. Levine p89-120

The **sound** of the mountain. Kawabata, Y.

The **sound** of thunder. Smith, W. A.

In Smith, W. A. The Courtneys p[297]-601

The **sound** of waves. Mishima, Y.

The **source** of light. Price, R.

SOUTH (U.S.) *See* Southern States

SOUTH AFRICA

See also Africa

Michener, J. A. The covenant

Paton, A. Tales from a troubled land

Smith, W. A. The Courtneys

19th century

Brink, A. P. A chain of voices

20th century

Bond, L. Vortex

Gordimer, N. Burger's daughter

Gordimer, N. The conservationist

Gordimer, N. July's people

Gordimer, N. Jump and other stories

Gordimer, N. None to accompany me

Gordimer, N. A sport of nature

Lessing, D. M. Children of violence

Lessing, D. M. The grass is singing

Paton, A. Ah, but your land is beautiful

Paton, A. Cry, the beloved country

Sheldon, S. Master of the game

Smith, W. A. The burning shore

Smith, W. A. Golden fox

Smith, W. A. Power of the sword

Smith, W. A. A time to die

Spark, M. The go-away bird

Swindells, M. Summer harvest

Communism

See Communism—South Africa

Farm life

See Farm life—South Africa

Frontier and pioneer life

See Frontier and pioneer life—South Africa

Native peoples

Coetzee, J. M. Life & times of Michael K.

Politics

See Politics—South Africa

Race relations

Brink, A. P. An act of terror

Brink, A. P. A chain of voices

Coetzee, J. M. Age of iron

Gordimer, N. Burger's daughter

Gordimer, N. The conservationist

Gordimer, N. July's people

Gordimer, N. My son's story

Gordimer, N. None to accompany me

Gordimer, N. A sport of nature

Lessing, D. M. The grass is singing

Michener, J. A. The covenant

Paton, A. Ah, but your land is beautiful

Paton, A. Cry, the beloved country

Paton, A. Too late the phalarope

Smith, W. A. Rage

Johannesburg

Paton, A. Too late the phalarope

SOUTH AFRICAN WAR, 1899-1902

Galsworthy, J. In chancery

Smith, W. A. The sound of thunder

SOUTH AFRICANS

See also Afrikaners

West Indies

Naipaul, V. S. Guerrillas

SOUTH AMERICA

See also Amazon River Valley

Allende, I. Eva Luna

Allende, I. The stories of Eva Luna

Conrad, J. Nostromo

Doyle, Sir A. C. The lost world

Hudson, W. H. Green mansions

Woolf, V. The voyage out

Politics

See Politics—South America

SOUTH CAROLINA

19th century

Fast, H. Freedom road

Jakes, J. Heaven and hell

Jakes, J. Love and war

Jakes, J. North and South

L'Engle, M. The other side of the sun

20th century

Allison, D. Bastard out of Carolina

Conroy, P. The lords of discipline

Conroy, P. The prince of tides

Humphreys, J. The fireman's fair

Humphreys, J. Rich in love

Straight, S. I been in sorrow's kitchen and licked out all the pots

Whitney, P. A. Woman without a past

Politics

See Politics—South Carolina

Charleston

Bristow, G. Celia Garth

Conroy, P. The lords of discipline

Shange, N. Sassafrass, Cypress & Indigo

SOUTH DAKOTA

19th century

Jones, D. C. A creek called Wounded Knee

Rölvaag, O. E. Giants in the earth

Rölvaag, O. E. Peder Victorious

20th century

Olsen, T. Yonnondio: from the thirties

Farm life

See Farm life—South Dakota

Frontier and pioneer life

See Frontier and pioneer life—South Dakota

South moon under. Rawlings, M. K.

also in Rawlings, M. K. The Marjorie Rawlings reader p3-270

SOUTH SEA ISLANDS *See* Islands of the Pacific

South Sea tales. London, J.

SOUTHAMPTON (N.Y.) *See* New York (State)—Southampton

SOUTHAMPTON INSURRECTION, 1831

Styron, W. The confessions of Nat Turner

SOUTHEAST ASIA

Browne, G. A. 18mm blues

Lederer, W. J. The ugly American

Straub, P. Koko

SOUTHERN AFRICA

Smith, W. A. The leopard hunts in darkness

Smith, W. A. Men of men

Southern cross. Greenleaf, S.
Southern discomfort. Brown, R. M.
Southern discomfort. Maron, M.
A Southern family. Godwin, G.
Southern ghost. Hart, C. G.
SOUTHERN RHODESIA *See* Zimbabwe
SOUTHERN STATES
    See also Old Southwest; Reconstruction; names of individual states
Faulkner, W. As I lay dying
Ferber, E. Show boat
Lester, J. Do Lord remember me
O'Connor, F. Everything that rises must converge
O'Connor, F. A good man is hard to find and other stories
Smith, L. The devil's dream
Smith, L. Oral history

            18th century
Robards, K. Nobody's angel

            19th century
Brown, R. M. High hearts
Mitchell, M. Gone with the wind
Price, E. Before the darkness falls
Price, E. Savannah
Price, E. To see your face again
Ripley, A. Scarlett
Walker, M. Jubilee

            20th century
Allison, D. Bastard out of Carolina
Alther, L. Original sins
Bambara, T. C. The salt eaters
Blair, L. The side of the angels
Brown, J. D. Addie Pray
Brown, R. M. Southern discomfort
Burns, O. A. Leaving Cold Sassy
Capote, T. The grass harp
Childress, M. Crazy in Alabama
Conroy, P. The prince of tides
Dexter, P. Paris Trout
Dickey, J. Deliverance
Fast, H. The trial of Abigail Goodman
Faulkner, W. Pylon
Flagg, F. Coming attractions
Flagg, F. Fried green tomatoes at the Whistle-Stop Cafe
Gaines, E. J. The gathering of old men
Gibbons, K. Charms for the easy life
Gibbons, K. Ellen Foster
Gibbons, K. A virtuous woman
Godwin, G. A Southern family
Grau, S. A. The keepers of the house
Grau, S. A. Roadwalkers
Lee, H. To kill a mockingbird
McCorkle, J. Crash diet
McCorkle, J. Ferris Beach
McCullers, C. Clock without hands
McCullers, C. The heart is a lonely hunter
McCullers, C. Reflections in a golden eye
Pearson, T. R. A short history of a small place
Percy, W. The last gentleman
Plain, B. Daybreak
Settle, M. L. Charley Bland
Siddons, A. R. Heartbreak Hotel
Siddons, A. R. Homeplace
Siddons, A. R. Outer banks
Siddons, A. R. Peachtree Road
Smith, L. Cakewalk
Smith, L. Me and my baby view the eclipse
Tyler, A. Earthly possessions
Warren, R. P. A place to come to
Westheimer, D. My sweet Charlie
Woods, S. Chiefs

            Frontier and pioneer life
    See Frontier and pioneer life—Southern States
            Mountain life
    See Mountain life—Southern States
            Politics
    See Politics—Southern States
SOUTHERN STATES DIALECT *See* Dialect stories—Southern States
Southern women. Battle, L.
Southshore. Tepper, S. S.
SOUTHWEST, NEW *See* Southwestern States
SOUTHWEST, OLD *See* Old Southwest
SOUTHWESTERN STATES
    See also Santa Fe Trail
Barrett, W. E. The lilies of the field
Horgan, P. A distant trumpet
Lehrer, J. Kick the can
McCarthy, C. The crossing
Thomas, R. Briarpatch
SOVIET UNION *See* Russia
Space. Michener, J. A.
SPACE AND TIME
    See also Time travel
Anderson, P. The shield of time
Benford, G. Timescape
De Hartog, J. The centurion
Heinlein, R. A. Job: a comedy of justice
SPACE COLONIES
Anderson, P. The sharing of flesh
Heinlein, R. A. The moon is a harsh mistress
Jenkins, W. F. Exploration team
Le Guin, U. K. The word for world is forest
McAuley, P. J. Red dust
Niven, L. The integral trees
Niven, L. Ringworld
Niven, L. The Ringworld engineers
Niven, L. The smoke ring
Pohl, F. Man Plus
Pohl, F. Mars Plus
Robinson, K. S. Green Mars
Robinson, K. S. Red Mars
SPACE FLIGHT
    See also Astronauts; Interplanetary voyages; Science fiction
Anderson, P. Tau Zero
Delany, S. R. The star pit
Pohl, F. Beyond the blue event horizon
Pohl, F. Gateway
Pohl, F. Heechee rendezvous
SPACE FLIGHT TO THE MOON
Clarke, A. C. Earthlight
Michener, J. A. Space
The space merchants. Pohl, F.
SPACE PROBES
Crichton, M. The Andromeda strain
Wilhelm, K. The dark door
SPACE SHIPS
Anderson, P. The longest voyage
Anderson, P. Tau Zero
Balmer, E. When worlds collide
Bova, B. Voyagers
Cherryh, C. J. Rimrunners
Clarke, A. C. The Garden of Rama
Clarke, A. C. Rama II
Clarke, A. C. Rama revealed
Clarke, A. C. Rendezvous with Rama
Crichton, M. Sphere
Harrison, P. Storming Intrepid
Leiber, F. Ship of shadows
Lem, S. Fiasco
McCaffrey, A. The city who fought
McCaffrey, A. The ship who won
Pohl, F. Homegoing

SPACE SHIPS—*Continued*
Smith, C. On the storm planet
Wolfe, G. Caldé of the long sun

SPACE STATIONS
Bova, B. The Trikon deception

SPACE TRAVEL *See* Space flight

SPAIN
Blasco Ibáñez, V. Blood and sand
Fuentes, C. Terra nostra
Fuentes, C. The two Numantias
Mérimée, P. Carmen

15th century
Lofts, N. Knight's Acre

16th century
Cervantes Saavedra, M. de. Don Quixote de la Mancha
Plaidy, J. The scarlet cloak

17th century
Cervantes Saavedra, M. de. Three exemplary novels

19th century
Cornwell, B. Sharpe's honour
Cornwell, B. Sharpe's sword
Pérez Galdós, B. Doña Perfecta
Pérez Galdós, B. Torquemada

20th century
Hemingway, E. For whom the bell tolls
Hemingway, E. The sun also rises
MacInnes, H. Message from Málaga
Malraux, A. Man's hope
Sheldon, S. The sands of time

Civil War, 1936-1939
Hemingway, E. For whom the bell tolls
Leavitt, D. While England sleeps

1939-
Greene, G. Monsignor Quixote

Kings and rulers
Fuentes, C. Terra nostra

Politics
See Politics—Spain

Rural life
Pérez Galdós, B. Doña Perfecta

Barcelona
Mortman, D. True colors

Granada
MacInnes, H. Message from Málaga

Madrid
Pérez Galdós, B. Torquemada

Málaga
MacInnes, H. Message from Málaga

Minorca
See Minorca (Spain)

Seville
Cervantes Saavedra, M. de. Man of glass
Cervantes Saavedra, M. de. Rinconete and Cortadillo

SPANIARDS

Mexico
Fuentes, C. The two shores

Netherlands
Holland, C. The Sea Beggars

SPANISH AMERICAN WAR, 1898 *See* United States—War of 1898

SPANISH CIVIL WAR, 1936-1939 *See* Spain—Civil War, 1936-1939

SPANISH INQUISITION *See* Inquisition

SPANISH MAIN
Sabatini, R. Captain Blood

The **spark**. Wharton, E.
In Wharton, E. Old New York
A **sparrow** falls. Smith, W. A.
In Smith, W. A. The Courtneys p[603]-938
Spartina. Casey, J.

SPAS *See* Health resorts
Speak for the dead. Yorke, M.
Speaker for the Dead. Card, O. S.
Speaker of Mandarin. Rendell, R.
Spearfield's daughter. Cleary, J.

SPECIAL FORCES (U.S. ARMY) *See* United States. Army. Special Forces

The **spectator** bird. Stegner, W. E.

SPECULATION
Norris, F. The pit

SPEECH DISORDERS
See also Stuttering
Spence + Lila. Mason, B. A.
Spencer's Mountain. Hamner, E.
Spencerville. DeMille, N.
Sphere. Crichton, M.
Spidertown. Rodriguez, A.

SPIES
See also International intrigue; Secret service
Aaron, D. Crossing by night
Abrahams, P. Hard rain
Allbeury, T. Deep purple
Allbeury, T. The Judas factor
Allbeury, T. A time without shadows
Anthony, E. Albatross
Anthony, E. The avenue of the dead
Anthony, E. The company of saints
Anthony, E. The Doll's House
Anthony, E. The tamarind seed
Block, L. The thief who couldn't sleep
Bosse, M. J. Fire in heaven
Bowen, E. The heat of the day
Bristow, G. Celia Garth
Buchan, J. The thirty-nine steps
Buckley, W. F. Mongoose, R.I.P
Buckley, W. F. Tucker's last stand
Buckley, W. F. A very private plot
Carr, P. Voices in a haunted room
Carroll, J. Family trade
Clancy, T. The Cardinal of the Kremlin
Clancy, T. Debt of honor
Clancy, T. The hunt for Red October
Clavell, J. Noble house
Coonts, S. The minotaur
Cooper, J. F. The spy
Cornwell, B. Sharpe's regiment
Cornwell, B. Sharpe's sword
Cussler, C. Deep six
Cussler, C. Night probe!
Cussler, C. Raise the Titanic!
Davies, R. What's bred in the bone
Deighton, L. Berlin game
Deighton, L. City of gold
Deighton, L. Faith
Deighton, L. Funeral in Berlin
Deighton, L. Game, set & match
Deighton, L. The Ipcress file
Deighton, L. London match
Deighton, L. Mexico set
Deighton, L. Spy hook
Deighton, L. Spy line
Deighton, L. Spy sinker
Deighton, L. SS-GB: Nazi-occupied Britain 1941
Deighton, L. XPD
DeMille, N. The charm school
Diehl, W. 27
Doctorow, E. L. The book of Daniel
Egleton, C. A double deception
Egleton, C. Hostile intent
Egleton, C. A killing in Moscow
Finder, J. The Moscow Club
Fleming, I. Bonded Fleming

SPIES—*Continued*

Fleming, I. Casino Royale
Fleming, I. Doctor No
Fleming, I. From Russia, with love
Fleming, I. Goldfinger
Fleming, I. The man with the golden gun
Fleming, I. More gilt-edged Bonds
Fleming, I. On Her Majesty's Secret Service
Fleming, I. You only live twice
Follett, K. Eye of the needle
Follett, K. The key to Rebecca
Follett, K. Lie down with lions
Forsyth, F. The deceiver
Forsyth, F. The devil's alternative
Forsyth, F. The fist of God
Francis, C. Wolf winter
Freemantle, B. Charlie's apprentice
Freemantle, B. Comrade Charlie
Fuentes, C. The Hydra head
Gardner, J. E. Brokenclaw
Gardner, J. E. Death is forever
Gardner, J. E. License renewed
Gardner, J. E. Maestro
Gardner, J. E. Never send flowers
Gardner, J. E. Seafire
Garfield, B. Hopscotch
Gifford, T. The Glendower legacy
Gilman, D. The amazing Mrs. Pollifax
Gilman, D. The elusive Mrs. Pollifax
Gilman, D. Mrs. Pollifax and the Hong Kong Buddha
Gilman, D. Mrs. Pollifax on safari
Gilman, D. Mrs. Pollifax on the China station
Gilman, D. A palm for Mrs. Pollifax
Gilman, D. The unexpected Mrs. Pollifax
Goldman, W. Marathon man
Grady, J. Six days of the condor
Grady, J. Thunder
Greene, G. 3: This gun for hire, The confidential agent, The ministry of fear
Greene, G. The human factor
Greene, G. The ministry of fear
Greene, G. Our man in Havana
Hall, A. Quiller bamboo
Hall, A. Quiller barracuda
Hall, A. The Quiller memorandum
Hall, A. Quiller meridian
Hall, A. Quiller Salamander
Hall, A. Quiller solitaire
Harrison, P. Black cipher
Higgins, J. The eagle has flown
Higgins, J. The eagle has landed
Hodge, J. A. The winding stair
Isaacs, S. Shining through
Jones, T. Hard road to Gettysburg
Kaye, M. M. Death in Kashmir
Keneally, T. Confederates
Koontz, D. R. Watchers
Le Carré, J. The honourable schoolboy
Le Carré, J. The little drummer girl
Le Carré, J. The looking glass war
Le Carré, J. The night manager
Le Carré, J. A perfect spy
Le Carré, J. The quest for Karla
Le Carré, J. The Russia house
Le Carré, J. The secret pilgrim
Le Carré, J. A small town in Germany
Le Carré, J. Smiley's people
Le Carré, J. The spy who came in from the cold
Le Carré, J. Tinker, tailor, soldier, spy
Ludlum, R. The Bourne identity
Ludlum, R. The Bourne supremacy
Ludlum, R. The Bourne ultimatum
Ludlum, R. The Parsifal mosaic
Lustbader, E. V. Jian
Lustbader, E. V. Shan
MacInnes, H. Agent in place
MacInnes, H. The double image
MacInnes, H. The hidden target
MacInnes, H. Message from Málaga
MacInnes, H. Prelude to terror
MacInnes, H. Ride a pale horse
MacInnes, H. The Salzburg connection
MacLean, A. Caravan to Vaccares
MacLean, A. Ice Station Zebra
MacLean, A. Where eagles dare
Mailer, N. Harlot's ghost
McEwan, I. The innocent
Morrell, D. Assumed identity
Morrell, D. The brotherhood of the rose
Ondaatje, M. The English patient
Rendell, R. Talking to strange men
Smith, M. C. Stallion Gate
Thomas, C. A hooded crow
Thomas, C. Playing with cobras
Trenhaile, J. The gates of exquisite view
Trevanian. The Eiger sanction
Uris, L. Topaz
Vonnegut, K. Mother night
Westlake, D. E. The spy in the ointment

Spindrift. Whitney, P. A.
Spinster. Ashton-Warner, S.

SPINSTERS *See* Single women

The **spire.** Golding, W.

SPIRITUALISM

Byatt, A. S. The conjugial angel
Colegate, I. The summer of the royal visit
Jackson, S. The haunting of Hill House
Whitney, P. A. Feather on the moon

A **splash** of red. Fraser, A.
Split images. Leonard, E.
Split infinity. Anthony, P.

SPLIT PERSONALITY *See* Dual personality

The **spoils** of Poynton. James, H.
A **sport** of nature. Gordimer, N.

SPORTS

See also Athletes; Games
Saul, J. Creature

Spring Moon. Lord, B. B.
The **spring** of the ram. Dunnett, D.
Spring snow. Mishima, Y.
The **spy.** Cooper, J. F.
Spy hook. Deighton, L.
A **spy** in the house of love. Nin, A.
In Nin, A. Cities of the interior p360-462
The **spy** in the ointment. Westlake, D. E.
Spy line. Deighton, L.
Spy sinker. Deighton, L.
The **spy** who came in from the cold. Le Carré, J.
The **spy** who loved me. Fleming, I.
In Fleming, I. Bonded Fleming p329-439

SQUIDS

Benchley, P. Beast
The **squirt** and the monkey. Stout, R.
In Stout, R. Kings full of aces p421-72

SS-GB: Nazi-occupied Britain 1941. Deighton, L.

ST. FRANCIS, ORDER OF *See* Franciscans

ST. PETERSBURG (RUSSIA) *See* Russia—St. Petersburg

St. Valentine's night. Greeley, A. M.

STAFFORDSHIRE DIALECT *See* Dialect stories—English—Staffordshire

STAGE LIFE *See* Theater life

A **stained** white radiance. Burke, J. L.
The **Stainless** Steel Rat sings the blues. Harrison, H.
Stainless steel visions. Harrison, H.
The **stalking** horse. McGown, J.
Stalking horse. Shoemaker, B.
Stallion Gate. Smith, M. C.
Stamboul train. See Greene, G. Orient Express

The **stand**. King, S.
Stand on Zanzibar. Brunner, J.
Stand we at last. Fairbairns, Z.
STANHOPE, LADY HESTER LUCY, 1776-1839
   Stewart, M. The Gabriel hounds
Star flight. Whitney, P. A.
Star of Peace. De Hartog, J.
Star of the sea. Anderson, P.
   In Anderson, P. The Time Patrol p291-398
The **star** pit. Delany, S. R.
   In Modern classic short novels of science fiction
   p164-220
The **star** rover. London, J.
A **star** shines over Mt. Morris Park. Roth, H.
The **Star** Trek reader [I]-IV. Blish, J.
Star trek, the next generation [series]
   David, P. Q-squared
   Duane, D. Dark mirror
Star wars [series]
   McIntyre, V. N. The crystal star
   Tyers, K. The truce at Bakura
   Wolverton, D. The courtship of Princess Leia
   Zahn, T. Dark force rising
   Zahn, T. The last command
Starbuck chronicles [series]
   Cornwell, B. Copperhead
   Cornwell, B. Rebel
Stardance [novelette]. Robinson, S.
   In The Hugo winners v4 p327-88
Stardust. Parker, R. B.
STARS
   Delany, S. R. The star pit
Stars. Harvey, K.
The **stars** are also fire. Anderson, P.
Stars in my pocket like grains of sand. Delany, S. R.
The **stars** shine down. Sheldon, S.
Starting over. Wakefield, D.
STARVATION
   Hamsun, K. Hunger
The **state** of Stony Lonesome. West, J.
STATUETTES *See* Art objects
Staying on. Scott, P.
The **steam** pig. McClure, J.
STEAMBOATS
   Forester, C. S. The African Queen
Steel guitar. Barnes, L.
STEEL INDUSTRY
   Marshall, C. Julie
   Porter, C. R. All-Bright Court
Steel tiger. Berent, M.
STEEPLECHASING *See* Horse racing
STEPBROTHERS
   See also Half-brothers
STEPCHILDREN
   See also Stepdaughters; Stepsons
   Aiken, J. Voices in an empty house
   Heyer, G. Bath tangle
   James, H. What Maisie knew
   Mukherjee, B. Jasmine
   Smith, W. A. Power of the sword
   Updike, J. Of the farm
STEPDAUGHTERS
   MacDonald, J. D. Slam the big door
   Wolitzer, H. Tunnel of love
STEPFATHERS
   Aiken, J. Voices in an empty house
   Dickens, C. David Copperfield
   Michael, J. Sleeping beauty

The **Stepford** wives. Levin, I.
Stephanie. Graham, W.
STEPMOTHERS
   Chase, J. The evening wolves
   Lee, G. China boy
   Smith, R. K. Jane's house
   Whitney, P. A. The singing stones
   Wolitzer, H. Hearts
Steppenwolf. Hesse, H.
STEPSISTERS
   See also Half-sisters
STEPSONS
   Wharton, E. The reef
The **sterile** cuckoo. Nichols, J. T.
STEVEDORES *See* Longshore workers
STEVENSON, ROBERT LOUIS, 1850-1894
   Martin, V. Mary Reilly
STEWARDS
   Stevenson, R. L. The master of Ballantrae
Stick. Leonard, E.
Stillwatch. Clark, M. H.
The **Stingaree**. Brand, M.
A **stitch** in time. Lathen, E.
STOCK EXCHANGE
   Archer, J. Not a penny more, not a penny less
   Galbraith, J. K. A tenured professor
   Robbins, T. Half asleep in frog pajamas
STOCKHOLM (SWEDEN) *See* Sweden—Stockholm
STOCKYARDS *See* Meat industry
The **stoic**. Auchincloss, L.
   In Auchincloss, L. Three lives
STOKER, BRAM, 1847-1912
         Parodies, travesties, etc.
   Newman, K. Anno-Dracula
STONE AGE
   Golding, W. Clonk clonk
   Harrison, S. Brother Wind
   Harrison, S. Mother earth, father sky
   Harrison, S. My sister the moon
   Thomas, E. M. The animal wife
The **stone** bull. Whitney, P. A.
STONE CARVING
   Pargeter, E. The green branch
   Pargeter, E. The heaven tree
   Pargeter, E. The heaven tree trilogy
   Pargeter, E. The scarlet seed
The **stone** diaries. Shields, C.
Stone heart. Rice, L.
Stonecutter's story. See Saberhagen, F. The third book
   of lost swords: Stonecutter's story
STONEHENGE (ENGLAND)
   Holland, C. Pillar of the Sky
Stones for Ibarra. Doerr, H.
Stories. Lessing, D. M.
STORIES ABOUT DIARIES *See* Diaries (Stories about)
STORIES ABOUT LETTERS *See* Letters (Stories about)
Stories and early novels. Chandler, R.
STORIES IN DIARY FORM *See* Diaries (Stories in
   diary form)
Stories not for the nervous. See Alfred Hitchcock
   presents: Stories not for the nervous

The **stories** of Bernard Malamud. Malamud, B.

The **stories** of Edith Wharton. Wharton, E.

The **stories** of Elizabeth Spencer. Spencer, E.

The **stories** of Eva Luna. Allende, I.

The **stories** of F. Scott Fitzgerald. Fitzgerald, F. S.

Stories of five decades. Hesse, H.

Stories of Hawaii. London, J.

The **stories** of Heinrich Böll. Böll, H.

The **stories** of John Cheever. Cheever, J.

The **stories** of John Edgar Wideman. Wideman, J. E.

The **stories** of Muriel Spark. Spark, M.

The **stories** of Ray Bradbury. Bradbury, R.

The **stories** of Stephen Dixon. Dixon, S.

STORIES OF THE FUTURE See Future

Stories of three decades. Mann, T.

STORIES WITHIN A NOVEL
> Agnon, S. Y. The bridal canopy
> Atwood, M. Lady Oracle
> Barnes, J. A history of the world in 10½ chapters
> Barth, J. The Tidewater tales
> Conley, R. J. Mountain windsong
> Dickinson, P. Hindsight
> Fowles, J. The magus
> Gardner, J. October light
> Hammett, D. Tulip
> King, S. The breathing method
> King, S. Misery
> Roth, P. The ghost writer
> Tan, A. The Joy Luck Club
> Vargas Llosa, M. Aunt Julia and the scriptwriter
> Vidal, G. Burr
> Waller, R. J. The bridges of Madison County
> Wiesel, E. The testament

The **Stork** Club. Dart, I. R.

Storm flight. Berent, M.

Storm in Shanghai. See Malraux, A. Man's fate (La condition humaine)

Storm in the village. Read, Miss
> *In* Read, Miss Chronicles of Fairacre p361-534

Storm warning. Higgins, J.

Storming heaven. Brown, D.

Storming Intrepid. Harrison, P.

STORMS
> *See also* Hurricanes; Typhoons
> Brand, M. Dust across the range
> Hailey, A. Airport

Stormswift. Brent, M.

The **stormy** petrel. Stewart, M.

The **story** of a lie. Stevenson, R. L.
> *In* Stevenson, R. L. The complete short stories v1 p361-408
> *In* Stevenson, R. L. The complete short stories of Robert Louis Stevenson

The **storyteller**. Vargas Llosa, M.

STORYTELLING
> Barth, J. The last voyage of somebody the sailor
> Erdrich, L. Tracks
> Gurganus, A. The oldest living Confederate widow tells all
> Maḥfūz, N. Arabian nights and days
> Mehta, G. A river Sutra
> Naylor, G. Bailey's Café
> Rushdie, S. Haroun and the sea of stories
> Vargas Llosa, M. The storyteller

Storyville. Battle, L.

STOUT, REX, 1886-1975
> **Parodies, travesties, etc.**
> Goldsborough, R. The bloodied ivy
> Goldsborough, R. The missing chapter

STRADIVARI, ANTONIO, 1644-1737
> Hersey, J. Antonietta

Straight. Francis, D.

Strait is the gate (La porte étroite). Gide, A.

The **strange** case of Dr. Jekyll and Mr. Hyde. Stevenson, R. L.
> *also in* Stevenson, R. L. The complete short stories of Robert Louis Stevenson
> *also in* Stevenson, R. L. The strange case of Dr. Jekyll and Mr. Hyde, and other famous tales p1-69

The **strange** case of Dr. Jekyll and Mr. Hyde, and other famous tales. Stevenson, R. L.

Strange fits of passion. Shreve, A.

Strange fruit. Smith, L. E.

The **strange** mutiny of Gunner Asch. See Kirst, H. H. The revolt of Gunner Asch

Strange pilgrims. García Márquez, G.

Strange things and stranger places. Campbell, R.

The **stranger**. Camus, A.

The **stranger** from the sea. Graham, W.

Stranger in a strange land. Heinlein, R. A.

Stranger in Savannah. Price, E.

A **stranger** is watching. Clark, M. H.

Strangers. Koontz, D. R.

Strangers and brothers. Snow, C. P.

Strangers and brothers [series]
> Snow, C. P. The affair
> Snow, C. P. The conscience of the rich
> Snow, C. P. Corridors of power
> Snow, C. P. Homecoming
> Snow, C. P. Last things
> Snow, C. P. The light and the dark
> Snow, C. P. The masters
> Snow, C. P. The new men
> Snow, C. P. The sleep of reason
> Snow, C. P. Strangers and brothers
> Snow, C. P. Time of hope

Strangers in company. Hodge, J. A.

STREAM OF CONSCIOUSNESS
> Aiken, C. Blue voyage
> Aiken, C. Great circle
> Ashton-Warner, S. Spinster
> Beauvoir, S. de. The monologue
> Beckett, S. Molloy, Malone dies, and The unnamable
> Böll, H. Billiards at half-past nine
> Böll, H. The clown
> Faulkner, W. As I lay dying
> Ford, F. M. The last post
> García Márquez, G. The autumn of the patriarch
> Hamsun, K. Hunger
> Hamsun, K. Mysteries
> Joyce, J. Finnegans wake
> Joyce, J. A shorter Finnegans wake
> Joyce, J. Ulysses
> Lessing, D. M. The golden notebook
> Lowry, M. Under the volcano
> Maḥfūz, N. The thief and the dogs
> Proust, M. The captive
> Proust, M. The captive [and] The fugitive
> Proust, M. The fugitive
> Proust, M. The Guermantes way
> Proust, M. Jean Santeuil
> Proust, M. Remembrance of things past
> Proust, M. Sodom and Gomorrah
> Proust, M. Swann's way
> Proust, M. Time regained
> Proust, M. Within a budding grove
> Pynchon, T. Gravity's rainbow
> Styron, W. Lie down in darkness
> Woolf, V. Jacob's room
> Woolf, V. Mrs. Dalloway
> Woolf, V. To the lighthouse
> Woolf, V. The waves
> Woolf, V. The years

The **street**. Petry, A. L.
The **streetbird**. Van de Wetering, J.
Streets of Laredo. McMurtry, L.
Strictly business. Henry, O.
    In Henry, O. The complete works of O. Henry
       p1484-1631

STRIKES AND LOCKOUTS
    Galsworthy, J. Swan song
    Kennedy, W. The ink truck
    Steinbeck, J. In dubious battle
Strip tease. Hiaasen, C.

STROLLING PLAYERS
    Sabatini, R. Scaramouche
Strong medicine. Hailey, A.
Strong poison. Sayers, D. L.

STUDENTS
    See also College life; School life; Youth
    Cather, W. The professor's house
    Cook, R. Coma
    Goldman, W. Marathon man
    Grass, G. Local anaesthetic
    King, S. Rage
    Knowles, J. Peace breaks out
    Ozick, C. The cannibal galaxy
    Peters, E. Legend in green velvet
    Segal, E. Doctors
    Wilson, F. P. The select
Studs Lonigan. Farrell, J. T.
A **study** in scarlet. Doyle, Sir A. C.
    also in Doyle, Sir A. C. The complete Sherlock
      Holmes
    also in Doyle, Sir A. C. Famous tales of Sherlock
      Holmes p1-131

STUTTERING
    Shields, D. Dead languages
SUBMARINE WARFARE *See* World War, 1939-1945—
    Naval operations—Submarine

SUBMARINES
    See also Nuclear submarines
    Beach, E. L. Run silent, run deep
    Buchheim, L.-G. The boat
    Hemingway, E. Islands in the stream
    Higgins, J. Thunder point
    McCutchan, P. The last farewell
    Verne, J. Twenty thousand leagues under the sea

SUBURBAN LIFE
    Beattie, A. Falling in place
    Berger, T. Neighbors
    Cheever, J. Bullet Park
    Connell, E. S. Mr. Bridge
    Connell, E. S. Mrs. Bridge
    De Vries, P. Reuben, Reuben
    Hoffman, A. Seventh heaven
    Levin, I. The Stepford wives
    McDermott, A. That night
    Oates, J. C. American appetites
    Oates, J. C. Expensive people
    Powers, J. F. Wheat that springeth green
    Shulman, M. Rally round the flag, boys!
    Stead, C. The man who loved children
    Updike, J. Rabbit is rich
    Updike, J. Rabbit redux
    Wilson, S. The man in the gray flannel suit

SUBURBS *See* Suburban life

SUBVERSIVE ACTIVITIES
    See also Terrorism

SUBWAYS
    Godey, J. The taking of Pelham one two three
    Vine, B. King Solomon's carpet

SUCCESS
    See also Ambition; Self-made men
    Adler, E. Fortune is a woman
    Archer, J. As the crow flies
    Archer, J. Kane & Abel

    Archer, J. The prodigal daughter
    Birmingham, S. The LeBaron secret
    Bradford, B. T. A woman of substance
    Bradford, B. T. The women in his life
    Carroll, J. Memorial bridge
    Delderfield, R. F. God is an Englishman
    Fitzgerald, F. S. The Great Gatsby
    Gage, E. Pandora's box
    Goudge, E. Such devoted sisters
    James, H. The American
    Jones, D. C. Come winter
    Lofts, N. The house at sunset
    Marsh, J. The House of Eliott
    O'Hara, J. Ten North Frederick
    Spencer, S. Men in black
    Steel, D. Jewels
    Thayer, N. Everlasting
    Thomas, R. A woman of our times
    West, N. A cool million
SUCCESSION *See* Inheritance and succession
Such devoted sisters. Goudge, E.
Sudden country. Estleman, L. D.
Sudden death. Brown, R. M.
Sudden death. Kienzle, W. X.
A **sudden**, fearful death. Perry, A.
Sudden vengeance. Crispin, E.
A **sudden** wild magic. Jones, D. W.

SUFFERING
    See also Good and evil
    Potok, C. I am the clay
The **sufferings** of young Werther. See Goethe, J. W. von.
    The sorrows of young Werther
SUFFOLK (ENGLAND) *See* England—Suffolk
The **sugar** pavilion. Laker, R.
Sugar Street. Maḥfūẓ, N.
Sugartown. Estleman, L. D.

SUICIDE
    Armstrong, C. A dram of poison
    Bambara, T. C. The salt eaters
    Barth, J. The floating opera
    Bass, R. Platte River
    Bausch, R. Rare & endangered species
    Caldwell, T. Ceremony of the innocent
    Didion, J. Play it as it lays
    Eugenides, J. The virgin suicides
    Flaubert, G. Madame Bovary
    Gilchrist, E. The Anna papers
    Gordon, M. The rest of life
    Horgan, P. Whitewater
    McFarland, D. The music room
    Mishima, Y. Runaway horses
    Oates, J. C. What I lived for
    Ōe, K. The silent cry
    Percy, W. The second coming
    Plath, S. The bell jar
    Roth, P. When she was good
    Saul, J. Shadows
    Styron, W. Lie down in darkness
    Turow, S. The burden of proof
    Tyler, A. The clock winder
A **suitable** boy. Seth, V.
A **suitable** vengeance. George, E.
Sula. Morrison, T.

SULLA, LUCIUS CORNELIUS
    McCullough, C. The first man in Rome
    McCullough, C. Fortune's favorites
    McCullough, C. The grass crown
Sullivan's sting. Sanders, L.
The **sum** of all fears. Clancy, T.

SUMERIANS
    Silverberg, R. Gilgamesh the king

SUMMER
    Bradbury, R. Dandelion wine

The **summer** before the dark. Lessing, D. M.

SUMMER CAMPS
Phillips, J. A. Shelter
Price, R. The tongues of angels
Swarthout, G. F. Bless the beasts and children
Wouk, H. The city boy, the adventures of Herbie Bookbinder and his cousin Cliff
Summer harvest. Swindells, M.
Summer of '42. Raucher, H.
Summer of fear. Parker, T. J.
The **summer** of Katya. Trevanian
The **summer** of the Barshinskeys. Pearson, D.
The **summer** of the Danes. Peters, E.
The **summer** of the royal visit. Colegate, I.
Summer people. Piercy, M.
The **Summer** Queen. Vinge, J. D.

SUMMER RESORTS
Appelfeld, A. Badenheim 1939
Benchley, P. Jaws
Kay, T. Shadow song
Raucher, H. Summer of '42
Siddons, A. R. Colony

SUMMER VACATIONS See Vacations
Summer's lease. Mortimer, J. C.
A **summons** to Memphis. Taylor, P. H.
The **sun** also rises. Hemingway, E.
also in Hemingway, E. The Hemingway reader p89-289
The **sun** dog. King, S.
In King, S. Four past midnight p605-763
Sunday the rabbi stayed home. Kemelman, H.
The **sundowners**. Cleary, J.
Sunflower. West, Dame R.
The **sunlight** dialogues. Gardner, J.
The **sunne** in splendour. Penman, S. K.
Sunshine. Klein, N.

SUPER BOWL GAME (FOOTBALL)
Harris, T. Black Sunday
Jenkins, D. Semi-tough
Superior women. Adams, A.

SUPERNATURAL PHENOMENA
See also Demoniac possession; Ghost stories; Horror stories
Ackroyd, P. English music
Allende, I. The house of the spirits
Amado, J. The war of the saints
Amis, K. The Green Man
Barker, C. The forbidden
Bradbury, R. Something wicked this way comes
Bradley, M. Z. The house between the worlds
Campbell, R. The long lost
Capote, T. A tree of night, and other stories
Card, O. S. Lost boys
Clark, M. H. Remember me
Davies, R. What's bred in the bone
Du Maurier, Dame D. Don't look now
Greeley, A. M. Angels of September
Hawthorne, N. Twice-told tales
Irving, W. Washington Irving's Tales of the supernatural
King, S. Carrie
King, S. Christine
King, S. The dark half
King, S. Firestarter
King, S. Insomnia
King, S. Needful things
King, S. Salem's Lot
King, S. The talisman
Koontz, D. R. Dragon tears
L'Amour, L. The haunted mesa
Leiber, F. Gonna roll the bones
Levin, I. Rosemary's baby
Lofts, N. Gad's Hall
Lovecraft, H. P. At the mountains of madness, and other novels
Lovecraft, H. P. The Dunwich horror, and others

Mysterious cat stories
Naylor, G. Mama Day
Poe, E. A. The narrative of Arthur Gordon Pym of Nantucket
Power, S. The grass dancer
Rice, A. Lasher
Rice, A. Taltos
Rice, A. The witching hour
Riley, J. M. In pursuit of the green lion
Spark, M. The comforters
Stoker, B. Dracula
Straub, P. Ghost story
Strieber, W. The forbidden zone
Thomas, E. M. Reindeer Moon
Whitney, P. A. The singing stones
Wilde, O. The picture of Dorian Gray
Wolfe, G. Castleview

SUPERSTITION
See also Occultism; Vampires; Voodooism; Werewolves
Naylor, G. Mama Day
Stevenson, R. L. The beach of Falesá

SURÊTÉ, FRENCH See Police—Paris (France)
Surfacing. Atwood, M.

SURGEONS
See also Physicians; Women physicians
Fielding, J. See Jane run
Greenberg, J. Age of consent
Hiaasen, C. Skin tight
Kundera, M. The unbearable lightness of being
Moore, B. The doctor's wife
Uris, L. QB VII

SURGERY
See also Transplantation of organs, tissues, etc.
Cook, R. Coma
Cook, R. Godplayer

SURREALISM
Berger, T. The houseguest
Childress, M. Crazy in Alabama
García Márquez, G. The autumn of the patriarch
Hoffman, A. Seventh heaven
Ishiguro, K. The unconsoled
Kingston, M. H. Tripmaster Monkey

SURREY (ENGLAND) See England—Surrey

SURROGATE MOTHERS
McCaffrey, A. The greatest love

SURVIVAL (AFTER AIRPLANE ACCIDENTS, SHIPWRECKS, ETC.)
See also Shipwrecks and castaways; Wilderness survival
Bosse, M. J. Mister Touch
Defoe, D. Robinson Crusoe
Dickey, J. To the white sea
Frank, P. Alas, Babylon
Gallico, P. The Poseidon adventure
Gann, E. K. The aviator
Golding, W. Lord of the Flies
MacLean, A. Night without end
Strieber, W. Warday
Trevor, E. The flight of the Phoenix
Vonnegut, K. Galápagos
Wiggins, M. John Dollar
Wilhelm, K. Where late the sweet birds sang
Survivor. Butler, O. E.

SURVIVORS, HOLOCAUST See Holocaust survivors
Suspects. Caunitz, W. J.

SUSPENSE NOVELS
See also Adventure; Conspiracies; Gothic romances; Horror stories; International intrigue; Kidnapping; Murder stories; Mystery and detective stories; Psychological novels; Secret service; Spies; Terrorism
Aaron, D. Crossing by night
Abrahams, P. Hard rain
Abrahams, P. Lights out
Alcott, L. M. A long fatal love chase

SUSPENSE NOVELS—*Continued*

Allbeury, T. The Judas factor
Allbeury, T. A time without shadows
Ambler, E. The Levanter
Anthony, E. The Doll's House
Anthony, E. Exposure
Anthony, E. Mission to Malaspiga
Anthony, E. The relic
Anthony, E. The tamarind seed
Archer, J. Honor among thieves
Bagley, D. Night of error
Ballard, M. F. Final curtain
Batchelor, J. C. Father's day
Block, L. The thief who couldn't sleep
Bond, L. Vortex
Bova, B. Death dream
Bova, B. The Trikon deception
Bradford, B. T. Remember
Brandon, J. Rules of evidence
Brett, S. Dead romantic
Brett, S. A shock to the system
Briskin, J. The other side of love
Brown, D. Chains of command
Brown, D. Flight of the Old Dog
Brown, D. Hammerheads
Brown, D. Night of the hawk
Brown, D. Sky masters
Brown, D. Storming heaven
Brown, S. Charade
Browne, G. A. 18mm blues
Browne, G. A. 19 Purchase Street
Browne, G. A. Hot Siberian
Buckley, C. T. Wet work
Byatt, A. S. Possession
Carr, C. The alienist
Clancy, T. The Cardinal of the Kremlin
Clancy, T. Clear and present danger
Clancy, T. Debt of honor
Clancy, T. The hunt for Red October
Clancy, T. Patriot games
Clancy, T. Red Storm rising
Clancy, T. The sum of all fears
Clancy, T. Without remorse
Clark, M. H. All around the town
Clark, M. H. The cradle will fall
Clark, M. H. A cry in the night
Clark, M. H. I'll be seeing you
Clark, M. H. Loves music, loves to dance
Clark, M. H. Remember me
Clark, M. H. Stillwatch
Clark, M. H. A stranger is watching
Clark, M. H. Where are the children?
Cleary, J. High road to China
Cody, L. Rift
Collins, L. The fifth horseman
Collins, W. The rationalist
Cook, R. Blindsight
Cook, R. Fatal cure
Cook, R. Harmful intent
Cook, R. Mindbend
Cook, R. Mortal fear
Cook, R. Mutation
Cook, R. Outbreak
Cook, R. Terminal
Cook, R. Vital signs
Cook, T. H. Evidence of blood
Coonts, S. Final flight
Coonts, S. The Intruders
Coonts, S. The minotaur
Coonts, S. The red horseman
Coonts, S. Under siege
Coscarelli, K. Heir apparent
Coulter, C. Impulse
Crichton, M. A case of need
Crichton, M. Disclosure
Crichton, M. Rising sun
Cussler, C. Cyclops
Cussler, C. Deep six

Cussler, C. Dragon
Cussler, C. Inca gold
Cussler, C. Night probe!
Cussler, C. Raise the Titanic!
Cussler, C. Sahara
Cussler, C. Treasure
Cussler, C. Vixen 03
Dailey, J. Masquerade
Deighton, L. Berlin game
Deighton, L. City of gold
Deighton, L. Faith
Deighton, L. Funeral in Berlin
Deighton, L. Game, set & match
Deighton, L. The Ipcress file
Deighton, L. London match
Deighton, L. Mexico set
Deighton, L. Spy hook
Deighton, L. Spy line
Deighton, L. Spy sinker
DeMille, N. Spencerville
Dickinson, P. Death of a unicorn
Dickinson, P. Hindsight
Dickinson, P. Perfect gallows
Dickinson, P. Play dead
Diehl, W. 27
Diehl, W. Primal fear
DiMercurio, M. Attack of the Seawolf
Easterman, D. Brotherhood of the tomb
Egleton, C. A double deception
Egleton, C. Hostile intent
Egleton, C. A killing in Moscow
Estleman, L. D. Kill zone
Fielding, J. See Jane run
Fielding, J. Tell me no secrets
Finder, J. The Moscow Club
Finney, P. Firedrake's eye
Fleming, I. Bonded Fleming
Fleming, I. Casino Royale
Fleming, I. Doctor No
Fleming, I. From Russia, with love
Fleming, I. Goldfinger
Fleming, I. The man with the golden gun
Fleming, I. More gilt-edged Bonds
Fleming, I. On Her Majesty's Secret Service
Fleming, I. You only live twice
Follett, K. Eye of the needle
Follett, K. The key to Rebecca
Follett, K. Lie down with lions
Follett, K. The man from St. Petersburg
Follett, K. Night over water
Follett, K. Paper money
Follett, K. Triple
Folsom, A. R. The day after tomorrow
Forsyth, F. The day of the jackal
Forsyth, F. The deceiver
Forsyth, F. The dogs of war
Forsyth, F. The fist of God
Forsyth, F. The fourth protocol
Forsyth, F. The negotiator
Forsyth, F. The Odessa file
Francis, C. Wolf winter
Francis, D. Bonecrack
Francis, D. Flying finish
Francis, D. For kicks
Francis, D. Forfeit
Francis, D. High stakes
Francis, D. Three to show
Francis, D. Twice shy
Freemantle, B. The button man
Freemantle, B. Charlie's apprentice
Freemantle, B. Comrade Charlie
Gardner, J. E. Brokenclaw
Gardner, J. E. Death is forever
Gardner, J. E. License renewed
Gardner, J. E. Maestro
Gardner, J. E. The man from Barbarossa
Gardner, J. E. Never send flowers
Gardner, J. E. Seafire

SUSPENSE NOVELS—_Continued_

Gardner, J. E. The secret families
Gardner, J. E. The secret generations
Gardner, J. E. The secret houses
Garfield, B. Hopscotch
Gash, J. The Vatican rip
Gifford, T. The Glendower legacy
Gill, B. M. Time and time again
Gilman, D. The amazing Mrs. Pollifax
Gilman, D. The elusive Mrs. Pollifax
Gilman, D. Incident at Badamya
Gilman, D. Mrs. Pollifax and the Hong Kong Buddha
Godey, J. The taking of Pelham one two three
Goldman, W. Marathon man
Grady, J. Six days of the condor
Grady, J. Thunder
Graham, W. Stephanie
Graham, W. The walking stick
Grant, M. Officer down
Gregory, P. The wise woman
Grisham, J. The client
Grisham, J. The firm
Grisham, J. The pelican brief
Guest, J. Killing time in St. Cloud
Hall, A. Quiller bamboo
Hall, A. Quiller barracuda
Hall, A. The Quiller memorandum
Hall, A. Quiller meridian
Hall, A. Quiller Salamander
Hall, A. Quiller solitaire
Harris, R. Fatherland
Harris, T. Black Sunday
Harris, T. Red Dragon
Harris, T. The silence of the lambs
Harrison, P. Black cipher
Harrison, P. Storming Intrepid
Higgins, J. Cold Harbour
Higgins, J. Confessional
Higgins, J. Day of judgment
Higgins, J. Exocet
Higgins, J. Eye of the storm
Higgins, J. Luciano's luck
Higgins, J. Night of the fox
Higgins, J. On dangerous ground
Higgins, J. A season in hell
Higgins, J. Thunder point
Higgins, J. Touch the devil
Highsmith, P. The boy who followed Ripley
Highsmith, P. Ripley's game
Hill, R. Dream of darkness
Hill, S. Mrs. de Winter
Hodge, J. A. Strangers in company
Hoeg, P. Smilla's sense of snow
Household, G. Rogue male
Hoving, T. Discovery
Hunter, E. Criminal conversation
Hunter, S. Dirty white boys
Iles, G. Black cross
Innes, H. Isvik
Innes, H. Medusa
Irving, C. Final argument
Katzenbach, J. Just cause
Kaye, M. M. Death in the Andamans
Kellerman, F. The quality of mercy
King, S. The dead zone
King, S. Dolores Claiborne
King, S. Gerald's game
King, S. Insomnia
King, S. Misery
Knebel, F. Seven days in May
Koontz, D. R. The bad place
Koontz, D. R. Dark rivers of the heart
Koontz, D. R. Lightning
Koontz, D. R. Mr. Murder
Koontz, D. R. Three complete novels
Krentz, J. A. Grand passion
Laker, R. The sugar pavilion
Le Carré, J. The honourable schoolboy
Le Carré, J. The little drummer girl

Le Carré, J. The night manager
Le Carré, J. A perfect spy
Le Carré, J. The quest for Karla
Le Carré, J. The Russia house
Le Carré, J. Smiley's people
Le Carré, J. The spy who came in from the cold
Le Carré, J. Tinker, tailor, soldier, spy
Leonard, E. Bandits
Leonard, E. Cat chaser
Leonard, E. Freaky Deaky
Leonard, E. Glitz
Leonard, E. The hunted
Leonard, E. Killshot
Leonard, E. LaBrava
Leonard, E. Split images
Leonard, E. Stick
Leonard, E. Touch
Lescroart, J. T. Hard evidence
Levin, I. The boys from Brazil
Levin, I. Sliver
Lindsey, D. L. An absence of light
Lindsey, D. L. Mercy
Lovesey, P. On the edge
Ludlum, R. The Aquitaine progression
Ludlum, R. The Bourne identity
Ludlum, R. The Bourne supremacy
Ludlum, R. The Bourne ultimatum
Ludlum, R. The Chancellor manuscript
Ludlum, R. The Gemini contenders
Ludlum, R. The Holcroft covenant
Ludlum, R. The Icarus agenda
Ludlum, R. The Matarese Circle
Ludlum, R. The Matlock paper
Ludlum, R. The Parsifal mosaic
Ludlum, R. The Rhinemann exchange
Ludlum, R. The road to Omaha
Ludlum, R. The Scarlatti inheritance
Ludlum, R. The scorpio illusion
Lustbader, E. V. Angel eyes
Lustbader, E. V. Black Blade
Lustbader, E. V. Floating city
Lustbader, E. V. French kiss
Lustbader, E. V. The Kaisho
Lustbader, E. V. White Ninja
Lutz, J. Dancing with the dead
Maas, P. China white
Maas, P. Father and son
MacInnes, H. Above suspicion
MacInnes, H. Agent in place
MacInnes, H. Assignment in Brittany
MacInnes, H. Cloak of darkness
MacInnes, H. Decision at Delphi
MacInnes, H. The double image
MacInnes, H. The hidden target
MacInnes, H. Message from Málaga
MacInnes, H. North from Rome
MacInnes, H. Prelude to terror
MacInnes, H. Ride a pale horse
MacInnes, H. The Salzburg connection
MacInnes, H. The snare of the hunter
MacInnes, H. The Venetian affair
MacLean, A. Caravan to Vaccares
MacLean, A. Floodgate
MacLean, A. Ice Station Zebra
MacLean, A. When eight bells toll
McCammon, R. R. Boy's life
McCammon, R. R. Gone south
McCammon, R. R. Mine
McCrumb, S. The hangman's beautiful daughter
McCrumb, S. If ever I return, pretty Peggy-O
McCrumb, S. She walks these hills
McCutchan, P. Halfhyde and the fleet review
McEwan, I. Black dogs
McEwan, I. The innocent
McMullen, M. A grave without flowers
McNaught, J. Perfect
Michaels, B. Houses of stone
Michaels, B. Into the darkness

SUSPENSE NOVELS—*Continued*

Moore, B. The color of blood
Moore, B. Lies of silence
Morrell, D. Assumed identity
Morrell, D. The covenant of the flame
Morrell, D. Desperate measures
Morrell, D. The fifth profession
Neville, K. The eight
Oates, J. C. Snake eyes
Ogilvie, E. When the music stopped
Palmer, M. Natural causes
Parker, T. J. Little Saigon
Patterson, J. Along came a spider
Patterson, J. Kiss the girls
Pearson, R. The angel maker
Pearson, R. Hard fall
Pearson, R. No witnesses
Perry, T. Metzger's dog
Perry, T. Vanishing act
Price, N. Night woman
Puzo, M. The fourth K
Reed, K. Gone
Rendell, R. The bridesmaid
Rendell, R. Heartstones
Rendell, R. A judgment in stone
Rendell, R. The killing doll
Rendell, R. Live flesh
Rendell, R. Make death love me
Rendell, R. Master of the moor
Rendell, R. Talking to strange men
Robards, K. Maggy's child
Robards, K. One summer
Roberts, N. Hidden riches
Roberts, N. Honest illusions
Roberts, N. Private scandals
Rosenberg, N. T. First offense
Rosenberg, N. T. Interest of justice
Sanders, L. The eighth commandment
Sanders, L. The first deadly sin
Sanders, L. The second deadly sin
Sanders, L. The seventh commandment
Sanders, L. The sixth commandment
Sanders, L. Sullivan's sting
Sanders, L. The tangent factor
Sanders, L. The tenth commandment
Sanders, L. The third deadly sin
Sandford, J. Rules of prey
Saul, J. Guardian
Saul, J. Shadows
Shannon, D. The Manson curse
Sheldon, S. The doomsday conspiracy
Sheldon, S. The sands of time
Smith, S. B. A simple plan
Smith, W. A. Elephant song
Smith, W. A. Golden fox
Steel, D. Vanished
Stewart, M. Airs above the ground
Stewart, M. The moon-spinners
Stewart, M. My brother Michael
Stewart, M. The stormy petrel
Stewart, M. This rough magic
Straub, P. Koko
Straub, P. The throat
Strieber, W. Majestic
Thomas, C. Firefox
Thomas, C. A hooded crow
Thomas, C. Playing with cobras
Thomas, M. M. Black money
Thomas, R. Ah, treachery!
Thomas, R. Briarpatch
Thomas, R. The fourth Durango
Trenhaile, J. The gates of exquisite view
Trevanian. The Eiger sanction
Trevor, W. Felicia's journey
Villars, E. Too close for comfort
Vine, B. Gallowglass
Vine, B. King Solomon's carpet
Vine, B. No night is too long
Wallace, I. The man

Walters, M. The sculptress
West, M. L. The clowns of God
West, M. L. Masterclass
Whitney, P. A. Black amber
Whitney, P. A. Columbella
Whitney, P. A. Daughter of the stars
Whitney, P. A. Domino
Whitney, P. A. Dream of orchids
Whitney, P. A. The ebony swan
Whitney, P. A. Emerald
Whitney, P. A. Feather on the moon
Whitney, P. A. Flaming Tree
Whitney, P. A. The glass flame
Whitney, P. A. Hunter's green
Whitney, P. A. Rainbow in the mist
Whitney, P. A. Sea Jade
Whitney, P. A. Silverhill
Whitney, P. A. The singing stones
Whitney, P. A. Spindrift
Whitney, P. A. Star flight
Whitney, P. A. The stone bull
Whitney, P. A. The turquoise mask
Whitney, P. A. Woman without a past
Wilhelm, K. The best defense
Wilson, F. P. The select
Woods, S. Dead eyes
Woods, S. Grass roots
Woods, S. Heat
Woods, S. Imperfect strangers
Woods, S. L.A. Times
Woods, S. Santa Fe rules
Yorke, M. Crime in question
Yorke, M. Dangerous to know
Yorke, M. Find me a villain
Yorke, M. Intimate kill

Suspicious characters. See Sayers, D. L. The five red herrings

Suspicious death. Simpson, D.

SUSSEX (ENGLAND) See England—Sussex

Swag. Leonard, E.
In Leonard, E. Elmore Leonard's Dutch treat: 3 novels

Swan song. Galsworthy, J.
In Galsworthy, J. A modern comedy

Swann's way. Proust, M.
also in Proust, M. Remembrance of things past v1 p3-462

Swan's chance. De Blasis, C.

SWEDEN

19th century
Moberg, V. The emigrants
Ross-Macdonald, M. Dancing on snowflakes

Farm life
See Farm life—Sweden

Rural life
Jönsson, R. My life as a dog
Strindberg, A. The scapegoat

Stockholm
Ozick, C. The Messiah of Stockholm
Ross-Macdonald, M. Dancing on snowflakes

SWEDES
See also Vikings

Denmark
Andersen Nexø, M. Pelle the conqueror: v1 Childhood
Andersen Nexø, M. Pelle the conqueror: v2 Apprenticeship

Islands of the Pacific
Conrad, J. Victory

United States
Cather, W. O pioneers!
Cather, W. The song of the lark
Moberg, V. The emigrants
Moberg, V. The last letter home
Moberg, V. Unto a good land

SWEDISH DIALECT *See* Dialect stories—Swedish
Sweet death, kind death. Cross, A.
The sweet dove died. Pym, B.
The sweet hereafter. Banks, R.
Sweet, sweet poison. Wilhelm, K.
Sweet Thursday. Steinbeck, J.
Sweet William. Hawkes, J.
Swimming in the volcano. Shacochis, B.

SWINDLERS AND SWINDLING
    See also Business—Unscrupulous methods
  Archer, J. Not a penny more, not a penny less
  Brown, J. D. Addie Pray
  Dickens, C. Martin Chuzzlewit
  Jhabvala, R. P. Three continents
  MacDonald, J. D. Barrier Island
  Melville, H. The confidence-man: his masquerade
  Shaw, I. Nightwork
  Yorke, M. The smooth face of evil

SWISS ALPS *See* Alps
Switch. Bayer, W.
Switchback. Wilcox, C.

SWITZERLAND
20th century
  Brookner, A. Hotel du Lac
  Cronin, A. J. A pocketful of rye
  Gilman, D. A palm for Mrs. Pollifax
  Stead, C. The little hotel
  Ullman, J. R. The White Tower
  Wharton, E. The children

Geneva
  Durrell, L. Sebastian

Lugano
  Kirst, H. H. The nights of the long knives

Zurich
  Davies, R. The manticore
The sword and the flame. Hill, P.
Sword at sunset. Sutcliff, R.
The sword in the stone. White, T. H.
  also in White, T. H. The once and future king p1-213
Sword of honour. See Waugh, E. Men at arms
The sword of Shannara. Brooks, T.
The sword of the Lictor. Wolfe, G.

SYMBOLISM
    See also Allegories; Parables
  Achebe, C. Anthills of the Savannah
  Atwood, M. Bodily harm
  Barth, J. Giles goat-boy
  Bellow, S. Henderson the rain king
  Böll, H. Billiards at half-past nine
  Coetzee, J. M. Foe
  Conrad, J. The Nigger of the Narcissus
  Dinesen, I. The angelic avengers
  Doctorow, E. L. Loon Lake
  Faulkner, W. A fable
  Fowles, J. The magus
  Fuentès, C. The campaign
  Fuentes, C. Terra nostra
  Gallico, P. The snow goose
  Gordimer, N. The conservationist
  Grass, G. Cat and mouse
  Grass, G. The Danzig trilogy
  Grass, G. Dog years
  Grass, G. Local anaesthetic
  Grass, G. The tin drum
  Handke, P. The left-handed woman
  Hawthorne, N. The scarlet letter
  Helprin, M. A soldier of the great war
  Hesse, H. Demian
  Hesse, H. The glass bead game (Magister Ludi)
  Hesse, H. Narcissus and Goldmund
  Hesse, H. Steppenwolf
  Hoban, R. Pilgermann
  Hulme, K. The bone people
  Irving, J. A prayer for Owen Meany

  Joyce, J. Ulysses
  Kafka, F. Metamorphosis
  Kafka, F. The trial
  Kawabata, Y. Thousand cranes
  Kingsolver, B. Animal dreams
  Lawrence, D. H. The plumed serpent (Quetzalcoatl)
  Mann, T. The black swan
  Mann, T. Death in Venice
  Mann, T. The magic mountain
  Martin, V. The great divorce
  Melville, H. Billy Budd, sailor
  Melville, H. Mardi: and a voyager thither
  Melville, H. Moby-Dick
  Momaday, N. S. The ancient child
  Morrison, T. Beloved
  Murdoch, I. Nuns and soldiers
  Nabokov, V. V. Ada
  Nabokov, V. V. Pale fire
  O'Brien, T. In the Lake of the Woods
  Ōe, K. The pinch runner memorandum
  Ōe, K. The silent cry
  Phillips, J. A. Shelter
  Plante, D. Annunciation
  Poe, E. A. The narrative of Arthur Gordon Pym of Nantucket
  Porter, K. A. Ship of fools
  Pynchon, T. V.
  Rushdie, S. The satanic verses
  Silverberg, R. Downward to the Earth
  Theroux, P. The Mosquito Coast
  Thomas, D. M. The white hotel
  Updike, J. Roger's version
  Wiesel, E. A beggar in Jerusalem
  Woiwode, L. Indian affairs
  Woiwode, L. What I'm going to do, I think
  Woolf, V. Between the acts
  Woolf, V. The waves
Symbols at your door. Fraser, A.

SYRACUSE (ITALY) *See* Italy—Syracuse

SYRIA
  Ambler, E. The Levanter
  Caldwell, T. Dear and glorious physician
  Werfel, F. The forty days of Musa Dagh

SYRIANS
Brazil
  Amado, J. Gabriela, clove and cinnamon

T

TA CH'ING DYNASTY *See* Manchus
Table money. Breslin, J.

TABOO *See* Superstition

TAHITI
  Maugham, W. S. The moon and sixpence
  Melville, H. Omoo: a narrative of adventures in the South Seas
Tai-Pan. Clavell, J.

TAILORS
  Markandaya, K. A handful of rice
Tainted evidence. Daley, R.

TAIPING REBELLION, 1850-1864
  Elegant, R. S. Mandarin
The taking of Pelham one two three. Godey, J.

TALAVERA CAMPAIGN, 1809 *See* Peninsular War, 1807-1814
The tale of Genji. Murasaki Shikibu
The tale of the body thief. Rice, A.
A tale of two cities. Dickens, C.
Tales from a troubled land. Paton, A.
Tales from the Drones Club. Wodehouse, P. G.
Tales of Alvin Maker [series]
  Card, O. S. Alvin Journeyman

Tales of Alvin Maker—[series]—*Continued*
  Card, O. S. Prentice Alvin
  Card, O. S. Red prophet
  Card, O. S. Seventh son
Tales of good and evil. See Gogol', N. V. The overcoat, and other tales of good and evil
The tales of Jacob. Mann, T.
  In Mann, T. Joseph and his brothers p3-258
Tales of land and sea. Conrad, J.
Tales of men and ghosts. Wharton, E.
  In Wharton, E. The collected short stories of Edith Wharton v2
Tales of terror and mystery. Doyle, Sir A. C.
Tales of the East and West. Conrad, J.
Tales of the Jewelled Men [series]
  Veryan, P. Ask me no questions
  Veryan, P. Had we never loved
  Veryan, P. Never doubt I love
  Veryan, P. A shadow's bliss
  Veryan, P. Time's fool
Tales of the South Pacific. Michener, J. A.
Tales of the supernatural, Washington Irving's. See Irving, W. Washington Irving's Tales of the supernatural
Tales of the Witch World [1]-3. Entered in Part I under title
Tales of yesteryear. Auchincloss, L.
The talisman. King, S.
The talisman. Scott, Sir W.
The talismans of Shannara. Brooks, T.
Talking God. Hillerman, T.
Talking to strange men. Rendell, R.
The talking trees and other stories. O'Faoláin, S.
  In O'Faolain, S. The collected stories of Sean O'Faolain p889-1060
The tall stranger. L'Amour, L.
  In L'Amour, L. Four complete novels p1-95
Taltos. Rice, A.
The tamarind seed. Anthony, E.
Taming a sea-horse. Parker, R. B.
Tamuli [series]
  Eddings, D. Domes of fire
  Eddings, D. The hidden city
  Eddings, D. The shining ones
A tan and sandy silence. MacDonald, J. D.
The tangent factor. Sanders, L.
The Tangle Box. Brooks, T.
Tangled vines. Dailey, J.
A tangled web. Michael, J.
The Tanglewood murders. See Kallen, L. C. B. Greenfield: the Tanglewood murders

TANNENBERG, BATTLE OF, 1914
  Solzhenitsyn, A. August 1914
Tapestry. Plain, B.
Tar: a midwest childhood. Anderson, S.
Tar baby. Morrison, T.
The tartan sell. Gash, J.
A taste for death. James, P. D.
Tau Zero. Anderson, P.
TAVERNS See Hotels, taverns, etc.
TEACHERS
  See also Students; Tutors
  Abe, K. The woman in the dunes
  Amis, K. Lucky Jim
  Ashton-Warner, S. Spinster
  Barth, J. The end of the road
  Bellow, S. The dean's December
  Boucher, A. The compleat werewolf
  Bradley, D. The Chaneysville incident
  Brett, S. Dead romantic
  Brontë, C. The professor
  Brontë, C. Villette
  Cheever, J. Falconer
  Colette. Claudine at school

Cronin, A. J. A song of sixpence
Davies, R. Fifth business
Delderfield, R. F. To serve them all my days
DeLillo, D. White noise
Dickens, C. Nicholas Nickleby
Dove, R. Through the ivory gate
Du Maurier, Dame D. The scapegoat
Durrell, L. Balthazar
Durrell, L. Clea
Durrell, L. Justine
Elkin, S. Her sense of timing
Elkin, S. Van Gogh's room at Arles
Fast, H. The trial of Abigail Goodman
Fowles, J. The magus
Gaines, E. J. A lesson before dying
Galbraith, J. K. A tenured professor
Godwin, G. The good husband
Godwin, G. The odd woman
Gordimer, N. My son's story
Gordon, M. The company of women
Grass, G. Local anaesthetic
Greenberg, J. No reck'ning made
Greene, G. The confidential agent
Hardy, T. Under the greenwood tree
Harrison, J. The beige dolorosa
Heller, J. Good as Gold
Hemingway, E. For whom the bell tolls
Hilton, J. Good-bye Mr. Chips
Holt, V. The Devil on horseback
Horgan, P. Whitewater
Hunter, E. The blackboard jungle
Irving, J. The 158-pound marriage
Kaufman, B. Up the down staircase
Kingsolver, B. Animal dreams
Knowles, J. Peace breaks out
Knowles, J. A separate peace
Lessing, D. M. Briefing for a descent into Hell
Lockridge, R. Raintree County
Ludlum, R. The Matlock paper
Lurie, A. Foreign affairs
Lurie, A. The war between the Tates
MacInnes, H. Above suspicion
Mapson, J.-A. Hank and Chloe
Marshall, C. Christy
McCarthy, M. The groves of Academe
Nabokov, V. V. Ada
Nabokov, V. V. Pale fire
Nabokov, V. V. Pnin
Oates, J. C. Solstice
Oates, J. C. Unholy loves
Patton, F. G. Good morning, Miss Dove
Pearce, M. E. Apple tree lean down
Pearce, M. E. The land endures
Peters, E. The murders of Richard III
Piercy, M. The longings of women
Price, N. Night woman
Price, R. The promise of rest
Price, R. The source of light
Pym, B. No fond return of love
Read, Miss. Battles at Thrush Green
Read, Miss. Chronicles of Fairacre
Read, Miss. The school at Thrush Green
Reed, I. Japanese by spring
Robards, K. One summer
Roiphe, A. R. If you knew me
Rossner, J. Looking for Mr. Goodbar
Roth, P. Letting go
Roth, P. The professor of desire
Sarton, M. As we are now
Sarton, M. A small room
Sartre, J. P. The age of reason
Shaw, I. Bread upon the waters
Siddons, A. R. Hill towns
Škvorecký, J. The engineer of human souls
Spark, M. The prime of Miss Jean Brodie
Thane, E. Dawn's early light
Trollope, J. The men and the girls
Updike, J. The centaur

TEACHERS—*Continued*
Updike, J. Memories of the Ford Administration
Waller, R. J. Slow waltz in Cedar Bend
Warren, R. P. A place to come to
Whitney, P. A. Columbella
Wiesel, E. Twilight
Wiggins, M. John Dollar
The **Teahouse** of the August Moon. Sneider, V.

TECHNOLOGY AND CIVILIZATION
Anderson, P. Orion shall rise
Anderson, S. Poor white
Burdick, E. Fail-safe
Huxley, A. Brave new world
Vonnegut, K. Cat's cradle
Vonnegut, K. Player piano
Vonnegut, K. The sirens of Titan

TECUMSEH, SHAWNEE CHIEF, 1768-1813
Thom, J. A. Panther in the sky

TEENAGERS *See* Adolescence; Youth

TELECOMMUNICATION
See also Television

TELEGRAPHERS
James, H. In the cage

TELEKINESIS *See* Psychokinesis

TELEPATHY
Le Guin, U. K. The left hand of darkness
McCaffrey, A. Damia
McCaffrey, A. Damia's children
McCaffrey, A. Lyon's pride
McCaffrey, A. Pegasus in flight
McCaffrey, A. The Rowan
Smith, C. On the storm planet
Vance, J. The miracle workers
Vinge, J. D. Catspaw

TELEVISION
Green, G. The last angry man
King, S. The running man
Kosinski, J. N. Being there
Roberts, N. Private scandals
Robinson, S. Stardance [novelette]
Thayer, S. The weatherman
Theroux, P. Millroy the Magician

TELEVISION PRODUCERS AND DIRECTORS
Clark, M. H. Stillwatch
McMurtry, L. Some can whistle
Steel, D. Heartbeat

TELEVISION PROGRAMS
Brown, S. Charade
Tell me a riddle. Olsen, T.
Tell me how long the train's been gone. Baldwin, J.
Tell me no secrets. Fielding, J.
Tell me that you love me, Junie Moon. Kellogg, M.
Telluride. Schofield, S. C.
The **Temple** of Dawn. Mishima, Y.
The **temple** of my familiar. Walker, A.
The **temple** of the golden pavilion. Mishima, Y.
Temporary kings. Powell, A.
In Powell, A. A dance to the music of time [v4]
Temporary shelter. Gordon, M.
Ten little Indians. Christie, A.
In Christie, A. Agatha Christie: five complete novels of murder and detection
Ten little niggers. See Christie, A. And then there were none
Ten little niggers. See Christie, A. Ten little Indians
Ten North Frederick. O'Hara, J.

TENANT FARMING
Delderfield, R. F. A horseman riding by
Faulkner, W. The mansion
Olsen, T. Yonnondio: from the thirties

The **tenant** of Wildfell Hall. Brontë, A.
The **tenants**. Malamud, B.
The **tenants** of time. Flanagan, T.
Tender. Childress, M.
Tender is the night. Fitzgerald, F. S.
also in Fitzgerald, F. S. The portable F. Scott Fitzgerald p169-545
Tender mercies. Brown, R.
Tender offerings. Rich, M.
The **tender** shoot. Colette
In Colette. The collected stories of Colette p421-48
Tending to Virginia. McCorkle, J.

TENNESSEE
See also Great Smoky Mountains (N.C. and Tenn.)

20th century
Alther, L. Kinflicks
Alther, L. Original sins
Marius, R. C. After the war
McCrumb, S. The hangman's beautiful daughter
McCrumb, S. If ever I return, pretty Peggy-O
McCrumb, S. She walks these hills
O'Connor, F. The violent bear it away
O'Connor, F. Wise blood
Warren, R. P. The cave
Whitney, P. A. The glass flame

Knoxville
Agee, J. A death in the family

Memphis
Faulkner, W. The reivers
Faulkner, W. Sanctuary
Grisham, J. The firm
Taylor, P. H. A summons to Memphis

TENNIS
Brown, R. M. Sudden death
The **tenth** commandment. Sanders, L.
The **tenth** man. Greene, G.
A **tenured** professor. Galbraith, J. K.
Teresa and other stories. O'Faoláin, S.
In O'Faolain, S. The collected stories of Sean O'Faolain p320-445
Terminal. Cook, R.

TERMINAL ILLNESS
Hood, A. Places to stay the night
L'Engle, M. Certain women
The **terminal** man. Crichton, M.
Terms of endearment. McMurtry, L.
Terra nostra. Fuentes, C.
The **terrible** threes. Reed, I.
The **terrible** twos. Reed, I.

TERRORISM
See also Violence
Anthony, E. The Doll's House
Brink, A. P. An act of terror
Brown, D. Storming heaven
Carr, P. The black swan
Clancy, T. Patriot games
Clancy, T. Red Storm rising
Clancy, T. The sum of all fears
Collins, L. The fifth horseman
Coonts, S. Final flight
Coonts, S. The red horseman
Coyle, H. W. Bright star
Drury, A. Preserve and protect
Estleman, L. D. Kill zone
Forsyth, F. The devil's alternative
Grady, J. Thunder
Grant, M. Officer down
Greene, G. The comedians
Harris, T. Black Sunday
Higgins, J. Confessional
Higgins, J. Eye of the storm
Higgins, J. Touch the devil
Kaye, M. M. Death in Kenya
Keneally, T. Flying hero class
Le Carré, J. The little drummer girl

TERRORISM—*Continued*

Lessing, D. M. The good terrorist
Ludlum, R. The Bourne ultimatum
Ludlum, R. The Icarus agenda
Ludlum, R. The Matarese Circle
Lustbader, E. V. Jian
MacInnes, H. Cloak of darkness
MacInnes, H. The hidden target
MacInnes, H. Prelude to terror
MacLean, A. Floodgate
McCarthy, M. Cannibals and missionaries
Moore, B. Lies of silence
O'Brien, E. House of splendid isolation
Pearson, R. Hard fall
Piercy, M. Vida
Puzo, M. The fourth K
Ruark, R. Something of value
Sheldon, S. Windmills of the gods
Smith, W. A. Golden fox
Smith, W. A. A time to die
Trevanian. Shibumi
Trevor, W. My house in Umbria
West, M. L. Lazarus
Westlake, D. E. The spy in the ointment

TERRORISTS *See* Terrorism

Tess of the D'Urbervilles. Hardy, T.

TEST PILOTS *See* Air pilots

TEST TUBE FERTILIZATION *See* Fertilization in vitro

The testament. Wiesel, E.

Testimony of two men. Caldwell, T.

TETRAPLEGICS *See* Quadriplegics

Tevye the dairyman and The railroad stories. Sholem Aleichem

Tevye's daughters. Sholem Aleichem

TEXAS

Michener, J. A. Texas

19th century

Bonner, C. Lily
Bonner, C. Looking after Lily
Estleman, L. D. Sudden country
Gipson, F. B. Old Yeller
Gipson, F. B. Savage Sam
Humphrey, W. The Ordways
Kelton, E. The far canyon
Kelton, E. Slaughter
Michener, J. A. The eagle and the raven
Rushing, J. G. Mary Dove

20th century

Brown, S. Where there's smoke
Dawson, C. Body of knowledge
Ferber, E. Giant
Hailey, E. F. A woman of independent means
Horgan, P. Whitewater
Hunter, S. Dirty white boys
McMurtry, L. Some can whistle
McMurtry, L. Texasville
Waller, R. J. Border music
Willocks, T. Green river rising
Wozencraft, K. Notes from the country club

Frontier and pioneer life

See Frontier and pioneer life—Texas

Politics

See Politics—Texas

Houston

Lindsey, D. L. An absence of light
Lindsey, D. L. Mercy
McMurtry, L. The evening star
McMurtry, L. Terms of endearment

San Antonio

Brown, S. Charade

Texas. Michener, J. A.

The Texas capitol murders. Crider, B.

Texasville. McMurtry, L.

TEXTILE INDUSTRY

See also Weavers

Singer, I. J. The brothers Ashkenazi

THAILAND

Somtow, S. P. Jasmine nights

18th century

Han, S. The enchantress

Bangkok

Bosse, M. J. Fire in heaven
Mishima, Y. The Temple of Dawn

The thanatos syndrome. Percy, W.

THANKSGIVING DAY

Capote, T. The Thanksgiving visitor

The Thanksgiving visitor. Capote, T.

That hideous strength. Lewis, C. S.

That night. McDermott, A.

That year of our war. Goldreich, G.

THEATER LIFE

See also Actors; Actresses; Strolling players; names of actors and actresses

Colette. Music-hall sidelights
Davies, R. World of wonders
Dickens, C. Nicholas Nickleby
Dreiser, T. Sister Carrie
Ferber, E. Show boat
Keneally, T. The playmaker
L'Engle, M. Certain women
Miller, W. M. The darfsteller
Priestley, J. B. The good companions
Prose, F. Hungry hearts
Renault, M. The mask of Apollo
Rhys, J. Voyage in the dark
Singer, I. B. The magician of Lublin
Unsworth, B. Morality play
Zola, É. Nana

THEATRICAL TROUPES *See* Strolling players; Theater life

The Theban mysteries. Cross, A.

THEFT

See also Embezzlement; Robbery; Thieves

Bausch, R. Rebel powers
Eliot, G. Silas Marner
Freedman, J. F. The obstacle course
Leonard, E. Bandits
Westlake, D. E. Don't ask

A theft. Bellow, S.

also in Bellow, S. Something to remember me by p[91]-181

Theirs was the kingdom. Delderfield, R. F.

Them. Oates, J. C.

THEODERIC *See* Theodoric, King of the Ostrogoths, 454?-526

THEODORA, EMPRESS, CONSORT OF JUSTINIAN I, EMPEROR OF THE EAST, D. 548

Bradshaw, G. The bearkeeper's daughter

THEODORIC, KING OF THE OSTROGOTHS, 454?-526

Jennings, G. Raptor

THEODOSIUS II, EMPEROR OF THE EAST, 401-450

Bradshaw, G. Imperial purple

Theophilus North. Wilder, T.

There was a little girl. McBain, E.

There's something in a Sunday. Muller, M.

These same long bones. Parker, G. M.

These thirteen. See Faulkner, W. Collected stories of William Faulkner

These thousand hills. Guthrie, A. B.

THESEUS (GREEK MYTHOLOGY)

Renault, M. The bull from the sea
Renault, M. The king must die

They do it with mirrors. See Christie, A. Murder with mirrors

They whisper. Butler, R. O.

Thicker than water. McInerny, R. M.

The **thief** and the dogs. Maḥfūẓ, N.

A **thief** of time. Hillerman, T.

The **thief** who couldn't sleep. Block, L.

THIEVES

See also Theft

Cervantes Saavedra, M. de. Rinconete and Cortadillo

Cussler, C. Inca gold

Defoe, D. Moll Flanders

Dickens, C. Oliver Twist

Gash, J. The Vatican rip

Gilman, D. A palm for Mrs. Pollifax

Herlihy, J. L. Midnight cowboy

Leiber, F. Ill met in Lankhmar

Leonard, E. Swag

Markandaya, K. A handful of rice

Michael, J. Inheritance

Pym, B. An academic question

Roberts, N. Honest illusions

Smith, S. B. A simple plan

Thomas, C. Firefox

Thomas, C. Firefox down

Wambaugh, J. The black marble

Westlake, D. E. Why me?

Thin air. Hammond, G.

The **thin** man. Hammett, D.

also in Hammett, D. The novels of Dashiell Hammett p589-726

The **thin** red line. Jones, J.

The **thin** woman. Cannell, D.

Things fall apart. Achebe, C.

The **things** they carried. O'Brien, T.

Think fast, Mr. Peters. Kaminsky, S. M.

Thinner. King, S.

Third and Indiana. Lopez, S.

The **third** book of lost swords: Stonecutter's story. Saberhagen, F.

The **third** deadly sin. Sanders, L.

The **third** violet. Crane, S.

In Crane, S. The complete novels of Stephen Crane p349-428

Thirteen at dinner. Christie, A.

Thirteen uncollected stories. Cheever, J.

The **thirteenth** juror. See Lescroart, J. T. The 13th juror

The **thirty-nine** steps. Buchan, J.

This gun for hire. Greene, G.

In Greene, G. 3: This gun for hire, The confidential agent, The ministry of fear

This real night. West, Dame R.

This rough magic. Stewart, M.

This savage race. Jones, D. C.

This shining land. Laker, R.

This side of glory. Bristow, G.

In Bristow, G. Gwen Bristow's Plantation trilogy p535-812

This side of paradise. Fitzgerald, F. S.

This was tomorrow. Thane, E.

This way out. Gardner, E. S.

In Gardner, E. S. Dead men's letters p147-87

This way out. Radley, S.

Thomas the imposter. See Cocteau, J. The impostor

The **thorn** birds. McCullough, C.

Thornyhold. Stewart, M.

Those extraordinary twins. Twain, M.

In Twain, M. The complete novels of Mark Twain v2 p609-60

Those who hunt the night. Hambly, B.

Those who love. Stone, I.

THOUGHT CONTROL See Brainwashing

THOUGHT TRANSFERENCE See Telepathy

A **thousand** acres. Smiley, J.

Thousand cranes. Kawabata, Y.

also in Kawabata, Y. Snow country and Thousand cranes p3-147

The **thousand** hour day. Kuniczak, W. S.

Three aces. Stout, R.

Three blind mice. Christie, A.

In Christie, A. Three blind mice, and other stories p1-91

Three blind mice. McBain, E.

Three blind mice, and other stories. Christie, A.

Three by Irving. See Irving, J. 3 by Irving

Three by Tey. Tey, J.

Three cases for Mr. Campion. Allingham, M.

Three complete novels. Koontz, D. R.

Three comrades. Remarque, E. M.

Three continents. Jhabvala, R. P.

Three doors to death. Stout, R.

In Stout, R. Five of a kind p307-441

Three exemplary novels. Cervantes Saavedra, M. de

Three faces of love. Zola, É.

Three from Galilee. Holmes, M.

The **three** guardsmen. See Dumas, A. The three musketeers

Three legends: The snow goose; The small miracle; Ludmila. Gallico, P.

Three lives. Auchincloss, L.

Three lives. Stein, G.

The **three** musketeers. Dumas, A.

A **three-pipe** problem. Symons, J.

Three to show. Francis, D.

Three witnesses. Stout, R.

In Stout, R. Royal flush p335-474

The **throat**. Straub, P.

Through a glass darkly. Koen, K.

Through the ivory gate. Dove, R.

Thrush Green. Read, Miss

Thunder. Grady, J.

Thunder on the right. Stewart, M.

Thunder point. Higgins, J.

Thunderball. Fleming, I.

In Fleming, I. Bonded Fleming p1-188

Thursday the rabbi walked out. Kemelman, H.

Thursday's children. Godden, R.

Thy brother death. Ferrars, E. X.

Thy brother's wife. Greeley, A. M.

TIBERIUS, EMPEROR OF ROME, 42 B.C.-37 A.D.

Douglas, L. C. The robe

TIBET (CHINA) See China—Tibet

A **ticket** to the boneyard. Block, L.

Tickled to death. Hess, J.

A **Tidewater** morning: three tales from youth. Styron, W.

The **Tidewater** tales. Barth, J.

The **ties** that bind. Adler, W.

Tight lines. Tapply, W. G.

The **tightrope** walker. Gilman, D.

Till morning comes. Han, S.

Till the butchers cut him down. Muller, M.

Till we have faces. Lewis, C. S.

Till we meet again. Krantz, J.

TIME

See also Clocks and watches

Amis, M. Time's arrow

Hoeg, P. Borderliners

TIME, TRAVELS IN *See* Time travel
Time and again. Finney, J.
TIME AND SPACE *See* Space and time
The time and the place and other stories. Maḥfūz, N.
Time and tide. Fleming, T. J.
Time and tide. O'Brien, E.
Time and time again. Gill, B. M.
Time bomb. Kellerman, J.
Time considered as a helix of semi-precious stones. Delany, S. R.
  In The Best of the Nebulas p329-57
Time enough for love. Heinlein, R. A.
A time for silence. Carr, P.
The time machine. Wells, H. G.
  also in Wells, H. G. The complete short stories of H. G. Wells
  also in Wells, H. G. Seven famous novels
Time of hope. Snow, C. P.
The Time Patrol. Anderson, P.
Time regained. [variant title: The past recaptured] Proust, M.
  also in Proust, M. Remembrance of things past v3 p709-1107
A time to die. Smith, W. A.
A time to kill. Grisham, J.
A time to love and a time to die. Remarque, E. M.
Time to murder and create. Block, L.

TIME TRAVEL
  Anderson, P. Star of the sea
  Anderson, P. The Time Patrol
  Bova, B. Orion and the conqueror
  De Hartog, J. The centurion
  Du Maurier, Dame D. The house on the strand
  Finney, J. From time to time
  Finney, J. Time and again
  Greenberg, J. With the Snow Queen
  Heinlein, R. A. Job: a comedy of justice
  Heinlein, R. A. Time enough for love
  Helprin, M. Winter's tale
  Koontz, D. R. Lightning
  Kress, N. And wild for to hold
  May, J. The adversary
  May, J. The golden torc
  May, J. The many-colored land
  May, J. The nonborn king
  McCaffrey, A. Dragonrider
  Moorcock, M. An alien heat
  Moorcock, M. Behold the man
  Moorcock, M. The end of all songs
  Moorcock, M. The hollow lands
  Niven, L. A world out of time
  Norton, A. Firehand
  Piercy, M. Woman on the edge of time
  Silverberg, R. Sailing to Byzantium
  Tiptree, J. Houston, Houston, do you read?
  Vonnegut, K. Slaughterhouse-five
  Wells, H. G. The time machine
A time without shadows. Allbeury, T.
Time's arrow. Amis, M.
Time's fool. Veryan, P.
Timescape. Benford, G.
The Timothy files. Sanders, L.
Timothy's game. Sanders, L.
The tin can tree. Tyler, A.
The tin drum. Grass, G.
  also in Grass, G. The Danzig trilogy
Tinker, tailor, soldier, spy. Le Carré, J.
  also in Le Carré, J. The quest for Karla p1-252
Titan. Varley, J.

TITANIC (STEAMSHIP)
  Cussler, C. Raise the Titanic!
  Finney, J. From time to time

TITUBA
  Condé, M. I, Tituba, black witch of Salem

To Asmara. Keneally, T.
To be the best. Bradford, B. T.
To dance with kings. Laker, R.
To have and have not. Hemingway, E.
To kill a mockingbird. Lee, H.
To know a woman. Oz, A.
To let. Galsworthy, J.
  In Galsworthy, J. The Forsyte saga p665-921
To love and be wise. Tey, J.
To save the sun. Bova, B.
To see your face again. Price, E.
To serve them all my days. Delderfield, R. F.
To skin a cat. McGuane, T.
To the end of her days. Ross-Macdonald, M.
To the far blue mountains. L'Amour, L.
To the Indies. Forester, C. S.
To the lighthouse. Woolf, V.
To the white sea. Dickey, J.
To your scattered bodies go. Farmer, P. J.
Tobacco road. Caldwell, E.
TOKYO (JAPAN) *See* Japan—Tokyo
Tom Jones. See Fielding, H. The history of Tom Jones, a foundling
Tom Sawyer. See Twain, M. The adventures of Tom Sawyer
Tom Sawyer abroad. Twain, M.
  In Twain, M. The adventures of Tom Sawyer; Tom Sawyer abroad; Tom Sawyer, detective p251-341
  In Twain, M. The complete novels of Mark Twain v2 p417-90
Tom Sawyer abroad, and other stories. Twain, M.
Tom Sawyer, detective. Twain, M.
  In Twain, M. The adventures of Tom Sawyer; Tom Sawyer abroad; Tom Sawyer, detective p357-415
  In Twain, M. The complete novels of Mark Twain v2 p999-1048
The **Tommyknockers.** King, S.
The **tongues** of angels. Price, R.
Tonio Kröger. Mann, T.
  In Mann, T. Stories of three decades
Tono-Bungay. Wells, H. G.
TONTO BASIN (ARIZ.)
  Grey, Z. The Arizona clan
Too close for comfort. Villars, E.
Too close to the edge. Dunlap, S.
Too late the phalarope. Paton, A.
Too many clients. Stout, R.
  In Stout, R. Three aces
Too many cooks. Stout, R.
  In Stout, R. Kings full of aces p1-187
Too many women. Stout, R.
  In Stout, R. All aces p155-302
Too much, too soon. Briskin, J.
Topaz. Uris, L.
TORIES, AMERICAN *See* American loyalists
TORONTO (ONT.) *See* Canada—Toronto
Torquemada. Pérez Galdós, B.
Torquemada and Saint Peter. Pérez Galdós, B.
  In Pérez Galdós, B. Torquemada p405-569
Torquemada at the stake. Pérez Galdós, B.
  In Pérez Galdós, B. Torquemada p1-60
Torquemada in Purgatory. Pérez Galdós, B.
  In Pérez Galdós, B. Torquemada p221-404
Torquemada on the cross. Pérez Galdós, B.
  In Pérez Galdós, B. Torquemada p61-220
The **torrents** of spring. Hemingway, E.
  also in Hemingway, E. The Hemingway reader p25-86
The **torrents** of spring. Turgenev, I. S.
TORRES CORTEZ, HERNÁN
  Fuentes, C. Sons of the Conquistador
  Fuentes, C. The two shores
Tortilla Flat. Steinbeck, J.
Total environment. Aldiss, B. W.
  In Modern classic short novels of science fiction p221-59

TOTALITARIANISM
> *See also* Communism; Dictators; Fascism; National
> socialism
Achebe, C. Anthills of the Savannah
Alvarez, J. In the time of the butterflies
Bellow, S. The dean's December
Chatwin, B. Utz
Del Vecchio, J. M. For the sake of all living things
James, P. D. The children of men
Koestler, A. Darkness at noon
Kundera, M. The joke
Miłosz, C. The seizure of power
Orwell, G. Animal farm
Orwell, G. Nineteen eighty-four
Wolf, C. What remains
Touch. Leonard, E.
Touch not the cat. Stewart, M.
Touch the devil. Higgins, J.
Tough guys don't dance. Mailer, N.

TOULOUSE, BATTLE OF, 1814
Cornwell, B. Sharpe's revenge

TOURIST TRADE
Gilman, D. Mrs. Pollifax on safari

TOURISTS *See* Tourist trade

TOUSSAINT LOUVERTURE, 1743?-1803
Bell, M. S. All souls' rising
Towards zero. Christie, A.
The **towers** of silence. Scott, P.
> *also in* Scott, P. The Raj quartet
The **town.** Faulkner, W.
> *also in* Faulkner, W. Snopes p351-671
The **town.** Richter, C.
> *also in* Richter, C. The awakening land p331-630
The **town** beyond the wall. Wiesel, E.
Town Crier exclusive, Confessions of a Princess manqué.
Elkin, S.
> *In* Elkin, S. Van Gogh's room at Arles: three novel-
> las p113-217
The **town** house. Lofts, N.
A **town** like Alice. See Shute, N. The legacy
Tracks. Erdrich, L.
Trade wind. Kaye, M. M.

TRADERS
Stevenson, R. L. The beach of Falesá

TRAFFIC ACCIDENTS
Agee, J. A death in the family
Banks, R. The sweet hereafter
Greenberg, J. The far side of victory
Oates, J. C. Black water
Read, Miss. Battles at Thrush Green
Steel, D. Accident
Wiesel, E. The accident
The **tragedy** of Pudd'nhead Wilson. See Twain, M. Pud-
d'nhead Wilson
The **tragedy** of X. Queen, E.
> *In* Queen, E. The XYZ murders p7-216
The **tragedy** of Y. Queen, E.
> *In* Queen, E. The XYZ murders p217-419
The **tragedy** of Z. Queen, E.
> *In* Queen, E. The XYZ murders p421-575
The **trail** driver. Grey, Z.
The **trail** to Seven Pines. L'Amour, L.

TRAIN TRAVEL *See* Railroads—Travel
The **train** was on time. Böll, H.
> *In* Böll, H. The stories of Heinrich Böll p165-250

TRAITORS *See* Treason
Traitor's purse. Allingham, M.
> *In* Allingham, M. Three cases for Mr. Campion
> p257-420

TRAMPS *See* Homeless persons
The **transformation.** See Hawthorne, N. The marble faun
The **transit** of Venus. Hazzard, S.

TRANSMIGRATION
> *See also* Reincarnation
Clark, M. H. The Anastasia syndrome

London, J. The star rover

TRANSPLANTATION OF ORGANS, TISSUES, ETC.
Brown, S. Charade
Cook, R. Coma
Pohl, F. The merchants of Venus

TRANSPORT PLANES
Francis, D. Flying finish

TRANSSEXUALS
Tremain, R. Sacred country
Vidal, G. Myra Breckinridge [and] Myron
Yoshimoto, B. Kitchen
A **trap** for fools. Cross, A.

TRAPPERS AND TRAPPING
Cooper, J. F. The Leatherstocking tales
Cooper, J. F. The pioneers
Cooper, J. F. The prairie
Fisher, V. Mountain man
Guthrie, A. B. The big sky

TRAPPING *See* Trappers and trapping

TRAVEL
Greenfeld, J. Harry and Tonto
Kerouac, J. On the road
Maugham, W. S. The razor's edge
Robertson, D. Praise the human season
Simpson, M. Anywhere but here
Smollett, T. G. Humphry Clinker
A **traveler's** tale. Shepard, L.
> *In* Modern classic short novels of science fiction
> p459-503

TRAVELS IN TIME *See* Time travel
The **travels** of Jaimie McPheeters. Taylor, R. L.
Travels with my aunt. Greene, G.

TREASON
> *See also* Defectors; Spies; World War, 1939-1945—
> Collaborationists
Bowen, E. The heat of the day
Treason's gift. Belle, P.
Treasure. Cussler, C.
The **treasure** of the Sierra Madre. Traven, B.

TREASURE-TROVE *See* Buried treasure
Treasures. Plain, B.
Treasury of great cat stories, Roger Caras'. See Roger
Caras' Treasury of great cat stories
Treasury of great dog stories, Roger Caras'. See Roger
Caras' Treasury of great dog stories

TREATIES
Cussler, C. Night probe!
A **tree** grows in Brooklyn. Smith, B.
The **tree** of hands. Rendell, R.
The **tree** of man. White, P.
A **tree** of night, and other stories. Capote, T.
The **trees.** Richter, C.
> *also in* Richter, C. The awakening land p1-167
Tregaron's daughter. Brent, M.
The **trembling** hills. Whitney, P. A.
The **trial.** Kafka, F.
Trial by fury. Ferrars, E. X.
The **trial** of Abigail Goodman. Fast, H.
Trial run. Francis, D.

TRIALS
> *See also* War crime trials; Witnesses
Amiel, J. A question of proof
Benét, S. V. The Devil and Daniel Webster
Brandon, J. Rules of evidence
Busch, F. Closing arguments
Campbell, B. M. Your blues ain't like mine
Coughlin, W. J. Death penalty
Coughlin, W. J. In the presence of enemies
Coughlin, W. J. Shadow of a doubt
Cozzens, J. G. By love possessed
Daley, R. Tainted evidence
De Felitta, F. Audrey Rose
Dershowitz, A. M. The advocate's devil
Dexter, P. Paris Trout

TRIALS—*Continued*

Dickens, C. Bleak House

Dickens, C. The posthumous papers of the Pickwick Club

Dickens, C. A tale of two cities

Diehl, W. Primal fear

Dostoyevsky, F. The brothers Karamazov

Dreiser, T. An American tragedy

Fast, H. The trial of Abigail Goodman

Faulkner, W. The mansion

Faulkner, W. Requiem for a nun

Fielding, J. Tell me no secrets

French, A. Billy

Friedman, P. Inadmissable evidence

Friedman, P. Reasonable doubt

Galsworthy, J. Maid in waiting

Galsworthy, J. Over the river

Galsworthy, J. The silver spoon

Grisham, J. A time to kill

Guterson, D. Snow falling on cedars

Hamilton, J. A map of the world

Higgins, G. V. Defending Billy Ryan

Hunter, E. Lizzie

Irving, C. Final argument

Jones, D. C. The court-martial of George Armstrong Custer

Katkov, N. Blood & orchids

Koestler, A. Darkness at noon

Latt, M. L. Powers of attorney

Lescroart, J. T. The 13th juror

Levin, M. Compulsion

Martini, S. P. Compelling evidence

Martini, S. P. Prime witness

Martini, S. P. Undue influence

Miller, S. The good mother

Oates, J. C. American appetites

Patterson, R. N. Degree of guilt

Patterson, R. N. Eyes of a child

Reed, B. The choice

Sinclair, U. Boston

Snow, C. P. The sleep of reason

Stirling, J. Lantern for the dark

Traver, R. Anatomy of a murder

Turow, S. Presumed innocent

Uris, L. QB VII

Warren, R. P. World enough and time

Welty, E. The Ponder heart

West, J. The massacre at Fall Creek

Wilhelm, K. The best defense

Wilhelm, K. Death qualified

Woods, S. Grass roots

TRIBES

See also Clans

Singer, I. B. The king of the fields

Tricks. McBain, E.

The **Trikon** deception. Bova, B.

Trillium [series]

Bradley, M. Z. Black Trillium

May, J. Blood Trillium

Norton, A. Golden Trillium

The **trimmed** lamp. Henry, O.

In Henry, O. The complete works of O. Henry p1365-1483

TRINIDAD AND TOBAGO

Naipaul, V. S. A house for Mr. Biswas

Naipaul, V. S. A way in the world

Trinity. Uris, L.

Trio for blunt instruments. Stout, R.

A **trip** to the center of the earth. See Verne, J. A journey to the centre of the earth

Triple. Follett, K.

Triple jeopardy. Stout, R.

In Stout, R. Kings full of aces p325-472

Tripmaster Monkey. Kingston, M. H.

Tripoint. Cherryh, C. J.

TRIPOLITAN WAR, 1801-1805 *See* United States—Tripolitan War, 1801-1805

Tristan. Mann, T.

In Mann, T. Stories of three decades

Tristram Shandy. See Sterne, L. The life and opinions of Tristram Shandy, gentleman

Trojan gold. Peters, E.

TROJAN WAR

Bradley, M. Z. The firebrand

The **troll** garden. Cather, W.

In Cather, W. Early novels and stories p1-132

In Cather, W. Willa Cather's collected short fiction, 1892-1912, v2

Trophies and dead things. Muller, M.

Tropic of Cancer. Miller, H.

Tropic of Capricorn. Miller, H.

Tropical night falling. Puig, M.

Trouble. Weldon, F.

Trouble for Lucia. Benson, E. F.

In Benson, E. F. Make way for Lucia p941-1119

Trouble in triplicate. Stout, R.

In Stout, R. All aces p303-442

A **trouble** of fools. Barnes, L.

Trouble shooter. L'Amour, L.

Troubled sleep. Sartre, J. P.

TROY (ANCIENT CITY)

See also Trojan War

Stone, I. The Greek treasure

The **truce** at Bakura. Tyers, K.

TRUCKS

Accidents

See Traffic accidents

True colors. Mortman, D.

True confessions. Dunne, J. G.

True grit. Portis, C.

TRUMPET PLAYERS

Baker, D. Young man with a horn

TRUMPETERS *See* Trumpet players

Trumps of doom. Zelazny, R.

Trust me. Updike, J.

Trust me on this. Westlake, D. E.

The **truth** about Bébé Donge. Simenon, G.

TRUTHFULNESS AND FALSEHOOD

Morrow, J. City of Truth

TUAMOTU ISLANDS *See* Islands of the Pacific

TUBERCULOSIS

Conrad, J. The Nigger of the Narcissus

Gide, A. The immoralist

Mann, T. The magic mountain

TUBMAN, HARRIET, 1815?-1913

Heidish, M. A woman called Moses

Tucker's last stand. Buckley, W. F.

TUDOR ENGLAND *See* England—16th century

Tuesday the rabbi saw red. Kemelman, H.

TUGBOATS

De Hartog, J. The captain

De Hartog, J. The Commodore

Tulip. Hammett, D.

In Hammett, D. The big knockover p238-74

Tumbleweed. Van de Wetering, J.

Tunnel of love. Wolitzer, H.

Tunnel vision. Paretsky, S.

TURIN (ITALY) *See* Italy—Turin

TURKEY

Kazan, E. America, America

Whitney, P. A. Black amber

Antioch

Oldenbourg, Z. The heirs of the kingdom

TURKEY—*Continued*

Istanbul

Bradshaw, G. The bearkeeper's daughter
Bradshaw, G. Imperial purple
Gilman, D. The amazing Mrs. Pollifax
Holt, V. The captive
L'Amour, L. The walking drum
The **turn** of the screw. James, H.
  also in James, H. The complete tales of Henry James v10
  also in James, H. The Henry James reader p255-356
  also in James, H. Short novels of Henry James p407-530

TURNCOATS *See* Defectors

TURNER, NAT, 1800?-1831

Styron, W. The confessions of Nat Turner
The **turquoise** lament. MacDonald, J. D.
The **turquoise** mask. Whitney, P. A.
The **turret** room. Armstrong, C.
  In Armstrong, C. The Charlotte Armstrong reader p345-501
Turtle diary. Hoban, R.
Turtle Moon. Hoffman, A.

TURTLES

Hoban, R. Turtle diary

TUSCANY (ITALY) *See* Italy—Tuscany

TUTORS

Barth, J. The sot-weed factor
Huxley, A. Antic hay
Mann, T. The black swan
Voltaire. Candide
Wilder, T. Theophilus North
Twenty-one stories. Greene, G.
  In Greene, G. Collected stories p325-562
The **twenty-seven** ingredient chili con carne murders. See Pickard, N. The 27 ingredient chili con carne murders
Twenty thousand leagues under the sea. Verne, J.
Twenty-two stories. See Gilliatt, P. 22 stories
Twenty years after. Dumas, A.
Twice in a blue moon. Moyes, P.
Twice shy. Francis, D.
Twice-told tales. Hawthorne, N.
Twilight. Wiesel, E.
The **twilight** of courage. Thoene, B.

TWINS

  See also Siamese twins
Barth, J. The sot-weed factor
Carr, P. We'll meet again
Carter, A. Wise children
Clark, M. H. I'll be seeing you
Golding, W. Darkness visible
Harvey, K. Stars
Howatch, S. The shrouded walls
Irving, J. A son of the circus
Jhabvala, R. P. Three continents
Jones, T. Hard road to Gettysburg
Michael, J. Deceptions
Michael, J. A tangled web
Singer, I. J. The brothers Ashkenazi
Stubbs, J. Light in summer
Thackeray, W. M. The Virginians
Thane, E. Kissing kin
Theroux, P. Doctor DeMarr
Trevanian. The summer of Katya
Tryon, T. The other
Woods, S. Palindrome
A **twist** in the tale. Archer, J.
A **twist** of the knife. Solomita, S.
The **twisted** sword. Graham, W.
The **two** Americas. Fuentes, C.
  In Fuentes, C. The orange tree p205-29
Two by Francis. Francis, D.
Two hundred years of great American short stories. See 200 years of great American short stories

Two hussars. Tolstoy, L., graf
  In Tolstoy, L. The portable Tolstoy p294-357
  In Tolstoy, L. The short novels of Tolstoy
Two lives: Reading Turgenev and My house in Umbria. Trevor, W.
The **two** Mrs. Grenvilles. Dunne, D.
The **two** Numantias. Fuentes, C.
  In Fuentes, C. The orange tree p101-47
The **two** shores. Fuentes, C.
  In Fuentes, C. The orange tree p3-49
Two thousand and sixty-one: odyssey three. See Clarke, A. C. 2061: odyssey three
Two thousand one: a space odyssey. See Clarke, A. C. 2001: a space odyssey
Two thousand ten: odyssey two. See Clarke, A. C. 2010: odyssey two
The **two** towers. Tolkien, J. R. R.
  also in Tolkien, J. R. R. The lord of the rings v2
Two women. Moravia, A.

TYCOONS *See* Millionaires

Typee: a peep at Polynesian life. Melville, H.
  also in Melville, H. Typee; Omoo; Mardi
Typee: a peep at Polynesian life; Omoo: a narrative of adventures in the South Seas; Mardi: and a voyager thither. Melville, H.
Typhoon. Conrad, J.
  In Conrad, J. Great short works of Joseph Conrad p259-328
  In Conrad, J. The portable Conrad p192-287
  In Conrad, J. Tales of land and sea p287-347

TYPHOONS

Conrad, J. Typhoon
Typical American. Jen, G.
Tzili, the story of a life. Appelfeld, A.

TZ'U-HSI, EMPRESS DOWAGER OF CHINA, 1835-1908

Buck, P. S. Imperial woman

U

U-boat. See Buchheim, L.-G. The boat

U-BOATS *See* Submarines

U.F.O.'S *See* Flying saucers

U.S.A.. Dos Passos, J.

The **ugly** American. Lederer, W. J.

Uhuru. Ruark, R.

UKRAINE

  See also Galicia (Poland and Ukraine)
Forsyth, F. The devil's alternative

Kiev

Anatoli, A. Babi Yar
Malamud, B. The fixer
Ultimate prizes. Howatch, S.
Ulysses. Joyce, J.
The **unbearable** lightness of being. Kundera, M.
Uncivil seasons. Malone, M.
Uncle Tom's cabin. Stowe, H. B.
  also in Stowe, H. B. Uncle Tom's cabin; The minister's wooing; Oldtown Folks p1-519
Uncle Tom's cabin: or, Life among the lowly; The minister's wooing; Oldtown folks. Stowe, H. B.
Uncle Tom's children. Wright, R.
  also in Wright, R. Works

UNCLES

  See also Nephews
Bellow, S. More die of heartbreak
Dickens, C. Nicholas Nickleby
Jackson, S. We have always lived in the castle
Norman, H. The bird artist
Trollope, J. The men and the girls
Welty, E. The Ponder heart
West, J. The state of Stony Lonesome

ATES. NAVY—*Continued*
J. A. The bridges at Toko-ri
The circle
The gulf
, J. Finnegan's week
Officers
L. Run silent, run deep
J. F. The obstacle course
. Blood & orchids
The Caine mutiny
War and remembrance
The winds of war
ATES MILITARY ACADEMY
onor & duty
. K. Dress gray
ATES NAVAL ACADEMY
J. F. The obstacle course
H. A sense of honor
Y LIFE *See* College life
Y OF CAMBRIDGE
P. The affair
P. The light and the dark
P. The masters
Y OF OXFORD
L. Gaudy Night
Y STUDENTS *See* College life
ss of ravens. Rendell, R.
d dream company. Ballard, J. G.

D COUPLES
Platte River
T. Disappearing acts

D MOTHERS
A time for silence
P. Slouching towards Kalamazoo
. The bingo palace
. Night sky
M. The company of women
ks, L. The L shaped room
S. Rage of angels
S. I been in sorrow's kitchen and licked out pots
er, D. My sweet Charlie
able. Beckett, S.
kett, S. Molloy, Malone dies, and The unable p400-577
auses. James, P. D.
es, P. D. Murder in triplicate v1
eath. See Sayers, D. L. The Dawson pedigree
lled adventure of one Hans Pfaall. Poe, E.

E. A. The imaginary voyages p366-506
santness at the Bellona Club. Sayers, D. L.
earth. Giardina, D.
le attachment. Pym, B.
le job for a woman. James, P. D.
James, P. D. Murder in triplicate v2
ected. Armstrong, C.
strong, C. The Charlotte Armstrong reader
-182
d land. Moberg, V.
oul. Appelfeld, A.
quished. Faulkner, W.
MOTHERS *See* Unmarried mothers
wn staircase. Kaufman, B.
dbox! Roiphe, A. R.
of the new sun. Wolfe, G.
United States. Air Force
ll. O'Donnell, L.
United States Military Academy

19th century
Riders of the purple sage

20th century
Mailer, N. The executioner's song
UTE INDIANS
Borland, H. When the legends die
UTILITARIANISM
Dickens, C. Hard times
UTOPIAS
Gilman, C. P. Herland
Hawthorne, N. The Blithedale romance
Hesse, H. The glass bead game (Magister Ludi)
Huxley, A. Brave new world
Huxley, A. Island
Le Guin, U. K. The dispossessed
Murdoch, I. The bell
Percy, W. The thanatos syndrome
Piercy, M. Woman on the edge of time
Rush, N. Mating
Skinner, B. F. Walden two
Unsworth, B. Sacred hunger
Weldon, F. Darcy's utopia
Wells, H. G. In the days of the comet
Utz. Chatwin, B.

V

V.. Pynchon, T.
VACATIONS
Brookner, A. Hotel du Lac
Mortimer, J. C. Summer's lease
Raucher, H. Summer of '42
Sarton, M. Joanna and Ulysses
Spark, M. The driver's seat
VAGABONDS *See* Rogues and vagabonds
VAGRANTS *See* Homeless persons
Valediction. Parker, R. B.
The **valentine** legacy. Coulter, C.
Valentine Pontifex. Silverberg, R.
VALETS
Parkinson, C. N. Jeeves: a gentleman's personal gentleman
Verne, J. Around the world in eighty days
Wodehouse, P. G. The code of the Woosters
Wodehouse, P. G. How right you are, Jeeves
Wodehouse, P. G. The inimitable Jeeves
Wodehouse, P. G. Jeeves and the tie that binds
The **Valhalla** exchange. Higgins, J.
VALLEY FORGE (PA.) *See* Pennsylvania—Valley Forge
Valley Forge. Kantor, M.
The **valley** of bones. Powell, A.
In Powell, A. A dance to the music of time [v3]
The **valley** of fear. Doyle, Sir A. C.
also in Doyle, Sir A. C. The complete Sherlock Holmes
The **Valley** of Horses. Auel, J. M.
The **vampire** Lestat. Rice, A.
VAMPIRES
Hambly, B. Those who hunt the night
King, S. Salem's lot
Leiber, F. Ship of shadows
Newman, K. Anno-Dracula
Pike, C. The season of passage
Rice, A. Interview with the vampire
Rice, A. The queen of the damned
Rice, A. The tale of the body thief
Rice, A. The vampire Lestat
Stoker, B. Dracula
Yarbro, C. Q. A candle for D'Artagnan
Yarbro, C. Q. Crusader's torch
VAN GOGH, VINCENT *See* Gogh, Vincent van, 1853-1890

Uncle's dream. Dostoyevsky, F.
In Dostoyevsky, F. The short novels of Dostoevsky p223-342
Uncollected stories. Doyle, Sir A. C.
Uncollected stories of William Faulkner. Faulkner, W.
Unconditional surrender. See Waugh, E. The end of the battle
The **unconquered.** Williams, B. A.
The **unconsoled.** Ishiguro, K.
Under siege. Coonts, S.
Under the banyan tree and other stories. Narayan, R. K.
Under the greenwood tree. Hardy, T.
Under the jaguar sun. Calvino, I.
Under the lake. Woods, S.
Under the volcano. Lowry, M.
Undercurrents. Pearson, R.
The **underground** man. Macdonald, R.
UNDERGROUND MOVEMENTS (WORLD WAR, 1939-1945) *See* World War, 1939-1945—Underground movements
UNDERGROUND RAILROAD
Bradley, D. The Chaneysville incident
Heidish, M. A woman called Moses
Stowe, H. B. Uncle Tom's cabin
West, J. Except for me and thee
UNDERWORLD
See also Crime and criminals; Gangsters; Mafia
Algren, N. The man with the golden arm
Dickens, C. Oliver Twist
Dos Passos, J. U.S.A.
Ellroy, J. L.A. confidential
Ellroy, J. White jazz
Puzo, M. The godfather
Singer, I. B. Scum
Steinbeck, J. Cannery Row
Underworld. Hill, R.
UNDOCUMENTED ALIENS
Prose, F. Primitive people
Undue influence. Martini, S. P.
UNEMPLOYED
Mahfūz, N. Autumn quail
Steinbeck, J. Cannery Row
Steinbeck, J. The grapes of wrath
Steinbeck, J. Sweet Thursday
An **unequal** marriage. Tennant, E.
The **unexpected** Mrs. Pollifax. Gilman, D.
UNFINISHED NOVELS
Burns, O. A. Leaving Cold Sassy
Camus, A. The first man
Capote, T. Answered prayers
Crane, S. The O'Ruddy
Dickens, C. The mystery of Edwin Drood
Fitzgerald, F. S. The last tycoon
Forester, C. S. Hornblower during the crisis, and two stories: Hornblower's temptation and The last encounter
Hammett, D. Tulip
Hawthorne, N. Doctor Grimshawe's secret
Hemingway, E. The garden of Eden
James, H. The ivory tower
Jones, J. Whistle
Kafka, F. Amerika
Kafka, F. The castle
Kafka, F. The trial
Mann, T. Confessions of Felix Krull, confidence man
Musil, R. The man without qualities
Olsen, T. Yonnondio: from the thirties
Proust, M. Jean Santeuil
Sterne, L. A sentimental journey through France and Italy
West, Dame R. Cousin Rosamund
West, Dame R. Sunflower
Wharton, E. The buccaneers
Wolfe, T. The good child's river

Unfinished tales of Númenor and Middle-earth. Tolkien, J. R. R.
The **Unforgetting** heart: an anthology of short stories by African American women (1859-1993). Entered in Part I under title
Unholy loves. Oates, J. C.
The **unicorn** hunt. Dunnett, D.
Unicorn point. Anthony, P.
UNICORNS
Beagle, P. S. The last unicorn
UNIDENTIFIED FLYING SAUCERS *See* Flying saucers
The **uninvited** corpse. Underwood, M.
Union Square. Tax, M.
UNITED STATES
See also Middle Western States; Southern States; Southwestern States; Western States; names of individual states
Sandburg, C. Remembrance Rock
Vonnegut, K. Hocus pocus
To 1776
L'Amour, L. Sackett's land
L'Amour, L. To the far blue mountains
Richter, C. The light in the forest
18th century
Stone, I. The President's lady
Thackeray, W. M. The Virginians
Vidal, G. Burr
French and Indian War, 1755-1763
Cooper, J. F. The last of the Mohicans
Cooper, J. F. The Leatherstocking tales
Cooper, J. F. The Pathfinder
Roberts, K. L. Northwest Passage
Revolution, 1775-1783
See also American loyalists
Bristow, G. Celia Garth
Cooper, J. F. The spy
Cornwell, B. Redcoat
Edmonds, W. D. Drums along the Mohawk
Fast, H. April morning
Fast, H. Citizen Tom Paine
Fast, H. Seven days in June
Kantor, M. Valley Forge
Roberts, K. L. Arundel
Stone, I. Those who love
Thane, E. Dawn's early light
Revolution, 1775-1783—Campaigns
Roberts, K. L. Oliver Wiswell
Roberts, K. L. Rabble in arms
Revolution, 1775-1783—Naval operations
Cooper, J. F. The pilot
1783-1809
Roberts, K. L. Lydia Bailey
19th century
De Blasis, C. Swan's chance
De Hartog, J. The peculiar people
Garwood, J. Prince Charming
Hill, R. B. Hanta yo
Jakes, J. Homeland
Jones, D. C. The barefoot brigade
Jones, D. C. Come winter
Jones, D. C. Elkhorn Tavern
Kantor, M. Andersonville
Keneally, T. Confederates
Lockridge, R. Raintree County
Mitchell, M. Gone with the wind
Oates, J. C. A Bloodsmoor romance
Plain, B. Crescent City
Price, E. Lighthouse
Price, E. Margaret's story
Price, E. New moon rising
Spellman, C. C. Paint the wind
Stone, I. Immortal wife
Stone, I. Love is eternal

UNITED STATES—19th century—*Continued*
Stone, I. The President's lady
Twain, M. The gilded age
Vidal, G. Burr
Vidal, G. Empire
Vidal, G. Lincoln

Tripolitan War, 1801-1805
Roberts, K. L. Lydia Bailey

War of 1812
Brown, R. M. Dolley

1815-1861
Dailey, J. The proud and the free
Richter, C. The town
Stowe, H. B. Uncle Tom's cabin
Updike, J. Memories of the Ford Administration

Civil War, 1861-1865
Brown, R. M. High hearts
Coleman, L. Look away, Beulah Land
Cornwell, B. Copperhead
Cornwell, B. Rebel
Crane, S. The red badge of courage
De Blasis, C. Swan's chance
Faulkner, W. The unvanquished
Gurganus, A. The oldest living Confederate widow tells all
Jakes, J. Love and war
Jakes, J. North and South
Johnston, T. C. Cry of the hawk
Jones, D. C. The barefoot brigade
Jones, D. C. Elkhorn Tavern
Jones, T. Hard road to Gettysburg
Kantor, M. Andersonville
Keneally, T. Confederates
Mitchell, M. Gone with the wind
Orde, L. Dreams of gold
Plain, B. Crescent City
Price, E. Beauty from ashes
Price, E. Margaret's story
Price, E. New moon rising
Price, E. Stranger in Savannah
Safire, W. Freedom
Shaara, M. The killer angels
Stewart, F. M. Pomp and circumstance
Thane, E. Yankee stranger
Vidal, G. Lincoln
Warren, R. P. Band of angels
Williams, B. A. House divided

1865-1898
Ferber, E. Saratoga trunk
Jakes, J. Heaven and hell
Twain, M. The gilded age
Wharton, E. The age of innocence

War of 1898
Jones, D. C. Remember Santiago
Thane, E. Ever after

20th century
Allende, I. The infinite plan
Auster, P. Mr. Vertigo
Berger, T. Sneaky people
Carroll, J. Memorial bridge
Carroll, J. Prince of peace
Céline, L.-F. Journey to the end of the night
DeLillo, D. Libra
Didion, J. Play it as it lays
Doctorow, E. L. Loon Lake
Doctorow, E. L. Ragtime
Dos Passos, J. The 42nd parallel
Dos Passos, J. 1919
Dos Passos, J. U.S.A.
Dunne, J. G. The red, white, and blue
Fast, H. The legacy
Fitzgerald, F. S. The beautiful and damned
Fitzgerald, F. S. The Great Gatsby
Gaddis, W. A frolic of his own
Gray, F. du P. Lovers and tyrants

Greenberg, J. In this sign
Hardwick, E. Sleepless nights
Harris, M. Lost and found
Heller, J. Something happened
Kerouac, J. The Dharma bums
Kerouac, J. On the road
Kosinski, J. N. Being there
Kosinski, J. N. Blind date
Lester, J. And all our wounds forgiven
Lewis, S. Babbitt
Mailer, N. Harlot's ghost
McGuane, T. The bushwhacked piano
Myrer, A. The last convertible
Nabokov, V. V. Lolita
Piercy, M. Vida
Proulx, A. Postcards
Reed, I. The last days of Louisiana Red
Reed, I. The terrible threes
Reed, I. The terrible twos
Roth, P. The great American novel
Shaw, I. Beggarman, thief
Shaw, I. Rich man, poor man
Stewart, F. M. Ellis Island
Theroux, P. Millroy the Magician
Updike, J. Memories of the Ford Administration
Vonnegut, K. Jailbird
Wouk, H. War and remembrance
Wouk, H. The winds of war

Armed forces
Batchelor, J. C. Father's day
Knebel, F. Seven days in May

College life
See College life—United States

Communism
See Communism—United States

Defenses
Cussler, C. Raise the Titanic!

Fascism
See Fascism—United States

Politics
See Politics—United States

Presidents
See Presidents—United States

Race relations
Baldwin, J. Another country
Baldwin, J. If Beale Street could talk
Bambara, T. C. The salt eaters
Banks, R. Continental drift
Bradley, D. The Chaneysville incident
Brandon, J. Rules of evidence
Brown, R. M. Southern discomfort
Brown, R. Civil wars
Campbell, B. M. Brothers and sisters
Campbell, B. M. Your blues ain't like mine
Carroll, J. The city below
Childress, A. A short walk
Childress, M. Crazy in Alabama
Davis, T. 1959
Dexter, P. Paris Trout
Dillard, A. The living
Doctorow, E. L. Ragtime
Ellison, R. Invisible man
Estleman, L. D. King of the corner
Estleman, L. D. Motown
Fairbairn, A. Five smooth stones
Fast, H. Freedom road
Faulkner, W. Intruder in the dust
Faulkner, W. Light in August
French, A. Billy
Gaines, E. J. The gathering of old men
Gaines, E. J. A lesson before dying
Goudge, E. Blessing in disguise
Grau, S. A. The keepers of the house

UNITED STATES—Race relations—*Continued*
Grey, Z. The vanishing American
Grisham, J. The chamber
Grisham, J. A time to kill
Gurganus, A. Blessed assurance: a moral tale
Harris, M. Lost and found
Hughes, L. Not without laughter
Hughes, L. Simple speaks his mind
Hughes, L. Simple stakes a claim
Hughes, L. Simple takes a wife
Hughes, L. Simple's Uncle Sam
Lee, H. To kill a mockingbird
L'Engle, M. The other side of the sun
Lester, J. And all our wounds forgiven
Lewis, S. Kingsblood royal
Marius, R. C. After the war
McCullers, C. Clock without hands
Michener, J. A. Chesapeake
Morrison, T. Tar baby
Nordan, L. Wolf whistle
Oates, J. C. Because it is bitter, and because it is my heart
Oates, J. C. What I lived for
Parker, G. M. These same long bones
Parks, G. The learning tree
Phillips, C. Crossing the river
Pinckney, D. High cotton
Porter, C. R. All-Bright Court
Price, R. The promise of rest
Rhodes, J. P. Voodoo dreams
Rice, A. The Feast of All Saints
Rushing, J. G. Mary Dove
Shange, N. Liliane
Shreve, S. R. A country of strangers
Siddons, A. R. Downtown
Smith, L. E. Strange fruit
Straight, S. Blacker than a thousand midnights
Styron, W. The confessions of Nat Turner
Wallace, I. The man
Warren, R. P. Band of angels
West, D. The wedding
Westheimer, D. My sweet Charlie
Wideman, J. E. Philadelphia fire
Williams, J. A. The man who cried I am
Woods, S. Chiefs
Wright, R. Native son

UNITED STATES. AIR FORCE
Berent, M. Storm flight
Dickey, J. To the white sea
Heller, J. Catch-22
Rosten, L. C. Captain Newman, M.D.
Westheimer, D. Von Ryan's Express

Officers
L'Amour, L. Last of the breed

UNITED STATES. ARMY
DeMille, N. The general's daughter
Fleming, T. J. The officers' wives
Hemingway, E. Across the river and into the trees
Hooker, R. MASH
Hyman, M. No time for sergeants
Jones, J. From here to eternity
Jones, J. The thin red line
McCullers, C. Reflections in a golden eye
O'Connor, R. Buffalo soldiers
Shaara, M. The killer angels
Carroll, J. Memorial bridge
Shulman, M. Rally round the flag, boys!

Officers
Brown, D. A. Killdeer Mountain
DeMille, N. Word of honor
Halberstam, D. One very hot day
Hersey, J. A bell for Adano
Hooker, R. MASH
Horgan, P. A distant trumpet
Nathanson, E. M. The dirty dozen
Pynchon, T. Gravity's rainbow
Sneider, V. The Teahouse of the August Moon
Traver, R. Anatomy of a murder

Uris, L. Armageddon
UNITED STATES. ARMY. CA
Jones, D. C. A creek called
UNITED STATES. ARMY. IN
Del Vecchio, J. M. The 13th
UNITED STATES. ARMY. SP
Griffin, W. E. B. The new
UNITED STATES. ARMY AIR
Griffin, W. E. B. The aviator
UNITED STATES. CENTR
AGENCY
Buckley, W. F. Mongoose, R
Buckley, W. F. A very priva
Clancy, T. The Cardinal of
Clancy, T. The hunt for Re
Garfield, B. Hopscotch
Gilman, D. The amazing M
Gilman, D. The elusive Mrs
Gilman, D. Mrs. Pollifax and
Gilman, D. Mrs. Pollifax on
Gilman, D. Mrs. Pollifax on
Gilman, D. A palm for Mr
Gilman, D. The unexpected
Grady, J. Six days of the
Grady, J. Thunder
Lustbader, E. V. Jian
Mailer, N. Harlot's ghost
Morrell, D. The brotherhood
Perry, T. Metzger's dog
Thomas, R. Ah, treachery!
Thomas, R. Briarpatch
Thomas, R. Missionary stew
Truman, M. Murder in the
UNITED STATES. CONGRES
Drury, A. Advise and cons
Goudge, E. Blessing in disg
Michael, J. Sleeping beauty
Oates, J. C. Black water
Vidal, G. Washington, D.C.
UNITED STATES. DEPT. C
BUREAU OF INVESTIGA
Federal Bureau of Inves
UNITED STATES. FEDERAL
GATION
Carroll, J. Memorial bridge
Grisham, J. The firm
Ludlum, R. The Chancello
Maas, P. Father and son
McMurtry, L. Pretty Boy
Reed, B. The indictment
Smith, A. North of Monta
UNITED STATES. MARINE
Griffin, W. E. B. Battlegr
Griffin, W. E. B. Close c
Griffin, W. E. B. Counter
Griffin, W. E. B. Honor
Griffin, W. E. B. Line of
Uris, L. Battle cry
Webb, J. H. A sense of
Styron, W. The long mar
UNITED STATES. NATION
SPACE ADMINISTRATI
Michener, J. A. Space
UNITED STATES. NATIO
Brown, D. Storming heav
UNITED STATES. NATIO
Clancy, T. Clear and pre
UNITED STATES. NAVAL
States Naval Academy
UNITED STATES. NAVY
Fleming, T. J. Time and
Heggen, T. Mister Rober
McBain, E. Death of a
McKenna, R. The Sand

Van Gogh's room at Arles. Elkin, S.
  In Elkin, S. Van Gogh's room at Arles: three novellas p221-312
Van Gogh's room at Arles: three novellas. Elkin, S.
Vane pursuit. MacLeod, C.
Vanish with the rose. Michaels, B.
Vanished. Steel, D.
Vanishing act. Perry, T.
The **vanishing** American. Grey, Z.
VANITY *See* Egoism
Vanity fair. Thackeray, W. M.
VANZETTI, BARTOLOMEO, 1888-1927
  Sinclair, U. Boston
VARIATION (BIOLOGY) *See* Mutation (Biology)
VASSAR COLLEGE
  McCarthy, M. The group
The **vast** memory of love. Bosse, M. J.
VATICAN
  Martin, M. Vatican
  West, M. L. Lazarus
Vatican. Martin, M.
The **Vatican** rip. Gash, J.
The **veil** of ignorance. Quill, M.
The **veiled** one. Rendell, R.
Vein of iron. Glasgow, E.
VENDETTA *See* Revenge
The **Venetian** affair. MacInnes, H.
The **Venetian** mask. Laker, R.
VENGEANCE *See* Revenge
VENICE (ITALY) *See* Italy—Venice
VENTRILOQUISTS
  Goldman, W. Magic
VENUS (PLANET)
  Lewis, C. S. Perelandra
  Pohl, F. The merchants of Venus
  Pohl, F. The merchants' war
  Pohl, F. The space merchants
  Zelazny, R. The doors of his face, the lamps of his mouth
Venus envy. Brown, R. M.
Venus in copper. Davis, L.
VERMONT
20th century
  Beattie, A. Love always
  Cook, R. Fatal cure
  Gardner, J. October light
  Higgins, G. V. Victories
  Morris, M. M. A dangerous woman
  Peck, R. N. A day no pigs would die
  Proulx, A. Postcards
Farm life
  See Farm life—Vermont
VERMOUTH *See* Wine and wine making
VERSAILLES (FRANCE) *See* France—Versailles
The **very** last gambado. Gash, J.
Very old bones. Kennedy, W.
A **very** particular murder. Haymon, S. T.
A **very** private plot. Buckley, W. F.
Vespers. McBain, E.
VETERANS (KOREAN WAR, 1950-1953)
  Percy, W. The moviegoer
  Warren, R. P. The cave
VETERANS (SOUTH AFRICAN WAR, 1899-1902)
  Delderfield, R. F. A horseman riding by
VETERANS (VIETNAMESE WAR, 1961-1975)
  Bausch, R. Rebel powers
  Busch, F. Closing arguments
  Butler, R. O. They whisper
  Clancy, T. Without remorse
  Del Vecchio, J. M. Carry me home
  Harris, T. Black Sunday
  Heinemann, L. Paco's story

  Kirkwood, J. Some kind of hero
  Mason, B. A. In country
  McCammon, R. R. Gone south
  O'Brien, T. In the Lake of the Woods
  Stone, R. Dog soldiers
  Straub, P. Koko
  Straub, P. The throat
  Thayer, S. The weatherman
  Thomas, R. Ah, treachery!
  Vonnegut, K. Hocus pocus
  Waller, R. J. Border music
  Webb, J. H. A sense of honor
VETERANS (WORLD WAR, 1914-1918)
  Faulkner, W. Soldiers' pay
  Ford, F. M. The last post
  Remarque, E. M. The road back
  Remarque, E. M. Three comrades
  Smith, W. A. A sparrow falls
VETERANS (WORLD WAR, 1939-1945)
  Algren, N. The man with the golden arm
  Battle, L. War brides
  Böll, H. The silent angel
  Fast, H. The outsider
  Guterson, D. Snow falling on cedars
  Heller, J. Closing time
  Jones, J. Whistle
  Knowles, J. Indian summer
  Knowles, J. Peace breaks out
  Lewis, S. Kingsblood royal
  Wharton, W. Birdy
  Wilson, S. The man in the gray flannel suit
VETERANS DAY
  Ford, F. M. A man could stand up
VETERINARIANS
  See also Women veterinarians
  Francis, D. Comeback
The **vicar** of sorrows. Wilson, A. N.
The **vicar** of tours. Balzac, H. de
  In Balzac, H. de. The short novels of Balzac
The **Vicar** of Wakefield. Goldsmith, O.
Victims. Uhnak, D.
VICTORIAN ENGLAND *See* England—19th century
Victories. Higgins, G. V.
Victory. Conrad, J.
Vida. Piercy, M.
VIENNA (AUSTRIA) *See* Austria—Vienna
VIETNAM
  Vida, N. Goodbye, Saigon
Army—Officers
  Halberstam, D. One very hot day
Communism
  See Communism—Vietnam
Ho Chi Minh City
  Greene, G. The quiet American
Saigon
  See Vietnam—Ho Chi Minh City
VIETNAMESE
United States
  Parker, T. J. Little Saigon
  Vida, N. Goodbye, Saigon
VIETNAMESE REFUGEES
  Vida, N. Goodbye, Saigon
VIETNAMESE SOLDIERS *See* Soldiers—Vietnam
VIETNAMESE WAR, 1961-1975
  Berent, M. Steel tiger
  Berent, M. Storm flight
  Buckley, W. F. Tucker's last stand
  Carroll, J. Memorial bridge
  Clancy, T. Without remorse
  Coonts, S. Flight of the Intruder
  Del Vecchio, J. M. The 13th valley

VIETNAMESE WAR, 1961-1975—_Continued_
DeMille, N. Word of honor
Duncan, D. J. The brothers K
Griffin, W. E. B. The aviators
Halberstam, D. One very hot day
Heinemann, L. Paco's story
Mason, B. A. In country
O'Brien, T. Going after Cacciato
O'Brien, T. The things they carried
Phillips, J. A. Machine dreams

Prisoners and prisons
Busch, F. Closing arguments

VIKINGS
Russ, J. Souls
Seton, A. Avalon
Smiley, J. The Greenlanders
Vile bodies. Waugh, E.
Village diary. Read, Miss
_In_ Read, Miss Chronicles of Fairacre p177-360
The village school. Read, Miss
_In_ Read, Miss Chronicles of Fairacre p9-176
Villette. Brontë, C.
Vindication. Sherwood, F.
Vineland. Pynchon, T.
The vines of Yarrabee. Eden, D.

VINEYARDS _See_ Wine and wine making
A vintage murder. Smith, J. L.

VIOLENCE
    See also Child abuse; Riots; Terrorism; Wife abuse
Banks, R. Affliction
Barker, C. Imajica
Bausch, R. Violence
Bell, M. S. All souls' rising
Berger, T. The houseguest
Bosse, M. J. Mister Touch
Brink, A. P. A chain of voices
Browne, G. A. 18mm blues
Busch, F. Closing arguments
Busch, F. Long way from home
Butler, O. E. Parable of the sower
Caputo, P. Horn of Africa
Coetzee, J. M. Life & times of Michael K.
Combs, H. Brules
Del Vecchio, J. M. For the sake of all living things
DeMille, N. Spencerville
Dexter, P. Brotherly love
Dickey, J. To the white sea
Dixon, S. Interstate
Ellison, H. A boy and his dog
Hunter, S. Dirty white boys
Jones, D. C. This savage race
Kosinski, J. N. Blind date
Lessing, D. M. The memoirs of a survivor
Lustbader, E. V. Angel eyes
Lustbader, E. V. Black Blade
Marius, R. C. After the war
Phillips, C. Cambridge
Rodriguez, A. Spidertown
Vida, N. Goodbye, Saigon
Vine, B. A fatal inversion
Vine, B. King Solomon's carpet
Walker, A. Possessing the secret of joy
Willocks, T. Green river rising
Woods, S. L.A. Times
Violence. Bausch, R.
The violent bear it away. O'Connor, F.
    also in O'Connor, F. Collected works p329-480
Violent ward. Deighton, L.
Violet Clay. Godwin, G.

VIOLINISTS
Hersey, J. Antonietta

The Virago book of ghost stories. Entered in Part I
    under title

The virgin in the ice. Peters, E.
VIRGIN ISLANDS OF THE UNITED STATES
    See also Saint Thomas (Virgin Islands of the U.S.)
VIRGIN MARY _See_ Mary, Blessed Virgin, Saint
The virgin suicides. Eugenides, J.
VIRGINIA
    See also Chesapeake Bay (Md. and Va.)

To 1800
L'Amour, L. To the far blue mountains
Thackeray, W. M. The Virginians

18th century
Settle, M. L. O Beulah Land

19th century
Brown, R. M. High hearts
Cather, W. Sapphira and the slave girl
Cornwell, B. Copperhead
Cornwell, B. Rebel
Styron, W. The confessions of Nat Turner
Williams, B. A. House divided

20th century
Adams, A. Families and survivors
Brown, R. M. Venus envy
Davis, T. 1959
Glasgow, E. Barren ground
Glasgow, E. In this our life
Glasgow, E. Vein of iron
Godwin, G. Father Melancholy's daughter
Hamner, E. The homecoming
Hamner, E. Spencer's Mountain
Pearson, T. R. Cry me a river
Shreve, S. R. A country of strangers
Smith, L. Fair and tender ladies
Smith, L. Family linen
Smith, L. Oral history
Styron, W. Lie down in darkness
Whitney, P. A. The ebony swan

Farm life
    See Farm life—Virginia

Frontier and pioneer life
    See Frontier and pioneer life—Virginia

Williamsburg
Thane, E. Dawn's early light
Thane, E. Ever after
Thane, E. Homing
Thane, E. The light heart
Thane, E. This was tomorrow
Thane, E. Yankee stranger
The Virginians. Thackeray, W. M.
Virgins of paradise. Wood, B.
Virtual light. Gibson, W.
Virtual mode. Anthony, P.

VIRTUAL REALITY
Anthony, P. Killobyte
Bova, B. Death dream
Gibson, W. Virtual light
A virtuous woman. Gibbons, K.

VIRUSES
Bosse, M. J. Mister Touch
The vision. Koontz, D. R.
    _In_ Koontz, D. R. Three complete novels p511-704
A vision of light. Riley, J. M.
VISIONS
    See also Dreams; Hallucinations and illusions
VISITORS FROM OUTER SPACE _See_ Interplanetary
    visitors
Vital parts. Berger, T.
Vital signs. Cook, R.
Vital signs. Wood, B.
VITICULTURE _See_ Wine and wine making
VITORIA CAMPAIGN, 1813 _See_ Peninsular War, 1807-
    1814

VIVISECTION *See* Medicine—Research
The **vivisector**. White, P.
Vixen 03. Cussler, C.
The **voice** of the city. Henry, O.
    In Henry, O. The complete works of O. Henry p1253-1364
Voice of the heart. Bradford, B. T.
Voices in a haunted room. Carr, P.
Voices in an empty house. Aiken, J.
Voices in summer. Pilcher, R.
Voices of summer. Pearson, D.
A **void** in hearts. Tapply, W. G.
The **volcano** lover. Sontag, S.

VOLCANOES
    Holt, V. The mask of the enchantress
    Lytton, E. B. L., Baron. The last days of Pompeii
    Verne, J. A journey to the centre of the earth
Vollands. Hill, P.
Voltaire's Candide, Zadig, and selected stories. Voltaire
Von Ryan's Express. Westheimer, D.
Voodoo dreams. Rhodes, J. P.
Voodoo, Ltd. Thomas, R.

VOODOOISM
    Rhodes, J. P. Voodoo dreams
Vortex. Bond, L.
A **vow** of sanctity. Black, V.
Voyage in the dark. Rhys, J.
The **voyage** out. Woolf, V.
Voyagers. Bova, B.

VOYAGES AND TRAVELS
    See also Adventure; Air travel; Railroads—Travel; Sea stories; Tourist trade
    Aiken, C. A heart for the gods of Mexico
    Barth, J. The last voyage of somebody the sailor
    Conrad, J. Youth
    Costain, T. B. The black rose
    De Hartog, J. The inspector
    De Hartog, J. Star of Peace
    Doig, I. The sea runners
    Dunnett, D. Scales of gold
    Dunnett, D. The unicorn hunt
    Endō, S. The samurai
    Fowles, J. A maggot
    Golding, W. Close quarters
    Golding, W. Fire down below
    Golding, W. Rites of passage
    Graves, R. Hercules, my shipmate
    Higgins, J. Storm warning
    Jennings, G. The journeyer
    Johnson, C. R. Middle passage
    MacInnes, H. Decision at Delphi
    Michener, J. A. Journey
    Moberg, V. The emigrants
    O'Brian, P. The golden ocean
    Pirsig, R. M. Lila
    Poe, E. A. The imaginary voyages: The narrative of Arthur Gordon Pym; The unparalleled adventure of one Hans Pfaall; The journal of Julius Rodman
    Sagan, F. The painted lady
    Seton, A. Avalon
    Stone, R. Outerbridge Reach
    Verne, J. Around the world in eighty days
    Villars, E. The Normandie affair
    Waltari, M. The Egyptian
    Waltari, M. The Etruscan

W

WAGON TRAINS
    Guthrie, A. B. The way West
    L'Amour, L. The tall stranger
Waifs and strays. Henry, O.
    In Henry, O. The complete works of O. Henry p1632-92

Waiting for orders. Ambler, E.
Waiting to exhale. McMillan, T.

WAITRESSES
    Hemingway, E. The torrents of spring
    Mapson, J.-A. Hank and Chloe
    Robbins, T. Skinny legs and all
    Steel, D. The gift
Wake the dead. Simpson, D.
Walden two. Skinner, B. F.

WALES
    Smollett, T. G. Humphry Clinker

           5th century
    Stewart, M. The crystal cave
    Stewart, M. Mary Stewart's Merlin trilogy

           13th century
    Pargeter, E. The green branch
    Pargeter, E. The heaven tree
    Pargeter, E. The scarlet seed
    Penman, S. K. Here be dragons
    Penman, S. K. The reckoning

           19th century
    Llewellyn, R. How green was my valley

           20th century
    Amis, K. The old devils
    Cronin, A. J. The citadel
    Gill, B. M. Nursery crimes
    Llewellyn, R. Green, green, my valley now
    Powell, A. The valley of bones

        Coal mines and mining
    See Coal mines and mining—Wales

            Farm life
    See Farm life—Wales

            Rural life
    Howatch, S. The wheel of fortune
A **walk** among the tombstones. Block, L.
A **walk** on the wild side. Algren, N.
Walking across Egypt. Edgerton, C.
The **walking** drum. L'Amour, L.
Walking shadow. Parker, R. B.
The **walking** stick. Graham, W.
Walks Far Woman. Stuart, C.
The **wall**. Hersey, J.
The **wall**, and other stories. See Sartre, J. P. Intimacy, and other stories
Wall of brass. Daley, R.

WALL STREET (NEW YORK, N.Y.)
    See also Stock exchange
    Plain, B. Treasures
    Thomas, M. M. Hanover Place
Wallis. Edwards, A.

WALTER, LUCY GOLD
    Goudge, E. The child from the sea
The **Wanderer**. Leiber, F.
The **wanderers**. Price, R.
The **Wapshot** chronicle. Cheever, J.
The **Wapshot** scandal. Cheever, J.

WAR
    See also Imaginary wars and battles; Interplanetary wars; Nuclear warfare; names of individual wars
    Anthony, P. Wielding a red sword
    Barker, P. The eye in the door
    Barker, P. Regeneration
    Bond, L. Vortex
    Brown, D. Flight of the Old Dog
    Brown, D. Sky masters
    Caputo, P. Horn of Africa
    Clancy, T. Red Storm rising
    Coonts, S. Flight of the Intruder
    Coyle, H. W. Bright star
    Coyle, H. W. Code of honor
    Faulkner, W. A fable
    Haasse, H. S. The scarlet city

WAR—*Continued*
Harrison, H. West of Eden
Llywelyn, M. Finn Mac Cool
Moravia, A. Two women
Pargeter, E. The scarlet seed
Sienkiewicz, H. The deluge
Sienkiewicz, H. Fire in the steppe
Tolkien, J. R. R. The Silmarillion
White, T. H. The book of Merlyn
War and peace. Tolstoy, L., graf
War and remembrance. Wouk, H.
The war between the Tates. Lurie, A.
War brides. Battle, L.

WAR CORRESPONDENTS *See* Journalists

WAR CRIME TRIALS
DeMille, N. Word of honor

WAR CRIMINALS
Forsyth, F. The Odessa file
King, S. Apt pupil
Levin, I. The boys from Brazil
Mortimer, J. C. Dunster
Uris, L. QB VII

WAR OF 1812 *See* United States—War of 1812
The war of the end of the world. Vargas Llosa, M.

WAR OF THE ROSES *See* England—15th century
The war of the saints. Amado, J.
The war of the worlds. Wells, H. G.
also in Wells, H. G. Seven famous novels

WARBECK, PERKIN, 1474-1499
Jarman, R. H. The courts of illusion
Warday. Strieber, W.
The warden. Trollope, A.

WARFIELD, WALLIS *See* Windsor, Wallis Warfield, Duchess of, 1896-1986

WARLOCKS *See* Witchcraft
The warlord. Bosse, M. J.
The warning bell. Reid Banks, L.
Wars of the heart. Villars, E.

WARSAW (POLAND) *See* Poland—Warsaw

WARSHIPS
See also Nuclear submarines
Fleming, T. J. Time and tide
McKenna, R. The Sand Pebbles
Reeman, D. A ship must die
Wartime lies. Begley, L.

WARWICKSHIRE (ENGLAND) *See* England—Warwickshire

WASHINGTON, GEORGE, 1732-1799
Kantor, M. Valley Forge

WASHINGTON (D.C.)

19th century
Adams, H. Democracy
Brown, R. M. Dolley
Vidal, G. 1876
Vidal, G. Empire
Vidal, G. Lincoln

20th century
Carroll, J. Family trade
Clark, M. H. Stillwatch
Coonts, S. Under siege
Drury, A. Advise and consent
Grisham, J. The pelican brief
Heller, J. Good as Gold
McMurtry, L. Cadillac Jack
Michaels, B. Shattered silk
Patterson, J. Along came a spider
Patterson, J. Kiss the girls
Quinn, S. Happy endings
Roberts, N. Honest illusions
Safire, W. Full disclosure
Stead, C. The man who loved children
Vidal, G. Hollywood
Vidal, G. Washington, D.C.

Viorst, J. Murdering Mr. Monti

Georgetown
Blatty, W. P. The exorcist

WASHINGTON (STATE)
Dillard, A. The living
Guterson, D. Snow falling on cedars

Frontier and pioneer life
See Frontier and pioneer life—Washington (State)

Seattle
Pearson, R. The angel maker
Pearson, R. No witnesses
Pearson, R. Undercurrents
Robbins, T. Half asleep in frog pajamas
Washington, D.C. Vidal, G.
Washington Irving's Tales of the supernatural. Irving. W.
Washington Square. James, H.
also in James, H. The American novels and stories of Henry James p162-295
also in James, H. The Henry James reader p1-163
also in James, H. Short novels of Henry James p59-256
Wasted years. Harvey, J.
Watchers. Koontz, D. R.
The water-method man. Irving, J.
In Irving, J. 3 by Irving p285-560
Water music. Boyle, T. C.
The waterfall. Drabble, M.
Waterfront. Schulberg, B.

WATERLOO, BATTLE OF, 1815
Cornwell, B. Sharpe's Waterloo
Watership Down. Adams, R.
The waterworks. Doctorow, E. L.

WATSON, EDGAR J., 1855-1910
Matthiessen, P. Killing Mister Watson
Waverly. Scott, Sir W.
Waverly Place. Brownmiller, S.
The waves. Woolf, V.
The wax dragon. Gardner, E. S.
In Gardner, E. S. The blonde in lower six p145-87
Waxwork. Lovesey, P.
A way in the world. Naipaul, V. S.
The way men act. Lipman, E.
The way of all flesh. Butler, S.
The way some people die. Macdonald, R.
In Macdonald, R. Archer in Hollywood p347-528
The way through the woods. Dexter, C.
The way up. See Hardwick, M. The Duchess of Duke Street
The way we live now. Trollope, A.
The way West. Guthrie, A. B.
Wayfinder's story. See Saberhagen, F. The seventh book of lost swords: Wayfinder's story
The wayward bus. Steinbeck, J.
We have always lived in the castle. Jackson, S.
We print the truth. Boucher, A.
In Boucher, A. The compleat werewolf and other stories of fantasy and science fiction p170-239
We the living. Rand, A.

WEALTH
See also Capitalists and financiers; Millionaires
Adler, E. Legacy of secrets
Adler, E. The secret of the Villa Mimosa
Archer, J. Kane & Abel
Archer, J. The prodigal daughter
Auchincloss, L. The dark lady
Auchincloss, L. The lady of situations
Auchincloss, L. Tales of yesteryear
Auchincloss, L. Three lives
Balzac, H. de. Eugénie Grandet
Birmingham, S. The Auerbach will
Birmingham, S. Carriage trade
Birmingham, S. The LeBaron secret
Birmingham, S. The Rothman scandal
Bradford, B. T. Angel
Bradford, B. T. Hold the dream

WEALTH—*Continued*
  Bradford, B. T. To be the best
  Bradford, B. T. The women in his life
  Capote, T. Answered prayers
  Dailey, J. Heiress
  DeMille, N. The Gold Coast
  Dickens, C. Great expectations
  Doctorow, E. L. The waterworks
  Donoso, J. A house in the country
  Dunne, D. An inconvenient woman
  Dunne, D. A season in purgatory
  Dunne, D. The two Mrs. Grenvilles
  Fast, H. Second generation
  Fitzgerald, F. S. The beautiful and damned
  Fitzgerald, F. S. The Great Gatsby
  Fitzgerald, F. S. The rich boy
  Fitzgerald, F. S. Tender is the night
  Follett, K. A dangerous fortune
  Freeman, C. The last princess
  Gage, E. Pandora's box
  Gould, J. Forever
  Grau, S. A. The condor passes
  Harris, R. Love and money
  Howatch, S. Sins of the fathers
  Isaacs, S. After all these years
  Jakes, J. California gold
  Kelly, J. P. Mr. Boy
  Kinsolving, W. Bred to win
  Knowles, J. Indian summer
  Korda, M. The fortune
  Korda, M. Worldly goods
  Kosinski, J. N. The devil tree
  Krantz, J. I'll take Manhattan
  Ludlum, R. The Scarlatti inheritance
  Malone, M. Uncivil seasons
  McMurtry, L. Some can whistle
  McNaught, J. Paradise
  Michael, J. Pot of gold
  Michael, J. A ruling passion
  Michael, J. Sleeping beauty
  Mitford, N. Love in a cold climate
  Mitford, N. The pursuit of love
  Murdoch, I. Henry and Cato
  O'Hara, J. From the terrace
  Pilcher, R. September
  Plain, B. Treasures
  Prose, F. Primitive people
  Quinn, S. Happy endings
  Ross-Macdonald, M. A woman possessed
  Shaw, I. Bread upon the waters
  Sheldon, S. The stars shine down
  Siddons, A. R. Colony
  Siddons, A. R. King's oak
  Siddons, A. R. Peachtree Road
  Steel, D. Jewels
  Stone, K. Happy endings
  Stone, K. Rainbows
  Tennenbaum, S. Yesterday's streets
  Thayer, N. Everlasting
  Thomas, M. M. Hanover Place
  Villars, E. Lipstick on his collar
  Voigt, C. Glass mountain
  Vonnegut, K. God bless you, Mr. Rosewater
  West, M. L. Masterclass
  Whitney, P. A. Poinciana
  Wilder, T. Theophilus North
  Wood, B. The dreaming
  Woods, S. Imperfect strangers
WEAPONS *See* Munitions; Nuclear weapons
WEATHER
      See also Storms
  The **weatherman**. Thayer, S.
WEAVERS
  Bradshaw, G. Imperial purple
  Eliot, G. Silas Marner
  Oldenbourg, Z. The heirs of the kingdom
  Singer, I. J. The brothers Ashkenazi

Weaveworld. Barker, C.
The **web** and the rock. Wolfe, T.
The **web** of earth. Wolfe, T.
      In Wolfe, T. The short novels of Thomas Wolfe
          p76-154
WEBSTER, DANIEL, 1782-1852
  Benét, S. V. The Devil and Daniel Webster
The **wedding**. West, D.
The **wedding** dress. Young, C.
Wedding song. Mahfūz, N.
WEDDINGS
  McCullers, C. The member of the wedding
  Streeter, E. Father of the bride
  Welty, E. Delta wedding
  West, D. The wedding
Wednesday the rabbi got wet. Kemelman, H.
Weep no more, my lady. Clark, M. H.
Wehr search. McCaffrey, A.
      In The Hugo winners v2 p329-87
Welcome, chaos. Wilhelm, K.
Welcome to Hard Times. Doctorow, E. L.
Welcome to the monkey house. Vonnegut, K.
We'll meet again. Carr, P.
The **well** of loneliness. Hall, R.
Well-schooled in murder. George, E.
WELSH
North America
  Thom, J. A. The children of first man
The **wench** is dead. Dexter, C.
WEREWOLVES
  Anderson, P. Operation Chaos
  Boucher, A. The compleat werewolf
  Michaels, B. The dark on the other side
  Strieber, W. The Wolfen
WERWOLVES *See* Werewolves
Wessex tales. Hardy, T.
WEST (U.S.) *See* Western States
WEST AFRICA
      See also Niger River
  Boyle, T. C. Water music
  Céline, L.-F. Journey to the end of the night
  Forsyth, F. The dogs of war
  Greene, G. The heart of the matter
Kings and rulers
  Sanders, L. The tangent factor
Politics
      See Politics—West Africa
The **West** End horror. Meyer, N.
WEST INDIANS
England
  Naipaul, V. S. The enigma of arrival
New York (N.Y.)
  Guy, R. Ruby
United States
  Condé, M. I, Tituba, black witch of Salem
  Kincaid, J. Lucy
WEST INDIES
      See also Trinidad and Tobago
  Atwood, M. Bodily harm
  Forester, C. S. Admiral Hornblower in the West Indies
  Fox, P. A servant's tale
  Gaskin, C. Fiona
  Guy, R. My love, my love
  Marshall, P. Praisesong for the widow
  Morrison, T. Tar baby
  Naipaul, V. S. Guerrillas
  Plain, B. Eden burning
  Rhys, J. Wide Sargasso Sea
  Shacochis, B. Swimming in the volcano

WEST INDIES—*Continued*
Politics
See Politics—West Indies

Race relations
Plain, B. Eden burning

WEST INDIES REGION *See* Caribbean region
West of Eden. Harrison, H.
West of the Pecos. Grey, Z.
WEST POINT (MILITARY ACADEMY) *See* United
States Military Academy

WEST VIRGINIA

20th century
Giardina, D. The unquiet earth
Phillips, J. A. Machine dreams
Phillips, J. A. Shelter
Settle, M. L. Charley Bland
Settle, M. L. The killing ground
Whitney, P. A. Daughter of the stars

Coal mines and mining
See Coal mines and mining—West Virginia

WESTCHESTER COUNTY (N.Y.) *See* New York
(State)—Westchester County

WESTERN STATES
Abbey, E. The fool's progress
Dexter, P. Deadwood
Doctorow, E. L. Welcome to Hard Times
Fisher, V. Mountain man
Guthrie, A. B. The big sky
Hoagland, E. Seven rivers west
Jones, D. C. Arrest Sitting Bull
Jones, D. C. A creek called Wounded Knee
McMurtry, L. Buffalo girls
McMurtry, L. Lonesome dove
McMurtry, L. Streets of Laredo
Michener, J. A. Centennial
Momaday, N. S. The ancient child
The Mysterious West
Spellman, C. C. Paint the wind
Spencer, L. Forgiving
Swarthout, G. F. The homesman

Farm life
See Farm life—Western States

Frontier and pioneer life
See Frontier and pioneer life—Western States
WESTERN STORIES
See also Adventure; Cowboys; Frontier and pioneer
life—Western States; Ranch life; Western States
Berger, T. Little Big Man
Bonner, C. Lily
Bonner, C. Looking after Lily
Brand, M. Dark Rosaleen
Brand, M. Fugitives' fire
Brand, M. The gentle desperado
Brand, M. Max Brand's best western stories
Brand, M. The Stingaree
Clark, W. V. T. The Ox-bow incident
Combs, H. Brules
Doctorow, E. L. Welcome to Hard Times
Durham, M. Dutch uncle
Durham, M. The man who loved Cat Dancing
Estleman, L. D. Bloody season
Estleman, L. D. City of widows
Estleman, L. D. Sudden country
Gorman, E. Death ground
Great stories of the American West
Grey, Z. The Arizona clan
Grey, Z. Knights of the range
Grey, Z. Riders of the purple sage
Grey, Z. The trail driver
Grey, Z. The vanishing American
Grey, Z. West of the Pecos
Guthrie, A. B. Fair land, fair land
Guthrie, A. B. The last valley

Guthrie, A. B. These thousand hills
Guthrie, A. B. The way West
Henry, W. Mackenna's gold
Houston, P. Cowboys are my weakness
Jakes, J. The best western stories of John Jakes
Johnston, T. C. Cry of the hawk
Jones, D. C. The search for Temperance Moon
Kelton, E. The far canyon
Kelton, E. Slaughter
L'Amour, L. Bendigo Shafter
L'Amour, L. The Californios
L'Amour, L. The Cherokee Trail
L'Amour, L. Four complete novels
L'Amour, L. The haunted mesa
L'Amour, L. Jubal Sackett
L'Amour, L. The lonesome gods
L'Amour, L. The man from the broken hills
L'Amour, L. The outlaws of Mesquite
L'Amour, L. Over on the dry side
L'Amour, L. The riders of High Rock
L'Amour, L. The rustlers of West Fork
L'Amour, L. The Sacketts: beginnings of a dynasty
L'Amour, L. The trail to Seven Pines
L'Amour, L. Trouble shooter
MacLean, A. Breakheart Pass
McMurtry, L. Anything for Billy
Portis, C. True grit
Schaefer, J. W. The collected stories of Jack Schaefer
Schaefer, J. W. Monte Walsh
Schaefer, J. W. Shane
Schofield, S. C. Telluride
Stegner, W. E. Angle of repose
Swarthout, G. F. The shootist
Wet work. Buckley, C. T.

WHALES
Melville, H. Moby-Dick

WHALING
Melville, H. Moby-Dick
What bloody man is that? Brett, S.
What I lived for. Oates, J. C.
What I'm going to do, I think. Woiwode, L.
What kind of day did you have? Bellow, S.
In Bellow, S. Him with his foot in his mouth and
other stories p61-163
What Maisie knew. James, H.
In James, H. What Maisie knew, In the cage, The
pupil
What Maisie knew, In the cage, The pupil. James, H.
What makes Sammy run? Schulberg, B.
What Mrs. McGillicuddy saw! Christie, A.
In Christie, A. Five complete Miss Marple novels
p409-553
What remains. Wolf, C.
In Wolf, C. What remains and other stories
What remains and other stories. Wolf, C.
What we talk about when we talk about love. Carver,
R.
What's bred in the bone. Davies, R.

WHEAT
Norris, F. The octopus
Norris, F. The pit
Wheat that springeth green. Powers, J. F.
The **wheel** of fortune. Howatch, S.
When a man murders. Stout, R.
In Stout, R. Royal flush p385-430
When all the world was young. Sams, F.
When eight bells toll. MacLean, A.
When in Rome. Marsh, Dame N.
When she was good. Roth, P.
When the bough breaks. Kellerman, J.
When the five moons rise. Vance, J.
When the legends die. Borland, H.
When the lion feeds. Smith, W. A.
In Smith, W. A. The Courtneys p[5]-295

When the music stopped. Ogilvie, E.
When the sacred ginmill closes. Block, L.
When the war broke out. Böll, H.
   In Böll, H. The stories of Heinrich Böll p568-81
When the war was over. Böll, H.
   In Böll, H. The stories of Heinrich Böll p582-96
When worlds collide. Balmer, E.
Where are the children? Clark, M. H.
Where are you going, where have you been? Oates, J. C.
Where eagles dare. MacLean, A.
Where echoes live. Muller, M.
Where I'm calling from. Carver, R.
Where is here? Oates, J. C.
Where is Joe Merchant? Buffett, J.
Where late the sweet birds sang. Wilhelm, K.
   also in Modern classic short novels of science fiction p373-414
Where or when. Shreve, A.
Where shadows go. Price, E.
Where there's smoke. Brown, S.
Where you'll find me and other stories. Beattie, A.
While England sleeps. Leavitt, D.
While my pretty one sleeps. Clark, M. H.
Whip hand. Francis, D.
Whirligigs. Henry, O.
   In Henry, O. The complete works of O. Henry p1094-1252
Whirlwind. Clavell, J.

WHISKEY
   Gaskin, C. A falcon for a queen
Whiskey River. Estleman, L. D.
Whispers. Plain, B.
Whistle. Jones, J.
White butterfly. Mosley, W.
The White Company. Doyle, Sir A. C.
The white dragon. McCaffrey, A.
White Fang. London, J.
White gold wielder. Donaldson, S. R.
The white hotel. Thomas, D. M.
The White House pantry murder. Roosevelt, E.
White jazz. Ellroy, J.
White Jenna. Yolen, J.
The white monkey. Galsworthy, J.
   In Galsworthy, J. A modern comedy
White Ninja. Lustbader, E. V.
White noise. DeLillo, D.
The white peacock. Lawrence, D. H.
White people. Gurganus, A.
The white plague. Herbert, F.
The White Tower. Ullman, J. R.
Whitewater. Horgan, P.

WHITTLING *See* Wood carving
Who goes home? Lemarchand, E.
Who is Simon Warwick? Moyes, P.
Who is Teddy Villanova? Berger, T.

WHODUNITS *See* Mystery and detective stories
Whose body? Sayers, D. L.
Why didn't they ask Evans? See Christie, A. The boomerang clue
Why me? Westlake, D. E.
The wicked day. Stewart, M.
Wide is the gate. Sinclair, U.
   In Sinclair, U. [Lanny Budd series]
The wide net and other stories. Welty, E.
   In Welty, E. The collected stories of Eudora Welty
Wide Sargasso Sea. Rhys, J.
The widening gyre. Parker, R. B.

WIDOWERS
   De Hartog, J. The outer buoy
   Friedman, P. Reasonable doubt
   Greenfeld, J. Harry and Tonto
   Kawabata, Y. The sound of the mountain
   Oz, A. To know a woman
   Proulx, A. The shipping news
   Sagan, F. Bonjour tristesse
   Smith, R. K. Jane's house

Whitney, P. A. Snowfire

WIDOWS
   Abe, K. The woman in the dunes
   Bawden, N. Family money
   Beagle, P. S. A fine and private place
   Böll, H. The silent angel
   Bowen, E. The heat of the day
   Bradford, B. T. Everything to gain
   Brookner, A. Dolly
   Collins, W. The rationalist
   Du Maurier, Dame D. My cousin Rachel
   Edgerton, C. Walking across Egypt
   Elkin, S. Mrs. Ted Bliss
   Faulkner, W. Soldiers' pay
   Godden, J. In her garden
   Grumbach, D. Chamber music
   Gurganus, A. The oldest living Confederate widow tells all
   Heyer, G. Bath tangle
   Holland, C. The Bear Flag
   Holt, V. Kirkland Revels
   Korda, M. The fortune
   L'Amour, L. The Cherokee Trail
   L'Engle, M. A severed wasp
   Leonard, E. Gold Coast
   Leslie, J. A. C. The ghost and Mrs. Muir
   Mann, T. The black swan
   Marshall, P. Praisesong for the widow
   McMurtry, L. The evening star
   McMurtry, L. Terms of endearment
   Murdoch, I. Nuns and soldiers
   O'Brien, E. House of splendid isolation
   Price, E. Beauty from ashes
   Price, E. Margaret's story
   Quinn, S. Happy endings
   Raucher, H. Summer of '42
   Ross-Macdonald, M. To the end of her days
   Sackville-West, V. All passion spent
   Sarton, M. A reckoning
   Settle, M. L. Celebration
   Smith, W. A. The burning shore
   Spark, M. A far cry from Kensington
   Spencer, L. Bitter sweet
   Spencer, L. Family blessings
   Stirling, J. Shadows on the shore
   Tyler, A. The clock winder
   Welty, E. The optimist's daughter
   Wharton, E. The reef
   Whitney, P. A. Woman without a past
   Williams, T. The Roman spring of Mrs. Stone
   Wolitzer, H. Hearts
   Wolitzer, H. Tunnel of love
   Yorke, M. The smooth face of evil
Widows. McBain, E.
The widows club. Cannell, D.
Wielding a red sword. Anthony, P.

WIFE ABUSE
   Allen, C. V. Dreaming in color
   Brownmiller, S. Waverly Place
   DeMille, N. Spencerville
   Freeman, C. Always and forever
   Greeley, A. M. Fall from grace
   King, S. Dolores Claiborne
   King, S. Insomnia
   Lescroart, J. T. The 13th juror
   Plain, B. Whispers
   Price, N. Sleeping with the enemy
   Robards, K. Maggy's child
   Shreve, A. Strange fits of passion
   Wilhelm, K. The best defense
   Wood, B. Virgins of paradise
   Wozencraft, K. Notes from the country club
   Yorke, M. Dangerous to know

WIFE AND HUSBAND *See* Husband and wife

WIFE BEATING *See* Wife abuse

WIFE SWAPPING *See* Marriage problems

Wild horses. Francis, D.

Wild Kat. Kijewski, K.

WILD MEN
Hoffman, A. Second nature

WILDERNESS SURVIVAL
Perry, T. Vanishing act

Wilderness tips. Atwood, M.

Wildest dreams. Blake, J.

Wildfire at midnight. Stewart, M.

Willa Cather, later novels. Cather, W.

Willa Cather's collected short fiction, 1892-1912. Cather, W.

WILLIAM III, KING OF GREAT BRITAIN, 1650-1702
Plaidy, J. William's wife

William's wife. Plaidy, J.

WILLIAMSBURG (VA.) *See* Virginia—Williamsburg

The willow pattern. Gulik, R. H. van

WILLS
Mortimer, J. C. Paradise postponed

WILTSHIRE (ENGLAND) *See* England—Wiltshire

The wind from the sea. Heaven, C.

The winding stair. Hodge, J. A.

Windmills of the gods. Sheldon, S.

Windover. Hodge, J. A.

Window on the square. Whitney, P. A.

Winds of change. Lackey, M.

Winds of fate. Lackey, M.

Winds of fury. Lackey, M.

The winds of war. Wouk, H.

WINDSOR, WALLIS WARFIELD, DUCHESS OF, 1896-1986
Edwards, A. Wallis

The Windsor knot. McCrumb, S.

WINE AND WINE MAKING
Crichton, R. The secret of Santa Vittoria
Dailey, J. Tangled vines
Eden, D. The vines of Yarrabee
Francis, D. Proof
Woods, S. Imperfect strangers

The wine-dark sea. O'Brian, P.

Winesburg, Ohio. Anderson, S.

Wings. Steel, D.

The wings of the dove. James, H.

The wings of the morning. Tryon, T.

WINNIPEG (MAN.) *See* Canada—Winnipeg

Winter in Eden. Harrison, H.

Winter in Thrush Green. Read, Miss

The winter of our discontent. Steinbeck, J.

Winter prey. Sandford, J.

Winter's tale. Helprin, M.

Winter's tales. Dinesen, I.

WINTHROP, ELIZABETH FONES *See* Hallet, Elizabeth Fones Winthrop Feake, b. 1610

The Winthrop woman. Seton, A.

WISCONSIN

20th century
Hamilton, J. A map of the world
Spencer, L. Bitter sweet

Farm life
See Farm life—Wisconsin

The wisdom of Father Brown. Chesterton, G. K.
In Chesterton, G. K. The Father Brown omnibus p227-431

Wise blood. O'Connor, F.
also in O'Connor, F. Collected works p1-132

Wise children. Carter, A.

The wise woman. Gregory, P.

Wish you were here. Brown, R. M.

The wishsong of Shannara. Brooks, T.

WIT *See* Humor

The witch in the wood. White, T. H.

WITCHCRAFT
See also Demoniac possession; Exorcism; Voodooism

Anderson, P. Operation Chaos
Barker, C. The Madonna
Brooks, T. The Elfstones of Shannara
Brooks, T. The sword of Shannara
Condé, M. I, Tituba, black witch of Salem
Gregory, P. The wise woman
Jones, D. W. A sudden wild magic
King, S. Thinner
Levin, I. Rosemary's baby
Lustbader, E. V. White Ninja
Rendell, R. The killing doll
Rice, A. Lasher
Rice, A. Taltos
Rice, A. The witching hour
Stewart, M. Thornyhold
Tryon, T. Harvest home
Updike, J. The witches of Eastwick
Weldon, F. Puffball

WITCHES *See* Witchcraft

The witches of Eastwick. Updike, J.

The witching hour. Rice, A.

With a tangled skein. Anthony, P.

With fire and sword. Sienkiewicz, H.

With the Snow Queen. Greenberg, J.

With the Snow Queen [novelette]. Greenberg, J.
In Greenberg, J. With the Snow Queen p3-78

The withdrawing room. MacLeod, C.

Within a budding grove. Proust, M.
also in Proust, M. Remembrance of things past v1 p465-1018

Without a hero. Boyle, T. C.

Without remorse. Clancy, T.

The witness. Uhnak, D.

The witness for the prosecution, and other stories. Christie, A.

WITNESSES
Leonard, E. Killshot

Wizard. Varley, J.

Wizard at large. Brooks, T.

WIZARDS *See* Magicians

WLT. Keillor, G.

WODEHOUSE, P. G. (PELHAM GRENVILLE), 1881-1975

Parodies, travesties, etc.
Parkinson, C. N. Jeeves: a gentleman's personal gentleman

WODEHOUSE, PELHAM GRENVILLE *See* Wodehouse, P. G. (Pelham Grenville), 1881-1975

A Wodehouse bestiary. Wodehouse, P. G.

Wolf and iron. Dickson, G. R.

Wolf in the shadows. Muller, M.

Wolf whistle. Nordan, L.

Wolf winter. Francis, C.

The Wolfen. Strieber, W.

WOLLSTONECRAFT, MARY, 1759-1797
Sherwood, F. Vindication

WOLVES
Dickson, G. R. Wolf and iron

A woman alone. Ross-Macdonald, M.

A woman called Moses. Heidish, M.

The woman destroyed. Beauvoir, S. de

The woman destroyed [novelette]. Beauvoir, S. de
In Beauvoir, S. de. The woman destroyed p121-254

Woman Hollering Creek and other stories. Cisneros, S.
Woman in the dark. Hammett, D.
The woman in the dunes. Abe, K.
The woman in white. Collins, W.
A woman of independent means. Hailey, E. F.
A woman of our times. Thomas, R.
A woman of substance. Bradford, B. T.
Woman of the inner sea. Keneally, T.
Woman on the edge of time. Piercy, M.
A woman possessed. Ross-Macdonald, M.
A woman scorned. Ross-Macdonald, M.
Woman slaughter. Ferrars, E. X.
Woman without a past. Whitney, P. A.
A Woman's eye. Entered in Part I under title
Woman's own. Carr, R.

WOMEN
See also Single women
Adams, A. Caroline's daughters
Adams, A. Superior women
Adler, E. Fortune is a woman
Adler, E. Legacy of secrets
Allen, C. V. Dream train
Allen, C. V. Painted lives
Alther, L. Kinflicks
Auchincloss, L. The book class
Auchincloss, L. The lady of situations
Bambara, T. C. The salt eaters
Battle, L. The past is another country
Beauvoir, S. de. The woman destroyed
Bellow, S. A theft
Blair, L. The side of the angels
Blake, J. Wildest dreams
Bowen, E. Eva Trout
Bradley, M. Z. The firebrand
Brookner, A. Brief lives
Brown, R. M. Six of one
Brown, S. Charade
Carr, R. Woman's own
Cather, W. Lucy Gayheart
Chase, J. During the reign of the Queen of Persia
Childress, A. A short walk
Clark, M. H. Loves music, loves to dance
Demetz, H. The journey from Prague Street
Didion, J. Democracy
Doerr, H. Consider this, señora
Dorris, M. A yellow raft in blue water
Esquivel, L. Like water for chocolate
Flagg, F. Fried green tomatoes at the Whistle-Stop Cafe
Fleming, T. J. Over there
French, M. Her mother's daughter
Gage, E. The master stroke
Garwood, J. Saving grace
Gibbons, K. Charms for the easy life
Gilman, D. Caravan
Glendinning, V. The grown-ups
Godwin, G. A mother and two daughters
Goldreich, G. Leah's journey
Goldsmith, O. The First Wives Club
Gordimer, N. A sport of nature
Gordon, M. The company of women
Goudge, E. Garden of lies
Hailey, E. F. Home free
Hailey, E. F. A woman of independent means
Hardwick, E. Sleepless nights
Harper, K. Circle of gold
Harris, R. Modern women
Hodge, J. A. Windover
Howatch, S. Scandalous risks
Isaacs, S. Close relations
Keneally, T. Woman of the inner sea
Kinsolving, W. Bred to win
Laker, R. Circle of pearls
Laker, R. The golden tulip
Laker, R. To dance with kings
Laker, R. The Venetian mask
Larsen, J. Silk road
L'Engle, M. Certain women

Lively, P. Moon tiger
Marshall, P. Daughters
McCorkle, J. Crash diet
McCorkle, J. Tending to Virginia
McDermott, A. At weddings and wakes
Mehta, G. Raj
Momaday, N. S. The ancient child
Munro, A. Open secrets
Naylor, G. The women of Brewster Place
Nin, A. Cities of the interior
Otto, W. How to make an American quilt
Pilcher, R. September
Pilcher, R. The shell seekers
Plain, B. Whispers
Pym, B. Excellent women
Reid Banks, L. The warning bell
Ross-Macdonald, M. An innocent woman
Sheldon, S. Windmills of the gods
Shields, C. The stone diaries
Shreve, S. R. Daughters of the new world
Siddons, A. R. Colony
Siddons, A. R. Hill towns
Siddons, A. R. Peachtree Road
Sienkiewicz, H. Fire in the steppe
Spellman, C. C. Paint the wind
Steel, D. Jewels
Steel, D. Vanished
Stone, K. Rainbows
Stubbs, J. Kelly Park
Swarthout, G. F. The homesman
Thayer, N. My dearest friend
Theroux, P. Doctor Slaughter
Thomas, E. M. The animal wife
Thomas, E. M. Reindeer Moon
Thomas, R. Bad girls, good women
Updike, J. S
Walker, A. Possessing the secret of joy
Weldon, F. The cloning of Joanna May
Weldon, F. Leader of the band
Wesley, M. A dubious legacy
West, Dame R. Sunflower
Wood, B. Green City in the sun

Psychology
Abbott, M. The last innocent hour
Alcott, L. M. A long fatal love chase
Appelfeld, A. Katerina
Auchincloss, L. The realist
Bausch, R. Rare & endangered species
Benedict, E. Safe conduct
Boyd, W. Brazzaville Beach
Bradford, B. T. Everything to gain
Bradford, B. T. Voice of the heart
Brookner, A. A closed eye
Brookner, A. Dolly
Busch, F. Long way from home
Byatt, A. S. The conjugial angel
Clark, M. H. All around the town
Clark, M. H. Remember me
Coetzee, J. M. Age of iron
Colwin, L. Goodbye without leaving
Corman, A. Prized possessions
Fox, P. A servant's tale
Gill, B. M. Time and time again
Godwin, G. Father Melancholy's daughter
Gordon, M. The rest of life
Greenberg, J. No reck'ning made
Hamilton, J. A map of the world
Hart, J. Sin
Hoeg, P. Smilla's sense of snow
Hood, A. Places to stay the night
Jong, E. Any woman's blues
Kincaid, J. Lucy
King, S. Dolores Claiborne
King, S. Gerald's game
Kingsolver, B. Animal dreams
Lessing, D. M. The good terrorist
Lively, P. The road to Lichfield
Martin, V. The great divorce

WOMEN—Psychology—*Continued*
Mason, B. A. Feather crowns
Michael, J. Sleeping beauty
Miller, S. For love
Morris, M. A mother's love
Morris, M. M. A dangerous woman
Oates, J. C. I lock my door upon myself
O'Brien, E. House of splendid isolation
O'Brien, E. Time and tide
Phillips, C. Cambridge
Price, N. Night woman
Quindlen, A. One true thing
Rossner, J. Olivia
Rush, N. Mating
Schwartz, L. S. Disturbances in the field
Shreve, A. Strange fits of passion
Simenon, G. Across the street
Simenon, G. The truth about Bébé Donge
Spencer, E. Knights and dragons
Steel, D. Accident
Stirling, J. Shadows on the shore
Stubbs, J. Light in summer
Symons, J. Something like a love affair
Szeman, S. The Kommandant's mistress
Tennant, E. Pemberley
Trevor, W. Felicia's journey
Trevor, W. Reading Turgenev
Villars, E. Too close for comfort
Waller, R. J. The bridges of Madison County
Weldon, F. Trouble
Wozencraft, K. Notes from the country club

Relation to other women
Allen, C. V. Dreaming in color
Atwood, M. The robber bride
Binchy, M. Circle of friends
Binchy, M. Light a penny candle
Brookner, A. Fraud
Fielding, J. Good intentions
Goldreich, G. Years of dreams
Hodge, J. A. Escapade
Kingsolver, B. The bean trees
McMillan, T. Waiting to exhale
Oates, J. C. Solstice
Piercy, M. Braided lives
Pym, B. Jane and Prudence
Ross-Macdonald, M. To the end of her days
Sarton, M. The magnificent spinster
Siddons, A. R. Outer banks
Updike, J. The witches of Eastwick
Vida, N. Goodbye, Saigon
Vine, B. The house of stairs
Weldon, F. Life force
Wolitzer, M. Friends for life
Wood, B. Vital signs

Social conditions
See also Feminism
Achebe, C. Anthills of the Savannah
Adams, A. Families and survivors
Aiken, J. Eliza's daughter
Alcott, L. M. A long fatal love chase
Alvarez, J. In the time of the butterflies
Atwood, M. The handmaid's tale
Atwood, M. Life before man
Banks, R. Continental drift
Battle, L. Southern women
Battle, L. Storyville
Battle, L. War brides
Binchy, M. Echoes
Böll, H. Group portrait with lady
Bradford, B. T. Act of will
Breslin, J. Table money
Brown, R. M. High hearts
Buck, P. S. Pavilion of women
Colwin, L. Family happiness
Cookson, C. The black velvet gown
Courter, G. The midwife
Courter, G. The midwife's advice

Drabble, M. The gates of ivory
Drabble, M. A natural curiosity
Drabble, M. The radiant way
Eden, D. The millionaire's daughter
Fairbairns, Z. Stand we at last
Fast, H. The immigrant's daughter
Fast, H. The trial of Abigail Goodman
Fleming, T. J. The officers' wives
Franklin, M. The end of my career
Franklin, M. My brilliant career
Freeman, C. Come pour the wine
Freeman, C. Fairytales
Freeman, C. Seasons of the heart
French, M. The women's room
Garcia, C. Dreaming in Cuban
Gaskin, C. The ambassador's women
Godwin, G. The odd woman
Godwin, G. Violet Clay
Gordimer, N. Burger's daughter
Grau, S. A. Roadwalkers
Gray, F. du P. Lovers and tyrants
Gross, J. The books of Rachel
Hailey, E. F. Life sentences
Handke, P. The left-handed woman
Harris, M. Lost and found
Hill, P. Artemia
Howard, M. Expensive habits
Irving, J. The world according to Garp
Isaacs, S. Shining through
Jaffe, R. Class reunion
James, H. The Bostonians
Laker, R. The silver touch
Lawrence, D. H. Women in love
Lessing, D. M. Children of violence
Lessing, D. M. The golden notebook
Lessing, D. M. The summer before the dark
Lofts, N. The day of the butterfly
Lord, B. B. Spring Moon
MacNeil, R. Burden of desire
McCarthy, M. The group
McCullough, C. The ladies of Missalonghi
Minot, S. Folly
Moore, B. I am Mary Dunne
Moravia, A. Two women
Mukherjee, B. The holder of the world
Mukherjee, B. Jasmine
Oates, J. C. A Bloodsmoor romance
Oates, J. C. Marya
Piercy, M. Braided lives
Piercy, M. Gone to soldiers
Piercy, M. The longings of women
Piercy, M. Small changes
Price, N. Sleeping with the enemy
Price, R. Kate Vaiden
Prose, F. Household saints
Ragen, N. Sotah
Rhys, J. After leaving Mr. Mackenzie
Rhys, J. Voyage in the dark
Richardson, S. Clarissa
Richardson, S. Pamela
Riley, J. M. In pursuit of the green lion
Riley, J. M. The oracle glass
Riley, J. M. A vision of light
Roiphe, A. R. Up the sandbox!
Ross-Macdonald, M. Dancing on snowflakes
Ross-Macdonald, M. Hell hath no fury
Sand, G. Lélia
Santmyer, H. H. "—and ladies of the club"
Sarton, M. The education of Harriet Hatfield
Sarton, M. Mrs. Stevens hears the mermaids singing
Shange, N. Sassafrass, Cypress & Indigo
Sherwood, F. Vindication
Shulman, A. K. Memoirs of an ex-prom queen
Stein, G. Three lives
Stirling, J. Lantern for the dark
Straight, S. I been in sorrow's kitchen and licked out all the pots
Tax, M. Rivington Street

WOMEN—*Continued*
Tax, M. Union Square
Trollope, A. Can you forgive her?
Trollope, J. The rector's wife
Tryon, T. The wings of the morning
Undset, S. Kristin Lavransdatter
Van Slyke, H. A necessary woman
Van Slyke, H. No love lost
Van Slyke, H. Public smiles, private tears
Villars, E. Wars of the heart
Walker, A. The color purple
Walker, A. The temple of my familiar
Weldon, F. The heart of the country
West, P. The women of Whitechapel and Jack the Ripper
West, Dame R. This real night
Wharton, E. The custom of the country
Wharton, E. Fast and loose
Wharton, E. The house of mirth
Wood, B. Virgins of paradise
Zaroulis, N. L. Call the darkness light
Zaroulis, N. L. The last waltz
Zola, É. Nana

WOMEN AIR PILOTS
Krantz, J. Till we meet again
Steel, D. Wings
Women and ghosts. Lurie, A.

WOMEN ARCHEOLOGISTS
Michaels, B. Search the shadows

WOMEN ARTISTS
Atwood, M. Cat's eye
Bradford, B. T. Act of will
De Lint, C. Memory and dream
Dove, R. Through the ivory gate
Mortman, D. True colors
Shange, N. Liliane

WOMEN ATHLETES
Brown, R. M. Sudden death

WOMEN AUTHORS
Allen, C. V. Dreaming in color
Atwood, M. Lady Oracle
Battle, L. Southern women
Brookner, A. Dolly
Brookner, A. Hotel du Lac
Carroll, J. Fault lines
Coward, N. Bon voyage
Dickinson, P. Death of a unicorn
Ephron, N. Heartburn
Fast, H. The establishment
Gilchrist, E. The Anna papers
Hailey, E. F. Joanna's husband and David's wife
Howard, M. Expensive habits
King, S. The Tommyknockers
Krentz, J. A. Grand passion
Lessing, D. M. The golden notebook
Oates, J. C. Marya
Oates, J. C. Unholy loves
Ogilvie, E. When the music stopped
Piercy, M. The longings of women
Rossner, J. His little women
Settle, M. L. Charley Bland
Settle, M. L. The killing ground
Shreve, A. Strange fits of passion
Stegner, W. E. Angle of repose
Thomas, R. All my sins remembered
Trevor, W. My house in Umbria
Weldon, F. Trouble
Whitney, P. A. Daughter of the stars
Whitney, P. A. Emerald
Wolf, C. What remains

WOMEN CLERGY
West, J. Except for me and thee

WOMEN EDITORS
Spark, M. A far cry from Kensington

WOMEN IN AGRICULTURE
Glasgow, E. Barren ground

WOMEN IN BUSINESS *See* Businesswomen
The **women** in his life. Bradford, B. T.
Women in love. Lawrence, D. H.

WOMEN IN POLITICS
Archer, J. The prodigal daughter
Didion, J. A book of common prayer
Ferber, E. Cimarron

WOMEN JOURNALISTS
Adams, A. Almost perfect
Anthony, E. Exposure
Atwood, M. Bodily harm
Bradford, B. T. Remember
Clark, M. H. I'll be seeing you
Cleary, J. The faraway drums
Cleary, J. Spearfield's daughter
Coulter, C. Impulse
Dailey, J. Tangled vines
Daley, R. A faint cold fear
Drabble, M. The middle ground
Gifford, T. The Glendower legacy
Gould, J. Forever
Lee, C. Y. Gate of rage
Lively, P. Cleopatra's sister
MacInnes, H. Ride a pale horse
Morrell, D. Assumed identity
Patterson, R. N. Degree of guilt
Quinn, S. Happy endings
Roberts, N. Private scandals
Siddons, A. R. Downtown
Thoene, B. The twilight of courage
Thomas, M. M. Black money
Villars, E. The Normandie affair
Walters, M. The sculptress

WOMEN LAWYERS
Clark, M. H. The cradle will fall
Crichton, M. Disclosure
Daley, R. Tainted evidence
Fielding, J. Tell me no secrets
Gordimer, N. None to accompany me
Latt, M. L. Powers of attorney
Michael, J. Sleeping beauty
Rosenberg, N. T. Interest of justice
Rosenberg, N. T. Mitigating circumstances
Rossner, J. His little women
Sheldon, S. Rage of angels
Stone, K. Happy endings
Uhnak, D. False witness
Wilhelm, K. The best defense
Wilhelm, K. Death qualified
The **women** of Brewster Place. Naylor, G.
The **women** of Whitechapel and Jack the Ripper. West, P.

WOMEN PHOTOGRAPHERS
Gage, E. Pandora's box
Woods, S. Palindrome

WOMEN PHYSICIANS
Brown, S. Where there's smoke
Cook, R. Blindsight
Cook, R. Outbreak
Cook, R. Vital signs
Gordon, M. Living at home
Palmer, M. Natural causes
Sheldon, S. Nothing lasts forever
Smith, W. A. Flight of the falcon
Wolitzer, M. Friends for life
Wood, B. Soul flame
Wood, B. Virgins of paradise
Wood, B. Vital signs

WOMEN POETS
Amis, K. The Russian girl
Conroy, P. The prince of tides
Jhabvala, R. P. Poet and dancer
Michaels, B. Houses of stone

WOMEN POETS—Continued
Shreve, A. Where or when

WOMEN SCIENTISTS
Roiphe, A. R. If you knew me

WOMEN VETERINARIANS
Stewart, M. Airs above the ground

WOMEN'S CLUBS See Clubs

WOMEN'S LIBERATION MOVEMENT See Feminism
The women's room. French, M.

WOOD CARVING
Arnow, H. L. S. The dollmaker

WORCESTERSHIRE (ENGLAND) See England—Worcestershire
The word for world is forest. Le Guin, U. K.
    also in The Hugo winners v3 p225-327
Word of honor. DeMille, N.
Working men. Dorris, M.
Works. Wright, R.
The works of Anton Chekhov. See Chekhov, A. P. The
    best known works of Anton Chekhov
The world according to Garp. Irving, J.
The world at the end of time. Pohl, F.
World enough and time. Warren, R. P.
The world from rough stones. Ross-Macdonald, M.
The world of Jeeves. Wodehouse, P. G.
The world of Nagaraj. Narayan, R. K.
The world of Suzie Wong. Mason, R.
World of wonders. Davies, R.
A world out of time. Niven, L.
World over. Maugham, W. S.
    In Maugham, W. S. Complete short stories v2
The world over. Wharton, E.
    In Wharton, E. The collected short stories of Edith
      Wharton v2

WORLD POLITICS
    See also Treaties
Clancy, T. Red Storm rising
Mailer, N. Harlot's ghost
West, M. L. The clowns of God
West, M. L. The shoes of the fisherman
A world to win. Sinclair, U.
    In Sinclair, U. [Lanny Budd series]

WORLD WAR, 1914-1918
Cather, W. One of ours
Delderfield, R. F. To serve them all my days
Ford, F. M. Parade's end
Hašek, J. The good soldier Svejk
Sholokhov, M. A. And quiet flows the Don
Smith, W. A. The burning shore
Solzhenitsyn, A. August 1914
Thane, E. Kissing kin
Trumbo, D. Johnny got his gun
West, P. Love's mansion

        Aerial operations
Gann, E. K. In the company of eagles

        Naval operations
Forester, C. S. The last nine days of the Bismarck
McCutchan, P. The last farewell

        Africa
Forester, C. S. The African Queen

        Canada
MacNeil, R. Burden of desire

        England
Barker, P. The eye in the door
Barker, P. Regeneration
Cookson, C. The Maltese Angel
Hilton, J. Random harvest
Thane, E. The light heart
West, Dame R. This real night

        France
Céline, L.-F. Journey to the end of the night
Cocteau, J. The impostor

Colette. Mitsou
Faulkner, W. A fable
Fleming, T. J. Over there
Ford, F. M. No more parades
Proust, M. Time regained
Remarque, E. M. All quiet on the western front

        Germany
Remarque, E. M. The road back

        Italy
Helprin, M. A soldier of the great war
Hemingway, E. A farewell to arms

        Middle East
Werfel, F. The forty days of Musa Dagh

        United States
Dos Passos, J. 1919
Dos Passos, J. Manhattan transfer

WORLD WAR, 1939-1945
Aaron, D. Crossing by night
Appelfeld, A. Tzili, the story of a life
Burnford, S. Bel Ria
Deighton, L. XPD
Delderfield, R. F. To serve them all my days
Fast, H. Second generation
Follett, K. Night over water
Higgins, J. The eagle has flown
Jones, J. The thin red line
Kirst, H. H. The night of the generals
Piercy, M. Gone to soldiers
Sinclair, U. [Lanny Budd series]
Steinbeck, J. The moon is down
Vonnegut, K. Mother night
Waugh, E. The end of the battle
Waugh, E. Men at arms
Waugh, E. Officers and gentlemen
Wouk, H. War and remembrance
Wouk, H. The winds of war

        Aerial operations
Heller, J. Catch-22
Vonnegut, K. Slaughterhouse-five

        Atrocities
    See also Holocaust, Jewish (1933-1945)
Anatoli, A. Babi Yar
De Hartog, J. The lamb's war
Hersey, J. The wall
Mortimer, J. C. Dunster
Uris, L. QB VII

        Collaborationists
Higgins, J. Thunder point

        Jews
    See also Holocaust, Jewish (1933-1945)
De Hartog, J. Star of Peace
Keneally, T. Schindler's list
Levi, P. If not now, when?
Remarque, E. M. The night in Lisbon

        Naval operations
De Hartog, J. The captain
Fleming, T. J. Time and tide
Heggen, T. Mister Roberts
MacLean, A. H.M.S. Ulysses
McCutchan, P. Cameron's crossing
McCutchan, P. Convoy homeward
McCutchan, P. Convoy north
McCutchan, P. Convoy of fear
McCutchan, P. Convoy south
Reeman, D. A ship must die

        Naval operations—Submarine
Beach, E. L. Run silent, run deep
Buchheim, L.-G. The boat

        Prisoners and prisons
    See also Concentration camps
Ballard, J. G. Empire of the Sun
Boulle, P. The bridge over the River Kwai

WORLD WAR, 1939-1945—Continued
Clavell, J. King Rat
Endō, S. The sea and poison
Higgins, J. The Valhalla exchange
Keneally, T. Schindler's list
Nathanson, E. M. The dirty dozen
Vonnegut, K. Slaughterhouse-five
Westheimer, D. Von Ryan's Express

Secret service
Follett, K. Eye of the needle
Follett, K. The key to Rebecca
Higgins, J. Cold Harbour
Iles, G. Black cross
Ludlum, R. The Rhinemann exchange

Underground movements
Allbeury, T. A time without shadows
Francis, C. Night sky
Gardner, J. E. The secret houses
Laker, R. This shining land
Sagan, F. A reluctant hero
Uris, L. Mila 18

Argentina
Griffin, W. E. B. Honor bound

Atlantic Ocean
MacLean, A. H.M.S. Ulysses
Monsarrat, N. The cruel sea

Australia
McCullough, C. An indecent obsession

Belgium
Hulme, K. The nun's story

China
Buck, P. S. Dragon seed

Czechoslovakia
Demetz, H. The house on Prague Street

Egypt
Deighton, L. City of gold
Mahfūz, N. Sugar Street

England
Barnard, R. Out of the blackout
Bowen, E. The heat of the day
Briskin, J. The other side of love
Carr, P. We'll meet again
Deighton, L. SS-GB: Nazi-occupied Britain 1941
Dickinson, P. Perfect gallows
Follett, K. Eye of the needle
Gallico, P. The snow goose
Gaskin, C. The charmed circle
Greene, G. The end of the affair
Greene, G. The ministry of fear
Higgins, J. Cold Harbour
Higgins, J. The eagle has landed
Howard, E. J. Confusion
Read, P. P. The free Frenchman
Renault, M. The charioteer
Snow, C. P. Homecoming
Spark, M. The girls of slender means
Thane, E. Homing
Waugh, E. Put out more flags

Europe
Shaw, I. The young lions
Thoene, B. The twilight of courage

France
Bates, H. E. Fair stood the wind for France
Durrell, L. Constance
Francis, C. Night sky
Greene, G. The tenth man
MacInnes, H. Assignment in Brittany
Read, P. P. The free Frenchman
Remarque, E. M. Arch of triumph
Sams, F. When all the world was young
Sartre, J. P. Troubled sleep

Germany
Böll, H. Group portrait with lady
Böll, H. The silent angel
Böll, H. A soldier's legacy
Briskin, J. The other side of love
Grass, G. Dog years
Iles, G. Black cross
Isaacs, S. Shining through
Kennedy, R. A. The bitterest age
Kirst, H. H. Forward, Gunner Asch!
Kirst, H. H. The return of Gunner Asch
Kirst, H. H. The revolt of Gunner Asch
Leffland, E. The knight, death, and the devil
MacLean, A. Where eagles dare
Remarque, E. M. A time to love and a time to die

Greece
De Bernières, L. Corelli's mandolin

Hungary
Korda, M. Worldly goods
Pearson, D. Csardas

Indian Ocean
Reeman, D. A ship must die

Ireland
Moore, B. The emperor of ice-cream

Italy
Crichton, R. The secret of Santa Vittoria
Moravia, A. Two women
Ondaatje, M. The English patient

Japan
Dickey, J. To the white sea

Jersey (Channel Islands)
Higgins, J. Night of the fox

Malaya
Shute, N. The legacy

Malta
Monsarrat, N. The kappillan of Malta

Mediterranean region
MacLean, A. The guns of Navarone

Norway
Laker, R. This shining land

Pacific Ocean
Beach, E. L. Run silent, run deep
Fleming, T. J. Time and tide
Griffin, W. E. B. Battleground
Griffin, W. E. B. Close combat
Griffin, W. E. B. Counterattack
Griffin, W. E. B. Line of fire
Heggen, T. Mister Roberts
Mailer, N. The naked and the dead
Michener, J. A. Tales of the South Pacific
Uris, L. Battle cry
Wouk, H. The Caine mutiny

Poland
Begley, L. Wartime lies
Hersey, J. The wall
Keneally, T. Schindler's list
Kosinski, J. N. The painted bird
Kuniczak, W. S. The thousand hour day
Miłosz, C. The seizure of power
Uris, L. Mila 18

Russia
Keneally, T. A family madness
Kirst, H. H. Forward, Gunner Asch!

Sicily
Hersey, J. A bell for Adano
Higgins, J. Luciano's luck

Solomon Islands
Griffin, W. E. B. Line of fire

WORLD WAR, 1939-1945—*Continued*
South Africa
Lessing, D. M. Landlocked
Lessing, D. M. A ripple from the storm

United States
Goldreich, G. That year of our war
Griffin, W. E. B. Counterattack
Guterson, D. Snow falling on cedars
Jones, J. Whistle
Leffland, E. Rumors of peace
Villars, E. Wars of the heart
Wouk, H. War and remembrance

Yugoslavia
MacLean, A. Force 10 from Navarone
World without end. Gray, F. du P.
Worldly goods. Korda, M.
World's end. Boyle, T. C.
World's end. Sinclair, U.
   In Sinclair, U. [Lanny Budd series]
World's end. Vinge, J. D.
World's end and other stories. Theroux, P.
The **worshipful** Lucia. Benson, E. F.
   In Benson, E. F. Make way for Lucia p763-940

WOUNDED KNEE CREEK, BATTLE OF, 1890
Jones, D. C. A creek called Wounded Knee
The **wounded** Land. Donaldson, S. R.
Woundhealer's story. See Saberhagen, F. The first book of lost swords: Woundhealer's story
A **wreath** for the bride. O'Donnell, L.
The **wreck** of the Mary Deare. Innes, H.

WRESTLING
Irving, J. The 158-pound marriage
WRITERS See Authors
Written on the body. Winterson, J.
The **wrong** rite. MacLeod, C.
Wuthering Heights. Brontë, E.
Wycliffe and the cycle of death. Burley, W. J.
Wycliffe and the dead flautist. Burley, W. J.
Wycliffe and the quiet virgin. Burley, W. J.
The **Wyndham** legacy. Coulter, C.

WYOMING

19th century
Durham, M. The man who loved Cat Dancing
L'Amour, L. Bendigo Shafter
Schaefer, J. W. Shane

20th century
Bausch, R. Rebel powers
Olsen, T. Yonnondio: from the thirties

Coal mines and mining
See Coal mines and mining—Wyoming

Frontier and pioneer life
See Frontier and pioneer life—Wyoming

X

Xenocide. Card, O. S.
Xenogenesis [series]
Butler, O. E. Adulthood rites
Butler, O. E. Dawn
Butler, O. E. Imago
Xingu. Wharton, E.
   In Wharton, E. The collected short stories of Edith Wharton v2

XPD. Deighton, L.
The **XYZ** murders. Queen, E.

Y

YACHTS AND YACHTING
Snow, C. P. Death under sail

YANGTZE RIVER (CHINA)
Hersey, J. A single pebble
Yankee at the court of King Arthur. See Twain, M. A Connecticut Yankee in King Arthur's court
Yankee stranger. Thane, E.
The **year** of the French. Flanagan, T.
The **year** of the ransom. Anderson, P.
   In Anderson, P. The Time Patrol p399-458
The **years.** Woolf, V.
The **Year's** best fantasy. See The Year's best fantasy and horror
The **Year's** best fantasy and horror. Entered in Part I under title
The **Year's** best science fiction. Entered in Part I under title
Years of dreams. Goldreich, G.
Yellow bird. Boyer, R.
A **yellow** raft in blue water. Dorris, M.
The **yellow** room conspiracy. Dickinson, P.
Yellow shadows. Gardner, E. S.
   In Gardner, E. S. The blonde in lower six p229-70
Yesterday's streets. Tennenbaum, S.
Yonnondio: from the thirties. Olsen, T.

YORKSHIRE (ENGLAND) *See* England—Yorkshire
You can't go home again. Wolfe, T.
You can't keep a good woman down. Walker, A.
You have the right to remain silent. Paul, B.
You know me, Al. Lardner, R.
   also in Lardner, R. Ring around the bases
You must remember this. Oates, J. C.
You only live twice. Fleming, I.
Young Bleys. Dickson, G. R.
Young Joseph. Mann, T.
   In Mann, T. Joseph and his brothers p261-444
The **young** lions. Shaw, I.
Young Lonigan. Farrell, J. T.
   In Farrell, J. T. Studs Lonigan
Young man with a horn. Baker, D.
The **young** manhood of Studs Lonigan. Farrell, J. T.
   In Farrell, J. T. Studs Lonigan
Youngblood Hawke. Wouk, H.
Your blues ain't like mine. Campbell, B. M.

YOUTH
   See also Adolescence; Boys; Girls; Students
Amado, J. The war of the saints
Bradford, R. Red sky at morning
Colette. Chéri
Conrad, J. Youth
Cronin, A. J. A song of sixpence
De Vries, P. Consenting adults
Fitzgerald, F. S. The beautiful and damned
Fitzgerald, F. S. This side of paradise
Galsworthy, J. The white monkey
Godden, R. Pippa passes
Guest, J. Ordinary people
Head, A. Mr. & Mrs. Bo Jo Jones
Hesse, H. Demian
Horowitz, E. Plain Jane
Malamud, B. Dubin's lives
McCarthy, M. Birds of America
Michener, J. A. The drifters
Mishima, Y. The sound of waves
Nichols, J. T. The sterile cuckoo
Salinger, J. D. The catcher in the rye
Sams, F. When all the world was young
Siddons, A. R. Heartbreak Hotel
Sillitoe, A. Saturday night and Sunday morning

YOUTH—*Continued*
  Singer, I. B. The certificate
  Smith, B. Joy in the morning
  Snow, C. P. The malcontents
  Spencer, S. Endless love
  Tarkington, B. Alice Adams
  Townsend, S. Adrian Mole: the lost years
  Turgenev, I. S. Fathers and sons
  Tyler, A. A slipping-down life
  Updike, J. Brazil
  Wolfe, T. Of time and the river
  Wolfe, T. The web and the rock
  Woolf, V. Jacob's room
Youth. Conrad, J.
  In Conrad, J. The complete short fiction of Joseph
    Conrad p151-80
  In Conrad, J. Great short works of Joseph Conrad
    p143-71
  In Conrad, J. The portable Conrad
  In Conrad, J. Tales of land and sea p7-32
You've got to read this. Entered in Part I under title
YUGOSLAVIA
  See also Bosnia and Hercegovina

20th century
  MacLean, A. Force 10 from Navarone
YUKON TERRITORY *See* Canada—Yukon Territory
Yvgenie. Cherryh, C. J.

Z

Zadig. Voltaire
  In Voltaire. Candide and other stories
  In Voltaire. Voltaire's Candide, Zadig, and selected
    stories p102-72
ZAIRE
  Griffin, W. E. B. The new breed
  Hulme, K. The nun's story

ZAMBIA
  Gilman, D. Mrs. Pollifax on safari
ZANZIBAR
  Kaye, M. M. Trade wind
The **zebra-striped** hearse. Macdonald, R.
  In Macdonald, R. Archer in jeopardy
ZEN BUDDHISM
  Kerouac, J. The Dharma bums
Zero eight fifteen v1. See Kirst, H. H. The revolt of
  Gunner Asch
Zero eight fifteen, v2. See Kirst, H. H. Forward, Gunner
  Asch!
Zero eight fifteen v3. See Kirst, H. H. The return of
  Gunner Asch
ZIMBABWE
  Smith, W. A. The angels weep
  Smith, W. A. The leopard hunts in darkness

Politics
  See Politics—Zimbabwe

ZIONISM
  Iles, G. Black cross
  Uris, L. Exodus
Zooey. Salinger, J. D.
  In Salinger, J. D. Franny and Zooey
ZOOLOGICAL GARDENS *See* Zoos
ZOOS
  Irving, J. Setting free the bears
  Martin, V. The great divorce
Zorba the Greek. Kazantzakis, N.
Zuckerman bound: a trilogy and epilogue. Roth, P.
Zuckerman unbound. Roth, P.
  also in Roth, P. Zuckerman bound: a trilogy and
    epilogue
ZULUS (AFRICAN PEOPLE)
  See also Matabele (African people)
  Paton, A. Cry, the beloved country
ZUÑI INDIANS
  Hillerman, T. Dance hall of the dead
ZURICH (SWITZERLAND) *See* Switzerland—Zurich

DIRECTORY OF PUBLISHERS AND DISTRIBUTORS

This list includes only publishers and distributors of in-print titles entered in this catalog

Academy Chicago Pubs., 363 W. Erie St., Chicago, Ill. 60610-3125 Tel 312-751-7300; 800-248-7323 (orders outside Ill.) Fax 312-751-7306

Ace Bks., 200 Madison Ave., New York, N.Y. 10016 Tel 212-951-8800; 800-631-8571 Fax 212-213-6706; refer orders to Berkley Pub. Group, P.O. Box 506, E. Rutherford, N.J. 07073 Tel 201-933-9292; 800-223-0510 (orders) Fax 201-933-4927

Algonquin Bks.: Algonquin Bks. of Chapel Hill, 307 W. Weaver St., Carrboro, N.C. 27510 Tel 919-967-0108 Fax 919-933-0272; refer orders to Workman Pub. Co. Inc., 708 Broadway, New York, N.Y. 10003 Tel 212-254-5900; 800-722-7202 Fax 212-254-8098; 800-521-1832 (orders)

Amereon Ltd., P.O. Box 1200, Mattituck, N.Y. 11952-9500 Tel 516-298-5100 Fax 516-298-5631

AMS Press, 56 E. 13th St., New York, N.Y. 10003 Tel 212-777-4700 Fax 212-995-5413

Anchor Bks. (NY): Anchor Bks., 1540 Broadway, New York, N.Y. 10036 Tel 212-354-6500; 800-223-6834 Fax 212-492-9698

Andrews & McMeel Inc., 4900 Main St., Kansas City, Mo. 64112 Tel 816-932-6700; 800-826-4216 Fax 816-932-6706

Andrews, McMeel & Parker See Andrews & McMeel

Arbor House Pub. Co., 1350 Ave. of the Americas, New York, N.Y. 10019 Tel 212-261-6500; 800-237-0657 Fax 212-261-6549

Arcade Pub., 141 5th Ave., New York, N.Y. 10010 Tel 212-475-2633; 800-343-9204 Fax 212-353-8148; refer orders to Little, Brown & Co., 200 West St., Waltham, Mass. 02254 Tel 617-890-0250; 800-343-9204 Fax 617-890-0875

Arkham House Pubs. Inc., P.O. Box 546, Sauk City, Wis. 53583 Tel 608-643-4500

Armchair Detective Lib., 129 W. 56th St., New York, N.Y. 10019-3881 Tel 212-765-0902; 800-352-2840 Fax 212-265-5478

Atheneum Pubs., 866 3rd Ave., New York, N.Y. 10022 Tel 212-702-2000; 800-257-5755; refer orders to Macmillan, 201 W. 103rd St., Indianapolis, Ind. 46290 Tel 800-428-5331 Fax 800-882-8583

Atlantic Monthly Press, 841 Broadway, New York, N.Y. 10003-4793 Tel 212-614-7850; 800-638-6460 Fax 212-614-7886; refer orders to Publishers Group West, P.O. Box 8843, Emeryville, Calif. 94662 Tel 800-788-3123

Aunt Lute Bks., P.O. Box 410687, San Francisco, Calif. 94141 Tel 415-826-1300 Fax 415-826-8300

Avenel Bks., 40 Engelhard Ave., Avenel, N.J. 07001 Tel 908-827-2700; 800-223-6804; refer orders to Random House

Ayer Co. Pubs. (The), Lower Mill Rd., N. Stratford, N.H. 03590 Tel 603-922-5105

Baen Pub. Enterprises, P.O. Box 1403, Riverdale, N.Y. 10471 Tel 718-548-3100 Fax 718-548-3102; refer orders to Simon & Schuster, 200 Old Tappan Rd., Old Tappan, N.J. 07675 Tel 800-223-2336 (orders)

Ballantine Bks., 201 E. 50th St., New York, N.Y. 10022 Tel 212-751-2713; 800-638-6460 Fax 212-572-4912; refer orders to 400 Hahn Rd., Westminster, Md. 21157 Tel 800-726-0600

Bantam Bks. Inc., 1540 Broadway, New York, N.Y. 10036 Tel 212-354-6500; 800-323-9872; 800-223-6834 (outside NY) Fax 212-492-9698

Bentley: Robert Bentley Inc. Pubs., 1000 Massachusetts Ave., Cambridge, Mass. 02138 Tel 617-547-4170; 800-423-4595

Berkley Pub. Group (The), 200 Madison Ave., New York, N.Y. 10016 Tel 212-951-8800; 800-631-8571 Fax 212-545-8917; refer orders to P.O. Box 506, E. Rutherford, N.J. 07073 Tel 201-933-9292; 800-223-0510 (orders) Fax 201-933-4927

Black Sparrow Press, 24 10th St., Santa Rosa, Calif. 95401 Tel 707-579-4011 Fax 707-579-0567

Bluejay Bks. Inc., 26 Douglas Rd., Chappequa, N.Y. 10514 Tel 914-238-3491; refer orders to St. Martin's Press

Borgo Press (The), P.O. Box 2845, San Bernardino, Calif. 92406-2845 Tel 909-884-5813 Fax 909-888-4942

Boyars, M.: Marion Boyars Pubs. Ltd., 24 Lacy Rd., London SW15 1NL, Eng. Tel (0181) 788 9522 Fax (0181) 789 8122

Branch offices

U.S.: Marion Boyars Pubs. Inc., 237 E. 39th St., No. 1A, New York, N.Y. 10016-2110 Tel 212-697-1599 Fax 212-808-0664; refer orders to Inland Bk. Co., 140 Commerce St., East Haven, Conn. 06512 Tel 203-467-4257; 800-243-0138 Fax 203-467-8364

Braziller: George Braziller Inc., 60 Madison Ave., Suite 1001, New York, N.Y. 10010 Tel 212-889-0909 Fax 212-689-5405

Buccaneer Bks. Inc., P.O. Box 168, Cutchogue, N.Y. 11935 Tel 516-734-5724; 800-791-0005 Fax 516-734-7920

Cambridge Univ. Press, Edinburgh Bldg., Shaftesbury Rd., Cambridge CB2 2RU, Eng. Tel (01223) 312 393 Fax (01223) 315 052

Branch offices

U.S.: Cambridge Univ. Press, 40 W. 20th St., New York, N.Y. 10011-4211 Tel 212-924-3900; refer orders to 110 Midland Ave., Port Chester, N.Y. 10573-4930 Tel 914-937-9600; 800-872-7423 (orders only) Fax 914-937-4712

Carol Pub. Group, 600 Madison Ave., 11th Floor, New York, N.Y. 10022 Tel 212-486-2200 Fax 212-486-2231; refer orders to 120 Enterprise Ave., Secaucus, N.J. 07094 Tel 201-866-8159

Carroll & Graf Pubs. Inc., 260 5th Ave., New York, N.Y. 10001 Tel 212-889-8772 Fax 212-545-7909; refer orders to Publishers Group West, P.O. Box 8843, Emeryville, Calif. 94662 Tel 800-788-3123

Caxton Ptrs. Ltd. (The), 312 Main St., Caldwell, Idaho 83605 Tel 208-459-7421; 800-657-6465 Fax 208-459-7450

Columbia Univ. Press, 562 W. 113th St., New York, N.Y. 10025 Tel 212-666-1000 Fax 212-316-3100; refer orders to 136 S. Broadway, Irvington, N.Y. 10533 Tel 914-591-9111; 800-944-8648 Fax 914-591-9201; 800-944-1844

Congdon & Weed, 180 N. Michigan Ave., Chicago, Ill. 60601-7401 Tel 312-782-9181; 800-221-7945; refer orders to Contemporary Bks.

Contemporary Bks. Inc., 2 Prudential Plaza, Suite 1200, Chicago, Ill. 60601 Tel 312-540-4500; 800-621-1918 Fax 312-540-4687

Copernicus Soc. of Am., P.O. Box 385, Fort Washington, Pa. 19034 Tel 215-628-3632

Countryman Press Inc. (The), P.O. Box 175, Woodstock, Vt. 05091-0175 Tel 802-457-1049; 800-245-4151

Coward-McCann Inc., 200 Madison Ave., New York, N.Y. 10016 Tel 212-951-8400; 800-631-8571; refer orders to 390 Murray Hill Parkway, East Rutherford, N.J. 07073

Coward, McCann & Geoghegan See Coward-McCann

Crown Pubs. Inc., 201 E. 50th St., New York, N.Y. 10022 Tel 212-751-2600 Fax 212-572-6192; refer orders to 400 Hahn Rd., Westminster, Md. 21157 Tel 410-848-1900; 800-733-3000 Fax 800-659-2436

Dark Harvest, P.O. Box 941, Arlington Heights, Ill. 60006 Tel 708-913-1114

DAW Bks. Inc., 375 Hudson St., New York, N.Y. 10014 Tel 212-366-2096; refer orders to Penguin USA, 375 Hudson St., New York, N.Y. 10014 Tel 212-366-2000 Fax 212-366-2666

Delacorte Press, 1540 Broadway, New York, N.Y. 10036 Tel 212-354-6500; 800-323-9872; 800-223-6834 (outside NY) Fax 212-492-9698

Dembner Bks., 61 4th Ave., New York, N.Y. 10011 Tel 212-228-8828; 800-365-3453; refer orders to Publishers Group West, P.O. Box 8843, Emeryville, Calif. 94662 Tel 800-788-3123

Dial Press (NY): The Dial Press, 1540 Broadway, New York, N.Y. 10036 Tel 212-354-6500; 800-323-9872; 800-223-6834 (outside NY) Fax 212-492-9698

Doherty Assocs.: Tom Doherty Assocs. Inc., 175 5th Ave., New York, N.Y. 10010 Tel 212-388-0100; 800-221-7945 Fax 212-420-9314; refer orders to St. Martin's Press Inc., 175 5th Ave., Room 1715, New York, N.Y. 10010 Tel 212-674-5151; 800-221-7945 Fax 212-420-9314

Doubleday, 1540 Broadway, 18th Floor, New York, N.Y. 10036 Tel 212-354-6500; 800-223-6834 (outside NY); 800-223-5780 (orders) Fax 212-302-7985; 800-258-4233 (orders)

Down East Bks., P.O. Box 679, Camden, Me. 04843 Tel 207-594-9544; 800-432-1670 (Me. only) Fax 207-594-7215

Dutton, 375 Hudson St., New York, N.Y. 10014-3657 Tel 212-366-2000 Fax 212-366-2020; refer orders to Penguin USA, P.O. Box 999, Dept. 17109, Bergenfield, N.J. 07621 Tel 800-253-6476

Ecco Press, 100 W. Broad St., Hopewell, N.J. 08525 Tel 609-466-4748; 800-223-2584; refer orders to W.W. Norton & Co. Inc., 500 5th Ave., New York, N.Y. 10110 Tel 212-354-5500; 800-233-4830 (orders) Fax 212-869-0856; 800-458-6515 (orders)

Eriksson: Paul S. Eriksson Pub., P.O. Box 62, I-54 Dunmore, Forest Dale, Vt. 05745 Tel 802-247-4210 Fax 802-247-4256

Evans & Co.: M. Evans & Co. Inc., 216 E. 49th St., New York, N.Y. 10017 Tel 212-688-2810 Fax 212-486-4544; refer orders to National Bk. Network, 4720 Boston Way, Lanham, Md. 20706 Tel 301-459-8696; 800-462-6420 Fax 301-459-2118

Everest House Pubs., 33 W. 60th St., New York, N.Y. 10023 Tel 212-685-6464

Faber & Faber Ltd., 3 Queen Sq., London WC1N 3AU, Eng. Tel (0171) 465 0045 Fax (0171) 465 0034; refer orders to 16 Burnt Mill, Elizabeth Way, Harlow, Essex CM20 2HX, Eng. Tel (01279) 417 134 Fax (01279) 417 366
Branch offices
U.S.: Faber & Faber Inc., 53 Shore Rd., Winchester, Mass. 01890 Tel 617-721-1427 Fax 617-721-1427; refer orders to C.U.P. Services, 750 Cascadilla St., Ithaca, N.Y. 14851 Tel 607-666-2211; 800-688-2877

Farrar, Straus & Giroux Inc., 19 Union Sq. W., New York, N.Y. 10003 Tel 212-741-6900; 800-631-8571 Fax 212-633-9385

Fawcett Columbine, 201 E. 50th St., New York, N.Y. 10022 Tel 212-572-2713; 800-733-0600 Fax 212-572-6046; refer orders to 400 Hahn Rd., Westminster, Md. 21157 Tel 800-733-3000

Fine, D.I.: Donald I. Fine Inc., 375 Hudson St., New York, N.Y. 10014-3657 Tel 212-366-2570 Fax 212-366-2933; refer orders to Penguin USA, P.O. Box 120, Bergenfield, N.J. 07621-0120 Tel 201-387-0600; 800-526-0275 Fax 201-385-6521; 800-227-9604

Fjord Press, P.O. Box 16349, Seattle, Wash. 98116 Tel 206-935-7376 Fax 206-938-1991; refer orders to Publishers Services, P.O. Box 2510, Novato, Calif. 94948 Tel 415-883-3530

Forge, 175 5th Ave., New York, N.Y. 10010 Tel 212-674-5151; 800-221-7945 Fax 212-420-9314; refer orders to St. Martin's Press Inc., 175 5th Ave., Room 1715, New York, N.Y. 10010 Tel 212-674-5151; 800-221-7945 Fax 212-420-9314

Four Walls Eight Windows Pub. Co., 39 W. 14th St., Room 503, New York, N.Y. 10011-7489 Tel 212-206-8965; 800-444-2524 Fax 212-206-8799

Fromm Int. Pub. Corp., 560 Lexington Ave., New York, N.Y. 10022 Tel 212-308-4010 Fax 212-371-5187

Godine: David R. Godine Pub., 9 Lewis St., Lincoln, Mass. 01773 Tel 617-259-0700; 800-344-4771 Fax 617-259-9198

Greenwood Press, 88 Post Road W., P.O. Box 5007, Westport, Conn. 06881 Tel 203-226-3571; 800-225-5800 Fax 203-222-1502

Grove/Atlantic 841 Broadway, New York, N.Y. 10003-4793 Tel 212-614-7850; 800-638-6460 Fax 212-614-7886; refer orders to Publishers Group West, P.O. Box 8843, Emeryville, Calif. 94662 Tel 800-788-3123

Grove Press See Grove/Atlantic

Grove Weidenfeld See Grove/Atlantic

Hall, G.K. & Co.: G. K. Hall & Co., P.O. Box 159, Thorndike, Me. 04921 Tel 800-223-6121; lib. & general ref. bks. available from 866 3rd Ave., New York, N.Y. 10022 Tel 212-702-6789; 800-257-5755

Harcourt Brace & Co., 1250 6th Ave., San Diego, Calif. 92101 Tel 619-231-6616; 800-543-1918 Fax 800-235-0256

Harcourt Brace Jovanovich See Harcourt Brace & Co.

Harmony Bks., 201 E. 50th St., New York, N.Y. 10022 Tel 212-751-2600 Fax 212-572-6192; refer orders to Random House Inc., 400 Hahn Rd., Westminster, Md. 21157 Tel 410-848-1900; 800-733-3000 Fax 800-659-2436

Harper & Row See HarperCollins Pubs.

HarperCollins Pubs., 10 E. 53rd St., New York, N.Y. 10022-5299 Tel 212-207-7000; 800-331-3761 Fax 212-207-7145; refer orders to 1000 Keystone Ind. Park, Scranton, Pa. 18512 Tel 717-343-4761; 800-982-4377; 800-242-7737 (outside Pa.) Fax 800-822-4090

HarperPerennial, 10 E. 53rd St., New York, N.Y. 10022-5299 Tel 212-207-7000; 800-331-3761 Fax 212-207-7145; refer orders to 1000 Keystone Ind. Park, Scranton, Pa. 18512-0588 Tel 717-343-4761; 800-982-4377; 800-242-7737 (outside Pa.) Fax 800-822-4090

HarperPrism, 10 E. 53rd St., New York, N.Y. 10022-5299 Tel 212-207-7000; 800-331-3761 Fax 212-207-7145; refer orders to 1000 Keystone Ind. Park, Scranton, Pa. 18512 Tel 717-343-4761; 800-982-4377; 800-242-7737 (outside Pa.) Fax 800-822-4090

Harvard Univ. Press, 79 Garden St., Cambridge, Mass. 02138 Tel 617-495-2600; 495-2480 (orders) Fax 617-495-8924; 800-962-4983

Hill & Wang Inc., 19 Union Sq. W., New York, N.Y. 10003 Tel 212-741-6900 Fax 212-741-6973; refer orders to P.O. Box 506, East Rutherford, N.J. 07073 Tel 800-631-8571 Fax 201-933-2316

Holt & Co.: Henry Holt & Co., 115 W. 18th St., New York, N.Y. 10011 Tel 212-886-9200 Fax 212-633-0748; refer orders to 4375 W. 1980 S., Salt Lake City, Utah 84104 Tel 800-488-5233 Fax 801-977-9712

Houghton Mifflin Co., 222 Berkeley St., Boston, Mass. 02116 Tel 617-351-5000; refer orders to Wayside Rd., Burlington, Mass. 01803 Tel 617-272-1500; 800-225-3362

Hyperion, 114 5th Ave., New York, N.Y. 10011 Tel 212-633-4400 Fax 212-633-4833; refer orders to Little, Brown & Co. Inc., 200 West St., Waltham, Mass. 02254 Tel 617-890-0250; 800-343-9204 Fax 617-890-0875

Indiana Univ. Press, 601 N. Morton St., Bloomington, Ind. 47404-3797 Tel 812-855-6804; 800-842-6796 (orders) Fax 812-855-7931

International Polygonics Ltd., P.O. Box 1563, Madison Sq. Station, New York, N.Y. 10159 Tel 212-683-2914

Kelley: Augustus M. Kelley Pubs., 1140 Broadway, Room 901, New York, N.Y. 10001-7504 Tel 212-685-7202 Fax 212-685-7202; refer orders to P.O. Box 1048, W. Caldwell, N.J. 07004-1048

Kensington Pub. Corp., 850 3rd Ave., New York, N.Y. 10022 Tel 212-407-1500; 800-221-2647 Fax 212-935-0699; refer orders to refer orders to Penguin USA, P.O. Box 120, Bergenfield, N.J. 07621-0120 Tel 201-387-0600; 800-526-0275

Knopf: Alfred A. Knopf Inc., 201 E. 50th St., New York, N.Y. 10022 Tel 212-751-2600; 800-726-0600; refer orders to Random House Inc., 400 Hahn Rd., Westminster, Md. 21157 Tel 410-848-1900

Kodansha Am., 114 5th Ave., 18th Floor, New York, N.Y. 10011 Tel 212-727-6460; 800-631-8571 Fax 212-727-9177; refer orders to Farrar, Straus & Giroux, 19 Union Sq. W., New York, N.Y. 10003 Tel 212-741-6900; 800-631-8571 Fax 212-633-9385

Kodansha Int./USA See Kodansha Am.

Krieger: Robert E. Krieger Pub. Co. Inc., P.O. Box 9542, Melbourne, Fla. 32902-9542 Tel 407-724-9542; 727-7270 (orders only) Fax 407-951-3671

Lawrence, S.: Seymour Lawrence Inc., 222 Berkeley St., Boston, Mass. 02116 Tel 617-351-5000; refer orders to Wayside Rd., Burlington, Mass. 01803 Tel 617-272-1500; 800-225-3362

Library of Am. (The), 14 E. 60th St., New York, N.Y. 10022 Tel 212-308-3360; 800-631-3577 Fax 212-750-8352; refer orders to Viking Penguin, P.O. Box 120, Bergenfield, N.J. 07621-0120 Tel 201-387-0600; 800-526-0275

Linden Press, Simon & Schuster Bldg., 1230 Ave. of the Americas, New York, N.Y. 10020 Tel 212-698-7000 Fax 212-698-7336

Little, Brown & Co. Inc., 34 Beacon St., Boston, Mass. 02108 Tel 617-227-0730 Fax 617-227-0790; refer orders to 200 West St., Waltham, Mass. 02254 Tel 617-890-0250; 800-343-9204 Fax 617-890-0875

Liveright Pub. Corp., 500 5th Ave., New York, N.Y. 10110 Tel 212-354-5500; 800-233-4830 Fax 212-869-0856

Longstreet Press Inc., 2140 Newmarket Parkway, Suite 118, Marietta, Ga. 30067 Tel 404-980-1488; 800-927-1488 Fax 404-859-9894

Louisiana State Univ. Press, French House, Room 207, Baton Rouge, La. 70893 Tel 504-388-6618 Fax 504-388-6461; refer orders to P.O. Box 25053, Baton Rouge, La. 70894-5053 Tel 800-861-3477 Fax 800-305-4416

Lyford Bks., c.o. Presidio Press, 505 B San Marin Dr., Suite 300, Novato, Calif. 94945-1340 Tel 415-898-1081 Fax 415-898-0383

Macmillan, 866 3rd Ave., New York, N.Y. 10022 Tel 212-702-2000; 800-835-3202; refer orders to 201 W. 103rd St., Indianapolis, Ind. 46290 Tel 800-428-5331 Fax 800-882-8583

McGraw-Hill Int. Bk. Co., 1221 Ave. of the Americas, New York, N.Y. 10020 Tel 212-512-2000; 800-722-4726; refer orders to McGraw-Hill/Tab Direct Marketing Orders, 860 Taylor Station Rd., Blacklick, Ohio 43004 Tel 800-822-8158 Fax 614-759-3641

McKay, D.: David McKay Co. Inc., 201 E. 50th St., New York, N.Y. 10022 Tel 212-751-2600; 800-638-6460 Fax 212-872-8026; refer orders to Random House

Modern Lib. (The), 201 E. 50th St., New York, N.Y. 10022 Tel 212-751-2600; 800-726-0600

Morrow: William Morrow & Co. Inc., 1350 Ave. of the Americas, New York, N.Y. 10019 Tel 212-261-6500; 800-237-0657 Fax 212-261-6549

Mysterious Press, 1271 Ave. of the Americas, New York, N.Y. 10020 Tel 212-522-7200 Fax 212-522-7158; refer orders to Little, Brown

Nautical & Aviation Pub. Co. of Am. Inc. (The), 8 W. Madison St., Suite 12, Baltimore, Md. 21201 Tel 410-659-0220

Naval Inst. Press, U.S. Naval Inst., Preble Hall, 118 Maryland Ave., Annapolis, Md. 21402-5035 Tel 410-268-6110 Fax 410-269-7940; refer orders to 2062 Generals Highway, Annapolis, Md. 21401-6780 Tel 410-224-3378; 800-233-8764 Fax 410-224-2406

Nelson, T.: Thomas Nelson Pubs., P.O. Box 14100, Nashville, Tenn. 37214 Tel 615-889-9000; 800-251-4000 Fax 615-883-7619; 391-5225 (orders)

New Am. Lib. Inc. (The), 375 Hudson St., New York, N.Y. 10014 Tel 212-366-2000; refer orders to Penguin USA, P.O. Box 120, Bergenfield, N.J. 07621 Tel 201-387-0600; 800-526-0275

New Directions Pub. Corp., 80 8th Ave., New York, N.Y. 10011 Tel 212-255-0230 Fax 212-255-0231; refer orders to W. W. Norton & Co. Inc., 500 5th Ave., New York, N.Y. 10110 Tel 212-354-5500; 800-233-4830 (orders) Fax 212-869-0856; 800-458-6515 (orders)

New Press (NY), 450 W. 41st St., 6th Floor, New York, N.Y. 10036 Tel 212-629-8802 Fax 212-268-6349; refer orders to Norton

Noonday Press, 19 Union Sq. W., New York, N.Y. 10003 Tel 212-741-6900; 800-631-8571 Fax 212-633-9385

Northwestern Univ. Press, 625 Colfax St., Evanston, Ill. 60201-2807 Tel 708-491-5313; 800-621-2736 Fax 708-491-8150

Norton: W. W. Norton & Co. Inc., 500 5th Ave., New York, N.Y. 10110 Tel 212-354-5500; 800-233-4830 (orders) Fax 212-869-0856; 800-458-6515 (orders)

Ohio State Univ. Press, 1070 Carmack Rd., 180 Pressey Hall, Columbus, Ohio 43210-1002 Tel 614-292-6930 Fax 614-292-2065

Ohio Univ. Press, Scott Quadrangle, Athens, Ohio 45701-2979 Tel 614-593-1155; 800-242-7737 Fax 614-563-4536; refer orders to Chicago Distr. Center, 11030 S. Langley Ave., Chicago, Ill. 60628 Tel 312-568-1550; 800-621-2736 (outside Ill.) Fax 312-660-2235

Ontario Review Press, 9 Honey Brook Dr., Princeton, N.J. 08540 Tel 609-737-7497; refer orders to George Braziller Inc., 60 Madison Ave., New York, N.Y. 10010 Tel 212-889-0909

Overlook Press (The), 149 Wooster St., 4th Floor, New York, N.Y. 10012 Tel 212-477-7162 Fax 212-477-7525; refer orders to 2568 Route 212, Woodstock, N.Y. 12498 Tel 914-679-6838 Fax 914-679-8571

Oxford Univ. Press, Walton St., Oxford OX2 6DP, Eng. Tel (01865) 56767 Fax (01865) 56646
Branch offices
U.S.: Oxford Univ. Press Inc., 198 Madison Ave., New York, N.Y. 10016-4314 Tel 212-726-6000; 800-334-4249 Fax 212-725-2972; refer orders to 2001 Evans Rd., Cary, N.C. 27513 Tel 919-677-1303; 800-451-7556 Fax 919-677-1303

Pantheon Bks. Inc., 201 E. 50th St., New York, N.Y. 10022 Tel 212-872-8238; 800-638-0600 Fax 212-572-6030; refer orders to Random House Inc., 400 Hahn Rd., Westminster, Md. 21157 Tel 410-848-1900; 800-733-3000 Fax 800-659-2436

Penguin Bks. See Penguin USA

Penguin USA, 375 Hudson St., New York, N.Y. 10014 Tel 212-366-2000; refer orders to Penguin USA, P.O. Box 120, Bergenfield, N.J. 07621 Tel 201-387-0600; 800-526-0275

Penzler Bks.: Otto Penzler Bks., 866 3rd Ave., New York, N.Y. 10022 Tel 212-702-2000; 800-257-5755; refer orders to Simon & Schuster

Phantasia Press, 5536 Crispin Way, W. Bloomfield, Mich. 48033

Pocket Bks., Simon & Schuster Bldg., 1230 Ave. of the Americas, New York, N.Y. 10020 Tel 212-698-7000; 800-223-2348; refer orders to Simon & Schuster Inc., 200 Old Tappan Rd., Old Tappan, N.J. 07675 Tel 201-767-5937; 800-223-2336

Poseidon Press, Simon & Schuster Bldg., 1230 Ave. of the Americas, New York, N.Y. 10020 Tel 212-698-7000; 800-223-2348; refer orders to Simon & Schuster Inc., 200 Old Tappan Rd., Old Tappan, N.J. 07675 Tel 201-767-5937; 800-223-2336

Prentice-Hall Inc., Route 9W, Englewood Cliffs, N.J. 07632 Tel 201-592-2000; 800-922-0579; refer orders to Prentice-Hall/Allyn & Bacon, 200 Old Tappan Rd., Old Tappan, N.J. 07675 Tel 800-223-1360 Fax 800-445-6991

Putnam: G. P. Putnam's Sons, 200 Madison Ave., New York, N.Y. 10016 Tel 212-951-8400; 800-631-8571; refer orders to 390 Murray Hill Parkway, East Rutherford, N.J. 07073

Random House Inc., 201 E. 50th St., New York, N.Y. 10022 Tel 212-751-2600; 800-726-0600; refer orders to 400 Hahn Rd., Westminster, Md. 21157 Tel 410-848-1900; 800-733-3000 Fax 800-659-2436

Regnery Bks., 422 1st St. S.E., Washington, D.C. 20003 Tel 202-546-5005 Fax 202-546-8759

ROC, 375 Hudson St., New York, N.Y. 10014-3657 Tel 212-366-2000 Fax 212-366-2888; refer orders to Penguin USA, P.O. Box 120, Bergenfield, N.J. 07621 Tel 201-387-0600; 800-526-0275

Rutgers Univ. Press, 109 Church St., New Brunswick, N.J. 08901 Tel 908-932-7764; 932-1070 (orders); 800-446-9323 Fax 908-932-7039; 932-1074 (orders)

Schocken Bks. Inc., 201 E. 50th St., New York, N.Y. 10022 Tel 212-572-2559; 800-726-0600 Fax 212-572-6030; refer orders to Random House Inc., 400 Hahn Rd., Westminster, Md. 21157 Tel 410-848-1900; 800-733-3000 Fax 800-659-2436

Scribner: Charles Scribner's Sons, 1230 Ave. of the Americas, New York, N.Y. 10020; refer orders to Simon & Schuster Inc. Pubs., 200 Old Tappan Rd., Old Tappan, N.J. 07675 Tel 800-223-2336 (orders) Fax 800-445-6991

Seaver Bks., c.o. Arcade Pub., 141 5th Ave., New York, N.Y. 10010 Tel 212-475-2633

Severn House Pubs. Ltd., 9-15 Sutton High St., 1st Floor, Sutton, Surrey SM1 1DF, Eng. Tel (0181) 770 3930 Fax (0181) 770 3850; refer orders to Tiptree Bk. Services Ltd., Church Rd., Tiptree, Colchester, CO5 0SR, Eng. Tel (01621) 816 362; 819 600 (orders) Fax (01621) 819 011
Branch offices
U.S.: Severn House Pubs. Ltd., 41 E. 57th St., 15th Floor, New York, N.Y. 10022 Tel 212-888-4042 Fax 212-759-5422

Sharpe, M.E.: M. E. Sharpe Inc., 80 Business Park Dr., Armonk, N.Y. 10504 Tel 914-273-1800; 800-541-6563 Fax 914-273-2106

Simon & Schuster Inc. Pubs., Simon & Schuster Bldg., 1230 Ave. of the Americas, New York, N.Y. 10020 Tel 212-698-7000; 800-223-2348; refer orders to Simon & Schuster, 200 Old Tappan Rd., Old Tappan, N.J. 07675 Tel 800-223-2336 (orders) Fax 800-445-6991

Smith, P.: Peter Smith Pub., Inc., 5 Lexington Ave., Magnolia, Mass. 01930 Tel 508-525-3562

Soho Press Inc., 853 Broadway, New York, N.Y. 10003 Tel 212-260-1900; 800-631-8571 Fax 212-260-1902; refer orders to Farrar, Straus & Giroux Inc., 19 Union Sq. W., New York, N.Y. 10003 Tel 212-741-6900; 800-631-8571 Fax 212-633-9385

Southern Ill. Univ. Press, P.O. Box 3697, Carbondale, Ill. 62902-3697 Tel 618-453-2281; 453-6619 (orders) Fax 618-453-1221

Southern Methodist Univ. Press, P.O. Box 415, Dallas, Tex. 75275 Tel 214-768-1432 Fax 214-768-1428; refer orders to Texas A&M Univ. Press

St. Martin's Press Inc., 175 5th Ave., Room 1715, New York, N.Y. 10010 Tel 212-674-5151; 800-221-7945 Fax 212-420-9314

Stanford Univ. Press, Stanford, Calif. 94305-2235 Tel 415-723-1593 Fax 415-725-3457

State House Press, 8906 Wall St., Suite 702, Austin, Tex. 78754 Tel 800-421-3378

State Univ. of N.Y. Press, State Univ. Plaza, Albany, N.Y. 12246-0001 Tel 518-472-5000 Fax 518-472-5038; refer orders to C.U.P. Services, P.O. Box 6525, Ithaca, N.Y. 14851 Tel 607-277-2211; 800-666-2211 Fax 607-277-6292; 800-688-2877

Stemmer House Pubs. Inc., 2627 Caves Rd., Owings Mills, Md. 21117 Tel 410-363-3690; 800-645-6958 (orders) Fax 410-363-8459

Summit Bks., 1230 Ave. of the Americas, New York, N.Y. 10020 Tel 212-698-7501; 800-223-2336; refer orders to Prentice Hall Trade, Simon & Schuster Inc., 200 Old Tappan Rd., Old Tappan, N.J. 07675 Tel 201-767-5937; 800-223-2336 (orders only)

Swallow Press, Scott Quadrangle, Athens, Ohio 45701-2979 Tel 614-593-1155; 800-242-7737 Fax 614-593-4536; refer orders to Chicago Distr. Center, 11030 S. Langley Ave., Chicago, Ill. 60628 Tel 312-568-1550; 800-621-2736 (outside Ill.) Fax 312-660-2235

Talese: Nan A. Talese, c.o. Doubleday, 1540 Broadway, New York, N.Y. 10036-4094 Tel 212-354-6500; 800-223-6834 Fax 212-492-9698; refer orders to Doubleday Consumer Services, P.O. Box 5071, Des Plains, Ill. 60017-5071

Taplinger Pub. Co. Inc., P.O. Box 1324, New York, N.Y. 10185; refer orders to Parkwest Publs. Inc., 451 Communipaw Ave., Jersey City, N.J. 07304 Tel 201-432-3257 Fax 201-432-3708

Thunder's Mouth Press, 632 Broadway, 7th Floor, New York, N.Y. 10012 Tel 212-780-0380 Fax 212-780-0388; refer orders to Publishers Group West, P.O. Box 8843, Emeryville, Calif. 94662 Tel 800-788-3123

Ticknor & Fields, 215 Park Ave. S., New York, N.Y. 10003 Tel 212-420-5800; 800-225-3362 Fax 212-420-5855; refer orders to Houghton Mifflin

Times Bks., 201 E. 50th St., New York, N.Y. 10022 Tel 212-751-2600; 800-726-0600; refer orders to Random House Inc., 400 Hahn Rd., Westminster, Md. 21157 Tel 410-848-1900; 800-733-3000 Fax 800-659-2436

Timescape Bks., 1230 Avenue of the Americas, New York, N.Y. 10020 Tel 212-245-6400

TOR Bks., 175 5th Ave., New York, N.Y. 10010 Tel 212-388-0100; 800-221-7945 Fax 212-420-9314; refer orders to St. Martin's Press

Trafalgar Sq. Inc., Howe Hill Rd., N. Pomfret, Vt. 05053 Tel 802-457-1911; 800-423-4525 Fax 802-457-1913

Turtle Bay Bks., 201 E. 50th St., New York, N.Y. 10022 Tel 212-751-2600; 800-726-0600

Twayne Pubs., 1633 Broadway, New York, N.Y. 10019 Tel 212-654-3000

Ultramarine Pub. Co. Inc., P.O. Box 303, Hastings-on-Hudson, N.Y. 10706 Tel 914-478-2522

Underwood/Miller, 708 Westover Dr., Lancaster, Pa. 17601 Tel 717-285-2255 Fax 717-285-2255

University of Calif. Press, 2120 Berkeley Way, Berkeley, Calif. 94720 Tel 510-642-6684; 800-822-6657 Fax 510-642-7127; refer orders to California-Princeton Fulfillment Services, 1445 Lower Ferry Rd., Ewing, N.J. 08618 Tel 609-883-1759; 800-822-6657 Fax 800-999-1958

University of Chicago Press, 5801 S. Ellis Ave., 4th Floor, Chicago, Ill. 60637 Tel 312-702-7700 Fax 312-702-9756; refer orders to 11030 S. Langley Ave., Chicago, Ill. 60628 Tel 312-568-1550; 800-621-2736 Fax 312-660-2235; 800-621-8476

University of Ga. Press (The), 330 Research Dr., Suite B-100, Athens, Ga. 30602-4901 Tel 706-369-6130 Fax 706-369-6131

University of Ill. Press, 1325 S. Oak St., Champaign, Ill. 61820 Tel 217-244-4689 Fax 217-244-8082; refer orders to P.O. Box 4856, Hampden Post Office, Baltimore, Md. 21211 Tel 800-545-4703 Fax 410-516-6969

University of Iowa Press, 119 W. Park Rd., 100 Kuhl House, Iowa City, Iowa 52242-1000 Tel 319-335-2000 Fax 319-335-2055; refer orders to Publications Order Dept., 100 Oakdale Campus, No. M105 OH, Iowa City, Iowa 52242-5000 Tel 319-335-4645; 800-235-2665 Fax 319-335-4039

University of N.C. Press (The), P.O. Box 2288, Chapel Hill, N.C. 27515-2288 Tel 919-966-3561; 800-848-6224 (orders) Fax 919-966-3829; 800-272-6817 (orders)

University of Neb. Press, 312 N. 14th St., P.O. Box 880484, Lincoln, Neb. 68588-0484 Tel 402-472-3581; 472-3584 (orders) Fax 402-472-6214; 800-526-2617 (orders)

University of Okla. Press, 1005 Asp Ave., Norman, Okla. 73019-0445 Tel 405-325-5111 Fax 405-325-4000; refer orders to P.O. Box 787, Norman, Okla. 73070-0787 Tel 405-325-2000; 800-627-7377 Fax 405-364-5798; 800-735-0476

University of Tex. Press, P.O. Box 7819, Austin, Tex. 78713-7819 Tel 512-471-7233; 800-252-3206 Fax 512-320-0668

University Press of Fla., 15 N.W. 15th St., Gainesville, Fla. 32611-2079 Tel 904-392-1351; 800-226-3822 Fax 904-392-7302

University Press of Ky., 663 S. Limestone St., Lexington, Ky. 40508-4008 Tel 606-257-2951; 800-666-2211; 800-839-6855 (orders) Fax 800-870-4981

University Press of Va., P.O. Box 3608, University Station, Charlottesville, Va. 22903-0608 Tel 804-924-3468 Fax 804-982-2655; 800-831-3406 (orders)

Vanguard Press Inc., 424 Madison Ave., New York, N.Y. 10017 Tel 212-753-3906

Viking See Penguin USA

Villard Bks., 201 E. 50th St., New York, N.Y. 10022 Tel 212-572-2720; 800-726-0600 Fax 212-572-6026; refer orders to Random House Inc., 400 Hahn Rd., Westminster, Md. 21157 Tel 410-848-1900; 800-733-3000 Fax 800-659-2436

Walker & Co., 435 Hudson St., New York, N.Y. 10014 Tel 212-727-8300; 800-289-2553 Fax 212-727-0984

Warner Bks., Time & Life Bldg., 1271 Ave. of the Americas, New York, N.Y. 10020 Tel 212-522-7200 Fax 212-522-7158; refer orders to Little, Brown

Washington Sq. Press, Simon & Schuster Bldg., 1230 Ave. of the Americas, New York, N.Y. 10020 Tel 212-698-7000; 800-223-2348; refer orders to Prentice Hall Trade, Simon & Schuster Inc., 200 Old Tappan Rd., Old Tappan, N.J. 07675 Tel 201-767-5937; 800-223-2336 (orders only)

Wesleyan Univ. Press, High St., Middletown, Conn. 06457 Tel 203-347-9411; refer orders to University Press of New England

Wyndham Bks., 1230 Ave. of the Americas, New York, N.Y. 10020 Tel 212-245-6400

Zebra Bks., 850 3rd Ave., New York, N.Y. 10022 Tel 212-407-1500; 800-221-2647 Fax 212-935-0699; refer orders to Penguin USA, P.O. Box 120, Bergenfield, N.J. 07621-0120 Tel 201-387-0600; 800-526-0275